Iceland: Vatnajökull Glacier
The huge ice tongue of the Vatnajökull Glacier extends into the coastal region of southern Iceland. The bluish-black areas are crevasses, glacial debris and ash from previous volcanic eruptions that occured over the past centuries. Filigreed areas at the bottom of the photograph were created by water melting from glaciers.

PLANET EARTH

MACMILLAN WORLD ATLAS

MACMILLAN • USA

U.S.A.: New York City
The Greater New York area is one of the world's largest metropolitan areas. Between the Hudson River and the East River lies the borough of Manhattan with the green rectangle of famous Central Park. Brooklyn, the most populous borough, lies on the western tip of Long Island. Sand-bars line the southern coast of Long Island.

Preface

A new Cartographic Worldview Shows our Planet in all its Glory

The Earth is our home, both in the region where we happen to live and on the entire planet. We travel to Antarctica or Bali, have friends in Brisbane and Yokohama, place telephone calls to Johannesburg or perhaps even to Tierra del Fuego. Our stereo system was manufactured in Korea, our whiskies were distilled in Scotland or Kentucky. The planet is fast becoming one, large global village.

For millions of years humankind has been wandering across the face of the Earth, and today global travel has become a familiar feature of life. An increasingly large number of people are spending ever more time and money visiting foreign places. Three decades ago, only seventy million people were counted at international frontier crossings; that number has since increased sevenfold: the world has become mobile.

Modern communication technology adds another dimension to this mobility. An event happening right now in Beijing appears without delay on video screens around the world. No spectacular event can occur without immediately attracting the attention of the world community. Distances have become irrelevant as the continents seem to move closer together. And yet, far too much of the world still remains unknown and foreign to us. The vast expanses of Siberia and Australia, the island world of Oceania, the landscapes of central Africa, the far north and the extreme south of the two American continents: who can claim to have a clear, detailed mental image of these fascinating regions of our planet?

Planet Earth Macmillan World Atlas is designed to meet the changing needs of a changing world. Although it follows in the tradition of Mercator and other cartographers, this new volume is a revolutionary innovation, a trailblazing geographic and cartographic databank. Its fundamental concept reflects two essential goals. First, it is a precise and detailed reference designed to meet the information needs of a contemporary people. It has been created with travelers, both business and leisure, in mind, and it also serves as an invaluable resource for families and students, politicians, scientists, and businesspeople. The maps in this volume have been drawn to depict the actual state of today's world with un-

precedented fidelity and accuracy.

But beyond all that, *Planet Earth Macmillan World Atlas* hopes to communicate a dream and a fascination: the fascination of our wonderful blue spaceship, a place where life is precious and worthwhile, a threatened oasis whose continued survival depends upon the cooperation and commitment of people around the world.

This book is the creation of the distinguished Bertelsmann Cartographic Institute, which has invested many years and many millions of dollars to create a revolutionary digital cartographic database for a major new atlas series. The 80 to 100 staff members and their expert advisers who have spent years designing (and who continually update) the cartographic database are passionately committed to the goals that define this atlas program. Worldwide cooperation is the guiding principle in all their work. To give just two examples: Chinese geographers and cartographers at the University of Nanking designed the cartography of China; and former employees of Sojus Karta in Moscow helped create the maps of the Commonwealth of Independent States that were born after the collapse of the Soviet Union. These collaborations are all the more remarkable in view of the fact that mapmakers have always been strongly influenced by the complex interplays of military and political forces.

The worldview embodied by *Planet Earth Macmillan World Atlas* provides other examples of cartographic collaboration as well. New techniques and innovations in cartography have been harnessed in a variety of ways. The revolutionary technique of computer cartography – all map designs were digitally scanned, and all individual map elements are stored in a central databank – permits rapid reaction to changes of every sort. This is a milestone on the path to creating a truly up-to-date cartography commensurate with the actual state of the world.

In creating *Planet Earth Macmillan World Atlas*, some antiquated cartographic conventions have been abandoned, new methods of representation have been developed, and different informational features have been emphasized. The most obvious example of these improvements lies in the new, more realistic use of color.

Subtle gradations of color represent fine distinctions in the world's ecological zones, which are depicted according to their particular climates and characteristic vegetation. Unlike the deserts and mountains in traditional atlases, where color is almost exclusively a function of elevation, the deserts in the *Planet Earth Macmillan World Atlas* are not green and mountains are not brown. Rather, coloration reflects more closely what you would see if you looked down at the Earth from the perspective of an orbiting spaceship.

The inclusion of a detailed network of transportation arteries is another important feature, and one that will no doubt prove useful to leisure travelers and businesspeople alike. For the first time ever, *Planet Earth Macmillan World Atlas* presents the world's entire continental network of roads and railways, complete with their exact routes, classifications and numbers. Emphasis has also been given to major cultural or natural sites that are likely to be of interest to tourists.

But perhaps the most important innovation of all has to do with the way we perceive the countries of the world in relation to one another. Previous atlases compel their readers to cope with maps whose scales vary from one page to the next. *Planet Earth Macmillan World Atlas* puts an end to that by depicting our planet's land surfaces in a single, unified and detailed scale of 1:5 million. The scale is the same everywhere, from Nordkapp to Capetown, from Siberia to Australia and Oceania. In order to satisfy the desire for precise and detailed information, *Planet Earth Macmillan World Atlas* also provides additional larger-scale maps depicting regions of particular interest to its primary audience: a detailed series of maps showing the United States and southern Canada in a scale of 1:2.5 million. As its users will quickly recognize, the policy of treating the continents and their countries with cartographic equality offers obvious practical advantages. Most of us grew up with atlases in which the map of England was nearly as big as the map of China and in which Europe was emphasized at the expense of marginally treated non-European continents. Cartographic misinformation has misled generations of atlas users into forming mistaken notions about the

relative sizes of the world's nations and cultural regions.

To deepen our understanding of our home planet and its topographic structures, *Planet Earth Macmillan World Atlas* offers much more than mere cartography. Selected satellite photographs at the beginning of the volume provide fascinating insights into the world's characteristic natural and cultural landscapes. These images also show the actual models which the map colorations faithfully represent.

Planet Earth Macmillan World Atlas is conceived to serve as the ideal tool for discriminating people with global perspectives in their professional work and personal lifestyles. The atlas sets new standards in graphic design, information density and practical usability. The foundation for this new worldview is an enlightened perspective on humankind's responsibility to the universe. This responsibility involves both an ecologically sensitive attitude and a respect for the fundamental equality of human rights throughout the world. What may seem like a utopia today can and must become a reality – step by step. We hope that *Planet Earth Macmillan World Atlas* will help to carry this message.

Table of Contents

Australia and Oceania

Africa

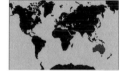

United States and Southern Canada

Index

Key to Maps: Continents

North and Middle America 1 : 5,000,000

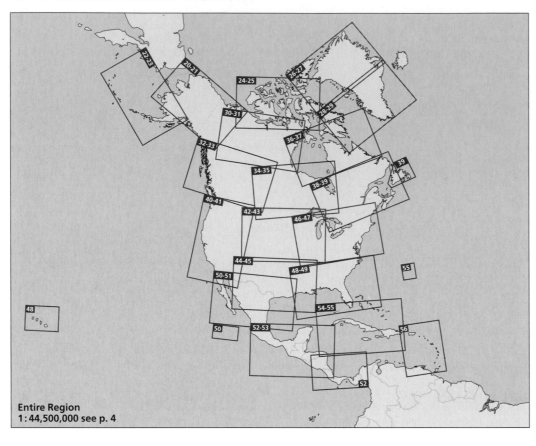

Entire Region
1 : 44,500,000 see p. 4

Europe 1 : 5,000,000

Entire Region
1 : 44,500,000 see p. 8

South America 1 : 5,000,000

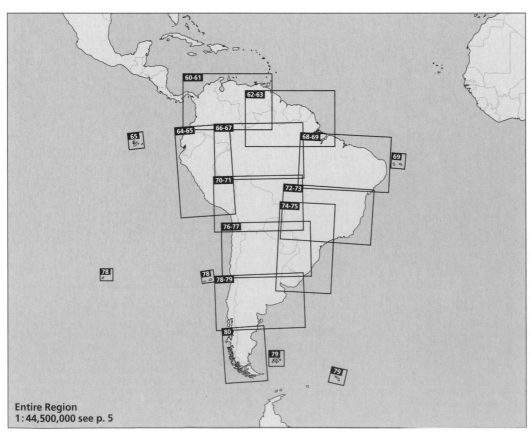

Entire Region
1 : 44,500,000 see p. 5

Asia 1 : 5,000,000

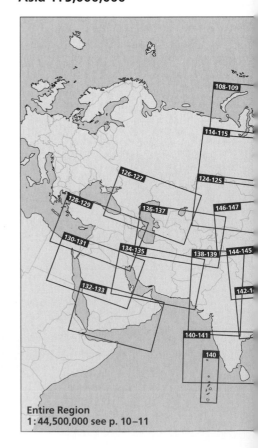

Entire Region
1 : 44,500,000 see p. 10–11

Australia and Oceania 1 : 5,000,000

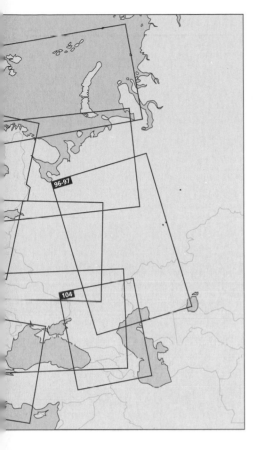

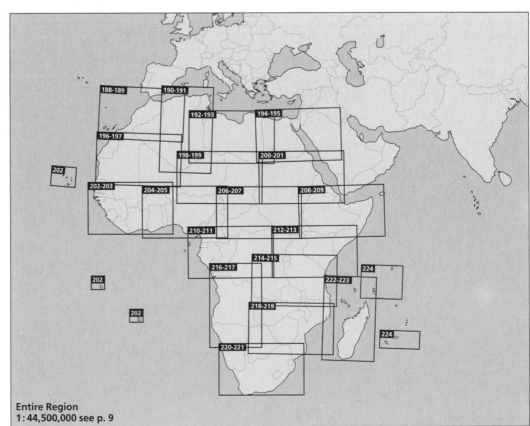

Entire Region
1 : 44,500,000 see p. 13

Africa 1 : 5,000,000

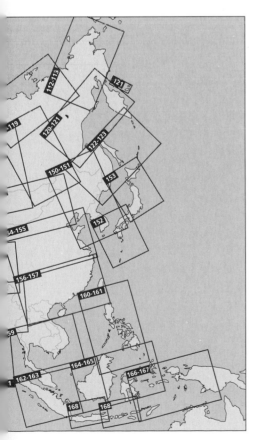

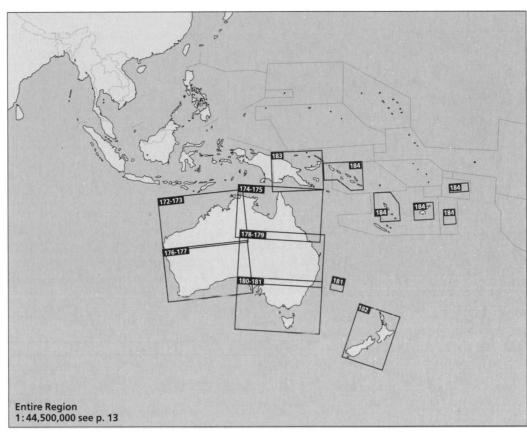

Entire Region
1 : 44,500,000 see p. 9

Key to Maps: United States of America and Southern Canada

United States of America and Southern Canada 1:2,500,000

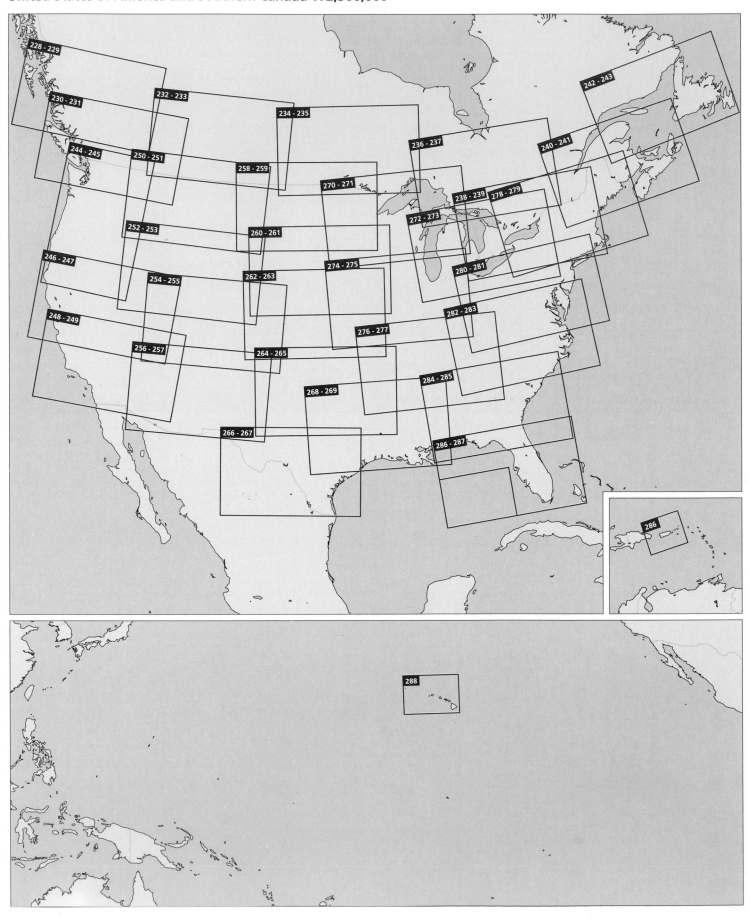

Map Samples

Satellite Imagery

Scale 1:44,500,000

Scale 1:5,000,000

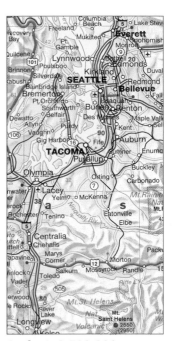

Scale 1:2,500,000

Space travel has provided us with a new image of the Earth. Earth observation satellites like those in the LANDSAT series orbit the Earth at an altitude of approximately 400 miles (700 kilometers). Sensors on board these satellites detect electromagnetic radiation reflected by the Earth, then transmit this information as photographic data to a global network of ground stations. But to arrive at brilliant satellite images like those selected for inclusion in this book, photographic data received from satellites must first be enhanced in a variety of ways.

Computers help make the gradations of color in the satellite images faithful renditions of their counterparts in nature. Various computer-assisted combinations of individually received spectral bands are used to achieve this accuracy. Filtering and contrast manipulation further enhance the images. Favorable photographic conditions are essential: optimum sunlight, ideal climatic conditions, and a minimum of cloud cover over the subject area.

Of course, satellite photographs are no substitute for maps, but their multifaceted images do serve as a valuable complement to the cartographic information expressed in maps. Their brilliance is fascinating, and they provide views of the Earth from new and fantastic perspectives.

Space probes can photograph the whole Earth in its entirety as a heavenly body. Satellites in orbit closer to the Earth can photograph areas the size of continents or subcontinents. The view from an airplane reveals individual landscapes. A map's scale expresses the distance between the Earth and an imaginary observer. It determines the extent and contents of the map.

The scale of 1:44,500,000 is suitable for representing the Earth as a whole. The world map shows the Earth's major structures, its division into oceans and landmasses, the continents and their relative geographical positions.

The various colors on the continents indicate major zones of vegetation. Bluish violet and yellowish red represent cold and dry deserts, green tones stand for various kinds of plant life. Since vegetation is largely a function of climate, a bluish green color indicates both coniferous forests and the colder climate of higher latitudes. Deep green, on the other hand, represents tropical rain forests in the hot, humid climate near the equator.

Shadings depict major topographic features of the Earth's crust: chains of folded mountains, highlands and basins, lowlands and low-mountain regions.

The majority of maps in this book are drawn in the scale of 1:5,000,000. All continents are thoroughly depicted in this scale, with the exception of Antarctica and some of the world's smaller islands. Maps on individual pages show parts of the continents. Settlements, transportation routes and political boundaries of various kinds are clearly visible against a color-coded background denoting the various topographies, climates and vegetation zones.

The spatial distribution and extent of settlements reflects population density. The few, widely spaced urban settlements in sparsely settled regions contrast with the urban sprawl of more densely populated regions. Maps also show the density of transportation networks, the presence or absence of roads and the accessibility of various places, as well as the distances between major intersections and the locations of railroads and airports. Political boundaries indicate international frontiers and national subdivisions.

The representation of cultural sights is more than just an aid to tourists and leisure travelers. These sites are often focal points of ethnocultural traditions, important places of worship or national identity.

As a complement to the maps of the world and its continents, a special section provides maps depicting the United States and southern Canada in detailed scale of 1:2,500,000.

At this scale, maps show a particular wealth of detail. It is possible to distinguish individual forms within the network of rivers and lakes, as well as within the represented relief. These forms range from gently undulating moraine landscapes and lakelands to resurgence valleys in low mountain ranges or individual mountain ranges among high mountains, including their degree of glaciation. The representation of traffic networks shows similar detail. These maps clearly portray the adaptation of towns to the relief or the relationship between their location and other topographic features such as rivers emerging from mountains or mouths of rivers or ocean bays. They also indicate how far cities extend their developed land into the surrounding region. The larger scale permits a greater degree of precision, for example, in the positioning of the numerous topographic map symbols. Other advantages of this scale are the improved definition of locations and greater precision for measuring distances. Large-scale maps are also useful for planning itineraries.

Explanation of Map Symbols Physical Aspects of the Earth

The Ocean

① Coastline, shoreline
② Island(s), archipelago
③ Tidal flat
④ Mangrove coast
⑤ Coral reef

Bathymetric Tints

⑥ 0 – 200 meters
⑦ 200 – 2,000 meters
⑧ 2,000 – 4,000 meters
⑨ 4,000 – 6,000 meters
⑩ 6,000 – 8,000 meters
⑪ 8,000 – 10,000 meters
⑫ Deeper than 10,000 meters
⑬ Water depth in meters

Coastlines are drawn with detail and precision in this atlas. As tides ebb and flow, certain sections of coast alternately belong to the mainland and the ocean. This is especially true of tidal flats and mangrove coasts, both of which are specially labeled on the maps.

Coral reefs in tropical oceans are remarkable features. Because of their low tolerance for changes in water temperature, salinity and deterioration in water quality, coral reefs are sensitive indicators of the quality of marine ecosystems.

Ocean depths are represented by bathymetric tints. The epicontinental shelf seas, which attain depths of 656 feet (200 m), are particularly important both politically and economically. During earlier geologic eras, some parts of these zones were dry land. Also known as continental shelves, these regions are rich in economically important resources. The ocean's deepest points are found near the edges of the continents. These deep sea trenches are depicted on individual map pages. Trenches are critical interfaces in the ongoing process of continental genesis and disappearance

Hydrographic Features

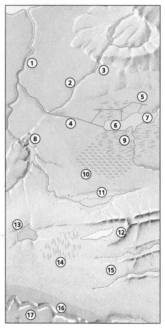

① Perennial stream or river
② Tributary river with headwaters
③ Waterfall, rapids
④ Navigable canal
⑤ Non-navigable canal
⑥ Freshwater lake
⑦ Elevation of lake above sea level and depth of lake
⑧ Reservoir with dam
⑨ Marsh, moor
⑩ Flood plain
⑪ Lake with variable shoreline

Mostly in Arid Regions

⑫ Seasonal lake
⑬ Salt lake
⑭ Salt swamp
⑮ River, drying up
⑯ Intermittent stream (wadi, arroyo)
⑰ Spring, well

The network of rivers and lakes provides a natural framework for the structures created by human beings in the process of developing and cultivating the land. Rivers and their mouths, bays and lake shores are preferred sites for human settlements. Rivers provide transportation routes, a source of hydroelectric power and water for irrigation. Above all, they supply us with our most basic need - potable water.

The maps depict the catchment areas of larger rivers with the treelike branching of their tributaries. Line thicknesses used in mapping the rivers correspond to their various sizes and to the hierarchy of main artery, major tributaries and headwaters. The paths of the blue lines represent the predominant characteristics of each natural watercourse with its meanders, branches, lakelike widenings and oxbows, as well as the comparatively rigid course of artificial waterways (canals). Agricultural and recreational uses are indicated by reservoirs and dams. The network of rivers and lakes reflects the world's gradient of water resources from abundance to aridity.

Glaciation

① Glacier in high-mountain range
② Glacial tongue

③ Continental ice sheet, icecap
④ Mean pack ice limit in summer
⑤ Mean pack ice limit in winter

The most recent ice age came to an end about 10,000 years ago. Its traces are still visible on roughly one-third of the Earth's landmasses, 11 percent of which are still covered by ice. The depiction of glaciers in the maps shows the worldwide distribution of these icy deserts. Continental ice sheets occupy by far the largest area, covering all of Antarctica and Greenland with sheets of ice as much as 10,000 feet (3,000 m) thick. Extensive surfaces of ocean, especially around the North Pole, are covered by sea or pack ice, and shelf ice is distributed along the edge of the Antarctic ice

sheet. Alpine glaciers cover only a relatively insignificant 1 percent of the landmasses.

Glaciers are almost always in motion, usually at a very slow pace. Glacial tongues tend to move more rapidly. Sometimes reaching lengths of more than 125 miles (200 km), these tongues of ice stretch from continental glaciers to the ocean, where they calve icebergs. Glacial tongues are often the most impressive features of alpine glaciers; larger examples of these ice tongues are shown on the maps.

The Topography of the Earth's Surface

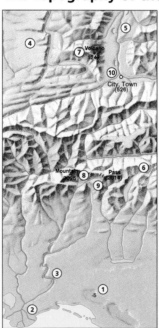

① Depressed region (land below sea level with depth in meters below sea level)
② River delta
③ Plain with depressed river valley
④ Hill country and highlands
⑤ Rift valley
⑥ Mountain range
⑦ Active volcano
⑧ Mountain (with elevation)
⑨ Pass (with elevation)
⑩ Approximate elevation of a city above sea level

Representing the third dimension – the topographic relief of the Earth's surface – is a special challenge for cartographers. The maps in this atlas derive their extraordinary dimensions from "relief shading." Gradations from pale to dark on the two-dimensional surface of the page help users visualize the Earth's actual three-dimensional topography. This impression is quantified with precise information about the elevations above sea level of mountains, passes and major cities.

The network of lakes and rivers is the counterpart to the relief depicted on the map. Waterways mark the locations of valleys that divide the topography. These two phenomena combine to provide an expressive picture of the geographic regions and their underlying tectonic structures.

Particularly clear examples include the Great Rift Valley (which runs from the Near East to southern East Africa), the gigantic basins and high plateaus of central Asia (surrounded by the world's highest mountains), the generously watered lowlands of North and South America, and the mighty ranges of corrugated mountains that form the Andes.

The Biosphere: Continental Ecological Zones

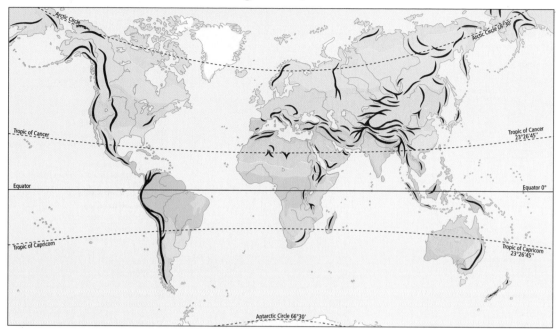

Tropics

I   Perennially humid climates
Tropical rain forest, moist savanna

II   Moist summer climates
Moist and dry savannas,
deciduous forests

Subtropics

III   Subtropical-tropical semidesert and
desert climates
Thorny scrub, desert

IV   Summer-humid to perennially moist
climates
Monsoon forest, shrubs

V   Mediterranean climates with dry
summers and moist winters
Shrubs, broadleaved evergreen forests

Temperature zones (middle latitudes)

VI   Winter-cold steppes, semidesert and
desert climates
Grasslands (steppe, prairie), desert

VII   Maritime to continental moist climates
Broadleaved deciduous forests, mixed
forests

Boreal zone

VIII   Taiga (needleleaved evergreen forests)

Polar and subpolar zone

IX   a: continental ice, ice cap
b: tundra (lichens, mosses, dwarf
shrubs)

High Mountains

Vertical arrangement of plant
communities by altitude

Macroclimates are among the most significant of the many factors affecting the distribution of life on Earth. Macroclimates influence soil formation and help shape surface topography, as well as affecting plant growth and animal communities, which in turn determine the suitability of a given geographic region for human habitation. All of these biotic and abiotic factors combine to create a complex web in which each factor influences the others in a variety of ways.

Based on climatic conditions and on the prevailing plant communities determined by those con-

ditions, the earth's landmasses can be subdivided into various habitats and ecozones. The boundaries between these zones, however, are not sharply defined. Instead, each zone emanates from a central region with characteristics typical of that zone, makes a transition across a boundary belt, and then more or less gradually changes into the adjacent landscape zone.

Although the limits of continental ecozones generally correspond to latitude, these zones exhibit two important asymmetries: regions of winter rainfall (Mediterranean climate) occur only along

the western edges of the continents; regions with moist summers (or perennially moist tropics) are located exclusively on the eastern edges (so-called "Shanghai climates").

Trees in Eurasia and America cannot grow beyond about 70 degrees of latitude; in South America tree-line occurs at 57 degrees, in New Zealand and Oceania at 48 degrees. The boreal or "northern" band of coniferous forests is entirely absent in the Southern Hemisphere because of the relatively limited extent of land area and the associated dominance of the ocean.

Arrangement of Ecological Zones by Altitude

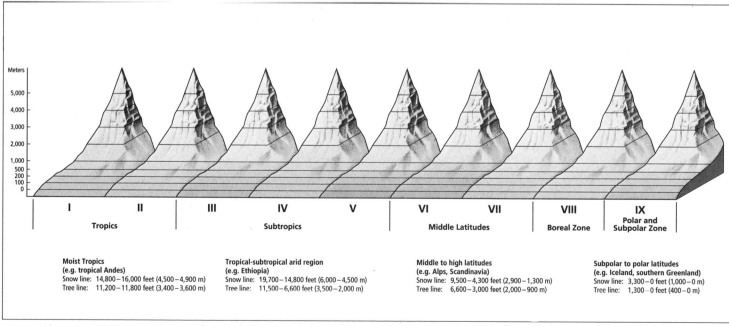

Moist Tropics
(e.g. tropical Andes)
Snow line: 14,800–16,000 feet (4,500–4,900 m)
Tree line: 11,200–11,800 feet (3,400–3,600 m)

Tropical-subtropical arid region
(e.g. Ethiopia)
Snow line: 19,700–14,800 feet (6,000–4,500 m)
Tree line: 11,500–6,600 feet (3,500–2,000 m)

Middle to high latitudes
(e.g. Alps, Scandinavia)
Snow line: 9,500–4,300 feet (2,900–1,300 m)
Tree line: 6,600–3,000 feet (2,000–900 m)

Subpolar to polar latitudes
(e.g. Iceland, southern Greenland)
Snow line: 3,300–0 feet (1,000–0 m)
Tree line: 1,300–0 feet (400–0 m)

An essential feature of geographic landscapes is their three-dimensional structure. The maps in this atlas provide clearly legible depictions of heights and depths on the face of the Earth. The arrangement of ecological zones is largely dependent upon latitude. This pattern, however, is overlaid by mountain ranges, which cut across latitudinally oriented climatic zones to create their own ecosystems where altitude creates characteristic ecological arrangements. A visible expression of the fact that biological conditions vary with altitude is the vertical arrangement of typical plant commu-

nities: generally forest (grassland) – meadows – cliffs (or talus) – ice (or glacier). This arrangement also creates characteristic ecological boundary lines: above the tree line and the (climatic) snow line; and in arid regions, the lower tree line as well depicts a boundary.

Elevations show typical climatic characteristics depending on a mountain range's location in the overall pattern of global climatic zones. Tropical mountains, for example, experience the same diurnal climatic variations typical of their neighboring lowlands.

The upper tree line in mountainous regions is caused by the lack of adequate warmth. The lower tree line found in arid regions is related to the lack of adequate moisture. This combination restricts the growth of forests in arid regions to more or less wide bands along the lower slopes of mountains.

Where a lower tree line is now found in humid high mountain regions, or where the band of forest is entirely absent in certain places, the causes of this deforestation are likely to be manmade.

Forests in mountainous regions provide abso-

lutely essential protection against avalanches and slope erosion.

The cultivation of crops in mountainous regions is likewise limited by prevailing climatic factors which, in turn, are primarily a function of elevation. In the Andes, for example, grains cannot be cultivated above 5,000 feet (1,500 m), although in the tropical Andes millet can be grown at elevations as high as 14,400 feet (4,400 m). With the exception of mining camps and settlements of shepherds at still higher elevations, these heights mark the upper limits of permanent human settlement.

Explanation of Map Symbols Manmade Features on Earth

The Map Margins

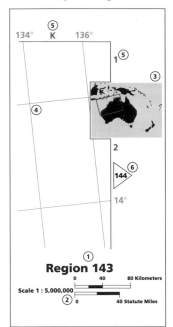

Region 143

Scale 1 : 5,000,000

① Page number and short title

② Numeric and graphic map scales (scales in kilometers and miles)

③ Locator map showing the position and extent of continental area covered by that particular map two page spread

④ Map grid (graticule) and its designation

0 degrees longitude (Meridian of Greenwich) = Gr.

Longitude 180 degrees to 1 degree west of Gr.	Longitude 1 degree to 180 degrees east of Gr.
Latitude 1 degree to 90 degrees north of the equator	Latitude 1 degree to 90 degrees north of the equator
Equator 0 degrees	**Equator 0 degrees**
Latitude 1 degree to 90 degrees south of the Equator	Latitude 1 degree to 90 degrees south of the Equator
Longitude 180 degrees to 1 degree west of Gr.	Longitude 1 degree to 180 degrees east of Gr.

0 degrees longitude of Greenwich = Gr.

⑤ Grid search key as specified for each index entry: Letters at top/bottom Numbers at left/right with graticule as searching grid

⑥ Page number of adjacent map page

Along with the short title and the page number, further aid in using the atlas is provided by the map overviews in the preface and by the locator maps at the beginning of each series of maps of individual continents. The number inside a small triangle on each map indicates the page where a map of the adjacent region can be found.

A locator map at the top right-hand corner of each double-page spread shows the area within the particular continent depicted by that particular map page. The scale notations in the lower margin are essential for determining geographic

distances. They express the relationship between a given distance on the map and a corresponding distance in the real world.

For centuries, the degree-calibrated latitude and longitude grid system has been used to define locations and plot courses on the face of the globe. The red letters along the top and bottom, together with the red numbers along the left and right margins, identify individual fields within the blue search grid.

Settlements and Transportation Routes

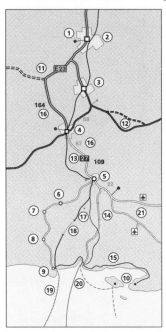

Town Symbols

① Urban area (normally surrounding cities with populations over 100,000)

② Population over 5 million

③ 1,000,000 – 5,000,000

④ 500,000 – 1,000,000

⑤ 100,000 – 500,000

⑥ 50,000 – 100,000

⑦ 10,000 – 50,000

⑧ 5,000 – 10,000

⑨ Population less than 5,000

⑩ Settlement, hamlet, research station (in remote areas often seasonally inhabited only)

Transportation Routes

⑪ Superhighway, four or more lanes, with number in blue

⑫ Highway under construction

⑬ Main road with number

⑭ Other road – road tunnel

⑮ Unpaved road, track

⑯ Distance in kilometers

⑰ Railway: main track – other track

⑱ Railway tunnel

⑲ Railway ferry

⑳ Car ferry – shipping line

㉑ International airport Domestic airport

Town symbols correspond to the populations of their respective places. The density of these symbols on the map combines with their relative values to indicate a region's population density and settlement structure (urban area or smaller, equally distributed towns).

The representation of urban areas sheds light on the increasing concentration of humanity in major metropolitan areas. According to UNESCO, by the year 2000 approximately half of the world's population will live in cities occupying only about four percent of the Earth's total land area.

In the depiction of transportation routes, special emphasis has been given to the representation of continental road networks. This corresponds to the importance of such networks on the threshold of the 21st century. Transportation of economically important goods, tourism, and the migrations of people searching for work or fleeing disasters all take place primarily over roads. These routes have been classified and numbered according to their relative importance. Distance specifications help map users make accurate calculations of distances.

Political and Other Boundaries

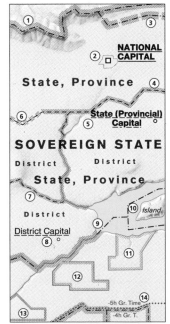

① International boundary

② Capital of a sovereign state

③ Disputed international boundary

④ 1st-order administrative boundary (e.g. region, state, autonomous region, province)

⑤ Capital city (1st-order administrative seat)

⑥ Disputed 1st-order administrative boundary

⑦ 2nd-order administrative boundary (e.g. region, area, province, country)

⑧ 2nd-order administrative seat

⑨ Boundary along watercourses or across bodies of water

⑩ Dependent region and specification of nation with jurisdiction

⑪ National park, national monument

⑫ Reservation

⑬ Restricted area

⑭ Boundary of a time zone with difference between local time and Greenwich Mean Time (GMT)

The documentation of territorial possessions was one of the reasons maps were invented. Maps play a central political role in border disputes and are an indispensable aid in interpreting or representing spatially related statistical data. The vast majority of statistical studies are based on national units or on regions within nations. Regardless of whether population distribution, buying power or cancer-incidence rates are measured, maps are the most convincing method of visually presenting and interpreting data.

International boundaries occupy first place in the hierarchy of political boundaries. They are therefore clearly marked in this atlas. First-order administrative boundaries, which define the limits of the major administrative units within a nation, come next in rank. Secondary boundaries are mapped when their political status merits it, providing their average surface area permits graphic representation on the scale involved. The maps also show capital cities or administrative seats of the depicted administrative entities.

Places and Points of Interest

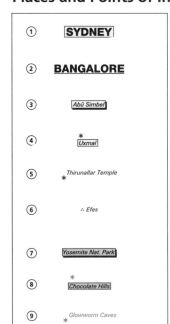

① Place of special interest

② Place of interest

③ UNESCO World Cultural Heritage Site

④ Cultural monument of special interest

⑤ Interesting cultural monument

⑥ Ancient monument or excavation

⑦ UNESCO World Natural Heritage Site

⑧ Natural monument of special interest

⑨ Interesting natural monument

The maps in this atlas provide the reader with a global view of the Blue Planet's most remarkable places and points of interest. These include exceptional monuments of natural or historical and cultural developments. Many of these places are important to national, ethnic or religious identity. This atlas places such sites in their geographical contexts. Graphic distinctions are made between natural and cultural monuments and according to their significance as magnets for tourism. UNESCO, a suborganization of the United Nations, has designated selected cultural sites and natural

monuments worldwide as part of the "heritage of mankind" and urged their special preservation. These sites are specially marked in the atlas. The volume thus provides not only an informative manual for globetrotters with widely ranging interests, but also serves as a helpful supplement for students of travel and nature guides or of relevant artistic and historical and cultural literature.

Lettering of Cities and Towns

① **TEHRĀN**
   MONTEVIDEO

② **MIAMI**
   LE HAVRE

③ MANHATTAN
   VAIHINGEN

④ **Darwin**
   Thimphu

⑤ Gallipolis
   Grindelwald
   Laugarvatn

⑥ **BOLZANO**
   BOZEN

⑦ **HALAP**
   (ALEPPO)

⑧ **FRANKFURT**
   am Main

Type size indicates the relative importance and population of the town

① City with a population over one million
② Large city
③ Boroughs of large cities or of cities with populations over one million
④ Medium-sized city
⑤ Small town, rural community
⑥ Place names in region with two official languages
⑦ Place name, alternate or earlier form
⑧ Official supplement to a place name

This atlas includes carefully selected place names. Type size corresponds to the number of inhabitants; type face indicates the particular significance or function of the place. Place names in capital letters indicate large cities with more than 100,000 inhabitants.

Some names of important places, landscape features and bodies of water are written in the accepted American form, but as a general rule, place names are written in the official national spelling. In the case of countries having two official languages, both versions are given. This rule also applies to all other geographic names.

Letter-oriented transliteration or phonetic transcription is used to spell names from languages with non-Roman alphabets. Wherever possible, the atlas has followed accepted standards for such procedures.

Geographic names can offer valuable insights into historical developments and relationships.

Topographic Typography

① **CHILE**   Réunion   (France)

② *GOBI* *Cappadocia* *Kimberley*

③ **ANDES** **Nan Ling** **Tibesti**

④ Mt. McKinley
   6194   **Simplonpass** (2005)   Cabo de Hornos

⑤ *JAVA* *Galápagos Islands* *York Peninsula*

⑥ *PACIFIC OCEAN*
   Finskij zaliv   *The Channel*

⑦ *Niger* *Panama Canal* *Taj Hu* *Niagara Falls*

⑧ *Yucatán Basin*   *Cayman Trench*

⑨ Nazca Ridge   Aves Ridge

⑩ *Aboriginal Land*   *Military Training Area*

⑪ 8848   *10540*   398

① Nation, administrative unit, designation of sovereignty
② Landscape, historical landscape
③ Mountains, mountain range, highland
④ Mountain with elevation above sea level, pass with elevation above sea level, cape
⑤ Island, archipelago, peninsula
⑥ Ocean, sea, gulf, bay, strait
⑦ River, canal, lake, waterfall
⑧ Undersea landscapes, trenches
⑨ Undersea mountains
⑩ Reservation, restricted areas
⑪ Elevation in meters above sea level Depth in oceans and lakes, elevation of lake surface

Lettering and typeface help explain the various features on a map. They also serve to structure geographic data according to significance and rank. These distinctions are reflected by the use of either all capital letters or mixtures of capital and lower-case letters, and by various type faces and sizes. Color also supports these distinctions: for example, rivers are labeled in blue, political units in gray, and sites of natural interest in green. Colored backgrounds or colored underlining indicates sites of interest to tourists.

Geographic names are one of the ways human beings express their possession of the land. People have given names to the remotest islands, to minor coves in the inhospitable Antarctic and to barely defined coastal promontories. The maps in this atlas, as in any other atlas, can include only the most important of these geographic names. All of them are listed in alphabetical order in the index of geographic names, together with search-grid designations that make it easy to pinpoint them on individual maps.

Sahara Desert/Algeria: Star Dunes
The photograph shows part of the Great Eastern Erg in eastern Algeria. The many-armed star dune formations are situated like pale yellow warts atop the flat, darker, faintly visible stripes of the longitudinal dunes. Star dunes attain heights of between 330 and 660 feet (100 and 200 meters).

The World

Among the planets of the solar system, the Earth is unique – not just because of its atmosphere, but above all because of its "face," whose features are the three oceans, occupying over two-thirds of the 196,911,000 square miles (510 million sq. km) of the surface of the Earth, and the seven continents. The Pacific Ocean alone is larger than all land areas together; the largest of these, in turn, is Eurasia, occupying a full third of the total. The highest elevations are reached in the Himalayas, where Mount Everest rises to 29,028 feet (8,848 m). Fourteen mountains over 26,000 feet can be found in this massive mountain range separating the Indian subcontinent from the rest of Asia. The longest mountain range is the Cordilleras, stretching the entire length of North and South

Not entirely up to date: This anonymous woodcut (1530) represents only the continents of the Old World and populates them with fantastic beasts taken from the prophecies of Daniel.

America. The deepest place on Earth is the Vitiaz Deep (–36,200 feet/–11,034 m) in the Mariana Trench near the southeast Asian archipelagos. The deepest depression on Earth lies 1,312 feet (400 m) below sea level and is part of a rift valley system that includes the East African faults and the Red Sea. A trench is also the home of the deepest lake with the greatest water volume, Lake Baikal, with a depth of 5,315 feet (1,620 m). The face of the Earth is given further character by volcano chains, such as the Hawaiian Islands, as well as by the icy masses of Antarctica, Greenland and high mountain glaciers.

North and Middle America
4

South America
5

Atlantic Ocean
6 – 7

Europe
8

Africa
9

Asia
10 – 11

Indian Ocean
12

Australia and Oceania
13

Pacific Ocean (1 : 55,500,000)
14 – 15

The Arctic · Antarctica
(1 : 30,000,000)   16

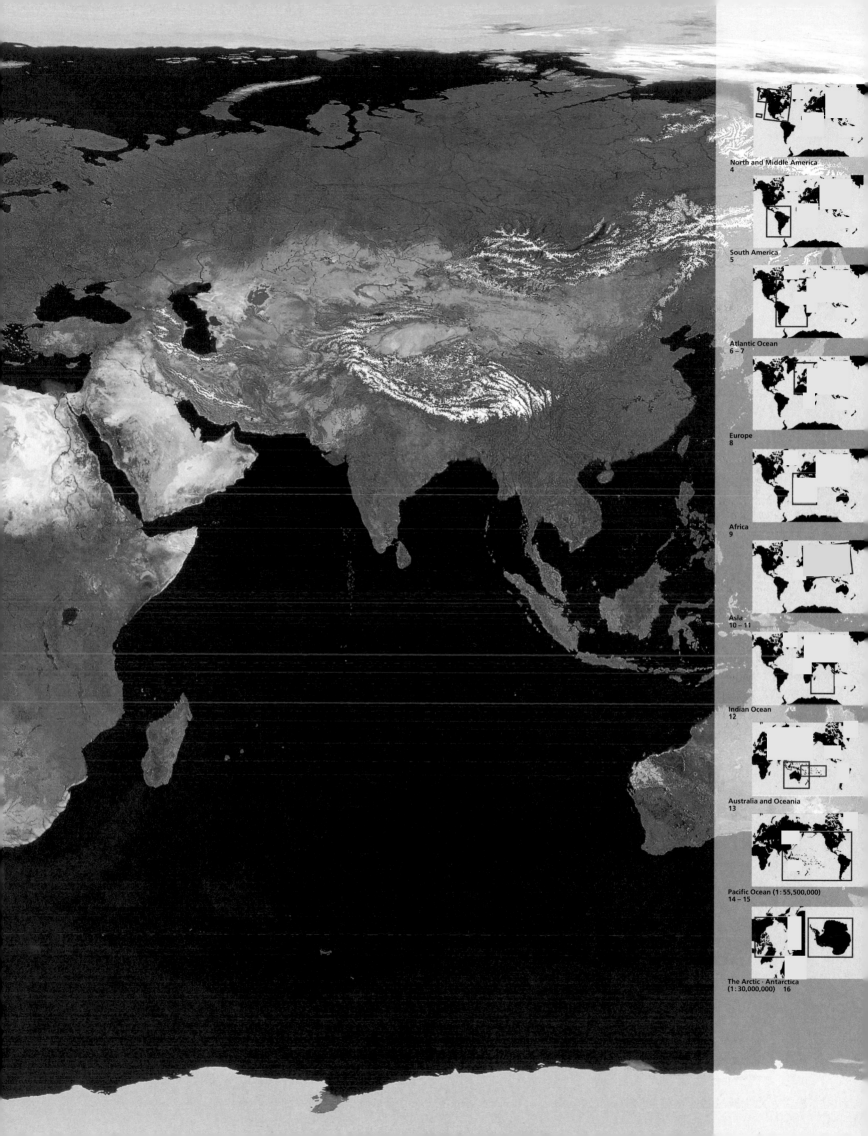

North and Middle America
4

South America
5

Atlantic Ocean
6 – 7

Europe
8

Africa
9

Asia
10 – 11

Indian Ocean
12

Australia and Oceania
13

Pacific Ocean (1 : 55,500,000)
14 – 15

The Arctic · Antarctica
(1 : 30,000,000)   16

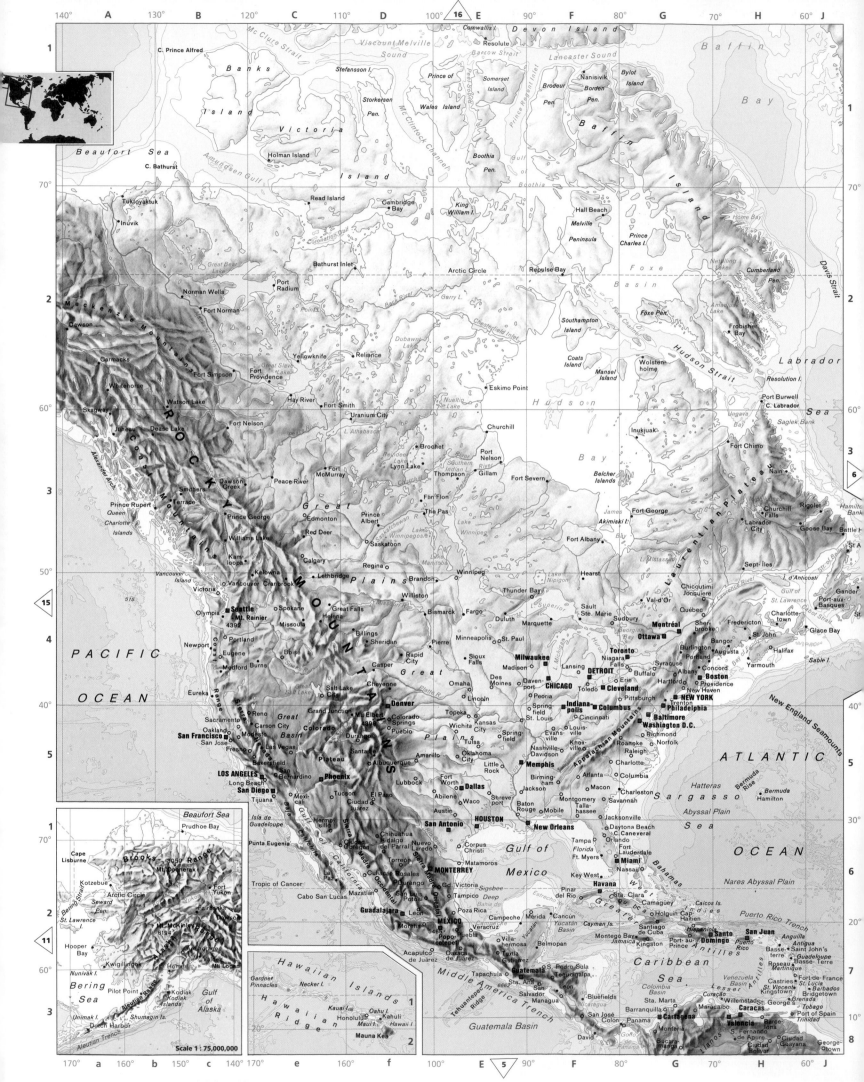

Scale at the equator 1 : 44,500,000

Scale at the equator 1 : 44,500,000

South America 5

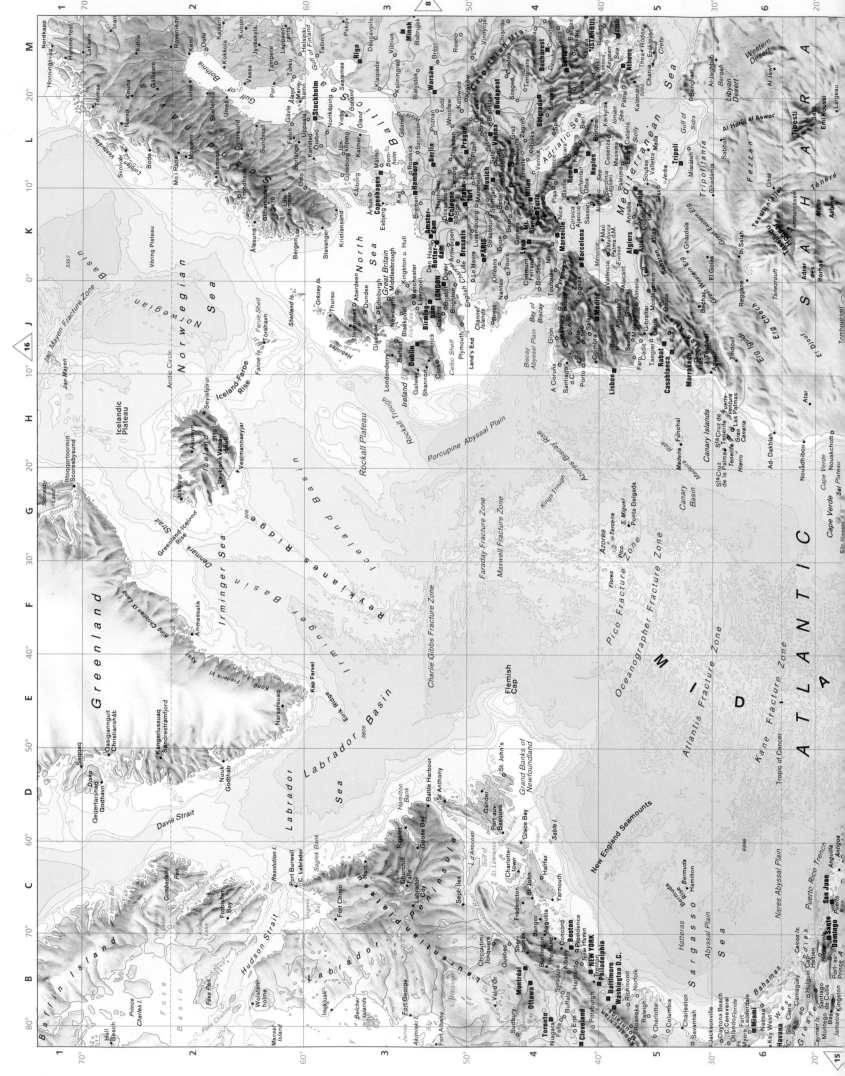

Scale at the equator 1 : 44,500,000

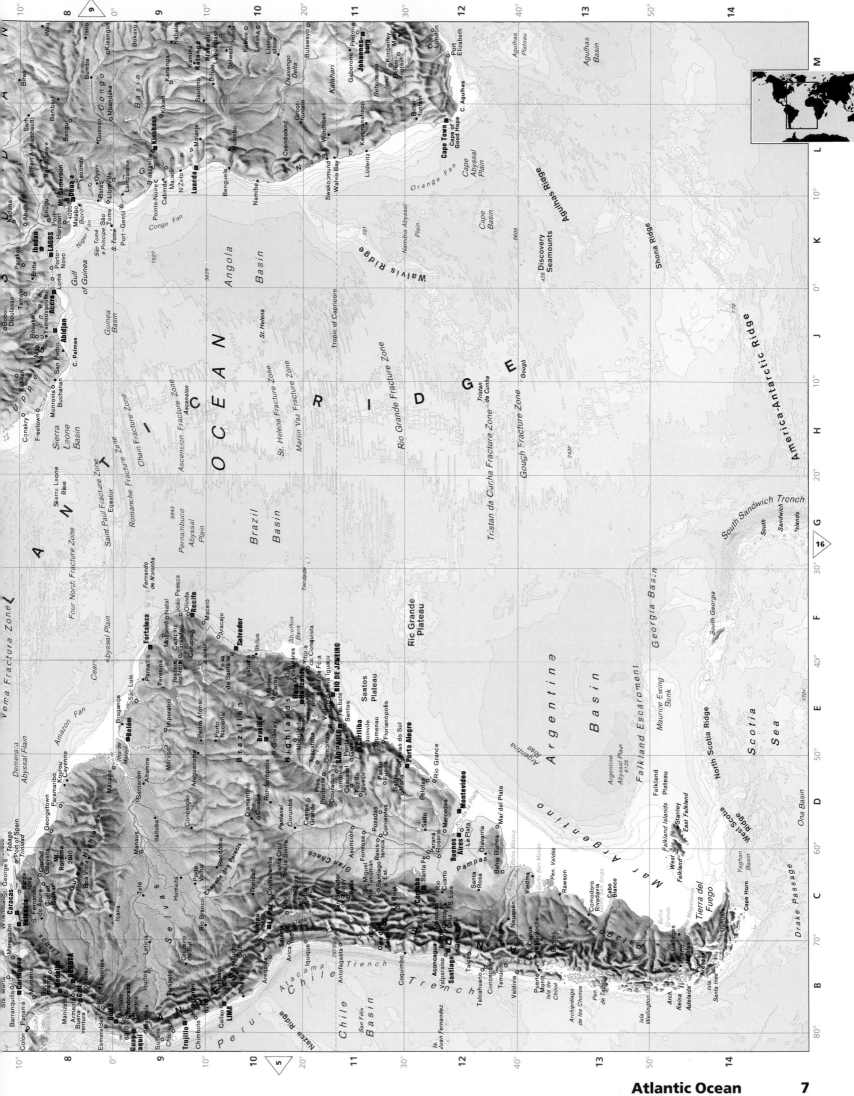

Scale at the equator 1 : 44,500,000

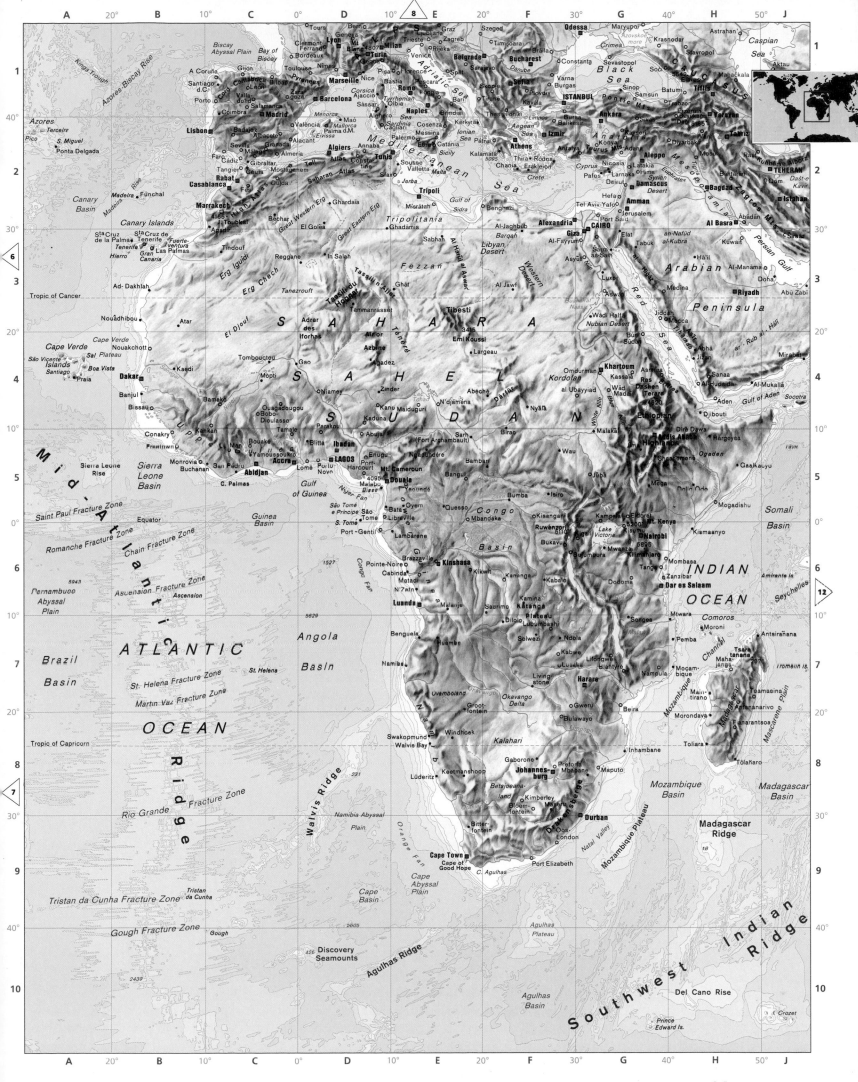

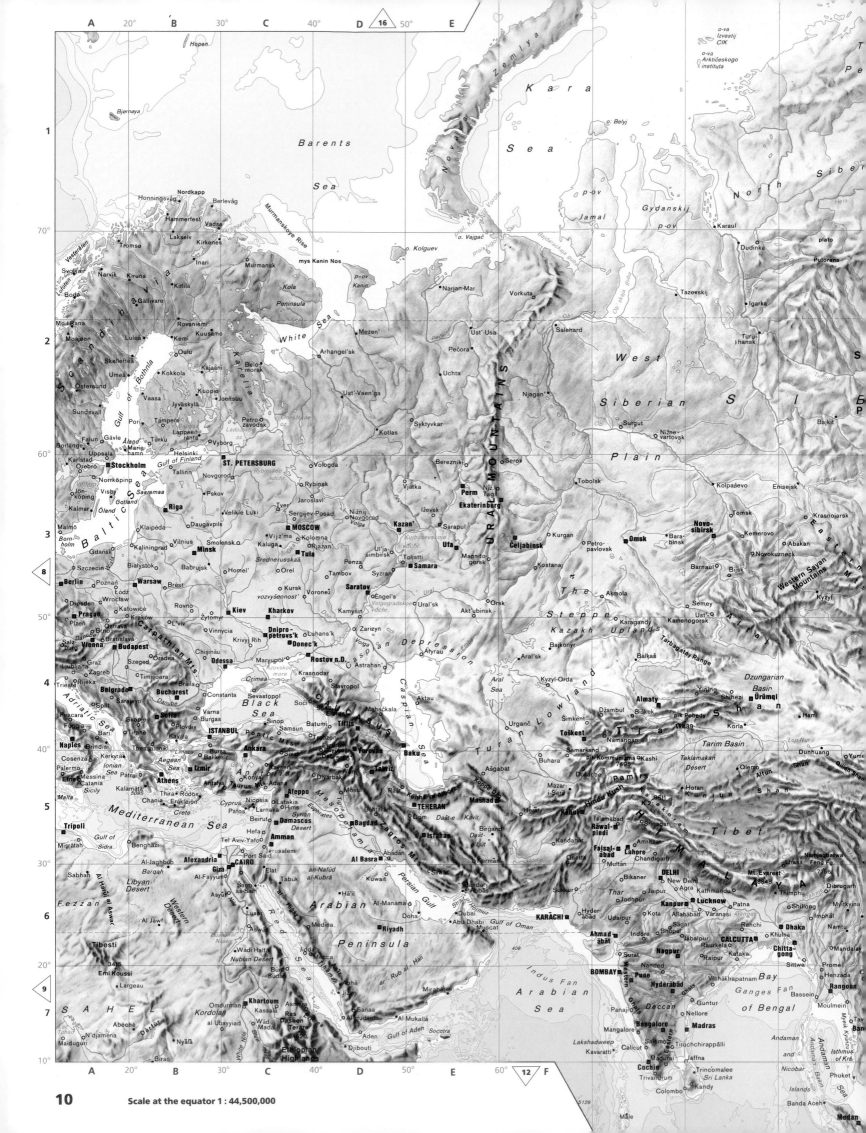

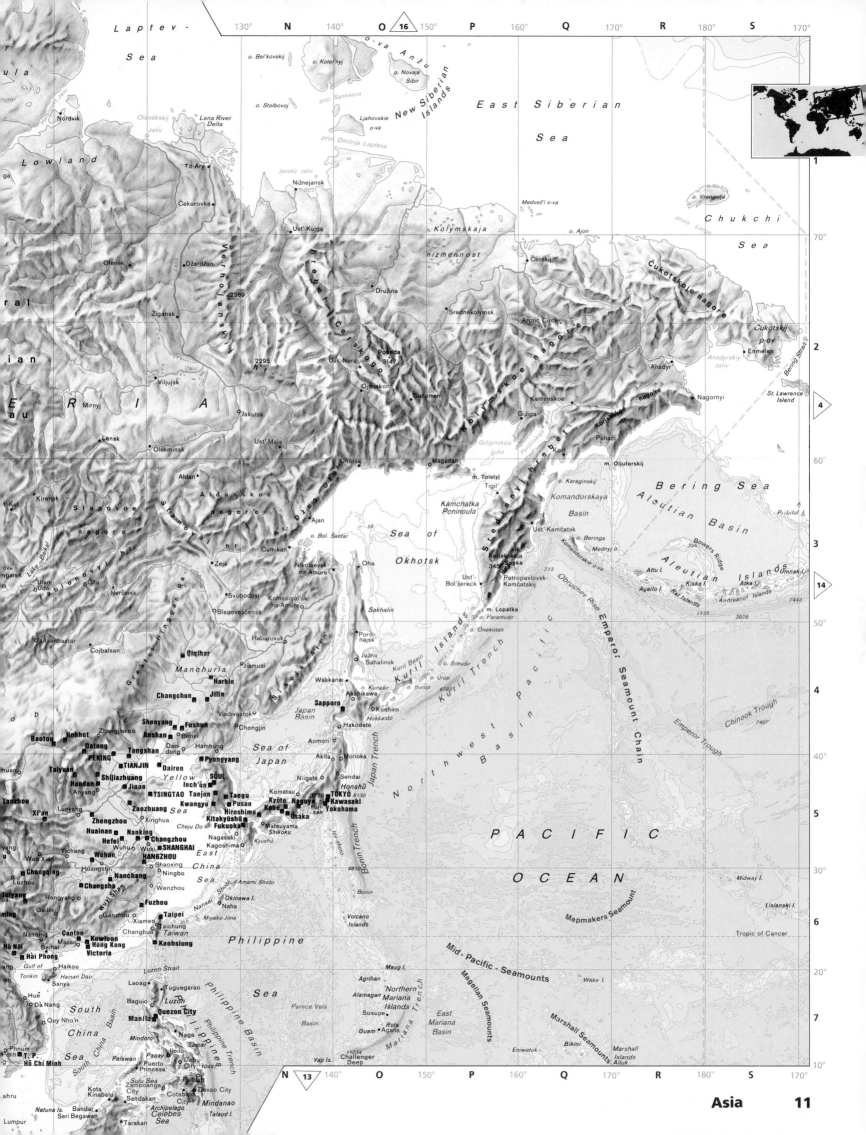

Laptev-
Sea

130° N O 140° 16 150° P 160° Q 170° R 180° S 170°

o. Bel'kovskij
o. Kotel'nyj
o-va Anžu
o. Novaja Sibir
New Siberian Islands
East Siberian Sea

Nordvik
o. Stolbovoj
prol. Sannikova
Ljahovskie o-va
prol. Dmitrija Lapteva

Lena River Delta
Oleněkskij zaliv

Lowland

Tit-Ary
Janskij zaliv
Medvež'i o-va
o. Vrangelja
Chukchi
Sea

Nižnejansk
prov. Longa

Čekurovka

Ust'-Kujga
Kolymskaja
o. Ajon
70°

Oleněk
Verhojanskij
nizmennost
Čerskij

2389
Družina
Arctic Circle
Čukotskoje nagore

Žigansk
Srednekolymsk
Čukotskij p-ov

2295
Pobeda
3147
Kamenskoe
Enmelen
2

Viljujsk
Ust'-Nera
Anadyrskiy zaliv
Bering Strait

Mirnyj
Ojmjakon
Susuman
Kamenskoe
Nagornyi
St. Lawrence Island
4

Jakutsk
Korjakskoe nagore
Korf

Lensk
Ust'-Maja
Gižiga
Pahači

Olëkminsk
Ohotsk
Magadan
m. Oljutorskij
60°

Aldan
m. Tolstyj
Tigil'
Bering Sea

Kirensk
Aldanskoe nagore
o. Karaginskij
Komandorskaya Basin
Aleutian Basin

Stanovoe nagore
Ajan
Kamchatka Poninoula
Ust'-Kamčatsk
o. Beringa
Komandorskije o-va
Pribilof I.

Lake Baikal
o. Bol. Šantar
Sea of Okhotsk
Mednyj
Bowers Ridge

Ulan-Ude
Čumikan
vlk.
Koriakskaja Sopka
713
Attu I.
Kiska I.
Umnak I.

Čita
Zeja
3456
Petropavlovsk-Kamčatskij
Ayattu I.
Rat Islands
Atka I.
14

Nerčinsk
Nikolaevsk-na-Amure
Ust'-Bol'šereck
Obručev Rise Emperor Seamount Chain
Andreanof Islands
7443

Ulaanbaatar
Svobodnyj
Oha
m. Lopatka
o. Paramušir
3078

Cojbalsan
Komsomol'sk-na-Amure
Sakhalin
50°

Blagoveščensk
Poronajsk
o. Onekotan
Simušir

Habarovsk
Južno Sahalinsk
Kuril Basin
Pacific

Qiqihar
Jiamusi
Kuril Islands
o. Urup

Manchuria
Wakkanai
Kuril Trench
Northwest
Basin

Harbin
Asahikawa
Iturup
9783

Changchun
Jilin
Sapporo
Kushiri
Ocean

Shenyang
Fushun
Vladivostok
Hokkaidō
Chinook Trough
7401

Baotou
Hohhot
Anshan
Chongjin
Hakodate
Japan Trench
40°

Datong
Benxi
Aomori
Morioka

PEKING
Tangshan
Dandong
Hamhung
Akita

Taiyuan
TIANJIN
Pyongyang
Niigata
Sendai

Handan
Dairen
SŎUL
Komatsu
3776
TOKYO
8130

Shijiazhuang
Inch'ŏn
Kyōto
Nagoya
KAWASAKI

Jinan
TSINGTAO
Taejon
Taegu
Ōsaka
Yokohama

Zaozhuang
Kwangyu
Pusan
Kōbe
Fuji-san

Zhengzhou
Xinghua
Kitakyūshū
Hiroshima
Bonin Trench

Huainan
Nanking
Fukuoka
Shikoku
30°

Hefei
Changzhou
Kagoshima
Kyūshū

Wuhan
SHANGHAI
Nagasaki
PACIFIC

Chongqing
HANGZHOU
East China Sea

Nanchang
Ningbo
OCEAN

Changsha
Wenzhou
Amami Shoto
Midway I.

Fuzhou
Nansei Shoto
Okinawa I.
Tropic of Cancer
Lisianski I.

Canton
Xiamen
Taipei
Naha
20°

Kowloon
Hong Kong
Taichung
Taiwan
Mapmakers Seamount

Victoria
Kaohsiung
Miyako Jima
Philippine

Hà Nôi
Hai Phong
Luzon Strait
Volcano Islands
Mid-Pacific Seamounts
Wake I.

Haikou
Hainan Dao
Bonin
Maug I.

Sanya
Laoag
Tuguegarao
Agrihan
Magellan Seamounts

Baguio
Luzon
Alamagan
Northern Mariana Islands
Marshall Seamounts
10°

Quezon City
Parece Vela
Supupe
East Mariana Basin

Manila
Rota
Agana
Guam

South China Sea
Mindoro
Naga
Iloilo
Samar
Yap Is.
11034
Challenger Deep
Eniwetok
Bikini
Marshall Islands
Alluk

Philippine Basin
Cebu City
10497

Puerto Princesa
Panay

Palawan
Butuan

Hô Chí Minh
Mindanao
Davao City

Kota Kinabalu
Zamboanga City
Cotabato City
Celebes Sea

Natuna Is.
Sandakan
Archipelago City
Talaud Is.

Tarakan
Talaud Is.

N 13 140° O 150° P 160° Q 170° R 180° S 170°

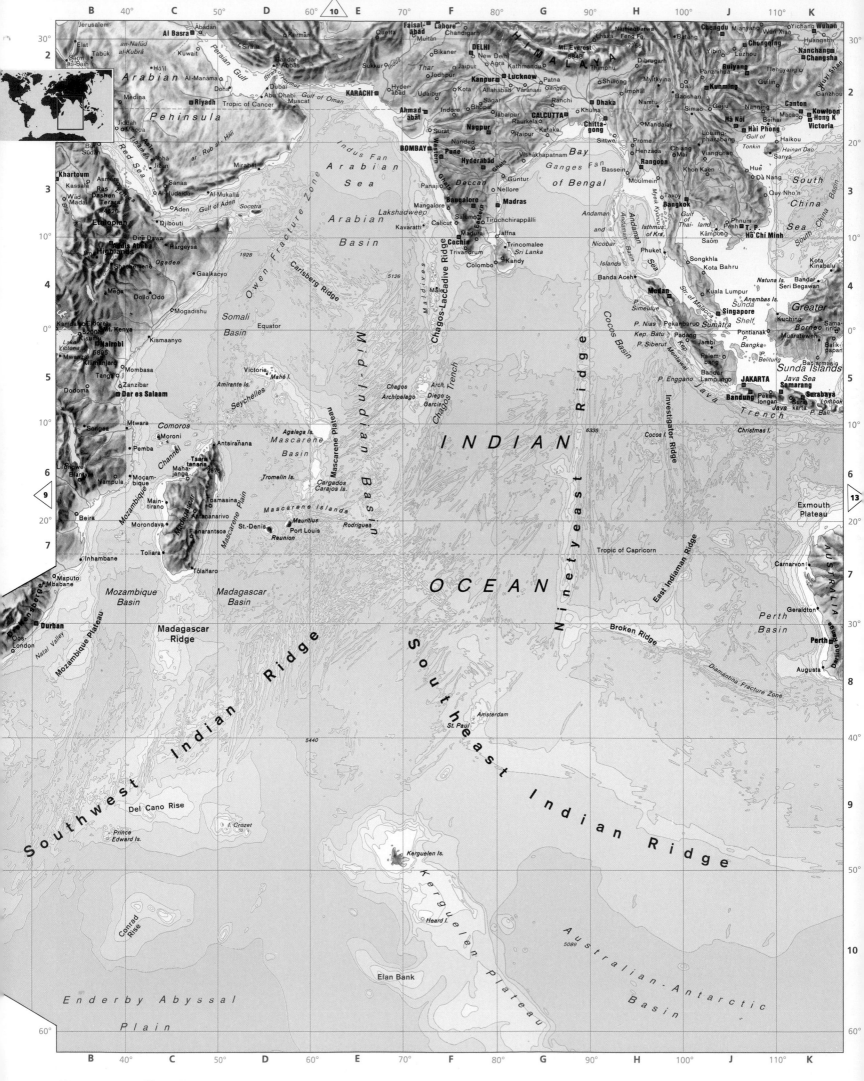

Scale at the equator 1 : 44,500,000

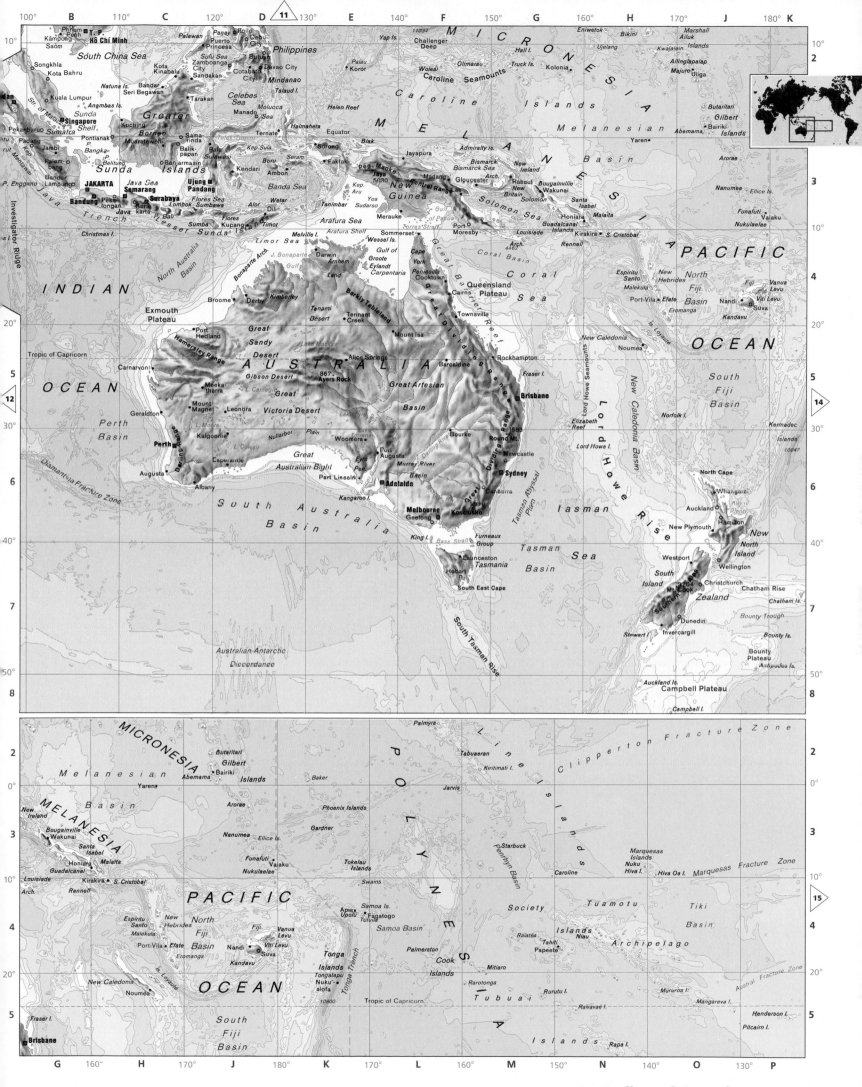

Scale at the equator 1 : 44,500,000

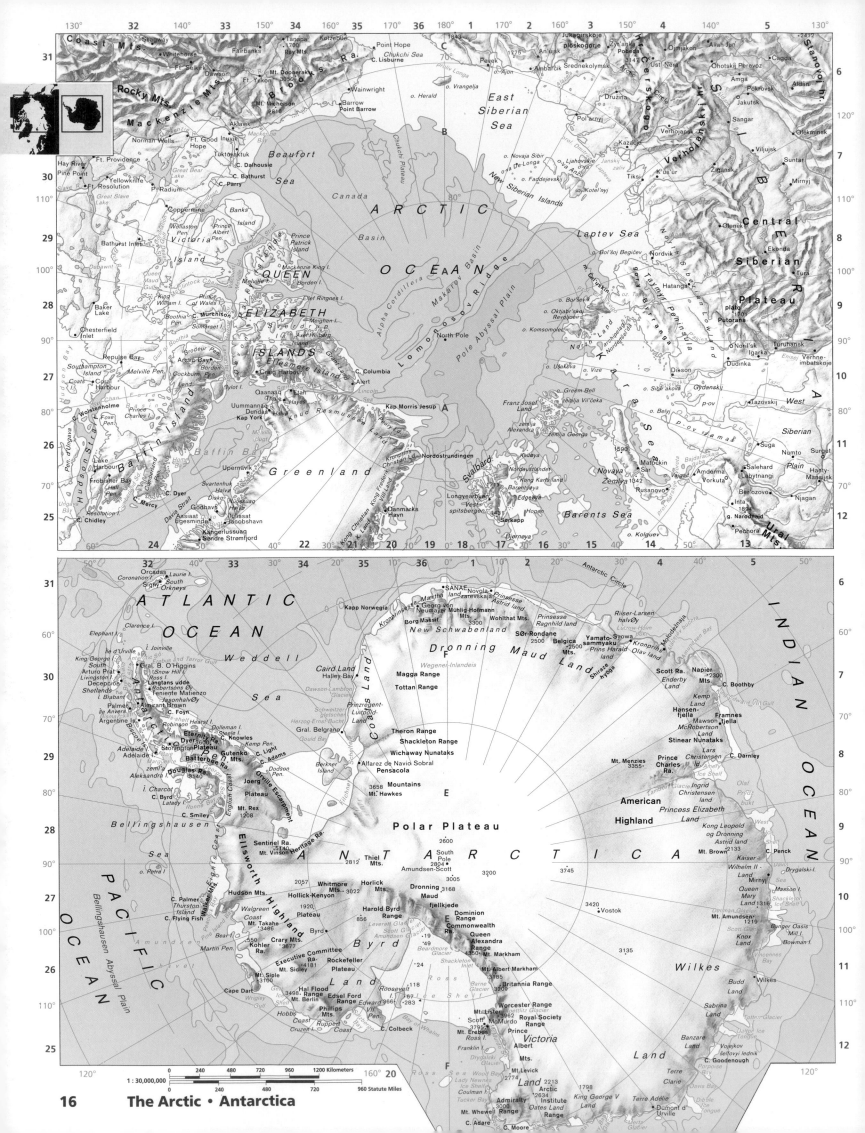

North and Middle America – one continent, two worlds

The North American continent, including Central America and the West Indian archipelago, covers an area of 9,266,400 square miles (24 million sq. km). Thus the continent extends from the icy climate of the North Pole to the hot and humid tropics. One-quarter of the area consists of islands and peninsulas: in the north, the Canadian islands and Greenland – the largest island in the world. South of the Tropic of Cancer lie the Greater and Lesser Antilles. The entire area is made up of five elements: the Canadian Shield, the low range of the Appalachian Mountains, the central plains, the high ranges of

"The Newe Islands That Lie Beyond Spain to the East By the Land of India." This depiction of America appeared in Sebastian Münster's "Cosmographia Universalis" (1550).

the Rocky Mountains, and the West Indian islands. Due to the North-South orientation of the mountain ranges, the continent has no mountain barriers to prevent the exchange of polar and tropical air masses. The original population of North, Central and South America originates from Asia and has been displaced, with the exception of a few remaining enclaves, by European immigrants and their descendants.

Alaska
20 – 21

Aleutians
22 – 23

Canada: Arctic Islands
24 – 25

Greenland: Northern Region
26 – 27

Greenland: Southern Region
28 – 29

Canada: Barren Grounds
30 – 31

Canada: British Columbia, Alberta,
Saskatchewan   32 – 33

Canada: Manitoba, Ontario
34 – 35

Canada: Labrador
36 – 37

Canada: Atlantic Provinces
38 – 39

U.S.A.: Pacific States
40 – 41

U.S.A.: Central States, North
42 – 43

U.S.A.: Central States, South
44 – 45

U.S.A.: Great Lakes, Northeastern
States   46 – 47

U.S.A.: Southeastern States
(Inset: Hawaii)   48 – 49

Mexico: Northern Region
50 – 51

Mexico: Southern Region ·
Central America   52 – 53

Greater Antilles
54 – 55

Lesser Antilles
56

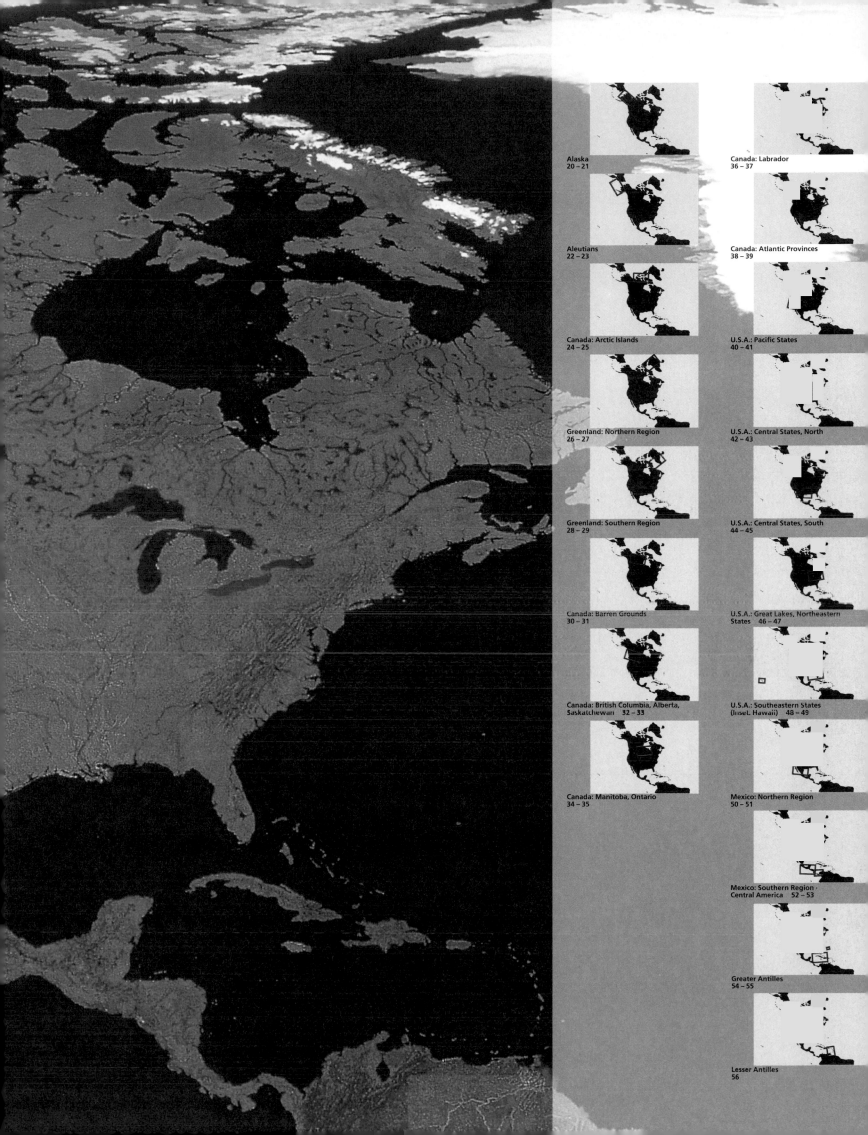

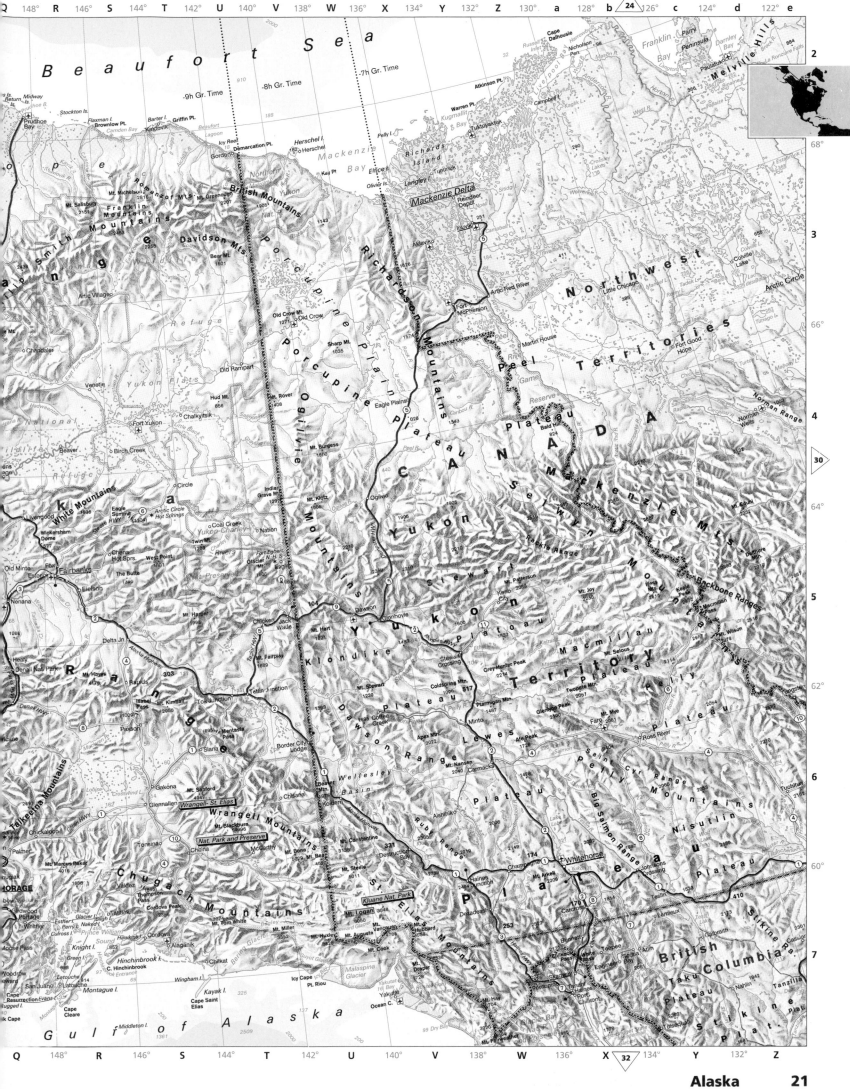

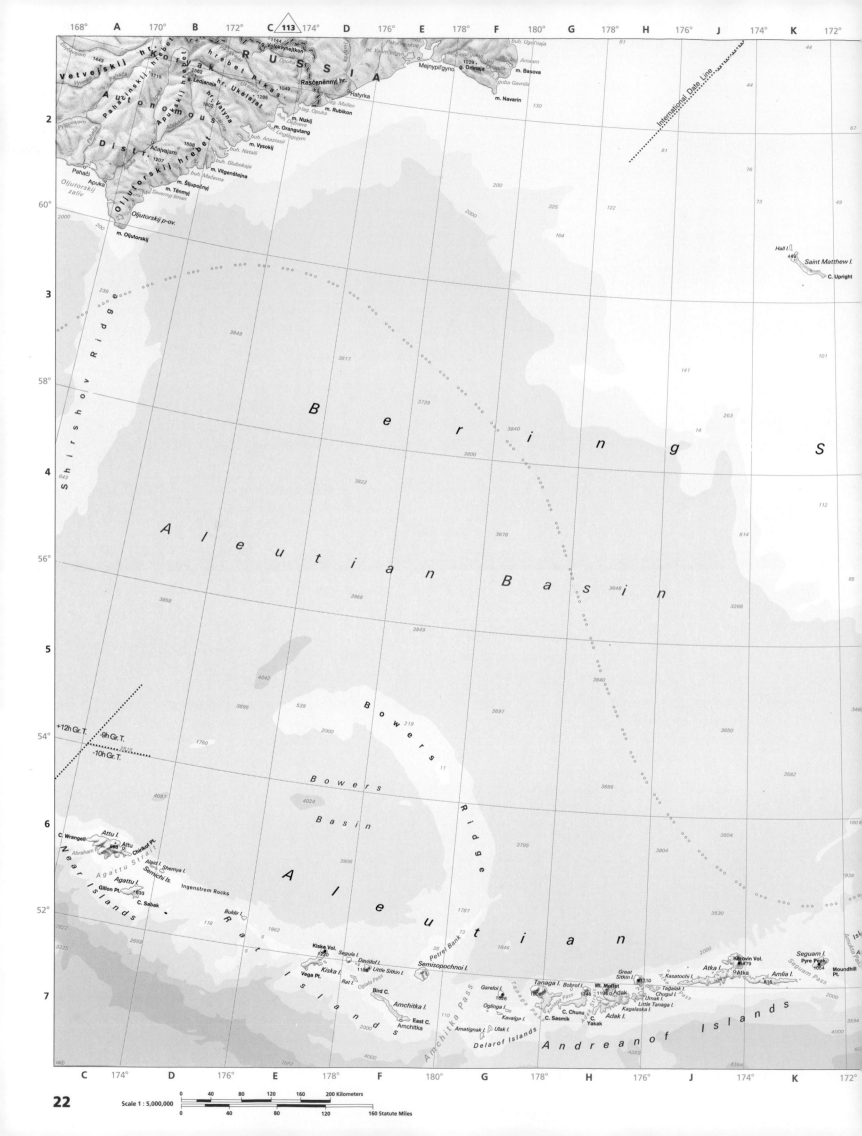

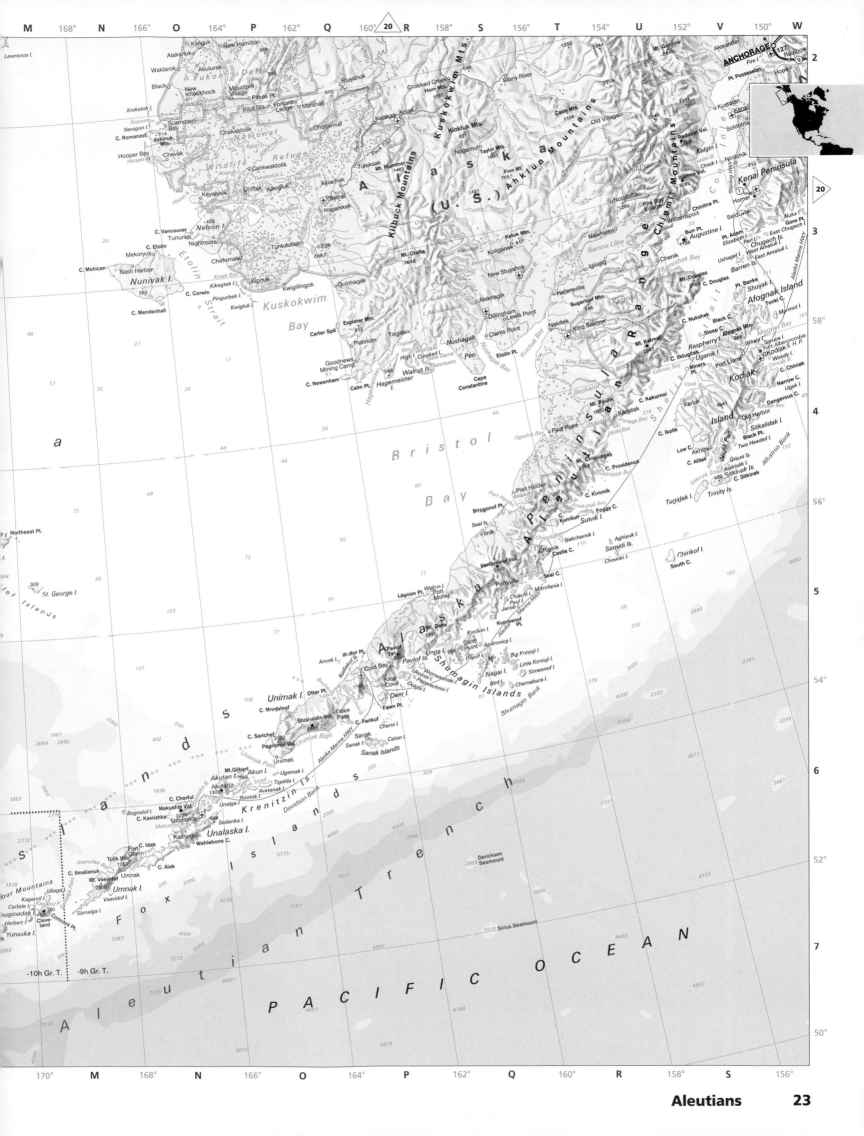

-8h Gr. Time -7h Gr. Time

A R C T I C

Canada Basin

O C E A N

76°
74°
72°
70°
68°
66°

Prince Gustav Adolf Sea

C. Isachsen
Isachsen Pen.
Ellef Ringnes
Deer Bay
Noice Pen.

C. Malloch

Borden Island 152

Brock I.
C. Murray
C. Leopold M'Clintock
C. Ludlow Rich
C. Hemphill
C. Scott
C. George Richards

Wilkins Strait

Mackenzie King Island 457

Emerald Isle 481

Hazen Strait

Findlay Group

Lougheed Island 248
Edmond Walker I.

Maclean Strait

Cameron I.

Vanier I.
Massey I.
Alexander I.

Byam Martin Channel

Q U E E N

Prince Patrick Island

Griffiths Pt.
Blossom
C. Manning
C. Mecham

Mould Bay 274
Dyer Bay

Eglington I. 152
Canrober Hills 562

C. Russell

Hecla and Griper

Sabine Pen.

Blue Hills 1067

M e l v i l l e   I s l a n d

Bailey Pt.
C. James Ross

Dundas Peninsula
Mt. Hamelin 335
Winter Harbour

Donett Pt.
Weatherall Bay
Sabine Bay

Walker Baldwin Ra.

Byam Martin 152

P a r r y   I s l a n d s

Cape Prince Alfred

Cape Wrottesley 512

Burnett Bay
Bernard I.

Bernard R.

B a n k s

Storkerson Bay
Meek Point

Thesiger Bay

Cape Kellett
Sachs Harbour 13

Cape Lambton 782

I s l a n d

457

Passage Pt.
Peel Pt.
Barnard Pt.

C. Elvira
Elvira I.

C. Storkerson 152

Stefansson Island

Goldsmith Channel

Storkerson Peninsula

M'Clintock Channel

C. John

Prince of Wales Strait

Deans Dundas B.

Prince Albert Peninsula

Berkeley Pt.
Walker B.
Fort Collinson

Wynniatt Bay

Narkusiak Pen.

Hadley Bay

Cape Cardwell
Cape Peter Richards

Minto Inlet

Shaler Mountains

640

V i c t o r i a

Amundsen Gulf

Cape Dalhousie
Baillie Is.
Cape Bathurst

Russell Inlet
Nicholson Pen.

Liverpool Bay

Franklin Bay

Parry Peninsula

Cape Parry
Booth Is.
Cape Parry

Darnley Bay

Paulatuk

Diamond Jennes Peninsula
Holman Island

Cape Pfarmigan
Albert Islands

Cape Lyon

Deas Thompson Pt.
Clinton Point
Brock Pt.

Melville Hills

Prince Albert Sound

Wollaston Peninsula

Mt. Bumpus 516

C. Stang
C. Michelsen

I s l a n d

Collins

Cape Baring

Clifton Pt.

Cape Young
C. Hope

Bluenose L.

Dolphin and Union Strait

Simpson Bay

Camping L.
Lady Franklin Pt.
Locker Pt.

Richardson Is.

Turnagain Pt.

Cambridge Bay

Dease Strait

140

Mt. George 183

Melbourne I.

Jenny Lind I.

N o r t h

Coville Lake
Arctic Circle

Coppermine
Berens Is.
Lawford Is.
Richardson Bay
Jameson Is.

C. Kendall
Duke of York Arch.
Northwest Passage

C o r o n a t i o n   Gulf

Kent Peninsula

Queen Maud

w e s t

C

A

N

Banks Pen.
Barry

Whitebear Pt.

Campbell Bay

Ritch I.
Dease Arm

Smith Arm

C. McDonnel
Ekka I. 552

Great Bear Lake

McTavish Arm

Kokeragl Pt.
Etacho Pt.

Fort Franklin
Fox Pt.

Pt. Leith
Sawmill Bay
Richardson I.
Fort Radium

Bathurst Inlet
MacAlpine Lake

21
30

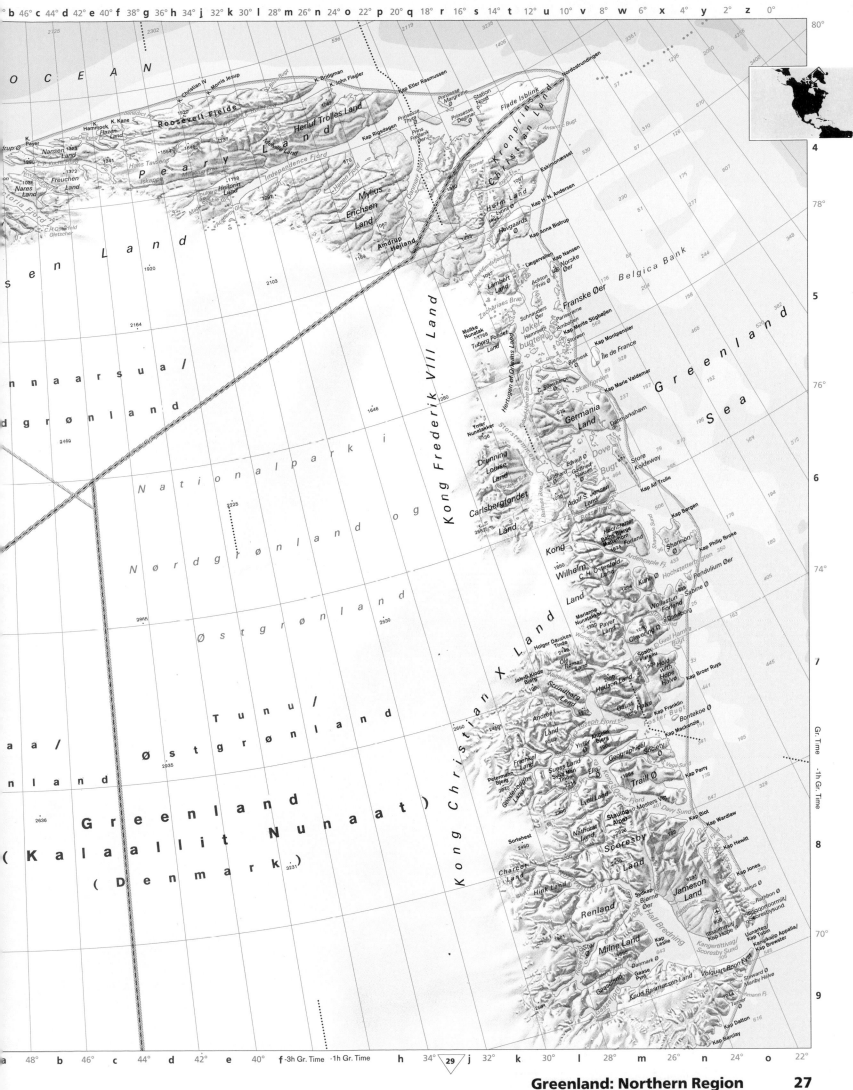

OCEAN

Christian IV · K. Morris Jesup
K. Benedict
Hammock K. Kane
Hozen
K. Payer
Roosevelt Fjelde
Nansen Land
1341 1372
Freuchen Land
Peary Land
Herluf Trolles Land
Melville Land
Hans Tavsens
Iskappe
Heilprin Land
Independence Fjord
Mylius Erichsen Land
Amdrup Højland

K. Bridgman
J. John Flagler
Kap Etter Rasmussen
Prinsesse Margrethe
Prinsesse Thyra
Prins Frederik Se
Kap Rigsdagen
Nordostrundingen
Station Nord
Flade Isblink
Kronprins Christian Land
Hovgaards
Kap Anna Bistrup
Kap H. N. Andersen
Holm Land
Lyon's
Eskimonæsset

sen Land Land

nnaarsua /
dgrønland

Ø s t g r ø n l a n d

Nationalpark i
Nørdgrønland og
Østgrønland

T u n u /
Ø s t g r ø n l a n d

G r e e n l a n d
(K a l a a l l i t N u n a a t)
(D e n m a r k)

Kong Frederik VIII Land

Kong Christian X Land

Greenland Sea

Germania Land
Danmarkshavn

Dronning Louise Land
Carlsbergfondet Land

Kong Wilhelm Land
C. H. Ostenfeld Land
Payer Land
Hochstetter Forland
Shannon Ø
Kap Philip Broke
Pendulum Øer
Hochstetterbugten
Kurm
Wollaston Forland
Sabine Ø
Clavering Ø

Holger Danckes Tinde
Ole Rømer Land
Spath Plateau
Hold With Hope
Halve
Kap Broer Ruys
Kap Franklin
Bontekoe Ø
Kap Mackenzie

Andrée Land
Ymer Ø
Suess Land
Ella Ø
Traill Ø
Geographical Society Ø
Kap Parry

Petermann Bjerg
Frænkel Land
Sortehest
Stauning Alper
Nathorst Land
Lyell Land
Davy Sund
Kap Biot
Kap Wardlaw
Kap Hewitt

Charcot Land
Hinks Land
Renland
Milne Land
Scoresby Land
Jameson Land
Kap Leslie
Kap Hope
Kangertittivag/
Scoresby Sund
Ittoqqortoormiit/ Scoresbysund
Kap Tobin
Kap Brewster
Volquart Boon Kyst
Knud Rasmussen Land
Kap Dalton
Kap Barclay

80°
4
78°
5
76°
6
74°
7
Gr. Time
-1h Gr. Time
8
70°
9

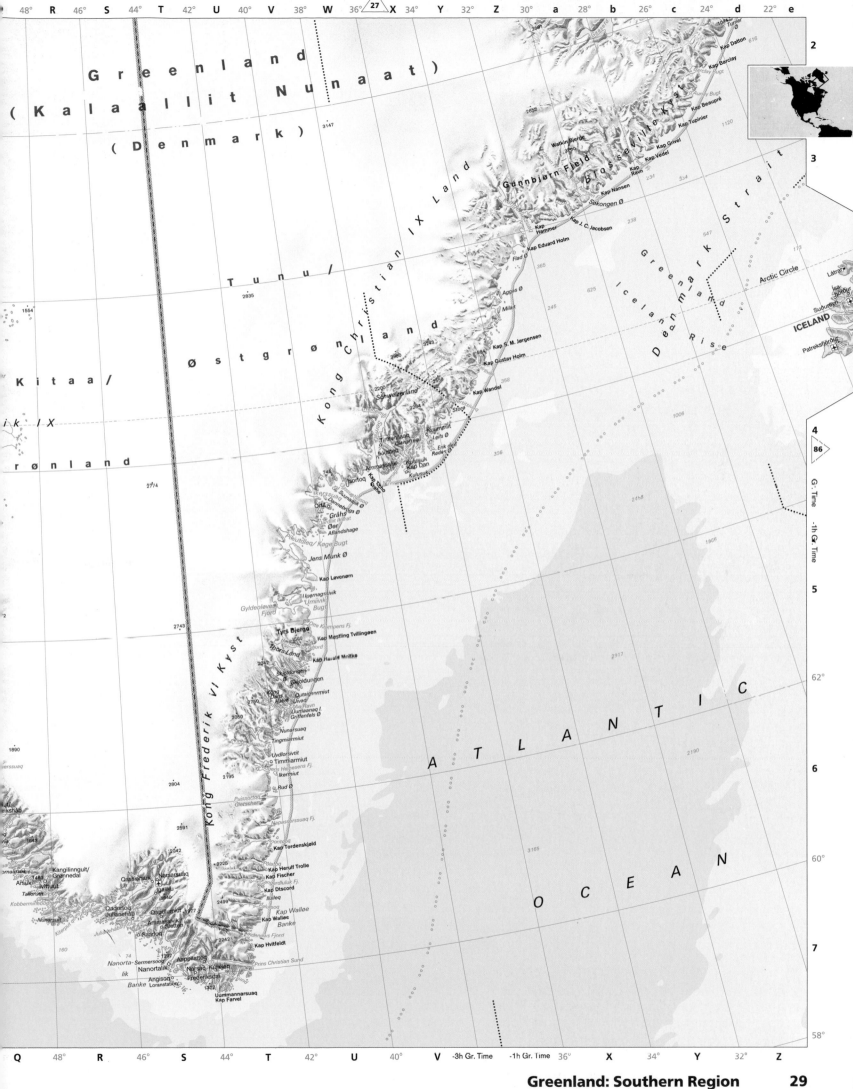

Greenland
(Kalaallit Nunaat)

(Denmark)

Tunu /

Østgrønland

Kitaa /

ik IX

rønland

Kong Christian IX Land

Gunnbjørn Field

Blosseville Kyst

Watkin Bjerge

Kap Nansen
Søkongen Ø
Kap J. C. Jacobsen
Kap Hammer
Kap Eduard Holm
Flad Ø

Aggas Ø
Milait

Kap S. M. Jørgensen
Kap Gustav Holm

Schweizerland
Kap Wandel
Storø

Tiniteqilaaq
Qaarmiit
Ikkatteq
Ammassalik
Jaortoq
Kulusuk Kap Dan
Kulusuk
Kap Dan

Kuummiit
Leifs Ø
Erik den Rødes

Kangeq
Sælvirsiag Ø
Grähs Ø
Ørli Ø
Hvidit Ikerat
Øer
Aflandshage

Pikiutdleq / Køge Bugt

Jens Munk Ø

Kap Løvenørn

Ikernagssivik
Umiivik
Bugt
Gyldenløves
Fjord
Otte Krumpens Fj.

Tyrs Bjerge
Kap Møsting Tvillingøen
Thors Land
Kap Harald Moltke

Skjoldungen
Ø Skjoldungen
Qutaigenrmiut
Kong
Oscar
Havn
Uivaq
Umanaq I.
Griffenfels Ø

Nunarsuaq
Tingmiarmiut

Uvdlorsivtit
Timmiarmiut
Iens Henesens Fj.
Ikermiut

Rud Ø

Puisortoq
Gletscher

Napassorssuaq Fj.

Kap Tordenskjøld
Kap Herull Trolle
Kap Fischer
Kanderdluluk Fj.
Kap Discord
Iluileq

Kong Frederik VI Kyst

Kap Walløe
Banke

Kap Walløe
Kap Hvitfeldt

Kangilinnguit / Grønnedal
Qassianuk
Narssarsuaq
Igaliku
Ivittuut
Arsuk
Talloruit
Qaqortoq
Julianehåb
Qagdlupat
Igdluuaq
Saarloq

Kobberminehytt

Nunarssuit

Nunarta- Sermersooq
Nanortalik
lik
Nanortalik
Banke
Appilattoq
Angisoq
Loranstation
Narsaq Kujalleq
Frederiksdal

Uummannarssuaq
Kap Farvel

Prins Christian Sund

Greenland
Rise
Denmark Strait
Iceland Rise

Arctic Circle

ICELAND
Látrar
Ísafjörður
Suðureyri
Patreksfjörður

ATLANTIC

OCEAN

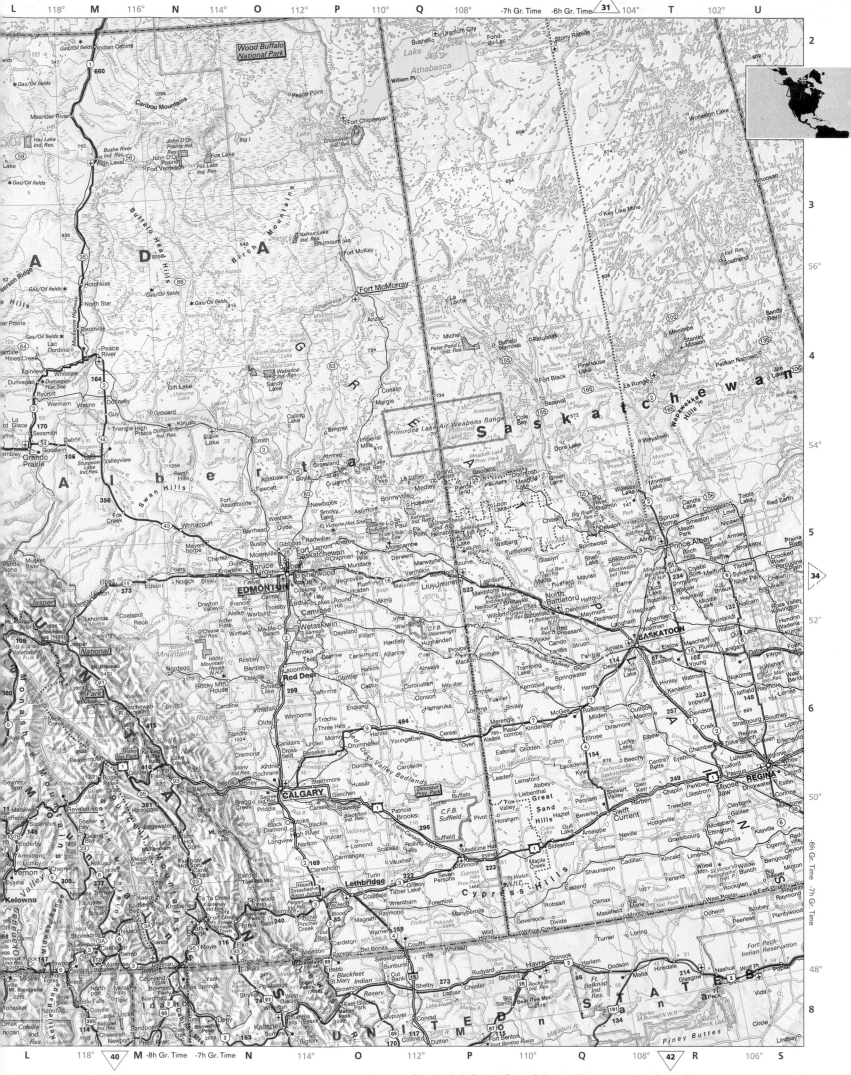

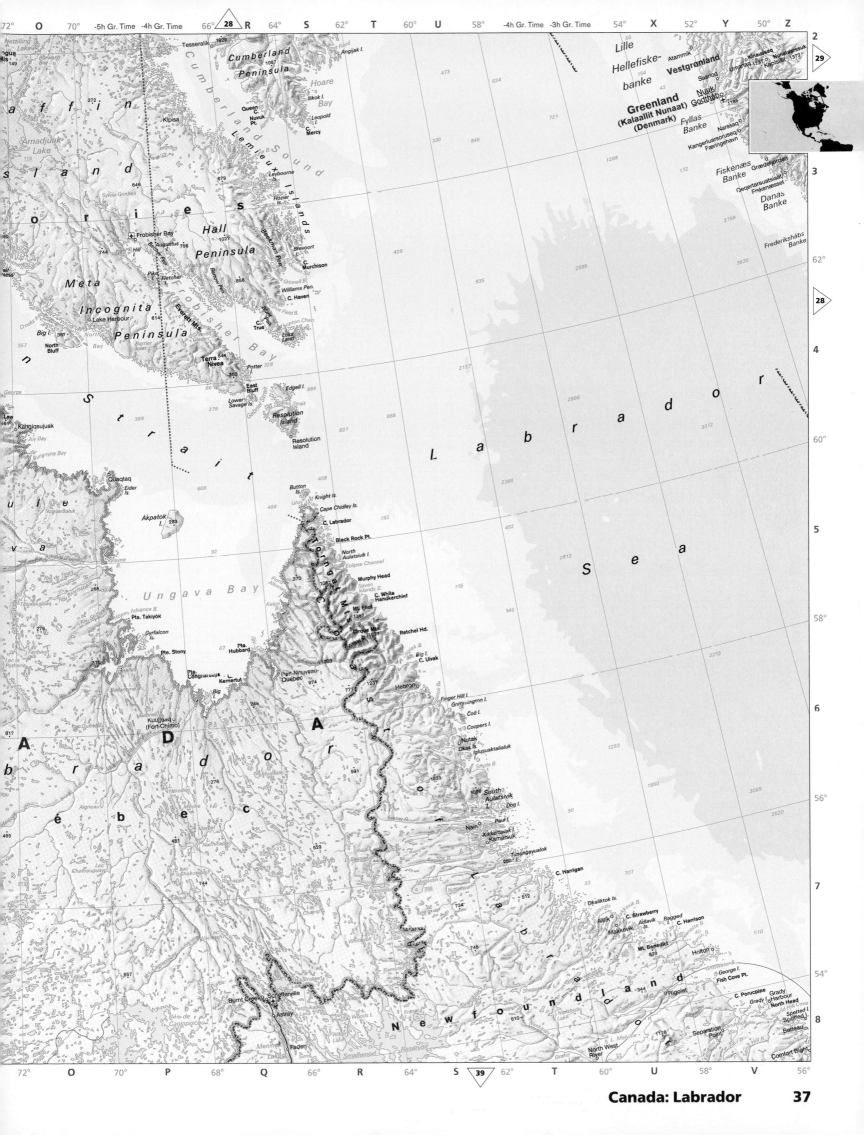

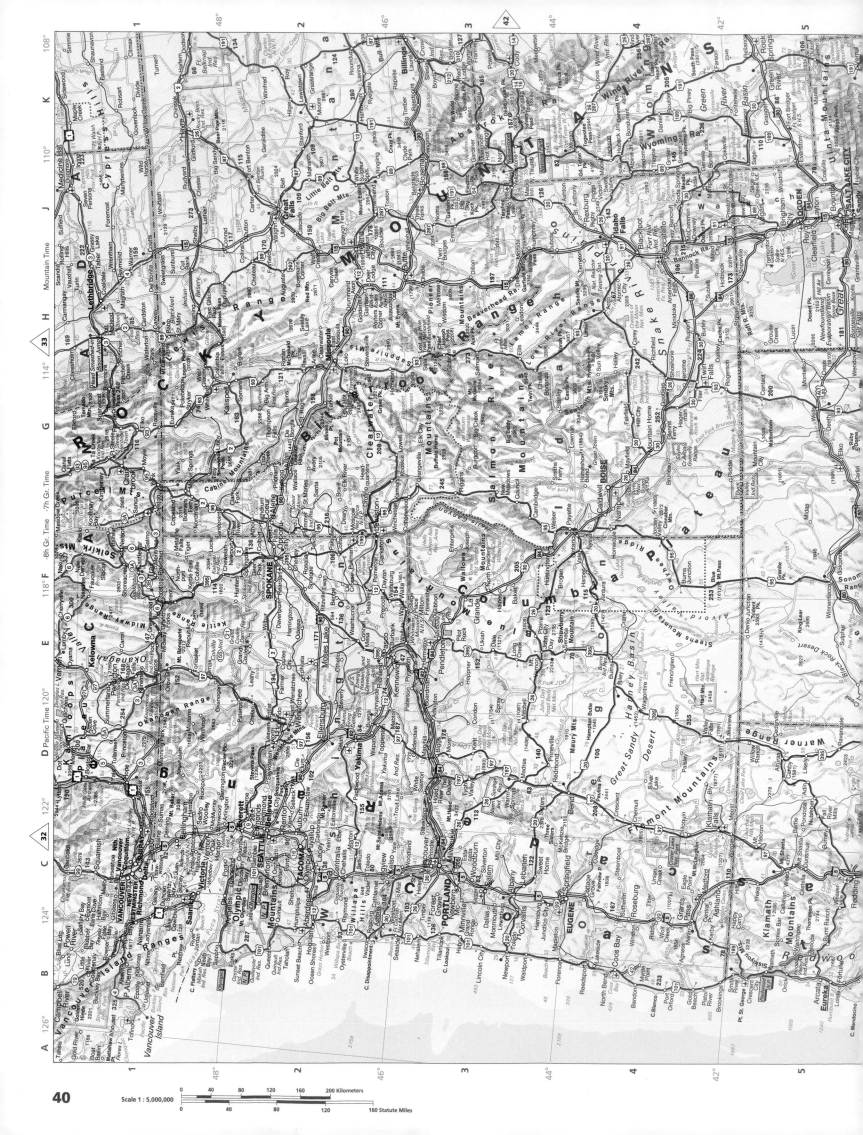

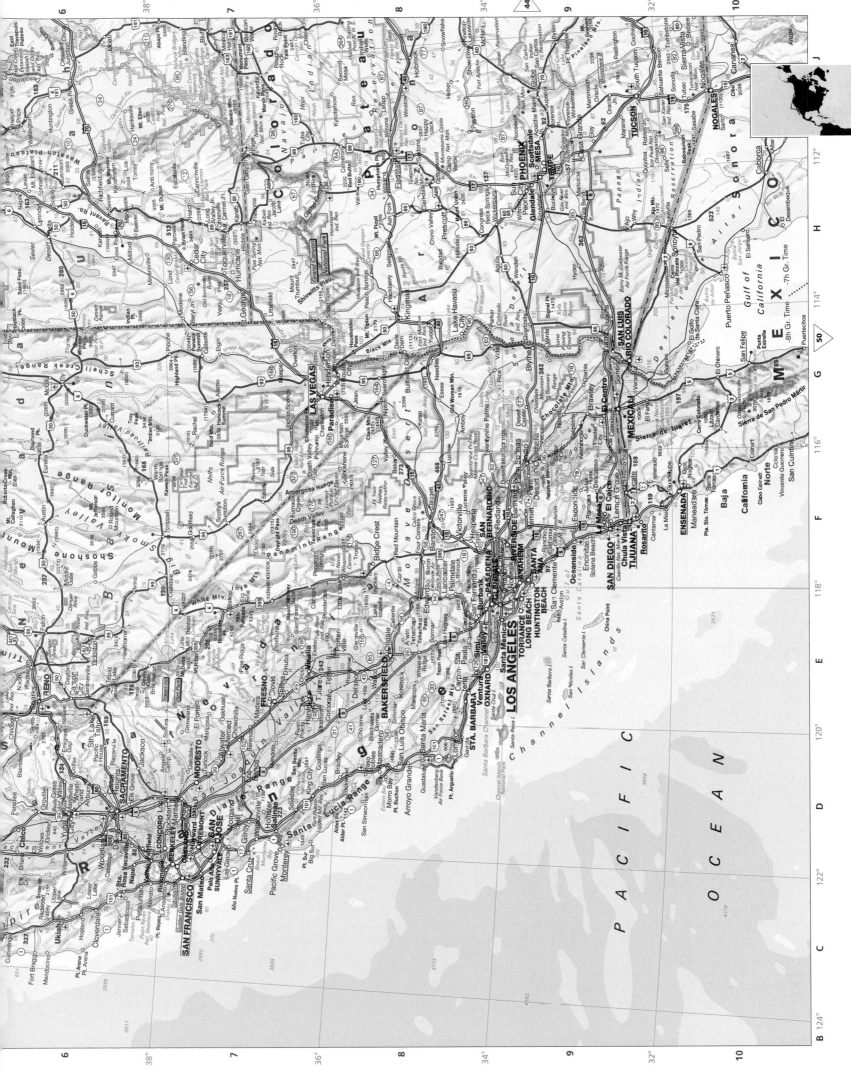

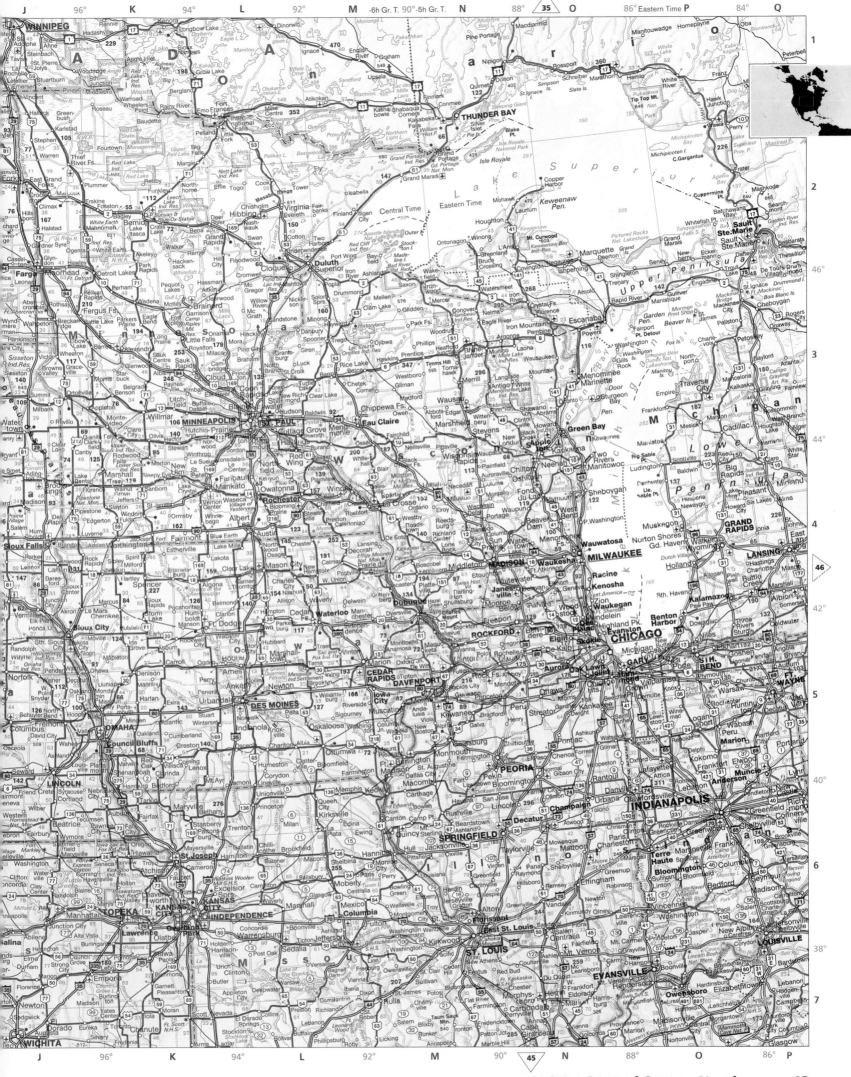

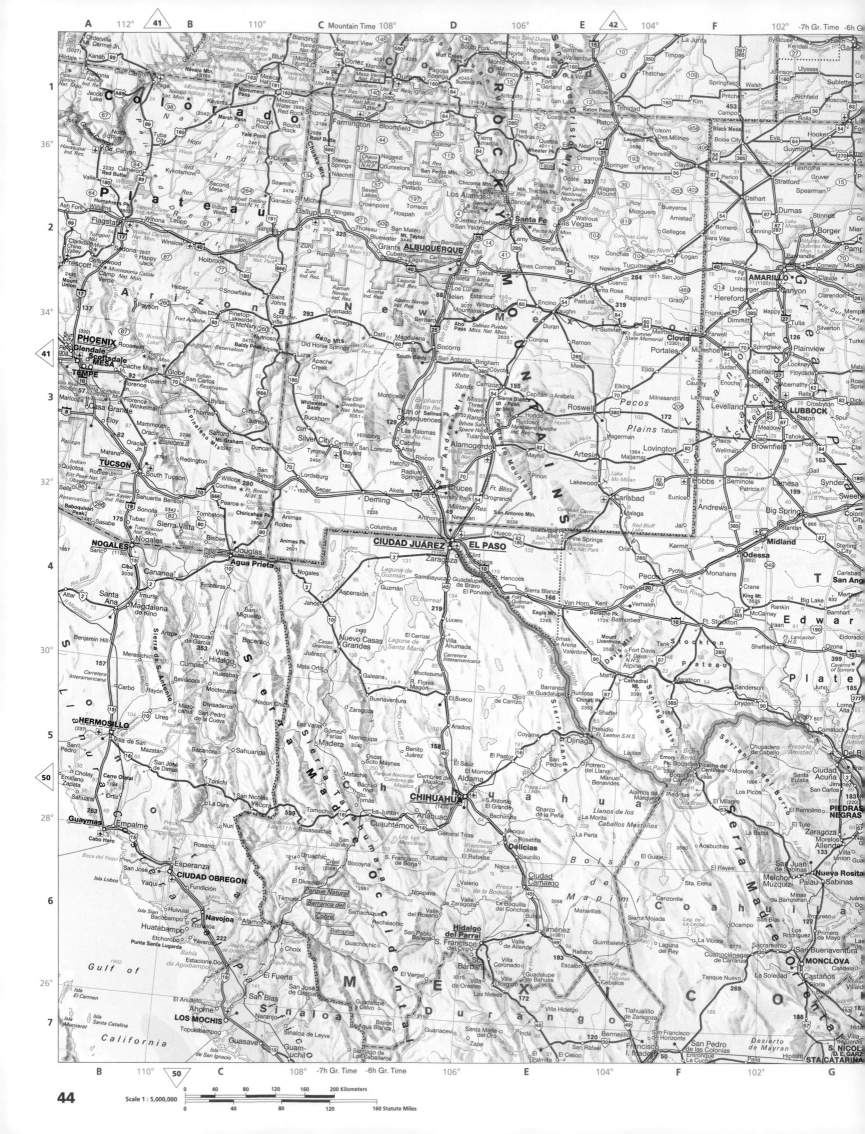

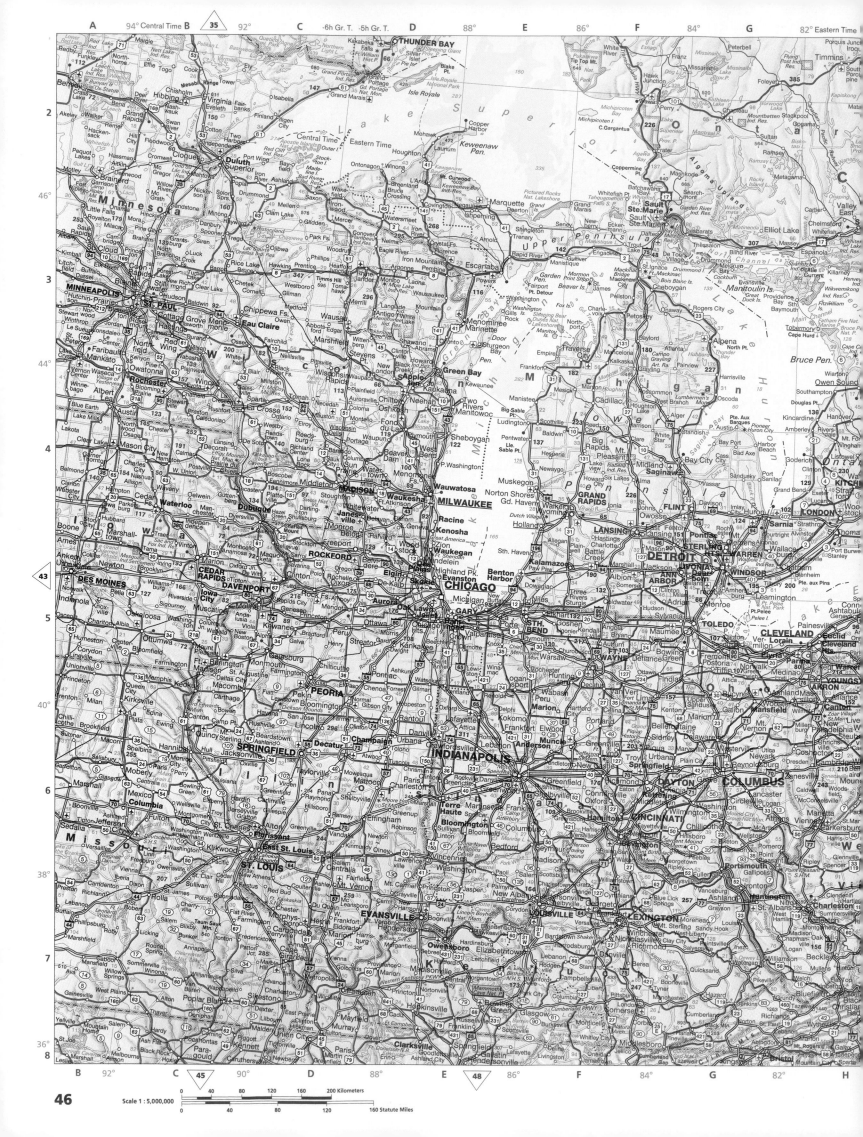

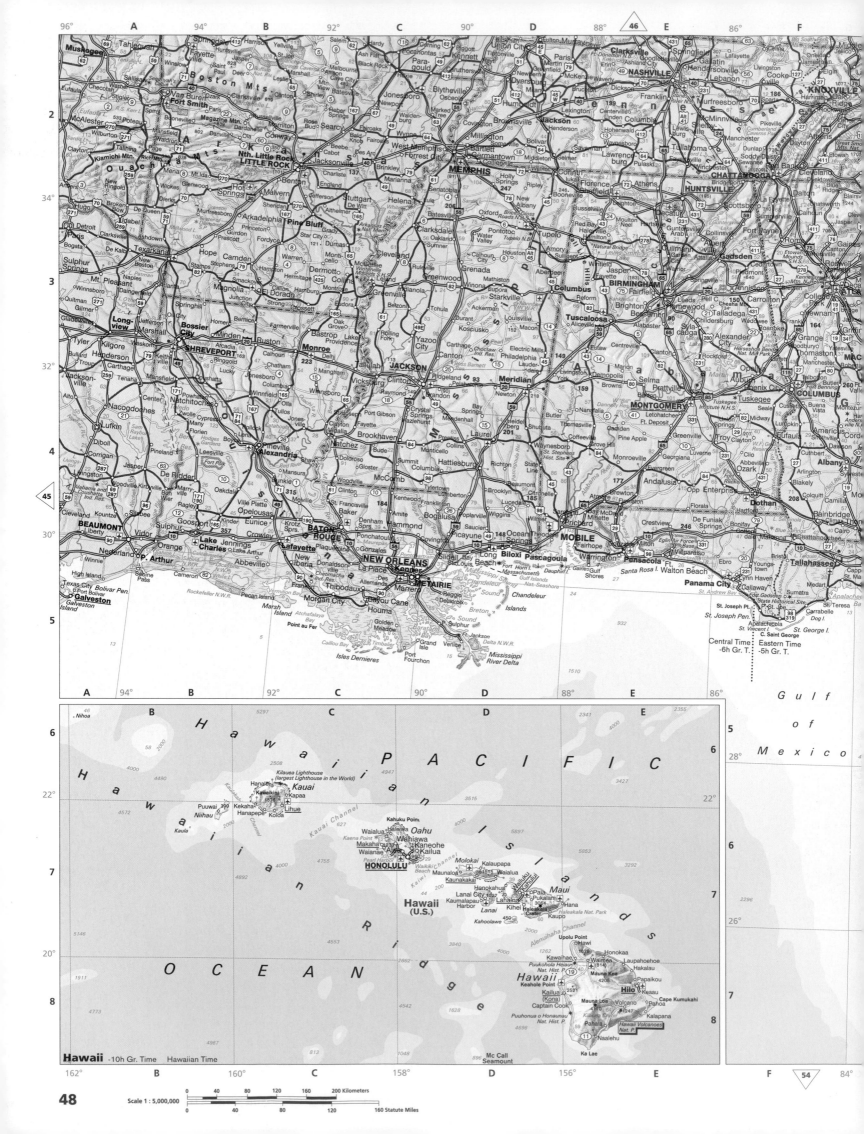

Scale 1 : 5,000,000

Revilla Gigedo Islands

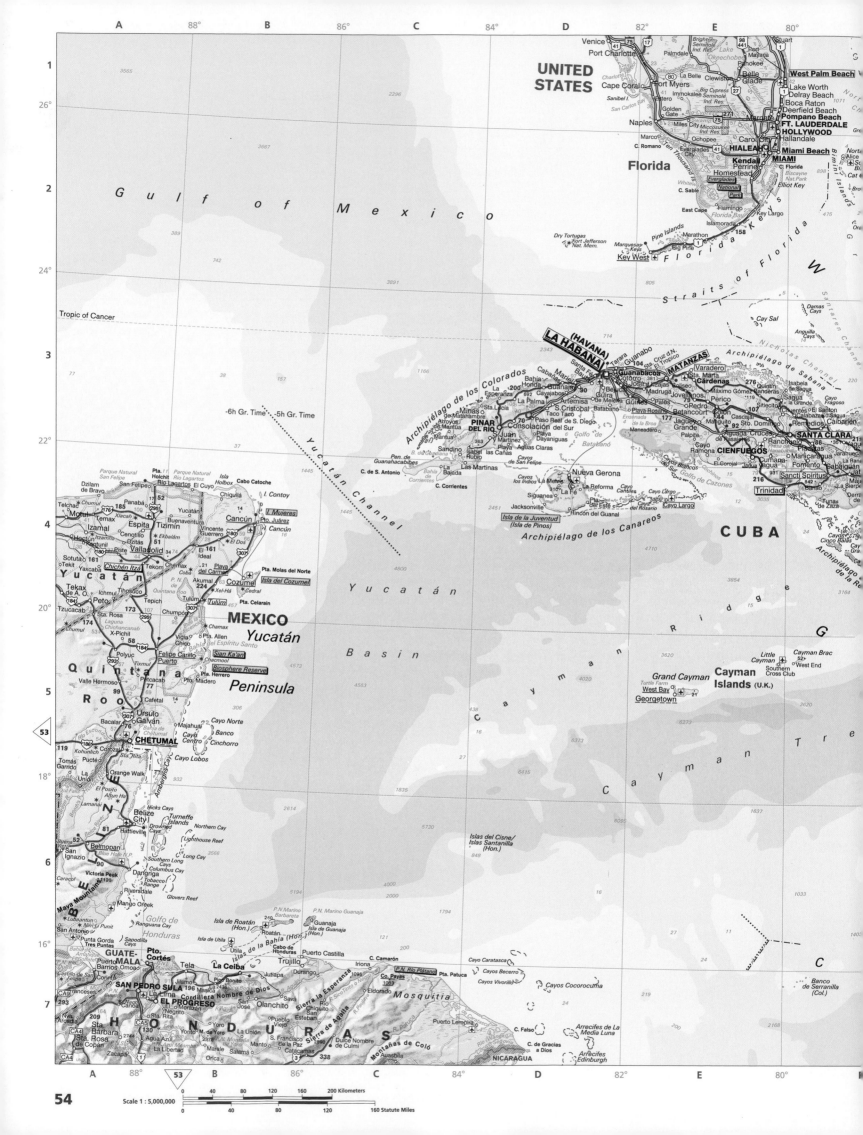

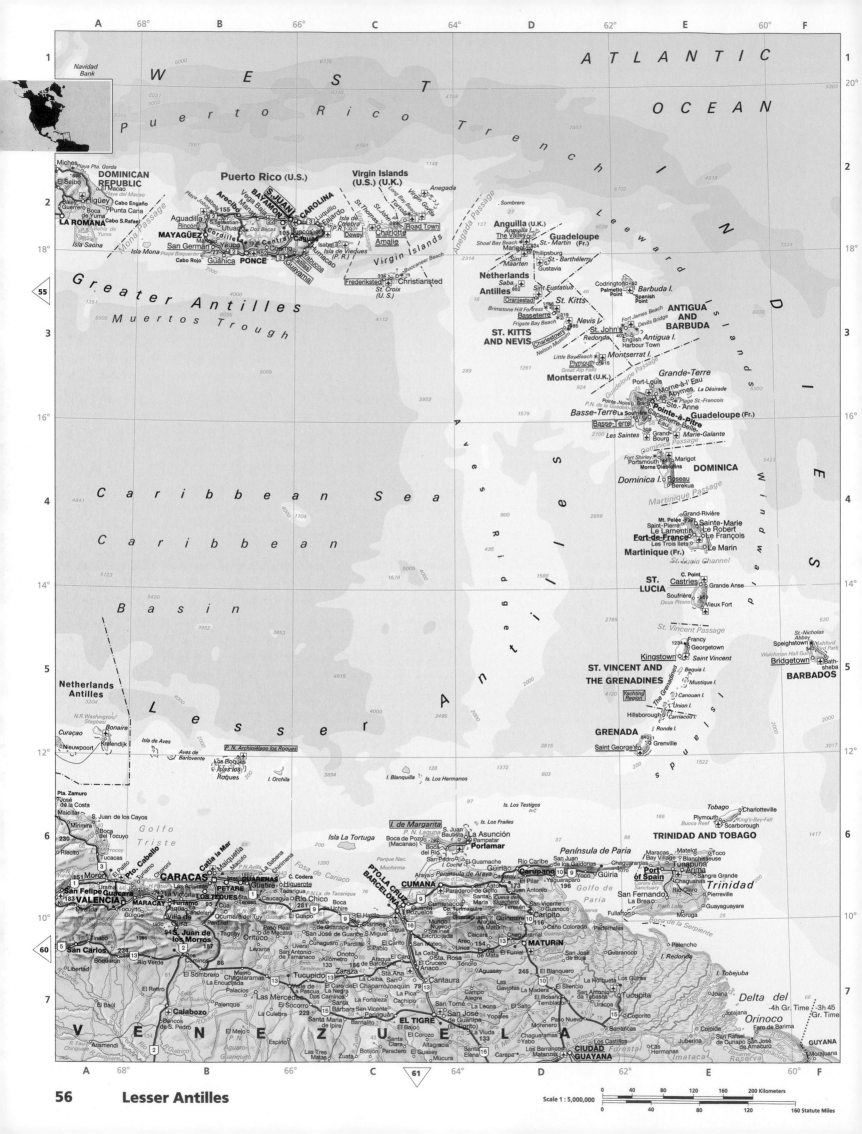

South America – continent of natural variety

Since most of South America's 6,872,580 square miles (17.8 million sq. km) are located in the Southern Hemisphere, it is considered a southern continent, like Africa. The continent is even connected with the Antarctic via the Southern Antilles and submarine rises. With the exception of the polar ice region, all climatic and vegetation zones are represented on the continent; the tropical climate is predominant, however. The western part of the continent is characterized by the volcano-studded mountain range of the Cordilleras de Los Andes, which is close to 4,660 miles (7,500 km) long and reaches a height of almost 23,000 feet (7,000 m). Parallel to them runs a continuous deep-sea trench in the Pacific Ocean. Over half

An early documentation of inter-cultural encounter: Zacharias Wagner created this depiction of an Indian dance during his sojourn in Brazil (1634–37) and subsequently published it in his "Bestiary."

of the continent's land mass is taken up by the giant lowlands of the Orinoco, the Amazon and the Paraná. Adjacent to the southeastern coast is a broad continental shelf cresting in the Falkland Islands (called Islas Malvinas by Argentina). More animal and plant species are found in South America than anywhere else in the world: More than 250 of the 350 known flowering plant families originate there; it is home to one-third of all bird species; and the number of insect species is beyond estimation. The Amazon Basin not only is the largest river region on Earth but also contains the greatest area of tropical forest.

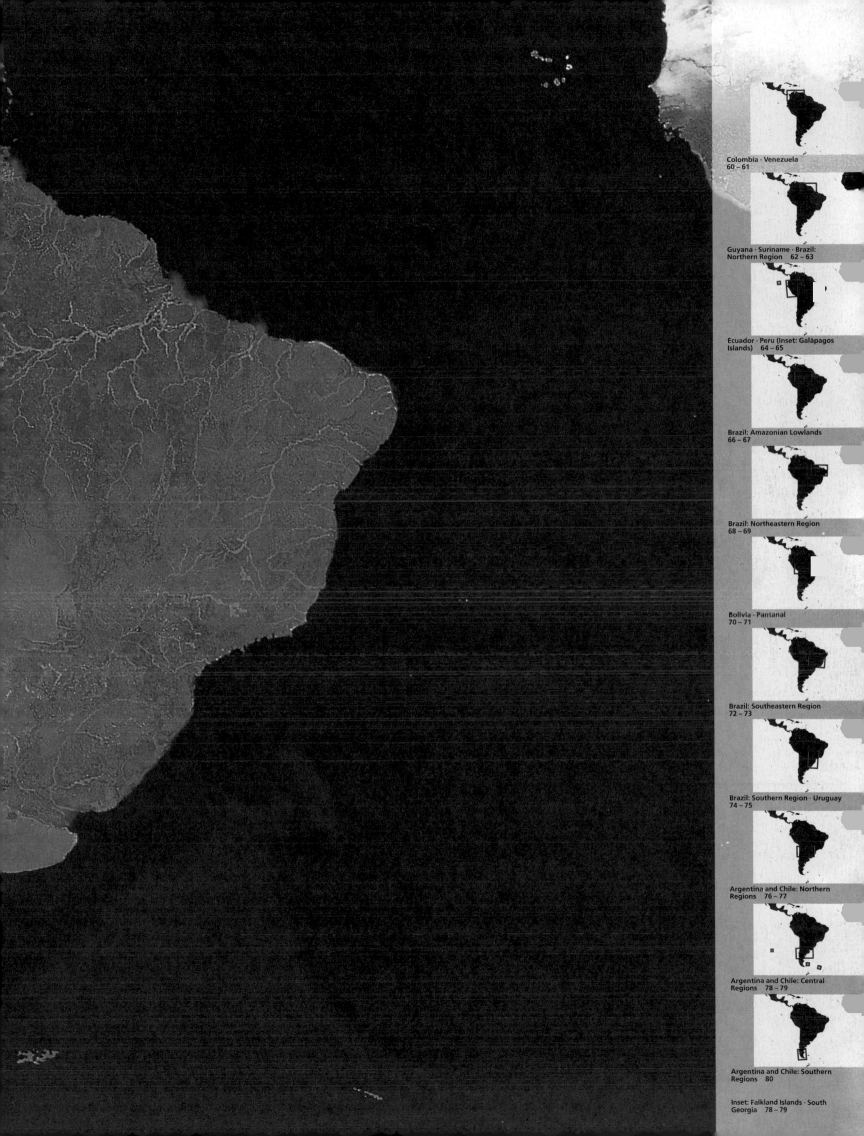

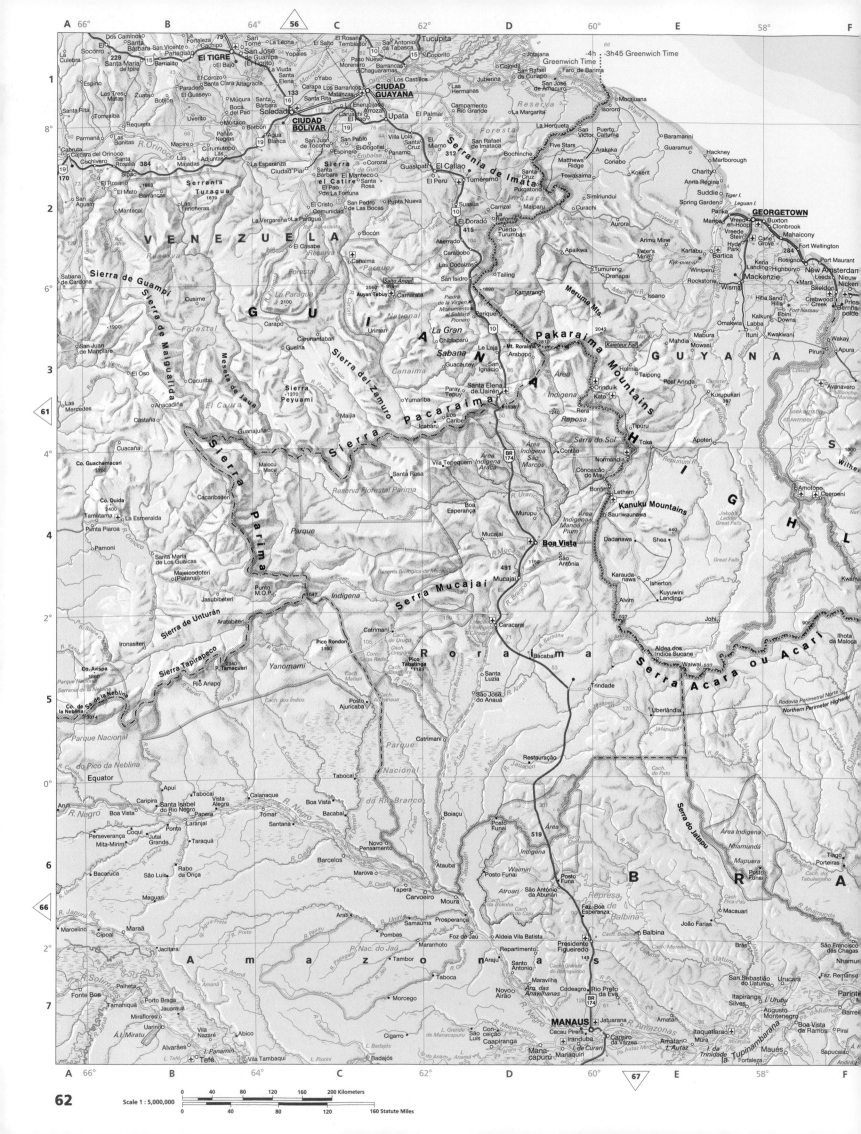

Scale 1 : 5,000,000

0   40   80   120   160   200 Kilometers

0   40   80   120   160 Statute Miles

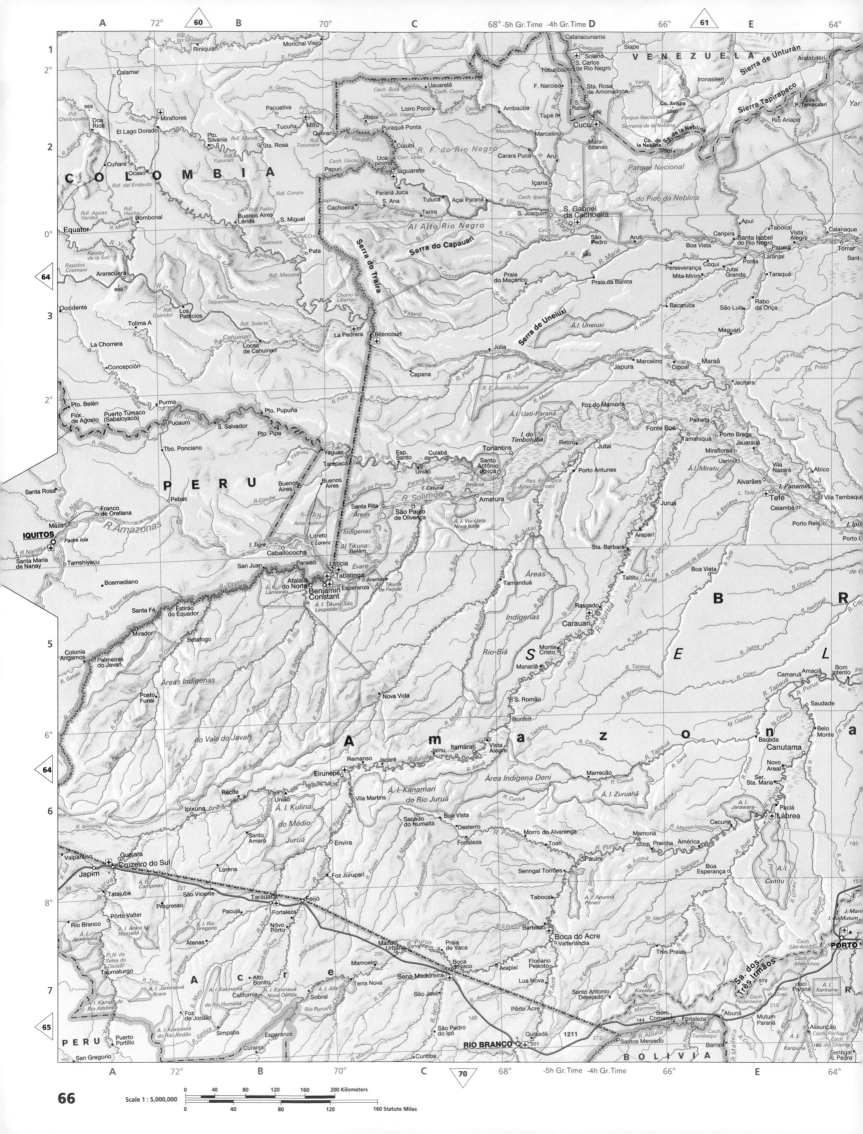

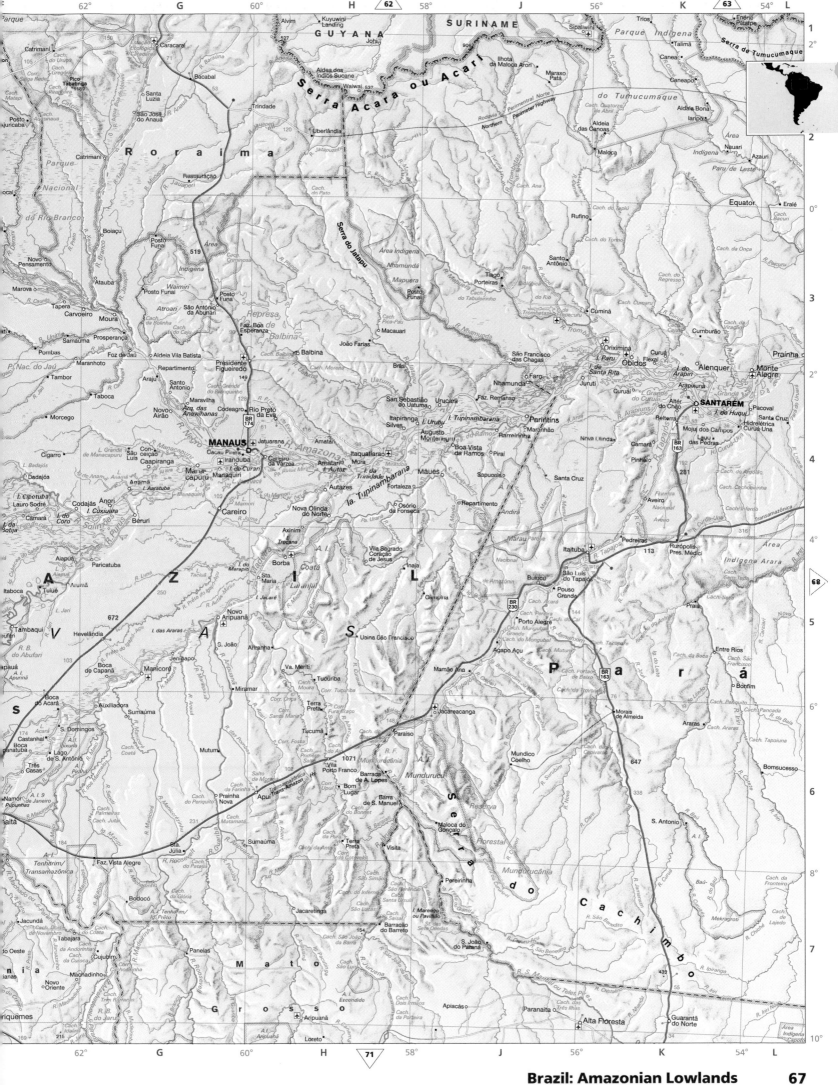

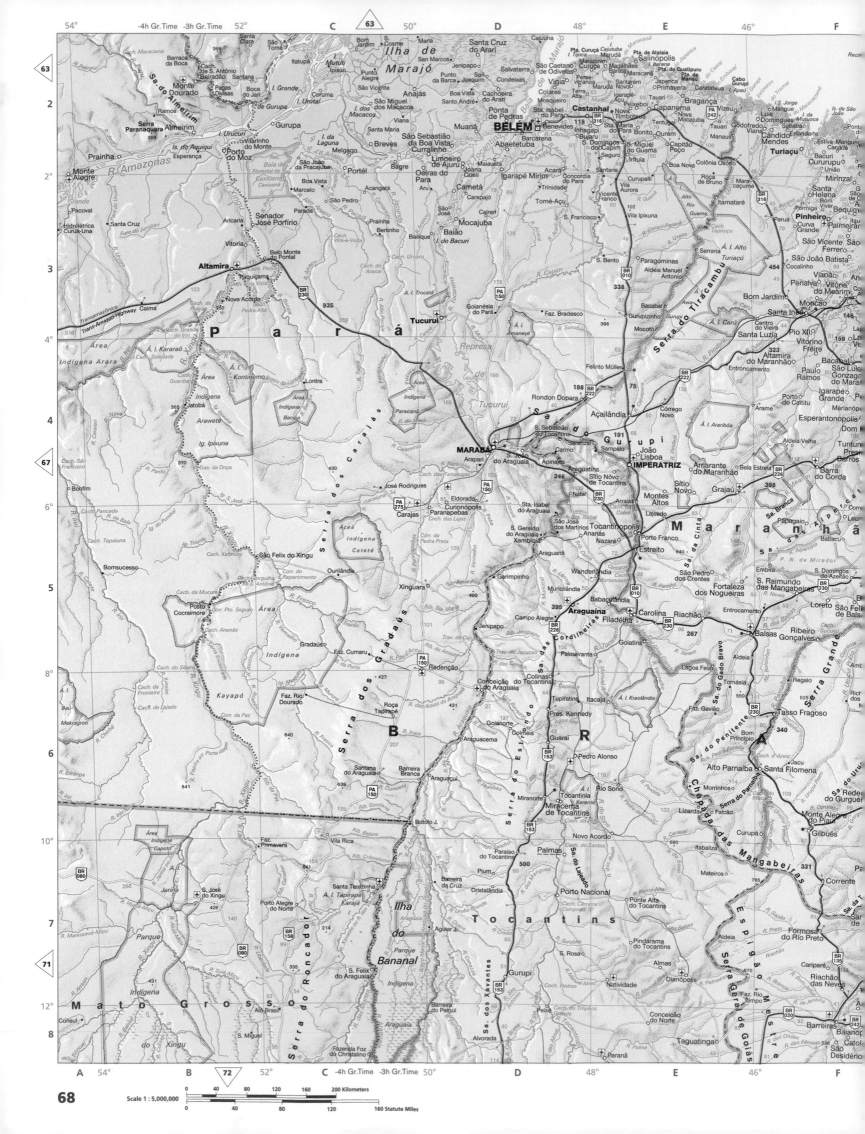

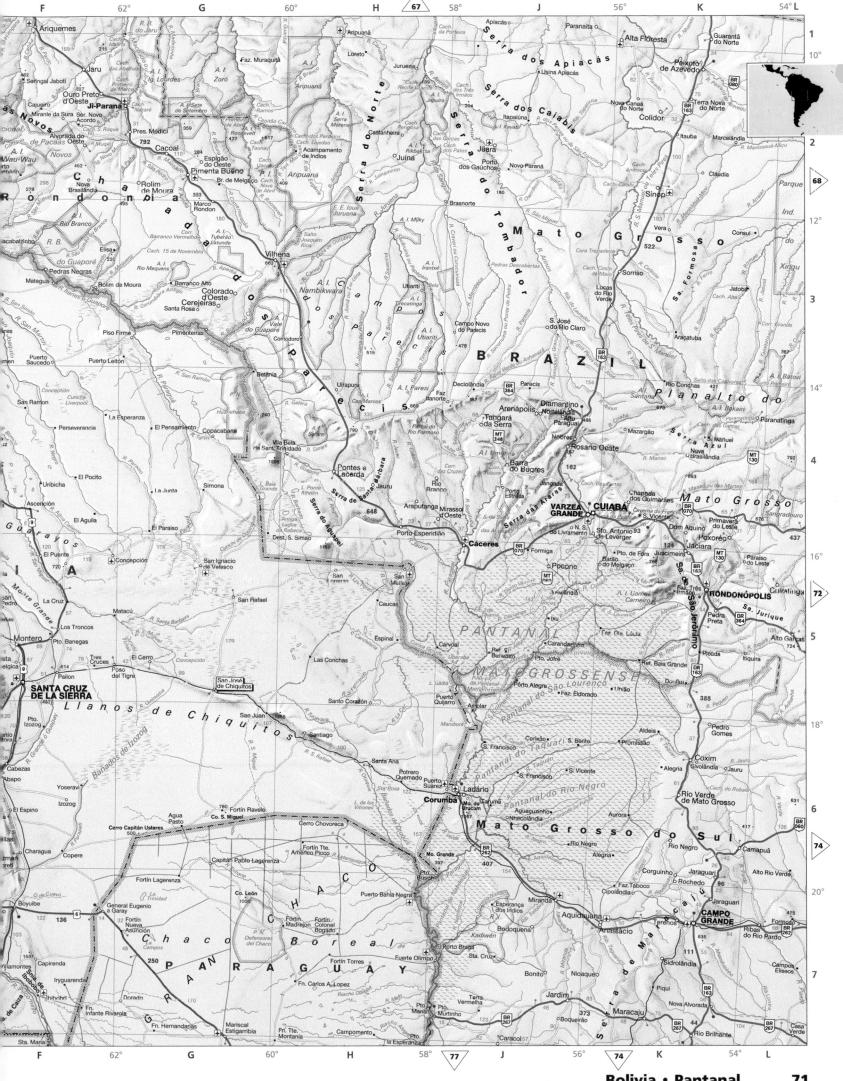

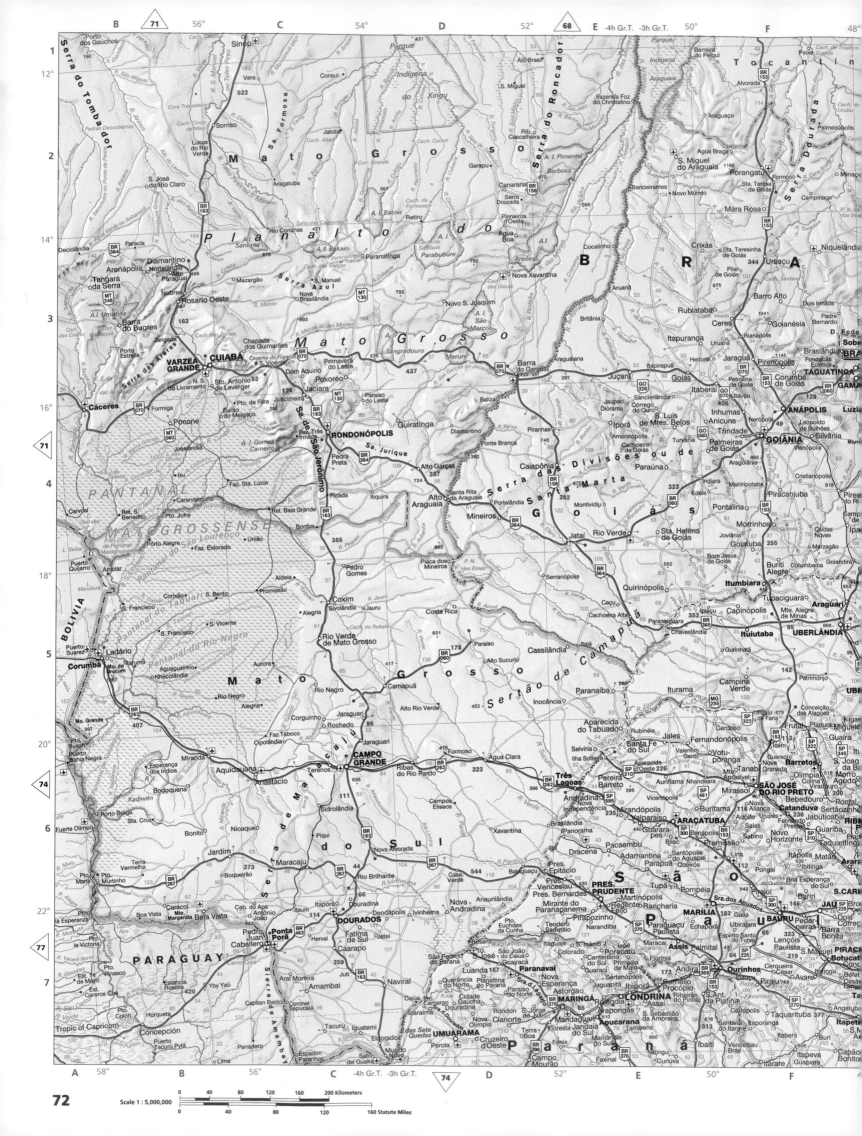

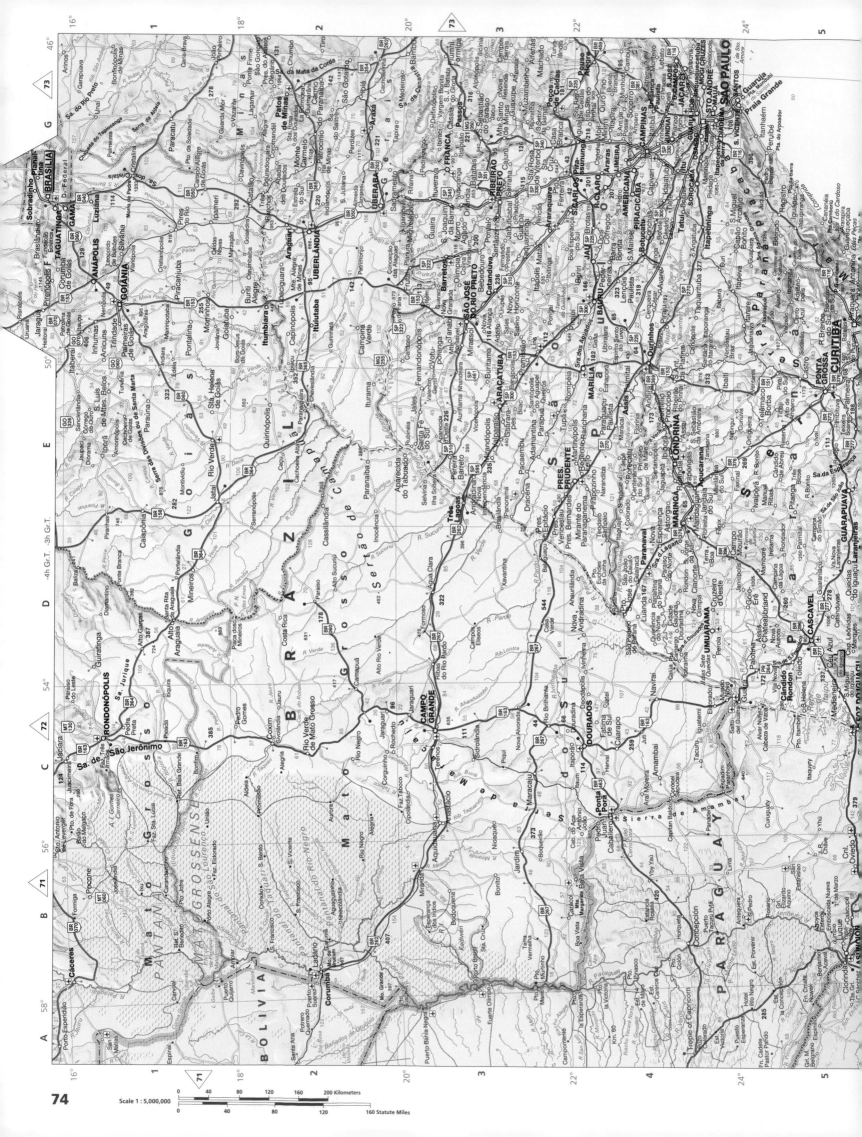

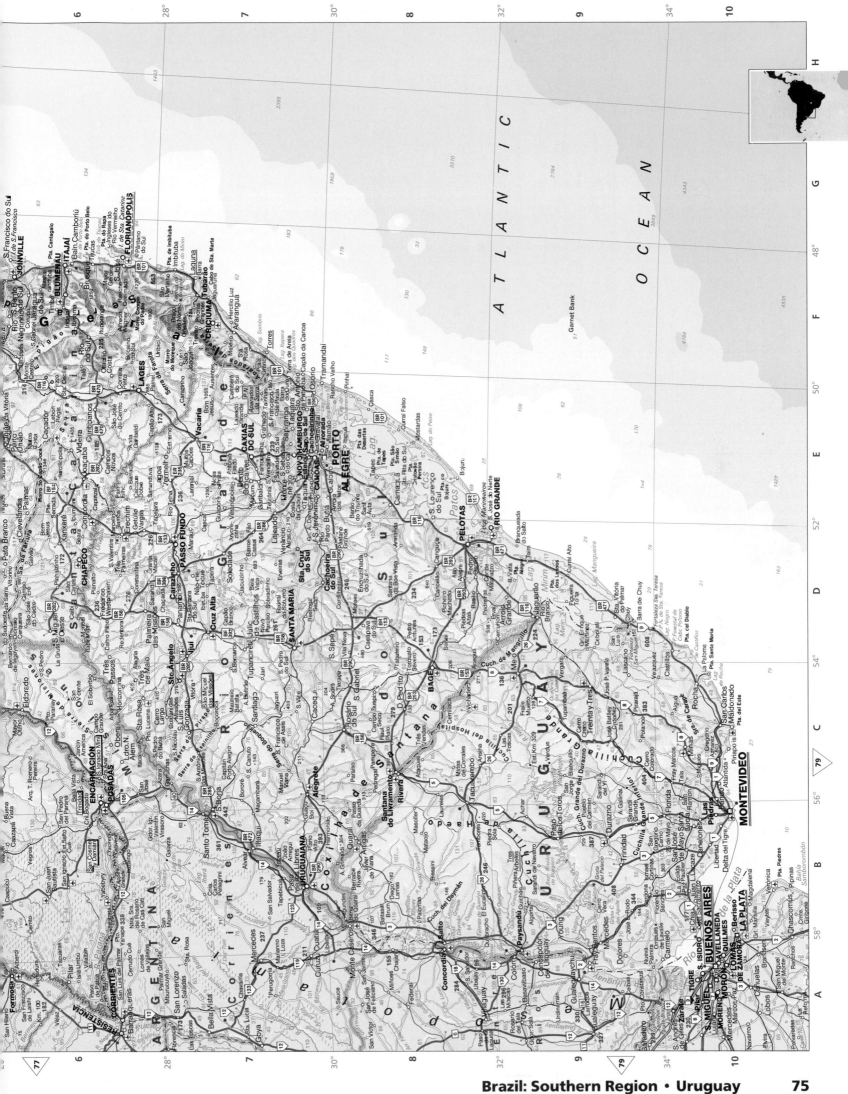

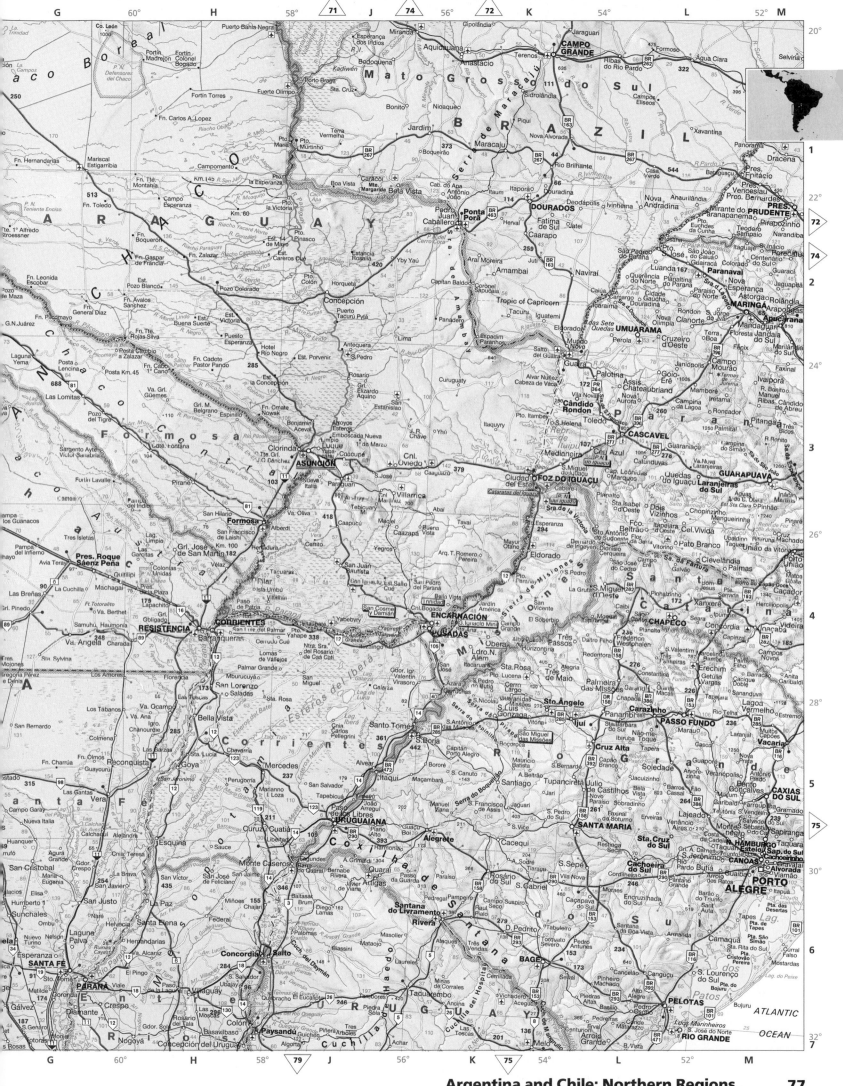

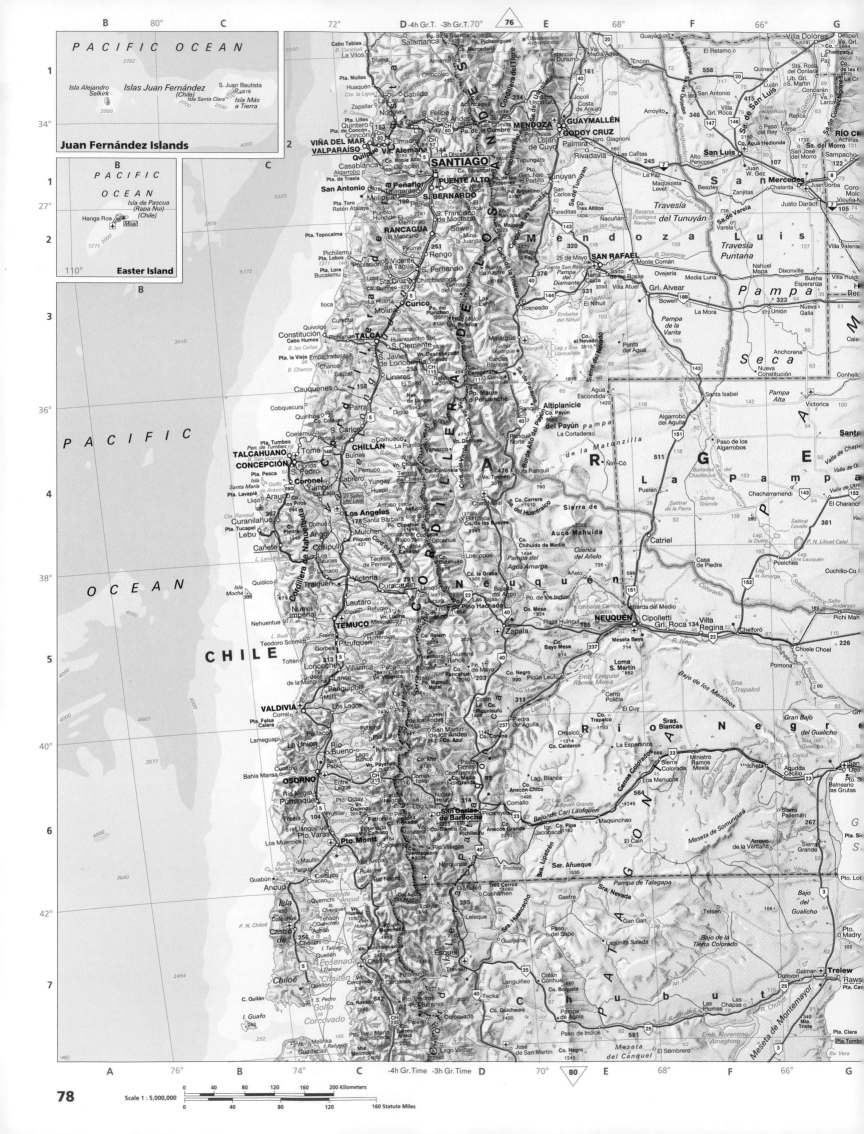

Argentina and Chile: Southern Regions

Scale 1 : 5,000,000

Europe – a continent of shifting political borders

With an area of 4,054,050 square miles (10.5 million sq. km), Europe is the fourth largest continent. From the point of view of physical geography it merely represents a peninsula of Eurasia, jutting out to the west. Europe and Asia have the least defined boundary among all continents. The traditional borderline runs along the Ural Mountains, the Ural River, the Caspian Sea, the northern edge of the Caucasus, the Black Sea, the Bosporus and the Aegean Sea. In Russia, which is part European and part Asian, this demarcation line is meaningless. A belt of high mountains in which the Alps are the highest range separates the South from the remainder of the continent. Adjacent to the North is the European

An aid to international trade: "New Map of Europe" including "the most noteworthy products and the foremost trading sites." J. Adams made this copperplate engraving in 1787.

medium-height mountainscape followed by a strip of lowlands that widens to the East. The British Isles are, geologically speaking, also part of the northern mountain areas. Its many islands and peninsulas interlace the continent with the Atlantic Ocean and the European Mediterranean Sea. Europe determined the destiny of the western world some years into the twentieth century: The scientific research of the planet, the industrial revolution, great inventions and discoveries, but also colonization and thus the transmission of European influences to other parts of the world had their origins here.

Svalbard · Novaya Zemlya
84 – 85

Scandinavia (Inset: Iceland)
86 –87

Finland · Northern Ural Mountains
88 – 89

Western Europe
90 – 91

Central Europe
92 – 93

Eastern Europe
94 – 95

Ural Mountains
96 – 97

Southwestern Europe
98 – 99

Southern Europe
100 – 101

Southeastern Europe
102 – 103

Caucasus
104

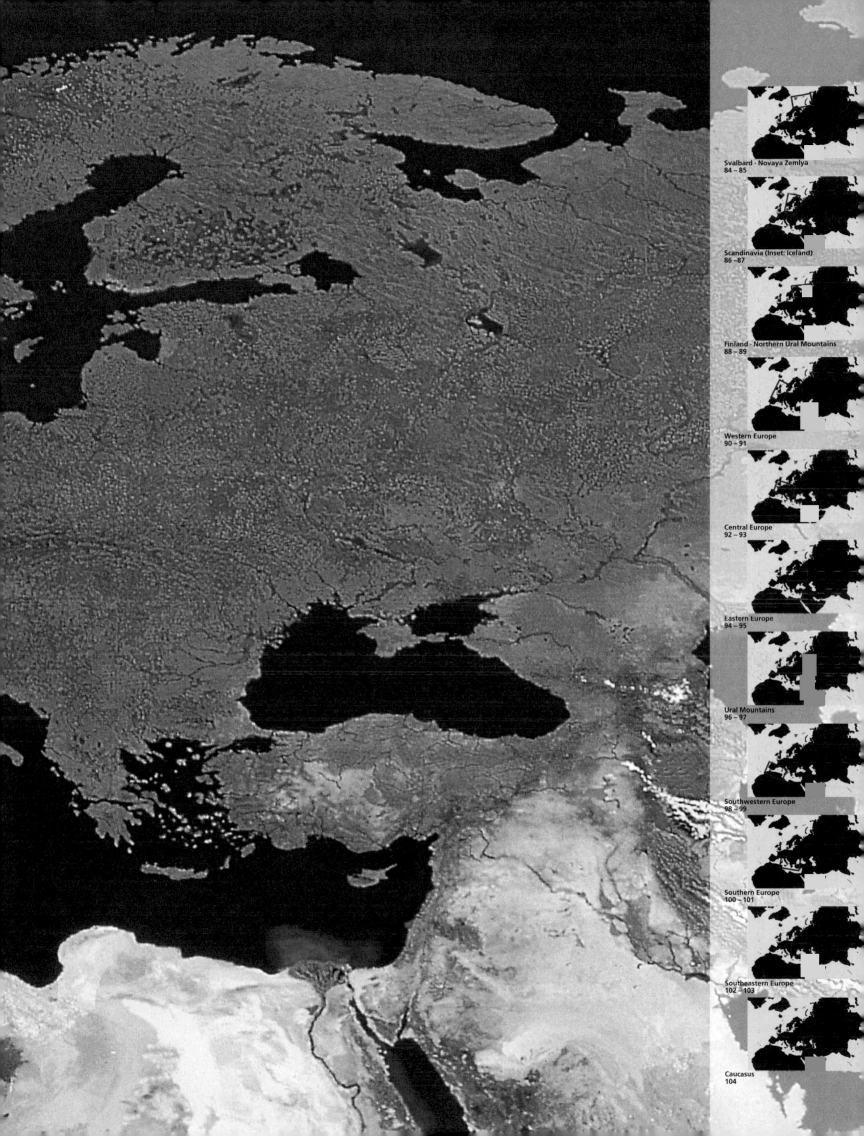

Greenwich Time +1h Greenwich Time

A R C T I C

+1h Greenwich Time +3h Gr. Time +4h Greenwich Time

Greenland Sea

Danskøya
Verlegen-huken
Phippsøya
Nordkapp
Parryøya
Sjuøyane
Martensøya
Kapp Platen

Fuglehuken
Ny-Ålesund
Longyearbyen
Prins Karls Forland
Daudmannsodden

Gustav V land
Nordaust-Svalbardnationalpark
Nordaust-Svalbardlandet

Spitsbergen

S v a l b a r d (Norway)

Olav V land

Kapp Laura
Storøya

Newtontoppen
1717

Kvitøya (Nor.)
Nasrelva

o. Viktorija (Rus.)

Isfjord Radio
Isfjorden
Barentsburg
Grønfjorden
Pyramiden

Hestberget
Barentsøya

Erik Eriksenstretet
Nordaust-Svalbard nat-res

Svenskøya
Kongsøya
Abeløya

Lågneset
Bellsund

Wedel Jarlsberg land
Tusen land

Kong Karls land

Boltodden
Storfjorden
Edgeøya
Stonepynten

Øyrlandsodden
Sørkappøya

Tjuvfjorden
Halvmåneøya

Storfjordrenna
Storfjordbanken

Hopen Radio
Hopen
370

Hopen banken

Bjørnøya Bank

Bjørnøy Radio
Bjørnøya (Nor.)
Tunheim
Perleporten

N o r w e g i a n

B a r e n t s

S e a

S e a

London

Fugløy Bank

Knivskjelodden
Magerøya
Nordkapp
Skarsvåg

Hammerfest
Havøysund
Rolvsøya

Mehamn
Gamvik

Sørøya
Breivikbotn
Hasvik

Kjøllefjord
Nordkinnhalvøya

Berlevåg
Båtsfjord

Andenes
Bergen
Kvaløy
Tromsø

Alta
Lakselv
Rastigaissa

Varangerhalvøya

Vardø
Vadsø

N O R W A Y
Finnmarksvidda

Hurtigrute

Murmanskoye Rise

Narvik

F I N L A N D

R U S S I A

Kirkenes
Nikel
Zapoljarnyj
Murmansk

Poljarnyj

S W E D E N
Kebnekaise

North Kap

Scale 1 : 5,000,000

0 40 80 120 160 200 Kilometers

0 40 80 120 160 Statute Miles

86

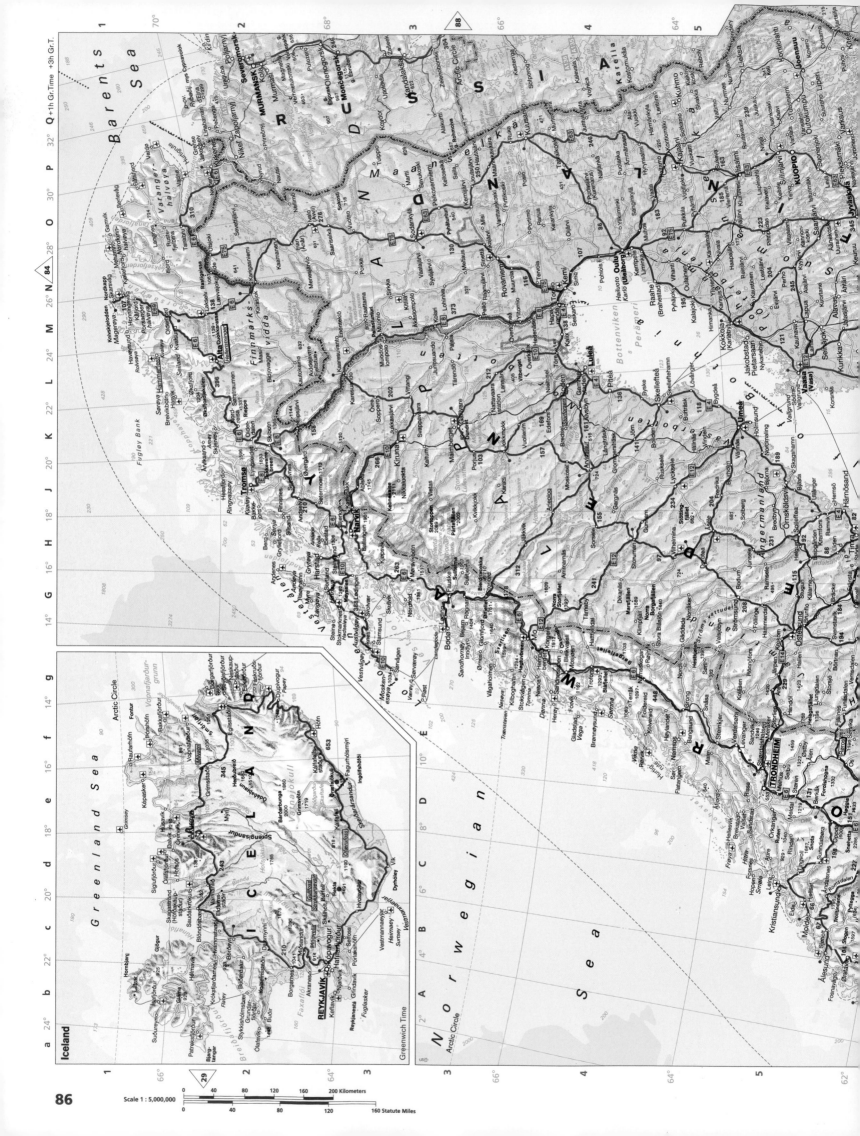

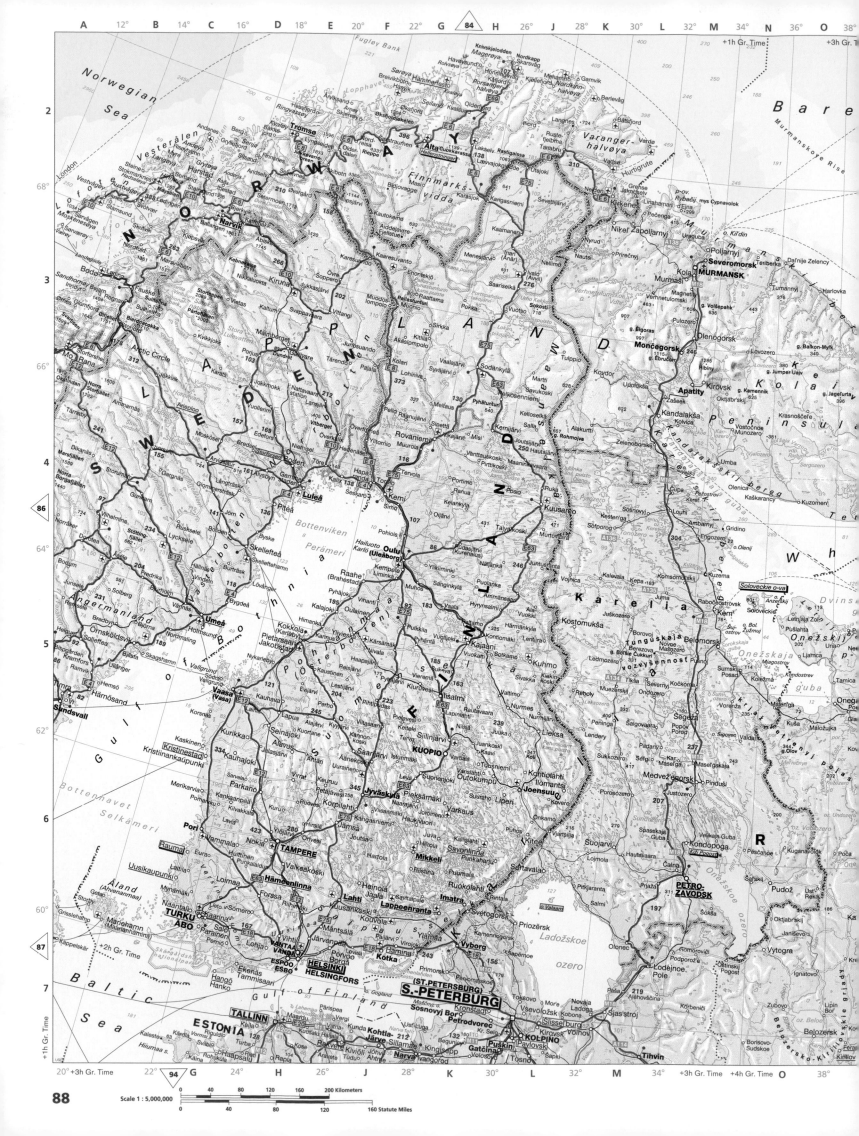

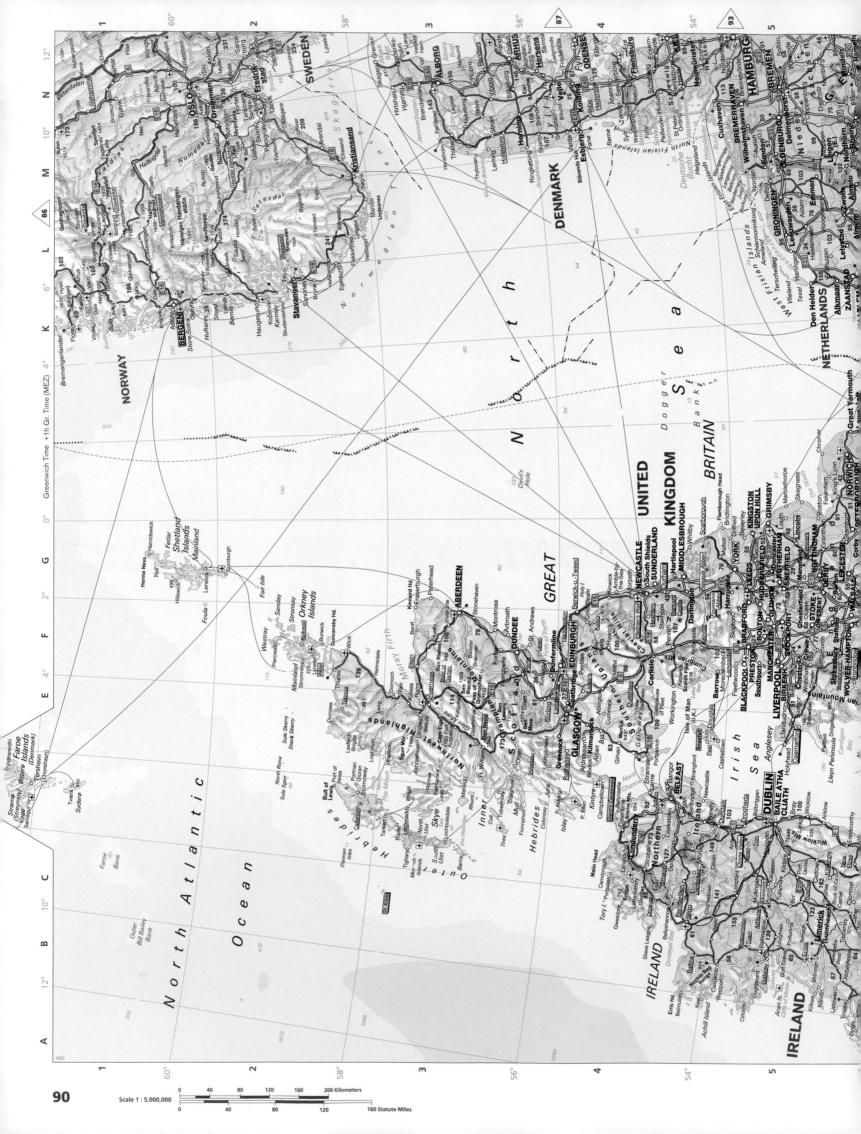

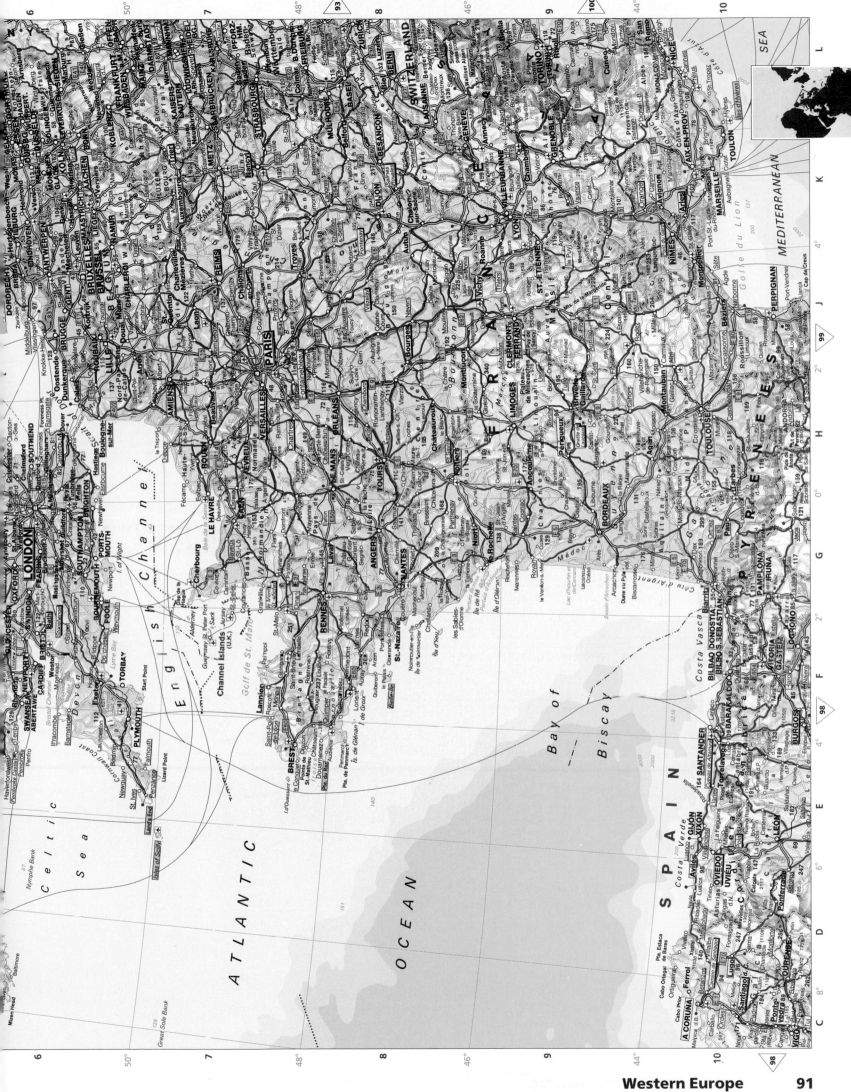

Gr. Time +1h Gr. Time (MEZ)

DENMARK

North Sea

Dogger Bank

UNITED KINGDOM

GREAT BRITAIN

IRELAND

DUBLIN / BAILE ATHA CLIATH

NETHERLANDS

AMSTERDAM
ROTTERDAM
's-GRAVENHAGE DEN HAAG

GRONINGEN
ENSCHEDE
OSNABRÜCK
MÜNSTER

BELGIUM
BRUXELLES / BRUSSEL
ANTWERPEN
GENT
BRUGGE
CHARLEROI
NAMUR
LIÈGE

LUXEMBOURG

KÖLN
DÜSSELDORF
ESSEN
DORTMUND
AACHEN
BONN
KOBLENZ
FRANKFURT
WIESBADEN
MAINZ
DARMSTADT
SAARBRÜCKEN
KARLSRUHE
STRASBOURG

Celtic Sea

St. George's Channel

Irish Sea

LIVERPOOL
MANCHESTER
LEEDS
BRADFORD
SHEFFIELD
NOTTINGHAM
LEICESTER
BIRMINGHAM
COVENTRY
NORWICH
CAMBRIDGE
PETERBOROUGH
LONDON
OXFORD
READING
SOUTHAMPTON
PORTSMOUTH
BRIGHTON
BRISTOL
CARDIFF
SWANSEA
NEWPORT
GLOUCESTER
SWINDON
PLYMOUTH
TORBAY
EXETER
BOURNEMOUTH
POOLE
SOUTHEND
MIDDLESBROUGH
SUNDERLAND
YORK
KINGSTON UPON HULL
GRIMSBY
IPSWICH
DOVER
HASTINGS
BOULOGNE-sur-Mer

English Channel

Channel Islands (U.K.)
Guernsey
Jersey

Cherbourg
Le Havre
ROUEN
CAEN
ÉVREUX
VERSAILLES
PARIS
AMIENS
LILLE
ROUBAIX
Calais
Dunkerque
Oostende

Arras
St.-Quentin
Laon
Charleville-Mézières
REIMS
METZ
NANCY

BREST
RENNES
Lorient
Quimper
St-Malo
St-Brieuc
Lannion

NANTES
ANGERS
LE MANS
TOURS
ORLÉANS
Chartres
Fontainebleau
Troyes
Chaumont

ATLANTIC OCEAN

Bay of Biscay

La Rochelle
Niort
POITIERS
Châteauroux
BOURGES
Nevers
DIJON
BESANÇON
MULHOUSE
BELFORT
BASEL

FRANCE

BORDEAUX
Angoulême
LIMOGES
CLERMONT-FERRAND
Périgueux
Brive-la-Gaillarde
ST-ÉTIENNE
LYON
VILLEURBANNE
Roanne
Vichy
Moulins
Montluçon

GRENOBLE
Chambéry
Annecy
GENÈVE / GENEVA
LAUSANNE
BERN
ZÜRICH
LUZERN

SWITZERLAND

TORINO (TURIN)
Rivoli
ALESSANDRIA
ASTI
Cúneo

SPAIN
SANTANDER
BILBAO / BILBO
DONOSTIA / S.SEBASTIAN
BARAKALDO
VITORIA / GASTEIZ
PAMPLONA / IRUÑA
Biarritz
Pau
Tarbes

TOULOUSE
Montauban
Albi
Agen
Cahors
Rodez
Millau
NÎMES
Avignon
ARLES
MARSEILLE
TOULON
AIX-EN-PROV.
NICE
MONACO
Cannes
MONTPELLIER
Béziers
Narbonne
Carcassonne
Perpignan

Pyrénées

Massif Central

Côte d'Azur

Golfe du Lion

MÉDITE...

Scale 1 : 5,000,000

0 40 80 120 160 200 Kilometers

0 40 80 120 160 Statute Miles

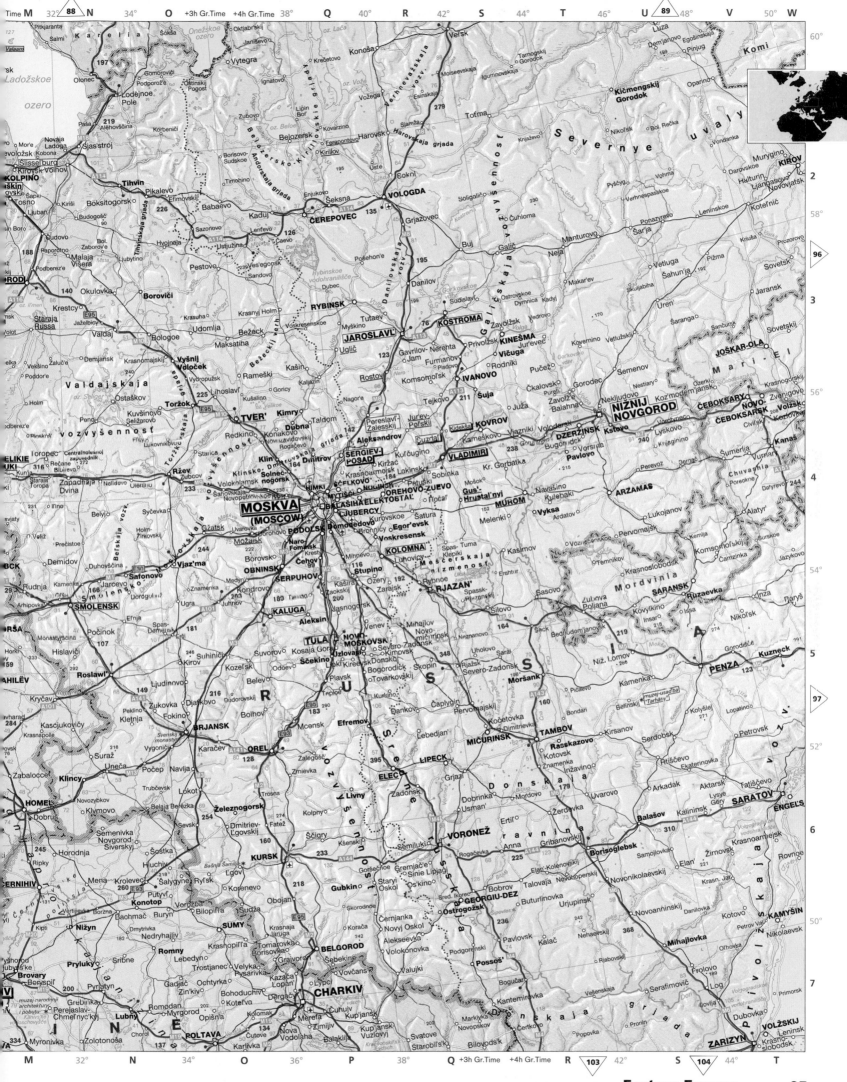

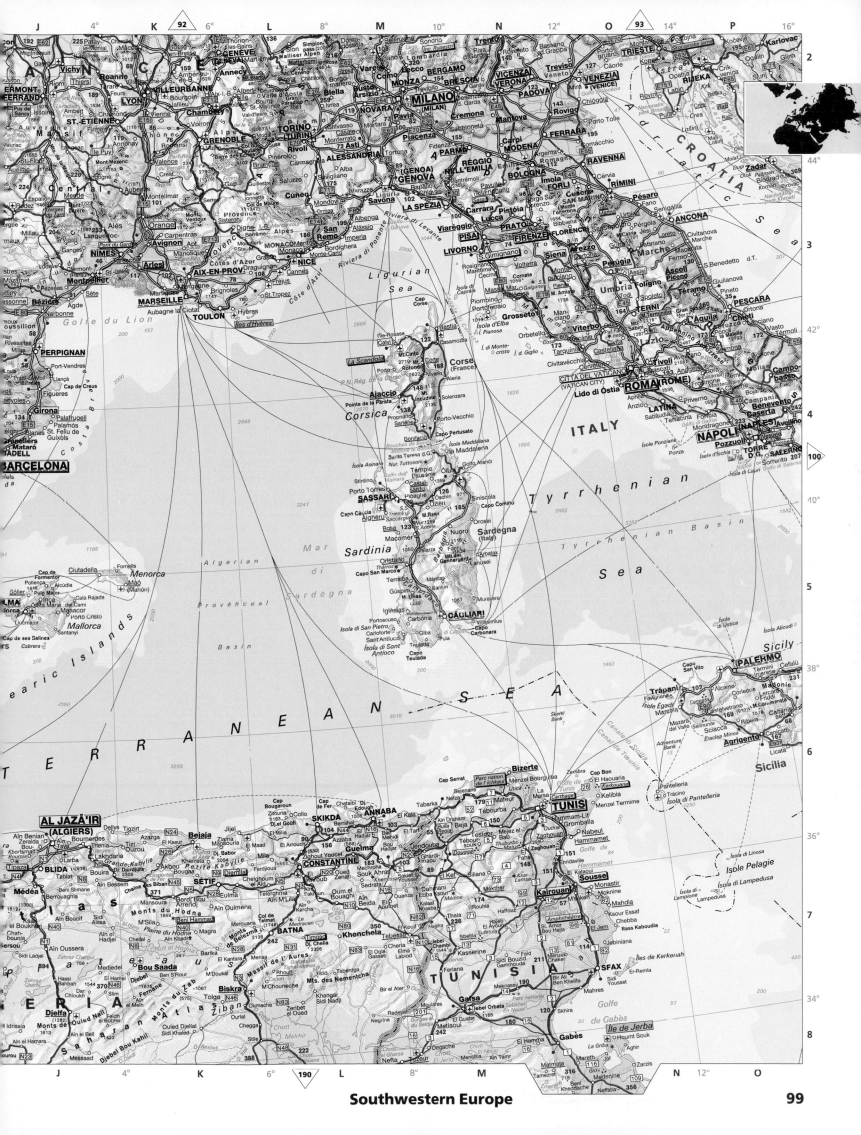

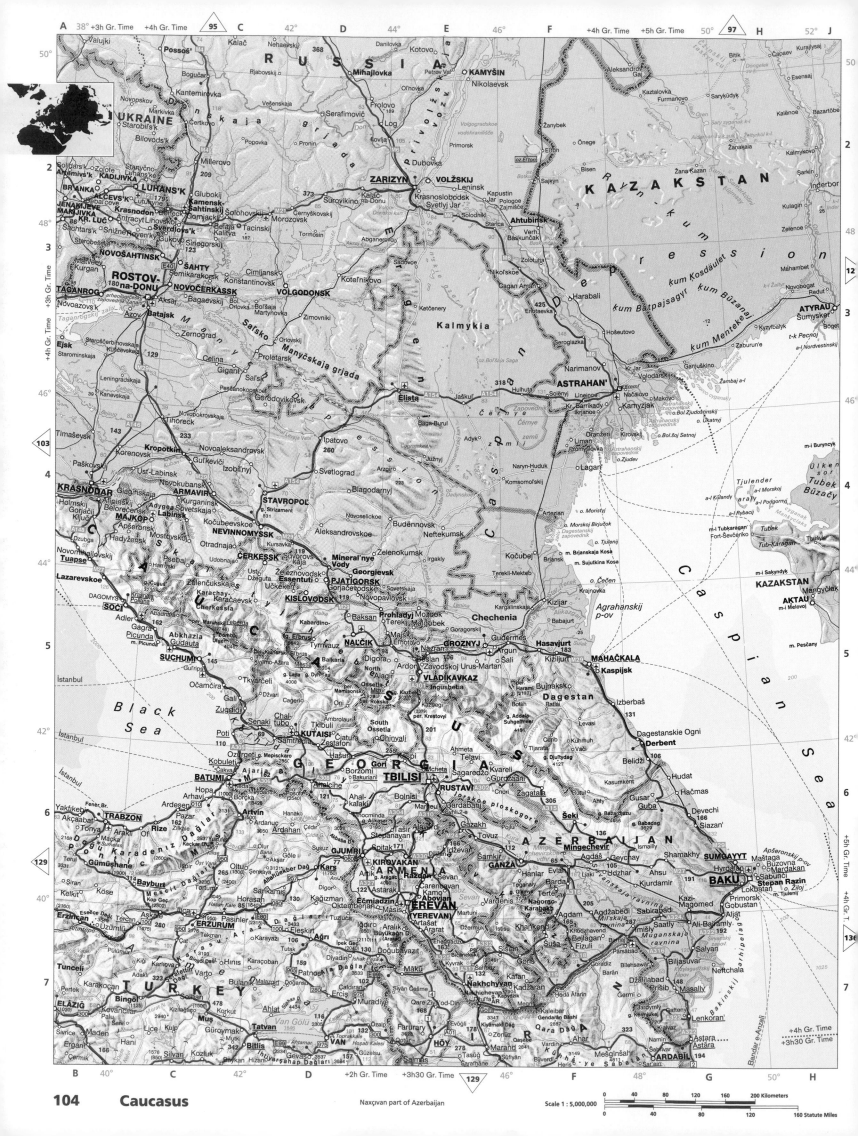

Naxçıvan part of Azerbaijan

Scale 1 : 5,000,000

Asia – continent of vivid contrasts

This 17,142,840-square-mile (4.4 million sq. km) continent, the largest in the world, incorporates all climatic and vegetation zones from the polar to the tropical region. The major landscapes of Europe continue in Asia to the East: in the North, the western Siberian lowlands, joined by the central Siberian ranges and the eastern Siberian mountains; farther South, the mountain chains converging on the node of Ararat, at

Asia in a copperplate engraving: This detailed map with boundaries and relief features in color was drawn by imperial cartographer Johann Baptist Homann in Nuremberg (circa 1700).

the Hindu Kush and in Indochina, encircling several plateaus, including the Tibetan highlands, the highest such feature on Earth at 14,764 feet (4,500 m). South of the mountain chains lie the plateaus of Arabia and the Indian subcontinent. Toward the Pacific the continent is bordered by garlands of islands and by sea trenches.

Russia: West Siberian Plain, Northern Region   108 – 109

Russia: Central Siberian Plateau, Northern Region   110 – 111

Russia: Siberia, Northeastern Region 112 – 113

Russia: West Siberian Plain, Southern Region   114 – 115

Sayan Mountains · Lake Baikal 116 – 117

Transbaikal Region 118 – 119

Far East: Northern Region · Kamchatka 120 – 121

Far East: Southern Region · Sakhalin 122 – 123

Kazakstan: The Steppe 124 – 125

Caspian Depression · Aral Sea 126 – 127

Near East 128 – 129

Arabian Peninsula: Northern Region 130 – 131

Arabian Peninsula: Southern Region 132 – 133

Persian Gulf · Plateau of Iran 134 – 135

Central Asia 136 – 137

India: Northwestern Region · Indus Valley   138 – 139

India: Southern Region · Maldives · Sri Lanka   140 – 141

India: Northeastern Region · Bangladesh 142 – 143

Tibet 144 – 145

Sinkiang 146 – 147

Mongolia 148 – 149

Manchuria · Korea 150 – 151

Japan 152 – 153

China: Northern Region 154 – 155

China: Southern Region 156 – 157

Thailand · Cambodia 158 – 159

Philippines 160 – 161

Malaysia · Sumatra 162 – 163

Borneo · Sulawesi 164 – 165

Moluccas · West Irian 166 – 167

Java · Lesser Sunda Islands 168

Russia: West Siberian Plain, Northern
Region   108 – 109

Caspian Depression · Aral Sea
126 – 127

Mongolia
148 – 149

Russia: Central Siberian Plateau,
Northern Region   110 – 111

Near East
128 – 129

Manchuria · Korea
150 – 151

Russia: Siberia, Northeastern Region
112 – 113

Arabian Peninsula: Northern Region
130 – 131

Japan
152 – 153

Russia: West Siberian Plain, Southern
Region   114 – 115

Arabian Peninsula: Southern Region
132 – 133

China: Northern Region
154 – 155

Sayan Mountains · Lake Baikal
116 – 117

Persian Gulf · Plateau of Iran
134 – 135

China: Southern Region
156 – 157

Transbaikal Region
118 – 119

Central Asia
136 – 137

Thailand · Cambodia
158 – 159

Far East: Northern Region · Kamchatka
120 – 121

India: Northwestern Region · Indus
Valley   138 – 139

Philippines
160 – 161

Far East: Southern Region · Sakhalin
122 – 123

India: Southern Region · Maldives · Sri
Lanka   140 – 141

Malaysia · Sumatra
162 – 163

Kazakstan: The Steppe
124 – 125

India: Northeastern Region · Bangladesh
142 – 143

Borneo · Sulawesi
164 – 165

Tibet
144 – 145

Moluccas · West Irian
166 – 167

Sinkiang
146 – 147

Java · Lesser Sunda Islands
168

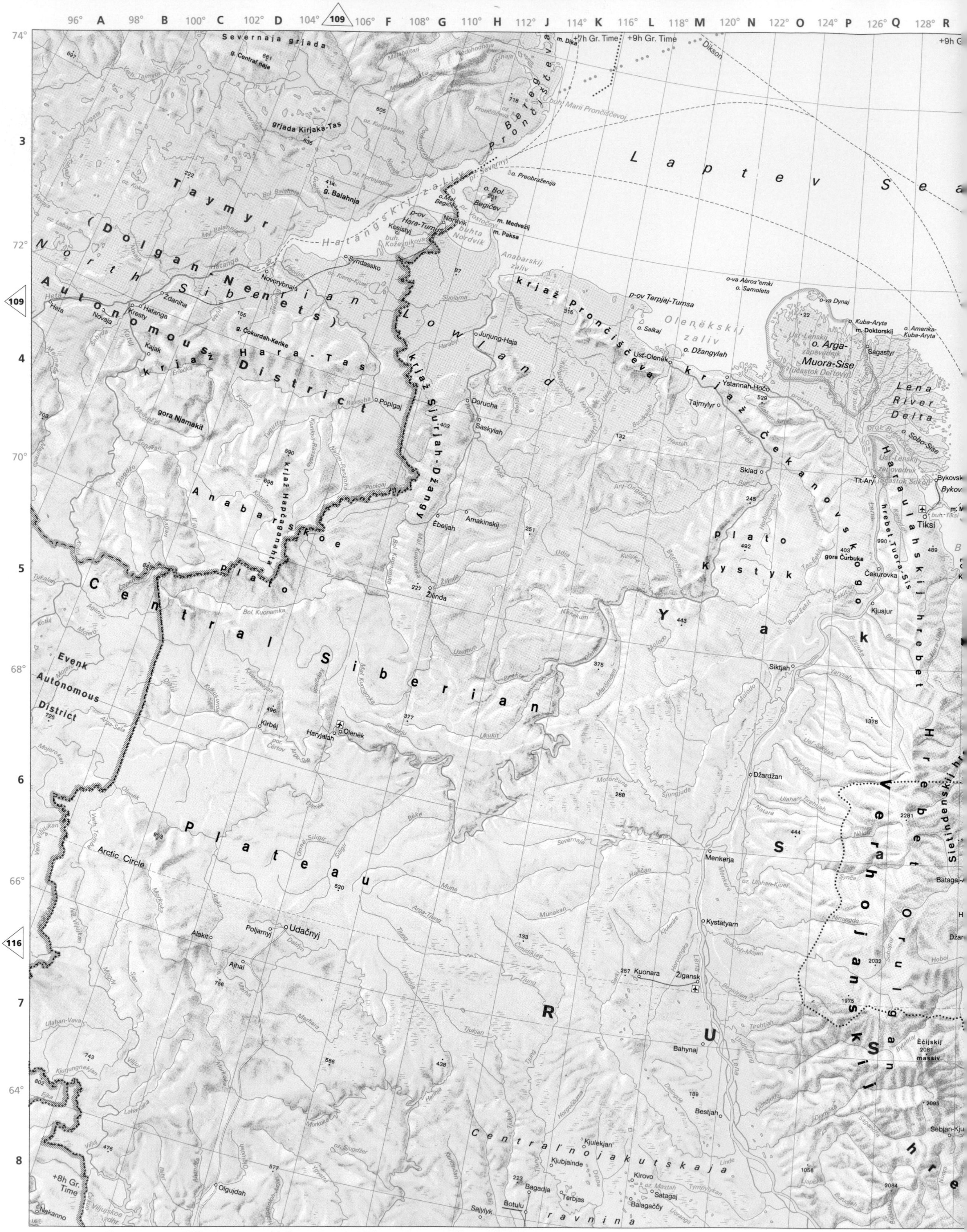

Laptev Sea

+7h Gr. Time +9h Gr. Time +9h G

Severnaja grjada

g. Central naja 661

grjada Kirjaka-Tas

Taymyr (Dolgan-Nenets) North Siberian Autonomous District

Hara-Tas krjaž

Central Siberian Plateau

Evenk Autonomous District

Anabarskoe plato

krjaž Sjujtah-Džangy

krjaž Hpčaganha

Lowland

Olenёkskij zaliv

krjaž prončiščeva

krjaž Čekanovskogo

Lena River Delta

plato Kystyk

Yak

Verahojanskij hrebet

Arctic Circle

Udačnyj

Poljarnyj

Alakit

Ajhal

Olenёk

Kirbej

Haryjalah

Menkerja

Kystatym

Džardžan

Žigansk

Kuonara

Bahynaj

Bestjah

Central'nojakutskaja ravnina

Hatanga

Kresty

Novaja

Hela

Čokurdah-Kёrikё

gora Njamakit

Popigaj

Dorucha

Saskylah

Ėbeljah

Amakinskij

Žilinda

Novorybnaja

Syndassko

Hara-Tumus

Nordvik

buhta Nordvik

Anabarskij zaliv

Jurjung-Haja

Usf-Olenёk

Salkaj

Džangylah

Ystannah-Hočo

Tajmylyr

Tiksi

Bykovskij

Bykov

Tit-Ary

gora Čurbuka

Čekurovka

Kjusjur

Siktjah

Sklad

Muora-Sise

o. Arga-

Kuba-Aryta

Sagastyr

Olgujdah

Nakanno

Scale 1 : 5,000,000

0 40 80 120 160 200 Kilometers

0 40 80 120 160 Statute Miles

+8h Gr. Time

a · o. Ėmmy · o. Žohova

+10h Gr. Time   +11h Gr. Time

r. Time

r o v a

s t

O m. Severnyj

Nanosnyj

m. Anisij

griada Šmidta

152

o. Beľkovskij

-127

o. Koteľnyj

m. Tolstova

m. Anžu

m. Malakatyn-Tas

374

Sannikova

m. Medvežij

Zemlja Bunge

m. Berëznyj

m. Nerpičij

61

o. Faddeevskij

guba Borša

guba Boršaj

m. Koževina

A n

ž

u

m. Vysokij

buhta Mira

o. Ploskij

42

o. Novaja Sibir'

m. Kamennyj

m. Nadëžnyj

N e w   S i b e r i a n   I s l a n d s

E a s t   S i b e r i a n

S e a

L j a h o v s k i e

pr. Sannikova

m. Skalistyj   o. Stolbovoj

-222

m. Povorotnyj

p-ov Kigiljah

m. Kigiljah   Kigiljah

43

o. Mal. Ljahovskij

pr. Ėterikan   241

g. Gavriša-Tas

o. Bol.

Ljahovskij   311

m. Malyj Van'kin

Šalaurova

m. Šalaurova

proliv Dmitrija Lapteva

m. Svjatoj Nos   -894   Bereg Djogos Jar

Ėbeljanskaja guba

m. Čurkin

p-ov Širokostan

o z. Bustah

p-ov Merkušina Strelka

52

p-ov Lopatka

o. Krestovyj

guba Gusinaja

Providenija

Medvežj'i o-va   o. Puškareva   o. Leont'eva

o. Krestovyj

70°

4

m. Buor-Haja

m. Makar   g. Turuktah

o. Jarok

Janskij zaliv

g. Muksunuoha-Tas

496

Poljarnoe

hr. Sunt-Ujala

o. Ulah-Tas

561

Logaškino

m. Krestovskij

70°

m. Krestovskij

Nižnejansk

J a n o - I n d i g i r s k a j a   n i z m e n n o s t'

Sagarye

Čokurdah

Kotenko

Ojotung

Kondakovskaja Vozvyšennost'

g. Hel-Amkanni   864

5

Entuziastov

Hajyr

Vlasovo

Kular

Ust-Jansk

Kazač'e

Severnyj   442

g. Madyl-Tasa

501

Tumat

284

Tenkeli   Krajnij

Čkalov

102

Nyčalah

Olenegorsk

hrebet Ulahan-Sis   754

Andrjuškino   m

Kolymekoe

68°

t

U

Namy

U s t - K u j g a

Kuiginskij krjaž

927

g. Semejka   1077

Selennjahskij hrebet

Nemkučenskij hrebet   1242

1025

1320

Irgičanskij hrebet

Deputatskij   1326

1221

g. Agra-Ėmeke

P o l o u s n y j   k r j a ž

678

oz. Ožogino

Aleko-Kjuèl'

Argahtah

K o l y m

Ebjah   g. Magan-Tas

241

Sylgy-Ytar

112

6

Momo-Selennjahskaja

g. Hadaranja

Sajlyk

Tommotskij massiv

Suturuoha

Belaja Gora   664

g. Kyjam

n   i   z   m   e   n

Druzina

Nelemp   Kul'dino

Lubuja

Srednekolymsk

Hatyrngnan

Arctic Circle

66°

h

a

807

r

hrebet Hadaranja

1919

hrebet Kurundja

2272

Syagannah

Kuberganja

A l a z e j s k o e

964

p l o s k o g o r i e

331

J u k a g i r s k o e

g. Čubukulah   1128

m. Selennjah

Hajysardah

Colbon

Batagaj   Betenkês

Ulahan-Kjuèl'

Momskij

2038

p l o s k o g o r i e

o. Sčigansk

Mačah

Boronuk

Verhojansk   Stolby

Ėsè-Hajja

1226

Kulun-Elbjut

Honuu   2633

Soboloh   Ugoľnoe

Nelemnoe

Oroek   1015

1185

64°

7

S

Bala

Junkjur

Tokuma

J a n s k o e

Lazo

Čibagalahskij hrebet

2647

2168

2533

g. Čubuka-Tala   9284

Zyrjanka

 Č

Gluharinyj

e

1615   Sejmčansko-Magadanskij

8

p l o s k o g o r i e

S   I

Barylas

Derbekinskaja vpadina

Nendeľginskij hrebet

Ė r g i n s k o e

1680

2304

2695

Čumpu-Kytyl

Predporožnyj

Zaharenko

g. Pobeda   3147

Sasyr

r

s

k

o

Poljarnyj hrebet

64°

1722

p l o s k o g o r i e

2763

Orčan

Ėrginskij

Usť-Nera

Nerskoe

Aľtyk   2080

2558

g. Ėzop   2038

t

g. Veršina-Tuoldah   1590

hrebet Tas-Kystabyt   2341

Neľkan

Sarylah

N e r s k o e   p l o s k o g o r i e

Ozernoe

Molodëžnyj

o Sejmčan

8

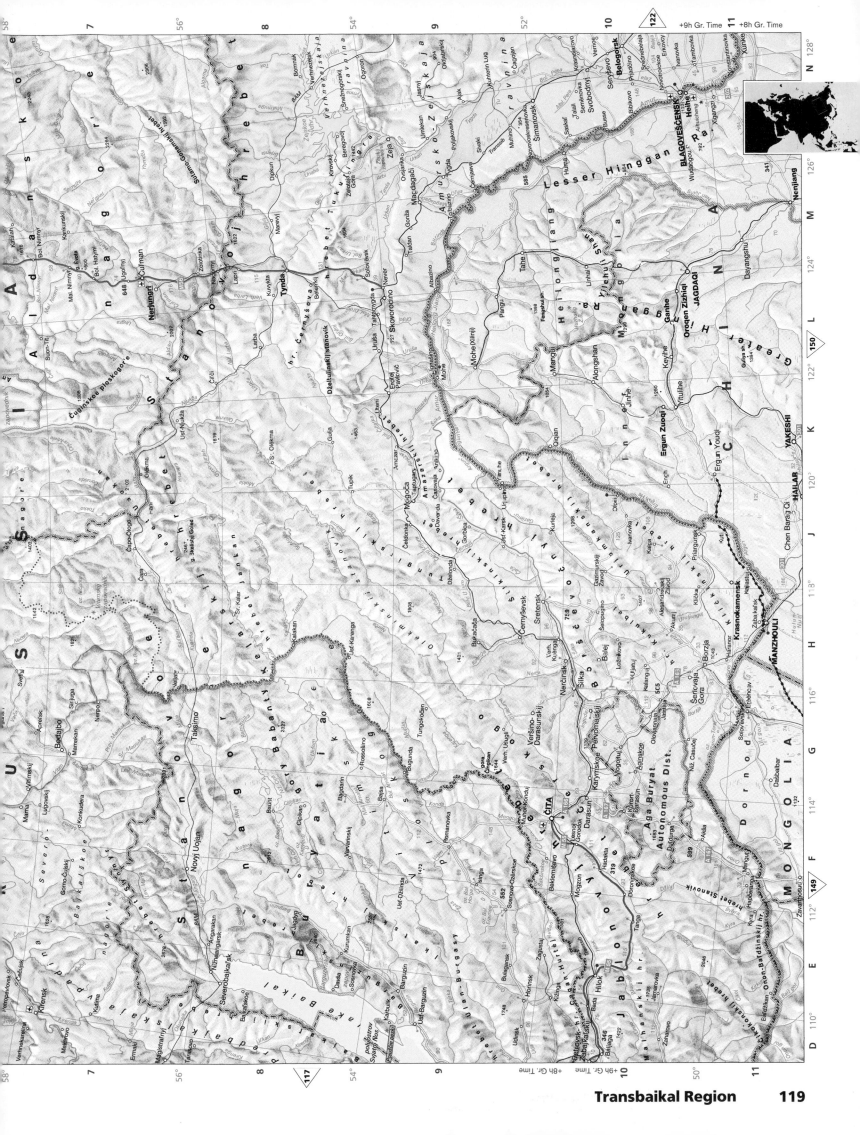

Scale 1 : 5,000,000

0   40   80   120   160   200 Kilometers

0   40   80   120   160 Statute Miles

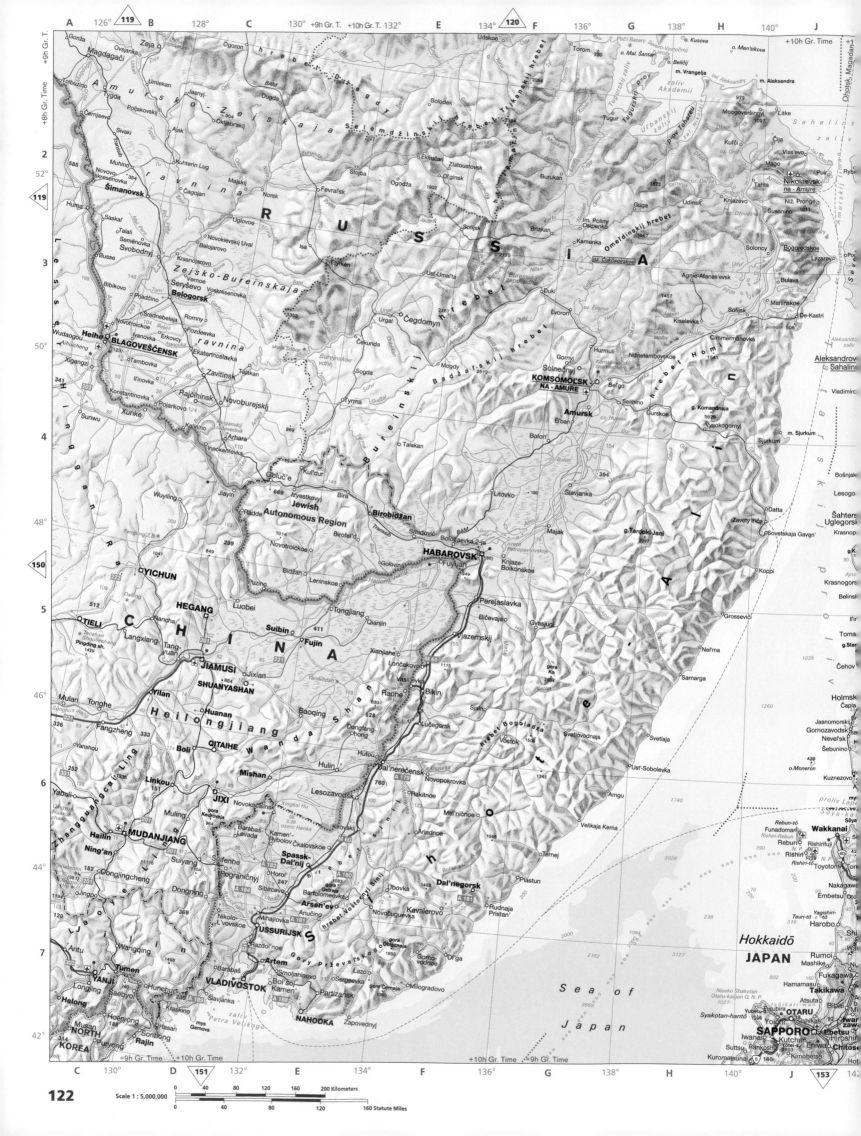

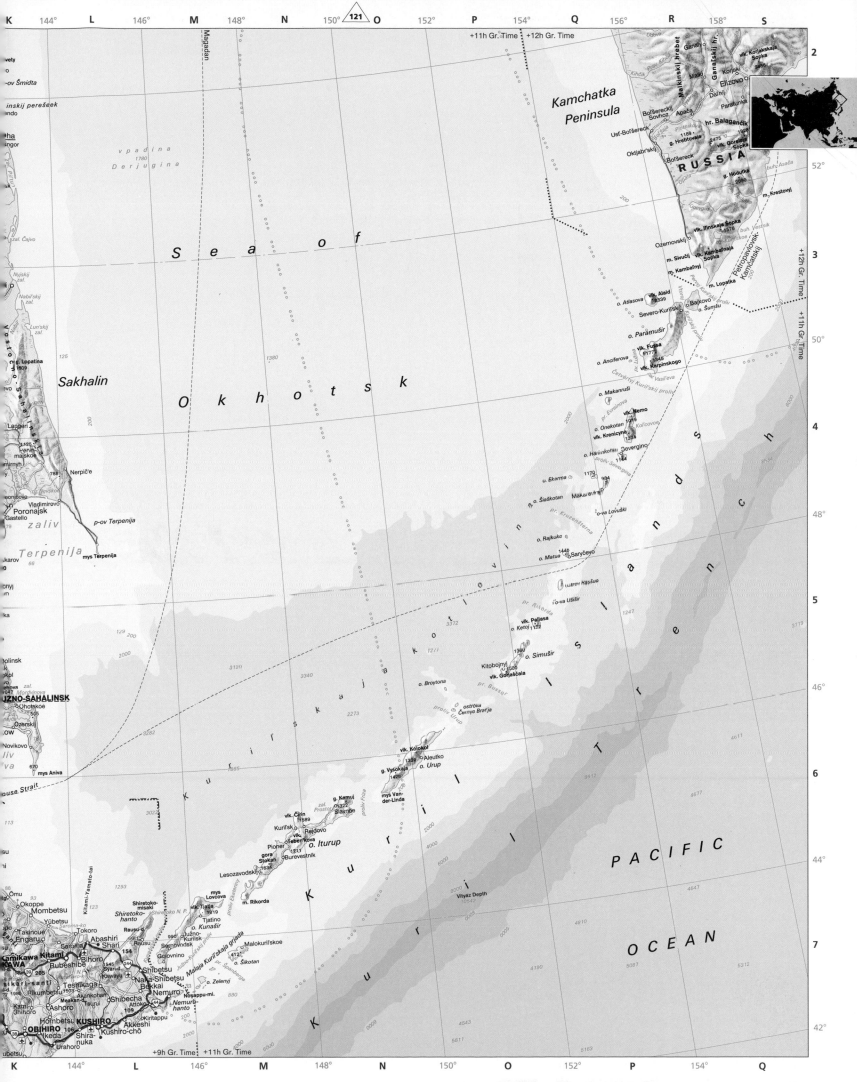

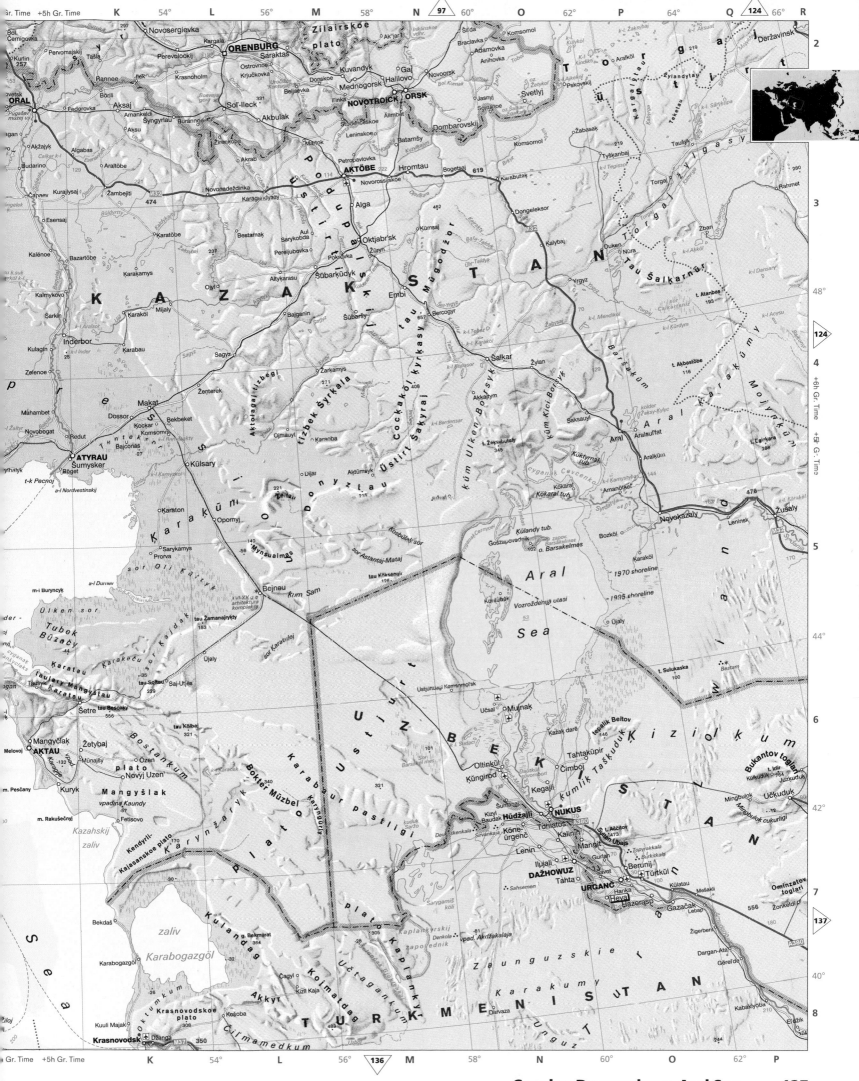

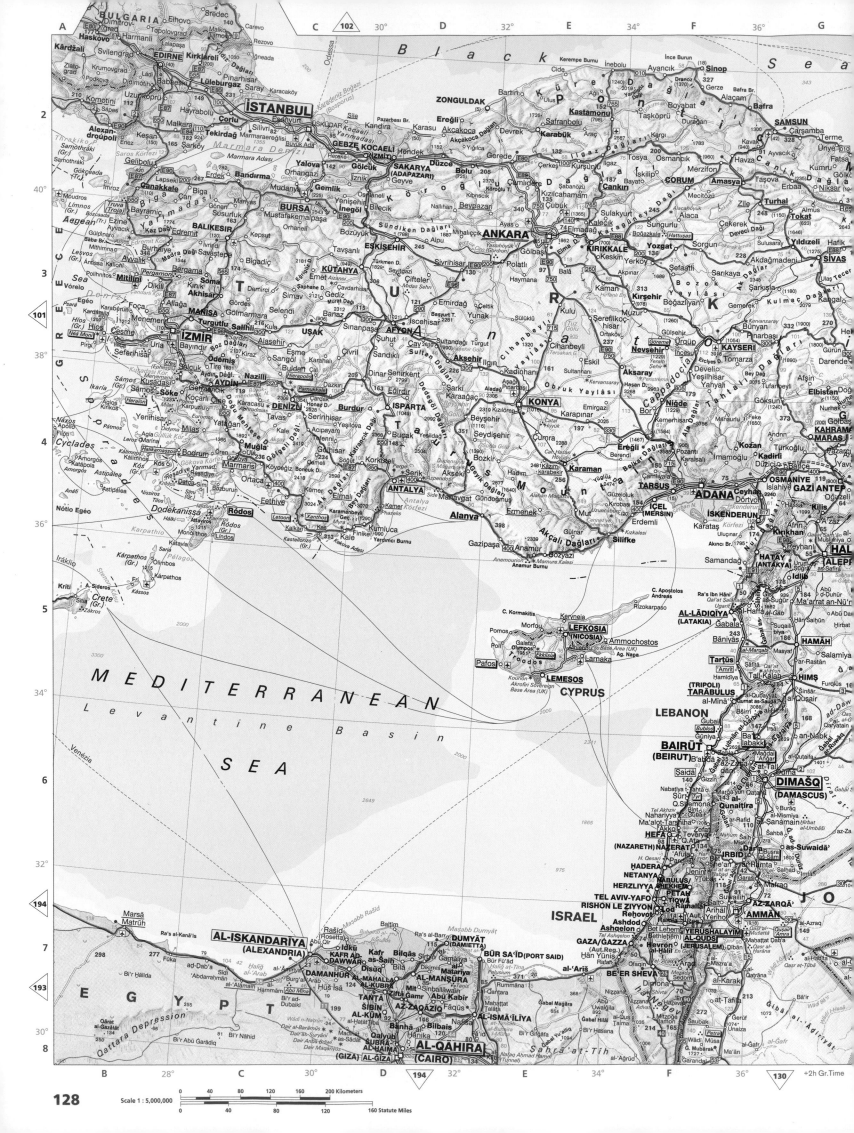

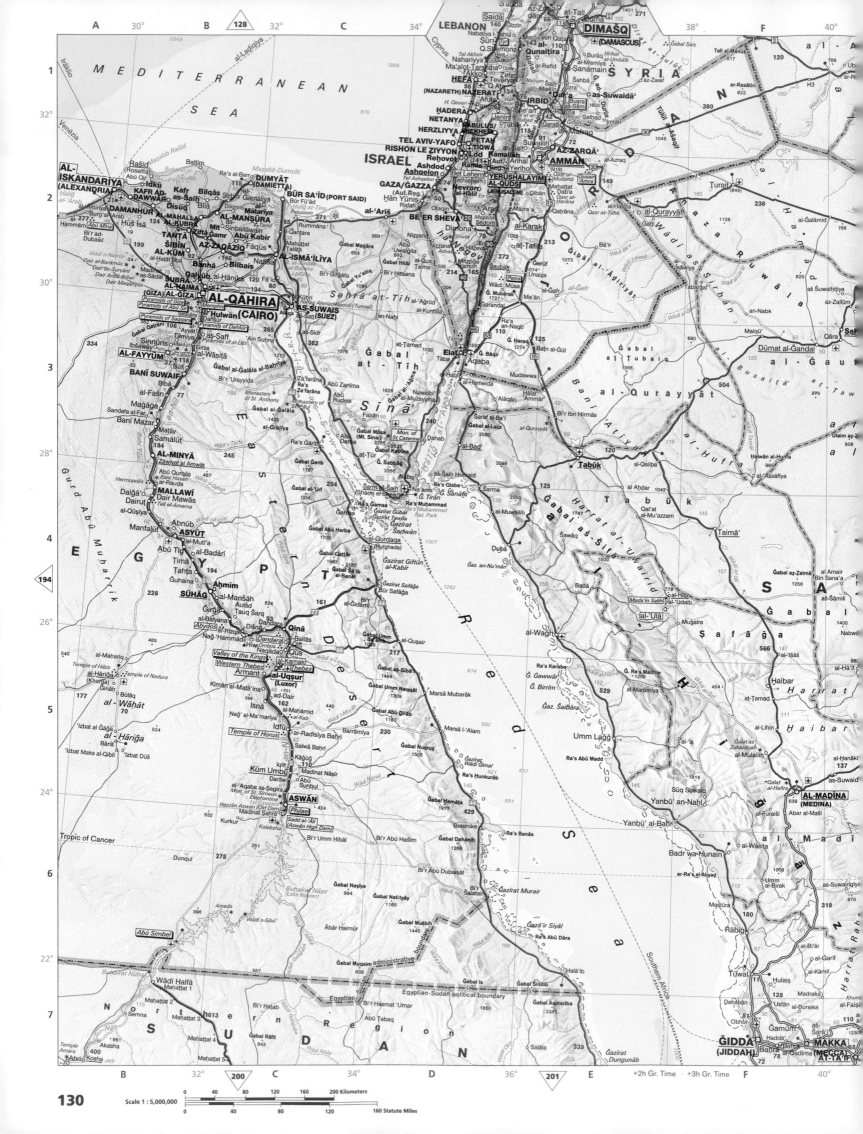

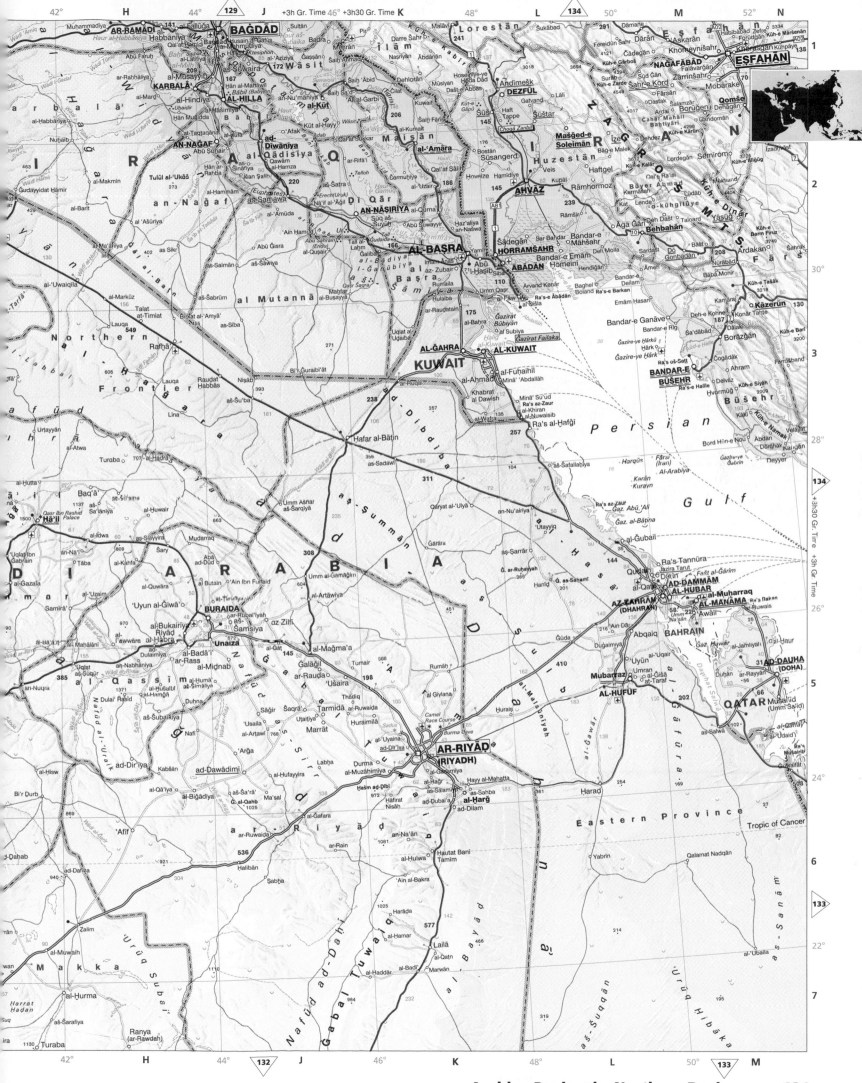

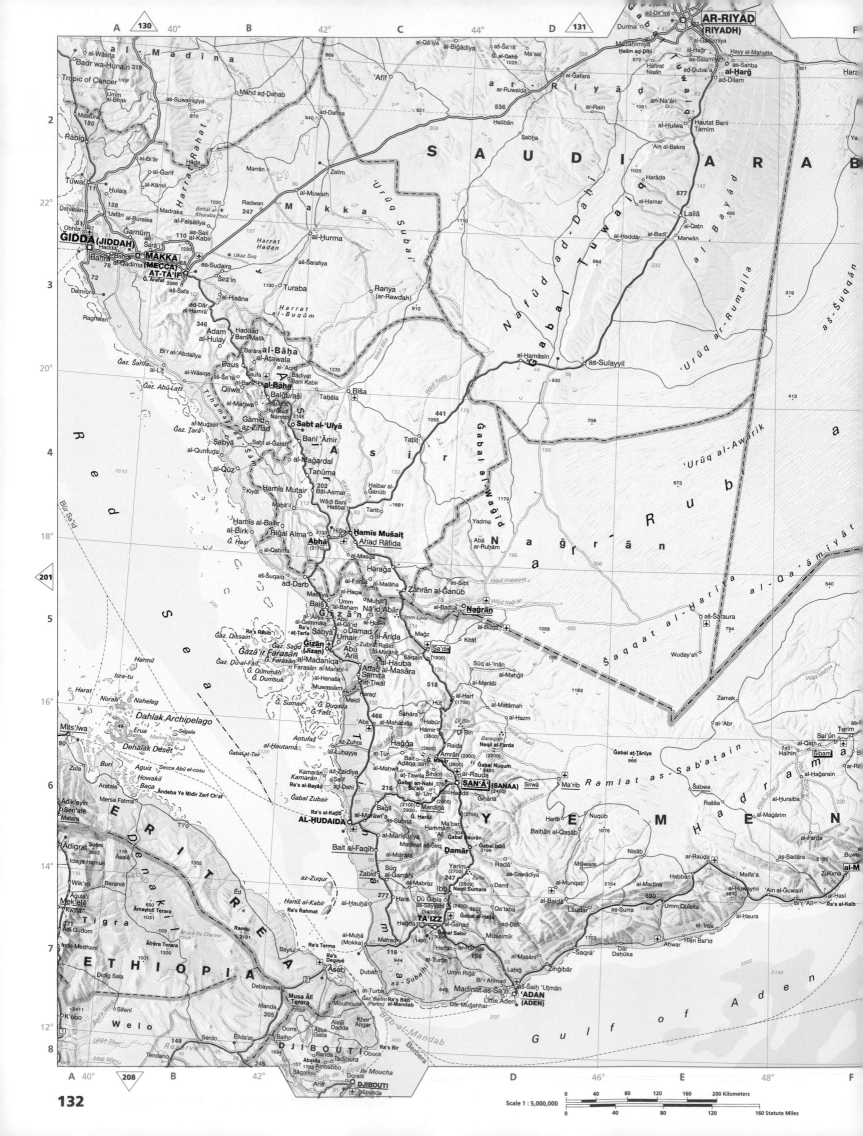

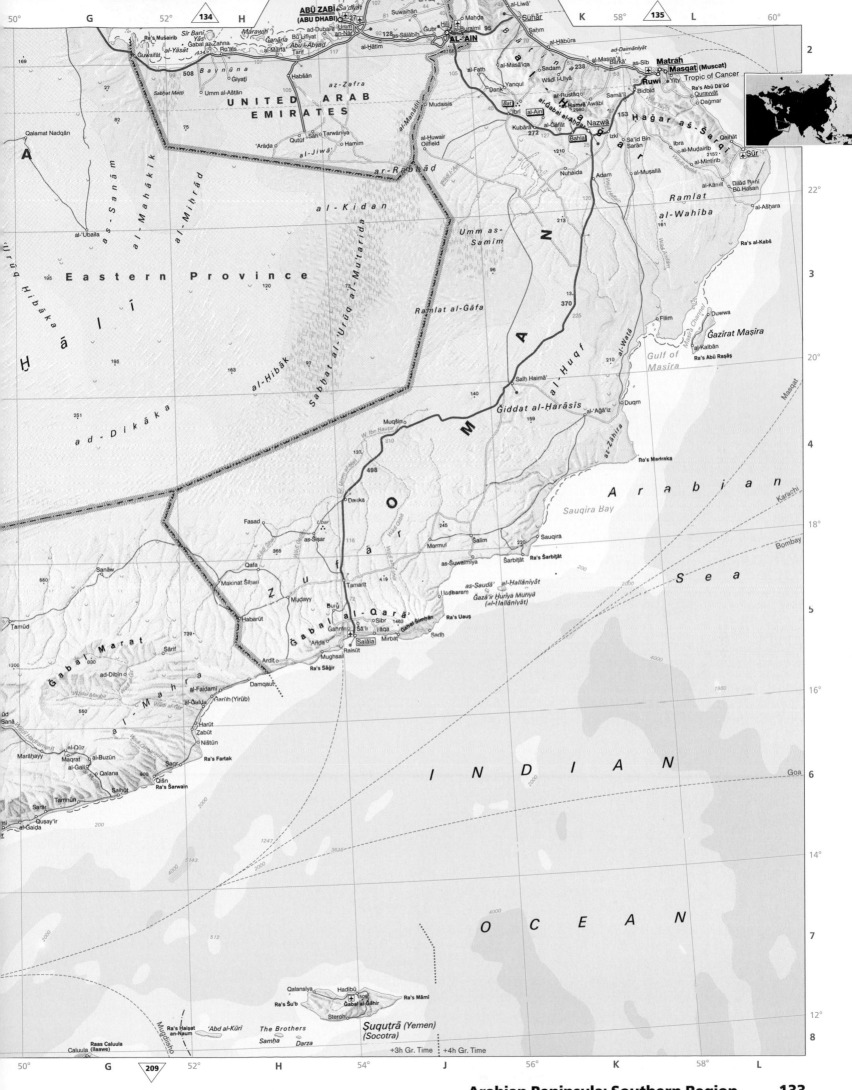

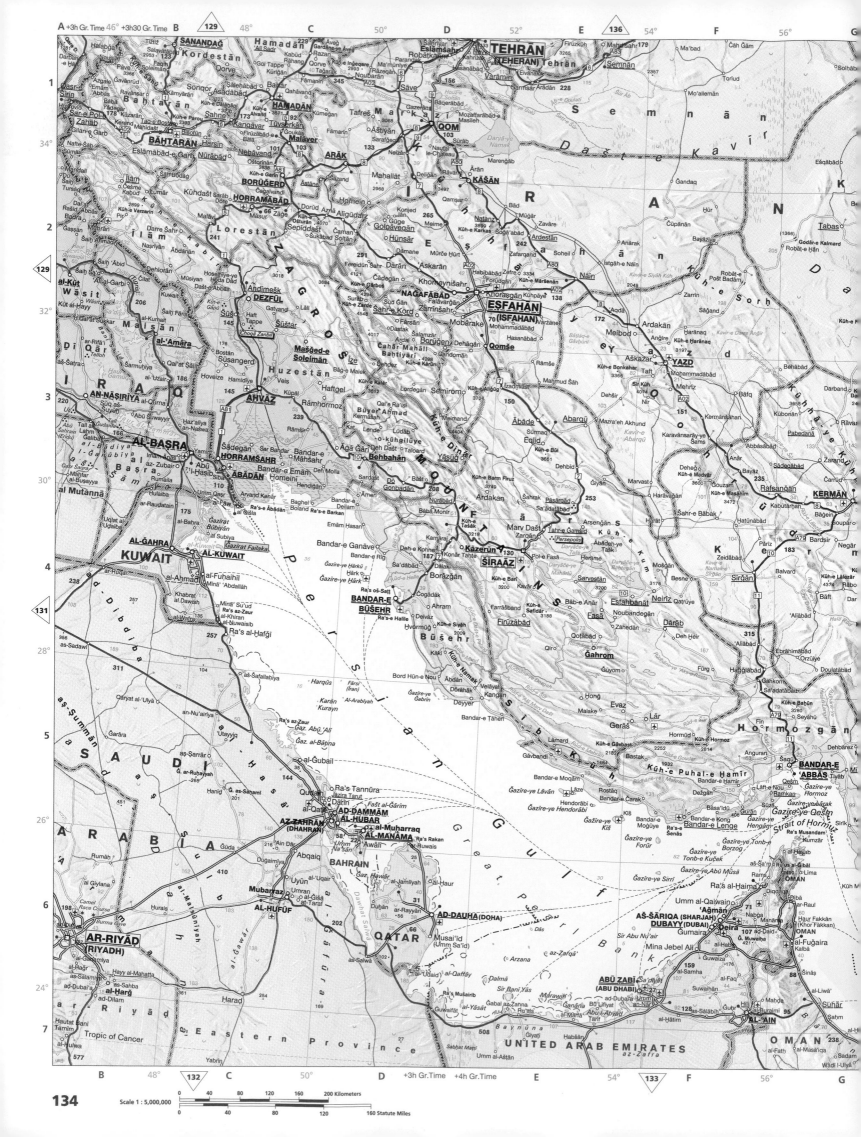

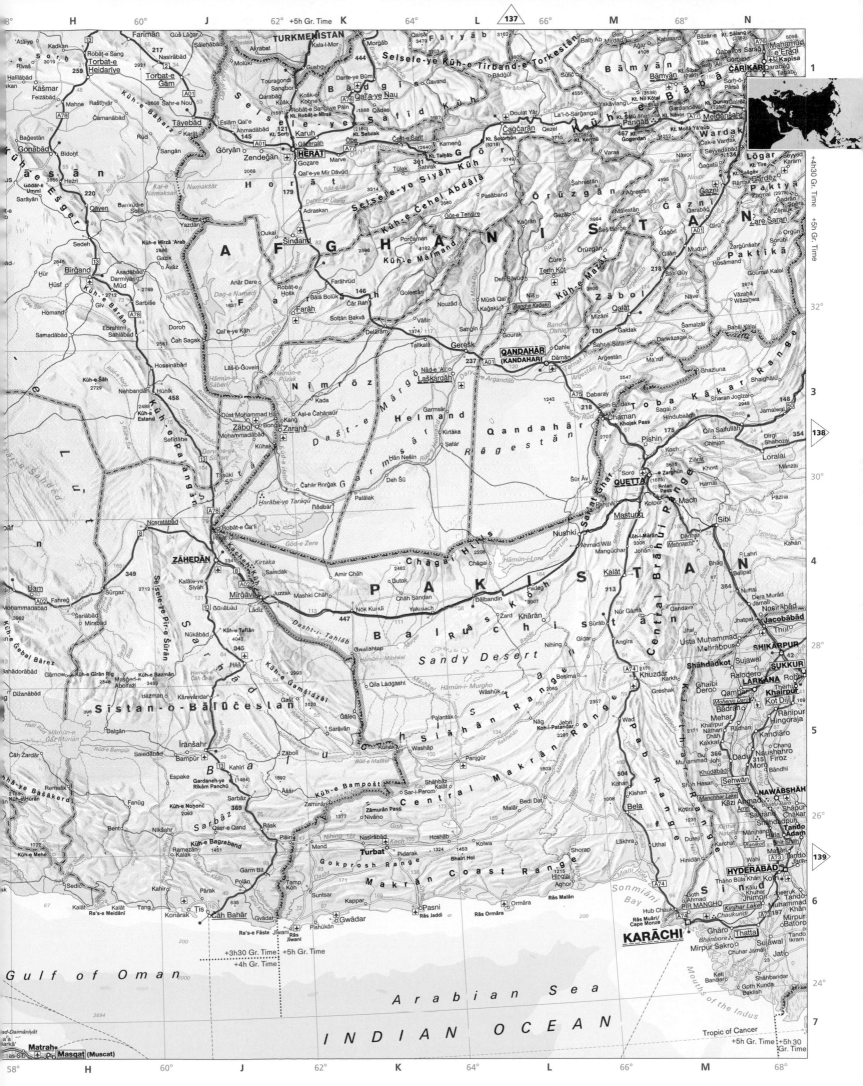

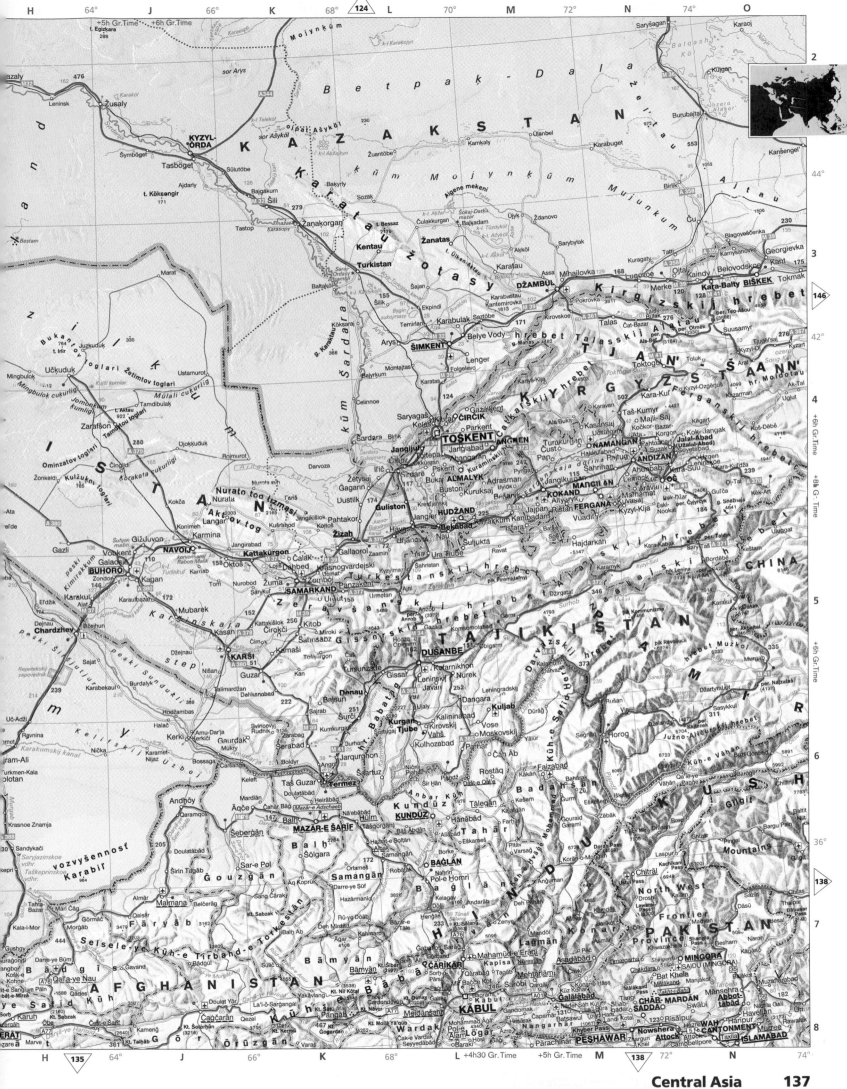

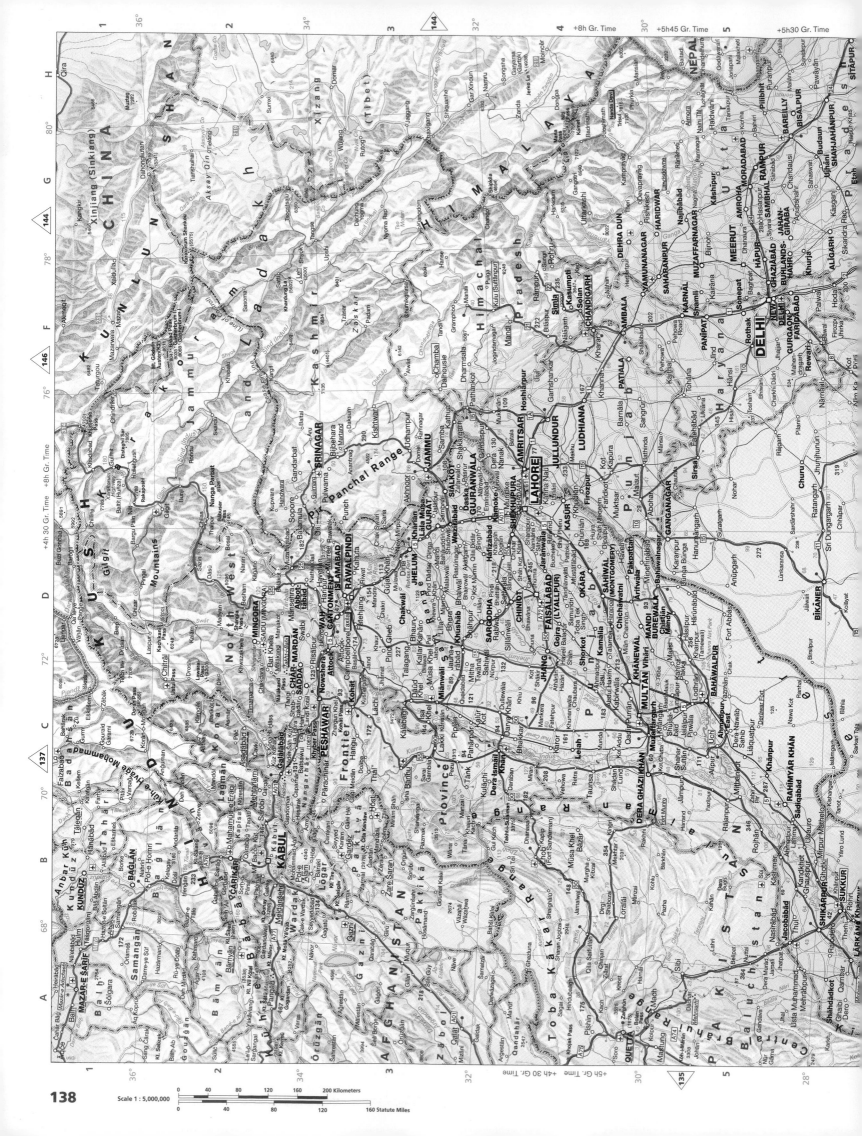

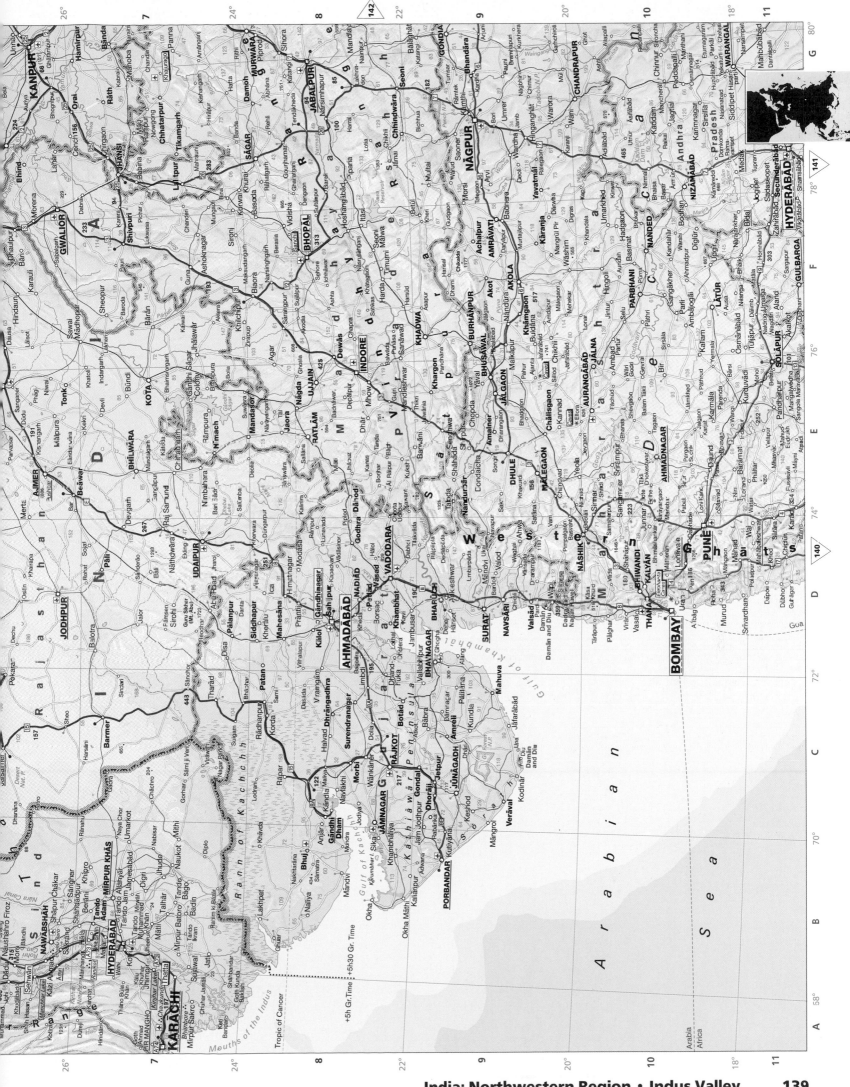

Map Grid — Left Panel (India: Southern Region)

| 78° | H | 80° | J | 82° | K |

Andhra Pradesh / Tamil Nadu region

Nizām Sugar, Siddipet, Huzūrābād, Elkaturti, Pāderu, **Orissa**, **Madhya Pradesh**, Chodavaram, **WARANGAL**, Gundala, 1440, Krishnadevipera, **Anakāpalle**

Medak, Gajwel, Jangaon, Narsampet, 742, Borgampād, Bhadrachalam, Chinturu, Narsipatnam, 652

Secunderābād, **HYDERĀBĀD**, Shamsābād, Suriāpet, Khammam, Ashwaraopet, Tuni, 232, **KAKINĀDA**

Tenāli, **MACHILĪPATNAM**, **VIJAYAWĀDA**, **ELŪRU**, **BHĪMAVARAM**, **GUNTUR**, **RĀJAHMUNDRY**, **SĀMALKOT**, Pithāpuram

Bay of Bengal

KURNOOL, **NELLORE**, **GUDDAPAH**, **PRODDATŪR**, **TIRUPATI**, **CHITTOOR**, **MADRAS**, **KĀNCHIPURAM**

Coromandel Coast

Pondicherry, **PONDICHERRY**, **CUDDALORE**, **SALEM**, **ERODE**, **TIRUCH- CHIRAPPALLI**, **THANJAVUR**, **KUMBAKONAM**, **DINDIGUL**, **MADURAI**

PALĀYANKOTTAI, **TUTICORIN**, **TIRUNELVELI**, **NĀGERCOIL**, Cape Comorin

Gulf of Mannar, *Palk Strait*, *Palk Bay*

JAFFNA, Rāmeswaram, **SRI LANKA**, **Anurādhapura**, **Polonnaruwa**, Trincomalee, Batticaloa

Negombo, **COLOMBO**, **MORATUWA**, **KANDY**, Nuwara Eliya, **Galle**, Matara, Hambantota

Sinharaja Forest Res.

Map Grid — Right Panel (Andaman and Nicobar Islands)

| L | 94° | M |

MYANMAR (BURMA), Bogale, Labutta, Kyonkadun, Galuzeik, Ama, Mawdin, *Erāwadī Myitwanā*, *Turtles*

Bay of Bengal

Great Coco Island, +5h30 Gr. Time, +6h30 Gr. Time, Narcondan I. (Ind.), Landfall I., Lakshmipur, *Coco Channel*, *Alexandra Channel*

North Andaman, Interview I., Mayabander, *Middle Andaman*, Barren I., *Andaman*

Bharatpur, Amkunj, *Andaman Is.*, Henry Lawrence I., Wilson I.

South Andaman, *Bilap Bay*, Shoal Bay, Havelock I., *Andaman Basin*

N. Sentinel I., *Constance Bay*, **Port Blair**, Rutland I., Cinque I.

Duncan Passage, Nachuge, Little Andaman, Tāmbeibui, *and Sea*

Sandy Point, Toibalewe, *Ten Degree Channel*

Keating Pt., Car Nicobar I., Malacca, **Nicobar Islands (India)**

Batti Malv I., Chaura I., Tarasa Dwip I., Bengāla, Tillanchang Dwip

Koimekeah, Katchall I., North Bay, Trinkat I., Koihoa, Nancowry I., *Nicobar Islands*

Enfok, *Sombrero Channel*, Little Nicobar Island, Dākoānk, 642, Tenlau

Indara Point, *Great Nicobar Island*, Indara Pt.

+5h30 Gr. Time, +7h Gr. Time

Tanjung Ba'u, P. Weh, P. Breueh, **Banda Aceh (Baiturahman)**, Lambaro Angan, **INDONESIA**, *SUMATRA*, Seulimeum, Jantho, Lam-panah, Lageuen, Calang

INDIAN OCEAN

Andaman and Nicobar Islands

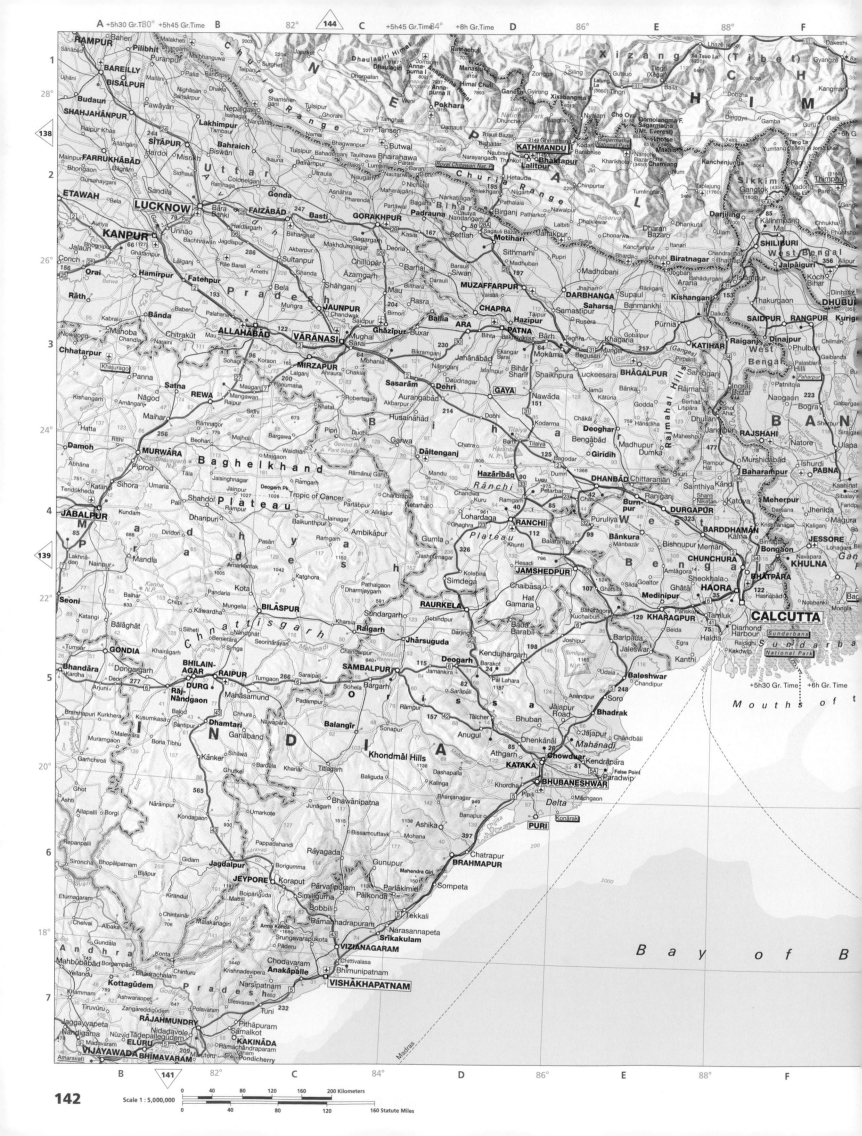

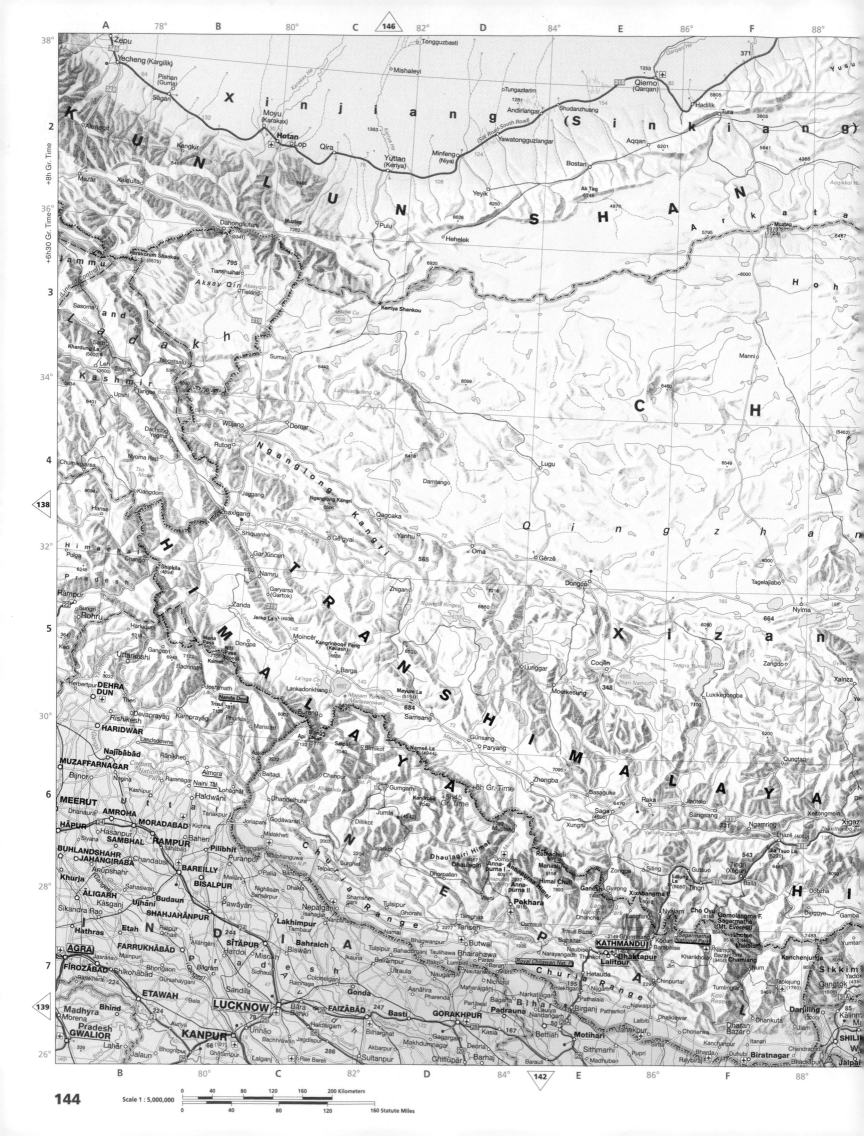

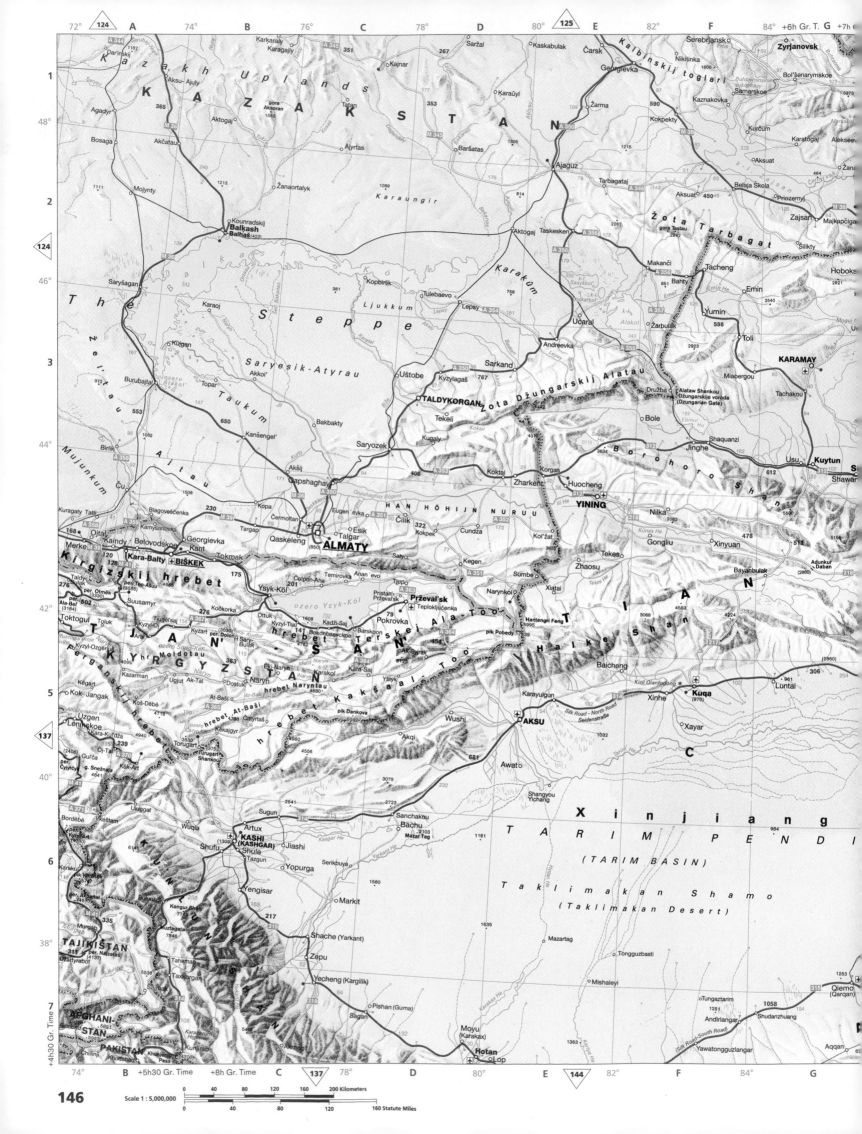

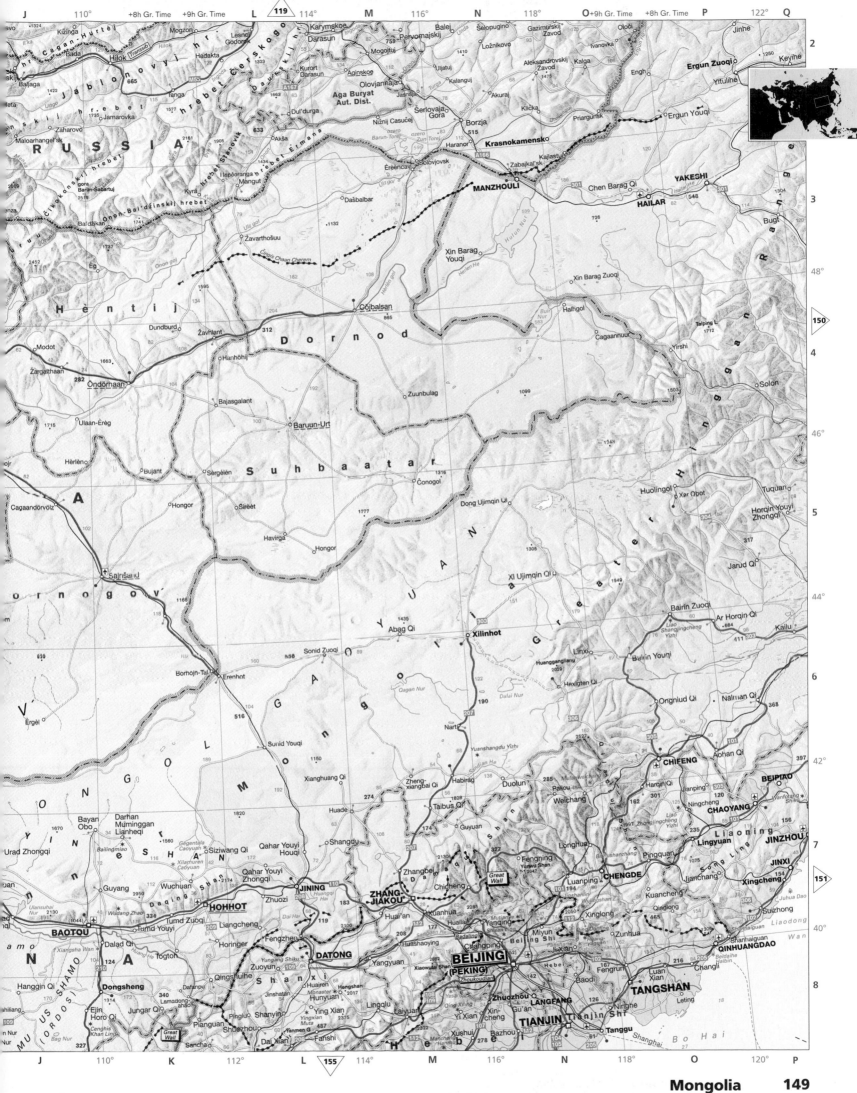

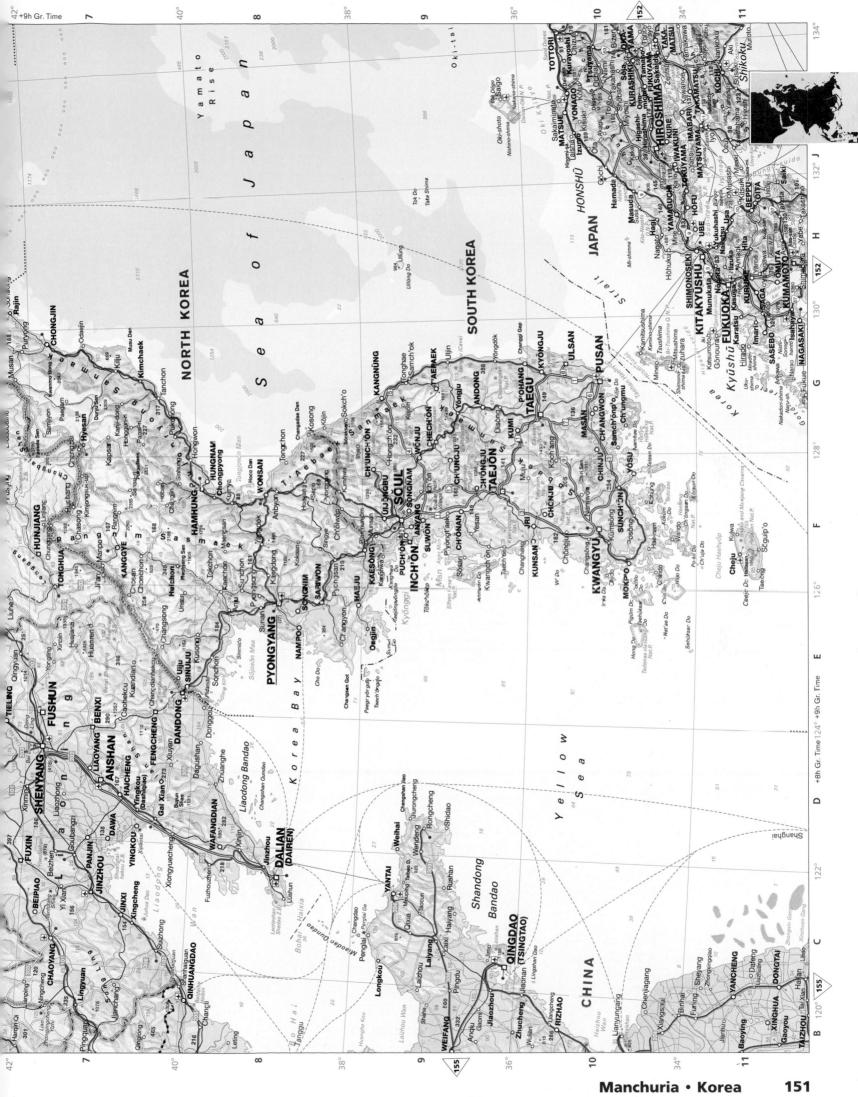

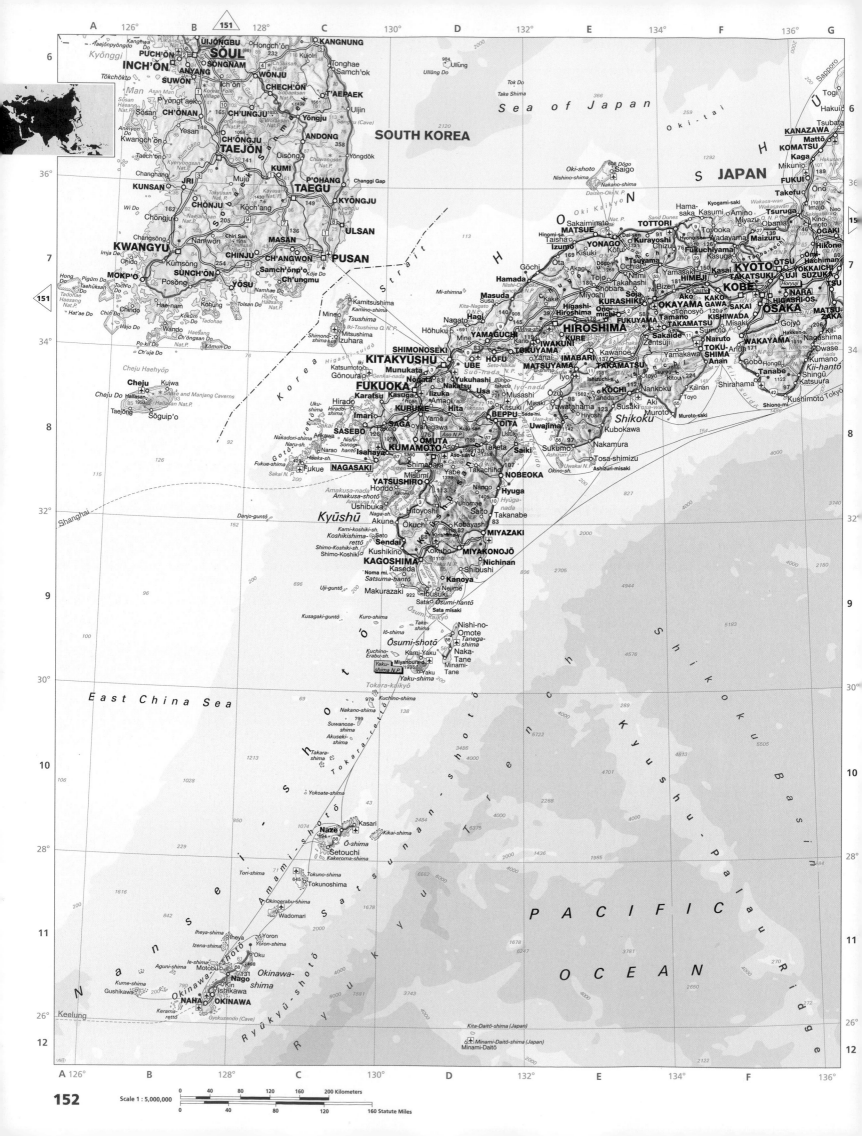

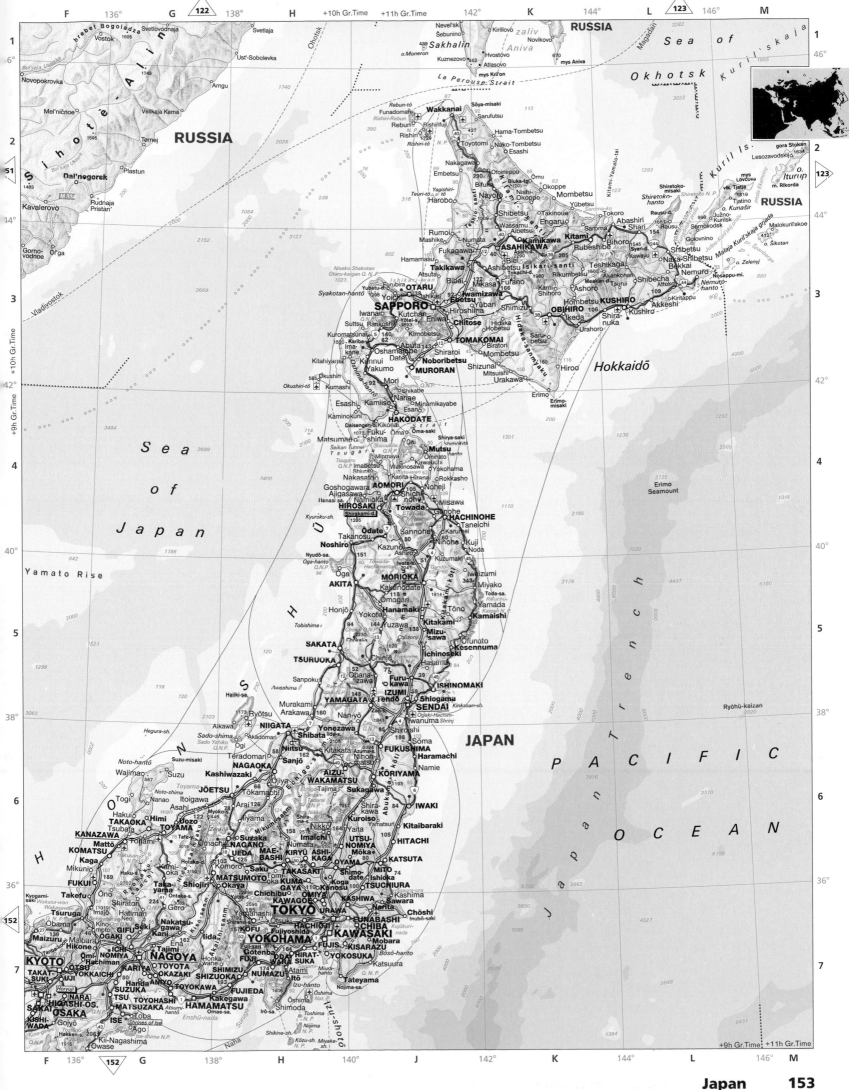

China: Northern Region 155

China: Southern Region   157

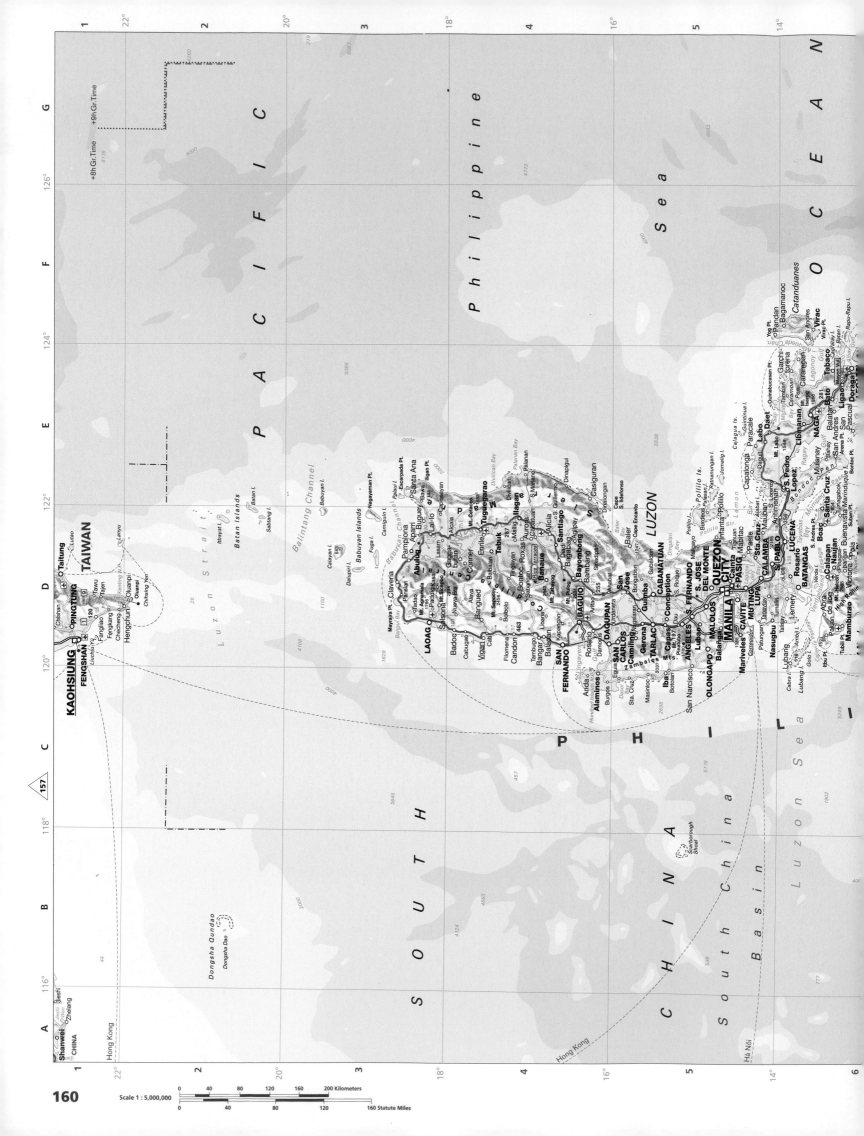

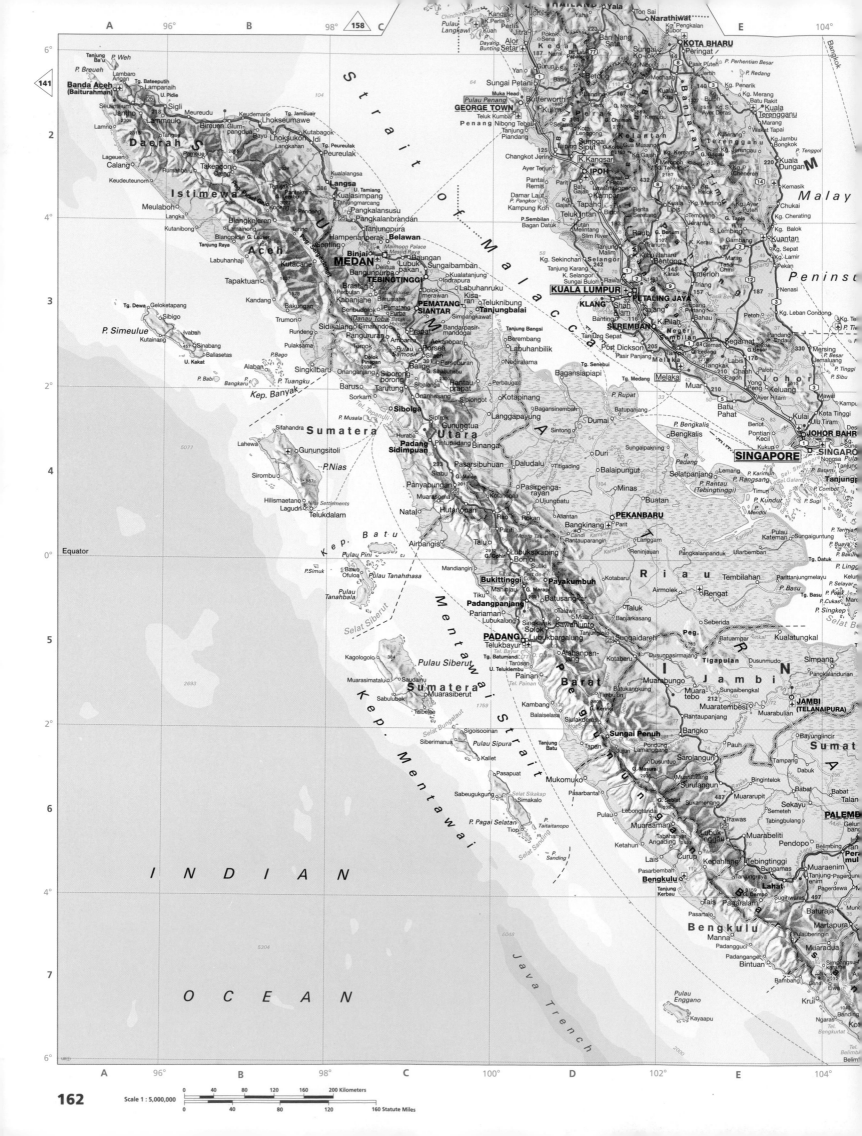

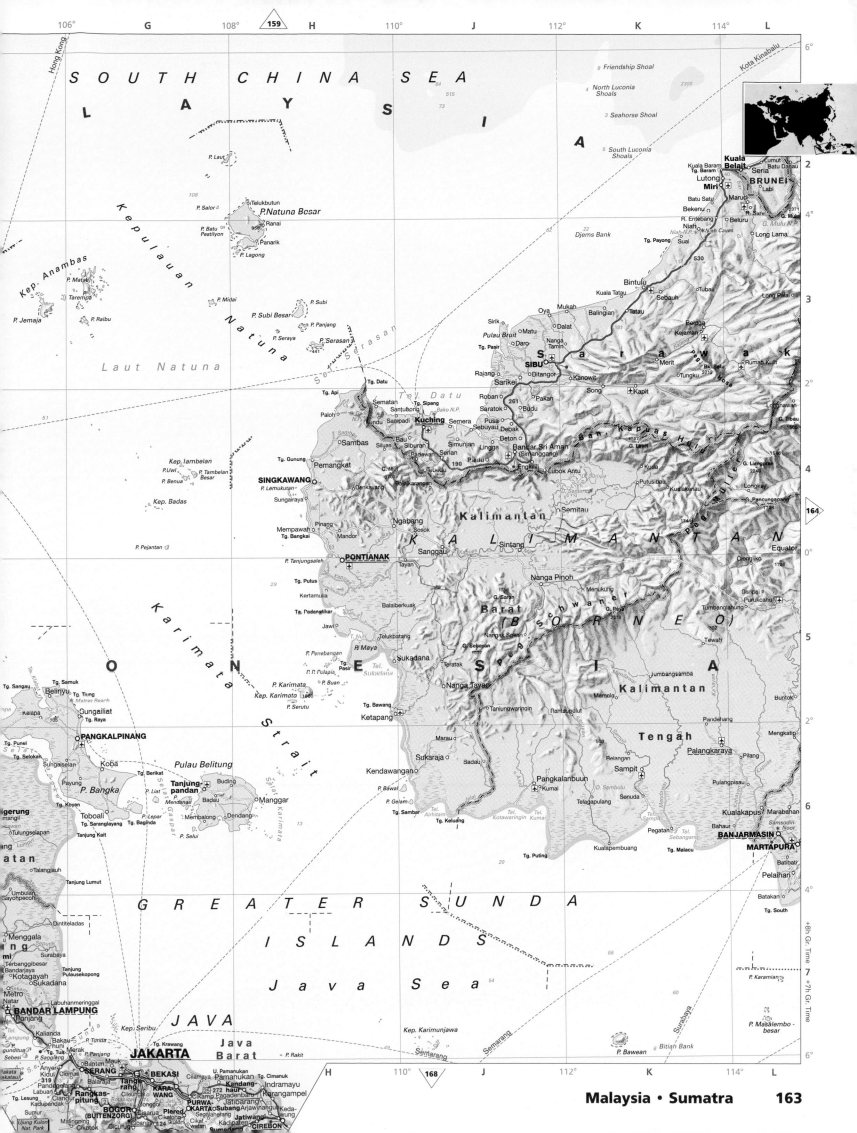

SOUTH CHINA SEA

M A L A Y S I A

Hong Kong

8 Friendship Shoal

North Luconia
Shoals

3 Seahorse Shoal

5 South Luconia
Shoals

Kota Kinabalu

Kuala Baram Tg. Baram
Lutong Seria
Miri **BRUNEI** Labi
Batu Satu
Bekenu R. Suai
R. Entebang Niah N.P.
Niah Niah Caves Long Lama

Kuala
Belait

Kep. Anambas

P. Matak
Tarempa

P. Jemaja P. Raibu

P. Salor
Telukbutun
P.Natuna Besar
Ranai
P. Batu
Pestilyon Panarik
P. Lagong

Kepulauan Natuna

P. Midai
P. Subi
P. Subi Besar P. Panjang
P. Seraya
P. Serasan

Laut Natuna

Djems Bank

Tg. Payong Suai
530

Bintulu
Kuala Tatau Tubau Long Palal
Oya Mukah Sebauh
Balingian Tatau
Sirik Dalat
Pulau Bruit Nanga 181
Daro Tamin
Tg. Pasir **S a r a w a k**
Rajang **SIBU** Bitangor Kanowit
Sarikei Song Kapit Rumah Kulit
Roban Pakan Merit Tungku Bk. Batu 2012
Saratok Budu
261 Kep. Anambas

Tg. Datu
Tg. Api Tel. Datu Bako N.P.
Sematan Tg. Sipang
Santubong
Paloh Sampadi **Kuching** Semera
Sungai Bau Siluas Siburan Padawan Serian
Sambas Beton
Simunjan Lingga
Singkawang Denkayang 190 Parilu Bandar Sri Aman
Balaikarangan Tebedu (Simanggang)
C. Niut Enkilili Lubok Antu
Sungairaya Kuda
Pemangkat Kep. Tambelan Semitau G. Lianggaran
P.Uwi Putusibau 2241
Kep. Badas Ngabang Sosok Kualakenau Longkay
Mempawah Mandor Sintang G. Pancungapang
Tg. Bangkai **K a l i m a n t a n**
P. Pejantan 1728
Pinang Olongliko
PONTIANAK Tayan Equator
P. Tanjungsaleh Sanggau Tumbanglahung Purukcahu
Tg. Putus Nanga Pinoh Tewah
Kertamulia Menukung
Tg. Padangtikar Balaiberkuak G. Saran Schwaner **B O R N E O**
Jawi **B a r a t** G. Raja
Telukbatang Nangak Sekan Jumbangsamba
T. Nuri G. Sebuyon Kalimantan
P. Maya Teratak Memala
P. Penebangan Sukadana Nanga Tayap Taniungwaringin Nantoupulut
P. Karimata **Tengah**
Kep. Karimata Buntok
P. Serutu Ketapang Marau Mengkatip
Tg. Bawang Sukaraja Sadau Pandehan
Kendawangan Palangkaraya Pilang
Pangkalanbuun Sampit Pulangpisau
P. Bawal Kumai D. Sembulu Senuda
P. Gelam Telagapulang Kualakapus Marabahan
Tg. Sambar Tel. Kualapembuang Bahaur **BANJARMASIN**
Airhitam Tg. Malacu Samsudin **MARTAPURA**
Tg. Keluang Kotawaringin Pegatan Noor
Tg. Puting Tel. Sebangau Pelaihari

Kuala Kapuas

Batu Danau
G. Mulu N.P.

Karimata Strait

P U L A U   B E L I T U N G

PANGKALPINANG

P. Bangka

Tanjung-
pandan Buding
Manggar

Toboali Membalong Dendang
P. Lepar
Tg. Saranglayang P. Selui

I N D O N E S I A

G R E A T E R   S U N D A

I S L A N D S

Java Sea

Kep. Karimunjawa
Semarang Surabaya

P. Bawean

P. Masalembo-
besar

P. Karamian

Bitiah Bank

Bandarjaya Surabaya
Kotagayah
Tanjung Pulausekopong

BANDAR LAMPUNG

Kep. Seribu

J A V A

JAKARTA Java
Barat
SERANG **BEKASI**
KARA-
WANG
BOGOR Subang Indramayu
(BUITENZORG) **PURWA-** Jatibarang
KARTA **CIREBON**

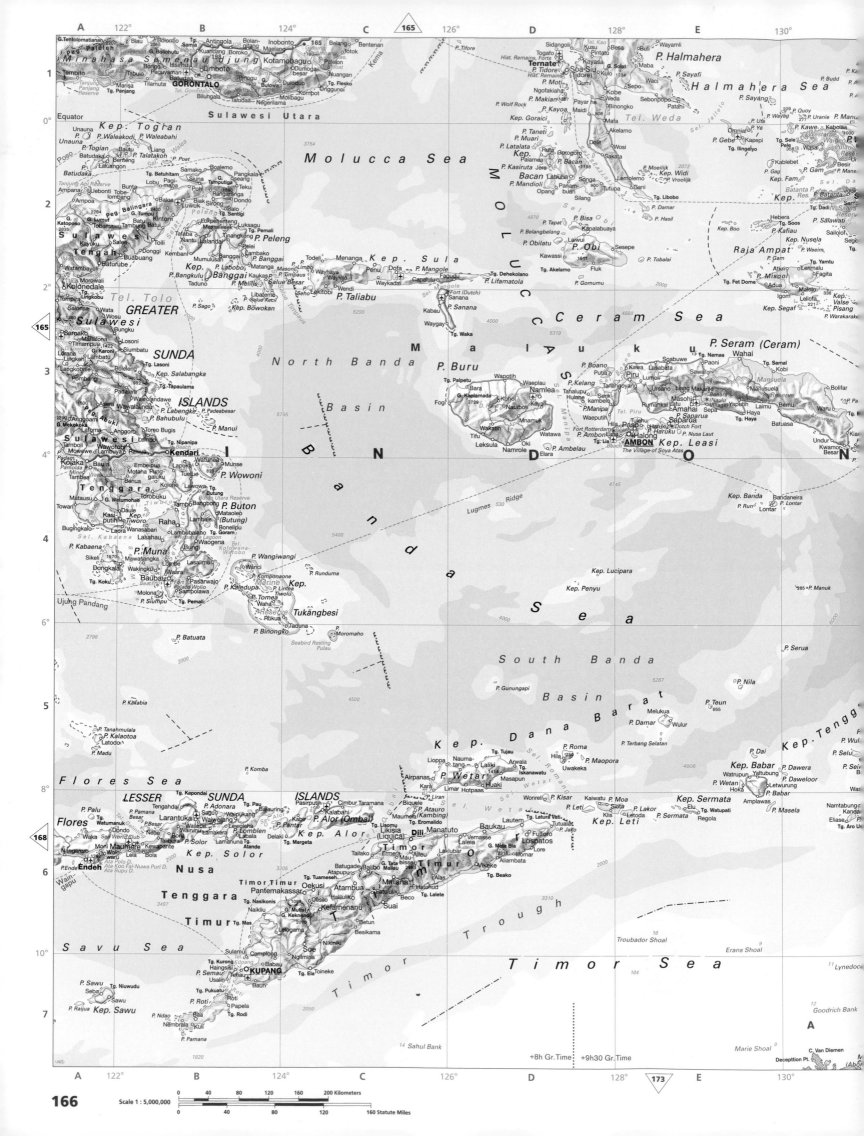

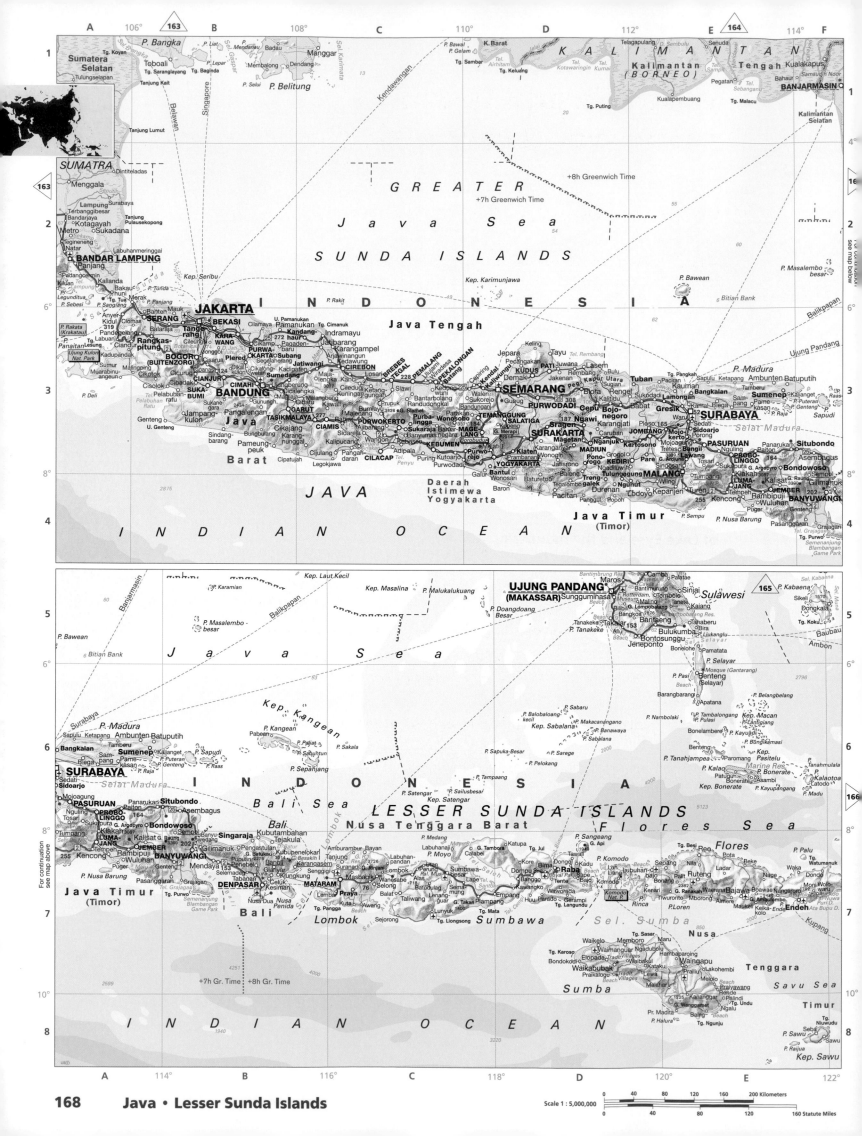

Australia and Oceania –
a new world in the Pacific

Australia: Northwestern Region
172 – 173

Australia: Northeastern Region
174 – 175

Australia: Southwestern Region
176 – 177

Australia: Eastern Region
178 – 179

Australia: Southeastern Region,
Tasmania   180 – 181

New Zealand
182

Papua New Guinea
183

Solomon Islands · Vanuatu · Fiji ·
Samoa · Tonga   184

The smallest continent (2,972,970 square miles/7.7 million sq. km) is

also the one farthest from all the others. Australia's distance from

Europe and the inaccessibility of its shores, due among other things

to the coral reefs that extend north and east, were among the

causes for its late exploration. Distinctive features are the western

plateau with average heights of between 656 and 1,640 feet

(200–500 m), the central lowlands with the internal drainage basin

of Lake Eyre and the mountain areas in the East including the

island of Tasmania. The archipelagos north and east of Australia,

including the world's second largest island, New Guinea, and the

Australia as it was charted in
1644 by the Dutch Abel Tasman.
It was not until 1770 that the
eastern coast was explored by
James Cook.

two-island nation of New Zealand, are sometImes called

Oceania, and comprise some 7,500 islands with an area

of 501,930 square miles (1.3 million sq. km) dispersed over

a sea area of 27,027,000 square miles (70 million sq. km).

Melanesia and New Zealand constitute the outer arc of islands,

Micronesia and Polynesia the inner. The islands sit partially on old

mountains of volcanic origin beneath the sea and partially on

elevated coral reefs. The 180th meridian, the dateline, runs through

the middle of the region.

Australia: Northwestern Region
172 – 173

Australia: Northeastern Region
174 – 175

Australia: Southwestern Region
176 – 177

Australia: Eastern Region
178 – 179

Australia: Southeastern Region,
Tasmania   180 – 181

New Zealand
182

Papua New Guinea
183

Solomon Islands · Vanuatu · Fiji ·
Samoa · Tonga   184

Scale 1 : 5,000,000

0 40 80 120 160 200 Kilometers

0 40 80 120 160 Statute Miles

Australia: Northwestern Region

Arafura Sea
Arafura Shelf

G u l f

o f

C a r p e n t a r i a

C. Wessel
Marchinbar I.
Wessel Is.
Mining Area (Bauxite)

Raragala I. Guluwuru I.
Drysdale I. Truant I.
N.W. Crocodile I. Elcho I. Cunningham's Is. C. Wilberforce
Bromby Is.

C. Croker
Croker I. McCluer I.
Minjilang
Mount
norman
Bay
Murgenella
North Goulburn I.
South Goulburn I.
Warruwi
Timber
Mill
Murgenella
Endyalgout
Wildlife
Sanctuary
Tor Rock
261

Hawkesbury Pt. C. Stewart
Castlereagh
Bay
Howard I.
Maningrida
Milingimbi
Napier Pen.
Buckingham Bay
67° Melville Bay
Yirrkala
Bremer I.
Nhulunbuy (Gove)
C. Arnhem

Nabarlek
Aborig.
Rock Art Oenpelli
Ubirr
Munmarlary
Mt. Howship
385
Nangalala
Ramingining
Mirrngadja Village
Gapuwiyak
Gove Pen.

Jabiru
Kakadu
Holiday
Village Burdulba
Ranger Uranium Mine
Nourlangie Rock
Camburinga
Pt. Alexander
Caledon Bay
C. Grey

Cooinda
Motel
Patonga
Kakadu Mt. Gilruth
436 Mt. Parsons
301
C. Shield
Blue Mud Bay Isle Woodah

National Park
El Sharana Mine Mt. Evelyn
366
Arnhem Aboriginal
Scott Pt.
Port Langdo
Bickerton I. Alyangula
Umbakumba
Groote
Eylandt
(Abor. Land)
C. Keer-weer

Sleisbeck Mine
295
Land
Angurugu
Rantyirrity Pt.
Tasman Pt.
Cape Beatrice

Mt. Lambell
318 Mountain
Valley
Mainoru
Numbulwar
Edward I.
Aborig.
Land

Nitmiluk
(Katherine Gorge
Nat. P.) Eva Valley
Three Graces
Edward R.
Stra

Edith
Falls
Katherine Beswick
Bamyili
Beswick
Aboriginal
Land
Roper Bar Ngukurr
St.Vidgeon
Warrakunta Pt.
Limmen Bight
Prawn Fishing Base
Maria I.
Kowany
Abori
Edward River

Cutta Cutta
Caves Moroak
Roper
Valley
Limmen Bight
Aboriginal
Land
Colee

Mataranka
(Hot Springs) Elsey
Elsey Cemetery
170 Hodgson Downs
Nathan River
The Four Archers
West I. North I.
Sir Edward
Pellew Group
Kowanyama

Gorrie Elsey Nat. P.
Hodgson River
Alawangandji
Aboriginal
Land Rosie Creek
Bing Bong
Centre I. Vanderlin I.
Rutland
Plains
Alli
Nassau R.

Birdum
Larrimah
Cox River
Bauhinia Downs
213
Borroloola
Abor. Land
Black Rocks
Landing
Manangoora
1 Borroloola
+9h 30
Greenwich Time +10h
Greenwich Time
Inkerman

Maryfield
227
Nutwood
Downs
O.T.Downs
Tanumbirini
1 Tawallah
Seven Emu
Wellesley Islands
(Mornington Is. Aboriginal Land Trust) Galbraith

Daly Waters
Roadhouse Carpentaria Hwy.
271 156
Pungalina
Mornington I.
C.Van Diemen (Big-Game Fishing)
Macaroni

Hidden Valley
39 Cape Crawford
106 McArthur
Robinson
River
Calvert
Gununa
Denham I. Bountiful Is.
Delta
Downs

Dunmarra
Roadhouse
190 Top Springs
(Aband.)
Mallapunyah
Kiana
Calvert Hills
Forsyth I.
Bentinck I. Point Austin
Stirli

Sir Charles Todo
Monument
128 Robinson
River
Wollogorang
Hells Gate
Roadhouse
Westmoreland
457 Sweers I.
Sweers I.Abor.Land)
Karumba

Beetaloo
270 Shadon Downs
Wallhallow
Creswell
Downs
Seigals Creek
Doomadgee
Aboriginal
Land
Escott Burketown
Maggieville
Normanton
(10)
Gulflander
(Hist. Railway)
Blackbul

Newcastle
Waters 652
Elliott
Uchanoidge Mungabroom
Anthony Lagoon
Fish River
Doomadgee
Armraynald
Wernadinga
Inverleigh
Glenore
East Haydon

Eva Downs
Waanyi-Garawa
Aboriginal
Land
Brinawa
Floraville
Macalister
Milgarra

Walmanpa-Warlpiri
16 224
Renner
Springs
Helen Springs
Brunette Downs
Mithebah
Connels Lagoon
Conservation Res.
Spring Vale
Highland Plains
Lawn Hill
Nat. P. Lawn
Hill
Gregory
Downs
Augustus-
Downs
Warren Vale
Old Coralie
(Ruins)
Yappar R.

Muckaty
Brunchilly
Rockhampton
Downs
226
11 Alexandria
Old Herbert Vale
Silver Star
Mine
Riversleigh
Lorraine
Cowan
Downs
Iffley
Clara

Banka
Banka
212 Gallipoli
Herbert Vale
Morstone
Gregory Downs 375
Burke
and Wills
Roadhouse
Myola
Sava
Dow

Phillip Creek
Station Stuart Memorial
86 Alroy Downs
Thorntonia
Gunpowder
Kamileroi
Alsace
Mining Area
(Iron Ore) Boomarra
Arizona
Numil Downs

Phillip Creek
John Flynn
Memorial
188 Frewena
Ranken Store
Camooweal Dobbyn
Kajabbi
Alcala
Kalmeta
Millunga

Warrego Mine
Three Ways
Roadhouse
Peko Mine
651 Barkly
Homestead
Roadhouse
Barkly Hwy.
66 Camooweal
Caves
Nat. P. Yelvertoft
Calton
Hills Mt.
Remarkable
475
Clonagh
Dalgonally
Manfred
Downs

Tennant Creek
(327) Nobles Nob Mine
436 Barry Caves
320 Soudan
Avon Downs
651 275 66
Austral
Downs Buckley R.
Hilton
Mining Area
(Silver, Uranium) Ford
Constantine
Quamby
Julia
Creek

Kaititja-Warlpiri
249 McLaren
Creek Kurundi
Epenarra
Burramurra
Out Station
Barkly Downs
Mary
Kathleen
Mount Isa Moondarra
Mining Area
(Silver, Uranium)
193 117
Cloncurry
Mt. Norna
418
Gilliat
Edith

Aboriginal
Davis Marbles
Scenic Reserve
Wauchope
Murchison Ra.
Mt.Cairns Kurinelli Out Station
Dempseys
Lake Nash Oban
Georgina
Downs Barkly
Tableland Bullecourt
Malbon
Vale Black Mtn.
566
Malbon
Oorindi

Willowra
Aboriginal
Land Trust 489 Warrabri
Old Ivy Mine
531 Murray
Downs Hatches Creek
506 Annitowa
Annotowa
339 577 Headingly
Sheila
Out Station
Warwick
Vale
O.S.
151 Duchess
Butru
McKinlay

Tanami
Desert
Wildlife
Sanctuary Willowra
Wirliyajarrayi
Abor. Land Barrow
Creek 557
Neutral Junction
Ammaroo
Derry Downs
Sandover Hwy.
Mt.Hogart
340
Argadargada
Urandangi
Ardmore
Dajarra
The Monument
83 Chats-
worth
Beaudesert
Selwyn P.O.
Answer
Downs
Arizona
Kynu

Central
Mt.Stuart
1140 Stirling
Mt.Tops
708 Mt.Octy
694
Utopia
Aboriginal Land
Ooratippra
Manners
Creek Carandotta
Buckingham
Downs
Noranside
Burnham
O.S.
Denbigh
Woods

Scale 1 : 5,000,000

0 40 80 120 160 200 Kilometers
0 40 80 120 160 Statute Miles

Scale 1 : 5,000,000

0   40   80   120   160   200 Kilometers

0   40   80   120   160 Statute Miles

H   126°   J   128°   173   K   130°   L   132°   M   134°   N

Tropic of Capricorn

Central

Windy Corner

Australia

L. MacDonald

Mt.Leisler
L. Anec
L. Cobb

McPhersons Pillar
530

Gibson Desert

L. Hancock

Charles
Knob
551

Browne
Ra.

Alfred and Marie Ra.

Nature
Reserve

L. Newell

L. Gruszka

Everard
Junction

Decker
Field

L. Sprenger

Mt. Johnson

Mt. Beadell

Mt. Charles
533

Baker Ra.

Herbert
Wash

L. Breaden

Sutherland Ra.

Mt. Charles

Blyth Lagoon

Mi Mi Rocks

Warburton Ra.

L. Gillen

574

Manton Knob
503

Baker Lake

Haasts Bluff Aboriginal Land

Mt.Russell
791

Johnstone Hill
701

Mt.Lieblg
1525

Papunya

Derwent

Narwietooma

Mt.Zeil
1166

Haast Bluff

Mt.Hay
1511

Mt.Soder
1250

Glen Helen

Mt.Ertwa

Hamilton
Downs

Alice Springs

Macdonnell Ranges

Northern

Hermannsburg

Undandita

Territory

Deep Well

Maryvale

Finke

S o u t h

Great Victoria Desert

INDIAN OCEAN

Australia: Southwestern Region   177

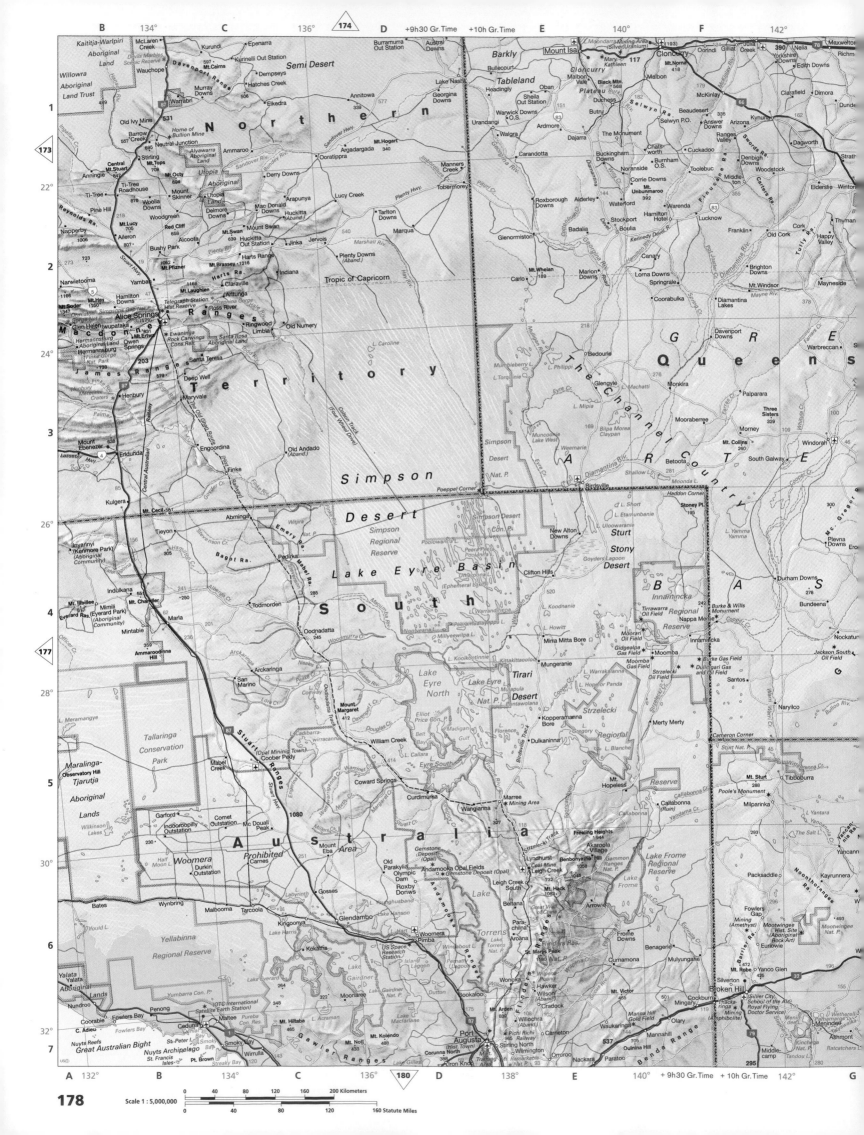

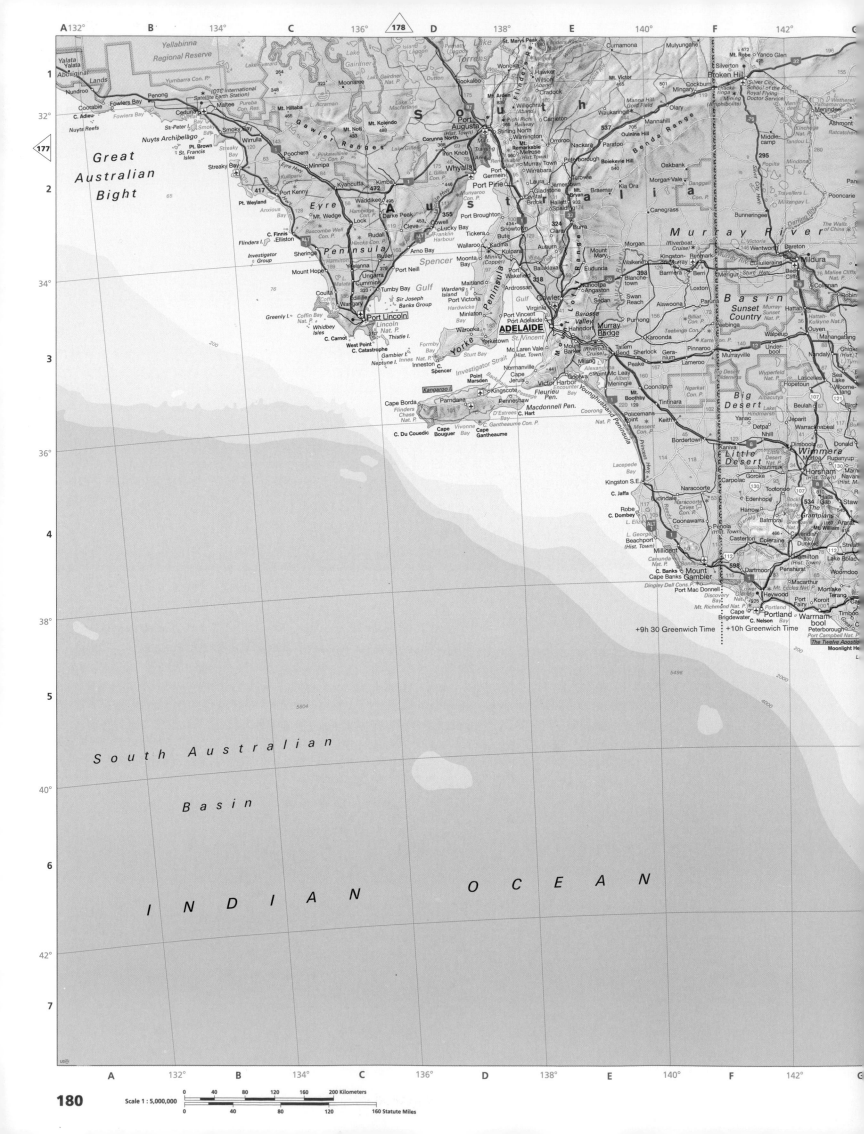

Scale 1 : 5,000,000

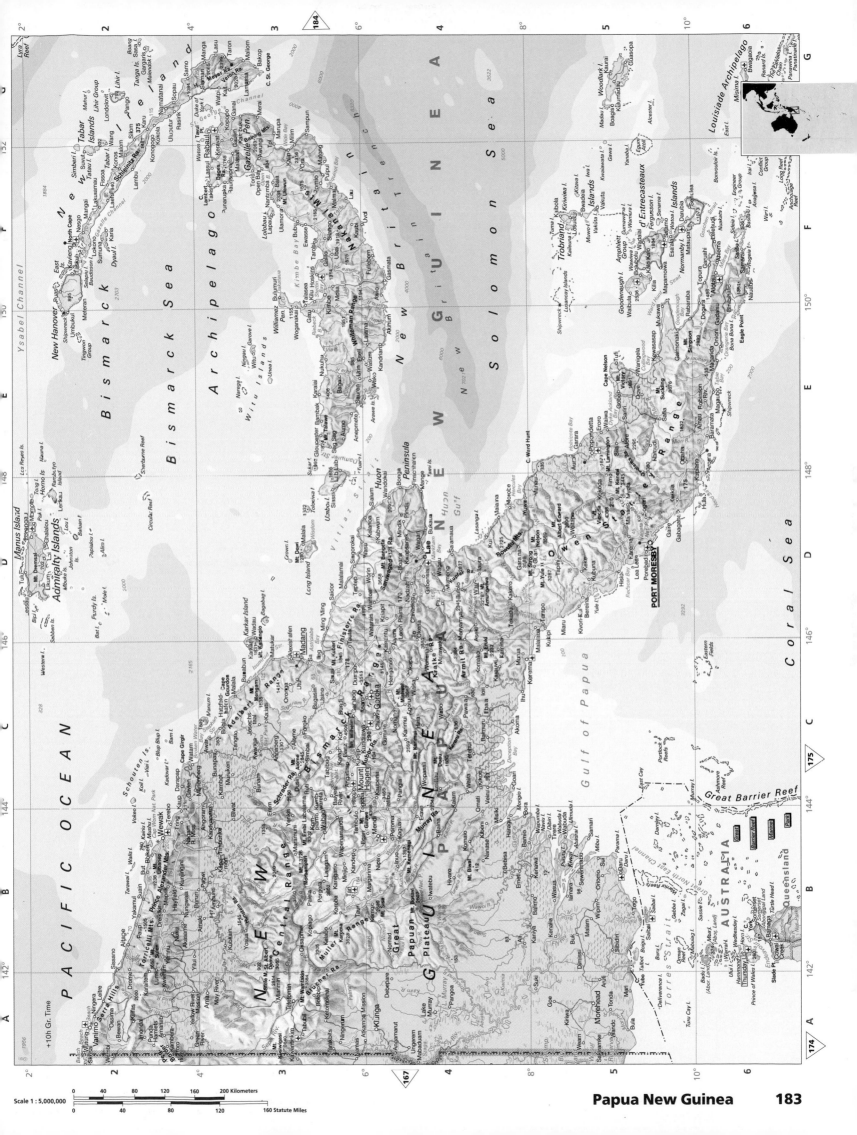

Scale 1 : 5,000,000

0 40 80 120 160 200 Kilometers

0 40 80 120 160 Statute Miles

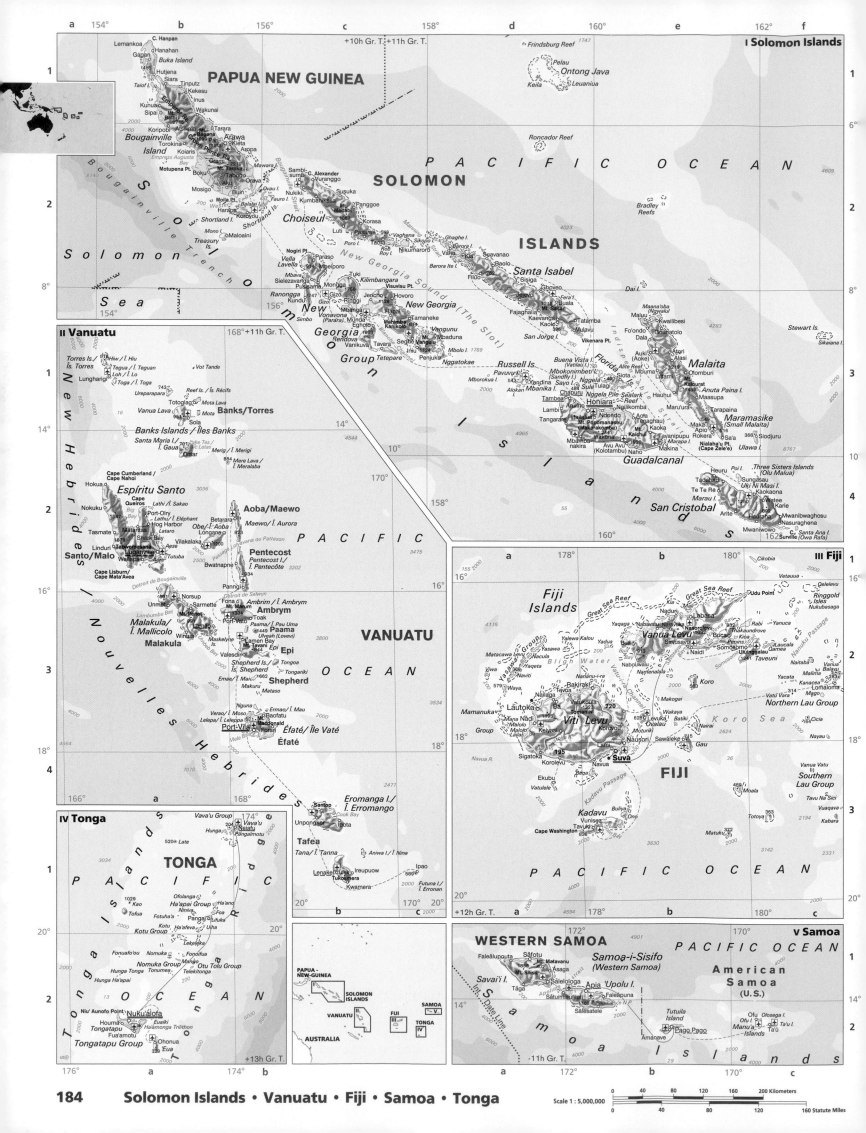

PAPUA NEW GUINEA

SOLOMON ISLANDS

I Solomon Islands

II Vanuatu

III Fiji

IV Tonga

V Samoa

WESTERN SAMOA

VANUATU

FIJI

TONGA

PACIFIC OCEAN

Fiji Islands

Viti Levu

Vanua Levu

Espíritu Santo

Malakula / Î. Mallicolo

Guadalcanal

San Cristobal

Malaita

Santa Isabel

New Georgia Group

Choiseul

Bougainville Island

Solomon Sea

New Hebrides / Nouvelles Hébrides

Banks Islands / Îles Banks

Pentecost / Î. Pentecôte

Ambrym

Shepherd Is.

Éfaté / Île Vaté

Eromanga I. / Î. Erromango

TONGA

Tonga Islands

Tongatapu Group

Vava'u Group

Ha'apai Group

Nomuka Group

Port-Vila

Suva

Honiara

Apia

Nuku'alofa

Nuku'alofa

Nukualofa

PACIFIC OCEAN

Scale 1 : 5,000,000

0   40   80   120   160   200 Kilometers

0   40   80   120   160 Statute Miles

Africa – a continent of vibrant culture and people

Africa, the second largest continent on Earth, takes up one-fifth of the total land mass on the planet. It is characterized by a coastline that contains few gulfs and peninsulas, the triangular southern cone, and the division into Upper Africa in the southeast and Lower Africa in the northwest. The highlands with basins and rises as well as an extended rift valley system shape its surface. Africa contains all tropical landscape and climatic areas of the world, distributed primarily along the latitude lines on both sides of the Equator. One-third of Africa is occupied by the largest desert on Earth, the Sahara. This

Johann Baptist Homann made this copperplate engraving of Africa around the year 1690, approximately 150 before Europeans first began to explore the continent's interior.

environment, hostile to life, separates white Africa, mostly settled by Islamic Arab peoples, from black Africa, characterized by the Sudanese and Bantu peoples. Contrary to the imaginary picture of the "dark continent," Africa has a vibrant culture and history. This is where, over three million years ago, our early ancestors learned to walk upright, and today its melange of peoples, races, languages and traditions is only beginning to be appreciated.

Morocco · Canary Islands
188 – 189

Algeria · Tunisia
190 – 191

Libya
192 – 193

Egypt
194 – 195

Mauritania · Mali: Northern Region
196 – 197

Niger · Chad
198 – 199

Sudan: Northern Region · Eritrea
200 – 201

Upper Guinea
202 – 203

Ghana · Togo · Benin · Nigeria · Cameroon   204 – 205

Central African Republic · Sudan: Southern Region   206 – 207

Ethiopia · Somali Peninsula
208 – 209

Lower Guinea
210 – 211

East Africa: Northern Region
212 – 213

East Africa: Southern Region
214 – 215

Angola · Namibia: Northern Region
216 – 217

Zambia · Zimbabwe · Mozambique
218 – 219

South Africa
220 – 221

Madagascar · Comoros
222 – 223

Seychelles · Réunion · Mauritius
224

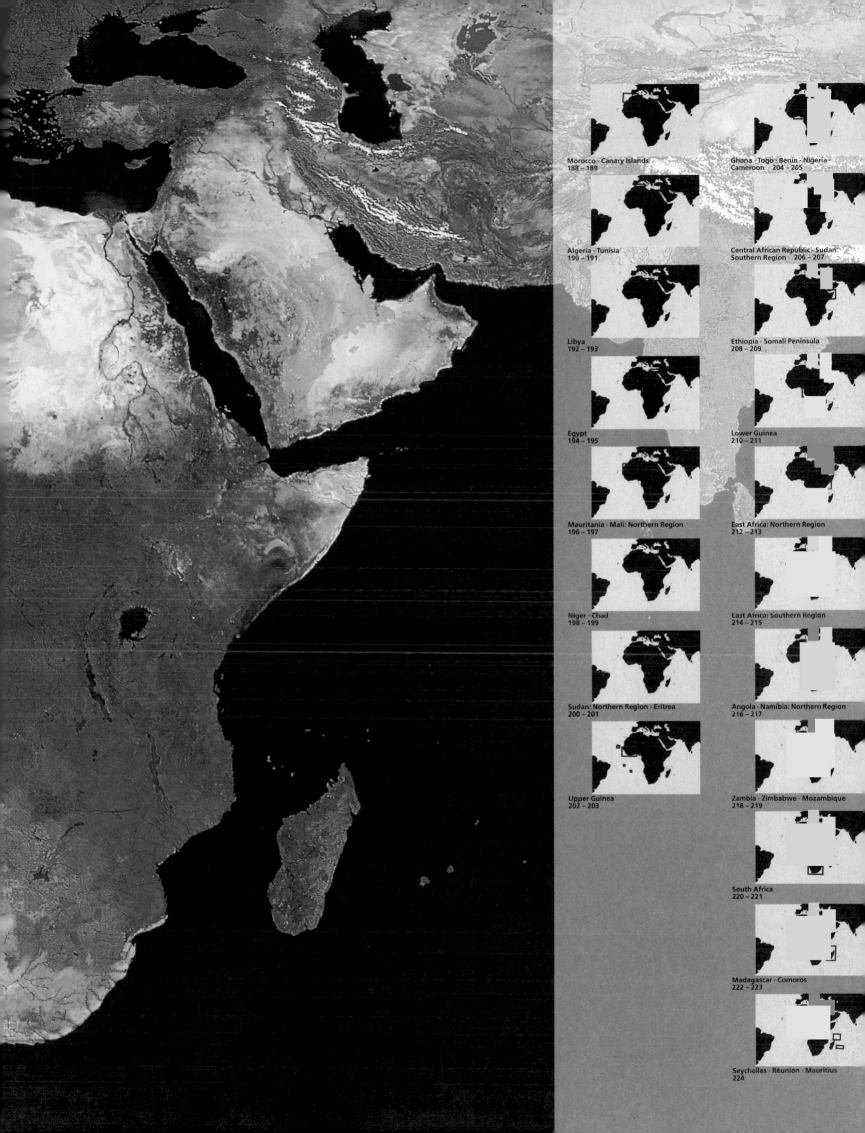

Morocco · Canary Islands
188 – 189

Algeria · Tunisia
190 – 191

Libya
192 – 193

Egypt
194 – 195

Mauritania · Mali: Northern Region
196 – 197

Niger · Chad
198 – 199

Sudan: Northern Region · Eritrea
200 – 201

Upper Guinea
202 – 203

Ghana · Togo · Benin · Nigeria ·
Cameroon   204 – 205

Central African Republic · Sudan:
Southern Region   206 – 207

Ethiopia · Somali Peninsula
208 – 209

Lower Guinea
210 – 211

East Africa: Northern Region
212 – 213

East Africa: Southern Region
214 – 215

Angola · Namibia: Northern Region
216 – 217

Zambia · Zimbabwe · Mozambique
218 – 219

South Africa
220 – 221

Madagascar · Comoros
222 – 223

Seychelles · Réunion · Mauritius
224

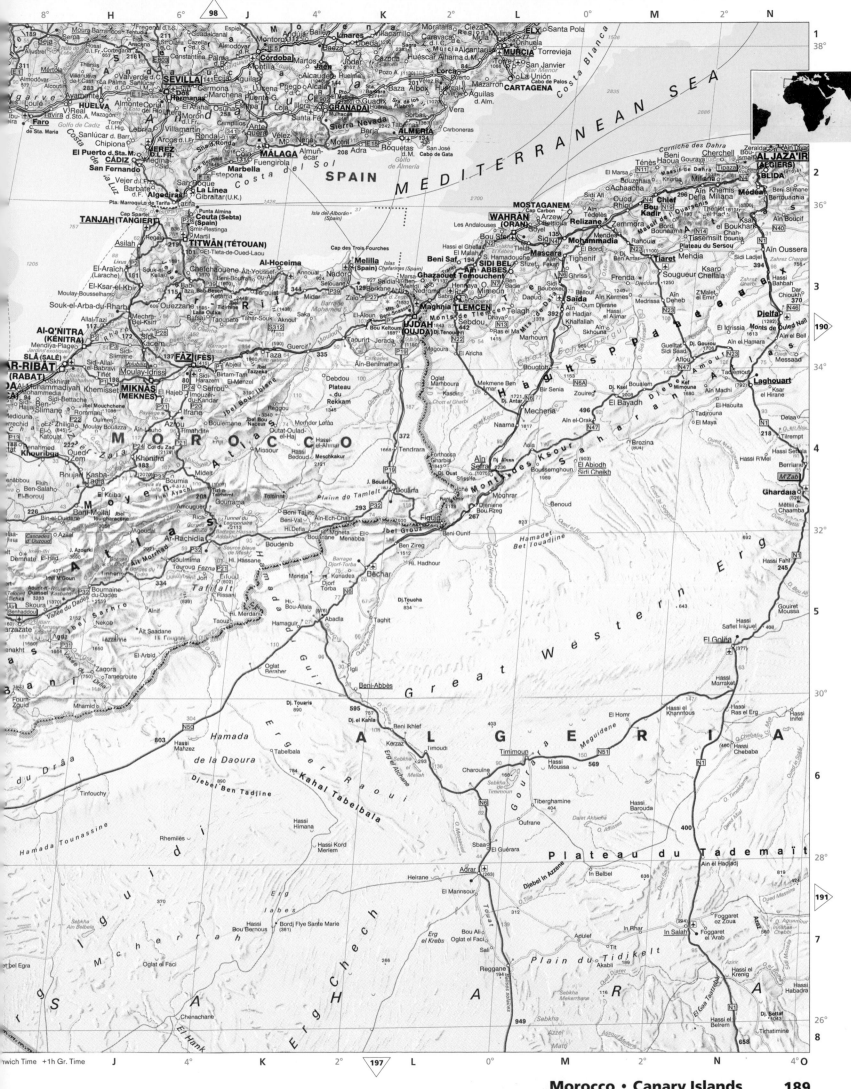

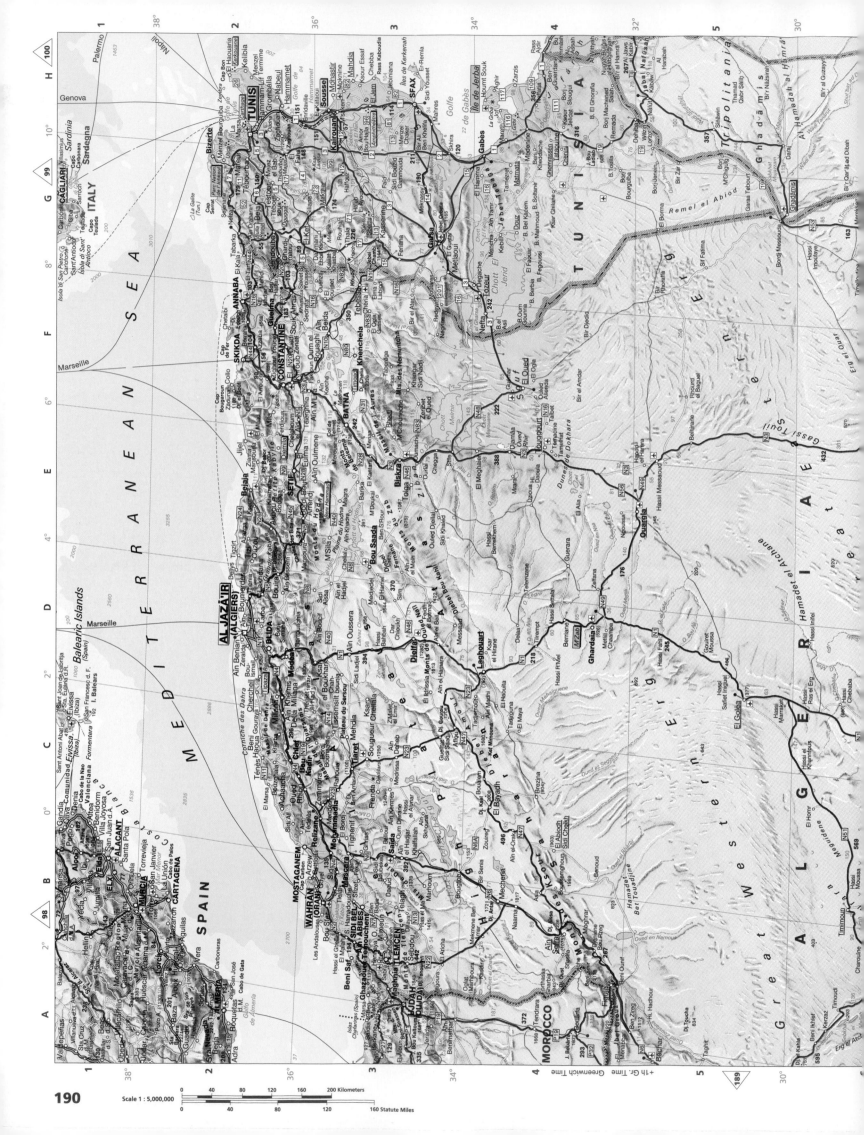

Algeria • Tunisia   191

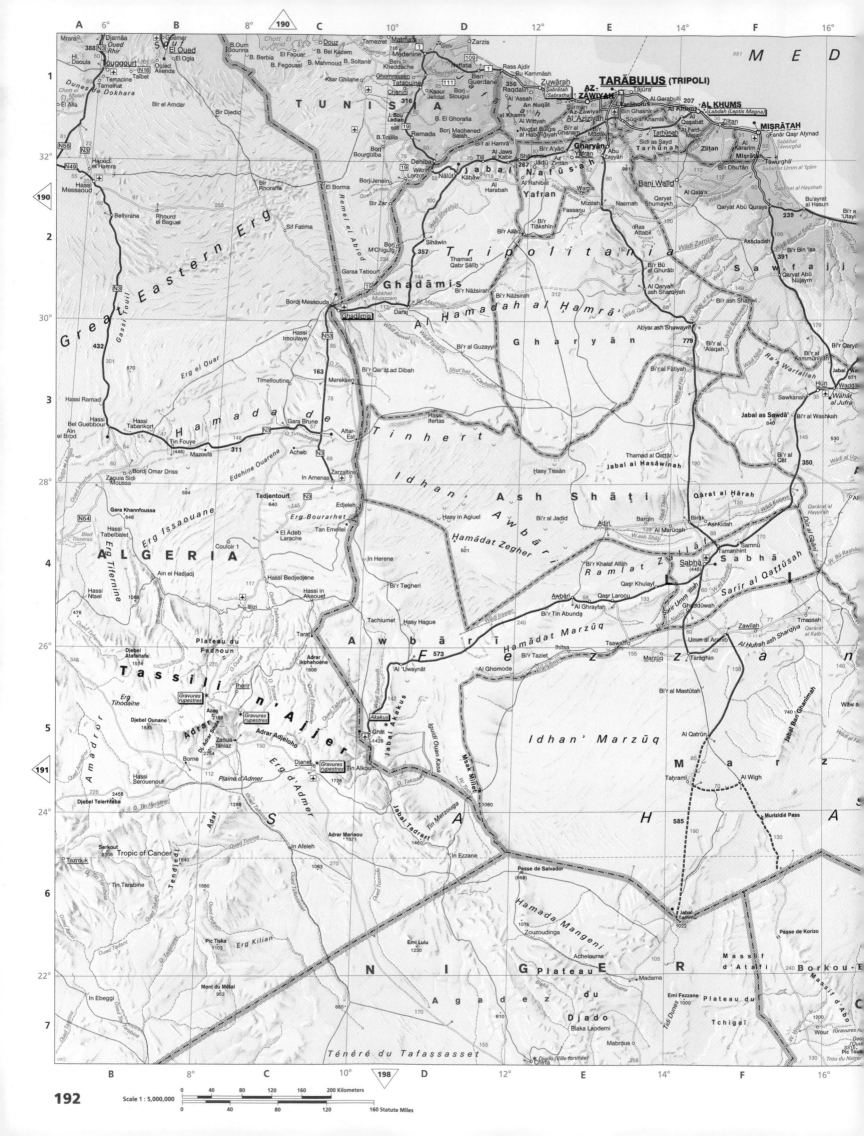

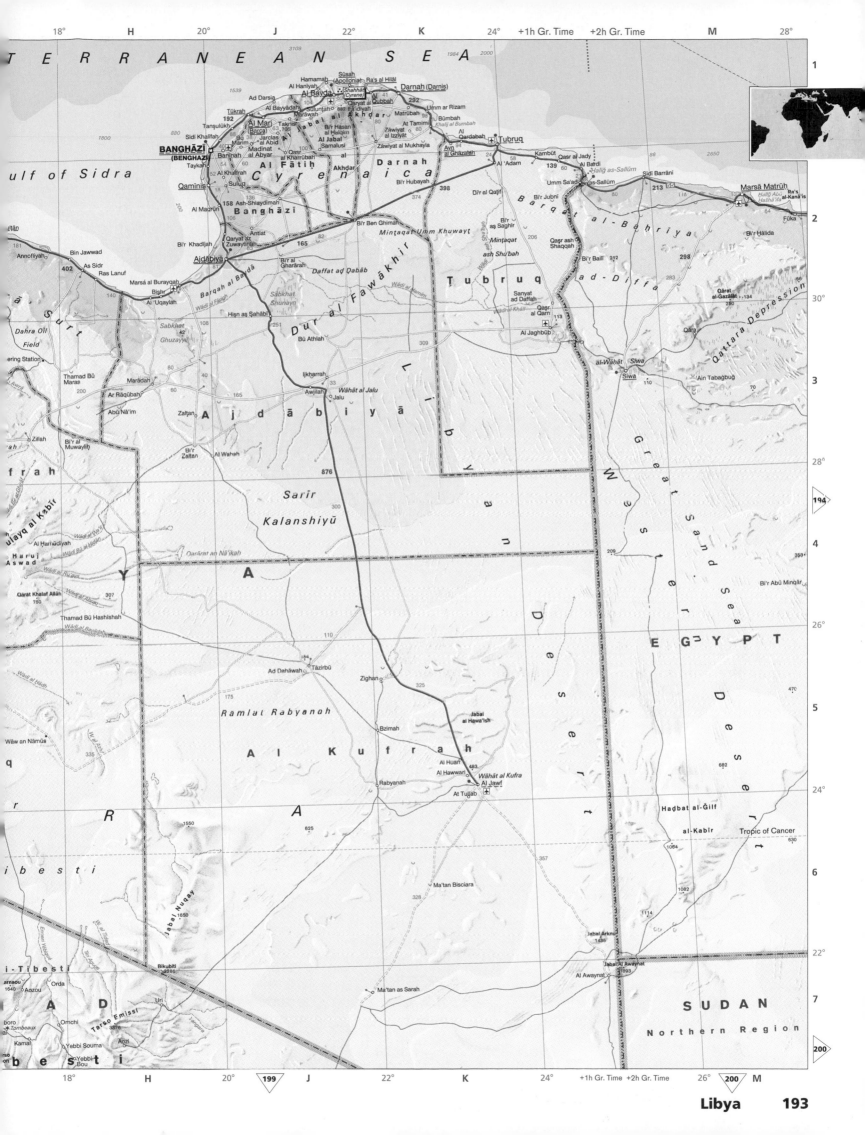

TERRANEAN SEA

Gulf of Sidra

Hamamah
Al Haniyah
Al Bayda
Ad Darsia
Al Bayyadiyah
Suluniah

Süsah (Apollonia)
Shahhāt (Cyrene)
Qaryat al Qubbah
Faidiyah

Ra's al Hilāl
Al
Qubbah

Darnah (Darnis)

Tukrah
Tanşulūkh
Al Marj (Barca)
Taknis
Jarclas
al Abid
Qasr
Marim
Banīnah
Madīnat al Abyar
al Kharrūbah

Bir Hasan al Haiqin
Al Jabal Samalusi

Umm ar Rizam
Matrūbah
At Tamimi

Bümbah
Khalīg al Bumbah
Zāwiyat al Izzīyāt
Zāwiyat al Mukhayla

Al Qardabah
Tubruq

BANGHĀZĪ (BENGHAZI)
Qaminis
Suluq
Al Khatrah
Al Madrūn
Ash-Shlaydīmah

Al Fātih
Banghāzī

Cyrenaica

Darnah

al Akhdar

Bir Hubayah

Ayn al Ghazālah
Al 'Adam
Kambūt
Qaşr al Jady
139
Halīg as-Sallūm
Sidī Barrāni

Marsā Matrūh

Fūka

Antlat
Qaryat az Zuwaytīnah

Bir Ben Ghimal

Minţaqat Umm Khuwayţ

Minţaqat ash Shu'bah
Qaşr ash Shaqqah
Bir Bailī
298

Bir aş Saghīr

Barqat al-Bahriya

Bir Halida

Ajdābiyā
Bir al Gharārah
Daffat aḍ Ḍabāb

Wādī al Namūs

Ţubruq

Qasr al Qarn
Sanyat ad Daffah
Al Jaghbūb

Umm Sa'ad
as-Sallūm

ad-Diffa

Barqah al Baydā
Wādī al Fārigh
Al 'Uqaylah
Bighr
Marsā al Burayqah

Hişn aş Şaḥābī
Sabkhat Shunayn
Bū Athlah

Dūr al Fawākhir

Libya

al-Wāḥāt
Siwa
Qārat al-Ghazālāt 134

Qārā

As Sidr
Ras Lanuf
Bin Jawwad
Annoflīyah
402

Sabkhat Ghuzayyil

Ijkharrah
Awjilah
Jalu
Wāḥāt al Jalu

Great Sand Sea

Qattara Depression

Dahra Oil Field
ering Station

Thamad Bū Maras
Marādah
Abū Nā'im
Ar Rāqūbah

Zaltan

Ajdābiyā

Bi'r Abū Minqār

Zillah
Bi'r al Muwaylih
Bi'r Zaltan
Al Wahah

Sarir

Kalanshiyū

Western Desert

EGYPT

Haruj Aswad
Qarat Khalaf Allāh
750
307

Thamad Bū Hashishah

Ramlat Rabyanah

Ad Dahāwah
Tāzirbū

Zighan

Jabal al Hawa'ish

Al Kufrah

Al Huari
Al Hawwari
At Tujjab

Wāḥāt al Kufra
Al Jawf

Tropic of Cancer

Haḍbat al-Ğilf al-Kabīr

Bzimah
Rabyanah

Wāw an Nāmūs

Tibesti

Jabal Nuqay

Ma'tan Bisciara

Jabal Arknu

Jabal At Awaynāt
Al Awaynat

SUDAN

Northern Region

Bikubiti
Tarso Emissi

Ma'tan as Sarah

Orda
Yebbi Souma

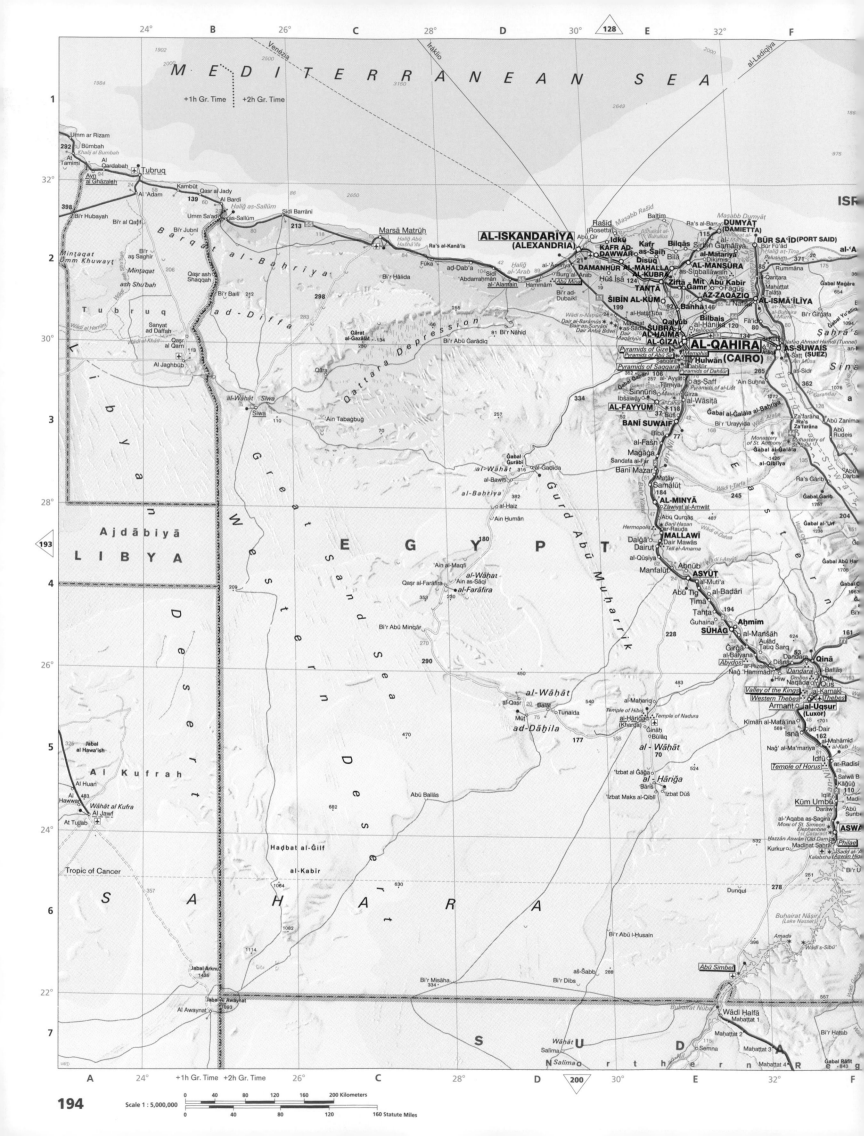

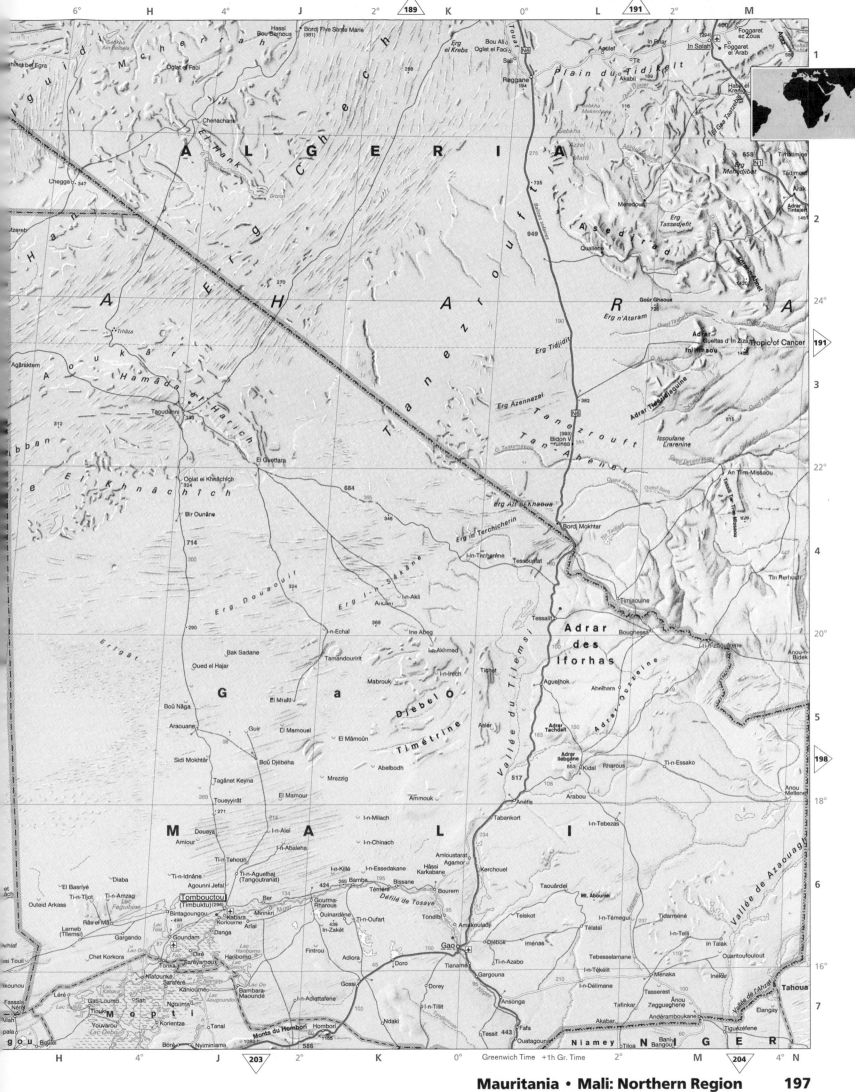

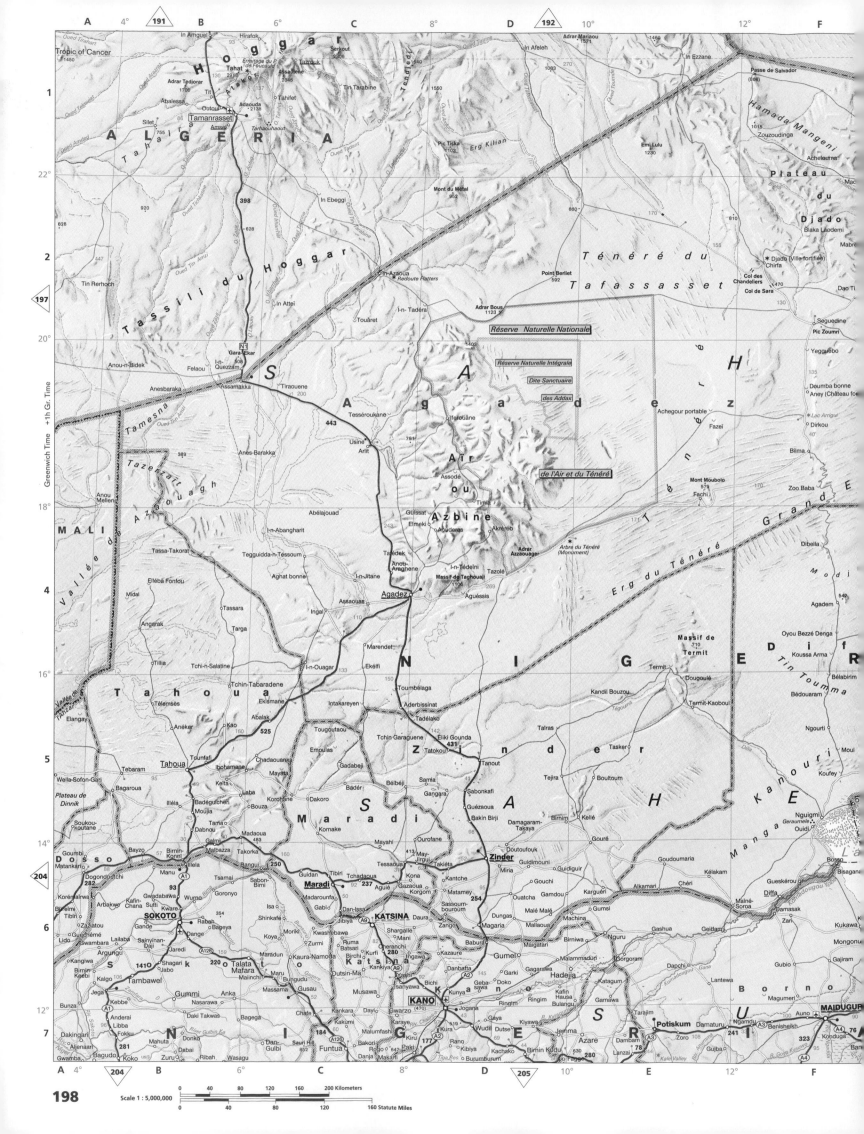

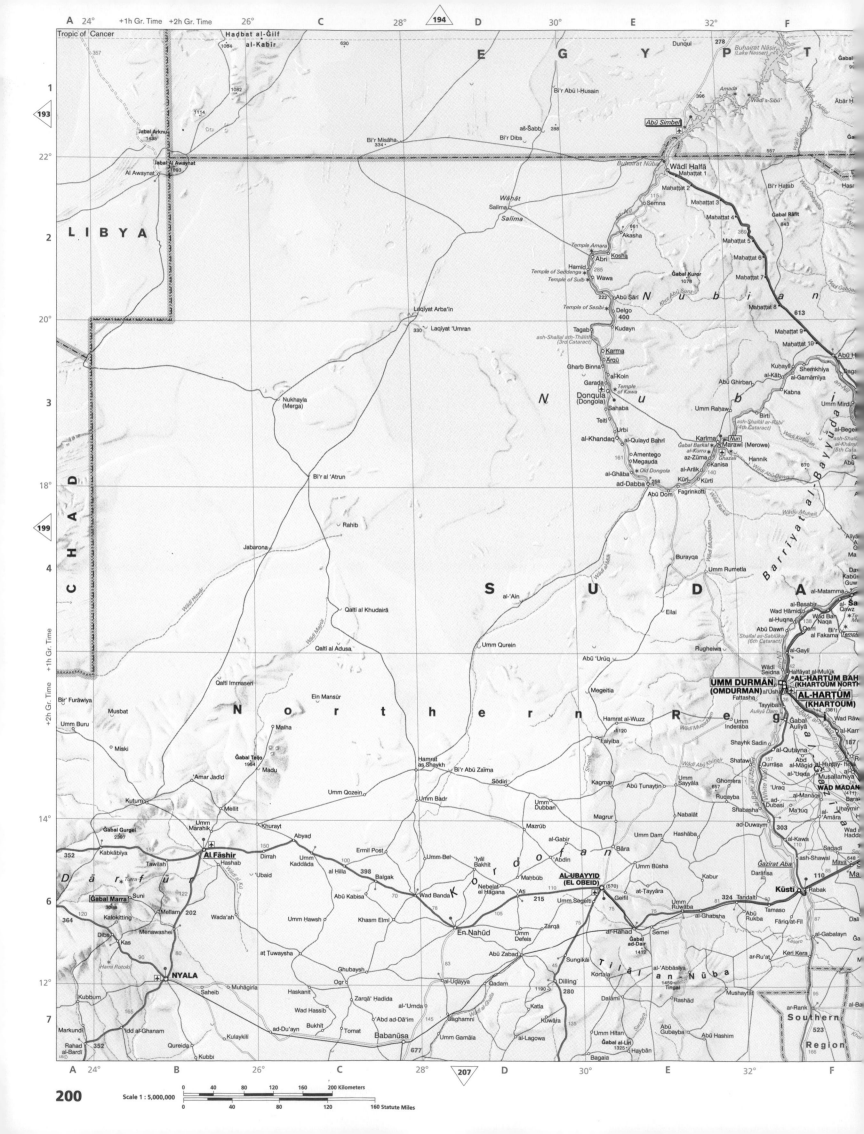

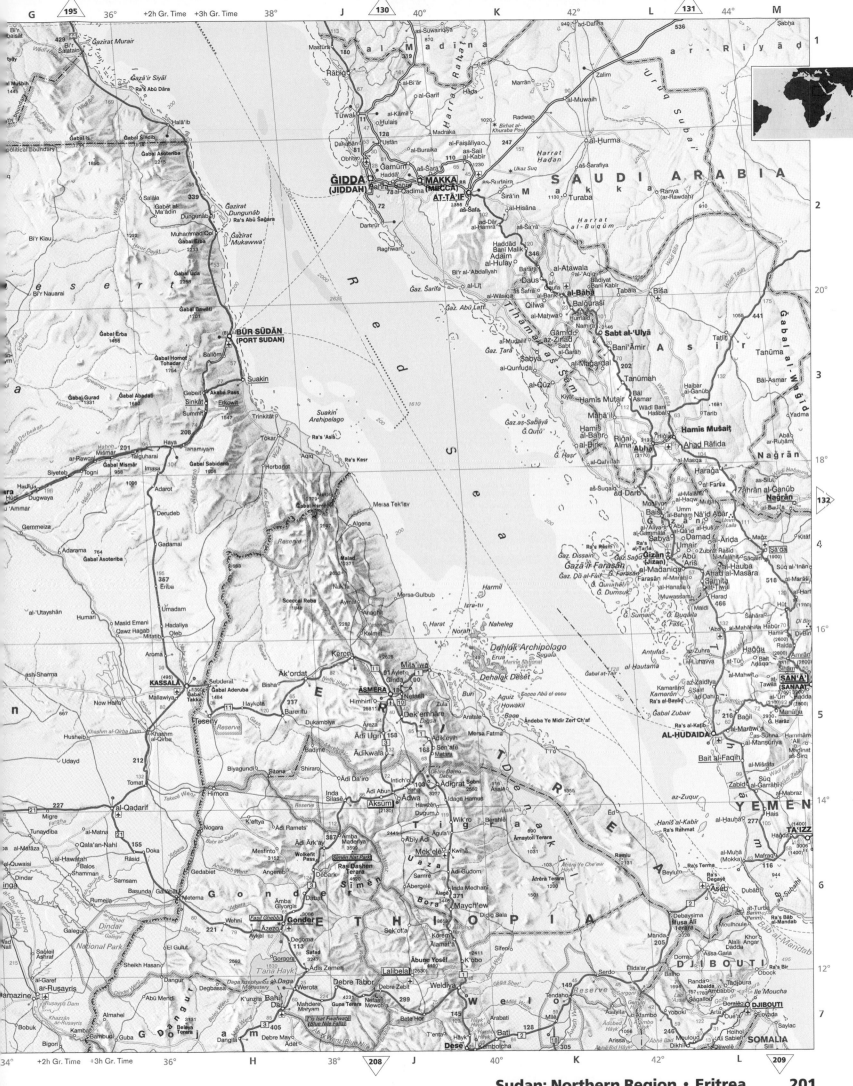

A
18°

B
16°

C
14°

D
12°

E
10°

F

MAURITANIA

DAKAR

SENEGAL

GAMBIA

GUINEA-BISSAU

BISSAU

ZIGUINCHOR

Arquipélago dos Bijagós

ATLANTIC

KAYES

BAMAKO

GUINEA

LABÉ

KANKAN

Djalo

Fouta

KINDIA

CONAKRY

Conakry

FARANAH

FREETOWN

SIERRA LEONE

Magburaka

Koidu

MONROVIA

LIBERIA

Buchanan

Grain Coast

OCEAN

Cape Verde

ATLANTIC OCEAN

−1h Gr. Time

Mindelo

CAPE VERDE

Cape Verde Islands

Praia

Ilhas de Sotavento

Ilhas de Barlavento

Ascension

Greenwich Time

ATLANTIC OCEAN

Georgetown Ascension
St. Helena (U.K.)

St. Helena

Greenwich Time

ATLANTIC OCEAN

Jamestown Saint Helena
St. Helena (U.K.)

Scale 1: 5,000,000

0   40   80   120   160   200 Kilometers

0   40   80   120   160 Statute Miles

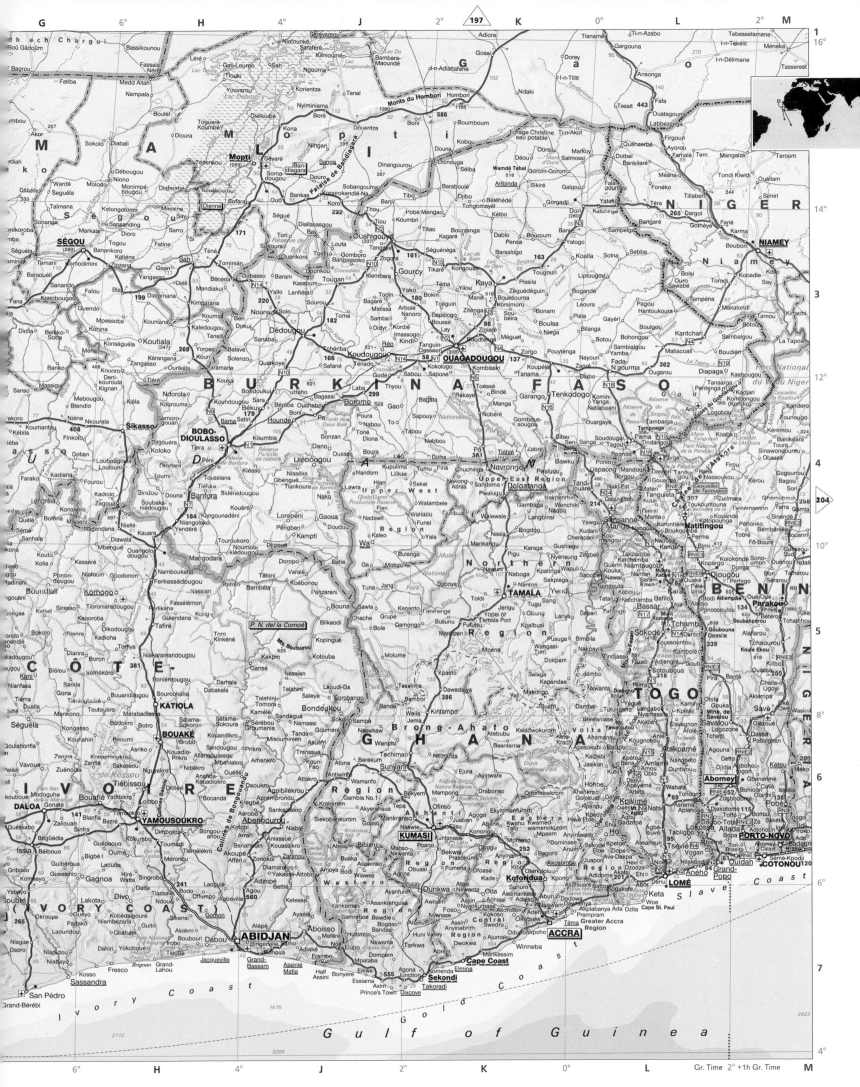

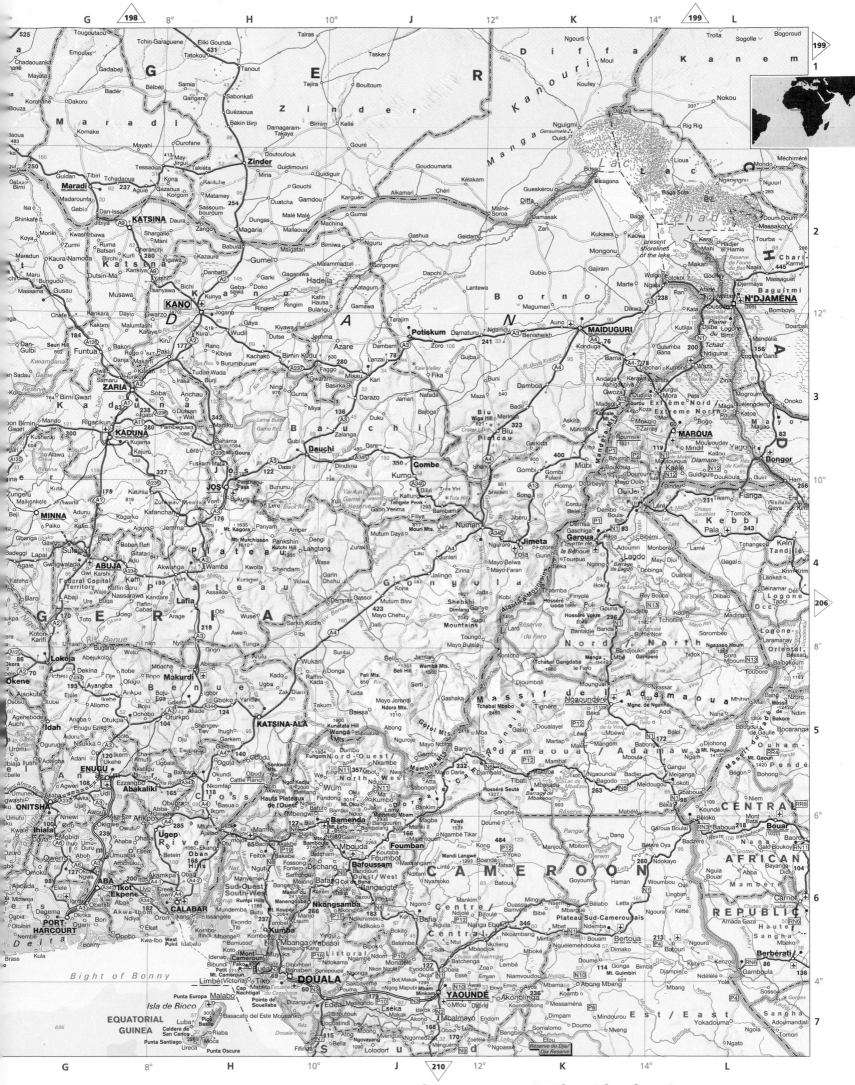

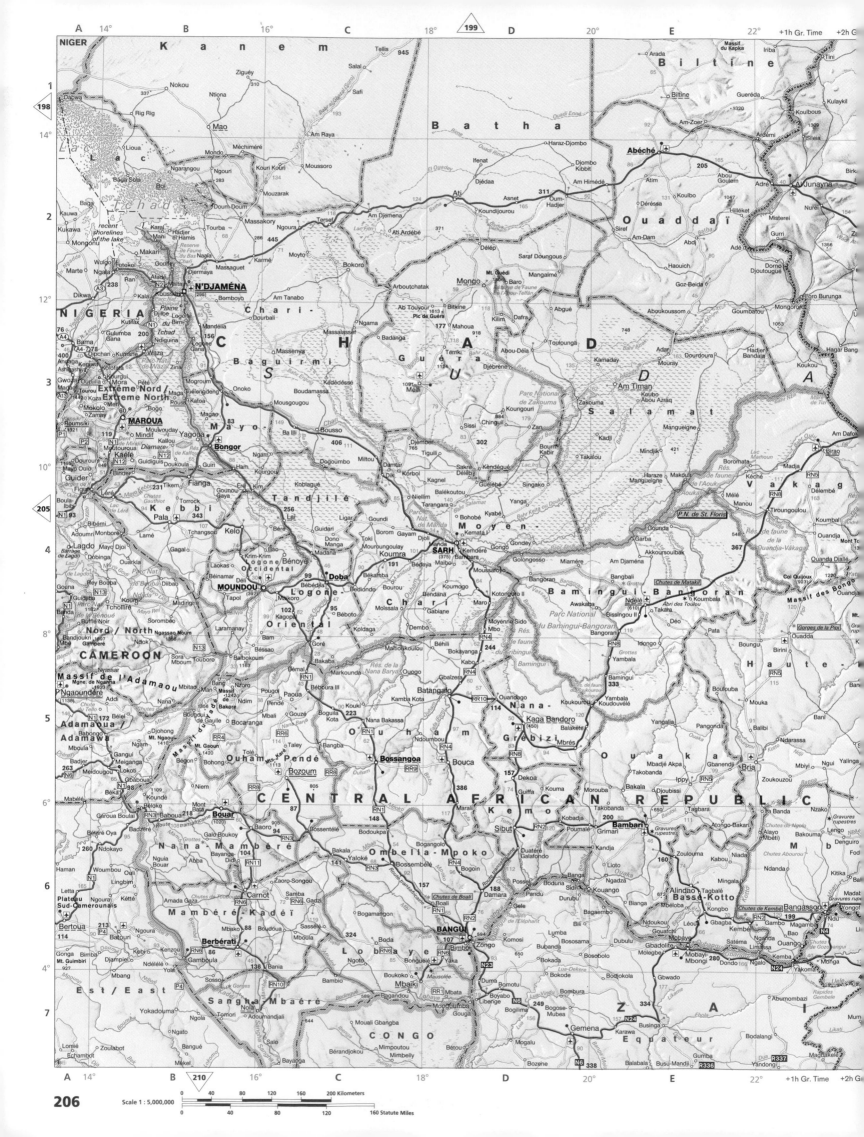

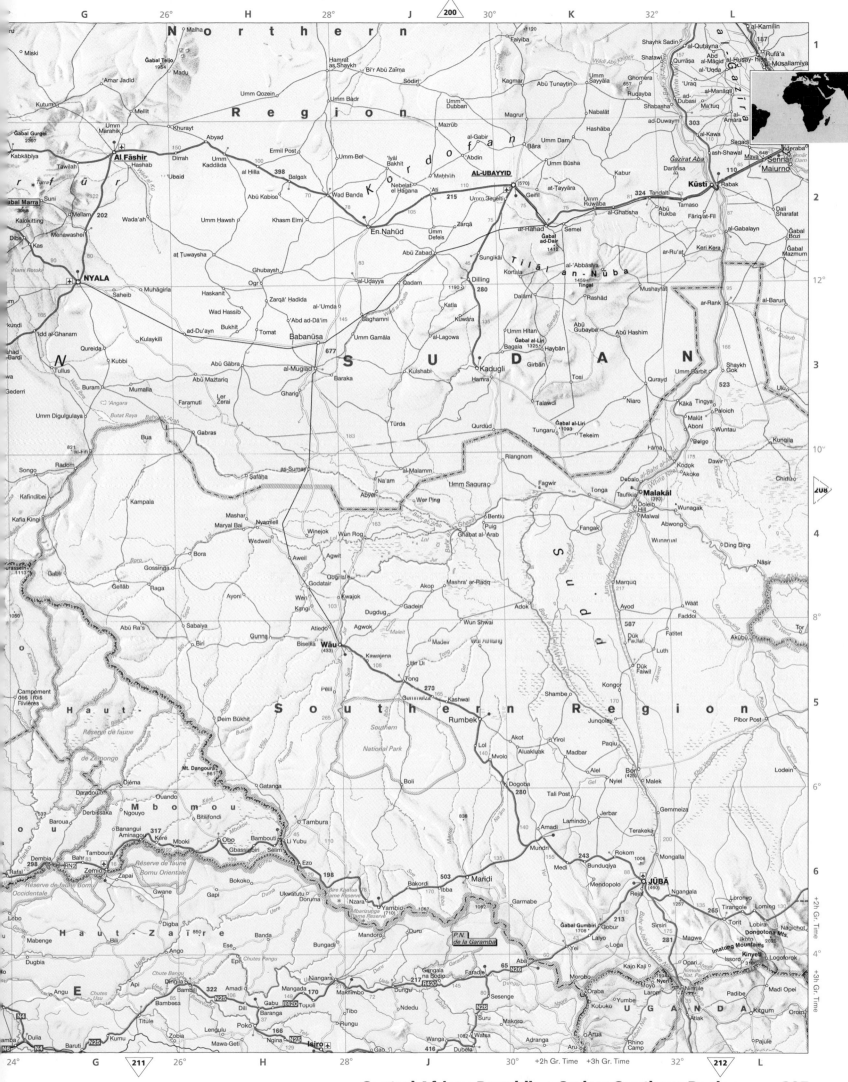

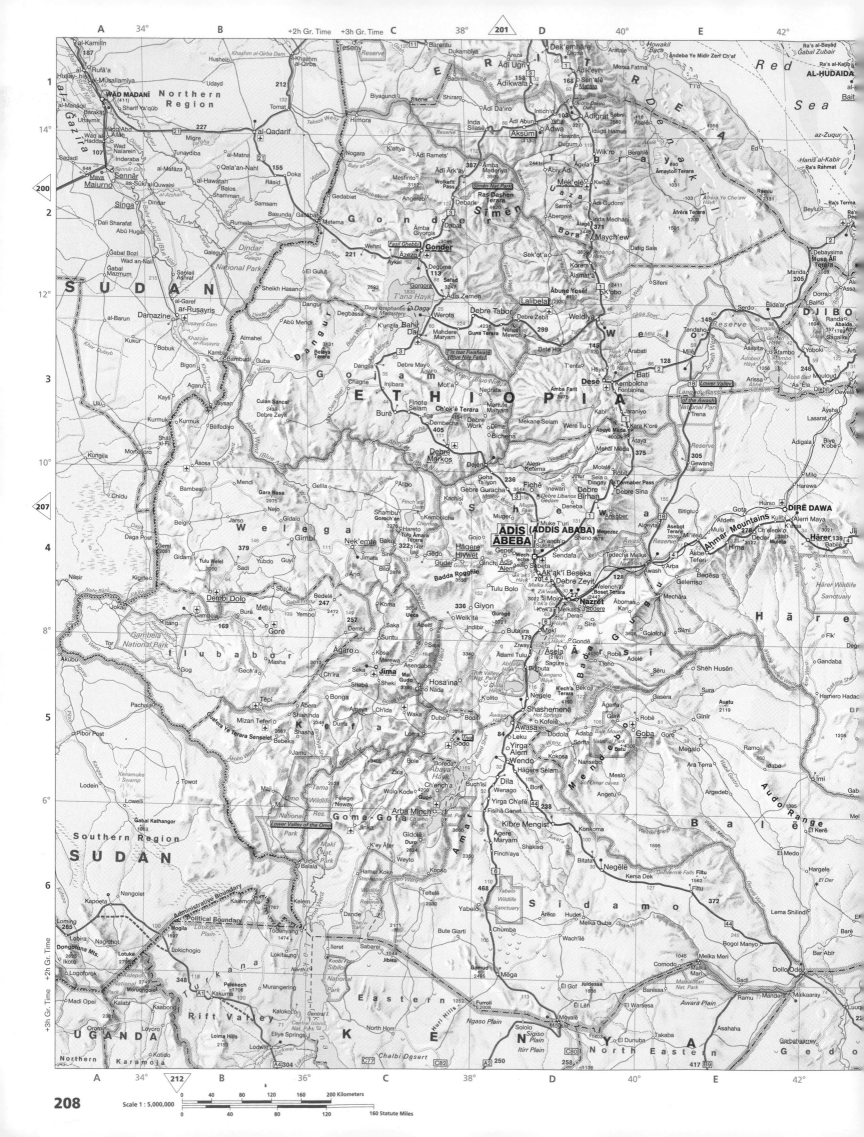

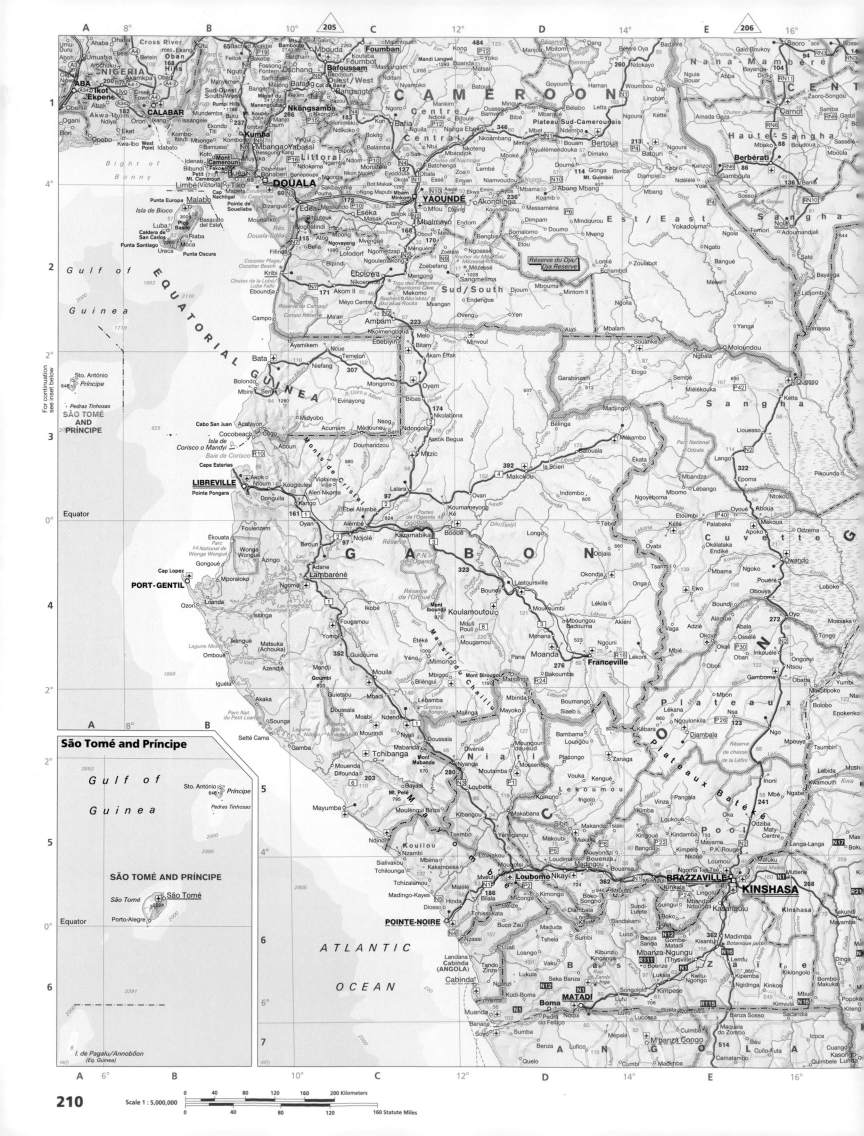

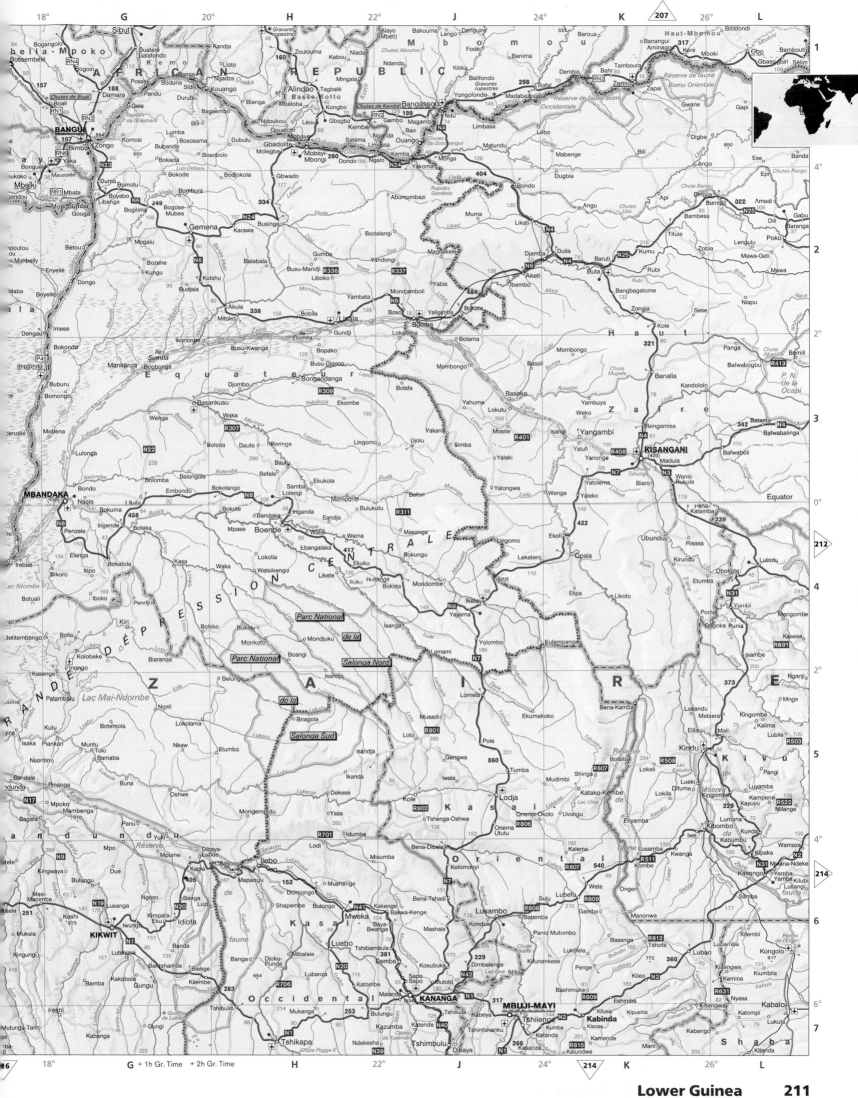

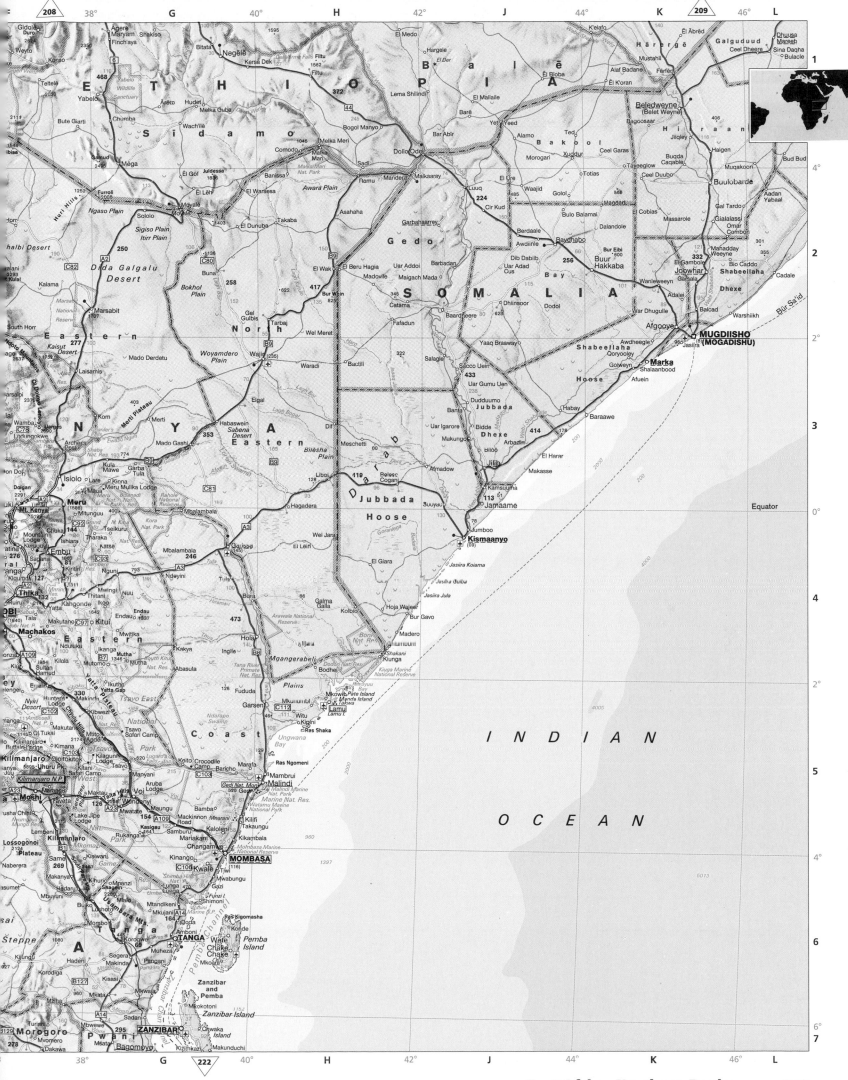

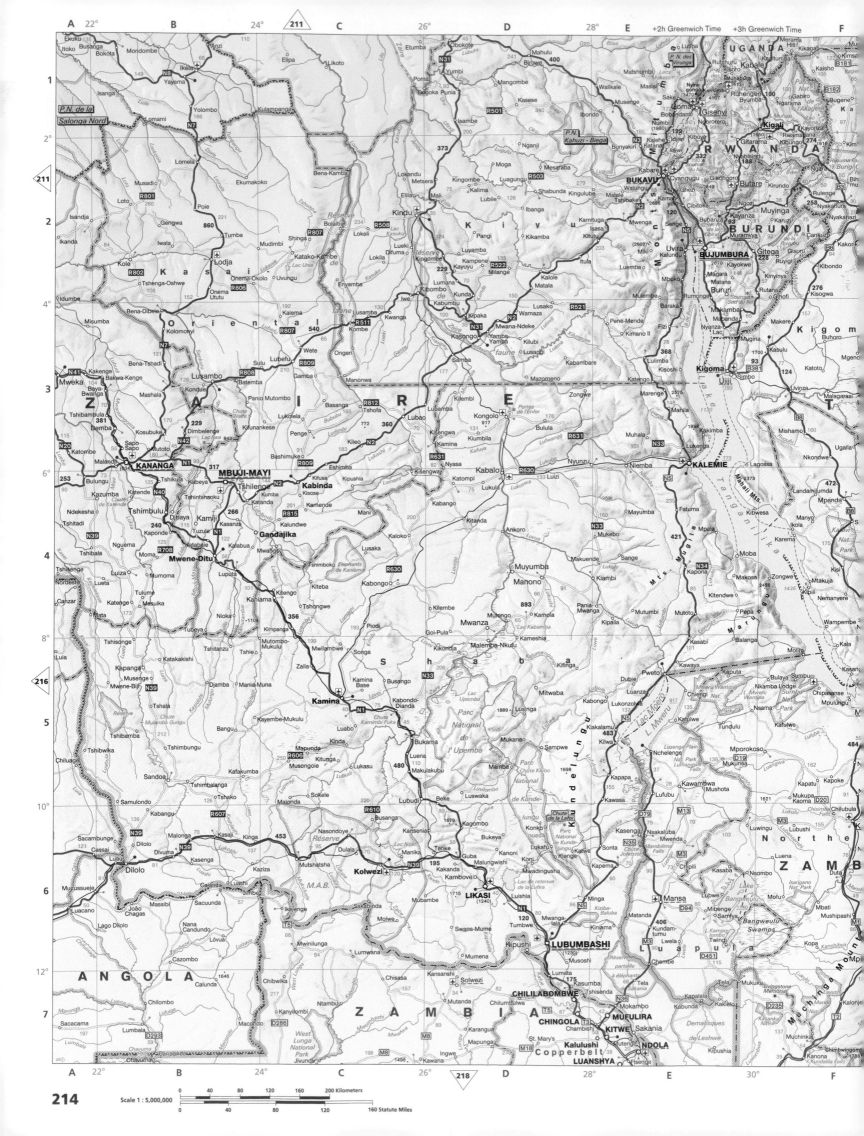

Scale 1 : 5,000,000

0 40 80 120 160 200 Kilometers

0   40   80   120   160 Statute Miles

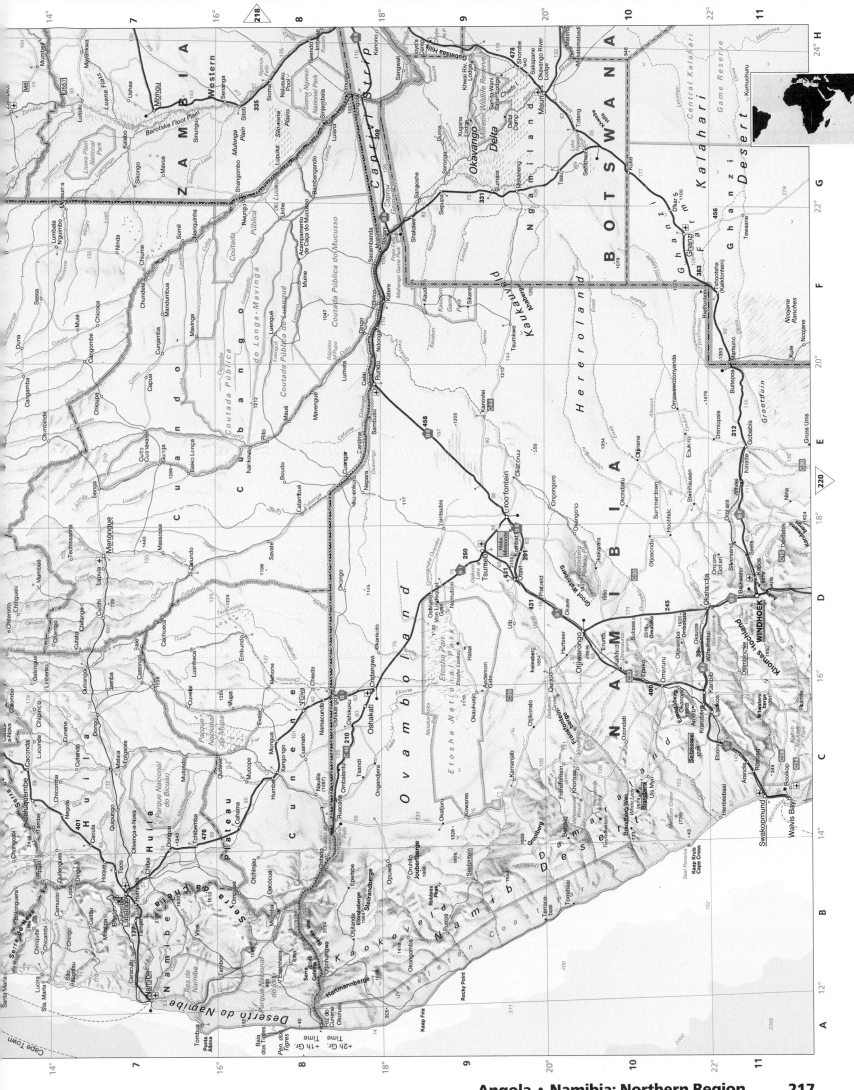

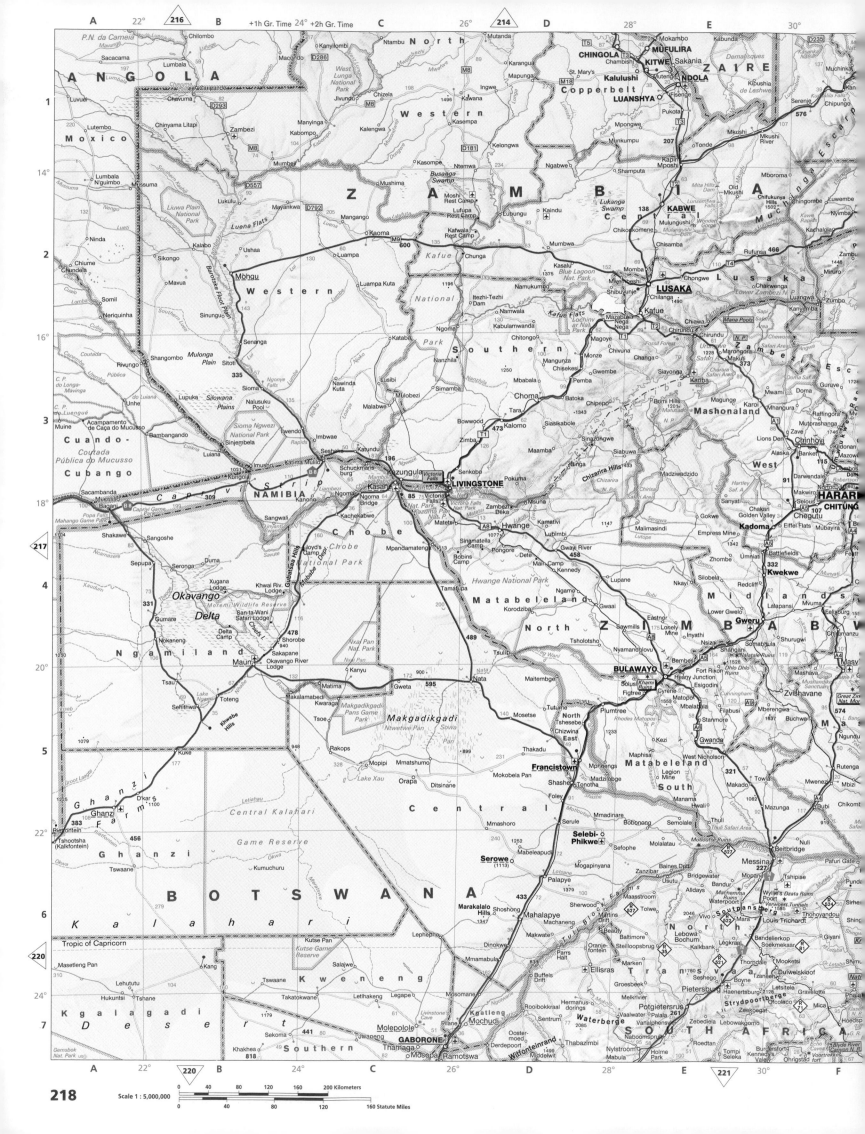

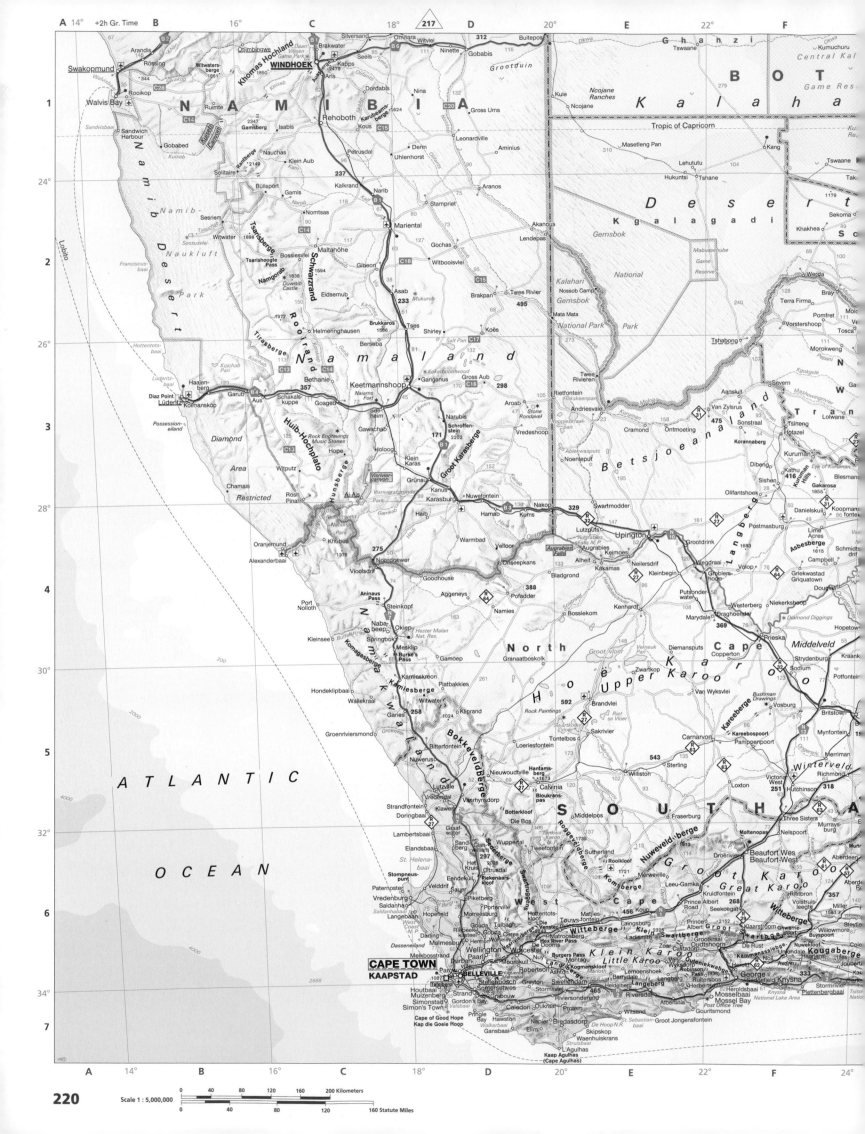

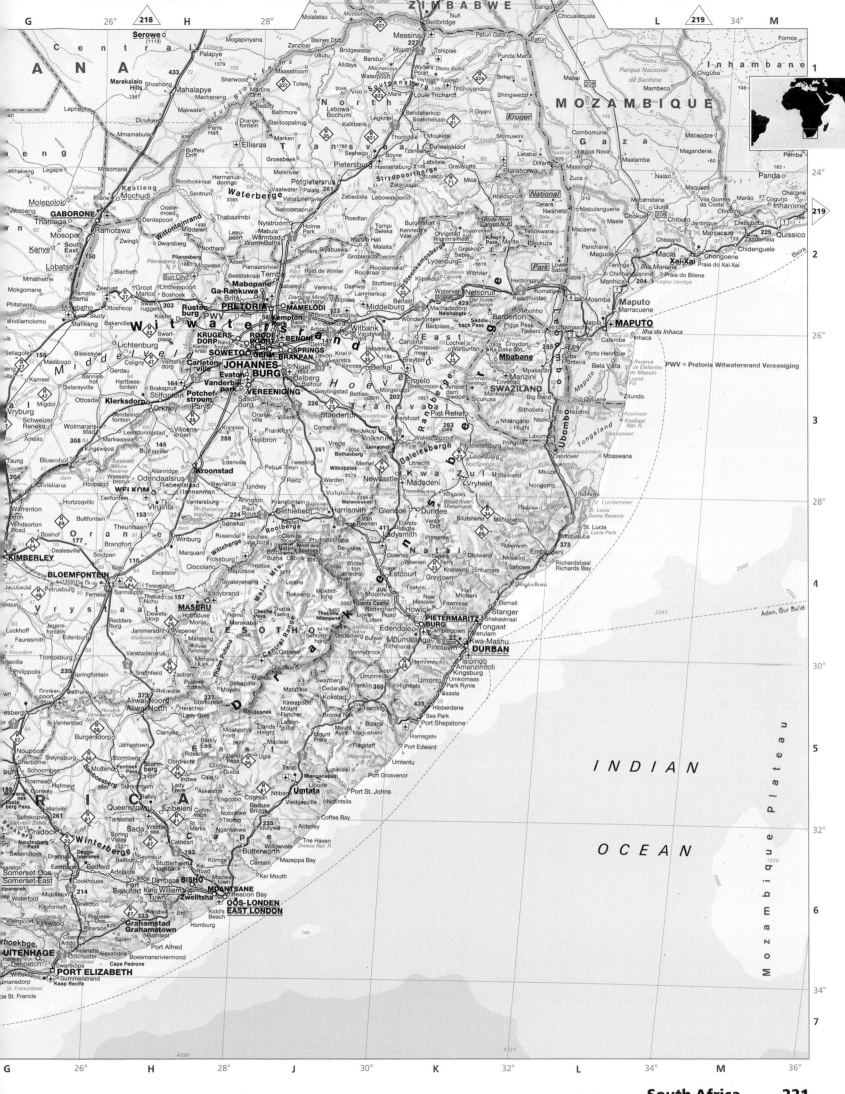

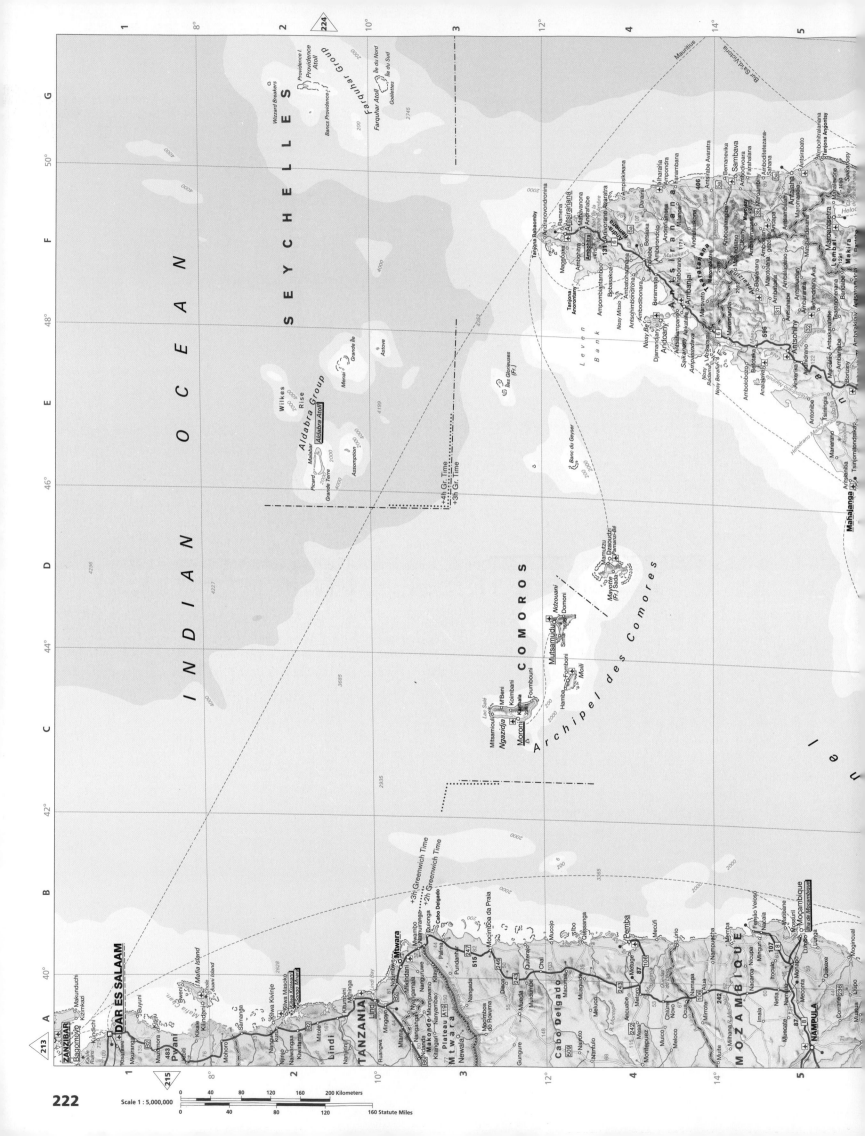

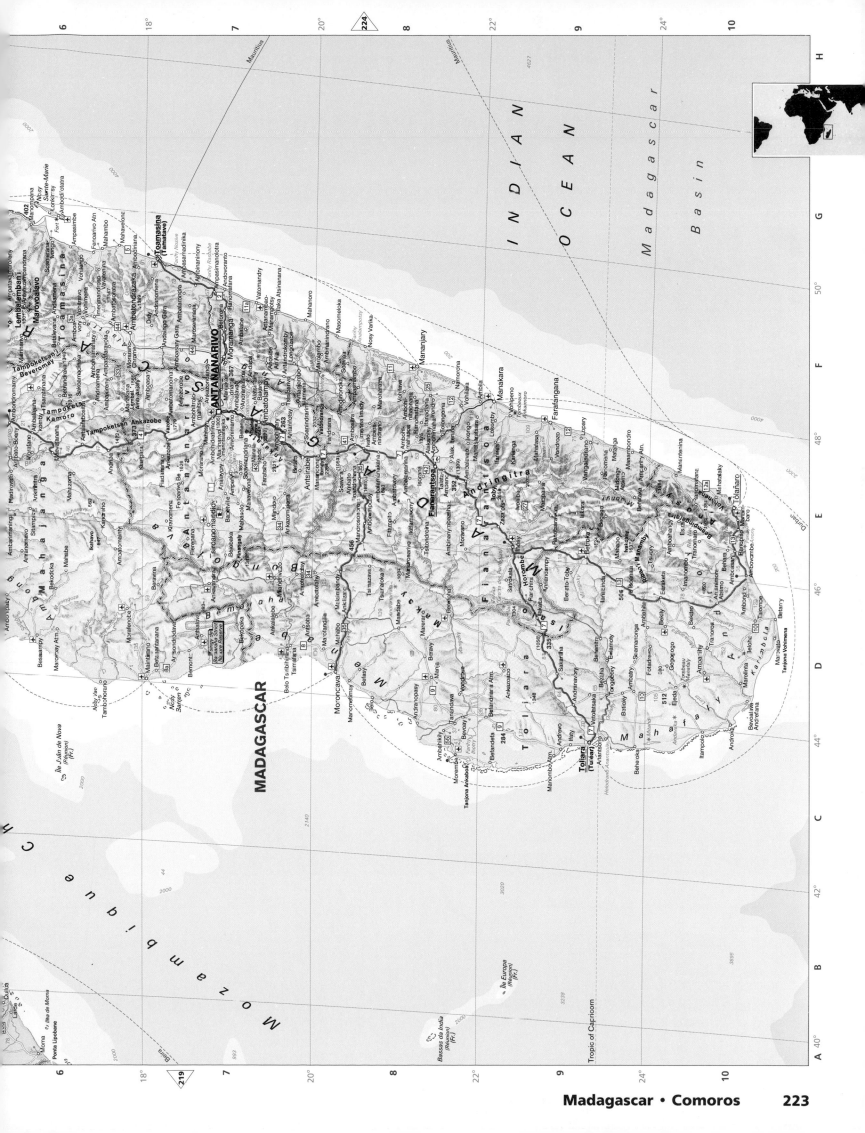

MADAGASCAR

Madagascar · Comoros   **223**

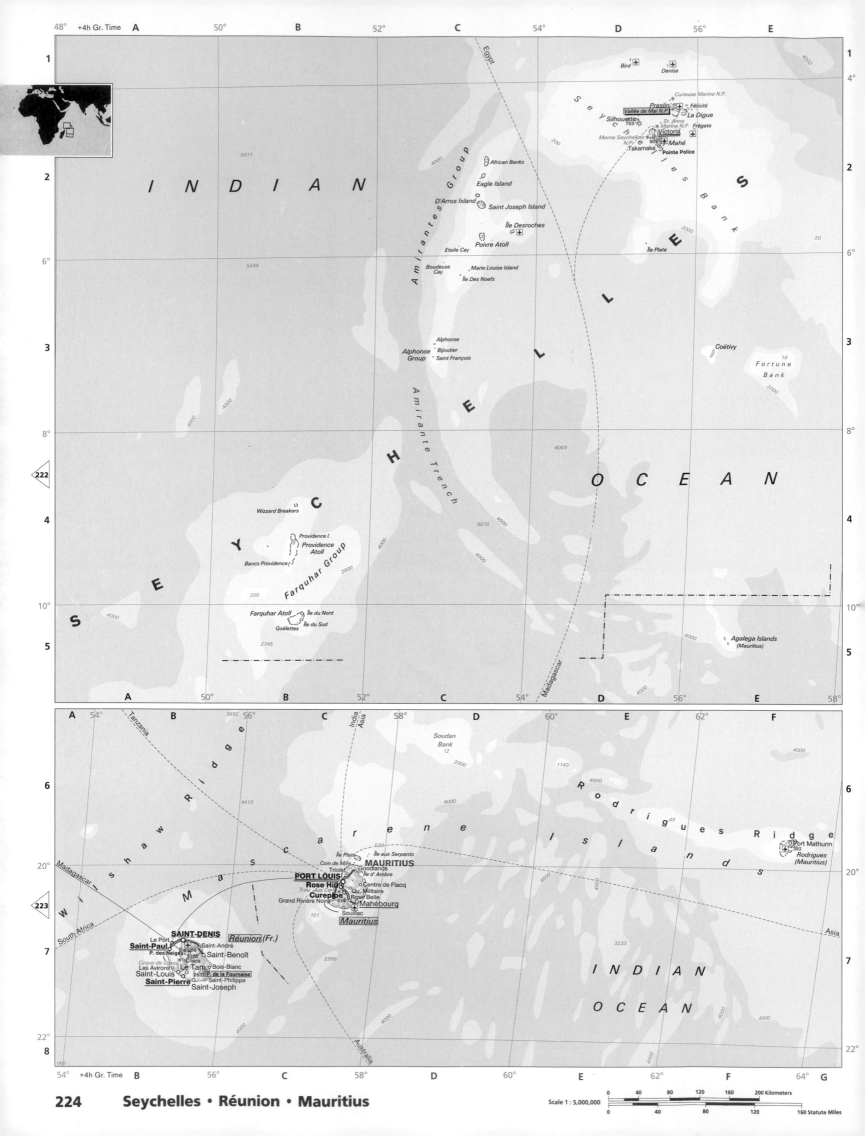

INDIAN

5011

5249

OCEAN

5070

Seychelles

Amirantes Group

Amirante Trench

African Banks

Eagle Island

D'Arros Island
Saint Joseph Island

Île Desroches

Poivre Atoll

Etoile Cay

Boudeuse
Cay
Marie Louise Island
Île Des Noefs

Alphonse
Alphonse
Group   Bijoutier
Saint François

Coëtivy

16
*Fortune
Bank*

4069

Wizzard Breakers

Providence I.
*Providence
Atoll*
Bancs Providence

Farquhar Group

200

2000

Farquhar Atoll   Île du Nord
Goélettes   Île du Sud

2745

Egypt

Bird
Denise

Curieuse Marine N.P.
Praslin   Félicité
Vallée de Mai N.P.   La Digue
Silhouette   753
St. Anne
Marine N.P.   Frégate
Morne Seychellois   906
N.P.   Mahé
Takamaka   Pointe Police
Victoria

Île Plate

20

2000

Madagascar

Agalega Islands
(Mauritius)

4000

222

Seychelles · Réunion · Mauritius

A   54°   B   3692   56°   C   India   58°   D   60°   E   62°   F   64°   G

Tanzania

shaw Ridge

Soudan
Bank   12

1143

Rodrigues   Ridge

4413

Mascarene

Madagascar

South Africa

India
Asia

Asia

530
Île Plate
Coin de Mire
Triolet   Île aux Serpents
MAURITIUS   Goodlands
Île d' Ambre
PORT LOUIS
Rose Hill   Centre de Flacq
Trou aux Cerfs   Qu. Militaire
Curepipe   Rose Belle
Grand Rivière Noire   828
Mahébourg
Souillac
101   *Mauritius*

Île Plate
Réunion (Fr.)

SAINT-DENIS
Le Port   Saint-André
Saint-Paul
P. des Neiges   3276
Cirque de Cilaos   3069
Cilaos   Saint-Benoît
Les Avirons   Le Tam   Bois-Blanc
Saint-Louis   2632   P. de la Fournaise
Saint-Pierre   Saint-Philippe
Saint-Joseph

Port Mathurin
392
*Rodrigues
(Mauritius)*

49

INDIAN

OCEAN

2350

3233

4000

Australia

223

54° +4h Gr. Time

Scale 1 : 5,000,000

0   40   80   120   160   200 Kilometers
0   40   80   120   160 Statute Miles

The U.S.A. and Southern Canada

The United States and the southern provinces of Canada occupy the entire center of North America. A clearly arranged topography characterizes this region between the Atlantic and Pacific Oceans. The mighty Rockies in the west and the narrow chain of the Appalachian Mountains in the east run more or less parallel to one another along their respective meridians of longitude. They enclose a huge plain whose expanse of arable land not only nourishes the native population, but also feeds millions of people in countries with less developed agriculture. Enormous coniferous and mixed forests and more than a million lakes are found in the north.

The Statue of Liberty, built "to glorify the Republic and Liberty," has become a symbol of freedom throughout the world. This lithograph was published in New York one year before "Lady Liberty" was unveiled on 28 October 1886.

British Columbia, Central
228 – 229

British Columbia, South
230 – 231

Alberta and Saskatchewan, South
232 – 233

Manitoba, South · Ontario, West
234 – 235

Ontario, Central · Québec, Southwest
236 – 237

Ontario and Québec, South
238 – 239

Québec, Southeast · Atlantic Provinces, West   240 – 241

Atlantic Provinces, East
242 – 243

Washington · Oregon
244 – 245

California, North · Nevada
246 – 247

California, South
248 – 249

Idaho, North · Montana
250 – 251

Idaho, South · Wyoming
252 – 253

Utah · Colorado
254 – 255

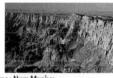

Arizona · New Mexico
256 – 257

North Dakota
258 – 259

South Dakota
260 – 261

Nebraska · Kansas
262 – 263

Oklahoma · Texas, North
264 – 265

Texas, South
266 – 267

Texas, East · Louisiana · Mississippi
268 – 269

Minnesota · Wisconsin and Michigan, North   270 – 271

Michigan, South · Southern Great Lakes Region   272 – 273

Iowa · Missouri and Illinois, North · Indiana   274 – 275

Missouri, South · Arkansas · Kentucky · Tennessee   276 – 277

New York · Northeastern States
278 – 279

Ohio · Pennsylvania · West Virginia · Maryland · Delaware   280 – 281

West Virginia · Virginia · North Carolina   282 – 283

Alabama · Georgia · South Carolina
284 – 285

Florida (Inset: Puerto Rico, Virgin Islands)   286 – 287

Hawaii
288

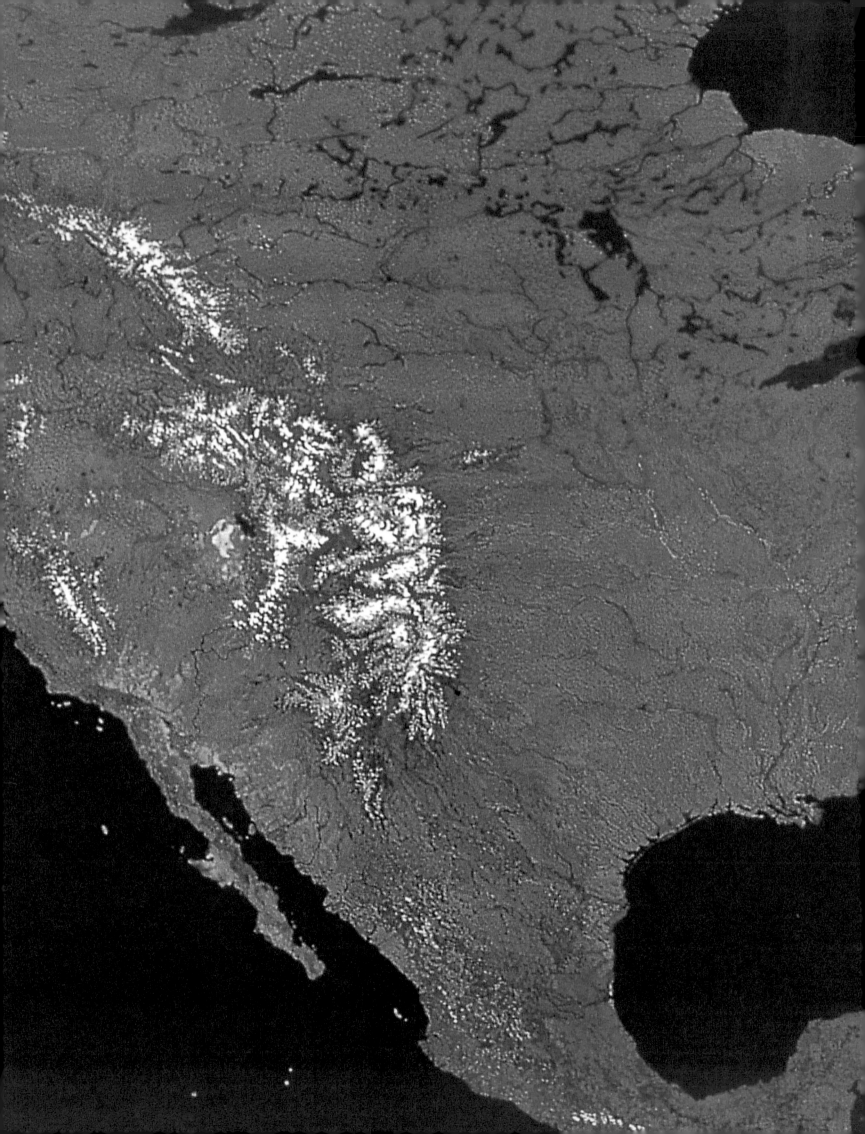

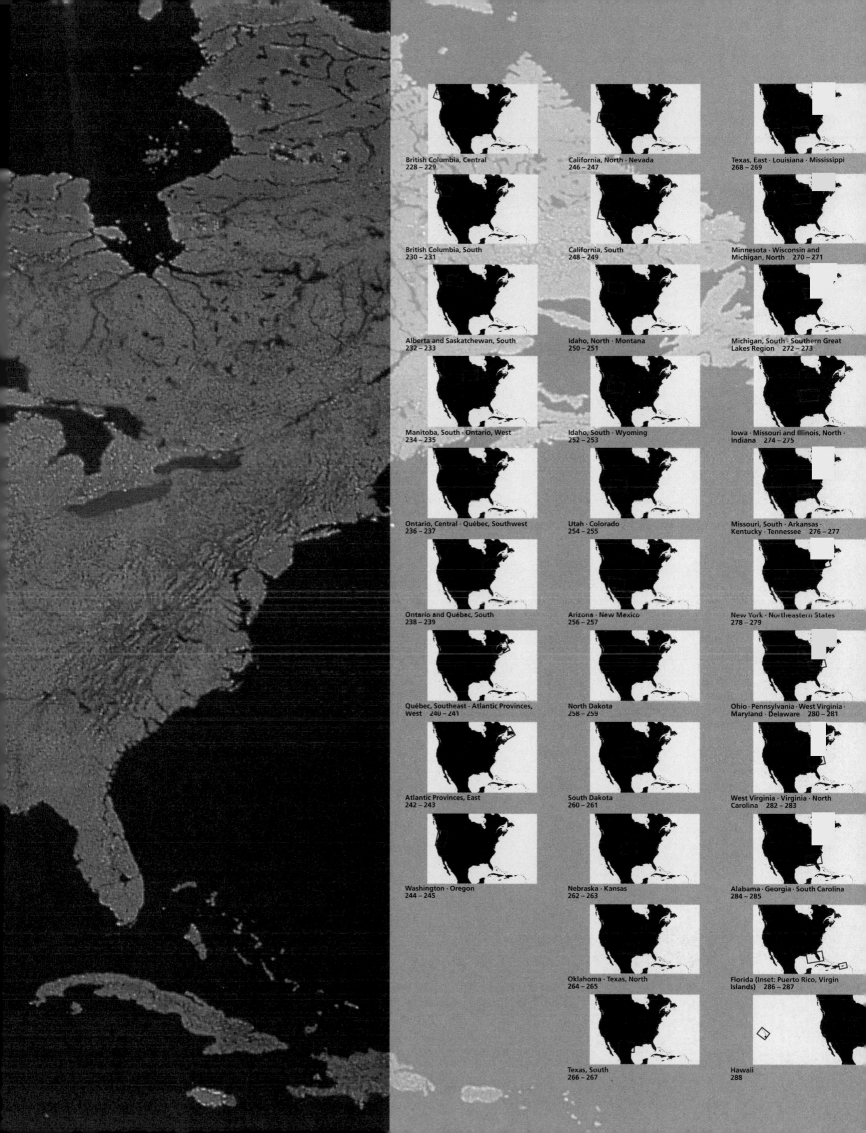

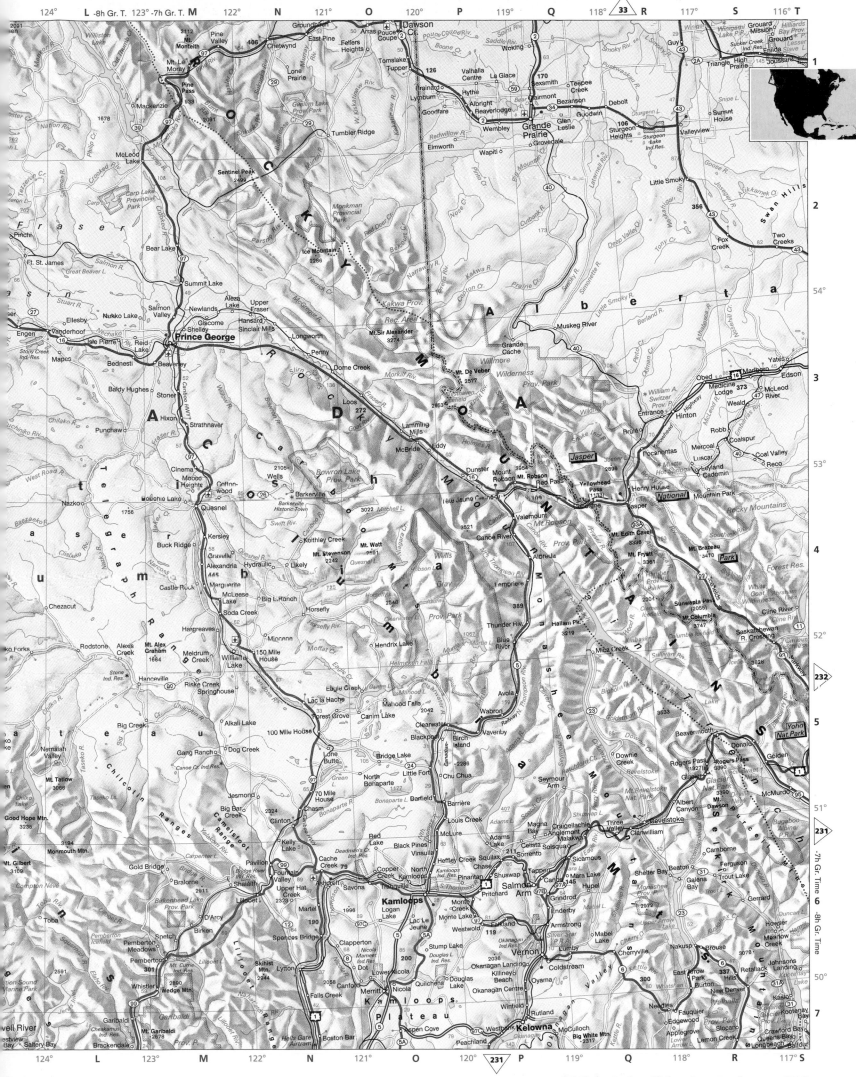

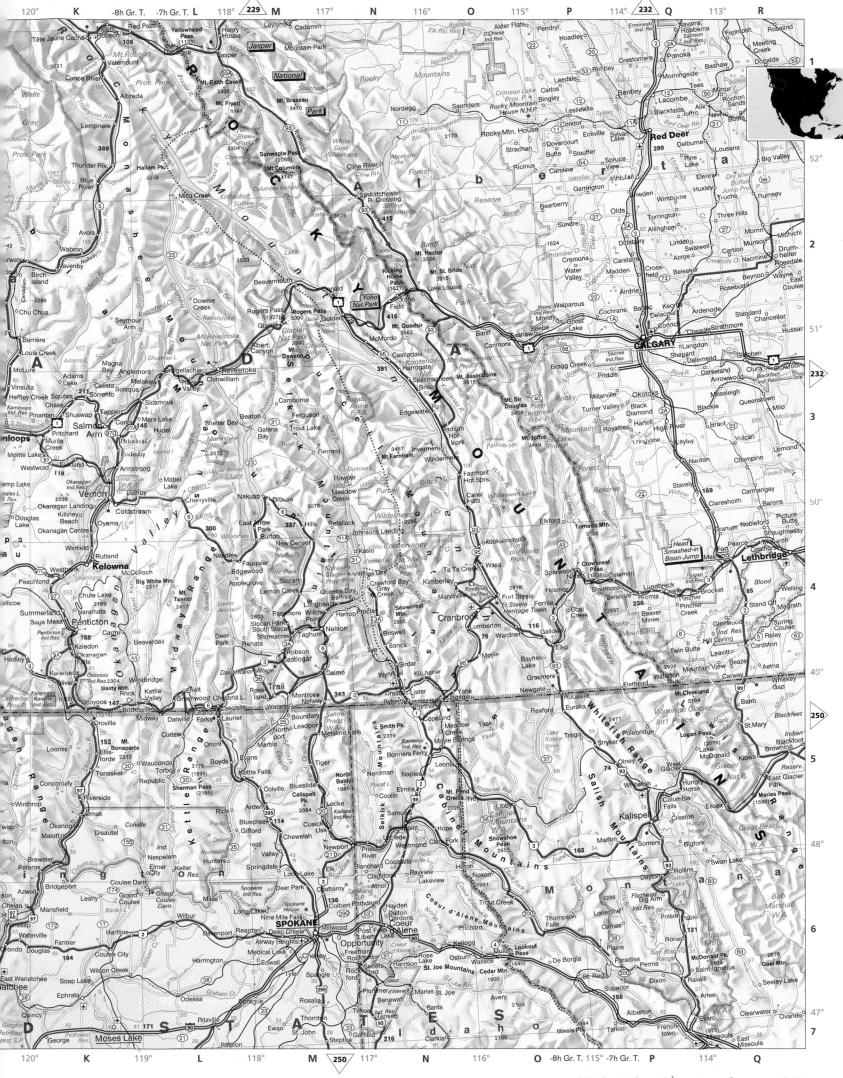

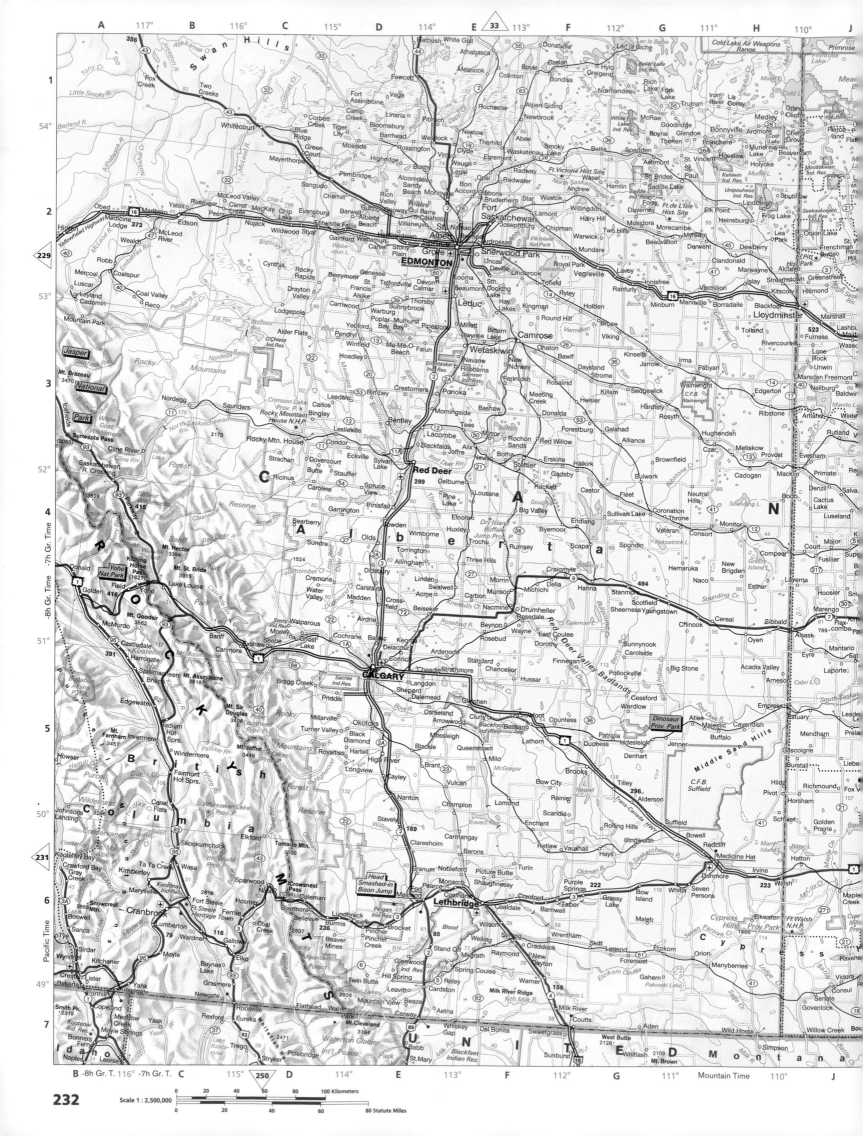

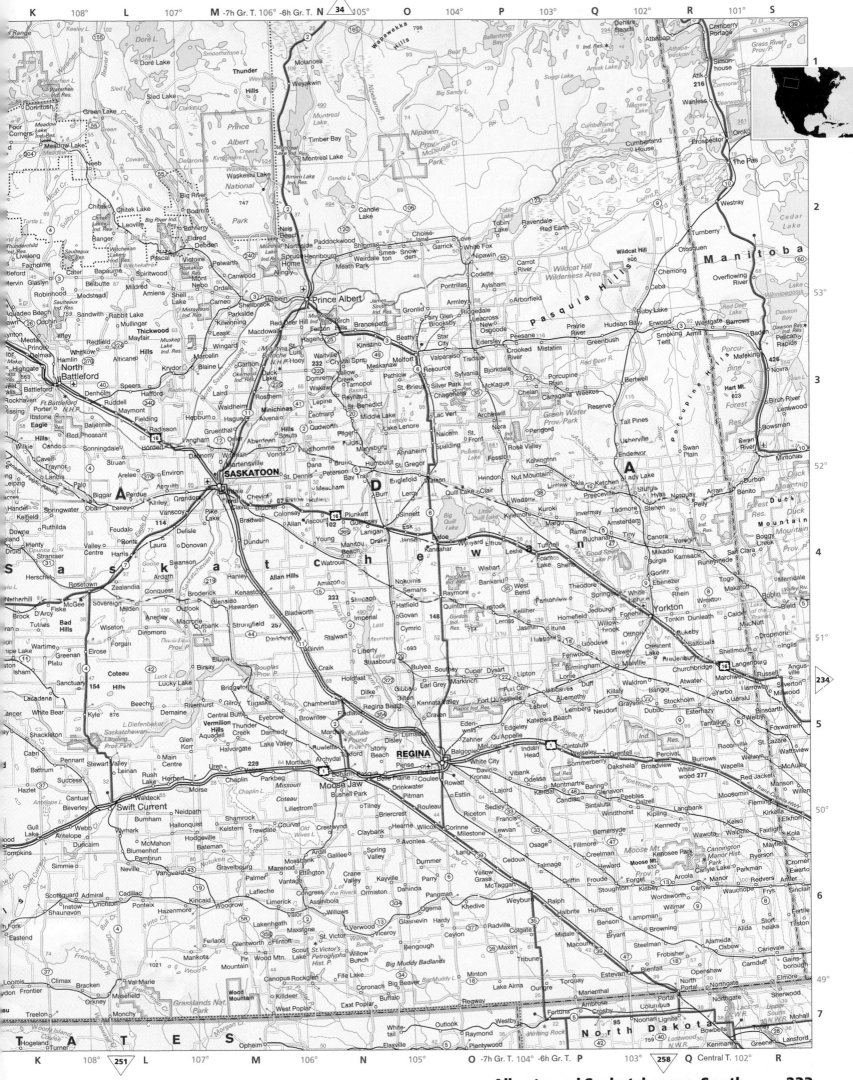

Alberta and Saskatchewan, South   233

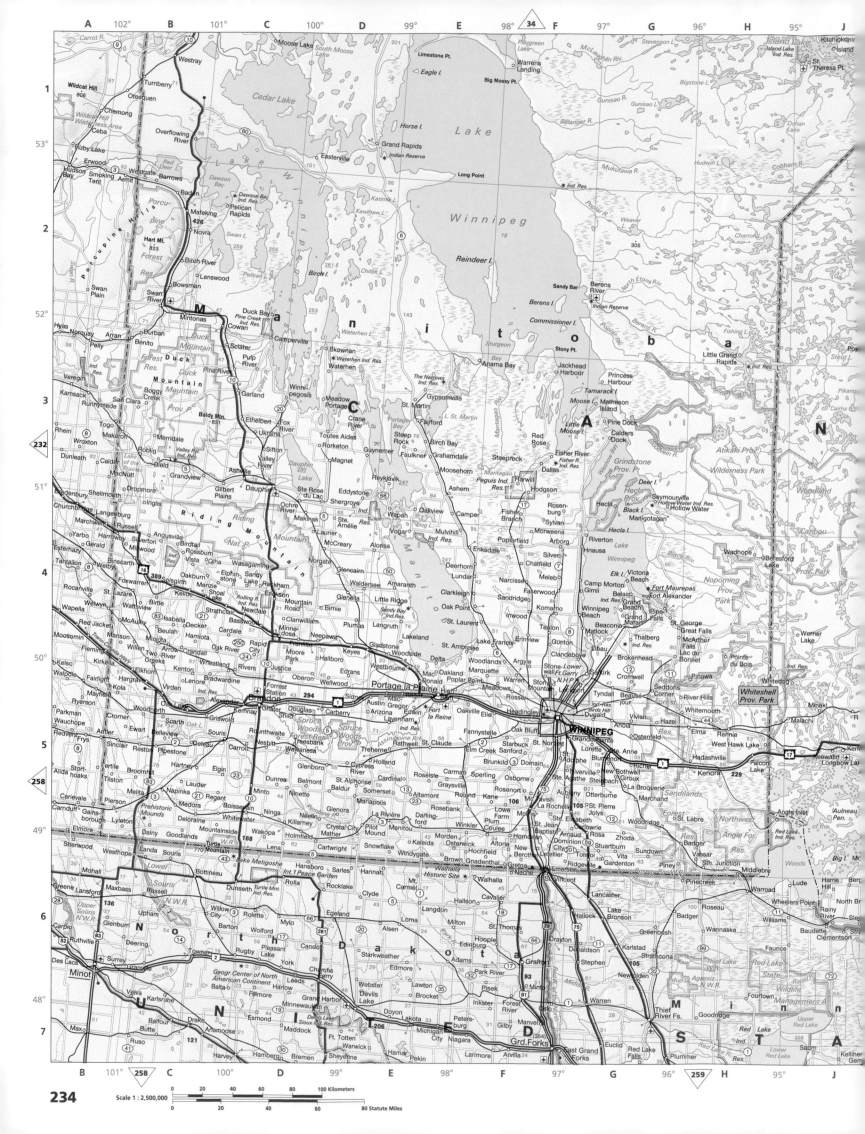

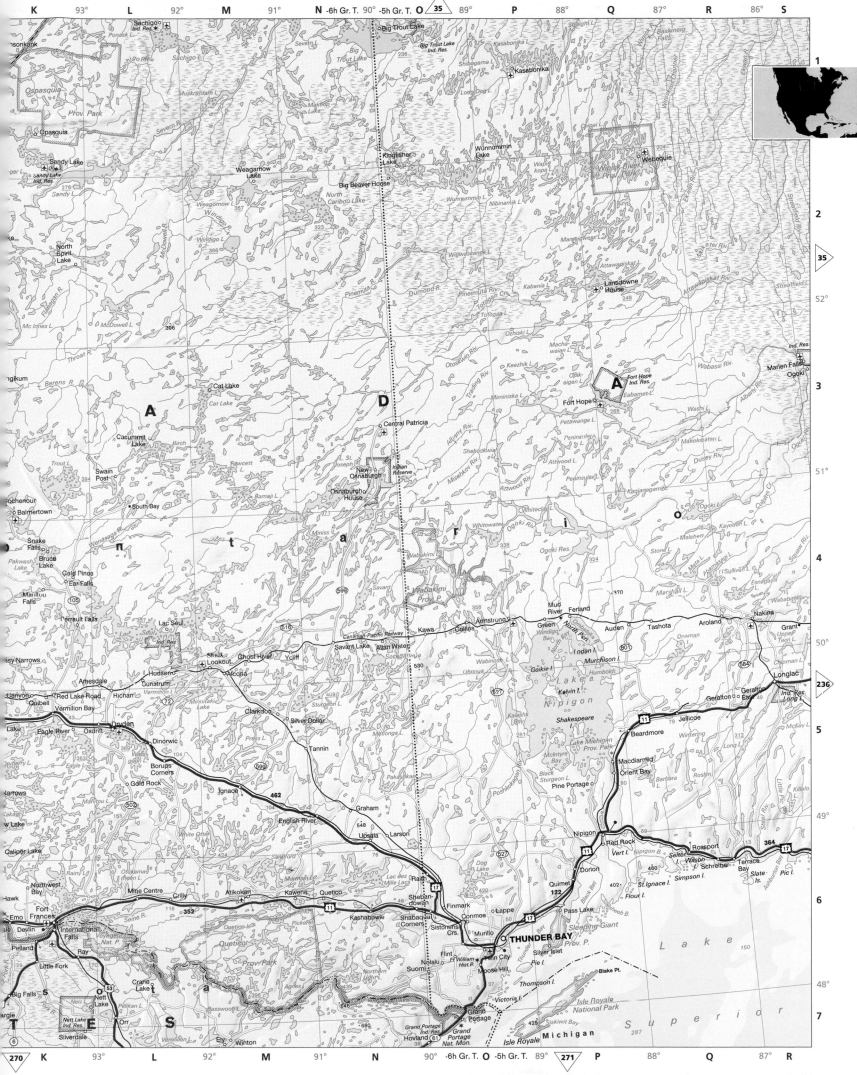

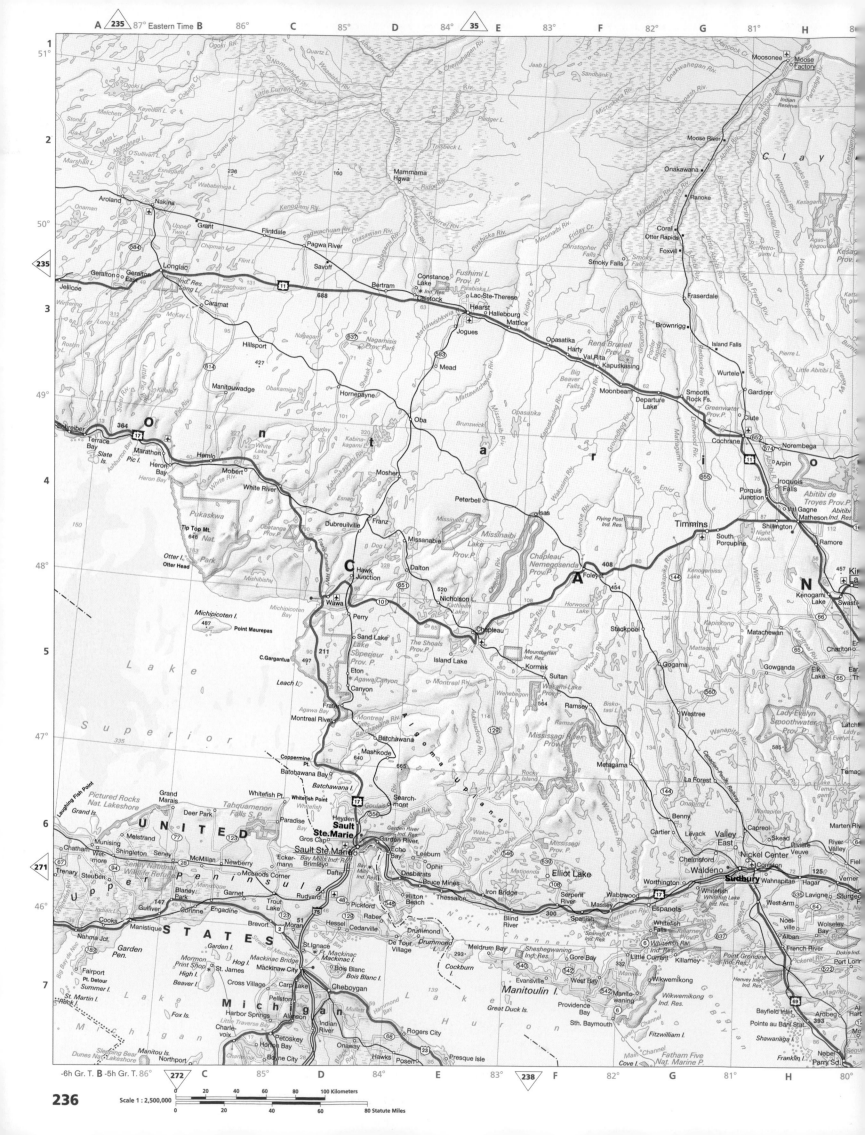

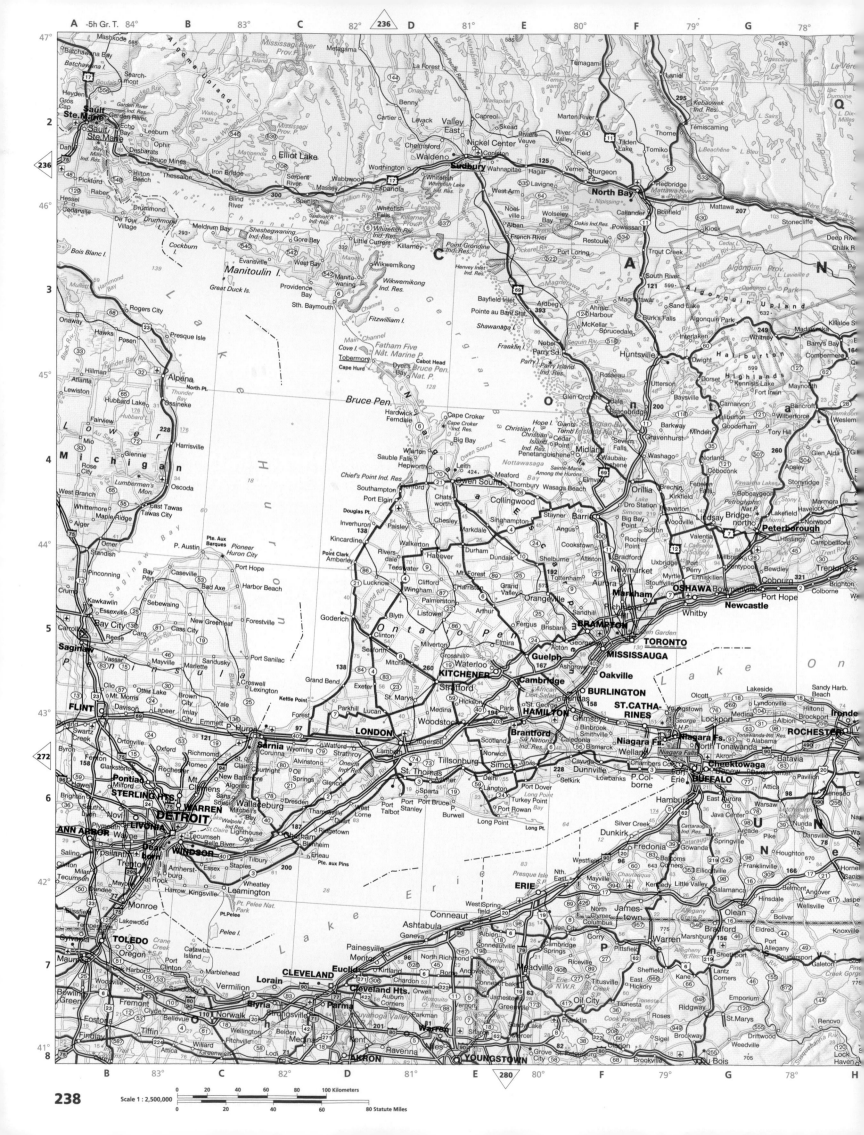

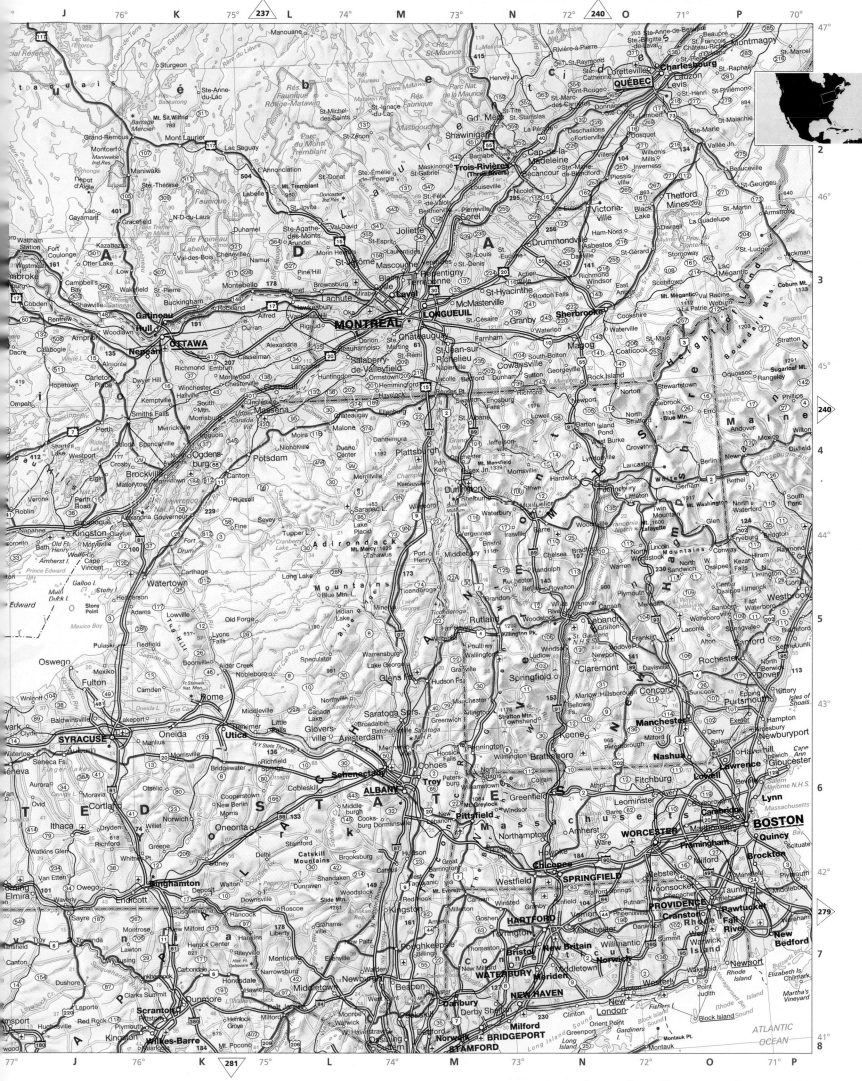

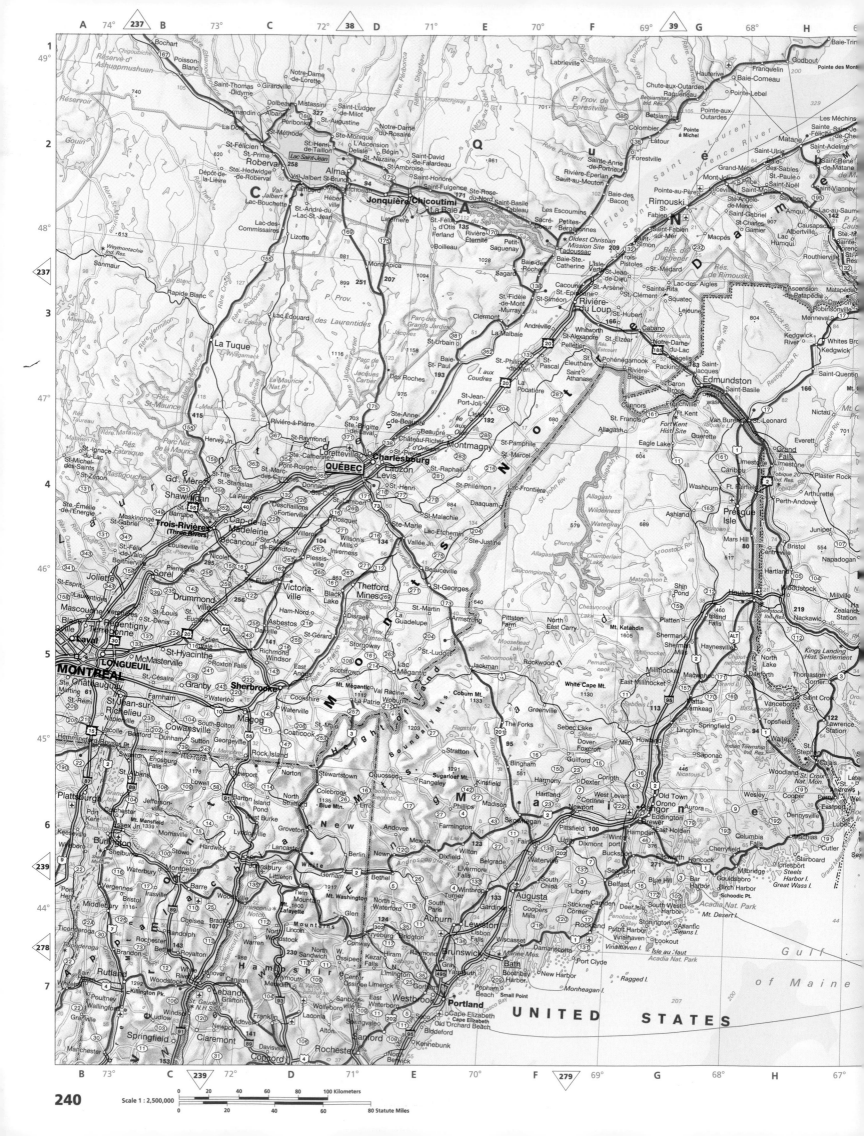

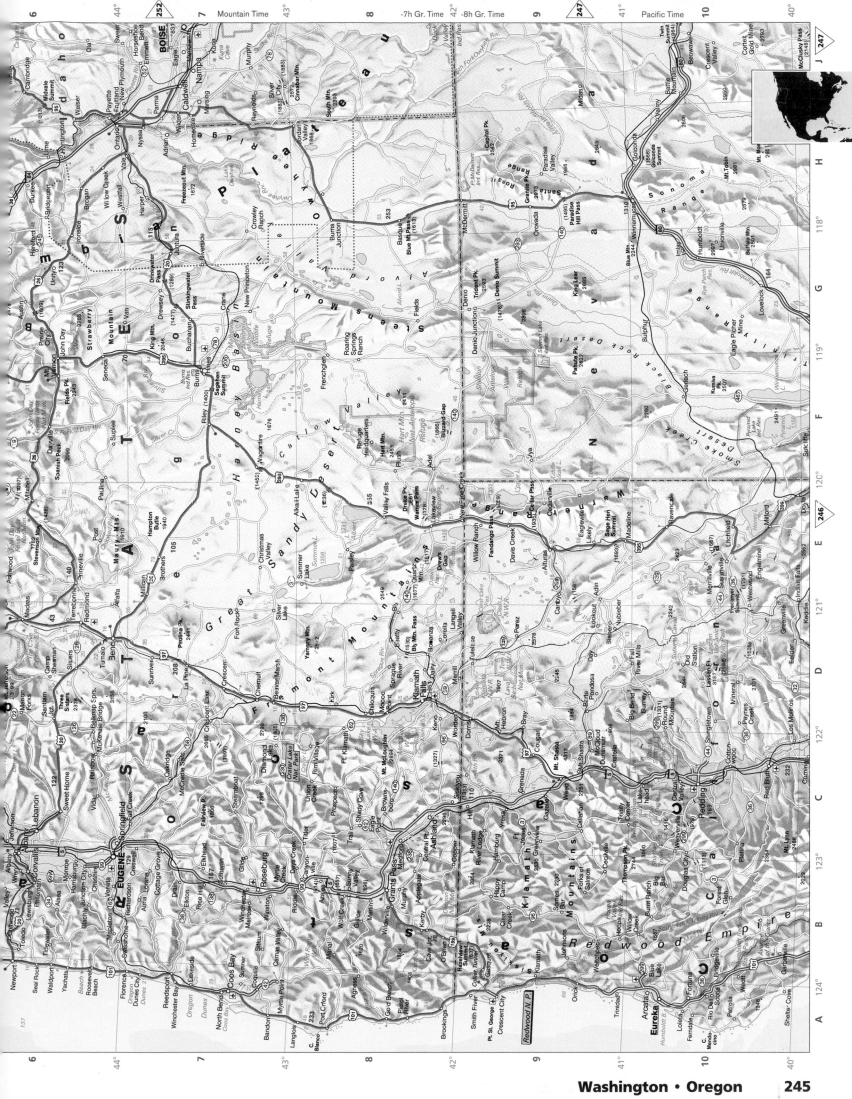

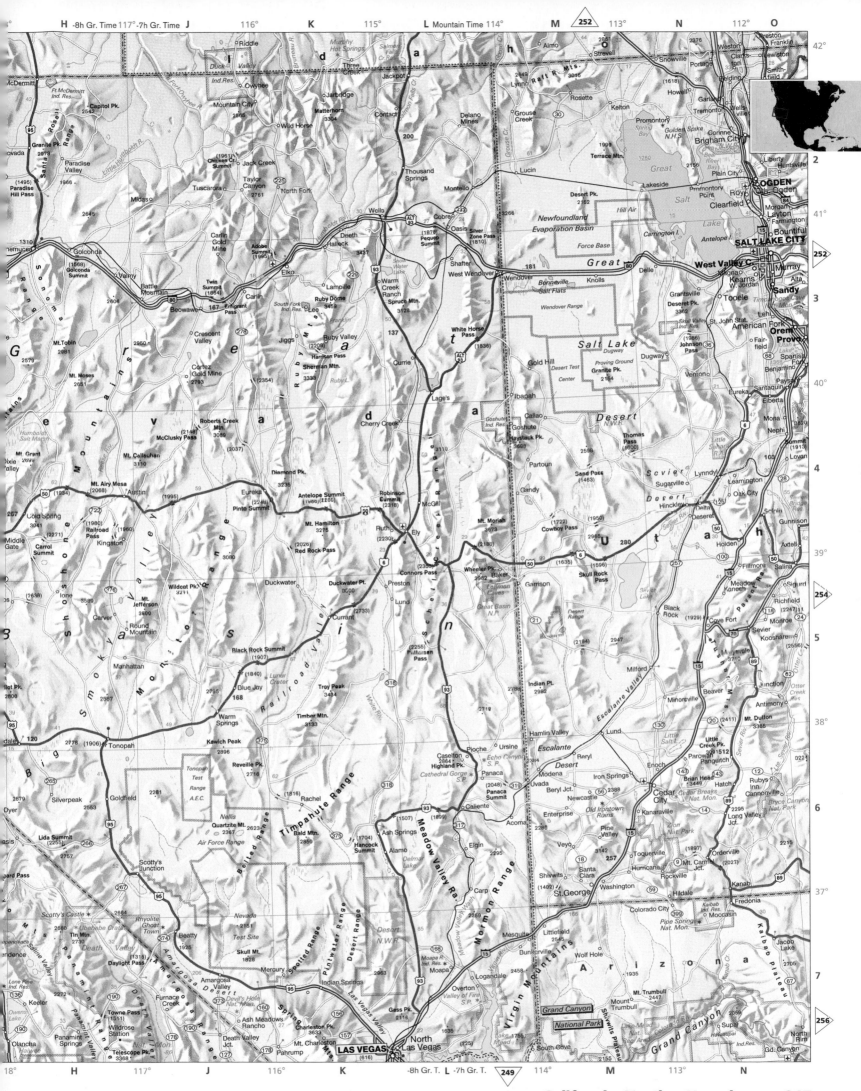

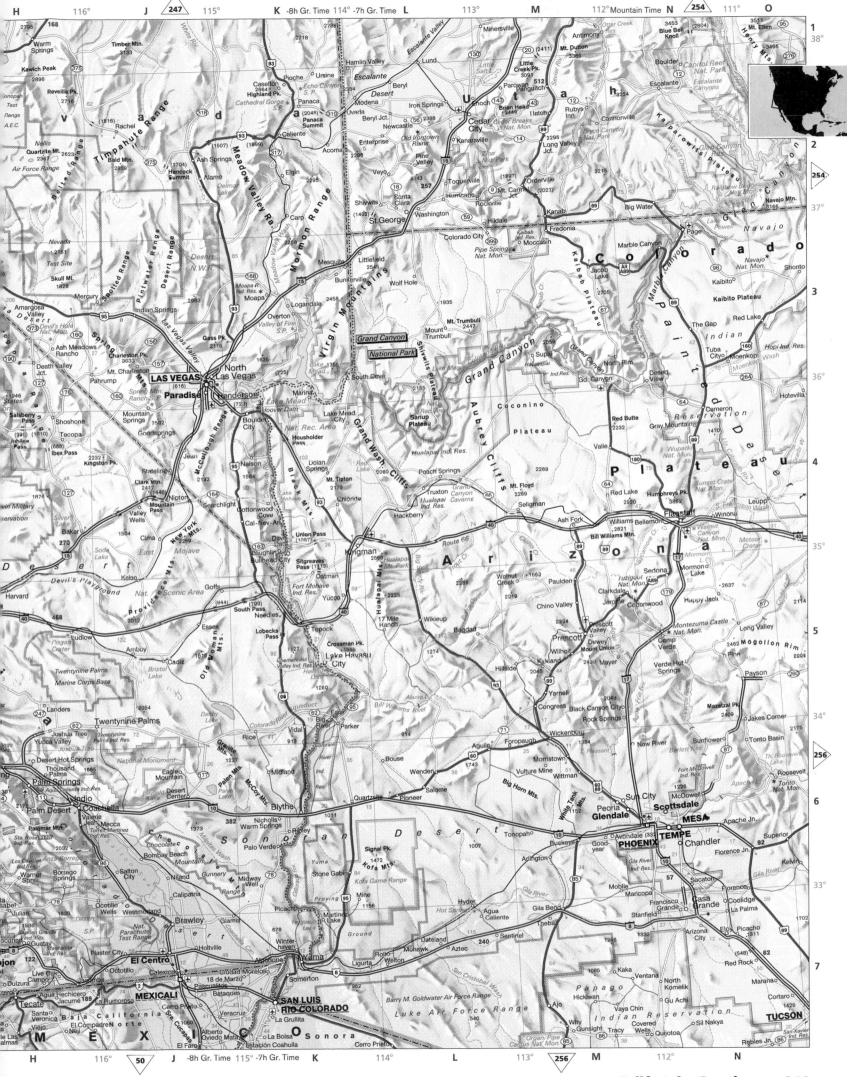

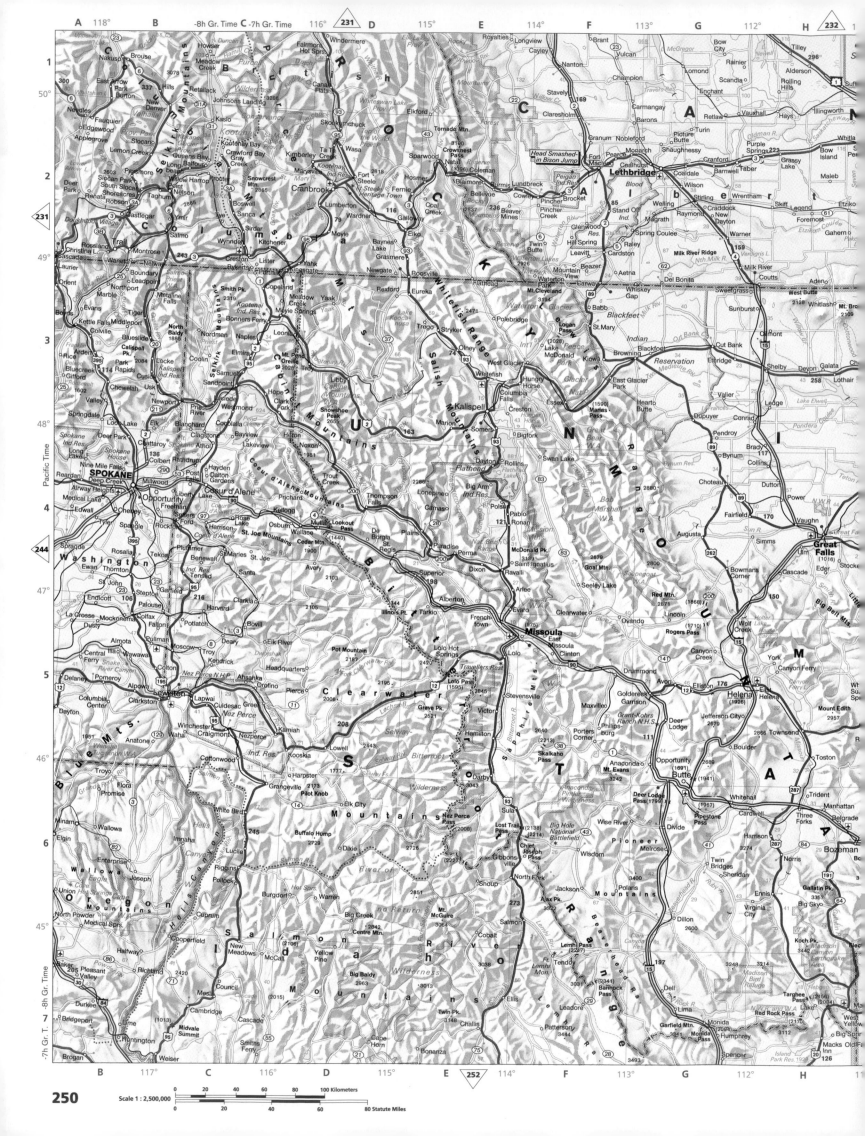

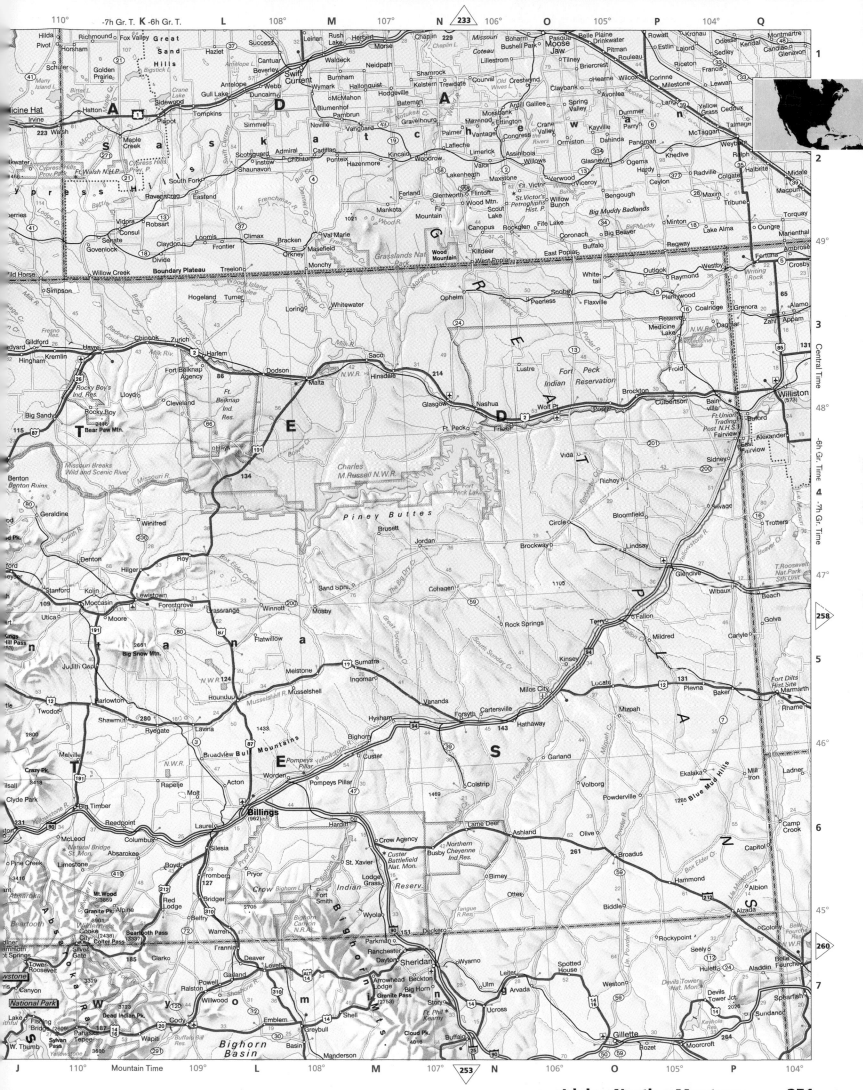

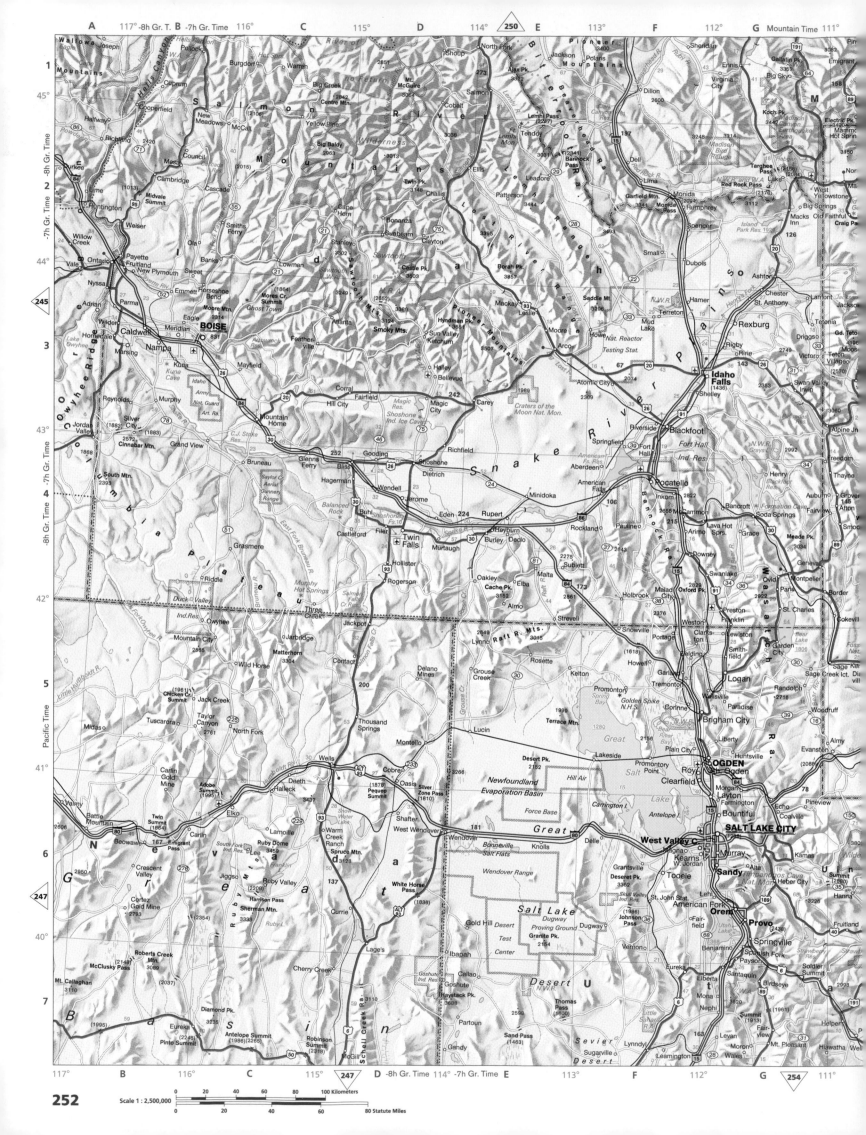

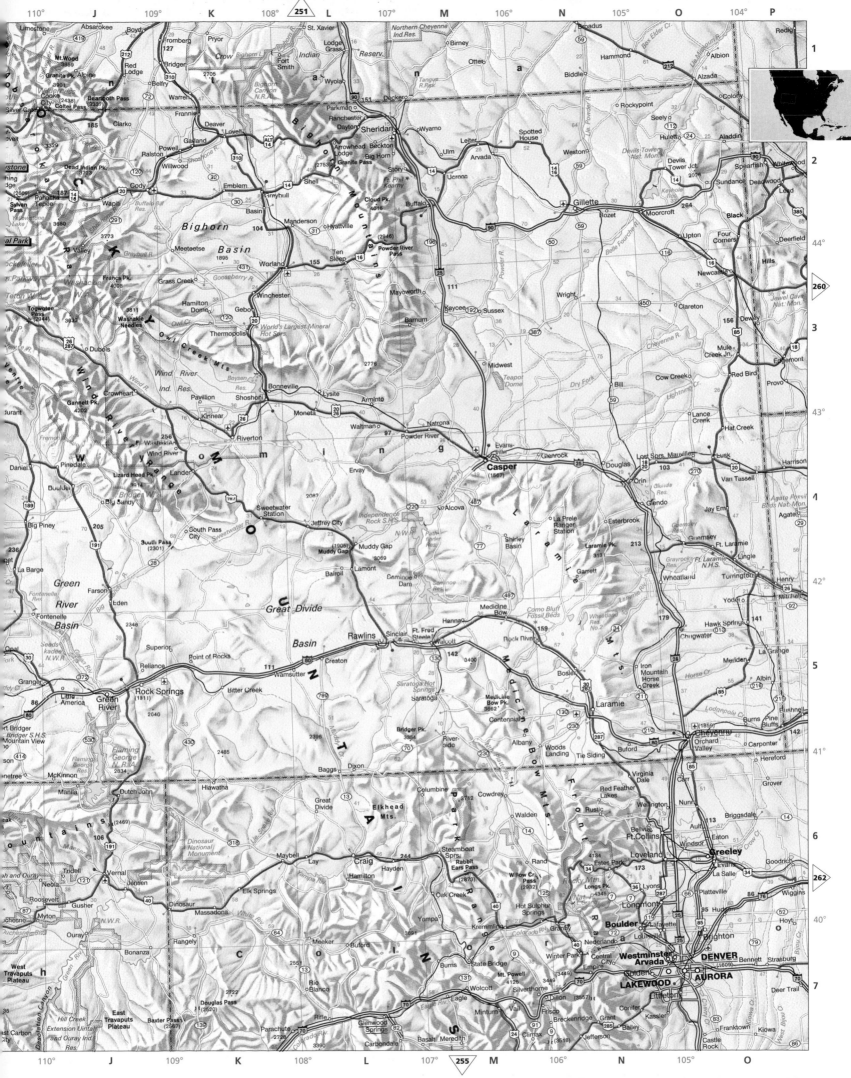

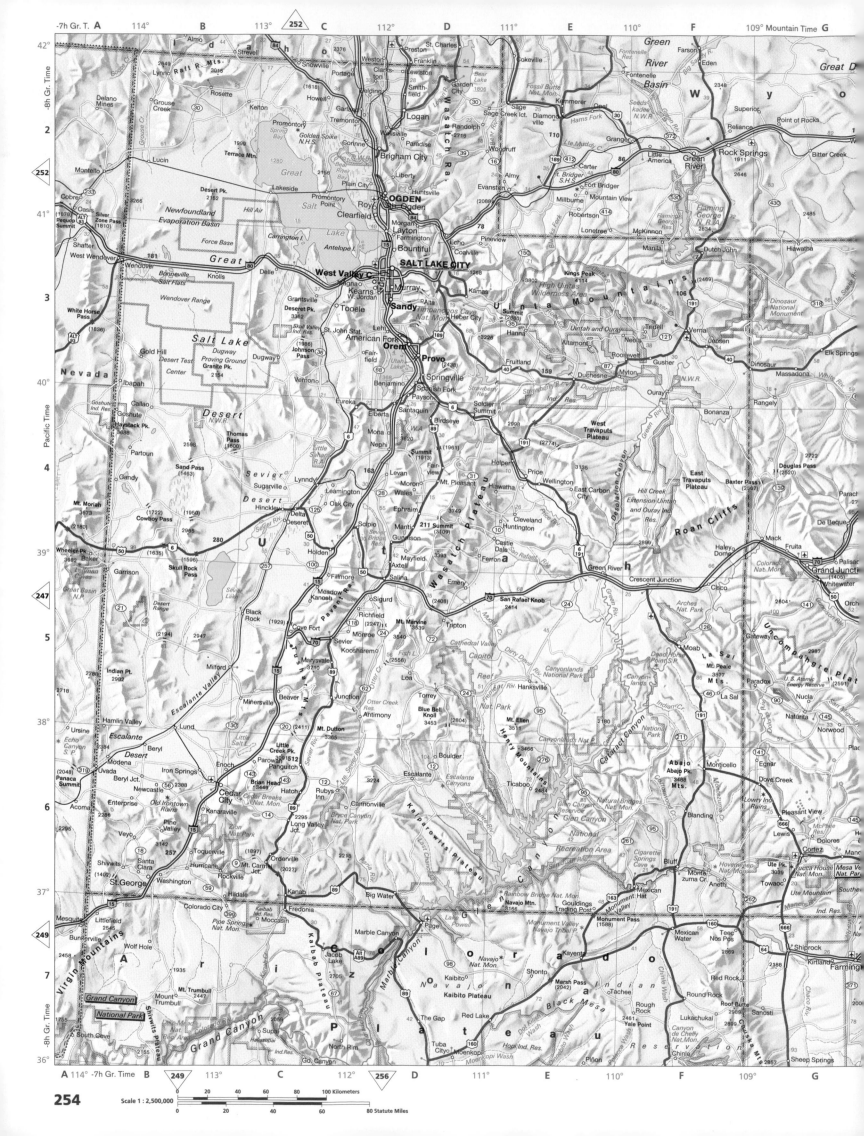

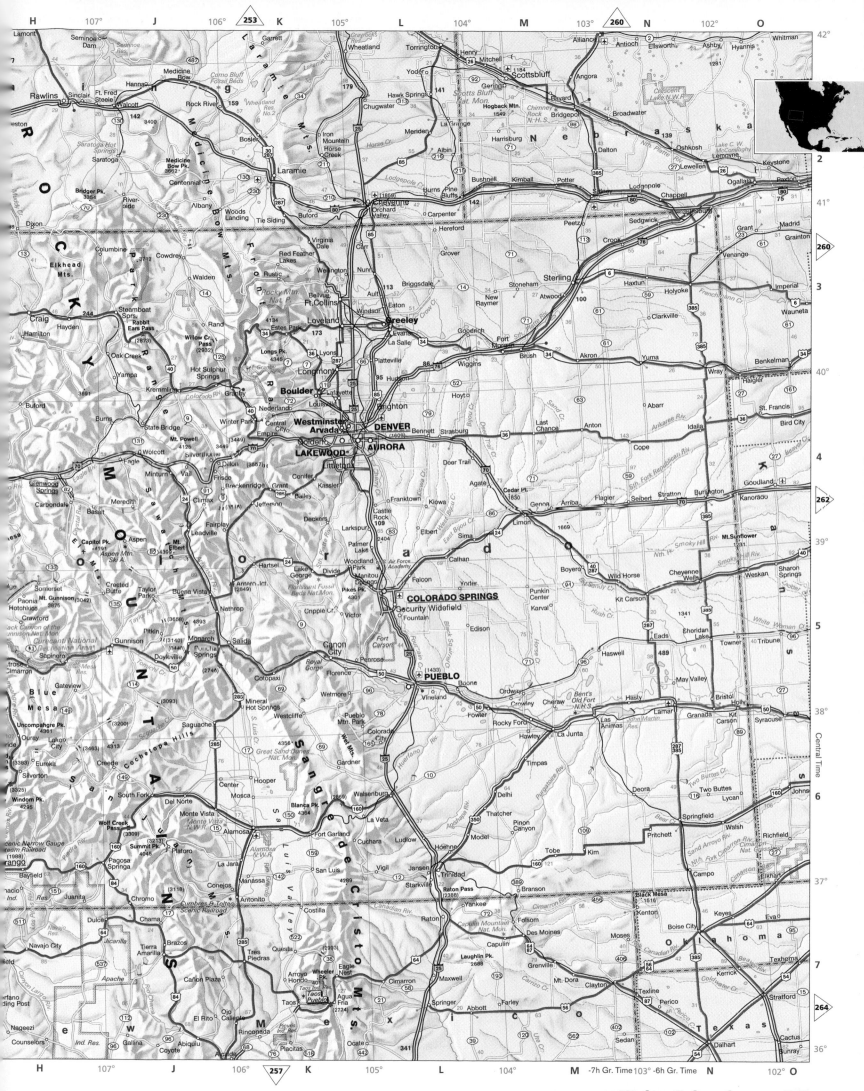

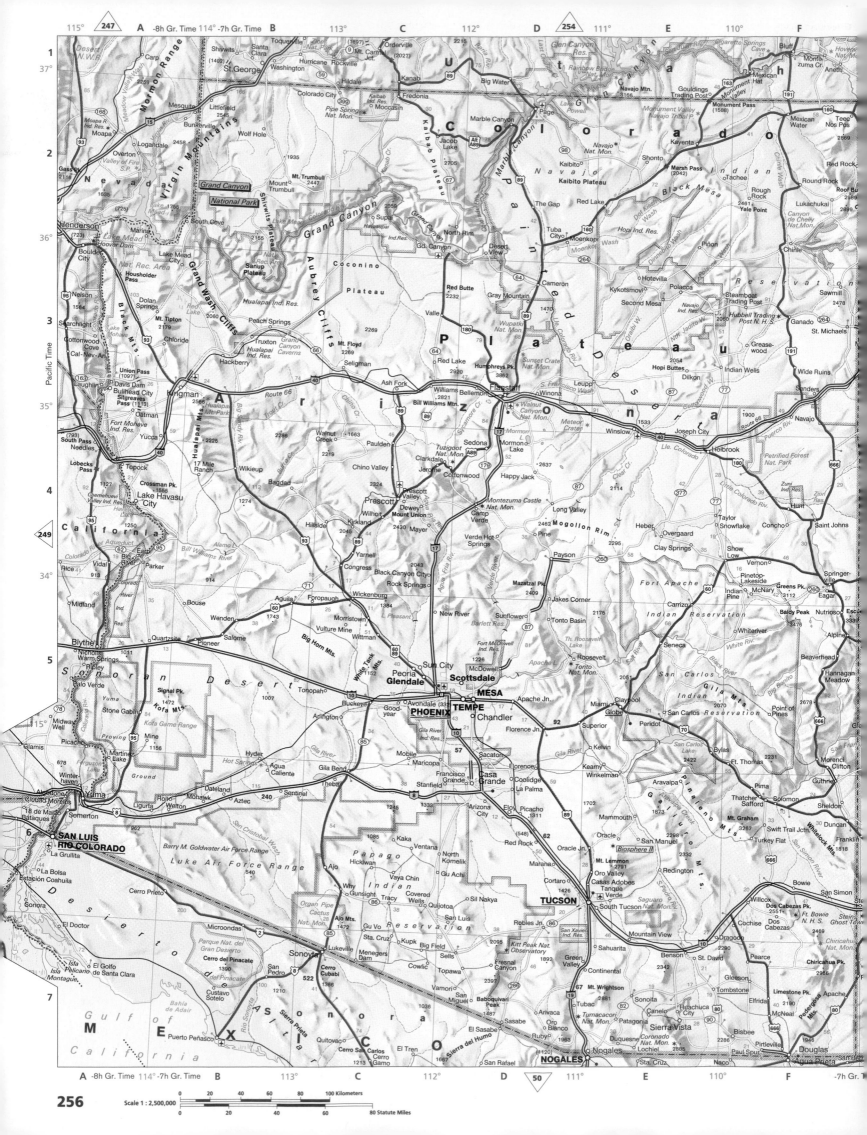

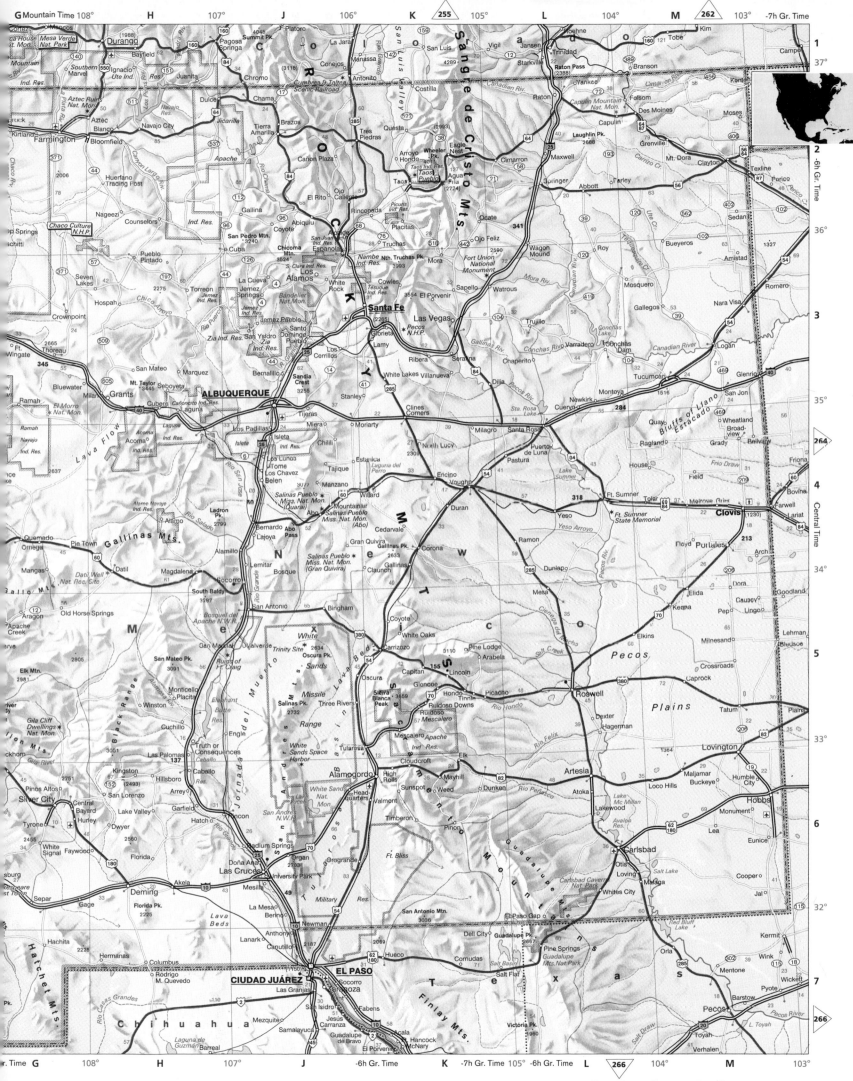

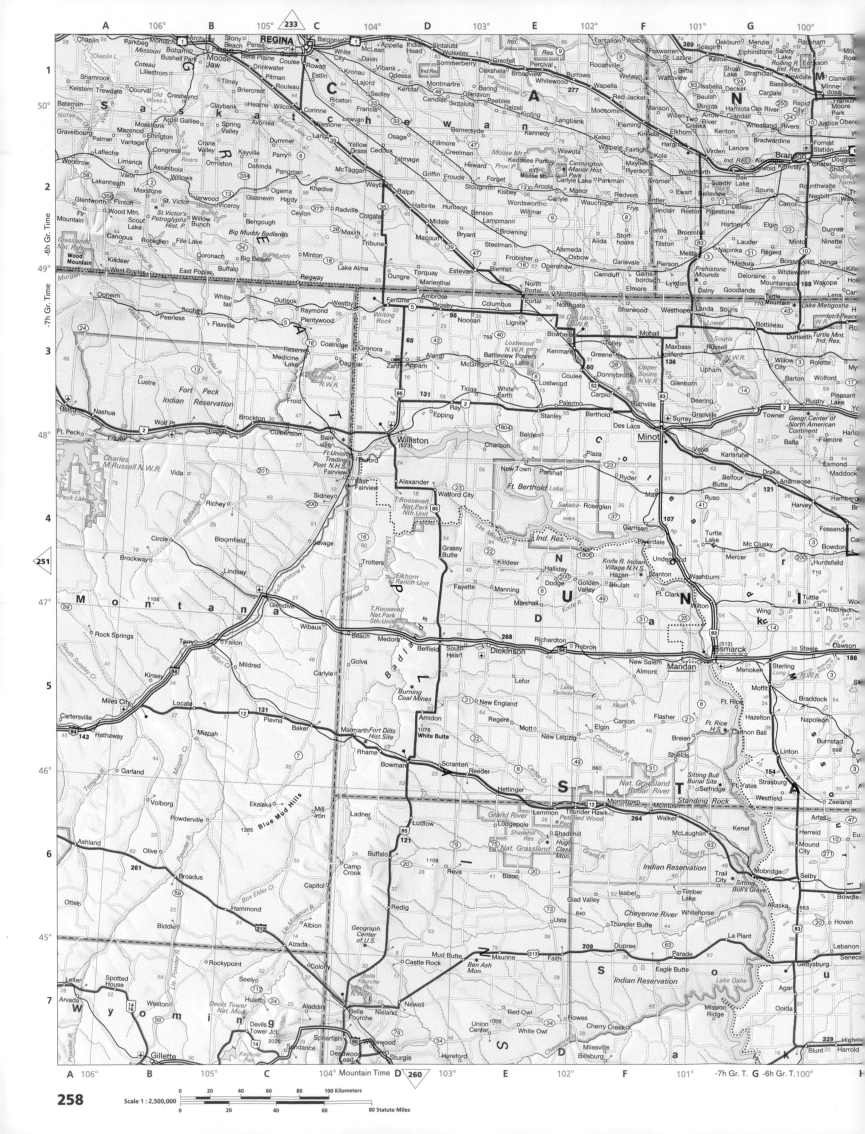

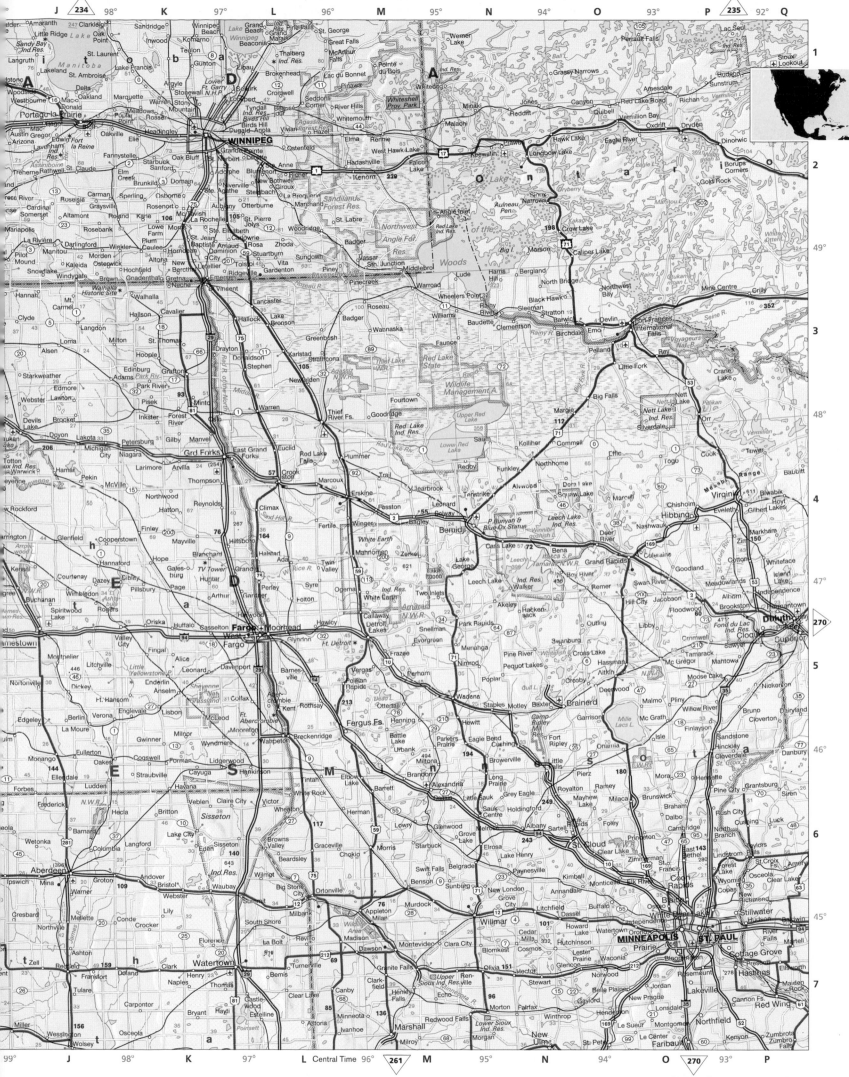

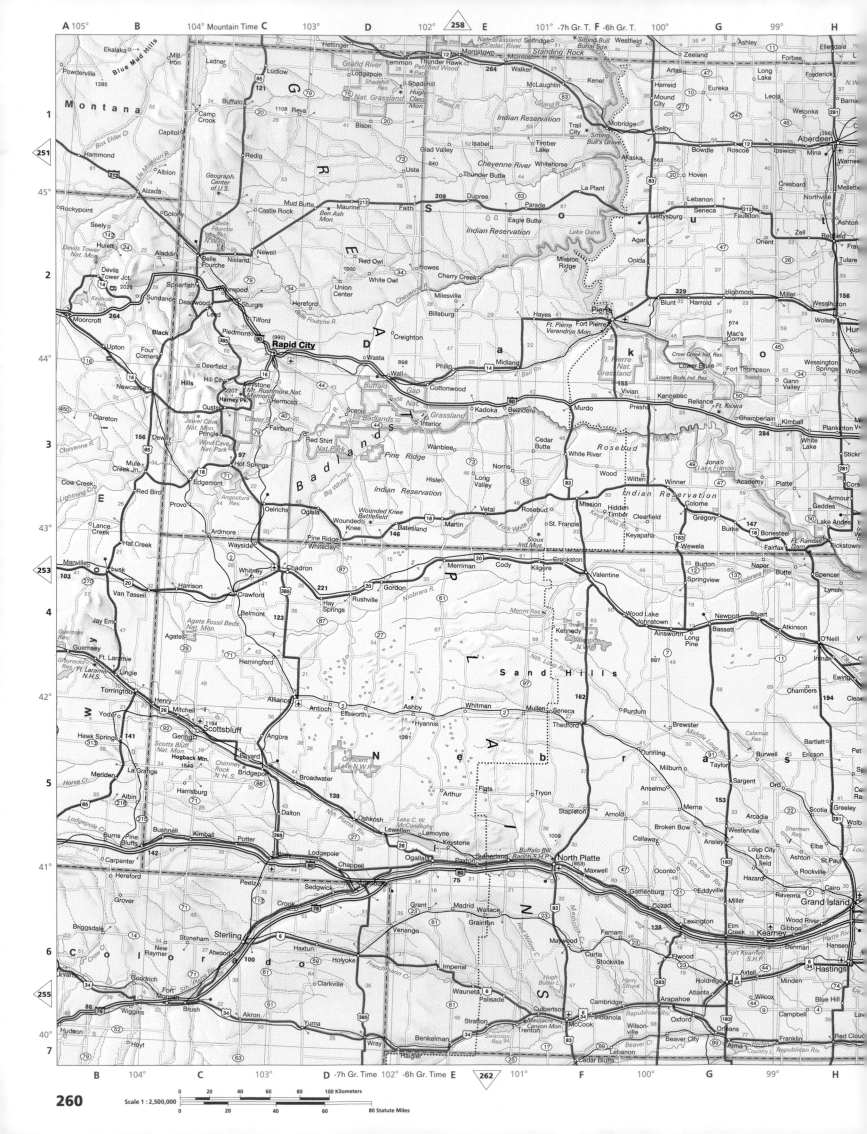

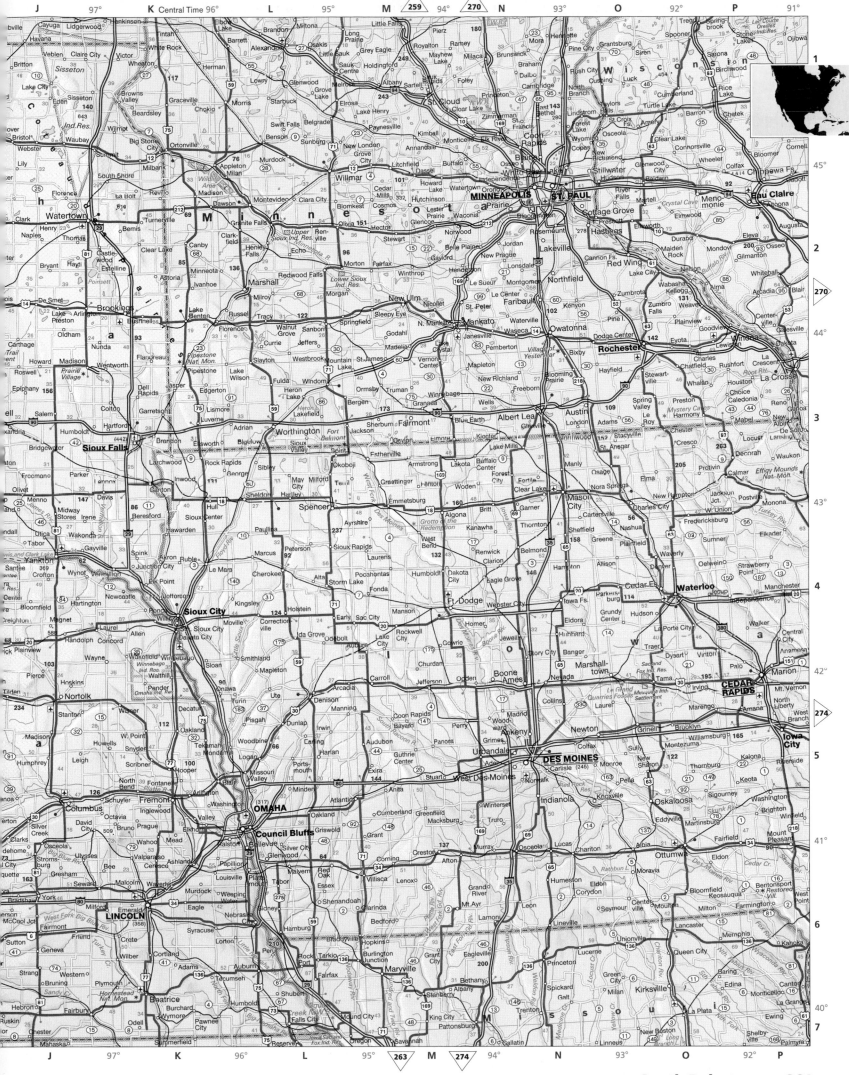

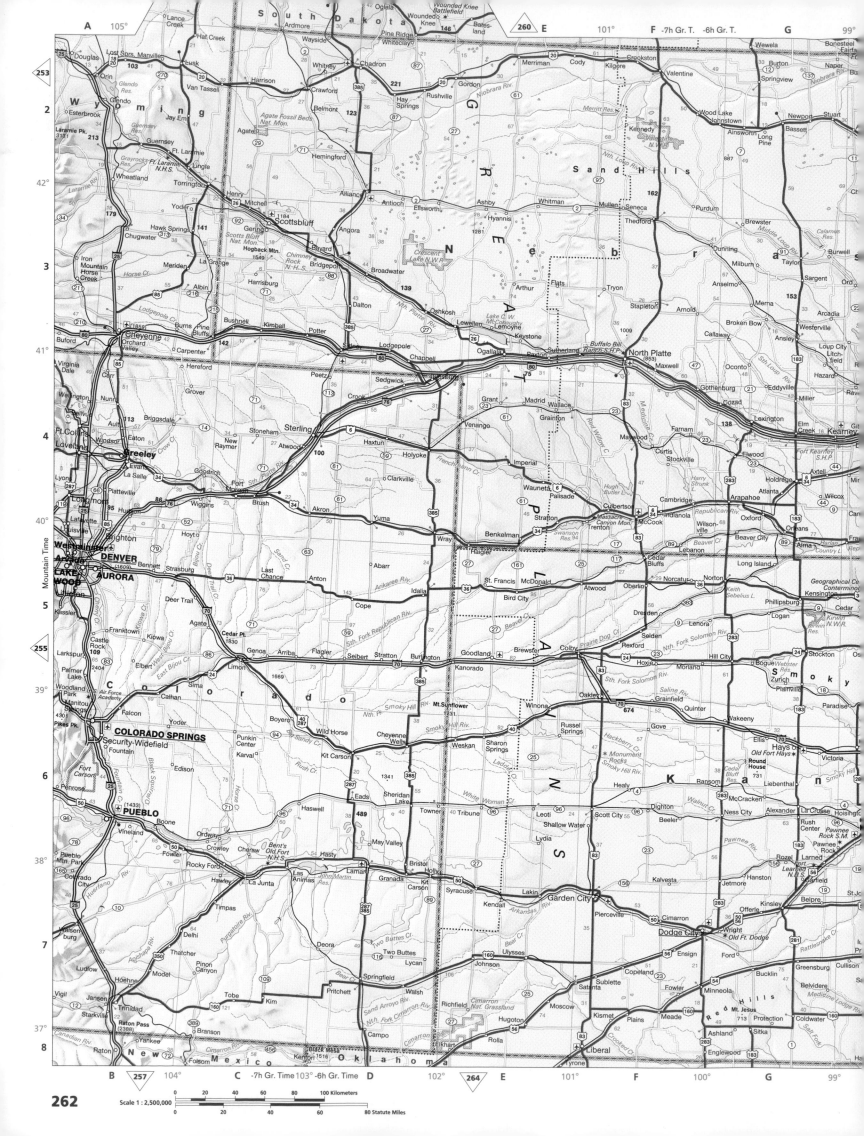

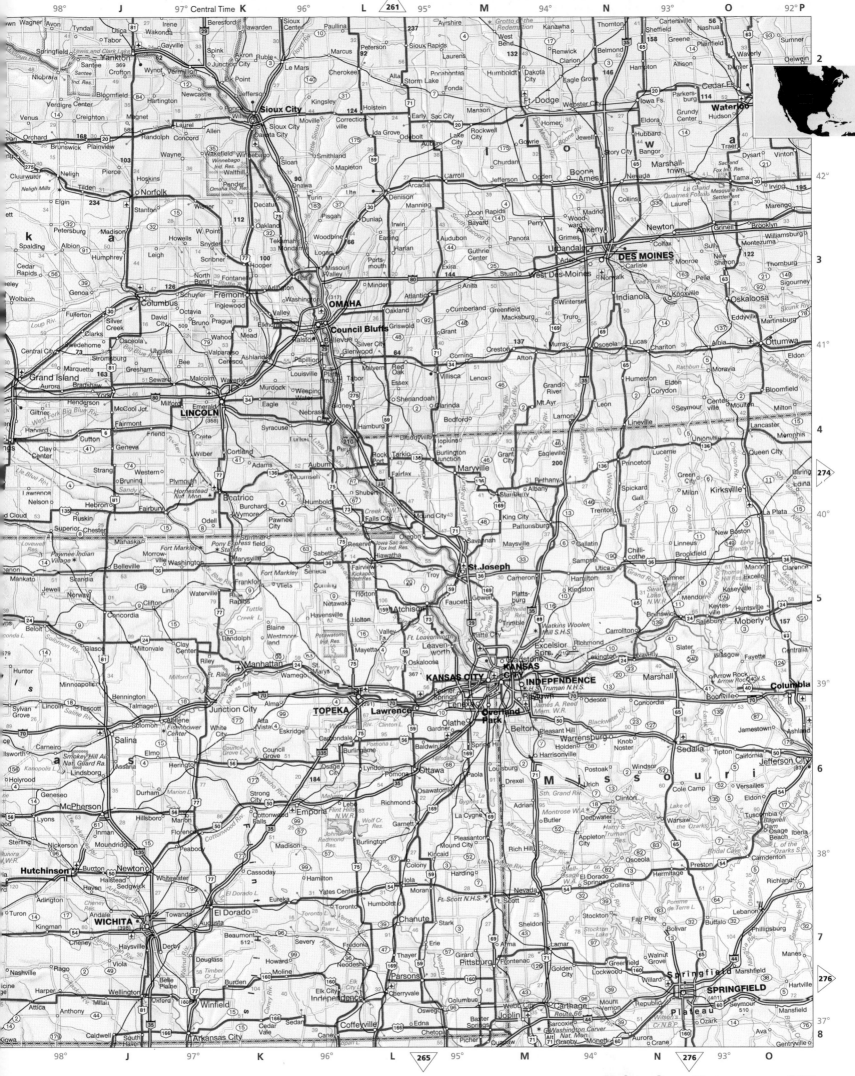

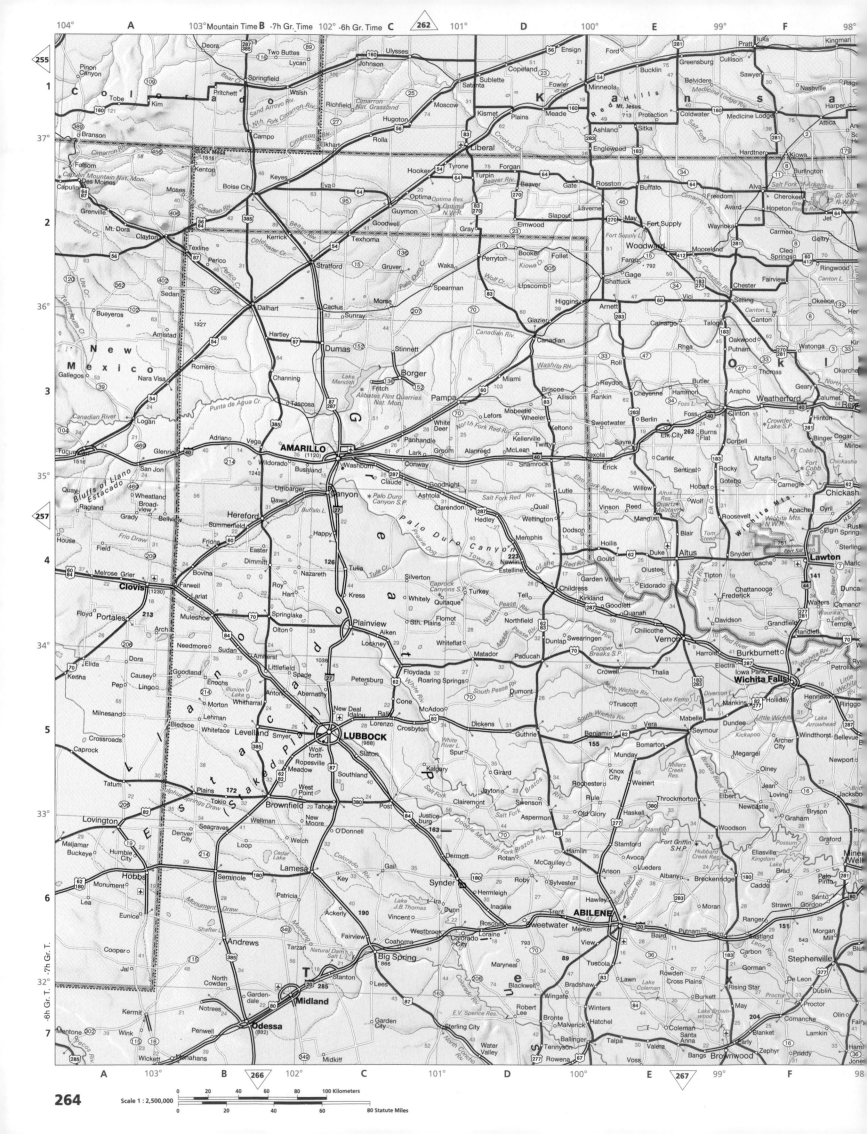

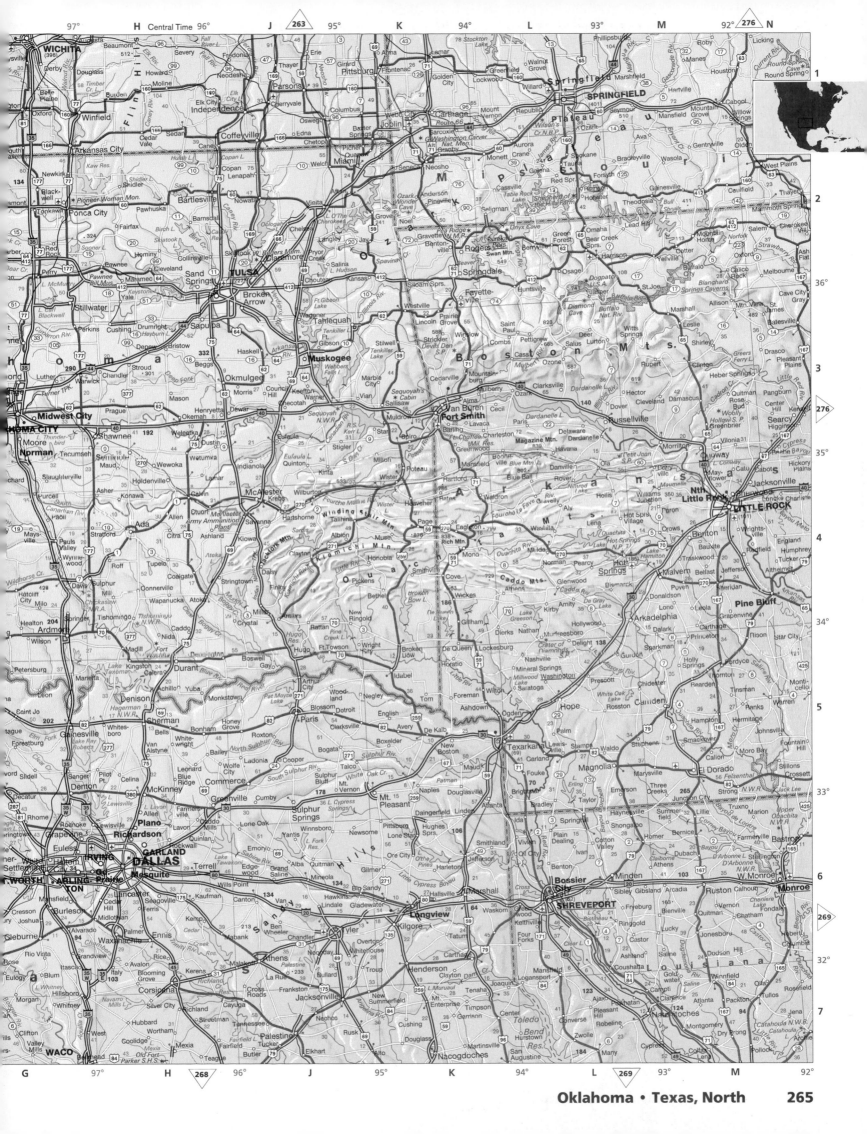

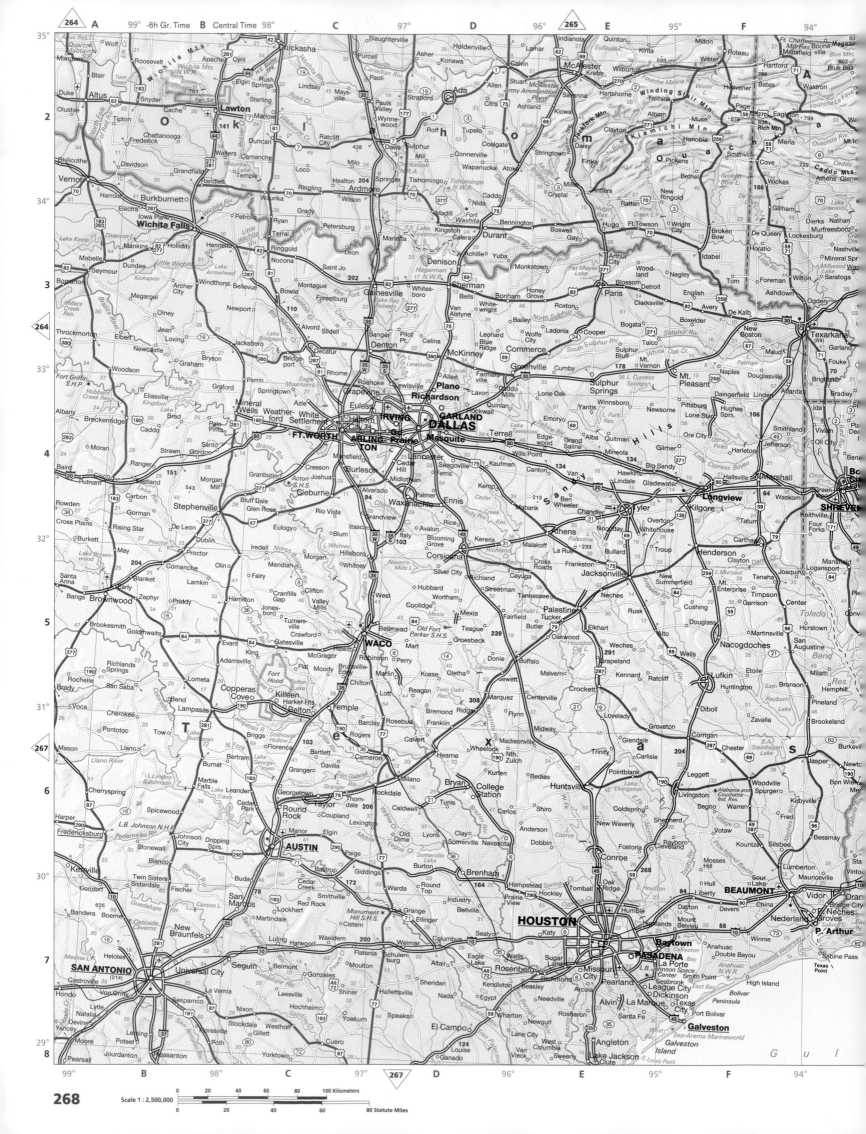

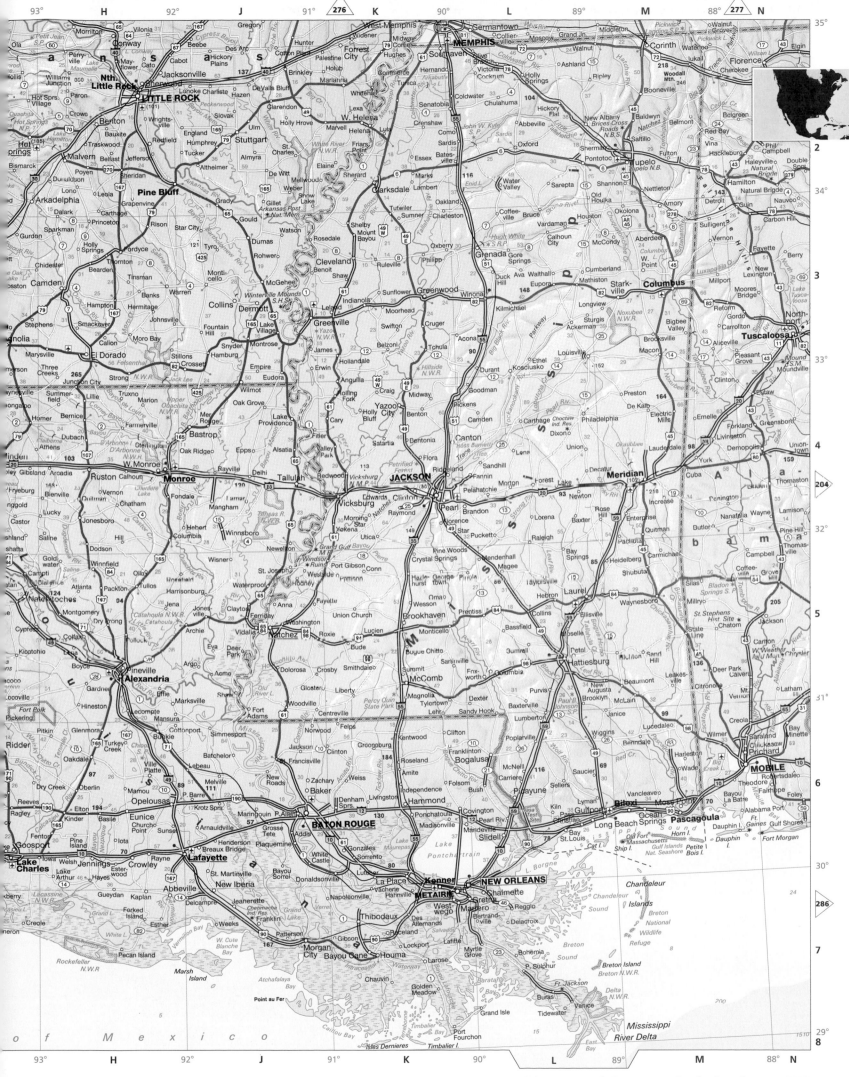

93° H 92° J 91° 276 K 90° L 89° M 88° 277 N
35°
2
34°
3
33°
32°
204
5
31°
286
7
29°
8

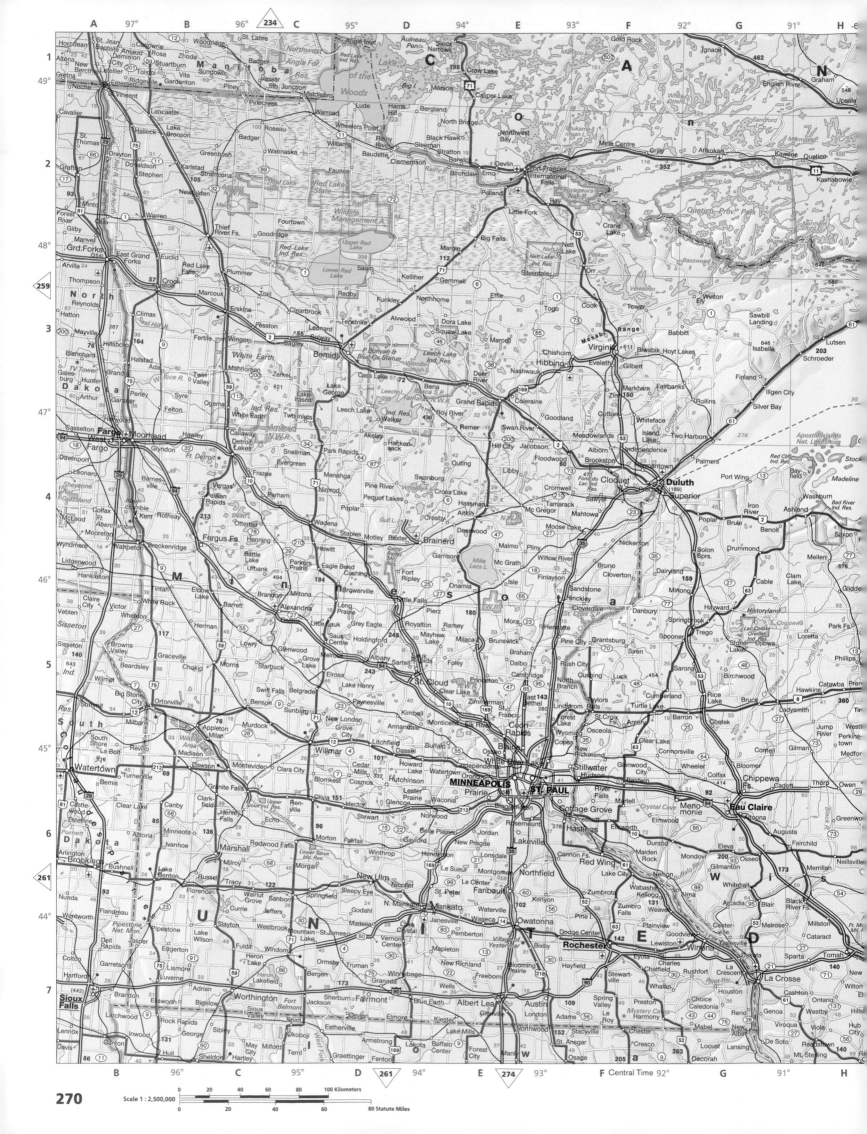

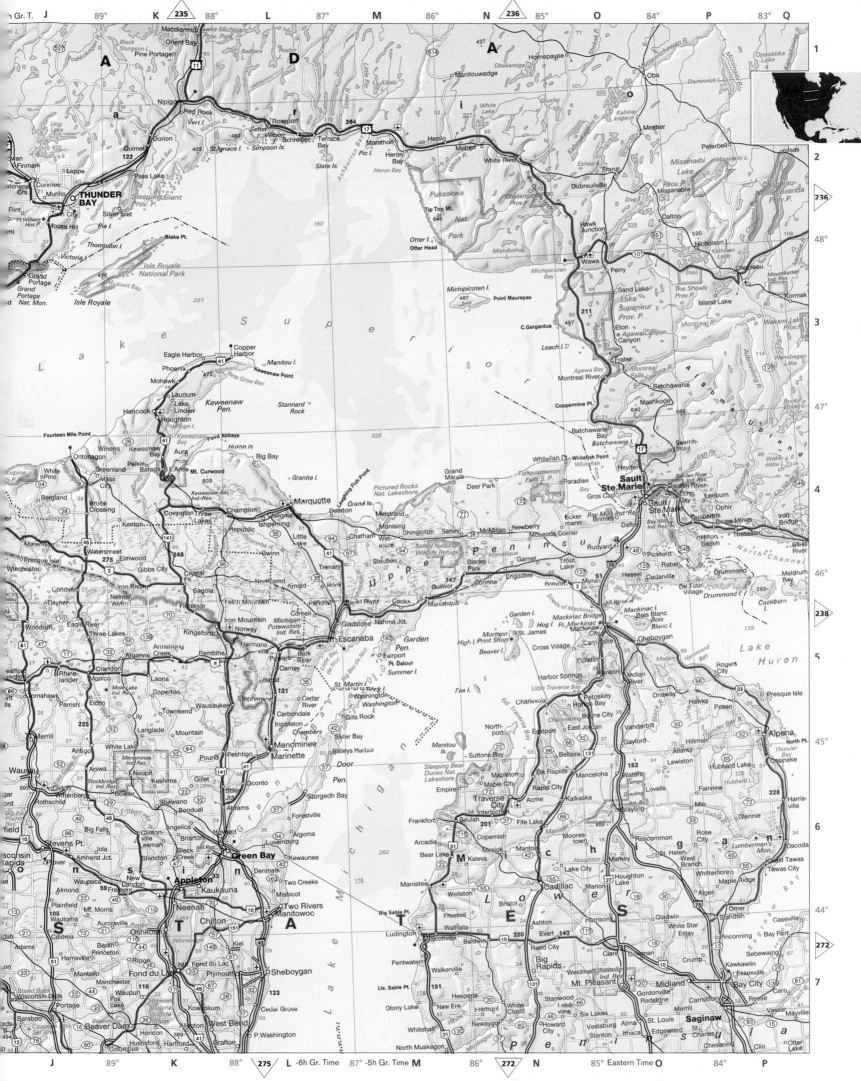

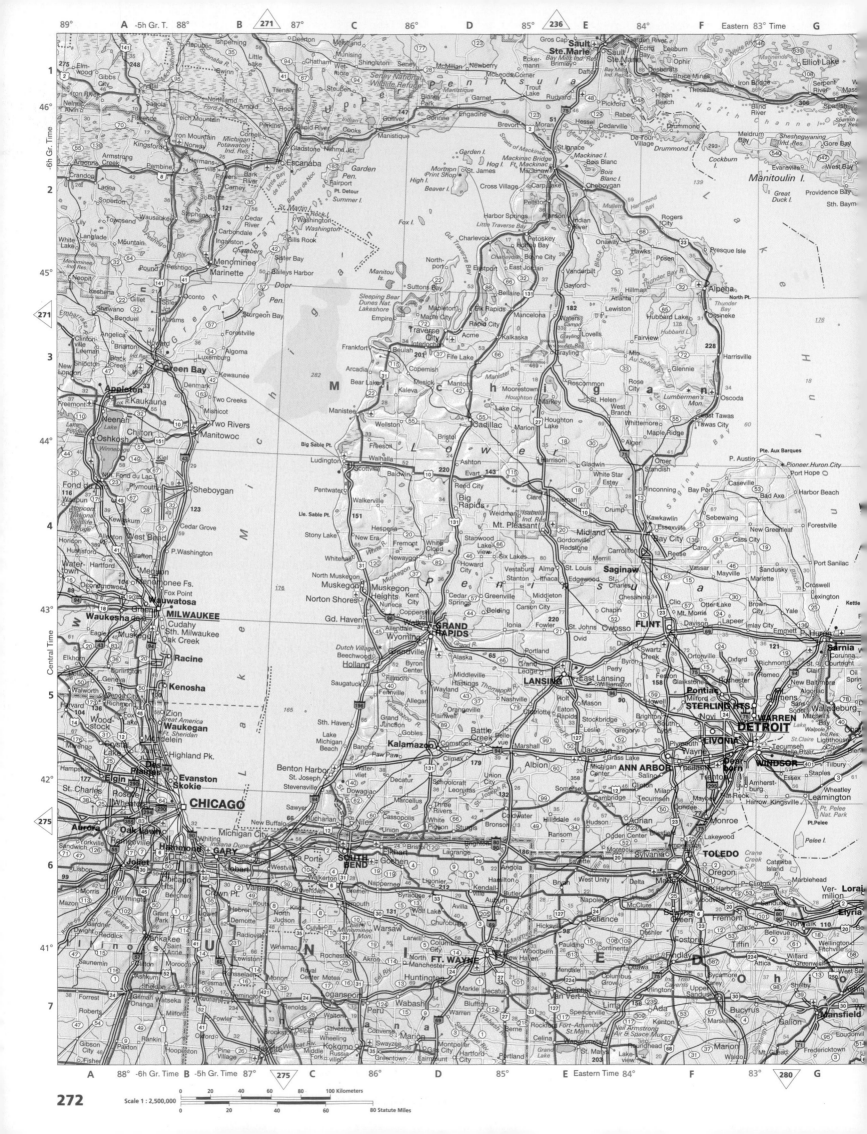

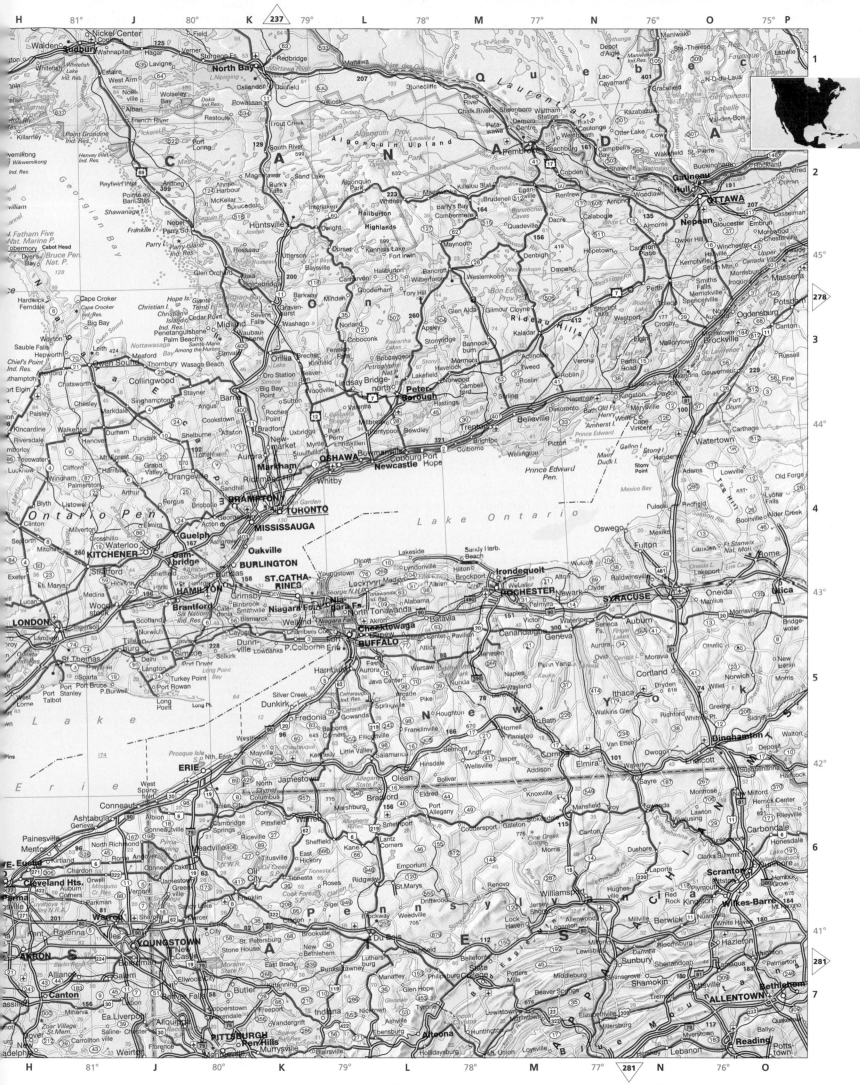

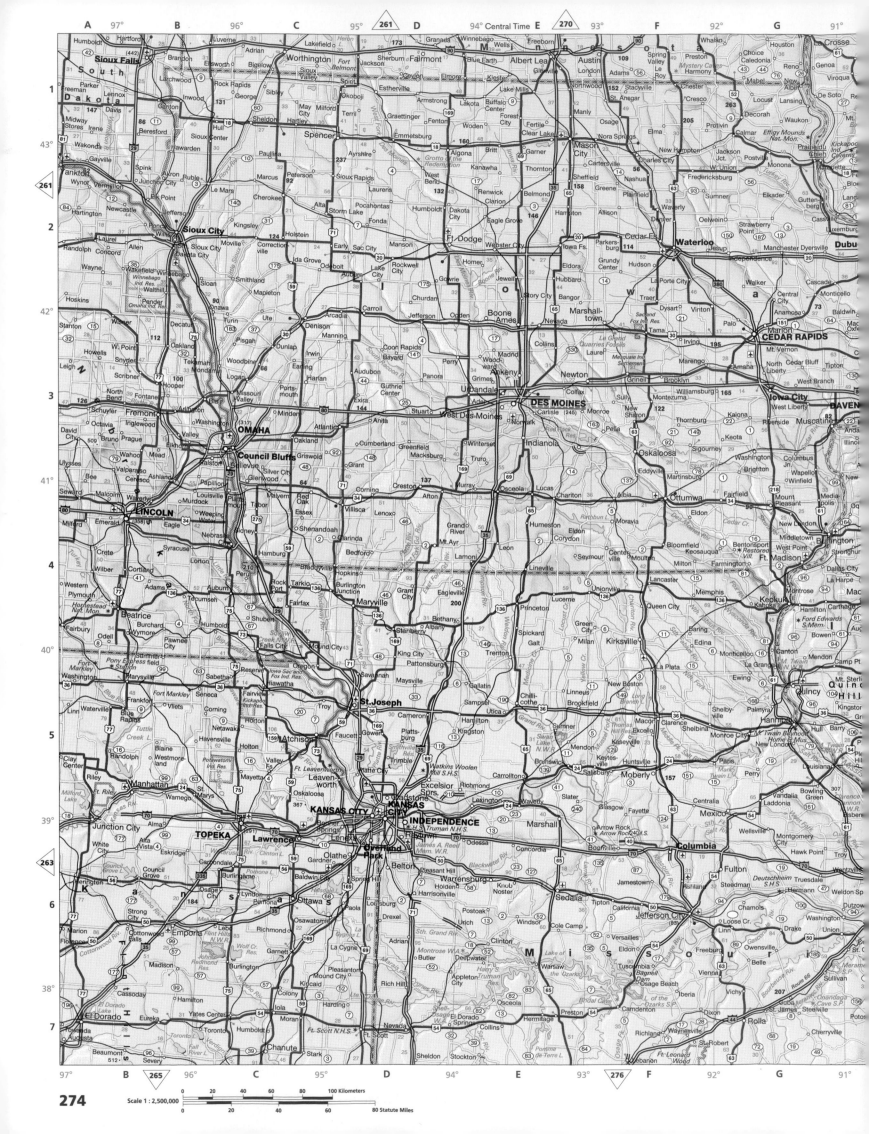

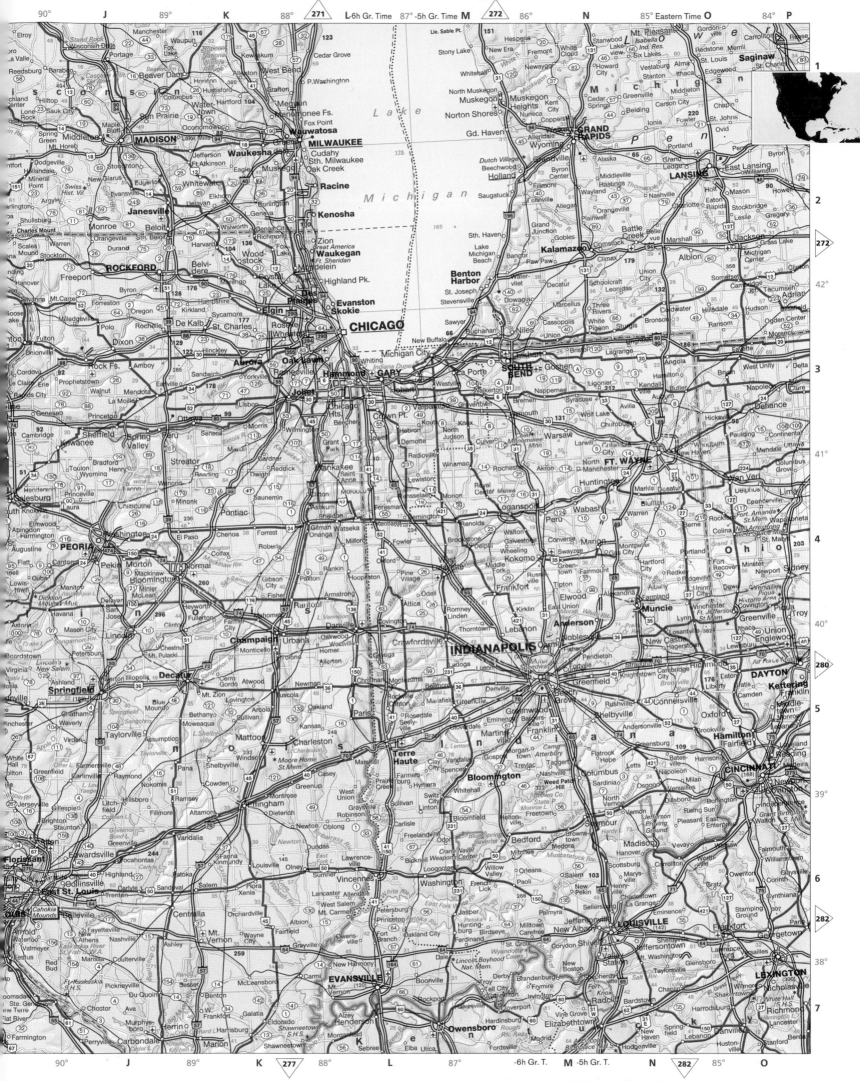

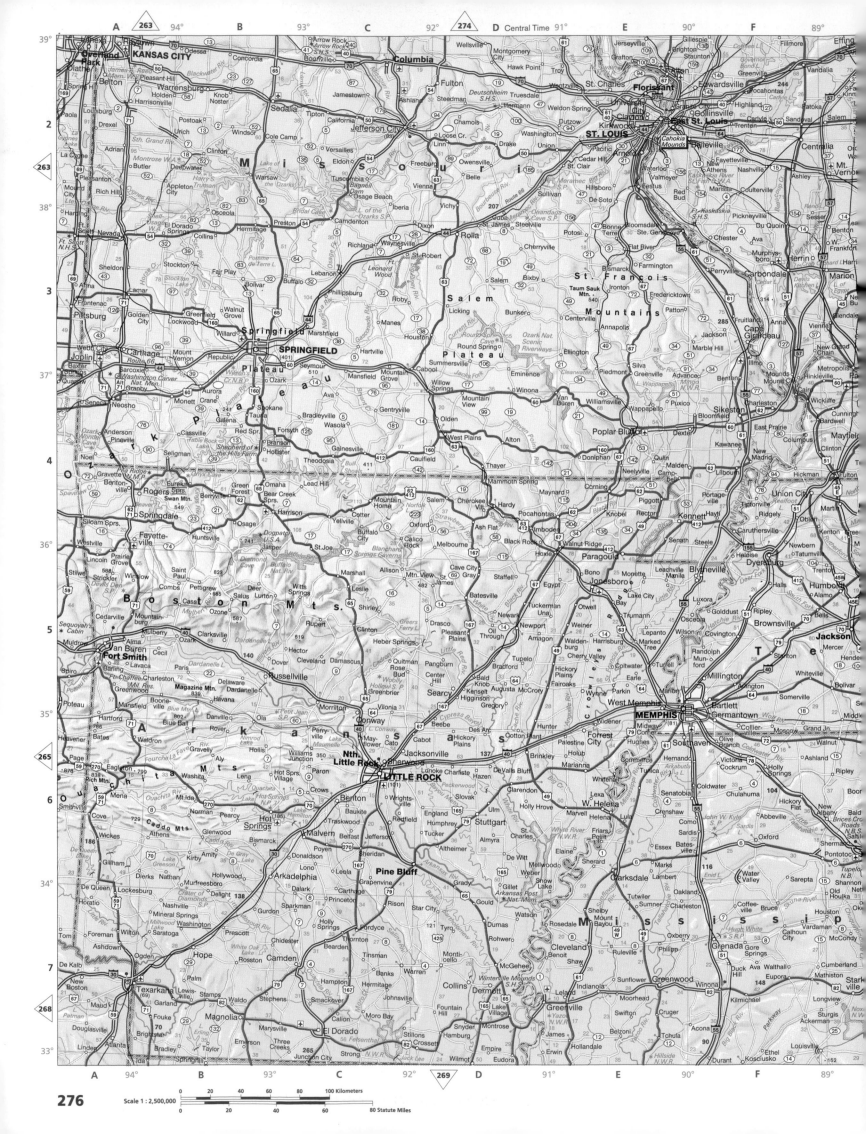

Missouri, South • Arkansas • Kentucky • Tennessee   277

Scale 1 : 2,500,000

| 0 | 20 | 40 | 60 | 80 | 100 Kilometers |

| 0 | 20 | 40 | 60 | 80 Statute Miles |

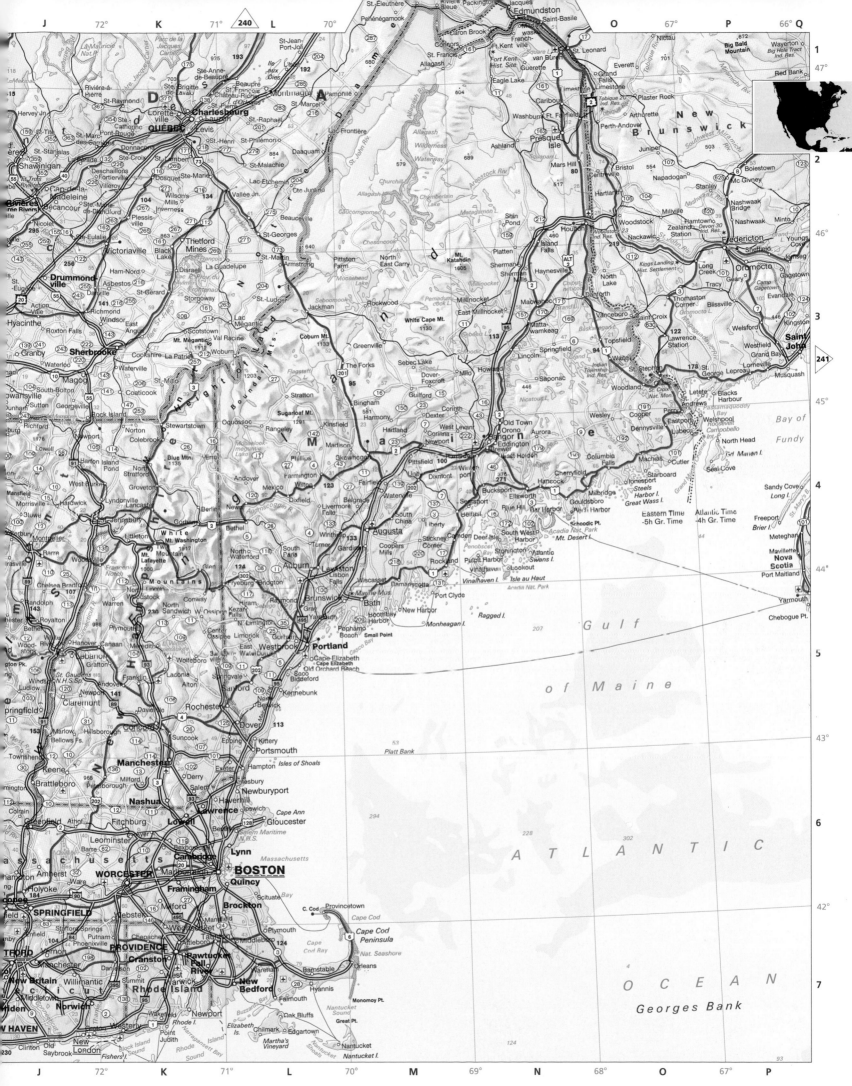

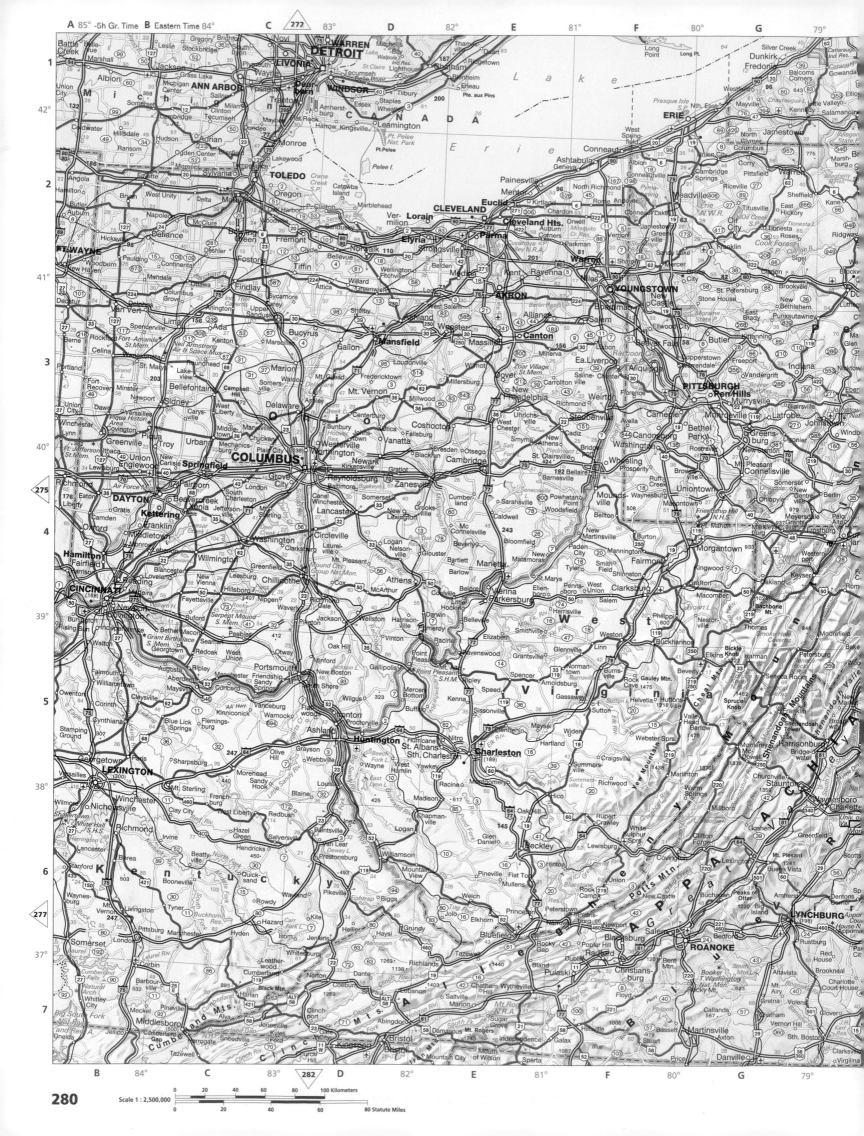

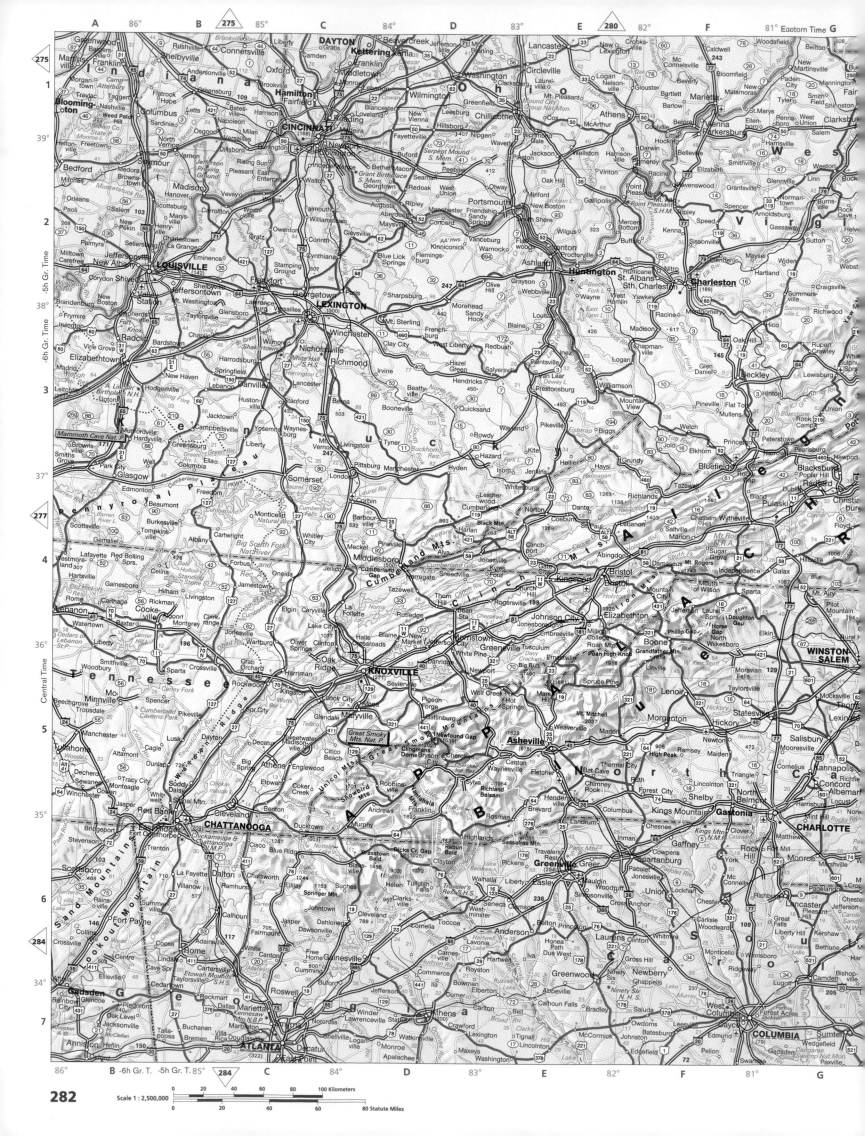

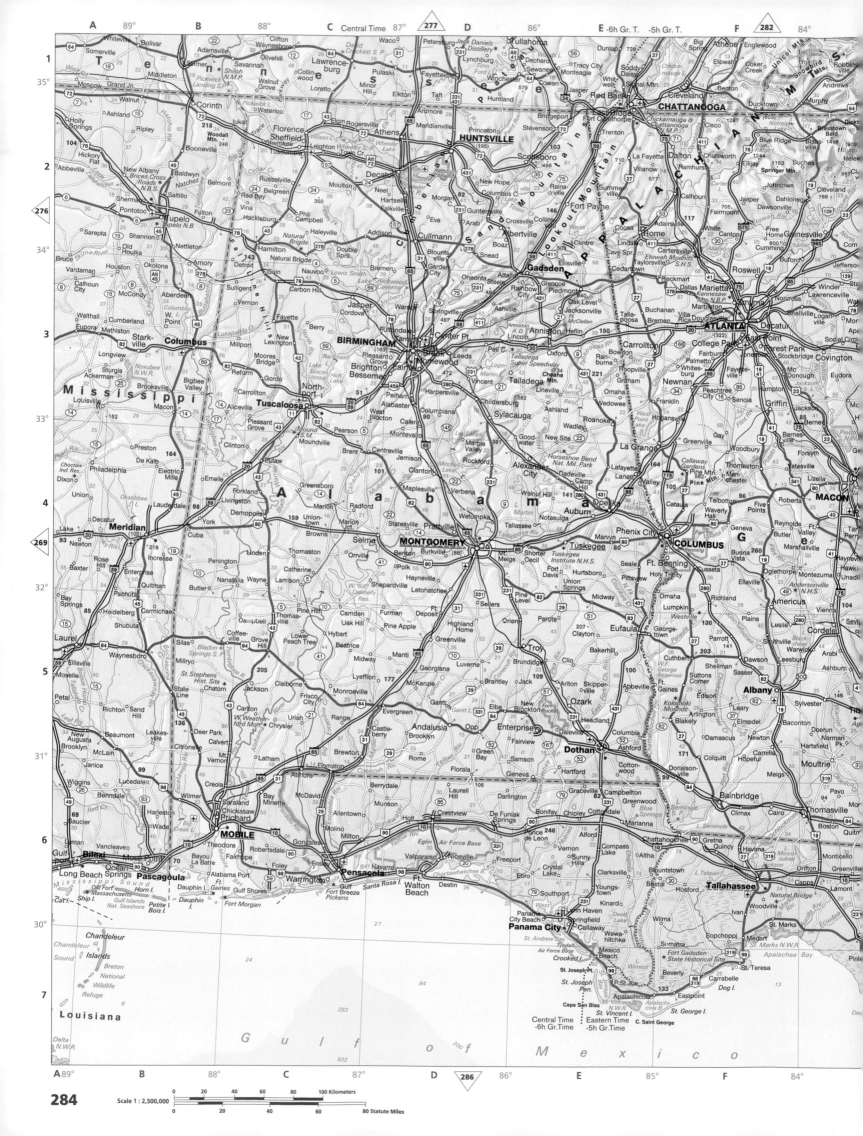

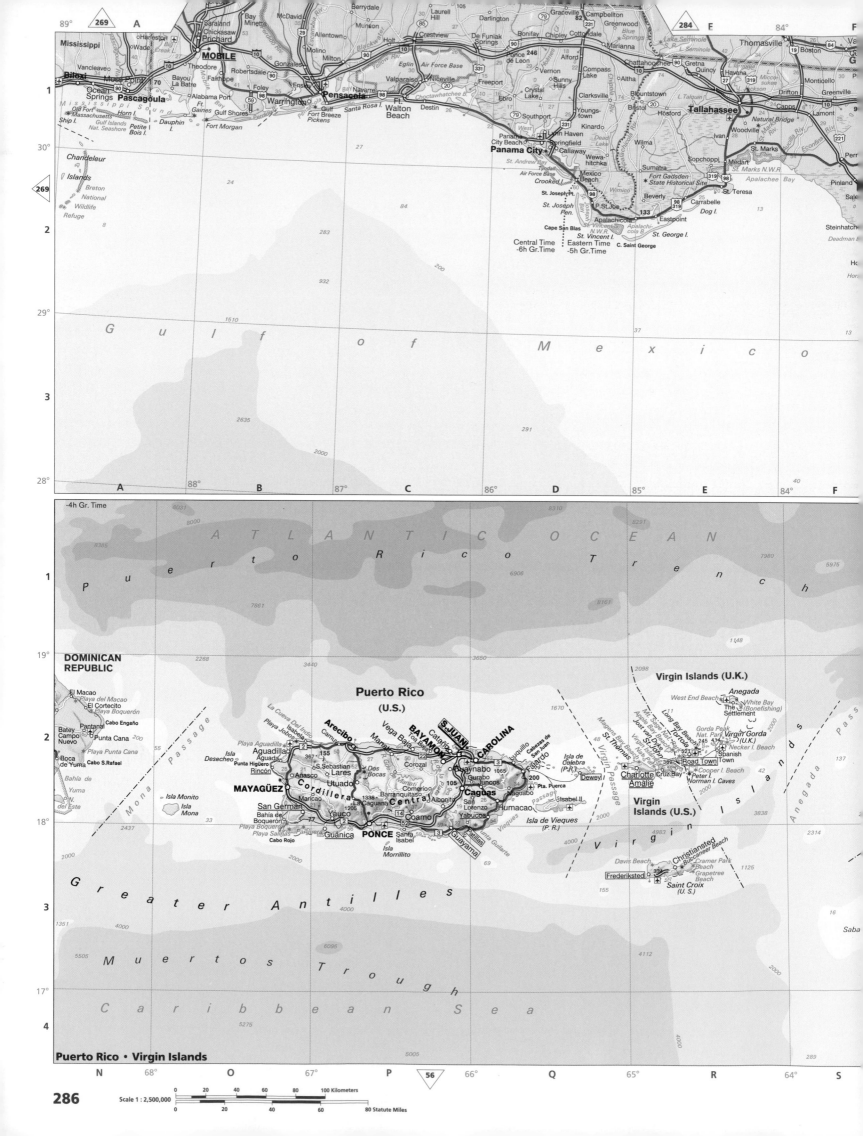

Mississippi

89° **269** A

Berrydale
Laurell Hill 105

Saraland McDavid Graceville 82 Campbellton
Chickasaw Munson Darlington 79 Greenwood 231 Greenwood
MOBILE Prichard 85 Crestview Bonifay Chipley Cottodale Blue Lake Seminole **284** F 84°
Theodore 29 Allentown De Funiak Marianna Springs Gretna Quincy Havana Thomasville 19 Boston Va
Biloxi Robertsdale Milton 90 90 90 Springs Chattahoochee 27 319 Monticello
Ocean Fairhope Foley Ensley 90 331 90 Alford Vernon Compass Quincy Tallahassee 24 Greenville
Springs **Pascagoula** Alabama Port Warrington **Pensacola** 98 Fort Santa Rosa Niceville 20 Freeport Ponce 246 Sunny Lake Drifton 9
Old Fort Gulf Shores Gulf Breeze Ft Pickens Walton Destin Southport Kinard Hosford Bristol Woodville 221
Horn I. Dauphin I. Fort Morgan Beach Youngstown 231 Natural Bridge

30° Chandeleur 27 Panama Springfield St. Marks
Islands Callaway Medart Sopchoppy
269 24 Panama City Mexico Beach Sumatra St. Marks N.W.R. Apalachee Bay
84 932 St. Joseph Pt. 98 Fort Gadsden 98
St. Joseph 98 State Historical Site Pinland
Cape San Blas Apalachicola Eastpoint 133 Carrabelle Dog I. St. Teresa Sale
2 St. Vincent I. St. George I. 13 Steinhatch

Central Time Eastern Time
-6h Gr.Time -5h Gr.Time

29° *G* 1510 *u* *l* *f* *o* *f* *M* *e* *x* *i* *c* *o* 37 13
2635
2000 291

28° A 88° B 87° C 86° D 85° E 84° F

-4h Gr. Time 8031 8000 8310 8291 7980 5975
A *T* *L* *A* *N* *T* *I* *C* *O* *C* *E* *A* *N*

8385 *P* *u* *e* *r* *t* *o* *R* *i* *c* *o* *T* *r* *e* *n* *c* *h*
1 *P* *u* *e* 7861 6906 8161 1148

19° **DOMINICAN** 2268 3440 3650 2098 **Virgin Islands (U.K.)**
REPUBLIC Anegada
El Macao West End Beach White Bay
El Cortecito **Puerto Rico** The (Bonefishing)
Batey Pantanal **(U.S.)** 1670 Settlement
Campo Cabo Engaño Gorda Peak Virgin Gorda
Nuevo Punta Cana La Cueva Del Indio Necker I. Beach
Boca Cabo S.Rafael Playa Jobos Isabela Arecibo **S. JUAN** Spanish Road Town
de Yuma Isla Aguadilla 155 Vega Baja **BAYAMON** **CAROLINA** Town
2 Desecheo 367 Camuy 27 50 3 Cooper I. Beach 137
Isla Monito Rincón Aguada Dos 22 Luquillo Peter I.
Bahia de Isla Añasco Lares Bocas Corozal Gurabo Isla de Charlotte Cruz Bay Norman I. Caves
Yuma Mona Utuado 1205 Comerio 105 Juncos Colebra Amalie 42
N. **MAYAGÜEZ** Maricao Barranquitaso (P.R.) Pta. Puerca **Virgin**
del Este San German 1338 Aibonito San Dewey 200 Isabel II **Islands (U.S.)**
18° Bahia de La Caguana **Central** Lorenzo Humacao
Boquerón Yauco 14 Coamo Yabucoa Isla de Vieques 4983 3838
2437 77 52 Santa Isabel (P. R.)
Playa Boquerón **Guánica** **PONCE** 19 Guayama Punta Guillarte Christiansted Buccaneer Park
Cabo Rojo Isla 69 4000 *V* *i* *r* *g* *i* *n* Davis Beach Beach Cramer Park 1125
Morrillito 2000 Frederiksted Grapetree
3 1351 5505 4000 6095 4112 155 Saint Croix 16
G **r** **e** **a** **t** **e** **r** **A** **n** **t** **i** **l** **l** **e** **s** 4000 (U. S.) Saba

17° **M** **u** **e** **r** **t** **o** **s** **T** **r** **o** **u** **g** **h**
5275

4 *C* *a* *r* *i* *b* *b* *e* *a* *n* *S* *e* *a*
5005 289

Puerto Rico • Virgin Islands

N 68° O 67° P **56** 66° Q 65° R 64° S

Scale 1 : 2,500,000

0 20 40 60 80 100 Kilometers

0 20 40 60 80 Statute Miles

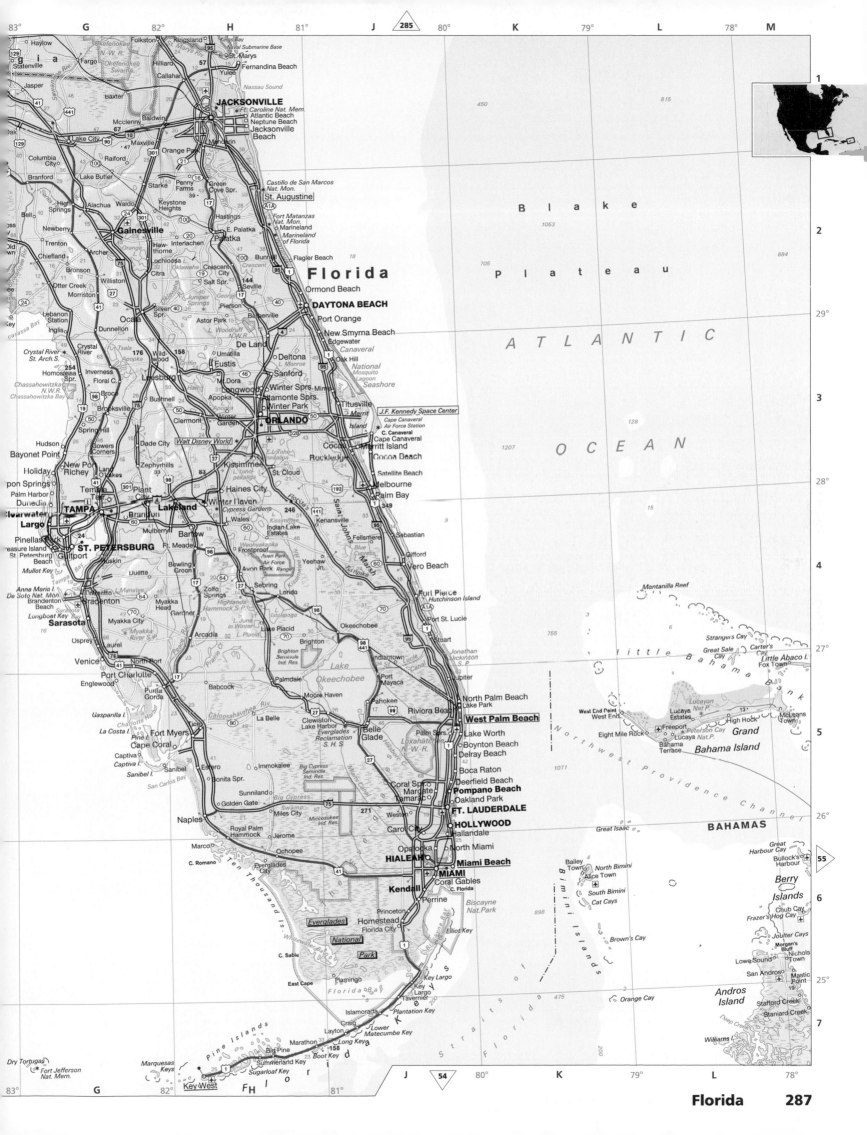

Florida 287

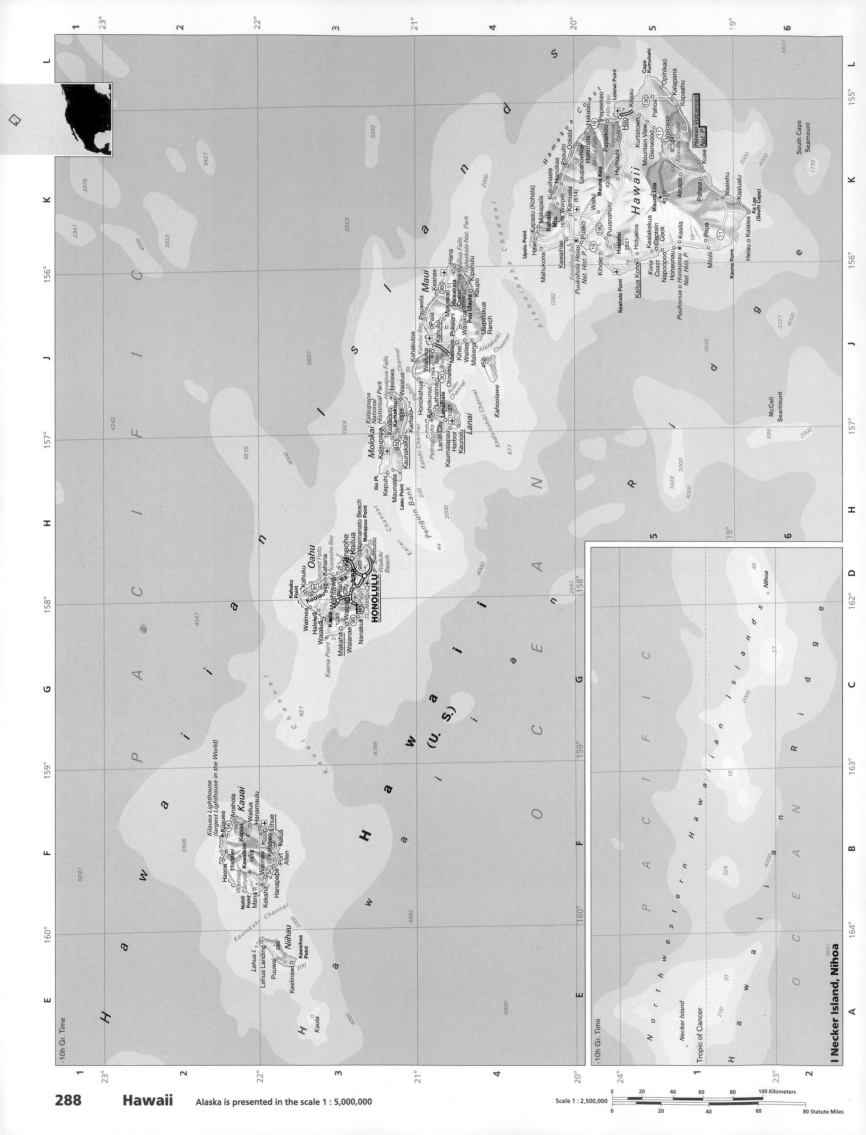

Scale 1 : 2,500,000

Hawaii

PACIFIC OCEAN

Kauai
Niihau
Oahu
HONOLULU
Molokai
Lanai
Maui
Kahoolawe
Hawaii
Hawaii Volcanoes Nat. P.

I Necker Island, Nihoa

Abbreviations

A.

A.	Alm (Ger.) mountain meadow
Abb.	Abbaye (Fr.) abbey
Abor.	(Engl.) aboriginal
Aç.	Açude (Port.) small reservoir
Ad.	Adası (Turk.) island
A.F.B.	(Engl.) Air Force Base
Ag.	Agios (Gr.) saint
A.I.	Área Indígena (Port.) Indian reservation
Ald.	Aldeia (Port.) village, hamlet
Arch.	(Engl.) archipelago
Arch.	Archipiélago (Span.) archipelago
Arg.	(Engl.) Argentina
Arh.	Arhipelag (Rus.) archipelago
Arq.	Arquipélago (Port.) archipelago
Arr.	Arroyo (Span.) brook
Art.Ra.	(Engl.) artillery range
Austr.	(Engl.) Australia
Aut.	(Engl.) autonomous
Aut.Dist.	(Engl.) autonomous district
Aut.Reg.	(Engl.) autonomous region

B

B.	Baie (Fr.) bay
B.	Biológica, -o (Port.) biological
Ba.	Bahía (Span.) bay
Bal.	Balka (Rus.) gorge
Ban.	Banjaran (Mal.) mountains
Bel.	Belo, -yj, -aja, -oe (Rus.) white
Bk.	Bukit (Mal.) mountain, hill
Bol.	Boloto (Rus.) swamp
Bol.	Bolšoj, -aja, -oe (Rus.) big
Bot.	(Engl.) botanical
B.P.	(Engl.) battlefield park
Br.	Brück, -e, -en (Ger.) bridge, -es
Braz.	(Engl.) Brazil
Brj.	Baraj (Turk.) dam
Buch.	Buchta (Ukr.) bay
Buh.	Buhta (Rus.) bay

C

C.	Cap (Fr.) cape, point
C.	Cabo (Port., Span.) cape, point
Cab.	Cabeça (Port.) heights, summit
Cach.	Cachoeira (Port.) rapids
Cal.	Caleta (Span.) bay
Can.	Canalul (Rom.) canal
Can.	Canal (Span.) canal
Cast.	Castello (Ital.) castle, palace
Cd.	Ciudad (Span.) city
Cga.	Ciénaga (Span.) swamp, moor
Ch.	Chenal (Fr.) canal
Chr.	Chrebet (Ukr.) mountains
Co.	Cerro (Span.) mountain, hill
Col.	Colonia (Span.) colony
Conv.	Convento (Span.) monastery
Cord.	Cordillera (Span.) mountain chain
Corr.	Corredeira (Port.) rapids
Cpo.	Campo (Port.) field
Cr.	(Engl.) creek
Cs.	Cerros (Span.) mountain, hill

D

D.	Dake (Jap.) mountain
Dağl.	Dağlar (Turk.) mountains
Dist.	(Engl.) district
Df.	Dorf (Ger.) village
Dl.	Deal (Rom.) heights, hill

E

Ea.	Estancia (Span.) ranch
Ej.	Ejido (Span.) common
Emb.	Embalse (Span.) reservoir
Ens.	Enseada (Port.) small bay
Erm.	Ermita (Span.) hermitage
Ero.	Estero (Span.) estuary
Esp.	España (Span.) Spain
Est.	Estación (Span.) railroad terminal
Estr.	Estrecho (Span.) straight, sound
Ez.	Ezero (Bulg.) lake

F

Faz.	Fazenda (Port.) ranch
Fin.	(Engl.) Finland
Fk.	(Engl.) fork
Fn.	Fortín (Span.) fort
Fr.	(Engl.) France
Fs.	(Engl.) falls, waterfall
Ft.	(Engl.) fort

G

Ğ.	Ğabal (Arab.) mountain
G.	Gawa (Jap.) lagoon
G.	Gîtul (Rom.) pass
G.	Golfo (Span.) bay, gulf
G.	Gora (Rus.) mountain
Gde.	Grande (Span.) big
Gds.	Grandes (Span.) big
Glac.	Glacier (Fr.) glacier
Gos.	Gosudarstvennyj, -aja (Rus.) national
Gr.	(Engl.) Greece
Gr.Br.	(Engl.) Great Britain
Grd.	Grand (Fr.) big
Grl.	General (Span.) general

H

H.	Hora (Ukr.) mountain
H.	Hütte (Ger.) mountain hut
Harb.	(Engl.) harbor
Hist.	(Engl.) historic
Hm.	Heim (Ger.) home
Hr.	Hrebet (Rus.) mountains
Hte.	Haute (Fr.) high
Hwy.	(Engl.) highway

I

I.	(Engl.) island
Î.	Île (Fr.) island
I.	Ilha (Port.) island
I.	Isla (Span.) island
Igl.	Iglesia (Span.) church
In.	Insulă (Rom.) island
Ind.	(Engl.) India
Ind.	(Engl.) Indian
Ind.Res.	(Engl.) Indian reservation
Int.	(Engl.) international
Is.	(Engl.) islands
Is.	Islas (Span.) islands
Îs.	Îles (Fr.) islands
It.	(Engl.) Italy

J

Jaz.	Jazovir (Bulg.) reservoir
Jct.	(Engl.) junction
Jez.	Jezero (Slovenian) lake
Juž.	Južnyj, -aja (Rus.) southern

K

Kan.	Kanal (Ger.) canal
Kep.	Kepulauan (Indon.) archipelago
Kg.	Kampong (Indon.) village
K-l.	Köli (Kazakh.) lake
K-l.	Küli (Uzbek.) lake
Kör.	Körfez (Turk.) gulf, bay
Kp.	Kólpos (Gr.) gulf, bay
Kr.	Krasno, -yj, -aja, -oe (Rus.) red

L

L.	(Engl.) lake
L.	Lac (Fr.) lake
L.	Lacul (Rom.) lake
L.	Lago (Span.) lake
Lag.	Laguna (Rus.) lagoon
Lag.	Laguna (Span.) lagoon
Lev.	Levyj, -aja (Rus.) left
Lim.	Liman (Rus.) lagoon
Lim.	Limni (Gr.) lake
Lte.	(Engl.) little

M

M.	Munte (Rom.) mountain
M.	Mys (Rus.) cape, point
Mal.	(Engl.) Malaysia
Mal.	Malo, -yj, -aja, -oe (Rus.) little
Man.	Manastir (Bulg.) monastery
Man.	Manastir (Turk.) monastery
Măn.	Mănăstire (Rom.) monastery
Mem.	(Engl.) memorial
Mgne.	Montagne (Fr.) mountain, mountains
Mi.	Misaki (Jap.) cape, point
Mil.Res.	(Engl.) military reservation
Milli P.	Milli Park (Turk.) national park
Min.	(Engl.) mineral
Mñas.	Montañas (Span.) mountains
Moh.	Mohyla (Ukr.) tomb
Mon.	Monasterio (Span.) monastery
M.P.	(Engl.) military park
Mt.	(Engl.) mount
Mte.	Monte (Span.) mountain
Mti.	Monti (Ital.) mountains
Mtn.	(Engl.) mountain
Mtns.	(Engl.) mountains
Mtn.S.P.	(Engl.) mountain state park
Mts.	(Engl.) mountains
Mts.	Montes (Span.) mountains
Munţ.	Munţii (Rom.) mountains
Mus.	(Engl.) museum

N

N.	Nehir/ Nehri (Turk.) river, stream
N.	Nudo (Span.) peak
Nac.	Nacional (Span.) national
Nac.	Nacional'nyj, -aja, -oe (Rus.) national
Nat.	(Engl.) national
Nat.Mon.	(Engl.) national monument
Nat.P.	(Engl.) national park
Nat.Seas.	(Engl.) national seashore
Naz.	Nazionale (Ital.) national
N.B.P.	(Engl.) national battlefield park
N.B.S.	(Engl.) national battlefield site
Ned.	Nederland (Neth.) Netherlands
Nev.	Nevado (Span.) snow-capped mountain
N.H.P.	(Engl.) national historic park
N.H.S.	(Engl.) national historic site
Niž.	Niže, -nij, -naja, -neje (Rus.) lower
Nizm.	Nizmennost' (Rus.) lowlands
N.M.P.	(Engl.) national military park
Nördl.	Nördlich (Ger.) northern
Nov.	Novo, -yj, -aja, -oe (Rus.) new
N.P.	(Engl.) national park
N.R.A.	(Engl.) national recreation area
Nsa.Sra.	Nossa Senhora (Port.) Our Lady
Nth.	(Engl.) north
Ntra.Sra.	Nuestra Señora (Span.) Our Lady
Nva.	Nueva (Span.) new
Nvo.	Nuevo (Span.) new
N.W.R.	(Engl.) national wildlife refuge

O

O.	Ostrov (Rus.) island
Obl.	Oblast (Rus.) district
Ö.	Östra (Swed.) eastern
Üv.	Üvre (Swed.) upper
Of.	Oficina (Span.) office
Ostr.	Ostrov (Rom.) island
O-va.	Ostrova (Rus.) islands
Oz.	Ozero (Rus.) lake

P

P.	(Engl.) port
P.	Passe (Fr.) pass
P.	Pico (Span.) peak
P.	Pulau (Indon.) island
Peg.	Pegunungan (Indon.) mountains
Pen.	(Engl.) peninsula
Pen.	Peninsula (Span.) peninsula
Per.	Pereval (Rus.) pass
Picc.	Piccolo (Ital.) little
P-iv.	Pivostriv (Ukr.) peninsula
Pk.	(Engl.) peak
Pkwy.	(Engl.) parkway
Pl.	Planina (Bulg.) mountain, mountains
P.N.	Parque Nacional (Span.) national park
Po.	Paso (Span.) pass
Pol.	(Engl.) Poland
Por.	Porog (Rus.) rapids
P-ov.	Poluostrov (Rus.) peninsula
Pr.	Proliv (Rus.) strait, sound
Pr.	Prohod (Bulg.) pass
Presq.	Presqu'île (Fr.) peninsula
Prov.	(Engl.) provincial
Prov.P.	(Engl.) provincial park
Pso.	Passo (Ital.) pass
Psto.	Puesto (Span.) outpost
Pt.	(Engl.) point
Pta.	Ponta (Port.) point
Pta.	Punta (Span.) point
Pte.	Pointe (Fr.) point
Pto.	Pôrto (Port.) port
Pto.	Puerto (Span.) port, pass
Pzo.	Pizzo (Ital.) point

Q

Q.N.P.	(Jap.) quasi national park

R

R.	Reka (Bulg.) river
R.	Reserva (Span.) reservation
R.	Rio (Port.) river
R.	Río (Span.) river
Ra.	(Engl.) range
Rch.	Riachão (Port.) small river
Rch.	Riacho (Span.) small river
Rdl.	Raudal (Span.) stream
Rep.	(Engl.) republic
Repr.	Represa (Span.) dam
Rère.	Rivière (Fr.) river
Res.	(Engl.) reservoir
Res.	Reserva (Port.) reservation
Resp.	Respublika (Rus.) republic
Rib.	Ribeira (Port.) shore
Rib.	Ribeiro (Port.) small river
Rif.	Rifugio (Ital.) mountain hut
Riv.	(Engl.) river
Rom.	(Engl.) Romania
Rom.	Romano, -na (Span.) Roman
Rus.	(Engl.) Russia

S

S.	San (Jap.) mountain, mountains
S.	San (Span.) saint
S.	São (Port.) saint
Sa.	Saki (Jap.) cape
Sa.	Serra (Port.) mountains
S.Afr.	(Engl.) South Africa
Sal.	Salar (Span.) salt desert, salt lagoon
Sanm.	Sanmyaku (Jap.) mountains
Sd.	(Engl.) sound
Sel.	Selat (Indon.) road
Sev.	Sever, -nyj, -naja, -noe (Rus.) north
Sf.	Sfintu (Rom.) holy
Sh.	Shima (Jap.) island
S.H.P.	(Engl.) state historic park
S.H.S.	(Engl.) state historic site
S.Kor.	(Engl.) South Korea
S.M.	(Engl.) state monument
Sna.	Salina (Span.) salt flat
Snas.	Salinas (Span.) salt flats
SNG.	Sodružestro Nezavisimyh Gosudarstv (Rus.) Commonwealth of independant states
Snía.	Serranía (Span.) ridge
S.P.	(Engl.) state park
Sr.	Sredne, -ij, -aja, -ee (Rus.) middle, central
Sra.	Sierra (Span.) mountains
St.	(Engl.) saint
St.	Saint (Fr., Span.) saint
Sta.	Santa (Span.) saint
Sta.	Staro, -ij, -aja, -oe (Rus.) old
Ste.	Sainte (Fr.) saint
Sth.	(Engl.) south
St.Mem.	(Engl.) state memorial
Sto.	Santo (Port.) saint
Str.	(Engl.) strait
Suh.	Suho, -aja (Rus.) dry
Sv	Svet, -a, -o (Bulg.) saint
Sv.	Sveti (Croatian) saint
Swed.	(Engl.) Sweden

T

T.	Take (Jap.) peak, heights
Tel.	Teluk (Indon.) bay
Tg.	Tanjung (Indon.) cape
Tg.	Töge (Jap.) pass
Tte.	Teniente (Span.) lieutenant

U

Ukr.	(Engl.) Ukraine
Ülk.	Ülken (Kazakh.) big
U.K.	(Engl.) United Kingdom
Urug.	(Engl.) Uruguay
U.S.	(Engl.) United States

V

V.	Vallée (Fr.) valley
Va.	Villa (Span.) market town
Vda.	Vereda (Port.) path
Vdhr.	Vodohranilišče (Rus.) reservoir
Vdp.	Vodospad (Ukr.) waterfall
Vel.	Veliko, -ij, -aja, -oe (Rus.) big
Verh.	Verhnie, -yj, -aja, -oe (Rus.) upper
Vf.	Vîrf (Rom.) peak, heights
Vill.	(Engl.) village
Vis.	Visočina (Bulg.) heights
Vjal.	Vjalikie (Belarus.) big
Vlk.	Vulkan (Ger.) volcano
Vn.	Volcán (Span.) volcano
Vod.	Vodopad (Rus.) waterfall
Vol.	Volcán (Span.) volcano
Vul.	Vulcano (Philip.) volcano

W

W.A.	(Engl.) wilderness area

Y

Y.	Yama (Jap.) mountain, mountains

Z

Zal.	Zaliv (Rus.) gulf, bay
Zap.	Zapadne, -ij, -aja, -noe (Rus.) west
Zapov.	Zapovednik (Rus.) protected area

Selected References

Index of Map Names

The index contains all names found on the maps in this atlas. The index's alphabetical listing corresponds to the sequence of letters in the Roman alphabet. Diacritical marks and special letters have been ignored in alphebetizing, e.g.:

A .... Á, À, Â, Ă, Å, Ą, Ā, Ã, Ä, Æ

The ligatures æ, œ are treated as ae and oe in the alphabetical listing.

Names that have been abbreviated on the maps are generally written in full in the index.

Generic concepts follow geographic names, e.g. Mexico, Gulf of; Ventoux, Mont. Exception: colors (e.g. Mount Blanc) and adjectives (e.g. Big, Little) come first. Official additions (e.g. Rothenburg ob der Tauber) are included in the alphabetizing.

To a certain degree, the index also includes

official alternate forms, linguistic variants, renamings and other secondary denominations. In such cases, the index refers to names as they appear on the maps, e.g. Merano = Meran, Leningrad = Sankt-Peterburg.

Abbreviations in parentheses help distinguish between places bearing the same names. Abbreviations as used on international motor-vehicle license plates have been given priority; where this is insufficient, ad-

ministrative informations like federal lands, provinces, regions, etc. are indicated.

Icons, which immediately follow the names, are used to indicate fundamental geographic concepts.

New York	○••	**USA**	(NY)	280-281	N 3	
①	②	③	④	⑤	⑥	
Search concept	Icon	Nation	Administrative unit	Page	Search grid designation	
Nihoa	⌒••	**USA**	(HI)	288	II	D 1
①	②	③	④	⑤	⑦	⑥
Search concept	Icon	Nation	Administrative unit	Page	Inset map	Search grid designation

② Icons

■ ......Sovereign nation	⌄ ......Depression	⊂ ......glacier	✈ ......Airport
▫ ......Administrative unit	▲ ......Mountains	⟨ ......dam	∴ ......Ruins, ruined city
★ ......Capital city (national capital)	▲ ......Mountain	≃ ......Undersea topography	••• ......World cultural or natural heritage site
☆ ......State (provincial) capital	▲ ......Active volcano	⊥ ......National park	
○ ......Place	≈ ......Ocean, part of an ocean	⤬ ......Reservation	⦂ ......Point of major interest
÷ ......Landscape	○ ......Lake, salt lake	×× ......Military installation	• ......Point of interest
⌒ ......Island	～ ......River, waterfall	II ......Transportation construction	

③ Souvereign States and Territories (Abbreviations in *italic:* Abbreviation not official)

A ......Austria	EST ......Estonia	LV ......Latvia	RT ......Togo
AFG ......Afghanistan	ET ......Egypt	M ......Malta	RUS ......Russia
AG ......Antigua and Barbuda	ETH ......Ethiopia	MA ......Morocco	RWA ......Rwanda
AL ......Albania	F ......France	*MAI* ......Marshall Islands	S ......Sweden
AND ......Andorra	FIN ......Finland	MAL ......Malaysia	SCV ......Vatican City
ANG ......Angola	FJI ......Fiji	*MAU* ......Mongolia	SD ......Swaziland
AR ......Armenia	FL ......Liechtenstein	MC ......Monaco	SGP ......Singapore
ARK ......Antarctica	FR ......Faroe Islands	MD ......Moldova	SK ......Slovakia
ARU ......Aruba	*FSM* ......Micronesia	MEX ......Mexico	SLO ......Slovenia
AUS ......Australia	G ......Gabon	MK ......Macedonia	SME ......Suriname
AUT ......Autonomous region	GB ......United Kingdom	MOC ......Mozambique	SN ......Senegal
AZ ......Azerbaijan	GBA ......Alderney	MS ......Mauritius	*SOL* ......Solomon Islands
B ......Belgium	GBG ......Guernsey	*MV* ......Maldives	SP ......Somalia
BD ......Bangladesh	GBJ ......Jersey	MW ......Malawi	*STP* ......São Tomé and Principe
BDS ......Barbados	GBM ......Isle of Man	MYA ......Myanmar (Burma)	*SUD* ......Sudan
BF ......Burkina Faso	GBZ ......Gibraltar	N ......Norway	SY ......Seychelles
BG ......Bulgaria	GCA ......Guatemala	NA ......Netherlands Antilles	SYR ......Syria
BH ......Belize	GE ......Georgia	NAM ......Namibia	*TCH* ......Chad
BHT ......Bhutan	GH ......Ghana	*NAU* ......Nauru	THA ......Thailand
BIH ......Bosnia and Herzegovina	GNB ......Guinea-Bissau	*NEP* ......Nepal	TJ ......Tajikistan
BOL ......Bolivia	GQ ......Equatorial Guinea	NIC ......Nicaragua	TM ......Turkmenistan
BR ......Brazil	GR ......Greece	NL ......Netherlands	TN ......Tunisia
BRN ......Bahrain	*GRØ* ......Greenland	NZ ......New Zealand	*TON* ......Tonga
BRU ......Brunei	GUY ......Guyana	OM ......Oman	TR ......Turkey
BS ......Bahamas	H ......Hungary	P ......Portugal	TT ......Trinidad and Tobago
BU ......Burundi	HK ......Hong Kong	PA ......Panama	*TUV* ......Tuvalu
BY ......Belarus	HN ......Honduras	*PAL* ......Palau	UA ......Ukraine
C ......Cuba	HR ......Croatia	PE ......Peru	UAE ......United Arab Emirates
CAM ......Cameroon	I ......Italy	PK ......Pakistan	USA ......United States
CDN ......Canada	IL ......Israel	PL ......Poland	UZ ......Uzbekistan
CH ......Switzerland	IND ......India	PNG ......Papua New Guinea	*VAN* ......Vanuatu
CI ......Côte d'Ivoire (Ivory Coast)	IR ......Iran	PY ......Paraguay	VN ......Vietnam
CL ......Sri Lanka	IRL ......Ireland	Q ......Qatar	*VRC* ......China
CO ......Colombia	IRQ ......Iraq	RA ......Argentina	WAG ......Gambia
COM ......Comoros	IS ......Iceland	RB ......Botswana	WAL ......Sierra Leone
CR ......Costa Rica	J ......Japan	RC ......Taiwan	WAN ......Nigeria
CV ......Cape Verde	JA ......Jamaika	RCA ......Central African Republic	*WB* ......West Bank
CY ......Cyprus	JOR ......Jordan	RCB ......Congo	WD ......Dominica
CZ ......Czech Republic	K ......Cambodia	RCH ......Chile	WG ......Grenada
D ......Germany	*KAN* ......Saint Kitts and Nevis	*RG* ......Guinea	WL ......Saint Lucia
DJI ......Djibouti	*KIB* ......Kiribati	RH ......Haiti	WS ......Western Samoa
DK ......Denmark	*KOR* ......North Korea	RI ......Indonesia	*WSA* ......Western Sahara
DOM ......Dominican Republic	KS ......Kyrgyzstan	RIM ......Mauritania	WV ......Saint Vincent and the Grenadines
DY ......Benin	KSA ......Saudi Arabia	RL ......Lebanon	Y ......Yemen
DZ ......Algeria	KWT ......Kuwait	RM ......Madagascar	YU ......Yugoslavia
E ......Spain	KZ ......Kazakhstan	RMM ......Mali	YV ......Venezuela
EAK ......Kenya	L ......Luxembourg	RN ......Niger	Z ......Zambia
EAT ......Tanzania	LAO ......Laos	RO ......Romania	ZA ......South Africa
EAU ......Uganda	*LAR* ......Libya	ROK ......South Korea	ZRE ......Zaire
EC ......Ecuador	*LB* ......Liberia	ROU ......Uruguay	ZW ......Zimbabwe
ER ......Eritrea	LS ......Lesotho	RP ......Philippines	
ES ......El Salvador	LT ......Lithuania	RSM ......San Marino	

AK	Alaska	IL	Illinois	NC	North Carolina	SC	South Carolina
AL	Alabama	IN	Indiana	ND	North Dakota	SD	South Dakota
AR	Arkansas	KS	Kansas	NE	Nebraska	TN	Tennessee
AZ	Arizona	KY	Kentucky	NH	New Hampshire	TX	Texas
CA	California	LA	Louisiana	NJ	New Jersey	UT	Utah
CO	Colorado	MA	Massachusetts	NM	New Mexico	VA	Virginia
CT	Connecticut	MD	Maryland	NV	Nevada	VT	Vermont
DE	Delaware	ME	Maine	NY	New York	WA	Washington
FL	Florida	MI	Michigan	OH	Ohio	WI	Wisconsin
GA	Georgia	MN	Minnesota	OK	Oklahoma	WV	West Virginia
HI	Hawaii	MO	Missouri	OR	Oregon	WY	Wyoming
IA	Iowa	MS	Mississippi	PA	Pennsylvania		
ID	Idaho	MT	Montana	RI	Rhode Island		

A

Aachen o •• D 92-93 J 3
Aačim, mys ▲ RUS 112-113 R 2
Aadan Yabaal o SP 212-213 L 2
'AA' Highway II USA (KY) 276-277 M 2
Äänekoski o FIN 88-89 H 5
Aansluit o ZA 220-221 F 3
Aappilattoq o GRØ (VGR) 26-27 X 7
Aappilattoq o GRØ (VGR) 28-29 S 6
Aar, De o ZA 220-221 G 6
Aaratuba, Ilha ~ BR 66-67 G 4
Aarau ☆ CH 92-93 K 5
Aare ~ CH 92-93 J 5
Aasiaat = Egedesminde o GRØ 28-29 O 2
Aba o VRC 154-155 B 5
Aba o WAN 204-205 G 6
Aba o ZRE 212-213 C 2
Aha, Gaziret ~ SUD 200-201 F 6
Abā ad-Dūd o KSA 130-131 J 4
Abá ar-Ruhām o KSA 132-133 D 4
Abacaxis, Rio ~ BR 66-67 H 5
Abadab, Gabal ▲ SUD 200-201 G 3
Äbādān o IR 134-135 C 3
'Ābādān, Ra'o o IR 134-135 C 4
Abāde o IR 134-135 E 3
Ahădehye Tašk o IR 134-135 F 4
Abadhara o GE 126-127 D 6
Abadla o DZ 188-189 K 5
Abaeté o BR 72-73 H 5
Abaeté, Rio ~ BR 72-73 H 5
Abaetetuba o BR 62-63 K 6
Abag Qi o VRC 148-149 M 5
Abaí o PY 70-77 K 4
Abaida ▲ DJI 208-209 F 3
Abaiara o BR 72-73 K 2
Abaji o WAN 204-205 G 4
Abajo Mountains ▲ USA 254-255 F 4
Ahejo Peak ▲ USA (UT) 254-255 F 6
Abaj Takalik ∴ GCA 52-53 J 4
Abak o WAN 204-205 G 6
Abakaliki o WAN 204-205 H 5
Abakan ∴ RUS (HKS) 116-117 E 9
Abakan ~ RUS 116-117 E 9
Abakan o RUS 124-125 Q 2
Abakanskij hrebet ▲ RUS 124-125 Q 2
Abala o RCB 210-211 E 4
Abala o RN 204-205 E 1
Abalessa o DZ 190-191 F 4
Abali, Bahr ~ TCH 206-207 D 3
Abamasagi Lake o CDN (ONT) 234-235 Q 4
Aban ~ RUS (KRN) 116-117 H 7
Abon ~ RUS 116-117 H 7
Abancay o PE 64-65 F 8
Abanga ~ G 210-211 C 4
Abangharit, ru ~ RN 198-199 C 4
Abapo o BOL 70-71 F 6
Abar al-Maši o KSA 130-131 F 5
Abaré o BR 68-69 J 6
Abãr Haimūr o ET 194-195 F 6
Abarqū o IR 134-135 E 3
Abarqū, Kavir-e o IR 134-135 E 3
Abarr o USA (CO) 254-255 N 4
Abashiri o J 152-153 L 5
Abasolo o MEX (DGO) 50-51 G 5
Abasolo o MEX (TAM) 50-51 K 5
Abasula o EAK 212-213 G 4
Abatskij ~ RUS 114-115 L 6
Abaucán, Rio ~ RA 76-77 D 5
Abaurai Island ~ PNG 183 B 5
Äbaya o ETH 208-209 E 5
Abaza o RUS 116-117 E 9
Abba o RCA 206-207 B 6
Abba-Omege o WAN 204-205 H 5
'Abbās, Bandar-e ☆ • IR 134-135 G 5
'Abbāsābād o IR (KER) 134-135 G 5
'Abbāsābād o IR (MAZ) 136-137 B 6
'Abbāsābād o IR (SEM) 134-135 F 2
Abbaye, Point ▲ USA (MI) 270-271 K 4
Abbazia della Monte Oliveto Maggiore • I 100-101 D 4
Abbazia di Casamari • I 100-101 D 4
Abbazia di Montecassino • I 100-101 D 4
Abbeville o F 90-91 H 6
Abbeville o USA (AL) 284-285 G 5
Abbeville o USA (GA) 284-285 G 5
Abbeville o USA (LA) 268-269 H 6
Abbeville o USA (MS) 268-269 L 2
Abbeville o USA (SC) 284-285 H 2
Abbey o CDN (SAS) 232-233 K 5

Abbeyfeale = Mainistir na Féile o IRL 90-91 C 5
Abbieglassie o AUS 178-179 J 4
Abbotsford o CDN (BC) 230-231 G 4
Abbotsford o USA (WI) 270-271 H 6
Abbott o USA (NM) 256-257 L 2
Abbottābād o PK 138-139 D 2
'Abd ad-Dā'im o SUD 206-207 H 3
'Abdal'aziz, Gabal ▲ SYR 128-129 J 4
'Abdaliyah, Bi'r al- o KSA 132-133 D 3
'Abd al-Kūri ~ Y 132-133 H 7
'Abdallāh, Mīnā' o KWT 130-131 L 3
Abdān o IR 134-135 D 4
Äbdānān o IR 134-135 B 1
Abdelcader o SP 208-209 F 3
'Abdin o SUD 200-201 D 6
Abdj o TCH 198-199 K 6
Abdon, Pulau ~ RI 166-167 F 1
Abdoulaye, Réserve d' ⊥ RT 202-203 L 5
Abdul Hakim o PK 138-139 F 4
Abdulino o RUS 96-97 H 7
Äbdy Werz ~ ETH 208-209 C 3
Ābe-e Bāzoft ~ IR 134-135 C 2
Abéché o TCH 198-199 K 6
Abe-e Estáde o AFG 134-135 M 2
Abeibara o RMM 196-197 L 5
Abejukolo o WAN 204-205 H 5
Äbo o Kührong ~ IR 134-135 D 2
Abélajouad o RN 198-199 C 4
Abelbodh o RMM 196-197 K 5
Abelhas, Cachoeira das ~ BR 70-71 G 2
Abelơya ~ N 84-85 R 3
Abel Tasman National Park ⊥ ·· NZ 182 D 4
Abeltι o ETH 208-209 C 4
Abemama Atoll ~ KIB 13 J 2
Abemarre o RI 166-167 L 5
Abono o GH 202-203 K 6
Abengourou o CI 202-203 J 6
Abenójar o E 98-99 E 5
Äbenrā o DK 86-87 D 7
Abeokuta o WAN 204-205 E 5
Ahepura o RI 166-167 L 3
Äbera o ETH 208-209 D 5
Aberaeron o GB 90-91 F 5
Abercrombie o USA (ND) 258-259 L 5
Abercrombie, Fort • USA (ND) 258-259 L 5
Abercrombie Caves • AUS 180-181 K 3
Abercrombie River ~ AUS 180-181 K 3
Aberdare National Park ⊥ EAK 212-213 F 4
Aberdeen o CDN (SAS) 232-233 M 3
Aberdeen ☆ GB 90-91 F 3
Aberdeen o USA (ID) 252-253 F 4
Aberdeen o USA (MD) 280-281 K 4
Aberdeen o USA (MS) 268-269 M 3
Aberdeen o USA (NC) 282-283 H 5
Aberdeen o USA (SD) 260-261 H 1
Aberdeen o ZA 220-221 G 6
Aberdeen Lake o CDN 30-31 U 3
Aberdeen Proving Ground xx USA (MD) 280-281 K 4
Aberdeen Road o ZA 220-221 G 6
Abergavenny-y-Fenni o GB 90-91 F 6
Äbergelê o ETH 200-201 J 6
Abergowrie o AUS 174-175 H 6
Abernethy o CDN (SAS) 232-233 P 5
Abertawe = Swansea o GB 90-91 F 6
Aberystwyth o GB 90-91 F 5
Äbe-e Seimarre ~ IR 134-135 B 2
Ābe-e Sūr ~ IR 134-135 F 4
Abez' o RUS 108-109 J 4
Äbe-e Zirmkān ~ IR 134-135 B 1
Abgarovo o RUS 96-97 D 9
Abgarm o IR 134-135 N 5
Abhá ☆ KSA 132-133 C 4
Abhāna o IND 138-139 G 8
Abhar Rūd ~ IR 128-129 N 4
Abhē Bid Hāyk' o ETH 208-209 E 3
Abico o BR 66-67 G 4
'Abidiyah o SUD 200-201 F 3
Abidjan ★ • CI 202-203 J 7
Abiekwasputs o ZA 220-221 G 3
Abii Hill o WAN 204-205 H 4
Abilene o USA (KS) 262-263 J 6
Abilene o USA (TX) 264-265 E 6
Abingdon o USA (IL) 274-275 H 4
Abingdon o USA (VA) 280-281 E 7

Abingdon o USA (VA) 280-281 E 7
Abingdon Downs o AUS 174-175 G 5
Abington o GB 90-91 F 4
Abinsi o WAN 204-205 H 5
Abiquiu o USA (NM) 256-257 J 2
Abirāmam o IND 140-141 H 6
Abisko o S 86-87 J 2
Abisko nationalpark ⊥ · S 86-87 J 2
Abitangka o VRC 144-145 G 5
Abitau River ~ CDN 30-31 P 5
Abitibi, Lake o CDN (ONT) 236-237 J 4
Abitibi de Troyes Provincial Park ⊥ CDN (ONT) 236-237 H 4
Abitibi Indian Reservation ✗ CDN (ONT) 236-237 H 4
Abitibi River ~ CDN 236-237 G 2
Äbiy Ädi o ETH 200-201 J 6
Abiyata Hāyk' o ETH 208-209 D 5
Abjeili o MA 188-189 J 3
Abkhazia = Abchazskaja Avtonomnaja Respublika o GE 126-127 D 6
Ahminga o AUS 178-179 C 4
Abnūb o ET 194-195 E 4
Abo o USA 256-257 J 4
Åbo = Turku ☆ FIN 88-89 G 6
Aboabo o RP 160-161 G 8
Aboh o WAN 204-205 G 6
Ahohyar o IND 138-139 F 4
Aboine, River ~ WAN 204-205 G 5
Aboisso o CI 202-203 J 7
Aboki o WAN 204-205 H 4
Abomey ☆ ··· DY 202-203 L 6
Abomey-Calavi o DY 204-205 E 5
Abomsa o ETH 208-209 E 4
Abong o WAN 204-205 J 5
Abong Mbang o CAM 210-211 D 2
Aboni o SUD 206-207 L 4
Abo Race ∴ USA (NM) 256-257 J 4
Abor o GH 202-203 L 6
Aboriginal Bora Ring ∴ AUS 178-179 N 4
Aborlan o RP 160-161 C 8
Aboua o G 210-211 E 3
Abou-Deïa o TCH 206-207 D 3
Abou Goulem o TCH 198-199 K 6
Ahroukroussom o TCH 206-207 F 2
Aboun o G 210-211 B 3
Abourak, Mont ▲ RMM 196-197 L 6
Abourou, Chutes ~ RCA 206-207 F 6
Abou-Telfán, Réserve de faune de l' ⊥ TCH 198-199 J 6
Abovjan o AR 128-129 L 2
Abqaiq o KSA 130-131 L 5
'Ahr, al- o Y 132-133 F 5
Abra, Lago del ~ BOL 70-71 D 2
Abra de Ilog o RP 160-161 D 5
Abra de Lizoite ▲ RA 76-77 D 2
Abraham Bay ~ BS 22-23 G 6
Abraham Bay o 36-37 R 2
Abraham Lake o CDN (ALB) 232-233 B 3
Abraham's Bay ~ BS 54-55 J 3
Abra Huashuaccasa ▲ PE 64-65 F 9
Abraka o WAN 204-205 G 6
Abra la Cruz Chica o BOL 76-77 E 1
Abrantes o P 98-99 C 5
Abra Pampa o RA 76-77 D 2
Abraq, Wādī al- ~ LAR 192-193 H 4
Abra Tapuna ▲ PE 64-65 F 8
Abrem o GH 202-203 K 7
Abrene = Pytalovo o LV 94-95 K 3
Abrejos, Punta ▲ MEX 50-51 C 4
Abreus o BR 68-69 H 7
Abri o SUD 200-201 E 2
Abril, 7 de o RA 76-77 E 3
Abrolhos, Arquipélago dos ~ BR 72-73 L 4
Abrolhos Bank ~ BR 72-73 L 4
Abrosimova o RUS 108-109 F 5
Abrud o RO 102-103 C 4
Abruzzo o I 100-101 D 3
Abruzzo, Parco Nazionale d' ⊥ I 100-101 D 4
'Abs o Y 132-133 D 5
Absaroka-Beartooth Wilderness ⊥ USA (MT) 250-251 J 4
Absaroka Range ▲ USA 252-253 H 1
Absarokee o USA (MT) 250-251 K 6
Absecon o USA (NJ) 280-281 M 4
Ab Touyour o TCH 206-207 D 3
Abu o IND 202-203 C 4
Abu 'Ali, Gazrat ~ KSA 130-131 L 4
Abū 'Ariš o KSA 132-133 C 5
Abū Ballás ∴ ET 194-195 C 5
Abū Dāra, Ra's o ET 194-195 H 6

Abū Darba o ET 194-195 F 3
Abū Dariha o SYR 128-129 G 5
Abū'Ud, Ra's o OM 132-133 G 5
Abū Dawn o SUD 200-201 F 4
Abū Dawn, Wādi ~ SUD 200-201 F 4
Abū Dhabi = Abū Zabi ★ • UAE 134-135 F 6
Abū Dī'āb, Gabal ▲ ET 194-195 F 3
Abū Dis o SUD 200-201 F 4
Abū Dom o SUD 200-201 E 4
Abū Dubaisat, Bi'r o ET 194-195 G 6
Abū Dulayq o SUD 200-201 F 4
Abufari o BR 66-67 F 5
Abū Faruh o IRQ 128-129 K 6
Abū Gābra o SUD 206-207 H 3
Abū Gārādiq, Bi'r o ET 194-195 D 2
Abū Ghirbān o SUD 200-201 F 3
Abugi o WAN 204-205 G 4
Abū Gubaybah o SUD 206-207 H 3
Abū Gulūd, Bi'r o SYR 128-129 H 5
Abū Hamad o SUD 200-201 F 3
Abū Harāz o SUD 200-201 F 3
Abū Harba, Gabal ▲ ET 194-195 F 3
Abū Hāšā'ifa, Halīğ ≈ ET 194-195 C 2
Ahū Haxhim o SUD 200-207 K 3
Abū Hāšim, Bi'r o ET 194-195 F 3
Abū Hugar o SUD 200-201 F 6
Abuja ☆ WAN 204-205 G 4
Abū Kabir o ET 194-195 E 2
Abū Kabisa o SUD 200-201 D 6
Abū Kamāl ★ SYR 128-129 J 5
Abū Khinzir, Wādi ~ SUD 200-201 E 5
Abuki, Pegunungan ▲ RI 164-165 G 5
Abukuma-gawa ~ J 152-153 J 6
Ahukuma-kuti ▲ J 152-153 J 6
Abū I-Abyad ~ UAE 134-135 E 6
Abū I-Husayn, Bi'r o ET 194-195 D 5
Abū Madd, Ra's o KSA 130-131 E 5
Abū Matariq o SUD 206-207 H 3
Abū Mendi o ETH 208-209 B 3
Abū Mina ∴··· ET 194-195 D 2
Abū Mingār, Bi'r o ET 194-195 C 4
Abū Mūsā, Gazire-ye ~ IR 134-135 F 6
Abunã o BR 66-67 E 7
Abuña, Rio ~ BOL 66-67 D 7
Abuná, Rio ~ BR 70-71 D 2
'Abune Yoséf ▲ ETH 200-201 J 6
Abū Qīr o ET 194-195 E 2
Abū Qurqas o ET 194-195 E 4
Abū Qurun o SUD 200-201 E 4
Abū Ra's o SUD 206-207 H 3
Abū Rāsas, Ra's ▲ OM 132-133 L 3
Abū Rudeis o ET 194-195 F 3
Abū Rukhah o SUD 200-201 F 4
Abū Saffar o SUD 200-201 F 4
Abū Sahrain, Bi'r o IRQ 130-131 J 4
Abū Šāri o SUD 200-201 E 2
Abū Simbel ∴··· ET 194-195 E 6
Abū Sir, Pyramids of ∴··· ET 194-195 E 3
Abū Suhair o IRQ 128-129 L 7
Abū Sunbul o ET 194-195 E 6
Abū Sunt, Khor ~ SUD 200-201 E 2
Abū Šuwayrir o SUD 200-201 K 2
Abuta o J 152-153 J 3
Abū Ţabbag o SUD 200-201 G 2
Abū Tig o ET 194-195 E 4
Abū Tunaytin o SUD 200-201 F 2
Abū 'Urūq o SUD 200-201 E 3
Abū 'Uwaiğīla o ET 194-195 E 2
Abūyie Meda ▲ ETH 208-209 D 3
Abuyog o RP 160-161 G 7
Abū Zabad o SUD 200-201 D 6
Abū Zabi ★ • UAE 134-135 E 6
Abū Zanima o ET 194-195 F 3
Abū Zayyan o SUD 200-201 F 4
Abwong o SUD 206-207 L 4
Aby, Lagune ~ CI 202-203 J 7
Abyad o SUD 200-201 J 7
Abyad, ar-Ra's ▲ SUD 200-201 G 2
Abyad, Tall al- o SYR 128-129 H 4
Abyar ash Shuwayrif o LAR 192-193 F 3

Abydos o AUS 172-173 D 6
Abydos ∴ ET 194-195 E 4
Abyei o SUD 206-207 J 4
Abyek o IR 136-137 B 6
Abyıj o RUS 110-111 Z 5
Abymes, Les o F 56 E 3
Abyrabit ~ RUS 110-111 U 5
Acacias o CO 60-61 G 6
Academy o USA (SD) 260-261 G 3
Academy, Cape ▲ CDN 36-37 K 4
Acadia National Park ⊥ USA (ME) 278-279 N 4
Acadia Valley o CDN (ALB) 232-233 H 4
Acadie ∴ CDN 240-241 J 2
Acadie Siding o CDN (NB) 240-241 K 4
Acahay o PY 76-77 J 3
Açailândia o BR 68-69 D 5
Acajutla o ES 52-53 K 5
Açajvajam ~ RUS (KOR) 112-113 M 3
Açajvajam ~ RUS 112-113 Q 6
Acala o MEX 52-53 H 3
Acala o USA (TX) 266-267 B 2
Acámbaro o MEX 52-53 D 1
Acampamento de Indios o BR 70-71 H 2
Acampamento Grande o BR 62-63 H 6
Acancéh o MEX 52-53 K 1
Acandi o CO 60-61 C 3
Acangatá ▲ BR 66-67 D 7
Acapetagua o MEX 52-53 H 4
Acaponeta o MEX 50-51 G 6
Acaponeta, Rio ~ MEX 50-51 G 6
Acapu o BR 68-69 D 3
Acapulco de Juárez o •• MEX 52-53 E 3
Acará o BR 62-63 K 6
Acará, Cachoeira ~ BR 66-67 G 2
Acará, Lago o BR 66-67 F 6
Acará, Rio ~ BR 68-69 D 2
Acarai, Rio ~ BR 68-69 D 3
Acará-Mirim, Rio ~ BR 68-69 D 3
Acaraú o BR 68-69 H 3
Acaraú, Rio ~ BR 72-73 H 3
Acarí o PE 64-65 E 9
Acari, Rio ~ BR 62-63 E 6
Acari, Rio ~ BR 66-67 E 6
Acari, Rio ~ BR 72-73 H 3
Acarigua o YV 60-61 G 3
Acasio o BOL 70-71 D 5
Acasta River ~ CDN 30-31 L 4
Acatayon o GQ 210-211 B 3
Acatic o MEX 52-53 C 1
Acatlán o MEX 52-53 F 3
Acatlán de Osorio o MEX 52-53 F 3
Acay, Nevado de ▲ RA 76-77 D 3
Acayucan o MEX 52-53 G 3
Accčen, ozero o RUS 112-113 X 4
Accomac o USA (VA) 280-281 L 6
Accra ★•• GH 204-205 L 6
Accygyj-Taryn-Jurjah ~ RUS 110-111 Y 7
Acebuches o MEX 50-51 H 3
Aceguá o BR 76-77 K 6
Acequias o YV 60-61 F 3
Acequias, Las o RA 76-77 F 4
Achaacha o DZ 190-191 C 4
Achacachi o BOL 70-71 C 5
Achaguas o YV 60-61 G 4
Achalpur o IND 138-139 F 9
Achao o RCH 78-79 C 7
Achar o ROU 76-77 J 6
Acheb o DZ 190-191 G 6
Achegtim o RMM 196-197 H 4
Achelouma o RN (AGA) 198-199 F 2
Achelouma ~ RN 198-199 F 2
Acheng o VRC 150-151 F 5
Acheron River ~ AUS 180-181 H 5
Achguig el Adam o RIM 196-197 E 5
Achiasi o GH 202-203 K 7
Achille o USA (OK) 264-265 H 5
Achim o USA (NE) 262-263 K 4
Achim, Oudi ~ TCH 198-199 J 5
Achinsk o RUS 116-117 F 7
Achiras o RA 78-79 G 2
Achiri o BOL 70-71 C 5
Achnasheen o GB 90-91 F 3
Achoma o PE 70-71 B 4
Achouka = Matsuka o G 210-211 B 4
Achton Friis Ø ~ GRØ 26-27 Q 4
Achwa ~ EAU 208-209 C 6

Adams Cove o CDN (NFL) 242-243 P 5
Adams Lake o CDN (BC) 230-231 K 3
Adams Lake o CDN (BC) 230-231 K 2
Adams River ~ CDN 230-231 K 2
Adamsville o USA (TN) 276-277 G 5
Adamsville o USA (TX) 266-267 J 2
'Adan ☆ Y 132-133 D 7
Adana ☆ TR 128-129 F 4
Adana, Wādi ~ Y 132-133 D 6
Adane o G 210-211 C 4
Adang, Teluk ≈ IND 164-165 E 4
Adani o WAN 204-205 G 5
Adaouda ▲ DZ 190-191 E 9
Adar o TCH 198-199 J 6
Adar, Khor ~ SUD 206-207 L 4
Adarama o SUD 200-201 G 4
Adare, Cape ▲ ARK 16 F 18
Adarot o SUD 200-201 H 4
Adaut o RI 166-167 J 6
Adavale o AUS 178-179 H 3
Adda ~ I 100-101 D 1
Adda ~ SUD 206-207 G 4
ad-Dab'a o ET 194-195 D 2
ad-Dabbu o SUD 200-201 E 3
ad-Dāḥila, al-Wāḥat ∴ ET 194-195 D 5
Ad-Dakhla o WSA 196-197 C 4
Addain Guhgel'morr, gom ▲ RUS 126-127 G 6
Ad Dāmir o SUD 200-201 F 4
ad-Dammām ☆ KSA 134-135 D 5
Addanki o IND 140-141 H 3
ad-Dār-al-Bayda o MA 188-189 H 4
Ad Darsia o LAR 192-193 J 1
ad-Dauha ☆ • Q 134-135 D 6
Addi o CAM 206-207 B 5
Addis o USA (LA) 268-269 J 6
Addis Ababa = Ādīs Ābeba ★ • ETH 208-209 D 4
Addison o USA (AL) 284-285 C 2
Addicon o USA (NY) 278-279 D 6
Addo o ZA 220-221 G 6
Addo, Uar o SP 212-213 H 2
Addo-Olifant National Park ⊥ ZA 220-221 G 6
ad-Du'ayn o SUD 206-207 H 3
ad-Dubais o SUD 200-201 F 5
ad-Duwaym o SUD 200-201 F 5
Adé o TCH 198-199 K 6
Adéane o SN 202-203 B 3
Adel o USA (GA) 284-285 G 5
Adel o USA (IA) 274-275 E 3
Adel o USA (OR) 244-245 H 4
Adelaide ☆ AUS 180-181 D 4
Adelaide o ZA 220-221 H 6
Adelaide Island ~ ARK 16 G 30
Adelaide Island ~ ARK 16 G 30
Adelaide Peninsula ∪ CDN 24-25 X 6
Adelaide River o AUS 172-173 K 2
Adelanto o USA (CA) 248-249 G 5
Adel Bagrou o RIM 196-197 G 7
Adelbert Range ▲ PNG 183 C 3
Adélie o ETH 208-209 D 5
Adele Island ~ AUS 172-173 F 3
Adelia María o RA 78-79 G 2
Adélie, Terre ∴ ARK 16 G 15
Adelong o AUS 178-179 H 7
Ademuz o E 98-99 G 4
Aden o CDN (ALB) 232-233 G 6
Aden = 'Adan o • Y 132-133 D 7
Aden, Gulf of ≈ 208-209 G 3
Adendorp o ZA 220-221 G 6
Adentan o GH 202-203 K 7
Ādama = Nazrét o ETH 208-209 D 4
Adam-Hulay o KSA 132-133 B 4
Adamantina o BR 72-73 D 6
Adamaoua o BR 72-73 D 6
Adamawa = Adamawa o CAM 204-205 K 5
Adamawa, Massif de l' ▲ CAM 204-205 K 5
Adamello ▲ I 100-101 C 1
Adaminaby o AUS 180-181 K 3
Ādami Tulu o ETH 208-209 D 5
Adamova o USA (CA) 246-247 C 3
Adams o USA (MN) 270-271 F 7
Adams o USA (NE) 262-263 K 4
Adams o USA (OR) 244-245 G 2
Adams, Fort • USA (MS) 268-269 J 5
Adams, Mount ▲ USA (WA) 244-245 D 3
Adin o USA (CA) 246-247 C 2
Adinsoone o SP 208-209 J 4

Adiora ○ **RMM** 196-197 K 6
Adipala ○ **RI** 168 C 3
Ādī Ramets' ○ **ETH** 200-201 H 6
Adiri ☆ **LAR** 192-193 E 4
'Ādiriyāt, Ǧibāl al- ▲ **JOR** 130-131 E 2
Adirondack Mountains ▲ **USA** 278-279 G 4
Ādīs Ābeba ★·· **ETH** 208-209 D 4
Ādīs 'Alem ○· **ETH** 208-209 D 4
Ādīs Zemen ○ **ETH** 200-201 H 6
Ādī Ugrī ○ **ER** 200-201 J 5
Adıyaman ☆ **TR** 128-129 H 4
Adjeloho, Adrar ▲ **DZ** 190-191 G 8
Adjengré ○ **RT** 202-203 L 5
Adjerar ▲ **DZ** 190-191 E 8
Adjiro ~ **DY** 202-203 L 5
Adjohoun ○ **DY** 204-205 E 5
Adjud ○ **RO** 102-103 E 4
Adjuntar, Presa de las < **MEX** 50-51 K 6
Adjuntas, Las ○ **YV** (BOL) 60-61 J 4
Adjuntas, Las ○ **YV** (FED) 60-61 H 2
Adlavik Islands ⌒ **CDN** 36-37 U 7
Adler ○ **RUS** 126-127 C 6
Admer, Erg d' ∸ **DZ** 190-191 G 8
Admer, Plaine d' ◡ **DZ** 190-191 G 8
Admiral ○ **CDN** (SAS) 232-233 L 6
Admiral Collinson, Cape ▲ **CDN** 24-25 V 5
Admiral's Beach ○ **CDN** (NFL) 242-243 P 5
Admiraltejstva, poluostrov ◡ **RUS** 108-109 G 4
Admiralty Gulf ≈ 172-173 G 3
Admiralty Gulf Aboriginal Land ✗ **AUS** 172-173 G 3
Admiralty Inlet ≈ 24-25 c 4
Admiralty Inlet ≈ 40-41 C 1
Admiralty Inlet ≈ 244-245 B 2
Admiralty Island ⌒ **CDN** 24-25 V 6
Admiralty Island ⌒ **USA** 32-33 C 3
Admiralty Island National Monument Kootznoowoo Wilderness ⊥· **USA** 32-33 C 3
Admiralty Islands ⌒ **PNG** 183 D 2
Admiralty Range ▲ **ARK** 16 F 17
Admont ○·· **A** 92-93 N 5
Ado ○ **WAN** (OGU) 204-205 E 5
Ado ○ **WAN** (PLA) 204-205 G 4
Ado Awaiye ○ **WAN** 204-205 E 5
Ādobed Häyk' ⬭ **ETH** 208-209 E 3
Adobes ○ **USA** (TX) 266-267 C 4
Adobe Summit ▲ **USA** (NV) 246-247 K 3
Ado-Ekiti ○ **WAN** 204-205 F 5
Adok ○ **SUD** 206-207 K 4
Adolfo ○ **BR** 72-73 F 6
Adolfo Gonzáles Chaves ○ **RA** 78-79 J 5
Adolfo López Mateos, Presa < **MEX** 50-51 F 5
Adolf S. Jensen Land ∸ **GRØ** 26-27 p 5
Adonara, Pulau ⌒ **RI** 166-167 B 6
Ādoni ○ **IND** 140-141 G 3
Adorf ○ **D** 92-93 M 3
Adoru ○ **WAN** 204-205 G 5
Ado-Tymovo ○ **RUS** 122-123 K 3
Adoumandjali ○ **RCA** 210-211 E 2
Adoumri ○ **CAM** 204-205 K 4
Adour ~ **F** 90-91 G 10
Adranga ○ **ZRE** 212-213 C 2
Adrar ☆· **DZ** (ADR) 188-189 L 7
Adrar ▲ **DZ** 190-191 F 8
Adrar □ **RIM** 196-197 E 4
Adrar Massif ▲ **RIM** 196-197 E 4
Adrar Soula, Djebel ▲ **DZ** 190-191 G 8
Adraskan ○ **AFG** 134-135 K 2
Adrasman ○ **TJ** 136-137 M 4
Adré ○ **TCH** 198-199 L 6
Adrian ○ **USA** (GA) 284-285 H 4
Adrian ○ **USA** (MI) 272-273 E 6
Adrian ○ **USA** (MN) 270-271 C 7
Adrian ○ **USA** (MO) 274-275 D 6
Adrian ○ **USA** (OR) 244-245 H 7
Adrian ○ **USA** (TX) 264-265 B 3
Adrianópolis ○ **BR** 74-75 F 5
Adriatic Sea ≈ 100-101 D 2
Adua ○ **RI** 166-167 E 2
Aduana ○ **RCH** 78-79 D 3
Aduana y Reten de Cuya ○ **RCH** 70-71 B 6
Aduku ○ **EAU** 212-213 D 2
Adunkur Daban ▲ **VRC** 146-147 G 4
Adunu ○ **WAN** 204-205 G 4
Adūr ○ **IND** 140-141 G 6
Adura ○ **WAN** 204-205 G 4
Adusa ○ **ZRE** 212-213 B 3
Advance ○ **USA** (MO) 276-277 F 3
Advat ∴· **IL** 130-131 D 2
Adventure, Bahía ≈ 80 C 2
Adventure Bank ≃ 100-101 C 6
Ādwa ○ **ETH** 200-201 J 5
Adwana ○ **IND** 138-139 B 9
Ady ○ **USA** (TX) 264-265 B 3
Adyča ~ **RUS** 110-111 U 5
Adygalah ○ **RUS** 120-121 M 2
Adygea = Adygè Respublikèm □ **RUS** 104 B 4
Adyk ○ **RUS** 104 E 4
Adzié ○ **RCB** 210-211 E 4
Adzopé ○ **CI** 202-203 J 6
Adz'va ~ **RUS** 108-109 H 8
Aegean Sea ≈ 100-101 K 5
Aegviidu ○ **EST** 94-95 J 2
Aekanopan ○ **RI** 162-163 C 3
Ærø ⌒ **DK** 86-87 E 9
Aérobo ○ **CI** 202-203 J 6
Aèros"emki, ostrova ⌒ **RUS** 110-111 N 3
Aesake, Lake ⬭ **PNG** 183 A 4
Aese ⌒ **VAN** 184 II a 2
Aetna ○ **CDN** (ALB) 232-233 E 6
Aetós ○ **GR** 100-101 H 4
Afadé ○ **CAM** 198-199 G 6
'Afak ☆ **IRQ** 128-129 L 6
Āfambo ○ **ETH** 208-209 E 3
Afanas'evo ☆ **RUS** 96-97 H 4
Afanas'evsk, Agnie- ○ **RUS** 122-123 H 3
'Afar, Tall ○ **IRQ** 128-129 K 4
Af Barwaarqo ○ **SP** 208-209 J 5
Āfdem ○ **ETH** 208-209 E 4
Afé ○ **SN** 202-203 C 2
Afe Peak ▲ **CDN** 20-21 X 5
Afféri ○ **CI** 202-203 J 6
Afflisses, Oued ~ **DZ** 190-191 C 6
Affollé ∸ **RIM** 196-197 E 6
Affon = Ouémé ~ **DY** 202-203 L 5
Afghanistan = Afghānistān ■ **AFG** 134-135 J 2
Afgooye ○ **SP** 212-213 K 2
'Afif ○ **KSA** 130-131 H 6
Afikpo ○ **WAN** 204-205 G 6
Afin, Rūd-e ~ **IR** 134-135 H 2
Afipinskij ○ **RUS** 126-127 C 5
Åfjord ○ **N** 86-87 E 5
Aflandshage ⌒ **GRØ** 28-29 V 4
Aflou ○ **DZ** 190-191 D 3
Afmadow ○ **SP** 212-213 J 3
Afobaka ○ **SME** 62-63 G 3
Afogados da Ingazeira ○ **BR** 68-69 K 5
Afognak Island ⌒ **USA** 22-23 U 3
Afognak Mountain ▲ **USA** 22-23 U 3
Afolé ○ **RT** 202-203 L 6
Afonso Cláudio ○ **BR** 72-73 K 6
Afore ○ **PNG** 183 E 5
Afouidich, Sebkhet ⬭ **WSA** 196-197 C 4
Afrânio ○ **BR** 68-69 H 6
Āfrēra Terara ▲ **ETH** 200-201 K 6
Āfrēra Ye Che'ew Häyk' ⬭ **ETH** 200-201 K 6
African Banks ⌒ **SY** 224 C 2
African Lion Safari ⊥ **CDN** (ONT) 238-239 E 5
Afridi Lake ⬭ **CDN** 30-31 P 3
Afrika, mys ▲ **RUS** 120-121 U 5
'Afrin ☆ **SYR** 128-129 G 4
Afşin ☆ **TR** 128-129 G 3
Afton ○ **USA** (IA) 274-275 D 3
Afton ○ **USA** (OK) 264-265 K 2
Afton ○ **USA** (WY) 252-253 H 4
Afua ○ **BR** 62-63 J 6
Afua, Rio ~ **BR** 62-63 K 6
Afuein < **SP** 212-213 K 3
'Afula ☆ **IL** 130-131 D 1
Afwein ~ **EAK** 212-213 G 3
Afyon ☆· **TR** 128-129 D 3
Aga ~ **RUS** 118-119 G 10
Aǧā', Ǧabal ▲ **KSA** 130-131 G 4
'Aǧabšīr ○ **IR** 128-129 L 4
Aga Buryat Autonomous District = Aginskij Burjatskij avtonom □ **RUS** 118-119 F 10
Agač, Koš ☆ **RUS** 124-125 Q 4
Agadem ○ **RN** 198-199 F 4
Agadez □ **RN** 198-199 C 3
Agadez ☆· **RN** (AGA) 198-199 C 4
Agādīr ☆· **MA** 188-189 G 5
Āǧā Ǧārī ○ **IR** 134-135 C 3
Agaho-gawa ~ **J** 152-153 H 6
Agaie ○ **WAN** 204-205 G 4
Again River ~ **CDN** 236-237 J 2
'Aǧā'iz, al- ○ **OM** 132-133 K 4
Agajakan ~ **RUS** 120-121 J 2
Agalega Islands ⌒ **MS** 224 E 5
Agamor ○ **RMM** 196-197 L 6
Agan ~ **RUS** 114-115 P 3
Agan ~ **RUS** 114-115 N 4
Aganyli ~ **RUS** 108-109 f 7
Agapa ~ **RUS** 108-109 X 6
Agapo Açu ○ **BR** 66-67 J 5
Agapovka ☆ **RUS** 96-97 L 7
Āǧar ○ **AFG** 136-137 K 7
Agar ○ **USA** (SD) 260-261 F 2
Agâraktem ○ **RIM** 196-197 G 3
Āgarfa ○ **ETH** 208-209 D 5
Agargar ∸ **WSA** 196-197 C 3
Āgaro ○ **ETH** 208-209 C 5
Āgarsararēn ○ **ETH** 208-209 G 5
Agartala ☆ **IND** 142-143 G 4
Agaru ○ **SUD** 208-209 B 3
Agaskagou Lake ⬭ **CDN** (ONT) 236-237 H 2
Agassiz ○ **CDN** (BC) 230-231 H 4
Agassiz Forest Reserve ⊥ **CDN** (MAN) 234-235 G 5
Agassiz Fracture Zone ≃ 14-15 P 11
Agassiz National Wildlife Refuge ⊥ **USA** (MN) 270-271 C 2
Agastya Malai ▲ **IND** 140-141 G 6
Agata (Nižnee), ozero ⬭ **RUS** 116-117 F 2
Agata (Verhnee), ozero ⬭ **RUS** 116-117 F 2
Agate ○ **USA** (CO) 254-255 M 4
Agate ○ **USA** (NE) 262-263 C 2
Agate Fossil Beds National Monument ∴ **USA** (NE) 262-263 C 2
Agats ○ **RI** 166-167 K 4
Agatti Island ⌒ **IND** 140-141 B 3
Agattu Island ⌒ **USA** 22-23 C 6
Agattu Strait ≈ 22-23 C 6
Agawa Bay ⬭ **CDN** (ONT) 236-237 D 5
Agawa Canyon · **CDN** (ONT) 236-237 D 5
Agawa River ~ **CDN** 236-237 D 5
Agbabu ○ **WAN** 204-205 F 5
Agbado ~ **DY** 204-205 E 4
Agbara ○ **WAN** 204-205 E 5
Agbarha-Otor ○ **WAN** 204-205 F 6
Agbélouvé ○ **RT** 202-203 L 6
Agbohoutogon ○ **DY** 204-205 E 5
Agbor-Bojiboji ○ **WAN** 204-205 G 5
Agboville ○ **CI** 202-203 H 7
Agdam ○ **AZ** 128-129 M 2
Agdaš = Ağdaş ○ **AZ** 128-129 M 2
Agde ○ **F** 90-91 J 10
Agdz ○ **MA** 188-189 H 5
Agdžabedi = Ağcabadi ○ **AZ** 128-129 M 2
Agege ○ **WAN** 204-205 E 5
Agen ○ **F** 90-91 H 9
Agenebode ○ **WAN** 204-205 G 5
Āgere Maryam ○ **ETH** 208-209 D 6
Aggas Ø ⌒ **GRØ** 28-29 Y 3
Aggeneys ○ **ZA** 220-221 D 4
Aggui ○ **RIM** 196-197 D 4
Aghat bonne ○ **RN** 198-199 C 4
Aghir ○ **TN** 190-191 H 4
Aghiyuk Island ⌒ **USA** 22-23 S 4
Aghor ○ **PK** 134-135 L 6
Aghouedir · **RIM** 196-197 E 4
Aghouinit ○ **WSA** 196-197 D 3
Aghreïjīt ○ **RIM** 196-197 D 4
Aghrijīt ∴· **RIM** 196-197 F 5
Aghzoumal, Sebkhet ⬭ **WSA** 196-197 D 2
Agiabampo, Bahia de ≈ 50-51 E 4
Agía Galíni ○ **GR** 100-101 K 7
Agia Napa ○· **CY** 128-129 E 5
Agiapuk River ~ **USA** 20-21 G 4
Agía Triáda ○ **GR** 100-101 H 6
Āǧi Čāy ~ **IR** 128-129 M 4
Agiert ○ **RIM** 196-197 F 6
Aginskoe ☆ **RUS** (AGN) 118-119 G 10
Aginskoe ☆ **RUS** (KRN) 116-117 G 8
Ágio Orous □ **GR** 100-101 K 4
Ágios Efstrátios ⌒ **GR** 100-101 K 5
Ágios Kírikos ○ **GR** 100-101 L 6
Ágios Konstantínos ○ **GR** 100-101 J 5
Agios Nikólaos ○· **GR** 100-101 K 7
Ágiou Orous, Kólpos ≈ 100-101 J 4
Agita ~ **RUS** 118-119 H 9
Agiuel, Hasy in < **LAR** 192-193 D 4
Ağlı ☆ **TR** 128-129 E 2
Aglipay ○ **RP** 160-161 D 4
'Aǧlūn, Ǧabal ▲ **JOR** 130-131 D 1
'Aǧmān ○ **UAE** 134-135 F 6
Agmar < **RIM** 196-197 E 2
Agnamala, Mount ▲ **RP** 160-161 D 3
Agnes ○ **USA** (TX) 264-265 G 6
Agnes Lake ⬭ **USA** (MN) 270-271 G 2
Agness ○ **USA** (OR) 244-245 A 8
Agnes Waters ○ **AUS** 178-179 L 3
Agnew ○ **AUS** 176-177 F 4
Agnibilékrou ○ **CI** 202-203 J 6
Agnie-Afanas'evsk ○ **RUS** 122-123 H 3
Agnita ○ **RO** 102-103 D 5
Agno ~ **RP** 160-161 D 5
Agnone ○ **I** 100-101 E 4
Ago ○ **J** 152-153 G 7
Ago-Are ○ **WAN** 204-205 E 4
Agogo ○ **GH** 202-203 K 6
Agona ○ **GH** 202-203 J 6
Agona Junction ○ **GH** 202-203 K 7
Agotu ○ **PNG** 183 C 4
Agou ○ **CI** 202-203 J 7
Agou, Mont ▲ **RT** 202-203 L 6
Agoudal ○ **MA** 188-189 J 4
Agoueïnīt ○ **RIM** 196-197 G 6
Agou Gadzépé ○ **RT** 202-203 L 6
Agouna ○ **DY** 202-203 L 6
Agounni Jefal ○ **RMM** 196-197 J 6
Agpamiut ○ **GRØ** 28-29 O 4
Agra ○⋯ **IND** 138-139 G 6
Agra-Emneke, gora ▲ **RUS** 110-111 X 5
Agrahanskij poluostrov ◡ **RUS** 126-127 G 6
Ágreda ○ **E** 98-99 G 4
Ağrestān ○ **AFG** 134-135 M 2
Ağrı ☆ **TR** 128-129 K 3
Agrigento ○ **I** 100-101 D 6
Agrínio ○ **GR** 100-101 H 5
Agrio, Río ~ **RA** 78-79 E 5
Agrirama · **USA** (GA) 284-285 G 5
Agrópoli ○ **I** 100-101 E 4
Agryz ☆ **RUS** 96-97 H 5
Agua Amarga, Pampa del ∸ **RA** 78-79 E 5
Agua Azúl ○ **HN** 52-53 L 4
Agua Azúl Cascades ~· **MEX** 52-53 H 3
Agua Azul Falls ~ **BH** 52-53 K 3
Agua Blanca ○ **YV** 60-61 K 4
Agua Boa ○ **BR** 72-73 D 3
Água Boa ○ **BR** 72-73 J 4
Agua Boa do Univini, Rio ~ **BR** 62-63 D 5
Agua Braga ○ **BR** 72-73 F 2
Água Branca ○ **BR** 68-69 K 5
Agua Branca, Igarapé ~ **BR** 66-67 H 7
Agua Caliente ∸ **PE** 64-65 E 6
Agua Caliente ○ **USA** (AZ) 256-257 B 6
Agua Caliente, Río ~ **BOL** 70-71 F 4
Agua Caliente Indian Reservation ✗ **USA** (CA) 248-249 H 6
Aguacatán ○ **GCA** 52-53 J 4
Aguachica ○ **CO** 60-61 E 3
Água Clara ○ **BR** 72-73 D 6
Aguaçuzinho ○ **BR** 70-71 J 6
Aguada ○ **USA** (PR) 286-287 O 2
Aguada de Pasajeros ○ **C** 54-55 E 3
Aguadas ○ **CO** 60-61 D 5
Aguadilla ○ **USA** (PR) 286-287 O 2
Aguados, Serra dos ▲ **BR** 72-73 E 7
Agua Duke, Caleta ≈ 76-77 B 3
Agua Dulce ○ **MEX** 52-53 G 2
Aguadulce ○ **PA** 52-53 D 7
Agua Dulce ○ **USA** (TX) 266-267 K 6
Agua Escondida ○ **RA** 78-79 E 4
Água Fria ○ **BR** 68-69 J 7
Agua Fria ○ **USA** (NM) 256-257 K 2
Água Fria, Ribeiro ~ **BR** 68-69 D 5
Agua Fria, Rio ~ **BR** 72-73 E 2
Agua Fria River ~ **USA** 256-257 C 4
Agua Hedionda, Cerro ▲ **RA** 78-79 F 2
Aguaí ○ **BR** 72-73 G 7
Agua Linda ○ **YV** 60-61 G 2
Aguán, Río ~ **HN** 52-53 L 4
Aguanaval, Río ~ **MEX** 50-51 H 5
Agua Negra, Río ~ **RA** 76-77 C 6
Aguanish ○ **CDN** (QUE) 242-243 F 2
Agua Nueva ○ **MEX** (COA) 50-51 J 5
Agua Nueva ○ **MEX** (TAM) 50-51 K 6
Agua Nueva ○ **USA** (TX) 266-267 J 7
Aguanus, Rivière ~ **CDN** 38-39 N 3
Aguapai, Rio ~ **BR** 70-71 H 4
Agua Pasto ○ **BOL** 70-71 G 6
Aguapei, Serra do ▲ **BR** 70-71 H 4
Aguapey, Río ~ **RA** 76-77 J 5
Água Preta, Igarapé ~ **BR** 66-67 E 3
Agua Prieta ○ **MEX** 50-51 E 2
Aguara, Río ~ **PY** 76-77 J 3
Aguaray ○ **RA** 76-77 F 2
Aguarico, Río ~ **EC** 64-65 D 1
Aguaro-Guariquito, Parque Nacional ⊥ **YV** 60-61 H 3
Aguasay ○ **YV** 60-61 K 3
Águas Belas ○ **BR** 68-69 K 6
Aguas Blancas ○ **BOL** 76-77 E 2
Aguas Blancas ○ **RCH** 76-77 C 3
Aguas Blancas, Cerro ▲ **RA** 76-77 C 3
Aguas Blancas, Quebrada de ~ **RCH** 76-77 D 2
Aguás Blancas y Aguás Negras, Reserva Faunística ⊥ **YV** 60-61 F 3
Aguascalientes □ **MEX** 50-51 H 6
Aguascalientes ☆· **MEX** (AGS) 50-51 H 7
Aguas Calientes, Salar ⬭ **RCH** 76-77 D 2
Aguas Calientes, Sierra de ▲ **RA** 76-77 D 3
Aguas Claras ○ **C** 54-55 D 3
Aguas Claraso ○ **C** 54-55 G 4
Águas de São Clara ○ **BR** 74-75 E 5
Águas Formosas ○ **BR** 72-73 K 4
Aguas Negras ○ **PE** 64-65 E 2
Aguateca ∴· **GCA** 52-53 J 3
Agua Verde ou Anhanazá, Rio ~ **BR** 70-71 J 4
Agua Viva ○ **YV** 60-61 F 3
Aguaytia ○ **PE** 64-65 E 6
Aguaytia, Río ~ **PE** 64-65 E 6
Aguazul ○ **CO** 60-61 E 5
Agu Bay ≈ 24-25 c 5
Agudda Cecilio ○ **RA** 78-79 G 6
Agudos do Sul ○ **BR** 74-75 F 5
Agudos Grandes, Serra ▲ **BR** 74-75 F 5
Águeda ○ **P** 98-99 C 4
Aguelhok ○ **RMM** 196-197 L 5
Aguelt ez Zerga ○ **RIM** 196-197 C 5
Aguemour ∸ **DZ** 190-191 E 7
Aguemour, Oued ~ **DZ** 190-191 E 7
Aguer-Tay, Falaise de l' ▲ **TCH** 198-199 H 2
Aguéssis ○ **RN** 198-199 D 4
Agues Verdes, Raudal ~ **CO** 64-65 F 1
Aguga ~ **EAU** 212-213 D 2
Águia Branca ○ **BR** 72-73 K 5
Aguiar Javaés ○ **BR** 68-69 D 7
Aguié ○ **RN** 198-199 C 6
Aguieira, Barragem da < **P** 98-99 C 4
Aguila ○ **USA** (AZ) 256-257 B 5
Aguila, El ○ **BOL** 70-71 F 4
Aguilal ○ **RIM** 196-197 C 6
Aguilâl Faï ○ **RIM** 196-197 C 5
Aguilar ○ **E** 98-99 E 6
Aguilar, Cerro ▲ **RA** 76-77 E 2
Aguilar, El ○ **RA** 76-77 E 2
Aguilar, Salar de ⬭ **RCH** 76-77 C 3
Aguilar de Campoo ○ **E** 98-99 E 3
Aguilares ○ **ES** 52-53 K 5
Aguilares ○ **USA** (TX) 266-267 H 6
Águilas ○ **E** 98-99 G 6
Aguililla ○ **MEX** 52-53 C 2
Aguirre, Bahía ≈ 80 H 7
Aguiz ⌒ **ER** 200-201 K 5
Aguja, Cerro ▲ **RA** 78-79 D 7
Aguja, Cerro ▲ **RCH** 80 F 7
Aguja, Punta ▲ **PE** 64-65 B 4
Agul ~ **RUS** 116-117 H 8
Āgula'i ○ **ETH** 200-201 J 6
Agulhas Basin ≃ 6-7 M 13
Agulhas Plateau ≃ 6-7 M 12
Agulhas Ridge ≃ 6-7 K 13
Agumbe ○ **IND** 140-141 F 4
Aguni-shima ⌒ **J** 152-153 B 11
Agur ○ **EAU** 212-213 D 2
Agurá Grande ○ **RA** 76-77 G 6
Agusan ~ **RP** 160-161 F 8
Agutaya Island ⌒ **RP** 160-161 D 7
Agwampt ~ **SUD** 200-201 G 3
Agwarra ○ **WAN** 204-205 F 3
Agwei ~ **SUD** 208-209 A 5
Agweri ○ **WAN** 204-205 G 5
Agwit ○ **SUD** 206-207 H 4
Agwok ○ **SUD** 206-207 J 5
Ahaba ○ **WAN** 204-205 G 6
Ahaberge ▲ **NAM** 216-217 F 9
Ahad al-Masāra ○ **KSA** 132-133 C 5
Aḥad Rāfida ○· **KSA** 132-133 C 4
Ahalcihe ○· **GE** 126-127 E 7
Ahalkalaki ○ **GE** 126-127 E 7
Ahamansu ○ **GH** 202-203 L 6
Ahanduizinho, Rio ~ **BR** 70-71 K 7
Ahangaran ○ **UZ** 136-137 L 4
Ahar ○· **IR** 128-129 M 3
Ahaura ○ **NZ** 182 C 5
Ahča-Kujma ○ **TM** 136-137 D 5
Aḥdar, al- ○ **KSA** 130-131 E 3
Aḥdar, al-Ǧabal al- ▲ **OM** 132-133 K 2
Ahellakane, Adrar ▲ **DZ** 190-191 E 7
Ahémè, Lac ⬭ **DY** 202-203 L 6
Ahenkro ○ **GH** 202-203 L 6
Ahero ○ **EAK** 212-213 E 4
Ahfir ○ **MA** 188-189 K 3
Ahíllio ○ **GR** 100-101 J 5
Ahioma ○ **PNG** 183 F 6
Ahiti ○ **NZ** 182 E 3
Ahklun Mountains ▲ **USA** 20-21 M 6
Ahlat ☆· **TR** 128-129 K 3
Aḥmad, Bi'r ○ **Y** 132-133 D 7
Aḥmadābād ○ **AFG** 134-135 J 1
Ahmadābād ○·· **IND** 138-139 D 8
Aḥmadal-Yāsin ○ **IRQ** 128-129 L 6
Aḥmadī, al- □ **KWT** 130-131 K 3
Aḥmadī, al- ☆ **KWT** (AMA) 130-131 L 3
Ahmadnagar ○· **IND** 138-139 E 10
Ahmadpur ○ **IND** 138-139 F 10
Ahmadpur East ○ **PK** 138-139 C 5
Ahmadpur Lamma ○ **PK** 138-139 C 5
Ahmadpur Siāl ○ **PK** 138-139 C 4
Ahmad Wāl ○ **PK** 134-135 L 4
Ahmar Mountains ▲ **ETH** 208-209 E 4
Ahmatova, zaliv ≈ 108-109 I e 2
Ahmeta ○ **GE** 126-127 F 7
Ahmic Harbour ○ **CDN** (ONT) 238-239 F 3
Aḥmīm ○· **ET** 194-195 E 4
Ahnet, Adrar n' ▲ **DZ** 190-191 D 8
Ahoada ○ **WAN** 204-205 G 6
Ahome ○ **MEX** 50-51 E 5
Ahoskie ○ **USA** (NC) 282-283 L 4
Ahousat ○ **CDN** (BC) 230-231 C 4
Ahram ○ **IR** 134-135 D 4
Ahraura ○ **IND** 142-143 C 3
Ahrweiler, Bad Neuenahr- ○ **D** 92-93 J 3
Ahsahka ○ **USA** (ID) 250-251 C 5
Ahsu = Ağsu ○ **AZ** 128-129 N 2
Ahtamar · **TR** 128-129 K 3
Ahtaranda ~ **RUS** 118-119 F 4
Ähtäri ○ **FIN** 88-89 H 5
Ahtarsk, Primorsko- ○ **RUS** 102-103 L 4
Ahtme, Jõhvi- ○ **EST** 94-95 K 2
Ahtuba ~ **RUS** 96-97 E 10
Ahtubinsk ☆ **RUS** 96-97 E 9
Ahty ○ **RUS** 126-127 G 7
Ahuacatlan ○ **MEX** 50-51 K 7
Ahuacatlán ○ **MEX** 52-53 F 1
Ahuachapán ☆ **ES** 52-53 K 5
Ahualulco ○ **MEX** 50-51 J 6
Ahualulco de Mercata ○ **MEX** 52-53 C 1
Ahuano ○ **EC** 64-65 D 2
Ahunba ○ **UZ** 136-137 N 4
Ahurjan ~ **AR** 128-129 K 2
Ahus, Pulau ⌒ **RI** 164-165 E 2
Ahvāz ☆· **IR** 134-135 C 3
Ahvenanmaa = Åland ⌒ **FIN** 88-89 F 6
Ahwa ○ **IND** 138-139 D 9
Ahwahnee ○ **USA** (CA) 248-249 E 2
Aḥwar ○ **Y** 132-133 E 7
Aḥwar, Wādī ~ **Y** 132-133 E 7
Ahzar, Vallée de l' ∸ **RMM** 196-197 M 7
Ai-Ais ○· **NAM** 220-221 C 3
Aiak, Cape ▲ **USA** 22-23 N 6
Aiaktalik Island ⌒ **USA** 22-23 U 4
Aialik Cape ▲ **USA** 20-21 Q 7
Aianí ○ **GR** 100-101 H 4
Aiapuá ○ **BR** 66-67 F 5
Aiapuá, Lago ⬭ **BR** 66-67 F 5
Aiari, Rio ~ **BR** 66-67 C 2
Aibak ☆· **AFG** 136-137 K 6
Aibetsu ○ **J** 152-153 K 3
Aibonito ○ **USA** (PR) 286-287 P 2
Aichilik River ~ **USA** 20-21 T 2
Aidarhan su koimašy suk < **KZ** 96-97 F 9
Aiddejavrre Fjellstue ○ **N** 86-87 L 2
Aiduma, Pulau ⌒ **RI** 166-167 H 3
Aiduna ○ **RI** 166-167 H 4
Aiea ○ **USA** (HI) 288 H 3
Aiema River ~ **PNG** 183 B 4
Aiere ○ **WAN** 204-205 G 5
Aigene mekeni ∸ **KZ** 124-125 F 6
Aigle, l' ○ **F** 90-91 H 7
Aigles, Lac-des- ○ **CDN** (QUE) 240-241 G 3
Aigneau, Lac ⬭ **CDN** 36-37 O 6
Aiguá ○ **ROU** 78-79 M 3
Aigues ~ **F** 90-91 K 9
Aiguilete, Cerro ▲ **RCH** 80 D 5
Aihuicheng · **VRC** 150-151 F 3
Aija ○ **PE** 64-65 D 6
Aikar, Tanjung ▲ **RI** 166-167 H 2
Aikawa ○ **J** 152-153 H 5
Aiken ○ **USA** (SC) 284-285 J 3
Aiken ○ **USA** (TX) 264-265 C 4
Aikima ○ **RI** 166-167 K 4
Ailaoshan Z.B. ⊥ **VRC** 156-157 B 4
Aileron ○ **AUS** 178-179 B 2
Aileu ○ **RI** 166-167 C 6
Ailigandí ○ **PA** 52-53 E 7
Ailinglapalag ⌒ **MAI** 13 J 2
Aillik ○ **CDN** 36-37 U 7
Aim ○ **RUS** (HBR) 120-121 F 4
Aim ~ **RUS** 120-121 E 4
Aimere ○ **RI** 168 E 7
Aimogasta ○ **RA** 76-77 D 5
Aimorés ○ **BR** 72-73 K 5
Aimorés, Serra dos ▲ **BR** 72-73 K 5
Aimorés, Serra dos ▲ **BR** 72-73 K 4
Ain ~ **F** 90-91 K 8
'Ain, al- ○ **UAE** 134-135 F 6
'Ain, Ra's al- ☆ **SYR** 128-129 J 4
'Ain, Wādī l- ~ **OM** 132-133 J 2
'Ain al-'Arab ○ **SYR** 128-129 H 4
'Ain al-Bakra ○ **KSA** 130-131 K 6
'Ain al-Ǧuwairī ○ **Y** 132-133 F 6
'Ain al-Maqfī ○ **ET** 194-195 D 4
'Ain al-Maqfī ○ **ET** 194-195 D 4
'Ain an-Nafṭ ○ **IRQ** 128-129 K 6
'Ain as-Sāqī ○ **ET** 194-195 D 4
'Ain as-Sāqī ○ **ET** 194-195 D 4
Ainaži ○ **LV** 94-95 J 3
Aïn Beida ○ **DZ** 190-191 F 3
Aïn Belbela, Sebkha ⬭ **DZ** 188-189 J 7
Aïn Benian ○ **DZ** 190-191 D 2
Âïn-Benîmathar ○ **MA** 188-189 K 3
Aïn Ben Tili ○ **RIM** 196-197 F 2
Aïn Bessem ○ **DZ** 190-191 D 2
'Aïn Bire ○ **RIM** 196-197 F 6
Âïn Boubat ○ **RIM** 196-197 D 6
Aïn Boucif ○ **DZ** 190-191 D 3
'Ain Dār ○ **KSA** 130-131 L 5
Aïn Defla ☆ **DZ** 190-191 C 2
Aïn Deheb ○ **DZ** 190-191 C 3
'Ain Diwār ○ **SYR** 128-129 K 4
Aïn Draham ○ **TN** 190-191 G 2
Âïn-Ech-Chair ○ **MA** 188-189 K 4
Aïn El Bell ○ **DZ** 190-191 D 3
Ain el Brod < **DZ** 190-191 E 6
Ain el Hadjadj < **DZ** 190-191 D 6
Ain el Hadjadj < **DZ** 190-191 F 7
Aïn el Hadjar ○ **DZ** 190-191 C 3
Aïn El Hadjel ○ **DZ** 190-191 D 3
Aïn el Hamara ○ **DZ** 190-191 D 3
Aïn el Melh ○ **DZ** 190-191 E 3
Aïn el-Orak ○ **DZ** 190-191 C 4
Aïn Fakroun ○ **DZ** 190-191 F 3
Aïn Fekan ○ **DZ** 190-191 C 3
Ainggyi ○ **MYA** 142-143 J 5
'Ain Ḥamūd ○ **IRQ** 130-131 J 2
'Ain Ḥumān ○ **ET** 194-195 D 4
'Ain Ibn Fuhaid ○ **KSA** 130-131 J 4
'Ain 'Īsā ○ **SYR** 128-129 H 4
Aïn Kercha ○ **DZ** 190-191 F 3
Aïn Kermes ○ **DZ** 190-191 C 3
Aïn Khadra ○ **DZ** 190-191 E 3
Âïn-Leuh ○ **MA** 188-189 J 4
Aïn Madhi ○ **DZ** 190-191 D 4
Ain Mansūr ○ **SUD** 200-201 C 5
Aïn M'Lila ○ **DZ** 190-191 F 2
Aïn Oulmene ○ **DZ** 190-191 E 3
Aïn Oussera ○ **DZ** 190-191 D 3
Ainsa-Sobrarbe ○ **E** 98-99 H 3
Aïn Sefra · **DZ** 188-189 L 4
'Ain Sifnī ○ **IRQ** 128-129 K 4
Aïn Skhouna ○ **DZ** 190-191 C 3
Ainslie, Lake ⬭ **CDN** (NS) 240-241 O 4
'Ain Suḫna ○ **ET** 194-195 F 3
Ainsworth ○ **USA** (NE) 262-263 G 2
Aïn Tamr ○ **TN** 190-191 G 4
Aïn Taya ○ **DZ** 190-191 D 2
Aïn Tédelès ○ **DZ** 190-191 C 3
Aïn Temouchent ☆ **DZ** 188-189 L 3
Aiome ○ **PNG** 183 C 3
Aiome, Mount ▲ **PNG** 183 C 3
Aiquebelle Provincial Park ⊥ **CDN** (QUE) 236-237 K 4
Aiquile ○ **BOL** 70-71 E 6
Aiquiri, Rio ~ **BR** 66-67 D 7
Airabu, Pulau = Raibu, Pulau ⌒ **RI** 162-163 G 3
Airbangis ○ **RI** 162-163 C 4
Aït Benhaddou ○⋯ **MA** 188-189 H 5
Airdrie ○ **CDN** (ALB) 232-233 D 4
Aire ~ **F** 90-91 K 7
Aire-sur-la-Lys ○ **F** 90-91 J 6
Aïr et du Ténéré, Réserve Naturelle Nationale de l' ⊥⋯ **RN** 198-199 D 2
Air Force Island ⌒ **CDN** 28-29 C 3
Air Force Museum · **USA** (OH) 280-281 B 4
Airhitam, Teluk ≈ 162-163 J 6
Airi, Cachoeira do ~ **BR** 66-67 H 6
Airlie Beach ○ **AUS** 174-175 K 7
Airlie Gardens · **USA** (NC) 282-283 K 6
Airmadidi ○· **RI** 164-165 J 3
Airmolek ○ **RI** 162-163 E 5
Aïr ou Azbine ▲ **RN** 198-199 D 3
Airpanas ○ **RI** 166-167 C 5
Air Papan ○ **MAL** 162-163 E 3
Airway Heights ○ **USA** (WA) 244-245 H 3
Airways ○ **CDN** (ALB) 232-233 G 3
Aisén, Seno ≈ 80 D 2
Aishihik ○ **CDN** 20-21 W 6
Aishihik Lake ⬭ **CDN** 20-21 W 6
Aisne, l' ~ **F** 90-91 K 7
Aïssa, Djebel ▲ **DZ** 188-189 L 4
Aitana ▲ **E** 98-99 G 5
Aitape ○ **PNG** 183 B 2
Âït-Baha ○ **MA** 188-189 G 5
Aït el Khaoua, Erg ∸ **RMM** 196-197 L 4
Aitkin ○ **USA** (MN) 270-271 E 4
Âït-Melloul ○ **MA** 188-189 G 5
Âït Morrhad ▲ **MA** 188-189 J 5
Âït Saadane ○ **MA** 188-189 J 5
Âït-Youssef-ou-Ali ○ **MA** 188-189 K 3
Aiuanã, Rio ~ **BR** 66-67 E 3
Aiuiá-Miçu, Rio ~ **BR** 68-69 B 7
Aiuruoca ○ **BR** 72-73 H 6
Aiwsa, Danau ⬭ **RI** 166-167 H 3
Aix-en-Provence ○· **F** 90-91 K 10
Aixiós ~ **GR** 100-101 J 4
Aix-les-Bains ○ **F** 90-91 K 9
Aiyetoro ○ **WAN** (KWA) 204-205 F 5
Aiyetoro ○ **WAN** (OGU) 204-205 E 5
Aiyura ○ **PNG** 183 C 4
Aizanoi ∴· **TR** 128-129 C 3
Āizawl ☆ **IND** 142-143 H 4
Aizpute ○·· **LV** 94-95 G 3
Aizuwakamatsu ○· **J** 152-153 H 6
Aj ~ **RUS** 96-97 L 6
Ajaccio ☆· **F** 98-99 M 4
Ajacuba ○ **MEX** 52-53 E 1
Ajajú, Río ~ **CO** 64-65 F 1
Ajak ○ **RUS** 118-119 N 9
Ajakli ~ **RUS** 108-109 b 6
Ajaköz ○ **KZ** 124-125 M 5
Ajaköz ~ **KZ** 124-125 L 5
Ajaktal, gory ▲ **RUS** 108-109 Z 7
Ajalpan ○ **MEX** 52-53 F 2
Ajan ○ **RUS** (IRK) 116-117 N 6
Ajan ☆ **RUS** (HBR) 120-121 H 5
Ajan ~ **RUS** 108-109 a 6
Ajan, ozero ~ **RUS** 108-109 a 7
Ajana ○ **AUS** 176-177 C 3
Ajan-Jurjah ~ **RUS** 120-121 M 2
Ajanka ○ **RUS** (KOR) 112-113 O 5
Ajanka ~ **RUS** 112-113 N 4
Ajanta ○· **IND** 138-139 E 9
Ajanta Caves ⋯ **IND** 138-139 E 9
Ajaokuta ○ **WAN** 204-205 G 5
Ajaria = Adžarskaja Avtonomnaja Respublika □ **GE** 126-127 D 7
Ajasse ○ **WAN** 204-205 F 4
Ajasso ○ **WAN** 204-205 H 6
Ājat ~ **KZ** 124-125 C 2
Ajaturku, ozero ⬭ **RUS** 108-109 Y 5
Ajava ~ **RUS** 116-117 L 6
Ajax ○ **USA** (TX) 268-269 G 5
Ajax Peak ▲ **USA** (ID) 250-251 F 6
Ajdābiyā □ **LAR** 192-193 H 3
Ajdābiyā ☆·· **LAR** (AJD) 192-193 J 2
Ajdar ~ **UA** 102-103 L 3
Ajdarkūl kūli ⬭ **UZ** 136-137 K 4
Ajdarkuly, kūli ⬭ **UZ** 136-137 K 4
Ajdarly ○ **KZ** 124-125 D 6
Ajer' Terjun ○ **MAL** 162-163 D 2
Ajgyržal, tau ▲ **KZ** 124-125 G 4
Ajhal ○ **RUS** 110-111 H 7
Aji, Isla ⌒ **CO** 60-61 C 6
Ajibarang ○ **RI** 168 C 3
Ajigasawa ○ **J** 152-153 J 4
Ajikagungan ○ **RI** 162-163 F 7
Ajjer, Tassili n' ▲⋯ **DZ** 190-191 F 8
Ajjuva ~ **RUS** 88-89 X 4
Ajkaegan ~ **RUS** 114-115 N 3
Ajkeköl ⬭ **KZ** 126-127 O 2
Ajkino ○ **RUS** 88-89 U 5
Ajmer ○· **IND** 138-139 E 6
Ajnabūlak ○ **KZ** 124-125 G 4
Ajni ○ **TJ** 136-137 L 5
Ajnskoe, ozero ⬭ **RUS** 122-123 K 4
Ajo ○ **USA** (AZ) 256-257 C 6
Ajoda ○ **WAN** 204-205 F 5
Ajo Mountains ▲ **USA** 256-257 C 6
Ajon ○ **RUS** 112-113 O 2
Ajon, ostrov ⌒ **RUS** 112-113 P 2
Aj-Pim ~ **RUS** 114-115 L 3
Ajrag = Cagaandörvölž ○ **MAU** 148-149 J 5
Ajryk ○ **KZ** 124-125 K 3
Ajsary ○ **KZ** 124-125 G 2
Ajtau ▲ **KZ** 124-125 J 6
Ajtor, ozero ⬭ **RUS** 114-115 J 4
Ajtos ○ **BG** 102-103 E 6
Ajuly, Aksu- ○ **KZ** 124-125 H 4
Ajumaku ○ **GH** 202-203 K 7
Ajumkan ~ **RUS** 120-121 D 6
Ajuy ○ **RP** 160-161 E 7
Ajvasedapur ~ **RUS** 114-115 O 2
Ajyrtas ○ **KZ** 124-125 K 4
Aka ~ **GH** 202-203 L 6
Akaba ○ **RT** 202-203 L 6
Akaba, Réservat d' ⊥ **RT** 202-203 L 6
Akaba Pass ▲ **SUD** 200-201 H 3
Akabli ○ **DZ** 190-191 C 7
Akačan ~ **RUS** 120-121 H 3
Akademii, zaliv ≈ 120-121 G 6
Akademii Nauk, lednik ⊂ **RUS** 108-109 I Z 1
Akademika Obručeva, hrebet ▲ **RUS** 116-117 G 9
Akadomari ○ **J** 152-153 H 6
Akadyr' ☆ **KZ** 124-125 H 4
Aka-Eze ○ **WAN** 204-205 G 6
Akagera ~ **RWA** 212-213 C 5
Akagera, Parc National de l' ⊥ **RWA** 212-213 C 4
Akagi ○ **J** 152-153 E 7
Akaishi-sanmyaku ▲ **J** 152-153 H 7
Akaka ○ **G** 210-211 B 5
Akaka Falls ~· **USA** 288 K 5
Āk'ak'ī Beseka ○ **ETH** 208-209 D 4
Akakro ○ **CI** 202-203 H 7
Akakus ⋯ **LAR** 190-191 H 8
Akakus, Jabal ▲ **LAR** 190-191 H 8
Akālgarh ○ **PK** 138-139 D 3
Akalkot ○ **IND** 140-141 G 2
Akamba, Chute ~ **ZRE** 210-211 L 3
Akam Éffak ○ **G** 210-211 C 3
Akamkpa ○ **WAN** 204-205 H 6
Akankohan ○ **J** 152-153 L 3
Akan National Park ⊥ **J** 152-153 L 3
Akanous ○ **NAM** 220-221 D 2
Akanyaru ~ **RWA** 212-213 B 5
Akaroa ○ **NZ** 182 D 5
Akasame ○ **PNG** 183 B 2
Akasha ○ **SUD** 200-201 E 2
Akashi ○ **J** 152-153 F 7
Akaska ○ **USA** (SD) 260-261 F 1
Äkäslompolo ○ **FIN** 88-89 H 3
Akassa ○ **WAN** 204-205 G 6
Akat Amnuai ○ **THA** 158-159 G 2
Akatsi ○ **GH** 202-203 L 6
Akbaba Dağı ▲ **TR** 128-129 K 2
Akbajtal, pereval ▲ **TJ** 136-137 N 5
Akbarpur ○ **IND** (BIH) 142-143 C 3
Akbarpur ○ **IND** (UTP) 142-143 C 2
Akbastöbe, tau ▲ **KZ** 126-127 P 4
Akbou ○ **DZ** 190-191 E 2
Akbulak ☆ **RUS** 96-97 J 8
Akçaabat ☆ **TR** 128-129 H 2
Akçadağ ☆ **TR** 128-129 G 3
Akçakale ☆ **TR** 128-129 H 4
Akçakoca ☆· **TR** 128-129 D 2
Akçakoca Dağları ▲ **TR** 128-129 D 2
Akçalı Dağları ▲ **TR** 128-129 E 4
Akčatau ○ **KZ** 124-125 J 5
Akçay ~ **TR** 128-129 C 4
Akchâr ∸ **RIM** 196-197 C 5
Ak Dağlar ▲ **TR** 128-129 F 3
Ak Dağlar ▲ **TR** 128-129 C 4
Akdağmadeni ☆ **TR** 128-129 F 3
Ak-Dovurak ○ **RUS** 116-117 E 10
Akdym, tau ▲ **KZ** 124-125 H 3
Akdžakala, vpadina ◡ **TM** 136-137 F 4
Akébou ∸ **RT** 202-203 L 6
Akela ○ **USA** (NM) 256-257 H 6
Akelama ~ **RI** 164-165 L 3
Akelamo ○ **RI** (MAL) 164-165 K 4
Akelamo ○ **RI** (MAL) 164-165 L 3
Akelamo, Tanjung ▲ **RI** 164-165 K 4
Akeley ○ **USA** (MN) 270-271 D 3
Akeonik ○ **USA** 20-21 K 1
Akeouet, Hassi in < **DZ** 190-191 G 7
Akera ~ **AZ** 128-129 M 3
Åkersberga ☆ **S** 86-87 J 7
Aketi ○ **ZRE** (HAU) 210-211 J 2
Aketi ~ **ZRE** 210-211 K 2
Akhiok ○ **USA** 22-23 T 4
Akhisar ☆ **TR** 128-129 B 3
Akhnoor ○ **IND** 138-139 E 3
Aki ○ **J** 152-153 E 8
Akiachak ○ **USA** 20-21 K 6
Akiéni ○ **G** 210-211 D 4
Akimiski Island ⌒ **CDN** 34-35 Q 4
Akıncı Burnu ▲ **TR** 128-129 F 4
Akinum ○ **PNG** 183 E 4
Akišma ~ **RUS** 122-123 E 2
Akita ☆ **J** 152-153 J 5
Ak"jar ☆ **RUS** 96-97 L 8
Akjoujt ☆ **RIM** 196-197 C 5
Akka ○ **MA** 188-189 G 6
Akkajaure ⬭ **S** 86-87 H 3
Akkajtym ○ **KZ** 126-127 N 4
Akkeshi ○ **J** 152-153 L 3
'Akko ☆·· **IL** 130-131 D 1
Akkol' ○ **KZ** 124-125 J 6
Akkol' ○ **KZ** (DZA) 136-137 M 3
Akköl ☆ **KZ** (DZM) 136-137 M 3
Akköl ⬭ **KZ** (DZM) 136-137 M 3
Akköl ⬭ **KZ** (KST) 126-127 P 3
Akkoursoulbak ○ **RCA** 206-207 E 4
Akkyr ▲ **TM** 136-137 D 4
Aklampa ○ **DY** 204-205 E 4
Aklavik ○ **CDN** 20-21 X 2
Aklera ○ **IND** 138-139 F 7
Aklim, Adrar-n- ▲ **MA** 188-189 G 5
Akloa, Cascade d' ~ **RT** 202-203 L 6
Akmeqit ○ **VRC** 146-147 C 7
Akmola ○ **KZ** 124-125 G 3
Akmola, tau ▲ **KZ** 124-125 F 4
Akniste ○ **LV** 94-95 J 3
Aknoul ○ **MA** 188-189 K 3
Akō ○ **J** 152-153 F 7
Ako'akas, Rochers = Ako'akas Rocks · **CAM** 210-211 C 2

294 Adiora — Ako'akas, Rochers

Ako'akas Rocks = Rochers Ako'akas • **CAM** 210-211 C 2
Ākobo Wenz ~ **ETH** 208-209 B 5
Ak-Ojuk, gora ▲ **RUS** 124-125 Q 3
Akok o **G** 210-211 B 3
Akoke o **SUD** 206-207 L 4
Akokora o **ZRE** 212-213 B 3
Akola o **IND** 138-139 F 9
Akoma o **PNG** 183 C 4
Akom II o **CAM** 210-211 C 2
Akono o **CAM** 210-211 C 2
Akonolinga o **CAM** 210-211 D 2
Akop o **SUD** 206-207 J 4
Akor o **RMM** 202-203 G 2
Āk'ordat o **ER** 200-201 H 5
Akoroso o **GH** 202-203 K 7
Akosombo o• **GH** 202-203 L 6
Akot o **IND** 138-139 F 9
Akot o **SUD** 206-207 K 5
Akoupé o **CI** 202-203 J 6
Akpatok Island ⌒ **CDN** 36-37 P 4
Akpınar ☆ **TR** 128-129 E 3
Akplabanya o **GH** 202-203 L 7
Akposso ∸ **RT** 202-203 L 6
Akqi o **VRC** 146-147 D 5
Akrab o **KZ** 126-127 L 2
Akrabat o **TM** 136-137 G 7
Akranes ☆ **IS** 86-87 b 2
Akráta o **GR** 100-101 J 5
Akra Ténaro ▲ **GR** 100-101 J 6
Akréréb o **RN** 198-199 D 4
Åkrestrømmen o **N** 86-87 E 6
Akrokorinthos ·· **GR** 100-101 J 6
Akron o **USA** (CO) 254-255 M 3
Akron o **USA** (IA) 274-275 B 2
Akron o **USA** (IN) 274-275 M 3
Akron o **USA** (NY) 278-279 C 5
Akron o **USA** (OH) 280-281 E 2
Akša ☆ **RUS** 118-119 F 10
Ak-Saj ~ **KS** 146-147 C 5
Akşaj ☆ **KZ** 96-97 H 8
Aksaj o **RUS** (ROS) 102-103 L 4
Aksaj ~ **RUS** 102-103 M 4
Aksaj ~ **RUS** 126-127 G 6
Aksaj Esaulovskij ~ **RUS** 102-103 N 4
Akşar o **TR** 128-129 K 2
Aksaray ☆ **TR** 128-129 F 3
Aksarka o **RUS** 108-109 N 8
Aksay o **VRC** 146-147 M 6
Aksay Qin ⌒ 144-145 B 3
Aksayqin Co o 144-145 B 3
Akşehir ☆ **TR** 128-129 D 3
Akşehir Gölü o **TR** 128-129 D 3
Akseki ☆ **TR** 128-129 D 4
'Aks-e Rostam, Rūdḫāne-ye ~ **IR** 134-135 F 4
Akši ~ **KZ** 124-125 D 5
Akšij o **KZ** 146-147 C 4
Aksoran tauy ▲ **KZ** 124-125 J 4
Aksu ~ **KS** 146-147 B 4
Aksu o **KZ** (AKM) 124-125 G 2
Aksu o **KZ** (7PK) 96-97 H 8
Aksu ☆ **KZ** 124-125 K 2
Aksu ~ **KZ** 124-125 L 5
Aksu o **VRC** 146-147 E 5
Aksu-Ajuly o **KZ** 124-125 H 4
Aksuat o **KZ** 124-125 N 4
Aksuat o **KZ** 124-125 N 5
Aksuat, köli o **KZ** 124-125 D 3
Aksubaevo ☆ **RUS** 96-97 G 6
Aksu Çayı ~ **TR** 128-129 D 4
Aksūm o··· **ETH** 208-209 D 1
Ak-Syjrak o **KS** 146-147 D 5
Ak-Tal o **KS** 146-147 B 5
Aktanyš ☆ **RUS** 96-97 J 6
Aktarsk o **RUS** 96-97 D 8
Aktaš o **RUS** 124-125 P 3
Aktau o **KZ** (KRG) 124-125 H 3
Aktau ☆ **KZ** 126-127 J 6
Aktau ☆ **KZ** (MNG) 126-127 J 6
Aktaz o **KZ** 124-125 H 4
Aktaz o **VRC** 146-147 H 6
Aktobe ☆ **KZ** 126-127 M 2
Aktogaj o **KZ** 124-125 J 4
Aktoġaj o **KZ** 124-125 L 5
Aktolagaj tizbegi ▲ **KZ** 126-127 L 4
Aktov tog ▲ **UZ** 136-137 J 4
Aktümsyk o **KZ** 126-127 M 4
Aku o **PNG** 184 I b 2
Akūbū o **SUD** 206-207 L 5
Akugdleq, Ikertooq ≈ 28-29 O 3
Akula o **ZRE** 210-211 H 2
Akuliarusinguaq ⌒ **GRØ** 26-27 Y 8
Akulurak o **USA** 20-21 H 5
Akumal o **MEX** 52-53 L 1
Akune o **J** 152-153 D 8
Akun Island ⌒ **USA** 22-23 O 5
Akuraj o **RUS** 118-119 H 10
Akure ☆ **WAN** 204-205 F 5
Akureyri ☆ **IS** 86-87 d 2
Akuš, ozero o **RUS** 114-115 K 7
Akuseki-shima ⌒ **J** 152-153 C 10
Akutan o **USA** 22-23 O 5
Akutan Pass ≈ 22-23 N 5
Akutukpa o **WAN** 204-205 G 4
Akwa-Ibom □ **WAN** 204-205 G 6
Akwanga o **WAN** 204-205 H 4
Akwatuk Bay ≈ 38-39 E 2
Akwaya o **CAM** 204-205 H 5
Akwot ~ **SUD** 206-207 K 5
Akyab = Sittwe ☆ **MYA** 142-143 H 5
Akžajkyn o **KZ** 124-125 E 6
Akžajyk o **KZ** 96-97 G 8
Akžar, k-l o **KZ** 136-137 L 3
Akžar, ozero o **KZ** 136-137 L 3
Alabama o **USA** (NY) 278-279 C 5
Alabama □ **USA** 284-285 C 4
Alabama Camp o **LB** 202-203 F 5
Alabama & Coushatta Indian Reservation X **USA** (TX) 268-269 F 6
Alabama Port o **USA** (AL) 284-285 B 6
Alabama River ~ **USA** 284-285 C 5
Alabaster o **USA** (AL) 284-285 D 3
Alabat Island ⌒ **RP** 160-161 D 5
al-'Abbāsīyah o **SUD** 200-201 E 6
Ala-Bel', pereval ▲ **KS** 136-137 N 3
Alabo ~ **GH** 202-203 L 6
Alabota, köli o **KZ** (KKC) 124-125 G 2
Alabota, köli o **KZ** (KST) 124-125 D 2
Ala Buka o **KS** 136-137 M 4
Ala-Buka ~ **KS** 146-147 B 5
Alaca ☆ **TR** 128-129 F 2
Alacahöyük ·· **TR** 128-129 F 2
Alacalufe, Reserva Florestal ⊥ **RCH** 80 C 6
Alaçam ☆ **TR** 128-129 F 2
Alacant o• **E** (ALI) 98-99 G 5
Alacant ☆ **E** 98-99 G 5
Alachua o **USA** (FL) 286-287 G 2
Alacranes, Presa < **C** 54-55 E 3
Aladağ ▲ **TR** 128-129 E 4
Ālādāg, Kūh-e ▲ **IR** 136-137 E 6
Ala Dağlar ▲ **TR** 128-129 F 4
Ala Dağlar ▲ **TR** 128-129 K 3
Aladdin o **USA** (WY) 252-253 O 2
Aladja o **WAN** 204-205 F 6
Aladža = Alağa o **TM** 136-137 C 5
Alaf Badane o **ETH** 208-209 G 6
Alafiarou o **DY** 204-205 E 4
Alaganik o **USA** 20-21 S 6
Alagapuram o **IND** 140-141 H 5
Ālagē ▲ **ETH** 200-201 J 6
Alagir o **RUS** 126-127 F 6
al-'Ağma, Ğabal ▲ **ET** 194-195 G 3
Alag nuur o **MAU** 146-147 M 3
Alagoa Grande o **BR** 68-69 L 5
Alagoas □ **BR** 68-69 K 6
Alagoinha o **BR** 68-69 K 6
Alagoinhas o **BR** 72-73 L 2
Alagón o **E** 98-99 G 4
Alagón, Río ~ **E** 98-99 D 4
al-'Ağrūd < **ET** 194-195 G 2
Alah ~ **RP** 160-161 F 9
Alahan Monastir ·· **TR** 128-129 E 4
Alahanpanjang o **RI** 162-163 D 5
Alaid, vulkan ▲ **RUS** 122-123 Q 3
Alaid Island ⌒ **USA** 22-23 C 6
Alaïli Dadda o **DJI** 208-209 F 2
al-Ain o··· **OM** 132-133 K 2
al-'Ain o **SUD** 200-201 D 4
Alajärvi o **FIN** 88-89 G 5
Alajskij hrebet ▲ **TJ** 136-137 M 5
Alajuela ☆ **CR** 52-53 B 6
Alakamisy Ambohimaha o **RM** 222-223 E 8
Alakamisy Itenina o **RM** 222-223 E 8
Alakanuk o **USA** 20-21 H 5
Alakit o **RUS** (SAH) 110-111 H 6
Alakit ~ **RUS** 110-111 H 6
Alaköl o **KZ** 124-125 J 6
Alaktak o **USA** 20-21 N 1
Alakuko o **WAN** 204-205 F 5
Alakurtti o **RUS** 88-89 L 3
Alalakeiki Channel ≈ 288 J 4
al-'Alamain o• **ET** 194-195 D 2
Alalaú, Rio ~ **BR** 62-63 D 6
'Alālī, al- o **RL** 128-129 F 6
Alamar o **C** 54-55 D 3
al-'Amārah o **SUD** 200-201 F 5
'Alā Marv Dašt, Rūd-e ~ **IR** 134-135 E 5
Ālamat'ā o **ETH** 200-201 J 6
Alameda o **CDN** (SAS) 232-233 Q 6
Alameda, La o **MEX** 50-51 G 5
Alamikamba o **NIC** 52-53 B 5
Alamillo o **USA** (NM) 256-257 J 4
Alaminos o **RP** 160-161 C 4
al-'Āmirīya o **ET** 194-195 D 2
Alamito Creek ~ **USA** 266-267 C 4
Alamo o **MEX** 52-53 F 1
Alamo o **SP** 208-209 F 6
Alamo o **USA** (ND) 258-259 D 3
Alamo o **USA** (NM) 256-257 H 4
Alamo o **USA** (NV) 248-249 J 2
Alamo o **USA** (TN) 276-277 F 5
Alamogordo o **USA** (NM) 256-257 K 6
Alamo Lake < **USA** (AZ) 256-257 B 4
Alamo Navajo Indian Reservation X **USA** (NM) 256-257 H 4
Alamor o **EC** 64-65 B 4
Alamos o **MEX** 50-51 E 4
Alamos, Los o **USA** (CA) 248-249 D 5
Alamos, Los o **USA** (NM) 256-257 J 3
Álamos, Río de los ~ **MEX** 50-51 J 3
Alamosa o **USA** (CO) 254-255 K 6
Alamosa National Wildlife Refuge ⊥ **USA** (CO) 254-255 K 6
Alamosa River ~ **USA** 256-257 H 5
Alamos de Márquez o **MEX** 50-51 H 3
Alampur o **IND** 140-141 H 3
Åland ⌒ **FIN** 88-89 F 6
Aland o **IND** 140-141 G 2
Ålands Hav ≈ 86-87 J 6
Alang o **IND** 138-139 D 9
Alange o **E** 98-99 D 5
Alanreed o **USA** (TX) 264-265 D 3
Alanson o **USA** (MI) 272-273 E 2
Alantika Mountains ▲ **WAN** 204-205 K 4
Alanya o **TR** 128-129 E 4
Alaolo ~ **SOL** 184 I e 3
Alaotra ∸ **RM** 222-223 F 6
Alaotra, Farihy o **RM** 222-223 F 6
Alapa o **WAN** 204-205 F 4
Alapaevsk o **RUS** 96-97 M 5
Alapaha o **USA** (GA) 284-285 G 5
Alapaha River ~ **USA** 284-285 G 6
Alapaha River ~ **USA** 286-287 F 1
al-'Aqaba, Ḫalīğ ≈ 194-195 G 3
al-'Aqaba aş-Şaġira o **ET** 194-195 F 5
'Alaqah, Bi'r al o **LAR** 192-193 F 3
'Alāqān o **KSA** 130-131 D 3
Alaquines o **MEX** 50-51 K 6
al-'Arab, Baḥr ~ **SUD** 206-207 J 4
al-Arab, Baḥr ~ **SUD** 206-207 G 3
al-Arāk o **SUD** 200-201 E 3
Alarcón, Embalse de < **E** 98-99 F 5
Alareak Island ⌒ **CDN** 36-37 M 2
Al-Argoub o **WSA** 196-197 C 3
al-'Arīš ☆ **ET** 194-195 F 2
al-'Arīš, Wādī ~ **ET** 194-195 F 2
Alas o **RI** (NBA) 168 C 7
Alas o **RI** (TIT) 166-167 C 6
Alas ~ **RI** 162-163 B 3
Alaš ~ **RUS** 124-125 Q 3
Alas, Hos- o **RUS** 110-111 S 6
Alas, Selat ≈ 168 C 7
Alaşehir ☆• **TR** 128-129 C 3
Alašejev buchta ≈ 16 G 5
Alashan Shamo ⌒ **VRC** 148-149 E 7
Alasi o **SOL** 184 I e 3
al-'Āṣī, Nahr ~ **SYR** 128-129 G 5
Alaska o **USA** (MI) 272-273 D 5
Alaska o **ZW** 218-219 F 3
Alaska, Gulf of ≈ 14-15 O 2
Alaska Highway II **CDN** 32-33 K 3
Alaska Peninsula ⌣ **USA** 22-23 P 5
Alaska Range ▲ **USA** 20-21 O 6
Alássio o• **I** 100-101 B 2
Alat o **UZ** 136-137 H 5
Alatau hrebet ▲ **RUS** 96-97 K 7
Alataw Shankou Žoṅġar Kakpasy ▲ 146-147 F 3
Al Atazar, Embalse de < **E** 98-99 F 4
Alati o **CAM** 210-211 D 2
Alatna River ~ **USA** 20-21 O 3
al-Atshan ~ **SUD** 200-201 G 6
Alatsinainy Bakaro o **RM** 222-223 E 7
Alatskivi o·· **EST** 94-95 K 2
Ālattur o **IND** 140-141 G 5
Alatyr' o **RUS** 96-97 E 6
Alausí o **EC** 64-65 C 3
Alava o **RP** 160-161 D 4
Alaverdi o **AR** 128-129 L 2
Ala-Vuokki o **FIN** 88-89 K 4
Alavus o **FIN** 88-89 G 5
Alawa o **WAN** 204-205 G 3
Alawa Game Reserve ⊥ **WAN** 204-205 G 3
Alawangandji Aboriginal Land X **AUS** 174-175 C 4
Al Awaynat o **LAR** 200-201 B 2
Al Awaynat, Jabal ▲ **SUD** 200-201 B 2
Alawoona o **AUS** 180-181 F 3
Alayo o **RCA** 206-207 F 6
Al-'Ayun ☆ **WSA** 188-189 E 7
al-'Ayyāt o **ET** 194-195 E 3
Alazani ~ **AZ** 128-129 M 2
Alazeja ~ **RUS** 110-111 b 5
Alazeja ~ **RUS** 112-113 H 1
Alazejskoe ploskogor'e ▲ **RUS** 110-111 a 6
Al 'Azīziyah ☆ **LAR** 192-193 E 1
Alba o• **I** 100-101 B 2
Alba o **USA** (TX) 264-265 J 6
Albacete o **E** 98-99 G 5
Albacutya, Lake o **AUS** 180-181 F 3
al-Badārī o **ET** 194-195 E 4
Alba de Tormes o **E** 98-99 E 4
Ålbæk Bugt ≈ 86-87 E 8
al-Baḥr al-Abyaḍ ~ **SUD** 200-201 F 5
al-Baḥr al-Azraq ~ **SUD** 200-201 F 5
al-Baḥr al-Azraq = Blue Nile ~ **SUD** 200-201 F 5
Alba Iulia ☆• **RO** 102-103 C 4
Albāka o **IND** 142-143 B 6
al-Balīḫ, Nahr ~ **SYR** 128-129 H 4
al-Ballāş o **ET** 194-195 F 4
al-Balyana o **ET** 194-195 E 4
Alban o **CDN** (ONT) 238-239 E 2
Alban o **CO** 60-61 D 5
Alban = San José o **CO** 64-65 D 1
Albanel o **CDN** (QUE) 240-241 C 2
Albanel, Lac o **CDN** 38-39 H 3
Albanel, Lac o **CDN** (QUE) 236-237 P 2
Albania = Shqipëri ■ **AL** 100-101 G 4
Albany o• **AUS** 176-177 D 7
Albany o **USA** (GA) 284-285 F 5
Albany o **USA** (IN) 274-275 N 4
Albany o **USA** (KY) 276-277 K 4
Albany o **USA** (MN) 270-271 D 5
Albany o **USA** (MO) 274-275 D 4
Albany o **USA** (OR) 244-245 B 6
Albany o **USA** (TX) 264-265 E 6
Albany o **USA** (WY) 252-253 M 5
Albany ☆• **USA** (NY) 278-279 H 6
Albany Downs o **AUS** 178-179 K 4
Albany Highway II **AUS** 176-177 D 6
Albany Island ⌒ **CDN** 34-35 Q 4
Albany River ~ **CDN** 234-235 O 3
Alba Posse o **RA** 76-77 K 4
Albarracín o• **E** 98-99 G 4
al-Barun o **SUD** 208-209 A 3
al-Basabir o **SUD** 200-201 F 4
al-Bāṭina, Ğazīrat ⌒ **KSA** 130-131 L 4
Albatros Bank ≃ 22-23 U 4
Albatross Bay ≈ 174-175 F 3
al-Bauga o **SUD** 200-201 F 3
al-Bawīṭī o **ET** 194-195 D 3
Al Bayda ☆ **LAR** 192-193 J 1
Albay Gulf ≈ 160-161 E 6
Albazino o **RUS** 118-119 M 9
al-Begeir o **SUD** 200-201 F 3
Albemarle o **USA** (NC) 282-283 G 5
Albemarle Sound ≈ 48-49 K 1
Albemarle Sound ≈ 282-283 L 4
Albenga o• **I** 100-101 B 2
Alberca, La o• **E** 98-99 D 4
Alberdi o **PY** 76-77 H 4
Alberfoyle o **AUS** 178-179 H 1
Alberga Creek ~ **AUS** 178-179 C 4
Albergaria-a-Velha o **P** 98-99 C 4
Alberni o **CDN** (BC) 230-231 E 4
Alberni Inlet ≈ 230-231 E 4
Alberobello o• **I** 100-101 F 4
Albert o **F** 90-91 J 6
Albert, Cape ▲ **CDN** 26-27 N 4
Albert, Lake o **AUS** 180-181 E 3
Albert, Lake o **USA** (OR) 244-245 E 8
Albert, Lake = Lac Mobutu-Sese-Seko o **EAU** 212-213 C 3
Alberta o **USA** (VA) 280-281 J 7
Alberta Beach o **CDN** (ALB) 232-233 D 2
Albert Canyon o **CDN** (BC) 230-231 M 2
Albert Edward, Mount ▲ **CDN** (BC) 230-231 D 4
Albert Edward, Mount ▲ **PNG** 183 D 5
Albert Edward Bay ≈ 24-25 U 6
Alberti o **RA** 78-79 J 3
Albert I Land ∸ **N** 84-85 G 3
Albertinia o **ZA** 220-221 E 7
Albert Islands ⌒ **CDN** (NWT) 24-25 N 5
Albert Law, Mont ▲ **CDN** 36-37 N 4
Albert Lea o **USA** (MN) 270-271 E 7
Albert Markham, Mount ▲ **ARK** 16 E 0
Albert Nile ~ **EAU** 212-213 C 2
Alberto de Agostini, Parque Nacional ⊥ **RCH** 80 E 7
Alberton o **CDN** (PEI) 240-241 L 4
Alberton o **USA** (MT) 250-251 E 4
Albert River ~ **AUS** 174-175 E 6
Albert Town o **BS** 54-55 H 3
Albert Town o **JA** 54-55 G 5
Albertville o **CDN** (QUE) 240-241 H 2
Albertville o• **F** 90-91 L 9
Albertville o **USA** (AL) 284-285 D 2
Albi ☆• **F** 90-91 J 10
Albia o **USA** (IA) 274-275 F 3
Albin o **USA** (WY) 252-253 O 5
Albina ☆ **SME** 62-63 G 3
Albina, Ponta ▲ **ANG** 216-217 A 7
Albion o **USA** (CA) 246-247 B 4
Albion o **USA** (IL) 274-275 K 6
Albion o **USA** (MI) 272-273 E 5
Albion o **USA** (MT) 250-251 P 6
Albion o **USA** (NE) 262-263 J 3
Albion o **USA** (NY) 278-279 C 5
Albion o **USA** (OK) 264-265 J 4
Albion o **USA** (PA) 280-281 F 2
Alborán, Isla del ⌒ **E** 98-99 F 7
Alborán, Isla del ⌒ **E** 188-189 K 3
Ålborg o·· **DK** 86-87 D 8
Ålborg Bugt ≈ 86-87 E 8
Alborn o **USA** (MN) 270-271 F 4
Alborz, Kūhhā-ye ▲ **IR** 136-137 B 6
Albox o **E** 98-99 F 6
Albreda o **CDN** (BC) 228-229 P 4
Albreda o• **WAG** 202-203 B 3
Albro o **AUS** 178-179 J 2
Albufeira o **P** 98-99 C 6
Albuquerque o• **E** 98-99 D 5
Albuquerque o• **USA** (NM) 256-257 J 3
Albury-Wodonga o **AUS** 180-181 J 4
Alcácer do Sal o **P** 98-99 C 5
Alcáçovas o **P** 98-99 C 5
Alcala o **AUS** 174-175 F 6
Alcala o **RP** 160-161 D 4
Alcalá de Chivert = Alcalà de Xivert o **E** 98-99 H 4
Alcalá de Henares o• **E** 98-99 F 4
Alcalá del Júcar o **E** 98-99 G 5
Alcalà de Xivert o **E** 98-99 H 4
Alcalá la Real o **E** 98-99 F 6
Alcalde o **USA** (NM) 256-257 J 2
Alcalde, Punta ▲ **RCH** 76-77 B 5
Álcamo o **I** 100-101 D 6
Alcañices o **E** 98-99 D 4
Alcañiz o **E** 98-99 G 4
Alcântara o **BR** 68-69 F 3
Alcántara o **E** 98-99 D 5
Alcantara Lake o **CDN** 30-31 P 5
Alcantarilla o **E** 98-99 G 6
Alcaracejos o **E** 98-99 E 5
Alcaraz o **E** 98-99 F 5
Alcaraz, Sierra de ▲ **E** 98-99 F 5
Alcatrazes, Ilha do ⌒ **BR** 72-73 H 8
Alcaudete o **E** 98-99 F 6
Alcázar ·· **E** 98-99 E 6
Alcázar de San Juan o **E** 98-99 F 5
Alcedo, Volcán ▲ **EC** 64-65 B 10
Alcester Island ⌒ **PNG** 183 G 5
Alčevs'k o **UA** 102-103 L 3
Alcira o **RA** 78-79 G 2
Alcoa o **USA** (TN) 282-283 D 5
Alcobaça o··· **P** 98-99 C 5
Alcoi o **E** 98-99 G 5
Alcolea del Pinar o **E** 98-99 F 4
Alcomdale o **CDN** (ALB) 232-233 E 2
Alcona o **CDN** (ONT) 234-235 M 4
Alcoota o **AUS** 178-179 C 2
Alcorcón o **E** 98-99 F 4
Alcorta o **RA** 78-79 J 2
Alcott Creek ~ **CDN** 232-233 K 2
Alcoutim o **P** 98-99 D 6
Alcova o **USA** (WY) 252-253 M 4
Alcovy River ~ **USA** 284-285 G 3
Alcoy o **RP** 160-161 E 8
Alcoy = Alcoi o **E** 98-99 G 5
Alcúdia o **E** 98-99 J 5
Alcúdia, l' o **E** 98-99 G 5
Alcurve o **CDN** (ALB) 232-233 H 2
Aldabra Atoll ∸··· **SY** 222-223 E 2
Aldabra Group ∸ **SY** 222-223 E 2
Aldaia Bona o **BR** 62-63 G 5
Aldama o **MEX** (CHA) 50-51 G 3
Aldama o **MEX** (TAM) 50-51 K 6
Aldamas, Los o **MEX** 50-51 K 4
Aldan ☆• **RUS** (SAH) 118-119 M 6
Aldan ~ **RUS** 118-119 P 4
Aldanskoe nagor'e ▲ **RUS** 118-119 L 6
Aldea, Isla ⌒ **RCH** 80 C 4
Aldea dos Indios Sucane o **GUY** 62-63 E 5
Aldehuela Gallinal o **ROU** 78-79 M 2
Aldeia o **BR** (BAH) 68-69 E 7
Aldeia o **BR** (GSU) 70-71 K 6
Aldeia o **BR** (MAR) 68-69 E 5
Aldeia, Serra da ▲ **BR** 72-73 G 4
Aldeia Beltrão o **BR** 76-77 K 5
Aldeia das Canoas o **BR** 62-63 G 5
Aldeia Grimaldi o **BR** 76-77 J 6
Aldeia Manuel Antonio o **BR** 68-69 E 3
Aldeia Velha o **BR** 68-69 F 4
Aldeia Viçosa o **ANG** 216-217 C 4
Aldeia Vila Batista o **BR** 62-63 D 6
Alder o **USA** (MT) 250-251 G 6
Alder Creek o **USA** (NY) 278-279 F 5
Alder Flats o **CDN** (ALB) 232-233 D 3
Alderley o **AUS** 178-179 E 2
Alderley o **ZA** 220-221 J 6
Alderney ⌒ **GBA** 90-91 F 7
Alder Peak ▲ **USA** (CA) 248-249 C 4
Alder Point ▲ **USA** (CA) 248-249 C 4
Alderson o **CDN** (ALB) 232-233 G 5
Aldoma o **RUS** (HBR) 120-121 H 5
Aldoma ~ **RUS** 120-121 G 5
Aldžer, ostrov ⌒ **RUS** 84-85 e 2
Alédjo o **DY** 202-203 L 5
Alédjo, Faille-d' ▲• **RT** 202-203 L 5
Aledo o **USA** (IL) 274-275 H 3
Aleg ☆ **RIM** 196-197 D 6
Aleg, Lac d' o **RIM** 196-197 D 6
Alegre o **BR** (ESP) 72-73 K 6
Alegre o **BR** (MIN) 72-73 G 5
Alegre, Rio ~ **BR** 70-71 H 4
Alegre, Rio ~ **BR** 70-71 J 5
Alegres Mountain ▲ **USA** (NM) 256-257 J 4
Alegrete o **BR** 76-77 K 5
Alegria o **BR** (GSU) 70-71 K 6
Alegria o **BR** (RSU) 76-77 K 4
Alegria o **RP** (CEB) 160-161 E 8
Alegria o **RP** (SUN) 160-161 G 7
Alegro, Ponta ▲ **BR** 74-75 D 9
Alëhovščina o **RUS** 94-95 N 1
Aleiandia o **CO** 60-61 D 3
Alej ~ **RUS** 124-125 N 2
Alejandra o **RA** 76-77 H 5
Alejandría o **BOL** 70-71 E 3
Alejandro Selkirk, Isla ⌒ **RCH** 78-79 B 1
Alejsk o **RUS** 124-125 N 2
Aleknagik o **USA** 22-23 R 3
Aleknagik, Lake o **USA** 22-23 R 3
Aleko-Kjuël' o **RUS** 110-111 d 5
Aleksandovskij, zaliv ≈ 122-123 J 3
Aleksandra, mys ▲ **RUS** 120-121 H 6
Aleksandra I, zeml'a ∸ **ARK** 16 G 29
Aleksandrija = Oleksandrivka o **UA** 102-103 H 3
Aleksandrov ☆·· **RUS** 94-95 Q 3
Aleksandrov Gaj ☆ **RUS** 96-97 F 8
Aleksandrovka ☆ **RUS** 96-97 J 7
Aleksandrovsk o **RUS** 114-115 D 5
Aleksandrovskij, Kus'e- o **RUS** 96-97 L 4
Aleksandrovskoe o **RUS** (STA) 126-127 E 5
Aleksandrovskoe o **RUS** (TOM) 114-115 O 4
Aleksandrovsk-Sahalinsij ☆• **RUS** 122-123 K 3
Aleksandry, zaliv ≈ 120-121 H 6
Aleksandry, Zemlja ⌒ **RUS** 84-85 Z 2
Alekseevaka o **RUS** 102-103 L 2
Alekseevka o **KZ** 124-125 O 4
Alekseevka ☆ **KZ** (AKM) 124-125 G 2
Alekseevka o **RUS** (SAH) 118-119 M 5
Alekseevka ☆ **RUS** (SAM) 96-97 G 7
Alekseevskoe ☆ **RUS** 96-97 G 6
Aleksin ☆• **RUS** 94-95 P 4
Aleksinac o **YU** 100-101 H 3
Alel o **SUD** 206-207 K 5
Ålem o **S** 86-87 H 8
Alemania o **EC** 64-65 B 10
Alèmbé o **G** 210-211 C 4
Alembé o **RCB** 210-211 E 4
'Alem Ketema o **ETH** 208-209 D 3
'Alem Maya o **ETH** 208-209 E 4
Além-Paraíba o **BR** 72-73 J 6
Ålen ☆ **N** 86-87 E 5
Alençon ☆ **F** 90-91 H 7
Alen Nkoma o **G** 210-211 C 3
Alenquer o **BR** 62-63 G 6
Alentejo ∸ **P** 98-99 C 6
Alenuihaha Channel ≈ 48-49 D 7
Alenuihaha Channel ≈ 288 J 4
Alépé o **CI** 202-203 J 7
Aleppo = Halab ☆··· **SYR** 128-129 G 4
Alerces, Parque Nacional los ⊥ **RA** 78-79 D 7
Aleria o **F** 98-99 M 3
Alerta o **PE** 70-71 B 2
Alert Bay o **CDN** (BC) 230-231 C 3
Alès o **F** 90-91 K 9
Alesandrovskij Zavod ☆ **RUS** 118-119 H 10
Alessándria ☆ **I** 100-101 B 2
Ålesund ☆• **N** 86-87 C 5
Aleutian Range ▲ **USA** 22-23 R 4
Aleutko o **RUS** 122-123 O 6
Alexander o **CDN** (MAN) 234-235 C 5
Alexander o **USA** (AK) 20-21 P 6
Alexander o **USA** (KS) 262-263 G 6
Alexander o **USA** (ND) 258-259 D 4
Alexander, Cape ▲ **SOL** 184 I c 2
Alexander, Kap ▲ **GRØ** 26-27 O 4
Alexander, Point ▲ **AUS** 174-175 D 3
Alexander Archipelago ⌒ **USA** 32-33 B 3
Alexanderbaai = Alexander Bay o **ZA** 220-221 C 4
Alexander Bay = Alexanderbaai o **ZA** 220-221 C 4
Alexander City o **USA** (AL) 284-285 E 4
Alexander Graham Bell National Historic Park ⊥• **CDN** (NS) 240-241 P 4
Alexander Inlet ≈ 28-29 G 2
Alexander Island ⌒ **CDN** 24-25 U 3
Alexandra o **AUS** 180-181 H 4
Alexandra o **NZ** 182 B 6
Alexandra, Cape ▲ **GB** 78-79 O 7
Alexandra Bay ≈ 174-175 H 5
Alexandra Channel ≈ 140-141 L 2
Alexandra Falls ~ **CDN** 30-31 L 5
Alexandra Fiord o **CDN** 26-27 N 4
Alexandra River ~ **AUS** 174-175 F 6
Alexandria o **AUS** 174-175 D 6
Alexandria o **BR** 68-69 J 5
Alexandria o **CDN** (BC) 228-229 M 4
Alexandria o **CDN** (ONT) 238-239 L 3
Alexándria o **GR** 100-101 J 4
Alexandria o **JA** 54-55 G 5
Alexandria ☆• **RO** 102-103 D 6
Alexandria o **USA** (IN) 274-275 N 4
Alexandria o **USA** (LA) 268-269 H 5
Alexandria o **USA** (MN) 270-271 C 5
Alexandria o **USA** (SD) 260-261 J 3
Alexandria o **USA** (VA) 280-281 J 5
Alexandria o **ZA** 220-221 H 6
Alexandria = al-Iskandarīya ☆·· **ET** 194-195 D 2
Alexandria Bay o **USA** (NY) 278-279 F 4
Alexandrina, Lake o **AUS** 180-181 E 3
Alexandroúpoli ☆ **GR** 100-101 K 4
Alexeck ~ **NAM** 216-217 E 10
Alex Graham, Mount ▲ **CDN** (BC) 228-229 M 4
Alexis o **USA** (IL) 274-275 H 3
Alexis Bay ≈ 38-39 Q 2
Alexis Creek o **CDN** (BC) 228-229 L 4
Alexishafen o **PNG** 183 C 3
Alexis River ~ **CDN** 38-39 Q 2
Alex Morrison National Park ⊥ **AUS** 176-177 C 4
Aleza Lake o **CDN** (BC) 228-229 M 2
Alfalfa o **USA** (OK) 264-265 F 3
Alfalfa o **USA** (OR) 244-245 D 6
Alfarez de Navio Sobral o **ARK** 16 E 0
Alfa River ~ **CDN** 24-25 f 4
Alfarràs o **E** 98-99 H 4
Al-Fāshir o• **SUD** 200-201 B 6
al-Fašn o **ET** 194-195 E 3
Alfatar o **BG** 102-103 E 6
Al Fātiḥ □ **LAR** 192-193 J 2
al-Fayyūm ☆·· **ET** 194-195 E 3
Alfenas o **BR** 72-73 H 6
al-Fifi o **SUD** 206-207 G 3
Alford o **USA** (FL) 286-287 D 1
Ålfotbreen ⊂ **N** 86-87 B 6
Alfred o **CDN** (ONT) 238-239 L 3
Alfred o **USA** (TX) 266-267 K 6
Alfred, Cape ▲ **CDN** 24-25 V 6
Alfred and Marie Range ▲ **AUS** 176-177 H 2
Alfredo Chaves o **BR** 72-73 K 6
Alfredo M. Terrazas o **MEX** 50-51 K 7
Alfredo Wagner o **BR** 74-75 F 6
Alfred Wegeners Halvø ⌣ **GRØ** 26-27 Z 8
Alf Trolle, Kap ▲ **GRØ** 26-27 q 6
Alga ☆ **KZ** 126-127 M 3
al-Gabalayn o **SUD** 200-201 F 6
Algabas o **KZ** 96-97 H 8
al-Gabir o **SUD** 200-201 D 6
al-Ğadīda o **ET** 194-195 D 3
al-Ğāhir, Ğabal ▲ **Y** 132-133 J 7
al-Ğalāla al-Baḥrīya, Ğabal ≈ 194-195 E 3
al-Ğalāla al-Qiblīya, Ğabal ▲ **ET** 194-195 F 3
Algama ~ **RUS** 118-119 O 8
Algama ~ **RUS** 120-121 D 5
al-Ğamālīya o **ET** 194-195 E 2
al-Gamāmiyah o **SUD** 200-201 F 3
Algan ~ **RUS** 112-113 Q 4
Alganskij krjaž ▲ **RUS** 112-113 Q 4
al-Garef o **SUD** 200-201 G 6
Al-Gargarat o **WSA** 196-197 B 4
Algarrobal, Quebrada ~ **RCH** 76-77 B 5
Algarrobo o• **RCH** 78-79 D 2
Algarrobo del Aguila o **RA** 78-79 F 4
Algarve ⌣ **E** 98-99 C 6
al-Ğauf □ **KSA** 130-131 F 3
al-Gaylī o **SUD** 200-201 F 4
al-Ğazīra ∸ **SUD** 200-201 F 5
Algeciras o **E** 98-99 E 6
Algena o **ER** 200-201 J 4
Alger o **USA** (MI) 272-273 E 3
Algeria = Al Jazā'ir ■ **DZ** 190-191 B 6
Algerian Provenceal Basin ≃ 98-99 K 4
Algeyta o **ETH** 208-209 E 4
al-Ghābah o **SUD** 200-201 E 3
al-Ghabshah o **SUD** 200-201 E 6
Alghero o• **I** 100-101 B 4
al-Ğidāmī, Bi'r o **ET** 194-195 F 4
Algiers = Al Jazā'ir ★··· **DZ** 190-191 D 2
al-Ğīza ☆·· **ET** 194-195 E 2
Algoabaai ≈ 220-221 G 6
Algoa Bay ≈ 220-221 G 6
Algodón, Río ~ **PE** 64-65 F 3
Algodone o **USA** (CA) 248-249 K 7
Algoma o **USA** (WI) 270-271 L 6
Algoma Upland ▲ **CDN** 236-237 E 5
Algona o **USA** (IA) 274-275 D 1
Algonac o **CDN** (ONT) 238-239 C 6
Algonquin Park o **CDN** (ONT) 238-239 G 3
Algonquin Provincial Park ⊥ **CDN** (ONT) 238-239 G 3
Algonquin Upland ▲ **CDN** 238-239 G 3
Algood o **USA** (TN) 276-277 K 4
Algorta o **ROU** 78-79 L 2
al-Ğurdaqa ☆• **ET** 194-195 F 4
al-Ḫābūr, Nahr ~ **IRQ** 128-129 K 4
al-Haiz o **ET** 194-195 D 3
Al Hamadah al Hamrā' ∸ **LAR** 192-193 D 2
Alhama de Murcia o **E** 98-99 G 6
Alhambra o **USA** (CA) 248-249 F 5
al-Ḥammām o **ET** 194-195 D 2
Alhančurtskij kanal < **RUS** 126-127 F 6
Alhandra o **BR** 68-69 L 5
al-Ḫānika o **ET** 194-195 E 2
al-Ḫāriğa o• **ET** 194-195 E 5
al-Ḫāriğa, al-Wāḥāt ∸• **ET** 194-195 E 5
al-Ḫarṭūm ★·· **SUD** 200-201 F 5
al-Ḫarṭūm Baḥrī o **SUD** 200-201 F 5
Al Haruj al Aswad ▲ **LAR** 192-193 G 4
Al Hassiane ∸ **WSA** 188-189 D 7
al-Ḫaṭāṭība o **ET** 194-195 E 2
al-Hawad, Wādī ~ **SUD** 200-201 F 4
al-Ḥawātah o **SUD** 200-201 G 6
Alheit o **ZA** 220-221 E 4
al Ḥilla o **SUD** 200-201 C 6
Al Hoceima ☆ **MA** 188-189 K 3
Al-Ḥudūd aš-Šamālīya □ **KSA** 130-131 H 3
Al-Ḥudūd aš-Šarqīya □ **KSA** 130-131 L 6
Al Hufrah ash Sharqīyah ∸ **LAR** 192-193 F 4
al-Ḥuqnah o **SUD** 200-201 F 4
Ålhus o **N** 86-87 C 6
al-Ḥuṣayḥiṣah o **SUD** 200-201 F 5
al-Ḥuwair Oilfield o **OM** 132-133 J 2
Ali o **PNG** 183 B 4
'Alī, Bi'r o **Y** 132-133 F 6
'Aliābād o **AFG** 136-137 L 6
'Aliābād o **IR** 134-135 F 4
Aliābād o **IR** 136-137 D 6
Aliade o **WAN** 204-205 H 5
Aliaga o **E** 98-99 G 4
Aliağa ☆ **TR** 128-129 B 3
Aliákmon ~ **GR** 100-101 J 4
'Alī al-Ğarbī ☆ **IRQ** 128-129 M 6
Aliambata o **RI** 166-167 D 6
Aliança o **BR** 66-67 F 7
Aliantan o **RI** 162-163 D 4
Alianza, La o **CO** 60-61 C 6
Alibāg o **IND** 138-139 D 10
Ali-Bajramly = Ali Bayramlı o **AZ** 128-129 N 3
Alibates Flint Quarries National Monument ∴ **USA** (TX) 264-265 C 3
Ālībo o **ETH** 208-209 C 4
Alibori ~ **DY** 204-205 E 3
Aliboy Knob ▲ **AUS** 172-173 J 4
Alicante = Alacant o• **E** 98-99 G 5
Alice o **AUS** 178-179 M 5
Alice o **USA** (ND) 258-259 K 5
Alice o **USA** (TX) 266-267 J 6
Alice o **ZA** 220-221 H 6
Alice, Punta ▲ **I** 100-101 F 5
Alice Arm o **CDN** 32-33 F 4
Alice River ~ **AUS** 174-175 G 4
Alice Springs o **AUS** 178-179 B 2
Alice Town o **BS** 54-55 G 2
Alice Town o **BS** 54-55 F 2
Aliceville o **USA** (AL) 284-285 B 3
Alicia o **RP** 160-161 D 4
Alicudi, Ísola di ⌒ **I** 100-101 E 5
Alida o **CDN** (SAS) 232-233 R 6
Alīgarh o **IND** 138-139 G 6
Alīgūdarz o **IR** 134-135 C 2
'Aliğūg, Kūh-e ▲ **IR** 134-135 D 3
Alikali o **WAL** 202-203 E 5
Alikazgan ~ **RUS** 126-127 G 6
Alikkod o **IND** 140-141 F 5
Alima ~ **RCB** 210-211 E 4
Älimbet o **KZ** 126-127 N 2
Alimbongo o **ZRE** 212-213 B 4
Alim Island ⌒ **PNG** 183 D 2
Alindao o **RCA** 206-207 E 6
Alingār, Darre-ye ~ **AFG** 136-137 M 7
Alingly o **CDN** (SAS) 232-233 N 2
Alingsås ☆ **S** 86-87 F 8
Alinshan ▲ **VRC** 144-145 C 4
Alīpur o **PK** 138-139 C 5
Alipur Duār o **IND** 142-143 F 2
Aliquippa o **USA** (PA) 280-281 F 3
Aliquisanda o **MOC** 214-215 H 7
Āli Rāipur o **IND** 138-139 E 8
Alirājpur o **IND** 142-143 C 4
Alisaang o **RI** 164-165 G 3
Ali Sabieh o **DJI** 208-209 F 3
'Alī Sadr o **IR** 128-129 N 5
Aliseda o **E** 98-99 D 5
Alishan o **RC** 156-157 M 5
Alishan • **RC** 156-157 M 5
Al-Iskandarīya ☆·· **ET** 194-195 D 2
al-Iskandarīya = Alexandria ☆·· **ET** 194-195 D 2
Aliskerovo o **RUS** 112-113 O 3
al-Ismā'īlīya ☆ **ET** 194-195 F 2
Alitak, Cape ▲ **USA** 22-23 T 4
Alitak Bay ≈ 22-23 T 4
Alite Reef ⌒ **SOL** 184 I e 3
Aliulik Peninsula ⌣ **USA** 22-23 U 4
Aliwal-Noord = Aliwal North o **ZA** 220-221 H 5
Aliwal North = Aliwal-Noord o **ZA** 220-221 H 5
Alix o **CDN** (ALB) 232-233 E 3
'Āliya, al- o **KSA** 132-133 C 5
Aliyābād o **IND** 140-141 H 4
'Aliyab Gharb o **SUD** 200-201 F 4
'Aliyāb Sharq o **SUD** 200-201 F 4
Alīyak, Godār-e ▲ **IR** 136-137 E 6
Al Jabal al Akhdar □ **LAR** 192-193 J 1
Al Jabal al Akhdar ▲ **LAR** 192-193 J 1
Aljat o **AZ** 128-129 N 3
Aljaty o **RUS** 116-117 L 9
Al Jawf ☆ **LAR** 192-193 K 5
Al Jazā'ir ★··· **DZ** 190-191 D 2
Aljenaari o **WAN** 204-205 E 3
Aljezur o **P** 98-99 C 6
Al Jufrah □ **LAR** 192-193 G 3
Aljustrel o **P** 98-99 C 6
al-Kab ∴• **ET** 194-195 F 5
al-Kāb o **SUD** 200-201 F 3
Alkali Lake o **CDN** (BC) 230-231 H 2
Alkali Lake o **USA** (OR) 244-245 F 8
Alkamari o **RN** 198-199 E 6
Alkamergen, köli o **KZ** 124-125 K 3
Alkamergen, köli o **KZ** 124-125 K 3
al-Kamilīn o **SUD** 200-201 F 5
al-Karnak o·· **ET** 194-195 F 5
al-Kawa o **SUD** 200-201 F 6
al-Khandaq o **SUD** 200-201 E 3
Al Khums □ **LAR** 192-193 E 1
Al Khums ☆ **LAR** (Akm) 192-193 F 1
Alkmaar o·· **NL** 92-93 H 2
al-Koin o **SUD** 200-201 E 3
al-Kūbrī o **ET** 194-195 F 2
Al Kufayfiyah o **KSA** 130-131 J 5
Al Kufrah □ **LAR** 192-193 J 5
al-Kuntilla o **ET** 194-195 G 3
al-Kurru • **SUD** 200-201 E 3
Allada o **DY** 204-205 E 5
al-Lāḏiqīya ☆ **SYR** 128-129 F 5
Allagash o **USA** (ME) 278-279 M 1
Allagash Lake o **USA** (ME) 278-279 M 2
Allagash River ~ **USA** 278-279 M 2
Allagash Wilderness Waterway ⊥ **USA** (ME) 278-279 M 2
al-Lagowa o **SUD** 206-207 J 3
Allagudda o **IND** 140-141 H 3
Allahābād o• **IND** 142-143 B 3
Allāhgānj o **IND** 138-139 G 6
Allah-Jun' o **RUS** (SAH) 120-121 H 3
Allah-Jun' ~ **RUS** 120-121 F 3
Allahüekber Dağlan ▲ **TR** 128-129 K 2
al-Lāhūn ∴• **ET** 194-195 E 3
Allaiha ~ **RUS** 110-111 Z 5
Allakaket o **USA** 20-21 O 3
Allal-bou-Fenzi o **MA** 188-189 G 5
Allal-Tazi o **MA** 188-189 H 3
Allamoore o **USA** (TX) 266-267 C 2
Allan o **CDN** (SAS) 232-233 M 4
Allangouassou o **CI** 202-203 H 6
Allan Hills ▲ **CDN** 232-233 M 4
Allanmyo o **MYA** 142-143 J 6
Allanridge o **ZA** 220-221 H 3
Allan Water o **CDN** (ONT) 234-235 N 4
Allapalli o **IND** 142-143 B 6
Allāq, Bi'r o **LAR** 192-193 D 2
'Allāqī, Wādī l- ~ **ET** 194-195 F 6
Allard, Lac o **CDN** (QUE) 242-243 E 2

Ako'akas Rocks — Allard, Lac **295**

Ampang o RI 168 C 7
Ampangalana, Lakandrano ⟨ RM 222-223 F 8
Ampanihy o RM 222-223 D 10
Amparafaravola o RM 222-223 F 6
Amparai o CL 140-141 J 7
Amparihy Atsinanana o RM 222-223 F 9
Amparo o BR 72-73 G 7
Amparo, El o YV 60-61 F 4
Ampasamadinika o RM 222-223 F 7
Ampasimanolotra o RM 222-223 F 8
Ampasimbe o RM 222-223 F 6
Ampasinambo o RM 222-223 F 7
Ampatakamaroreny o RM 222-223 E 5
Ampato, Cordillera de ▲ PE 64-65 F 9
Ampato, Nevado ▲ PE 70-71 B 4
Ampefy o RM 222-223 E 7
Amper o WAN 204-205 H 4
Ampére Seamount ≃ 188-189 E 3
Amphithéâtre (El Jem) ··· TN 190-191 II 3
Amphlett Group ᴧ PNG 183 F 5
Ampibako o RI 164-165 G 4
Ampisikinana o RM 222-223 E 8
Ampiyacu, Rio ∿ PE 64-65 F 3
Amplawas o RI 166-167 E 6
Ampoa o RI 164-165 G 4
Ampombiantambo o RM 222-223 F 4
Ampondra o RM 222-223 F 4
Amputa ∿ RUS 114-115 O 3
Amqui o CDN (QUE) 240-241 H 2
'Amrān o Y 132-133 C 6
Amrâne, Bîr' o RIM 196-197 F 3
Amrävati o IND 138-139 F 5
Amreli o IND 138-139 C 9
Ämri o· PK 138-139 B 6
'Amrit o· SYR 128-129 F 5
Amritsar o· IND 138-139 E 4
Amroha o IND 138-139 G 5
Amsãga ⋆ RIM 196-197 C 5
Amsel o· DZ 190-191 J 9
Amsterdam o CDN (SAS) 232-233 X 3
Amsterdam ⋆★ NL 92-93 H 2
Amsterdam o USA (NY) 278-279 G 6
Amsterdam o ZA 220-221 K 3
Amsterdam, Ile ∿ F 12 F 8
Amstetten o A 92-93 N 4
Am Tanabo o TCH 198-199 H 6
Amu-Buharskij kanal ⟨ UZ 136-137 H 5
'Amūdā o IRQ 120-129 L 7
Amu-Dar'ja o TM 136-137 H 4
Amudarjo ∿ UZ 136-137 H 3
Amudat o EAU 212-213 E 3
Amukta Island ᴧ 22-23 L 6
Amukta Pass ≋ 22-23 L 6
Åmund Ringnes Island ᴧ CDN 24-25 X 1
Amundsen, Mount ▲ ARK 16 G 11
Amundsen Bay ≋ 16 G 5
Amundsen Glacier ⟨ ARK 16 E 0
Amundsen Gulf ≋ 24-25 J 5
Amundsen havet ≋ 16 G 26
Amundsen-Scott o ARK 16 F 0
Amungwiwa, Mount ▲ PNG 183 D 4
Amuntai o RI 164-165 D 5
Amur ∿ RUS 122-123 J 2
'Amūr, Wādi ∿ SUD 200-201 G 3
Amurang o RI 164-165 J 3
Amursk o RUS 122-123 K 3
Amurskie stolby · RUS 122-123 H 3
Amurskij liman ≋ 122-123 J 2
Amurko Zejzkaja ravnina ⥈ RUS 118-119 N 8
Amutu-Besar, Pulau ᴧ RI 166-167 G 3
Amyderya ∿ TM 136-137 H 5
Amyl ∿ RUS 116-117 F 9
Amzi, Oued Tin ∿ DZ 190-199 D 2
Amzi, Oued Ti-n ∿ RN 198-199 B 3
Am-Zoer o TCH 198-199 H 5
'Äna ⋆ IRQ 128-129 J 5
Ana, Cachoeira ∿ BR 62-63 F 5
Anabanua o RI 164-165 G 5
Anabar ∿ RUS 110-111 J 4
Anabarskij zaliv ≋ 110-111 J 3
Anabarskoe plato ▲ RUS 110-111 F 4
Anaborano o RM 222-223 F 4
Anacadiña o YV 60-61 J 5
Anaco o YV 60-61 J 3
Anacoco o USA (LA) 268-269 G 5
Anacoco, Bayou ∿ USA 268-269 G 6
Anaconda o USA (MT) 250-251 G 5
Anaconda-Pintler Wilderness ⊥ USA (MT) 250-251 F 5
Anacortes o USA (WA) 244-245 C 2
Anadarko o USA (OK) 264-265 F 3
Anadolu = Anatolia ⋆ 128-129 D 3
Anadyr' ⋆★ RUS (CUK) 112-113 T 4
Anadyr ∿ RUS 112-113 Q 3
Anadyr' o RUS 112-113 S 4
Anadyr' ∿ RUS 112-113 T 4
Anadyrskaja nizmennost' ∿ RUS 112-113 S 4
Anadyrskij liman ≋ 112-113 T 4
Anadyrskij zaliv ≋ 112-113 U 4
Anadyrskoe ploskogor'e ▲ RUS 112-113 P 3
Anadyrskoye Ploskogor'ye = Anadyrskoe ploskogor'e ▲ RUS 112-113 P 3
Anáfi ∿ GR 100-101 K 6
Anagni o· I 100-101 D 4
Anagua Island ᴧ PNG 183 F 6
Anaharãvi o GR 100-101 G 5
Anaheim o USA (CA) 248-249 G 6
Anahidrano o RM 222-223 F 5
Anahim Lake o CDN (BC) 228-229 J 4
Anahola o USA (HI) 288 F 2
Anáhuac o· MEX (CHA) 50-51 F 3
Anahuac o MEX (NL) 50-51 J 4
Anahuac o USA (TX) 268-269 F 4
Anahuac National Wildlife Refuge ⊥ USA (TX) 268-269 F 7

Anaimalai ∿ IND 140-141 G 5
Anai Mudi ▲ IND 140-141 G 5
Anaj o RUS 116-117 N 9
Anajás o BR 62-63 K 6
Anajatuba o BR 68-69 F 3
Anajé o BR 72-73 K 3
Anakalang o RI 168 D 7
Anakâpalle o IND 142-143 C 7
Anakchon o WSA 188-189 E 7
Anakdara o RI 164-165 G 5
Anakie o USA 178-179 J 2
Anaktuk o USA 20-21 L 1
Anaktuvuk Pass o USA 20-21 P 2
Anaktuvuk River ∿ USA 20-21 P 2
Analalava o RM 222-223 F 5
Analamaitso ▲ RM 222-223 F 6
Analampotsy, Farihy ≋ RM 222-223 F 7
Analavory o RM 222-223 E 7
Anamã o BR 66-67 G 4
Anamã, Igarapé do ∿ BR 66-67 G 4
Anamã, Lago o BR 66-67 G 4
Anama, ozero o RUS 116-117 Q 6
Ana Maria o BR 62-63 K 6
Ana María, Golfo de ≋ 54-55 F 4
Anambas, Kepulauan ∿ RI 162-163 F 3
Anambra ∿ WAN 204-205 G 4
Anambra, River ∿ WAN 204-205 G 5
Anamoose o USA (ND) 258-259 G 4
Anamu, Rio ∿ BR 62-63 F 5
Anamur ⋆ TR 128-129 E 4
Anamur Burnu ▲ TR 128-129 E 4
Anan o J 152-153 F 8
Ananás o BR 68-69 E 5
Ananás, Cachoeira ∿ BR 68-69 B 5
Ananda-Kouadiokro o CI 202-203 H 6
Anandpur o IND 142-143 E 5
Anan'evo o KS 146-147 C 4
Ananta, Lago o PE 70-71 B 4
Anantapur o IND 140-141 G 5
Anantnag o IND 138-139 E 3
Anantsono o RM 222-223 D 9
Anantsono, Helodrano ≋ 222-223 C 9
Anapka, zaliv ≋ 120-121 V 3
Anápolis o BR 72-73 F 4
Anapu, Rio ∿ BR 62-63 J 6
Anär o IR 134-135 F 3
Anárak o IR 134-135 E 2
Anárbár, Rüd-e ∿ IR 134-135 D 2
Anär Dare o AFG 134-135 J 2
Añarjärvi = Inari ≋ FIN 88-89 J 2
Añanjohka ∿ FIN 88-89 H 2
Anamitsog o GRØ 28-29 Q 6
Anastácio o BR 70-71 K 7
Anastácio, Rio ∿ BR 72-73 E 4
Anastasij, bunta ≋ 112-113 H 6
Anatolia = Anadolu ⋆ TR 128-129 D 3
Anatolikí Makedonía Kai Thráki ⋆ GR 100-101 K 4
Andróžanske vzdněhranilišče ⟨ KS 136-137 N 4
Andoain o E 98-99 F 3
Andoany o RM 222-223 F 4
Anaúá, Rio ∿ BR 62-63 G 5
Anáunethát Lake o CDN 30-31 H 5
Anaurilândia o BR 72-73 D 7
Anavga o RUS 120-121 S 5
Anavilhanas, Arquipélago das ᴧ BR 66-67 G 4
'Anaza Ruwäla ⥈ KSA 130-131 G 2
Anbâ Bišwi, Dair ∴ ET 194-195 E 2
Anbār, al- ⋆ IRQ 128-129 H 6
Anbyon o KOR 150-151 F 8
Anča ∿ RUS 120-121 H 3
An Cabhán = Cavan ⋆ IRL 90-91 D 5
An Caisleán Nua = Newcastle West o IRL 90-91 C 5
An Caol = Keel o IRL 90-91 B 4
Ancasti o del Alto, Sierra de ▲ RA 76-77 E 5
Ancenis o F 90-91 G 8
Ancha, Canal ≋ 80 C 4
Anchorage o USA 20-21 Q 6
Anchorena o RA 76-77 E 5
Ancien o RMM 196-197 K 4
Anciferova, ostrov ᴧ RUS 122-123 Q 3
Anclitas, Cayos ᴧ C 54-55 F 4
An Clochán = Clifden o· IRL 90-91 B 5
Anclote Keys ᴧ USA (FL) 286-287 G 5
An Cóbh = Cobh o IRL 90-91 C 6
Ancohuma, Nevado ▲ BOL 70-71 C 4
An Coiréan = Waterville o IRL 90-91 B 6
Ancon o PE 64-65 D 7
Ancon, Punta ▲ EC 64-65 B 3
Ancona o· I 100-101 D 3
Anconcito o EC 64-65 B 3
Ancuabe o MOC 218-219 H 3
Ancuaze o MOC 218-219 H 1
Ancud o RCH 78-79 C 6
Ancud, Golfo de ≋ 78-79 C 7
Anda o RCH 78-79 C 6
Andacollo o RCH 76-77 B 6
Andaga o WAN 204-205 H 4
Andahuaylas o PE 64-65 F 8
Andaii, Rio ∿ BR 62-63 F 6
An Daingean = Dingle o· IRL 90-91 B 6
Andaingo Gara o RM 222-223 F 6
Andakalaka o RM 222-223 E 5
Andale o USA (KS) 262-263 J 7
Andalgala o RA 76-77 E 5
Andalouses, Les o DZ 188-189 L 3
Åndalsnes ⋆ N 86-87 C 5
Andalucia ⋆ E 98-99 D 6
Andalusia o USA (AL) 284-285 D 5
Andalusia o USA (IL) 274-275 H 3
Andam, Wādi ∿ OM 132-133 L 3
Andaman and Nicobar Islands ∿ IND 140-141 L 4
Andaman Basin ≃ 158-159 C 5
Andaman Islands ᴧ IND 140-141 L 3
Andaman Sea ≋ 158-159 C 4

Andamarca o BOL 70-71 D 6
Andamooka Opal Fields o AUS 178-179 D 6
Andamooka Ranges ▲ AUS 178-179 D 6
Andapa o RM 222-223 F 5
Andapa o RM (IMA) 222-223 F 5
Andarab o AFG 138-139 L 7
Andaraí o BR 72-73 K 2
Andarma ∿ RUS 114-115 Q 5
Andavaka o RM 222-223 D 10
Andavake o RM 222-223 F 7
Andekie o USA 178-179 J 2
Ândeba Ye Midir Zerf Ch'af ▲ ER 200-201 K 5
Andelys, les o F 90-91 H 7
Andenes ⋆ N 86-87 H 2
Anderai o WAN 204-205 H 2
Ánderamboukane o RMM 196-197 M 4
Ânderdalen nasjonalpark ⊥ N 86-87 H 2
Andermatt o CH 92-93 K 5
Anderson, Salto ∿ RA 78-79 G 5
Anderson o USA (ASA) 222-223 F 5
Anderson o USA (MO) 276-277 A 4
Anderson o USA (IN) 274-275 N 4
Anderson o USA (TX) 268-269 E 6
Anderson Bay ≋ USA 264-265 K 5
Anderson Channel ≋ 36-37 R 3
Anderson Creek o USA 264-265 K 5
Anderson Gate o NAM 216-217 C 7
Anderson Island ᴧ CDN 36-37 U 6
Anderson Point ▲ CDN (NWT) 26-27 A 4
Anderson River ∿ CDN 20-21 a 2
Anderson River ∿ USA 274-275 M 6
Andersonville o USA (IN) 274-275 N 5
Andersonville National Historic Site · USA (GA) 284-285 F 5
Andes o CO 60-61 D 5
Andes = Andes, Cordillera de los ▲ 5 D 8
Andes, Cordillera de los ▲ 5 D 8
Andes, Los o RCH 78-79 D 2
Andfjorden ≋ 86-87 H 2
Andhøy o AFG 136-137 J 6
Andhra Pradesh ⋆ IND 140-141 H 2
Andijskoe Kojsu ∿ RUS 126-127 G 6
Andikithira ∿ GR 100-101 J 7
Andilamena o RM 222-223 F 6
Andimešk o· IR 134-135 C 2
Anding o VRC 156-157 F 6
Andino, Parque Nacional ⊥ RCH 78-79 C 6
Andiparos ∿ GR 100-101 K 6
Andira o BR 72-73 E 7
Andiru, Rio ∿ BR 66-67 D 5
Andirá, Rio ∿ BR 66-67 D 5
Andirlangar o VRC 144-145 D 2
Andižan o· UZ 136-137 M 4
Andižanskaja oblast' ⋆ UZ 136-137 M 4
Andižanskoe vodohranilišče ⟨ KS 136-137 N 4
Andoain o E 98-99 F 3
Andoany o RM 222-223 F 4
Andōas ∿ PE 64-65 D 3
Andohajango o RM 222-223 F 5
Andoi o RI 166-167 G 2
Andong o ROK 150-151 G 9
Androm o AUS 174-175 F 3
Andorinha o BR 68-69 J 7
Andorinha, Cachoeira do ∿ BR 66-67 F 7
Andørja ∿ N 86-87 H 2
Andorra ■ AND 98-99 H 3
Andorra La Vella ⋆ AND 98-99 H 3
Andorskaja grjada ▲ RUS 94-95 P 2
Andover o USA (ME) 278-279 L 4
Andover o USA (NH) 278-279 N 4
Andover o USA (OII) 200-201 Γ 2
Andover o USA (SD) 260-261 J 1
Andovoranto o RM 222-223 F 6
Andøya ∿ N 86-87 G 2
Andrada o ANG 216-217 F 3
Andradina o BR 72-73 E 6
Andrafainkona o RM 222-223 F 4
Andrafiabe o RM 222-223 F 4
Andraframena ▲ RM 222-223 E 5
Andranavory o RM 222-223 D 9
Andranomena o RM 222-223 E 7
Andranomitra o RM 222-223 D 8
Andranopasy o RM 222-223 D 8
Andranovondronina o RM 222-223 F 5
Andreafsky River ∿ USA 20-21 J 5
Andreanof Islands ᴧ USA 22-23 H 7
Andrecyk Lake o CDN 30-31 O 7
Andrée Land ⊥ GRØ 26-27 m 7
Andrée o N 84-85 J 3
Andreevka o KZ 124-125 M 6
Andreevka o RUS 96-97 G 7
Andreevskij, ozero o RUS 114-115 J 5
André Felix, Parc National ⊥ RCA 206-207 F 4
Andre Lake o CDN 36-37 R 7
Andrelândia o BR 72-73 H 6
Andrequicé o BR 76-77 B 6
Andréville o CDN (QUE) 240-241 F 3
Andrevo o RM 222-223 E 6
Andrew o CDN (ALB) 232-233 F 2
Andrew Gordon Bay ≋ 36-37 M 2
Andrew River ∿ CDN 30-31 O 6
Andrews o USA (NC) 282-283 D 3
Andrews o USA (SC) 284-285 G 2
Andrews o USA (TX) 264-265 B 6
Andria o· I 100-101 F 4
Andriamena o RM 222-223 E 6
Andriamena, Lavarie d' · RM 222-223 E 6
Andriba o RM 222-223 E 6
Andrieswille o ZA 220-221 G 6
Andujevica o YU 100-101 G 3
Andringitra ▲ RM 222-223 F 7
Andrjuškino o RUS 112-113 J 3
Androfiamena o RM 222-223 F 5
Androka o RM 222-223 D 10

Androna ⊥ RM 222-223 E 5
Andronica Island ᴧ USA 22-23 R 5
Andropov = Rybinsk o RUS 94-95 Q 2
Androranga ∿ RM 222-223 F 5
Andros o GR 100-101 K 6
Andros (ASA) 222-223 F 5
Androscoggin River ∿ USA 278-279 M 4
Andrába o BS 54-55 F 2
Andros Town o· BS 54-55 G 2
Androth Island ᴧ IND 140-141 F 4
Andry ∿ BR 62-63 J 7
Androy ⋆ RM 222-223 D 10
Andru River ∿ PNG 183 E 4
Andselv o N 86-87 J 2
Andudu o ZRE 212-213 D 2
Andújar o E 98-99 E 5
Andulo o ANG 216-217 D 5
Andylivan ∿ RUS 112-113 M 4
Anec, Lake o AUS 176-177 K 1
Anecón Chico, Cerro ▲ RA 78-79 D 6
Anecón Grande, Cerro ▲ RA 78-79 D 6
Anefis o RMM 196-197 L 5
Anegada o GB 56 C 2
Anegada o· BS 286-287 B 2
Anegada, Bahía ≋ 78-79 H 6
Anegada, Punta ▲ PA 52-53 D 8
Anegada Passage ≋ 56 C 2
Aného o RT 202-203 L 6
Anekal o IND 140-141 G 4
Anéker o RN 198-199 B 5
Añelo o RA 78-79 D 5
Anemounon ∴ TR 128-129 E 4
Anepahan o RP 160-161 C 8
Anepmete o PNG 183 F 4
Anerley o CDN (SAS) 232-233 L 4
Anesbaraka o DZ 198-199 B 3
Aneth o USA (UT) 254-255 F 6
Aneto, Pico de ▲ E 98-99 H 3
Anette Island ⊥ USA 32-33 M 4
Anette Island Indian Reservation ⅄ USA 32-33 E 4
Aney o RN 198-199 F 3
Anfeg, Oued ∿ DZ 190-191 E 9
Anfu o VRC 156-157 J 3
Anga, Bol'šaja ∿ RUS 116-117 M 6
Anga ∿ RUS 116-117 P 6
Anga ∿ RUS 116-117 L 9
Ang'angXi ∿ VRC 150-151 D 4
Angara ∿ RUS 116-117 N 6
Angarsk o RUS 116-117 L 7
Angas o BR 68-69 F 3
Angaston o AUS 180-181 E 3
Angatuba o BR 72-73 F 7
Angaur ᴧ 222-223 E 7
Angba o WAN 204-205 G 5
Angel, El o EC 64-65 D 5
Ángel de la Guarda, Isla ᴧ MEX 50-51 C 3
Angeles o RP 160-161 D 5
Angeles, Los o RCH 78-79 C 4
Angeles, Los o USA (TX) 266-267 H 5
Angeles, Port o USA (WA) 244-245 B 2
Ångelholm o S 86-87 F 8
Angélica o RA 76-77 G 6
Angelica o USA (WI) 270-271 K 6
Angelim o BR 68-69 K 6
Angelina River ∿ USA 268-269 G 5
Angellala Creek ∿ AUS 178-179 J 4
Angelo River ∿ AUS 176-177 D 1
Angels Camp o USA (CA) 246-247 E 5
Angel's Cove o CDN (NFL) 242-243 O 4
Angelus Oaks o USA (CA) 248-249 H 5
Angemuk, Gunung ▲ RI 166-167 K 3
Angerburg = Węgorzewo o PL 92-93 T 1
Angereb o ETH 200-201 H 6
Angereb Wenz ∿ ETH 200-201 H 6
Ångermanälven ∿ S 86-87 H 5
Ångermanland ⋆ S 86-87 H 5
Angermünde o D 92-93 N 2
Angers o F 90-91 G 8
Ångesån ∿ S 86-87 L 3
Angetu o ETH 208-209 E 3
Anggoami o RI 164-165 G 5
Anggoro o RI 164-165 G 5
Angical o BR 68-69 F 4
Angicos o BR 68-69 K 4
Angier o USA (NC) 282-283 J 5
Angijak Island ᴧ CDN 36-37 T 2
Angikuni Lake o CDN 30-31 U 4
Angira o PK 134-135 M 4
Angïre o IR 134-135 F 2
Angisoq = Loransatien o GRØ 28-29 S 7
Angkor Wat ··· K 158-159 H 4
Angle Inlet o USA (MN) 270-271 C 1
Anglem, Mount ▲ NZ 182 A 7
Anglemont o CDN (BC) 230-231 K 3
Anglesea o AUS 180-181 H 5
Anglesey ᴧ GB 90-91 E 5
Angleton o USA (TX) 268-269 E 6
Angliers o CDN (QUE) 236-237 J 5
Angmagssalik Fjord ≋ 28-29 W 4
Ango o ZRE 206-207 G 6
Angoche o MOC 218-219 H 3
Angôhrán o IR 134-135 G 4
Angol o RCH 78-79 C 4
Angola ■ ANG 216-217 C 5
Angola o USA (IN) 274-275 N 3

Angola Abyssal Plain = Namibia Abyssal Plain ≃ 6-7 K 11
Angola Basin ≃ 6-7 K 10
Angola Swamp o USA (NC) 282-283 K 5
Angolin o RM 142-143 J 1
Angóngó, Hánaïto de ▲ MOC 218-219 G 2
Angontsy, Tanjona ▲ RM 222-223 F 5
Angoon o USA 32-33 C 3
Angor o UZ 136-137 K 6
Angora o USA (NE) 262-263 C 3
Angostura, Presa de la ⟨ MEX (CHI) 52-53 H 3
Angostura, Presa de la ⟨ MEX (SON) 50-51 E 2
Angostura Reservoir ⟨ USA (SD) 260-261 E 3
Angoulême ★· F 90-91 H 9
Angpawing Bum ▲ MYA 142-143 J 3
Angra dos Reis o· BR 72-73 H 7
Angramios, Pulau ᴧ RI 166-167 H 3
Ang Thong Marine National Park ⊥ THA 158-159 E 6
Angu o ZRE 210-211 K 2
Anguang o VRC 154-155 J 2
Anguilla o GB 56 D 2
Anguilla o USA (MS) 268-269 K 3
Anguilla Cays ᴧ BS 54-55 F 3
Anguille, Cape ▲ CDN (NFL) 242-243 L 5
Anguille Mountains ▲ CDN 242-243 L 5
Anguman o AFG 136-137 M 7
Anguo o VRC 154-155 J 2
Anguran o IR 134-135 L 5
Angurugu o AUS 174-175 D 3
Angusko Point ▲ CDN 30-31 X 5
Angusville o CDN (MAN) 234-235 D 4
Angwa ∿ ZW 218-219 F 3
Anhai o VRC 156-157 K 6
Anhandui-Guaçu, Rio ∿ BR 76-77 K 3
Anholt ∿ DK 86-87 E 8
Anhua o VRC 156-157 G 4
Anhui □ VRC 154-155 K 5
Ani · TR 128-129 K 2
Aniak o USA 20-21 L 6
Aniakchak Crater ⟨ USA 22-23 R 4
Anakchak National Monument and Preserve ⊥ USA 22-23 S 4
Aniak River ∿ USA 20-21 M 2
Aniakshak Bay ≋ 22-23 R 4
Anibaré o CI 202-203 J 6
Ánibal Pinto, Lago o RCH 80 C 5
Anicuns o BR 72-73 F 4
Anié o RT 202-203 L 6
Anié, Pic d' ▲ F 90-91 G 10
Anie o RO 102-103 H 4
Anihovka o RUS 124-125 J 3
Anikino o RUS 118-119 K 9
An Iobhar = Newry o GB 90-91 D 4
Anil, Igarapé o ∿ BR 66-67 J 7
Animas o USA (NM) 256-257 G 7
Animas, Las o USA (CO) 262-263 D 6
Animas, Punta ▲ RCH 76-77 B 4
Animas, Quebrada de las ∿ RCH 76-77 R 4
Animas Peak ▲ USA (NM) 256-257 G 7
Animas River ∿ USA 254-255 H 6
Anina o RO 102-103 H 4
Aninaus Pass ≋ ZA 220-221 C 4
Anisij, mys ▲ RUS 110-111 W 1
Anita o USA (IA) 274-275 D 2
Anita Garibaldi o BR 74-75 E 6
Aniuk River ∿ USA 20-21 M 2
Aniva o RUS 122-123 K 5
Aniva, mys ▲ RUS 122-123 K 5
Anivorano Avaratra o RM 222-223 F 4
Aniwa o USA (WI) 270-271 J 6
Aniwa Island ∿ ∿ La Nina ∿ VAN 184 II b 4
Aniyo o J 152-153 G 7
Anjar o IND 138-139 C 8
Anji o VRC 154-155 L 6
Anjohibe o RM 222-223 E 5
Anjombony ∿ RM 222-223 E 5
Anjou ⋆ F 90-91 G 8
Anjozorobe o RM 222-223 E 7
Anju o KOR 150-151 E 8
Anjuj, Bol'šoj ∿ RUS 112-113 M 3
Anjuj, Malyj ∿ RUS 112-113 L 2
Anjujskij hrebet ▲ RUS 112-113 M 3
Anka o WAN 198-199 B 6
Ankaboa, Tanjona ▲ RM 222-223 C 8
Ankaimoro, Tombeaux · RM 222-223 E 6
Ankaizina ∿ RM 222-223 F 5
Ankalobe o RM 222-223 D 7
Ankang o VRC 154-155 F 5
Ankara ★· TR 128-129 E 3
Ankaramy o RM 222-223 E 5
Ankarana ⊥ RM 222-223 F 4
Ankasa National Park ⊥ GH 202-203 H 7
Ankatafa o RM 222-223 F 4
Ankavandra o RM 222-223 D 7
Ankavanibe o RM 222-223 E 5
Ankazoabo o RM 222-223 D 8
Ankazobe o RM 222-223 E 7
Ankazoroa o RM 222-223 E 6
Ankazomiriotra o RM 222-223 E 6
Ankazondandy o RM 222-223 E 7
Ankery o USA (IA) 274-275 E 3
Ankerika o IND 140-141 F 4
Ankhali o IND 140-141 F 4

Ankilizato o RM 222-223 D 8
Ankirihitra o RM 222-223 E 6
Anklam o D 92-93 M 2
Ankleshwar o IND 138-139 D 6
Ankli o IND 140-141 F 4
Ankober o ETH 208-209 D 3
Ankofrototsy o RM 222-223 D 7
Ankpa o WAN 204-205 G 4
An Láithreach = Laragh o· IRL 90-91 D 5
Anliu o VRC 154-155 J 2
Anliu o VRC 156-157 G 4
Anloga o GH 202-203 J 7
Ankola o RM 222-223 E 7
Ankoro o ZRE 214-215 D 4
Ankumen-gCearr = Mullingar o IRL 90-91 D 5
Anmyŏn Do ∿ ROK 150-151 F 9
Ann, Cape ▲ USA (MA) 278-279 L 4
Anna o RUS 102-103 M 2
Anna o USA (IL) 276-277 F 3
Anna o USA (MS) 268-269 J 5
Anna, Lake o USA (VA) 280-281 J 5
Anna, Lake o USA (VA) 280-281 K 5
Annaberg o PNG 183 C 2
Anna Bistrup, Kap ▲ GRØ 26-27 a 4
Annaheim o CDN (SAS) 232-233 O 3
Annaheim o CDN (SAS) 232-233 O 3
an-Nabl = Nabl o SYR 128-129 G 5
an-Nahl o ET 194-195 F 3
Anna Maria Island ∿ USA (FL) 286-287 G 4
Annandale o USA (MN) 270-271 D 5
Anna Plains o AUS 172-173 H 3
Annapolis ★· USA (MD) 280-281 K 5
Annapolis o USA (MO) 276-277 E 3
Annapolis Royal o CDN (NS) 240-241 K 6
Annapurna Himal ▲ NEP 144-145 D 6
Annapurna I ▲ NEP 144-145 D 6
Annapurna Sanctuary ⊥ NEP 144-145 D 6
Ann Arbor o USA (MI) 272-273 F 5
Anna Regina o GUY 62-63 H 2
Annaville o CDN (QUE) 238-239 N 2
Anne, Mount o AUS 180-181 J 7
Anne Marie o CDN (QUE) 238-239 N 2
Annecy o· F 90-91 L 9
Annecy, Lake o USA 176-177 E 3
Annen-gCearr = Mullingar o IRL 90-91 D 5
Annecieu Francis o PNG 183 C 2
Annenkov Island ᴧ GB 78-79 O 7
Annigeri o IND 140-141 F 3
an-Nil ⋆ ET 194-195 E 3
an-Nil ∿ SUD 200-201 G 3
Anning o VRC 156-157 C 4
Anniston o USA (AL) 284-285 E 3
Anniston Army Depot ×× USA (AL) 284-285 E 3
Annitowa o AUS 178-179 D 1
Annofiiyah o LAR 192-193 G 4
Annona o USA (TX) 264-265 H 4
Annonay o· F 90-91 K 9
Annotto Bay o JA 54-55 G 5
Annual o MA 188-189 K 3
an-Nugaym, Bi'r o SUD 200-201 G 3
An Nuqāt al Khams o LAR 192-193 D 1
Anola o CDN (MAN) 234-235 G 5
An Ómaigh = Omagh ★· GB 90-91 D 4
Año Nuevo, Seno ≋ 80 F 7
Año Nuevo Point ▲ USA (CA) 248-249 B 2
Anony, Farihy ≋ RM 222-223 E 10
Anor o BR 66-67 G 4
Anori o BR 66-67 G 4
Anorontany, Tanjona ▲ RM 222-223 F 4
Anosy ∿ RM 222-223 E 10
Anou-n-Bidek o DZ 198-199 B 3
an-Nugaym, Bi'r o SUD 200-201 G 3
Anpo Gang ∿ 156-157 F 6
Anping o VRC 154-155 K 6
Anqing o VRC 154-155 L 3
Anqiu o VRC 154-155 K 3
Anquincila o RA 76-77 E 5
Anranomavo ∿ RM 222-223 D 6
Anranomavo ∿ RM 222-223 D 6
Anriandampy ∿ RM 222-223 E 9
Ansai o VRC 154-155 F 3
Ansas o RI 166-167 G 3
Ansbach o· D 92-93 L 4
Anse-à-Galets o RH 54-55 J 5
Anse-à-Veau o RH 54-55 J 5
Anjozorobe o RM 222-223 E 7
Anse-Pleureuse o CDN (QUE) 242-243 J 2
Anserma o CO 60-61 D 5
Anse Rouge o RH 54-55 J 5
Anshan o VRC 150-151 D 7
Anshi o IND 140-141 F 3
Anshun o VRC 156-157 D 3
Ansitta, Cerro de ▲ RA 76-77 C 6
Ansitta, Cordillera de ▲ RA 76-77 C 6
Ankara ★· TR 128-129 E 3
Ankara ⋆ ROU 76-77 K 6
Ankarama, Tombeaux · RM 222-223 E 6
Anson Bay ≋ 172-173 J 2
Ansonga o RMM 196-197 M 4
Answer Downs o AUS 174-175 F 7
Anta o PE 64-65 F 9
Anta, Cachoeira da ∿ BR 66-67 J 7
Antakya = Hatay ⋆ TR 128-129 G 4
Antalya o TR 128-129 D 4
Antalya Körfezi ≋ 128-129 D 4
Antanambao Manampotsy o RM 222-223 F 7
Antananarivo ★ RM (ATN) 222-223 E 7
Antandrokomby o RM 222-223 F 7

Antanifotsy o RM 222-223 E 7
Antanimora Atsimo ★ RM 222-223 D 10
Antanjombolamena o RM 222-223 E 7
An tAonach = Nenagh o· IRL 90-91 C 5
Antar, Djebel ▲ DZ 188-189 L 4
Antarctica ⋆ AKK 16 F 28
Antarctic Bugt ≋ 26-27 s 3
Antarctic Peninsula ⋆ ARK 16 G 30
Antarctic Sound ≋ 16 G 31
Antares, Gunung ▲ RI 166-167 L 4
Antas o BR 68-69 J 5
Antécume Pata ∿ F 62-63 G 4
Antelope o CDN (SAS) 232-233 K 5
Antelope o USA (OR) 244-245 E 6
Antelope Island ᴧ USA (UT) 254-255 C 2
Antelope Lake o CDN (SAS) 232-233 K 5
Antelope Mine o ZW 218-219 E 5
Antelope Summit ▲ USA (NV) 246-247 K 4
Antelope Valley Indian Museum · USA (CA) 248-249 G 5
Antenor Navarro o BR 68-69 J 5
Antequera o E 98-99 E 6
Antequera o PY 76-77 J 3
Antero Junction o USA (CO) 254-255 K 5
Antetezampandrana o RM 222-223 F 6
Anthony o USA (KS) 262-263 H 7
Anthony o USA (TX) 256-257 A 2
Anthony Island ∿ ··· CDN (BC) 228-229 C 4
Anthony Lagoon o AUS 174-175 C 5
Anti Atlas ▲ MA 188-189 G 5
Anticosti, Île d' ᴧ CDN (QUE) 242-243 E 3
Antiga Lagoa da Rabeca o BR 70-71 H 4
Antigo o USA (WI) 270-271 J 5
Antigonish o CDN (NS) 240-241 N 5
Antigua o MEX 52-53 F 2
Antigua, Salina la ∿ RA 76-77 F 5
Antigua and Barbuda ■ AG 56 E 3
Antigua Guatemala ··· GCA 52-53 J 4
Antigua Cauce del Río Bermejo ∿ RA 76-77 H 2
Antiguo Morelos o MEX 50-51 K 6
Antilla o C 54-55 H 4
Antimari, Rio ∿ BR 66-67 C 7
An Ti-m-Missaou o DZ 196-197 M 4
Antimonán o RP 160-161 D 6
Antimony o USA (UT) 254-255 D 5
Antinaotajoha ∿ RUS 108-100 R 7
An tInbhear Mór = Arklow o· IRL 90-91 D 5
Antingola o RI 164-165 H 3
Antioch o USA (NE) 262-263 D 2
Antioquia □ CO 60-61 D 5
Antipajuta o RUS 108-109 R 7
Antipodes Islands ᴧ NZ 13 J 7
Antisana, Volcán ▲ EC 64-65 D 5
Ántissa o GR 100-101 K 5
an tiúr = Newry o GB 90-91 D 4
Antiwinfo o GH 202-203 J 7
Antler o CDN (SAS) 232-233 R 6
Antlers o USA (OK) 264-265 J 4
Antofagasta ⋆ RCH 76-77 D 4
Antofagasta de la Sierra o RA 76-77 D 4
Antofalla, Salar de o RA 76-77 D 4
Antofalla, Volcán ▲ RA 76-77 D 3
Antoinette Bay ≋ 26-27 L 3
Anton o USA (TX) 264-265 M 4
Antongila, Helodrano ≋ 222-223 F 5
Antongomena-Bevary o RM 222-223 E 6
Antonibé o RM 222-223 E 5
Antonina o BR (CEA) 68-69 J 4
Antonina o BR (PAR) 74-75 F 5
Antonio de Biedma o RA 80 G 3
António Dias o BR 72-73 J 7
Antônio Gonçalves o BR 68-69 H 7
António João o BR 76-77 K 2
António Martins o BR 68-69 J 5
Antônio Prado o BR 74-75 E 7
Antonio Varas, Península o RCH 80 D 5
Antonito o USA (CO) 254-255 J 6
Antón Lizardo o MEX 52-53 F 2
Antracyt o UA 102-103 L 3
Antrim ⋆ GB 90-91 D 4
Antrim Mountains ▲ GB 90-91 D 4
Antsahabe o RM 222-223 F 4
Antsahampano o RM 222-223 F 4
Antsakabary o RM 222-223 F 5
Antsakanalabe o RM 222-223 E 6
Antsalova o RM 222-223 D 7
Antsambalahy o RM 222-223 F 5
Antsaravibe o RM 222-223 E 4
Antsatramidola o RM 222-223 E 6
Antsiafabositra o RM 222-223 E 6
Antsianitia o RM 222-223 E 5
Antsirabato o RM 222-223 F 5
Antsirabe o RM 222-223 E 7
Antsirabe Afovoany o RM 222-223 F 5
Antsirabe Avaratra o RM 222-223 F 4
Antsiranana ⋆ RM (ASA) 222-223 F 4
Antsla o EST 94-95 K 3
Antsoha o RM 222-223 F 5
Antsohihy o RM 222-223 E 5
Antsohimbondrona o RM 222-223 F 4
Antsondrodava o RM 222-223 D 7
Antu o VRC 150-151 G 6
Antuco o RCH 78-79 D 4
Antucu, Volcán ▲ RCH 78-79 D 4
Antufaš ∿ Y 132-133 C 6
Antwerpen ★· B 90-91 J 3
Antykan o RUS 120-121 F 6
An Uaimh = Navan o· IRL 90-91 D 5
Anuajito, El o MEX 50-51 G 5
Anučino o RUS 122-123 E 7
Añueque, Sierra ▲ RA 78-79 E 6
Anugul o IND 142-143 D 5

Anuj ~ **RUS** 124-125 O 2
Anum o **GH** 202-203 L 6
Anumma, River ~ **WAN** 204-205 J 3
Anūpgarh o **IND** 138-139 D 5
Anūpshahr o **IND** 138-139 G 5
Anuradhapura o··· **CL** 140-141 J 6
Anvak Island ⌒ **USA** 22-23 P 5
Anvers = Antwerpen ☆·· **B** 92-93 H 3
Anvers, Île ⌒ **ARK** 16 G 30
Anvik o **USA** 20-21 K 5
Anvik River ~ **USA** 20-21 K 5
Anxi o **VRC** (GAN) 146-147 M 5
Anxi o **VRC** (JXI) 156-157 J 2
An Xian o **VRC** 154-155 D 6
Anxious Bay ≈ 180-181 C 2
Anyang o **ROK** 150-151 F 9
Anyang o **VRC** 154-155 J 3
A'nyêmaqên Shan ▲ **VRC** 144-145 M 3
Anyer-Kidul o **RI** 168 A 3
Anyinam o **GH** 202-203 K 6
Anyirawase o **GH** 202-203 L 6
Anykščiai ☆·· **LT** 94-95 J 4
Anyuan o **VRC** 156-157 J 4
Anyue o **VRC** 154-155 D 6
Anza-Borrego Desert State Park ⊥ **USA** (CA) 248-249 H 6
Anzac o **CDN** 32-33 P 3
Anzalī, Bandar-e o· **IR** 128-129 N 4
Anze o **VRC** 154-155 H 3
Anžero-Sudžensk o **RUS** 114-115 T 6
Anzerskij, ostrov ⌒ **RUS** 88-89 O 4
Anzhero Sudzhensk = Anžero-Sudžensk o **RUS** 114-115 T 6
Anzi o **ZRE** 210-211 J 4
Ánzio o **I** 100-101 D 4
Anzoategui o **CO** 60-61 D 5
Anzob o **TJ** 136-137 L 5
Anzob, pereval ▲ **TJ** 136-137 L 5
Anžu, mys ▲ **RUS** 110-111 V 2
Anžu, ostrova ⌒ **RUS** 110-111 U 2
Aoba, Île = Obe ⌒ **VAN** 184 II a 2
Aoba/ Maewo □ **VAN** 184 II b 2
Ao Ban Don ≈ 158-159 E 6
Aodanga o **TCH** 198-199 H 4
Aohan Qi o **VRC** 148-149 O 6
'Aoînât ez Zbil o **RIM** 196-197 F 6
Aoiz o **E** 98-99 G 3
Aoke = Auki ☆ **SOL** 184 I e 3
Aola = Tenaghau o **SOL** 184 I e 3
Aomen = Macao ☆·· **P** 156-157 H 5
Aomori o **J** 152-153 J 4
Aonia o **USA** (GA) 284-285 H 3
Ao Phangnga National Park ⊥ **THA** 158-159 E 6
Aore ⌒ **VAN** 184 II a 2
Ao Sawi ≈ 158-159 E 5
Aosta o **I** 100-101 A 2
Aosta, Valle d' = Vallé d'Aoste □ **I** 100-101 A 2
Aoste, Vallée d' = Valle d'Aosta □ **I** 100-101 A 2
Ao Trat ≈ 158-159 G 4
Aouara o **F** 62-63 H 3
Aoudaghost ∴· **RIM** 196-197 E 6
Aoudech o **RIM** 196-197 C 6
Aouderas o **RN** 198-199 D 4
Aoufirst · **WSA** 196-197 C 2
Aougoundou, Lac ⊖ **RMM** 202-203 J 2
Aouhinet bel Egra o **DZ** 188-189 H 7
Aouînat Sarrag o **RIM** 196-197 D 5
Aouk, Bahr ~ **TCH** 206-207 D 4
Aoukalé ~ **TCH** 206-207 E 3
Aouk-Aoukale, Réserve de faune de l' ⊥ **RCA** 206-207 F 4
Aoukâr ∸ **RIM** 196-197 E 5
Aoukâr ∸ **RMM** 196-197 H 3
Aoulef o **DZ** 190-191 C 7
Aoulime, Ibel ▲ **MA** 188-189 G 5
Aoulouz o **MA** 188-189 G 5
Aourir n' Ouassel ▲ **MA** 188-189 H 5
Aourou o **RMM** 202-203 E 2
Aousard o **WSA** 196-197 C 3
Aozi o **TCH** 198-199 J 2
Aozou o· **TCH** 198-199 H 2
Apa, Cachoeira ~ **PY** 76-77 J 2
Apa, Río ~ **PY** 76-77 J 2
Apača o **RUS** 122-123 R 2
Apache o **USA** (AZ) 256-257 F 7
Apache o **USA** (OK) 264-265 F 4
Apache Creek o **USA** (NM) 256-257 G 5
Apache Junction o **USA** (AZ) 256-257 D 5
Apache Lake o **USA** (AZ) 256-257 D 5
Apache Mountains ▲ **USA** (TX) 266-267 C 2
Apacheta Cruz Grande ▲ **BOL** 76-77 E 1
Apaikwa o **GUY** 62-63 D 2
Apakapur ~ **RUS** 114-115 O 3
Apalachee o **USA** (GA) 284-285 G 3
Apalachee Bay ≈ 286-287 E 2
Apalachee River ~ **USA** 284-285 G 3
Apalachicola o **USA** (FL) 286-287 E 2
Apalachicola Bay ≈ 286-287 D 2
Apalachicola River ~ **USA** 286-287 D 1
Apan o **MEX** 52-53 E 2
Apapel'gino o **RUS** 112-113 Q 2
Apaporis, Río ~ **CO** 66-67 B 3
Aparados da Serra ▲ **BR** 74-75 E 7
Aparados da Serra, Parque Nacional ⊥·· **BR** 74-75 E 7
Aparecida d'Oeste o **BR** 72-73 E 6
Aparecida do Tabuado o **BR** 72-73 E 6
Aparri o **RP** 160-161 D 3
Apastovo ☆ **RUS** 96-97 F 6
Apatana o **RI** 168 E 6
Apatity o **RUS** 88-89 M 3
Apatou o **F** 62-63 G 3
Apatzingán de la Constitución o **MEX** 52-53 C 2
Apauwar o **RI** (IRJ) 166-167 K 2
Apauwar ~ **RI** 166-167 K 3
Apawanza o **ZRE** 212-213 B 3
Apaxtla de Castrejón o **MEX** 52-53 E 2
Ape o **LV** 94-95 K 3
Apediá, Rio ~ **BR** 70-71 G 3
Apeldoorn o· **NL** 92-93 H 2
Apeleg, Arroyo ~ **RA** 80 E 2
Apennines = Appennini ▲ **I** 100-101 B 2
Apere, Río ~ **BOL** 70-71 E 4
Apesokubi o **GH** 202-203 L 6
Apetina = Puleowine o **SME** 62-63 G 4
Apeú, Ilha ⌒ **BR** 68-69 E 2
Apex o **USA** (NC) 282-283 J 5
Apex Mountain ▲ **CDN** 20-21 V 5
Aphrodisias ·· **TR** 128-129 C 4
Api ▲ **NEP** 144-145 C 5
Api o **ZRE** 210-211 K 2
Api, Gunung ▲ **RI** 168 D 7
Api, Tanjung □ **RI** 162-163 H 4
Apia o **CO** 60-61 D 5
Āpia ★ **WS** 184 V b 1
Apiacás o **BR** 66-67 J 7
Apiaí o **BR** 74-75 F 5
Apinaco, Cachoeira ~ **BR** 70-71 K 2
Apiñacoccha, Lago ⊖ **PE** 64-65 F 9
Apinajes o **BR** 68-69 D 4
Apio o **SOL** 184 I e 3
Apishapa River ~ **USA** 254-255 L 6
Apitpac o **MEX** 52-53 H 3
Aplahoué o **DY** 202-203 L 6
Aplao o **PE** 70-71 A 5
Apo, Mount ▲ **RP** 160-161 F 9
Apódaca o **MEX** 50-51 J 5
Apodi o **BR** 68-69 K 4
Apodi, Chapada do ▲ **BR** 68-69 J 4
Apodi, Rio ~ **BR** 68-69 J 4
Apo East Pass ≈ 160-161 D 6
Apoko o **RCB** 210-211 E 4
Apolima Strait ≈ 184 V a 1
Apolinario Saravia o **RA** 76-77 F 3
Apollo Bay o **AUS** 180-181 G 5
Apollonia = Sūsah o·· **LAR** 192-193 J 1
Apolo o **BOL** 70-71 C 4
Apolu o **WAN** 204-205 F 4
Apopa o **ES** 52-53 K 5
Apopka o **USA** (FL) 286-287 H 3
Apopka, Lake ⊖ **USA** (FL) 286-287 H 3
Apoquitaua, Rio ~ **BR** 66-67 J 5
Aporá o **BR** 68-69 J 7
Aporé, Rio ~ **BR** 72-73 E 5
Apo Reef National Park ⊥ **RP** 160-161 D 6
Aporema o **BR** 62-63 J 5
Apostle Islands National Lakeshore ⊥ **USA** (WI) 270-271 H 3
Apostoles Andreas, Cape ▲ **TR** 128-129 F 5
Apostolove o **UA** 102-103 H 4
Apoteri o **GUY** 62-63 E 3
Appam o **USA** (ND) 258-259 D 3
Appat ⌒ **GRØ** 26-27 Z 8
Appé Grande, Ilha ⌒ **RA** 76-77 J 4
Appelton City o **USA** (MO) 274-275 D 6
Appennino Abruzzese ▲ **I** 100-101 D 3
Apple Creek ~ **USA** 274-275 H 5
Applegate o **USA** (OR) 244-245 B 8
Applegrove o **CDN** (BC) 230-231 L 4
Apple River o **CDN** (NS) 240-241 L 5
Apple Springs o **USA** (TX) 268-269 F 5
Appleton o· **JA** 54-55 G 5
Appleton o **USA** (MN) 270-271 B 5
Appleton o **USA** (WI) 270-271 K 6
Appleton City o **USA** (MO) 274-275 E 6
Apple Valley o **USA** (CA) 248-249 G 5
Appomattox o **USA** (VA) 280-281 H 6
Appomattox Court House National Historic Park · **USA** (VA) 280-281 H 6
Appomattox River o **USA** (VA) 280-281 H 6
Approuague ~ **F** 62-63 H 4
Apraksin Bor o **RUS** 94-95 M 2
Apreľsk o **RUS** 118-119 G 6
Apricena o **I** 100-101 E 4
Aprília o **I** 100-101 D 4
April River ~ **PNG** 183 B 3
Aprompronou o **CI** 202-203 J 6
Apšeronsk o **RUS** 126-127 C 5
Apšeronskij poluostrov ⌒ **AZ** 128-129 N 2
Apsley o **CDN** (ONT) 238-239 G 4
Apsley River ~ **AUS** 178-179 L 6
Apsley Strait ≈ 172-173 K 1
Apt o **F** 90-91 K 10
Aptos o **USA** (CA) 248-249 C 3
Apu ~ **RI** 166-167 D 3
Apucarana o **BR** 72-73 E 7
Apuí o **BR** (AMA) 66-67 E 3
Apuí o **BR** (AMA) 66-67 H 6
Apuka o **RUS** (KOR) 112-113 P 6
Apuka ~ **RUS** 112-113 Q 6
Apukskij hrebet ▲ **RUS** 112-113 Q 6
Apura o **SME** 62-63 F 3
Apurahuan o **RP** 160-161 C 8
Apure o **CO** 60-61 D 3
Apure, Río ~ **YV** 60-61 F 4
Apurimac, Río ~ **PE** 64-65 F 8
Apurinã, Área Indígena X **BR** 66-67 F 5
Apurinã Peneri, Área Indígena X **BR** 66-67 D 7
Apurito o **YV** 60-61 G 4
Apurlec · **PE** 64-65 C 5
Apuseni, Munții ▲ **RO** 102-103 C 4
'Aqaba ☆ **JOR** 130-131 D 3
Aqaba, Gulf of = al-'Aqaba, Ḫalīǧ ≈ 194-195 G 3
Āqā Bābā o **IR** 128-129 N 4
Āqče o **AFG** 136-137 K 6
'Aqdā o **IR** 134-135 E 2
'Aqiq o **SUD** 200-201 J 3
'Aqīq, al- o **KSA** 132-133 B 3
'Aqīq, Wādī al- ~ **KSA** 130-131 G 5
Aqisserniaq o **GRØ** 28-29 O 3
Aqitag ▲ **VRC** 146-147 K 5
Āq Kand o **IR** 128-129 N 4
Āq Koprūk o **AFG** 136-137 K 6
Āq Qal'e o **IR** 136-137 D 6
Aqqan o **VRC** 144-145 E 2
Aqqikkol Hu ⊖ **VRC** 144-145 G 2
'Aqra ☆ **IRQ** 128-129 K 4
Āq Şū ~ **IRQ** 128-129 L 5
Aqtaū = Aktau ☆ **KZ** 126-127 J 6
Aqtöbe = Aktöbe ☆ **KZ** 126-127 M 2
Aqua Caliente Indian Reservation X **USA** (CA) 248-249 H 6
Aquacanta, Raudal ~ **YV** 60-61 K 4
Aquadell o **CDN** (SAS) 232-233 M 5
Aquadeo Beach o **CDN** (SAS) 232-233 K 2
Água Fria, Ribeiro ~ **BR** 68-69 D 6
Aquanga o **USA** (CA) 248-249 H 6
Água Quente, Rio ~ **BR** 68-69 F 6
Aquatuk River ~ **CDN** 34-35 O 3
Aquidabán, Río ~ **PY** 76-77 J 2
Aquidauana o **BR** 70-71 K 7
Aquidauana, Rio ~ **BR** 70-71 J 6
Aquijes, Los o **PE** 64-65 E 9
Aquila o **MEX** 52-53 C 2
Aquilla Creek ~ **USA** 266-267 K 2
Aquin o **RH** 54-55 J 5
Aquiqui, Ilhas do ⌒ **BR** 62-63 H 6
Aquitaine □ **F** 90-91 G 10
Ara o **IND** 142-143 D 3
'Arab ~ **SUD** 200-201 G 4
Arab o **USA** (AL) 284-285 D 2
'Arab, 'Ain al- o **SYR** 128-129 H 4
'Araba, Wādī ~ **ET** 194-195 F 3
'Araba, Wādī l- ~ **JOR** 130-131 D 2
'Arabābād o **IR** 134-135 G 2
Araban ☆ **TR** 128-129 G 4
Arabati o **ETH** 208-209 D 3
Arabats'ka zatoka ≈ 102-103 J 5
Arabela o **USA** (NM) 256-257 K 5
Arabi o **USA** (GA) 284-285 G 5
Arabian Basin ≃ 12 E 3
Arabian Oryx Sanctuary ⊥··· **OM** 132-133 K 4
Arabian Peninsula ∸ **KSA** 10-11 C 6
Arabian Sea ≈ 12 E 3
Arabīya, al- ⌒ **KSA** 134-135 D 5
Arabopó o **YV** 62-63 D 3
Arabos, Los o **C** 54-55 E 3
Arabou o **RMM** 196-197 L 5
Araç ☆ **TR** 128-129 E 2
Araca o **BOL** 70-71 D 5
Aracá, Área Indígena X **BR** 62-63 D 4
Araçá, Rio ~ **BR** 66-67 F 2
Aracai, Cachoeira do ~ **BR** 68-69 C 3
Aracaju ☆· **BR** 68-69 K 7
Aracati o **BR** 68-69 K 4
Aracatu o **BR** 72-73 K 3
Araçatuba o **BR** (MAT) 70-71 K 3
Araçatuba o **BR** (PAU) 72-73 E 6
Araceli o **RP** 160-161 C 7
Aracena o **E** 98-99 D 6
Araci o **BR** 68-69 J 7
Araçu, Rio ~ **BR** 66-67 H 5
Araçuaí o **BR** 72-73 J 4
Araçuaí, Rio ~ **BR** 72-73 J 4
'Arad o **IL** 130-131 D 2
Arad ☆· **RO** 102-103 B 4
Arad, Tel ∴· **IL** 130-131 D 2
Arada o **TCH** 198-199 K 5
'Arāḍa o **UAE** 132-133 H 2
Ārādān o **IR** 136-137 C 7
Aradan o **RUS** 116-117 F 9
Arados o **MEX** 50-51 F 3
Arafura, Laut ≈ 166-167 G 6
Arafura Sea ≈ 166-167 G 6
Arafura Shelf ≃ 13 E 4
Aragac o **AR** 128-129 K 2
Aragac, gora ▲ **AR** 128-129 L 2
Arage o **WAN** 204-205 H 4
Araghene, Anou- o **RN** 198-199 C 4
Aragoiânia o **BR** 72-73 F 4
Aragón □ **E** 98-99 G 4
Aragon o **USA** (NM) 256-257 G 5
Aragón, Río ~ **E** 98-99 G 3
Araguacema o **BR** 68-69 D 6
Araguaçu o **BR** 72-73 F 2
Araguaçui o **BR** 68-69 D 6
Aragua de Barcelona o **YV** 60-61 J 3
Aragua de Maturín o **YV** 60-61 K 3
Araguaia, Parque Indígena X **YV** 68-69 C 7
Araguaia, Parque Nacional do X **BR** 68-69 C 7
Araguaia, Rio ~ **BR** 68-69 D 5
Araguaiana o **BR** 72-73 E 3
Araguaimujo, Caño ~ **YV** 60-61 L 3
Araguaína o **BR** 68-69 D 5
Araguanã o **BR** 68-69 D 5
Araguari o **BR** 72-73 F 5
Araguari, Rio ~ **BR** 62-63 J 5
Araguari, Rio ~ **BR** 72-73 F 5
Araguatins o **BR** 68-69 D 4
Arahal o **E** 98-99 E 6
Arai o **BR** 72-73 G 2
Arai o **J** 152-153 H 6
Araias do Araguaia, Rio das ~ **BR** 68-69 C 6
Araioses o **BR** 68-69 H 3
Araju o **BR** 66-67 G 4
Arak o **DZ** 190-191 D 8
Arāk ☆· **IR** 134-135 C 1
Arakaka o **GUY** 62-63 D 2
Arakamčečen, ostrov ⌒ **RUS** 112-113 Y 4
Arakan Yoma = Ragaing Yōma ▲ **MYA** 142-143 J 6
Arakawa o **J** 152-153 H 5
Arakawa-gawa ~ **J** 152-153 H 5
Araklı ☆ **TR** 128-129 J 2
Arak's ~ **AR** 128-129 L 2
Aral o **KS** 146-147 B 5
Aral ☆ **KZ** 126-127 O 4
Ara Lake ⊖ **CDN** (ONT) 234-235 Q 4
Aralık ☆ **TR** 128-129 L 3
Aral karakūmy ⌣ **KZ** 126-127 P 4
Aralköl o **KZ** 124-125 C 3
Aralkūm o **KZ** 126-127 P 4
Aral Moreira o **BR** 76-77 K 2
Aral Sea ⊖ 126-127 N 5
Aral'sk ☆ **KZ** 126-127 O 4
Aralsor, köl ⊖ **KZ** (ZPK) 96-97 F 9
Aralsor, köl ⊖ **KZ** (ZPK) 96-97 H 9
Aralsul'fat o **KZ** 126-127 O 4
Araltöbe o **KZ** 96-97 H 8
Aramac o **AUS** 178-179 H 2
Aramaca, Ilha ⌒ **BR** 66-67 C 5
Arame o **BR** 68-69 E 4
Aramia River ~ **PNG** 183 B 4
Aramil' o **RUS** 96-97 M 5
Ārān o **IR** 134-135 D 1
Arancay o **PE** 64-65 D 6
Aranda de Duero o **E** 98-99 F 4
Arandai o **RI** 166-167 G 3
Arandas o **MEX** 52-53 C 1
Arandis o **NAM** 216-217 C 11
Arani o **BOL** 70-71 E 5
Ārani o **IND** 140-141 H 4
Aran Islands ⌒· **IRL** 90-91 C 5
Aranjuez o **E** 98-99 F 4
Aranos o **NAM** 220-221 D 2
Aransas Bay ≈ 266-267 K 6
Aransas National Wildlife Refuge ⊥ **USA** (TX) 266-267 L 5
Aransas Pass o **USA** (TX) 266-267 K 6
Aransas River ~ **USA** 266-267 K 5
Arantangi o **IND** 140-141 H 5
Arantes, Ribeiro ~ **BR** 72-73 E 5
Aranyaprathet o **THA** 158-159 G 4
Araouane o **RMM** 196-197 J 5
Aráoz o **RA** 76-77 E 4
Arapa o **PE** 70-71 B 4
Arapa, Lago de ⊖ **PE** 70-71 B 4
Arapahoe o **USA** (NE) 262-263 G 4
Arapari o **BR** (AMA) 66-67 D 4
Arapari o **BR** (P) 68-69 D 4
Arapey Grande, Río ~ **ROU** 76-77 J 6
Arapho o **USA** (OK) 264-265 F 3
Arapicos o **EC** 64-65 D 2
Arapiraca o **BR** 68-69 K 6
Arapiri, Ilha do ⌒ **BR** 66-67 K 4
Arapiuns, Rio ~ **BR** 66-67 K 4
Arapixi o **BR** 66-67 C 7
Arapixuna o **BR** 66-67 K 4
Arapkir ☆ **TR** 128-129 H 3
Arapongas o **BR** 72-73 E 7
Arapunya o **AUS** 178-179 C 2
Araputanga o **BR** 70-71 H 4
Araquaia, Rio ~ **BR** 68-69 D 6
'Ar'ar ☆ **KSA** 130-131 G 2
'Ar'ar, Wādī ~ **KSA** 130-131 G 2
Arara, Área Indígena X **BR** 66-67 K 5
Arara, Paraná ~ **BR** 66-67 G 4
Araracuara o **CO** 64-65 F 2
Arara Igarapé Humaitá, Área Indígena X **BR** 64-65 F 6
Araranguá o **BR** 74-75 F 7
Ararapira o **BR** 74-75 F 5
Araraquara o **BR** 72-73 F 6
Araras o **BR** (P) 66-67 K 6
Araras o **BR** (PAU) 72-73 G 7
Araras, Cachoeira ~ **BR** 66-67 K 6
Araras, Ilha das ⌒ **BR** 66-67 G 5
Araras, Serra das ▲ **BR** 70-71 J 4
Ararat o **AR** 128-129 L 3
Ararat o **AUS** 180-181 G 4
Ararat o **BR** 68-69 H 3
Ararenda o **BR** 68-69 H 4
Arari o **BR** 68-69 F 3
Araria o **IND** 142-143 E 2
Araribóa, Área Indígena X **BR** 68-69 E 4
Araripe o **BR** 68-69 H 5
Araripe, Chapada do ▲ **BR** 68-69 H 5
Araripina o **BR** 68-69 H 5
Araruama o **BR** 72-73 J 7
Araruama, Lagoa ⊖ **BR** 72-73 J 7
Aras, Rūd-e ~ **IR** 128-129 M 3
Arasālu o **IND** 140-141 F 4
Aras Nehri ~ **TR** 128-129 K 2
Aras Nehri ~ **TR** 128-129 J 3
Aratabiteri o **YV** 66-67 E 2
Aratale o **ER** 200-201 K 5
Araṭâne o **RIM** 196-197 F 5
Ara Terra o **ETH** 208-209 E 5
Arati o **BR** 66-67 F 3
Araticu, Rio ~ **BR** 68-69 D 3
Araua, Rio ~ **BR** 66-67 E 7
Arauá, Rio ~ **BR** 66-67 G 6
Arauá, Rio ~ **BR** 66-67 E 5
Arauca ☆ **CO** 60-61 F 4
Arauca, Río ~ **YV** 60-61 H 4
Araucária o **BR** 74-75 F 5
Arauco o **RCH** 78-79 C 4
Arauco, Golfo de ≈ 78-79 C 4
Araure o **YV** 60-61 G 3
'Arava, ha ∸ **IL** 130-131 D 2
Aravaipa o **USA** (AZ) 256-257 E 6
Aravaipa Creek ~ **USA** 256-257 E 6
Aravan o **KS** 136-137 N 4
Aravete o **EST** 94-95 J 2
Arawa ☆ **PNG** 184 I b 2
Arawale National Reserve ⊥ **EAK** 212-213 H 4
Arawe Islands ⌒ **PNG** 183 E 4
Araweté Igarapé Ipixuna, Área Indígena X **BR** 68-69 B 4
Araxá o **BR** 72-73 G 5
Araya o **YV** 60-61 J 2
Araya, Península de ⌣ **YV** 60-61 J 2
Arayé, Wādī ~ **TCH** 192-193 G 6
Araz ~ **AZ** 128-129 N 3
Arazraz, Oued ~ **DZ** 190-191 E 9
Arbadin o **SP** 212-213 J 3
Arbakwe o **WAN** 198-199 B 6
Arba Minch ☆ **ETH** 208-209 C 6
'Arbat o **IRQ** 128-129 L 5
Árbatax o· **I** 100-101 B 5
Arbaṭ Dāġ ▲ **IR** 128-129 M 4
Arbau o **RI** 166-167 F 4
Arbi ~ **RUS** 118-119 N 9
Arbīl □ **IRQ** 128-129 K 4
Arbīl ☆ **IRQ** (ARB) 128-129 L 4
Arboga ☆· **S** 86-87 G 7
Arbolé o **BF** 202-203 J 3
Arboledas o **CO** 60-61 E 4
Arboledas o **RA** 78-79 J 4
Arboletes o **CO** 60-61 C 3
Arbor o **ZA** 220-221 J 3
Arborfield o **CDN** (SAS) 232-233 P 2
Arborg o **CDN** (MAN) 234-235 F 4
Arboutchatak o **TCH** 198-199 H 6
Arbre du Ténéré · **RN** 198-199 D 4
Arbroath o **GB** 90-91 F 3
Arbuckle o **USA** (CA) 246-247 C 4
Arbutla ~ **RUS** 120-121 Q 3
Arc, Des o **USA** (AR) 276-277 D 6
Arcabuco o **CO** 60-61 E 5
Arcachon o **F** 90-91 G 9
Arcade o **USA** (NY) 278-279 C 6
Arcadia o **USA** (FL) 286-287 H 4
Arcadia o **USA** (IA) 274-275 C 2
Arcadia o **USA** (LA) 268-269 H 4
Arcadia o **USA** (MI) 272-273 C 3
Arcadia o **USA** (NE) 262-263 G 3
Arcadia o **USA** (WI) 270-271 G 6
Arčagly-Ajat ~ **RUS** 124-125 B 2
Arcahaie o **RH** 54-55 J 5
Arcaly ~ **KZ** 124-125 F 2
Arcángelo, Monte ▲ **I** 100-101 E 4
Arcas, Quebradas de ~ **RCH** 76-77 C 1
Arcata o **USA** (CA) 246-247 A 3
Arcelia o **MEX** 52-53 D 2
Arc-et-Senans o··· **F** 90-91 K 8
Arch o **USA** (NM) 256-257 M 4
Arch Cape o **USA** (OR) 244-245 B 5
Archdale o **USA** (NC) 282-283 H 5
Archer o **USA** (FL) 286-287 G 2
Archer Bay ≈ 174-175 F 3
Archer Bend National Park ⊥ **AUS** 174-175 G 3
Archer City o **USA** (TX) 264-265 F 5
Archer Fiord ≈ 26-27 Q 3
Archer River ~ **AUS** 174-175 F 3
Archer's Post o **EAK** 212-213 F 3
Archerwill o **CDN** (SAS) 232-233 P 3
Arches National Park ⊥ **USA** (UT) 254-255 F 5
Archie o **USA** (LA) 268-269 J 5
Archipel-de-Mingan, Réserve de Parc Nacional de L' ⊥ **CDN** (QUE) 242-243 E 2
Archipiélago de las Guaitecas, Parque Nacional ⊥ **RCH** 80 C 2
Archipiélago los Roques, Parque Nacional ⊥·· **YV** 60-61 H 2
Archydal o **CDN** (SAS) 232-233 N 5
Arckaringa o **AUS** 178-179 C 4
Arckaringa Creek ~ **AUS** 178-179 C 4
Arčman o **TM** 136-137 E 5
Arco o **USA** (ID) 252-253 E 3
Arco, El o **MEX** 50-51 C 3
Arcola o **CDN** (SAS) 232-233 Q 6
Arcola o **USA** (IL) 274-275 K 5
Arcola o **USA** (TX) 268-269 E 7
Arcos o **BR** 72-73 H 6
Arcos de la Frontera o **E** 98-99 E 6
Arcoverde o **BR** 68-69 K 6
Arctic Bay o **CDN** 24-25 d 4
Arctic Circle Hot Springs · **USA** 20-21 S 4
Arctic Harbour ≈ 28-29 G 2
Arctic Institute Range ▲ **ARK** 16 F 16
Arctic Ocean ≈ 16 B 33
Arctic Red River ~ **CDN** 20-21 Z 4
Arcturus o **ZW** 218-219 F 3
Arcyz ☆ **UA** 102-103 F 5
Ardabīl o· **IR** 128-129 N 3
Ardahan o· **TR** 128-129 K 2
Ardakan o **IR** 134-135 D 3
Ardakān o **IR** 134-135 E 2
Ardal o **IR** 134-135 D 3
Ardanuç o **TR** 128-129 K 2
Ardath o **CDN** (SAS) 232-233 L 4
Ardatov o **RUS** 94-95 S 4
Ardavidu o **IND** 140-141 H 3
Ardbeg o **CDN** (ONT) 238-239 E 3
Ardébé, Ati o **TCH** 198-199 H 6
Ardee = Baile Átha Fhirdhia o **IRL** 90-91 D 5
Ardémi o **TCH** 198-199 L 5
Arden o **USA** (TX) 266-267 G 2
Arden o **USA** (WA) 244-245 H 2
Arden, Mount ▲ **AUS** 180-181 D 2
Ardencaple Fjord ≈ 26-27 p 6
Ardennes ▲ **B** 92-93 H 4
Ardenode o **CDN** (ALB) 232-233 E 4
Ardenvoir o **USA** (WA) 244-245 E 3
Ardeşen ☆ **TR** 128-129 J 2
Ardestān o· **IR** 134-135 E 2
Ardila, Ribeira de ~ **P** 98-99 D 5
Ardila, Río ~ **E** 98-99 D 5
Ardiles o **RA** 76-77 E 4
Ardill o **CDN** (SAS) 232-233 N 6
Ardilla, Cerro La ▲ **MEX** 50-51 H 6
Ardīṭ o **OM** 132-133 H 5
Ardlethan o **AUS** 180-181 J 3
Ard Mhacha = Armagh ☆· **GB** 90-91 D 4
Ardmore o **AUS** 178-179 E 1
Ardmore o **USA** (AL) 284-285 D 2
Ardmore o **USA** (OK) 264-265 G 4
Ardmore o **USA** (SD) 260-261 C 3
Ardon o **RUS** 126-127 F 6
Ardon ~ **RUS** 126-127 F 6
Ardrossan o **AUS** 180-181 D 3
Ardrossan o **CDN** (ALB) 232-233 E 2
Ardrossan o **GB** 90-91 E 4
Åre o· **S** 86-87 F 5
Arebi o **ZRE** 212-213 B 2
Arecibo o **USA** (PR) 286-287 P 2
Areco, Río ~ **RA** 78-79 K 3
Aredo o **RI** 166-167 G 3
Aregičinski, mys ▲ **RUS** 120-121 Q 3
Areia, Cachoeira d' ~ **BR** 68-69 F 6
Areia, Ribeira da ~ **BR** 72-73 H 3
Areia Branca o **BR** 68-69 K 4
Arelee o **CDN** (SAS) 232-233 L 3
Arena, Isla ⌒ **MEX** 50-51 C 4
Arena, La o **RCH** 78-79 C 6
Arena, Point o **USA** (CA) 246-247 B 5
Arena, Point ▲ **USA** (CA) 246-247 B 5
Arenal, Volcán ▲ **CR** 52-53 B 6
Arenales o **RCH** 76-77 D 2
Arenales, Cerro ▲ **RCH** 80 D 3
Arena Point ▲ **RP** 160-161 E 6
Arenápolis o **BR** 70-71 J 4
Arenas o **PA** 52-53 D 8
Arenas, Punta ▲ **RCH** 76-77 B 1
Arenas, Punta de ▲ **RA** 80 F 6
Arendal ☆ **N** 86-87 D 7
Arenillas o **EC** 64-65 B 3
Arenosa o **PA** 52-53 E 7
Areo o **YV** 60-61 K 3
Areópoli o **GR** 100-101 J 6
Areōs, Área Indígena X **BR** 72-73 D 3
Arequipa ☆· **PE** 70-71 B 5
Ārēro o **ETH** 208-209 D 6
Arestruz, Pampa del ∸ **RCH** 76-77 C 1
Arévalo o **E** 98-99 E 4
Āreza o **ER** 200-201 J 5
Arezzo o **I** 100-101 C 3
Arfersiorfik ≈ 28-29 O 2
'Arǧa o **KSA** 130-131 J 5
Argada ~ **RUS** 118-119 E 8
Argadargada o **AUS** 178-179 D 1
Argahtah o **RUS** 110-111 d 5
Argajas ☆ **RUS** 96-97 M 6
Arga-Jurjah ~ **RUS** 110-111 S 5
Arga Jurjah ~ **RUS** 110-111 c 5
Argalant o **MAU** 148-149 G 4
Argalastí o **GR** 100-101 J 5
Arga-Muora-Sise, ostrov ⌒ **RUS** 110-111 P 3
Argan o **VRC** 146-147 J 5
Arganda o **E** 98-99 F 4
Arġandāb, Daryā-ye ~ **AFG** 134-135 M 2
Arġandāb, Daryā-ye ~ **AFG** 134-135 L 3
Argao o **RP** 160-161 E 8
Argas o **RUS** 118-119 N 4
Arga Sala ~ **RUS** 110-111 H 5
Arga-Sala ~ **RUS** 116-117 M 2
Arga-Tjung ~ **RUS** 110-111 K 6
Argaybulak Daban ▲ **VRC** 146-147 J 4
Argazinskoe vodohranilišče < **RUS** 96-97 M 6
Argedeb o **ETH** 208-209 E 5
Argelia o **CO** 60-61 C 6
Argent, Côte d' ⌣ **F** 90-91 G 10
Argenta o **I** 100-101 C 2
Argentan o **F** 90-91 G 7
Argentia o **CDN** (NFL) 242-243 P 5
Argentina o **RA** 76-77 F 5
Argentina ■ **RA** 78-79 E 4
Argentina, La o **CO** 60-61 C 6
Argentina, Laguna la ⊖ **RA** 78-79 L 4
Argentina Rise ≃ 6-7 D 13
Argentine Abyssal Plain ≃ 6-7 D 13
Argentine Basin ≃ 6-7 D 13
Argentine Islands o **ARK** 16 G 30
Argentino, Lago ⊖ **RA** 80 D 5
Argentino, Mar ≈ 5 E 10
Argentino, Paso ▲ **RA** 78-79 E 2
Argenton-sur-Creuse o **F** 90-91 H 8
Argeş ~ **RO** 102-103 E 5
Arġestān o **AFG** 134-135 M 3
Arġestān Rūd ~ **AFG** 134-135 M 3
Argi ~ **RUS** 120-121 C 6
Argo o **USA** (LA) 268-269 J 5
Argoim o **BR** 72-73 L 2
Argolão, Cachoeira do ~ **BR** 66-67 K 4
Argolikos Kólpos ≈ 100-101 J 6
Argonne o **USA** (WI) 270-271 K 5
Argopyro, Gunung ▲ **RI** 168 E 3
Árgos o· **GR** 100-101 J 6
Argos o **USA** (IN) 274-275 M 3
Árgos Orestikó o **GR** 100-101 H 4
Argostóli o **GR** 100-101 H 5
Arguello, Point ▲ **USA** (CA) 248-249 D 5
Arguelo Canyon ≃ 248-249 C 5
Argun o **RUS** (CEC) 126-127 F 6
Argun' ~ **RUS** 118-119 K 9
Argun ~ **RUS** 126-127 F 6
Argungu o **WAN** 198-199 B 6
Arguut o **MAU** 148-149 F 5
Arguvan ☆ **TR** 128-129 H 3
Arguyartu Point ▲ **CDN** 28-29 G 2
Argyle o **CDN** (MAN) 234-235 F 4
Argyle o **USA** (WI) 274-275 J 2
Argyle, Lake ⊖ **AUS** 172-173 J 4
Arhangaj □ **MAU** 148-149 D 4
Arhangel'sk ☆ **RUS** 88-89 Q 4
Arhangel'skoe ☆ **RUS** 96-97 K 6
Arhanzel'skaja Guba o **RUS** 108-109 H 4
Arhara o **RUS** (AMR) 122-123 D 4
Arhara ~ **RUS** 122-123 D 4
Arhavi o **TR** 128-129 J 2
arheologičeskij zapovednik Tanais · **RUS** 102-103 L 4
Arhipelag Sedova ⌒ **RUS** 108-109 I Y 2
Arhipovka o **RUS** 94-95 M 4
Ar Horqin Qi o **VRC** 150-151 C 6
Århus o **DK** 86-87 E 8
Ariadnoe o **RUS** 122-123 F 6
Ariake-kai ≈ 152-153 D 8
Ariamsvlei o **NAM** 220-221 D 4
Ariano Irpino o **I** 100-101 E 4
Ariari, Río ~ **CO** 60-61 E 6
Aria River ~ **PNG** 183 E 3
Arias o **RA** 78-79 H 2
Ari Atoll ⌒ **MV** 140-141 B 6
Aribinda o· **BF** 202-203 K 2
Arica o **RCH** 70-71 B 6
Aricapampa o **PE** 64-65 D 5
Aricaria o **BR** 68-69 B 3
Arichat o **CDN** (NS) 240-241 O 5
Arichuna o **YV** 60-61 H 4
Aricota, Lago ⊖ **PE** 70-71 B 5
Arid, Cape ▲ **AUS** 176-177 G 7
Arida o **J** 152-153 F 7
'Ariḍa o **OM** 132-133 H 5
Āriḍa, al- o **KSA** 132-133 C 5
Aridéa o **GR** 100-101 J 4
Ariège ~ **F** 90-91 H 10
Ariel o **RA** 78-79 K 4
Ārifwāla o **PK** 138-139 D 4
Arig gol ~ **MAU** 148-149 E 2
Arihāl ☆·· **AUT** 130-131 D 2
Arihanha, Rio ~ **BR** 72-73 D 4
Arikaree River ~ **USA** 254-255 N 4
Arikawa o **J** 152-153 C 8
Arikok Nationaal Park ⊥ **ARU** 60-61 G 1
Arima o· **TT** 60-61 L 2
Arimo o **USA** (ID) 252-253 F 4
Arimu Mine o **GUY** 62-63 E 2
Arinos o **BR** 72-73 G 3
Arinos, Rio ~ **BR** 70-71 J 3
Ariogala o **LT** 94-95 H 4
Aripeka o **USA** (FL) 286-287 G 3
Ariporo, Río ~ **CO** 60-61 F 4
Aripuanã o **BR** 66-67 H 7
Aripuanã, Área Indígena X **BR** 70-71 H 2
Aripuanã, Parque Indígena X **BR** 70-71 G 2
Aripuanã, Rio ~ **BR** 66-67 G 5
Ariquemes o **BR** 66-67 F 7
Ariranha o **BR** 66-67 H 5
Aris o **NAM** 216-217 D 11
'Ariš, Wādī l- ~ **ET** 194-195 F 3
Arismendi o **YV** 60-61 G 3
Arissa o **ETH** 208-209 E 3
Aristazabal Island ⌒ **CDN** (BC) 228-229 E 4
Aristizábal, Cabo ▲ **RA** 80 G 2
Aristoménis o **GR** 100-101 H 6
Aritao o **RP** 160-161 D 4
Arite o **SOL** 184 I e 4
Ariton o **USA** (AL) 284-285 E 5
Arivaca o **USA** (AZ) 256-257 D 7
Arivaca Junction o **USA** (AZ) 256-257 D 7
Arivonimamo o **RM** 222-223 E 7
Ariyadka o **IND** 140-141 F 4
Ariyalur o **IND** 140-141 H 5
Ariza o **E** 98-99 F 4
Arizaro, Salar de ⊖ **RA** 76-77 D 3
Arizona o **AUS** (QLD) 174-175 F 6
Arizona o **AUS** (QLD) 178-179 F 1
Arizona o **CDN** (MAN) 234-235 E 5
Arizona □ **USA** 256-257 B 3
Arizona City o **USA** (AZ) 256-257 D 6
Arizpe o **MEX** 50-51 D 2
Årjäng ☆ **S** 86-87 F 7
Arjawinangun o **RI** 168 C 3
Arjeplog o **S** 86-87 H 3
Ārjo o **ETH** 208-209 C 4
Arjona o **CO** 60-61 D 2
Arjuna, Gunung ▲ **RI** 168 E 3
Arjuni o **IND** 142-143 B 5
Arka o **RUS** (HBR) 120-121 K 3
Arka ~ **RUS** 120-121 J 3
Arkabutla Lake < **USA** (MS) 268-269 K 2
Arkadak o **RUS** 102-103 N 2
Arkadelphia o **USA** (AR) 276-277 B 6
Arkalgūd o **IND** 140-141 G 4
Arkalyk ☆ **KZ** 124-125 E 3
Arkansas □ **USA** 276-277 B 6
Arkansas City o **USA** (AR) 276-277 D 7
Arkansas City o **USA** (KS) 262-263 K 7
Arkansas Post National Memorial · **USA** (AR) 276-277 D 6
Arkansas River ~ **USA** 254-255 J 4
Arkansas River ~ **USA** 262-263 E 7
Arkansas River ~ **USA** 264-265 J 3
Arkansas River ~ **USA** 276-277 D 6
Arka-Pojlovajaha ~ **RUS** 108-109 Q 8
Arkaroola Village o **AUS** 178-179 E 6
Arka-Tab"jaha ~ **RUS** 108-109 Q 8
Arkatag ▲ **VRC** 144-145 F 2
Arkell, Mount ▲ **CDN** 20-21 X 6
Arkhangel'sk = Arhangel'sk ☆ **RUS** 88-89 Q 4
Arklow = An tInbhear Mór o **IRL** 90-91 D 5
Arknu, Jabal ▲ **LAR** 192-193 L 6
Arkona, Kap ▲· **D** 92-93 M 1
Arkonam o **IND** 140-141 H 4
Arktičeskij, mys ▲ **RUS** 108-109 I b 1
Arktičeskogo instituta, ostrova ⌒ **RUS** 108-109 T 4
Arktik Hoyland ∸ **GRØ** 26-27 R 5
Arlal o **RMM** 196-197 J 6
Arlan, gora ▲ **TM** 136-137 D 5
Arlanza, Río ~ **E** 98-99 F 3
Arlanzón o **E** 98-99 F 3
Arlanzón, Río ~ **E** 98-99 E 3
Arlee o **USA** (MT) 250-251 E 4
Arles o··· **F** 90-91 K 10
Arli o **BF** 202-203 L 4
Arli, Parc National de l' ⊥ **BF** 202-203 L 4
Arli, Réserve de l' ⊥ **BF** 202-203 L 4
Arlington o **USA** (AZ) 256-257 C 5
Arlington o **USA** (GA) 284-285 F 5
Arlington o **USA** (KS) 262-263 H 7
Arlington o **USA** (NE) 262-263 K 3
Arlington o **USA** (OH) 280-281 C 3
Arlington o **USA** (OR) 244-245 E 5
Arlington o **USA** (SD) 260-261 J 2
Arlington o **USA** (TN) 276-277 F 5
Arlington o **USA** (TX) 264-265 G 6
Arlington o **USA** (VA) 280-281 J 5
Arlington o **USA** (VT) 278-279 H 5
Arlington o **USA** (WA) 244-245 C 2
Arlington o **ZA** 220-221 H 4
Arlit o **RN** 198-199 C 3
Arlon ☆· **B** 92-93 H 4
Arltunga o **AUS** 178-179 C 2
'Armā' ▲ **KSA** 130-131 K 5
Arma o **USA** (KS) 262-263 M 7
Armacão dos Búzios o **BR** 72-73 K 7
Armagh ☆· **GB** 90-91 D 4
Armagnac ∸ **F** 90-91 H 10
Arma Konda ▲ **IND** 142-143 C 6
Arman' o **RUS** (MAG) 120-121 O 4
Arman' ~ **RUS** 120-121 O 3
Armanda o **BR** 74-75 D 8
Armando Bermúdes, Parque Nacional ⊥ **DOM** 54-55 K 5
Armant o· **ET** 194-195 F 5
Armark Lake ⊖ **CDN** 30-31 T 2
Armark River ~ **CDN** 30-31 T 2
Armas, Las o **RA** 78-79 L 4
Armavir o **RUS** 126-127 D 5
Armavir o **RUS** (STV) 102-103 M 5
Armenia ☆ **CO** 60-61 D 5
Armenia = Armenija ∸ 128-129 J 3
Armenia = Armenija ■ **AR** 128-129 L 2
Armería o **MEX** 52-53 C 2
Armero o **CO** 60-61 D 5
Armidale o **AUS** 178-179 L 6
Armil Lake ⊖ **CDN** 30-31 Y 3
Arminavallen = Saut la Moitie ~ **SME** 62-63 G 3
Arminto o **USA** (WY) 252-253 L 3
Armit o **CDN** (SAS) 232-233 R 3
Armitidž, poluostrov ⌣ **RUS** 84-85 a 2
Armit Range ▲ **PNG** 183 C 4
Armjans'k o **UA** 102-103 H 4
Armley o **CDN** (SAS) 232-233 O 2
Armour o **USA** (SD) 260-261 H 3
Armraynald o **AUS** 174-175 E 5

298 **Anuj — Armraynald**

Arm River ~ CDN 232-233 N 5
Armstrong o CDN (BC) 230-231 K 3
Armstrong o CDN (ONT) 234-235 O 4
Armstrong o CDN (QUE) 240-241 E 5
Armstrong o USA (IA) 274-275 D 1
Armstrong o USA (IL) 274-275 L 4
Armstrong o USA (TX) 266-267 K 7
Armstrong Creek o USA (WI) 270-271 K 5
Armstrong River ~ AUS 172-173 K 4
Ārmūr o IND 138-139 G 10
Arnaud o CDN (MAN) 234-235 F 5
Arnaud (Payne), Rivière ~ CDN 36-37 O 4
Arnaudville o USA (LA) 268-269 J 6
Arnedo o E 98-99 F 3
Arneiroz o BR 68-69 H 5
Arneson o CDN (ALB) 232-233 H 4
Arnett o USA (OK) 264-265 E 2
Arnhem ☆• NL 92-93 H 2
Arnhem, Cape ▲ AUS 174-175 D 3
Arnhem Aboriginal Land ⊥ AUS 174-175 B 3
Arnhem Bay ≈ 174-175 D 3
Arnhem Highway II AUS 172-173 K 2
Arnhem Land ⊥ AUS 174-175 B 3
Arno ~ I 100-101 C 3
Arno Bay o AUS 180-181 D 2
Arnold o USA (CA) 246-247 E 5
Arnold o USA (MI) 270-271 L 4
Arnold o USA (MO) 274-275 H 6
Arnold o USA (NE) 262-263 F 3
Arnold River ~ AUS 174-175 C 5
Arnoldsburg o USA (WV) 280-281 E 5
Arnold's Cove o CDN (NFL) 242-243 P 5
Arnott Strait ≈ 24-25 U 2
Arnøy ⌒ N 86-87 K 1
Arnprior o CDN (ONT) 238-239 J 3
Arnsberg o• D 92-93 K 3
Arnstadt o• D 92-93 L 3
Arntfield o CDN (QUE) 236-237 J 4
Aro, Río ~ YV 60-61 J 4
Aroa o YV 60-61 G 2
Aroab o NAM 220-221 D 3
Arochuku o WAN 204-205 G 6
Aroeiras o BR 68-69 L 5
Arokam, Oued ~ DZ 190-191 G 9
Aroland o CDN (ONT) 236-237 B 2
Arolik River ~ USA 22-23 Q 3
Aroma o PNG 183 E 6
Aroma o RCH 70-71 C 6
Aroma o SUD 200-201 H 5
Aroma, Quebrada de ~ RCH 70-71 C 6
Aroona o AUS 178-179 E 6
Aroostook River ~ USA 278-279 N 2
Aropa o PNG 184 I b 2
Aropuk Lake ⬭ USA 20-21 H 6
Arorae ⌒ KIB 13 J 3
Arowy ⌒ RP 100-101 F 0
Aro Usu, Tanjung ▲ RI 166-167 F 6
Arpa Çayı ~ TR 128-129 K 2
Arpajon o F 90-91 J 7
Arpangasia ~ BD 142-143 F 4
Arpin o CDN (ONT) 236-237 H 4
Arpoador, Ponta do ▲ BR 74-75 G 5
Arq. T. Romero Pereira o PY 76-77 K 4
Arqū o SUD 200-201 E 3
Arque, Río ~ BOL 70-71 D 5
Arra ~ PK 134-135 L 5
Ar-Rachidia ☆ MA 188-189 J 5
ar-Radd, Wādī ~ SYR 128-129 J 4
ar-Radiyya Bahri o ET 194-195 F 5
ar-Rafid o SYR 128-129 F 6
Arraga o RA 76-77 E 5
Arrah o CI 202-203 J 6
ar-Rahad o SUD (Sku) 200-201 E 6
ar-Rahad ~ SUD 200-201 G 6
Arraial do Cabo o BR 72-73 J 7
Arraias o BR (MAR) 68-69 E 4
Arraias o BR (TOC) 72-73 G 2
Arraias, Rio ~ BR 70-71 K 2
Arraida o OM 132-133 J 5
Arran o CDN (SAS) 232-233 R 4
Arran ⌒ GB 90-91 E 4
Arrandale o CDN (BC) 228-229 E 2
ar-Rank o SUD 206-207 L 3
Arras o CDN 32-33 K 4
Arras ☆• F 90-91 J 6
Ar Rashidiyah = Ar Rachidia ☆ MA 188-189 J 5
ar-Rauḍa o ET 194-195 E 4
ar-Rawdah = Ranya o KSA 132-133 C 3
ar-Rawdah, Sabhat ⬭ SYR 128-129 J 5
ar-Rawgal o SUD 200-201 G 3
Arrecife o• E 188-189 E 6
Arrecife Edinburgh ⌒ NIC 54-55 D 7
Arrecifes o RA 78-79 J 3
Arrecifes, Río ~ RA 78-79 J 3
Arrecifes de la Media Luna ⌒ NIC 54-55 D 7
Arreti o PA 52-53 F 8
Arrey o USA (NM) 256-257 H 6
Arriaga o• MEX 52-53 H 3
Arrias, Los o RA 76-77 F 6
Arriba o USA (CO) 254-255 M 4
Ar-Ribāt ☆•• MA 188-189 H 4
Arrieros, Quebrada de los ~ RCH 76-77 C 2
Ar-Rif ▲ MA 188-189 J 3
Arrigetch Peaks ▲ USA 20-21 N 3
Arrigui, Lac • RN 198-199 F 3
Ar-Riyāḍ ☆•• KSA 130-131 K 5
ar-Rizqa o ET 194-195 F 4
Arroio dos Ratos o BR 74-75 E 8
Arroio Grande o BR 74-75 D 9
Arrojado, Rio ~ BR 72-73 H 2
Arrojolândia o BR 72-73 H 2
Arrowhead, Lake < USA (TX) 264-265 F 5
Arrowhead Lodge o USA (WY) 252-253 L 2
Arrowhead River ~ CDN 30-31 H 5
Arrowie o AUS 178-179 E 6
Arrow River o CDN (MAN) 234-235 C 4
Arrow Rock o USA (MO) 274-275 F 5
Arrowrock Reservoir ⬭ USA (ID) 252-253 C 3
Arrow Rock State Historic Site ∴ USA (MO) 274-275 F 5
Arrowsmith, Mount ▲ CDN (BC) 230-231 F 4
Arrowsmith River ~ CDN 30-31 Y 2
Arrowwood o CDN (ALB) 232-233 E 5
Arrowwood Lake ⬭ USA (ND) 258-259 J 4
Arroyito o RA (COD) 76-77 F 6
Arroyito o RA (MEN) 78-79 F 2
Arroyo Acambuco ~ RA 76-77 F 2
Arroyo Batelito ~ RA 76-77 H 5
Arroyo Bueno o C 54-55 H 4
Arroyo de la Iglesia ~ RA 76-77 C 6
Arroyo de la Ventana o RA 78-79 F 6
Arroyo de los Huesos o RA 78-79 K 4
Arroyo El Asustado ~ RA 76-77 G 4
Arroyo Grande o USA (CA) 248-249 D 4
Arroyo Hondo o USA (NM) 256-257 K 2
Arroyo Ituyuro ~ RA 76-77 F 2
Arroyo Santa Rita ~ RA 76-77 E 2
Arroyos de Mantua o C 54-55 C 3
Arroyos Esteros o PY 76-77 J 3
Arroyo Teuquito ~ RA 76-77 G 3
Arrozal o YV 60-61 K 3
ar-Ru'at o SUD 200-201 F 6
Arrufó o RA 76-77 G 6
ar-Ruṣayriṣ o SUD 208-209 B 3
Arsameia • TR 128-129 H 4
Aršan o RUS 116-117 J 9
Arsen'ev o RUS 122-123 E 6
Arsenğān o IR 134-135 E 4
Arsent'evka o RUS 122-123 K 5
Ārsī ■ ETH 208-209 D 5
Arsikeri o IND 140-141 G 4
Arsk ☆ RUS 96-97 F 5
Arso o RI 166-167 L 3
Arsuk o GRØ 28-29 Q 6
Arta o DJI 208-209 F 3
Árta o GR 100-101 H 5
Artas o USA (SD) 260-261 G 1
Artašat o AR 128-129 L 3
Artawi, al- o KSA 130-131 J 5
Artāwiya, al- o KSA 130-131 J 4
Arteaga o MEX (COA) 50-51 J 5
Arteaga o MEX (MIC) 52-53 C 2
Arteaga o RA 78-79 J 2
Artem o RUS 122-123 E 7
Artemisa o C 54-55 D 3
Artemivs'k o UA 102-103 L 3
Artem-Ostrov o AZ 128-129 O 2
Artemou o RIM 196-197 D 7
Artëmovsk o RUS 116-117 F 8
Artemovsk = Artemivs'k o UA 102-103 L 3
Artëmovskij ☆ RUS 96-97 M 5
Artesia o USA (NM) 256-257 L 6
Artesian o USA (SD) 260-261 J 2
Artesian Bore Baths • AUS 178-179 K 5
Artesia Wells o USA (TX) 266-267 H 5
Artezian o RUS 126-127 G 5
Arthur o CDN (ONT) 238-239 E 5
Arthur o USA (ND) 258-259 K 4
Arthur o USA (NE) 262-263 E 3
Arthur City o USA (TX) 264-265 J 5
Arthurette o CDN (NB) 240-241 H 4
Arthur Point ▲ AUS 178-179 L 2
Arthur River o AUS 176-177 D 6
Arthur's Pass o NZ 182 C 5
Arthur's Pass ▲ NZ 182 C 5
Arthur's Pass National Park ⊥ NZ 182 C 5
Arthur's Town o BS 54-55 H 2
Arti ☆ RUS 96-97 L 5
Artic o USA (OR) 244-245 B 4
Artic National Wildlife Refuge ⊥ USA 20-21 R 2
Artic Red River ~ CDN 20-21 Y 3
Artic Village o USA 20-21 S 2
Artigas ☆ ROU 76-77 J 6
Artik o AR 128-129 K 2
Artillery Lake ⬭ CDN 30-31 Q 4
Artjugina ~ RUS 114-115 T 3
Artland o CDN (SAS) 232-233 J 3
Artois ⊥ F 90-91 H 6
Artur, ostrov ⌒ RUS 84-85 b 2
Arturo Prat o ARK 16 G 30
Artux o VRC 146-147 C 6
Artvin ☆ TR 128-129 J 2
Artybaš o RUS 124-125 P 3
Artyk o RUS (SAH) 110-111 Z 7
Artyk ~ RUS 110-111 a 7
Artyk o TM 136-137 F 6
Artyšta o RUS 124-125 P 1
Aru o BR (AMA) 66-67 D 2
Aru o BR (P) 68-69 D 3
Aru o IND 138-139 E 2
Aru o ZRE 212-213 C 2
Aru, Kepulauan ⌒ RI 166-167 H 5
Aru, Tanjung ▲ RI 164-165 E 5
Arua ☆ EAU 212-213 C 2
Aruã, Rio ~ BR 66-67 J 4
Aruanã o BR 72-73 E 3
Aruba ⌒ ARU 60-61 F 1
Aruba Lodge o EAK 212-213 G 5
Arufi o PNG 183 A 5
Arufu o WAN 204-205 H 5
Aruja o BR 72-73 G 7
Aruliho o SOL 184 I d 3
Arumã o BR 66-67 F 5
Arumã, Rio ~ BR 66-67 E 4
Arumbi o ZRE 212-213 C 2
Ārumuganeri o IND 140-141 H 6
Arun ~ NEP 142-143 E 2
Arunāchal Pradesh ■ IND 142-143 H 1
Arundel o CDN (QUE) 238-239 L 3
Arundel = Kohinggo ⌒ SOL 184 I c 3
Arun Qi o VRC 150-151 D 3
Arupukottai o IND 140-141 H 6
Aruri, Rio ~ BR 66-67 K 5
Arusi, Selat ≈ 166-167 H 2
Arus, Tanjung ▲ RI 164-165 G 3
Arusha ■ EAT 212-213 E 5
Arusha ☆ EAT (ARU) 212-213 F 5
Arusha Chini o EAT 212-213 F 5
Arusha National Park ⊥ EAT 212-213 F 5
Aruti o BR 66-67 D 3
Aruwimi ~ ZRE 210-211 L 3
Arvada o USA (CO) 254-255 K 4
Arvada o USA (WY) 252-253 M 2
Arvajhèèr ☆ MAU 148-149 F 4
Arvand Kenār o IR 134-135 C 3
Arvi o IND 138-139 G 9
Arvidsjaur o• S 86-87 J 4
Arvika ☆• S 86-87 F 7
Årviksand o N 86-87 K 1
Arvilla o USA (ND) 258-259 K 4
Arvorezinha o BR 74-75 D 7
Arwala o RI 166-167 D 5
Arwin o USA (CA) 248-249 F 4
Ary, Tit- o RUS (SAH) 110-111 Q 3
Ary, Tit- o RUS (SAH) 118-119 N 5
Aryg-Uzju o RUS 116-117 F 10
Aryktah o RUS 118-119 M 4
Ary-Ongorbut ⌒ RUS 110-111 M 4
Arys o KZ 136-137 L 3
Arys' o KZ 136-137 L 3
Arys ~ KZ 136-137 L 3
Arys, sor ⬭ KZ 124-125 E 6
Arys-Turkistan kanal < KZ 136-137 L 3
Arzamas o RUS 94-95 S 4
Arzana ⌒ UAE 134-135 E 6
Arzew o DZ 188-189 L 3
Arzgir o RUS 126-127 F 5
Arzon o F 90-91 F 8
As o B 92-93 H 3
Aša ☆ RUS 96-97 K 6
Asa ~ ZRE 206-207 G 6
Asab o NAM 220-221 C 2
Asaba o WAN 204-205 G 5
Asača, buhta ≈ 122-123 S 2
Asadābād ☆• AFG 138-139 C 2
Asadābād o IR (HAM) 134-135 C 1
Asadābād o IR (HOR) 134-135 J 2
Asad Buhairat al- < SYR 128-129 H 4
Āsaga o WS 184 V a 1
Aşağı Pınarbaşı o TR 128-129 E 3
Asagny, Parc National d' ⊥ CI 202-203 H 7
Asahaha o EAK 212-213 H 2
Asahi o J 152-153 G 6
Asahi-dake ▲ J 152-153 K 3
Asahi-gawa ~ J 152-153 E 7
Asahikawa o J 152-153 K 3
Asalē o ETH 200-201 K 5
Asālem o IR 128-129 N 4
Asamankese o GH 202-203 K 7
Asambi o RI 168 E 6
Asankranguaa o GH 202-203 J 7
Asan Man ≈ 150-151 F 9
Āsār o IR 134-135 J 5
'Asara, al- o SYR 128-129 J 5
Asaro o PNG 183 C 4
Asaro River ~ PNG 183 C 4
Asawinso o GH 202-203 J 6
Āsayita o ETH 208-209 F 3
Asbesberge ▲ ZA 220-221 F 4
Asbest o RUS 96-97 M 5
Asbestos o CDN (QUE) 238-239 O 3
Asbe Teferi o ETH 208-209 E 4
Asbury Park o USA (NJ) 280-281 M 3
Ascención o BOL 70-71 F 4
Ascención, Bahía de la ≈ 52-53 L 2
Ascension ⌒ GB 202-203 B 7
Ascensión o MEX 50-51 F 2
Ascension Fracture Zone ≃ 6-7 H 9
Aschaffenburg o D 92-93 K 4
Aschersleben o• D 92-93 L 3
Ascochinga o RA 76-77 E 6
Ascoli Piceno ☆• I 100-101 D 3
Ascope o PE 64-65 C 5
Ascotán o RCH 76-77 C 1
Ascotán, Salar de ⬭ RCH 76-77 C 1
Ascunción o BOL 70-71 D 2
Aščykōl ⬭ KZ 124-125 E 6
Aščykōl, ojpat ⊥ KZ 124-125 E 6
Aščykol', ozero ⬭ KZ 136-137 M 3
Aščyšu ~ KZ 124-125 J 3
Ascysu ~ KZ 124-125 L 4
Āše o RUS 126-127 C 6
Āseb o ER 200-201 L 6
Asebot Terara ▲ ETH 208-209 E 4
Asedjrad ▲ DZ 190-191 C 8
Asekeevo ☆ RUS 96-97 H 7
Aseki o PNG 183 D 4
As Ela o DJI 208-209 F 3
Āsela ☆ ETH 208-209 D 5
Āsele o• S 86-87 H 4
Asembagus o RI 168 B 6
Asembo o EAK 212-213 E 4
Asendabo o ETH 208-209 C 5
Asenovgrad o BG 102-103 D 6
Asera o RI 164-165 G 5
Asermanuevo o CO 60-61 D 5
Aserrado o YV 62-63 D 2
Asfi ☆ MA 188-189 G 4
Ašgabat ☆• TM 136-137 F 6
Åsgårdfonna ⊂ N 84-85 K 3
Ash o USA (NC) 282-283 J 6
Asha o WAN 204-205 E 5
Ašhāne o IR 136-137 E 6
Ashangē Hayk' ⬭ ETH 200-201 J 6
Ashanti Region ■ GH 202-203 J 6
Ashara, al- o OM 132-133 L 3
Ashburn o USA (GA) 284-285 G 5
Ashburton o NZ 182 C 5
Ashburton Bay ≈ 236-237 B 4
Ashburton Downs o AUS 176-177 D 1
Ashburton River ~ AUS 172-173 B 7
Ashby o USA (NE) 262-263 E 2
Ashcroft o CDN (BC) 230-231 H 3
Ashdod ☆ IL 130-131 D 2
Ashdown o USA (AR) 276-277 A 7
Asheboro o USA (NC) 282-283 H 5
Asher o USA (OK) 264-265 H 4
Asheron o CDN (MAN) 234-235 E 3
Asherton o USA (TX) 266-267 H 5
Asheville o• USA (NC) 282-283 E 5
Asheweig River ~ CDN 34-35 N 3
Ashewele o WAN 204-205 F 5
Ash Flat o USA (AR) 276-277 D 4
Ashford o AUS 178-179 L 5
Ashford o USA (AL) 284-285 E 5
Ashford Bird Park ⊥• BDS 56 F 5
Ash Fork o USA (AZ) 256-257 C 3
Ashgabat = Ašgabat ☆• TM 136-137 F 6
Ashgrove o CDN (ONT) 238-239 F 5
Ashibetsu o J 152-153 K 3
Ashigashiya o WAN 204-205 K 3
Ashika o IND 142-143 D 6
Ashikaga o J 152-153 H 6
Ashiro o J 152-153 J 4
Ashizuri-misaki ▲ J 152-153 E 8
Ashizuri-Uwakai National Park ⊥ J 152-153 E 8
Ashkidah o LAR 192-193 F 4
Ashkum o USA (IL) 274-275 L 4
Ashland o USA (AL) 284-285 E 3
Ashland o USA (IL) 274-275 H 5
Ashland o USA (KS) 262-263 G 7
Ashland o USA (KY) 276-277 N 2
Ashland o USA (LA) 268-269 G 4
Ashland o USA (ME) 278-279 N 2
Ashland o USA (MO) 274-275 F 6
Ashland o USA (MS) 268-269 L 2
Ashland o USA (MT) 250-251 N 6
Ashland o USA (NE) 262-263 K 3
Ashland o USA (OH) 280-281 D 3
Ashland o USA (OK) 264-265 H 4
Ashland o USA (OR) 244-245 C 8
Ashland o USA (VA) 280-281 J 6
Ashland o USA (WI) 270-271 H 4
Ashland City o USA (TN) 276-277 H 4
Ashley o USA (IL) 274-275 J 6
Ashley o USA (ND) 258-259 H 5
Ashley o USA (OH) 280-281 D 3
Ash Meadows Rancho o USA (NV) 248-249 H 3
Ashmont o AUS 180-181 G 2
Ashmore Reef ⌒ AUS 172-173 F 2
Ashmore Reef ⌒ PNG 183 C 6
Ashokan Reservoir ⬭ USA (NY) 280-281 M 2
Ashoknagar o IND 138-139 F 7
Ashoro o J 152-153 K 3
Ashqelon ☆• IL 130-131 D 2
Ashqelon, Tel ∴• IL 130-131 D 2
ash-Shallāl al-Khāmis = 5th Cataract ~ SUD 200-201 F 3
ash-Shallāl ar-Rābi' = 4th Cataract ~ SUD 200-201 F 3
ash-Shallal as-Sablūkah = 6th Cataract ~ SUD 200-201 F 4
ash-Shallāl ath-Thālith = 3rd Cataract ~ SUD 200-201 E 3
ash-Sharmah o SUD 200-201 G 5
Ash Shatt ■ LAR 192-193 D 4
ash-Shawal o SUD 200-201 F 6
ash-Shiaydimah o LAR 192-193 J 2
ash-Shuheit ~ SUD 200-201 G 6
ash-Shurayk o SUD 200-201 F 3
Ash Springs o USA (NV) 248-249 J 2
Ashta o IND 138-139 F 8
Ashtabula o USA (OH) 280-281 F 2
Ashtabula, Lake ⬭ USA (ND) 258-259 J 4
Ashtola o USA (TX) 264-265 C 3
Ashton o USA (ID) 252-253 G 2
Ashton o USA (NE) 262-263 H 3
Ashton o USA (SD) 260-261 H 1
Ashton o ZA 220-221 E 6
Ashuanipi Lake ⬭ CDN 38-39 L 2
Ashville o CDN (MAN) 234-235 C 3
Ashville o USA (AL) 284-285 D 3
Ashville o USA (PA) 280-281 H 3
Ashwaraopet o IND 142-143 B 7
Ashwood o USA (OR) 244-245 E 6
Asia o PE 64-65 D 8
Asia, Estrecho ≈ 80 C 5
Asiak River ~ CDN 30-31 N 2
Asid Gulf ≈ 160-161 E 6
Asientos, Los o PA 52-53 D 8
Asif Melloul ~ MA 188-189 H 4
Asilah o• MA 188-189 H 3
Asile, L' o RH 54-55 J 5
Asillo o PE 70-71 B 4
Asinara, Golfo dell' ≈ 100-101 B 4
Asinara, Isola ⌒ I 100-101 B 4
Asindonhopo o SME 62-63 G 4
Asi Nehri ~ TR 128-129 G 4
Asino ☆ RUS 114-115 T 6
Asir ■ KSA 132-133 C 4
'Asis, Ra's ▲ SUD 200-201 J 3
Aşkale ☆ TR 128-129 J 3
'Askarān o IR 134-135 D 2
Askarly ☆ KZ 124-125 H 3
Askarovo ☆ RUS 96-97 L 7
Aškazar o IR 134-135 F 3
Askeaton o ZA 220-221 H 5
Asker ☆ N 86-87 E 7
Askersund ☆• S 86-87 G 7
Askim ☆ N 86-87 E 7
Askino ☆ RUS 96-97 K 5
Askinuk Mountains ▲ USA 20-21 H 6
Askira o WAN 204-205 K 3
Askiz ☆ RUS 116-117 E 9
Asköping o S 86-87 H 7
Askot o IND 144-145 C 6
Askøy ⌒ N 86-87 B 6
Asla o DZ 188-189 L 4
Aşl-e Čaḫānsūr o AFG 134-135 K 3
Asler o RMM 196-197 L 5
Asmār o AFG 136-137 M 7
Āsmara ☆• ER 200-201 J 5
Asmara, Wādī ~ KSA 130-131 G 4
Asmat Woodcarvings o• RI 166-167 K 4
Āsmera = Āsmara ☆• ER 200-201 J 5
Ašmjany ☆ BY 94-95 K 4
Asnāhra o IND 142-143 C 2
Asnet o TCH 198-199 J 6
Āsni o MA 188-189 H 5
Aso o J 152-153 D 8
Aso National Park ⊥• J 152-153 D 8
Asori o RI 166-167 J 3
Āsosa o ETH 208-209 B 3
Aso-san ▲ J 152-153 D 8
Asoteriba, Gabal ▲ SUD 200-201 H 2
Aspen o CDN (NS) 240-241 N 5
Aspen o USA (CO) 254-255 J 4
Aspen Cove o CDN (BC) 230-231 J 4
Aspendos •• TR 128-129 D 4
Aspen Mountain Ski Area • USA (CO) 254-255 J 4
Aspermont o USA (TX) 264-265 D 5
Aspiring, Mount ▲ NZ 182 B 6
Aspy Bay ≈ 240-241 P 4
Asquith o CDN (SAS) 232-233 L 3
Asrama o RT 202-203 L 6
Asriko o CI 202-203 H 6
Assa o KZ 136-137 M 3
Assa ~ KZ 136-137 M 3
Assa o MA 188-189 G 6
Assaba ■ RIM 196-197 D 6
aš-Šabb o ET 194-195 D 6
Assadjene ▲ DZ 190-191 F 9
aṣ-Ṣaff o ET 194-195 E 3
'Assāfiya, al- o KSA 130-131 F 3
Assa Galla o DJI 208-209 F 2
'Assah, Al o LAR 192-193 D 1
aṣ-Ṣāḥiliya, Ǧabal ▲ SYR 128-129 G 5
Assahoun o RT 202-203 L 6
Assai o BR 72-73 E 7
Assaikio o WAN 204-205 H 4
Assaka o MA 188-189 G 6
Assal, Lac o DJI 208-209 F 3
as-Salam, Bahr ~ SUD 200-201 H 6
Assam ■ IND 142-143 H 2
aš-Šām, Ǧabal ▲ OM 132-133 K 2
Assamakka o RN 198-199 B 3
Assaouas o RN 198-199 C 4
Assaq, Oued ~ WSA 196-197 C 2
Assaré o BR 68-69 J 5
Assaria o USA (KS) 262-263 J 6
Assateague Islands National Seashore ⊥ USA (VA) 280-281 L 5
aṣ-Ṣaṭṭ o ET 194-195 F 3
As-Sawirah ☆• MA 188-189 G 5
Assdadah o LAR 192-193 F 2
Asse, River ~ WAN 204-205 G 6
Assegai ~ SD 220-221 K 3
Assen ☆ NL 92-93 J 2
Assen o ZA 220-221 H 2
As Siba'n o KSA 130-131 G 4
as-Sidr o ET 194-195 F 3
As Sidr o LAR 192-193 H 2
Assin Anyinabrim o GH 202-203 K 7
Assina River ~ PNG 183 B 2
as-Sinbalāwain o ET 194-195 E 2
Assiniboia o CDN (SAS) 232-233 N 6
Assiniboine, Mount ▲ CDN (BC) 230-231 O 3
Assiniboine River ~ CDN 232-233 Q 3
Assiniboine River ~ CDN 234-235 E 5
Assiniboine River ~ CDN 234-235 B 4
Assinica, Lac ⬭ CDN 38-39 G 3
Assinica, Lac ⬭ CDN (QUE) 236-237 N 2
Assinica, La Réserve de ⊥ CDN (QUE) 236-237 O 2
Assinié Mafia o• CI 202-203 J 7
Assin Nyankumase o GH 202-203 K 7
Assis o BR 72-73 E 7
Assis Brasil o BR 70-71 C 2
Assis Chateaubriand o BR 74-75 D 5
Assisi o•• I 100-101 D 3
Assodé o RN 198-199 D 3
Assok Begua o G 210-211 C 3
Assomption ⌒ SY 222-223 E 2
Assomption, Rivière l' ~ CDN 238-239 M 2
Assos •• TR 128-129 B 3
Assu o BR 68-69 K 4
Assu, Rio ~ BR 68-69 K 4
as-Sukki o SUD 200-201 F 6
As Sultān o• LAR 192-193 G 2
as-Sumay o SUD 206-207 H 4
Assumption o USA (IL) 274-275 J 5
Assunção o BR 66-67 E 7
Assur ∴•• IRQ 128-129 K 5
As Sūs ~ MA 188-189 G 5
as-Suwais ☆ ET 194-195 F 3
as-Suwais, Ḫalīǧ ≈ 194-195 F 3
as-Suwais, Qunāt < ET 194-195 F 2
Assyni ~ RUS 122-123 F 2
Astakóe o GR 100-101 H 5
Astān, Umm al- o UAE 132-133 H 2
Astane o IR 128-129 N 4
Āstāne o IR 134-135 C 2
Astantaj-Mataj, sor ⊥ KZ 126-127 M 5
Astara o AZ 128-129 N 3
Āstara o IR 128-129 N 3
Astarak o AR 128-129 L 2
Asti ☆• I 100-101 B 2
Astillero,El o E 98-99 F 3
Astipálea o GR 100-101 L 6
Astipálea ⌒ GR 100-101 L 6
Astivay o AFG 136-137 M 7
Astiyān o IR 134-135 C 1
Astorga o BR 72-73 E 7
Astorga o• E 98-99 D 3
Astoria o USA (IL) 274-275 H 4
Astoria o USA (SD) 260-261 K 2
Astoria o• USA (OR) 244-245 B 4
Astor Park o USA (FL) 286-287 H 2
Astove Island ⌒ SY 222-223 E 3
Astrahan' o KZ 124-125 G 3
Astrahan' ☆ RUS 96-97 E 10
Astrahanskij zapovednik ⊥ RUS 126-127 G 5
Astrahanskij zapovednik ⊥ RUS (AST) 96-97 F 10
Astrakhan' = Astrahan' ☆ RUS 96-97 E 10
Astray o CDN 36-37 Q 7
Astrolabe Bay ≈ 183 C 3
Astronomical Society Islands ⌒ CDN 24-25 a 6
Ástros o GR 100-101 J 6
Astrovna o BY 94-95 L 4
Astura, gora ▲ RUS 108-109 e 3
Asturias ■ E 98-99 D 3
Asuéfri o CI 202-203 J 6
Asunción o CR 52-53 C 7
Asunción ☆• PY 76-77 J 3
Asuncion, Río de la ~ MEX 50-51 C 2
Asunción Nochixtlán o MEX 52-53 F 3
Asundi o IND 140-141 G 3
'Asūriya, al- o IRQ 128-129 K 7
Asutsuare o GH 202-203 L 6
Aswa ~ EAU 212-213 D 2
Aswān ☆•• ET 194-195 F 5
Aswān = Aswān ☆•• ET 194-195 F 5
Aswān High Dam = Sadd al-'Āli <•• ET (ASW) 194-195 F 6
Asyma o RUS 118-119 N 4
Asyūṭ ☆• ET 194-195 E 4
Asyūṭī, Wādī l- ~ ET 194-195 E 4
Ata, Qiryat o IL 130-131 D 1
Ataa o GRØ 28-29 P 2
Ata Bupu Danau • RI 168 E 7
Atacama, Desierto de ⊥ RCH 76-77 B 4
Atacama, Puna de ⊥ RA 76-77 C 4
Atacama, Salar de ⬭• RCH 76-77 C 2
Atacama Trench = Atacama Trench/ Peru-Chile Trench ≃ 70-71 A 5
Atacames o EC 64-65 C 1
Atafaitafa, Djebel ▲ DZ 190-191 F 8
Atafi, Massif d' ▲ RN 192-193 F 6
'Ataiye o IR 136-137 F 7
Atajaña, Cerro ▲ RCH 70-71 B 6
Atakakup Indian Reservation ⊥ CDN (SAS) 232-233 M 2
Ata Koo Fai-Nuwa Puri Danau • RI 168 E 7
Atakor ▲ DZ 190-191 E 9
Atakora, Chaîne de l' ▲ DY 202-203 L 4
Atakora, Zone Cynégétique de l' ⊥ DY 202-203 L 4
Atakpamé ☆ RT 202-203 L 6
Atalaia o BR 68-69 K 6
Atalaia, Ponta de ▲ BR 68-69 E 2
Atalaia do Norte o BR 66-67 B 5
Atalaya o PE 64-65 F 7
Atalaya, Cerro ▲ PE 70-71 B 3
Ataléia o BR 72-73 K 5
Atamanovo o RUS 116-117 F 7
Atambua o RI 166-167 C 6
Atami o• J 152-153 H 7
Atammik o GRØ 28-29 O 4
Atanbas, tau ▲ KZ 126-127 P 3
Atande, Tanjung ▲ RI 166-167 B 6
Atanik o USA 20-21 L 1
Atapange o RI 164-165 G 6
Ata Polo Danau • RI 168 E 7
Atapupu o RI 166-167 C 6
'Atāqa, Ǧabal ▲ ET 194-195 F 3
Ataques o ROU 76-77 K 6
Atâr ☆ RIM 196-197 D 4
Atar, Khor ~ SUD 206-207 K 4
Ataram, Erg n' ⊥ DZ 190-191 C 9
Atas Bogd ▲ MAU 148-149 C 6
Atascadero o PE 64-65 B 4
Atascadero o USA (CA) 248-249 D 4
Atascosa River ~ USA 266-267 J 4
Atasi Nkwanta o GH 202-203 K 7
Atasta o MEX 52-53 H 2
Atasu ☆ KZ 124-125 G 4
Atatürk Barajı < TR 128-129 H 4
Atauba o BR 62-63 D 6
Ataúro, Pulau ⌒ RI 166-167 ?
Atauro, Pulau (Kambing) ⌒ RI 166-167 C 6
Atawala, al- o KSA 132-133 B 3
Ātaya o ETH 208-209 D 3
'Atbara ~ ETH 200-201 H 6
'Atbara o SUD (Nil) 200-201 G 4
'Atbara ~ SUD 200-201 G 4
Atbasar ☆ KZ 124-125 F 3
At-Baši, hrebet ▲ KS 146-147 B 5
Atchafalaya Bay ≈ 268-269 J 7
Atchafalaya River ~ USA 268-269 J 6
Atchane, Erg el ⊥ DZ 188-189 L 6
Atchane, Hamadet el ⊥ DZ 190-191 E 6
Atchison o USA (KS) 262-263 L 5
Atchuelinguk River ~ USA 20-21 K 6
Atebubu o GH 202-203 K 6
Ateiku o GH 202-203 K 7
Aten, Río ~ BOL 70-71 C 4
Atenango del Río o MEX 52-53 E 2
Atenas o BR 66-67 B 7
Atencingo o MEX 52-53 E 2
Atequiza o MEX 52-53 C 1
Aterau ☆ KZ 96-97 H 10
Aterau = Aterau ☆ KZ 96-97 H 10
Atesa o GH 202-203 J 6
Athabasca, Lake ⬭ CDN 30-31 P 6
Athabasca River ~ CDN 228-229 R 3
Athamar • TR 128-129 K 3
Athārān Hazārī o PK 138-139 D 4
Athenia Lake ⬭ CDN 30-31 O 4
Athens o USA (AL) 284-285 D 2
Athens o USA (AR) 276-277 B 6
Athens o USA (GA) 284-285 G 3
Athens o USA (LA) 268-269 G 4
Athens o USA (OH) 280-281 D 4
Athens o USA (TN) 282-283 C 5
Athens o USA (TX) 264-265 J 6
Athens = Athína ☆••• GR 100-101 J 5
Atherton o AUS 174-175 H 5
Atherton Tableland ⊥ AUS 174-175 H 5
Athgarh o IND 142-143 D 5
Athi ~ EAK 212-213 G 3
Athiémè o DY 202-203 L 6
Athienou o CY 128-129 E 5
Athína ☆••• GR 100-101 J 5
Athi River o EAK 212-213 F 4
Athl, Wādī al ~ LAR 192-193 H 5
Athlone = Baile Átha Luain o IRL 90-91 D 5
Athni o IND 140-141 F 2
Athol o USA (ID) 250-251 C 4
Athol o USA (MA) 278-279 J 6
Atholl, Kap ▲ GRØ 26-27 P 5
Áthos ▲••• GR 100-101 K 4
'Ati o SUD 200-201 D 6
Ati ☆ TCH 198-199 J 6
Atiak o EAU 212-213 D 2
Atiamuri o NZ 182 F 3
Atibaia o BR 72-73 G 7
Atico o PE 70-71 A 5
Atiedo o SUD 206-207 H 5
Atienza o E 98-99 F 4
Atijere o WAN 204-205 F 5
Atik o CDN (MAN) 234-235 B 2
Atikaki Provincial Wilderness Park ⊥ CDN (MAN) 234-235 H 3
Atikameg River ~ CDN 34-35 P 4
Atiki ■ GR 100-101 J 6
Atikokan o CDN (ONT) 234-235 M 6
Atikonak Lake ⬭ CDN 38-39 M 2
Atim o TCH 198-199 K 6
Atinia, Nakong- o GH 202-203 K 4
Atitlán, Lago de ⬭• GCA 52-53 J 4
Atitlán, Volcán ▲ GCA 52-53 J 4
Atka o RUS 120-121 O 3
Atka o USA 22-23 J 6
Atka Island ⌒ USA 22-23 J 6
Atkamba Mission o PNG 183 A 3
Atka Pass ≈ 22-23 J 6
Atkins o USA (AR) 276-277 C 5
Atkinson o USA (NC) 282-283 J 6
Atkinson o USA (NE) 262-263 H 2
Atkinson Lake ⬭ CDN 30-31 R 5
Atkinson Point ▲ CDN 20-21 Z 2
Atkot o IND 138-139 C 8
Atkri o RI 166-167 F 2
Atlacomulco o MEX 52-53 E 2
Atlanta o USA (ID) 252-253 C 3
Atlanta o USA (LA) 268-269 H 5
Atlanta o USA (MI) 272-273 E 2
Atlanta o USA (NE) 262-263 G 4
Atlanta o USA (TX) 264-265 K 5
Atlanta ☆• USA (GA) 284-285 F 3
Atlantic o USA (IA) 274-275 C 3
Atlantic o USA (ME) 278-279 N 4
Atlantic o USA (NC) 282-283 L 6
Atlantic Beach o USA (FL) 286-287 H 1
Atlantic City o• USA (NJ) 280-281 M 4
Atlantic Ocean ≈ 6-7 D 6
Atlantida o ROU 78-79 M 3
Atlantis Fracture Zone ≃ 6-7 E 5
Atlasova, ostrov ⌒ RUS 122-123 Q 3
Atlasovo o RUS (KMC) 120-121 S 6
Atlasovo o RUS (SHL) 122-123 K 5
Atlee o CDN (ALB) 232-233 H 5
Atlee Creek ~ AUS 172-173 K 6
Atlin o CDN 20-21 Y 7
Atlin Lake ⬭ CDN 20-21 Y 7
Atlin Provincial Park ⊥ CDN 32-33 D 2
Atlixco o MEX 52-53 E 2
Atmakūr o IND 140-141 H 3
Atmakur o IND (ANP) 140-141 G 2
Atmakur o IND (ANP) 140-141 H 3
Atmis ~ RUS 94-95 S 5
Atmore o USA (AL) 284-285 C 5
Atna Peak ▲ CDN (BC) 228-229 F 3
Atnarko o CDN (BC) 228-229 J 4
Atnbrua o N 86-87 E 6
Atocha o BOL 70-71 D 7
Atog o CAM 210-211 C 2
Atoka o USA (NM) 256-257 L 6
Atoka o USA (OK) 264-265 H 4
Atoka Lake < USA (OK) 264-265 H 4
Atome o ANG 216-217 C 5
Atomic City o USA (ID) 252-253 F 3
Atongo-Bakari o RCA 206-207 E 6
Atonyia o WSA 188-189 G 7
Atori o SOL 184 I e 3
Atotonilco el Alto o MEX 52-53 C 1
Atotonilco el Alto o MEX 52-53 C 1
Atotonilco El Grande o MEX 52-53 E 1
Atouat, Mount ▲ LAO 158-159 J 3
Atoyac, Río ~ MEX 52-53 E 2
Atoyac, Río ~ MEX 52-53 F 3
Atoyac de Alvarez o MEX 52-53 D 3
Atoyatempan o MEX 52-53 F 2
Atpadi o IND 140-141 F 2
Atqasuk o USA 20-21 M 1
Atrai ~ BD 142-143 F 3
Atrak, Rūd-e ~ IR 136-137 E 6
Åtran ~ S 86-87 F 8
Atrato, Río ~ CO 60-61 C 4
Atrek ~ TM 136-137 D 6
'Atrun, Bi'r al- o SUD 200-201 C 3
Atsion o USA (NJ) 280-281 M 4
Atsumi-hantō ⌒ J 152-153 G 7
Atsuta o J 152-153 J 3
Atsy o RI 166-167 K 4
Atta o CAM 204-205 J 5
Attakro o CI 202-203 J 6
Attalla o USA (AL) 284-285 D 2
aṭ-Ṭamad o ET 194-195 G 3
At Tamimi o LAR 192-193 K 1
aṭ-Ṭanf, Ǧabal ▲ SYR 128-129 H 6
Attāni o IND 140-141 G 5
Attapu o LAO 158-159 J 3
Attar, Oued el ~ DZ 190-191 E 4
Attawapiskat o CDN 34-35 P 4
Attawapiskat Lake ⬭ CDN (ONT) 234-235 Q 2
Attawapiskat River ~ CDN 234-235 R 2
Attayampatti o IND 140-141 H 5
aṭ-Ṭayyārah o SUD 200-201 E 6
Atteï, In o DZ 198-199 C 2
Atterbury Reserve Training Center ✕✕ USA (IN) 274-275 M 5
Attica o USA (IN) 274-275 L 4
Attica o USA (KS) 262-263 H 7
Attica o USA (NY) 278-279 C 6
Attica o USA (OH) 280-281 D 2
at-Tih, Ǧabal ▲ ET 194-195 F 3
at-Tih, Ṣahrā' ⊥ ET 194-195 F 2
Attikamagen Lake ⬭ CDN 36-37 Q 7
aṭ-Ṭina, Ḫalīǧ ≈ 194-195 F 2
Attingal o IND 140-141 G 6
Attippāra o IND 140-141 G 6
Attleboro o USA (RI) 278-279 K 7
Attobrou, Yakass- o CI 202-203 J 6
Attock o• PK 138-139 D 3
Attock-Campbellpore o PK 138-139 D 3
Attoko o J 152-153 L 3
Attoyac River ~ USA 268-269 F 5
Attu o GRØ 28-29 O 3
Attu o USA 22-23 C 6
Attu Island ⌒ USA 22-23 C 6
at-Ṭūr ☆ ET 194-195 F 3
Attur o IND 140-141 H 5
aṭ Ṭuwayshah o SUD 200-201 C 6
Attwood Lake ⬭ CDN (ONT) 234-235 P 3
Attwood River ~ CDN 234-235 P 3
Attykeveem ~ RUS 112-113 N 2
Atucatiquini, Rio ~ BR 66-67 C 6
Atuel, Río ~ RA 78-79 E 3
Atuka o RI 166-167 J 4
Atuna o GH 202-203 J 6
Atuntaqui o EC 64-65 C 1
Atura o EAU 212-213 D 2

Arm River — Atura 299

Atures o **YV** 60-61 H 5
Atutia, Rio ~ **RA** 76-77 B 6
Ätvidaberg o **S** 86-87 H 7
Atwa, al- o **KSA** 130-131 H 3
Atwater o **CDN** (SAS) 232-233 Q 5
Atwater o **USA** (CA) 248-249 D 2
Atwood o **USA** (IL) 274-275 K 5
Atwood o **USA** (KS) 262-263 E 5
Atykan, ostrov ~ **RUS** 120-121 Q 4
Atžaksy o **KZ** 126-127 M 3
Atzinging Lake o **CDN** 30-31 S 5
Aua River ~ **CDN** 24-25 e 7
Auasberge ▲ **NAM** 216-217 D 11
Auasinaua, Cachoeira ~ **BR** 66-67 F 2
Auatu ▲ **ETH** 208-209 E 5
Auau Channel ≈ **USA** 288 J 4
Aubagne o **F** 90-91 K 10
Aube ~ **F** 90-91 K 8
Aúbe o **MOC** 218-219 K 3
Aubenas o **F** 90-91 K 9
Aubigny o **CDN** (MAN) 234-235 F 5
Aubigny-sur-Nère o **F** 90-91 J 8
Aubinadong River ~ **CDN** 236-237 E 5
Aubrey Cliffs ▲ **USA** 256-257 B 3
Aubry Lake o **CDN** 30-31 S 2
Auburn o **AUS** (QLD) 178-179 L 3
Auburn o **AUS** (SA) 180-181 D 3
Auburn o **USA** (AL) 284-285 E 4
Auburn o **USA** (CA) 246-247 D 2
Auburn o **USA** (IA) 274-275 D 2
Auburn o **USA** (IN) 274-275 N 3
Auburn o **USA** (ME) 278-279 M 4
Auburn o **USA** (NE) 262-263 L 4
Auburn o **USA** (NY) 278-279 E 6
Auburn o **USA** (WA) 244-245 C 3
Auburn o **USA** (WY) 252-253 H 4
Auburn Corners o **USA** (OH) 280-281 E 2
Auburndale o **USA** (FL) 286-287 H 3
Auburn Range ▲ **AUS** 178-179 L 3
Auburn River ~ **AUS** 178-179 L 3
Aubusson o **F** 90-91 J 9
Auca Mahuida, Sierra de ▲ **RA** 78-79 E 4
Auçan, Cerro ▲ **RCH** 76-77 C 1
Aucara o **PE** 64-65 E 9
Aucayacu o **PE** 64-65 D 6
Auch ☆ **F** 90-91 H 10
Auchi o **WAN** 204-205 G 5
Aucilla River ~ **USA** 286-287 F 1
Auckland ☆ **NZ** 182 E 2
Auckland Bay ≈ 158-159 E 4
Auckland Islands ⌒ **NZ** 13 H 8
Aude ~ **F** 90-91 J 10
Auden o **CDN** (ONT) 234-235 Q 4
Audhild Bay ≈ 26-27 E 3
Audierne o **F** 90-91 E 7
Audo Range ▲ **ETH** 208-209 E 5
Audru o • **EST** 94-95 J 2
Audubon o **USA** (IA) 274-275 D 3
Aue o **D** 92-93 M 3
Augathella o **AUS** 178-179 J 3
Augrabies o **ZA** 220-221 E 4
Augrabies Falls ~ •• **ZA** 220-221 E 4
Augrabies Falls National Park ⊥ **ZA** 220-221 E 4
Augsburg o • **D** 92-93 L 4
Aug Thong o **THA** 158-159 F 3
Augusta o **AUS** 176-177 C 7
Augusta o **I** 100-101 E 6
Augusta o **USA** (AR) 276-277 D 5
Augusta o **USA** (GA) 284-285 J 3
Augusta o **USA** (IL) 274-275 H 4
Augusta o **USA** (KS) 262-263 K 7
Augusta o **USA** (MT) 250-251 G 4
Augusta o **USA** (OH) 280-281 B 5
Augusta o **USA** (WI) 270-271 G 6
Augusta ☆ **USA** (ME) 278-279 M 4
Augustina Libarona o **RA** 76-77 F 4
Augustin Codazzi o **CO** 60-61 E 2
Augustine Island ⌒ **USA** 22-23 U 3
Augusto Montenegro o **BR** 66-67 J 4
Augusto Severo o **BR** 68-69 K 4
Augustów o **PL** 92-93 R 2
Augustus, Mount ▲ **AUS** 176-177 D 2
Augustus Downs o **AUS** 174-175 G 4
Augustus Island ⌒ **AUS** 172-173 G 3
Augustus Island o **CDN** 36-37 G 3
Auilta, Rio ~ **BR** 72-73 D 2
Auke Bay o **USA** 32-33 C 2
Auki o **SOL** 184 I e 3
Aukpar River ~ **CDN** 36-37 N 2
Aulåd Tauq Šarq o • **ET** 194-195 F 4
Aulander o **USA** (NC) 282-283 K 4
Auld, Lake o **AUS** 172-173 F 7
Auliräipära o **IND** 142-143 G 4
Aulitivik Island ~ **CDN** 28-29 G 2
Auliya Dam o **SUD** 200-201 F 5
Aulneau Peninsula ~ **CDN** (ONT) 234-235 J 5
Aul Sarykobda o **KZ** 126-127 M 3
Ault o **USA** (CO) 254-255 L 3
Aumo o **PNG** 183 E 3
Auna o **WAN** 204-205 F 4
Aundah o **IND** 138-139 F 10
Auno o **WAN** 204-205 K 3
Auob ~ **NAM** 220-221 D 4
Aupwel o **PNG** 183 D 3
Aur, Pulau ⌒ **MAL** 162-163 F 3
Aura o **USA** (MI) 270-271 K 4
Aurahua o **PE** 64-65 E 8
Auram ~ **NAM** 220-221 D 4
Aurangābād o **IND** 138-139 E 10
Aurangābād o **IND** 142-143 D 3
Auras o **C** 54-55 G 4
Auray o **F** 90-91 F 8
Aurbunak, Gunung ▲ **RI** 164-165 D 5
Aure ~ **N** 86-87 D 5
Aure River ~ **PNG** 183 E 4
Aures, Massif de l' ▲ **DZ** 190-191 F 3
Aure Scarp ≈ **PNG** 183 C 4
Auri, utes • **RUS** 122-123 J 2
Aurich (Ostfriesland) o **D** 92-93 J 2
Auriflama o **BR** 72-73 E 6

Aurillac ☆ **F** 90-91 J 9
Auriya o **IND** 138-139 G 6
Aurlandsvangen o **N** 86-87 C 6
Auro o **PNG** 183 E 5
Aurora o **BR** (CEA) 68-69 J 5
Aurora o **BR** (GSU) 70-71 K 6
Aurora o **CDN** (ONT) 238-239 E 6
Aurora o **CDN** (ONT) 238-239 F 4
Aurora o **GUY** 62-63 E 2
Aurora o **RP** (ISA) 160-161 D 4
Aurora o **RP** (ZAS) 160-161 E 9
Aurora o **USA** (AK) 20-21 H 4
Aurora o **USA** (CO) 254-255 L 4
Aurora o **USA** (KY) 276-277 G 4
Aurora o **USA** (ME) 278-279 N 4
Aurora o **USA** (MN) 270-271 B 4
Aurora o **USA** (NE) 262-263 J 4
Aurora o **USA** (NY) 278-279 E 6
Aurora, Île ⌒ **Maewo** = **VAN** 184 II b 2
Aurora, La o **RA** 76-77 E 4
Aurora do Tocantins o **BR** 72-73 G 2
Auroraville o **USA** (WI) 270-271 H 6
Aurukun Aboriginal Land ⅄ **AUS** 174-175 F 3
Aus o **NAM** 220-221 C 3
Ausa o **IND** 138-139 F 10
Au Sable River ~ **USA** 272-273 K 3
Ausangate, Nudo ▲ **PE** 70-71 B 3
Auschwitz = Oświęcim o ••• **PL** 92-93 P 3
Ausentes o **BR** 74-75 E 7
Ausis < **NAM** 216-217 B 9
Aussig = Ústí nad Labem o **CZ** 92-93 N 3
Austerlitz = Slavkov u Brna o **CZ** 92-93 O 4
Austfonna ⌒ **N** 84-85 N 3
Austin o **CDN** (MAN) 234-235 E 5
Austin o **USA** (MN) 270-271 F 7
Austin o **USA** (NV) 244-245 G 6
Austin ☆ **USA** (TX) 266-267 K 3
Austin, Lake o **AUS** 176-177 E 3
Austin Channel ≈ 24-25 U 3
Austin Island ⌒ **CDN** 30-31 X 5
Austral Downs o **AUS** 174-175 G 4
Australia ☆ **AUS** 176-177 F 4
Australia ⊥ **AUS** 13 D 5
Australian-Antarctic Basin ≃ 12 G 10
Australian-Antarctic Discordance ≃ 13 D 7
Australian Capital Territory ◻ **AUS** 180-181 K 5
Australian Fossil Mammal Sites ⊥ ••• **AUS** (QLD) 174-175 E 6
Australian Fossil Mammal Sites ⊥ ••• **AUS** (SA) 180-181 F 4
Australind o **AUS** 176-177 C 6
Austria = Österreich ■ **A** 92-93 N 5
Austvågøy ⌒ **N** 86-87 G 2
Austwell o **USA** (TX) 266-267 L 5
Autás-Mirim, Rio ~ **BR** 66-67 G 5
Autaz, Ilha ⌒ **BR** 66-67 H 4
Autazes o **BR** 66-67 H 4
Autaz Mirim, Paraná ~ **BR** 66-67 H 4
Autec ◦ • **BS** 54-55 G 2
Authier-Nord o **CDN** (QUE) 236-237 K 4
Autlán de Navarro o **MEX** 52-53 B 2
Autridge Bay ≈ 24-25 Q 5
Autun o **F** 90-91 K 8
Auvergne o **AUS** (SC) 284-285 L 3
Auvergne ▲ **F** 90-91 J 9
Aux Barques, Pointe ▲ **USA** (MI) 272-273 L 3
Auxerre ☆ **F** 90-91 J 8
Auxiliadora o **BR** 66-67 G 6
Auyan Tebuy ▲ **YV** 60-61 K 5
Auyuittuq National Park ⊥ **CDN** 28-29 Q 3
Ava o **MYA** 142-143 J 5
Ava o **USA** (IL) 276-277 F 3
Ava o **USA** (MO) 276-277 D 4
Ava o **USA** (MS) 268-269 L 3
Avača ~ **RUS** 120-121 T 6
Avá-Canoeiro, Área Indígena ⅄ **BR** 72-73 F 2
Avačinskaja, guba ≈ 120-121 S 7
Avačinskij zaliv ≈ 120-121 S 7
Avadh ~ **IND** 142-143 B 2
Avadi o **IND** 140-141 J 4
Avakubi o **ZRE** 210-211 L 3
Avalik River ~ **USA** 20-21 L 1
Avaljak hrebet ▲ **RUS** 96-97 L 6
Avallon o **F** 90-91 J 8
Avalon o **USA** (CA) 248-249 F 6
Avalon o **USA** (TX) 264-265 H 6
Avalon Peninsula ~ **CDN** 242-243 P 5
Avalon Reservoir o **USA** 256-257 C 6
Avalos, Arroyo ~ **RA** 76-77 H 5
Avanavero o **SME** 62-63 F 3
Avannaarsua = Nordgrønland ~ **GRØ** 26-27 V 4
Avard o **USA** (OK) 264-265 F 2
Avare o **BR** 72-73 F 7
Avarskoe Kojsu ~ **RUS** 126-127 G 6
Avatanak Island ⌒ **USA** 22-23 O 5
Avatanak Strait ≈ 22-23 O 5
Ave, Rio ~ **P** 98-99 C 4
Ave-Dakpa o **GH** 202-203 L 6
Aveğ o **IR** 128-129 N 5
Aveğ, Gardáne-ye ▲ **IR** 128-129 N 5
Aveiro o **BR** 66-67 K 4
Aveiro ☆ • **P** 98-99 C 4
Aveiro, Floresta Nacional ⊥ **BR** 66-67 K 4
Avekova ~ **RUS** 112-113 L 5
Avelino Lopes o **BR** 68-69 G 7
Avella o **USA** (PA) 280-281 F 3
Avellaneda o **RA** 78-79 K 3
Avellino o **I** 100-101 E 4
Avenal o **USA** (CA) 248-249 D 3
Avenne of the Giants • **USA** (CA) 246-247 B 3
Avery o **USA** (ID) 250-251 D 4
Avery o **USA** (TX) 264-265 K 5

Aves, Isla ⌒ **YV** 56 D 4
Aves, Islas de ⌒ **YV** 60-61 H 1
Aves de Barlovento ⌒ **YV** 60-61 H 2
Aves Ridge ≈ 56 D 5
Aveyron ~ **F** 90-91 J 9
Avezzano o **I** 100-101 D 3
Avia Teray o **RA** 76-77 G 4
Avignon o • **F** 90-91 K 10
Ávila de los Caballeros o ••• **E** 98-99 E 4
Avilés o • • **E** 98-99 E 2
Avilla o **USA** (IN) 274-275 N 3
Avilla, Parque Nacional ⊥ **YV** 60-61 H 2
Avinurme o **EST** 94-95 K 2
Avirons, Les o **F** 224 B 7
Avis o **P** 98-99 D 5
Avispa, Cerro ▲ **YV** 66-67 E 2
Avissawella o **CL** 140-141 J 6
Avoca o **AUS** (TAS) 180-181 J 6
Avoca o **AUS** (VIC) 180-181 G 4
Avoca o **USA** (TX) 264-265 E 6
Avola o **CDN** (BC) 230-231 K 2
Avola o **I** 100-101 E 6
Avon ~ **USA** (MT) 250-251 G 5
Avon ~ **USA** (SD) 260-261 H 4
Avondale o **USA** (AZ) 256-257 C 6
Avon Downs o **AUS** (NT) 174-175 G 3
Avon Downs o **AUS** (QLD) 178-179 J 1
Avonia o **USA** (PA) 280-281 F 1
Avon Park o **USA** (FL) 286-287 H 4
Avon Park Air Force Range ✕✕ **USA** (FL) 286-287 H 4
Avon River ~ **AUS** 176-177 D 5
Avondale o **AUS** 180-181 L 3
Avontuur o **ZA** 220-221 F 6
Avranches o **F** 90-91 G 7
Avstrijskij proliv ≈ 84-85 f 2
Avu, Lake o **PNG** 183 A 4
Avu Avu = Kolotambu o **SOL** 184 I e 3
'Awábi o **OM** 132-133 K 2
Awaē o **CAM** 210-211 C 2
Awagakama River ~ **CDN** 236-237 E 2
Awa Gurupi, Área Indígena ⅄ **BR** 68-69 E 3
Awai, Pulau ⌒ **RI** 166-167 J 2
Awaji-shima ⌒ **J** 152-153 F 7
Awakaba o **RCA** 206-207 H 4
Awang o **RI** 168 C 7
Awanui o **NZ** 182 D 1
Awar o **PNG** 183 C 3
Awara Plain ~ **EAK** 212-213 H 2
Awara soela ~ **SME** 62-63 G 4
Awaré o **RA** point ▲ **NZ** 182 B 6
Āwasa o **ETH** 208-209 D 5
Āwasa Hāyk' o **ETH** 208-209 D 5
Awash o **ETH** 208-209 E 4
Awashima ⌒ **J** 152-153 H 5
Āwash National Park ⊥ **ETH** 208-209 D 4
Āwash Reserve ⊥ **ETH** 208-209 D 4
Āwash Wenz ~ **ETH** 208-209 D 4
Awat o **VRC** 146-147 E 5
Āwat'a Shet' ~ **ETH** 208-209 D 6
Awatere River ~ **NZ** 182 D 4
Awbāri o **LAR** 190-191 H 7
Awbāri ~ **LAR** 192-193 E 4
Awdheegle o **SP** 212-213 K 3
Awdiinle o **SP** 212-213 J 2
Awe o **WAN** 204-205 H 4
Aweil o **SUD** 206-207 H 4
Awendaw o **USA** (SC) 284-285 L 3
Awgu o **WAN** 204-205 G 5
Awio o **PNG** 183 F 4
Awira Wenz ~ **ETH** 200-201 K 6
Awisam o **GH** 202-203 K 7
Awisang o **RI** 164-165 F 4
Awjilah o **LAR** 192-193 J 3
Awka o **WAN** 204-205 G 5
Awrā, Wādī al ~ **LAR** 192-193 G 3
Awu, Gunung ▲ **RI** 164-165 J 2
Awun, River ~ **WAN** 204-205 F 4
Awuna River ~ **USA** 20-21 M 2
Awungi o **PNG** 183 F 3
Awura, Tanjung ▲ **RI** 166-167 H 4
Awwal, Wādī ~ **LAR** 190-191 H 6
Axe Hill ▲ **AUS** 176-177 J 3
Axel Heiberg Island ⌒ **CDN** 26-27 P 2
Axim o **GH** 202-203 J 7
Axinim o **BR** 66-67 H 5
Axtell o **USA** (NE) 262-263 G 4
Axtell o **USA** (UT) 254-255 D 4
Axton o **USA** (VA) 280-281 G 7
Axui o **BR** 68-69 G 3
Ayabaca o **PE** 64-65 C 4
Ayachi, Jbel ▲ **MA** 188-189 J 4
Ayacucho o **PE** 64-65 E 8
Ayacucho o **RA** 78-79 K 4
A'yäd, Bi'r o **LAR** 192-193 E 1
Ayakkum Hu o **VRC** 144-145 G 2
Ayamé o **CI** 202-203 J 7
Ayami, Tanjung ▲ **RI** 166-167 H 4
Ayamonte o • **E** 98-99 D 6
Ayan0k o **TR** 128-129 F 2
Ayanfure o **GH** 202-203 K 7
Ayangba o **WAN** 204-205 G 5
Ayapata o **PE** 70-71 B 3
Ayapel o **CO** 60-61 D 2
Ayapunga, Cerro ▲ **EC** 64-65 C 3
Ayarde, Laguna o **RA** 76-77 G 3
Ayaviri o **PE** (LIM) 64-65 D 8
Ayaviri o **PE** (PUN) 70-71 B 3
Ayden o **USA** (NC) 282-283 K 5
Aydin ☆ **TR** 128-129 B 4
Aydin Dağları ▲ **TR** 128-129 B 4
Aydingol Hu o **VRC** 146-147 J 4
Ayer o **USA** (MA) 278-279 K 6
Ayer Deras, Kampung Sungai o **MAL** 162-163 E 2
Ayer Hitam o **MAL** 162-163 E 4
Ayer Puteh, Kampung o **MAL** 162-163 E 2
Ayers Rock ▲ • **AUS** 176-177 L 2

Ayilür o **IND** 140-141 H 5
Ayina ~ **G** 210-211 D 2
Ayinwafe o **GH** 202-203 K 6
Ayiyak River ~ **USA** 20-21 O 2
Aykel o **ETH** 200-201 H 5
Aykino o **RUS** 88-89 O 4
Aýlon o **E** 98-99 F 4
Aylmer o **CDN** (ONT) 238-239 E 6
Aylmer, Lac o **CDN** (QUE) 238-239 O 3
Aylmer Lake o **CDN** 30-31 P 3
Aylsham o **CDN** (SAS) 232-233 P 2
Aymat o **USA** 244-245 K 2
Ayn al Ghāzalah o **LAR** 192-193 K 1
Ayn az-Zaraf, Bahr ~ **SUD** 206-207 K 4
Aynor o **USA** (SC) 284-285 L 3
Ayo o **PE** 64-65 F 9
Ayod o **SUD** 206-207 H 4
Ayoni o **SUD** 206-207 H 4
Ayopaya, Rio ~ **BOL** 70-71 D 5
Ayon, ostrov ⌒ **RUS** 112-113 N 4
Ayos o **CAM** 210-211 D 2
'Ayoūn el 'Atroûs o **RIM** 196-197 F 5
Ayr o **AUS** 174-175 J 6
Ayr o • **GB** 90-91 E 4
Ayr Lake o **CDN** 26-27 Q 8
Ayrshire o **USA** (IA) 274-275 D 2
Āysha o **ETH** 208-209 F 3
Ayu, Kepulauan ⌒ **RI** 166-167 F 1
Ayu, Pulau ⌒ **RI** 166-167 F 1
Ayu, Tanjung ▲ **RI** 164-165 E 4
Ayungon o **RP** 160-161 E 8
Ayutla de los Libres o **MEX** 52-53 E 3
Ayutthaya o • **THA** 158-159 F 3
Ayuy o **EC** 64-65 D 3
Ayvacık o **TR** 128-129 B 3
Ayvalık o **TR** 128-129 B 3
Ayyampettai o **IND** 140-141 H 5
Azad Kashmir ~ **IND** 138-139 D 3
Azahar, Costa del ~ **E** 98-99 H 4
Azaila o **E** 98-99 G 4
Azamgarh o **IND** 138-139 H 4
Azanaques, Cerro ▲ **BOL** 70-71 D 6
Azanaques, Cordillera de ▲ **BOL** 70-71 D 6
Azangaro o **PE** 70-71 B 4
Azao ▲ **DZ** 190-191 G 6
Azaoua, In~ o **RN** 198-199 C 2
Azaouak, Vallée de l' ~ **RMM** 196-197 M 6
Azara o **RA** 76-77 K 5
Āžarbāyğān-e Ḡarbi □ **IR** 128-129 L 3
Āžarbāyğān-e Šarqi □ **IR** 128-129 M 4
Azare o **WAN** 204-205 J 3
Āžaršahr o **IR** 128-129 L 4
Azas ~ **RUS** 116-117 H 9
Azas, ozero = Todža, ozero o **RUS** 116-117 H 9
Azauri o **BR** 62-63 K 3
Azaz ▲ **DZ** 190-191 G 4
Azazga o **DZ** 190-191 F 3
Az Bogd ▲ **MAU** 146-147 M 3
Azeffāl ⌒ **RIM** 196-197 C 5
Azemmour o **MA** 188-189 G 3
Azendjé o **DZ** 190-191 G 6
Azennezal, Erg ≃ **DZ** 190-191 C 9
Azerbaijan = Azerbajdžan ■ **AZ** 128-129 M 7
Azero ~ **BOL** 70-71 E 6
Azevedo Sodré o **BR** 76-77 K 6
Āzezo o **ETH** 200-201 H 5
Azgale o **IR** 128-129 L 5
Azilal ☆ **MA** 188-189 H 4
Azingo o **G** 210-211 B 4
Azingo, Lac o **G** 210-211 B 4
Aziri o **DZ** 190-191 F 7
Aziz o **TCH** 198-199 H 4
'Aziziya, al- o **IRQ** 128-129 L 6
Azlam, Wādī ~ **KSA** 130-131 E 4
Azle o **USA** (TX) 264-265 G 6
Aznã o **IR** 134-135 H 5
'Aẓmakaevo o **RUS** 96-97 H 6
Aznakaevo o **RUS** 96-97 H 6
Azogues o **EC** 64-65 C 3
Azores = Açores, Archipélago dos ⌒ **P** 6-7 G 5
Azores-Biscaya Rise ≈ 6-7 G 4
Azores-Cape Saint Vincent Ridge ≃ 188-189 D 2
Azoum, Bahr ~ **TCH** 206-207 E 3
Azourki, Jbel ▲ **MA** 188-189 H 5
Azov o **USA** (KS) 280-281 D 7
Azov, Sea of = Azovskoe more ≈ 102-103 J 4
Azovy o **RUS** 114-115 H 2
Azpeitia o • **E** 98-99 F 3
Azrak, Bahr ~ **TCH** 206-207 E 3
Azraq, al- o **JOR** 130-131 D 2
Āžre o **AFG** 138-139 D 2
Azrou o **MA** 188-189 J 4
Azrou, Oued ~ **DZ** 190-191 F 9
Aztec o **USA** (NM) 256-257 H 2
Aztec Ruins National Monument ∴ **USA** (NM) 256-257 H 2
Aztecas, Los o **MEX** 50-51 K 6
Azua ☆ **DOM** 54-55 K 5
Azuaga o **E** 98-99 E 5
Azúcar o **EC** 64-65 C 3
Azuer, Rio ~ **DZ** 190-191 F 9
Azuero, Peninsula de ~ **PA** 52-53 Q 8
Azufral, Volcán ▲ **CO** 60-61 C 6
Azufre ó Copiapo, Cerro ▲ **RCH** 76-77 C 2
Azul o **MEX** 50-51 J 4
Azul ☆ **RA** 78-79 K 4
Azul, Arroyo del ~ **RA** 78-79 K 4
Azul, Cerro ▲ **CR** 52-53 B 7
Azul, Cerro ▲ **EC** 64-65 B 10
Azul, Cerro ▲ **RA** 78-79 D 6
Azul, Rio ~ **BR** 64-65 F 5
Azul, Rio ~ **MEX** 52-53 G 3
Azul, Rio ~ **MEX** 52-53 G 3
Azul, Serra ▲ **BR** 70-71 K 4

Azúl Meambar, Parque Nacional ⊥ **HN** 52-53 L 4
Azucar o • **C** 54-55 H 5
Azcalar o **MEX** 52-53 K 2
Bacan, Kepulauan ⌒ **RI** 164-165 K 4
Bacanora o **MEX** 50-51 E 3
Bacateiro o **BR** 68-69 F 3
Bacău ☆ **RO** 102-103 E 4
Bắc Bình o **VN** 158-159 J 6
Bắc Giang o **VN** 156-157 E 6
Bắc Hà o • **VN** 156-157 E 6
Bachaguero o **YV** 60-61 F 2
Bachčysaraj o **UA** 102-103 H 5
Bache Peninsula ~ 26-27 M 4
Bachhrawān o **IND** 142-143 B 2
Bachinga o **MEX** 50-51 G 3
Báchiniva o **MEX** 50-51 F 3
Bachu o **VRC** 146-147 D 6
Bachu Akabe o **CAM** 204-205 H 6
Bačka Palanka o **YU** 100-101 G 3
Bačka Topola o **YU** 100-101 G 2
Back Bay o **RP** 280-281 L 7
Back Bay National Wildlife Refuge ⊥ **USA** (VA) 280-281 L 7
Backbone Mountain ▲ **USA** (MD) 280-281 G 4
Backbone Ranges ▲ **CDN** 30-31 E 4
Bäckefors o **S** 86-87 F 7
Bäckhammar o **S** 86-87 G 7
Back River ~ **CDN** 30-31 S 3
Backstairs Passage ≈ 180-181 D 3
Bắc Lac o **VN** 156-157 D 5
Bắc Mê o **VN** 156-157 D 5
Bắc Ngư'ờ'n o **VN** 156-157 D 5
Bắc Ninh ☆ • **VN** 156-157 E 6
Baco, Mount ▲ **RP** 160-161 D 6
Bacobampo o **MEX** 50-51 E 4
Bacolod o **RP** 160-161 E 7
Baconton o **USA** (GA) 284-285 F 5
Bacqueville, Lac o **CDN** 36-37 M 5
Bactii o **SP** 212-213 H 3
Bacuag o **RP** 160-161 F 8
Bacuati o **BR** 62-63 H 6
Bacuaga ~ **RP** 160-161 G 8
Bacuri o **BR** 68-69 F 3
Bacuri, Cachoeira ~ **BR** 62-63 H 6
Bacuri, Ilha do ⌒ **BR** 68-69 G 3
Bacuri, Lago de ~ **BR** 68-69 G 3
Bad o **IR** 134-135 G 4
Bad', al- o **KSA** 130-131 D 3
Badā o **ETH** 208-209 D 5
Badā o **KSA** 130-131 E 4
Bada o **RUS** 118-119 D 10
Bada Barabil o **IND** 142-143 D 4
Badagangshan Z.B. ⅄ **VRC** 156-157 F 2
Badagara o **IND** 140-141 F 5
Badago o **RMM** 202-203 F 4
Badagri o **WAN** 204-205 E 5
Badahšān □ **AFG** 136-137 M 6
Badā'i, al- o **KSA** 130-131 H 4
Badain Jaran Shamo ⌒ **VRC** 148-149 E 7
Badajós o **BR** 66-67 F 4
Badajós, Lago o **BR** 66-67 F 4
Badajoz ☆ • • **E** 98-99 D 5
Badaling • **VRC** 154-155 J 1
Badam ~ **KZ** 136-137 L 3
Badan, Kepulauan ⌒ **RI** 162-163 G 4
Badau o **RI** 162-163 H 4
Bada Valley ∴ • **RI** 164-165 G 4
Bad Axe o **USA** (MI) 272-273 G 4
Baddeck o **CDN** (NS) 240-241 P 7
Baddo ~ **PK** 134-135 J 4
Bad Dürrheim o **D** 92-93 K 4
Badegi o **WAN** 204-205 G 4
Badēguicheri o **RN** 198-199 B 5
Baden o **A** 92-93 O 5
Baden o **CDN** (MAN) 234-235 B 4
Baden-Baden o • **D** 92-93 K 4
Baden-Württemberg □ **D** 92-93 K 4
Bädepalli o **IND** 140-141 H 5
Bäder o **RN** 198-199 C 5
Badgastein o **A** 92-93 M 5
Badger o **CDN** (NFL) 242-243 M 4
Badger o **USA** (MN) 270-271 B 3
Badgingarra o **AUS** 176-177 C 5
Badgingarra National Park ⊥ **AUS** 176-177 C 5
Bādgīs □ **AFG** 136-137 J 7
Bādğūl o **AFG** 136-137 J 7
Bağestān o **IR** 134-135 H 3
Badghel o **IR** 136-137 F 6
Bad Hersfeld o • **D** 92-93 K 3
Bad Hills o **CDN** (SAS) 232-233 K 4
Badhyskij zapovednik ⊥ **TM** 136-137 G 7
Bādi, al- o **IRQ** 128-129 J 5
Badī', al- o **KSA** 130-131 K 6
Badi'a, al- o **KSA** 132-133 D 3
Badiara ~ **SN** 202-203 D 3
Badikaha o **CI** 202-203 H 5
Badin o **ETH** 200-201 H 5
Badin o **PK** 138-139 B 6
Badinko, Réserve du ⊥ **RMM** 202-203 F 3
Badin Lake o **USA** (NC) 282-283 G 5
Badin-Ko ~ **RMM** 202-203 F 3
Badir ~ **RN** 198-199 C 5
Bad Ischl o • **A** 92-93 M 5
Bādiyat Bani Kabir ~ **KSA** 132-133 B 3
Badjarīha ~ **RUS** 110-111 a 5
Badjer o **CAM** 204-205 K 6
Badland o **ETH** 200-201 H 5
Badlands ⅄ **USA** 260-261 D 3
Badlands ⊥ **USA** 260-261 D 3
Badlands National Park ⊥ **USA** (SD) 260-261 D 3

Badnāwar o **IND** 138-139 E 8
Badnera o **IND** 138-139 F 9
Bad Neuenahr-Ahrweiler o • **D** 92-93 J 3
Bado o **RI** 166-167 K 5
Badoc o **RP** 160-161 D 4
Ba Động o **VN** 158-159 J 6
Badong o **VRC** 154-155 G 6
Badou o **RT** 202-203 L 6
Baraccaro o **CDN** (NS) 240-241 K 7
Bacerac o **MEX** 50-51 F 2
Bắc Giang o **VN** 156-157 E 6
Bacha o **IRQ** 128-129 L 2
Bachalo o **WAL** 202-203 D 6
Bâdrah o **IR** 128-129 L 6
Badrānlū o **IR** 136-137 G 6
Bad Rapids ~ **USA** 260-261 E 2
Bad Reichenhall o • **D** 92-93 M 5
Badrinath o **IND** 138-139 G 3
Bad River ~ **USA** 260-261 E 2
Bad River Indian Reservation ⅄ **USA** (WI) 270-271 H 4
Badr wa-Hunain o **KSA** 130-131 F 6
Bad Segeberg o **D** 92-93 L 2
Bad Tölz o **D** 92-93 L 5
Badu o **VRC** 156-157 J 3
Badu Island ⌒ **AUS** 174-175 G 2
Badulla o **CL** 140-141 J 7
Badvel o **IND** 140-141 H 3
Badwater River ~ **CDN** 30-31 H 5
Badžal ~ **RUS** 122-123 H 3
Badžal'skij hrebet ▲ **RUS** 122-123 E 3
Baediam o **RIM** 202-203 E 2
Baeza o **EC** 64-65 D 2
Baeza o • **E** 98-99 F 6
Baezaeko River ~ **CDN** 228-229 K 4
Bafang o **CAM** 204-205 J 6
Bafata o **GNB** 202-203 C 3
Baffin Basin ≃ 26-27 P 7
Baffin Bay ≈ 266-267 L 6
Baffin Bay ≈ 266-267 O 5
Baffin-Greenland Rise ≃ 28-29 L 3
Baffin Island ⌒ **CDN** 24-25 O 4
Bafia o **CAM** 204-205 J 6
Bafilo o **RT** 202-203 L 5
Bafing ~ **RMM** 202-203 D 3
Bafing-Makana o **RMM** 202-203 D 3
Bafodia o **WAL** 202-203 D 5
Bafoulabé o **RMM** 202-203 D 3
Bafoussam ☆ **CAM** 204-205 J 6
Bāfq o **IR** 134-135 H 4
Bafra o **TR** 128-129 F 2
Bafra Burnu ▲ **TR** 128-129 F 2
Bäft o **IR** 134-135 G 4
Bafu Bay ≈ 202-203 F 7
Bafut o • **CAM** 204-205 J 5
Bafwabalinga o **ZRE** 212-213 A 3
Bafwaboğo o **ZRE** 210-211 L 3
Bafwaboli o **ZRE** 210-211 L 3
Bafwasende o **ZRE** 212-213 A 3
Baga o **WAN** 198-199 H 5
Bagabag o **RP** 160-161 D 4
Bagabag Island ⌒ **PNG** 183 D 3
Baga-Burul o **RUS** 126-127 F 5
Bagaces o **CR** 52-53 B 6
Bagadja o **RUS** 118-119 J 3
Bagaembo o **ZRE** 206-207 C 6
Bagaevskij = stanica Bagaevskaja o **RUS** 102-103 M 4
Bagai o **PNG** 183 E 4
Bagaia o **SUD** 206-207 K 3
Bagalkot o **IND** 140-141 F 2
Bāğalūr o **IND** 140-141 G 4
Bagamanoc o **RP** 160-161 E 6
Bagan Datuk o **MAL** 162-163 D 2
Bagandou o **RCA** 210-211 J 2
Baganga o **RP** 160-161 G 9
Bagani o **NAM** 216-217 G 9
Bagansiapiapi o **RI** 162-163 D 3
Baganuur = Nuurst o **MAU** 148-149 J 4
Bagaré o **BF** 202-203 J 3
Bagaroua o **RN** 198-199 B 5
Bagasin o **PNG** 183 C 3
Bagata o **BF** 202-203 H 4
Bagata o **ZRE** 210-211 F 5
Bagazan o **PE** 64-65 E 5
Bagbe ~ **WAL** 202-203 E 5
Bagdad o **IRQ** 128-129 L 6
Bagdad o **USA** (AZ) 256-257 C 5
Bagdarin o **RUS** 118-119 E 8
Bagé o **BR** 76-77 K 6
Bagega o **WAN** 204-205 F 3
Bägen o **IR** 134-135 G 4
Bäg-e Malek o **IR** 134-135 F 3
Bägerhat o • **BD** 142-143 F 4
Bagheria o **I** 100-101 D 6
Baghlan ☆ **AFG** 136-137 L 6
Baghelkhand Plateau ▲ **IND** 142-143 A 4
Baghpat o **IND** 138-139 F 4
Bağil o **Y** 132-133 E 6
Baginda, Tanjung ▲ **RI** 162-163 G 6
Bäğlän ▲ **AFG** 136-137 L 6
Bagley o **USA** (MN) 270-271 C 3
Bagley Icefield ⌒ **USA** 20-21 T 6
Bagnères-de-Bigorre o **F** 90-91 H 10
Bago o **RP** 160-161 E 7
Bago, Pulau ⌒ **RI** 164-165 H 3
Bagodar o **IND** 142-143 D 3
Bagodra o **IND** 138-139 D 8
Bagoé ~ **RMM** 202-203 G 3
Bagomoyo o • **EAT** 214-215 K 4
Bagoosar o **SP** 208-209 G 6
Bagot o **CDN** (MAN) 234-235 E 5

Bagot Range ▲ AUS 178-179 C 4
Bagou ○ DY 204-205 E 3
Bagraband, Kūh-e ▲ IR 134-135 J 5
Bagrāmī ○ AFG 138-139 B 2
Bagrationovsk ☆•• RUS 94-95 G 4
Bagre ○ BR 62-63 J 6
Bag Tug ∼ VRC 154-155 F 2
Bagua ○ PE 64-65 C 4
Bagua Grande ○ PE 64-65 C 4
Baguales, Cerro ▲ RA 80 F 4
Bāguanos ○ C 54-55 G 4
Bagudo ○ WAN 204-205 F 3
Baguinéda ○ RMM 202-203 G 3
Baguio ○ RP (DAO) 160-161 F 9
Baguio ○•• RP (BEN) 160-161 D 4
Bagyrlaj ∼ KZ 96-97 G 9
Bāha, al- ◘ KSA 132-133 B 3
Bāha, al- ☆ KSA (BAH) 132-133 B 3
Bahādorābād ○ IR 134-135 G 4
Bahadurganj ○ IND 142-143 E 2
Bahadurganj ○ NEP 144-145 D 7
Baham, Umm al- ○ KSA 132-133 C 5
Bahamas ▲ BS 54-55 H 2
Bahamas, The ■ BS 54-55 J 4
Bahamas National Trust Park ⊥ BS 54-55 J 4
Bahapča ∼ RUS 120-121 O 2
Bahār ○ IR 134-135 C 1
Bahārāgora ○ IND 142-143 E 4
Bahārak ○ AFG 136-137 M 6
Baharampur ○• IND 142-143 F 3
Baharden ○ TM 136-137 E 5
Bahardok ○ TM 136-137 F 5
Bahariya Oasis = al-Wāhāt al-Baḥriya ∴• ET 194-195 D 3
Bāḥarz, Kūh-e ▲ IR 136-137 F 7
Bahau ○ MAL 162-163 E 3
Bahaur ○ RI 164-165 D 5
Bahāwalnagar ○ PK 138-139 D 5
Bahāwalpur ○• PK 138-139 C 5
Bahay ○ RP 160-161 E 6
Bahçe ☆ TR 128-129 G 4
Baheri ○ IND 138-139 G 5
Bahi ○ EAT 212-213 E 6
Bahia ◘ BR 68-69 H 7
Bahía, Islas de la ⌒ HN 52-53 L 3
Bahia, Tanjung ▲ RI 166-167 H 4
Bahía Asunción ○ MEX 50-51 B 4
Bahía Blanca ≈ 78-79 J 5
Bahía Blanca ○ RA (BUA) 78-79 H 5
Bahía Bustamante ○ RA 80 G 2
Bahia Creek ○ RA 78-79 H 6
Bahía de Caráquez ○ EC 64-65 B 2
Bahía de Los Angeles ○ MEX 50-51 C 3
Bahía Grande ≈ 80 F 5
Bahía Honda ○ C 54-55 D 3
Bahía Kino ○ MEX 50-51 D 3
Bahía Laura ○ RA 80 G 4
Bahía Mansa ○ RCH 78-79 C 6
Bahías, Cabo dos ▲ RA 80 H 2
Bahía Solano ○ CO 60-61 C 4
Bahía Tortugas ○ MEX 50-51 B 4
Bahir Dar ○ ETH 208-209 C 3
Bāhla ○ IND 138-139 C 6
Bahlo ○••• OM 132-133 K 2
Baḥma ○ IRQ 128-129 L 4
Bahn ○ LB 202-203 F 6
Bahr ○ RCA 206-207 G 6
Bahra ○ KSA 132-133 A 3
Bahra, al- ○ KWT 130-131 K 3
Bahra al-Qadīma ○ KSA 132-133 A 3
Bahraich ○ IND 142-143 B 2
Bahrain = al-Bahrain ■ BRN 134-135 D 6
Bahr al-Milh < IRQ 128-129 K 6
Bahret Lut = Yam Hamelah ○ JOR 130-131 D 2
Baḥriya, Barqat al- ∴ ET 192-193 L 2
Baḥšī Kalai ○ AFG 138-139 B 4
Bahta ∼ RUS 114-115 U 3
Bahta ∼ RUS 116-117 F 4
Baḥtarān ◘ IR 134-135 B 1
Baḥtarān ☆• IR (BAH) 134-135 B 1
Baḥtegān, Daryāče-ye ○ IR 134-135 E 4
Bahtemir ∼ RUS 126-127 G 5
Baḥtiyārī, Čahār Maḥāll-o- ◘ IR 134-135 D 3
Bahty ○ KZ 124-125 N 5
Bahubulu, Pulau ⌒ RI 164-165 H 5
Bāhū Kalāt, Rūdḥāne-ye ∼ IR 134-135 J 6
Bahusuai ○ RI 164-165 G 5
Bahynaj ○ RUS 110-111 O 6
Baia ○ PNG 183 F 3
Baía, Rio da ∼ BR 68-69 B 5
Baía dos Tigres ○ ANG 216-217 A 8
Baía Farta ○ ANG 216-217 B 6
Baía Formosa ○ BR 68-69 L 5
Baia Grande, Lago ○ BR 70-71 G 4
Baia Mare ☆• RO 102-103 C 4
Baianópolis ○ BR 72-73 H 2
Baião ○ BR 68-69 D 3
Baia River ∼ PNG 183 B 4
Baibokoum ○ TCH 206-207 B 5
Baicheng ○ VRC (JIL) 150-151 D 5
Baicheng ○ VRC (XUZ) 146-147 E 5
Băicoi ○ RO 102-103 D 5
Baidā', al- ○ Y 132-133 D 7
Baidā' Natīl ○ KSA 130-131 G 4
Baidi Cheng • VRC 154-155 F 6
Baidou ∼ RCA 206-207 E 6
Baie, La ○ CDN (QUE) 240-241 E 2
Baie-des-Bacon ○ CDN (QUE) 240-241 F 2
Baie-des-Rochers ○ CDN (QUE) 240-241 F 3
Baie-des-Sables ○ CDN (QUE) 240-241 H 2
Baie-du-Poste ○ CDN (QUE) 236-237 P 2
Baie-du-Renard ○ CDN (QUE) 242-243 G 3
Baie Johan Beetz ○ CDN (QUE) 242-243 F 2
Baie-Sainte-Catherine ○ CDN (QUE) 240-241 F 2
Baie-Sainte-Claire ○ CDN (QUE) 242-243 D 3
Baie-Trinité ○ CDN (QUE) 242-243 A 3
Ba'īğī ○ IRQ 128-129 K 5
Baiḥān al-Qaṣāb ○ Y 132-133 D 6
Baihe ○ VRC (JIL) 150-151 G 6
Baihe ○ VRC (SXI) 154-155 G 5
Baikal, Lake = Bajkal, ozero ○ RUS 116-117 N 9
Baikal-Amur-Magistrale = BAM II RUS 118-119 E 7
Baikoré, Bahr ∼ TCH 206-207 E 3
Baikunthpur ○ IND 142-143 C 4
Baila ○ SN 202-203 B 3
Baila ○ VRC 144-145 F 6
Bailang ○ VRC 156-157 E 4
Baile Átha Cliath = Dublin ★•• IRL 90-91 D 5
Baile Átha Fhirdhia = Ardee ○ IRL 90-91 D 5
Baile Átha Luain = Athlone ○ IRL 90-91 D 5
Baile Átha Troim = Trim ☆• IRL 90-91 D 5
Baile Brigín = Balbriggan ○ IRL 90-91 D 5
Baile Chaisleáin Bhéarra = Castletown Bearhaven ○ IRL 90-91 C 6
Baile Chathail = Charlestown ○ IRL 90-91 C 5
Băile Herculane ○ RO 102-103 C 5
Baile Locha Riach = Loughrea ○ IRL 90-91 C 5
Baile Mhistéala = Mitchelstown ○ IRL 90-91 C 5
Bailén ○ E 98-99 F 5
Băileşti ○ RO 102-103 C 5
Bailey ○ USA (CO) 254-255 K 4
Bailey ○ USA (TX) 264-265 H 5
Bailey ○ ZA 220-221 H 5
Bailey Point ▲ CDN 24-25 O 3
Bailey Range ▲ AUS 176-177 G 4
Baileys Harbor ○ USA (WI) 270-271 L 5
Bail Hongal ○ IND 140-141 F 3
Baili, Bi'r ○ ET 192-193 L 2
Bailidujuan • VRC 156-157 E 3
Bailin ○ VRC 156-157 H 3
Bailingmiao • VRC 148-149 K 7
Bailique ○ BR (APA) 62-63 J 5
Bailique ○ BR (P) 68-69 D 3
Bailique, Ilha ⌒ BR 62-63 K 5
Baillargeon, Réserve ⊥ CDN (QUE) 240-241 L 2
Bailleul ○ F 90-91 J 6
Ba Illi ○ TCH (CHB) 206-207 C 3
Ba Illi ∼ TCH 206-207 C 3
Baillie Hamilton Island ⌒ CDN 24-25 Z 3
Baillie Islands ⌒ CDN 24-25 G 5
Baillie River ∼ CDN 30-31 R 3
Bailong Jiang ∼ VRC 154-155 D 5
Bailundo ○ ANG 216-217 C 6
Baima ○ VRC 154-155 B 5
Baimaxue Shan Z.B. ⊥• VRC 144-145 M 6
Baimka ○ RUS 112-113 N 3
Baimun ○ RI 166-167 H 5
Baimuru ○ PNG 183 C 4
Baino ○ PNG 183 B 4
Bainbridge ○ USA (GA) 284-285 F 6
Bainbridge Island ○ USA (WA) 244-245 C 3
Baines Drift ○ RB 218-219 E 6
Bainet ○ RH 54-55 J 5
Baing ○ RI 168 E 8
Baingoin ○ VRC 144-145 H 5
Baining Mountains ▲ PNG 183 G 3
Bainville ○ USA (MT) 250-251 P 3
Baiona ○ E 98-99 C 3
Baiquan ○ VRC 150-151 F 4
Bā'ir ○ JOR 130-131 E 2
Bā'ir, Wādī ∼ JOR 130-131 E 2
Baird ○ USA (TX) 264-265 E 6
Baird Inlet ≈ 20-21 H 6
Baird Mountains ▲ USA 20-21 K 3
Baird Peninsula ⌣ CDN 24-25 h 6
Bairds Table Mountain ▲ AUS 174-175 G 6
Baire ○ C 54-55 G 4
Bairiki ★ KIB 13 J 2
Bairin Youqi ○ VRC 148-149 O 6
Bairin Zuoqi ○ VRC 148-149 O 5
Bairnsdale ○ AUS 180-181 J 4
Bairoil ○ USA (WY) 252-253 L 4
Bairūt ★ RL 128-129 F 6
Baiš ○ KSA 132-133 C 5
Bais ○ RP 160-161 E 8
Baiš, Wādī ∼ KSA 132-133 C 5
Baise ∼ F 90-91 H 10
Baisha ○ VRC (HAI) 156-157 F 7
Baisha ○ VRC (SIC) 156-157 E 2
Baishan ○ VRC 150-151 F 6
Bai Shan ▲ VRC 146-147 L 5
Baishanzu ▲ VRC 156-157 L 3
Baishilazi Z.B. ⊥• VRC 150-151 E 7
Baishiling • VRC 156-157 G 7
Baishui ○ VRC 154-155 F 4
Baishuijiang Z.B. ⊥• VRC 154-155 D 5
Baisogala ○•• LT 94-95 H 4
Baissa ○ WAN 204-205 J 5
Bait Adaqa ○ Y 132-133 C 6
Baitadi ○ NEP 144-145 C 6
Bait al-Faqih ○• Y 132-133 C 6
Bait Lahm = Bet Lehem ☆•• WB 130-131 D 2
Bait Range ▲ CDN 32-33 G 4
Baiturahman = Banda Aceh ☆ RI 162-163 A 2
Baixa do Tubarā, Rio ∼ BR 68-69 J 7
Baixa Grande ○ BR 68-69 H 7
Baixão ○ BR 72-73 K 2
Baixo Guandu ○ BR 72-73 K 5
Baixo Longa ○ ANG 216-217 E 7
Baiyang Gou • VRC 146-147 H 4
Baiyan Temple • VRC 154-155 G 3
Baiyer River ○ PNG 183 C 3
Baiyer River National Park ⊥ PNG 183 C 3
Baiyi ○ VRC 154-155 E 6
Baiyin ○ VRC 154-155 D 3
Baizeklik Qianfodong • VRC 146-147 J 4
Baja ○ H 92-93 P 5
Baja, Punta ▲ MEX (BCN) 50-51 B 3
Baja, Punta ▲ MEX (SON) 50-51 D 3
Baja California ⌣ MEX 50-51 B 2
Baja California Norte ◘ MEX 50-51 B 2
Baja California Sur ◘ MEX 50-51 C 4
Bajada, La ○ C 54-55 C 4
Bajada del Agrio ○ RA 78-79 D 5
Bajaga ∼ RUS 120-121 E 2
Bajan ○ MAU 146-147 M 2
Baján ○ MEX 50-51 J 4
Bajanaul ○•• KZ 124-125 J 3
Bajanbulag ○ MAU 148-149 D 4
Bajančandman = Ih suuž ○ MAU 148-149 H 3
Bajandaj ☆ RUS 116-117 M 9
Bajandèlgèr =Širèèt ○ MAU 148-149 L 5
Bajangol=Baruunharaa ○ MAU 148-149 H 3
Bajan-Hongor ◘ MAU 148-149 D 4
Bajanhongor ☆ MAU 148-149 E 4
Bajanhošuu ○ MAU 146-147 K 1
Bajanlig = Hatansuudal ○ MAU 148-149 E 5
Bajanmönh = Ulaan-Èrèg ○ MAU 148-149 J 4
Bajan-Ölgij ◘ MAU 146-147 J 1
Bajan-Öndör = Bumbat ○ MAU 148-149 G 4
Bajan-Önžuul = Ihhaírhan ○ MAU 148-149 H 4
Bajan-Ovoo ○ MAU 146-147 M 3
Bajan-Ovoo = Žavhlant ○ MAU 148-149 L 4
Bajantèèg ○ MAU 148-149 E 5
Bajan Uul = Bajan ○ MAU 146-147 M 2
Bajan-Uul = Žavarthošuu ○ MAU 148-149 L 3
Bajasgalant ○ MAU 148-149 L 4
Bajawa ○ RI 168 E 7
Bajdarackaja guba ≈ 108-109 L 7
Bajdarata ∼ RUS 108-109 M 8
Bajdrag gol ∼ MAU 148-149 D 4
Bajganin ☆ KZ 126-127 M 3
Bajie ○ VRC 156-157 C 4
Bajimba, Mount ▲ AUS 178-179 M 5
Bajina Bašta ○• YU 100-101 G 3
Bajío de Ahuichila ○ MEX 50-51 H 5
Bajíos de Agua Blanca ○ MEX 50-51 F 5
Bajkadam ○ KZ 136-137 L 3
Bajkal ○ RUS 116-117 M 10
Bajkal, zaliv ≈ 122-123 K 2
Bajkalovo ○ RUS 114-115 J 6
Bajkalovsk ○ RUS 108-109 U 6
Bajkal'sk ○ RUS 116-117 L 10
Bajkal'skij hrebet ▲ RUS 116-117 O 8
Bajkal'skij zapovednik ⊥ RUS 116-117 M 10
Bajkal'skoe ○ RUS 118-119 D 8
Bajki ○ RUS 96-97 K 6
Bajkit ○ RUS 116-117 H 5
Bajkonyr ○ KZ 124-125 E 5
Bajkovo ○ RUS 122-123 R 3
Bajmak ☆ RUS 96-97 L 7
Bajo ○ RI 168 D 7
Bajo Caracoles ○ RA 80 E 3
Bajo de Carl Laufquen ∴ RA 78-79 E 6
Bajo de la Tierra Colorada ∴ RA 78-79 F 7
Bajo del Gualicho ∴ RA 78-79 G 7
Bajo de los Menucos ∴ RA 78-79 F 5
Bajoga ○ WAN 204-205 J 3
Bajo Hondo ○ RA 76-77 D 6
Bajo Nuevo ⌒ CO 54-55 F 7
Bajool ○ AUS 178-179 L 2
Bajo Pichanaquí ○ PE 64-65 E 7
Bajos de Haina ○ DOM 54-55 K 5
Bajram-Ali ○ TM 136-137 H 6
Bajsa ○ RUS 118-119 F 8
Bajsun ○ UZ 136-137 K 5
Bajugan ○ RI 164-165 G 3
Bajyrküm ○ KZ 136-137 L 3
Baká ○ NIC 52-53 B 5
Bakaba ○ TCH 206-207 C 5
Bakairi, Área Indígena ⚔ BR 70-71 K 4
Bakal ○ RUS 96-97 L 6
Bakala ○ RCA (OMB) 206-207 C 6
Bakala ○ RCA (Oua) 206-207 E 5
Bakali ∼ ZRE 210-211 F 6
Bakaly ☆ RUS 96-97 H 6
Bakanas ∼ KZ 124-125 L 6
Bakaoré ○ TCH 198-199 K 5
Bakau ○• WAG 202-203 B 3
Bakaucengal ○ RI 164-165 E 5
Bakauhuni ○ RI 162-163 F 7
Bakayan, Gunung ▲ RI 164-165 E 2
Bakbakty ○ KZ 124-125 K 6
Bakčar ○ RUS (TOM) 114-115 R 6
Bakčar ∼ RUS 114-115 R 6
Bakebe ○ CAM 204-205 H 6
Bakel ○ SN 202-203 D 2
Bakelalan ○ MAL 164-165 D 2
Baker ○ USA (CA) 248-249 H 4
Baker ○ USA (LA) 268-269 J 6
Baker ○ USA (MT) 250-251 P 5
Baker ○ USA (NV) 246-247 L 4
Baker ○ USA (OR) 244-245 H 6
Baker ○ USA (WV) 280-281 H 4
Baker, Canal ≈ 80 C 3
Baker, Mount ▲ USA (WA) 244-245 D 2
Baker Creek ∼ CDN 228-229 M 4
Bakerhill ○ USA (AL) 284-285 E 5
Baker Island ⌒ USA 13 K 2
Baker Island ⌒ USA 32-33 D 4
Baker Lake ○ AUS 176-177 J 3
Baker Lake ○ CDN (NWT) 30-31 V 3
Baker Lake ○ CDN (NWT) 30-31 W 3
Baker Lake ○ USA (WA) 244-245 D 2
Baker Range ▲ AUS 176-177 H 2
Bakers Dozen Islands ⌒ CDN 36-37 K 6
Baker Settlement ○ CDN (NS) 240-241 L 6
Bakersfield ○ USA (CA) 248-249 F 4
Bakersfield ○ USA (TX) 266-267 E 3
Bakerville ○ ZA 220-221 H 2
Ba Kha ○ VN 156-157 D 6
Bakhtiyārpur ○ IND 142-143 D 3
Bakı ★• AZ 128-129 N 2
Bakin Birji ○ RN 198-199 D 5
Bakinskij arhipelago ⌒ AZ 128-129 N 3
Bakırçay ∼ TR 128-129 B 3
Bakkafjörður ○ IS 86-87 f 1
Bakkejord ○ N 86-87 J 2
Bako ○ CI 202-203 G 5
Bako ○ ETH 208-209 C 4
Bako National Park ⊥ MAL 162-163 J 4
Bakong, Pulau ⌒ RI 162-163 F 4
Bakongan ○ RI 162-163 B 3
Bakool ◘ SP 208-209 F 6
Bakop ○ PNG 183 G 3
Bakordi ○ SUD 206-207 J 6
Bakore, Massif de ▲ RCA 206-207 B 5
Bakori ○ WAN 204-205 G 3
Bakouma ○ RCA 206-207 F 6
Bakoumba ○ G 210-211 D 4
Bakoye ∼ RMM 202-203 F 3
Baksa ∼ RUS 114-115 R 7
Bak Sadane ○ RMM 196-197 J 5
Bakşaj ∼ KZ 96-97 G 10
Baksan ○• RUS 104 E 6
Baksan ∼ RUS 126-127 E 6
Baktalórántháza ○ H 92-93 R 5
Baku = Bakı ★• AZ 128-129 N 2
Bakulu ○ RI 164-165 K 3
Bakung, Pulau ⌒ RI 162-163 F 4
Bakuriani ○ GE 126-127 E 7
Bakwa-Kenge ○ ZRE 210-211 J 6
Baky ∼ RUS 110-111 X 5
Bakyrly ○ KZ 124-125 E 6
Bala ○ CDN (ONT) 238-239 F 3
Bala ○ RUS 110-111 T 6
Bala ○ SN 202-203 D 2
Balâ ☆ TR 128-129 E 3
Bala ○ WAN 204-205 F 4
Bala, Cerros de ▲ BOL 70-71 C 3
Balabac ○ RP 160-161 B 9
Balabac Island ⌒ RP 160-161 B 9
Balabac Strait ≈ 160-161 B 9
Balabagan ○ RP 160-161 F 9
Balabaiba ○ ANG 216-217 B 6
Ba'labakk ☆•• RL 128-129 G 5
Balabala ○ ZRE 210-211 H 2
Balabalangan, Kepulauan ⌒ RI 164-165 E 5
Bālā Bolūk ○ AFG 134-135 K 2
Balad al-Mala ○ IRQ 128-129 L 5
Balade ○ IR 136-137 B 6
Baladjie Lake ○ AUS 176-177 E 5
Balad Rūz ○ IRQ 128-129 L 6
Balad Sinǧār ○ IRQ 128-129 J 4
Balagaččy ○ RUS 110-119 L 3
Balaganah ○ RUS 118-119 H 6
Balagančik, hrebet ▲ RUS 122-123 R 2
Balagannoe ○ RUS 120-121 N 4
Balaganoï ○ RUS 116 117 L 0
Balagan-Taas • RUS 110-111 Z 6
Balaghat ○ IND 142-143 B 5
Balaguer ○ E 98-99 H 4
Balahna ○ RUS 94-95 S 3
Balahnja, gora ▲ RUS 110-111 F 3
Balahta ☆ RUS 116-117 E 8
Ba Loi, Công ∼ VN 158 159 J 5
Balai Berkuak ○ RI 162-163 J 5
Balaikarangan ○ RI 162-163 J 4
Balaipungut ○ RI 162-163 D 4
Balaiselasa ○ RI 162-163 D 5
Balaka ○ MW 218-219 H 2
Balakbal ∴• MEX 52-53 K 3
Balakété ○ RCA 206-207 D 5
Balaki ○ RG 202-203 E 3
Balaklava ○ AUS 180-181 E 3
Balaklija ○ UA 102-103 K 3
Bālākot ○ PK 138-139 D 2
Balakovo ☆ RUS 96-97 E 7
Balala ○ ETH 208-209 B 6
Balalai Island ⌒ SOL 184 I b 2
Balama ○ MOC 218-219 K 1
Balamba ○ CAM 204-205 J 6
Balambangan, Pulau ⌒ MAL 160-161 B 9
Balam Tākli ○ IND 138-139 E 10
Balancán de Domínguez ○ MEX 52-53 J 3
Balanced Rock ∴ USA (ID) 252-253 D 4
Balandou ○ RG 202-203 F 4
Balanga ☆ RP 160-161 D 5
Balanga ○ ZRE 214-215 C 5
Balangala ○ ZRE 210-211 G 3
Ba Làng An, Mũi ▲ VN 158-159 K 3
Balāngir ○ IND 142-143 C 5
Balangkayan ○ RP 160-161 F 7
Balangoda ○ CL 140-141 J 7
Balao ○ EC 64-65 C 3
Balaoan ○ RP 160-161 D 4
Balapitiya ○ CL 140-141 J 7
Balaraja ○ RI 168 B 3
Balarāmpur ○ IND 142-143 E 4
Balasan ○ RP 160-161 E 7
Balašiha ☆ RUS 94-95 P 4
Bāl-Asmar ○ KSA 132-133 C 4
Balašov ○ RUS 102-103 N 2
Balassagyarmat ○ H 92-93 P 4
Balāt ○ ET 194-195 D 5
Balat (Labuhanbalat) ○ RI 168 C 7
Bala-Taldyk ∼ KZ 126-127 N 3
Balatan ○ RP 160-161 E 6
Balaton ○ H 92-93 O 5
Balatonfüred ○ H 92-93 O 5
Balauring ○ RI 166-167 B 6
Balavé ○ BF 202-203 H 3
Balaya ○ RG 202-203 D 4
Balazote ○ E 98-99 F 5
Balbalan ○ RP 160-161 D 4
Balbalasang ○ RP 160-161 D 4
Balbi, Mount ▲ PNG 184 I b 1
Balbina ○ BR 62-63 E 6
Balbina, Cachoeira ∼ BR 62-63 E 6
Balbina, Represa de < BR 62-63 E 6
Balboa ○ CO 60-61 D 5
Balboa ○• PA 52-53 E 7
Balbriggan = Baile Brigín ○ IRL 90-91 D 5
Balcad ○ SP 212-213 K 2
Balcarce ○ RA 78-79 K 4
Balcarres ○ CDN (SAS) 232-233 P 5
Bălceşti ○ RO 102-103 C 5
Balčik ○ BG 102-103 F 6
Balclutha ○ NZ 182 B 7
Balcoms Corners ○ USA (NY) 278-279 B 6
Balcones Escarpment ▲ USA 266-267 H 4
Bald Eagle Mountain ▲ USA 280-281 J 3
Balde de la Mora ○ RA 76-77 E 6
Baldenburg = Biały Bór ○• PL 92-93 O 2
Bald Head ▲ AUS 176-177 E 7
Bald Hill ▲ CDN 20-21 Z 4
Bald Hill No. 2 ▲ AUS 178-179 L 4
Bald Knob ○ USA (AR) 276-277 D 5
Bald Mountain ▲ USA 248-249 J 2
Baldock Lake ○ CDN 34-35 H 2
Baldur ○ CDN (MAN) 234-235 D 5
Baldwin ○ USA (FL) 286-287 H 1
Baldwin ○ USA (IA) 274-275 H 2
Baldwin ○ USA (MI) 272-273 D 4
Baldwin ○ USA (WI) 270-271 F 6
Baldwin, Parc Provincial ⊥ CDN (QUE) 240-241 K 2
Baldwin Bank ⌒ AUS 172-173 H 2
Baldwin City ○ USA (KS) 262-263 L 6
Baldwin Peninsula ⌣ USA 20-21 J 3
Baldwinsville ○ USA (NY) 278-279 E 5
Baldwinton ○ CDN (SAS) 232-233 J 3
Baldwyn ○ USA (MS) 268-269 M 2
Baldy Hughes ○ CDN (BC) 228-229 M 3
Baldy Mountain ▲ CDN (BC) 230-231 K 4
Baldy Mountain ▲ CDN (MAN) 234-235 C 3
Baldy Peak ▲ USA (AZ) 256-257 F 5
Bal'džikan ○ RUS 118-119 E 11
Bale ○ ANG 216-217 D 7
Balē ◘ ETH 208-209 E 6
Balé ∼ RG 202-203 E 4
Bale ∼ RMM 202-203 F 4
Bâle = Basel ○• CH 92-93 J 5
Baleares, Islas ◘ E 98-99 H 5
Balearic Islands = Balears, Illes ⌒ E 98-99 H 5
Balease ∼ RI 164-165 G 5
Balease, Gunung ▲ RI 164-165 G 5
Baleh ∼ MAL 162-163 K 4
Baleia, Ponta da ▲ BR 72-73 L 4
Baleine, Rivière à la ∼ CDN 36-37 Q 5
Balej ☆ RUS 118-119 H 10
Balékoutou ○ TCH 206-207 D 4
Baleleshberge ▲ ZA 220-221 K 3
Bale Mount National Park ⊥ ETH 208-209 D 5
Balene ○ RP 160-161 E 6
Baler ○ RP 160-161 D 5
Baler Bay ≈ 160-161 D 5
Baleshwar ○ IND 142-143 E 5
Balestrand ☆• N 86-87 C 6
Baléya ○ RMM 202-203 F 3
Baleyara ○ RN 204-205 E 2
Baley Guerrero ○ DOM 54-55 L 5
Balezino ☆ RUS 96-97 H 5
Balfour ○ AUS 180-181 H 6
Balfour ○ CDN (BC) 230-231 N 4
Balfour ○ USA (ND) 258-259 G 4
Balfour ○ ZA (CAP) 220-221 H 6
Balfour ○ ZA (TRA) 220-221 J 3
Balfour Downs ○ AUS 172-173 E 7
Balgak ○ SUD 200-201 C 6
Balgazyn ○ RUS 116-117 G 10
Balgo ○ AUS 172-173 J 6
Balgonie ○ CDN (SAS) 232-233 O 5
Balguntay ○ VRC 146-147 H 4
Balğurasi ○ KSA 132-133 B 4
Balḫ ○ AFG 136-137 K 6
Balḫ ◘ AFG 136-137 K 6
Balḫ, Daryā-ye ∼ AFG 136-137 K 6
Balḫ Āb ○ AFG 136-137 K 7
Balḫ Āb, Rūd-e ∼ AFG 136-137 K 7
Balho ○ DJI 200-201 L 6
Bali ○ CAM 204-205 J 6
Bali ◘ RI 168 B 6
Bali, Laut ≈ 168 B 6
Bali, Pulau ⌒ RI 168 B 7
Bali, Selat ≈ 168 B 7
Balibi ○ RCA 206-207 E 5
Balibo ○ RI 166-167 C 6
Baliem ∼ RI 166-167 K 4
Baliem Valley ⌣ RI 166-167 K 3
Balifondo ○ RCA 206-207 F 6
Balige ○ RI 162-163 C 3
Baliguda ○ IND 142-143 C 5
Balıkesir ☆ TR 128-129 B 3
Balikpapan ○ RI 164-165 E 4
Balikpapan, Teluk ≈ 164-165 E 4
Balimela Reservoir ○ IND 142-143 C 6
Balimo ○ PNG 183 B 5
Baling ○ MAL 162-163 D 2
Balingara, Pegunungan ▲ RI 164-165 G 4
Balingian ○ MAL 162-163 K 3
Balinn ∼ RMM 202-203 E 3
Balintang Channel ≈ 160-161 D 3
Balises solaires II• DZ 190-191 C 8
Baliza ○ BR 72-73 D 4
Baljaga ○ RUS 116-117 O 10
Baljennie ○ CDN (SAS) 232-233 L 3
Balkan Mountains = Stara Planina ▲ BG 102-103 C 6
Balkaš ○ KZ 124-125 J 5
Balkašin ☆ KZ 124-125 F 2
Balkon-Myřk, gora ▲ RUS 88-89 O 2
Ball, Mount ▲ AUS 172-173 H 5
Balladonia Motel ○ AUS 176-177 G 6
Ballangen ○ N 86-87 H 2
Ballantyne, Lac ○ CDN 36-37 P 5
Ballantyne Strait ≈ 24-25 O 2
Ballarat ○ AUS 180-181 G 4
Ballard, Lake ○ AUS 176-177 F 4
Ballaroo ○ AUS 178-179 K 4
Ballasetas ○ RI 162-163 B 3
Ballater ○ GB 90-91 F 3
Ballé ○ RMM 202-203 F 2
Ballena, Punta ▲ EC 64-65 B 2
Ballenas, Canal de ≈ 50-51 C 3
Ballenero, Canal ≈ 80 E 7
Ballia ○ IND 142-143 D 3
Ballidu ○ AUS 176-177 D 5
Ballina ○ AUS 178-179 M 5
Ballina = Béal an Átha ○ IRL 90-91 C 4
Ballinasloe = Béal Átha na Sluaighe ○ IRL 90-91 C 5
Ballinger ○ USA (TX) 266-267 H 2
Ball Lake ○ CDN (ONT) 234-235 K 4
Ballone Highway II AUS 178-179 J 4
Balloul ○ DZ 190-191 C 3
Ball's Pyramid ⌒ AUS 180-181 N 7
Bally ○ USA (PA) 280-281 L 3
Ballycastle ○ GB 90-91 D 4
Ballyshannon ○ IRL 90-91 C 4
Balmacara ○ GB 90-91 E 3
Balmaceda ○ RCH 80 D 5
Balmaceda, Cerro ▲ RCH 80 D 5
Balmaceda, Parque Nacional ⊥ RCH 80 D 5
Balmaceda, Sierra ▲ RCH 80 F 6
Balmertown ○ CDN (ONT) 234-235 K 3
Balmoral ○ AUS 180-181 F 4
Balmoral ○ ZA 220-221 J 2
Balmorhea ○ USA (TX) 266-267 D 2
Balnearia ○ RA 76-77 F 6
Balneário Camboriú ○ BR 74-75 F 6
Balneario del Sol ○• C 54-55 H 5
Balneario las Grutas ○ RA 78-79 G 6
Balneario Massini ○ RA 78-79 H 6
Balo ○ RI 164-165 H 4
Baloa ○ RI 164-165 H 4
Balobaloang-Kecil, Pulau ⌒ RI 168 D 6
Balod ○ IND 142-143 B 5
Balohan, Teluk ≈ 162-163 A 2
Balok, Kampung ○ MAL 162-163 E 3
Balombo ○ ANG (BGU) 216-217 C 6
Balombo ∼ ANG 216-217 C 6
Balong ○ RI 168 D 3
Balong ○ VRC 144-145 L 2
Balonne River ∼ AUS 178-179 K 5
Balotra ○ IND 138-139 D 7
Balqash Köl = Balkaš köli ○ KZ 124-125 H 6
Balrāmpur ○ IND 142-143 C 2
Balranald ○ AUS 180-181 G 3
Balş ○ RO 102-103 D 5
Balsa Nova ○ BR 74-75 F 5
Balsapuerto ○ PE 64-65 D 4
Balsas ○ BR 68-69 E 5
Balsas ○ MEX 52-53 E 2
Balsas ○ PE 64-65 D 5
Balsas, Río ∼ MEX 52-53 E 3
Balsas, Rio das ∼ BR 68-69 E 7
Balsas, Rio das ∼ BR 68-69 F 5
Balsinhas, Ribeiro ∼ BR 68-69 F 5
Balta ☆ UA 102-103 F 4
Balta ○ USA (ND) 258-259 G 3
Balta Brăilei ∴ RO 102-103 E 5
Baltakol ○ KZ 136-137 K 3
Baltal ○ IND 138-139 E 2
Baltasar Brum ○ ROU 76-77 J 6
Baltasi ☆ RUS 96-97 G 5
Baltazar ○ YV 60-61 H 6
Bălţi ☆ MD 102-103 E 4
Baltic Sea ≈ 86-87 H 9
Baltijsk ○ RUS 94-95 F 4
Balṭīm ○ ET 194-195 E 2
Baltimore ○ USA (OH) 280-281 D 4
Baltimore ○• USA (MD) 280-281 K 4
Baltimore ○ ZA 218-219 E 6
Baltimore = Dún na Séad ○ IRL 90-91 C 6
Baltit ○ PK 138-139 E 1
Baltiysk = Baltijsk ○ RUS 94-95 F 4
Baltra, Isla ⌒ EC 64-65 B 10
Baltrum ⌒ D 92-93 J 2
Baluan Island ⌒ PNG 183 D 2
Baluarte, Arroyo ∼ USA 266-267 J 6
Balūčestān ∴ IR 134-135 J 5
Balūčestān, Sīstān -ō- ◘ IR 134-135 H 5
Baluchistan = Baluchistān ∴ 134-135 J 5
Baluchistan = Baluchistān ◘ PK 134-135 K 4
Balud ○ RP 160-161 E 6
Balui ∼ MAL 164-165 D 2
Balūr ○ IND 140-141 F 4
Baluran Game Park ⊥ RI 168 B 6
Balut Island ⌒ RP 160-161 F 10
Balvard ○ IR 134-135 G 4
Balvi ☆•• LV 94-95 K 3
Balwāda ○ IND 138-139 E 8
Balwina Aboriginal Land ⚔ AUS 172-173 J 6
Balygyčan ○ RUS (MAG) 112-113 H 5
Balygyčan ∼ RUS 112-113 H 5
Balygyčan, Verhnij ○ RUS 112-113 H 5
Balyhta ○ RUS 116-117 M 8
Balykča ○ RUS 124-125 P 3
Balyktah ∼ RUS 110-111 W 2
Balyktyg-Hem ∼ RUS 116-117 H 10
Balzac ○ CDN (ALB) 232-233 D 4
Balzar ○ EC 64-65 C 2
Balzas ○ EC 64-65 C 3
Balž gol ∼ MAU 148-149 K 3
Bam ○ IR 134-135 H 4
Bam ○ TCH 206-207 C 4
BAM = Baikal-Amur-Magistrale II RUS 118-119 E 7
Bam, Lac de ○• BF 202-203 K 3
Bama ○• BF 202-203 H 4
Bama ○ VRC 156-157 E 4
Bama ○ WAN 204-205 K 3
Bamaba ○ ZRE 210-211 G 5
Bamaga ⚔ AUS 174-175 G 2
Bamaji Lake ○ CDN (ONT) 234-235 M 3
Bamake ○ LB 202-203 G 7
Bamako ◘ RMM 202-203 G 3
Bamako ★• RMM (BAM) 202-203 F 3
Bamba ○ EAK 212-213 G 5
Bamba ∼ RCA 206-207 D 6
Bamba ○ RMM 196-197 K 6
Bamba ○ ZRE 210-211 G 6
Bambadinca ○ GNB 202-203 C 3
Bambak ○ PNG 183 E 3
Bambalang ○ CAM 204-205 J 5
Bambam ○ WAN 204-205 J 4
Bambama ○ RCB 210-211 D 5
Bambamarca ○ PE 64-65 C 5
Bambana, Río ∼ NIC 52-53 B 5
Bambang ○ RI 162-163 E 7
Bambang ○ RP 160-161 D 4
Bambangan ○ MAL 160-161 B 10
Bambangando ○ ANG 218-219 B 3
Bambara ○ TCH 206-207 D 4
Bambara-Maoundé ○ RMM 202-203 J 2
Bambari ☆ RCA 206-207 E 6
Bambaroo ○ AUS 174-175 J 6
Bambéla ○ CI 202-203 J 5
Bamberg ○•• D 92-93 L 4
Bamberg ○ USA (SC) 284-285 J 3
Bambesa ○ ZRE 210-211 K 2
Bambesi ○ ETH 208-209 B 4
Bambey ○• SN 202-203 B 2
Bambila ○ RMM 202-203 E 2
Bambili ○ ZRE 210-211 L 2
Bambio ○ RCA 210-211 F 2
Bamboesberg ▲ ZA 220-221 G 5
Bamboi ○ GH 202-203 J 5
Bamboo Creek ○ AUS 172-173 E 6
Bambouk ∴ RMM 202-203 E 2
Bambouti ○ RCA 206-207 H 6
Bamboutos, Monts ▲ CAM 204-205 J 6
Bambudi ○ ETH 208-209 B 3
Bambuí ○ BR 72-73 H 6
Bambui ○ CAM 204-205 J 5
Bambujka ∼ RUS 118-119 G 8
Bamenda ☆ CAM 204-205 J 6
Bamendjing, Lac de < CAM 204-205 J 6
Bame Town ○ LB 202-203 F 7
Bamfield ○ CDN (BC) 230-231 D 5
Bami ○ TM 136-137 E 5
Bamingui ○ RCA (Bam) 206-207 E 5
Bamingui ∼ RCA 206-207 E 5
Bamingui-Bangoran ◘ RCA 206-207 D 4
Bamingui-Bangoran, Parc National du ⊥ RCA 206-207 D 4
Bamio ○ PNG 183 B 4
Bam Island ⌒ PNG 183 C 2
Bamkeri ○ RI 166-167 F 2
Bampošt, Kūh-e ▲ IR 134-135 K 5
Bampūr ○ IR 134-135 J 5
Bampūr, Rūd-e ∼ IR 134-135 H 5
Bamrūd-e Soflā ○ IR 134-135 J 2
Bamu River ∼ PNG 183 B 4
Bamusso ○ CAM 204-205 H 6
Bāmyān ◘ AFG 134-135 M 1
Bamyan ☆• AFG (BM) 134-135 M 1
Bāmyān ∼ AFG 136-137 K 7
Bamyili ○ AUS 172-173 L 3
Ban ○ BF 202-203 J 2
Bana ○ CAM 204-205 J 6
Bana ∴ TM 136-137 K 2
Bana, Col de ▲ CAM 204-205 J 6
Banā, Wādī ∼ Y 132-133 D 7
Banabuiú, Açude < BR 68-69 J 4
Banabuiú, Rio ∼ BR 68-69 J 4
Bana Daniéd ○ SN 202-203 D 2
Bañadas del Chadileuvá ∴ RA 70-79 F 4
Banagi ○ EAT 212-213 E 5
Banalia ○ ZRE 210-211 K 3
Banama ○ RG 202-203 F 5
Banamba ○ RMM 202-203 G 3
Banana ○ AUS 178-179 L 3
Banana ○ ZRE 216-217 B 3
Bananal, Ilha do ⌒ BR 68-69 C 7
Bananal, Rio ∼ BR 68-69 D 6
Banana Range ▲ AUS 178-179 L 3
Banana River ≈ 286-287 J 3
Banandjé ○ CI 202-203 G 5
Bananeiras ○ BR 68-69 L 5
Banantara ○ RG 202-203 F 4
Banangui ○ RCA 206-207 E 6
Banankoro ○ RG 202-203 F 5
Banankoro ○ RMM (SÉ) 202-203 G 3
Banankoro ○ RMM (SIK) 202-203 F 4
Banao ○ C (CG) 54-55 G 4
Banao ○ C (SS) 54-55 F 4
Banapur ○ IND 142-143 D 6
Banās, Ra's ▲ ET 194-195 G 6
Banat ∴ 102-103 B 5
Banat ○ USA (MI) 270-271 L 5
Banaue ☆ RP 160-161 D 4
Banaz ☆ TR 128-129 C 3
Banaz Çayı ∼ TR 128-129 C 3
Banba ○ RMM 202-203 G 4
Ban Bakha ○ LAO 156-157 D 7
Ban Ban ○ AUS 178-179 G 3
Ban Ban ○ LAO 156-157 C 7
Ban Ban ○ VN 156-157 D 7
Banbar ○ VRC 144-145 K 5
Banbaran ○ RMM 202-203 F 3
Banbirpur ○ IND 144-145 C 6
Ban Boun Tai ○ LAO 156-157 B 6
Banbridge ○ GB 90-91 D 4
Banbury ○ GB 90-91 G 5
Bancauan Island ⌒ RP 160-161 C 9
Banc d'Arguin, Parc National du ⊥•• RIM 196-197 B 4
Ban Chamrung ○ THA 158-159 G 4
Ban Chiang ○••• THA 158-159 G 2
Banco, El ○ CO 60-61 E 3
Bancoran Island ⌒ RP 160-161 C 9
Bancos de San Pedro ○ YV 60-61 H 3
Bancroft ○ CDN (ONT) 238-239 H 3
Bancroft ○ USA (ID) 252-253 G 4
Bancs Providence ⌒ SY 224 B 4
Banda ○ CAM 204-205 K 4
Banda ○ GH 202-203 J 5
Banda ○ IND 138-139 G 7
Bānda ○ IND 142-143 B 3
Banda ○ ZRE (BAN) 210-211 G 6
Banda ○ ZRE (Hau) 206-207 H 6
Banda, Kepulauan (Nutmeg Kepulauan) ⌒•• RI 166-167 E 4
Banda, La ○ RA 76-77 E 4
Banda Aceh ☆ RI 162-163 A 2
Banda Banda, Mount ▲ AUS 178-179 M 6
Bandabe ○ RM 222-223 F 5
Banda del Río Salí ○ RA 76-77 E 4
Bandae ○ GH 202-203 J 7

Bagot Range — Bandae 301

Bartica ☆ GUY 62-63 E 2
Bartın ☆ TR 128-129 E 2
Bartle o USA (CA) 246-247 D 2
Bartle Frere ▲ AUS 174-175 H 5
Bartlesville o USA (OK) 264-265 J 2
Bartlett o USA (NE) 262-263 H 3
Bartlett o USA (OH) 280-281 E 4
Bartlett o USA (TN) 276-277 F 5
Bartlett o USA (TX) 266-267 K 3
Bartlett, Cape ▲ CDN 36-37 K 6
Bartlett Lake ⬭ CDN 30-31 K 4
Bartletts Harbour o CDN (NFL) 242-243 L 2
Bartok Lake, De ⬭ CDN 30-31 U 5
Bartolomé Masó o C 54-55 G 4
Barton o RP 160-161 C 7
Barton o USA (ND) 258-259 G 3
Barton o USA (VT) 278-279 J 4
Bartoszyce o PL 92-93 Q 1
Bartow o USA (FL) 286-287 H 4
Bartow o USA (WV) 280-281 G 5
Bartylaakty, köl ⬭ KZ 96-97 H 10
Baru o CO 60-61 D 2
Baru o RI (IRJ) 166-167 G 2
Baru o RI (MAL) 164-165 K 3
Bārū, Nahr ~ SUD 208-209 A 4
Baru, Punta ▲ CO 60-61 D 2
Barukova, mys ▲ RUS 112-113 U 5
Barumun ~ RI 162-163 D 3
Barun-Torej, ozero ⬭ RUS 118-119 G 10
Barus o RI 162-163 C 3
Barusiahe o RI 162-163 C 3
Baruti o ZRE 210-211 K 2
Baruunharaa o MAU 148-149 H 3
Baruunturuun o MAU 116-117 G 11
Baruun-Urt ☆ MAU 148-149 L 4
Barva, Volcán ▲ CR 52-53 B 6
Barvinkove o UA 102-103 K 3
Barwāni o IND 138-139 E 8
Barwick o CDN (ONT) 234-235 K 6
Barwidgi o AUS 174-175 H 5
Barwon River ~ AUS 178-179 J 5
Barycz ~ PL 92-93 O 3
Barylas o RUS 110-111 T 7
Baryš o RUS 96-97 E 7
Barysav ☆ BY 94-95 L 4
Barysaw = Barysav ☆ BY 94-95 L 4
Bāš Ābdān o AFG 136-137 L 6
Basacato del Este o GQ 210-211 B 2
Basaguke o VRC 144-145 E 6
Bāsa'īdū o IR 134-135 F 5
Basăk ~ K 158-159 H 5
Basakan, Gunung ▲ RI 164-165 E 2
Bašākerd, Kūhhā-ye ⛰ IR 134-135 G 5
Basāl o PK 138-139 D 3
Baš-Alatau hrebet ⛰ RUS 96-97 K 7
Basali o ZRE 210-211 J 3
Basalt o USA (CO) 254-255 H 4
Basanga o ZRE 210-211 K 6
Basankusu o ZRE 210-211 G 3
Basar o IND 138-139 F 10
Basarabi o RO 102-103 F 5
Basaseachic o MEX 50-51 E 3
Basaseachi Falls ~ MEX 50-51 E 3
Basavana Bāgevādi o IND 140-141 F 2
Basavilbaso o RA 78-79 K 2
Basay o RP 160-161 E 8
Bascán, Río ~ MEX 52-53 H 3
Baščelakskij hrebet ⛰ RUS 124-125 N 3
Bas-Chari, Réserve animale du ⊥ TCH 198-199 G 6
Bascombe Well Conservation Park ⊥ AUS 180-181 C 2
Base Casamance, Parc National du ⊥ SN 202-203 B 3
Basel ☆ • CH 92-93 J 5
Basettihalli o IND 140-141 G 4
Bashaw o CDN (ALB) 232-233 F 3
Bashee Bridge o ZA 220-221 J 5
Basheerivier ~ ZA 220-221 H 5
Bashi Haixia ≈ 156-157 M 6
Bashimuke o ZRE 210-211 K 6
Bashkortostan = Respublika Baškortostan □ RUS 96-97 J 6
Basiano o RI 164-165 H 4
Basilaki Island ⌒ PNG 183 F 6
Basilan Island ⌒ RP 160-161 D 9
Basilan Strait ≈ 160-161 D 9
Basile o USA (LA) 268-269 H 6
Basile, Pico ▲ GQ 210-211 B 2
Basilicata □ I 100-101 E 4
Basílio o BR 74-75 D 8
Basin o USA (WY) 252-253 K 2
Basingstoke o GB 90-91 G 6
Basin Lake ⬭ CDN (SAS) 232-233 N 3
Basīrī, al- o SYR 128-129 G 5
Basirka o WAN 204-205 J 3
Baška o HR 100-101 E 2
Baskahegan Lake ⬭ USA (ME) 278-279 O 3
Başkale ☆ TR 128-129 L 3
Baskan ~ KZ 124-125 L 6
Baskatong, Réservoir ⬭ CDN (QUE) 238-239 K 2
Baškaus ~ RUS 124-125 Q 3
Baskerville, Cape ▲ AUS 172-173 F 4
Baskineig Falls ~ CDN 34-35 N 4
Baškirskij zapovednik ⊥ RUS 96-97 K 7
Baskunčak, ozero ⬭ RUS 96-97 E 9
Basler Lake ⬭ CDN 30-31 M 4
Basmat o IND 138-139 F 10
Bašnja Šamilja • RUS 102-103 J 2
Bāsoda o IND 138-139 F 8
Basoko o ZRE 210-211 J 3
Basongo o ZRE 210-211 H 6
Basotu o EAT 212-213 E 6
Basova, mys ▲ RUS 112-113 U 5
Basque o USA (OR) 244-245 H 8
Başra, al- □ IRQ 130-131 K 2
Başra, al- ☆ IRQ (BAS) 130-131 K 2
Bassano o CDN (ALB) 232-233 F 5
Bassano del Grappa o I 100-101 C 2
Bassar o RT 202-203 L 5
Bassas da India ⌒ F 218-219 K 5
Bassaula o WAN 204-205 J 5
Bassein ~ MYA 158-159 C 2
Bassein = Puthein o MYA 158-159 C 2
Basse-Kotto □ RCA 206-207 E 6
Basse-Normandie □ F 90-91 G 7
Basse Santa Su ☆ • WAG 202-203 C 3
Basse-Terre ☆ ·· F 56 E 3
Basseterre ★ KAN 56 D 3
Bassett o USA (NE) 262-263 G 2
Bassett o USA (VA) 280-281 G 7
Bassfield o USA (MS) 268-269 L 5
Bass Highway II AUS 180-181 H 6
Bassikounou o RIM 196-197 H 7
Bassila o DY 202-203 L 5
Basso o DY 204-205 E 3
Basso ▲ TCH 198-199 L 4
Bass River o CDN (NS) 240-241 M 5
Bass Strait ≈ 180-181 H 5
Basswood o CDN (MAN) 234-235 C 4
Basswood Lake ⬭ USA (MN) 270-271 G 2
Bāšt o IR 134-135 D 3
Bastak o IR 134-135 F 5
Baštanka o UA 102-103 H 4
Baštau hrebet ⛰ RUS 96-97 K 7
Bastenaken = Bastogne o B 92-93 H 3
Basti o IND 142-143 C 2
Bastia ☆ • F 98-99 M 3
Basti Maluk o PK 138-139 C 5
Bastogne o B 92-93 H 3
Bastrop o USA (LA) 268-269 J 4
Bastrop o USA (TX) 266-267 K 3
Basu, Pulau ⌒ RI 162-163 E 5
Basu, Tanjung ▲ RI 162-163 E 5
Basua o WAN 204-205 H 5
Basunda o SUD 200-201 G 6
Başyurt Tepe ▲ TR 128-129 D 3
Bas-Zaïre □ ZRE 210-211 D 6
Bat ··· OM 132-133 K 2
Bata ☆ GQ 210-211 B 3
Batabanó o C 54-55 D 3
Batabanó, Golfo de ≈ 54-55 D 3
Batabi o WAN 204-205 F 4
Bataf o RI 166-167 K 3
Batagaj o RUS 110-111 U 6
Batagaj-Alyta o RUS 110-111 S 6
Batag Island ⌒ RP 160-161 F 6
Bataguaçu o BR 72-73 D 6
Batajka ~ RUS 108-109 Z 6
Batajsk o RUS 102-103 L 4
Batakan o RI 164-165 D 6
Bataker Palace • RI 162-163 C 3
Batak Houses • RI 162-163 C 3
Batala o IND 138-139 E 4
Batalha o BR (ALA) 68-69 K 6
Batalha o BR (PIA) 68-69 G 4
Batalha, Mosteiro de ··· P 98-99 C 5
Batam, Pulau ⌒ RI 162-163 E 4
Batama o ZRE 210-211 L 3
Batamaj o RUS 118-119 O 4
Batâmbali Beafada o GNB 202-203 C 4
Batamšy ☆ KZ 126-127 N 2
Batan o VRC 154-155 B 4
Batang o RI 168 C 3
Batang o VRC 144-145 M 6
Batangafo o RCA 206-207 D 5
Batangas ☆ RP 160-161 D 6
Batan Island ⌒ RP (ALB) 160-161 F 6
Batan Island ⌒ RP (BTN) 160-161 E 2
Batan Islands ⌒ RP 160-161 D 2
Batanta, Pulau ⌒ RI 166-167 F 2
Batanta Pulau Reserve ⊥ • RI 166-167 F 2
Batas Island ⌒ RP 160-161 C 7
Batatais o BR 72-73 G 6
Batavia o USA (NY) 278-279 C 5
Batavia = Jakarta ★ RI 168 B 3
Batavia Downs o AUS 174-175 G 3
Bat Cave o USA (NC) 282-283 E 5
Batcham o CAM 204-205 J 6
Batchawana o CDN (ONT) 236-237 D 5
Batchawana Bay o CDN (ONT) 236-237 D 6
Batchawana Island ⌒ CDN (ONT) 236-237 D 6
Batchawana River ~ CDN 236-237 D 5
Batchellerville o USA (NY) 278-279 H 5
Batchelor o AUS 172-173 K 2
Batchelor o USA (LA) 268-269 J 6
Batchenga o CAM 204-205 J 6
Bătdâmbâng o K 158-159 G 4
Bateckij o RUS 94-95 M 2
Bateeputih, Tanjung ▲ RI 162-163 A 2
Bateias o BR 74-75 F 5
Batéké, Plateaux ⛰ RCB 210-211 E 5
Batel, Esteros del ⬭ RA 76-77 H 5
Bateman o CDN (SAS) 232-233 M 6
Batemans Bay o AUS 180-181 L 3
Batemba o ZRE 210-211 J 6
Baté-Nafadj o RG 202-203 F 4
Batería, Cerro de la • RA 78-79 D 4
Bates o AUS 176-177 M 5
Bates o USA (AR) 276-277 A 6
Batesburg o USA (SC) 284-285 J 3
Batesland o USA (SD) 260-261 D 3
Batesville o USA (AR) 276-277 D 5
Batesville o USA (IN) 274-275 N 5
Batesville o USA (MS) 268-269 L 2
Batesville o USA (TX) 266-267 H 5
Bath o CDN (ONT) 238-239 J 4
Bath o ··· GB 90-91 F 6
Bath o USA (NC) 282-283 L 5
Bath o USA (NY) 278-279 D 6
Bath o • USA (ME) 278-279 M 5
Batha □ TCH 198-199 J 5
Batha ~ TCH 198-199 J 6
Bathā, Wādil- ~ OM 132-133 L 2
Batha de Lairi ~ TCH 206-207 C 3
Batheaston o AUS 178-179 K 2
Bathinda o IND 138-139 E 4
Baths, The ∸ GB 56 C 2
Baths Bjerge Matterhorn ▲ GRØ 26-27 p 6
Bathsheba o BDS 56 F 5
Bath Springs o USA (TN) 276-277 G 5
Bá Thu'ó'c ☆ VN 156-157 D 6
Bathurst o AUS 180-181 K 2
Bathurst o CDN (NB) 240-241 K 3
Bathurst o ZA 220-221 H 6
Bathurst = Banjul ★ • WAG 202-203 B 3
Bathurst, Cape ▲ CDN 24-25 H 5
Bathurst Inlet ≈ 30-31 P 2
Bathurst Inlet o CDN 30-31 P 2
Bathurst Island ⌒ AUS 172-173 K 1
Bathurst Island ⌒ CDN 24-25 V 3
Bathurst Mines o CDN (NB) 240-241 K 3
Bati o ETH 208-209 E 3
Batia o DY 202-203 L 4
Batibati o RI 164-165 D 5
Batibo o CAM 204-205 H 6
Batié o BF 202-203 J 5
Batiki ⌒ FJI 184 III b 2
Bāṭin, Wādī al- ~ KSA 130-131 J 3
Bāṭina ∸ OM 132-133 K 1
Batinga o BR 72-73 K 4
Batiscan, Rivière ~ CDN 240-241 C 3
Bat Island ⌒ PNG 183 D 2
Batkanu o WAL 202-203 D 5
Batken o KS 136-137 M 4
Batkes o RI 166-167 F 5
Bat Khela o PK 138-139 C 2
Batlai o RUS 126-127 G 6
Bāṭlāq-e Gāvḫūni ⬭ IR 134-135 E 2
Batlow o AUS 180-181 K 3
Batman ☆ TR 128-129 J 4
Baṭn, Ğāl al- ⛰ IRQ 130-131 H 2
Batna ☆ DZ 190-191 F 3
Baṭn al-Ġūl o JOR 130-131 D 3
Batnorov = Dundburd o MAU 148-149 K 4
Bato o RP 160-161 E 6
Ba To' o VN 158-159 K 3
Bato Bato ☆ RP 160-161 C 10
Batoka o Z 218-219 D 3
Bat-Ölzijt o MAU 148-149 G 3
Batomga o RUS (HBR) 120-121 G 5
Batomga ~ RUS 120-121 F 5
Baton Rouge ☆ • USA (LA) 268-269 J 6
Batopilas o • MEX 50-51 F 4
Batoua o CAM 204-205 K 6
Batouala o G 210-211 D 3
Batouri o CAM 206-207 B 6
Batovi, Área Indígena ✕ BR 72-73 D 2
Batovil, Rio ~ BR 72-73 D 2
Ba Town o LB 202-203 F 6
Batpajsagyr, kum ∸ KZ 96-97 F 10
Ba Tri o VN 158-159 J 5
Batsari o WAN 198-199 C 6
Batsawul o AFG 138-139 C 2
Båtsfjord o N 86-87 O 1
Batteau o CDN 38-39 R 2
Batterbee Range ⛰ ARK 16 F 30
Batticaloa o • CL 140-141 J 7
Batti Malv Island ⌒ IND 140-141 L 5
Battleboro o USA (NC) 282-283 K 4
Battle Camp o AUS 174-175 H 4
Battle Creek ~ CDN 232-233 J 6
Battle Creek o USA (MI) 272-273 E 5
Battle Creek ~ USA 250-251 K 3
Battlefields o ZW 218-219 E 4
Battleford o CDN (SAS) 232-233 K 3
Battle Ground o USA (WA) 244-245 C 5
Battle Harbour o CDN 38-39 R 2
Battle Lake o USA (MN) 270-271 C 4
Battle Mountain o USA (NV) 246-247 J 3
Battle River ~ CDN 232-233 H 3
Battleview o USA (ND) 258-259 E 3
Battor o GH 202-203 L 6
Battrum o CDN (SAS) 232-233 K 5
Batu ▲ ETH 208-209 D 5
Batu, Bukit ▲ MAL 162-163 K 3
Batu, Kepulauan ⌒ RI 162-163 C 4
Batu, Tanjung ▲ RI (KTI) 164-165 F 2
Batu, Tanjung ▲ RI (SUB) 162-163 D 6
Batuaga o RI 164-165 H 6
Batuampar o RI 162-163 E 5
Batuamparan o RI 164-165 D 5
Batuasa o RI 166-167 F 3
Batuata, Pulau ⌒ RI 166-167 B 5
Batubatu o RI 164-165 F 6
Batuberagam, Tanjung ▲ RI 162-163 F 7
Batu Buteh, Gunung ▲ MAL 162-163 D 2
Batudaa o RI 164-165 H 3
Batudaka o RI 164-165 G 4
Batudaka, Pulau ⌒ RI 164-165 G 4
Batu Danau o MAL 164-165 D 1
Batudulag o RI 168 C 7
Batugade o RI 166-167 C 6
Batu Gajah o MAL 162-163 D 2
Batuhitam, Tanjung ▲ RI 164-165 H 4
Batui o RI 164-165 H 4
Batukangkung o RI 162-163 D 5
Batukau, Gunung ▲ RI 168 B 7
Batulicin o RI 164-165 D 5
Batumandi, Tanjung ▲ RI 162-163 D 5
Batumi ☆ • GE 126-127 D 7
Batu Pahat o • MAL 162-163 E 4
Batupanjang o RI 162-163 D 4
Batuputih o RI (JTI) 168 E 3
Batuputih o RI (KTI) 164-165 F 3
Batur, Danau ⬭ RI 168 B 7
Baturaja o RI 162-163 F 7
Batu Rakit o MAL 162-163 E 2
Baturetno o RI 168 D 3
Baturi o MEX 50-51 E 5
Baturube o RI 164-165 G 4
Batusangkar o • RI 162-163 D 5
Batu Satu o MAL 162-163 K 2
Batusitanduk o RI 164-165 G 5
Batu Tambung o RI 164-165 H 4
Batutua o RI 166-167 B 7
Baty-Jurjah ~ RUS 108-109 c 6
Batyr ~ RUS 118-119 E 4
Batyrevo o RUS 96-97 E 6
Bau o MAL 162-163 J 4
Bau o RI 164-165 F 5
Baú, Rio ~ BR 66-67 K 6
Baú, Rio do ~ BR 66-67 K 7
Ba'u, Tanjung ▲ RI 162-163 A 2
Bauana, Rio ~ BR 66-67 F 4
Baubau o RI 164-165 H 6
Bauchi □ WAN 204-205 H 3
Bauchi ☆ WAN (BAU) 204-205 H 3
Baudette o USA (MN) 270-271 D 2
Baudisson Island ⌒ PNG 183 F 2
Baudo, Río ~ CO 60-61 C 5
Bauer Basin ≃ 14-15 S 9
Baugé o F 62-63 H 3
Bauhinia Downs o AUS (NT) 174-175 C 5
Bauhinia Downs o AUS (QLD) 178-179 K 3
Bauia o RI 164-165 G 6
Baukau o RI 166-167 D 6
Baúl, El ∴ • GCA 52-53 J 4
Baúl, El o YV 60-61 G 3
Bauld, Cape ▲ CDN (NFL) 242-243 N 1
Baule-Escoublac, la o • F 90-91 F 8
Baumann Fiord ≈ 24-25 d 2
Baú-Mekragroti, Área Indígena ✕ BR 66-67 K 6
Baun o RI 166-167 B 7
Baungan o RI 162-163 C 3
Baun Pulau Reserve ⊥ • RI 166-167 H 5
Baunt o RUS 118-119 F 8
Baunt, ozero ⬭ RUS 118-119 F 8
Baures o BOL 70-71 F 3
Bauru o BR 72-73 F 7
Bauru o ZRE 210-211 H 3
Bauska ☆ ·· LV 94-95 J 3
Bauta o C 54-55 D 3
Bauta o ZRE 210-211 H 3
Bautu o RI 164-165 H 4
Bautzen o ·· D 92-93 N 3
Bauxite o USA (AR) 276-277 C 6
Baviácora o MEX 50-51 D 3
Bavispe, Rio ~ MEX 50-51 E 2
Bavly ☆ RUS 96-97 H 6
Bavon o USA (VA) 280-281 K 6
Bawa o RP 160-161 E 3
Bāwal o IND 138-139 F 5
Bawal, Pulau ⌒ RI 162-163 J 6
Bawang, Tanjung ▲ RI 162-163 H 5
Bawangling Z.B. ⊥ VRC 156-157 F 7
Bawātī, Ğabal ▲ SUD 200-201 H 3
Baw Baw, Mount ▲ AUS 180-181 J 4
Baw Baw National Park ⊥ AUS 180-181 J 4
Bawdie o GH 202-203 J 7
Bawe o RI (IRJ) 166-167 F 2
Bawe o RI (IRJ) 166-167 H 3
Bawean, Pulau ⌒ RI 168 E 2
Bawen o RI 168 D 3
Bawku o GH 202-203 K 4
Bawlake o MYA 142-143 K 6
Bawlf o CDN (ALB) 232-233 F 3
Bawo o LB 202-203 F 7
Bawo Ofuloa o RI 162-163 C 5
Baxkorgan o VRC 146-147 K 6
Baxley o USA (GA) 284-285 H 5
Baxoi o VRC 144-145 L 5
Baxter o USA (FL) 286-287 G 1
Baxter o USA (MN) 270-271 D 4
Baxter o USA (MS) 268-269 L 4
Baxter o USA (TN) 276-277 K 4
Baxter Cliffs ∸ AUS 176-177 H 6
Baxter Pass ▲ USA (CO) 254-255 G 4
Baxter Springs o USA (KS) 262-263 M 7
Baxterville o USA (MS) 268-269 L 5
Bay o RMM 202-203 J 3
Bay □ SP 212-213 J 2
Bay o USA (AR) 276-277 E 5
Bay, Réserve de ⊥ RMM 202-203 J 3
Baya-Bwanga o ZRE 210-211 J 6
Bayāḍ, al- ∸ KSA 132-133 E 3
Bayāḍ, Ra's al- ▲ Y 132-133 C 6
Bayādah, Wādī al ~ LAR 192-193 H 4
Bayadi o G 210-211 C 5
Bayaguana o DOM 54-55 L 5
Bayamo ☆ C 54-55 G 4
Bayamón o USA (PR) 286-287 P 2
Bayan o VRC 150-151 F 4
Bayanbulak o VRC 146-147 G 4
Bayanbulak Z.B. II VRC 146-147 G 4
Bayanga o RCA 210-211 F 2
Bayanga-Didi o RCA 206-207 B 6
Bayan Har Shan ⛰ VRC 144-145 K 3
Bayan Har Shan ▲ VRC (QIN) 144-145 L 3
Bayan Har Shankou ▲ VRC 144-145 L 3
Bayan Obo o VRC 148-149 J 7
Bayan Olji o VRC 154-155 D 1
Bayan Shan ▲ VRC 144-145 L 2
Bayard o USA (IA) 274-275 D 3
Bayard o USA (NE) 262-263 C 3
Bayard o USA (NM) 256-257 G 6
Bayat ☆ TR 128-129 F 2
Bayawan o RP 160-161 E 8
Bayāż o IR 134-135 F 3
Bayāżīye o IR 134-135 F 2
Baybay o RP 160-161 F 7
Bayboro o USA (NC) 282-283 L 5
Bay Bulls o CDN (NFL) 242-243 Q 5
Bayburt ☆ • TR 128-129 J 2
Bay City o USA (MI) 272-273 F 4
Bay City o USA (OR) 244-245 B 5
Bay de Verde o CDN (NFL) 242-243 Q 4
Baydhabo ☆ SP 212-213 J 2
Bay du Vin o CDN (NB) 240-241 K 3
Bayerischer Wald ∸ D 92-93 M 4
Bayern □ D 92-93 L 4
Bayeux o BR 68-69 L 5
Bayeux o • F 90-91 G 7
Bayfield o USA (CO) 254-255 H 6
Bayfield o USA (WI) 270-271 H 4
Bayfield Inlet o CDN (ONT) 238-239 E 3
Bay Fiord ≈ 26-27 J 4
Bāy Háp, Cḥu'a Sông ≈ 158-159 H 6
Bayındır ☆ TR 128-129 B 3
Bāyir Ğovein, Kūh-e ⛰ IR 136-137 E 6
Bayizhen o VRC 144-145 K 6
Baykan ☆ TR 128-129 J 3
Baykonyr = Bajkoŋyr o KZ 124-125 E 5
Bay Mills Indian Reservation ✕ USA (MI) 270-271 O 4
Baynes Lake o CDN (BC) 230-231 O 4
Baynes Mountains ⛰ NAM 216-217 B 8
Baynūna ∸ UAE 132-133 H 2
Bayo, Cerro ▲ RCH 80 D 2
Bayobar o PE 64-65 B 4
Bay of Whales ≈ 16 F 20
Bayog o RP 160-161 E 9
Bayombong ☆ RP 160-161 D 4
Bayo Mesa, Cerro ▲ RA 78-79 E 5
Bayonet Point o USA (FL) 286-287 G 3
Bayon Macon ~ USA 268-269 J 4
Bayonne o • F 90-91 G 10
Bayou Bartholomew River ~ USA 276-277 D 7
Bayou Cane o USA (LA) 268-269 K 7
Bayou D'Arbonne Lake < USA (LA) 268-269 H 4
Bayou de Loutre ~ USA 268-269 H 4
Bayou de View ~ USA 276-277 D 5
Bayou Dorcheat ~ USA 268-269 G 4
Bayou La Batre o USA (AL) 284-285 B 6
Bayou La Grune ~ USA 276-277 D 6
Bayou Meto o USA (AR) 276-277 D 6
Bayou Pierre ~ USA 268-269 K 4
Bayou Sorrel o USA (LA) 268-269 J 6
Bay Port o USA (MI) 272-273 F 4
Bayramiç ☆ TR 128-129 B 3
Bayreuth o D 92-93 L 4
Bays, Lake of ⬭ CDN (ONT) 238-239 F 3
Bay Shore o USA (NY) 280-281 N 3
Bayside o USA (TX) 266-267 K 5
Bay Springs o USA (MS) 268-269 L 5
Baysville o CDN (ONT) 238-239 F 3
Baytik Shan ⛰ VRC 146-147 K 3
Baytown o USA (TX) 268-269 E 7
Bay Trail o CDN (SAS) 232-233 N 3
Bay Tree o CDN 32-33 L 4
Bayu o RI (ACE) 162-163 B 2
Bayu o RI (STG) 164-165 H 5
Bayugan o RP 160-161 F 8
Bayunglincir o RI 162-163 E 6
Bayun Gol He ~ VRC 144-145 L 2
Bayur, Tanjung ▲ RI 164-165 E 4
Bayur, Teluk ≈ 162-163 D 5
Bay View o NZ 182 F 3
Bayview o USA (ID) 250-251 C 4
Bay View o USA (MI) 272-273 E 2
Bayyādah, Al o LAR 192-193 J 1
Bayy al Kabír, Wādī ~ LAR 192-193 F 2
Bayzo o RN 198-199 B 6
Bazardjuzu, gora ▲ RUS 126-127 G 7
Bazar-e Tale o AFG 136-137 L 7
Bāzargān o IR 128-129 L 3
Bazar-Korgon o KS 136-137 N 4
Bazarnye Mataki ☆ RUS 96-97 F 6
Bazartöbe o KZ 96-97 H 9
Bazaruto, Ilhas do ⌒ MOC 218-219 H 5
Bazaruto, Parque Nacional de ⊥ MOC 218-219 H 5
Bazavluk ~ UA 102-103 J 4
Baženovo o RUS 96-97 J 6
Bazhong o VRC 154-155 E 6
Bazhou o VRC 154-155 K 2
Bazin, Rivière ~ CDN 236-237 N 5
Bazmān o IR 134-135 J 5
Bazmān, Kūh-e ▲ IR 134-135 H 4
Bazou o CAM 204-205 J 6
Bazré o CI 202-203 H 6
Be, Nosy ⌒ RM 222-223 F 4
Beach ∸ CDN 240-241 L 4
Beach o USA (ND) 258-259 D 6
Beach • USA (DE) 280-281 L 5
Beachburg o CDN (ONT) 238-239 J 3
Beachêne, Lac ⬭ CDN (QUE) 238-239 G 2
Beach Point ▲ CDN 24-25 d 7
Beachport o AUS 180-181 E 4
Beach River ~ USA 276-277 G 5
Beacon o AUS 176-177 D 5
Beacon o USA (NY) 280-281 N 2
Beacon Bay o ZA 220-221 H 6
Beaconia o CDN (MAN) 234-235 G 4
Beadell, Mount ▲ AUS 176-177 H 2
Beadle o CDN (SAS) 232-233 K 4
Beadon Point ▲ AUS 172-173 D 6
Beafada, Batâmbali o GNB 202-203 C 4
Beagle, Canal ≈ 80 F 7
Beagle Bay ≈ 172-173 F 4
Beagle Bay ✕ AUS (WA) 172-173 F 4
Beagle Bay Aboriginal Land ✕ AUS 172-173 F 4
Beagle Gulf ≈ 172-173 J 2
Beagle Island ⌒ AUS 176-177 C 4
Beagle Reef ⌒ AUS 172-173 F 3
Beako, Tanjung ▲ RI 166-167 D 6
Bealanana o RM 222-223 F 5
Béal an Atha = Ballina o IRL 90-91 C 4
Béal an Mhuirthead = Belmullet o IRL 90-91 C 4
Béal Átha na Sluaighe = Ballinasloe o IRL 90-91 C 5
Beale Air Force Base • USA (CA) 246-247 D 4
Bealeton o USA (VA) 280-281 J 5
Beals Creek ~ USA 264-265 C 6
Beampingaratra ⛰ RM 222-223 E 10
Beanntraí = Bantry o IRL 90-91 C 6
Bean Station o USA (TN) 282-283 D 4
Bear, Mount ▲ USA 20-21 U 6
Bear Bay ≈ 24-25 c 3
Bearberry o CDN (ALB) 232-233 D 4
Bear Cove o CDN (BC) 230-231 B 3
Bear Cove o CDN (NFL) 242-243 M 3
Bear Creek ~ USA 254-255 N 6
Bear Creek ~ USA 262-263 E 7
Bear Creek ~ USA 284-285 C 2
Bear Creek Springs o USA (AR) 276-277 B 4
Bearden o USA (AR) 276-277 C 7
Beardmore o CDN (ONT) 234-235 Q 5
Beardmore Glacier ⊂ ARK 16 E 0
Beardmore Reservoir < AUS 178-179 K 4
Beardsley o USA (MN) 270-271 B 5
Beardstown o USA (IL) 274-275 H 4
Beardy River ~ AUS 178-179 L 5
Bearhead Creek ~ CDN 32-33 M 4
Bear Island ⌒ ARK 16 F 26
Bear Island ⌒ CDN 34-35 Q 3
Bear Islands = Medvež'i ostrova ⌒ RUS 112-113 L 1
Bear Lake o CDN (BC) 228-229 M 2
Bear Lake o USA (MI) 272-273 C 3
Bear Lake ⬭ USA (ID) 252-253 G 5
Bear Lake ⬭ USA (UT) 254-255 D 2
Bear Mount ▲ USA 20-21 T 2
Bearpaw Mount ▲ USA 20-21 P 4
Bear Paw Mountain ▲ USA (MT) 250-251 K 3
Bear River ~ USA 252-253 G 4
Bear River ~ USA 254-255 D 2
Bear River Bay ≈ 254-255 C 2
Bearskin Lake o CDN 34-35 L 4
Beartooth Pass ▲ USA (MT) 250-251 K 6
Bear Valley o USA (CA) 246-247 E 5
Beas ~ IND 138-139 E 4
Beas de Segura o E 98-99 F 5
Beasley o USA (TX) 268-269 E 7
Beata, Cabo ▲ DOM 54-55 K 6
Beata, Isla ⌒ DOM 54-55 K 6
Beaton o CDN (BC) 230-231 M 3
Beatrice o USA (AL) 284-285 C 5
Beatrice o USA (NE) 262-263 K 4
Beatrice o ZW 218-219 F 4
Beatrice, Cape ▲ AUS 174-175 D 4
Beatton River o CDN 32-33 K 3
Beatty o CDN (SAS) 232-233 O 3
Beatty o USA (NV) 248-249 H 3
Beatty o USA (OR) 244-245 D 8
Beattyville o CDN (QUE) 236-237 L 4
Beattyville o USA (KY) 276-277 M 3
Beauceville o CDN (QUE) 240-241 E 4
Beauchêne Island ⌒ GB 78-79 L 7
Beaucoup Creek ~ USA 276-277 F 3
Beaudesert o AUS (QLD) 178-179 F 1
Beaudesert o AUS (QLD) 178-179 M 5
Beaufield o CDN (SAS) 232-233 J 4
Beaufort o AUS 180-181 G 4
Beaufort o MAL 160-161 A 10
Beaufort o USA (NC) 282-283 L 6
Beaufort o USA (SC) 284-285 K 4
Beaufort Lagoon ⬭ USA 20-21 U 2
Beaufort-Wes = Beaufort West o ZA 220-221 F 6
Beaufort West = Beaufort-Wes o ZA 220-221 F 6
Beaugency o F 90-91 H 8
Beauharnois o CDN (QUE) 238-239 M 3
Beaulieu River ~ CDN 30-31 N 4
Beauly o • GB 90-91 F 3
Beaumont o CDN (ALB) 232-233 E 2
Beaumont o USA (CA) 248-249 H 6
Beaumont o USA (KS) 262-263 K 7
Beaumont o USA (KY) 276-277 K 4
Beaumont o USA (MS) 268-269 M 5
Beaumont o USA (TX) 268-269 F 6
Beaumont-de-Lomagne o F 90-91 H 10
Beaumont-sur-Oise o F 90-91 J 7
Beaune o F 90-91 K 8
Beaupré o CDN (QUE) 240-241 E 3
Beaupré, Kap ▲ GRØ 28-29 c 2
Beauséjour o CDN (MAN) 234-235 G 4
Beauséjour National Historical Park, Fort • CDN (NB) 240-241 L 5
Beauty o ZA 218-219 D 6
Beauvais ☆ • F 90-91 J 7
Beauvais Lake ⬭ CDN 30-31 R 5
Beauvallon o CDN (ALB) 232-233 G 2
Beaver o USA (AK) 20-21 R 3
Beaver o USA (OK) 264-265 D 2
Beaver o USA (OR) 244-245 B 5
Beaver o USA (UT) 254-255 C 5
Beaver Brook Station o CDN (NB) 240-241 K 3
Beaver City o USA (NE) 262-263 G 4
Beaver Cove o CDN (BC) 230-231 C 3
Beavercreek o USA (OH) 280-281 B 4
Beaver Creek ~ USA 20-21 R 4
Beaver Creek ~ USA 250-251 L 4
Beaver Creek ~ USA 258-259 D 4
Beaver Creek ~ USA 262-263 F 4
Beaver Creek ~ USA 262-263 E 5
Beaver Creek ~ USA 264-265 F 4
Beaver Creek Mountain ⛰ USA 284-285 D 3
Beaver Dam o USA (KY) 276-277 J 3
Beaver Dam o USA (WI) 274-275 K 1
Beaverdam Lake ⬭ USA (WI) 274-275 K 1
Beaverdell o CDN (BC) 230-231 K 4
Beaver Falls o USA (PA) 280-281 F 3
Beaverhead o USA (AZ) 256-257 F 5
Beaverhead Range ⛰ USA 250-251 F 6
Beaverhead River ~ USA 250-251 G 6
Beaverhill Lake ⬭ CDN (ALB) 232-233 F 2
Beaverhill Lake ⬭ CDN (NWT) 30-31 R 4
Beaver Island ⌒ USA (MI) 272-273 D 2
Beaver Lake ⬭ CDN 30-31 L 5
Beaver Lake ⬭ USA (AR) 276-277 A 4
Beaverley o CDN (BC) 228-229 M 3
Beaverlodge Lake ⬭ CDN (NWT) 30-31 K 3
Beaverlodge Lake ⬭ CDN (SAS) 30-31 P 6
Beaver Marsh o USA (OR) 244-245 D 7
Beaver Mines o CDN (ALB) 232-233 D 6
Beaver Mountain ▲ CDN 20-21 U 5
Beavermouth o CDN (BC) 230-231 M 2
Beaver River ~ CDN 30-31 G 5
Beaver River ~ CDN 34-35 M 3
Beaver River ~ CDN 38-39 E 2
Beaver River ~ USA 264-265 D 2
Beaver Run Reservoir ⬭ USA (PA) 280-281 G 3
Beaver Springs o USA (PA) 280-281 J 3
Beaverstone River ~ CDN 34-35 L 3
Beaverton o CDN (ONT) 238-239 F 4
Beaverton o USA (OR) 244-245 C 5
Beāwar o IND 138-139 E 6
Beazer o CDN (ALB) 232-233 E 6
Beazley o RA 78-79 F 2
Bebarama o CO 60-61 C 4
Bébédjia o TCH 206-207 C 4
Bebedouro o BR 72-73 F 6
Bebeka o ETH 208-209 B 5
Bebenaro o RI 166-167 C 6
Bebisa o PNG 183 B 4
Béboto o TCH 206-207 C 4
Béboura III o RCA 206-207 C 5
Bebra o D 92-93 K 3
Becal o • MEX 52-53 J 1
Becan ∴ • MEX 52-53 K 2
Becanchén o MEX 52-53 K 2
Bécancour o CDN (QUE) 238-239 N 2
Bécard, Lac ⬭ CDN 36-37 N 4
Bečenča o RUS 118-119 G 5
Becerreá o E 98-99 D 3
Becerro, Cayos ⌒ HN 54-55 D 7
Béchar ☆ DZ 188-189 K 5
Becharof Lake ⬭ USA 22-23 S 4
Becher, Cape ▲ CDN 24-25 Y 2
Becher Peninsula ⌣ CDN 36-37 P 3
Bechevin Bay ≈ 22-23 P 5
Becilla de Valderaduey o E 98-99 E 3
Beckley o USA (WV) 280-281 E 6
Becks o NZ 182 B 6
Beckton o USA (WY) 252-253 L 2
Beckwourth Pass ▲ USA (CA) 246-247 E 4
Beco o RI 166-167 C 6
Bedarra Island ⌒ AUS 174-175 J 6
Bédaya o TCH 206-207 C 4
Beddouza, Cap ▲ MA 188-189 G 4
Bedelē o ETH 208-209 C 4
Bedēsa o ETH 208-209 E 4
Bedford o CDN (QUE) 238-239 N 3
Bedford o GB 90-91 G 5
Bedford o USA (IA) 274-275 D 4
Bedford o USA (IN) 274-275 M 6
Bedford o USA (NY) 280-281 N 2
Bedford o USA (PA) 280-281 H 4
Bedford o USA (VA) 280-281 G 6
Bedford o ZA 220-221 H 6
Bedford, Cape ▲ AUS 174-175 H 4
Bedford, Lake ⬭ AUS 176-177 G 3
Bedford, Mount ▲ AUS 172-173 H 4
Bedford Downs o AUS 172-173 H 4
Bediako o GH 202-203 J 6
Bediani o GE 126-127 F 7
Bedias o USA (TX) 268-269 E 6
Bedi Dat o PK 134-135 L 5
Bediondo o TCH 206-207 C 4
Bedjedjene, Hassi < DZ 190-191 G 7
Bednesti o CDN (BC) 228-229 L 3
Bednodem'janovsk o RUS 94-95 S 5
Bédo o TCH 198-199 J 3
Bedoba o RUS 116-117 H 6
Bédouaram o RN 198-199 F 5
Bedoud, Hassi o MA 188-189 K 4
Bedourie o AUS 178-179 E 3
Bee o USA (NE) 262-263 J 4
Beebe o USA (AR) 276-277 D 5
Beechal River ~ AUS 178-179 H 4
Beecher o USA (IL) 274-275 L 3
Beechey Lake ⬭ CDN 30-31 Q 3
Beechey Point o USA 20-21 Q 1
Beech Fork Lake ⬭ USA (WV) 280-281 D 5
Beech Grove o USA (IN) 274-275 M 5
Beechgrove o USA (TN) 276-277 J 5
Beech Island o USA (SC) 284-285 J 3
Beechwood o USA (MI) 272-273 C 5
Beechworth o AUS 180-181 J 4
Beechy o CDN (SAS) 232-233 L 5
Beekman Peninsula ⌣ CDN 36-37 R 3
Beeler o USA (KS) 262-263 F 6
Beenčime ~ RUS 110-111 N 4
Beenleigh o AUS 178-179 M 4
Be'ér Sheva' ☆ IL 130-131 D 2
Beerwah o AUS 178-179 M 4
Beeskow o • D 92-93 N 2
Beestekraal o ZA 220-221 H 2
Beetaloo o AUS 174-175 B 5
Beeville o USA (TX) 266-267 K 5
Befale o ZRE 210-211 H 3
Befandefa o RM 222-223 C 9
Befandriana Atsimo o RM 222-223 C 9
Befandriana Avaratra o RM 222-223 F 5
Befasy o RM 222-223 D 8
Beffa ~ DY 204-205 E 4
Befori o ZRE 210-211 J 3
Beforona o RM 222-223 F 7
Befotaka o RM (FNS) 222-223 E 9
Befotaka o RM (MJG) 222-223 F 5
Bega o AUS 180-181 K 4
Beggs o USA (OK) 264-265 H 3
Begičeva, grjada ⛰ RUS 108-109 X 5
Begidzjan ~ RUS 110-111 P 6
Bégin o CDN (QUE) 240-241 D 2
Begna ~ N 86-87 D 6
Begogo o RM 222-223 E 9
Bégon o RCA 206-207 B 5
Begoro o GH 202-203 K 6
Begunicy o RUS 94-95 L 2
Begusarai o IND 142-143 E 3
Beh ~ RI 168 C 7
Behābād o IR 134-135 G 3
Béhague, Pointe ▲ F 62-63 J 3
Behara o RM 222-223 E 10
Behbahān o • IR 134-135 D 3
Beheloka o RM 222-223 C 9
Behenjy o RM 222-223 E 7
Béhili o RCA 206-207 D 5
Behm Canal ≈ 32-33 E 4
Behring Point o BS 54-55 G 2
Behšahr o • IR 136-137 C 6
Bei'an o VRC 150-151 F 3
Béibouo o CI 202-203 G 6
Beibu Wan ≈ 156-157 E 6
Beichuan o VRC 154-155 D 6
Beid, El ~ 198-199 G 6
Beida = Goz o TCH 198-199 K 6
Beidaihe Haibin • VRC 154-155 L 2
Beidaneikechuke o VRC 144-145 F 5
Beidou o VRC 156-157 H 6
Beigi o ETH 208-209 B 4
Beihai o VRC 156-157 F 6
Bei Jiang ~ VRC 156-157 H 4
Bei Jiao ⌒ VRC 158-159 L 2

Bartica — Bei Jiao 303

Beijing ★••• VRC 154-155 K 2
Beijin Gang ≈ 156-157 H 6
Beijing Shi ▫ VRC 154-155 K 2
Bei Ling • VRC 150-151 D 7
Beiliu o VRC 156-157 G 5
Béinamar o TCH 206-207 B 4
Beipan Jiang ~ VRC 156-157 D 4
Beipiao o VRC 150-151 C 7
Beira ☆ MOC 218-219 H 4
Beira Alta o ANG 216-217 C 4
Beiradão o BR 62-63 H 6
Beirut = Bairūt ★ RL 128-129 F 6
Beiseker o CDN (ALB) 232-233 E 4
Bei Shan ▲ VRC 146-147 M 5
Beishan • VRC (JIL) 150-151 E 6
Beishan • VRC (ZHE) 156-157 L 2
Beitan o VRC 156-157 F 6
Beitau o VRC 156-157 F 6
Beitbridge o ZW 218-219 F 6
Beitstadfjorden ≈ 86-87 E 5
Beitun o VRC 146-147 H 2
Beizhangdian o VRC 154-155 H 3
Beizhen o VRC 150-151 C 7
Beja o•• P 98-99 D 5
Beja ☆ TN 190-191 G 2
Bejaja ☆• DZ 190-191 E 2
Béjar o• E 98-99 E 4
Bejarn o N 86-87 G 3
Beji ~ PK 138-139 B 5
Beji o WAN 204-205 G 4
Bejlagan = Beylagan o AZ 128-129 M 3
Bejneu ☆ KZ 126-127 L 5
B.E. Jordan Lake ⊂ USA (NC) 282-283 H 5
Bejsug ~ RUS 102-103 L 5
Bejsugskij liman ≈ 102-103 L 4
Bejucal o C 54-55 D 3
Bek ~ CAM 210-211 E 2
Béka o CAM (ADA) 204-205 K 5
Béka o CAM (ADA) 206-207 B 5
Béka o CAM (NOR) 204-205 K 4
Bekabad o UZ 136-137 L 4
Békamba o TCH 206-207 C 4
Bekasi o RI 168 B 3
Bekati o UZ 136-137 K 4
Bekbeket o KZ 96-97 H 10
Bekdaš o TM 136-137 C 4
Bek-Džar o KS 136-137 N 4
Beke o RI 168 E 7
Bèkè ~ RUS 110-111 K 6
Beke o ZRE 214-215 D 5
Bekenu o MAL 162-163 K 2
Békés o H 92-93 Q 5
Békéscsaba o H 92-93 Q 5
Bekily o RM 222-223 D 10
Bekipay o RM 222-223 E 6
Bekitro o RM 222-223 D 10
Bekkai o J 152-153 L 3
Bekmurat, gora ▲ TM 136-137 D 4
Bekodoka o RM 222-223 D 6
Bek'oji o ETH 208-209 D 5
Bekopaka o RM 222-223 D 7
Békuy o BF 202-203 J 4
Bekwai o GH 202-203 K 6
Bekyem o GH 202-203 J 6
Bela ~ BR 70-71 H 3
Bela o IND 142-143 C 3
Bela o PK 134-135 M 5
Bélabirim o RN 198-199 F 5
Bélabo o CAM 204-205 K 6
Bela Estrela o BR 68-69 E 4
Belaga o MAL 162-163 K 3
Belair o CDN (MAN) 234-235 G 4
Bel Air o USA (MD) 280-281 K 4
Belaja ~ RUS 96-97 L 6
Belaja ~ RUS 112-113 R 4
Belaja ~ RUS 112-113 O 5
Belaja ~ RUS 116-117 L 9
Belaja ~ RUS 122-123 C 3
Belaja ~ RUS 126-127 D 5
Belaja, gora ▲ RUS 112-113 S 4
Belaja, Ust'- o RUS 112-113 R 4
Belaja Berëzka o RUS 94-95 N 5
Belaja Cerkov' = Bila Cerkva ☆ UA 102-103 G 3
Belaja Gora o RUS 110-111 a 5
Belaja Holunica ☆ RUS 96-97 G 4
Belaja Kalitva o RUS 102-103 M 3
Belaja Škola o KZ 124-125 N 5
Belajau, Danau o RI 162-163 K 6
Belaja Zemlja, ostrova ⌒ RUS 84-85 g 2
Belalcázar o E 98-99 E 5
Bela Lorena o BR 72-73 G 3
Belamoty o RM 222-223 D 9
Belang o RI 164-165 J 3
Belangan o RI 162-163 K 6
Belangbelang, Pulau ⌒ RI (MAL) 164-165 D 2
Belangbelang, Pulau ⌒ RI (SSE) 168 E 6
Belanger Island ⌒ CDN 36-37 L 6
Bela Palanka o• YU 100-101 J 3
Belarus = Belarus' ■ BY 94-95 K 5
Belas o ANG 216-217 B 4
Belāti o IND 140-141 F 2
Bela Vista o ANG (BGO) 216-217 B 3
Bela Vista o ANG (HBO) 216-217 D 6
Bela Vista o BR (APA) 62-63 J 4
Bela Vista o BR (GSU) 76-77 J 2
Bela Vista o BR (RSU) 74-75 D 7
Bela Vista o MOC 220-221 L 3
Bela Vista, Cachoeira ~ BR 68-69 C 3
Belawan o RI 162-163 C 3
Belayan ~ RI 164-165 E 3
Bélbéji o RN 198-199 C 5
Belbutte o CDN (SAS) 232-233 L 2
Bel'c' = Bălţi ☆ MD 102-103 E 4
Belčeräg o AFG 136-137 J 7
Bełchatów o PL 92-93 P 3
Belcher Channel ≈ 24-25 X 2
Belcher Islands o CDN (NWT) 36-37 K 6
Belcher Point ▲ CDN 24-25 g 3
Belchite o E 98-99 G 4
Belcourt Creek ~ CDN 228-229 O 2
Bel'cy = Bălţi ☆ MD 102-103 E 4
Belda o IND 142-143 E 4
Belden o USA (CA) 246-247 D 3
Belden o USA (ND) 258-259 E 3
Belden o USA (OH) 280-281 D 2
Beldene Gas Field • AUS 178-179 K 4
Belding o USA (MI) 272-273 D 4
Bel'dunčana, ozero o RUS 116-117 G 2
Bele, ozero o RUS 116-117 E 8
Belebej ☆ RUS 96-97 J 6
Belebelka o RUS 94-95 M 3
Beledweyne ☆ SP 208-209 G 6
Béléhédé o BF 202-203 K 2
Beléko-Soba o RMM 202-203 G 3
Bélel o CAM 206-207 B 5
Belel o WAN 204-205 K 4
Belele o AUS 176-177 D 3
Belém ☆ BR (AMA) 66-67 C 5
Belém o BR (PA) 68-69 L 5
Belém ☆• BR (P) 62-63 K 6
Belem o PE 70-71 C 4
Belem de São Francisco o BR 68-69 J 6
Belen o CO 60-61 E 4
Belen ~ PA 52-53 D 7
Belén o RA 76-77 D 4
Belén o RCH 70-71 C 6
Belen o USA (NM) 256-257 J 4
Belén, Río ~ RA 76-77 D 4
Belen'kij o RUS 118-119 M 8
Belesc Cogani o SP 212-213 H 3
Beles Wenz ~ ETH 208-209 C 3
Belet Weyne = Beledweyne ☆ SP 208-209 G 6
Beleuli ∴• UZ 136-137 E 2
Belev ☆ RUS 94-95 P 5
Bélèya o RG 202-203 E 4
Beleya Terara ▲ ETH 208-209 C 3
Beleza, Ribeiro ~ BR 68-69 C 6
Belezma, Monts de ▲ DZ 190-191 E 3
Belfast ☆• GB 90-91 E 4
Belfast o USA (AR) 276-277 C 6
Belfast o USA (ME) 278-279 M 4
Belfast o USA (OH) 280-281 C 4
Belfast o ZA 220-221 K 2
Belfield o USA (ND) 258-259 D 5
Bēlfodiyo o ETH 208-209 B 3
Belfort ☆• F 90-91 L 8
Belfry o USA (MT) 250-251 K 6
Belgaum o• IND 140-141 F 3
Belgica Bank ≃ 26-27 s 4
Belgica Mountains ▲ ARK 16 F 3
Belgium = België/ Belgique ■ B 92-93 G 3
Bel'go o RUS 122-123 G 3
Belgo o SUD 206-207 L 3
Belgorod ☆ RUS 102-103 K 2
Belgorod-Dnestrovskij ☆ UA 102-103 G 4
Belgrade o USA (ME) 278-279 M 4
Belgrade o USA (MN) 270-271 C 5
Belgrade o USA (MT) 250-251 H 6
Belgrade = Beograd ★ YU 100-101 H 2
Belgrano o RA 76-77 F 3
Belgrano, Cerro ▲ RA 80 E 3
Belgreen o USA (AL) 284-285 B 2
Bel Guebbour, Hassi o DZ 190-191 F 6
Bel Guerdâne, Bir o RIM 196-197 E 2
Belhatti o IND 140-141 F 3
Belhaven o USA (NC) 282-283 L 5
Belhe o IND 138-139 E 10
Belhirane o DZ 190-191 F 5
Béli ~ BF 202-203 K 2
Béli o GNB 202-203 D 4
Beli o WAN 204-205 J 5
Belic o C 54-55 G 5
Bélice ~ I 100-101 D 6
Beličij, ostrov ⌒ RUS 120-121 G 6
Belidži o RUS 126-127 H 7
Belifang o CAM 204-205 J 5
Beli Hill ▲ WAN 204-205 J 5
Belimbing o RI (LAM) 162-163 F 7
Belimbing o RI (SUS) 162-163 F 6
Belimbing, Tanjung ▲ RI 162-163 F 7
Belimbing, Teluk ≈ 162-163 F 7
Bélinga o G 210-211 D 3
Belinskij o RUS 94-95 R 5
Belinskoe o RUS 122-123 K 4
Belinyu o RI 162-163 F 5
Belitung, Pulau ⌒ RI 162-163 G 6
Belize o ANG 210-211 D 6
Belize ■ BH 52-53 K 3
Belize City o BH 52-53 K 3
Belize River ~ BH 52-53 K 3
Bélizon o F 62-63 H 3
Beljaevka ☆ RUS 96-97 K 8
Beljaka, kosa ~ RUS 112-113 X 3
Beljanica ▲ YU 100-101 H 2
Beljanka ~ RUS 118-119 O 4
Bel Kacem, Bir o TN 190-191 G 4
Bel'kači o RUS (SAH) 120-121 D 4
Bel'kači ~ RUS 120-121 D 4
Belkar o IND 140-141 E 2
Belknap Springs o USA (OR) 244-245 C 6
Bel'kovskij, ostrov ⌒ RUS 110-111 U 2
Bel'kovskij Nos, mys ▲ RUS 108-109 J 7
Bell o USA (FL) 286-287 G 2
Bell o USA (GA) 284-285 H 3
Bell o ZA 220-221 H 6
Bell, Rivière ~ CDN 236-237 L 3
Bella o CAM 210-211 C 2
Bella, Laguna la o RA 76-77 G 3
Bella Bella o CDN (BC) 228-229 F 4
Bellac o F 90-91 H 8
Bella Coola o CDN (BC) 228-229 H 4
Bella Coola River ~ CDN 228-229 H 4
Belladère o RH 54-55 J 5
Bella Flor o BOL 70-71 D 2
Bellaire o USA (MI) 272-273 D 3
Bellaire o USA (OH) 280-281 F 3
Bellary o IND 140-141 G 3
Bellata o AUS 178-179 K 5
Bellavista o PE (CAJ) 64-65 C 4
Bellavista o PE (MAR) 64-65 D 5
Bella Vista o PY 76-77 K 4
Bella Vista o RA 76-77 H 5
Bella Vista, Salar de o RCH 70-71 C 7
Bell Bay ≈ 24-25 e 5
Bellburns o CDN (NFL) 242-243 L 2
Belle, La o USA (FL) 286-287 H 5
Belle Anse o RH 54-55 J 5
Belle Côte o CDN (NS) 240-241 O 4
Belledune o CDN (NB) 240-241 K 3
Bellefontaine o USA (OH) 280-281 C 3
Bellefonte o USA (PA) 280-281 J 3
Belle Fourche o USA (SD) 260-261 C 2
Belle Fourche Reservoir ⊂ USA (SD) 260-261 C 2
Belle Fourche River ~ USA 252-253 N 3
Belle Glade o USA (FL) 286-287 J 5
Belle-Île ⌒ F 90-91 F 8
Belle Isle o CDN (NFL) 242-243 N 1
Belle Isle, Strait of ≈ 242-243 M 1
Bellemont o USA (AZ) 256-257 D 3
Bellenden Ker o AUS 174-175 H 5
Belleoram o CDN (NFL) 242-243 N 5
Belle Plaine o CDN (SAS) 232-233 N 5
Belle Plaine o USA (KS) 262-263 J 7
Belle Plaine o USA (MN) 270-271 E 6
Belle River o CDN (ONT) 238-239 C 6
Belle River o CDN (PEI) 240-241 N 4
Belleterre o CDN (QUE) 236-237 K 5
Belleview o CDN (MAN) 234-235 C 5
Belleville o CDN (NS) 240-241 K 7
Belleville o CDN (ONT) 238-239 H 4
Belleville o USA (IL) 274-275 J 6
Belleville o USA (KS) 262-263 J 5
Belleville o USA (TX) 266-267 L 4
Belleville o USA (WV) 280-281 E 4
Belleville o ZA 220-221 D 6
Bellevue o AUS 174-175 H 5
Bellevue o CDN (ALB) 232-233 D 6
Bellevue o USA (IA) 274-275 H 2
Bellevue o USA (ID) 252-253 D 3
Bellevue o USA (MI) 272-273 D 5
Bellevue o USA (NE) 262-263 L 3
Bellevue o USA (OH) 280-281 D 2
Bellevue o USA (TX) 264-265 F 5
Bellevue o USA (WA) 244-245 C 3
Bellevue de l'Inini, Mont ▲ F 62-63 H 4
Bellingen o AUS 178-179 M 6
Bellinger, Lac o CDN 38-39 G 3
Bellingham o USA (WA) 244-245 C 2
Bellingshausen Abyssal Plain ≈ 16 G 27
Bellingshausen Sea ≈ 16 G 28
Bellinzona ☆• CH 92-93 K 5
Bell-Irving River ~ CDN 32-33 F 3
Bell Island ⌒ CDN (NFL) 242-243 N 2
Bell Island ⌒ CDN (NFL) 242-243 P 5
Bell Island Hot Springs o USA 32-33 E 4
Bellmead o USA (TX) 266-267 K 2
Bellmore o USA (IN) 274-275 L 5
Bell National Historic Park, Alexander Graham • CDN (NS) 240-241 P 4
Bello o CO 60-61 D 4
Bellocq o RA 78-79 J 3
Bellona Island ⌒ SOL 184 I d 4
Bellota o USA (CA) 246-247 D 5
Bellows Falls o USA (NH) 278-279 J 5
Bellpat o PK 138-139 B 5
Bell River ~ AUS 180-181 K 2
Bell River ~ CDN 20-21 W 3
Bells o USA (TN) 276-277 F 5
Bells o USA (TX) 264-265 H 5
Bellsund ≈ 84-85 H 4
Bellton o USA (WV) 280-281 F 4
Belluno ☆ I 100-101 D 1
Bellview o USA (NM) 256-257 M 4
Bell Ville o RA 78-79 H 2
Bellvue o USA (CO) 254-255 K 3
Belly River ~ CDN 232-233 E 6
Belmond o USA (IA) 274-275 E 2
Belmont o AUS 180-181 L 2
Belmont o CDN (MAN) 234-235 D 5
Belmont o USA (MS) 268-269 M 2
Belmont o USA (NE) 262-263 C 2
Belmont o USA (NY) 278-279 C 6
Belmont o USA (TX) 266-267 K 4
Belmont o ZA 220-221 G 4
Belmont, Fort • USA (MN) 270-271 G 7
Belmonte o BR 72-73 L 3
Belmopan ★ BH 52-53 K 3
Belmore Creek ~ AUS 174-175 F 5
Belmullet = Béal an Mhuirthead o IRL 90-91 C 4
Belo o RM 222-223 D 8
Belobaka o RM 222-223 D 7
Belobrova, proliv ≈ 108-109 I Z 1
Belo Campo o BR 72-73 K 3
Beloe, ozero o RUS 94-95 P 1
Beloe, ozero o RUS 114-115 U 7
Belogolovaja ~ RUS 120-121 R 5
Belogorsk o RUS (AMR) 122-123 C 3
Belogorsk o RUS (KMR) 114-115 U 7
Belogorskij materik ∸ RUS 114-115 J 3
Belogorskij materik, vozvyšennost' ▲ RUS 114-115 J 3
Beloha o RM 222-223 D 10
Belo Horizonte ☆ BR 72-73 J 5
Beloit o USA (KS) 262-263 H 5
Beloit o USA (WI) 274-275 J 2
Belo Jardim o BR 68-69 K 6
Belojarovo o RUS 122-123 C 3
Belojarskij o RUS (HMN) 114-115 J 3
Belojarskij ☆ RUS (SVR) 96-97 M 5
Béloko o RCA 206-207 B 6
Belokuriha o RUS 124-125 O 3
Belo Monte o BR (ALA) 68-69 K 6
Belo Monte o BR (AMA) 66-67 E 6
Belo Monte do Pontal o BR 68-69 C 3
Belomorsk o RUS 88-89 N 4
Belomorsko-Baltijskij kanal < RUS 88-89 N 4
Belomorsko-Kulojskoje-plato ▲ RUS 88-89 Q 4
Belonge o ZRE 210-211 H 5
Belopa o RI 164-165 G 5
Beloreček ☆ RUS 126-127 C 5
Beloreck ☆ RUS 96-97 L 7
Belot, Lac o CDN 30-31 G 2
Belo Tsiribihina o RM 222-223 D 7
Belousovka o KZ 124-125 N 3
Belovo ☆ RUS 114-115 T 7
Beloye Ozero = Beloe, ozero o RUS 94-95 P 1
Belozersk o RUS 94-95 P 1
Belozerskoe ☆ RUS 114-115 H 7
Belozersko-Kirillovskie grjady ▲ RUS 94-95 P 1
Belpre o USA (KS) 262-263 G 7
Belpre o USA (OH) 280-281 E 4
Belrem, Hassi el < DZ 190-191 D 7
Bel'skaja vozvyšennost' ▲ RUS 94-95 N 4
Bel'skie, Ust'-gory ▲ RUS 112-113 R 4
Bel'skoe o RUS 116-117 F 7
Belt o USA (MT) 250-251 J 4
Belt Bay ⊂ AUS 178-179 D 5
Belted Range ▲ USA 248-249 H 2
Belterra o BR 66-67 K 4
Belton o USA (MO) 274-275 D 6
Belton o USA (SC) 284-285 H 2
Belton o USA (TX) 266-267 K 2
Belton Lake < USA (TX) 266-267 K 2
Beltov tepalik ∸ UZ 136-137 G 3
Beluga Lake ⊂ USA 20-21 P 6
Beluha, gora ▲ KZ 124-125 P 4
Beluran o MAL 160-161 B 10
Beluru o MAL 164-165 D 2
Beluš'e o RUS 88-89 T 3
Beluš'ja Guba o RUS 108-109 E 6
Beluži̇j Nos, mys ▲ RUS 108-109 M 6
Belvedere Marittimo o I 100-101 E 5
Belvidere o USA (IL) 274-275 K 2
Belvidere o USA (KS) 262-263 G 7
Belvidere o USA (SD) 260-261 E 3
Belwa, River ~ WAN 204-205 J 4
Belwali o LB 202-203 F 6
Belyando River ~ AUS 178-179 J 2
Belye Vody ☆ KZ 136-137 L 3
Belyj ☆ RUS 94-95 N 4
Belyj, ostrov ⌒ RUS 108-109 O 5
Belyj Čulym ~ RUS 114-115 U 7
Belyj Jar ☆ RUS 114-115 S 5
Belyj Urjum ~ RUS 118-119 H 9
Belyy, Ostrov = Belyj, ostrov ⌒ RUS 108-109 O 5
Bełżec o PL 92-93 R 3
Belzoni o USA (MS) 268-269 K 3
Béma o RMM 202-203 F 2
Bémal o RCA 206-207 C 5
Bemanevika o RM 222-223 G 5
Bemaraha ∸ RM 222-223 D 7
Bemarivo ~ RM 222-223 F 5
Bembe o ANG 216-217 C 3
Bembeche ∸ TCH 198-199 J 3
Bembèrèkè o DY 204-205 E 3
Bembesi o ZW 218-219 E 4
Bemersyde o CDN (SAS) 232-233 Q 6
Bemetāra o IND 142-143 B 5
Bemidji o USA (MN) 270-271 D 3
Bemis o USA (SD) 260-261 K 2
Bemonto o RM 222-223 D 7
Bemu o RI 166-167 E 3
Ben o BF 202-203 H 3
Bena o USA (MN) 270-271 D 3
Bena o WAN 204-205 F 3
Benabarre o• E 98-99 H 3
Bena-Dibele o ZRE 210-211 J 6
Benagerie o AUS 178-179 F 6
Benahmed o MA 188-189 H 4
Benahouin o CI 202-203 J 6
Benain ~ RI 166-167 C 6
Bena-Kamba o ZRE 210-211 K 5
Benalla o AUS 180-181 H 4
Ben Ash Monument • USA (SD) 260-261 D 1
Benato-Toby o RM 222-223 D 9
Bena-Tshadi o ZRE 210-211 J 6
Benaule o PNG 183 F 3
Benavente o E 98-99 E 3
Benavides o USA (TX) 266-267 J 6
Ben Badis o DZ 188-189 L 3
Ben Bolt o USA (TX) 266-267 J 6
Benbonyathe Hill ▲ AUS 178-179 E 6
Ben Boyd National Park ⊥ AUS 180-181 K 4
Benbrook Lake < USA (TX) 264-265 G 6
Bencubbin o AUS 176-177 D 5
Bend o USA (OR) 244-245 D 6
Bend o USA (TX) 266-267 J 2
Bèndana o TCH 206-207 D 4
Benda Range ▲ AUS 180-181 E 2
Bendel ■ WAN 204-205 F 5
Bendela o ZRE 210-211 F 5
Bendeleben Mountains ▲ USA 20-21 H 4
Bendemeer o AUS 178-179 L 6
Bender = Tighina o MD 102-103 F 4
Bender Qaasim = Boosaaso ☆ SP 208-209 J 3
Bendery = Tighina o MD 102-103 F 4
Bendieuta Creek ~ AUS 178-179 E 6
Bendigo o AUS 180-181 H 4
Bend of the Boyne ••• IRL 90-91 D 5
Bendugu o WAL 202-203 E 5
Bene o MOC 218-219 G 2
Benedict, Mount ▲ CDN 36-37 U 7
Benedict Fjord ≈ 26-27 f 2
Benedictine Monastery • AUS 176-177 D 5
Benedito Leite o BR 68-69 F 5
Bénéna o RMM 202-203 H 3
Benenitra o RM 222-223 D 9
Benešov o CZ 92-93 N 4
Benevento ☆• I 100-101 E 4
Benevides o BR 62-63 K 6
Benewah o USA (ID) 250-251 C 4
Benfica o BR 72-73 J 6
Benga o MOC 218-219 G 3
Benga o MW 218-219 H 1
Bengābād o IND 142-143 E 3
Bengal, Bay of ≈ 10-11 H 7
Bengala o CO 60-61 E 5
Bengāla o IND 140-141 L 5
Bengalun, Tanjung ▲ RI 164-165 E 3
Bengamisa o ZRE 210-211 K 3
Bengawan ~ RI 168 E 3
Bengbis o CAM 210-211 D 2
Bengbu o VRC 154-155 K 5
Benge o USA (WA) 244-245 G 4
Benghazi = Banghāzi ☆ LAR 192-193 J 1
Ben Ghimah, Bi'r o LAR 192-193 J 2
Bengkalis o RI 162-163 E 4
Bengkalis, Pulau ⌒ RI 162-163 E 4
Bengkayang o RI 162-163 H 4
Bengkulu ▫ RI 162-163 E 7
Bengkulu ☆ RI 162-163 E 6
Bengkunat, Teluk ≈ 162-163 F 7
Bengo ▫ ANG 216-217 B 4
Bengo ~ ANG 216-217 B 4
Bengo, Baia do ≈ 216-217 B 4
Bengough o CDN (SAS) 232-233 N 6
Benguela ▫ ANG 216-217 B 6
Benguela ☆• ANG (BGU) 216-217 B 6
Ben Guerdane o TN 192-193 D 1
Benguerir o MA 188-189 H 4
Beni o ZRE 212-213 B 3
Beni, Río ~ BOL 70-71 D 3
Beni-Abbès o• DZ 188-189 K 5
Beniah Lake o CDN 30-31 N 4
Beni-Boufrah o MA 188-189 J 3
Benicarló o E 98-99 H 4
Benicasim = Benicàssim o E 98-99 H 4
Benicia o USA (CA) 246-247 C 5
Benicito, Río ~ BOL 70-71 E 2
Benidorm o E 98-99 G 5
Beni Hammad ••• DZ 190-191 E 3
Beni Haoua o DZ 190-191 C 2
Beni Ikhlef o DZ 188-189 L 6
Beni Kheddache o TN 190-191 H 4
Beni-Mellal ☆ MA 188-189 H 4
Benin ■ DY 204-205 E 4
Benin, Bight of ≈ 204-205 E 6
Benin, River ~ WAN 204-205 F 6
Benin City ☆• WAN 204-205 F 5
Beni Ounif o DZ 188-189 L 4
Beni Saf o DZ 188-189 L 3
Benisheikh o WAN 204-205 K 3
Beni Slimane o DZ 190-191 D 2
Beni-Smir ▲ DZ 188-189 L 4
Beni-Snassen, Monts des ▲ MA 188-189 K 3
Beni Tajjite o MA 188-189 K 4
Benito o CDN (MAN) 234-235 B 3
Benito Juárez o MEX 50-51 F 3
Benito Juárez o RA 78-79 K 4
Benito Juárez, Parque Nacional ⊥ MEX 52-53 F 3
Benito Juárez, Presa < MEX 52-53 G 3
Beni-Val o MA 188-189 K 4
Benjamin o USA (TX) 264-265 E 5
Benjamin o USA (UT) 254-255 D 3
Benjamin, Isla ⌒ RCH 80 C 2
Benjamin Aceval o PY 76-77 J 3
Benjamin Constant o BR 66-67 B 5
Benjamin Hill o MEX 50-51 D 2
Benjamin River o CDN (NB) 240-241 J 3
Benjina o RI 166-167 H 5
Benkelman o USA (NE) 262-263 E 4
Ben Lawers ▲ GB 90-91 E 3
Ben Loganbli o LB 202-203 E 6
Ben Lomond ▲ AUS 180-181 J 6
Ben Macdui ▲ GB 90-91 F 3
Ben Mehidi o DZ 190-191 F 2
Ben More ▲ GB 90-91 E 3
Benmore, Lake o NZ 182 C 6
Benndale o USA (MS) 268-269 M 6
Bennett o USA (CO) 254-255 L 4
Bennett o USA (NC) 282-283 H 5
Bennett o USA (NM) 256-257 M 6
Bennett, Lake o AUS 172-173 K 7
Bennett, Mount ▲ AUS 172-173 C 7
Bennetta, ostrov ⌒ RUS 110-111 b 1
Bennett Lake o CDN 20-21 X 6
Bennettsville o USA (SC) 284-285 L 2
Ben Nevis ▲•• GB 90-91 E 3
Bennichāb o RIM 196-197 C 5
Bennington o USA (KS) 262-263 J 6
Bennington o USA (OK) 264-265 H 4
Bennington o USA (VT) 278-279 H 6
Benny o CDN (ONT) 238-239 D 2
Benoit o USA (MS) 268-269 J 3
Benoit o USA (WI) 270-271 G 4
Benoit's Cove o CDN (NFL) 242-243 K 3
Benoni o ZA 220-221 J 3
Benoud o DZ 190-191 C 4
Bénoué ~ CAM 204-205 K 4
Bénoué, Cuvette de la ∸ CAM 204-205 K 4
Bénoué, Parc National de la ⊥ CAM 204-205 K 4
Bénoye o TCH 206-207 C 4
Bến Quang o VN 158-159 J 2
Ben Rinnes ▲ GB 90-91 F 3
Bensékou o DY 204-205 E 3
Ben-Slimane ☆ MA 188-189 H 4
Benson o CDN (SAS) 232-233 P 6
Benson o USA (AZ) 256-257 E 7
Benson o USA (MN) 270-271 C 5
Ben S'Rour o DZ 190-191 E 3
Bent o IR 134-135 H 5
Bent, Rūdhāne-ye ~ IR 134-135 H 5
Ben Tadjine, Djebel ▲ DZ 188-189 K 6
Benta Seberang o MAL 162-163 D 2
Bentenan o RI 164-165 J 3
Benteng o RI (SLT) 164-165 G 4
Benteng o RI (SSE) 168 E 6
Bentiaba ~ ANG 216-217 B 7
Bentick Island ⌒ MYA 158-159 E 5
Bentinck Island ⌒ AUS 174-175 E 5
Bentinck Sound ≈ 158-159 D 3
Bentiu o SUD 206-207 J 4
Bentley o CDN (ALB) 232-233 D 3
Bent Mountain o USA (VA) 280-281 F 6
Bento Gomes, Rio ~ BR 70-71 J 5
Bento Gonçalves o BR 74-75 E 7
Benton o USA (AL) 284-285 D 4
Benton o USA (AR) 276-277 C 6
Benton o USA (CA) 248-249 F 2
Benton o USA (IL) 276-277 G 3
Benton o USA (KY) 276-277 G 4
Benton o USA (LA) 268-269 G 4
Benton o USA (MO) 276-277 F 3
Benton o USA (MS) 268-269 K 4
Benton o USA (TN) 282-283 C 5
Benton City o USA (WA) 244-245 F 4
Bentong o MAL 162-163 D 3
Benton Harbor o USA (MI) 272-273 C 5
Bentonia o USA (MS) 268-269 K 4
Bentonsport o USA (IA) 274-275 G 4
Bentonville o USA (AR) 276-277 A 4
Bentonville o• USA (NC) 282-283 J 5
Bentota o CL 140-141 H 7
Bến Tre ☆ VN 158-159 J 5
Bents o CDN (SAS) 232-233 L 4
Bent's Old Fort National Historic Site • USA (CO) 254-255 M 5
Bentuka o MAL 160-161 A 10
Benty o RG 202-203 D 5
Benua o RI 164-165 H 6
Benua, Pulau ⌒ RI 162-163 G 4
Benualawas o RI 164-165 D 4
Benue ▫ WAN 204-205 G 5
Benue, River • WAN 204-205 G 4
Benum, Gunung ▲ MAL 162-163 E 3
Benut o MAL 162-163 E 4
Ben Wheeler o USA (TX) 264-265 J 6
Benxi o VRC 150-151 D 7
Benxi Shuidong • VRC 150-151 E 7
Benye o ZRE 210-211 F 4
Benza o ANG 216-217 B 3
Ben Zireg o DZ 188-189 L 5
Beo o RI 164-165 K 1
Beoga o RI 166-167 J 3
Beograd ★ YU 100-101 H 2
Beohari o IND 142-143 B 3
Beoumi o CI 202-203 H 6
Beowawe o USA (NV) 246-247 J 3
Bepondi, Pulau ⌒ RI 166-167 H 2
Beppu o• J 152-153 D 8
Beqa ⌒ FJI 184 III b 3
Beque, De o USA (CO) 254-255 G 4
Bequia Island ⌒ WV 56 E 5
Bequimão o BR 68-69 F 3
Ber o RMM 196-197 J 6
Berabevú o RA 78-79 J 2
Berafia, Nosy ⌒ RM 222-223 E 5
Berahlê o ETH 200-201 K 6
Beraketa o RM 222-223 D 10
Beramanja o RM 222-223 F 4
Bérandjokou o RCB 210-211 F 2
Berangas o RI 164-165 E 5
Berāni o PK 138-139 B 7
Berat ☆•• AL 100-101 G 4
Berau ~ RI 164-165 E 2
Berau, Teluk ≈ 166-167 G 3
Beraun = Beroun o CZ 92-93 N 4
Beravina o RM 222-223 D 7
Beravy o RM 222-223 D 8
Berazino ☆ BY 94-95 L 5
Berbera o SP 208-209 G 3
Berbérati ☆ RCA 206-207 B 6
Berbia, Bir o TN 190-191 G 4
Berbice ~ GUY 62-63 E 4
Berchtesgaden o D 92-93 M 5
Berclair o USA (TX) 266-267 K 5
Bercogyi o KZ 126-127 N 3
Berd' ~ RUS 114-115 S 7
Berd' ~ RUS 124-125 N 1
Berdaale o SP 212-213 J 2
Berd'ans'ka kosa ~ UA 102-103 K 4
Berdensar, köl o KZ 126-127 M 4
Berdičev = Berdyčiv ☆ UA 102-103 F 3
Berdigestjah ☆ RUS 118-119 N 4
Berdjans'k o UA 102-103 K 4
Berdsk o RUS 124-125 N 1
Berdyans'k = Berdjans'k o UA 102-103 K 4
Berdyčiv ☆ UA 102-103 F 3
Béré o TCH 206-207 C 4
Berea o USA (KY) 276-277 L 3
Berea o USA (NC) 282-283 J 4
Béréba o BF 202-203 J 4
Berebere o RI 164-165 L 2
Bereeda o SP 208-209 K 3
Beregovoe o RUS 124-125 M 2
Beregovoj o RUS 118-119 K 8
Berehove ☆ UA 102-103 C 3
Bereina o PNG 183 D 5
Bereja ~ RUS 122-123 B 3
Bereku o EAT 212-213 E 6
Berekua o WD 56 E 4
Berekum o GH 202-203 J 6
Bérëlëh ~ RUS 110-111 b 4
Bérëlëh ~ RUS 120-121 M 2
Berembang o RI 162-163 D 3
Berenda o USA (CA) 248-249 D 2
Berendi o TR 128-129 F 4
Berenike o ET 194-195 G 6
Berens Island ⌒ CDN (MAN) 234-235 F 2
Berens Islands ⌒ CDN 30-31 N 2
Berens River o CDN (MAN) 234-235 F 2
Berens River ~ CDN 234-235 F 2
Berens River ~ CDN 234-235 K 3
Bereš ~ RUS 114-115 U 7
Beresford o CDN (NB) 240-241 K 3
Beresford o USA (SD) 260-261 K 3
Beresford Lake o CDN (MAN) 234-235 H 4
Berettyóújfalu o H 92-93 Q 5
Berezivka o UA 102-103 G 4
Berežnaja o RUS 88-89 R 6
Bereznehuvate o UA 102-103 H 4
Berezník o RUS 88-89 R 5
Berezniki o RUS 114-115 D 5
Berežnyh, mys ▲ RUS 110-111 X 1
Berëzova o RUS 88-89 M 4
Berëzovaja ~ RUS 116-117 F 8
Berëzovaja ~ RUS 112-113 R 5
Berëzovka ☆ RUS (KRN) 116-117 F 7
Berëzovka ☆ RUS (PRM) 96-97 K 5
Berëzovka ~ RUS 112-113 J 3
Berëzovka ~ RUS 112-113 H 3
Berëzovka ~ RUS 114-115 R 5
Berëzovka ~ RUS 114-115 D 4
Berëzovo ☆ RUS 114-115 H 3
Berëzovskij o RUS 114-115 T 7
Berëzovskij ☆ RUS 96-97 M 5
Berg o N 86-87 H 2
Berga o E 98-99 H 3
Berga, mys ▲ RUS 108-109 I c 1
Bergama ☆• TR 128-129 B 3
Bérgamo ☆• I 100-101 B 2
Bergara o E 98-99 F 3
Bergen ☆••• N 86-87 B 6
Bergen o• NL 92-93 H 2
Bergen o USA (MN) 270-271 D 7
Bergen (Rügen) o D 92-93 M 1
Berg en Dal o SME 62-63 G 3
Bergerac o F 90-91 H 9
Bergland o CDN (ONT) 234-235 J 6
Bergland o USA (MI) 270-271 J 4
Bergsig o NAM 216-217 C 10
Bergville o ZA 220-221 J 4
Berhait o IND 142-143 E 3
Berhala, Selat ≈ 162-163 F 5
Berhampur = Brahmapur o IND 142-143 D 6
Berikat, Tanjung ▲ RI 162-163 F 6
Berilo o BR 72-73 J 4
Beringa, mogila • RUS 120-121 V 6
Beringa, mys ▲ RUS 112-113 X 4
Beringa, ostrov ⌒ RUS 120-121 W 6
Beringarra o AUS 176-177 D 3
Bering Glacier ⊂ USA 20-21 T 6
Bering Land Bridge Nature Reserve ⊥ USA 20-21 G 4
Beringov proliv ≈ 112-113 a 4
Berino o USA (NM) 256-257 J 6
Beripeta o IND 140-141 J 4
Beris ~ RUS 110-111 Q 4
Berisso o RA 78-79 L 3
Beriza o BR 72-73 K 3
Berkåk ☆ N 86-87 E 5
Berkane o MA 188-189 K 3
Berkeley o USA (CA) 248-249 B 2
Berkeley, Cape ▲ CDN 24-25 V 4
Berkeley Point ▲ CDN 24-25 M 5
Berkeley River ~ AUS 172-173 H 3
Berkeley Sound ≈ 78-79 M 6
Berkeley Group ⌒ CDN 24-25 V 2
Berkner Island ⌒ ARK 16 F 30
Berkovica o BG 102-103 C 6
Berland River ~ CDN 228-229 R 3
Berlengas, Rio ~ BR 68-69 G 5
Berlevåg o N 86-87 O 1
Berliet, Point ▲ RN 198-199 D 2
Berlin ★••• D 92-93 M 2
Berlin o USA (MD) 280-281 L 5
Berlin o USA (ND) 258-259 J 5
Berlin o USA (NH) 278-279 K 4
Berlin o USA (NJ) 280-281 M 4
Berlin o USA (OK) 264-265 E 3
Berlin o USA (PA) 280-281 H 4
Berlin o USA (WI) 270-271 K 7
Berlin, Mount ▲ ARK 16 F 23
Berlinguet Inlet ≈ 24-25 d 5
Berlin Reservoir < USA (OH) 280-281 E 3
Bermagui o AUS 180-181 L 4
Bermego, Río ~ RA 76-77 C 5
Bermeja, Sierra ▲ E 98-99 E 6
Bermejillo o MEX 50-51 H 5
Bermejo, Isla ⌒ RA 78-79 J 5
Bermejo, Río ~ RA 76-77 D 6
Bermejo, Río ~ RA 76-77 H 4
Bermejo, Río ~ RA 76-77 F 2
Bermuda ▫ GB 54-55 L 1
Bermuda Island ⌒ GB 54-55 L 1
Bermuda Islands ⌒ GB 54-55 L 2
Bern ★••• CH 92-93 J 5
Bernabe Rivera o ROU 76-77 J 6
Bernalillo o USA (NM) 256-257 J 3
Bernam ~ MAL 162-163 D 3
Bernard Island ⌒ CDN 24-25 J 4
Bernardo o USA (NM) 256-257 J 4
Bernardo de Irigoyen o RA 74-75 D 6
Bernardo O'Higgins, Parque Nacional ⊥ RCH 80 C 5
Bernardo Sacuita, Ponta do ▲ BR 68-69 F 2
Bernard River ~ CDN 24-25 K 4
Bernay o F 90-91 H 7
Bernburg (Saale) o• D 92-93 L 3
Berne o USA (IN) 274-275 O 4
Berne o USA (WA) 244-245 D 3
Berner o USA (GA) 284-285 G 3
Berner Alpen ▲ CH 92-93 J 5
Bernice o USA (LA) 268-269 H 4
Bernier, Cape ▲ AUS 172-173 H 3
Bernier Bay ≈ 24-25 b 5
Bernier Island ⌒ AUS 176-177 B 2
Bernina, Piz ▲ CH 92-93 K 5
Berninapass ▲ CH 92-93 L 5
Bernstorffs Isfjord ≈ 28-29 U 5
Bero ~ ANG 216-217 B 7
Beroroha o RM 222-223 D 8
Beroun o CZ 92-93 N 4
Berounka ~ CZ 92-93 M 4
Berrahal o DZ 190-191 F 2
Berrechid o MA 188-189 H 4
Berrekhem, Hassi o DZ 190-191 E 4
Berri o AUS 180-181 F 3
Berriane o DZ 190-191 D 4
Berridale o AUS 180-181 K 4
Berrigan o AUS 180-181 H 3
Berriwillock o AUS 180-181 G 3
Berrouaghia o DZ 190-191 D 2
Berrugas o CO 60-61 D 3
Berry ▲ F 90-91 H 8
Berry o USA (AL) 284-285 C 3
Berry, De o USA (TX) 264-265 K 6
Berry Creek ~ CDN 232-233 G 4
Berrydale o USA (FL) 286-287 B 1
Berryessa, Lake o USA (CA) 246-247 C 5
Berry Head o CDN (NFL) 242-243 K 4
Berry Islands ⌒ BS 54-55 F 2
Berrymoor o CDN (ALB) 232-233 D 2
Berryville o USA (AR) 276-277 B 4
Berryville o USA (VA) 280-281 J 4
Berseba o NAM 220-221 C 3
Berthierville o CDN (QUE) 238-239 M 2
Berthold o USA (ND) 258-259 F 3
Berthierhaugh o AUS 174-175 G 3
Bertinho o BR 68-69 C 3
Bertolínia o BR 68-69 G 5
Bertoua ☆ CAM 204-205 K 6
Bertram o CDN (ONT) 236-237 D 3
Bertram o USA (TX) 266-267 J 3
Bertrand o CDN (NB) 240-241 K 3
Bertrandville o USA (LA) 268-269 L 7
Bertwell o CDN (SAS) 232-233 Q 3
Berunij ☆ UZ 136-137 G 4

304 Beijing — Berunij

Birsilpur ○ **IND** 138-139 D 5
Birsk ☆ **RUS** 96-97 J 6
Birsuat ∼ **RUS** 124-125 B 2
Birtam-Tam ○ **MA** 188-189 J 4
Bi'r Ṭarfāwī < **IRQ** 128-129 K 6
Birti ○ **SUD** 200-201 F 3
Birtle ○ **CDN** (SAS) 232-233 R 5
Biruaca ○ **YV** 60-61 H 4
Birufu ○ **RI** 166-167 K 4
Birūr ○ **IND** 140-141 F 4
Biržai ☆ ·· **LT** 94-95 J 3
Bir Zar ○ **TN** 190-191 H 5
Biša ○ **KSA** 132-133 C 3
Bisa, Pulau ⌒ **RI** 164-165 K 4
Biša, Wādī ∼ **KSA** 132-133 C 3
Bisagana ○ **WAN** 198-199 F 6
Bisalpur ○ **IND** 138-139 G 5
Bisanadi National Reserve ⊥ **EAK** 212-213 G 3
Bisbee ○ **USA** (AZ) 256-257 F 7
Biscarrosse ○ **F** 90-91 G 9
Biscay, Bay of ≈ 90-91 E 9
Biscay Abyssal Plain ≃ 6-7 J 4
Biscayne Bay ≈ 286-287 J 6
Biscayne National Park ⊥ **USA** (FL) 286-287 J 6
Bischofshofen ○ **A** 92-93 M 5
Biscoe ○ **USA** (NC) 282-283 H 5
Biscoe Islands ⌒ **ARK** 16 G 30
Biscucuy ○ **YV** 60-61 G 3
Bisellia ○ **SUD** 206-207 H 5
Bisen ○ **KZ** 96-97 E 9
Bisert' ○ **RUS** 96-97 L 5
Bisha ○ **ER** 200-201 H 5
Bishaltar ○ **NEP** 144-145 E 7
Bishan ○ **VRC** 156-157 E 2
Bishkek = Biškek ★ **KS** 146-147 B 4
Bishkhali ∼ **BD** 142-143 G 4
Bishnupur ○ **IND** 142-143 E 4
Bisho ○ **ZA** 220-221 H 6
Bishop ○ **USA** (CA) 248-249 F 2
Bishop ○ **USA** (TX) 266-267 K 6
Bishop Hill State Historic Park • **USA** (IL) 274-275 H 3
Bishop Range ▲▲ **AUS** 172-173 H 6
Bishop's Falls ○ **CDN** (NFL) 242-243 N 3
Bishopville ○ **USA** (SC) 284-285 K 2
Bişhr ○ **LAR** 192-193 H 2
Bishushanzhang • **VRC** 148-149 N 7
Bisina, Lake ⬭ **EAU** 212-213 E 3
Bisiu ○ **EAU** 212-213 E 3
Biškek ★ **KS** 146-147 B 4
Biskotasi Lake ⬭ **CDN** (ONT) 236-237 G 5
Biskra ☆ • **DZ** 190-191 E 3
Biskupiec ○ **PL** 92-93 Q 2
Bislig ○ **RP** 160-161 G 8
Bismarck ○ **CDN** (ONT) 238-239 F 5
Bismarck ○ **USA** (AR) 276-277 B 6
Bismarck ○ **USA** (MO) 276-277 E 3
Bismarck ☆ **USA** (ND) 258-259 G 5
Bismarck Archipelago ⌒ **PNG** 183 E 2
Bismarck Range ▲▲ **PNG** 183 C 3
Bismarck Sea ≈ 183 E 2
Bismarckstraße ≈ 16 G 30
Bismil ☆ **TR** 128-129 J 4
Biso ○ **EAU** 212-213 C 3
Bison ○ **USA** (SD) 260-261 D 1
Bisonó ○ **DOM** 54-55 K 5
Bisotūn ○ **IR** 134-135 B 1
Bispgården ○ **S** 86-87 H 5
Bissamcuttack ○ **IND** 142-143 C 6
Bissane ○ **RMM** 196-197 K 6
Bissau ★ • **GNB** 202-203 C 4
Bissikrima ○ **RG** 202-203 E 4
Bissingou II ○ **RCA** 206-207 E 4
Bissora ☆ **GNB** 202-203 C 3
Bistcho Lake ⬭ **CDN** 30-31 K 6
Bistineau, Lake ⬭ **USA** (LA) 268-269 G 4
Bistrița ☆ • **RO** 102-103 D 4
Biswān ○ **IND** 142-143 B 2
Bita ∼ **RCA** 206-207 G 5
Bita, Río ∼ **CO** 60-61 G 4
Bitam ○ **G** 210-211 C 2
Bitangor ○ **MAL** 162-163 J 3
Bitata ○ **ETH** 208-209 D 6
Bitencourt ○ **BR** 66-67 C 3
Bitian Bank ≃ 168 E 2
Bitigiu ○ **ETH** 208-209 E 4
Bitik ○ **KZ** 96-97 G 8
Bitilifondi ○ **RCA** 206-207 H 6
Bitjug ∼ **RUS** 94-95 R 5
Bitjug ∼ **RUS** 102-103 M 2
Bitkine ○ **TCH** 206-207 D 3
Bitlis ☆ • **TR** 128-129 K 3
Bitola ○ ·· **MK** 100-101 H 4
Bitou ○ **BF** 202-203 K 4
Bitoutouk ○ **CAM** 210-211 C 2
Bitter Creek ○ **USA** (WY) 252-253 K 5
Bitter Creek ∼ **USA** 252-253 J 5
Bitterfeld ○ **D** 92-93 M 3
Bitterfontein ○ **ZA** 220-221 D 5
Bitter Lake ⬭ **CDN** (SAS) 232-233 J 5
Bittern Lake ○ **CDN** (ALB) 232-233 E 3
Bittern Lake Indian Reservation ✕ **CDN** (SAS) 232-233 N 2
Bitterroot Range ▲▲ **USA** 250-251 D 4
Bitterroot River ∼ **USA** 250-251 E 5
Bitui River ∼ **PNG** 183 B 5
Bitumount ○ **CDN** 32-33 P 3
Bitung ○ **RI** 164-165 J 3
Bituruna ○ **BR** 74-75 E 6
Bitzshtini Mount ▲ **USA** 20-21 P 4
Biu ○ **WAN** 204-205 K 3
Biuka-tōge ▲ **J** 152-153 K 2
Biu Plateau ▲▲ **WAN** 204-205 K 3
Biwabik ○ **USA** (MN) 270-271 F 3
Biwai, Mount ▲ **PNG** 183 B 4
Biwa-ko ⬭ **J** 152-153 G 7
Biwako Quasi National Park ⊥ **J** 152-153 F 7
Biwat ○ **PNG** 183 B 3
Bixby ○ **USA** (MN) 270-271 E 7
Bixby ○ **USA** (MO) 276-277 D 3
Biyagundi ○ **ER** 200-201 H 5
Biyang ○ **VRC** 154-155 H 5
Biye K'obē ○ **ETH** 208-209 F 3
Biysk = Bijsk ☆ **RUS** 124-125 O 2
Bizana ○ **ZA** 220-221 J 5
Bižanābād ○ **IR** 134-135 H 5
Bižbuljak ☆ **RUS** 96-97 J 7
Bize ∼ **KZ** 124-125 K 6
Bizen ○ **J** 152-153 F 7
Bizerte ☆ • **TN** 190-191 G 2
Bizigui ∼ **BF** 202-203 K 3
Bjahoml' ○ **BY** 94-95 L 4
Bjala ○ **BG** 102-103 D 6
Bjala Slatina ○ **BG** 102-103 C 6
Bjarèzina ∼ **BY** 94-95 L 5
Bjarezinski zapavednik ⊥ **BY** 94-95 L 4
Bjargtangar ▲ **IS** 86-87 a 2
Bjaroza ○ **BY** 94-95 J 5
Bjas'-Kjuël' ○ **RUS** (SAH) 118-119 N 4
Bjas'-Kjuël' ○ **RUS** (SAH) 118-119 J 6
Bjästa ○ **S** 86-87 J 5
Bjelašnica ▲ **BIH** 100-101 G 3
Bjelovar ○ **HR** 100-101 F 2
Bjerkvik ○ **N** 86-87 H 2
Bjorkdale ○ **CDN** (SAS) 232-233 P 3
Björna ○ **S** 86-87 J 5
Bjørnafjorden ≈ 86-87 B 6
Bjørne Øer ⌒ **GRØ** 26-27 n 8
Bjorne Peninsula ⌒ **CDN** 24-25 c 2
Bjørnesk Ø ⌒ **GRØ** 26-27 q 5
Bjørnøya ⌒ **N** 84-85 L 5
Bjørnøya Bank ≃ 84-85 M 5
Bjørnøy Radio ○ **N** 84-85 L 5
Bjurholm ○ • **S** 86-87 J 5
Bjutejdjah ○ • **RUS** 120-121 D 3
Bla ○ **RMM** 202-203 H 3
Blachly ○ **USA** (OR) 244-245 B 6
Black ○ **USA** 20-21 H 5
Blackall ○ **AUS** 178-179 H 3
Black Bay ⬭ **CDN** (ONT) 234-235 P 6
Black Bear Creek ∼ **USA** 264-265 G 2
Black Bear River ∼ **CDN** 34-35 L 3
Blackbear River ∼ **CDN** 34-35 M 3
Black Birch Lake ⬭ **CDN** 34-35 C 2
Black Braes ○ **AUS** 174-175 H 6
Blackbull ○ **AUS** 174-175 F 5
Blackburn, Mount ▲ **USA** 20-21 T 6
Black Canyon City ○ **USA** (AZ) 256-257 C 4
Black Canyon of the Gunnison National Monument ∴ **USA** (CO) 254-255 H 5
Black Cape ▲ **USA** 22-23 U 3
Black Creek ○ **CDN** (BC) 230-231 D 4
Black Creek ○ **USA** (WI) 270-271 K 6
Black Creek ∼ **USA** 268-269 L 5
Black Diamond ○ **CDN** (ALB) 232-233 D 5
Blackdown ○ **AUS** 174-175 G 5
Blackdown Tableland National Park ⊥ **AUS** 178-179 K 2
Black Duck River ∼ **CDN** (ONT) 34-35 M 2
Blackfalds ○ **CDN** (ALB) 232-233 E 3
Blackfeet Indian Reservation ✕ **USA** (MT) 250-251 F 3
Blackfoot ○ **CDN** (ALB) 232-233 H 2
Blackfoot ○ **USA** (ID) 252-253 F 3
Blackfoot ○ **USA** (MT) 250-251 G 3
Blackfoot Indian Reserve ✕ **CDN** (ALB) 232-233 F 5
Blackfoot Reservoir ⬭ **USA** (ID) 252-253 G 4
Blackfoot River ∼ **USA** 250-251 F 5
Black Forest = Schwarzwald ▲▲ **D** 92-93 K 4
Black Hawk ○ **CDN** (ONT) 234-235 K 6
Black Hills ▲▲ **USA** 260-261 B 2
Blackie ○ **CDN** (ALB) 232-233 E 5
Black Island ⌒ • **CDN** (MAN) 234-235 G 3
Black Lake ○ **CDN** (QUE) 238-239 O 2
Black Lake ⬭ **CDN** (SAS) 30-31 R 6
Black Lake ⬭ **USA** 22-23 R 4
Black Mesa ▲ **USA** (OK) 264-265 B 2
Black Mesa ∸ **USA** 256-257 E 2
Black Mountain ▲ **AUS** 178-179 E 1
Black Mountain ▲ **CDN** 26-27 G 3
Black Mountain ▲ **USA** (VA) 280-281 D 7
Black Mountains ▲▲ **USA** 256-257 A 3
Black Nossob ∼ **NAM** 216-217 E 10
Black Pines ○ **CDN** (BC) 230-231 K 3
Black Point ▲ **AUS** 176-177 C 7
Black Point ○ **BS** 54-55 G 2
Black Point ▲ **USA** 22-23 U 4
Blackpool ○ **CDN** (BC) 230-231 J 2
Blackpool ○ • **GB** 90-91 F 5
Black Range ▲▲ **USA** 256-257 H 5
Black River ○ **CDN** (NS) 240-241 O 4
Black River ∼ **CDN** 20-21 Z 6
Black River ∼ **CDN** 234-235 G 4
Black River ∼ **CDN** 238-239 F 4
Black River ○ ·· **JA** 54-55 G 5
Black River ∼ **USA** 20-21 T 3
Black River ∼ **USA** 256-257 E 5
Black River ∼ **USA** 256-257 L 6
Black River ∼ **USA** 270-271 H 6
Black River ∼ **USA** 272-273 E 2
Black River ∼ **USA** 272-273 G 4
Black River ∼ **USA** 276-277 E 4
Black River ∼ **USA** 276-277 D 5
Black River ∼ **USA** 278-279 F 5
Black River ∼ **USA** 280-281 D 2
Black River ∼ **USA** 282-283 J 6
Black River ∼ **USA** 284-285 L 3
Black River ∼ **USA** 284-285 K 2
Black River ∼ **USA** 286-287 H 1
Black River Falls ○ **USA** (WI) 270-271 H 6
Black Rock ○ **USA** (AR) 276-277 D 4
Black Rock ○ **USA** (UT) 254-255 C 5
Black Rock Desert ∸ **USA** 246-247 F 3
Black Rock Point ▲ **CDN** 36-37 R 4
Black Rocks ▲ • **WAN** 204-205 H 4
Black Rocks Landing ○ **AUS** 174-175 D 4
Black Rock Summit ▲ **USA** (NV) 246-247 J 5
Blackrun ○ **USA** (OH) 280-281 D 3
Blacksburg ○ **USA** (VA) 280-281 F 6
Black Sea ≈ 102-103 G 6
Blacks Fork ∼ **USA** 254-255 E 3
Blacks Harbour ○ **CDN** (NB) 240-241 J 5
Blackshear ○ **USA** (GA) 284-285 H 5
Blackshear, Lake < **USA** (GA) 284-285 G 5
Black Squirrel Creek ∼ **USA** 254-255 L 5
Blackstone ○ **USA** (VA) 280-281 H 6
Blackstone River ∼ **CDN** 20-21 V 4
Blackstone River ∼ **CDN** 30-31 H 5
Blackstone River ∼ **CDN** 232-233 B 3
Black Sturgeon Lake ⬭ **CDN** (ONT) 234-235 P 5
Blackville ○ **AUS** 178-179 L 6
Blackville ○ **CDN** (NB) 240-241 K 4
Blackville ○ **USA** (SC) 284-285 J 3
Black Volta ∼ **GH** 202-203 J 5
Black Warrior River ∼ **USA** 284-285 C 4
Blackwater ○ **AUS** 178-179 K 2
Blackwater ∼ **USA** 286-287 C 1
Blackwater Creek ∼ **AUS** 178-179 H 3
Blackwater Creek ∼ **AUS** 180-181 L 2
Blackwater Lake ⬭ **CDN** 30-31 H 3
Blackwater National Wildlife Refuge ✕ **USA** (MD) 280-281 K 5
Blackwater River ∼ **CDN** 30-31 H 4
Blackwater River ∼ **USA** 274-275 E 6
Blackwell ○ **USA** (OK) 264-265 G 2
Blackwell ○ **USA** (TX) 264-265 D 6
Blackwells Corner ○ **USA** (CA) 248-249 E 4
Blackwood River ∼ **AUS** 176-177 D 6
Bladenboro ○ **USA** (NC) 282-283 J 6
Bladensburg National Park ⊥ **AUS** 178-179 G 2
Bladgrond ○ **ZA** 220-221 D 4
Bladon Springs State Park ⊥ • **USA** (AL) 284-285 B 5
Bladworth ○ **CDN** (SAS) 232-233 M 4
Blaeberry River ∼ **CDN** 230-231 N 2
Blåfjellet ▲ **N** 86-87 F 4
Blagodarnyj ○ **RUS** 102-103 N 5
Blagoevgrad ○ **BG** 102-103 C 6
Blagoevo ○ **RUS** 88-89 T 5
Blagopolučija, zaliv ≈ 108-109 K 4
Blagoveščenka ○ **KZ** 146-147 B 4
Blagoveščenka ☆ **RUS** 124-125 L 2
Blagoveščensk ☆ **RUS** (BAS) 96-97 J 6
Blagoveščensk ☆ • **RUS** (AMR) 122-123 B 3
Blagoveščenskij proliv ≈ 110-111 Z 2
Blagoveshchensk = Blagoveščensk ☆ • **RUS** 122-123 B 3
Blaine ○ **USA** (KS) 262-263 K 5
Blaine ○ **USA** (KY) 276-277 N 2
Blaine ○ **USA** (MN) 270-271 E 5
Blaine ○ **USA** (TN) 282-283 D 4
Blaine ○ **USA** (WA) 244-245 C 2
Blaine Lake ○ **CDN** (SAS) 232-233 M 3
Blainville ○ **CDN** (QUE) 238-239 M 3
Blair ○ **USA** (NE) 262-263 K 3
Blair ○ **USA** (OK) 264-265 E 4
Blair ○ **USA** (WI) 270-271 G 6
Blair Athol ○ **AUS** 178-179 J 2
Blairbeth ○ **ZA** 220-221 H 2
Blairgowrie ○ **GB** 90-91 F 3
Blairmore ○ **CDN** (ALB) 232-233 D 6
Blairsden ○ **USA** (CA) 246-247 E 4
Blairsville ○ **USA** (GA) 284-285 G 2
Blairsville ○ **USA** (PA) 280-281 G 3
Blaka ∼ **RN** 198-199 F 2
Blaka Laodemi ○ **RN** 198-199 F 2
Blake Bay ≈ 24-25 e 7
Blakely ○ **USA** (GA) 284-285 F 5
Blake Plateau ≃ 286-287 K 1
Blake Point ▲ **USA** (MI) 270-271 K 2
Blama ○ **WAL** 202-203 E 6
Blanc, Lac ⬭ **CDN** (QUE) 236-237 P 5
Blanc, le ○ **F** 90-91 H 8
Blanca, Cordillera ▲▲ **PE** 64-65 D 6
Blanca, Lago ⬭ **RCH** 70-71 C 5
Blanca, Laguna ⬭ **RCH** 80 E 6
Blanca, Punta ▲ **MEX** 50-51 B 3
Blanca, Rio ∼ **BOL** 70-71 D 7
Blanca, Sierra ▲ **USA** (NM) 256-257 K 5
Blanca Grande, Laguna la ⬭ **RA** 78-79 H 5
Blanca Peak ▲ **USA** (CO) 254-255 K 6
Blancas, Sierras ▲▲ **RA** 78-79 F 6
Blancester ○ **USA** (OH) 280-281 C 4
Blanchard ○ **USA** (ID) 250-251 C 3
Blanchard ○ **USA** (ND) 258-259 K 4
Blanchard ○ **USA** (OK) 264-265 G 3
Blanchard River ∼ **USA** 280-281 C 2
Blanchard Springs Caverns ∴ **USA** (AR) 276-277 C 5
Blanche, Lake ⬭ **AUS** (SA) 178-179 E 5
Blanche, Lake ⬭ **AUS** (WA) 172-173 F 7
Blanche Channel ≈ 184 I c 3
Blanche-Marievallen ∼ **SME** 62-63 F 3
Blanchet Island ⌒ **CDN** 30-31 N 4
Blanchetown ○ **AUS** 180-181 E 3
Blanchisseuse ○ **TT** 60-61 L 2
Blanco ○ **USA** (NM) 256-257 H 2
Blanco ○ **USA** (TX) 266-267 J 3
Blanco, Cabo ▲ **CR** 52-53 B 7
Blanco, Cape ▲ **USA** (OR) 244-245 A 8
Blanco, Cerro ▲ **RA** 78-79 D 6
Blanco, Lago ⬭ **RA** 80 E 2
Blanco, Lago ⬭ **RCH** 80 F 7
Blanco, Río ∼ **BOL** 70-71 E 3
Blanco, Río ∼ **PE** 64-65 F 4
Blanco, Río ∼ **RA** 76-77 C 6
Blanco, Río ∼ **RA** 76-77 C 5
Blanco, Río ∼ **RA** 76-77 B 6
Blanco, Río ∼ **RA** 78-79 D 2
Blanco, Río ∼ **RA** 80 E 3
Blanco, Río ∼ **RCH** 80 D 2
Blanco Creek ∼ **USA** 266-267 K 5
Blanco River ∼ **USA** 266-267 J 3
Blancos, Los ○ **RA** 76-77 F 2
Blancos del Sur, Cayos ⌒ **C** 54-55 E 3
Bland ○ **USA** (VA) 280-281 E 6
Blandá ∼ **IS** 86-87 d 2
Bland Creek ∼ **AUS** 180-181 J 2
Blandford ○ **CDN** (NS) 240-241 L 6
Blanding ○ **USA** (IL) 274-275 H 2
Blanding ○ **USA** (UT) 254-255 F 6
Blanes ○ **E** 98-99 J 4
Blaney Park ○ **USA** (MI) 270-271 N 4
Blanfla ○ **CI** 202-203 H 6
Blangkejeren ○ **RI** 162-163 B 2
Blangpidie ○ **RI** 162-163 B 3
Blanket ○ **USA** (TX) 266-267 J 2
Blanquero, El ○ **YV** 60-61 K 3
Blanquilla, Isla ⌒ **YV** 60-61 J 2
Blanquillo ○ **ROU** 78-79 M 2
Blantyre ☆ • **MW** 218-219 H 2
Blåsjøen ⬭ **N** 86-87 C 7
Blau ○ **RI** 164-165 H 3
Blauer Nil = Ābay Wenz ∼ **ETH** 208-209 C 3
Blauer Nil = al-Baḥr al-Azraq ∼ **SUD** 200-201 G 6
Blåvands Huk ⌒ **DK** 86-87 D 9
Blaye ○ **F** 90-91 G 9
Blayney ○ **AUS** 180-181 K 2
Bleaker Island ⌒ **GB** 78-79 L 7
Blebo ○ **LB** 202-203 G 7
Blednaja, gory ▲▲ **RUS** 108-109 L 3
Bledsoe ○ **USA** (TX) 264-265 A 5
Bled Tisseras ⬭ **DZ** 190-191 F 7
Blega ○ **RI** 168 E 3
Bleikvassli ○ **N** 86-87 F 4
Blendio ○ **RMM** 202-203 G 4
Blenheim ○ **CDN** (ONT) 238-239 D 6
Blenheim ○ **NZ** 182 D 4
Blenheim ○ **USA** (SC) 284-285 L 2
Blenheim Palace ••• **GB** 90-91 G 6
Blesmanspos ○ **ZA** 220-221 G 3
Blessing ○ **USA** (TX) 266-267 L 5
Bleu, Lac ⬭ **CDN** (QUE) 238-239 G 2
Bleus, Monts ▲▲ **ZRE** 212-213 C 3
Blewett ○ **USA** (WA) 244-245 E 3
Blicade ○ **F** 62-63 H 4
Blida ☆ **DZ** 190-191 D 2
Bligh Island ⌒ **USA** 20-21 R 6
Bligh Water ≈ 184 III a 2
Blikaodi ○ **CI** 202-203 J 5
Blina ○ **AUS** 172-173 G 4
Blina Oil Field • **AUS** 172-173 G 4
Blind Channel ○ **CDN** (BC) 230-231 D 3
Blindman River ∼ **CDN** 232-233 D 3
Blind River ○ **CDN** (ONT) 238-239 C 2
Blinisht ○ **AL** 100-101 G 4
Blipi ○ **LB** 202-203 F 6
Bliss ○ **USA** (ID) 252-253 D 4
Bliss Bugt ≈ 26-27 I 2
Blissfield ○ **USA** (MI) 272-273 F 6
Bliss Landing ○ **CDN** (BC) 230-231 E 3
Blissville ○ **CDN** (NB) 240-241 J 5
Blitchton ○ **USA** (GA) 284-285 J 4
Blitta ○ **RT** 202-203 L 5
Blizzard Gap ▲ **USA** (OR) 244-245 F 8
Bloedel ○ **CDN** (BC) 230-231 D 3
Bloemfontein ☆ **ZA** 220-221 H 4
Bloemhof ○ **ZA** 220-221 G 3
Bloemhof Dam < **ZA** 220-221 G 3
Blois ☆ • **F** 90-91 H 8
Blolékin ○ **CI** 202-203 G 6
Blomkest ○ **USA** (MN) 270-271 C 6
Blöndósbær ☆ **IS** 86-87 c 2
Blood Indian Creek ∼ **CDN** 232-233 G 4
Blood Indian Reserve ✕ **CDN** (ALB) 232-233 E 6
Blood River Monument • **ZA** 220-221 K 4
Bloodvein River ∼ **CDN** 234-235 G 3
Bloody Falls ∼ **CDN** 30-31 M 2
Bloomer ○ **USA** (WI) 270-271 G 5
Bloomfield ○ **USA** (IA) 274-275 F 4
Bloomfield ○ **USA** (IN) 274-275 M 5
Bloomfield ○ **USA** (MO) 276-277 F 4
Bloomfield ○ **USA** (MT) 250-251 P 4
Bloomfield ○ **USA** (NE) 262-263 J 2
Bloomfield ○ **USA** (NM) 256-257 H 2
Bloomfield ○ **USA** (OH) 280-281 E 4
Bloomfield River ✕ **AUS** 174-175 H 4
Blooming Grove ○ **USA** (TX) 264-265 H 6
Blooming Prairie ○ **USA** (MN) 270-271 E 7
Bloomington ○ **USA** (IL) 274-275 J 4
Bloomington ○ **USA** (IN) 274-275 M 5
Bloomington ○ **USA** (MN) 270-271 E 6
Bloomington ○ **USA** (TX) 266-267 L 5
Bloomington ○ **USA** (WI) 274-275 H 2
Bloomington, Lake ⬭ **USA** (IL) 274-275 K 4
Bloomsburg ○ **USA** (PA) 280-281 K 2
Bloomsbury ○ **AUS** 174-175 K 7
Bloomsdale ○ **USA** (MO) 274-275 H 6
Blora ○ **RI** 168 D 3
Blosseville Kyst ∸ **GRØ** 28-29 a 2
Blossom ○ **USA** (TX) 264-265 J 5
Blossom, mys ▲ **RUS** 112-113 U 1
Bloukranspas ▲ **ZA** 220-221 D 5
Blount Mountains ▲▲ **USA** 284-285 D 3
Blountstown ○ **USA** (FL) 286-287 D 1
Blountsville ○ **USA** (AL) 284-285 D 2
Blowering Reservoir < **AUS** 180-181 K 3
Blow River ∼ **CDN** 20-21 W 2
Bloxsome Bay ≈ 24-25 K 2
Blubber Bay ○ **CDN** (BC) 230-231 E 4
Blucher ○ **CDN** (SAS) 232-233 M 3
Blucher Range ▲▲ **PNG** 183 A 3
Bludnaja ∼ **RUS** 110-111 F 3
Bludnaja ∼ **RUS** 118-119 E 10
Blue Ball ○ **USA** (AR) 276-277 B 6
Blue Bell Knoll ▲ **USA** (UT) 254-255 D 5
Blueberry River ∼ **CDN** 32-33 K 3
Bluecreek ○ **USA** (WA) 244-245 H 2
Blue Cypress Lake ⬭ **USA** (FL) 286-287 J 4
Blue Earth ○ **USA** (MN) 270-271 D 7
Bluefield ○ **USA** (WV) 280-281 E 6
Bluefields ☆ **NIC** 52-53 C 5
Bluefields, Bahía de ≈ 52-53 C 6
Bluefish River ∼ **CDN** 30-31 F 2
Bluegoose Prairie ∸ **CDN** 36-37 N 2
Bluegoose River ∼ **CDN** 36-37 N 2
Blue Grass Parkway II **USA** (KY) 276-277 L 3
Blue Hill ○ **USA** (ME) 278-279 N 4
Blue Hill ○ **USA** (NE) 262-263 H 4
Blue Hills ▲▲ **CDN** 24-25 O 3
Blue Hills of Couteau ▲▲ **CDN** 242-243 L 5
Blue Hole National Park ⊥ **BH** 52-53 K 3
Blue Jay ○ **USA** (NV) 246-247 J 5
Blue Knob ▲ **AUS** 178-179 M 6
Blue Lagoon National Park ⊥ **Z** 218-219 D 2
Blue Lake ○ **USA** (CA) 246-247 B 3
Blue Licks Spring ○ **USA** (KY) 276-277 L 2
Blue Mesa ▲▲ **USA** 254-255 H 5
Blue Mesa Reservoir ⬭ **USA** (CO) 254-255 H 5
Blue Mound ○ **USA** (IL) 274-275 J 5
Blue Mountain ▲ **IND** 142-143 H 4
Blue Mountain ▲▲ **USA** 276-277 A 6
Blue Mountain ▲ **USA** (NH) 278-279 K 4
Blue Mountain ▲ **USA** (NV) 246-247 G 3
Blue Mountain Lake ○ **USA** (NY) 278-279 G 5
Blue Mountain Lake < **USA** (AR) 276-277 B 5
Blue Mountains ▲▲ **JA** 54-55 G 5
Blue Mountains ▲▲ **USA** 244-245 G 6
Blue Mountains ▲▲ **USA** 280-281 J 3
Blue Mountains ▲ **USA** (TX) 266-267 H 3
Blue Mountains National Park ⊥ ·· **AUS** 180-181 L 2
Blue Mount Pass ▲ **USA** (OR) 244-245 H 8
Blue Mud Bay ≈ 174-175 C 3
Blue Mud Hills ▲▲ **USA** 250-251 P 6
Blue Nile = Ābay Wenz ∼ **ETH** 208-209 C 3
Blue Nile Falls = T'is Isat Fwafwatē ∼ ·· **ETH** 208-209 C 3
Bluenose Lake ⬭ **CDN** 24-25 M 6
Blue Rapids ○ **USA** (KS) 262-263 K 5
Blue Ridge ○ **USA** (GA) 284-285 F 2
Blue Ridge ○ **USA** (TX) 264-265 H 5
Blue Ridge ▲ **USA** (NY) 278-279 G 5
Blue Ridge Lake < **USA** (GA) 284-285 F 2
Blue Ridge Parkway II **USA** (NC) 282-283 F 4
Blue Ridge Parkway II **USA** (VA) 280-281 F 7
Blue River ○ **CDN** (BC) 228-229 P 4
Blue River ∼ **USA** 256-257 F 5
Blue River ∼ **USA** 264-265 H 5
Blue River ∼ **USA** 274-275 M 6
Blue Robin Hill ○ **AUS** 176-177 H 4
Blueslide ○ **USA** (WA) 244-245 H 2
Blue Springs ∴ **USA** (FL) 286-287 D 1
Blue Springs Caverns • **USA** (IN) 274-275 M 6
Bluestone Reservoir < **USA** (WV) 280-281 F 6
Bluewater ○ **AUS** 174-175 J 6
Bluewater ○ **USA** (NM) 256-257 H 3
Bluff ○ **AUS** 178-179 K 2
Bluff ○ **NZ** 182 B 7
Bluff ○ **USA** (AK) 20-21 J 4
Bluff ○ **USA** (UT) 254-255 F 6
Bluff, Cape ▲ **CDN** 38-39 R 2
Bluff, The ○ **BS** 54-55 G 2
Bluff Dale ○ **USA** (TX) 264-265 F 6
Bluff Face Range ▲▲ **AUS** 172-173 H 4
Bluff Point ▲ **AUS** 176-177 C 3
Bluff Point ▲ **USA** (NC) 282-283 L 5
Bluffs of Llano Estacado ∸ **USA** 256-257 M 4
Bluffton ○ **USA** (IN) 274-275 N 4
Blukwa ○ **ZRE** 212-213 C 3
Blum ○ **USA** (TX) 264-265 G 6
Blumenau ○ • **BR** 74-75 F 6
Blumenhof ○ **CDN** (SAS) 232-233 L 5
Blumenort ○ **CDN** (MAN) 234-235 G 5
Blunt ○ **USA** (SD) 260-261 G 2
Blunt Peninsula ◡ **CDN** 36-37 R 3
Blup Blup Island ⌒ **PNG** 183 C 2
Bly ○ **USA** (OR) 244-245 D 8
Blyde River Canyon Nature Reserve ⊥ ·· **ZA** 220-221 K 2
Bly Mountain Pass ▲ **USA** (OR) 244-245 D 8
Blyth ○ **CDN** (ONT) 238-239 D 5
Blythe ○ **USA** (CA) 248-249 K 6
Blytheville ○ **USA** (AR) 276-277 F 5
Blyth Lagoon ⬭ **AUS** 176-177 H 2
Blyth River ∼ **AUS** 174-175 C 3
Bnagola ○ **ZRE** 210-211 H 5
Bø ☆ **N** 86-87 D 7
Bo ☆ **WAL** 202-203 E 6
Boa ∼ **CI** 202-203 G 5
Boac ☆ **RP** 160-161 D 6
Boaco ☆ **NIC** 52-53 B 5
Boa Esperança ○ **BR** (AMA) 66-67 E 6
Boa Esperança ○ **BR** (MIN) 72-73 H 6
Boa Esperança ○ **BR** (ROR) 62-63 D 4
Boa Esperança do Sul ○ **BR** 72-73 F 6
Boa Fé ○ **BR** 66-67 F 4
Boagis ○ **PNG** 183 G 5
Boalemo ○ **RI** 164-165 H 4
Boali ○ **RCA** 206-207 D 6
Boali, Chutes de ∼ ·· **RCA** 206-207 D 6
Boanamary ○ **RM** 222-223 E 5
Boanda ○ **CAM** 204-205 K 6
Boane ○ **MOC** 220-221 L 3
Boangi ○ **ZRE** 210-211 H 4
Boang Island ⌒ **PNG** 183 G 2
Boano, Pulau ⌒ **RI** 166-167 D 3
Boano, Selat ≈ 166-167 D 3
Boa Nova ○ **BR** (P) 68-69 E 2
Boa Nova ○ **BR** (RON) 66-67 F 7
Boardman ○ **USA** (OH) 280-281 F 2
Boardman ○ **USA** (OR) 244-245 F 5
Boat Basin ○ **CDN** (BC) 230-231 C 4
Boatman ○ **AUS** 178-179 J 4
Boat of Garten ○ • **GB** 90-91 F 3
Boatswain, Baie ≈ 38-39 E 3
Boa Viagem ○ **BR** 68-69 J 4
Boa Vista ○ **BR** (AMA) 66-67 E 3
Boa Vista ○ **BR** (AMA) 66-67 F 3
Boa Vista ○ **BR** (AMA) 66-67 E 5
Boa Vista ○ **BR** (AMA) 66-67 C 6
Boa Vista ○ **BR** (GSU) 76-77 J 2
Boa Vista ○ **BR** (P) 62-63 K 6
Boa Vista ○ **BR** (P) 68-69 C 3
Boa Vista ○ **BR** (RSU) 74-75 D 9
Boa Vista ☆ **BR** (ROR) 62-63 D 4
Boa Vista, Ilha de ⌒ **CV** 202-203 C 5
Boa Vista da Ramos ○ **BR** 66-67 J 4
Boa Vista das Palmas ○ **BR** 72-73 H 4
Boa Vista do Tupim ○ **BR** 72-73 K 2
Boawae ○ **RI** 168 E 7
Boaz ○ **USA** (AL) 284-285 D 2
Bobadah ○ **AUS** 180-181 J 2
Bobai ○ **VRC** 156-157 F 5
Bobandana ○ **ZRE** 212-213 B 4
Bobasakoa ○ **RM** 222-223 F 4
Bobbie Burns Creek ∼ **CDN** 230-231 N 3
Bobbili ○ **IND** 142-143 C 6
Bobcaygeon ○ **CDN** (ONT) 238-239 G 4
Bobila ○ **ZRE** 210-211 H 2
Bob Marshall Wilderness Area ⊥ **USA** (MT) 250-251 F 3
Bob Marshall Wilderness Area ⊥ **USA** (MT) 250-251 F 4
Bobo ∼ **RCA** 206-207 C 5
Bobo-Dioulasso ☆ **BF** 202-203 H 4
Bobolice ○ **PL** 92-93 O 2
Bobonaza, Río ∼ **EC** 64-65 D 2
Bobonong ○ **RB** 218-219 E 5
Bobopayo ○ **RI** 164-165 K 3
Bobr ○ **BY** 94-95 L 4
Bóbr ∼ **PL** 92-93 N 3
Bobrof Island ⌒ **USA** 22-23 H 7
Bobrov ○ **RUS** 102-103 L 2
Bobrujsk = Babrujsk ☆ **BY** 94-95 L 5
Bobrynec' ○ **UA** 102-103 H 3
Bobuk ○ **SUD** 208-209 B 3
Bobures ○ **YV** 60-61 F 3
Boby ▲ **RM** 222-223 E 9
Boca, Cachoeira da ∼ **BR** 66-67 K 5
Boca, La ○ **BOL** 70-71 E 4
Boca Arenal ○ **CR** 52-53 B 6
Boca Candelaria ⌒ **CO** 60-61 C 6
Boca Caragual ⌒ **CO** 60-61 C 5
Boca Chica ○ • **DOM** 54-55 L 5
Boca de Anaro ○ **YV** 60-61 F 4
Boca de Arguaca ○ **YV** 60-61 H 4
Boca de la Serpiente ≈ 60-61 L 3
Boca del Pao ○ **YV** 60-61 J 3
Boca del Río ○ **MEX** 52-53 F 2
Boca del Rio ○ **YV** 60-61 J 2
Boca del Rio Indio ○ **PA** 52-53 D 7
Boca del Tocuyo ○ **YV** 60-61 G 2
Boca de Pozo ○ **YV** 60-61 J 2
Boca de Sábelo ○ **PA** 52-53 E 7
Boca de Uchire ○ **YV** 60-61 J 2
Boca de Yuma ○ **DOM** 54-55 L 5
Boca do Acará ○ **BR** 66-67 F 6
Boca do Acre ○ **BR** 66-67 D 7
Boca do Capanã ○ **BR** 66-67 G 5
Boca do Carapanatuba ○ **BR** 66-67 F 6
Boca do Iaco ○ **BR** 66-67 C 7
Boca do Jari ○ **BR** 62-63 J 6
Bocaina de Minas ○ **BR** 72-73 H 7
Bocaino do Sul ○ **BR** 74-75 F 6
Bocaiúva ○ **BR** 72-73 J 4
Bocaiúva do Sul ○ **BR** 74-75 F 5
Docana, La ○ **MEX** 50-51 B 3
Bocanda ○ **CI** 202-203 H 6
Bocaranga ○ **RCA** 206-207 B 5
Boca Raton ○ **USA** (FL) 286-287 J 5
Bocas del Toro ☆ **PA** 52-53 C 7
Bocas del Toro, Archipiélago de ⌒ **PA** 52-53 C 7
Bocay, Río ∼ **NIC** 52-53 B 5
Bochart ○ **CDN** 38-39 H 4
Bochart ○ **CDN** (QUE) 236-237 P 3
Bochinche ○ **YV** 62-63 D 2
Bocholt ○ **D** 92-93 J 3
Bocoio ○ **ANG** 216-217 C 6
Bocón ○ **YV** 60-61 K 4
Bocono ○ **YV** 60-61 F 3
Boçoroca ○ **BR** 76-77 K 5
Bocoyna ○ **MEX** 50-51 F 4
Boda ○ **RCA** 206-207 C 6
Böda ○ **S** 86-87 H 8
Bodajbo ☆ **RUS** 118-119 G 7
Bodalangi ○ **ZRE** 210-211 J 2
Bodalla ○ **AUS** 180-181 L 4
Bodallin ○ **AUS** 176-177 E 5
Bodangora, Mount ▲ **AUS** 180-181 K 2
Boddington ○ **AUS** 176-177 D 6
Bodega Bay ○ **USA** (CA) 246-247 B 5
Bodélé ∸ **TCH** 198-199 H 4
Boden ○ • **S** 86-87 K 4
Bodensee ⬭ **CH** 92-93 K 5
Bode-Shadu ○ **WAN** 204-205 F 4
Bodfish ○ **USA** (CA) 248-249 F 4
Bodhan ○ **IND** (ANP) 138-139 F 10
Bodhan ○ **IND** (KAR) 140-141 G 2
Bodhei ○ **EAK** 212-213 H 4
Bodi ○ **DY** 202-203 L 5
Bodi ○ **GH** 202-203 J 6
Bodie ○ **USA** (CA) 246-247 F 5
Bodingué ∼ **RCA** 210-211 F 2
Bodīti ○ **ETH** 208-209 C 5
Bod'ja, Jaškur- ☆ **RUS** 96-97 H 5
Bodjokola ○ **ZRE** 210-211 H 2
Bodmin ○ **CDN** (SAS) 232-233 M 2
Bodmin ○ **GB** 90-91 E 6
Bodo ○ **CDN** (ALB) 232-233 H 3
Bodo ○ **CI** 202-203 H 7
Bodø ☆ **N** 86-87 G 3
Bodocó ○ **BR** (AMA) 66-67 G 7
Bodocó ○ **BR** (PER) 68-69 J 5
Bodokro ○ **CI** 202-203 H 6
Bodoquena ○ **BR** 70-71 J 7
Bodoukpa ○ **RCA** 206-207 C 6
Bodrum ☆ • **TR** 128-129 B 4
Bodum ○ **S** 86-87 H 5
Boduna ○ **RCA** 206-207 D 6
Boé ○ • **GNB** 202-203 C 4
Boëkovo ∼ **RUS** 112-113 L 2
Boende ○ **ZRE** 210-211 H 4
Boenze ○ **ZRE** 210-211 E 6
Boerne ○ **USA** (TX) 266-267 J 4
Boesmansrivier ∼ **ZA** 220-221 H 6
Boesmansriviermond ○ **ZA** 220-221 H 6
Boeuf River ∼ **USA** 268-269 J 4
Boevaja gora • **RUS** 96-97 J 8
Bofete ○ **BR** 72-73 F 7
Boffa ○ **RG** 202-203 C 4
Bofossou ○ **RG** 202-203 F 5
Boga ○ **ZRE** 212-213 B 3
Bogal, Lagh ∼ **EAK** 212-213 H 3
Bogale ○ **MYA** 158-159 C 2
Bogalusa ○ **USA** (LA) 268-269 L 6
Bogamangon ○ **RCA** 206-207 C 6
Bogandé ○ **BF** 202-203 K 3
Bogan Gate ○ **AUS** 180-181 J 2
Bogangolo ○ **RCA** 206-207 D 6
Boganida ∼ **RUS** 108-109 b 6
Bogan River ∼ **AUS** 178-179 J 6
Bogantungan ○ **AUS** 178-179 J 2
Bogaševo ○ **RUS** 114-115 S 6
Bogata ○ **USA** (TX) 264-265 J 5
Bogatoe ☆ **RUS** 96-97 G 7
Bogatye Saby ☆ **RUS** 96-97 G 6
Boğazkale ☆ • **TR** 128-129 F 2
Boğazlıyan ☆ **TR** 128-129 F 3
Bogbonga ○ **ZRE** 210-211 G 3
Bogd = Hovd ○ **MAU** 148-149 F 5
Bogda Feng ▲ **VRC** 146-147 J 4
Bogdanovič ☆ **RUS** 114-115 G 6
Bogdanovka ○ **RUS** 96-97 G 7
Bogda Shan ▲▲ **VRC** 146-147 J 4
Bogdoo ○ **GH** 202-203 K 4
Böget ○ **KZ** 96-97 G 10
Bogetsaj ○ **KZ** 126-127 N 2
Boggabilla ○ **AUS** 178-179 L 5
Boggabri ○ **AUS** 178-179 L 6
Boggola, Mount ▲ **AUS** 176-177 D 1
Boggy Creek ○ **CDN** (MAN) 234-235 B 3
Bogia ○ **PNG** 183 C 3
Bogilima ○ **ZRE** 210-211 G 2
Boğnürd ○ • **IR** 136-137 E 6
Bogo ○ **CAM** 206-207 B 3
Bogo ○ **RP** 160-161 F 7
Bogoin ○ **RCA** 206-207 D 6
Bogoladza, hrebet ▲▲ **RUS** 122-123 F 5
Bogol Manyo ○ **ETH** 208-209 E 6
Bogong, Mount ▲ **AUS** 180-181 J 4
Bogong National Park ⊥ **AUS** 180-181 J 4
Bogor (Buitenzorg) ○ **RI** 168 B 3
Bogoria, Lake ⬭ • **EAK** 212-213 F 3
Bogorodick ☆ ·· **RUS** 94-95 Q 5
Bogorodsk ○ **RUS** 94-95 S 3
Bogorodsk ○ **RUS** 96-97 K 5
Bogorodskoe ☆ **RUS** (KIR) 96-97 G 5
Bogorodskoe ☆ • **RUS** (HBR) 122-123 J 2
Bogoroud ○ **TCH** 198-199 G 5
Bogose-Mubea ○ **ZRE** 210-211 G 2
Bogoslof Island ⌒ **USA** 22-23 N 6
Bogoso ○ **GH** 202-203 J 7
Bogotá ★ • **CO** 60-61 D 5
Bogotol ☆ **RUS** 114-115 U 6
Bogra ○ **BD** 142-143 F 3
Bogučany ☆ **RUS** 116-117 H 6
Bogučar ○ **RUS** 102-103 M 3
Bogué ○ **RIM** 196-197 C 6
Bogue ○ **USA** (KS) 262-263 G 5
Bogue Banks ≃ 282-283 L 6
Bogue Chitto ○ **USA** (MS) 268-269 K 5
Bogue Chitto River ∼ **USA** 268-269 K 6
Bogüédia ○ **CI** 202-203 G 6
Bogue Homo ∼ **USA** 268-269 L 5
Bogueloosa Creek ∼ **USA** 284-285 B 5
Boguila Kota ○ **RCA** 206-207 C 5
Bogunda ○ **AUS** 178-179 H 1
Bo Hai ≈ 154-155 L 2
Bohai Haixia ≈ 150-151 C 8
Bohai Wan ≈ 154-155 K 2
Boharm ○ **CDN** (SAS) 232-233 N 5
Bohemia ○ **USA** (LA) 268-269 L 7
Bohemia Downs ○ **AUS** 172-173 H 5
Bohena Creek ∼ **AUS** 178-179 K 6
Bohicon ○ **DY** 204-205 E 5
Böhmisch-Trübau = Česká Třebová ○ • **CZ** 92-93 O 4
Bohobé ○ **TCH** 206-207 D 4
Bohodou ○ **RG** 202-203 F 5
Bohoduchiv ○ **UA** 102-103 J 2
Bohol ⌒ **RP** 160-161 F 8
Bohol Sea ≈ 160-161 F 8
Bohol Strait ≈ 160-161 E 8
Bohong ○ **RCA** 206-207 B 5
Bohongou ○ **BF** 202-203 L 3
Böhönye ○ **H** 92-93 O 5
Bohorods'kyj Kostel • **UA** 102-103 D 2
Böhöt ○ **MAU** 148-149 J 5
Boi ○ **WAN** 204-205 H 4
Boi, Ponta do ▲ **BR** 72-73 H 7
Bóia, Rio ∼ **BR** 66-67 C 5
Boiaçu ○ **BR** 62-63 D 6
Boiekevie Hill ▲ **AUS** 180-181 E 2
Boiestown ○ **CDN** (NB) 240-241 J 4
Boigu Island ⌒ **AUS** 174-175 G 1
Boiken ○ **PNG** 183 B 2
Boila ○ **MOC** 218-219 K 3
Boilleau ○ **CDN** (QUE) 240-241 E 2
Boina ∸ **RM** 222-223 E 6
Boipārigūda ○ **IND** 142-143 C 6
Boipeba, Ilha de ⌒ **BR** 72-73 L 2
Bois, Lac des ⬭ **CDN** 30-31 G 2
Bois, Ribeiro dos ∼ **BR** 68-69 D 6
Bois, Rio dos ∼ **BR** 72-73 F 2
Bois, Rio dos ∼ **BR** 72-73 F 4
Bois-Blanc ○ **F** 224 B 7
Bois Blanc ○ **USA** (MI) 272-273 E 2
Bois Blanc Island ⌒ **USA** (MI) 272-273 E 2
Bois d'Arc Creek ∼ **USA** 264-265 H 5
Boise ☆ • **USA** (ID) 252-253 B 3
Boise City ○ **USA** (OK) 264-265 B 2
Boissevain ○ **CDN** (MAN) 234-235 C 5
Boituva ○ **BR** 72-73 G 7
Boja ○ **RI** 168 D 3
Bojano ○ **I** 100-101 E 4
Bojarka ∼ **RUS** 108-109 b 6

306 Birsilpur — Bojarka

Bojarsk ○ RUS 116-117 N 7
Bojčinovci ○ BG 102-103 C 6
Bojkov, liman ≈ 102-103 K 5
Bojmurot ○ UZ 136-137 K 4
Bojonegoro ○ RI 168 D 3
Boju ○ WAN 204-205 G 5
Boju-Ega ○ WAN 204-205 H 5
Bojuru ○ BR 74-75 E 8
Bojuru, Ponta do ▲ BR 74-75 E 8
Bokada ○ ZRE 206-207 D 6
Bokākhāt ○ IND 142-143 H 2
Boka Kotorska ≈ ··· 100-101 G 3
Bokala ○ ZRE 210-211 F 5
Bokata ○ ZRE 210-211 J 2
Bokatola ○ ZRE 210-211 G 4
Bokayanga ○ RCA 206-207 D 5
Boké ■ RG 202-203 C 4
Boké ☆ RG (BOK) 202-203 C 4
Bokele ○ ZRE 210-211 H 4
Bokhara River ∼ AUS 178-179 J 5
Bokh el Mâ ○ RIM 196-197 E 5
Bokhol Plain ⊥ EAK 212-213 G 2
Boki ○ CAM 204-205 K 4
Bokin ○ BF 202-203 K 3
Boki Saboudo ○ SN 196-197 D 7
Bokito ○ CAM 204-205 J 6
Bokkeveldberge ▲ ZA 220-221 D 5
Boknafjorden ≈ 86-87 B 7
Boko ○ RCB 210-211 E 6
Bokode ○ ZRE 210-211 G 2
Bokoko ○ ZRE 206-207 H 6
Bokolako ○ SN 202-203 D 3
Bokolango ○ ZRE 210-211 H 3
Bokolo ○ CI 202-203 G 5
Bokonbaevskoe ○ KS 146-147 C 4
Bokondo ○ ZRE 210-211 G 3
Bokoro ○ TCH 198-199 H 6
Boko-Songho ○ RCB 210-211 D 6
Bokota ○ ZRE 210-211 J 4
Bokote ○ ZRE 210-211 H 4
Boksburg ○ ZA 220-221 J 3
Boksitogorsk ☆ RUS 94-95 N 2
Bokter Müzbel ▲ KZ 126-127 L 6
Boktor ∼ RUS 122-123 G 3
Boku ○ PNG 184 I b 2
Boku ○ ZRE 210-211 F 5
Bokuma ○ ZRE 210-211 G 4
Bokungu ○ ZRE 210-211 J 4
Bol ☆ TCH 198-199 G 6
Bola ○ RI 166-167 B 6
Bola, Bahr ∼ TCH 206-207 D 3
Bolafa ○ ZRE 210-211 J 3
Bolaiti ○ ZRE 210-211 K 5
Bolama ☆• GNB 202-203 C 4
Bolama ○ ZRE 210-211 J 3
Bolān ∼ PK 134-135 M 4
Boland Lake ⊖ CDN 30-31 U 5
Bolangitang ○ RI 164-165 H 3
Bolaños, Río ∼ MEX 50-51 H 7
Bolon Pass ▲ PK 134-135 M 4
Bolbec ○ F 90-91 H 7
Bolbolo ○ RP 160-161 D 4
Bolčiha ○ RUS 124-125 M 2
Bold Point ▲ RP 160-161 C 7
Bold Spring ○ USA (TN) 276-277 H 5
Boldyr ○ UZ 136-137 K 6
Bole ○ ETH 208-209 C 5
Bole ○ GH 202-203 J 5
Bole ○ VRC 146-147 F 3
Boleko ○ ZRE 210-211 G 4
Bolena ○ ZRE 210-211 G 3
Bolesławiec ○• PL 92-93 N 3
Bolgart ○ AUS 176-177 D 5
Bolgatanga ☆• GH 202-203 K 4
Bolger ○ CDN (QUE) 236-237 M 4
Bolhov ☆• RUS 94-95 O 5
Bolhrad ☆ UA 102-103 F 5
Boli ○ SUD 206-207 J 5
Boli ○ VRC 150-151 H 5
Boli ○ ZRE 212-213 A 4
Bolia ○ IND 138-139 E 7
Bolia ○ ZRE 210-211 G 4
Boliche = Pedro J. Montero ○ EC 64-65 C 3
Boliden ○ S 86-87 K 4
Bolifar ○ RI 166-167 F 3
Bolinha, Cachoeira da ∼ BR 62-63 D 6
Bolintin-Vale ○ RO 102-103 D 5
Boliohutu, Gunung ▲ RI 164-165 H 3
Bolívar ○ BOL (COC) 70-71 D 5
Bolívar ○ BOL (PAN) 70-71 D 3
Bolívar ○ CO 60-61 C 7
Bolívar ○ PE 64-65 D 5
Bolívar ○ USA (MO) 276-277 B 3
Bolivar ○ USA (NY) 278-279 C 6
Bolivar ○ USA (TN) 276-277 G 5
Bolívar, Pico ▲•• YV 60-61 F 3
Bolivar Peninsula ⌣ USA 268-269 F 7
Bolivia ■ BOL 70-71 D 5
Bolivia ○ C 54-55 F 3
Boljevac ○ YU 100-101 H 3
Boljoon ○ RP 160-161 E 8
Bolkar Dağları ▲ TR 128-129 F 4
Bollène ○ F 90-91 K 9
Bollnäs ○ S 86-87 H 6
Bollock, Mount ▲ CDN 24-25 W 3
Bollon ○ AUS 178-179 J 5
Bollons Seamount ≃ 14-15 L 13
Bolmen ⊖ S 86-87 F 8
Bolnisi ○ GE 126-127 F 7
Bolobo ○ ZRE 210-211 F 5
Boločaevka 2-ja ○ RUS 122-123 F 4
Bolodek ○ RUS 122-123 E 2
Bologna ☆•• I 100-101 C 2
Bolognesi ○ PE 64-65 E 7
Bologoe ☆ RUS 94-95 O 3
Boloiedi ∼ EAT 212-213 E 5
Bolomba ○ ZRE 210-211 G 3
Bolombo ∼ ZRE 210-211 H 3
Bolon' ○ RUS 122-123 G 4
Bolon', ozero ⊖ RUS 122-123 G 4
Bolona ○ BF 202-203 G 4
Bolonchén ∴• MEX 52-53 K 2
Bolonchén de Rejón ○• MEX 52-53 K 1
Bolondo ○ GQ 210-211 B 3
Bolongongo ○ ANG 216-217 C 4
Bolonguera ○ ANG 216-217 B 6
Bolontio ○ RI 164-165 H 3
Bolotnoe ☆ RUS 114-115 S 7
Bolovens, Plateau des ▲ LAO 158-159 J 3
Bol'šaja ∼ RUS 110-111 a 2
Bol'šaja ∼ RUS 122-123 R 2
Bol'šaja ∼ RUS 122-123 K 2
Bol'šaja, guba ≈ 110-111 X 2
Bol'šaja Balahnja ∼ RUS 108-109 f 5
Bol'šaja Belaja ∼ RUS 116-117 K 9
Bol'šaja Biča ∼ RUS 114-115 L 6
Bol'šaja Bootankaga ∼ RUS 108-109 b 4
Bol'šaja Černigovka ☆ RUS 96-97 G 7
Bol'šaja Glušica ☆ RUS 96-97 G 7
Bol'šaja Horga, ozero ⊖ RUS 118-119 E 9
Bol'šaja Kof-Tajga, gora ▲ RUS 124-125 Q 2
Bol'šaja Kuonamka ∼ RUS 110-111 J 4
Bol'šaja Kuropatoč'ja ∼ RUS 112-113 J 1
Bol'šaja Lebjaž'ja ∼ RUS 116-117 E 5
Bol'šaja Martynovka = Slobodа Bol'šaja Martynovka ○ RUS 102-103 M 4
Bol'šaja Murata ☆ RUS 116-117 F 7
Bol'šaja Mutnaja ∼ RUS 88-89 X 3
Bol'šaja Nisogora ○ RUS 88-89 S 4
Bol'šaja Orlovka ○ RUS 102-103 M 4
Bol'šaja Padeja, gora ▲ RUS 108-109 J 7
Bol'šaja Pula ∼ RUS 88-89 V 3
Bol'šaja Rečka ○ RUS 96-97 E 4
Bol'šaja Saga, ozero ⊖ RUS 96-97 D 10
Bol'šaja Sosnovka ☆ RUS 96-97 J 5
Bol'šaja Usa ○ RUS 96-97 J 5
Bol'šaja Uzen' ∼ RUS 96-97 F 8
Bol'šakovo ○ RUS 94-95 G 4
Bolsena, Lago di ⊖ I 100-101 C 3
Bol'šenarymskoe ○ KZ 124-125 O 4
Bol'šereče ☆ RUS 114-115 N 6
Bol'šereck ○ RUS 122-123 R 2
Bol'šereck, Ust'- ☆ RUS 122-123 R 2
Bol'šereckij Sovhoz ○ RUS 122-123 R 2
Bol'šeustinskoe ☆ RUS 96-97 L 6
Bol'ševik ○ RUS 120-121 M 2
Bol'ševik, ostrov ⌒ RUS 108-109 I d 2
Bol'šezemel'skaja tundra ⊥ RUS 88-89 W 3
Bolsi ○ RN 202-203 L 3
Bolsico ○ RCH 76-77 B 2
Bol'šie Čukkuri, gora ▲ RUS 88-89 M 4
Bol'šie Hatymi ○ RUS 118-119 M 7
Bol'šoe Eravnoe, ozero ⊖ RUS 118-119 F 9
Bol'šoe Jarovoe ozero ⊖ RUS 124-125 L 2
Bol'šoe Jasavėjto, ozero ⊖ RUS 108-109 M 7
Bol'šoe Kizi, ozero ⊖ RUS 122-123 J 3
Bol'šoe Morskoe, ozero ⊖ RUS 112-113 K 1
Bol'šoe Nagatkino ☆ RUS 96-97 F 6
Bol'šoe Sorokino ☆ RUS 114-115 K 6
Bol'šoe Toko, ozero ⊖ RUS 120-121 D 6
Bol'šoe Topol'noe ozero ⊖ RUS 124-125 K 2
Bol'šoe Zaborov'e ○ RUS 94-95 N 2
Bol'šoj, ostrov ⌒ RUS 108-109 U 4
Bol'šoj Abakan ∼ RUS 124-125 Q 2
Bol'šoj Aim ∼ RUS 120-121 E 5
Bol'šoj Amalat ∼ RUS 118-119 F 9
Bol'šoj Anjuj ∼ RUS 112-113 L 2
Bol'šoj Atlym ∼ RUS 114-115 J 3
Bol'šoj Avam ∼ RUS 108-109 Z 6
Bol'šoj Balhan, hrebet ▲ TM 136-137 D 5
Bol'šoj Baranov, mys ▲ RUS 112-113 M 2
Bol'šoj Begičev, ostrov ⌒ RUS 110-111 J 2
Bol'šoj Čeremšan ∼ RUS 96-97 G 6
Bol'šoj Čurki ○ RUS 88-89 T 5
Bol'šoj Dubčes ∼ RUS 114-115 T 4
Bol'šoj Homus-Jurjah ∼ RUS 110-111 d 4
Bol'šoj Ik ∼ RUS 96-97 L 6
Bol'šoj Ik ∼ RUS 96-97 K 7
Bol'šoj Iremel', gora ▲ RUS 96-97 L 6
Bol'šoj Irgiz ∼ RUS 96-97 F 8
Bol'šoj Jarhodon ∼ RUS 112-113 H 4
Bol'šoj Jarudej ∼ RUS 108-109 P 8
Bol'šoj Kamen' ○ RUS 122-123 E 7
Bol'šoj Karaman ∼ RUS 96-97 E 8
Bol'šoj Kas ∼ RUS 116-117 E 6
Bol'šoj Kazymskij Sor, ozero ⊖ RUS 114-115 J 3
Bol'šoj Kėpėrveem ∼ RUS 112-113 O 2
Bol'šoj Kinel' ∼ RUS 96-97 H 7
Bol'šoj Kujbiveem ∼ RUS 112-113 P 5
Bol'šoj Kumak ∼ RUS 96-97 L 8
Bol'šoj Kun"jak ∼ RUS 114-115 L 5
Bol'šoj Ljahovskij, ostrov ⌒ RUS 110-111 X 3
Bol'šoj Ljamčin Nos, mys ▲ RUS 108-109 H 7
Bol'šoj Loptjuga ∼ RUS 88-89 U 5
Bol'šoj Megtyg"egan ∼ RUS 114-115 R 4
Bol'šoj Nimnyr ○ RUS (SAH) 118-119 M 6
Bol'šoj Nimnyr ∼ RUS 118-119 M 6
Bol'šoj Oju ∼ RUS 108-109 J 7
Bol'šoj Ol'doj ∼ RUS 118-119 L 8
Bol'šoj On ○ RUS 124-125 Q 2
Bol'šoj Ous ∼ RUS 114-115 F 4
Bol'šoj Peledon ∼ RUS 112-113 O 3
Bol'šoj Pykarvaam ∼ RUS 112-113 S 3
Bol'šoj Rautan, ostrov ⌒ RUS 112-113 Q 2
Bol'šoj Sajan ▲ RUS 116-117 J 9
Bol'šoj Salym ∼ RUS 114-115 L 4
Bol'šoj Šantar ○ RUS 120-121 G 6
Bol'šoj Šantar, ostrov ⌒ RUS 120-121 G 6
Bol'šoj Selerikan ∼ RUS 110-111 X 7
Bol'šoj Setnoj, ostrov ⌒ RUS 126-127 H 5
Bol'šoj Šiskaryn, ozero ⊖ RUS 114-115 K 6
Bol'šoj Šor ⊖ KZ 126-127 J 5
Bol'šoj Tap ∼ RUS 114-115 H 4
Bol'šoj Turtas ∼ RUS 114-115 L 5
Bol'šoj Tyrkan ∼ RUS 120-121 E 5
Bol'šoj Uluj ☆ RUS 116-117 E 7
Bol'šoj Urkan ∼ RUS 118-119 M 8
Bol'šoj Uvat, ozero ⊖ RUS 114-115 L 6
Bol'šoj Uzen' ∼ RUS 96-97 F 8
Bol'šoj Yllymah ∼ RUS 118-119 N 6
Bol'šoj Zelenec, ostrov ⌒ RUS 108-109 H 7
Bol'šoj Zelenzuk ∼ RUS 126-127 D 5
Bol'šoj Zjudostinskij, ostrov ⌒ RUS 126-127 H 5
Bol'šoj Žužmuj, ostrov ⌒ RUS 88-89 N 4
Bolsón de Mapimí ⊥ MEX 50-51 G 3
Boltodden ▲ N 84-85 L 4
Bolton ○ GB 90-91 F 5
Bolton ○ USA (NC) 282-283 J 6
Bolu ☆ TR 128-129 D 2
Bolubolu ○ PNG 183 F 5
Bolvaninka ∼ RUS 116-117 N 6
Bolvanskij Nos ▲ RUS 108-109 H 6
Bolyston ○ CDN (NS) 240-241 O 5
Bolzano = Bozen ☆ I 100-101 C 1
Boma ○ ZRE 210-211 D 6
Bomaderry, Nowra- ○ AUS 180-181 L 3
Bomadi ○ WAN 204-205 F 6
Bomarton ○ USA (TX) 264-265 E 5
Bomassa ○ RCB 210-211 F 2
Bombabasua ○ RI 164-165 F 4
Bombala ○ AUS 180-181 K 4
Bombay ☆•• IND 138-139 D 10
Bombay Beach ○ USA (CA) 248-249 J 6
Bomberai ∼ RI 166-167 G 3
Bomberai Peninsula ⌣ RI 166-167 G 3
Bombo ☆ EAU 212-213 D 3
Bombo ∼ ZRE 210-211 E 6
Bömbögör = Zadgaj ○ MAU 148-149 D 4
Bombo-Makuka ○ ZRE 210-211 F 6
Bombonal ○ CO 64-65 F 1
Bomboyo ○ TCH 198-199 G 6
Bombura ○ ZRE 210-211 G 2
Bom Comercio ○ BR 66-67 E 7
Bom Conselho ○ BR 68-69 K 6
Bom Despacho ○ BR 72-73 H 5
Bomdila ○• IND 142-143 H 2
Bomet ○ EAK 212-213 E 4
Bomi ○ AUS 178-179 K 5
Bomi ○ VRC 144-145 K 6
Bomili ○ ZRE 212-213 A 3
Bom Intento ○ BR 66-67 F 5
Bom Jardim ○ BR (MAR) 68-69 F 3
Bom Jardim ○ BR (P) 62-63 J 6
Bom Jardim ○ BR (RIO) 72-73 J 7
Bom Jardim de Minas ○ BR 72-73 H 6
Bom Jardim ou Bacabal, Igarapé ∼ BR 66-67 J 5
Bom Jesus ○ ANG 216-217 B 4
Bom Jesus ○ BR (CAT) 74-75 D 6
Bom Jesus ○ BR (PIA) 68-69 F 6
Bom Jesus ○ BR (RSU) 74-75 E 7
Bom Jesus, Rio ∼ BR 68-69 F 7
Bom Jesus da Gurguéia, Serra ▲ BR 68-69 G 6
Bom Jesus da Lapa ○ BR 72-73 J 2
Bom Jesus da Penha ○ BR 72-73 G 6
Bom Jesus de Goiás ○ BR 72-73 F 5
Bom Jesus do Amparo ○ BR 72-73 J 5
Bom Jesus do Galho ○ BR 72-73 J 5
Bom Jesus do Itabapoana ○ BR 72-73 K 6
Bømlo ⌒ N 86-87 B 7
Bom Lugar ○ BR 66-67 H 6
Bomnak ○ RUS 118-119 O 8
Bomokandi ∼ ZRE 210-211 L 2
Bomongo ○ ZRE 210-211 G 3
Bomotu ○ ZRE 210-211 G 2
Bom Princípio ○ BR 68-69 E 6
Bom Sucesso ○ BR 68-69 B 5
Bom Sucesso ○ BR (MIN) 72-73 H 6
Bom Sucesso ○ BR (PA) 68-69 K 5
Bomu ∼ ZRE 206-207 F 6
Bomu Occidentale, Réserve de faune ⊥ ZRE 206-207 G 6
Bomu Orientale, Réserve de faune ⊥ ZRE 206-207 G 6
Bom Viver ○ BR 68-69 F 3
Bon, Cap ▲ TN 190-191 H 2
Bona, Mount ▲ USA 20-21 U 6
Bonāb ○ IR 128-129 M 4
Bonaberi ○ CAM 204-205 H 6
Bona Bona Island ⌒ PNG 183 E 6
Bon Accord ○ CDN (ALB) 232-233 E 2
Bonaire ⌒ NA 60-61 G 1
Bonam ○ BF 202-203 K 3
Bonampak ∴• MEX 52-53 J 3
Bonang ○ AUS 180-181 K 4
Bonang ○ RI 168 E 7
Bonanza ○ NIC 52-53 B 4
Bonanza ○ USA (ID) 252-253 D 2
Bonanza ○ USA (OR) 244-245 D 8
Bonanza ○ USA (UT) 254-255 F 3
Bonao ☆ DOM 54-55 K 5
Bonapabli ○ LB 202-203 F 6
Bonaparte, Mount ▲ USA (WA) 244-245 F 2
Bonaparte Archipelago ⌒ AUS 172-173 G 3
Bonaparte Lake ⊖ CDN (BC) 230-231 J 2
Bonaparte River ∼ CDN 230-231 H 2
Bonar ○ E 98-99 E 3
Bonara (Naulu Village) ⚔• RI 166-167 E 3
Bonaventure ○ CDN (QUE) 240-241 K 2
Bonaventure, Rivière ∼ CDN 240-241 K 2
Bonavista ○ CDN (NFL) 242-243 P 4
Bonavista, Cape ▲•• CDN (NFL) 242-243 P 4
Bonavista Bay ≈ 242-243 P 4
Bonavista Peninsula ⌣•• CDN 242-243 P 4
Boncuk Dağı ▲ TR 128-129 C 4
Bondari ○ RUS 94-95 S 5
Bond Lake, Governor ⊖ USA (IL) 274-275 J 6
Bondo ○ ZRE (EQU) 210-211 G 3
Bondo ○ ZRE (Hau) 210-211 J 2
Bondoc Peninsula ⌣ RP 160-161 E 6
Bondokodi ○ RI 168 D 7
Bondoukou ☆• CI 202-203 J 5
Bondoukui ○ BF 202-203 J 4
Bondowoso ○ RI 168 E 3
Bonds Cay ⌒ BS 54-55 G 2
Bonduel ○ USA (WI) 270-271 K 6
Bondurant ○ USA (WY) 252-253 H 3
Boné ○ RG 202-203 E 4
Bone ∼ RI 164-165 H 3
Bone, Teluk ≈ 164-165 G 5
Bone = Watampone ○ RI 164-165 G 6
Bonebone ○•• RI 164-165 G 5
Bon Echo Provincial Park ⊥ CDN (ONT) 238-239 H 4
Bone Creek ∼ CDN 232-233 K 6
Bone-Dumoga National Park ⊥•• RI 164-165 H 3
Bonelambere ○ RI 168 E 6
Bonelipu ○ RI 164-165 H 6
Bonelohe ○ RI 164-165 G 6
Bonépoupa ○ CAM 204-205 J 6
Bonerate ○ RI 168 E 6
Bonerate, Kepulauan ⌒ RI 168 E 6
Bonerate, Pulau ⌒ RI 168 E 6
Bonesteel ○ USA (SD) 260-261 H 3
Bonete, Cerro ▲ RA 76-77 C 4
Bonete, Río ∼ RA 76-77 C 5
Bonfield ○ CDN (ONT) 238-239 F 2
Bonfim ○ BR (AMA) 66-67 D 6
Bonfim ○ BR (MAT) 70-71 K 5
Bonfim ○ BR (P) 66-67 K 5
Bonfim ○ BR (ROR) 62-63 E 4
Bonfinópolis de Minas ○ BR 72-73 H 4
Bonga ○ ETH 208-209 C 5
Bonga ○ PNG 183 D 4
Bongabon ○ RP 160-161 D 5
Bongandanga ○ ZRE 210-211 H 3
Bongaon ○ IND 142-143 F 4
Bongār ○ IR 134-135 J 3
Bông Hu'ng ☆ VN 156-157 E 6
Bongka ∼ RI 164-165 G 4
Bongo ○ RI 164-165 H 3
Bongo, Massif des ▲ RCA 206-207 F 4
Bongolava ⊥ RM 222-223 D 7
Bongolo, Grottes de • G 210-211 C 5
Bongor ☆ TCH 206-207 B 3
Bongouanou ☆ CI 202-203 H 6
Bongouanou, Collines de ▲ CI 202-203 H 6
Bongué ○ RCA 206-207 D 6
Bonham ○ USA (TX) 264-265 H 5
Boni ○ BF 202-203 J 4
Boni ○ RMM 202-203 J 2
Boniérdougou ○ CI 202-203 H 5
Bonifacio ○ • F 98-99 M 4
Bonifacio ○ RP 160-161 E 8
Bonifacio, Bocche di ≈ 98-99 M 4
Bonifacio, Bouches de ≈ 98-99 M 4
Bonifay ○ USA (FL) 286-287 D 1
Boninal ○ BR 72-73 K 2
Boni National Reserve ⊥ EAK 212-213 H 4
Bonin National Park ⊥ GH 202-203 J 7
Bonin Trench ≃ 14-15 G 4
Bonita ○ USA (AZ) 256-257 F 6
Bonita, La ○ EC 64-65 D 1
Bonitas, Las ○ YV 60-61 J 4
Bonita Springs ○ USA (FL) 286-287 H 5
Bonito ○ BR (BAH) 68-69 H 7
Bonito ○ BR (GSU) 76-77 J 1
Bonito ○ BR (MIN) 72-73 H 3
Bonito ○ BR (P) 68-69 F 2
Bonito ○ BR (PER) 68-69 L 6
Bonito, Pico ▲ HN 52-53 L 4
Bonito, Rio ∼ BR 72-73 E 4
Bonito Pico, Parque Nacional ⊥ HN 52-53 L 4
Bonjol ○ RI 162-163 D 4
Bonkahar, Kūh-e ▲ IR 134-135 E 3
Bonkoukou ○ RN 204-205 E 1
Bonn ○• D 92-93 J 3
Bonneau ○ USA (SC) 284-285 L 3
Bonne Bay ≈ 242-243 K 3
Bonnechere Caves ∴• CDN (ONT) 238-239 H 3
Bonners Ferry ○ USA (ID) 250-251 C 3
Bonner Springs ○ USA (KS) 262-263 M 5
Bonnet, Cachoeira do ∼ BR 66-67 H 6
Bonne Terre ○ USA (MO) 276-277 E 3
Bonnet Plume River ∼ CDN 20-21 Y 4
Bonneville ○ USA (OR) 244-245 D 5
Bonneville ○ USA (WY) 252-253 K 3
Bonneville Salt Flats ⊥ USA 254-255 B 3
Bonney, Lake ⊖ AUS 180-181 F 4
Bonney Downs ○ AUS 172-173 D 7
Bonnie Rock ○ AUS 176-177 E 5
Bonnissant, Pointe ▲ CDN 36-37 K 5
Bonny ○ WAN 204-205 G 6
Bonny, Bight of ≈ 204-205 G 6
Bono ○ USA (AR) 276-277 E 5
Bonoi ○ RI 166-167 J 2
Bonou ○ DY 204-205 E 5
Bonoua ○ CI 202-203 J 7
Bonsall ○ USA (CA) 248-249 G 6
Bon Secour Bay ≈ 284-285 C 6
Bonshaw ○ AUS 178-179 L 5
Bonshaw ○ CDN (PEI) 240-241 M 4
Bonsoaga ∼ BF 202-203 L 3
Bontang ○ RI 164-165 E 3
Bontekoe Ø ⌒ GRØ 26-27 p 7
Bonthe ○ WAL 202-203 D 6
Bontoc ☆ RP 160-161 D 4
Bontoc Point ▲ RP 160-161 E 6
Bontosunggu Jeneponto ○ RI 164-165 F 6
Bonvouloir Islands ⌒ PNG 183 F 6
Bon Wier ○ USA (TX) 268-269 G 6
Bonyere ○ GH 202-203 J 7
Bonyhád ○ H 92-93 P 5
Bonzan ○ BF 202-203 J 4
Boo, Kepulauan ⌒ RI 166-167 E 2
Boobare ○ AUS 178-179 H 4
Boodi Boodi Range ▲ AUS 176-177 G 2
Bookaloo ○ AUS 178-179 D 6
Booker ○ USA (TX) 264-265 D 2
Booko ○ CI 202-203 G 5
Boola ○ RG 202-203 F 5
Boolardy ○ AUS 176-177 D 3
Boolba ○ AUS 178-179 K 4
Booligal ○ AUS 180-181 H 2
Boolitharda Hill ▲ AUS 176-177 D 3
Boomarra ○ AUS 174-175 F 6
Boomi River ∼ AUS 178-179 K 5
Boonah ○ AUS 178-179 M 5
Bööncagaan nuur ⊖ MAU 148-149 D 5
Boondooma Reservoir ⊖ AUS 178-179 L 4
Boone ○ USA (CO) 254-255 L 5
Boone ○ USA (IA) 274-275 E 2
Boone ○ USA (NC) 282-283 F 4
Boone Reservoir ⊖ USA (TN) 282-283 E 4
Boone River ∼ USA 274-275 E 2
Booneville ○ USA (AR) 276-277 B 5
Booneville ○ USA (KY) 276-277 M 3
Booneville ○ USA (MS) 268-269 M 2
Boongaree Island ⌒ AUS 172-173 G 3
Boonsboro ○ USA (MD) 280-281 J 4
Boonville ○ USA (CA) 246-247 B 4
Boonville ○ USA (IN) 274-275 L 6
Boonville ○ USA (MO) 274-275 F 6
Boonville ○ USA (NY) 278-279 F 5
Boopi, Río ∼ BOL 70-71 D 4
Boorabbin ○ AUS 176-177 F 5
Boorabbin National Park ⊥ AUS 176-177 F 5
Boorama ○ SP 208-209 F 4
Böörög Dėlijn Ėls ⊥ MAU 116-117 F 10
Booroondara, Mount ▲ AUS 178-179 H 6
Boorowa ○ AUS 180-181 K 3
Boort ○ AUS 180-181 G 4
Boosaaso = Bender Qaasim ☆ SP 208-209 J 3
Boothbay Harbor ○ USA (ME) 278-279 M 5
Boothby, Cape ▲ ARK 16 G 6
Boothby, Mount ▲ AUS 180-181 E 3
Boothia, Gulf of ≈ 24-25 a 5
Boothia Isthmus ⌣ CDN 24-25 Z 6
Boothia Peninsula ⌣ CDN 24-25 Y 5
Booth Islands ⌒ CDN 24-25 J 5
Booth's River ∼ BH 52-53 K 3
Boothulla ○ AUS 178-179 H 4
Booti Booti National Park ⊥ AUS 180-181 M 2
Boot Key ⌒ USA (FL) 286-287 H 7
Booué ○ G 210-211 C 4
Boqiyiyo Spring ○ AUS 176-177 E 3
Bopa ○ DY 202-203 L 6
Bopako ○ ZRE 210-211 H 3
Bophuthatswana (former Homel, now part of North-West) ■ ZA 220-221 F 3
Bopo ○ WAN 204-205 G 5
Boqên ○ VRC 144-145 K 5
Boqueirão ○ BR (ACR) 64-65 F 5
Boqueirão ○ BR (BAH) 68-69 G 7
Boqueirão ○ BR (GSU) 76-77 J 1
Boqueirão ○ BR (PA) 68-69 K 5
Boqueirão, Serra do ▲ BR 68-69 G 7
Boqueirão, Serra do ▲ BR 72-73 H 2
Boqueirão, Serra do ▲ BR 76-77 K 5
Boqueirão Cesário ○ BR 68-69 J 4
Boquerón ○ C 54-55 H 5
Boquerón ○ USA (PR) 286-287 O 2
Boqueron ○ YV 60-61 G 3
Boquerón, Playa ⊥ USA 286-287 O 2
Boquete, Cerro ▲ RA 78-79 E 7
Boquilla, Presa de la ⊂ MEX 50-51 G 4
Boquilla del Conchos, La ○ MEX 50-51 G 4
Boquillas ○ USA (TX) 266-267 E 4
Boquillas del Carmen ○ MEX 50-51 H 3
Boquira ○ BR 72-73 J 2
Bor ○ RUS (GOR) 96-97 D 5
Bor ○ RUS (KRN) 116-117 E 5
Bor ○ SUD 206-207 K 5
Bor ☆• TR 128-129 F 4
Bor, Lagh ∼ EAK 212-213 G 2
Bora ▲ ETH 200-201 J 6
Bora ○ PNG 183 B 4
Bora ○ SUD 206-207 H 4
Borabu ○ THA 158-159 G 2
Borabu Park ⊥• THA 158-159 G 2
Boracho Peak ▲ USA (TX) 266-267 C 3
Borah Peak ▲ USA (ID) 252-253 E 2
Boraldaj ∼ KZ 136-137 L 3
Boraldaj, žota ▲ KZ 136-137 L 3
Borang, Tanjung ▲ RI 166-167 G 4
Borås ☆ S 86-87 F 8
Borāzǧān ○ IR 134-135 D 4
Borba ○ BR 66-67 H 5
Borbon ○ RP 160-161 F 7
Borbón ○ YV 60-61 J 4
Borborema, Planalto da ⊥ BR 68-69 K 5
Borçka ☆ TR 128-129 J 2
Borde Alto del Payún ▲ RA 78-79 E 4
Bordeaux ☆• F 90-91 G 9
Bordėbė ○ KS 136-137 N 5
Borden ○ AUS 176-177 E 7
Borden ○ CDN (PEI) 240-241 M 4
Borden ○ CDN (SAS) 232-233 L 3
Borden Island ⌒ CDN 24-25 Q 1
Borden Peninsula ⌣ CDN 24-25 e 4
Borden River ∼ CDN 30-31 Z 3
Border ○ USA (WY) 252-253 H 4
Border, Pegunungan ▲ RI 166-167 L 3
Border City Lodge ○ USA 20-21 U 5
Bordertown ○ AUS 180-181 F 4
Borðeyri ○ IS 86-87 c 2
Bord Hūn-e Nou ○ IR 134-135 D 4
Bordighera ○ I 100-101 A 3
Bordj Bou Arreridj ☆ DZ 190-191 E 2
Bordj Bounaama ○ DZ 190-191 C 3
Bordj Flye Sainte Marie ○ DZ 188-189 K 7
Bordj Messouda ○ DZ 190-191 G 5
Bordj Mokhtar ○ DZ 196-197 L 4
Bordj Omar Driss ○ DZ 190-191 F 6
Bordoloni ○ IND 142-143 J 2
Borē ○ ETH 208-209 D 5
Boré ○ RMM 202-203 J 2
Boreda ○ ETH 208-209 C 5
Borensberg ○ S 86-87 G 7
Boren Xuanguan ∴• VRC 156-157 D 2
Borgå = Porvoo ○ FIN 88-89 H 6
Borgampād ○ IND 142-143 B 7
Borgarfjörður ○ IS 86-87 g 2
Borgarnes ☆ IS 86-87 c 2
Børgefjellet ▲ N 86-87 F 4
Børgefjell nasjonalpark ⊥ N 86-87 F 4
Børgen, Kap ▲ GRØ 26-27 q 6
Borger ○ USA (TX) 264-265 C 3
Borgholm ☆• S 86-87 H 8
Borgi ○ IND 142-143 B 6
Borgia, De ○ USA (MT) 250-251 D 4
Borg Jøkel Bræ ⊂ GRØ 26-27 n 5
Borg Massif = Borgmassivet ▲ ARK 16 F 36
Borgne, Lake ⊖ USA (MS) 268-269 L 6
Borgne, Le ○ RH 54-55 J 5
Borgomanero ○ I 100-101 B 2
Borgo San Lorenzo ○ I 100-101 C 3
Borgou ○ RT 202-203 L 4
Borgu ⊥ DY 204-205 E 4
Borgu Game Reserve ⊥ WAN 204-205 E 3
Borgund ○ N 86-87 C 6
Borgund stavkirke •• N 86-87 C 6
Borhojn-Tal ○ MAU 148-149 K 6
Bori ○ DY 204-205 E 4
Bori ○ IND 138-139 G 9
Bori ○ WAN 204-205 G 6
Boria Tibhu ○ IND 142-143 B 5
Borigumma ○ IND 142-143 C 6
Börili ○ KZ 96-97 H 8
Borisoglebsk ○ RUS 102-103 N 2
Borisov = Barysav ☆ BY 94-95 L 4
Borisova, mys ▲ RUS 120-121 G 6
Borisovka ○ RUS 102-103 K 2
Borisovo-Sudskoe ○ RUS 94-95 P 2
Boriziny ○ RM 222-223 E 5
Borja ○ PE 64-65 D 4
Borj Bourguiba ○ TN 190-191 G 4
Borjhar ○ IND 138-139 E 8
Borj Jenein ○ TN 190-191 H 5
Borj Machened Salah ○ TN 192-193 D 1
Borj M'Chiguig ○ TN 190-191 H 5
Borj Slougui ○ TN 190-191 H 4
Borko ○ AFG 136-137 L 6
Borkou ⊥ TCH 198-199 H 3
Borkou-Ennedi-Tibesti ■ TCH 198-199 H 4
Borkum ⌒ D 92-93 J 2
Borlänge ☆ S 86-87 G 6
Borne ○ DZ 190-191 F 8
Borneo = Kalimantan ⌒ 164-165 B 4
Bornholm ⌒• DK 86-87 G 9
Bornholmsgattet ≈ 86-87 G 9
Borno ■ WAN 198-199 E 6
Boro ∼ RB 218-219 B 4
Boro ∼ SUD 206-207 G 4
Borobudur ••• RI 168 D 3
Borodale Creek ∼ AUS 176-177 G 4
Borodino ○ RUS 116-117 G 8
Borogoncy ☆• RUS 118-119 P 4
Borohoro Shan ▲ VRC 146-147 E 3
Borojó ○ YV 60-61 F 2
Boroko ○ RI 164-165 H 3
Boroli ∼ TCH 200-207 C 3
Borom ○ TCH 206-207 C 4
Boromata ○ RCA 206-207 E 3
Boromo ○• BF 202-203 J 4
Boron ○ CI 202-203 H 5
Boron ○ RMM 202-203 G 3
Boron ○ USA (CA) 248-249 G 5
Bor-Öndör = Hėrlėn ○ MAU 148-149 J 4
Borong, hrebet ▲ RUS 110-111 V 6
Borononо ○ RM 222-223 E 5
Boroňuk ○ RUS 110-111 T 6
Bororé ○ RB 76-77 K 5
Borovići ○ RUS (PSK) 94-95 L 3
Borovići ☆ RUS (NVG) 94-95 N 2
Borovo ○ RUS 88-89 U 5
Borovoj ○ RUS 88-89 M 4
Borovsk ○• RUS 94-95 P 4
Borovskoj ☆ KZ 124-125 C 2
Borradaile ○ CDN (ALB) 232-233 H 2
Borrego Springs ○ USA (CA) 248-249 H 6
Borrero ○ EC 64-65 C 3
Borroloola ⚔ AUS 174-175 D 5
Borroloola Aboriginal Land ⚔ AUS 174-175 C 4
Borşa ○ RO 102-103 D 4
Borsad ○ IND 138-139 D 8
Borsa-kelmas šuri ⊖ UZ 136-137 E 3
Borščevočnyj, hrebet ▲ RUS 118-119 H 10
Borskoe ☆ RUS 96-97 G 7
Bort-les-Orgues ○ F 90-91 J 9
Börtnan ○ S 86-87 F 5
Boru ○ RI 166-167 D 6
Boruambe ∼ ZRE 210-211 F 4
Borūǧen ○• IR 134-135 D 3
Borūǧerd ○• IR 134-135 C 2
Borulah ∼ RUS 110-111 U 6
Borulah ∼ RUS 118-119 O 5
Borups Corners ○ CDN (ONT) 234-235 L 5
Bor-Üzüür ○ MAU 146-147 L 3
Bory, Tiangue- ○ RG 202-203 D 4
Boryspil' ○ UA 102-103 G 2
Borzja ☆ RUS (CTN) 118-119 H 10
Borzja ∼ RUS 118-119 G 10
Borzna ○ UA 102-103 H 2
Boržomi ○• GE 126-127 E 7
Borzongijn Gov' ⊥ MAU 148-149 G 6
Borzova, zaliv ≈ 108-109 J 3
Bosa ○• I 100-101 B 4
Bosaga ○ KZ 124-125 H 5
Bosanska Brod ○ BIH 100-101 G 2
Bosanska Krupa ○ BIH 100-101 F 2
Bosanski Novi ○ BIH 100-101 F 2
Bosanski Petrovac ○ BIH 100-101 F 2
Bosanski Šamac ○ BIH 100-101 G 2
Bosavi, Mount ▲ PNG 183 B 4
Boscobel ○ USA (WI) 274-275 H 1
Bosconia ○ CO 60-61 E 2
Bose ○ VRC 156-157 E 5
Bosencheve, Parque Nacional ⊥ MEX 52-53 D 2
Boset Terara ▲ ETH 208-209 D 4
Boshoek ○ ZA 220-221 H 2
Boshof ○ ZA 220-221 G 4
Bô Sinh ○ VN 156-157 C 6
Boskamp ○ SME 62-63 G 3
Boslanti ○ SME 62-63 G 3
Bosler ○ USA (WY) 252-253 N 5
Bosmediano ○ PE 64-65 F 4
Bosna ∼ BIH 100-101 G 2
Bosnia and Herzegovina = Bosna i Hercegovina ■ BIH 100-101 F 2
Bosnik ○ RI 166-167 J 2
Bošnjakovo ○ RUS 122-123 K 4
Boso ○ ZRE 210-211 J 2
Bosobolo ○ ZRE 206-207 D 6
Bosoboso ○ RP 160-161 G 9
Bōsō-hanto ⌣ J 152-153 H 7
Bososama ○ ZRE 206-207 E 6
Bosporus = İstanbul Boğazı ≈ 128-129 C 2
Bosporus = Karadeniz Boğazı ≈ 128-129 C 2
Bosque ○ USA (NM) 256-257 J 4
Bosque de Proteccion ⊥ PE 64-65 E 7
Bosquel del Apache National Wildlife Refuge ⊥• USA (NM) 256-257 H 5
Bosque Petrificado J. Ormachea • RA 80 F 2
Bošrūye ○ IR 134-135 G 2
Bossaga ○ TM 136-137 J 6
Bossangoa ☆ RCA 206-207 C 5
Bossembélé ○ RCA 206-207 C 6
Bossentélé ○ RCA 206-207 C 6
Bossiekom ○ ZA 220-221 E 4
Bossier City ○ USA (LA) 268-269 G 4
Bossiesvlei ○ NAM 220-221 C 2
Bosso ○ RN (DIF) 198-199 F 6
Bosso ∼ RN 204-205 E 1
Bosso, Dallol ∼ BF 204-205 E 2
Bossut, Cape ▲ AUS 172-173 E 5
Bostān ○ IR 134-135 B 3
Bostan ○ VRC 144-145 E 2
Bostānābād ○ IR 128-129 M 4
Bostankum ⊥ KZ 126-127 K 6
Bosten Hu • VRC 146-147 H 5
Boston ○ GB 90-91 G 5
Boston ○ RP 160-161 G 9
Boston ○ USA (GA) 284-285 G 6
Boston ☆• USA (MA) 278-279 K 6
Boston Bar ○ CDN (BC) 230-231 H 4
Boston Mountains ▲ USA 276-277 A 5
Bostonnais, Rivière ∼ CDN 240-241 C 3
Bosumba ∼ ZRE 210-211 G 3
Bosumtwi, Lake ⊖ GH 202-203 K 6
Boswell ○ CDN (BC) 230-231 N 4
Boswell ○ USA (OK) 264-265 J 4
Botād ○ IND 138-139 C 8
Botafogo ○ BR 66-67 B 5
Botalón, El ○ YV 60-61 F 2
Botan Çayı ∼ TR 128-129 K 4
Botanique Jardin • ZRE 210-211 E 6
Botany Bay ≈ 180-181 L 2
Botare ○ RI 166-167 G 3
Botata ○ LB 202-203 F 6
Bote ○ IND 138-139 E 10
Boteka ○ ZRE 210-211 G 4
Botemola ○ ZRE 210-211 G 5
Boteti ∼ RB 218-219 B 5
Botev ▲ BG 102-103 D 6
Botha ○ CDN (ALB) 232-233 F 3
Botha, Oued el ∼ DZ 190-191 D 7
Bothasberg ▲ ZA 220-221 J 3
Bothaville ○ ZA 220-221 H 3
Bothell ○ USA (WA) 244-245 C 3
Bothnia, Gulf of ≈ 86-87 J 5
Bothwell ○ AUS 180-181 J 7
Botija, Ilha da ⌒ BR 66-67 F 4
Botijón ○ YV 60-61 J 3
Botitembongo ○ ZRE 210-211 G 4
Botkul', ozero ⊖ RUS 96-97 E 9
Botlih ○ RUS 126-127 G 6
Bot Makak ○ CAM 210-211 C 2
Botolan ○ RP 160-161 D 5
Botomoju ∼ RUS 118-119 J 4
Botopasi ○ SME 62-63 G 3
Botoşani ☆• RO 102-103 E 4
Botou ○ BF (EST) 202-203 L 3
Botou ○ BF (EST) 204-205 E 2
Botou ○ VRC 154-155 K 2
Botro ○ CI 202-203 H 6
Botswana ■ RB 218-219 B 6
Bottenhavet ≈ 86-87 J 6
Bottenviken ≈ 86-87 L 4
Botterkloof ▲ ZA 220-221 D 5
Bottineau ○ USA (ND) 258-259 G 3
Bottle Creek ○ GB 54-55 K 4
Botuali ○ ZRE 210-211 F 4
Botucatu ○ BR 72-73 F 7
Botulu ○• RUS 118-119 J 3
Botumirim ○ BR 72-73 J 4
Botuobuja, Ulahan ∼ RUS 118-119 E 5
Botwood ○ CDN (NFL) 242-243 N 3
Bou ∼ CI 202-203 H 5
Bou ○ RI 164-165 G 3
Bouaflé ☆ CI 202-203 H 6
Bou Akba ○ DZ 188-189 H 6
Bouaké ☆• CI 202-203 H 6
Bou Aleb ○ RIM 196-197 F 6
Boualem ○ DZ 190-191 C 4
Bou Ali ○ DZ 188-189 L 7
Bou Ali, Oued ∼ DZ 190-191 D 5
Bou-Allala, Hassi ○ DZ 188-189 K 5
Bouam ○ CAM 204-205 K 6
Bouânane ○ MA 188-189 K 4
Bouandougou ○ CI 202-203 H 5
Bouanri ○ DY 204-205 E 3
Bouansa ○ RCB 210-211 D 6
Bouar ☆• RCA 206-207 B 6
Bouârfa ○ MA 188-189 L 4
Bouârfa, Jbel ▲ MA 188-189 L 4
Bouba Ndjida, Parc National de ⊥ CAM 206-207 B 4

Bojarsk — Bouba Ndjida, Parc National de 307

Boubela ○ CI 202-203 G 7
Bou Bernous, Hassi ○ DZ 188-189 K 7
Boubon ○ RN 202-203 L 3
Boubouri ○ CI 202-203 H 7
Bouca ○ RCA 206-207 D 5
Boucaut Bay ≈ 174-175 C 2
Bouchard ○ RA 78-79 H 3
Bouchette, Lac- ○ CDN (QUE) 240-241 C 2
Bouchie Lake ○ CDN (BC) 228-229 M 3
Bouchouaymiy ○ WSA 196-197 B 3
Boucle du Baoulé, Parc National de la ⊥ RMM 202-203 F 2
Boû Cṭaïla ○ RIM 196-197 E 7
Boudamassa ○ TCH 206-207 C 3
Boudbouda ○ RIM 196-197 C 5
Boudenib ○ MA 188-189 K 5
Boudeuse Cay ⌒ SY 224 C 3
Boû Dîb ○ RIM 196-197 F 5
Boudiéri ○ BF 202-203 L 3
Boû Djébéha ○ RMM 196-197 J 5
Boudo ○ ANG 216-217 E 8
Boudoua ○ RCA 206-207 C 6
Boudtenga ○ BF 202-203 K 3
Bouénguidi ~ G 210-211 D 4
Bouenza □ RCB 210-211 D 6
Bouenza ~ RCB 210-211 D 5
Bougaa ○ DZ 190-191 E 2
Boû Gâdoûm ○ RIM 196-197 G 7
Bougainville, Cape ▲ AUS 172-173 H 2
Bougainville, Cape ▲ GB 78-79 L 6
Bougainville, Détroit de ≈ 184 II a 2
Bougainville Island ⌒ PNG 184 I b 2
Bougainville Reef ⌒ AUS 174-175 J 4
Bougainville Strait ≈ 184 I c 2
Bougainville Trench ≃ 183 G 3
Bougaroun, Cap ▲ DZ 190-191 F 2
Boughessa ○ RMM 196-197 M 4
Bougoui ○ RCA 206-207 B 5
Bougouni ○ RMM 202-203 G 4
Bougouriba ~ BF 202-203 J 4
Bougouso ○ CI 202-203 G 5
Bougtob ○ DZ 190-191 C 3
Bouguer, Cape ▲ AUS 180-181 D 4
Boû Guettâra ○ RIM 196-197 C 5
Bou Hadjar ○ DZ 190-191 G 2
Bou Iblane, Jbel ▲ MA 188-189 J 4
Bouira ☆ DZ 190-191 D 2
Bou-Izakarn ○ MA 188-189 G 6
Boujad ○ MA 188-189 H 4
Boujdour ○ WSA 188-189 D 7
Boujdour, Cap ▲ WSA 188-189 D 7
Bou Kadir ○ DZ 190-191 C 2
Bou Kahil, Djebel ▲ DZ 190-191 D 3
Boukān ○ IR 128-129 M 4
Bou Keltoum, Jbel ▲ MA 188-189 K 3
Boukoko ○ RCA 210-211 F 2
Boukoula ○ CAM 204-205 K 3
Boukoumbé ○ DY 202-203 L 4
Boukra ○ WSA 188-189 E 7
Bou Ladiab, Jebel ▲ TN 190-191 H 4
Boula-Ibib ○ CAM 204-205 K 4
Boulal ○ RMM 202-203 F 2
Boulal ○ SN 202-203 C 2
Boû Lanouâr ○ RIM 196-197 B 4
Boulâouane • MA 188-189 G 4
Boulder ○ USA (CO) 254-255 K 3
Boulder ○ USA (MT) 250-251 G 5
Boulder ○ USA (UT) 254-255 D 6
Boulder ○ USA (WY) 252-253 J 4
Boulder, Kalgoorli- ○ AUS 176-177 F 5
Boulder City ○ USA (NV) 248-249 K 4
Boulder Creek ○ USA (CA) 248-249 B 2
Boulel ○ RMM 202-203 H 2
Boulél ○ SN 202-203 C 2
Boulemane ☆ MA 188-189 J 4
Boulgou ○ BF 202-203 L 3
Bouli ~ DY 204-205 E 3
Bouli ○ RIM 196-197 E 7
Boulia ○ AUS 178-179 E 2
Boulogne-sur-Mer ○• F 90-91 H 6
Boulouba ○ RCA 206-207 E 5
Boulouli ○ RMM 202-203 F 3
Boulsa ○ BF 202-203 K 3
Boulsmaïl ○ DZ 190-191 D 2
Boultoum ○ RN 198-199 E 5
Boumaine-du-Dades ○ MA 188-189 J 5
Boumango ○ G 210-211 D 5
Boumba ~ CAM 210-211 E 2
Boumbé I ~ RCA 206-207 B 6
Boumbé II ~ CAM 206-207 B 6
Boumbia ○ CI 202-203 G 7
Boumboum ○ RMM 202-203 K 2
Boumda National Park ⊥ AUS 180-181 K 4
Boûmdeïd ○ RIM 196-197 E 6
Boumerdes ☆ DZ 190-191 D 2
Bou Mertala ○ RIM 196-197 F 4
Boumia ○ MA 188-189 J 4
Boum Kabir ○ TCH 206-207 D 3
Bou Mréga ○ RIM 196-197 E 6
Bouna ☆ CI 202-203 J 5
Bou Naceur, Ibel ▲ MA 188-189 K 4
Boû Nâga ○ RIM 196-197 D 5
Boû Nâga ○ RMM 196-197 J 5
Boundary ○ CDN 32-33 E 3
Boundary ○ USA (WA) 244-245 H 2
Boundary Mountains ▲ USA 278-279 L 3
Boundary Peak ▲ USA (CA) 248-249 F 2
Boundary Plateau ▲ CDN 232-233 J 6
Boundary Ranges ▲ CDN 32-33 E 3
Boundiali ☆ CI 202-203 G 5
Boundji ○ G 210-211 D 4
Boundji ○ RCB 210-211 E 4
Boungo ~ RCA 206-207 F 4
Boungou ~ RCA 206-207 E 5
Boungu ○ RCA 206-207 F 5
Bouniandjé ~ G 210-211 D 3
Bounkiling ○ SN 202-203 C 3
Boun Nua ○ LAO 156-157 B 6
Bounoum ~ SN 202-203 C 2
Bountiful ○ USA (UT) 254-255 D 3
Bountiful Islands ⌒ AUS 174-175 E 5
Bounty Islands ⌒ NZ 13 J 7
Bounty Plateau ≃ 13 J 7
Bounty Trough ≃ 14-15 K 12
Bouquet ○ RA 78-79 J 2
Boura ○ BF 202-203 J 4
Bourarhet, Erg ∸ DZ 190-191 G 7
Bourbeuse River ~ USA 274-275 G 6
Bourbonnais ∸ F 90-91 J 8
Bourdel, Lac ○ CDN 36-37 M 6
Bourem ○ RMM 196-197 K 6
Bourg, Lac ○ CDN 36-37 N 6
Bourg-en-Bresse ☆• F 90-91 K 8
Bourges ☆··· F 90-91 J 8
Bourgogne □ F 90-91 J 8
Bourgogne ∸ F 90-91 K 8
Bourgoin-Jallieu ○ F 90-91 K 9
Bourg-Saint-Maurice ○ F 90-91 L 9
Boû Rjeimât ○ RIM 196-197 C 5
Bourke ○ AUS 178-179 H 6
Bournemouth ○ GB 90-91 G 6
Bourou ○ TCH 206-207 C 4
Bouroum ○ BF 202-203 K 3
Bourrah ○ CAM 204-205 K 3
Bourzanga ○ BF 202-203 K 3
Bous, Adrar ▲ RN 198-199 D 2
Bou Saada ○• DZ 190-191 E 3
Bouse ○ USA (AZ) 256-257 B 5
Bou Sellam ~ DZ 190-191 E 2
Bou Sfer ○ DZ 188-189 L 3
Boussé ○ BF 202-203 K 3
Boussemghoun ○ DZ 190-191 C 4
Bousso ○ TCH 206-207 C 3
Bousso River ~ CDN 30-31 M 4
Boussouma ○ BF 202-203 K 3
Boutilimit ○ RIM 196-197 C 6
Boutougou Fara ○ SN 202-203 D 3
Boutourou, Monts ▲ CI 202-203 J 5
Bouza ○ RN 198-199 C 5
Bouzghaïa ☆ DZ 190-191 C 2
Bovill ○ USA (ID) 250-251 C 5
Bovina ○ USA (TX) 264-265 B 4
Bowbells ○ USA (ND) 258-259 E 3
Bow City ○ CDN (ALB) 232-233 F 5
Bowden ○ CDN (ALB) 232-233 D 4
Bowdle ○ USA (SD) 260-261 G 1
Bowdon ○ USA (GA) 284-285 E 3
Bowdon ○ USA (ND) 258-259 H 4
Bowell ○ CDN (ALB) 232-233 H 5
Bowell Islands ⌒ CDN 30-31 W 3
Bowen ○ AUS 174-175 K 7
Bowen ○ RA 78-79 F 3
Bowen ○ USA (IL) 274-275 G 4
Bowen, Cape ▲ AUS 174-175 H 4
Bowen Island ○ CDN (BC) 230-231 F 4
Bowens Hill ○ USA (GA) 284-285 G 5
Bowenville ○ AUS 178-179 L 4
Bowers Basin ≃ 22-23 E 5
Bowie ○ USA (AZ) 256-257 F 6
Bowie ○ USA (MD) 280-281 K 5
Bowie ○ USA (TX) 264-265 G 5
Bowie National Historic Site, Fort • USA (AZ) 256-257 F 6
Bow Island ○ CDN (ALB) 232-233 G 6
Bowler ○ USA (WI) 270-271 K 6
Bowling Green ○ USA (FL) 286-287 H 4
Bowling Green ○ USA (KY) 276-277 J 4
Bowling Green ○ USA (MO) 274-275 G 5
Bowling Green ○ USA (OH) 280-281 C 2
Bowling Green ○ USA (VA) 280-281 J 5
Bowling Green Bay ≈ 174-175 J 6
Bowling Green Bay National Park ⊥ AUS 174-175 J 6
Bowman ○ USA (GA) 284-285 G 2
Bowman ○ USA (ND) 258-259 D 5
Bowman Bay ≈ 36-37 N 2
Bowman Island ⌒ ARK 16 G 11
Bowmans Corner ○ USA (MT) 250-251 G 4
Bowmanville ○ CDN (ONT) 238-239 G 5
Bowokan, Kepulauan ⌒ RI 164-165 H 5
Bowral ○ AUS 180-181 L 3
Bow River ~ AUS 172-173 J 4
Bow River ~ CDN 232-233 E 5
Bowron Lake Provincial Park ⊥ CDN (BC) 228-229 N 3
Bowron Lake Provincial Park ⊥ CDN (BC) 228-229 O 3
Bowron River ~ CDN 228-229 N 3
Bowser ○ CDN (BC) 230-231 E 4
Bowsman ○ CDN (MAN) 234-235 B 2
Bowutu Mountains ▲ PNG 183 D 4
Bow Valley Provincial Park ⊥ CDN (ALB) 232-233 C 4
Bowwood ○ Z 218-219 D 3
Boxborough ○ USA (MA) 278-279 K 6
Boxelder ○ USA (TX) 264-265 K 5
Box Elder Creek ~ USA 250-251 L 4
Box Elder Creek ~ USA 250-251 P 6
Box Lake ○ CDN 30-31 Q 6
Boxwood Hill ○ AUS 176-177 E 7
Boyabat ○ TR 128-129 F 2
Boyabo ○ ZRE 210-211 G 2
Boyacá ○ CO (BOL) 60-61 D 3
Boyacá ○ CO (BOY) 60-61 E 5
Boyang ○ VRC 156-157 K 2
Boyce ○ USA (LA) 268-269 H 5
Boyce Thompson Arboretum • USA (AZ) 256-257 D 5
Boyd ○ USA (MT) 250-251 K 6
Boyd, Lac ○ CDN 38-39 F 2
Boyd Lake ○ CDN 30-31 S 5
Boyd River ~ AUS 178-179 M 5
Boyds ○ USA (WA) 244-245 G 2
Boyellé ○ RCB 210-211 G 2
Boyero ○ USA (CO) 254-255 M 5
Boyer River ~ CDN 30-31 L 6
Boyer River ~ USA 274-275 C 3
Boykin ○ USA (AL) 284-285 C 4
Boykins ○ USA (VA) 280-281 J 7
Boyle = Mainistir na Búille ○ IRL 90-91 C 5
Boylston ○ CDN (NS) 240-241 O 5
Boyne ○ ZA 218-219 E 6
Boyne City ○ USA (MI) 272-273 E 2
Boyne Valley ··· IRL 90-91 D 5
Boynton Beach ○ USA (FL) 286-287 J 5
Boyolali ○ RI 168 D 3
Boy River ○ USA (MN) 270-271 D 3
Boysen Reservoir ○ USA (WY) 252-253 K 3
Boys Ranch ○ USA (TX) 264-265 B 3
Boyuibe ○ BOL 70-71 F 7
Boyup Brook ○ AUS 176-177 D 6
Bozburun ○ TR 128-129 C 4
Bozcaada ⌒ TR 128-129 B 3
Bozdağlar ▲ TR 128-129 B 3
Božedomova, mys ▲ RUS 120-121 T 3
Bozeman ○ USA (MT) 250-251 H 6
Bozeman Pass ▲ USA (MT) 250-251 J 6
Bozen = Bolzano ☆ I 100-101 C 1
Bozene ○ ZRE 210-211 G 2
Bożgān ○ IR 136-137 F 6
Bozhou ○ VRC 154-155 J 5
Bozkır ☆ TR 128-129 E 4
Bozköl ○ KZ 126-127 O 5
Bozok Yaylâsı ▲ TR 128-129 F 3
Bozoum ☆• RCA 206-207 C 5
Bozova ☆ TR 128-129 H 4
Bozüyük ☆ TR 128-129 D 3
Bozyazı ☆ TR 128-129 E 4
Brabant, Île ⌒ ARK 16 G 30
Brač ⌒ HR 100-101 F 3
Bracciano, Lago di ○ I 100-101 D 3
Bracebridge ○ CDN (ONT) 238-239 F 3
Bräcke ○ S 86-87 G 5
Bracken ○ CDN (SAS) 232-233 K 6
Brackendale ○ CDN (BC) 230-231 F 4
Brackett Lake ○ CDN 30-31 G 3
Brackettville ○ USA (TX) 266-267 G 4
Bracknell ○ GB 90-91 G 6
Braclavka ○ RUS 124-125 B 3
Braço do Lontra ~ BR 68-69 C 4
Braço do Norte ○ BR 74-75 F 7
Braço Menor do Araguaia ou Jauaés ~ BR 68-69 D 7
Brad ○ RO 102-103 C 4
Brad ○ USA (TX) 264-265 F 6
Brádano ~ I 100-101 E 4
Braddock ○ USA (ND) 258-259 G 5
Braddyville ○ USA (IA) 274-275 C 4
Bradenton ○ USA (FL) 286-287 G 4
Bradford ○ CDN (ONT) 238-239 F 4
Bradford ○ GB 90-91 G 5
Bradford ○ USA (AR) 276-277 D 5
Bradford ○ USA (IL) 274-275 J 3
Bradford ○ USA (PA) 280-281 H 2
Bradford ○ USA (VT) 278-279 J 4
Bradley ○ USA (AR) 276-277 B 7
Bradley ○ USA (CA) 248-249 D 4
Bradley ○ USA (SC) 284-285 H 2
Bradley Reefs ⌒ SOL 184 I e 2
Bradleyville ○ USA (MO) 276-277 C 4
Bradore, Baie ≈ 38-39 Q 3
Bradshaw ○ USA (NE) 262-263 J 4
Bradshaw ○ USA (TX) 264-265 E 6
Bradwardine ○ CDN (MAN) 234-235 C 5
Bradwell ○ CDN (SAS) 232-233 M 4
Brady ○ USA (MT) 250-251 H 3
Brady ○ USA (TX) 266-267 H 2
Brady Creek ~ USA 266-267 H 2
Brady Glacier ⊂ USA 32-33 B 2
Brady Reservoir < USA (TX) 266-267 H 2
Braemar ○ AUS 180-181 E 2
Braemar ○ GB 90-91 F 3
Braga ○·· P 98-99 C 4
Bragado ○ RA 78-79 J 3
Bragança ○ BR 68-69 E 2
Bragança ○ P 98-99 D 4
Bragança Paulista ○ BR 72-73 G 7
Bragg, Fort ○ USA (CA) 246-247 B 4
Bragg Creek ○ CDN (ALB) 232-233 D 5
Braham ○ USA (MN) 270-271 E 5
Brahestad ○ FIN 88-89 H 4
Brahim, Hassi ○ MA 188-189 G 6
Brahmakund ○ IND 142-143 K 2
Brahmani ~ IND 142-143 D 5
Brahmapur ○ IND 142-143 D 6
Brahmaputra ~ IND 142-143 H 2
Braidwood ○ AUS 180-181 K 3
Brăila ☆• RO 102-103 E 5
Brainard ○ CDN 32-33 L 4
Brainerd ○ USA (MN) 270-271 D 4
Braintree ○ GB 90-91 H 6
Brakna □ RIM 196-197 D 6
Brakpan ○ NAM 220-221 D 2
Brakpan ○ ZA 220-221 J 3
Brakspruit ○ ZA 220-221 H 3
Brakwater ○ NAM 216-217 D 11
Bralorne ○ CDN (BC) 230-231 G 3
Brálos ○ GR 100-101 J 5
Bramhapuri ○ IND 138-139 G 9
Brampton ○ CDN (ONT) 238-239 F 5
Brampton Islands ⌒ AUS 174-175 K 7
Bramwell ○ AUS 174-175 G 3
Branca, Serra ▲ BR 68-69 F 5
Brancepeth ○ CDN (SAS) 232-233 N 2
Branch ○ CDN (NFL) 242-243 P 6
Branch Creek ~ AUS 174-175 E 5
Branchville ○ USA (SC) 284-285 K 3
Branco, Ilhéu ⌒ CV 202-203 B 5
Branco, Rio ~ BR 62-63 D 6
Branco, Rio ~ BR 66-67 E 7
Branco, Rio ~ BR 66-67 B 5
Branco, Rio ~ BR 66-67 D 5
Branco, Rio ~ BR 66-67 G 7
Branco, Rio ~ BR 68-69 F 7
Branco, Rio ~ BR 70-71 F 3
Branco, Rio ~ BR 70-71 H 2
Branco ou Cabixi, Rio ~ BR 70-71 G 3
Brandberg ·· NAM 216-217 C 10
Brandberg Wes ○ NAM 216-217 C 10
Brandbu ☆ N 86-87 E 6
Brande ○ DK 86-87 D 9
Brandenburg □ D 92-93 M 3
Brandenburg ○ USA (KY) 276-277 J 3
Brandenburg an der Havel ○• D 92-93 M 2
Brandenton Beach ○ USA (FL) 286-287 G 4
Brandfort ○ ZA 220-221 H 4
Brandon ○ CDN (MAN) 234-235 D 5
Brandon ○ USA (FL) 286-287 G 4
Brandon ○ USA (MN) 270-271 C 5
Brandon ○ USA (MS) 268-269 L 4
Brandon ○ USA (SD) 260-261 K 3
Brandon ○ USA (VT) 278-279 H 5
Brandsen ○ RA 78-79 K 3
Brandvlei ○ ZA 220-221 E 5
Brandýs nad Labem-Stará Boleslav ○ CZ 92-93 N 3
Brandywine ○ USA (MD) 280-281 K 5
Branford ○ USA (FL) 286-287 G 2
Brang, Kuala ○ MAL 162-163 E 2
Braniewo ○• PL 92-93 P 1
Br'anka ○ UA 102-103 L 3
Branqueada do Salto ○ BR 74-75 D 9
Bransan ○ SN 202-203 D 3
Bransfield Strait ≈ 16 G 30
Branson ○ USA (CO) 254-255 M 6
Branson ○ USA (MO) 276-277 B 4
Brant ○ CDN (ALB) 232-233 E 5
Brantford ○ CDN (ONT) 238-239 E 5
Brantley ○ USA (AL) 284-285 D 5
Brantôme ○ F 90-91 H 9
Brantville ○ CDN (NB) 240-241 L 3
Brás ○ BR 66-67 H 4
Bras d'Or Lake ○ CDN (NS) 240-241 P 5
Brasil ○ C 54-55 G 4
Brasilândia ○ BR 72-73 D 6
Brasiléia ○ BR 70-71 C 2
Brasília ★··· BR 72-73 G 3
Brasília, Lago de ○ BR 72-73 G 3
Brasília de Minas ○ BR 72-73 H 4
Braslândia ○ BR 72-73 F 3
Braslav ○ BY 94-95 K 4
Brasnorte ○ BR 70-71 H 2
Braşov ☆• RO 102-103 D 5
Brass ○ WAN 204-205 G 6
Brasschaat ○ B 92-93 H 3
Brassey, Banjaran ▲ MAL 160-161 B 10
Brassey, Mount ▲ AUS 178-179 C 2
Brassey Range ▲ AUS 176-177 G 2
Brasstown Bald ▲ USA (GA) 284-285 G 2
Brastagi ○• RI 162-163 C 3
Bratislava ★·· SK 92-93 O 4
Bratovoeşti ○ RO 102-103 C 5
Bratsk ☆ RUS 116-117 K 7
Bratskoe vodohraniliščе < RUS 116-117 L 8
Bratskoye Vodokhranilishche = Bratskoe vodohraniliščе < RUS 116-117 L 8
Brattleboro ○ USA (VT) 278-279 J 6
Braulio Carrillo, Parque Nacional ⊥ CR 52-53 C 6
Braúnas ○ BR 72-73 J 5
Braunau am Inn ○ A 92-93 M 4
Braunlage ○ D 92-93 L 3
Braunschweig ○·· D 92-93 L 2
Brava, Ilha ⌒ CV 202-203 B 6
Brava, La ○ RA 76-77 G 6
Brava, Laguna la ○ RA 78-79 H 2
Bravo, Cerro ▲ BOL (COC) 70-71 E 5
Bravo, Cerro ▲ BOL (POT) 76-77 D 2
Bravo, Cerro ▲ RCH 76-77 C 4
Bravo, El ○ RA 76-77 F 4
Bravo del Norte, Río ~ MEX 50-51 J 3
Bravo River ~ BH 52-53 K 3
Brawley ○ USA (CA) 248-249 J 7
Bray ○ USA (CA) 246-247 D 2
Bray ○ ZA 220-221 F 2
Bray = Bré ○ IRL 90-91 D 5
Bray Island ⌒ CDN 24-25 h 6
Bray-sur-Seine ○ F 90-91 J 7
Brazeau, Mount ▲ CDN (ALB) 228-229 R 4
Brazeau Reservoir < CDN (ALB) 232-233 C 3
Brazeau River ~ CDN 228-229 R 4
Brazeau River ~ CDN 232-233 C 3
Brazil ○ USA (IN) 274-275 L 5
Brazil = Brasil ■ BR 74-75 C 2
Brazil Basin ≃ 6-7 G 10
Brazilian Highlands = Brasileiro, Planalto ∸ BR 72-73 H 3
Brazo Aná Cuá ~ PY 76-77 J 4
Brazo de Loba ~ CO 60-61 D 3
Brazos ○ USA (NM) 256-257 J 2
Brazos River ~ USA 264-265 E 5
Brazos River ~ USA 266-267 L 3
Brazo Sur del Río Coig (Coyle) ~ RA 80 E 5
Brazzaville ★• RCB 210-211 E 6
Brčko ○ BIH 100-101 G 2
Brdy ▲ CZ 92-93 M 4
Bré = Bray ○ IRL 90-91 D 5
Brea, Cordillera de la ▲ RA 76-77 C 5
Breaden, Lake ○ AUS 176-177 H 2
Breaksea Sound ≈ 182 A 6
Brea Pozo ○ RA 76-77 F 5
Breas, Las ○ RCH 76-77 B 5
Breaux Bridge ○ USA (LA) 268-269 J 6
Brebes ○ RI 168 C 3
Brechin ○ CDN (ONT) 238-239 F 4
Breckenridge ○ USA (CO) 254-255 J 4
Breckenridge ○ USA (MN) 270-271 B 4
Breckenridge ○ USA (TX) 264-265 F 6
Breckinridge Mountain ▲ USA (CA) 248-249 F 4
Brecknock, Península ⌣ RCH 80 E 7
Brecon ○• GB 90-91 F 6
Brecon Beacons National Park ⊥ GB 90-91 F 6
Breda ○• NL 92-93 H 3
Bredasdorp ○ ZA 220-221 E 7
Bredbo ○ AUS 180-181 K 3
Bredbyn ○ S 86-87 J 5
Bredenbury ○ CDN (SAS) 232-233 Q 5
Brèdi, ostrov ⌒ RUS 84-85 d 2
Bredsel ○ S 86-87 K 4
Bredy ☆ RUS 124-125 B 2
Breede ~ ZA 220-221 E 7
Breeza Plains Out Station ○ AUS 174-175 H 4
Bregalnica ~ MK 100-101 J 4
Bregenz ☆ A 92-93 K 5
Bregovo ○ BG 102-103 C 5
Bréhal ○ F 90-91 G 7
Brehat ○ CDN (NFL) 242-243 N 1
Brehovskie ostrova ⌒ RUS 108-109 U 6
Breiðafjörður ≈ 86-87 b 2
Breien ○ USA (ND) 258-259 G 5
Breivikbotn ○ N 86-87 L 1
Brejão da Caatinga ○ BR 68-69 H 7
Brejo ○ BR 68-69 G 3
Brejo, Riachão do ~ BR 68-69 G 6
Brejo da Madre de Deus ○ BR 68-69 K 6
Brejo de São Félix ○ BR 68-69 G 4
Brejo do Cruz ○ BR 68-69 K 5
Brejo do Serra ○ BR 68-69 G 7
Brejo Grande ○ BR (CEA) 68-69 J 5
Brejo Grande ○ BR (SER) 68-69 K 7
Brejolândia ○ BR 72-73 J 2
Brejo Velho, Riachão ~ BR 72-73 J 2
Brekken ○ N 86-87 E 5
Brekstad ○ N 86-87 D 5
Brelen ○ USA (ND) 258-259 G 5
Bremangerlandet ⌒ N 86-87 B 6
Bremen ☆·· D 92-93 K 2
Bremen ○ USA (AL) 284-285 D 3
Bremen ○ USA (GA) 284-285 E 3
Bremen ○ USA (IN) 274-275 M 3
Bremen ○ USA (ND) 258-259 H 4
Bremer Bay ≈ 176-177 E 7
Bremer Bay ○ AUS (WA) 176-177 E 7
Bremerhaven ○ D 92-93 K 2
Bremer Island ⌒ AUS 174-175 D 3
Bremer Range ▲ AUS 176-177 F 6
Bremerton ○ USA (WA) 244-245 C 3
Bremervörde ○ D 92-93 K 2
Bremner ○ CDN (ALB) 232-233 E 2
Bremond ○ USA (TX) 266-267 L 2
Brenãs, Las ○ RA 76-77 G 4
Brenham ○ USA (TX) 266-267 L 3
Brennerpaß = Passo del Brennero ▲ A 92-93 L 5
Brennevinsfjorden ≈ 84-85 L 2
Brent ○ USA (AL) 284-285 C 4
Brenta ~ I 100-101 C 2
Brentford Bay ≈ 24-25 Z 5
Brentwood ○ USA (TN) 276-277 J 4
Brenzia ○ DZ 190-191 C 4
Brep ○ PK 138-139 D 1
Bresaylor ○ CDN (SAS) 232-233 K 3
Bréscia ○• I 100-101 C 2
Bresnahan, Mount ▲ AUS 176-177 D 1
Bressanone = Brixen ○ I 100-101 C 1
Bressuire ○ F 90-91 G 8
Brèst ○ BY 94-95 H 5
Brest ○ F 90-91 E 7
Brest = Brèst ○ BY 94-95 H 5
Bretagne □ F 90-91 E 7
Bretaña ○ PE 64-65 E 4
Breteuil ○ F 90-91 J 7
Breton, Cape ▲ CDN (NS) 240-241 Q 5
Breton Cove ○ CDN (NS) 240-241 P 4
Breton Island ⌒ USA (LA) 268-269 L 7
Breton National Wildlife Refuge ⊥ USA (LA) 268-269 M 7
Breton N. W. R. ⊥ USA (LA) 268-269 L 7
Breton Sound ≈ 48-49 D 5
Breton Sound ≈ 268-269 L 7
Brett, Cape ▲ NZ 182 E 1
Breueh, Pulau ⌒ RI 162-163 A 2
Brevard ○ USA (NC) 282-283 E 5
Breverville ○ LB 202-203 E 6
Breves ○ BR 62-63 J 6
Brevoort, Kap ▲ GRØ 26-27 U 3
Brevoort Island ⌒ CDN 36-37 R 3
Brevort ○ USA (MI) 270-271 N 4
Brewaniase ○ GH 202-203 L 5
Brewarrina ○ AUS 178-179 J 5
Brewer ○ CDN (SAS) 232-233 Q 4
Brewer ○ USA (ME) 278-279 N 4
Brewster ○ USA (KS) 262-263 E 5
Brewster ○ USA (NE) 262-263 G 3
Brewster ○ USA (NY) 280-281 N 2
Brewster ○ USA (WA) 244-245 F 2
Brewster, Lake ○ AUS 180-181 J 2
Brewton ○ USA (AL) 284-285 C 5
Breyten ○ ZA 220-221 J 3
Brezina ○ DZ 190-191 C 4
Brežnev = Naberežnye Čelny ☆ RUS 96-97 H 6
Brezovo Polje ▲ HR 100-101 F 2
Bria ☆ RCA 206-207 E 5
Briakan ○ RUS 122-123 F 2
Briançon ○• F 90-91 L 9
Brian Head ▲ USA (UT) 254-255 C 6
Briarton ○ USA (WI) 270-271 K 6
Bribie Island ⌒ AUS 178-179 M 4
Bribri ○ CR 52-53 C 7
Bričany = Briceni ☆ MD 102-103 E 3
Bričen' = Briceni ☆ MD 102-103 E 3
Briceni ☆ MD 102-103 E 3
Brices Cross Roads National Battlefield Site ∴ USA (MS) 268-269 M 2
Briconnet, Lac ○ CDN 38-39 O 3
Bridal Cave ∴ USA (MO) 274-275 F 6
Bridesville ○ CDN (BC) 230-231 K 4
Bridge City ○ USA (TX) 268-269 G 6
Bridgeford ○ CDN (SAS) 232-233 M 5
Bridge Lake ○ CDN (BC) 230-231 J 2
Bridgenorth ○ CDN (ONT) 238-239 G 4
Bridge over the River Kwai • THA 158-159 E 3
Bridge Point ▲ BS 54-55 G 2
Bridgeport ○ USA (AL) 284-285 E 2
Bridgeport ○ USA (CA) 246-247 F 5
Bridgeport ○ USA (CT) 280-281 N 2
Bridgeport ○ USA (NE) 262-263 C 3
Bridgeport ○ USA (OH) 280-281 F 3
Bridgeport ○ USA (OR) 244-245 H 6
Bridgeport ○ USA (TX) 264-265 G 5
Bridgeport ○ USA (WA) 244-245 F 2
Bridgeport, Lake ⊂ USA (TX) 264-265 G 5
Bridger ○ USA (MT) 250-251 L 6
Bridge River ~ CDN 230-231 G 3
Bridge River Indian Reservation X CDN (BC) 230-231 G 3
Bridger Peak ▲ USA (WY) 252-253 L 5
Bridger State Historic Site, Fort • USA (WY) 252-253 H 5
Bridger Wilderness Area ⊥ USA (WY) 252-253 J 4
Bridgeton ○ USA (NJ) 280-281 L 4
Bridgetown ○ AUS 176-177 D 6
Bridgetown ★ BDS 56 F 5
Bridgetown ○ CDN (NS) 240-241 K 6
Bridgeville ○ CDN (QUE) 240-241 L 2
Bridgeville ○ USA (CA) 246-247 B 3
Bridgewater ○ AUS (TAS) 180-181 J 7
Bridgewater ○ AUS (VIC) 180-181 G 4
Bridgewater ○ CDN (NS) 240-241 L 6
Bridgewater ○ USA (NY) 278-279 F 6
Bridgewater ○ USA (SD) 260-261 J 3
Bridgewater ○ USA (VA) 280-281 H 5
Bridgewater ○ ZA 218-219 E 6
Bridgewater, Cape ○ AUS 180-181 F 5
Bridgman, Kap ▲ GRØ 26-27 m 2
Bridgton ○ USA (ME) 278-279 L 4
Bridlington ○ GB 90-91 G 4
Bridport ○ AUS 180-181 J 6
Bridport ○ GB 90-91 F 6
Bridport Inlet ≈ 24-25 R 3
Brie ∸• F 90-91 J 7
Brieg = Brzeg ○• PL 92-93 O 3
Brier Creek ~ USA 284-285 H 3
Briercrest ○ CDN (SAS) 232-233 N 5
Brier Island ⌒ CDN (NS) 240-241 J 6
Brig ○• CH 92-93 J 5
Brig Bay ○ CDN (NFL) 242-243 M 1
Briggs ○ USA (TX) 266-267 K 3
Briggs, Cape ▲ CDN 24-25 Y 4
Briggsdale ○ USA (CO) 254-255 L 3
Brigham City ○ USA (UT) 254-255 C 2
Bright ○ AUS 180-181 J 4
Brighton ○ CDN (ONT) 238-239 H 4
Brighton ○ GB 90-91 G 6
Brighton ○ USA (AL) 284-285 C 3
Brighton ○ USA (CO) 254-255 L 4
Brighton ○ USA (FL) 286-287 H 4
Brighton ○ USA (IA) 274-275 G 3
Brighton ○ USA (IL) 274-275 H 5
Brighton ○ USA (IN) 274-275 N 3
Brighton ○ USA (MI) 272-273 F 5
Brighton Downs ○ AUS 178-179 F 2
Brighton Seminole Indian Reservation X USA (FL) 286-287 H 4
Brightsand Lake ○ CDN (SAS) 232-233 K 2
Brightstar ○ USA (AR) 276-277 B 7
Brigida, Riachão ou ~ BR 68-69 J 6
Brignan ⌣ CI 202-203 H 7
Brignoles ○ F 90-91 L 10
Brikama ○ WAG 202-203 B 3
Brilhante, Rio ~ BR 76-77 K 1
Brilon ○ D 92-93 K 3
Brimley ○ USA (MI) 270-271 O 4
Brimstone Hill Fortress ∴ KAN 56 D 3
Brinawa ○ AUS 174-175 E 6
Brinckheuvel, National Reservaat ⊥ SME 62-63 G 3
Brindakit ○ RUS 120-121 G 3
Bríndisi ☆• I 100-101 F 4
Brinkley ○ USA (AR) 276-277 D 6
Brinkleyville ○ USA (NC) 282-283 K 4
Brin-Navolok ○ RUS 88-89 Q 5
Brinnon ○ USA (WA) 244-245 C 3
Brion, Île ⌒ CDN (QUE) 242-243 G 5
Brioni, Nacionalni park ⊥ HR 100-101 D 2
Brisbane ☆• AUS 178-179 M 4
Brisbane ○ CDN (ONT) 238-239 E 5
Brisbane River ~ AUS 178-179 M 4
Brisco ○ CDN (BC) 230-231 N 3
Briscoe ○ USA (TX) 264-265 D 3
Brisson, Lac ○ CDN 36-37 R 6
Bristol ○ CDN (NB) 240-241 H 4
Bristol ○• GB 90-91 F 6
Bristol ○ USA (CO) 254-255 N 5
Bristol ○ USA (CT) 280-281 O 2
Bristol ○ USA (FL) 286-287 E 1
Bristol ○ USA (GA) 284-285 H 5
Bristol ○ USA (IN) 274-275 N 3
Bristol ○ USA (MI) 272-273 D 3
Bristol ○ USA (SD) 260-261 J 1
Bristol ○ USA (TN) 282-283 E 4
Bristol ○ USA (VA) 280-281 D 7
Bristol ○ USA (VT) 278-279 H 4
Bristol Bay ≈ 22-23 Q 4
Bristol Channel ≈ 90-91 E 6
Bristol Lake ○ USA (CA) 248-249 J 5
Bristow ○ USA (OK) 264-265 H 3
Britânia ○ BR 72-73 E 3
Britannia ○ CDN (NFL) 242-243 P 4
Britannia, Mount ▲ CDN 24-25 Y 2
Britannia Beach ○ CDN (BC) 230-231 F 4
Britannia Range ▲ ARK 16 E 0
Britanskij kanal ≈ 84-85 b 2
British Columbia □ CDN 32-33 F 3
British Mountains ▲ USA 20-21 U 2
British Virgin Islands □ GB 56 C 2
Brito Godins ○ ANG 216-217 D 4
Brits ○ ZA 220-221 H 2
Britstown ○ ZA 220-221 F 5
Britt ○ USA (IA) 274-275 E 1
Britton ○ USA (SD) 260-261 J 1
Britvin, mys ▲ RUS 108-109 F 5
Brive-la-Gaillarde ○ F 90-91 H 9
Brixen = Bressanone ○ I 100-101 C 1
Brjanka = Br'anka ○ UA 102-103 L 3
Brjansk ○ RUS 94-95 O 5
Brjansk ○ RUS 126-127 G 5
Brjanskaja Kosa, mys ▲ RUS 126-127 G 5
Brjanskoe ○ RUS 122-123 K 5
Brjanta ~ RUS 118-119 N 8
Brjungjade ~ RUS 120-121 J 2
Brjusa, ostrov ⌒ RUS 84-85 b 2
Brno ○• CZ 92-93 O 4
Broa, Ensenada de la ≈ 54-55 D 3
Broadacres ○ CDN (SAS) 232-233 K 3
Broadalbin ○ USA (NY) 278-279 G 5
Broad Arrow ∴ AUS 176-177 F 5
Broadback Rivière ~ CDN 38-39 F 3
Broadback Rivière ~ CDN 236-237 M 2
Broadford ○ AUS 180-181 H 4
Broad Peak ▲ IND 138-139 F 2
Broad River ~ USA 284-285 J 2
Broad River ~ USA 284-285 H 3
Broad River ~ USA 284-285 G 2
Broad Sound ≈ 178-179 K 2
Broadsound Range ▲ AUS 178-179 K 2
Broadus ○ USA (MT) 250-251 O 6
Broadview ○ CDN (SAS) 232-233 Q 5
Broadview ○ USA (MT) 250-251 L 5
Broadview ○ USA (NM) 256-257 M 4
Broadview Acton ○ USA (MT) 250-251 L 5
Broadwater ○ USA (NE) 262-263 D 3
Broadway ○ USA (VA) 280-281 H 5
Brobo ○ CI 202-203 H 6
Brochant, Rivière ~ CDN 36-37 O 5
Brochet ○ CDN 34-35 F 2
Brochet, Lac ○ CDN 30-31 T 6
Brock ○ CDN (SAS) 232-233 K 4
Brocken ▲ D 92-93 L 3
Brocket ○ CDN (ALB) 232-233 E 6
Brocket ○ USA (ND) 258-259 J 3
Brock Island ⌒ CDN 24-25 O 2
Brockman, Mount ▲ AUS 172-173 C 7
Brockport ○ USA (NY) 278-279 D 5
Brock River ~ CDN 24-25 L 6
Brockton ○ USA (MA) 278-279 K 6
Brockton ○ USA (MT) 250-251 P 3
Brockville ○ CDN (ONT) 238-239 K 4
Brockway ○ USA (MT) 250-251 O 4
Brockway ○ USA (PA) 280-281 H 2
Broco ○ USA (FL) 286-287 G 3
Brodec'ke ○ UA 102-103 F 3
Broderick ○ CDN (SAS) 232-233 M 4
Brodeur Peninsula ⌣ CDN 24-25 b 4
Brodeur River ~ CDN 24-25 b 4
Brodick ○ GB 90-91 E 4
Brodie Bay ≈ 28-29 G 2
Brodnica ○• PL 92-93 P 2
Brodokalmak ○ RUS 114-115 G 7
Brody ○ UA 102-103 D 2
Broer Ruys, Kap ▲ GRØ 26-27 p 7
Brogan ○ USA (OR) 244-245 H 6
Broke Inlet ≈ 176-177 D 7
Broken Arrow ○ USA (OK) 264-265 J 2
Broken Bay ≈ 180-181 L 2
Broken Bow ○ USA (NE) 262-263 G 3
Broken Bow ○ USA (OK) 264-265 K 4
Broken Bow Lake ○ USA (OK) 264-265 K 4
Brokenburg ○ USA (VA) 280-281 J 5
Brokenhead ○ CDN (MAN) 234-235 G 4
Broken Hill ○ AUS 180-181 F 2
Broken Ridge ≃ 12 H 8
Broken River ~ AUS 180-181 H 4
Broken Skull River ~ CDN 30-31 E 4
Broken Water Bay ≈ 183 C 2
Brokopondo ☆ SME 62-63 G 3
Bromby Islands ⌒ AUS 174-175 D 2
Bromley ○ ZW 218-219 F 3
Bromo, Gunung ▲ RI 168 E 3
Bromo-Tengger-Semeru National Park ⊥ RI 168 E 3
Bromsi, Pulau ⌒ RI 166-167 J 2
Brønderslev ○ DK 86-87 D 8
Brong-Ahafo Region □ GH 202-203 J 6
Bronkhorstspruit ○ ZA 220-221 J 2
Bronnicy ○• RUS 94-95 Q 4
Brønnøysund ○ N 86-87 F 4
Bronson ○ USA (FL) 286-287 G 2
Bronson ○ USA (MI) 272-273 D 6
Bronson ○ USA (TX) 268-269 F 5
Bronte ○ USA (TX) 266-267 G 2
Brookeland ○ USA (TX) 268-269 G 5
Brookesmith ○ USA (TX) 266-267 H 2
Brooke's Point ○ RP 160-161 B 8
Brookfield ○ USA (MO) 274-275 E 5
Brookgreen Gardens • USA (SC) 284-285 L 3
Brookhaven ○ USA (MS) 268-269 K 5
Brookings ○ USA (OR) 244-245 A 8
Brookings ○ USA (SD) 260-261 K 2
Brooklet ○ USA (GA) 284-285 J 4
Brooklyn ○ CDN (NS) 240-241 L 5
Brooklyn ○ USA (AL) 284-285 D 5
Brooklyn ○ USA (IA) 274-275 F 3
Brooklyn ○ USA (MS) 268-269 L 5
Brooklyn (River cruises) • AUS 180-181 L 2
Brookneal ○ USA (VA) 280-281 H 6
Brooks ○ CDN (ALB) 232-233 G 5
Brooksburg ○ USA (NY) 278-279 G 6
Brooksby ○ CDN (SAS) 232-233 O 3
Brooks Mount ▲ USA 20-21 G 4
Brooks Nek ○ ZA 220-221 J 5
Brooks Peninsula Provincial Recreation Area ⊥ CDN (BC) 230-231 B 3
Brooks Range ▲ USA 20-21 K 2
Brookston ○ USA (MN) 270-271 F 4
Brookstone ○ USA (IN) 274-275 M 4
Brooksville ○ USA (FL) 286-287 G 3
Brooksville ○ USA (MS) 268-269 M 3
Brookton ○ AUS 176-177 D 6
Brookville ○ AUS 174-175 J 7
Brookville ○ USA (IN) 274-275 N 5
Brookville ○ USA (PA) 280-281 G 2
Brookville Reservoir < USA (IN) 274-275 O 5
Broome ○ AUS 172-173 F 4
Broomhill ○ CDN (MAN) 234-235 B 5
Brooms Head ○ AUS 178-179 M 5
Brotas ○ BR 72-73 F 7
Brotas de Macaúbas ○ BR 68-69 G 7
Brother John Gletscher ⊂ GRØ 26-27 O 4
Brothers ○ USA (OR) 244-245 E 7
Brothers, The ⌒ Y 132-133 H 7
Broughton Island ⌒ CDN (NWT) 28-29 J 3
Broughton Island ⌒ CDN (NWT) 36-37 L 6
Broulkou ○ TCH 198-199 J 4
Brouse ○ CDN (BC) 230-231 M 3
Brovary ○ UA 102-103 G 2
Brovinia ○ AUS 178-179 L 3
Browder ○ USA (KY) 276-277 H 3
Browerville ○ USA (MN) 270-271 D 4
Brown ○ CDN (MAN) 234-235 E 5
Brown, Mount ▲ ARK 16 F 9

308 Boubela — Brown, Mount

Brown, Mount ▲ USA (MT) 250-251 H 3
Brown, Point ▲ AUS 180-181 B 2
Brown Bank ≃ 160-161 B 7
Brown City o USA (MI) 272-273 G 4
Brown Co. State Park ⊥ USA (IN) 274-275 M 5
Browne o USA 20-21 Q 4
Browne Bay ≈ 24-25 X 4
Browne Range ▲▲ AUS 176-177 H 2
Brownfield o CDN (ALB) 232-233 G 3
Brownfield o USA (TX) 264-265 B 5
Browning o CDN (SAS) 232-233 Q 6
Browning o USA (MT) 250-251 G 3
Brown Lake o CDN 30-31 Y 3
Brownlee o CDN (SAS) 232-233 N 5
Brownlow Point ▲ USA 20-21 S 1
Brownrigg o CDN (ONT) 236-237 G 3
Brown River ~ AUS 178-179 K 3
Brown River ~ PNG 183 D 5
Browns o USA (AL) 284-285 C 4
Brownsberg, National Reservaat ⊥ SME 62-63 G 3
Brownsboro o USA (OR) 244-245 C 8
Brownsburg o CDN (QUE) 238-239 L 3
Brownsburg o USA (IN) 274-275 M 5
Brown's Cay ⌒ BS 54-55 F 2
Brown's Cove o CDN (NFL) 242-243 M 3
Browns Town o JA 54-55 G 5
Brownstown o USA (IN) 274-275 M 6
Browns Valley o USA (MN) 270-271 B 5
Brownsville o USA (KY) 276-277 J 3
Brownsville o USA (TN) 276-277 F 5
Brownsville o USA (TX) 266-267 K 8
Brownsweg o SME 62-63 G 3
Brownton o USA (GA) 284-285 J 5
Brownwood o USA (TX) 266-267 J 2
Brownwood, Lake < USA (TX) 266-267 H 2
Browse Island ⌒ AUS 172-173 F 3
Broxton o USA (GA) 284-285 H 5
Broytona, ostrov ⌒ RUS 122-123 Q 5
Bruce o CDN (ALB) 232-233 F 2
Bruce o USA (MS) 268-269 L 3
Bruce o USA (WI) 270-271 G 5
Bruce, Mount ▲ AUS 172-173 D 7
Bruce Crossing o USA (MI) 270-271 J 4
Bruce Highway II AUS 178-179 K 2
Bruce Lake o CDN (ONT) 234-235 K 4
Bruce Mines o CDN (ONT) 238-239 D 2
Bruce Peninsula ~ CDN 238-239 D 3
Bruce Peninsula National Park ⊥ CDN (ONT) 238-239 D 3
Bruce Rock o AUS 176-177 E 5
Bruceton o USA (TN) 276-277 G 4
Bruceville-Eddy o USA (TX) 266-267 K 2
Bruck an der Leitha o A 92-93 O 5
Bruck an der Mur o A 92-93 N 5
Brudenell o CDN (ONT) 238-239 H 3
Bruderheim o CDN (ALB) 232-233 F 2
Brug, De o ZA 220-221 G 4
Bruges = Brugge ☆•• B 92-93 G 3
Brugge ☆•• B 92-93 G 3
Brühl o•• D 92-93 J 3
Bruini o IND 142-143 K 1
Bruit, Pulau ⌒ MAL 162-163 J 3
Brujas o CO 60-61 G 6
Brujas, Las o MEX 50-51 K 6
Brukkaros ▲ NAM 220-221 C 2
Brûlé o CDN (ALB) 228-229 R 3
Brule o USA (WI) 270-271 G 4
Brûle, Lac = Burnt Lake o CDN 38-39 N 2
Brumadinho o BR 72-73 H 6
Brumado o BR 72-73 K 3
Brumunddal ☆ N 86-87 E 6
Brunchilly o AUS 174-175 C 6
Brundage o USA (TX) 266-267 H 5
Brundidge o USA (AL) 284-285 E 5
Bruneau o USA (ID) 252-253 C 4
Bruneau River ~ USA 252-253 C 4
Brunei ■ BRU 164-165 D 1
Brunei, Teluk ≈ 164-165 D 1
Brunette Downs o AUS 174-175 C 6
Brunette Island ⌒ CDN (NFL) 242-243 M 5
Brunflo o S 86-87 G 5
Bruni o USA (TX) 266-267 J 6
Bruning o USA (NE) 262-263 J 4
Brunkild o CDN (MAN) 234-235 F 5
Brünn = Brno o• CZ 92-93 O 4
Bruno o CDN (SAS) 232-233 N 3
Bruno o USA (MN) 270-271 F 4
Bruno o USA (NE) 262-263 K 3
Brunswick o USA (GA) 284-285 J 5
Brunswick o USA (MD) 280-281 J 4
Brunswick o USA (ME) 278-279 M 5
Brunswick o USA (MN) 270-271 E 5
Brunswick o USA (MO) 274-275 E 5
Brunswick o USA (NE) 262-263 J 2
Brunswick = Braunschweig o•• D 92-93 L 2
Brunswick, Península ~ RCH 80 E 6
Brunswick Bay ≈ 172-173 G 3
Brunswick Heads o AUS 178-179 M 5
Brunswick Lake o CDN (ONT) 236-237 E 4
Bruntál o CZ 92-93 O 4
Bruny Island ⌒ AUS 180-181 J 7
Brus o YU 100-101 H 3
Brusett o USA (MT) 250-251 M 4
Brush o USA (CO) 254-255 M 3
Brus-Kamen' ▲▲ RUS 108-109 X 8
Brusque o BR 74-75 F 6
Brussel = Bruxelles ★•• B 92-93 H 3
Brussels = Bruxelles/ Brussel ★•• B 92-93 H 3
Brüx = Most o CZ 92-93 M 3
Bruxelles = Brussel ★•• B 92-93 H 3
Bruzual o YV 60-61 G 3
Bryan o USA (OH) 280-281 B 2
Bryan o USA (TX) 266-267 L 3
Bryan, Mount ▲ AUS 180-181 E 2
Bryansk = Brjansk o RUS 94-95 O 5
Bryant o CDN (SAS) 232-233 P 6
Bryant o USA (AR) 276-277 C 6
Bryant o USA (SD) 260-261 J 2
Bryant Creek ~ USA 276-277 C 4
Bryce Canyon National Park ∴ USA (UT) 254-255 C 6
Bryden, Mount ▲ AUS 178-179 K 1
Brylivka o UA 102-103 H 4
Bryne ☆ N 86-87 B 7
Bryson o USA (TX) 264-265 F 5
Bryson City o USA (NC) 282-283 D 5
Brzeg o• PL 92-93 O 3
Brześć Kujawski o PL 92-93 P 2
Brzesko o PL 92-93 Q 4
Bširri ☆ RL 128-129 G 5
Bảo Lôc o VN 158-159 J 5
Bảo Yên o VN 156-157 D 5
Bua o FJI 184 III b 2
Bua ~ MW 218-219 G 1
Bua ~ SUD 206-207 G 3
Bua Bay ≈ 184 III b 2
Buabuang o RI 164-165 H 4
Buafri o GH 202-203 K 5
Buaka o GH 202-203 J 6
Buala o SOL 184 I d 3
Bū al Ghirāf, Wādī ~ LAR 192-193 G 4
Bū al Gharāb, Bi'r < LAR 192-193 E 2
Bū al Hidān, Wādī ~ LAR 192-193 H 4
Buan, Pulau ⌒ RI 162-163 H 5
Buatan o RI 162-163 D 4
Bū Athlah o LAR 192-193 J 3
Buaya, Pulau ⌒ RI 162-163 F 4
Buaya Channel ≈ 166-167 K 6
Bua Yai o THA 158-159 G 3
Bu'ayrat al Hasun o LAR 192-193 F 2
Buba o GNB 202-203 C 4
Bubanda o ZRE 206-207 D 6
Bubanza o BU 212-213 C 5
Bubaque o• GNB 202-203 C 4
Bubi o ZW (Mvi) 218-219 F 5
Bubi ~ ZW 218-219 E 4
Bubi ~ ZW 218-219 F 5
Bubiai o• LT 94-95 H 4
Bubiki o EAT 212-213 D 5
Būbiyān, Ğazīrat ⌒ KWT 130-131 L 3
Bublitz = Bobolice o PL 92-93 O 2
Bublos ∴••• RL 128-129 F 5
Bubu ~ EAT 214-215 H 4
Bubu o PNG 183 F 3
Bububu ~ ZRE 210-211 K 6
Bubuya ~ ZRE 210-211 G 3
Buca o FJI 184 III b 2
Buçaco o ANG 216-217 F 5
Bucak ☆ TR 128-129 D 4
Bucalemu o RCH 78-79 C 3
Bucaramanga ☆ CO 60-61 E 4
Bucareli Bay ≈ 32-33 D 4
Bucas Grande Island ⌒ RP 160-161 F 8
Buccaneer Archipelago ⌒ AUS 172-173 F 3
Buccaneer Beach ≃ USA 286-287 R 3
Bucca Reef ≃• TT 60-61 L 2
Buchan o AUS 180-181 K 4
Buchanan o CDN (SAS) 232-233 Q 4
Buchanan ☆ LB 202-203 E 7
Buchanan o USA (GA) 284-285 F 3
Buchanan o USA (MI) 272-273 C 6
Buchanan o USA (ND) 258-259 J 4
Buchanan o USA (OR) 244-245 G 7
Buchanan o USA (VA) 280-281 G 6
Buchanan, Lake o AUS 178-179 H 1
Buchanan, Lake < USA (TX) 266-267 J 3
Buchanan Bay ≈ 26-27 N 4
Buchanan Highway II AUS 172-173 J 4
Buchanan Caves • AUS 180-181 K 4
Buchan Gulf ≈ 26-27 Q 8
Buchans o CDN (NFL) 242-243 M 4
Buchans Junction o CDN (NFL) 242-243 M 4
Bucharest = București ★• RO 102-103 E 5
Bucheke o PK 138-139 D 4
Buchenwald o• D 92-93 L 3
Buch'isi o ETH 208-209 C 5
Buchon, Point ▲ USA (CA) 248-249 D 4
Buchwa o ZW 218-219 F 5
Buck, Lake o AUS 172-173 K 5
Buckambool Mountain ▲ AUS 178-179 H 6
Buckatunna Creek ~ USA 268-269 M 5
Buck Creek ~ CDN 228-229 H 2
Buck Creek ~ USA 264-265 D 4
Buck Creek ~ USA 276-277 L 3
Buckeye o USA (AZ) 256-257 C 5
Buckeye o USA (NM) 256-257 M 6
Buckeye Lake o USA (OH) 280-281 D 4
Buckhannon o USA (WV) 280-281 F 4
Buckhorn o USA (NM) 256-257 G 5
Buckhorn Draw ~ USA 266-267 G 3
Buckhorn Lake o CDN (ONT) 238-239 G 4
Buckhorn Reservoir < USA (KY) 276-277 M 3
Buckingham o CDN (QUE) 238-239 K 3
Buckingham Bay ≈ 174-175 C 3
Buckingham Downs o AUS 178-179 E 2
Buckingham Island ⌒ CDN 24-25 a 2
Buck Lake o CDN (ALB) 232-233 D 2
Buckland o USA 20-21 K 4
Buckland, Monte ▲ RA 80 H 7
Buckland River ~ USA 20-21 K 4
Buckley o USA (WA) 244-245 C 3
Buckley Bay ≈ 16 G 15
Buckley Bay o CDN (BC) 230-231 E 4
Buckley River ~ AUS 174-175 E 7
Bucklin o USA (KS) 262-263 G 7
Buckmuische = Ezemieki o LV 94-95 K 3
Buckner Creek ~ USA 262-263 F 7
Buck Ridge o CDN (BC) 228-229 M 4
Bucksport o USA (ME) 278-279 N 4
Buck Valley o USA (PA) 280-281 H 4
Buco Zau o ANG 210-211 D 6
Buctouche o CDN (NB) 240-241 L 4
București ★• RO 102-103 E 5
Bucyrus o USA (OH) 280-281 D 3
Buda o USA (TX) 266-267 K 3
Budaka o EAU 212-213 D 3
Budalin o MYA 142-143 J 4
Bù Đăng o VN 158-159 J 5
Budapest ★•• H 92-93 P 5
Búðardalur ☆ IS 86-87 c 2
Budarino o KZ 96-97 G 8
Budaun o IND 138-139 G 5
Budawang Range ▲▲ AUS 180-181 L 3
Bud Bud o SP 208-209 H 6
Budd, Pulau ⌒ RI 166-167 F 1
Buddabadah o AUS 178-179 J 6
Buddha Park • THA 158-159 H 3
Budd Land ≃ ARK 16 G 12
Bude o USA (MS) 268-269 K 5
Budënnovsk o RUS 126-127 F 5
Budi, Lago o RCH 78-79 C 5
Budibudi Islands ⌒ PNG 183 G 5
Buding o RI 162-163 G 6
Búðir o IS 86-87 b 2
Budjala o ZRE 210-211 G 2
Budogošč' o RUS 94-95 N 2
Budongquan o VRC 144-145 J 3
Budu o MAL 162-163 J 4
Budu, Tanjung ▲ MAL 162-163 J 3
Budungbudung ~ RI 164-165 F 5
Budva o• YU 100-101 G 3
Budweis = České Budějovice o CZ 92-93 N 4
Buéa ☆• CAM 204-205 H 6
Buedu o WAL 202-203 E 5
Buefjorden ≈ 86-87 B 6
Buela o ANG 216-217 C 2
Buena o USA (WA) 244-245 E 4
Buena Esperanza o RA 78-79 G 3
Buena Hora o BOL 70-71 D 3
Buenaventura o C 54-55 G 4
Buenaventura o CO 60-61 C 6
Buenaventura o MEX (CHA) 50-51 F 3
Buenaventura o MEX (YUC) 52-53 L 1
Buenaventura, Bahía de ≈ 60-61 C 6
Buena Vista ∴• BH 52-53 K 3
Buena Vista o BOL (PAN) 70-71 D 2
Buena Vista o BOL (SAC) 70-71 F 5
Buenavista o CO 60-61 E 5
Buena-vista o CO 60-61 D 3
Buenavista o MEX (CHI) 52-53 H 3
Buenavista o MEX (SIN) 50-51 E 5
Buena Vista o PY 76-77 J 4
Buena Vista o RA 76-77 D 4
Buenavista o RP (MAR) 160-161 D 6
Buenavista o RP (ZAS) 160-161 E 9
Buena Vista o USA (CO) 254-255 J 5
Buena Vista o USA (GA) 284-285 F 4
Buena Vista o USA (VA) 280-281 G 6
Buena Vista o YV 60-61 G 4
Buena Vista, Bahía ≈ 54-55 F 3
Buena Vista Alta o PE 64-65 C 6
Buena Vista Island = Vatilau Island ⌒ SOL 184 I d 3
Buena Vista Lake o USA (CA) 248-249 E 4
Buenavista Tomatlán o MEX 52-53 C 2
Buendía, Embalse de < E 98-99 F 4
Buenga ~ ANG 216-217 C 3
Bueno, Río ~ RCH 78-79 C 6
Bueno Brandão o BR 72-73 G 7
Buenópolis o BR 72-73 H 4
Buenos Aires o CO (AMA) 66-67 B 4
Buenos Aires o CO (MET) 60-61 E 6
Buenos Aires o CO (TOL) 60-61 D 5
Buenos Aires o CO (VAU) 64-65 F 1
Buenos Aires o CR 52-53 C 7
Buenos Aires □ RA 78-79 H 3
Buenos Aires ★•• RA (BUA) 78-79 K 3
Buenos Aires, Lago o RA 80 E 3
Buenos Aires Lérida o CO 66-67 B 2
Buen Pasto o RA 80 F 2
Buesaco o CO 64-65 D 1
Buet, Rivière ~ CDN 36-37 O 4
Buey o CO 60-61 C 4
Buey Arriba o C 54-55 G 4
Bueyeros o USA (NM) 256-257 M 3
Bueyes, Cerro de los ▲ RA 78-79 D 4
Búfala o MEX 50-51 G 4
Bufalo, Reserva Parcial do ⊥ ANG 216-217 B 6
Bufareh o RI 166-167 K 3
Buffalo o CDN (ALB) 232-233 H 5
Buffalo o CDN (SAS) 232-233 N 6
Buffalo o USA (IA) 274-275 H 3
Buffalo o USA (MN) 270-271 E 5
Buffalo o USA (MO) 276-277 B 3
Buffalo o USA (ND) 258-259 K 5
Buffalo o USA (OK) 264-265 E 2
Buffalo o USA (SD) 260-261 C 1
Buffalo o USA (TN) 276-277 G 5
Buffalo o USA (TX) 266-267 L 2
Buffalo o USA (WV) 280-281 E 5
Buffalo o USA (WY) 252-253 M 2
Buffalo o• USA (NY) 278-279 C 6
Buffalo Bill Ranch State Historic Park ∴ USA (NE) 262-263 F 3
Buffalo Bill Reservoir o USA (WY) 252-253 J 2
Buffalo Center o USA (IA) 274-275 E 1
Buffalo City o USA (AR) 276-277 C 4
Buffalo Creek ~ CDN 32-33 O 3
Buffalo Gap National Grassland ⊥ USA (SD) 260-261 D 3
Buffalo Head Hills ▲▲ CDN 32-33 M 3
Buffalo Hump ▲ USA (ID) 250-251 D 6
Buffalo Lake o CDN (ALB) 232-233 F 3
Buffalo Lake o CDN (NWT) 30-31 M 5
Buffalo Lake o USA (TX) 264-265 B 4
Buffalo Mountain ▲ USA (NV) 246-247 G 3
Buffalo National River ⊥ USA (AR) 276-277 C 5
Buffalo Pound Provincial Park ⊥ CDN (SAS) 232-233 N 5
Buffalo River ~ CDN 30-31 M 6
Buffalo River ~ CDN 32-33 M 3
Buffalo River ~ USA 268-269 J 5
Buffalo River ~ USA 270-271 G 6
Buffalo River ~ USA 276-277 C 4
Buffalo River ~ USA 276-277 G 5
Buffalo Springs National Reserve ⊥ EAK 212-213 F 3
Buff Bay o JA 54-55 G 5
Buffels Drift o ZA 218-219 D 6
Buffelsrivier ~ ZA 220-221 J 5
Buffelsrivier ~ ZA 220-221 K 4
Bufflé Noir o CAM 204-205 K 5
Buford o USA (CO) 254-255 H 4
Buford o USA (GA) 284-285 F 2
Buford o USA (ND) 258-259 D 4
Buford o USA (OH) 280-281 C 4
Buford o USA (WY) 252-253 N 5
Buftea o RO 102-103 D 5
Bug ~ PL 92-93 R 2
Buga o CO 60-61 C 6
Buga o MAU 146-147 M 2
Buga o WAN 204-205 G 4
Bugaboo Alpine Provincial Recreation Area ⊥ CDN (BC) 230-231 N 3
Bugadi o EAU 212-213 D 3
Bugala Island ⌒ EAU 212-213 D 4
Bugana o WAN 204-205 G 5
Bugant o MAU 148-149 H 3
Bugdajly o TM 136-137 D 5
Buge o VRC 144-145 M 5
Bugembe o EAU 212-213 D 3
Bugene o EAT 212-213 C 4
Buggs Island Lake o USA (VA) 280-281 H 7
Bugi o• RI 166-167 K 3
Bugingkalo o RI 164-165 G 6
Bugiri o EAU 212-213 D 3
Bugojno o BIH 100-101 F 2
Bugrino o RUS 88-89 U 2
Bugsuk Island ⌒ RP 160-161 B 8
Bugt o VRC 150-151 C 3
Buguey o RP 160-161 D 3
Bugui Point ▲ RP 160-161 E 6
Bugul'ma ☆ RUS 96-97 H 6
Bugul'minsko-Belebeevskaja vozvyšennost' ▲▲ RUS 96-97 H 6
Bugunda o RUS 118-119 G 9
Buguruslan ☆ RUS 96-97 H 7
Buhara = Buhoro ☆•• UZ 136-137 J 5
Buharskaja oblast' □ UZ 136-137 H 4
Bu He ~ VRC 144-145 M 2
Buhera o ZW 218-219 F 4
Buhl o USA (ID) 252-253 D 4
Buhlandshahr o IND 138-139 F 5
Buhoro ☆•• UZ 136-137 J 5
Buhtarma ~ KZ 124-125 O 4
Buhta Sytygan-Tala ≈ 110-111 S 4
Buhu ~ EAT 212-213 E 6
Buick o CDN 32-33 K 3
Buiko o EAT 212-213 G 6
Builth Wells o GB 90-91 F 5
Bū'in o IR 136-137 B 7
Buin o PNG 184 I b 2
Bui National Park ⊥ GH 202-203 J 5
Buinsk ☆ RUS 96-97 F 6
Buir Nur ~ VRC 148-149 N 4
Buitenzorg = Bogor o RI 168 B 3
Buitepos o NAM 216-217 E 11
Buiucu o BR 66-67 J 5
Buj o RUS 94-95 R 2
Buj ~ RUS 96-97 J 5
Bujanovac o YU 100-101 H 3
Bujant o MAU 148-149 H 4
Bujant gol ~ MAU 148-149 C 4
Bujaraloz o E 98-99 G 4
Bujaru o BR 62-63 K 6
Bujaru, Rio ~ BR 68-69 E 2
Bujnaksk o RUS 126-127 G 6
Bujukly o RUS 122-123 K 4
Bujumbura ★• BU 212-213 B 5
Bujunda ~ RUS 120-121 P 2
Buk o PNG 183 B 5
Buka o UZ 136-137 L 4
Bukadan o RI 164-165 G 3
Bukačača o RUS 118-119 H 9
Bukadaban Feng ▲ VRC 144-145 H 2
Bukairiya, al- o KSA 130-131 H 4
Buka Island ⌒ PNG 184 I b 1
Bukama o ZRE 214-215 C 5
Bu Kammāsh o LAR 192-193 D 1
Bukantov toglari ▲▲ UZ 136-137 H 3
Bukasa Island ⌒ EAU 212-213 D 4
Bukat, Pulau ⌒ RI 164-165 E 2
Bukaua o PNG 183 D 4
Bukavu ☆ ZRE 212-213 B 5
Bukedea o EAU 212-213 E 3
Bukene o EAT 212-213 D 6
Bukeya o ZRE 214-215 D 6
Bukhit o SUD 206-207 H 3
Bukhoro = Buhoro ☆•• UZ 136-137 J 5
Bukima o EAT 212-213 D 4
Bukitkemuning o RI 162-163 F 7
Bukit Lata Papalang ▲ MAL 162-163 D 2
Bukittinggi •• RI 162-163 D 5
Bükk ▲▲ H 92-93 Q 4
Bukkāpatna o IND 140-141 G 4
Bukken Fiord ≈ 26-27 C 3
Bükki Nemzeti Park ⊥ H 92-93 Q 4
Bukoba ☆ EAT 212-213 C 4
Bukoloto o EAU 212-213 D 3
Bukombe o EAT 212-213 D 5
Bukrane o RI 166-167 F 5
Büktyrma bögeni < KZ 124-125 N 4
Bukuru o WAN 204-205 H 4
Būl, Kūh-e ▲ IR 134-135 E 3
Bula o GNB 202-203 C 3
Bula o PNG 183 A 5
Bula o ZRE 212-213 B 3
Bula, Cachoeira ~ BR 66-67 C 2
Bula Atumba o ANG 216-217 C 4
Bulacaue Point ▲ RP 160-161 E 7
Bulacle o SP 208-209 H 6
Bulaevo ☆ KZ 124-125 G 1
Bulag o MAU 148-149 J 3
Bulagansk o RUS 118-119 E 9
Bulagi o RI 164-165 H 4
Bulahdelah o AUS 180-181 M 2
Bulaka ~ RI 166-167 K 5
Bulalacao Island ⌒ RP 160-161 D 7
Bulalakao o RP 160-161 D 6
Bulan o RP 160-161 E 6
Bulanaš o RUS 96-97 M 5
Bulancak ☆ TR 128-129 H 2
Bulanghe o VRC 154-155 F 2
Bulangu o WAN 198-199 E 6
Bulanık ☆ TR 128-129 K 3
Būlāq o ET 194-195 E 5
Bulava o RUS 122-123 J 3
Bulawa, Gunung ▲ RI 164-165 H 3
Bulawayo ☆• ZW 218-219 E 5
Bulaya o Z 214-215 F 5
Bulbodney Creek ~ AUS 180-181 J 2
Bul'buhta o RUS 118-119 H 6
Bulbula o ETH 208-209 D 5
Buldan ☆ TR 128-129 C 3
Buldāna o IND 138-139 F 9
Buldibuyo o PE 64-65 D 6
Buldir Island ⌒ USA 22-23 D 6
Büldyrtty ~ KZ 96-97 H 9
Buleleng o RI 164-165 H 5
Bulenga o GH 202-203 J 5
Bulga Downs o AUS 176-177 E 4
Bulgan o MAU 146-147 L 2
Bulgan o MAU (ÖMN) 148-149 F 5
Bulgan □ MAU 148-149 F 3
Bulgan ☆ MAU (BUL) 148-149 F 3
Bulgan = Burènhajrhan o MAU 146-147 K 2
Bulgan = Šargalant o MAU 146-147 K 2
Bulgan gol ~ MAU 146-147 K 2
Bulgar ☆ RUS 96-97 F 6
Bulgaria = Bălgarija ■ BG 102-103 C 6
Bulgnéville o F 90-91 K 7
Buli o RI 164-165 L 3
Bū Lifiyat o UAE 134-135 E 6
Buliluyan, Cape ▲ RP 160-161 B 8
Bulimba o AUS 174-175 G 5
Bulisa o EAU 212-213 C 2
Buliya ⌒ FJI 184 III b 3
Bulkley Ranges ▲▲ CDN 228-229 G 2
Bulkley River ~ CDN 32-33 G 4
Bullabulling o AUS 176-177 F 5
Bullara o AUS 172-173 B 7
Bullard o USA (TX) 264-265 J 6
Bulla Regia ∴•• TN 190-191 G 2
Bullaxaar o SP 208-209 G 3
Bull Creek ~ CDN 232-233 L 6
Bullecourt o AUS 174-175 E 7
Bullen, Cape ▲ CDN 24-25 d 3
Bullen River ~ CDN 30-31 S 3
Buller, Mount ▲ AUS 180-181 J 4
Bullfinch o AUS 176-177 E 5
Bull Harbour o CDN (BC) 230-231 B 3
Bullhead City o USA (AZ) 256-257 A 3
Bulli o AUS 180-181 L 3
Bull Island ⌒ USA (SC) 284-285 L 4
Bullita Out Station o AUS 172-173 K 4
Bull Lake o CDN 30-31 R 5
Bull Mountains ▲▲ USA 250-251 L 5
Bullock o USA (NC) 282-283 J 4
Bullock's Harbour o BS 54-55 G 2
Bulloo Downs o AUS 176-177 E 2
Bulloo River ~ AUS 178-179 H 4
Bullo River o AUS 172-173 J 3
Bullpound Creek ~ CDN 232-233 G 4
Bull River ~ CDN 230-231 O 4
Bulls o NZ 182 E 4
Bulls Bay ≈ 284-285 L 4
Bull Shoals Lake o USA (AR) 276-277 C 4
Büllsport o NAM 220-221 C 2
Bulmer Lake o CDN 30-31 J 4
Bulnajn Nuruu ▲▲ MAU 148-149 C 3
Bulnes o RCH 78-79 C 4
Bulo Balamal o SP 212-213 J 2
Buloke, Lake o AUS 180-181 G 4
Bulolo o PNG 183 D 4
Bulolo River ~ PNG 183 D 4
Bulongo o ZRE 210-211 H 6
Buloo River ~ AUS 178-179 H 3
Bulqizë o• AL 100-101 H 4
Bultfontein o ZA 220-221 H 4
Bulu o RI 168 D 3
Buluan o RP 160-161 F 9
Buluan ~ RP 160-161 F 9
Buluan Lake o RP 160-161 F 9
Bulukumba o RI 164-165 G 6
Bulukutu o ZRE 210-211 H 4
Bulula o ZRE 212-213 A 6
Bulumuri o PNG 183 F 3
Bulun o RUS (SAH) 120-121 E 2
Bulun ~ RUS 112-113 H 4
Bulungu o ZRE (Ban) 210-211 G 6
Bulungu o ZRE (KOC) 216-217 F 3
Bulunkol o VRC 146-147 B 6
Bulupulu, Tanjung ▲ RI 164-165 G 5
Bulus o RUS 118-119 O 4
Bulusan o RP 160-161 F 6
Bulusan Vulcano ▲ RP 160-161 F 6
Bulwark o CDN (ALB) 232-233 G 3
Bulwer o ZA 220-221 J 4
Bulyea o CDN (SAS) 232-233 O 4
Buma ~ ZRE 210-211 F 5
Bū Marim o LAR 192-193 J 1
Bumba o ZRE 210-211 J 2
Bümbah o LAR 192-193 K 1
Bumbat o MAU 148-149 G 4
Bumbire Island ⌒ EAT 212-213 C 4
Bumble Bee o USA (AZ) 256-257 C 4
Bum Bum, Pulau ⌒ MAL 160-161 C 10
Bumbuna o WAL 202-203 E 5
Bumi Hills o ZW 218-219 E 3
Bumijawa o RI 168 C 3
Bumpus, Mount ▲ CDN 24-25 P 6
Buna o EAK 212-213 G 3
Buna o ZRE 210-211 G 5
Bunabun o PNG 183 C 3
Bunam o PNG 183 C 3
Bunapas o PNG 183 C 3
Bunbury o AUS 176-177 C 6
Bunda o EAT 212-213 D 5
Bundaberg o AUS 178-179 M 3
Bunda Bunda o AUS 174-175 G 7
Bundarra o AUS 178-179 L 6
Bundeena o AUS 178-179 G 4
Bundey, Mount ▲ AUS 172-173 K 2
Bundey River ~ AUS 178-179 C 1
Bündi o IND 138-139 E 7
Bundi o PNG 183 C 3
Bundibugyo o EAU 212-213 C 3
Bundick Creek ~ USA 268-269 G 6
Bundjalung National Park ⊥ AUS 178-179 M 5
Bunduqiya o SUD 206-207 K 6
Bunga ~ ZRE 210-211 K 3
Bunga, River ~ WAN 204-205 H 3
Bungadi o ZRE 206-207 H 6
Bungalaut, Selat ≈ 162-163 C 6
Bungamas o RI 162-163 E 6
Bungbulang o RI 168 B 3
Bunger Oasis ⌒ ARK 16 G 11
Bungi o RI 164-165 H 6
Bungikamasi, Pulau ⌒ RI 168 E 6
Bungil Creek ~ AUS 178-179 K 4
Bungku o RI 164-165 G 5
Bungle Bungle National Park ⊥ AUS 172-173 J 4
Bungle Bungle Range ▲▲ AUS 172-173 J 4
Bungo o ANG 216-217 C 3
Bungoma o EAK 212-213 E 3
Bungo-suido ≈ 152-153 E 8
Bungo-takada o J 152-153 D 8
Bung Sam Phan o THA 158-159 F 3
Bungtlang o IND 142-143 H 4
Bungudu o WAN 198-199 C 6
Bungunya o AUS 178-179 K 5
Buni o WAN 204-205 K 3
Bunia o ZRE 212-213 C 3
Bunie o ZRE 212-213 A 2
Buninyong o AUS 180-181 G 4
Bunji o IND 138-139 E 2
Bunker o USA (MO) 276-277 D 3
Bunker Group ⌒ AUS 178-179 M 2
Bunker Hill o USA 20-21 H 4
Bunkerville o USA (NV) 248-249 K 3
Bunkie o USA (LA) 268-269 H 6
Bunnell o USA (FL) 286-287 H 2
Bunneringee o AUS 180-181 F 2
Bunsuru ~ WAN 198-199 C 6
Bunta o RI 164-165 H 4
Buntharig o THA 158-159 H 3
Buntu o RI 168 C 3
Bununu o WAN 204-205 H 4
Bunut o BRU 164-165 D 1
Bunyakiri o ZRE 212-213 B 5
Bünyan ☆ TR 128-129 F 3
Bunyan, Paul & Blue Ox Statue • USA (MN) 270-271 D 3
Bunyanyi, Lake o EAU 212-213 B 4
Bunyu, Pulau ⌒ RI 164-165 E 2
Bunza o WAN 204-205 E 2
Buolkalah ~ RUS 110-111 M 3
Buôn Ma Thuôt ☆• VN 158-159 K 4
Buor-Ėekit ~ RUS 110-111 P 4
Buor-Haja, guba ≈ 110-111 S 4
Buor-Haja, mys ▲ RUS 110-111 T 4
Buor-Jurjah ~ RUS 110-111 Z 6
Buotama ~ RUS 118-119 N 5
Bupul o RI 166-167 L 5
Buqa', al- o KSA 132-133 D 5
Buqda Caqable o SP 208-209 G 6
Bur o RUS (IRK) 116-117 N 6
Bur ~ RUS 110-111 O 4
Bura o EAK 212-213 G 4
Buraan o SP 208-209 J 3
Buraatyn davaa ▲ MAU 146-147 K 1
Buraevo ☆ RUS 96-97 J 6
Buraida ☆ KSA 130-131 H 4
Buraika, al- o KSA 132-133 A 3
Buraimi, al- o OM 134-135 F 6
Burakin o AUS 176-177 D 5
Būrālān o IR 128-129 L 3
Buram o SUD 206-207 G 3
Burang o VRC 144-145 C 5
Buranhem, Rio ~ BR 72-73 L 4
Burannoe o RUS 96-97 J 8
Buras o USA (LA) 268-269 L 7
Bū Rashādah, Wādī < LAR 192-193 G 4
Burauen o RP 160-161 F 7
Buraydah = Buraida ☆ KSA 130-131 H 4
Burayqah o SUD 200-201 E 4
Burbank o USA (CA) 248-249 F 5
Burbank o USA (WA) 244-245 G 4
Burchard o USA (NE) 262-263 K 4
Burcher o AUS 180-181 J 2
Burco ☆ SP 208-209 G 4
Burdalyk o TM 136-137 J 5
Burdekin Dam < AUS 174-175 J 7
Burden o USA (KS) 262-263 K 7
Burdulba o AUS 172-173 L 2
Burdur ☆• TR 128-129 D 4
Burdur Gölü o TR 128-129 D 4
Burē o ETH (Ilu) 208-209 B 4
Burē o ETH (Wel) 208-209 C 3
Bureau, Lac o CDN (QUE) 236-237 N 4
Bureimi o RN 204-205 E 2
Bureinskij hrebet ▲▲ RUS 122-123 E 4
Bureinskiy Khrebet = Bureinskij hrebet ▲▲ RUS 122-123 E 4
Bureja ~ RUS 122-123 C 4
Burejnskij zapovednik ⊥ RUS 122-123 F 3
Burejnskoe vodohranilišče < RUS 122-123 D 3
Burengapara o IND 142-143 G 3
Burènhajrhan o MAU 146-147 K 2
Bureo, Río ~ RCH 78-79 C 4
Burera, Lac o RWA 212-213 B 4
Burevestnik o RUS 122-123 M 6
Bürfell o IS 86-87 d 2
Būr Fu'ād o ET 194-195 F 2
Burğ o OM 132-133 H 5
Burgagylkan ~ RUS 120-121 M 3
Burgal-'Arab o ET 194-195 D 2
Burgas o BG 102-103 E 6
Bur Gavo o SP 212-213 H 4
Burgaw o USA (NC) 282-283 K 6
Burgdorf o USA (ID) 250-251 D 6
Burgdorf Hot Springs • USA (ID) 250-251 D 6
Burgenland □ A 92-93 O 5
Burgeo o CDN (NFL) 242-243 L 5
Burgeo Bank ≃ 242-243 L 5
Burgersdorp o ZA 220-221 H 5
Burgersfort o ZA 220-221 K 2
Burgers Pass ▲ ZA 220-221 D 6
Burges, Mount ▲ AUS 176-177 F 5
Burgess o USA (VA) 280-281 J 6
Burgess, Mount ▲ CDN 20-21 V 3
Burgis o CDN (SAS) 232-233 Q 4
Burgo de Osma, El o E 98-99 F 4
Burgos o•• E 98-99 F 3
Burgos o RP 160-161 C 4
Burgoyne Bay ≈ 36-37 O 4
Burgsvik o S 86-87 J 8
Burgundy = Bourgogne □ F 90-91 K 8
Burhala o RUS 120-121 N 2
Burhan Budai Shan ▲▲ VRC 144-145 K 3
Burhan buudaj ▲ MAU 148-149 C 5
Burhaniye ☆ TR 128-129 B 3
Burhānpur o IND 138-139 F 9
Burhi Rapti ~ IND 142-143 C 2
Buri o BR 72-73 F 7
Buri ⌒ ER 200-201 J 5
Burias Island ⌒ RP 160-161 E 6
Burias Passage ≈ 160-161 E 6
Burica, Punta ▲ PA 52-53 C 7
Buried Village • NZ 182 F 3
Burien o USA (WA) 244-245 C 3
Burigi, Lake o EAT 212-213 C 5
Burigi Game Reservat ⊥ EAT 212-213 C 5
Burin o CDN (NFL) 242-243 N 5
Burin Peninsula ~ CDN 242-243 N 5
Buri Ram o THA 158-159 G 3
Buritaca • CO 60-61 E 2
Buritama o BR 72-73 E 6
Buriti, Ribeiro ~ BR 70-71 K 7
Buriti, Rio ~ BR 68-69 G 3
Buriti, Rio ~ BR 70-71 H 3
Buriti Alegre o BR 72-73 F 5
Buriti Bravo o BR 68-69 G 4
Buriticupu, Rio ~ BR 68-69 E 4
Buriti dos Lopes o BR 68-69 H 3
Buritirama o BR 68-69 G 7
Buritis o BR 72-73 G 3
Burjassot o E 98-99 G 5
Burji o WAN 204-205 H 3
Burkand'ja o RUS 120-121 M 2
Burkanoko, Lake o AUS 178-179 H 5
Burkburnett o USA (TX) 264-265 F 4
Burke o USA (SD) 260-261 G 3
Burke and Wills Roadhouse o AUS 174-175 F 6
Burke Channel ≈ 230-231 B 2
Burke Development Road II AUS 174-175 F 6
Burke River ~ AUS 178-179 E 1
Burke's Pass ▲ ZA 220-221 C 4
Burkesville o USA (KY) 276-277 K 4
Burketown o AUS 174-175 E 5
Burkett o USA (TX) 264-265 E 6
Burkeville o USA (TX) 268-269 G 6
Burkeville o USA (VA) 280-281 H 6
Burke & Wills Monument • AUS 178-179 F 4
Burkina Faso ■ BF 202-203 H 4
Burkitkala ∴• UZ 136-137 G 4
Bürkitti, tau ▲ KZ 124-125 H 4
Burkot o RUS 120-121 P 3
Burk's Falls o CDN (ONT) 238-239 F 3
Burkville o USA (AL) 284-285 D 4
Burla ~ RUS 124-125 L 2
Burleigh o AUS 174-175 G 7
Burleson o USA (TX) 264-265 G 6
Burley o USA (ID) 252-253 E 4
Burlingame o USA (KS) 262-263 L 6
Burlington o CDN (NFL) 242-243 M 3
Burlington o CDN (ONT) 238-239 F 5
Burlington o USA (CO) 254-255 N 4
Burlington o USA (IA) 274-275 G 4
Burlington o USA (KS) 262-263 L 6
Burlington o USA (KY) 276-277 L 1
Burlington o USA (NC) 282-283 H 4
Burlington o USA (OK) 264-265 F 2
Burlington o USA (VT) 278-279 H 4
Burlington o USA (WA) 244-245 C 2
Burlington o USA (WI) 274-275 K 2
Burlington Junction o USA (MO) 274-275 C 4
Burma = Myanmar ■ MYA 142-143 J 4
Burma Cave • KSA 130-131 K 5
Burmantovo o RUS 114-115 F 4
Burmis o CDN (ALB) 232-233 D 6
Burnaby o CDN (BC) 230-231 G 4
Burndoo o AUS 180-181 G 2
Burnet o USA (TX) 266-267 J 3
Burnett Bay ≈ 24-25 J 4
Burnett Highway II AUS 178-179 L 3
Burnett Lake o CDN 30-31 S 6
Burnett Range ▲▲ AUS 178-179 L 3
Burnett River ~ AUS 178-179 L 3
Burney o USA (CA) 246-247 D 3
Burney, Monte ▲ RCH 80 D 6
Burnham o CDN (SAS) 232-233 L 5
Burnham Out Station o AUS 178-179 F 2
Burnie-Somerset o AUS 180-181 H 6
Burning Coal Mines ∴ USA (ND) 258-259 D 5
Burnley o GB 90-91 F 5
Burnpur o IND 142-143 E 4
Burns o USA (CO) 254-255 J 4
Burns o USA (OR) 244-245 F 7
Burns o USA (WY) 252-253 O 5
Burns Flat o USA (OK) 264-265 E 3
Burnside o CDN (NFL) 242-243 P 4
Burnside, Lake o AUS 176-177 G 2
Burnside River ~ CDN 30-31 P 2
Burns Indian Reservation X USA (OR) 244-245 F 7
Burns Junction o USA (OR) 244-245 H 8
Burns Lake o CDN (BC) 228-229 J 2
Burnsville o USA (WV) 280-281 F 5
Burnsville Lake o USA (WV) 280-281 F 5
Burntbush River ~ CDN 236-237 J 3
Burnt Creek o CDN 36-37 Q 7
Burnt Ground o BS 54-55 H 3
Burnt Islands o CDN (NFL) 242-243 K 5
Burnt Lake o CDN 38-39 N 2
Burnt Lake = Lac Brulê o CDN 38-39 N 2
Burnt Ranch o USA (CA) 246-247 B 3

Brown, Mount — Burnt Ranch 309

Buro ~ **RUS** 108-109 W 6
Burpee, Cape ▲ **CDN** 24-25 j 6
Burqin o **VRC** 146-147 H 2
Burr o **CDN** (SAS) 232-233 N 3
Burra o **AUS** 180-181 E 2
Burracoppin o **AUS** 176-177 E 5
Burramurra Out Station o **AUS** 174-175 D 7
Burras, Río de las ~ **RA** 76-77 D 2
Burrel ☆ •• **AL** 100-101 H 4
Burrell Creek ~ **CDN** 230-231 L 4
Burrendong Reservoir < **AUS** 180-181 K 2
Burren Junction o **AUS** 178-179 K 6
Burr Ferry o **USA** (LA) 268-269 G 5
Burrgum Hill ▲ **AUS** 178-179 M 3
Burrinjuck Reservoir < **AUS** 180-181 K 3
Burro, El o **YV** 60-61 H 4
Burro, Serranías del ▲ **MEX** 50-51 H 3
Burr Oak Reservoir o **USA** (OH) 280-281 D 4
Burro Creek ~ **USA** 256-257 B 4
Burro Peak ▲ **USA** (NM) 256-257 G 6
Burrows o **CDN** (SAS) 232-233 Q 5
Burr Point ▲ **USA** 22-23 U 3
Burrton o **USA** (KS) 262-263 J 6
Burrumbeet, Lake o **AUS** 180-181 G 4
Burrum Heads o **AUS** 178-179 M 3
Burrwood o **USA** (LA) 268-269 L 8
Bursa ☆ •• **TR** 128-129 C 2
Būr Safāğa o **ET** 194-195 F 4
Būr Sa'īd ☆ **ET** 194-195 F 2
Burstall o **CDN** (SAS) 232-233 J 5
Būr Sūdān ☆ • **SUD** 200-201 H 3
Bur Tinle o **SP** 208-209 H 5
Burton o **CDN** (BC) 230-231 M 3
Burton o **USA** (NE) 262-263 G 2
Burton o **USA** (TX) 266-267 L 3
Burton o **USA** (WV) 280-281 F 4
Burton, Baie de o **ZRE** 212-213 B 6
Burton, Lac o **CDN** 36-37 K 7
Burton, Lake < **USA** (GA) 284-285 G 2
Burton upon Trent o **GB** 90-91 G 5
Burträsk o **S** 86-87 K 4
Buru, Pulau ⌒ **RI** 166-167 D 3
Burubajtal o **KZ** 124-125 J 6
Buru Island ⌒ **AUS** 183 B 5
Burukan o **RUS** 122-123 F 2
Burullus, Buhairat al- o **ET** 194-195 E 2
Burumburum o **WAN** 204-205 H 3
Burunda ~ **RUS** 122-123 D 2
Burundi ■ **BU** 212-213 B 5
Buruntuma o **GNB** 202-203 D 3
Buruolah ~ **RUS** 118-119 N 3
Bururi o **BU** 212-213 B 5
Bururi o **PNG** 183 B 2
Burutu o **WAN** 204-205 F 6
Burwash Bay ≈ 36-37 O 2
Burwell o **USA** (NE) 262-263 G 3
Burwick o **GB** 90-91 F 2
Buryatia = Respublika Burjatija ■ **RUS** 116-117 K 9
Buryn' o **UA** 102-103 H 2
Buryncyk mujisi ▲ **KZ** 126-127 J 5
Burynšik, mys ▲ **KZ** 126-127 J 5
Bury Saint Edmunds o • **GB** 90-91 H 5
Būš o **ET** 194-195 E 3
Busaira o **SYR** 128-129 J 5
Busaitā', al- ⊥ **KSA** 130-131 F 3
Busang ~ **RI** 162-163 K 4
Busanga o **ZRE** (EQU) 210-211 J 4
Busanga o **ZRE** (SHA) 214-215 C 6
Busanga Swamp ⌄ **Z** 218-219 C 2
Busanqo o **ZRE** 214-215 C 5
Busby o **CDN** (ALB) 232-233 E 2
Busby o **USA** (MT) 250-251 N 6
Būšehr ■ **IR** 134-135 D 4
Būšehr, Bandar-e ☆ • **IR** 134-135 D 4
Busembatia o **EAU** 212-213 D 3
Bush o **USA** (LA) 268-269 L 6
Bushat o **AL** 100-101 G 4
Bushell o **CDN** 30-31 P 6
Bushell Park o **CDN** (SAS) 232-233 N 5
Bushenyi o **EAU** 212-213 C 4
Bushe River Indian Reserve ✗ **CDN** 30-31 L 6
Bushland o **USA** (TX) 264-265 B 3
Bushman Drawings • **ZA** 220-221 F 5
Bushman Paintings • **SD** 220-221 K 3
Bushman Paintings • **ZA** 220-221 J 4
Bushnell o **USA** (FL) 286-287 G 3
Bushnell o **USA** (IL) 274-275 H 4
Bushnell o **USA** (NE) 262-263 C 3
Bushnell o **USA** (SD) 260-261 K 2
Bush River ~ **CDN** 228-229 R 4
Bushy Park o **AUS** 178-179 B 2
Busia o **EAU** 212-213 E 3
Businga o **ZRE** 210-211 H 2
Busira ~ **ZRE** 210-211 G 4
Busisi o **EAT** 212-213 D 5
Bus'k ☆ **UA** 102-103 D 3
Busoga ■ **EAU** 212-213 D 3
Busonga o **EAK** 212-213 E 3
Buṣra aš-šām o •• **SYR** 128-129 G 6
Busse o **RUS** 122-123 B 3
Busselton o **AUS** 176-177 C 6
Busseri ~ **SUD** 206-207 H 5
Bussol', proliv ≈ 122-123 O 5
Bustah, ozero o **RUS** 110-111 Y 3
Bustamante o **MEX** 50-51 K 6
Bustamante o **USA** (TX) 266-267 H 7
Bustamante, Punta ▲ **RA** 80 F 5
Busto Arsizio o **I** 100-101 B 2
Buston o **TJ** 136-137 L 4
Busu o **RI** 164-165 L 4
Busuanga o **RP** 160-161 C 6
Busuanga Island ⌒ **RP** 160-161 D 6
Busu-Djanoa o **ZRE** 210-211 H 3
Busu-Kwanga o **ZRE** 210-211 H 3
Busu-Mandji o **ZRE** 210-211 H 2
Busungwe o **EAU** 212-213 C 4
Busunju o **EAU** 212-213 D 3
Busunu o **GH** 202-203 K 5
But o **PNG** 183 B 2
Buta o **ZRE** 210-211 K 2
Butahuao, Cerro ▲ **RA** 78-79 D 5
Butain, al o **KSA** 130-131 H 4
Butajira o **ETH** 208-209 D 4
Butak o **PK** 134-135 K 4
Buta Ranquil o **RA** 78-79 E 4
Butare o • **RWA** 212-213 B 5
Butaritari Island ⌒ **KIB** 13 J 2
Butaš, ozero o **RUS** 114-115 G 7
Butat Raya o **SUD** 206-207 G 3
Bute o **AUS** 180-181 D 2
Butedale o **CDN** (BC) 228-229 F 3
Bute Giarti o **ETH** 208-209 C 6
Bute Inlet ≈ 230-231 D 3
Butemba o **EAU** 212-213 C 3
Butembo o **ZRE** 212-213 B 3
Butha-Buthe o **LS** 220-221 J 4
Buthidaung o **MYA** 142-143 H 5
Butiá o **BR** 74-75 E 8
Butiaba o **EAU** 212-213 C 3
Butler o **USA** (AL) 284-285 B 4
Butler o **USA** (GA) 284-285 F 4
Butler o **USA** (IN) 274-275 O 3
Butler o **USA** (MO) 274-275 D 6
Butler o **USA** (OK) 264-265 E 3
Butler o **USA** (PA) 280-281 G 3
Butler o **USA** (TX) 268-269 E 5
Butolo J. o **BR** 68-69 C 6
Buton, Pulau ⌒ **RI** 164-165 H 6
Buton, Selat ≈ 164-165 H 6
Buton Utara Reserve ⊥ **RI** 164-165 H 6
Buto River ~ **LB** 202-203 F 7
Butrint ∴ ••• **AL** 100-101 H 5
Butru o **AUS** 178-179 E 1
Buttahatchee River ~ **USA** 268-269 M 3
Butte o **CDN** (ALB) 232-233 D 3
Butte o **USA** (MT) 250-251 G 5
Butte o **USA** (ND) 258-259 G 4
Butte o **USA** (NE) 262-263 H 2
Butte, The ▲ **USA** 20-21 S 4
Butte Creek ~ **USA** 246-247 D 4
Butter Creek Pass ▲ **USA** (OR) 244-245 E 6
Butterpot Provincial Park ⊥ **CDN** (NFL) 242-243 P 5
Butterworth o **MAL** 162-163 D 2
Butterworth o **ZA** 220-221 J 6
Buttle Lake o **CDN** (BC) 230-231 D 4
Butt of Lewis ▲ **GB** 90-91 D 2
Button Islands ⌒ **CDN** 36-37 R 4
Buttonwillow o **USA** (CA) 248-249 E 4
Butu o **CAM** 204-205 H 6
Butu o **RI** 164-165 F 5
Butuan ☆ **RP** 160-161 F 8
Butuan Bay ≈ 160-161 F 8
Butuí, Rio ~ **BR** 76-77 J 5
Butung = Pulau Buton ⌒ **RI** 164-165 H 6
Butung, Tanjung ▲ **RI** 164-165 H 6
Butuo o **VRC** 156-157 C 3
Buturlinovka o **RUS** 102-103 M 2
Butwal o **NEP** 144-145 D 7
Buucagaan o **MAU** 148-149 D 4
Buulobarde o **SP** 212-213 K 2
Buur Hakkaba o **SP** 212-213 K 2
Buvuma Island ⌒ **EAU** 212-213 D 3
Buwaiš o **Y** 132-133 F 6
Buwenge o **EAU** 212-213 D 3
Buxar o **IND** 142-143 D 3
Buxton o **GUY** 62-63 E 2
Buxton o **USA** (OR) 244-245 B 5
Büyer Ahmad-o-Kūhgīlūye ■ **IR** 134-135 D 3
Buyo o **CI** 202-203 G 6
Buyo, Lac du < **CI** 202-203 G 6
Buyspoort ▲ **ZA** 220-221 F 6
Büyük Ada o **TR** 128-129 C 2
Büyükağrı Dağı (Ararat) ▲ •• **TR** 128-129 L 3
Büyük menderes Nehri ~ **TR** 128-129 C 3
Buyuni o **EAT** 214-215 K 4
Buyun Shan ▲ **VRC** 150-151 D 7
Buzači, poluostrov ⌄ **KZ** 126-127 J 5
Buzan ~ **RUS** 96-97 F 10
Būzanaj, kum ⊥ **KZ** 96-97 F 10
Buzău ☆ • **RO** 102-103 E 5
Buzdjak ☆ **RUS** 96-97 J 6
Buzi o **MOC** 218-219 H 4
Buzi, Rio ~ **MOC** 218-219 H 4
Buzi Gonbad o **AFG** 146-147 B 7
Búzios o **BR** 68-69 L 5
Búzios, Cabo dos ▲ **BR** 72-73 K 7
Buzluk Mağarası • **TR** 128-129 H 3
Buzovna o **AZ** 128-129 O 2
Buzuluk ☆ **RUS** 96-97 H 7
Buzuluk ~ **RUS** 102-103 N 2
Buzūn, al- o **Y** 132-133 G 6
Büzyldyk o **KZ** 124-125 E 3
Bwadela o **PNG** 183 F 5
Bwagaoia o **PNG** 183 G 6
Bwana-Mutombo o **ZRE** 216-217 E 3
Bwanga o **EAT** 212-213 C 5
Bwari o **WAN** 204-205 G 4
Bwatnapne o **VAN** 184 II b 2
Bwea Town o **LB** 202-203 F 7
Bwele-Milonda ~ **ZRE** 216-217 E 3
Bweni o **EAT** 214-215 K 4
Bwiam o **WAG** 202-203 B 3
Byadgi o **IND** 140-141 F 3
Byam Channel ≈ 24-25 T 3
Byam Martin Channel ≈ 24-25 S 2
Byam Martin Island ⌒ **CDN** 24-25 T 3
Bydgoszcz ☆ • **PL** 92-93 P 2
Byemoor o **CDN** (ALB) 232-233 F 4
Byers o **USA** (TX) 264-265 F 4
Byfield o **AUS** 178-179 L 2
Byfield National Park ⊥ **AUS** 178-179 L 2
Byford o **AUS** 176-177 D 6
Bygdeå o • **S** 86-87 K 4
Bygin ~ **KZ** 136-137 L 3
Bygin sukojmasy < **KZ** 136-137 L 3
Bygland ☆ **N** 86-87 C 7
Bykle o **N** 86-87 C 7
Bykovskaja, protoka ~ **RUS** 110-111 Q 3
Bykovskij o **RUS** 110-111 R 3
Bykovskij poluostrov ⌄ **RUS** 110-111 R 4
Bylas o **USA** (AZ) 256-257 E 5
Bylok o **TJ** 136-137 M 4
Bylong o **AUS** 180-181 L 2
Bylot Island ⌒ **CDN** 24-25 g 4
Bylyra ~ **RUS** 118-119 E 11
Bynoe River ~ **AUS** 174-175 F 5
Bynum o **USA** (MT) 250-251 G 4
Bynum Reservoir o **USA** (MT) 250-251 G 4
Byrakan ~ **RUS** 118-119 K 4
Byrd o **ARK** 16 F 25
Byrd Land ⊥ **ARK** 16 E 0
Byro o **AUS** 176-177 D 3
Byrock o **AUS** 178-179 J 6
Byron o **USA** (IL) 274-275 J 2
Byron o **USA** (MI) 272-273 F 5
Byron, Cape ▲ **AUS** 178-179 M 5
Byron, Isla ⌒ **RCH** 80 C 3
Byron Bay ≈ 36-37 V 7
Byron Bay ≈ 178-179 M 5
Byron Center o **USA** (MI) 272-273 D 5
Byron Sound ≈ 78-79 K 6
Byrranga, Gory ▲ **RUS** 108-109 U 5
Byske o **S** 86-87 K 4
Byskeälven ~ **S** 86-87 K 4
Byssa ~ **RUS** 122-123 D 2
Bystraja ~ **RUS** 108-109 V 5
Bystraja ~ **RUS** 120-121 R 7
Bystraja ~ **RUS** 120-121 S 6
Bystraja ~ **RUS** 120-121 R 5
Bystrinskij hrebet ▲ **RUS** 120-121 S 5
Bystrjanka o **RUS** 124-125 O 2
Bystryj Istok ☆ **RUS** 124-125 O 2
Bystryj Tanyp ~ **RUS** 96-97 J 6
Bystrzyca ~ **PL** 92-93 O 3
Bysyttah o **RUS** 118-119 H 4
Bytantaj ~ **RUS** 110-111 T 5
Bytom o **PL** 92-93 P 3
Bytów o • **PL** 92-93 O 1
Byumba o **RWA** 212-213 C 4
Byxelkrok o **S** 86-87 H 8
Byzanz = İstanbul ☆ ••• **TR** 128-129 C 2
Bzimah o **LAR** 192-193 K 5
Bzyb' ~ **GE** 126-127 D 6

C

Caaća o **TM** 136-137 G 6
Caacupé ☆ **PY** 76-77 J 3
Caaguazú o **PY** 76-77 J 3
Caala o **ANG** 216-217 C 6
Caamaño Sound ≈ 32-33 F 5
Caamaño Sound ≈ 228-229 E 4
Caapiranga o **BR** 66-67 G 4
Caapucu o **PY** 76-77 J 4
Caarapo o **BR** 76-77 K 2
Caatiba o **BR** 72-73 K 3
Caatingas ⊥ **BR** 68-69 G 7
Caazapá ☆ **PY** 76-77 J 4
Cab o **RP** 160-161 D 4
Cabaad, Raas ▲ **SP** 208-209 J 5
Cabacal, Rio ~ **BR** 70-71 H 4
Cabaceiras o **BR** 68-69 K 5
Cabadbaran o **RP** 160-161 F 8
Cabaiguán o **C** 54-55 F 3
Caballo o **USA** (NM) 256-257 H 6
Caballococha o **PE** 66-67 B 4
Caballones, Cayo ⌒ **C** 54-55 F 4
Caballo Reservoir < **USA** (NM) 256-257 H 5
Caballos, Bahia de ≈ 64-65 E 9
Caballos Mesteños, Llanos de los ⊥ **MEX** 50-51 G 3
Cabañas o **C** 54-55 D 3
Cabanatuan o **RP** 160-161 D 5
Cabangtohan o **RP** 160-161 D 7
Cabano o • **CDN** (QUE) 240-241 G 3
Cabarete o **DOM** 54-55 K 5
Cabarete, Punta ▲ • **DOM** 54-55 K 5
Cabatuan o **RP** 160-161 D 4
Čabda ~ **RUS** 120-121 F 4
Cabecea do Salsa, Igarapé ~ **BR** 66-67 F 5
Cabeceiras o **BR** (GOI) 72-73 G 3
Cabeceiras o **BR** (PIA) 68-69 G 4
Cabeceiras de Basto o **P** 98-99 D 4
Cabeço do Apa o **BR** 76-77 K 2
Cabedelo o **BR** 68-69 L 5
Cabelelo da Velha, Baía ≈ 68-69 F 2
Cabeza del Este, Cayo ⌒ **C** 54-55 F 4
Cabeza del Mar o **RCH** 80 E 6
Cabeza Mechuda, Punta ▲ **MEX** 50-51 D 5
Cabezas o **BOL** 70-71 F 6
Cabezas de San Juan ▲ **USA** (PR) 286-287 Q 2
Cabildo o **RCH** 78-79 D 2
Cabimas o **YV** 60-61 F 2
Cabinda ■ **ANG** 210-211 D 6
Cabinda ☆ **ANG** (Cab) 210-211 D 6
Cabinet Mountains ▲ **USA** 250-251 C 3
Cabinet Mountains Wilderness Area ⊥ **USA** (MT) 250-251 D 3
Cabingaan Island ⌒ **RP** 160-161 D 10
Cabitutu, Rio ~ **BR** 66-67 J 6
Cable o **USA** (WI) 270-271 G 4
Cable Beach ⊥ **AUS** 172-173 F 5
Cabo o **BR** 68-69 L 6
Cabo Blanco o **RA** 80 H 3
Cabo de Hornos, Parque Nacional ⊥ **RCH** 80 G 7
Cabo Delgado ■ **MOC** 214-215 K 7
Cabo Frio, Ilha do ⌒ **BR** 72-73 K 7
Čaboksar o **IR** 136-137 B 6
Cabo Ledo o **ANG** 216-217 B 4
Cabonga, Réservoir o **CDN** (QUE) 236-237 M 5
Cabool o **USA** (MO) 276-277 C 3
Caboolture o **AUS** 178-179 M 4
Cabo Orange, Parque Nacional do ⊥ **BR** 62-63 J 3
Cabo Polonio, Parque Forestal de ⊥ **ROU** 74-75 D 10
Cabora Bassa, Lago de < **MOC** 218-219 F 2
Caborca o • **MEX** 50-51 C 2
Cabo San Lucas o **MEX** 50-51 E 6
Cabot o **USA** (AR) 276-277 C 6
Cabot Head ▲ **CDN** (ONT) 238-239 D 3
Cabot Strait ≈ 38-39 O 5
Cabra Corral, Embalse < **RA** 76-77 E 3
Cabra Island ⌒ **RP** 160-161 D 6
Cabral o **DOM** 54-55 K 5
Cabral, Serra do ▲ **BR** 72-73 H 4
Cabramurra o **AUS** 180-181 K 3
Cabrera o **CO** 60-61 D 6
Cabrera o • **DOM** 54-55 L 5
Cabreras, Las ~ **C** 54-55 G 4
Cabrero o **RCH** 78-79 C 4
Cabreúva o **BR** 72-73 G 7
Cabri o **CDN** (SAS) 232-233 K 5
Cabri Lake o **CDN** (SAS) 232-233 J 4
Cabrillo National Monument • **USA** (CA) 248-249 G 7
Cabrobó o **BR** 68-69 J 6
Cabruta o **YV** 60-61 H 4
Cabuca o **GNB** 202-203 C 3
Cabudare o **YV** 60-61 G 2
Cabugao o **RP** 160-161 D 4
Cabure o **YV** 60-61 G 2
Cabure, El o **RA** 76-77 F 4
Cabure-i o **RA** 76-77 K 3
Caburgua, Lago o **RCH** 78-79 D 5
Cabuyaro o **CO** 60-61 E 5
Čača ~ **RUS** 118-119 J 9
Caçador o **BR** 74-75 E 6
Čačak o • **YU** 100-101 H 3
Cacao o **F** 62-63 H 3
Caçapava do Sul o **BR** 74-75 D 8
Cacaribaiteri o **YV** 60-61 J 6
Cacau Pirera o **BR** 66-67 G 4
Cáccia, Capo ▲ **I** 100-101 B 4
Cacequi o **BR** 76-77 K 5
Cáceres o **BR** 70-71 J 5
Cáceres o ••• **E** 98-99 D 5
Čačevičy o **BY** 94-95 L 5
Cachachi o **PE** 64-65 C 5
Cachapoal, Río ~ **RCH** 78-79 D 3
Cachari o **RA** 78-79 K 4
Cache o **USA** (OK) 264-265 F 4
Cache Creek o **CDN** (BC) 230-231 H 3
Cache Creek ~ **USA** 264-265 F 4
Cache Creek, West ~ **USA** 264-265 F 4
Cachendo o **PE** 70-71 B 5
Cache Peak ▲ **USA** (ID) 252-253 E 4
Cache River ~ **USA** 276-277 D 5
Cacheu ☆ **GNB** 202-203 B 3
Cacheu, Rio ~ **GNB** 202-203 C 3
Cachi o • **RA** 76-77 D 3
Cachí, Nevado de ▲ **RA** 76-77 D 3
Ca Chiên, Sông ~ **VN** 158-159 J 6
Cachimbo o **ANG** 216-217 F 4
Cachimbo, Serra do ▲ **BR** 66-67 J 6
Cachina, Quebrada ~ **RCH** 76-77 B 3
Cachingues o **ANG** 216-217 D 6
Cachipo o **YV** 60-61 J 3
Cachira o **CO** 60-61 E 4
Cachoeira o **BR** (AMA) 66-67 C 2
Cachoeira o **BR** (BAH) 72-73 L 2
Cachoeira Alta o **BR** 72-73 E 5
Cachoeira de Goiás o **BR** 72-73 E 4
Cachoeira do Arari o **BR** 62-63 K 6
Cachoeira do Sul o **BR** 74-75 D 8
Cachoeiras de Macacu o **BR** 72-73 J 7
Cachoeirinha o **BR** 72-73 G 5
Cachoeirinha, Cachoeira ~ **BR** 66-67 K 4
Cachoeirinha, Corredeira ~ **BR** 66-67 G 7
Cachoeirinho o **BR** 74-75 E 7
Cachoeiro de Itapemirim o **BR** 72-73 K 6
Cachos, Punta ▲ **RCH** 76-77 B 4
Cachueca o **ANG** 216-217 D 7
Cachuela Esperanza o **BOL** 70-71 E 2
Cachuma, Lake o **USA** (CA) 248-249 E 5
Cacimba de Dentro o **BR** 68-69 L 5
Cacina o **GNB** 202-203 C 4
Caciporé, Cabo ▲ **BR** 62-63 J 4
Caciporé, Rio ~ **BR** 62-63 J 4
Cacique Doble o **BR** 74-75 E 6
Cacoal o **BR** 70-71 G 2
Cacocum o **C** 54-55 G 4
Cacolo o **ANG** 216-217 E 5
Caconda o **ANG** 216-217 C 6
Cacouna o **CDN** (QUE) 240-241 F 3
Cactus o **USA** (TX) 264-265 C 2
Cactus Lake o **CDN** (SAS) 232-233 J 3
Caçu o **BR** 72-73 E 5
Cacuaco o **ANG** 216-217 B 4
Cacuchi ~ **ANG** 216-217 D 6
Cacuilo ~ **ANG** 216-217 E 4
Cacula o **ANG** 216-217 C 7
Caculé o **BR** 72-73 J 3
Cacumba, Ilha ⌒ **BR** 72-73 L 4
Cacumbi o **ANG** 216-217 E 5
Cacuria o **BR** 66-67 E 6
Cacuso o **ANG** 216-217 C 4
Cada, Río ~ **CO** 60-61 E 4
Cadaadley o **SP** 208-209 G 4
Cadaado o **SP** 208-209 H 5
Cadale o **SP** 212-213 L 2
Čadan ☆ **RUS** 116-117 E 10
Cadariri, Río ~ **BR** 66-67 J 6
Caddo o **USA** (OK) 264-265 H 4
Caddo o **USA** (TX) 264-265 F 6
Caddo Mills o **USA** (TX) 264-265 H 5
Caddo Mountains ▲ **USA** 276-277 B 6
Caddo River ~ **USA** 276-277 B 6
Čādegān o **IR** 134-135 D 2
Cadena, Arroyo de la ~ **MEX** 50-51 G 5
Cadereyta o **MEX** 50-51 J 5
Cadibarrawirracanna, Lake o **AUS** 178-179 C 5
Cadillac o **CDN** (QUE) 236-237 K 4
Cadillac o **CDN** (SAS) 232-233 L 6
Cadillac o **USA** (MI) 272-273 D 3
Cadillal, Embalse el < **RA** 76-77 E 4
Cádiz o **E** 98-99 D 6
Cadiz o **RP** 160-161 E 7
Cadiz o **USA** (CA) 248-249 J 5
Cadiz o **USA** (KY) 276-277 H 4
Cadiz o **USA** (OH) 280-281 F 3
Cádiz, Golfo de ≈ 98-99 D 6
Cadlao Island ⌒ **RP** 160-161 C 7
Cadman = Urd gol o **MAU** 146-147 L 2
Čadobec ~ **RUS** 116-117 J 6
Cadogan o **CDN** (ALB) 232-233 H 3
Cadogan Glacier ⊂ **CDN** 26-27 L 4
Cadogan Inlet ≈ 26-27 H 4
Cadomin o **CDN** (ALB) 228-229 R 3
Cadott o **USA** (WI) 270-271 G 6
Cadotte Lake o **CDN** 32-33 M 3
Cadotte River ~ **CDN** 32-33 M 3
Cadoux o **AUS** 176-177 D 5
Cadron Creek ~ **USA** 276-277 C 5
Caduman Point ▲ **RP** 160-161 F 7
Cadwell o **USA** (GA) 284-285 G 4
Caen ☆ • **F** 90-91 G 7
Caerdydd = Cardiff o **GB** 90-91 F 6
Caerfyrddin = Carmarthen o **GB** 90-91 E 6
Caernarfon o ••• **GB** 90-91 E 5
Caerphilly Castle •• **GB** 90-91 F 6
Caesaera Scugog, Lake o **CDN** (ONT) 238-239 G 4
Caesar Creek Lake < **USA** (OH) 280-281 C 4
Caetas o **BR** 68-69 K 6
Caeté o **BR** 72-73 J 5
Caeté, Baía do ≈ 68-69 E 2
Caeté, Rio ~ **BR** 66-67 C 7
Caetité o **BR** 72-73 J 3
Čaevo o **RUS** 94-95 P 2
Cafamaum o **BR** 68-69 H 7
Cafayate o • **RA** 76-77 E 4
Cafema, Serra ▲ **ANG** 216-217 B 8
Cafetal o **MEX** 52-53 K 2
Cafuma ~ **ANG** 216-217 E 8
Cagaan Bogd ▲ **MAU** 148-149 D 6
Cagaandörvölž o **MAU** 148-149 J 5
Cagaannuur o **MAU** 146-147 J 1
Cagaan-Ovoo o **MAU** 148-149 E 5
Cagaan-Uul = Šarga o **MAU** 148-149 D 3
Čagalvandi o **IR** 134-135 C 2
Čagan ~ **RUS** 96-97 G 8
Cagan Aman ☆ **RUS** 96-97 E 10
Cagayan ~ **RP** 160-161 D 4
Cagayan de Oro ☆ **RP** 160-161 F 8
Cagayan de Tawi Tawi Island ⌒ **RP** 160-161 C 9
Cagayan Islands ⌒ **RP** 160-161 D 8
Čagčarān o • **AFG** 134-135 L 1
Čagda o **RUS** (SAH) 118-119 M 4
Čagda o **RUS** (SAH) 120-121 D 4
Cageri o **GE** 126-127 E 6
Cagle o **USA** (TN) 276-277 K 5
Cagles Mill Lake o **USA** (IN) 274-275 M 5
Cágliari o **I** 100-101 B 5
Cágliari, Golfo di ≈ 100-101 B 5
Cagnano Varano o **I** 100-101 E 4
Čagojan o **RUS** 122-123 C 2
Čagra ~ **RUS** 96-97 F 7
Cagraray Island ⌒ **RP** 160-161 E 6
Caguán, Río ~ **CO** 64-65 E 1
Caguana, La o **USA** (PR) 286-287 P 2
Caguas o **USA** (PR) 286-287 P 2
Čagyl o **TM** 136-137 D 4
Čagyl'teniz, köli o **KZ** 124-125 F 1
Čāh Āb o **AFG** 136-137 L 6
Cahaba River ~ **USA** 284-285 C 4
Cahabón, Río ~ **GCA** 52-53 K 4
Cahama o **ANG** 216-217 C 8
Čahār Bāg o **AFG** 136-137 K 6
Čahār Borğak o **AFG** 134-135 K 3
Čāh Bahār o • **IR** 134-135 J 6
Čāh Bahār, Ra's-e ▲ **IR** 134-135 J 6
Čāh Čeibi, Hāmūn-e o **IR** 134-135 J 4
Caher = An Chathair o **IRL** 90-91 D 5
Čāh Gām o **IR** 136-137 D 7
Cahkwaktolik o **USA** 20-21 J 6
Cahobas, Las o **RH** 54-55 K 5
Cahokia Mounds ••• **USA** (IL) 274-275 H 6
Cahors ☆ • **F** 90-91 H 9
Cahotal o **C** 54-55 G 4
Čāh Sagak o **IR** 134-135 J 2
Cahuacho o **PE** 64-65 F 9
Cahuapanas o **PE** 64-65 D 4
Cahuilla Indian Reservation ✗ **USA** (CA) 248-249 H 6
Cahuinari, Río ~ **CO** 66-67 B 3
Cahul ☆ **MD** 102-103 F 5
Čāh Zardār o **IR** 134-135 H 5
Caí, Cachoeira do ~ **BR** 66-67 J 5
Caia o **MOC** 218-219 H 3
Caiabi, Cachoeira ~ **BR** 70-71 K 2
Caiabis, Serra dos ▲ **BR** 70-71 J 2
Caiambé o **BR** 66-67 E 4
Caianda o **ANG** 214-215 B 6
Caiapó, Rio ~ **BR** 68-69 D 6
Caiapó, Rio ~ **BR** 72-73 E 4
Caiapônia o **BR** 72-73 E 4
Caibarién o **C** 54-55 F 3
Caibi o **BR** 74-75 D 6
Caibiran o **RP** 160-161 F 7
Caicara o **YV** 60-61 K 3
Caiçara do Rio do Vento o **BR** 68-69 K 4
Caicedo o **CO** 60-61 D 4
Caicedonia o **CO** 60-61 D 5
Caico o **BR** 68-69 K 5
Caicos Islands ⌒ **GB** 54-55 J 4
Caicos Passage ≈ 54-55 J 3
Caicumbo o **ANG** 216-217 F 5
Cái Đầu o **VN** 158-159 H 5
Caigua o **YV** 60-61 J 3
Cái Lậy o **VN** 158-159 J 5
Caillou Bay ≈ 268-269 J 7
Caima o **BR** 68-69 B 3
Caimanero o **MEX** 50-51 F 6
Caimanero, Laguna del o **MEX** 50-51 F 6
Caimbambo o **ANG** (BGU) 216-217 C 6
Caimbambo ~ **ANG** 216-217 B 6
Caimito o **CO** 60-61 D 3
Caín, El o **RA** 78-79 E 6
Caine, Río ~ **BOL** 70-71 E 6
Cainta o **RP** 160-161 D 5
Caiongo o **ANG** 216-217 C 3
Caipe o **RA** 76-77 C 3
Caipupa o **ANG** 216-217 E 5
Cairari o **BR** 68-69 D 3
Cairn, Île ⌒ **CDN** 36-37 L 6
Cairn Mountain ▲ **USA** 20-21 N 6
Cairns o •• **AUS** 174-175 H 5
Cairns, Mount ▲ **AUS** 174-175 C 7
Cairns Lake o **CDN** (ONT) 234-235 J 3
Cairns Section ⊥ **AUS** 174-175 J 4
Cairo o **USA** (GA) 284-285 F 6
Cairo o **USA** (KY) 276-277 F 4
Cairo o **USA** (WV) 262-263 H 4
Cairo = al-Qāhira ☆ ••• **ET** 194-195 E 2
Cairo, Cape ▲ **CDN** 24-25 V 1
Cairu o **BR** 72-73 L 2
Caiseal = Cashel o • **IRL** 90-91 D 5
Caisleán an Bharraigh = Castlebar ☆ **IRL** 90-91 C 5
Caititu, Área Indígena ✗ **BR** 66-67 E 6
Caitou o **ANG** 216-217 B 7
Caiúa o **BR** 72-73 D 7
Caiundo o **ANG** 216-217 D 7
Caixa, Rio de ~ **BR** 72-73 J 2
Caiyuan o **VRC** 156-157 C 3
Caizi Hu o **VRC** 154-155 K 6
Čaja ~ **RUS** 114-115 R 5
Čaja ~ **RUS** 118-119 D 6
Čaja-Ajan, gory ▲ **RUS** 108-109 Z 7
Cajabamba o **EC** 64-65 C 2
Cajabamba o **PE** 64-65 C 5
Cajacay o **PE** 64-65 D 7
Cajamarca ☆ • **PE** 64-65 C 5
Cajamarquilla o **PE** 64-65 D 7
Čajan o **KZ** 136-137 L 3
Čajanda ~ **RUS** 118-119 F 5
Cajatambo o **PE** 64-65 D 7
Cajazeiras o **BR** 68-69 J 5
Cajazeiras, Rio ~ **BR** 68-69 C 4
Čajbuha o **RUS** 120-121 T 3
Cajcara del Orinoco o **YV** 60-61 H 4
Čajcyns'kij Kamen' ▲ **RUS** 88-89 U 3
Čajetina o **YU** 100-101 G 3
Cajidiocan o **RP** 160-161 E 6
Čajkovskij ☆ **RUS** 96-97 J 5
Cajobabo o **C** 54-55 H 4
Cajon o **USA** (CA) 248-249 G 5
Cajon, El o **USA** (CA) 248-249 H 7
Cajón, Embalse el < **HN** 52-53 L 4
Cajón del Maipo • **RCH** 78-79 D 2
Cajones, Río ~ **MEX** 52-53 F 3
Cajon Pass ▲ **USA** (CA) 248-249 G 5
Cajon Troncoso ~ **RCH** 78-79 D 4
Caju, Cachoeira do ~ **BR** 62-63 D 6
Cajuapara, Rio ~ **BR** 68-69 E 4
Cajuata o **BOL** 70-71 D 5
Cajueiro o **BR** (MIN) 72-73 H 3
Cajueiro o **BR** (RON) 70-71 F 2
Cajuru o **BR** 72-73 G 6
Cajutuba, Ilha ⌒ **BR** 62-63 G 6
Cajutuba, Ilha ⌒ **BR** 68-69 E 2
Cajuuna o **BR** 62-63 K 6
Čajvo, zaliv ≈ 122-123 K 2
Caka o **VRC** 144-145 M 2
Caka Yanhu o **VRC** 144-145 M 2
Čak-e Vardak o **AFG** 138-139 B 2
Čakne-ye Pāin o **IR** 136-137 F 6
Cakranegara o • **RI** 168 C 7
Čakva o • **GE** 126-127 D 7
Čakyja ~ **RUS** 118-119 O 4
Čal o **AFG** 136-137 L 6
Çal ☆ **TR** 128-129 C 3
Cal, Río La ~ **BOL** 70-71 H 6
Cala o **ZA** 220-221 H 5
Calabar ☆ **WAN** 204-205 H 6
Calabazar de Sagua o **C** 54-55 F 3
Calabei o **RI** 168 C 7
Calabogie o **CDN** (ONT) 238-239 J 3
Calabozo o **YV** 60-61 H 3
Calabria ■ **I** 100-101 F 5
Calabria, Parco Nazionale della ⊥ **I** 100-101 F 5
Calacoa o **PE** 70-71 B 5
Calacoto o **BOL** 70-71 C 5
Calafate, El o **RA** 80 D 5
Calafquen, Lago o **RCH** 78-79 C 5
Calagua Islands ⌒ **RP** 160-161 E 5
Calahoo o **CDN** (ALB) 232-233 E 2
Calahorra o • **E** 98-99 G 3
Calai o **ANG** 216-217 E 8
Calais o • **F** 90-91 H 6
Calais o **USA** (ME) 278-279 O 3
Čalak o **UZ** 136-137 K 5
Calalaste, Sierra de ▲ **RA** 76-77 D 4
Calalzo di Cadore o **I** 100-101 D 1
Calama o **BR** 66-67 F 7
Calama o **RCH** 76-77 C 2
Calamar o **CO** (ATL) 60-61 D 2
Calamar o **CO** (VAU) 60-61 E 7
Calamarca o **BOL** 70-71 C 5
Calamba o • **RP** 160-161 D 5
Calamian Group ⌒ **RP** 160-161 C 6
Calamocha o **E** 98-99 G 4
Calamus o **USA** (IA) 274-275 H 3
Calamus Reservoir o **USA** (NE) 262-263 G 3
Calamuya ∴ • **HN** 52-53 L 4
Calanaque o **BR** 66-67 E 3
Calandula o **ANG** 216-217 C 4
Calandula, Quedas do ~ •• **ANG** 216-217 D 4
Calang o **RI** 162-163 A 2
Calanga o **PE** 64-65 D 8
Calapan ☆ **RP** 160-161 D 6
Cala Rajada o **E** 98-99 J 5
Călăraşi ☆ **MD** 102-103 F 4
Călăraşi ☆ **RO** 102-103 E 5
Calarca o **CO** 60-61 D 5
Calatambo o **RCH** 70-71 C 6
Calatayud o **E** 98-99 G 4
Calatrava o **RP** 160-161 E 7
Calavite Passage ≈ 160-161 D 6
Calayan Island ⌒ **RP** 160-161 D 3
Calbayog o **RP** 160-161 F 6
Calbore o **PA** 52-53 D 7
Calbuco o **RCH** 78-79 C 6
Calbuco, Volcán ▲ **RCH** 78-79 C 6
Calca o **PE** 70-71 B 3
Calcasieu Lake o **USA** (LA) 268-269 G 7
Calcasieu River ~ **USA** 268-269 H 6
Calceta o **EC** 64-65 B 2
Calchaquí o **RA** 76-77 G 5
Calchaquí, Río ~ **RA** 76-77 G 6
Calchaquí, Río ~ **RA** 76-77 D 3
Calchaquí las Aves, Laguna o **RA** 76-77 G 5
Calçoene o **BR** 62-63 J 4
Calçoene, Rio ~ **BR** 62-63 J 4
Calcutta ☆ •• **IND** 142-143 F 4
Caldas o **CO** 60-61 D 4
Caldas Novas o **BR** 72-73 F 4
Caldeiras o **BR** 72-73 J 2
Calder o **CDN** (SAS) 232-233 R 4
Caldera o **CR** 52-53 B 7
Caldera o **RCH** 76-77 B 4
Caldera de Taburiente, Parque Nacional de la ⊥ **E** 188-189 C 6
Calderon, Cerro ▲ **RA** 78-79 E 6
Calder River ~ **CDN** 30-31 M 3
Calders Dock o **CDN** (MAN) 234-235 G 3
Çaldıran ☆ **TR** 128-129 K 3
Caldonia o **USA** (MN) 270-271 G 7
Caldwell o **USA** (ID) 252-253 B 3
Caldwell o **USA** (KS) 262-263 J 7
Caldwell o **USA** (NC) 282-283 H 4
Caldwell o **USA** (OH) 280-281 E 4
Caldwell o **USA** (TX) 266-267 L 3
Calebee Creek ~ **USA** 284-285 E 4
Caledon o **ZA** 220-221 D 7
Caledon Bay ≈ 174-175 D 3
Caledonia o **CDN** (NS) 240-241 N 5
Caledonia o **CDN** (ONT) 238-239 F 5
Caledonia o **USA** (MN) 270-271 G 7
Caledonia Hills ▲ **CDN** 240-241 K 5
Caledonrivier ~ **ZA** 220-221 H 4
Calen o **AUS** 174-175 K 7
Calequisse o **GNB** 202-203 B 3
Calera o **USA** (AL) 284-285 D 3
Calera o **USA** (OK) 264-265 H 5
Calera, La o **RCH** 78-79 D 2
Caleta Josefina o **RCH** 80 F 6
Caleta Olivia o **RA** 80 G 3
Caleta Vitor o **RCH** 70-71 B 6
Caleufú o **RA** 78-79 G 3
Caleufú, Río ~ **RA** 78-79 D 6
Calexico o **USA** (CA) 248-249 J 7
Calfpen Swamp o **USA** (SC) 284-285 K 4
Calgary o • **CDN** (ALB) 232-233 D 4
Calhan o **USA** (CO) 254-255 L 4
Calhoun o **USA** (GA) 284-285 F 2
Calhoun o **USA** (KY) 276-277 H 3
Calhoun o **USA** (LA) 268-269 H 4
Calhoun City o **USA** (MS) 268-269 L 3
Calhoun Falls o **USA** (SC) 284-285 H 2
Calhua o **PE** 64-65 F 9
Cali ☆ **CO** 60-61 C 6
Calicoan Island ⌒ **RP** 160-161 F 7
Calico Ghost Town • **USA** (CA) 248-249 H 5
Calico Rock o **USA** (AR) 276-277 C 4
Calicut o • **IND** 140-141 F 5
Caliente o **USA** (CA) 248-249 F 4
Caliente o **USA** (NV) 248-249 K 2
California o **BR** 66-67 B 7
California o **CO** 60-61 E 4
California o **USA** (MO) 274-275 F 6
California ■ **USA** 246-247 D 3
California Aqueduct < **USA** (CA) 248-249 C 2
California City o **USA** (CA) 248-249 G 4
Calik ~ **RI** 162-163 F 6
Calilegua, Parque Nacional ⊥ **RA** 76-77 E 2
Calima = Darien o **CO** 60-61 C 6
Călimani, Munții ▲ **RO** 102-103 D 4
Calimere, Point ▲ **IND** 140-141 H 5
Calingasta o **RA** 76-77 C 6
Calingiri o **AUS** 176-177 D 5
Calintaan o **RP** 160-161 D 6
Calion o **USA** (AR) 276-277 C 7
Calipatria o **USA** (CA) 248-249 J 6
Caliper Lake o **CDN** (ONT) 234-235 K 5
Calipuy, Reserva Nacional ⊥ **PE** 64-65 C 6
Calispell Peak ▲ **USA** (WA) 244-245 H 2
Calistoga o **USA** (CA) 246-247 C 5
Calitzdorp o **ZA** 220-221 E 6
Calkar köl o **KZ** 96-97 G 8
Calkarteniz, sor o **KZ** 126-127 P 3
Calkiní o **MEX** 52-53 J 1
Callabonna o **AUS** 178-179 F 5
Callabonna, Lake o **AUS** 178-179 F 5
Callabonna Creek ~ **AUS** 178-179 F 5
Callaghan o **USA** (TX) 266-267 H 6
Callagiddy o **AUS** 176-177 C 2
Callahan o **USA** (CA) 246-247 C 2
Callahan o **USA** (FL) 286-287 H 1
Callahan, Mount ▲ **USA** (NV) 246-247 J 4
Callama ó Quirce, Río ~ **BOL** 70-71 D 7
Callana, Río ~ **PE** 64-65 E 5
Callander o **CDN** (ONT) 238-239 F 2
Callands o **USA** (VA) 280-281 G 7
Callanish o **GB** 90-91 D 2
Callao o **PE** 64-65 D 8
Callao o **USA** (UT) 254-255 B 4
Callao o **USA** (VA) 280-281 K 6
Callao, El o **YV** 62-63 D 2
Callaqui, Volcán ▲ **RCH** 78-79 D 4
Callara, Lake o **AUS** 178-179 D 5
Callatharra Springs o **AUS** 176-177 C 2
Callawa o **AUS** 172-173 E 6
Callaway o **USA** (FL) 286-287 D 1
Callaway o **USA** (MN) 270-271 C 4
Callaway o **USA** (NE) 262-263 G 3
Callaway Gardens • **USA** (GA) 284-285 F 4
Calle Calle, Río ~ **RCH** 78-79 C 5
Calles o **MEX** 50-51 K 6
Calliope o **AUS** 178-179 L 3
Callon o **USA** (WI) 270-271 J 6
Cal Madow, Buuraha ▲ **SP** 208-209 J 3
Calmar o **CDN** (ALB) 232-233 E 2
Calmar o **USA** (IA) 274-275 G 1
Cal Miskaat, Buuraha ▲ **SP** 208-209 J 3
Calm Point ▲ **USA** 22-23 Q 3
Čalna o **RUS** 88-89 N 6

Cal-Nev-Ari o USA (NV) 248-249 K 4
Calombo o ANG 216-217 C 6
Calonda o ANG 216-217 F 4
Calonga ~ ANG 216-217 C 7
Caloosahatchee River ~ USA 286-287 H 5
Caloto o CO 60-61 C 6
Caloundra o AUS 178-179 M 4
Calpet o USA (WY) 252-253 H 4
Calpon, Cerro ▲ PE 64-65 C 5
Calpulalpan o MEX 52-53 E 1
Calstock o CDN (ONT) 236-237 D 3
Caltagirone o I 100-101 E 6
Caltama, Cerro ▲ BOL 70-71 C 7
Caltanissetta o I 100-101 E 6
Calton Hills o AUS 174-175 E 7
Ca Lu o VN 158-159 J 2
Caluango o ANG 216-217 E 4
Calucinga o ANG 216-217 D 5
Calulo o ANG 216-217 C 4
Calumet o USA (OK) 264-265 F 3
Calunda o ANG 214-215 B 7
Caluquembe o ANG 216-217 C 6
Čalūs o• IR 136-137 B 6
Caluula o SP 208-209 K 3
Calvert o USA (AL) 284-285 B 5
Calvert o USA (TX) 266-267 L 2
Calvert, Cape ▲ CDN (BC) 230-231 B 2
Calvert Hills o AUS 174-175 D 5
Calvert Island ⌒ CDN (BC) 230-231 A 2
Calvi o•• F 98-99 M 3
Calvillo o MEX 50-51 H 7
Calvin o USA (OK) 264-265 H 4
Calvinia o ZA 220-221 D 5
Calwa o USA (CA) 248-249 E 3
Calzada de Calatrava o E 98-99 F 5
Camabatela o ANG 216-217 C 4
Camacã o BR 72-73 L 3
Camaçã, Rio ~ BR 66-67 D 6
Camaçari o BR 68-69 K 7
Camachi, Lac o CDN (QUE) 236-237 M 5
Camacupa o ANG 216-217 D 6
Camaguan o YV 60-61 H 3
Camagüey ☆• C 54-55 G 4
Camagüey, Archipiélago de ⌒ C 54-55 F 3
Camaipi o BR 62-63 J 5
Camaiú, Rio ~ BR 66-67 H 5
Camalote o C 54-55 G 4
Camamu o BR 72-73 L 2
Camana o PE 70-71 A 5
Čamanābād o IR 134-135 H 1
Camanau, Rio ~ BR 62-63 D 6
Čaman Bid o IR 136-137 E 6
Camandog Island ⌒ RP 160-161 F 7
Čaman Soltān o IR 134-135 C 2
Camapuã o BR 70-71 K 6
Camaquã o BR 74-75 E 8
Camará o BR (AMA) 66-67 F 4
Camará o BR (P) 66-67 K 4
Camaragibe o BR 68-69 L 6
Camaraipi, Rio ~ BR 68-69 C 3
Camararé, Rio ~ BR 70-71 H 3
Camarata o YV 60-61 K 5
Camargo o MEX 50-51 K 4
Camargo o USA (OK) 264-265 E 2
Camaron o BOL 76-77 E 1
Camarón, Cabo ▲ HN 54-55 C 7
Camarones o RA 80 H 2
Camarones, Bahía ≈ 80 H 2
Camarones, Río ~ RCH 70-71 C 6
Camaruã o BR 66-67 E 5
Camarvik Creek ~ CDN 30-31 Z 3
Camas o USA (MT) 250-251 E 4
Camas o USA (WA) 244-245 C 5
Camas Valley o USA (OR) 244-245 B 7
Camata, Río ~ BOL 70-71 C 4
Camatambo o ANG 216-217 C 3
Cà Mau o VN 158-159 H 6
Cà Mau, Mũi ▲ VN 158-159 H 6
Camaxilo o ANG 216-217 E 4
Camba o RI 164-165 F 6
Čamba ~ RUS 116-117 L 5
Cambahee River ~ USA 284-285 K 4
Cambaju o GNB 202-203 C 3
Camballin o AUS 172-173 G 4
Cambândua o ANG 216-217 D 6
Cambange o ANG 216-217 F 4
Cambao o CO 60-61 D 5
Cambará do Sul o BR 74-75 E 7
Cambaxi o ANG 216-217 E 4
Cambellford o CDN (ONT) 238-239 H 4
Cambo ~ ANG 216-217 D 4
Cambodia = Kâmpŭchéa ■ K 158-159 G 4
Camboeiro, Riachão do ~ BR 68-69 F 7
Cambombo o ANG 216-217 C 5
Camboon P.O. o AUS 178-179 L 3
Camboriú, Ponta ▲ BR 74-75 G 5
Camborne o CDN (BC) 230-231 M 3
Cambrai o• F 90-91 J 6
Cambria o USA (CA) 248-249 C 4
Cambrian Mountains ▲ GB 90-91 F 5
Cambridge o CDN (NS) 240-241 N 4
Cambridge o CDN (ONT) 238-239 E 5
Cambridge o•• GB 90-91 H 5
Cambridge o JA 54-55 G 5
Cambridge o NZ 182 E 2
Cambridge o USA (ID) 252-253 B 2
Cambridge o USA (IL) 274-275 H 3
Cambridge o USA (MA) 278-279 K 6
Cambridge o USA (MD) 280-281 K 5
Cambridge o USA (MN) 270-271 E 5
Cambridge o USA (NE) 262-263 F 4
Cambridge o USA (OH) 280-281 E 3
Cambridge Bay ≈ 24-25 T 6
Cambridge Bay o CDN 24-25 U 6
Cambridge City o USA (IN) 274-275 N 5
Cambridge Gulf ≈ 172-173 J 3
Cambridge Junction o USA (MI) 272-273 E 5
Cambridge Point ▲ CDN 24-25 g 3
Cambridge Springs o USA (PA) 280-281 F 2
Cambrils o E 98-99 H 4
Cambu, Rio ~ BR 62-63 K 6
Cambuí o BR 72-73 G 7
Cambulo o ANG 216-217 F 3
Camburinga ⅄ AUS 174-175 D 3
Cambutal o PA 52-53 D 8
Camden o USA (AL) 284-285 C 5
Camden o USA (AR) 276-277 C 7
Camden o USA (ME) 278-279 M 4
Camden o USA (MS) 268-269 L 4
Camden o USA (NC) 282-283 L 4
Camden o USA (NJ) 280-281 L 4
Camden o USA (NY) 278-279 F 5
Camden o USA (OH) 280-281 B 4
Camden o USA (TN) 276-277 G 4
Camden o• USA (SC) 284-285 K 2
Camden Bay ≈ 20-21 S 1
Camdenton o USA (MO) 274-275 F 6
Cameia, Acampamento da o ANG 216-217 F 5
Cameia, Parque Nacional da ⊥ ANG 216-217 F 5
Camel Back Mountain ▲ CDN (NB) 240-241 J 3
Camel Creek o AUS 174-175 H 6
Çameli o TR 128-129 C 4
Camel Race Course • KSA 130-131 K 5
Camelsfoot Range ▲ CDN 230-231 G 2
Cameo o CDN (SAS) 232-233 M 2
Cameron o USA (AZ) 256-257 D 3
Cameron o USA (LA) 268-269 G 7
Cameron o USA (MO) 274-275 D 5
Cameron o USA (SC) 284-285 K 3
Cameron o USA (TX) 266-267 L 3
Cameron Corner • AUS 178-179 F 5
Cameron Island ⌒ CDN 24-25 U 2
Cameron River ~ CDN 30-31 N 4
Cameroon ■ CAM 204-205 J 6
Cameroon, Mount = Mont Cameroun ▲• CAM 204-205 H 6
Cameroun, Estuaire du ≈ 210-211 B 2
Cametá o BR 68-69 D 3
Camfield o AUS 172-173 K 4
Camiaco o BOL 70-71 E 4
Camiguin Island ⌒ RP (CAG) 160-161 D 3
Camiguin Island ⌒ RP (MSO) 160-161 F 8
Camiling o RP 160-161 D 5
Camilla o USA (GA) 284-285 F 5
Camiña o RCH 70-71 C 6
Caming o RI 164-165 G 6
Caminha o P 98-99 C 4
Camino de Santiago ••• E 98-99 D 3
Caminos, Dos o YV 60-61 J 3
Camisea o PE 64-65 F 7
Çamkani o AFG 138-139 B 3
Camlidere ☆ TR 128-129 E 2
Cammarata, Monte ▲ I 100-101 D 6
Cammoo Caves • AUS 178-179 L 2
Camocim o BR 68-69 H 3
Camocim de São Félix o BR 68-69 L 6
Camogtong o RP 160-161 E 6
Camongua o ANG 216-217 D 5
Camooweal o AUS 174-175 E 6
Camooweal Caves National Park ⊥ AUS 174-175 E 6
Camopi o F 62-63 H 4
Camopi ~ F 62-63 H 4
Camorta Island ⌒ IND 140-141 L 5
Camotes Islands ⌒ RP 160-161 F 7
Camotes Sea ≈ 160-161 F 7
Čamp, ostrov ⌒ RUS 84-85 e 2
Campamento o HN 52-53 L 4
Campamento Río Grande o YV 60-61 L 3
Campana, Cerro la ▲ RCH 80 D 5
Campana, Isla ⌒ RCH 80 C 4
Campana, Monte ▲ RA 80 H 7
Campana, Parque Nacional la ⊥ RCH 78-79 D 2
Campanario o BR 72-73 K 5
Campanario, Cerro ▲ RA 78-79 D 3
Campanas o RA 76-77 D 5
Campania ◘ I 100-101 E 4
Campania Island ⌒ CDN (BC) 228-229 E 3
Campanilla o PE 64-65 D 5
Campanquiz, Cerros ▲ PE 64-65 D 4
Campaspe o AUS 174-175 J 7
Campbell o USA (AL) 284-285 C 5
Campbell o USA (MO) 276-277 E 4
Campbell o USA (NE) 262-263 H 4
Campbell o ZA 220-221 F 4
Campbell, Cape ▲ NZ 182 E 4
Campbell Bay ≈ 24-25 U 6
Campbell Hill ▲ USA (OH) 280-281 C 3
Campbell Island ⌒ CDN 24-25 G 6
Campbell Island ⌒ NZ 13 H 8
Campbell Lake o CDN (NWT) 20-21 Y 2
Campbell Lake o CDN (NWT) 30-31 Q 4
Campbell Plateau ≃ 13 J 7
Campbell River o CDN (BC) 230-231 D 3
Campbell's Bay o CDN (QUE) 238-239 J 3
Campbellsville o USA (KY) 276-277 K 3
Campbellton o CDN (NB) 240-241 J 3
Campbellton o CDN (PEI) 240-241 L 4
Campbellton o USA (FL) 286-287 D 1
Campbellton o USA (TX) 266-267 J 5
Campbell Town o AUS 180-181 J 6
Campbeltown o GB 90-91 E 4
Camp Century o GRØ 26-27 U 5
Camp Crook o USA (SD) 260-261 C 1
Campeana o GNB 202-203 C 4
Campeche ☆• MEX 52-53 J 2
Campeche, Bahía de ≈ 52-53 G 2
Campechuela o C 54-55 G 4
Campement des Trois Rivières o RCA 206-207 G 5
Camper o CDN (MAN) 234-235 E 3
Camperdown o AUS 180-181 G 5
Camperdown o ZA 220-221 K 4
Camperville o CDN (MAN) 234-235 C 3
Camp Gagetown xx CDN (NB) 240-241 J 5
Camp Hill o USA (AL) 284-285 E 4
Cẩm Phả o VN 156-157 E 6
Campidano ⌣ I 100-101 B 5
Campillos o E 98-99 E 6
Campina o BR 66-67 J 5
Campina da Lagoa o BR 74-75 D 5
Campina do Simão o BR 74-75 E 5
Campina Grande o BR 68-69 L 5
Campinas o BR (BAH) 72-73 J 2
Campinas o BR (PAU) 72-73 G 7
Campinas, Área Indígena ⅄ BR 64-65 F 5
Campina Verde o BR 72-73 F 5
Camping Island ⌒ CDN 24-25 P 6
Campinho o BR (BAH) 72-73 J 2
Campinho o BR (BAH) 72-73 L 2
Camp Kalao o RP 160-161 G 9
Camp Lloyd o GRØ 28-29 P 3
Camplong o RI 166-167 B 7
Campo o• CAM 210-211 B 2
Campo o MOC 218-219 J 3
Campo o USA (CA) 248-249 H 7
Campo o USA (CO) 254-255 N 6
Campo, El o USA (TX) 266-267 L 4
Campo, Réserve de = Campo Reserve ⊥ CAM 210-211 B 2
Campo Alegre o BR (ALA) 68-69 K 6
Campo Alegre o BR (PIA) 68-69 H 6
Campo Alegre o BR (TOC) 68-69 D 5
Campoalegre o CO 60-61 D 6
Campo Alegre o YV 60-61 K 3
Campo Alegre de Goiás o BR 72-73 G 4
Campo Alegre de Lourdes o BR 68-69 G 6
Campobasso ☆ I 100-101 E 4
Campo Belo o BR 72-73 H 6
Campo Bernal o YV 60-61 E 3
Campo Camalajue o MEX 50-51 B 3
Campo de Carabobo, Parque ⊥• YV 60-61 G 2
Campo de Talampaya • RA 76-77 D 5
Campo do Padre, Morro ▲ BR 74-75 F 6
Campo Erê o BR 74-75 D 6
Campo Esperanza o PY 76-77 H 2
Campo Gallo o RA 76-77 F 4
Campo Garay o RA 76-77 G 5
Campo Grande ☆ BR 70-71 K 7
Campo Grande o RA 76-77 K 4
Campo Grande, Cachoeira ~ BR 70-71 F 2
Campo Grayling Artillery Range xx USA (MI) 272-273 E 3
Campo Largo o BR 74-75 F 5
Campo Maior o BR 68-69 G 4
Campo Maior o P 98-99 D 5
Campomento o PY 76-77 H 1
Campo Mourão o BR 74-75 D 5
Campo Novo do Parecis o BR 70-71 J 3
Campo Nuevo o MEX 50-51 B 3
Campo Reserve = Réserve de Campo ⊥ CAM 210-211 B 2
Campos o BR 72-73 K 6
Campos, Laguna o PY 70-71 G 7
Campos, Tierra de ▲ E 98-99 E 4
Campos Belos o BR 72-73 G 2
Campos do Jordão o BR 72-73 H 7
Campos dos Parecis ⌣ BR 70-71 H 3
Campo Seco o BR 76-77 K 6
Campos Eliseos o BR 72-73 D 6
Campo Serio o PE 64-65 E 2
Campos Gerais o BR 72-73 H 6
Campos Novos o BR 74-75 E 6
Campos Sales o BR 68-69 H 5
Camp Peary xx USA (VA) 280-281 K 6
Camp Pendleton Marine Corps Base • USA (CA) 248-249 G 6
Camp Point o USA (IL) 274-275 G 4
Camp Ripley Military Reservation xx USA (MN) 270-271 D 4
Camp Roberts Military Reservation xx USA (CA) 248-249 D 4
Camp Scenic o USA (TX) 266-267 H 3
Camp Sherman o USA (OR) 244-245 D 6
Campti o USA (LA) 268-269 G 5
Camp Verde o USA (AZ) 256-257 D 4
Camp Wood o USA (TX) 266-267 H 4
Cam Ranh o VN 158-159 K 5
Camrose o CDN (ALB) 232-233 F 2
Camsell Bay o CDN 28-29 F 3
Camsell Lake o CDN 30-31 O 4
Camú, Río ~ DOM 54-55 K 5
Camucio o ANG 216-217 B 7
Camulemba, Capenda- o ANG 216-217 E 4
Camuy o USA (PR) 286-287 P 2
Camuya, Río ~ CO 64-65 F 1
Čamzinka o RUS 96-97 D 6
Čamzinka o RUS 96-97 D 6
Çan ☆ TR 128-129 B 2
Cana o BOL 70-71 C 7
Caña, La o CO 60-61 C 3
Canaã o BR 68-69 F 5
Canaã, Rio ~ BR 70-71 F 2
Canaan o USA (NH) 278-279 J 5
Canaan River ~ CDN 240-241 K 4
Canaan Station o CDN (NB) 240-241 K 4
Canabal o E 98-99 D 3
Cana-Brava o BR 72-73 H 4
Cana Brava, Rio ~ BR 72-73 F 2
Cana-Brava, Serra da ▲ BR 72-73 K 4
Canada o BR 68-69 F 2
Canada ■ CDN 38-39 D 3
Cañada, La o RA (COD) 76-77 F 6
Cañada, La o RA (SAE) 76-77 F 4
Canada Basin ≃ 16 B 33
Canada Bay ≈ 242-243 M 2
Cañada Condal ~ RA 76-77 F 2
Cañada de Gómez o RA 78-79 J 2
Cañada de Luque o RA 76-77 F 6
Cañada de Media Luna ~ RA 76-77 F 2
Cañada El Rosillo ~ RA 76-77 F 2
Cañada Grande ~ RA 76-77 F 2
Canada Harbour o CDN (NFL) 242-243 M 2
Canada Lake o USA (NY) 278-279 G 5
Cañada Rica ~ RA 76-77 F 2
Cañada Rosquín o RA 78-79 J 2
Cañada Seca o RA 78-79 H 3
Canadian o USA (TX) 264-265 D 3
Canadian-Pacific-Railway II CDN 232-233 K 3
Canadian River ~ USA 256-257 M 3
Canadian River ~ USA 264-265 J 3
Canadian River ~ USA 264-265 D 3
Cañadón El Pluma ~ RA 80 E 3
Cañadón Lagarto o RA 80 F 2
Cañadón Sacho ~ RA 80 E 2
Cañadón Seco ~ RA 80 E 2
Canadys o USA (SC) 284-285 K 3
Canagu, Río ~ YV 60-61 H 3
Canaima o YV 60-61 K 4
Canaima, Parque Nacional ⊥••• YV 60-61 K 4
Çanakkale ☆• TR 128-129 B 2
Çanakkale Boğazı ≈ 128-129 B 2
Canal al Desierto < RA 76-77 F 4
Canal de Dios < RA 76-77 F 3
Canal de Tûnis ≃ 100-101 C 6
Canale di Sicilia ≃ 100-101 C 6
Canal Flats o CDN (BC) 230-231 O 3
Canali o MEX 52-53 E 1
Canal No.1 < RA 78-79 L 4
Canal No.2 < RA 78-79 L 4
Canal No.5 < RA 78-79 L 4
Canal No.9 < RA 78-79 K 4
Canal No. 11 < RA 78-79 K 4
Canal No. 12 < RA 78-79 K 4
Canal No. 16 < RA 78-79 K 3
Canal P.O. o AUS 178-179 K 3
Canals o RA 78-79 H 2
Canal Virgen del Carmen < RA 76-77 F 3
Canal Winchester o USA (OH) 280-281 D 4
Canamã, Rio ~ BR 70-71 H 2
Cananari, Río ~ CO 66-67 B 2
Canandaigua o USA (NY) 278-279 D 6
Cananea o MEX 50-51 D 2
Cananéia o BR 74-75 G 5
Cañar o EC 64-65 C 3
Canarana o BR (BAH) 68-69 H 7
Canarana o BR (MAT) 72-73 D 2
Canárias, Ilha das ⌒ BR 68-69 H 3
Canarreos, Archipiélago de los ⌒ C 54-55 D 4
Canary o AUS 178-179 F 2
Canary Basin ≃ 188-189 E 3
Canary Islands = Canarias, Islas ⌒ E 188-189 C 6
Cañas o MEX 52-53 D 2
Cañas, Bahía las ≈ 78-79 C 3
Cañas, Las o CR 52-53 B 6
Cañas, Playa las o C 54-55 D 3
Cañas, Río ~ RA 76-77 E 2
Cañasgordas o CO 60-61 C 4
Canastra, Rio ~ BR 68-69 D 7
Canastra, Serra da ▲ BR 68-69 J 7
Canastra, Serra da ▲ BR 72-73 G 6
Canatián o MEX 50-51 G 5
Canatiba o BR 72-73 J 2
Canaveral o EC 64-65 B 3
Canaveral, Cape ▲ USA (FL) 286-287 J 3
Canaveral National Seashore ⊥ USA (FL) 286-287 J 3
Cañaveras o E 98-99 F 4
Canavieiras o BR 72-73 L 3
Canayan o RP 160-161 E 8
Cañazas o PA (Pan) 52-53 F 7
Cañazas o PA (Ver) 52-53 D 7
Canberra ★• AUS 180-181 K 3
Canberra Space Centre • AUS 180-181 K 3
Canby o USA (CA) 246-247 F 2
Canby o USA (MN) 270-271 B 6
Canby o USA (OR) 244-245 C 5
Cancela o BR 68-69 G 3
Cancelão o BR 74-75 D 8
Canchaylo o PE 64-65 E 7
Canchungo o GNB 202-203 B 3
Canconga o ANG 216-217 E 6
Cancosa o RCH 70-71 C 6
Cancuc o MEX 52-53 H 3
Cancuén ∴• GCA 52-53 J 3
Cancún o• MEX 52-53 L 1
Cancún, Isla ⌒ MEX 52-53 L 1
Candarave o PE 70-71 B 5
Çandarlı Körfezi ≈ 128-129 B 3
Candeado o MOC 218-219 G 4
Candeias o BR 72-73 L 2
Candeias, Rio ~ BR 66-67 F 7
Candela o MEX 50-51 J 4
Candelaria o• MEX 52-53 J 2
Candelaria o USA (TX) 266-267 C 3
Candelaria, La o YV 60-61 H 2
Candelaria, Río ~ BOL 70-71 H 5
Candelaria, Río ~ MEX 52-53 J 2
Candeleda o E 98-99 E 4
Candelwood, Lake o USA (CT) 280-281 N 2
Candi • RI (LAM) 162-163 E 7
Candi • RI (RIA) 162-163 D 4
Candiac o CDN (SAS) 232-233 P 5
Candi Besakih • RI 168 B 7
Cândido de Abreu o BR 74-75 E 5
Cándido González o C 54-55 F 4
Cândido Mendes o BR 68-69 F 2
Cândido Rondon o BR 76-77 K 3
Cândido Sales o BR 72-73 K 3
Candi Mendut • RI 168 D 3
Candi Pura • RI 168 B 7
Candi Sukuh • RI 168 D 3
Candle o USA 20-21 K 4
Candle Lake o CDN (SAS) 232-233 N 2
Candle Lake o CDN (SAS) 232-233 N 2
Čandman' = Talšand o MAU 148-149 C 5
Cando o CDN (SAS) 232-233 K 3
Cando o USA (ND) 258-259 H 3
Candon o RP 160-161 D 4
Candover o ZA 220-221 K 3
Candulo o MOC 214-215 J 6
Cần Đước o VN 158-159 J 5
Candy Reservoir o USA (OK) 264-265 H 2
Canea o BR 62-63 G 5
Caneapo o BR 62-63 G 5
Canegrass o AUS 180-181 F 2
Cane Grove o GUY 62-63 F 2
Canela, La o C 54-55 H 4
Canela Baja o RCH 76-77 B 6
Canelo o USA (AZ) 256-257 E 7
Canelones ☆ ROU 78-79 L 3
Canelos o EC 64-65 D 2
Canelos, Los o RCH 80 E 6
Cane River o AUS (WA) 172-173 B 7
Cane River ~ AUS 172-173 B 7
Cañete o E 98-99 G 4
Cañete o• RCH 78-79 C 4
Cañete, Río de ~ PE 64-65 D 8
Caney o USA (KS) 262-263 L 7
Caney Fork ~ USA 276-277 K 5
Caney River ~ USA 202-203 K 1
Caney River ~ USA 264-265 J 2
Caneyville o USA (KY) 276-277 J 3
Canford o CDN (BC) 230-231 J 3
Čangada ~ RUS 108-109 c 7
Cangaime, Río ~ EC 64-65 D 3
Cangala o ANG 216-217 D 6
Cangallo o PE 64-65 E 8
Cangalo o ANG 216-217 D 5
Cangamba o ANG 216-217 E 6
Cangandala o ANG 216-217 D 4
Cangandala, Parque Nacional de ⊥ ANG 216-217 D 4
Cangas o E 98-99 C 3
Cangas del Narcea o E 98-99 D 3
Cangoa o ANG 216-217 E 6
Cango Caves • ZA 220-221 F 6
Cangombe o ANG 216-217 F 7
Çangrâfa o RIM 196-197 D 6
Cangrejo, Cerro ▲ RA 80 D 4
Cangshan o VRC 154-155 L 4
Canguaretama o BR 68-69 L 5
Canguçu o BR 74-75 D 8
Čangüle, Rūdhāne-ye ~ IRQ 128-129 M 6
Cangumbe o ANG 216-217 E 5
Cangxi o VRC 154-155 D 6
Cangyanshan • VRC 154-155 J 3
Cangyuan o VRC 142-143 L 4
Cangzhou o VRC 154-155 K 2
Can Hasan Höyüğü ∴• TR 128-129 E 4
Canhotinho o BR 68-69 K 6
Caniapiscau, Réservoir de < CDN 36-37 P 7
Caniapiscau, Rivière ~ CDN 36-37 P 7
Canicattì o I 100-101 D 6
Canigao Channel ≈ 160-161 F 7
Canik Dağları ▲ TR 128-129 G 2
Canim Lake o CDN (BC) 230-231 J 2
Canim Lake o CDN (BC) 230-231 J 2
Canindé o BR 68-69 J 4
Canindé, Rio ~ BR 68-69 G 5
Caninde de São Francisco o BR 68-69 K 6
Canipo Island ⌒ RP 160-161 D 7
Canisteo o USA (NY) 278-279 D 6
Canisteo River ~ USA 278-279 D 6
Canister Fall ~ GUY 62-63 E 3
Canit Point ▲ RP (ROM) 160-161 E 6
Canit Point ▲ RP (SUS) 160-161 G 8
Canjime o ANG 216-217 E 8
Çankırı ☆• TR 128-129 E 2
Cankuzo o BU 212-213 C 5
Canlaon, Mount ▲ RP 160-161 E 7
Canmang o VRC 156-157 G 2
Canmore o CDN (ALB) 232-233 C 4
Cann, Mount ▲ AUS 180-181 K 4
Cannac Island ⌒ PNG 183 G 5
Cannanore o• IND 140-141 F 5
Cannanore Islands ⌒ IND 140-141 E 5
Cannelton o USA (IN) 274-275 M 7
Cannes o• F 90-91 L 10
Canning Hill ▲ AUS 176-177 D 4
Canning River ~ USA 20-21 R 2
Canning Stock Route II AUS 172-173 G 7
Cannon Ball o USA (ND) 258-259 G 5
Cannonball River ~ USA 258-259 F 5
Cannon Beach o USA (OR) 244-245 B 5
Cannondale Mount ▲ AUS 178-179 K 3
Cannon Falls o USA (MN) 270-271 F 6
Cannonville o USA (UT) 254-255 C 6
Cann River o AUS (VIC) 180-181 K 4
Cann River ~ AUS 180-181 K 4
Caño, El o PA 52-53 D 7
Caño, Isla de ⌒ CR 52-53 C 7
Cano, Pico do ▲ CV 202-203 B 6
Canoa o HN 52-53 K 4
Canoas o BR 74-75 E 7
Canoas o MEX 50-51 K 6
Canoas, Punta ▲ MEX 50-51 B 3
Caño Basame ~ YV 60-61 L 3
Canobie o AUS 174-175 F 6
Caño Bocon ~ CO 60-61 G 5
Canobolas, Mount ▲ AUS 180-181 K 2
Canochee River ~ USA 284-285 J 4
Caño Chupabe ~ CO 60-61 G 6
Caño Colorado o YV 60-61 K 3
Canoe o CDN (BC) 230-231 K 3
Canoe Creek Indian Reserve ⅄ CDN (BC) 230-231 G 2
Caño el Pinal ~ CO 60-61 F 5
Canoe Reach ~ CDN 228-229 Q 4
Canoe River o CDN (BC) 228-229 P 4
Canoe River ~ CDN 228-229 P 4
Canoinhas o BR 74-75 E 6
Cañon • DZ 190-191 F 3
Canonaco, Río ~ EC 64-65 D 2
Canonba o AUS 178-179 J 6
Cañoncito Indian Reservation ⅄ USA (NM) 256-257 H 3
Canon City o USA (CO) 254-255 K 5
Cañon del Majes-Colca • PE 64-65 F 9
Cañon del Sumidero, Parque Nacional ⊥ MEX 52-53 H 3
Cañon de Río Blanco, Parque Nacional ⊥ MEX 52-53 F 2
Cañon Fiord ≈ 26-27 J 3
Cañon Plaza o USA (NM) 256-257 J 2
Canonsburg o USA (PA) 280-281 F 3
Canoochee o USA (GA) 284-285 H 4
Canopus o CDN (SAS) 232-233 M 6
Canora o CDN (SAS) 232-233 Q 4
Canosa di Puglia o• I 100-101 F 4
Canouan Island ⌒ WV 56 E 5
Canowindra o AUS 180-181 K 2
Canrober Hills ▲ CDN 24-25 N 2
Canso o CDN (NS) 240-241 O 5
Canso, Strait of ≈ 240-241 O 5
Canso Channel ≈ 28-29 J 3
Canta o PE 64-65 D 7
Cantabria ◘ E 98-99 E 3
Cantábrica, Cordillera ▲ E 98-99 D 3
Cantador, Cerro el ▲ MEX 52-53 C 2
Cantagalo, Ponta ▲ BR 74-75 F 6
Cantalejo o E 98-99 F 4
Cantalpino o E 98-99 E 4
Čantal'skij hrebet ▲ RUS 112-113 T 3
Čantal'vergyrgyn ~ RUS 112-113 U 3
Cantamar o MEX 50-51 A 1
Cantanal, Sierra de ▲ RA 76-77 D 6
Cantário, Rio ~ BR 70-71 F 2
Cantaura o YV 60-61 J 3
Canterbury o••• GB 90-91 H 6
Canterbury Bight ≈ 182 D 5
Cần Thơ' o• VN 158-159 H 5
Canthyuaya, Cerros de ▲ PE 64-65 E 5
Cantil o USA (CA) 248-249 G 4
Cantilan o RP 160-161 F 8
Cantiles, Cayo ⌒ C 54-55 D 4
Canto del Agua o RCH 76-77 B 5
Canto do Buriti o BR 68-69 G 6
Canton o USA (GA) 284-285 F 2
Canton o USA (IL) 274-275 J 4
Canton o USA (MO) 274-275 G 4
Canton o USA (MS) 268-269 K 4
Canton o USA (NC) 282-283 E 5
Canton o USA (NY) 278-279 F 4
Canton o USA (OK) 264-265 F 2
Canton o USA (PA) 280-281 K 2
Canton o USA (SD) 260-261 K 3
Canton o USA (TX) 264-265 J 6
Canton o• USA (OH) 280-281 E 3
Canton = Guangzhou ☆•• VRC 156-157 H 5
Canton Lake o USA (OK) 264-265 F 2
Cantuar o CDN (SAS) 232-233 K 5
Cantwell o USA 20-21 Q 5
Canudos o BR 68-69 J 6
Cañuelas o RA 78-79 K 3
Canumã, Rio ~ BR 66-67 H 5
Canunda National Park ⊥ AUS 180-181 F 4
Canutama o BR 66-67 E 6
Canutillo o USA (TX) 266-267 A 2
Canwood o CDN (SAS) 232-233 M 2
Canxixe o MOC 218-219 H 3
Čany ☆ RUS 114-115 O 7
Čany, ozero o RUS 124-125 K 1
Canyon o CDN (ONT) 234-235 K 5
Canyon o CDN (ONT) 236-237 D 5
Canyon ∴~ RI 166-167 K 4
Canyon o USA (TX) 264-265 C 4
Canyon o USA (WY) 252-253 H 2
Canyon Creek o USA (MT) 250-251 G 5
Canyon de Chelly National Monument ∴ USA (AZ) 256-257 F 2
Canyon Ferry o USA (MT) 250-251 H 5
Canyon Ferry Lake o USA (MT) 250-251 H 5
Canyon Lake o USA (TX) 266-267 J 4
Canyonlands National Park ⊥ USA (UT) 254-255 F 5
Canyon Largo River ~ USA 256-257 H 2
Canyon Ranges ▲ CDN 30-31 G 4
Canyon River ~ CDN 36-37 G 2
Canyonville o USA (OR) 244-245 B 8
Canzar o ANG 216-217 F 3
Cao Bằng ☆• VN 156-157 E 5
Caohekou o VRC 150-151 D 7
Caojian o VRC 142-143 L 3
Cao Lãnh o VN 158-159 H 5
Caombo o ANG 216-217 D 4
Caonao ~ C 54-55 F 4
Caoqiao o VRC 154-155 L 6
Càorle o I 100-101 D 2
Cao Xian o VRC 154-155 J 4
Čapa ~ RUS 116-117 F 5
Capachica o PE 70-71 C 4
Čapaev = Čapaevo ☆ KZ 96-97 G 8
Čapaevka ~ RUS 96-97 G 7
Čapaevo ☆ KZ 96-97 G 8
Čapaevo o RUS 118-119 H 5
Čapaevskoe o KZ 124-125 H 2
Capahuari, Río ~ EC 64-65 D 3
Capaias o RP 160-161 C 7
Capalonga o RP 160-161 E 5
Capalulu o RI 164-165 J 4
Capana o BR 66-67 C 3
Capana, Punta ▲ YV 60-61 F 2
Capanema o BR 68-69 E 2
Capão Alto o BR 74-75 E 6
Capão Bonito o BR 72-73 F 7
Capão Branco o BR 74-75 D 7
Capão da Canoa o BR 74-75 E 7
Capão Doce, Morro do ▲ BR 74-75 E 6
Caparaó, Parque Nacional do ⊥ BR 72-73 K 6
Čaparhār o AFG 138-139 C 2
Capas o RP 160-161 D 5
Capauari, Rio ~ BR 66-67 C 3
Capauari, Serra do ▲ BR 66-67 C 3
Cap-aux-Meules o CDN (QUE) 242-243 G 5
Capay o RP 160-161 E 6
Capbreton o F 90-91 G 10
Cap-Chat o CDN (QUE) 242-243 B 3
Cap-de-la-Madeleine o CDN (QUE) 238-239 N 2
Cap-de-Rabast o CDN (QUE) 242-243 D 3
Cap-d'Espoir o CDN (QUE) 240-241 L 2
Cape Abyssal Plain ≃ 6-7 L 12
Cape Anguille o CDN (NFL) 242-243 J 5
Cape Arid National Park ⊥ AUS 176-177 G 6
Cape Banks o AUS 180-181 F 4
Cape Barren Island ⌒ AUS 180-181 K 6
Cape Basin ≃ 6-7 K 12
Cape Bertholet Wildlife Sanctuary ⊥ AUS 172-173 F 4
Cape Borda o AUS 180-181 D 3
Cape Breton Highlands National Park ⊥ CDN (NS) 240-241 O 4
Cape Breton Island ⌒ CDN (NS) 240-241 P 4
Cape Byrd ▲ ARK 16 G 8
Cape Canaveral o USA (FL) 286-287 J 3
Cape Canaveral Air Force Station xx USA (FL) 286-287 J 3
Cape Charles o USA (VA) 280-281 K 6
Cape Chidley Islands ⌒ CDN 36-37 R 4
Cape Coast ☆• GH 202-203 K 7
Cape Cod Bay ≈ 278-279 L 7
Cape Cod Peninsula ⌣ USA 278-279 M 7
Cape Colbeck ▲ ARK 16 F 21
Cape Coral o USA (FL) 286-287 H 5
Cape Crawford o AUS 174-175 C 5
Cape Croker o CDN (ONT) 238-239 D 4
Cape Croker Indian Reserve ⅄ CDN (ONT) 238-239 E 4
Cape Dart ▲ ARK 16 F 24
Cape Dorset o CDN 36-37 L 2
Cape Elizabeth o USA (ME) 278-279 L 5
Cape Fear River ~ USA 282-283 J 6
Cape Fear River ~ USA 282-283 J 5
Cape Flying Fish ▲ ARK 16 F 26
Cape Freshfield ▲ ARK 16 G 16
Cape Gantheaume Conservation Park ⊥ AUS 180-181 D 4
Cape George o CDN (NS) 240-241 O 5
Cape Girardeau o USA (MO) 276-277 F 3
Cape Girgir ▲ PNG 183 C 2
Cape Hope Islands ⌒ CDN 38-39 E 2
Cape Horn o USA (ID) 252-253 C 2
Cape Horn = Hornos, Cabo de ▲ RCH 80 G 8
Cape Island ⌒ USA (SC) 284-285 L 3
Cape Jervis o AUS 180-181 E 3
Cape Krusenstern National Monument ⊥ USA 20-21 H 3
Capel o AUS 176-177 C 6
Capel, Cape ▲ CDN 24-25 X 3
Capela do Alto Verde o BR 72-73 H 4
Cape Le Grand National Park ⊥ AUS 176-177 G 6
Capelinha o BR 72-73 J 4
Capelka o RUS 94-95 L 2
Capella o AUS 178-179 K 2
Capello, Is o F 00-01 J 7
Cape Lookout National Seashore ⊥ USA (NC) 282-283 L 6
Cape May o USA (NJ) 280-281 M 5
Capembe ~ ANG 216-217 F 8
Cape Melville National Park ⊥ AUS 174-175 H 4
Cape Monze = Rās Muari ▲ PK 134-135 M 6
Cape Moore ▲ ARK 16 F 21
Capenda-Camulemba o ANG 216-217 E 4
Cape Palmer ▲ ARK 16 F 27
Cape Parry o CDN 24-25 K 5
Cape-Pele o CDN (NB) 240-241 L 4
Cape Peninsula ⌣ ZA 220-221 D 7
Cape Pole o USA 32-33 D 3
Cape Race o CDN (NFL) 242-243 P 6
Cape Rama o IND 140-141 E 3
Cape Range ▲ AUS 172-173 A 7
Cape Range National Park ⊥ AUS 172-173 A 7
Cape Ray o CDN (NFL) 242-243 J 5
Cape River ~ AUS 174-175 H 7
Cape Romain National Wildlife Refuge ⊥ USA (SC) 284-285 L 4
Cape Sable Island ⌒ CDN (NS) 240-241 K 7
Cape Saint Francis ▲ CDN (NFL) 242-243 Q 5
Cape Saint Francis o ZA 220-221 G 7
Cape Saint John ▲ CDN (NFL) 242-243 N 2
Cape Scott Provincial Park ⊥ CDN (BC) 230-231 A 3
Čāpešlū o IR 136-137 F 6
Cape Smiley ▲ ARK 16 F 29
Capesterre-Belle-Eau o F 56 E 3
Cape Surville ▲ SOL 184 I f 4
Cape Tormentine o CDN (NB) 240-241 M 4
Cape Upstart National Park ⊥ AUS 174-175 J 6
Cape Verde = Cabo Verde ■ CV 202-203 B 6
Cape Verde Islands = Cabo Verde, Arquipélago de ⌒ CV 202-203 B 6
Cape Verde Plateau ≃ 6-7 G 7
Cape Vincent o USA (NY) 278-279 E 4
Cape Washington ▲ FJI 184 III a 3
Cape York Peninsula ⌣ AUS 174-175 G 3
Cape Young o CDN 24-25 O 6
Cape Zele'e = Nialaha'u Point ▲ SOL 184 I e 3
Cap-Haïtien ☆• RH 54-55 J 5
Capiá, Rio ~ BR 68-69 K 6
Capibaribe, Rio ~ BR 68-69 L 5
Capilla del Monte o RA 76-77 E 6
Capim, Rio ~ BR 68-69 D 2
Capim Grosso o BR 68-69 H 7
Capinópolis o BR 72-73 F 5
Capinzal o BR 74-75 E 6
Capirenda o BOL 76-77 F 1
Cap Island ⌒ RP 160-161 D 10
Capissayan o RP 160-161 D 3
Capistrano o BR 68-69 J 4
Capitachouane, Rivière ~ CDN 236-237 M 5

Cal-Nev-Ari — Capitachouane, Rivière 311

Capitan ○ **USA** (NM) 256-257 K 5
Capitán Aracena, Isla ⌒ **RCH** 80 E 7
Capitan Baldo ○ **PY** 76-77 K 2
Capitan Grande Indian Reservation X **USA** (CA) 248-249 H 7
Capitán Pablo Lagerenza ☆ **PY** 70-71 G 6
Capitán Porto Alegro ○ **BR** 76-77 K 5
Capitán Sarmiente ○ **RA** 78-79 K 3
Capitán Ustares, Cerro ▲ **BOL** 70-71 G 6
Capitão, Igarapé ~ **BR** 66-67 E 6
Capitão Cardoso, Rio ~ **BR** 70-71 G 2
Capitão de Campos ○ **BR** 68-69 H 4
Capitão Enéas ○ **BR** 72-73 J 4
Capitão Leônidas Marques ○ **BR** 74-75 D 5
Capitão Poço ○ **BR** 68-69 E 2
Capitão Rivadenaira ○ **EC** 64-65 E 2
Capitol ○ **USA** (MT) 250-251 P 6
Capitol Peak ▲ **USA** (CO) 254-255 H 4
Capitol Peak ▲ **USA** (NV) 246-247 H 2
Capitol Reef National Park ⊥ **USA** (UT) 254-255 D 5
Capivara, Represa < **BR** 72-73 E 7
Capivara, Rio ~ **BR** 68-69 D 6
Capivaras, Cachoeira das ~ **BR** 66-67 K 6
Capivaras, Salto das ~ **BR** 70-71 K 3
Capivarí ○ **BR** 72-73 G 7
Capivari, Rio ~ **BR** 70-71 J 6
Capixaba ○ **BR** 68-69 G 7
Čaplanovo ○ **RUS** 122-123 K 5
Čaplino ○ **RUS** 112-113 Y 4
Čaplino, Novoe ○ **RUS** 112-113 Y 4
Čapljina ○ **BIH** 100-101 F 3
Čaplygin ○ **RUS** 94-95 Q 5
Čaplynka ○ **UA** 102-103 H 4
Cap Marcos, Área Indígena X **BR** 70-71 H 4
Cap Mountain ▲ **CDN** 30-31 H 4
Capoche ~ **MOC** 218-219 G 2
Capoeira do Rei ○ **BR** 62-63 J 5
Capolo ○ **ANG** 216-217 B 5
Čapoma ~ **RUS** 88-89 P 3
Caponda ○ **MOC** 218-219 F 2
Čapo-Ologo ○ **RUS** 118-119 J 7
Capo Rizzuto ○ **I** 100-101 F 5
Capot Blanc, Lac ⬭ **CDN** 30-31 O 4
Capoto, Área Indígena X **BR** 68-69 B 6
Capotoah, Mount ▲ **RP** 160-161 F 6
Cappadocia = Capadocia ⏊ **TR** 128-129 F 3
Cappahayden ○ **CDN** (NFL) 242-243 Q 6
Capps ○ **USA** (FL) 286-287 F 1
Capráia, Ísola di ⌒ **I** 100-101 B 3
Capreol ○ **CDN** (ONT) 238-239 E 2
Capri, Ísola di ⌒ •• **I** 100-101 E 4
Capricorn, Cape ▲ **AUS** 178-179 L 2
Capricorn Group ⌒ **AUS** 178-179 L 2
Capricorn Highway II **AUS** 178-179 H 2
Capricorn Section ⊥ **AUS** 178-179 M 2
Caprivi Game Park ⊥ **NAM** 218-219 B 4
Caprivi Strip = Caprivistrook ⏊ **NAM** 218-219 B 3
Caprock ○ **USA** (NM) 256-257 M 5
Caprock Canyons State Park ⊥ • **USA** (TX) 264-265 C 4
Capron ○ **USA** (VA) 280-281 J 7
Cap Seize ○ **CDN** (QUE) 242-243 B 3
Captain Cook ○ **USA** (HI) 288 K 5
Captains Flat ○ **AUS** 180-181 K 3
Captiva ○ **USA** (FL) 286-287 G 5
Captiva Island ⌒ **USA** (FL) 286-287 G 5
Capua ○ **ANG** 216-217 E 7
Capucapu, Rio ~ **BR** 62-63 E 6
Capulin ○ **USA** (NM) 256-257 M 2
Capulin Mountain National Monument • **USA** (NM) 256-257 M 2
Capul Island ⌒ **RP** 160-161 F 6
Capunda ○ **ANG** 216-217 D 5
Cap Wom National Park ⊥ **PNG** 183 B 2
Čaqlāve, Čam-e ~ **IRQ** 128-129 L 5
Caqua ○ **YV** 60-61 H 2
Caquena ○ **RCH** 70-71 C 6
Caquetá, Río ~ **CO** 66-67 B 3
Caqueza ○ **CO** 60-61 E 5
Čara ☆ **RUS** (CTN) 118-119 J 7
Čara ~ **RUS** 118-119 J 6
Carabao Island ⌒ **RP** 160-161 D 6
Carabaya, Cordillera de ▲ **PE** 70-71 B 3
Carabaya, Río ~ **PE** 70-71 C 4
Carabayllo ○ **PE** 64-65 D 7
Carabinani, Rio ~ **BR** 66-67 G 4
Carabobo ○ **YV** 62-63 D 2
Caracal ○ **RO** 102-103 D 5
Caracal, Rio ~ **BR** 68-69 E 6
Caracarai ○ **BR** 62-63 D 5
Caracaraí, Estação Ecológica ⊥ **BR** 62-63 D 5
Caracas ★ • **YV** 60-61 H 2
Caracol ∴ • **BH** 52-53 K 3
Caracól ○ **BR** 68-69 G 6
Caracol ○ **BR** 76-77 J 2
Caracol ~ **MEX** 50-51 D 5
Caracoli ○ **CO** 60-61 E 2
Caracuja Falls ~ **CDN** 30-31 F 3
Caraculo ○ **ANG** 216-217 B 7
Carad ○ **RH** 54-55 J 5
Carai ○ **BR** 72-73 K 4
Caraiari, Rio ~ **BR** 68-69 B 4
Caraíva ○ **BR** 72-73 L 4
Carajas ○ **BR** 68-69 C 5
Carajás, Serra dos ▲ **BR** 68-69 C 5
Čarak, Bandar-e ○ **IR** 134-135 F 5
Caramat ○ **CDN** (ONT) 236-237 B 3
Caramelo ○ **CO** 60-61 D 3
Caramoan ○ **RP** 160-161 E 6
Caramoan Peninsula ⌣ **RP** 160-161 E 6
Caraná, Rio ~ **BR** 70-71 H 3
Caranavi ○ **BOL** 70-71 D 4
Carandaí ○ **BR** 72-73 J 6
Carandazinho ○ **BR** 70-71 J 5
Carandotta ○ **AUS** 178-179 E 1
Carangola ○ **BR** 72-73 J 6
Caransebeş ○ **RO** 102-103 C 5
Carapa ○ **YV** 60-61 K 3
Carapajó ○ **BR** 68-69 D 3
Carapán ○ **MEX** 52-53 C 2
Cara-Paraná, Río ~ **CO** 64-65 F 2
Carapé, Sierra de ▲ **ROU** 78-79 M 3
Carapebus ○ **BR** 72-73 K 7
Carapo ○ **YV** 60-61 K 5
Caraquet ○ • **CDN** (NB) 240-241 L 3
Carara Puca ○ **BR** 66-67 D 2
Carat, Tanjung ▲ **RI** 162-163 F 6
Caratasca, Cayo ⌒ **HN** 54-55 D 6
Caratasca, Laguna de ≈ 54-55 C 7
Carateua ○ **BR** 68-69 E 2
Caratinga ○ **BR** 72-73 J 5
Carauari ○ **BR** 66-67 D 5
Caraúbas ○ **BR** 68-69 K 4
Caravela ○ **GNB** 202-203 B 4
Caravelas ○ **BR** 72-73 L 4
Caraveli ○ **PE** 64-65 F 9
Caraz ○ **PE** 64-65 D 6
Carazinho ○ **BR** (CAT) 74-75 E 7
Carazinho ○ **BR** (RSU) 74-75 D 7
Carballino, O ○ **E** 98-99 C 3
Carballo ○ **E** 98-99 C 3
Carberry ○ **CDN** (MAN) 234-235 D 5
Carbine ○ **AUS** 176-177 F 5
Carbó ○ **MEX** 50-51 D 3
Carbon ○ **CDN** (ALB) 232-233 E 4
Carbon ○ **USA** (TX) 264-265 F 6
Carbon, Cap ▲ **DZ** 188-189 L 3
Carbonado ○ **USA** (WA) 244-245 C 3
Carbonara, Capo ▲ **I** 100-101 B 5
Carbondale ○ **USA** (CO) 254-255 H 4
Carbondale ○ **USA** (IL) 276-277 F 3
Carbondale ○ **USA** (KS) 262-263 L 6
Carbondale ○ **USA** (MI) 270-271 L 5
Carbondale ○ **USA** (PA) 280-281 L 2
Carbonear ○ **CDN** (NFL) 242-243 P 5
Carbonera, La ○ **MEX** 50-51 L 5
Carboneras ○ **E** 98-99 G 6
Carbon Hill ○ **USA** (AL) 284-285 C 3
Carbónia ○ **I** 100-101 B 5
Carbonita ○ **BR** 72-73 J 4
Carcajou Lake ⬭ **CDN** 30-31 F 2
Carcajou River ~ **CDN** 30-31 F 3
Carcar ○ **RP** 160-161 E 7
Carcarañá, Río ~ **RA** 78-79 J 2
Carcassonne ☆ •• **F** 90-91 J 10
Carcross ○ **CDN** 20-21 X 6
Çardak ☆ **TR** 128-129 C 4
Cardale ○ **CDN** (MAN) 234-235 C 4
Cardamon Hills ▲ **IND** 140-141 G 5
Cardamum Island ⌒ **IND** 140-141 E 5
Cardeña ○ **E** 98-99 E 5
Cardenas ○ **C** 54-55 E 3
Cárdenas ○ **C** 54-55 E 3
Cárdenas ○ **MEX** (SLP) 50-51 K 6
Cárdenas ○ • **MEX** (TAB) 52-53 H 2
Cardenyabba Creek ~ **AUS** 178-179 G 5
Cardiel, Lago ⬭ **RA** 80 E 4
Cardiff ○ **GB** 90-91 F 6
Cardigan ○ **CDN** (NS) 240-241 N 4
Cardigan ○ **GB** 90-91 E 5
Cardigan Bay ≈ 90-91 E 5
Cardigan Strait ≈ 24-25 a 2
Cardinal ○ **CDN** (MAN) 234-235 E 5
Cardona ○ **ROU** 78-79 L 2
Cardón del Plata ▲ **RA** 78-79 E 2
Cardoso ○ **BR** 72-73 F 6
Cardoso, Ilha do ⌒ **BR** 74-75 G 5
Cardston ○ **CDN** (ALB) 232-233 E 6
Cardwell ○ **AUS** 174-175 J 6
Cardwell ○ **USA** (MT) 250-251 H 6
Čardwell, Čape ▲ **CDN** 24-25 L 5
Cardwell Range ▲ **AUS** 174-175 H 6
Čardzouskaja oblast' ▫ **TM** 136-137 G 4
Careen Lake ⬭ **CDN** 32-33 Q 3
Carefree ○ **USA** (IN) 274-275 M 6
Carei ○ **RO** 102-103 C 4
Careiro ○ **BR** 66-67 G 4
Careiro da Várzea ○ **BR** 66-67 H 4
Carén ○ **RCH** 76-77 B 6
Čarencavan ○ **AR** 128-129 L 2
Carentan ○ **F** 90-91 G 7
Carevo ○ **BG** 102-103 E 6
Carey ○ **USA** (ID) 252-253 E 3
Carey ○ **USA** (OH) 280-281 C 3
Carey, Lake ⬭ **AUS** 176-177 G 4
Carey Downs ○ **AUS** 176-177 C 2
Carey Lake ⬭ **CDN** 30-31 S 4
Carey Øer ⌒ **GRØ** 26-27 O 5
Careysburg ○ **LB** 202-203 E 6
Careys Cave • **AUS** 180-181 K 3
Cargados Carajos Islands ⏊ **MS** 12 D 6
Carhaix-Plouguer ○ **F** 90-91 F 7
Carhuamayo ○ **PE** 64-65 D 7
Carhuanca ○ **PE** 64-65 F 8
Carhuaz ○ **PE** 64-65 D 6
Carhué ○ **RA** 78-79 H 4
Cariaco, Golfo de ≈ 60-61 J 2
Cariamanga ○ **EC** 64-65 C 4
Cariango ○ **ANG** 216-217 C 5
Cariati ○ **I** 100-101 F 5
Caribaná, Punta ▲ **CO** 60-61 C 3
Caribbean Basin ≃ 56 A 4
Caribbean Marine Research Centre Lee Stocking Island ∴ • **BS** 54-55 G 3
Caribbean Sea ≈ 5 D 3
Caribe, Río ~ **MEX** 52-53 J 2
Caribes, Los ○ **YV** 62-63 D 3
Caribia ○ **CO** 60-61 C 3
Cariboo Highway • **CDN** (BC) 230-231 H 2
Cariboo Mountains ▲ **CDN** 228-229 N 3
Caribou ○ **CDN** 30-31 V 6
Caribou ○ **USA** (ME) 278-279 O 2
Caribou Depot ○ **CDN** (NB) 240-241 J 3
Caribou Island ⌒ **CDN** 36-37 J 2
Caribou Lake ⬭ **CDN** (MAN) 30-31 W 6
Caribou Lake ⬭ **CDN** (NWT) 20-21 Y 2
Caribou Lake ⬭ **CDN** (ONT) 234-235 O 4
Caribou Mount ▲ **USA** 20-21 P 3
Caribou Mountains ▲ **CDN** 30-31 M 6
Caribou River ~ **CDN** 20-21 X 3
Caribou River ~ **CDN** 30-31 W 6
Caribou River ~ **CDN** 30-31 F 5
Caribou River ~ **CDN** 228-229 N 4
Caribou River ~ **USA** 22-23 Q 5
Caricaca, Rio ~ **BR** 68-69 E 5
Carié ○ **BR** 68-69 K 6
Carievale ○ **CDN** (SAS) 232-233 R 6
Carigara ○ **RP** 160-161 F 7
Čārikār ☆ **AFG** 138-139 B 2
Cari Laufquen Grande, Laguna ⬭ **RA** 78-79 E 6
Carinda ○ **AUS** 178-179 J 6
Cariñena ○ **E** 98-99 G 4
Carinhanha ○ **BR** 72-73 J 3
Carinhanha, Rio ~ **BR** 72-73 H 3
Caripande ○ **ANG** 214-215 B 7
Caripare ○ **BR** 68-69 F 7
Caripé, Rio ~ **BR** 68-69 D 3
Caripira ○ **BR** 66-67 E 3
Caripito ○ **YV** 60-61 K 2
Cariquima ○ **RCH** 70-71 C 6
Carira ○ **BR** 68-69 K 7
Cariré ○ **BR** 68-69 H 3
Cariris Novos, Serra dos ▲ **BR** 68-69 H 5
Caris, Río ~ **YV** 60-61 K 3
Caritaya, Embalse de < **RCH** 70-71 C 6
Caritianas ○ **BR** 66-67 F 7
Carito, El ○ **YV** 60-61 J 3
Carius ○ **BR** 68-69 J 5
Čarky (Muolakan) ~ **RUS** 110-111 V 6
Carl Blackwell, Lake ⬭ **USA** (OK) 264-265 G 2
Carleton ○ **CDN** (NS) 240-241 K 6
Carleton, Mount ▲ **CDN** (NB) 240-241 J 3
Carleton Place ○ **CDN** (ONT) 238-239 J 3
Carletonville ○ **ZA** 220-221 H 3
Carlin ○ **USA** (NV) 246-247 J 3
Carlindi ○ **AUS** 172-173 D 6
Carlin Gold Mine ○ **USA** (NV) 246-247 J 3
Carlinville ○ **USA** (IL) 274-275 J 5
Carlisle ○ **GB** 90-91 F 4
Carlisle ○ **USA** (IA) 274-275 E 3
Carlisle ○ **USA** (IN) 274-275 L 6
Carlisle ○ **USA** (PA) 280-281 J 3
Carlisle ○ **USA** (SC) 284-285 J 2
Carlisle ○ **USA** (TX) 268-269 E 6
Carlisle Island ⌒ **USA** 22-23 L 6
Carlisle Lakes ⬭ **AUS** 176-177 J 4
Carlo ○ **AUS** 178-179 E 2
Carloforte ○ **I** 100-101 B 5
Carlópolis ○ **BR** 72-73 F 7
Carlos ○ **CDN** (ALB) 232-233 D 3
Carlos ○ **USA** (TX) 266-267 L 3
Carlos Casares ○ **RA** 78-79 J 3
Carlos Chagas ○ **BR** 72-73 K 4
Carlos Tejedor ○ **RA** 78-79 H 3
Carlota, La ○ **RA** 78-79 H 2
Carlow = Ceatharlach ○ **IRL** 90-91 D 5
Carlowrie ○ **CDN** (MAN) 234-235 G 5
Carlsbad ○ **USA** (CA) 248-249 G 6
Carlsbad ○ **USA** (NM) 256-257 L 6
Carlsbad ○ **USA** (TX) 266-267 G 2
Carlsbad Caverns National Park ⊥ **USA** (NM) 256-257 L 6
Carlsberg Fjord ≈ 26-27 o 8
Carlsbergfondet Land ⏊ **GRØ** 26-27 n 5
Carlsberg Ridge ≃ 12 D 4
Carlton ○ **CDN** (SAS) 232-233 M 3
Carlton ○ **USA** (AL) 284-285 C 5
Carlton ○ **USA** (GA) 284-285 G 2
Carlton ○ **USA** (OR) 244-245 B 5
Carlton ○ **USA** (WA) 244-245 E 2
Carlyle ○ **CDN** (SAS) 232-233 Q 6
Carlyle ○ **USA** (IL) 274-275 J 6
Carlyle ○ **USA** (MT) 250-251 P 5
Carlyle Lake ○ **CDN** (SAS) 232-233 Q 6
Carlyle Lake ⬭ **USA** (IL) 274-275 J 6
Carmacks ○ **CDN** 20-21 W 5
Carmagnola ○ **I** 100-101 A 2
Carman ○ **CDN** (MAN) 234-235 E 5
Carmangay ○ **CDN** (ALB) 232-233 E 5
Carmanville ○ **CDN** (NFL) 242-243 O 3
Carmarthen ○ **GB** 90-91 E 6
Carmaux ○ **F** 90-91 J 9
Carmel ○ **USA** (IN) 274-275 M 5
Carmelita ○ **GCA** 52-53 J 3
Carmelo ○ **ROU** 78-79 K 3
Carmen ○ **RP** 160-161 F 8
Carmen ○ **USA** (OK) 264-265 F 2
Carmen, El ○ **BOL** 70-71 F 3
Carmen, El ○ **CO** 60-61 B 6
Carmen, El ○ **EC** 64-65 C 2
Carmen, El ○ **GCA** 52-53 H 4
Carmen, El ○ **RA** 76-77 E 3
Carmen, Isla del ⌒ **MEX** 52-53 J 2
Carmen, Isla El ⌒ **MEX** 50-51 D 5
Carmen, Laguna del ≈ 52-53 H 2
Carmen, Río del ~ **RCH** 76-77 B 5
Carmen de Areco ○ **RA** 78-79 K 3
Carmen de Bolivar, El ○ **CO** 60-61 D 3
Carmen de Patagones ○ **RA** 78-79 H 6
Carmen Silva, Sierra de ▲ **RCH** 80 F 6
Carmi ○ **CDN** (BC) 230-231 K 4
Carmi ○ **USA** (IL) 274-275 K 6
Carmichael ○ **AUS** 178-179 J 1
Carmichael ○ **USA** (CA) 246-247 D 5
Carmichael ○ **USA** (MS) 268-269 M 5
Carmichael Crag ▲ **AUS** 176-177 L 2
Carmichael River ~ **AUS** 178-179 J 2
Carmila ○ **AUS** 178-179 K 1
Carmo ○ **BR** 68-69 D 4
Carmo de Mata ○ **BR** 72-73 H 6
Carmo de Minas ○ **BR** 72-73 H 7
Carmo do Paranaíba ○ **BR** 72-73 G 5
Carmody, Lake ⬭ **AUS** 176-177 E 6
Carmona ○ **CR** 52-53 B 7
Carmona ○ •• **E** 98-99 E 6
Carnage, Mount ▲ **AUS** 176-177 F 5
Carnaíba ○ **BR** 68-69 K 5
Carnamah ○ **AUS** 176-177 C 4
Carnarvon ○ **AUS** (QLD) 178-179 J 3
Carnarvon ○ **AUS** (WA) 176-177 B 2
Carnarvon ○ **CDN** (ONT) 238-239 G 3
Carnarvon ○ **ZA** 220-221 F 5
Carnarvon National Park ⊥ **AUS** 178-179 J 3
Carnarvon Range ▲ **AUS** 176-177 F 2
Carnarvon Range ▲ **AUS** 178-179 K 3
Carnatic Shoal ≃ 160-161 B 7
Carndonagh ○ **IRL** 90-91 D 4
Carnduff ○ **CDN** (SAS) 232-233 R 6
Carnegie ○ **AUS** 176-177 G 2
Carnegie ○ **USA** (OK) 264-265 F 3
Carnegie ○ **USA** (PA) 280-281 G 3
Carnegie ○ **USA** (PA) 280-281 F 3
Carnegie, Lake ⬭ **AUS** 176-177 G 3
Carn Eige ▲ **GB** 90-91 E 3
Carneiro ○ **USA** (KS) 262-263 H 6
Carnera, Punta ▲ **EC** 64-65 B 3
Carnes ○ **AUS** 178-179 C 6
Carnesville ○ **USA** (GA) 284-285 G 2
Carney ○ **USA** (MI) 270-271 L 5
Car Nicobar Island ⌒ **IND** 140-141 L 5
Carnikava ○ **LV** 94-95 J 3
Carnot ○ • **RCA** 206-207 B 6
Carnot, Cape ▲ **AUS** 180-181 C 3
Carnot Bay ≈ 172-173 F 4
Carnsore Point ▲ **IRL** 90-91 D 5
Carnwath River ~ **CDN** 30-31 F 2
Carnwood ○ **CDN** (ALB) 232-233 D 2
Caro ○ **USA** (MI) 272-273 F 4
Caro, El ○ **YV** 60-61 J 3
Caro de La Negra, El ○ **YV** 60-61 J 3
Carol City ○ **USA** (FL) 286-287 J 6
Carolina ○ **BR** 68-69 E 5
Carolina ○ **CO** 60-61 D 4
Carolina ○ **E** 98-99 F 5
Carolina ○ **RCH** 76-77 B 2
Carolina ○ **USA** (PR) 286-287 Q 2
Carolina ○ **ZA** 220-221 K 3
Carolina Sandhills National Wildlife Refuge ⊥ **USA** (SC) 284-285 K 2
Caroline ○ **CDN** (ALB) 232-233 D 3
Caroline, Lake ⬭ **AUS** 178-179 D 3
Caroline Beach ○ **USA** (NC) 282-283 K 6
Caroline Island ⌒ **KIB** 13 M 3
Caroline Islands ⌒ **FSM** 13 F 2
Caroline National Memorial, Fort • **USA** (FL) 286-287 H 1
Caroline Seamounts ≃ 13 F 2
Carolside ○ **CDN** (ALB) 232-233 G 4
Caron ○ **AUS** 176-177 D 4
Caron Brook ○ **CDN** (NB) 240-241 G 3
Caroni, Río ~ **YV** 60-61 K 5
Carora ○ **YV** 60-61 F 2
Carp ○ **USA** (NV) 248-249 K 2
Carpathian Mountains = Karpaty ▲ 102-103 B 3
Carpaţii Orientali ▲ **RO** 102-103 D 4
Carpentaria, Gulf of ≈ 174-175 E 3
Carpentaria Highway II **AUS** 174-175 B 5
Carpenter ○ **USA** (SD) 260-261 J 2
Carpenter ○ **USA** (WY) 252-253 O 5
Carpenter Lake ⬭ **CDN** (BC) 230-231 G 3
Carpentras ○ **F** 90-91 K 9
Carpi ○ **I** 100-101 C 2
Carpina ○ **BR** 68-69 L 5
Carpinteria ○ **USA** (CA) 248-249 E 5
Carpio ○ **USA** (ND) 258-259 F 3
Carp Lake ⬭ **CDN** (BC) 228-229 L 2
Carp Lake ○ **USA** (MI) 272-273 E 2
Carp Lake Provincial Park ⊥ **CDN** (BC) 228-229 L 2
Carpolac ○ **AUS** 180-181 F 4
Carr ○ **USA** (CO) 254-255 L 3
Carrabelle ○ **USA** (FL) 286-287 E 2
Carracollo ○ **BOL** 70-71 D 5
Carragana ○ **CDN** (SAS) 232-233 P 3
Čār Rāh ○ **AFG** 134-135 K 2
Carraipia ○ **CO** 60-61 E 2
Carranya ○ **AUS** 172-173 H 5
Carrapatal ○ **BR** 68-69 G 3
Carrapatal, Ilha ⌒ **BR** 68-69 G 3
Carrara ○ **I** 100-101 C 2
Carrasquero ○ **YV** 60-61 E 2
Carr Boyd Ranges ▲ **AUS** 172-173 J 4
Carreira Comprida, Cachoeira ~ **BR** 68-69 D 7
Carrere, Cerro ▲ **RA** 78-79 E 4
Carreta, Punta ▲ **PE** 64-65 D 9
Carretera Interamericana II **MEX** 50-51 F 2
Carretero, Puerto de ▲ **E** 98-99 F 6
Carr Fork Lake ⬭ **USA** (KY) 276-277 M 3
Carriacou Island ⌒ **WG** 56 E 5
Carrical ○ **CV** 202-203 B 5
Carrick ○ **IRL** 90-91 C 4
Carriere ○ **USA** (MS) 268-269 L 6
Carrieton ○ **AUS** 180-181 E 2
Carrington ○ **USA** (ND) 258-259 H 4
Carrington Island ⌒ **USA** (UT) 254-255 C 3
Carrión, Río ~ **E** 98-99 E 3
Carriringue ○ **RCH** 78-79 D 5
Carrizal ○ **CO** 60-61 E 1
Carrizal ○ **RA** 76-77 D 5
Carrizal ○ **YV** 62-63 D 2
Carrizal, Alto de ▲ **CO** 60-61 C 4
Carrizal, El ○ **MEX** 50-51 F 2
Carrizal, Punta ▲ **RCH** 76-77 B 5
Carrizal, Quebrada ~ **RCH** 76-77 B 5
Carrizal Bajo ○ **RCH** 76-77 B 5
Carrizo ○ **USA** (AZ) 256-257 E 5
Carrizo, Quebrada del ~ **RCH** 76-77 C 3
Carrizo Creek ~ **USA** 256-257 M 2
Carrizo Springs ○ **USA** (TX) 266-267 H 5
Carrizozo ○ **USA** (NM) 256-257 K 5
Carroll ○ **CDN** (MAN) 234-235 C 5
Carroll ○ **USA** (IA) 274-275 D 2
Carrollton ○ **USA** (AL) 284-285 B 3
Carrollton ○ **USA** (GA) 284-285 E 3
Carrollton ○ **USA** (IL) 274-275 H 5
Carrollton ○ **USA** (KY) 276-277 K 2
Carrollton ○ **USA** (MI) 272-273 F 4
Carrollton ○ **USA** (MO) 274-275 E 5
Carrollton ○ **USA** (MS) 268-269 L 3
Carrollton ○ **USA** (OH) 280-281 E 3
Carrol Summit ▲ **USA** (NV) 246-247 H 4
Carrot Creek ○ **CDN** (ALB) 232-233 C 2
Carrot River ○ **CDN** (SAS) 232-233 P 2
Carrot River ~ **CDN** 232-233 Q 2
Carrozas ○ **CO** 60-61 E 6
Čarrūd ○ **IR** 134-135 G 3
Carruthers ○ **CDN** (SAS) 232-233 J 3
Çarşamba ☆ **TR** 128-129 G 2
Čaršanga ○ **TM** 136-137 K 6
Carseland ○ **CDN** (ALB) 232-233 E 5
Carson ○ **USA** (ND) 258-259 F 5
Carson, Fort • **USA** (CO) 254-255 L 5
Carson City ○ **USA** (MI) 272-273 E 4
Carson City ☆ **USA** (NV) 246-247 F 4
Carson River ~ **AUS** 172-173 H 3
Carson Sink ⬭ **USA** (NV) 246-247 G 4
Carstairs ○ **CDN** (ALB) 232-233 D 4
Cartagena ☆ ••• **CO** 60-61 D 2
Cartagena ○ **E** 98-99 G 6
Cartagena del Chaira ○ **CO** 64-65 E 1
Cartago ○ **CO** 60-61 D 5
Cartago ☆ **CR** 52-53 C 7
Cartago ○ **USA** (CA) 248-249 F 3
Carta Valley ○ **USA** (TX) 266-267 G 4
Carter ○ **USA** (MT) 250-251 J 4
Carter ○ **USA** (OK) 264-265 E 3
Carter ○ **USA** (WY) 252-253 H 5
Carter, Mount ▲ **AUS** 174-175 G 3
Carters Lake < **USA** (GA) 284-285 F 2
Carter Spit ▲ **USA** 22-23 P 3
Carters Range ▲ **AUS** 178-179 F 2
Cartersville ○ **USA** (GA) 284-285 F 2
Cartersville ○ **USA** (IA) 274-275 E 2
Cartersville ○ **USA** (MT) 250-251 N 5
Carthage ∴ ••• **TN** 190-191 H 2
Carthage ○ **USA** (AR) 276-277 C 6
Carthage ○ **USA** (IL) 274-275 G 4
Carthage ○ **USA** (MO) 276-277 A 3
Carthage ○ **USA** (MS) 268-269 L 4
Carthage ○ **USA** (NC) 282-283 H 5
Carthage ○ **USA** (NY) 278-279 F 5
Carthage ○ **USA** (SD) 260-261 J 2
Carthage ○ **USA** (TN) 276-277 K 4
Carthage ○ **USA** (TX) 264-265 K 6
Cartier ○ **CDN** (ONT) 238-239 D 2
Cartier, Port- ○ **CDN** (QUE) 242-243 B 2
Cartier Islet ⌒ **AUS** 172-173 F 2
Carti Suitupo ○ **PA** 52-53 E 7
Cartridge Mount ▲ **CDN** 30-31 K 4
Cartwright ○ **CDN** (MAN) 234-235 D 5
Cartwright ○ **USA** (KY) 276-277 K 4
Carú, Área Indígena X **BR** 68-69 E 3
Caru, Rio ~ **BR** 68-69 E 3
Caruachi ○ **YV** 60-61 K 3
Caruaru ○ **BR** 68-69 L 6
Caruban ○ **RI** 168 D 3
Carún, Río ~ **YV** 60-61 K 5
Carunantabari ○ **YV** 60-61 K 5
Carúpano ○ **YV** 60-61 K 2
Carurai ○ **RP** 160-161 C 7
Caruthersville ○ **USA** (MO) 276-277 F 4
Čarvakskoe vodohranilišče < **UZ** 136-137 M 4
Carvel ○ **CDN** (ALB) 232-233 D 2
Carver ○ **USA** (NV) 246-247 H 5
Carvinas ○ **BOL** 70-71 D 3
Carvoal ○ **BR** 70-71 J 5
Carvoeiro ○ **BR** 62-63 D 6
Carway ○ **CDN** (ALB) 232-233 E 6
Cary ○ **USA** (MS) 268-269 K 4
Cary ○ **USA** (NC) 282-283 J 5
Caryčanka ○ **UA** 102-103 J 3
Caryš ~ **KZ** 124-125 O 3
Čaryš ~ **RUS** 124-125 N 2
Carysfort, Cape ▲ **GB** 78-79 M 6
Caryšskoe ○ **RUS** 124-125 N 3
Carysville ○ **USA** (OH) 280-281 C 3
Caryville ○ **USA** (TN) 282-283 C 4
Čaš ○ **UZ** 136-137 K 5
Casabe, El ○ **YV** 60-61 K 4
Casabindo ○ **RA** 76-77 D 2
Casablanca ○ **RCH** 78-79 D 2
Casablanca = Ad-Dār-al-Bayda ☆ **MA** (CAS) 188-189 H 4
Casablanca = Ad-Dār-al-Bayda ☆ • **MA** (Cas) 188-189 H 4
Casa Branca ○ **BR** 72-73 G 6
Casa da Pedra • **BR** 70-71 K 4
Casadepaga ○ **USA** 20-21 H 4
Casa de Piedra ○ **RA** 78-79 F 5
Casa Grande ○ **USA** (AZ) 256-257 D 6
Casa Grandes Ruins National Monument • **USA** (AZ) 256-257 D 5
Casale Monferrato ○ • **I** 100-101 B 2
Casalins ○ **RA** 78-79 K 4
Casamance ⏊ **SN** 202-203 C 3
Casamance ~ **SN** 202-203 C 3
Casamento, Lagoa do ⬭ **BR** 74-75 E 8
Casamozza ○ **F** 98-99 M 3
Casanare ○ **CO** 60-61 G 5
Casanare, Río ~ **CO** 60-61 F 4
Casanay ○ **YV** 60-61 K 2
Casa Nova ○ **BR** 68-69 H 6
Casa Piedra ○ **USA** (TX) 266-267 C 4
Casarabi ○ **BOL** 70-71 E 4
Casares ○ **NIC** 52-53 L 6
Casas ○ **MEX** 50-51 K 6
Casas Adobes ○ **USA** (AZ) 256-257 E 6
Casas Grandes ∴ **MEX** 50-51 F 2
Casas Grandes, Río ~ **MEX** 50-51 F 2
Casa Verde ○ **BR** 72-73 D 6
Casavieja ○ • **E** 98-99 E 4
Casazinc ○ **CO** 60-61 E 6
Casca ○ **BR** (RSU) 74-75 E 7
Casca ○ **BR** (RSU) 74-75 E 8
Cascadas del Río Queguay ~ • **ROU** 78-79 K 2
Cascade ○ **CDN** (BC) 230-231 L 4
Cascade ○ **USA** (IA) 274-275 G 2
Cascade ○ **USA** (ID) 252-253 B 2
Cascade ○ **USA** (MT) 250-251 H 4
Cascade Caverns ∴ **USA** (TX) 266-267 J 4
Cascade Mountain Ski Area • **USA** (WI) 274-275 J 1
Cascade Range ▲ **USA** 244-245 C 10
Cascade Reservoir ⬭ **USA** (ID) 252-253 B 2
Cascade River ~ **CDN** 232-233 C 4
Cascades ○ **AUS** 176-177 F 6
Cascais ○ **P** 98-99 C 5
Cascajal ○ **C** 54-55 E 3
Cascajal, Río ~ **PE** 64-65 B 4
Cascapédia, Rivière ~ **CDN** 240-241 J 2
Cascas ○ **PE** 64-65 C 5
Cascavel ○ **BR** (CEA) 68-69 J 4
Cascavel ○ **BR** (PAR) 74-75 D 5
Casco, El ○ **MEX** 50-51 G 5
Casco Bay ≈ 278-279 L 5
Cascorro ○ **C** 54-55 G.4
Cascumpeque Bay ≈ 38-39 N 5
Cascumpeque Bay ≈ 240-241 M 4
Časeľka ~ **RUS** 114-115 Q 2
Časeľskoe, ozero ⬭ **RUS** 114-115 P 2
Caselton ○ **USA** (NV) 248-249 K 2
Caserta ☆ **I** 100-101 E 4
Caseville ○ **USA** (MI) 272-273 F 4
Casey ○ **USA** (IL) 274-275 L 5
Caseyr, Raas = Cap Gwardafuy ▲ **SP** 208-209 K 3
Cashel ○ **ZW** 218-219 G 4
Cashel = Caiseal ○ • **IRL** 90-91 D 5
Cashmere Downs ○ **AUS** 176-177 E 4
Cashton ○ **USA** (WI) 270-271 H 7
Casian Island ⌒ **RP** 160-161 C 7
Casigua ○ **YV** 60-61 F 2
Casiguran ○ **RP** 160-161 E 4
Casilda ○ **RA** 78-79 J 2
Casimiro de Abreu ○ **BR** 72-73 J 7
Casino ○ **AUS** 178-179 M 5
Casinos ○ **E** 98-99 G 5
Casiquiare, Río ~ **YV** 60-61 H 6
Casma ○ **PE** 64-65 C 6
Čašniki ☆ **BY** 94-95 L 4
Časovaja ○ **RUS** 118-119 J 9
Časovo ○ **RUS** 88-89 V 5
Caspana ○ **RCH** 76-77 C 2
Caspe ○ **E** 98-99 G 4
Casper ○ **USA** (WY) 252-253 M 4
Caspian ○ **USA** (MI) 270-271 K 4
Caspian Depression ⌣ 126-127 F 5
Caspian Sea ≈ 126-127 H 5
Cass ○ **RCH** 76-77 D 2
Cass ○ **USA** (AR) 276-277 B 5
Cassacatiza ○ **MOC** 218-219 G 2
Cassai ○ **ANG** (LUS) 216-217 F 5
Cassai ~ **ANG** 216-217 F 5
Cassamba ○ **ANG** 216-217 F 6
Cassange, Rio ~ **BR** 70-71 J 5
Cassango ○ **ANG** 216-217 D 4
Cassasala ○ **ANG** 216-217 E 5
Cass City ○ **USA** (MI) 272-273 F 4
Casselman ○ **CDN** (ONT) 238-239 K 3
Casselton ○ **USA** (ND) 258-259 K 5
Cass Fjord ≈ 26-27 S 3
Cássia ○ **BR** 72-73 G 6
Cassiar ○ **CDN** 30-31 E 6
Cassiar Mountains ▲ **CDN** 30-31 D 5
Cassiar-Stewart Highway II **CDN** 32-33 E 3
Cassidy ○ **CDN** (BC) 230-231 F 4
Cassilândia ○ **BR** 72-73 E 5
Cassilis ○ **AUS** 180-181 K 2
Cassinga ○ **ANG** 216-217 D 7
Cassino ○ **I** 100-101 D 4
Cass Lake ○ **USA** (MN) 270-271 D 3
Cassoday ○ **USA** (KS) 262-263 K 6
Cassongue ○ **ANG** 216-217 C 5
Cassopolis ○ **USA** (MI) 272-273 C 6
Cass River ~ **USA** 272-273 F 4
Cassville ○ **USA** (MO) 276-277 B 4
Cassville ○ **USA** (WI) 274-275 H 2
Cast ▲ **MAU** 146-147 K 1
Castaic ○ **USA** (CA) 248-249 F 5
Castana ○ **YV** 60-61 J 5
Castanhal ○ **BR** (AMA) 66-67 F 6
Castanhal ○ **BR** (P) 68-69 E 2
Castanheira ○ **BR** 70-71 H 2
Castaños ○ **MEX** 50-51 J 4
Castaño Viejo ○ **RA** 76-77 C 6
Castèl del Monte •• **I** 100-101 F 4
Castelhanos, Ponta dos ▲ **BR** (ESP) 72-73 K 6
Castelhanos, Ponta dos ▲ **BR** (RIO) 72-73 H 7
Casteljaloux ○ **F** 90-91 H 9
Castella ○ **USA** (CA) 246-247 C 2
Castellana, Grotte di •• **I** 100-101 F 4
Castellana, La ○ **RP** 160-161 E 7
Castellar de Santisteban ○ **E** 98-99 F 5
Castelldefels ○ **E** 98-99 H 4
Castelli ○ **RA** (BUA) 78-79 L 4
Castelli ○ **RA** (CHA) 76-77 G 3
Castelló de la Plana ○ **E** 98-99 G 5
Castellón de la Plana = Castelló de la Plana ○ **E** 98-99 G 5
Castelnaudary ○ • **F** 90-91 H 10
Castelnau-Magnoac ○ **F** 90-91 H 10
Castelo ○ **BR** 72-73 K 6
Castelo Branco ☆ • **P** 98-99 D 5
Castelo do Piauí ○ **BR** 68-69 H 4
Castelsardo ○ • **I** 100-101 B 4
Castelsarrasin ○ **F** 90-91 H 9
Castelvetrano ○ **I** 100-101 D 6
Casterton ○ **AUS** 180-181 F 4
Castilla ○ **PE** 64-65 B 4
Castilla ○ **RA** 78-79 K 3
Castilla la Mancha ▫ **E** 98-99 F 5
Castilla y León ▫ **E** 98-99 D 3
Castilletes ○ **CO** 60-61 F 2
Castillo, El ∴ • **NIC** 52-53 B 6
Castillo, Pampa del ⏊ **RA** 80 F 2
Castillo de Bayuela ○ **E** 98-99 E 4
Castillo de San Felipe • **CO** 60-61 D 2
Castillo de San Marcos National Monument • **USA** (FL) 286-287 H 2
Castillos ○ **ROU** 74-75 D 10
Castillos, Laguna de ⬭ **ROU** 74-75 D 10
Castillos, Los ○ • **YV** 60-61 K 3
Castle ○ **USA** (MT) 250-251 J 5
Castlebar = Caisleán an Bharraigh ○ **IRL** 90-91 C 5
Castleberry ○ **USA** (AL) 284-285 C 5
Castle Cape ▲ **USA** 22-23 R 4
Castle Creek ~ **CDN** 228-229 O 3
Castledale ○ **CDN** (BC) 230-231 N 2
Castle Dale ○ **USA** (UT) 254-255 E 4
Castleford ○ **USA** (ID) 252-253 D 4
Castlegar ○ **CDN** (BC) 230-231 M 4
Castle Island ⌒ **BS** 54-55 H 3
Castle Island ○ **CDN** (NFL) 242-243 N 1
Castle Island ⌒ **CDN** (NWT) 36-37 L 7
Castlemaine ○ **AUS** 180-181 H 4
Castle Mountain ▲ **USA** (CA) 248-249 D 4
Castle Peak ▲ **USA** (ID) 252-253 D 2
Castlepoint ○ **NZ** 182 F 4
Castlereagh Bay ≈ 174-175 C 3
Castlereagh River ~ **AUS** 178-179 K 6
Castle Rock ○ **CDN** (BC) 228-229 M 4
Castle Rock ○ **USA** (CO) 254-255 L 4
Castle Rock ○ **USA** (SD) 260-261 C 2
Castle Rock ○ **USA** (WA) 244-245 C 4
Castletown ○ **GBM** 90-91 E 4
Castletown Bearhaven = Baile Chaisleáin Bhéarra ○ **IRL** 90-91 C 6
Castle Windsor •• **GB** 90-91 G 6
Castlewood ○ **USA** (SD) 260-261 J 2
Castolon ○ **USA** (TX) 266-267 D 4
Castor ○ **CDN** (ALB) 232-233 G 3
Castor ○ **USA** (LA) 268-269 G 4
Castor Creek ~ **USA** 268-269 H 4
Castor River ~ **USA** 276-277 E 3
Castres ○ **F** 90-91 J 10
Castries ★ **WL** 56 E 4
Castro ○ **BR** (BAH) 72-73 L 2
Castro ○ **BR** (PAR) 74-75 E 5
Castro ○ **RCH** 78-79 C 7
Castro, Canal ≈ 80 C 5
Castro, Punta ▲ **RA** 78-79 G 7
Castro Barras ○ **RA** 76-77 E 6
Castro Daire ○ **P** 98-99 D 4
Castrovillari ○ **I** 100-101 F 5
Castroville ○ **USA** (TX) 266-267 J 4
Castrovirreyna ○ **PE** 64-65 E 8
Castuera ○ **E** 98-99 E 5
Častye ☆ **RUS** 96-97 J 5
Častyh ○ **RUS** 118-119 E 6
Casuarina Coast ⌣ **RI** 166-167 J 4
Casummit Lake ○ **CDN** (ONT) 234-235 L 3
Caswell ○ **USA** 20-21 Q 6
Çat ☆ **TR** 128-129 J 3
Catabola ○ **ANG** (BIE) 216-217 D 6
Catabola ○ **ANG** (HBO) 216-217 C 6
Cataby Roadhouse ○ **AUS** 176-177 C 5
Catacamas ○ **HN** 52-53 B 4
Catacaos ○ **PE** 64-65 B 4
Catache ○ **PE** 64-65 C 5
Catacocha ○ **EC** 64-65 C 4
Cataguases ○ **BR** 72-73 J 6
Catahoula Lake ⬭ **USA** (LA) 268-269 H 5
Catahoula National Wildlife Refuge ⊥ **USA** (LA) 268-269 H 5
Catahuasi ○ **PE** 64-65 E 8
Cataingan ○ **RP** 160-161 E 6
Çatak ☆ **TR** 128-129 K 3
Çatak Çayı ~ **TR** 128-129 K 3
Catalão ○ **BR** 72-73 G 5
Çatalhöyük ∴ • **TR** 128-129 E 4
Catalina ○ **CDN** (NFL) 242-243 P 4
Catalina ○ **RCH** 76-77 C 3
Catalina, Punta ▲ **RCH** 80 F 6
Catalunya ▫ **E** 98-99 J 4
Catama ○ **SP** 212-213 H 2
Catamarca ▫ **RA** 76-77 D 4
Catamayo ○ **EC** 64-65 C 3
Catambué ○ **ANG** 216-217 E 8
Catanacuname ○ **CO** 60-61 H 6
Catandica ○ **MOC** 218-219 G 4
Catanduanes ⌒ **RP** 160-161 F 6
Catanduva ○ **BR** 72-73 F 6
Catanduvas ○ **BR** 74-75 D 5
Catánia ○ **I** 100-101 E 6
Catán Lil ○ **RA** 78-79 D 5
Cataño ○ **USA** (PR) 286-287 P 2
Catanzaro ○ **I** 100-101 F 5
Cataract ○ **USA** (WI) 270-271 H 6
Cataract, 1st ~ • **ET** 194-195 F 5
Cataract, 3rd = ash-Shallāl ath-Thālith ~ **SUD** 200-201 E 3
Cataract, 4th = ash Shallāl ar-Rābi' ~ **SUD** 200-201 F 3
Cataract, 5th = ash-Shallāl al-Khāmis ~ **SUD** 200-201 F 3
Cataract, 6th = Shallal as-Sablūkah ~ **SUD** 200-201 F 4
Cataract Canyon ⌣ **USA** 254-255 E 6
Cataractes • **RM** 222-223 F 7
Cataratas del Iguazú ~ •• **RA** 76-77 K 3
Catarate de San Rafael ~ • **EC** 64-65 D 2
Cataraugus Creek ~ **USA** 278-279 C 6
Catarina ○ **USA** (TX) 266-267 H 5
Catarman ☆ **RP** 160-161 F 6
Catastrophe, Cape ▲ **AUS** 180-181 D 3
Catata-a-Nova ○ **ANG** 216-217 C 6
Catatumbo, Río ~ **YV** 60-61 E 3
Cataula ○ **USA** (GA) 284-285 F 4
Cataviña ○ **MEX** 50-51 B 3
Catawba ○ **USA** (WI) 270-271 H 5
Catawba Island ○ **USA** (OH) 280-281 D 2
Catawba Lake < **USA** (NC) 282-283 F 5
Catawba River ~ **USA** 284-285 K 2
Cataxa ○ **MOC** 218-219 G 2
Catazaja ○ **MEX** 52-53 H 3
Catbalogan ☆ **RP** 160-161 F 7
Čat-Bazar ○ **KS** 136-137 N 3
Cat Cays ⌒ **BS** 54-55 F 2
Cateco Cangola ○ **ANG** 216-217 C 4
Catedral de Sol • **CO** 60-61 E 5
Cateel Bay ≈ 160-161 G 9
Catemaco ○ **MEX** 52-53 G 2
Catemaco, Laguna de ⬭ • **MEX** 52-53 G 2
Catembe ○ **MOC** 220-221 L 3
Catende ○ **BR** 68-69 L 6
Catengue ○ **ANG** 216-217 B 6
Cater ○ **CDN** (SAS) 232-233 K 2
Catete ○ **ANG** 216-217 B 4
Cateté, Área Indígena X **BR** 68-69 C 5
Catete, Rio ~ **BR** 66-67 K 6
Cathair na Mart = Westport ○ • **IRL** 90-91 C 5
Cathay ○ **USA** (ND) 258-259 H 4
Cathcart ○ **ZA** 220-221 H 6

312 Capitan — Cathcart

Cathedral Gorge State Park • USA (NV) 248-249 K 2
Cathedral Mountain ▲ USA (TX) 266-267 D 3
Cathedral Peak o ZA 220-221 J 4
Cathedral Provincial Park ⊥ CDN (BC) 230-231 J 4
Cathedral Valley ∴ USA (UT) 254-255 D 5
Catherine o USA (AL) 284-285 C 4
Catherine, Mount ▲ AUS 178-179 K 3
Cathlamet o USA (WA) 244-245 B 4
Catia la Mar o YV 60-61 H 2
Catió ☆ GNB 202-203 C 4
Catire, Sierra el ▲ YV 60-61 K 4
Cat Island ⌒ BS 54-55 H 2
Cat Island ⌒ USA (MS) 268-269 L 6
Čatkal'skij hrebet ▲ UZ 136-137 M 4
Catkaly Kamyclovskij Log ⊥ KZ 124-125 F 1
Cat Lake o CDN (ONT) 234-235 M 3
Cat Lake ○ CDN (ONT) 234-235 M 3
Catlettsburg o USA (KY) 276-277 N 2
Catlow Valley ⌣ USA 244-245 F 7
Cato o USA (AR) 276-277 C 6
Catoche, Cabo ▲ MEX 52-53 L 1
Catolândia o BR 72-73 H 2
Catolé do Rocha o BR 68-69 K 5
Catolo o ANG 216-217 D 4
Caton Island ⌒ USA 22-23 P 5
Catoute ▲ E 98-99 D 3
Cátria, Monte ▲ I 100-101 D 3
Catriel o RA 78-79 F 4
Catrilo o RA 78-79 H 4
Catrimani o BR (ROR) 62-63 D 5
Catrimani o BR (ROR) 66-67 F 2
Catrimani, Rio ~ BR 66-67 F 2
Catskill o USA (NY) 278-279 H 6
Catskill Mountains ▲ USA 278-279 G 6
Cattaraugus Indian Reservation ✗ USA (NY) 278-279 C 6
Cattle Creek ~ AUS 172-173 K 4
Cattle Creek Out Station o AUS 172-173 K 4
Catuane o MOC 220-221 L 3
Catumbela ~ ANG 216-217 C 6
Caturiá, Ilha ⌒ BR 66-67 C 4
Cauaburi, Rio ~ BR 66-67 D 2
Cauale ~ ANG 216-217 D 3
Cauayan o RP 160-161 E 7
Cauca o ANG 216-217 C 4
Cauca, Río ~ CO 60-61 D 3
Caucagua o YV 60-61 H 2
Caucaia o BR 68-69 J 3
Caucas o BOL 70-71 H 5
Caucasia o CO 60-61 D 3
Caucasus = Bol'šoj Kavkaz ▲ 104 B 4
Cauce Seco del Río Pilcomayo ~ RA 76-77 G 2
Caucete o RA 76-77 C 6
Cauchari o RA 76-77 D 3
Cauchari, Salar de o RA 76-77 D 2
Caucomgomoc Lake o USA (ME) 278-279 M 2
Caulfield o USA (MO) 276-277 C 4
Caumbue o ANG 216-217 F 4
Čaun ~ RUS 112-113 Q 2
Čaunskaja guba ≈ 112-113 P 2
Caupolicán ⊥ BOL 70-71 C 4
Cauquenes o RCH 78-79 C 3
Caurés, Rio ~ BR 66-67 F 3
Causabiscau, Lac o CDN 38-39 F 2
Causapscal o CDN (QUE) 240-241 H 2
Causapscal, Parc Provincial ⊥ CDN (QUE) 240-241 H 2
Căușeni ☆ MD 102-103 F 4
Causey o USA (NM) 256-257 M 5
Cautário, Rio ~ BR 70-71 E 3
Cautín, Río ~ RCH 78-79 C 6
Caution, Cape ▲ CDN (BC) 230-231 B 2
Caution Point ▲ AUS 172-173 K 1
Cauto ~ C 54-55 G 4
Cauto Cristo o C 54-55 G 4
Cauto Embarcadero o C 54-55 G 4
Cauvery ~ IND 140-141 G 5
Cauvery ~ IND 140-141 F 4
Cavalier o USA (ND) 258-259 K 3
Cavalla River ~ LB 202-203 G 7
Cavallo Passage ≈ 266-267 L 5
Cavalonga, Sierra ▲ RA 76-77 D 2
Cavan = An Cabhán ☆ IRL 90-91 D 5
Cavdan o MAU 148-149 C 3
Çavdarhisar ☆ TR 128-129 C 3
Cave o NZ 182 C 6
Cave City o USA (AR) 276-277 D 5
Cave Junction o USA (OR) 244-245 B 8
Cavendish o AUS 180-181 G 4
Cavendish o CDN (ALB) 232-233 H 5
Cavendish o CDN (PEI) 240-241 M 4
Caverna de Santana • BR 74-75 F 5
Caverna do Diabo • BR 74-75 F 5
Caverna do Francês • BR 70-71 K 4
Caverns of Sonora ∴ • USA (TX) 266-267 G 3
Cave Spring o USA (GA) 284-285 E 2
Caviana de Dentro, Ilha ⌒ BR 62-63 J 5
Caviana de Fora, Ilha ⌒ BR 62-63 J 5
Cavite o RP 160-161 D 5
Čavki o AFG 138-139 C 2
Cawayan o RP 160-161 E 7
Caxambu o BR 72-73 H 6
Caxias o BR 68-69 G 4
Caxias do Sul o BR 74-75 E 7
Caxito ☆ ANG 216-217 B 4
Caxiuanã, Baía de o BR 62-63 J 6
Caxiuanã, Reserva Florestal de ⊥ BR 62-63 J 6
Caxuxa o BR 68-69 F 4
Çay ☆ • TR 128-129 D 3
Cayajabos o C 54-55 D 3
Cayambe o EC 64-65 C 1
Cayambe, Volcán ▲ EC 64-65 D 1
Cayambre, Isla ⌒ CO 60-61 C 6
Cayara o PE 64-65 F 8
Cayce o USA (SC) 284-285 J 3
Cây Du'o'ng, Vüng ≈ 158-159 H 5
Cayenne ☆ F 62-63 H 3
Cayes, Les ☆ • RH 54-55 J 5
Cayley o CDN (ALB) 232-233 E 5
Cayman Brac ⌒ GB 54-55 F 5
Cayman Islands ▫ GB 54-55 E 5
Caynabo o SP 208-209 J 3
Cayo, El ∴ • MEX 52-53 J 3
Cayo Guillerme o •• C 54-55 F 3
Cayo Güin o C 54-55 H 4
Cayo Largo o •• C 54-55 E 4
Cayo Mambi o C 54-55 H 4
Cayo Ramona o C 54-55 E 3
Cayos Arcas, Isla ⌒ MEX 52-53 J 1
Cay Sal Bank ⌒ BS 54-55 E 3
Cayucos o USA (CA) 248-249 D 4
Cayuga o CDN (ONT) 238-239 F 6
Cayuga o USA (IN) 274-275 L 5
Cayuga o USA (ND) 258-259 K 5
Cayuga o USA (TX) 268-269 E 5
Cayuga Lake ○ USA (NY) 278-279 E 6
Cayuse Pass ▲ USA (WA) 244-245 D 4
Cazage o ANG 216-217 F 5
Cazalla de la Sierra o E 98-99 E 6
Čažma, mys ▲ RUS 120-121 T 6
Cazombo o ANG 214-215 B 6
Cazones, Golfo de ≈ 54-55 E 4
Cazorla o E 98-99 F 6
Cazorla o YV 60-61 H 3
Cazorla, Segura y Las Villas Parque Nacional de ⊥ E 98-99 F 5
Cazula o MOC 218-219 G 2
Ccatca o PE 70-71 B 3
Cea, Río ~ E 98-99 E 3
Ceará ▫ BR 68-69 H 4
Ceara Abyssal Plain = Ceará Abyssal Plain ≃ 6-7 E 8
Ceará-Mirim o BR 68-69 L 4
Ceatharlach = Carlow o IRL 90-91 D 5
Ceba o CDN (SAS) 232-233 Q 2
Ceballos o MEX 50-51 G 4
Čebarkul' ☆ RUS 96-97 M 6
Čeboksarskoe vodohranilišče < RUS 96-97 E 5
Čeboksary ☆ RUS 96-97 F 5
Cebollati o ROU 74-75 D 9
Ceboruco, Cerro ▲ MEX 52-53 B 2
Cebu ⌒ RP 160-161 E 8
Cebu City ☆ •• RP 160-161 E 7
Čečeljugjun ~ RUS 110-111 a 6
Čečen, ostrov ⌒ RUS 126-127 G 5
Cècèrlèg ☆ MAU 148-149 E 4
Čechy ⊥ CZ 92-93 M 4
Cecil o USA (AL) 284-285 E 4
Cecil o USA (AR) 276-277 B 5
Cecil o USA (OR) 244-245 E 5
Cecil, Mount ▲ AUS 176-177 M 2
Cecil Goodman o AUS 172-173 K 2
Cecil Plains o AUS 178-179 L 4
Cecil Rhodes, Mount ▲ AUS 176-177 F 2
Cecilville o USA (CA) 246-247 B 2
Cecina o I 100-101 C 3
Čečuj ~ RUS 118-119 D 7
Čečujsk o RUS 116-117 O 6
Cedar o CDN (BC) 230-231 F 4
Cedar o USA (KS) 262-263 H 5
Cedar Bluff o USA (IA) 274-275 G 3
Cedar Bluff Reservoir ~ USA 262-263 G 6
Cedar Bluffs o USA (KS) 262-263 F 5
Cedar Breaks National Monument ∴ USA (UT) 254-255 C 6
Cedar Butte o USA (SD) 260-261 E 3
Cedar City o USA (UT) 254-255 B 6
Cedar Creek ~ USA (TX) 266-267 K 3
Cedar Creek ~ USA 258-259 F 5
Cedar Creek ~ USA 274-275 G 4
Cedar Creek ~ USA 284-285 B 2
Cedar Creek ~ USA 284-285 D 4
Cedar Creek Reservoir ○ USA (TX) 264-265 H 6
Cedaredge o USA (CO) 254-255 H 5
Cedar Falls o USA (IA) 274-275 F 2
Cedar Grove o USA (TN) 276-277 G 5
Cedar Grove o USA (WI) 274-275 L 1
Cedar Hill o USA (MO) 274-275 H 6
Cedar Hill o USA (TX) 264-265 H 6
Cedar Island ⌒ USA (NC) 282-283 L 6
Cedar Island National Wildlife Refuge ⊥ USA (NC) 282-283 L 6
Cedar Key o USA (FL) 286-287 F 2
Cedar Lake ○ CDN (QUE) 238-239 G 2
Cedar Lake ○ USA (IL) 276-277 F 3
Cedar Lake ○ USA (TX) 264-265 B 6
Cedar Mills o USA (MN) 270-271 D 6
Cedar Mountain ▲ USA (MT) 250-251 D 4
Cedar Park o USA (TX) 266-267 K 3
Cedar Pass ▲ USA (CA) 246-247 E 2
Cedar Point o CDN (ONT) 238-239 E 4
Cedar Point ▲ USA (CO) 254-255 M 4
Cedar Rapids o USA (IA) 274-275 G 3
Cedar Rapids o USA (NE) 262-263 H 3
Cedar River ~ CDN 228-229 F 2
Cedar River ~ USA (MI) 270-271 L 5
Cedar River ~ USA 274-275 G 3
Cedar River National Grassland ⊥ USA (ND) 258-259 F 5
Cedars of Lebanon State Park ⊥ USA (TN) 276-277 J 4
Cedar Springs o USA (MI) 272-273 D 4
Cedartown o USA (GA) 284-285 E 2
Cedar Vale o USA (KS) 262-263 K 7
Cedarvale o USA (NM) 256-257 K 4
Cedarville o USA (AR) 276-277 A 5
Cedarville o USA (CA) 246-247 E 2
Cedarville o USA (MI) 270-271 O 4
Cedarville o ZA 220-221 J 5
Cedeño o HN 52-53 L 5
Cedoux o CDN (SAS) 232-233 P 6
Cedral o BR 68-69 F 3
Cedral o MEX (SLP) 50-51 J 6
Cedral ∴ • MEX (QR) 52-53 L 1
Cèdres, Parque National des ⊥ DZ 190-191 C 3
Cedro o BR 68-69 J 5
Cedros o MEX (DGO) 50-51 J 5
Cedros o MEX (SON) 50-51 E 4
Cedros, Isla ⌒ MEX 50-51 B 3
Ceduna o AUS 180-181 B 2
Ceek o SP 208-209 G 4
Ceel Afweyn o SP 208-209 H 4
Ceelaayo o SP 208-209 J 3
Ceelbuur o SP 208-209 H 6
Ceel Dheere o SP 208-209 H 6
Ceel Duubo o SP 212-213 K 2
Ceel Gaal o SP 208-209 K 3
Ceel Garas o SP 208-209 G 6
Ceel Huur o SP 208-209 J 6
Ceel Madoobe, togga ~ SP 208-209 J 4
Ceepeecee o CDN (BC) 230-231 C 4
Ceerigaabo ☆ SP 208-209 H 3
Cefalù o I 100-101 E 5
Cega, Río ~ E 98-99 E 4
Čegdomyn o RUS 122-123 E 3
Čegitun ~ RUS 112-113 Z 3
Cegléd o H 92-93 P 5
Cegonha, Corredeira da ~ BR 72-73 E 7
Čehel Abdālān, Kūh-e ▲ AFG 134-135 K 2
Ceheng o VRC 156-157 D 4
Čehov o RUS (SHL) 122-123 K 5
Čehov ☆ • RUS (Mos) 94-95 P 4
Čehova, gora ▲ RUS 122-123 K 5
Ceiba, La ☆ HN 52-53 L 4
Ceiba, La o YV (ANZ) 60-61 J 3
Ceiba, La o YV (TRU) 60-61 F 3
Ceibal, El ∴ • GCA 52-53 J 3
Ceibalito o RA 76-77 E 3
Ceibas o RA 78-79 K 2
Ceja, La o CO 60-61 D 4
Cejas, Las o RA 76-77 E 4
Čeka ~ RUS 114-115 O 6
Čekanovskij o RUS 116-117 K 7
Čekanovskogo, krjaž ▲ RUS 110-111 N 3
Çekerek ☆ TR 128-129 F 2
Çekerek Irmağı ~ TR 128-129 F 2
Çekerek Irmağı ~ TR 128-129 G 2
Čekmaguš ☆ RUS 96-97 J 6
Čekunda o RUS 122-123 E 3
Čekurdah o RUS 110-111 a 4
Čekurovka o RUS 110-111 Q 4
Celaque, Parque Nacional ⊥ HN 52-53 K 4
Celarain, Punta ▲ MEX 52-53 L 1
Čelasin ~ RUS 120-121 G 5
Celaya o MEX 52-53 D 1
Čelbas ~ RUS 102-103 M 5
Čeldonka o RUS 118-119 J 9
Celebes Basin ▲ 14-15 D 7
Celebes Sea ≈ 164-165 G 2
Celeiro Murta o BR 72-73 J 4
Čelekon o TM 136-137 C 5
Celendín o PE 64-65 C 5
Celeste, Rio ~ BR 70-71 K 3
Celestún o • MEX 52-53 J 1
Celica o EC 64-65 C 4
Čelina o RUS 102-103 M 4
Celina o USA (OH) 280-281 B 3
Celina o USA (TN) 276-277 K 4
Celina o USA (TX) 264-265 H 5
Celinnoe o KZ 136-137 L 4
Celinnoe ☆ RUS (ALT) 124-125 O 2
Celinnoe ☆ RUS (KRG) 114-115 G 7
Celinograd = Akmola ☆ KZ 124-125 G 3
Celista o CDN (BC) 230-231 K 3
Čeljabinsk ☆ RUS 96-97 M 6
Celje o SLO 100-101 E 1
Čeljuskin, mys ▲ RUS 108-109 f 3
Čeljuskin, poluostrov ⌒ RUS 108-109 e 3
Celle o •• D 92-93 L 2
Čel'mana, ostrova ⌒ RUS 108-109 V 4
Čelno-Veršiny ☆ RUS 96-97 G 6
Čelomdža ~ RUS 120-121 M 3
Čölonöön ~ RUS 118-119 G 6
Celorico da Beira o P 98-99 D 4
Celtic Sea ≈ 90-91 D 6
Celtic Shelf ≃ 6-7 J 3
Çeltik ☆ TR 128-129 D 3
Čeluk o RI 168 B 7
Cema ~ RUS 88-89 T 4
Čemal o RUS 124-125 P 3
Cemara ~ RI 166-167 J 4
Čemdal'sk o RUS 116-117 L 6
Cemoltan o KZ 146-147 C 4
Cempi, Teluk ≈ 168 D 7
Cenajo, Embalse del < E 98-99 G 5
Čenārān o IR 136-137 F 6
Čenāreh o IR 128-129 M 5
Cenderawasih, Teluk ≈ 166-167 H 3
Cenderawasih Marine Reserve ⊥ • RI 166-167 H 3
Cenepa, Río ~ PE 64-65 C 4
Cengel = Hösööt o MAU 146-147 J 1
Cenghis Khan Ling • VRC 154-155 F 2
Cènhèr = Altan Ovoo o MAU 148-149 E 4
Cènhèrmandal = Modot o MAU 148-149 J 4
Cennet ve Cehennem • TR 128-129 F 4
Cenotillo o MEX 52-53 K 1
Centani o ZA 220-221 J 6
Centenario, El o MEX 50-51 D 5
Centenário do Sul o BR 72-73 E 7
Centenary o USA (SC) 284-285 L 2
Centenary o ZW 218-219 F 3
Centennial o USA (WY) 252-253 M 5
Center o USA (CO) 254-255 J 6
Center o USA (NE) 262-263 J 2
Center o USA (TX) 268-269 F 5
Center, Le o USA (MN) 270-271 E 6
Centerburg o USA (OH) 280-281 D 3
Center Hill o USA (AR) 276-277 D 5
Center Hill Lake ○ USA (TN) 276-277 K 4
Center Ossipee o USA (NH) 278-279 K 5
Center Point o USA (AL) 284-285 D 3
Centerville o USA (IA) 274-275 F 4
Centerville o USA (MO) 276-277 E 3
Centerville o USA (NC) 282-283 J 4
Centerville o USA (TN) 276-277 H 5
Centerville o USA (TX) 268-269 E 5
Centerville o USA (WI) 270-271 G 6
Centinela, Cerro ▲ RA 78-79 D 4
Centinela, Picacho del ▲ MEX 50-51 H 3
Centinela, Sierra del ▲ RA 76-77 E 3
Central o BR 68-69 G 7
Central ▫ EAK 212-213 F 4
Central ▫ EAU 212-213 C 3
Central ▫ MW 218-219 G 1
Central ▫ RB 218-219 C 5
Central o USA (AL) 284-285 E 2
Central o USA (NM) 256-257 G 6
Central ▫ Z 218-219 D 2
Central = Centre ▫ CAM 204-205 J 6
Central, Cordillera ▲ CR 52-53 B 6
Central, Cordillera ▲ DOM 54-55 K 5
Central, Cordillera ▲ USA 286-287 P 2
Central African Republic = Centrafricaine, République ■ RCA 206-207 C 5
Central Australia Aboriginal Land ✗ AUS 172-173 J 6
Central Australian Railway II AUS 176-177 M 2
Central Bedeque o CDN (PEI) 240-241 M 4
Central Brāhui Range ▲ PK 134-135 M 4
Central Butte o CDN (SAS) 232-233 M 5
Central City o USA (CO) 254-255 K 4
Central City o USA (IA) 274-275 G 2
Central City o USA (KY) 276-277 H 3
Central City o USA (NE) 262-263 J 3
Central Deborah Mine • AUS 180-181 H 4
Central de Minas o BR 72-73 K 5
Central Desert Aboriginal Land ✗ AUS 172-173 K 5
Central Eastern Australian Rainforest ⊥ ••• AUS 178-179 M 5
Central Ferry o USA (WA) 244-245 H 4
Centralia o USA (IL) 274-275 J 6
Centralia o USA (MO) 274-275 F 5
Centralia o USA (WA) 244-245 C 4
Central Island ⌒ EAK 212-213 F 2
Central Island National Park ⊥ EAK 212-213 F 2
Central Kalahari Game Reserve ⊥ RB 218-219 B 5
Central los Molles o RCH 76-77 B 6
Central Makrān Range ▲ PK 134-135 K 5
Central Mount Stuart ▲ AUS 172-173 L 6
Central Mount Wedge ▲ AUS 172-173 K 7
Central'naja, gora ▲ RUS 108-109 e 4
Central'nojakutskaja ravnina ⌣ RUS 118-119 J 3
Central'nolesnoj zapovednik ▲ RUS 94-95 N 3
Central'nosibirskij zapovednik učastok Elogujskij ⊥ RUS 114-115 S 4
Central'nosibirskij zapovednik učastok Enisejsko-Stolbovoj ⊥ RUS 114-115 V 3
Central'no-Tungusskoe, plato ⊥ RUS 116-117 K 5
Central'nye Karakumy ⊥ TM 136-137 E 5
Central'nyj o RUS 114-115 T 7
Central Pacific Basin ≃ 14-15 K 6
Central Patricia o CDN (ONT) 234-235 N 3
Central Point o USA (OR) 244-245 C 8
Central Range ▲ LS 220-221 J 4
Central Range ▲ PNG 183 B 3
Central Region ▫ GH 202-203 K 7
Central Saanich o CDN (BC) 230-231 F 5
Central Siberian Plateau = Srednesibirskoe ploskogor'e ⊥ RUS 10-11 J 2
Central Valley o USA (CA) 246-247 C 3
Central West Goldfields • AUS 180-181 K 2
Central West River o CDN (NS) 240-241 N 5
Centre ▫ F 90-91 H 8
Centre o USA (AL) 284-285 E 2
Centre = Central ▫ CAM 204-205 J 6
Centre de Flacq o MS 224 C 7
Centre Island ⌒ AUS 174-175 D 4
Centre Mountain ▲ USA (ID) 250-251 D 6
Centre Spatial Guyanais • F 62-63 H 3
Centreville o CDN (NB) 240-241 H 4
Centreville o CDN (NFL) 242-243 P 4
Centreville o USA (AL) 284-285 C 4
Centreville o USA (MD) 280-281 K 4
Centreville o USA (MS) 268-269 J 5
Centro, Cayo ⌒ MEX 52-53 L 2
Centro, El o USA (CA) 248-249 J 7
Centro do Vieira o BR 68-69 F 3
Centurion o ROU 74-75 D 9
Century o USA (FL) 286-287 B 1
Cenxi o VRC 156-157 G 5
Cenzontle o MEX 50-51 H 4
Čepca ~ RUS 96-97 J 5
Čepeck, Kirovo- ☆ RUS 96-97 G 4
Cepiring o RI 168 D 3
Cepu o RI 168 D 3
Ceram = Pulau Seram ⌒ RI 166-167 E 3
Ceram Sea = Seram, Laut ≈ 166-167 D 3
Cerbatana, Serrania de la ▲ YV 60-61 H 4
Cercado, El o DOM 54-55 K 5
Čerdakly ☆ RUS 96-97 F 6
Čerdyn' ☆ RUS 114-115 D 4
Cereal o CDN (ALB) 232-233 H 4
Cerejeiras o BR 70-71 G 3
Čeremhovo ☆ RUS 116-117 L 9
Čeremhovskaja, Irkutsko, ravnina ⌣ RUS 116-117 K 8
Čeremšan ☆ RUS 96-97 G 6
Čeremuhovo o RUS 114-115 F 4
Čeremšiki o RUS 116-117 E 9
Čerendej ~ RUS 118-119 J 5
Čerepanovo ☆ RUS 124-125 N 1
Čerepovec ☆ RUS 94-95 P 2
Ceres o BR 72-73 F 3
Ceres o RA 76-77 G 5
Ceres o ZA 220-221 D 6
Ceresco o USA (NE) 262-263 K 3
Cerete o CO 60-61 D 3
Cerezo de Abajo o E 98-99 F 4
Čerga o RUS 124-125 O 3
Cerignola o I 100-101 E 4
Čeriktej o RUS 118-119 P 4
Čerkasskoe o RUS 96-97 E 7
Čerkassy = Čerkasy ☆ UA 102-103 H 3
Čerkasy ☆ UA 102-103 H 3
Çerkeş ☆ TR 128-129 E 2
Čerkessk ☆ RUS 126-127 E 5
cerkva Česnoho chresta • UA 102-103 C 3
Čerlak ☆ RUS 124-125 J 1
Çermik ☆ TR 128-129 H 3
Cerna o RO 102-103 F 5
Černaja ~ RUS 112-113 P 5
Černaja ~ RUS 112-113 L 5
Černaja ~ RUS 118-119 J 9
Černaja, Bol'šaja ~ RUS 116-117 E 5
Černaja, gora ▲ RUS 122-123 F 7
Cernavodă o RO 102-103 F 5
Černenko = Šarypovo o RUS 114-115 U 7
Černigov = Černihiv o • UA 102-103 G 2
Černihiv o • UA 102-103 G 2
Černihivs'ke polissja ⊥ UA 102-103 G 2
Černivci ☆ UA 102-103 D 3
Černjachiv o UA 102-103 G 2
Černjaevo o RUS 118-119 N 9
Černjahovsk ☆ •• RUS 94-95 G 4
Černjanka o RUS 102-103 K 2
Černogorsk o RUS 116-117 E 9
Černorečenskij o RUS 96-97 H 3
Černovcy = Černivci ☆ UA 102-103 D 3
Černovka o RUS 124-125 M 1
Černozemel'skij kanal o RUS 126-127 F 5
Černuška ☆ RUS 96-97 K 5
Černut'evo o RUS 88-89 U 5
Černycev cyganak ≈ 126-127 N 5
Černye Brat'ja, ostrova ⌒ RUS 122-123 O 5
Černye zemli ⊥ RUS 96-97 D 10
Černyj Čulym ~ RUS 114-115 U 7
Černyj Urjum ~ RUS 118-119 J 9
Černyševa, grjada ▲ RUS 108-109 H 9
Černyševsk o RUS 118-119 F 4
Černyševskij o RUS 102-103 N 3
Černyševa, hrebet ▲ RUS 118-119 L 8
Cero, Corredeira ~ BR 70-71 J 5
Cerqueira César o BR 72-73 F 7
Cerralvo o MEX 50-51 K 4
Cerralvo, Isla ⌒ MEX 50-51 E 5
Čërrik o • AL 100-101 G 4
Cerrillada o ROU 76-77 J 6
Cerrillos o RCH 76-77 C 2
Cerrito o PY 76-77 J 4
Cerrito, El o CO 60-61 C 6
Cerritos o MEX 50-51 J 6
Cerro, El o BOL 70-71 G 7
Cerro Azul o BR 74-75 F 5
Cerro Blanco o RA 80 G 3
Cerro Blanco o RCH 76-77 B 5
Cerro Chato o ROU 78-79 M 2
Cerro Chovoreca o PY 70-71 H 6
Cerro Colorado o ROU 78-79 M 2
Cerro-Cora o BR 68-69 K 5
Cerro Cora, Parque Nacional del ⊥ PY 76-77 J 2
Cerro de Pasco ☆ PE 64-65 D 7
Cerro Gordo o USA (IL) 274-275 K 5
Cerro Largo o BR 76-77 K 5
Cerro Mangote ∴ PA 52-53 D 7
Cerrón, Cerro ▲ YV 60-61 F 2
Cerro Pintado • YV 60-61 H 6
Cerro Policía o RA 78-79 E 5
Cerro Punta o PA 52-53 C 7
Cerro Rico o RA 76-77 E 5
Cerros Colorados, Embalse < RA 78-79 E 5
Cerros de Amotape, Parque Nacional ⊥ PE 64-65 B 3
Cerro Vera o ROU 78-79 L 2
Cerrudo Cué o RA 76-77 J 4
Čerskij o RUS 112-113 L 2
Čerskogo, hrebet ▲ RUS 118-119 E 10
Čertala ~ RUS 114-115 O 6
Certaldo o I 100-101 C 3
Cértegui o CO 60-61 C 5
Čertkovo o RUS 102-103 M 3
Čertov, porog ~ RUS 110-111 H 5
Čertovo, ozero o RUS 114-115 Q 2
Čerubaj-Nūra ~ KZ 124-125 H 4
Cervantes o AUS 176-177 C 5
Cervati, Monte ▲ I 100-101 E 4
Červen' ☆ BY 94-95 L 5
Cervera o E 98-99 H 4
Cervera de Pisuerga o E 98-99 E 3
Cervéteri o • I 100-101 D 4
Cérvia o I 100-101 D 2
Cervino, Monte = Matterhorn ▲ •• I 100-101 A 1
Červjanka o RUS 116-117 J 7
Červonograd = Červonohrad o UA 102-103 D 2
Červonohrad o UA 102-103 D 2
Červonoznam'janka o UA 102-103 G 4
Cerwa o VRC 144-145 M 3
Čeryševsk o RUS 118-119 H 9
César, Río ~ CO 60-61 E 3
Césares, Isla de los ⌒ RA 78-79 H 5
Cesário Lange o BR 72-73 G 7
Cesena o I 100-101 D 2
Cesira, La o RA 78-79 H 2
Cēsis ☆ •• LV 94-95 J 3
Česká Třebová o CZ 92-93 O 4
České Budějovice o CZ 92-93 N 4
Českomoravská vrchovina ▲ CZ 92-93 N 4
Český Krumlov o ••• CZ 92-93 N 4
Český Šternberk •• CZ 92-93 N 4
Český Těšín o CZ 92-93 P 4
Česma ☆ RUS 124-125 B 2
Çeşme ☆ TR 128-129 B 3
Češme Biğār o IR 128-129 M 5
Češme Kabūd o IR 134-135 B 2
Cess, River o LB 202-203 F 7
Cessford o CDN (ALB) 232-233 G 5
Čëšskaja guba ≈ 88-89 S 3
Cessnock o AUS 180-181 L 2
Češt-e Šarif o • AFG 134-135 K 1
Cestos Bay ≈ 202-203 F 7
Cestos River ~ LB 202-203 F 7
Cesvaine ☆ •• LV 94-95 K 3
Čet' ~ RUS 114-115 T 6
Cetaceo, Mount ▲ RP 160-161 E 4
Cětar o VRC 154-155 B 3
Četlasskij Kamen' ▲ RUS 88-89 U 4
Cetraro o I 100-101 E 5
Četvërtyj Kuril'skij proliv ≈ 122-123 Q 3
Četyrëhstolbovoj, ostrov ⌒ RUS 112-113 M 1
Céu Azul o BR 74-75 D 5
Ceuta o E 98-99 E 7
Ceuta o YV 60-61 F 3
Cevcenko, cyganak ≈ 126-127 O 4
Cevennen = Cévennes ▲ F 90-91 J 9
Cévennes ▲ F 90-91 J 9
Cévennes, Parc National des ⊥ • F 90-91 J 9
Ceyhan ☆ TR 128-129 F 4
Ceyhan Nehri ~ TR 128-129 F 4
Ceylanpinar ☆ TR 128-129 J 4
Ceylon o CDN (SAS) 232-233 O 6
Ceylon o USA (MN) 270-271 D 7
Ceylon Plain ≃ 12 F 4
Chaah o MAL 162-163 E 3
Cha-am o THA 158-159 E 4
Cha'anpu o VRC 156-157 G 2
Chabbie Lake ○ CDN (ONT) 236-237 J 3
Chabet El Akra • DZ 190-191 E 2
Chablé o MEX 52-53 J 3
Chabyêr Caka ○ VRC 144-145 E 5
Chacabuco o RA 78-79 J 3
Chacala o BOL 70-71 D 5
Chacane o MOC 218-219 H 7
Chacao o RCH 78-79 C 6
Chacao, Canal de ≈ 78-79 C 6
Chacarilla, Quebrada de ~ RCH 70-71 C 7
Chacarrão, Cachoeira do ~ BR 66-67 H 6
Chacas o PE 64-65 D 6
Chacay, Arroyo el ~ RA 78-79 E 3
Chacay Alto o RCH 76-77 B 5
Chacayan o PE 64-65 D 7
Chachani, Volcán ▲ PE 70-71 B 5
Chachapoyas ☆ PE 64-65 D 5
Chacharramendi o RA 78-79 G 4
Chacho o GH 202-203 J 5
Chacho, El o RA 76-77 E 6
Chachoengsao o THA 158-159 F 4
Cháchro o • PK 138-139 C 7
Chacmool ∴ • MEX 52-53 L 2
Chaco ▫ RA 76-77 G 3
Chaco, Quebrada de ~ RCH 76-77 C 3
Chaco Austral ⊥ RA 76-77 G 3
Chaco Boreal ⊥ PY 70-71 G 7
Chaco Central ⊥ PY 76-77 G 3
Chaco Culture National Historic Park ⊥ ••• USA (NM) 256-257 H 2
Chacon, Cape ▲ USA 32-33 E 4
Chacopaya o BOL 70-71 C 4
Chaco River ~ USA 256-257 G 2
Chacras, Cerro ▲ EC 64-65 B 10
Chad, Lake = Tchad, Lac ○ 198-199 F 6
Chad = Tchad ■ TCH 198-199 G 5
Chadaouanka o RN 198-199 C 5
Chadayang o VRC 156-157 K 5
Chadbourn o USA (NC) 282-283 J 6
Chadin o PE 64-65 C 5
Chadiza o Z 218-219 G 2
Chadron o USA (NE) 262-263 D 2
Chafarinas, Islas ⌒ E 188-189 K 3
Chafe o WAN 204-205 G 3
Chaffee Military Reservation, Fort ✗✗ • USA (AR) 276-277 A 5
Chaffers, Isla ⌒ RCH 80 C 2
Chafo o WAN 204-205 F 3
Chafurray o CO 60-61 E 6
Chāgai o PK 134-135 L 4
Chāgai Hills ▲ PK 134-135 K 4
Chāgalamarri o IND 140-141 H 3
Chaghat ~ BD 142-143 F 3
Chagne o ETH 208-209 C 3
Chagoness o CDN (SAS) 232-233 O 3
Chagos Archipelago ⌒ GB 12 F 5
Chagos-Laccadive Ridge ≃ 12 F 5
Chagos Trench ≃ 12 F 5
Chaguanas o TT 60-61 L 2
Chaguaramal o YV 60-61 K 3
Chaguaramas o TT 60-61 L 2
Chaguaramas o YV (GUA) 60-61 H 3
Chaguaramas o YV (MON) 60-61 K 3
Chaguarpambo o EC 64-65 C 3
Chagulak Island ⌒ USA 22-23 L 6
Chahbounia o DZ 190-191 D 3
Chāh Sandan o PK 134-135 K 4
Chai o MOC 214-215 L 6
Chaibāsa o IND 142-143 D 4
Chaigneau, Islas ⌒ RCH 80 C 6
Chaillu, Massif du ▲ G 210-211 C 4
Chai Nat o THA 158-159 F 3
Chain Fracture Zone ≃ 6-7 H 9
Chaira, La o CO 64-65 E 1
Chaitén o RCH 78-79 C 7
Chaiwopu o VRC 146-147 H 4
Chaiya o THA 158-159 E 6
Chaiyaphum o THA 158-159 G 3
Chajarí o RA 76-77 H 6
Chak o PK 138-139 D 5
Chakachamna Lake ○ USA 20-21 O 6
Chakachatna River ~ USA 20-21 O 6
Chākāi o IND 142-143 E 3
Chakaktolik o USA 20-21 J 6
Chākar ~ PK 138-139 B 5
Chakari o ZW 218-219 E 4
Chakdarra o • PK 138-139 D 2
Chake Chake o EAT 212-213 G 6
Chakia o IND 142-143 C 3
Chak Jhumra o PK 138-139 D 4
Chakkrarat o THA 158-159 G 3
Chakonipau, Lac ○ CDN 36-37 P 6
Chakri o PK 138-139 D 3
Chak Swari o IND 138-139 D 3
Chakwāl o PK 138-139 D 3
Chakwenga o Z 218-219 E 2
Chala o EAT 214-215 F 4
Chala o PE 64-65 E 9
Chalaco o PE 64-65 C 4
Chalais o F 90-91 H 9
Chalalou o PNG 183 D 2
Chalanta o RA 78-79 G 2
Chalatenango ☆ ES 52-53 K 4
Chalaua o MOC 218-219 K 3
Chalawa, River ~ WAN 204-205 H 3
Chalbi Desert ⌣ EAK 212-213 F 2
Chalchuapa o ES 52-53 K 5
Chalengkou o VRC 146-147 L 6
Chaleur Bay ≈ 240-241 K 3
Chaleurs, Baie des ≈ 240-241 K 3
Chalhuanca o PE 64-65 F 9
Chalía o Shehuen, Río ~ RA 80 E 4
Chaling o VRC 156-157 H 3
Chalinze o EAT 214-215 K 4
Chālisgaon o IND 138-139 E 9
Chalk River o CDN (ONT) 238-239 H 2
Chalky Inlet ≈ 182 A 7
Chalkyitsik o USA 20-21 T 3
Challakere o IND 140-141 G 3
Challans o F 90-91 G 8
Challa-Ogoyi o DY 204-205 E 4
Challapata o BOL 70-71 D 6
Challenger Deep ≃ 14-15 G 6
Challenger Plateau ≃ 182 B 3
Challis o USA (ID) 252-253 D 2
Chalmette o USA (LA) 268-269 L 7
Châlons-en-Champagne (-sur-Marne) ☆ • F 90-91 K 7
Chalon-sur-Saône o F 90-91 K 8
Chalouba = Oum o TCH 198-199 K 5
Chaltel o Fitz Roy, Cerro ▲ RA 80 D 4
Chaltubo o • GE 104 D 5
Chá Lugela o MOC 218-219 J 3
Cham o D 92-93 M 4
Chàm ⌒ VN 158-159 K 3
Chama o USA (NM) 256-257 J 2
Chama o Z 214-215 G 6
Chama, Rio ~ USA 256-257 J 2
Chamah, Gunung ▲ MAL 162-163 D 2
Chamais o NAM 220-221 B 3
Chaman o PK 134-135 M 3
Chamax ∴ • MEX 52-53 L 2
Chamaya, Río ~ PE 64-65 C 5
Chamba o EAT 214-215 H 6
Chamba o •• IND 138-139 F 3
Chambal ~ IND 138-139 G 6
Chambas o C 54-55 F 3
Chamberlain o CDN (SAS) 232-233 N 5
Chamberlain o USA (SD) 260-261 G 3
Chamberlain Island ⌒ CDN 36-37 M 2
Chamberlain Lake ○ USA (ME) 278-279 M 2
Chamberlain River ~ AUS 172-173 H 4
Chambers o USA (NE) 262-263 H 2
Chambers Bay ≈ 172-173 K 2
Chambersburg o USA (PA) 280-281 J 4
Chambers Cois o CDN (ONT) 238-239 F 6
Chambers Creek ~ USA 264-265 H 6
Chambers Island ⌒ USA (WI) 270-271 L 5
Chambéry ☆ • F 90-91 K 9
Chambeshi ~ Z 214-215 F 6
Chambi, Jebel ▲ TN 190-191 G 3
Chambira, Río ~ PE 64-65 E 4
Chambishi o Z 214-215 E 7
Chambo o EC 64-65 C 2
Chambord o CDN (QUE) 240-241 C 2
Chambord, Château ••• F 90-91 H 8
Chambrey o RP 160-161 E 7
Chambri Lakes ○ PNG 183 B 3
Chame o PA 52-53 E 7
Chamelecón, Río ~ HN 52-53 K 4
Chametengo o MOC 218-219 H 3
Chameza o CO 60-61 E 5
Chāmi o RIM 196-197 C 4
Chamical o RA 76-77 D 6
Chamiss Bay o CDN (BC) 230-231 B 3
Cham Kha o THA 142-143 L 6
Chamlang ▲ NEP 144-145 F 7
Ch'amo Hāyk' ○ ETH 208-209 C 6
Chamois o USA (MO) 274-275 G 6
Chamouchouane, Rivière ~ CDN 38-39 H 4
Chamouchouane, Rivière ~ CDN 236-237 P 3
Champ, Lac ○ CDN 36-37 R 7
Champagne o CDN 20-21 W 6
Champagne ⊥ • F 90-91 K 7
Champagne-Ardenne ▫ F 90-91 K 8
Champaign o USA (IL) 274-275 K 4
Champaquí, Cerro ▲ RA 76-77 E 6
Champasak o LAO 158-159 H 3
Champerico o GCA 52-53 J 4
Champhai o IND 142-143 H 4
Champion o CDN (ALB) 232-233 E 5
Champion o USA (MI) 270-271 L 4
Champlain o USA (NY) 278-279 H 4
Champlain, Lake ○ USA (NY) 278-279 H 4
Champotón o • MEX 52-53 J 2
Chāmrājnagar o IND 140-141 G 5
Chana, Kafin- o WAN 198-199 B 6
Chanachane, Oued ~ DZ 196-197 H 2
Chañaral o RCH 76-77 B 4
Chañaral, Isla ⌒ RCH 76-77 B 5
Chança, Rio ~ P 98-99 D 6
Chancani o RA 76-77 E 6
Chancay o PE 64-65 D 7
Chancay, Río ~ PE 64-65 C 5
Chancaybaños o PE 64-65 C 5
Chancellor o CDN (ALB) 232-233 F 4
Chan-Chan ••• PE 64-65 C 6
Ch'anch'o o ETH 208-209 D 4
Chanco o RCH 78-79 C 3
Chanco, Bahía ≈ 78-79 C 3
Chanda o IND 142-143 B 4
Chandalar River ~ USA 20-21 Q 3
Chandaler o USA 20-21 Q 3

Cathedral Gorge State Park — Chandaler 313

Chandarpur o **IND** 142-143 C 5
Chandausi o **IND** 138-139 G 5
Chāndbāli o **IND** 142-143 E 5
Chandeleur Islands ⌒ **USA** (LA) 268-269 M 7
Chandeleur Sound ≈ 268-269 L 7
Chandeliers, Col des ▲ **RN** 198-199 F 2
Chanderi o **IND** 138-139 G 7
Chandgad o **IND** 140-141 F 3
Chandigarh ☆ ·· **IND** 138-139 F 4
Chandipur o **IND** 142-143 E 5
Chandla o **IND** 142-143 B 3
Chandler o **CDN** (QUE) 240-241 L 2
Chandler o **USA** (AZ) 256-257 D 5
Chandler o **USA** (OK) 264-265 H 3
Chandler o **USA** (TX) 264-265 J 6
Chandler, Mount ▲ **AUS** 176-177 M 3
Chandler Lake ⊖ **USA** 20-21 O 2
Chandler River ~ **USA** 20-21 P 2
Chandless, Rio ~ **BR** 66-67 C 7
Chandless, Rio ~ **BR** 70-71 J 2
Chandpur o **BD** 142-143 G 4
Chandrabhāga ~ **IND** 138-139 F 3
Chandragadi o **NEP** 144-145 G 7
Chandrapur o **IND** (MAH) 138-139 G 10
Chandrapur o **IND** (MAP) 142-143 C 4
Chandrasekbarapuram o **IND** 140-141 H 3
Chanduy o **EC** 64-65 B 3
Chandvad o **IND** 138-139 E 9
Chandwa o **IND** 142-143 D 4
Chandwak o **IND** 142-143 C 3
Chang o **PK** 138-139 B 6
Changa o **Z** 218-219 E 3
Changadae Dan ▲ **KOR** 150-151 G 8
Changamba o **ANG** 216-217 E 6
Changamwe o **EAK** 212-213 G 6
Changanācheri o **IND** 140-141 G 6
Changane, Rio ~ **MOC** 220-221 L 2
Changara o **MOC** 218-219 G 3
Changbai o **VRC** 150-151 G 7
Changbai Shan ▲ **VRC** 150-151 F 7
Changbaishan · **VRC** 150-151 G 6
Changbaishan Z.B. ⊥ · **VRC** 150-151 F 6
Changcheng o **VRC** 156-157 F 7
Changchun ☆ **VRC** 150-151 E 6
Changdao o **VRC** 154-155 M 3
Changde o **VRC** 156-157 G 2
Changdianhekou o **VRC** 150-151 E 7
Changfeng o **VRC** 154-155 K 5
Changgi Gap ▲ **ROK** 150-151 G 9
Changhang o **ROK** 150-151 F 9
Changhua o **RC** 156-157 M 4
Changji o **VRC** 146-147 H 3
Changjiang o **VRC** 156-157 F 7
Chang Jiang ~ **VRC** 154-155 F 6
Changjiang Kou ≈ 154-155 N 6
Changjiang Sanxia ⌣ ·· **VRC** 154-155 F 6
Changjie Temple · **VRC** 154-155 F 4
Changjin o **KOR** 150-151 F 7
Changjin Gang ~ **KOR** 150-151 F 7
Changjin Ho ⊖ **KOR** 150-151 F 7
Changkat Jering o **MAL** 162-163 D 2
Changle o **VRC** (FUJ) 156-157 L 4
Changle o **VRC** (SIC) 154-155 E 6
Changli o **VRC** 154-155 L 2
Changling o **VRC** (HUB) 154-155 H 6
Changling o **VRC** (JIL) 150-151 E 5
Changlun o **MAL** 162-163 D 1
Changning o **VRC** (HUN) 156-157 H 3
Changning o **VRC** (SIC) 156-157 D 2
Changning o **VRC** (YUN) 142-143 L 3
Chango o **IND** 138-139 G 4
Changphu o **IND** 142-143 K 2
Changpin o **RC** 156-157 M 5
Changping o **VRC** 154-155 K 1
Changsan Got ▲ **KOR** 150-151 E 8
Changsha ☆ · **VRC** 156-157 H 2
Changshan o **VRC** 156-157 L 2
Changshan Qundao ⌒ **VRC** 150-151 D 8
Changshou o **VRC** 156-157 E 2
Changshu o **VRC** 154-155 M 6
Changshun o **VRC** 156-157 E 3
Changsong o **KOR** 150-151 E 7
Changsŏng o **ROK** 150-151 F 10
Changtai o **VRC** 156-157 K 4
Changting o **VRC** 156-157 K 4
Changtu o **VRC** 150-151 E 6
Changuillo o **PE** 64-65 E 9
Ch'angwon o **ROK** 150-151 G 10
Changwu o **VRC** 156-157 G 5
Changxing o **VRC** 154-155 L 6
Changyang o **VRC** 156-157 D 3
Changyon o **KOR** 150-151 E 8
Changyuan o **VRC** 154-155 J 4
Changzhi o **VRC** 154-155 H 3
Changzhou o **VRC** 154-155 L 6
Chankanai o **CL** 140-141 H 6
Chanler's Falls ~ **EAK** 212-213 G 3
Chân Mây, Mũi ▲ **VN** 158-159 K 2
Channapatna o **IND** 140-141 G 4
Channarāyapatna o **IND** 140-141 G 4
Channel Country, The ⌣ **AUS** 178-179 E 3
Channel Islands □ **GB** 90-91 F 7
Channel Islands ∸ **GB** 90-91 F 7
Channel Islands ⌒ **USA** (CA) 248-249 D 6
Channel Islands National Park ∴ **USA** (CA) 248-249 D 6
Channel-Port-aux-Basques o **CDN** (NFL) 242-243 J 5
Channel Rock ⌒ **BS** 54-55 G 3
Channing o **USA** (TX) 264-265 B 3
Chantada o **E** 98-99 D 3
Chanthaburi o **THA** 158-159 G 4
Chantrey Inlet ≈ 30-31 W 2
Chanu Daro ∴ · **PK** 138-139 B 6
Chanute o **USA** (KS) 262-263 L 7
Chany, Ozero = Čany, ozero ⊖ **RUS** 124-125 K 1
Chao, Isla ⌒ **PE** 64-65 C 6
Chaohu o **VRC** 154-155 K 6
Chao Hu · **VRC** 154-155 K 6
Chaouià ∸ **MA** 188-189 H 4
Chaoyang o **VRC** 150-151 C 7
Chaozhou o **VRC** 156-157 K 5
Chapacura, Cachoeira ~ **BOL** 70-71 F 4
Chapada o **BR** 74-75 D 7
Chapada Diamantina, Parque Nacional ⊥ **BR** 72-73 K 2
Chapada dos Guimarães o **BR** 70-71 K 4
Chapada dos Veadeiros, Parque Nacional da ⊥ **BR** 72-73 G 3
Chapada Grande ▲ **BR** 68-69 G 5
Chapadinha o **BR** 68-69 G 3
Chapais o **CDN** 38-39 G 4
Chapais o **CDN** (QUE) 236-237 O 3
Chapala o **MEX** 52-53 C 1
Chapala, Lago de ⊖ **MEX** 52-53 C 1
Chapalcó, Valle de ⌣ **RA** 78-79 G 4
Chaparaó, Serra do ▲ **BR** 72-73 J 6
Chapare, Río ~ **BOL** 70-71 E 5
Chaparra o **PE** 64-65 F 9
Chaparral o **CO** 60-61 D 6
Chaparrito o **CO** 60-61 F 5
Chaparro, El o **YV** 60-61 J 3
Chapas, Las o **RA** 78-79 F 7
Chapeco o **BR** 74-75 D 6
Chapel Hill o **USA** (NC) 282-283 H 5
Chapel Hill o **USA** (TN) 276-277 J 5
Chapel Island Indian Reserve X · **CDN** (NS) 240-241 P 5
Chapelle, La o **RH** 54-55 J 5
Chapelton o **JA** 54-55 G 5
Chaperito o **USA** (NM) 256-257 L 3
Chapin o **USA** (MI) 272-273 E 4
Chapleau o **CDN** (ONT) 236-237 E 5
Chapleau-Nemegosenda Provincial Park ⊥ **CDN** (ONT) 236-237 F 4
Chapleau River ~ **CDN** 236-237 E 4
Chaplin o **CDN** (SAS) 232-233 M 5
Chaplin o **USA** (KY) 276-277 K 3
Chaplin Lake ⊖ **CDN** (SAS) 232-233 M 5
Chapman, Cape ▲ **CDN** 24-25 b 6
Chapman, Lac ⊖ **CDN** (QUE) 236-237 O 4
Chapman Ranch o **USA** (TX) 266-267 K 6
Chapmanville o **USA** (WV) 280-281 D 6
Chapo, Lago ⊖ **RCH** 78-79 C 6
Chappell o **USA** (NE) 262-263 D 3
Chappells o **USA** (SC) 284-285 J 2
Chapra o **IND** (BIH) 142-143 D 3
Chapra o **IND** (MAP) 138-139 F 8
Chã Preta o **BR** 68-69 K 6
Chaptico o **USA** (MD) 280-281 K 5
Chapuru o · **SOL** 184 I d 3
Chapuy o **RA** 78-79 J 2
Châr o **RIM** 196-197 D 4
Charache o **YV** 60-61 F 3
Charadai o **RA** 76-77 H 4
Charagua o **BOL** 70-71 F 6
Charala o **CO** 60-61 E 4
Charancho, El o **RA** 78-79 G 4
Charara Safari Area ⊥ **ZW** 218-219 E 3
Charcas o **MEX** 50-51 J 6
Charco o **USA** (TX) 266-267 K 5
Charco, El o **RA** 76-77 E 4
Charco de la Peña o **MEX** 50-51 G 3
Charcot, Île ⌒ **ARK** 16 G 23
Charcot Land ∸ **GRØ** 26-27 I 7
Chardon o **USA** (OH) 280-281 E 2
Chardzhev ☆ **TM** 136-137 H 5
Charef, Oued ~ **MA** 188-189 K 4
Charente ~ **F** 90-91 H 8
Charentes ~ **F** 90-91 G 9
Chari ~ **TCH** 206-207 B 3
Chari-Baguirmi □ **TCH** 206-207 C 3
Charité-sur-Loire, la o **F** 90-91 J 8
Chariton o **USA** (IA) 274-275 E 3
Chariton River ~ **USA** 274-275 F 4
Charity o **GUY** 62-63 E 2
Charkhi Dādri o **IND** 138-139 F 5
Charkiv o **UA** 102-103 K 3
Charleroi o **B** 92-93 H 3
Charles, Cape ▲ **USA** (VA) 280-281 L 6
Charles, Mount ▲ **AUS** (WA) 176-177 D 3
Charles, Mount ▲ **AUS** (WA) 176-177 J 2
Charles, Peak ▲ **AUS** 176-177 F 6
Charles Bay ≈ 36-37 M 3
Charlesbourg o **CDN** (QUE) 238-239 O 2
Charles City o **USA** (IA) 274-275 F 1
Charles City o **USA** (VA) 280-281 J 6
Charles Dickens Point ▲ **CDN** 24-25 X 5
Charles Fuhr o **RA** 80 E 5
Charles Island ⌒ **CDN** 36-37 M 3
Charles Knob ▲ **AUS** 176-177 H 2
Charles Lake ⊖ **CDN** 30-31 O 6
Charles Lighthouse, Cape · **USA** (VA) 280-281 L 6
Charles Mount ▲ **USA** (IL) 274-275 H 2
Charles M. Russell National Wildlife Refuge ⊥ **USA** (MT) 250-251 M 4
Charleston o · **NZ** 182 C 4
Charleston o **USA** (AR) 276-277 A 5
Charleston o **USA** (IL) 274-275 K 5
Charleston o **USA** (MO) 276-277 F 4
Charleston o **USA** (MS) 268-269 K 2
Charleston o · **USA** (SC) 284-285 L 4
Charleston ☆ **USA** (WV) 280-281 E 5
Charleston, Lake ⊖ **USA** (IL) 274-275 L 5
Charleston Peak ▲ **USA** (NV) 248-249 J 3
Charlestown o ·· **KAN** 56 D 3
Charlestown o **USA** (IN) 274-275 N 6
Charles Town o **USA** (WV) 280-281 J 4
Charlestown = Baile Chathail o **IRL** 90-91 C 5
Charles Yorke, Cape ▲ **CDN** 24-25 f 4
Charleville o **AUS** 178-179 J 4
Charleville-Mézières ☆ **F** 90-91 K 7
Charlevoix o **USA** (MI) 272-273 D 2
Charlevoix, Lake ⊖ **USA** (MI) 272-273 D 2
Charlie Gibbs Fracture Zone ≃ 6-7 E 3
Charliste o **USA** (AR) 276-277 D 6
Charlo o **CDN** (NB) 240-241 J 3
Charloit, Lac de ⊖ **CDN** 30-31 Q 4
Charlotte o **USA** (MI) 272-273 E 5
Charlotte o **USA** (NC) 282-283 G 5
Charlotte o **USA** (TN) 276-277 H 4
Charlotte o **USA** (TX) 266-267 J 5
Charlotte, Lake ⊖ **CDN** (NS) 240-241 M 6
Charlotte Amalie ☆ · **USA** (VI) 286-287 R 2
Charlotte Bank ≃ 158-159 J 7
Charlotte Court House o **USA** (VA) 280-281 H 6
Charlotte Harbor ≈ 286-287 G 5
Charlotte Lake ⊖ **CDN** (BC) 228-229 J 4
Charlottesville o ··· **USA** (VA) 280-281 H 5
Charlottetown ☆ · **CDN** (PEI) 240-241 M 4
Charlotteville o **TT** 60-61 L 2
Charlson o **USA** (ND) 258-259 E 3
Charlton o **AUS** 180-181 G 4
Charlton o **CDN** (ONT) 236-237 J 5
Charlton Island ⌒ **CDN** 38-39 E 2
Charnley River ~ **AUS** 172-173 G 4
Charouïne o **DZ** 188-189 L 6
Charron Lake ⊖ **CDN** (MAN) 234-235 H 2
Chārsadda o · **PK** 138-139 C 2
Charters Towers o · **AUS** 174-175 J 7
Chartres ☆ ··· **F** 90-91 H 7
Chās o **IND** 142-143 E 4
Chaschuil o **RA** 76-77 C 4
Chaschuil o Guanchin, Río ~ **RA** 76-77 C 4
Chascomús o **RA** 78-79 K 3
Chase o **CDN** (BC) 230-231 K 3
Chase City o **USA** (VA) 280-281 H 7
Chasicó o **RA** (BUA) 78-79 H 5
Chasicó o **RA** (RIN) 78-79 E 6
Chasicó, Arroyo ~ **RA** 78-79 H 5
Chasicó, Laguna ⊖ **RA** 78-79 H 5
Chasm o **CDN** (BC) 230-231 H 2
Chasong o **KOR** 150-151 F 7
Chasquitambo o **PE** 64-65 D 7
Chassahowitzka o **USA** (FL) 286-287 G 3
Chassahowitzka Bay ≈ 286-287 G 3
Chassahowitzka National Wildlife Refuge ⊥ **USA** (FL) 286-287 G 3
Châtaigneraie, la o **F** 90-91 G 8
Chatanika River ~ **USA** 20-21 R 4
Chateau o **CDN** (NFL) 242-243 N 1
Châteaubriant o **F** 90-91 G 8
Château Chambord ··· **F** 90-91 H 8
Château-d'Oex o **CH** 92-93 J 5
Châteaudun o **F** 90-91 H 7
Chateaugay o **USA** (NY) 278-279 G 4
Château-Gontier o **F** 90-91 G 8
Châteauguay o **CDN** (QUE) 238-239 M 3
Chateauguay, Lac ⊖ **CDN** 36-37 P 6
Châteaulin o **F** 90-91 E 7
Châteauneuf-sur-Charente o **F** 90-91 G 9
Châteauneuf-sur-Loire o **F** 90-91 J 8
Château-Renault o **F** 90-91 H 8
Château-Richer o **CDN** (QUE) 238-239 O 2
Châteauroux ☆ **F** 90-91 H 8
Château-Thierry o **F** 90-91 J 7
Châtellerault o **F** 90-91 H 8
Chater o **CDN** (MAN) 234-235 D 5
Chatfield o **CDN** (MAN) 234-235 F 4
Chatfield o **USA** (MN) 270-271 F 7
Chatham o **CDN** (NB) 240-241 K 3
Chatham o **CDN** (ONT) 238-239 C 6
Chatham o **USA** (AK) 32-33 C 3
Chatham o **USA** (IL) 274-275 J 5
Chatham o **USA** (LA) 268-269 H 4
Chatham o **USA** (MI) 270-271 M 4
Chatham o **USA** (VA) 280-281 G 7
Chatham, Isla ⌒ **RCH** 80 C 5
Chatham Hill o **USA** (VA) 280-281 E 7
Chatham Island ⌒ **AUS** 176-177 D 7
Chatham Island ⌒ **NZ** 14-15 L 12
Chatham Rise ≃ 14-15 K 12
Chatham Sound ≈ 228-229 D 2
Chatham Strait ≈ 32-33 C 3
Châtillon o **I** 100-101 A 2
Châtillon-sur-Seine o · **F** 90-91 K 8
Chato, Cerro ▲ **RA** 78-79 C 7
Chatom o **USA** (AL) 284-285 B 5
Chatra o **IND** 142-143 D 3
Chatrapur o **IND** 142-143 D 6
Chatsworth o **AUS** 178-179 F 1
Chatsworth o **CDN** (ONT) 238-239 E 4
Chatsworth o **USA** (GA) 284-285 F 2
Chattahoochee o **USA** (FL) 286-287 E 1
Chattahoochee River ~ **USA** 284-285 E 3
Chattahoochee River ~ **USA** 284-285 E 5
Chattanooga o **USA** (OK) 264-265 F 4
Chattanooga o · **USA** (TN) 276-277 K 5
Chattaroy o **USA** (WA) 244-245 H 3
Chattoga River ~ **USA** 284-285 E 2
Chattooga River ~ **USA** 284-285 G 2
Chatuge Lake < **USA** (GA) 284-285 G 2
Chaua o **ANG** 216-217 E 4
Chaubara o **PK** 138-139 C 4
Chaudepalle o **IND** 140-141 H 4
Chaudière, Rivière ~ **CDN** 238-239 O 2
Châu Đốc o · **VN** 158-159 H 5
Chauk o **MYA** 142-143 J 5
Chaukundi ∴ · **PK** 134-135 M 6
Chaumont o **F** 90-91 K 7
Chaumont o **F** 90-91 H 8
Chauncey o **USA** (GA) 284-285 G 4
Chauques, Islas ⌒ **RCH** 78-79 C 7
Chaura Island ⌒ **IND** 140-141 L 5
Chauri o · **IND** 140-141 F 3
Chautauqua Lake ⊖ **USA** (IL) 274-275 J 4
Chautauqua Lake ⊖ **USA** (NY) 278-279 B 6
Chauvin o **USA** (LA) 268-269 K 7
Chavakachcheri o **CL** 140-141 J 6
Chāvakkād o **IND** 140-141 G 5
Chaval o **BR** 68-69 H 3
Chavarría o **RA** 76-77 H 5
Cha-Vat o **THA** 158-159 F 7
Chaves o **BR** 62-63 K 6
Chaves o · **P** 98-99 D 4
Chaveslândia o **BR** 72-73 E 5
Chavez, Los o **USA** (NM) 256-257 J 4
Chavigny, Lac ⊖ **CDN** 36-37 M 5
Chavín de Huántar ··· **PE** 64-65 D 6
Chavinillo o **PE** 64-65 D 6
Chavón, Río ~ **DOM** 54-55 L 5
Chavuma o **Z** 218-219 B 1
Chavuma Falls ~ **Z** 218-219 B 1
Chavuna o **EAT** 212-213 D 6
Chayanta, Río ~ **BOL** 70-71 D 6
Chazón o **RA** 78-79 H 2
Chazón, Arroyo ~ **RA** 78-79 H 2
Cheadle o **CDN** (ALB) 232-233 E 4
Cheaha Mountain ▲ **USA** (AL) 284-285 E 3
Cheakamus Indian Reserve X **CDN** (BC) 230-231 F 4
Cheat Lake ⊖ **USA** (WV) 280-281 G 4
Cheat Mountain ▲ **USA** 280-281 G 5
Cheat River ~ **USA** 280-281 G 4
Cheb o **CZ** 92-93 M 3
Chebaba, Hassi < **DZ** 190-191 D 6
Chebba o **TN** 190-191 H 3
Chebbi, Erg ∸ **MA** 188-189 K 5
Chebogue Point o **CDN** (NS) 240-241 J 7
Cheboksary = Čeboksary ☆ **RUS** 96-97 E 5
Cheboygan o **USA** (MI) 272-273 E 2
Checa o **E** 98-99 G 4
Chech, Erg ∸ **DZ** 196-197 J 2
Chech, Erg ∸ **RIM** 196-197 G 3
Chechaouèn = Shifshawn ☆ **MA** 188-189 J 3
Ché Ché o **GNB** 202-203 C 4
Checheng o **RC** 156-157 M 5
Chechenia = Nohčijčo' Respublika □ **RUS** 126-127 F 6
Cheche Pass ▲ **LS** 220-221 J 4
Chech'ŏn o **ROK** 150-151 G 9
Checotah o **USA** (OK) 264-265 J 3
Chedabucto Bay ≈ 240-241 O 5
Cheding o **VRC** 144-145 G 6
Cheduba = Man'aung o **MYA** 142-143 H 6
Cheduba Island = Man'aung Kyun ⌒ **MYA** 142-143 H 6
Cheduba Strait ≈ 142-143 H 6
Cheecham o **CDN** 32-33 P 3
Cheektowaga o **USA** (NY) 278-279 C 6
Cheepash River ~ **CDN** 236-237 G 2
Cheepie o **AUS** 178-179 H 4
Cheesman Peak ▲ **AUS** 176-177 L 3
Chefornak o **USA** 20-21 H 6
Chéfu, Rio ~ **MOC** 194-195 F 6
Chegga o **DZ** 190-191 E 3
Chegga o **RIM** 196-197 H 2
Chegge o **RIM** 196-197 E 5
Chegutu o **ZW** 218-219 F 4
Chehalis o **USA** (WA) 244-245 C 4
Chehalis River ~ **USA** 244-245 B 4
Chehaw Indian Monument · **USA** (GA) 284-285 F 5
Chehong Jiang ~ **VRC** 156-157 C 3
Chejchila, La o **RA** 76-77 E 4
Cheju o **ROK** 150-151 F 11
Cheju Do ⌒ **ROK** 150-151 F 11
Cheju Haehyŏp ≈ 150-151 F 11
Chela, Serra da ▲ **ANG** 216-217 B 8
Chelan o **CDN** (SAS) 232-233 P 3
Chelan o **USA** (WA) 244-245 E 3
Chelan, Lake ⊖ **USA** (WA) 244-245 E 2
Chelaslie River ~ **CDN** 228-229 H 3
Chelatna Lake ⊖ **USA** 20-21 P 5
Ch'elenk'o o **ETH** 208-209 E 4
Chelforó o **RA** 78-79 F 5
Chelforo, Arroyo ~ **RA** 78-79 K 4
Chelghoum El Aïd o **DZ** 190-191 F 2
Chelia, Djebel ▲ **DZ** 190-191 F 3
Chelif, Oued ~ **DZ** 190-191 C 2
Chelinda o **MW** 214-215 G 6
Cheline o **MOC** 218-219 H 6
Chellal o **DZ** 190-191 E 3
Chełm ☆ **PL** 92-93 R 3
Chełmno o · **PL** 92-93 P 2
Chelmsford o **CDN** (ONT) 238-239 D 2
Chelmsford Dam < **ZA** 220-221 J 4
Chełmża o · **PL** 92-93 P 2
Chelsea o **USA** (OK) 264-265 J 2
Chelsea o **USA** (VT) 278-279 J 5
Cheltenham o · **GB** 90-91 F 6
Chelvai o **IND** 142-143 B 6
Chelyabinsk = Čeljabinsk ☆ **RUS** 96-97 M 6
Chemaïa o **MA** 188-189 G 4
Chemainus o **CDN** (BC) 230-231 F 5
Chemax o **MEX** 52-53 L 1
Chemba o **MOC** 218-219 H 3
Chembe o **Z** 214-215 E 6
Chemchâm, Sebkhet ⊖ **RIM** 196-197 D 4
Chemehuevi Valley Indian Reservation X **USA** (CA) 248-249 K 5
Chemillé o **F** 90-91 G 8
Chemnitz o **D** 92-93 M 3
Chemong o **CDN** (SAS) 232-233 Q 2
Chemult o **USA** (OR) 244-245 D 7
Chemung River ~ **USA** 278-279 E 6
Chenab ~ **IND** 138-139 E 3
Chenāb ~ **PK** 138-139 D 3
Chenachen o **DZ** 188-189 J 7
Chena Hot Springs o **USA** 20-21 R 4
Chenango River ~ **USA** 278-279 F 6
Chena River ~ **USA** 20-21 R 4
Chen Barag Qi o **VRC** 150-151 B 3
Ch'ench'a o **ETH** 208-209 C 5
Chencoyi o **MEX** 52-53 J 2
Chenereh, Kampung o **MAL** 162-163 E 2
Chénéville o **CDN** (QUE) 238-239 K 3
Cheney o **USA** (KS) 262-263 J 7
Cheney o **USA** (WA) 244-245 H 3
Cheney Reservoir ⊖ **USA** (KS) 262-263 J 7
Chengalpattu o **IND** 140-141 H 4
Chengam o **IND** 140-141 H 4
Chengannūr o **IND** 140-141 G 6
Chengbu o **VRC** 156-157 F 3
Chengcheng o **VRC** 154-155 F 4
Chengde o ··· **VRC** 154-155 K 1
Chengdu ☆ **VRC** 154-155 D 6
Chenggu o **VRC** 154-155 E 5
Chenghai o **VRC** 156-157 K 5
Cheng Hai ⊖ **VRC** 142-143 M 2
Chengkung o **RC** 156-157 M 5
Chengmai o **VRC** 156-157 G 7
Chengqian o **VRC** 154-155 K 4
Chengshan Jiao ▲ **VRC** 154-155 N 3
Chengwu o **VRC** 154-155 J 4
Cheng Xian o **VRC** 154-155 D 5
Cheniere Lake < **USA** (LA) 268-269 H 4
Chenik o **USA** 22-23 T 3
Chenini o · **TN** 190-191 H 4
Chenjiagang o **VRC** 154-155 L 4
Chenoa o **USA** (IL) 274-275 K 4
Chenpur o **NEP** 144-145 C 6
Chenque, Cerro ▲ **RA** 80 G 2
Chenxi o **VRC** (HUN) 156-157 G 2
Chenxi o **VRC** (SIC) 154-155 E 6
Chenzhou o **VRC** 156-157 H 4
Cheo Reo o **VN** 158-159 K 4
Chepachet o **USA** (RI) 278-279 K 7
Chepen o **PE** 64-65 C 5
Chepes o **RA** 76-77 D 6
Chepes, Sierra de ▲ **RA** 76-77 D 6
Chepo o · **PA** 52-53 E 7
Chepstow o **GB** 90-91 F 6
Chequamegon Bay ⊖ **USA** (WI) 270-271 H 4
Cheran o **MEX** 52-53 D 2
Cheranchi o **WAN** 198-199 C 6
Cherangany Hills ▲ **EAK** 212-213 E 3
Cheraw o **USA** (CO) 254-255 M 5
Cheraw o **USA** (SC) 284-285 L 2
Cherbourg o **F** 90-91 G 7
Cherchell o · **DZ** 190-191 D 2
Cherepani o **GH** 202-203 L 4
Cherepovets = Čerepovec ☆ **RUS** 94-95 P 2
Cherful, Cape ▲ **USA** 22-23 N 5
Chergui, Aftoût ech ∸ **RIM** 196-197 C 6
Chergui, Zahrez ⊖ **DZ** 190-191 D 3
Cherhill o **CDN** (ALB) 232-233 D 2
Chéri o **RN** 198-199 E 6
Cheria o **DZ** 190-191 F 3
Cheriāl o **IND** 140-141 H 2
Cherkasy = Čerkasy ☆ **UA** 102-103 H 3
Chernabura Island ⌒ **USA** 22-23 R 5
Chernihiv = Černihiv o · **UA** 102-103 G 2
Cherni Island ⌒ **USA** 22-23 P 5
Chernivtsi = Černivci ☆ **UA** 102-103 D 3
Chernobyl = Čornobyl' o **UA** 102-103 G 2
Chernyakhovsk = Černjahovsk ☆ ·· **RUS** 94-95 G 4
Cherokee o **USA** (AL) 284-285 B 2
Cherokee o **USA** (IA) 274-275 C 2
Cherokee o **USA** (NC) 282-283 D 5
Cherokee o **USA** (OK) 264-265 F 2
Cherokee o **USA** (TX) 266-267 J 2
Cherokee Indian Reservation X **USA** (NC) 282-283 D 5
Cherokee Lake ⊖ **USA** (TN) 282-283 D 4
Cherokee Sound o **BS** 54-55 G 1
Cherokee Village o **USA** (AR) 276-277 D 4
Cherrabun o **AUS** 172-173 G 5
Chérrepe, Punta de ▲ **PE** 64-65 C 5
Cherry Creek ~ **CDN** 230-231 L 3
Cherry Creek o **USA** (NV) 246-247 L 4
Cherry Creek o **USA** (SD) 260-261 E 2
Cherry Creek ~ **USA** 254-255 L 4
Cherryfield o **USA** (ME) 278-279 O 4
Cherry Hill o **USA** (VA) 280-281 J 7
Cherryspring o **USA** (TX) 266-267 J 3
Cherryvale o **USA** (KS) 262-263 L 7
Cherry Valley o **USA** (AR) 276-277 E 5
Cherryville o **CDN** (BC) 230-231 L 3
Cherryville o **USA** (MO) 276-277 D 3
Cherskogo, Khrebet = Čerskogo, hrebet ▲ **RUS** 110-111 W 5
Cherson ☆ · **UA** 102-103 H 4
Chesaning o **USA** (MI) 272-273 E 4
Chesapeak Bay Bridge Tunnel II **USA** (VA) 280-281 L 6
Chesapeake o **USA** (VA) 280-281 K 7
Chesapeake Bay ≈ 280-281 K 5
Chesapeake Beach o **USA** (MD) 280-281 K 5
Chesea, Río ~ **PE** 64-65 F 6
Cheshire o **USA** (OR) 244-245 B 6
Chëshskaya Guba = Čëšskaja guba ≈ 88-89 S 3
Cheslatta Lake ⊖ **CDN** (BC) 228-229 J 3
Chesley o **CDN** (ONT) 238-239 D 4
Chesnee o **USA** (SC) 284-285 J 1
Chester o **CDN** (NS) 240-241 L 6
Chester o ·· **GB** 90-91 F 5
Chester o **USA** (IA) 274-275 F 1
Chester o **USA** (ID) 252-253 G 3
Chester o **USA** (IL) 276-277 F 3
Chester o **USA** (MT) 250-251 J 3
Chester o **USA** (NE) 262-263 J 4
Chester o **USA** (OH) 280-281 F 3
Chester o **USA** (OK) 264-265 F 2
Chester o **USA** (PA) 280-281 L 4
Chester o **USA** (SC) 284-285 J 2
Chester o **USA** (TX) 268-269 F 6
Chester o **USA** (VA) 280-281 J 6
Chesterfield o **GB** 90-91 G 5
Chesterfield o **USA** (SC) 284-285 K 2
Chesterfield Inlet ≈ 30-31 X 4
Chesterton o **USA** (IN) 274-275 L 3
Chesterton Range ▲ **AUS** 178-179 J 3
Chestertown o **USA** (MD) 280-281 K 4
Chesterville o **CDN** (ONT) 238-239 K 3
Chestnut o **USA** (IL) 274-275 J 4
Chesuncook Lake ⊖ **USA** (ME) 278-279 M 3
Chetaibi o · **DZ** 190-191 F 2
Chetek o **USA** (WI) 270-271 G 5
Chéticamp o **CDN** (NS) 240-241 P 4
Cheticamp River ~ **CDN** 240-241 P 4
Chetimacha Indian Reservation X **USA** 268-269 J 7
Chet Korkora o **RMM** 196-197 H 6
Chetlat Island ⌒ **IND** 140-141 E 5
Chetopa o **USA** (KS) 262-263 L 7
Chetumal ☆ · **MEX** 52-53 K 2
Chetumal, Bahía de ≈ 52-53 K 2
Chetwynd o **CDN** 32-33 K 4
Chevak o **USA** 20-21 H 6
Chevejecure, Río ~ **BOL** 70-71 D 4
Cheviot o **CDN** (SAS) 232-233 M 3
Cheviot Hills, The ▲ **GB** 90-91 F 4
Cheviot Range ▲ **AUS** 178-179 G 3
Chewack River ~ **USA** 244-245 E 2
Che'w Bahir ⊖ **ETH** 208-209 C 6
Chewelah o **USA** (WA) 244-245 H 2
Chewore Safari Area ⊥ **ZW** 218-219 E 3
Cheyenne o **USA** (OK) 264-265 E 3
Cheyenne ☆ **USA** (WY) 252-253 O 5
Cheyenne Bottoms ⊖ **USA** (KS) 262-263 H 6
Cheyenne River ~ **USA** 252-253 O 3
Cheyenne River ~ **USA** 260-261 D 2
Cheyenne River Indian Reservation X **USA** (SD) 260-261 E 1
Cheyenne Wells o **USA** (CO) 254-255 N 5
Cheyūr o **IND** 140-141 J 4
Chezacut o **CDN** (BC) 228-229 L 4
Chhāpar o **IND** 138-139 E 6
Chhatak o **BD** 142-143 G 3
Chhatarpur o **IND** 138-139 G 7
Chhattisgarh ∸ **IND** 142-143 B 5
Chhaygaon o **IND** 142-143 G 2
Chhindwāra o **IND** 138-139 G 8
Chhota Udepur o **IND** 138-139 E 8
Chhukha o **BHT** 142-143 F 2
Chhura o **IND** 142-143 C 5
Chiachi Island ⌒ **USA** 22-23 R 5
Ch'iaksan National Park ⊥ **ROK** 150-151 G 9
Chiamboni o **SP** 212-213 H 4
Chiangchün o **RC** 156-157 M 5
Chiang Dao o **THA** 142-143 L 6
Chiang Kan o **THA** 158-159 F 2
Chíang Kham o **THA** 142-143 M 6
Chiang Khong o **THA** 142-143 M 5
Chiang Mai ☆ **THA** 142-143 L 6
Chiang Rai o **THA** 142-143 L 6
Chian Muan o **THA** 142-143 M 6
Chiapa, Río ~ **MEX** 52-53 H 3
Chiapa de Corzo o · **MEX** 52-53 H 3
Chiapas □ **MEX** 52-53 H 3
Chiari o **I** 100-101 B 2
Chiasien o **RC** 156-157 M 5
Chiautla o **MEX** 52-53 E 2
Chiávari o · **I** 100-101 B 2
Chiavenna o **I** 100-101 B 1
Chiawa o **Z** 218-219 E 2
Chiayi o **RC** 156-157 M 5
Chiba ☆ **J** 152-153 J 7
Chibabava o **MOC** 218-219 G 5
Chibembe o **Z** 218-219 G 1
Chibia o **ANG** 216-217 B 7
Chibiaparú o **YV** 62-63 D 3
Chibi Moya · **VRC** 156-157 H 2
Chibougamau o **CDN** (QUE) 236-237 O 3
Chibougamau, Lac ⊖ **CDN** (QUE) 236-237 O 3
Chibougamau, Rivière ~ **CDN** 236-237 N 3
Chibuto o **MOC** 220-221 L 2
Chibuzhanghu ⊖ **VRC** 144-145 H 4
Chibwika o **Z** 214-215 C 7
Chica, Sierra ▲ **RA** 76-77 E 6
Chicago o · **USA** (IL) 274-275 L 3
Chicago Heights o **USA** (IL) 274-275 L 3
Chicala o **ANG** (BIE) 216-217 D 6
Chicala o **ANG** (MOX) 216-217 E 5
Chicamba o **MOC** 218-219 G 4
Chicamba Real, Barragem de < **MOC** 218-219 G 4
Chicambi o **ANG** 216-217 B 6
Chicaná ∴ · **MEX** 52-53 K 2
Chicapa ~ **ANG** 216-217 F 3
Chicas, Salinas ⊖ **RA** 78-79 H 5
Chicbul o **MEX** 52-53 J 2
Chic-Choc, Parc Provincial ⊥ **CDN** (QUE) 240-241 K 2
Chic-Chocs, Monts ▲ **CDN** 240-241 H 2
Chicha o **TCH** 198-199 J 4
Chichagof o **USA** 32-33 B 3
Chichagof Island ⌒ **USA** 32-33 B 3
Chichancanab, Laguna ⊖ · **MEX** 52-53 K 2
Chichaoua o **MA** 188-189 G 5
Chicharrona, La o **MEX** 50-51 H 6
Chīchāwatni o **PK** 138-139 D 4
Chiché, Rio ~ **BR** 68-69 B 6
Chicheng o **VRC** 154-155 J 1
Chichén Itzá ∴ ··· **MEX** 52-53 K 1
Chichester Range ▲ **AUS** 172-173 D 7
Chichibu o **J** 152-153 H 6
Chichibu-Tama National Park ⊥ **J** 152-153 H 7
Chichigalpa o **NIC** 52-53 L 5
Chichirate o **EC** 64-65 D 3
Chichón, Volcan ▲ **MEX** 52-53 H 3
Chickaloon o **USA** 20-21 Q 6
Chickamauga & Chattanooga National Military Park · **USA** (GA) 284-285 E 2
Chickamauga Lake < **USA** (TN) 282-283 C 5
Chickasaw o **USA** (AL) 284-285 B 6
Chickasaw Bogue ~ **USA** 284-285 C 4
Chickasawhatchee Creek ~ **USA** 284-285 F 5
Chickasawhay River ~ **USA** 268-269 M 5
Chickasaw National Recreation Area ⊥ · **USA** (OK) 264-265 H 4
Chickasha o **USA** (OK) 264-265 G 3
Chickasha, Lake < **USA** (OK) 264-265 F 3
Chic Kata o **RH** 54-55 J 5
Chicken o **USA** 20-21 U 4
Chicken Creek Summit ▲ **USA** (NV) 246-247 J 2
Chick Lake ⊖ **CDN** 30-31 F 3
Chiclayo ☆ **PE** 64-65 C 5
Chico o **MOC** 218-219 G 5
Chico o **USA** (CA) 246-247 D 4
Chico, Arroyo ~ **RA** 78-79 L 4
Chico, Río ~ **RA** 76-77 E 4
Chico, Río ~ **RA** 78-79 D 7
Chico, Río ~ **RA** 80 F 5
Chico, Río ~ **RA** 80 F 4
Chico, Río ~ **RA** 80 G 2
Chicoa o **MOC** 218-219 G 2
Chico Arroyo ~ **USA** 256-257 H 3
Chicoasén o **MEX** 52-53 H 3
Chicoasén, Presa < · **MEX** 52-53 H 3
Chicoca o **ANG** 216-217 F 7
Chicomba o **ANG** 216-217 C 7
Chicomo o **MOC** 220-221 M 2
Chicomoztoc ∴ · **MEX** 50-51 H 6
Chicomuselo o **MEX** 52-53 H 4
Chicondua ~ **ANG** 216-217 B 7
Chicontepec de Tejeda o **MEX** 52-53 E 1
Chicopee o **USA** (MA) 278-279 J 6
Chicoral o **CO** 60-61 D 5
Chicot State Park ⊥ **USA** (LA) 268-269 H 6
Chicotte o **CDN** (QUE) 242-243 E 3
Chicoutimi o **CDN** (QUE) 240-241 D 2
Chicualacuala o **MOC** 218-219 F 6
Chicuma o **ANG** 216-217 C 6
Chicundo o **ANG** 216-217 D 6
Chicupa o **ANG** 216-217 E 7
Ch'ida o **ETH** 208-209 C 5
Chidambaram o ·· **IND** 140-141 H 5
Chidenguele o **MOC** 220-221 M 2
Chidester o **USA** (AR) 276-277 B 7
Chido o **ROK** 150-151 F 10
Chidu o **SUD** 208-209 A 4
Chiede o **ANG** 216-217 C 8
Chief Joseph Pass ▲ **USA** (MT) 250-251 F 6
Chiefland o **USA** (FL) 286-287 G 2
Chief Menominee Monument · **USA** (IN) 274-275 M 3
Chiefs Island ⌒ **RB** 218-219 B 4
Chief's Point Indian Reservation X **CDN** (ONT) 238-239 D 4
Chiemsee ⊖ **D** 92-93 M 5
Chiengi o **Z** 214-215 E 5
Chiềng Khu'o'ng o **VN** 156-157 C 6
Chiengo o **ANG** 216-217 D 7
Chieo Lan Reservoir < **THA** 158-159 E 6
Chiese ~ **I** 100-101 C 2
Chieti ☆ **I** 100-101 E 3
Chifango o **ANG** 216-217 D 7
Chifeng o **VRC** 148-149 O 6
Chiftak o **USA** (AK) 20-21 J 6
Chifu o **WAN** 204-205 F 3
Chifukunya Hills ▲ **Z** 218-219 E 2
Chifumage ~ **ANG** 216-217 F 5
Chifunda o **Z** 214-215 G 6
Chifunde o **MOC** 218-219 G 2
Chig o **RIM** 196-197 D 5
Chigamane o **MOC** 218-219 G 5
Chiginagak, Mount ▲ **USA** 22-23 S 4
Chiginagak Bay ≈ 22-23 S 4
Chigmit Mountains ▲ **USA** 22-23 U 3
Chignecto, Cape ▲ **CDN** (NB) 240-241 K 5
Chignecto Bay ≈ 240-241 L 5
Chignecto Game Sanctuary ⊥ **CDN** (NS) 240-241 L 5
Chignik o **USA** 22-23 R 4
Chignik Bay ≈ 22-23 R 4
Chigombe, Rio ~ **MOC** 218-219 G 6
Chigorodo o **CO** 60-61 C 4
Chigoubiche, Lac ⊖ **CDN** (QUE) 236-237 P 3
Chiguana o **BOL** 70-71 D 7
Chigubo o **MOC** 218-219 G 6
Chihli, Gulf of = Bo Hai ≈ 154-155 L 2
Chihsing Yen ⌒ **RC** 156-157 M 6
Chihuahua □ **MEX** 50-51 F 3
Chihuido de Medio, Cerro ▲ **RA** 78-79 E 5
Chijmuni o **BOL** 70-71 D 5
Chikanda o **WAN** 204-205 E 4
Chikaskia River ~ **USA** 262-263 J 7
Chik Ballāpur o **IND** 140-141 G 4
Chikhli o **IND** (GUJ) 138-139 D 9
Chikhli o **IND** (MAH) 138-139 F 9
Chikhli o **IND** (MAP) 138-139 G 8
Chikjajur o **IND** 140-141 G 3
Chikmagalūr o **IND** 140-141 F 4
Chiknāyakanhalli o **IND** 140-141 G 4
Chikodi o **IND** 140-141 F 2
Chikombedzi o **ZW** 218-219 F 5
Chikonkomene o **Z** 218-219 E 2
Chikuma-gawa ~ **J** 152-153 H 6
Chikuminuk Lake ⊖ **USA** 20-21 L 6
Chikwa o **Z** 214-215 G 6
Chikwawa o **MW** 218-219 H 3
Chikwina o **MW** 214-215 H 6
Chikyu-misaki ▲ **J** 152-153 J 3
Chila o **ANG** 216-217 C 6
Chila o **MEX** 52-53 F 3
Chila, Laguna ⊖ **MEX** 50-51 K 6
Chilakalūrupet o **IND** 140-141 J 2
Chilako River ~ **CDN** 228-229 L 3
Chilan o **RC** 156-157 M 4
Chi Lăng o **VN** 156-157 E 6
Chilanga o **Z** 218-219 E 2
Chilanko Forks o **CDN** (BC) 228-229 K 4
Chilanko River ~ **CDN** 228-229 K 4
Chilapa o **MEX** 52-53 E 3
Chilapa de Díaz o **MEX** 52-53 F 3
Chilas o · **IND** 138-139 E 2
Chilaw o **CL** 140-141 H 7
Chilca o **PE** 64-65 D 8

314 Chandarpur — Chilca

Chilca, Cordillera de ▲ PE 64-65 F 9
Chilca, Punta ∧ PE 64-65 D 8
Chilcas ○ RA 76-77 E 4
Chilcaya ○ RCH 70-71 C 6
Chilcoot ○ USA (CA) 246-247 E 4
Chilcotin River ~ CDN 230-231 E 2
Chilcotin Ranges ▲ CDN 230-231 F 2
Chilcott Island ∧ AUS 174-175 L 5
Childers ○ AUS 178-179 M 3
Childersburg ○ USA (AL) 284-285 E 4
Childress ○ USA (TX) 264-265 D 4
Chile ■ RCH 78-79 C 5
Chile ○• RA 76-77 D 5
Chileka ○ MW 218-219 H 2
Chilembwe ○ Z 218-219 F 1
Chilena, Punta ∧ RCH 80 D 6
Chilengue, Serra do ▲ ANG 216-217 C 6
Chile Rise ≃ 5 B 8
Chiles, Los ○ CR 52-53 B 6
Chilesburg ○ USA (VA) 280-281 J 5
Chilete ○ PE 64-65 C 6
Chilikadrotna River ~ USA 20-21 N 6
Chililabombwe ○ Z 214-215 D 7
Chilili ○ USA (NM) 256-257 J 4
Chilkat ○ USA 20-21 S 6
Chilkat Bald Eagle Preserve ⊥ USA 20-21 W 7
Chilkat Inlet ≈ 20-21 X 7
Chilko Lake ○ CDN (BC) 230-231 G 4
Chilkoot Pass ▲ USA 20-21 X 7
Chilko River ~ CDN 230-231 E 2
Chilla ○ EC 64-65 C 3
Chillagoe ○ AUS 174-175 H 5
Chillajara ○ BOL 70-71 E 7
Chillán ○ RCH 78-79 C 4
Chillán, Río ~ RCH 78-79 D 4
Chillán, Volcán ▲ RCH 78-79 D 4
Chillar ○ RA 78-79 J 4
Chilla Well ○ AUS 172-173 K 6
Chillicothe ○ USA (IL) 274-275 J 4
Chillicothe ○ USA (MO) 274-275 E 5
Chillicothe ○ USA (OH) 280-281 D 4
Chillicothe ○ USA (TX) 264-265 E 4
Chillinji ○ IND 138-139 E 1
Chilliwack ○ CDN (BC) 230-231 H 4
Chillupar ○ IND 142-143 G 2
Chilmari ○ BD 142-143 F 3
Chilmark ○ USA (MA) 278-279 L 7
Chiloango ~ ANG 210-211 D 6
Chilobwe ○ MW 218-219 H 2
Chiloé, Isla de ∧ RCH 70-79 C 7
Chiloé, Parque Nacional ⊥ RCH 78-79 B 7
Chilombo ○ ANG 214-215 B 7
Chilongozi ○ Z 218-219 F 1
Chiloquin ○ USA (OR) 244-245 D 8
Chilpancingo de los Bravos ★ MEX 52-53 K 4
Chilpi ○ IND 142-143 F 4
Chiltepec ○ MEX 52-53 H 2
Chilticothe ○ USA (IL) 274-275 J 4
Chilton ○ USA (TX) 266-267 K 2
Chilton ○ USA (WI) 270-271 K 6
Chiluage ○ ANG 216-217 F 4
Chilubula ○ Z 214-215 F 6
Chilumba ○ MW 214-215 H 6
Chilumbuwo ○ Z 214-215 D 7
Chilwa, Lake ○ MW 218-219 H 2
Chimala ○ EAT 214-215 H 5
Chimaliro ○ MW 214-215 H 6
Chimaltenango ★ GCA 52-53 J 4
Chimán ○ PA 52-53 E 7
Chimanimani ○• Z 218-219 G 4
Chimanimani National Park ⊥ ZW 218-219 G 4
Chimbán ○ PE 64-65 C 5
Chimbangombe ○ ANG 216-217 D 6
Chimbarongo ○ RCH 78-79 D 3
Chimbinde ○ ANG 216-217 D 6
Chimbo, Río ~ EC 64-65 C 2
Chimboin ○ ZW 216-217 B 7
Chimborazo, Volcán ▲ EC 64-65 C 2
Chimbote ○ PE 64-65 C 6
Chimbwingombi ▲ Z 218-219 F 1
Chiméal ○ K 158-159 G 5
Chimney Rock • USA (NC) 282-283 E 5
Chimney Rock National Historic Site • USA (NE) 262-263 C 2
Chimoio ○ MOC 218-219 H 4
Chimumo ○ ANG 216-217 D 6
Chi'ra ○ ETH 208-209 C 5
Chinacota ○ CO 60-61 E 4
Chinake ○ IND 140-141 F 2
China Lake ○ USA (CA) 248-249 G 4
China Lake Naval Weapons Center xx USA (CA) 248-249 G 4
Chinampas ○ MEX 50-51 J 7
China Muerte, Arroyo ~ RA 78-79 D 5
Chinandega ○ NIC 52-53 L 5
China Point ≃ 248-249 F 7
Chinati Peak ▲ USA (TX) 266-267 C 4
Chincha, Islas de ∧ PE 64-65 D 8
Chincha Alta ○ PE 64-65 D 8
Chinchaga River ~ CDN 30-31 K 6
Chinchilla ○ AUS 178-179 L 4
Chinchilla de Monte Aragón ○ E 98-99 G 5
Chinchina ○ CO 60-61 D 5
Chinchin Straits ≈ 162-163 U 7
Chinchorro, Banco ≈ MEX 52-53 L 3
Chincolco ○ RCH 78-79 D 2
Chincoteague ○ USA (VA) 280-281 L 6
Chincoteague Bay ≈ 280-281 L 5
Chincultic ∴ MEX 52-53 J 3
Chinde ○ MOC 218-219 H 4
Chindo ○ ROK 150-151 F 10
Chindwin Myit ~ MYA 142-143 H 4
Chinegue ○ MOC 218-219 H 1
Chinero, Río ~ RCH 50-51 B 2
Chingaza, Parque Nacional ⊥ CO 60-61 E 5
Chingo ○ ANG 216-217 B 7
Chingola ○ Z 214-215 D 7

Chingombe ○ Z 218-219 F 2
Chinguar ○ ANG 216-217 D 6
Chinguetia ○ ANG 216-217 D 5
Chinguetti ○ RIM 196-197 D 4
Chingul ○ TCH 206-207 D 3
Chinhama ○ ANG 216-217 D 6
Chinhanda ○ MOC 220-221 L 2
Chin Hills ▲ MYA 142-143 H 4
Chinhoyi ★ ZW 218-219 F 3
Chiniak, Cape ∧ USA 22-23 U 4
Chiniak Bay ≈ 22-23 U 4
Chiniot ○ PK 138-139 D 4
Chinitna Point ∧ USA 20-21 O 3
Chinjan ○ PK 134-135 M 3
Chinkapook ○ AUS 180-181 G 3
Chinko ~ RCA 206-207 G 6
Chinle ○ USA (AZ) 256-257 F 2
Chinle Wash ~ USA 256-257 F 2
Chinmen ○ RC 156-157 L 4
Chinmen Tao ∧ RC 156-157 L 4
Chinnür ○ IND 138-139 G 10
Chino ○ USA (CA) 248-249 G 5
Chino Creek ~ USA 256-257 C 3
Chinon ○ F 90-91 H 8
Chinook ○ CDN (ALB) 232-233 H 4
Chinook ○ USA (MN) 256-257 K 3
Chinook ○ USA (WA) 244-245 C 3
Chinook Trough ≃ 14-15 L 3
Chinook Valley ○ CDN 32-33 M 3
Chino Valley ○ USA (AZ) 256-257 C 4
Chinpurtar ○ NEP 144-145 E 7
Chinquite ○ ANG 216-217 B 6
Chinsali ○ Z 214-215 G 6
Chintalnar ○ IND 142-143 E 5
Chintámani ○ IND 140-141 H 4
Chinteche ○ MW 214-215 H 6
Chinturu ○ IND 142-143 B 7
Chinvali ○ GE 126-127 F 6
Chinyama Litapi ○ Z 218-219 B 1
Chioco ○ MOC 218-219 G 3
Chióggia ○ I 100-101 D 2
Chipai Lake ○ CDN 34-35 N 4
Chipanga ○ MOC 218-219 H 3
Chipasanse ○ Z 214-215 F 5
Chipata ○ Z 218-219 G 1
Chipepo ○ Z 218-219 D 3
Chiperone, Monte ▲ MOC 218-219 H 3
Chipewyan Indian Reserve ✕ CDN 30-31 O 6
Chipewyan River ~ CDN 32-33 O 3
Chipili ○ Z 214-215 E 6
Chipinda Pools ○ ZW 218-219 F 5
Chipindo ○ ANG 216-217 D 6
Chipinga Safari Area ⊥ ZW 218-219 G 5
Chipinge ○ ZW 218-219 G 5
Chipinna ○ ANG 216-217 C 6
Chipoka ○ MW 218-219 H 1
Chipitola River ~ USA 286-287 D I
Chippenham ○ GB 90-91 H 6
Chipley ○ USA (FL) 286-287 D 1
Chipman ○ CDN (NB) 240-241 K 4
Chipman Lake ○ CDN (ONT) 236-237 B 3
Chipman River ~ CDN 30-31 R 6
Chippewa, Lake ○ USA (WI) 270-271 G 5
Chippewa Falls ○ USA (WI) 270-271 G 6
Chippewa River ~ USA 270-271 G 5
Chipungo ○ Z 218-219 F 1
Chiputneticook Lakes ○ USA 278-279 O 3
Chiputo ○ MOC 218-219 G 2
Chiquian ○ PE 64-65 C 6
Chiquilá ○ MEX 52-53 L 1
Chiquimula ○ GCA 52-53 K 4
Chiquinata, Bahía ≈ 70-71 B 7
Chiquinquirá ○ CO 60-61 E 4
Chiquitina, Isla ∧ PE 64-65 D 7
Chiquitos, Llanos de ∧ BOL 70-71 F 6
Chira, Río ~ PE 64-65 B 4
Chiramba ○ MOC 218-219 H 3
Chiredzi ○ ZW 218-219 F 5
Chireno ○ USA (TX) 268-269 F 5
Chirfa ○ RN 198-199 F 2
Chiriacu ○ PE 64-65 C 4
Chiribiquete, Raudal ~ CO 64-65 F 1
Chiricahua Peak ▲ USA (AZ) 256-257 F 7
Chiriguare, Reserva Faunística ⊥ YV 60-61 G 3
Chirikof Island ∧ USA 22-23 T 5
Chirikof Point ∧ USA 22-23 U 6
Chirimena ○ YV 60-61 H 2
Chiriquí, Golfo de ≈ 52-53 C 7
Chiriqui, Laguna de ≈ 52-53 D 7
Chiriquí Grande ○ PA 52-53 D 7
Chiris, Río ∧ PE 64-65 E 8
Chiri San ▲ ROK 150-151 F 10
Chirisan National Park ⊥ ROK 150-151 F 10
Chirma Safari Area ⊥ ZW 218-219 E 3
Chiromo ○ MW 218-219 H 3
Chirripó, Río ~ CR 52-53 C 7
Chirripó Grande, Cerro ▲ CR 52-53 C 7
Chirumanzu ○ ZW 218-219 F 3
Chirundu ○ Z 218-219 E 3
Chisamba ○ Z 218-219 E 2
Chisana ○ USA 20-21 U 5
Chisana River ~ USA 20-21 U 5
Chisasa ○ Z 214-215 C 7

Chisasibi ○ CDN 38-39 E 2
Chisec ○ GCA 52-53 J 4
Chisekesi ○ Z 218-219 E 2
Chisenga ○ MW 214-215 G 5
Chishan ○ RC 156-157 M 5
Chishang ○ RC 156-157 M 5
Chisholm ○ USA (MN) 270-271 F 3
Chishui ○ VRC 156-157 D 3
Chishuihe ○ VRC 156-157 D 3
Chishui He ~ VRC 156-157 D 2
Chisik Island ∧ USA 20-21 O 6
Chisimba Falls ~ Z 214-215 F 6
Chişinău ★ MD 102-103 F 4
Chişineu-Criş ○ RO 102-103 B 4
Chisos Mountains ▲ USA 266-267 D 4
Chissano ○ MOC 220-221 L 2
Chissibuca ○ MOC 220-221 M 2
Chissinguane ○ MOC 220-221 M 2
Chistián Mandy ○ PK 138-139 D 5
Chisumbanje ○ MOC 218-219 H 5
Chita ○ BOL 70-71 D 6
Chita ○ EAT 214-215 H 5
Chitado ○ ANG 216-217 B 8
Chitaga ○ CO 60-61 E 4
Chităpur ○ IND 140-141 G 2
Chitek ○ CDN (SAS) 232-233 K 3
Chitek Lake ○ CDN (SAS) 232-233 L 2
Chitek Lake ○ CDN (MAN) 234-235 D 2
Chitek Lake Indian Reservation ✕ CDN (SAS) 232-233 L 2
Chitembo ○ ANG 216-217 D 6
Chi Thanh ○ VN 158-159 K 4
Chitina ○ USA 20-21 S 6
Chitina River ~ USA 20-21 S 6
Chitipa ○ MW 214-215 G 5
Chito ○ EC 64-65 C 3
Chitobe ○ MOC 218-219 G 5
Chitongo ○ Z 218-219 D 3
Chitose ○ J 152-153 J 3
Chitowe ○ EAT 214-215 H 5
Chitradurga ○ IND 140-141 G 3
Chitrakūt ○ IND 142-143 B 3
Chitrál ○ PK 138-139 C 2
Chitré ○ PA 52-53 D 8
Chitre, Serra do ▲ BR 72-73 K 4
Chittagong ○ BD 142-143 G 4
Chittaurgarh ○ IND 138-139 E 7
Chittivalasa ○ IND 142-143 C 7
Chittoor ○ IND 140-141 H 4
Chitungwiza ○ ZW 218-219 F 3
Chitwood ○ USA (OR) 244-245 B 6
Chityal ○ IND 140-141 H 2
Chiu Chiu ○ RCH 70-71 C 7
Chiulezi, Río ~ MOC 214-215 J 6
Chiumbe ~ ANG 216-217 F 4
Chiumbo ○ ANG 216-217 D 6
Chiu Oyu ▲ NEP 144-145 F 6
Chiúre ○ MOC 218-219 K 1
Chiúre Novo ○ MOC 218-219 K 1
Chivacoa ○ YV 60-61 G 2
Chivasing ○ PNG 183 D 4
Chivasso ○ I 100-101 A 2
Chivato ○ RCH 76-77 B 7
Chivay ○ PE 70-71 B 4
Chivé ○ BOL 70-71 C 4
Chivhu ○ ZW 218-219 F 4
Chivilingoy ○ RA 78-79 K 3
Chivilcoo ○ C 54-55 G 5
Chiweta ○ MW 214-215 H 6
Chixoy o Negro, Río ~ GCA 52-53 J 4
Chizarira Hills ▲ ZW 218-219 D 3
Chizarira National Park ⊥ ZW 218-219 D 3
Chizu ○ J 152-153 F 7
Chizwina ○ RB 218-219 D 5
Chlef ○ DZ 190-191 G 2
Chloride ○ USA (AZ) 256-257 A 3
Chmel'nyc'kyj ★ UA 102-103 E 3
Chmel'nyc'kyj, Perejaslav- ○ UA 102-103 G 2
Chôăm Khsant ○ K 158-159 H 3
Choapa, Río ~ RCH 76-77 B 6
Choapan ○ MEX 52-53 G 3
Choapas, Las ○ MEX 52-53 G 3
Choate ○ CDN (BC) 230-231 H 4
Chobe ~ NAM 218-219 C 4
Chobe National Park ⊥ RB 218-219 C 4
Chocaman ○ MEX 52-53 F 3
Chocamán, Cerro ▲ PE 64-65 E 8
Chochó ○ Z 214-215 G 8
Chochó ○ YV 60-61 H 2
Chocó ○ USA (NC) 282-283 K 5
Choctawhatchee Bay ≈ 286-287 C 1
Choctawhatchee River ~ USA 286-287 C 1
Choctawhatchee River, East Fork ~ USA 284-285 C 5
Choctawhatchee River, West Fork ~ USA 284-285 C 5
Choctaw Indian Reservation ✕ USA (MS) 268-269 L 4
Chodavaram ○ IND 142-143 C 7
Cho Do ~ KOR 150-151 E 8
Chodzież ○ PL 92-93 O 2
Choele Choel ○ RA 78-79 G 5
Chofombo ○ MOC 218-219 F 2
Choice ○ USA (MN) 270-271 G 7
Choichuff, Lagh ~ EAK 212-213 F 2
Choiseul ○ SOL 184 I c 2
Choiseul ∧ SOL 184 I c 2
Choix ○ MEX 50-51 G 4
Choix, Port aux ○ CDN (NFL) 242-243 L 2
Chojnice ○ PL 92-93 O 2
Chojnoki ○ BY 94-95 M 6
Chōkai Quasi National Park ⊥ J 152-153 J 5

Chōkai-san ▲ J 152-153 J 5
Chok Chai ○ THA 158-159 G 3
Choke Canyon Lake ○ USA (TX) 266-267 H 4
Ch'ok'ē Terara ▲ ETH 208-209 C 3
Chokio ○ USA (MN) 270-271 B 5
Chókué ○ MOC 220-221 L 2
Cholame ○ USA (CA) 248-249 E 4
Chola Shan ▲ VRC 144-145 M 4
Chola Shan ▲ VRC (SIC) 144-145 M 5
Chola Shankou ▲ VRC 144-145 M 5
Cholay ○ MEX 50-51 D 3
Cholchol, Río ~ RCH 78-79 C 5
Chole ∧ EAT 214-215 K 4
Choluteca ○ HN 52-53 L 5
Choluteca, Río ~ HN 52-53 L 5
Ch'ōlwōn ○ ROK 150-151 F 8
Choma ○ Z 218-219 D 3
Chom Bung ○ THA 158-159 F 4
Chomen ○ ETH 208-209 C 4
Chom Phra ○ THA 158-159 G 3
Chom Tong ○ THA 142-143 L 6
Chomūn ○ IND 138-139 E 6
Chon ○ IND 138-139 E 6
Chona ~ EAT 212-213 D 6
Chonan ○ PK 138-139 D 4
Chonchi ○ RCH 78-79 C 6
Chonchón Gang ~ KOR 150-151 E 8
Chongiin ★ KOR 150-151 G 7
Chongju ○ ROK 150-151 F 10
Chongming ○ VRC 154-155 M 6
Chongoene ○ MOC 220-221 L 2
Chongorói ○ ANG 216-217 B 6
Chongoyape ○ PE 64-65 B 6
Chongpyong ○ KOR 150-151 F 8
Chongqing ○ VRC (SIC) 154-155 C 6
Chongqing ○• VRC (SIC) 156-157 C 2
Chongren ○ VRC 156-157 K 3
Chong Samui ○ THA 158-159 E 6
Chong Tao ○ THA 158-159 E 6
Chongwe ~ Z 218-219 E 2
Chongyang ○ VRC 156-157 J 2
Chongyi ○ VRC 156-157 J 4
Chŏnju ○ ROK 150-151 F 10
Chonos, Archipiélago de los ∧ RCH 80 C 2
Chontaleña, Cordillera ▲ NIC 52-53 B 6
Chontali ○ PE 64-65 C 5
Chontalpa ○ MEX 52-53 H 3
Cho'n Thành ○ VN 158-159 J 5
Chon Buri ○ THA 158-159 G 2
Chonphon ○ THA 158-159 F 5
Chompi ○ PE 64-65 E 5
Chompon ○ THA 158-159 F 3
Chumsaeng ○ THA 158-159 F 3
Chumul ∴ MEX (YUC) 52-53 K 1
Chumul ∴ MEX (YUC) 52-53 K 2
Chun ○ THA 142-143 M 6
Chuna ○ PK 138-139 E 2
Chunán ○ VRC 156-157 L 2
Chuncar ○ PE 64-65 B 4
Chunchanga, Pampa de ⊥ PE 64-65 D 8
Chunchi ○ EC 64-65 C 3
Ch'unch'ŏn ○ ROK 150-151 F 9
Chunchura ○ IND 142-143 F 4
Chundela ○ ANG 216-217 B 7
Chunga ○ Z 218-219 D 2
Chungara, Lago ○ RCH 70-71 C 6
Chunggang ○ KOR 150-151 F 7
Ch'ungju ○ ROK 150-151 F 9
Ch'ungmu ○ ROK 150-151 G 10
Chungui ○ PE 64-65 E 8
Chungyang Shanmo ▲ RC 156-157 M 5
Chünjin ○ PK 138-130 D 4
Chunky River ~ USA 268-269 M 4
Chunshui ○ VRC 154-155 H 5
Chunu, Cape ▲ USA 22-23 II 7
Chunwan ○ VRC 156-157 G 5
Chunya ○ EAT 214-215 G 5
Chuŏr Phnum Dăngrek ▲ K 158-159 G 3
Chuŏr Phnum Kravanh ▲ K 158-159 G 4
Chupadero de Caballo ○ MEX 50-51 J 3
Chupadero Springs ○ USA (TX) 266-267 J 4
Chuquibamba ○ PE 64-65 F 9
Chuquicamata ○ RCH 76-77 C 2
Chuquicara ○ PE 64-65 C 6
Chuquiribamba ○ EC 64-65 C 3
Chuquis ○ PE 64-65 D 6
Chur ★ CH 92-93 K 5
Churachándpur ○ IND 142-143 H 4
Churcampa ○ PE 64-65 E 8
Church ○ USA (VA) 280-281 J 6
Churchbridge ○ CDN (SAS) 232-233 R 5
Church Hill ○ USA (TN) 282-283 E 4
Churchill ○ CDN 30-31 W 6
Churchill Cap ∧ CDN 30-31 X 6
Churchill Falls ○ CDN 38-39 M 2
Churchill Lake ○ CDN 32-33 G 3
Churchill Lake ○ USA (ME) 278-279 M 2
Churchill Reef ∧ USA 172-173 F 3
Churchill River ~ CDN 34-35 J 2
Churchill River ~ CDN 38-39 N 2
Church Point ○ USA (LA) 268-269 H 6
Churchs Ferry ○ USA (ND) 258-259 H 3
Churchville ○ USA (VA) 280-281 G 5
Churdan ○ USA (IA) 274-275 D 2
Churia Range ▲ NEP 144-145 F 7

Chrome ○ USA (CA) 246-247 C 4
Chromer ○• GB 90-91 H 5
Chromo ○ USA (CO) 254-255 J 6
Chrysler ○ USA (AL) 284-285 C 5
Chuali, Lagoa ○ MOC 220-221 L 2
Chuave ○ PNG 183 C 4
Chub Cay ∧ BS 54-55 G 2
Chubu-Sangaku National Park ⊥ J 152-153 J 6
Chubut ■ RA 78-79 D 7
Chubut, Río ~ RA 78-79 F 7
Chuchi Lake ○ CDN (BC) 230-231 J 2
Chuchiliga ○ GH 202-203 K 4
Chucul ~ RA 78-79 G 3
Chucunaque ~ PA 52-53 E 7
Chuckery ○ USA (OH) 280-281 C 3
Chucul, Río ~ RCH 76-77 C 2
Chucul, Quebrada ~ RCH 76-77 C 2
Chugiak ○ USA 20-21 O 6
Chuginadak Island ∧ USA 22-23 L 6
Chugoku-sanchi ▲ J 152-153 E 7
Chugul Island ∧ USA 22-23 L 6
Chugwater ○ USA (WY) 252-253 O 5
Chuhar Jamali ○ PK 134-135 M 6
Ch'uhar Kána ○ PK 138-139 D 4
Chuka ○ EAK 212-213 F 4
Chukai ○ MAL 162-163 E 2
Chukchi Autonomous District = Čukotskij avtonomnyj okrug ▣ RUS 112-113 O 3
Chukchi Plateau ≃ 16 B 35
Chukchi Sea ≈ 112-113 X 1
Chukotat, Rivière ~ CDN 36-37 L 4
Chukotskiy Poluostrov = Čukotskij poluostrov ∧ RUS 112-113 W 3
Chula ○ USA (GA) 284-285 G 5
Chulahuma ○ USA (MS) 268-269 L 2
Chulas, Raudal las ~ CO 60-61 F 4
Chula Vista ○ USA (CA) 248-249 G 7
Chulitna River ~ USA 20-21 Q 5
Chuma ○ BOL 70-71 C 4
Chuma Shankou ▲ VRC 144-145 L 6
Chumba ○ ETH 208-209 D 6
Chumbicha ○ RA 76-77 D 5
Chumbo ~ RA 72-73 G 5
Chumikgiarsa ○ IND 138-139 F 3
Chuphae ○ THA 158-159 G 2
Chuphon ○ THA 158-159 F 5
Churín ○ PE 64-65 D 7
Churobusco ○ USA (IN) 274-275 N 3
Churu ○ IND 138-139 E 5
Churuguara ○ YV 60-61 G 2
Chu' Sê ○ VN 158-159 K 4
Chuska Mountains ▲ USA 256-257 F 3
Chusmisa ○ RCH 70-71 C 6
Chūsonji • J 152-153 J 5
Chust ○ UZ 102-103 O 3
Chute-des-Passes ○ CDN 38-39 J 2
Chute Lake ○ CDN (BC) 230-231 K 4
Chutine Landing ○ CDN 32-33 J 4
Chuvashia = Čavaš respubliki ▣ RUS 96-97 E 6
Chuwangsan National Park ⊥ ROK 150-151 G 9
Chuxiong ○ VRC 156-157 B 4
Chuy ○ ROU 74-75 D 2
Chuzhou ○ VRC 154-155 L 5
Chwaka ○ EAT 214-215 K 4
Chyulu Hills ▲ EAK 212-213 F 5
Ciácoola, Monte ▲ I 100-101 C 5
Ciamis ○ RI 168 B 3
Ciandur ○ RI 168 B 3
Cianjur ○ RI 168 B 3
Ciano ○ EC 64-65 C 3
Cianorte ○ BR 72-73 H 7
Ciasmin ○ CO 60-61 D 2
Ciatura ○ GE 126-127 E 6
Cibadak ○ RI 168 B 3
Cibagalahskij hrebet ▲ RUS 110-111 W 6
Cibatu ○ RI 168 B 3
Cibit ○ RUS 124-125 P 3
Cibitoke ○ BU 212-213 B 5
Čičatka, Bol'šaja ~ RUS 118-119 K 8
Cícero Dantas ○ BR 68-69 J 7
Cicia ∧ FJI 184 III c 2
Čičkajúl ~ RUS 114-115 T 6
Cicurug ○ RI 168 B 3
Cidade Gaúcha ○ BR 72-73 D 7
Cide ★ TR 128-129 E 2
Ciechanów ○ PL 92-93 Q 2
Ciego, El ○ C 54-55 L 3
Ciego de Ávila ★ C 54-55 G 4
Ciempozuelos ○ E 98-99 F 4
Ciénaga ○ CO 60-61 D 2
Ciénaga, La ○ RA 76-77 C 5
Ciénaga Grande de Santa Marta ≈ 60-61 D 2
Cienéguillas ○ RA 76-77 C 5
Cienéguillas ○ MEX (ZAC) 50-51 J 5
Cienfuegos ★ C 54-55 E 3
Cieza ○ E 98-99 G 5
Çifteler ★ TR 128-129 D 3
Cifuentes ○ C 54-55 E 3
Cifuncho ○ RCH 76-77 B 3
Cigarro ○ BR 66-67 E 4
Çiğdikóy ○ RUS 84-85 e 2
Cihanbeyli ★ TR 128-129 E 3
Cihanbeyli Yaylási ▲ TR 128-129 E 3
Cihuatlán ○ MEX 52-53 F 3
Cijara, Reserva Nacional de ⊥ E 98-99 E 5
Cijulung ○ RI 168 B 3
Cikalongkulon ○ RI 168 B 3
Cikalongwetan ○ RI 168 B 3
Cikampek ○ RI 168 B 3
Cikobia ∧ FJI 184 III c 1
Čikoj ~ RUS 116-117 N 10
Čikoj ~ RUS 116-117 N 10
Čikokon ~ RUS 118-119 N 8
Čikokonskij hrebet ▲ RUS 118-119 N 8
Cikotok ○ RI 168 B 3
Čikšina ○ RUS 88-89 Y 4
Čikting ~ RUS 114-115 D 2
Cilacap ○ RI 168 B 3
Cilamaya ○ RI 168 B 3
Cilaos, Cirque de ~• F 224 B 7
Çilat ○ IRQ 128-129 M 5
Čil'či ○ RUS 118-119 L 7
Çıldır ○ TR 128-129 K 2
Cileungsi ○ RI 168 B 3
Čili ~ KZ 112-113 P 5
Cilibia ○ RO 102-103 E 5
Čilili ○ HR 100-101 G 3
Cill Airne = Killarney ○• IRL 90-91 B 5
Cill Bheagáin = Kilbeggan ○ IRL 90-91 D 5
Cill Chainnigh = Kilkenny ★• IRL 90-91 D 5
Cill Choaí = Kilkee ○ IRL 90-91 B 5
Cill Dara = Kildare ○ IRL 90-91 D 5
Cill Mhantáin = Wicklow ○ IRL 90-91 D 5
Cill Orglan = Killorglin ○ IRL 90-91 B 5
Cill Rois = Kilrush ○ IRL 90-91 B 5
Cil'ma ~ RUS 88-89 V 4
Čil'mamedkum ⊥ TM 134-135 J 4
Čima ○ RUS 116-117 J 9
Cimanggu ○ RI 168 A 3
Cimanuk, Tanjung ∧ RI 168 C 3
Cimarron ○ USA (CO) 254-255 H 5
Cimarron ○ USA (KS) 262-263 F 7
Cimarron ○ USA (NM) 256-257 C 2
Cimarron National Grassland ⊥ USA (KS) 262-263 E 7
Cimarron River ~ USA 254-255 N 6
Cimarron River ~ USA 256-257 G 2
Cimarron River ~ USA 264-265 G 3
Čimbaj ○ UZ 136-137 G 4
Čimboj ○ UZ 136-137 F 4
Čimčememel' ~ RUS 112-113 O 3
Cimia ○ MD 102-103 F 4
Čimkent ○ UZ 112-113 N 4
Čimljansk ○ RUS 102-103 N 4
Čimljanskoe vodohranilišče ≺ RUS 102-103 N 4
Cimmermanovka ○ RUS 122-123 H 3
Cîmpeni ○ RO 102-103 C 4
Cîmpina ○ RO 102-103 D 5
Cîmpu ○ RI 164-165 G 5
Cîmpulung ○ RO 102-103 D 5
Cîmpulung Moldovenesc ○• RO 102-103 D 4
Čina ~ RUS 116-117 L 3
Čina ~ RUS 118-119 F 8
Cina, Tanjung ∧ RI 162-163 F 7
Çınar ★ TR 128-129 J 4
Cinaruco, Río ~ YV 60-61 F 4
Cincel, Río ~ RA 76-77 D 7
Cincinnati ○ USA (OH) 280-281 B 4
Cinco Balas, Cayos ∧ C 54-55 F 4
Cinco de Maio, Cachoeira ~ BR 70-71 K 3
Çine ★ TR 128-129 C 4
Cinejevem ~ RUS 112-113 Q 3
Cinema ○ CDN (BC) 228-229 M 3
Cingaly ○ RUS 114-115 K 4
Çingandžá, gora ∧ RUS 112-113 H 4
Cingera, mys ∧ RUS 108-109 I f 2
Çingildi ○ UZ 136-137 J 4
Çingirlau ○ KZ 96-97 H 8
Çíngis Chaan Cherem ∴• MAU 148-149 L 3
Cinnabar Mountain ▲ USA (ID) 252-253 B 4
Činoz ○ UZ 136-137 L 4
Činozero, ozero ~ RUS 88-89 M 5
Cinque Island ~ IND 140-141 L 4
Cinta, Serra da ▲ BR 68-69 E 5
Cintalapa de Figueroa ○ MEX 52-53 H 3
Cinto, Monte ▲ F 98-99 M 3
Cintra, Golfo de ≈ 196-197 B 3
Cinuaskos, Los ○ DOM 54-55 K 5
Ciotat, la ○ F 90-91 K 10
Cipa ~ RUS 118-119 K 8
Cipanda ○ RUS 120-121 F 4
Cipatujah ○ RI 168 C 3
Cipikan ○ RUS (BUR) 118-119 F 8
Cipikan ~ RUS 118-119 F 8
Cipo, Rio ~ BR 72-73 J 5
Cipó ○ BR 66-67 E 3
Cipolândia ○ BR 70-71 K 7
Cipolletti ○ RA 78-79 F 5
Cipotuba, Ilha ∧ BR 66-67 F 4
Čir ~ RUS 102-103 N 3
Circa ○ PE 64-65 F 8
Čirčik ○ UZ 136-137 L 4
Čirčik ~ UZ 136-137 L 4
Circle ○ USA (MT) 250-251 O 4
Circleville ○ USA (OH) 280-281 D 4
Circleville ○ USA (UT) 254-255 E 6
Circular Head ∧ AUS 180-181 H 6
Circular Reef ∧ PNG 183 D 2
Cirebon ○ RI 168 C 3
Čirikovo ○ RUS 94-95 P 4
Čirin, vulkan ▲ RUS 122-123 M 6
Čirinda ○ RUS 116-117 K 3
Ciriquiri, Río ~ BR 66-67 F 1
Čirka Kem' ~ RUS 88-89 M 5
Cir Kud ○ SP 212-213 J 2
Čirkuovo ○ RUS 118-119 P 8
Cirò ○ I 100-101 F 5
Čirò ~ UZ 136-137 K 5
Čirpan ○ BG 102-103 D 6
Cirque, Cerro ▲ BOL 70-71 C 5
Ciruelo, El ○ MEX 50-51 D 5
Cisarua ○ RI 168 B 3
Cisco ○ USA (GA) 284-285 F 2
Cisco ○ USA (TX) 264-265 F 6
Cisco ○ USA (UT) 254-255 F 5
Ciskei (former Homeland, now part of East-Cape) ▣ ZA 220-221 H 5
Čiskova ∧ RUS 116-117 G 3
Cišmy ★ RUS 96-97 J 6
Cisne, Islas del = Islas Santanilla ∧ HN 54-55 D 6
Cisne, Laguna del ○ RA 70-77 F 5
Cisnes, Río ~ RCH 80 C 2
Cisnes Medio ○ RCH 80 C 2
Cisolok ○ RI 168 B 3
Cissala ○ RG 202-203 E 4
Cistern ○ USA (TX) 266-267 J 4
Cistern Point ∧ BS 54-55 G 3
Cisterna ○ E 98-99 E 3
Čistoe, ozero ~ RUS 120-121 O 4
Čistopol' ○ RUS 96-97 G 6
Čistopol'e ★ KZ 124-125 E 2
Čitá ~ RUS (CTN) 118-119 F 9
Čita ~ RUS 118-119 F 9
Citadelle, La ∴ • RH 54-55 J 5
Čita Kandaw, Kôtal-e ▲ AFG 138-139 B 3
Citaré, Río ~ BR 62-63 G 5
Citiari, Igarapé ~ BR 66-67 E 6
Citico Beach ○ USA (TN) 282-283 C 5
Citra ○ USA (FL) 284-285 H 5
Citra ○ USA (OK) 264-265 H 4
Citronelle ○ USA (AL) 284-285 B 5
Citrusdal ○ ZA 220-221 D 6
Citrus Heights ○ USA (CA) 246-247 D 5
Città del Vaticano ★ ••• SCV 100-101 D 4
Cittanova ○ I 100-101 F 5
Ciu ○ RI 164-165 G 7
Ciudad ○ MEX 50-51 G 6
Ciudad Acuña ○ MEX 50-51 J 3
Ciudad Altamirano ○ MEX 52-53 D 2
Ciudad Bolívar ★• YV 60-61 H 3
Ciudad Camargo ○ MEX 50-51 G 4
Ciudad Colón ○ CR 52-53 B 7
Ciudad Constitución ○ MEX 50-51 D 5
Ciudad Cuauhtémoc ○ MEX 52-53 J 3
Ciudad Cortes ○ CR 52-53 C 7
Ciudad Darío ○ NIC 52-53 L 5
Ciudad de Guatemala = Guatemala ★ ••• GCA 52-53 J 4
Ciudad del Carmen ○ MEX 52-53 J 2
Ciudad del Este ○ PY 76-77 K 3
Ciudad del Maíz ○ MEX 50-51 K 6

Colorado River ~ USA 254-255 G 4
Colorado River ~ USA 256-257 B 2
Colorado River ~ USA 264-265 D 6
Colorado River ~ USA 266-267 J 2
Colorado River Aqueduct < USA (CA)
248-249 H 2
Colorado River Indian Reservation ⅄ USA
(AZ) 256-257 A 5
Colorados, Archipiélago de los ∩ C
54-55 C 3
Colorados, Cerros ▲ RA 78-79 E 6
Colorado Springs ○ • USA (CO)
254-255 L 2
Colotlán ○ MEX 50-51 H 6
Colotlipa ○ MEX 52-53 E 3
Colpitts Creek ∩ CDN 236-237 B 2
Colpon-Ata ○ KS 146-147 C 4
Colquechaca ○ BOL 70-71 D 6
Colquen, Cerro ▲ RCH 78-79 C 4
Colquiri ○ BOL 70-71 D 5
Colquitt ○ USA (GA) 284-285 E 3
Colrain ○ USA (MA) 278-279 J 6
Colson Track II USA 178-179 D 3
Colstrip ○ USA (MT) 250-251 N 6
Colter Pass ○ USA (MT) 250-251 K 6
Colton ○ USA (SD) 260-261 K 3
Colton ○ USA (UT) 254-255 E 4
Colton ○ USA (WA) 244-245 H 4
Coltons Point ○ USA (MD) 280-281 K 5
Coltwater ○ USA (AR) 276-277 E 5
Columbia ○ USA (AL) 284-285 E 5
Columbia ○ USA (KY) 276-277 E 5
Columbia ○ USA (LA) 268-269 H 4
Columbia ○ USA (MD) 280-281 K 4
Columbia ○ USA (MO) 274-275 F 6
Columbia ○ USA (MS) 268-269 G 5
Columbia ○ USA (NC) 282-283 L 5
Columbia ○ USA (PA) 280-281 K 3
Columbia ○ USA (SD) 260-261 H 1
Columbia ○ USA (TN) 276-277 H 5
Columbia ☆ USA (SC) 284-285 J 3
Columbia, Mount ▲ CDN (BC)
228-229 R 4
Columbia Beach ○ USA (WA)
244-245 G 3
Columbia Center ○ USA (WA)
244-245 H 4
Columbia City ○ USA (FL) 286-287 G 1
Columbia City ○ USA (IN) 274-275 N 3
Columbia Falls ○ USA (ME)
278 279 O 4
Columbia Falls ○ USA (MT)
250-251 E 3
Columbia Glacier ⊂ USA 20-21 R 6
Columbia Icefield ⊂ CDN (ALB)
228-229 R 4
Columbia Mountains ▲ CDN
228-229 M 3
Columbiana ○ USA (AL) 284-285 D 3
Columbia National Wildlife Refuge ⊥
USA (WA) 244-245 F 4
Columbia Reach ○ CDN 230-231 M 2
Columbia River ~ CDN 230-231 L 2
Columbia River ~ USA 244-245 D 2
Columbine ○ USA (CO) 254-255 J 3
Columbus ○ USA (GA) 284-285 E 4
Columbus ○ USA (IN) 274-275 N 5
Columbus ○ USA (KS) 262-263 M 7
Columbus ○ USA (KY) 276-277 F 4
Columbus ○ USA (MS) 268-269 G 4
Columbus ○ USA (MT) 250-251 K 6
Columbus ○ USA (NC) 282-283 E 3
Columbus ○ USA (NE) 262-263 H 3
Columbus ○ USA (NM) 256-257 H 7
Columbus ○ USA (TX) 266-267 L 4
Columbus ○ USA (WI) 274-275 J 1
Columbus ☆ USA (OH) 280-281 D 2
Columbus Cay ∩ BH 52-53 L 3
Columbus City ○ USA (AL)
284-285 D 2
Columbus Grove ○ USA (OH)
280-281 B 2
Columbus Junction ○ USA (IA)
274-275 G 3
Columbus Lake < USA (MS)
268-269 H 4
Columbus Landing 5/ 4th/ 1494 • JA
54-55 G 5
Columbus Monument • BS 54-55 H 2
Columna, Pico ▲ PA 52-53 E 7
Coluna ○ BR 72-73 J 5
Colup, Cerro ▲ RCH 76-77 C 2
Colusa ○ USA (CA) 246-247 C 4
Colville ○ USA (WA) 244-245 H 2
Colville Channel ≈ 182 E 2
Colville Indian Reservation ⅄ USA (WA)
244-245 F 2
Colville Lake ○ CDN (NWT) 30-31 F 2
Colville Lake < CDN (NWT) 30-31 G 2
Colville River ~ USA 20-21 N 4
Coma, La ○ MEX 50-51 F 5
Comácchio ○ I 100-101 D 2
Comácha ○ MOC 218-219 G 3
Comalcalco ○ MEX 52-53 H 2
Comallo ○ RA 78-79 D 6
Comallo, Arroyo ~ RA 78-79 D 6
Comanche ○ USA (OK) 264-265 G 4
Comanche ○ USA (TX) 266-267 J 3
Comandante Fontana ○ RA 76-77 H 3
Comandante Girbone ○ RA 78-79 L 3
Comandante Luis Piedra Buena ○ RA
80 F 4
Comănești ○ RO 102-103 E 4
Comarapa ○ BOL 70-71 E 5
Comas ○ PE 64-65 C 7
Comau, Fiordo ≈ 78-79 C 7
Comayagua ☆ • HN 52-53 L 4
Comayagua, Montañas de ▲ HN
52-53 L 4
Comayagüela ○ HN 52-53 L 4
Combapata ○ PE 70-71 B 4
Combarbalá ○ RCH 78-79 B 6
Combermere ○ CDN (ONT)
238-239 H 3
Combermere, Cape ▲ CDN 24-25 a 2
Combermere Bay ≈ 142-143 H 6

Combo, Selat ≈ 162-163 F 4
Combol, Pulau ∩ RI 162-163 E 4
Combs ○ USA (AR) 276-277 B 5
Comè ○ DY 202-203 L 6
Comeby Chance ○ AUS 178-179 K 6
Comechingón, Sierra de ▲ RA
78-79 G 2
Comedero ○ MEX 50-51 F 5
Comemoração, Rio ~ BR 70-71 G 2
Comer ○ USA (GA) 284-285 G 2
Comerío ○ USA (PR) 286-287 P 2
Comer Strait ≈ 36-37 G 2
Comerzinho ○ BR 72-73 K 4
Comet Downs ○ AUS 178-179 K 2
Comet Outstation ○ AUS 178-179 C 5
Comet River ~ AUS 178-179 K 3
Comfort ○ USA (TX) 266-267 J 4
Comfort, Cape ▲ CDN 36-37 K 2
Comfort, Point < USA (TX) 266-267 L 5
Comfort Bight ○ CDN 38-39 R 2
Comicó, Arroyo ~ RA 78-79 F 6
Comilla ○ BD 142-143 G 4
Comino, Capo ▲ I 100-101 B 4
Comitán de Domínguez ○ MEX
52-53 H 3
Comite River ~ USA 268-269 J 6
Commander Islands = Komandorskie
ostrova ∩ RUS 120-121 I W 6
Commee ○ CDN (ONT) 234-235 O 6
Commerce ○ USA (GA) 284-285 G 2
Commerce ○ USA (MS) 268-269 K 2
Commerce ○ USA (TX) 264-265 J 5
Commissioner Island ∩ CDN (MAN)
234-235 F 2
Committee Bay ≈ 24-25 c 6
Commodore Reef ∩ 160-161 A 8
Commonwealth Meteorological Station •
AUS 178-179 H 6
Commonwealth Range ▲ ARK 16 E 0
Commoron Creek ~ AUS 178-179 L 5
Como ~ RCB 210-211 E 3
Como ∩ USA (MS) 268-269 L 2
Como ○ USA (TX) 264-265 J 5
Como, Lago di ○ I 100-101 B 2
Comoapa ○ NIC 52-53 B 5
Como Bluff Fossil Beds ∴ USA (WY)
252-253 K 6
Comodoro ○ ETH 208-209 E 6
Comodoro ○ RO 70-71 H 3
Comodoro Rivadavia ○ RA 80 G 2
Comoé, Parc National de la ⊥ •••• CI
202-203 J 6
Comonfort ○ MEX 52-53 D 1
Comorin, Cape ▲ IND 140-141 G 6
Comoros = Comores • COM
222-223 G 3
Comoros = Comores, Archipel des ∩
COM 222-223 G 3
Comox ○ CDN (BC) 230-231 L 2
Compass Lake ○ USA (FL)
286-287 D 1
Compeer ○ CDN (ALB) 232-233 H 4
Compiègne ○ F 90-91 J 7
Complejo Ferroviair Zárate-Brazo Largo ~
RA 78-79 K 2
Cómpris ∩ RUS 118-119 L 6
Compostela ○ MEX 50-51 G 7
Compostela ○ RP 160-161 G 9
Comprida, Ilha ∩ BR 74-75 G 6
Compton ○ USA (CA) 248-249 F 6
Compton North ○ USA (CA) 248-249 F 6
Comrat ○ MD 102-103 F 4
Comstock ○ USA (MI) 272-273 D 5
Comstock ○ USA (TX) 266-267 K 3
Comunidad ○ CR 52-53 B 6
Comunidad ○ YV (AMA) 60-61 H 6
Comunidad ○ YV (BOL) 60-61 K 4
Comunidad de Madrid □ E 98-99 F 4
Côria ~ RUS 118-119 D 4
Cona ○ VRC 144-145 H 7
Conakry ☆ RG 202-203 D 5
Conambo, Río ~ EC 64-65 C 5
Conasauga River ~ USA 284-285 F 2
Conay, Río ~ RCH 76-77 B 5
Concan ○ USA (TX) 266-267 H 4
Concarán ○ RA 78-79 F 3
Concarneau ○ F 90-91 F 8
Conceição ○ BR (AMA) 66-67 G 4
Conceição ○ BR (PA) 68-69 J 5
Conceição, Riachão ~ BR 68-69 H 5
Conceição da Barra ○ BR 72-73 M 4
Conceição das Alagoas ○ BR 72-73 F 5
Conceição de Macabu ○ BR 72-73 K 7
Conceição do Araguaia ○ BR 68-69 H 6
Conceição do Canindé ○ BR 68-69 J 5
Conceição do Coité ○ BR 68-69 J 5
Conceição do Mato Dentro ○ BR
72-73 J 5
Conceição do Mau ○ BR 62-63 E 4
Conceição do Norte ○ BR 72-73 G 2
Concepción ○ BOL 70-71 F 5
Concepción ○ CO 64-65 E 7
Concepción ○ PE 64-65 E 7
Concepción ☆ PY 76-77 J 2
Concepción ○ RA 76-77 E 4
Concepción, Cape ▲ USA 178-179 H 6
Concepción, La ○ EC 64-65 C 1
Concepción, La ○ PA 52-53 C 7
Concepción, Punta ▲ MEX 50-51 D 4
Concepción, Volcán ▲ NIC 52-53 B 5
Concepción de Buenos Aires ○ MEX
52-53 C 2
Concepción del Oro ○ MEX 50-51 J 5
Concepción del Uruguay ○ RA
78-79 K 2
Conception Island ∩ BS 54-55 H 3
Conception, Canal ≈ 80 C 3
Conception, Lago ○ BOL 70-71 F 5
Conception, Point ▲ USA (CA)
248-249 D 5
Conception Bay ≈ 242-243 P 5

Conch ○ IND 138-139 G 7
Conchal ○ BR 72-73 G 7
Conchal, Bahía ≈ 76-77 B 6
Conchas ○ USA (NM) 256-257 L 3
Conchas, La ○ BOL 70-71 H 5
Conchas Lake < USA (NM)
256-257 L 3
Conchas River ~ USA 256-257 L 3
Conch Bar ○ CDN (NFL) 242-243 N 2
Conche ○ CDN (NFL) 242-243 N 2
Conchi ○ RCH 76-77 C 2
Concho ○ USA (AZ) 256-257 F 4
Concho River, Middle ~ USA
266-267 F 3
Concho River, North ~ USA
266-267 G 2
Conchos, Río ~ MEX 50-51 K 5
Conchos, Río ~ MEX 50-51 F 4
Concón ○ RCH 78-79 B 6
Concón, Punta de ▲ RCH 78-79 D 2
Conconully ○ USA (WA) 244-245 F 2
Concord ○ USA (CA) 248-249 C 2
Concord ○ USA (MI) 272-273 M 2
Concord ○ USA (NC) 282-283 F 5
Concord ☆ USA (NH) 278-279 K 5
Concórdia ○ BR 74-75 D 6
Concordia ○ MEX 50-51 F 6
Concordia ○ PE 64-65 E 4
Concordia ○ RA 76-77 H 8
Concordia ○ USA (KS) 262-263 J 5
Concordia ○ USA (MO) 274-275 E 5
Concordia, La ○ MEX 52-53 H 3
Concórdia do Pará ○ BR 68-69 G 2
Concord Point < USA 280-281 K 4
Conda ○ ANG 216-217 C 5
Conda ○ USA (ID) 252-253 G 4
Condamine ○ AUS 178-179 L 4
Condamine River ~ AUS 178-179 L 4
Côn Đao ∩ VN 158-159 J 6
Condé ○ AUS 216-217 C 5
Conde ○ BR 68-69 K 7
Conde ○ USA (SD) 260-261 H 1
Condédezi, Rio ~ MOC 218-219 G 2
Condega ○ NIC 52-53 L 5
Condeixas ○ BR 62-63 K 6
Conde Loca ○ ANG 216-217 B 4
Conde Matarazzo ○ BR 74-75 D 9
Condeúba ○ BR 72-73 K 3
Condoblin ○ AUS 180-181 J 2
Condom ○ F 90-91 H 10
Condon ○ RUS 110-111 W 4
Condon ○ USA (OR) 244-245 E 5
Condor ○ USA (SAS) 232-233 D 3
Cóndor, Cerro El ▲ RA 76-77 C 3
Cóndor, Cordillera del ▲ PE 64-65 C 4
Côn Đảo = Poulo Condor ∩ VN
158-159 J 6
Côn Đảo ∩ VN (Con) 158-159 J 6
Cone ○ USA (TX) 264-265 C 5
Conecuh River ~ USA 284-285 C 5
Conecuh River ~ USA 284-285 C 5
Conejo, El ○ MEX 50-51 D 5
Conejos ○ USA (CO) 254-255 J 6
Cone Peak ▲ USA 174-175 G 3
Conesa ○ RA 78-79 J 2
Conestoga River ~ CDN 238-239 E 5
Conflict Group ∩ PNG 183 F 6
Confluencia ○ RA 78-79 D 6
Confolens ○ F 90-91 H 8
Confusion Bay ≈ 242-243 N 2
Confuso, Río ~ PY 76-77 H 3
Congaree River ~ USA 284-285 K 3
Congaree Swamp National Monument ⊥
USA (SC) 284-285 K 3
Congaz ○ MD 102-103 F 4
Congenerge ○ MOC 218-219 H 2
Conger Range ▲ USA 26-27 J 5
Conghua ○ VRC 156-157 H 5
Congjiang ○ VRC 156-157 F 4
Congnaraya, Pointe ▲ CDN 36-37 Q 5
Congo ○ BR 68-69 K 5
Congo ○ RCB 210-211 D 5
Congo ○ RCB 210-211 D 5
Congo Basin = Grande Dépression
Centrale ⊇ ZRE 9 E 5
Congo Fan ≃ 6-7 K 9
Congonhas ○ BR 72-73 H 6
Congonhas do Norte ○ BR 72-73 J 5
Congo Town ○ BS 54-55 G 4
Congress ○ CDN (SAS) 232-233 N 6
Conguillo los Paraguas, Parque Nacional
⊥ RCH 78-79 D 5
Conhelo ○ RA 78-79 G 4
Conifer ○ USA (CO) 254-255 L 4
Coniston ○ AUS 172-173 L 7
Coniston ○ CDN (ONT) 238-239 F 4
Conjtaca ○ MEX 50-51 F 5
Conjo ○ ANG 216-217 D 5
Conjuboy ○ AUS 174-175 H 4
Conjuror Bay ○ CDN 30-31 K 3
Conkal ○ MEX 52-53 K 1
Conlara, Río ~ RA 78-79 G 2
Conmee ○ CDN (ONT) 234-235 O 6
Conn ○ USA (MI) 268-269 K 5
Connaughton, Mount ▲ AUS
172-173 F 7
Conneaut ○ USA (OH) 280-281 F 2
Conneaut Lake ○ USA (PA)
280-281 F 2
Conneautville ○ USA (PA) 280-281 F 2
Connecticut □ USA 280-281 N 2
Connecticut River ~ USA 278-279 J 6
Connecticut River ~ USA 280-281 O 2
Connell ○ USA (WA) 244-245 G 4
Connellsville ○ USA (PA) 280-281 G 3
Connelly, Mount ▲ USA 20-21 U 5
Connels Lagoon Conservation Reserve ⊥
AUS 174-175 D 6
Conner ○ RP 160-161 D 2
Conner, Mount ▲ AUS 176-177 L 2
Conne River ○ CDN (NFL) 242-243 N 5
Connemara ⊇ IRL 90-91 B 5

Conn Lake < CDN 26-27 O 8
Connor, Mount ▲ AUS 172-173 H 3
Connors ○ CDN (NB) 240-241 G 3
Connors Range ▲ AUS (NV) 246-247 L 4
Connors Range ▲ AUS 178-179 K 1
Connors River ~ AUS 178-179 K 2
Conoble Lake ○ AUS 180-181 H 2
Conodoguinet Creek ~ USA
280-281 J 3
Conogol ○ MAU 148-149 M 5
Cononaco ○ EC 64-65 E 2
Conover ○ USA (MI) 270-271 J 4
Conquest ○ CDN (SAS) 232-233 L 4
Conquet ○ F 90-91 E 7
Conquista ○ BOL 70-71 D 4
Conrad ○ USA (MT) 250-251 H 3
Conran, Cape ▲ AUS 180 101 K 4
Conrich ○ USA (ALB) 232-233 G 4
Conroe ○ USA (TX) 268-269 E 6
Conroe, Lake < USA (TX) 268-269 E 6
Consata, Río ~ BOL 70-71 D 4
Conselheiro Lafaiete ○ BR 72-73 J 6
Conselho, Ponta de ▲ BR 72-73 L 2
Consett ○ GB 90-91 F 4
Consolación del Sur ○ C 54-55 D 3
Consol Lake ○ USA 30-31 M 5
Consort ○ CDN (ALB) 232-233 H 4
Constance, Lac de = Bodensee ○ CH
92-93 K 5
Constance Bay ≈ 140-141 L 4
Constance Headland ▲ AUS
176-177 G 2
Constance Lake ○ CDN (ONT)
236-237 D 3
Constancia, Cerro ▲ RCH 70-71 C 4
Constanța ☆ • RO 102-103 F 5
Constantina ○ BR 74-75 D 6
Constantina ○ E 98-99 E 6
Constantine ☆ • DZ 190-191 F 2
Constantine, Cape ▲ USA 22-23 R 3
Constantine, Mount ▲ CDN 20-21 U 6
Constanza ○ DOM 54-55 K 5
Constitución ○ RCH 78-79 C 4
Constitución de 1857, Parque Nacional
⊥ MEX 50-51 B 1
Consuelo Peak ▲ AUS 178-179 K 3
Consul ○ CDN (SAS) 232-233 J 6
Consul ○ PE 64-65 E 4
Consul River ~ CDN 30-31 T 3
Contact ○ USA (NV) 246-247 L 2
Contagem ○ BR 72-73 H 5
Contamana ○ PE 64-65 E 6
Contamana, Sierra ▲ PE 64-65 F 6
Contão ○ BR 62-63 D 4
Contas, Rio de ~ BR 72-73 L 3
Contendas do Sincorá ○ BR 72-73 K 2
Continental ○ USA (AZ) 256-257 E 7
Continental ○ USA (OH) 280-281 B 2
Contoy, Isla ∩ MEX 52-53 L 1
Contramaestre ○ C 54-55 G 4
Contrato, Rio ~ BR 68-69 H 5
Con Trau, Hòn ∩ VN 158-159 K 4
Contreras, Isla ∩ RCH 80 C 6
Contuboel ○ GNB 202-203 C 3
Conturmaza ○ PE 64-65 C 5
Convención ○ CO 60-61 E 3
Convento, Cerro ▲ RA 80 F 5
Convento, Montañas de ▲ EC
64-65 C 2
Converse ○ USA (IN) 274-275 N 4
Converse ○ USA (LA) 268-269 G 5
Conway ○ USA (AR) 276-277 C 5
Conway ○ USA (NH) 278-279 K 5
Conway ○ USA (SC) 284-285 L 3
Conway ○ USA (TX) 264-265 C 3
Conway, Lake < USA (AR) 276-277 C 5
Conway National Park ⊥ AUS
174-175 K 7
Coober Pedy ○ AUS 178-179 C 5
Coocoran Lake ○ AUS 178-179 J 5
Cooinda Motel ○ AUS 172-173 L 2
Cook ○ AUS 176-177 L 5
Cook ○ USA (MN) 270-271 F 3
Cook, Cape ▲ CDN (BC) 230-231 A 3
Cook, Mount ▲ NZ 182 C 5
Cook, Mount ▲ USA 20-21 U 6
Cook Bay ≈ 16 G 16
Cook Bay ≈ 184 II b 4
Cooke, Mount ▲ AUS (WA)
172-173 E 7
Cooke, Mount ▲ AUS (WA)
176-177 D 6
Cooke City ○ USA (MT) 250-251 K 6
Cookeville ○ USA (TN) 276-277 K 4
Cook Forest State Park ⊥ USA (PA)
280-281 G 2
Cookhouse ○ ZA 220-221 G 6
Cooking Lake ○ CDN (ALB)
232-233 G 3
Cook Inlet ≈ 22-23 U 3
Cook Islands □ NZ 13 L 4
Cook Lake ○ CDN 30-31 P 4
Cook Peninsula ∪ CDN 30-31 M 2
Cooks ○ USA (MI) 270-271 M 5
Cooksburg ○ USA (PA) 278-279 G 6
Cooks Harbour ○ CDN (NFL)
242-243 N 1
Cookshire ○ CDN (QUE) 238-239 O 4
Cookstown ○ CDN (ONT) 238-239 F 4
Cookstown ○ GB 90-91 D 4
Cooktown ○ AUS 174-175 H 4
Cool ○ RO 102-103 D 6
Cool, Tanjung ▲ RI 166-167 K 6
Coolabah ○ AUS 178-179 H 6
Cooladdi ○ AUS 178-179 H 4
Coolah ○ AUS 180-181 K 3
Coolamon ○ AUS 180-181 J 3
Coolangatta ○ AUS 178-179 M b
Coolgardie ○ AUS 176-177 F 5
Coolibah ○ AUS 172-173 L 4
Coolidge ○ USA (AZ) 256-257 D 6
Coolidge ○ USA (TX) 266-267 L 2
Coolin ○ USA (ID) 250-251 C 3

Coolmunda Reservoir < AUS
178-179 L 5
Cooloola National Park ⊥ AUS
178-179 M 4
Coolville ○ USA (OH) 280-281 E 4
Cooma ○ AUS 180-181 K 4
Coombes Cove ○ CDN (NFL)
242-243 N 5
Coomera ○ AUS 178-179 M 4
Coonabarabran ○ AUS 180-181 K 3
Coonalpyn ○ AUS 180-181 E 3
Coonamble ○ AUS 178-179 K 6
Coonawarra ○ AUS 180-181 E 4
Coondapoor ○ IND 140-141 F 4
Coongan River ~ AUS 172-173 D 6
Coongoola ○ AUS 178-179 H 4
Coon Rapids ○ USA (IA) 274-275 D 3
Coon Rapids ○ USA (MN) 270-271 E 6
Cooper ○ USA (TX) 264-265 J 5
Cooper ○ USA (NM) 256-257 M 4
Cooper ○ USA (TX) 264-265 J 5
Cooper Creek ~ AUS 178-179 F 4
Cooper Creek ~ AUS 178-179 E 4
Cooperfield ○ USA (OR) 244-245 J 5
Cooper River ~ USA 284-285 L 3
Coopers Island ○ CDN 36-37 T 6
Coopers Mills ○ USA (ME)
278-279 M 4
Cooper's Town ○ BS 54-55 G 1
Cooperstown ○ USA (ND) 258-259 J 4
Cooperstown ○ USA (NY) 278-279 G 6
Coop Lake ○ USA 30-31 M 5
Coorabie ○ AUS 176-177 M 5
Coorabulka ○ AUS 178-179 K 2
Coorada ○ AUS 178-179 K 3
Coordewandy ▲ AUS 176-177 D 4
Coorong National Park ⊥ AUS
180-181 E 3
Coorow ○ AUS 176-177 D 4
Cooroy ○ AUS 178-179 M 4
Coosa ○ USA (GA) 284-285 E 2
Coosa River ~ USA 284-285 D 3
Coosawattee River ~ USA 284-285 F 2
Coosawhatchie River ~ USA
284-285 J 4
Coos Bay ≈ 244-245 A 7
Coos Bay ○ USA (OR) 244-245 A 7
Cootamundra ○ AUS 180-181 K 3
Coover Creek ~ USA 280-281 D 7
Copa, Cerro ▲ BOL 70-71 C 7
Copacabana ○ BOL (PAZ) 70-71 C 5
Copacabana ○ CO 60-61 D 4
Copacabana, Península de ∪ BOL
70-71 C 5
Copahue ○ RA 78-79 D 4
Copahue, Volcán ▲ RCH 78-79 D 4
Copal Urco ○ PE 64-65 D 4
Copán ∴ ••• HN 52-53 K 4
Copan ○ USA (OK) 264-265 J 2
Copan Lake < USA (OK) 264-265 J 2
Copano Bay ≈ 266-267 K 5
Copán Ruinas ○ HN 52-53 K 4
Copas ○ USA (MN) 270-271 F 5
Cope ○ USA (CO) 254-255 N 3
Cope, El ○ PA 52-53 D 7
Copeland ○ USA (ID) 250-251 C 3
Copeland ○ USA (KS) 262-263 F 7
Copeland Islands ∩ USA 286-287 H 5
Copemish ○ USA (MI) 272-273 D 3
Copenhagen = København ☆ • DK
86-87 Q 9
Copere ○ BOL 70-71 F 6
Copeton Reservoir < AUS 178-179 L 5
Copetón ○ YV 60-61 J 4
Copiapó ☆ RCH 76-77 B 4
Copiapó, Río ~ RCH 76-77 B 4
Copko ○ RUS 108-109 Z 6
Copko ○ RUS 108-109 I 7
Coporito ○ YV 60-61 L 3
Coporolo ○ ANG 216-217 B 6
Coposa, Cerro ▲ RCH 70-71 C 7
Coppabella ○ AUS 178-179 K 1
Coppename Monding, National Reservaat
⊥ SME 62-63 G 2
Coppenamerivier ~ SME 62-63 F 3
Copper ○ USA (OR) 244-245 B 8
Copperas Cove ○ USA (TX)
266-267 K 2
Copperbelt □ Z 218-219 D 7
Copper Breaks State Park ⊥ USA (TX)
264-265 E 4
Copper Creek ○ CDN (BC) 230-231 J 3
Copper Harbor ○ USA (WI)
270-271 K 4
Coppermine ○ CDN 30-31 M 2
Coppermine Point ○ CDN (ONT)
236-237 D 5
Coppermine River ~ CDN 30-31 M 2
Copper Mines ○ AUS 180-181 H 7
Copperneedle River ~ CDN 30-31 W 4
Copper River ~ USA 20-21 S 5
Copperstown ○ USA (PA) 280-281 G 3
Coppersville ○ USA (MI) 272-273 D 4
Copperton ○ ZA 220-221 F 4
Copton Creek ~ USA 228-229 P 2
Coqên ○ VRC 144-145 G 5
Coqueiro, Ribeiro ~ BR 70-71 J 5
Coqueiros, Ponta dos ▲ BR 68-69 L 5
Coqui ○ USA (WI) 270-271 G 5
Coquí ○ RH 54-55 F 3
Coquí ○ USA (PR) 286-287 P 2
Coquilhatville = Mbandaka ☆ ZRE
210-211 D 3
Coquille ○ USA (OR) 244-245 A 7
Coquille River ~ USA 236-237 J 2
Coquimatlán ○ MEX 52-53 C 2
Coquimbo ☆ RCH 76-77 B 6
Coquimbo, Bahía ≈ 76-77 B 5
Corabia ○ RO 102-103 D 6
Coração de Jesus ○ BR 72-73 H 4
Coraci-Paraná, Rio ~ BR 66-67 G 3
Coracora ○ PE 64-65 D 8
Corail ○ RH 54-55 H 5
Corais, Ilha dos ∩ BR 74-75 F 5
Coral ○ USA (MI) 272-273 D 4
Coralaique, Río ~ RCH 78-79 B 5
Coral Basin ≃ 13 F 4
Coral Bay ≈ 160-161 B 8
Coral Bay ○ AUS 172-173 A 7

Coral Gables ○ USA (FL) 286-287 J 6
Coral Harbour ○ CDN 36-37 H 2
Coral Heights ○ BS 54-55 G 1
Coral Sea ≈ 13 G 4
Coral Sea Islands Territory □ AUS
174-175 K 4
Coral Springs ○ USA (FL) 286-287 J 5
Corangamite, Lake ○ AUS 180-181 G 5
Coranzuli ○ RA 76-77 D 2
Coro, Golfete de ≈ 60-61 F 2
Coro, Ilha do ∩ BR 66-67 F 4
Coro Trepadeira ○ BR 70-71 K 3
Corazón, El ○ EC 64-65 C 2
Corberríe ○ CDN (NS) 240-241 K 6
Corbett Inlet ≈ 30-31 X 4
Corbett National Park ⊥ • IND
138-139 G 2
Corbin ○ USA (KY) 276-277 L 4
Corby ○ GB 90-91 G 5
Corcaigh = Cork ☆ IRL 00 01 C 6
Corcoran ○ USA (CA) 248-249 E 3
Corcovada, Park National ⊥ CR
52-53 C 7
Corcovado ○ RA 78-79 D 7
Corcovado, Golfo ≈ 78-79 C 7
Corcovado, Volcán ▲ RCH 78-79 C 7
Corcubión ○ E 98-99 C 3
Corda, Ribeiro ~ BR 68-69 D 5
Corda, Rio ~ BR 68-69 F 5
Cordeiro ○ BR 72-73 J 7
Cordeiro, Rio ~ BR 68-69 K 6
Cordele ○ USA (GA) 284-285 F 4
Cordell ○ USA (OK) 264-265 F 3
Cordilheira ○ BR (ALB) 232-233 G 3
Cordilheiras, Serra das ▲ BR 68-69 D 5
Cordillera Cantábrica ▲ E 98-99 D 3
Cordillera Central ▲ PE 64-65 C 4
Cordillera Central ▲ PE 64-65 C 4
Cordillera Central ▲ RP 160-161 D 2
Cordillera de los Picachos, Parque
Nacional ⊥ CO 60-61 D 5
Cordillera Occidental ▲ PE 64-65 C 4
Cordillera Oriental ▲ PE 64-65 D 4
Cordilleras Range ▲ RP 160-161 F 7
Cordisburgo ○ BR 72-73 H 5
Córdoba ○ MEX 52-53 F 2
Córdoba ☆ RA 78-79 G 2
Córdoba ☆ • RA (COD) 76-77 E 6
Córdoba, Sierra de ▲ RA 78-79 G 2
Córdoba ☆ • E 98-99 E 6
Cordobés, Cerro ▲ RA 76-77 C 5
Cordón Alto ▲ RA 80 F 4
Cordón de las Llarretas ▲ RA
78-79 E 3
Cordón Seler ▲ RCH 80 E 4
Cordova ○ USA 20-21 S 6
Cordova ○ USA (AL) 284-285 C 3
Cordova ○ USA (IA) 274-275 H 3
Cordova Bay ≈ 32-33 D 4
Cordova Peak ▲ USA 20-21 S 6
Coreaú, Rio ~ BR 68-69 H 4
Coremas ○ BR 68-69 K 5
Corfield ○ AUS 178-179 G 1
Corfu = Kérkira ∩ GR 100-101 G 5
Corguinho ○ BR 70-71 K 6
Coria ~ E 98-99 D 5
Coria del Río ○ E 98-99 D 6
Corigue ☆ GUY 62-63 E 2
Coribe ○ BR 72-73 J 2
Coricudgy, Mount ▲ AUS 180-181 L 2
Corinna ○ AUS 180-181 H 6
Corinne ○ USA (MI) 278-279 M 4
Corinne ○ CDN (SAS) 232-233 O 5
Corinne ○ USA (MI) 270-271 N 4
Corinne ○ USA (UT) 254-255 C 2
Corinth ○ USA (KY) 276-277 L 2
Corinth ○ USA (ME) 278-279 N 3
Corinth ○ USA (MS) 268-269 M 2
Corinto ○ BR 72-73 H 5
Corinto ○ CO 60-61 C 6
Corinto ○ HN 52-53 K 4
Corinto ○ NIC 52-53 L 5
Corio Bay ≈ 178-179 L 2
Corixa Grande ~ BR 70-71 J 5
Corixão, Rio ~ BR 70-71 J 6
Cork ○ AUS 178-179 G 2
Cork ☆ IRL 90-91 C 6
Corleone ○ I 100-101 D 6
Cornae, vozero ○ BY 94-95 J 5
Corn Creek ~ USA 256-257 E 3
Cornelia ○ USA (GA) 284-285 G 2
Cornélio Procópio ○ BR 72-73 E 7
Cornelius ○ USA (NC) 282-283 G 5
Cornelius Grinnell Bay ≈ 36-37 R 3
Cornell ○ USA (WI) 270-271 G 5
Corner Brook ○ CDN (NFL)
242-243 N 4
Corner Inlet ≈ 180-181 K 5
Corner Point ○ USA 236-237 J 2
Corney Bayou ~ USA 268-269 H 4
Corning ○ USA (AR) 276-277 E 4
Corning ○ USA (CA) 246-247 C 4
Corning ○ USA (IA) 274-275 D 4
Corning ○ USA (KS) 262-263 K 5
Corning ○ USA (NY) 278-279 E 6
Cornish, Mount ▲ AUS 172-173 H 4
Corn Islands = Islas del Maíz ∩ NIC
52-53 C 5
Cornobyľ ○ UA 102-103 G 2
Cornomors'ke ○ UA 102-103 H 5
Cornouaille ⊥ F 90-91 E 7
Cornudas ○ USA (TX) 266-267 B 2

Cornwall ○ BS 54-55 G 2
Cornwall ○ CDN (ONT) 238-239 L 3
Cornwall ⊥ GB 90-91 E 6
Cornwall Coast ≈ AUS 90-91 E 6
Cornwall Island ∩ CDN 24-25 Y 3
Cornwallis Island ∩ CDN 24-25 Y 3
Çornyj Čeremoš ~ UA 102-103 D 3
Coro ☆ ••• YV 60-61 G 2
Coro, Golfete de ≈ 60-61 F 2
Coro, Ilha do ∩ BR 66-67 F 4
Coro, Raudal ~ CO 66-67 B 3
Coroa, Cachoeira da ~ BR 68-69 E 5
Coroatá ○ BR 68-69 F 4
Corocoro ○ BOL 70-71 C 5
Coroico ○ BOL 70-71 D 4
Coroico, Río ~ BOL 70-71 D 4
Corojal, El ○ YV 60-61 H 3
Corolla ○ USA (NC) 282-283 M 4
Coromandel ○ BR 72-73 G 5
Coromandel ○ NZ 182 E 2
Coromandel Coast ≈ IND 140-141 J 6
Coromandel Peninsula ∪ ••• NZ 182 E 2
Corona ○ RP 160-161 D 2
Corona ○ USA (CA) 248-249 G 6
Corona ○ USA (NM) 256-257 K 4
Corona, Hv. ~ MEX 50-51 F 5
Coronach ○ CDN (SAS) 232-233 N 6
Coronado, Bahía de ≈ 52-53 C 7
Coronado National Monument • USA
(AZ) 256-257 E 7
Coronation ○ CDN (ALB) 232-233 G 3
Coronation Island ∩ ARK 16 G 32
Coronation Island ∩ USA 172-173 G 3
Coronation Island Wilderness ⊥ USA
32-33 C 4
Coron Bay ≈ 160-161 D 7
Coronda ○ RA 76-77 G 6
Coronel ○ RCH 78-79 C 4
Coronel Bogado ○ PY 76-77 J 4
Coronel Dorrego ○ RA 78-79 J 5
Coronel Martínez ○ PY 76-77 J 3
Coronel Moldes ○ RA 78-79 G 6
Coronel Oviedo ☆ PY 76-77 J 3
Coronel Pringles ○ RA 78-79 J 4
Coronel Rodolfo Bunge ○ RA 78-79 J 4
Coronel Sapucaia ○ BR 76-77 K 2
Coronel Suárez ○ RA 78-79 J 4
Coronel Vidal ○ RA 78-79 J 4
Coronel Vivida ○ BR 74-75 D 5
Coroni Bird Sanctuary ⊥ TT 60-61 L 2
Coron Island ∩ RP 160-161 D 7
Coropuna, Nevado ▲ PE 64-65 F 9
Corowa-Wahgunyah ○ AUS
180-181 J 4
Corozal ○ BH 52-53 K 2
Corozal ○ YV 60-61 K 4
Corpus Christi ○ USA (TX) 266-267 K 6
Corpus Christi, Lake < USA (TX)
266-267 K 6
Corpus Christi Bay ≈ 266-267 K 6
Corque ○ BOL 70-71 D 6
Corral ○ RCH 78-79 C 4
Corral de Bustos ○ RA 78-79 H 2
Corralejo ○ E 188-189 C 8
Corrales ○ CO 60-61 E 5
Corrales, Los (Los Corrales de Buelna) ○
E 98-99 E 3
Corrella ○ 054-55 C 0
Correne ○ MOC 218-219 K 2
Correctionville ○ USA (IA) 274-275 C 2
Corregidor Island ∩ RP 160-161 D 5
Córrego do Ouro ○ BR 72-73 E 4
Córrego Niutaca ~ BR 70-71 J 7
Córrego Novo ○ BR 68-69 F 4
Correia Pinto ○ BR 74-75 E 6
Corrente ○ BR 68-69 F 7
Corrente, Rio ~ BR 68-69 G 4
Corrente, Rio ~ BR 68-69 F 5
Corrente, Rio ~ BR 72-73 J 3
Corrente, Rio ~ BR 72-73 G 5
Correntes ○ BR 68-69 K 6
Correntes, Riachão ~ BR 68-69 H 4
Correntes, Rio ~ BR 70-71 K 5
Correntina ○ BR 72-73 H 2
Correntoso ○ BR 68-69 F 4
Correntoso ○ RA 78-79 D 5
Corrib, Lough ○ IRL 90-91 C 4
Corrida de Cori ▲ RA 76-77 C 3
Corrie Downs ○ AUS 178-179 F 2
Corrientes ○ RA 76-77 H 4
Corrientes, Bahía de ≈ 54-55 C 4
Corrientes, Cabo ▲ C 54-55 C 4
Corrientes, Cabo ▲ CO 60-61 C 4
Corrientes, Cabo ▲ MEX 52-53 B 1
Corrientes, Río ~ PE 64-65 E 3
Corrientes, Río ~ RA 78-79 H 5
Corrigan ○ USA (TX) 268-269 F 5
Corrigin ○ AUS 176-177 D 6
Corry ○ USA (PA) 280-281 G 2
Corryong ○ AUS 180-181 J 4
Corse □ F 98-99 M 3
Corse, Cap ▲ F 98-99 M 3
Corsica ○ USA (SD) 260-261 H 3
Corsica = Corse ∩ F 100-101 B 4
Corsicana ○ USA (TX) 264-265 H 6
Cortadera, La ○ RCH 76-77 C 2
Cortaderal, Cerro ▲ RCH 76-77 C 5
Cortaderas, Pampa de ⊇ PE 70-71 A 5
Cortazar ○ MEX (AZ) 256-257 D 6
Corte ○ F 98-99 M 3
Cortegana ○ E 98-99 D 6
Cortés ○ RP 160-161 G 8
Cortez ○ USA (CO) 254-255 G 6
Cortez Gold Mine ○ USA (NV)
246-247 J 3
Cortina d'Ampezzo ○ I 100-101 D 1
Cortkiv ○ UA 102-103 D 3
Cortland ○ USA (NE) 262-263 K 4
Cortland ○ USA (NY) 278-279 E 6
Cortona ○ I 100-101 C 3
Corubal, Rio ~ GNB 202-203 C 4
Coruche ○ P 98-99 C 5
Çoruh Nehri ~ TR 128-129 J 2
Çorum ☆ • TR 128-129 F 2

Coruma ○ BR 62-63 J 6
Corumbá ○ BR 70-71 J 6
Corumba, Rio ~ BR 72-73 G 4
Corumbá de Goiás ○ BR 72-73 F 3
Corumbaíba ○ BR 72-73 F 5
Corumbaú, Ponta de ▲ BR 72-73 L 4
Corumbiara Antigo, Rio ~ BR 70-71 G 3
Coruña, A ☆ •• E 98-99 C 3
Corunna ○ CDN (ONT) 238-239 C 6
Corunna North ▲ AUS 180-181 D 2
Čoruoda ~ RUS 118-119 K 7
Corupá ○ BR 74-75 F 6
Coruto, Laguna ⊖ BOL 76-77 D 2
Corutuba, Rio ~ BR 72-73 J 3
Corvallis ○ USA (OR) 244-245 B 6
Corvette, Rivière ~ CDN 38-39 G 2
Corwen ○ GB 90-91 F 5
Corwin ○ USA 20-21 H 2
Cory Bay ≈ 36-37 M 2
Corydon ○ USA (IA) 274-275 E 4
Corydon ○ USA (IN) 274-275 M 6
Cosa • I 100-101 C 3
Cosamaloapan ○ MEX 52-53 G 2
Cosapa ○ BOL 70-71 C 6
Cosapilla ○ RCH 70-71 C 5
Coscaya ○ RCH 70-71 C 6
Cosenza ○ I 100-101 F 5
Coşeşti ○ RO 102-103 D 5
Coshocton ○ USA (OH) 280-281 E 3
Cosigüina, Punta ▲ NIC 52-53 L 5
Cosigüina, Volcán ▲ NIC 52-53 L 5
Cosmoledo Atoll ⊥ SY 222-223 E 2
Cosmo Newbery Aboriginal Land ✕ AUS 176-177 G 4
Cosmo Newbery Mission ✕ AUS 176-177 G 4
Cosmópolis ○ BR 72-73 G 7
Cosmos ○ USA (MN) 270-271 D 6
Cosne-Cours-sur-Loire ○ F 90-91 J 8
Cosoleacaque ○ MEX 52-53 G 2
Costa, Cordillera de la ▲ RCH 78-79 C 4
Costa, La ○ MEX 52-53 J 1
Costa, Ponta do ▲ BR 62-63 J 3
Costa Blanca ⌣ E 98-99 G 6
Costa Brava ⌣ E 98-99 J 4
Costa da Cadeia ○ BR 74-75 E 7
Costa Daurada ⌣ E 98-99 H 4
Costa de Araujo ○ RA 78-79 E 2
Costa de la Luz ⌣ E 98-99 D 6
Costa del Sol ⌣ E 98-99 E 6
Costa de Prata ⌣ P 98-99 C 5
Costa Island, La ⌒ USA (FL) 286-287 G 5
Costa Marques ○ BR 70-71 E 3
Costa Rica ○ BR 72-73 D 5
Costa Rica ○ C 54-55 H 4
Costa Rica ■ CR 52-53 B 7
Costa Vasca ⌣ E 98-99 F 3
Costa Verde ⌣ E 98-99 D 3
Costera del Golfo, Llanura ⌣ MEX 50-51 K 5
Costera del Pacífico, Llanura ⌣ MEX 50-51 D 3
Costeşti ○ MD 102-103 E 4
Costeşti ○ RO 102-103 D 5
Costilla ○ USA (NM) 256-257 K 2
Cota ○ CO 60-61 D 5
Cotabambas ○ PE 64-65 F 8
Cotabato City ☆ RP 160-161 F 9
Cotacachi, Cerro ▲ EC 64-65 C 1
Cotacachi-Cayapas, Reserva Ecológica ⊥ EC 64-65 C 1
Cotacajes, Río ~ BOL 70-71 D 5
Cotagaita ○ BOL 70-71 E 7
Cotahuasi ○ PE 64-65 F 9
Cotahuasi, Río ~ PE 64-65 F 9
Cotaxe, Rio ~ BR 72-73 K 5
Cotazar ○ MEX 52-53 D 1
Coteau des Prairies ▲ USA 260-261 J 1
Coteau du Missouri ▲ USA 258-259 F 3
Coteau Hills ▲ CDN 232-233 L 4
Côteaux ○ RH 54-55 H 5
Côte d'Azur ⌣ • F 90-91 L 10
Côte-d'Ivoire ■ CI 202-203 G 5
Cotejipe ○ BR 72-73 H 2
Cotentin ⊥ F 90-91 G 7
Côtes de Fer ○ RH 54-55 J 5
Coti, Rio ~ BR 66-67 E 7
Cotia ○ BR 72-73 G 7
Cotia, Rio ~ BR 66-67 E 7
Cotija de la Paz ○ MEX 52-53 C 2
Cotingo, Rio ~ BR 62-63 D 3
Coto de Doñana, Parque Nacional ⊥ ••• E 98-99 D 6
Cotonou ☆ DY 204-205 E 5
Cotopaxi ○ USA (CO) 254-255 K 5
Cotopaxi, Volcán ▲ EC 64-65 C 2
Cotorro ○ C 54-55 D 3
Cotovelo, Corredeira do ~ BR 66-67 H 6
Cotronei ○ I 100-101 F 5
Cottage Grove ○ USA (MN) 270-271 F 6
Cottage Grove ○ USA (OR) 244-245 B 7
Cottageville ○ USA (SC) 284-285 K 4
Cottar's Mara Camp ○ EAK 212-213 E 4
Cottbus ○ D 92-93 N 3
Cotter ○ USA (AR) 276-277 C 4
Cottica, Mont ▲ F 62-63 G 4
Cotton ○ USA (MN) 270-271 F 3
Cottonbush Creek ~ AUS 178-179 E 2
Cottondale ○ USA (FL) 286-287 D 1
Cotton Draw ~ USA 266-267 C 2
Cotton Plant ○ USA (AR) 276-277 D 5
Cottonport ○ USA (LA) 268-269 H 6
Cotton Valley ○ USA (LA) 268-269 G 4
Cottonwood ○ CDN (BC) 228-229 M 3
Cottonwood ○ USA (AL) 284-285 E 5
Cottonwood ○ USA (AZ) 256-257 C 4
Cottonwood ○ USA (CA) 246-247 C 3
Cottonwood ○ USA (ID) 250-251 C 5
Cottonwood ○ USA (SD) 260-261 E 3
Cottonwood Cove ○ USA (NV) 248-249 K 4
Cottonwood Creek ~ USA 250-251 H 3
Cottonwood Creek ~ USA 254-255 F 6
Cottonwood Falls ○ USA (KS) 262-263 K 6
Cottonwood River ~ USA 262-263 K 6
Cottonwood River ~ USA 270-271 C 6
Cottonwood Wash ~ USA 256-257 E 3
Cotuhe, Río ~ PE 66-67 B 4
Cotuí ☆ DOM 54-55 K 5
Cotulla ○ USA (TX) 266-267 H 5
Couchman Range ▲ AUS 172-173 H 3
Coudersport ○ USA (PA) 280-281 H 2
Coudres, Île aux ⌒ CDN (QUE) 240-241 E 3
Couëron ○ F 90-91 G 8
Cougar ○ USA (CA) 246-247 C 2
Couhé ○ F 90-91 H 8
Coulee ○ USA (ND) 258-259 F 3
Coulee City ○ USA (WA) 244-245 F 3
Coulee Dam ○ USA (WA) 244-245 G 3
Coulman Island ⌒ ARK 16 F 18
Couloir 1 < DZ 190-191 G 7
Coulomb Point ▲ AUS 172-173 F 4
Coulommiers ○ F 90-91 J 7
Coulonge, Rivière ~ CDN 238-239 J 2
Coulta ○ AUS 180-181 C 3
Coulterville ○ USA (CA) 248-249 D 2
Coulterville ○ USA (IL) 274-275 J 6
Council ○ USA (AK) 20-21 J 4
Council ○ USA (ID) 252-253 B 2
Council Bluffs ○ USA (IA) 274-275 C 3
Council Grove ○ USA (KS) 262-263 K 6
Council Grove Lake ⊖ USA (KS) 262-263 K 6
Council Hill ○ USA (OK) 264-265 J 3
Counselors ○ USA (NM) 256-257 H 2
Countess ○ CDN (ALB) 232-233 F 5
Country Force Base Suffield ✕✕ CDN (ALB) 232-233 H 5
Country Harbour ≈ 240-241 O 5
Coupeville ○ USA (WA) 244-245 C 2
Coupland ○ USA (TX) 266-267 K 3
Courageous Lake ⊖ CDN 30-31 O 3
Courantyne ~ GUY 62-63 F 4
Courmayeur ○ I 100-101 A 2
Cours-sur-Loire, Cosne ○ F 90-91 J 8
Court ○ CDN (SAS) 232-233 J 4
Courtenay ○ CDN (BC) 230-231 E 4
Courtenay ○ USA (ND) 258-259 J 4
Courtright ○ CDN (ONT) 238-239 C 6
Courval ○ CDN (SAS) 232-233 M 5
Coushatta ○ USA (LA) 268-269 G 4
Coushatta Indian Reservation, & Alabama ✕ USA (TX) 268-269 F 6
Coutances ○ F 90-91 G 7
Couto de Magalhães, Rio ~ BR 72-73 D 2
Couto de Magelhães de Minas ○ BR 72-73 J 5
Coutras ○ F 90-91 G 9
Coutts ○ CDN (ALB) 232-233 G 6
Couture, Lac ⊖ CDN 36-37 M 4
Cova Figueira ○ CV 202-203 B 6
Covè ○ DY 204-205 E 5
Cove ○ USA (AR) 276-277 A 6
Cove Fort ○ USA (UT) 254-255 C 5
Cove Island ⌒ CDN (ONT) 238-239 D 3
Covelo ○ USA (CA) 246-247 B 4
Coventry ○ GB 90-91 G 5
Coventry Lake ⊖ CDN 30-31 R 5
Cove Palisades State Park, The ⊥ • USA (OR) 244-245 D 6
Covered Wells ○ USA (AZ) 256-257 C 6
Covilhã ○ P 98-99 D 4
Covington ○ USA (GA) 284-285 G 3
Covington ○ USA (IN) 274-275 L 4
Covington ○ USA (KY) 276-277 L 1
Covington ○ USA (LA) 268-269 K 6
Covington ○ USA (MI) 270-271 K 4
Covington ○ USA (OH) 280-281 B 3
Covington ○ USA (OK) 264-265 G 2
Covington ○ USA (TN) 276-277 F 5
Covington ○ USA (VA) 280-281 F 6
Covunco, Arroyo ~ RA 78-79 E 5
Cowal, Lake ⊖ AUS 180-181 J 2
Cowal Creek ✕ AUS 174-175 G 2
Cowan ○ CDN (MAN) 234-235 C 2
Cowan ○ USA (TN) 276-277 K 5
Cowan, Cerro ▲ EC 64-65 B 10
Cowan, Lake ⊖ AUS 176-177 G 5
Cowan Downs ○ AUS 174-175 F 6
Cowan Hill ▲ AUS 176-177 E 5
Cowan Lake ⊖ USA (OH) 280-281 C 4
Cowansville ○ CDN (QUE) 238-239 N 3
Coward ○ USA (SC) 284-285 L 3
Coward Springs ○ AUS 178-179 D 5
Cow Bay ○ CDN (NS) 240-241 M 6
Cowboy Pass ▲ USA (UT) 254-255 B 4
Cowcowing Lakes ⊖ AUS 176-177 D 5
Cow Creek ○ USA (WY) 252-253 O 3
Cow Creek ~ USA 244-245 G 4
Cowden ○ USA (IL) 274-275 K 5
Cowdrey ○ USA (CO) 254-255 J 3
Cowell ○ AUS 180-181 D 2
Cow Head ○ CDN (NFL) 242-243 L 3
Cowhouse Creek ~ USA 266-267 K 2
Cowichan Lake ⊖ CDN (BC) 230-231 E 5
Cowie Point ▲ CDN 24-25 c 7
Cowles ○ USA (NM) 256-257 K 3
Cowley ○ CDN (ALB) 232-233 D 6
Cowlic ○ USA (AZ) 256-257 C 7
Cowlitz River ~ USA 244-245 C 4
Cowpasture River ~ USA 280-281 G 5
Cowpens ○ USA (SC) 284-285 J 1
Cowra ○ AUS 180-181 K 2
Cowval ~ GUY 62-63 F 3
Cox ○ USA (OH) 280-281 D 4
Coxilha de Santana ▲ BR 76-77 J 5
Coxim ○ BR 70-71 K 6
Cox Island ⌒ CDN 36-37 K 5
Cox River ○ AUS 174-175 C 4
Cox's Bazar ○ • BD 142-143 H 5
Cox's Cove ○ CDN (NFL) 242-243 K 3
Coxs Creek ~ AUS 178-179 K 6
Coyaguaima, Cerro ▲ RA 76-77 D 2
Coyah ○ RG 202-203 D 5
Coyaima ○ CO 60-61 D 6
Coyame ○ MEX 50-51 G 3
Coyanosa Draw ~ USA 266-267 D 3
Coy City ○ USA (TX) 266-267 J 5
Coyoacán ○ MEX 52-53 E 2
Coyolate, Río ~ GCA 52-53 J 4
Coyolito ○ HN 52-53 L 5
Coyote ○ USA (NM) 256-257 J 2
Coyote ○ USA (NM) 256-257 K 5
Coyote, Bahía ≈ 50-51 D 5
Coyote, Río ~ MEX 50-51 C 2
Coyotitán ○ MEX 50-51 F 6
Coyte, El ○ RA 80 E 2
Coyuca de Benítez ○ MEX 52-53 D 3
Cozad ○ USA (NE) 262-263 G 4
Cozes ○ F 90-91 G 9
Cozumel ○ • MEX 52-53 L 1
Cozumel, Isla del ⌒ •• MEX 52-53 L 1
Crab Orchard ○ USA (TN) 282-283 C 5
Crab Orchard Lake ⊖ USA (IL) 276-277 F 3
Crabwood Creek ○ GUY 62-63 F 3
Cracow ○ AUS 178-179 L 3
Cracroft Island ⌒ CDN (BC) 230-231 D 3
Craddock ○ CDN (ALB) 232-233 F 6
Cradle Mountain Lake St. Clair National Park ⊥ AUS 180-181 H 6
Cradle Valley ○ AUS 180-181 H 6
Cradock ○ AUS 180-181 E 2
Cradock ○ ZA 220-221 G 6
Craig ○ USA (AK) 32-33 D 4
Craig ○ USA (CO) 254-255 H 3
Craig ○ USA (FL) 286-287 J 7
Craig ○ USA (MS) 268-269 K 4
Craig Creek ~ USA 280-281 F 6
Craigellachie ○ CDN (BC) 230-231 L 3
Craigie ○ AUS 174-175 H 6
Craigieburn ○ AUS 180-181 H 4
Craigmont ○ USA (ID) 250-251 C 5
Craigmore ○ CDN (NS) 240-241 O 5
Craigmyle ○ CDN (ALB) 232-233 F 4
Craignure ○ GB 90-91 E 3
Craig Pass ▲ USA (WY) 252-253 H 2
Craigsville ○ USA (WV) 280-281 F 5
Craik ○ CDN (SAS) 232-233 N 4
Craiova ☆ • RO 102-103 C 5
Cramond ○ ZA 220-221 E 3
Cranberry Junction ○ CDN 32-33 F 4
Cranberry Lake ⊖ USA (NY) 278-279 G 4
Cranbourne ○ AUS 180-181 H 5
Cranbrook ○ AUS 176-177 D 7
Cranbrook ○ CDN (BC) 230-231 O 4
Crandall ○ CDN (MAN) 234-235 C 4
Crandon ○ USA (WI) 270-271 K 5
Crane ○ USA (MO) 276-277 B 4
Crane ○ USA (OR) 244-245 G 7
Crane ○ USA (TX) 266-267 E 2
Crane Creek State Park ⊥ USA (OH) 280-281 C 2
Crane Lake ⊖ CDN (SAS) 232-233 J 5
Crane Lake ○ USA (MN) 270-271 F 2
Crane Lake ⊖ USA (IL) 274-275 H 4
Crane River ○ CDN (MAN) 234-235 D 3
Crane Valley ○ CDN (SAS) 232-233 N 6
Cranfills Gap ○ USA (TX) 266-267 K 2
Cranford ○ CDN (ALB) 232-233 F 6
Cranston ○ USA (RI) 278-279 K 7
Cranstown, Kap ▲ GRØ 26-27 X 8
Cranswick River ~ CDN 20-21 Y 4
Crapaud ○ CDN (PEI) 240-241 M 4
Crary Mountains ▲ ARK 16 F 25
Crasna ~ RO 102-103 C 4
Crater Lake ⊖ USA (OR) 244-245 C 8
Crater Lake ⊥ • WAN 204-205 K 3
Crater Lake National Monument ∴ USA (OR) 244-245 C 8
Crater Lake National Park ⊥ •• USA (OR) 244-245 C 8
Crater Mountain ▲ USA 20-21 M 5
Crater of Diamonds State Park ∴ • USA (AR) 276-277 B 6
Craters of the Moon National Monument ∴ USA (ID) 252-253 E 3
Cratéus ○ BR 68-69 H 4
Crati ~ I 100-101 F 5
Crato ○ BR 68-69 J 5
Crauford, Cape ▲ CDN 24-25 e 4
Cravari ou Curucuinazá, Rio ~ BR 70-71 J 3
Craven ○ CDN (SAS) 232-233 O 5
Cravo Norte ○ CO 60-61 F 4
Crawford ○ USA (CO) 254-255 H 5
Crawford ○ USA (GA) 284-285 G 3
Crawford ○ USA (NE) 262-263 C 2
Crawford ○ USA (TX) 266-267 K 2
Crawford Bay ○ CDN (BC) 230-231 N 4
Crawfordsville ○ USA (IN) 274-275 M 4
Crawley ○ USA (WV) 280-281 F 6
Crazy Peak ▲ USA (MT) 250-251 J 5
Creede ○ USA (CO) 254-255 J 6
Creedmoor ○ USA (NC) 282-283 J 4
Creek Town ○ WAN 204-205 H 6
Creel ○ • MEX 50-51 F 4
Cree Lake ⊖ CDN 34-35 C 2
Creelman ○ CDN (SAS) 232-233 P 6
Creighton ○ USA (NE) 262-263 J 2
Creighton ○ USA (SD) 260-261 D 2
Creil ○ F 90-91 J 7
Cremona ○ CDN (ALB) 232-233 D 4
Cremona ☆ I 100-101 C 2
Crenshaw ○ USA (MS) 268-269 K 2
Creola ○ USA (AL) 284-285 B 6
Creole ○ USA (LA) 268-269 G 7
Crepori, Rio ~ BR 66-67 J 6
Cres ○ HR 100-101 E 2
Cres ⊥ HR 100-101 E 2
Cresbard ○ USA (SD) 260-261 H 1
Crescent ○ USA (OK) 264-265 G 3
Crescent ○ USA (OR) 244-245 D 7
Crescent, La ○ USA (MN) 270-271 G 7
Crescent City ○ USA (CA) 246-247 A 2
Crescent City ○ USA (FL) 286-287 H 2
Crescent Group = Yongle Qundao ⌒ VRC 158-159 L 2
Crescent Head ○ AUS 178-179 M 6
Crescent Junction ○ USA (UT) 254-255 F 5
Crescent Lake ○ CDN (SAS) 232-233 Q 5
Crescent Lake ○ USA (OR) 244-245 D 7
Crescent Lake ⊖ USA (FL) 286-287 H 2
Crescent Lake National Wildlife Refuge ⊥ USA (NE) 262-263 D 3
Crescent Valley ○ USA (NV) 246-247 J 3
Cresco ○ USA (IA) 274-275 F 1
Crespo ○ RA 78-79 J 2
Cresson ○ USA (TX) 264-265 G 6
Crest ○ F 90-91 K 9
Crested Butte ○ USA (CO) 254-255 J 5
Crestline ○ USA (CA) 248-249 G 5
Crestomere ○ CDN (ALB) 232-233 E 3
Creston ○ CDN (BC) 230-231 N 4
Creston ○ USA (CA) 248-249 D 4
Creston ○ USA (IA) 274-275 D 3
Creston ○ USA (MT) 250-251 E 3
Creston ○ USA (WY) 252-253 L 5
Crestón, Cerro ▲ RA 76-77 E 3
Crestview ○ USA (FL) 286-287 C 1
Crestwynd ○ CDN (SAS) 232-233 N 5
Creswell ○ USA (OR) 244-245 B 7
Creswell Bay ≈ 24-25 Z 4
Creswell Downs ○ AUS 174-175 C 5
Crete ○ USA (NE) 262-263 K 4
Crete = Kríti ⌒ GR 100-101 K 7
Crete, Sea of = Kritiko Pelagos ≈ 100-101 K 6
Creus, Cap de ▲ E 98-99 J 3
Creuse ~ F 90-91 J 8
Crewe ○ GB 90-91 F 5
Crewe ○ USA (VA) 280-281 H 6
Crichton ○ CDN (SAS) 232-233 L 6
Criciúma ○ BR 74-75 F 7
Crieff ○ GB 90-91 F 3
Crikvenica ○ HR 100-101 E 2
Crilly ○ CDN (ONT) 234-235 L 6
Crimea = Krym ⊥ UA 102-103 H 5
Crimea = Krym, Respublika ◘ UA 102-103 H 5
Crimea = Kryms'kyj pivostriv ⌣ UA 102-103 H 5
Criminosa, Cachoeira ~ BR 62-63 D 6
Criminosa, Cachoeira ~ BR 70-71 E 2
Crimson Cliffs ▲ GRØ 26-27 R 5
Crimson Lake Provincial Park ⊥ CDN (ALB) 232-233 C 3
Criolla, Cerro la ▲ RA 80 E 5
Cripple ○ USA 20-21 M 5
Cripple Creek ○ USA (CO) 254-255 K 5
Criş, Chişineu- ○ RO 102-103 B 4
Crisfield ○ USA (MD) 280-281 L 6
Crisóstomo, Ribeiro ~ BR 68-69 C 7
Crispín, El ○ RA 76-77 F 6
Cristais, Serra dos ▲ BR 72-73 G 4
Cristal, Monts de ▲ G 210-211 C 3
Cristalândia ○ BR 68-69 D 7
Cristalina ○ BR 72-73 G 4
Cristalino, Rio ~ BR 66-67 K 7
Cristalino, Rio ~ BR 72-73 E 3
Cristiano Muerto, Arroyo ~ RA 78-79 K 5
Cristianópolis ○ BR 72-73 F 4
Cristianos, Los ○ E 188-189 C 6
Cristo, El ○ YV 60-61 K 4
Cristóbal, Punta ▲ EC 64-65 B 10
Cristóbal Cólon, Pico ▲ •• CO 60-61 E 2
Cristoffel National Park ⊥ NA 60-61 G 1
Cristópolis ○ BR 72-73 H 2
Cristovão Pereira, Ponta ▲ BR 74-75 E 8
Criterion, Cerro ▲ PE 64-65 E 9
Criterion Pass ▲ USA (OR) 244-245 D 5
Crixás ○ BR 72-73 F 3
Crixás, Rio ~ BR 68-69 D 7
Crixas Açu, Rio ~ BR 72-73 F 3
Crixas Mirim, Rio ~ BR 72-73 E 2
Crna gora ▲ MK 100-101 H 3
Crni vrh ▲ BIH 100-101 F 2
Croajingolong National Park ⊥ AUS 180-181 K 4
Croatá ○ BR 68-69 H 4
Croatan Sound ≈ 282-283 M 5
Croatia = Hrvatska ■ HR 100-101 E 2
Croche, Rivière ~ CDN 240-241 C 3
Crocker ○ USA (SD) 260-261 J 1
Crocker, Banjaran ▲ MAL 160-161 A 10
Crocker Range National Park ⊥ MAL 160-161 B 10
Crockett ○ USA (TX) 268-269 E 5
Crocodile Camp ○ EAK 212-213 G 5
Crocodile Farm • AUS 172-173 K 2
Crocodiles • BF (CTO) 202-203 J 3
Crocodiles • BF (VNE) 202-203 J 3
Crofton ○ USA (NE) 262-263 J 2
Croharé ○ USA (KY) 276-277 J 3
Croher River ~ CDN 24-25 M 6
Croix, Lac à la ⊖ CDN 38-39 J 3
Croix des Bouquets ○ RH 54-55 J 5
Croix-de-Vie, Saint-Gilles- ○ F 90-91 G 8
Croker, Cape ▲ AUS 172-173 L 1
Croker Bay ≈ 24-25 e 3
Croker Island ⌒ AUS 172-173 L 1
Cromer ○ CDN (MAN) 234-235 B 5
Cromwell ○ CDN (MAN) 234-235 G 4
Cromwell ○ NZ 182 B 6
Cromwell ○ USA (MN) 270-271 F 4
Crông Kno ~ VN 158-159 K 4
Cronin, Mount ▲ CDN (BC) 228-229 H 2
Crook ○ USA (CO) 254-255 N 3
Crooked Creek ○ USA 20-21 L 6
Crooked Creek ~ USA 262-263 F 7
Crooked Island ⌒ BS 54-55 H 3
Crooked Island ⌒ USA 22-23 Q 3
Crooked Island ⌒ USA (FL) 286-287 D 2
Crooked Lake ⊖ CDN 24-25 X 4
Crooked River ○ CDN (SAS) 232-233 P 3
Crooked River ~ CDN 228-229 M 2
Crooked River ~ USA 244-245 E 6
Crooks Inlet ≈ 36-37 O 3
Crookston ○ USA (MN) 270-271 B 3
Crookston ○ USA (NE) 262-263 F 2
Crooksville ○ USA (OH) 280-281 D 4
Crookwell ○ AUS 180-181 K 3
Croppa Creek ~ AUS 178-179 L 5
Croque ○ CDN (NFL) 242-243 N 1
Crosby ○ CDN (ONT) 238-239 J 4
Crosby ○ USA (MN) 270-271 E 4
Crosby ○ USA (MS) 268-269 J 5
Crosby ○ USA (ND) 258-259 D 3
Crosbyton ○ USA (TX) 264-265 C 5
Cross ○ USA (SC) 284-285 K 3
Cross ○ USA (TX) 266-267 J 5
Cross, Cape = Kruis, Kaap ▲ NAM 216-217 B 10
Cross Anchor ○ USA (SC) 284-285 J 2
Cross City ○ USA (FL) 286-287 F 2
Crosse, La ○ USA (WA) 244-245 H 4
Crossett ○ USA (AR) 276-277 D 7
Crossfield ○ CDN (ALB) 232-233 D 4
Crosshill ○ CDN (ONT) 238-239 E 5
Cross Hill ○ USA (SC) 284-285 J 2
Cross Lake ○ USA (MN) 270-271 D 4
Cross Lake ⊖ USA (LA) 268-269 G 4
Crossley Lakes ⊖ CDN 20-21 a 2
Crossman Peak ▲ USA (AZ) 256-257 A 4
Cross Plains ○ USA (TX) 264-265 E 6
Cross River ◘ WAN 204-205 H 5
Cross River ~ WAN 204-205 H 6
Crossroads ○ USA (NM) 256-257 M 5
Cross Roads ○ USA (TX) 264-265 J 6
Cross Sound ≈ 32-33 B 2
Cross Village ○ USA (MI) 272-273 D 2
Crossville ○ USA (AL) 284-285 E 2
Crossville ○ USA (TN) 276-277 K 5
Crosswind Lake ⊖ USA 20-21 S 5
Croswell ○ USA (MI) 272-273 G 4
Croton Creek ~ USA 264-265 D 5
Crotone ○ I 100-101 F 5
Crouse ○ CDN (NFL) 242-243 N 2
Crow Agency ○ USA (MT) 250-251 M 6
Crow Creek ~ USA 254-255 L 3
Crow Creek Indian Reservation ✕ USA (SD) 260-261 G 2
Crowder Lake State Park ⊥ • USA (OK) 264-265 F 3
Crowdy Bay National Park ⊥ AUS 178-179 M 6
Crowell ○ USA (TX) 264-265 E 5
Crowe River ~ CDN 238-239 H 4
Crowfoot ○ CDN (ALB) 232-233 F 5
Crowfoot Creek ~ CDN 232-233 F 5
Crowheart ○ USA (WY) 252-253 J 3
Crow Indian Reservation ✕ USA (MT) 250-251 L 6
Crow Lake ○ CDN (ONT) 234-235 K 5
Crowl Creek ~ AUS 180-181 H 2
Crowley ○ USA (CO) 254-255 M 5
Crowley ○ USA (LA) 268-269 H 6
Crowley, Lake ⊖ USA (CA) 248-249 F 2
Crowley Ranch ○ USA (OR) 244-245 H 7
Crowleys Ridge ▲ USA 276-277 E 5
Crown Island ⌒ PNG 183 D 3
Crown Point ○ USA (IN) 274-275 L 3
Crownpoint ○ USA (NM) 256-257 G 3
Crown Prince Frederik Island ⌒ CDN 24-25 c 6
Crown Prince Range ▲ PNG 184 I b 2
Crow River ~ CDN 30-31 G 6
Crows ○ USA (AR) 276-277 C 6
Crows Nest ○ AUS 178-179 M 4
Crowsnest Pass ▲ CDN (BC) 230-231 P 4
Croydon ○ AUS 174-175 G 6
Croydon ○ SD 220-221 K 3
Crozet, Îles ⌒ F 9 J 10
Crozier Channel ≈ 24-25 M 3
Crozon ○ F 90-91 E 7
Cruce, El ○ GCA 52-53 K 3
Cruce de la Jagua ○ DOM 54-55 L 5
Crucero ○ PE 70-71 B 4
Crucero, El ○ MEX 50-51 B 3
Crucero, El ○ YV 60-61 J 3
Cruces ○ C 54-55 E 3
Cruces, Las ○ MEX 52-53 H 3
Cruces, Las ○ USA (NM) 256-257 J 6
Cruces, Punta ▲ CO 60-61 C 4
Crucetillas, Puerto de las ▲ E 98-99 F 5
Crucita ○ EC 64-65 B 2
Cruger ○ USA (MS) 268-269 K 3
Cruilas ○ MEX 50-51 K 5
Crump ○ USA (MI) 272-273 E 4
Crump Lake ⊖ USA (OR) 244-245 F 8
Cruz, Bahía ≈ 80 H 2
Cruz, Cabo ▲ C 54-55 G 5
Cruz, Ilha ⌒ BR 72-73 L 3
Cruz, La ○ BOL (SAC) 70-71 F 4
Cruz, La ○ BOL (SAC) 70-71 F 5
Cruz, La ○ CR 52-53 B 6
Cruz, La ○ MEX (SIN) 50-51 F 6
Cruz, La ○ MEX (TAM) 50-51 L 6
Cruz, La ○ RA 78-79 G 2
Cruz Alta ○ BR 74-75 D 7
Cruz Bay ○ USA (VI) 286-287 R 2
Cruz de Elorza ○ MEX 50-51 J 6
Cruz del Eje ○ RA 76-77 E 6
Cruz de Loreto, La ○ MEX 52-53 B 2
Cruz de Taratara, La ○ YV 60-61 G 2
Cruzeiro ○ BR 72-73 H 7
Cruzeiro ○ MOC 218-219 H 5
Cruzeiro d'Oeste ○ BR 72-73 D 7
Cruzeiro do Nordeste ○ BR 68-69 K 6
Cruzeiro do Sul ○ BR 64-65 F 5
Cruzen Island ⌒ ARK 16 F 23
Cruzes, Corredeira das ~ BR 70-71 J 4
Cruz Grande ○ MEX 52-53 E 3
Cruzinha da Garca ○ CV 202-203 B 5
Cruz Machado ○ BR 74-75 E 6
Crysdale, Mount ▲ CDN 32-33 J 4
Crystal ○ USA (OK) 264-265 J 4
Crystal Bay ≈ 286-287 G 3
Crystal Brook ○ AUS 180-181 E 2
Crystal Cave ∴ USA (WI) 270-271 F 6
Crystal City ○ CDN (MAN) 234-235 E 5
Crystal City ○ USA (TX) 266-267 H 5
Crystal Creek National Park ⊥ AUS 174-175 J 6
Crystal Falls ○ USA (MI) 270-271 K 4
Crystal Lake ○ USA (FL) 286-287 D 1
Crystal Lake ○ USA (IL) 274-275 K 2
Crystal Lake Cave ∴ USA (IA) 274-275 H 2
Crystal River ○ USA (FL) 286-287 G 3
Crystal River ~ USA 254-255 H 4
Crystal River State Archaeological Site • USA (FL) 286-287 G 3
Crystal Springs ○ CDN (SAS) 232-233 N 3
Crystal Springs ○ USA (MS) 268-269 K 5
Cserhát ⊥ H 92-93 P 5
C. Silverberge Ø ⌒ GRØ 26-27 p 5
Csorna ○ H 92-93 O 5
Cḥu'u Long, Cḥu'a Sông ⊥ VN 158-159 J 6
Cúa ○ YV 60-61 H 2
Cù'a Bày Hóp ≈ 158-159 H 6
Cuacaña ○ YV 60-61 J 5
Cuacua, Rio ~ MOC 218-219 J 3
Cù'a Cung Hầu ≈ 158-159 J 6
Cuaio ~ ANG 216-217 F 7
Cuajinicuilapa ○ MEX 52-53 E 3
Cuale ○ ANG 216-217 D 4
Cuamato ○ ANG 216-217 C 8
Cuamba ○ MOC 218-219 J 2
Cuanavale ~ ANG 216-217 E 7
Cuando ~ ANG 218-219 B 3
Cuando-Cubango ◘ ANG 216-217 E 7
Cuangar ○ ANG 216-217 E 8
Cuango ○ ANG (LUN) 216-217 E 4
Cuango ○ ANG (UIG) 216-217 D 3
Cuango ~ ANG 216-217 D 4
Cuanza ○ ANG (BIE) 216-217 D 5
Cuanza ~ ANG 216-217 B 4
Cuanza Norte ◘ ANG 216-217 C 4
Cuanza Sul ◘ ANG 216-217 C 5
Cuao, Río ~ YV 60-61 H 5
Cuareim, Río ~ ROU 76-77 J 6
Cuarinuma ○ CO 60-61 G 6
Cuarto, Río ~ RA 78-79 G 2
Cù'a Soi Rap ≈ 158-159 J 5
Cuatir ~ ANG 216-217 E 8
Cuatro Caminos ○ C 54-55 G 4
Cuatrociénegas de Carranza ○ MEX 50-51 H 4
Cuauhtémoc ○ MEX (CHA) 50-51 F 3
Cuauhtémoc ○ MEX (TAM) 50-51 K 6
Cuautitlán ○ MEX 52-53 E 2
Cuautla ○ MEX 52-53 B 1
Cuautla de Morelos ○ MEX 52-53 E 2
Cuba ■ C 54-55 E 4
Cuba ○ USA (AL) 284-285 B 4
Cuba ○ USA (IL) 274-275 H 4
Cuba ○ USA (MO) 274-275 G 6
Cuba ○ USA (NM) 256-257 J 2
Cuba City ○ USA (WI) 274-275 H 2
Cù Bai ○ VN 158-159 J 2
Cubal ○ ANG (BGU) 216-217 C 6
Cubal ~ ANG 216-217 C 5
Cubal ~ ANG 216-217 B 7
Cubango ○ ANG (HUA) 216-217 D 7
Cubango ~ ANG 216-217 D 8
Cubaté, Rio ~ BR 66-67 D 2
Cubati ~ ANG 216-217 D 7
Cube ○ EC 64-65 C 1
Cubero ○ USA (NM) 256-257 H 3
Cubia ~ ANG 216-217 F 7
Cubitas ○ C 54-55 G 4
Čubłas ○ RUS 88-89 Q 4
Çubuk ☆ TR 128-129 E 2
Čubuka-Tala, gora ▲ RUS 110-111 a 7
Čubukulah, gora ▲ RUS 110-111 d 6
Čubukulah, krjaž ▲ RUS 110-111 d 7
Cubulco ○ GCA 52-53 J 4
Cuchara ○ USA (CO) 254-255 K 6
Cuchi ○ ANG (CUA) 216-217 D 7
Cuchi ~ ANG 216-217 D 7
Cuchilla, La ○ RA 76-77 G 4
Cuchilla de Haedo ▲ ROU 78-79 L 2
Cuchilla de la Tristeza ▲ RA 78-79 E 3
Cuchilla del Hospital ▲ ROU 78-79 M 2
Cuchilla Grande ▲ ROU 78-79 M 2
Cuchilla Grande del Durazno ▲ ROU 78-79 L 2
Cuchilla Grande Inferior ▲ ROU 78-79 L 2
Cuchillo ○ USA (NM) 256-257 H 5
Cuchillo-Co ○ RA 78-79 G 5
Cuchivero ○ YV 60-61 J 4
Cuchivero, Río ~ YV 60-61 J 4
Cucho Ingenio ○ BOL 70-71 E 6
Cuchumatanas, Parque Nacional Los ⊥ • GCA 52-53 J 4
Cuchumatanas, Sierra de los ▲ GCA 52-53 J 4
Cuckadoo ○ AUS 178-179 F 1
Cuckoo ○ USA (VA) 280-281 J 6
Cucuí ○ BR 66-67 D 2
Cucumbi ~ ANG 216-217 E 4
Cucurici, Cachoeira ~ BR 72-73 D 2
Cucurital ○ YV 60-61 J 5
Cucuta ☆ CO 60-61 E 4
Cudahy ○ USA (WI) 274-275 L 2
Cuddalore ○ IND 140-141 H 5
Cuddapah ○ IND 140-141 H 3
Čudovo ☆ RUS 94-95 M 2
Čudskoe ozero ⊖ RUS 94-95 K 2
Cudworth ○ CDN (SAS) 232-233 N 3
Čudzjavr, ozero ⊖ RUS 88-89 N 2
Cue ○ AUS 176-177 D 3
Cuebe ~ ANG 216-217 D 7
Cueio ~ ANG 216-217 D 7
Cueiras, Rio ~ BR 66-67 G 4
Cuélab • PE 64-65 D 5
Cuelei ~ ANG 216-217 D 7
Cuéllar ○ E 98-99 E 4
Cuemba ○ ANG 216-217 E 6
Cuenca ○ E 98-99 F 4
Cuenca ☆ •• EC 64-65 C 3
Cuenca, Serranía de ▲ E 98-99 F 4
Cuenca del Añelo ⊥ RA 78-79 E 5
Cuencamé ○ MEX 50-51 H 5
Cuengo ~ ANG 216-217 E 4
Cuerámaro ○ MEX 52-53 D 1
Cuernavaca ☆ • MEX 52-53 E 2
Cuero ○ C 54-55 H 5
Cuero ○ USA (TX) 266-267 K 4
Cuervo ○ USA (NM) 256-257 L 3
Cueto ○ C 54-55 H 4
Cuetzalan ○ • MEX 52-53 F 1
Cueva de la Quebrada del Toro, Parque Nacional ⊥ YV 60-61 G 2
Cueva de las Brujas • RA 78-79 E 3
Cueva de las Manos • RA 80 E 3
Cueva del Guacharo •• YV 60-61 K 2
Cueva del Milodón • RCH 80 D 5
Cuevas ○ RP 160-161 G 8
Cuevas, Las ○ RA 78-79 D 2
Cuevas de Jumandi • EC 64-65 D 2
Cuevas o de las Cañas, Río ~ RA 76-77 E 3
Cuevo ○ BOL 70-71 F 7
Cuevo, Quebrada de ~ BOL 70-71 F 7
Čuga ~ RUS 118-119 L 7
Čuginskoe ploskogor'e ▲ RUS 118-119 K 7
Cugo ~ ANG 216-217 D 3
Čugor', mys ▲ RUS 108-109 Q 7
Čugor'jaha ~ RUS 108-109 Q 7
Čuguš, gora ▲ RUS 126-127 D 6
Čuhloma ○ RUS 94-95 S 2
Čuhujiv ○ UA 102-103 K 3
Cuiabá ○ BR (AMA) 66-67 C 4
Cuiabá ☆ BR (MAT) 70-71 J 4
Cuiabá, Rio ~ BR 70-71 J 5
Cuije ~ ANG 216-217 D 4
Cuilapa ☆ GCA 52-53 J 4
Cuilo ○ ANG (LUN) 216-217 E 4
Cuilo ~ ANG 216-217 E 4
Cuilo ~ ANG 216-217 C 3
Cuilo ~ ANG 216-217 E 5
Cuilo-Futa ○ ANG 216-217 C 3
Cuilo Pombo ○ ANG 216-217 C 3
Cuima ○ ANG 216-217 C 6
Cuimba ○ ANG 216-217 C 3
Cuio ○ ANG 216-217 B 6
Cuira o Monos ○ CO 64-65 F 2
Cuiriri ~ ANG 216-217 E 7
Cuito ~ ANG 216-217 F 8
Cuito Cuanavale ○ ANG 216-217 E 7
Cuiubi ○ BR 66-67 C 2
Cuiuni, Rio ~ BR 66-67 F 3
Cuivre River ~ USA 274-275 H 5
Cuiyun Lang • VRC 154-155 D 5
Čuja ~ RUS 118-119 F 6
Čuja ~ RUS 124-125 Q 3
Čuja ~ RUS 124-125 P 3
Čuja, Boľšaja ~ RUS 118-119 F 6
Cujar, Río ~ PE 64-65 F 7
Čujskij, Gorno ○ RUS 118-119 E 7
Cujubim ○ BR 66-67 G 7
Čukar ○ RUS 118-119 H 4
Cukas, Pulau ⌒ RI 162-163 F 5
Čukča ~ RUS 110-111 Z 6
Čukčagirskoe, ozero ⊖ •• RUS 122-123 G 3
Čukočje, ozero ○ RUS 112-113 L 2
Čukočja, Boľšaja ~ RUS 112-113 K 2
Čukotskij, mys ▲ RUS 112-113 Y 4
Čukotskij poluostrov ⌣ RUS 112-113 W 3
Čukotskoe more ≈ 112-113 X 1
Čukša ~ RUS 116-117 J 7
Çukurca ☆ TR 128-129 K 4
Cula ~ MD 102-103 F 4
Čulakan ~ RUS 116-117 M 6
Čulakkurgan ○ KZ 136-137 L 3
Culamagia ○ ANG 216-217 D 4
Culan Sancai ▲ ETH 208-209 B 3
Cù Lao Thu = Phù Qùy ⌒ VN 158-159 K 5
Čulas ~ RUS 88-89 T 4
Čulasa ○ RUS 88-89 T 4
Culasi ○ RP 160-161 E 7
Culbertson ○ USA (MT) 250-251 P 3
Culbertson ○ USA (NE) 262-263 F 4
Culdesac ○ USA (ID) 250-251 C 5
Culebra, Isla de ⌒ USA (PR) 286-287 Q 2
Culebras ○ PE 64-65 C 6
Culebras, Punta ▲ PE 64-65 C 6
Culgoa River ~ AUS 178-179 J 5
Culiacán Rosales ☆ MEX 50-51 F 5
Culion ○ RP 160-161 D 7
Culion Island ⌒ RP 160-161 C 7
Culiseu, Rio ~ BR 72-73 D 2
Cullen Garden • CDN (ONT) 238-239 F 5
Cullera ○ E 98-99 G 5
Cullinan ○ ZA 220-221 J 2
Cullison ○ USA (KS) 262-263 H 7
Cullmann ○ USA (AL) 284-285 D 2
Cullulleraine ○ AUS 180-181 F 3
Čuľman ○ RUS (SAH) 118-119 M 7
Čuľman ~ RUS 118-119 M 7
Culpeper ○ USA (VA) 280-281 J 5
Culpina ○ BOL 70-71 E 7
Culross Island ⌒ USA 20-21 R 6
Culuene, Rio ~ BR 72-73 D 2
Čuluunhoroom = Èrèèncav ○ MAU 148-149 M 3
Čuluut gol ~ MAU 148-149 E 3
Culver ○ USA (IN) 274-275 M 3
Culver, Point ▲ AUS 176-177 H 6
Culverden ○ NZ 182 D 5
Čulym ☆ RUS (NVS) 114-115 Q 7
Čulym ~ RUS 114-115 S 6
Čulym ~ RUS 114-115 Q 7
Čulymskaja ravnina ⌣ RUS 114-115 T 6
Čulyšman ~ RUS 124-125 Q 3
Čulyšmanskoe nagorie ▲ RUS 124-125 P 3
Cuma ○ ANG 216-217 C 6
Cumã, Baía do ≈ 68-69 F 3
Cuma, Cachoeira ~ BR 66-67 C 2
Cumaná ☆ • YV 60-61 J 2
Cumanacoa ○ YV 60-61 K 2
Cumanayagua ○ C 54-55 E 3
Cumanda ○ EC 64-65 C 3
Cumaral ○ CO 60-61 E 5
Cumaral = Barranca de Upía ○ CO 60-61 E 5
Cumaral, Raudal ~ CO 60-61 F 6

318 Coruma — Cumaral, Raudal

Cumaribo o CO 60-61 G 5
Cumaru, Cachoeira ~ BR 62-63 G 6
Cumbal, Nevado de ▲ CO 64-65 D 1
Cumbe o EC 64-65 C 3
Cumberland o CDN (BC) 230-231 D 4
Cumberland o USA (IA) 274-275 D 3
Cumberland o USA (IN) 274-275 N 5
Cumberland o USA (KY) 276-277 N 4
Cumberland o USA (MD) 280-281 H 4
Cumberland o USA (MS) 268-269 L 3
Cumberland o USA (OH) 280-281 E 4
Cumberland o USA (VA) 280-281 H 6
Cumberland o USA (WI) 270-271 F 5
Cumberland, Cape = Cape Nahoi ▲ VAN 184 II a 2
Cumberland, Lake < USA (KY) 276-277 K 4
Cumberland Bay ≈ 78-79 0 7
Cumberland Caverns Park ⅄ USA (TN) 276-277 K 5
Cumberland City Reservoir < USA (PA) 280 281 H 4
Cumberland Downs o AUS 178-179 J 2
Cumberland Falls ~ USA 276-277 L 4
Cumberland Gap ▲ USA (TN) 282-283 D 4
Cumberland Gap National Historic Park ∴ USA (KY) 276-277 M 4
Cumberland House o CDN (SAS) 232-233 Q 2
Cumberland Island ⌒ USA (GA) 284-285 J 6
Cumberland Island National Seashore ⊥ USA (GA) 284-285 J 6
Cumberland Islands ⌒ AUS 174-175 K 7
Cumberland Mountains ▲ USA 282-283 D 4
Cumberland Parkway II USA (KY) 276-277 K 3
Cumberland Peninsula ⌣ CDN 28-29 G 3
Cumberland River ~ USA 276-277 K 4
Cumberland River ~ USA 276-277 M 4
Cumberland Sound ≈ 36-37 R 2
Cumbi o ANG 216-217 B 3
Cumborah o AUS 178-179 J 5
Cumbre, Paso de la ▲ RA 78-79 E 2
Cumbre, Volcán La ▲ EC 64-65 B 10
Cumbrera, Cerro ▲ RCH 80 D 4
Cumbres and Toltec Scenic Railroad • USA (CO) 254-255 J 6
Cumbres de Majalca o MEX 50-51 F 3
Cumbres de Majalca, Parque Nacional ⊥ MEX 50-51 F 3
Cumbrian Mountains ▲ GB 90-91 F 4
Cumbum o IND 140-141 H 3
Cumburão o BR 62-63 G 6
Cumby o USA (TX) 264-265 J 5
Čumikan ☆ RUS (HBR) 120-121 F 6
Čumikan ~ RUS 120-121 F 5
Cuminá o BR 62-63 F 6
Cuminá, Rio ~ BR 62-63 F 5
Cuminapanema, Rio ~ BR 62-63 G 6
Cumming o USA (GA) 284-285 F 2
Cummings o USA (CA) 246-247 B 4
Cummins o AUS 180-181 C 3
Cummins Range ▲ AUS 172-173 H 5
Cumnock o GB 90-91 E 4
Čumpu-Kytyl o RUS 110-111 Y 7
Çumra ☆ TR 128-129 E 4
Cumshewa Head ▲ CDN (BC) 228-229 C 3
Cumshewa Inlet ≈ 228-229 C 3
Cumuté, Rio ~ BR 68-69 C 4
Čumyš ~ RUS 124-125 N 2
Čuna ~ RUS 116-117 H 7
Cunaguaro o YV 60-61 J 3
Cunani o BR 62-63 J 4
Cuñare o CO 64-65 F 1
Cunamo o RCH 78-79 C 6
Cunauaru, Rio ~ BR 66-67 F 4
Cund ~ ANG 216-217 D 6
Cunday o CO 60-61 D 5
Cundeelee ⅄ AUS 176-177 G 5
Cundeelee Aboriginal Land ⅄ AUS 176-177 G 5
Cunderdin o AUS 176-177 D 5
Cunduacán o MEX 52-53 H 2
Cunene o ANG (HUA) 216-217 C 7
Cunene ▪ ANG 216-217 C 8
Cunene ~ ANG 216-217 D 7
Cunene ~ ANG 216-217 B 8
Cúneo ☆ I 100-101 A 2
Cung Hầu, Cửa ≈ 158-159 J 6
Cunha o BR 72-73 H 7
Cunhãs, Rio das ~ BR 68-69 D 5
Cunhinga ~ ANG 216-217 D 5
Cuniã, Estação Ecológica ⊥ BR 66-67 F 7
Cuniuá, Rio ~ BR 66-67 D 6
Čunja ~ RUS 116-117 H 5
Čunja, Strelka o RUS 116-117 L 5
Cunjamba o ANG 216-217 F 7
Cunnamulla o AUS 178-179 H 5
Cunningham o USA (KY) 276-277 G 4
Cunningham o USA (TN) 276-277 H 4
Cunningham o USA (TX) 264-265 J 5
Cunningham, Lake ⊙ ZW 218-219 E 5
Cunningham Islands ⌒ AUS 174-175 D 2
Cunningham Lake ⊙ CDN (BC) 228-229 J 2
Čunskij o RUS 116-117 H 7
Čun'skij ☆ RUS 116-117 J 7
Cuntima o GNB 202-203 C 3
Čuokkarašša ▲ N 86-87 M 2
Čupa o RUS 88-89 M 3
Čūpānān o IR 134-135 F 2
Cupar o CDN (SAS) 232-233 O 5
Cupari, Rio ~ BR 66-67 K 4
Cupertino o USA (CA) 248-249 B 2
Cupica o CO 60-61 C 4
Cupica, Golfo de ≈ 60-61 C 4
Cupisnique, Cerro ▲ PE 64-65 C 5
Cupixi o BR 62-63 J 5
Čuprovo o RUS 88-89 T 4
Cuprum o USA (ID) 250-251 C 6
Cuptano, Isla ⌒ RCH 80 D 2
Curaça o BR 68-69 J 6
Curaça, Rio ~ BR 68-69 J 6
Curaçao ⌒ NA 60-61 G 1
Curacautín o RCH 78-79 D 5
Curacaví o RCH 78-79 D 2
Curachi o GUY 62-63 D 2
Curácuaro de Morelos o MEX 52-53 D 2
Curahuara de Carangas o BOL 70-71 C 5
Curale o ETH 208-209 G 5
Cura Malal, Sierra de ▲ RA 78-79 H 4
Curanilahué o RCH 78-79 C 4
Curanja o BR 66-67 B 7
Curanja, Río ~ PE 70-71 B 2
Čurapča ☆• RUS 120-121 E 3
Curaray o EC 64-65 D 2
Curaray o PE 64-65 E 3
Curaray, Río ~ PE 64-65 E 3
Curari, Ilha de ⌒ BR 66-67 G 4
Curaru o RA 78-79 H 3
Curauaí, Rio ~ BR 66-67 H 5
Čurbuka, gora ▲ RUS 110-111 Q 4
Čurbukan ~ RUS 116-117 H 2
Curdimurka o AUS 178-179 D 5
Čūre o AFG 134-135 M 2
Curecanti National Recreation Area ⊥• USA (CO) 254-255 H 5
Curepipe o MS 224 C 7
Curepto o RCH 78-79 C 3
Curib o RUS 126-127 G 6
Curibaya o PE 70-71 B 5
Curiche Liverpool ⊙ BOL 70-71 F 4
Curichi de Oquiriquia ~ BOL 70-71 G 5
Curichi Tunas ~ BOL 70-71 G 5
Curico o RCH 78-79 D 3
Curicuriari, Rio ~ BR 66-67 C 3
Curieuse Marine National Park ⊥ SY 224 D 2
Curi Leuvú, Arroyo ~ RA 78-79 D 4
Curimatá o BR 68-69 F 7
Curimatá, Rio ~ BR 68-69 F 6
Curimatá de Baixo, Rio ~ BR 66-67 E 5
Curimávida, Cerro de ▲ RCH 76-77 B 6
Curionópolis o BR 68-69 D 5
Curitiba o BR (ACR) 70-71 C 2
Curitiba ☆• BR (PAR) 74-75 F 5
Curitibanos o BR 74-75 E 6
Curiúva o BR 74-75 E 5
Čurkin, mys ▲ RUS 110-111 W 3
Curlew o USA (WA) 244-245 G 2
Curly Cut Cays ⌒ BS 54-55 G 3
Curnamona o AUS 178-179 E 6
Čuro ~ RUS 118-119 F 7
Curoca ~ ANG 216-217 B 8
Curoca, Cachoeira da ~ BR 66-67 G 7
Currais Novos o BR 68-69 K 5
Currais o BR 74-75 D 9
Curral Falso o BR 74-75 E 8
Curralinho o BR 62-63 K 6
Curral Novo o BR 68-69 H 6
Curral Velho o BR 72-73 H 2
Curral Velho o CV 202-203 C 5
Curran o CDN (ONT) 238-239 L 3
Currant o USA (NV) 246-247 K 5
Currarehue o RCH 78-79 D 5
Currawinya o AUS 178-179 H 5
Currawinya National Park ⊥ AUS 178-179 H 5
Current Island ⌒ BS 54-55 G 2
Current River ~ USA 276-277 D 3
Currie o AUS 180-181 G 5
Currie o USA (MN) 270-271 C 6
Currie o USA (NV) 246-247 L 3
Currie Indian Reserve, Mount ⅄ CDN (BC) 230-231 G 3
Currituck o USA (NC) 282-283 L 4
Currituck Sound ≈ 282-283 M 4
Curtea de Argeș o• RO 102-103 D 5
Čūrtī o IR 136-137 B 6
Curtin o AUS 176-177 G 5
Curtin Springs o AUS 176-177 L 2
Curtis o USA (NE) 262-263 F 4
Curtis Island ⌒ AUS 178-179 L 2
Curtis Lake ⊙ CDN 30-31 Z 2
Curtis River ~ CDN 30-31 Z 2
Curu, Rio ~ BR 68-69 J 3
Curuá o BR 62-63 G 6
Curuá, Ilha do ⌒ BR 62-63 J 5
Curuá, Rio ~ BR 62-63 G 6
Curuá, Rio ~ BR 66-67 K 7
Curuaés, Rio ~ BR 66-67 K 7
Curuaí o BR 66-67 K 4
Curuá ou Cururu, Rio ~ BR 72-73 D 3
Curuá-Una, Rio ~ BR 66-67 K 4
Curuça o BR 68-69 E 2
Curuçá, Ponta ▲ BR 68-69 E 2
Curuçá, Rio ~ BR 64-65 F 4
Curuduri, Rio ~ BR 66-67 F 2
Curuguaty o PY 76-77 K 3
Curuma la Grande, Cerro ▲ RA 78-79 H 4
Curumutopo o YV 60-61 J 4
Curup o RI 162-163 E 6
Curupá o BR 68-69 F 6
Curupaiti o BR 68-69 E 3
Curupira o BR 68-69 J 4
Curuquetê, Rio ~ BR 66-67 E 7
Cururu, Raudal ~ CO 66-67 B 2
Cururu-Açu, Rio ~ BR 66-67 J 7
Cururu ou Cururu-ri, Rio ~ BR 66-67 J 7
Cururupu o BR 68-69 F 2
Curuzú Cuatiá o RA 76-77 H 5
Curva del Turco o RA 76-77 F 3
Curva Grande o BR 68-69 F 3
Curvelo o BR 72-73 H 5
Curwood, Mount ▲ USA (MI) 270-271 K 4
Cushabatay, Río ~ PE 64-65 E 5
Cushamen o RA 78-79 D 7
Cushing o USA (MN) 270-271 D 4
Cushing o USA (OK) 264-265 H 3
Cushing o USA (TX) 268-269 F 5
Cushing o USA (WI) 270-271 F 5
Cusick o USA (WA) 244-245 H 2
Cusime o YV 60-61 J 5
Cusipata o PE 70-71 B 3
Cusis, Río ~ BOL 70-71 H 5
Čusovaja ~ RUS 96-97 L 5
Čusovoj ☆ RUS 96-97 K 4
Čusovskoe, ozero ⊙ RUS 114-115 D 4
Cusseta o USA (GA) 284-285 F 4
Cussivi ~ ANG 216-217 F 7
Cusso ~ ANG 216-217 C 7
Cusson, Pointe ▲ CDN 36-37 K 4
Čust o UZ 136-137 M 4
Custer o USA (MT) 250-251 M 5
Custer o USA (SD) 260-261 C 3
Custer Battlefield National Monument ∴ USA (MT) 250-251 M 6
Custer State Park ⊥ USA (SD) 260-261 C 3
Custódia o BR 68-69 K 6
Cusuco, Parque Nacional ⊥ HN 52-53 K 4
Cutato o ANG (BIE) 216-217 D 6
Cutato o ANG (CUA) 216-217 D 7
Cutato ~ ANG 216-217 D 5
Cutbank o CDN (SAS) 232-233 M 4
Cut Bank o USA (MT) 250-251 G 3
Cut Bank Creek ~ USA 250-251 G 3
Cutbank River ~ CDN 228-229 P 2
Cutenda o ANG 216-217 C 7
Cutervo o PE 64-65 C 5
Cutervo, Parque Nacional de ⊥ PE 64-65 C 5
Cuthbert o USA (GA) 284-285 F 5
Cutknife o CDN (SAS) 232-233 K 3
Cutler o USA (ME) 278-279 O 4
Čutove o UA 102-103 J 3
Cuttaburra Creek ~ AUS 178-179 H 5
Cutta Cutta Caves • AUS 172-173 L 3
Cuttack=Kataka o IND 142-143 D 5
Cutzamala de Pinzón o MEX 52-53 D 2
Čuvanajskie gory ▲ RUS 112-113 O 3
Čuvanskij hrebet ▲ RUS 112-113 O 4
Čuvanskoe o RUS 112-113 O 4
Cuvelai o ANG (CUN) 216-217 C 7
Cuvelai ~ ANG 216-217 D 7
Cuvette ▪ RCB 210-211 E 4
Cuvo ~ ANG 216-217 C 5
Cuxhaven o D 92-93 K 2
Cuxiuara, Ilha ⌒ BR 66-67 G 4
Cuy, El o RA 78-79 E 5
Cuyabeno, Reserva Faunística ⊥ EC 64-65 E 2
Cuyahoga Valley National Recreation Area ⊥ USA (OH) 280-281 E 2
Cuyama o USA (CA) 248-249 E 5
Cuyo, El o MEX 52-53 L 1
Cuyo East Passage ≈ 160-161 D 7
Cuyo "English Game" Subterranean National Park ⊥ RP 160-161 D 7
Cuyo Island ⌒ RP 160-161 D 7
Cuyo Islands ⌒ RP 160-161 D 7
Cuyo West Passage ≈ 160-161 D 7
Cuyuni River ~ GUY 62-63 E 2
Čuzco ☆••• PE 70-71 B 3
Čuzik ~ RUS 114-115 P 5
Čvrsnica ▲ BIH 100-101 F 3
Cyamo River ~ USA 248-249 E 4
Cyangugu o RWA 212-213 B 5
Čyappara o RUS 118-119 P 4
Čyb ~ RUS 88-89 V 5
Čybyda ~ RUS 118-119 K 4
Cyclades = Kikládes ⌒ GR 100-101 K 6
Cycloop, Pegunungan ▲ RI 166-167 L 3
Cycloop Mountains Reserve ⊥• RI 166 167 L 3
Čyhyryn o UA 102-103 H 3
Čyjyrčyk, pereval ▲ KS 136-137 N 4
Čym o RUS 108-109 K 8
Cymric o CDN (SAS) 232-233 O 4
Čyna ~ RUS 118-119 M 5
Cynthia o AUS 178-179 L 3
Cynthia o CDN (ALB) 232-233 C 2
Cynthiana o USA (KY) 276-277 L 2
Cyohoha Sud, Lac ⊙ BU 212-213 C 5
Cypnavolok, mys ▲ RUS 88-89 M 2
Cypress o USA (LA) 268-269 G 5
Cypress Bayou ~ USA 276-277 D 5
Cypress Creek ~ USA 268-269 E 7
Cypress Gardens ∴• USA (FL) 286-287 H 4
Cypress Hills ▲ CDN 232-233 H 6
Cypress Hills Provincial Park ⊥ CDN (ALB) 232-233 H 6
Cypress Hills Provincial Park ⊥ CDN (SAS) 232-233 J 6
Cypress Provincial Park ⊥ CDN (BC) 230-231 F 4
Cypress River o CDN (MAN) 234-235 D 5
Cypress Springs, Lake < USA (TX) 264-265 J 5
Cyprus = Kypros ▪ CY 128-129 E 5
Čyra ~ RUS 118-119 M 4
Cyrene o ZW 218-219 E 5
Cyrene = Shahhāt ∴••• LAR 192-193 J 1
Cyril o USA (OK) 264-265 F 4
Cyrus Field Bay ≈ 36-37 R 3
Čyrvonae, vozero ⊙ BY 94-95 L 5
Cytherea o AUS 178-179 J 4
Czaplinek o• PL 92-93 O 2
Czar o CDN (ALB) 232-233 H 3
Czarnków o PL 92-93 O 2
Czech Republic = Česká Republika ▪ CZ 92-93 M 4
Czersk o PL 92-93 O 2
Częstochowa ☆• PL 92-93 P 3
Człuchów o• 92-93 O 2

D

Da'an o VRC 150-151 E 5
Daanbantayan o RP 160-161 F 7
Daan Viljoen Game Park ⊥ NAM 216-217 D 11
Daaquam o CDN (QUE) 240-241 E 4
Dab'a, Mahaṭṭat o JOR 130-131 E 2
Dabadougou o CI 202-203 G 5
Dabaga o EAT 214-215 H 5
Dabai o WAN 204-205 F 3
Dabajuro o YV 60-61 F 2
Dabakala ☆ CI 202-203 H 5
Dabancheng o VRC 146-147 J 4
Dabaray o AFG 134-135 M 3
Dabaro o SP 208-209 J 5
Daba Shan ▲ VRC 154-155 F 5
Dabassi o RG 202-203 C 4
Dabat o ETH 200-201 H 6
Dabatou o RG 202-203 E 4
Dabeiba o CO 60-61 C 4
Daben o VRC 156-157 F 7
Dābhāde o IND 138-139 D 10
Dabhoi o IND 138-139 D 8
Dābhol o IND 140-141 E 2
Dabie Shan ▲ VRC 154-155 J 6
Dablo o BF 202-203 K 3
Dabnou o RN 198-199 B 5
Dabo o SN 202-203 C 3
Dabola o RG 202-203 F 4
Dabou o CI 202-203 H 7
Daboya o GH 202-203 K 5
Dabra o IND 138-139 G 7
Dabsan Hu ⊙ VRC 144-145 K 2
Dabuk o RI 162-163 E 6
Dabus Wenz ~ ETH 208-209 B 3
Dabwa o TCH 198-199 F 5
Dacca = Dhaka ★•• BD 142-143 G 4
Đắc Glei o VN 158-159 J 3
Dachau o D 92-93 L 4
Dacheng o VRC 156-157 J 2
Dachenzhuang o VRC 154-155 K 2
Dachigam National Park ⊥ IND 138-139 E 2
Dachsteingruppe ▲ A 92-93 M 5
Dachung Yogma o IND 138-139 G 3
Dacia Seamount ≈ 188-189 E 5
Đắc Mil o VN 158-159 J 4
Dacre o CDN (ONT) 238-239 J 3
Đắc Song o VN 158-159 J 4
Đắc Tô o VN 158-159 J 3
Dadanawa o GUY 62-63 E 4
Dade City o USA (FL) 286-287 G 3
Dades, Gorges du •• MA 188-189 J 5
Dades, Oued ~ MA 188-189 J 5
Dadès, Vallée du ⩣ MA 188-189 H 5
Dadeville o USA (AL) 284-285 E 4
Dādhar o PK 134-135 M 4
Dadi, Tanjung ▲ RI 166-167 F 2
Dadong o VRC 156-157 F 5
Dadonghai • VRC 156-157 F 7
Dadra and Nagar Haveli ▪ IND 138-139 D 9
Dādu o PK 134-135 M 5
Daduan o VRC 156-157 J 2
Dādu Canal ~ PK 134-135 M 5
Dadu He ~ VRC 154-155 C 6
Dadukou o VRC 154-155 K 6
Dadynskoe, ozero ⊙ RUS 126-127 F 5
Daerah Istimewa Aceh ▪ RI 162-163 A 2
Daerah Istimewa Yogyakarta ▪ RI 168 C 4
Daet ☆ RP 160-161 E 5
Dafang o VRC 156-157 D 3
Dafanpu o VRC 154-155 G 2
Dafeng o VRC 154-155 M 5
Dafengding National Ecosystem Reserves ⊥ VRC 156-157 C 2
Daffat ad Dabāb ⩣ LAR 192-193 J 2
Dafina, ad- o KSA 130-131 H 6
Dafoe o CDN (SAS) 232-233 O 4
Dafor o GH 202-203 L 6
Dafra o TCH 206-207 D 3
Dafter o USA (MI) 270-271 O 4
Daga o BHT 142-143 F 2
Daga ⌒ ETH 208-209 C 3
Daga ~ SUD 208-209 A 4
Dagaari o SP 208-209 H 6
Daga Istephanos Monastery • ETH 208-209 C 3
Dagaldyn ~ RUS 108-109 c 7
Dagami o RP 160-161 F 7
Dagana o• SN 196-197 C 6
Dagandely ~ KZ 124-125 K 4
Daga Post o SUD 208-209 A 4
Dagash o SUD 200-201 F 3
Dagasuli, Pulau ⌒ RI 164-165 K 2
Dagda o LV 94-95 K 3
Dages Range ▲ PNG 183 F 3
Dagestan = Dagestan, Respublika ▪ RUS 126-127 G 5
Dagestanskie Ogni o RUS 126-127 H 6
Dagestanskij zapovednik ⊥ RUS 126-127 G 5
Daggaboersnek ▲ ZA 220-221 G 6
Daggett o USA (CA) 248-249 H 5
Daggyai Co ⊙ VRC 144-145 E 6
Dagida Game Reserve ⊥ WAN 204-205 F 4
Dagingggou ⊥• VRC 150-151 C 6
Daglung o VRC 144-145 H 6
Dagmar o OM 132-133 L 2
Dagmar o USA (MT) 250-251 P 3
Dagö = Hiiumaa saar ⌒ EST 94-95 H 2
Dagomys o RUS 126-127 C 6
Dagoudane-Pickine o SN 202-203 B 2
Dagua o CO 60-61 C 6
Daguan o VRC (SIC) 156-157 C 2
Daguan o VRC (YUN) 156-157 C 3
D'Aguilar Range ▲ AUS 178-179 M 4
Daguit o RP 160-161 E 5
Daguragu-Kurintji Aboriginal Land ⅄ AUS 172-173 K 4
Dagushan o VRC 150-151 D 8
Dagworth o AUS (QLD) 174-175 G 5
Dagworth o AUS (QLD) 178-179 G 1
Dagzhuka o VRC 144-145 G 6
Dah o RI 166-167 K 5
Dahab o ET 194-195 G 3
Dahabān o KSA 132-133 A 3
Dahadinni River ~ CDN 30-31 G 4
Dahānib, Ǧabal ▲ ET 194-195 G 6
Dahāwah, Ad o LAR 192-193 J 5
Dahbed o UZ 136-137 K 5
Daheba o VRC 144-145 M 3
Dahequ o VRC 154-155 C 3
Dahi, ad- o Y 132-133 C 6
Dahinda o CDN (SAS) 232-233 N 6
Dahiri o CI 202-203 H 7
Dahlak Archipelago ⌒ ER 200-201 K 5
Dahle o AFG 134-135 L 3
Dahle, Band-e < AFG 134-135 M 3
Dahlonega o USA (GA) 284-285 G 2
Dahmani o TN 190-191 G 3
Dahnā', ad- ▲ KSA 130-131 H 3
Dahnā', ad- ⩣ KSA 130-131 J 4
Dāhod o IND 138-139 E 8
Dahongliutan o VRC 144-145 B 3
Dahra, Corniche des ⌣ DZ 190-191 C 2
Dahra, Massif de ▲ DZ 190-191 C 2
Dahra Oil Field ⩣ LAR 192-193 G 2
Dahr Oualâta ⩣ RIM 196-197 G 6
Dahr Tîchît ⩣ RIM 196-197 F 5
Dahsa, Wādī d- ~ ET 194-195 E 4
Dahšūr o ET 194-195 E 3
Dahšūr, Pyramids of ∴••• ET 194-195 E 3
Dahūk ▪ IRQ 128-129 K 4
Dahūk ☆ IRQ (DAH) 128-129 K 4
Đại, Cửa ≈ 158-159 J 5
Dai, Pulau ⌒ RI 166-167 E 5
Daïa, Monts de ▲ DZ 188-189 L 3
Ḍaid, ad- o UAE 134-135 F 6
Daïet Akhicha ⊙ DZ 190-191 C 6
Dai Hai ⊙ VRC 154-155 H 1
Dai Island ⌒ SOL 184 I e 2
Dailing • VRC 150-151 G 4
Đại Lo'i o VN 156-157 D 7
Daimāniyāt, ad- ⌒ OM 132-133 K 2
Daimiel o E 98-99 F 5
Daingerfield o USA (TX) 264-265 K 5
Daintree o AUS 174-175 H 5
Daintree National Park ⊥ AUS 174-175 H 5
Dair, ad- o ET 194-195 F 5
Dair, Ǧabal ad- ▲ SUD 200-201 E 6
Dair al-Barāmūs ∴ ET 194-195 E 2
Dairana o RM 222-223 F 4
Dair as-Suryānī ∴• ET 194-195 E 2
Dā'irat ar-Riyy o IRQ 128-129 L 6
Dair az-Zaur ☆ SYR 128-129 J 5
Daireaux o RA 78-79 J 4
Dairen = Dalian o VRC 150-151 C 8
Dair Hāfir o SYR 128-129 G 4
Dair Mawās o ET 194-195 E 4
Dairūṭ o ET 194-195 E 4
Dairy o USA (OR) 244-245 D 8
Dairy Creek o AUS 176-177 C 2
Dairyland o USA (WI) 270-271 F 4
Dai-sen ▲ J 152-153 E 7
Daisengen-dake ▲ J 152-153 J 4
Daisen-Oki National Park ⊥ J 152-153 E 6
Daisetsuzan National Park ⊥ J 152-153 K 3
Dai Shan ⌒ VRC 154-155 N 6
Daisy o USA (OK) 264-265 J 4
Dai Xian o VRC 154-155 H 2
Daiyun Shan ▲ VRC 156-157 K 4
Dajabón ☆ DOM 54-55 K 5
Dajan nuur ⊙ MAU 146-147 J 1
Dajarra o AUS 178-179 E 1
Dajiuba o VRC 144-145 G 2
Daka ~ GH 202-203 K 5
Dakar ★• SN 202-203 B 2
Dakataua, Lake ⊙ PNG 183 F 3
Dakawa o EAT 214-215 J 4
Dakelangsi o VRC 144-145 G 6
Dakeshi o VRC 144-145 G 6
Dakata Shet' ~ ETH 208-209 F 5
Dakhla o RIM 196-197 E 4
Dakhlet Nouâdhibou ≈ 196-197 B 4
Dakhlet Nouâdhibou ▪ RIM 196-197 B 4
Dakingari o WAN 204-205 F 3
Daki Takwas o WAN 204-205 F 3
Đắk Nông o VN 158-159 J 4
Dako, Gunung ▲ RI 164-165 G 3
Dākoank o IND 140-141 L 6
Dakoro o RN 198-199 C 5
Dakota o USA (MN) 270-271 G 7
Dakota City o USA (IA) 274-275 D 2
Dakota City o USA (NE) 262-263 K 2
Dakovica o YU 100-101 H 3
Đakovo o• HR 100-101 G 2
Daksum o IND 138-139 E 3
Dala o ANG (LUS) 216-217 F 4
Dala o ANG (LUS) 216-217 F 5
Dala o SOL 184 I e 3
Dalaba o• RG 202-203 D 4
Dalaba o SN 202-203 D 3
Dalad Qi o VRC 154-155 G 1
Dalahaj o RUS 116-117 L 10
Dālahānī, Kūh-e ▲ IR 134-135 B 1
Dalai Nur ⊙ VRC 148-149 N 6
Dālakī o IR 134-135 D 4
Dālakī, Rūdhāne-ye ~ IR 134-135 D 4
Dalälven ~ S 86-87 H 6
Dalaman Çayı ~ TR 128-129 C 4
D'Alembert o CDN (QUE) 236-237 J 4
Dalāmī o SUD 206-207 K 3
Dalandole o SP 212-213 K 2
Dalangyun o MYA 142-143 J 6
Dalanzadgad ☆ MAU 148-149 G 6
Dala River ~ CDN 228-229 F 3
Dalark o USA (AR) 276-277 C 6
Dalarna ⩣ S 86-87 F 6
Dalat o MAL 162-163 J 3
Đà Lạt ☆•• VN 158-159 K 5
Dal'at Rašīd 'Abbās o IRQ 128-129 L 6
Dālbandin o PK 134-135 L 4
Dalbeg o AUS 174-175 J 7
Dalbo o USA (MN) 270-271 E 5
Dalby o AUS 178-179 L 4
Dalcahue o RCH 78-79 C 7
Dale o N (HOR) 86-87 B 6
Dale ☆ N (FJO) 86-87 B 6
Dale o USA (IN) 274-275 M 6
Dale o USA (OR) 244-245 E 6
Dale Hollow Lake ⊙ USA (TN) 276-277 K 4
Dalei Shan ▲ VRC 146-147 N 6
Dalemead o CDN (ALB) 232-233 E 5
Dalet o MYA 142-143 H 5
Daleville o USA (AL) 284-285 E 5
Dalgā' o ET 194-195 E 4
Dalgān o IR 134-135 H 5
Dalgaranga Hill ▲ AUS 176-177 D 3
Dalgety Brook ~ AUS 176-177 D 2
Dalgonally o AUS 174-175 F 7
Dălgopol o BG 102-103 E 6
Dalgyn ~ RUS 110-111 J 6
Dalhart o USA (TX) 264-265 B 2
Dalhousie o CDN (NB) 240-241 J 2
Dalhousie o IND 138-139 F 3
Dalhousie, Cape ▲ CDN 24-25 G 5
Dalhousie Road o CDN (NS) 240-241 L 6
Dalhousie West o CDN (NS) 240-241 K 6
Dali o RMM 202-203 G 2
Dali o VRC (SXI) 154-155 F 4
Dali o• VRC (YUN) 142-143 M 3
Ḍāli', aḍ- o• Y 132-133 D 7
Dalian o VRC 150-151 C 8
Daliang Shan ▲ VRC 156-157 C 2
Dālimb o IND 140-141 G 2
Dali Sharafat o SUD 200-201 F 6
Dalkola o IND 142-143 E 3
Dall, Mount ▲ USA 20-21 O 5
Dallas o CDN (MAN) 234-235 F 3
Dallas o USA (GA) 284-285 F 3
Dallas o USA (OR) 244-245 B 6
Dallas o• USA (TX) 264-265 H 6
Dallas City o USA (IL) 274-275 G 4
Dalles, The o USA (OR) 244-245 D 5
Dalli o WAN 204-205 J 4
Dall Island ⌒ USA 32-33 D 4
Dall Lake ⊙ USA 20-21 J 6
Dalmā ⌒ UAE 134-135 E 6
Dalmacija ⩣ HR 100-101 E 3
Dalmacio Vélez Sarsfield o RA 78-79 H 2
Dalmas, Lac ⊙ CDN 38-39 J 2
Dalmatia = Dalmacija ⩣ HR 100-101 E 3
Dalmatovo ☆ RUS 114-115 G 6
Dalmeny o CDN (SAS) 232-233 M 3
Dalmǧ, Haur ⊙ IRQ 128-129 L 6
Dal'nee o RUS 122-123 K 5
Dal'negorsk o RUS 122-123 F 6
Dal'nerečensk o RUS 122-123 E 6
Dal'nij o RUS 120-121 R 7
Dal'nije Zelency o RUS 88-89 O 2
Dalñoe o KZ 124-125 E 2
Dalny o CDN (MAN) 234-235 C 5
Daloa ☆ CI 202-203 G 6
Dalong o VRC 156-157 F 3
Dalrymple, Mount ▲ AUS 178-179 K 1
Dalrymple Lake < AUS 174-175 J 7
Dalsland ⩣ S 86-87 F 7
Dalsmynni o IS 86-87 c 2
Daltenganj o IND 142-143 D 3
Dalton o CDN (ONT) 236-237 D 4
Dalton o USA (GA) 284-285 F 2
Dalton o USA (NE) 262-263 D 3
Dalton Gardens o USA (ID) 250-251 C 4
Dalton Ice Tongue ⊂ ARK 16 G 13
Daltro Filho o BR 74-75 D 6
Dalu o VRC 154-155 D 3
Daludalu o RI 162-163 D 4
Dalugama o CL 140-141 H 7
Dalupiri Island ⌒ RP (CAG) 160-161 D 3
Dalupiri Island ⌒ RP (NSA) 160-161 F 6
Dalu Shan ▲ VRC 156-157 E 2
Dalvík o IS 86-87 d 2
Dalwallinu o AUS 176-177 D 5
Dalwhinnie o GB 90-91 E 3
Dalyr o RUS 110-111 R 4
Daly River ⅄ AUS (NT) 172-173 K 2
Daly River ~ AUS 172-173 K 2
Daly River Aboriginal Land ⅄ AUS 172-173 J 2
Daly River Wildlife Sanctuary ⊥ AUS 172-173 J 2
Daly Waters o AUS 174-175 B 5
Dal'za, ozero ⊙ RUS 122-123 H 2
Dalzell o CDN (SAS) 232-233 Q 5
Dam, Am- o TCH 198-199 K 6
Damā, Wādī ~ KSA 130-131 E 4
Damad o KSA 132-133 C 5
Damagarete ☆ RP 160-161 E 8
Dāmān o AFG 134-135 L 3
Dāmān ☆ IND 138-139 D 9
Damān and Diu ▪ IND 138-139 D 9
Damān and Diu ▪ IND 138-139 C 9
Dāmane o IR 134-135 D 2
Damanhūr ☆ ET 194-195 E 2
Damant Lake ⊙ CDN 30-31 R 5
Damaqun Shan ▲ VRC 148-149 M 7
Ḍamār ☆ Y 132-133 D 6
Damar, Kepulauan ⌒ RI 166-167 E 5
Damar, Pulau ⌒ RI (MAL) 164-165 L 4
Damar, Pulau ⌒ RI (MAL) 166-167 E 5
Damara o RCA 206-207 D 6
Damaraland ⩣ NAM 216-217 B 9
Damardatar o RI 164-165 D 5
Damariscotta o USA (ME) 278-279 M 4
Damar Laut o MAL 162-163 D 2
Damasak o WAN 198-199 F 6
Damas Cays ⌒ BS 54-55 F 3
Damascus o USA (AR) 276-277 C 5
Damascus o USA (GA) 284-285 F 5
Damascus o USA (VA) 280-281 E 7
Damascus = Dimašq ★••• SYR 128-129 G 6
Damaturu o WAN 204-205 J 3
Damauli o NEP 144-145 E 7
Damāvand o IR 136-137 C 7
Damāvand, Kūh-e ▲•• IR 136-137 C 7
Damazine o SUD 208-209 B 3
Damba o ANG 216-217 C 3
Dambai o GH 202-203 L 5
Dambam o WAN 204-205 J 3
Damboa o WAN 204-205 K 3
Dambulla o••• CL 140-141 J 7
Dam Creek ~ USA 264-265 K 6
Dame Marie o RH 54-55 H 5
Dame Marie, Cape ▲ RH 54-55 H 5
Dāmgān o• IR 136-137 D 6
Damietta = Dumyāṭ ☆ ET (DUM) 194-195 E 2
Dāmin, Rūdhāne-ye ~ IR 134-135 J 5
Dammām, ad- ☆ KSA 134-135 D 5
Dāmnagar o IND 138-139 C 9
Dāmodar ~ IND 142-143 E 4
Damoh o IND 138-139 G 8
Damongo o GH 202-203 K 5
Damortis o RP 160-161 D 4
Dampar o WAN 204-205 J 4
Dampelas, Tanjung ▲ RI 164-165 F 3
Damphu o BHT 142-143 G 2
Dampier o AUS 172-173 C 6
Dampier Archipelago ⌒ AUS 172-173 C 6
Dampier Downs o AUS 172-173 F 5
Dampier Land ⩣ AUS 172-173 F 4
Dampier Strait ≈ 183 E 3
Dampir, Selat ≈ 166-167 F 2
Damqaut o Y 132-133 H 5
Dam Qu ~ VRC 144-145 J 4
Damrūr o KSA 132-133 A 3
Damt o Y 132-133 D 6
Damtang o VRC 144-145 D 4
Damtar o TCH 206-207 C 3
Damwal o ZA 220-221 J 2
Damxung o VRC 144-145 H 5
Dana o CDN (SAS) 232-233 N 3
Dana, Lac ⊙ CDN (QUE) 236-237 L 2
Dana, Mount ▲ USA (CA) 248-249 E 2
Dana Barat, Kepulauan ⌒ RI 166-167 C 5
Danané ☆ CI 202-203 F 6
Đà Nẵng ☆• VN 158-159 K 2
Danao o RP 160-161 F 7
Danas Banke ≈ 28-29 P 5
Danau Rombebai ⊙ RI 166-167 J 2
Danau Toba ⊙•• RI 162-163 C 3
Danba o VRC 154-155 B 6
Danbatta o WAN 198-199 D 6
Danbury o USA (CT) 280-281 N 2
Danbury o USA (WI) 270-271 F 4
Danby Lake ⊙ USA (CA) 248-249 J 6
Dan Chang o THA 158-159 E 3
Dancheng o VRC 154-155 J 5
Dandara o ET (QIN) 194-195 F 4
Dandara ∴•• ET (QIN) 194-195 F 4
Dandaragan o AUS 176-177 C 5
Dandau o ANG 216-217 D 5
Dande o ETH 208-209 C 6
Dandeli o IND 140-141 F 3
Dandenong o AUS 180-181 H 4
Dandenong Park o AUS 174-175 J 7
Dando o ANG 216-217 D 5
Dandong o VRC 150-151 E 7
Daneborg o GRØ 26-27 p 6
Danesfahan o IR 128-129 N 5
Danfeng o VRC 154-155 G 5
Danforth o USA (ME) 278-279 O 3
Dang o CAM 204-205 K 6
Danga o RMM 196-197 J 6
Dangara o TJ 136-137 L 5
Dangar Falls ~• AUS 178-179 L 6
Dangchang o VRC 154-155 D 4
Danger Point ▲ ZA 220-221 D 7
Dange o WAN 198-199 B 6
Danger Area ⅹⅹ USA (NV) 246-247 G 4
Dangerous Cape ▲ USA 22-23 U 4
Danggali Conservation Park ⊥ AUS 180-181 F 2
Dangila o ETH 208-209 C 3
Dangjin Shankou ▲ VRC 146-147 M 6
Dangoura, Mont ▲ RCA 206-207 H 5
Dangriga o BH 52-53 K 3
Dangshan o VRC 154-155 K 4
Dangtu o VRC 154-155 L 6
Dan-Gulbi o WAN 204-205 G 3
Dangur o ETH (Goj) 200-201 G 6
Dangur ▲ ETH 208-209 B 3
Dangyang o VRC 154-155 G 6
Daniel o USA (WY) 252-253 H 4
Daniel's Harbour o CDN (NFL) 242-243 L 2
Danielskuil o ZA 220-221 F 4
Danielson o USA (CT) 278-279 K 7
Danielson Provincial Park ⊥ CDN (SAS) 232-233 M 4
Danilov o RUS 94-95 R 2
Danilovka o RUS 96-97 D 8
Danilovskaja vozvyšennost' ▲ RUS 94-95 Q 2
Daning o VRC 154-155 G 3
Daninghe • VRC 154-155 F 6
Danja o WAN 204-205 G 3
Danjiangkou o••• VRC 154-155 G 5
Danjiankou Sk. ⊙ VRC 154-155 G 5
Danjo-guntō ⌒ J 152-153 C 8
Dank o OM 132-133 K 2
Dankov o RUS 94-95 Q 5
Danli o HN 52-53 L 4
Danmark Fjord ≈ 26-27 n 2
Danmark Ø ⌒ GRØ 26-27 m 8
Danmarkshavn o GRØ 26-27 q 5
Dannebrogs Ø ⌒ GRØ 28-29 V 4
Dannemora o USA (NY) 278-279 H 4
Dannenberg (Elbe) o D 92-93 L 2
Dannevirke o NZ 182 F 4
Dannhauser o ZA 220-221 K 4
Dano o BF 202-203 J 4
Danot o ETH 208-209 G 5
Danridge o USA (TN) 282-283 D 4
Dan River ~ USA 282-283 H 4
Dan Sadau o WAN 204-205 G 3
Dansary, köl ⊙ KZ 124-125 D 4
Danskøya ⌒ N 84-85 G 3
Dansville o USA (NY) 278-279 D 6
Dānta o IND 138-139 D 7
Dantalpalli o IND 140-141 H 2
Dantcho o RT 202-203 L 5
Dante o USA (VA) 280-281 D 7
Dante = Xaafuun o SP 208-209 K 3
Danube = Donau ~ D 8 F 4
Danubyu o MYA 158-159 C 2
Danum Valley Conservation Area ⊥ MAL 160-161 B 10
Danville o CDN (QUE) 238-239 N 3
Danville o USA (AR) 276-277 B 5
Danville o USA (GA) 284-285 G 4
Danville o USA (IL) 274-275 L 4
Danville o USA (IN) 274-275 M 5
Danville o USA (KY) 276-277 L 3
Danville o USA (PA) 280-281 K 3
Danville o USA (VA) 280-281 G 7

Cumaribo — Danville 319

Danville o **USA** (WA) 244-245 G 2
Dan Xian o **VRC** 156-157 F 7
Danxiashan • **VRC** 156-157 H 4
Danyang o **VRC** 154-155 L 5
Danyi-Apéyémé o **RT** 202-203 L 6
Danzhai o **VRC** 156-157 E 3
Danzhou o **VRC** 156-157 F 4
Đao Lý So'n ⌒ **VN** 158-159 K 3
Daoro o **CI** 202-203 G 7
Daotanghe o **VRC** 154-155 B 3
Dao Thổ Chu' ⌒ **VN** 158-159 G 6
Daoud o **DZ** 188-189 L 3
Daoukro o **CI** 202-203 J 6
Daoula, Hassi o **DZ** 190-191 E 4
Daoura, Hamada de la ⊥ **DZ** 188-189 K 6
Daoura, Oued ~ **DZ** 188-189 J 5
Dao Xian o **VRC** 156-157 G 4
Daozhen o **VRC** 156-157 E 2
Dapa o **RP** 160-161 G 8
Dapaong ☆ **RT** 202-203 L 4
Dapchi o **WAN** 198-199 E 6
Dapélogo o **BF** 202-203 K 3
Đa Phúc ☆ **VN** 156-157 D 6
Dapitan o **RP** 160-161 E 8
Dāpoli o **IND** 140-141 E 2
Dapolinė o **IND** 142-143 J 2
Dapsang = K2 ▲ **PK** 138-139 F 2
Dapuchaihe o **VRC** 150-151 G 6
Da Qaidam o **VRC** 144-145 K 2
Daqiao o **VRC** 156-157 C 3
Daqing o **VRC** 150-151 E 4
Daqinggou ⊥ • **VRC** 150-151 C 6
Daqing Shan ▲ **VRC** 154-155 G 1
Dara o **SN** 202-203 C 2
Dar'a ☆ **SYR** 128-129 G 6
Dārāb o • **IR** 134-135 F 4
Darab ⊥ **SP** 212-213 H 3
Darāban o **PK** 138-139 C 4
Daradou o **RCA** 206-207 G 6
Darāfisa o **SUD** 200-201 F 6
Daraj o **LAR** 190-191 H 5
Dār al-Hamrā', ad- o **KSA** 132-133 B 3
Dārān o **IR** 134-135 D 2
Darapap o **PNG** 183 C 2
Darasun o **RUS** 118-119 F 10
Darasun, Kurort o **RUS** 118-119 F 10
Darasunskij, Veršino o **RUS** 118-119 G 9
Darauli o **IND** 142-143 D 2
Darāw o **ET** 194-195 F 5
Darazo o **WAN** 204-205 J 3
Darb, ad- o **KSA** 132-133 C 5
Darband o **IR** 134-135 G 3
Darband, Kūh-e ▲ **IR** 134-135 G 3
Darband-e Hān o **IRQ** 128-129 M 5
Darband Sar ▲ **IR** 136-137 B 6
Darbhanga o **IND** 142-143 D 2
D'Arbonne National Wildlife Refuge ⊥ **USA** (LA) 268-269 H 4
Darby o **USA** (MT) 250-251 E 5
Darby, Cape ▲ **USA** 20-21 J 4
Darby Creek ~ **USA** 280-281 C 4
Darby Mountains ▲ **USA** 20-21 J 4
Dar Chioukh o **DZ** 190-191 D 3
D'Arcy o **CDN** (BC) 230-231 G 3
D'Arcy o **CDN** (SAS) 232-233 K 4
Darda o **AUS** 176-177 F 3
Dār Dahūka o **Y** 132-133 E 7
Dardanelle o **USA** (AR) 276-277 B 5
Dardanelle Lake o **USA** (AR) 276-277 B 5
Dareda o **EAT** 212-213 E 6
Dar el Barka o **RIM** 196-197 C 6
Dar el Beida = Ad-Dār-al-Bayda ☆ • **MA** 188-189 H 4
Darende ☆ **TR** 128-129 G 3
Dar es Salaam ☆ • **EAT** 214-215 K 4
Dareton o **AUS** 180-181 G 3
Darfield o **CDN** (BC) 230-231 J 2
Dārfūr ⊥ **SUD** 206-207 F 2
Dargan-Ata o **UZ** 136-137 H 4
Dargaville o **NZ** 182 D 1
Dargeçit ☆ **TR** 128-129 J 4
Dargo o **AUS** 180-181 J 4
Dargol o **RN** 202-203 L 3
Darhala o **CI** 202-203 H 5
Darhan o **MAU** 148-149 G 3
Darhan Muminggan Lianheqi o **VRC** 148-149 K 7
Darién ⊥ **PA** 60-61 B 3
Darien o **USA** (GA) 284-285 J 5
Darien = Calima o **CO** 60-61 C 6
Darién, Golfo del ≈ 60-61 C 3
Darién, Parque Nacional de ⊥ ••• **PA** 52-53 F 8
Darién, Serranía del ▲ **PA** 52-53 E 7
Darien Center o **USA** (NY) 278-279 C 6
Dariha, Abū o **SYR** 128-129 G 5
Dārīn o **KSA** 134-135 D 5
Dar'inskij ☆ **KZ** 124-125 H 4
Dario Meira o **BR** 72-73 L 3
Dārjiling o **IND** 142-143 F 2
Dārjing o **IND** 142-143 D 5
Darkan o **AUS** 176-177 D 6
Darke Peak o **AUS** 180-181 D 2
Darkylah o **RUS** 120-121 D 3
Darling o **ZA** 220-221 D 6
Darling, Mount ▲ **AUS** 180-181 K 3
Darling Downs ⊥ **AUS** 178-179 L 4
Darlingford o **CDN** (MAN) 234-235 E 5
Darling Peninsula ~ **CDN** 26-27 O 4
Darling Range ▲ **AUS** 176-177 D 5
Darling River ~ **AUS** 178-179 H 6
Darling River ~ **AUS** 180-181 G 2
Darlington o **GB** 90-91 G 4
Darlington o **USA** (FL) 286-287 C 1
Darlington o **USA** (SC) 284-285 L 2
Darlington o **USA** (WI) 274-275 H 2
Darlington Point o **AUS** 180-181 H 3
Darlot, Lake o **AUS** 176-177 F 3
Darłowo o • **PL** 92-93 O 1
Darmazār o **IR** 134-135 G 4
Darmiyān o **IR** 134-135 H 2
Darmody o **CDN** (SAS) 232-233 M 5
Darmstadt o • **D** 92-93 K 4
Darnah ▫ **LAR** 192-193 K 1
Darnah ☆ **LAR** (DAR) 192-193 K 1
Darnall o **ZA** 220-221 K 4
Darnétal o **F** 90-91 H 7
Darnick o **AUS** 180-181 G 2
Darnis = Darnah ☆ **LAR** 192-193 K 1
Darnley, Cape ▲ **ARK** 16 G 7
Darnley Bay ≈ 24-25 K 6
Darnley Island ⌒ **AUS** 183 B 5
Daro o **MAL** 162-163 J 3
Daroca o **E** 98-99 G 4
Darouma ~ **RMM** 202-203 F 2
Darou-Mousti o **SN** 202-203 B 2
Darovskoe o **RUS** 96-97 E 4
Darre Angīr, Kavīr-e o **IR** 134-135 F 2
Darregaz o **IR** 136-137 F 6
Darregueira o **RA** 78-79 H 4
Darre Qeyād ~ **IR** 134-135 C 2
Darre Šahr o **IR** 134-135 B 2
Darre-ye Būm o **AFG** 136-137 H 7
Darre-ye Ṣūf o **AFG** 136-137 K 7
Darrington o **USA** (WA) 244-245 D 2
D'Arros Island ⌒ **SY** 224 C 2
Darr River ~ **AUS** 178-179 G 2
Darrūd o **IR** 136-137 F 6
Darsana o **BD** 142-143 F 4
Dartford o **GB** 90-91 H 6
Dartmoor o **AUS** 180-181 F 4
Dartmoor National Park ⊥ **GB** 90-91 F 6
Dartmouth o **CDN** (NS) 240-241 M 6
Dartmouth, Lake o **AUS** 178-179 H 4
Dartmouth Reservoir < **AUS** 180-181 J 4
Daru o **PNG** 183 B 5
Daru o **WAL** 202-203 E 6
Daruba o **RI** 164-165 L 2
Darubia o **PNG** 183 F 5
Daru Island ⌒ **PNG** 183 B 5
Daruvar o **HR** 100-101 F 2
Darvaza o **TM** 136-137 F 4
Darvazskij hrebet ▲ **TJ** 136-137 M 5
Darvel, Teluk ≈ 160-161 C 10
Darvi = Bulgan o **MAU** 146-147 L 2
Darvills o **USA** (VA) 280-281 J 6
Darvinskij zapovednik ⊥ **RUS** 94-95 P 2
Darvoza o **UZ** 136-137 K 4
Darwaz o **AFG** 136-137 M 5
Darwāzagai o **AFG** 134-135 M 3
Darwell o **CDN** (ALB) 232-233 D 2
Darwendale o **ZW** 218-219 F 3
Dārwha o **IND** 138-139 F 9
Darwin ☆ **AUS** 172-173 K 2
Darwin o **GB** 78-79 L 6
Darwin o **USA** (OH) 280-281 D 4
Darwin, Bahía ≈ 80 C 2
Darwin, Canal ≈ 80 C 2
Darwin, Cordillera ▲ **RCH** 80 E 7
Darwin, Cordillera de ▲ **RCH** 76-77 C 4
Darwin, Isla ⌒ **EC** 64-65 B 9
Darwin, Mont o **ZW** 218-219 F 3
Darwin, Volcán ▲ **EC** 64-65 B 10
Darwin River o **AUS** 172-173 K 2
Daryāče-ye Taškoi **IR** 134-135 E 4
Darya Khān o **PK** 138-139 C 4
Daryaleh o **SP** 208-209 G 4
Daryāpur o **IND** 138-139 F 9
Daryā-ye Hazar ≈ 136-137 B 7
Daryā-ye Vāhān ~ **AFG** 136-137 N 6
Darza ⌒ **Y** 132-133 H 7
Dārzīn o **IR** 134-135 H 4
Dās ⌒ **UAE** 134-135 E 6
Dasāda o **IND** 138-139 C 8
Dašbalbar o **MAU** 148-149 M 3
Dashan o **VRC** 156-157 D 3
Dashapalla o **IND** 142-143 D 5
Dashennongjia ▲ **VRC** 154-155 G 6
Dashennongjia ▲ **VRC** 154-155 G 6
Dashhowuz = Dažhovuz ☆ **TM** 136-137 F 4
Dashuikeng o **VRC** 154-155 E 3
Dashwood o **CDN** (BC) 230-231 E 4
Dašinčilėn = Suuž o **MAU** 148-149 G 4
Daska o **PK** 138-139 E 3
Dasol Bay ≈ 160-161 C 5
Dass o **WAN** 204-205 H 3
Dassa o **DY** 204-205 E 5
Dassabolo ~ **RIM** 202-203 E 3
Dassari o **DY** 202-203 L 4
Dassel o **USA** (MN) 270-271 D 5
Dasseneiland ⌒ **ZA** 220-221 D 6
Dastak o **IR** 134-135 D 2
Dašt-e 'Abbās o **IR** 134-135 B 1
Dašt-e Palang, Rūd-e ~ **IR** 134-135 D 4
Dašt-e Qal'e o • **AFG** 136-137 L 6
Dāsū o **PK** 138-139 D 2
Datang o **VRC** (GXI) 156-157 F 4
Datang o **VRC** (GXI) 156-157 F 5
Datça ☆ **TR** 128-129 B 4
Date o **J** 152-153 J 3
Dateland o **USA** (AZ) 256-257 B 6
Datian o **VRC** 156-157 K 4
Datian Ding ▲ **VRC** 156-157 G 5
Datian Z.B. ⊥ • **VRC** 156-157 F 7
Datil o **USA** (NM) 256-257 H 4
Datil Well National Recreation Site • **USA** (NM) 256-257 H 4
Dating o **VRC** 156-157 E 4
Datkan o **MYA** 142-143 J 6
Datong o **VRC** (QIN) 154-155 B 3
Datong o **VRC** (SHA) 154-155 H 1
Datong o **VRC** (XUZ) 146-147 C 7
Datong He ~ **VRC** 154-155 B 3
Datong Shan ▲ **VRC** 144-145 M 2
Datori o **DY** 202-203 L 4
Dato Temple • **VRC** (SIC) 156-157 C 2
Dato Temple • **VRC** (SIC) 156-157 D 2
Datta o **CI** 202-203 H 7
Datta o **RUS** 122-123 J 4
Datton, Kap ▲ **GRØ** 28-29 c 2
Datu, Tanjung ▲ **RI** 162-163 H 3
Datu, Teluk ≈ 162-163 J 4
Datuk, Tanjung ▲ **RI** 162-163 E 4
Datu Piang o **RP** 160-161 F 9
Dau o **RP** 160-161 D 5
Daub o **RI** 166-167 L 6
Dāūd Khel o **PK** 138-139 C 3
Daudmannsodden ▲ **N** 84-85 H 3
Daudnagar o **IND** 142-143 D 3
Daugaard Jensen Land ⊥ **GRØ** 26-27 T 3
Daugava ~ **LV** 94-95 K 3
Daugavpils ☆ • **LV** 94-95 K 4
Dauka o **OM** 132-133 J 4
Daule o **EC** 64-65 C 2
Daule o **RI** 164-165 H 6
Daule, Río ~ **EC** 64-65 B 2
D'Aunay Bugt ≈ 28-29 c 2
Daund o **IND** 138-139 E 10
Daung Kyun ⌒ **MYA** 158-159 E 4
Dauphin o **CDN** (MAN) 234-235 C 3
Dauphiné ⊥ **F** 90-91 K 9
Dauphin Island o **USA** (AL) 284-285 B 6
Dauphin Island ⌒ **USA** (AL) 284-285 B 6
Dauphin Lake o **CDN** (MAN) 234-235 D 3
Dauphin River ~ **CDN** 234-235 E 3
Daura o **WAN** 198-199 D 6
Daurān, Ǧabal ▲ **Y** 132-133 D 6
Daur'an, Wādī ~ **Y** 132-133 F 6
Daurkina, poluostrov ⌣ **RUS** 112-113 Y 3
Daus o **KSA** 132-133 B 3
Dausa o **IND** 138-139 F 6
Dâu Tiêng o **VN** 158-159 J 5
Dautkŭl suvombori < **UZ** 136-137 F 3
Dāvangere o **IND** 140-141 F 3
Davao City o **RP** 160-161 F 9
Davao Gulf ≈ 160-161 F 9
Dāvari o **IR** 134-135 G 5
Dāvarzan o **IR** 136-137 E 6
Davenda o **RUS** 118-119 J 9
Davenport o **USA** (CA) 248-249 B 2
Davenport o **USA** (IA) 274-275 H 3
Davenport o **USA** (ND) 258-259 K 5
Davenport o **USA** (WA) 244-245 G 3
Davenport Creek ~ **AUS** 178-179 D 5
Davenport Downs o **AUS** 178-179 F 3
Davenport Range ▲ **AUS** 174-175 C 7
David ☆ •• **PA** 52-53 C 7
David City o **USA** (NE) 262-263 J 3
David Crockett State Park ⊥ **USA** (TN) 276-277 H 5
Davidof Island ⌒ **USA** 22-23 F 7
Davidson o **CDN** (SAS) 232-233 N 4
Davidson o **USA** (OK) 264-265 E 4
Davidson, Mount ▲ **AUS** 172-173 K 6
Davidson Bank ≃ 22-23 O 6
Davidson Mountains ▲ **USA** 20-21 T 2
Davieau Island ⌒ **CDN** 36-37 L 6
Davilla o **USA** (TX) 266-267 K 3
Davin o **CDN** (SAS) 232-233 O 5
Davinópolis o **BR** 72-73 G 5
Davis o **USA** (CA) 246-247 D 5
Davis o **USA** (OK) 264-265 G 4
Davis o **USA** (SD) 260-261 J 3
Davis, Fort o **USA** (TX) 266-267 D 3
Davis Bay ≈ 16 G 14
Davis Creek o **USA** (CA) 246-247 E 2
Davis Dam o **USA** (AZ) 256-257 A 3
Davis Mountains ▲ **USA** 266-267 C 3
Davis National Historic Site, Fort ∴ **USA** (TX) 266-267 D 3
Davison o **USA** (MI) 272-273 F 4
Davis River ~ **AUS** 172-173 E 7
Davis Sea ≈ 16 G 10
Davisville o **USA** (NH) 278-279 K 5
Davlekanovo ☆ **RUS** 96-97 J 6
Davo ~ **CI** 202-203 G 7
Davos o • **CH** 92-93 K 5
Davša o **RUS** 118-119 D 8
Davy Crockett Lake o **USA** (TN) 282-283 E 4
Davy Lake o **CDN** 30-31 P 6
Davy Sund ≈ 26-27 o 7
Dawa o **VRC** 150-151 D 7
Dawab o **SUD** 200-201 F 4
Dawadawa o **GH** 202-203 K 5
Dawa Dawa o **RP** 160-161 E 9
Dawādimī, ad- o • **KSA** 130-131 J 5
Dawangstan SK o **VRC** 156-157 F 5
Dawa Wenz ~ **ETH** 208-209 D 6
Dawelor, Pulau ⌒ **RI** 166-167 F 5
Dawera, Pulau ⌒ **RI** 166-167 E 5
Dawes Range ▲ **AUS** 178-179 L 3
Dawhat Salwā ≈ 134-135 D 6
Dawhenya o **GH** 202-203 L 7
Dawir o **SUD** 206-207 L 4
Dawn o **USA** (OH) 280-281 B 3
Dawn o **USA** (TX) 264-265 B 4
Dawn o **USA** (VA) 280-281 J 6
Dawson o **CDN** 20-21 V 4
Dawson o **USA** (GA) 284-285 F 5
Dawson o **USA** (MN) 270-271 B 6
Dawson o **USA** (ND) 258-259 H 5
Dawson, Isla ⌒ **RCH** 80 E 6
Dawson, Mount ▲ **CDN** (BC) 230-231 M 2
Dawson Bay o **CDN** (MAN) 234-235 C 2
Dawson Bay Indian Reserve ✕ **CDN** (MAN) 234-235 C 2
Dawson Creek o **CDN** 32-33 K 4
Dawson Highway ll **AUS** 178-179 K 3
Dawson-Lambton Glacier ⊂ **ARK** 16 F 33
Dawson Range ▲ **AUS** 178-179 K 2
Dawson Range ▲ **CDN** 20-21 V 5
Dawson River ~ **AUS** 178-179 K 3
Dawsons Landing o **CDN** (BC) 230-231 B 2
Dawson Springs o **USA** (KY) 276-277 H 3
Dawsonville o **CDN** (NB) 240-241 J 3
Dawsonville o **USA** (GA) 284-285 F 2
Dawu o **VRC** (HUB) 154-155 J 6
Dawu o **VRC** (SIC) 154-155 B 6
Daww, ad- ☆ **SYR** 128-129 G 5
Dax o **F** 90-91 G 10
Daxi o **VRC** 156-157 M 2
Da Xian o **VRC** 154-155 E 6
Daxin o **VRC** 156-157 E 5
Daxue Shan ▲ **VRC** 154-155 B 6
Day o **USA** (CA) 246-247 D 2
Daya o **RIM** 196-197 E 5
Dayang Bunting, Pulau ⌒ **MAL** 162-163 C 1
Dayangshu o **VRC** 150-151 E 3
Dayao o **VRC** 156-157 B 4
Daya Wan ≈ 156-157 J 5
Dayaxa o **SP** 208-209 H 3
Daybabān, Shut'bat ad ~ **LAR** 192-193 D 3
Dayi ~ **GH** 202-203 L 6
Dayi o **VRC** 154-155 C 6
Dayi o **WAN** 204-205 G 3
Daylesford o **AUS** 180-181 H 4
Daylight Pass ▲ **USA** (CA) 248-249 H 3
Daymán, Cuchilla del ▲ **ROU** 76-77 J 6
Daymán, Río ~ **ROU** 76-77 J 6
Dayong o **VRC** 156-157 G 2
Days Creek o **USA** (OR) 244-245 B 8
Daysland o **CDN** (ALB) 232-233 F 3
Dayton o **USA** (MT) 250-251 E 4
Dayton o **USA** (NV) 246-247 F 4
Dayton o **USA** (OH) 280-281 B 4
Dayton o **USA** (OR) 244-245 B 5
Dayton o **USA** (TN) 276-277 K 5
Dayton o **USA** (TX) 268-269 F 6
Dayton o **USA** (WA) 244-245 H 4
Dayton o **USA** (WY) 252-253 L 2
Daytona Beach o **USA** (FL) 286-287 H 2
Dayu o **RI** 164-165 D 4
Dayu o **VRC** 156-157 J 4
Dayul Gömpa o **VRC** 144-145 M 6
Da Yunhe ~ **VRC** 154-155 M 6
Dayville o **USA** (OR) 244-245 F 6
Dazey o **USA** (ND) 258-259 J 4
Dazhou Dao ⌒ **VRC** 156-157 G 7
Dažhovuz ☆ **TM** 136-137 F 4
Dazhu o **VRC** 154-155 E 6
Dazkırı ☆ **TR** 128-129 C 4
Dazu o **VRC** 156-157 D 2
Dazu Shike • **VRC** 156-157 D 2
Dchira o **WSA** 188-189 E 7
Dead Horse Point State Park • **USA** (UT) 254-255 F 5
Dead Indian Peak ▲ **USA** (WY) 252-253 J 2
Dead Lake o **USA** (MN) 270-271 C 4
Dead Lake < **USA** (FL) 286-287 D 1
Deadman Bay ≈ 286-287 F 2
Deadman's Bay o **CDN** (NFL) 242-243 P 3
Deadman's Cay o • **BS** 54-55 H 3
Deadmans Cove o **CDN** (NFL) 242-243 M 1
Deadman's Creek Indian Reserve ✕ **CDN** (BC) 230-231 J 3
Deadman Summit ▲ **USA** (CA) 248-249 E 2
Deadwood o **USA** (SD) 260-261 C 2
Deakin o **AUS** 176-177 K 5
Dealesville o **ZA** 220-221 G 4
Déali o **SN** 202-203 C 2
De'an o **VRC** 156-157 J 2
Dean, Mount ▲ **AUS** 176-177 G 6
Dean Channel ≈ 228-229 G 4
Deán Funes o **RA** 76-77 E 6
Dean River ~ **CDN** 228-229 J 4
Deans Dundas Bay ≈ 24-25 N 4
Dearborn o **USA** (MI) 272-273 F 5
Deary o **USA** (ID) 250-251 C 5
Dease Arm o **CDN** 30-31 J 2
Dease Inlet ≈ 20-21 N 1
Dease Lake o **CDN** (BC) 32-33 E 2
Dease River ~ **CDN** 30-31 L 2
Dease River ~ **CDN** 30-31 E 6
Dease Strait ≈ 24-25 S 6
Deas Thompson Point ▲ **CDN** 24-25 L 6
Death Valley ⌣ **USA** 248-249 G 3
Death Valley Junction o **USA** (CA) 248-249 H 3
Death Valley National Monument ⊥ • **USA** (CA) 248-249 G 3
Deatsville o **USA** (AL) 284-285 D 4
Deauville o • **F** 90-91 H 7
Deaver o **USA** (WY) 252-253 K 2
Debak o **MAL** 162-163 J 4
Debal'ceve o **UA** 102-103 L 3
Debalo o **SUD** 206-207 K 4
Debao o **VRC** 156-157 E 5
Debar o • **MK** 100-101 H 4
Debark o **ETH** 200-201 H 6
Debauch Mountain ▲ **USA** 20-21 L 4
Debaysima o **ER** 200-201 L 6
Debden o **CDN** (SAS) 232-233 M 2
Debdirge o **RUS** 120-121 E 2
Debdou o **MA** 188-189 K 4
Debed ~ **AR** 128-129 L 2
Debepare o **PNG** 183 A 4
Débéré ~ **BF** 202-203 J 3
Debesa o **AUS** 172-173 G 4
Debessy ☆ **RUS** 96-97 H 5
Debin o **RUS** (MAG) 120-121 O 2
Debin ~ **RUS** 120-121 N 2
Debo, Lac o **RMM** 202-203 H 2
Debolt o **CDN** 32-33 M 4
Deborah East, Lake o **AUS** 176-177 E 5
Deborah West, Lake o **AUS** 176-177 E 5
Débougou o **RMM** 202-203 H 2
Debre Birhan o **ETH** 208-209 D 4
Debrecen o **H** 92-93 Q 5
Debre Damo Debir • **ETH** 200-201 J 5
Debre Libanos Gedam • **ETH** 208-209 D 4
Debre Markos ☆ **ETH** 208-209 C 3
Debre May o **ETH** 208-209 C 3
Debre Sina o **ETH** 208-209 D 4
Debre Tabor o **ETH** 208-209 D 3
Debre Work' o **ETH** 208-209 D 3
Debre Zebit o **ETH** 208-209 D 3
Debre Zeyit o **ETH** (Goj) 208-209 B 3
Debre Zeyit o **ETH** (She) 208-209 D 4
Decatur o **USA** (AL) 284-285 D 2
Decatur o **USA** (GA) 284-285 F 3
Decatur o **USA** (IL) 274-275 K 5
Decatur o **USA** (IN) 274-275 O 4
Decatur o **USA** (MI) 272-273 D 5
Decatur o **USA** (MS) 268-269 L 4
Decatur o **USA** (NE) 262-263 K 3
Decatur o **USA** (TN) 282-283 C 5
Decatur o **USA** (TX) 264-265 G 5
Decaturville o **USA** (TN) 276-277 G 5
Decazeville o **F** 90-91 J 9
Deccan ⊥ **IND** 10-11 G 7
Decelles, Lac o **CDN** (QUE) 236-237 O 4
Decelles, Réservoir o **CDN** (QUE) 236-237 L 5
Decepcion o **ARK** 16 G 30
Déception o **CDN** 36-37 M 3
Déception, Rivière ~ **CDN** 36-37 M 3
Déception Bay ≈ 36-37 M 3
Deception Bay ≈ 183 C 4
Deception Lake o **CDN** 34-35 D 2
Deception Point ▲ **AUS** 172-173 K 1
Dechang o **VRC** 156-157 C 3
Decherd o **USA** (TN) 276-277 J 5
Dechu o **IND** 138-139 D 6
Děčín o **CZ** 92-93 N 3
Deciolândia o **BR** 70-71 J 4
Decize o **F** 90-91 J 8
Decker o **CDN** (MAN) 234-235 C 4
Decker o **USA** (MT) 250-251 N 6
Decker Field o **AUS** 176-177 H 2
Decker Lake o **CDN** (BC) 228-229 J 2
Deckers o **USA** (CO) 254-255 K 4
Declo o **USA** (ID) 252-253 E 4
Decoigne o **CDN** (ALB) 228-229 Q 4
Decorah o **USA** (IA) 274-275 G 1
Dedegöl Dağları ▲ **TR** 128-129 D 4
Deder o **ETH** 208-209 E 4
Dediāpāda o **IND** 138-139 D 9
Dedo, Cerro ▲ **RA** 80 E 2
Dédougou ☆ **BF** 202-203 J 3
Dedoviči ☆ **RUS** 94-95 L 3
Dedza o **MW** 218-219 H 2
Dee ~ **GB** 90-91 F 3
Dee ~ **GB** 90-91 F 5
Deep Bay o **CDN** 30-31 L 5
Deep Cove o **NZ** 182 A 6
Deep Creek o **USA** (WA) 244-245 H 3
Deep Creek, South Fork ~ **USA** 244-245 H 2
Deep Creek Lake < **USA** (MD) 280-281 G 4
Deep Fork ~ **USA** 264-265 H 3
Deep River o **CDN** (ONT) 238-239 H 2
Deep River ~ **CDN** 242-243 M 2
Deep River ~ **USA** 282-283 H 5
Deep Rose Lake o **CDN** 30-31 U 3
Deep Valley Creek ~ **CDN** 228-229 R 2
Deepwater o **AUS** 178-179 L 5
Deepwater o **USA** (MO) 274-275 E 6
Deep Well o **AUS** 178-179 C 3
Deer o **USA** (AR) 276-277 B 5
Deer Bay ≈ 24-25 T 1
Deer Creek ~ **USA** 268-269 K 4
Deer Creek Lake o **USA** (OH) 280-281 C 4
Deerfield o **USA** (SD) 260-261 C 2
Deerfield Beach o **USA** (FL) 286-287 J 5
Deerfield River ~ **USA** 278-279 J 6
Deer Fork ~ **USA** 276-277 F 5
Deerhorn o **CDN** (MAN) 234-235 E 4
Deering o **USA** 20-21 J 3
Deering o **USA** (ND) 258-259 F 3
Deering, Mount ▲ **AUS** 176-177 K 2
Deer Island ⌒ **CDN** (MAN) 234-235 G 3
Deer Island ⌒ **USA** 22-23 P 5
Deer Isle o **USA** (ME) 278-279 N 4
Deer Lake o **CDN** (NFL) 242-243 L 3
Deer Lake o **CDN** (ONT) 34-35 J 4
Deer Lake o **CDN** (ONT) 234-235 J 2
Deer Lake o **CDN** (NFL) 242-243 L 3
Deer Lodge o **USA** (MT) 250-251 G 5
Deer Lodge Pass ▲ **USA** (MT) 250-251 G 6
Deer Park o **CDN** (BC) 230-231 L 4
Deer Park o **USA** (AL) 284-285 B 5
Deer Park o **USA** (LA) 268-269 J 5
Deer Park o **USA** (MI) 270-271 N 4
Deer Park o **USA** (WA) 244-245 H 3
Deerpass Bay o **CDN** 30-31 J 3
Deer Pond o **CDN** (NFL) 242-243 O 4
Deer River ~ **CDN** 34-35 J 2
Deer River o **USA** (MN) 270-271 E 3
Deerton o **USA** (MI) 270-271 L 4
Deer Trail o **USA** (CO) 254-255 L 4
Deer Trail Creek ~ **USA** 254-255 M 4
Deerwood o **USA** (MN) 270-271 E 4
Deeth o **USA** (NV) 246-247 K 2
Defensores del Chaco, Parque Nacional ⊥ **PY** 70-71 G 7
Defferrari o **RA** 78-79 K 5
Defia, Hassi o **MA** 188-189 K 4
Defiance o **USA** (OH) 280-281 B 2
Défilé de Tosaye ⊥ **RMM** 196-197 K 6
Degache o **TN** 190-191 G 4
Degali ~ **RUS** 116-117 F 4
Degayê, Ra's ▲ **ER** 200-201 L 6
Dêgê o **VRC** 144-145 M 5
Degeh Bur o **ETH** 208-209 F 4
Degeh Medo o **ETH** 208-209 F 5
Dégelis o **CDN** (QUE) 240-241 G 3
Degema o **WAN** 204-205 G 6
Deggendorf o **D** 92-93 M 4
Degollado o **MEX** 52-53 C 1
Degoma o **ETH** 200-201 H 6
Dégrad Claude = Dégrad des Emerillon o **F** 62-63 H 4
Dégrad des Emerillon = Dégrad Claude o **F** 62-63 H 4
Dégrad Haut Camopi o **F** 62-63 H 4
Dégrad Saint-Léon o **F** 62-63 H 4
Dégrad Vitalo o **F** 62-63 H 4
De Grau o **CDN** (NFL) 242-243 J 4
De Grey River ~ **AUS** 172-173 D 6
Dehalak Desēt ⌒ **ER** 200-201 K 5
Dehāqān o **IR** 134-135 D 3
Dehbārez o **IR** 134-135 G 5
Dehbid o **IR** 134-135 E 3
Deh Dašt o **IR** 134-135 D 3
Dehdez o **IR** 134-135 D 3
Deheg o **IR** 134-135 F 3
Dehej o **IND** 138-139 D 9
Deh-e Kohne o **IR** 134-135 D 4
Dehekolano, Tanjung ▲ **RI** 164-165 K 4
Dehepodo o **RI** 164-165 K 3
Dehgaon o **IND** 138-139 G 8
Deh Ḥeir o **IR** 134-135 F 4
Dehiba o **TN** 190-191 H 4
Dehkanabad o **UZ** 136-137 K 5
Dehlorān o **IR** 134-135 B 1
Deh Mirdād o **AFG** 136-137 K 7
Deh Molla o **IR** 134-135 C 3
Deh Parān o **AFG** 136-137 L 7
Dehra Dun o • **IND** 138-139 G 4
Deh Rāvūd o **AFG** 134-135 L 2
Dehri o **IND** 142-143 D 3
Dehšir o **IR** 134-135 E 3
Deh Šū o **AFG** 134-135 K 3
Dehua o **VRC** 156-157 L 4
Dehui o **VRC** 150-151 E 5
Deichmann Fjord ≈ 26-27 o 9
Deilam, Bandar-e o **IR** 134-135 D 3
Deim Bûkhit o **SUD** 206-207 H 5
Deira o **UAE** 134-135 F 6
Dej o **RO** 102-103 C 4
Dejen o **ETH** 208-209 D 3
Dejian o **VRC** 156-157 F 2
Dejnau o **TM** 136-137 H 5
De Jongs, Tanjung ▲ **RI** 166-167 K 5
De-Kastri o **RUS** 122-123 J 3
Dek'emhāre o **ER** 200-201 J 5
Dekese o **ZRE** 210-211 H 5
Dekina o **WAN** 204-205 G 5
Dekoa o **RCA** 206-207 D 5
Delaa o **DZ** 190-191 D 4
Delacour o **CDN** (ALB) 232-233 E 4
Delacroix o **USA** (LA) 268-269 L 7
Delaki o **RI** 166-167 C 6
Delaney o **USA** (WA) 244-245 H 4
Delanggu o **RI** 168 D 3
Delano o **USA** (CA) 248-249 E 4
Delārām o **AFG** 134-135 K 2
Delareyville o **ZA** 220-221 G 3
Delarof Islands ⌒ **USA** 22-23 G 7
Delavan o **USA** (IL) 274-275 J 4
Delavan o **USA** (WI) 274-275 K 2
Delaware o **USA** (AR) 276-277 B 5
Delaware o **USA** (OH) 280-281 C 3
Delaware ▫ **USA** 280-281 L 4
Delaware Bay ≈ 280-281 L 4
Delaware Creek ~ **USA** 266-267 C 2
Delaware Lake o **USA** (OH) 280-281 C 3
Delaware River ~ **USA** 262-263 L 5
Delaware River ~ **USA** 278-279 F 6
Delaware River ~ **USA** 280-281 M 2
Delbi o **SN** 202-203 C 2
Del Bonita o **CDN** (ALB) 232-233 F 6
Delburne o **CDN** (ALB) 232-233 E 3
Delcambre o **USA** (LA) 268-269 J 7
Del Cano Rise ≃ 9 H 10
Delčevo o • **MK** 100-101 J 4
Delco o **USA** (NC) 282-283 J 6
Deleau o **CDN** (MAN) 234-235 C 5
Deleg o **EC** 64-65 C 3
Delegate River o **AUS** 180-181 K 4
Délembé o **RCA** 206-207 F 4
Délép o **TCH** 198-199 J 6
Delfino o **BR** 68-69 H 7
Delfinópolis o **BR** 72-73 G 6
Delft o • **NL** 92-93 H 2
Delfus o **PE** 64-65 D 4
Delfzijl o **NL** 92-93 J 2
Delgado, Cabo ▲ **MOC** 214-215 L 6
Dėlgėr = Tajgan o **MAU** 148-149 C 4
Dėlgėrėh = Hongor o **MAU** 148-149 K 5
Dėlgėrhangaj = Hašaat o **MAU** 148-149 G 5
Dėlgėr mörön ~ **MAU** 148-149 D 3
Delgo o **SUD** 200-201 E 2
Delhi o **CDN** (ONT) 238-239 E 6
Delhi ☆ ••• **IND** 138 130 F 5
Delhi o **USA** (CO) 254-255 L 6
Delhi o **USA** (LA) 268-269 J 4
Delhi o **USA** (NY) 278-279 G 6
Déli o **TCH** 206-207 B 4
Deli, Pulau ⌒ **RI** 168 A 3
Delia o **CDN** (ALB) 232-233 F 4
Delicias o **CO** 64-65 E 2
Delicias o **MEX** 50-51 G 3
Delicias, Las o **CO** 60-61 F 5
Delījān o **IR** 134-135 D 1
Delight o **USA** (AR) 276-277 B 6
Delingdè ~ **RUS** 110-111 O 7
Delingdèkèn ~ **RUS** 116-117 H 3
Delingha o **VRC** 144-145 L 2
Delin'ja ~ **RUS** 110-111 V 7
Delisle o **CDN** (QUE) 240-241 D 2
Delisle o **CDN** (SAS) 232-233 L 4
Delissaville ✕ **AUS** 172-173 K 2
Delitua o **RI** 162-163 C 3
Deliverence Island ⌒ **AUS** 183 A 5
Deljankir ~ **RUS** 110-111 a 7
Del'kju-Ohotskaja ~ **RUS** 120-121 J 3
Del'ku ~ **RUS** 110-111 a 6
Dell o **USA** (MT) 250-251 G 7
Dell City o **USA** (TX) 266-267 B 2
Delle o **USA** (UT) 254-255 C 3
Dell Rapids o **USA** (SD) 260-261 K 3
Dellys o **DZ** 190-191 D 2
Delmar Lake o **USA** (NV) 248-249 K 2
Delmarva Peninsula ⌣ **USA** 280-281 L 4
Delmas o **CDN** (SAS) 232-233 K 3
Delmas o **ZA** 220-221 J 3
Delmenhorst o **D** 92-93 K 2
Delmont o **USA** (NJ) 280-281 M 4
Delmore Downs o **AUS** 178-179 C 2
Del Norte o **USA** (CO) 254-255 J 6
de-Longa, ostrova ⌒ **RUS** 110-111 b 1
Deloraine o **AUS** 180-181 J 6
Deloraine o **CDN** (MAN) 234-235 C 5
Delos ••• **GR** 100-101 K 6
Delphi ••• **GR** 100-101 J 5
Delphi o **USA** (IN) 274-275 M 4
Delphos o **USA** (OH) 280-281 B 3
Delportshoop o **ZA** 220-221 G 4
Delray Beach o **USA** (FL) 286-287 J 5
Del Rio o **USA** (TX) 266-267 F 4
Delsbo o **S** 86-87 H 6
Del Sur o **USA** (CA) 248-249 F 5
Delta o **CDN** (BC) 230-231 G 4
Delta o **CDN** (MAN) 234-235 E 4
Delta o **USA** (CO) 254-255 G 5
Delta o **USA** (OH) 280-281 B 2
Delta o **USA** (UT) 254-255 C 4
Delta Camp o **RB** 218-219 B 4
Delta del Tigre o **ROU** 78-79 L 3
Delta Downs o **AUS** 174-175 F 5
Delta Dunării ⊥ ••• **RO** 102-103 F 5
Delta Junction o **USA** 20-21 S 4
Delta Mendota Canal < **USA** (CA) 248-249 D 3
Delta National Wildlife Refuge ⊥ **USA** (LA) 268-269 L 7
Delthore Mountain ▲ **CDN** 30-31 F 4
Deltona o **USA** (FL) 286-287 H 3
Del'tula ~ **RUS** 116-117 E 3
Delungra o **AUS** 178-179 L 5
Dėluun = Rašaant o **MAU** 146-147 K 2
Del Verme Falls ~ **ETH** 208-209 E 6
Dèm, Lac de o • **BF** 202-203 K 3
Dema ~ **RUS** 96-97 J 6
Demagiri o **IND** 142-143 H 4
Demaine o **CDN** (SAS) 232-233 L 5
Demak o **RI** 168 D 3
Demalisques de Leshwe ⊥ **ZRE** 214-215 E 7
Demaraisville o **CDN** (ONT) 236-237 M 3
Demarcation Point ▲ **USA** 20-21 U 2
Demba o **ZRE** 210-211 J 6
Demba Koli o **SN** 202-203 D 3
Dembecha o **ETH** 208-209 C 3
Dembi o **ETH** 208-209 C 4
Dembia o **RCA** 206-207 G 6
Dembi Dolo o • **ETH** 208-209 B 4
Dembo o **CAM** 204-205 K 4
Dembo o **TCH** 206-207 C 4
Demensk, Spas- o **RUS** 94-95 O 4
Demerara Abyssal Plain ≃ 6-7 D 7
Demers, Pointe ▲ **CDN** 36-37 K 4
Demers Centre o **CDN** (QUE) 238-239 H 3
Demidov ☆ **RUS** 94-95 M 4
Deming o **USA** (NM) 256-257 H 6
Deming o **USA** (WA) 244-245 C 2
Demini, Rio ~ **BR** 66-67 F 3
Demirci ☆ **TR** 128-129 C 3
Dem'janka ~ **RUS** 114-115 K 5
Dem'janka ~ **RUS** 114-115 N 5
Dem'janovo ☆ **RUS** 96-97 E 3
Demjansk ☆ **RUS** 94-95 N 3
Dem'janskoe o **RUS** 114-115 K 5
Demmin o **D** 92-93 M 2
Demnate o **MA** 188-189 H 5
Demopolis o **USA** (AL) 284-285 C 4
Demotte o **USA** (IN) 274-275 L 3
Dempo, Gunung ▲ **RI** 162-163 E 6
Dempo, Selat ≈ 162-163 F 4
Dempseys o **AUS** 174-175 C 7
Dempster Highway ll **CDN** 20-21 V 4
Demsa o **CAM** 204-205 K 4
Demta o **RI** 166-167 L 3
Denakil ⊥ **ETH** 200-201 K 5
Denali Highway ll **USA** 20-21 Q 5
Denali National Park o **USA** 20-21 Q 5
Denali National Park and Preserve ⊥ **USA** 20-21 P 5
Denan o **ETH** 208-209 F 5
Denau o **UZ** 136-137 K 5
Denbigh o **CDN** (ONT) 238-239 H 3
Denbigh, Cape ▲ **USA** 20-21 K 4
Denbigh Downs o **AUS** 178-179 F 2
Den Chai o **THA** 158-159 F 2
Dendang o **RI** 162-163 G 6
Dendâra o **RIM** 196-197 G 6
Déndoudi o **SN** 202-203 D 2
Deneba o **ETH** 208-209 D 4
Deneżkin Kamen', gora ▲ **RUS** 114-115 E 4
Dengfeng o **VRC** 154-155 H 4
Dengi o **WAN** 204-205 H 4
Dengkou o **VRC** 154-155 E 1
Dengqên o **VRC** 144-145 K 5
Denguiro o **RCA** 206-207 F 6
Dengyuan o **VRC** 156-157 D 2
Dengzhou o **VRC** 154-155 H 5
Den Haag = 's-Gravenhage ☆ •• **NL** 92-93 H 2
Denham o **AUS** 176-177 B 2
Denham, Mount ▲ **JA** 54-55 G 5
Denham Island ⌒ **AUS** 174-175 E 5
Denham Range ▲ **AUS** 178-179 J 2
Denham Sound ≈ 176-177 B 2
Denham Springs o **USA** (LA) 268-269 K 6
Denhart o **CDN** (ALB) 232-233 G 5
Den Helder o **NL** 92-93 H 2
Denholm o **CDN** (SAS) 232-233 L 3
Deni, Área Indígena ✕ **BR** 66-67 C 6
Denia o **E** 98-99 H 5
Denial Bay ≈ 180-181 B 2
Denikouroula o **RMM** 202-203 H 4
Deniliquin o **AUS** 180-181 H 3
Denio o **USA** (NV) 246-247 G 2
Denio Junction o **USA** (NV) 246-247 G 2
Denio Summit ▲ **USA** (NV) 246-247 G 2
Denise Island ⌒ **SY** 224 D 1
Denison o **USA** (IA) 274-275 C 2
Denison o **USA** (TX) 264-265 H 5
Denison Range ▲ **AUS** 172-173 J 5
Denizli ☆ **TR** 128-129 C 4
Denkanikota o **IND** 140-141 G 4
Denkola ∴ • **TM** 136-137 E 4
Denman o **AUS** 180-181 L 2
Denman o **USA** (NE) 262-263 H 4
Denman Glacier ⊂ **ARK** 16 G 10
Denman Island o **CDN** (BC) 230-231 E 4
Denmark o **AUS** 176-177 D 7
Denmark o **USA** (SC) 284-285 J 3
Denmark o **USA** (WI) 270-271 L 6
Denmark = Danmark ■ **DK** 86-87 C 9
Denmark Strait ≈ 6-7 F 2
Denniel Creek ~ **CDN** 232-233 L 6
Dennis, Lake o **AUS** 172-173 J 6
Dennysville o **USA** (ME) 278-279 O 4
Den Oever o **NL** 92-93 H 2
Denpasar ☆ **RI** 168 B 7
Dent, La ▲ **CI** 202-203 G 6
Denton o **USA** (GA) 284-285 H 5
Denton o **USA** (MD) 280-281 L 5
Denton o **USA** (MT) 250-251 K 4

320 Danville — Denton

Denton o **USA** (NC) 282-283 G 5
Denton o **USA** (TX) 264-265 G 5
Denton Creek ~ **USA** 264-265 G 5
Dentons Corner o **USA** (VA) 280-281 H 6
D'Entrecasteaux, Point ▲ **AUS** 176-177 C 7
D'Entrecasteaux Islands ⌒ **PNG** 183 F 5
D'Entrecasteaux National Park ⊥ **AUS** 176-177 C 7
Denu o **GH** 202-203 L 6
Denver o **USA** (IA) 274-275 F 2
Denver ☆• **USA** (CO) 254-255 L 4
Denver City o **USA** (TX) 264-265 B 6
Denzil o **CDN** (SAS) 232-233 J 3
Déo o **RCA** 206-207 E 4
Déo, Mayo ~ **CAM** 204-205 K 5
Deodápolis o **BR** 76-77 K 2
Deoqarh Peak ▲ **IND** 142-143 C 4
Deoghar o **IND** 142-143 E 3
Deolāli o **IND** 138-139 D 10
Deoli o **IND** 138-139 G 9
Deolia o **IND** 138-139 E 7
Deora o **USA** (CO) 254-255 N 6
Deori o **IND** 142-143 B 5
Deoria o **IND** 142-143 C 2
Deo Tu Na ▲ **K** 158-159 J 4
Déou o **BF** 202-203 K 2
Dep ~ **RUS** 118-119 N 9
Dep ~ **RUS** 122-123 C 2
Dep, River ~ **WAN** 204-205 H 4
Depālpur o **IND** 138-139 E 8
De Panne o **B** 92-93 G 3
Depapre o **RI** 166-167 L 3
Departure Bay o **CDN** (BC) 230-231 F 4
Departure Lake o **CDN** (ONT) 236-237 G 3
Depew o **USA** (NY) 278-279 C 6
Depew o **USA** (OK) 264-265 H 3
Deposit o **USA** (NY) 278-279 F 6
Depot d'Aigle o **CDN** (QUE) 238-239 J 2
Dépôt-de-la-Lièvre o **CDN** (QUE) 240-241 C 2
Dépôt Lézard Rnes o **F** 62-63 H 3
Deptumala ~ **RUS** 108-109 a 5
Deputatskij ☆ **RUS** 110-111 W 5
Dêqên o **VRC** (XIZ) 144-145 H 5
Dêqên o **VRC** (YUN) 144-145 M 6
Deqing o **VRC** 156-157 G 5
Dera o **ETH** 208-209 D 4
Dera ~ **SP** 212-213 J 3
Dera Bugti o **PK** 138-139 B 5
Dera Ghazi Khan o• **PK** 138-139 C 4
Dera Ismāīl Khān o **PK** 138-139 C 4
Derale ▲ **AUS** 180-181 K 2
Dera Murād Jamali o **PK** 138-139 B 5
Dera Nānak o **IND** 138-139 E 3
Dera Nawāb Sahib o **PK** 138-139 C 5
Derāwar Fort o• **PK** 138-139 C 5
Derbeikan, Wādī ~ **SUD** 200-201 G 3
Derbeke ~ **RUS** 110-111 V 7
Derbekinskaja vpadina ◡ **RUS** 110-111 U 7
Derbent o **RUS** 126-127 H 6
Derbissaka o **RCA** 206-207 G 6
Derby o **AUS** (TAS) 180-181 J 6
Derby o **AUS** (WA) 172-173 F 4
Derby o **CDN** (PEI) 240-241 L 4
Derby o **GB** 90-91 G 5
Derby o **USA** (IN) 274-275 M 6
Derby o **USA** (KS) 262-263 J 7
Derby o **ZA** 220-221 H 2
Derby Lake o **CDN** 30-31 X 2
Derby Shelton o **USA** (CT) 280-281 N 2
Derdepoort o **ZA** 220-221 H 2
Dereli ☆ **TR** 128-129 H 2
Deren, Adrar-n- ▲ **MA** 188-189 G 5
Déréssa o **TCH** 198-199 K 6
Derewo ~ **RI** 166-167 J 3
Derg, Lough o **IRL** 90-91 C 5
Dergači ☆ **RUS** 96-97 F 8
Derhačy o **UA** 102-103 K 2
Derickson Seamount ≃ 22-23 Q 6
Derik ☆ **TR** 128-129 J 4
Derjugina, vpadina ≃ 122-123 L 2
Derkül ~ **KZ** 96-97 G 8
Derm o **NAM** 220-221 D 1
Dermitt o **USA** (TX) 264-265 C 6
Dermott o **USA** (AR) 276-277 D 7
Dernieres, Isles ⌒ **USA** (LA) 268-269 K 7
Deroche o **CDN** (BC) 230-231 G 4
Deror o **ETH** 208-209 G 4
Derramadero o **C** 54-55 F 4
Derre o **MOC** 218-219 J 3
Derri o **SP** 208-209 H 6
Derry o **USA** (NH) 278-279 K 6
Derry Doire = Londonderry ☆• **GB** 90-91 D 4
Derry Downs o **AUS** 178-179 C 2
Derudeb o **SUD** 200-201 H 4
De Rust o **ZA** 220-221 F 6
Derval o **F** 90-91 G 8
Derwent o **AUS** 172-173 L 7
Derwent o **CDN** (ALB) 232-233 H 2
Derwent, River ~ **AUS** 180-181 J 7
Deržavinsk ☆ **KZ** 124-125 E 3
Deržavnyj zapovednyk Dunajskie plavni •• **UA** 102-103 F 5
Desaguadero, Río ~ **BOL** 70-71 D 5
Desaguadero, Río ~ **RA** 78-79 F 2
Desagües de los Colorados o **RA** 76-77 D 5
Desaru o **MAL** 162-163 F 4
Desbarats o **CDN** (ONT) 238-239 B 2
Desbarats Strait ≈ 24-25 T 2
Descabezado Grande, Volcán ▲ **RCH** 78-79 D 3
Descanso o **USA** (CA) 248-249 H 7
Descanso, El o **PE** 70-71 B 4
Deschaillons o **CDN** (QUE) 238-239 N 2
Descharme River ~ **CDN** 32-33 Q 3
Deschutes River ~ **USA** 244-245 D 6
Deschutes River ~ **USA** 244-245 E 5
Descoberto o **BR** 72-73 H 2
Descubierta, La o **DOM** 54-55 K 5
Desē ☆ **ETH** 208-209 D 3
Deseado, Cabo ▲ **RCH** 80 C 6
Deseado, Río ~ **RA** 80 G 3
Desecheo, Isla ⌒ **USA** (PR) 286-287 O 2
Desecho o **YV** 60-61 H 6
Desemboque, El o **MEX** 50-51 C 2
Desengaño, Punta ▲ **RA** 80 G 4
Desenzano del Garda o **I** 100-101 C 2
Deseret o **USA** (UT) 254-255 C 4
Deseret Peak ▲ **USA** (UT) 254-255 C 3
Desertas, Ilhas ⌒ **P** (Ma) 188-189 C 4
Desertas, Ilhas ⌒ **P** (MAD) 188-189 C 4
Desertas, Ponta das ▲ **BR** 74-75 E 8
Desert Center o **USA** (CA) 248-249 J 6
Desert Hot Springs o **USA** (CA) 248-249 H 6
Desert National Park ⊥ **IND** 138-139 C 6
Desert National Wildlife Refuge ⊥ **USA** (NV) 248-249 J 3
Desert Peak ▲ **USA** (UT) 254-255 B 2
Desert Range ▲ **USA** 240-249 J 3
Desert Range xx **USA** (UT) 254-255 B 5
Desert Test Center xx **USA** (UT) 254-255 B 3
Desert View o **USA** (AZ) 256-257 D 2
Deshler o **USA** (OH) 280-281 C 2
Desiderio Tello o **RA** 76-77 D 6
Desierto Central de Baja California, Parque Nacional del ⊥ **MEX** 50-51 B 3
Desirade, La ⌒ **F** 56 E 3
Des Lacs o **USA** (ND) 258-259 F 3
Des Lacs National Wildlife Refuge ⊥ **USA** (ND) 258-259 E 3
Desmarais Lake o **CDN** 30-31 R 5
Des Moines o **USA** (WA) 244-245 C 3
Des Moines ☆• **USA** (IA) 274-275 E 3
Des Moines River ~ **USA** 274-275 F 4
Desna ~ **RUS** 94-95 N 4
Desna ~ **UA** 102-103 G 2
Desnățui ~ **RO** 102-103 C 5
Desolatión, Isla ⌒ **RCH** 80 C 6
Desolation Canyon ◡ **USA** 254-255 E 4
Desolation Point ▲ **RP** 160-161 F 7
Desolation Sound Provincial Marine Park ⊥ **CDN** (BC) 230-231 E 3
Desoronto o **CDN** (ONT) 238-239 H 4
De Soto National Monument • **USA** (FL) 286-287 G 4
Despatch o **ZA** 220-221 G 6
Despeñaderos o **RA** 76-77 E 6
Des Plaines o **USA** (IL) 274-275 L 2
Despotovac o **YU** 100-101 H 2
Des Roches o **CDN** (QUE) 240-241 D 3
Desroches, Île ⌒ **SY** 224 C 2
Dessau o•• **D** 92-93 M 3
Destacado Island ⌒ **RP** 160-161 F 6
Destacamento São Simão o **BR** 70-71 G 4
Desterro o **BR** 66-67 C 6
Destin o **USA** (FL) 286-287 C 1
D'Estrees Bay ≈ 180-181 D 3
Destruction Bay o **CDN** 20-21 V 6
Desvelos, Bahía ≈ 80 G 4
Dete o **ZW** 218-219 D 4
Detmold o• **D** 92-93 K 3
Detour, Point ▲ **USA** (MI) 270-271 M 5
Detpa o **AUS** 180-181 F 4
Detrin ~ **RUS** 120-121 N 3
Detroit o **USA** (AL) 284-285 B 2
Detroit o **USA** (OR) 244-245 C 6
Detroit o **USA** (TX) 264-265 J 5
Detroit o• **USA** (MI) 272-273 F 5
Detroit, Fort ∴ **USA** (MN) 270-271 C 4
Détroit de Jacques Cartier ≈ 38-39 N 4
Détroit d'Honguedo ≈ 38-39 M 4
Detroit Lake o **USA** (OR) 244-245 C 6
Detroit Lakes o **USA** (MN) 270-271 C 4
Dettifoss ~ **IS** 86-87 e 2
Det Udom o **THA** 158-159 H 3
Detuo o **VRC** 156-157 C 2
Deua National Park ⊥ **AUS** 180-181 K 3
Deukeskenkala ∴• **TM** 136-137 F 3
Deustua o **PE** 70-71 B 4
Deutsch Brod = Havlíčkův Brod o• **CZ** 92-93 N 4
Deutsche Bucht ≈ 92-93 J 1
Deutschheim State Historic Site • **USA** (MO) 274-275 G 6
Deux Balé, Forét des ⊥ **BF** 202-203 J 4
Deux Bassins, Col de ▲ **DZ** 190-191 D 2
Deux Pitons • **WL** 56 E 5
Deva ☆• **RO** 102-103 C 5
Devadurg o **IND** 140-141 G 2
Devakottai o **IND** 140-141 H 6
Devanhalli o **IND** 140-141 G 4
Devar Hipparg o **IND** 140-141 G 2
Devarkonda o **IND** 140-141 H 2
Devarshola o **IND** 140-141 G 5
De Veber, Mount ▲ **CDN** (ALB) 228-229 P 3
Devechi = Davaçi o **AZ** 128-129 N 2
Deveci Dağı ▲ **TR** 128-129 F 2
Develi ☆ **TR** 128-129 F 3
Deveril o **AUS** 178-179 K 2
Devers o **USA** (TX) 268-269 F 6
Devgarh o **IND** 138-139 D 7
Deviation Peak ▲ **USA** 20-21 K 3
Devica ~ **RUS** 102-103 L 2
Deville o **CDN** (ALB) 232-233 F 2
Deville Névé ~ **CDN** 230-231 M 2
Devil Mountain ▲ **USA** 20-21 H 3
Devil Mountain Lake o **USA** 20-21 H 3
Devils Bridge ⩦ **AG** 56 E 3
Devils Den o **USA** (CA) 248-249 E 4
Devils Den State Parks ⊥ **USA** (AR) 276-277 A 5
Devils Gate ▲ **USA** (CA) 246-247 F 5
Devil's Hole ≃ 90-91 H 3
Devil's Hole National Monument ∴ **USA** (NV) 248-249 H 3
Devil's Island = Diable, Île du ⌒ **F** 62-63 H 3
Devils Kitchen Lake o **USA** (IL) 276-277 F 3
Devils Lake o **USA** (ND) 258-259 J 3
Devils Lake Sioux Indian Reservation ⅹ **USA** (ND) 258-259 J 4
Devils Marbles Scenic Reserve • **AUS** 174-175 C 7
Devil's Playground ⩦ **USA** 248-249 H 4
Devil's Point ▲ **BS** 54-55 J 3
Devils Postpile National Monument ∴ **USA** (CA) 248-249 E 2
Devils River ~ **USA** 266-267 F 3
Devils Tower Junction o **USA** (WY) 252-253 O 2
Devils Tower National Monument ∴ **USA** (WY) 252-253 O 2
Devin o **BG** 102-103 D 7
Devine o **USA** (TX) 266-267 J 4
Devipattinam o **IND** 140-141 H 6
Devli o **IND** 138-139 E 7
Devlin o **CDN** (ONT) 234-235 K 6
Devnja o **BG** 102-103 F 6
Devoll, Lumi ~ **AL** 100-101 H 4
Devon o **CDN** (ALB) 232-233 E 2
Devon ⩦ **GB** 90-91 E 6
Devon o **USA** (MT) 250-251 H 3
Devon o **ZA** 220-221 J 3
Devon 30 Indian Reserve ⅹ• **CDN** (NB) 240-241 J 4
Devon Island ⌒ **CDN** 24-25 b 3
Devonport o **AUS** 180-181 J 6
Devonshire o **AUS** 178-179 H 2
Devrek ☆ **TR** 128-129 D 2
Devure ~ **ZW** 218-219 F 4
Dewa, Tanjung ▲ **RI** (ACE) 162-163 A 3
Dewa, Tanjung ▲ **RI** (KSE) 164-165 E 5
Dewar o **USA** (OK) 264-265 J 3
Dewās o **IND** 138-139 F 8
Dewatto o **USA** (WA) 244-245 C 3
Dewberry o **CDN** (ALB) 232-233 H 2
Dewdney o **CDN** (BC) 230-231 G 4
Dewelē o **ETH** 208-209 F 3
Dewetsdorp o **ZA** 220-221 H 4
Dewey o **USA** (AZ) 256-257 C 4
Dewey o **USA** (SD) 260-261 B 3
Dewey o•• **USA** (PR) 286-287 Q 2
Dewey Lake o **USA** (KY) 276-277 N 3
Dexing o **VRC** 156-157 K 2
D. Expedito Lopes Francisco Santos o **BR** 68-69 H 5
Dexter o **USA** (ME) 278-279 M 3
Dexter o **USA** (MO) 276-277 F 4
Dexter o **USA** (MS) 268-269 L 5
Dexter o **USA** (NM) 256-257 L 5
Dexterity Island ⌒ **CDN** 26-27 O 8
Deyang o **VRC** 154-155 D 6
Dey-Dey, Lake o **AUS** 176-177 L 4
Deyhūk o **IR** 134-135 G 2
Deyyer o **IR** 134-135 D 5
Dez, Rūd-e ~ **IR** 134-135 C 2
Dezadeash o **CDN** 20-21 W 6
Dezadeash Lake o **CDN** 20-21 W 6
Dezfūl o• **IR** 134-135 C 2
Dežgān o **IR** 134-135 F 5
Dezhneva, Mys = Dežneva, mys ▲ **RUS** 112-113 a 3
Dezhou o **VRC** 154-155 K 3
Dežneva, buhta ≈ 112-113 R 6
Dežneva, mys ▲ **RUS** 112-113 a 3
Dhahran = az-Zahrān o **KSA** 134-135 D 5
Dhahran = Zahrān, az- o **KSA** 134-135 D 5
Dhaka ★•• **BD** 142-143 G 4
Dhakia o **IND** 144-145 C 6
Dhaleswari ~ **BD** 142-143 F 3
Dhamtari o **IND** 142-143 B 5
Dhanāna o **IND** 138-139 C 6
Dhanasar o **PK** 138-139 B 4
Dhanaura o **IND** 138-139 G 5
Dhanbād o **IND** 142-143 E 4
Dhandelhura o **NEP** 144-145 C 6
Dhandhuka o **IND** 138-139 C 8
D'Hanis o **USA** (TX) 266-267 H 4
Dhankuta o **NEP** 144-145 F 7
Dhanpuri o **IND** 142-143 B 4
Dhanushkodi o **IND** 140-141 H 6
Dhār o **IND** 138-139 E 8
Dharampur o **IND** 138-139 D 9
Dharan Bazar o **NEP** 144-145 F 7
Dhārapuram o **IND** 140-141 G 5
Dhāri o **IND** 138-139 C 9
Dharmapuri o **IND** 140-141 H 4
Dharmastala o **IND** 140-141 F 4
Dharmavaram o **IND** 140-141 G 3
Dharmjaygarh o **IND** 142-143 C 4
Dharmsala o **IND** 138-139 F 3
Dhārni o **IND** 138-139 F 9
Dharwad o **IND** 140-141 F 3
Dhaulagiri ▲ **NEP** 144-145 D 6
Dhaulagiri Himal ▲ **NEP** 144-145 D 6
Dhauliganga ~ **IND** 138-139 G 4
Dhaulpur o **IND** 138-139 F 6
Dhaya o **DZ** 188-189 L 3
Dhaym-al-Khayl o **WSA** 196-197 D 2
Dhebar Lake o **IND** 138-139 D 7
Dhekelia Sovereign Base Area (GB) xx **CY** 128-129 E 5
Dhenkānāl o **IND** 142-143 D 5
Dhiinsoor o **SP** 212-213 J 2
Dhing o **IND** 142-143 H 2
Dhlo Dhlo Ruins ∴• **ZW** 218-219 E 4
Dholera o **IND** 138-139 D 8
Dhone o **IND** 140-141 G 3
Dhoodi, Bannaanka ⩦ **SP** 208-209 H 4
Dhorpatan o **NEP** 144-145 D 6
Dhrāngadhra o **IND** 138-139 C 8
Dhubbato o **SP** 208-209 G 4
Dhuburi o **IND** 142-143 F 2
Dhud, togga ~ **SP** 208-209 J 3
Dhule o **IND** 138-139 E 9
Dhulian o **BD** 142-143 F 3
Dhunche o **NEP** 144-145 E 6
Dhurbo o **SP** 208-209 K 3
Dhuudo o **SP** 208-209 K 4
Dhuudo, togga ~ **SP** 208-209 K 4
Dhuusa Mareeb ☆ **SP** 208-209 H 6
Di o **BF** 202-203 J 3
Dia o **LB** 202-203 E 6
Diaba o **RMM** 196-197 H 6
Diabakania o **RG** 202-203 E 4
Diabali o **RMM** 202-203 G 2
Diablo, Punta del ▲ **ROU** 74-75 D 10
Diablo Range ▲ **USA** 248-249 C 2
Diablotins, Morne ▲ **WD** 56 E 4
Diabo o **BF** 202-203 K 3
Diabugu o **WAG** 202-203 C 3
Diaca o **MOC** 214-215 K 6
Diadema o **BR** 72-73 G 7
Diadi o **RP** 160-161 D 4
Diadioumbéra o **RMM** 202-203 E 2
Diafarabé o **RMM** 202-203 H 2
Diaka ~ **RMM** 202-203 H 2
Diakon o **RMM** 202-203 E 2
Dialafara o **RMM** 202-203 E 3
Dialaka o **RMM** 202-203 E 2
Dialakoto o **SN** 202-203 D 3
Diallassagou o **RMM** 202-203 J 3
Dialloubé o **RMM** 202-203 H 2
Diamante o **RA** 78-79 J 2
Diamante, Pampa del ⩦ **RA** 78-79 F 3
Diamante, Río ~ **RA** 78-79 F 3
Diamantina o• **BR** 72-73 J 5
Diamantina, Chapada ▲ **BR** 72-73 J 2
Diamantina, Chapada da ▲ **BR** 68-69 H 7
Diamantina Development Road II **AUS** 178-179 E 2
Diamantina Fracture Zone ≃ 13 B 6
Diamantina Lakes o **AUS** 178-179 F 2
Diamantina River ~ **AUS** 178-179 E 3
Diamantino o **BR** (MAT) 70-71 J 4
Diamantino o **BR** (MAT) 72-73 D 4
Diamantino, Rio ~ **BR** 72-73 D 4
Diamarakro o **CI** 202-203 J 6
Diamare ⩦ **CAM** 206-207 B 3
Diambala o **RCB** 210-211 D 6
Diamond Area Restricted xx **NAM** 220-221 B 3
Diamond Cave • **USA** (AR) 276-277 B 5
Diamond Diggings • **ZA** 220-221 F 4
Diamond Islands ⌒ **CDN** 36-37 M 2
Diamond Jennes Peninsula ◡ **CDN** 24-25 N 5
Diamond Lake o **USA** (OR) 244-245 C 7
Diamond Peak ▲ **USA** (NV) 246-247 K 4
Diamondville o **USA** (WY) 252-253 H 5
Diamou o **RMM** 202-203 E 2
Diamounguél o **SN** 202-203 D 2
Diana o **SN** 202-203 D 3
Diana Bay ≈ 36-37 P 4
Dianbai o **VRC** 156-157 G 6
Diancang Shan ▲ **VRC** 142-143 M 3
Dian Chi o **VRC** 156-157 C 4
Dianda, Kabondo- o **ZRE** 214-215 C 5
Diandian o **RG** 202-203 D 4
Diandioumé o **RMM** 202-203 F 2
Diangouté Kamara o **RMM** 202-203 F 2
Dianké Makam o **SN** 202-203 D 3
Dianópolis o **BR** 68-69 E 7
Dianra o **CI** 202-203 G 5
Diapaga o **BF** 202-203 L 3
Diaramana o **RMM** 202-203 H 3
Dias o **MOC** 218-219 H 1
Diassa = Madina o **RMM** 202-203 G 4
Diatas, Danau o **RI** 162-163 D 5
Díavlos Zakinthou ≈ 100-101 H 6
Diawala o **CI** 202-203 H 4
Díaz Ordaz o **MEX** 50-51 C 4
Díaz Point ▲• **NAM** 220-221 B 3
Dibā o **UAE** 134-135 G 6
Dibage o **IRQ** 128-129 K 5
Dībān o **JOR** 130-131 D 2
Dibaru, Danau o **RI** 162-163 D 5
Dibaya o **ZRE** 214-215 B 4
Dibaya-Lubue o **ZRE** 210-211 G 6
Dibble Ice Tongue ⊂ **ARK** 16 G 14
Dib Dabiib < **SP** 212-213 J 2
Dibdiba, ad- ▲ **KSA** 130-131 K 3
Dibella o **RN** 198-199 F 4
Dibeng o **ZA** 220-221 F 3
Dibia o **WAL** 202-203 E 6
Di Bīn o **Y** 132-133 D 6
Di Bīn ∴• **Y** 132-133 D 5
Dibin, ad- o **Y** 132-133 G 5
Dibiri Island ⌒ **PNG** 183 B 5
Dibni o **NEP** 144-145 D 7
Diboll o **USA** (TX) 268-269 F 5
Dibombari o **CAM** 204-205 H 6
Dibrugarh o **IND** 142-143 J 2
Dibs o **SUD** 200-201 B 6
Dibs, Bi'r o **ET** 194-195 D 6
Dick, Mount ▲ **AUS** 174-175 H 7
Dickens o **USA** (TX) 264-265 D 5
Dickey o **USA** (ND) 258-259 J 5
Dickeyville o **USA** (WI) 274-275 H 2
Dickinson o **USA** (ND) 258-259 E 5
Dickinson o **USA** (TX) 268-269 E 7
Dicks Creek Gap ▲ **USA** (GA) 284-285 G 2
Dickson o **USA** (AK) 20-21 H 4
Dickson o **USA** (TN) 276-277 H 4
Dickson Land ⩦ **N** 84-85 J 3
Dickson Mounds Museum • **USA** (IL) 274-275 H 4
Dicle Nehri ~ **TR** 128-129 J 4
Dico Leopoldino o **BR** 68-69 H 4
Dida Galgalu Desert ⩦ **EAK** 212-213 G 2
Didah o **KSA** 130-131 H 4
Didēsa Wenz ~ **ETH** 208-209 B 4
Didiéni o **RMM** 202-203 F 3
Didiévi o **CI** 202-203 H 6
Didig Sala o **ETH** 200-201 K 6
Didimótiho o **GR** 100-101 L 4
Didsbury o **CDN** (ALB) 232-233 D 4
Didwāna o **IND** 138-139 E 6
Didy o **RM** 222-223 F 7
Didyma ∴•• **TR** 128-129 B 4
Didyr o **BF** 202-203 J 3
Die Bos o **ZA** 220-221 D 5
Diébougou o **BF** 202-203 J 4
Dieciocho de Marzo o **MEX** 50-51 L 5
Dieciocho de Marzo o **MEX** 52-53 J 2
Diecké o **RG** 202-203 F 6
Diefenbaker, Lake o **CDN** (SAS) 232-233 L 5
Diego de Almagro o **RCH** 76-77 B 4
Diego de Alvear o **RA** 78-79 H 3
Diego Garcia ⌒ **GB** 12 F 5
Diego Lamas o **ROU** 76-77 J 6
Diégo Suarez = Antsiranana ☆ **RM** 222-223 F 4
Diéli o **RMM** 202-203 H 3
Diéma o **RMM** 202-203 F 2
Diemals o **AUS** 176-177 E 4
Diemansputs o **ZA** 220-221 E 4
Điên Biên ☆• **VN** 156-157 C 6
Diễn Châu ☆ **VN** 156-157 D 7
Dieng Plateau • **RI** 168 C 3
Dienné o••• **RMM** 202-203 H 3
Diên Phu'ó'c o **VN** 158-159 K 4
Diepholz o **D** 92-93 K 2
Dieppe o• **F** 90-91 H 7
Dierks o **USA** (AR) 276-277 A 6
Dieterich o **USA** (IL) 274-275 K 5
Dietrich o **USA** (ID) 252-253 D 4
Die Venster ▲ **ZA** 220-221 D 6
Dif o **EAK** 212-213 H 3
Diffa ◘ **RN** 198-199 F 4
Diffa ☆ **RN** (DIF) 198-199 F 6
Diffa, ad- ⩦ **ET** 192-193 L 2
Difounda o **G** 210-211 C 5
Difuma o **ZRE** 210-211 K 5
Dig o **IND** 138-139 F 6
Digba o **ZRE** 206-207 G 6
Digboi o **IND** 142-143 J 2
Digby o **CDN** (NS) 240-241 K 6
Digges o **CDN** 30-31 W 6
Digges Islands ⌒ **CDN** 36-37 K 3
Digges Sound ⌒ **CDN** 36-37 K 3
Dighanchi o **IND** 140-141 F 2
Dighton o **USA** (KS) 262-263 F 6
Diğla ~ **IRQ** 128-129 M 6
Diglūr o **IND** 138-139 F 10
Digne-les-Bains o• **F** 90-91 L 9
Digoin o **F** 90-91 K 8
Digor ☆ **TR** 128-129 K 2
Digora o **RUS** 126-127 F 6
Digos ☆ **RP** 160-161 F 9
Digri o **PK** 138-139 B 7
Digsa • **ER** 200-201 J 5
Digua o **RCH** 78-79 D 4
Diguillín, Río ~ **RCH** 78-79 D 4
Digul ~ **RI** 166-167 K 5
Digya National Park ⊥ **GH** 202-203 K 6
Dihang or Siang ~ **IND** 142-143 J 1
Diibao o **CAM** 206-207 B 4
Dijar o **KZ** 126-127 M 4
Dijmphna Sund ≈ 26-27 p 4
Dijon ☆•• **F** 90-91 K 8
Dijun ~ **RG** 202-203 F 5
Dijur o **RUS** 88-89 W 4
Dik o **TCH** 206-207 C 4
Dika, mys ▲ **RUS** 108-109 k 3
Dikāka, ad- ⩦ **KSA** 132-133 G 4
Dikanäs o **S** 86-87 G 4
Dikhil o **DJI** 208-209 F 3
Dikhu ~ **IND** 142-143 J 2
Dikili ☆ **TR** 128-129 B 3
Dikimdja o **RUS** 118-119 K 6
Dikirnis o **ET** 194-195 E 2
Dikodougou o **CI** 202-203 H 5
Dikson ☆ **RUS** 108-109 T 5
Dikson, ostrov ⌒ **RUS** 108-109 T 5
Dikulwe ~ **ZRE** 214-215 D 6
Dikwa o **WAN** 198-199 F 6
Dila o **ETH** 208-209 D 5
Dilam, ad- o **KSA** 130-131 K 6
Dilezi Geçidi ▲ **TR** 128-129 L 4
Dili ☆ **RI** 166-167 C 6
Dili o **ZRE** 210-211 L 2
Dilia ~ **RN** 198-199 F 5
Dilia o **USA** (NM) 256-257 K 3
Di Linh o• **VN** 158-159 K 5
Diližan o **AR** 128-129 L 2
Diližanskij zapovednik ⊥ **AR** 128-129 L 2
Dilj ▲ **HR** 100-101 F 2
Dilke o **CDN** (SAS) 232-233 N 5
Dilkon o **USA** (AZ) 256-257 E 3
Dilley o **USA** (TX) 266-267 H 5
Dilli o **RMM** 202-203 G 2
Dillikot o **NEP** 144-145 C 6
Dilling o **SUD** 200-201 D 6
Dillingham o **USA** 22-23 R 3
Dillon o **USA** (CO) 254-255 J 4
Dillon o **USA** (MT) 250-251 G 6
Dillon o **USA** (SC) 284-285 L 2
Dillon Lake o **USA** (OH) 280-281 E 3
Dillsboro o **USA** (IN) 274-275 N 5
Dillsburg o **USA** (PA) 280-281 J 3
Dilo = Djidji ~ **G** 210-211 D 4
Dilolo o **ZRE** 214-215 B 6
Dilts Historic Site, Fort ∴ **USA** (ND) 258-259 D 5
Dima o **ETH** 208-209 D 3
Dimako o **CAM** 204-205 K 6
Dimalla o **RIM** 196-197 E 6
Dimāpur o **IND** 142-143 H 3
Dimašq ★••• **SYR** 128-129 G 6
Dimbaza o **ZA** 220-221 H 6
Dimbelenge o **ZRE** 210-211 J 6
Dimbokro ☆ **CI** 202-203 H 6
Dimboola o **AUS** 180-181 G 4
Dimbulah o **AUS** 174-175 H 5
Dimissi o **PNG** 183 B 5
Dimitrievka o **RUS** 94-95 R 5
Dimitrovgrad o **BG** 102-103 D 6
Dimitrovgrad ☆ **RUS** 96-97 F 6
Dimitrovgrad o• **YU** 100-101 J 3
Dimlang ▲ **WAN** 204-205 J 4
Dimlao o **RP** 160-161 F 8
Dimlik ~ **TCH** 206-207 C 4
Dimma Lake o **CDN** 30-31 T 5
Dimmitt o **USA** (TX) 264-265 B 4
Dimona ☆ **IL** 130-131 D 2
Dimora o **AUS** 178-179 G 1
Dimpam o **CAM** 210-211 D 2
Dina o **PK** 138-139 D 3
Dinagat o **RP** 160-161 F 8
Dinagat Island ⌒ **RP** 160-161 F 7
Dinajpur o **BD** 142-143 F 3
Dinalongan o **RP** 160-161 D 4
Dinan o•• **F** 90-91 F 7
Dinangourou o **RMM** 202-203 J 2
Dinant o• **B** 92-93 H 3
Dinapigui o **RP** 160-161 E 4
Dinar ☆ **TR** 128-129 D 3
Dinār, Kūh-e ▲ **IR** 134-135 D 3
Dinara ▲ **YU** 100-101 F 2
Dinchiya Shet' ~ **ETH** 208-209 C 5
Dindar o **SUD** (Kas) 200-201 G 6
Dindar ~ **SUD** 200-201 G 6
Dindar National Park ⊥ **SUD** 200-201 G 6
Dinder Wenz ~ **ETH** 208-209 B 3
Dindi o **ZW** 218-219 G 3
Dindigul o **IND** 140-141 G 5
Dindima o **WAN** 204-205 J 3
Dindori o **IND** 142-143 B 4
Dindoudi Séydi o **SN** 202-203 D 2
Dinga o **PK** 138-139 D 3
Dinga o **ZRE** 210-211 F 6
Dingalan Bay ≈ 160-161 D 5
Ding'an o **VRC** 156-157 D 4
Dingbian o **VRC** 154-155 E 3
Ding Ding o **SUD** 206-207 L 4
Dinge o **ANG** 216-217 B 7
Dinggye o **VRC** 144-145 F 6
Dinghushan • **VRC** 156-157 H 5
Dinghushan Z.B. ⊥ **VRC** 156-157 H 5
Dingila o **ZRE** 210-211 L 2
Dingle = An Daingean o **IRL** 90-91 B 5
Dingle Bay ≈ 90-91 B 5
Dingley Dell Cons. P. • **AUS** 180-181 F 5
Dingnan o **VRC** 156-157 J 4
Dingo o **ANG** 216-217 F 8
Dingo o **AUS** 178-179 K 2
Dingtao o **VRC** 154-155 J 4
Dinguirayé o **RG** 202-203 E 4
Dingwall o **CDN** (NS) 240-241 P 4
Dingwall o **GB** 90-91 E 3
Dingwells Mills o **CDN** (NS) 240-241 N 4
Dingxi o **VRC** 154-155 D 4
Dingxiang o **VRC** 154-155 H 2
Dingyuan o **VRC** 154-155 K 5
Dingzhou o **VRC** 154-155 J 2
Dingzikou o **VRC** 146-147 L 6
Dinhata o **IND** 142-143 F 2
Đinh Lap ☆ **VN** 156-157 E 6
Dinnebito Wash ~ **USA** 256-257 E 2
Dinnik, Plateau de ▲ **RN** 204-205 E 1
Dinokwe o **RB** 218-219 D 6
Dinorwic o **CDN** (ONT) 234-235 L 5
Dinosaur o **USA** (CO) 254-255 G 3
Dinosaur National Monument ∴ **USA** (CO) 254-255 G 3
Dinosaur Provincial Park ⊥••• **CDN** (ALB) 232-233 G 5
Dinosaurusspore • **NAM** 216-217 D 10
Dinsmore o **CDN** (SAS) 232-233 L 4
Dintiteladas o **RI** 162-163 F 7
Dinuba o **USA** (CA) 248-249 E 3
Dioïla o **RMM** 202-203 G 3
Diomandou o **RG** 202-203 F 5
Dinna o **BF** 202-203 J 4
Diona o **TCH** 198-199 L 4
Diongoï o **RMM** 202-203 F 2
Dionisio o **BR** 72-73 J 5
Dionísio Cerqueira o **BR** 74-75 D 6
Dionouga o **BF** 202-203 K 2
Diorama o **BR** 72-73 E 4
Diosso o **RCB** 210-211 C 6
Diou o **F** 90-91 J 8
Dioulatiédougou o **CI** 202-203 G 5
Diouloulou o **SN** 202-203 B 3
Dioumara o **RMM** 202-203 F 2
Dioundiou o **RN** 204-205 E 2
Dioura o **RMM** 202-203 H 2
Diourbel ☆• **SN** 202-203 B 2
Diourou o **RMM** 202-203 H 3
Dipālpur o **PK** 138-139 D 4
Dipchari o **WAN** 204-205 K 3
Diphu o **IND** 142-143 H 3
Dipkun o **RUS** 118-119 N 8
Diplo o **PK** 138-139 B 7
Dipolog ☆ **RP** 160-161 E 8
Dippa ~ **RUS** 118-119 K 3
Dipperu National Park ⊥ **AUS** 178-179 K 1
Di Qār ◘ **IRQ** 128-129 M 7
Diqdāqa o **UAE** 134-135 F 6
Dir o **PK** 138-139 C 2
Dira o **TCH** 198-199 G 5
Dirangzong o **IND** 142-143 H 2
Dirat at-Tulūl ⩦ **SYR** 128-129 G 6
Dire o **IRQ** 128-129 L 4
Diré o **RMM** 196-197 J 6
Direction, Cape ▲ **AUS** 174-175 G 3
Dirē Dawa o• **ETH** 208-209 E 4
Dirgi Shabozai o **PK** 138-139 B 4
Diriamba o **NIC** 52-53 L 6
Dirico o **ANG** 216-217 F 8
Dir'iya, ad- o **KSA** (QAS) 130-131 H 5
Dir'iya, ad- o• **KSA** (RIY) 130-131 K 5
Dirk Hartog Island ⌒•• **AUS** 176-177 B 2
Dirkou o **RN** 198-199 F 3
Dirrah o **SUD** 200-201 C 6
Dirranbandi o **AUS** 178-179 K 5
Dirty Devil River ~ **USA** 254-255 E 5
Disa o **IND** 138-139 D 7
Disang ~ **IND** 142-143 J 2
Disappointment, Cape ▲ **GB** 78-79 O 7
Disappointment, Cape ▲ **USA** (WA) 244-245 A 4
Disappointment, Lake o **AUS** 172-173 F 7
Disautel o **USA** (WA) 244-245 F 2
Discovery Bay ≈ 180-181 F 5
Discovery Bay o **USA** (WA) 244-245 C 3
Discovery Reef = Huaguang Jiao ⌒ **VRC** 158-159 L 2
Discovery Seamounts ≃ 6-7 K 13
Dishkakat o **USA** 20-21 M 5
Dishna River ~ **USA** 20-21 M 5
Disko Banke ≃ 28-29 M 2
Disko Bugt ≈ 28-29 O 2
Disko Fjord ≈ 28-29 N 2
Diskotjord = Kangerluk o **GRØ** 28-29 N 2
Disko Ø ⌒ **GRØ** 28-29 N 2
Disley o **CDN** (SAS) 232-233 N 5
Dismal Creek ~ **CDN** 232-233 B 2
Dismal Lakes o **CDN** 30-31 L 2
Dišnā o **ET** 194-195 F 4
Disney o **AUS** 178-179 J 1
Disneyland • **USA** (CA) 248-249 G 6
Disney World, Walt •• **USA** (FL) 286-287 H 3
display structure o **CDN** 32-33 Q 3
Dispur ☆ **IND** 142-143 G 2
Disputada, La o **RCH** 78-79 D 2
Disraeli o **CDN** (QUE) 238-239 O 3
Disraeli Fiord ≈ 26-27 O 2
Diss o **GB** 90-91 H 5
Dissain, Ğazirat ⌒ **KSA** 132-133 B 5
Disteghil Sar ▲ **IND** 138-139 E 1
Distrito Federal ◘ **BR** 72-73 F 3
Distrito Federal ◘ **MEX** 52-53 E 2
Disūq o **ET** 194-195 E 2
Ditang o **VRC** 156-157 F 2
Dite Sanctuaire des Addax, Réserve Naturelle Intégrale ⊥ **RN** 198-199 D 3
Ditinn o **RG** 202-203 D 4
Ditsinane < **RB** 218-219 C 5
Diu o **IND** 138-139 C 9
Divāndarre o **IR** 128-129 M 5
Divénié o **RCB** 210-211 D 5
Diverson Lake < **USA** (TX) 264-265 F 5
Divide o **CDN** (SAS) 232-233 J 6
Divide o **USA** (CO) 254-255 K 5
Divide o **USA** (MT) 250-251 G 6
Divilican o **RP** 160-161 E 4
Divilican Bay ≈ 160-161 E 4
Divinhe o **MOC** 218-219 H 5
Divinolândia de Minas o **BR** 72-73 J 5
Divinópolis o **BR** 72-73 H 6
Divisa o **PA** 52-53 D 7
Divisadero, El o **MEX** 50-51 F 4
Divisaderos o **MEX** 50-51 E 3
Divisões ou de Santa Marta, Serra das ▲ **BR** 72-73 D 4
Divisópolis o **BR** 72-73 K 3
Divisor, Serra de ▲ **BR** 64-65 F 5
Divisoria o **RP** 160-161 F 7
Divisorio, El o **RA** 78-79 J 5
Divnogorsk o **RUS** 116-117 F 8
Divo ☆ **CI** 202-203 H 7
Divor, Ribeira do ~ **P** 98-99 C 5
Divot o **USA** (TX) 266-267 H 5
Divriği ☆••• **TR** 128-129 H 3
Divuma o **ZRE** 214-215 B 6
Diwāniya, ad- ☆ **IRQ** 128-129 L 7
Diwopu J. II **VRC** 146-147 H 4
Diwouni, Mare o **DY** 202-203 L 4
Dixcove o **GH** 202-203 K 7
Dixfield o **USA** (ME) 278-279 L 4
Dixiasenlin • **VRC** 150-151 G 5
Dixie o **USA** (ID) 250-251 D 6
Dixie o **USA** (WA) 244-245 G 4
Dixie Valley o **USA** (NV) 246-247 G 4
Dix-Milles, Lac o **CDN** (QUE) 238-239 H 2
Dixmont o **USA** (ME) 278-279 M 4
Dixon o **USA** (CA) 246-247 D 5
Dixon o **USA** (IL) 274-275 J 3
Dixon o **USA** (KY) 276-277 H 3
Dixon o **USA** (MO) 276-277 C 3
Dixon o **USA** (MS) 268-269 L 4
Dixon o **USA** (MT) 250-251 E 4
Dixon o **USA** (WY) 252-253 L 5
Dixon Entrance ≈ 228-229 D 2
Dixonville o **CDN** 32-33 M 3
Dixonville o **RA** 78-79 G 3
Diyadin ☆ **TR** 128-129 K 3
Diyālā ◘ **IRQ** 128-129 L 6
Diyarbakır o•• **TR** 128-129 J 4
Dizangué o **CAM** 210-211 C 2
Dize o **IR** 128-129 L 4
Dizhipoumian ⊥ **VRC** 154-155 K 1
Dja ~ **CAM** 210-211 E 2
Dja, Réserve du = Dja Reserve ⊥••• **CAM** 210-211 D 2
Djado, Plateau du ▲ **RN** 198-199 F 1
Djado (Ville fortifiée) ∴• **RN** 198-199 F 2
Djakarta = Jakarta ★ **RI** 168 B 3
Djakotomè o **DY** 202-203 L 6
Djalasiga o **ZRE** 212-213 C 2
Djale ~ **ZRE** 210-211 J 5
Djaluwon Creek ~ **AUS** 172-173 H 6
Djamâa o **DZ** 190-191 E 4
Djamandjary o **RM** 222-223 F 4
Djamba o **ZRE** (HAU) 210-211 K 2
Djamba o **ZRE** (SHA) 214-215 B 5
Djambala o **CAM** 204-205 K 5
Djambala ☆ **RCB** 210-211 E 5
Djampiel o **CAM** 206-207 B 6
Djanet ☆• **DZ** 190-191 G 8
Djangylah, ostrov ⌒ **RUS** 110-111 N 3
Djanyška ~ **RUS** 110-111 Q 7
Djara ~ **RUS** 110-111 F 5
Dja Reserve = Réserve du Dja ⊥••• **CAM** 210-211 D 2
Djaret, Oued ~ **DZ** 190-191 C 7
Djarua ~ **RI** 166-167 G 3
Djat'kovo o **RUS** 94-95 O 5
Djeboho ▲ **GH** 202-203 L 5
Djebok o **RMM** 196-197 L 6
Djébrène o **TCH** 206-207 D 3
Djédaa o **TCH** 198-199 J 6
Djeddars • **DZ** 190-191 C 3
Djedi, Oued ~ **DZ** 190-191 E 3
Djedid, Bir o **DZ** 190-191 F 4
Djelfa ☆• **DZ** 190-191 D 3
Djéma o **RCA** 206-207 G 5
Djemadja, Pulau = Jemaja, Pulau ⌒ **RI** 162-163 F 3
Djèmber o **TCH** 206-207 C 3
Djemena, Am o **TCH** 198-199 H 6
Djemila ∴••• **DZ** 190-191 E 2
Djems Bank ≃ 162-163 K 3
Djeniene Bou Rzeg o **DZ** 188-189 L 4
Djerem ~ **CAM** 204-205 K 6
Djérem ~ **CAM** 204-205 K 5
Djermaya o **TCH** 198-199 G 6
Djibasso o **BF** 202-203 H 3
Djibo o **BF** 202-203 K 2
Djiborosso o **CI** 202-203 G 5
Djibouti ■ **DJI** 208-209 F 3
Djibouti ★ **DJI** 208-209 F 3

Denton — Djibouti 321

Djidja ○ DY 202-203 L 6
Djidji = Dilo ~ G 210-211 D 4
Djigoué ○ BF 202-203 J 4
Djigouéra ○ BF 202-203 H 4
Djiguéni ○ RIM 196-197 F 7
Djilbe ○ CAM 206-207 B 3
Djillali Ben Amar ○ DZ 190-191 C 3
Djiroutou ○ CI 202-203 G 7
Djogos Jar, Bereg ⌣ RUS 110-111 X 3
Djohong ○ CAM 206-207 B 5
Djoku-Punda ○ ZRE 210-211 H 6
Djoli ○ TCH 206-207 D 4
Djolu ○ ZRE 210-211 J 3
Djombo ○ ZRE 210-211 H 3
Djombo = Haraz ○ TCH 198-199 J 6
Djombo Kibbit ○ TCH 198-199 J 6
Djona, Zone Cynégétique de ⊥ DY 204-205 E 3
Djonâba ○ RIM 196-197 D 6
Djorf Torba ○ DZ 188-189 K 5
Djorf-Torba, Barrage < DZ 188-189 K 5
Djoua ~ G 210-211 D 3
Djoubissi ○ RCA 206-207 E 5
Djoudj, Parc National des oiseaux du ⊥ ••• SN 196-197 B 6
Djoué ~ RCB 210-211 E 5
Djougou ○ DY 202-203 L 5
Djoûk, Passe de ▲ RIM 196-197 D 6
Djoum ○ CAM 210-211 D 2
Djoumboli ○ CAM 204-205 K 5
Djourab, Erg du ⩡ TCH 198-199 H 4
Djoutou-Pétel ○ RG 202-203 D 4
Djugadjak ~ RUS 112-113 K 4
Djugu ○ ZRE 212-213 C 3
Djulljukju ○ RUS 118-119 K 4
Djul'tydag, gora ▲ RUS 126-127 G 7
Djúpivogur ○ IS 86-87 f 2
Djupkun, ozero ⌓ RUS (EVN) 108-109 c 7
Djupkun, ozero ⌓ RUS (EVN) 116-117 F 2
Djura, Kytyl- ○ RUS 118-119 M 5
Djurdjura, Djebel ▲ DZ 190-191 E 2
Djurtjuli ☆ RUS 96-97 J 6
D'kar ○ RB 216-217 F 10
Dla ~ RMM 202-203 F 3
Dlinnyj, ostrov ⌒ RUS 108-109 I Y 2
Dlolwana ○ ZA 220-221 K 4
Dmitrievka ○ KZ 124-125 E 2
Dmitriev-L'govskij ○ RUS 94-95 O 5
Dmitrija Lapteva, proliv ≈ 110-111 W 3
Dmitrov ☆• RUS 94-95 P 3
Dmytrivka ○ UA 102-103 H 2
Dnepr ~ RUS 94-95 M 4
Dneprodzeržinsk = Dniprodzeržyns'k ○ UA 102-103 J 3
Dnepropetrovsk = Dnipropetrovs'k ☆ UA 102-103 J 3
Dnestr = Dnister ~ UA 102-103 E 3
Dnestr = Nistru ~ MD 102-103 F 4
Dnipro ~ UA 102-103 J 3
Dnipro ~ UA 102-103 G 2
Dniprodzeržyns'k ○ UA 102-103 J 3
Dniprodzherzhyns'k = Dniprodzeržyns'k ○ UA 102-103 J 3
Dnipropetrovs'k ☆ UA 102-103 J 3
Dniprorudne ○ UA 102-103 J 4
Dniprovskyj lyman ≈ 102-103 G 4
Dniprovs'kyj lyman ≈ 102-103 H 4
Dnister ~ UA 102-103 E 3
Dnistrovs'kyj lyman ≈ 102-103 G 4
Dnjapro ~ BY 94-95 M 5
Dnjaprovska-Buhski, Kanal < BY 94-95 J 5
Dno ☆ RUS 94-95 L 3
Do, Lac ⌓ RMM 202-203 J 2
Doa ○ MOC 218-219 H 3
Doäba ○ PK 138-139 C 3
Doaktown ○ CDN (NB) 240-241 J 4
Doangdoangan Besar, Pulau ⌒ RI 164-165 E 6
Doany ○ RM 222-223 F 5
Doba ☆ TCH 206-207 C 4
Doba ○ VRC 144-145 G 5
Dobbiaco = Toblach ○ I 100-101 D 1
Dobbin ○ USA (TX) 268-269 E 6
Dobbin Bay ≈ 26-27 N 4
Dobbs, Cape ▲ CDN 36-37 F 2
Dobbspet ○ IND 140-141 G 4
Dobbyn ○ AUS 174-175 F 6
Dobele ○•• LV 94-95 H 3
Doberai Peninsula ⌣ RI 166-167 F 2
Dobie River ~ CDN 234-235 N 3
Dobinga ○ CAM 204-205 K 4
Doblas ○ RA 78-79 G 4
Dobo ○•• RI 166-167 H 4
Doboj ○• BIH 100-101 G 2
Doboy Sound ≈ 284-285 J 5
Dobre Miasto ○• PL 92-93 Q 2
Dobrič ○ BG 102-103 E 6
Dobrich = Dobrič ○ BG 102-103 E 6
Dobrinka ○ RUS 94-95 R 5
Dobrjanka ☆ RUS 96-97 K 4
Dobromyl' ○ UA 102-103 C 3
Dobron' ○ UA 102-103 C 3
Dobropil'la ○ UA 102-103 K 3
Dobroteşti ○ RO 102-103 D 5
Dobruči ○ RUS 94-95 K 2
Dobruš ○ BY 94-95 M 5
Dobržanskogo, ostrov ⌒ RUS 112-113 M 5
Dobzha ○ VRC 144-145 G 6
Đốc, Mũi ▲ VN 158-159 J 2
Docas, Cachoeira das ~ BR 72-73 D 3
Doc Can Island ⌒ RP 160-161 C 10
Doce, Rio ~ BR 72-73 E 4
Doce, Rio ~ BR 72-73 K 5
Docker River ⵅ AUS (NT) 176-177 K 2
Docker River ~ AUS 176-177 K 2
Docking ○ GB 90-91 H 5
Dock Junction ○ USA (GA) 284-285 J 5
Dockrell, Mount ▲ AUS 172-173 H 5
Dockyard, The ⩡ AG 56 E 3
Doctor Arroyo ○ MEX 50-51 J 6
Doctor González ○ MEX 50-51 K 5
Doctor Mora ○ MEX 50-51 J 7
Doctor Pedro P. Peña ☆ PY 76-77 F 2
Doda ○ EAT 212-213 G 6
Doda ○ RI 164-165 G 4
Dodaga ○ RI 164-165 L 3
Dod Ballapur ○ IND 140-141 G 4
Dodecanese = Dodekanissa ⌒ GR 100-101 L 6
Dødes Fjord, De ≈ 26-27 R 5
Dodge ○ USA (ND) 258-259 E 4
Dodge Center ○ USA (MN) 270-271 F 6
Dodge City ○• USA (KS) 262-263 F 7
Dodge Lake ⌓ CDN 30-31 R 6
Dodinga ○ RI 164-165 K 3
Dodji ○ SN 202-203 C 2
Dodol < SP 212-213 J 2
Dodola ○ ETH 208-209 D 5
Dodoma ⊡ EAT 212-213 E 6
Dodoma ★• EAT (DOD) 214-215 H 4
Dodori ~ EAK 212-213 H 4
Dodori National Reserve ⊥ EAK 212-213 H 4
Dodowa ○ GH 202-203 K 7
Dodsland ○ CDN (SAS) 232-233 K 4
Dodson ○ USA (LA) 268-269 H 4
Dodson ○ USA (MT) 250-251 L 3
Dodson ○ USA (TX) 264-265 D 4
Dodson Peninsula ⌣ ARK 16 F 30
Doege ○ ANG 216-217 F 4
Doembang Nangbuat ○ THA 158-159 F 3
Doerun ○ USA (GA) 284-285 G 5
Dofa ○ RI 164-165 J 4
Dögāʾī ○ IR 136-137 F 6
Dogai Coring ⌓ VRC 144-145 G 3
Dogal'dyn ~ RUS 108-109 a 7
Doğanşehir ☆ TR 128-129 G 3
Doğansu ○ TR 128-129 K 3
Dogbo-Tota ○ DY 202-203 L 6
Dog Creek ○ CDN (BC) 230-231 G 2
Dogdo ~ RUS 110-111 V 6
Dogger Bank ≃ 90-91 H 4
Dog Island ⌒ CDN 36-37 T 6
Dog Island ⌒ USA (FL) 286-287 E 2
Dog Lake ⌓ CDN (MAN) 234-235 E 4
Dog Lake ⌓ CDN (ONT) 234-235 O 6
Dog Lake ⌓ CDN (ONT) 236-237 D 4
Dōgo ⌒ J 152-153 E 6
Dogo ○ RMM 202-203 G 4
Dogoba ○ SUD 206-207 J 5
Dō Gonbadān ○• IR 134-135 D 3
Dogondoutchi ○ RN 198-199 B 6
Dogoumbo ○ TCH 206-207 C 3
Dōgo-yama ▲ J 152-153 E 7
Dogpatch U.S.A. • USA (AR) 276-277 B 4
Dogpound Creek ~ CDN 232-233 D 4
Dog Salmon River ~ USA 22-23 S 4
Doğubayazıt ☆ TR 128-129 L 3
Doğu Karadeniz Dağlari ▲ TR 128-129 H 2
Doğu Menteşe Dağları ▲ TR 128-129 C 4
Dogura ○ PNG 183 F 6
Dogwalo, River ~ WAN 204-205 H 3
Dogwood Creek ~ AUS 178-179 K 4
Dogyaling ○ VRC 144-145 G 5
Dogyldo ~ RUS 114-115 U 4
Doha = ad-Dauha ★ Q 134-135 D 6
Doi, Pulau ⌒ RI 164-165 K 2
Doigan ▲ EAK 212-213 F 3
Doig River ~ CDN 32-33 K 3
Doi Inthanon ▲ THA 142-143 L 6
Doi Inthanon National Park ⊥ THA 142-143 L 6
Đồi Mồi, Hòn ⌒ VN 158-159 H 6
Dois Córregos ○ BR 72-73 F 7
Dois de Novembro, Cachoeira ~ BR 66-67 F 7
Dois Irmãos ○ BR 72-73 F 3
Dois Irmãos, Cachoeira ~ BR 66-67 H 7
Dois Riachos, Rio ~ BR 68-69 K 6
Doi Suthep-Poi National Park ⊥ THA 142-143 L 6
Dois Vizinhos ○ BR 74-75 D 5
Doi Tachi ▲ THA 158-159 E 2
Doka ○ RI 166-167 H 5
Doka ○ SUD 200-201 G 6
Dokhara, Dunes de ⩡ DZ 190-191 E 4
Dokis Indian Reserve ⵅ CDN (ONT) 238-239 F 2
Doko ○ RG 202-203 F 4
Doko ○ WAN 198-199 D 6
Dokpam ○ GH 202-203 K 5
Doktorskij, mys ▲ RUS 110-111 Q 3
Dokučaevs'k ○ UA 102-103 K 4
Dokui ○ BF 202-203 H 3
Dolak, Pulau ⌒ RI 166-167 K 5
Dolak Pulau Reserve ⊥ • RI 166-167 J 5
Doland ○ USA (SD) 260-261 H 2
Dolan Springs ○ USA (AZ) 256-257 A 3
Dolavon ○ RA 78-79 G 7
Dolbeau ○ CDN (QUE) 240-241 C 2
Dolbel ○ RN 202-203 L 2
Dolby Lake ⌓ CDN 30-31 R 5
Doldrums Fracture Zone ≃ 6-7 F 8
Dole ○ F 90-91 K 8
Doleib Hill ○ SUD 206-207 K 4
Dolenci ○ MK 100-101 H 4
Dolgellau ○ GB 90-91 F 5
Dolgij, ostrov ⌒ RUS (NAO) 88-89 X 2
Dolgij, ostrov ⌒ RUS (NNC) 108-109 H 7
Dolgij Most ○ RUS 116-117 H 7
Dolgoderevenskoe ☆ RUS 96-97 M 6
Dolgoi Island ⌒ USA 22-23 Q 5
Dolia ○ IND 138-139 C 8
Dolina gejzerov •• RUS 120-121 S 6
Dolinovka ○ RUS 120-121 S 6
Dolinsk ○ RUS 122-123 K 5
Dolit ○ RI 164-165 K 4
Dolleman Island ⌒ ARK 16 F 30
Dollo Odo ○ ETH 208-209 F 6
Dolni Lom ○ BG 102-103 C 6
Dolný Kubín ○ SK 92-93 P 4
Dolo ○ RI 164-165 F 4
Dolokmerawan ○ RI 162-163 C 3
Dolok Pinapan ▲ RI 162-163 C 3
Dolomite Caves • NAM 216-217 C 10
Dolomiti = Dolomiten ▲ I 100-101 C 1
Dolong ○ RI 164-165 H 4
Doloon ○ MAU 148-149 G 5
Dolores ○ CO 60-61 D 6
Dolores ○ GCA 52-53 K 3
Dolores ○ RA 78-79 L 4
Dolores ○ ROU 78-79 K 2
Dolores ~ RP 160-161 F 6
Dolores ○ USA (CO) 254-255 G 6
Dolores ○ YV 60-61 G 3
Dolores Creek ~ USA 266-267 H 6
Dolores Hidalgo ○• MEX 50-51 J 7
Dolores River ~ USA 254-255 G 5
Doloroso ○ USA (MS) 268-269 J 5
Dolphin, Cape ▲ GB 78-79 L 6
Dolphin and Union Strait ≈ 24-25 O 6
Dolphins • AUS 176-177 B 2
Đỗ Lư'ơng ☆ VN 156-157 D 7
Dolyna ☆ UA 102-103 D 3
Dolyns'ka ○ UA 102-103 H 3
Dom, Gunung ▲ RI 166-167 J 3
Doma ○ ZW 218-219 F 3
Domain ○ CDN (MAN) 234-235 F 5
Domaine de chasse d'Iguéla ⊥ G 210-211 B 4
Dom Aquino ○ BR 70-71 K 4
Domar ○ VRC 144-145 C 4
Doma Safari Area ⊥ ZW 218-219 F 3
Domažlice ○ CZ 92-93 M 4
Dombaj Ul'gen, gora ▲ RUS 126-127 D 6
Dombarovskij ☆ RUS 126-127 N 2
Dombås ○ N 86-87 D 5
Dombe ○ MOC 218-219 G 4
Dombe Grande ○ ANG 216-217 B 6
Dombey, Cape ▲ AUS 180-181 E 4
Dombo ○ RI 166-167 J 2
Domboshawa ○• ZW (Mle) 218-219 F 3
Domboshawa ▲ ZW (Mle) 218-219 F 3
Dombóvár ○ H 92-93 P 5
Dom Cavat ○ BR 72-73 J 5
Dome Bay ≈ 24-25 U 1
Dome Creek ○ CDN (BC) 228-229 N 3
Domel ○ IND 138-139 E 3
Domeyko ○ RCH 76-77 B 5
Domeyko, Cordillera de ▲ RCH 76-77 C 3
Domfront ○ F 90-91 G 7
Dominase ○ GH 202-203 K 6
Domingos Martins ○ BR 72-73 K 6
Domingos Mourão ○ BR 68-69 H 4
Dominica ■ WD 56 E 4
Dominica Island ⌒ WD 56 E 4
Dominical ○ CR 52-53 C 7
Dominican Republic = Republica Dominicana ■ DOM 54-55 K 5
Dominica Passage ≈ 56 E 4
Dominion, Cape ▲ CDN (NWM) 28-29 C 3
Dominion City ○ CDN (MAN) 234-235 F 5
Dominion Range ▲ ARK 16 E 0
Domiongo ○ ZRE 210-211 H 6
Domkonda ○ IND 138-139 G 10
Domo ○ ETH 208-209 H 5
Domodedovo ☆ RUS 94-95 P 4
Domodóssola ○ I 100-101 B 1
Domoni ○ COM 222-223 D 4
Dom Pedrito ○ BR 76-77 K 6
Dom Pedro ○ BR 68-69 F 4
Dompem ○ GH 202-203 J 7
Dompu ○ RI 168 D 7
Domremy ○ CDN (SAS) 232-233 N 3
Dom Silvério ○ BR 72-73 J 6
Domuyo, Volcán ▲ RA 78-79 D 4
Don ~ GB 90-91 F 3
Don ~ RUS 94-95 Q 5
Don ~ RUS 102-103 L 2
Doña Ana ○ USA (NM) 256-257 J 6
Doña Ana, Cerro ▲ RCH 76-77 B 5
Doña Inés, Cerro ▲ RCH 76-77 C 4
Doña Juana, Volcán ▲ CO 64-65 D 1
Donald ○ AUS 180-181 G 4
Donald ○ CDN (BC) 230-231 M 2
Donalda ○ CDN (ALB) 232-233 F 3
Donald Landing ○ CDN (BC) 228-229 J 2
Donaldson ○ USA (AR) 276-277 C 6
Donaldson ○ USA (MN) 270-271 B 2
Donaldsonville ○ USA (LA) 268-269 K 6
Donalsonville ○ USA (GA) 284-285 F 5
Doña Rosa, Cordillera ▲ RCH 76-77 B 6
Donauwörth ○• D 92-93 L 4
Don Benito ○ E 98-99 E 5
Doncaster ○ AUS 174-175 G 7
Doncaster ○ GB 90-91 G 5
Doncaster Indian Réserve ⵅ CDN (QUE) 238-239 L 2
Doncello, El ○ CO 64-65 E 1
Dondaicha ○ IND 138-139 E 9
Donderkamp ○ SME 62-63 F 3
Don Diego ○ CO 60-61 E 2
Dondo ○ ANG 216-217 C 4
Dondo ○ MOC 218-219 H 4
Dondo ○ RI (NTI) 168 E 7
Dondo ○ RI (SLT) 164-165 H 4
Dondo ○ ZRE 206-207 E 6
Dondo, Teluk ≈ 164-165 G 3
Dondon ○ RH 54-55 J 5
Đo'n Du'o'ng ○ VN 158-159 K 5
Donec ~ RUS 102-103 K 2
Doneck ○ RUS 102-103 L 3
Donec'k ☆ UA 102-103 K 4
Doneck = Donec'k ☆ UA 102-103 K 4
Donec'kyj krjaž ▲ UA 102-103 K 3
Donegal ○• IRL 90-91 C 4
Donegal Bay ≈ 90-91 C 4
Donelson National Battlefield, Fort • USA (AR) 276-277 H 4
Don Esteban, Arroyo ~ ROU 78-79 L 2
Donets'k = Donec'k ☆ UA 102-103 K 4
Donett Point ▲ CDN 24-25 S 2
Dong ○ IND 142-143 K 1
Donga ○ DY 202-203 L 5
Donga ○ WAN 204-205 J 5
Donga, River ~ WAN 204-205 J 5
Dong'an ○ VRC 156-157 G 3
Dongane, Lagoa ⌓ MOC 218-219 H 7
Dongara ○ AUS 176-177 C 4
Dongargarh ○ IND 142-143 B 5
Dongchuan ○ VRC 156-157 C 3
Dongco ○ VRC 144-145 E 4
Đong Đăng ○ VN 156-157 E 6
Dongeleksor ○ KZ 126-127 O 3
Döngelek su kojmasy < KZ 96-97 G 8
Dongfang ○ VRC (HAI) 156-157 F 7
Dongfang ○ VRC (HUN) 156-157 F 2
Dongfanghong ○ VRC 150-151 J 4
Dongfeng ○ VRC 150-151 E 6
Donggala ○•• RI 164-165 F 4
Donggi ○ RI 164-165 H 4
Donggi Cona ⌓ VRC 144-145 M 3
Donggou ○ VRC 150-151 E 8
Dongguan ○ VRC (MS) 156-157 F 5
Dongguan ○ VRC (GDG) 156-157 H 5
Đồng Hà ☆ VN 158-159 J 2
Dong Hai ≈ 154-155 N 6
Donghai ○ VRC 154-155 L 4
Donghai Dao ⌒ VRC 156-157 G 6
Đong Hới ☆ VN 158-159 J 2
Dong Jiang ~ VRC 156-157 J 5
Dongjingcheng ○ VRC 150-151 G 5
Dongkait, Tanjung ▲ RI 164-165 F 5
Dongkala ○ RI 164-165 H 6
Dongkeng ○ VRC 156-157 L 3
Dongkou ○ VRC 156-157 G 3
Donglan ○ VRC 156-157 E 4
Dongliang ○ VRC 154-155 H 2
Dong Ling • VRC 150-151 D 7
Dongmen ○ VRC 156-157 E 5
Dongming ○ VRC 154-155 J 4
Dongnan Qiuling ▲ VRC 156-157 H 4
Dongning ○ VRC 150-151 H 5
Dongo ○ ANG 216-217 C 7
Dongo ○ ZRE 210-211 G 2
Dongola = Donqula ☆ SUD 200-201 E 3
Dongotona Mountains ▲ SUD 206-207 L 6
Dongou ○ RCB 210-211 G 2
Dong Phaya Yen ▲ THA 158-159 F 2
Đồng Phú ○ VN 158-159 J 5
Dongpo ○ VRC 144-145 C 5
Dongqiao ○ VRC 144-145 H 5
Dongsha Dao ⌒ VRC 156-157 K 6
Dongshanling • VRC 156-157 G 7
Dongshan Wan ≈ 156-157 K 5
Dongsha Qundao ⌒ VRC 156-157 K 6
Dongsheng ○ VRC 154-155 F 2
Dongtai ○ VRC 154-155 M 5
Dong Taijnar Hu ⌓ VRC 144-145 K 2
Dongting Hu ⌓ VRC 156-157 H 2
Đồng Triều ☆ VN 156-157 E 6
Dongue ○ ANG 216-217 C 7
Donguila ○ G 210-211 B 3
Dong Ujimqin Qi ○ VRC 148-149 N 5
Dongui ~ RUS 96-97 J 8
Dongwe ~ Z 218-219 C 1
Dongxing ○ VRC 156-157 F 7
Dongyang ○ VRC 156-157 M 2
Dongying ○ VRC 154-155 L 3
Dongzhai ○ VRC 154-155 J 5
Dongzhaigang Z.B. ⊥ VRC 156-157 G 7
Dongzhi ○ VRC 154-155 K 6
Donie ○ USA (TX) 266-267 L 2
Doniphan ○ USA (MO) 276-277 E 4
Donjek River ~ CDN 20-21 V 6
Donji Vakuf ○ BIH 100-101 F 2
Don Juan ○ DOM 54-55 L 5
Donkar ○ BHT 142-143 G 2
Donkerpoort ○ ZA 220-221 G 5
Donko ○ WAN 204-205 F 3
Don Martin ○ MEX 50-51 J 4
Donmatia ○ IND 142-143 G 3
Dønna ⌒ N 86-87 F 3
Donnacona ○ CDN (QUE) 238-239 O 2
Donnelly ○ CDN 32-33 M 4
Donner Pass ▲ USA (CA) 246-247 E 4
Donnybrook ○ AUS 176-177 C 6
Donnybrook ○ USA (ND) 258-259 F 3
Donnybrook ○ ZA 220-221 J 4
Dono Manga ○ TCH 206-207 C 4
Donon ▲ F 90-91 L 7
Donostia-San Sebastián ○•• E 98-99 G 3
Donovan ○ CDN (SAS) 232-233 L 4
Đon Quê ○ VN 158-159 J 2
Donqula ☆ SUD 200-201 E 3
Don River ~ AUS 174-175 J 7
Donskaja grjada ▲ RUS 102-103 L 3
Donskaja ravnina ▲ RUS 94-95 R 5
Donskoe ○ RUS 96-97 K 8
Donskoj ○ RUS 94-95 Q 5
Donyztau ▲ KZ 126-127 M 4
Doolgunna ○ AUS 176-177 E 2
Doomadgee ⵅ AUS 174-175 E 5
Doomadgee Aboriginal Land ⵅ AUS 174-175 E 5
Doonerak, Mount ▲ USA (AK) 20-21 P 3
Doongmabulla ○ AUS 178-179 J 2
Doornik = Tournai ○• B 92-93 G 3
Doorns, De ○ ZA 220-221 D 6
Door Peninsula ⌣ USA 270-271 L 6
Dora ○ USA (NM) 256-257 M 5
Dora, Lake ⌓ AUS 172-173 F 7
Dora, Mount ▲ AUS 176-177 G 3
Dorada, La ○ CO 60-61 D 5
Dorado ○ PY 76-77 G 1
Dorado, El ○ MEX 50-51 F 5
Dorado, El ○ YV 62-63 D 2
Dorado, Río ~ RA 76-77 F 3
Doraga ○ RP 160-161 E 6
Dörähäk ○ IR 134-135 D 5
Dora Lake ○ USA (MN) 270-271 D 3
Doralé ○ DJI 208-209 F 3
Doranäla ○ IND 140-141 H 3
Doran Lake ⌓ CDN 30-31 Q 5
Dorbod ○ VRC 150-151 E 4
Dorchester ○ CDN (NB) 240-241 L 5
Dorchester ☆• GB 90-91 F 6
Dorchester, Cape ▲ CDN 36-37 L 2
Dordabis ○ NAM 216-217 D 11
Dordogne ~ F 90-91 H 9
Dordrecht ○• NL 92-93 H 3
Dordrecht ○ ZA 220-221 H 5
Doreen, Mount ▲ AUS 172-173 K 7
Dores do Indaiá ○ BR 72-73 H 5
Dores do Rio Preto ○ BR 72-73 K 6
Dores Turvo ○ BR 72-73 J 6
Dorey ○ RMM 202-203 K 2
Dörgön = Seer ○ MAU 146-147 L 1
Dori ☆ BF 202-203 K 2
Doringbaai ○ ZA 220-221 D 5
Doringrivier ~ ZA 220-221 D 6
Dorion ○ CDN (ONT) 234-235 P 6
Dorion ○ CDN (QUE) 238-239 L 3
Dorisvale ○ AUS 172-173 K 3
Dorlin ○ F 62-63 H 4
Dormansville ○ USA (NY) 278-279 H 6
Dormentes ○ BR 68-69 H 6
Dornoch ○ GB 90-91 E 3
Dornod ⊡ MAU 148-149 L 4
Doro Djoutougué ○ TCH 198-199 L 6
Dorogov' ⊡ MAU 148-149 J 5
Doro ○ RMM 196-197 K 6
Dorogobuž ○ RUS 94-95 N 4
Doroh ○ IR 134-135 J 2
Dorohoi ○ RO 102-103 E 4
Dorohovo ○ RUS 94-95 P 4
Dorolamo ○ RI 164-165 L 3
Doroninskoe ○ RUS 118-119 F 10
Döröö nuur ⌓ MAU 146-147 L 2
Doropo ○ CI 202-203 J 5
Dorotea ○ S 86-87 H 4
Dorothy ○ CDN (ALB) 232-233 F 4
Dorowa ○ ZW 218-219 F 4
Dorožnyj ○ RUS 118-119 G 5
Dorra ○ DJI 200-201 L 6
Dorrance ○ USA (KS) 262-263 H 6
Dorreen ○ CDN (BC) 228-229 F 2
Dorre Island ⌒ AUS 176-177 B 2
Dorrigo ○ AUS 178-179 M 6
Dorrigo National Park ⊥ AUS 178-179 M 6
Dorris ○ USA (CA) 246-247 D 2
Dorsale Camerounaise ▲ CAM 204-205 J 5
Dorset ○ CDN (ONT) 238-239 J 3
Dorset ○ CDN (ONT) 238-239 G 3
Dorset Island ⌒ CDN 36-37 L 2
Dört Kilise ∴• TR 128-129 J 2
Dortmund ○• D 92-93 J 3
Dörtyol ☆• TR 128-129 G 4
Dorucha ○ RUS 110-111 J 3
Dorüd ○ IR 134-135 C 2
Doruma ○ ZRE 206-207 H 6
Dörvölzin = Buga ○ MAU 146-147 M 2
Dos, El ∴• MEX 52-53 L 1
Dos Bocas ∴ USA (PR) 286-287 P 2
Dos Cabezas ○ USA (AZ) 256-257 F 6
Dos Cabezas Peak ▲ USA (AZ) 256-257 F 6
Dos Caminos ○ C 54-55 H 4
Dos Caminos ○ YV 60-61 H 3
Dos de Mayo ○ PE 64-65 E 5
Doseo, Bahr ~ TCH 206-207 D 4
Dos Hermanas ○ E 98-99 E 6
Dōši ○ AFG 136-137 L 7
Dos Lagunas ○ GCA 52-53 K 3
Dos Lagunas, Parque Nacional ⊥ RCH 80 E 2
Đỗ So'n ☆ VN 156-157 E 6
Dospat ○ BG 102-103 D 7
Dosquet ○ CDN (QUE) 238-239 O 2
Dos Ríos ○ CO 64-65 F 1
Dos Rios ○ USA (CA) 246-247 B 4
Dosso ⊡ RN 204-205 E 2
Dosso ☆ RN (DOS) 204-205 E 2
Dossor ○ KZ 96-97 H 10
Dostuk ○ KS 146-147 B 5
Doswell ○ USA (VA) 280-281 J 6
Dot ○ CDN (BC) 230-231 H 3
Dothan ○ USA (AL) 284-285 E 5
Dot Klish Wash ~ USA 256-257 E 2
Dotswood ○ AUS 174-175 J 6
Douai ○ F 90-91 J 6
Douala ☆ CAM 204-205 H 6
Douala-Edéa, Réserve ⊥ CAM 210-211 B 2
Doualayel ○ CAM 204-205 K 5
Douaouir, Erg ⩡ RMM 196-197 J 4
Douarnenez ○ F 90-91 E 7
Douaya ○ RMM 196-197 J 6
Doubabougou ○ RMM 202-203 G 2
Double Bayou ○ USA (TX) 268-269 F 7
Double Island Point ▲ AUS 178-179 M 3
Double Mer ⌓ CDN 36-37 U 7
Double Mountain ▲ AUS 178-179 L 2
Double Mountain Fork Brazos River ~ USA 264-265 C 5
Double Springs ○ USA (AL) 284-285 C 2
Doubodo ~ BF 202-203 L 4
Doubs ~ F 90-91 L 8
Doubtful Bay ≈ 172-173 G 4
Doubtful Island Bay ≈ 176-177 E 7
Doubtful Sound ≈ 182 A 6
Douchuishan • VRC 154-155 D 5
Doudou ○ BF 202-203 J 4
Doué ~ SN 196-197 C 6
Douélé ○ CI 202-203 G 6
Douentza ○ RMM 202-203 J 2
Dougga ∴• TN 190-191 G 2
Doughboy Bay ≈ 182 A 7
Dougherty ○ USA (TX) 264-265 C 5
Doughton Gap ▲ USA (NC) 282-283 F 4
Douglas ○ AUS 172-173 K 2
Douglas ○ CDN (MAN) 234-235 D 5
Douglas ○ GB 78-79 L 6
Douglas ☆• GBM 90-91 E 4
Douglas ○ USA (AK) 32-33 C 2
Douglas ○ USA (AZ) 256-257 F 7
Douglas ○ USA (GA) 284-285 H 5
Douglas ○ USA (WA) 244-245 E 3
Douglas ○ USA (WY) 252-253 N 4
Douglas ○ ZA 220-221 F 4
Douglas, Cape ▲ USA 22-23 U 3
Douglas, Mount ▲ USA 22-23 U 3
Douglas Channel ≈ 228-229 E 3
Douglas City ○ USA (CA) 246-247 C 3
Douglas Creek ~ AUS 178-179 D 5
Douglas Flat ○ USA (CA) 246-247 E 5
Douglas Lake ○ CDN (BC) 230-231 J 3
Douglas Lake ⌓ CDN 30-31 Q 4
Douglas Lake ⌓ USA (TN) 282-283 D 5
Douglas Lake Indian Reserve ⵅ CDN (BC) 230-231 J 3
Douglas Pass ▲ USA (CO) 254-255 G 4
Douglas Peninsula ⌣ CDN 30-31 P 4
Douglas Point ▲ CDN (ONT) 238-239 D 4
Douglas Ponds Creek ~ AUS 178-179 H 3
Douglas Provincial Park ⊥ CDN (SAS) 232-233 M 4
Douglas Range ▲ ARK 16 G 29
Douglass ○ USA (KS) 262-263 J 7
Douglass ○ USA (TX) 268-269 F 5
Douglastown ○ CDN (QUE) 240-241 L 2
Douglasville ○ USA (GA) 284-285 F 3
Douglasville ○ USA (TX) 264-265 K 5
Dougmuge ○ VRC 156-157 C 5
Dougoulé ○ RN 198-199 E 5
Douhongpo ▲ VRC 156-157 D 4
Douka ○ RG 202-203 E 5
Douka, Bahr Kelta ou ~ TCH 206-207 D 4
Doukhobor Village • CDN (BC) 230-231 M 4
Doukoula ○ CAM 206-207 B 3
Doulatābād ○ AFG (BAL) 136-137 K 6
Doulatābād ○ AFG (FĀ) 136-137 J 6
Doulatābād ○ IR 134-135 G 4
Doulati, Āb-e ~ IR 136-137 C 7
Doulat Yār ○ AFG 134-135 L 1
Doullens ○ F 90-91 J 6
Doumandzou ○ G 210-211 C 3
Doumba bonne ○ RN 198-199 F 3
Doum Doum ○ TCH 198-199 G 6
Doumé ○ CAM (CEN) 204-205 K 6
Doumé ○ CAM (EST) 204-205 K 6
Doumé ~ CAM 206-207 B 6
Doumen ○ VRC 156-157 H 5
Doumo ○ CAM 210-211 D 2
Douna ○ BF 202-203 H 4
Douna ○ RMM 202-203 K 2
Doundé Bagué ○ SN 202-203 D 2
Dounet ○ RG 202-203 E 4
Dounguél-Sigon ○ RG 202-203 D 4
Dounkassa ○ DY 204-205 E 3
Dounkou ○ BF 202-203 J 3
Duqing ○ VRC 156-157 D 3
Dourada, Serra ▲ BR 72-73 F 2
Douradina ○ BR (GSU) 76-77 K 2
Douradina ○ BR (PAR) 72-73 D 7
Douradoquara ○ BR 72-73 G 5
Dourados ○ BR 76-77 K 2
Dourados, Rio ~ BR 76-77 K 2
Dourados, Serra dos ▲ BR 72-73 D 7
Dourbali ○ TCH 206-207 B 3
Dourbeye ○ CAM 204-205 K 4
Dourdoura ○ TCH 206-207 E 3
Douro ○ RMM (MOP) 202-203 J 2
Douro ~ RMM 202-203 J 2
Douro, Rio ~ P 98-99 D 4
Douroum ○ CAM 204-205 K 3
Doussala ○ G (Ngo) 210-211 C 5
Doussala ○ G (Nya) 210-211 C 5
Doutoufouk ○ RN 198-199 D 6
Douz ○• TN 190-191 G 4
Dove ○ PNG 183 E 5
Dove Bugt ≈ 26-27 q 5
Dove Creek ○ USA (CO) 254-255 G 6
Dover ○ AUS 180-181 J 7
Dover ○ CDN (NFL) 242-243 P 4
Dover ○• GB 90-91 H 6
Dover ○ USA (AR) 276-277 B 5
Dover ○ USA (NH) 278-279 L 5
Dover ○ USA (NJ) 280-281 M 3
Dover ○ USA (OH) 280-281 E 3
Dover ○ USA (TN) 276-277 H 4
Dover ☆ USA (DE) 280-281 L 4
Dover, Point ▲ AUS 176-177 H 6
Dover, Strait of ≈ 90-91 H 6
Dovercourt ○ CDN (ALB) 232-233 D 3
Dover-Foxcroft ○ USA (ME) 278-279 M 3
Dover River ~ CDN 32-33 O 3
Dovrefjell ▲ N 84-85 H 3
Dovsk ○ BY 94-95 M 5
Dowa ○ MW 218-219 G 1
Dowagiac ○ USA (MI) 272-273 C 6
Dowerin ○ AUS 176-177 D 5
Dowi, Mount ▲ PNG 183 D 3
Dowling Lake ⌓ CDN (ALB) 232-233 F 4
Downe ○ CDN (SAS) 232-233 K 4
Downey ○ USA (ID) 252-253 F 4
Downie Creek ○ CDN (BC) 230-231 L 2
Downie Creek ~ CDN 230-231 L 2
Downieville ○ USA (CA) 246-247 E 4
Downs ○ USA (KS) 262-263 H 5
Downsville ○ USA (NY) 278-279 F 6
Downton, Mount ▲ CDN (BC) 228-229 K 4
Doyle ○ USA (CA) 246-247 E 3
Doylestown ○ USA (PA) 280-281 L 3
Doyleville ○ USA (CO) 254-255 J 5
Doyon ○ USA (ND) 258-259 J 3
Doze de Outubro, Rio ~ BR 70-71 H 3
Dozgah, Rūdḫāne-ye ~ IR 134-135 E 4
Dozois, Réservoir ⌓ CDN (QUE) 236-237 L 5
Drâa, Cap ▲ MA 188-189 F 6
Drâa, Hamada du ⩡ DZ 188-189 H 6
Drâa, Oued ~ MA 188-189 G 6
Drâa, Vallée du ⌣•• MA 188-189 H 5
Dra Afratir ⩡ WSA 196-197 D 2
Drabonso ○ GH 202-203 K 6
Dracena ○ BR 72-73 E 6
Drachten ○ NL 92-93 J 2
Drăgăneşti-Olt ○ RO 102-103 D 5
Drăgăneşti-Vlaşca ○ RO 102-103 D 5
Drăgăşani ○ RO 102-103 D 5
Draghoender ○ ZA 220-221 F 4
Dragocennaja, guba ≈ 110-111 W 1
Dragon, Kap ▲ GRØ 26-27 Y 2
Dragoon ○ USA (AZ) 256-257 E 6
Draguignan ○ F 90-91 L 10
Drahičyn ○ BY 94-95 J 5
Drain ○ USA (OR) 244-245 B 7
Drake ○ CDN (SAS) 232-233 N 4
Drake ○ USA (MO) 274-275 G 6
Drake ○ USA (ND) 258-259 G 4
Drakensberge ▲ ZA 220-221 J 4
Drake Passage ≈ 5 E 10
Drake Peak ▲ USA (OR) 244-245 E 8
Drakes Bay ≈ 248-249 B 2
Dráma ○ GR 100-101 K 4
Drammen ☆ N 86-87 E 7
Drangajökull ⊂ IS 86-87 b 1
Dranoz ▲ TR 128-129 F 2
Draper, Mount ▲ USA 20-21 V 7
Drar Souttouf ⩡ WSA 196-197 C 4
Drāsan ○ PK 138-139 D 1
Drasco ○ USA (AR) 276-277 C 5
Drava ~ HR 100-101 F 2
Drawa ~ PL 92-93 N 2
Drawsko Pomorskie ○ PL 92-93 N 2
Drayton ○ USA (ND) 258-259 K 3
Drayton Valley ○ CDN (ALB) 232-233 D 2
Dreamworld • AUS 178-179 M 4
Dreikikir ○ PNG 183 B 2
Dremsel, Mount ▲ PNG 183 D 2
Drennan ○ ZA 220-221 G 6
Dresden ○ CDN (ONT) 238-239 C 6
Dresden ☆•• D 92-93 M 3
Dresden ○ USA (KS) 262-263 F 5
Dresden ○ USA (OH) 280-281 D 3
Dresden ○ USA (TN) 276-277 G 4
Dreux ○ F 90-91 H 7
Drevsjø ○ N 86-87 F 6
Drew ○ USA (MS) 268-269 K 3
Drewsey ○ USA (OR) 244-245 G 7
Drew's Gap ▲ USA (OR) 244-245 E 8
Drews Reservoir ⌓ USA (OR) 244-245 E 8
Drexel ○ USA (MO) 274-275 D 6
Drezdenko ○ PL 92-93 N 2
Driffield ○ GB 90-91 G 4
Drifton ○ USA (FL) 286-287 F 1
Driftpile River ~ CDN 32-33 N 4
Driftpile River Indian Reserve ⵅ CDN 32-33 N 4
Driftwood ○ CDN 32-33 G 4
Driftwood ○ USA (PA) 280-281 H 2
Driftwood Creek ~ CDN 228-229 G 2
Driftwood River ~ CDN 32-33 N 4
Driftwood River ~ CDN 236-237 G 3
Driggs ○ USA (ID) 252-253 G 3
Drimiopsis ○ NAM 216-217 E 11
Drin, Lumi ~ AL 100-101 G 3
Drina ~ YU 100-101 G 3
Drinkwater ○ CDN (SAS) 232-233 N 5
Drinkwater Pass ▲ USA (OR) 244-245 G 7
Dripping Springs ○ USA (TX) 266-267 J 3
Driscoll ○ USA (TX) 266-267 K 6
Drniš ○ HR 100-101 F 3
Drobeta-Turnu Severin ○• RO 102-103 C 5
Drobin ○ PL 92-93 P 2
Drogerivier ○ ZA 220-221 F 6
Drogheda = Droichead Átha ○ IRL 90-91 D 5
Drogobyč = Drohobyč ☆ UA 102-103 C 3
Drohobyč ☆ UA 102-103 C 3
Droichead Átha = Drogheda ○ IRL 90-91 D 5
Droichead na Bandan = Bandan ○ IRL 90-91 C 6
Drôme ~ F 90-91 K 9
Drome ○ PNG 183 B 2
Dromedary, Cape ▲ AUS 180-181 L 4
Dronne ~ F 90-91 H 9
Dronning Ingrid Land ⩡ GRØ 28-29 P 4
Dronning Louise Land ⩡ GRØ 26-27 n 5
Dronning Maud fjellkjede ▲ ARK 16 E 0
Dronning Maud land ⩡ ARK 16 F 36
Dronten ○ NL 92-93 H 2
Dropmore ○ CDN (MAN) 234-235 B 3
Drosh ○ PK 138-139 C 2
Dro Station ○ CDN (ONT) 238-239 F 4
Drottningholm ••• S 86-87 H 7
Drovers Cave National Park ⊥ AUS 176-177 C 5
Drovjanoj ○ RUS 108-109 P 5
Drowned Cays ⌒ BH 52-53 K 3
Drowning River ~ CDN 236-237 C 2
Dr. Petru Groza = Ştei ○ RO 102-103 C 4
Druid ○ CDN (SAS) 232-233 K 4
Drumduff ○ AUS 174-175 G 5
Drume ○ YU 100-101 G 3
Drumheller ○ CDN (ALB) 232-233 F 4
Drummond ○ USA (MI) 270-271 P 4
Drummond ○ USA (MT) 250-251 F 5
Drummond ○ USA (WI) 270-271 G 4
Drummond Island ⌒ USA (MI) 272-273 F 2
Drummond Range ▲ AUS 178-179 J 2
Drummondville ○ CDN (QUE) 238-239 N 3
Drumochter, Pass of ▲ GB 90-91 E 3
Drumright ○ USA (OK) 264-265 H 3
Druskininkai ○•• LT 94-95 H 4
Druza, gora ▲ RUS 120-121 K 3
Druzba ○ KZ 124-125 N 6
Družina ○ RUS 110-111 Z 5
Družkivka ○ UA 102-103 K 3
Družkovka = Družkivka ○ UA 102-103 K 3
Družnyj ○ RUS 114-115 T 5
Dry Bay ≈ 20-21 V 7
Dryberry Lake ⌓ CDN (ONT) 234-235 K 5
Drybrough ○ CDN 34-35 F 2
Dry Creek ○ USA (LA) 268-269 G 6
Dry Creek ~ USA 252-253 J 3
Dryden ○ CDN (ONT) 234-235 L 5
Dryden ○ USA (NY) 278-279 E 6
Dryden ○ USA (TX) 266-267 E 3
Dry Fork ~ USA 252-253 N 3
Drygalski Glacier ⊂ ARK 16 F 17

322 Djidja — Drygalski Glacier

Drygalski-Island ⌒ ARK 16 G 10
Drygalskis Halvø ⌣ GRØ 28-29 P 1
Dry Hartsrivier ~ ZA 220-221 G 3
Dry Island Buffalo Jump Provincial Park ⊥ CDN (ALB) 232-233 F 4
Dry Prong o USA (LA) 268-269 H 5
Dry River ~ AUS 172-173 L 3
Drysdale Island ⌒ AUS 174-175 C 2
Drysdale River o AUS (WA) 172-173 H 3
Drysdale River ~ AUS 172-173 H 3
Drysdale River National Park ⊥ AUS 172-173 H 3
Dry Tortugas ⌒ USA (FL) 286-287 G 7
Drytown o USA (CA) 246-247 E 5
Dschang o CAM 204-205 J 6
Dtscord, Kap ▲ GRØ 28-29 T 6
Dua ~ ZRE 210-211 J 2
Duaca o YV 60-61 G 2
Duale ~ ZRE 210-211 J 3
Ḍū al-Faif, Ġazirat ⌒ KSA 132-133 B 5
Dualla o CI 202-203 G 5
Du'an o VRC 156-157 F 5
Duane Center o USA (NY) 278-279 G 4
Duangua, Rio ~ MOC 218-219 F 2
Duansban o VRC 156-157 E 4
Duaringa o AUS 178-179 K 2
Duart o CDN (ONT) 238-239 D 6
Duarte o MEX 50-51 J 7
Duas Barras do Morro o BR 68-69 H 7
Duau, Mount ▲ PNG 183 C 4
Dubā o KSA 130-131 D 4
Duba o WAN 204-205 F 4
Ḍubāb o Y 132-133 C 7
Dubach o USA (LA) 268-269 H 4
Dubai = Dubayy o • UAE 134-135 F 6
Dubai'a, ad- o KSA 130-131 K 5
Dubai'a, ad- o UAE 134-135 F 6
Dubaiki, Bi'r ad- o ET 194-195 D 2
Dubăsari ☆ MD 102-103 F 4
Dubawnt Lake ⊂ CDN 30-31 S 4
Dubawnt River ~ CDN 30-31 T 3
Dubayy o • UAE 134-135 F 6
Dubbo o AUS 180-181 K 2
Dubčes ~ RUS 114-115 U 4
Dubec o RUS 94-95 Q 2
Dubela o ZRE 212-213 B 2
Dubėsar' = Dubăsari ☆ MD 102-103 F 4
Dubie o ZRE 214-215 E 5
Dublikan ~ RUS 122-123 E 3
Dublin o USA (GA) 284-285 H 4
Dublin o USA (TX) 264-265 F 6
Dublin o USA (VA) 280-281 F 6
Dublin = Baile Átha Cliath ★ •• IRL 90-91 D 5
Dubli River ~ USA 20-21 N 4
Dubna o RUS 94-95 P 3
Dubno o UA 102-103 D 2
Dubo o ETH 208-209 C 5
Dubois o USA (ID) 252-253 F 2
Du Bois o USA (PA) 280-281 H 2
Dubois o USA (WY) 252-253 J 3
Du Bose o CDN (BC) 228-229 F 2
Dubossary = Dubăsari ☆ MD 102-103 F 4
Dubovka o RUS 96-97 D 9
Dubréka o RG 202-203 D 5
Dubreuilville o CDN (ONT) 236-237 D 4
Dubrovnik o ••• HR 100-101 G 3
Dubrovycja o UA 102-103 E 2
Dubulu o ZRE 206-207 E 6
Dubuque o • USA (IA) 274-275 H 2
Dubwe o LB 202-203 G 7
Duchener, Réserve de ⊥ CDN (QUE) 240-241 G 2
Duchesne o USA (UT) 254-255 E 3
Duchesne River ~ USA 254-255 E 3
Duchess o AUS 178-179 E 1
Duchess o CDN (ALB) 232-233 G 5
Duck Bay o CDN (MAN) 234-235 C 2
Duck Creek ~ AUS 172-173 C 7
Duck Hill o USA (MS) 268-269 L 3
Duck Islands ⌒ CDN (NWT) 28-29 J 3
Duck Islands ⌒ CDN (ONT) 238-239 C 3
Duck Lake o CDN (SAS) 232-233 M 3
Duck Mountain ▲ CDN 234-235 B 3
Duck Mountain Forest Reserve ⊥ CDN (MAN) 234-235 B 3
Duck Mountain Provincial Park ⊥ CDN (MAN) 234-235 B 3
Duck River o USA (TN) 276-277 H 5
Duck River ~ USA 276-277 H 5
Ducktown o USA (TN) 282-283 C 5
Duck Valley Indian Reservation ⚔ USA (NV) 246-247 J 1
Duckwater o USA (NV) 246-247 K 5
Duckwater Point ▲ USA (NV) 246-247 K 5
Duc Lập ☆ VN 158-159 J 2
Đức Liêu o VN 158-159 J 5
Dục Myo o VN 158-159 K 4
Ducor o USA (CA) 248-249 E 4
Du Couedic, Cape ▲ AUS 180-181 D 4
Đức Phổ o VN 158-159 K 3
Đức Tho ☆ VN 156-157 D 7
Đức Trọng o VN 158-159 K 5
Duda, Río ~ CO 60-61 D 6
Dudduumo o SP 212-213 J 3
Düdensuyu Mağarası •• TR 128-129 D 4
Dudhani o IND 140-141 G 2
Dūdhi o IND 142-143 C 3
Dudh Kosi ~ NEP 144-145 F 7
Dudhwa National Park ⊥ IND 144-145 C 6
Dudignac o RA 78-79 J 3
Dudinka ☆ RUS (TMR) 108-109 W 7
Dudinka ~ RUS 108-109 W 7
Dudley o GB 90-91 F 5
Dudorovskij o RUS 94-95 O 5
Dūdu o IND 138-139 E 6
Dudub o ETH 208-209 H 5
Dudypta ~ RUS 108-109 Y 6
Due o ZRE 210-211 G 6
Duékoué o CI 202-203 G 6
Duere, Rio ~ BR 68-69 D 7
Duero, Río ~ E 98-99 F 4
Duette o USA (FL) 286-287 G 4
Due West o USA (SC) 284-285 H 2
Duff o CDN (SAS) 232-233 P 5
Dufreboy, Lac ⊂ CDN 36-37 O 5
Dufrost, Pointe ▲ CDN 36-37 L 4
Dufur o USA (OR) 244-245 D 5
Duğail, ad- o IRQ 128-129 L 6
Duğaimiya o KSA 130-131 L 5
Dugal o CDN (QUE) 240-241 J 2
Dugald o CDN (MAN) 234-235 G 5
Dugbia o ZRE 210-211 K 2
Dugda o RUS (AMR) 122-123 C 2
Dugda ~ RUS 122-123 D 2
Dugdemona River ~ USA 268-269 H 4
Dugdug o SUD 206-207 J 4
Duge o LB 202-203 F 6
Dugi Otok ⌒ HR 100-101 E 2
Dugum o ETH 200-201 J 6
Dugway o USA (UT) 254-255 C 3
Dugwaya o SUD 200-201 G 4
Dugway Proving Ground xx USA (UT) 254-255 B 3
Duhamel o CDN (QUE) 238-239 K 2
Duḥān o Q 134-135 D 6
Duhau o RA 78-79 H 4
Du He ~ VRC 154-155 G 5
Duḥna o KSA 130-131 H 5
Duhovnickoe ☆ RUS 96-97 F 7
Duhovščina ☆ RUS 94-95 N 4
Duhubi o NEP 144-145 F 7
Ḍuḥūr, Abū ♂- o SYR 128-129 G 5
Duida, Cerro ▲ YV 60-61 J 6
Duifken Point ▲ AUS 174-175 F 3
Duisburg o D 92-93 J 3
Duitama o CO 60-61 E 5
Duiwelskloof o ZA 218-219 F 6
Dujiangyan o VRC 154-155 C 6
Dujiang Yan • VRC 154-155 C 6
Dukambiya o ER 200-201 H 5
Dūkān o IRQ 128-129 L 5
Dūkān Buhairat < IRQ 128-129 L 4
Duke o USA (OK) 264-265 E 4
Duke Island ⌒ USA 32-33 E 4
Dukelen o KZ 126-127 O 3
Duke of York Archipelago ⌒ CDN 24-25 P 6
Duke of York Bay ≈ 36-37 G 2
Duke of York Island ⌒ PNG 183 G 3
Dūk Fadiat o SUD 206-207 K 5
Dūk Faiwil o SUD 206-207 K 5
Duki o RUS 122-123 F 3
Duki ~ RUS 122-123 F 3
Dukkālah ⊥ MA 188-189 G 4
Dukku o WAN 204-205 F 3
Dukoa, ozero ⊂ RUS 112-113 J 2
Dūkštas o LT 94-95 K 4
Duku o WAN 204-205 J 3
Dulac o USA (LA) 268-269 K 7
Dulaihān o KSA 130-131 G 4
Dulaimiya, ad- o KSA 130-131 H 4
Dulqi' Rašid o KSA 130-131 H 5
Dulala o ZRE 214-215 C 6
Dulamaya o RI 164-165 H 3
Dulan o VRC 144-145 M 2
Dulayb, Khor ~ SUD 208-209 A 3
Dulce o USA (NM) 256-257 J 2
Dulce, Arroyo ~ RA 78-79 L 4
Dulce, Golfo ≈ 52-53 C 7
Dulce, Laguna la ⊂ RA 78-79 F 4
Dulce, Río ~ GCA 52-53 K 4
Dulce, Río ~ RA 76-77 F 5
Dulce Nombre de Culmí o HN 54-55 C 7
Dul'durga ☆ RUS 118-119 F 10
Dul'galah ~ RUS 110-111 T 6
Dulhunty River ~ AUS 174-175 G 2
Dulia o ZRE (HAU) 210-211 K 2
Dulia o ZRE (KIV) 212-213 B 3
Dulkaninna o AUS 178-179 E 5
Dullewāla o PK 138-139 C 4
Dullingari Gas and Oil Field • AUS 178-179 F 5
Dulovo o BG 102-103 E 6
Duluth o USA (MN) 270-271 F 4
Dulzura o USA (CA) 248-249 H 7
Duma ~ EAT 212-213 D 5
Duma o RB 218-219 B 4
Dūmā ☆ SYR 128-129 G 6
Duma o ZRE (Equ) 210-211 G 2
Duma ~ ZRE 206-207 H 6
Dumai o RI 162-163 D 4
Dumalag o RP 160-161 E 7
Dumaran Island ⌒ RP 160-161 C 7
Dumaresq River ~ AUS 178-179 L 5
Dumas o USA (AR) 276-277 D 7
Dumas o USA (TX) 264-265 C 3
Dumas, Península ⌒ RCH 80 F 7
Dūmat al-Ǧandal o • KSA 130-131 F 3
Dumba Cambango o ANG 216-217 D 5
Dumbleyung o AUS 176-177 D 6
Dumbleyung Lake ⊂ AUS 176-177 D 6
Dumbo o CAM 204-205 J 5
Dum Duma o IND 142-143 J 2
Dume, Point ▲ USA (CA) 248-249 F 5
Dumfries o • GB 90-91 F 4
Dumfries o USA (VA) 280-281 J 5
Dummer o CDN (SAS) 232-233 O 6
Dumogabesar o RI 164-165 J 3
Dumoine, Lac ⊂ CDN (QUE) 238-239 H 2
Dumoine, Rivière ~ CDN 238-239 H 2
Dumond River ~ CDN 34-35 M 4
Dumond River ~ CDN 234-235 O 2
Dumont o USA (TX) 264-265 D 5
Dumont d'Urville o ARK 16 G 15
Dumpore o USA (PA) 280-281 L 2
Dumpu o PNG 183 C 3
Dumrān, Wādī ad ~ LAR 192-193 F 4
Dumri o IND 142-143 E 4
Dumsuk, Ǧazīrat ⌒ KSA 132-133 C 5
Dumyāṭ ☆ ET 194-195 E 2
Dumyāṭ, Maṣabb ~ ET 194-195 E 2
Duna ~ ANG 216-217 F 6
Dunaföldvár o H 92-93 P 5
Dunaj ~ UA 102-103 F 5
Dunajivci ☆ UA 102-103 E 3
Dunajská Streda o SK 92-93 O 5
Dunalley o AUS 180-181 J 7
Dunărea ~ RO 102-103 C 5
Dunaújváros o H 92-93 P 5
Dunav ~ BG 102-103 D 6
Dunav ~ YU 100-101 G 2
Dunbar o AUS 174-175 G 5
Dunbar o GB 90-91 F 4
Dunbrody Abbey •• IRL 90-91 D 5
Duncairn o CDN (SAS) 232-233 K 5
Duncan o CDN (BC) 230-231 F 5
Duncan o USA (AZ) 256-257 F 6
Duncan o USA (OK) 264-265 G 4
Duncan, Cape ▲ CDN 34-35 Q 4
Duncan, Lac ⊂ CDN 38-39 E 2
Duncanby Landing o CDN (BC) 230-231 B 2
Duncan Highway II AUS 172-173 H 5
Duncan Lake ⊂ CDN 30-31 N 4
Duncan Lake ⊂ CDN (BC) 230-231 N 3
Duncan Passage ≈ 140-141 L 4
Duncan River ~ CDN 230-231 M 3
Duncansby Head ▲ GB 90-91 F 2
Duncan Town o BS 54-55 H 3
Dundaga o • LV 94-95 H 3
Dundalk o CDN (ONT) 238-239 E 4
Dundalk o • IRL 90-91 D 4
Dundalk o USA (MD) 280-281 K 4
Dundangan Island ⌒ RP 160-161 D 10
Dundas o CDN (ONT) 238-239 F 5
Dundas o GRØ 26-27 Q 5
Dundas o USA (IL) 274-275 K 6
Dundas, Lake ⊂ AUS 176-177 F 6
Dundas Harbour o CDN 24-25 f 3
Dundas Island ⌒ CDN (BC) 228-229 C 2
Dundas Island ⌒ CDN (BC) 228-229 D 2
Dundas Peninsula ⌣ CDN 24-25 P 3
Dundas Strait ≈ 172-173 K 1
Dundburd o MAU 148-149 K 4
Dún Dealgan = Dundalk o • IRL 90-91 D 4
Dundee o AUS 178-179 G 1
Dundee o GB 90-91 F 3
Dundee o USA (MI) 272-273 F 6
Dundee o USA (TX) 264-265 F 5
Dundee o ZA 220-221 K 4
Dundgov' ◘ MAU 148-149 G 5
Dundo o ANG 216-217 F 3
Dundooboo Range ▲ AUS 180-181 H 2
Dundret ▲ • S 86-87 K 3
Dundurn o CDN (SAS) 232-233 M 4
Dunedin o NZ 182 C 6
Dunedin o USA (FL) 286-287 G 3
Dunedin River ~ CDN 30-31 G 6
Dunedoo o AUS 180-181 K 2
Dunes City o USA (OR) 244-245 A 7
Dunfermline o GB 90-91 F 3
Dünga Bünga o PK 138-139 D 5
Dungan, Kuala o • MAL 162-163 E 2
Dungannon o GB 90-91 D 4
Dún Garbhán = Dungarvan o IRL 90-91 D 5
Düngarpur o IND 138-139 D 8
Dungarvan = Dún Garbhán o IRL 90-91 D 5
Dungas o RN 198-199 D 6
Dungeness, Punta ▲ RA 80 F 6
Dungeness Spit ▲ USA (WA) 244-245 B 2
Dungog o AUS 180-181 L 2
Dungu o ZRE (Hau) 212-213 B 2
Dungu ~ ZRE 212-213 B 2
Dungunāb o SUD 200-201 H 2
Dungunāb, Ǧazirat ⌣ SUD 200 201 H 2
Dunham o CDN (QUE) 238-239 N 3
Dunham River o AUS (WA) 172-173 J 4
Dunham River ~ AUS 172-173 J 4
Dunhua o VRC 150-151 G 6
Dunhuang = Minghoshan o • VRC 146-147 M 5
Dunière, Parc Provincial de ⊥ CDN (QUE) 240-241 J 2
Dunkeld o AUS 180-181 G 4
Dunken o USA (NM) 256-257 K 6
Dunkerque o F 90-91 J 6
Dunkirk o USA (NY) 278-279 B 6
Dunk Island ⌒ AUS 174-175 J 5
Dunkwa o GH 202-203 K 7
Dun Laoghaire o IRL 90-91 D 5
Dunlap o USA (IA) 274-275 C 3
Dunlap o USA (NM) 256-257 L 4
Dunlap o USA (TN) 276-277 K 5
Dunlap o USA (TX) 264-265 D 4
Dunleath o CDN (SAS) 232-233 Q 4
Dunmarra o AUS 174-175 B 5
Dunmore o CDN (ALB) 232-233 H 6
Dunmore o USA (PA) 280-281 L 2
Dunmore Town o • BS 54-55 G 2
Dunn o USA (NC) 282-283 J 5
Dunn o USA (TX) 264-265 D 6
Dún na Séad = Baltimore o IRL 90-91 C 6
Dunnellon o USA (FL) 286-287 G 2
Dunne River ~ CDN 36-37 L 2
Dunnigan o USA (CA) 246-247 D 5
Dunning o USA (NE) 262-263 F 3
Dunns River Falls ~ • JA 54-55 G 5
Dunnville o CDN (ONT) 238-239 F 6
Dunolly o AUS 180-181 G 4
Dunqul o ET 194-195 E 6
Dunraven o USA (NY) 278-279 G 6
Dunrea o CDN (MAN) 234-235 D 5
Dunrobin o AUS 178-179 J 2
Dunsborough o AUS 176-177 C 6
Dunseith o USA (ND) 258-259 G 3
Dunster o CDN (BC) 228-229 P 3
Dunvegan o CDN 32-33 L 4
Dunvegan o CDN (NS) 240-241 O 4
Dunvegan Historic Site ∴ CDN 32-33 L 4
Dunvegan Lake ⊂ CDN 30-31 Q 5
Dunville o CDN (NFL) 242-243 P 5
Dunyāpur o PK 138-139 C 5
Duolun o VRC 148-149 N 6
Dư'ơng Đông o • VN 158-159 G 5
Duparquet o CDN (QUE) 236-237 J 4
Duparquet, Lac ⊂ CDN (QUE) 236-237 J 4
Dupnica o BG 102-103 C 6
Du Pont o USA (GA) 284-285 H 6
Dupree o USA (SD) 260-261 E 1
Dupuy, Cape ▲ AUS 172-173 B 6
Dupuyer o USA (MT) 250-251 G 3
Duqaila, Ǧazīrat ⌒ KSA 132-133 C 5
Duqm o OM 132-133 K 4
Duque de York, Isla ⌒ RCH 80 C 5
Duquesne o USA (AZ) 256-257 E 7
Dura, La o MEX 50-51 E 3
Durack Range ▲ AUS 172-173 H 4
Durack River ~ AUS 172-173 H 4
Dūrāğ o AFG 136-137 M 6
Durağan ☆ TR 128-129 F 2
Dur al Fawākhir ⊥ LAR 192-193 J 3
Dūr al Ghānī ⊥ LAR 192-193 F 4
Duran o USA (NM) 256-257 K 4
Durán = Eloy Alfaro o EC 64-65 C 3
Durance ~ F 90-91 L 9
Durand o USA (IL) 274-275 J 2
Durand o USA (MI) 272-273 F 5
Durand o USA (WI) 270-271 G 6
Durango o • E 98-99 F 3
Durango o HN 54-55 C 7
Durango ◘ MEX 50-51 G 5
Durango o USA (CO) 254-255 H 6
Durango, Victoria de = Durango ☆ • MEX 50-51 G 5
Durañona o RA 78-79 J 4
Durant o USA (MS) 268-269 L 3
Durant o USA (OK) 264-265 H 5
Durazno ☆ ROU 78-79 L 2
Durban o CDN (MAN) 234-235 B 3
Durban ☆ • ZA 220-221 K 4
Durban Island ⌒ CDN 28-29 J 3
Durbanville o ZA 220-221 D 6
Durbet-Daba, pereval ▲ MAU 146-147 J 1
Durbet-Daba, pereval ▲ RUS 146-147 J 1
Durdur ~ SP 208-209 F 3
Dureji o PK 134-135 M 6
Durenan o RI 168 D 4
Durg o IND 142-143 B 5
Durgāpur o • IND 142-143 E 4
Durgarajupatnam o IND 140-141 J 4
Durham o CDN (ONT) 238-239 E 4
Durham ☆ ••• GB 90-91 G 4
Durham o USA (KS) 262-263 J 6
Durham o USA (NC) 282-283 J 4
Durham Downs o AUS 178-179 F 4
Duri o RI 162-163 D 4
Durian, Selat ≈ 162-163 E 4
Durika, Cerro ▲ CR 52-53 C 7
Durjela o RI 166-167 H 4
Durkee o USA (OR) 244-245 H 6
Durkin Outstation o AUS 176-177 M 5
Durlas = Thurles o IRL 90-91 D 5
Durma o KSA 130-131 K 5
Durmitor ▲ YU 100-101 G 3
Durmitor Nacionalni park ⊥ ••• YU 100-101 G 3
Durness o GB 90-91 E 2
Durnev, aral ⌒ KZ 96-97 H 10
Duro ▲ ETH 208-209 C 6
Duroa o RI 166-167 G 4
Durong South o AUS 178-179 L 4
Durra o ETH 208-209 C 5
Durrandella o AUS 178-179 J 3
Durrës ☆ •• AL 100-101 G 4
Duru o ZRE (Hau) 206-207 J 6
Duru ~ ZRE 212-213 B 2
Durubu o ZRE 206-207 E 6
Durukhsi o ETH 208-209 G 4
Durūz, Ǧabal ad ▲ SYR 128-129 G 6
D'Urville, Tanjung ▲ RI 166-167 J 2
D'Urville Island ⌒ NZ 182 D 4
Duryu San ▲ KOR 150-151 G 7
Dūš, 'Izbat o ET 194-195 E 5
Ḍū Šaiḥ o IRQ 128-129 L 6
Dušak o TM 136-137 G 6
Dušanbe ☆ TJ 136-137 L 5
Dusey River ~ CDN 234-235 Q 3
Dushan o VRC 156-157 E 4
Dushanbe = Dušanbe ☆ TJ 136-137 L 5
Dushore o USA (PA) 280-281 K 2
Dusin o PNG 183 C 3
Dusky Sound ≈ 182 A 6
Dusséjour, Cape ▲ AUS 172-173 J 3
Düsseldorf ☆ • D 92-93 J 3
Dussoumbidiagna o RMM 202-203 E 2
Dustin o USA (OK) 264-265 H 3
Düstlik ☆ UZ 136-137 L 4
Düst Mohammad Hān o IR 134-135 J 3
Dusty o USA (WA) 244-245 H 4
Dusunmudo o RI 162-163 E 5
Dusunpasirmayang o RI 162-163 E 5
Dusuntuo o RI 162-163 D 6
Duta o Z 214-215 F 6
Dutch Creek o CDN 230-231 N 3
Dutch Fort ∴ • RI (MAL) 166-167 E 3
Dutch Fort ∴ • RI (SLT) 164-165 G 3
Dutch Village • USA (MI) 272-273 C 5
Dutsan Wai o WAN 204-205 H 3
Dutse o WAN 204-205 H 3
Dutsin-Ma o WAN 198-199 C 6
Duttaluru o IND 140-141 H 3
Dutton o USA (MT) 250-251 H 4
Dutton, Lake ⊂ AUS 178-179 D 6
Dutton, Mount ▲ USA (UT) 254-255 C 5
Dutzow o USA (MO) 274-275 H 6
Duvall o USA (WA) 244-245 D 3
Duvefjorden ≈ 84-85 N 2
Duvernay o CDN (ALB) 232-233 G 2
Duvno o BIH 100-101 F 3
Duwisib Castle • NAM 220-221 C 2
Duwwa o OM 132-133 L 3
Duxbury, Lac ⊂ CDN 38-39 F 2
Duye ~ ZRE 212-213 B 3
Duyun o VRC 156-157 E 3
Düzce ☆ TR 128-129 D 2
Düzdüzān o IR 128-129 M 4
Düziçi o TR 128-129 G 4
Duzigou Gang ▲ VRC 156-157 C 2
Dvinskaja guba ≈ 88-89 P 4
Dvinskaya Guba = Dvinskaja guba ≈ 88-89 P 4
Dwarsberg o ZA 220-221 H 2
Dwellingup o AUS 176-177 D 6
Dwesa-natuurreservaat ⊥ ZA 220-221 J 6
Dwight o CDN (ONT) 238-239 G 3
Dwight o USA (IL) 274-275 K 3
Dwokwa o GH 202-203 K 7
Dworshak Reservoir ⊂ USA (ID) 250-251 C 5
Dwyer o USA (NM) 256-257 H 6
Dwyer Hill o CDN (ONT) 238-239 K 3
Dwyka ~ ZA 220-221 E 6
Dyaul Island ⌒ PNG 183 F 2
Dyer o USA (NV) 248-249 F 2
Dyer, Cabo ▲ RCH 80 C 4
Dyer, Cape ▲ CDN 28-29 K 3
Dyer Bay ≈ 24-25 L 3
Dyer Plateau ▲ ARK 16 G 30
Dyer's Bay o CDN (ONT) 238-239 D 3
Dyersburg o USA (TN) 276-277 F 4
Dyersville o USA (IA) 274-275 G 2
Dygdal o RUS 118-119 P 4
Dyh-Tau, gora ▲ RUS 126 127 E 6
Dyje ~ CZ 92-93 N 4
Dyjsembaj ~ KZ 124-125 E 5
Dyke Ackland Bay ≈ 183 E 5
Dymond Lake ⊂ CDN 30-31 Q 5
Dynaj, ostrova ⌒ RUS 110-111 P 3
Dyrhóley ▲ IS 86-87 d 3
Dyryn-Jurjah ~ RUS 118-119 K 7
Dysart o AUS 178-179 K 2
Dysart o CDN (SAS) 232-233 O 5
Dysart o USA (IA) 274-275 F 2
Dytiki ◘ GR 100-101 H 5
Dytiki Macedonia ◘ GR 100-101 H 4
Džagdy, hrebet ▲ RUS 122-123 C 2
Džagyn ~ RUS 112-113 H 5
Džalal-Abad = Jalal-Abad o KS 136-137 N 4
Džalilabad = Cǝlilabad o AZ 128-129 N 3
Džambul ☆ KZ 136-137 M 3
Džana ~ RUS 120-121 F 6
Džanda ~ RUS 120-121 D 4
Džanga o TM 136-137 C 4
Džangylah, ostrov ⌒ RUS 110-111 N 3
Džankoj ☆ UA 102-103 J 5
Dzaoudzi o F 222-223 D 4
Džapi ~ RUS 122-123 H 2
Džardžan o RUS (SAH) 110-111 P 5
Džardžan ~ RUS 110-111 P 5
Džargalah o RUS 110-111 S 6
Džarkurgan = Jarqurghon o UZ 136-137 K 6
Džartyrabot o TJ 136-137 N 6
Dzata Ruins ∴ • ZA 218-219 F 6
Džaur ~ RUS 122 123 H 4
Džebariki-Haja o RUS 120-121 F 2
Džebel = Ǧebel o TM 136-137 D 5
Džebrail o AZ 128-129 M 3
Džejhun o TM 136-137 H 5
Dželnau o UZ 136-137 J 5
Džeksona, ostrov ⌒ RUS 84-85 d 2
Dželandy o TJ 136-137 N 6
Dželgala o RUS 120-121 N 6
Dželonda o RUS 118-119 J 9
Dželtulah ~ RUS 118-119 N 6
Dželtulinskij stanovik ▲ RUS 118-119 L 8
Dzeng o CAM 210-211 C 2
Džerba ~ RUS 118-119 H 5
Džermuk o AR 128-129 L 3
Dž'ernjur, bololo ⊥ RUS 88-89 X 5
Dzerzhinsk = Dzeržinsk o RUS 94-95 S 3
Dzeržinsk o RUS 94-95 S 3
Dzeržyns'k o UA 102-103 K 3
Dzevdaha, ozero ⊂ RUS 122-123 H 2
Dzhugdzhur, Khrebet = Džug-Džur, hrebet ▲ RUS 120-121 F 6
Działdowo o • PL 92-93 Q 2
Dzibalchén o MEX 52-53 K 2
Dzibilchaltún ∴ • MEX 52-53 K 1
Džida o RUS (BUR) 116-117 N-10
Džida ~ RUS 116-117 M 10
Džidinskij hrebet ▲ MAU 148-149 F 2
Dzierżoniów o • PL 92-93 O 3
Džigda o RUS 120-121 F 5
Džila ~ RUS 118-119 F 10
Dzilam de Bravo o MEX 52-53 K 1
Džilinda, Ust'- o RUS 118-119 E 9
Dzioua o DZ 190-191 E 4
Džirgatal' o TJ 136-137 M 5
Dzisna ~ BY 94-95 L 4
Dzisna ~ BY 94-95 K 4
Dzita o GH 202-203 L 7
Dzitás o MEX 52-53 K 1
Džizakskaja oblast' ◘ UZ 136-137 K 4
Dzjaržynsk ☆ BY 94-95 K 5
Džjunekjan ~ RUS 120-121 F 3
Dzodze o GH 202-203 L 6
Džogdžo ~ RUS 108-109 e 6
Džubga o RUS 126-127 C 5
Džug-Džur, hrebet ▲ RUS 120-121 F 6
Džugdžurskij zapovednik ⊥ RUS (HBR) 120-121 G 5
Džuk ~ RUS 122-123 H 2
Džul'fa = Culfa o AZ 128-129 L 3
Dzungarian Basin = Junggar Pendi ⊥ VRC 146-147 H 3
Dzungarian Gate = Alataw Shankow Žongar Kakpasy ▲ 146-147 F 3
Džurak-Sal ~ RUS 102-103 N 4
Džuryn o UA 102-103 F 3
Dzvari o GE 126-127 E 6
Dźwierzuty o PL 92-93 Q 2

E

Ea A Dun ~ VN 158-159 K 3
Eabamet Lake ⊂ CDN (ONT) 234-235 Q 3
Eades o CDN (ONT) 236-237 J 4
Eads o USA (CO) 254-255 N 5
Eadytown o USA (SC) 284-285 K 3
Eagar o USA (AZ) 256-257 F 4
Eagle o USA (AK) 20-21 T 4
Eagle o USA (CO) 254-255 J 4
Eagle o USA (ID) 252-253 B 3
Eagle o USA (NE) 262-263 K 4
Eagle o USA (WI) 274-275 K 2
Eagle Bend o USA (MN) 270-271 C 4
Eagle Butte o USA (SD) 260-261 E 2
Eagle Cape Wilderness Area ⊥ USA (OR) 244-245 H 5
Eagle Cap Wilderness Area • USA (OR) 244-245 H 5
Eagle Cave ∴ USA (WI) 274-275 H 1
Eagle Creek o CDN (BC) 230-231 J 2
Eagle Creek ~ CDN 228-229 N 4
Eagle Creek ~ CDN 232-233 L 4
Eagle Creek o USA (OR) 244-245 C 5
Eagle Creek ~ USA 276-277 L 2
Eagle Grove o USA (IA) 274-275 E 2
Eagle Harbor o USA (MI) 270-271 K 3
Eagle Hills ▲ CDN 232-233 K 3
Eagle Island ⌒ SY 224 C 2
Eagle Lake o CDN (ONT) 234-235 K 5
Eagle Lake o USA (ME) 278-279 N 1
Eagle Lake o USA (TX) 266-267 L 4
Eagle Lake ⊂ USA (CA) 246-247 E 3
Eagle Mountain o USA (CA) 248-249 J 6
Eagle Mountain Lake < USA (TX) 264-265 G 6
Eagle Mountains ▲ USA (TX) 266-267 B 3
Eagle Nest o USA (NM) 256-257 K 2
Eagle Pass o USA (TX) 266-267 G 5
Eagle Passage ≈ 78-79 L 7
Eagle Picher Mine o USA (NV) 246-247 G 3
Eagle Plains o CDN 20-21 W 3
Eagle Point ▲ PNG 183 E 6
Eagle Point o USA (OR) 244-245 C 8
Eagle River o CDN (ONT) 234-235 K 5
Eagle River ~ CDN 20-21 W 3
Eagle River ~ CDN 38-39 P 2
Eagle River ~ CDN 230-231 L 3
Eagle River o USA (WI) 270-271 J 5
Eagle River ~ USA 254-255 H 4
Eagle Summit ▲ USA 20-21 S 4
Eagleton o USA (AR) 276-277 A 6
Eagleville o USA (CA) 246-247 E 2
Eagleville o USA (MO) 274-275 E 4
Eagleville o USA (TN) 276-277 J 5
Ea H'leo o VN 158-159 K 4
Eandja o ZRE 210-211 H 4
Earaheedy o AUS 176-177 F 2
Ear Falls o CDN (ONT) 234-235 K 4
Earle o USA (AR) 276-277 E 5
Earl Grey o CDN (SAS) 232-233 O 5
Earling o USA (IA) 274-275 C 3
Earls Cove o CDN (BC) 230-231 F 4
Earlton o CDN (ONT) 236-237 J 5
Earltown o CDN (NS) 240-241 M 5
Earlville o USA (IL) 274-275 K 3
Early o USA (IA) 274-275 C 2
Early o USA (TX) 266-267 J 2
Earn ~ GB 90-91 F 3
Earn Lake o CDN 20-21 X 5
Earp o USA (CA) 248-249 K 5
Easley o USA (SC) 284-285 H 2
East = Est ◘ CAM 210-211 D 2
East, Mount ▲ AUS 176-177 G 4
East Alligator River ~ AUS 174-175 B 3
East Amatuli Island ⌒ USA 22-23 V 3
East Anguo o CDN (QUE) 238-239 O 3
East Arm ⊂ CDN 30-31 E 5
East Arrow Park o CDN (BC) 230-231 M 3
East Aurora o USA (NY) 278-279 C 6
East Bay ≈ 36-37 J 2
East Bay ≈ 268-269 L 7
East Bay ≈ 268-269 F 7
East Bay ⊂ CDN (ONT) 234-235 P 5
East Bethel o USA (MN) 270-271 E 5
East Bijou Creek ~ USA 254-255 L 4
East Bluff ▲ CDN 36-37 H 4
Eastbourne o GB 90-91 H 6
East Brady o USA (PA) 280-281 G 3
East Broughton o CDN (QUE) 238-239 O 2
East Caicos ⌒ GB 54-55 K 4
East Cape ▲ NZ 182 G 2
East Cape ▲ USA (AK) 22-23 F 7
East Cape ▲ USA (FL) 286-287 H 6
East-Cape Province ◘ ZA 220-221 H 5
East Carbon City o USA (UT) 254-255 E 4
East Cay ⌒ AUS 183 C 5
East Channel ~ CDN 20-21 Y 3
East China Sea ≈ 10-11 M 5
East Chugach Island ⌒ USA 22-23 V 3
East Coulee o CDN (ALB) 232-233 F 4
East Dereham o GB 90-91 H 5
Eastend o CDN (SAS) 232-233 K 6
East End Point ▲ BS 54-55 G 2
East Enterprise o USA (IN) 274-275 O 6
Easter o USA (TX) 264-265 B 4
Easter Cape ▲ CDN 24-25 b 5
Easter Group ⌒ AUS 176-177 B 4
Easter Island = Pascua, Isla de ⌒ RCH 78-79 B 2
Eastern ◘ EAK 212-213 F 4
Eastern ◘ EAU 212-213 D 3
Eastern ◘ Z 218-219 F 1
Eastern Bay ≈ 280-281 K 5
Eastern Blue Pond ⊂ CDN (NFL) 242-243 L 2
Eastern Desert = Ṣaḥrā' aš-Šarqīya, as- ⊥ ET 194-195 E 3
Eastern Fields ⌒ PNG 183 C 6
Eastern Ghāts ▲ IND 140-141 G 5
Eastern Group ⌒ AUS 176-177 H 6
Eastern Meelpaeg ⊂ CDN (NFL) 242-243 O 4
Eastern Neck Island National Wildlife Refuge ⚔ USA (MD) 280-281 K 5
Eastern Province = Al-Ḥudūd aš-Šarqīya ◘ KSA 130-131 L 6
Eastern Province = Aš Šarqīya ◘ KSA 132-133 G 3
Eastern Region ◘ GH 202-203 K 6
Eastern Sayan Mountains = Vostočnyj Sajan ▲ RUS 116-117 F 8
East Fairview o USA (ND) 258-259 D 4
East Falkland ⌒ GB 78-79 L 6
East Fork ~ USA 284-285 C 2
East Fork Andreafsky ~ USA 20-21 J 5
East Fork Bruneau River ~ USA 252-253 C 4
East Fork Chandalar ~ USA 20-21 S 2
East Fork Grand River ~ USA 274-275 D 4
East Fork Lake ⊂ USA (IL) 274-275 K 6
East Fork White River ~ USA 274-275 M 6
East Frisian Islands = Ostfriesische Inseln ⌒ D 92-93 J 2
East Glacier Park o USA (MT) 250-251 F 3
East Grand Forks o USA (MN) 270-271 A 3
East Hampton o USA (NY) 280-281 O 3
East Haydon o AUS 174-175 F 5
East Helena o USA (MT) 250-251 H 5
East Hickory o USA (PA) 280-281 G 2
East Holden o USA (ME) 278-279 N 4
East Holothuria Reef ⌒ AUS 172-173 H 2
East Hyden Wheat Bin o AUS 176-177 E 6
East Indiaman Ridge ≃ 12 H 7
East Island ⌒ PNG 183 G 6
East Islands ⌒ PNG 183 F 2
East Jeddore o CDN (NS) 240-241 M 6
East Jordan o USA (MI) 272-273 D 2
East Lake Tohopekaliga ⊂ USA (FL) 286-287 H 3
Eastland o USA (TX) 264-265 F 6
East Lansing o USA (MI) 272-273 E 5
East Liverpool o USA (OH) 280-281 F 3
East London = Oos-Londen ☆ • ZA 220-221 H 6
East Lynn Lake o USA (WV) 280-281 D 5
Eastmain o CDN 38-39 E 2
Eastmain, Rivière ~ CDN 38-39 F 2
Eastman o USA (GA) 284-285 G 4
East Mariana Basin ≃ 14-15 H 6
Eastmere o AUS 178-179 H 2
East Millinocket o USA (ME) 278-279 N 3
East Missoula o USA (MT) 250-251 F 5
East Mojave National Scenic Area ⊥ • USA (CA) 248-249 J 4
Eastnor o ZW 218-219 E 4
East Novaya Zemlya Trough = Novozemel'skaja vpadina ≃ 108-109 G 6
Easton o USA (MD) 280-281 K 5
Easton o USA (PA) 280-281 L 3
East Pacific Rise ≃ 14-15 Q 12
East Palatka o USA (FL) 286-287 H 2
East Point ▲ CDN (PEI) 240-241 O 4
Eastpoint o USA (FL) 286-287 E 2
East Point o USA (GA) 284-285 F 3
Eastpoort o ZA 220-221 G 6
East Poplar o CDN (SAS) 232-233 N 6
East Porcupine River ~ CDN 20-21 V 4
Eastport o CDN (NFL) 242-243 P 4
Eastport o USA (ME) 278-279 O 4
Eastport o USA (MI) 272-273 D 2
East Port Hébert o CDN (NS) 240-241 L 7
East Prairie o USA (MO) 276-277 F 4
East Prairie River ~ CDN 32-33 M 4
East Ridge o USA (TN) 276-277 K 5
East River ~ CDN 238-239 F 3
East Saint Louis o USA (IL) 274-275 H 6
East Siberian Sea = Vostočno-Sibirskoe more ≈ 10-11 Q 1
East Tawas o USA (MI) 272-273 F 3
East Transvaal Province ◘ ZA 220-221 J 3
East Travaputs Plateau ▲ USA 254-255 F 4
East Union o USA (IN) 274-275 M 4
East Waterboro o USA (ME) 278-279 L 5
East Wenatchee o USA (WA) 244-245 E 3
Ea Sup o VN 158-159 J 4
Eateringinna Creek ~ AUS 176-177 M 3
Eaton o USA (CO) 254-255 L 3
Eaton o USA (OH) 280-281 B 4
Eatonia o CDN (SAS) 232-233 J 4
Eaton Rapids o USA (MI) 272-273 E 5
Eatonton o USA (GA) 284-285 G 3
Eatonville o USA (WA) 244-245 C 4
Eau Claire o USA (WI) 270-271 G 6
Eau Claire, Lac à l' ⊂ CDN 36-37 M 6
Eau Claire, Rivière à l' ~ CDN 36-37 M 6
Eau Claire River ~ USA 270-271 J 5
Eau de Boynes o RH 54-55 J 5
Eauripik Rise ≃ 166-167 K 1
Ebagoola o AUS 174-175 G 4
Ebalo o PNG 183 C 4
Eban o WAN 204-205 F 4
Ebanga o ANG 216-217 C 6
Ebangalaka o ZRE 210-211 H 4
Ebano o MEX 50-51 K 6
Ebba Havn ≈ 28-29 U 5
Ebba Ksour = Dahmani o TN 190-191 G 3
Ebe o RI 166-167 J 3
Ebebiyin o G 210-211 C 2
Ebejty, ozero ⊂ RUS 124-125 G 1
Ebel Alembe o G 210-211 C 3
Ebeljah o RUS 110-111 J 4
Ebeljanskaja guba ≈ 110-111 W 3
Ebelle o WAN 204-205 G 5
Ebeltoft o DK 86-87 E 8
Ebem o WAN 204-205 G 6
Ebenezer o CDN (SAS) 232-233 Q 4
Ebensburg o • USA (PA) 280-281 H 3
Ebe River ~ WAN 204-205 H 6
Eberswalde o D 92-93 M 2
Ebetsu o J 152-153 J 3
Ebian o VRC 156-157 C 2

Drygalski-Island — Ebian 323

Ebini Downs o GUY 62-63 F 3
Ebinur Hu o VRC 146-147 F 3
Ébja o RUS 118-119 L 4
Ébjah o RUS 110-111 c 5
Ebo o ANG 216-217 C 5
Ebola o ZRE 210-211 H 2
Éboli o I 100-101 E 4
Ebolowa ★ CAM 210-211 D 2
Ebony o NAM 216-217 C 11
Eboundja o CAM 210-211 D 2
Ebrähimäbäd o IR 134-135 G 4
Ebrahimi o IR 134-135 H 2
Ebre, l' ~ E 98-99 H 4
Ebrié, Lagune ≈ 202-203 H 7
Ebro ~ USA (FL) 286-287 D 1
Ebro, Río ~ E 98-99 G 4
Ébručore, gora ▲ RUS 88-89 M 3
Ecatepec de Morelos o MEX 52-53 E 2
Echambot o CAM 210-211 D 2
Echaporã o BR 72-73 E 7
Ech Chergui, Chott o DZ 190-191 D 2
Echeconnee Creek ~ USA 284-285 G 4
Echigo-sanmyaku ▲ J 152-153 H 6
Echigo-Sanzan-Tadami Quasi National Park ⊥ J 152-153 H 6
Echo ~ USA (MN) 270-271 C 6
Echo o USA (UT) 254-255 D 2
Echo Bay o CDN (ONT) 236-237 D 6
Echo Bay o CDN 30-31 L 2
Echo Canyon State Park ⊥ · USA (NV) 248-249 K 2
Echo Caves · ZA 220-221 K 2
Echoing River ~ CDN 34-35 L 3
Echouani, Lac o CDN (QUE) 236-237 H 6
Echuca-Moama o AUS 180-181 H 4
Écija o E 98-99 E 6
Éçijskij massiv ▲ RUS 110-111 R 6
Ecilda Paullier o ROU 78-79 L 3
Eckengrafen = Viesite o LV 94-95 J 3
Ecker, Río ~ RA 80 E 3
Eckemförde o D 92-93 K 1
Eckerö o FIN 88-89 F 6
Eckville o CDN (ALB) 232-233 D 3
Eclectic o USA (AL) 284-285 D 4
Eclipse Channel ≈ 36-37 R 5
Eclipse Island ∩ AUS 176-177 D 7
Eclipse River ~ CDN 36-37 R 5
Eclipse Sound ≈ 24-25 g 4
Éçmiadzin o AR 128-129 L 2
Econfina Creek ~ USA 286-287 D 1
Econfina River ~ USA 286-287 F 1
Ecoole o CDN (BC) 230-231 D 5
Écorce, Lac de l' ~ CDN (QUE) 236-237 M 5
Écrins, Barre des ▲ F 90-91 L 9
Écrins, Parc National des ⊥ · F 90-91 L 9
Ecstall River ~ CDN 228-229 E 3
Ecuador ■ EC 64-65 B 2
Écuils, Pointe aux ▲ CDN 36-37 K 5
Éd o ER 200-201 N 4
Edaläbäd o IND 138-139 F 9
Edam o CDN (SAS) 232-233 K 2
Edam o NL 92-93 H 2
Edappalli o IND 140-141 G 5
Edarma ~ USA 116-117 K 6
Edcouch o USA (TX) 266-267 K 7
Eddies Cove o CDN (NFL) 242-243 M 1
Eddies Cove West o CDN (NFL) 242-243 L 2
Eddington o USA (ME) 278-279 N 4
ed Úouakel, Hamada ⊥ DZ 188-189 H 7
Eddy o CDN (BC) 228-229 O 3
Eddystone o CDN (MAN) 234-235 D 3
Eddyville o USA (IA) 274-275 F 3
Eddyville o USA (KY) 276-277 G 3
Eddyville o USA (NE) 262-263 G 3
Ede o WAN 204-205 F 5
Edéa o CAM 210-211 D 2
Edefors o S 86-87 K 3
Edehine Ouarene ⊥ DZ 190-191 G 6
Edehon Lake o CDN 30-31 V 5
Edéia o BR 72-73 F 4
Eden o AUS 180-181 K 4
Eden o USA (ID) 252-253 D 4
Eden o USA (NC) 282-283 H 4
Eden o USA (SD) 260-261 J 1
Eden o USA (TX) 266-267 H 2
Eden o USA (WY) 252-253 J 4
Edenburg o ZA 220-221 G 4
Edendale o NZ 182 B 7
Edendale o CDN (BC) 230-231 K 4
Edenhope o AUS 180-181 F 4
Edenton o USA (NC) 282-283 L 4
Edenville o ZA 220-221 H 3
Edenwold o CDN (SAS) 232-233 O 5
Ede Point o CDN 24-25 V 4
Eder ~ USA (MT) 250-251 H 4
Edersley o CDN (SAS) 232-233 P 3
Édessa o · GR 100-101 J 4
Edgar o USA (MN) 270-271 G 6
Edgar, Mount ▲ AUS 172-173 F 6
Edgar Ranges ▲ AUS 172-173 L 7
Edgecumbe o NZ 182 E 2
Edgefield o USA (SC) 284-285 J 3
Edgeley o CDN (SAS) 232-233 O 5
Edgeley o USA (ND) 258-259 J 5
Edgell Island ∩ CDN 36-37 R 4
Edgemont o USA (SD) 260-261 C 3
Edgeøya ∩ N 84-85 M 4
Edgeyjakulen ∩ N 84-85 N 4
Edgerton o CDN (ALB) 232-233 H 3
Edgerton o USA (MN) 270-271 F 5
Edgerton o USA (WI) 274-275 J 4
Edgertown o USA (VA) 280-281 J 7
Edgewater o CDN (BC) 230-231 N 3
Edgewater o USA (FL) 286-287 H 5
Edgewood o CDN (BC) 230-231 L 4
Edgewood o USA (MI) 272-273 H 4
Edgewood o USA (TX) 264-265 J 6
Ediessane, Oued ~ DZ 190-191 G 8
Edillilie o AUS 180-181 C 3
Edina o USA (MO) 274-275 F 3
Edinburg o USA (ND) 258-259 K 3

Edinburg o USA (TX) 266-267 J 7
Edinburgh ★ ··· GB 90-91 F 4
Edinburgh o USA (IN) 274-275 N 5
Edincy = Edineţ ★ MD 102-103 E 3
Edinec = Edineţ ★ MD 102-103 E 3
Edineţ ★ MD 102-103 E 3
Edingeni o MW 214-215 G 7
Edirne ★ ··· TR 128-129 B 2
Edison o CDN (ALB) 232-233 B 2
Edison o USA (GA) 284-285 F 4
Edisto Beach o USA (SC) 284-285 K 4
Edisto Island o USA (SC) 284-285 K 4
Edisto River ~ USA 284-285 K 3
Edisto River, North Fork ~ USA 284-285 J 3
Edisto River, South Fork ~ USA 284-285 J 3
Edith, Mount ▲ USA (MT) 250-251 H 5
Edith Cavell, Mount ▲ CDN (ALB) 228-229 O 4
Edith Downs o AUS 174-175 G 7
Edith Falls o AUS 172-173 L 3
Edithvale o AUS 172-173 K 3
Edjeleh o DZ 190-191 G 7
Edkins Range ▲ AUS 172-173 G 4
Edmond o USA (OK) 264-265 G 3
Edmonds o USA (WA) 244-245 C 3
Edmond Walker Island ∩ CDN 24-25 U 2
Edmonton ★ · CDN (ALB) 232-233 E 2
Edmonton o USA (KY) 276-277 K 4
Edmore o USA (ND) 258-259 J 3
Edmund o USA (SC) 284-285 J 3
Edmund Lake o CDN 34-35 N 3
Edmundston o CDN (NB) 240-241 G 3
Edna o CDN (BC) 230-231 L 4
Edna o USA (TX) 266-267 L 4
Édolo o I 100-101 C 1
Edouard, Lac o CDN (QUE) 240-241 C 3
Édouard, Lac o CDN (QUE) 240-241 C 3
Edouard, Lac = Lake Edward o ZRE 212-213 B 4
Edough, Djebel ▲ DZ 190-191 F 2
Edrans o CDN (MAN) 234-235 D 4
Edremit o TR 128-129 K 3
Edremit · TR 128-129 B 3
Edremit Körfezi ≈ 128-129 B 3
Edsbyn o S 86-87 G 6
Edsel Ford Range ▲ ARK 16 F 23
Edson o CDN (ALB) 232-233 B 2
Edson River ~ CDN 232-233 B 2
Eduard Holm, Kap ▲ GRØ 28-29 Y 3
Eduni, Mount ▲ CDN 30-31 E 3
Edvard Ø ∩ GRØ 26-27 P 5
Edwall o USA (WA) 244-245 H 3
Edward, Lake = Lac Édouard o ZRE 212-213 B 4
Edward Island ∩ USA 174-175 C 4
Edward River ⚓ AUS (QLD) 174-175 F 4
Edward River ~ AUS 180-181 J 3
Edward River Kowanyama Aboriginal Land ⚓ AUS 174-175 F 4
Edwards o USA (CA) 248-249 G 5
Edwards o USA (MS) 268-269 K 4
Edwards Air Force Base · USA (CA) 248-249 G 5
Edwards Plateau ▲ USA 266-267 F 2
Edwards State Memorial, Fort ⚓ · USA (IL) 274-275 G 4
Edwardsville o USA (IL) 274-275 J 6
Edward Vilith Peninsula ∩ ARK 16 F 22
Edwin o CDN (MAN) 234-235 E 5
Edziza Peak ▲ CDN 32-33 E 3
Eisenhower Center · USA (KS) 262-263 J 6
Edzo o CDN 30-31 N 4
Eek o USA 20-21 J 4
Eek Island ∩ USA 20-21 J 6
Eekit ~ RUS 110-111 P 4
Eeklo o B 92-93 G 3
Eek River ~ USA 20-21 K 6
Eel River ~ USA 246-247 B 3
Eel River ~ USA 274-275 N 4
Eel River ~ USA 274-275 L 5
Eel River Bridge o CDN (NB) 240-241 H 3
Eendekuil o ZA 220-221 D 6
Eêvijn buudal o MAU 146-147 M 2
Éfaté ∩ VAN 184 II b 3
Éfaté = Île Vaté ∩ VAN 184 II b 3
Efes · ··· TR 128-129 B 3
Effie o USA (MN) 270-271 E 3
Effigy Mounds National Monument · USA (IA) 274-275 G 1
Effingham o USA (IL) 274-275 K 5
Efimovskij o RUS 94-95 O 2
Efon Alaye o WAN 204-205 F 5
Eforie Nord o RO 102-103 F 5
Efremov o RUS 94-95 Q 5
Efremova ~ RUS 108-109 T 5
Efremova, buhta ≈ 108-109 T 5
Eg o MAU 148-149 K 3
Égadi, Ísole ∩ I 100-101 D 6
Eganville o CDN (ONT) 238-239 H 4
Egari o PNG 183 B 4
Egayit o MYA 142-143 J 6
Egbe o WAN 204-205 F 4
Egbunda o ZRE 210-211 L 2
Ege Denizi ≈ 128-129 A 3
Egedesminde ≈ 28-29 O 2
Egedesminde = Aasiaat o GRØ 28-29 O 2
Egeland o USA (ND) 258-259 H 3
Egenolf Lake o CDN 30-31 U 6
Egeo Pelagos ≈ 100-101 K 5
Eger o H 92-93 Q 5
Eger = Ohře ~ CZ 92-93 M 3
Egersund o N 86-87 C 7
Egerton, Mount ▲ AUS 176-177 D 2
Eggenfelden o D 92-93 M 4
Èg gol ~ MAU 148-149 F 3
Egholo o SOL 184 I c 3
Egilsstadir o IS 86-87 F 2
Egina o GR 100-101 J 6
Egina ~ GR 100-101 J 6
Eginbah o AUS 172-173 D 6

Egindybulak o KZ 124-125 K 4
Égio o GR 100-101 J 5
Eğirdir o TR 128-129 D 4
Eğirdir Gölü o TR 128-129 D 3
Égito Praia o ANG 216-217 B 5
Egizkara, tau ▲ KZ 124-125 H 6
Égletons o F 90-91 J 8
Eglin Air Force Base xx USA (FL) 286-287 C 1
Eglington Island ∩ CDN 24-25 M 3
Eglinton Fiord ≈ 26-27 Q 8
Egmont o CDN (BC) 230-231 F 4
Egmont, Cape ▲ NZ 182 D 3
Egmont, Mount ▲ NZ 182 E 3
Egmont National Park ⊥ NZ 182 E 3
Egoi''jah ~ RUS 114-115 N 5
Egorovsk o RUS 94-95 Q 4
Egorlyk ~ RUS 102-103 M 5
Egošinskaja o RUS 96-97 F 3
Egra o IND 142-143 E 5
Egrgiz Dağı ▲ TR 128-129 C 3
Egua o RP 160-161 C 5
Egujja, gora o KZ 120-121 P 4
Egum Atoll ∩ PNG 183 F 5
Egvekinot o RUS 112-113 V 3
Egypt o USA (AR) 276-277 E 5
Egypt o USA (TX) 266-267 L 4
Egypt, Lake of o USA (IL) 276-277 G 3
Eha-Amufu o WAN 204-205 G 5
Ehegnadzor o AR 128-129 L 3
Eh-Eh, Riacho ~ RA 76-77 H 3
Ehi o GH 202-203 K 6
Ehodak o N 86-87 L 2
Eholt o CDN (BC) 230-231 L 4
Ehrhardt o USA (SC) 284-285 J 3
Eibi, Bur ▲ SP 212-213 K 2
Eichstätt o D 92-93 L 4
Eide o N 86-87 C 5
Eider Island ∩ CDN 36-37 R 4
Eidsbotn West Fiord ≈ 24-25 b 2
Eidsemub o NAM 220-221 C 2
Eidsvold o AUS 178-179 L 2
Eidukal ~ SUD 200-201 G 3
Eielson o USA 20-21 R 4
Eifel ▲ D 92-93 J 3
Eiffel Flats o ZW 218-219 E 4
Eiger ▲ CH 92-93 J 5
Eight Degree Channel ≈ 140-141 E 6
Eights Coast ▲ ARK 16 F 27
Eighty Mile Beach ⌣ AUS 172-173 G 5
Eikefjord o N 86-87 B 6
Eikwe o GH 202-203 J 7
Eilai o SUD 200-201 E 4
Eildon, Lake o AUS 180-181 H 4
Eileen Lake o CDN 30-31 R 5
Eilerts de Haan, National Reservaat ⊥ SME 62-63 F 4
Eilerts de Haan Gebergte ▲ SME 62-63 F 4
Einasleigh o AUS 174-175 H 6
Einasleigh River ~ AUS 174-175 G 5
Eindayaza o MYA 158-159 E 3
Eindhoven o NL 92-93 H 3
Einme o MYA 158-159 C 2
Eirik Ridge ≈ 6-7 E 33
Eiriksjökull ⌒ IS 86-87 d 2
Eirunepé o BR 66-67 C 6
Eiseb ~ NAM 216-217 F 10
Eisenach o D 92-93 L 3
Eisenerz o A 92-93 N 5
Eisenhower, Mount ▲ CDN (ALB) 232-233 C 4
Eisenstadt ★ A 92-93 O 5
Eišiškés o LT 94-95 J 4
Eivánaki o IR 136-137 C 7
Eivissa o E 98-99 H 5
Eivissa ∩ E (BAL) 98-99 H 5
Eja ~ RUS 102-103 L 4
Ejea de los Caballeros o E 98-99 G 3
Ejeda o RM 222-223 D 10
Ejer Bavnehøj ▲ DK 86-87 D 9
Ejido o YV 60-61 F 3
Ejidogari o WAN 204-205 F 4
Ejim ~ RUS 118-119 L 4
Ejin Horo Qi o VRC 154-155 F 2
Ejin Qi o VRC 148-149 E 7
Ejisu o GH 202-203 K 6
Ej-Jemâa o MA 188-189 G 5
ej Jill, Sebkhet o RIM 196-197 D 2
Ejka ~ RUS 116-117 M 4
Ejna o RUS 88-89 M 2
Ejsk o RUS 102-103 L 4
Ejtja ~ RUS 114-115 G 4
Ejule o WAN 204-205 G 5
Ejura o GH 202-203 K 6
Ejutla o MEX 52-53 F 3
Ekalaka o USA (MT) 250-251 P 6
Ekaluit River ~ CDN 24-25 T 5
Ekalugad Fiord ≈ 28-29 F 2
Ekamour o RIM 196-197 E 6
Ekang o WAN 204-205 H 6
Ekarjaujaha ~ RUS 108-109 T 6
Ekarma, ostrov ∩ RUS 122-123 P 4
Éката o G 210-211 E 5
Ekbálam · MEX 52-53 K 1
Ekblaw Glacier ⌒ CDN 26-27 M 4
Ekélfi o RN 198-199 C 4
Ekenäs o FIN 88-89 G 6
Eket o WAN 204-205 G 6
Ekibastuz ☆ KZ 124-125 L 3
Ekibastuz = Ekibastüz ☆ KZ 124-125 J 3
Ekiti, ozero o RUS 122-123 E 6
Ékityki ~ RUS 112-113 U 3

Éktyktšiz hrebet ▲ RUS 112-113 T 3
Ekuyčju o RUS 110-111 S 6
Ekkan''egan ~ RUS 114-115 P 4
Ekok o CAM 204-205 H 6
Ekoli o ZRE 210-211 K 4
Ekom, Chutes, d' ~ CAM 204-205 J 6
Ekondo Titi o CAM 204-205 H 6
Ekor o RI 164-165 K 3
Ekouata o G 210-211 B 4
Ekpindi o KZ 136-137 L 3
Ekshärad o S 86-87 F 6
Eksjö ★ S 86-87 G 7
Eku, River ~ WAN 204-205 M 7
Ekubu o FJI 184 III a 3
Ekukola o ZRE 210-211 H 4
Ekuma ~ NAM 216-217 E 9
Ekumakoko o ZRE 210-211 H 4
Ékvyvatapskij hrebet ▲ RUS 112-113 S 2
Ékvyvatop ~ RUS 112-113 T 2
Ekwa o CAM 210-211 D 2
Ekwan Point ▲ CDN 34-35 P 4
Ekwan River ~ CDN 34-35 O 4
Ekwan River ~ CDN 234-235 R 2
Ekyiomenfurom o GH 202-203 K 6
Ela, Tanjung ▲ RI 166-167 C 7
El Abiodh Sidi Cheikh o DZ 190-191 E 4
Él Âbrêd o ETH 208-209 Q 6
Elabuga o RUS 96-97 H 6
El 'Açâba ▲ RIM 196-197 D 6
Elada o GR 100-101 H 5
Élada Steireá o GR 100-101 J 5
El Adeb Larache o DZ 190-191 G 7
El Agrado o CO 60-61 D 6
Elaho River ~ CDN 230-231 F 3
El-Àîoun o MA 188-189 K 3
El Alia o DZ 190-191 F 3
El Alimar, Hassi o DZ 190-191 C 3
El Alto o PE 64-65 B 4
El Amdar, Bir o DZ 190-191 D 6
Elan' o RUS 102-103 N 2
Elan Bank = Élan Bank ≈ 12 F 10
Elandsbaai o ZA 220-221 D 6
Elands Height o ZA 220-221 H 4
Elandslaagte o ZA 220-221 J 2
Elandsrivier ~ ZA 220-221 J 2
Elangay o RN 196-197 M 7
Elanka o RUS 114-115 N 5
Elan'-Kolenovskij o RUS 102-103 M 2
El Aouinet o DZ 190-191 G 3
El Âquer ▲ RIM 196-197 E 6
Elara o RI 166-167 D 3
El Arab, Oued ~ DZ 190-191 F 3
El-Araich o MA 188-189 H 3
El-Arbid o MA 188-189 J 5
El Aricha o DZ 188-189 L 3
El Arish o AUS 174-175 J 5
El Arrouch o DZ 190-191 F 2
El Asli, Bir ~ DZ 190-191 F 2
Elassóna o GR 100-101 J 5
Elat o IL 130-131 D 3
Élavagnon o RT 202-203 L 6
El Âquer ▲ RIM 196-197 E 6
Elba o USA (AL) 284-285 D 5
Elba o USA (ID) 252-253 E 4
Elba o USA (KY) 276-277 H 3
Elba o USA (NE) 262-263 H 3
Elba, Ísola d' ∩ I 100-101 C 3
El Bajo o YV 60-61 J 3
Élban o RUS 122-123 G 3
Elbasan ★ AL 100-101 H 4
El Basriyé o RMM 196-197 E 4
El Bayadh o DZ 190-191 C 4
Elbe o D 92-93 K 2
Elbe = Labe ~ CZ 92-93 N 3
El Béher o RIM 196-197 F 7
El Beid ~ WAN 198-199 G 4
El Ghorafia, Bir o TN 192-193 D 1
Efga ~ RUS 120-121 H 1
El Giara o SP 212-213 H 8
Elburt o USA (TX) 264-265 F 5
Elbert, Mount ▲ USA (CO) 254-255 J 4
Elberta o USA (UT) 254-255 D 4
Elberton o USA (GA) 284-285 H 2
El Beru Hagia o SP 212-213 H 2
Elbeuf o F 90-91 H 7
El Bioba o DZ 190-191 E 3
Elbistan o TR 128-129 G 3
El-Bjut, Kulun o RUS 110-111 Y 6
Elblag ★ PL 92-93 P 1
El Bordj o DZ 190-191 E 3
El Bordo o CO 60-61 C 6
El Borma o TN 190-191 G 4
El-Borouj o MA 188-189 H 4
El Botín o YV 60-61 F 4
El Bouz o RIM 196-197 G 6
Elbow o CDN (SAS) 232-233 M 4
Elbow Lake o USA (MN) 270-271 C 5
Elbow River ~ CDN 232-233 D 5
El'brus o RUS 126-127 E 6
Efbrus, gora ▲ RUS 104 D 5
El Bur o ETH 208-209 D 7
El Campin o CO 60-61 E 4
El Canton o YV 60-61 F 4
El Capitan Peak ▲ USA (NM) 256-257 K 5
El Capitan Reservoir ~ USA (CA) 248-249 H 7
El Carril o RA 76-77 E 3
El Caura, Reserva Forestal ⊥ YV 60-61 J 4
El Cerrito o USA (CA) 248-249 B 2
El Chaco, Parque Nacional ⊥ RA 76-77 H 4
Elche = Elx o E 98-99 G 5
Elche de la Sierra o E 98-99 F 5
Elcho o USA (WI) 270-271 J 5

Elcho Island ∩ AUS 174-175 C 2
El Cobias o SP 212-213 K 2
El Cocuy, Parque Nacional ⊥ CO 60-61 E 4
El Corozo o YV 60-61 J 3
Elda o E 98-99 G 5
Eldama Ravine o EAK 212-213 E 3
El Darien o CO 60-61 D 4
El Der · ETH 208-209 D 7
El Dere o SP 208-209 H 7
Elderslie o AUS 178-179 G 2
El Dorado o BR (GSU) 76-77 K 2
Eldorado o BR (PAU) 74-75 F 5
Eldorado o RA 76-77 K 4
El Dorado o USA (AR) 276-277 C 7
Eldorado o USA (IL) 276-277 G 3
El Dorado o USA (KS) 262-263 K 7
Eldorado o USA (OK) 264-265 E 3
El Dorado o USA (TX) 266-267 G 3
El Dorado Lake o USA (KS) 262-263 K 7
El Dorado Springs o USA (MO) 276-277 A 3
Eldoret o EAK 212-213 E 3
Eldred o USA (IA) 274-275 F 4
Eldred o USA (PA) 280-281 H 5
Eldridge o USA (IA) 274-275 H 3
El Dunuba o EAK 212-213 G 2
El'džik ~ TM 136-137 H 5
Elec ~ RUS 94-95 Q 4
Eleckij o RUS 108-109 M 5
Elečej o RUS 120-121 D 3
Electra o USA (TX) 264-265 F 4
Electric Mills o USA (MS) 268-269 M 4
Electric Peak ▲ USA (MT) 250-251 J 6
Elefantes, Fiordo ≈ 80 C 3
Elefantes, Rio dos ~ MOC 220-221 L 1
Eleja o · LV 94-95 H 3
Elektrénai o LT 94-95 J 4
Elektrostal ★ RUS 94-95 Q 4
Elektrostal' = Élektrostal' o RUS 94-95 Q 4
Eleku ~ ZRE 210-211 G 3
Elele o WAN 204-205 G 6
Elephant Island ∩ ARK 16 G 31
Elephant Point ▲ USA 20-21 K 3
Éléphant, Île = Lathu o VAN 184 II a 2
Elephanta Caves · ··· IND 138-139 D 10
Elephant Butte Reservoir < USA (NM) 256-257 H 5
Elephantine · ET 194-195 F 5
Éléphants de Kaniama, Réserve ⊥ ZRE 214-215 C 4
Elephant Training Centre · THA 142-143 L 6
Elesbão Veloso o BR 68-69 G 5
Eleskirt o TR 128-129 K 3
El Espino o BOL 70-71 F 6
El Estrecho o CO 60-61 C 7
Elesvaram o IND 142-143 C 7
El Eulma o DZ 190-191 F 2
Eleuthera Island ∩ BS 54-55 G 2
Eleva o USA (WI) 270-271 G 6
Eleven Point River ~ USA 276-277 D 4
El Fahs o TN 190-191 G 3
El Faouar o TN 190-191 G 4
El Farcya o WSA 188-189 G 7
El Fedjaj, Chott o TN 190-191 G 4
Elfin Cove o USA 32-33 B 2
Elfrida o USA (AZ) 256-257 F 7
El Fud o ETH 208-209 F 5
El Gaa Taatzebar ⊥ DZ 190-191 D 7
Elgal < EAK 212-213 G 2
El Gallãoulya o RIM 196-197 E 4
El Gambole < SP 212-213 K 2
el Gareb, Bir o RIM 196-197 B 4
Efgen ~ RUS 120-121 Q 2
El Gharsa, Chott o TN 190-191 F 3
El Gheddiya o RIM 196-197 F 3
El Ghorafia, Bir o TN 192-193 D 1
El Gleita o RIM 196-197 E 7
El Gof o ETH 208-209 D 7
El Golëa o DZ 190-191 D 5
Elgon, Mount ▲ EAU 212-213 E 3
Élgoras, gora ▲ RUS 88-89 L 2
El Guamache o YV 60-61 H 2
El Guasey o YV 60-61 H 3
El Guérara o DZ 188-189 L 6
El Guettara o RMM 196-197 J 4
El Gulut o ETH 200-201 G 6
Ei K'oran o ETH 208-209 G 6
El Korima, Oued ~ DZ 188-189 L 4
Elk City o USA (ID) 250-251 F 5
Elk City o USA (KS) 262-263 L 7
Elk City o USA (OK) 264-265 E 3
Elk City Lake o USA (KS) 262-263 L 7
Elk Creek o USA (CA) 246-247 C 4
Elk Creek o USA (NE) 262-263 L 4
Elk Creek ~ USA 264-265 D 3
El Kebir, Oued ~ TN 190-191 E 3
El Kébira, Sebkha o DZ 188-189 L 3
El Kef o TN 190-191 G 3
El-Kelaa-des-Srarhna o MA 188-189 H 4
Él Kerë o ETH 208-209 F 6
el-Kerma, Hassi o MA 188-189 G 6
Elkford o CDN (BC) 230-231 P 3
El-Khaoula o MA 188-189 H 5
Elkhart o USA (IN) 274-275 N 3
Elkhart o USA (KS) 262-263 E 7
Elkhart o USA (TX) 268-269 E 5
Elkhart Lake o USA (WI) 272-273 D 5
el Khatt, Oued ~ RIM 196-197 E 4
Elkhead o USA (OR) 244-245 B 7
Elkhead Mounts ▲ USA 254-255 H 3
El Khnâchich ▲ RMM 196-197 H 3
Elkhorn o CDN (MAN) 234-235 B 5
Elkhorn o USA (NE) 262-263 K 3
Elkhorn o USA (WI) 274-275 K 2
Elkhorn Ranch Unit ⊥ USA (ND) 258-259 D 4
El Khroub o DZ 190-191 F 2
Elkin o USA (NC) 282-283 G 4
Elkins o USA (NM) 256-257 L 5
Elkins o USA (WV) 280-281 G 5
Elk Island ∩ CDN (MAN) 234-235 G 4
Elk Island National Park ⊥ CDN (ALB) 232-233 F 2
Elk Lake o CDN (ONT) 236-237 H 5
Elk Lakes Provincial Park ⊥ CDN (BC) 230-231 O 3
Elk Mountain ▲ USA (NM) 254-255 H 4
Elk Mountains ▲ USA 254-255 H 4
Elko o CDN (BC) 230-231 P 3
Elko o USA (NV) 246-247 K 3
Èlkonka o RUS 118-119 N 6
El Koran o ETH 208-209 G 6
Elk Point o CDN (ALB) 232-233 H 2
Elk Point o USA (SD) 260-261 K 4
Elk Rapids o USA (MI) 272-273 D 3
Elk River ~ CDN 230-231 O 4
Elk River o CDN 232-233 C 3
Elk River ~ USA (ID) 250-251 C 5

Elk River ~ USA (MN) 270-271 D 5
Elk River ~ USA 262-263 K 7
Elk River ~ USA 276-277 A 4
Elk River ~ USA 280-281 E 5
Elk River ~ USA 284-285 D 4
El Ksar el Kbir o MA 188-189 J 3
El Kseur o DZ 190-191 F 2
El Ksiba o MA 188-189 J 4
Elk Springs o USA (KY) 276-277 H 4
Elkton o USA (MD) 280-281 L 4
Elkton o USA (OR) 244-245 B 7
Elkton o USA (TN) 284-285 D 1
Elkton o USA (VA) 280-281 H 5
Elkton o USA (WA) 280-281 J 5
El Kуar el Kbir o MA 188-189 J 3
Elkwater o CDN (ALB) 232-233 H 6
Ehotovo o RUS 126-127 K 3
Ella Ø ∩ GRØ 26-27 n 7
Elaville o USA (FL) 286-287 F 1
Ellaville o USA (GA) 284-285 F 4
Ell Bay ≈ 36-37 F 2
Elléba Fonfou o RN 198-199 B 4
Ellef Ringnes Island ∩ CDN 24-25 U 1
Él Lêh o ETH 208-209 D 7
El Lein o EAK 212-213 H 4
Éléloyé o TCH 198-199 J 4
Ellen, Mount ▲ USA (UT) 254-255 E 5
Ellenboro o USA (WV) 280-281 E 4
Ellenburg o USA (NY) 278-279 H 4
Ellendale o USA (ND) 258-259 J 5
Ellensburg o USA (WA) 244-245 E 3
Ellenville o USA (NY) 280-281 M 2
Ellepugol-Émtor, ozero o RUS 114-115 Q 4
Ellerbe o USA (NC) 282-283 H 5
Ellery, Mount ▲ AUS 180-181 K 4
Ellesby o USA (NC) 228-229 L 2
Ellesmere Island ∩ CDN 24-25 e 2
Ellice River ~ CDN 30-31 R 2
Ellice Islands = Tuvalu Islands ∩ TUV 13 J 3
Ellicott City o USA (MD) 280-281 K 4
Ellicottville o USA (NY) 278-279 C 6
Ellijay o USA (GA) 284-285 F 2
Ellinger o USA (TX) 266-267 L 4
Ellington o USA (MO) 276-277 D 4
Ellinwood o USA (KS) 262-263 H 6
Elliot o ZA 220-221 H 5
Elliot, Mount ▲ AUS 174-175 J 6
Elliot Lake o CDN (ONT) 238-239 C 2
Elliot Price Conservation Park ⊥ AUS 178-179 D 6
Elliott o AUS 174-175 B 5
Elliott o USA (MD) 280-281 L 5
Elliott, Mount ▲ AUS 172-173 H 6
Elliott Key ~ USA (FL) 286-287 J 6
Ellis o USA (ID) 252-253 D 2
Ellisras o ZA 218-219 D 6
Elliston o AUS 180-181 C 2
Elliston o USA (MT) 250-251 G 5
Ellisville o USA (AL) 284-285 E 2
Ellisville o USA (MS) 268-269 L 5
Ellora Caves ··· IND 138-139 E 9
Ellsworth o USA (KS) 262-263 H 6
Ellsworth o USA (ME) 278-279 N 4
Ellsworth o USA (MN) 270-271 B 7
Ellsworth o USA (WI) 270-271 F 6
Ellsworth Highland ▲ ARK 16 F 28
Ellwood City o UGA 100-201 D 3
Elma o CDN (MAN) 234-235 H 6
Elma o USA (IA) 274-275 F 1
Elma o USA (WA) 244-245 B 3
el Ma, Oued ~ RIM 196-197 F 2
El Maad o DZ 190-191 E 2
El Mabrouk o RIM 196-197 C 6
Elmadağ o TR 128-129 E 3
Elma Daği ▲ TR 128-129 E 3
El Mahbas o WSA 188-189 G 7
Elma Labiod o DZ 190-191 G 3
El Malah o DZ 190-191 D 3
Elmali ★ · TR 128-129 C 4
El Mallaile o ETH 208-209 F 6
El Mamouel o RMM 196-197 J 5
El Mâmoûn o RMM 196-197 K 5
El Mamour o RMM 196-197 J 5
El-Mansour-Eddahbi, Barrage < MA 188-189 H 5
El Marsa o DZ 190-191 C 2
El Maya o DZ 190-191 D 2
Elm Creek o CDN (MAN) 234-235 F 5
Elm Creek o USA (NE) 262-263 G 4
El Medo o ETH 208-209 E 6
El Meghaier o DZ 190-191 F 3
El Mejo o YV 60-61 F 3
Elmeki o RN 198-199 D 4
El Melhes o RIM 196-197 D 5
El Menabba o DZ 188-189 L 4
El Ménia = El Golëa o DZ 190-191 D 5
El-Menzel o MA 188-189 J 4
Elmer o USA (OK) 264-265 E 4
Elmer City o USA (WA) 244-245 G 2
Elmer Creek ~ USA 118-119 N 6
El Mojàn = San Rafael o YV 60-61 F 2
El Molzar o RA 76-77 E 4
Elmore o AUS 180-181 H 4
Elmore o USA (MN) 270-271 D 7
El Morro National Monument · · USA (NM) 256-257 G 3
El Mounir, Hassi o DZ 188-189 H 6

El Mraïti o **RMM** 196-197 J 5
El Mreïti o **RIM** 196-197 G 3
Elmvale o **CDN** (ONT) 238-239 F 4
Elmwood o **USA** (IL) 274-275 J 4
Elmwood o **USA** (OK) 264-265 D 2
Elmwood o **USA** (WI) 270-271 F 6
El Nido o **RP** 160-161 G 2
Elnja o **RUS** 94-95 N 4
Elnora o **CDN** (ALB) 232-233 F 4
El Nula o **YV** 60-61 F 4
El Obeid = al-Ubayyid ✰ **SUD**
200-201 A 4
Elogbatindi o **CAM** 210-211 C 2
El Ogla o **DZ** 190-191 F 4
El Ogla Gasses o **DZ** 190-191 F 3
Elogo o **RCB** 210-211 B 5
Eloguj o **RUS** 114-115 T 3
Eloguiskij, učastok ⊥ **RUS** 114-115 S 4
Eiojana o **RUS** 100-109 H 8
Elopada o **RI** 168 D 7
Elora o **USA** (TN) 276-277 J 5
Elorza o **YV** 60-61 G 4
Elota o **MEX** 50-51 F 6
El-Oualidia o **MA** 188-189 G 4
El Ouassât ⊥ **RIM** 196-197 E 3
El Oued ✰ **DZ** 190-191 F 4
Elovaja, Bolšaja (Tet) ∼ **RUS**
114-115 U 5
Elovka ∼ **RUS** 120-121 T 5
Elovo o **RUS** 88-89 Q 5
Eloy o **USA** (AZ) 256-257 D 6
Eloy Alfaro o **EC** (GUA) 64-65 C 3
Eloy Alfaro o **EC** (MAN) 64-65 B 2
El Paso o **USA** (TX) 266-267 A 2
El Paso Gap o **USA** (NM) 256-257 L 6
El Paso Mountains ▲ **USA** 248-249 G 4
Elphant, Rapides de l' ∼ **ZRE**
206-207 D 6
Elphinstone o **AUS** 178-179 K 1
Elphinstone o **CDN** (MAN) 234-235 C 4
El Pilar o **YV** 60-61 K 2
Elpitiya o **CL** 140-141 J 7
El Portal o **USA** (CA) 248-249 E 2
El Porvenir o **USA** (NM) 256-257 K 3
El Questro o **AUS** 172-173 H 4
Eiqui, Rio ∼ **RCH** 76-77 B 6
El Respiro o **YV** 60-61 G 4
El Rey, Parque Nacional ⊥ **RA**
76-77 F 4
el Rharbi, Oued ∼ **DZ** 190-191 G 4
Elrosa o **USA** (MN) 270-271 D 5
El Rosario o **YV** 60-61 K 3
Eiro5è o **CDN** (SAS) 232-233 K 4
Elroy o **USA** (WI) 270-271 H 7
El Salto o **YV** 60-61 H 4
El Salvador ■ **ES** 52-53 K 5
Elsamere National Park ⊥ **EAK**
212-213 F 4
Elsberry o **USA** (MO) 274-275 H 5
Elsey o **AUS** 174-175 B 4
Elsey Cemetery • **AUS** 174-175 B 4
Elsey National Park ⊥ **AUS**
174-175 B 4
El Sharana Mine • **AUS** 172-173 L 2
Elsio Hills o **AUS** 178-170 J 3
Elsie Island ∼ **CDN** 36-37 K 5
El Silencio o **YV** 60-61 K 3
Elsinore, Lake o **USA** (CA)
248-249 G 6
El Socorro o **YV** 60-61 J 3
Elstad o **N** 86-87 E 6
Elstow o **CDN** (SAS) 232-233 M 3
Eltanin Fracture Zone System ≃
14-15 O 13
El Tarf o **DZ** 190-191 G 2
Eltice Island ∼ **CDN** 20-21 X 2
El Tichilt o **RIM** 196-197 D 4
El Tigre o **YV** 60-61 J 3
El Tigre, Arroyo ∼ **RA** 76-77 H 6
El Tigrito = San José de Guanipa o **YV**
60-61 J 3
El Toba, Arroyo ∼ **RA** 76-77 E 2
Elton o **RUS** 96-97 E 9
Elton o **USA** (LA) 268-269 H 6
Elton, ozero o **RUS** 96-97 E 9
Eltopia o **USA** (WA) 244-245 F 4
El Tuparro, Parque Nacional (Reserva
Biológica) ⊥ **CO** 60-61 G 5
Eityreva ∼ **RUS** 114-115 R 5
Elu o **RI** 166-167 K 6
Elubo o **GH** 202 203 J 7
Elu Inlet ≈ **CDN** 24-25 T 6
El Ure o **SP** 212-213 J 2
Elùru o **IND** 140-141 J 2
Elva o **EST** 94-95 K 2
Elva ∼ **RUS** 88-89 V 5
Elvas o⋅⋅ **P** 98-99 D 5
Elverum o **N** 86-87 E 6
Elvira o **RA** 78-79 K 3
Elvira, Cape ▲ **CDN** 24-25 S 4
Elvire Island ∼ **CDN** 24-25 S 4
Elvire Mount ▲ **AUS** 172-173 J 5
Elvita, Rio ∼ **CO** 60-61 G 4
El Vivero o **YV** 60-61 H 4
El Wak o **EAK** 212-213 H 2
El Warsesa o **EAK** 212-213 G 2
Elwell, Lake o **USA** (MT) 250-251 H 3
El Wenz o **WAN** 204-205 N 4
Elwood o **USA** (NE) 262-263 G 4
Elx o **E** 98-99 G 5
Ely o **GB** 90-91 H 5
Ely o **USA** (MN) 270-271 G 3
Ely o **USA** (NV) 246-247 L 4
Elyria o **USA** (OH) 280-281 D 2
Elyru ∼ ** île Mai** o **VAN** 184 II b 3
Emali o **EAK** 212-213 F 4
Emám 'Abbâs o **IR** 134-135 A 1
Emám Hasan o **IR** 134-135 D 4
Emám Homeini, Bandar-e o **IR**
134-135 C 3
Emám Tâqi o **IR** 136-137 F 7
Emân o **S** 86-87 G 8
Emandžrovka o **RUS** 110-111 I 7
Emas, Parque Nacional das ⊥ **BR**
72-73 D 6
Embarcación o **RA** 76-77 E 2

Embarras River ∼ **CDN** 228-229 R 3
Embarrass River ∼ **USA** 270-271 K 6
Embarrass River ∼ **USA** 274-275 H 4
Èmbenčimê ∼ **RUS** 116-117 J 3
Embetsu o **J** 152-153 J 2
Embi o **KZ** 126-127 N 3
Embi ∼ **RUS** 96-97 H 10
Embilipitiya o **CL** 140-141 J 7
Embira o **BR** 68-69 E 5
Embira, Rio ∼ **BR** 66-67 B 6
Emblem o **USA** (WY) 252-253 G 4
Embocada o **BOL** 70-71 F 4
Embondo o **ZRE** 210-211 G 3
Emboracação, Represa o **BR** 72-73 G 5
Emboral, Baía do ≈ 68-69 G 2
Emboscada o **BOL** 70-71 E 2
Emboscada, La o **BOL** 70-71 D 2
Emboscada Nueva o **PY** 76-77 J 3
Embreeville o **USA** (TN) 280-281 H 4
Embrun o **CDN** (ONT) 238-239 K 3
Embu o **EAK** 212-213 F 4
Embudo, Raudal del ∼ **CO** 64-65 F 1
Embundu o **ANG** 216-217 D 8
Emca o **RUS** 88-89 Q 5
Emca ∼ **RUS** 88-89 Q 5
Emcisweni o **RUS** 214-215 G 6
Emden o **D** 92-93 J 2
Emden Deep ≃ 160-161 G 7
Emeck o **RUS** 88-89 Q 5
Emeishan o **VRC** 156-157 C 2
Èmel' o **KZ** 124-125 N 5
Emeljanovskaja o **RUS** 88-89 Q 4
Emelle o **USA** (AL) 284-285 B 4
Emerald o **AUS** 178-179 K 2
Emerald Bank ≃ 38-39 N 7
Emerald Isle ∼ **CDN** 24-25 P 2
Emeriau Point ▲ **AUS** 172-173 F 4
Emenillon o **F** 62-63 H 4
Emersen o **CDN** (MAN) 234-235 F 5
Emerson o **USA** (GA) 276-277 B 7
Emory o **USA** (UT) 254-255 D 3
Emery Range ▲ **AUS** 178-179 C 4
Emet o **TR** 128-129 C 3
Emeti o **PNG** 183 B 4
Emi Fezzane ▲ **TCH** 198-199 G 2
Emi Koussi ▲ **TCH** 198-199 J 3
Emiliano Zapata o **MEX** (CHI) 52-53 J 3
Emiliano Zapata o **MEX** (COA)
50-51 H 5
Emiliano Zapata o **MEX** (SON)
50-51 D 3
Emin o **VRC** 146-147 F 2
Eminäbâd o **PK** 138-139 E 3
Eminee o **USA** (IN) 274-275 M 5
Eminence o **USA** (KY) 276-277 K 2
Eminence o **USA** (MO) 274-275 H 3
Emin He ∼ **VRC** 146-147 F 2
Emini o **CAM** 210-211 D 2
Emigdehard o **USA** (NC) 282-283 M 5
Emigdumo, La o **CA** 246-247 C 4
Emlichheim o **D** 92-93 H 2
Emma, Mount ▲ **CDN** 24-25 g 4
Emmaboda o **S** 86-87 G 8
Emme ∼ **CH** 92-93 K 3
Emmen o **NL** 92-93 J 2
Emmet o **AUS** 178-179 H 3
Emmetsburg o **USA** (IA) 274-275 D 1
Emmett o **USA** (ID) 252-253 B 3
Emmett o **USA** (MI) 272-273 G 5
Emmingdum o **IND** 140-141 G 3
Emmitsburg o **USA** (MD) 280-281 J 4
Emmonak o **USA** 20-21 H 5
Èmmy, mys ▲ **RUS** 110-111 b 1
Emo o **CDN** (ONT) 234-235 K 6
Emory o **USA** (TX) 266-267 D 3
Emory Pass ▲ **USA** (NM) 256-257 H 5
Emory Peak ▲ **USA** (TX) 200-207 D 4
Emoulas o **MEX** 50-51 D 4
Empalme o **MEX** 50-51 D 4
Empangeni o **ZA** 220-221 K 4
Empedrado o **RCH** 78-79 C 3
Emperado, El o **YV** 60-61 F 3
Emperor Range ▲ **PNG** 184 I b 1
Emperor Seamount Chain ≃ 14-15 K 3
Emperor Trough ≃ 14-15 K 3
Empexa, Salar de o **BOL** 70-71 E 5
Empire o **RA** 276-277 D 7
Empire o **USA** (CA) 248-249 D 2
Empire o **USA** (OR) 244-245 B 3
Emporia o **USA** (KS) 262-263 K 6
Emporia o **USA** (VA) 280-281 J 7
Emporium o **USA** (PA) 280-281 H 3
Empress o **CDN** (ALB) 232-233 H 5
Empress Augusta Bay ≈ 184 I b 2
Empress Mine o **ZW** 218-219 E 4
Ems ∼ **D** 92-93 J 2
Emu Park o **AUS** 178-179 L 2
Emure o **WAN** 204-205 F 5
Emva o **RUS** 88-89 U 5
Emwan o **CAM** 204-205 K 6
Ena o **J** 152-153 H 3
Enakievo = Jenakíjeve o **UA**
102-103 L 3
Enangipani o **EAK** 212-213 G 4
Enarotali o **RI** 166-167 J 3
Enate o **RUS** 116-117 F 5
Encaitedo o **BR** 68-69 J 4
Encantado, Cape ▲ **CDN** 30-31 T 5
Encanto o **CO** 60-61 E 3
Encaración ✰ **PY** 76-77 K 4
Encarnacion de Díaz o **MEX** 50-51 H 7
Encinal o **USA** (TX) 266-267 B 5
Encinal, El o **MEX** 50-51 K 5
Encinitas o **USA** (CA) 248-249 G 7
Encino o **CO** 60-61 E 4
Encino o **USA** (NM) 256-257 K 4
Encino o **USA** (TX) 266-267 C 6
Enco o **RA** 76-77 E 2

Encon o **RA** 78-79 F 2
Encontrados o **YV** 60-61 E 3
Encounter Bay ≈ 180-181 E 5
Encrucijada, La o **YV** 60-61 J 3
Encruzilhada o **BR** 72-73 K 5
Encruzilhada do Sul o **BR** 74-75 D 8
Encudcijada, La o **YV** 60-61 H 3
Enda o **VRC** 144-145 L 5
Endako o **CDN** (BC) 228-229 J 2
Endau o **EAK** (EAS) 212-213 G 4
Endau ▲ **EAK** (EAS) 212-213 G 4
Endè ∼ **RUS** 116-117 E 2
Ende, Pulau o **RI** 168 E 7
Endeavor o **USA** (WI) 270-271 H 6
Endeavour Strait ≈ 174-175 G 2
Endebes o **EAK** 212-213 E 3
Endeh o **RI** 168 E 7
Endengue o **CAM** 210-211 D 2
Enderby o **CDN** (BC) 230-231 M 2
Enderby Abyssal Plain ≃ 12 B 10
Enderby Land ⊡ **ARK** 16 G 6
Enderlin o **USA** (ND) 258-259 K 5
Endiang o **CDN** (ALB) 232-233 F 4
Endicott o **USA** (NY) 278-279 E 6
Endicott o **USA** (WA) 244-245 H 4
Endicott Arm ≈ 32-33 D 3
Endicott Mountains ▲ **USA** 20-21 N 3
Endicott Mountains Range ▲ **USA**
20-21 N 3
Endiké o **RCB** 210-211 E 4
Endimari, Rio ∼ **BR** 66-67 D 7
Endom o **CAM** 210-211 D 2
Endra, ozero o **RUS** 114-115 L 4
Endyalgout Island ∼ **AUS** 172-173 L 1
Ene, Rio ∼ **PE** 64-65 E 7
Eneaba o **AUS** 176-177 C 4
Enemawira o **RI** 164-165 J 1
Enemy, Lake of the o **CDN** 30-31 O 4
Enéné Patatpe o **F** 62-63 G 4
Energia o **RA** 78-79 K 5
Enerucijada, La o **YV** 60-61 K 3
Enez o **TR** 128-129 B 2
Enfield o **CDN** (NS) 240-241 M 6
Enfield o **USA** (CT) 280-281 N 2
Enfield o **USA** (NC) 282-283 K 4
Enfok o **IND** 140-141 L 6
Emi Fezzane ▲ **TCH** 198-199 G 2
Engadin ⊡ **CH** 92-93 N 5
Engadine o **USA** (MI) 270-271 N 4
Engaño, Cabo ▲ **DOM** 54-55 L 5
Engaru o **J** 152-153 K 2
Engaruka o **EAT** (ARV) 212-213 E 5
Engaruka ∴⋅ **EAT** (ARV) 212-213 E 5
Engaruka Basin ⊡ **EAT** 212-213 F 5
Engcobo o **ZA** 220-221 H 5
Engelhard o **USA** (NC) 282-283 M 5
Engelmine o **USA** (CA) 246-247 C 4
Engel's = Èngel's o **RUS** 96-97 F 8
Engelsbergs bruk ∴ **S** 86-87 H 7
Engen o **CDN** (BC) 228-229 K 2
Engenheiro Navarro o **BR** 72-73 J 4
Engenho, El o **PE** 64-65 E 9
Engerina Creek ∼ **AUS** 178-179 C 4
Enggano, Pulau ∼ **RI** 162-163 F 7
Engh o **VRC** 150-151 M 3
Engida ∼ **RUS** 116-117 E 2
Engineer Group ∼ **PNG** 183 F 0
Engkilili o **MAL** 162-163 J 4
England ■ **GB** 90-91 H 5
England, Cape ▲ **CDN** (AII) 276-277 D 6
Engle o **USA** (NM) 256-257 H 5
Englee o **CDN** (NFL) 242-243 M 2
Englefeld o **CDN** (SAS) 232-233 O 3
Englefield, Cape ▲ **CDN** 24-25 g 6
Englefield Bay ≈ 228-229 B 4
Englehart o **CDN** (ONT) 236-237 G 3
Englevale o **USA** (ND) 258-259 K 5
Englewood o **USA** (FL) 280-281 G 6
Englewood o **USA** (KS) 262-263 G 7
Englewood o **USA** (OH) 280-281 B 4
Englewood o **USA** (TN) 282-283 C 5
English o **USA** (IN) 274-275 M 5
English Bay o **CDN** 36-37 J 7
English Channel ≈ 90-91 G 6
English Coast ⊡ **ARK** 16 F 29
English Harbour East o **CDN** (NFL)
242-243 N 4
English Harbour Town o **AG** 56 E 3
English Harbour West o **CDN** (NFL)
242-243 N 5
English River o **CDN** (ONT)
234-235 N 5
Engoordina o **AUS** 178-179 C 3
Engozero o **RUS** 88-89 M 4
Engure o **LV** 94-95 H 3
Enid o **USA** (OK) 264-265 G 2
Enid Creek ∼ **AUS** 172-173 K 2
Enid Lake o **USA** (MS) 268-269 L 2
Enid Mining Area, Mount • **AUS**
172-173 E 4
Enisej ∼ **RUS** 10-11 H 2
Enisej, Bol'šoj ∼ **RUS** 116-117 G 10
Enisejsk ✰ **RUS** 116-117 F 8
Enisejskij zaliv ≈ 108-109 S 5
Enisejsko-Stolbovoj, učastok ⊥ **RUS**
114-115 U 3
Eniwa o **J** 152-153 J 3
Enjil o **MA** 188-189 J 4
Enjukovo o **RUS** 94-95 P 2
Ènkën, mys ▲ **RUS** 120-121 J 5
Enkhuizen o **NL** 92-93 H 2
Enköping o **S** 86-87 H 7
Ènmelen o **RUS** 112-113 T 4
Ènmelen o **RUS** 112-113 X 4
Ènmyvaam ∼ **RUS** 112-113 N 3
Enna o **I** 100-101 E 6
Ennadai o **CDN** 30-31 T 5
Ennadai Lake o **CDN** 30-31 S 5
En Naga, Oued ∼ **DZ** 188-189 J 5
En Nahûd o **SUD** 200-201 D 6
En Namous, Oued ∼ **DZ** 188-189 J 4
Enné, Ouadi ∼ **TCH** 198-199 J 5
Enneri Mi ∼ **TCH** 198-199 G 2
Enneri Tésé ∼ **TCH** 198-199 H 2
Enneri Yébiqué ∼ **TCH** 192-193 G 6
Ennery o **RH** 54-55 J 4
Enngonia o **AUS** 178-179 H 5
Ennis o **USA** (MT) 250-251 H 6

Ennis o **USA** (TX) 264-265 H 6
Ennis = Inis o **IRL** 90-91 C 5
Enniscorthy = Inis Córthaidh o **IRL**
90-91 D 5
Enniskillen o **USA** (ND) 238-239 G 4
Enniskillen ✰ **GB** 90-91 D 4
Enochs o **USA** (TX) 264-265 B 5
Enoch o **USA** (UT) 254-255 B 6
Enonkoski o **FIN** 88-89 G 2
Enontekiö o **FIN** 88-89 G 2
Enore River ∼ **USA** 284-285 J 2
Enosburg Falls o **USA** (VT) 278-279 J 4
Enozero o **RUS** 96-97 E 10
Enping o **VRC** 156-157 H 5
Enrekang o **RI** 164-165 G 6
Enridaville o **USA** (IN) 190-191 H 3
Enrile o **RP** 160-161 H 2
Enriquillo, Lago o **DOM** 54-55 K 5
Enschede o **NL** 92-93 J 2
Enseada de Tijucas ≈ 74-75 F 6
Ensenada • **MEX** 50-51 A 2
Ensenada o **USA** (NM) 256-257 K 3
Ensenada Chaitén ≈ 78-79 C 7
Ensenada de Tumaco ≈ 60-61 B 7
Enshi o **VRC** 154-155 F 3
Enshû-nada ≈ 152-153 H 3
Ensign o **USA** (KS) 262-263 F 7
Ensley o **USA** (FL) 286-287 B 1
Ènstor, ozero o **RUS** 114-115 K 4
Entebbing, Rumah o **MAL** 162-163 K 3
Entebbe o **EAU** 212-213 D 3
Entel o **USA** (MS) 268-269 M 4
Enterprise o **CDN** 30-31 S 5
Enterprise o **USA** (AL) 284-285 D 5
Enterprise o **USA** (MS) 268-269 M 4
Enterprise o **USA** (OR) 244-245 H 5
Enterprise o **USA** (UT) 254-255 B 6
Enterprise Point ▲ **RP** 160-161 C 7
Entiako River ∼ **CDN** 228-229 J 2
Entico o **USA** (WA) 244-245 H 3
Entrada, Punta ▲ **RA** 80 F 5
Entrance o **CDN** (ALB) 228-229 R 3-4
Entreré o **BR** 68-69 J 7
Entre Lagos o **RCH** 78-79 C 6
Entre Rios o **BOL** 76-77 E 1
Entre-Ríos o **BR** 66-67 K 5
Entre-Ríos o **BR** 68-69 J 7
Entre Ríos, Cordillera ▲ **HN** 52-53 M 4
Entriken o **USA** (PA) 280-281 H 3
Entroncamento o **BR** 68-69 F 5
Entroncamento o **BR** 68-69 E 4
Entronque La Cuchilla o **MEX**
50-51 H 5
Enu o **RI** 166-167 L 3
Enugu ∼ **ZA** 220-221 K 4
Enugu o **WAN** 204-205 G 5
Enugu Ezike o **WAN** 204-205 G 5
Enumclaw o **USA** (WA) 244-245 D 4
Ènurmino o **RUS** 112-113 X 2
Envigado o **CO** 60-61 D 4
Envira o **BR** 68-69 D 7
Enyamba o **ZRE** 210-211 K 5
Enyčavajam ∼ **RUS** 112-113 O 6
Enyelli o **RCB** 210-211 E 4
Enyngvajam ∼ **RUS** 120-121 V 3
Eo, Rio ∼ **E** 98-99 D 3
Eochaill = Youghal o **IRL** 90-91 D 6
Eola o **USA** (TX) 266-267 C 3
Eólie o Lipari, Isole ∼ **I** 100-101 E 5
Èpako o **NAM** 216-217 D 10
Epanomi o **GR** 100-101 J 4
Epatlán o **MEX** 52-53 G 2
Epe o **WAN** 204-205 E 5
Epécuén, Laguna o **RA** 78-79 H 4
Epéna o **RCB** 210-211 F 3
Epenarra o **AUS** 174-175 C 7
Epesus = Efes ∴⋅ **TR** 128-129 B 3
Ephraim o **USA** (UT) 254-255 D 4
Ephrata o **USA** (PA) 280-281 J 4
Ephrata o **USA** (WA) 244-245 F 3
Epi o **VAN** 184 II b 3
Epi ∼ **VAN** (EPI) 184 II b 3
Epi o **ZRE** 210-211 L 2
Epidaurus ⋅⋅⋅ **GR** 100-101 J 6
Épinal ✰ **F** 90-91 L 7
Epini o **ZRE** 212-213 B 3
Epiphany o **USA** (SD) 260-261 J 4
Epizana o **BOL** 70-71 E 5
Epokenkoso o **ZRE** 210-211 F 5
Epoma o **RCB** 210-211 E 3
Epping o **USA** (ND) 258-259 D 3
Epping o **USA** (NH) 278-279 L 5
Epping Forest o **AUS** 178-179 J 2
Epping Forest National Park ⊥ **AUS**
178-179 J 2
Epps o **USA** (LA) 268-269 J 4
Epsom o **AUS** 178-179 H 5
Epu, River ∼ **WAN** 204-205 G 4
Epukiro o **NAM** (GOB) 216-217 E 10
Epukiro ∼ **NAM** 216-217 E 10
Epulu o **ZRE** 212-213 B 3
Epulu, Station de capture d' ∼ **ZRE**
212-213 B 3
Eupa Falls ∼ **NAM** 216-217 B 8
Epuyén o **RA** 78-79 D 7
Eqlid o **IR** 134-135 D 3
Equateur ⊡ **ZRE** 210-211 G 3
Equator ∼ **Äquator** 6-7 O 3
Equatorial Guinea = Guinea Ecuatorial ■
GQ 210-211 C 2
Eračimo o **RUS** 116-117 E 3
Erahtur o **RUS** 94-95 N 4
Eralé o **BR** 62-63 H 5
Fram o **PNG** 183 C 4
Eran Bay ≈ 160-161 B 8
Era River ∼ **PNG** 183 C 4
Erátini o **GR** 100-101 J 5
Erode o **IND** 140-141 G 5
Erofej Pavlovič o **RUS** 118-119 L 8
Erave o **PNG** 183 B 4

Eromalido, Tanjung ▲ **RI** 166-167 C 6
Eromanga o **AUS** 178-179 G 4
Eromanga ∼ **VAN** 13 H 4
Eromanga Island = Île Erromango ∼ **VAN**
184 II b 4
Eromohon o **RUS** 116-117 L 2
Eromgoberg ▲ **NAM** 216-217 C 10
Erong Springs o **AUS** 176-177 D 3
Eröö o Bugant o **MAU** 148-149 H 3
Eröö gol ∼ **MAU** 148-149 H 3
Eropol ∼ **RUS** 112-113 P 4
Eroro o **PNG** 183 E 5
Erba, Gabal ▲ **SUD** (Ahm) 200-201 H 2
Erba, Gabal ▲ **SUD** (Ahm) 200-201 H 2
Erawadi = Îrrawaddy ∼ **MYA**
158-159 C 3
Erawadi Myitwanyâ ᴗ **MYA**
158-159 E 3
Erawan National Park ⊥⋅ **THA**
158-159 E 3
Erbaa ✰ **TR** 128-129 H 2
Erbogačen o **RUS** 116-117 N 5
Èrča, Bol'šaja ∼ **RUS** 116-117 b 5
Erçek Gölü o **TR** 128-129 L 3
Erciş o **TR** 128-129 L 3
Erciyes Daği ▲ **TR** 128-129 F 3
Erdaobaihe o **VRC** 150-151 G 6
Erdek ✰ **TR** 128-129 C 2
Erdemli o **TR** 128-129 F 3
Er-Remla o **TN** 190-191 H 3
Èrdènècagaan = Čonogol o **MAU**
148-149 K 3
Èrdènècogt o **MAU** 148-149 E 4
Èrdènèdalaj = Sanqijin Dalaj o **MAU**
148-149 G 4
Èrdènèmandal = Ölziym o **MAU**
148-149 G 4
Èrdènèsant = Ulaanhudag o **MAU**
148-149 G 4
Èrdènèt o **MAU** 148-149 G 3
Enshû-nada ≈ 152-153 H 3
Èrdènì Cu ∴⋅ **MAU** 148-149 F 4
Erdi ⊡ **TCH** 198-199 J 3
Eré o **ER** 200-201 H 5
Erebus, Mount ▲ **ARK** 16 F 17
Erebus and Terror Gulf ≈ 16 G 31
Erebus Bay ≈ 24-25 W 2
Erech ∴⋅ **IRQ** 128-129 L 7
Erechim o **BR** 74-75 D 6
Èrèèncav o **MAU** 148-149 M 3
Ereğli o **TR** 128-129 E 2
Ereğli ✰ **TR** 128-129 F 3
Erejmentau o **KZ** 122-123 C 3
Èrèké o **RCA** 206-207 C 5
Èrema o **RUS** 116-117 N 5
Èrema, Bol'šaja ∼ **RUS** 116-117 N 5
Erenhot o **VRC** 148-149 K 6
Erepecuru, Lago de o **BR** 62-63 F 4
Ereré o **BR** 68-69 J 4
Èrer Wenz ∼ **ETH** 208-209 F 5
Èrevan ✰ **AR** 128-129 L 2
Erfenisdam ⊂ **ZA** 220-221 G 4
Erfoud o **MA** 188-189 J 5
Erfurt ✰⋅ **D** 92-93 L 3
Ergani o **TR** 128-129 H 3
Èrgel o **MAU** 148-149 J 6
Èrgeni ▲ **RUS** 118-119 O 4
Ergene Nehri ∼ **TR** 128-129 B 2
Èrgeni ▲ **RUS** 96-97 E 10
Èrgig, Bahr ∼ **VRC** 118-119 L 9
Ergun He ∼ **VRC** 118-119 L 9
Èrgun Youqi o **VRC** 150-151 O 1
Èrgun Zuoqi o **VRC** 150-151 C 2
Èrgueveem ∼ **RUS** 112-113 X 4
Er Hai o **VRC** 142-143 M 3
Eri, River ∼ **WAN** 204-205 E 4
Erì, Rio ∼ **E** 98-99 D 3
Èaashi o **J** (IIOK) 152-153 J 4
Èaashi o **J** (HOK) 152-153 J 4
Fsayon Bay ≈ 26-27 J 3
Esbjerg o **DK** 86-87 D 9
Esbo = Espoo o **FIN** 88-89 H 6
Escada o **BR** 68-69 L 6
Escalante o **USA** (UT) 254-255 D 4
Escalante River ∼ **USA** 254-255 D 6
Escalante Valley o **USA** 254-255 B 5
Escalón o **MEX** 50-51 G 4
Escambia River ∼ **USA** 286-287 B 1
Escanaba o **USA** (MI) 270-271 M 4
Escanaba River ∼ **USA** 270-271 L 4
Escara o **BOL** 70-71 E 4
Escárcega o **MEX** 52-53 J 2
Escarpada Point ▲ **RP** 160-161 J 1
Escatawpa River ∼ **USA** 284-285 B 5
Eschscholtz Bay ≈ 20-21 J 3
Eschwege o⋅ **D** 92-93 L 3
Eschweiler o **D** 92-93 H 3
Escobas o **USA** (TX) 266-267 C 6
Escocesa, Bahía ≈ 54-55 L 5
Escocia o **USA** (CA) 246-247 B 3
Escoga, La o **BOL** 70-71 E 4
Escola o **BOL** 70-71 D 5
Escondida, La o **MEX** 50-51 G 6
Escondido o **USA** (CA) 248-249 G 6
Escondido, Rio ∼ **NIC** 52-53 B 5
Escoporanga o **BR** 72-73 K 5
Escoria, El o⋅⋅⋅ **E** 98-99 E 4
Escott o **AUS** 174-175 C 7
Escoumins, Les o **CDN** (QUE)
240-241 J 2
Escravos o **WAN** 204-205 F 6
Escudilla Mountain ▲ **USA** (AZ)
256-257 F 5
Escuinapa de Hidalgo o **MEX** 50-51 G 6
Escuintla o **GCA** 52-53 J 4
Escuintla o **MEX** 50-51 G 6
Escuminac o **CDN** (NB) 240-241 L 3
Escuminac, Point ▲ **CDN** (NB)
240-241 L 3

Eshan o **VRC** 156-157 C 4
Eshimba o **ZRE** 210-211 K 6
Esigodini o **ZW** 218-219 E 5
Esil ∼ **KZ** (TRG) 124-125 E 3
Esil ∼ **KZ** 124-125 F 1
Esinskaja o **RUS** 94-95 N 1
Esira o **RM** 222-223 E 10
Esk o **AUS** 178-179 M 3
Esk o **CDN** (SAS) 232-233 O 4
Èškameš o **AFG** 136-137 L 4
Èškâšem o **AFG** 136-137 M 6
Eskdale o **AUS** 180-181 J 4
Esker o **CDN** 38-39 L 2
Eskifjörður o **IS** 86-87 f 2
Eskil ✰ **TR** 128-129 E 3
Eskilstuna o **S** 86-87 H 7
Eskimo Lakes o **CDN** 20-21 S 3
Eskimonæsset ∼ **GRO** 20-27 s 3
Eskimo Point ▲ **CDN** (NWT) 30-31 W 5
Eskimo Point ▲ **CDN** (MAN) 30-31 W 6
Èski-Nookat o **KS** 136-137 N 4
Èskişehir ✰ **TR** 128-129 D 3
Eskridge o **USA** (KS) 262-263 K 6
Esla, Rio ∼ **E** 98-99 D 3
Eslâmâbâd-e Garb o **IR** 134-135 A 2
Eslâm Qal'e o **AFG** 134-135 J 1
Eslâm Qal'e o **AFG** 134-135 J 1
Eslâmšahr o **IR** 136-137 B 7
Eslöv o **S** 86-87 F 9
Eşme ✰ **TR** 128-129 C 3
Esmeralda o **AUS** 174-175 G 6
Esmeralda, Isla ∼ **RCH** 80 C 4
Esmeralda, La o **RCH** 76-77 C 4
Esmeralda, La o **YV** (AMA) 60-61 J 4
Esmeralda, La o **YV** (BAR) 60-61 J 5
Esmeralda, Rio ∼ **BOL** 70-71 D 3
Esmeraldas ✰ **EC** 64-65 C 10
Esmeraldas o **BR** 72-73 H 5
Esmeraldas ⊡ **EC** 64-65 C 1
Esmeraldas, Rio ∼ **EC** 64-65 C 1
Esmond o **USA** (ND) 258-259 H 3
Esnagami Lake o **CDN** (ONT)
236-237 B 2
Esnagi Lake o **CDN** (ONT) 236-237 D 4
Espadim Paranhos o **BR** 76-77 K 2
Espake o **IR** 134-135 J 5
Espalion o **F** 90-91 J 9
España o **RP** 160-161 J 8
España ∼ **USA** 254-255 D 5
Espanola o **CDN** (ONT) 238-239 D 2
Espanola o **USA** (NM) 256-257 J 3
Española, Isla ∼ **EC** 64-65 C 10
Esparto o **USA** (CA) 246-247 C 5
Espaevilla o **PA** 52-53 D 8
Espenberg o **USA** 20-21 J 3
Espenberg, Cape ▲ **USA** 20-21 J 3
Esperança o **BR** (PA) 62-63 H 6
Esperança o **BR** (PB) 68-69 L 5
Esperança, Serra da ▲ **BR** 74-75 E 5
Esperança dos Indios o **BR** 70-71 J 7
Esperance o **AUS** 176-177 F 6
Esperance Bay ≈ 176-177 F 6
Esperantina o **BR** 68-69 G 3
Esperantonopolis o **BR** 68-69 F 4
Esperanza o **MEX** 66-67 C 5
Esperanza o **RA** (UCA) 66-67 B 7
Esperanza o **C** 54-55 E 3
Esperanza o **MEX** 50-51 T 4
Esperanza o **RA** (SAC) 80 E 5
Esperanza o **RA** (SAF) 76-77 G 6
Esperanza o **USA** (TX) 266-267 B 2
Esperanza, La o **BOL** 70-71 F 4
Esperanza, La o **C** 54-55 D 3
Esperanza, La o **HN** 52-53 K 4
Esperanza, La o **RA** 78-79 E 6
Esperanza, La o **YV** 60-61 J 5
Esperanza, Sierra la o **HN** 54-55 C 7
Esperanza Inlet ≈ 230-231 D 4
Espichel, Cabo ▲ **P** 98-99 C 5
Espigão, Serra do ▲ **BR** 74-75 D 6
Espigão do Oeste o **BR** 70-71 G 2
Espigão Mestre ▲ **BR** 68-69 E 7
Espinal o **BOL** 70-71 H 5
Espinal o **CO** 60-61 D 5
Espinar o **PA** 52-53 D 9
Espinero o **YV** 60-61 K 4
Espinheira o **ANG** 216-217 D 8
Espinho o **P** 98-99 C 4
Espinilho, Serra do ▲ **BR** 76-77 K 5
Espinillo o **RA** 76-77 H 3
Espino o **CO** 60-61 H 4
Espino, El o **RA** 76-77 D 2
Espinosa o **BR** 72-73 J 3
Espinosa o **BR** 72-73 J 3
Espírito Santo o **BR** (AMA) 66-67 J 4
Espírito Santo do Turvo o **BR** 72-73 F 7
Espírito Santo o **BR** (AMA) 66-67 J 4
Espírito Santo, Área Indígena ⊥ **BR**
66-67 H 7
Espíritu Santo ∼ **VAN** 184 II a 2
Espíritu Santo, Bahía del ≈ 52-53 L 2
Espíritu Santo, Isla ∼ **MEX** 50-51 D 5
Espírito Santo do Pinhal o **BR**
72-73 G 7
Espita o **MEX** 52-53 K 1
Esplanada o **BR** 68-69 K 7
Espoo o **FIN** 88-89 H 6
Espungabera o **MOC** 218-219 G 5
Esqâbâd o **IR** 134-135 G 1
Esquel o **RA** 220-221 C 4
Esquibel, Gulf of ≈ 32-33 D 4
Esquina o **RA** 76-77 H 6
Esquina o **RCH** 70-71 C 6
Esquiú o **RA** 76-77 E 5
Ess ∼ **RUS** 114-115 Q 4
Essaouira = As-Gawîrah ✰ **MA** (Ess)
188-189 G 5
Essé o **CAM** 204-205 J 6
Es-Sed, Oued ∼ **TN** 190-191 H 4
Es Seggeur, Oued ∼ **DZ** 190-191 G 4
Essej o **RUS** 108-109 e 7
Essej, ozero o **RUS** 108-109 e 7
Essen o **B** 92-93 H 3
Essendon, Mount ▲ **AUS** 176-177 F 3
Essentuki o **RUS** 126-127 E 5
Esséquibo ∼ **GUY** 62-63 F 3
Essequibo River ∼ **GUY** 62-63 E 2

Fatitet ○ **SUD** 206-207 K 5
Fātiyah, Bi'r al ○ **LAR** 192-193 F 3
Fat'janiha ∼ **RUS** 114-115 U 2
Fat'janiha, Bol'šaja ∼ **RUS** 114-115 U 3
Fatki ∼ **BD** 142-143 F 4
Fatolulik ○ **RI** 166-167 C 6
Fatsa ☆ **TR** 128-129 G 2
Fatujuring (Village of pearl trade) ○ ·· **RI** 166-167 H 5
Fatuma ○ **ZRE** 214-215 E 4
Fatunda ○ **ZRE** 210-211 F 6
Fatural ○ **RI** 166-167 H 5
Faucett ○ **USA** (MO) 274-275 D 5
Faulkner ○ **CDN** (MAN) 234-235 E 3
Faulkton ○ **USA** (SD) 260-261 G 1
Faunce ○ **USA** (MN) 270-271 D 2
Fauquier ○ **CDN** (BC) 230-231 L 4
Faure Island ⌒ **AUS** 176-177 B 2
Fauresmith ○ **ZA** 220-221 G 4
Fauro Island ⌒ **SOL** 184 I c 2
Fauske ○ **N** 86-87 G 3
Faux Cap = Betanty ○ **RM** 222-223 D 10
Favignana ○ **I** 100-101 D 6
Fāw, al- ☆ **IRQ** 130-131 L 3
Fawcett Lake ⊖ **CDN** (ONT) 234-235 M 3
Fawnie Range ▲ **CDN** 228-229 J 3
Fawnleas ○ **ZA** 220-221 K 4
Fawn Point ▲ **USA** 22-23 P 5
Fawn River ∼ **CDN** 34-35 M 3
Fawwāra, al- ○ **KSA** 130-131 H 4
Faxaflói ≈ 86-87 b 2
Faxälven ∼ **S** 86-87 H 5
Faxinal ○ **BR** 74-75 E 5
Faxinal do Soturno ○ **BR** 74-75 D 7
Faya ∼ **RMM** 202-203 G 3
Faya = Largeau ☆ **TCH** 198-199 J 4
Fayala ○ **ZRE** 210-211 F 5
Fayette ○ **USA** (AL) 284-285 C 3
Fayette ○ **USA** (MO) 274-275 F 5
Fayette ○ **USA** (MS) 268-269 J 5
Fayette ○ **USA** (ND) 258-259 E 4
Fayette ○ **USA** (OH) 280-281 B 2
Fayette, La ○ **USA** (GA) 284-285 E 2
Fayetteville ○ **USA** (AR) 276-277 A 4
Fayetteville ○ **USA** (GA) 284-285 F 3
Fayetteville ○ **USA** (IL) 274-275 J 6
Fayetteville ○ **USA** (NC) 282-283 J 5
Fayetteville ○ **USA** (OH) 280-281 C 4
Fayetteville ○ **USA** (TN) 276-277 J 5
Fayḥān, Wādī ∼ **KSA** 130-131 H 3
Faysal, Wādī ∼ **LAR** 192-193 E 2
Faywood ○ **USA** (NM) 256-257 G 6
Fāz ☆ ··· **MA** 188-189 J 3
Fazao ○ **RT** 202-203 L 5
Fazao, Monts du ▲ **RT** 202-203 L 5
Fazao Malfakassa, Parc National de ⊥ **RT** 202-203 L 5
Fazeï ○ **RN** 198-199 E 3
Fazenda Boa Esperança ○ **BR** 62-63 D 6
Fazenda Bradesco ○ **BR** 68-69 D 3
Fazenda Cumaru ○ **BR** 68-69 C 5
Fazenda Eldorado ○ **BR** 70-71 J 5
Fazenda Foz do Christalino ○ **BR** 72-73 E 2
Fazenda Gavião ○ **BR** 68-69 E 6
Fazenda Itanorte ○ **BR** 70-71 J 4
Fazenda Muraquitã ○ **BR** 70-71 G 2
Fazenda Narciso ○ **BR** 66-67 D 2
Fazenda Primavera ○ **BR** 68-69 B 7
Fazenda Remanso ○ **BR** 66-67 J 4
Fazenda Rio Dourado ○ **BR** 68-69 C 6
Fazenda Rio Limpo ○ **BR** 68-69 F 7
Fazenda Santa Lúcia ○ **BR** 70-71 K 5
Fazenda São Sebastião ○ **BR** 70-71 E 2
Fazenda Taboco ○ **BR** 70-71 K 7
Fazenda Três Irmãos ○ **BR** 70-71 K 5
Fazenda Vista Alegre ○ **BR** 66-67 G 7
Fazilpur ○ **PK** 138-139 C 5
Fdérik ☆ **RIM** 196-197 D 3
Fé, La ○ **C** 54-55 D 4
Fear, Cape ▲ **USA** (NC) 282-283 K 7
Feather Falls ○ **USA** (CA) 246-247 D 4
Featherston ○ **NZ** 182 E 4
Feathertop, Mount ▲ **AUS** 180-181 J 4
Featherville ○ **USA** (ID) 252-253 C 3
Fécamp ○ **F** 90-91 H 7
Federal ○ **RA** 76-77 H 6
Federal Capital Territory □ **WAN** 204-205 G 4
Federalsburg ○ **USA** (MD) 280-281 L 5
Fedjour, Col de ▲ **DZ** 190-191 F 2
Fedorovka ○ **KZ** (KST) 124-125 D 1
Fedorovka ☆ **KZ** (KST) 124-125 C 2
Fedorovka ☆ **KZ** (ZPK) 96-97 H 8
Fedorovka ☆ **RUS** 96-97 J 7
Fedotova kosa ⌣ **UA** 102-103 J 4
Feestone ○ **USA** (CA) 246-247 B 5
Féfiné, Rio ∼ **GNB** 202-203 D 4
Fegoh, Wādī ∼ **ET** 194-195 G 6
Fegoussi, Bir ○ **TN** 190-191 G 4
Fehmarn ⌒ **D** 92-93 L 1
Feia, Lagoa ⊖ **BR** 72-73 K 6
Feidh el Botma ○ **DZ** 190-191 D 3
Feidong ○ **VRC** 154-155 K 6
Feijó ○ **BR** 66-67 B 7
Feilai Xia • **VRC** 156-157 H 5
Feilding ○ **NZ** 182 E 4
Feio ou Aguapei, Rio ∼ **BR** 72-73 E 6
Feira de Santana ○ **BR** 72-73 L 2
Feitok ○ **CAM** 204-205 H 6
Feixi ○ **VRC** 154-155 K 6
Fei Xian ○ **VRC** 154-155 K 4
Feiżābād ○ **IR** 134-135 H 1
Feke ☆ **TR** 128-129 F 4
Feklistova, ostrov ⌒ **RUS** 120-121 G 6
Felaou ○ **DZ** 198-199 B 3
Felch Mountain ○ **USA** (MI) 270-271 L 4
Feldberg ▲ ·· **D** 92-93 J 5
Feldioara ○ • **RO** 102-103 D 5
Feldkirch ○ **A** 92-93 K 5
Felege Neway ○ **ETH** 208-209 C 6
Felguera, La ○ **E** 98-99 E 3
Feliciano, Arroyo ∼ **RA** 76-77 H 6
Félicité Island ⌒ **SY** 224 D 2
Felidu Atoll ⌒ **MV** 140-141 B 6
Felinto Müller ○ **BR** 68-69 E 4
Felipe, San ∼ **USA** 248-249 H 6
Felipe Carillo Puerto ○ • **MEX** 52-53 K 2
Felix, Cape ▲ **CDN** 24-25 X 6
Felix, Rio ∼ **USA** 256-257 L 5
Felixburg ○ **ZW** 218-219 F 4
Felixlândia ○ **BR** 72-73 H 5
Felixstowe ○ **GB** 90-91 H 6
Felizardo ○ **BR** 68-69 J 5
Fellfoot Point ▲ **CDN** 24-25 b 3
Fellsmere ○ **USA** (FL) 286-287 J 4
Félou, Chutes de ∼ • **RMM** 202-203 E 2
Felps ○ **USA** (LA) 268-269 K 6
Felsenthal, Lake < **USA** (AR) 276-277 C 7
Felton ○ **USA** (MN) 270-271 B 3
Feltre ○ **I** 100-101 C 1
Fêmeas, Rio das ∼ **BR** 72-73 H 2
Femund ⊖ **N** 86-87 E 5
Femundsmarka nationalpark ⊥ **N** 86-87 F 5
Fence Lake ○ **USA** (NM) 256-257 G 4
Fenelon Falls ○ **CDN** (ONT) 238-239 G 4
Fener Burnu ▲ **TR** 128-129 H 2
Feng'an ○ **VRC** 156-157 J 5
Fengcheng ○ **VRC** (JXI) 156-157 J 2
Fengcheng ○ **VRC** (LIA) 150-151 E 7
Fengdu ○ **VRC** 156-157 E 2
Fenggang ○ **VRC** 156-157 E 3
Fenghua ○ **VRC** 156-157 M 2
Fenghuang ○ **VRC** (GDG) 156-157 K 5
Fenghuang ○ **VRC** (HUB) 154-155 J 6
Fenghuang ○ **VRC** (HUN) 156-157 F 3
Fenghuangshan • **VRC** 150-151 E 7
Fengjie ○ **VRC** 154-155 F 6
Fengkang ○ **RC** 156-157 M 5
Fengliang ○ **VRC** 156-157 K 5
Fengling Guan ▲ **VRC** 156-157 L 2
Fengling Z.B. ⊥ • **VRC** 150-151 G 3
Fengning ○ **VRC** 148-149 N 7
Fengpin ○ **RC** 156-157 M 5
Fengpo ○ **VRC** 156-157 B 5
Fengqiu ○ **VRC** 154-155 J 4
Fengrun ○ **VRC** 154-155 L 2
Fengshan ○ **RC** 156-157 M 5
Fengshan ○ **VRC** 156-157 E 4
Fengshui Shan ▲ **VRC** 150-151 D 1
Fengshun ○ **VRC** 156-157 K 5
Fengstan SK ⊖ **VRC** 156-157 F 2
Fengtongzhai Giant panda Reserves ⊥ **VRC** 154-155 C 6
Fengxian ○ **VRC** 154-155 M 6
Feng Xian ○ **VRC** (JIA) 154-155 K 4
Feng Xian ○ **VRC** (SXI) 154-155 F 5
Fengxiang ○ **VRC** 154-155 E 4
Fengxin ○ **VRC** 156-157 J 2
Fengxue Si • **VRC** 154-155 H 4
Fengyang ○ **VRC** 154-155 K 5
Fengyuan ○ **RC** 156-157 M 4
Fengzhen ○ **VRC** 154-155 H 1
Fen He ∼ **VRC** 154-155 G 3
Feni ○ **BD** 142-143 G 4
Feniak Lake ⊖ **USA** 20-21 L 2
Feni Islands ⌒ **PNG** 183 G 3
Fênix ○ **BR** 72-73 E 7
Fennimore ○ **USA** (WI) 274-275 H 2
Fennville ○ **USA** (MI) 272-273 C 5
Fenoarivo Atsinanana ○ **RM** 222-223 F 6
Fenoarivo Be ○ **RM** 222-223 E 7
Fenshui Guan ▲ **VRC** 156-157 K 3
Fenton ○ **CDN** (SAS) 232-233 N 2
Fenton ○ **USA** (IA) 274-275 D 1
Fenton ○ **USA** (LA) 268-269 H 6
Fenton ○ **USA** (MI) 272-273 F 5
Fenwood ○ **CDN** (SAS) 232-233 P 4
Fenyang ○ **VRC** 154-155 G 3
Feodosija ☆ • **UA** 102-103 J 5
Feodosijs'ka zatoka ≈ 102-103 J 5
Fer, Cap de ▲ **DZ** 190-191 F 2
Fer, Lesportes de • **DZ** 190-191 E 2
Fera Island ⌒ **SOL** 184 I d 3
Ferapontovo ○ **RUS** 94-95 Q 2
Ferdé ○ **RIM** 196-197 C 6
Ferdinand ○ **USA** (IN) 274-275 M 6
Ferdjioua ○ **DZ** 190-191 E 2
Ferdo, Le ∸ **SN** 202-203 C 2
Ferdous ○ **IR** 134-135 H 1
Fereidūnkenār ○ **IR** 136-137 C 6
Fereidūn Šahr ○ **IR** 134-135 D 2
Fērfēr ○ **ETH** 208-209 G 6
Fergana ☆ **UZ** 136-137 M 4
Ferganskaja dolina ∸ **UZ** 136-137 M 4
Ferganskaja oblast □ **UZ** 136-137 M 4
Ferganskij hrebet ▲ **KS** 136-137 N 4
Fergus ○ **CDN** (ONT) 238-239 E 5
Fergus Falls ○ **USA** (MN) 270-271 B 4
Ferguson ○ **CDN** (BC) 230-231 M 3
Ferguson Lake ⊖ **CDN** (NWT) 24-25 T 6
Ferguson Lake ⊖ **CDN** (NWT) 30-31 V 4
Ferguson Lake ⊖ **USA** (CA) 248-249 K 7
Ferguson River ∼ **CDN** 30-31 X 4
Fergusson Island ⌒ **PNG** 183 F 5
Fergusson River ○ **AUS** 172-173 K 3
Feriana ○ **TN** 190-191 G 3
Ferintosh ○ **CDN** (ALB) 232-233 F 3
Ferkessédougou ☆ **CI** 202-203 H 5
Ferland ○ **CDN** (ONT) 234-235 P 4
Ferland ○ **CDN** (QUE) 240-241 E 2
Ferland ○ **CDN** (SAS) 232-233 M 6
Ferlo, Vallée du ∼ **SN** 202-203 C 2
Ferma ○ **LT** 94-95 J 4
Fermeuse ○ **CDN** (NFL) 242-243 Q 6
Fermoselle ○ **E** 98-99 D 4
Fermoy = Mainistir Fhear Maí ○ **IRL** 90-91 C 5
Fernandez Bay ∸ • **BS** 54-55 H 2
Fernandina, Isla ⌒ **EC** 64-65 B 10
Fernandina Beach ○ **USA** (FL) 286-287 H 1
Fernando de Magallanes, Parque Nacional ⊥ **RCH** 80 D 6
Fernando de Noronha, Ilha ⌒ **BR** 68-69 L 1
Fernandónopolis ○ **BR** 72-73 E 6
Fernando Prestes ○ **BR** 72-73 F 6
Fernane, Djebel ▲ **DZ** 190-191 E 3
Fernan Vaz = Lagune Nkomi ⊖ **G** 210-211 B 4
Fernão Veloso ○ **MOC** 218-219 L 2
Ferndale ○ **USA** (CA) 246-247 A 3
Ferndale ○ **USA** (WA) 244-245 C 2
Fernie ○ **CDN** (BC) 230-231 O 4
Fernley ○ **USA** (NV) 246-247 F 4
Ferokh ○ **IND** 140-141 F 5
Ferrara ☆ • **I** 100-101 C 2
Ferreira ○ **ZA** 220-221 H 4
Ferreira do Alentejo ○ **P** 98-99 C 5
Ferreira Gomes ○ **BR** 62-63 J 5
Ferreñave ○ **PE** 64-65 C 5
Ferriday ○ **USA** (LA) 268-269 J 5
Ferris ○ **USA** (TX) 264-265 H 6
Ferro, Corredeira do ∼ **BR** 72-73 D 7
Ferro, Rio ∼ **BR** 70-71 K 3
Ferrol ○ **E** 98-99 C 3
Ferrol, Isla ⌒ **PE** 64-65 C 6
Ferron ○ **USA** (UT) 254-255 D 4
Ferryland ○ **CDN** (NFL) 242-243 Q 5
Feršampenuaz ☆ **RUS** 96-97 L 7
Ferté-Bernard, la ○ **F** 90-91 H 7
Fertile ○ **CDN** (SAS) 232-233 R 6
Fertile ○ **USA** (IA) 274-275 E 1
Fertile ○ **USA** (MN) 270-271 B 3
Fertő ⊖ **H** 92-93 O 5
Fès = Fāz ☆ ··· **MA** (Fes) 188-189 J 3
Feshi ○ **ZRE** 216-217 E 3
Fessenden ○ **USA** (ND) 258-259 H 4
Fessi, Oued ∼ **TN** 190-191 H 4
Festus ○ **USA** (MO) 274-275 H 6
Fet Dome, Tanjung ▲ **RI** 166-167 E 2
Fété Bowé ○ **SN** 202-203 D 2
Feteşti ○ **RO** 102-103 F 5
Fethiye ☆ • **TR** 128-129 C 4
Fetisovo ○ **KZ** 126-127 K 6
Fetlar ⌒ **GB** 90-91 G 1
Feudal ○ **CDN** (SAS) 232-233 L 4
Feuilles, Lac aux ⊖ **CDN** 36-37 P 5
Feuilles, Rivière aux ∼ **CDN** 36-37 O 5
Feurs ○ **F** 90-91 K 9
Fevral'sk ○ **RUS** 122-123 D 2
Fezna ⌒ **MA** 188-189 J 5
Fezzan = Fazzān ∸ **LAR** 192-193 D 5
F.G. Villarreal ○ **MEX** 50-51 L 5
Fiadanana ○ **RM** 222-223 E 7
Fiambalá ○ **RA** 76-77 D 4
Fiambala, Río ∼ **RA** 76-77 D 4
Fian ○ **GH** 202-203 J 4
Fianarantsoa □ **RM** 222-223 D 8
Fianarantsoa ☆ • **RM** (Fna) 222-223 E 8
Fianga ○ **TCH** 206-207 B 4
Fiatt ○ **USA** (IL) 274-275 H 4
Fichē ○ **ETH** 208-209 D 4
Fichot Islands ○ **CDN** (NFL) 242-243 N 1
Fichtelgebirge ▲ **D** 92-93 L 3
Ficksburg ○ **ZA** 220-221 H 4
Fidenza ○ • **I** 100-101 C 2
Field ○ **CDN** (BC) 230-231 N 2
Field ○ **CDN** (ONT) 238-239 E 2
Field ○ **USA** (NM) 256-257 M 4
Fielding ○ **CDN** (SAS) 232-233 L 3
Fielding ○ **USA** (UT) 254-255 C 2
Fields ○ **USA** (OR) 244-245 G 8
Fields Peak ▲ **USA** (OR) 244-245 F 6
Fier ☆ ·· **AL** 100-101 G 4
Fierenana ○ **RM** 222-223 D 7
Fiery Creek ∼ **AUS** 180-181 G 4
Fierzë, Liqeni i ∼ **AL** 100-101 H 3
Fifa ○ **RG** 202-203 F 4
Fife ○ **USA** (TX) 266-267 H 2
Fife ○ **USA** (WA) 244-245 C 3
Fife Lake ○ **CDN** (SAS) 232-233 N 6
Fife Lake ○ **USA** (MI) 272-273 D 3
Fifinda ○ **CAM** 210-211 C 2
Figeac ○ **F** 90-91 J 9
Figtree ○ **ZW** 218-219 E 5
Figueira da Foz ○ **P** 98-99 C 4
Figueira de Castelo Rodrigo ○ **P** 98-99 D 4
Figueira Torta ○ **BR** 74-75 D 9
Figueres ○ **E** 98-99 J 3
Figueroa, Bañado de ⊖ **RA** 76-77 F 4
Figuig ○ **MA** 188-189 L 4
Figuil ○ **CAM** 204-205 K 4
Fiherenana ∼ **RM** 222-223 D 9
Fiji ■ **FJI** 184 III b 3
Fiji = Fiji Islands ⌒ **FJI** 184 III a 2
Fik' ○ **ETH** 208-209 F 4
Fika ○ **WAN** 204-205 J 3
Filabres, Sierra de los ▲ **E** 98-99 F 6
Filabusi ○ **ZW** 218-219 E 5
Filadelfia ○ **BOL** 70-71 C 2
Filadélfia ○ **BR** (BAH) 68-69 H 7
Filadélfia ○ **BR** (TOC) 68-69 E 5
Filadelfia ○ **CR** 52-53 B 6
Filadelfia ○ **PE** 70-71 C 3
Filamane ○ **RMM** 202-203 G 4
Filchner-Schelfeis ⊂ **ARK** 16 E 30
Filer ○ **USA** (ID) 252-253 D 4
Filiaşi ○ **RO** 102-103 C 5
Filiatrá ○ **GR** 100-101 H 6
Filicudi, Ísola ⌒ **I** 100-101 E 5
Filim ○ **OM** 132-133 L 3
Filingué ○ **RN** 204-205 E 1
Filippova ∼ **RUS** 112-113 L 2
Filipstad ☆ **S** 86-87 G 7
Filiya ○ **WAN** 204-205 J 4
Fillmore ○ **CDN** (SAS) 232-233 P 6
Fillmore ○ **USA** (CA) 248-249 F 5
Fillmore ○ **USA** (IL) 274-275 J 5
Fillmore ○ **USA** (MI) 272-273 C 5
Fillmore ○ **USA** (ND) 258-259 H 3
Fillmore ○ **USA** (UT) 254-255 C 5
Filomena ○ **RP** 160-161 D 4
Filtu ○ **ETH** 208-209 E 6
Filuo ○ **SOL** 184 I d 2
Fimi ∼ **ZRE** 210-211 F 5
Fin ○ **IR** 134-135 F 5
Fina, Réserve de ⊥ **RMM** 202-203 F 3
Finca 7 ○ **CR** 52-53 C 7
Finca de Chañaral ○ **RCH** 76-77 C 4
Finch'a'ā Dam < **ETH** 208-209 C 4
Finch'aya ○ **ETH** 208-209 D 6
Finchburg ○ **USA** (AL) 284-285 C 5
Fındık ○ **TR** 128-129 J 4
Findlater ○ **CDN** (SAS) 232-233 N 5
Findlay ○ **USA** (OH) 280-281 C 2
Findlay Group ⌒ **CDN** 24-25 S 2
Fine ○ **USA** (NY) 278-279 F 4
Fingal ○ **AUS** 180-181 J 6
Fingal ○ **USA** (ND) 258-259 K 5
Finger Hill Island ⌒ **CDN** 36-37 S 5
Finger Lake ⊖ **CDN** 34-35 K 4
Finger Lakes ⊖ **USA** (NY) 278-279 E 6
Fingoe ○ **MOC** 218-219 F 2
Finike ☆ • **TR** 128-129 D 4
Finisterra, Cabo ▲ **E** 98-99 C 3
Finisterre Range ▲ **PNG** 183 D 3
Fink Creek ○ **USA** 20-21 J 4
Finke ○ **AUS** 178-179 C 3
Finke Bay ≈ 172-173 K 2
Finke Gorge National Park ⊥ **AUS** 176-177 M 2
Finke River ∼ **AUS** 176-177 M 2
Finke River ∼ **AUS** 178-179 C 4
Finkolo ○ **RMM** 202-203 G 4
Finland ○ **USA** (MN) 270-271 G 3
Finland, Gulf of ≈ 86-87 M 7
Finland = Suomi ■ **FIN** 88-89 G 5
Finlay Forks ○ **CDN** 32-33 J 4
Finlay Mountains ▲ **USA** 266-267 B 2
Finlay Ranges ▲ **CDN** 32-33 H 3
Finlay River ∼ **CDN** 32-33 H 3
Finlayson ○ **USA** (MN) 270-271 F 4
Finlayson Channel < **CDN** (BC) 228-229 F 4
Finley ○ **AUS** 180-181 H 3
Finley ○ **USA** (ND) 258-259 K 4
Finley ○ **USA** (OK) 264-265 J 4
Finmark ○ **CDN** (ONT) 234-235 O 6
Finnegan ○ **CDN** (ALB) 232-233 F 4
Finnie Bay ≈ 36-37 L 2
Finnigan, Mount ▲ **AUS** 174-175 H 4
Finnis, Cape ▲ **AUS** 180-181 C 2
Finnmarksvidda ∸ **N** 86-87 L 2
Finn Mount ▲ **USA** 20-21 M 6
Finnsnes ○ **N** 86-87 H 2
Finote Selam ○ **ETH** 208-209 C 3
Finschhafen ○ **PNG** 183 D 4
Finspång ☆ **S** 86-87 G 7
Finsteraarhorn ▲ **CH** 92-93 K 5
Finsterwalde ○ **D** 92-93 M 3
Fintrou ○ **RMM** 196-197 K 6
Finucane Range ▲ **AUS** 178-179 F 2
Finyolé ○ **CAM** 204-205 K 4
Fiordland National Park ··· **NZ** 182 A 6
Fiordland Provincial Recreation Area ⊥ **CDN** (BC) 228-229 F 4
Firebag River ∼ **CDN** 32-33 P 3
Firebaugh ○ **USA** (CA) 248-249 D 3
Firedrake Lake ⊖ **CDN** 30-31 R 5
Fire Island ⌒ **USA** 20-21 P 6
Fire Island National Seashore ⊥ **USA** (NY) 280-281 O 3
Firenze ☆ ··· **I** 100-101 C 3
Firestone Plantation • **LB** 202-203 E 6
Firgoun ○ **RN** 202-203 L 2
Firjuza ○ **TM** 136-137 F 6
Firk, Ša'īb ∼ **IRQ** 130-131 J 2
Firmat ○ **RA** 78-79 J 2
Firmeza ○ **PE** 70-71 C 2
Firminy ○ **F** 90-91 K 9
Fir Mountain ○ **CDN** (SAS) 232-233 M 6
Firou ○ **DY** 202-203 L 4
Firozābād ○ **IND** 138-139 G 6
Firozpur ○ **IND** 138-139 E 4
Firsovo ○ **RUS** 122-123 K 5
First Broad River ∼ **USA** 282-283 F 5
Firth of Clyde ≈ 90-91 E 4
Firth of Forth ≈ 90-91 F 3
Firth of Tay ≈ 90-91 F 3
Firth River ∼ **CDN** 20-21 V 2
Fīrūzābād ○ • **IR** 134-135 E 4
Fīrūzābād-e Bālā ○ **IR** 134-135 C 1
Fīrūzkūh ○ **IR** 136-137 C 7
Firvale ○ **CDN** (BC) 228-229 H 4
Fischell ○ **CDN** (NFL) 242-243 K 4
Fischer ○ **USA** (TX) 266-267 J 4
Fischer, Kap ▲ **GRØ** 28-29 T 6
Fisenge ○ **Z** 218-219 E 1
Fish Camp ○ **USA** (CA) 248-249 E 2
Fish Cove Point ▲ **CDN** 36-37 V 7
Fish Creek ∼ **USA** 20-21 P 1
Fisheating Creek ∼ **USA** 286-287 H 4
Fisher ○ **AUS** 176-177 L 5
Fisher ○ **USA** (AR) 276-277 E 5
Fisher ○ **USA** (IL) 274-275 K 4
Fisher, Lake O.C. < **USA** (TX) 266-267 G 2
Fisher Branch ○ **CDN** (MAN) 234-235 F 3
Fisher Øer ⌒ **GRØ** 26-27 U 5
Fisher River ○ **CDN** (MAN) 234-235 F 3
Fisher River ∼ **USA** 250-251 D 3
Fisher River Indian Reserve X **CDN** (MAN) 234-235 F 3
Fishers ○ **USA** (IN) 274-275 M 5
Fishers Island ⌒ **USA** (NY) 280-281 P 2
Fishguard ○ **GB** 90-91 E 6
Fishing Bridge ○ **USA** (WY) 252-253 H 2
Fishing Creek ○ **USA** (MD) 280-281 K 5
Fishing Lake ⊖ **CDN** (MAN) 234-235 H 2
Fishing Lakes ⊖ **CDN** 20-21 Y 3
Fishing River ∼ **USA** 282-283 K 4
Fish Lake ⊖ **CDN** 30-31 H 4
Fish Lake ⊖ **USA** (UT) 254-255 D 5
Fish River ○ **AUS** 174-175 D 5
Fish River ∼ **USA** 20-21 J 4
Fish River ∼ **USA** 284-285 C 6
Fishtrap Lake ⊖ **USA** (KY) 276-277 N 3
Fisihā Genet ○ **ETH** 208-209 D 5
Fiskå ☆ **N** 86-87 B 5
Fiske ○ **CDN** (SAS) 232-233 K 4
Fiskenæs Banke ≃ 28-29 O 5
Fiskenæsset = Qeqertarsuatsiaat ○ **GRØ** 28-29 P 5
Fissoa ○ **PNG** 183 F 2
Fišt, gora ▲ **RUS** 126-127 C 6
Fitampito ○ **RM** 222-223 E 8
Fitchburg ○ **USA** (MA) 278-279 K 6
Fitchville ○ **USA** (OH) 280-281 D 2
Fitler ○ **USA** (MS) 268-269 J 4
Fitri, Lac ⊖ **TCH** 198-199 H 6
Fitzcarrald ○ **PE** 64-65 F 7
Fitzgerald ○ **USA** (GA) 284-285 G 5
Fitzgerald River National Park ⊥ **AUS** 176-177 E 6
Fitzmaurice River ∼ **AUS** 172-173 K 3
Fitzroy ○ **AUS** 172-173 K 3
Fitzroy ○ **GB** 78-79 L 6
Fitz Roy ○ **RA** 80 G 3
Fitz Roy, Cape ▲ **CDN** 24-25 g 3
Fitzroy Crossing ○ **AUS** 172-173 G 5
Fitzroy Island ⌒ **AUS** 174-175 J 5
Fitzroy River ∼ **AUS** 172-173 F 4
Fitzroy River ∼ **AUS** 172-173 H 4
Fitzroy River ∼ **AUS** 178-179 K 2
Fitzwilliam Island ⌒ **CDN** (ONT) 238-239 D 3
Fitzwilliam Strait ≈ 24-25 N 2
Fiume = Rijeka ○ **HR** 100-101 E 2
Five Cays Settlements ○ **GB** 54-55 J 4
Five Mile Hill ▲ **AUS** 172-173 E 6
Five Points ○ **USA** (CA) 248-249 D 3
Five Points ○ **USA** (GA) 284-285 F 4
Five Stars ○ **GUY** 62-63 D 2
Fizi ○ **ZRE** 212-213 B 6
Fizuli = Füzuli ○ **AZ** 128-129 M 3
Fjällnes ○ **S** 86-87 F 5
Fjerritslev ○ **DK** 86-87 D 8
Fkih-Ben-Salah ○ **MA** 188-189 H 4
Flade Isblink ∸ **GRØ** 26-27 r 3
Flad Ø ⌒ **GRØ** 28-29 Y 3
Flagler ○ **USA** (CO) 254-255 M 4
Flagler Beach ○ **USA** (FL) 286-287 H 2
Flagstaff ○ • **USA** (AZ) 256-257 D 3
Flagstaff ○ **ZA** 220-221 J 5
Flagstaff Lake ⊖ **USA** (ME) 278-279 L 3
Flaherty Island ⌒ **CDN** 36-37 J 7
Flåm ○ **N** 86-87 C 6
Flamborough Head ▲ **GB** 90-91 G 4
Flamenco, Isla ⌒ **RA** 78-79 H 6
Flamencos, Parque Nacional los ⊥ ·· **CO** 60-61 E 2
Fläming ∸ **D** 92-93 M 2
Flaming Gorge National Rercreation Area ⊥ **USA** (WY) 252-253 J 5
Flaming Gorge Reservoir ∼ **USA** 252-253 J 5
Flamingo ○ **USA** (FL) 286-287 J 6
Flampleu ○ **CI** 202-203 F 6
Flanagan River ∼ **CDN** 34-35 K 4
Flanagan River ∼ **CDN** 234-235 K 2
Flandreau ○ **USA** (SD) 260-261 K 2
Flannagan Reservoir ⊖ **USA** (VA) 280-281 D 6
Flasher ○ **USA** (ND) 258-259 F 5
Flåsjön ⊖ **S** 86-87 G 4
Flat ○ **USA** 20-21 L 5
Flat ○ **USA** (TX) 266-267 K 2
Flat Bay ○ **CDN** (NFL) 242-243 K 4
Flatey ⌒ **IS** 86-87 b 2
Flathead ○ **CDN** (BC) 230-231 P 4
Flathead Indian Reservation X **USA** (MT) 250-251 E 4
Flathead Lake ⊖ **USA** (MT) 250-251 E 4
Flathead River ∼ **CDN** 230-231 P 4
Flathead River ∼ **USA** 250-251 F 4
Flathead River, South Fork ∼ **USA** 250-251 F 4
Flat Island ⌒ 160-161 A 7
Flatonia ○ **USA** (TX) 266-267 K 4
Flatow = Złotów ○ • **PL** 92-93 O 2
Flat Point ▲ **NZ** 182 E 4
Flat River ∼ **CDN** 30-31 F 5
Flat River ○ **USA** (MO) 276-277 E 3
Flatrock ○ **USA** (IN) 274-275 N 5
Flat Rock ○ **USA** (MI) 272-273 F 5
Flats ○ **USA** (NE) 262-263 E 3
Flattery, Cape ▲ **AUS** 174-175 H 4
Flattery, Cape ▲ **USA** (WA) 244-245 A 2
Flat Top ○ **USA** (WV) 280-281 E 6
Flatwillow ○ **USA** (MT) 250-251 L 5
Flatwoods ○ **USA** (KY) 276-277 N 2
Flaxcombe ○ **CDN** (SAS) 232-233 J 4
Flaxman Island ⌒ **USA** 20-21 S 1
Flaxville ○ **USA** (MT) 250-251 O 3
Flé ∼ **RG** 202-203 F 4
Flecha Point ▲ **RP** 160-161 E 9
Flèche, la ○ **F** 90-91 G 8
Fleet ○ **CDN** (ALB) 232-233 G 3
Fleetwood ○ **GB** 90-91 F 5
Flekkefjord ☆ **N** 86-87 C 7
Fleming ○ **CDN** (SAS) 232-233 R 5
Flemingsburg ○ **USA** (KY) 276-277 M 2
Flemington ○ **USA** (NJ) 280-281 M 3
Flemish Cap ≃ 6-7 E 4
Flenelon Falls ○ **CDN** (ONT) 238-239 G 4
Flensburg ○ • **D** 92-93 K 1
Flers ○ **F** 90-91 G 7
Flesko, Tanjung ▲ **RI** 164-165 J 3
Fletcher Island ⌒ **CDN** 36-37 Q 3
Fletcher Lake ⊖ **CDN** 30-31 P 4
Fletscher ○ **USA** (NC) 282-283 E 5
Flett Lake ⊖ **CDN** 30-31 R 5
Fleurance ○ **F** 90-91 H 10
Fleur de Lys ○ **CDN** (NFL) 242-243 M 2
Fleur de May, Lac ⊖ **CDN** 38-39 M 3
Fleurieu Peninsula ⌒ **AUS** 180-181 E 3
Flexal ○ **BR** 62-63 G 6
Flinders Bay ≈ 176-177 C 7
Flinders Chase National Park ⊥ **AUS** 180-181 D 3
Flinders Group ⌒ **AUS** 174-175 H 4
Flinders Highway II **AUS** (QLD) 174-175 H 7
Flinders Highway II **AUS** (SA) 180-181 C 2
Flinders Island ⌒ **AUS** (SA) 180-181 C 2
Flinders Island ⌒ **AUS** (TAS) 180-181 J 5
Flinders Peak ▲ **AUS** 178-179 M 4
Flinders Ranges ▲ **AUS** 180-181 E 2
Flinders Ranges National Park ⊥ **AUS** 178-179 E 6
Flinders Reef ⌒ **AUS** 174-175 K 5
Flinders River ∼ **AUS** 174-175 F 5
Flint ○ **CDN** (ONT) 234-235 O 6
Flint ○ **USA** (MI) 272-273 F 4
Flintdale ○ **CDN** (ONT) 236-237 C 2
Flint Hills ▲ **USA** 262-263 K 6
Flint Hills National Wildlife Refuge • **USA** (KS) 262-263 L 6
Flint Lake ⊖ **CDN** 28-29 C 2
Flint Lake ⊖ **CDN** (ONT) 236-237 C 3
Flintoft ○ **CDN** (SAS) 232-233 M 6
Flint Rapids ∼ **CDN** 34-35 P 4
Flint River ∼ **USA** 284-285 F 5
Flint River ∼ **USA** 284-285 D 2
Flint River ∼ **USA** 284-285 F 3
Flint River ∼ **USA** 284-285 F 4
Flisa ☆ **N** 86-87 F 6
Flix ○ **E** 98-99 H 4
Flomaton ○ **USA** (AL) 284-285 C 5
Flomot ○ **USA** (TX) 264-265 D 4
Floods ○ **CDN** (BC) 230-231 H 4
Floodwood ○ **USA** (MN) 270-271 F 4
Flora ○ **USA** (IL) 274-275 K 6
Flora ○ **USA** (MS) 268-269 K 4
Flora ○ **USA** (OR) 244-245 H 5
Floral ○ **CDN** (SAS) 232-233 M 3
Florala ○ **USA** (AL) 284-285 D 5
Floral City ○ **USA** (FL) 286-287 G 3
Flora Valley ○ **AUS** 172-173 J 5
Floraville ○ **AUS** 174-175 E 6
Flor da Serra ○ **BR** 74-75 D 6
Flor de Agosto ○ **PE** 64-65 F 3
Flor del Desierto ○ **RCH** 76-77 C 2
Flor de Punga ○ **PE** 64-65 E 4
Florence ○ **USA** (AL) 284-285 C 2
Florence ○ **USA** (AZ) 256-257 D 5
Florence ○ **USA** (CO) 254-255 K 5
Florence ○ **USA** (KS) 262-263 K 6
Florence ○ **USA** (MN) 270-271 B 6
Florence ○ **USA** (MS) 268-269 K 4
Florence ○ **USA** (OR) 244-245 A 6
Florence ○ **USA** (PA) 280-281 F 3
Florence ○ **USA** (SC) 284-285 L 2
Florence ○ **USA** (SD) 260-261 J 1
Florence ○ **USA** (TX) 266-267 K 3
Florence ○ **USA** (WI) 270-271 K 5
Florence = Firenze ☆ ··· **I** 100-101 C 3
Florence, Lake ⊖ **AUS** 178-179 E 5
Florence Junction ○ **USA** (AZ) 256-257 D 5
Florencia ☆ **CO** 64-65 E 1
Florencia ○ **RA** 76-77 H 5
Florencio Sanches ○ **ROU** 78-79 L 2
Florens, mys ▲ **RUS** 112-113 U 1
Florentino Ameghino, Embalse < **RA** 78-79 F 7
Flores ○ **BR** 68-69 K 5
Flores ☆ • **GCA** 52-53 K 3
Flores ⌒ **RI** 168 E 7
Flores, Arroyo de las ∼ **RA** 78-79 J 4
Flôres, Igarapé ∼ **BR** 70-71 F 3
Flores, Ilha das ⌒ **P** 6-7 F 5
Flores, Las ○ **CO** 60-61 E 2
Flores, Las ○ **RA** (BUA) 78-79 K 4
Flores, Las ○ **RA** (SAJ) 76-77 C 6
Flores de Goiás ○ **BR** 72-73 G 3
Flores do Piauí ○ **BR** 68-69 G 5
Flores Gracía ○ **MEX** 50-51 H 6
Flores Island ⌒ **CDN** (BC) 230-231 C 4
Flores Sea = Flores, Laut ≈ 168 D 6
Florešt' = Floreşti ☆ **MD** 102-103 F 4
Floresta ○ **BR** (PAR) 72-73 D 7
Floresta ○ **BR** (PER) 68-69 J 6
Floreşti ☆ **MD** 102-103 F 4
Florešty = Floreşti ☆ **MD** 102-103 F 4
Floresville ○ **USA** (TX) 266-267 J 4
Florian ○ **CO** 60-61 E 5
Floriano ○ **BR** 68-69 G 5
Floriano Peixoto ○ **BR** 66-67 D 7
Florianópolis ☆ • **BR** 74-75 F 6
Florida ○ **C** 54-55 F 4
Florida ○ **CO** 60-61 C 6
Florida ○ **RCH** 78-79 C 4
Florida ☆ **ROU** 78-79 L 3
Florida ○ **USA** (NM) 256-257 H 6
Florida □ **USA** 286-287 J 2
Florida, Cape ▲ **USA** (FL) 286-287 J 6
Florida, La ○ **CO** 64-65 D 1
Florida, La ∴ • **GCA** 52-53 J 3
Florida, La ○ **YV** 60-61 G 3
Florida Bay ≈ 286-287 J 6
Floridablanca ○ **CO** 60-61 E 4
Florida City ○ **USA** (FL) 286-287 J 6
Florida Islands ⌒ **SOL** 184 I e 3
Florida Keys ⌒ **USA** (FL) 286-287 H 7
Florida Peak ▲ **USA** (NM) 256-257 H 6
Florida's Turnpike II **USA** (FL) 286-287 H 3
Florido, Río ∼ **MEX** 50-51 G 4
Florien ○ **USA** (LA) 268-269 G 5
Florin ○ **USA** (CA) 246-247 D 5
Flórina ○ **GR** 100-101 H 4
Florínia ○ **BR** 72-73 E 7
Florissant ○ **USA** (MO) 274-275 H 6
Florissant Fossil Beds National Monument ∴ **USA** (CO) 254-255 K 5
Florø ☆ **N** 86-87 B 6
Flour Island ⌒ **CDN** (ONT) 234-235 P 6
Floyd ○ **USA** (NM) 256-257 M 4
Floyd ○ **USA** (VA) 280-281 F 7
Floyd, Mount ▲ **USA** (AZ) 256-257 C 3
Floydada ○ **USA** (TX) 264-265 C 5
Floyd River ∼ **USA** 274-275 B 2
Flu ○ **LB** 202-203 G 7
Fluk ○ **RI** 164-165 K 4
Flumendosa ∼ **I** 100-101 B 5
Fluvanna ○ **USA** (TX) 264-265 C 6
Flying Fox Creek ∼ **AUS** 174-175 B 4
Flying Post Indian Reserve X **CDN** (ONT) 236-237 F 4
Flynn ○ **USA** (TX) 266-267 L 2
Fly River ∼ **PNG** 183 B 5
Foa ⌒ **TON** 184 IV a 1
Foam Lake ○ **CDN** (SAS) 232-233 P 4
Fô-Bouré ○ **DY** 204-205 E 3
Foča ○ • **BIH** 100-101 G 3
Foça ☆ **TR** 128-129 B 3
Foca, Isla ⌒ **PE** 64-65 B 4
Foca, Punta ▲ **RA** 80 H 3
Fochi ∸ **TCH** 198-199 G 3
Focşani ☆ **RO** 102-103 E 5
Fodé ○ **RCA** 206-207 F 6
Fodekaria ○ **RG** 202-203 F 4
Fofore ○ **WAN** 204-205 K 4
Fogang ○ **VRC** 156-157 H 5
Fog Bay ≈ 172-173 K 2
Fogelevo ○ **KZ** 136-137 L 3
Foggaret el 'Arab ○ **DZ** 190-191 D 7
Foggaret ez Zoua ○ **DZ** 190-191 D 7
Fóggia ☆ **I** 100-101 E 4
Foggy Cape ▲ **USA** 22-23 S 4
Fogi ○ **RI** 166-167 D 3
Fogo ○ **CDN** (NFL) 242-243 O 3
Fogo, Ilha de ⌒ **CV** 202-203 B 6
Fogo Island ⌒ **CDN** (NFL) 242-243 O 3
Føhn Fjord ≈ 26-27 m 8
Föhr ⌒ **D** 92-93 K 1
Fóia ▲ **P** 98-99 C 6
Foisy ○ **CDN** (ALB) 232-233 G 2
Foix ○ **F** 90-91 H 10
Foja, Pegunungan ▲ **RI** 166-167 K 3
Fokina ∼ **RUS** 108-109 W 7
Fokino ○ **RUS** 94-95 O 5
Fokku ○ **WAN** 204-205 F 3
Folda ≈ 86-87 G 3
Foldereid ○ **N** 86-87 F 4
Foley ○ **RB** 218-219 D 5
Foley ○ **USA** (AL) 284-285 C 6
Foley ○ **USA** (MN) 270-271 E 5
Foleyet ○ **CDN** (ONT) 236-237 F 4
Foley Island ⌒ **CDN** 24-25 j 6
Folgares ○ **ANG** 216-217 C 7
Folgefonni ⊂ **N** 86-87 C 7
Foligno ○ **I** 100-101 D 3
Folkestone ○ • **GB** 90-91 H 6
Folkston ○ **USA** (GA) 284-285 H 6
Folkstone ○ **USA** (NC) 282-283 K 6
Folldal ☆ **N** 86-87 D 5
Follett ○ **USA** (TX) 264-265 D 2
Follette, La ○ **USA** (TN) 282-283 C 4
Föllinge ○ **S** 86-87 G 5
Follónica ○ **I** 100-101 C 3
Folly Beach ○ **USA** (SC) 284-285 L 4
Folly Island ⌒ **USA** (SC) 284-285 L 4
Folsom ○ **USA** (LA) 268-269 K 6
Folsom ○ **USA** (NM) 256-257 M 2
Fomboni ○ **COM** 222-223 C 4
Fome, Rio da ∼ **BR** 68-69 G 3
Fomena ○ **GH** 202-203 K 6
Fomento ○ **C** 54-55 F 3
Fomič ∼ **RUS** 110-111 F 4
Fona ○ **VAN** 184 II b 3
Fonda ○ **USA** (IA) 274-275 D 2
Fondale ○ **USA** (LA) 268-269 H 4
Fond-du-Lac ○ **CDN** 30-31 Q 6
Fond du Lac ⊖ **CDN** 30-31 Q 6
Fond du Lac ○ **USA** (WI) 270-271 K 7
Fond du Lac Indian Reservation X **USA** (MN) 270-271 F 4
Fond du Lac River ∼ **CDN** 30-31 R 6
Fonehill ○ **CDN** (SAS) 232-233 Q 4
Fonéko ○ **RN** 202-203 L 2
Fongolembi ○ **SN** 202-203 D 3
Fonni ○ **I** 100-101 B 4
Fonoifua ⌒ **TON** 184 IV a 2
Fonsagrada, A ○ **E** 98-99 D 3
Fonseca ○ **CO** 60-61 E 2
Fonseca, Golfo de ≈ 52-53 L 5
Fonsecas, Serra dos ▲ **BR** 72-73 H 4
Fontaine Lake ⊖ **CDN** 30-31 Q 6
Fontana, Lago ⊖ **RA** 80 E 2
Fontana Lake < **USA** (NC) 282-283 D 5
Fontanelle ○ **USA** (NE) 262-263 K 3
Fontanina ○ **ETH** 208-209 D 3
Fontas ○ **CDN** 30-31 J 6
Fontas River ∼ **CDN** 30-31 J 6
Fonte Boa ○ **BR** 66-67 D 4
Fontenay, Abbaye de ··· **F** 90-91 K 8
Fontenay-le-Comte ○ **F** 90-91 G 8
Fonteneau, Lac ⊖ **CDN** 38-39 O 3
Fontenelle ○ **CDN** (QUE) 240-241 L 2
Fontenelle ○ **USA** (WY) 252-253 H 5
Fontenelle Reservoir ⊖ **USA** (WY) 252-253 H 4
Fontibón ○ **CO** 60-61 D 5
Fontur ▲ **IS** 86-87 f 1
Fonuafo'ou ⌒ **TON** 184 IV a 2
Fonualei ⌒ **TON** 184 IV a 1
Fo'ondo ○ **SOL** 184 I e 3
Foping ○ **VRC** 154-155 E 5
Foping Z.B. ⊥ • **VRC** 154-155 E 5
Forage Christine eau potable ○ **BF** 202-203 K 2
Forari ○ **VAN** 184 II b 3
Forbes ○ **AUS** 180-181 K 2
Forbes ○ **USA** (ND) 258-259 J 6
Forbes, Kap ▲ **GRØ** 26-27 R 4
Forbus ○ **USA** (TN) 276-277 K 4
Forcados ○ **WAN** 204-205 F 6
Ford ○ **USA** (ID) 250-251 B 4
Ford ○ **USA** (KS) 262-263 G 7
Ford, Cape ▲ **AUS** 172-173 J 2
Ford, Cerro el ▲ **RCH** 80 E 6
Fordate, Pulau ⌒ **RI** 166-167 F 5
Ford Costantine ○ **AUS** 174-175 F 7
Førde ☆ **N** 86-87 B 6
Ford Falls ∼ **CDN** 30-31 R 4
Fording River ∼ **CDN** 230-231 P 4
Ford River ∼ **CDN** 36-37 H 2
Ford River ∼ **USA** 270-271 L 5
Fordsville ○ **USA** (KY) 276-277 J 3
Fordyce ○ **USA** (AR) 276-277 C 7
Forécariah ○ **RG** 202-203 D 5
Forel, Mont ▲ **GRØ** 28-29 W 3
Foreman ○ **USA** (AR) 276-277 A 7
Foremost ○ **CDN** (ALB) 232-233 G 6
Foresman ○ **USA** (IN) 274-275 L 4
Forest ○ **CDN** (ONT) 238-239 D 5
Forest ○ **USA** (MS) 268-269 L 4
Forest, Lac la ⊖ **CDN** 36-37 O 7
Forest Acres ○ **USA** (SC) 284-285 K 2
Forestburg ○ **CDN** (ALB) 232-233 F 3
Forestburg ○ **USA** (TX) 264-265 G 5
Forest City ○ **USA** (IA) 274-275 E 1
Forest City ○ **USA** (NC) 282-283 F 5
Forestdale ○ **CDN** (BC) 228-229 H 2

Fatitet — Forestdale 327

Forest Glen ○ **USA** (CA) 246-247 B 3
Forest Grove ○ **CDN** (BC) 230-231 H 2
Forestgrove ○ **USA** (MT) 250-251 K 4
Forest Grove ○ **USA** (OR) 244-245 B 5
Forest Home ○ **AUS** 174-175 G 6
Forestier, Cape ▲ **AUS** 180-181 K 7
Forest Lake ○ **USA** (MN) 270-271 F 5
Forest Park ○ **USA** (GA) 284-285 F 3
Forest River ○ **USA** (ND) 258-259 K 3
Forest Strait ≈ 158-159 E 5
Forestville ○ **CDN** (QUE) 240-241 F 2
Forestville ○ **USA** (MI) 272-273 G 4
Forestville ○ **USA** (WI) 270-271 L 6
Forfar ○ **GB** 90-91 F 3
Forgan ○ **CDN** (SAS) 232-233 L 4
Forgan ○ **USA** (OK) 264-265 D 2
Forges-les-Eaux ○ **F** 90-91 H 7
Forget ○ **CDN** (SAS) 232-233 Q 6
Forillon, Parc Nacional de ⊥ **CDN** (QUE) 240-241 L 2
Fork ○ **USA** (SC) 284-285 L 2
Forked Island ○ **USA** (LA) 268-269 H 7
Forkland ○ **USA** (AL) 284-285 C 4
Fork Reservoir, Lake ⬭ **USA** (TX) 264-265 J 6
Forks ○ **USA** (WA) 244-245 A 3
Forks of Cacapon ○ **USA** (WV) 280-281 H 4
Forks of Salmon ○ **USA** (CA) 246-247 B 2
Fork Union ○ **USA** (VA) 280-281 H 6
Forlandet nasjonalpark ⊥ **N** 84-85 G 3
Forlandsundet ≈ 84-85 G 3
Forli ○ **I** 100-101 D 2
Forman ○ **USA** (ND) 258-259 K 5
Formation Cave ∴ **USA** (ID) 252-253 G 4
Formby Bay ≈ 180-181 D 3
Formentera, Illa de ⌒ **E** 98-99 H 5
Formentor, Cap de ▲·· **E** 98-99 J 5
Formia ○ **I** 100-101 D 4
Formiga ○ **BR** (MAR) 68-69 F 3
Formiga ○ **BR** (MIN) 72-73 H 6
Formosa ○ **BR** 72-73 G 3
Formosa ◘ **RA** 76-77 G 3
Formosa ☆ **RA** (FOR) 76-77 H 4
Formosa, Cachoeira da ∼ **BR** 72-73 D 2
Formosa, Ilha ⌒ **GNB** 202-203 B 4
Formosa, La ○ **BR** 72-73 G 5
Formosa, Parque Nacional ⊥ **RA** 76-77 G 3
Formosa, Serra ▲ **BR** 70-71 K 3
Formosa do Rio Preto ○ **BR** 68-69 F 7
Formoso ○ **BR** (GOI) 72-73 F 2
Formoso ○ **BR** (GSU) 72-73 D 6
Formoso ○ **BR** (MIN) 72-73 G 3
Formoso, Cape ▲ **WAN** 204-205 G 6
Formoso, Rio ∼ **BR** 68-69 D 7
Formoso, Rio ∼ **BR** 72-73 H 2
Formoso, Rio ∼ **BR** 72-73 H 4
Formoso, Rio ∼ **BR** 72-73 D 5
Fornæs ▲ **DK** 86-87 E 8
Fornells ○ **E** 98-99 K 4
Fornos ○ **MOC** 218-219 H 6
Foro Burunga ○ **SUD** 198-199 L 6
Foroko ○ **PNG** 183 C 3
Forolshogna ▲ **N** 86-87 E 5
Foropaugh ○ **USA** (AZ) 256-257 B 5
Foros ○· **UA** 102-103 H 5
Forpost-Kargat ○ **RUS** 114-115 Q 7
Forres ○ **RA** 76-77 F 4
Forrest ○ **AUS** (VIC) 180-181 G 5
Forrest ○ **AUS** (WA) 176-177 K 5
Forrest ○ **USA** (IL) 274-275 K 4
Forrest, Mount ▲ **AUS** 176-177 E 4
Forrest City ○ **USA** (AR) 276-277 E 5
Forrest Lakes ⬭ **AUS** 176-177 K 4
Forreston ○ **USA** (IL) 274-275 J 2
Forrest River Aboriginal Land ✕ **AUS** 172-173 H 3
Forrest Station ○ **CDN** (MAN) 234-235 D 5
Forsayth ○ **AUS** 174-175 G 6
Forshaga ☆ **S** 86-87 F 7
Forsnes ○ **N** 86-87 D 5
Forssa ○ **FIN** 88-89 G 6
Forsyth ○ **USA** (GA) 284-285 G 3
Forsyth ○ **USA** (MO) 276-277 B 4
Forsyth ○ **USA** (MT) 250-251 N 5
Forsyth Island ⌒ **AUS** 174-175 E 5
Forsyth Range ▲ **AUS** 178-179 G 2
Fort (Dutch) ∴· **RI** 164-165 J 5
Fort Abbās ○ **PK** 138-139 D 5
Fort Abercrombie · **USA** (ND) 258-259 L 5
Fort Albany ○ **CDN** 34-35 Q 4
Fort Albercrombie State Historical Park · **USA** 22-23 U 4
Fortale, Caño la ∼ **CO** 60-61 F 5
Fort Alexander ○ **CDN** (MAN) 234-235 G 4
Fortaleza ○ **BOL** 70-71 D 3
Fortaleza ○ **BR** (ACR) 66-67 B 7
Fortaleza ○ **BR** (AMA) 66-67 C 6
Fortaleza ○ **BR** (AMA) 66-67 H 4
Fortaleza ○ **BR** (RON) 66-67 E 7
Fortaleza ☆· **BR** (CEA) 68-69 J 3
Fortaleza, La ○ **YV** 60-61 J 3
Fortaleza dos Nogueiras ○ **BR** 68-69 E 5
Fortaleza San Miguel · **ROU** 74-75 D 9
Fortaleza Santa Teresa · **ROU** 74-75 D 9
Fort Amanda State Memorial · **USA** (OH) 280-281 B 3
Fort Amherst National Historic Park · **CDN** (PEI) 240-241 M 4
Fort Anne National Historic Park · **CDN** (NS) 240-241 K 6
Fort Apache Indian Reservation ✕ **USA** (AZ) 256-257 E 4
Fort Atkinson ○ **USA** (WI) 274-275 K 2
Fort Augustus ○· **GB** 90-91 E 3
Fort Battleford National Historic Park · **CDN** (SAS) 232-233 K 3
Fort Beaufort ○ **ZA** 220-221 H 6
Fort Belknap Agency ○ **USA** (MT) 250-251 L 3
Fort Belknap Indian Reservation ✕ **USA** (MT) 250-251 L 3
Fort Belmont · **USA** (MN) 270-271 C 7
Fort Belvoir xx **USA** (VA) 280-281 J 5
Fort Benning ○ **USA** (GA) 284-285 F 4
Fort Benning xx **USA** (GA) 284-285 F 4
Fort Benton ○ **USA** (MT) 250-251 J 4
Fort Benton Ruins · **USA** (MT) 250-251 J 4
Fort Berthold Indian Reservation ✕ **USA** (ND) 258-259 E 4
Fort Bliss Military Reservation xx **USA** (NM) 256-257 J 6
Fort Bragg ○ **USA** (NC) 282-283 J 5
Fort Bragg Military Reservation xx **USA** (NC) 282-283 H 5
Fort Branch ○ **USA** (IN) 274-275 L 6
Fort Bridger ○ **USA** (WY) 252-253 H 5
Fort-Chimo = Kuujjuaq ○ **CDN** 36-37 P 5
Fort Chipewyan ○ **CDN** 30-31 O 6
Fort Churchill ○ **CDN** 30-31 X 6
Fort Clark ○ **USA** (ND) 258-259 F 4
Fort Cobb ○ **USA** (OK) 264-265 F 3
Fort Cobb Reservoir < **USA** (OK) 264-265 F 3
Fort Cobb State Park ⊥· **USA** (OK) 264-265 F 3
Fort Collins ○ **USA** (CO) 254-255 K 3
Fort Collinson ○ **CDN** 24-25 N 5
Fort Coulonge ○ **CDN** (QUE) 238-239 J 3
Fort Craig, Ruins of · **USA** (NM) 256-257 H 5
Fort-Dauphin = Tôlanaro ○· **RM** 222-223 E 10
Fort Davis ○ **USA** (AL) 284-285 E 4
Fort de Cock · **RI** 162-163 D 5
Fort-de-France ☆ **F** 56 E 4
Fort Deposit ○ **USA** (AL) 284-285 D 5
Fort Dodge ○ **USA** (IA) 274-275 D 2
Fort Drum · **USA** (NY) 278-279 F 4
Forteau ○ **CDN** (NFL) 242-243 M 1
Fort Edward National Historic Site · **CDN** (NS) 240-241 L 6
Fort Egbert National Historic Site · **USA** 20-21 U 4
Fort Erie ○ **CDN** (ONT) 238-239 G 6
Fortescue River ∼ **AUS** 172-173 C 6
Fortescue River Roadhouse ○ **AUS** 172-173 C 6
Fort Eustis xx **USA** (VA) 280-281 K 6
Fort Fisher · **USA** (NC) 282-283 K 7
Fort Frances ○ **CDN** (ONT) 234-235 K 6
Fort Franklin ○ **CDN** 30-31 H 3
Fort Fraser ○ **CDN** (BC) 228-229 K 2
Fort Fred Steele ○ **USA** (WY) 252-253 M 5
Fort Gadsden State Historical Site · **USA** (FL) 286-287 E 2
Fort Gaines ○ **USA** (GA) 284-285 E 5
Fort Garland ○ **USA** (CO) 254-255 K 6
Fort George ○ **CDN** 38-39 E 2
Fort George National Historic Park · **CDN** (ONT) 238-239 F 5
Fort George River = La Grande Rivière ∼ **CDN** 38-39 G 2
Fort Gibson ○ **USA** (OK) 264-265 J 3
Fort Gibson Lake ⬭ **USA** (OK) 264-265 J 2
Fort Glenn ○ **USA** 22-23 N 6
Fort Good Hope ○ **CDN** 30-31 E 2
Fort Gordon xx **USA** (GA) 284-285 H 3
Fort Griffin State Historic Park ⩦ **USA** 264-265 E 6
Fort Hall ○ **CDN** 30-31 T 6
Fort Hall ○ **USA** (ID) 252-253 F 3
Fort Hall Indian Reservation ✕ **USA** (ID) 252-253 F 3
Fort Hancock ○ **USA** (TX) 266-267 B 2
Forthassa Gharbia ○ **DZ** 188-189 L 4
Fort Hope ○ **CDN** (ONT) 234-235 P 3
Fort Hope Indian Reserve ✕ **CDN** (ONT) 234-235 Q 3
Fort Huachuca · **USA** (AZ) 256-257 E 7
Fort Hunter Liggett Military Reservation xx **USA** (CA) 248-249 C 3
Fortierville ○ **CDN** (QUE) 238-239 N 2
Fortín 1° de Mayo ○ **RA** 78-79 D 5
Fortín, El ○ **RA** 76-77 F 6
Fortín Avalos Sanchez ○ **PY** 76-77 G 2
Fortín Boquerón ○ **PY** 76-77 H 2
Fortín Cabo 1° Cano ○ **PY** 76-77 H 3
Fortín Cadete Pastor Pando ○ **PY** 76-77 H 3
Fortín Carlos A. Lopez ○ **PY** 76-77 H 1
Fortín Charrúa ○ **RA** 76-77 G 5
Fortín Cmate Nowak ○ **PY** 76-77 H 3
Fortín Colonel Bogado ○ **PY** 70-71 H 7
Fortín de las Flores ○ **MEX** 52-53 F 2
Fort Independence Indian Reservation ✕ **USA** (CA) 248-249 F 3
Fortín Gaspar de Francia ○ **PY** 76-77 H 2
Fortín General Diaz ○ **PY** 76-77 G 2
Fortín Guanacos · **RA** 78-79 D 4
Fortín Hernandarias ○ **PY** 76-77 G 1
Fortín Infante Rivarola ○ **PY** 76-77 F 1
Fortín Lagerenza ○ **PY** 70-71 G 7
Fortín Lavalle ○ **RA** 76-77 G 3
Fortín Leonida Escobar ○ **PY** 76-77 G 2
Fortín Madrejon ○ **PY** 70-71 H 7
Fortín Malargüe · **RA** 78-79 E 3
Fortín Nueva Asunción ○ **PY** 70-71 G 7
Fortín Olmos ○ **RA** 76-77 G 5
Fortín Pilcomayo ○ **RA** 76-77 G 2
Fortín Pozo Hondo ○ **PY** 76-77 F 2
Fortín Ravelo ○ **BOL** 70-71 G 6
Fortín Teniente Américo Picco ○ **PY** 70-71 H 6
Fortín Teniente Montanía ○ **PY** 76-77 H 2
Fortín Teniente Rojas Silva ○ **PY** 76-77 G 2
Fortín Toledo ○ **PY** 76-77 G 2
Fortín Torres ○ **PY** 76-77 H 1
Fortín Zalazar ○ **PY** 76-77 H 2
Fort Irwin ○ **CDN** (ONT) 238-239 G 3
Fort Jackson ∴ **USA** (SC) 284-285 K 2
Fort Jones ○ **USA** (CA) 246-247 C 2
Fort Kearney State Historic Park ∴· **USA** (NE) 262-263 G 4
Fort Kent ○ **USA** (ME) 278-279 N 1
Fort Kent Historic Site · **USA** (ME) 278-279 N 1
Fort Kissimmee ○ **USA** (FL) 286-287 H 4
Fort Klamath ○ **USA** (OR) 244-245 C 8
Fort Knox xx **USA** (KY) 276-277 K 3
Fort Langley National Historic Park · **CDN** (BC) 230-231 G 4
Fort Laramie ○ **USA** (WY) 252-253 O 4
Fort la Reine · **CDN** (MAN) 234-235 E 5
Fort Lauderdale ○ **USA** (FL) 286-287 J 5
Fort Lemhi Monument · **USA** (ID) 252-253 E 2
Fort Lewis · **USA** (WA) 244-245 C 4
Fort Liard ○ **CDN** 30-31 H 5
Fort Liberté ☆ **RH** 54-55 K 5
Fort MacKavett ○ **USA** (TX) 266-267 G 3
Fort MacKay ○ **CDN** 32-33 P 3
Fort Mackinac · **USA** (MI) 272-273 E 2
Fort Madison ○ **USA** (IA) 274-275 G 4
Fort Matanzas National Monument · **USA** (FL) 286-287 H 2
Fort Maurepas · **CDN** (MAN) 234-235 G 4
Fort McClellan xx **USA** (AL) 284-285 E 3
Fort McCoy Military Reservation xx **USA** (WI) 270-271 H 6
Fort McHenry · **USA** (MD) 280-281 K 4
Fort McKavett State Historic Site · **USA** (TX) 266-267 G 3
Fort McMurray ○· **CDN** 32-33 P 3
Fort McPherson ○ **CDN** 20-21 Y 3
Fort Meade ○ **USA** (FL) 286-287 H 4
Fort Mill ○ **USA** (SC) 284-285 K 1
Fort Mohave Indian Reservation ✕ **USA** (AZ) 256-257 A 4
Fort Morgan ○ **USA** (CO) 254-255 M 3
Fort Morgan · **USA** (AL) 284-285 B 6
Fort Mtobeni ○ **ZA** 220-221 K 4
Fort Munro ○· **PK** 138-139 B 5
Fort Myers ○ **USA** (FL) 286-287 H 5
Fort Nassau · **GUY** 62-63 F 3
Fort Nelson ○ **CDN** 30-31 H 6
Fort Nelson Indian Reserve ✕ **CDN** 30-31 H 6
Fort Nelson River ∼ **CDN** 30-31 H 6
Fort Norman ○ **CDN** 30-31 G 3
Fort Oglethorpe ○ **USA** (GA) 284-285 E 2
Fort Payne ○ **USA** (AL) 284-285 E 2
Fort Peck ○ **USA** (MT) 250-251 N 3
Fort Peck Indian Reservation ✕ **USA** (MT) 250-251 O 3
Fort Pickett xx **USA** (VA) 280-281 J 6
Fort Pierce ○ **USA** (FL) 286-287 J 4
Fort Pierre ○ **USA** (SD) 260-261 F 2
Fort Pierre National Grassland ⊥ **USA** (SD) 260-261 F 2
Fort Pierre Verendrye Monument · **USA** (SD) 260-261 F 2
Fort Pitt Historic Park · **CDN** (SAS) 232-233 J 2
Fort Portal ☆ **EAU** 212-213 C 3
Fort Prince of Wales National Historic Park · **CDN** 30-31 W 6
Fort Providence ○ **CDN** 30-31 L 5
Fort Qu'Appelle ○ **CDN** (SAS) 232-233 P 5
Fort Ransom ○ **USA** (ND) 258-259 K 5
Fort Recovery ○ **USA** (OH) 280-281 B 3
Fort Resolution ○ **CDN** 30-31 N 5
Fortress · **RI** 162-163 C 3
Fortress of Louisbourg National History Park · **CDN** (NS) 240-241 P 5
Fort Rice ○ **USA** (ND) 258-259 G 5
Fort Rice Historic Site · **USA** (ND) 258-259 G 5
Fort Ripley ○ **USA** (MN) 270-271 D 4
Fort Rixon ○ **ZW** 218-219 E 5
Fort Rock ○ **USA** (OR) 244-245 D 7
Fortrose ○ **NZ** 182 B 7
Fort Rotterdam ∴· **RI** 166-167 D 3
Fort Rotterdam, Museum ∴· **RI** 164-165 F 6
Fort Rucker xx **USA** (AL) 284-285 E 5
Fort Rupert ○ **CDN** 38-39 E 3
Fort Rupert ○ **CDN** (BC) 230-231 B 3
Fort Saint James ○ **CDN** (BC) 228-229 K 2
Fort Saint James · **CDN** (BC) 228-229 K 2
Fort Saint James National Historic Park ∴· **CDN** (BC) 228-229 K 2
Fort Saint John ○ **CDN** 32-33 K 3
Fort San ○ **CDN** (SAS) 232-233 P 5
Fort Sandeman = Zhob ○ **PK** 138-139 B 4
Fort Saskatchewan ○ **CDN** (ALB) 232-233 E 2
Fort Scott ○ **USA** (KS) 262-263 M 7
Fort-Ševčenko ○ **KZ** 126-127 J 5
Fort Severn ○ **CDN** 34-35 N 3
Fort Sheridan · **USA** (IL) 274-275 L 2
Fort Simpson ○ **CDN** 30-31 J 5
Fort Smith ○ **CDN** 30-31 O 5
Fort Smith ○ **USA** (AR) 276-277 A 5
Fort Smith ○ **USA** (MT) 250-251 M 6
Fort Steele Heritage Town · **CDN** (BC) 230-231 O 4
Fort Stewart xx **USA** (GA) 284-285 J 4
Fort Stockton ○ **USA** (TX) 266-267 E 3
Fort Supply ○ **USA** (OK) 264-265 E 2
Fort Supply Lake ⬭ **USA** (OK) 264-265 E 2
Fort Témiscamingue National Historic Park · **CDN** (QUE) 236-237 J 5
Fort Thomas ○ **USA** (AZ) 256-257 F 5
Fort Thompson ○ **USA** (SD) 260-261 G 2
Fort Totten ○ **USA** (ND) 258-259 J 4
Fort Towson ○ **USA** (OK) 264-265 J 4
Fort Trois Riviéres · **CDN** (QUE) 238-239 N 2
Fortuna ○ **BR** 68-69 F 4
Fortuna ○ **USA** (CA) 246-247 A 3
Fortuna ○ **USA** (ND) 258-259 D 3
Fortuna, La ○ **MEX** 50-51 E 6
Fortuna, Rio ∼ **BR** 70-71 G 2
Fortuna de Minas ○ **BR** 72-73 H 5
Fortuna de San Carlos ○ **CR** 52-53 B 6
Fortuna Ledge ○ **USA** 20-21 J 6
Fortune ○ **CDN** (NFL) 242-243 N 5
Fortune Bank ≃ 224 E 3
Fortune Bay ≈ 242-243 N 5
Fortune Harbour ○ **CDN** (NFL) 242-243 N 3
Fort Union Trading Post National Historic Site ∴ **USA** (MT) 250-251 P 3
Fort Valley ○ **USA** (GA) 284-285 G 4
Fort Vasquez State Museum · **USA** (CO) 254-255 L 3
Fort Vermilion ○ **CDN** 30-31 M 6
Fortville ○ **USA** (IN) 274-275 N 5
Fort Walsh National Historic Park · **CDN** (SAS) 232-233 J 6
Fort Walton Beach ○ **USA** (FL) 286-287 C 1
Fort Washakie ○ **USA** (WY) 252-253 K 4
Fort Wayne ○ **USA** (IN) 274-275 N 3
Fort Wellington ○ **GUY** 62-63 F 2
Fort William ○ **GB** 90-91 E 3
Fort William Historic Park · **CDN** (ONT) 234-235 O 6
Fort Wingate ○ **USA** (NM) 256-257 G 3
Fort Worth ○ **USA** (TX) 264-265 G 6
Fort Yates ○ **USA** (ND) 258-259 G 5
Fortymile River ∼ **USA** 20-21 U 4
Fort Yukon ○ **USA** 20-21 S 3
Fort Yuma Indian Reservation ✕ **USA** (CA) 248-249 K 7
Forūdgān ○ **IR** 134-135 D 2
Forūmad ○ **IR** 136-137 E 6
Forūr, Ğazire-ye ⌒ **IR** 134-135 F 5
Forvik ○ **N** 86-87 F 4
Fosa de Cariaco ≈ 60-61 J 2
Fosca ○ **CO** 60-61 E 5
Foshan ○· **VRC** 156-157 H 5
Fosheim Peninsula ◡ **CDN** 26-27 H 4
Fosnavåg ☆ **N** 86-87 B 5
Foso ○ **GH** 202-203 K 7
Foss ○ **USA** (OK) 264-265 E 3
Fossa, Corredeira ∼ **BR** 66-67 H 6
Fossil ○ **USA** (OR) 244-245 E 5
Fossil Butte National Monument ∴ **USA** (WY) 252-253 H 5
Fossil Downs ○ **AUS** 172-173 G 5
Fossil Forest ⊥· **Z** 218-219 E 3
Foss Lake < **USA** (OK) 264-265 E 3
Fossong Fontem ○ **CAM** 204-205 H 6
Fosston ○ **CDN** (SAS) 232-233 P 3
Fosston ○ **USA** (MN) 270-271 C 3
Foster ○ **AUS** 180-181 J 5
Foster Bay ≈ 24-25 f 6
Foster Bugt ≈ 26-27 o 7
Fostoria ○ **USA** (OH) 280-281 C 2
Fostoria ○ **USA** (TX) 268-269 E 6
Fotadrevo ○ **RM** 222-223 D 10
Fotiná ○ **GR** 100-101 J 4
Fotokol ○ **CAM** 198-199 G 6
Fotuha'a ⌒ **TON** 184 IV a 1
Fouénan ○ **CI** 202-203 G 5
Fougamou ○ **G** 210-211 C 4
Fougani, Hassi ○ **MA** 188-189 J 5
Fougères ○· **F** 90-91 G 7
Fouke ○ **USA** (AR) 276-277 B 7
Foula ⌒ **GB** 90-91 F 1
Foulabala ○ **RMM** 202-203 G 4
Foulamory ○ **RG** 202-203 D 3
Foul Bay ≈ 36-37 N 3
Foulenzem ○ **G** 210-211 B 4
Foulwind, Cape ▲ **NZ** 182 C 4
Fouman ○ **IR** 128-129 N 4
Foumbadou ○ **RG** 202-203 F 5
Foumban ○·· **CAM** 204-205 J 6
Foumbot ○ **CAM** 204-205 J 6
Foumbouni ○ **COM** 222-223 C 3
Foum-el-Hassan · **MA** 188-189 G 6
Foum-Zguid ○ **MA** 188-189 H 5
Foundiougne ○ **SN** 202-203 B 2
Founougo ○ **DY** 204-205 E 3
Fountain ○ **USA** (CO) 254-255 L 5
Fountain Creek ∼ **USA** 254-255 L 5
Fountain Hill ○ **USA** (AR) 276-277 D 7
Fountain Inn ○ **USA** (SC) 284-285 H 2
Fountains Abbey ··· **GB** 90-91 G 4
Fountain Valley ○ **CDN** (BC) 230-231 H 3
Fouquet ○ **RH** 54-55 J 5
Fourche La Fave River ∼ **USA** 276-277 B 6
Fourche Maline River ∼ **USA** 264-265 J 4
Fourche Mountain ▲ **USA** 276-277 B 6
Fourchu ○ **CDN** (NS) 240-241 P 5
Four Corners ○ **USA** (CA) 248-249 G 5
Four Corners ○ **USA** (WY) 252-253 O 2
Fourcroy, Cape ▲ **AUS** 172-173 K 1
Four Forks ○ **USA** (LA) 268-269 G 4
Fouriesburg ○ **ZA** 220-221 J 4
Four Mountains, Islands of the ⌒ **USA** 22-23 L 6
Fournaise, Piton de la ▲·· **F** 224 B 7
Four North Fracture Zone ≃ 6-7 F 8
Fourou ○ **RMM** 202-203 G 4
Fourteen Mile Point ▲ **USA** (MI) 270-271 J 3
Fourtown ○ **USA** (MN) 270-271 C 2
Fouta Djalon ▲ **RG** 202-203 D 4
Foveaux Strait ≈ 182 A 7
Fowler ○ **USA** (CO) 254-255 L 5
Fowler ○ **USA** (IN) 274-275 L 4
Fowler ○ **USA** (KS) 262-263 F 7
Fowler ○ **USA** (MI) 272-273 E 4
Fowler ○ **USA** (SC) 284-285 L 3
Fowlers Bay ≈ 180-181 B 2
Fowlers Bay ○ **AUS** (SA) 176-177 M 5
Fowlers Gap ○ **AUS** 178-179 F 6
Fowlerton ○ **USA** (TX) 266-267 J 5
Fox ○ **USA** 20-21 R 4
Fox Cove ○ **CDN** (NFL) 242-243 N 5
Foxe Basin ≈ 24-25 g 6
Foxe Channel ≈ 36-37 J 2
Foxe Peninsula ◡ **CDN** 36-37 L 2
Fox Glacier ○ **NZ** 182 C 5
Fox Islands ⌒ **USA** (AK) 22-23 M 6
Fox Islands ⌒ **USA** (MI) 272-273 D 2
Fox Lake ○ **CDN** 30-31 M 6
Fox Lake ○ **USA** (IL) 274-275 K 2
Fox Lake ○ **USA** (WI) 274-275 K 1
Fox Lake Indian Reserve ✕ **CDN** 30-31 M 6
Fox Point ▲ **CDN** 30-31 J 3
Fox Point ○ **USA** (WI) 274-275 L 1
Fox River ○ **CDN** (MAN) 234-235 C 3
Fox River ∼ **CDN** 34-35 J 3
Fox River ∼ **USA** 270-271 K 6
Fox River ∼ **USA** 274-275 K 3
Fox River ∼ **USA** 274-275 G 4
Foxton Beach ○ **NZ** 182 E 4
Fox Valley ○ **CDN** (SAS) 232-233 J 5
Foxvill ○ **CDN** (ONT) 236-237 G 2
Foxwarren ○ **CDN** (MAN) 234-235 B 4
Foxworth ○ **USA** (MS) 268-269 L 5
Foyle, Lough ≈ 90-91 D 4
Foyn, Cape ▲ **ARK** 16 G 30
Foynøya ⌒ **N** 84-85 P 2
Foz de Areala, Represa de < **BR** 74-75 E 5
Foz de Jaú ○ **BR** 62-63 D 6
Foz do Cunene ○ **ANG** 216-217 A 8
Foz do Iguaçu ○ **BR** 76-77 K 3
Foz do Jordão ○ **BR** 66-67 B 7
Foz do Mamoriá ○ **BR** 66-67 D 4
Foz Jurupari ○ **BR** 66-67 B 6
Frænkel Land ⩦ **GRØ** 26-27 m 7
Fraga ○ **E** 98-99 H 4
Fragoso, Cayo ⌒ **C** 54-55 F 3
Fraile Muerto ○ **ROU** 78-79 M 2
Frailes, Islas Los ⌒ **YV** 60-61 K 2
Frambo ○ **CI** 202-203 J 7
Framingham ○ **USA** (MA) 278-279 K 6
Framnesfjella ▲ **ARK** 16 G 7
Franca ○ **BR** 72-73 G 6
Francavilla Fontana ○ **I** 100-101 F 4
France ■ **F** 92-93 E 5
France, Glacier de ⊂ **GRØ** 28-29 X 3
France, Île de ⌒ 26-27 r 5
Frances, Lake ⬭ **USA** (MT) 250-251 G 3
Franceses ○ **GCA** 52-53 K 4
Frances Lake ⬭ **CDN** 30-31 E 5
Frances River ∼ **CDN** 30-31 E 5
Franceville ☆ **G** 210-211 D 4
Franche-Comté ◘ **F** 90-91 K 8
Francia, La ○ **RA** 76-77 F 6
Francis ○ **CDN** (SAS) 232-233 P 5
Francis Case, Lake ⬭ **USA** (SD) 260-261 G 3
Francisco Aires ○ **BR** 68-69 G 5
Francisco Beltrão ○ **BR** 74-75 D 6
Francisco de Vitoria ○ **RA** 78-79 H 3
Francisco Dumont ○ **BR** 72-73 H 4
Francisco Grande ○ **USA** (AZ) 256-257 D 6
Francisco I. Madero ○ **MEX** (COA) 50-51 H 5
Francisco I. Madero ○ **MEX** (DGO) 50-51 G 5
Francisco I. Madero, Presa < **MEX** 50-51 G 3
Francisco Perito Moreno, Parque Nacional ⊥ **RA** 80 D 3
Francisco Rueda ○ **MEX** 52-53 H 3
Francisco Sá ○ **BR** 72-73 J 4
Franciscusbaai ≈ 220-221 B 2
Francistown ☆ **RB** 218-219 D 5
Franco da Rocha ○ **BR** 72-73 G 7
Franco de Orellana ○ **PE** 64-65 F 3
François ○ **CDN** (NFL) 242-243 M 5
François, Le ○ **F** 56 E 4
Francois Lake ○ **CDN** (BC) 228-229 J 2
Francois Lake ⬭ **CDN** (BC) 228-229 J 3
Franconia Notch · **USA** (NH) 278-279 K 4
Francs Peak ▲ **USA** (WY) 252-253 J 3
Frankel City ○ **USA** (TX) 264-265 B 6
Frankfield ○ **AUS** 178-179 J 2
Frankfort ○ **USA** (IN) 274-275 M 4
Frankfort ○ **USA** (KS) 262-263 K 5
Frankfort ○ **USA** (MI) 272-273 C 3
Frankfort ○ **USA** (SD) 260-261 H 2
Frankfort ☆ **USA** (KY) 276-277 L 2
Frankfort ○ **ZA** 220-221 J 3
Frankfurt (Oder) ○· **D** 92-93 N 2
Frankfurt am Main ○ **D** 92-93 K 3
Frank Hann National Park ⊥ **AUS** 176-177 F 6
Fränkische Alb ▲ **D** 92-93 L 4
Fränkische Saale ∼ **D** 92-93 K 3
Franklin ○ **AUS** 178-179 F 2
Franklin ○ **CDN** (MAN) 234-235 D 4
Franklin ○ **USA** (GA) 284-285 E 3
Franklin ○ **USA** (ID) 252-253 G 4
Franklin ○ **USA** (IN) 274-275 M 5
Franklin ○ **USA** (KY) 276-277 J 4
Franklin ○ **USA** (LA) 268-269 J 7
Franklin ○ **USA** (NC) 282-283 D 5
Franklin ○ **USA** (NE) 262-263 H 4
Franklin ○ **USA** (NH) 278-279 K 5
Franklin ○ **USA** (NM) 256-257 F 6
Franklin ○ **USA** (OH) 280-281 B 4
Franklin ○ **USA** (PA) 280-281 G 2
Franklin ○ **USA** (TN) 276-277 J 5
Franklin ○ **USA** (TX) 266-267 L 2
Franklin ○ **USA** (VA) 280-281 K 7
Franklin ○ **USA** (WV) 280-281 G 5
Franklin ○ **ZA** 220-221 J 5
Franklin, Kap ▲ **GRØ** 26-27 o 7
Franklin, Point ▲ **USA** 20-21 L 1
Franklin Bay ≈ 24-25 J 6
Franklin D. Roosevelt Lake ⬭ **USA** (WA) 244-245 G 2
Franklin Glacier ⊂ **CDN** (BC) 230-231 D 2
Franklin Harbour ≈ 180-181 D 2
Franklin Island ⌒ **ARK** 16 F 17
Franklin Island ⌒ **CDN** (ONT) 238-239 E 3
Franklin Lake ⬭ **CDN** (NWT) 30-31 V 2
Franklin Lake ⬭ **CDN** (SAS) 30-31 S 6
Franklin Lake ⬭ **USA** (NV) 246-247 K 3
Franklin Lower Gordon Wild Rivers Nationalpark ⊥ **AUS** 180-181 H 7
Franklin Mountains ▲ **CDN** 30-31 F 3
Franklin Mountains ▲ **USA** 20-21 S 2
Franklin Ø ⌒ **GRØ** 26-27 R 3
Franklin Point ▲ **CDN** 24-25 W 6
Franklin Strait ≈ 24-25 X 5
Franklinton ○ **USA** (LA) 268-269 K 6
Franklinton ○ **USA** (NC) 282-283 J 4
Franklinville ○ **USA** (NY) 278-279 C 6
Frankston ○ **USA** (TX) 264-265 J 6
Frankton ○ **NZ** 182 B 6
Franktown ○ **USA** (CO) 254-255 L 4
Frannie ○ **USA** (WY) 252-253 K 2
Franquelin ○ **CDN** (QUE) 242-243 A 3
Fransfontein ○ **NAM** 216-217 C 10
Fransfonteinberge ▲ **NAM** 216-217 C 10
Franske Øer ⌒ **GRØ** 26-27 q 4
Fränsta ○ **S** 86-87 H 5
Franz ○ **CDN** (ONT) 236-237 D 4
Franz Josef Glacier ○ **NZ** 182 C 5
Franz Josef Land = Franca-Iosifa, Zemlja ⌒ **RUS** 84-85 Y 3
Frascati ○ **I** 100-101 D 4
Fraser, Mount ▲ **AUS** 176-177 E 2
Fraser Basin ◡ **CDN** 228-229 K 2
Fraserburg ○ **ZA** 220-221 E 5
Fraserburgh ○ **GB** 90-91 F 3
Fraserdale ○ **CDN** (ONT) 236-237 G 3
Fraser Island ⌒··· **AUS** 178-179 M 3
Fraser Island National Park ⊥ **AUS** 178-179 M 3
Fraser Lake ○ **CDN** (BC) 228-229 K 2
Fraser Lake ⬭ **CDN** (BC) 228-229 K 2
Fraser Lake ⬭ **CDN** (NFL) 36-37 S 7
Fraser National Park ⊥ **AUS** 180-181 H 4
Fraser Plateau ▲ **CDN** 228-229 J 4
Fraser Range ○ **AUS** 176-177 G 6
Fraser River ∼ **CDN** 36-37 S 6
Fraser River ∼ **CDN** 228-229 M 3
Fraser River ∼ **CDN** 228-229 Q 4
Fraser River ∼ **CDN** 230-231 H 4
Frater ○ **CDN** (ONT) 236-237 D 5
Fraternidad, Parque Nacional La ⊥ **ES** 52-53 K 4
Fraustro ○ **MEX** 50-51 J 5
Fray Bentos ☆ **ROU** 78-79 K 2
Fray Jorge ○ **RCH** 76-77 B 6
Fray Jorge, Parque Nacional ⊥ **RCH** 76-77 B 6
Fray Marcos ○ **ROU** 78-79 M 3
Frazee ○ **USA** (MN) 270-271 C 4
Frazer ○ **USA** (MT) 250-251 N 3
Frazier Park ○ **USA** (CA) 248-249 F 5
Freakly Point ▲ **CDN** 36-37 K 7
Frebag River ∼ **CDN** 32-33 Q 3
Fred ○ **USA** (TX) 268-269 F 6
Freden, ostrov ⌒ **RUS** 84-85 g 2
Frederica National Monument, Fort · **USA** (GA) 284-285 J 5
Fredericia ○· **DK** 86-87 D 9
Frederick ○ **USA** (MD) 280-281 J 4
Frederick ○ **USA** (OK) 264-265 E 4
Frederick ○ **USA** (SD) 260-261 H 1
Frederick, Mount ▲ **AUS** (NT) 172-173 J 5
Frederick, Mount ▲ **AUS** (WA) 172-173 D 7
Frederick E. Hyde Fjord ≈ 26-27 j 2
Fredericksburg ○ **USA** (IA) 274-275 F 2
Fredericksburg ○ **USA** (TX) 266-267 J 3
Fredericksburg ○ **USA** (VA) 280-281 J 5
Frederick Sound ≈ 32-33 C 3
Frederickton ○ **CDN** (NFL) 242-243 O 3
Fredericktown ○ **USA** (MD) 280-281 L 4
Fredericktown ○ **USA** (MO) 276-277 E 3
Fredericktown ○ **USA** (OH) 280-281 D 3
Frederico Westphalen ○ **BR** 74-75 D 6
Fredericton ☆ **CDN** (NB) 240-241 J 5
Frederik Henrik Island = Pulau Dolak ⌒ **RI** 166-167 K 5
Frederiksdal = Narsaq Kujalleg ○ **GRØ** 28-29 S 6
Frederikshåb = Paamiut ○ **GRØ** 28-29 Q 5
Frederikshåbs Banke ≃ 28-29 P 5
Frederikshavn ○ **DK** 86-87 E 8
Frederiksted ○·· **USA** (VI) 286-287 R 3
Fredonia ○ **CO** 60-61 D 5
Fredonia ○ **USA** (AZ) 256-257 C 2
Fredonia ○ **USA** (KS) 262-263 L 7
Fredonia ○ **USA** (NY) 278-279 B 6
Fredonyer Summit ▲ **USA** (CA) 246-247 E 3
Fredrika ○ **S** 86-87 J 4
Fredriksberg ○ **S** 86-87 G 6
Fredrikstad ☆ **N** 86-87 E 7
Freeborn ○ **USA** (MN) 270-271 E 7
Freeburg ○ **USA** (MO) 274-275 G 6
Freedom ○ **USA** (CA) 248-249 C 3
Freedom ○ **USA** (KY) 276-277 K 4
Freedom ○ **USA** (OK) 264-265 E 2
Freedom ○ **USA** (WY) 252-253 H 4
Freehold ○ **USA** (NJ) 280-281 M 3
Free Home ○ **USA** (GA) 284-285 F 2
Freeland ○ **USA** (WA) 244-245 C 2
Freelandville ○ **USA** (IN) 274-275 L 6
Freeling Heights ▲ **AUS** 178-179 E 6
Freels, Cape ▲ **CDN** (NFL) 242-243 P 3
Freeman ○ **USA** (SD) 260-261 J 3
Freeman ○ **USA** (WA) 244-245 H 3
Freemansundet ≈ 84-85 M 3
Freemont ○ **CDN** (SAS) 232-233 J 3
Freeport ○ **BS** 54-55 F 1
Freeport ○ **CDN** (NS) 240-241 J 6
Freeport ○ **USA** (FL) 286-287 C 1
Freeport ○ **USA** (IL) 274-275 J 2
Freeport ○ **USA** (PA) 280-281 G 3
Freeport ○ **USA** (TX) 266-267 M 5
Freer ○ **USA** (TX) 266-267 J 6
Freesoil ○ **USA** (MI) 272-273 C 3
Freetown ○ **USA** (IN) 274-275 M 6
Freetown ★· **WAL** 202-203 D 5
Freezeout Mountain ▲ **USA** (OR) 244-245 H 7
Frégate Island ⌒ **SY** 224 D 2
Fregenal de la Sierra ○· **E** 98-99 D 5
Fregon ○ **AUS** 176-177 M 3
Freiberg ○· **D** 92-93 M 3
Freiburg im Breisgau ○· **D** 92-93 J 5
Frei Inocêncio ○ **BR** 72-73 K 5
Frei Orlando ○ **BR** 72-73 H 5
Freire ○ **RCH** 78-79 C 5
Freirina ○ **RCH** 76-77 B 5
Freising ○ **D** 92-93 L 4
Freiwaldau = Jeseník ○ **CZ** 92-93 O 3
Fréjus ○ **F** 90-91 L 10
Fremantle ○ **AUS** 176-177 C 6
Fremont ○ **USA** (CA) 248-249 C 2
Fremont ○ **USA** (MI) 272-273 D 4
Fremont ○ **USA** (NC) 282-283 K 5
Fremont ○ **USA** (NE) 262-263 K 3
Fremont ○ **USA** (OH) 280-281 C 2
Fremont ○ **USA** (WI) 270-271 K 6
Fremont Lake ⬭ **USA** (WY) 252-253 J 3
Fremont Mountains ▲ **USA** 244-245 D 7
Fremont River ∼ **USA** 254-255 D 5
French Bay ⩦· **BS** 54-55 H 3
Frenchburg ○ **USA** (KY) 276-277 M 3
French Cove ○ **CDN** (NFL) 242-243 N 2
French Creek ∼ **USA** 280-281 F 2
Frenchglen ○ **USA** (OR) 244-245 G 8
French Guiana = Guyane française ◘ **F** 62-63 H 3
French Hills ▲ **AUS** 172-173 H 6
French Lick ○ **USA** (IN) 274-275 M 6
Frenchman Butte ○ **CDN** (SAS) 232-233 J 2
Frenchman Creek ∼ **CDN** 232-233 L 6
Frenchman Creek ∼ **USA** 262-263 D 4
Frenchman River ∼ **CDN** 232-233 K 6
Frenchman's Bay ≈· 54-55 G 6
Frenchman's Cove Provincial Park ⊥ **CDN** (NFL) 242-243 N 5
French Pass ○ **NZ** 182 D 4
French River ○ **CDN** (ONT) 238-239 E 2
French River ∼ **CDN** 238-239 E 2
Frenchtown ○ **USA** (MT) 250-251 E 4
Frenchville ○ **USA** (ME) 278-279 N 1
Frenda ○ **DZ** 190-191 C 3
Frere ○ **ZA** 220-221 J 4
Fresco ○ **CI** 202-203 H 7
Fresco, Rio ∼ **BR** 68-69 C 5
Freshfield Icefield ⊂ **CDN** (ALB) 232-233 B 4
Freshwater ○ **CDN** (NFL) 242-243 P 5
Freshwater Point ▲ **AUS** 176-177 C 4
Fresia ○ **RCH** 78-79 C 6
Fresnal Canyon ○ **USA** (AZ) 256-257 D 7
Fresnillo de González Echeverría ○ **MEX** 50-51 H 6
Fresno ○ **USA** (CA) 248-249 E 3
Fresno Reservoir ⬭ **USA** (MT) 250-251 J 3
Freuchen Bay ≈ 24-25 f 7
Freuchen Land ⩦ **GRØ** 26-27 c 2
Freudenthal = Bruntál ○ **CZ** 92-93 O 4
Frewena ○ **AUS** 174-175 C 6
Freycinet Estuary ≈ 176-177 B 3
Freycinet National Park ⊥ **AUS** 180-181 K 7
Freycinet Peninsula ◡ **AUS** 180-181 J 7
Fria ○ **RG** 202-203 D 4
Fria, Kaap ▲ **NAM** 216-217 A 9
Friant ○ **USA** (CA) 248-249 E 3
Friars Point ○ **USA** (MS) 268-269 K 2
Frías ○ **RA** 76-77 E 5
Friday Creek ∼ **CDN** 236-237 F 2
Friday Harbour ○ **USA** (WA) 244-245 B 2
Fridtjof Nansen Halvø ◡ **GRØ** 28-29 U 4
Friedberg (Hessen) ○ **D** 92-93 K 3
Friedrichshafen ○ **D** 92-93 K 5
Friend ○ **USA** (NE) 262-263 J 4
Friendship ○ **USA** (AR) 276-277 B 6
Friendship ○ **USA** (OH) 280-281 C 5
Friendship Hill National Historic Site · **USA** (PA) 280-281 G 4
Friendship Shoal ≃ 162-163 K 2
Friesach ○ **A** 92-93 N 5
Frigate, Lac ⬭ **CDN** 38-39 G 2
Frigate Bay Beach ⩦ **KAN** 56 D 3
Friggesund ○ **S** 86-87 H 6
Frindsburg Reef ⌒ **SOL** 184 I d 1
Frio, Cabo ▲ **BR** 72-73 K 7
Frio Draw ∼ **USA** 256-257 M 4
Friona ○ **USA** (TX) 264-265 B 4
Frio River ∼ **USA** 266-267 J 5
Frisco ○ **USA** (CO) 254-255 J 4
Frisco City ○ **USA** (AL) 284-285 C 5
Fritch ○ **USA** (TX) 264-265 C 3
Fritz Hugh Sound ≈ 230-231 B 2
Friuli-Venézia Giúlia ◘ **I** 100-101 D 1
Friza, proliv ≈ 122-123 N 6
Frobisher ○ **CDN** (SAS) 232-233 Q 6
Frobisher Bay ≈ 36-37 Q 3
Frobisher Bay ○ **CDN** 36-37 P 3
Frobisher Lake ⬭ **CDN** 32-33 Q 3
Frog Lake ○ **CDN** (ALB) 232-233 H 2
Frog Lake ⬭ **CDN** (ALB) 232-233 H 2
Frog River ∼ **CDN** 32-33 G 3
Frog River ∼ **CDN** 34-35 M 3
Frohavet ≈ 86-87 D 5
Froid ○ **USA** (MT) 250-251 P 3
Frolovo ○ **RUS** (KRN) 116-117 L 6
Frolovo ○ **RUS** (VLG) 102-103 N 3
Fromberg ○ **USA** (MT) 250-251 L 6
Frome, Lake ⬭ **AUS** 178-179 E 6
Frome Downs ○ **AUS** 178-179 E 6
Fronteiro, Cachoeira da ∼ **BR** 68-69 B 6
Frontenac ○ **USA** (KS) 262-263 M 7
Frontera ○ **E** 188-189 C 7
Frontera ○· **MEX** 52-53 H 2
Frontera, Punta ▲ **MEX** 52-53 H 2
Frontera Comalapa ○ **MEX** 52-53 H 4
Fronteras ○ **MEX** 50-51 E 2

328 Forest Glen — Fronteras

Frontier o CDN (SAS) 232-233 K 6
Front Range ▲ USA 254-255 K 3
Front Royal o USA (VA) 280-281 H 5
Frosinone ☆ I 100-101 D 4
Frostburg o USA (MD) 280-281 H 4
Frostproof o USA (FL) 286-287 H 4
Froude o CDN (SAS) 232-233 P 6
Frøya ⌒ N 86-87 D 5
Frozen Strait ≈ 24-25 d 7
Fruita o USA (CO) 254-255 G 4
Fruitland o USA (ID) 252-253 B 3
Fruitland o USA (MO) 276-277 F 3
Fruitland o USA (UT) 254-255 E 3
Frunze = Biškek ★ KS 146-147 B 4
Frunze, mys ▲ RUS 108-109 I Y 1
Fruta de Leite o BR 72-73 J 4
Frutal o BR 72-73 F 6
Frutillar o RCH 78-79 C 6
Fryatt, Mount ▲ CDN (ALB) 228-229 R 4
Fryeburg o USA (LA) 268-269 G 4
Fryeburg o USA (ME) 278-279 L 4
Frymire o USA (KY) 276-277 J 3
Frys o CDN (SAS) 232-233 R 6
Fua'amotu o TON 184 IV a 2
Fucheng o VRC 154-155 K 3
Fuding o VRC 156-157 M 3
Fududa < EAK 212-213 G 5
Fuencaliente o E 188-189 C 6
Fuencaliente de la Palma o E 188-189 C 6
Fuengirola o E 98-99 E 6
Fuente de Cantos o E 98-99 D 5
Fuente del Fresno o E 98-99 F 5
Fuente de San Esteban, La o E 98-99 D 4
Fuente Obejuna o E 98-99 E 5
Fuentesaúco o E 98-99 E 4
Fuerte o BOL 70-71 E 7
Fuerte, El o MEX 50-51 E 4
Fuerte, Río ~ MEX 50-51 E 4
Fuerte Bulnes o RCH 80 E 6
Fuerte Olimpo ☆ PY 76-77 J 1
Fuerte Quemado o RA 76-77 D 4
Fuerte San Lorenzo ∴ ··· PA 52-53 E 7
Fuerte San Rafael • RA 78-79 E 3
Fuerteventura ⌒ E 188-189 D 6
Fufeng o VRC 154-155 E 4
Fufulsu o GH 202-203 K 5
Fuğaira, al- o UAE 134-135 G 6
Fuga Island ⌒ RP 160-161 D 3
Fuglasker ⌒ IS 86-87 b 3
Fuglohukon ▲ N 84-85 G 3
Fugløy Bank ≃ 86-87 J 1
Fuğma o Y 132-133 F 5
Fugong o VRC 142-143 L 2
Fugou o VRC 154-155 J 4
Fugu o VRC 154-155 G 2
Fuhai o VRC 146-147 H 2
Fuhaihil, al- o KWT 130-131 L 3
Fuji o J 152-153 H 7
Fujian ▫ VRC 156-157 K 3
Fu Jiang ~ VRC 154-155 D 6
Fujieda o J 152-153 H 7
Fuji-gawa ~ J 152-153 H 7
Fuji-Hakone-Izu National Park ⊥ J 152-153 H 7
Fujin o VRC 150-151 J 4
Fuji-san ▲ • J 152-153 H 7
Fujisawa o J 152-153 H 7
Fujiyoshida o J 152-153 H 7
Fūka o ET 194-195 C 2
Fukagawa o J 152-153 K 3
Fukang o VRC 146-147 H 3
Fukuchiyama o J 152-153 F 7
Fukue o J 152-153 C 8
Fukuei Chiao ▲ RC 156-157 M 4
Fukue-shima ⌒ J 152-153 C 8
Fukui ☆ J 152-153 G 6
Fukuoka ☆ • J 152-153 D 8
Fukushima ☆ J (HOK) 152-153 J 4
Fukushima ☆ J (FUK) 152-153 J 6
Fukuyama o J 152-153 E 7
Fulacunda o GNB 202-203 C 4
Fulda o CDN (SAS) 232-233 N 3
Fulda o •• D (HES) 92-93 K 3
Fulda ~ D 92-93 K 3
Fulda o USA (MN) 270-271 C 7
Fulford Harbour o CDN (BC) 230-231 F 5
Fuli o RC 156-157 M 5
Fuling o VRC 156-157 E 2
Fullarton o TT 60-61 L 2
Fulleborn o PNG 183 F 4
Fullerton o USA (IL) 274-275 K 4
Fullerton o USA (ND) 258-259 J 5
Fullerton o USA (NE) 262-263 J 3
Fulton o USA (AR) 276-277 B 7
Fulton o USA (IL) 274-275 H 3
Fulton o USA (KY) 276-277 G 4
Fulton o USA (MO) 274-275 G 6
Fulton o USA (MS) 268-269 M 2
Fulton o USA (NY) 278-279 E 5
Fultondale o USA (AL) 284-285 D 3
Fulton River ~ CDN 228-229 H 2
Fultoro o RI 166-167 D 6
Fulula ~ ZRE 210-211 F 6
Fulunäs o S 86-87 F 6
Fumbelo o ANG 216-217 E 5
Fumel o F 90-91 H 9
Fumiela o ANG 216-217 D 3
Funabashi o J 152-153 H 7
Funadomari o J 152-153 J 2
Funafuti Atoll ⌒ TUV 13 J 3
Funan o VRC 154-155 J 5
Funäsdalen o S 86-87 F 5
Funchal o P 188-189 C 4
Fundacão Eclética o BR 72-73 F 3
Fundación o CO 60-61 D 2
Fundão o BR 72-73 K 5
Fundão o P 98-99 D 4
Fundo, Rio ~ BR 68-69 G 6
Fundong o CAM 204-205 J 5
Fundy, Bay of ≈ 240-241 J 6
Fundy National Park ⊥ CDN (NB) 240-241 K 5
Fungom ▲ CAM 204-205 H 5
Funhalouro o MOC 218-219 H 6
Funiak Springs, De o USA (FL) 286-287 C 1
Funing o VRC (JIA) 154-155 L 5
Funing o VRC (YUN) 156-157 D 5
Funkley o USA (MN) 270-271 D 3
Funsi o GH 202-203 K 4
Funtua o WAN 204-205 G 3
Funzi Island ⌒ EAK 212-213 G 6
Fuping o VRC (HEB) 154-155 J 2
Fuping o VRC (SXI) 154-155 F 4
Fuqāhā', Al o LAR 192-193 G 4
Fuqing o VRC 156-157 L 4
Fuquan o VRC 156-157 E 3
Fuquay Varina o USA (NC) 282-283 H 5
Fura Braço, Corredeira ~ BR 66-67 H 6
Furaiši, al- o KSA 130-131 F 5
Furancungo o MOC 218-219 G 2
Furano o J 152-153 K 3
Furano, Kami- o J 152-153 K 3
Furāt, al- ~ SYR 128-129 L 7
Furāwiya, Bi'r o SUD 198-199 L 5
Furdale o CDN (SAS) 232-233 M 3
Fūrg o IR 134-135 F 4
Furkwa o EAT 212-213 E 6
Furman o USA (AL) 284-285 D 5
Furmanov ☆ RUS 94-95 R 3
Furmanovo ☆ KZ 96-97 F 9
Furnace Creek o USA (CA) 248-249 H 3
Furnas, Represa de < BR 72-73 G 6
Furneaux Group ⌒ AUS 180-181 K 6
Furness o CDN (SAS) 232-233 J 2
Furo Carandazinho ~ BR 70-71 J 5
Furo do Jurupari ~ BR 68-69 B 3
Furo do Tajapuru ~ BR 62-63 J 6
Furqlūs o SYR 128-129 G 5
Furral, El o YV 60-61 K 3
Furroli ▲ ETH 208-209 D 7
Fürstenfeld o A 92-93 O 5
Fürstenwalde (Spree) o • D 92-93 N 2
Fürth o D 92-93 L 4
Furubira o J 152-153 J 3
Furukawa o J 152-153 J 5
Fury and Hecla Strait ≈ 24-25 e 6
Fury Point ▲ CDN 24-25 a 4
Fusagasuga o CO 60-61 D 5
Fushimi Lake Provincial Park ⊥ CDN (ONT) 236-237 E 3
Fushui o VRC 154-155 F 4
Fushun o VRC 150-151 D 7
Fusilier o CDN (SAS) 232-233 J 4
Fuskam Mata o WAN 204-205 H 3
Fusong o VRC 150-151 F 6
Fussa, vulkan ▲ RUS 122-123 Q 3
Füssen o • D 92-93 L 5
Fusui o VRC 156-157 E 5
Futa, Cuilo- o ANG 216-217 C 3
Futalaufquen, Lago o RA 78-79 D 7
Futaleufú o RCH 78-79 D 7
Futaleufú, Río ~ RA 78-79 D 7
Futrono o RCH 78-79 C 6
Futuna Island = Île Erronan ⌒ VAN 184 II c 4
Fu Xian o VRC 154-155 F 4
Fuxian Hu o VRC 156-157 C 4
Fuxin o VRC 150-151 C 6
Fuxing o VRC 156-157 J 2
Fuyang o VRC 154-155 J 5
Fuyu o VRC (HEI) 150-151 E 4
Fuyu o VRC (JIL) 150-151 E 5
Fuyuan o VRC (HEI) 150-151 K 3
Fuyuan o VRC (YUN) 156-157 D 4
Fuyun o VRC 146-147 J 2
Fuzhou ☆ • VRC 156-157 L 3
Fuzhouzhen o VRC 150-151 C 8
Fwa, Lac o • ZRE 210-211 J 6
Fyllas Banke ≃ 28-29 O 5
Fyn ⌒ DK 86-87 E 9
Fyresvatn o N 86-87 D 7

G

Ga o GH 202-203 J 5
Gaalkacyo ☆ SP 208-209 H 5
Gaamodebli o LB 202-203 F 6
Gaasefjord ≈ 26-27 m 8
Gaaseland ⊥ GRØ 26-27 m 8
Gaase Pynt ▲ GRØ 26-27 m 8
Gāb, al- ⊥ SYR 128-129 G 5
Gaba o ETH 208-209 F 5
Gabagaba o PNG 183 D 5
Ǧabal, al-Ahḍar ▲ OM 132-133 K 2
Ǧabala o • SYR 128-129 F 5
Ǧabal 'Abdal'azīz ▲ SYR 128-129 J 4
Gabalatuai o LB 202-203 F 6
Ǧabal Auliyā o SUD 200-201 F 5
Ǧabal Bozi o SUD 200-201 F 6
Gabaldon o RP 160-161 D 5
Ǧabal Mazmum o SUD 200-201 F 6
Ǧabal os Sarāǧ o AFG 136-137 L 7
Gabargaon o BD 142-143 F 3
Gabarouse o CDN (NS) 240-241 P 5
Gabbac, Raas ▲ SP 208-209 K 4
Gabba Island ⌒ AUS 183 B 5
Gabbro Lake o CDN 38-39 M 2
Gabbs o USA (NV) 246-247 H 5
Ǧabbūl, Sabḫat al- o SYR 128-129 G 4
Gabela o ANG 216-217 C 5
Gabensis o PNG 183 D 4
Gabès ☆ TN 190-191 H 4
Gabès, Gulf of = Gabès, Golfe de ≈ 190-191 H 3
Gabēt al-Ma'ādin o SUD 200-201 H 2
Ǧabǧaba, Wādī ~ SUD 194-195 F 6
Gabi o RN 198-199 C 6
Gabia o ZRE 210-211 F 6
Gabiane o TCH 206-207 D 4
Gabir o SUD 206-207 G 4
Ǧābir, Qal'at • SYR 128-129 H 5
Gabiro o RWA 212-213 C 4
Gabo Island ⌒ AUS 180-181 K 4
Gabon ■ G 210-211 C 4
Gabon, Estuaire de ≈ 210-211 B 3
Gaborone ★ RB 220-221 G 2
Gabras o SUD 206-207 H 3
Gabreševci o BG 102-103 C 6
Gabriel, Lac o CDN 36-37 P 5
Gabriel Strait ≈ 36-37 R 4
Gabriel Vera o BOL 70-71 E 6
Gabriel Zamora o MEX 52-53 C 2
Ǧābrik, Rūd-e ~ IR 134-135 H 5
Ǧabrīn, Ǧazīre-ye ⌒ IR 134-135 D 5
Gabriola o CDN (BC) 230-231 F 4
Gabrovo o BG 102-103 D 6
Gabú ☆ GNB 202-203 C 3
Gabu o ZRE 212-213 A 2
Gacheta o CO 60-61 E 5
Gackle o USA (ND) 258-259 H 5
Gacko o BIH 100-101 G 3
Gačsar o IR 136-137 B 6
Gadabeji o RN 198-199 C 5
Ǧadaf, Wādī l- ~ JOR 130-131 E 2
Gadag o IND 140-141 F 3
Gadaisu o PNG 183 E 6
Gadamai o SUD 200-201 H 4
Gada Oundou o RG 202-203 E 4
Gäddede o S 86-87 G 4
Gadein o SUD 206-207 J 4
Ǧadīd, al-Wādī l- ⊥ ET 194-195 D 5
Gado Bravo, Serra do ▲ BR 68-69 E 6
Gādra o PK 138-139 C 7
Ǧadrān o AFG 138-139 B 3
Gadsby o CDN (ALB) 232-233 F 3
Gadsden o USA (AL) 284-285 D 3
Gadsden o USA (SC) 284-285 K 3
Ǧadūn, Wādī ~ OM 132-133 H 4
Gadwāl o IND 140-141 G 2
Gadzi o RCA 206-207 C 6
Gael Hamke Bugt ≈ 26-27 p 6
Găeşti o RO 102-103 D 5
Gaeta, Golfo di ≈ 100-101 D 4
Ǧafara, al- o KSA 130-131 J 6
Ǧa'farābād = Abgarm o IR 128-129 N 5
Ǧafāt, al- o OM 132-133 K 2
Gaffney o USA (SC) 284-285 J 1
Ǧafr, al- o JOR (MAA) 130-131 E 2
Ǧafr, al- o JOR (MAA) 130-131 E 2
Gafsa ☆ • TN 190-191 G 3
Gaftony o AZ 128-129 N 3
Ǧāfūra, al- ⊥ KSA 134-135 D 6
Gag, Pulau ⌒ RI 166-167 E 2
Gagal o TCH 206-207 B 4
Gagan o PNG 184 I b 1
Gagarawa o WAN 198-199 D 6
Gagargarh o IND 142-143 C 2
Gagarin o • RUS 94-95 O 4
Gagarin ☆ UZ 136-137 L 4
Ǧāǧarm o IR 136-137 E 6
Ǧaǧarm, Kal-e Šur ~ IR 136-137 E 6
Ǧaǧatū o AFG 138-139 B 3
Gagau, Gunung ▲ MAL 162-163 E 2
Gago o USA (NM) 256-257 G 6
Gage o USA (OK) 264-265 E 2
Gagere ~ WAN 198-199 C 6
Gagetown o CDN (NB) 240-241 J 5
Gaggabutan o RP 160-161 D 4
Ǧaǧǧaga, Nahr ~ SYR 128-129 J 4
Gaghamni o SUD 206-207 J 3
Gāǧi o AFG 138-139 B 3
Gāǧi Meidān o AFG 138-139 C 3
Ǧaǧin, Rūd-e ~ IR 134-135 G 6
Gagnoa ☆ CI 202-203 H 6
Gagnon o CDN 38-39 K 3
Gagnon, Lac o CDN (QUE) 238-239 K 2
Ǧāǧōri o AFG 134-135 M 2
Gagra o • GE 120-127 D 6
Ǧāǧūd, Rūdḫāne-ye ~ IR 100-107 D 7
Ga Hai o VRC 144-145 L 2
Gahern o CDN (ALB) 232-233 G 6
Gahkom o IR 134-135 F 4
Ǧahnin o OM 132-133 J 5
Ǧahra, al- o • KWT 130-131 K 3
Ǧahrom o • IR 134-135 E 4
Gaiba, Lago o BOL 70-71 J 6
Gaibanda o BD 142-143 F 3
Gaida, al- o Y 132-133 G 6
Gaida, al- o Y 132-133 H 5
Gaigou o BF 202-203 K 2
Gail ~ A 92-93 M 5
Gail o USA (TX) 264-265 C 6
Gail, al- o Y 132-133 G 6
Gail Bāwazīr o • Y 132-133 F 6
Gaillac o F 90-91 H 10
Gaillimh = Galway ☆ • IRL 90-91 C 5
Gaiman o RA 78-79 G 7
Gaimonaki o PNG 183 E 5
Gaines, Fort • USA (AL) 284-285 B 6
Gainesboro o USA (TN) 276-277 K 4
Gainesville o USA (FL) 286-287 G 2
Gainesville o USA (GA) 284-285 G 2
Gainesville o USA (MO) 276-277 C 4
Gainesville o USA (TX) 264-265 G 5
Gainford o CDN (ALB) 232-233 D 2
Gainsborough o CDN (SAS) 232-233 R 6
Gairdner, Lake o AUS 178-179 C 6
Gairdner River ~ AUS 176-177 E 6
Gaire o PNG 183 D 5
Gairesi ~ ZW 218-219 G 3
Gairo o EAT 214-215 J 4
Gaital, Cerro ▲ PA 52-53 D 7
Gaithersburg o USA (MD) 280-281 J 4
Gaivota o BR 62-63 J 5
Gai Xian o VRC 150-151 D 7
Gaj ☆ RUS 96-97 L 8
Gaja, Pulau ⌒ MAL 160-161 C 10
Gajah, Kampung o MAL (KEL) 162-163 D 2
Gajah, Kampung o MAL (PER) 162-163 D 2
Gajahmungkur, Danau o RI 168 D 3
Gajčaveem ~ RUS 112-113 O 5
Gajendragarh o IND 140-141 F 3
Gaji, River ~ WAN 204-205 J 3
Gajiram o WAN 198-199 F 6
Gajny ☆ RUS 96-97 J 3
Gajwel o IND 140-141 H 2
Gakarosa ▲ ZA 220-221 F 3
Gakem o WAN (BEN) 204-205 H 5
Gakem o WAN (CRI) 204-205 H 5
Gakona o USA 20-21 S 5
Gakona River ~ USA 20-21 S 5
Gakou o RMM 202-203 F 2
Gala o VRC 144-145 G 6
Gal Adhale o SP 208-209 H 5
Ǧalāǧil o KSA 130-131 J 5
Galahad o CDN (ALB) 232-233 G 3
Galal, togga ~ SP 208-209 K 3
Ǧalālābād ☆ • AFG 138-139 C 2
Galam ~ RUS 122-123 E 2
Galam, Selat ≈ 162-163 E 4
Ǧalāmīd, al- o KSA 130-131 G 2
Galán o CO 60-61 E 4
Galán, Cerro ▲ RA 76-77 D 3
Galana ~ EAK 212-213 G 5
Galandūk o IR 136-137 B 7
Galanga o ANG 216-217 C 6
Galangachi o RT 202-203 L 4
Galangue o ANG 216-217 D 6
Galaosiё o UZ 136-137 J 5
Galápagos, Islas = Colón, Archipiélago de ⌒ EC 64-65 B 9
Galápagos, Parque Nacional de ⊥ ··· EC 64 65 B 0
Galápagos Fracture Zone = Galapagos Fracture Zone ≃ 14-15 P 8
Galápagos Islands = Colón, Archipiélago de ⌒ EC 64-65 B 9
Galapagos Rise = Galápagos Rise ≃ 5 B 6
Galarza o RA 76-77 J 5
Galarza, Laguna o RA 76-77 J 5
Galas ~ MAL 162-163 D 2
Galashiels o GB 90-91 F 4
Galata o CY 128-129 E 5
Galata o USA (MT) 250-251 H 3
Galaţi ☆ • RO 102-103 F 5
Galatia o USA (IL) 276-277 G 3
Galax o USA (VA) 280-281 F 7
Galbraith o AUS 174-175 F 5
Galbraith o CDN 20-21 Y 7
Galbyn Gov' ⊥ MAU 148-149 H 6
Ǧaldak o AFG 134-135 M 3
Gáldar o E 188-189 D 6
Galdhøpiggen ▲ •• N 86-87 D 6
Ǧaldiyan o IR 128-129 L 4
Galé o RMM 202-203 F 3
Galeana o MEX (CHA) 50-51 F 2
Galeana o MEX (NL) 50-51 J 5
Galečnyj, mys ▲ RUS 110-111 d 1
Galegu o SUD (Naz) 200-201 G 6
Galegu ~ SUD 200-201 G 6
Galela o RI 164-165 K 3
Galela, Teluk ≈ 164-165 K 3
Galena o USA (AK) 20-21 M 4
Galena o USA (IL) 274-275 H 2
Galena o USA (MO) 276-277 B 4
Galena Bay o CDN (BC) 230-231 M 3
Galenbindunuwewa o CL 140-141 J 6
Galeo o LB 202-203 G 7
Ǧāleq o IR 134-135 K 5
Galera o EC 64-65 B 1
Galera, Punta ▲ EC 64-65 B 1
Galera, Río ~ BR 70-71 H 4
Galesburg o USA (IL) 274-275 H 4
Galesburg o USA (ND) 258-259 K 4
Galesong o RI 164-165 F 6
Galesville o USA (WI) 270-271 G 6
Galēti Shet' ~ ETH 208-209 E 4
Galeton o USA (PA) 280-281 J 2
Galgamuwa o CL 140-141 J 7
Gal'gavaam ~ RUS 112-113 J 1
Galguduud ▫ SP 208-209 H 6
Gal Hareeri o SP 208-209 H 6
Galheirão, Rio ~ BR 68-69 C 7
Galheiros, Serra da ▲ BR 68-69 G 5
Galheiros da Lapa o BR 72-73 J 2
Galheiros o BR 70-70 H 4
Galheteira, Riachão ~ BR 68-69 H 6
Ǧalǧamid ▲ IRQ 128-129 L 5
Gali o GE 126-127 D 6
Galia o BR 72-73 F 7
Galiano o CDN (BC) 230-231 F 5
Ǧaliba o IRQ 130-131 K 2
Galibi o SME 62-63 G 3
Galibi, National Reservaat ⊥ SME 62-63 H 3
Galič o • RUS 94-95 S 2
Galice o USA (OR) 244-245 B 8
Galicia ▫ E 98-99 C 3
Galičskaja vozvyšennosť ▲ RUS 94-95 R 3
Galilee o CDN (SAS) 232-233 N 6
Galilee, Lake o AUS 178-179 H 2
Galiléia o BR 72-73 K 5
Galilo o PNG 183 F 3
Galim o CAM (ADA) 204-205 K 5
Galim o CAM (OUE) 204-205 J 6
Galimovskij hrebet ▲ RUS 112-113 H 5
Galimyj o RUS 112-113 H 5
Galinda o ANG 216-217 B 4
Galinhas, Ilha das ⌒ GNB 202-203 C 4
Galion o USA (OH) 280-281 D 3
Galiuro Mountains ▲ USA 256-257 E 6
Galivedu o IND 140-141 H 4
Galiwinku ⚔ AUS 174-175 C 3
Gallābāt o SUD 200-201 H 6
Gallants o CDN (NFL) 242-243 K 4
Gallaorol ☆ UZ 136-137 K 5
Gallatin o USA (MO) 274-275 E 5
Gallatin o USA (TN) 276-277 J 4
Gallatin Peak ▲ USA (MT) 250-251 H 6
Gallatin River ~ USA 250-251 H 6
Galle o ··· CL 140-141 J 7
Gállego, Río ~ E 98-99 G 4
Gallego Rise ≃ 14-15 R 8
Gallegos o USA (NM) 256-257 M 3
Gallegos, Río ~ RA 80 F 5
Galleguillos o RCH 76-77 B 4
Gallina o USA (NM) 256-257 J 2
Gallinas o USA (NM) 256-257 K 4
Gallinas Mountains ▲ USA 256-257 H 4
Gallinas Peak ▲ USA (NM) 256-257 K 4
Gallinas River ~ USA 256-257 K 3
Gallinero, Cerro ▲ YV 60-61 H 5
Gallipoli o AUS 174-175 D 6
Gallipoli o I 100-101 F 4
Gallipolis o USA (OH) 280-281 D 5
Gällivare o • S 86-87 K 3
Gallix o CDN (QUE) 242-243 B 2
Gallja, ostrov ⌒ RUS 84-85 e 2
Galljaaral o UZ 136-137 K 5
Gallo Arroyo ~ USA 256-257 K 4
Gallo Mountains ▲ USA 256-257 G 4
Galloo Island ⌒ USA (NY) 278-279 E 5
Galloway o CDN (BC) 230-231 O 4
Galloway ⊥ GB 90-91 E 4
Gallup o USA (NM) 256-257 G 3
Galma, River ~ WAN 204-205 H 3
Galma Galla o EAK 212-213 H 4
Galmi o RN 198-199 B 6
Galo Boukoy o RCA 206-207 B 6
Gal Oya National Park ⊥ CL 140-141 J 7
Galpón, El o RA 76-77 E 3
Ǧalrēz o AFG 138-139 B 2
Galšar = Bujant o MAU 148-149 K 4
Galt o USA (CA) 246-247 D 5
Galt o USA (MO) 274-275 E 4
Gal Tardo o SP 212-213 K 2
Galtat-Zemmour o WSA 196-197 D 2
Galūgāh o IR 136-137 C 6
Ǧalūlā' o IRQ 128-129 L 5
Galung o RI 164-165 F 5
Galur o RI 168 D 3
Galuzeik o MYA 158-159 C 3
Galva o USA (IL) 274-275 H 3
Galvão o BR 74-75 D 6
Galves o RA 78-79 J 2
Galveston o • USA (TX) 268-269 F 7
Galveston Bay ≈ 268-269 F 7
Galvestone o USA (IN) 274-275 M 4
Galveston Island ⌒ USA (TX) 268-269 F 7
Galvez, Río ~ PE 64-65 F 4
Galway = Gaillimh ☆ • IRL 90-91 C 5
Galway Bay ≈ 90-91 C 5
Gam, Pulau ⌒ RI (IRJ) 166-167 F 2
Gam, Pulau ⌒ RI (IRJ) 166-167 E 2
Gama o BR 72-73 F 3
Gama o RG 202-203 F 6
Gama, Isla ⌒ RA 78-79 H 6
Gamaches o F 90-91 H 7
Ǧamāǧim, Umm al- o KSA 130-131 J 4
Gamana, River ~ WAN 204-205 H 5
Gama River ~ PNG 183 B 4
Gāmāsiāb, Rūd-e ~ IR 134-135 B 1
Gamawa o WAN 198-199 E 6
Gamba o ANG 216-217 D 5
Gamba o G 210-211 C 5
Gamba o VRC 144-145 G 6
Gamba o ZRE 210-211 K 6
Gambaga o GH 202-203 K 4
Gambang o MAL 162-163 E 3
Gambara o MEX 52-53 C 2
Gambēla o ETH 208-209 B 4
Gambela National Park ⊥ ETH 208-209 A 5
Gambell o USA 20-21 E 5
Gambia ■ WAG 202-203 B 3
Gambia, River ~ WAG 202-203 B 3
Gambia No.1 o GH 202-203 J 6
Gambie ~ SN 202-203 D 3
Gambier Islands ⌒ AUS 180-181 D 3
Gambo o ANG 216-217 F 4
Gambo o CDN (NFL) 242-243 O 4
Gambo o RCA 206-207 F 6
Gamboa o PA 52-53 E 7
Gamboma o RCB 210-211 E 4
Gamboula o RCA 206-207 B 6
Gamčen, hrebet ▲ RUS 120-121 T 6
Gamčen, vulkan ▲ RUS 120-121 T 6
Gamdou o RN 198-199 D 6
Gameleir, Ribeiro ~ BR 68-69 C 7
Gameleira, Serra da ▲ BR 68-69 G 5
Gameleira da Lapa o BR 72-73 J 2
Gameleira o BR 70-70 H 4
Gameteira, Riachão ~ BR 68-69 H 6
Ǧamǧamāl ▲ IRQ 128-129 L 5
Gamia o DY 204-205 E 3
Ǧāmid az-Zināď o KSA 132-133 B 4
Ǧamīl al-'Imrān o IRQ 128-129 L 6
Gamis o NAM 220-221 C 2
Gamkab ~ NAM 220-221 C 4
Gamkahe o RI 164-165 K 3
Gamkarivier ~ ZA 220-221 E 6
Ǧammāla, al- o KSA 132-133 C 5
Gammelstaden o • S 86-87 L 4
Gammel Sukkertoppen = Kangaamiut o GRØ 28-29 O 4
Gammon Ranges National Park ⊥ AUS 178-179 E 6
Gammouda = Sidi Bouzid ☆ TN 190-191 G 3
Gamoep o ZA 220-221 D 4
Gamova, mys ▲ RUS 122-123 D 7
Gamperé ▲ CAM 206-207 B 5
Gamping o RI 168 D 3
Gamra o RIM 196-197 D 6
Ǧamsa o ET 194-195 F 4
Ǧamsa, Ra's ▲ ET 194-195 F 4
Gamsberg ▲ NAM 220-221 C 1
Gamsby River ~ CDN 228-229 G 3
Ǧamšīdzāī, Kūh-e ▲ IR 134-135 J 4
Gamūd ▲ ETH 208-209 D 6
Ǧamūm o KSA 132-133 A 3
Gamvik o N 86-87 O 1
G'amys, gora ▲ AZ 128-129 M 2
Gana, Komadougou ~ WAN 198-199 E 6
Ǧanad, al- o Y 132-133 D 7
Ganado o USA (AZ) 256-257 F 3
Ganado o USA (TX) 266-267 L 4
Ganai o PNG 183 E 3
Ganal'skij hrebet ▲ RUS 120-121 R 7
Ganaly o RUS 120-121 R 7
Ganamiya, al- o KSA 130-131 K 5
Ǧanāna ⌒ UAE 134-135 E 6
Gananita o SUD 200-201 F 3
Gananoque o CDN (ONT) 238-239 J 4
Ganāve, Bandar-e o IR 134-135 D 4
Gancheng o VRC 156-157 F 7
Gand = Gent ☆ • B 92-93 G 3
Ganda o ANG 216-217 C 6
Gandaba o ETH 208-209 F 4
Gandadiwata, Gunung ▲ RI 164-165 F 5
Gandajika o ZRE 214-215 B 4
Ǧandaq o IR 134-135 F 1
Gandara o RP 160-161 F 6
Gandarbal o IND 138-139 E 2
Gandāva o PK 134-135 M 4
Gande o WAN 198-199 B 6
Ganden • VRC 144-145 H 6
Gander o CDN (NFL) 242-243 O 4
Gander Bay o CDN (NFL) 242-243 O 3
Gander Lake o CDN (NFL) 242-243 O 4
Gander River ~ CDN 242-243 O 3
Gāndhi Dhām o • IND 138-139 C 8
Gāndhinagar ☆ •• IND 138-139 D 8
Gāndhi Sāgar o IND 138-139 E 7
Gandía o E 98-99 G 5
Gandiaye o SN 202-203 B 2
Gandō-ko < J 152-153 J 5
Gandomak o AFG 138-139 C 2
Gandomān o IR 134-135 D 3
Gandu o BR 72-73 L 2
Gandy o USA (UT) 254-255 B 4
Gāneb o RIM 196-197 E 5
Ganesh ▲ NEP 144-145 E 6
Ganga ~ IND 142-143 E 3
Gangačin o IR 128-129 L 4
Gangākher o IND 138-139 F 10
Gangala na Bodio o ZRE 212-213 B 2
Gan Gan o RA 78-79 E 7
Gangan ▲ RG 202-203 D 4
Ganganagar o IND 138-139 D 5
Gangāpur o IND 138-139 E 7
Gangara o RN 198-199 D 5
Gangaw o MYA 142-143 J 4
Gangca o VRC 154-155 B 3
Gangchang o VRC 154-155 D 6
Ganges o CDN (BC) 230-231 F 5
Ganges o F 90-91 J 10
Ganges = Ganga ~ IND 142-143 E 3
Ganges, Mouths of the ≈ 142-143 F 5
Ganges Fan = Bengal Fan ≃ 10-11 H 7
Ganges River Delta = Ganga Delta ⊥ IND 142-143 F 4
Gangīr, Rūdḫāne-ye ~ IR 134-135 A 2
Gangkha o BHT 142-143 F 2
Gango ~ ANG 216-217 C 5
Gangoli o IND 140-141 F 4
Gangotri o IND 138-139 G 4
Gang Ranch o CDN (BC) 230-231 G 2
Gangtok ☆ • IND 142-143 F 2
Gangu ~ ZRE 206-207 F 6
Gangui o CAM 206-207 B 5
Gangula o ANG 216-217 B 5
Ganhe o VRC 150-151 D 2
Gani o RI 164-165 L 4
Gāni Hel o AFG 138-139 B 3
Gan Jiang ~ VRC 156-157 J 3
Ganjuškino ☆ KZ 96-97 F 10
Ganlanba • VRC 156-157 B 6
Ganluo o VRC 156-157 C 2
Gannan o VRC 150-151 D 4
Gannat o F 90-91 J 8
Gannett Peak ▲ USA (WY) 252-253 J 3
Ganquan o VRC 154-155 F 3
Gansbaai o ZA 220-221 D 7
Gansé o CI 202-203 J 5
Gansen o VRC 144-145 J 2
Gansu ▫ VRC 148-149 D 7
Ganta o LB 202-203 F 6
Gantang o VRC 154-155 D 3
Gantas, Las o RA 76-77 G 5
Gantheaume, Cape ▲ AUS 180-181 D 4
Gantheaume Bay ≈ 176-177 C 3
Gantheaume Point ▲ AUS 172-173 F 4
Ganti o RI 168 C 7
Gantira o RI 164-165 G 5
Gantisan o MAL 160-161 B 9
Gantt o USA (AL) 284-285 D 5
Gantt Lake < USA (AL) 284-285 D 5
Ǧanūbiya, al Bādiya l ⊥ IRQ 130-131 K 2
Ganxi o VRC 156-157 F 2
Ganye o WAN 204-205 K 4
Ganyesa o ZA 220-221 G 3
Ganyli ~ AZ 128-129 M 2
Ganyu o VRC 154-155 L 4
Ganža o • AZ 128-129 M 2
Ganze ~ ZRE 210-211 K 6
Ganzhou o VRC 156-157 J 4
Gao o BF 202-203 J 4
Gao ▫ RMM 196-197 J 5
Gao ☆ • RMM (GAO) 196-197 K 6
Gao o ZRE 212-213 B 2
Gao'an o VRC 156-157 J 2
Gaochang Gucheng ∴ • VRC 146-147 J 4
Gaochun o VRC 154-155 L 6
Gaofengtao o VRC 154-155 L 4
Gaogou o VRC 154-155 L 4
Gaohezhen o VRC 154-155 K 6
Gaojiabu o VRC 154-155 G 2
Gaolan o VRC (GAN) 154-155 C 3
Gaolan • VRC (HUB) 154-155 G 6
Gaoligong Shan ▲ 142-143 L 2
Gaomi o VRC 154-155 L 3
Gaoping o VRC 154-155 H 4
Gaotai o VRC 154-155 A 2
Gaotang o VRC 154-155 K 3
Gaoua ☆ BF 202-203 J 4
Gaoual o RG 202-203 D 3
Gaoun, Mont ▲ RCA 206-207 B 5
Gao Xian o VRC 156-157 D 2
Gaoyi o VRC 154-155 J 3
Gaozhou o VRC 156-157 G 6
Gap o F 90-91 L 9
Gap, Pico ▲ RCH 80 F 6
Gapi o ZRE 206-207 H 6
Gapuwiyak ⚔ AUS 174-175 C 3
Gar' ~ RUS 122-123 C 2
Garaa Tebourt o TN 190-191 H 5
Garabinzam o RCB 210-211 D 3
Garāblus ☆ SYR 128-129 H 4
Garabogazköl o TM 136-137 C 4
Gara Brune o DZ 190-191 G 6
Garabulli, Al o LAR 192-193 E 1
Garacad o SP 208-209 J 5
Garachico o E 188-189 C 6
Garada o SUD 200-201 E 3
Garadag o SP 208-209 H 4
Gara Dragoman o BG 102-103 C 6
Gara-Ekar ▲ DZ 198-199 B 3
Ǧarāǧir, Wādi al- ~ KSA 130-131 H 4
Garagoa o CO 60-61 E 5
Garaguene, Tchin o RN 198-199 D 5
Garagum ⊥ TM 136-137 E 4
Garah o AUS 178-179 K 5
Garaina o PNG 183 D 4
Garajonay, Parque Nacional de ⊥ ··· E 188-189 C 6
Garalo o RMM 202-203 G 4
Garamba ~ ZRE 212-213 B 2
Garamba, Parc National de la ⊥ ··· ZRE 206-207 J 6
Garampani o IND 142-143 H 2
Gara Nasa ▲ ETH 208-209 B 4
Ǧarandal o JOR 130-131 D 2
Ǧarandal, Wādī ~ ET 194-195 F 3
Garango o BF 202-203 K 4
Garanhuns o BR 68-69 K 6
Ga-Rankuwa o ZA 220-221 H 2
Garapa, Serra do ▲ BR 72-73 J 2
Garapu o BR 72-73 D 2
Garapuava o BR 72-73 G 4
Ǧarārā o KSA 130-131 K 4
Garara o PNG 183 E 5
Ǧaraš o •• JOR 130-131 D 1
Garawe o LB 202-203 G 7
Garayalde o RA 80 G 2
Garba o RCA 206-207 E 4
Garbahaarrey ☆ SP 212-213 J 2
Garba Tula o EAK 212-213 G 3
Garber o USA (OK) 264-265 G 2
Garberville o USA (CA) 246-247 B 3
Ǧarbi, 'Ali al- ☆ IRQ 128-129 M 6
Gārboš, Kūh-e ▲ IR 134-135 D 2
Garças, Cachoeira das ~ BR 70-71 H 2
Garças, Cachoeira das ~ BR 70-71 K 4
Garças ou Jacarégueau, Rio das ~ BR 72-73 D 3
Garchitorena o RP 160-161 E 6
Garciasville o USA (TX) 266-267 J 7
Garcitas, Las o RA 76-77 H 4
Garda o I 100-101 C 2
Gardabani o GE 126-127 F 7
Gardandēvāl o AFG 138-139 B 2
Garde Lake o CDN 30-31 Q 4
Gardelegen o • D 92-93 L 2
Garden City o USA (AL) 284-285 D 2
Garden City o USA (GA) 284-285 J 4
Garden City o USA (KS) 262-263 F 7
Garden City o USA (TX) 266-267 F 2
Garden City o USA (UT) 254-255 D 2
Garden Cove o CDN (NFL) 242-243 O 5
Gardendale o USA (TX) 264-265 B 6
Gardenia Lake o CDN 30-31 R 4
Garden Island ⌒ USA (MI) 272-273 D 2
Garden Peninsula ~ USA 270-271 M 5
Garden River o CDN (ONT) 236-237 D 6
Garden River ~ CDN 238-239 B 2
Garden River Indian Reserve ✕ CDN (ONT) 236-237 D 6
Gardens Corner o USA (SC) 284-285 K 4
Garden State Parkway II USA (NJ) 280-281 M 4
Gardenton o CDN (MAN) 234-235 G 5
Garden Valley o USA (TX) 264-265 D 4
Gardēz ☆ AFG 138-139 B 3
Gardi o USA (GA) 284-285 J 5
Gardiner o CDN (ONT) 236-237 G 3
Gardiner o USA (ME) 278-279 M 4
Gardiner o USA (MT) 250-251 J 6
Gardiner, Mount ▲ AUS 178-179 K 2
Gardiners Island ⌒ USA (NY) 280-281 O 2
Gardner o USA (CO) 254-255 K 6
Gardner o USA (FL) 286-287 H 4
Gardner o USA (IL) 274-275 K 3
Gardner o USA (KS) 262-263 M 6
Gardner o USA (LA) 268-269 H 5
Gardner o USA (ND) 258-259 L 4
Gardner Canal < CDN (BC) 228-229 F 3
Gardner Island ⌒ KIB 13 K 3
Gardner Pinnacles ⌒ USA 14-15 M 5
Gardner Plateau ▲ AUS 172-173 G 3
Gardner Range ▲ AUS 172-173 J 5
Gardnerville o USA (NV) 246-247 F 5
Gardunha, Serra da ▲ P 98-99 D 4
Garei ~ BD 142-143 F 4
Gareloi Island ⌒ USA 22-23 G 7
Gare Tigre o F 62-63 H 3
Garfa, Oued ~ RIM 196-197 D 7
Garfield o AUS 178-179 H 2
Garfield o USA (KS) 262-263 G 6
Garfield o USA (NM) 256-257 H 6
Garfield o USA (WA) 244-245 H 3
Garfield Mountain ▲ USA (MT) 250-251 G 7
Garford o AUS 176-177 M 4
Gargamelle o CDN (NFL) 242-243 L 2
Gargando o RMM 196-197 H 6
Gargano, Promontorio del ▲ I 100-101 E 4
Gargantua, Cape ▲ CDN (ONT) 236-237 C 5
Gargaris o PNG 183 G 2
Gargnäs o S 86-87 H 4
Gargouna o RMM 202-203 L 2
Gargždai ☆ •• LT 94-95 G 4
Garhchiroli o IND 142-143 B 5
Garhshankar o IND 138-139 F 4
Gari ☆ RUS 114-115 G 5
Gariāband o IND 142-143 C 5
Garian o RI 166-167 H 3
Ǧarib, Ǧabal ▲ ET 194-195 F 3
Garibaldi o BR 74-75 E 7
Garibaldi o CDN (BC) 230-231 F 4
Garibaldi o USA (OR) 244-245 B 5
Garibaldi, Mount ▲ CDN (BC) 230-231 F 4
Garibaldi Provincial Park ⊥ CDN (BC) 230-231 G 4
Garies o ZA 220-221 C 5
Garif, al- o KSA 130-131 F 6
Gariganus o NAM 220-221 D 3
Garimpinho o BR 68-69 D 5
Garin, Kūh-e ▲ IR 134-135 C 2
Garin Shehu o WAN 204-205 J 4
Garin Yerima o WAN 204-205 J 4
Ǧarīr, Wādi al- ~ KSA 130-131 H 5
Garissa ☆ EAK 212-213 G 4
Garkem o WAN 204-205 H 5
Garki o WAN 198-199 D 6
Garkida o WAN 204-205 K 3

Frontier — Garkida 329

Garladinne o **IND** 140-141 G 3
Garland o **CDN** (MAN) 234-235 C 3
Garland o **USA** (AR) 276-277 B 7
Garland o **USA** (MT) 250-251 O 5
Garland o **USA** (NC) 282-283 J 6
Garland o **USA** (TX) 264-265 H 6
Garland o **USA** (UT) 254-255 C 2
Garland o **USA** (WY) 252-253 K 2
Garm o **TJ** 136-137 M 5
Garmāb o **IR** 128-129 N 5
Garmabe o **SUD** 206-207 K 6
Garmanda o **RUS** 112-113 K 5
Garmanda, Bol'šaja ~ **RUS** 112-113 K 5
Garm Bīt o **IR** 134-135 J 6
Garme o **IR** 136-137 E 6
Garmisch-Partenkirchen o• **D** 92-93 L 5
Garmsār o **AFG** (HL) 134-135 L 3
Garmsār ∸ **AFG** 134-135 K 3
Garmsār o **IR** 136-137 C 7
Garner o **USA** (IA) 274-275 E 1
Garner o **USA** (NC) 282-283 J 5
Garnet o **USA** (MI) 270-271 N 4
Garnet Bank ≃ 74-75 F 9
Garnet Bay ≈ 36-37 M 2
Garnett o **USA** (KS) 262-263 L 6
Garnett o **USA** (SC) 284-285 J 4
Garnish o **CDN** (NFL) 242-243 N 5
Garnpung, Lake o **AUS** 180-181 G 2
Garonne ~ **F** 90-91 H 9
Garoowe ☆ **SP** 208-209 J 4
Garou o **DY** 204-205 E 3
Garou, Lac o **RMM** 196-197 J 6
Garoua ☆ **CAM** 204-205 K 4
Garoua Boulai o **CAM** 206-207 B 6
Garove Island ⌒ **PNG** 183 E 3
Garré o **RA** 78-79 H 4
Garretson o **USA** (SD) 260-261 K 3
Garrett o **USA** (WY) 252-253 N 4
Garrett Fracture Zone ≃ 14-15 R 9
Garrick o **CDN** (SAS) 232-233 O 2
Garrido, Isla ⌒ **RCH** 80 C 2
Garrington o **CDN** (ALB) 232-233 D 4
Garrison o **USA** (MN) 270-271 E 4
Garrison o **USA** (MT) 250-251 G 5
Garrison o **USA** (ND) 258-259 F 4
Garrison o **USA** (NV) 246-247 M 5
Garrison o **USA** (TX) 268-269 F 5
Garro o **MEX** 52-53 G 2
Garrobo, El o **NIC** 52-53 B 5
Garruchas o **BR** 76-77 K 5
Garry, Cape ▲ **CDN** 24-25 Z 4
Garry Bay ≈ 24-25 d 6
Garry Lake o **CDN** 30-31 T 3
Garsala o **SP** 212-213 K 2
Garsen o **EAK** 212-213 H 5
Garsila o **SUD** 198-199 L 6
Gartempe ~ **F** 90-91 H 8
Gartok = Garyarsa o **VRC** 144-145 C 5
Garu o **PNG** 183 E 3
Garuahi o **PNG** 183 F 6
Garub o **NAM** 220-221 C 3
Ğarūb o **Y** 132-133 H 5
Garuma o **RCH** 76-77 C 2
Garupá, Rio ~ **BR** 76-77 J 6
Garut o• **RI** 168 B 3
Garuva o **BR** 74-75 F 6
Garwa o **IND** 142-143 C 3
Garwolin o **PL** 92-93 Q 3
Gar Xincun o **VRC** 144-145 C 4
Gary o **USA** (IN) 274-275 L 3
Garyarsa o **VRC** 144-145 C 5
Garysburg o **USA** (NC) 282-283 K 4
Garza o **RA** 76-77 F 5
Garza Garcia o **MEX** 50-51 J 5
Garzas, Las o **RA** 76-77 H 5
Garzê o **VRC** 144-145 M 5
Garzon o **CO** 60-61 D 6
Gasan Kuli o **TM** 136-137 C 6
Gasan-Kulijskijučastok Krasnovodskogo zapovednik ⊥ **TM** 136-137 C 6
Gaschiga o **CAM** 204-205 K 4
Gas City o **USA** (IN) 274-275 N 4
Gascogne ∸ **F** 90-91 G 10
Gascoigne o **CDN** (SAS) 232-233 J 5
Gasconade River ~ **USA** 274-275 G 6
Gasconade River ~ **USA** 276-277 C 3
Gascoyne, Mount ▲ **AUS** 176-177 D 2
Gascoyne Junction o **AUS** 176-177 C 2
Gascoyne River ~ **AUS** 176-177 C 2
Gasera o **ETH** 208-209 E 5
Gash ~ **ER** 200-201 H 5
Gashaka o **WAN** 204-205 J 5
Gasherbrum I ▲ **PK** 138-139 F 2
Gasherbrum II ▲ **PK** 138-139 F 2
Gas Hu o **VRC** 146-147 K 6
Gashua o **WAN** 198-199 E 6
Gashunchaka o **VRC** 144-145 K 2
Gasim o **RI** 166-167 F 2
Ğāsk o **IR** 134-135 G 6
Ğāsk, Ḫalīğ-e ≈ 134-135 G 6
Gaskačokka ▲ **N** 86-87 H 3
Gasmata o **PNG** 183 F 4
Gaspar, Selat ≈ 162-163 G 6
Gaspar Hernández o **DOM** 54-55 K 5
Gasparilla Island ⌒ **USA** (FL) 286-287 G 5
Gaspé o **CDN** (QUE) 240-241 L 2
Gaspé, Baie de ≈ 240-241 L 2
Gaspé, Cape ▲ **CDN** (QUE) 240-241 L 2
Gaspé, Péninsule de ⌣ **CDN** 240-241 J 2
Gaspereau Forks o **CDN** (NB) 240-241 K 4
Gaspésie, Parc de la ⊥ **CDN** (QUE) 240-241 J 2
Gasquet o **USA** (CA) 246-247 B 2
Gassan o **BF** 202-203 J 3
Ğaşşān o **IRQ** 128-129 L 6
Gassan ▲ **J** 152-153 H 5
Gassane o **SN** 202-203 C 2
Gassaway o **USA** (WV) 280-281 F 5
Gassend Lake o **CDN** 24-25 J 6
Gassi Touil ∸ **DZ** 190-191 F 6
Gassol o **WAN** 204-205 J 4
Gass Peak ▲ **USA** (NV) 248-249 J 3
Gašt o **IR** 134-135 J 5
Gastello o **RUS** 122-123 K 4
Gastón o **C** 54-55 G 4
Gastona, Río ~ **RA** 76-77 E 4
Gastonia o **USA** (NC) 282-283 F 5
Gastre o **RA** 78-79 E 7
Ġāṭ, al- o **KSA** 130-131 J 4
Gata o **CV** 202-203 C 5
Gata, Sierra de ▲ **E** 98-99 D 4
Gataga River ~ **CDN** 30-31 F 6
Gatanga o **SUD** 206-207 H 5
Gatčina ☆ **RUS** 94-95 M 2
Gate o **USA** (OK) 264-265 D 2
Gate City o **USA** (VA) 280-281 D 7
Gatehouse of Fleet o **GB** 90-91 E 4
Gatentiri o **RI** 166-167 L 5
Gates o **USA** (NC) 282-283 L 4
Gateshead Island ⌒ **CDN** 24-25 W 5
Gates of the Artic National Park and Preserve ⊥ **USA** 20-21 N 2
Gatesville o **USA** (TX) 266-267 K 2
Gateview o **USA** (CO) 254-255 H 5
Gateway o **USA** (CO) 254-255 G 5
Gateway National Recreation Area • **USA** (NY) 280-281 N 3
Gathto Creek ~ **CDN** 30-31 G 6
Gati-Loumo o **RMM** 202-203 H 2
Gatin, Rivière ~ **CDN** 36-37 M 4
Gatineau o **CDN** (QUE) 238-239 K 3
Gatineau, Rivière ~ **CDN** 236-237 N 5
Gatineau, Rivière ~ **CDN** 238-239 K 3
Gatlinburg o **USA** (TN) 282-283 D 5
Gatos, Los o **USA** (CA) 248-249 C 2
Ġaṭṭī o **KSA** 130-131 E 2
Gatton o **AUS** 178-179 M 4
Gatún, Lago o• **PA** 52-53 E 7
Gatuncito o **PA** 52-53 D 7
Gatvand o **IR** 134-135 C 2
Gau ⌒ **FJI** 184 III b 3
Gaua, Île = Santa Maria Island ⌒ **VAN** 184 II a 2
Gaudan o **TM** 136-137 F 6
Gaudan, pereval ▲ **TM** 136-137 F 6
Gauer Lake o **CDN** 34-35 H 2
Ğauf, Wādī al- ~ **Y** 132-133 D 5
Ğaufa, al- o **KSA** 132-133 B 3
Gaujas nacionālais parks ⊥ **LV** 94-95 J 3
Gaula ~ **N** 86-87 E 5
Gaulay River ~ **USA** 280-281 E 5
Gauley Mountain ▲ **USA** (WV) 280-281 F 5
Gaulim o **PNG** 183 G 3
Gaulle, De o **RCA** 206-207 B 5
Gaultois o **CDN** (NFL) 242-243 N 5
Gaurdak o **TM** 136-137 K 6
Gauribidanur o **IND** 140-141 G 4
Gauss Halvø ∸ **GRØ** 26-27 o 7
Gausta ▲ **N** 86-87 D 7
Gauthiot, Chutes ~• **TCH** 206-207 B 4
Gauttier, Pegunungan ▲ **RI** 166-167 K 3
Ğavāher Deh o **IR** 136-137 B 6
Ğavand o **AFG** 136-137 J 7
Ğavānrūd o **IR** 134-135 B 1
Gāvbandī o **IR** 134-135 E 5
Gāvbast, Kūh-e ▲ **IR** 134-135 E 5
Gávdos ⌒ **GR** 100-101 K 7
Gave de Pau ~ **F** 90-91 G 10
Gāve Rūd ~ **IR** 134-135 B 1
Gāvgān o **IR** 128-129 L 4
Gavião o **BR** 68-69 J 7
Gavião o **P** 98-99 D 5
Gavião, Rio ~ **BR** 72-73 K 3
Gavien o **PNG** 183 C 2
Gaviota o **USA** (CA) 248-249 D 5
Gaviota Beach • **USA** (CA) 248-249 D 5
Gaviota Pass ▲ **USA** (CA) 248-249 D 5
Gaviotas, Las o **YV** 60-61 K 3
Gävle ☆ **S** 86-87 H 6
Gavriila, guba ≈ 112-113 U 5
Gavrilov -Jam ☆ **RUS** 94-95 Q 3
Gávrio o **GR** 100-101 K 6
Gavriša-Tas, gora ▲ **RUS** 110-111 X 3
Gavunipalli o **IND** 140-141 H 4
Gawachab o **NAM** 220-221 C 3
Gawa Island ⌒ **PNG** 183 F 5
Gawalisi, Gunung ▲ **RI** 164-165 F 4
Gawa Obo o **VRC** 144-145 M 3
Ğawār,al- ∸ **UAE** 130-131 L 5
Gawler o **AUS** 180-181 E 3
Gawler Ranges ▲ **AUS** 180-181 C 2
Gawu o **WAN** 204-205 G 4
Ġawwār, Ğazīrat ⌒ **KSA** 130-131 E 5
Gaxun Nur o **VRC** 148-149 E 6
Gay o **USA** (GA) 284-285 F 3
Gay o **USA** (OK) 264-265 J 5
Gaya o•• **IND** 142-143 D 3
Gaya o **MAL** 160-161 B 9
Gaya o **RN** 204-205 E 3
Gaya o **WAN** 204-205 H 3
Gaya, Pulau ⌒ **MAL** 160-161 B 9
Gayam o **TCH** 206-207 C 4
Gayamcam o **RP** 160-161 E 9
Gayaza o **EAU** 212-213 C 4
G'Aydat Al Ihoucha ∸ **WSA** 188-189 F 7
Gayéri o **BF** 202-203 L 3
Gay Head ▲ **USA** (MA) 278-279 L 7
Gaylord o **USA** (MI) 272-273 E 2
Gaylord o **USA** (MN) 270-271 D 6
Gaylord o **USA** (VA) 280-281 J 4
Gayna River ~ **CDN** 30-31 E 3
Gays River o **CDN** (NS) 240-241 M 5
Gayville o **USA** (SD) 260-261 J 4
Ġayyāda, Šu'aib ~ **IRQ** 128-129 J 6
Gaz, Rūd-e ~ **AFG** 134-135 K 2
Gaza □ **MOC** 218-219 G 6
Gaza/ Ġazza ☆ **AUT** 130-131 D 2
Gazačak o **TM** 136-137 G 4
Gaz-Ačak = Gazačak o **TM** 136-137 G 4
Gazakh = Qazax o• **AZ** 128-129 L 2
Ġazala, al- o **KSA** 130-131 G 4
Ġazālāt, Qārat al- ▲ **ET** 194-195 C 2
Gazalkent o **UZ** 136-137 L 4
Gazanak o **IR** 136-137 C 7
Gazankulu (früheres Homeland, jetzt zu North-Transvaal □ **ZA** 220-221 J 1
Gazaoua o **RN** 198-199 C 6
Gazara o **TJ** 136-137 L 5
Gazelle o **USA** (CA) 246-247 C 2
Gazelle Channel ≈ 183 F 2
Gazelle Peninsula ⌣ **PNG** 183 F 3
Gazerān o **IR** 134-135 D 1
Gāzergāh o• **AFG** 134-135 K 1
Gazi o **EAK** 212-213 G 6
Gazi Antep ☆ **TR** 128-129 G 4
Gazīk o **IR** 134-135 J 2
Gazimur ~ **RUS** 118-119 J 9
Gazimurskij Zavod ☆ **RUS** 118-119 J 10
Gazipaşa ☆ **TR** 128-129 E 4
Gazipur o **BD** 142-143 G 4
Gazli o **UZ** 136-137 H 4
Ğaz Mūriān, Hāmūn-e o **IR** 134-135 H 5
Ġaznī □ **AFG** 134-135 M 2
Ġaznī ☆• **AFG** (ĠA) 138-139 B 3
Ġaznī, Daryā-ye ~ **AFG** 138-139 B 3
Gbabam o **CI** 202-203 H 7
Gbaboua o **CAM** 206-207 B 5
Gbadolite o **ZRE** 206-207 E 6
Gbagba o **RCA** 206-207 E 6
Gbaïzera o **RCA** 206-207 D 5
Gbako, River ~ **WAN** 204-205 G 4
Gbananmè o **DY** 204-205 E 5
Gbanendji o **RCA** 206-207 E 5
Gbanga ☆ **LB** 202-203 F 6
Gbanga o **WAN** 204-205 G 4
Gbangbatok o **WAL** 202-203 D 6
Gbanhala ~ **RG** 202-203 F 5
Gbapleu o **CI** 202-203 F 6
Gbarnga o **WAN** 202-203 F 6
Gbassa o **DY** 204-205 E 3
Gbassigbiri o **RCA** 206-207 H 6
Gbatala o **LB** 202-203 F 6
Gbele Game Production Reserve ⊥ **GH** 202-203 J 4
Gbengué o **BF** 202-203 J 4
Gbentu o **WAL** 202-203 E 5
Gberia Timbako o **WAL** 202-203 E 5
Gbéroubouè o **DY** 204-205 E 3
Gbibo o **LB** 202-203 F 7
Gbodonon o **CI** 202-203 H 5
Gboko o **WAN** 204-205 H 5
Gbongaa o **CI** 202-203 G 5
Gbongan o **WAN** 204-205 F 5
Gbung o **GH** 202-203 K 5
Gbwado o **ZRE** 210-211 H 2
Gdańsk ☆•• **PL** 92-93 P 1
Gdańsk, Gulf of = Gdańska, Zatoka ≈ 92-93 P 1
Gdańska, Zatoka ≈ 92-93 P 1
Gdov ☆ **RUS** 94-95 K 2
Gdyel o **DZ** 188-189 L 3
Gdynia o•• **PL** 92-93 P 1
Geary o **CDN** (NB) 240-241 J 5
Geary o **USA** (OK) 264-265 F 3
Gêba, Canal do ≈ 202-203 B 4
Geba, Rio ~ **GNB** 202-203 C 3
Ğebal Bārez, Kūh-e ▲ **IR** 134-135 G 4
Gebasawa o **WAN** 198-199 D 6
Geba Wenz ~ **ETH** 208-209 B 4
Gebe, Pulau ⌒ **RI** 166-167 E 2
Gebeit o **SUD** 200-201 H 3
Gebeledan o **CI** 202-203 F 5
Gebituolatuo o **VRC** 146-147 L 6
Gebo o **USA** (WY) 252-253 K 3
Gebre Guracha o **ETH** 208-209 D 4
Gebze ☆ **TR** 128-129 C 2
Gech'a o **ETH** 208-209 B 5
Gedabiet o **ETH** 200-201 H 6
Geddes o **USA** (SD) 260-261 H 3
Gedenštroma, zaliv ≈ 110-111 Y 2
Gedi o **EAK** 212-213 H 5
Gedi National Monument • **EAK** 212-213 H 5
Gediz ☆ **TR** 128-129 C 3
Gediz Nehri ~ **TR** 128-129 C 3
Gedlegube o **ETH** 208-209 G 5
Gēdo o **ETH** 208-209 C 4
Gedo □ **SP** 212-213 H 2
Gedongratu o **RI** 162-163 F 7
Gedser o **DK** 86-87 E 9
Geegully Creek ~ **AUS** 172-173 F 5
Geel o **B** 92-93 H 3
Geelong o• **AUS** 180-181 H 5
Geelvink Channel ≈ 176-177 B 4
Geesaley o **SP** 208-209 K 3
Geese Islands ⌒ **USA** 22-23 U 4
Geeveston o **AUS** 180-181 J 7
Gēga Shet' ~ **ETH** 208-209 E 3
Gegbwema o **WAL** 202-203 E 6
Gegentala Caoyuan • **VRC** 148-149 K 7
Gê'gyai o **VRC** 144-145 C 4
Geidam o **WAN** 198-199 E 6
Geifil o **SUD** 200-201 E 6
Geikie Island ⌒ **CDN** (ONT) 234-235 P 4
Geikie River ~ **CDN** 34-35 D 2
Geiki Gorge National Park ⊥ **AUS** 172-173 G 5
Geillini Lake o **CDN** 30-31 W 5
Geillini River ~ **CDN** 30-31 W 5
Geilo o **N** 86-87 D 6
Geirangerfjorden ≈•• 86-87 C 5
Geiser del Tatio o• **RCH** 76-77 C 2
Geita o **EAT** 212-213 D 5
Gejberga, ostrova ⌒ **RUS** 108-109 c 3
Gejiu o **VRC** 156-157 C 5
Geka, mys ▲ **RUS** 112-113 U 4
Gel ~ **SUD** 206-207 J 5
Gela o **I** 100-101 E 6
Geladangong ▲ **VRC** 144-145 H 4
Geladī o **ETH** 208-209 H 5
Gelai ▲ **EAT** 212-213 F 5
Gelam, Pulau ⌒ **RI** 162-163 J 6
Gele o **ZRE** 206-207 D 6
Gelemso o **ETH** 208-209 E 4
Gelendžik o **RUS** 126-127 C 5
Gel Gulbis < **EAK** 212-213 G 2
Gelibolu ☆• **TR** 128-129 B 2
Gelīla o **ETH** 208-209 C 4
Gelinting, Teluk ≈ 166-167 B 6
Gelläb o **SUD** 206-207 G 4
Gellinsor o **SP** 208-209 H 5
Geloketapang o **RI** 162-163 A 3
Gelot' o **RUS** 116-117 L 7
Gelsenkirchen o **D** 92-93 J 3
Gelumbang o **RI** 162-163 F 6
Gemaliel o **USA** (KY) 276-277 K 4
Gemas o **MAL** 162-163 E 3
Gembele, Rapides ~ **ZRE** 210-211 J 2
Gembogl o **PNG** 183 C 3
Gembu o **WAN** 204-205 J 5
Geme o **RI** 164-165 K 1
Gemena o **ZRE** 210-211 G 2
Gemerek ☆ **TR** 128-129 G 3
Gemerī Hāyk' o **ETH** 208-209 E 3
Gemi ▲ **ETH** 208-209 B 4
Gemlik ☆ **TR** 128-129 C 2
Gemlik Körfezi ≈ 128-129 C 2
Gemmeiza o **SUD** 200-201 G 4
Gemmell o **USA** (MN) 270-271 D 3
Gemona del Friuli o **I** 100-101 D 1
Gempol o **RI** 168 E 3
Gemsbok National Park ⊥ **RB** 220-221 E 2
Gemsbokvlakte o **ZA** 220-221 G 2
Genalē Wenz ~ **ETH** 208-209 E 6
Gendarān Bāshī ▲ **IR** 128-129 M 3
Genémasson o **DY** 204-205 E 3
General Acha o **RA** 78-79 G 4
General A. Darnes o **BR** 74-75 E 7
General Alvear o **RA** (BUA) 78-79 J 4
General Alvear o **RA** (MEN) 78-79 F 3
General Arenales o **RA** 78-79 J 3
General Arnulfo R. Gómez o **MEX** 50-51 G 5
General Ballivián o **RA** 76-77 F 2
General Belgrano o **RA** 78-79 K 3
General Bravo o **MEX** 50-51 K 5
General Cabrera o **RA** 78-79 H 2
General Camacho o **BOL** 70-71 C 5
General Carrera, Lago o **RCH** 80 D 3
General Cepeda o **MEX** 50-51 J 5
General Conesa o **RA** (BUA) 78-79 L 4
General Conesa o **RA** (RIN) 78-79 G 6
General Elizardo Aquino o **PY** 76-77 J 3
General Enrique Martinez o **ROU** 74-75 D 9
General Enrique Mosconi o **RA** 76-77 F 2
General Eugenio A. Garay ☆ **PY** 70-71 F 7
General Francisco Murguía o **MEX** 50-51 H 5
General Güemes o **RA** 76-77 E 3
General Ignacio Zaragoza o **MEX** 50-51 K 6
General José de San Martín o **RA** 76-77 H 4
General Juan Madariaga o **RA** 78-79 L 4
General la Madrid o **RA** 78-79 J 4
General Levalle o **RA** 78-79 H 3
General L. Plaza Gutiérrez o **EC** 64-65 C 3
General Luna o **RP** 160-161 G 8
General Luz o **BR** 74-75 E 7
General Mansilla o **RA** 78-79 L 3
General M. Belgrano o **RA** 76-77 H 3
General Mosconi o **RA** 76-77 F 2
General Obligado o **RA** 76-77 H 4
General Pico o **RA** 78-79 H 3
General Pinedo o **RA** 76-77 G 4
General Roca o **RA** 78-79 F 5
General Sampaio o **BR** 68-69 J 4
General San Martin o **RA** 78-79 H 4
General Santos ☆ **RP** 160-161 F 9
General Simón Bolivar o **MEX** 50-51 H 5
General Terán o **MEX** 50-51 K 5
General Tiburcio o **BR** 68-69 H 3
General Toševo o **BG** 102-103 F 6
General Treviño o **MEX** 50-51 K 4
General Trías o **MEX** 50-51 F 3
General Villegas o **RA** 78-79 H 3
General Vintter, Lago o **RA** 78-79 D 7
Genesee o **CDN** (ALB) 232-233 D 2
Geneseo o **USA** (IL) 274-275 H 3
Geneseo o **USA** (KS) 262-263 H 6
Geneseo o **USA** (NY) 278-279 D 6
Genet o **ETH** 208-209 D 4
Geneva o **USA** (AL) 284-285 E 5
Geneva o **USA** (GA) 284-285 F 4
Geneva o **USA** (ID) 252-253 G 4
Geneva o **USA** (NE) 262-263 J 4
Geneva o **USA** (NY) 278-279 E 6
Geneva o **USA** (OH) 280-281 F 2
Geneva = Genève ☆• **CH** 92-93 J 5
Geneva, Lake = Léman, Lac o **CH** 92-93 J 5
Genève ☆• **CH** 92-93 J 5
Gengma o **VRC** 142-143 L 4
Gengwa o **ZRE** 210-211 J 5
Genil, Río ~ **E** 98-99 E 6
Genk o **B** 92-93 H 3
Genkai-nada ≈ 152-153 D 8
Genkanyj, hrebet ▲ **RUS** 112-113 Y 3
Gennargentu, Monti del ▲ **I** 100-101 B 4
Genoa o **AUS** 180-181 K 4
Genoa o **USA** (CO) 254-255 M 4
Genoa o **USA** (NE) 262-263 J 3
Genoa o **USA** (NV) 246-247 F 4
Genoa o **USA** (WI) 270-271 G 7
Genoa = Genova ☆•• **I** 100-101 B 2
Genoa City o **USA** (WI) 274-275 K 2
Genova ☆•• **I** 100-101 B 2
Genova, Golfo di ≈ 100-101 B 2
Genovesa, Isla ⌒ **EC** 64-65 C 9
Gens-de-Terre, Rivière ~ **CDN** 236-237 M 5
Gent ☆•• **B** 92-93 G 3
Genteng o **RI** 168 B 3
Genteng, Pulau ⌒ **RI** 168 E 3
Genteng, Ujung ▲ **RI** 168 B 3
Genteng Game Park ⊥ **RI** 168 B 3
Genting o **RI** 162-163 C 3
Gentios, Isla dos ⌒ **BR** 70-71 E 3
Gentryville o **USA** (MO) 276-277 C 4
Genyem o **RI** 166-167 L 3
Geographe Bay ≈ 176-177 C 6
Geographe Channel ≈ 176-177 B 2
Geographical Center of Conterminous United States • **USA** (KS) 262-263 H 5
Geographical Center of North American Continent ∴ **USA** (ND) 258-259 H 3
Geographical Center of the United States ∴ **USA** (SD) 260-261 C 1
Geographical Society Ø ⌒ **GRØ** 26-27 o 7
Geok-Tepe o **TM** 136-137 E 5
Geologičeskaja, grjada ▲ **RUS** 108-109 Z 4
Geologičeskij o **RUS** 112-113 V 3
Georga, Zemlja ⌒ **RUS** 84-85 a 2
George o **USA** (IA) 274-275 C 1
George o **USA** (WA) 244-245 F 3
George o **ZA** 220-221 F 6
George, Cape ▲ **CDN** (BC) 228-229 D 3
George, Cape ▲ **CDN** (NS) 240-241 N 5
George, Lake o **AUS** (NSW) 180-181 K 3
George, Lake o **AUS** (SA) 180-181 E 4
George, Lake o **AUS** (WA) 172-173 F 7
George, Lake o **EAU** 212-213 C 3
George, Lake o **USA** (FL) 286-287 H 2
George, Lake o **USA** (NY) 278-279 H 5
George, Mount ▲ **AUS** 172-173 D 7
George, Mount ▲ **CDN** 24-25 S 6
George, Rivière ~ **CDN** 36-37 R 6
George Gill Range ▲ **AUS** 176-177 L 2
George Island ⌒ **CDN** 36-37 V 7
George Island ⌒ **GB** 78-79 L 7
George National Historic Park, Fort • **CDN** (ONT) 238-239 F 5
George Reservoir, Walter F. < **USA** (AL) 284-285 E 5
George Richards, Cape ▲ **CDN** 24-25 R 2
George River ~ **USA** 20-21 M 5
George R. Parks Highway II **USA** 20-21 P 5
Georges Bank ≃ 278-279 O 7
George Sound ≈ 182 A 6
Georges Tavern o **USA** (VA) 280-281 H 6
Georgetown o **AUS** 174-175 G 6
George Town o **AUS** 180-181 J 6
George Town o• **BS** 54-55 H 3
Georgetown o **CDN** (NS) 240-241 N 4
Georgetown o **CDN** (ONT) 238-239 F 5
Georgetown o **GB** 202-203 B 7
Georgetown ☆ **GB** 54-55 E 5
Georgetown ★ **GUY** 62-63 E 2
George Town ☆•• **MAL** 162-163 D 2
Georgetown o **USA** (CA) 246-247 E 5
Georgetown o **USA** (DE) 280-281 L 5
Georgetown o **USA** (GA) 284-285 E 5
Georgetown o **USA** (KY) 276-277 L 2
Georgetown o **USA** (MS) 268-269 K 5
Georgetown o **USA** (OH) 280-281 C 5
Georgetown o **USA** (TX) 266-267 K 3
Georgetown o• **USA** (SC) 284-285 L 3
Georgetown ☆• **WAG** 202-203 C 3
Georgetown o **WV** 56 E 5
Georgetown, Lake < **USA** (TX) 266-267 K 3
Georgeville o **CDN** (QUE) 238-239 N 3
George Washington Carver National Monument ∴ **USA** (MO) 276-277 A 3
George West o **USA** (TX) 266-267 J 5
Georgia □ **USA** 284-285 F 4
Georgia = Gruzija ■ **GE** 126-127 E 7
Georgia, Strait of ≈ 230-231 E 4
Georgia Basin ≃ 6-7 F 14
Georgiana o **USA** (AL) 284-285 D 5
Georgian Bay o **CDN** (ONT) 238-239 D 3
Georgian Bay Island National Park ⊥ **CDN** (ONT) 238-239 F 4
Georgievka o **KZ** 124-125 M 4
Georgievka o **KZ** 146-147 B 4
Georgievsk o **RUS** 126-127 E 5
Georgina Downs o **AUS** 178-179 D 1
Georgina River ~ **AUS** 178-179 E 2
Georgiu-Dež = Liski o **RUS** 102-103 L 2
Georg von Neumayer o **ARK** 16 F 36
Gera o• **D** 92-93 M 3
Gerace o **I** 100-101 F 5
Gerachiné o **PA** 52-53 E 7
Geráki o **GR** 100-101 J 6
Geral, Serra ▲ **BR** 72-73 K 2
Geral, Serra ▲ **BR** 74-75 E 5
Gerald o **CDN** (SAS) 232-233 R 5
Geral'd, ostrov ⌒ **RUS** 112-113 X 1
Geral de Goiás, Serra ▲ **BR** 72-73 G 2
Geraldine o **NZ** 182 C 6
Geraldine o **USA** (MT) 250-251 J 4
Geraldo, Furo do ~ **BR** 66-67 F 5
Geral do Paranã ou do Veadeiros, Serra ▲ **BR** 72-73 G 3
Geraldton o **AUS** 176-177 C 4
Geraldton o **CDN** (ONT) 236-237 B 3
Geralton o **CDN** (ONT) 236-237 B 3
Geralton East o **CDN** (ONT) 236-237 B 3
Geralzinho o **BR** 72-73 K 3
Gerampi o **RI** 168 D 7
Geranium o **AUS** 180-181 F 3
Gerāš o **IR** 134-135 F 5
Geraumele ∴• **RN** 198-199 F 5
Gèrbiči, gora ▲ **RUS** 116-117 M 2
Gerdau o **ZA** 220-221 H 3
Gerdine, Mount ▲ **USA** 20-21 O 6
Gerede ☆ **TR** 128-129 E 2
Gerede Çayı ~ **TR** 128-129 E 2
Gërel'de o **UZ** 136-137 H 4
Gerešk o **AFG** 134-135 L 3
Gerger ☆ **TR** 128-129 H 3
Gerihun o **WAL** 202-203 E 6
Gerik o• **MAL** 162-163 D 2
Gering o **USA** (NE) 262-263 C 3
Gerlach o **USA** (NV) 246-247 F 3
Germakolo o **RI** 166-167 G 2
German Busch, Reserva Natural ⊥ **BOL** 70-71 F 5
German Creek o **AUS** 178-179 K 2
Germania o **RA** 78-79 H 3
Germania Land ∸ **GRØ** 26-27 p 5
Germansen Landing o **CDN** 32-33 H 4
Germantown o **USA** (TN) 276-277 F 5
Germany = Deutschland ■ **D** 92-93 J 4
Germencik ☆ **TR** 128-129 B 4
Ğermī o **IR** 128-129 N 3
Germiston o **ZA** 220-221 J 3
Gernika-Lumo o **E** 98-99 F 3
Gero o **J** 152-153 G 7
Geroliménas o **GR** 100-101 J 6
Gerona o **RP** 160-161 D 5
Gerona = Girona o **E** 98-99 J 4
Gerrard o **CDN** (BC) 230-231 M 3
Gers ~ **F** 90-91 H 10
Ğerūf o **JOR** 130-131 D 2
Gerung o **RI** 168 C 7
Gerze ☆ **TR** 128-129 F 2
Gêrzê o **VRC** 144-145 E 4
Gesa ~ **RI** 166-167 J 3
Gestro, Wabē ~ **ETH** 208-209 E 5
Getafe o **E** 98-99 F 4
Geti o **ZRE** 212-213 C 3
Getkan ~ **RUS** 118-119 L 8
Gètljangèn, laguna ≈ 112-113 Y 4
Gettysburg o **USA** (PA) 280-281 J 4
Gettysburg o **USA** (SD) 260-261 G 1
Gettysburg National Military Park • **USA** (PA) 280-281 J 4
Getúlio Vargas o **BR** 74-75 D 6
Getz Ice Shelf ⊂ **ARK** 16 F 24
Gevaş ☆ **TR** 128-129 K 3
Gevgelija o **MK** 100-101 J 4
Gevrai o **IND** 138-139 E 10
Gewanē o **ETH** 208-209 E 3
Geychay = Göyçay o **AZ** 128-129 M 2
Geyik Dağları ▲ **TR** 128-129 D 4
Geylegphug o **BHT** 142-143 G 2
Geyser o **USA** (MT) 250-251 J 4
Geyser, Banc du ⌒ **RM** 222-223 E 4
Geyserville o **USA** (CA) 246-247 C 5
Geyve ☆ **TR** 128-129 D 2
Gezāb o **AFG** 134-135 M 2
Gezhou Ba • **VRC** 154-155 G 6
Ghābat al-'Arab o **SUD** 206-207 J 4
Ghadāmis □ **LAR** 190-191 H 5
Ghadāmis ☆••• **LAR** (GHD) 190-191 G 5
Ghaddūwah o **LAR** 192-193 F 4
Ghaghara ~ **IND** 142-143 C 2
Ghaghe Island ⌒ **SOL** 184 I d 2
Ghāghra o **IND** 142-143 D 4
Ghaibi Dero o **PK** 134-135 M 5
Ghairatganj o **IND** 138-139 G 8
Ghalla, Wādī al- ~ **SUD** 206-207 J 3
Ghallamane ∸ **RIM** 196-197 E 3
Ghallamane, Sebkhet o **RIM** 196-197 F 3
Ghana ■ **GH** 204-205 B 5
Ghangmi o **RI** 166-167 K 4
Ghanzi □ **RB** 216-217 F 11
Ghanzi ☆ **RB** (GHA) 216-217 F 10
Ghanzi Farms ∸ **RB** 216-217 F 10
Ghaoua, Goûr ▲ **DZ** 190-191 D 9
Gharārah, Bi'r al o **LAR** 192-193 J 2
Gharb Binna o **SUD** 200-201 E 3
Gharbi, Chott el o **DZ** 188-189 L 4
Gharbi, Zahrez o **DZ** 190-191 D 3
Ghardaïa ☆• **DZ** 190-191 D 4
Ghardimaou o **TN** 190-191 G 2
Gharig o **SUD** 206-207 H 3
Ghāro o **PK** 134-135 M 6
Gharyān □ **LAR** 192-193 E 3
Gharyān ☆ **LAR** (Ghr) 192-193 E 1
Ghāt o **LAR** 190-191 H 8
Ghātāl o **IND** 142-143 E 4
Ghātampur o **IND** 142-143 B 2
Ghātsila o **IND** 142-143 E 4
Ghauspur o **PK** 138-139 B 5
Ghawdex = Gozo ⌒ **M** 100-101 E 6
Ghazāl, Bahr al- ~ **SUD** 206-207 J 4
Ghazāl, Bahr el ~ **TCH** 198-199 H 5
Ghazaouet o **DZ** 188-189 L 3
Ghaziābād o **IND** 138-139 F 5
Ghāzipur o **IND** 142-143 C 3
Ghazluna o **PK** 134-135 M 3
Gheorghe Gheorghiu-Dej = Oneşti o **RO** 102-103 E 4
Gheorgheni o **RO** 102-103 D 4
Gherdi o **IND** 140-141 F 2
Gherla o **RO** 102-103 C 4
Ghilarza o **I** 100-101 B 4
Ghimpaţi o **RO** 102-103 D 5
Ghio, Lago o **RA** 80 E 3
Ghizar o **IND** (JAK) 138-139 D 1
Ghizar ~ **IND** 138-139 D 1
Gho Dôn o **VN** 156-157 D 5
Ghogha o **IND** 138-139 D 9
Ghomera o **SUD** 200-201 E 5
Ghomode, Al o **LAR** 192-193 D 5
Ghomrassen o **TN** 190-191 H 4
Ghorahi o **NEP** 144-145 D 6
Ghosla o **IND** 138-139 E 8
Ghost Lake o **CDN** (ALB) 232-233 D 4
Ghost Lake o **CDN** 30-31 M 4
Ghost River o **CDN** (ONT) 234-235 M 4
Ghost River Wilderness ⊥ **CDN** (ALB) 232-233 C 4
Ghost Town • **USA** (ID) 252-253 C 3
Ghot o **IND** 142-143 B 6
Ghotanu o **IND** 138-139 C 6
Ghotki o• **PK** 138-139 B 6
Ghoveo o **SOL** 184 I d 3
Ghrayfah, Al o **LAR** 192-193 E 4
Ghriss o **DZ** 190-191 C 3
Ghuar o **IND** 138-139 B 8
Ghubaysh o **SUD** 200-201 C 6
Ghutkel o **IND** 142-143 B 5
Ghwarriepoort ▲ **ZA** 220-221 F 6
Giai Tru'o'ng So'n ▲ **VN** 156-157 D 7
Gialalassi o **SP** 212-213 K 2
Giàng o **VN** 158-159 J 3
Giang Trung ▲ **VN** 158-159 K 4
Giannitsá o **GR** 100-101 J 4
Giant Forest o **USA** (CA) 248-249 F 3
Giants Castle ▲•• **ZA** 220-221 J 4
Giants Castle Game Reserve ⊥ **ZA** 220-221 J 4
Giant's Causeway ••• **GB** 90-91 D 4
Giants Tomb Island ⌒ **CDN** (ONT) 238-239 E 4
Giant Yellowknife Mine • **CDN** 30-31 M 4
Gianyar o **RI** 168 B 7
Giá Rai o **VN** 158-159 H 6
Giarre o **I** 100-101 E 6
Gia Vu'c o **VN** 158-159 K 3
Giba o **I** 100-101 B 5
Gibara o **C** 54-55 G 4
Gibbon o **USA** (NE) 262-263 H 4
Gibbon o **USA** (OR) 244-245 G 5
Gibbons o **CDN** (ALB) 232-233 E 2
Gibbonsville o **USA** (ID) 250-251 F 6
Gibb River o **AUS** (WA) 172-173 H 4
Gibb River ~ **AUS** 172-173 H 3
Gibbs o **CDN** (SAS) 232-233 O 5
Gibbs City o **USA** (MI) 270-271 K 4
Gibeon o **NAM** 220-221 C 2
Gibeon Station o **NAM** 220-221 C 2
Gībe Shet' ~ **ETH** 208-209 C 5
Gībē Wenz ~ **ETH** 208-209 C 4
Ğibla, Ḏū o• **Y** 132-133 D 7
Gibraltar o **CDN** (NS) 240-241 M 6
Gibraltar o **GBZ** 98-99 E 6
Gibraltar, Estrecho de ≈ 188-189 J 3
Gibraltar Range National Park ⊥ **AUS** 178-179 M 5
Gibsland o **USA** (LA) 268-269 G 4
Gibson o **USA** (LA) 268-269 K 7
Gibson City o **USA** (IL) 274-275 K 4
Gibson Desert ∸ **AUS** 172-173 G 7
Gibson Desert Nature Reserve ⊥ **AUS** 176-177 H 2
Gibson Island o **USA** (MD) 280-281 K 4
Gibson Lake o **CDN** 30-31 X 4
Gibsons o **CDN** (BC) 230-231 F 4
Gibsonville o **USA** (NC) 282-283 H 4
Gida o **WAN** 204-205 J 5
Gīdalo o **ETH** 208-209 B 4
Gīdam o **IND** 142-143 B 6
Gīdamī o **ETH** 208-209 B 4
Gīdar o **PK** 134-135 M 4
Gīdar Dhor ~ **PK** 134-135 M 4
Ğidda o• **KSA** 132-133 A 3
Giddalur o **IND** 140-141 H 3
Ğiddat al-Ḥarāsis ∸ **OM** 132-133 K 4
Giddings o **USA** (TX) 266-267 L 3
Gideån ~ **S** 86-87 J 5
Gidgealpa Gas Field • **AUS** 178-179 F 4
Gidgee o **AUS** 176-177 E 3
Gidgi, Lake o **AUS** 176-177 H 4
Gīdolē o **ETH** 208-209 C 6
Gielnaga del Coro o **RA** 76-77 E 6
Gien o **F** 90-91 J 8
Gieseckes Isfjord ≈ 26-27 X 7
Gießen o **D** 92-93 K 3
Gifford o **USA** (FL) 286-287 J 4
Gifford o **USA** (WA) 244-245 G 2
Gifford Creek o **AUS** 176-177 D 2
Gifford Fiord ≈ 24-25 f 5
Gifford River ~ **CDN** 24-25 f 5
Ğifğāfa, Bi'r < **ET** 194-195 F 2
Gift Lake o **CDN** 32-33 N 4
Giftūn al-Kabīr, Ğazīrat ⌒ **ET** 194-195 F 4
Gifu ☆ **J** 152-153 G 7
Gigant o **RUS** 102-103 M 4
Giganta, Cerro ▲ **MEX** 50-51 D 4
Giganta, Sierra de la ▲ **MEX** 50-51 D 4
Gigante o **CO** 60-61 D 6
Gig Harbor o **USA** (WA) 244-245 C 3
Gigi, Danau o **RI** 166-167 G 2
Giglio, Ísola del ⌒ **I** 100-101 C 3
Gigüela, Río ~ **E** 98-99 F 5
Ğiḥāna o **Y** 132-133 D 6
Gihofi o **BU** 212-213 C 5
Giir Forest National Park ⊥ **IND** 138-139 C 9
Gijón = Xixón o• **E** 98-99 E 3
Gikongoro o **RWA** 212-213 B 5
Gila o **USA** (NM) 256-257 G 6
Gila, Tanjung ▲ **RI** 164-165 L 3
Gila Bend o **USA** (AZ) 256-257 C 6
Gila Cliff Dwellings National Monument • **USA** (NM) 256-257 G 5
Gila Mountains ▲ **USA** 256-257 E 5
Gilān o **AFG** 134-135 M 2
Ğīlān o **IR** 136-137 D 6
Gīlān □ **IR** 128-129 N 3
Gīlan-e Garb o **IR** 134-135 A 1
Gila River ~ **USA** 256-257 G 6
Gila River ~ **USA** 256-257 D 5
Gila River Indian Reservation X **USA** (AZ) 256-257 C 5
Gilbert o **USA** (MN) 270-271 F 3
Gilbert, Islas ⌒ **RCH** 80 E 7
Gilbert, Mount ▲ **CDN** (BC) 230-231 E 3
Gilbert Islands ⌒ **KIB** 13 J 2
Gilberton o **AUS** 174-175 G 6
Gilbert Plains o **CDN** (MAN) 234-235 C 3
Gilbert River o **AUS** (QLD) 174-175 G 6
Gilbert River ~ **AUS** 174-175 F 5
Gilbert River ~ **CDN** (NFL) 38-39 Q 2
Gilberts Dome ▲ **AUS** 178-179 J 2
Gilbués o **BR** 68-69 F 6
Gilby o **USA** (ND) 258-259 K 3
Gildford o **USA** (MT) 250-251 J 3
Gilé o **MOC** 218-219 K 3
Giles, Lake o **AUS** 176-177 E 4
Giles Meteorological Station o **AUS** 176-177 K 2
Ğilf al-Kabīr, Haḍbat al- ▲ **ET** 192-193 L 6
Gilford Island ⌒ **CDN** (BC) 230-231 C 3
Gilgandra o **AUS** 178-179 K 6
Gilgil o **EAK** 212-213 F 4
Gil Gil Creek ~ **AUS** 178-179 K 5
Gilgit o **IND** (JAK) 138-139 E 2
Gilgit ~ **IND** 138-139 E 2
Gilgit Mountains ▲ **IND** 138-139 D 1
Gilgunnia o **AUS** 180-181 J 2
Gilgunnia Range ▲ **AUS** 180-181 H 2
Gili, Reserva do ⊥ **MOC** 218-219 K 3
Gilimanuk o **RI** 168 B 7
Gil Island ⌒ **CDN** (BC) 228-229 E 3
Giljuj ~ **RUS** 118-119 N 8
Gillam o **AUS** 172-173 D 6
Gillam o **CDN** 34-35 J 2
Gillams o **CDN** (NFL) 242-243 K 3
Gilleleje o **DK** 86-87 F 8
Gillen, Lake o **AUS** 176-177 H 3
Gilles, Lake o **AUS** 180-181 D 2
Gillespie o **USA** (IL) 274-275 J 5

330 Garladinne — Gillespie

Gornozavodsk ○ **RUS** (SHL) 122-123 J 5
Gornozavodsk ☆ **RUS** (PRM) 96-97 L 4
Gornyj ○ **RUS** (HBR) 122-123 G 3
Gornyj ○ **RUS** (NVS) 114-115 R 7
Gornyj ☆ **RUS** (SAR) 96-97 F 8
Gornyj Altaj, Respublika □ **RUS** 124-125 P 3
Goro ○ **ETH** 208-209 E 5
Goroch'an ▲ **ETH** 208-209 C 4
Gorodec ○ **RUS** 94-95 S 3
Gorodeck ○ **RUS** 88-89 S 5
Gorodišče ○ **RUS** 96-97 D 7
Gorodok, Lesnoj ○ **RUS** 118-119 F 10
Gorodovikovsk ○ **RUS** 102-103 M 4
Gorogoro ○ **RI** 164-165 K 4
Goroh, Tanjung ▲ **RI** 162-163 F 5
Gorohovec ○ **RUS** 94-95 S 3
Goroka ☆ • **PNG** 183 C 4
Goroke ○ **AUS** 180-181 F 4
Gorom-Gorom ○ **BF** 202-203 K 2
Gorong, Kepulauan ⌒ **RI** 166-167 F 4
Gorong, Pulau ⌒ **RI** 166-167 F 3
Gorongosa ○ **MOC** (Sof) 218-219 H 4
Gorongosa ▲ **MOC** (Sof) 218-219 H 4
Gorongosa, Parque Nacional de ⊥ **MOC** 218-219 H 4
Gorongosa, Rio ~ **MOC** 218-219 H 5
Gorontalo ○ **RI** 164-165 H 3
Gorontalo, Teluk ≈ 164-165 H 3
Goronyo ○ **WAN** 198-199 B 6
Gororos ○ **BR** 72-73 J 5
Goroubi ~ **RN** 202-203 L 3
Gorouol ~ **BF** 202-203 K 2
Gorrie ○ **AUS** 172-173 L 3
Goršečnoe ○ **RUS** 102-103 L 2
Gort = An Gort ○ **IRL** 90-91 C 5
Ġōryān ○ **AFG** 134-135 J 1
Gorzów Wielkopolski ☆ • **PL** 92-93 N 2
Goschen Strait ≈ 183 F 6
Gosford-Woy Woy ○ **AUS** 180-181 L 2
Goshen ○ **USA** (CA) 248-249 E 3
Goshen ○ **USA** (CT) 280-281 N 2
Goshen ○ **USA** (IN) 274-275 N 3
Goshen ○ **USA** (VA) 280-281 G 6
Goshogawara ○ **J** 152-153 J 4
Goshute ○ **USA** (NV) 246-247 L 4
Goshute Indian Reservation ✕ **USA** (NV) 246-247 L 4
Goslar ○ ··· **D** 92-93 L 3
Gospić ○ **HR** 100-101 E 2
Gosport ○ **USA** (IN) 274-275 M 5
Gossas ○ **SN** 202-203 B 2
Gosses ○ **AUS** 178-179 C 6
Gossi ○ **RMM** 202-203 K 2
Gossinga ○ **SUD** 206-207 G 4
Gostivar ○ • **MK** 100-101 H 4
Gostynin ○ **PL** 92-93 P 2
Goszapovednik ○ **KZ** 126-127 N 5
Gota ○ • **ETH** 208-209 E 4
Göta älv ~ **S** 86-87 F 8
Götaland ∸ **S** 86-87 F 8
Gotebo ○ **USA** (OK) 264-265 F 3
Göteborg ☆ ·· **S** 86-87 E 8
Gotel Mountains ⛰ **WAN** 204-205 J 5
Gotenba ○ **J** 152-153 H 7
Gotera = San Francisco ☆ **ES** 52-53 K 5
Gotha ○ • **D** 92-93 L 3
Goth Ahmad ○ **PK** 134-135 M 6
Gothenburg ○ **USA** (NE) 262-263 F 4
Gothèye ○ **RN** 202-203 L 3
Goth Kunda Baklish ○ **PK** 134-135 M 6
Gotland ⌒ ·· **S** 86-87 J 8
Gotō-rettō ⌒ **J** 152-153 C 8
Gotska Sandön ⌒ • **S** 86-87 J 7
Gotska Sandön Nationalpark ⊥ **S** 86-87 J 7
Göttingen ○ • **D** 92-93 K 3
Gottwaldov = Zlín ○ **CZ** 92-93 O 4
Gotvaľd = Zimijiv ○ **UA** 102-103 K 3
Gouandé ○ **DY** 202-203 L 4
Gouatchi ○ **RCA** 206-207 E 6
Gouaya ~ **BF** 202-203 K 3
Goubangzi ○ **VRC** 150-151 C 7
Goubi ○ **RT** 202-203 L 5
Goubouna ▲ **DY** 202-203 L 5
Gouburn River ~ **AUS** 180-181 L 2
Gouchi ○ **RN** 198-199 D 6
Gouda ○ • **NL** 92-93 H 2
Gouda ○ **ZA** 220-221 D 6
Goudar, Rūd-e ~ **IR** 134-135 F 5
Goudiri ○ **SN** 202-203 D 2
Goudoumaria ○ **RN** 198-199 E 6
Goûfi, Djebel el ▲ **DZ** 190-191 F 2
Gouga ○ **RCA** 210-211 G 2
Gough Fracture Zone ≃ 6-7 H 13
Gough Lake ⬭ **CDN** (ALB) 232-233 F 3
Gouin, Réservoir ⊥ **CDN** (QUE) 236-237 O 4
Gouin, Réservoir ⬭ **CDN** (QUE) 236-237 O 4
Gouina, Chutes de ~ • **RMM** 202-203 E 2
Gouiret Moussa ○ **DZ** 190-191 D 5
Gouka ○ **DY** 202-203 L 5
Ğoukār ○ **IR** 134-135 C 1
Goulahonfla ○ **CI** 202-203 G 6
Goulais River ~ **CDN** 236-237 D 6
Goulburn ○ **AUS** 180-181 K 3
Goulburn Island, North ⌒ **AUS** 174-175 B 2
Goulburn Island, South ⌒ **AUS** 174-175 B 2
Goulburn River ~ **AUS** 180-181 H 4
Goulburn River National Park ⊥ **AUS** 180-181 K 2
Gould ○ **USA** (AR) 276-277 D 7
Gould ○ **USA** (OK) 264-265 E 4
Gould, Mount ▲ **AUS** 176-177 D 2
Gould Bay ≈ 16 F 32
Gouldings Trading Post ○ **USA** (UT) 254-255 E 6
Gouldsboro ○ **USA** (ME) 278-279 N 4
Goulfey ○ **CAM** 198-199 G 6
Goulia ○ **CI** 202-203 G 4
Goulimine ☆ **MA** 188-189 F 6
Goulmima ○ **MA** 188-189 J 5
Goulou D. • **VRC** 156-157 G 5
Goumal Kalai ○ **AFG** 138-139 B 3
Goumal Rūd ~ **AFG** 138-139 B 3
Goumbatou ○ **TCH** 206-207 F 3
Goumbi ▲ **G** 210-211 C 4
Goumbi ○ **RN** 198-199 B 6
Goumbou ○ **RMM** 202-203 G 2
Gouméré ○ **CI** 202-203 J 6
Gouna ○ **CAM** 204-205 K 4
Gounatolo ○ **SOL** 184 I e 3
Gounda ○ **RCA** (Bam) 206-207 E 4
Gounda ~ **RCA** 206-207 E 4
Goundam ○ **RMM** 196-197 J 6
Goundi ○ **TCH** 206-207 C 4
Gounou-Gaya ○ **TCH** 206-207 B 4
Ğoupār ○ **IR** 134-135 G 3
Goúra ○ **GR** 100-101 J 6
Goura, Mount ▲ **WAN** 204-205 H 3
Ġouraid Ġaramī ○ **AFG** 136-137 M 6
Ġourak ○ **AFG** 134-135 L 2
Gourara ∸ **DZ** 190-191 C 6
Gouraya ○ **DZ** 190-191 C 2
Gourcy ○ **BF** 202-203 J 3
Gourdon ○ **F** 90-91 H 9
Gourdon, Cape ▲ **PNG** 183 C 3
Gouré ○ **RN** 198-199 E 6
Gourey ○ **RIM** 202-203 D 2
Gourie ○ • **JA** 54-55 G 5
Gourits ~ **ZA** 220-221 E 6
Gouritsmond ○ **ZA** 220-221 E 7
Gourjhamar ○ **IND** 138-139 G 8
Gourlay Lake ⬭ **CDN** (ONT) 236-237 D 4
Gourma ∸ **BF** 202-203 L 4
Gourma-Rharous ○ **RMM** 196-197 K 6
Gourmeur ○ **TCH** 198-199 K 4
Gouro ○ **TCH** 198-199 J 3
Gourou, Djebel ▲ **DZ** 190-191 D 3
Gourrama ○ **MA** 188-189 J 4
Gouvêa ○ **BR** 72-73 J 5
Gouverneur ○ **USA** (NY) 278-279 F 4
Ğouzam ○ **IR** 134-135 F 3
Gouzé ○ **RCA** 206-207 C 5
Ğouzğān □ **AFG** 136-137 J 6
Gouzon ○ **F** 90-91 J 8
Gov' ∸ **MAU** 148-149 F 6
Gov'-Altaj □ **MAU** 146-147 M 3
Gov' Altajn nuruu ⛰ **MAU** 148-149 D 5
Govan ○ **CDN** (SAS) 232-233 O 4
Gove ○ **USA** (KS) 262-263 F 6
Govena, mys ▲ **RUS** 112-113 O 7
Govena, poluostrov ⌣ **RUS** 112-113 O 7
Govenlock ○ **CDN** (SAS) 232-233 J 6
Gove Peninsula ⌣ **AUS** 174-175 D 3
Governador Eugênio ○ **BR** 68-69 F 4
Governador Valadares ○ **BR** 72-73 K 5
Governor Generoso ○ **RP** 160-161 G 9
Governor's Camp ○ **EAK** 212-213 E 4
Governor's Harbour ○ • **BS** 54-55 G 2
Govind Ballabh Pant Sāgar < **IND** 142-143 C 3
Gowanda ○ **USA** (NY) 278-279 C 6
Gowan Range ⛰ **AUS** 178-179 H 3
Gowan River ~ **CDN** 34-35 J 3
Gower ○ **USA** (MO) 274-275 D 5
Gowers Corners ○ **USA** (FL) 286-287 G 3
Gowganda ○ **CDN** (ONT) 236-237 H 5
Gowrie ○ **USA** (IA) 274-275 D 2
Goya ○ **RA** 76-77 H 5
Goyder Creek ~ **AUS** 178-179 C 3
Goyder River ~ **AUS** 174-175 C 3
Goyders Lagoon ⬭ **AUS** 178-179 E 4
Goyelle, Lac ⬭ **CDN** (QUE) 242-243 H 2
Goyllarisquizga ○ **PE** 64-65 D 7
Goyo Kyauwo, River ~ **WAN** 204-205 K 3
Goyoum ○ **CAM** 204-205 K 6
Goẓare ○ **AFG** 134-135 K 1
Goz-Beida ○ **TCH** 198-199 K 6
Gozha Co ⬭ **VRC** 144-145 C 3
Gozo ⌒ **M** 100-101 E 6
Gozobangui, Chutes de ~ **ZRE** 206-207 F 6
Graaff-Reinet ○ • **ZA** 220-221 G 6
Graafwater ○ **ZA** 220-221 D 6
Grabo ○ **CI** 202-203 G 7
Grabo, Collines de ⛰ **CI** 202-203 G 7
Grabouw ○ **ZA** 220-221 D 7
Grace ○ **USA** (ID) 252-253 G 4
Grace (South), Lake ⬭ **AUS** 176-177 E 6
Gracefield ○ **CDN** (QUE) 238-239 J 2
Graceville ○ **USA** (FL) 286-287 D 1
Graceville ○ **USA** (MN) 270-271 B 5
Gračevka ☆ **RUS** 96-97 H 7
Gracho Cardoso ○ **BR** 68-69 K 7
Gracias ☆ **HN** 52-53 K 4
Gracias a Dios, Cabo de ▲ **HN** 54-55 D 7
Gradaús ○ **BR** 68-69 C 5
Gradaús, Serra dos ⛰ **BR** 68-69 C 6
Grado, Embalse de El < **E** 98-99 H 3
Gradsko ○ **MK** 100-101 H 4
Grady ○ **USA** (AR) 276-277 D 6
Grady ○ **USA** (NM) 256-257 M 4
Grady ○ **USA** (OK) 264-265 G 4
Grady Harbour ○ **CDN** 38-39 Q 2
Grady Island ⌒ **CDN** 38-39 Q 2
Grædefjorden ○ **GRØ** 28-29 P 5
Graettinger ○ **USA** (IA) 274-275 D 1
Graford ○ **USA** (TX) 264-265 F 6
Grafton ○ **AUS** 178-179 M 5
Grafton ○ **USA** (IL) 274-275 H 6
Grafton ○ **USA** (ND) 258-259 K 3
Grafton ○ **USA** (NH) 278-279 K 5
Grafton ○ **USA** (WI) 274-275 L 1
Grafton ○ **USA** (WV) 280-281 F 4
Gragnon Lake ⬭ **CDN** 30-31 O 5
Graham ○ **CDN** (ONT) 234-235 N 5
Graham ○ **USA** (AL) 284-285 E 3
Graham ○ **USA** (TX) 264-265 F 5
Graham, Mount ▲ **USA** (AZ) 256-257 F 6
Graham Creek ~ **USA** 244-245 G 3
Grahamdale ○ **CDN** (MAN) 234-235 E 3
Graham Head ▲ **CDN** (NS) 240-241 M 6
Graham Island ⌒ **CDN** (BC) 228-229 B 3
Graham Island ⌒ **CDN** (NWT) 24-25 a 2
Graham Lake ⬭ **CDN** 32-33 N 3
Graham Lake ⬭ **USA** (ME) 278-279 N 4
Graham Moore, Cape ▲ **CDN** 24-25 j 4
Graham Moore Bay ≈ 24-25 V 3
Graham River ~ **CDN** 32-33 J 3
Grahamstad = Grahamstown ○ **ZA** 220-221 H 6
Grahamstown = Grahamstad ○ **ZA** 220-221 H 6
Grahamsville ○ **USA** (NY) 280-281 M 2
Grahovo ☆ **RUS** 96-97 H 5
Gråhs Øer ⌒ **GRØ** 28-29 V 4
Grain Coast ⌣ **LB** 202-203 E 7
Graines, Rivière-aux- ○ **CDN** (QUE) 242-243 C 2
Grainfield ○ **USA** (KS) 262-263 F 5
Grainton ○ **USA** (NE) 262-263 E 4
Grajagan ○ **RI** 168 B 7
Grajagan, Teluk ≈ 168 B 7
Grajaú ○ **BR** 68-69 E 4
Grajaú, Rio ~ **BR** 68-69 F 3
Grajewo ○ **PL** 92-93 R 2
Grajvoron ○ **RUS** 102-103 J 2
Gramado ○ • **BR** 74-75 E 7
Gramilla ○ **RA** 76-77 E 4
Grammos ⛰ **GR** 100-101 H 4
Gramoteino ○ **RUS** 114-115 T 7
Gramphoo ○ **IND** 138-139 F 3
Grampianfjella ▲ **N** 84-85 G 3
Grampian Mountains ⛰ **GB** 90-91 E 3
Grampians, The ⛰ **AUS** 180-181 G 4
Grampians National Park ⊥ **AUS** 180-181 G 4
Gramsh ☆ • **AL** 100-101 H 4
Granaatboskolk ○ **ZA** 220-221 D 5
Granada ○ **CO** (ANT) 60-61 D 4
Granada ○ **CO** (MET) 60-61 E 6
Granada ○ ··· **E** 98-99 F 6
Granada ☆ ·· **NIC** 52-53 B 6
Granada ○ **USA** (CO) 254-255 N 5
Granada ○ **USA** (MN) 270-271 D 7
Granada II, Cerro ▲ **RA** 76-77 D 2
Gran Altiplanicie Central ∸ **RA** 80 E 4
Gran Bahía ∸ • **DOM** 54-55 L 5
Gran Bajo del Gualicho ∸ **RA** 78-79 G 6
Gran Bajo de San Julián ∸ **RA** 80 F 4
Granbury ○ **USA** (TX) 264-265 G 6
Granby ○ **CDN** (QUE) 238-239 N 3
Granby ○ **USA** (CO) 254-255 K 3
Granby ○ **USA** (CT) 280-281 O 2
Granby ○ **USA** (MO) 276-277 A 4
Granby River ~ **CDN** 230-231 L 4
Gran Canaria ⌒ **E** 188-189 D 7
Gran Chaco ∸ **RA** 76-77 F 3
Grand Bahama Island ⌒ **BS** 54-55 F 1
Grand Ballon, le ▲ **F** 90-91 L 8
Grand Bank ○ **CDN** (NFL) 242-243 N 5
Grand-Bassam ○ • **CI** 202-203 J 7
Grand Bay ○ **CDN** (NB) 240-241 J 5
Grand Beach ○ **CDN** (MAN) 234-235 G 4
Grand Bend ○ **CDN** (ONT) 238-239 D 5
Grand-Bérébi ○ **CI** 202-203 G 7
Grand-Bourg ○ **F** 56 E 4
Grand Bruit ○ **CDN** (NFL) 242-243 K 5
Grandby, Lake ⬭ **USA** (CO) 254-255 K 3
Grand Caicos ⌒ **GB** 54-55 K 4
Grand Canal < **IRL** 90-91 D 5
Grand Canyon ○ **USA** (AZ) 256-257 C 2
Grand Canyon ⌣ **USA** 256-257 B 2
Grand Canyon Caverns ∴ **USA** (AZ) 256-257 B 3
Grand Canyon National Park ⊥ ··· **USA** (AZ) 256-257 B 2
Grand Canyon of the Liard ⌣ **CDN** 30-31 G 6
Grand Cayman ⌒ **GB** 54-55 E 5
Grand Cess ○ **LB** 202-203 F 7
Grand-Combe, la ○ **F** 90-91 K 9
Grand Coulee ○ **CDN** (SAS) 232-233 O 5
Grand Coulee ○ **USA** (WA) 244-245 G 3
Grand Coulee Dam < • **USA** (WA) 244-245 G 3
Grand Desert ○ **CDN** (NS) 240-241 M 6
Grande, Arroyo ~ **RA** 78-79 K 4
Grande, Arroyo ~ **ROU** 78-79 L 2
Grande, Cayo ⌒ **C** 54-55 F 4
Grande, Ciénaga ⬭ **CO** 60-61 D 3
Grande, Corredeira ~ **BR** 70-71 K 3
Grande, Ilha ⌒ **BR** 72-73 H 7
Grande, La ○ **USA** (OR) 244-245 G 5
Grande, Lago ⬭ **BR** 66-67 K 4
Grande, Lago ⬭ **RA** 80 G 3
Grande, Monte ▲ **BR** 70-71 J 6
Grande, Playa ∸ • **DOM** 54-55 L 5
Grande, Ponta ▲ **CV** 202-203 B 5
Grande, Punta ▲ **PE** 64-65 D 9
Grande, Punta ▲ **RCH** 76-77 B 3
Grande, Río ~ **BOL** 70-71 E 6
Grande, Rio ~ **BR** 68-69 G 7
Grande, Rio ~ **BR** 72-73 H 2
Grande, Rio ~ **BR** 72-73 F 6
Grande, Río ~ **GCA** 52-53 J 4
Grande, Río ~ **PE** 64-65 E 9
Grande, Río ~ **RA** 76-77 E 2
Grande, Río ~ **RA** 76-77 D 4
Grande, Río ~ **RA** 78-79 E 4
Grande, Río ~ **RA** 80 F 6
Grande, Río ~ **RCH** 76-77 B 6
Grande, Rio ~ **USA** 266-267 G 5
Grande, Río ~ **YV** 60-61 L 3
Grande, Rivière la ~ **CDN** 38-39 E 2
Grande, Salar ⬭ **RCH** 76-77 C 4
Grande, Serra ⛰ **BR** 68-69 H 4
Grande, Serra ⛰ **BR** 68-69 F 6
Grande, Sierra ⛰ **MEX** 50-51 G 3
Grande, Sierra ⛰ **RA** 76-77 E 6
Grande-Anse ○ **CDN** (NB) 240-241 K 3
Grande Anse ○ **WL** 56 E 4
Grande Anse, Plage ∸ • **RH** 54-55 J 5
Grande Cache ○ **CDN** (ALB) 228-229 P 3
Grande Casse, Pointe de la ▲ **F** 90-91 L 9
Grande Cayemite ⌒ **RH** 54-55 J 5
Grande de Gurupa, Ilha ⌒ **BR** 62-63 J 6
Grande de Lipez, Río ~ **BOL** 76-77 D 1
Grande de Manacapuru, Lago ⬭ **BR** 66-67 G 4
Grande de Manati, Rio ~ **USA** 286-287 P 2
Grande de Matagalpa, Río ~ **NIC** 52-53 C 5
Grande de Santiago, Río ~ **MEX** 50-51 G 7
Grande de São Isabel, Ilha ⌒ **BR** 68-69 H 3
Grande de Tarija, Río ~ **RA** 76-77 E 2
Grande do Branquinho, Cachoeira ~ **BR** 66-67 G 4
Grande do Curuai, Lago ⬭ **BR** 66-67 K 4
Grande do Iriri, Cachoeira ~ **BR** 68-69 B 3
Grande-Entrée ○ **CDN** (QUE) 242-243 G 5
Grande Île ⌒ **SY** 222-223 E 2
Grande Kabylie ⛰ **DZ** 190-191 D 2
Grande Miquelon ⌒ **F** 242-243 M 6
Grande o Guapay, Río ~ **BOL** 70-71 E 5
Grande o Guasamayo, Río ~ **RA** 76-77 D 4
Grande Pointe ○ **CDN** (MAN) 234-235 G 5
Grande Prairie ○ **CDN** 32-33 L 4
Grande Quatre, Réservoir de la < **CDN** 36-37 N 7
Grand Erg de Bilma ∸ **RN** 198-199 F 4
Grande Rivière, La = Fort George River ~ **CDN** 38-39 G 2
Grande Rivière de la Baleine ~ **CDN** 36-37 L 7
Grande Ronde River ~ **USA** 244-245 H 5
Grandes, Salinas ⬭ **RA** (CHU) 78-79 H 7
Grandes, Salinas ⬭ **RA** (LAP) 78-79 H 4
Grandes, Salinas ⬭ **RA** (LAP) 78-79 H 5
Grandes Cascades ~ **MA** 188-189 K 3
Grande Sido ~ **TCH** 206-207 D 4
Gran Desierto Del Pinacate, Parque Natural del ⊥ **MEX** 50-51 C 2
Grand Étang ○ **CDN** (NS) 240-241 O 4
Grande-Terre ⌒ **F** 56 E 3
Grande Terre ⌒ **SY** 222-223 E 2
Grande-Vallée ○ **CDN** (QUE) 242-243 C 3
Grand Falls ○ **CDN** (NFL) 242-243 N 4
Grand Falls ○ • **CDN** (NB) 240-241 H 3
Grandfalls ○ **USA** (TX) 266-267 E 2
Grandfather Mountain ▲ **USA** (NC) 282-283 F 4
Grandfield ○ **USA** (OK) 264-265 F 4
Grand Forks ○ **CDN** (BC) 230-231 L 4
Grand Forks ○ **USA** (ND) 258-259 K 4
Grand Gulf Military Park • **USA** (MS) 268-269 J 4
Grand Harbor ○ **USA** (ND) 258-259 J 3
Grand Haven ○ **USA** (MI) 272-273 C 4
Grandin ○ **USA** (ND) 258-259 L 4
Grandin, Lac ⬭ **CDN** 30-31 K 3
Grandioznyj, pik ▲ **RUS** 116-117 G 9
Grand Island ○ **USA** (NE) 262-263 H 4
Grand Island ⌒ **USA** (MI) 270-271 M 4
Grand Isle ○ **USA** (LA) 268-269 L 7
Grand Isle ⊥ **USA** (VT) 278-279 H 4
Grand Junction ○ **USA** (MI) 272-273 C 5
Grand Junction ○ **USA** (TN) 276-277 F 5
Grand Junction ○ • **USA** (CO) 254-255 G 4
Grand Lac Victoria ⬭ **CDN** (QUE) 236-237 L 5
Grand-Lahou ○ **CI** 202-203 H 7
Grand Lake ⬭ **CDN** (NB) 240-241 J 5
Grand Lake ⬭ **CDN** (NFL) 38-39 O 2
Grand Lake ⬭ **CDN** (NFL) 242-243 L 4
Grand Lake ⬭ **USA** (LA) 268-269 H 7
Grand Lake ⬭ **USA** (ME) 278-279 O 3
Grand Lake ⬭ **USA** (OH) 280-281 B 3
Grand Ledge ○ **USA** (MI) 272-273 E 5
Grand le Pierre ○ **CDN** (NFL) 242-243 O 5
Grand Manan Channel ≈ 240-241 H 6
Grand Manan Island ⌒ **CDN** (NB) 240-241 J 6
Grand Marais ○ **CDN** (MAN) 234-235 G 4
Grand Marais ○ **USA** (MI) 270-271 N 4
Grand Marais ○ **USA** (MN) 270-271 H 3
Grand Mécatina, Ile du ⌒ **CDN** (QUE) 242-243 K 2
Grand-Mère ○ **CDN** (QUE) 238-239 N 2
Grand Mesa ⛰ **USA** 254-255 H 4
Grand-Métis ○ **CDN** (QUE) 240-241 G 2
Grandois ○ **CDN** (NFL) 242-243 N 1
Grândola ○ **P** 98-99 C 5
Grandora ○ **CDN** (SAS) 232-233 M 3
Grand-Popo ○ • **DY** 202-203 L 6
Grand Portage ○ **USA** (MN) 270-271 J 3
Grand Portage Indian Reservation ✕ **USA** (MN) 270-271 J 3
Grand Portage National Monument ∴ **USA** (MN) 270-271 J 3
Grand Prairie ○ **USA** (TX) 264-265 G 6
Grand Pré National Historical Park • **CDN** (NS) 240-241 L 5
Grand Quarries Fossils, Le • **USA** (IA) 274-275 F 2
Grand Rapids ~ **CDN** 32-33 O 3
Grand Rapids ○ **USA** (MI) 272-273 D 5
Grand Rapids ○ **USA** (MN) 270-271 E 3
Grand-Remous ○ **CDN** (QUE) 238-239 K 2
Grand River ○ **USA** (IA) 274-275 E 4
Grand River ~ **USA** 260-261 E 1
Grand River ~ **USA** 272-273 E 5
Grand River ~ **USA** 272-273 D 5
Grand River ~ **USA** 272-273 D 4
Grand River ~ **USA** 274-275 E 5
Grand River National Grassland ⊥ **USA** (SD) 260-261 D 1
Grand-Riviere ○ **F** 56 E 4
Grand Rivière Noire ○ **MS** 224 C 7
Grand Ronde ○ **USA** (OR) 244-245 B 5
Grand Saline ○ **USA** (TX) 264-265 J 6
Grand-Santi ○ **F** 62-63 G 3
Grands Jardins, Parc des ⊥ **CDN** (QUE) 240-241 E 3
Grand Teton National Park ⊥ **USA** (WY) 252-253 H 3
Grand Teton Peak ▲ **USA** (WY) 252-253 H 3
Grand Traverse Bay ⬭ **USA** (MI) 272-273 D 2
Grand Turk Island ⌒ **GB** 54-55 K 4
Grand Valley ○ **CDN** (ONT) 238-239 E 5
Grandview ○ **CDN** (MAN) 234-235 C 3
Grand View ○ **USA** (ID) 252-253 B 4
Grandview ○ **USA** (TX) 264-265 G 6
Grandview ○ **USA** (WA) 244-245 F 4
Grandville ○ **USA** (MI) 272-273 D 5
Grand Wash Cliffs ⛰ **USA** 256-257 B 3
Granet, Lac ⬭ **CDN** (QUE) 236-237 L 5
Granet Lake ⬭ **CDN** 24-25 J 6
Grange ○ **USA** (GA) 284-285 H 3
Grange, La ○ **USA** (GA) 284-285 E 3
Grange, La ○ **USA** (KY) 276-277 K 2
Grange, La ○ **USA** (MO) 274-275 G 4
Grange, La ○ **USA** (NC) 282-283 K 5
Grange, La ○ **USA** (TX) 266-267 L 4
Grange Hill ○ **JA** 54-55 F 5
Granger ○ **USA** (TX) 266-267 K 3
Granger ○ **USA** (WA) 244-245 E 4
Granger ○ **USA** (WY) 252-253 J 5
Granger, Lake < **USA** (TX) 266-267 K 3
Grangeville ○ **USA** (ID) 250-251 C 6
Granisle ○ **CDN** (BC) 228-229 H 2
Granite ○ **USA** (OR) 244-245 G 6
Granite Bay ○ **CDN** (BC) 230-231 D 3
Granite City ○ **USA** (IL) 274-275 H 6
Granite Falls ○ **USA** (MN) 270-271 C 6
Granite Island ⌒ **USA** (MI) 270-271 L 4
Granite Lake ⬭ **CDN** (NFL) 242-243 L 4
Granite Mountains ⛰ **USA** 248-249 J 5
Granite Pass ▲ **USA** (WY) 252-253 L 2
Granite Peak ▲ **AUS** 176-177 D 7
Granite Peak ▲ **USA** (MT) 250-251 K 6
Granite Peak ▲ **USA** (NV) 246-247 H 2
Granite Peak ▲ **USA** (UT) 254-255 B 3
Granites Mine, The ∴ • **AUS** 172-173 K 6
Granito ○ **BR** 68-69 J 5
Granja ○ **BR** 68-69 H 3
Granja Macali ○ **BR** 74-75 D 6
Gran Laguna Salada ⬭ **RA** 80 G 2
Gran Muralla • **PE** 64-65 C 6
Gränna ○ • **S** 86-87 G 7
Granollers ○ **E** 98-99 J 4
Gran Pajatén ··· **PE** 64-65 D 5
Gran Pajonal ⛰ **PE** 64-65 E 7
Gran Pampa Pelada ∸ **BOL** 76-77 D 1
Gran Pampa Salada ∸ **BOL** 70-71 D 7
Gran Paradiso ▲ **I** 100-101 A 2
Gran Quivira ○ **USA** (NM) 256-257 J 4
Gran Rio ~ **SME** 62-63 F 4
Gran Sabana, La ∸ **YV** 62-63 D 3
Gran Sasso d'Italia ⛰ **I** 100-101 D 3
Grant ○ **CDN** (ONT) 236-237 B 2
Grant ○ **USA** (CO) 254-255 K 4
Grant ○ **USA** (IA) 274-275 D 3
Grant ○ **USA** (NE) 262-263 E 4
Grant, Lake ⬭ **USA** (OH) 280-281 C 5
Grant, Mount ▲ **USA** (NV) 246-247 H 4
Grant, Mount ▲ **USA** (NV) 246-247 G 5
Granta, mys ▲ **RUS** 84-85 Z 2
Gran Tarajal ○ **E** 188-189 D 6
Grant City ○ **USA** (MO) 274-275 D 4
Grantham ○ **GB** 90-91 G 5
Grant-Kohrs Ranch National Historic Site • **USA** (MT) 250-251 G 5
Grant Lake ⬭ **CDN** 30-31 L 3
Grant Park ○ **USA** (IL) 274-275 L 3
Grant Point ▲ **CDN** 24-25 X 6
Grant River ○ **CDN** (NS) 240-241 P 5
Grants ○ **USA** (NM) 256-257 H 3
Grant's Birthplace, U.S. • **USA** (OH) 280-281 B 5
Grantsburg ○ **USA** (WI) 270-271 F 5
Grants Pass ○ **USA** (OR) 244-245 B 8
Grant Suttie Bay ≈ 24-25 h 6
Grantsville ○ **USA** (MD) 280-281 G 4
Grantsville ○ **USA** (UT) 254-255 C 3
Grantsville ○ **USA** (WV) 280-281 E 5
Granum ○ **CDN** (ALB) 232-233 E 6
Granville ○ **F** 90-91 G 7
Granville ○ **USA** (ND) 258-259 G 3
Granville ○ **USA** (NY) 278-279 H 5
Granville Lake ⬭ **CDN** 34-35 F 2
Grão-Mogol ○ **BR** 72-73 J 4
Grapeland ○ **USA** (TX) 268-269 E 5
Grapenvine ○ **USA** (AR) 276-277 C 6
Grapevine ○ **USA** (CA) 248-249 F 5
Grapevine ○ **USA** (TX) 264-265 G 6
Gras, Lac de ⬭ **CDN** 30-31 O 3
Grasa, Cerro la ▲ **RA** 78-79 D 5
Graskop ○ **ZA** 220-221 K 2
Grasmere ○ **CDN** (BC) 230-231 O 4
Grasmere ○ **USA** (ID) 252-253 C 4
Grass Creek ○ **USA** (WY) 252-253 K 3
Grasse ○ **F** 90-91 L 10
Grasset, Lac ⬭ **CDN** (QUE) 236-237 K 3
Grass Lake ○ **USA** (MI) 272-273 E 5
Grassland ○ **USA** (TX) 264-265 C 5
Grasslands National Park ⊥ **CDN** (SAS) 232-233 L 6
Grassrange ○ **USA** (MT) 250-251 L 4
Grassridgedam < **ZA** 220-221 G 5
Grass Valley ○ **USA** (CA) 246-247 D 4
Grass Valley ○ **USA** (OR) 244-245 E 5
Grassy ○ **AUS** 180-181 H 6
Grassy Butte ○ **USA** (ND) 258-259 D 4
Grassy Island Lake ⬭ **CDN** (ALB) 232-233 H 4
Grassy Lake ○ **CDN** (ALB) 232-233 G 6
Grassy Narrows ○ **CDN** (ONT) 234-235 K 4
Grassy Plains ○ **CDN** (BC) 228-229 J 3
Grates Cove ○ **CDN** (NFL) 242-243 Q 4
Grates Point ▲ **CDN** (NFL) 242-243 Q 4
Gratiot ○ **USA** (OH) 280-281 D 4
Gratis ○ **USA** (OH) 280-281 B 4
Gratwick, Mount ▲ **AUS** 172-173 D 6
Gratz ○ **USA** (KY) 276-277 L 2
Gravata ○ **BR** 68-69 L 6
Gravataí ○ **BR** 74-75 E 7
Gravelbourg ○ **CDN** (SAS) 232-233 M 6
Gravel Hill Lake ⬭ **CDN** 30-31 S 4
Gravelle ○ **CDN** (BC) 228-229 M 4
Gravelly ○ **USA** (AR) 276-277 B 6
Gravelotte ○ **ZA** 218-219 F 6
Gravenhage, 's-= Den Haag ☆ ·· **NL** 92-93 H 2
Gravenhurst ○ **CDN** (ONT) 238-239 F 4
Grave Peak ▲ **USA** (ID) 250-251 E 5
Gravesend ○ **AUS** 178-179 L 5
Graves Strait ≈ 36-37 R 4
Gravette ○ **USA** (AR) 276-277 A 4
Gravures rupestres ··· **DZ** 190-191 G 8
Gray ○ **F** 90-91 K 8
Gray ○ **USA** (AR) 276-277 D 5
Gray ○ **USA** (GA) 284-285 G 3
Gray ○ **USA** (ME) 278-279 L 5
Gray ○ **USA** (OK) 264-265 D 2
Gray ○ **USA** (TX) 264-265 K 6
Gray Creek ○ **CDN** (BC) 230-231 N 4
Gray Lake, De < **USA** (AR) 276-277 B 6
Grayland ○ **USA** (WA) 244-245 A 4
Grayling ○ **USA** (MI) 272-273 E 3
Grayling Fork ~ **USA** 20-21 U 3
Grayling River ~ **CDN** 30-31 G 6
Gray Mountain ○ **USA** (AZ) 256-257 D 3
Grayr-Nagel • **WSA** 196-197 C 2
Grayrocks Reservoir < **USA** (WY) 252-253 O 4
Grays ○ **USA** (SC) 284-285 J 4
Grays Harbor ≈ 244-245 A 4
Grays Lake ⬭ **USA** (ID) 252-253 G 3
Grayson ○ **CDN** (SAS) 232-233 Q 5
Grayson ○ **USA** (KY) 276-277 N 2
Grays River ○ **USA** (WA) 244-245 B 4
Gray Strait ≈ 36-37 R 4
Graysville ○ **CDN** (MAN) 234-235 E 5
Graysville ○ **USA** (IN) 274-275 L 5
Grayville ○ **USA** (IL) 274-275 K 6
Graz ☆ ·· **A** 92-93 N 5
Grease River ~ **CDN** 30-31 Q 6
Greasewood ○ **USA** (AZ) 256-257 F 3
Greasy Lake ⬭ **CDN** 30-31 H 4
Great Alp Falls ∸ **GB** 56 D 3
Great America ∴ • **USA** (IL) 274-275 L 2
Great Artesian Basin ⌣ **AUS** 178-179 F 3
Great Australian Bight ≈ 176-177 J 6
Great Bahama Bank ≃ 54-55 F 2
Great Barasway ○ **CDN** (NFL) 242-243 O 5
Great Barrier Island ⌒ **NZ** 182 E 2
Great Barrier Reef ∸ **AUS** 174-175 G 2
Great Barrier Reef Marine Park ⊥ ··· **AUS** 174-175 H 3
Great Barrington ○ **USA** (MA) 278-279 H 6
Great Basalt Wall National Park ⊥ **AUS** 174-175 H 6
Great Basin ⌣ **USA** 246-247 H 3
Great Basin National Park ⊥ **USA** (NV) 246-247 L 5
Great Bear Lake ⬭ **CDN** 30-31 J 2
Great Bear River ~ **CDN** 30-31 H 3
Great Bear Wilderness Area ⊥ **USA** (MT) 250-251 F 3
Great Beaver Lake ⬭ **CDN** (BC) 228-229 L 2
Great Bend ○ **USA** (KS) 262-263 H 6
Great Bend ○ **USA** (ND) 258-259 L 5
Great Bitter Lake = Murra, al-Buḥaira l- < **ET** 194-195 F 2
Great Britain ∸ **GB** 90-91 G 3
Great Central ○ **CDN** (BC) 230-231 E 4
Great Coco Island ⌒ **MYA** 140-141 L 2
Great Dismal Swamp National Wildlife Refuge ⊥ **USA** (VA) 280-281 K 7
Great Divide ○ **USA** (CO) 254-255 H 3
Great Divide Basin ⌣ **USA** 252-253 K 4
Great Dividing Range ⛰ **AUS** 13 F 4
Great Duck Islands ⌒ **CDN** (ONT) 238-239 B 3
Great Eastern Erg = Grand Erg Oriental ∸ **DZ** 190-191 E 6
Great Eastern Highway II **AUS** 176-177 E 5
Greater Accra Region □ **GH** 202-203 K 7
Greater Hinggan Range = Da Hinggan Ling ⛰ **VRC** 150-151 B 5
Greater Sunda Islands = Sunda Besar, Kepulauan ⌒ **RI** 164-165 E 2
Great Exhibition Bay ≈ 182 D 1
Great Exuma Island ⌒ **BS** 54-55 G 3
Great Falls ○ **CDN** (MAN) 234-235 G 4
Great Falls ~ **GUY** 62-63 E 4
Great Falls ○ **USA** (MT) 250-251 H 4
Great Falls ○ **USA** (SC) 284-285 K 2
Great Falls ~ **USA** 250-251 H 4
Great Falls ~ **USA** 280-281 J 4
Great Guana Cay ⌒ **BS** 54-55 G 2
Great Harbour Cay ⌒ **BS** 54-55 F 2
Great Inagua Island ⌒ **BS** 54-55 J 4
Great Isaac ⌒ **BS** 54-55 F 1
Great Kambung Swamp ⬭ **AUS** 180-181 G 3
Great Karoo = Groot Karoo ∸ **ZA** 220-221 E 6
Great Keppel Island ⌒ ·· **AUS** 178-179 L 2
Great Lake ⬭ **AUS** 180-181 J 6
Great Lake ⬭ **USA** (NC) 282-283 K 6
Great Mercury Island ⌒ **NZ** 182 E 2
Great Nicobar Island ⌒ **IND** 140-141 L 6
Great North East Channel ≈ 183 B 6
Great Northern Highway II **AUS** 172-173 H 5
Great Ocean Road • **AUS** 180-181 G 5
Great Ouse ~ **GB** 90-91 G 5
Great Palm Island ⌒ **AUS** 174-175 J 6
Great Papuan Plateau ⛰ **PNG** 183 B 4
Great Pearl Bank ⌒ **UAE** 134-135 D 5
Great Plains ∸ 4 C 3
Great Point ▲ **USA** (MA) 278-279 L 7
Great Porcupine Creek ~ **USA** 250-251 M 5
Great Rattling Brook ~ **CDN** 242-243 N 4
Great Ruaha ~ **EAT** 214-215 J 4
Great Sacandaga Lake ⬭ **USA** (NY) 278-279 G 5
Great Salt Lake ⬭ **USA** (UT) 254-255 C 2
Great Salt Lake Desert ∸ **USA** 254-255 B 3
Great Salt Plains National Wildlife Refuge ⊥ **USA** (OK) 264-265 F 2
Great Salt Plains Reservoir ⬭ **USA** (OK) 264-265 F 2
Great Sand Dunes National Monument ∴ **USA** (CO) 254-255 K 6
Great Sand Hills ⛰ **CDN** 232-233 J 5
Great Sand Sea = Baḥr ar Ramla al Kabir ∸ **ET** 194-195 B 3
Great Sandy Desert ∸ **AUS** 172-173 F 6
Great Sandy Desert ∸ **USA** 244-245 D 7
Great Sea Reef ⌒ **FJI** 184 III b 2
Great Sitkin Island ⌒ **USA** 22-23 H 6
Great Slave Lake ⬭ **CDN** 30-31 M 5
Great Smoky Mountains ⛰ **USA** 282-283 D 5
Great Smoky Mountains National Park ⊥ ··· **USA** (TN) 282-283 D 5
Great Sole Bank ≃ 90-91 B 7
Great Swamp ⬭ **USA** (NC) 282-283 L 5
Great Valley ⌣ **USA** 280-281 F 6
Great Victoria Desert ∸ **AUS** 176-177 J 3
Great Victoria Desert Flora and Fauna Reserve ⊥ **AUS** 176-177 K 4
Great Wall = Great Wall, The ··· **VRC** 154-155 K 1
Great Wall of China • **AUS** 178-179 E 6
Great Wass Island ⌒ **USA** (ME) 278-279 O 4
Great Western Erg = Grand Erg Occidental ∸ **DZ** 188-189 L 5
Great Western Torres Island ⌒ **MYA** 158-159 D 5
Great Yarmouth ○ **GB** 90-91 H 5
Gredos, Coto Nacional de ⊥ **E** 98-99 E 4
Greece = Ellás ■ **GR** 100-101 H 5
Greeley ○ **USA** (CO) 254-255 L 3
Greeley ○ **USA** (NE) 262-263 H 3
Greeleyville ○ **USA** (SC) 284-285 L 3
Greely Fiord ≈ 26-27 H 3
Greèm Bell, ostrov ⌒ **RUS** 84-85 h 2
Green ○ **CDN** (ONT) 234-235 P 4
Greenan ○ **CDN** (SAS) 232-233 K 4
Green Bay ≈ 242-243 N 3
Green Bay ○ **USA** (AL) 284-285 D 5
Green Bay ○ **USA** (WI) 270-271 K 6
Green Bay ⬭ **USA** (WI) 270-271 L 6
Greenbrier ○ **USA** (AR) 276-277 C 5
Greenbrier River ~ **USA** 280-281 F 5
Greenbrier River ~ **USA** 280-281 F 6
Greenbush ○ **CDN** (SAS) 232-233 Q 3
Greenbush ○ **USA** (MN) 270-271 B 2
Green Cape ▲ **AUS** 180-181 K 4
Greencastle ○ **USA** (IN) 274-275 M 5
Greencastle ○ **USA** (PA) 280-281 J 4
Green Cay ⌒ **BS** 54-55 G 2
Green City ○ **USA** (MO) 274-275 F 4
Green Cove Springs ○ **USA** (FL) 286-287 H 2
Greendale ○ **USA** (OH) 280-281 B 4
Greendale ○ **USA** (WI) 274-275 K 2
Greene ○ **USA** (IA) 274-275 F 2
Greene ○ **USA** (ND) 258-259 F 3
Greene ○ **USA** (NY) 278-279 F 6
Greeneville ○ **USA** (TN) 282-283 E 4
Greenfield ○ **USA** (CA) 248-249 C 3
Greenfield ○ **USA** (IA) 274-275 D 3
Greenfield ○ **USA** (IL) 274-275 H 5
Greenfield ○ **USA** (IN) 274-275 N 5
Greenfield ○ **USA** (MA) 278-279 J 6
Greenfield ○ **USA** (MO) 276-277 B 3
Greenfield ○ **USA** (OH) 280-281 C 4
Greenfield ○ **USA** (TN) 276-277 G 4
Greenfield ○ **USA** (VA) 280-281 H 6
Green Forest ○ **USA** (AR) 276-277 B 4
Green Head ○ **AUS** 176-177 C 5
Greenhill River ~ **CDN** 236-237 E 4
Greenhorn Mountains ⛰ **USA** 248-249 F 4
Green Island ⌒ **AUS** 174-175 J 5
Green Island ⌒ **USA** 20-21 R 6
Green Island Bay ≈ 160-161 C 7
Green Lake ⬭ **CDN** (BC) 230-231 H 2
Green Lake ○ **USA** (TX) 266-267 L 5
Greenland ○ **USA** (MI) 270-271 J 4
Greenland-Iceland Rise ≃ 6-7 G 2
Greenly Island ⌒ **AUS** 180-181 C 3
Green Mountain ⛰ **USA** 278-279 J 5
Greenock ○ **GB** 90-91 E 4
Greenough ○ **AUS** 176-177 C 4
Greenough, Mount ▲ **USA** 20-21 U 2
Greenough River ~ **AUS** 176-177 C 4
Greenport ○ **USA** (NY) 280-281 O 2
Green River ○ **PNG** 183 A 2
Green River ○ **USA** (UT) 254-255 E 4
Green River ○ **USA** (WY) 252-253 J 5
Green River ~ **USA** 252-253 J 5
Green River ~ **USA** 254-255 F 4
Green River ~ **USA** 274-275 J 3
Green River ~ **USA** 276-277 K 3
Green River Basin ⌣ **USA** 252-253 J 4
Green River Lake ⬭ **USA** (KY) 276-277 K 3
Green River Parkway II **USA** (KY) 276-277 J 3
Greensboro ○ **USA** (AL) 284-285 C 4
Greensboro ○ **USA** (FL) 286-287 E 1
Greensboro ○ **USA** (GA) 284-285 G 3
Greensboro ○ **USA** (NC) 282-283 H 4

332 Gornozavodsk — Greensboro

Greensburg ○ USA (IN) 274-275 N 5
Greensburg ○ USA (KS) 262-263 G 7
Greensburg ○ USA (KY) 276-277 K 3
Greensburg ○ USA (LA) 268-269 K 6
Greensburg ○ USA (PA) 280-281 G 3
Greens Peak ▲ USA (AZ) 256-257 F 4
Greenstreet ○ CDN (SAS) 232-233 J 2
Green Swamp ⊂ USA (NC) 282-283 J 6
Greentown ○ USA (IN) 274-275 N 4
Greenup ○ USA (IL) 274-275 K 5
Greenvale ○ AUS 174-175 H 6
Green Valley ○ USA (AZ) 256-257 E 7
Greenview ○ USA (CA) 246-247 C 2
Greenville ☆ LB 202-203 F 7
Greenville ○ USA (AL) 284-285 D 5
Greenville ○ USA (CA) 246-247 E 3
Greenville ○ USA (FL) 286-287 F 1
Greenville ○ USA (GA) 284-285 F 3
Greenville ○ USA (IL) 274-275 J 6
Greenville ○ USA (KY) 276-277 H 3
Greenville ○ USA (ME) 278-279 M 3
Greenville ○ USA (MI) 272-273 D 4
Greenville ○ USA (MO) 276-277 E 3
Greenville ○ USA (MS) 268-269 J 3
Greenville ○ USA (OH) 280-281 B 3
Greenville ○ USA (PA) 280-281 F 2
Greenville ○ USA (SC) 284-285 H 2
Greenville ○ USA (TN) 282-283 K 5
Greenville ○ USA (TX) 264-265 H 5
Greenwater ○ USA (WA) 244-245 D 3
Green Water Provincial Park ⊥ CDN (SAS) 232-233 P 3
Greenwater Provincial Park ⊥ • CDN (ONT) 236-237 G 3
Greenwich ○ GB 90-91 H 6
Greenwich ○ USA (CT) 280-281 N 2
Greenwich ○ USA (NJ) 280-281 L 4
Greenwich ○ USA (NY) 278-279 H 5
Greenwich ○ USA (OH) 280-281 D 2
Greenwood ○ CDN (BC) 230-231 L 4
Greenwood ○ USA (AR) 276-277 A 5
Greenwood ○ USA (FL) 286-287 D 1
Greenwood ○ USA (IN) 274-275 M 5
Greenwood ○ USA (LA) 268-269 G 4
Greenwood ○ USA (MS) 268-269 K 3
Greenwood ○ USA (SC) 284-285 H 2
Greenwood ○ USA (WI) 270-271 H 6
Greenwood, Lake < USA (SC) 284-285 H 2
Greer ○ USA (ID) 250-251 C 5
Greer ○ USA (SC) 284-285 H 2
Greers Ferry Lake ⊂ USA (AR) 276-277 C 5
Greeshield Lake ⊂ CDN 28-29 G 3
Greeson, Lake ⊂ USA (AR) 276-277 B 6
Gregoria Pérez de Denis ○ RA 76-77 G 5
Gregório, Cachoeira ∼ BR 66-67 F 2
Gregório, Rio ∼ BR 66-67 B 6
Gregorio Aznarez ○ ROU 78-79 M 3
Gregorio Méndez ○ MEX 52-53 J 3
Gregory ○ USA (AR) 276-277 D 5
Gregory ○ USA (MI) 272-273 E 5
Gregory ○ USA (SD) 260-261 G 3
Gregory, Lake ⊂ AUS (SA) 178-179 E 5
Gregory, Lake ⊂ AUS (WA) 176-177 E 2
Gregory Creek ∼ AUS 178-179 D 5
Gregory Development Road II AUS 174-175 J 7
Gregory Downs ○ AUS 174-175 E 6
Gregory Lake ⊂ AUS 172-173 H 6
Gregory National Park ⊥ AUS 172-173 K 4
Gregory Range ▲ AUS 172-173 E 6
Gregory Range ▲ AUS 174-175 G 6
Gregory River ∼ AUS 174-175 E 6
Gregory Springs ○ AUS 174-175 H 6
Greïlif ○ RIM 196-197 E 6
Greifswald ○ • D 92-93 M 1
Greig Bank ≃ 162-163 H 5
Greiz ○ • D 92-93 M 3
Gremiha ○ RUS 88-89 P 2
Gremjač'e ○ RUS 102-103 L 2
Gremjačinsk ☆ RUS 96-97 K 4
Grenå ○ DK 86-87 E 8
Grenada ○ USA (CA) 246-247 C 2
Grenada ○ USA (MS) 268-269 L 3
Grenada ■ WG 56 E 5
Grenadines, The ∩ WV 56 E 5
Grenen ∸ •• DK 86-87 E 8
Grenfell ○ AUS 180-181 K 2
Grenfell ○ CDN (SAS) 232-233 Q 5
Grenfell, Mount ▲ AUS 178-179 H 6
Grenivík ○ IS 86-87 d 2
Grenoble ☆ F 90-91 K 9
Grenora ○ USA (ND) 258-259 D 3
Grense Jakobselv ○ N 86-87 P 2
Grenville ○ USA (NM) 256-257 M 2
Grenville ○ WG 56 E 5
Grenville, Cape ▲ AUS 174-175 G 2
Grenville Channel ≈ 228-229 D 3
Greshak ○ PK 134-135 M 5
Gresham ○ USA (NE) 262-263 J 3
Gresham ○ USA (OR) 244-245 C 5
Gresik ○ RI 168 E 3
Gressåmoen nasjonalpark ⊥ N 86-87 F 4
Gretna ○ CDN (MAN) 234-235 F 5
Gretna ○ USA (FL) 286-287 E 1
Gretna ○ USA (LA) 268-269 K 7
Gretna ○ USA (VA) 280-281 G 7
Grevená ○ GR 100-101 H 4
Grevy, Isla ∩ RCH 80 G 7
Grey, Cape ▲ AUS 174-175 D 3
Greybull ○ USA (WY) 252-253 K 2
Greybull River ∼ USA 252-253 J 2
Grey Eagle ○ USA (MN) 270-271 D 5
Grey Hunter Peak ▲ CDN 20-21 X 5
Greylingstad ○ ZA 220-221 J 3
Greylock, Mount ▲ USA (MA) 278-279 H 6
Greymouth ○ NZ 182 C 5
Grey Range ▲ AUS 178-179 G 5
Grey River ○ CDN (NFL) 242-243 L 5
Grey River ∼ CDN 242-243 L 5
Greys Point ○ USA (VA) 280-281 K 6
Greyton ○ ZA 220-221 D 7
Greytown ○ ZA 220-221 K 4
Griba, La • TN 190-191 H 4
Gribanovskij ○ RUS 102-103 M 2
Gribbell Island ∩ CDN (BC) 228-229 E 3
Gribingui ∼ RCA 206-207 D 5
Gribingui-Bamingui, Réserve de faune du ⊥ RCA 206-207 D 5
Griboue ○ CI 202-203 G 6
Gridino ○ RUS 88-89 N 4
Gridley ○ USA (CA) 246-247 D 4
Griekwastad = Griquatown ○ ZA 220-221 F 4
Grier ○ USA (NM) 256-257 M 4
Griffenfelds Ø = Uumaanaq ∩ GRØ 28-29 I 5
Griffin ○ CDN (SAS) 232-233 P 6
Griffin ○ USA (GA) 284-285 F 3
Griffin, Lake ⊂ USA (FL) 286-287 H 3
Griffin Lake ⊂ CDN 30-31 U 5
Griffin Point ▲ USA 20-21 T 1
Griffith ○ AUS 180-181 J 3
Griffith Island ∩ CDN 24-25 Y 3
Griffiths Point ▲ CDN 24-25 K 2
Grifton ○ USA (NC) 282-283 K 5
Griggsville ○ USA (IL) 274-275 H 5
Grigor'evka ○ RUS 116-117 F 9
Grigor'evskaja ○ RUS 96-97 J 4
Grijalva, Monte ▲ MEX 50-51 C 7
Grijalva, Río ∼ MEX 52-53 H 2
Grili, ostrov ∩ RUS 84-85 f 2
Grillon, Mount ▲ USA 32-33 B 2
Grimes ○ USA (IA) 274-275 E 3
Grimari ○ RCA 206-207 E 6
Grimma ○ D 92-93 M 3
Grimmington Island ∩ CDN 36-37 T 6
Grimsby ○ CDN (ONT) 238-239 F 5
Grimsby ○ • GB 90-91 G 5
Grimselpass ▲ •• CH 92-93 K 5
Grimsey ∩ IS 86-87 e 1
Grímsstaðir ○ IS 86-87 e 2
Grímsvötn ▲ IS 86-87 e 2
Grindavík ○ IS 86-87 b 3
Grindrod ○ CDN (BC) 230-231 K 3
Grindsted ○ DK 86-87 D 9
Grindstone Provincial Park ⊥ CDN (MAN) 234-235 G 3
Grinell ○ USA (IA) 274-275 F 3
Grinnah, Sebkhet ⊂ WSA 196-197 C 3
Grinnel Land ∸ CDN 26-27 L 3
Grinnell Glacier ⊂ CDN 36-37 Q 3
Grinnel Peninsula ⊂ CDN 24-25 Y 2
Griquatown = Griekwastad ○ ZA 220-221 F 4
Griquet ○ CDN (NFL) 242-243 N 1
Grise Fiord ○ CDN 24-25 f 2
Grisslehamn ○ S 86-87 J 6
Griswold ○ CDN (MAN) 234-235 C 5
Griswold ○ USA (IA) 274-275 C 3
Grivel, Kap ▲ GRØ 28-29 b 2
Grivița ○ RO 102-103 E 5
Grizim ○ DZ 196-197 J 2
Grizzly Bear Creek ∼ CDN 232-233 H 2
Grizzly Bear Mountain ▲ CDN 30-31 K 3
Grjazi ○ RUS 94-95 Q 5
Grjazovec ○ RUS 94-95 R 2
Groais Island ∩ CDN (NFL) 242-243 N 2
Groauras, Rio ∼ BR 68-69 H 4
Grobin = Grobiņa ☆ •• LV 94-95 G 3
Grobiņa ☆ •• LV 94-95 G 3
Groblersdal ○ ZA 220-221 J 2
Groblershoop ○ ZA 220-221 E 4
Grodno = Hrodna ☆ BY 94-95 H 5
Groenlo ○ NL 92-93 J 2
Groenrivier ∼ ZA 220-221 C 5
Groenriviermond ○ ZA 220-221 C 5
Groesbeck ○ USA (TX) 266-267 L 2
Groesbeek ○ ZA 218-219 E 6
Grogol ○ RI 168 D 3
Groix, Île de ∩ F 90-91 F 8
Grójec ○ PL 92-93 Q 3
Grombalia ○ TN 190-191 H 2
Grong ○ N 86-87 F 4
Groningen ☆ • NL 92-93 J 2
Gronlid ○ CDN (SAS) 232-233 O 2
Grønlingrotten • N 86-87 G 3
Grønnedal = Kangilinnguit ○ GRØ 28-29 Q 6
Groom ○ USA (TX) 264-265 C 3
Grootberg ▲ NAM 216-217 C 9
Groot Bergrivier ∼ ZA 220-221 D 6
Grootdraaidam < ZA 220-221 J 3
Grootdrink ○ ZA 220-221 E 4
Grootduin ∸ NAM 216-217 E 11
Groote Eylandt ∩ AUS 174-175 D 3
Grootfontein ☆ NAM 216-217 E 9
Groot Henarpolder ○ SME 62-63 F 3
Groot Jongensfontein ○ ZA 220-221 E 7
Groot Karasberge ▲ NAM 220-221 D 3
Groot Karoo = Great Karoo ∸ ZA 220-221 E 6
Groot Kei ∼ ZA 220-221 H 6
Grootkraal ○ ZA 220-221 F 6
Groot Laagte ∼ RB 216-217 F 10
Groot Marico ○ ZA 220-221 H 2
Groot Rietrivier ∼ ZA 220-221 E 5
Grootrivier ∼ ZA 220-221 F 6
Groot Visrivier ∼ ZA 220-221 H 6
Grootvloer ⊂ ZA 220-221 E 4
Groot Waterberg ▲ NAM 216-217 D 10
Groot Winterhoekberge ▲ ZA 220-221 G 6
Gropakehn ○ LB 202-203 G 7
Gros Cap ○ CDN (ONT) 236-237 D 6
Gros Morne ▲ CDN (NFL) 242-243 L 3
Gros-Morne ○ RH 54-55 J 5
Gros Morne National Park ⊥ ••• CDN (NFL) 242-243 L 3
Gros Pate ▲ CDN (NFL) 242-243 L 2
Grossa da Marambaia, Ponta ▲ BR 72-73 J 7
Gross Aub ○ NAM 220-221 D 3
Gross Barmen, Warmbron • NAM 216-217 D 11
Großer Arber ▲ D 92-93 M 4
Großer Ötscher ▲ A 92-93 N 5
Großer Schwielowsee ⊂ D 92-93 N 2
Grosse Tete ○ USA (LA) 268-269 J 6
Grosseto ☆ I 100-101 C 3
Grossevići ○ RUS 122-123 H 5
Großglockner ▲ •• A 92-93 M 5
Gross Ums ○ NAM 220-221 D 1
Gros Ventre Range ▲ USA 252-253 H 3
Gros Ventre River ∼ USA 252-253 H 3
Groswater Bay ≈ 36-37 V 7
Groton ○ USA (CT) 280-281 O 2
Groton ○ USA (SD) 260-261 H 1
Groton ○ USA (WA) 244-245 D 3
Grotto of the Redemption • USA (ID) 274-275 D 2
Grou, Oued ∼ MA 188-189 H 4
Grouard ○ CDN 32-33 M 4
Groumania ○ CI 202-203 J 6
Groundbirch ○ CDN 32-33 K 4
Groundhog River ∼ CDN 236-237 F 4
Grouse Creek ○ USA (UT) 254-255 B 2
Grouse Creek ∼ USA 254-255 B 2
Groust, Rivière ∼ CDN 36-37 N 4
Grouz, Ibel ▲ DZ 188-189 L 4
Grove ○ USA (OK) 264-265 K 2
Grove City ○ USA (MN) 270-271 D 5
Grove City ○ USA (OH) 280-281 C 4
Grove City ○ USA (PA) 280-281 F 2
Grove Hill ○ USA (AL) 284-285 C 5
Grove Lake ○ USA (MN) 270-271 C 5
Groveland ○ USA (CA) 248-249 D 2
Grover ○ USA (CO) 254-255 L 3
Grover ○ USA (WY) 252-253 H 4
Grovertown ○ USA (IN) 274-275 M 3
Groves ○ USA (TX) 268-269 G 7
Groveton ○ USA (NH) 278-279 K 4
Groveton ○ USA (TX) 268-269 E 5
Groznyj ☆ RUS 104 E 5
Grudovo = Sredec ○ BG 102-103 E 6
Grudziądz ○ • PL 92-93 P 2
Gruenthal ○ CDN (SAS) 232-233 M 3
Gruesa, Cerro Punta ▲ RA 80 D 5
Gruesa, Punta ▲ RCH 70-71 B 7
Grulla ○ USA (TX) 266-267 J 7
Grullo, El ○ MEX 52-53 B 2
Grumantbyen ○ N 84-85 J 3
Grumo Áppula ○ I 100-101 F 4
Grums ☆ S 86-87 F 7
Grünau ○ NAM 220-221 D 3
Grundarfjörður ○ IS 86-87 b 2
Grundy ○ USA (VA) 280-281 D 6
Grundy Center ○ USA (IA) 274-275 F 2
Grupe ○ GH 202-203 J 5
Gruszka, Lake ⊂ AUS 176-177 H 2
Gruta ○ BR 68-69 H 7
Gruta, La ○ RA 74-75 D 6
Gruta C. del Aguila • ROU 78-79 L 2
Gruta de Intihuasi • RA 78-79 G 2
Gruta del Palacio • ROU 78-79 L 2
Gruta Paz • EC 64-65 D 1
Grutas de Juxtlahuaca, Parque Natural ⊥ MEX 52-53 E 3
Gruver ○ USA (TX) 264-265 C 2
Grūzdžiai ○ LT 94-95 H 3
Gryfice ○ PL 92-93 N 2
Gryllefjord ○ N 86-87 H 2
Gryt ○ S 86-87 H 7
Grytøya ∩ N 86-87 H 2
Grytviken ○ GB 78-79 O 7
Guabito ○ PA 52-53 C 7
Guabo, El ○ PA 52-53 D 7
Guabrún ○ RCH 78-79 C 6
Guacamaya, Raudal ∼ CO 60-61 G 6
Guacamayas ○ CO (CA) 60-61 D 6
Guacamayas ○ CO (VIC) 60-61 F 5
Guacara ○ YV 60-61 H 2
Guacautey ○ YV 62-63 D 3
Guachamacari, Cerro ▲ YV 60-61 J 6
Guachara ○ YV 60-61 G 4
Guácharo, Parque Nacional ⊥ YV 60-61 K 2
Gu Achi ○ USA (AZ) 256-257 C 6
Guachochic ○ MEX 50-51 F 4
Guachucal ○ CO 64-65 D 1
Guaco ○ CO 60-61 F 6
Guaçu Boi ○ BR 76-77 J 5
Guadajoz, Río ∼ E 98-99 E 6
Guadalajara ☆ E 98-99 F 4
Guadalajara ☆ •• MEX 52-53 C 1
Guadalcanal ○ E 98-99 E 5
Guadalcanal ∩ SOL 184 I d 3
Guadalcázar ○ MEX 50-51 J 6
Guadalimar, Río ∼ E 98-99 F 5
Guadalmez, Río ∼ E 98-99 E 5
Guadalope, Río ∼ E 98-99 G 4
Guadalupe ○ BR 68-69 G 5
Guadalupe ○ E 98-99 E 5
Guadalupe ○ ••• E 98-99 E 5
Guadalupe ○ MEX (COA) 50-51 J 3
Guadalupe ○ MEX (NL) 50-51 J 5
Guadalupe ○ MEX (ZAC) 50-51 H 6
Guadalupe ∼ MEX 50-51 D 5
Guadalupe ○ PE 64-65 C 5
Guadalupe ○ USA (CA) 248-249 D 5
Guadalupe de Bahues ○ MEX 50-51 G 4
Guadalupe de Bravo ○ MEX 50-51 F 2
Guadalupe Mountains ▲ USA 256-257 L 6
Guadalupe Mountains National Park ⊥ USA (TX) 266-267 C 2
Guadalupe Peak ▲ USA (TX) 266-267 C 2
Guadalupe River ∼ USA 266-267 K 4
Guadalupe Victoria ○ MEX (DGO) 50-51 G 5
Guadalupe Victoria ○ MEX (TAM) 50-51 L 5
Guadalupe y Calvo ○ MEX 50-51 F 4
Guadarrama, Sierra de ▲ E 98-99 E 4
Guadeloupe ∩ F 56 D 2
Guadeloupe, Parc National de la ⊥ F 56 E 3
Guadeloupe Passage ≈ 56 E 3
Guadelupe ○ MEX 50-51 A I
Guadelupe, La ○ CDN (QUE) 240-241 E 5
Guadiana, Bahía de ≈ 54-55 C 3
Guadiana, Río ∼ E 98-99 E 5
Guadiana Menor, Río ∼ E 98-99 F 6
Guaduas ○ CO 60-61 D 5
Guafera Ye Terara Senselet ▲ ETH 208-209 B 5
Guafo, Isla ∩ RCH 78-79 B 7
Guaíba ○ BR 74-75 E 8
Guaicuí ○ BR 72-73 H 4
Guáimaro ○ C 54-55 G 4
Guaina ○ YV 60-61 K 5
Guainía, Río ∼ CO 60-61 G 6
Guaiquinima, Cerro ▲ YV 60-61 K 5
Guaíra ○ BR (PAR) 76-77 K 3
Guaíra ○ BR (PAU) 72-73 F 6
Guairacá ○ BR 72-73 D 7
Guaitecas, Islas ∩ RCH 80 D 1
Guajaba, Cayo ∩ C 54-55 G 4
Guajará ○ BR 64-65 F 5
Guajará-Mirim ○ BR 70-71 E 2
Guaje, El ○ MEX 50-51 H 3
Guajeru ○ BR 72-73 K 3
Guajira, Península de la ∪ CO 60-61 F 1
Gualaceo ○ EC 64-65 C 3
Gualala ○ USA (CA) 246-247 B 5
Gualán ○ GCA 52-53 K 4
Gualaquiza ○ EC 64-65 C 3
Gualcuna ○ RCH 76-77 B 5
Gualeguay ○ RA 78-79 K 2
Gualeguay, Río ∼ RA 78-79 K 2
Gualeguaychu ○ RA 78-79 K 2
Gualeguaychu, Río ∼ RA 78-79 K 2
Gualjaina ○ RA 78-79 D 7
Guallatiri ○ RCH 70-71 C 6
Guallatiri, Volcán ▲ RCH 70-71 C 6
Gualmatan ○ CO 64-65 D 1
Guamal ○ CO (MAG) 60-61 D 3
Guamal ○ CO (MET) 60-61 E 6
Guamani, Cordillera de ▲ PE 64-65 C 4
Guamblin, Isla ∩ RCH 80 C 2
Guamini ○ RA 78-79 H 4
Guamo ○ CO 60-61 D 5
Guamo, El ○ CO 60-61 C 3
Guamote ○ EC 64-65 C 2
Guampí, Sierra de ▲ YV 60-61 J 4
Guamúchil ○ MEX 50-51 E 5
Guamués, Río ∼ CO 64-65 D 1
Gua Musang ○ MAL 162-163 E 2
Gu'an ○ VRC 154-155 K 2
Guanabacoa ○ C 54-55 D 3
Guanabo ○ C 54-55 D 3
Guanacaste, Cordillera de ▲ CR 52-53 B 6
Guanacayabo, Golfo de ≈ 54-55 G 4
Guanaceví ○ MEX 50-51 G 5
Guanaco Muerto ○ RA 76-77 E 6
Guanaco Sombriana ○ RA 76-77 E 5
Guanaguana ○ YV 60-61 K 2
Guanahacabibes, Península de ∪ C 54-55 C 4
Guanahani Island = San Salvador ∩ BS 54-55 H 3
Guanaja ○ HN 54-55 C 6
Guanaja, Isla de ∩ HN 54-55 C 6
Guanajay ○ C 54-55 D 3
Guanajuato ☆ ••• MEX 50-51 J 7
Guanajuña ○ YV 60-61 K 3
Guanambi ○ BR 72-73 J 3
Guañape, Islas de ∩ PE 64-65 C 6
Guañape, Punta ▲ 64-65 C 6
Guanaquero, Bahía ≈ 76-77 B 6
Guanare ☆ YV 60-61 G 3
Guanare, Río ∼ YV 60-61 G 3
Guanarito ○ YV 60-61 G 3
Guanay ○ BOL 70-71 D 4
Guanay, Cerro ▲ YV 60-61 H 5
Guandacol ○ RA 76-77 C 5
Guandi, Rio ∼ BR 72-73 K 5
Guandiping ○ VRC 156-157 G 2
Guang'an ○ VRC 154-155 E 6
Guangchang ○ VRC 156-157 K 3
Guangde ○ VRC 154-155 L 6
Guangdong □ VRC 156-157 H 4
Guanghai ○ VRC 156-157 H 6
Guanghan ○ VRC 154-155 D 6
Guangji ○ VRC 154-155 D 6
Guangmao Shan ▲ VRC 142-143 M 2
Guangning ○ VRC 156-157 H 5
Guangrao ○ VRC 154-155 L 3
Guangsheng Si • VRC 154-155 G 3
Guangshui ○ VRC 154-155 H 6
Guangshun ○ VRC 156-157 E 3
Guangxi Zhuangzu Zizhiqu □ VRC 156-157 E 4
Guangyang ○ VRC 156-157 K 2
Guangyuan ○ VRC 154-155 D 5
Guangze ○ VRC 156-157 K 3
Guangzhou ☆ •• VRC 156-157 H 5
Guanhães ○ BR 72-73 J 5
Guaniamo, Río ∼ YV 60-61 J 4
Guánica ○ • USA (PR) 286-287 P 3
Guanipa, Río ∼ YV 60-61 K 3
Guanling ○ VRC 156-157 D 4
Guanocó ○ YV 60-61 K 2
Guanqiao ○ VRC 154-155 D 3
Guanta ○ RCH 76-77 B 5
Guanta ○ YV 60-61 J 2
Guantánamo ☆ C 54-55 H 4
Guantánamo Bay xx USA 54-55 H 5
Guantao ○ VRC 154-155 J 3
Guanumbi ○ BR 68-69 K 5
Guanyun ○ VRC 154-155 L 4
Guapa ○ CO 60-61 C 4
Guapí ○ CO 60-61 C 6
Guapiara ○ BR 74-75 F 5
Guápiles ○ CR 52-53 C 6
Guapo, El ○ YV 60-61 J 2
Guaporé ○ BR 74-75 E 7
Guaporé, Reserva Biológica do ⊥ BR 70-71 F 3
Guaporé, Río ∼ BOL 70-71 G 3
Guaqui ○ BOL 70-71 C 5
Guará, Rio ∼ BR 72-73 H 2
Guarabira ○ BR 68-69 L 5
Guaraci ○ BR (PAR) 72-73 E 7
Guaraci ○ BR (PAU) 72-73 F 6
Guaraí ○ BR 68-69 D 6
Guarajambala, Río ∼ HN 52-53 K 4
Guaramurí ○ GUY 62-63 E 2
Guaranda ☆ EC 64-65 C 2
Guaraniaçu ○ BR 74-75 D 5
Guarani das Missões ○ BR 76-77 K 5
Guaranoco ○ YV 60-61 K 3
Guarantã do Norte ○ BR 66-67 K 7
Guarapari ○ BR 72-73 K 6
Guarapiche, Reserva Forestal ⊥ YV 60-61 K 2
Guarapuava ○ BR 74-75 E 5
Guaraqueçaba ○ BR 74-75 F 5
Guararã ○ BR 72-73 J 6
Guararapes ○ BR 72-73 E 6
Guaratinga ○ BR 72-73 L 4
Guaratinguetá ○ BR 72-73 H 7
Guaratuba ○ BR 74-75 F 5
Guarayos ○ BOL 70-71 C 3
Guarda ☆ • P 98-99 D 4
Guarda, A ○ E 98-99 C 4
Guarda Mor ○ BR 72-73 G 4
Guardia, La ○ RA 76-77 E 5
Guardia, La ○ RCH 76-77 C 4
Guardia Mitre ○ RA 78-79 H 6
Guardián, Cabo ▲ RA 80 G 4
Guardian Brito, Isla ∩ RCH 80 D 7
Guardo ○ E 98-99 E 3
Guarei, Rio ∼ BR 72-73 D 7
Guarenas ○ YV 60-61 H 2
Guari ○ PNG 183 D 5
Guaria ○ CR 52-53 C 7
Guariba ○ BR 72-73 F 6
Guariba, Rio ∼ BR 66-67 G 6
Guaribas, Cachoeira ∼ BR 68-69 B 4
Guaricana, Pico ▲ BR 74-75 F 5
Guárico, Embalse del < YV 60-61 H 3
Guárico, Río ∼ YV 60-61 H 3
Guaritico, Caño ∼ YV 60-61 G 4
Guarujá ○ BR 74-75 G 5
Guarulhos ○ BR 72-73 G 7
Guasave ○ MEX 50-51 E 5
Guasca ○ CO 60-61 E 5
Guascama, Punta ▲ CO 60-61 B 6
Guasipati ○ YV 62-63 D 2
Guasopa ○ PNG 183 G 5
Guatacondo ○ RCH 70-71 C 7
Guatacondo, Quebrada de ∼ RCH 70-71 C 7
Guataquí ○ CO 60-61 D 5
Guatay ○ USA (CA) 248-249 H 7
Guatemala ■ GCA 52-53 J 4
Guatemala, Ciudad de = Guatemala ★ •• GCA 52-53 J 4
Guatemala Basin ≃ 5 B 4
Guatimape, Laguna ○ MEX 50-51 G 5
Guatín ○ RCH 76-77 C 2
Guatire ○ YV 60-61 H 2
Guatopo, Parque Nacionale ⊥ YV 60-61 H 2
Guaviare, Río ∼ CO 60-61 G 6
Guaxupé ○ BR 72-73 G 6
Guayabal ○ C 54-55 G 4
Guayabal ○ YV 60-61 H 3
Guayabero, Río ∼ CO 60-61 E 6
Guayabo, El ○ YV 60-61 E 3
Guayaguas ○ RA 76-77 D 6
Guayaguayare ○ TT 60-61 L 2
Guayalejo, Río ∼ MEX 50-51 K 6
Guayama ○ • USA (PR) 286-287 P 3
Guayaneco, Archipiélago ∩ RCH 80 C 3
Guayapán, Quebrada de ∼ MEX 50-51 F 5
Guayape, Río ∼ HN 52-53 L 4
Guayapo, Río ∼ YV 60-61 H 5
Guayaquil ☆ EC 64-65 C 3
Guayaquil, Golfo de ≈ 64-65 B 3
Guayaramerín ○ BOL 70-71 E 2
Guayas, Río ∼ EC 64-65 E 1
Guayatayoc, Salinas de ⊂ RA 76-77 E 2
Guaycurú ○ RA 76-77 G 5
Guayllabamba, Río ∼ EC 64-65 C 1
Guayllabamba ○ EC 64-65 C 2
Guaymallén ○ RA 78-79 E 2
Guaymas ○ • MEX 50-51 D 4
Guaynabo ○ USA (PR) 286-287 P 2
Guayquiraró, Río ∼ RA 76-77 H 6
Guayubín ○ DOM 54-55 K 5
Guayzimi ○ EC 64-65 C 4
Guba ○ ETH 208-209 B 3
Guba ○ ZRE 214-215 D 6
Guba = Quba ○ • AZ 128-129 N 2
Guba Dolgaja ○ RUS 108-109 H 6
Gubaha ☆ RUS 96-97 K 4
Ġubail ☆ • RL 128-129 F 5
Ġubail, al- ○ KSA 130-131 L 4
Ġubāl, Ġazirat ∩ ET 194-195 F 4
Guban ∸ ETH 208-209 F 3
Gubat ○ RP 160-161 F 6
Gubato, Bannaanka ∸ SP 208-209 H 4
Gubatsaa Hills ▲ RB 218-219 B 4
Ġubba ○ KSA 130-131 G 3
Gubbi ○ IND 140-141 G 4
Gúbbio ○ I 100-101 D 3
Guben ○ D 92-93 N 3
Gubi ○ WAN 204-205 H 3
Gubio ○ WAN 198-199 F 6
Gubkin ○ RUS 102-103 K 2
Gubug ○ RI 168 D 3
Gucha ∼ EAK 212-213 E 4
Gucheng ○ VRC (HUB) 154-155 G 5
Gucheng ○ VRC (SHA) 154-155 G 4
Gučin-Us = Arguut ○ MAU 148-149 F 5
Ġūda ○ KSA 130-131 L 5
Gūdalūr ○ IND 140-141 G 5
Gudalur ○ IND 140-141 G 5
Gudauta ○ • GE 126-127 D 6
Ġudayyidat 'Ar'ar ○ KSA 130-131 G 2
Ġudayyidat Ḥāmir ○ IRQ 128-129 J 7
Gudbrandsdalen ∸ N 86-87 D 6
Guddekoppa ○ IND 140-141 F 4
Gudekota ○ IND 140-141 G 3
Gudenå ∼ DK 86-87 D 8
Guder ○ ETH 208-209 C 4
Guder Falls ∼ ETH 208-209 C 4
Gudermes ○ RUS 126-127 G 6
Gudgaon ○ IND 138-139 F 9
Gudi ○ WAN 204-205 H 4
Gudibanda ○ IND 140-141 G 4
Gudiña, A ○ E 98-99 D 3
Gudivāda ○ IND 140-141 J 2
Gudiyattam ○ IND 140-141 H 4
Gudong ○ VRC 142-143 L 3
Gudryolum ○ TM 136-137 D 6
Güdür ○ IND 140-141 H 3
Gudvangen ○ N 86-87 C 6
Gudžal ∼ RUS 122-123 E 3
Gue, Rivière du ∼ CDN 36-37 N 6
Guechémé ○ RN 204-205 E 2
Guéckedou ○ WAL 202-203 E 5
Guédi, Mont ▲ TCH 198-199 J 6
Güéjar, Río ∼ CO 60-61 E 6
Guéké ○ RG 202-203 F 5
Guélaour, Oued ∼ RIM 196-197 D 6
Guelb er Rîchât ▲ RIM 196-197 E 4
Guéléhé ○ TCH 206-207 D 4
Guélengdeng ○ TCH 206-207 B 3
Guéléninkoro ○ RMM 202-203 F 4
Guelma ☆ DZ 190-191 F 2
Guelph ○ CDN (ONT) 238-239 E 5
Guelta d'Archei • TCH 198-199 K 4
Gueltat Sidi Saad ○ DZ 190-191 C 3
Guémar ○ DZ 190-191 F 4
Guembou, Te-n- ○ RIM 196-197 F 6
Guendel ○ RIM 196-197 E 6
Guéndo ○ RMM 202-203 G 3
Guéné ○ DY 204-205 E 3
Guénéto ○ SN 202-203 D 3
Guenguel, Río ∼ RA 80 E 3
Guenté Paté ○ SN 202-203 C 2
Guépaouo ○ CI 202-203 H 6
Güeppí ○ PE 64-65 E 2
Guéra □ TCH 206-207 C 3
Guéra, Pic de ▲ TCH 206-207 D 3
Güer Aike ○ RA 80 F 5
Guérande ○ F 90-91 F 8
Guerara ○ DZ 190-191 E 4
Guercif ○ MA 188-189 K 3
Guéréda ○ TCH 198-199 L 5
Guéret ☆ F 90-91 H 8
Guerette ○ USA (ME) 278-279 N 1
Guérin Kouka ○ RT 202-203 L 5
Guerneville ○ USA (CA) 246-247 B 5
Guernsey ○ CDN (SAS) 232-233 N 4
Guernsey ∩ GBG 90-91 F 7
Guernsey ○ USA (WY) 252-253 O 4
Guernsey Reservoir < USA (WY) 252-253 O 4
Guérou ○ RIM 196-197 E 6
Guerra ○ USA (TX) 266-267 J 7
Guerrero ○ MEX (COA) 50-51 J 3
Guerrero ○ MEX (TAM) 50-51 K 4
Guerrero □ MEX 52-53 D 3
Guerrero, Cayos ∩ NIC 52-53 C 5
Guerrero Negro ○ • MEX 50-51 B 4
Gueskérou ○ RN 198-199 F 6
Guéssabo ○ CI 202-203 G 6
Guéssésso ○ CI 202-203 G 6
Guessihio ○ CI 202-203 H 6
Guessou-Sud ○ DY 204-205 E 3
Guesteclitas ○ CO 60-61 E 2
Guétéma ○ RMM 202-203 F 2
Gueydan ○ USA (LA) 268-269 H 6
Guévo ○ CI 202-203 G 7
Guézaoua ○ RN 198-199 D 5
Guga ○ RUS 122-123 G 2
Gugê ▲ ETH 208-209 C 5
Güge ○ IR 134-135 D 2
Gugu ▲ ETH 208-209 D 4
Guguang, Gunung ▲ RI 164-165 E 2
Guhāgar ○ IND 140-141 E 2
Ġuhaina ○ ET 194-195 E 4
Ġuhr ○ UAE 134-135 F 6
Guiana Highlands = Guayana, Macizo de ▲ 62-63 C 3
Guiana Plateau ≃ 62-63 G 1
Guiba, Jasiira ∩ SP 212-213 J 4
Guibéroua ○ CI 202-203 G 6
Guichaud, Rivière ∼ CDN 36-37 L 3
Guichi ○ VRC 154-155 K 6
Guichón ○ ROU 78-79 L 2
Guidan ○ RN 198-199 C 6
Guidari ○ TCH 206-207 C 4
Guider ○ CAM 204-205 K 4
Guidiguir ○ RN 198-199 D 6
Guidiguis ○ CAM 206-207 B 3
Guidimaka □ RIM 196-197 D 7
Guidimouni ○ RN 198-199 D 6
Guiding ○ VRC 156-157 E 3
Guidjiba ○ CAM 204-205 K 4
Guidong ○ VRC 156-157 H 3
Guidouma ○ G 210-211 C 4
Guiendana ○ CI 202-203 H 5
Guier, Lac de ⊂ SN 196-197 C 6
Guietsou ○ G 210-211 C 5
Guifeng • VRC 156-157 K 2
Guiffa ○ RCA 206-207 D 5
Guigang ○ VRC 156-157 F 5
Guiglo ○ CI 202-203 G 6
Güigüe ○ YV 60-61 H 2
Guihua ○ VRC 156-157 D 6
Guihulngan ○ RP 160-161 E 7
Guijá ○ MOC 220-221 L 2
Guijuelo ○ E 98-99 E 4
Guilderton ○ AUS 176-177 C 5
Guildford ○ • GB 90-91 G 6
Guilford ○ USA (ME) 278-279 M 3
Guilford Courthouse National Military Park • USA (NC) 282-283 H 4
Guilin ○ • VRC 156-157 G 4
Guillaume-Delisle, Lac ⊂ CDN 36-37 L 6
Guillé ○ RIM 196-197 E 6
Guillemard Bay ≈ 24-25 X 5
Guillestre ○ F 90-91 L 9
Guilmaro ○ DY 202-203 L 4
Guimarães ○ BR 68-69 F 3
Guimarães ○ P 98-99 C 4
Guimarânia ○ BR 72-73 G 5
Guimaras Island ∩ RP 160-161 E 7
Guimaras Strait ≈ 160-161 E 7
Guimba ○ RP 160-161 D 5
Guimbaleta ○ MEX 50-51 H 4
Guimbiri, Mont ▲ CAM 204-205 K 6
Guin ○ USA (AL) 284-285 C 3
Guinagourou ○ DY 204-205 E 4
Guinchos Cay ∩ BS 54-55 G 3
Guinda ○ USA (CA) 246-247 C 5
Guindelman ○ RP 160-161 F 8
Guiné ○ BR 72-73 K 2
Guinea = Guinée ■ RG 202-203 D 4
Guinea, Gulf of ≈ 9 D 5
Guinea Basin ≃ 6-7 J 8
Guinea-Bissau ■ GNB 202-203 B 3
Güines ○ C 54-55 D 3
Guingamp ○ F 90-91 F 7
Guinguinéo ○ SN 202-203 C 2
Guintinua Island ∩ RP 160-161 E 5
Guiones, Punta ▲ CR 52-53 B 7
Guiping ○ VRC 156-157 G 5
Guir ○ RMM 196-197 J 5
Guir, Hamada du ∸ DZ 188-189 K 5
Guir, Oued ∼ MA 188-189 K 5
Güira de Melena ○ C 54-55 D 3
Guiratinga ○ BR 72-73 D 4
Güires, Los ○ YV 60-61 L 3
Guiri ○ CAM 206-207 B 3
Güiria ○ YV 60-61 K 2
Guirripa, Caño ∼ CO 60-61 F 5
Guirvas ○ SN 196-197 C 7
Guisa ○ C 54-55 G 4
Guishanfeng • VRC 154-155 J 6
Guishi SK ⊂ VRC 156-157 G 4
Guissat ○ RN 198-199 D 4
Guissèr ○ MA 188-189 H 4
Guissouumalé ○ RMM 202-203 F 3
Guitri ○ CI 202-203 H 7
Guiuan ○ RP 160-161 F 7
Guixi ○ VRC 156-157 K 2
Guiyang ○ VRC (HUN) 156-157 H 4
Guiyang ☆ VRC (GZH) 156-157 E 3
Guizhou □ VRC 156-157 D 3
Gujarat □ IND 138-139 C 8
Gūjar Khān ○ PK 138-139 D 3
Gujba ○ WAN 204-205 J 3
Gujiao ○ VRC 154-155 H 3
Gujrānwāla ○ PK 138-139 E 3
Gujrāt ○ PK 138-139 E 3
Gujri ○ IND 138-139 E 8
Gukera, ostrov ∩ RUS 84-85 c 2
Gulang ○ VRC 154-155 C 3
Gulargambone ○ AUS 178-179 K 6
Gulbarga ○ • IND 140-141 G 2
Gulbene ☆ LV 94-95 K 3
Gulbin Ka, River ∼ WAN 204-205 F 3
Gul'ča ○ KS 136-137 N 4
Gul'ča ∼ KS 136-137 N 5
Guledagudda ○ IND 140-141 F 2
Gulf Breeze ○ USA (FL) 286-287 B 1
Gulf Development Road II AUS 174-175 G 6
Gulf Islands National Seashore ⊥ USA (MS) 268-269 M 6
Gulflander (Historical Railway) • AUS 174-175 F 5
Gulfport ○ USA (FL) 286-287 G 4
Gulfport ○ USA (MS) 268-269 L 6
Gulf Shores ○ USA (AL) 284-285 C 6
Gulgong ○ AUS 180-181 K 2
Gulir ○ RI 166-167 F 4
Gulistan = Gulistón ☆ UZ 136-137 L 4
Guliston ☆ UZ 136-137 L 4
Guliya Shan ▲ VRC 150-151 D 3
Gulja ○ RUS 118-119 K 8
Guljaevskie Koški, ostrova ∩ RUS 88-89 X 2
Guljanci ○ BG 102-103 D 6
Gul Kach ○ PK 138-139 B 4
Gulkana River ∼ USA 20-21 S 5
Gul'kevĭči ○ RUS 102-103 M 5
Güllab Dere ∼ TR 128-129 H 4
Gull Bay ○ CDN (ONT) 234-235 O 5
Gullfoss • IS 86-87 c 2
Gull Lake ○ CDN (SAS) 232-233 K 5
Gull Lake ⊂ CDN (ALB) 232-233 E 3
Gull Lake ⊂ USA (MN) 270-271 D 4
Gull Pond ⊂ CDN (NFL) 242-243 M 3
Gullrock Lake ⊂ CDN (ONT) 234-235 K 4
Güllük Körfezi ≈ 128-129 D 4
Gulmarg ○ • IND 138-139 E 2
Gulmar Kalo ∴ •• TR 128-129 K 4
Gulmit ○ PK 138-139 E 1
Gul Muhammad ○ PK 134-135 M 5
Gülnar ☆ TR 128-129 E 4
Gülpınar ☆ TR 128-129 B 3
Gul'rips ○ GE 126-127 D 6
Gülşehir ☆ TR 128-129 F 3
Gulu ☆ EAU 212-213 D 2
Gulumba Gana ○ WAN 206-207 B 3
Gulūr ○ IND 140-141 G 4
Guluwuru Island ∩ AUS 174-175 D 2
Gulwe ○ EAT 214-215 J 4
Ġumaira ○ UAE 134-135 F 6
Gumal ∼ PK 138-139 C 3
Gumani Hurasagar ∼ BD 142-143 F 3
Gumare ○ RB 218-219 B 4
Gumawana Island ∩ PNG 183 F 5
Gumba ○ ANG 216-217 C 5
Gumba ○ ZRE 210-211 H 2
Gumbiri, Ġabal ▲ SUD 206-207 K 6
Gumbiro ○ EAT 214-215 H 6
Gumbo Gumbo Creek ∼ AUS 178-179 G 4
Gumel ○ WAN 198-199 D 6
Gumgarhi ○ NEP 144-145 D 6
Gumi ○ RI 164-165 K 3
Gumine ○ PNG 183 C 4
Gumla ○ IND 142-143 D 4
Gumlu ○ AUS 174-175 J 6
Gummersbach ○ D 92-93 J 3
Gummi ○ WAN 198-199 B 6
Gumpolds = Humpolec ○ CZ 92-93 N 4
Gumsi ○ WAN 198-199 E 6
Gum Swamp Creek ∼ USA 284-285 G 4
Gümüşhane ☆ TR 128-129 H 2
Gumu Uen, Uar < SP 212-213 J 3
Gumzai ○ RI 166-167 H 4
Guna ○ IND 138-139 F 7
Gūnābād ○ IR 134-135 J 4
Guna Terara ▲ ETH 208-209 D 3
Gunbar ○ AUS 180-181 H 3
Gundagai ○ • AUS 180-181 K 3
Gundāla ○ IND 142-143 B 7
Gundji ○ ZRE 210-211 H 2
Gundlupet ○ IND 140-141 G 5
Gündoğmuş ☆ TR 128-129 E 4
Guneydogu Toroslar ▲ TR 128-129 G 4
Gunga ○ ANG 216-217 E 7
Gungi ○ ZRE 216-217 E 3
Gungo ○ ANG 216-217 C 5
Gungu ○ ZRE 210-211 G 6

Greensburg — Gungu 333

Gungure o MOC 214-215 K 6
Guniujiang Z.B. ⊥ VRC 156-157 K 2
Gūniya ★ RL 128-129 F 6
Gunn o CDN (ALB) 232-233 D 2
Gunnarramby Swamp ≈ AUS 180-181 G 2
Gunnam o S 86-87 H 4
Gunnawarra ★ AUS 174-175 H 5
Gunnbjørn Fjeld ▲ GRØ 28-29 X 3
Gunnedah o AUS 178-179 L 6
Gunning o AUS 180-181 K 3
Gunningbar Creek ~ AUS 178-179 J 6
Gunnison o CDN (CO) 254-255 J 5
Gunnison o USA (UT) 254-255 D 4
Gunnison, Mount ▲ USA (CO) 254-255 H 5
Gunnison River ~ USA 254-255 G 5
Gunpowder o AUS 174-175 E 6
Günsang o VRC 144-145 D 5
Gunsight o USA (AZ) 256-257 C 6
Gunt ~ TJ 136-137 N 6
Gunta o WAN 204-205 H 3
Guntakal o IND 140-141 G 3
Guntersville o USA (AL) 284-285 D 2
Guntersville Lake ⊂ USA (AL) 284-285 D 2
Gunton o CDN (MAN) 234-235 F 4
Guntur o IND 140-141 J 2
Gununa o AUS 174-175 E 5
Gunung, Tanjung ▲ RI 162-163 H 4
Gunung Ambang Reserve ⊥ RI 164-165 J 3
Gunungapi, Pulau ▲ RI 166-167 D 5
Gunung Gading National Park ⊥ MAL 162-163 H 4
Gununghalum o RI 168 B 3
Gunung Lompobatang Reserve ⊥ • RI 164-165 G 6
Gunung Meja Reserve ⊥ • RI 166-167 G 2
Gunung Mulu National Park ⊥ MAL 164-165 D 1
Gunung Rinjani Reserve ⊥ • RI 168 C 7
Gunungsitoli o RI 162-163 B 4
Gunungtua o RI 162-163 C 4
Gunupur o IND 142-143 C 6
Gunyan, Mount ▲ AUS 178-179 L 5
Gunzenhausen o D 92-93 L 4
Guocheng o VRC 154-155 D 3
Guocun o VRC 154-155 B 5
Guodao o VRC 154-155 H 5
Guoguo Wenwu • VRC 154-155 G 4
Guo He ~ VRC 154-155 G 4
Guoju o VRC 156-157 N 2
Guoquanyan ▲ VRC 154-155 C 4
Guoyang o VRC 154-155 K 5
Gur ~ RUS 122-123 H 3
Ġurābī, Ġabal ⊥ ET 194-195 D 3
Gurabo o USA (PR) 286-287 Q 2
Guragė ▲ ETH 208-209 D 4
Gúrán o IR 134-135 F 5
Gurara, River ~ WAN 204-205 G 4
Gurba o ZRE 206-207 H 6
Gurbantünggüt Shamo ⊥ VRC 146-147 H 3
Gurdáspur o IND 138-139 E 3
Gurdon o USA (AR) 276-277 D 7
Gurdzaani o GE 126-127 F 7
Gurë o ETH 208-209 D 5
Gur'ev'sk ★ RUS 94-95 R 4
Gur'evsk = Atyrau ★ KZ 96-97 H 10
Gurgaon o IND 138-139 F 5
Gurgei, Ġabal ▲ SUD 200-201 B 6
Gurguéira, Rio ~ BR 68-69 G 6
Gurguéira, Rio ~ BR 68-69 F 6
Guri, Embalse de ⊂ YV 60-61 K 4
Gurib ~ NAM 220-221 C 3
Gurig National Park ⊥ AUS 172-173 L 1
Gurijuba, Canal do ~ BR 62-63 J 5
Ġúrín o IRQ 128-129 K 4
Gurinhatã o BR 72-73 F 5
Gurlan o UZ 136-137 G 4
Ġurm o AFG 136-137 M 6
Gurner o AUS 172-173 K 7
Guro o MOC 218-219 G 3
Güroymak ★ TR 128-129 K 3
Gurri o SUD 198-199 L 6
Gurskoe o RUS 122-123 G 3
Gurué o MOC 218-219 J 2
Gurumeti ~ EAT 212-213 E 5
Gurun o MAL 162-163 D 2
Gürün ★ TR 128-129 G 3
Gurupa o BR 62-63 J 6
Gurupi o BR 68-69 D 7
Gurupi, Baía do ≈ BR 68-69 E 3
Gurupi, Cabo ▲ BR 68-69 E 2
Gurupi, Rio ~ BR 68-69 D 3
Gurupi, Serra do ▲ BR 68-69 D 4
Gurupizinho o BR 68-69 E 3
Guru Sikhar ▲ IND 138-139 D 7
Guruve o ZW 218-219 F 3
Guruzália o MW 140-141 H 2
Gurvan Sajchan ▲ MAU 148-149 F 6
Gurvansajhan = Suugaant o MAU 148-149 H 5
Gurvantės = Urt o MAU 148-149 E 6
Gurydangdan, peski ⊥ TM 136-137 F 6
Gusar o Qusar o AZ 128-129 N 2
Gusau o WAN 198-199 C 6
Gusev o RUS 94-95 H 4
Gushan ~ VRC 156-157 L 1
Gusher o USA (UT) 254-255 F 3
Gushgy o TM 136-137 H 7
Gushgy ~ TM 136-137 H 7
Gushi o VRC (HEN) 154-155 J 5
Gushi o VRC (QIN) 144-145 L 5
Gushiegu o GH 202-203 K 5
Gushie Point ▲ CDN 36-37 K 6
Gushikawa o J 152-153 B 11
Gushikawa o J 152-153 B 11
Gusi o RI 166-167 G 3
Gusika ~ RUS 110-111 a 4
Gusinaja ~ RUS 110-111 b 4
Gusinaja, guba ≈ RUS 110-111 b 4
Gusinaja Vadega, ~ RUS 108-109 E 5

Gusinaja Zemlja, poluostrov ⌣ RUS 108-109 D 6
Gusinoe, ozero o~ RUS 116-117 M 10
Gusinoozërsk o RUS 116-117 N 10
Gūš Lāġar ~ IR 136-137 G 7
Güstrow o D 92-93 M 2
Gutah o CDN 32-33 K 3
Gutara ~ RUS 116-117 H 8
Gutarskij hrebet ▲ RUS 116-117 H 8
Gutenko Mountains ▲ ARK 16 F 30
Gütersloh o D 92-93 K 3
Guthalungra o AUS 174-175 J 6
Guthrie o USA (AZ) 256-257 F 6
Guthrie o USA (OK) 264-265 G 3
Guthrie o USA (TX) 264-265 D 5
Guthrie Center o USA (IA) 274-275 D 3
Gutian o VRC 156-157 L 3
Gutiérrez Zamora o MEX 52-53 F 1
Gutsuo o VRC 144-145 F 6
Guttaiyūr o IND 140-141 G 5
Guttenberg o USA (IA) 274-275 G 2
Guttstadt = Dobre Miasto o~ PL 92-93 Q 2
Gutu o ZW 218-219 F 4
Gu Vo o USA (AZ) 256-257 C 6
Guwahati o IND 142-143 G 2
Guwaifât o UAE 134-135 G 5
Gûwaiza o UAE 134-135 F 6
Guwayr o SUD 200-201 F 4
Guy o CDN 32-33 M 4
Guyana ■ GUY 62-63 E 3
Guyandot River ~ USA 280-281 D 5
Guyang o VRC 148-149 J 7
Guyenne o F 90-91 G 9
Guy Fawkes River National Park ⊥ AUS 178-179 M 6
Guyi o ETH 208-209 B 4
Guymon o USA (OK) 264-265 C 2
Gûyom o IR 134-135 E 4
Guyot Glacier ⊂ USA 20-21 U 6
Guyra o AUS 178-179 L 6
Guyton o USA (GA) 284-285 J 4
Guzar o UZ 136-137 K 5
Guzayyil, Bi'r al • LAR 192-193 K 4
Güzeloluk o TR 128-129 F 4
Güzelsu o TR 128-129 K 3
Guzhen o VRC (ANH) 154-155 K 5
Guzhen o VRC (FUJ) 156-157 M 3
Guzmán o MEX 50-51 F 2
Guzmán, Laguna de ⊂ MEX 50-51 F 2
Gvadar o IR 134-135 J 6
Gvardejsk o RUS 94-95 G 4
Gvardejsk = Gvardejsk ★ RUS 94-95 G 4
Gvasjugi o RUS 122-123 G 5
Gwa o MYA 158-159 C 2
Gwaai o ZW 218-219 F 4
Gwabegar o AUS 178-179 K 6
Gwada o WAN 204-205 G 4
Gwadabawa o WAN 198-199 B 6
Gwädär o PK 134-135 K 6
Gwagwalada o WAN 204-205 G 4
Gwalia ∴ AUS 176-177 F 4
Gwalior o IND 138-139 G 6
Gwalishtap o PK 134-135 K 4
Gwamba o WAN 204-205 F 3
Gwambara o WAN 198-199 B 6
Gwanda o ZW 218-219 E 5
Gwane o ZRE 206-207 H 6
Gwaram o WAN 204-205 H 4
Gwardafuy, Cap = Raas Caseyr ▲ SP 208-209 K 3
Gwarif o RI 166-167 K 3
Gwarzo o WAN 204-205 G 3
Gwasero o WAN 204-205 G 4
Gwayi ~ ZW 218-219 D 4
Gwayi River o ZW 218-219 D 4
Gweedore o IRL 90-91 D 4
Gwembe o ZW 218-219 D 3
Gweru o ZW (Mid) 218-219 E 4
Gweru o ZW 218-219 E 4
Gweta o RB 218-219 C 5
Gwi o WAN 204-205 G 4
Gwillim River ~ CDN 34-35 C 2
Gwinn o USA (MI) 270-271 L 4
Gwinner o USA (ND) 258-259 K 5
Gwoza o WAN 204-205 K 4
Gwydir Highway II AUS 178-179 L 6
Gwydir River ~ AUS 178-179 L 6
Gwynne o CDN (ALB) 232-233 E 2
Gwynn Island ⌣ USA (VA) 280-281 K 6
Gyaca o VRC 144-145 G 4
Gya'gya = Saga o VRC 144-145 E 6
Gyandzha = Ganza o AZ 128-129 M 2
Gyangzê o VRC 144-145 G 5
Gyaring Co ⊂ VRC 144-145 G 5
Gyaring Hu ⊂ VRC 144-145 L 3
Gyda o RUS 108-109 N 4
Gydanskaja grjada ▲ RUS 108-109 Q 7
Gydanskaja guba ≈ RUS 108-109 R 5
Gydanskij poluostrov ⌣ RUS 108-109 Q 6
Gydanskij proliv ≈ 108-109 Q 5
Gydanskiy Poluostrov = Gydanskij poluostrov ⌣ RUS 108-109 Q 6
Gyêbar Co ⊂ VRC 144-145 E 6
Gyirong o VRC 144-145 E 6
Gyitang o VRC 144-145 L 3
Gyldenløves Fjord ≈ 28-29 U 4
Gympie o AUS 178-179 M 4
Gynym ~ RUS 118-119 O 7
Gynym ~ RUS 120-121 D 5
Gyobingauk o MYA 142-143 J 6
Gyokusendo • J 152-153 B 11
Gyöngyös o H 92-93 P 5
Győr o H 92-93 O 5

Gypsum Palace o AUS 180-181 G 3
Gypsum Point ▲ CDN 30-31 M 5
Gypsumville o CDN (MAN) 234-235 E 3
Gyrfalcon Islands ▲ CDN 36-37 P 5
Gyrgyčan o RUS 112-113 Q 2

H

H1 o IRQ 128-129 J 6
H3 o IRQ 128-129 J 6
Häädemeeste o EST 94-95 J 2
Ha'afeva ▲ TON 184 IV a 1
Haag, Den = 's-Gravenhage ★ ★ NL 92-93 H 2
Haakon VII Land ⊥ N 84-85 H 3
Haalenberg o NAM 220-221 B 3
Ha'amonga Triiithon • TON 184 IV a 2
Ha'ano ▲ TON 184 IV a 1
Ha'apai Group ▲ TON 184 IV a 1
Haapajärvi o FIN 88-89 H 5
Haapsalu ★ EST 94-95 H 2
Haarlem ★ ★★ NL 92-93 H 2
Haarlem o ZA 220-221 F 6
Haast o NZ 182 B 5
Haastbergat ▲ N 84-85 M 3
Haast Bluff o AUS 176-177 L 1
Haast Pass ▲ NZ 182 B 6
Haasts Bluff Aboriginal Land ⊥ AUS 176-177 K 1
Hab ~ PK 134-135 M 6
Haba, al- o UAE 134-135 G 6
Habadra, Hassi • DZ 190-191 E 7
Habahe o VRC 146-147 H 1
Habana, La ★ C 54-55 D 3
Habarane o CL 140-141 J 6
Habar Cirir o SP 208-209 H 6
Habarovsk o RUS 122-123 F 4
Habarût o OM 132-133 K 5
Habaswein o EAK 212-213 G 3
Habay o SP 212-213 J 3
Ḩabbā, al- o KSA 130-131 G 4
Habbân o Y 132-133 G 6
Ḩabbāniya, al- o IRQ 128-129 K 6
Ḩabbāniya, al- o IRQ 128-129 K 6
Habeljaha ~ RUS 108-109 O 5
Habibābād o IR 134-135 D 3
Habirag o VRC 148-149 M 6
Habšān o UAE 132-133 H 2
Habūr ~ Y 132-133 C 5
Ḩābūr, al- ~ SYR 128-129 J 4
Ḩābūr, Nahr al- ~ SYR 128-129 J 4
Hacari o CO 60-61 E 3
Hacha, Raudal ~ CO 64-65 F 1
Hachinohe o J 152-153 J 4
Hachiōji ★ J 152-153 H 7
Hachita-gota-ko o J 152-153 J 5
Hachita o USA (NM) 256-257 G 7
Hack, Mount ▲ AUS 178-179 F 5
Hackberry o USA (AZ) 256-257 B 3
Hackberry o USA (LA) 268-269 G 7
Hackberry Creek ~ USA 262-263 F 6
Hackensack o USA (MN) 270-271 D 4
Hackett o CDN (ALB) 232-233 F 3
Hacketstown o USA (NJ) 280-281 M 3
Hoolobburg o USA (AL) 284-285 B 2
Hackney o GUY 62-63 F 2
Ḩaḍmas ~ Xaqmaz o AZ 128-129 N 2
Haco o ANG 216-217 C 5
Hacufera o MOC 218-219 G 5
Hadaaftimo o SP 208-209 J 3
Hadagali o IND 140-141 F 3
Hadakta o RUS 118-119 F 10
Hadaliya o SUD 200-201 H 4
Hadama o RUS 116-117 J 9
Hadaran'ja, hrebet ▲ RUS 110-111 V 5
Hadashville o CDN (MAN) 234-235 H 5
Ḩadbaram o OM 132-133 J 5
Ḩadbat al-Ġilf al-Kabīr ▲ ET 192-193 L 6
Hadd, al- o OM 132-133 L 2
Hadd, Ra's al- ▲ OM 132-133 L 2
Hadda ∴ AFG 138-139 C 2
Haddād o Y 132-133 H 7
Haddād Bani Malik o KSA 132-133 C 3
Haddār, al- o KSA 132-133 C 2
Haddington • GB 90-91 F 4
Haddon Corner • AUS 178-179 F 4
Haddummati Atoll ▲ MV 140-141 B 7
Hadejia o WAN (KAN) 198-199 E 6
Hadejia ~ WAN 198-199 D 6
Hadera o IL 130-131 D 1
Haderslev o DK 86-87 K 5
Hadgaon o IND 138-139 F 10
Hādh, Wādī ~ LAR 192-193 G 5
Hadht o NZ 134-135 G 6
Hadhour, Hassi o DZ 188-189 L 5
Hadibū o Y 132-133 H 7
Hadiga o SUD 200-201 E 4
Hadilik o VRC 144-145 F 2
Hadita ★ TR 128-129 E 4
Hadita, al- o KSA 130-131 G 4
Hadseløya ▲ N 86-87 G 2
Hadsten o DK 86-87 D 7
Hadsund o DK 86-87 D 7
Hadudpur ~ RUS 114-115 P 3
Haduttê ~ RUS 108-109 R 8

Hadweenzie River ~ USA 20-21 Q 3
Hadyjah ~ KSA 114-115 K 2
Hadyr'jaha, Bol'šaja ~ RUS 114-115 P 2
Hadytajaha ~ RUS 108-109 N 8
Hae o THA 142-143 M 6
Haeju o KOR 150-151 E 8
Haena o USA (HI) 288 F 2
Haenam o ROK 150-151 F 10
Haenertsburg o ZA 218-219 E 6
Hafar al-Bāṭin o KSA 130-131 J 3
Hafeira, Oued el- ~ RIM 196-197 E 2
Haffa, al- o SYR 128-129 G 5
Haffner Bjerg ▲ GRØ 26-27 T 5
Hafford o CDN (SAS) 232-233 L 4
Haffouz o TN 190-191 G 3
Hafik ★ TR 128-129 G 2
Ḩafīrat Nisāh o KSA 130-131 K 5
Ḩāfizābād o PK 138-139 D 3
Hafnarfjörður ★ IS 86-87 c 2
Haftgel o IR 134-135 D 3
Haft Tappe ∴ IR 134-135 C 2
Hagadera o EAK 212-213 H 3
Ḩaḡal Bi'r • SYR 128-129 H 5
Hagar o CDN (ONT) 238-239 E 2
Ḩaḡar, al- o OM 132-133 K 2
Ḩaḡara, al- o IRQ 128-129 K 6
Ḩaḡāra, al- ⊥ KSA 130-131 H 3
Ḩaḡar Banga o SUD 206-207 F 3
Hagari ~ IND 140-141 G 3
Ḩaḡḍa o Y 132-133 C 7
Hagemeister Island ⌣ USA 22-23 Q 3
Hagemeister Strait ≈ 22-23 Q 3
Hagen o CDN (SAS) 232-233 N 3
Hagen o D 92-93 J 3
Hagen, Mount ▲ PNG 183 C 3
Hagensborg o CDN (BC) 228-229 H 4
Hägere Hiywet o ETH 208-209 C 4
Hägere Selam o ETH 208-209 D 5
Hagerman o USA (ID) 252-253 D 4
Hagerman o USA (NM) 256-257 L 5
Hagerman National Wildlife Refuge ⊥ USA (TX) 264-265 H 5
Hagerstown o USA (IN) 274-275 N 6
Hagerstown o USA (MD) 280-281 J 4
Ḩaġḡa o Y 132-133 G 7
Hägg 'Abd Allāh o SUD 200-201 F 6
Ḩāḡḡ 'Alī Qoli, Kavīr-e o IR 136-137 D 7
Hagi o J 152-153 D 7
Hà Giang o VN 156-157 D 5
Ḩaġr, al- o KSA 130-131 K 5
Hague o CDN (SAS) 232-233 M 4
Hague, Cap de la ▲ F 90-91 G 7
Haguenau o F 90-91 L 7
Hahan ~ RUS 120-121 D 4
Ḩaḥčan ~ RUS 110-111 N 6
Hahira o USA (GA) 284-285 G 6
Hahndorf o AUS 180-181 E 3
Hahnville o USA (LA) 268-269 K 7
Haho ~ RT 202-203 L 6
Haho o RT 202-203 L 6
Haia o PNG 183 C 4
Ḩai'an o VRC (GDG) 156-157 G 6
Hai'an o VRC (JIA) 154-155 M 5
Haib o NAM (KAB) 220-221 D 4
Haibar o KSA 130-131 F 5
Haicheng o VRC 150-151 D 7
Haida o CDN (BC) 228-229 B 2
Haidarah o TN 190-191 G 3
Haifa = Hefa o IL 130-131 D 1
Haifeng o VRC 156-157 J 5
Haig o AUS 176-177 J 5
Haigler o USA (NE) 262-263 E 4
Haikang o VRC 156-157 G 6
Haikou ★ VRC 156-157 G 6
Ḩā'il ★ KSA 130-131 G 4
Ḩā'il, Wādī ~ KSA 130-131 G 4
Hailakandi o IND 142-143 H 3
Hailar o VRC 150-151 C 3
Hailar He ~ VRC 150-151 C 3
Hailey o USA (ID) 252-253 D 3
Haileybury o CDN (ONT) 236-237 J 5
Hailin o RUS 112-113 O 6
Hailing o VRC 154-155 M 6
Hailong o RUS 96-97 L 8
Hailun o VRC 150-151 F 4
Hailuoto (Karlö) ▲ FIN 88-89 H 4
Ḩaima, Ra's al- o UAE 134-135 F 6
Haimen o VRC 154-155 M 6
Hainan o VRC 156-157 F 7
Hainan Dao ⌣ VRC 156-157 G 7
Hainan Strait = Qiongzhou Haixia ≈ 156-157 F 6
Hainault Tourist Mine • AUS 176-177 F 5
Haindi o LB 202-203 E 6
Haines o USA (AK) 20-21 X 7
Haines o USA (OR) 244-245 H 2
Haines City o USA (FL) 286-287 H 3
Haines Highway II CDN 20-21 W 6
Haines Junction o CDN 20-21 W 6
Haingsisi o RI 166-167 H 7
Haining o VRC 154-155 M 6
Hair, Qasr al- ∴ SYR 128-129 H 5
Hair al-Garbi, Qasr al- ∴ SYR 128-129 G 5
Hairé Lao o SN 196-197 C 6
Hairjuzova ~ RUS 120-121 U 3
Hairy Hill o CDN (ALB) 232-233 F 2
Ḩaḏramaut ⊥ Y 132-133 G 6
Ḩaḏramaut, Wādī ~ Y 132-133 F 5
Haiṣat an-Naum, Ra's ▲ Y 132-133 H 7
Ḩā'it, al- o KSA 130-131 G 5
Haitan Dao ⌣ VRC 156-157 L 4
Haiti ■ RH 54-55 J 5
Haiwee Reservoir ⊂ USA (CA) 248-249 G 3
Haiyan o VRC (QIN) 154-155 B 3

Haiyan o VRC (ZHE) 154-155 M 6
Haiyang o VRC 154-155 M 3
Haiyuan o VRC 154-155 D 3
Haizhou Wan ≈ 154-155 L 4
Haja, Džebariki- o RUS 120-121 F 2
Haja, Jurjung- o RUS 110-111 J 3
Hajata, Suntar-hrebet ▲ RUS 110-111 V 7
Hajdarkan o KS 136-137 M 5
Hajeb El Ayoun o TN 190-191 G 3
Hajiki-saki ▲ J 152-153 H 5
Hajja, Eje- o RUS 110-111 U 6
Hajjah o Y 132-133 C 6
Hajjiulja o RUS 120-121 T 4
Hajnówka o PL 92-93 R 2
Hajo o ROK 150-151 F 10
Hajpudyrskaja, guba o 108-109 H 7
Hajrjuzovo, Ust'- o RUS 120-121 R 5
Hajsn ★ UA 102-103 K 3
Hajyr o RUS 110-111 T 4
Haysardah o RUS 118-119 O 5
Haka o MYA 142-143 H 4
Hakai Recreation Area ⊥ CDN (BC) 230-231 A 2
Hakalau o USA (HI) 288 K 5
Hakčan, Ust'- o RUS 120-121 M 2
Hakkari ★ TR 128-129 K 4
Hakkari Dağları ▲ TR 128-129 K 4
Hakken-san ▲ J 152-153 F 7
Hakkoda-san ▲ J 152-153 J 4
Hakkulabad o UZ 136-137 N 4
Hakodate o J 152-153 J 4
Hakoma o RUS 116-117 J 2
Hakskeenpan o ZA 220-221 E 5
Hakui o J 152-153 G 6
Haku-san ▲ J 152-153 G 6
Hakusan National Park ⊥ J 152-153 G 6
Häla ~ PK 138-139 B 7
Halab (Aleppo) ★ ★★★ SYR 128-129 G 4
Halaban o RI 162-163 B 3
Halabǰa ~ IRQ 128-129 M 5
Halač o TM 136-137 J 5
Ḩalā'ib o ET 194-195 H 6
Halali o NAM 216-217 D 9
Ḩalāt 'Ammār o KSA 130-131 E 3
Halawa o USA (HI) 288 J 3
Halberstadt o D 92-93 L 3
Halbrite o CDN (SAS) 232-233 N 5
Halčaganahta, krjaž ▲ RUS 110-111 G 4
Halcon, Mount ▲ RP 160-161 D 6
Haldane River ~ CDN 30-31 J 2
Halden ★ N 86-87 E 7
Haldia o IND 142-143 F 4
Haldwani o IND 138-139 G 5
Hale Center o USA (TX) 264-265 C 4
Haleiwa o USA (HI) 288 G 3
Hale River ~ AUS 178-179 C 2
Haley Dome o USA (UT) 254-255 F 4
Haleyville o USA (AL) 284-285 C 2
Half Assini o GH 202-203 J 7
Ḩalfāyat al-Mulūk o SUD 200-201 F 5
Hal Flood Range ▲ ARK 16 F 23
Halfmoon Bay o CDN (BC) 230-231 F 4
Halfmoon Bay o NZ 182 B 7
Half Moon Bay o USA (CA) 248-249 B 2
Half Moon Lake ⊂ AUS 176-177 M 4
Halfway o USA (OR) 244-245 H 6
Half Way Hills ▲ CDN 30-31 V 3
Halfway River ~ CDN 32-33 J 3
Halgen o SP 208-209 G 6
Ḩalḥāl o Y 132-133 D 7
Halhgol o MAU 148-149 O 4
Haliban o KSA 130-131 J 4
Haliburton o CDN (ONT) 238-239 G 4
Haliburton Highlands ▲ CDN 238-239 G 3
Ḩālidi o IRQ 128-129 L 6
Ḩālida, Bi'r o ET 194-195 H 6
Halifax o AUS 174-175 J 6
Halifax ★ CDN (NS) 240-241 M 6
Halifax, Mount ▲ AUS 174-175 J 6
Halifax Bay ≈ 174-175 J 6
Ḩaliǧ al-'Arab ≈ 194-195 D 2
Halikarnassos ∴ TR 128-129 B 4
Ḩalil, al- = Hevron o WB 130-131 D 2
Ḩalīlābād o IR 136-137 F 7
Halle, Ra's e ▲ IR 134-135 D 4
Hallovo o RUS 96-97 L 8
Halli Rūd ~ IR 134-135 H 6
Hallukik o RU 166-167 C 6
Ḩālis, al- o IRQ 128-129 L 6
Ḩalyal o IND 140-141 F 3
Haljala o EST 94-95 K 2
Haljango, ostrov ⌣ RUS 108-109 P 5
Halkanskij hrebet ▲ RUS 120-121 L 3
Halke Shan ▲ VRC 146-147 K 4
Halkett, Cape ▲ USA 20-21 O 1
Ḩālki ~ GR 100-101 L 6
Halkida o GR 100-101 J 4
Halkidikí ⌣ GR 100-101 J 4
Halkirk o CDN (ALB) 232-233 F 3
Hallam Peak ▲ CDN (BC) 228-229 Q 4
Halland ⊥ S 86-87 F 8
Hallandale o USA (FL) 286-287 J 6
Ḩallānīyāt, al- ⌣ OM 132-133 K 5
Hallasan ▲ ROK 150-151 F 11
Hallasan National Park ⊥ ROK 150-151 F 11
Hallboro o CDN (MAN) 234-235 D 4
Hall Beach o CDN 24-25 f 6
Hall Bredning ≈ 26-27 n 8
Ḩallé, al- o KSA 130-131 G 5
Halle (Saale) o D 92-93 L 3
Halleck o USA (NV) 246-247 K 3
Hallein o A 92-93 M 5
Halls o S 86-87 G 5

Hallett o AUS 180-181 E 2
Hallettsville o USA (TX) 266-267 L 4
Halley Bay ⌂ ARK 16 F 34
Halliday o USA (ND) 258-259 E 4
Halliday Lake o CDN 30-31 P 5
Hall Indian Reservation, Fort ⊥ USA (ID) 252-253 F 3
Hallingdal ⌣ N 86-87 D 6
Hallingdalselvi ~ N 86-87 D 6
Hallingskarvet ▲ N 86-87 C 6
Hall Island ⌣ USA 48-49 Y 6
Hall Island ⌣ USA 112-113 V 6
Hall Islands ⌣ FSM 13 G 2
Hall Lake o CDN 24-25 f 6
Hall Land ⊥ GRØ 26-27 U 3
Hällnäs o S 86-87 J 4
Hallock o USA (MN) 270-271 B 3
Hallonquist o CDN (SAS) 232-233 M 5
Hallowell, Cape ▲ CDN 24-25 d 6
Hall Peninsula ⌣ CDN 36-37 Q 3
Hall Point ▲ AUS 174-175 F 3
Hallson o USA (ND) 258-259 K 3
Hallsville o USA (TX) 268-269 F 4
Hallville o CDN (ONT) 238-239 K 3
Hallyŏ Haesang National Park ⊥ ROK 150-151 G 10
Halmahera ⌣ RI 166-167 H 3
Halmahera, Laut ≈ 166-167 H 4
Halmahera Sea = Halmahera, Laut ≈ 166-167 E 1
Ḩal'merno, ozero o RUS 108-109 N 7
Halmstad o S 86-87 F 8
Hälöl o IND 138-139 D 8
Halong o RI 166-167 E 3
Hal'šany o BY 94-95 K 4
Halstad o USA (MN) 270-271 B 3
Halstead o USA (KS) 262-263 J 4
Haltom City o USA (TX) 264-265 G 6
Halturin o RUS 96-97 F 4
Halura, Pulau ⌣ RI 168 E 8
Halvad o IND 138-139 C 8
Halverson Ridge ▲ CDN 32-33 L 3
Halvmåneøya ⌣ N 84-85 L 3
Halvorgate o CDN (SAS) 232-233 M 4
Halzan Sogootyn davaa ▲ MAU 148-149 D 3
Ham ~ NAM 220-221 D 4
Ham o TCH 206-207 B 3
Hamab o NAM 220-221 D 4
Hamād, al- ⊥ KSA 130-131 F 2
Hamada o J 152-153 E 7
Hamadān ★ IR 134-135 C 1
Hamaguir o DZ 188-189 K 5
Ḩamāh ★ ★★★ SYR 128-129 G 4
Hamakua Coast ⌣ USA 288 K 4
Hamamah o LAR 192-193 J 1
Hamamasu o J 152-153 J 3
Hamamatsu o J 152-153 G 7
Haman o CAM 204-205 K 6
Hamar ★ N 86-87 E 6
Hamar o USA (ND) 258-259 J 4
Hamar, al- o KSA 132-133 E 3
Hamar-Daban, hrebet ▲ RUS 116-117 L 10
Ḩamāsīn, al- o KSA 132-133 D 3
Ḩamāṭa, Ġabal ▲ ET 194-195 H 5
Hama-Tombetsu o J 152-153 K 2
Hamba o COM 222-223 C 4
Hambantota o CL 140-141 J 7
Hambaparoing o RI 168 E 7
Hamberg o USA (ND) 258-259 H 4
Hamber Provincial Park ⊥ CDN (BC) 228-229 R 4
Hambidge Conservation Park ⊥ AUS 180-181 C 2
Hamborgerland ⌣ GRØ 28-29 Z 3
Hamburg o D 92-93 L 2
Hamburg o SME 62-63 G 3
Hamburg o USA (AR) 276-277 D 7
Hamburg o USA (IA) 274-275 C 4
Hamburg o USA (NY) 278-279 C 6
Hamburg o ZA 220-221 H 6
Hamd, Wādī al- ~ KSA 130-131 E 4
Hämeenlinna ★ FIN 88-89 H 6
Hamelin o AUS 176-177 D 3
Hamelin, Mount ▲ USA 24-25 P 3
Hamelin Pool o AUS 176-177 B 3
Hameln o D 92-93 K 3
Hamen Wan ≈ 156-157 K 3
Hamer o USA (ID) 252-253 F 3
Hamer Koke o ETH 208-209 D 5
Hamero Hadad o ETH 208-209 F 5
Hamersley o AUS 172-173 C 7
Hamersley Lakes o AUS 176-177 E 5
Hamersley Range ▲ AUS 172-173 C 6
Hamersley Range National Park ⊥ AUS 172-173 C 7
Hamgåä, al- o KSA 130-131 H 5
Hamhung o KOR 150-151 F 8
Hami o VRC 146-147 L 4
Hämi, al- o Y 132-133 F 6
Hamidiya o SYR 128-129 G 5
Hamidiye o IR 134-135 C 3
Hamilton Creek ~ AUS 174-175 F 3
Hamilton o AUS (TAS) 180-181 J 7
Hamilton o CDN (ONT) 238-239 F 5
Hamilton ★ NZ 182 E 2
Hamilton o NZ 182 E 2
Hamilton ★ GB 54-55 L 1
Hamilton o USA (AK) 20-21 J 5
Hamilton o USA (AL) 284-285 C 2
Hamilton o USA (CO) 254-255 H 3
Hamilton o USA (IL) 274-275 H 3
Hamilton o USA (IN) 274-275 N 4
Hamilton o USA (KS) 262-263 K 7
Hamilton o USA (MO) 274-275 D 5

Hamilton o USA (MT) 250-251 E 5
Hamilton o USA (OH) 280-281 B 4
Hamilton o USA (TX) 266-267 J 5
Hamilton o USA (WA) 244-245 D 2
Hamilton, Lake ⊂ USA 180-181 C 3
Hamilton, Lake ⊂ USA 276-277 C 6
Hamilton, Mount ▲ USA (NV) 246-247 K 4
Hamilton Bank ≃ 6-7 D 3
Hamilton City o USA (CA) 246-247 C 4
Hamilton Creek ~ AUS 176-177 M 3
Hamilton Dome o USA (WY) 252-253 F 3
Hamilton Downs o AUS 176-177 M 1
Hamilton Hotel o AUS 178-179 F 2
Hamilton Island o AUS 174-175 K 7
Hamilton River ~ AUS 174-175 F 3
Hamim o UAE 132-133 J 2
Hamim, Wādī al- ~ LAR 192-193 K 2
Hamina o FIN 88-89 J 6
Hamiota o CDN (MAN) 234-235 C 4
Hami Pendi ⌣ VRC 146-147 L 4
Hamir o ★ Y 132-133 C 6
Hämir, Wādī ~ IRQ 128-129 J 7
Ḩāmir, al- o KSA 130-131 G 2
Ḩāmir, Wādī ~ Y 132-133 F 6
Hami Rotoki • SUD 200-201 B 6
Hamirpur o IND 142-143 B 3
Hamis, Hadjer el o TCH 198-199 G 6
Ḩāmis al-Bahr o KSA 132-133 B 4
Ḩāmis Mušait o KSA 132-133 C 4
Ḩāmis, Wādī al- ~ KSA 132-133 C 4
Hamlen Bay ≈ 36-37 Q 3
Hamlet o USA (NC) 282-283 H 6
Hamlet, Mount ▲ USA 20-21 M 2
Hamlin o CDN (ALB) 232-233 G 2
Hamlin o USA (SAS) 232-233 K 3
Hamlin o USA (TX) 264-265 D 6
Hamlin Valley ~ USA (UT) 254-255 B 6
Hamm o D 92-93 J 3
Hammām, al- o IRQ 128-129 L 7
Ḩammām 'Alī o Y 132-133 G 6
Hammamet o TN 190-191 H 2
Hammamet, Golfe de ≈ 190-191 H 2
Hammam-Lif o TN 190-191 H 2
Hamman, Oued ~ DZ 190-191 G 2
Hammer, Kap ▲ GRØ 28-29 Z 2
Hammerdal o S 86-87 G 5
Hammerfest o N 86-87 L 1
Hammern ~ GRØ 26-27 q 4
Hammilton Sound ≈ 242-243 O 3
Hammock, Kap ▲ GRØ 26-27 q 4
Hammon o USA (OK) 264-265 E 3
Hammond o USA (LA) 268-269 K 7
Hammond o USA (MT) 258-259 D 4
Hammond Bay ≈ 272-273 E 2
Hammond Island ⌣ AUS 183 B 6
Hammondvale o CDN (NB) 240-241 K 5
Hammonton o USA (NJ) 280-281 M 4
Hamna ~ RUS 120-121 F 3
Hamnej ~ RUS 116-117 L 10
Ham-Nord o CDN (QUE) 238-239 O 3
Hamoud o RIM 196-197 E 3
Hamoyet, Ġabal ▲ SUD 200-201 J 4
Hampa o RUS 118-119 L 4
Hampden o CDN (NFL) 242-243 M 3
Hampden o USA (ME) 278-279 N 4
Hampenanperak o RI 162-163 C 3
Hampi o ∴ IND 140-141 G 4
Hampshire o USA (IL) 274-275 K 2
Hampton o CDN (NB) 240-241 K 5
Hampton o CDN (NS) 240-241 K 6
Hampton o USA (AR) 276-277 D 7
Hampton o USA (IA) 274-275 E 2
Hampton o USA (NB) 262-263 J 3
Hampton o USA (SC) 284-285 J 3
Hampton o USA (VA) 280-281 K 6
Hampton Butte ▲ USA (OR) 244-245 E 7
Hampton Roads ≈ 280-281 K 7
Hamra o RUS 118-119 F 5
Hamra o SUD 206-207 J 3
Ḩamrā', al- o LAR 192-193 H 1
Hamra, Oued el ~ LAR 188-189 G 7
Ḩamrān, Bi'r o IRQ 128-129 K 5
Hamränge o S 86-87 H 6
Hamrat al-Wuzz o SUD 200-201 E 5
Hamrin, Ġabal ▲ IRQ 128-129 L 6
Hamsara ~ RUS 116-117 H 9
Hams Fork ~ USA 252-253 H 5
Hamstead o USA (NC) 282-283 K 6
Hàm Thuận Nam o VN 156-157 J 6
Hamtown o CDN (NB) 240-241 J 4
Hamūd, 'Ain o IRQ 128-129 J 2
Hamūdiyah, Al o LAR 192-193 G 3
Hamuku o RI 166-167 H 3
Hämün-e Ġaz Mūrīãn o IR 134-135 H 5
Ham Yên o VN 156-157 D 5
Hamyskij o RUS 126-127 D 5
Hana o USA (HI) 288 J 4
Ḩanabanilla, Presa de ⊂ C 54-55 E 3
Hanahan o PNG 184 I b 1
Hanak o TR 128-129 K 2
Hanäkiya, al o KSA 130-131 G 5
Hanäkiya, Wädi al- ~ KSA 130-131 G 5
Hanalei o USA (HI) 288 F 2
Hà Nam o VN 156-157 D 6
Hanamaki o J 152-153 J 5
Hanamaulu o USA (HI) 288 F 2
Hanapepe o USA (HI) 288 F 2
Hänaqin ★ IRQ 128-129 L 6
Hanarasalja, mys ▲ RUS 108-109 P 8
Hän ar-Rahba o IRQ 128-129 K 5
Hanaša, al- o KSA 132-133 C 5
Hanåtir o SYR 128-129 G 5
Hän Beben o IR 136-137 D 6

Hazīpur o IND 142-143 D 3
Hazlehurst o USA (GA) 284-285 H 5
Hazlehurst o USA (MS) 268-269 K 5
Hazlet o CDN (SAS) 232-233 K 5
Hazleton o USA (PA) 280-281 L 3
Hazlett, Lake o AUS 172-173 J 6
Ḥazm, al- o Y 132-133 D 5
Hazorasp ☆ UZ 136-137 G 4
Ḥażrat-e Solṭān o AFG 136-137 K 6
Hazro o PK 138-139 D 3
Hažuu-Us o MAU 148-149 H 5
Ḫazzān Aswān (Old Dam) < • ET 194-195 F 5
Headingley o CDN (MAN) 234-235 F 5
Headingly o AUS 178-179 E 1
Headland o USA (AL) 284-285 E 5
Headlands o ZW 218-219 G 4
Head of Bay d'Espoir o CDN (NFL) 242-243 N 5
Head of Bight ≈ 176-177 L 5
Headquarters o USA (ID) 250-251 D 5
Headquarters o USA (NM) 256-257 J 6
Head Smashed-in Bison Jump ••• CDN (ALB) 232-233 E 6
Heafford Junction o USA (WI) 270-271 J 5
Healesville o AUS 180-181 H 4
Healey Lake o CDN 30-31 Q 3
Healton o USA (OK) 264-265 G 4
Healy o USA 20-21 Q 5
Healy o USA (KS) 262-263 F 6
Heany Junction o ZW 218-219 E 5
Heard Island ⌒ AUS 12 F 10
Hearne o CDN (SAS) 232-233 N 5
Hearne o USA (TX) 266-267 L 3
Hearst o CDN (ONT) 236-237 E 3
Hearst Island ⌒ ARK 16 G 30
Hearst San Simeon State Historic Monument • USA (CA) 248-249 C 4
Heart Butte o USA (MT) 250-251 G 3
Heart River ~ USA 258-259 F 5
Heart's Content o CDN (NFL) 242-243 P 5
Heath, Río ~ BOL 70-71 C 3
Heathcote o AUS 180-181 H 4
Heatherdown o CDN (ALB) 232-233 D 2
Heath Steele o CDN (NB) 240-241 J 3
Heavener o USA (OK) 264-265 K 4
H. E. Bailey Turnpike II USA (OK) 264-265 F 4
Hebbale o IND 140-141 F 4
Hebbronville o USA (TX) 266-267 J 6
Hebburli o IND 140-141 F 4
Hebei ◘ VRC 154-155 J 2
Hebel o AUS 178-179 J 5
Heber o USA (AZ) 256-257 E 4
Hebera o RI 166-167 E 2
Heber City o USA (UT) 254-255 D 3
Heber Springs o USA (AR) 276-277 C 5
Hebert o USA (LA) 268-269 J 4
Hébertville o CDN (QUE) 240-241 D 2
Hebgen Lake o USA (MT) 250-251 H 7
Hebi o VRC 154-155 J 4
Hebo o USA (OR) 244-245 B 5
Hebri o IND 140-141 F 4
Hebrides, Sea of the ≈ 90-91 D 3
Hebrides or Western Isles ⌒ GB 90-91 D 3
Hebron o CDN 36-37 S 5
Hebron o USA (IN) 274-275 L 3
Hebron o USA (MS) 268-269 L 5
Hebron o USA (ND) 258-259 E 5
Hebron o USA (NE) 262-263 J 4
Hebron = Hevron ☆ WB 130-131 D 2
Hebron, Mount o USA (CA) 246-247 C 2
Hebron Fiord ≈ 36-37 S 5
Heby ☆ S 86-87 H 7
Hecate o CDN (BC) 230-231 C 4
Hecate Strait ≈ 228-229 C 2
Hecelchakán o • MEX 52-53 J 1
Heceta Island ⌒ USA 32-33 D 4
Hechevarria o C 54-55 H 4
Hechi o VRC 156-157 F 4
Hechuan o VRC 154-155 E 6
Hechun o VRC 156-157 G 6
Heckford Bank ≃ 158-159 D 5
Hecla o CDN (MAN) 234-235 G 3
Hecla o USA (SD) 260-261 H 1
Hecla and Griper Bay ≈ 24-25 P 2
Hecla Island ⌒ CDN (MAN) 234-235 G 3
Hecla Provincial Park ⊥ CDN (MAN) 234-235 G 3
Hectanooga o CDN (NS) 240-241 J 6
Hector o USA (AR) 276-277 C 5
Hector o USA (MN) 270-271 D 6
Hector, Mount ▲ CDN (ALB) 232-233 B 4
Hectorspruit o ZA 220-221 K 2
Hector Tejada o PE 70-71 B 4
Hedaru o EAT 212-213 F 6
Heddal stavkirke •• N 86-87 D 7
Hede o S 86-87 F 5
Hedenäset o S 86-87 L 3
Hedgesville o USA (WV) 280-281 J 4
Hediondas, Las o RCH 76-77 C 5
Hedley o CDN (BC) 230-231 J 4
Hedley o USA (TX) 264-265 D 4
Heerenveen o NL 92-93 H 2
Heer Land ⊥ N 84-85 K 4
Heerlen o NL 92-93 H 3
Heezen Fracture Zone ≃ 14-15 Q 13
Hefa ☆ • IL 130-131 D 1
Hefar Qesari ∴ • IL 130-131 D 1
Hefei ☆ VRC 154-155 K 6
Hefeng o VRC 156-157 G 2
Heffley Creek o CDN (BC) 230-231 J 3
Heflin o USA (AL) 284-285 E 3
Hegang o VRC 150-151 H 4
Heggadadevankote o IND 140-141 G 4
Hegigio River ~ PNG 183 B 4
Hegura-shima ⌒ J 152-153 G 6
Heho o MYA 142-143 K 5
Hehua o VRC 154-155 G 6
Heiau o Kalalea o USA (HI) 288 K 6
Heide o D 92-93 K 1
Heidelberg o • D 92-93 K 4
Heidelberg o USA (MS) 268-269 M 5
Heidelberg o ZA (CAP) 220-221 E 7
Heidelberg o ZA (TRA) 220-221 J 3
Heiden, Port ≈ 22-23 R 4
Heidenheim an der Brenz o D 92-93 L 4
Hei-gawa ~ J 152-153 J 5
Height of Land ▲ USA 278-279 K 3
Heihe o VRC 150-151 F 2
Hei He ~ VRC 154-155 A 2
Heilbron o ZA 220-221 H 3
Heilbronn o • D 92-93 K 4
Heilongjiang ◘ VRC 150-151 E 4
Heilong Jiang ~ VRC 150-151 F 3
Heilprin Gletscher ⊂ GRØ 26-27 S 5
Heilprin Land ⊥ GRØ 26-27 h 3
Heilsberg = Lidzbark Warmiński o • PL 92-93 Q 1
Heimaey ⌒ IS 86-87 c 3
Heimahe o VRC 144-145 M 2
Heinola o FIN 88-89 J 6
Heinsburg o CDN (ALB) 232-233 H 2
Heinze Chaung ≈ 158-159 D 3
Ḥeirābād o AFG 136-137 K 6
Heirane < DZ 188-189 L 7
Heishan SK o VRC 154-155 J 6
Heisler o CDN (ALB) 232-233 F 3
Heist, Knokke- o • B 92-93 G 3
Heitoraí o BR 72-73 F 3
Heitske o RI 166-167 K 5
Hejaz = al-Ḥiǧāz ▲ KSA 130-131 E 4
Hejdžanskij hrebet ▲ RUS 120-121 L 4
Hejgijaha ~ RUS 114-115 L 2
Hejian o VRC 154-155 K 2
Hejiang o VRC (GDG) 156-157 G 6
Hejiang o VRC (SIC) 156-157 D 2
Hejin o VRC 154-155 G 4
Hejing o VRC 146-147 H 4
Hèjjaha ~ RUS 108-109 K 7
Hejsa, ostrov ⌒ RUS 84-85 e 2
Hèkčekit-Sene ~ RUS 108-109 d 7
Hekimhan ☆ TR 128-129 G 3
Hekla ▲ IS 86-87 d 2
Hekou o VRC (GAN) 154-155 C 3
Hekou o VRC (HUB) 154-155 H 6
Hekou o VRC (YUN) 156-157 C 5
Helagsfjället ▲ S 86-87 F 5
Helaliturku, ozero o RUS 108-109 X 5
Hel-Amkanni, gora ▲ RUS 110-111 c 5
Helan o VRC 154-155 E 2
Helan Shan ▲ VRC 154-155 D 2
Helanshan Z.B. • VRC 154-155 D 2
Helder, Den o NL 92-93 H 2
Helen o USA (GA) 284-285 G 2
Helena o USA (AR) 276-277 E 6
Helena ☆ USA (MT) 250-251 G 5
Helena Island ⌒ USA (SC) 284-285 K 4
Helendale o USA (CA) 248-249 G 5
Helen Springs o AUS 174-175 B 6
Helensville o NZ 182 E 2
Helgoland ⌒ D 92-93 J 1
Helgoländer Bucht ≈ 92-93 J 1
Helgum o S 86-87 H 5
Helheimfjord ≈ 28-29 V 3
Heliopolis ∴ • ET 194-195 E 2
Helleland o N 86-87 C 7
Hellerstninger ••• N 86-87 L 2
Hellesvik o N 86-87 D 5
Hellier o USA (KY) 276-277 N 3
Hellín o • E 98-99 G 5
Hells Canyon • USA (OR) 244-245 J 5
Hells Canyon National Recreation Area • USA (OR) 244-245 J 5
Hells Canyon Wilderness Area ⊥ USA (OR) 244-245 J 5
Hells Gate Airtram • CDN (BC) 230-231 H 4
Hells Gate Roadhouse o AUS 174-175 E 5
Hell Ville = Andoany o RM 222-223 F 4
Helmand ◘ AFG 134-135 K 3
Helmand, Rūd-e ~ AFG 134-135 J 3
Helmcken Falls ~ CDN 230-231 J 2
Helmeringhausen o NAM 220-221 C 2
Helmond o NL 92-93 H 3
Helmsdale o GB 90-91 F 2
Helmstedt o • D 92-93 L 2
Heloise o USA (TN) 276-277 F 4
Helong o VRC 150-151 G 6
Helotes o USA (TX) 266-267 J 4
Helper o USA (UT) 254-255 E 4
Helsingborg o • S 86-87 F 8
Helsingfors = Helsinki ★ ••• FIN 88-89 H 6
Helsingør o • DK 86-87 F 8
Helsinki ★ ••• FIN 88-89 H 6
Helska, Mierzeja ⌣ PL 92-93 P 1
Heltonville o USA (IN) 274-275 M 6
Helvecia o RA 76-77 G 6
Helvetia o USA (WV) 280-281 F 5
Hemando o RA 78-79 H 2
Hemaruka o CDN (ALB) 232-233 G 4
Hemčik ~ RUS 116-117 E 10
Hemčik ~ RUS 124-125 Q 3
Hemet o USA (CA) 248-249 H 6
Hemingford o USA (NE) 262-263 C 2
Hemingway o USA (SC) 284-285 L 3
Hemlo o CDN (ONT) 236-237 C 4
Hemlock o USA (OR) 244-245 B 5
Hemlock Grove o USA (PA) 280-281 L 2
Hemmingford o CDN (QUE) 238-239 M 3
Hemnesberget o N 86-87 F 3
Hemphill o USA (TX) 268-269 G 5
Hemphill, Cape ▲ CDN 24-25 O 2
Hempstead o USA (NY) 280-281 N 3
Hempstead o USA (TX) 266-267 L 3
Hemse o S 86-87 J 8
Hemsö o S 86-87 J 5
Hemudu Wenhua Yizhi ∴ VRC 156-157 M 2
Henan ◘ VRC 154-155 H 5
Hen and Chicken Islands ⌒ NZ 182 E 1
Henares, Río ~ E 98-99 F 4
Henasi-saki ▲ J 152-153 H 4
Henbury o AUS 176-177 M 2
Henbury Meteorite Craters • AUS 176-177 M 2
Hendek ☆ TR 128-129 D 2
Henderson o RA 78-79 J 4
Henderson o USA (IL) 274-275 H 3
Henderson o USA (KY) 276-277 H 3
Henderson o USA (LA) 268-269 J 6
Henderson o USA (MN) 270-271 E 6
Henderson o USA (NC) 282-283 J 4
Henderson o USA (NE) 262-263 J 4
Henderson o USA (NV) 248-249 K 3
Henderson o USA (NY) 278-279 E 5
Henderson o USA (TN) 276-277 G 5
Henderson o USA (TX) 264-265 K 6
Hendersonville o USA (NC) 282-283 E 5
Hendersonville o USA (TN) 276-277 J 4
Hendīǧān o IR 134-135 C 3
Hendīǧān, Rūdḫāne-ye ~ IR 134-135 C 3
Hendon o CDN (SAS) 232-233 P 3
Hendorābī o IR 134-135 E 5
Hendorābī, Ǧazīre-ye ⌒ IR 134-135 E 5
Hendricks o USA (KY) 276-277 M 3
Hendrik Ø ⌒ GRØ 26-27 Y 2
Hendriksen Strait ≈ 24-25 X 2
Hendrik Verwoerddam < ZA 220-221 G 5
Hendrik Verwoerd Dam Nature Reserve ⊥ ZA 220-221 G 5
Hendrina o ZA 220-221 J 3
Hendrix Lake o CDN (BC) 228-229 O 4
Hengām, Ǧazīre-ye ⌒ IR 134-135 F 5
Ḥengān o AFG 136-137 L 7
Henganofi o PNG 183 C 4
Hengchun o RC 156-157 M 5
Hengduan Shan ▲ VRC 144-145 M 7
Hengelo o NL 92-93 J 2
Hengshan o VRC (HUN) 156-157 H 3
Hengshan ▲ VRC (HUN) 156-157 H 3
Hengshan • VRC (HUN) 156-157 H 3
Hengshan • VRC (SHA) 154-155 H 2
Hengshui o VRC 154-155 J 3
Heng Xian o VRC 156-157 F 5
Hengyang o VRC 156-157 H 3
Heničes'k o UA 102-103 J 4
Henley Falls o USA (MN) 270-271 C 6
Henlopen, Cape ▲ USA (DE) 280-281 L 5
Hennaya o DZ 188-189 L 3
Hennebont o F 90-91 F 8
Hennenman o ZA 220-221 H 3
Hennessey o USA (OK) 264-265 G 2
Hennigsdorf o D 92-93 M 2
Henning o USA (MN) 270-271 C 4
Henribourg o CDN (SAS) 232-233 N 2
Henrietta o USA (TX) 264-265 F 5
Henrietta Maria, Cape ▲ CDN 34-35 P 3
Henriette o USA (MN) 270-271 E 5
Henri Pittier, Parque Nacional ⊥ YV 60-61 H 2
Henry o USA (ID) 252-253 G 4
Henry o USA (IL) 274-275 J 3
Henry o USA (NE) 262-263 B 3
Henry o USA (SD) 260-261 J 2
Henry, Cape ▲ CDN (BC) 228-229 B 4
Henry, Cape ▲ USA (NC) 282-283 M 4
Henryetta o USA (OK) 264-265 J 3
Henry Horton State Park ⊥ USA (TN) 276-277 J 5
Henry House o CDN (ALB) 228-229 Q 4
Henry Kater, Cape ▲ CDN 28-29 G 2
Henry Kater Peninsula ⌣ CDN 28-29 F 2
Henry Lawrence Island ⌒ IND 140-141 L 3
Henry Mountains ▲ USA 254-255 E 5
Henry River ~ AUS 172-173 B 7
Henry's Fork ~ USA 252-253 G 3
Henryville o USA (IN) 274-275 N 6
Henshaw, Lake ⌣ USA 248-249 H 6
Hentėjn nuruu ▲ MAU 148-149 H 3
Hentiesbaai o NAM 216-217 C 11
Hentij ◘ MAU 148-149 J 3
Henvey Inlet Indian Reserve ⵅ CDN (ONT) 238-239 E 3
Henzada o MYA 158-159 C 2
Hepburn o CDN (SAS) 232-233 M 3
Hepburn Lake o CDN 30-31 M 2
Hephzibah o USA (GA) 284-285 H 3
Heping o VRC 156-157 J 4
Heppner o USA (OR) 244-245 F 5
Hepu o VRC 156-157 F 6
Hepworth o CDN (ONT) 238-239 D 4
Heqing o VRC 142-143 M 2
Heraclea ∴ MK 100-101 H 4
Héraðsvötn ~ IS 86-87 d 2
Heraion ∴ ••• GR 128-129 B 4
Ḥerāme o IR 134-135 J 1
Herāt ◘ AFG 134-135 J 1
Herāt ☆ •• AFG (HE) 134-135 K 1
Heraz, Rūdḫāne-ye ~ IR 136-137 B 6
Herbagat o SUD 200-201 H 3
Herbang o BD 142-143 H 5
Herbert o CDN (SAS) 232-233 L 5
Herbert o NZ 182 C 6
Herbert, Mount ▲ AUS 172-173 G 4
Herbert Hoover National Historic Site • USA (IA) 274-275 G 3
Herbert Island ⌒ USA 22-23 L 6
Herbert Lake o CDN 30-31 R 6
Herbert Ø ⌒ GRØ 26-27 P 5
Herberton o AUS 174-175 H 5
Herbertpur o IND 138-139 F 4
Herbert River ~ AUS 174-175 H 6
Herbert River Falls • AUS 174-175 H 6
Herbertsdale o ZA 220-221 E 7
Herbert Vale o AUS 174-175 E 6
Herbert Wash ⌣ AUS 176-177 H 2
Herbiers, les o F 90-91 G 8
Herceg-Novi o • YU 100-101 G 3
Herchmer o CDN 34-35 J 2
Herclio Luz o BR 74-75 F 7
Hercilópolis o BR 74-75 F 5
Hercules Bay ≈ 183 D 4
Hercules Gemstone Deposit • AUS 176-177 D 3
Herdlak ⌒ GRØ 28-29 Q 5
Herðubreið ▲ IS 86-87 e 2
Hereda, Punta ▲ PE 64-65 B 4
Heredia ☆ CR 52-53 B 6
Hereford • GB 90-91 F 5
Hereford o USA (CO) 254-255 L 3
Hereford o USA (OR) 244-245 G 6
Hereford o USA (SD) 260-261 D 2
Hereford o USA (TX) 264-265 B 4
Hereke o TR 128-129 C 2
Hereroland ⊥ NAM 216-217 E 10
Herford o • D 92-93 K 2
Hèrgu ~ RUS 122-123 E 2
Herington o USA (KS) 262-263 K 6
Heriot Bay o CDN (BC) 230-231 D 3
Heris o IR 128-129 M 3
Heritage Range ▲ ARK 16 F 28
Herkimer o USA (NY) 278-279 F 5
Hèrlèn o MAU 148-149 J 4
Hèrlèn gol ~ MAU 148-149 M 3
Herlen He ~ VRC 148-149 N 3
Herluf Trolles Land ⊥ GRØ 26-27 l 2
Herman o USA (MN) 270-271 B 5
Hermanas o USA (NM) 256-257 H 7
Hermanas, Las o YV 60-61 L 3
Herma Ness ▲ GB 90-91 G 1
Hermann o USA (MO) 274-275 G 6
Hermannsburg o AUS 176-177 M 1
Hermannsburg Aboriginal Land ⵅ AUS 176-177 M 1
Hermanos, Cerro ▲ RCH 80 D 3
Hermanos, Islas Los ⌒ YV 60-61 J 2
Hermansville o USA (MI) 270-271 L 5
Hermantown o USA (MN) 270-271 F 4
Hermanusdorings o ZA 220-221 H 2
Hermidale o AUS 178-179 J 6
Hermiston o USA (OR) 244-245 F 5
Hermitage o USA (AR) 276-277 C 7
Hermitage o USA (MO) 276-277 B 3
Hermitage Bay ≈ 242-243 M 5
Hermleigh o USA (TX) 264-265 D 6
Hermon o ZA 220-221 D 6
Hermopolis ∴ • ET 194-195 E 4
Hermosa o USA (SD) 260-261 C 3
Hermosas, Parque Nacional las ⊥ CO 60-61 D 6
Hermosillo ☆ MEX 50-51 D 3
Hernandarias o RA 76-77 H 6
Hernando o USA (MS) 268-269 L 2
Hernán Mejía Miraval o RA 76-77 F 4
Herndon o USA (VA) 280-281 J 5
Herning o DK 86-87 D 8
Hérodier, Lac o CDN 36-37 P 6
Heroica Zitácuaro o MEX 52-53 D 2
Herold o ZA 220-221 F 6
Heroldsbaai o ZA 220-221 F 7
Heron o USA (MT) 250-251 D 3
Heron Bay ≈ 236-237 B 4
Heron Bay o CDN (ONT) 236-237 B 4
Heron Island ⌒ AUS 178-179 L 2
Heron Lake o USA (MN) 270-271 C 7
Heron Lake ⌣ USA (MN) 270-271 C 7
Herøy o N 86-87 F 4
Herradura o MEX 50-51 J 6
Herradura o RA 76-77 H 4
Herreid o USA (SD) 260-261 F 1
Herrera del Duque o • E 98-99 E 5
Herrera de Pisuerga o E 98-99 E 3
Herreras, Las o MEX 50-51 G 5
Herreras, Los o MEX 50-51 K 5
Herrero, Punta ▲ MEX 52-53 L 2
Herrick Center o USA (PA) 280-281 L 2
Herrick Creek ~ CDN 228-229 N 2
Herries Range ▲ AUS 178-179 L 5
Herrin o USA (IL) 276-277 F 3
Herring Cove o CDN (NS) 240-241 M 6
Herrington Lake ⌣ USA (KY) 276-277 L 3
Herschel o CDN 20-21 W 2
Herschel o CDN (SAS) 232-233 K 4
Herschel o ZA 220-221 H 5
Herschel Island ⌒ CDN 20-21 W 2
Hersfeld, Bad o • D 92-93 K 3
Hershey o USA (PA) 280-281 K 3
Herson = Cherson ☆ • UA 102-103 H 4
Hertford o USA (NC) 282-283 L 4
Hertogenbosch, 's- ☆ • NL 92-93 H 3
Hertugen of Orleans Land ⊥ GRØ 26-27 o 5
Hertzogville o ZA 220-221 G 4
Heruff Trolle, Kap ▲ GRØ 28-29 T 6
Herval o BR 76-77 K 2
Hervey Bay ≈ 178-179 M 3
Hervey Bay o AUS (QLD) 178-179 M 3
Hervey Junction o CDN (QUE) 238-239 N 2
Herveys Range ▲ AUS 180-181 K 2
Herzliyya o IL 130-131 D 1
Herzog-Ernst-Bucht ≈ 16 F 33
Hesadi o IND 142-143 D 4
Heşarak o AFG 138-139 B 2
Heshan o VRC (GDG) 156-157 H 5
Heshan o VRC (GXI) 156-157 F 5
Heshun o VRC 154-155 H 3
Hesperia o USA (CA) 248-249 G 5
Hesperia o USA (MI) 272-273 C 4
Hesperus Mountain ▲ USA (CO) 254-255 G 6
Hessel o USA (MI) 270-271 O 4
Hessen ◘ D 92-93 K 3
Hessfjord o N 86-87 J 2
Hess Mountains ▲ CDN 20-21 Z 5
Hess River ~ CDN 20-21 Y 5
Hester, Peak ▲ AUS 172-173 D 7
Hester Malan Natural Reserve ⊥ ZA 220-221 D 4
Hestkjølen ▲ N 86-87 F 4
Heta o RUS (SAH) 108-109 c 6
Heta ~ RUS 108-109 c 6
Heta, Boľšaja ~ RUS 108-109 V 7
Hetagčan ~ RUS 112-113 K 5
Hetagima o RI 166-167 K 4
Hetauda o NEP 144-145 E 7
Hetch Hetchy Aqueduct < USA (CA) 248-249 C 2
Het Kruis o ZA 220-221 D 6
Hetovo o RUS 88-89 R 5
Hettinger o USA (ND) 258-259 E 5
Hètyľky ~ RUS 114-115 R 2
Heuru o SOL 184 I e 4
Heva ☆ ••• UZ 136-137 G 4
Héva, Rivière- o CDN (QUE) 236-237 K 4
Heveländia o BR 66-67 G 5
Hevi o GH 202-203 L 6
Hevron ☆ WB 130-131 D 2
Heward o CDN (SAS) 232-233 P 6
Hewitt o USA (MN) 270-271 C 4
Hewitt o USA (TX) 266-267 K 2
Hewitt, Kap ▲ GRØ 26-27 p 8
Hexham o • GB 90-91 F 4
He Xian o VRC (ANH) 154-155 L 6
He Xian o VRC (GXI) 156-157 G 4
Hexigten Qi o VRC 148-149 N 6
Hex River Pass ▲ ZA 220-221 D 6
Hexrivierberge ▲ ZA 220-221 D 6
Hext o USA (TX) 266-267 H 3
Heyang o VRC 154-155 G 4
Heyburn o USA (ID) 252-253 E 4
Heyburn Lake ⌣ USA (OK) 264-265 H 3
Heyden o CDN (ONT) 236-237 D 6
Heydon o ZA 220-221 G 5
Heyfield o AUS 180-181 J 4
Heyu o VRC 154-155 G 5
Heyuan o VRC 156-157 J 5
Heywood o AUS 180-181 F 5
Heywood Islands ⌒ AUS 172-173 G 3
Heywood Shoal ⌒ AUS 172-173 G 2
Heyworth o USA (IL) 274-275 K 4
Hezār, Kūh-e ▲ IR 134-135 G 4
Heze o VRC 154-155 J 4
Hezhang o VRC 156-157 D 3
Hezrī o IR 134-135 H 1
Hezuozhen o VRC 154-155 C 4
Hhohho o SD 220-221 K 2
Hiagtin Gol ~ VRC 144-145 L 2
Hialeah o USA (FL) 286-287 J 6
Hian o GH 202-203 J 4
Hiawatha o USA (CO) 254-255 G 3
Hiawatha o USA (KS) 262-263 L 5
Hiawatha o USA (UT) 254-255 D 4
Hibāk, al- ⊥ KSA 132-133 H 3
Hibarba ~ RUS 108-109 b 7
Hibberdene o ZA 220-221 K 5
Hibbing o USA (MN) 270-271 F 3
Hibbs, Point ▲ AUS 180-181 H 7
Hibernia Reef ⌒ AUS 172-173 F 1
Hibiny ▲ RUS 88-89 M 3
Hibis, Temple of ∴ • ET 194-195 E 5
Hickiwan o USA (AZ) 256-257 C 6
Hickman o USA (KY) 276-277 F 4
Hickman o USA (NM) 256-257 H 4
Hickman, Mount ▲ CDN 32-33 E 3
Hickmann o RA 76-77 E 2
Hickory o USA (NC) 282-283 F 5
Hickory, Lake ⌣ USA (NC) 282-283 F 5
Hickory Flat o USA (MS) 268-269 L 2
Hickory Plains o USA (AR) 276-277 D 5
Hickory Ridge o USA (AR) 276-277 E 5
Hicks, Point ▲ AUS 180-181 K 4
Hicks Cays ⌒ BH 52-53 K 3
Hicks Lake o CDN 30-31 T 5
Hickson o CDN (ONT) 238-239 E 5
Hickson Lake o CDN 34-35 D 2
Hicksville o USA (OH) 280-281 B 2
Hico o USA (TX) 266-267 J 2
Hico o USA (WV) 280-281 E 5
Hida-gawa ~ J 152-153 G 7
Hidaka o J 152-153 K 3
Hidaka-sanmyaku ▲ J 152-153 K 3
Hidaldo o MEX 50-51 K 5
Hidalgo o MEX (DGO) 50-51 G 5
Hidalgo o MEX (NL) 50-51 J 5
Hidalgo ◘ MEX 52-53 E 1
Hidalgo del Parral o • MEX 50-51 G 4
Hida-sanmyaku ▲ J 152-153 G 6
Hidden Peak = Gasherbrum I ▲ PK 138-139 F 2
Hiddensee ⌒ D 92-93 M 1
Hidden Timber o USA (SD) 260-261 F 3
Hidden Valley o AUS (NT) 172-173 L 4
Hidden Valley o AUS (QLD) 174-175 J 6
Hidden Valley o AUS (QLD) 174-175 J 7
Hidden Valley National Park ⊥ AUS 172-173 J 3
Hidrelétrica Curuá-Una o BR 66-67 K 4
Hidrolândia o BR 68-69 H 4
Hiệ n o VN 158-159 J 3
Hierapolis ••• TR 128-129 C 4
Hierro ⌒ E 188-189 B 7
Higashi-Hiroshima o J 152-153 E 7
Higashikagura o J 152-153 K 3
Higashi-Ōsaka o J 152-153 F 7
Higashi Shina Kai = Dong Hai ≈ 154-155 N 6
Higashi-suidō ≈ 152-153 C 8
Hiǧāz, al- ▲ KSA 130-131 E 4
Higgins o USA (TX) 264-265 D 2
Higginson o USA (AR) 276-277 D 5
Higginsville o AUS 176-177 F 5
High Atlas = Haut Atlas ▲ MA 188-189 G 5
High Bank o CDN (NS) 240-241 N 5
High Bluff o CDN (MAN) 234-235 E 4
Highbourn Cay ⌒ BS 54-55 G 2
Highbury o AUS (QLD) 174-175 G 5
Highbury o AUS (QLD) 178-179 H 2
Highbury o GUY 62-63 F 2
Highflats o ZA 220-221 K 5
Highgate o CDN (SAS) 232-233 K 3
High Hill River ~ CDN 32-33 P 3
High Island o USA (TX) 268-269 F 7
High Island ⌒ USA 22-23 G 4
High Island ⌒ USA (MI) 272-273 D 2
Highland o USA (CA) 248-249 G 5
Highland o USA (IL) 274-275 J 6
Highland Home o USA (AL) 284-285 D 5
Highland Park o USA (IL) 274-275 L 2
Highland Peak ▲ USA (NV) 248-249 K 2
Highland Plains o AUS 174-175 D 6
Highlands o CDN (NFL) 242-243 K 4
Highlands o USA (NC) 282-283 D 5
Highlands o USA (NJ) 280-281 M 3
Highlands o USA (TX) 268-269 E 7
Highlands Hammock State Park ⊥ • USA (FL) 286-287 H 4
Highland Springs o USA (VA) 280-281 J 6
High Level o CDN 30-31 L 6
Highmore o USA (SD) 260-261 G 2
High Peak ▲ GB 90-91 G 5
High Peak ▲ USA (NC) 282-283 F 5
High Plateaux = Hauts Plateaux ▲ DZ 188-189 L 4
High Point o USA (NC) 282-283 G 5
High Prairie o CDN 32-33 M 4
High River o CDN (ALB) 232-233 E 5
High Rock o BS 54-55 F 1
Highrock Lake < CDN (SAS) 34-35 D 2
High Rock Lake < USA (NC) 282-283 G 5
High Rolling Mountains ▲ RP 160-161 D 6
High Rolls o USA (NM) 256-257 K 6
High Springs o USA (FL) 286-287 G 2
Hightowers o USA (NC) 282-283 H 4
High Uintas Wilderness Area ⊥ USA (UT) 254-255 E 3
Highwood o USA (MT) 250-251 J 4
Highwood Peak ▲ USA (MT) 250-251 J 4
Highwood River ~ CDN 232-233 D 5
Higirio, El o RCH 76-77 B 5
Hiǧla o KSA 132-133 C 4
Hiǧr, al- o • KSA 130-131 E 4
Higuera, La o RCH 76-77 B 5
Higüero, Punta ▲ USA (PR) 286-287 O 2
Higuerote o • YV 60-61 H 2
Higüey ☆ DOM 54-55 L 5
Hiiraan ◘ SP 208-209 G 6
Hiiumaa saar ⊥ EST 94-95 H 2
Hijar o E 98-99 G 4
Hikone o J 152-153 G 7
Hikurangi o NZ 182 E 1
Hikurangi ▲ NZ 182 G 2
Hikurangi Trench ≃ 182 F 4
Hila o RI (MAL) 166-167 E 3
Hila o RI (MAL) 166-167 D 5
Hilakondji o DY 202-203 L 6
Hilāl, Ǧabal ▲ ET 194-195 F 2
Hiland Park o USA (FL) 286-287 D 1
Hilda o CDN (ALB) 232-233 H 5
Hildale o USA (UT) 254-255 C 6
Hildesheim o ••• D 92-93 K 2
Hilger o USA (MT) 250-251 K 4
Hilham o USA (TN) 276-277 K 4
Hili o UAE 134-135 F 6
Hiliardton o CDN (ONT) 236-237 J 5
Hiliomódi o GR 100-101 J 6
Hilismaetano o • RI 162-163 B 4
Hill o USA (LA) 268-269 H 4
Hill, Fort A.P. • USA (VA) 280-281 J 5
Ḥilla, al- ☆ IRQ 128-129 L 6
Hillabee Creek ~ USA 284-285 E 3
Hill Air Force Base xx USA (UT) 254-255 B 2
Hill City o USA (ID) 252-253 C 3
Hill City o USA (KS) 262-263 G 5
Hill City o USA (MN) 270-271 E 4
Hill City o USA (SD) 260-261 C 3
Hill Creek Extension Uintah and Ouray Indian Reservation ⵅ USA (UT) 254-255 F 4
Hillékét o TCH 198-199 K 6
Hill End o • AUS 180-181 K 2
Hillerød o • DK 86-87 F 9
Hilli o IND 142-143 F 3
Hilliard o USA (FL) 286-287 H 1
Hill Island ⌒ CDN 36-37 P 3
Hill Island Lake o CDN 30-31 P 5
Hillman o USA (MI) 272-273 F 2
Hillman, Lake ⌣ AUS 176-177 D 5
Hillmond o CDN (SAS) 232-233 J 2
Hills o CDN (BC) 230-231 M 4
Hillsboro o USA (GA) 284-285 G 3
Hillsboro o USA (IL) 274-275 J 5
Hillsboro o USA (KS) 262-263 J 6
Hillsboro o USA (MO) 274-275 H 6
Hillsboro o USA (ND) 258-259 K 4
Hillsboro o USA (NM) 256-257 H 6
Hillsboro o USA (OH) 280-281 C 4
Hillsboro o USA (OR) 244-245 C 5
Hillsboro o USA (TX) 264-265 G 6
Hillsboro o USA (WI) 270-271 H 7
Hillsboro Canal < USA (FL) 286-287 J 5
Hillsborough o USA (NC) 282-283 H 4
Hillsborough o USA (NH) 278-279 K 5
Hillsborough o WG 56 E 5
Hillsborough Bay ≈ 240-241 M 4
Hillsdale o USA (MI) 272-273 E 6
Hillsdale Lake ⌣ USA (KS) 262-263 M 6
Hillside o AUS 172-173 D 6
Hillside o USA (AZ) 256-257 C 4
Hillside National Wildlife Refuge ⊥ USA (MS) 268-269 K 3
Hillsport o CDN (ONT) 236-237 C 3
Hill Spring o CDN (ALB) 232-233 E 6
Hillston o AUS 180-181 H 2
Hillsville o USA (VA) 280-281 F 7
Hillswick o GB 90-91 G 1
Hilltop o USA (WI) 274-275 H 1
Hilo o • USA (HI) 288 K 5
Hilo Bay ≈ 288 K 5
Hilok ☆ RUS (CTN) 118-119 E 10
Hilok ~ RUS 116-117 N 10
Hilt o USA (CA) 246-247 C 2
Hiltaba, Mount ▲ AUS 180-181 C 2
Hilton o AUS 174-175 E 7
Hilton o USA (NY) 278-279 D 5
Hilton Beach o CDN (ONT) 238-239 B 2
Hilton Head Island o USA (SC) 284-285 K 4
Hilton Head Island ⌒ USA (SC) 284-285 K 4
Hilvan ☆ TR 128-129 H 4
Hilversum o NL 92-93 H 2
Himachal Pradesh ◘ IND 138-139 F 3
Himalaya = Himalaya Shan ▲ 144-145 B 4
Himal Chuli ▲ NEP 144-145 E 6
Himana, Hassi o DZ 188-189 K 6
Himanka o FIN 88-89 G 4
Himarë o • AL 100-101 G 4
Himatnagar o IND 138-139 D 8
Himbirti o ER 200-201 J 5
Himeji o J 152-153 F 7
Himeji-jo Castle ••• J 152-153 F 7
Himi o J 152-153 G 6
Himki ☆ RUS 94-95 P 4
Himora o ETH 200-201 H 5
Ḥimṣ ☆ SYR 128-129 G 5
Hinatuan o RP 160-161 G 8
Hinatuan Passage ≈ 160-161 F 8
Hînceşti ☆ MD 102-103 F 4
Hinche ☆ RH 54-55 J 5
Hinchinbrook, Cape ▲ USA 20-21 R 6
Hinchinbrook Entrance ≈ 20-21 R 6
Hinchinbrook Island ⌒ AUS 174-175 J 6
Hinchinbrook Island ⌒ USA 20-21 R 6
Hinchinbrook Island National Park ⊥ AUS 174-175 J 6
Hinckley o USA (IL) 274-275 K 3
Hinckley o USA (MN) 270-271 F 4
Hinckley o USA (MN) 270-271 F 5
Hinckley o USA (UT) 254-255 C 4
Hinckley, Mount ▲ AUS 176-177 K 3
Hincks Conservation Park ⊥ AUS 180-181 C 2
Hinda o RCB 210-211 D 6
Hindan ~ IND 138-139 F 5
Hindaun o IND 138-139 F 6
Hindes o USA (TX) 266-267 J 5
Hindiktig-Hol', ozero o RUS 124-125 Q 3
Hindiya, al- ☆ IRQ 128-129 L 6
Hindmarsh, Lake ⌣ AUS 180-181 F 4
Hinds Lake o CDN (NFL) 242-243 M 4
Hindubaāgh o PK 134-135 M 3
Hindu Kush = Hendūkoš ▲ 138-139 B 2
Hindupur o IND 140-141 G 4
Hindustan ⌣ IND 142-143 B 2
Hines o USA (FL) 286-287 F 2
Hines o USA (OR) 244-245 F 7
Hines Creek o CDN 32-33 L 3
Hinesville o USA (GA) 284-285 J 5
Hinganghāt o IND 138-139 G 9
Hinganskij zapovednik ⊥ RUS 122-123 C 4
Hingham o USA (MT) 250-251 J 3
Hinglaj o PK (BEL) 134-135 L 6
Hinglaj o • PK (BEL) 138-139 E 7
Hingol ~ PK 134-135 L 6
Hingoli o IND 138-139 F 10
Hingoraja o PK 138-139 B 6
Hinidān o PK 134-135 M 6
Hinike ~ RUS 120-121 L 2
Hinis ☆ TR 128-129 J 3
Hink Land ⊥ GRØ 26-27 l 8
Hinkleville o USA (KY) 276-277 G 3
Hinlopenrenna ≃ 84-85 J 2
Hinlopenstretet ≈ 84-85 K 2
Hinnøya ⌒ N 86-87 G 2
Hinoba-an o RP 160-161 E 8
Hino-gawa ~ J 152-153 E 7
Hinogyaung o MYA 158-159 C 2
Hinojo o RA 78-79 J 4
Hinojosa del Duque o • E 98-99 E 5
Hinomi-saki ▲ J 152-153 E 7
Hinsdale o USA (MT) 250-251 M 3
Hinsdale o USA (NY) 278-279 C 6
Hinton o CDN (ALB) 228-229 R 3
Hinton o USA (OK) 264-265 F 3
Hinton o USA (WV) 280-281 F 6
Híos o GR 100-101 L 5
Híos ⌒ GR 100-101 L 5
Hipólito o MEX 50-51 J 5
Hipuapua Falls ~ • USA 288 J 4
Hir o IR 136-137 B 6
Hira o IND 140-141 G 2
Hirado o • J 152-153 C 8
Hirado-shima ⌒ J 152-153 C 8
Hirafok o DZ 190-191 E 9
Hirākūd Reservoir < IND 142-143 C 5
Hiram o USA (ME) 278-279 L 5
Hiraman ~ EAK 212-213 G 4
Hiranai o J 152-153 J 4
Hiratsuka o J 152-153 H 7
Ḫirbat al-Umbāšī ∴ • SYR 128-129 G 6
Ḫirbat Isriya o SYR 128-129 G 5
Hirehadagalli o IND 140-141 F 3
Hiré-Watta o CI 202-203 H 6
Hirfanlı Barajı < TR 128-129 E 3
Hiripitiya o CL 140-141 J 7
Hiriyur o IND 140-141 G 4
Hirmās, Bi'r Ibn o KSA 130-131 E 3
Hirmil, al- ☆ RL 128-129 G 5
Hirna o ETH 208-209 E 4
Hiroo o J 152-153 K 3
Hirosaki o • J 152-153 J 4
Hiroshima o J (HOK) 152-153 J 3
Hiroshima ☆ • J (HIR) 152-153 E 7
Ḥirr, Wādī ⊢ ~ IRQ 128-129 K 7
hirs'ka miscevisc' • UA 102-103 G 3
Hirs'kyj Tikyč ~ UA 102-103 F 3
Hirson o F 90-91 K 7
Hirşova o • RO 102-103 F 5
Hirtshals o DK 86-87 D 8
Hisaka-shima ⌒ J 152-153 C 8
Hisāna, al- o KSA 132-133 B 3
Hisār o IND 138-139 E 5
Ḥisb, Šaʿīb ~ IRQ 128-129 K 7
Hišig-Öndör = Maan't o MAU 148-149 F 3
Hisiu o PNG 183 D 5
Hislaviči o RUS 94-95 N 4
Hisle o USA (SD) 260-261 E 3
Ḥiṣn, Qal'at al- • SYR 128-129 G 5
Hişn aş Şahābī o LAR 192-193 J 2
Hispaniola ⌒ 54-55 K 6
Historic Fort Delaware • USA (NY) 280-281 M 2
Historic Remains ∴ • RI 164-165 K 3

336 Hazīpur — Historic Remains

Historic Remains, Forts ∴• RI 164-165 K 3
Historyland ∴• USA (WI) 270-271 G 5
Hisw, al- o KSA 130-131 G 5
Hit o IRQ 128-129 K 6
Hitachi o J 152-153 J 6
Hitia Sand Hills o GUY 62-63 F 3
Hitoyoshi o J 152-153 D 8
Hitra ⌒ N 86-87 D 5
Hiu, Île = Hiw ⌒ VAN 184 II a 1
Hiuchi-nada ≈ 152-153 E 7
Hiva-Oa ⌒ F 13 O 3
Hivaro o PNG 183 B 4
Hiw o ET 194-195 F 4
Hiw = Île Hiu ⌒ VAN 184 II a 1
Hiwassee Lake < USA (NC) 282-283 C 5
Hiwassee River ~ USA 282-283 C 5
Hixon o CDN (BC) 228-229 M 3
Hiyoshi o J 152-153 E 8
Hiyyon, Nāal ~ IL 130-131 D 2
Hizan ☆ TR 128-129 K 3
Hjälmaren o S 86-87 G 7
Hjalmar Lake o CDN 30-31 P 5
Hjargas nuur o MAU 116-117 F 11
Hjelset o N 86-87 C 5
Hjerkinn o N 86-87 D 5
Hjørring o DK 86-87 E 8
Hkākabo Rāzi ▲ MYA 142-143 K 1
Hkqingzi o MYA 142-143 H 5
Hkyenhpa o MYA 142-143 K 2
Hlabisa o ZA 220-221 K 4
Hlebarovo = Car Kalojan o BG 102-103 E 6
Hlegu o MYA 158-159 D 2
Hlobyne o UA 102-103 H 3
Hlotse o LS 220-221 J 4
Hluchiv o UA 102-103 H 2
Hluhluwe o ZA 220-221 L 4
Hluhluwe Game Reserve ⊥ ZA 220-221 L 4
Hluthi o SD 220-221 K 3
Hlybokae o BY 94-95 K 4
Hmel'nickij = Chmel'nyc'kyj ☆ UA 102-103 E 3
Hmitevskogo, poluostrov ⌒ RUS 120-121 N 4
Hnalān o IND 142-143 H 4
H. N. Andersen, Kap ▲ GRØ 26-27 r 3
Hnausa o CDN (MAN) 234-235 G 4
Hnilij Tikič ~ UA 102-103 G 3
Ho ☆ GH 202-203 L 6
Hòa Bình o VN 158-159 J 2
Hòa Bình ☆ VN 156-157 D 6
Hoadley o CDN (ALB) 232-233 D 3
Hoài Nhơn o VN 158-159 K 3
Hoanib ~ NAM 216-217 B 9
Hoar, Lake o AUS 176-177 G 2
Hoare Bay ≈ 36-37 S 2
Hoarusib ~ NAM 216-217 B 9
Hoback Junction o USA (WY) 252-253 H 3
Hoba Meteorite •• NAM 216-217 D 9
Hoban o KOR 150-151 F 7
Hobart ☆• AUS 180-181 J 7
Hobart o USA (IN) 274-275 L 3
Hobart o USA (OK) 264-265 E 3
Hobart Island ⌒ CDN 36-37 N 2
Hobbema o CDN (ALB) 232-233 E 3
Hobbs o USA (NM) 256-257 M 6
Hobbs Coast ✓ ARK 16 F 23
Hōbetsu o J 152-153 K 3
Hobhouse o ZA 220-221 H 4
Hobo o CO 60-61 D 6
Hoboken o USA (GA) 284-285 H 5
Hoboksar o VRC 146-147 G 2
Hobol ~ RUS 110-111 R 6
Hobro o DK 86-87 D 8
Hobson, Cape ▲ CDN 24-25 X 5
Hobson Lake o CDN (BC) 228-229 O 4
Hobucken o USA (NC) 282-283 L 5
Hobyo o SP 208-209 J 6
Hochalmspitze ▲ A 92-93 M 5
Hochberry Draw ~ USA 266-267 D 2
Hochfeld o NAM 216-217 D 10
Hochfield o CDN (MAN) 234-235 F 5
Hochheim o USA (TX) 266-267 K 4
Hồ Chí Minh, Thành Phố = Thành Phố Hồ Chí Minh ☆•• VN 158-159 J 5
Hochstetterbugten ≈ 26-27 q 6
Hochstetter Forland ⌒ GRØ 26-27 p 6
Hocking River ~ USA 280-281 D 4
Hockley o USA (TX) 268-269 E 6
Hóc Môn o VN 158-159 J 5
Hočo o RUS 120-121 D 3
Hočo, Ystannah- o RUS 110-111 N 3
Hoctún o MEX 52-53 K 1
Ḩodā Āfarīn o IR 128-129 M 3
Hodal o IND 138-139 F 6
Hodar, utes • RUS 122-123 H 3
Hodgenville o USA (KY) 276-277 K 3
Hodges Gardens ∴ USA (LA) 268-269 G 5
Hodges Hill ▲ CDN (NFL) 242-243 N 3
Hodgeville o CDN (SAS) 232-233 M 5
Hodgson o CDN (MAN) 234-235 F 3
Hodgson Downs o AUS 174-175 C 4
Hodgson River o AUS 174-175 C 4
Hodh ⌒ RIM 196-197 F 6
Hodh ech-Chargui ◘ RIM 196-197 G 5
Hodh el-Gharbi ◘ RIM 196-197 E 6
Hodigere o IND 140-141 G 4
Hodna ~ SP 208-209 J 6
Hódmezővásárhely o H 92-93 Q 5
Hodna, Chott el o DZ 190-191 E 3
Hodna, Monts du ▲ DZ 190-191 E 3
Hodna, Plaine du ⌒ DZ 190-191 E 3
Hodo Dan ▲ KOR 150-151 F 8
Hồ Đơn Dương o VN 158-159 K 5
Hodonín o CZ 92-93 O 4
Hodq Shamo ⌒ VRC 154-155 E 1
Hodutka, gora ▲ RUS 122-123 R 2
Hodžambas o TM 136-137 J 5
Hodzana River ~ USA 20-21 Q 3
Hodža-Obigarm o TJ 136-137 L 5
Hodžejli = Hŭdžajli ☆• UZ 136-137 F 3
Hoë o RUS 122-123 K 3
Hoedspruit o ZA 220-221 K 2
Hoehne o USA (CO) 254-255 L 6
Hoë Karoo = Upper Karoo ⌒ ZA 220-221 D 5
Hoek van Holland o NL 92-93 H 3
Hoeryong o KOR 150-151 G 6
Hoëveld ⌒ ZA 220-221 J 3
Hoey o CDN (SAS) 232-233 N 3
Hoeyang o KOR 150-151 F 8
Hof o D 92-93 L 3
Höfðakaupstaður = Skagaströnd o IS 86-87 c 2
Hoffmans Cay ⌒ BS 54-55 G 2
Hofmarkt = Odorheiu Secuiesc o RO 102-103 D 4
Hofmeyr o ZA 220-221 G 5
Höfn o IS 86-87 f 2
Hofsjökull ⊂ IS 86-87 d 2
Hofsós o IS 86-87 d 2
Hōfu o J 152-153 D 7
Hoğalak, Kūh-e ▲ IR 128-129 M 5
Höganäs o S 86-87 F 8
Hogan Group ⌒ AUS 180-181 J 5
Hogansville o USA (GA) 284-285 F 3
Hogart, Mount ▲ AUS 178-179 D 1
Hogatza River ~ USA 20-21 N 3
Hogback Mountain ▲ USA (NE) 262-263 C 3
Hog Cay ⌒ BS 54-55 H 3
Hogeland o USA (MT) 250-251 L 3
Høgeloft ▲ N 86-87 D 6
Hogem Ranges ▲ CDN 32-33 G 4
Hoggar ▲ DZ 190-191 E 9
Hoggar, Tassili du ⌒ DZ 190-191 E 10
Høggia ▲ N 86-87 E 5
Hog Harbor o VAN 184 II a 2
Hog Island ⌒ USA (MI) 272-273 D 2
Hog Island ⌒ USA (VA) 280-281 L 6
Hog Landing o USA 20-21 N 4
Hogsback o ZA 220-221 H 6
Högsby ☆ S 86-87 H 8
Høgtuvbreen ▲ N 86-87 F 3
Hohenstein = Olsztynek o PL 92-93 Q 2
Hohenwald o USA (TN) 276-277 H 5
Hohe Tatra = Tatry ▲ SK 92-93 P 4
Hohe Tauern ▲ A 92-93 M 5
Hohhot ☆ VRC 154-155 G 1
Hoh Indian Reservation ✗ USA (WA) 244-245 A 3
Hohoe o GH 202-203 L 6
Hoholitna River ~ USA 20-21 M 6
Hoh Sai Hu o VRC 144-145 J 3
Hōhuku o J 152-153 D 7
Hoh Xil Hu o VRC 144-145 H 3
Hoh Xil Shan ▲ VRC 144-145 F 3
Hôi An o•• VN 158-159 K 3
Hoima o EAU 212-213 C 3
Hoisington o USA (KS) 262-263 H 6
Hoj, vozvyšennosť ▲ RUS 108-109 O 7
Hoja Wajeer o SP 212-213 H 4
Hojd Tamir gol ~ MAU 148-149 C 4
Hoka o RI 166-167 E 5
Hokitika o NZ 182 C 5
Hokkaidō ⌒ J 152-153 K 3
Hokksund ☆ N 86-87 D 7
Ḩokmābād o IR 136-137 E 6
Hokua o VAN 184 II a 2
Hola o EAK 212-213 H 4
Holalagondi o IND 140-141 G 3
Holanda Rous, Reserva Florestal ⊥ RCH 80 F 7
Hola Prystan' o UA 102-103 H 4
Holbæk o DK 86-87 E 9
Holbein o CDN (SAS) 232-233 M 2
Holberg o CDN (BC) 230-231 A 3
Holberg Inlet ≈ 230-231 B 3
Holbox, Isla ⌒ MEX 52-53 L 1
Holbrook o AUS 180-181 J 3
Holbrook o USA (AZ) 256-257 E 4
Holbrook o USA (ID) 252-253 F 4
Holchit, Punta ▲ MEX 52-53 K 1
Holcomb o USA (MS) 268-269 L 3
Holden o CDN (ALB) 232-233 F 2
Holden o USA (MO) 274-275 E 6
Holden o USA (UT) 254-255 C 4
Holdenville o USA (OK) 264-265 H 3
Holdfast o CDN (SAS) 232-233 N 5
Holdingford o USA (MN) 270-271 D 5
Holdman o USA (OR) 244-245 G 5
Holdrege o USA (NE) 262-263 G 4
Hold with Hope Halvø ⌒ GRØ 26-27 p 7
Hole in the Wall ☆• BS 54-55 G 2
Holejaha ~ RUS 108-109 O 5
Holešov o CZ 92-93 O 4
Holger Danskes Tinde ▲ GRØ 26-27 n 6
Holguín ☆ C 54-55 G 4
Holhol o DJI 208-209 F 3
Holiday o USA (FL) 286-287 G 3
Holiday Resort • AUS 176-177 E 7
Holitna River ~ USA 20-21 M 6
Hollabrunn o A 92-93 O 4
Holland o CDN (MAN) 234-235 E 5
Holland o• USA (MI) 272-273 C 5
Hollandale o USA (MS) 268-269 K 3
Hollandale o USA (WI) 274-275 J 2
Holland Bay ≈ 54-55 G 6
Hollat o RI 166-167 G 4
Holleschau = Holešov o CZ 92-93 O 4
Hollick-Kenyon Plateau ▲ ARK 16 F 26
Holliday o USA (TX) 264-265 F 5
Hollidaysburg o USA (PA) 280-281 H 3
Hollis o USA (AK) 32-33 D 4
Hollis o USA (AR) 276-277 B 6
Hollis o USA (OK) 264-265 E 4
Hollister o USA (CA) 248-249 C 3
Hollister o USA (ID) 252-253 D 4
Hollister o USA (MO) 276-277 B 4
Hollister o USA (OK) 264-265 F 4
Hollister, Mount ▲ AUS 172-173 B 7
Hollókő o••• H 92-93 P 4
Hollow Water o CDN (MAN) 234-235 G 3
Hollow Water Indian Reserve ✗ CDN (MAN) 234-235 G 3
Holly o USA (CO) 254-255 N 5
Holly Beach o USA (LA) 268-269 G 7
Holly Bluff o USA (MS) 268-269 K 4
Holly Hill o USA (SC) 284-285 K 3
Holly Hrove o USA (AR) 276-277 D 6
Holly Ridge o USA (NC) 282-283 K 6
Holly Springs o USA (AR) 276-277 C 7
Holly Springs o USA (MS) 268-269 L 2
Hollywood o USA (AR) 276-277 B 6
Hollywood o USA (FL) 286-287 J 5
Hollywood, Los Angeles •• USA (CA) 248-249 F 5
Holm ☆ RUS 94-95 M 3
Holma o WAN 204-205 K 4
Holman Island o CDN 24-25 N 5
Hólmavík ☆ IS 86-87 c 2
Holme Park o ZA 220-221 J 2
Holmes Creek ~ USA 286-287 D 1
Holmes Reef ⌒ AUS 174-175 J 5
Holmes River ~ CDN 228-229 P 3
Holmfield o CDN (MAN) 234-235 D 5
Holmia o GUY 62-63 E 3
Holm Land ⌒ GRØ 26-27 q 3
Holmogorskaja o RUS 88-89 Q 5
Holmogory o RUS 88-89 Q 4
Holmsk o RUS 122-123 K 5
Holmskj o RUS 126-127 C 5
Holms Ø ⌒ GRØ 26-27 W 6
Holmsund o S 86-87 K 5
Holm-Žirkovskij o RUS 94-95 N 4
Holnicote Bay ≈ 183 E 5
Holohovčan ~ RUS 112-113 N 5
Holoj ~ RUS 118-119 F 9
Holokit ~ RUS 108-109 a 7
Holomoloh-Jurjah ~ RUS 118-119 G 4
Holoog o NAM 220-221 C 3
Holroyd River ~ AUS 174-175 F 4
Holstebro o•• DK 86-87 D 8
Holstein o USA (IA) 274-275 C 2
Holsteinsborg = Sisimiut o GRØ 28-29 O 3
Holston Lake o USA (TN) 282-283 E 4
Holston River ~ USA 280-281 D 7
Holston River ~ USA 282-283 D 4
Holt o USA (AL) 284-285 C 3
Holt o USA (FL) 286-287 C 1
Holt o USA (MI) 272-273 E 5
Holter Lake o USA (MT) 250-251 H 5
Holt Lake < USA (AL) 284-285 C 3
Holton o CDN 36-37 V 7
Holton o USA (KS) 262-263 L 5
Holt Rock o AUS 176-177 E 6
Holtville o USA (CA) 248-249 J 7
Holualoa o USA (HI) 288 K 5
Holub o USA (AR) 276-277 E 6
Holuwon o RI 166-167 K 4
Holyhead o GB 90-91 E 5
Holy Island o GB 90-91 G 4
Holyoke o USA (CO) 254-255 N 3
Holyoke o USA (MA) 278-279 J 6
Holyrood o CDN (NFL) 242-243 P 5
Holyrood o USA (KS) 262-263 H 6
Holy Trinity o USA (AL) 284-285 E 4
Hom ~ NAM 220-221 D 4
Homa Bay o EAK 212-213 E 4
Ḩomām o IR 128-129 N 4
Homand o IR 134-135 H 2
Hománe o MOC 218-219 H 6
Homathko Icefield ⊂ CDN (BC) 230-231 E 2
Homathko River ~ CDN 230-231 E 2
Hombetsu o J 152-153 K 3
Hombori o RMM 202-203 K 2
Hombori, Monts du ▲ RMM 202-203 J 2
Hombre Muerto, Salar del o RA 76-77 D 3
Home Bay ≈ 36-37 R 2
Homedale o USA (ID) 252-253 B 3
Homefield o CDN (SAS) 232-233 P 4
Home Hill o AUS 174-175 J 6
Ḩomein o IR 134-135 D 2
Homel' ☆ BY 94-95 M 5
Home of Bullion Mine • AUS 178-179 C 1
Homer o USA (AK) 22-23 V 3
Homer o USA (IA) 274-275 E 2
Homer o USA (IL) 274-275 L 4
Homer o USA (LA) 268-269 G 4
Homer Tunnel ▲ NZ 182 A 6
Homerville o USA (GA) 284-285 H 5
Homestead o AUS 174-175 H 7
Homestead o USA (FL) 286-287 J 6
Homestead National Monument ∴ USA (NE) 262-263 K 4
Homewood o USA (AL) 284-285 D 3
Homi, hrebet ▲ RUS 122-123 H 3
Hominy o USA (OK) 264-265 H 2
Homnābād o IND 140-141 G 2
Homo, Cerro el ▲ HN 52-53 L 4
Homochitto River ~ USA 268-269 J 5
Homodji o RN 198-199 F 4
Homolha o RUS 118-119 G 6
Homolho ~ RUS 118-119 H 6
Homonhon Island ⌒ RP 160-161 F 7
Homosassa Springs o USA (FL) 286-287 G 3
Homot Tohadar, Ğabal ▲ SUD 200-201 H 3
Homustah o RUS 118-119 P 4
Homyel' = Homel' ☆ BY 94-95 M 5
Honaunau o USA (HI) 288 K 5
Honāvar o IND 140-141 F 3
Honaz Dağ ▲ TR 128-129 C 4
Honda o CO 60-61 D 5
Honda Bay ≈ 160-161 C 8
Hòn Đất o VN 158-159 H 5
Hondeklipbaai o ZA 220-221 C 5
Hondo ~ C 54-55 D 3
Hondo o J 152-153 D 8
Hondo o USA (NM) 256-257 K 5
Hondo o USA (TX) 266-267 H 4
Hondo, Río ~ USA 256-257 K 5
Hondo Creek ~ USA 266-267 H 4
Hondo River ~ BH 52-53 K 3
Honduras ■ HN 52-53 K 4
Honduras, Cabo de ▲ HN 52-53 L 3
Honduras, Golfo de ≈ 52-53 L 3
Hone o CDN 34-35 F 2
Honea Path o USA (SC) 284-285 H 2
Hønefoss ☆ N 86-87 E 6
Hone River ~ CDN 36-37 O 2
Honesdale o USA (PA) 280-281 L 2
Honey Grove o USA (TX) 264-265 J 5
Honey Lake o USA (CA) 246-247 E 3
Honeymoon Bay o CDN (BC) 230-231 E 5
Ḩonğ o IR 134-135 E 5
Hong'an o VRC 154-155 J 6
Hongch'ŏn o ROK 150-151 F 9
Hongde o VRC 154-155 E 3
Hong Do ⌒ ROK 150-151 E 10
Hongdong o VRC 154-155 G 3
Hongfeng Hu o VRC 156-157 E 3
Hồng Gai ☆ VN 156-157 E 6
Honggun-ri o KOR 150-151 G 7
Hongguqu o VRC 154-155 C 3
Honghu o VRC 156-157 H 2
Hong Hu o VRC 156-157 H 2
Hongjiang o VRC 156-157 F 3
Hongkong ◘ HK 156-157 J 5
Hongliuyuan o VRC (GAN) 146-147 M 5
Hongliuyuan o VRC (GAN) 154-155 B 2
Hongmen o VRC 154-155 L 6
Hongmenhe o VRC 154-155 F 5
Hồng Ngự o VN 158 150 H 5
Hòn Gốm, B. D. ⌒ VN 158-159 K 4
Hongor o MAU (DOG) 148-149 K 5
Hongor o MAU (SUH) 148-149 L 5
Hongshan o VRC 154-155 H 6
Hongshishan o VRC 148-149 C 6
Hongshui He ~ VRC 156-157 E 4
Hongū o J 152-153 F 8
Hongueda, Détroit d' ≈ 242-243 D 3
Hongwei o VRC 156-157 K 2
Hongwon o KOR 150-151 F 7
Hongya o VRC 156-157 C 2
Hongyuan o VRC 154-155 C 5
Hongze o VRC 154-155 L 5
Hongze Hu o VRC 154-155 L 5
Hongzhi Liang ▲ VRC 154-155 F 4
Honi o GE 126-127 E 6
Honiara ★• SOL 184 I d 3
Honiton o GB 90-91 F 6
Honjō o J 152-153 J 5
Honkawane o J 152-153 H 7
Hon Minh Hoa ⌒ VN 158-159 J 5
Honnali o IND 140-141 F 3
Honningsvåg o N 86-87 M 1
Honobia o USA (OK) 264-265 K 4
Honohina o USA (HI) 288 K 5
Honokaa o USA (HI) 288 K 4
Honokahua o USA (HI) 288 J 4
Honolulu ☆• USA (HI) 288 H 3
Honoria o PE 64-65 E 6
Hon Rái ⌒ VN 158-159 H 6
Honshū ⌒ J 152-153 F 6
Hontorbé o SN 202-203 D 2
Honuu ☆ RUS 110-111 Y 6
Hood, Fort xx USA (TX) 266-267 K 2
Hood, Mount ▲ USA 244-245 D 5
Hood Bay ≈ 183 D 6
Hood Canal ~ USA 244-245 B 3
Hood Point ▲ AUS 176-177 E 7
Hood Point ▲ PNG 183 D 6
Hood River ~ CDN 30-31 P 2
Hood River o USA (OR) 244-245 D 5
Hoodsport o USA (WA) 244-245 B 3
Hoogeveen o NL 92-93 J 2
Hooker o USA (OK) 264-265 C 2
Hooker Creek Aboriginal Land ✗ AUS 172-173 K 5
Hook Island ⌒ AUS 174-175 K 7
Hook Point ▲ CDN 34-35 P 3
Hool o MEX 52-53 J 2
Hoonah o USA 32-33 C 2
Hoopa o USA (CA) 246-247 B 2
Hoopa Valley Indian Reservation ✗ USA (CA) 246-247 B 2
Hooper o USA (CO) 254-255 K 6
Hooper o USA (NE) 262-263 K 3
Hooper o USA (WA) 244-245 G 4
Hooper, Cape ▲ CDN 28-29 G 2
Hooper Bay ≈ 20-21 G 6
Hooper Bay o USA 20-21 G 6
Hooper Inlet ≈ 24-25 f 6
Hooper Point ▲ CDN (BC) 228-229 D 2
Hooper Strait ≈ 280-281 K 5
Hoopeston o USA (IL) 274-275 L 4
Hooping Harbour o CDN (NFL) 242-243 M 2
Hoople o USA (ND) 258-259 K 3
Hoop Nature Reserve, De ⊥ ZA 220-221 E 7
Hoopstad o ZA 220-221 G 3
Hoosick Falls o USA (NY) 278-279 H 6
Hoosier o CDN (SAS) 232-233 J 4
Hoover o USA (TX) 264-265 D 3
Hoover Dam <• USA (NV) 248-249 K 3
Hoover Reservoir o USA (OH) 280-281 D 3
Hopa ☆ TR 128-129 J 2
Ho-pang o MYA 142-143 L 4
Hope o CDN (BC) 230-231 H 4
Hope o NAM 220-221 C 3
Hope o USA (AK) 20-21 Q 6
Hope o USA (AR) 276-277 B 7
Hope o USA (ID) 250-251 C 3
Hope o USA (IN) 274-275 N 5
Hope o USA (ND) 258-259 K 4
Hope o USA (NM) 256-257 L 6
Hope, Cape ▲ CDN 24-25 O 6
Hope, Kap = Ittaajimmiit o GRØ 26-27 o 8
Hope, Lake o AUS 176-177 F 6
Hope Campbell Lake o AUS 176-177 G 4
Hopefield o ZA 220-221 D 6
Hopeful o USA (GA) 284-285 F 5
Hope Island ⌒ CDN (ONT) 238-239 E 4
Hopelchén o• MEX 52-53 K 2
Hopeless, Mount ▲ AUS 178-179 E 5
Hope Mills o USA (NC) 282-283 J 6
Hopen o N (ROM) 86-87 D 5
Hopen ⌒ N (SVA) 84-85 O 4
Hopenbanken ≈ 84-85 P 4
Hopen Radio o N 84-85 O 4
Hope or Panda, Lake o AUS 178-179 E 5
Hoper ~ RUS 94-95 S 5
Hoper ~ RUS 102-103 N 2
Hope River ~ AUS 176-177 E 3
Hopes Advance Bay ≈ 36-37 P 5
Hopeton o USA (OK) 264-265 F 2
Hopetoun o AUS (VIC) 180-181 G 3
Hopetoun o AUS (WA) 176-177 F 6
Hopetown o CDN (ONT) 238-239 J 3
Hopetown o ZA 220-221 G 4
Hope Vale ✗ AUS 174-175 H 4
Hope Vale Aboriginal Land ✗ AUS 174-175 H 4
Hopewell o USA (VA) 280-281 J 6
Hopewell Cape o CDN (NB) 240-241 L 5
Hopewell Islands ⌒ CDN 36-37 K 5
Hồ Phú Ninh o VN 158-159 K 3
Hopi Buttes ▲ USA (AZ) 256-257 E 3
Hopi Indian Reservation ✗ USA (AZ) 256-257 E 2
Hopin o MYA 142-143 K 3
Hopkins o USA (MO) 274-275 D 4
Hopkins, Lake o AUS 176-177 K 2
Hopkinsville o USA (KY) 276-277 H 4
Hopland o USA (CA) 246-247 B 5
Ho-pong o MYA 142-143 K 5
Hoppner Inlet ≈ 24-25 e 7
Hopton Lake o CDN 30-31 V 5
Hoque o ANG 216-217 B 7
Hoquiam o USA (WA) 244-245 B 4
Hor ~ RUS 122-123 F 5
Horace Mount ▲ USA 20-21 Q 3
Horana o CL 140-141 J 7
Ḩorāsān ◘ IR 134-135 G 2
Horasan ☆ TR 128-129 K 2
Horatio o USA (AR) 276-277 A 7
Horbusuonka ~ RUS 110-111 P 4
Hörby o S 86-87 F 9
Horcajo de los Montes o E 98-99 E 5
Horcones, Río ~ RA 76-77 E 3
Horden, Lac o CDN (ONT) 236-237 L 2
Hor'dil Sar'dag ▲ MAU 148-149 D 2
Hordogoj o RUS 118-119 G 4
Horej-Ver o RUS 88-89 Y 3
Horezmskaja oblast' ◘ UZ 136-137 G 4
Horezu • RO 102-103 C 5
Horgo o MAU 148-149 D 3
Horgoččuma ~ RUS 110-111 N 7
Horicon o USA (WI) 274-275 K 1
Horicon National Wildlife Refuge ⊥ USA (WI) 274-275 K 1
Horincy o RUS 118-119 K 5
Horinger o VRC 154-155 G 1
Horinsk ☆ RUS 118-119 D 9
Horizontina o BR 76-77 K 4
Horki ☆ BY 94-95 M 4
Horlick Mountains ▲ ARK 16 E 0
Horlivka o UA 102-103 L 3
Horlog Hu o VRC 144-145 L 2
Hormigas, Las o PE 70-71 C 3
Hormoz o IR 134-135 F 5
Hormoz, Ğazīr-ye ⌒ IR 134-135 G 5
Hormoz, Kūh-e ▲ IR 134-135 F 5
Hormozgān ◘ IR 134-135 F 5
Hormud ◘ IR 134-135 F 5
Hormuz, Strait of = Hormoz, Tange-ye ≈ 134-135 G 5
Horn, Van o USA (TX) 266-267 C 2
Horna o RI 166-167 G 2
Hornachos o E 98-99 D 5
Hornaday River ~ CDN 24-25 K 6
Hornavan o S 86-87 H 3
Hornbjarg ▲ IS 86-87 b 1
Hornby Bay o CDN 30-31 L 2
Hornby Island o CDN (BC) 230-231 E 4
Horncastle o PA 62-63 C 7
Horndal o S 86-87 H 6
Horndean o CDN (MAN) 234-235 F 5
Hornell o USA (NY) 278-279 D 6
Hornell Lake o CDN 30-31 K 4
Hornepayne o CDN (ONT) 236-237 D 3
Hornillos, Punta ▲ PE 70-71 A 5
Horn Island ⌒ AUS 174-175 G 2
Horn Island ⌒ USA (MS) 268-269 M 6
Horn Mountains ▲ USA 20-21 L 6
Hornos Islands ⌒ PNG 183 D 2
Hornos, Caleta los ≈ 70-77 B 5
Horn Plateau ▲ CDN 30-31 J 4
Horn River ~ CDN 30-31 K 4
Hornsby o AUS 180-181 L 2
Hornslandet ⌒ S 86-87 H 6
Hornsund ≈ 84-85 J 4
Hornsundtind ▲ N 84-85 K 4
Horodnja o UA 102-103 G 2
Horodok ☆ UA 102-103 C 3
Horog ▲ TJ 136-137 M 6
Horol' o RUS 122-123 E 6
Horombe ▲ RM 222-223 D 9
Horošee ozero o RUS 124-125 L 2
Horoshiri-dake ▲ J 152-153 K 3
Horowupotana o CL 140-141 J 6
Horqin Youji Zhongqi o VRC 150-151 C 5
Horqin Zuoyi Houqi o VRC 150-151 D 6
Horqueta o PY 76-77 J 2
Horqueta, La o YV 62-63 D 2
Horquetas, Las o CR 52-53 C 6
Horra o VRC 144-145 H 5
Ḩorramābād ☆• IR 134-135 C 2
Ḩorram Darre o IR 128-129 N 4
Ḩorramšahr o• IR 134-135 C 3
Horrocks o AUS 176-177 C 4
Horsburgh Atoll ⌒ MV 140-141 B 5
Horse (Saint Barbe) Islands ⌒ CDN (NFL) 242-243 N 2
Horse Creek o USA (WY) 252-253 N 5
Horse Creek ~ USA 252-253 O 5
Horse Creek ~ USA 254 255 M 5
Horse Creek ~ USA 276-277 A 3
Horse Creek ~ USA 284-285 G 5
Horse Creek ~ USA 286-287 H 4
Horsefly o CDN (BC) 228-229 N 4
Horsefly Lake o CDN (BC) 228-229 N 4
Horsefly River ~ CDN 228-229 N 4
Horse Gap ▲ USA (NC) 282-283 F 4
Horsens o DK 86-87 D 9
Horse River ~ CDN 32-33 P 3
Horseshoe Bay ≈ 280-287 F 2
Horseshoe Bay o CDN (BC) 230-231 F 4
Horseshoe Beach o USA (FL) 286-287 F 2
Horseshoe Bend o USA (ID) 252-253 B 3
Horseshoe Bend National Military Park • USA (AL) 284-285 E 4
Horsham o AUS 180-181 G 4
Horsham o CDN (SAS) 232-233 J 5
Horten ☆ N 86-87 E 7
Hortense o USA (GA) 284-285 J 5
Hortensias, Las o RCH 78-79 C 5
Horti o IND 140-141 F 2
Hortobágy o H 92-93 Q 5
Hortobágyi Nemzeti Park ⊥ H 92-93 Q 5
Horton o USA (KS) 262-263 L 5
Horton Bay o USA (MI) 272-273 D 2
Horton Lake o CDN 30-31 H 2
Horton River ~ CDN 24-25 H 6
Horumnug-Tajga, hrebet ▲ RUS 116-117 G 10
Horungka ~ RUS 110-111 O 6
Horus, Temple of ∴•• ET 194-195 F 5
Horwood Lake o CDN (ONT) 236-237 F 5
Horyn' ~ UA 102-103 E 2
Horyuji ••• J 152-153 F 7
Hoşab Kalesi • TR 128-129 K 3
Hosahalli o IND 140-141 F 4
Hosa'ina o ETH 208-209 C 5
Hosakote o IND 140-141 G 3
Hos-Alas o RUS 110-111 S 6
Ḩosāmand o AFG 138-139 B 3
Hosanagara o IND 140-141 F 4
Hosato, ozero o RUS 108-109 T 6
Hosdrug o IND 140-141 F 4
Hosdurga o IND 140-141 G 4
Hose, Pegunungan ▲ MAL 162-163 K 3
Hosedaju ~ RUS 108-109 H 8
Hoseinābād o IR 128-129 M 5
Hoseinābād o IR 134-135 J 3
Hoseinābād, Rūdḩāne-ye ~ IR 134-135 J 3
Hoseinīye-ye Ḩoda Dād o IR 134-135 C 2
Hošeutovo o RUS 96-97 E 10
Hosford o USA (FL) 286-287 E 1
Hoshāb o PK 134-135 K 5
Hoshangābād o IND 138-139 F 8
Hoshiārpur o IND 138-139 E 4
Ḩōsī o AFG 138-139 B 2
Hoska ~ RUS 110-111 c 6
Hoskins o PNG 183 F 3
Hoskins o USA (NE) 262-263 J 2
Hoskote o IND 140-141 G 4
Hosmer o CDN (BC) 230-231 P 4
Hōsōōt o MAU 146-147 J 1
Hospah o USA (NM) 256-257 H 3
Hospās Rūd ~ AFG 134-135 K 3
Hospet o IND 140-141 G 3
Hospicio o PE 70-71 B 6
Hospicio o PE 70-71 B 5
Ḩosrovī o IR 134-135 A 1
Hosrovskij zapovednik ⊥ AR 128-129 L 2
Ḩōst o AFG 138-139 B 3
Hoste, Isla ⌒ RCH 80 F 7
Hostomel' o UA 102-103 G 2
Hosūr o IND 140-141 G 4
Ḩōš Yeilāq o IR 136-137 D 6
Hot o THA 142-143 L 6
Hotakadake ▲ J 152-153 G 6
Hotamış Gölü o TR 128-129 E 4
Hotan o VRC 144-145 B 2
Hotan He ~ VRC 146-147 E 6
Hotazel o ZA 220-221 F 3
Ḩotbe Sarā o IR 128-129 N 3
Hotchkiss o CDN 32-33 M 3
Hotchkiss o USA (CO) 254-255 H 5
Hotchkiss River ~ CDN 32-33 L 3
Hotel dos Manantiales o RA 80 F 4
Hotel el Cerrito o RA 80 E 5
Hotel las Horquetas o RA 80 E 4
Hotel Río Negro o PY 76-77 H 3
Hotevilla o USA (AZ) 256-257 F 3
Hồ Thác Bà < VN 156-157 D 6
Hotham, Cape ▲ AUS 172-173 K 2
Hotham, Cape ▲ CDN 24-25 Z 3
Hotham Inlet ≈ 20-21 J 3
Hotham River ~ AUS 176-177 D 6
Hotoho ~ RUS 118-119 F 6
Hotpaas o RI 166-167 D 5
Hot Springs o USA (NC) 282-283 E 5
Hot Springs o USA (SD) 260-261 C 3
Hot Springs o• USA (AR) 276-277 B 6
Hot Springs • USA (AZ) 256-257 B 6
Hot Springs • USA (OR) 244-245 E 8
Hot Springs o ZW 218-219 G 4
Hot Springs, Cove • USA (OR) 244-245 H 5
Hot Springs Cove o CDN (BC) 230-231 C 4
Hot Springs National Park ⊥ USA (AR) 276-277 B 6
Hot Springs Village o USA (AR) 276-277 B 6
Hotspur Seamount ≃ 72-73 M 4
Hot Sulphur Springs o USA (CO) 254-255 J 3
Hottah Lake o CDN 30-31 K 3
Hottentotsbaai ≈ 220-221 B 3
Hottentotskloof o ZA 220-221 D 6
Hot Water Beach • NZ 182 E 2
Hot Wells o USA (TX) 266-267 C 3
Houėgbo o DY 204-205 E 5
Houeïriye o RIM 196-197 G 6
Houghton o USA (NY) 278-279 C 6
Houghton o USA (WI) 270-271 K 3
Houghton Lake o USA (MI) 272-273 E 3
Houghton Lake o USA (MI) 272-273 E 3
Houhai o VRC 156-157 G 6
Houhora o NZ 182 D 1
Houhu o VRC 156-157 G 6
Houlton o USA (ME) 278-279 O 2
Houma o TON 184 IV a 2
Houma o USA (LA) 268-269 K 7
Houma o VRC 154-155 G 4
Houmt Souk o TN 190-191 H 4
Houndé o• BF 202-203 J 4
Hounien, Zouan- o CI 202-203 F 6
Hourtin et de Carcans, Lac d' o F 90-91 G 9
Housatonic River ~ USA 280-281 N 2
House o USA (NM) 256-257 M 4
Householder Pass ▲ USA (AZ) 256-257 A 3
Houshui Wan ≈ 156-157 F 7
Houston o CDN (BC) 228-229 H 2
Houston o USA (AK) 20-21 Q 6
Houston o USA (MN) 270-271 G 7
Houston o USA (MO) 276-277 D 3
Houston o USA (MS) 268-269 M 3
Houston o• USA (TX) 268-269 E 7
Houston, Lake < USA (TX) 268-269 E 6
Houston Co. Lake < USA (TX) 268-269 E 5
Houston Point ▲ CDN 34-35 Q 4
Houston River ~ USA 268-269 G 6
Houtman Abrolhos ⌒ AUS 176-177 B 4
Houtton Island ⌒ CDN (NS) 240-241 L 7
Houxia o VRC 146-147 H 4
Houz-e Solṭān o IR 134-135 D 1
Hova o S 86-87 G 7
Hovd o MAU (ÖVÖ) 148-149 F 5
Hovd ~ MAU 146-147 L 2
Hovd ☆ MAU 146-147 K 1
Hovden o N 86-87 C 7
Hovd gol ~ MAU 146-147 K 1
Ḩoveize o IR 134-135 C 3
Hoven o USA (SD) 260-261 G 1
Hovenweep National Monument ∴ USA (UT) 254-255 F 6
Hoverla, hora ▲ UA 102-103 D 3
Hovgaards Ø ⌒ GRØ 26-27 q 4
Hovland o USA (MN) 270-271 H 3
Hovoro o SOL 184 I c 3
Hövsgöl ◘ MAU 148-149 D 3
Hövsgöl nuur o MAU 148-149 E 2
Hovu-Aksy o RUS 116-117 F 10
Howakil ⌒ ER 200-201 K 5
Howakil Bay ≈ 200-201 K 5
Howard o USA (KS) 262-263 K 7
Howard o USA (SD) 260-261 J 2
Howard o USA (WI) 270-271 K 6
Howard City o USA (MI) 272-273 D 4
Howard Island ⌒ AUS 174-175 C 3
Howard Junction o NZ 182 D 4
Howard Lake o CDN 30-31 Q 4
Howard Lake o USA (MN) 270-271 D 5
Howards Creek ~ USA 266-267 F 3
Howard Springs o AUS 172-173 K 2
Howe, Cape ▲ AUS 180-181 K 4
Howe o USA (ID) 252-253 F 3
Howell o USA (MI) 272-273 F 5
Howell o USA (UT) 254-255 C 2
Howells o USA (NE) 262-263 K 3
Howes o USA (SD) 260-261 D 2
Howe Sound ≈ 230-231 F 4
Howick o ZA 220-221 K 4
Howick Group ⌒ AUS 174-175 H 4
Howitt, Lake o AUS 178-179 E 4
Howland o USA (ME) 278-279 N 3
Howley o CDN (NFL) 242-243 L 3
Howlong o AUS 180-181 J 3
Howser o CDN (BC) 230-231 N 3
Howship, Mount ▲ AUS 174-175 B 3
Hoxie o USA (AR) 276-277 E 4
Hoxie o USA (KS) 262-263 F 5
Hoxtolgay o VRC 146-147 H 3
Hoxud o VRC 146-147 H 4
Hōy o• IR 128 129 L 3
Høyanger ☆ N 86-87 C 6
Hoyé, Bin- o CI 202-203 F 6
Hoyerswerda o D 92-93 N 3
Høylandet o N 86-87 F 4
Hoyo, Mont ▲ ZRE 212-213 B 3
Hoyt o USA (CO) 254-255 L 4
Hoyt Lakes o USA (MN) 270-271 F 3
Hozier Islands ⌒ CDN 36-37 R 2
Hpangpai o MYA 142-143 L 4
Hpawngtut o MYA 142-143 K 3
Hradec Králové o CZ 92-93 N 3
Hradyz'k o UA 102-103 H 3
Hrami ~ GE 126-127 F 7
Hrebinka o UA 102-103 H 2
Hrebtovaja gora ▲ RUS 122-123 R 2
Hristais o BR 68-69 J 4
Hrodna ☆ BY 94-95 H 5
Hroma ~ RUS 110-111 Z 4
Hromskaja guba ≈ 110-111 Z 4
Hromtau ☆ KZ 126-127 N 2
Hron ~ SK 92-93 P 4
Hrubieszów o PL 92-93 R 3
Hsenwi o MYA 142-143 K 4
Hsinchu o RC 156-157 M 4
Hsingying o RC 156-157 M 5
Hsipaw o MYA 142-143 K 4
Hsuen Shan ▲ RC 156-157 M 4
Hṭai Đu'o'ng ☆ VN 156-157 E 6
Hṭai Ninh ☆ VN 156-157 E 6
Hṭai Phong ☆• VN 156-157 E 6
Htingu o MYA 142-143 K 3
Hua'an o VRC 156-157 K 4
Huab ~ NAM 216-217 C 9
Huabuzhen o VRC 156-157 L 2
Huaca o EC 64-65 D 1
Huacalera o RA 76-77 E 2
Huacaña o PE 64-65 E 9
Huacas, Las ⌒• CR 52-53 B 6
Huacaya o BOL 70-71 F 7
Huacaya, Río ~ BOL 76-77 F 1
Huacaybamba o PE 64-65 D 6
Huachacalla o BOL 70-71 C 6
Huachi o VRC 154-155 F 3
Huachi, Lago o BOL 70-71 F 4
Huacho o PE 64-65 D 7
Huachos o PE 64-65 E 8
Huachuca City o USA (AZ) 256-257 E 7
Huacrachuco o PE 64-65 D 6
Huacullani o PE 70-71 C 5
Huade o VRC 148-149 M 7
Huadian o VRC 150-151 F 6
Huaguang Jiao ⌒ VRC 158-159 L 2
Huahaizi o VRC 146-147 M 6
Hua Hin o• THA 158-159 E 4
Huahua, Río = Río Wawa ~ NIC 52-53 B 4

Historic Remains, Forts — Huahua, Río 337

Huaiá-Miçu, Rio ~ BR 68-69 B 7
Huai'an o VRC (HEB) 154-155 J 1
Huai'an o VRC (JIA) 154-155 L 5
Huaibei o VRC 154-155 K 5
Huaibin o VRC 154-155 J 5
Huai He ~ VRC 154-155 K 5
Huaihua o VRC 156-157 F 3
Huaiji o VRC 156-157 H 5
Huailai o VRC 154-155 J 1
Huaillas, Cerro ▲ BOL 70-71 D 5
Huai Na o THA 158-159 F 2
Huainan o VRC 154-155 K 5
Huairen o VRC 154-155 H 2
Huaiyang o VRC 154-155 J 5
Huaiyin o VRC 154-155 L 5
Huai Yot o THA 158-159 E 7
Huaiyuan o VRC 154-155 K 5
Huajialing o VRC 154-155 D 4
Huajianzi o VRC 150-151 E 7
Huajuapan o MEX 50-51 G 5
Huajuapan de León o• MEX 52-53 F 3
Huaki o• RI 166-167 D 5
Hualalai ▲ USA (HI) 288 K 5
Hualapai Indian Reservation ⅹ USA (AZ) 256-257 B 3
Hualapai Mountain Park ⊥• USA (AZ) 256-257 B 3
Hualapai Mountains ▲ USA 256-257 B 4
Hualiangting SK o VRC 154-155 K 6
Hualien o RC 156-157 M 5
Huallaga, Río ~ PE 64-65 D 4
Huallanca o PE 64-65 D 6
Hualong o VRC 154-155 C 3
Huamachuco o PE 64-65 C 5
Huamali o PE 64-65 E 7
Huamani o PE 64-65 E 8
Huamantla o MEX 52-53 F 2
Huambo ◻ ANG 216-217 C 6
Huambo ☆ ANG (HBO) 216-217 C 6
Huambo o PE 64-65 F 9
Huamboya o EC 64-65 C 2
Huampami o PE 64-65 C 4
Huamuxtitlán o MEX 52-53 E 3
Huan, Al o LAR 192-193 K 5
Huañamarca o PE 70-71 A 5
Huanan o VRC 150-151 H 4
Huancabamba o PE 64-65 C 4
Huancabamba, Río ~ PE 64-65 C 4
Huancache, Sierra de ▲ RA 78-79 D 7
Huancane o PE 70-71 C 4
Huancano o PE 64-65 E 8
Huancapallac o PE 64-65 D 6
Huanca Sancos o PE 64-65 E 8
Huancavelica ☆ PE 64-65 E 8
Huancayo ☆• PE 64-65 E 8
Huanchaca, Cerro ▲ BOL 70-71 D 7
Huanchaca, Parque Nacional ⊥ BOL 70-71 G 4
Huanchon o PE 64-65 E 7
Huangcangyu • VRC 154-155 K 5
Huangchuan o VRC 154-155 J 5
Huangdi Ling • VRC 154-155 F 4
Huanggang o VRC 154-155 J 6
Huangganggliang ▲ VRC 148-149 N 6
Huanggang Shan ▲ VRC 156-157 K 3
Huangguoshu Pubu • VRC 156-157 D 3
Huang He ~ VRC 154-155 K 3
Huanghe Kou ≈ 154-155 L 3
Huanghua o VRC 154-155 K 2
Huanglianyu ▲ VRC 156-157 K 4
Huangling o VRC 154-155 F 4
Huanglong o VRC 154-155 F 4
Huanglonggong ∴ VRC 154-155 M 6
Huanglong Si • VRC 154-155 C 5
Huangmei o VRC 154-155 J 6
Huangpi o VRC 154-155 J 6
Huangping o VRC 156-157 E 3
Huangqi Hai o VRC 154-155 H 1
Huangsha o VRC 156-157 L 3
Huangshan o• VRC (ANH) 156-157 L 2
Huangshan ∴ VRC (ANH) 154-155 L 6
Huangshi o VRC 154-155 J 6
Huang Shui ~ VRC 154-155 C 3
Huangtu Gaoyuan ⊥ VRC 154-155 E 3
Huangyaguan • VRC 154-155 K 1
Huangyan o VRC 156-157 M 2
Huangyuan o VRC 154-155 B 3
Huangzhong o VRC 154-155 B 3
Huaninaoyuan o VRC 156-157 G 3
Huaning o VRC 156-157 C 4
Huaniqueo o MEX 52-53 D 2
Huanquelén o RA 78-79 J 4
Huanquer o RA 76-77 G 6
Huanren o VRC 150-151 E 7
Huanta o PE 64-65 E 8
Huantacareo o MEX 52-53 D 2
Huantraico, Sierra del ▲ RA 78-79 E 4
Huánuco ☆ PE 64-65 D 6
Huanuni o BOL 70-71 D 6
Huanusco o MEX 50-51 H 7
Huan Xian o VRC 154-155 E 3
Huanza o PE 64-65 D 7
Huanzo, Cordillera de ▲ PE 64-65 F 9
Huapí, Serranías ▲ NIC 52-53 B 5
Huaping o VRC 156-157 B 3
Huaping Yü ⌒ RC 156-157 M 4
Huaping Z.B. ⊥ VRC 156-157 F 4
Huaqiao o VRC 154-155 E 6
Huaqingchi • VRC 154-155 F 4
Huaquén o RCH 78-79 D 2
Huaquillas o EC 64-65 B 3
Huara o RCH 70-71 C 7
Huaral o PE 64-65 D 7
Huaraz ☆ PE 64-65 D 6
Huari o PE 64-65 D 6
Huarina o BOL 70-71 C 5
Huarmey o PE 64-65 C 7
Huarochirí o PE 64-65 D 8
Huarocondo o PE 64-65 F 8
Huarong o VRC 156-157 H 2
Huarquehue, Parque Nacional ⊥ RCH 78-79 D 5
Huasabas o MEX 50-51 E 3
Huasaga o EC 64-65 D 3
Huasago, Río ~ PE 64-65 D 3
Hua Sai o THA 158-159 F 6
Huascarán, Parque Nacional ⊥ ∴ PE 64-65 D 6
Huasco o RCH 76-77 B 5
Huasco, Río ~ RCH 76-77 B 5
Huasco, Salar de o RCH 70-71 C 7
Huashan o VRC (GXI) 156-157 F 4
Hushan • VRC (SXI) 154-155 G 4
Huashan-Yabihua • VRC 156-157 E 6
Huashaoying o VRC 154-155 J 1
Huashixia o VRC 144-145 M 3
Huata, Península de ⌣ BOL 70-71 C 5
Huatabampo o MEX 50-51 E 4
Huatugou o VRC 146-147 K 6
Huatunas, Lago o BOL 70-71 E 3
Huatusco de Chicuellar o MEX 52-53 F 2
Huaura, Río ~ PE 64-65 D 7
Huautla o MEX 50-51 K 7
Huautla de Jiménez o MEX 52-53 F 2
Huaxi • VRC 156-157 E 3
Hua Xian o VRC (GDG) 156-157 H 5
Hua Xian o VRC (HEN) 154-155 J 4
Huayabamba, Río ~ PE 64-65 D 5
Huayacocotla o MEX 52-53 E 1
Huayasa, Nevado ▲ PE 70-71 B 5
Huaying o VRC (SIC) 154-155 E 6
Huaying o VRC (SXI) 154-155 F 4
Huayllacayan o PE 64-65 D 7
Huayllay o PE 64-65 D 7
Huaynamota, Río ~ MEX 50-51 G 6
Huayna Potosí, Nevado ▲ BOL 70-71 C 5
Huaytiquina o RA 76-77 D 2
Huayuan o VRC 156-157 F 2
Huayucachi o PE 64-65 E 8
Huayuri, Pampa de ⊥ PE 64-65 E 9
Huazhou o VRC 156-157 G 6
Ḩubar, al- o KSA 134-135 D 5
Hubayah, Bi'r o LAR 192-193 K 2
Hubbard o CDN (SAS) 232-233 P 4
Hubbard o USA (IA) 274-275 E 2
Hubbard o USA (TX) 266-267 L 2
Hubbard, Mount ▲ CDN 20-21 V 6
Hubbard, Pointe ▲ CDN 36-37 Q 5
Hubbard Creek Reservoir o USA (TX) 264-265 E 6
Hubbard Glacier ⊂ CDN 20-21 V 6
Hubbard Lake o USA (MI) 272-273 F 3
Hubbard Lake o USA (MI) 272-273 F 3
Hubbards o CDN (NS) 240-241 L 6
Hub Chauki o PK 134-135 M 6
Hub City o USA (WI) 274-275 H 1
Hubei ◻ VRC 154-155 G 6
Hubli o IND 140-141 F 3
Hubynycha o UA 102-103 J 3
Hucal o RA 78-79 G 4
Hucal, Valle de ⌣ RA 78-79 G 4
Hučeto, ozero o RUS 108-109 S 6
Huckitta o AUS 178-179 C 2
Huckitta Creek ~ AUS 178-179 C 2
Huckitta Out Station o AUS 178-179 C 2
Hudaida, al- o Y 132-133 C 6
Hudain, Wādī ~ ET 194-195 G 6
Hudan ~ RUS 118-119 E 10
Hudat = Xudat o AZ 128-129 N 2
Huddersfield o GB 90-91 G 5
Hudet o ETH 208-209 D 6
Hudgin Creek ~ USA 276-277 D 7
Hūdi o SUD 200-201 G 4
Hudie Quan • VRC 142-143 L 2
Hudiksvall o S 86-87 H 6
Hud Mount ▲ USA 20-21 T 3
Hudosej ~ RUS 114-115 R 2
Ḩudra, Wādī ~ Y 132-133 F 5
Hudson o CDN (ONT) 234-235 L 4
Hudson o USA (CO) 254-255 L 3
Hudson o USA (FL) 286-287 G 3
Hudson o USA (IA) 274-275 F 2
Hudson o USA (MD) 280-281 K 5
Hudson o USA (MI) 272-273 E 6
Hudson o USA (NY) 278-279 H 6
Hudson o USA (TX) 268-269 F 5
Hudson o USA (WI) 270-271 F 6
Hudson, Cerro ▲ RCH 80 D 3
Hudson, Lake o USA (OK) 264-265 J 2
Hudson Bay o CDN (SAS) 232-233 Q 3
Hudson Canyon ≃ 46-47 M 6
Hudson Falls o USA (NY) 278-279 H 5
Hudson Land ⊥ GRØ 26-27 o 7
Hudson Mountains ▲ ARK 16 F 27
Hudson River ~ USA 284-285 G 2
Hudson's Hope o CDN 32-33 K 3
Huduk, Naryn- o RUS 126-127 G 5
Hudžah ~ RUS 120-121 M 2
Hŭdžajli ☆• UZ 136-137 F 3
Huě ☆∴ VN 158-159 J 2
Huechulafquén, Lago o RA 78-79 D 5
Hueco o USA (TX) 266-267 B 2
Huecu, El o RA 78-79 D 4
Huedin o RO 102-103 C 4
Huehuetenango ☆ GCA 52-53 J 4
Huehuetla o MEX 52-53 E 1
Huejotzingo o MEX 52-53 E 2
Huejúcar o MEX 50-51 H 6
Huejuquilla El Alto o MEX 50-51 H 6
Huejutla de Reyes o MEX 50-51 K 7
Huelma o E 98-99 F 6
Huelva o• E 98-99 D 6
Huencuecho Sur o RCH 78-79 D 3
Huenque, Río ~ PE 70-71 C 5
Huepil o RCH 78-79 D 4
Hueque, Río ~ YV 60-61 G 2
Huequi, Península ⌣ RCH 78-79 C 7
Huequi, Volcán ▲ RCH 78-79 C 7
Huércal-Overa o E 98-99 G 6
Huerfano River ~ USA 254-255 L 6
Huerfano Trading Post o USA (NM) 256-257 H 2
Huerra, La o MEX 52-53 B 2
Huerta, La o RCH 78-79 D 3
Huerta, Sierra de la ▲ RA 76-77 D 6
Huertecillas o MEX 50-51 J 5
Huesca o• E 98-99 G 3
Huéscar o E 98-99 F 6
Huesos, Arroyo de los ~ RA 78-79 K 4
Huetamo de Nuñez o MEX 52-53 D 2
Huey Yang Waterfall ⊥• THA 158-159 E 5
Hufayyira, al- o KSA 130-131 J 5
Ḩufra, al- o KSA 130-131 F 3
Huftarøy ⌒ N 86-87 B 6
Hufūf, al- o KSA 130-131 L 5
Hufuma o RI 166-167 G 2
Ḩuǧand ☆ TJ 136-137 L 4
Hugdjakit ~ RUS 108-109 b 7
Hugdjungda, hrebet ▲ RUS 116-117 H 2
Huger o USA (SC) 284-285 L 3
Hugh Butler Lake o USA (NE) 262-263 F 4
Hughenden o AUS 174-175 H 7
Hughenden o CDN (ALB) 232-233 H 3
Hughes o RA 78-79 J 2
Hughes o USA 20-21 N 3
Hughes o USA (AR) 276-277 E 6
Hughes Springs o USA (TX) 264-265 K 6
Hughesville o USA (MD) 280-281 K 5
Hughesville o USA (PA) 280-281 K 2
Hugh Glass Monument • USA (SD) 260-261 D 1
Hugh River ~ AUS 176-177 M 2
Hugh White State Recreational Park • USA (MS) 268-269 L 3
Hugli ~ IND 142-143 E 5
Hugo o USA (OK) 264-265 J 4
Hugo Reservoir o USA (OK) 264-265 J 4
Hugoton o USA (KS) 262-263 E 7
Huguangyan • VRC 156-157 G 6
Huguenot Memorial • ZA 220-221 D 6
Huguo o VRC 156-157 D 2
Huia o NZ 182 E 2
Hui'an o VRC 156-157 L 4
Hui'anpu o VRC 154-155 E 3
Huib-Hochplato ⊥ NAM 220-221 C 3
Huichang o VRC 156-157 J 4
Huichapan o MEX 52-53 E 1
Huichon o KOR 150-151 F 7
Huichuan o VRC 154-155 C 4
Huidong o VRC (GDG) 156-157 J 5
Huidong o VRC (SIC) 156-157 C 3
Huila ◻ ANG 216-217 C 7
Huila, Nevado del ▲ CO 60-61 D 6
Huilai o VRC 156-157 K 5
Huila Plateau ▲ ANG 216-217 C 7
Huili o VRC 156-157 C 3
Huillapima o RA 76-77 E 5
Huilong o VRC 156-157 G 3
Huimbayoc o PE 64-65 E 5
Huimilpan o MEX 52-53 D 1
Huimin o VRC 154-155 K 3
Huiñaimarca, Lago o PE 70-71 C 5
Huinan o VRC 150-151 F 6
Huinca Renancó o RA 78-79 G 3
Huining o VRC 154-155 D 4
Huishui o VRC 156-157 E 3
Huisne ~ F 90-91 H 7
Huitimbo o GH 202-203 J 7
Huitong o VRC 156-157 F 3
Huitoto, Raudal ~ CO 64-65 F 1
Huitoyacu, Río ~ PE 64-65 D 3
Huittinen o FIN 88-89 G 6
Huitzo o MEX 52-53 F 3
Huivulai o MEX 50-51 E 4
Huixtepec o MEX 52-53 F 3
Huixtla o MEX 52-53 H 4
Huiyang o VRC 156-157 J 5
Huize o VRC 156-157 C 3
Huizhou o VRC 156-157 J 5
Huji o VRC 154-155 H 6
Hujra Shāh Meqeem o PK 138-139 D 4
Hukeri o IND 140-141 F 2
Hukou o VRC 156-157 K 2
Hukou Pubu • VRC 154-155 G 4
Hukovo o UA 102-103 L 3
Hukuntsi o RB 220-221 E 1
Hula o PNG 183 D 6
Hulah Lake o USA (OK) 264-265 H 2
Hulaiba o KWT 130-131 K 2
Hulaifa as-Sufla, al- o KSA 130-131 G 5
Ḩulaiş o KSA 130-131 F 6
Hul'ajpole o UA 102-103 K 4
Hulan o VRC 150-151 F 5
Hulane o RI 166-167 D 3
Hulayq al Kabir, Al ▲ LAR 192-193 G 4
Hulekal o IND 140-141 F 3
Hulett o USA (WY) 252-253 O 2
Hulga ~ RUS 114-115 G 2
Hulhuta o RUS 96-97 E 10
Hulin o VRC 150-151 J 5
Huliyar o IND 140-141 G 4
Hull o CDN (QUE) 238-239 K 3
Hull o USA (IA) 274-275 B 1
Hull o USA (IL) 274-275 G 5
Hull o USA (TX) 268-269 F 6
Hullehgush o IND 138-139 E 1
Ḩülm o• AFG 136-137 K 6
Hulo o GE 126-127 E 7
Hultsfred ☆ S 86-87 G 8
Hulun Nur o VRC (NMZ) 148-149 N 3
Ḩulwa, al- o KSA 130-131 K 6
Ḩulwān o• ET 194-195 E 3
Ḩuma o VRC 150-151 F 2
Ḩumā' aš-Šimāliya, al- o KSA 130-131 J 5
Humacao o USA (PR) 286-287 Q 2
Humahuaca o RA 76-77 E 2
Ḩumaid, al- o KSA 132-133 B 4
Humaitá o BOL 70-71 D 2
Humaitá o BR 66-67 F 6
Humansdorp o ZA 220-221 G 7
Humari o SUD 200-201 G 4
Humay o PE 64-65 E 8
Humbe o ANG 216-217 C 8
Humber ≈ 90-91 G 5
Humberto 1 o RA 76-77 G 6
Humberto de Campas o BR 68-69 G 3
Humbert River o AUS 172-173 K 4
Humble o USA (TX) 268-269 E 7
Humble City o USA (NM) 256-257 M 6
Humboldt o CDN (SAS) 232-233 N 3
Humboldt o USA (IA) 274-275 D 2
Humboldt o USA (KS) 262-263 L 7
Humboldt o USA (NE) 262-263 L 4
Humboldt o USA (NV) 246-247 G 3
Humboldt o USA (SD) 260-261 J 3
Humboldt o USA (TN) 276-277 G 5
Humboldt Bay ≈ 246-247 A 3
Humboldt Bay o CDN (ONT) 234-235 P 5
Humboldt Gletscher ⊂ GRØ 26-27 S 4
Humboldt Redwoods State Park ⊥ USA (CA) 246-247 B 3
Humboldt River ~ USA 246-247 G 3
Humboldt Salt Marsh o USA (NV) 246-247 H 4
Hume, Lake < AUS 180-181 J 4
Húmeda, Pampa ⊥ RA 78-79 H 3
Hume Highway II AUS 180-181 J 3
Ḩumeida, al- o KSA 130-131 D 3
Humenné o SK 92-93 Q 4
Hume River ~ CDN 30-31 E 3
Humeston o USA (IA) 274-275 E 4
Hummi, ozero o RUS 122-123 G 3
Humocaro Bajo o YV 60-61 G 3
Humos, Cabo ▲ RCH 78-79 C 3
Humos, Isla ⌒ RCH 80 C 2
Humpata o ANG 216-217 B 7
Humphrey o USA (AR) 276-277 D 6
Humphrey o USA (ID) 252-253 F 2
Humphrey o USA (NE) 262-263 J 3
Humphreys Peak ▲ USA (AZ) 256-257 D 3
Humpolec o CZ 92-93 N 4
Humptulips o USA (WA) 244-245 B 3
Humpty Doo o AUS 172-173 K 2
Humuula o USA (HI) 288 K 5
Hūn ☆• LAR 192-193 F 4
Húnaflói ≈ 86-87 c 2
Hunan ◻ VRC 156-157 G 3
Hunchun o VRC 150-151 H 6
Hundested o DK 86-87 E 9
Hundred and Two River ~ USA 274-275 D 4
Hundred Islands National Park • RP 160-161 D 4
Hunedoara o• RO 102-103 C 5
Hunga ⌒ TON 184 IV a 1
Hunga Ha'apai ⌒ TON 184 IV a 2
Hungary = Magyarország ■ H 92-93 O 5
Hunga Tonga ⌒ TON 184 IV a 2
Hungerford o AUS 178-179 H 5
Hungiji o MAU 146-147 M 1
Hungnam o KOR 150-151 F 8
Hungry Horse o USA (MT) 250-251 E 3
Hungry Horse Reservoir o USA (MT) 250-251 F 3
Hunguj gol ~ MAU 146-147 L 1
Hungund o IND 140-141 G 2
Hu'ng Yên ☆ VN 156-157 E 6
Hunhada ~ RUS 110-111 U 7
Ḩunik o IR 134-135 J 3
Huni Valley o GH 202-203 K 7
Hunjiang o VRC 150-151 F 7
Ḩunkurāb, Ra's ▲ ET 194-195 G 5
Hunkuyi o WAN 204-205 G 3
Ḩūnsār o• IR 134-135 D 2
Hunsberge ▲ NAM 220-221 C 3
Hunsrück ▲ D 92-93 J 4
Hunstein Range ▲ PNG 183 B 3
Hunsūr o IND 140-141 G 4
Hunt o USA (AZ) 256-257 F 4
Hunte ~ D 92-93 K 2
Hunter o USA (AR) 276-277 D 5
Hunter o USA (KS) 262-263 H 5
Hunter o USA (ND) 258-259 K 4
Hunter Island ⌒ AUS 180-181 H 6
Hunter Island ⌒ CDN (BC) 230-231 A 2
Hunter Liggett Military Reservation, Fort xx USA (CA) 248-249 C 4
Hunter River ~ AUS 180-181 L 2
Hunter River o CDN (PEI) 240-241 M 4
Hunters o USA (WA) 244-245 G 2
Hunter's Lodge o EAK 212-213 F 5
Huntingburg o USA (IN) 274-275 M 6
Huntingdon o CDN (QUE) 238-239 L 3
Huntingdon o USA (TN) 276-277 G 5
Hunting Island ⌒ USA (SC) 284-285 K 4
Huntington o USA (IN) 274-275 N 4
Huntington o USA (MA) 278-279 J 6
Huntington o USA (NY) 280-281 N 3
Huntington o USA (OR) 244-245 H 6
Huntington o USA (PA) 280-281 J 3
Huntington o USA (TX) 268-269 F 5
Huntington o USA (UT) 254-255 E 4
Huntington o USA (WV) 280-281 D 5
Huntington Beach o USA (CA) 248-249 G 6
Huntland o USA (TN) 276-277 J 5
Huntly o GB 90-91 F 3
Huntly o NZ 182 E 2
Huntoon o CDN (SAS) 232-233 P 6
Hunts Inlet o CDN (BC) 228-229 D 2
Huntsville o CDN (ONT) 238-239 F 3
Huntsville o USA (AR) 276-277 B 4
Huntsville o USA (MO) 274-275 F 5
Huntsville o USA (TX) 268-269 E 6
Huntsville o USA (UT) 254-255 D 2
Huntsville o• USA (AL) 284-285 D 2
Hunucma o MEX 52-53 K 1
Hunyuan o VRC 154-155 H 2
Hunza ~ PK 138-139 E 1
Huocheng o VRC 146-147 E 3
Huoi Mo o LAO 156-157 C 7
Huolingol o VRC 148-149 O 5
Huonfels o AUS 174-175 G 6
Hu'o'ng Diên o VN 158-159 J 2
Huong He o LAO 156-157 D 6
Hu'o'ng Khê ☆ VN 156-157 D 7
Hu'o'ng So'n ☆ VN 156-157 D 7
Huon Gulf ≈ 183 D 4
Huon Peninsula ⌣ PNG 183 D 4
Hūon Rāi ~ VN 158-159 H 6
Huonville-Ranelagh o AUS 180-181 J 7
Huoqiu o VRC 154-155 K 5
Huoshan o VRC 154-155 K 6
Huoshou o VRC 154-155 G 3
Hupel o CDN (BC) 230-231 L 3
Ḩuqf, al- ⊥ OM 132-133 K 4
Ḩuqna, Tall o IRQ 128-129 K 4
Huqui, Ilha do ⌒ BR 66-67 K 4
Ḩūr o IR (ESF) 134-135 F 2
Ḩūr o IR (HOR) 134-135 H 2
Huraba o RI 162-163 C 4
Ḩuraiba,al- o Y 132-133 F 6
Ḩuraimilā o KSA 130-131 K 5
Ḩuraiş o KSA 130-131 K 5
Ḩūrān ≈ 134-135 F 5
Hurd, Cape ▲ CDN (ONT) 238-239 D 3
Hurdiyo o SP 208-209 K 3
Hurdsfield o USA (ND) 258-259 H 4
Hurén ~ RUS 120-121 M 3
Hure Qi o VRC 150-151 C 6
Hurghada = al-Gurdaqa ☆• ET 194-195 F 4
Huri Hills ▲ EAK 212-213 F 2
Huringda ~ RUS 114-115 U 2
Huringda ~ RUS 116-117 F 2
Ḩuriyā Muriyā, Ǧazā'ir ⌒ Y 132-133 J 5
Hurki o BY 94-95 M 4
Hurley o USA (NM) 256-257 G 6
Hurley o USA (WI) 270-271 H 4
Ḩurma, al- o KSA 132-133 C 3
Hurman Çayı ~ TR 128-129 G 3
Hurmuli o RUS 122-123 G 3
Huron o USA (CA) 248-249 D 3
Huron o USA (SD) 260-261 H 2
Huron, Lake o 46-47 G 3
Huron, Lake o 272-273 F 2
Huron Islands ⌒ USA (MI) 270-271 L 4
Ḩurr, Wādī al- ~ KSA 130-131 H 2
Hurricane o USA (AK) 20-21 Q 5
Hurricane o USA (UT) 254-255 B 6
Hurricane o USA (WV) 280-281 D 5
Hurricane Creek ~ USA 284-285 H 5
Hurry Fjord ≈ 26-27 o 8
Hurso o ETH 208-209 E 4
Hurstown o USA (TX) 268-269 F 5
Hurtado o RCH 76-77 B 6
Hurtado, Río ~ RCH 76-77 B 6
Hurtsboro o USA (AL) 284-285 E 4
Hurwitz Lake o CDN 30-31 V 5
Ḩuš'a, al- o KSA 132-133 C 5
Ḩušaibi, al- o KSA 130-131 H 5
Husainābād o IND 142-143 D 3
Husain al-Ǧāfūs o IRQ 128-129 L 6
Husana ~ RUS 108-109 b 7
Húsavík ☆ IS 86-87 e 1
Ḩūsf o IR 134-135 H 2
Husheib o SUD 200-201 G 5
Huşi o RO 102-103 F 4
Ḩūš Īsā o ET 194-195 E 2
Huskisson o AUS 180-181 L 3
Huskvarna o S 86-87 G 8
Huslia o USA 20-21 M 4
Huslia River ~ USA 20-21 M 4
Husmund ~ RUS 116-117 K 2
Hussar o CDN (ALB) 232-233 F 4
Hustisford o USA (WI) 274-275 K 1
Hustonville o USA (KY) 276-277 L 3
Husum o D 92-93 K 1
Husum o USA (WA) 244-245 D 5
Ḩūţ o Y 132-133 C 5
Hutag o MAU 148-149 F 3
Hutan Melintang o MAL 162-163 D 3
Hutanopan o RI 162-163 C 4
Hutchinson o USA (KS) 262-263 J 6
Hutchinson o USA (MN) 270-271 D 6
Hutchinson o ZA 220-221 F 5
Hutchinson Island ⌒ USA (FL) 286-287 J 4
Hutch Mountain ▲ USA (AZ) 256-257 D 4
Hutjena o PNG 184 I b 1
Hutou o VRC 150-151 J 5
Ḩutta, al- o KSA 130-131 G 3
Hutton Range ▲ AUS 176-177 G 2
Huttonsville o USA (WV) 280-281 G 5
Hutubi o VRC 146-147 H 4
Hutudabiga ~ RUS 108-109 W 4
Huu o RI 168 D 7
Hữu Lũ'ng ☆ VN 156-157 E 6
Huvin Hippargi o IND 140-141 G 2
Ḩuwair, al- o KSA 130-131 H 4
Huwairah, Wādī ~ Y 132-133 F 6
Huwār, Wādī ~ SUD 200-201 B 4
Ḩuwaymī, al- o Y 132-133 E 6
Huwayt, Wādī ~ SUD 200-201 F 2
Huxi Xincun o VRC 148-149 E 7
Huxley o CDN (ALB) 232-233 E 4
Huxley, Mount ▲ USA 20-21 U 6
Huyuyun He ~ VRC 144-145 M 2
Ḩūzestān ◻ IR 134-135 B 3
Huzhong Z.B. ⊥• VRC 150-151 D 2
Huzhou o VRC 154-155 M 6
Huzhu Tuzu Zizhixian o VRC 154-155 B 3
Hužir o RUS 116-117 N 9
Hužirt o MAU 148-149 F 4
Huzūrābād o IND 138-139 G 10
Ḩvāğe o IR 128-129 M 3
Ḩvāğe Mohammad, Kūh-e ▲ AFG 136-137 M 7
Hvalynsk ☆ RUS 96-97 F 7
Hvammstangi o IS 86-87 c 2
Hvar o• HR 100-101 F 3
Hvar ⌒ HR 100-101 F 3
Hvitfeldt, Kap ▲ GRØ 28-29 T 6
Hvojnaja o RUS 94-95 O 2
Hvolsvöllur ☆ IS 86-87 c 3
Ḩvormūğ o IR 134-135 D 4
Hvorostjanka ☆ RUS 96-97 F 7
Hvostovo o RUS 122-123 K 5
Hwali o ZW 218-219 E 5
Hwange o ZW 218-219 D 4
Hwange National Park ⊥ ZW 218-219 D 4
Hwedza o ZW 218-219 F 4
Hyades, Cerro ▲ RCH 80 D 3
Hyak o USA (WA) 244-245 D 3
Hyannis o USA (MA) 278-279 L 7
Hyannis o USA (NE) 262-263 E 3
Hyas o CDN (SAS) 232-233 Q 4
Hyattsville o USA (MD) 280-281 K 5
Hyattville o USA (WY) 252-253 L 2
Hybart o USA (AL) 284-285 C 5
Hyco Reservoir o USA (NC) 282-283 H 4
Hyco River ~ USA 280-281 G 7
Hydaburg o USA 32-33 D 4
Hyde Inlet ≈ 24-25 g 3
Hyde Lake o CDN 30-31 W 5
Hyden o AUS 176-177 E 6
Hyden o USA (KY) 276-277 M 3
Hyde Park o GUY 62-63 E 2
Hyder o USA (AK) 32-33 E 4
Hyder o USA (AZ) 256-257 B 5
Hyderābād ☆• IND 140-141 H 2
Hyderābād o• PK 138-139 B 7
Hydraulic o CDN (BC) 228-229 N 4
Hyen o N 86-87 B 6
Hyères o F 90-91 L 10
Hyères, Îles d' ⌒• F 90-91 L 10
Hyesan ☆ KOR 150-151 G 7
Hyland Bay ≈ 172-173 J 2
Hyland Plateau ▲ CDN 30-31 E 5
Hyland River ~ CDN 30-31 E 5
Hyl'čuju ~ RUS 88-89 X 2
Hylly o AZ 128-129 N 3
Hymera o USA (IN) 274-275 L 5
Hynčešt' = Hînceşti ☆ MD 102-103 F 4
Hyndman Peak ▲ USA (ID) 252-253 D 3
Hyono-sen ▲ J 152-153 F 7
Hyrax Hill ∴• EAK 212-213 F 4
Hyrdalan = Xırdalan o AZ 128-129 N 2
Hyrynsalmi o FIN 88-89 K 4
Hysham o USA (MT) 250-251 M 5
Hythe o CDN 32-33 L 4
Hyuga o J 152-153 D 8
Hyūga-nada ≈ 152-153 D 8

I

Iá, Rio ~ BR 66-67 D 3
Iabes, Erg ⊥ DZ 188-189 K 7
Iaciara o BR 72-73 G 3
Iaco, Rio ~ BR 66-67 C 7
Iaco, Rio ~ PE 70-71 B 2
Iaçu o BR 72-73 K 2
Iakora o RM 222-223 E 9
Ia Krăng Po' Cô ~ VN 158-159 J 3
Ialibu o PNG 183 B 4
Ialomiţa ~ RO 102-103 E 5
Ialpug ~ MD 102-103 F 4
Iamara o PNG 183 B 5
Iamonia, Lake o USA (FL) 286-287 E 1
Ianabinda o RM 222-223 D 9
Ianca o RO 102-103 E 5
Ian Lake o CDN (BC) 228-229 B 3
Iao Valley ⌣• USA 288 J 4
Iaripo o BR 62-63 G 5
Iaşi ☆• RO 102-103 E 4
Iauaretê o BR 66-67 C 2
Iauaretê, Cachoeira ~ BR 66-67 D 3
Iauiari, Igarapé ~ BR 66-67 C 2
Iba ☆ RP 160-161 C 5
Ibadan ☆ WAN 204-205 E 5
Ibagué ☆ CO 60-61 D 5
Ibaiti o BR 72-73 E 7
Ibanabuiú o BR 68-69 J 4
Ibanda o EAU 212-213 C 4
Ibáñez, Río ~ RCH 80 D 3
Ibanga o ZRE 212-213 A 5
Ibapah o USA (UT) 254-255 B 3
Ibar ~ YU 100-101 H 3
Ibarej, Río ~ BOL 70-71 E 4
Ibarra ☆ EC 64-65 C 1
Ibb o• Y 132-133 D 6
Ibba o SUD (SR) 206-207 J 6
Ibba ~ SUD 206-207 J 5
Ibembo o ZRE 210-211 J 2
Ibenga ~ RCB 210-211 F 2
Iberá, Esteros del o RA 76-77 J 5
Iberá, Laguna o RA 76-77 J 5
Iberia o PE (LOR) 64-65 E 4
Iberia o PE (MDI) 70-71 C 2
Iberia o USA (MO) 274-275 F 6
Iberville, Lac d' o CDN 36-37 N 7
Ibestad o N 86-87 H 2
Ibeto o WAN 204-205 F 3
Ibex Pass ▲ USA (CA) 248-249 H 4
Ibi o E 98-99 G 5
Ibi o WAN 204-205 H 4
Ibiá o BR 72-73 G 5
Ibiaí o BR 72-73 H 4
Ibiapaba, Serra da ▲ BR 68-69 H 3
Ibiapina o BR 68-69 H 3
Ibiara o BR 68-69 J 5
Ibib, Wādī ~ ET 194-195 G 6
Ibibobo o BOL 76-77 F 1
Ibicaraí o BR 72-73 L 3
Ibicuitinga o BR 68-69 J 4
Ibimirim o BR 68-69 K 6
Ibina ~ ZRE 212-213 B 3
Ibindy ▲ RM 222-223 E 8
Ibipeba o BR 68-69 G 7
Ibipira o BR 68-69 F 5
Ibipitanga o BR 72-73 J 2
Ibiporã o BR 72-73 E 7
Ibiquera o BR 72-73 K 2
Ibiraba o BR 68-69 G 7
Ibiraci o BR 72-73 G 6
Ibirama o BR 74-75 F 6
Ibiraçal, Rio ~ BR 76-77 J 5
Ibiruba o BR 74-75 D 7
Ibitiara o BR 72-73 J 2
Ibitinga o BR 72-73 F 6
Ibitinga, Represa < BR 72-73 F 6
Ibitira o BR 72-73 J 3
Ibitirama o BR 72-73 K 6
Ibn Ḩauṭar, Wādī = Umm al-Ḩalt, Wādī ~ OM 132-133 J 4
Ibo o BR (BAH) 68-69 J 6
Ibó o BR (PER) 68-69 J 6
Ibo o MOC 214-215 L 7
Ibohamane o RN 198-199 C 5
Iboko o ZRE 210-211 G 4
Ibondo o ZRE 212-213 B 4
Ibonma o RI 166-167 G 3
Iboro o WAN 204-205 E 5
Ibotirama o BR 72-73 J 2
Iboundji, Mont ▲ G 210-211 C 4
Ibra o OM 132-133 L 2
Ibra o RI 166-167 G 4
Ibra, Wādī ~ SUD 206-207 G 3
'Ibrī o OM 132-133 K 2
Ibšawāy o ET 194-195 E 3
Ibstone o CDN (SAS) 232-233 K 3
Ibuaçu o BR 68-69 J 4
Ibuguaçu o BR 68-69 H 3
Ibusuki o• J 152-153 D 9
Ica o PE 64-65 E 9
Ičа ~ RUS 114-115 P 6
Iča ~ RUS 120-121 R 6
Içá, Rio ~ BR 66-67 C 4
Ica, Río de ~ PE 64-65 E 9
Icabarú o YV 62-63 D 3
Icalma, Paso de ▲ RA 78-79 D 5
Içana o BR 66-67 D 2
Içana, Rio ~ BR 66-67 D 2
Icaño o RA 76-77 E 5
Icapuí o BR 68-69 K 4
Icaraí o BR 68-69 J 3
Icaraíma o BR 72-73 D 7
Icatu o BR 68-69 F 3
Iceberg Point ▲ CDN 26-27 G 3
Ice Caves ∴ USA (WA) 244-245 D 5
Icefields Parkway o CDN (ALB) 228-229 R 4
Iceland = Ísland ■ IS 86-87 b 2
Iceland = Ísland ⌒ IS 86-87 c 2
Iceland Basin ≃ 6-7 G 3
Iceland-Faroe Rise = Iceland-Færoe Rise ≃ 6-7 H 2
Icelandic Plateau ≃ 6-7 H 2
Icém o BR 72-73 F 6
Ice Mountain ▲ CDN (BC) 228-229 N 2
Ičera ~ RUS 118-119 D 6
Ichalkaranji o IND 140-141 F 2
Iche o MA 188-189 L 4
Icheu o WAN 204-205 G 5
Ichi-gawa ~ J 152-153 F 7
Ichilo, Río ~ BOL 70-71 E 5
Ichinomiya o J 152-153 G 7
Ichinoseki o J 152-153 J 5
Ichkeul, Parc National de l' ⊥∴ TN 190-191 G 2
Ichmul o MEX 52-53 K 1
Ichoa, Río ~ BOL 70-71 E 4
Ichocan o PE 64-65 C 5
Ich'ŏn o ROK 150-151 F 9
Icht o MA 188-189 H 6
Ichuña o PE 70-71 B 5
Ičigemskij hrebet ▲ RUS 112-113 L 5
Ičinskaja Sopka, vulkan ▲ RUS 120-121 R 6
Ičinskij o RUS 120-121 Q 6
Icó o BR 68-69 J 5
Icoca o ANG 216-217 D 3
Ičoda ~ RUS 118-119 E 5
Ičuveem ~ RUS 112-113 Q 2
Icy Bay ≈ 20-21 U 7
Icy Cape ▲ USA 20-21 J 1
Icy Cape ▲ USA 20-21 T 7
Icy Reef ⌒ USA 20-21 U 2
Icy Strait ≈ 32-33 C 2
Ida ~ RUS 116-117 M 9
Ida o USA (LA) 268-269 G 4
Idabato o CAM 204-205 H 6
Idabel o USA (OK) 264-265 K 5
Idabo o ETH 208-209 E 5
Idaga Hamus o ETH 200-201 J 5
Ida Grove o USA (IA) 274-275 C 2
Idah o WAN 204-205 G 5
Idaho ◻ USA 252-253 B 2
Idaho Army National Guard Artillery Range xx USA (ID) 252-253 B 3
Idaho Falls o USA (ID) 252-253 F 3
Idaho National Engineering Laboratory • USA (ID) 252-253 F 3
Idaiatuba o BR 72-73 G 7
Idak, Cape ▲ USA 22-23 N 6
Idalia o USA (CO) 254-255 N 4
Idalia National Park ⊥ AUS 178-179 H 3
Idalina, Cachoeira ~ BR 70-71 G 2
Idalou o USA (TX) 264-265 C 5
Idanre o• WAN 204-205 F 5
Ida-Oumarkt o MA 188-189 G 6
Idappādi o IND 140-141 G 5
Idar o IND 138-139 D 8
Idar-Oberstein o D 92-93 J 4
Ida Valley o AUS 176-177 F 4
'Idd al-Ghanam o SUD 206-207 G 3
Iddesleigh o CDN (ALB) 232-233 G 5
Ideal, El o MEX 52-53 L 1
Ideles o DZ 190-191 E 9
Idenao o CAM 204-205 H 6
Idèr gol ~ MAU 148-149 D 3
Idfū o• ET 194-195 F 5
Idhan' Awbārī ⊥ LAR 192-193 D 3
Idhan' Marzūq ⊥ LAR 192-193 E 5
Idi o RI 162-163 B 2
Idi-Iroko o WAN 204-205 E 5
Idil ☆ TR 128-129 J 4
Idini o RIM 196-197 C 6
Idiofa o ZRE 210-211 G 6
Idiriya o WSA 188-189 F 7
Idjwi o ZRE 212-213 B 5
Idjwi, Ile ⌒ ZRE 212-213 B 5
Idjum ~ RUS 120-121 F 5
Idkū o ET 194-195 E 2
Idlib ☆ SYR 128-129 G 5
Idoani o WAN 204-205 F 5
Idodi o EAT 214-215 H 4
Idogo o WAN 204-205 E 5
Idolo, Isla del ⌒ MEX 50-51 L 7
Idongo o RCA 206-207 E 5
Ídra ⌒ GR 100-101 J 6
Idre o S 86-87 F 6
Idrigill o GB 90-91 D 3
Idrija o SLO 100-101 D 2
Idrinskoe ☆ RUS 116-117 F 8
Idriss 1., Barrage < MA 188-189 J 3
Idumbe o ZRE 210-211 H 5
Idutywa o ZA 220-221 J 6
Idwa, al- o KSA 130-131 H 4
Idževan o AR 128-129 L 2
Iecava o LV 94-95 J 3
Iengra ~ RUS 118-119 M 7
Iepê o BR 72-73 E 7
Ieper o• B 92-93 G 3
Ierápetra o GR 100-101 K 7
Ie-shima ⌒ J 152-153 B 11
Ievlevo o RUS 114-115 J 6
Ifakara o EAT 214-215 J 5
Ifaki o WAN 204-205 F 5
'Ifāl, Wādī ~ KSA 130-131 D 3
Ifanadiana o RM 222-223 E 8
Ifanirea o RM 222-223 E 9

338 Huaiá-Miçu, Rio — Ifanirea

Ifaty o ~ **RM** 222-223 C 9
Ife o • **WAN** 204-205 F 5
Ifenat o **TCH** 198-199 J 6
Iferouâne o **RN** 198-199 D 3
Ifertas, Hassi < **LAR** 190-191 H 6
Ifetedo o **WAN** 204-205 E 5
Ifetesene ▲ **DZ** 190-191 E 8
Iffley o **CDN** 174-175 F 6
Iffley o **CDN** (SAS) 232-233 K 2
Ifjord o **N** 86-87 N 1
Ifon o **WAN** 204-205 F 5
Iforhas, Adrar des ▲ **RMM** 196-197 L 4
Ifould Lake o **AUS** 176-177 M 5
Ifrane ☆ **MA** 188-189 J 4
Ifunda o **EAT** 214-215 H 4
Iga ~ **RUS** 116-117 N 7
Igabi o **EAU** 212-213 D 3
Igaliku o **GRØ** 28-29 S 6
Igaliku Fjord ≈ 28-29 S 6
Igalula o **EAT** 212-213 D 3
Iganga o **EAU** 212-213 D 3
Igangan o **WAN** 204-205 E 5
Igapó o **BR** 68-69 K 6
Igapora o **BR** 72-73 J 2
Igara Paraná, Río ~ **CO** 64-65 F 2
Igarapava o **BR** 72-73 G 6
Igarapé-Açu o **BR** 68-69 E 2
Igarapé Grande o **BR** 68-69 F 4
Igarapé Lage, Área Indígena ⅄ **BR** 70-71 E 2
Igarapé Lourdes, Área Indígena ⅄ **BR** 70-71 G 2
Igarapé Mirim o **BR** 62-63 K 6
Igarka o **RUS** 108-109 W 8
Igarka-Lybangajaha ~ **RUS** 108-109 R 7
Igarra o **WAN** 204-205 F 5
Igbeti o **WAN** 204-205 E 5
Igawa o **EAT** 214-215 H 5
Igboho o **WAN** 204-205 E 4
Igbo-Ora o **WAN** 204-205 E 5
Igbor o **WAN** 204-205 H 5
Iğdır ☆ **TR** 128-129 L 3
Igdlorssuit Sund ≈ 26-27 Y 8
Igdlulik o **GRØ** 26-27 W 6
Igėfveem ~ **RUS** 112-113 Y 4
Igichuk Hills ▲ **USA** 20-21 J 3
Igirma o **RUS** 116-117 L 7
Igiugig o **USA** 22-23 T 3
Iglau = Jihlava o **CZ** 92-93 N 4
Igle, Cerro ▲ **RA** 80 D 5
Iglesia o **I** 100-101 D 7
Iglesias, Cerro ▲ **RA** 80 G 3
Igli o **DZ** 188-189 K 5
Igloolik o **CDN** 24-25 f 6
Igloolik Island ∩ **CDN** 24-25 f 6
Iglusuaktalaluk Island ∩ **CDN** 36-37 T 6
Ignace o **CDN** (UNI) 234-235 M 5
Ignacio o **USA** (CO) 254-255 H 6
Ignalina o **LT** 94-95 K 4
Ignašino o **RUS** 118-119 L 9
Ignatovo o **RUS** 94-95 P 1
Iğneada o **TR** 120-129 H 2
Ignit Fiord ≈ 36-37 T 2
Igom ☆ **RI** 166-167 F 2
Igoma o **EAT** 214-215 G 4
Igombe ~ **EAT** 212-213 F 3
Igornachoix Bay ≈ 38-39 Q 3
Igornachoix Bay ≈ 242-243 L 2
Igoumenitsa o **GR** 100-101 H 5
Igporin o **WAN** 204-205 F 4
Igra ☆ **RUS** 96-97 H 5
Igrim o **RUS** 114-115 M 4
Igrita o **WAN** 204-205 F 5
Iguache, Mesas de ▲ **CU** 64-65 F 1
Iguaçu, Parque Nacional do ⊥ ••• **BR** 74-75 D 5
Iguaçu, Río ~ **BR** 74-75 D 5
Igual o **BR** 72-73 K 3
Iguala de la Independencia o **MEX** 52-53 E 2
Iguape o **BR** 74-75 G 5
Iguará, Río ~ **BR** 68-69 G 3
Iguatemi o **BR** 76-77 K 2
Iguatemi, Río ~ **BR** 76-77 K 2
Iguatu o **BR** 68-69 J 5
Iguazú, Parque Nacional del ⊥ ••• **RA** 76-77 K 3
Iguéla o **G** 210-211 B 4
Iguetti ∠ **RIM** 196-197 F 2
Iguetti, Sebkhet o **RIM** 196-197 F 2
Iguguno o **EAT** 212-213 E 6
Iguidi, Erg ∠ **DZ** 196-197 G 2
Iguidi Ouan Kasa ∠ **LAR** 190-191 H 8
Iguitu o **BR** 68-69 G 7
Igumnovskaja o **RUS** 94-95 S 1
Igunga o **EAT** 212-213 D 6
Igurubi o **EAT** 212-213 D 5
Iğtej o **RUS** 116-117 L 8
Iharana o **RM** 222-223 G 4
Ihavandifulu Atoll ∩ **MV** 140-141 A 9
Ihbulag o **MAU** 148-149 G 6
Ihema, Lac o **RWA** 212-213 C 4
Iherir ~ **DZ** 190-191 G 8
Iheya o **J** 152-153 B 11
Iheya-shima ∩ **J** 152-153 B 11
Ihhairhan o **MAU** 148-149 J 4
Ihiala o **WAN** 204-205 G 6
Ihitsa o **LAR** 192-193 G 5
Ihosy o **RM** 222-223 E 9
Ihotry, Farihy o **RM** 222-223 C 8
Ih o **MAU** 102-103 C 6
Ihtiyarşahap Dağları ▲ **TR** 128-129 K 3
Ihtiman o **BG** 102-103 C 5
Ihu o **PNG** 183 C 4
Ihuari o **PE** 64-65 D 7
Ihugh o **WAN** 204-205 H 5
Ih-Uul = Selenge o **MAU** 148-149 K 3
Iida o **J** 152-153 G 7
Iide-san ▲ **J** 152-153 H 6
Iijoki ~ **FIN** 88-89 J 4
Iisaku o **EST** 94-95 K 2

Iisalmi o **FIN** 88-89 J 5
Iiyama o **J** 152-153 H 6
Iizuka o **J** 152-153 D 8
İj o **IND** 140-141 G 2
Ijebu-Igbo o **WAN** 204-205 E 5
Ijebu-Ode o **WAN** 204-205 E 5
Ijero o **WAN** 204-205 E 5
Ijkharran o **LAR** 192-193 J 3
Ijoubban ☆ **RIM** 196-197 G 4
Ijouak o **MA** 188-189 G 5
IJsselmeer o **J** 92-93 H 2
Iju o **BR** 74-75 D 7
Ik ~ **RUS** 96-97 H 7
Ik, ozero o **RUS** 114-115 L 6
Ika o **RUS** 116-117 K 8
Ikahavo ▲ **RM** 222-223 D 6
Ikalamavony o **RM** 222-223 E 8
Ikamiut o **GRØ** 28-29 N 3
Ikanbujimal o **VRC** 146-147 J 6
Ikanda o **ZRE** 210-211 J 5
Ikang o **WAN** 204-205 H 6
Ikanga o **EAK** 212-213 G 4
Ikare o **WAN** 204-205 F 5
Ikaría ∩ **GR** 100-101 L 6
Ikatskij hrebet ▲ **RUS** 118-119 E 9
Ikauna o **IND** 142-143 D 4
Ik'inskaja Sopka, vulkan ▲ **RUS** 122-123 R 3
Ikeda o **J** 152-153 K 3
Ikej o **RUS** (IRK) 116-117 K 8
Ikej ~ **RUS** 116-117 J 8
Ikeja ☆ **WAN** 204-205 E 5
Ikela o **ZRE** 210-211 J 4
Ikelemba o **ZRE** 210-211 H 3
Ikelenge o **Z** 214-215 C 6
Ikem o **WAN** 204-205 G 5
Ikėn ~ **RUS** 108-109 X 6
Ikèngué o **G** 210-211 B 4
Ikeq Sund ≈ 28-29 T 6
Ikerasârssuk o **GRØ** (VGR) 26-27 W 7
Ikere o **WAN** 204-205 F 5
Ikermiut o **GRØ** 28-29 U 5
Ikerssuaq ≈ 28-29 V 4
Ikertlvaq ≈ 28-29 X 5
Iki ∩ **J** 152-153 C 8
Ikimba Kamachumu, Lake o **EAT** 212-213 C 4
Ikire o **WAN** 204-205 E 5
Ikirun o **WAN** 204-205 F 5
Ikkalileu o **GRØ** 28-29 W 4
Ikobé o **G** 210-211 C 4
Ikohahoene, Adrar ▲ **DZ** 190-191 G 8
Ikola o **EAT** 214-215 F 4
Ikule o **WAN** 204-205 F 5
Iknlik, Cape ▲ **USA** 22-23 T 4
Ikoma o **WAN** 204-205 H 6
Ikomu o **WAN** 198-199 B 6
Ikongo o **RM** 222-223 E 8
Ikonongo o **ZRE** 210-211 G 3
Ikoo o **EAK** 212-213 G 4
Ikopa ~ **RM** 222-223 E 7
Ikorodu o **WAN** 204-205 E 5
Ikot Ekpene o **WAN** 204-205 G 6
Ikoto o **SUD** 208-209 A 6
Ikoy ~ **G** 210-211 C 4
Ikpik Bay ≈ 24-25 J 6
Ikpikpuk River ~ **USA** 20-21 N 1
Ikrianoe o **RUS** 96-97 E 10
Iksa ~ **RUS** 114-115 N 6
Ikutha o **EAK** 212-213 G 5
Ila o **USA** (GA) 284-285 G 2
Ilafergh, Oued ~ **DZ** 196-197 L 4
Ilaga o **RI** 166-167 J 4
Ilagan ☆ **RP** 160-161 D 4
Ilaiyánkudi o **IND** 140-141 C 7
Ilaji o **WAN** 204-205 E 5
Ilaka Atsinanana o **RM** 222-223 F 7
Ilakaka o **RM** 222-223 D 9
Ilakana Patatpe o **F** 62-63 G 4
Ilám ☆ **IR** 134-135 F 2
Ilām • **IR** (ILA) 134-135 B 2
Ilanskiľ o **RUS** 116-117 H 7
Ila-Orangun o **WAN** 204-205 F 5
Ilaro o **WAN** 204-205 E 5
Ilaura o **PNG** 183 D 4
Ilave o **PE** 70-71 C 5
Ilave, Río ~ **PE** 70-71 C 5
Ilawe o **WAN** 204-205 F 5
Ilbenge o **RUS** 118-119 M 4
Ilbilbie o **AUS** 178-179 K 1
Île ~ **KZ** 124-125 K 6
Ilebġâne, Adrar ▲ **RMM** 196-197 L 5
Ilebo o **ZRE** 210-211 H 4
Ileck, Sol'- o **RUS** 96-97 H 7
Île-de-France ∠ **F** 90-91 J 7
Île-d'Entrée o **CDN** (QUE) 242-243 G 5
Île Des Noefs o **SY** 224 B 5
Ile du Nord o **SY** 224 D 1
Ile du Sud o **SY** 224 D 1
Ileg o **PNG** 183 D 3
Ilek ~ **KZ** 126-127 H 8
Ilek o **RUS** (ORB) 96-97 H 8
Ilek ~ **RUS** 96-97 H 8
Ileksa ~ **RUS** 88-89 O 5
Ileret o **EAK** 212-213 G 2
Île-Rousse, L' o **F** 98-99 M 3
Iles, Lac des o **CDN** (QUE) 238-239 H 2
Ilesa o **WAN** 204-205 F 5
Ilesa o **RUS** 88-89 T 5
Ilesa o **WAN** (KWA) 204-205 E 4
Ileža ~ **RUS** 94-95 J 2
Ilford o **CDN** 34-35 J 2
Ilfracombe o **AUS** 178-179 H 2
Ilfracombe o **GB** 90-91 H 6
Ilga ~ **RUS** 116-117 M 9
Ilgaz ☆ **TR** 128-129 F 2
Ilgaz Dağları ▲ **TR** 128-129 F 2
Ilgin o **TR** 128-129 D 3
Ilha Grande, Baía de ≈ 72-73 H 7
Ilhas Selvagens ∩ **P** 188-189 D 5
Ilhéus o • **BR** 72-73 L 3

Ilhota da Maloca Arori o **BR** 62-63 F 5
Ili ~ **KZ** 146-147 D 4
Ilia o **RO** 102-103 C 5
Ilia (WA) o **USA** 244-245 H 4
Iliamna Lake o **USA** 22-23 T 3
Iliamna Volcano ▲ **USA** 20-21 O 6
Ilić o **KZ** 136-137 L 4
Ilica o **TR** 128-129 J 3
Ilica o **TR** 128-129 J 3
Ilicínia o **BR** 72-73 H 6
Ilidža o **BIH** 100-101 G 3
Ilig, Raas ▲ **SP** 208-209 J 5
Iligan o **RP** (LAN) 160-161 F 8
Iligan o **RP** 160-161 D 4
Iligan Bay ≈ 160-161 E 8
Iligan Point ▲ **RP** 160-161 E 3
Ili He ~ **VRC** 146-147 E 4
Ilikok Island ∩ **CDN** 36-37 S 2
Ilim ~ **RUS** 116-117 M 7
Ilimanaq = Claushavn o **GRØ** 28-29 P 2
Ilimo o **PNG** 183 D 5
Ilimpeja ~ **RUS** 116 117 M 4
Ilimsk o **RUS** 116-117 L 7
Ilin-Dželi ~ **RUS** 118-119 N 4
Iling o **RUS** 96-97 K 8
Ilino o **RUS** 94-95 M 4
Ili'novka o **RUS** 122-123 C 4
Il'inskaja Sopka, vulkan ▲ **RUS** 122-123 R 3
Il'inskij o **RUS** 96-97 J 4
Il'inskij o **RUS** 122-123 K 5
Iliomar o **RI** 166-167 D 6
Ilio Point ▲ **USA** (HI) 288 H 3
Ilir ~ **RUS** (IRK) 116-117 K 8
Ilir ~ **RUS** 116-117 K 8
Ilirgytgyn, ozero o **RUS** 112-113 K 1
Ilirnej o **RUS** 112-113 P 3
Ilirnej, ozero o **RUS** 112-113 P 3
Ilirnejskij krjaž ▲ **RUS** 112-113 P 3
Ilistaja ~ **RUS** 122-123 G 6
Ilitsu Baraji o **TR** 128-129 J 4
Il'ja ~ **RUS** 114-115 O 4
Ilja ~ **RUS** 118-119 F 10
Il'jak ~ **RUS** 114-115 O 4
Il'jali o **TM** 136-137 G 4
Iljalinskij kanal < **TM** 136-137 E 4
Iljara o **EAK** 212-213 H 4
Ilkutgitak, Cape ▲ **USA** 22-23 T 3
Ill ~ **F** 90-91 L 7
Ilapel o **RCH** 76-77 B 6
Ilapel, Río ~ **RCH** 76-77 B 6
Illara Creek ~ **AUS** 176-177 M 2
Illawarra, Lake o **AUS** 180-181 J 5
Illawong o **AUS** 176-177 M 3
Illbillee, Mount ▲ **AUS** 176-177 M 3
Illeullewaat Névé ▲ **CDN** 230-231 M 2
Illéla o **RN** 198-199 F 5
Illela o **WAN** 198-199 B 6
Iller ~ **D** 92-93 L 4
Illes Balears ∩ **E** 98-99 H 5
Illescas, Cerro ▲ **PE** 64-65 B 4
Illescas o **MEX** 50-51 F 6
Ilīgeri City o **USA** (MN) 270-271 J 7
Illimani, Nevado del ▲ **BOL** 70-71 D 5
Ilimo o **PE** 64-65 C 5
Illingworth o **CDN** (ALB) 232-233 P 5
Illiniza, Volcán ▲ **EC** 64-65 C 2
Illinois o **USA** 274-275 H 4
Illinois City o **USA** (IL) 274-275 H 3
Illinois Point ▲ **USA** (MT) 250-251 O 4
Illinois River ~ **USA** 244-245 D 8
Illinois River ~ **USA** 264-265 K 2
Illinois River ~ **USA** 274-275 H 5
Illinois River ~ **USA** 276-277 B 5
Illiopolis o **USA** (IL) 274-275 J 5
Illiwa ~ **GUY** 62-63 E 4
Illizi o **DZ** 190-191 G 7
Illmo o **USA** (MO) 276-277 F 3
Illorsuit o **GRØ** 26-27 Y 8
Illueca o **E** 98-99 G 4
Illusion Lake o **USA** (TX) 264-265 B 5
Ilma, Lake o **AUS** 176-177 J 4
Ilmalianuk, Cape ▲ **USA** 22-23 M 6
Il'men', ozero o **RUS** 94-95 M 6
Ilnik o **USA** 22-23 R 4
Ilo o **PE** 70-71 D 5
Ilobasco o • **ES** 52-53 K 5
Ilobu o **WAN** 204-205 F 5
Iloca o **RCH** 78-79 C 3
Ilofa o **WAN** 204-205 F 5
Ilog o **RP** 160-161 E 8
Iloilo City o • **RP** 160-161 E 7
Ilomantsi o **FIN** 88-89 L 5
Ilonga o **EAT** 214-215 J 5
Ilorin ☆ **WAN** 204-205 F 5
Ilovlja o **RUS** 96-97 F 8
Il'pinskij, mys ▲ **RUS** 120-121 V 4
Il'pinskij, poluostrov ⟩ **RUS** 120-121 V 4
Il'pyr, poluostrov ⟩ **RUS** 120-121 V 4
Il'pyrskij o **RUS** 120-121 V 4
Ilua Fjord ≈ 28-29 S 6
Iluabor o **ETH** 208-209 B 5
Iluġwa o **RI** 166-167 K 3
Iluileq o **GRØ** 28-29 T 6
Iluġkste o **LV** 94-95 K 4
Ilula o **EAT** 212-213 D 5
Ilulissat = Jakobshavn o **GRØ** 28-29 P 2
Ilur o **RI** 166-167 H 3
Ilushi o **WAN** 204-205 F 5
Ilwaco o **USA** (WA) 244-245 B 4
Ilwendo o **Z** 214-215 D 3
Ilyč ~ **RUS** 114-115 K 3
Ilza ~ **RUS** 118-119 G 11
Imabari o **J** 152-153 E 7
Imabetsu o **J** 152-153 J 4
Imajó o **J** 152-153 G 7
Imakane o **J** 152-153 H 3
Imala o **MOC** 218-219 K 2
Imám Änas o **INQ** 130-131 K 2
Imamoġlu ▲ **TR** 128-129 F 3
Imanbulak ~ **KZ** 124-125 E 2
Imandi o **RI** 164-165 H 3
Imandra, ozero o **RUS** 88-89 M 3

Imangra o **RUS** 118-119 K 7
Imanombo o **RM** 222-223 D 10
Imantau, köli o **KZ** 124-125 F 2
Imari o **J** 152-153 C 8
Imasa o **SUD** 200-201 H 3
Imassogo o **BF** 202-203 J 3
Imata o **PE** 70-71 D 4
Imata, Serrania de ▲ **YV** 62-63 D 2
Imataca, Reserva Forestal ⊥ **YV** 62-63 D 1
Imatong Mountains ▲ **SUD** 206-207 L 6
Imatra o **FIN** 88-89 K 6
Imbituba o **BR** 74-75 F 7
Imbituba, Ponta de ▲ **BR** 74-75 F 7
Imbitura o **BR** 72-73 H 5
Imdaw o **MYA** 142-143 K 5
Indé o **MEX** 50-51 G 5
Imboden o **USA** (AR) 276-277 D 4
Imbrodture Creek ~ **AUS** 178-179 G 2
Imbwae o **Z** 218-219 C 3
Iménas o **RMM** 196-197 M 4
Imerina Imady o **RM** 222-223 L 7
Imerintsiatesika o **RM** 222-223 E 7
Imese o **ZRE** 210-211 G 2
Imessouane, Pointe ▲ **MA** 188-189 G 5
Imġyt ~ **RUS** 114-115 L 5
Imġytskoe, boloto ⊥ **RUS** 114-115 L 5
Imi o **ETH** 208-209 D 5
Imin-n-Ifri • **MA** 188-189 H 5
Imin-n-Tanoute o **MA** 188-189 G 5
Imišly = Imişli o **AZ** 128-129 N 3
Imjan Gang ~ **KOR** 150-151 F 8
Imjan o **USA** (NV) 246-247 J 7
Imlay City o **USA** (MI) 272-273 F 4
Imlily o **WSA** 196-197 C 3
Immokalee o **USA** (FL) 286-287 H 5
Immouzzer-des-Ida-Outanane o **MA** 188-189 G 5
Imnaha o **USA** (OR) 244-245 J 5
Imnaha River ~ **USA** 244-245 J 5
Imnlor, ozero o **RUS** 114-115 N 4
Imo o **WAN** 204-205 G 6
Imo River ~ **WAN** 204-205 G 6
Imotski o **HR** 100-101 F 3
Imoulaye, Hassi < **DZ** 190-191 G 6
Imouzer-du-Kandar o **MA** 188-189 J 4
Impenvdom ~ **RUS** 112-113 P 5
India ∎ **IND** 138-139 C 7
Indiana o **USA** (PA) 280-281 G 3
Indiana Dunes • **USA** (IN) 274-275 L 3
Indiana Trail Caverns ∴ **USA** (OH) 280-281 C 3
Indian Bay o **CDN** (NFL) 242-243 P 3
Indian Bayou ~ **USA** (LA) 276-277 D 6
Indian Brook o **CDN** 240-241 P 4
Indian Cabins o **CDN** 30-31 L 1
Indian Community ~ **USA** (AZ) 256-257 F 4
Indian Creek ~ **USA** (254-255 F 5
Indian Falls o **USA** (CA) 246-247 E 4
Indian Gardens o **CDN** (NS) 240-241 M 6
Indian Harbour o **CDN** (NS) 240-241 M 6
Indian Head o **CDN** (SAS) 232-233 P 5
Indian Head o **USA** (MD) 280-281 J 5
Indian Heaven Wilderness ⊥ **USA** (WA) 244-245 D 4
Indian Lake o **USA** (NY) 278-279 G 5
Indian Lake o **USA** (MI) 270-271 M 4
In-Abaleha o **RMM** 196-197 J 6
Inabu o **J** 152-153 G 7
Inácio Dias, Ponta ▲ **BR** 74-75 F 5
Inácio Martins o **BR** 74-75 E 5
Inadale o **USA** (TX) 264-265 D 6
In-Adiattafene o **RMM** 202-203 J 2
Inaja o **BR** 66-67 H 5
Inajá, Río ~ **BR** 68-69 C 6
In-Akhmed o **RMM** 196-197 K 5
In-Akli o **RMM** 196-197 K 4
Indí o **RIM** 196-197 E 2
Inamabari ~ **PE** 70-71 D 4
Inambari, Río ~ **PE** 70-71 D 4
In Amenas o **DZ** 190-191 G 6
In Amguel o **DZ** 190-191 F 8
Inangahua o **NZ** 182 C 4
Inan'ja ~ **RUS** 120-121 N 2
Inanudak Bay ≈ 22-23 M 6
Inanwatan o **RI** 166-167 G 3
Iñapari o **PE** 70-71 D 4
Inarajan o **USA** 184 I b 2
Inari • **FIN** 88-89 J 2
Inari ☆ **FIN** 88-89 J 2
Inarigda o **RUS** 116-117 N 4
Inarijärvi ~ **FIN** 86-87 N 2
Inaru River ~ **USA** 20-21 N 1
Inauini, Río ~ **BR** 66-67 C 7
Inawashiro-ko o **J** 152-153 J 6
In Azzene, Djebel ▲ **DZ** 190-191 C 7
In Belbel o **DZ** 190-191 C 7
Inca o **E** 98-99 J 5
Inca, Cerro del ▲ **RCH** 76-77 C 1
Inca, Río del ~ **RCH** 76-77 C 1
Inca de Oro o **RCH** 76-77 C 4
Incahuasi o **PE** 64-65 C 5
Incahuasi o **RA** 76-77 D 1
Incahuasi, Nevado de ▲ **RA** 76-77 C 4
Incé Burnu ▲ **TR** 128-129 F 1
Ince Burnu ▲ **TR** 128-129 D 2
Incesu ☆ **TR** 128-129 F 3
Inchini o **ETH** 208-209 C 4
Inchiri ☆ **RMM** 196-197 K 6
Inch'ŏn • **ROK** 150-151 F 9
Inchope o **MOC** 218-219 G 4
Inchul o **UA** 102-103 H 3
Inchulec' o **UA** 102-103 H 4
Inca o **O** 98-99 J 5
Indio, El o **USA** (TX) 266-267 G 5
Indio, Río ~ **NIC** 52-53 B 6

Indio Rico o **RA** 78-79 J 5
Indio Rico, Arroyo ~ **RA** 78-79 J 5
Índios, Cachoeira dos ▲ **BR** 66-67 F 2
Indios, Cayos los ∩ **C** 54-55 D 4
Indios, Los ∩ **C** 54-55 H 4
Indios, Río dos o **BR** 72-73 D 6
Indiskaja guba ≈ 88-89 U 3
Indispensable Strait ≈ 184 I e 3
Inda Medhani o **ETH** 200-201 J 5
Indara Point ▲ **IND** 140-141 G 9
Indargarh o **IND** 138-139 F 7
Inda Silasê o **ETH** 200-201 J 5
Indaw o **MYA** 142-143 K 5
Indé o **MEX** 50-51 G 5
Indombo o **G** 210-211 D 4
Indore o •• **IND** 138-139 E 8
Indore o • **IND** 138-139 E 8
Indrapur o **IND** 138-139 E 10
Indramayu o **RI** 162-163 F 8
Indrapura o **RI** 162-163 C 6
Indravati ~ **IND** 142-143 C 6
Indre ~ **F** 90-91 H 8
Indulkana ⅄ **AUS** 176-177 M 3
Indus ~ **PK** 138-139 C 5
Indus, Mouths of the ≈ **PK** 138-139 A 7
Indus Fan ≃ 12 F 6
Industry o **USA** (IL) 274-275 H 4
Industry o **USA** (TX) 266-267 L 4
Indwe o **ZA** 220-221 H 5
Ine Abeg o **RMM** 196-197 K 4
Inebolu ☆ **TR** 128-129 F 1
Injune o **AUS** 178-179 K 3
Inkanwaya o **BOL** 70-71 D 5
Inkerman o **AUS** 174-175 F 5
In-Killé o **RMM** 196-197 K 6
Inkisi ~ **ZRE** 210-211 E 6
In Ekker o **DZ** 190-191 E 8
Inklin River ~ **CDN** 32-33 D 2
Inkom o **USA** (ID) 252-253 F 4
Inkouele o **RCB** 210-211 E 4
Inkster o **USA** (ND) 258-259 K 3
Inlander II **USA** 174-175 F 5
Inland Kaikoura Range ▲ **NZ** 182 D 5
Inland Lake o **USA** 20-21 L 3
Inle Lake o •• **MYA** 142-143 K 5
Inman o **USA** (KS) 262-263 J 6
Inman o **USA** (NE) 262-263 H 4
Inman o **USA** (SC) 284-285 H 1
In-Milach o **RMM** 196-197 K 6
Inn ~ **D** 92-93 M 4
Innabba o **DZ** 190-191 D 7
Innahas Chebbi o **DZ** 190-191 D 7
Innalik o **GRØ** 28-29 O 2
Innamincka o **AUS** 178-179 F 4
Innamincka Regional Reserve ⊥ **AUS** 178-179 F 4
Inndyr o **N** 86-87 G 3
Inner Hebrides ∩ **GB** 90-91 D 3
Inner Mongolia = Nei Mongol Zizhiqu □ **VRC** 154-155 D 2
Innes National Park ⊥ **AUS** 180-181 D 3
Inneston o **AUS** 180-181 D 3
Innesvale o **AUS** 172-173 K 3
Innetalling Island ∩ **CDN** 36-37 K 7
Innisfail o **AUS** 174-175 J 5
Innisfail o **CDN** (ALB) 232-233 M 4
Innisfree o **CDN** (ALB) 232-233 O 2
Innjah o **RUS** 118-119 J 6
Inokonent'evka o **RUS** 122-123 C 4
Innoko River ~ **USA** 20-21 L 5
Innsbruck ☆ **A** 92-93 L 5
Innuksuac, Rivière ~ **CDN** 36-37 L 5
Inobonto o **RI** 164-165 J 3
Inoca o **BOL** 70-71 C 6
Inocência o **BR** 72-73 E 5
Inongo o **ZRE** 210-211 G 4
Inoni o **RCB** 210-211 D 4
Inostrancava, zaliv ≈ 108-109 L 3
Inowroclaw o **PL** 92-93 P 2
Inpynékuľ ~ **RUS** 112-113 Y 4
Inquisivi o **BOL** 70-71 D 5
In Rhar o **DZ** 190-191 C 7
Inriville o **RA** 78-79 H 7
In-Sākâne, Erg ∠ **RMM** 196-197 K 4
In Salah o **DZ** 190-191 D 7
Insar o **RUS** 96-97 F 7
Inscription, Cape ▲ **AUS** 176-177 B 3
Insculas o **PE** 64-65 C 4
Insein o **MYA** 158-159 F 7
Inskip Point ▲ **AUS** 178-179 M 3
In Sokki, Oued ~ **DZ** 190-191 D 7
Inster o **CDN** (SAS) 258-259 K 3
Instow o **CDN** (SAS) 232-233 K 6
Insurăţei o **RO** 102-103 E 5
Inta o 108-109 J 8
Intakareyen o **RN** 198-199 C 5
In Talak o **RMM** 196-197 M 6
In-Tebezas o **RMM** 196-197 M 6
Intendente Alvear o **RA** 78-79 H 3
Intercoastal Waterway ~ **USA** 280-281 K 7
Interlachen o **USA** (FL) 286-287 H 2
Interlaken o **CDN** (ONT) 238-239 G 3
Interlaken o • **CH** 92-93 J 5
Interlochen o **USA** (MI) 272-273 D 3
International Amistad Reservoir < **USA** (TX) 266-267 F 4
International Falcon Reservoir < **USA** (TX) 266-267 H 7
International Falls o **USA** (MN) 270-271 J 2
Intervew Island ∩ **IND** 140-141 L 3
Intʼich'o o **ETH** 200-201 J 5
In-Tillit o **RMM** 202-203 K 2
Intracoastal Waterway < **USA** (Fl.) 286-287 H 1
Intracoastal Waterway < **USA** (LA) 268-269 K 7
Intracoastal Waterway < **USA** (SC) 284-285 K 3
Intracoastal Waterway < **USA** (TX) 268-269 F 7
Intrepid Inlet ≈ 24-25 M 2
Intutu o **PE** 64-65 E 4
Inuarfigssuaq o **GRØ** 26-27 Q 4
Inúbia o **BR** 72-73 L 3
Inûbō-saki ▲ **J** 152-153 J 7
Inugsuin Fiord ≈ 28-29 F 2

Inukjuak ○ CDN 36-37 K 5
Inulik Lake ○ CDN 30-31 N 2
Inulterg Sø ○ GRØ 26-27 h 3
Inuo ○ PNG 183 B 4
Inuria, Lago ○ PE 64-65 E 6
Inútil, Bahia ≈ 80 E 6
Inuvik ○ CDN 20-21 Y 2
Inuya, Rio ~ PE 64-65 F 7
In'va ~ RUS 96-97 J 4
Inveraray ○ GB 90-91 E 3
Invercargill ○ NZ 182 B 7
Inverell ○ AUS 178-179 L 5
Inverhuron ○ CDN (ONT) 238-239 D 4
Inverleigh ○ AUS (QLD) 174-175 F 6
Inverleigh ○ AUS (VIC) 180-181 H 5
Inverloch ○ AUS 180-181 H 5
Invermay ○ CDN (SAS) 232-233 P 4
Invermere ○ CDN 230-231 N 3
Inverness ○ CDN (NS) 240-241 O 4
Inverness ○ CDN (QUE) 238-239 O 2
Inverness ○ GB 90-91 E 3
Inverness ○ USA (FL) 286-287 G 3
Inverurie ○ GB 90-91 F 3
Inverway ○ AUS 172-173 J 4
Investigator Channel ≈ 158-159 E 5
Investigator Group ⌢ AUS 180-181 C 2
Investigator Passage ≈ 158-159 D 4
Investigator Ridge ≃ 13 A 3
Investigator Strait ≈ 180-181 D 3
Inwood ○ CDN (MAN) 234-235 F 4
Inwood ○ USA (IA) 274-275 B 1
Inyangani ▲ ZW 218-219 G 4
Inyarinyi (Kenmore Park) ○ AUS 176-177 M 3
Inyathi ○ ZW 218-219 E 4
Inyokern ○ USA (CA) 248-249 G 4
Inyo Mountains ⌢ USA 248-249 F 2
Inyonga ○ EAT 214-215 G 4
Inza ○ RUS 96-97 G 7
Inza ~ RUS 96-97 D 7
In-Zakêt ○ RMM 196-197 K 6
Inzavino ○ RUS 94-95 S 5
Inzia ~ ZRE 210-211 F 6
In Ziza, Gueltas d' < DZ 190-191 D 9
Ioánnina ○ GR 100-101 H 5
Iokanga ~ RUS 88-89 O 3
Iola (KS) 262-263 L 7
Iola ○ USA (WI) 270-271 J 6
Iolgo, hrebet ▲ RUS 124-125 P 3
Iolotan ○ TM 136-137 H 6
Iomi, ostrov ⌢ RUS 112-113 Y 4
Iona ○ ANG 216-217 B 8
Iona, Parque Nacional de ⊥ ANG 216-217 B 8
Ionava ○ LT 94-95 J 4
Ione ○ USA (CA) 246-247 H 5
Ione ○ USA (CA) 246-247 E 5
Iones, Cap ▲ USA 36-37 N 5
Ionesport ○ USA (ME) 278-279 O 4
Iongo ○ ANG 216-217 D 4
Ionia ○ USA (MI) 272-273 D 4
Ionian Islands = Iónioi Nísoi ⌢ GR 100-101 G 5
Ionian Sea = Iónio, Mare ≈ 100-101 F 6
Iónioi Nísoi ⌢ GR 100-101 H 5
Iónio Pélagos ≈ 100-101 F 6
Ionivéem ~ RUS 112-113 Y 4
Ión Nísoi ⌢ GR 100-101 G 5
Iony, ostrov ⌢ RUS 120-121 K 5
Iori ~ GE 126-127 F 4
Iori ○ PNG 183 C 4
ius ⌢ GR 100-101 K 6
Iô-shima ⌢ J 152-153 D 9
Iota ○ USA (LA) 268-269 H 6
Ioué Juruena, Estação Ecológica ⊥ BR 70-71 H 3
Iouigharacène, Ibel ▲ MA 188-189 J 4
Ioulik ○ RIM 196-197 B 5
Iowa ○ USA (LA) 268-269 H 6
Iowa ▣ USA 274-275 D 2
Iowa City ○ USA (IA) 274-275 G 3
Iowa Falls ○ USA (IA) 274-275 E 1
Iowa Park ○ USA (TX) 264-265 F 5
Iowa River ~ USA 274-275 E 1
Iowa River ~ USA 274-275 G 3
Iowa Sac and Fox Indian Reservation ⌖ USA (KS) 262-263 L 5
Ipadu, Cachoeira ~ BR 66-67 D 2
Ipala ○ GCA 52-53 K 4
Ipameri ○ BR 72-73 K 4
Ipanema ○ BR 72-73 K 5
Ipao ○ VAN 184 II c 4
Iparia ○ PE 64-65 E 6
Ipatinga ○ BR 72-73 J 5
Ipatovo ~ RUS 102-103 N 5
Ipauçu ○ BR 72-73 F 7
Ipaumirim ○ BR 68-69 J 5
Ipek Geçidi ▲ TR 128-129 K 3
Iperu ○ WAN 204-205 F 5
Ipetu-Ijesha ○ WAN 204-205 F 5
Ipewik River ~ USA 20-21 H 2
Iphigenia Bay ≈ 32-33 C 4
Ipiaçara, Rio ○ BR 68-69 B 4
Ipiaçu ○ BR 72-73 F 5
Ipiales ○ CO 64-65 D 1
Ipiaú ○ BR 72-73 L 3
Ipil ○ RP 160-161 E 9
Ipira ○ BR 72-73 L 2
Ipiranga, Rio ~ BR 66-67 K 7
Ipiros ○ BR 100-101 H 5
Ipita ○ BOL 70-71 F 6
Ipitinga, Rio ~ BR 62-63 H 3
Ipixuna, Igarapé ~ BR 66-67 D 5
Ipixuna, Rio ~ BR 66-67 F 6
Ipixun ○ BR 62-63 J 6
Ipixuna ○ BR 66-67 B 6
Ipixuna, Área Indigena ⌖ BR 66-67 F 4
Ipixuna, Igarapé ~ BR 68-69 B 4
Ipixuna, Rio ~ BR 66-67 F 6
Ipixuna, Rio ~ BR 66-67 F 6
Ipixuna ou Paraná Pixuna, Rio ~ BR 66-67 F 6
i pobutu • UA 102-103 G 2
Ipoh ☆ MAL 162-163 D 2
Iporá ○ BR 72-73 G 4
Iporanga ○ BR 74-75 F 5
Ipota ○ VAN 184 II b 4

Ippy ○ RCA 206-207 E 5
Ipsári ▲ GR 100-101 K 4
Ipswich ○ AUS 178-179 M 4
Ipswich ○ GB 90-91 H 5
Ipswich ○ USA (MA) 278-279 L 6
Ipswich ○ USA (SD) 260-261 G 1
Ipu ○ BR 68-69 H 4
Ipumirim ○ BR 74-75 D 6
Ipun, Isla ⌢ RCH 80 C 2
Iqe ○ VRC 146-147 M 6
Iqlit ○ ET 194-195 F 6
Iquipi ○ PE 64-65 F 9
Iquique ☆ RCH 70-71 B 7
Iquitos ☆ • PE 64-65 F 7
Ira ○ USA (TX) 264-265 D 5
Irá, Igarapé ~ BR 66-67 C 3
Iraan ○ USA (TX) 266-267 E 3
Ira Banda ○ RCA 206-207 F 6
Iracaja, Cachoeira do ~ BR 70-71 E 2
Iracoubo ○ F 62-63 H 3
Iraé ○ BR 68-69 X 4
Iraí de Minas ○ BR 72-73 G 5
Iraília ○ WSA 196-197 C 2
Irai Island ⌢ PNG 183 F 6
Irajuba ○ BR 72-73 K 2
Iraka ○ WAN 204-205 H 3
Irakan, Bol'šoj ~ RUS 120-121 C 6
Iráklio ☆ GR 100-101 K 7
Iramaia ○ BR 72-73 K 2
Iran = Irân ■ IR 134-135 D 2
Iranduba ○ BR 66-67 G 4
Irânšahr ○ IR 134-135 J 5
Irapuato ○ MEX 52-53 D 1
Iraq = 'Irâq ■ IRQ 128-129 J 6
Iraquara ○ BR 72-73 K 2
Irará ○ BR 72-73 L 2
Irarraren ⊥ DZ 190-191 E 7
Irasville ○ USA (VT) 278-279 J 4
Irati ○ BR 74-75 E 5
Irau, Gunung ▲ RI 166-167 G 2
Iraucuba ○ BR 68-69 J 3
Irawan, Wâdi < LAR 192-193 D 4
Irbejskoe ~ RUS 116-117 G 8
Irbeni vâin ≈ 94-95 G 3
Irbes Šaurums ≈ 94-95 G 3
Irbid ○ JOR 130-131 D 1
Irbit ~ RUS 114-115 G 6
Irebue ○ ZRE 210-211 F 4
Irecê ○ BR 68-69 H 7
Iredell ○ USA (TX) 264-265 G 6
Ireland = Éire ■ IRL 90-91 B 5
Ireland = Éire ⌢ IRL 90-91 C 4
Irendyk hrebet ▲ RUS 96-97 L 7
Irène ○ F 62-63 H 3
Irene ○ RA 78-79 J 5
Irene ○ USA (SD) 260-261 J 3
Iretama ○ BR 74-75 D 5
Iretskij, mys ▲ RUS 120-121 Q 4
Iretskij liman < RUS 120-121 Q 3
Ireupouw ○ VAN 184 II b 4
Irgakly ○ RUS 126-127 F 5
Irgičan ~ RUS 110-111 W 5
Irgičanskij hrebet ▲ RUS 110-111 V 5
Irharhar, Oued ~ DZ 190-191 E 8
Irharhar, Oued ~ DZ 198-199 C 2
Irherm ○ MA 188-189 G 5
Irhil M'Goun ▲ MA 188-189 H 5
Iri ○ ROK 150-151 F 10
Iriaki ○ RI 166-167 H 3
Irian Jaya ⌢ RI 166-167 H 4
Iriba ○ TCH 198-199 L 5
Irié ○ RG 202-203 F 5
Iriji ○ RIM 196-197 D 5
Iriki ○ MA 188-189 H 6
Iriklinskoe vodohranilišče < RUS 96-97 L 8
Irimi ○ RI 166-167 G 2
Iringa ○ EAT 214-215 H 4
Iringa ☆ EAT (IRI) 214-215 H 4
Iriona ○ HN 54-55 C 7
Iriri, Rio ~ BR 68-69 B 4
Iririmirim, Baía ≈ 68-69 F 2
Iriri Nôvo, Rio ~ BR 68-69 B 6
Irish Sea ≈ 90-91 E 5
Iritka ~ RUS 116-117 M 4
Irituia ○ BR 68-69 E 2
Irkeštam ○ KS 136-137 N 5
Irkineeva ~ RUS 116-117 H 6
Irkineevo ○ RUS 116-117 H 6
Irkut ~ RUS 116-117 L 10
Irkutsk ☆ • RUS 116-117 M 9
Irkutsko-Čeremhovskaja ravnina ⌣ RUS 116-117 K 8
Irlir, togi ▲ UZ 136-137 H 5
Irma ○ USA (ALB) 232-233 G 3
Irminger Basin ≃ 6-7 E 3
Irminger Sea ≈ 6-7 F 2
Irmo ○ USA (SC) 284-285 J 2
Imogou ~ CI 202-203 J 5
Iro, Lac ○ TCH 206-207 D 3
Irobo ○ CI 202-203 H 7
Iroise ≈ 90-91 E 7
Ironasiteri ○ YV 66-67 G 2
Iron Bridge ○ CDN (ONT) 238-239 B 2
Ironbridge • • • GB 90-91 F 5
Iron Creek ○ CDN 232-233 G 3
Iron Creek ○ USA 20-21 H 4
Irondequoit ○ USA (NY) 278-279 D 5
Irondro ○ EAT 214-215 J 4
Irondro ○ RM 222-223 E 8
Iron Knob ○ AUS 180-181 D 2
Iron Mountain ○ USA (MI) 270-271 K 5
Iron Mountain ○ USA (WY) 252-253 N 5
Iron Mountains ▲ USA 282-283 C 4
Iron Range National Park ⊥ AUS 174-175 G 3
Iron River ○ USA (MI) 270-271 K 4
Iron River ○ USA (WI) 270-271 H 4
Ironside ○ USA (OR) 244-245 H 4
Ironton ○ USA (MO) 276-277 D 3
Ironton ○ USA (OH) 280-281 D 5
Ironwood ○ USA (MI) 270-271 G 3
Iroquois ○ CDN (ONT) 238-239 K 4
Iroquois ○ USA (SD) 260-261 J 2

Iroquois Falls ○ CDN (ONT) 236-237 H 4
Iroquois River ~ USA 30-31 L 2
Irô-saki ▲ J 152-153 H 7
'Irqa, al- ○ Y 132-133 E 7
Irrawaddy ~ MYA 142-143 J 6
'Irsâl ○ RL 128-129 G 5
Irsina ○ I 100-101 F 4
Irtjaš, ozero ○ RUS 96-97 M 6
Irtyš ~ RUS 114-115 K 4
Irtyš = Ertis ~ KZ 124-125 K 2
Irtyšsk ○ KZ 124-125 J 2
Irumu ○ ZRE 212-213 B 3
Irún ○ E 98-99 G 3
Irupana ○ BOL 70-71 D 5
Irurzun ○ E 98-99 G 3
Iruya, Rio ~ RA 76-77 E 2
Irva ~ RUS 88-89 N 3
Irvine ○ CDN (ALB) 232-233 H 6
Irvine ○ USA (CA) 248-249 G 6
Irvine ○ USA (KY) 276-277 M 3
Irvine Inlet ≈ 36-37 Q 2
Irvines Landing ○ CDN (BC) 230-231 F 4
Irving ○ USA (TX) 264-265 G 6
Irving ○ USA (KY) 276-277 J 3
Irvington ○ USA (AL) 274-275 C 5
Irwin ○ USA (TX) 274-275 C 5
Irwin Military Reservation, Fort • USA (CA) 248-249 H 4
Irwin River ~ AUS 176-177 C 4
Irwinton ○ USA (GA) 284-285 G 4
Iryguareindé ○ BOL 70-71 F 1
'Iš, al- ○ KSA 130-131 F 5
Is, Ğabal ▲ ET 194-195 G 6
Isa ~ RUS 122-123 D 3
Isa ○ WAN 198-199 G 6
'Isâ, 'Ain ○ SYR 128-129 H 4
Isaac River ~ AUS 176-177 K 6
Isaac Jililbe ~ SP 212-213 H 3
Isabal, Lago ○ USA (SD) 260-261 E 1
Isabel, Bahía ≈ 64-65 B 10
Isabela ○ RP 160-161 D 9
Isabela ○ RP (286-287 O 2
Isabela, Cabo ▲ DOM 54-55 K 5
Isabela, Canal ≈ 64-65 B 10
Isabela, Isla ⌢ EC 64-65 B 10
Isabela, La ○ C 54-55 K 3
Isabela, La ○ DOM 54-55 K 5
Isabela, Ruinas de la ∴ DOM 54-55 K 5
Isabela de Sagua ○ C 54-55 G 3
Isabela II ○ USA (PR) 286-287 O 2
Isabella ○ CDN (MAN) 234-235 C 4
Isabella ○ USA (MN) 270-271 G 3
Isabella, Bahía de la ≈ 54-55 K 5
Isabella ○ USA (PR) 286-287 O 2
Isabella, Cordillera ▲ NIC 52-53 M 7
Isabella Indian Reservation ⌖ USA (MI) 272-273 E 4
Isabella Reservoir ~ USA (CA) 248-249 F 4
Isabelle Range ▲ AUS 172-173 E 6
Isabel Pass ▲ USA 20-21 S 5
Isabel Rubio ○ C 54-55 C 3
Isabis ○ NAM 220-221 C 1
Isaccea ○ RO 102-103 F 5
Isačenko, ostrov ⌢ RUS 108-109 Y 3
Isachsen ○ CDN 24-25 U 1
Isachsen, Cape ▲ CDN 24-25 T 1
Isachsen Peninsula ⌢ CDN 24-25 T 1
Isafjördur ○ IS 86-87 b 1
Isahaya ○ J 152-153 D 5
Isaka ○ ZRE 210-211 D 5
Isa Khel ○ PK 138-139 C 3
Isakly ○ RUS 96-97 G 6
Isalo ▲ RM 222-223 D 7
Isalo, Parc National de l' ⊥ RM 222-223 D 9
Isambe ○ ZRE 210-211 L 4
Isandja ○ ZRE (EQU) 210-211 H 4
Isandja ○ ZRE (KOC) 210-211 H 5
Isanga ○ ZRE 210-211 J 4
Isangano National Park ⊥ Z 214-215 F 6
Isangi ○ ZRE 210-211 K 3
Isango ○ ZRE 212-213 B 4
Isanlu ○ WAN 204-205 G 5
Isanlu-Esa ○ WAN 204-205 F 4
Išan Šalib ○ IRQ 128-129 L 7
Isar ~ D 92-93 M 4
Isas ○ CDN (ONT) 236-237 H 4
'Išâš, al- ○ KSA 130-131 F 5
Isasa ○ ZRE 212-213 B 5
'Isâwiya, al- ○ KSA 130-131 F 2
Isbil, Ğabal ▲ Y 132-133 D 6
Isbjorn Strait ≈ 26-27 O 1
Iscayachi ○ BOL 76-77 E 1
Ischersiar ○ TR 128-129 D 3
Ischia ○ I 100-101 C 1
Íschia ⌢ I 100-101 E 7
Íschia, Ísola d' ⌢ I 100-101 D 4
Ischiguilasto, Parque Natural Provincial ⊥ ~ RA 76-77 C 3
Iscuande, Rio ~ CO 60-61 C 6
Isdell River ~ AUS 172-173 G 4
Ise ○ J 152-153 G 7
Iševka ~ RUS 96-97 F 6
Iseke ○ EAT 214-215 H 4
Iseo, Lago d' ○ I 100-101 D 2
Isérnia ○ I 100-101 E 4
Ise-shima National Park ⊥ J 152-153 G 7
Isert ~ RUS 114-115 M 5
Isetskoe ☆ RUS 114-115 H 6
Ise-wan ≈ 152-153 G 7
Iseyin ○ WAN 204-205 E 5
Isfahan ○ IR 136-137 M 4
Isfjorden ○ N 84-85 D 3
Isfjord Radio ○ N 84-85 H 1
Isfjordrenna ≈ 26-27 N 2
Isha ○ PK 138-139 C 3
Ishak Paşa Sarayı ∴ TR 128-129 L 3

Isham ○ CDN (SAS) 232-233 K 4
Ishasha ○ EAU 212-213 B 4
Isherton ○ GUY 62-63 F 4
Ishiara ○ EAK 212-213 F 4
Ishikari ○ J 152-153 J 7
Ishikari-wan ≈ 152-153 J 3
Ishikawa ○ J 152-153 B 11
Ishinomaki ○ J 152-153 J 6
Ishioka ○ J 152-153 J 6
Ishpeming ○ USA (MI) 270-271 L 4
Ishurdi ○ BD 142-143 F 3
Isiboro Securé, Parque Nacional ⊥ BOL 70-71 D 5
Isikari-santi ~ J 152-153 K 3
Isilkul' ○ RUS 124-125 G 1
Išim ~ RUS 114-115 K 5
Išim, Ust'- ○ RUS 114-115 L 6
Isimala • EAT 214-215 H 4
Išimbaj ○ RUS 96-97 K 7
Isimbira ○ EAT 214-215 G 4
Išimskaja ravnina ⌣ RUS 114-115 J 6
Isinga ○ RUS 118-119 X 8
Isiolo ○ EAK 212-213 F 3
Isiolo, Lagh ~ EAK 212-213 F 3
Isiovo, Rio ~ BOL 70-71 F 5
Isipingo ○ ZA 220-221 K 5
Isiro ○ ZRE 212-213 A 2
Isisford ○ AUS 178-179 H 3
Isit ○ RUS 118-119 M 5
Isjangulovo ~ RUS 96-97 K 7
Iska ~ RUS 114-115 H 6
Iskanawatu, Tanjung ▲ RI 166-167 D 5
Iskâr ~ BG 102-103 C 6
Iskaten', hrebet ▲ RUS 112-113 V 3
Iskenderun ○ TR 128-129 G 4
Iskenderun Körfezi ≈ 128-129 F 4
Iskilip ○ TR 128-129 E 2
Iskitim ○ RUS 124-125 N 1
Iskushuban ○ SP 208-209 K 3
Iskut River ~ CDN 32-33 E 3
Iskut ~ CDN 32-33 E 3
Isla ~ RUS 92-93 X 3
Isla, Salar de la ~ RCH 76-77 C 3
Isla Angel de la Guarda, Parque Natural ⊥ MEX (BCN) 50-51 D 3
Isla de Aguada ○ MEX 52-53 J 2
Isla de Salamanca, Parque Nacional ⊥ ~ CO 60-61 D 2
Isla Guamblín, Parque Nacional ⊥ RCH 80 C 2
Islahiye ○ TR 128-129 G 4
Islamabad • ★ PK 138-139 D 3
Isla Magdalena, Parque Nacional ⊥ RCH 80 C 2
Islâmgarh ○ PK 138-139 C 6
Isla Mona ~ USA (PR) 286-287 O 2
Islamorada ○ USA (FL) 286-287 J 7
Islâmpur ○ IND 142-143 F 3
Islâmpur ○ IND 142-143 F 2
Island ~ N 86-89 A 3
Island Bay ≈ 160-161 C 8
Island City ○ USA (OR) 244-245 G 5
Island Falls ○ CDN (ONT) 236-237 G 3
Island Falls ○ USA (ME) 278-279 O 2
Island Lagoon ○ AUS 180-181 D 1
Island Lake ○ CDN (ONT) 236-237 F 3
Island Lake ○ CDN 34-35 K 4
Island Lake ○ USA (MN) 270-271 F 3
Island Park Reservoir ~ USA 252-253 J 2
Island Pond ○ CDN (NFL) 242-243 H 4
Island Pond ○ USA (VT) 278-279 K 4
Island River ~ CDN 30-31 J 5
Islands, Bay of ≈ 36-37 U 7
Islands, Bay of ≈ 182 E 1
Islands, Bay of ≈ 242-243 K 3
Isla Riesco, Reserva Florestal ⊥ RCH 80 C 6
Islas Columbretes ~ E 98-99 H 5
Isla Umbú ○ PY 76-77 H 4
Islay ○ CDN (ALB) 232-233 H 2
Islay ⌢ GB 90-91 D 4
Islay ○ PE 70-71 A 5
Islaz ○ RO 102-103 D 6
Isle aux Morts ○ CDN (NFL) 242-243 K 5
Isle Historic Site, Fort de L' • CDN (ALB) 232-233 G 2
Isle of Man ◆ GBM 90-91 E 4
Isle of Wight ⌢ GB 90-91 F 6
Isle Pierre ○ CDN (BC) 228-229 F 3
Isle Royale National Park ⊥ USA (MI) 270-271 K 2
Isles of Scilly ⌢ • GB 90-91 D 7
Isleta ○ CO 60-61 H 6
Isleta ○ USA (NM) 256-257 J 4
Isleta Indian Reservation ⌖ USA (NM) 256-257 J 4
Isle Woodah ⌢ AUS 174-175 D 3
Islington ○ CDN (NFL) 242-243 P 5
Isluga, Parque Nacional ⊥ RCH 70-71 C 7
Isly, Oued ~ MA 188-189 K 3
Ismael Cortinas ○ ROU 78-79 J 2
Ismâ'iliya, al- ○ ET 194-195 F 2
Ismailly = Ismayıllı ○ AZ 128-129 N 2
Ismaning ○ D 92-93 L 4
Isná ~ ET 194-195 F 5
Isoanala ○ RM 222-223 D 9
Isoka ○ Z 214-215 G 6
Isola ○ USA (MS) 268-269 K 3
Isom ○ USA (KY) 276-277 M 3
Isonga ○ PNG 183 F 3
Isopa ○ EAT 214-215 G 5
Isorana ○ RM 222-223 E 8
Isororo ○ GUY 62-63 E 1
Isortoq ○ GRØ 28-29 P 4
Isortoq ○ GRØ (ØGR) 28-29 O 3
Isortoq ○ GRØ (VGR) 28-29 O 3
Iso-Vietonen ○ FIN 88-89 H 3
Isparta ○ TR 128-129 C 3
Isperih ○ BG 102-103 E 6
Íspica ○ I 100-101 E 6
Ispir ○ TR 128-129 J 2
Isquiliac, Isla ⌢ RCH 80 C 2
Israel = Yisrâ'el ■ IL 130-131 D 2

Isra ≈ 176-177 G 6
Israelite Bay ○ AUS (WA) 176-177 G 5
Isra-tu ○ ER 200-201 J 4
Issa ~ RUS 96-97 D 7
Issabba, Dan- ○ WAN 198-199 C 6
Issano ○ GUY 62-63 E 3
Issangele ○ CAM 204-205 H 6
Issaouane, Erg ⌣ DZ 190-191 F 7
Issasquah ○ USA (MA) 244-245 C 2
Isseke ○ EAT 214-215 H 4
Issia ○ CI 202-203 G 6
Issimu ○ RI 164-165 H 3
Issoire ○ F 90-91 J 9
Issono ○ SUD 207-213 D 2
Issoudun ○ F 90-91 H 8
Issoulane Erarenine ⊥ DZ 190-191 D 7
Istanbul ☆ • TR 128-129 C 2
Istanbul Boğazı ≈ 128-129 C 2
Istgah-e Nāin ○ IR 134-135 E 2
Isthmus of Kra ⌣ THA 158-159 E 5
Istiéa ○ GR 100-101 J 5
Istisu ~ AZ 128-129 M 3
Istmina ○ CO 60-61 C 5
Istmo de Ofqui ⌣ RCH 80 C 3
Istmo Malagua ~ CO 60-61 C 5
Istokpoga, Lake ○ USA (FL) 286-287 H 4
Istra ☆ • RUS 94-95 P 4
Istra ≈ SLO 100-101 D 1
Istunmäki ○ FIN 88-89 J 5
Isumrud Strait ≈ 183 C 3
Isuna ○ EAT 212-213 D 6
Iswepe ○ ZA 220-221 K 3
Itabaiana ○ BR (PA) 68-69 L 5
Itabaiana ○ BR (SER) 68-69 K 7
Itabaianinha ○ BR 68-69 K 7
Itabaliza ○ BR 68-69 F 5
Itabapoana ○ BR 72-73 K 6
Itabapoana, Rio ~ BR 72-73 K 6
Itaberá ○ BR 72-73 F 7
Itaberaba ○ BR 72-73 K 2
Itaberaí ○ BR 72-73 H 4
Itabira ○ BR 72-73 J 5
Itabirinha de Mantena ○ BR 72-73 K 5
Itaboca ○ BR 66-67 F 5
Itaboraí ○ BR 72-73 J 7
Itabuna ○ BR 72-73 L 3
Itacaiúna, Rio ~ BR 68-69 D 4
Itacaja ○ BR 68-69 E 5
Itacambira ○ BR 72-73 J 3
Itacaré ○ BR 72-73 L 3
Itacaruaré ○ RA 76-77 K 3
Itaetê ○ BR 72-73 K 2
Itaguaí ○ BR 72-73 J 7
Itaguajé ○ BR 72-73 E 7
Itaguara, Rio ~ BR 72-73 H 6
Itaguari, Rio ~ BR 72-73 H 3
Itagüí ○ CO 60-61 D 4
Itah Gale ○ AUS 180-181 H 3
Itaí ○ BR 72-73 F 7
Itaim, Rio ~ BR 68-69 H 5
Itainópolis ○ BR 68-69 H 5
Itainzinho, Rio ~ BR 68-69 H 5
Itaiópolis ○ BR 74-75 F 6
Itaipu, Represa de < BR 76-77 K 3
Itaipu ○ BR 70-71 K 5
Itaituba ○ BR (AMA) 66-67 F 5
Itaituba ○ BR (PA) 66-67 K 5
Itajaí ○ BR 70-71 K 5
Itajaí ○ BR 74-75 F 6
Itaji ○ BR 72-73 K 3
Itajubá ○ BR 72-73 H 7
Itajubaquara ○ BR 68-69 G 7
Itaju do Colônia ○ BR 72-73 L 3
Itaju da Colônia ○ BR 72-73 L 3
Itakhoia ○ BD 142-143 G 3
Itala Nature Reserve ⊥ ZA 220-221 K 3
Italy = Italia ■ I 100-101 C 4
Italy = Italia ■ I 100-101 C 4
Itamaraju ○ BR 72-73 L 4
Itamarandiba ○ BR 72-73 J 4
Itamarati ○ BR 66-67 C 6
Itamarati de Minas ○ BR 72-73 J 6
Itambacuri ○ BR 72-73 K 5
Itambé ○ BR 72-73 L 3
Itamirim ○ BR 72-73 J 3
Itampolo ○ RM 222-223 D 10
Itanagar ☆ IND 142-143 H 2
Itanagra ○ BR 72-73 L 2
Itanhaém ○ BR 74-75 G 5
Itanhauã, Rio ~ BR 66-67 E 5
Itanhém ○ BR 72-73 K 4
Itanhém, Rio ~ BR 72-73 L 4
Itaobim ○ BR 72-73 K 4
Itaocara ○ BR 72-73 J 6
Itapaci ○ BR 72-73 H 3
Itapacurá, Rio ~ BR 66-67 G 5
Itapaiúna ○ BR 70-71 J 2
Itapajé ○ BR 68-69 J 3
Itaparaná, Rio ~ BR 66-67 F 5
Itaparica ○ BR 72-73 L 3
Itaparica, Ilha ~ BR 72-73 L 2
Itapebi ○ BR 72-73 L 3
Itapecerica ○ BR 72-73 H 6
Itapecuru, Rio ~ BR 68-69 G 3
Itapecurumirim ○ BR 68-69 G 3
Itapejara d'Oeste ○ BR 74-75 D 5
Itapemirim, Rio ~ BR 72-73 K 6
Itapera ○ BR 68-69 G 3
Itaperuna, Lagoa ≈ BR 74-75 F 7
Itaperuna ○ BR 72-73 K 6
Itapetinga ○ BR 72-73 K 3
Itapetininga ~ BR 72-73 F 7
Itapeva ○ BR 72-73 F 7
Itapevi ○ BR 72-73 G 7

Itapicuru, Rio ~ BR 68-69 G 4
Itapicuru, Rio ~ BR 68-69 J 7
Itapicuru-Açu, Rio ~ BR 68-69 H 7
Itapicuru-Mirim, Rio ~ BR 68-69 H 7
Itapipoca ○ BR 68-69 J 3
Itapira ○ BR 72-73 G 7
Itapiranga ○ BR (AMA) 66-67 H 4
Itapiranga ○ BR (CAT) 74-75 D 6
Itapirapuã ○ BR 72-73 G 4
Itapirapuã, Pico ▲ BR 74-75 F 5
Itapiúna ○ BR 68-69 J 2
Itápolis ○ BR 72-73 F 7
Itapora ○ BR 76-77 K 2
Itaporanga ○ BR (PA) 68-69 J 5
Itaporanga ○ BR (PAU) 72-73 F 7
Itapuã do Oeste ○ BR 66-67 F 2
Itapuranga ○ BR 72-73 H 3
Itaquai, Rio ~ BR 66-67 B 5
Itaquaquecetuba ○ BR 72-73 G 7
Itaqui ○ BR 76-77 J 5
Itaquyry ○ PY 76-77 K 3
Itarana ○ BR 72-73 K 5
Itarana, Ilha ~ BR 68-69 F 2
Itararé ○ BR 74-75 F 6
Itararé, Rio ~ BR 74-75 E 6
Itarema ○ BR 68-69 J 3
Itârsi ○ IND 138-139 F 5
Itasca ○ USA (TX) 264-265 G 6
Itasca State Park ⊥ USA (MN) 270-271 C 3
Itasy ○ RM 222-223 E 7
Itata ○ RCH 78-79 C 4
Itati ○ RA 76-77 H 4
Itatiaia, Parque Nacional do ⊥ BR 72-73 H 7
Itatiba ○ BR 72-73 G 7
Itatinga ○ BR 72-73 F 7
Itatingui ○ BR 72-73 L 3
Itatira ○ BR 68-69 J 4
Itatupã ○ BR 62-63 J 6
Itaú ○ BR 68-69 K 4
Itaú, Rio ~ BOL 70-71 F 2
Itauba ○ BR 70-71 K 2
Itaúçu ○ BR 72-73 F 4
Itaueira ○ BR 68-69 G 5
Itaueira, Rio ~ BR 68-69 G 5
Itaum ○ BR 76-77 K 2
Itauna ○ BR 68-69 F 3
Itaúnas ○ BR 72-73 L 5
Itbayat ~ RP 160-161 D 2
Itbu Point ~ RP 160-161 D 6
Itche Lake ○ CDN 30-31 N 3
Ite ○ PE 70-71 B 5
Itéa ○ GR 100-101 J 5
Itemgen, köli ~ KZ 124-125 Q 2
Iten ○ EAK 212-213 E 3
Itenectito, Rio de USA 20-21 P 2
Itenes o Guaporé, Río ~ BOL 70-71 F 3
Iterh, Oued ~ DZ 196-197 M 4
Itete ○ EAT 214-215 J 5
Itezhi-Tezhi Dam < Z 218-219 D 2
Ithaca ○ USA (MI) 272-273 E 4
Ithaca ○ USA (NY) 278-279 E 6
Ithaca ○ USA (OH) 280-281 B 4
Itháki ⌢ GR 100-101 H 5
Itigi ○ EAT 212-213 E 6
Itiki ○ IND 140-141 G 3
Itilleq ○ GRØ 28-29 O 3
Itimbiri ~ ZRE 210-211 J 2
Itinga, Rio ~ BR 68-69 E 4
Itipo ○ ZRE 210-211 G 4
Itiquira ○ BR 70-71 K 5
Itiquira ou Piquiri ~ BR 70-71 J 5
Itirapuão ○ BR 72-73 G 7
Itirr Plain ~ EAK 212-213 G 2
Itiúba ○ BR 68-69 J 7
Itkillik River ~ USA 20-21 P 2
Itó ○ J 152-153 H 7
Ito, Paysage d' • MA 188-189 J 4
Itobe ○ WAN 204-205 G 5
Itobo ○ EAT 212-213 D 6
Itoculo ○ MOC 218-219 L 2
Itoigawa ○ J 152-153 G 6
Itoko ○ ZRE 210-211 H 4
Itomampy ~ RM 222-223 E 9
Itonamas, Rio ~ BOL 70-71 E 3
Itoquois River ~ USA 274-275 L 4
Itquiy ○ WSA 188-189 E 7
Ittaajimmiit = Kap Hope ○ GRØ 26-27 O 8
Ittel, Oued ~ DZ 190-191 E 3
Ittoqqortoormiit = Scoresbysund ○ GRØ 26-27 p 8
Itu ○ BR 72-73 G 7
Itu ○ WAN 204-205 G 6
Ituaçu ○ BR 72-73 K 2
Ituango ○ CO 60-61 D 4
Ituberá ○ BR 72-73 L 2
Itui, Rio ~ BR 66-67 B 5
Ituiutaba ○ BR 72-73 F 5
Itula ○ ZRE 212-213 A 5
Ituma ○ EAT (MBE) 214-215 G 5
Ituma ○ EAT (SIN) 214-215 G 4
Itumbiara ○ BR 72-73 G 5
Ituna ○ CDN (SAS) 232-233 P 4
Itungi ○ EAT 214-215 G 5
Ituporanga ○ BR 74-75 F 6
Iturama ○ BR 72-73 F 5
Ituri ~ ZRE 212-213 A 3
Iturup, ostrov ~ RUS 122-123 H 6
Ituruna ○ BR 72-73 H 6
Ituverava ○ BR 72-73 G 6
Ituxi, Rio ~ BR 66-67 E 6
Ituzaingo ○ RA 76-77 J 4
Itwangi ○ EAT 212-213 D 5
Itzmanna ∴ MEX 52-53 K 1
Iztapa ○ GCA 52-53 K 3
Iuka ○ USA (MS) 262-263 H 7
Iultin ○ RUS 112-113 V 3
Iululú ○ MOC 218-219 K 2

Iva ○ USA (SC) 284-285 H 2
Ivacevičy ○ BY 94-95 J 5
Ival ○ BR 74-75 E 5
Ival, Rio ~ BR 74-75 D 4
Ivaiporã ○ BR 74-75 E 5
Ivakoany ▲ RM 222-223 E 9
Ivalo ○ FIN 88-89 J 2
Ivalojoki ~ FIN 88-89 J 2
Ivanava ○ BY 94-95 H 5
Ivančice ○ CZ 92-93 N 4
Ivangorod ○ RUS 94-95 L 2
Ivangrad ○ YU 100-101 G 3
Ivanhoe ○ AUS 180-181 H 4
Ivanhoe ○ USA (MN) 270-271 B 6
Ivanhoe River ~ CDN 236-237 G 4
Ivanivka ○ UA 102-103 J 3
Ivankiv ○ UA 102-103 C 3
Ivano-Frankivs'k ☆ UA 102-103 B 3
Ivano-Frankivsk = Ivano-Frankivs'k ☆ UA 102-103 B 3
Ivanovka ○ RUS (AMR) 122-123 B 3
Ivanovka ○ RUS (CTN) 118-119 J 10
Ivanovka ○ RUS (ORB) 96-97 H 7
Ivanovka ~ RUS 122-123 C 3
Ivanovo ○ • • BG 102-103 D 6
Ivanovo ○ RUS (PSK) 94-95 M 3
Ivanovo ○ RUS (IVN) 94-95 S 3
Ivanovsk, Katav- ○ RUS 96-97 L 6
Ivanteevka ~ RUS 96-97 F 7
Ivaška ○ RUS 120-121 U 4
Ivato ○ RM 222-223 E 8
Ivdel' ○ RUS 114-115 F 4
Iveetok Camp ○ USA 20-21 E 5
Ivindo ~ G 210-211 D 3
Ivinheima ○ BR 72-73 E 6
Ivinheima, Rio ~ BR 76-77 K 1
Ivisaartoq ≃ GRØ 28-29 P 4
Ivisan ○ RP 160-161 E 7
Ivisaruk River ~ USA 20-21 H 2
Ivittuut ○ GRØ 28-29 Q 6
Ivnarganek ○ GRØ 26-27 R 6
Ivohibe ○ RM 222-223 E 9
Ivnarssuit ○ GRØ 26-27 W 7
Ivolginsk ○ RUS 116-117 N 10
Ivon, Rio ~ BOL 70-71 D 2
Ivondro ~ RM 222-223 F 6
Ivongo, Soanierana- ○ RM 222-223 F 6
Ivori River ~ PNG 183 C 4
Ivorogbo ○ WAN 204-205 G 6
Ivory Coast = CI 202-203 G 7
Ivrea ○ I 100-101 A 2
Ivrindi ☆ TR 128-129 B 3
Ivujivik ○ CDN 36-37 L 3
Ivuna ○ EAT 214-215 G 5
Iwa Island ⌢ PNG 183 F 4
Iwaizumi ○ J 152-153 K 5
Iwaki ○ J 152-153 J 6
Iwaki ~ J 152-153 J 4
Iwakuni ○ J 152-153 E 7
Iwala ○ ZRE 210-211 J 5
Iwamizawa ○ J 152-153 J 3
Iwanai ○ J 152-153 J 3
Iwanuma ○ J 152-153 J 6
Iwatebu ○ PNG 183 B 4
Iwate-san ▲ J 152-153 K 5
Iwe ○ ZRE 210-211 K 5
Iwo ○ WAN 204-205 F 5
Iwopin ○ WAN 204-205 F 5
Iwungu ○ ZRE 210-211 G 5
Iwupataka ○ AUS 178-179 B 2
Ixcún ∴ GCA 52-53 K 3
Ixiamas ○ BOL 70-71 C 3
Ixmiquilpan ○ MEX 52-53 E 1
Ixopo ○ ZA 220-221 K 5
Ixtapa ○ MEX (GRO) 52-53 D 3
Ixtapa ○ MEX (OAX) 52-53 F 3
Ixtapan de la Sal ○ MEX 52-53 E 2
Ixtlahuaca ○ MEX 52-53 F 2
Ixtlahuacan del Rio ○ MEX 52-53 C 1
Ixtlán ∴ MEX 52-53 B 1
Ixtlán de Juárez ○ MEX 52-53 F 3
Ixtlán del Rio ○ MEX 50-51 G 7
Ixu ○ BR 70-71 J 5
'Iyâl Bakhit ○ SUD 200-201 D 6
Iyapa ○ WAN 204-205 F 5
Iyayi ○ EAT 214-215 H 5
Iyo ○ J 152-153 E 7
Iyo-nada ○ J 152-153 D 7
Iž ~ RUS 96-97 H 5
Izabal, Lago de ○ GCA 52-53 K 4
Izadhvāst ○ IR 134-135 E 3
Izaguéne ○ RIM 196-197 C 6
Izamal ○ MEX 52-53 K 1
Izapa ∴ MEX 52-53 H 4
'Izbat al-Ğâğa ○ ET 194-195 E 3
Izberbaš ○ RUS 126-127 G 6
Izborsk ○ • RUS 94-95 K 3
Iže ○ IR 134-135 C 3
Izena-shima ⌢ J 152-153 B 11
Izhevsk = Iževsk ○ RUS 96-97 H 5
Iževsk = Iževsk ○ RUS 96-97 H 5
Ižma = Ižma ~ RUS 88-89 W 4
Izjum ○ UA 102-103 J 5
Izki ○ OM 132-133 K 2
Izfistan = Žizah ☆ UZ 136-137 K 4
Ižma ○ RUS 88-89 W 4
Ižma ~ RUS 88-89 W 4
Izmail ○ UA 102-103 F 5
Izmajil ☆ UA 102-103 F 5
Izmir ☆ • TR 128-129 B 3
Izmorskij ☆ RUS 114-115 T 6
Iznik Gölü ○ TR 128-129 C 2
Iznik ○ TR 128-129 C 2
Izobil'noe ○ KZ 124-125 H 2
Izobil'nyj ○ RUS 102-103 M 5
Izozog ○ BOL 70-71 F 6
Izozog, Bañados de ○ BOL 70-71 F 6
Izra' ○ SYR 128-129 G 6
Izu-hanto ~ J 152-153 H 7
Izuhara ○ J 152-153 C 7
Izumi ○ J 152-153 E 7
Izumo ○ J 152-153 E 7
Izu-shotō ~ J 152-153 H 7
Izvestij CIK, ostrova ⌢ RUS 108-109 T 4
Izvestkovyj ○ RUS 122-123 D 4

Jaala o **FIN** 88-89 J 6
Jaba o **PK** 138-139 D 3
Jabal, Bahr al-(White Nile) ~ **SUD** 206-207 K 4
Jabal al Hawa'ish **LAR** 192-193 K 5
Jabali, Isla ~ **RA** 78-79 H 6
Jabalón, Río o **E** 98-99 F 5
Jabalpur o **IND** 138-139 G 8
Jabarona o **SUD** 200-201 C 4
Jabillo o **CR** 52-53 C 7
Jabiru o **AUS** 172-173 L 2
Jabiru Oil Field • **AUS** 172-173 G 1
Jabitaca o **BG** 102-103 D 6
Jablanica o **BIH** 100-101 F 3
Jablon o **RUS** 112-113 P 4
Jablonovyj o **RUS** 120-121 O 3
Jhhinnvwj hrebet **RUS** 118-119 D 10
Jabo o **RI** 168 E 3
Jabon o **RI** 168 E 3
Jaboncillos Creek ~ **USA** 266-267 J 6
Jabotá, Rio o **BR** 70-71 K 3
Jabung, Tanjung **RI** 162-163 F 6
Jaburu, Rio o **BR** 68-69 C 7
Jabuticabal o **BR** 72-73 J 5
Jabuticatubas o **BR** 72-73 J 5
Jaca o **E** 98-99 G 3
Jacaf, Canal o **RCH** 80 D 2
Jacaí o **SP** 208-209 H 6
Jacala o **MEX** 50-51 K 7
Jacana o **BR** 68-69 L 5
Jacaraí o **BR** 68-69 L 5
Jacaré o **BR** 66-67 C 6
Jacaré, Ilha **BR** 66-67 H 5
Jacaré, Rio o **BR** 66-67 H 4
Jacaré, Rio o **BR** 66-67 H 7
Jacaré, Rio o **BR** 72-73 H 6
Jacareacanga o **BR** 66-67 J 6
Jacaré Grande o **BR** 72-73 J 3
Jacaré Guaçu, Rio o **BR** 72-73 F 6
Jacareí o **BR** 72-73 H 7
Jacaré Pepira, Rio o **BR** 72-73 F 6
Jacaretinga o **BR** 68-69 J 3
Jacas Grande o **PE** 64-65 D 6
Jacaúna o **BR** 68-69 L 3
Jaceel, togga ~ **SP** 208-209 K 3
Jaceyl ~ **SP** 208-209 K 3
Jáchal, Río o **RA** 76-77 C 6
Jáchymov o **CZ** 92-93 M 3
Jaciara o **BR** 70-71 K 4
Jacinto o **BR** 72-73 K 4
Jacinto, San o **USA** (CA) 248-249 H 6
Jari Paraná, Rio o **BR** 66-67 E 7
Jaciparaná, Rio o **BR** 66-67 E 7
Jaottara o **BR** 66-67 F 7
Jack o **USA** (AL) 284-285 D 5
Jack Creek o **USA** (NV) 246-247 F 4
Jack Daniels Distillery • **USA** (TN) 276-277 J 5
Jackfish Creek ~ **CDN** 30-31 N 4
Jackfork Mountain **USA** 264-265 J 4
Jackhead Harbour o **CDN** (MAN) 234-235 F 3
Jack Lee, Lake o **USA** (AR) 276-277 G 7
Jackman o **USA** (ME) 278-279 H 4
Jackpint River ~ **CDN** 228-229 P 3
Jackpot o **USA** (NV) 246-247 J 2
Jacksboro o **USA** (TX) 264-265 F 5
Jacks Fork ~ **USA** 276-277 D 3
Jackson o **AUS** 178-179 K 4
Jackson o **CDN** (NS) 240-241 M 5
Jackson o **USA** (AL) 284-285 C 5
Jackson o **USA** (CA) 246-247 E 5
Jackson o **USA** (GA) 284-285 G 3
Jackson o **USA** (KY) 276-277 M 3
Jackson o **USA** (LA) 268-269 J 6
Jackson o **USA** (MI) 272-273 E 5
Jackson o **USA** (MN) 270-271 D 7
Jackson o **USA** (MO) 276-277 F 3
Jackson o **USA** (MT) 250-251 F 4
Jackson o **USA** (NC) 282-283 K 4
Jackson o **USA** (OH) 280-281 D 4
Jackson o **USA** (TN) 276-277 G 3
Jackson o **USA** (WY) 252-253 H 3
Jackson • • **USA** (MS) 268-269 K 4
Jackson, Fort xx **USA** (LA) 268-269 L 7
Jackson, Kap **GRØ** 26-27 R 3
Jackson, Lake o **USA** (FL) 286-287 E 1
Jackson, Mount **AUS** 176-177 E 6
Jackson, Port o **AUS** 180-181 L 2
Jackson Arm o **CDN** (NFL) 242-243 M 3
Jackson Bay o **CDN** (BC) 230-231 D 3
Jacksonboro o **USA** (SC) 284-285 K 4
Jackson Junction o **USA** (IA) 274-275 F 1
Jackson Lake o **USA** (OH) 280-281 D 5
Jackson Lake o **USA** (WY) 252-253 H 3
Jackson Lake o **USA** (GA) 284-285 G 3
Jackson Lake Lodge o **USA** (WY) 252-253 H 3
Jackson River ~ **USA** 280-281 G 6
Jacksonville o **C** 54-55 D 4
Jacksonville o **USA** (AL) 284-285 E 4
Jacksonville o **USA** (AR) 276-277 C 6
Jacksonville o **USA** (FL) 286-287 H 1
Jacksonville o **USA** (IL) 274-275 H 5
Jacksonville o **USA** (NC) 282-283 K 6
Jacksonville o **USA** (TX) 268-269 E 5
Jacksonville Beach o **USA** (FL) 286-287 H 1
Jacktown o **USA** (KY) 276-277 K 3
Jack Wade o **USA** 20-21 U 4
Jacmel ☆• **RH** 54-55 J 5
Jacó o **CR** 52-53 C 7
Jacobábád o **PK** 138-139 B 5
Jacob Lake o **USA** 22-23 H 5
Jacob Lake o **USA** (AZ) 256-257 C 4
Jacobsdal o **ZA** 220-221 G 4

Jacobson o **USA** (MN) 270-271 E 4
Jacobsville o **USA** (MI) 270-271 K 4
Jacona o **MEX** 52-53 C 2
Jacques, Lac o **CDN** 240-241 F 3
Jacques, Lac à o **CDN** 30-31 F 2
Jacques Cartier, Mont **CDN** (QUE) 240-241 K 2
Jacques Cartier, Parc de la **CDN** (QUE) 240-241 J 2
Jacques Cartier, Rivière ~ **CDN** 240-241 D 3
Jacqueville o • **CI** 202-203 H 7
Jacquinot Bay ≈ 183 F 3
Jacu o **BR** 68-69 F 6
Jacuba, Rio o **BR** (TAB) 70-71 J 8
Jacuí o **BR** 72-73 G 6
Jacuí, Rio o **BR** 74-75 D 7
Jacuípe o **BR** 72-73 L 2
Jacuipinho o **BR** 74-75 D 7
Jacumba o **USA** (CA) 248-249 H 7
Jacundá o **BR** 66-67 F 7
Jacundá, Rio o **BR** 66-67 F 6
Jacunici o **BR** 68-69 C 3
Jacup o **AUS** 176-177 E 6
Jacupiranga o **BR** 72-73 G 7
Jacurici, Açude < **BR** 68-69 J 7
Jacurici, Rio o **BR** 68-69 J 7
Jada o **WAN** 204-205 K 4
Jadajahodyjaha ~ **RUS** 108-109 O 8
Jaddi, Ras **PK** 134-135 K 6
Jadebusen ≈ 92-93 K 2
Jadid, Bi'r al o **LAR** 192-193 E 4
J. A. D. Jensens Nunatakker **GRØ** 28-29 Q 5
Jadkal o **IND** 140-141 H 4
Jadranska magistrala II **HR** 100-101 F 3
Jadransko more ≈ 100-101 D 2
Jädü o **LAR** 192-193 E 2
Jaén o **E** 98-99 F 6
Jaen o **PE** 64-65 C 4
Jafarābād o **IND** 138-139 F 9
Jáfarābād o **IND** 138-139 C 9
Jafärah o **TN** 190-191 H 4
Jaffa, Cape **AUS** 180-181 E 4
Jaffa, Cirque de **MA** 188-189 J 4
Jaffna o **CL** 140-141 J 6
Jagalür o **IND** 140-141 F 3
Jagbahun o **WAL** 202-203 D 5
Jagdaqi o **VRC** 150-151 F 2
Jagdalpur o **IND** 142-143 C 6
Jagfiburn o **IND** 142-143 R 2
Jagdyg ~ **RUS** 118-119 E 8
Jagefurra, gora **RUS** 88-89 P 3
Jagersfontein o **ZA** 220-221 G 4
Jaggayyapeta o **IND** 142-143 C 4
Joghbüb, Al o **LAR** 190-190 L 0
Jagodnoe o **RUS** 120-121 N 2
Jago Hiver ~ **USA** 20-21 T 2
Jagtial o **IND** 138-139 G 10
Jagua o **C** 54-55 E 3
Jaguapití o **BR** 72-73 E 7
Jaguaquara o **BR** 72-73 K 2
Jaguarão o **BR** 74-75 D 9
Jaguarão, Rio ~ **BR** 74-75 D 9
Jaguarari o **BR** 68-69 H 7
Jaguaralva o **BR** 74-75 D 5
Jaguaribe o **BR** 68-69 J 4
Jaguaribe, Rio ~ **BR** 68-69 J 5
Jaguaruana o **BR** 68-69 K 4
Jaguaruna o **BR** (SA-5-5) H 7
Jagüé, Rio ~ **RA** 76-77 C 5
Jagüey Grande o **C** 54-55 E 3
Jagvi o **IND** 140-141 F 3
Jagyja ~ **RUS** 114-115 N 5
Jah, Pyt'- o **RUS** 114-115 M 4
Jahadyjaha ~ **RUS** 108-109 O 5
Jahanabad o **IND** 142-143 D 3
Jahangiraba o **IND** 138-139 G 5
Jahleel, Point **AUS** 172-173 K 1
Jahuey Creek ~ **USA** 266-267 H 5
Jaicós o **BR** 68-69 H 6
Jailleu, Bourgoin- o **F** 90-91 K 9
Jailolo o **RI** 164-165 K 3
Jailolo, Selat ≈ 166-167 E 2
Jainagar o **IND** 142-143 B 4
Jaipur o **IND** 142-143 B 4
Jaipur ☆• **IND** 138-139 E 6
Jaisalmer o **IND** 138-139 C 6
Jaisinghnagar o **IND** 142-143 B 4
Jaj ~ **RUS** 122-123 H 4
Jaja ☆ **RUS** (KMR) 114-115 T 6
Jaja ~ **RUS** 114-115 T 6
Jájapur o **IND** 142-143 E 5
Jäjapur Road o **IND** 142-143 E 5
Jajarkot o **NEP** 144-145 B 4
Jajce o **BIH** 100-101 F 2
Jajpan o **UZ** 136-137 M 4
Jajva ~ **RUS** 114-115 O 5
Jákar o **BHT** 142-143 G 2
Jakarta ☆ • **RI** 168 B 3
Jakarta, Teluk ≈ 168 B 3
Jaken o **RI** 168 D 3
Jakes Corner o **USA** (AZ) 256-257 D 4
Jakhau o **IND** 138-139 A 8
Jäkkvik o **S** 86-87 H 3
Jako, Pulau ~ **RI** 166-167 D 6
Jakob Kjode Bjerg **GRØ** 26-27 m 6
Jakobshavn = Ilulissat o **GRØ** 28-29 P 2
Jakob's Ladder Great Falls ~ **GUY** 62-63 G 4
Jakobstad o **FIN** 88-89 G 5
Jakójä o **S** 86-87 G 8
Jam Jodhpur o **IND** 138-139 C 9
Jakhandi o **IND** 140-141 F 2
Jakovleva ~ **RUS** 108-109 U 6
Jakpa o **WAN** 204-205 F 6

Jakšino o **RUS** 88-89 W 3
Jaktali ~ **RUS** 116-117 H 2
Jaktali, plato **RUS** 116-117 H 2
Jakutsk = Respublika = Respublika Saha **RUS** 110-111 M 4
Jakutsk ☆ **RUS** 118-119 O 4
Jal o **USA** (NM) 256-257 M 6
Jalaid Qi o **VRC** 150-151 G 2
Jalal-Abad o **KS** 136-137 N 4
Jalälpur o **PK** 138-139 D 3
Jalälpur Pirwäla o **PK** 138-139 C 5
Ja'tän o **OM** 132-133 L 2
Jalán, Rio o **HN** 52-53 L 4
Jalang o **RI** 164-165 G 6
Jalapa ☆ **GCA** 52-53 K 4
Jalapa o **MEX** (TAB) 52-53 H 3
Jalapa ☆ • **MEX** (VER) 52-53 F 2
Jalapa de Díaz o **MEX** 52-53 F 2
Jalapa Enríquez = Jalapa ☆ • **MEX** 52-53 F 2
Jalasjärvi o **FIN** 88-89 G 5
Jalaté, Rio ~ **MEX** 52-53 J 3
Jalaud ~ **RP** 160-161 E 7
Jales o **BR** 72-73 E 7
Jaleswar o **IND** 142-143 E 5
Jalgaon o **IND** (MAH) 138-139 E 10
Jälgaon o • **IND** (MAH) 138-139 E 9
Jalingo o **WAN** 204-205 J 4
Jalisco o **MEX** 52-53 B 2
Jälna o **IND** 138-139 E 10
Jälor o **IND** 138-139 D 7
Jalostotitlan o **MEX** 50-51 H 7
Jalpa o **MEX** 50-51 H 7
Jalpa de Méndez o **MEX** 52-53 H 3
Jalpaiguri o **IND** 142-143 F 2
Jalpan o **MEX** 50-51 K 7
Jalpuh, ozero o **UA** 102-103 F 5
Jalta ~ **UA** 102-103 J 5
Játipan de Morelos o **MEX** 52-53 G 3
Jalu o **LAR** 192-193 L 3
Jalu, Wähät al o **LAR** 192-193 J 3
Jalutorovsk o **RUS** 114-115 J 6
Jama o **EC** 64-65 B 2
Jama ~ **RUS** 120-121 P 4
Jamaame o **SP** 212-213 J 3
Jámai o **IND** 138-139 G 8
Jamaica o **JA** 54-55 G 6
Jamaica Channel ≈ 54-55 H 6
Jamal o **C** 54-55 H 4
Jamal, poluostrov ~ **RUS** 108-109 N 7
Jamalin', hrebet **RUS** 122-123 F 2
Jamalpur o **BD** 142-143 F 3
Jamaliwal o **PK** 138-139 B 4
Jamanxim, Rio ~ **BR** 66-67 K 6
Jamari o **WAN** 204-205 J 3
Jamari, Rio ~ **BR** 00-07 I 7
Jamarovka o **RUS** 118-119 E 10
Jämbö o **IND** 138-139 G 10
Jamba o **BR** (HUA) 216-217 D 7
Jamba ~ **ANG** 216-217 E 4
Jambeli, Canal de ≈ 64-65 B 3
Jambi o **RI** 162-163 E 5
Jambi ☆ **RI** (JAM) 102-103 E 5
Jamboeye o **RI** 162-163 B 2
Jambol o **BG** 102-103 G 6
Jambon, Pointe **CDN** (QUE) 240-241 J 2
Jambongan, Pulau ~ **MAL** 160-161 B 9
Jambuar, Tanjung **RI** 162-163 B 2
Jambu Bongkok, Kampung o **MAL** 162-163 F 3
Jambukan ~ **RUS** 116-117 J 3
Jambusar o **IND** 138-139 D 8
Jambuto, ozero o **RUS** (JAN) 108-109 Q 6
Jambuto, ozero o **RUS** (JAN) 108-109 N 7
James o **USA** (MS) 268-269 J 3
James, Isla ~ **RCH** 80 C 2
James, Lake < **USA** (NC) 282-283 F 5
Jamesaddak o **PK** 138-139 C 4
James A. Reed Memorial Wildlife Refuge **USA** (MO) 274-275 D 6
James Bay ≈ 34-35 Q 4
James Beach, Fort • **AG** 56 E 3
James Cook Monument • **AUS** 174-175 H 4
James Creek o **CDN** 30-31 N 4
James Dalton Highway II **USA** 20-21 P 3
James Island o **USA** (SC) 284-285 L 4
Jameson, Cape **CDN** 24-25 h 6
Jameson Land **GRØ** 26-27 o 8
James Ranges **AUS** 176-177 M 2
James River ~ **CDN** 30-31 D 4
James River ~ **CDN** 232-233 C 4
James River ~ **USA** 258-259 H 4
James River ~ **USA** 260-261 J 3
James River ~ **USA** 276-277 B 4
James Ross, Cape **CDN** 24-25 O 3
James Ross Island ~ 24-25 Y 6
James Ross Strait ≈ 24-25 V 6
James Smith Indian Reservation **CDN** (SAS) 232-233 O 2
Jamestown o **AUS** 180-181 E 2
Jamestown o **GB** 202-203 C 7
Jamestown o **USA** (MO) 274-275 F 6
Jamestown o **USA** (NY) 278-279 B 6
Jamestown o **USA** (SC) 284-285 L 3
Jamestown o **USA** (ND) 258-259 J 5
Jamestown o • **USA** (ND) 258-259 J 5
Jamestown o **USA** (TN) 282-283 D 4
Jamestown o **ZA** 220-221 H 5
Jamestown Reservoir < **USA** (ND) 258-259 J 4
Jamesville o **USA** (NC) 282-283 L 5
Jamieson o **AUS** 180-181 J 4
Jaminawá Arara, Área Indígena **BR** 64-65 F 6
Jämjö o **S** 86-87 G 8
Jamkhandi o **IND** 140-141 F 2
Jamkie, Verchnie o **RUS** 112-113 L 3
Jara ~ **RUS** 108-109 T 7

Jamliyah, al- o **IND** 134-135 D 6
Jamm o **RUS** 94-95 L 2
Jammalamadugu o **IND** 140-141 H 3
Jammerbugten ≈ 86-87 D 8
Jammersdirf o **ZA** 220-221 H 4
Jammu o **IND** 138-139 E 3
Jammu and Kashmir **IND** 138-139 E 2
Jamnagar o • **IND** 138-139 C 8
Jämner o **IND** 138-139 E 10
Jamozero o **RUS** 88-89 V 4
Jaránwäla o **PK** 138-139 D 4
Jampampgukulon o **RI** 168 B 3
Jampur o **PK** 138-139 C 5
Jämsä o **FIN** 88-89 J 6
Jamsävej ~ **RUS** 114-115 O 2
Jamshedpur o • **IND** 142-143 E 4
Jamsk o **RUS** 120-121 Q 4
Jamtari o **WAN** 204-205 J 5
Jämtland **S** 86-87 F 5
Jamu o **ETH** 208-209 B 5
Jamui o **IND** 142-143 E 3
Jamul o **USA** (CA) 248-249 H 7
Jamuna ~ **BD** 142-143 F 3
Jamundí o **CO** 60-61 C 6
Jamutarida ~ **RUS** 108-109 e 4
Jana o **BR** (MAG) 120-121 N 3
Jana ~ **RUS** 110-111 V 4
Jana ~ **RUS** 120-121 N 3
Janakpur o **NEP** 144-145 E 7
Janauacá, Lago o **BR** 66-67 G 4
Janaúba o **BR** 72-73 J 3
Janauçu, Ilha ~ **BR** 62-63 J 5
Janaul o **RUS** 96-97 J 5
Jand o **PK** 138-139 D 3
Jandaíra do Sul o **BR** 72-73 E 7
Jandaíra o **BR** 68-69 K 5
Jandía Playa o **E** 188-189 D 6
Jandiatuba, Rio ~ **BR** 66-67 C 5
Jandowae o **AUS** 178-179 L 4
Janeiro, 31 de o **BR** 68-69 F 7
Janeiro, Área Indígena 9 de **BR** 66-67 F 6
Janesville o **USA** (MN) 270-271 F 6
Janesville o **USA** (WI) 274-275 J 2
Janeville o **CDN** (NB) 240-241 M 4
Jang o **IND** 142-143 G 2
Jang, plato **RUS** 108-109 b 7
Jangada o **BR** 70-71 J 4
Janggi **VRC** 144-145 F 4
Jangiabad o **UZ** 136-137 M 4
Jangier o **UZ** 136-137 L 4
Jangijül' o **UZ** 136-137 L 4
JangkiSíkok o **UZ** 136-137 L 4
Jangkurgan o **UZ** 136-137 M 4
Jangil', hrebet **RUS** 116-117 M 4
Jangipur o **IND** 142-143 E 3
Jangirabad o **UZ** 136-137 J 4
Jonngai Shen **VRC** 144-145 F 4
Jangoda ~ **RUS** 108-109 Z 5
Jangoda ~ **RUS** 108-109 X 6
Jangozero, ozero ~ **RUS** 88-89 M 5
Janice o **USA** (MS) 268-269 L 5
Janiopolis o **BR** 72-73 E 7
Jánivevo o **RUS** 88-89 D 5
Janjuay o **RP** 160-161 E 7
Jankan, hrebet **RUS** 118-119 H 9
Jan Kempdorp o **ZA** 220-221 G 3
Jan Mayen Fracture Zone ≈ 6-7 J 1
Jannaye, Lac à o **CDN** 38-39 L 2
Janów Lubelski o **PL** 92-93 R 3
Janrakynnot o **RUS** 120-121 Y 4
Janranaj o **RUS** 112-113 Q 2
Jansen o **CDN** (SAS) 232-233 O 4
Janseville o **ZA** 220-221 G 6
Jansk, Ust'- o **RUS** 110-111 V 4
Janskie porugi ~ **RUS** 110-111 T 5
Janskij zaliv ≈ 110-111 U 4
Janskoe ploskogor'e **RUS** 110-111 T 6
Jantan o **RI** 166-167 H 3
Jantetelco o **MEX** 52-53 E 2
Janthoe o **RI** 162-163 A 2
Jantingue o **MOC** 220-221 L 2
Januária o **BR** 72-73 H 3
Janúario Cicco o **BR** 68-69 L 5
Janus Ø ~ **GRØ** 26-27 p 8
Janykurgan o **KZ** 136-137 K 3
Jaora o **IND** 138-139 E 7
Japan = Nippon **J** 152-153 J 6
Japan, Sea of (J) ≈ 152-153 J 6
Japan Basin ≈ 10-11 N 4
Japanese War Cemetery • **AUS** 180-181 K 4
Japanese World War II Bunker ∴• **RI** 166-167 K 7
Japan Trench ≈ 152-153 K 7
Japaratinga o **BR** 68-69 L 5
Japaratuba o **BR** 68-69 K 7
Japerica o **BR** 68-69 F 2
Japerica, Baía do ≈ 68-69 E 2
Japim o **BR** 64-65 F 5
Japom, mys **RUS** 120-121 Q 4
Japtikaale o **RUS** 108-109 O 7
Japurá, Área Indígena **BR** 70-71 H 2
Japurá, Rio o **BR** 66-67 E 4
Jaqué o **PA** 52-53 G 8
Jar o **RUS** (SVK) 114-115 H 6
Jar o **RUS** (UDM) 96-97 H 4
Jar, Krasnyj o **RUS** 114-115 T 7
Jara o **RUS** 108-109 T 7

Jara, La o **USA** (CO) 254-255 K 6
Jarabacoa o •• **DOM** 54-55 K 5
Jaraguá o **BR** 72-73 F 3
Jaraguá o **C** 54-55 G 3
Jaraguá do Sul o **BR** 74-75 F 6
Jaraguari o **BR** (GSU) 70-71 L 7
Jaraguari o **BR** (GSU) 70-71 K 7
Jarahueca o **C** 54-55 F 4
Jaranjuco o **ETH** 208-209 D 3
Jaransk o **RUS** 96-97 F 5
Jaránwäla o **PK** 138-139 D 4
Jarato, campo de **RUS** 108-109 Q 6
Jaraucu, Rio ~ **BR** 68-69 B 3
Jarawara, Área Indígena **BR** 66-67 E 6
Jaú, Parque Nacional do **BR** 66-67 G 3
Jaú, Rio o **BR** 66-67 G 3
Jarbidge o **USA** (NV) 246-247 K 2
Jarbo Pass **USA** (CA) 246-247 D 4
Jarceyo o **RUS** 116-117 E 5
Jarcevo o **RUS** (SML) 94-95 M 4
Jarclas al Abid o **LAR** 192-193 G 3
Jardim o **BR** (CEA) 68-69 J 5
Jardim do Serido o **BR** 68-69 K 5
Jardín, Sierra del **RCH** 76-77 D 4
Jardín América o **RA** 76-77 K 4
Jardines de la Reina, Archipiélago de los ~ **C** 54-55 F 4
Jardywai = Yardimik o **AZ** 128-129 N 3
Jarega o **RUS** 88-89 W 5
Jarenga o **RUS** 88-89 U 5
Jarenga ~ **RUS** 88-89 U 5
Jari, Estação Ecológica do **BR** 62-63 H 5
Jari, Lago o **BR** 66-67 F 5
Jari, Rio ~ **BR** 62-63 H 6
Jari, Rio o **BR** 66-67 H 5
Jarif, Wädï **LAR** 192-193 G 2
Jarina, Área Indígena **BR** 68-69 B 7
Jarina ou Juruna, Rio ~ **BR** 68-69 B 7
Jarkovo ~ **RUS** 114-115 J 6
Jarnema o **RUS** 88-89 P 5
Jarny o **F** 90-91 K 7
Jarocin o **PL** 92-93 O 3
Jarok, ostrov ~ **RUS** 110-111 V 4
Jaroslavl' ☆•• **RUS** 94-95 Q 3
Jaroslaw o **PL** 92-93 R 3
Jaroto pervoe, ozero o **RUS** 108-109 O 8
Jaroto vtoroe, ozero o **RUS** 108-109 O 8
Jarotschin = Jarocin o **PL** 92-93 O 3
Jarovaja ~ **RUS** 112-113 L 3
Jarqurghon o **UZ** 136-137 K 6
Jarrahdale o **AUS** 176-177 D 6
Jarrow o **CDN** (ALB) 232-233 G 3
Jar-Sale o **RUS** 108-109 O 8
Jartai o **VRC** 154-155 D 2
Jartai Yanchi o **VRC** 154-155 D 2
Jaru o **BR** 70-71 F 2
Jaru, Reserva Biológica do **BR** 66-67 G 7
Jaru, Rio ~ **BR** 70-71 F 2
Jarudei ~ **RUS** 114-115 L 2
Jarud Qi o **VRC** 150-151 C 5
Jaruma o **BOL** 70-71 F 5
Jaruqe o **ETH** 208-209 B 4
Jarvie o **CDN** (ALB) 232-233 E 3
Jarvis o **CDN** (ONT) 238-239 E 6
Jarvis Island o **USA** 13 C 3
Jarvsö o **S** 86-87 H 6
Järwäli o **IND** 138-139 D 5
Jary o **RUS** 108-109 M 7
Jasaan o **RP** 160-161 H 8
Jasacanajá ~ **RUS** 110-111 c 7
Jasacanajá ~ **RUS** 120-121 O 2
Jasavéjjaha ~ **RUS** 108-109 N 7
Jasavéjjaha ~ **RUS** 108-109 N 7
Jasavéjto, ozero o **RUS** 108-109 N 7
Jasel'da ~ **BY** 94-95 J 5
Jashpurnagar o **IND** 142-143 D 4
Jasilira ☆ **SP** 212-213 K 3
Jasikan o **GH** 202-203 K 6
Jaší'kul', ozero o **TJ** 136-137 N 6
Jaśliúnai o **LT** 94-95 J 4
Jaškino ~ **RUS** 114-115 S 7
Jaškul' o **RUS** 96-97 D 10
Jaškur-Boð'ja o **RUS** 96-97 H 5
Jasmin o **CDN** (SAS) 232-233 P 4
Jasnaja o **RUS** 118-119 G 10
Jasnoe o **RUS** 94-95 G 4
Jasnogorsk ☆• **RUS** 94-95 P 4
Jasnomorski o **RUS** 122-123 Q 2
Jasnyj o **RUS** (AMR) 122-123 C 2
Jasnyj o **RUS** (ORB) 126-127 N 2
JasonhalvØy **ARK** 16 G 30
Jason Islands ~ **GB** 78-79 K 6
Jasper o **CDN** (ALB) 228-229 Q 4
Jasper o **USA** (AL) 284-285 C 3
Jasper o **USA** (AR) 276-277 C 6
Jasper o **USA** (FL) 286-287 G 1
Jasper o **USA** (GA) 284-285 F 2
Jasper o **USA** (MN) 274-275 M 6
Jasper o **USA** (MN) 270-271 B 7
Jasper o **USA** (NY) 278-279 D 6
Jasper o **USA** (TX) 268-269 F 5
Jasper Lake o **CDN** (ALB) 228-229 R 3
Jasper National Park ⊥ ••• **CDN** (ALB) 228-229 Q 3
Jasrána o **IND** 138-139 G 6
Jastrow = Jastrowie o **PL** 92-93 O 2
Jastrowie o **PL** 92-93 O 2
Jasuibitobori o **YV** 60 61 J 6
Jataí o **BR** 72-73 E 4
Jatapu, Rio do **BR** 62-63 F 6
Jatapu, Serra do **BR** 62-63 E 6
Jatapuzinho, Rio ~ **BR** 62-63 E 6
Jelai ~ **RI** 162-163 G 7

Jatei o **BR** 76-77 K 2
Jath o **IND** 140-141 F 2
Jati o **PK** 138-139 B 7
Jati o **RI** 168 J 5
Jatibarang o **RI** 168 C 3
Jatibonico o **C** 54-55 F 4
Jatiluhur, Danau o **RI** 168 B 3
Jatirogo o **RI** 168 D 3
Jatiwangi o **RI** 168 C 3
Jatobá o **BR** (MAT) 70-71 J 4
Jatobá o **BR** (PA) 70-71 K 6
Jaú o **BR** 72-73 F 7
Jauaperi, Rio ~ **BR** 62-63 F 5
Jauaraua o **BR** 66-67 E 4
Jaucha, Arroyo de ~ **RA** 78-79 E 3
Jauharäbad o **PK** 138-139 D 3
Jauja o • **PE** 64-65 E 7
Jaumave o **MEX** 50-51 K 6
Jaunpiebalga o • **LV** 94-95 K 3
Jaunpur o **IND** 142-143 C 3
Jaupaci o **BR** 72-73 E 4
Jauquara, Rio o **BR** 70-71 J 4
Jaurdi o **AUS** 176-177 E 5
Jaurin ~ **RUS** 122-123 D 4
Jauru o **BR** (GSU) 70-71 K 6
Jauru o **BR** (MAT) 70-71 H 5
Jauru, Rio ~ **BR** 70-71 K 6
Jauru, Rio ~ **BR** 70-71 H 5
Java o **RI** 168 D 4
Java ~ **LA** (LA) 268-269 H 5
Java Barat o **RI** 168 B 3
Java Center o **USA** (NY) 278-279 C 6
Javaj, poluostrov ~ **RUS** 108-109 Q 5
Javan o **TJ** 136-137 L 5
Java Sea = Java, Laut ≈ 14-15 D 8
Java Tengah o **RI** 168 D 4
Java Timur o **RI** 168 D 4
Java Trench ≈ 12-13 J 6
Javari, Rio ~ **BR** 66-67 C 5
Javer de Viana o **ROU** 76-77 J 6
Javier, Isla ~ **RCH** 80 C 3
Javier de Viana o **ROU** 76-77 J 6
Javlenka o **KZ** 124-125 F 1
Jawi o **RI** 162-163 H 5
Jaworzno o **PL** 92-93 P 3
Jaws al Kabir, Al o **LAR** 192-193 D 2
Jay o **USA** (OK) 264-265 J 2
Jay o **USA** (FL) 286-287 B 2
Jay Em o **USA** (WY) 252-253 O 4
Jayton o **USA** (TX) 264-265 D 5
Jazira Tarut o • **KSA** 130-131 M 4
Jazykovo o **RUS** 114-115 J 6
Jazykovo ☆ **RUS** (BAS) 96-97 J 6
J. C. Jacobsen, Kap **GRØ** 28-29 Z 2
Jean o **USA** (TX) 264-265 F 5
Jean de Daie o **CDN** (NFL) 242-243 L 1
Jeanerette o **USA** (LA) 268-269 J 7
Jeanette Ray ☆ 36-37 V 7
Jeavons, Lake o **AUS** 172-173 J 6
Jean Rabel o •• **RH** 54-55 J 5
Jebba o **WAN** 204-205 F 4
Jeberos o **PE** 64-65 D 4
Jebiniana o **TN** 190-191 H 4
Jebri o **PK** 134-135 L 5
Jëdburgh o **CDN** (SAS) 232-233 P 4
Jeddah = Gidda ☆• **KSA** 132-133 A 3
Jeddore Cape **CDN** (NS) 240-241 M 6
Jedrzejów o **PL** 92-93 Q 3
Jedway o **CDN** (BC) 230-231 C 3
Jefe, Cerro **PA** 52-53 G 8
Jeffara o **TN** 190-191 H 4
Jeffers o **USA** (MN) 270-271 C 6
Jefferson o **USA** (GA) 284-285 G 2
Jefferson o **USA** (GA) 284-285 G 2
Jefferson o **USA** (IA) 274-275 D 2
Jefferson o **USA** (NC) 282-283 F 4
Jefferson o **USA** (OR) 244-245 B 6
Jefferson o **USA** (SD) 260-261 K 4
Jefferson o **USA** (TX) 268-269 F 4
Jefferson, Fort • **USA** (OH) 280-281 C 4
Jefferson, Mount **USA** (NV) 246-247 J 2
Jefferson, Mount **USA** (OR) 244-245 D 6
Jefferson City o **USA** (MO) 274-275 F 6
Jefferson City o **USA** (TN) 250-251 G 5
Jefferson City o **USA** (TN) 282-283 D 4
Jefferson National Memorial, Fort **USA** (MO) 286-287 G 7
Jefferson Proving Ground xx **USA** (IN) 274-275 N 6
Jefferson State Memorial, Fort • **USA** (OH) 280-281 D 3
Jeffersonton o **USA** (KY) 276-277 K 2
Jeffersonville o **USA** (GA) 284-285 G 3
Jeffersonville o **USA** (IN) 274-275 N 6
Jeffersonville o **USA** (OH) 280-281 C 4
Jeffersonville o **USA** (NY) 278-279 D 6
Jeffersonville o **USA** (TX) 268-269 J 6
Jeffrey City o **USA** (WY) 252-253 L 4
Jeffries, Lake o **USA** 246-247 D 4
Jef-Jef el Kébir **TCH** 198-199 K 2
Jega o **WAN** 198-199 B 6
Jege o **WAN** 198-199 B 6
Jeinemeni, Cerro **RCH** 80 C 3
Jejui-Guazú, Río o **PY** 76-77 J 3
Jékabpils o • **LV** 94-95 J 3
Jekyll Island o **USA** (GA) 284-285 J 5
Jelai ~ **RI** 162-163 G 7

Jelap La **BHT** 142-143 F 2
Jelenia Góra ☆ • **PL** 92-93 N 3
Jelgava o • **LV** 94-95 H 3
Jeli o **MAL** 162-163 E 3
Jellico o **USA** (TN) 282-283 C 4
Jellicoe o **CDN** (BC) 230-231 J 4
Jellicoe o **CDN** (ONT) 234-235 Q 5
Jelly Bean Crystals • **AUS** 178-179 L 4
Jelmusibak o **RI** 164-165 D 4
Jelsa o **HR** 100-101 F 3
Jema o **GH** 202-203 J 6
Jemaja, Pulau ~ **RI** 162-163 F 3
Jemalung o **MAL** 162-163 E 3
Jema Shet' ~ **ETH** 208-209 D 4
Jembawan, Danau o **RI** 162-163 F 6
Jember o **RI** 168 E 4
Jemez Indian Reservation **USA** (NM) 256-257 J 2
Jemez Pueblo o **USA** (NM) 256-257 J 3
Jemez Springc o **USA** (NM) 256-257 J 3
Jemilčyne o **UA** 102-103 E 2
Jeminay o **VRC** 146-147 G 2
Jemison o **USA** (AL) 284-285 D 4
Jemma o **WAN** (BAU) 204-205 H 3
Jemma o **WAN** (KAD) 204-205 H 3
Jempang, Danau o **RI** 164-165 F 6
Jemseg o **CDN** (NB) 240-241 J 5
Jen o **WAN** 204-205 J 4
Jena o **D** 92-93 L 3
Jena o **USA** (LA) 268-269 H 5
Jenakijeve o **UA** 102-103 L 3
Jenda o **MW** 214-215 G 7
Jendouba o **TN** 190-191 G 2
Jenerhodar o **UA** 102-103 J 4
Jeneshuaya, Arroyo ~ **BOL** 70-71 D 3
Jenin o **WB** 130-131 D 1
Jenipapo o **BR** (AMA) 66-67 G 5
Jenipapo o **BR** (P) 62-63 H 5
Jenipapo o **BR** (TOC) 68-69 D 5
Jenipapo, Ribeiro ~ **BR** 68-69 G 5
Jenipapo, Rio ~ **BR** 68-69 G 4
Jenkins o **USA** (KY) 276-277 N 3
Jenkins o **USA** (NJ) 280-281 M 4
Jenner o **CDN** (ALB) 232-233 G 5
Jenner o **USA** (CA) 246-247 B 5
Jennings ~ **CDN** 20-21 N 2
Jennings o **USA** (LA) 268-269 H 6
Jennings Randolph Lake o **USA** (MD) 280-281 G 4
Jenny o **SME** 62-63 G 3
Jenny Lind Island ~ **CDN** 24-25 V 6
Jenolan Caves • **AUS** 180-181 J 4
Jensen o **USA** (UT) 254-255 F 3
Jensen, Cape **CDN** 24-25 h 6
Jens Munk Island ~ **CDN** 24-25 U 8
Jens Munk Ø ~ **GRØ** 28-29 U 4
Jepara o **RI** 168 D 3
Jeparit o **AUS** 180-181 G 4
Jequié o **BR** 72-73 K 2
Jequinhonha, Rio ~ **BR** 72-73 L 3
Jequiriçá o **BR** 72-73 L 2
Jequitaí o **BR** 72-73 H 4
Jequital, Rio ~ **BR** 72-73 H 4
Jequitiba o **BR** 72-73 J 5
Jequitinhonha o **BR** 72-73 K 4
Jequitinhonha, Rio ~ **BR** 72-73 J 4
Jerada o **MA** 188-189 K 3
Jerangau, Kampung o **MAL** 162-163 E 3
Jerangle o **AUS** 180-181 K 3
Jerantut o **MAL** 162-163 E 3
Jerba, Île de ~ **TN** 190-191 H 4
Jerbar o **SUD** 206-207 K 8
Jerdera o **RI** 166-167 H 5
Jere o **RI** 164-165 K 4
Jerecuaro o **MEX** 52-53 D 1
Jérôme o • **RH** 54-55 J 5
Jeremoabo o **BR** 68-69 J 7
Jerer Shet' ~ **ETH** 208-209 D 4
Jerez, Rio ~ **MEX** 50-51 H 6
Jerez de García Salinas o • **MEX** 50-51 H 6
Jerez de la Frontera o **E** 98-99 D 6
Jerez de los Caballeros o **E** 98-99 D 5
Jericho o **AUS** 178-179 J 2
Jericho o **SOL** 184 I d 3
Jericho = Arihā o • **AUT** 130-131 D 2
Jericho Dam < **ZA** 220-221 K 3
Jericoacoara o **BR** 68-69 H 3
Jericoacoara, Ponta **BR** 68-69 H 3
Jerigu o **GH** 202-203 K 5
Jerliderie o **AUS** 180-181 H 3
Jerko La o **VRC** 144-145 C 5
Jerome o **USA** (AZ) 256-257 C 4
Jerome o **USA** (ID) 286-287 H 6
Jerome o **USA** (ID) 252-253 D 4
Jerori o **BOL** 70-71 E 4
Jerramungup o **AUS** 176-177 E 6
Jersey **GBJ** 90-91 F 7
Jersey City o **USA** (NJ) 280-281 M 3
Jersey Cove o **CDN** (QUE) 240-241 L 2
Jersey Shore o **USA** (PA) 280-281 J 2
Jerseyville o **USA** (IL) 274-275 H 5
Jertih o **MAL** 162-163 E 2
Jerumenha o **BR** 68-69 G 5
Jerusalem = Yerushalayim / al-Quds ★ ••• **IL** 130-131 D 2
Jervis, Monte **RCH** 80 C 4
Jervis Bay ≈ **AUS** 180-181 L 3
Jervis Inlet ≈ 230-231 F 4
Jervois o **AUS** 178-179 D 2
Jesenice o **SLO** 100-101 E 1
Jesenik o **CZ** 92-93 O 3
Jesi, Monte **MOC** 214-215 H 7
Jesmond o **CDN** (BC) 230-231 G 3
Jessama o **USA** (NC) 282-283 L 5
Jesselstown = Kota Kinabalu ★ • **MAL** 160-161 B 10
Jessheim ☆ **N** 86-87 D 6
Jessore o **BD** 142-143 F 4
Jesup o **USA** (GA) 284-285 J 5
Jesup o **USA** (IA) 274-275 F 2

Južnyj ○ KZ 126-127 N 4
Južnyj ○ RUS 112-113 Q 2
Južnyj, mys ▲ RUS (KMC) 120-121 I X 6
Južnyj, mys ▲ RUS (KOR) 120-121 R 5
Južnyj, mys ▲ RUS (KOR) 120-121 U 5
Južnyj, ostrov ⌒ RUS 108-109 k 3
Južnyj Ergalah ~ RUS 108-109 W 7
Južnyj Ural ▲ RUS 96-97 K 8
Juzzak ○ PK 134-135 J 4
Jwaneng ○ RB 220-221 G 2
Jylland ⊥ DK 86-87 D 9
Jyllandsfjældet ▲ GRØ 28-29 U 4
Jyväskylä ☆ FIN 88-89 H 5
Jzaviknek River ~ USA 20-21 J 6

K

K2 ▲ PK 138-139 F 2
Kaabong ○ EAU 212-213 E 2
Kaabougou ○ BF 204-205 E 3
Kaahka ○ TM 136-137 F 6
Kaala ▲ USA (HI) 288 G 3
Kaalualu ○ USA (HI) 288 K 6
Kaamanen ○ FIN 88-89 J 2
Kaap die Goeie Hoop = Cape of Good Hope ▲ · ZA 220-221 D 7
Kaapmuiden ○ ZA 220-221 K 2
Kaapstad = Cape Town ☆ ·· ZA 220-221 D 6
Kaaresuvanto ○ FIN 88-89 G 2
Kaart ⊥ RMM 202-203 F 3
Kaavi ○ FIN 88-89 K 5
Kabacan ○ RP 160-161 F 9
Kabaena, Pulau ⌒ RI 164-165 G 6
Kabaena, Selat ≈ 164-165 G 6
Kabah ∴ · MEX 52-53 K 1
Kabaklyoba ○ TM 136-137 H 5
Kabala ○ WAL 202-203 E 5
Kabale ○ EAU 212-213 B 4
Kabalo ○ ZRE 214-215 D 4
Kabamba, Lac ○ ZRE 214-215 D 4
Kabambare ○ ZRE 212-213 A 6
Kabanga ○ ZRE 216-217 E 3
Kabango ○ ZRE 214-215 D 4
Kabangu ○ ZRE 214-215 B 6
Kabania Lake ○ CDN (ONT) 234-235 P 2
Kabanjahe ○ RI 162-163 C 3
Kabankalan ○ RP 160-161 E 8
Kabara ⌒ FJI 184 III c 3
Kabara ○ RMM 196-197 J 6
Kabara, Lac ○ RMM 202-203 H 2
Kabarai ○ RI 166-167 F 2
Kabardino-Balkaria = Kėbėrdej-Balkėr Respublikėm ◻ RUS 104 D 5
Kabardino-Balkarskaja Respublika ◻ RUS 104 D 5
Kabare ○ ZRE 212-213 B 5
Kabarnet ○ EAK 212-213 E 3
Kabasalan ○ RP 160-161 E 9
Kabau ○ RI 164-165 J 5
Kābāw ○ LAR 192-193 D 2
Kabba ○ WAN 204-205 G 5
Kabe ○ WAN 204-205 F 3
Kaberamaido ○ EAU 212-213 D 3
Kabetogama Lake ○ USA (MN) 270-271 F 2
Kabeya ○ ZRE 214-215 B 4
Kabi ○ ETH 208-209 D 3
Kabla ~ TCH 206-207 B 4
Kabika River ~ CDN 236-237 J 3
Kabinakagami Lake ○ CDN (ONT) 236-237 D 4
Kabinakagami River ~ CDN 236-237 D 2
Kabin Buri ○ THA 158-159 F 3
Kabinda ○ ZRE 214-215 C 4
Kabir ○ RI 166-167 C 6
Kabīr, Kūh-e ▲ IR 134-135 B 2
Kabīr, Nahr az-Zāb al ~ IRQ 128-129 K 4
Kabir, Wāw al ○ LAR 192-193 G 5
Kabīrwāla ○ PK 138-139 C 4
Kabkābīyah ○ SUD 200-201 B 6
Kablebet ○ RI 166-167 E 2
Kabna ○ SUD 200-201 F 3
Kabo ○ RCA 206-207 D 5
Kabolaa ○ RI 166-167 F 2
Kabompo ○ Z (NTW) 218-219 C 1
Kabompo ~ Z 218-219 C 1
Kabondo-Dianda ○ ZRE 214-215 C 5
Kabongo ○ ZRE (SHA) 214-215 C 4
Kabongo ○ ZRE (SHA) 214-215 E 5
Kabou ○ RCA 206-207 E 6
Kabou ○ RT 202-203 L 5
Kaboudia, Rass ▲ TN 190-191 H 3
Kabrousse ○ SN 202-203 B 3
Kabš, Ra's al- ▲ OM 132-133 L 3
Kabšān ○ KSA 130-131 H 5
Kabūd Rāhang ○ IR 128-129 N 5
Kābul ◻ AFG 138-139 B 2
Kābul ★ AFG (KB) 138-139 B 2
Kābul, Daryā-ye ~ AFG 138-139 B 2
Kabul = Kābul ★ AFG 138-139 B 2
Kabulamwanda ○ Z 218-219 D 2
Kabumbu ○ ZRE 210-211 L 6
Kabunda ○ ZRE 214-215 E 7
Kabunduk ○ RI 168 D 7
Kabur ○ SUD 200-201 E 6
Kaburuang ○ RI 164-165 K 2
Kaburuang, Pulau ⌒ RI 164-165 K 2
Kabūshiya ○ SUD 200-201 F 4
Kabūtarhān ○ IR 134-135 G 3
Kabuzai Island ⌒ MYA 158-159 D 4
Kabwe ☆ Z 218-219 E 2
Kabwum ○ PNG 183 D 4
Kabyé, Monts ▲ RT 202-203 L 5
Kabyrga ~ KZ 126-127 P 2
Kačanik ○ · YU 100-101 H 3
Kacepi ○ RI 166-167 E 2
Kačerikova ○ RUS 116-117 N 9
Kach ○ PK 134-135 M 3
Kachako ○ WAN 204-205 H 3
Kachalola ○ Z 218-219 F 2
Kachchh, Gulf of ≈ 138-139 B 8
Kacheh Kūh ▲ PK 134-135 J 4
Kachekabwe ○ RB 218-219 C 4
Kachemak Bay ≈ 22-23 V 3
Kachia ○ WAN 204-205 G 4
Kachikani Pass ▲ PK 138-139 D 2
Kachisi ○ ETH 208-209 C 4
Kachovka ○ UA 102-103 H 4
Kachovs'ke vodoschovyšče < UA 102-103 H 4
Kachovs'kyj kanal < UA 102-103 J 4
Kachulu ○ MW 218-219 H 2
Kachung ○ EAU 212-213 D 3
Kačikatcy ○ RUS 118-119 O 5
Kačiry ☆ KZ 124-125 K 2
Kačkanar ○ RUS 96-97 L 4
Kaçkar Dağı ▲ TR 128-129 J 2
Kačug ☆ RUS 116-117 M 9
Kačul = Cahul ☆ MD 102-103 F 5
Kaczawa ~ PL 92-93 N 3
Kada ○ AFG 134-135 K 3
Ka Dake Station ○ SD 220-221 K 3
Kadaly, Ust'e ○ RUS 118-119 E 6
Kadambūr ○ IND 140-141 G 6
Kadaney Rūd ~ AFG 134-135 M 3
Kadangan ○ RI 168 E 3
Kadan Kyun ⌒ MYA 158-159 E 4
Kadavu ⌒ FJI 184 III b 3
Kadavu Passage ≈ 184 III b 3
Kaddam ○ IND 138-139 G 10
Kaddam Dam < IND 138-139 G 10
Kade ○ GH 202-203 K 6
Kadéï ~ RCA 210-211 E 2
Kadepur ○ IND 140-141 F 2
Kadi, ozero ○ RUS 122-123 J 3
Kadiana ○ RMM 202-203 G 4
Kadiaso ○ CI 202-203 G 5
Kadijivka ○ UA 102-103 L 3
Kadina ○ AUS 180-181 D 2
Kadınhanı ○ TR 128-129 E 3
Kadioha ○ CI 202-203 H 5
Kadiolo ○ RMM 202-203 H 4
Kadiondola ▲ RG 202-203 E 4
Kadipaten ○ RI 168 C 3
Kadiri ○ IND 140-141 H 3
Kadirli ☆ TR 128-129 G 4
Kadiwēn, Reserva Indígena ✗ BR 70-71 J 7
Kadjebi ○ GH 202-203 L 6
Kadji ○ TCH 206-207 E 3
Kadkan ○ IR 136-137 F 7
Kado ○ WAN 204-205 H 5
Kadoka ○ USA (SD) 260-261 E 3
Kadoma ○ ZW 218-219 E 4
Kadovar Island ⌒ PNG 183 C 2
Kadu ○ RI 168 D 7
Kadugli ○ SUD 206-207 J 3
Kaduj ○ RUS 94-95 P 2
Kaduna ◻ WAN 204-205 G 3
Kaduna ☆ · WAN (KAD) 204-205 G 3
Kaduna, River ~ WAN 204-205 F 4
Kadung Ga ○ MYA 142-143 K 2
Kadupandak ○ RI 168 A 3
Kadūr ○ IND 140-141 G 4
Kadyj ○ RUS 94-95 S 3
Kadykčan ○ RUS 120-121 O 2
Kadžaran ○ AR 128-129 M 3
Kadžerom ○ RUS 88-89 X 4
Kaechon ○ KOR 150-151 E 8
Kaédi ☆ RIM 196-197 D 6
Kaélé ○ CAM 206-207 B 3
Kaena Point ▲ · USA (HI) 288 G 3
Kaeng Khlo ○ THA 158-159 G 2
Kaeo ○ NZ 182 D 1
Kaesŏng ○ ROK 150-151 F 9
Kaevanga ○ SOL 184 I d 3
Kafakumba ○ ZRE 214-215 B 5
Kafan ○ AR 128-129 M 3
Kafanchan ○ WAN 204-205 H 4
Kafferrivier ~ ZA 220-221 G 4
Kaffin-Saru ○ WAN 204-205 G 4
Kaffrine ○ SN 202-203 C 2
Kafia Kingi ○ SUD 206-207 G 4
Kafiau, Pulau ⌒ RI 166-167 E 2
Kafin ○ WAN 204-205 G 4
Kafindibei ○ SUD 206-207 G 4
Kafirnigan ~ TJ 136-137 L 6
Kåfjord ○ N 86-87 M 1
Kafolo ○ CI 202-203 H 5
Kafountine ○ SN 202-203 B 3
Kafr ad-Dawwār ○ ET 194-195 E 2
Kafr aš-Šaiḫ ☆ ET 194-195 E 2
Kafu ~ EAU 212-213 C 3
Kafubu ~ ZRE 214-215 E 6
Kafue ○ Z (Lus) 218-219 E 2
Kafue ~ Z 218-219 E 2
Kafue Flats ⊥ Z 218-219 D 2
Kafue National Park ⊥ Z 218-219 C 2
Kafukule ○ MW 214-215 G 6
Kafulwe ○ Z 214-215 E 5
Kafuya ~ ZRE 210-211 L 6
Kafwala Rest Camp ○ Z 218-219 D 2
Kaga ○ J 152-153 G 6
Kaga Bandoro ☆ RCA 206-207 D 5
Kagadi ○ EAU 212-213 C 3
Kaǵaki ○ AFG 134-135 L 2
Kaǵaki, Band-e ○ ·· AFG 134-135 L 2
Kagalaska Island ⌒ USA 22-23 H 7
Kagal'nik ~ RUS 102-103 M 4
Kagamil Island ⌒ USA 22-23 L 6
Kagamil Pass ≈ 22-23 M 6
Kāgān ○ PK 138-139 D 2
Kagan ☆ UZ 136-137 J 5
Kagangan, Pulau ⌒ RI 164-165 F 6
Kagaré ○ BF 202-203 K 3
Kagarko ○ WAN 204-205 G 4
Kagegawa ○ J 152-153 H 7
Kagera ◻ EAT 212-213 C 4
Kagera ~ EAT 212-213 C 4
Kaggi ○ IND 140-141 F 4
Kagianagami Lake ○ CDN (ONT) 234-235 Q 4
Kağızman ☆ TR 128-129 K 2
Kaglik Lake ○ CDN 20-21 a 2
Kagloryuak River ~ CDN 24-25 Q 5
Kagmar ○ SUD 200-201 E 5
Kagnel ○ TCH 206-207 D 4
Kagologolo ○ RI 162-163 C 5
Kagombo ○ ZRE 214-215 D 6
Kagopal ○ TCH 206-207 C 4
Kagora, Mount ▲ WAN 204-205 H 4
Kagoshima ☆ J 152-153 D 9
Kagoshima-wan ≈ 152-153 D 9
Kağrān ○ AFG 134-135 L 2
Kāğū, Rūdḫāne-ye ~ IR 134-135 J 6
Kagua ○ PNG 183 B 4
Kāğūğ ○ ET 194-195 F 5
Kahakuloa ○ USA (HI) 288 J 4
Kahal Tabelbala ▲ DZ 188-189 K 6
Kahama ○ EAT 212-213 D 5
Kahān ○ PK 138-139 B 5
Kahana ○ USA (HI) 288 H 3
Kahatola, Pulau ⌒ RI 164-165 K 3
Kahayan ~ RI 162-163 K 5
Kahayan ~ RI 164-165 D 5
Kahemba ○ ZRE 216-217 E 3
Kahfa, al- ○ KSA 130-131 H 4
Kahir ○ IR 134-135 J 6
Kahiri ○ IR 134-135 J 5
Kahla, Djebel el ▲ DZ 188-189 L 6
Kahlotus ○ USA (WA) 244-245 G 4
Kahmard ○ AFG 136-137 K 7
Kāhna Nau ○ PK 138-139 E 4
Kahnple ○ LB 202-203 F 6
Kahnūğ ○ IR 134-135 G 5
Kahnwia ○ LB 202-203 F 7
Kahoka ○ USA (MO) 274-275 G 4
Kahokunui ○ USA (HI) 288 J 4
Kahone ○ SN 202-203 C 2
Kahoolawe ⌒ USA (HI) 288 J 4
Kahramanmaraş ☆ · TR 128-129 G 4
Kahrizak ○ IR 136-137 B 7
Kahror Pakka ○ PK 138-139 C 5
Kāhta ☆ TR 128-129 H 4
Kahtana ~ RUS 120-121 T 4
Kahuku ○ USA (HI) 288 H 3
Kahuku Point ▲ USA (HI) 288 H 3
Kahul = Cahul ☆ MD 102-103 F 5
Kahului ○ · USA (HI) 288 J 4
Kahului Bay ≈ 288 J 4
Kahuzi ○ EAU 212-213 C 3
Kahūta ○ PK 138-139 D 3
Kahuzi-Biega, Parc National du ⊥ ··· ZRE 212-213 A 4
Kai, Kepulauan ⌒ RI 166-167 G 4
Kaiam ○ PNG 183 B 4
Kaiama ○ WAN 204-205 E 4
Kaiapit ○ PNG 183 D 4
Kaiapoi ○ NZ 182 D 5
Kaiashk Bay ≈ 234-235 O 5
Kaibab Indian Reservation ✗ USA (AZ) 256-257 C 2
Kaibab Plateau ▲ USA 256-257 C 2
Kai Besar ○ RI 166-167 K 5
Kai Besar, Pulau ⌒ RI 166-167 G 4
Kaibito ○ USA (AZ) 256-257 D 2
Kaibito Plateau ▲ USA 256-257 D 2
Kaibola ○ PNG 183 F 5
Kaibus, Teluk ≈ 166-167 F 2
Kaidu He ~ VRC 146-147 G 4
Kai Dulah, Pulau ⌒ RI 166-167 G 4
Kalemolhila ○ SUD 208-209 B 6
Kaieteur Fall ~ ·· GUY 62-63 E 3
Kaieteur National Park ⊥ · GUY 62-63 E 3
Kaifeng ○ · VRC 154-155 J 4
Kaigani ○ USA 32-33 D 4
Kaihu ○ NZ 182 D 1
Kaihua ○ VRC 156-157 L 2
Kai Ketjil, Pulau ⌒ RI 166-167 G 4
Kaikohe ○ NZ 182 D 1
Kaikoura ○ NZ 182 D 5
Kailahun ○ WAL 202-203 E 5
Kailash = Kangrinboqê Feng ▲ VRC 144-145 C 5
Kailashahar ○ IND 142-143 H 3
Kaileuna Island ⌒ PNG 183 F 5
Kaili ○ VRC 156-157 E 3
Kailu ○ VRC 150-151 C 6
Kailua Kona ○ · USA (HI) 288 K 5
Kaima ○ RI 166-167 K 4
Kaimana ○ RI 166-167 G 3
Kaimeer, Pulau ⌒ RI 166-167 G 4
Käina ○ ·· EST 94-95 H 2
Kainab ~ NAM 220-221 D 3
Kainan ○ J 152-153 F 8
Kainantu ○ PNG 183 C 4
Kaindu ○ Z 218-219 D 2
Kaindy ○ KS 136-137 N 3
Kainji Dam < WAN 204-205 F 4
Kainji Lake National Park ⊥ WAN 204-205 E 3
Kainji Reservoir < WAN 204-205 F 3
Kaipara Harbour ≈ 182 E 2
Kaiparowits Plateau ▲ USA 254-255 D 6
Kaiping ○ VRC 156-157 H 5
Kaipotok Bay ≈ 36-37 U 7
Kaipuri, Pulau ⌒ RI 166-167 J 2
Kairāna ○ IND 138-139 F 5
Kairiru Island ⌒ PNG 183 B 2
Kaironi ○ RI 166-167 G 2
Kairouan ☆ ··· TN 190-191 H 3
Kais ~ RI 166-167 G 2
Kaiserslautern ○ D 92-93 J 4
Kaiserstuhl ▲ D 92-93 J 4
Kaiser Wilhelm II.-Land ⊥ ARK 16 G 9
Kaišho ○ EAT 212-213 C 4
Kaišiadorys ☆ LT 94-95 J 4
Kaisu ○ EAU 212-213 C 3
Kaisut Desert ⊥ EAK 212-213 F 3
Kait ○ PNG 183 G 3
Kait, Tanjung ▲ RI 162-163 G 6
Kaita ○ EAU 212-213 C 3
Kaitaia ○ NZ 182 D 1
Kaitangata ○ NZ 182 B 7
Kaitanimbar, Pulau ⌒ RI 166-167 G 5
Kaiteriteri ○ NZ 182 D 4
Kaithal ○ IND 138-139 F 5
Kaititja-Warlpiri Aboriginal Land ✗ AUS 174-175 B 6
Kaitum ○ S 86-87 K 3
Kaitumälven ~ S 86-87 J 3
Kaiwatu ○ RI 166-167 D 6
Kaiwi Channel ≈ 288 H 3
Kai Xian ○ VRC 154-155 F 6
Kaiyang ○ VRC 156-157 E 3
Kaiyuan ○ VRC (LIA) 150-151 E 6
Kaiyuan ○ VRC (YUN) 156-157 C 5
Kaiyuh Mountains ▲ USA 20-21 L 5
Kaja, Wādī ~ SUD 198-199 L 6
Kajaani ○ FIN 88-89 J 4
Kajabbi ○ AUS 174-175 F 7
Kajak ○ RUS 108-109 e 6
Kajang ○ MAL 162-163 D 3
Kajang (Typical Amatowa Village) ○ ·· RI 164-165 G 6
Kajasan National Park ⊥ · ROK 150-151 G 10
Ķajdak, sor ⊥ KZ 126-127 K 5
Kajdak, Sor ○ KZ 126-127 K 5
Kajerkan ○ RUS 108-109 W 7
Kajiado ○ EAK 212-213 F 4
Kajlastuj ○ RUS 118-119 J 11
Kajmonovo ○ RUS 116-117 M 7
Kajnar ○ KZ 124-125 K 4
Kajo Kaji ○ SUD 212-213 C 2
Kajola ○ WAN 204-205 F 5
Kajpiĝakuj, ozero ○ RUS 112-113 I 5
Kajrakkum ○ TJ 136-137 L 4
Kajrakkumskoe vodohranilišče < TJ 136-137 M 4
Ķajraķty ~ KZ 126-127 N 3
Kajser Franz Joseph Fjord ≈ 26-27 m 7
Kajtezek, pereval ▲ TJ 136-137 N 6
Kajuru ○ WAN 204-205 G 3
Ķak, köli ○ KZ 124-125 E 2
Kākā ○ SUD 206-207 L 3
Kaka ○ USA (AZ) 256-257 C 6
Kakaban, Pulau ⌒ RI 164-165 F 2
Kakabeka Falls ○ · CDN (ONT) 234-235 O 6
Kakabia, Pulau ⌒ RI 166-167 B 5
Kakachischuan, Pointe ▲ CDN 36-37 K 7
Kakadu Holiday Village · AUS 172-173 L 2
Kakadu National Park ⊥ ··· AUS 172-173 L 2
Kakagi Lake ○ CDN (ONT) 234-235 K 5
Kakali ○ RI 164-165 F 4
Kakamas ○ ZA 220-221 E 4
Kakamega ☆ EAK 212-213 E 3
Kakamenga Forest Reserve ⊥ EAK 212-213 E 3
Kaka Mundi Section ⊥ AUS 178-179 J 3
Kākān ○ AFG 136-137 M 6
Kakanda ○ ZRE 214-215 D 6
Kakat, Ujung ▲ RI 162-163 B 3
Kakata ○ LB 202-203 E 6
Kakavi Theollogu ○ GR 100-101 H 5
Kakching ○ MYA 142-143 J 3
Kakdwip ○ IND 142-143 F 5
Kake ○ J 152-153 E 7
Kake ○ USA 32-33 D 3
Kakenge ○ ZRE 210-211 H 6
Kakeroma-shima ⌒ J 152-153 C 10
Kāki ○ IR 134-135 D 4
Kaklelu ○ ZRE 214-215 E 7
Kakimba ○ ZRE 212-213 B 6
Kakināda ○ IND 140-141 K 2
Kakisa River ~ CDN 30-31 K 5
Kakkar ○ PK 134-135 M 5
Kakobola ○ ZRE 210-211 G 6
Kakogawa ○ J 152-153 F 7
Kakonko ○ EAT 212-213 C 5
Kakoro ○ PNG 183 D 4
Kakpin ○ CI 202-203 J 5
Kakrima ~ RG 202-203 D 4
Kaktovik ○ USA 20-21 T 1
Kakuma ○ EAK 212-213 E 2
Kakumbi ○ Z 218-219 F 1
Kakumi ○ WAN 204-205 G 3
Kakumiro ○ EAU 212-213 C 3
Kakunodate ○ J 152-153 J 5
Kakwa Provincial Recreation Area ⊥ CDN (BC) 228-229 O 2
Kakwa River ~ CDN 228-229 P 2
Kakya ○ EAK 212-213 G 4
Ķakyl, tau ▲ KZ 124-125 F 4
Kala ○ EAT 214-215 F 5
Kala ○ WAN 198-199 G 6
Kalaallit Nunaat = Grønland ◻ GRØ 26-27 c 8
Kalaat Khasba ○ TN 190-191 G 3
Kālābāgh ○ PK 138-139 C 3
Kalabahi ○ RI 166-167 C 6
Kalabakan ○ MAL 160-161 B 10
Kalabi ○ EAU 212-213 D 2
Kalabo ○ Z 218-219 B 2
Kalabsha ∴ · ET 194-195 F 6
Kalabua ○ ZRE 214-215 B 4
Kalač ○ RUS 102-103 M 2
Kalāčāy ○ IR 136-137 B 6
Kalačinsk ☆ RUS 114-115 N 7
Kalač-na-Donu ○ RUS 102-103 N 3
Kaladan ○ IND (MIZ) 142-143 H 4
Kaladan ~ IND 142-143 H 5
Kaladar ○ CDN (ONT) 238-239 H 4
Ka Lae ▲ USA (HI) 288 K 6
Kalafgān ○ AFG 136-137 L 6
Kalafilia ○ RG 202-203 F 5
Kalahari Desert ⊥ RB 220-221 E 1
Kalahari Gemsbok National Park ⊥ ZA 220-221 E 2
Kalaheo ○ USA (HI) 288 F 3
Kalaigaon ○ IND 142-143 G 2
Kalaihum ○ TJ 136-137 M 5
Kalaji ○ WAG 202-203 C 3
Kalajoki ○ FIN 88-89 G 4
Kalakala · BOL 70-71 D 6
Kalakan ○ RUS (CTN) 118-119 H 8
Kalakan ~ RUS 118-119 H 8
Kalalé ○ DY 204-205 E 3
Kalāle ○ IR 136-137 D 6
Kala-I-Mor ○ TM 136-137 H 7
Kalaloch ○ USA (WA) 244-245 A 3
Kalām ○ PK 138-139 D 2
Kalama < EAK 212-213 F 2
Kalama ○ USA (WA) 244-245 C 4
Kalamalouė, Parc National de ⊥ CAM 198-199 G 6
Kalamariá ○ GR 100-101 J 4
Kalamáta ○ GR 100-101 J 6
Kalamazoo ○ USA (MI) 272-273 D 5
Kalamazoo River ~ USA 272-273 D 5
Kalambáka ○ · GR 100-101 H 5
Kalambo ~ EAT 214-215 F 5
Kalambo Falls ~ · EAT 214-215 F 5
Kalamits'ka zatoka ≈ 102-103 H 5
Kalana ○ EST 94-95 H 2
Kalana ○ RMM 202-203 F 4
Kalangali ○ EAT 214-215 G 4
Kalanguj ○ RUS 118-119 H 10
Kalao, Pulau ⌒ RI 168 E 6
Kalaotoa, Pulau ⌒ RI 168 E 6
Kala Oya ~ CL 140-141 J 6
Kalapana ○ USA (HI) 288 L 5
Kalar ~ RUS 118-119 H 8
Kalār, Kūh-e ▲ IR 134-135 D 3
Kalar, Srednij ○ RUS 118-119 H 8
Kalaraš = Călăraşi ☆ MD 102-103 F 4
Kalāme ○ S 86-87 H 5
Kalarskij hrebet ▲ RUS 118-119 H 8
Kalasin ○ THA 158-159 G 2
Kalāt ○ · PK 134-135 M 4
Kalāte ○ IR 136-137 D 6
Kalāte-ye Siyāh ○ IR 134-135 J 4
Kalatungan Mountains ▲ RP 160-161 F 9
Kalaupapa ○ USA (HI) 288 J 3
Kalaupapa National Historical Park ⊥ · USA (HI) 288 J 3
Kalaus ~ RUS 102-103 N 5
Kalaus ~ RUS 126-127 E 5
Kalaw ○ MYA 142-143 K 5
Kalb, De ○ USA (IL) 274-275 K 3
Kalb, De ○ USA (MS) 268-269 M 4
Kalb, De ○ USA (TX) 264-265 K 5
Kalb, Qarārat al ○ LAR 192-193 F 4
Kalb, Ra's al- ▲ Y 132-133 F 6
Kalbā ○ UAE 134-135 G 6
Kalbān, al- ○ OM 132-133 L 3
Kalbarri ○ · AUS 176-177 C 3
Kalbarri National Park ⊥ AUS 176-177 C 3
Kalbinskij hrebet ▲ KZ 124-125 M 4
Kaldakvistl ~ IS 86-87 d 2
Ķaldyķajty ~ KZ 96-97 H 9
Ķaldyķöl ○ KZ 136-137 L 3
Kaldykol', ozero ○ KZ 136-137 L 3
Kalé ○ RMM 202-203 E 3
Kale ☆ TR 128-129 C 4
Kalecik ☆ · TR 128-129 E 2
Kaledon ○ CDN (BC) 230-231 K 4
Kaledougou ○ RMM 202-203 H 3
Kaledupa, Pulau ⌒ RI 164-165 H 6
Kalegauk ⌒ MYA 158-159 D 3
Kalogosilik River ~ USA 20-21 Q 2
Kalehe ○ ZRE 212-213 B 5
Kaleibar ○ IR 128-129 M 3
Kaleida ○ CDN (MAN) 234-235 E 5
Kalema ○ ZRE 210-211 P 5
Kalemie ○ ZRE 212-213 B 6
Kalemyo ○ MYA 142-143 J 4
Kalengwa ○ Z 218-219 C 1
Kalėnnoe ○ KZ 96-97 G 9
Kaleo ○ GH 202-203 J 4
Kaleste ○ EST 94-95 H 2
Kāl-e Šūr ~ IR 134-135 G 1
Kāl-e Šūr, Rūd-e ~ IR 136-137 F 6
Kaleva ○ USA (MI) 272-273 C 3
Kalevala ○ RUS 88-89 L 4
Kale Valley ~ · WAN 204-205 J 3
Kalewa ○ MYA 142-143 J 4
Kalf ~ NAM 220-221 C 2
Kálfafell ○ IS 86-87 e 3
Kálfafellsstaður ○ IS 86-87 f 2
Kalfou ○ CAM 206-207 B 3
Kalfou, Réserve de ⊥ CAM 206-207 B 3
Kalga ☆ RUS 118-119 J 10
Kalgalakša, guba ≈ 88-89 N 4
Kalgary ○ USA (TX) 264-265 C 5
Kalghatgi ○ IND 140-141 F 3
Kalginčevajam ~ RUS 120-121 T 5
Kalgin Island ⌒ USA 20-21 O 6
Kalgo ○ WAN 198-199 B 6
Kalgoorlie-Boulder ○ AUS 176-177 F 5
Kali ~ NEP 144-145 C 6
Kali ○ RMM 202-203 E 3
Kali ○ RUS 88-89 R 5
Kalia ~ CAM 206-207 B 3
Kaliakair ○ BD 142-143 G 3
Kaliakra, Nos ▲ BG 102-103 F 6
Kalian ○ RP 160-161 F 9
Kalianda ○ RI 162-163 F 7
Kalianget ○ RI 168 E 3
Kaliānpur ○ IND 138-139 B 8
Kalibo ☆ RP 160-161 E 7
Kaliet ○ RI 162-163 C 6
Kali Gandaki ~ NEP 144-145 D 7
Kaliganj ○ BD 142-143 F 4
Kaligondang ○ RI 168 C 3
Kalima ○ ZRE 210-211 L 5
Kalimantan ⌒ 164-165 B 4
Kalimantan Barat ◻ RI 162-163 J 4
Kalimantan Selatan ◻ RI 164-165 D 5
Kalimantan Tengah ◻ RI 162-163 K 5
Kalimantan Timur ◻ RI 164-165 D 3
Kálimnos ○ · GR 100-101 L 6
Kálimnos ⌒ GR 100-101 L 6
Kālimpang ○ IND 142-143 F 2
Kalinga ○ AUS 174-175 G 4
Kalinga ○ IND 142-143 D 5
Kalingupatti ○ IND 140-141 H 6
Kalinin ☆ TM 136-137 F 3
Kalinin = Tver' ☆ RUS 94-95 O 3
Kalinina ○ RUS 116-117 O 6
Kalinina, zaliv ≈ 108-109 I Y 2
Kalininabad ○ TJ 136-137 L 6
Kaliningrad ☆ ·· RUS 94-95 G 4
Kalinino ○ RUS 122-123 C 4
Kalinino = Tašir ○ AR 128-129 L 2
Kalininsk ○ RUS 96-97 D 8
Kalinjra ○ IND 138-139 E 8
Kalinkavičy ○ BY 94-95 L 5
Kalinko ○ RG 202-203 E 4
Kalip ○ PNG 183 F 3
Kalipagan ○ RP 160-161 F 10
Kalipucang ○ RI 168 C 3
Kaliro ○ EAU 212-213 D 3
Kalis ○ SP 208-209 J 4
Kalisat ○ RI 168 E 4
Kalisizo ○ EAU 212-213 C 4
Kalispel Indian Reservation ✗ USA (WA) 244-245 H 2
Kalispell ○ USA (MT) 250-251 E 3
Kalisz ☆ ·· PL 92-93 P 3
Kalitidu ○ RI 168 D 3
Kalitva ~ RUS 102-103 M 3
Kalitua ○ EAT 212-213 C 6
Kalivia ○ GR 100-101 J 6
Kalivita ~ RUS 102-103 M 3
Kaliwiro ○ RI 168 C 3
Kaliwungu ○ RI 168 D 3
Kalix ○ S 86-87 L 4
Kalixälven ~ S 86-87 L 3
Kaljazin ☆ ·· RUS 94-95 P 3
Ķalkaman ○ KZ 124-125 K 3
Kalkan ○ TR 128-129 C 4
Kalkaringi ○ AUS 172-173 K 4
Kalkaska ○ USA (MI) 272-273 D 3
Kalkbank ○ ZA 218-219 E 6
Kalkfeld ○ NAM 216-217 D 10
Kalkfontein = Tshootsha ○ RB 216-217 F 11
Kalkrand ○ NAM 220-221 C 2
Kalkuni ○ GUY 62-63 F 3
Ķalķūtan ~ KZ 124-125 G 3
Kallakkurichchi ○ IND 140-141 H 5
Kallam ○ IND 138-139 F 10
Kallambella ○ IND 140-141 G 4
Källandsö ⌒ S 86-87 F 7
Kallar ○ IND 140-141 F 4
Kallār ○ IRQ 128-129 L 5
Kallar Kahār ○ PK 138-139 D 3
Kalli ○ AUS 176-177 D 3
Kalli ○ EST 94-95 J 2
Kallidaikurichchi ○ IND 140-141 G 6
Kallislahti ○ FIN 88-89 K 6
Kallsjön ○ S 86-87 F 5
Ķalmaķķol, köli ○ KZ 124-125 E 2
Kalmakkyrğan ~ KZ 124-125 E 5
Kalmali ○ IND 140-141 G 2
Kalmanka ☆ RUS 124-125 N 2
Kalmar ☆ S 86-87 H 8
Kalmard ○ IR 134-135 G 2
Kalmard, Godār-e ▲ IR 134-135 G 2
Kalmarsund ≈ 86-87 H 8
Kalmeta ○ AUS 174-175 F 6
Kalmiopsis Wilderness Area ⊥ USA (OR) 244-245 B 8
Kal'mius ~ UA 102-103 K 4
Kalmunai ○ CL 140-141 J 7
Kalmykia = Hal'mg Tangč ◻ RUS 126-127 F 4
Kalmykovo ☆ KZ 96-97 G 9
Kalna ○ IND 142-143 F 4
Kalnciems ○ LV 94-95 H 3
Kalni ~ BD 142-143 G 3
Kalocsa ○ H 92-93 P 5
Kalohi Channel ≈ 288 H 4
Kalo Kalo ○ PNG 183 F 5
Kaloke ○ LB 202-203 G 7
Kalokitting ○ SUD 200-201 B 6
Kaloko ○ ZRE 214-215 C 4
Kalokol ○ EAK 212-213 E 2
Kālol ○ IND 138-139 D 8
Kalole ○ ZRE 212-213 A 5
Kalomo ○ Z (SOU) 218-219 D 3
Kalomo ~ Z 218-219 D 3
Kalona ○ USA (IA) 274-275 G 3
Kalone Peak ▲ CDN (BC) 228-229 H 4
Kalonje ○ Z 214-215 F 7
Kalosi ○ RI 164-165 F 5
Kalossia ○ EAK 212-213 E 3
Kalounka ○ RG 202-203 C 4
Kalourat, Mount ▲ SOL 184 I e 3
Kalpáki ○ GR 100-101 H 5
Kalpeni Island ⌒ IND 140-141 B 3
Kalpitiya ○ CL 140-141 H 6
Kalskag ○ USA 20-21 K 6
Kaltag ○ USA 20-21 L 4
Kaltamy ~ RUS 108-109 Z 7
Kaltasy ☆ RUS 96-97 J 6
Kaltinėnai ○ LT 94-95 H 4
Kaltuk ○ RUS 116-117 K 8
Kaltungo ○ WAN 204-205 J 4
Kaluga ☆ ·· RUS 94-95 P 4
Kalugumalai ○ IND 140-141 G 6
Kalu hrebet ▲ RUS 96-97 K 7
Kālu Khuhar ○ PK 134-135 M 6
Kaluluma ○ MW 214-215 G 7
Kalulushi ○ Z 214-215 E 7
Kaluma-Kanda ○ BD 142-143 G 3
Kalumbu, Mwadi- ○ ZRE 216-217 E 3
Kalumburu ✗ AUS 172-173 H 3
Kalumburu Aboriginal Land ✗ AUS 172-173 H 3
Kalumengongo ~ ZRE 214-215 D 5
Kalumpang ○ RI 164-165 F 5
Kalundborg ○ · DK 86-87 E 9
Kalundu ○ ZRE 212-213 B 5
Kalundwe ○ ZRE 214-215 C 4
Kalungu ~ Z 214-215 G 5
Kalungwishi ~ Z 214-215 E 5
Kalūr Kot ○ PK 138-139 C 3
Kaluš ☆ UA 102-103 D 3
Kalvakurti ○ IND 140-141 H 2
Kalvarija ○ ·· LT 94-95 H 4
Kalvesta ○ USA (KS) 262-263 F 6
Kalyān ○ IND 138-139 D 10
Kalyandrug ○ IND 140-141 G 3
Ķalybaj ○ KZ 126-127 O 3
Ķalybek, köli ○ KZ 124-125 G 2
Kalygir', buhta ≈ 120-121 S 7
Kalynivka ☆ UA 102-103 F 3
Kam ~ NAM 220-221 C 2
Kam, River ~ WAN 204-205 J 4
Kama ○ RMM 202-203 E 3
Kama ~ RUS 96-97 G 6
Kama ~ RUS 114-115 J 4
Kamada ○ TCH 198-199 G 4
Kamaday ○ TCH 206-207 E 3
Kamaishi ○ J 152-153 J 5
Kamakawalar, Danau ○ RI 166-167 H 3
Kamakwie ○ WAL 202-203 D 5
Kamal ○ RI 168 E 3
Kamal ○ TCH 198-199 H 2
Kamāl, Abū ☆ SYR 128-129 J 5
Kamale Mountain ▲ WAN 204-205 K 3
Kamālia ○ PK 138-139 D 4
Kamalo ○ USA (HI) 288 J 3
Kamalpur ○ IND 142-143 G 3
Kaman ☆ TR 128-129 E 3
Kamanga ○ EAT 212-213 D 5
Kamangu ○ Z 214-215 F 6
Kamanyola ○ ZRE 212-213 B 5
Kamāraj ○ IR 134-135 D 4
Kamarān ○ Y 132-133 C 6
Kamarān ⌒ Y 132-133 C 6
Kamarang ○ GUY 62-63 D 3
Kāmāreddi ○ IND 138-139 G 10
Kamaron ○ WAL 202-203 E 5
Kamarsuk ○ CDN 36-37 T 6
Kamas ○ USA (UT) 254-255 D 3
Kamaši ○ UZ 136-137 K 5
Kamativi ○ ZW 218-219 D 4
Kamba ○ WAN 204-205 E 3
Kamba Kota ○ RCA 206-207 C 5
Kambal ○ SUD 208-209 B 3
Kambalda ○ AUS 176-177 F 5
Kambal'naja Sopka, vulkan ▲ RUS 122-123 R 3
Kambal'nickie Koški, ostrova ⌒ RUS 88-89 T 2
Kambal'nyj, mys ▲ RUS 122-123 R 3
Kambang ○ RI 162-163 D 5
Kambarka ☆ RUS 96-97 J 5
Kamberatoro ○ PNG 183 A 2
Kambia ○ WAL 202-203 D 5
Kambolé ○ RT 202-203 L 5
Kambot ○ PNG 183 C 3
Kambove ○ ZRE 214-215 D 6
Kambuku ○ PNG 183 G 3
Kambūt ○ LAR 192-193 L 2
Kamčatka ~ RUS 120-121 T 5
Kamčatskij, mys ▲ RUS 120-121 U 5
Kamčatskij poluostrov ⌣ RUS 120-121 U 5
Kamčatsk, Ust'- ☆ RUS 120-121 U 5
Kamčatskij, Petropavlovsk- ☆ · RUS 120-121 S 7
Kamčatskij proliv ≈ 120-121 U 6
Kamčatskij zaliv ≈ 120-121 T 6
Kamchatka Peninsula = Kamčatka, poluostrov ⌣ RUS 120-121 Q 5
Kamdēš ○ · AFG 136-137 M 7
Kameasi ○ RI 164-165 G 4
Kameel ○ ZA 220-221 G 3
Kamélé ○ CI 202-203 J 5
Kamelik ~ RUS 96-97 F 8
Kamen' ○ BY 94-95 L 4
Kamende ○ ZRE 214-215 C 4
Kamenec-Podol'skij = Kam'janec'-Podil's'kyj ☆ UA 102-103 E 3
Kameng ○ AFG 134-135 L 1
Kameng ~ IND 142-143 H 2
Kamenica ○ BIH 100-101 G 3
Kamenka ☆ KZ 96-97 G 8
Kamenka ○ RUS (ARH) 88-89 S 4
Kamenka ○ RUS (IRK) 122-123 O 2
Kamenka ○ RUS (KRN) 116-117 G 6
Kamenka ○ RUS (PEN) 96-97 D 7
Kamenka ○ RUS (SML) 94-95 N 4
Kamenka ~ RUS 108-109 I d 2
Kamenka ~ RUS 110-111 d 6
Kamenka ~ RUS 116-117 G 6
Kamenka ~ RUS 124-125 O 2
Kamennaja, kosa ⊥ RUS 108-109 P 7
Kamennaja tundra ⊥ RUS 108-109 a 7
Kamen'-na-Obi ☆ RUS 124-125 M 2
Kamennik, gora ▲ RUS 88-89 N 3
Kamennogorsk ○ RUS 94-95 L 1
Kamennyj, Mys- ○ RUS 108-109 P 7
Kamennyj, mys ▲ RUS 110-111 c 2
Kamennyj Dubčes ~ RUS 114-115 T 4
Kamennyj Stolb, mys ▲ RUS 110-111 S 4
Kameno ○ BG 102-103 E 6
Kamen'-Rybolov ○ RUS 122-123 E 6
Kamenskoe ☆ RUS 112-113 U 5
Kamensk-Šahtinskij ○ RUS 102-103 M 3
Kamensk-Ural'skij ☆ RUS 96-97 M 5
Kamensk Ural'skiy = Kamensk-Ural'skij ☆ RUS 96-97 M 5
Kamenz ○ D 92-93 N 3
Kameshla ○ ZRE 214-215 D 5
Kameškova ~ RUS 112-113 M 3
Kameškovo ☆ RUS 94-95 R 3
Kāmet ▲ IND 138-139 G 4
Kameur, Bahr ~ RCA 206-207 E 4
Kamiah ○ USA (ID) 250-251 C 5
Kamienna, Skarżysko- ○ PL 92-93 Q 3
Kamiesberge ▲ ZA 220-221 C 5
Kamieskroon ○ ZA 220-221 C 5
Kami-Furano ○ J 152-153 K 3
Kamiiso ○ J 152-153 J 4
Kamiji ○ ZRE 214-215 B 4
Kamikawa ○ J 152-153 K 3
Kami-koshiki-shima ⌒ J 152-153 C 9
Kāmil, al- ○ KSA 130-131 F 6
Kāmil, al- ○ OM 132-133 L 2
Kamileroi ○ AUS 174-175 F 6
Kamilukuak Lake ○ CDN 30-31 T 4
Kamilukuak River ~ CDN 30-31 S 5
Kamimbi Fuka, Chute ~ ZRE 214-215 C 5
Kamina ○ PNG 183 C 4
Kamina ○ RT 202-203 L 5
Kamina ○ ZRE (SHA) 210-211 L 6
Kamina ○ ZRE (SHA) 214-215 C 5
Kamina Base ○ ZRE 214-215 C 5
Kaminak Lake ○ CDN 30-31 W 4
Kamin'-Kašyrs'kyj ○ UA 102-103 D 2
Kaminokuni ○ J 152-153 J 4
Kamino-shima ⌒ J 152-153 C 7
Kaminuriak Lake ○ CDN 30-31 W 4
Kamioka ○ J 152-153 G 6
Kamishak Bay ≈ 22-23 T 3
Kamishak River ~ USA 22-23 T 3
Kami-Shihoro ○ J 152-153 K 3
Kami-shima ⌒ J 152-153 D 8
Kamitsushima ○ J 152-153 C 7
Kamituga ○ ZRE 212-213 B 5
Kami-Yaku ○ J 152-153 D 9
Kamjana mohyla · UA 102-103 J 4
Kam'janec'-Podil's'kyj ☆ UA 102-103 E 3
Kamjani Mohyly · UA 102-103 K 4
Kamjanka ○ UA 102-103 H 3
Kam'janka ○ UA 102-103 G 4

Južnyj — Kam'janka 343

Kam'janske o UA 102-103 C 3
Kamjong o IND 142-143 J 3
Kamkaly o KZ 124-125 G 6
Kamloops o CDN (BC) 230-231 J 3
Kamloops Indian Reserve Ⅹ CDN (BC) 230-231 J 3
Kamloops Plateau ▲ CDN 230-231 J 3
Kammanassieberge ▲ ZA 220-221 F 6
Kammūniyah, Bi'r al o LAR 192-193 G 3
Kamo o AR 128-129 L 2
Kamo ~ RUS 116-117 H 5
Kāmoke o PK 138-139 E 4
Kamola o ZRE 214-215 D 4
Kamoro ▲ RM 222-223 E 6
Kamoro ~ RM 222-223 E 6
Kamoro, Tampoketsan'i ▲ RM 222-223 E 6
Kamoto o Z 218-219 G 1
Kamp 52 o SME 62-63 F 3
Kampa, Teluk ≈ 162-163 F 5
Kampa do Rio Amônea, Área Indígena Ⅹ BR 64-65 F 6
Kampala ★• EAU 212-213 D 3
Kampala o SUD 206-207 G 4
Kampar o MAL 162-163 D 2
Kampar ~ RI 162-163 E 4
Kamparkan ~ RI 162-163 D 4
Kamparkiri ~ RI 162-163 D 4
Kampene o ZRE 210-211 L 5
Kamphaeng Phet o THA 158-159 E 2
Kamphambale o MW 214-215 G 7
Kampi Katoto o EAT 214-215 G 4
Kampi Ya Moto o EAK 212-213 E 4
Kampli o IND 140-141 G 3
Kampolombo, Lake ⊂ Z 214-215 E 6
Kâmpóng Cham o K 158-159 H 4
Kâmpóng Chhnăng o K 158-159 H 4
Kâmpóng Saôm ≈ 158-159 G 5
Kâmpóng Saôm o K 158-159 G 5
Kâmpóng Spoe o K 158-159 H 5
Kâmpóng Thum o K 158-159 H 4
Kâmpóng Trach o K 158-159 H 5
Kâmpôt o K 158-159 H 5
Kampsville o USA (IL) 274-275 H 5
Kampti o BF 202-203 J 4
Kampumbu o Z 214-215 G 6
Kampung ~ RI 166-167 K 4
Kampung Ayer Puteh o MAL 162-163 E 2
Kampung Balok o MAL 162-163 E 3
Kampung Berawan o MAL 164-165 D 1
Kampung Buloh o MAL 162-163 E 2
Kampung Chenereh o MAL 162-163 E 2
Kampung Cherating o MAL 162-163 E 2
Kampung Jambu Bongkok o MAL 162-163 E 2
Kampung Jerangau o MAL 162-163 E 2
Kampung Kemara o MAL 162-163 E 2
Kampung Koh o MAL 162-163 D 2
Kampung Lamir o MAL 162-163 E 3
Kampung Laut o MAL 162-163 F 4
Kampung Leban Condong o MAL 162-163 E 3
Kampung Merang o MAL 162-163 E 2
Kampung Merting o MAL 162-163 E 2
Kampung Nibong o MAL 162-163 D 2
Kampung Penarik o MAL 162-163 E 2
Kampung Relok o MAL 162-163 E 2
Kampung Sekinchan o MAL 162-163 D 3
Kampung Sepat o MAL 162-163 E 3
Kampung Sook o MAL 160-161 B 10
Kampung Sungai Ayer Deras o MAL 162-163 E 2
Kampung Sungai Rengit o MAL 162-163 F 4
Kampung Tebingtinggi o RI 162-163 H 3
Kampung Tekek o• MAL 162-163 F 3
Kampung Tengah o MAL 162-163 F 4
Kampung Terolak o MAL 162-163 D 2
Kamrau, Teluk ≈ 166-167 G 3
Kamsack o CDN (SAS) 232-233 R 4
Kamsar o RG 202-203 C 4
Kamskoe Ust'e ☆ RUS 96-97 F 6
Kamskoe vodohranilišče < RUS 96-97 K 4
Kamskoye Vodokhranilishche = Kamskoe vodohranilišče < RUS 96-97 K 4
Kamsuuma o SP 212-213 J 3
Kāmthi o IND 138-139 G 9
Kamtsha ~ ZRE 210-211 G 6
Kamuchawi Lake ⊂ CDN 34-35 E 2
Kamudi o IND 140-141 H 6
Kamuela o USA (HI) 288 K 4
Kamuj, gora ▲ RUS 122-123 N 6
Kámuk, Cerro ▲ CR 52-53 C 7
Kamuli o EAU 212-213 D 3
Kamušnyj ☆ KZ 124-125 B 3
Kamutambai ~ ZRE 214-215 B 4
Kam'yanets'-Podil'skyy = Kam'janec'-Podil'skyj ☆ UA 102-103 E 3
Kāmyārān o IR 134-135 B 1
Kamyšanovka o KS 146-147 B 4
Kamyšet o RUS 116-117 J 8
Kamyševatskaja o RUS 102-103 K 4
Kamyševka o RUS 114-115 H 6
Kamyshin = Kamyšin o RUS 96-97 D 8
Kamyšin o RUS 96-97 D 8
Kamysköl o KZ 96-97 H 10
Kamyšlov ☆ RUS 114-115 G 6
Kamyšovyj, Južno-, hrebet ▲ RUS 122-123 K 5
Kamyšovyj hrebet ▲ RUS 122-123 K 3
Kamys-Samarkölinin kujmasy ⊂ KZ 96-97 G 9
Kamysty-Ajat ~ KZ 124-125 B 2
Kamystybas, köl ⊂ KZ 126-127 O 4
Kamyzjak ☆ RUS (AST) 96-97 F 10
Kamyzjak ~ RUS 126-127 H 5
Kan ~ RUS 116-117 G 7
Kan o UZ 136-137 K 5
Kanaaupscow, Rivière ~ CDN 36-37 M 7
Kanab o USA (UT) 254-255 C 6
Kanab Creek ~ USA 256-257 C 2
Kanacea ⌒ FJI 184 III c 2
Kanadej o RUS 96-97 E 7
Kanaga Pass ≈ 22-23 H 7
Kanagi o J 152-153 J 4
Kanaima Fall ~ GUY 62-63 D 2
Kanairiktok River ~ CDN 36-37 S 7
Kanā'is, Ra's al- ▲ ET 194-195 C 2
Kanaka o RI 166-167 G 3
Kanakakee River ~ USA 274-275 L 3
Kanakapura o IND 140-141 G 4
Kanakatte o IND 140-141 G 4
Kanakoro o BF 202-203 G 4
Kanaktok Mount ▲ USA 20-21 L 3
Kanamari do Rio Juruá, Área Indígena Ⅹ BR 66-67 C 6
Kananaskis River ~ CDN 232-233 C 5
Kananga ☆ ZRE 210-211 J 6
Kananggar o RI 168 E 8
Kanangio, Mount ▲ PNG 183 C 3
Kanangra Boyd National Park ⊥ AUS 180-181 L 2
Kananto o GH 202-203 K 5
Kananyga ~ RUS 120-121 Q 3
Kanaraville o USA (UT) 254-255 B 6
Kanas o IND 138-139 E 8
Kanaš o RUS 96-97 E 6
Kanatak o USA 22-23 S 4
Kanawha o USA (IA) 274-275 E 2
Kanawha River ~ USA 280-281 D 5
Kanawi, Pulau ⌒ MAL 160-161 B 10
Kanazawa ☆• J 152-153 G 6
Kanazi o EAT 212-213 C 4
Kanbalu o MYA 142-143 J 4
Kanbe o MYA 158-159 D 2
Kanbi ~ BF 202-203 K 3
Kančalan o RUS (CUK) 112-113 T 4
Kančalan ~ RUS 112-113 T 4
Kanchana Buri o THA 158-159 E 3
Kanchanadit o THA 158-159 E 6
Kanchanpur o NEP 144-145 F 7
Kanchenjunga ▲ NEP 144-145 G 7
Kanchibya ~ Z 214-215 F 6
Kānchipuram o•• IND 140-141 H 4
Kanci o RI 168 C 3
Kandahar o CDN (SAS) 232-233 O 4
Kandahār o IND 138-139 F 10
Kandahar = Qandahār ☆•• AFG 134-135 L 3
Kandalakša o RUS 88-89 M 3
Kandalakshskaya Guba = Kandalakšskaja guba ≈ 88-89 M 3
Kandalakšskaja guba ≈ 88-89 M 3
Kandalakšskij bereg ⌣ RUS 88-89 M 3
Kandang o RI 162-163 B 3
Kandangan o RI 164-165 D 5
Kandanghaur o RI 168 C 3
Kandar o RI 166-167 F 6
Kandare o WAN 204-205 H 4
Kandé o RT 202-203 L 5
Kandéko ~ RCB 210-211 F 3
Kandep o PNG 183 B 3
Kandero o DY 204-205 E 3
Kandi o DY 204-205 E 3
Kāndi o IND 142-143 F 4
Kandi, Tanjung ▲ RI 164-165 G 3
Kandiadiou o SN 202-203 B 3
Kandiāro o PK 138-139 B 6
Kandika o RG 202-203 D 3
Kandik River ~ USA 20-21 T 4
Kandil Bouzou o RN 198-199 E 5
Kandıra ☆ TR 128-129 D 2
Kandja ö RCA 206-207 E 6
Kandkhot o PK 138-139 B 5
Kāndla o IND 138-139 C 8
Kando ~ ZRE 214-215 D 6
Kandololo o ZRE 210-211 K 3
Kandos o AUS 180-181 K 2
Kandreho o RM 222-223 E 6
Kandrian o PNG 183 E 4
Kandry ☆ RUS 96-97 J 6
Kanduanam o PNG 183 B 3
Kandukūr o IND 140-141 H 3
Kandy o••• CL 140-141 J 7
Kane o CDN (MAN) 234-235 F 5
Kane, Kap ▲ GRØ 26-27 e 2
Kane Basin ≈ 26-27 P 4
Kane Fracture Zone ≃ 6-7 D 6
Kanektok River ~ USA 22-23 Q 3
Kanel o SN 202-203 D 2
Kanem ◘ TCH 198-199 G 5
Kaneohe o USA (HI) 288 H 3
Kaneohe Bay ≈ 288 H 3
Kanevka o RUS 88-89 P 3
Kanevskaja o RUS 102-103 L 4
Kanferandé o RG 202-203 C 4
Kang o AFG 134-135 J 3
Kang o RB 218-219 B 6
Kangaamiut = Gammel Sukkertoppen o GRØ 28-29 O 4
Kangaatsiaq o GRØ 28-29 O 2
Kangahun o WAL 202-203 D 5
Kangal ☆ TR 128-129 G 3
Kangalassy o RUS 118-119 O 4
Kangalas-Uėle ~ RUS 110-111 L 3
Kangān o IR 134-135 E 5
Kangān Čam ~ IR 134-135 B 2
Kangar ☆ MAL 162-163 D 1
Kangara o RMM 202-203 F 4
Kangaré o RMM 202-203 F 4
Kangaroo Island ⌒•• AUS 180-181 D 3
Kangaroo Valley ⌣ AUS 180-181 L 3
Kangasniemi o FIN 88-89 J 6
Kangāvar o• IR 134-135 B 1
Kangding o VRC 154-155 B 6
Kangdong o KOR 150-151 F 8
Kangean, Kepulauan ⌒ RI 168 B 6
Kangean, Pulau ⌒ RI 168 B 6
Kangeeak Point ▲ CDN 28-29 H 3
Kangen ~ SUD 208-209 A 5
Kangeq ⌒ GRØ 26-27 X 7
Kangerdluarssuk ≈ 26-27 Y 8
Kangerdlugssuaq ≈ 26-27 Y 8
Kangerdluluk Fjord ≈ 28-29 T 6
Kangerluarsoruseq = Færingehavn o GRØ 28-29 P 5
Kangerluarsuk o GRØ 28-29 O 4
Kangerluk = Diskofjord o GRØ 28-29 N 2
Kangerlussuaq ≈ 26-27 Y 8
Kangerlussuaq ≈ 28-29 O 3
Kangerlussuaq ≈ 28-29 Y 2
Kangerlussuaq = Søndrestrømfjord o GRØ 28-29 P 3
Kangersuneq ≈ 28-29 P 4
Kangertitsivaq ≈ 28-29 X 3
Kangertittivag = Scoresby Sund ≈ 26-27 o 8
Kanghwa o ROK 150-151 F 9
Kanghwa Do ⌒ ROK 150-151 F 9
Kangi o SUD 206-207 H 4
Kangik o USA 20-21 L 1
Kangikajip Appalia = Brewster, Kap ▲ GRØ 26-27 p 8
Kangilinnguit = Grønnedal o GRØ 28-29 Q 6
Kangilo Fiord ≈ 28-29 G 3
Kangiqsujuak o CDN 36-37 O 4
Kangiwa o WAN 204-205 E 2
Kangkir o VRC 144-145 B 2
Kang Kra Chan National Park ⊥• THA 158-159 E 4
Kangmar o VRC 144-145 G 6
Kangnŭng o ROK 150-151 G 9
Kango o G 210-211 C 3
Kangole o EAU 212-213 E 2
Kangonde o EAK 212-213 F 4
Kangounadéni o BF 202-203 H 4
Kangping o VRC 150-151 D 6
Kangrinboqê Feng ▲ VRC 144-145 C 5
Kangsar, Kuala o• MAL 162-163 D 2
Kangto ▲ IND 142-143 H 2
Kangye ☆ KOR 150-151 F 7
Kangzigyai ▲ VRC 146-147 N 6
Kanha National Park ⊥• IND 142-143 B 4
Kanhar ~ IND 142-143 C 4
Kani o• CI 202-203 G 5
Kani o J 152-153 G 7
Kani o MYA 142-143 J 4
Kaniama o ZRE 214-215 C 4
Kaniasso o CI 202-203 G 5
Kanibadam o TJ 136-137 M 4
Kanibes ~ NAM 220-221 C 2
Kanigiri o IND 140-141 H 3
Kanimeh o UZ 136-137 J 4
Kanin, poluostrov ⌣ RUS 88-89 S 3
Kanin Kamen' ▲ RUS 88-89 R 2
Kanin Nos o RUS 88-89 R 2
Kanin Nos, mys ▲ RUS 88-89 R 2
Kaninskaja tundra ⊥ RUS 88-89 S 3
Kanioumé o RMM 202-203 J 2
Kanisa o SUD 200-201 E 3
Kanita o J 152-153 J 4
Kaniva o AUS 180-181 F 4
Kanivs'ke vodoschovyšče < UA 102-103 G 2
Kaniya o PNG 183 B 4
Kanji-dong o KOR 150-151 G 7
Kanjirapalli o IND 140-141 G 6
Kanjiroba ▲ NEP 144-145 D 6
Kankaanpää o FIN 88-89 G 6
Kankakee o USA (IL) 274-275 L 3
Kankakee River ~ USA 274-275 K 3
Kankalabé o RG 202-203 E 4
Kankan ◘ RG 202-203 E 4
Kankan ☆ RG (KAN) 202-203 F 4
Kankara o WAN 204-205 G 3
Kankelaba ~ RMM 202-203 G 4
Kānker o IND 142-143 B 5
Kankesanturai o CL 140-141 J 6
Kankiya o WAN 198-199 C 6
Kankossa o RIM 196-197 E 7
Kankunskij o RUS 118-119 N 7
Kanmaw Kyun ⌒ MYA 158-159 E 5
Kann o IR 136-137 B 7
Kanna o MYA 142-143 K 6
Kannad o IND 138-139 E 9
Kannapolis o USA (NC) 282-283 G 5
Kannata Valley o CDN (SAS) 232-233 O 5
Kannavam o IND 140-141 F 5
Kannoka = Sillamäe o EST 94-95 K 2
Kannonkoski o FIN 88-89 H 5
Kannonsaha o FIN 88-89 H 5
Kannus o FIN 88-89 G 5
Kano o J 152-153 D 7
Kano o RMM 202-203 F 3
Kano ◘ WAN 204-205 H 3
Kano ☆•• WAN (KAN) 198-199 D 6
Kano, River ~ WAN 204-205 H 3
Kanobe, Pulau ⌒ RI 166-167 F 1
Kanona o Z 218-219 F 1
Kanon Nak o VN 158-159 K 3
Kanoni o ZRE 214-215 D 6
Kanono o NAM 218-219 C 3
Kanopolis Lake ⊂ USA (KS) 262-263 H 6
Kanorado o USA (KS) 262-263 D 5
Kanoroba o CI 202-203 G 5
Kanosh o USA (UT) 254-255 C 5
Kanouri ⊥ RN 198-199 F 5
Kanovlei o NAM 216-217 E 9
Kanowit o MAL 162-163 K 3
Kanowna ∴ AUS 176-177 F 5
Kanoya o J 152-153 D 9
Kanozero o RUS 88-89 N 3
Kanpur o IND 142-143 B 2
Kansanshi o Z 214-215 D 7
Kansas o USA (IL) 274-275 L 5
Kansas o USA (OK) 264-265 K 2
Kansas ◘ USA 262-263 F 6
Kansas City o USA (KS) 262-263 M 5
Kansas City o USA (MO) 274-275 D 5
Kansas River ~ USA 262-263 K 5
Kanšengel' o KZ 124-125 J 6
Kansenia o ZRE 214-215 D 6
Kansk ☆ RUS 116-117 G 7
Kantah o CDN 30-31 J 6
Kantah River ~ CDN 32-33 K 3
Kantalai o CL 140-141 J 6
Kantang o THA 158-159 E 7
Kantchari o BF 202-203 L 3
Kantche o RN 198-199 D 6
Kantegir ~ RUS 116-117 E 9
Kantemirovka o KZ 136-137 M 3
Kantemirovka o RUS 102-103 L 3
Kantharalak o THA 158-159 H 3
Kānthi o IND 142-143 E 5
Kantishna o USA 20-21 P 5
Kantishna River ~ USA 20-21 P 4
Kanto-sanchi ▲ J 152-153 H 6
Kantunil o MEX 52-53 K 1
Kanuku Mountains ▲ GUY 62-63 E 4
Kanur o IND 140-141 G 3
Kanus o NAM 220-221 D 3
Kanuti River ~ USA (AK) 20-21 O 3
Kanu Woralaksaburi o THA 158-159 E 2
Kanye ☆ RB 220-221 G 2
Kanyemba o ZW 218-219 F 2
Kanyilombi o Z 214-215 C 7
Kanym Bol'šoj, gora ▲ RUS 114-115 U 7
Kanyš-Kija o KS 136-137 M 4
Kanyu o RB 218-219 C 5
Kao o RN 198-199 B 5
Kao ⌒ TON 184 IV a 1
Kaoboul, Termit- o RN 198-199 E 5
Kaôh Kŏng ⌒ K 158-159 G 5
Kaôh Rŭng ⌒ K 158-159 G 5
Kaôh Rŭng Sâmlŏem ⌒ K 158-159 G 5
Kaohsiung o RC 156-157 M 5
Kaôh Tang ⌒ K 158-159 G 5
Kaôh Thmei ⌒ K 158-159 G 5
Kaoka o SOL 184 I e 3
Kaokaona ☆ SOL 184 I e 4
Kaokoveld ⊥ NAM 216-217 B 8
Kaolack ☆ SN 202-203 B 2
Kaolak River ~ USA 20-21 K 2
Kaolé o RIM 196-197 F 6
Kaoleni o EAK 212-213 G 5
Kaole Ruins • EAT 214-215 K 4
Kaolinovo o BG 102-103 E 6
Kaolo o SOL 184 I d 3
Kaoma o Z 218-219 C 2
Kaouadja o RCA (Kot) 206-207 F 5
Kaouadja ~ RCA 206-207 F 4
Kaouadja ~ RCA 206-207 G 5
Kap o IND 138-139 G 10
Kap o PK 134-135 K 5
Kapa o MYA 158-159 E 4
Kapaa o USA (HI) 288 F 2
Kapaahu o USA (HI) 288 K 5
Kapaau o USA (HI) 288 K 4
Kapadokya ⊥ TR 128-129 F 4
Kapadvanj o IND 138-139 D 8
Kapaimeri o PNG 183 B 3
Kapalabuaya o RI 164-165 K 4
Kapalala o Z 214-215 E 7
Kapandae o GH 202-203 K 5
Kapande ~ ZRE 214-215 D 6
Kapanga o ZRE 214-215 B 5
Kapangan o RP 160-161 D 4
Kapapa o ZRE 214-215 E 5
Kapatu ~ EAT 212-213 E 6
Kapatu o Z 214-215 F 5
Kapau River ~ PNG 183 D 4
Kapchorwa o EAU 212-213 E 3
Kapčiamiestis o LT 94-95 H 4
Kapedo o EAK 212-213 F 3
Kapema o ZRE 214-215 E 6
Kapenguria o EAK 212-213 E 3
Kapia o ZRE 210-211 G 6
Kapichira Falls ~ MW 218-219 H 2
Kapini o LV 94-95 K 3
Kapip o PK 138-139 B 4
Kapiri Mposhi o Z 218-219 E 1
Kāpīsā ◘ AFG 138-139 B 2
Kapisillit o GRØ 28-29 P 4
Kapiskau River ~ CDN 34-35 O 4
Kapiskong Lake ⊂ CDN (ONT) 236-237 G 5
Kapit o MAL 162-163 K 3
Kapiti Island ⌒ NZ 182 E 4
Kapiura River ~ PNG 183 E 3
Kapka, Massif du ▲ TCH 198-199 K 5
Kaplamada, Gunung ▲ RI 166-167 D 3
Kaplan o USA (LA) 268-269 H 7
Kaplankyr, plato ▲ UZ 136-137 E 4
Kaplankyrskij zapovednik ⊥ TM 136-137 E 4
Kapoe o THA 158-159 E 6
Kapoeta o SUD 208-209 A 6
Ka Poh National Park ⊥• THA 158-159 E 5
Kapoke o Z 214-215 F 5
Kapona o ZRE 214-215 E 4
Kapondai, Tanjung ▲ RI 166-167 B 6
Kaponde o ZRE 214-215 B 4
Kapong o THA 158-159 E 6
Kapoposang, Pulau ⌒ RI 164-165 F 6
Kaporo o MW 214-215 G 5
Kaposvár o H 92-93 O 5
Kapotakshi ~ BD 142-143 F 4
Kappar o PK 134-135 K 6
Kappelskär o S 86-87 J 7
Kappelshamn o S 86-87 J 8
Kapp Platen ▲ N 84-85 N 2
Kapps o NAM 216-217 D 11
Kapsabet o EAK 212-213 E 3
Kapsan o KOR 150-151 G 7
Kapsaouis, Rivière ~ CDN 36-37 K 7
Kāpsi o IND 140-141 F 2
Kapsiki ▲• CAM 204-205 K 3
Kaptai o BD 142-143 H 4
Kaptai Lake ⊂ BD 142-143 H 4
Kaptiau o RI 166-167 K 3
Kapuas ~ RI 162-163 H 5
Kapuas ~ RI 164-165 D 5
Kapuas Hulu, Banjaran ▲ MAL 162-163 K 4
Kapur Utara, Pegunungan ▲ RI 168 D 3
Kapuskasing o CDN (ONT) 236-237 F 3
Kapuskasing River ~ CDN 236-237 F 3
Kapuskasing River ~ CDN 236-237 F 4
Kapustin Jar o RUS 96-97 D 9
Kaputa o Z 214-215 E 5
Kaputar National Park, Mount ⊥ AUS 178-179 L 6
Kaputirr o EAK 212-213 E 2
Kap Walløe Banke ≃ 28-29 T 6
Kapydžik, gora ▲ AZ 128-129 L 3
Kapyljuši, ozero ⊂ RUS 118-119 F 8
Kara o RI 166-167 C 5
Kara ☆ RT (DLK) 202-203 L 5
Kara ~ RT 202-203 L 5
Kara, Ust'- o RUS 108-109 L 7
Kara ~ RUS 108-109 L 7
Karaba, Ra's ▲ KSA 130-131 E 5
Kara-Balta = Kara-Balty o KS 136-137 N 3
Kara-Balty o KS 136-137 N 3
Karabaš ☆ RUS 96-97 M 6
Karabastau o KZ 136-137 M 3
Karabau o KZ 96-97 H 9
Karabaur, pastiligi ▲ KZ 126-127 L 6
Karabekaul o TM 136-137 J 5
Karabil', vozvyšennost' ▲ TM 136-137 H 6
Karabinka o RUS 124-125 P 2
Kara-Bogaz-Gol = Garabogazköl ≈ 136-137 C 4
Karabogazköl, zaliv ≈ 136-137 C 4
Karabuget o KZ 124-125 H 6
Karabük ☆ TR 128-129 E 2
Karabula o RUS (KRN) 116-117 H 6
Karabula ~ RUS 116-117 H 7
Karabulak o KZ 136-137 L 3
Karaburun ☆ TR 128-129 B 3
Karabutak ☆ KZ 126-127 O 3
Karaca Dağ ▲ TR 128-129 H 4
Karačaevsk o RUS 126-127 D 6
Karacaköy o TR 128-129 C 2
Karacasu ☆ TR 128-129 C 4
Karacek, köl ⊂ KZ 126-127 L 6
Karačev o RUS 94-95 O 5
Karachay-Cherkessia = Karačaj-Čerkes Respublika ◘ RUS 126-127 D 6
Karāchi ☆• PK (SIN) 134-135 M 6
Karāchi ☆• PK (SIN) 138-139 A 7
Karaçoban ☆ TR 128-129 K 3
Karād o IND 140-141 F 2
Kara Deniz ≈ 128-129 D 1
Karadeniz Boğazi = Bosporus ≈ 128-129 C 2
Karaespe ~ KZ 124-125 E 5
Karağ o IR 136-137 B 7
Karaga o GH 202-203 K 5
Karaga, buhta ≈ 120-121 U 4
Karagaj ☆ RUS 96-97 J 4
Karagajly o KZ 124-125 J 4
Karagajly-Ajat ~ RUS 124-125 B 2
Karagandy ☆ KZ 124-125 H 4
Karagandysay o KZ 126-127 L 2
Karagaz, hrebet ▲ TM 136-137 D 5
Karagije, vpadina ⌣ KZ 126-127 J 6
Karaginskij, ostrov ⌒ RUS 120-121 V 4
Karaginskij zaliv ≈ 120-121 U 4
Karagoš, gora ▲ RUS 124-125 Q 3
Karagüney Dağı ▲ TR 128-129 E 2
Karahalli ☆ TR 128-129 C 3
Kara Hobda ~ KZ 126-127 M 2
Karaiai o PNG 183 E 3
Karaidel' ☆ RUS 96-97 K 6
Karaisalı ☆ TR 128-129 F 4
Karaitem o PNG 183 B 2
Karajagi o IND 140-141 F 2
Karaja Masel'ga o RUS 88-89 N 5
Karak o MAL 162-163 E 3
Karak, al- ☆• JOR 130-131 D 2
Kara-Kabak o KS 136-137 N 5
Kara-Kala o TM 136-137 E 5
Karakamys o KZ 96-97 H 9
Karakax He ~ VRC 144-145 C 2
Karakaya Barajı < TR 128-129 H 3
Karakeçi o TR 128-129 H 4
Karakeču ⊥ KZ 126-127 K 5
Karakelong, Kepulauan ⌒ RI 164-165 K 1
Kara-Kengir ~ KZ 124-125 E 4
Karaketang, Pulau ⌒ RI 164-165 J 2
Karaklis o AR 128-129 L 2
Karakoçan ☆ TR 128-129 J 3
Karakojyn köli ⊂ KZ 124-125 F 5
Karakol o KS 146-147 C 5
Karaköl o KZ (GUR) 96-97 H 9
Karaköl o KZ (KZL) 126-127 O 5
Karaköl o KZ (KZL) 124-125 D 6
Karaköl, köl ⊂ KZ 126-127 N 3
Karakoram ▲ IND 138-139 E 1
Kara K'orē o ETH 208-209 D 3
Karakoro ~ RMM 202-203 E 2
Karakorum Highway II PK 138-139 E 1
Karakorum Shankou ▲ VRC 138-139 F 2
Karakovaja ~ RUS 120-121 S 6
Karaktau, gory ▲ KZ 136-137 K 3
Kara-Kudzur ~ KS 146-147 C 5
Kara-Kul' o KS 136-137 N 4
Karakul' o KS 136-137 H 5
Karakul' o UZ 136-137 H 5
Karakul', ozero ⊂ TJ 136-137 N 5
Kara-Kul'dža o KS 136-137 N 4
Karakulino o RUS 96-97 H 5
Karakum = KZ 126-127 M 4
Kara Kum = Garagum ⊥ TM 136-137 E 4
Karakumskij kanal < TM (ASH) 136-137 F 5
Karakumskij kanal < TM (MAR) 136-137 H 6
Karal o TCH 198-199 G 6
Karal'ka ~ RUS 114-115 R 3
Karalundi Mission o AUS 176-177 E 3
Karam o RUS 116-117 N 8
Karama ~ RI 164-165 F 5
Karamadai o IND 140-141 G 5
Karaman ☆• TR 128-129 E 4
Karamanbeyli Geçidi ▲ TR 128-129 D 4
Karamay o VRC 146-147 G 3
Karambu o RI 164-165 E 5
Karamea o NZ 182 D 4
Karamea Bight ≈ 182 C 4
Karamet-Nijaz o TM 136-137 J 6
Karami, River ~ WAN 204-205 H 3
Karamian, Pulau ⌒ RI 164-165 D 6
Karamiran o VRC 144-145 E 2
Karamiran He ~ VRC 144-145 E 2
Karamken o RUS 120-121 O 3
Karamoja ◘ EAU 212-213 D 2
Karamor, Pegunungan ▲ RI 166-167 K 3
Karamyk o KS 136-137 M 5
Karamyševo o RUS 116-117 K 7
Karān ⌒ KSA 130-131 L 4
Karang o SN 202-203 B 3
Karangampel o RI 168 C 3
Karanganyar o RI 168 D 3
Karangasem = Amlapura o• RI 168 B 7
Karangboto, Tanjung ▲ RI 168 C 3
Karanggede o RI 168 D 3
Karangjati o RI 168 D 3
Karangnunggal o RI 168 C 3
Karangoua ~ RCB 210-211 D 3
Karangpandan o RI 168 D 3
Karangua o Z 214-215 D 7
Karanguana o RMM 202-203 H 3
Kāranja o IND 138-139 F 9
Karanji o IND 138-139 G 9
Karanpur o IND 138-139 D 5
Karaoba o KZ 126-127 M 4
Karaoj o KZ 124-125 J 6
Karap o PNG 183 C 3
Karapınar ☆ TR 128-129 E 4
Karapuz ~ RUS 114-115 P 7
Karara o AUS 178-179 L 5
Kararaô, Área Indígena Ⅹ BR 68-69 B 4
Kararim, Al o LAR 192-193 F 1
Karas, Pulau ⌒ RI 166-167 G 3
Kara-Saj o KS 146-147 C 5
Kara-Sal ~ RUS 126-127 F 5
Karasavvon o FIN 88-89 G 2
Karasburg ☆ NAM 220-221 D 4
Karas'e, ozero Bol'šoe ⊂ RUS 114-115 J 5
Kara Sea = Karskoe more ≈ 108-109 J 6
Karašek, Ozero = köl Karacek ⊂ KZ 126-127 L 6
Karasjok o N 86-87 M 2
Karašjokka ~ N 86-87 M 2
Karasor, köli ⊂ KZ 124-125 K 3
Karasor, köli ⊂ KZ (KRG) 124-125 J 4
Karasor, köli ⊂ KZ (PVL) 124-125 J 3
Karasu ☆ TR 128-129 D 2
Karasu ~ TR 128-129 K 3
Karasu-Aras Dağları ▲ TR 128-129 J 3
Karasu Çayı ~ TR 128-129 G 4
Karasuk ☆ RUS 124-125 L 2
Karasuk Hills ▲ EAK 212-213 E 2
Kara-Suu o KS 136-137 N 4
Karāt o IR 134-135 J 1
Karatajka o RUS 108-109 J 7
Karatal ~ KZ 124-125 K 6
Karatas o KZ 136-137 L 4
Karataş ☆ TR 128-129 F 4
Karataš, gora ▲ RUS 96-97 L 7
Karatau o KZ (DZM) 136-137 M 3
Karatau ▲ KZ 126-127 J 6
Karatau hrebet ▲ RUS 96-97 K 6
Karatau žotasy ▲ KZ 124-125 E 6
Karatina o EAK 212-213 F 4
Karatöbe ☆ KZ 96-97 H 9
Karatogaj o KZ 124-125 O 4
Karaton o KZ 96-97 H 10
Kara-Torgaj ~ KZ 124-125 E 4
Karats o S 86-87 J 3
Karatschi = Karāchi ☆• PK 138-139 A 7
Karatsu o J 152-153 C 8
Karatu o EAT 212-213 E 5
Karatulej, sor ⊥ KZ 126-127 L 5
Karatung, Pulau ⌒ RI 164-165 K 1
Karatürk o KZ 146-147 C 4
Karaudanawa o GUY 62-63 E 4
Karaul o RUS 108-109 U 6
Karaulbazar o UZ 136-137 J 5
Karauli o IND 138-139 F 6
Karaungir ⊥ KZ 124-125 K 5
Karauwi o PNG 183 C 4
Karaülj o KZ 124-125 L 4
Karavan o KS 136-137 M 4
Karavānsarāy-ye Šams o IR 134-135 F 3
Karavās o GR 100-101 J 6
Karawa o ZRE 210-211 H 2
Karawanella o CL 140-141 J 7
Karawang o RI 168 B 3
Karawang, Tanjung ▲ RI 168 B 2
Karawanken ▲ A 92-93 M 5
Karawari River ~ PNG 183 B 3
Karayazı ☆ TR 128-129 K 3
Karaye o WAN 204-205 H 3
Karayulgun o VRC 146-147 E 5
Karažal o KZ 124-125 G 5
Karažal ☆ KZ 124-125 G 4
Karbalā' ◘ IRQ 128-129 J 6
Karbalā' ☆• IRQ (KAR) 128-129 L 6
Kårböle o S 86-87 G 6
Karbulik o RUS 116-117 O 9
Karchat o PK 134-135 M 6
Karda o RUS 116-117 L 8
Kardakáta o GR 100-101 H 5
Kardeljevo = Ploče o HR 100-101 F 3
Karditsa o GR 100-101 H 5
Kardiva Channel ≈ 140-141 B 5
Kärdla ☆ EST 94-95 H 2
Kărdžali o BG 102-103 D 7
Kărdžali o BG 102-103 D 7
Karé, Monts ▲ RCA 206-207 C 5
Kareeberge ▲ ZA 220-221 E 5
Kareebospoort ▲ ZA 220-221 F 5
Karegari o PNG 183 B 3
Karelia = Karelija ⊥ RUS 88-89 L 6
Karelia = Karelija, Respublika ◘ RUS 88-89 M 5
Karelka ~ RUS 108-109 E 5
Karel'skij bereg ⌣ RUS 88-89 M 3
Karema o EAT 214-215 F 4
Karema o PNG 183 D 5
Karenga ~ RUS 118-119 H 8
Karenga, Ust'- o RUS 118-119 H 8
Karengi o WAN 204-205 E 3
Karera o IND 138-139 G 7
Karesuando o S 86-87 L 2
Kārevāndar o IR 134-135 J 5
Kargal o IND 140-141 F 3
Kargala o RUS (ORB) 96-97 J 8
Kargala o RUS (TOM) 114-115 R 6
Kargalinskaja o RUS 126-127 G 6
Kargalytau ▲ KZ 126-127 J 2
Kargapol'e ☆ RUS 114-115 H 6
Kargasok ☆ RUS 114-115 Q 5
Kargat ☆ RUS (NVS) 114-115 Q 7
Kargat ~ RUS 114-115 Q 7
Kargat, Forpost- o RUS 114-115 Q 7
Kargı ☆ TR 128-129 F 2
Kargil o IND 138-139 F 2
Kargopol' ☆ RUS 88-89 P 6
Karguéri o RN 198-199 E 6
Karhe, Rūd-e ~ IR 134-135 C 3
Karhe, Rūdhāne-ye ~ IR 134-135 D 3
Kari o WAN 204-205 J 3
Karia o PNG 183 F 2
Karianga o RM 222-223 E 9
Kariba o ZW 218-219 E 3
Kariba, Lake < Z 218-219 D 3
Kariba-yama ▲ J 152-153 H 3
Karibib ☆ NAM 216-217 C 10
Karie o SOL 184 I f 4
Kariega ~ ZA 220-221 F 6
Kariés o GR 100-101 K 4
Karigasniemi o FIN 88-89 H 2
Karikachi-tōge ▲ J 152-153 K 3
Kārikāl o IND 140-141 H 5
Karikari, Cape ▲ NZ 182 D 1
Karilatsi o EST 94-95 K 2
Karima o SUD 200-201 E 3
Karimabad o• IND 138-139 E 1
Karimama o DY 204-205 E 2
Karimata, Kepulauan ⌒ RI 162-163 H 5
Karimata, Pulau ⌒ RI 162-163 H 5
Karimata Strait = Karimata, Selat ≈ 162-163 G 5
Karimbola ⊥ RM 222-223 D 10
Karimganj o IND 142-143 H 3
Karimnagar o IND 138-139 G 10
Karimui o PNG 183 C 4
Karimui, Mount ▲ PNG 183 C 4
Karimun, Pulau ⌒ RI 162-163 E 4
Karimunjawa, Kepulauan ⌒ RI 168 D 2
Karin o SP 208-209 G 3
Karina o WAL 202-203 E 5
Karipuna, Área Indígena Ⅹ BR 66-67 E 7
Karisimbi, Mount ▲ RWA 212-213 B 4
Káristos o GR 100-101 K 5
Karitiana, Área Indígena Ⅹ BR 66-67 E 7
Kariya o J 152-153 G 7
Kāriyāpatti o IND 140-141 H 6
Karjala ⊥ FIN 88-89 K 6
Karjat o IND 138-139 E 10
Kārkal o IND 140-141 F 4
Karkar o PNG 183 C 3
Karkaraly o KZ 124-125 J 4
Karkar Island ⌒ PNG 183 D 3
Karkas, Kūh-e ▲ IR 134-135 D 2
Karkh o PK 134-135 M 5
Karkinits'ka zatoka ≈ 102-103 H 5
Karkonosze ▲ PL 92-93 N 3
Karksi-Nuia o•• EST 94-95 J 2
Karla-Aleksandra, ostrov ⌒ RUS 84-85 e 2
Karlaralong, Kepulauan ⌒ RI 164-165 J 1
Karleby = Kokkola o FIN 88-89 G 5
Karlik ▲ VRC 146-147 L 4
Karlıova ☆ TR 128-129 J 3
Karlivka o UA 102-103 J 3
Karl-Marx-Stadt = Chemnitz o D 92-93 M 3
Karlobag o HR 100-101 E 2
Karlo-Libknehtovsk = Soledar o UA 102-103 L 3
Karlovac o HR 100-101 E 2
Karlovássi o GR 100-101 L 6
Karlovo o BG 102-103 D 6
Karlovy Vary o CZ 92-93 M 3
Karlsbad = Karlovy Vary o CZ 92-93 M 3
Karlsborg ☆ S 86-87 G 7
Karlsena, mys ▲ RUS 108-109 M 3
Karlshamn ☆ S 86-87 G 8
Karlskoga ☆ S 86-87 G 7
Karlskrona ☆ S 86-87 G 8
Karlsruhe o• D 92-93 K 4
Karlsruhe o USA (ND) 258-259 G 3
Karlstad ☆•• S 86-87 F 7
Karlstad o USA (MN) 270-271 B 2
Karlštejn • CZ 92-93 O 4
Karluk o USA 22-23 U 4
Karma o RN 202-203 L 3
Karma o• SUD 200-201 E 3
Karma ~ TCH 206-207 C 3
Karmāla o• IND 138-139 E 10
Karmaskaly ☆ RUS 96-97 K 6
Karmé o TCH 198-199 G 6
Karmeliťskyj monastyr • UA 102-103 E 3
Karmina ☆ UZ 136-137 J 4
Karmøy ⌒ N 86-87 B 7
Karnak, al- o•• ET 194-195 F 5
Karnāl o IND 138-139 F 5
Karnali ~ NEP 144-145 C 6
Karnaou ▲ TCH 198-199 H 2
Karnaphuli ~ BD 142-143 G 4
Karnataka ◘ IND 140-141 F 3
Karnataka Plateau ▲ IND 140-141 F 2
Karnes City o USA (TX) 266-267 K 5
Karnobat o BG 102-103 E 6
Karnprayāg o IND 138-139 G 4
Kärnten ◘ A 92-93 M 5
Karo Batak House • RI 162-163 C 3
Karoi o ZW 218-219 E 3
Karo La ▲ VRC 144-145 H 6
Karoma, Mount ▲ PNG 183 B 3
Karonga o MW 214-215 G 5
Karoni, Gunung ▲ RI 164-165 G 5
Karonie o AUS 176-177 G 5
Karoo National Park ⊥ ZA 220-221 F 6
Karoonda o AUS 180-181 E 3
Karor o PK 138-139 C 4
Karora o SUD 200-201 J 4
Karosa o RI 164-165 F 4
Karoso, Tanjung ▲ RI 168 D 7
Karpathio Pélagos ≈ 100-101 L 6
Kárpathos o GR 100-101 L 7
Kárpathos ⌒ GR 100-101 L 7
Karpenissi o GR 100-101 H 5
Karpinsk o RUS 114-115 F 5

344 Kam'janske — Karpinsk

Karpinskogo, vulkan ▲ RUS 122-123 Q 3
Karpogory o RUS 88-89 S 4
Karpuzlu ☆ TR 128-129 B 4
Karpysak o RUS 114-115 R 7
Karratha o AUS 172-173 C 6
Karratha Roadhouse o AUS 172-173 C 6
Karrats Fjord ≈ 26-27 Y 8
Karredouw o ZA 220-221 G 6
Karridale o AUS 176-177 C 7
Kars ☆• TR 128-129 K 2
Karsakbaj o KZ 124-125 E 5
Kärsämäki o FIN 88-89 H 5
Kārsava o LV 94-95 K 3
Karshi o WAN 204-205 G 4
Karši ☆ UZ 136-137 J 5
Karšinskaja step' ⚍ UZ 136-137 J 5
Karsk, Ust'- o RUS 118-119 J 9
Karskie Vorota, proliv ≈ 108-109 G 6
Karskiye Vorota, Proliv = Karskie Vorota, proliv ≈ 108-109 G 6
Karsrivierviei o ZA 220-221 E 7
Kartabu o GUY 62-63 E 2
Kartabyz, ozero o RUS 114-115 G 7
Kartaël o RUS 88-89 W 4
Kartaly ☆ RUS 124-125 B 2
Karte Conservation Park ⊥ AUS 180-181 F 3
Karthala ▲ COM 222-223 C 3
Karti o IR 134-135 H 6
Kartosuro o RI 168 D 3
Kartuzy o• PL 92-93 P 1
Karu o PNG 183 G 2
Karubaga o RI 166-167 K 3
Karubeamsberge ▲ NAM 220-221 C 1
Karufa o RI 166-167 G 3
Karuh o• AFG 134-135 K 1
Karumba o AUS 174-175 F 5
Kārumbhar Island ⌒ IND 138-139 B 8
Karumei o J 152-153 J 4
Karumwa o EAT 212-213 D 5
Kārūn, Kūh-e ▲ IR 134-135 D 3
Kārūn, Rūd-e ~ IR 134-135 C 3
Karungu o EAK 212-213 E 4
Karūr o IND 140-141 H 5
Karuzi o BU 212-213 C 5
Karval o USA (CO) 254-255 M 5
Karviná o CZ 92-93 P 4
Karwai o RI 166-167 H 4
Kārwār o IND 140-141 F 3
Karwin = Karviná o CZ 92-93 P 4
Karymskoe ☆ RUS 118-119 G 10
Karyngúrly ⚍ KZ 126-127 L 6
Karynžaryk ⚍ KZ 126-127 K 6
Kas ~ RUS 116-117 E 6
Kas o SUD 200-201 B 6
Kaş ☆•• TR 128-129 C 4
Kasa o RP 160-161 D 3
Kasa o VRC 154-155 B 6
Kasai o ZRE 210-211 G 4
Kasaan Bay ≈ 32-33 D 4
Kasaba o Z 214-215 E 6
Kasabi o ZRE 214-215 E 5
Kasabonika o CDN 34-35 M 4
Kašaf Rūd ~ IR 136-137 G 6
Kasah ~ AR 128-129 L 2
Kasai o J 152-153 F 7
Kasai ~ ZRE 210-211 G 5
Kasai-Occidental ■ ZRE 210-211 H 6
Kasai-Oriental ■ ZRE 210-211 J 5
Kasaji o ZRE 214-215 B 6
Kāsa Khurd o IND 138-139 D 10
Kasāl o IND 140-141 E 2
Kasalu o Z 218-219 D 2
Kasama ☆ Z 214-215 F 6
Kāšān o• IR 134-135 D 2
Kašan ~ TM 136-137 H 7
Kasan o UZ 136-137 J 5
Kasane ☆ RB 218-219 C 3
Kasanga o EAT 214-215 F 5
Kasangulu o ZRE 210-211 E 6
Kasanka National Park ⊥ Z 214-215 F 7
Kasansaj o UZ 136-137 M 4
Kasanza o ZRE 214-215 B 4
Kāsaragod o IND 140-141 F 4
Kasari o J 152-153 C 10
Kasaro ~ SUD 200-201 F 6
Kasasi o WAL 202-203 E 5
Kasatochi Island ⌒ USA 22-23 J 6
Kasba Lake o CDN 30-31 S 5
Kasba-Tadla o MA 188-189 H 4
Kascjukovičy o BY 94-95 N 5
Kasdir o DZ 188-189 L 4
Kaseda o J 152-153 D 9
Kasegaluk Lagoon ≈ 20-21 J 2
Kasei ~ ZRE 216-217 F 3
Kasempa o Z 218-219 C 1
Kasenga o ZRE (SHA) 214-215 E 6
Kasenga o ZRE (SHA) 214-215 B 6
Kasenge o ZRE 210-211 G 4
Kasengu o ZRE 212-213 C 2
Kasenye o ZRE 212-213 C 3
Kasese o EAU 212-213 C 3
Kasese o ZRE 212-213 A 4
Kaset Wisai o THA 158-159 G 3
Kaseyville o USA (MO) 274-275 F 5
Kashabowie o CDN (ONT) 234-235 N 6
Kashechewan o CDN 34-35 Q 4
Kashega o USA 22-23 N 6
Kashi o• VRC 146-147 C 6
Kashileshi ~ ZRE 214-215 B 6
Kashima o J 152-153 J 7
Kashima-nada ≈ 152-153 J 6
Kashinatpur o BD 142-143 F 4
Kāshīpur o IND 138-139 G 5
Kashiwa o J 152-153 H 7
Kashiwazaki o J 152-153 H 6
Kāshmor o PK 138-139 B 5
Kashnuk River ~ USA 20-21 H 6
Kashwal o SUD 206-207 J 5
Kasi ~ RI 166-167 G 2
Kasia o IND 142-143 C 2
Kasidishi ~ ZRE 214-215 B 5
Kasigau ▲ EAK 212-213 G 5
Kasigluk o USA 20-21 J 6
Kasimbar o RI 164-165 G 4
Kasimov o RUS 94-95 R 4
Kašin ☆• RUS 94-95 P 3
Kasindi o ZRE 212-213 B 3
Kasinje o MW 218-219 H 2
Kašira ☆• RUS 94-95 Q 4
Kasiruta, Pulau ⌒ RI 164-165 K 4
Kasiui, Pulau ⌒ RI 166-167 F 4
Kaskabulak o KZ 124-125 L 4
Kaškadar'inskaja oblast' ■ UZ 136-137 J 5
Kaškadar'ja ~ UZ 136-137 J 5
Kaškān, Rūdhāne-ye ~ IR 134-135 B 2
Kaškarancy o RUS 88-89 O 3
Kaskas o SN 196-197 C 6
Kaskaskia River ~ USA 274-275 J 6
Kaskaskia River State Fish and Wildlife Area ⊥ USA (IL) 274-275 J 6
Kaskaskia State Historic Site, Fort • USA (IL) 274-275 J 6
Kaskattama River ~ CDN 34-35 L 2
Kaskinen o FIN 88-89 F 5
Kaskö = Kaskinen o FIN 88-89 F 5
Kasli ☆ RUS 96-97 M 6
Kaslo o CDN (BC) 230-231 N 4
Kāšmar o IR 136-137 F 7
Kasmere Lake o CDN 30-31 T 6
Kasompe o Z 218-219 C 1
Kasongo o ZRE 210-211 L 6
Kasongo-Lunda o ZRE 216-217 D 3
Kasongo-Lunda, Chutes ~ ZRE 216-217 D 3
Kaspi o GE 126-127 F 7
Kaspijsk o RUS 126-127 G 6
Kaspijskij = Lagan' ☆ RUS 126-127 G 5
Kasr, Ra's ▲ SUD 200-201 J 3
Kassa o DY 204-205 E 3
Kassalā ☆• SUD 200-201 H 5
Kassama o RMM 202-203 E 3
Kassándra ⌒ GR 100-101 J 5
Kassándras, Kólpos ≈ 100-101 J 4
Kassándria o GR 100-101 J 4
Kassel o• D 92-93 K 3
Kasséré o CI 202-203 G 5
Kasserine ☆ TN 190-191 G 3
Kassipute o RI 164-165 H 6
Kassler o USA (CO) 254-255 K 4
Kássos ⌒ GR 100-101 L 7
Kassoum o BF 202-203 J 3
Kastamonu ☆• TR 128-129 E 2
Kastéli o GR 100-101 J 7
Kastoriá o GR 100-101 H 4
Kasuga o J (FKA) 152-153 D 8
Kasuga o J (HYO) 152-153 F 7
Kasuku ~ ZRE 210-211 K 4
Kasuku, Lac o ZRE 210-211 K 5
Kasulu o EAT 212-213 C 6
Kasumba o ZRE 214-215 D 7
Kasumi o J 152-153 F 7
Kasumigaura-ura o J 152-153 J 6
Kasumkent o RUS 126-127 H 7
Kasumpti o IND 138-139 F 4
Kasungu o MW 218-219 G 1
Kasungu National Park ⊥ MW 214-215 G 7
Kasūr o PK 138-139 E 4
Kat o IR 134-135 C 3
Kata ~ RUS 116-117 L 6
Kataba o Z 218-219 C 3
Katabaie o ZRE 214-215 B 4
Katagum o WAN 198-199 E 6
Katagum, River ~ WAN 204-205 H 3
Katahdin, Mount ▲ USA (ME) 278-279 N 3
Katajsk ☆ RUS 114-115 G 6
Kataka o IND 142-143 D 5
Katakokishi o ZRE 214-215 B 5
Katako-Kombe o ZRE 210-211 K 5
Kataku o RI 168 D 7
Katakwi o EAU 212-213 D 3
Katalah o RUS 118-119 N 6
Katamatite o AUS 180-181 H 4
Katana o RI 164-165 L 3
Katana o ZRE 212-213 B 5
Katanda o ZRE 214-215 B 4
Katanga ~ RUS 116-117 L 6
Katanga Plateau ⚍ ZRE 9 F 6
Katangi o IND 138-139 G 8
Katāngi o IND 138-139 G 9
Katanning o AUS 176-177 D 6
Kaṭaouâne o RIM 196-197 G 6
Kataramba ~ RUS 116-117 H 4
Katavi National Park ⊥ EAT 214-215 F 4
Katav-Ivanovsk ☆ RUS 96-97 L 6
Katcha o WAN 204-205 G 4
Katchall Island ⌒ IND 140-141 L 6
Katchamba o RT 202-203 L 5
Katchirga o BF 202-203 L 2
Kateel River ~ USA 20-21 K 4
Kateman, Pulau ⌒ RI 162-163 E 4
Katemcy o USA (TX) 266-267 H 3
Katende o ZRE 214-215 B 4
Katende, Chutes de ~ ZRE 214-215 B 4
Katenge o ZRE 214-215 B 4
Katengo o ZRE 212-213 B 6
Katepwa Beach o CDN (SAS) 232-233 P 5
Katere o NAM 216-217 F 9
Katerini o GR 100-101 J 4
Katesh o EAT 212-213 E 6
Katete o Z 218-219 G 2
Katghora o IND 142-143 C 4
Katha o MYA 142-143 K 3
Kathang o IND 142-143 K 2
Kathangor, Gabal ▲ SUD 208-209 A 6
Kathawachaga Lake o CDN 30-31 O 2
Katherine o AUS 172-173 L 3
Katherine River ~ AUS 172-173 K 3
Kāthiāwār Peninsula ᴗ IND 138-139 B 8
Kathleen Lake o CDN (ONT) 236-237 E 5
Kathmandu ★••• NEP 144-145 E 7
Kathu o ZA 220-221 F 3
Kathua o IND 138-139 E 3
Kati o RMM 202-203 F 3
Katiali o CI 202-203 G 5
Katiati o PNG 183 C 3
Katib, Ra's al- ▲ Y 132-133 C 6
Katiéna o RMM 202-203 H 3
Katihar o IND 142-143 E 3
Katima Mulilo ☆ NAM 218-219 C 3
Katimik Lake o CDN (MAN) 234-235 D 2
Katini o ZRE 216-217 E 3
Katiola ☆ CI 202-203 H 5
Katios, Parque Nacional los ⊥••• CO 60-61 C 4
Katiti Aboriginal Land ⚔ AUS 176-177 L 2
Katla o SUD 206-207 J 3
Katlanovo o MK 100-101 H 4
Katmai, Mount ▲ USA 22-23 T 3
Katmai National Park and Preserve ⊥ USA 22-23 T 3
Katmay Bay ≈ 22-23 T 4
Kato o GUY 62-63 E 3
Katoa o TCH 206-207 D 3
Kātoda o IND 138-139 E 7
Káto Glikóvrisi o GR 100-101 J 6
Katombe o ZRE 210-211 H 6
Katompi o ZRE 214-215 D 4
Katonga ~ EAU 212-213 C 3
Katonkaragaj o KZ 124-125 O 4
Katoomba-Wentworth Falls o AUS 180-181 L 2
Katoposo, Gunung ▲ RI 164-165 G 4
Káto Soúnio o GR 100-101 K 6
Katoto o EAT 212-213 C 6
Katowice ☆ PL 92-93 P 3
Katoya o IND 142-143 F 4
Katrancık Dağı ▲ TR 128-129 D 4
Katrina, Gabal ▲ ET 194-195 F 3
Katrineholm ☆ S 86-87 H 7
Katse o EAK 212-213 G 4
Katsena ~ CAM 204-205 J 5
Katsepy o RM 222-223 E 5
Katsina o WAN (KAD) 198-199 C 6
Katsina ■ WAN 198-199 C 6
Katsina-Ala o WAN 204-205 H 5
Katsina-Ala, River ~ WAN 204-205 H 5
Katsumoto o J 152-153 C 8
Katsuta o J 152-153 J 6
Katsuura o J (CHI) 152-153 J 7
Katsuura o J (WAK) 152-153 F 8
Kattakišlok o UZ 136-137 K 5
Kattakurgan = Kattakŭrgon o UZ 136-137 K 5
Kattaqŭrgon o UZ 136-137 K 5
Kattankudi o CL 140-141 J 7
Kattarakara o IND 140-141 G 6
Kattavía o GR 100-101 L 7
Kattawagami Lake o CDN (ONT) 236-237 H 3
Kattawagami River ~ CDN 236-237 J 2
Kattegat ≈ 86-87 E 8
Katterjåkk o S 86-87 J 2
Kāttupputtūr o IND 140-141 H 5
Katumbi o MW 214-215 G 6
Katun' ~ RUS 124-125 O 2
Katunda o Z 218-219 C 3
Katunguru o EAU 212-213 C 4
Katunskij hrebet ▲ RUS 124-125 O 3
Katupa o RI 168 D 7
Kātūria o IND 142-143 E 3
Katwe o EAU 212-213 B 4
Katwe o ZRE 214-215 D 6
Katy o USA (TX) 268-269 E 7
Katym ~ RUS 114-115 K 5
Kau o RI 164-165 K 3
Kau, Teluk ≈ 164-165 K 3
Kauai ⌒ USA (HI) 288 F 2
Kauai Channel ≈ 288 G 3
Kauara o CI 202-203 H 4
Kaubi o PNG 183 F 3
Kaudom o NAM 216-217 F 9
Kaudom ~ NAM 216-217 F 9
Kaudom Game Park ⊥ NAM 216-217 F 9
Kaufbeuren o• D 92-93 L 5
Kaufman o USA (TX) 264-265 H 6
Kaugel River ~ PNG 183 C 4
Kauhajoki o FIN 88-89 G 5
Kauhava o FIN 88-89 G 5
Kaukas o RI 164-165 H 4
Kaukauna o USA (WI) 270-271 K 6
Kaukauveld ⚍ NAM 216-217 F 9
Kauksi o• EST 94-95 K 2
Kaula ⌒ USA (HI) 288 E 3
Kaulakahi Channel ≈ 288 E 2
Kaulžur ~ KZ 126-127 N 3
Kaumalapau Harbor o USA (HI) 288 J 4
Kauman o RI 168 E 3
Kaunakakai o• USA (HI) 288 H 3
Kauna Point ▲ USA (HI) 288 K 5
Kaunas ☆•• LT 94-95 H 4
Kaundy, vpadina ᴗ KZ 126-127 K 6
Kaunolu o• USA (HI) 288 J 4
Kaup o PNG 183 B 2
Kaupanger o N 86-87 C 6
Kaupena o PNG 183 C 4
Kaupo o USA (HI) 288 J 4
Kaurai o PNG 183 G 5
Kauro ~ EAK 212-213 F 3
Kaušany = Căuşeni ☆ MD 102-103 F 4
Kaustinen o FIN 88-89 G 5
Kautokeino o N 86-87 L 2
Kauur o WAG 202-203 C 3
Kauwa o WAN 198-199 F 6
Kau-Ye Kyun ⌒ MYA 158-159 E 5
Kava ~ RUS 120-121 M 4
Kavadarci o MK 100-101 J 4
Kavak ☆ TR 128-129 G 2
Kavála o GR 100-101 K 4
Kavalerovo o RUS 122-123 F 6
Kavalga Island ⌒ USA 22-23 G 7
Kāvali o IND 140-141 J 3
Kavār o IR 134-135 E 4
Kavaratti o IND 140-141 E 5
Kavendu ▲ RG 202-203 D 4
Kavi o IND 138-139 D 8
Kavieng ☆ PNG 183 F 2
Kavigvalik Lake o USA 20-21 J 6
Kavik River ~ USA 20-21 R 2
Kavinga o Z 214-215 F 7
Kavir, Dašt-e ⚍ IR 134-135 E 1
Kavkazkij zapovednik ⊥ RUS 126-127 D 6
Kávos o GR 100-101 H 5
Kavrizhka, Cape ▲ USA 22-23 N 6
Kavuu ~ EAT 214-215 F 4
Kawa o CDN (ONT) 234-235 O 4
Kawa o RI (MAL) 166-167 E 3
Kawa ~ RI 166-167 E 3
Kawa, Temple of • SUD 200-201 E 3
Kawagit o RI 166-167 L 4
Kawagoe o J 152-153 H 7
Kawaguchi o J 152-153 H 7
Kawai o IND 138-139 F 7
Kawaihae o• USA (HI) 288 K 4
Kawaihae Bay ≈ 288 L 4
Kawaihoa Point ▲ USA (HI) 288 E 3
Kawaikini ▲ USA (HI) 288 F 2
Kawajena o SUD 206-207 J 5
Kawakawa o NZ 182 E 1
Kawala o MYA 142-143 J 2
Kawali o RI 168 C 3
Kawambwa o Z 214-215 E 5
Kawana o Z 218-219 C 1
Kawanee o USA (MO) 276-277 F 4
Kawangko o RI 168 D 7
Kawangkoan o RI 164-165 J 3
Kawanoe o J 152-153 E 7
Kawant o IND 138-139 E 8
Kawardha o IND 142-143 B 4
Kawarga ~ RI 166-167 K 5
Kawartha Lakes o CDN (ONT) 238-239 G 4
Kawasa o ZRE 214-215 E 5
Kawasaki o J 152-153 H 7
Kawatipoli o MYA 142-143 K 6
Kawauchi o J 152-153 J 4
Kawau Island ⌒ NZ 182 E 2
Kawaya o ZRE 214-215 E 5
Kawayan o RP 160-161 F 7
Kawayu o J 152-153 L 3
Kawe, Pulau ⌒ RI 166-167 F 2
Kaweah, Lake o USA (CA) 248-249 F 3
Kaweka ▲ NZ 182 F 3
Kawembwe o Z 214-215 F 6
Kawene o CDN (ONT) 234-235 M 6
Kawentinkim o RI 166-167 L 4
Kawe Rapids ~ Z 218-219 F 2
Kawhia o NZ 182 E 3
Kawich Peak ▲ USA 246-247 J 5
Kawich Peak ▲ USA (NV) 248-249 H 2
Kawinaw Lake o CDN (MAN) 234-235 D 2
Kawkareik o MYA 158-159 E 2
Kawkawlin o USA (MI) 272-273 F 4
Kawkpalut o MYA 158-159 E 2
Kawlin o MYA 142-143 J 4
Kawtang o MYA 142-143 J 3
Kaw Reservoir o USA (OK) 264-265 H 2
Kaxarari, Área Indígena ⚔ BR 66-67 D 7
Kaxgar He ~ VRC 146-147 C 6
Kax He ~ VRC 146-147 F 4
Kaxian D. ∴ VRC 150-151 D 2
Kaxinauá Nova Olinda, Área Indígena ⚔ BR 66-67 B 7
Kaxinawá do Rio Humaitá, Área Indígena ⚔ BR 66-67 B 7
Kaxinawá do Rio Jordão, Área Indígena ⚔ BR 64-65 F 6
Kaya ☆ BF 202-203 K 3
Kayaapu o RI 162-163 E 7
Kayabi, Área Indígena ⚔ BR 70-71 J 2
Kayak Island ⌒ USA 20-21 S 7
Kayambi o Z 214-215 G 6
Kayan ~ RI 164-165 E 2
Kayanga ~ SN 202-203 C 3
Kāyankulam o IND 140-141 G 6
Kayanza o BU 212-213 B 5
Kayapó, Área Indígena ⚔ BR 68-69 B 5
Kayar o SN 202-203 B 2
Kayasa o RI 164-165 K 3
Kayattār o IND 140-141 G 6
Kaycee o USA (WY) 252-253 M 3
Kaye, Mount ▲ AUS 180-181 K 4
Kaydon Lake o CDN (ONT) 236-237 D 2
Kayeli o RI 166-167 D 3
Kayembe-Mukulu o ZRE 214-215 D 5
Kayenta o USA (AZ) 256-257 E 2
Kayenzi o EAT 212-213 D 5
Kayes ■ RMM 202-203 E 3
Kayes ☆ RMM (KAY) 202-203 E 2
Kayima o WAL 202-203 E 5
Kayli o SUD 208-209 B 3
Kaymor o SN 202-203 C 3
Kaynabayongo o ZRE 212-213 B 4
Kayoa, Pulau ⌒ RI 164-165 K 3
Kayokwe o BU 212-213 B 5
Kayonza o RWA 212-213 C 4
Kay Point ▲ CDN 20-21 W 2
Kayrunnera o AUS 178-179 G 6
Kayseri ☆•• TR 128-129 F 3
Kayuadi, Pulau ⌒ RI 168 E 6
Kayuagung o RI 162-163 F 6
Kayuku o RI 164-165 G 4
Kayupangang, Pulau ⌒ RI 168 D 6
Kayuyu o ZRE 210-211 L 5
Kayville o CDN (SAS) 232-233 N 6
Kazabazua o CDN (QUE) 238-239 J 3
Kazača Lopan' o UA 102-103 K 2
Kazače o RUS 110-111 V 4
Kazačinskoe ☆ RUS 116-117 F 7
Kazah o• AZ 128-129 L 2
Kazahdar'ja o UZ 136-137 F 3
Kazahskij zaliv ≈ 126-127 K 6
Kazakh Uplands = Saryarka ⚍ KZ 124-125 G 4
Kazak'jaha ~ RUS 108-109 V 6
Kazakstan = Kazakstan ■ KZ 126-127 J 3
Kazamabika o G 210-211 C 4
Kazan' ☆•• RUS 96-97 F 6
Kazandžik = Gazanǧyk o TM 136-137 D 5
Kazanlăk o•• BG 102-103 D 6
Kazan River ~ CDN 30-31 V 4
Kazanskoe ☆ RUS 114-115 K 7
Kazantips'ka zatoka ≈ 102-103 J 5
Kazarman o KS 146-147 B 5
Kazas ~ RUS 116-117 H 9
Kazaure o WAN 198-199 D 6
Kazbegi o GE 126-127 F 6
Kazbek, gora ▲ GE 126-127 F 6
Kaz Dağı ▲ TR 128-129 B 3
Kazer • TCH 198-199 J 3
Kazer, Pico ▲ RCH 80 G 7
Kāzerūn o IR 134-135 D 4
Kāzi Ahmad o PK 138-139 B 6
Kazibacna ~ BD 142-143 F 4
Kazıklı Çayı ~ TR 128-129 G 3
Kazil'skoe ☆ RUS 96-97 L 7
Kazi-Magomed o AZ 128-129 N 2
Kāzimiya, al- o IRQ 128-129 L 6
Kāzımkarabekir ☆• TR 128-129 E 4
Kaziranga National Park ⊥••• IND 142-143 H 2
Kaziza o ZRE 214-215 B 6
Kaznakovka o KZ 124-125 N 4
Kaztalovka ☆ KZ 96-97 F 9
Kažukas = Marijampole ☆•• LT 94-95 H 4
Kazuma Pan National Park ⊥ ZW 218-219 C 4
Kazumba o ZRE 214-215 B 4
Kazungula o Z 218-219 C 3
Kazuno o J 152-153 J 4
Kazym ~ RUS 114-115 J 3
Kazyr ~ RUS 116-117 G 9
Kbombole o SN 202-203 B 2
Kbor Roumia • DZ 190-191 D 2
Ké o G 210-211 C 3
Ke ~ IND 142-143 B 3
Ké, Enneri ~ TCH 198-199 H 3
Kéa ⌒ GR 100-101 K 6
Keaau o USA (HI) 288 K 5
Keahole Point ▲ USA (HI) 288 J 5
Kealaikahiki Channel ≈ 288 H 4
Kealakekua o USA (HI) 288 K 5
Kealia o USA (HI) 288 F 3
Keanae o USA (HI) 288 J 4
Keansburg o USA (NJ) 280-281 M 3
Kearney o USA (NE) 262-263 G 4
Kearns o USA (UT) 254-255 C 3
Kearny o USA (AZ) 256-257 E 5
Kearsarge Pass ▲ USA (CA) 248-249 F 3
Keating Point ▲ IND 140-141 L 5
Kébaly o RG 202-203 D 4
Keban ☆ TR 128-129 H 3
Keban Barajı < TR 128-129 H 3
Kebaowek Indian Reservation ⚔ CDN (QUE) 238-239 G 2
Kébara o RCB 210-211 E 5
Kebasen o RI 168 C 3
Kebbe o WAN 198-199 B 6
Kebbi, Mayo ~ TCH 206-207 B 4
Kébémèr o SN 202-203 B 2
Kébi, Mayo ~ CAM 204-205 K 4
Kébila o RMM 202-203 G 4
Kebili ☆ TN 190-191 G 4
Kebnekaise ▲•• S 86-87 J 3
Kebri Dehar o ETH 208-209 G 5
Kebumen o RI 168 C 3
Kech ~ PK 134-135 K 5
K'ech'a Terara ▲ ETH 208-209 D 5
Kéché o RCA 206-207 E 3
Kechika Ranges ▲ CDN 30-31 F 6
Kechika River ~ CDN 30-31 F 6
Kecskemét o H 92-93 P 5
Keda o GE 126-127 D 7
Kedah ■ MAL 162-163 D 1
Kedainiai ☆• LT 94-95 H 4
Kedawung o RI 168 C 3
Keddie o USA (CA) 246-247 E 3
Kédédéssé o TCH 206-207 C 3
Kedgwick o CDN (NB) 240-241 H 3
Kedgwick River o CDN (NB) 240-241 H 3
Kedgwick River ~ CDN 240-241 H 3
Kedi o IND 138-139 F 4
Kedi o RI 164-165 K 3
Kediet ej Jill ▲ RIM 196-197 D 3
Kedir o RI 166-167 K 3
Kediri o RI 168 E 3
Kedon o RUS (MAG) 112-113 K 4
Kedon ~ RUS 112-113 K 4
Kedonskij hrebet ▲ RUS 112-113 K 4
Kédougou o SN 202-203 D 3
Kedrovaja, gora ▲ RUS 122-123 D 6
Kedrovyj o RUS 114-115 P 6
Kedungwuni o RI 168 C 3
Kedva ~ RUS 88-89 W 4
Kędzierzyn o PL 92-93 P 3
Kędzierzyn-Koźle o• PL 92-93 P 3
Keebi, Birnin- o WAN 198-199 B 6
Keefton o USA (OK) 264-265 J 3
Keekorok Lodge o EAK 212-213 E 4
Keel = An Caol o IRL 90-91 B 5
Keele Peak ▲ CDN 30-31 E 4
Keeler o USA (CA) 248-249 G 3
Keele River ~ CDN 30-31 F 3
Keelinawi o USA (HI) 288 E 3
Keelung o• RC 156-157 M 4
Keene o USA (CA) 248-249 F 4
Keene o USA (NH) 278-279 J 6
Keene, Lake o AUS 176-177 G 2
Keenjhar Lake o•• PK 138-139 B 7
Keepit, Lake < AUS 178-179 L 6
Keep River ~ AUS 172-173 J 3
Keep River National Park ⊥ AUS 172-173 J 3
Keerweer, Cape ▲ AUS 174-175 F 3
Keeseville o USA (NY) 278-279 H 4
Keetmannshoop ☆ NAM 220-221 D 3
Keewatin o CDN (ONT) 234-235 J 5
Keewatin River ~ CDN 34-35 F 2
Keezhik Lake o CDN (ONT) 234-235 P 3
Kefa ■ ETH 208-209 B 5
Kefalonia ⌒ GR 100-101 H 5
Kefamenanu o RI 166-167 C 6
Keffi o WAN 204-205 G 4
Keflavík o IS 86-87 b 2
Kef Mimouna ▲ DZ 190-191 D 4
K'eftya o ETH 200-201 H 6
Kê Gà, Mũi ▲ VN 158-159 K 5
Kegajli ☆ UZ 136-137 F 3
Kegali ~ RUS 112-113 L 4
Kēgart o KS 136-137 N 4
Kegaska o CDN (QUE) 242-243 G 2
Kegdal o IND 140-141 F 3
Kegen o KZ 146-147 D 4
Kegworth o CDN (SAS) 232-233 P 5
Kehl o D 92-93 J 4
Keibul-Lamjoa National Park ⊥ IND 142-143 H 3
Keikakolo o RI 168 E 7
Keila o•• EST 94-95 J 2
Keila ⌒ SOL 184 I d 1
Keimoes o ZA 220-221 E 4
Kei Mouth o ZA 220-221 J 6
Keipene o LV 94-95 J 3
Kei Road o ZA 220-221 H 6
Keiskammarivier ~ ZA 220-221 H 6
Keita o RN 198-199 B 5
Keita ou Douka, Bahr ~ TCH 206-207 D 4
Keitele o FIN (KPN) 88-89 J 5
Keitele o FIN (KSS) 88-89 H 5
Keith o AUS 180-181 F 4
Keith, Cape ▲ AUS 172-173 K 1
Keith Arm o CDN 30-31 J 3
Keithley Creek o CDN (BC) 228-229 N 4
Keith Sebelius Lake o USA (KS) 262-263 G 5
Keithville o USA (LA) 268-269 G 4
Keiyasi o FJI 184 III a 2
Keizer o USA (OR) 244-245 C 5
Kejaman o MAL 162-163 K 3
Kejimkujik National Park ⊥ CDN (NS) 240-241 K 6
Kéjngypil'gyn, laguna ≈ 112-113 U 5
Kejobon o RI 168 C 3
Kejvy ▲ RUS 88-89 O 3
Kekaha o USA (HI) 288 F 3
Këkajgyr o KS 146-147 B 5
Këk-Art o KS 146-147 B 5
Keke o PNG 183 D 5
Kékem o CAM 204-205 J 6
Kekertuk o CDN 28-29 J 3
Kekesu o PNG 184 I b 1
Kekirawa o CL 140-141 J 6
Kekneno, Gunung ▲ RI 166-167 C 6
Kekova Adası ⌒ TR 128-129 C 4
Kekovandasi ~ TR 128-129 C 4
Kekri o IND 138-139 E 7
Kekurnoi, Cape ▲ USA 22-23 T 4
Kekurnyj, zaliv ≈ 120-121 Q 4
Keku Strait ≈ 32-33 D 3
Kelabo o PNG 183 B 3
K'elafo o ETH 208-209 G 6
Kelag o VRC 154-155 E 6
Kelagay o AFG 136-137 L 7
Kelai ~ RI 164-165 E 3
Kélakam o RN 198-199 E 6
Kelambakkam o IND 140-141 J 4
Kelan o VRC 154-155 G 2
Kelandic Plateau ⚍ 86-87 g 1
Kelang, Pulau ⌒ RI 166-167 D 3
Kelankylä o FIN 88-89 J 4
Kelanoa o PNG 183 D 4
Kelantan ■ MAL 162-163 D 2
Kelapa o RI 162-163 F 5
Kélbo o BF 202-203 K 3
Këlcyrë o• AL 100-101 H 4
Kel'da ~ RUS 88-89 R 4
Kele ~ RUS 118-119 P 4
Keleft o AFG 136-137 K 6
Kelem o ETH 208-209 B 6
Kelema o EAT 212-213 E 6
Keleraš = Călăraşi ☆ MD 102-103 F 4
Keles ☆ UZ 136-137 L 4
Kéléya o RMM 202-203 G 4
Kelež ~ RUS 116-117 F 9
Kelfield o CDN (SAS) 232-233 K 4
Kelford o USA (NC) 282-283 K 4
Kelgo Bay ≈ 36-37 R 5
Kelibia o TN 190-191 H 2
Kelifskij Uzboj ⚍ TM 136-137 H 6
Kelifvun, gora ▲ RUS 112-113 O 2
Kelimjar ~ RUS 110-111 P 4
Keling o RI 168 D 3
Kelkit ☆ TR 128-129 H 2
Kelkit Çayı ~ TR 128-129 G 2
Kéllé o RCB 210-211 E 4
Kellé o RN 198-199 E 5
Keller o USA (WA) 244-245 G 2
Kellerberrin o AUS 176-177 D 5
Keller Lake o CDN 30-31 G 4
Kellerville o USA (TX) 264-265 D 3
Kellet, Canal de ≈ 50-51 B 4
Kellet, Cape ▲ CDN 24-25 H 5
Kellet River ~ CDN 24-25 b 6
Kellett River ~ CDN 24-25 K 5
Kellett River ~ CDN 30-31 Y 2
Kellett Strait ≈ 24-25 M 3
Kelliher o CDN (SAS) 232-233 P 4
Kelliher o USA (MN) 270-271 D 3
Kelloe o CDN (MAN) 234-235 C 4
Kellog o RUS (KRN) 114-115 T 3
Kellog ~ RUS 114-115 S 3
Kellogg o USA (ID) 250-251 C 4
Kellogg o USA (MN) 270-271 F 6
Kelloselkä o FIN 88-89 K 3
Kelly, Mount ▲ USA 20-21 J 2
Kelly Lake o CDN (BC) 230-231 H 2
Kelly Lake o CDN 30-31 G 3
Kelly Range ▲ AUS 176-177 F 2
Kelly River ~ USA 20-21 J 2
Kel'ma ~ RUS 114-115 U 5
Kelmė ☆ LT 94-95 H 4
Kelmet o ER 200-201 J 4
Kelo o TCH 206-207 B 4
Kelongwa o Z 218-219 D 1
Kelowna o CDN (BC) 230-231 K 4
Kelsey o CDN 34-35 H 2
Kelsey Bay o CDN (BC) 230-231 C 3
Kelso o CDN (SAS) 232-233 R 6
Kelso o• GB 90-91 F 4
Kelso o USA (CA) 248-249 J 4
Kelso o USA (WA) 244-245 C 4
Kelstern o CDN (SAS) 232-233 M 5
Keltie Bugt ≈ 26-27 Z 2
Kelton o USA (TX) 264-265 D 3
Kelton o USA (UT) 254-255 B 2
Kelu o VRC 156-157 F 6
Kelua o RI 164-165 D 5
Keluang, Tanjung ▲ RI 162-163 H 5
Kelume o RI 162-163 F 5
Kel'vat ~ RUS 114-115 N 5
Kelvin o USA (AZ) 256-257 E 5
Kelvington o CDN (SAS) 232-233 P 3
Kem' o RUS (KAR) 88-89 N 4
Kem' ~ RUS 88-89 M 4
Kem' ~ RUS 116-117 E 6
Kemah ☆• TR 128-129 H 3
Kemal, Gunung ▲ RI 164-165 E 3
Kemâliye ☆ TR 128-129 H 3
Kemano o CDN (BC) 228-229 G 3
Kemano River ~ CDN 228-229 G 3
Kemara, Kampung o MAL 162-163 E 2
Kemasik o MAL 162-163 E 2
Kemata I o TCH 206-207 D 4
Kemba o RCA 206-207 F 6
Kembani o RI 164-165 H 4
Kembapi o RI 166-167 L 6
Kembé o RCA 206-207 E 6
Kembé, Chutes de ~ RCA 206-207 E 6
Kembéra o RG 202-203 D 4
Kembolcha o ETH (Wel) 208-209 C 4
Kembolcha o ETH (Weo) 208-209 D 3
Kemčug ~ RUS 116-117 E 7
Kemčug, Bol'šoj ~ RUS 116-117 E 7
Kemdéré o TCH 206-207 D 4
Kemenagi, Mount ▲ PNG 183 B 4
Kemer o TR 128-129 C 4
Kemer ☆ TR 128-129 D 4
Kemerhisar o TR 128-129 F 4
Kemerovo ☆ RUS 114-115 T 7
Kemi o FIN 88-89 H 4
Kemijärvi o FIN (LAP) 88-89 J 3
Kemijärvi o FIN (LAP) 88-89 J 3
Kemijoki ~ FIN 88-89 H 3
Kemkara o RUS 120-121 H 5
Kemlja o RUS 96-97 D 6
Kemmerer o USA (WY) 252-253 H 5
Kemnay o CDN (MAN) 234-235 C 5
Kémo ■ RCA 206-207 D 6
Kemp o USA (TX) 264-265 H 6
Kemp, Lake < USA (TX) 264-265 E 5
Kempaž ~ RUS 114-115 F 2
Kempe Fjord ≈ 26-27 m 7
Kempele o FIN 88-89 H 4
Kempendjaj o RUS 118-119 J 4
Kempendjaji ~ RUS 118-119 J 4
Kemp Land ⚍ ARK 16 G 6
Kemp Peninsula ᴗ ARK 16 F 30
Kemps Bay o BS 54-55 G 2
Kempsey o AUS 178-179 M 6
Kempt, Lac o CDN (QUE) 236-237 O 5
Kempten (Allgäu) o• D 92-93 L 5
Kempton o AUS 180-181 J 7
Kempton Park o ZA 220-221 J 2
Kemptown o CDN (NS) 240-241 M 5
Kemptville o CDN (NS) 240-241 K 6
Kemptville o CDN (ONT) 238-239 K 3
Kemubu o MAL 162-163 E 2
Ken ~ IND 142-143 B 3
Kenadsa o DZ 188-189 K 5
Kenai o• USA 20-21 P 6
Kenai Fjords National Park ⊥ USA 22-23 V 3
Kenai Mountains ▲ USA 20-21 P 7
Kenai National Wildlife Refuge ⊥ USA 20-21 P 6
Kenai Peninsula ᴗ USA 20-21 P 6
Kenalia o PNG 183 B 5
Kenamuke Swamp o SUD 208-209 A 5
Kenamu River ~ CDN 38-39 O 2
Kenamu River ~ CDN 38-39 P 2
Kenansville o USA (FL) 286-287 J 4
Kenapuru Head o NZ 182 E 4
Kenār Daryā o IR 136-137 B 6
Kenari o RI 168 D 7
Kenaston o CDN (SAS) 232-233 M 4
Kenawa o PNG 183 B 5
Kenbridge o USA (VA) 280-281 H 7
Kencong o RI 168 E 4
Kendal o CDN (SAS) 232-233 P 5
Kendal o• GB 90-91 F 4
Kendal o RI 168 D 3
Kendall o USA (FL) 286-287 J 6
Kendall o USA (KS) 262-263 E 7
Kendall o USA (WA) 244-245 C 2
Kendall, Cape ▲ CDN (NWT) 24-25 O 6
Kendall, Mount ▲ NZ 182 D 4
Kendall, Point ▲ CDN 24-25 d 6
Kendall River ~ AUS 174-175 F 4
Kendallville o USA (IN) 274-275 N 3
Kendari ☆ RI 164-165 H 5
Kendawangan o RI 162-163 J 6
Kendégué o TCH 206-207 D 3
Kendeng, Pegunungan ▲ RI 168 D 3
Kendenup o AUS 176-177 D 7
Kendleton o USA (TX) 266-267 L 4
Kendrāpāra o IND 142-143 E 5
Kendrew o ZA 220-221 G 6
Kendrick o USA (ID) 250-251 C 5
Kendu Bay o EAK 212-213 E 4
Kendujhargarh o IND 142-143 D 5
Kendyrli-Kajasanskoe plato ▲ KZ 126-127 K 6
Kenedy o USA (TX) 266-267 K 5
Kenel o USA (SD) 260-261 F 1
Kenema ☆ WAL 202-203 E 6
Kenenikjan ~ RUS 118-119 J 5
Kenenkou o RMM 202-203 G 3
Kenevi, Mount ▲ PNG 183 D 5
Kenga ~ RUS 114-115 Q 6
Kengdaj ~ RUS 110-111 Q 4
Kenge o ZRE 210-211 F 6
Kengirli sukojmasy < KZ 124-125 E 5
Kengjade ~ RUS 110-111 H 5
Kengkeme ~ RUS 118-119 N 5
Keng Tung o MYA 142-143 L 5
Kengué o RCB 210-211 D 5
Kenhardt o ZA 220-221 E 4
Kéniéba o RMM 202-203 E 3
Kénié'bandi o RMM 202-203 E 3
Kéniébaoulé, Réserve de ⊥ RMM 202-203 F 3
Keningau o MAL 160-161 B 10
Kénitra = Al-Q'nitra ☆ MA (Knt) 188-189 H 3
Kenli o VRC 154-155 L 3
Kenly o USA (NC) 282-283 J 5
Kenmare o USA (ND) 258-259 E 3

Karpinskogo, vulkan — Kenmare 345

Kenmare = Neidín ○ **IRL** 90-91 C 6
Kenmare River ≈ 90-91 C 6
Kenna ○ **USA** (NM) 256-257 M 5
Kenna ○ **USA** (WV) 280-281 E 5
Kennard ○ **USA** (TX) 268-269 E 5
Kennebec ○ **USA** (SD) 260-261 G 3
Kennebecasis River ~ **CDN** 240-241 K 5
Kennebec River ~ **USA** 278-279 M 3
Kennebunk ○ **USA** (ME) 278-279 L 5
Kennedy ○ **AUS** 174-175 H 6
Kennedy ○ **CDN** (SAS) 232-233 Q 5
Kennedy ○ **USA** (NE) 262-263 F 2
Kennedy ○ **USA** (NY) 278-279 B 6
Kennedy ○ **ZW** 218-219 D 4
Kennedy Channel ≈ 26-27 Q 3
Kennedy Development Road II **AUS** 174-175 H 6
Kennedy Hill ▲ **AUS** 174-175 G 3
Kennedy Kanal ≈ 26-27 R 3
Kennedy Peak ▲ **MYA** 142-143 H 4
Kennedy Range ▲▲ **AUS** 176-177 C 2
Kennedy River ~ **AUS** 174-175 H 4
Kennedy Space Center, John Fitzgerald xx **USA** (FL) 286-287 J 3
Kennedy's Vale ○ **ZA** 220-221 K 2
Kenner ○ **USA** (LA) 268-269 K 6
Kennesaw Mountain National Battlefield Park · **USA** (GA) 284-285 F 3
Kennetcook ○ **CDN** (NS) 240-241 M 5
Kenneth Range ▲▲ **AUS** 176-177 D 1
Kennett ○ **USA** (MO) 276-277 E 4
Kennewick ○ **USA** (WA) 244-245 F 4
Kenney Dam · **CDN** (BC) 228-229 K 3
Kennisis Lake ○ **CDN** (ONT) 238-239 G 3
Keno ○ **USA** (OR) 244-245 D 8
Keno City ○ **CDN** 20-21 X 5
Kenogami Lake ○ **CDN** (ONT) 236-237 H 4
Kenogami River ~ **CDN** 236-237 D 2
Kenogami River ~ **CDN** 236-237 C 2
Kenogamissi Lake ⬭ **CDN** (ONT) 236-237 G 5
Kenora ○ **CDN** (ONT) 234-235 J 5
Kenosee Park ○ **CDN** (SAS) 232-233 Q 6
Kenosha ○ **USA** (WI) 274-275 L 2
Kensal ○ **USA** (ND) 258-259 J 4
Kenscoff ○·· **RH** 54-55 J 5
Kenselt ○ **USA** (AR) 276-277 D 5
Kensington ○ **CDN** (PEI) 240-241 M 4
Kensington ○ **USA** (KS) 262-263 G 5
Kensington Downs ○ **AUS** 178-179 H 2
Kent ○ **USA** (MN) 270-271 B 4
Kent ○ **USA** (OH) 280-281 E 2
Kent ○ **USA** (OR) 244-245 E 5
Kent ○ **USA** (TX) 266-267 C 2
Kent ○ **USA** (WA) 244-245 C 3
Kentau ○ **KZ** 136-137 L 3
Kenṭau ○ **KZ** 136-137 L 3
Kent City ○ **USA** (MI) 272-273 D 4
Kent Group ⌒ **AUS** 180-181 J 5
Ken Thao ○ **LAO** 158-159 F 2
Kenting National Park ⊥ · **RC** 156-157 M 5
Kent Island ⌒ **USA** (MD) 280-281 K 5
Kent Junction ○ **CDN** (NB) 240-241 K 4
Kentland ○ **USA** (IN) 274-275 L 4
Kenton ○ **CDN** (MAN) 234-235 C 5
Kenton ○ **USA** (MI) 270-271 K 4
Kenton ○ **USA** (OH) 280-281 C 3
Kenton ○ **USA** (OK) 264-265 B 2
Kenton ○ **USA** (TN) 276-277 F 4
Kent Peninsula ◡ **CDN** 24-25 S 6
Kentrikí Macedonía ◘ **GR** 100-101 J 4
Kentucky ◘ **USA** 276-277 H 3
Kentucky Lake < **USA** (KY) 276-277 G 4
Kentucky River ~ **USA** 276-277 L 3
Kentville ○ **CDN** (NS) 240-241 L 5
Kentwood ○ **USA** (LA) 268-269 K 6
Kenya ■ **EAK** 212-213 E 3
Kenya, Mount ▲·· **EAK** 212-213 F 4
Kenya National Park, Mount ⊥ **EAK** 212-213 F 4
Kenyon ○ **USA** (MN) 270-271 E 6
Kenzou ○ **CAM** 206-207 B 6
Keokuk ○ **USA** (IA) 274-275 G 4
Keoladeo National Park ⊥··· **IND** 138-139 F 6
Keoma ○ **CDN** (ALB) 232-233 E 4
Keosauqua ○ **USA** (IA) 274-275 G 4
Keota ○ **USA** (IA) 274-275 G 3
Keowee, Lake ⬭ **USA** (SC) 284-285 H 2
Kepa ○ **RUS** 88-89 M 4
Kepahiang ○ **RI** 162-163 E 6
Kepanjen ○ **RI** 168 E 4
Kepelekese ~ **ZRE** 216-217 F 3
Keperveem ○ **RUS** 112-113 N 3
Kepi ○ **RI** 166-167 K 5
Kepina ~ **RUS** 88-89 Q 4
Kepino ○ **RUS** 88-89 Q 4
Kępno ○ **PL** 92-93 O 3
Keppe ○ **RI** 164-165 G 5
Keppel Bay ≈ 178-179 L 2
Keppel Island ⌒ **GB** 78-79 L 6
Kepsut ☆ **TR** 128-129 C 3
Kepteni ○ **RUS** 118-119 P 4
Keptin ○ **RUS** 118-119 M 4
Kepudori ○ **RI** 166-167 H 2
Kepuhi ○ **USA** (HI) 288 H 3
Kerai, Kuala ○ **MAL** 162-163 E 2
Kerala ◘ **IND** 140-141 F 5
Kerama-rettō ⌒ **J** 152-153 B 11
Keram River ~ **PNG** 183 C 3
Kéran ~ **RT** 202-203 L 4
Kéran, Gorges du ◡· **RT** 202-203 L 5
Kéran, Parc National de la ⊥ **RT** 202-203 L 4
Kerang ○ **AUS** 180-181 G 3
Kerang ○ **RI** 164-165 E 5
Keranirhat ○ **BD** 142-143 H 4
Keraudren, Cape ▲ **AUS** 172-173 D 5
Keravat ○ **PNG** 183 G 3
Kerawa ○ **CAM** 204-205 K 3
Kerba, Col de ▲ **DZ** 190-191 D 3
Kerbau, Tanjung ▲ **RI** 162-163 E 6
Kerbi ~ **RUS** 122-123 F 2
Kerby ○ **USA** (OR) 244-245 B 8
Kerč ○ **UA** 102-103 K 5
Kerčens'ka Protoka ≈ 102-103 K 5
Kerch = Kerč ○· **UA** 102-103 K 5
Kerchouel ○ **RMM** 196-197 L 6
Kerdëm ○· **RUS** 118-119 O 5
Kéré ○ **RCA** (Hau) 206-207 G 6
Kéré ~ **RCA** 206-207 H 6
Kerec, mys ▲ **RUS** 88-89 P 4
Kerein Hills ○ **AUS** 180-181 J 2
Kerej, köli ⬭ **KZ** 124-125 F 3
Kerema ☆ **PNG** 183 C 4
Keremeos ○ **CDN** (BC) 230-231 K 4
Keremeos Ranche Indian Reserve X **CDN** (BC) 230-231 K 4
Keremesit ~ **RUS** 110-111 b 4
Kérémou ○ **DY** 204-205 E 3
Kerempe Burnu ▲ **TR** 128-129 E 1
Keren ○ **ER** 200-201 J 5
Kerend ○ **IR** 134-135 B 1
Kerens ○ **USA** (TX) 264-265 H 6
Kereru Range ▲▲ **PNG** 183 C 4
Keret' ○ **RUS** 88-89 M 3
Keret', ozero ⬭ **RUS** 88-89 M 4
Kerewan ☆ **WAG** 202-203 B 3
Kerguelen, Îles ⌒ **F** 12 E 9
Kerguélen Plateau ≃ 12 F 10
Keria Landing ○ **GUY** 62-63 F 2
Kericho ○· **EAK** 212-213 E 4
Keri Kera ○ **SUD** 200-201 F 6
Kerikeri ○ **NZ** 182 D 1
Kerinci, Danau ⬭ **RI** 162-163 D 6
Kerinci, Gunung ▲ **RI** 162-163 D 5
Kerio ~ **EAK** 212-213 F 2
Keriya He ~ **VRC** 144-145 C 2
Kerkenah, Îles de ⌒ **TN** 190-191 H 3
Kerkertaluk Island ⌒ **CDN** 28-29 G 2
Kerki ○ **TM** 136-137 J 6
Kerkiči ○ **TM** 136-137 J 6
Kérkira ☆·· **GR** 100-101 G 5
Kérkira ⌒ **GR** 100-101 G 5
Kerkouane ∴··· **TN** 190-191 H 2
Kermadec Islands ⌒ **NZ** 13 K 5
Kermadec Trench ≃ 14-15 L 11
Kermān ◘ **IR** 134-135 F 4
Kermān ☆· **IR** (KER) 134-135 G 3
Kermānšāhan ○ **IR** 134-135 F 3
Kermāšah ○ **IR** 134-135 D 3
Kermit ○ **USA** (TX) 266-267 D 2
Kërmjukej, gora ▲ **AZ** 128-129 N 3
Kermū, Kōtal-e ▲ **AFG** 134-135 M 1
Kernay ∸ **TM** 136-137 F 3
Kernersville ○ **USA** (NC) 282-283 G 4
Kernertut, Cap ▲ **CDN** 36-37 Q 5
Kern National Wildlife Refuge ⊥ · **USA** (CA) 248-249 E 4
Kern River ~ **USA** 248-249 F 3
Kernville ○ **USA** (CA) 248-249 F 4
Kernville ○ **USA** (OR) 244-245 B 6
Kérou ○ **DY** 204-205 E 3
Kérouané ○ **RG** 202-203 F 5
Kerrick ○ **USA** (TX) 264-265 B 2
Kerriya Shankou ▲ **VRC** 144-145 C 3
Kerr Lake, Robert S. ⬭ **USA** (OK) 264-265 J 3
Kerrobert ○ **CDN** (SAS) 232-233 J 4
Kerr Scott Reservoir, W. ⬭ **USA** (NC) 282-283 F 4
Kerrville ○ **USA** (TX) 266-267 H 3
K'ersa ○ **ETH** 208-209 E 4
Kersa Dek ○ **ETH** 208-209 D 6
Kershaw ○ **USA** (SC) 284-285 K 2
Kersinyané ○ **RMM** 202-203 E 2
Kersley ○ **CDN** (BC) 228-229 M 4
Kertamulia ○ **RI** 162-163 H 5
Kerteh ○ **MAL** 162-163 E 2
Kerteminde ○· **DK** 86-87 E 9
Kertosono ○ **RI** 168 E 3
Keruak ○ **RI** 168 C 7
Kerugoya ○ **EAK** 212-213 F 4
Kervansaray ∴·· **TR** 128-129 E 3
Keryneia ○· **TR** 128-129 E 5
Kerzaz ○ **DZ** 188-189 L 6
Kesagami Lake ⬭ **CDN** (ONT) 236-237 H 2
Kesagami Lake Provincial Park ⊥ **CDN** (ONT) 236-237 H 2
Kesagami River ~ **CDN** 236-237 H 2
Keşan ☆ **TR** 128-129 B 2
Kešem ○ **AFG** 136-137 M 6
Kesem Wenz ~ **ETH** 208-209 D 4
Kesennuma ○ **J** 152-153 J 5
Keshena ○ **USA** (WI) 270-271 K 6
Keshod ○ **IND** 138-139 C 9
Kesiman ○ **RI** 168 B 7
Keskin ○ **TR** 128-129 E 3
Kestell ○ **ZA** 220-221 J 4
Kestenğa ○ **RUS** 88-89 L 4
Keswick ○ **GB** 90-91 F 4
Keszthely ○ **H** 92-93 O 5
Ket' ~ **RUS** 114-115 R 5
Ket', Bol'šaja ~ **RUS** 114-115 V 6
Keta ○ **GH** 202-203 L 7
Keta, gory ▲▲ **RUS** 108-109 Y 7
Keta, ozero ⬭ **RUS** 108-109 X 7
Ketahun ○ **RI** 162-163 D 6
Keta Lagoon ⬭ **GH** 202-203 L 7
Ketama ○ **MA** 188-189 J 3
Ketanda ○ **RUS** (HBR) 120-121 J 3
Ketanda ~ **RUS** 120-121 J 3
Ketanggungan ○ **RI** 168 C 3
Ketapang ○ **RI** (JTI) 168 E 3
Ketapang ○ **RI** (KBA) 162-163 H 5
Ketčenery ○ **RUS** 96-97 D 10
Ketchen ○ **CDN** (SAS) 232-233 Q 4
Ketchikan ○ **USA** 32-33 E 4
Ketchum ○ **USA** (ID) 252-253 D 3
Kete-Krachi ○ **GH** 202-203 K 6
Ketesso ○ **CI** 202-203 J 7
Keti Bandar ○ **PK** 134-135 M 6
Ketlica, ostrov ⌒ **RUS** 84-85 c 2
Ketlik River ~ **USA** 20-21 L 2
Ketoj, ostrov ⌒ **RUS** 122-123 P 5
Ketok Mountain ▲ **USA** 22-23 S 3
Ketomoknai ○ **PNG** 183 A 3
Ketoria, Cape ▲ **CDN** 36-37 M 2
Kétou ○· **DY** 204-205 E 5
Ketovo ☆ **RUS** 114-115 H 7
Ke Town ○ **LB** 202-203 F 6
Kętrzyn ○ **PL** 92-93 Q 1
Ketsko-Tymskaja, ravnina ◡ **RUS** 114-115 S 4
Ketta ○ **RCB** 210-211 E 3
Kétté ○ **CAM** 206-207 B 6
Kettering ○ **USA** (OH) 280-281 B 4
Kettle Falls ○ **USA** (WA) 244-245 G 2
Kettleman City ○ **USA** (CA) 248-249 E 3
Kettleman Hills ▲▲ **USA** 248-249 D 3
Kettle Point ▲ **CDN** (ONT) 238-239 C 5
Kettle Range ▲▲ **USA** 244-245 G 2
Kettle River ~ **CDN** 34-35 M 2
Kettle River ~ **CDN** 230-231 L 4
Kettle River ~ **USA** 244-245 G 2
Kettle River ~ **USA** 270-271 F 4
Kettle Valley ○ **CDN** (BC) 230-231 L 4
Keudeuteunom ○ **RI** 162-163 A 2
Keuka Lake ⬭ **USA** (NY) 278-279 D 6
Keul' ○ **RUS** 116-117 L 6
Keum ~ **RUS** 114-115 L 5
Keur Madiabel ○ **SN** 202-203 B 3
Keur Masséne ○ **RIM** 196-197 B 6
Keur Momar Sar ○ **SN** 196-197 C 7
Keuruu ○ **FIN** 88-89 H 5
Kèušen' = Căuseni ☆ **MD** 102-103 F 4
Kévé ○ **RT** 202-203 L 6
Kèveem ~ **RUS** 112-113 R 2
Kewanee ○ **USA** (IL) 274-275 J 3
Kewapante ○ **RI** 166-167 B 6
Kewasasap ○ **PNG** 183 E 5
Kewaskum ○ **USA** (WI) 274-275 K 1
Kewaunee ○ **USA** (WI) 270-271 L 6
Keweenaw Bay ○ **USA** (MI) 270-271 K 4
Keweenaw Bay ⬭ **USA** (MI) 270-271 K 4
Keweenaw Bay Indian Reservation X **USA** (MI) 270-271 K 4
Keweenaw Peninsula ◡ **USA** 270-271 K 3
Keweenaw Point ▲ **USA** (MI) 270-271 L 3
Key ○ **USA** (TX) 264-265 C 6
K'ey Āfer ○ **ETH** 208-209 C 6
Keyaluvik ○ **USA** 20-21 H 6
Keyapaha ○ **USA** (SD) 260-261 F 3
Keya Paha River ~ **USA** 260-261 F 3
Keyes ○ **CDN** (MAN) 234-235 D 4
Keyes ○ **USA** (OK) 264-265 B 2
Keyhole Reservoir ⬭ **USA** (WY) 252-253 O 2
Keyihe ○ **VRC** 150-151 D 2
Key Largo ○ **USA** (FL) 286-287 J 6
Key Largo ⌒ **USA** (FL) 286-287 J 6
Key Like Mine ○ **CDN** 34-35 D 2
Keyling Inlet ≈ 172-173 J 3
Keyser ○ **USA** (WV) 280-281 H 4
Keystone ○ **USA** (CA) 248-249 D 2
Keystone ○ **USA** (NE) 262-263 E 3
Keystone ○ **USA** (SD) 260-261 C 3
Keystone ○ **USA** (WA) 244-245 C 2
Keystone Heights ○ **USA** (FL) 286-287 G 2
Keystone Lake ⬭ **USA** (OK) 264-265 H 2
Keysville ○ **USA** (VA) 280-281 H 6
Keytesville ○ **USA** (MO) 274-275 F 5
Key West ○· **USA** (FL) 286-287 H 7
Kez ☆ **RUS** 96-97 H 5
Kezar Falls ○ **USA** (ME) 278-279 L 5
Kezi ○ **ZW** 218-219 E 5
Kežma ○ **RUS** 116-117 K 6
Kežmarok ○ **SK** 92-93 Q 4
Kgalagadi ◘ **RB** 220-221 E 2
Kgatleng ◘ **RB** 220-221 H 2
Kgokgole ~ **ZA** 220-221 F 3
Kgun Lake ⬭ **USA** 20-21 H 6
Khabou ○ **RIM** 202-203 D 2
Khabrat al Dawish ○ **KWT** 130-131 K 3
Khachbiyine, Oued al- ~ **WSA** 188-189 F 7
Khadrah, Al ○ **LAR** 192-193 J 2
Khadwa ○ **IND** 138-139 F 9
Khagaria ○ **IND** 142-143 E 3
Khairāgarh ○ **IND** 142-143 B 5
Khairapa ○ **IND** 138-139 D 6
Khairpur ○ **PK** (PU) 138-139 D 5
Khairpur ○· **PK** (SIN) 138-139 B 6
Khairpur Nāthan Shāh ○ **PK** 134-135 M 5
Khajurago ○··· **IND** 138-139 G 7
Khajuri Kach ○ **PK** 138-139 B 3
Khakassia = Hakasija, Respublika ◘ **RUS** 124-125 Q 2
Khakhea ○ **RB** 220-221 F 2
Khakurdi ○ **IND** 138-139 E 9
Khalaf Allāh, Bi'r < **LAR** 192-193 E 4
Khalaf Allāh, Qārat ▲ **LAR** 192-193 G 4
Khalfallah ○ **DZ** 190-191 C 3
Khālī, Wādī al ~ **LAR** 192-193 K 2
Khalij al-Baḥrain ≈ 134-135 D 6
Khalij al Bumbah ≈ 192-193 K 1
Khalīj Surt ≈ 192-193 G 2
Khambhāliya ○ **IND** 138-139 B 8
Khambhat ○ **IND** 138-139 D 8
Khambhāt, Gulf of ≈ 138-139 C 9
Khāmgaon ○ **IND** 138-139 F 9
Khami Ruins ∴··· **ZW** 218-219 E 5
Khamis Mushayt = Ḫamīs Mušait ○ **KSA** 132-133 C 4
Kham Khuan Kaeo ○ **THA** 158-159 H 3
Khammam ○ **IND** 142-143 B 7
Khampat ○ **MYA** 142-143 J 4
Kham Ta Kla ○ **THA** 158-159 G 2
Khan ~ **NAM** 216-217 C 11
Khānāpur ○ **IND** 140-141 F 3
Khandala ○ **IND** 138-139 F 10
Khānewāl ○ **PK** 138-139 C 4
Khāngāh Dogrān ○ **PK** 138-139 D 4
Khāngarh ○ **PK** 138-139 C 5
Khangar Sidi Nadji ○ **DZ** 190-191 F 3
Khanka, Ozero = Hanka, ozero ⬭ **RUS** 122-123 E 6
Khankendi = Xankandı ☆ **AZ** 128-129 M 3
Khanna ○ **IND** 138-139 F 4
Khannfous, Hassi el ○ **DZ** 190-191 D 6
Khannfoussa, Gara ▲ **DZ** 190-191 F 7
Khanom ○ **THA** 158-159 E 6
Khānpur ○ **PK** (PU) 138-139 C 5
Khānpur ○ **PK** (SIN) 138-139 B 6
Khansiir, Raas ▲ **SP** 208-209 G 3
Khanty-Mansi Autonomous District=Hanty-Mansijskij avt. okrug ◘ **RUS** 114-115 G 3
Khao Chmao National Park ⊥ · **THA** 158-159 F 4
Khao Kha Khaeng ▲ **THA** 158-159 E 2
Khao Kheaw National Park ⊥ · **THA** 158-159 F 3
Khao Khieo Open Zoo · **THA** 158-159 F 4
Khao Laem Reservoir < **THA** 158-159 E 3
Khao Sok National Park ⊥ **THA** 158-159 E 6
Khapalu ○ **IND** 138-139 F 2
Khaptada National Park ⊥ **NEP** 144-145 C 6
Kharagpur ○ **IND** 142-143 E 4
Khārān ○ **PK** 134-135 L 4
Kharar ○ **IND** 138-139 F 4
Khardung La ▲ **IND** 138-139 F 2
Kharepātan ○ **IND** 140-141 E 2
Khârga, El = al-Ḫāriğa ○· **ET** 194-195 E 5
Khargon ○ **IND** 138-139 E 9
Khāriān ○ **PK** 138-139 D 3
Khariār ○ **IND** 142-143 C 5
Kharikhola ○ **NEP** 144-145 F 7
Kharj, al = Ḫarǧ, al ○ **KSA** 130-131 K 5
Kharkiv = Charkiv ○ **UA** 102-103 K 3
Khârroûb, Oued ~ **RIM** 196-197 F 3
Kharsia ○ **IND** 142-143 C 5
Khartoum = al-Harṭūm ★·· **SUD** 200-201 F 5
Khartoum North = al-Harṭūm Baḥrī ○ **SUD** 200-201 F 5
Khāsi-Jaintia Hills ▲▲ **IND** 142-143 G 3
Khasm Elmi ○ **SUD** 200-201 C 6
Khatai ○ **IND** 142-143 C 3
Khātegaon ○ **IND** 138-139 F 8
Khatima ○ **IND** 138-139 G 5
Khatoli ○ **IND** 138-139 F 7
Khatt Atoui ~ **RIM** 196-197 C 4
Khatt et Toueïrja ~ **RIM** 196-197 C 5
Khaur ○ **PK** 138-139 D 3
Khāvda ○ **IND** 138-139 B 8
Khazzān ar-Ruṣayri < **SUD** 208-209 B 3
Khed ○ **IND** 140-141 E 2
Kheda ○ **IND** 138-139 D 8
Khedive ○ **CDN** (SAS) 232-233 O 6
Khèmis-des-Zèmamra ○ **MA** 188-189 G 4
Khemis Miliana ○ **DZ** 190-191 D 2
Khemissa ∴· **DZ** 190-191 F 2
Khemisset ☆ **MA** 188-189 H 4
Khemmarat ○ **THA** 158-159 H 2
Khenchela ☆ **DZ** 190-191 F 3
Khenifra ☆ **MA** 188-189 J 4
Kherālu ○ **IND** 138-139 D 8
Kherba ○ **DZ** 190-191 C 2
Kheri ○ **IND** 138-139 F 9
Kherir, Oued ~ **RIM** 196-197 F 2
Kherrata ○ **DZ** 190-191 E 2
Kherson = Cherson ☆· **UA** 102-103 H 4
Kherwāra ○ **IND** 138-139 D 8
Khe Sanh ☆· **VN** 158-159 J 2
Khe Ve ○ **VN** 158-159 H 2
Khewra ○ **PK** 138-139 D 3
Khezmir ○ **RIM** 196-197 E 5
Khimki = Himki ☆ **RUS** 94-95 P 4
Khipro ○ **PK** 138-139 B 7
Khiran, al- ○ **KWT** 130-131 L 3
Khiu ○ **PK** 138-139 C 4
Khlong Ngae ○ **THA** 158-159 F 7
Khlong Thom ○ **THA** 158-159 E 7
Khmel'nyts'kyy = Chmel'nyc'kyj ☆ **UA** 102-103 E 3
Khodzhavend = Xocavand ○ **AZ** 128-129 M 3
Khogué Tobène ○ **SN** 202-203 C 2
Khojak Pass ▲ **PK** 134-135 M 3
Khok Chang ○ **THA** 158-159 G 2
Khok Kloi ○ **THA** 158-159 E 6
Khok Phek ○ **THA** 158-159 G 3
Khok Pho ○ **THA** 158-159 F 7
Khok Samrong ○ **THA** 158-159 F 3
Khomas Hochland ▲▲ **NAM** 216-217 D 11
Khomeynišahr ○ **IR** 134-135 D 2
Khon ○ **THA** 158-159 E 2
Khondmāl Hills ▲▲ **IND** 142-143 C 5
Khong Chiam ○ **THA** 158-159 H 3
Khong Khi Sua ○ **THA** 158-159 F 3
Khon Kaen ○ **THA** 158-159 G 2
Khôr Anyâr ○ **DJI** 200-201 L 6
Khorāsān ◘ **IR** 134-135 G 1
Khorasgān ○ **IR** 134-135 D 2
Khordha ○ **IND** 142-143 D 5
Khor Fakkan = Ḫaur Fakkān ○ **UAE** 134-135 G 6
Khor Gamdze ○ **VRC** 144-145 M 5
Khorixas ☆ **NAM** 216-217 C 10
Khor Khor ○ **IR** 128-129 L 4
Khossanto ○ **SN** 202-203 E 3
Khost ○ **PK** 134-135 M 3
Khotol Mount ▲ **USA** 20-21 M 4
Khouribga ☆ **MA** 188-189 H 4
Khreum ○ **MYA** 142-143 H 5
Khswan Mountain ▲ **CDN** 32-33 F 4
Khuang Nai ○ **THA** 158-159 H 3
Khubus ○ **ZA** 220-221 C 4
Khuchinarai ○ **THA** 158-159 H 2
Khudabad ○ **IND** 138-139 E 1
Khudābād ○ **PK** 134-135 M 5
Khudiān ○ **PK** 138-139 E 4
Khudzhand = Ḫuǧand ☆ **TJ** 136-137 L 4
Khukhan ○ **THA** 158-159 H 3
Khulayf, Qaṣr ○ **LAR** 192-193 E 4
Khulna ○ **BD** 142-143 F 4
Khunaniwāla ○ **PK** 138-139 C 4
Khunjerab Pass ▲ **PK** 138-139 E 1
Khun Yuam ○ **THA** 142-143 K 6
Khuraburi ○ **THA** 158-159 E 6
Khurai ○ **IND** 138-139 G 7
Khurayt ○ **SUD** 200-201 B 6
Khurībgah = Khouribga ☆ **MA** 188-189 H 4
Khurja ○ **IND** 138-139 F 5
Khushāb ○ **PK** 138-139 D 3
Khutzeymateen Inlet ≈ 228-229 D 2
Khuzdār ○ **PK** 134-135 M 5
Khwai River Lodge ○ **RB** 218-219 B 4
Khwane ○ **MYA** 158-159 E 3
Khwazakhela ○ **PK** 138-139 D 2
Khwebe Hills ▲▲ **RB** 218-219 B 5
Khyber Pass ▲·· **PK** 138-139 C 2
Kia ⌒ **FJI** 184 III b 2
Kia ○ **SOL** 184 I d 2
Kiakalamu ○ **ZRE** 214-215 E 5
Ķiakty, köli ⬭ **KZ** 124-125 F 3
Kiama ○ **AUS** 180-181 L 3
Kiamba ○ **RP** 160-161 F 9
Kiambere Reservoir < **EAK** 212-213 F 4
Kiambi ○ **ZRE** 214-215 E 4
Kiambu ○ **EAK** 212-213 F 4
Kiamichi Mountain ▲▲ **USA** 264-265 J 4
Kiamichi River ~ **USA** 264-265 J 4
Kiampanjang ○ **RI** 164-165 E 2
Kiana ○ **AUS** 174-175 D 5
Kiana ○ **USA** 20-21 K 3
Kiandarat ○ **RI** 166-167 F 3
Kiandra ○ **AUS** 180-181 K 3
Kiangara ○ **RM** 222-223 E 6
Kiangarow, Mount ▲ **AUS** 178-179 L 4
Kiangdom ○ **IND** 138-139 G 3
Kiangwe ~ **ZRE** 210-211 L 6
Kiantajärvi ⬭ **FIN** 88-89 K 4
Kia Ora ○ **AUS** 180-181 E 2
Kiasko River ~ **CDN** 236-237 H 2
Kiatai ○ **VRC** 146-147 E 4
Kiáto ○ **GR** 100-101 J 5
Kiau, Bi'r ○ **SUD** 200-201 G 2
Kiawah Island ⌒ **USA** (SC) 284-285 K 4
Kibakwe ○ **EAT** 214-215 J 4
Kibale ○ **EAU** 212-213 C 3
Kibali ~ **ZRE** 212-213 C 2
Kibangou ○ **RCB** 210-211 D 5
Kibau ○ **EAT** 214-215 H 5
Kibawe ○ **RP** 160-161 F 9
Kibaya ○ **EAT** 212-213 F 6
Kibbanahalli ○ **IND** 140-141 G 4
Kibeni ○ **PNG** 183 B 4
Kiberege ○ **EAT** 214-215 J 4
Kibi ○ **GH** 202-203 K 6
Kibira, Parc National de la ⊥ **BU** 212-213 B 5
Kibiti ○ **EAT** 214-215 K 4
Kibiya ○ **WAN** 204-205 H 3
Kiboga ○ **EAU** 212-213 C 3
Kiboko ~ **EAK** 212-213 F 5
Kibombo ○ **ZRE** 210-211 K 5
Kibondo ○ **EAT** 212-213 C 5
Ķibraj ☆ **UZ** 136-137 L 4
Kibre Mengist ○ **ETH** 208-209 D 6
Kıbrıscık ☆ **TR** 128-129 D 2
Kibungo ○ **RWA** 212-213 C 5
Kibunzi ○ **ZRE** 210-211 D 6
Kibuye ○ **RWA** 212-213 B 5
Kibwesa ○ **EAT** 214-215 E 4
Kibwezi ○ **EAK** 212-213 F 5
Kičevo ○ **MK** 100-101 H 4
Kichha ○ **IND** 138-139 G 5
Kichi-Kichi ○ **TCH** 198-199 H 4
Kichimiloo Claypan ⬭ **AUS** 178-179 H 5
Kichwamba ○ **EAU** 212-213 C 4
Kici Borsyķ, ķúm ∸ **KZ** 126-127 O 4
Kickapoo, Lake < **USA** (TX) 264-265 F 5
Kickapoo Indian Caverns ∴ **USA** (WI) 274-275 H 1
Kickapoo Indian Reservation X **USA** (KS) 262-263 L 5
Kickene Özen ~ **KZ** 96-97 F 9
Kicking Horse Pass ▲ **CDN** (ALB) 232-233 B 4
Kičmengskij Gorodok ☆ **RUS** 96-97 D 4
Kidal ○ **RMM** 196-197 L 5
Kidan, al- ∸ **KSA** 132-133 H 2
Kidapawan ☆ **RP** 160-161 F 9
Kidatu ○ **EAT** 214-215 J 4
Kidd's Beach ○ **ZA** 220-221 H 6
Kidekša ○··· **RUS** 94-95 R 3
Kidepo ~ **SUD** 208-209 A 6
Kidepo National Park ⊥ **EAU** 212-213 D 2
Kidete ○ **EAT** 214-215 J 4
Kidira ○ **SN** 202-203 D 2
Kidnappers, Cape ▲ **NZ** 182 F 3
Kidney Island ⌒ **CDN** 36-37 J 6
Kidston ○ **AUS** 174-175 H 6
Kiekinkoski ○ **FIN** 88-89 L 4
Kiel ☆· **D** 92-93 L 1
Kiel ○ **USA** (WI) 270-271 K 7
Kielce ☆· **PL** 92-93 Q 3
Kieler Bucht ≈ 92-93 L 1
Kiembara ○ **BF** 202-203 J 3
Kienge ○ **ZRE** 214-215 D 6
Kieng-Kjuel', ozero ⬭ **RUS** 110-111 G 3
Kiên Lu'o'ng ○ **VN** 158-159 H 5
Kiester ○ **USA** (MN) 270-271 E 7
Kieta ○ **PNG** 184 I b 2
Kiev = Kyjiv ★··· **UA** 102-103 G 2
Kievka ☆ **KZ** 124-125 G 3
Kievka ~ **RUS** 122-123 E 7
Kievskij Egan ~ **RUS** 114-115 Q 4
Kifaya ○ **RG** 202-203 D 3
Kiffa ☆ **RIM** 196-197 E 6
Kifinga ○ **ZRE** 214-215 D 5
Kifissiá ○ **GR** 100-101 J 5
Kifrī ☆ **IRQ** 128-129 L 5
Kifunankese ○ **ZRE** 210-211 K 6
Kifusa ○ **ZRE** 214-215 C 4
Kigač ~ **RUS** 96-97 F 10
Kigali ★ **RWA** 212-213 C 4
Kigalik River ~ **USA** 20-21 N 2
Kigataq ⌒ **GRØ** 26-27 X 7
Kiği ☆ **TR** 128-129 J 3
Kigiljah ○ **RUS** 110-111 W 3
Kigiljah, mys ▲ **RUS** 110-111 W 3
Kigiljah, poluostrov ◡ **RUS** 110-111 W 3
Kigluaik Mountains ▲▲ **USA** 20-21 H 4
Kignan ○ **RMM** 202-203 H 4
Kigoma ◘ **EAT** 212-213 C 6
Kigoma ☆ **EAT** (KIG) 212-213 B 6
Kigomasha, Ras ▲ **EAT** 212-213 G 6
Kigosi ~ **EAT** 212-213 C 5
Kigumo ○ **EAK** 212-213 F 4
Kihčik ~ **RUS** 120-121 R 7
Kihei ○ **USA** (HI) 288 J 4
Kihelkona ○ **EST** 94-95 H 2
Kihnu saar ⌒ **EST** 94-95 J 2
Kiholo ○ **USA** (HI) 288 K 5
Kihurio ○ **EAT** 212-213 G 6
Kii-hantō ◡ **J** 152-153 G 8
Kii-Nagashima ○ **J** 152-153 G 7
Kii-sanchi ▲▲ **J** 152-153 F 8
Kii-suidō ≈ 152-153 F 8
Kija ~ **RUS** 114-115 W 5
Kija ~ **RUS** 114-115 T 6
Kija ~ **RUS** 118-119 G 9
Ķijaly-Būrta ~ **KZ** 126-127 M 2
Kijanebalola, Lake ⬭ **EAU** 212-213 C 4
Kijang ○ **RI** 162-163 F 4
Kijasovo ○ **RUS** 96-97 H 5
Kiji, Île ⌒ **RIM** 196-197 B 5
Kijungu ○ **EAT** 212-213 F 6
Kika ○ **DY** 204-205 E 4
Kikagati ○ **EAU** 212-213 C 4
Kikai-shima ⌒ **J** 152-153 C 10
Kikale ○ **EAT** 214-215 K 4
Kikamba ○ **ZRE** 210-211 L 5
Kikambala ○ **EAK** 212-213 G 5
Kikegtek Island ⌒ **USA** 22-23 O 3
Kikert Lake ⬭ **CDN** 30-31 N 2
Kikiakrovak River ~ **USA** 20-21 O 2
Kikinda ○· **YU** 100-101 H 2
Kikiongolo ○ **ZRE** 210-211 E 6
Kikkertavak Island ⌒ **CDN** 36-37 T 6
Kikombo ○ **EAT** 214-215 H 4
Kikonai ○ **J** 152-153 J 4
Kikondja ○ **ZRE** 214-215 D 5
Kikori ○ **PNG** 183 C 4
Kikori River ~ **PNG** 183 B 4
Kikwit ○ **ZRE** 210-211 G 6
Kil ☆ **S** 86-87 F 7
Kilaguni Lodge ○ **EAK** 212-213 G 5
Kilakkarai ○ **IND** 140-141 H 6
Kilala ○ **EAK** 212-213 F 4
Kilauea ○ **USA** (HI) 288 F 2
Kilauea Crater ▲ **USA** (HI) 288 K 5
Kilauea Lighthouse (Largest Lighthose in the World) II · **USA** (HI) 288 F 2
Kilbeggan = Cill Bheagáin ○ **IRL** 90-91 D 5
Kilbella River ~ **CDN** 230-231 B 2
Kilboghamn ○ **N** 86-87 F 3
Kilbuck Mountains ▲▲ **USA** 20-21 K 6
Kilcoy ○ **AUS** 178-179 M 4
Kildala River ~ **CDN** 228-229 F 3
Kildare = Cill Dara ○ **IRL** 90-91 D 5
Kil'din, ostrov ⌒ **RUS** 88-89 M 2
Kildonan ○ **CDN** (BC) 230-231 E 5
Kildonan ○ **ZW** 218-219 F 3
Kildurk ○ **AUS** 172-173 J 4
Kilekale Lake ⬭ **CDN** 30-31 H 2
Kilembe ○ **ZRE** (BAN) 210-211 G 6
Kilembe ○ **ZRE** (SHA) 214-215 D 4
Kilembi ○ **ZRE** 210-211 L 6
Kileo ○ **ZRE** 210-211 K 6
Kilgana ~ **RUS** 120-121 P 3
Kilganskij massiv ▲▲ **RUS** 120-121 P 3
Kilgore ○ **USA** (NE) 262-263 F 2
Kilgore ○ **USA** (TX) 264-265 K 6
Kilgoris ○ **EAK** 212-213 E 4
Kili ~ **UZ** 136-137 K 4
Kilia ○ **PNG** 183 F 5
Kilian, Erg ∸ **DZ** 190-191 G 9
Kilibo ○ **DY** 204-205 E 4
Kili Bulak ○ **VRC** 144-145 J 4
Kilifarevo ○ **BG** 102-103 D 6
Kilifas ○ **PNG** 183 A 2
Kilifi ○ **EAK** 212-213 G 5
Kiligwa River ~ **USA** 20-21 L 2
Kilija ☆ **UA** 102-103 F 5
Kilikkollūr ○ **IND** 140-141 G 6
Kilim ○ **TCH** 206-207 D 3
Kilimanjaro ◘ **EAT** 212-213 F 5
Kilimanjaro ▲▲·· **EAT** 212-213 F 5
Kilimanjaro Buffalo Lodge ○ **EAK** 212-213 F 5
Kilimanjaro National Park ⊥··· **EAT** 212-213 F 5
Kilimatinde ○ **EAT** 212-213 E 6
Kilimbangara ⌒ **SOL** 184 I c 2
Kilindoni ○ **EAT** 214-215 K 4
Kilingi-Nõmme ○ **EST** 94-95 J 2
Kilíni ○· **GR** 100-101 H 6
Kilinochchi ○ **CL** 140-141 J 6
Kilipsjärvi ○ **FIN** 88-89 F 2
Kilis ☆ **TR** 128-129 G 4
Kiliuda Bay ≈ 22-23 U 4
Kiljanki ○ **RUS** 120-121 E 2
Kilju ○ **KOR** 150-151 G 7
Kilkee = Cill Chaoi ○ **IRL** 90-91 C 5
Kilkenny = Cill Chainnigh ☆· **IRL** 90-91 D 5
Kilkís ○ **GR** 100-101 J 4
Killaloe Station ○ **CDN** (ONT) 238-239 H 3
Killalo Lake ⬭ **CDN** (ONT) 236-237 B 3
Killaly ○ **CDN** (SAS) 232-233 Q 5
Killam ○ **CDN** (ALB) 232-233 G 3
Killarney ○ **AUS** (NT) 172-173 K 4
Killarney ○ **AUS** (QLD) 178-179 H 2
Killarney ○ **CDN** (MAN) 234-235 D 5
Killarney ○ **CDN** (ONT) 238-239 D 3
Killarney = Cill Airne ○· **IRL** 90-91 C 5
Killarney Provincial Park ⊥ **CDN** (ONT) 238-239 D 2
Killdeer ○ **CDN** (SAS) 232-233 M 6
Killdeer ○ **USA** (ND) 258-259 E 4
Kill Devil Hills ○ **USA** (NC) 282-283 M 4
Killeen ○ **USA** (TX) 266-267 K 2
Killik River ~ **USA** 20-21 N 2
Killiney Beach ○ **CDN** (BC) 230-231 K 3
Killington Peak ▲ **USA** (VT) 278-279 J 5
Killorglin = Cill Orglan ○ **IRL** 90-91 C 5
Kilmarnock ○ **GB** 90-91 E 4
Kilmarnock ○ **USA** (VA) 280-281 K 6
Kil'mez' ☆ **RUS** 96-97 G 5
Kil'mez' ~ **RUS** 96-97 H 5
Kilmichael ○ **USA** (MS) 268-269 L 3
Kilmore ○ **AUS** 180-181 H 4
Kiln ○ **USA** (MS) 268-269 L 6
Kilogbe ○ **WAN** 204-205 E 3
Kilombero ~ **EAT** 214-215 J 5
Kilómetro 133 ○ **YV** 60-61 J 3
Kilosa ○ **EAT** 214-215 J 4
Kilrush = Cill Rois ○ **IRL** 90-91 C 5
Kilto ○ **AUS** 172-173 F 4
Kilu ○ **PNG** 183 F 3
Kiluan ○ **RI** 162-163 F 7
Kilubi ○ **ZRE** (KIV) 210-211 L 6
Kilubi ~ **ZRE** 214-215 C 5
Kilunguye ~ **ZRE** 212-213 A 6
Kilwa ○ **ZRE** 214-215 E 5
Kilwa Kisiwani ∴··· **EAT** 214-215 K 5
Kilwa Kivinje ○ **EAT** 214-215 K 5
Kilwa Masoko ○ **EAT** 214-215 K 5
Kilwat ○ **RI** 166-167 G 4
Kilwinning ○ **CDN** (SAS) 232-233 M 2
Kim ~ **CAM** 204-205 J 6
Kim ○ **TCH** 206-207 B 4
Kim ○ **USA** (CO) 254-255 M 6
Ķima ☆ **KZ** 124-125 E 3
Kimaan ○ **RI** 166-167 K 5
Kimamba ○ **EAT** 214-215 J 4
Kimana ○ **EAK** 212-213 F 5
Kimān al-Maṭā'ina ○ **ET** 194-195 F 5
Kimanis, Teluk ≈ 160-161 A 10
Kimano II ○ **ZRE** 212-213 B 6
Kimba ○ **AUS** (QLD) 174-175 G 4
Kimba ○ **AUS** (SA) 180-181 D 2
Kimba ○ **RCB** 210-211 E 5
Kimball ○ **USA** (MN) 270-271 D 5
Kimball ○ **USA** (NE) 262-263 C 3
Kimball ○ **USA** (SD) 260-261 H 3
Kimball, Mount ▲ **USA** 20-21 S 5
Kimbao ○ **ZRE** 210-211 F 6
Kimbe ☆ **PNG** 183 F 3
Kimbe Bay ≈ 183 F 3
Kimberley ∸ **AUS** 172-173 G 4
Kimberley ○ **CDN** (BC) 230-231 O 4
Kimberley ☆ **ZA** 220-221 G 4
Kimberley Aboriginal Land X **AUS** 172-173 H 3
Kimberley Downs ○ **AUS** 172-173 G 4
Kimberley Plateau ∸ **AUS** 172-173 G 4
Kimberly ○ **USA** (OR) 244-245 F 6
Kimbirila Sud ○ **CI** 202-203 G 5
Kimchaek ○ **KOR** 150-151 G 7
Kimču ~ **RUS** 116-117 K 5
Kimenga ~ **RCB** 210-211 D 5
Kími ○ **GR** 100-101 K 5
Kimilili ○ **EAK** 212-213 E 3
Kimirekkum, peski ∸ **UZ** 136-137 H 5
Kimjongsuk-up ○ **KOR** 150-151 F 7
Kimobetsu ○ **J** 152-153 J 3
Kimongo ○ **RCB** 210-211 D 6
Kimovsk ☆ **RUS** 94-95 Q 5
Kimowin River ~ **CDN** 32-33 Q 3
Kimpanga ○ **ZRE** 214-215 C 4
Kimparana ○ **RMM** 202-203 H 3
Kimpata-Eku ○ **ZRE** 210-211 G 6
Kimpelo ○ **RCB** 210-211 E 5
Kimpese ○ **ZRE** 210-211 E 6
Kimry ☆ **RUS** 94-95 P 3
Kimsambi ○ **EAT** 212-213 C 4
Kimsi ○ **EAT** 212-213 C 5
Kim So'n ☆· **VN** 156-157 E 6
Kimsquit ○ **CDN** (BC) 228-229 H 4
Kimsquit River ~ **CDN** 228-229 G 3
Kimvula ○ **ZRE** 210-211 E 6
Kimža ~ **RUS** 88-89 S 4
Kin ○ **J** 152-153 D 11
Kinabalu, Gunung ▲·· **MAL** 160-161 B 9
Kinabalu National Park ⊥ **MAL** 160-161 B 9
Kinabulu National Park ⊥ **MAL** 160-161 B 9
Kinak Bay ≈ 22-23 O 3
Kinangaly ▲ **RM** 222-223 D 7
Kinango ○ **EAK** 212-213 G 6
Kinara ○ **RI** 166-167 G 3
Kinard ○ **USA** (FL) 286-287 D 1
Kinaussaq ▲ **GRØ** 28-29 P 4
Kinbasket Lake ⬭ **CDN** (BC) 228-229 Q 4
Kincaid ○ **CDN** (SAS) 232-233 M 6
Kincaid ○ **USA** (KS) 262-263 L 6
Kincardine ○ **CDN** (ONT) 238-239 D 4
Kinchafoonee Creek ~ **USA** 284-285 F 5
Kinchega National Park ⊥ **AUS** 180-181 G 2
Kinchil ○ **MEX** 52-53 K 1
Kincolith ○ **CDN** 32-33 F 4
Kinda ○ **ZRE** 214-215 C 5
Kindakun Point ▲ **CDN** (BC) 228-229 B 3
Kindamba ○ **RCB** 210-211 E 5
Kinder ○ **USA** (LA) 268-269 H 6
Kindersley ○ **CDN** (SAS) 232-233 J 4
Kindi ○ **BF** 202-203 J 3
Kindi ○ **ZRE** 210-211 F 6
Kindia ◘ **RG** 202-203 D 4
Kindia ☆ **RG** (KIN) 202-203 D 4
Kindikti, köli ⬭ **KZ** 124-125 C 3
Kindu ○ **ZRE** 210-211 K 5
Kinel' ☆ **RUS** 96-97 G 7
Kinel'-Čerkasy ☆ **RUS** 96-97 G 7
Kinel'skie jary ▲▲ **RUS** 96-97 G 7
Kineshma = Kinešma ☆ **RUS** 94-95 S 3
Kinesi ○ **EAT** 212-213 D 4
Kinešma ☆ **RUS** 94-95 S 3
King ○ **USA** (TX) 266-267 K 2
King, Cayo ⌒ **NIC** 52-53 C 5
King, Lake ⬭ **AUS** (WA) 176-177 E 6
King, Lake ⬭ **AUS** (WA) 176-177 F 2
King, Mount ▲ **AUS** 178-179 J 3
Kinga ○ **ZRE** 214-215 B 6
Kinganga ○ **ZRE** 210-211 D 6
Kingaroy ○ **AUS** 178-179 L 4
King Charles Cape ▲ **CDN** 36-37 K 2
King Christian Island ⌒ **CDN** 24-25 U 2
King City ○ **USA** (CA) 248-249 C 3
King City ○ **USA** (MO) 274-275 D 4
Kingcome Inlet ≈ 230-231 C 3

346 Kenmare — Kingcome Inlet

Kingcome Inlet ○ **CDN** (BC)
230-231 C 3
King Cove ○ **USA** 22-23 P 5
King Edward River ≈ **AUS** 172-173 H 3
King Edward VIth Gulf ≋ 16 G 6
Kingfisher ○ **USA** (OK) 264-265 G 3
Kingfisher Lake ○ **CDN** (ONT)
234-235 O 2
King George Bay ≈ 78-79 K 6
King George Island ↷ **ARK** 16 G 31
King George Islands ↷ **CDN** 36-37 K 6
King George Sound ≈ 36-37 N 4
King George Sound ≈ 176-177 D 7
King George VIth Sound ≋ 16 F 30
King George VIth Land ⊥ **ARK** 16 F 16
King Haakon Bay ≈ 78-79 O 7
Kingisepp ☆ **RUS** 94-95 L 2
Kingisepp = Kuressaare ○•= **EST**
94-95 H 2
King Island ▲ **AUS** 180-181 H 5
King Island ↷ **CDN** (BC) 228-229 G 4
King Island ↷ **USA** 20-21 F 4
King Junction ○ **AUS** 174-175 G 4
King Lear ▲ **USA** (NV) 246-247 G 2
King Leopold Ranges ▲ **AUS**
172-173 H 2
Kingman ○ **CDN** (ALB) 232-233 F 2
Kingman ○ **USA** (AZ) 256-257 A 3
Kingman ↷ **USA** (KS) 262-263 H 7
King Mountain ▲ **USA** (OR)
244-245 C 2
King Mountain ▲ **USA** (TX)
266-267 E 2
Kingnait Fiord ≋ 36-37 R 2
Kingnait Range ▲ **CDN** 36-37 L 2
Kingombe ○ **ZRE** 210-211 L 5
Kingoonya ○ **AUS** 178-179 C 6
Kingora River ~ **CDN** 24-25 e 6
Kingoué ○ **RCB** 210-211 E 5
Kingri ○ **PK** 138-139 B 4
King River ~ **AUS** 172-173 L 3
King River ~ **AUS** 180-181 J 4
King Salmon ○ **USA** 22-23 S 3
King Salmon River ~ **USA** 22-23 S 3
King Salmon River ~ **USA** 22-23 S 4
King's-Bay-Fall • **TT** 60-61 L 2
Kings Bay Naval Submarine Base xx
USA (GA) 284-285 J 6
Kingsburg ○ **CDN** (NS) 240-241 L 6
Kingsburg ○ **USA** (CA) 248-249 E 3
Kingsburg ○ **USA** (SC) 284-285 L 3
Kingsburg ○ **ZA** 220-221 H 7
Kings Canyon ⌂ **AUS** 176-177 L 2
Kings Canyon National Park ⊥ **USA** (CA)
240-249 F 2
Kings Canyon National Park ⊥ **USA** (CA)
248-249 F 3
Kingscote ○ **AUS** 180-181 D 3
Kinga Cove ○ **CDN** (NFL) 242-243 P 4
Kingsfield ○ **USA** (ME) 278-279 L 4
Kingsford ○ **USA** (WI) 270-271 K 5
Kingsgate ○ **CDN** (BC) 230-231 N 4
Kings Hill Pass ▲ **USA** (MT)
250-251 J 5
Kingslake National Park ⊥ **AUS**
100-101 I 4
Kingsland ○ **USA** (GA) 284-285 J 6
Kingsland ○ **USA** (TX) 266-267 H 3
Kings Landing Historical Settlement •
CDN (NB) 240-241 H 5
Kingsley ○ **USA** (IA) 274-275 C 2
Kingsley ○ **ZA** 220-221 K 3
King's Lynn ○ **GB** 90-91 H 5
Kings Mountain ○ **USA** (NC)
282-283 F 5
Kings Mountain National Military Park •
USA (SC) 284-285 J 1
Kings Sound ≈ 172-173 F 4
Kings Peak ▲ **USA** (UT) 252-253 K 5
King's Point ○ **CDN** (NFL) 242-243 M 3
Kingsport ○ **USA** (TN) 282-283 E 4
Kings River ~ **USA** 276-277 B 4
Kingston ○ **AUS** 180-181 J 7
Kingston ○ **CDN** (NB) 240-241 H 5
Kingston ○ **CDN** (ONT) 238-239 J 4
Kingston ★ • **JA** 54-55 G 5
Kingston ○ **USA** (IL) 274-275 G 5
Kingston ○ **USA** (MO) 274-275 D 5
Kingston ○ **USA** (NM) 256-257 H 4
Kingston ○ **USA** (NY) 246-247 H 4
Kingston ○ **USA** (NY) 280-281 M 2
Kingston ○ **USA** (OK) 264-205 H 5
Kingston ○ **USA** (PA) 280-281 L 2
Kingston ○ **USA** (TN) 282-283 D 5
Kingston-on-Murray ○ **AUS** 180-181 F 3
Kingston Peak ▲ **USA** (CA)
248-249 J 4
Kingston S.E. ○ **AUS** 180-181 E 4
Kingston upon Hull ○ **GB** 90-91 G 5
Kingstown ○ **WV** 56 E 5
Kingstree ○ **USA** (SC) 284-285 L 3
Kings Valley ○ **USA** (OR) 244-245 B 6
Kingsville ○ **USA** (TX) 266-267 K 6
Kingswood ○ **ZA** 220-221 G 3
Kingulube ○ **ZRE** 212-213 B 5
Kingungi ○ **ZRE** 210-211 F 6
Kingurutik Lake ○ **CDN** 36-37 S 6
Kingurutik River ~ **CDN** 36-37 S 6
Kingussie ○ **GB** 90-91 E 3
Kingwaya ○ **ZRE** 210-211 G 6
King William Island ↷ **CDN** 24-25 X 6
King Williams Town ○ **ZA** 220-221 H 6
King William's Town ○ • **ZA**
220-221 H 6
Kingwood ○ **USA** (WV) 280-281 G 4
Kinama ○ **ZRE** 214-215 E 6
Kinik ○ **TR** 128-129 B 3
Kinipaghulghat Mountains ▲ **USA**
20-21 H 5
Kinirapoort ○ **ZA** 220-221 J 5
Kinistino ○ **CDN** (SAS) 232-233 N 3
Kinkala ○ **RCB** 210-211 E 5
Kinkasan-shima ↷ **J** 152-153 J 5
Kinkon, Chutes de ⌂ **RG** 202-203 D 4
Kinkony, Farihy ⬦ **RM** 222-223 D 6
Kinkosi ○ **ZRE** 210-211 E 6
Kinley ○ **CDN** (SAS) 232-233 L 3
Kinley Point ▲ **CDN** 26-27 L 3

Kinmundy ○ **USA** (IL) 274-275 K 6
Kinna ○ **EAK** 212-213 G 3
Kinna ○ **S** 86-87 F 8
Kinnaird Head ⌒ **GB** 90-91 G 3
Kinnear ○ **USA** (WY) 252-253 K 3
Kinnegad ○ **IRL** 90-91 D 5
Kinnekulle ▲• **S** 86-87 F 7
Kinniconick ○ **USA** (KY) 276-277 M 2
Kinniya ○ **CL** 140-141 J 6
Kino, Bahia ≈ **MEX** 50-51 C 3
Kinomoto ○ **J** 152-153 K 7
Kinoosao ○ **CDN** 34-35 F 2
Kinrara ○ **AUS** 174-175 H 6
Kinross ○ **ZA** 220-221 J 3
Kinsarvik ○ **N** 86-87 C 6
Kinsella ○ **CDN** (ALB) 232-233 G 3
Kinsey ○ **USA** (MT) 250-251 O 5
Kinshasa ○ **ZRE** 210-211 E 6
Kinshasa ● ★ • **ZRE** (Kin) 210-211 E 6
Kinsley ○ **USA** (KS) 262-263 G 7
Kinston ○ **USA** (NC) 282-283 K 5
Kinta ○ **USA** (OK) 264-265 J 3
Kintampo ○ **GH** 202-203 K 5
Kintinnian ○ **RG** 202-203 F 4
Kintom ○ **RI** 164-165 H 4
Kintop ○ **RI** 164-165 D 5
Kintore, Mount ▲ **AUS** 176-177 L 3
Kintore Range ▲ **AUS** 176-177 K 1
Kintyre ⌒ **GB** 90-91 E 4
Kinu-gawa ~ **J** 152-153 H 6
Kinushseo River ~ **CDN** 34-35 P 3
Kinuso ○ **CDN** 32-33 N 4
Kinwat ○ **IND** 138-139 G 10
Kinyéran ○ **RG** 202-203 F 4
Kinyeti ▲ **SUD** 212-213 D 2
Kinyinya ○ **BU** 212-213 C 5
Kioa ↷ **FJI** 184 III b 2
Kiokluk Mountains ▲ **USA** 20-21 L 6
Kiona ○ **USA** (WA) 244-245 D 4
Kiosk ○ **CDN** (ONT) 238-239 G 2
Kiowa ○ **USA** (CO) 254-255 L 4
Kiowa ○ **USA** (KS) 262-263 H 7
Kiowa ○ **USA** (MT) 250-251 F 3
Kiowa ○ **USA** (OK) 264-265 J 4
Kiowa, Fort • **USA** (SD) 260-261 G 3
Kiowa Creek ~ **USA** 254-255 L 4
Kiowa Creek ~ **USA** 264-265 D 2
Kipahulu ○ **USA** (HI) 288 J 4
Kipaila ○ **ZRE** 214-215 E 4
Kipaka ○ **ZRE** 210-211 L 6
Kiparissia ○ **GR** 100-101 H 6
Kipiawa, Lac ○ **CDN** (QUE) 238-239 G 2
Kipemba ○ **ZRE** 210-211 F 6
Kipembawe ○ **EAT** 214-215 G 4
Kipengere Range ▲ **EAT** 214-215 G 5
Kipievo ○ **RUS** 88-89 X 4
Kipili ○ **EAT** 214-215 F 4
Kipini ○ **EAK** 212-213 H 5
Kipkelion ○ **EAK** 212-213 E 4
Kipling ○ **CDN** (SAS) 232-233 Q 5
Kipnuk ○ **USA** 22-23 O 3
Kipti ○ **UA** 102-103 G 2
Kipushi ○ **ZRE** 214-215 D 6
Kipushia ○ **ZRE** (KOR) 214-215 C 4
Kipushia ○ **ZRE** (SHA) 214-215 E 7
Kiran ~ **RUS** 120-121 F 6
Kirana, Tanjung ⌒ **RI** 166-167 G 3
Kirandul ○ **IND** 140-141 D 6
Kirane ○ **RMM** 202-203 E 3
Kiranomena ○ **RM** 222-223 E 7
Kiranur ○ **IND** 140-141 H 5
Kiranür ○ **IND** 140-141 H 5
Kirbej ○ **RUS** 110-111 H 5
Kirbikán, Wádi ~ **SUD** 200-201 F 3
Kirby Villé ○ **USA** (TX) 266-269 U 6
Kirchhoffer River ~ **CDN** 36-37 G 2
Kireevsk ○ **RUS** 94-95 P 5
Kirej ~ **RUS** 116-117 K 9
Kirenga ~ **RUS** 116-117 N 7
Kirensk ▲ **RUS** 116-117 O 7
Kirevna ~ **RUS** 120-121 T 5
Kirganik ○ **RUS** (KMC) 120-121 S 6
Kirganik ~ **RUS** 120-121 S 6
Kirgiz-Mijaki ○ **RUS** 96-97 J 7
Kirgizskij hrebet ▲ **KZ** 136-137 N 3
Kiri ○ **ZRE** 210-211 G 4
Kirlab ○ **RI** 166-167 J 2
Kiriaini ○ **EAK** 212-213 F 4
Kinkhan ○ **TR** 128-129 G 4
Kirikkale ○ **TR** 128-129 E 3
Kirillov ○ **RUS** 94-95 P 5
Kirillovo ○ **RUS** 122-123 K 5
Kirinda ○ **CL** 140-141 J 7
Kirishima-Yaku National Park ⊥ **J**
152-153 D 9
Kirishima-yama ▲ **J** 152-153 D 9
Kiriši ○ **RUS** 94-95 N 2
Kirit ○ **SP** 208-209 H 4
Kiritappu ○ **J** 152-153 L 3
Kiritimati Island ↷ **KIB** 13 M 2
Kiritiri ○ **EAK** 212-213 F 4
Kiriwa ○ **PNG** 183 A 5
Kiriwina Island ↷ **PNG** 183 F 5
Kirjaka-Tas, grjada ▲ **RUS** 108-109 f 4
Kirk ○ **USA** (OH) 244-245 D 4
Kirkalocka ○ **AUS** 176-177 D 4
Kirkcaldy ○ **GB** 90-91 F 3
Kirkella ○ **CDN** (MAN) 234-235 B 4
Kirkenes ○ **N** 86-87 P 2
Kirkensville ○ **USA** (OH) 280-281 D 4
Kirkfield ○ **CDN** (ONT) 238-239 F 3
Kirkçeçit ○ **TR** 128-129 K 3
Kirk Gemstone Deposit, Mount • **AUS**
176-177 F 6
Kirkimbie ○ **AUS** 172-173 J 4
Kirk Lake ○ **CDN** 30-31 P 4
Kirkland ○ **USA** (AZ) 256-257 C 4
Kirkland ○ **USA** (IL) 274-275 K 2
Kirkland ○ **USA** (NM) 244-245 C 3
Kirkland Lake ○ • **CDN** (ONT)
236-237 J 4
Kirklareli ○ **TR** 128-129 B 2
Kirklin ○ **USA** (IN) 274-275 M 4

Kirkpatrick Lake ○ **CDN** (ALB)
232-233 G 4
Kirksville ○ **USA** (MO) 274-275 F 4
Kirkûk ☆ **IRQ** 128-129 L 5
Kirkun ○ **USA** (WY) 128-129 E 11
Kirkwall ○ **GB** 90-91 F 2
Kirkwood ○ **USA** (IL) 274-275 H 4
Kirkwood ○ **USA** (MO) 274-275 H 6
Kirkwood ○ **ZA** 220-221 G 6
Kirobasi ○ **TR** 128-129 E 4
Kirov ○ **RUS** 94-95 O 4
Kirov ○ **RUS** (KIR) 96-97 L 5
Kirova, ostrov ↷ **RUS** 108-109 Z 3
Kirovabad = Ganža ○ **AZ** 128-129 M 2
Kirovakan = Karaklis ○ **AR** 128-129 M 2
Kirovo ○ **RUS** 118-119 L 5
Kirovo-Čepeck ○ **RUS** 96-97 G 4
Kirovograd = Kirovohrad ☆ **UA**
102-103 H 3
Kirovohrad ☆ **UA** 102-103 H 3
Kirovsk ○ **RUS** (LEN) 94-95 M 2
Kirovsk ○ **RUS** (MUR) 88-89 M 3
Kirovsk = Babadayhan ○ **TM**
136-137 F 4
Kirovs'ke ○ **UA** 102-103 J 4
Kirovs'kan ○ **RUS** (AMR) 118-119 N 8
Kirovskij ○ **RUS** (AST) 126-127 H 5
Kirovskij ○ **RUS** (KMC) 120-121 Q 6
Kirovskij ○ **RUS** (ROS) 122-123 G 4
Kirovskij ○ **TJ** 136-137 L 6
Kirovskoe ○ **KS** 136-137 M 3
Kirov su kojmasy ⬦ **KZ** 96-97 G 8
Kirpili ~ **RUS** 102-103 L 5
Kirs ○ **RUS** 96-97 H 4
Kirsanov ○ **RUS** 94-95 S 5
Kirşehir ☆ **TR** 128-129 F 3
Kirtachi ○ **RN** 204-205 F 2
Kirtâka ○ **AFG** 134-135 J 5
Kirtaka ~ **PK** 134-135 J 4
Kirthar National Park ⊥ **PK**
134-135 M 6
Kirthar Range ▲ **PK** 134-135 M 5
Kirtland ○ **USA** (NM) 256-257 G 2
Kirtland ○ **USA** (OH) 280-281 E 2
Kiru ○ **WAN** 204-205 J 4
Kiruna ○ • **S** 86-87 K 3
Kirundo ○ **BU** 212-213 C 5
Kirundu ○ **EAT** 214-215 K 4
Kirwan National Wildlife Refuge ⊥ **USA**
(KS) 262-263 G 5
Kirwin Reservoir ○ **USA** (KS)
262-263 G 5
Kiryandongo ○ **EAU** 212-213 E 3
Kiryû ○ **J** 152-153 H 0
Kiržač ☆ **RUS** 94-95 Q 3
Kiš ○ **IR** 134-135 G 5
Kisama ○ **RM** 222-223 E 7
Kisangani ○ **ZRE** 214-215 J 4
Kisangire ○ **EAT** 214-215 K 4
Kisantete ○ **ZRE** 210-211 F 6
Kisantu ○ • **ZRE** 210-211 E 6
Kisar, Pulau ↷ **RI** 160-167 J 6
Kisaralik River ~ **USA** 20-21 K 6
Kisârân ○ **RI** 162-163 C 3
Kisarawe ○ **EAT** 214-215 K 4
Kisarazu ○ **J** 152-153 H 7
Kisasi ○ **EAT** 212-213 G 6
Kisatchie ○ **USA** (LA) 268-269 G 5
Kisbey ○ **CDN** (SAS) 232-233 Q 6
Kiselevka ○ **RUS** 122-123 H 3
Kiselevsk ○ **RUS** 124-125 P 1
Kiselevsk = Kiselëvsk ○ **RUS**
124-125 P 1
Kisengi ○ **EAT** 212-213 D 6
Kisengwa ○ **ZRE** 214-215 C 4
Kisengwa ○ **ZRE** (KOR) 214-215 C 4
Kishangani ○ **IND** 142-143 K 4
Kishangar ○ **IND** 138-139 C 6
Kishangarh ○ **IND** (MAP) 138-139 G 7
Kishangarh ○ **IND** (RAJ) 138-139 E 6
Kishari ○ **PK** 134-135 M 5
Kishiwada ○ **J** 152-153 F 7
Kishtwar ○ **IND** 138-139 E 3
Kisi ○ **EAT** 214-215 H 4
Kisi ○ **WAN** 204-205 E 4
Kisigo ~ **EAT** 214-215 G 4
Kisigo Game Reserve ⊥ **EAT**
214-215 H 4
Kisii ○ **EAK** 212-213 E 4
Kisiju ○ **EAT** 214-215 K 5
Kisima ○ **EAK** 212-213 G 3
Kišinev = Chişinău ★ **MD** 102-103 F 4
Kisiwani ○ **EAT** 212-213 G 5
Kisiwani, Kilwa ~ **EAT** 214-215 K 5
Kiska Island ↷ **USA** 22-23 H 5
Kiska Volcan ▲ **USA** 22-23 E 6
Kiskörös ○ **H** 92-93 P 5
Kiskunfélegyháza ○ **H** 92-93 P 5
Kiskunhalas ○ **H** 92-93 P 5
Kislovodsk ○ **RUS** 104 D 5
Kismayo ○ **SP** 212-213 J 4
Kismet ○ **USA** (KS) 262-263 F 7
Kiso-gawa ~ **J** 152-153 K 7
Kisogwa ○ **EAT** 212-213 C 3
Kisomoro ○ **EAU** 212-213 B 4
Kiso-sanmyaku ▲ **J** 152-153 G 7
Kisose ○ **EAT** 214-215 H 4
Kisoshi ○ **ZRE** 212-213 B 5
Kispiox River ~ **CDN** 32-33 F 4
Kissen ~ **RG** 202-203 E 3
Kissidougou ○ **RG** 202-203 E 5
Kissimmee ○ **USA** (FL) 286-287 H 3
Kissimmee, Lake ○ **USA** (FL)
286-287 H 4
Kissimmee River ~ **USA** 286-287 H 4
Kissingen, Bad ○ **D** 92-93 L 3
Kistanje ○ **HR** 100-101 I 3
Kistigan Lake ○ **CDN** 34-35 K 3
Kisuki ○ **J** 152-153 E 7
Kisvárda ○ **H** 92-93 R 4
Kita ○ **RMM** 202-203 F 3
Kitaa = Vestgrønland ⊥ **GRØ** 26-27 Z 6

Kita-Daitō-shima ↷ **J** 152-153 D 12
Kitäf ○ **Y** 132-133 D 5
Kitahiyama ○ **J** 152-153 H 3
Kitaibaraki ○ **J** 152-153 J 6
Kitakami ○ **J** 152-153 J 5
Kitakami-gawa ~ **J** 152-153 J 5
Kitakami-kōti ▲ **J** 152-153 J 5
Kitakyūshū ○ **J** 152-153 D 8
Kitale ○ **EAK** 212-213 E 4
Kitamaat Village ○ **CDN** (BC)
228-229 D 3
Kitami ○ **J** 152-153 K 3
Kitami-santi ▲ **J** 152-153 K 2
Kitami-tōge ▲ **J** 152-153 K 3
Kitanda ○ **ZRE** 214-215 D 4
Kitangari ○ **EAT** 214-215 K 6
Kitangiri, Lake ○ **EAT** 212-213 E 6
Kitani Safari Camp ⌂ **EAK** 212-213 F 5
Kitava Island ↷ **PNG** 183 F 5
Kitaya ○ **EAT** 214-215 L 6
Kit Carson ○ **USA** (CO) 254-255 N 5
Kitchener ○ **AUS** 176-177 H 5
Kitchener ○ **CDN** (BC) 230-231 N 4
Kitchener ○ **CDN** (ONT) 238-239 E 5
Kitchigama, Rivière ~ **CDN** 236-237 H 2
Kitchings Mill ○ **USA** (SC) 284-285 J 3
Kite ○ **USA** (GA) 284-285 H 4
Kite ○ **USA** (KY) 276-277 N 3
Kiteba ○ **ZRE** 214-215 C 4
Kitee ○ **FIN** 88-89 L 4
Kitendwe ○ **ZRE** 214-215 E 4
Kitenga ○ **ZRE** 210-211 F 6
Kitengo ○ **ZRE** 214-215 C 4
Kitgum ○ **EAU** 212-213 D 2
Kithira ○ **GR** 100-101 J 6
Kithira ↷ **GR** 100-101 J 6
Kithnos ↷ **GR** 100-101 K 6
Kitika ○ **RCA** 206-207 F 6
Kitimat ○ **CDN** (BC) 228-229 D 3
Kitimat Ranges ▲ **CDN** 228-229 E 3
Kitimat River ~ **CDN** 228-229 F 2
Kitinen ~ **FIN** 88-89 J 3
Kitiwaka ~ **EAT** 214-215 H 6
Kitkatla ○ **CDN** (BC) 228-229 D 3
Kitilä ○ **FIN** 88-89 H 4
Kitlope River ~ **CDN** 228-229 G 2
Kitob ○ **UZ** 136-137 L 3
Kitobojnyi ○ **RUS** 122-123 O 5
Kitoj ~ **RUS** 116-117 L 9
Kitou ○ **J** 152-153 E 7
Kitsamby ~ **RM** 222-223 E 7
Kitscoty ○ **CDN** (ALB) 232-233 H 2
Kitsuki ○ **J** 152-153 D 8
Kitsumkalum Lake ○ **CDN** (BC)
228-229 F 2
Kitsumkalum River ~ **CDN** 228-229 E 2
Kittakittaooloo, Lake ⬦ **AUS**
178-179 F 5
Kittanning ○ **USA** (PA) 280-281 G 3
Kittery ○ **USA** (ME) 278-279 L 5
Kitt Peak National Observatory • **USA**
(AZ) 256-257 F 7
Kitty Hawk ○ **USA** (NC) 282-283 M 4
Kitui ○ **EAK** 212-213 G 4
Kitumbeino ○ **EAT** 212-213 F 5
Kitumbini ○ **EAT** 214-215 K 4
Kitunda ○ **EAT** 214-215 G 4
Kitunga ○ **EAT** 214-215 C 5
Kitutu ○ **ZRE** 212-213 B 5
Kitwanga ○ **CDN** 32-33 F 4
Kitwe ○ **Z** 214-215 E 7
Kitzbühel ○ **A** 92-93 M 5
Kitzingen ○ **D** 92-93 L 4
Kiu ○ **PLW** 212-213 F 4
Kiubo, Chute ⌂ **ZRE** 214-215 D 5
Kiuga Marine National Reserve ⊥ **EAK**
212-213 H 4
Kiu Lom Reservoir ○ **THA** 142-143 L 6
Kiumbila ○ **ZRE** 210-211 L 6
Kiunga ○ **EAK** 212-213 H 4
Kiunga ○ **PNG** 183 A 4
Kiuruvesi ○ **FIN** 88-89 J 5
Kivalina ○ **USA** 20-21 H 3
Kivalina River ~ **USA** 20-21 H 3
Kivu ○ **IR** 128-129 N 4
Kivijärvi ○ **FIN** 88-89 H 5
Kivioli ○ **EST** 94-95 K 2
Kivori-Kui ○ **PNG** 183 D 5
Kivu, Lac ○ **ZRE** 212-213 B 4
Kiwai Island ↷ **PNG** 183 B 5
Kiwalik ○ **USA** 20-21 K 3
Kiwatama ○ **EAT** 214-215 K 5
Kiwayuu Bay ≈ 212-213 H 5
Kiwi House • **NZ** 182 E 3
Kiworo ○ **RI** 166-167 K 5
Kiyámaki Dâğ ▲ **IR** 128-129 L 3
Kiyâsar ○ **IR** 136-137 G 4
Kiyât ○ **KSA** 132-133 B 4
Kiyawa ○ **WAN** 204-205 J 3
Kiyiu Lake ○ **CDN** (SAS) 232-233 K 4
Kiyl ~ **KZ** 96-97 J 5
Kizel ○ **RUS** 114-115 D 5
Kizema ○ **RUS** 88-89 V 4
Kizhake Chalakudi ○ **IND** 140-141 G 5
Kiziba-Baluba ⊥ **ZRE** 214-215 D 6
Kizi-Hem ~ **RUS** 116-117 J 7
Kizlagaç ○ **TR** 128-129 J 3
Kizilcahamam ○ **TR** 128-129 E 2
Kizilirmak ~ **TR** 128-129 F 2
Kiziljurt ○ **RUS** 126-127 G 6
Kizilkum ⊥ **UZ** 136-137 J 2
Kizilören ○ **TR** 128-129 D 4
Kizil Qianfodonga ○ **VRC** 146-147 G 5
Kiziltepe ○ **TR** 128-129 J 4
Kizimkazi ○ **EAT** 214-215 K 5
Kizir ~ **RUS** 116-117 G 7
Kizkalesi ~ **TR** 128-129 F 4
Kiznêr ☆ **RUS** 96-97 G 5

Kizyl Arvat ○ **TM** 136-137 E 5
Kizyl Atrek = Gyzyletrek ○ **TM**
136-137 D 6
Kizyl Baudak ○ **TM** 136-137 F 3
Kjahta ○ **RUS** 116-117 N 10
Kjalvaz ○ **AZ** 128-129 N 3
Kjær, Ytyk ~ **RUS** 120-121 L 2
Kjøpsvik ○ **N** 86-87 H 2
Km. 60 ○ **PY** 76-77 H 2
Km. 100 ○ **RA** 76-77 H 4
Km. 145 ○ **PY** 76-77 H 2
Knarvik ○ **N** 86-87 B 6
Kneehills Creek ~ **CDN** 232-233 F 4
Knee Lake ○ **CDN** (MAN) 34-35 J 3
Knewstubb Lake ○ **CDN** (BC)
228-229 K 3
Kneža ○ **BG** 102-103 D 6
Knickerbocker ○ **USA** (TX) 266-267 H 4
Knidos • **TR** 128-129 B 4
Kniepblade Ridge ▲ **USA** 20-21 L 2
Knife Delta ≋ 30-31 W 6
Knife River ~ **USA** 258-259 E 4
Knife River Indian Village National Historic
Site ∴ **USA** (ND) 258-259 F 4
Knight Inlet ≋ 230-231 D 3
Knight Islands ↷ **CDN** 36-37 R 4
Knights Landing ○ **USA** (CA)
246-247 D 5
Knightstown ○ **USA** (IN) 274-275 N 5
Knin ○ **HR** 100-101 F 2
Knippa ○ **USA** (TX) 266-267 H 4
Knivskjelodden ⌒ **N** 86-87 M 1
Knjaginino ○ **RUS** 96-97 D 6
Knjaze-Bolkonskoe ○ **RUS** 122-123 H 2
Knjaževac ○ **YU** 100-101 J 3
Knjazevo ○ **RUS** 88-89 H 2
Knjazevo ○ **RUS** 122-123 P 2
Knob, Cape ⌒ **AUS** 176-177 D 7
Knobby Head ⌒ **AUS** 176-177 C 4
Knobel ○ **USA** (AR) 276-277 E 4
Knob Noster ○ **USA** (MO) 274-275 E 5
Knokke-Heist ○ • **B** 92-93 G 3
Knolls ○ **USA** (UT) 254-255 B 5
Knorr, Cape ▲ **CDN** 26-27 P 4
Knott ○ **USA** (TX) 266-267 H 4
Knotts Island ○ **USA** (NC) 282-283 M 4
Knowles, Cape ▲ **ARK** 16 F 30
Knowles Lake ○ **CDN** 30-31 R 5
Knox ○ **USA** (IN) 274-275 M 3
Knox, Cape ▲ **CDN** (BC) 228-229 B 2
Knox City ○ **USA** (TX) 264-265 E 5
Knox Land ⊥ **ARK** 16 F 11
Knoxville ○ **USA** (IA) 274-275 E 3
Knoxville ○ **USA** (IL) 274-275 H 4
Knoxville ○ **USA** (PA) 280-281 J 2
Knoxville ☆ **USA** (TN) 282-283 D 5
Knuckles ▲ **CL** 140-141 J 7
Knud Rasmussen Land ⊥ **GRØ**
26-27 V 4
Knud Rasmussen Land ⊥ **GRØ**
26-27 m 8
Knysna ○ **ZA** 220-221 F 7
Knysna National Lake Area ⊥ **ZA**
220-221 F 7
Ko, gora ▲ **RUS** 122-123 J 3
Koaba ○ **DY** 202-203 L 4
Koagas ○ **RI** 166-167 G 3
Koala ○ **BF** 202-203 L 4
Koamb ○ **CAM** 210-211 D 2
Koaties de Pan ○ **ZA** 220-221 D 5
Kob' ○ **RUS** 116-117 K 8
Koba ○ **RI** (MAL) 166-167 H 5
Koba ○ **RI** 162-163 G 6
Kobadie ○ **RN** 202-203 L 3
Kobayashi ○ **J** 152-153 D 9
Kobbermineb ⌂ **GRØ** 28-29 Q 6
Kobe ○ **RI** 166-167 K 4
Kobe ★ **J** 152-153 F 7
Kobedaigouré ○ **CI** 202-203 H 7
Kobefaky ○ **UA** 102-103 J 3
Kobenni ○ **RIM** 196-197 F 7
København ● ★ • **DK** 86-87 E 9
Kobi ○ **RI** 166-167 G 2
Kobi ○ **WAN** 204-205 K 4
Kobjai ○ **RUS** 118-119 N 4
Koblenz ○ • **D** 92-93 J 3
Kobleve ○ **UA** 102-103 G 4
Kobli ○ **DY** 202-203 L 4
K'obo ○ **ETH** 200-201 J 6
Koboko ○ **EAU** 212-213 C 2
Kobona ○ **RUS** 94-95 M 1
Koborr, Pulau ↷ **RI** 166-167 H 5
Kobra ○ **RUS** 96-97 G 4
Kobryn ○ **BY** 94-95 J 5
Kobuk ○ **USA** 20-21 M 3
Kobuk River ~ **USA** 20-21 M 3
Kobuk Valley National Park ⊥ **USA**
20-21 L 3
Kobuleti ○ **GE** 126-127 D 7
Koca Deresi ~ **TR** 128-129 B 3
Kocaeli (Izmit) ☆ **TR** 128-129 C 2
Kocaeli Yarımadası ▲ **TR** 128-129 C 2
Kocaköy ○ **TR** 128-129 J 3
Koçarlı ○ **TR** 128-129 B 4
Koçani ○ **MK** 100-101 J 4
Koçarlı ○ **TR** 128-129 B 4
Koçcum ~ **RUS** 116-117 K 3
Koček ○ **RUS** 118-119 J 6
Kočenevo ○ **RUS** 114-115 N 7
Kočenga ~ **RUS** 116-117 M 8
Kočerinovo ○ **BG** 102-103 C 6
Kočevje ○ **YU** 100-101 E 2
Kočevo ○ **RUS** 96-97 J 4
Kôch'ang ○ **ROK** 150-151 F 10
Ko Chang ↷ **THA** 158-159 G 4
Ko Chang ▲ **THA** 158-159 G 4
Kochbārdo ○ **CL** 140-141 H 7
Koch Creek ○ **CDN** 230-231 M 4
Kôchi ★ • **J** 152-153 E 8
Koch Island ↷ **CDN** 24-25 h 6

Klotz, Mount ▲ **CDN** 20-21 U 4
Kluane Lake ○ **CDN** 20-21 V 6
Kluang ○ **MAL** 162-163 E 3
Kludang ○ **BRU** 164-165 D 1
Klumbang River ~ **CDN** 126-127 D 6
Klungkung ○ • **RI** 168 B 7
Klutlan Glacier ⊂ **CDN** 20-21 U 6
Klymovo ○ **RUS** 94-95 N 5
Km.60 ○ **PY** 76-77 H 2
Km.100 ○ **RA** 76-77 H 4
Km.145 ○ **PY** 76-77 H 2
Kjøllefjord ○ **N** 86-87 N 1
Kjøpsvik ○ **N** 86-87 N 1
Kjuel, Aleko- ○ **RUS** 110-111 K 3
Kjuel, Bjas'- ○ **RUS** 118-119 N 4
Kjuel, Bjas'- ○ **RUS** 118-119 N 4
Kjuel, Bjas'- ○ **RUS** 118-119 N 4
Kjuel, Kudu- ○ **RUS** 118-119 N 4
Kjuel, Sebjan- ○ **RUS** 110-111 R 7
Kjuel, Segjan- ○ **RUS** 118-119 P 4
Kjuel, Ulahan- ○ **RUS** 110-111 V 6
Kjuel, Us- ○ **RUS** 118-119 P 4
Kjuel, Usun- ○ **RUS** 118-119 H 4
Kjuenelekjan ~ **RUS** 110-111 G 5
Kjuente ~ **RUS** 120-121 J 2
Kjuereljah ○ **RUS** 118-119 N 4
Kjulekjan' ○ **RUS** 118-119 K 3
Kjulenke ~ **RUS** 110-111 O 6
Kjudjae ~ **RUS** 118-119 J 4
Kjunkju ~ **RUS** 118-119 N 5
Kjunkjuj-Rassoha ~ **RUS** 110-111 G 4
Kjupcy ○ **RUS** 120-121 F 3
Kjurdamir = Kürdamir ○ **AZ**
128-129 N 2
Kjurjungnekjan ~ **RUS** 116-117 O 3
Kjusjur ○ **RUS** 110-111 J 3
Kjustendil ○ • **BG** 102-103 C 6
Kiterput gornu ≋ 28-29 R 6
Kjutgum ○ **EAU** 212-213 D 6
Klaarstroom ○ **ZA** 220-221 F 6
Klabat, Teluk ≈ 162-163 F 5
Kladanj ○ **BIH** 100-101 G 2
Kladno ○ **CZ** 92-93 N 3
Klaeng ○ **THA** 158-159 F 4
Klagenfurt ☆ **A** 92-93 N 5
Klaipėda ○ • **LT** 94-95 G 4
Klakah ○ **RI** 168 E 3
Klamath Falls ○ **USA** (OR) 244-245 D 8
Klamath Mountains ▲ **USA**
246-247 C 2
Klamath River ~ **USA** 246-247 B 2
Klamath River Lodge ⌂ **USA** (CA)
240-247 C 2
Klamono ○ **RI** 166-167 F 2
Klang ○ **MAL** 162-163 D 3
Klappan River ~ **CDN** 32-33 F 3
Klarälven ~ **S** 86-87 F 6
Klark ~ **RUS** 112-113 V 1
Kläsene Nature Reserve ⊥ **ZA**
178-179 T 6
Klaten ○ **RI** 168 D 3
Klatovy ○ **CZ** 92-93 N 4
Klattau = Klatovy ○ **CZ** 92-93 M 4
Klawer ○ **ZA** 220-221 D 5
Klawock ○ **USA** 32-33 D 4
Kle ○ **LB** 202-203 E 6
Kleena Kleene ○ **CDN** (BC)
230-231 E 2
Klein Aub ○ **NAM** 220-221 D 3
Kleinbegin ○ **ZA** 220-221 E 5
Klein Doringrivier ~ **ZA** 220-221 D 5
Kleiner Kaukasus = Malyj Kavkaz ▲ **GE**
126-127 D 7
Kleiner Khingan ▲ **VRC** 150-151 P 1
Klein Karas ○ **NAM** 220-221 D 4
Klein Karoo = Little Karoo ⊥ **ZA**
220-221 F 6
Kleinpoort ○ **ZA** 220-221 G 6
Klein Rietrivier ~ **ZA** 220-221 E 5
Klein's Camp ⌂ **EAT** 212-213 E 4
Kiekovača ▲ **BIH** 100-101 F 2
Klèla ○ **RMM** 202-203 H 4
Klemtu ○ **CDN** (BC) 228-229 F 2
Klerksdorp ○ **ZA** 220-221 H 3
Klerkskraal ○ **ZA** 220-221 H 3
Klery Creek ○ **USA** 20-21 H 3
Klésso ○ **BF** 202-203 J 4
Kletnja ○ **RUS** 94-95 N 5
Kleve ○ **D** 92-93 J 3
Klička ○ **RUS** 118-119 J 10
Kličkinskij, hrebet ▲ **RUS** 118-119 H 10
Klickitat ○ **USA** (WA) 244-245 D 5
Klickitat River ~ **USA** 244-245 D 4
Klimino ○ **RUS** 116-117 J 6
Klimpfjäll ○ **S** 86-87 G 4
Klin ○ **RUS** 94-95 N 3
Klina ○ **YU** 100-101 H 3
Klinaklini Glacier ⊂ **CDN** (BC)
230-231 D 3
Klinaklini River ~ **CDN** 230-231 D 2
Klincy ○ **RUS** 94-95 M 5
Klinovec ▲ **CZ** 92-93 M 3
Klinsko-Dmitrovskaja grjada ▲ **RUS**
94-95 O 3
Klintehamn ○ **S** 86-87 J 8
Klipfontein ○ **ZA** 220-221 G 6
Klipplaat ○ **ZA** 220-221 G 6
Kliprand ○ **ZA** 220-221 D 5
Kliprivier ~ **ZA** 220-221 D 5
Klipskool ○ **ZA** 220-221 K 2
Kliis ○ **RI** 166-167 D 6
Kljavino ○ **RUS** 96-97 H 6
Kljaz'ma ~ **RUS** 94-95 Q 3
Ključ ○ **BIH** 100-101 F 2
Ključ ○ **RUS** 120-121 Q 2
Ključevaja Sopka, vulkan ▲ **RUS**
120-121 T 5
Ključi ○ **RUS** (KMC) 120-121 T 5
Ključi ○ **RUS** (ALT) 124-125 L 2
Kljukva ○ **RUS** 108-109 h 3
Ključi ○ **RUS** 118-119 D 10
Klobuk ○ **THA** 158-159 G 4
Ko Chang ▲ • **THA**
158-159 G 4
Klobučký iiman ≈ 102-103 K 5
Klodzko ○ • **PL** 92-93 O 3
Klondike Highway II **CDN** 20-21 W 5
Klondike Plateau ▲ **CDN** 20-21 V 5
Klondike River ~ **CDN** 20-21 V 4
Klosterneuburg ○ • **A** 92-93 O 4

Koch Peak ▲ **USA** (MT) 250-251 H 5
Kochtale = Kohtla ○ **EST** 94-95 K 2
Kocjubyns'ke ○ **UA** 102-103 E 3
Kočki ☆ **RUS** 124-125 M 1
Kočkoma ○ **RUS** 88-89 N 4
Kočkor-Ata ○ **KS** 136-137 N 4
Kočubeevskoe ○ **RUS** 126-127 D 5
Kočubej ○ **RUS** 126-127 G 5
Koda ~ **RUS** 116-117 F 3
Kodâr ○ **IND** 140-141 H 7
Kodari ○ **NEP** 142-143 L 3
Kodarma ○ **IND** 142-143 F 5
Kodiak ○ **USA** 22-23 U 4
Kodina ~ **RUS** 88-89 U 4
Kodino ○ **RUS** 88-89 H 5
Kodiyakkarai ○ **IND** 140-141 H 5
Kodjari ○ **BF** 202-203 L 4
Kodmo, togga ~ **SP** 208-209 H 4
Kodok ○ **SUD** 206-207 L 4
Kodumuru ○ **IND** 140-141 G 3
Kodyma ~ **UA** 102-103 F 3
Koébonou ○ **CI** 202-203 H 6
Koës ○ **NAM** 220-221 D 2
Koettlitz Glacier ⊂ **ARK** 16 F 16
Kofa Game Range ⊥ **USA** (AZ)
256-257 A 5
Kofa Mountains ▲ **USA** 256-257 A 5
Kofarnihon ○ **TJ** 136-137 L 5
Koforidua ○ **GH** 202-203 K 6
Koffiefontein ○ **ZA** 220-221 G 4
Koforidua ○ **GH** 202-203 K 6
Kofu ○ **J** (TOT) 152-153 E 7
Kofu ○ **J** (YMN) 152-153 H 7
Koga ○ **J** 152-153 H 6
Kogaluc, Lac ○ **CDN** 36-37 L 5
Kogaluc, Rivière ~ **CDN** 36-37 L 5
Kogaluk Bay ≈ 36-37 K 5
Kogaluk River ~ **CDN** 36-37 S 6
Kogalym ○ **RUS** 114-115 N 3
Køge ○ **DK** 86-87 F 9
Køge Bugt ≈ 86-87 F 9
Køge Bugt = Pikiutdleq ≋ 28-29 U 4
Kogel' ~ **RUS** 114-115 D 3
Kogmanskloof ▲ **ZA** 220-221 F 6
Kogon River ~ **CDN** 30-31 V 5
Kogon ~ **RG** 202-203 C 4
Kogrukluk River ~ **USA** 20-21 M 3
Kogtok River ~ **CDN** 30-31 V 4
Koğur ○ **IR** 136-137 B 6
Kuuyae Strikt Nature Reserve ⊥ **GH**
202-203 K 6
Kohala Mountains ▲ **USA** 288 K 4
Kohan ○ **PK** 134-135 M 5
Kulıäl ○ • **PK** 138-139 B 5
Kohät Pass ▲ **PK** 138-139 C 2
Kohila ○ **EST** 94-95 J 2
Kohil'nik ~ **UA** 102-103 F 5
Kohima ★ • **IND** 142-143 J 3
Kohingoo = Arundel ↷ **SOL** 184 I c 3
Ko Hinh ○ **LAO** 156-157 C 6
Kut-i-Palandar ▲ **PK** 134-135 L 5
Kohler Range ▲ **ARK** 16 F 25
Kohlu ○ **PK** 138-139 B 5
Kohtla-Järve ○•= **EST** 94-95 K 2
Kohung ○ **ROK** 150-151 F 10
Kohunlich ↷ **MEX** 52-53 K 2
Koiama, Jasiira ↷ **SP** 212-213 J 4
Koichab ~ **NAM** 220-221 B 2
Kôje Do ↷ **ROK** 150-151 G 10
Koigorodok ○ **RUS** 96-97 G 3
Kôjin ○ **ROK** 150-151 G 9
Kojmatdag ▲ **TM** 136-137 D 4
Kojnathun, ozero ○ **RUS** 112-113 V 4
Kojonup ○ **AUS** 176-177 D 6
Kojtaš ○ **UZ** 136-137 K 4
Kojū ○ **UZ** 136-137 J 4
Kojvčaren ~ **RUS** 112-113 V 1
Kojvêrelanskij krjaž ▲ **RUS**
112-113 R 5
K'ok'a ○ **ETH** 208-209 D 4
K'ok'a Gidib ○ **ETH** 208-209 D 4
K'ok'a Häyk' ○ **ETH** 208-209 D 4
Kokand ○ **UZ** 136-137 M 4
Kokanee Glacier Provincial Park ⊥ **CDN**
(BC) 230-231 M 4
Kokani ~ **EAK** 212-213 G 5
Kôkaral ○ **KZ** 124-125 H 2
Kôkaral, tubegi ~ **KZ** 126-127 O 4
Kokas ○ **RI** 166-167 G 3
Kokatha ○ **AUS** 178-179 C 6
Kokča ○ **UZ** 136-137 J 4
Kökcengirsor, köli ~ **KZ** 124-125 G 2
Kokenau ○ **RI** 166-167 J 4
Kokeragi Point ▲ **USA** 30-31 H 3
Kokerboomwoud ○ **NAM** 220-221 D 3
Kokerit ○ **GUY** 62-63 K 3
Ko Kho Khao ↷ **THA** 158-159 E 6
Kokish ○ **CDN** (BC) 230-231 C 3
Ko-Jangak ○ **KS** 136-137 M 4
Kokkola ○ **FIN** 88-89 H 5
Koklappeme ~ **GRØ** 28-29 U 4
Koko ~ **WAN** (BEL) 204-205 D 4
Koko ○ **WAN** (SOK) 204-205 F 3
Kokoda ○ **PNG** 183 D 5
Kokoda Trail • **PNG** 183 D 5
Kokofu ○ **PNG** 183 G 2
Kokologo ○ **BF** 202-203 K 3

Kokomo ○ **USA** (IN) 274-275 M 4
Kokonselkä ⊖ **FIN** 88-89 H 5
Kokopo ○ **PNG** 183 G 3
Kokora, ozero ⊖ **RUS** 108-109 d 5
Kokoro ~ **RG** 202-203 F 3
Kokosa ○ **ETH** 208-209 D 5
Kokoso ○ **GH** 202-203 K 7
Kokoula ~ **RG** 202-203 D 4
Kokpek ○ **KZ** 146-147 D 4
Kökpektí ○ **KZ** 124-125 N 4
Kokrajhar ○ **IND** 142-143 G 2
Kokrines Hills ▲ **USA** 20-21 N 4
Kokruagarok ○ **USA** 20-21 O 1
Koksa ~ **RUS** 124-125 O 3
Koksan ○ **KOR** 150-151 F 8
Köksaraj ○ **KZ** 136-137 L 3
Köksengir, tau ▲ **KZ** (AKT) 126-127 M 5
Köksengir, tau ▲ **KZ** (KZL) 124-125 D 6
Kökšetau ☆ **KZ** 124-125 F 2
Kökšetau üstírtí ▲ **KZ** 124-125 F 2
Koksoak, Rivière ~ **CDN** 36-37 P 6
Kokstad ○ **ZA** 220-221 J 5
Köksu ○ **KZ** 136-137 L 4
Koksu ~ **KZ** 124-125 L 6
Koktac, Rivière ~ **CDN** 36-37 L 5
Köktal ○ **KZ** 124-125 L 6
Köktas ~ **KZ** 124-125 G 5
Köktöbe, tau ▲ **KZ** 124-125 E 5
Koktokay ○ **VRC** 146-147 J 2
Köktyrnak, tubegi ⌣ **KZ** 126-127 O 4
Koku, Tanjung ▲ **RI** 164-165 G 6
Kokubo ○ **J** 152-153 D 9
Kokumbo ○ **CI** 202-203 H 6
Kŏkŭm Do ⌒ **ROK** 150-151 F 10
Ko Kut ⌒ **THA** 158-159 G 5
Kol ○ **PNG** 183 C 3
Kola ○ **CDN** (MAN) 234-235 B 5
Kola ○ **RI** 166-167 H 4
Kola ○ **RUS** 88-89 M 2
Kola, Gorges de ⌣ • **CAM** 204-205 K 4
Kola, Pulau ⌒ **RI** 166-167 H 4
Kolachel ○ **IND** 140-141 G 6
Kolāchi ~ **PK** 134-135 M 5
Kolahun ○ **LB** 202-203 E 5
Kolaka ○ **RI** 164-165 G 6
Kolan River ~ **AUS** 178-179 L 3
Ko Lanta ⌒ **THA** 158-159 E 7
Kola Peninsula = Kol'skij poluostrov ⌣ **RUS** 88-89 N 3
Kolār ○ • **IND** 140-141 H 4
Kolar Gold Fields ○ **IND** 140-141 H 4
Kolari ○ **FIN** 88-89 G 3
Kolåsen ○ **S** 86-87 F 5
Kolasib ○ **IND** 142-143 H 3
Kolašin ○ • **YU** 100-101 G 3
Kola Town ○ **LB** 202-203 G 6
Kolattupuzha ○ **IND** 140-141 G 6
Kolāyat ○ **IND** 138-139 D 6
Kölbaj, tau ▲ **KZ** 126-127 K 6
Kolbeinsstaðir ○ **IS** 86-87 b 2
Kolbio ○ **EAK** 212-213 H 4
Kol'covoe, ozero ⊖ **RUS** 122-123 Q 4
Kol'čugino ☆ **RUS** 94-95 Q 3
Kol'čum ~ **RUS** 114-115 U 5
Kolda ☆ **SN** 202-203 C 3
Koldaga ○ **TCH** 206-207 C 4
Köldenen-Temir ~ **KZ** 126-127 M 3
Kolding ○ • **DK** 86-87 D 9
Kole ○ **ZRE** (HAU) 210-211 K 2
Kole ○ **ZRE** (KOR) 210-211 J 5
Kolebira ○ **IND** 142-143 D 4
Kolek"egan ~ **RUS** 114-115 P 4
Kolendo ○ **RUS** 122-123 K 2
Kolendo, Mount ▲ **AUS** 180-181 D 2
Kolenovskij, Elan'- ○ **RUS** 102-103 M 2
Kolenté ○ **RG** 202-203 D 4
Kolente ~ **RG** 202-203 D 5
Koležma ○ **RUS** 88-89 N 4
Kolgarin ○ **AUS** 176-177 E 6
Kolguev, ostrov ⌒ **RUS** 88-89 U 2
Kolhāpur ○ **IND** (ANP) 140-141 H 2
Kolhāpur ○ •• **IND** (MAH) 140-141 F 2
Kolhida ☆ **GE** 126-127 D 6
Kolhozabad ○ **TJ** 136-137 L 6
Koli ▲ **FIN** 88-89 K 5
Kolia ○ **CI** 202-203 G 5
Koliba ~ **RG** 202-203 D 3
Ko Libong ⌒ **THA** 158-159 E 7
Koliganek ○ **USA** 22-23 S 3
Kolín ○ •• **CZ** 92-93 N 3
Kolin ○ **USA** (MT) 250-251 K 4
Kolinbiné ~ **RMM** 202-203 E 2
K'olīto ○ **ETH** 208-209 D 5
Koljučaja, gora ▲ **RUS** 112-113 S 3
Koljučin, ostrov ⌒ **RUS** 112-113 X 3
Koljučinskaja guba ≈ 112-113 X 3
Kolka ○ •• **LV** 94-95 H 3
Kolky ○ **UA** 102-103 D 2
Kollegal ○ **IND** 140-141 G 4
Kolleru Lake ⊖ **IND** 140-141 J 2
Kollipara ○ **IND** 140-141 J 2
Kollo ○ **RN** 204-205 E 2
Kolmackij, porog ~ **RUS** 88-89 P 3
Kolmakovo ○ **RUS** 114-115 P 7
Kolmanskop ○ **NAM** 220-221 B 3
Kolmar = Chodzież ○ • **PL** 92-93 O 2
Kolno ○ **PL** 92-93 Q 2
Kolo ○ **EAT** 212-213 E 6
Koło ○ **PL** 92-93 P 2
Koloa ○ **USA** (HI) 288 F 3
Kolobane ○ **SN** 202-203 C 2
Kolobeke ○ **ZRE** 210-211 G 4
Kołobrzeg ○ **PL** 92-93 N 1
Kolofata ○ **CAM** 206-207 B 3
Ko-lok, Sungai ○ **THA** 158-159 F 7
Kolokani ○ **RMM** 202-203 F 3
Koloko ○ **BF** 202-203 H 4
Kolokol, vulkan ▲ **RUS** 122-123 O 5
Kolokolkova guba ≈ 88-89 W 2
Kolokondé ○ **DY** 202-203 L 5
Kolomak ○ **UA** 102-103 J 3
Kolomino ○ **RUS** 114-115 R 6
Kolomna ☆ •• **RUS** 94-95 Q 4
Kolomoki Mounds • **USA** (GA) 284-285 F 5
Kolomonyi ○ **ZRE** 210-211 J 6
Kolomyja ☆ **UA** 102-103 D 3
Kolondiéba ○ **RMM** 202-203 G 4
Kolonedale ○ **RI** 164-165 G 5
Kolongotomo ○ **RMM** 202-203 H 3
Kolonia = Pohnpei ★ **FSM** 13 G 2
Kolono ○ **RI** 164-165 H 6
Kolonodale ○ **RI** 164-165 G 4
Kolosovyh, ostrov ⌒ **RUS** 108-109 W 4
Kolossa ~ **RMM** 202-203 G 3
Kolotambu = Avu Avu ○ **SOL** 184 I e 3
Kolowana-Watobo, Teluk ≈ 164-165 H 6
Kolozero ⊖ **RUS** 88-89 M 2
Kolp' ~ **RUS** 94-95 O 2
Kolpakova ~ **RUS** 120-121 R 6
Kolpaševo ☆ **RUS** 114-115 R 5
Kolpino ○ **RUS** 94-95 M 2
Kolpny ○ **RUS** 94-95 P 5
Kólpos Hanión ≈ 100-101 J 7
Kólpos Kissámou ≈ 100-101 J 7
Kolpur ○ **PK** 134-135 M 4
Kol'skij zaliv ≈ 88-89 M 2
Kolubara ~ **YU** 100-101 H 2
Kolumadulu Atoll ⌒ **MV** 140-141 B 6
Kolva ~ **RUS** 88-89 Y 3
Kolva ~ **RUS** 114-115 E 4
Kolvavis ~ **RUS** 108-109 H 8
Kolvereid ○ **N** 86-87 E 4
Kolvica ○ **RUS** 88-89 M 3
Kolvickoe, ozero ⊖ **RUS** 88-89 M 3
Kolwa ○ **PK** 134-135 L 5
Kolwezi ○ **ZRE** 214-215 C 6
Kolyma ~ **RUS** 112-113 L 2
Kolymak ~ **RUS** 112-113 M 5
Kolymskaja guba ≈ 110-111 d 4
Kolymskaja nizmennost' ⌣ **RUS** 110-111 c 5
Kolymskoe ○ **RUS** 112-113 K 2
Kolymskoe, vodohranilišče < **RUS** 120-121 N 3
Kolymskoe nagor'e ▲ **RUS** 112-113 H 6
Kolymskoye Nagor'ye = Kolymskoe nagor'e ▲ **RUS** 112-113 H 6
Kolyšlej ○ **RUS** 96-97 D 7
Kolyvan' ☆ **RUS** 114-115 R 7
Kom ▲ **BG** 102-103 C 6
Kom ○ **EAK** 212-213 G 3
Kom ~ **G** 210-211 C 2
Koma ○ **ETH** 208-209 C 4
Komagasberge ▲ **ZA** 220-221 C 4
Komaio ○ **PNG** 183 B 4
Komako ○ **PNG** 183 C 4
Komanda ○ **ZRE** 212-213 B 3
Komandnaja, gora ▲ **RUS** 122-123 H 3
Komandorskaja kotlovina = Komandorskaya Basin ≃ 120-121 V 5
Komandorskie ostrova ⌒ **RUS** 120-121 I W 6
Komandorskij Basin ≃ 120-121 V 5
Komarno ○ **CDN** (MAN) 234-235 F 4
Komárno ○ **SK** 92-93 P 5
Komárom ○ **H** 92-93 P 5
Komarovka ○ **RUS** 116-117 E 7
Komatipoort ○ **ZA** 220-221 K 2
Komatirivier ~ **ZA** 220-221 K 2
Komatsu ○ **J** 152-153 G 6
Komba, Pulau ⌒ **RI** 166-167 B 5
Kombat ○ **NAM** 216-217 D 9
Kombe ○ **ZRE** 210-211 K 6
Kombile ○ **WAL** 202-203 E 5
Kombissiri ○ **BF** 202-203 K 3
Kombo-Itindi ○ **CAM** 204-205 H 6
Kombone ○ **CAM** 204-205 H 6
Kombongou = Kondio ○ **BF** 204-205 E 3
Koméayo ○ **CI** 202-203 G 6
Kome Island ⌒ **EAT** 212-213 D 5
Komenda ○ **GH** 202-203 K 7
Komering ~ **RI** 162-163 F 6
Komfane ○ **RI** 166-167 H 4
Komga ○ **ZA** 220-221 H 6
Komi = Komi, Respublika ■ **RUS** 96-97 G 1
Komin-Yanga ○ **BF** 202-203 L 4
Komi-Permyak Autonomous District=Komi-Permjackij avt. okrug ■ **RUS** 96-97 H 3
Kommunarsk = Alčevs'k ○ **UA** 102-103 L 3
Kommunizma, pik ▲ **TJ** 136-137 N 5
Komo ~ **G** 210-211 C 3
Komo ○ **PNG** 183 B 4
Komodimini ○ **RMM** 202-203 G 3
Komodo ○ **RI** 168 D 7
Komodo, Pulau ⌒ **RI** 168 D 7
Komodo National Park ⊥ ••• **RI** 168 D 7
Komodou ○ **RG** 202-203 F 5
Komono ○ **RCB** 210-211 D 5
Komoran, Pulau ⌒ **RI** 166-167 K 6
Komorane ○ **YU** 100-101 H 3
Komoro ○ **J** 152-153 H 6
Komosi ○ **ZRE** 206-207 D 6
Komotiní ○ **GR** 100-101 K 4
Kompa ○ **DY** 204-205 E 2
Kompiam ○ **PNG** 183 B 3
Komponaone, Pulau ⌒ **RI** 164-165 H 6
Kompot ○ **RI** 164-165 J 3
Komrat = Comrat ○ **MD** 102-103 F 4
Komsberge ▲ **ZA** 220-221 E 6
Komsomol ○ **KZ** (AKT) 126-127 O 2
Komsomol ○ **KZ** (KST) 124-125 B 3
Komsomolabad ○ **TJ** 136-137 M 5
Komsomol cyganaky ≈ 126-127 K 5
Komsomolec, ostrov ⌒ **RUS** 108-109 I Z 1
Komsomol'sk ☆ • **RUS** 94-95 R 3
Komsomol'sk, Ustjurtdagi ○ **UZ** 136-137 F 2
Komsomol'skij ○ **RUS** (CUK) 112-113 R 2
Komsomol'skij ○ **RUS** (HMN) 114-115 G 4
Komsomol'skij ○ **RUS** (KAR) 88-89 M 4
Komsomol'skij ○ **RUS** (KLM) 126-127 G 5
Komsomol'skij ○ **RUS** (KOM) 108-109 K 8
Komsomol'skij ○ **RUS** (MOR) 96-97 D 6
Komsomol'skij zapovednik ⊥ **RUS** 122-123 G 3
Komsomol'sk-na-Amure ○ • **RUS** 122-123 G 3
Komsomol'sk na Amure = Komsomol'sk-na-Amure ○ • **RUS** 122-123 G 3
Komsomol'sk-na-Pečore ○ **RUS** 114-115 D 3
Komsomol'skoj Pravdy, ostrova ⌒ **RUS** 108-109 g 3
Kŏmun Do ⌒ **ROK** 150-151 F 11
Kon ○ **CAM** 204-205 J 6
Kön ~ **KZ** 124-125 F 4
Kona ○ **RMM** 202-203 J 2
Kona ○ **RN** 198-199 D 6
Kona ○ **WAN** 204-205 J 4
Kona = Kailua ○ **USA** (HI) 288 K 5
Kona Coast ⌣ **USA** 288 K 5
Konakovo ☆ **RUS** 94-95 P 3
Konanmoukro ○ **CI** 202-203 H 6
Konar ■ **AFG** 136-137 M 7
Konar, Daryā-ye ~ **AFG** 138-139 C 2
Konārak ○ ••• **IND** 142-143 E 6
Konārak ○ **IR** 134-135 J 6
Konar-e Ḫāṣṣ ○ **AFG** 138-139 C 2
Konār Tahte ○ **IR** 134-135 D 4
Konawa ○ **USA** (OK) 264-265 H 4
Konaweha ~ **RI** 164-165 G 5
Konda ○ **RI** 166-167 F 2
Konda ~ **RUS** 114-115 K 5
Konda ~ **RUS** 118-119 F 9
Kondagaon ○ **IND** 142-143 B 6
Kondakovskaja vozvyšennost' ▲ **RUS** 110-111 b 4
Kondan, ozero ⊖ **RUS** 114-115 K 6
Konde ○ **EAT** 212-213 G 6
Kondembaia ○ **WAL** 202-203 E 5
Kondinin ○ **AUS** 176-177 E 6
Kondinskaja nizmennost' ⌣ **RUS** 114-115 H 4
Kondinskoe ☆ **RUS** 114-115 J 5
Kondio = Kombongou ○ **BF** 204-205 E 3
Kondoa ○ **EAT** 212-213 E 6
Kondoma ~ **RUS** 124-125 P 2
Kondopoga ☆ **RUS** 88-89 N 5
Kondostrov ⌒ **RUS** 88-89 O 4
Kondratovskaja ○ **RUS** 88-89 R 5
Kondromo ~ **RUS** 116-117 G 4
Kondrovo ☆ **RUS** 94-95 O 4
Kondue ○ **ZRE** 210-211 J 6
Konduga ○ **WAN** 204-205 K 3
Konduj-Muhor ○ **RUS** 118-119 F 9
Kondyreva ~ **RUS** 112-113 O 5
Konecbor ○ **RUS** 88-89 Y 4
Koneng ○ **RI** 162-163 B 2
Konènmyveem ~ **RUS** 112-113 V 3
Konergino ○ **RUS** 112-113 V 4
Köneürgenč ☆ **TM** 136-137 F 3
Konevaam ~ **RUS** 112-113 P 2
Konevo ○ **RUS** 88-89 P 5
Kong ○ **CAM** 204-205 K 6
Kong ○ • **CI** 202-203 H 5
Kŏng ~ **K** 158-159 J 4
Kong, Bandar-e ○ **IR** 134-135 F 5
Kongakut River ~ **USA** 20-21 U 2
Kongasso ○ **CI** 202-203 G 6
Kongbeng Caves • **RI** 164-165 E 3
Kongbo ○ **RCA** 206-207 E 6
Kong Christian IX Land ∸ **GRØ** 28-29 V 3
Kong Christian X Land ∸ **GRØ** 26-27 k 7
Kong Dans Halvø ⌣ **GRØ** 28-29 U 5
Kongelai ○ **EAK** 212-213 E 3
Kong Frederik IX Land ∸ **GRØ** 28-29 P 3
Kong Frederik VIII Land ∸ **GRØ** 26-27 m 5
Kong Frederik VI Kyst ∸ **GRØ** 28-29 T 6
Kong Fu • **VRC** 154-155 K 4
Konginskij hrebet ▲ **RUS** 112-113 K 4
Kong Karls Land ⌒ **N** 84-85 P 3
Kong Leopold og Dronning Astrid land ∸ **ARK** 16 F 9
Kongola ○ **NAM** 218-219 B 3
Kongolo ○ **ZRE** 210-211 L 6
Kongor ○ **LB** 202-203 E 6
Kongor ○ **SUD** 206-207 K 5
Kong Oscar Fjord ≈ 26-27 n 7
Kongoussi ○ **BF** 202-203 K 3
Kongsberg ☆ **N** 86-87 D 7
Kongsfjorden ≈ 84-85 G 3
Kongsøya ⌒ **N** 84-85 Q 3
Kongsvinger ☆ • **N** 86-87 F 6
Kongtongshan • **VRC** 154-155 E 4
Kongur Shan ▲ **VRC** 146-147 B 6
Kongwa ○ **EAT** 214-215 J 4
Kong Wilhelm Land ∸ **GRØ** 26-27 o 6
Koni ○ **ZRE** 214-215 D 6
Koni, poluostrov ⌣ **RUS** 120-121 O 4
Konig, Cape ▲ **CDN** 24-25 g 6
Königgrätz = Hradec Králové ○ **CZ** 92-93 N 3
Konimeh ☆ **UZ** 136-137 J 4
Konin ☆ • **PL** 92-93 P 2
Konin ~ **RUS** 122-123 G 2
Konina ○ **RMM** 202-203 G 3
Konjed Jān ○ **IR** 134-135 D 2
Konka ~ **UA** 102-103 K 4
Könkamäälven ~ **S** 86-87 K 2
Könkämäeno ~ **FIN** 88-89 F 2
Konkče, Daryā-ye ~ **AFG** 136-137 L 6
Konkiep ~ **NAM** 220-221 C 3
Konko ○ **ZRE** 214-215 D 6
Konkoma ○ **ETH** 208-209 D 6
Konkouré ○ **RG** (KIN) 202-203 D 4
Konkouré ~ **RG** 202-203 D 4
Kon'kovaja ~ **RUS** 112-113 K 2
Kon'kovaja, Bol'šaja ~ **RUS** 112-113 J 2
Konkudera ○ **RUS** 118-119 F 7
Konkwesso ○ **WAN** 204-205 F 3
Konni, Birnin- ○ **RN** 198-199 B 6
Konnūr ○ **IND** 140-141 F 2
Konobougou ○ **RMM** 202-203 G 3
Konogogo ○ **PNG** 183 G 2
Konololo ○ **ZRE** 210-211 K 3
Konomerume = Donderkamp ○ **SME** 62-63 F 3
Konončan ~ **RUS** 118-119 H 3
Kononda ~ **RUS** 116-117 M 3
Konongo ○ **GH** 202-203 K 6
Konos ○ **PNG** 183 F 2
Konoša ○ **RUS** 94-95 R 1
Kōnosu ○ **J** 152-153 H 6
Konotop ○ **UA** 102-103 H 2
Kon Plong ○ **VN** 158-159 K 3
Konqi He ~ **VRC** 146-147 J 5
Konsankoro ○ **RG** 202-203 F 5
Konséguéla ○ **RMM** 202-203 H 3
Końskie ○ • **PL** 92-93 Q 3
Konso ○ **ETH** 208-209 C 6
Konstantina, mys ▲ **RUS** 108-109 N 3
Konstantinopel = İstanbul ☆ ••• **TR** 128-129 C 2
Konstantinovka ☆ **RUS** 122-123 B 4
Konstantinovsk ○ **RUS** 102-103 M 4
Konstanz ○ • **D** 92-93 K 5
Konta ○ **IND** 142-143 B 7
Kontagora ○ **WAN** 204-205 F 3
Kontagora, River ~ **WAN** 204-205 F 3
Kontcha ○ **CAM** 204-205 K 5
Kontinemo, Área Indígena X **BR** 68-69 B 4
Kontiolahti ○ **FIN** 88-89 K 5
Kontiomäki ○ **FIN** 88-89 K 4
Kontubek ○ **UZ** 136-137 F 2
Kon Tum ○ **VN** 158-159 K 3
Konus, gora ▲ **RUS** (CUK) 112-113 U 3
Konus, gora ▲ **RUS** (HBR) 120-121 D 5
Konus, ostrov ⌒ **RUS** 120-121 U 3
Konušin, mys ▲ **RUS** 88-89 R 3
Konya ☆ •• **TR** 128-129 E 4
Konyrat ○ **KZ** 124-125 J 5
Konza ○ **EAK** 212-213 F 4
Konžakovskij Kamen', gora ▲ **RUS** 114-115 E 5
Konzi ~ **ZRE** 210-211 F 6
Koobi Fora ∴ • **EAK** 212-213 C 6
Koocanusa, Lake ⊖ **USA** (MT) 250-251 D 3
Koodnanie, Lake ⊖ **AUS** 178-179 E 4
Kookooligit Mountains ▲ **USA** 20-21 E 5
Kookynie ○ **AUS** 176-177 F 4
Koolatah ○ **AUS** 174-175 G 4
Koolau Range ▲ **USA** 288 G 3
Koolen', ozero ⊖ **RUS** 112-113 Z 4
Kooline ○ **AUS** 172-173 C 7
Koolkootinnie, Lake ⊖ **AUS** 178-179 D 4
Koolpinyah ○ **AUS** 172-173 K 2
Koolyanobbing ○ **AUS** 176-177 E 5
Koombooloomba ○ **AUS** 174-175 H 5
Koonalda Cave • **AUS** 176-177 K 5
Koondoo ○ **AUS** 178-179 H 3
Koongie Park ○ **AUS** 172-173 H 5
Koopmansfontein ○ **ZA** 220-221 G 4
Koor ○ **RI** 166-167 G 2
Koorawatha ○ **AUS** 180-181 K 3
Koorda ○ **AUS** 176-177 D 5
Koordarrie ○ **AUS** 172-173 B 7
Koosharem ○ **USA** (UT) 254-255 D 5
Kooskia ○ **USA** (ID) 250-251 D 5
Kootenai Indian Reservation X **USA** (ID) 250-251 C 3
Kootenai River ~ **USA** 250-251 D 3
Kootenay Bay ○ **CDN** (BC) 230-231 N 4
Kootenay Indian Reserve X **CDN** (BC) 230-231 O 4
Kootenay Lake ⊖ **CDN** (BC) 230-231 N 4
Kootenay National Park ⊥ **CDN** (BC) 230-231 N 2
Kootenay River ~ **CDN** 230-231 O 3
Koo Wee Rup ○ **AUS** 180-181 H 5
Koozata Lagoon ≈ 20-21 E 5
Kopa ○ **Z** 214-215 F 6
Kopang ○ **RI** 168 C 7
Kopanzu ○ **LB** 202-203 F 6
Kopaonik ▲ **YU** 100-101 G 3
Kopargo ○ **DY** 202-203 L 5
Kópasker ○ **IS** 86-87 e 1
Kopasor, köl ⊖ **KZ** 126-127 N 4
Kópavogur ○ **IS** 86-87 c 2
Ko Payang ⌒ **THA** 158-159 D 6
Kopbirlik ○ **KZ** 124-125 K 5
Kopé, Mont ▲ **CI** 202-203 G 7
Kopejsk ○ **RUS** 96-97 M 6
Kopeng ○ **RI** 168 D 3
Koper ○ **SLO** 100-101 D 2
Kopervik ○ **N** 86-87 B 7
Kop'evo ☆ **RUS** 114-115 U 7
Kop Geçidi ▲ **TR** 128-129 J 2
Ko Phangan ○ **THA** 158-159 E 6
Ko Phangan ⌒ **THA** 158-159 F 6
Ko Phi ⌒ **THA** 158-159 E 7
Ko Phra Thong ⌒ **MYA** 158-159 E 6
Ko Phuket ⌒ •• **THA** 158-159 E 7
Kopi, Ugol'nye ○ **RUS** 112-113 T 4
Kopiago ○ **PNG** 183 B 3
Köping ☆ • **S** 86-87 G 7
Kopingué ○ **CI** 202-203 J 5
Koporokendié-Na ○ **RMM** 202-203 J 2
Koppa ○ **IND** 140-141 F 4
Koppal ○ **IND** 140-141 G 3
Koppang ☆ **N** 86-87 E 6
Kopparberg ○ **S** 86-87 G 7
Koppe Dāğ ▲ **IR** 136-137 E 5
Kopperamanna Bore ○ **AUS** 178-179 E 5
Koppi ○ **RUS** 122-123 J 4
Koppies ○ **ZA** 220-221 H 3
Koppieskraalpan ⊖ **ZA** 220-221 E 3
Koprivnica ○ **HR** 100-101 F 1
Köprüçay ~ **TR** 128-129 D 4
Kor, Rūd-e ~ **IR** 134-135 E 4
Ko Ra ⌒ **THA** 158-159 E 6
Korab ▲ **AL** 100-101 H 4
Korabavur pastligi ∸ **UZ** 136-137 E 3
Korača ○ **RUS** 102-103 K 2
Ko Racha Noi ⌒ **THA** 158-159 E 7
Ko Racha Yai ⌒ **THA** 158-159 E 7
K'orahē ○ **ETH** 208-209 G 5
Korakata cukurligi ∸ **UZ** 136-137 J 4
Korakülka ∸ **UZ** 136-137 E 3
Kora National Park ⊥ **EAK** 212-213 G 4
Korangal ○ **IND** 140-141 G 2
Korannaberg ▲ **ZA** 220-221 F 3
Korān-o-Mongān ○ **AFG** 136-137 M 6
Koraon ○ **IND** 142-143 C 3
Koraput ○ **IND** 142-143 C 6
Korasa ○ **SOL** 184 I c 2
Koratagere ○ **IND** 140-141 G 4
Ko Rawi ⌒ **THA** 158-159 E 7
Korbèndja, hrebet ▲ **RUS** 112-113 K 5
Korbeniči ○ **RUS** 94-95 O 1
Korbol ○ **TCH** 206-207 C 4
Korbol, Bahr ~ **TCH** 206-207 C 3
Korbu, Gunung ▲ **MAL** 162-163 D 2
Korbunčana ~ **RUS** 116-117 L 3
Korçë ☆ •• **AL** 100-101 H 4
Korčula ○ • **HR** 100-101 F 3
Korčula ⌒ **HR** 100-101 F 3
Korda ○ **IND** 138-139 C 8
Kordestān ■ **IR** 128-129 M 5
Kordié ○ **BF** 202-203 J 3
Kord-Kuy ○ **IR** 136-137 D 6
Kord Meriem, Hassi ○ **DZ** 188-189 K 6
Kordofan = Kurdufān ∸ **SUD** 198-199 D 6
Kore ○ **RI** 168 D 7
Korea Bay ≈ 150-151 D 8
Korean Folk Village • **ROK** 150-151 F 9
Koreare ○ **RI** 166-167 F 5
Korea Strait ≈ 152-153 C 8
Korec' ○ **UA** 102-103 E 2
Korem ○ **ETH** 200-201 J 6
Korémaïrwa ○ **RN** 204-205 E 2
Korenevo ○ **RUS** 102-103 J 2
Korenovsk ○ **RUS** 102-103 L 5
Korepino ○ **RUS** 114-115 D 4
Korf ○ **RUS** 120-121 V 3
Korfa, zaliv ≈ 120-121 V 3
Korǵalžyn ☆ **KZ** 124-125 G 3
Korgas ○ **VRC** 146-147 E 3
Korgen ○ **N** 86-87 F 3
Korgom ○ **RN** 198-199 D 6
Korhogo ☆ • **CI** 202-203 H 5
Koribundu ○ **WAL** 202-203 E 6
Korientze ○ **RMM** 202-203 J 2
Korim ○ **RI** 166-167 J 2
Korinthiakós Kólpos ≈ 100-101 J 5
Kórinthos ○ **GR** 100-101 J 6
Korioume ○ **RMM** 196-197 J 6
Koripobi ○ **PNG** 184 I b 2
Kőris-hegy ▲ • **H** 92-93 O 5
Korissía ○ **GR** 100-101 K 6
Kōriyama ○ **J** 152-153 J 6
Korizo, Passe de ▲ **TCH** 192-193 F 6
Korjaki ○ **RUS** 120-121 S 7
Korjakskaja Sopka, vulkan ▲ **RUS** 120-121 S 7
Korjakskoe nagor'e ▲ **RUS** 112-113 N 6
Korjažma ☆ **RUS** 88-89 T 6
Korkodon ○ **RUS** (MAG) 112-113 H 4
Korkodon ~ **RUS** 112-113 H 4
Korkodonskij hrebet ▲ **RUS** 112-113 J 4
Korkut ☆ **TR** 128-129 J 3
Korkuteli ☆ **TR** 128-129 D 4
Korla ○ **VRC** 146-147 H 5
Korliki ○ **RUS** 114-115 R 4
Kormak ○ **CDN** (ONT) 236-237 F 5
Kormakitis, Cape ▲ **TR** 128-129 E 5
Kornake ○ **RN** 198-199 C 5
Kornati ⌒ **HR** 100-101 E 3
Kornati, Nacionalni park ⊥ **HR** 100-101 E 3
Korneevka ○ **KZ** 124-125 J 3
Kórnik ○ • **PL** 92-93 O 2
Koro ○ **CI** 202-203 G 5
Koro ⌒ **FJI** 184 III b 2
Koro ○ **RMM** 202-203 J 2
Koroba ○ **PNG** 183 B 3
Koroc, Rivière ~ **CDN** 36-37 R 5
Korodiga ○ **EAT** 212-213 F 6
Korodziba ○ **RB** 218-219 D 4
Köroğlu Dağlari ▲ **TR** 128-129 D 2
Köroğlu Tepe ▲ **TR** 128-129 D 2
Korogwe ○ **EAT** 212-213 G 6
Korohane ○ **RN** 198-199 C 5
Koroit ○ **AUS** 180-181 G 5
Korolevu ○ **FJI** 184 III a 3
Korom, Bahr ~ **TCH** 206-207 D 3
Koronadal ○ **RP** 160-161 F 9
Korondougou ○ **CI** 202-203 G 5
Koronga ○ **RMM** 202-203 G 2
Koronga, Mont ▲ **RT** 202-203 L 5
Koróni ○ **GR** 100-101 H 6
Korónia, Limni ⊖ **GR** 100-101 J 4
Korontière ○ **DY** 202-203 L 4
Koror ★ **PAL** 13 E 2
Körös ~ **H** 92-93 Q 5
Koro Sea ≈ 184 III b 2
Korosten' ○ **UA** 102-103 F 2
Korostyšiv ○ **UA** 102-103 F 2
Korotaiha ~ **RUS** 108-109 K 7
Korotčaevo ○ **RUS** 114-115 P 2
Koro Toro ○ **TCH** 198-199 J 4
Korovin Island ⌒ **USA** 22-23 Q 5
Korovin Volcan ▲ **USA** 22-23 J 6
Korovou ○ **FJI** 184 III b 2
Korovou ○ **SOL** 184 I b 2
Korpilahti ○ **FIN** 88-89 H 5
Korpun ○ **PNG** 183 G 3
Korsakow ○ **RUS** 122-123 K 5
Korsimoro ○ **BF** 202-203 K 3
Korskrogen ○ **S** 86-87 G 6
Korsnäs ○ **FIN** 88-89 F 5
Korsør ○ **DK** 86-87 E 9
Koršunovo ○ **RUS** 118-119 E 6
Kortala ○ **SUD** 200-201 E 6
Kortkeros ○ **RUS** 96-97 G 3
Kortrijk ○ **B** 92-93 G 3
Korumburra ○ **AUS** 180-181 H 5
Korup, Park National de ⊥ **CAM** 204-205 H 6
Korvonsaroj Raboti Malik • **UZ** 136-137 J 4
Korwai ○ **IND** 138-139 G 7
Koryak Autonomous District = Korjakskij avtonomnyi okrug ■ **RUS** 112-113 N 5
Koryl'ky ~ **RUS** 108-109 T 8
Kós ○ •• **GR** 100-101 L 6
Kós ⌒ **GR** 100-101 L 6
Kosa ○ **ETH** 208-209 C 5
Kosa ☆ **RUS** 96-97 J 4
Kosa Arabats'ka Strilka ⌣ **UA** 102-103 J 4
Kosa Byr'učyj Ostriv ⌣ **UA** 102-103 J 4
Koš-Agač ○ **RUS** (ROS) 124-125 Q 3
Koš-Agač ☆ **RUS** (GOR) 124-125 Q 4
Kosaja Gora ○ • **RUS** 94-95 P 4
Kosa-Mèèčkyn, ostrov ⌒ **RUS** 112-113 V 4
Ko Samet National Park • **THA** 158-159 F 4
Ko Samui ⌒ •• **THA** 158-159 F 6
Kosbūlak sor ∸ **KZ** 126-127 M 5
Kościan ○ • **PL** 92-93 O 2
Kościerzyna ○ • **PL** 92-93 O 1
Kosciusko ○ **USA** (MS) 268-269 L 3
Kosciusko, Mount ▲ **AUS** 180-181 K 4
Kosciusko Island ⌒ **USA** 32-33 D 3
Kosciusko National Park ⊥ **AUS** 180-181 K 4
Kosdäulet, kum ∸ **KZ** 96-97 F 10
Koš-Dëbë ○ **KS** 146-147 B 5
Kose ○ •• **EST** 94-95 J 2
Köse ☆ **TR** 128-129 H 2
Köse Dağları ▲ **TR** 128-129 G 2
Koses ~ **RUS** 114-115 R 4
Kosha ○ **SUD** 200-201 E 2
Köshetau = Kökšetau ☆ **KZ** 124-125 F 2
Koshi ○ **ZRE** 210-211 G 6
Koshikishima-rettō ⌒ **J** 152-153 C 9
Kosibaai-natuurreservaat ⊥ **ZA** 220-221 L 3
Kosi Bay ≈ 220-221 L 3
Ko Si Boya ⌒ **THA** 158-159 E 7
Košice ○ **SK** 92-93 Q 4
Kösim ~ **KZ** 96-97 G 9
Kosimeer ⊖ **ZA** 220-221 L 3
Ko Similan ⌒ **THA** 158-159 D 6
Kosi Reservoir < **NEP** 144-145 F 7
Kosistyj ○ **RUS** 110-111 G 3
Kosjerić ○ **YU** 100-101 G 2
Kos'ju ~ **RUS** 108-109 H 9
Koskaecodde Lake ⊖ **CDN** (NFL) 242-243 N 5
Koskarköl ⊖ **KZ** 124-125 M 5
Košk-e Kohne ○ **AFG** 134-135 K 1
Koški ☆ **RUS** 96-97 G 6
Koskol ○ **KZ** 124-125 E 4
Koslan ○ **RUS** 88-89 U 5
Kosma ~ **RUS** 88-89 U 4
Kosminskij Kamen' ▲ **RUS** 88-89 U 3
Kosminskoe, ozero ⊖ **RUS** 88-89 U 3
Košoba ○ **TM** 136-137 D 4
Kosong ○ **KOR** 150-151 G 8
Kosovo Polje ∸ **YU** 100-101 H 3
Kosovska Mitrovica ○ • **YU** 100-101 H 3
Kosse ○ **USA** (TX) 266-267 L 2
Kosso ○ **CI** 202-203 H 7
Kossou, Lac de < **CI** 202-203 H 6
Kossuth ○ **USA** (MS) 268-269 M 2
Kósta ○ **GR** 100-101 J 6
Kostanaj ☆ **KZ** 124-125 C 2
Koster ○ **ZA** 220-221 H 2
Kostinbrod ○ **BG** 102-103 C 6
Kostin Nos, mys ▲ **RUS** 108-109 E 6
Kostomukša ○ **RUS** 88-89 L 4
Kostopil' ○ **UA** 102-103 E 2
Kostroma ○ **RUS** (KOR) 120-121 U 4
Kostroma ○ • **RUS** 94-95 R 3
Kostroma ~ **RUS** 94-95 R 2
Kostrzyn ○ • **PL** 92-93 N 2
Kostyantynivka = Južnoukrains'k = Južnoukrains'k ○ **UA** 102-103 K 3
Kosubosu ○ **WAN** 204-205 E 4
Kosubuke ○ **ZRE** 210-211 J 6
Ko Surin Nua ⌒ **THA** 158-159 D 6
Ko Surin Tai ⌒ **THA** 158-159 D 6
Kos'va ~ **RUS** 96-97 K 4
Kos'va, Bol'šaja ~ **RUS** 114-115 E 5
Kosvinskij Kamen', gora ▲ **RUS** 114-115 E 5
Koszalin ☆ • **PL** 92-93 O 1
Kőszeg ○ •• **H** 92-93 O 5
Kota ○ **IND** (MAP) 142-143 C 4
Kota ○ **IND** (RAJ) 138-139 E 7
Kota, Cascades de la ~ • **DY** 202-203 L 4
Kotaagung ○ **RI** 162-163 F 7
Kotabangun ○ **RI** 164-165 E 4
Kotabaru ○ **RI** (KSE) 164-165 E 5
Kotabaru ○ **RI** (RIA) 162-163 D 5
Kotabaru ○ **RI** (SUB) 162-163 D 5
Kota Belud ○ **MAL** 160-161 B 9
Kota Bharu ☆ **MAL** 162-163 E 1
Kota Bumi ○ **RI** 162-163 F 7
Kot Addu ○ **PK** 138-139 C 4
Kotagayah ○ **RI** 162-163 F 7
Kotagede ○ **RI** 168 D 3
Kota Kinabalu ☆ • **MAL** 160-161 B 10
Kōtal-e Mollā Yā'qūb ▲ **AFG** 134-135 M 1
Kota Lenggong ○ **MAL** 162-163 D 2
Kotamangalam ○ **IND** 140-141 G 5
Kota Marudu ○ **MAL** 160-161 B 9
Kotamobagu ○ **RI** 164-165 J 3
Kotanopan ○ **RI** 162-163 C 4
Ko Tao ⌒ **THA** 158-159 E 5
Kotapinang ○ **RI** 162-163 D 4
Ko Tarutao ⌒ **THA** 158-159 E 7
Kota Tinggi ○ • **MAL** 162-163 E 4
Kotawaringin Teluk ≈ 162-163 J 6
Kotcho Lake ⊖ **CDN** 30-31 J 6
Kotcho River ~ **CDN** 30-31 J 6
Kot Chutta ○ **PK** 138-139 C 5
Kot Diji ○ •• **PK** 138-139 B 6
Koteľnič ○ **RUS** 96-97 F 4
Koteľnikovo ○ **RUS** 102-103 N 4
Koteľnyj, ostrov ⌒ **RUS** 110-111 V 2
Koteľva ○ **UA** 102-103 J 2
Kotenko ○ **RUS** 110-111 a 4
Kotera ~ **RUS** 118-119 F 8
Kotiari ○ **SN** 202-203 D 3
Kotido ○ **EAU** 212-213 E 2
Kotira ○ **PK** 134-135 M 5
Kotjukan ~ **RUS** 108-109 f 6
Kotjukan ~ **RUS** 110-111 G 4
Kotka ☆ **FIN** 88-89 J 6
Kot Kapūra ○ **IND** 138-139 E 4
Kotlas ☆ **RUS** 88-89 T 6
Kotlik ○ **USA** 20-21 J 5
Kot Mūmin ○ **PK** 138-139 D 3
Koto ○ **CAM** 204-205 H 6
Kotobi ○ **CI** 202-203 H 6
Kotongoro II ○ **TCH** 206-207 D 4
Koton-Karifi ○ **WAN** 204-205 G 4
Koton-Koro ○ **WAN** 204-205 F 3
Kotopounga ○ **DY** 202-203 L 4
Kotor ○ •• **YU** 100-101 G 3
Kotor Varoš ○ **BIH** 100-101 F 2
Kotouba ○ **CI** 202-203 J 5
Kotoula ○ **BF** 202-203 G 4
Kotovo ○ **RUS** 96-97 D 8
Kotovsk ○ **RUS** 94-95 R 5
Kotovs'k ☆ **UA** 102-103 F 4
Kotovsk = Hînceşti ☆ **MD** 102-103 F 4
Kot Pūtli ○ **IND** 138-139 F 6
Kotri ~ **IND** 142-143 B 6
Kotri ○ **PK** 138-139 B 7
Kot Shākir ○ **PK** 138-139 D 4
Kottagūdem ○ **IND** 142-143 B 7
Kottakota ○ **IND** 140-141 H 4
Kottayam ○ • **IND** 140-141 G 6
Kotto ~ **RCA** 206-207 E 6
Kottūru ○ **IND** 140-141 G 3
Kotu ⌒ **TON** 184 IV a 1
Kotu Group ⌒ **TON** 184 IV a 1
Kotuj ~ **RUS** 108-109 e 6
Kotujkan ~ **RUS** 116-117 J 2
Koturdepe ○ **TM** 136-137 C 5
Kotwa ○ **ZW** 218-219 G 3
Kotzebue ○ **USA** 20-21 J 3
Kotzebue Sound ≈ 20-21 J 3
Kouadio-Prikro ○ **CI** 202-203 H 6
Kouaga ~ **RMM** 202-203 E 2
Kouakourou ○ **RMM** 202-203 H 2
Kouandé ○ **DY** 202-203 L 4
Kouandikro ○ **CI** 202-203 H 6
Kouango ○ **RCA** 206-207 D 6
Kouankan ○ **RG** 202-203 F 5
Kouassikro ○ **CI** 202-203 J 6
Kouba Olanga ○ **TCH** 198-199 J 5
Koubia ○ **RG** 202-203 E 4
Koubo Abou Azraq ○ **TCH** 206-207 E 3
Kouchibouguac National Park ⊥ **CDN** (NB) 240-241 L 4
Koudou, Cascades de ~ • **DY** 204-205 E 3
Koudougou ☆ **BF** 202-203 J 3
Kouéré ○ **BF** 202-203 J 4
Koufey ○ **RN** 198-199 F 5
Kouffo ~ **DY** 202-203 L 6
Kouga ~ **ZA** 220-221 F 6
Kougaberge ▲ **ZA** 220-221 F 6
Kougnohou ○ **RT** 202-203 L 6
Kougouleu ○ **G** 210-211 B 3
Kouibli ○ **CI** 202-203 G 6
Kouif, El ○ **TN** 190-191 G 3
Kouilou ■ **RCB** 210-211 C 5
Kouilou ~ **RCB** 210-211 C 6
Kouka ○ **BF** 202-203 H 4
Koukdjuak, Great Plain of the ∸ **CDN** 28-29 D 3
Koukdjuak River ~ **CDN** 28-29 D 3
Kouki ○ **RCA** 206-207 C 5
Kouklia ○ **CY** 128-129 E 5
Koukou ○ **TCH** 206-207 F 3
Koukourou ○ **RCA** (Bam) 206-207 E 5
Koukourou ~ **RCA** 206-207 E 5
Koukourou-Bamingui, Réserve de faune du ⊥ **RCA** 206-207 D 5
Koula ○ **RMM** 202-203 G 3
Koulamoutou ☆ **G** 210-211 D 4
Koulbo ○ **TCH** 198-199 K 6
Koulbous ○ **SUD** 198-199 L 5
Koulé ○ **RG** 202-203 F 5
Koulé Ekou ▲ **DY** 204-205 E 4
Koulikoro ○ **RMM** 202-203 G 3
Koulou ○ **RN** 204-205 E 2
Koulouguidi ○ **RMM** 202-203 E 3
Koulountou ~ **SN** 202-203 D 3
Koulouoko ~ **BF** 202-203 K 3
Koum ○ **CAM** 206-207 B 4
Kouma ○ **RCA** (Kem) 206-207 D 5
Kouma ~ **RCA** 206-207 D 6
Koumamevong ○ **G** 210-211 C 3
Koumantou ○ **RMM** 202-203 G 4
Koumba ~ **RG** 202-203 D 4
Koumbal ○ **RCA** 206-207 F 4
Koumbala ○ **RCA** (Bam) 206-207 E 4
Koumbala ~ **RCA** 206-207 E 4
Koumbia ○ **BF** 202-203 J 4
Koumbia ○ **RG** 202-203 D 4
Koumbi Saleh ∴ • **RIM** 196-197 G 7
Koumbo ○ **BF** 202-203 K 4
Koumbri ○ **BF** 202-203 J 3
Koumia ○ **RMM** 202-203 H 3
Koumogo ○ **TCH** 206-207 D 4
Koumongou ○ **RT** (DSA) 202-203 L 4
Koumongou ~ **RT** 202-203 L 4
Koumou ~ **RCA** 206-207 F 4
Koumpentoum ○ **SN** 202-203 C 2
Koumra ○ **TCH** 206-207 C 4
Kounahiri ○ **CI** 202-203 H 6
Koundara ○ **RG** 202-203 D 3
Koundé ○ **RCA** 206-207 B 5
Koundessong ○ **CAM** 210-211 D 2
Koundian ○ **RMM** 202-203 E 3
Koundian ○ **RN** 202-203 F 4
Koundijourou ○ **TCH** 198-199 J 6
Koundou ○ **RG** 202-203 E 5
Koundougou ○ **BF** 202-203 H 4
Koun-Fao ○ **CI** 202-203 J 6
Koungheul ○ **SN** 202-203 C 3
Koungouri ○ **TCH** 206-207 D 3
Kouniana ○ **RMM** 202-203 H 3
Kounkané ○ **SN** 202-203 C 3
Kountouata ○ **SN** 202-203 C 3
Kountze ○ **USA** (TX) 268-269 F 6
Kouoro ○ **RMM** 202-203 H 3
Koup ○ **ZA** 220-221 E 6
Koupé, Mont ▲ **CAM** 204-205 H 6
Koupéla ○ **BF** 202-203 K 3
Kouraï ~ **RG** 202-203 F 5
Kouraqué ○ **RMM** 202-203 E 3
Kourémalé ○ **RMM** 202-203 F 4
Kourgou ○ **TCH** 206-207 C 3
Kourgui ○ **CAM** 206-207 B 3

348 Kokomo — Kourgui

L

Lajedo, Cachoeira de ~ BR 68-69 B 6
Lajes o BR 68-69 K 4
Lajes, Cachoeira das ~ BR 68-69 D 5
Lajinha o BR 72-73 K 6
Lajitas o USA (TX) 266-267 D 4
Lajitas, Las o RA 76-77 E 3
Lajla, gora ▲ GE 126-127 E 6
Lajma ~ RUS 114-115 J 5
La Jolla Indian Reservation ✗ USA (CA) 248-249 G 6
Lajord o CDN (SAS) 232-233 O 5
Lajoya o USA (NM) 256-257 J 4
La Joya o USA (TX) 266-267 J 7
Laka ~ RUS 88-89 R 4
Lakamané o RMM 202-203 F 2
Lake o USA (MS) 268-269 L 4
Lake o USA (MT) 250-251 H 7
Lake o USA (WY) 252-253 H 2
Lake Alma o CDN (SAS) 232-233 O 6
Lake Andes o USA (SD) 260-261 H 3
Lake Argyle Tourist Village o AUS 172-173 J 4
Lake Arthur o USA (LA) 268-269 H 6
Lake Arthur o USA (NM) 256-257 L 6
Lake Benton o USA (MN) 270-271 B 6
Lake Biddy o AUS 176-177 E 6
Lake Boga o AUS 180-181 G 3
Lake Bolac o AUS 180-181 G 4
Lake Bronson o USA (MN) 270-271 B 2
Lake Butler o USA (FL) 286-287 G 1
Lake Cargelligo o AUS 180-181 J 2
Lake Charles o USA (LA) 268-269 G 6
Lake Chelan National Recreation Area ⊥ USA (WA) 244-245 E 2
Lake City o USA (AR) 276-277 E 5
Lake City o USA (CO) 254-255 H 5
Lake City o USA (FL) 286-287 G 1
Lake City o USA (IA) 274-275 D 2
Lake City o USA (MI) 272-273 D 3
Lake City o USA (MN) 270-271 F 6
Lake City o USA (SC) 284-285 L 3
Lake City o USA (SD) 260-261 J 1
Lake City o USA (TN) 282-283 C 4
Lake Clark National Park and Preserve ⊥ USA 20-21 O 6
Lake Cormorant o USA (MS) 268-269 K 2
Lake Cowichan o CDN (BC) 230-231 E 5
Lake Crystal o USA (MN) 270-271 D 6
Lake District National Park ⊥ GB 90-91 E 4
Lake Errock o CDN (BC) 230-231 G 4
Lake Eyre Basin ⌣ AUS 178-179 D 4
Lake Eyre National Park ⊥ AUS 178-179 D 5
Lakefield o AUS 174-175 H 4
Lakefield o CDN (ONT) 238-239 G 4
Lakefield o USA (MN) 270-271 C 7
Lakefield National Park ⊥ AUS 174-175 H 4
Lake Francis o CDN (MAN) 234-235 F 4
Lake Frome Regional Reserve ⊥ AUS 178-179 F 6
Lake Gairdner National Park ⊥ AUS 178-179 C 6
Lake Geneva o USA (WI) 274-275 K 2
Lake George o USA (CO) 254-255 K 5
Lake George o USA (MN) 270-271 C 3
Lake George o USA (NY) 278-279 H 5
Lake Gilles Conservation Park ⊥ AUS 180-181 D 2
Lake Grace o AUS 176-177 E 6
Lakehamu River ~ PNG 183 D 5
Lake Harbor o USA (FL) 286-287 J 5
Lake Harbour o CDN 36-37 P 3
Lake Havasu City o USA (AZ) 256-257 A 4
Lake Hawea o NZ 182 B 6
Lakehead o USA (CA) 246-247 C 3
Lake Helen o USA (FL) 286-287 H 3
Lake Henry o USA (MN) 270-271 D 5
Lake Hughes o USA (CA) 248-249 F 5
Lakehurst o USA (NJ) 280-281 M 4
Lake Isabella o USA (CA) 248-249 F 4
Lake Itasca o USA (MN) 270-271 C 3
Lake Jackson o USA (TX) 268-269 E 7
Lake Jipe Lodge o EAK 212-213 F 5
Lake King o AUS 176-177 E 6
Lakeland o CDN (MAN) 234-235 E 4
Lakeland o USA (FL) 286-287 H 3
Lakeland o USA (GA) 284-285 G 5
Lakeland Downs o AUS 174-175 H 4
Lake Lenore o CDN (SAS) 232-233 O 3
Lake Linden o USA (MI) 270-271 K 3
Lake Louise o CDN (ALB) 232-233 B 4
Lakelse Lake o CDN (BC) 228-229 F 2
Lake Mackay Aboriginal Land ✗ AUS 172-173 J 6
Lake Mason o AUS 176-177 E 3
Lake Mattamuskeet National Wildlife Refuge ⊥ USA (NC) 282-283 L 5
Lake Mburo National Park ⊥ EAU 212-213 C 4
Lake McDonald o USA (MT) 250-251 F 3
Lake Mead City o USA (AZ) 256-257 A 3
Lake Mead National Recreation Area • USA (AZ) 256-257 B 2
Lake Mead National Recreation Area • USA (NV) 248-249 K 3
Lake Metigoshe International Peace Garden • USA (ND) 258-259 G 3
Lake Michigan Beach o USA (MI) 272-273 C 5
Lake Michigan Provincial Park ⊥ CDN (ONT) 234-235 P 5
Lake Mills o USA (IA) 274-275 E 1
Lake Mills o USA (WI) 274-275 K 1
Lake Minchumina o USA 20-21 O 5
Lake Murray o PNG 183 A 4
Lake Nash o AUS 178-179 D 1
Lakenheath o CDN (SAS) 232-233 M 6
Lake O'Brien o CDN (NFL) 242-243 O 3
Lake of the Ozarks State Park ⊥ USA (MO) 274-275 F 6
Lake of the Prairies o CDN (MAN) 234-235 B 3
Lake Oswego o USA (OR) 244-245 C 5
Lake Paringa o NZ 182 B 5
Lake Park o USA (FL) 286-287 J 5
Lake Park o USA (GA) 284-285 G 6
Lake Placid o USA (FL) 286-287 H 4
Lake Placid o USA (NY) 278-279 H 4
Lakeport o USA (NY) 278-279 F 5
Lake Preston o USA (SD) 260-261 J 2
Lake Providence o USA (LA) 268-269 J 4
Lake Rara National Park ⊥ NEP 144-145 C 6
Lake Seminole State Park ⊥ • USA (GA) 284-285 F 6
Lake Shasta Caverns ⊥ USA (CA) 246-247 C 3
Lakeshore o USA (CA) 248-249 E 2
Lakeside o USA (NY) 278-279 C 5
Lakeside o USA (OR) 244-245 A 7
Lakeside o USA (UT) 254-255 C 2
Lakeside o USA (VA) 280-281 J 6
Lake Stevens o USA (WA) 244-245 C 2
Lake Superior Provincial Park ⊥ CDN (ONT) 236-237 D 5
Lake Tekapo o NZ 182 C 6
Lake Torrens National Park ⊥ AUS 178-179 D 6
Lake Valley o CDN (SAS) 232-233 M 5
Lake Valley o USA (NM) 256-257 H 6
Lake Victor o USA (TX) 266-267 J 3
Lakeview o USA (ID) 250-251 C 4
Lakeview o USA (MI) 272-273 D 4
Lakeview o USA (OH) 280-281 C 3
Lakeview o USA (OR) 244-245 E 8
Lake View o USA (SC) 284-285 L 2
Lake Village o USA (AR) 276-277 D 7
Lakeville o USA (MN) 270-271 E 6
Lake Wales o USA (FL) 286-287 H 4
Lake Way o AUS 176-177 F 3
Lake Wilson o USA (MN) 270-271 C 6
Lakewood o USA (CO) 254-255 K 4
Lakewood o USA (MI) 272-273 F 6
Lakewood o USA (NJ) 280-281 M 3
Lakewood o USA (NM) 256-257 L 6
Lake Woodruff National Wildlife Refuge ⊥ USA (FL) 286-287 H 2
Lake Worth o USA (FL) 286-287 J 5
Lake Zurich o USA (IL) 274-275 K 2
Lakhdaria o DZ 190-191 D 2
Lākheri o IND 138-139 F 7
Lakhimpur o IND 142-143 B 2
Lakhipur o IND 142-143 H 3
Lakhnādon o IND 138-139 G 8
Lakhpat o IND 138-139 B 8
Lākhra o PK 134-135 M 6
Lakin o USA (KS) 262-263 E 7
Lakinsk o RUS 94-95 Q 3
Lakitusaki River ~ CDN 34-35 P 3
Lakki o PK 138-139 C 3
Lákkoma o GR 100-101 K 4
Laklo ~ RI 166-167 C 6
Laklubar o RI 166-167 C 6
Lakohembi o RI 168 E 7
Lakonikós Kólpos ≈ 100-101 J 6
Lakor, Pulau ⌒ RI 166-167 E 6
Lakota ☆ CI 202-203 H 7
Lakota o USA (IA) 274-275 D 1
Lakota o USA (ND) 258-259 J 3
Laksefjorden ≈ 86-87 N 1
Lakselv o N 86-87 M 1
Laksfossen ~ •• N 86-87 F 4
Lakshadweep ▫ IND 140-141 E 5
Lakshadweep Sea ≈ 140-141 F 6
Lakshimpur o BD 142-143 G 4
Lakshmipur o IND 140-141 L 3
Laktaši o BIH 100-101 F 2
Lakuan o RI 164-165 G 3
Lakuramau o PNG 183 F 2
Lalafuta ~ Z 218-219 C 2
Lalago o EAT 212-213 D 5
Lāla Mūsa o PK 138-139 D 3
Lalandai o RI 164-165 H 4
Lalapansi o ZW 218-219 F 4
Lalapaşa ☆ TR 128-129 B 2
Lalara o G 210-211 C 3
Lalaua o MOC 218-219 K 2
Lalaua, Rio ~ MOC 218-219 K 2
Lalbert o AUS 180-181 G 3
Lalbiti o NEP 144-145 E 7
Laleham o AUS 178-179 K 2
Laleia o RI 166-167 D 6
La Leona o YV 60-61 K 3
Lalete, Tanjung ▲ RI 166-167 C 6
Lālezār, Kūh-e ▲ IR 134-135 G 4
Lālezār, Rūd-e ~ IR 134-135 G 3
Lalganj o IND 142-143 B 2
Lalganj o IND 142-143 C 3
Lālī o IR 134-135 C 2
Lalibela o ••• ETH 208-209 D 2
Laliki o RI 166-167 D 5
Lalik River ~ PNG 183 F 3
Lalin o E 98-99 C 3
Lalin o VRC 150-151 F 5
Lalindu ~ RI 164-165 G 5
Lalitpur o IND 138-139 G 7
Lalitpur o •• NEP 144-145 E 7
Lalla Outka ▲ MA 188-189 J 3
Lalla Rookh o AUS 172-173 D 6
La-Lo o RP 160-161 D 3
Lalo o DY 202-203 L 6
La'l-ō-Sarğangal o AFG 134-135 M 1
La'l Pūra o AFG 138-139 C 2
Laluangon o RI 164-165 G 4
Lalung La ▲ VRC 144-145 F 6
Lalyo o SUD 206-207 K 6
Lam o CAM 204-205 J 5
Lama o BD 142-143 H 5
Lama, ozero o RUS 108-109 Y 7
La Macarena o CO 60-61 E 6
La Macolla o YV 60-61 F 1
La Madera o YV 60-61 K 3
Lamadongzhao o VRC 154-155 G 2
Lamainong o RI 162-163 B 3
Lamakera o RI 166-167 B 6
Lamalaga ⊥ WSA 196-197 B 3
Lamaline o CDN (NFL) 242-243 N 6
Lamanai ∴ • BH 52-53 K 3
Lamanche Valley Provincial Park ⊥ CDN (NFL) 242-243 Q 5
Lamanuna o RI 166-167 B 6
Lamap ☆ VAN 184 II a 3
Lamar o USA (CO) 254-255 N 5
Lamar o USA (LA) 268-269 J 4
Lamar o USA (MO) 276-277 A 3
Lamar o USA (OK) 264-265 H 3
Lamar o USA (SC) 284-285 K 2
Lāmard o IR 134-135 E 5
Lamari River ~ PNG 183 C 4
La Martre o CDN (QUE) 242-243 B 3
Lamas o PE (LOR) 64-65 F 3
Lamas o PE (MAR) 64-65 D 5
Lamassa o PNG 183 G 3
La Mauricie National Park ⊥ CDN (QUE) 240-241 C 3
Lambako o RI 164-165 H 4
Lambale o RI 164-165 H 6
Lamballe o F 90-91 F 7
Lambaréné ☆ • G 210-211 C 4
Lambari o BR 72-73 H 6
Lambari, Rio ~ BR 72-73 H 5
Lambaro Angan o RI 162-163 A 2
Lambatu o RI 164-165 G 5
Lambayeque o PE 64-65 C 5
Lambell, Mount ▲ AUS 172-173 L 2
Lambert o USA (MS) 268-269 K 2
Lambert, Cape ▲ AUS 172-173 C 6
Lambert, Cape ▲ PNG 183 F 3
Lambert Glacier ⊂ ARK 16 F 8
Lambert Land ⊥ GRØ 26-27 p 4
Lambertsbaai o ZA 220-221 D 6
Lamberts Bay = Lambertsbaai o ZA 220-221 D 6
Lambeth o CDN (ONT) 238-239 D 6
Lambi o SOL 184 I d 3
Lambom o S 86-87 G 6
Lambrama o PE 64-65 F 8
Lambton, Cape ▲ CDN 24-25 K 5
Lambu o PNG 183 F 2
Lambubalano o RI 164-165 H 6
Lambumbu Bay ≈ 184 II a 3
Lambunao o RP 160-161 E 7
Lambuya o RI 164-165 H 5
Lamdesar o RI 166-167 F 5
Lamé o TCH 206-207 B 4
Lame Burra Game Reserve ⊥ WAN 204-205 H 3
Lame Deer o USA (MT) 250-251 N 6
Lamego o • 98-99 D 4
Lameguapi o RCH 78-79 C 6
Lameirão, Área Indígena ✗ BR 66-67 B 5
Lamen Bay o VAN 184 II b 3
Lamentin, Le o F 56 E 4
Lameroo o AUS 180-181 F 3
Lamesa o USA (TX) 264-265 C 6
Lami o FJI 184 III b 3
Lamia o GR 100-101 J 5
Lamie River ~ USA 274-275 E 6
Lamigan Point ▲ RP 160-161 G 9
Lamindo o SUD 206-207 K 6
Lamington, Mount ▲ PNG 183 E 5
Lamington National Park ⊥ AUS 178-179 M 5
Lamir, Kampung o MAL 162-163 E 3
Lamison o USA (AL) 284-285 C 4
Lamitan o RP 160-161 E 9
Lam Kachuan o THA 158-159 F 3
Lamkin o USA (TX) 266-267 J 2
Lammerkop o ZA 220-221 J 2
Lammeulo o RI 162-163 A 2
Lamming Mills o CDN (BC) 228-229 O 3
La Moille o USA (IL) 274-275 J 3
Lamoille o USA (NV) 246-247 K 3
Lamoille River ~ USA 278-279 H 4
La Moine River ~ USA 274-275 H 4
Lamon Bay ≈ 160-161 D 5
Lamongan o RI 168 E 3
Lamoni o USA (IA) 274-275 E 4
Lamont o CDN (ALB) 232-233 F 2
Lamont o USA (CA) 248-249 F 4
Lamont o USA (FL) 286-287 F 1
Lamont o USA (ID) 252-253 G 3
Lamont o USA (OK) 264-265 G 2
Lamont o USA (WY) 252-253 L 4
La Motte, Lac o CDN (QUE) 236-237 K 4
La Moure o USA (ND) 258-259 J 5
Lampa o PE 70-71 B 4
Lampa, Río ~ PE 64-65 F 9
Lampanaih o RI 162-163 A 2
Lampang o THA 142-143 L 6
Lam Pao Reservoir o THA 158-159 G 2
Lampasas o USA (TX) 266-267 J 2
Lampasas River ~ USA 266-267 K 3
Lampazos de Naranjo o MEX 50-51 J 4
Lampedusa o I 100-101 D 7
Lampedusa, Ísola di ⌒ I 100-101 D 7
Lamper o RI 164-165 E 4
Lamphun o THA 142-143 L 6
Lampione, Ísola di ⌒ I 100-101 D 7
Lam Plaimat o THA 158-159 G 3
Lampman o CDN (SAS) 232-233 Q 6
Lamprey o CDN 30-31 W 6
Lampung ▫ RI 162-163 F 7
Lampung, Teluk ≈ 162-163 F 7
Lamu o • EAK 212-213 H 5
Lamud o PE 64-65 D 5
Lamu Island ⌒ EAK 212-213 H 5
Lamutskaja ~ RUS 112-113 R 4
Lamutskoe o RUS 112-113 P 4
Lamy o USA (NM) 256-257 K 3
Lan' ~ BY 94-95 K 5
Lana, Río de la ~ MEX 52-53 G 3
Lanagan, Lake o AUS 172-173 H 5
Lanai ⌒ USA (HI) 288 J 4
Lanai City o USA (HI) 288 J 4
Lanaihale ▲ USA (HI) 288 J 4
Lanalhué, Lago o RCH 78-79 C 4
Lanao, Lake o RP 160-161 F 9
Lanark o GB 90-91 F 4
Lanark o USA (NM) 256-257 J 7
Lanas o MAL 160-161 B 10
Lanbi Kyun ⌒ MYA 158-159 E 5
Lancang o VRC 142-143 M 4
Lancang Jiang ~ VRC 142-143 M 4
Lancang Jiang ~ VRC 144-145 L 5
Lancaster o CDN (ONT) 238-239 L 3
Lancaster o • GB 90-91 F 4
Lancaster o USA (CA) 248-249 F 5
Lancaster o USA (IL) 274-275 L 6
Lancaster o USA (MN) 270-271 B 2
Lancaster o USA (MO) 274-275 F 4
Lancaster o USA (NH) 278-279 K 4
Lancaster o USA (OH) 280-281 D 4
Lancaster o USA (PA) 280-281 K 3
Lancaster o USA (SC) 284-285 K 2
Lancaster o USA (TX) 264-265 H 6
Lancaster o USA (WI) 274-275 H 2
Lancaster Sound ≈ 24-25 c 3
Lancaster State Historic Site, Fort ∴ USA (TX) 266-267 F 3
Lance Creek o USA (WY) 252-253 O 3
Lancelin o AUS 176-177 C 5
Lancer o CDN (SAS) 232-233 K 5
Lancester o USA (KY) 276-277 L 3
Lanciano o I 100-101 E 3
Lanco o RCH 78-79 C 5
Lancones o PE 64-65 B 4
Lancrenon, Chutes de ~ • CAM 206-207 B 5
Land, De o USA (FL) 286-287 H 2
Landa o USA (ND) 258-259 G 3
Landak ~ RI 162-163 H 4
Landana o ANG 210-211 D 6
Land Between The Lakes ⊥ USA (KY) 276-277 G 4
Landeck o A 92-93 L 5
Landegode ⌒ N 86-87 G 3
Lander o USA (WY) 252-253 K 4
Lander River ~ AUS 172-173 L 6
Landers o USA (CA) 248-249 H 5
Landete o E 98-99 G 5
Landfall Island ⌒ IND 140-141 L 3
Landi o RG 202-203 E 4
Landi Kotal o PK 138-139 C 2
Landis o CDN (SAS) 232-233 K 3
Land O'Lakes o USA (FL) 286-287 G 3
Landor o AUS 176-177 D 2
Landri Sales o BR 68-69 G 5
Landrum o USA (SC) 284-285 H 1
Landry, Lac o CDN (QUE) 242-243 G 2
Landšaftnyj park "Sofijivka" • UA 102-103 G 3
Land's End ▲ •• GB 90-91 E 6
Landshut o • D 92-93 M 4
Landskrona o •• S 86-87 F 9
Lanďštejn • CZ 92-93 N 4
Lane City o USA (TX) 266-267 L 4
Lanett o USA (AL) 284-285 E 4
Lanfiéra o BF 202-203 J 3
Lang o CDN (SAS) 232-233 O 6
Langa o PE 64-65 D 8
Langaboo o RT 202-203 L 5
Langadás o GR 100-101 J 4
Langa-Langa ☆ ZRE 210-211 E 5
Langano Häyk' ~ ETH 208-209 D 5
Langar o UZ 136-137 J 4
Langara, Bahía ≈ 80 G 3
Langara Island ⌒ CDN (BC) 228-229 A 2
Langarūd o IR 136-137 B 6
Langatabiki o SME 62-63 G 3
Langbank o CDN (SAS) 232-233 Q 5
Lang Bay o CDN (BC) 230-231 E 4
Langberg ▲ ZA (CAP) 220-221 E 4
Langberg ▲ ZA 220-221 F 4
Langberge ▲ ZA 220-221 D 6
Langbinsi o GH 202-203 K 4
Langdale o CDN (BC) 230-231 F 4
Lang Dinh o VN 156-157 D 7
Langdon o CDN (ALB) 232-233 E 5
Langdon o USA (ND) 258-259 J 3
Langeac o F 90-91 J 9
Langeb, Wādī ~ SUD 200-201 H 4
Langebaan o ZA 220-221 D 6
Langeberg ▲ ZA 220-221 E 6
Langeland ⌒ DK 86-87 E 9
Langell Valley o USA (OR) 244-245 D 8
Langenburg o CDN (SAS) 232-233 R 5
Langeoog ⌒ D 92-93 J 2
Langepas o RUS 114-115 N 4
Langeri o RUS (SHL) 122-123 K 3
Langeri ~ RUS 122-123 K 3
Langfang o VRC 154-155 K 2
Langford o CDN (BC) 230-231 F 5
Langford o USA (SD) 260-261 J 1
Langgam o RI 162-163 D 4
Langgapayung o RI 162-163 C 4
Langgur o RI 166-167 G 4
Langham o CDN (SAS) 232-233 M 3
Langjökull ⊂ IS 86-87 d 2
Langka o RI 162-163 B 2
Langkadonkhang o VRC 144-145 C 5
Langkahan o RI 162-163 B 2
Langkawi, Pulau ⌒ MAL 162-163 C 1
Langkesi, Kepulauan ⌒ RI 164-165 J 6
Langkobale o RI 164-165 G 5
Langkon o MAL 160-161 B 9
Langlade o USA (WI) 270-271 K 5
Langlade, Isthme de ⊥ F 242-243 M 6
Langlade ou Petit Miquelon ⌒ F 242-243 M 6
Langley o CDN (BC) 230-231 G 4
Langley o USA (OK) 264-265 J 2
Langley Island ⌒ CDN 20-21 X 2
Langlo Crossing P.O. o AUS 178-179 H 4
Langlois o USA (OR) 244-245 A 8
Langlo River ~ AUS 178-179 H 3
Langmusi o VRC 154-155 C 4
Langnes o N 86-87 O 1
Lango o G 210-211 E 3
Lango, Tarso ▲ TCH 198-199 J 2
Langogne o F 90-91 J 9
Langon o F 90-91 G 9
Langøya ⌒ N 86-87 G 2
Langqên Zangbo ~ VRC 144-145 C 5
Langres o • F 90-91 K 8
Langruth o CDN (MAN) 234-235 E 4
Langry ~ RUS 122-123 K 2
Langsa o RI 162-163 B 2
Långseleån ~ S 86-87 G 4
Lang Shan ▲ VRC 148-149 H 7
Lang So'n ☆ VN 156-157 E 6
Lang Suan o THA 158-159 E 6
Langtang o NEP 144-145 E 6
Langtang o WAN 204-205 H 4
Langtang National Park ⊥ NEP 144-145 E 6
Långtans udde ▲ ARK 16 G 31
Langtao o MYA 142-143 K 2
Langton o CDN (ONT) 238-239 E 6
Langton Bay ≈ 24-25 J 6
Långträsk o S 86-87 K 4
Langtry o USA (TX) 266-267 F 4
Langu o THA 158-159 E 7
Langudi Rassa National Park ⊥ ETH 208-209 E 3
Languedoc ⊥ F 90-91 J 10
Languedoc-Roussillon ▫ F 90-91 J 10
Langueyú, Arroyo ~ RA 78-79 K 4
Langui Layo, Lago o PE 70-71 B 4
L'Anguille River ~ USA 276-277 E 5
Languiñeo o RA 78-79 D 7
Langxi o VRC 154-155 L 6
Langxiang o VRC 150-151 G 4
Langzhong o VRC 154-155 D 6
Laniel o CDN (QUE) 236-237 J 5
Lanigan o CDN (SAS) 232-233 N 4
Lanigan Creek ~ CDN 232-233 N 4
Lanín, Parque Nacional ⊥ RA 78-79 D 5
Lanjut o RI 162-163 F 5
Lankao o VRC 154-155 J 4
Lankapatti o IND 142-143 H 3
Lankovaja ~ RUS 120-121 O 4
Lanlacuni Bajo o PE 70-71 B 3
Lannemezan o F 90-91 H 10
Lannion o F 90-91 F 7
L'Annonciation o CDN (QUE) 238-239 L 2
Lanquín o • GCA 52-53 K 4
Lansdale o USA (PA) 280-281 L 3
Lansdowne o AUS 172-173 H 4
Lansdowne o IND 138-139 G 5
Lansdowne House o CDN (ONT) 234-235 Q 2
L'Anse o USA (MI) 270-271 K 4
L'Anse-au-Griffon o CDN (QUE) 240-241 L 2
L'Anse-au-Loup o CDN (NFL) 242-243 M 1
L'Anse-aux-Gascons o CDN (QUE) 240-241 L 2
L'Anse aux Meadows National Historic Park ⊥ ••• CDN (NFL) 242-243 N 1
L'Anse-à-Valleau o CDN (QUE) 242-243 D 3
Lansford o USA (ND) 258-259 F 3
Lansing o USA (IA) 274-275 G 1
Lansing ☆ USA (MI) 272-273 E 5
Lansjärv o S 86-87 L 3
Lantewa o WAN 198-199 E 6
Lanthenay, Romorantin- o F 90-91 H 8
Lantian o VRC 154-155 F 4
Lantigiang, Pulau ⌒ RI 168 E 6
Lantz Corners o USA (PA) 280-281 H 2
Lantzville o CDN (BC) 230-231 E 4
Lanu o RI 164-165 G 3
Lanuhza Bay ≈ 160-161 G 8
Lanusei o I 100-101 B 5
Lanxi o VRC (HEI) 150-151 F 4
Lanxi o VRC (ZHE) 156-157 L 2
Lan Xian o VRC 154-155 G 2
Lanya o GH 202-203 L 5
Lanyu o RC 156-157 M 5
Lanyu ⌒ RC 156-157 M 5
Lanza o BOL 70-71 D 2
Lanza, Río ~ PE 70-71 C 4
Lanzai o WAN 204-205 J 3
Lanzarote ⌒ E 188-189 E 6
Lanzhou ☆ • VRC 154-155 C 3
Laoag ☆ RP 160-161 D 3
Lào Cai ☆ VN 156-157 C 5
Laoguié o CI 202-203 H 7
Laohekou o VRC 154-155 G 5
Laokas o TCH 206-207 B 4
Laon ☆ • F 90-91 J 7
Laona o USA (WI) 270-271 K 5
Laoong o RP 160-161 F 6
Laora o RI 164-165 H 6
Laos = Lao ▪ LAO 158-159 H 2
Laoshan • VRC 154-155 M 3
Laotieshan Shedao Z.B. ⊥ • VRC 150-151 C 8
Laouda o CI 202-203 H 6
Laoudi-Ba o CI 202-203 J 5
La'oueissi o RIM 196-197 D 6
Laouni, Oued ~ DZ 198-199 B 2
Laouridou o CI 202-203 H 7
Lao Xanh, Cù ⌒ VN 158-159 K 4
Laoye Ling ▲ VRC 150-151 G 6
Lapa o BR 74-75 F 5
Lapachito o RA 76-77 H 4
Lapac Island ⌒ RP 160-161 D 10
Lapai o WAN 204-205 G 4
Lapalisse o F 90-91 J 8
La Palma ⌒ E 188-189 C 6
La Palma o USA (AZ) 256-257 D 6
La Pampa ▫ RA 78-79 F 4
La Panza Range ▲ USA 248-249 D 4
Laparan Island ⌒ RP 160-161 D 10
Lapata o RA 80 F 7
La Patrie o CDN (QUE) 238-239 O 3
Lapau o PNG 183 F 3
La Paz ☆ • BOL 70-71 C 5
Lape o RI 168 C 7
Lapeer o USA (MI) 272-273 F 4
Lapie River ~ CDN 20-21 Y 6
Lapihunghanan o RI 164-165 D 5
La Pine o USA (OR) 244-245 D 7
Lapining Island ⌒ RP 160-161 F 7
Lapinlahti o FIN 88-89 J 5
La Plata o CO 60-61 D 6
La Plata ☆ • RA 78-79 L 3
La Plata o USA (MD) 280-281 K 5
La Plata River ~ USA 254-255 G 6
La Poile River ~ CDN 242-243 K 5
Laporte o CDN (SAS) 232-233 J 4
La Porte o USA (CA) 246-247 D 4
Laporte o USA (PA) 280-281 K 2
La Porte City o USA (IA) 274-275 F 2
Lappa o RUS 120-121 D 4
Lappajärvi o FIN 88-89 G 5
Lappe o CDN (ONT) 234-235 O 6
Lappeenranta o • FIN 88-89 K 6
Lappland ⊥ 86-87 H 3
Lappy ~ RUS 120-121 D 4
Lapri o RUS 118-119 M 8
Laprida o RA 78-79 J 4
Lapseki ☆ TR 128-129 B 2
Lapševo ☆ RUS 96-97 F 6
Laptev Sea = Laptevyh, more ≈ 110-111 L 3
Lapua o FIN 88-89 G 5
Lapuko o RI 164-165 H 6
La Purísima Mission State Historic Park • USA (CA) 248-249 D 5
Lapus, Munții ▲ RO 102-103 C 4
La Push o USA (WA) 244-245 A 3
Lapwai o USA (ID) 250-251 C 5
Laqiyat Arba'in o SUD 200-201 D 2
Laqiyat 'Umran o SUD 200-201 D 3
L'Àquila ☆ •• I 100-101 D 3
Lār o IR 134-135 F 5
Lara o AUS 180-181 H 5
Lara ~ G 210-211 C 3
Larabanga o GH 202-203 K 5
Larache = El-Araïch o MA (Tet) 188-189 H 3
Laragh = An Láithreach o • IRL 90-91 D 5
Lārak, Ğazīre-ye ⌒ IR 134-135 G 5
Laramanay o TCH 206-207 B 4
Laramate o PE 64-65 E 9
Laramie o USA (WY) 252-253 N 5
Laramie Mountains ▲ USA 252-253 M 4
Laramie National Historic Site, Fort ∴ USA (WY) 252-253 O 4
Laramie Peak ▲ USA (WY) 252-253 N 4
Laramie River ~ USA 252-253 N 5
Laranjal o BR (AMA) 66-67 E 3
Laranjal o BR (RSU) 74-75 E 7
Laranjeiras do Sul o BR 74-75 D 5
Laranjinha, Rio ~ BR 72-73 E 7
Larantuka o RI 166-167 B 6
Larat o RI 166-167 F 5
Larat, Pulau ⌒ RI 166-167 F 5
Larba o DZ 190-191 D 2
Larba o RUS 118-119 L 8
Lärbro o S 86-87 J 8
Larchwood o USA (IA) 274-275 B 1
Larde o MOC 218-219 K 3
Lardeau River ~ CDN 230-231 M 3
Larder Lake o CDN (ONT) 236-237 J 4
Larder River Provincial Park ⊥ CDN (ONT) 236-237 J 5
Lare o EAK 212-213 F 3
Laredo o E 98-99 F 3
Laredo o USA (TX) 266-267 H 6
Laredo Sound ≈ 32-33 F 5
Laredo Sound ≈ 228-229 F 4
Lar'egan ~ RUS 114-115 O 4
Lār-e Polūr o IR 136-137 C 7
Lares o PE 64-65 F 8
Lares o • USA (PR) 286-287 P 2
Larga, Laguna o RA 76-77 F 6
Largeau ☆ TCH 198-199 J 4
Largest Lighthouse in the World (Kilauea Lighthouse) II • USA (HI) 288 F 2
Largo o BR 68-69 H 7
Largo o USA (FL) 286-287 G 4
Largo, Cayo ⌒ C 54-55 E 4
Lariang o RI 164-165 F 4
Lariang ~ RI 164-165 F 4
Lariat o USA (TX) 264-265 B 4
Larimore o USA (ND) 258-259 K 4
Larino o RUS 96-97 L 6
Lario = Lago di Como o I 100-101 B 2
La Rioja ▫ RA 76-77 D 5
Lárissa o GR 100-101 J 5
La Rivière o CDN (MAN) 234-235 E 5
Lar'jak o RUS 114-115 Q 4
Lark o USA (TX) 264-265 C 3
Larkāna o • PK 138-139 B 6
Lark Harbour o CDN (NFL) 242-243 K 3
Larkspur o USA (CO) 254-255 L 4
Larnaka o • CY 128-129 E 5
Larne o • GB 90-91 E 4
Larned o USA (KS) 262-263 G 6
Larned National Historic Site, Fort ∴ USA (KS) 262-263 G 6
Laro o CAM 204-205 K 4
Larocu, Qasr o LAR 192-193 E 4
La Ronser, ostrov ⌒ RUS 84-85 g 2
Laropi o EAU 212-213 C 2
Larose o USA (LA) 268-269 K 7
Larrainzar o MEX 52-53 H 3
Larrey Point ▲ AUS 172-173 D 5
Larrimah o AUS 174-175 B 4
Larroque o RA 78-79 K 2
Larry's River o CDN (NS) 240-241 O 5
Lars Christensen land ⊥ ARK 16 G 7
Larsen is-shelf ⊂ ARK 16 G 30
Larson o CDN (ONT) 234-235 N 5
Laru Mat, Tanjung ▲ RI 166-167 F 5
Larvik ☆ N 86-87 E 7
Larwill o USA (IN) 274-275 N 3
Lasahata o RI 166-167 E 3
Lasahau o RI 164-165 H 6
La Sal o USA (UT) 254-255 F 5
Lasalimu o RI 164-165 H 6
La Sal Mountains ▲ USA 254-255 F 5
Lasam o RP 160-161 D 3
Lasanga Island ⌒ PNG 183 D 4
Las Animas o USA (CO) 254-255 M 5
Lasara o USA (TX) 266-267 K 7
Lasarat o ETH 208-209 F 3
Lascar, Volcán ▲ RCH 76-77 D 2
Lascano o EC 64-65 B 2
Lascano o ROU 78-79 M 2
Las Catitas o RA 78-79 E 2
Lascaux, Grotte de ••• F 90-91 H 9
Lascelles o AUS 180-181 G 3
L'Ascension o CDN (QUE) 240-241 D 2
L'Ascension-de-Patapédia o CDN (QUE) 240-241 H 3
La Scieri o G 210-211 D 3
Las Cuatro Bocas o YV 60-61 F 2
Lasem o RI 168 D 3
Lashburn o CDN (SAS) 232-233 J 2
Las Heras o RA 80 F 3
Lashio o MYA 142-143 K 4
La Silla o CO 60-61 E 3
Łask o PL 92-93 P 3
Laškargāh ☆ • AFG 134-135 L 3
Laskeek Bay ≈ 228-229 C 4
Lāš-ō-Ğovein o AFG 134-135 J 3
Lasolo ~ RI 164-165 G 5
Lasoni, Tanjung ▲ RI 164-165 H 5
La Spézia o •• I 100-101 B 2
Las Piedras, Río de ~ PE 70-71 B 2
Las Plumas o RA 78-79 F 7
Laspur o PK 138-139 D 1
Las Ramas = Salitre o EC 64-65 C 2
Lassance o BR 72-73 H 4
Lassen Peak ▲ USA (CA) 246-247 D 3
Lassen Volcanic National Park ⊥ USA (CA) 246-247 D 3
Lasseter Highway II AUS 176-177 M 2
Lassio ~ G 210-211 D 4
Lassul o PNG 183 F 3
Last Chance o USA (CO) 254-255 M 4
Last Chance Creek ~ USA 254-255 D 6
Last Mountain Lake o CDN (SAS) 232-233 N 4
Lastoursville o G 210-211 D 4
Lastovo o HR 100-101 F 3
Lastovo ⌒ HR 100-101 F 3
Las Tres Matas o YV 60-61 J 3
Lasu o PNG 183 G 3
Las Vegas o USA (NM) 256-257 K 3
Las Vegas o •• USA (NV) 248-249 J 3
Las Vegas Valley ⌣ USA 248-249 J 3
Latacunga ☆ EC 64-65 C 2
Latady Island ⌒ ARK 16 F 29
Latah Creek ~ USA 244-245 H 3
Latakia = al-Lādiqīya ☆ SYR 128-129 F 5
Latalata, Pulau ⌒ RI 164-165 K 4
Lata Papalang, Bukit ▲ MAL 162-163 D 2
La Tapoa ~ BF 202-203 L 3
Lataro ⌒ VAN 184 II a 2
Latas o RCH 76-77 C 2
Lātāseno ~ FIN 88-89 G 2
Latchford o CDN (ONT) 236-237 J 5
Late ⌒ TON 184 IV a 1
Lateriquique, Río ~ PY 70-71 H 6
Laterriere o CDN (QUE) 240-241 D 2
Latham o AUS 176-177 D 4
Latham o USA (AL) 284-285 C 5
Lathan o IND 142-143 J 2
Lathi = Île Sakao ⌒ VAN 184 II a 2
Lathom o CDN (ALB) 232-233 F 5
Lathu = Île Éléphant ⌒ VAN 184 II a 2
Latiffiya, al- o IRQ 128-129 L 6
Latik o RIM 196-197 G 6
Latimojong Mountains Reserve ⊥ • RI 164-165 F 5
Latina ☆ I 100-101 D 4
Latinos, Ponta dos ▲ BR 74-75 D 9
Lat'juga o RUS 88-89 U 4
Latodo o RI 168 E 6
Latoma o RI 164-165 G 5
Latornell River ~ CDN 228-229 Q 2
Latorre o RCH 76-77 B 5
Latou o RI 164-165 G 5
Latouche o USA 20-21 R 6
Latouche Island ⌒ USA 20-21 R 6
Latouche Treville, Cape ▲ AUS 172-173 E 5
Latour o CDN (QUE) 240-241 G 2
Látrar o IS 86-87 b 1
Latrobe o AUS 180-181 J 6
Latrobe o USA (PA) 280-281 G 3
La Trochita II • RA 78-79 D 6
Latta o USA (SC) 284-285 L 2
Latu o RI 166-167 E 3
Latulipe o CDN (QUE) 236-237 J 5
Lātūr o IND 138-139 F 10
Latura Vatı, Tanjung ▲ RI 166-167 D 6
Latvia = Latvija ▪ LV 94-95 J 3
Lau o PNG 183 F 3
Lau o WAN 204-205 J 4
Lauca, Parque Nacional ⊥ RCH 70-71 C 6
Laucala ⌒ FJI 184 III c 2
Laudar o Y 132-133 D 7
Lauder o CDN (MAN) 234-235 C 5
Lauderdale o USA (MS) 268-269 M 4
Lauenburg/ Elbe o D 92-93 L 2
Lauge Koch Kyst ⊥ GRØ 26-27 U 5
Laughing Fish Point ▲ USA (MI) 270-271 M 4
Laughland Lake o CDN 30-31 X 2
Laughlen, Mount ▲ AUS 178-179 C 2
Laughlin o USA (NV) 248-249 K 4
Laughlin Peak ▲ USA (NM) 256-257 L 2
Lau Group, Northern ⌒ FJI 184 III c 2
Lau Group, Southern ⌒ FJI 184 III c 3
Lauhkaung o MYA 142-143 L 3
Lauiya Nandangarh o IND 142-143 D 2
Launceston o AUS 180-181 J 6
Launceston o GB 90-91 E 6
Launglon o MYA 158-159 E 4
Launglonbok Islands ⌒ MYA 158-159 D 4
Laungmasu o IND 142-143 H 4
La Unión o CO (NAR) 64-65 D 1
La Unión o CO (VCA) 60-61 C 5
La Unión o EC 64-65 B 2
La Unión o PE 64-65 D 6
Laupahoehoe o USA (HI) 288 K 5
Lauqa o KSA 130-131 H 3
Laura o AUS (QLD) 174-175 H 4
Laura o AUS (SA) 180-181 E 2
Laura o CDN (SAS) 232-233 L 4
Laura o USA (IL) 274-275 J 4
Laura, Kapp ▲ N 84-85 P 2
La Urbana o YV 60-61 H 4
Laurel o USA (DE) 280-281 L 5
Laurel o USA (FL) 286-287 G 4
Laurel o USA (IA) 274-275 F 3
Laurel o USA (MD) 280-281 K 4
Laurel o USA (MS) 268-269 L 5
Laurel o USA (MT) 250-251 L 6

Lajedo, Cachoeira de — Laurel 351

Laurel o USA (NE) 262-263 J 2
Laurel o USA (VA) 280-281 J 6
Laurel, Cerro ▲ MEX 52-53 L 2
Laureles o ROU 76-77 K 6
Laurel Hill o USA (FL) 286-287 C 1
Laurel River ~ USA 276-277 L 3
Laurel River Lake < USA (KY) 276-277 L 3
Laurel Springs o USA (NC) 282-283 F 4
Laureliville o USA (OH) 280-281 D 4
Laurenceton o CDN (NFL) 242-243 N 3
Laurens o USA (IA) 274-275 D 2
Laurens o USA (SC) 284-285 F 2
Laurentians ⊥ CDN 238-239 H 2
Laurentides ⊥ CDN (QUE) 238-239 M 3
Laurentides ⊥ CDN 238-239 M 2
Lauri o MYA 142-143 J 3
La Uribe o CO 60-61 C 5
Laurie, Mont ▲ AUS 176-177 G 3
Laurie Island o ARK 16 G 32
Laurie Lake o CDN 34-35 E 2
Laurier o CDN (MAN) 234-235 D 4
Laurier o USA (WA) 244-245 G 2
Laurier, Mont ☆ CDN (QUE) 238-239 K 2
Laurie River o CDN 34-35 F 2
Laurinburg o USA (NC) 282-283 H 6
Laurium o USA (WI) 270-271 K 3
Lauro de Freitas o BR 72-73 L 2
Lauro Sodré o BR 66-67 F 4
Lausanne ☆ CH 92-93 J 5
Laut, Kampung o MAL 162-163 F 4
Laut, Pulau ∧ RI 162-163 G 4
Laut, Pulau ∧ RI (KSE) 164-165 E 5
Laut, Selat ≈ 164-165 E 5
Lautaret, Col du ▲ F 90-91 L 9
Lautaro o RCH 78-79 C 5
Lautem o RI 166-167 D 6
Laut Kecil, Kepulauan ∧ RI 164-165 D 6
Lautoka o FJI 184 III a 2
Lauttawar, Danau o RI 162-163 B 2
Lauz, Ǧabal al- ▲ KSA 130-131 D 3
Lauzon o CDN (QUE) 238-239 O 2
Lava Beds ⊥ USA 256-257 H 6
Lava Beds ⊥ USA 256-257 J 5
Lava Beds National Monument ∴ USA (CA) 246-247 B 4
Lavaca o USA (AR) 276-277 A 5
Lavaca, Port o USA (TX) 266-267 L 5
Lavaca Bay ≈ 266-267 L 5
Lavacicle Creek ∴ USA (OR) 244-245 E 7
Lava Flow ∟ USA 256-257 H 4
Lava Hot Springs o USA (ID) 252-253 F 4
Laval ☆ • F 90-91 G 7
Lavalle o RA 76-77 F 2
La Valle o USA (WI) 270-271 H 7
Lăvän, Ğazïre-ye ∧ IR 134-135 E 5
Lavapié, Punta ▲ RCH 78-79 C 4
Lavaur o F 90-91 H 10
Lavenham o CDN (MAN) 234-235 E 5
La Vérendrye Provincial Réserve ⊥ CDN (QUE) 236-237 L 5
Laverlochère o CDN (QUE) 236-237 J 5
Laverne o USA (OK) 264-265 C 2
Laverton o AUS 176-177 G 4
Lavieille, Lake o CDN (ONT) 238-239 G 3
Laviera o EAT 212-213 F 6
Lavigne o CDN (ONT) 238-239 E 2
Lavik o N 86-87 B 6
Lavillette o CDN (NB) 240-241 K 3
Lavina o USA (MT) 250-251 L 5
La Viuda o YV 60-61 K 3
Lavon o USA (TX) 264-265 H 5
Lavon, Lake o USA (TX) 264-265 H 5
Lavonia o USA (GA) 284-285 G 2
Lavoy o CDN (ALB) 232-233 G 2
Lavrador, Ribeiro do ∧ BR 70-71 J 3
Lavras o BR 72-73 H 6
Lavrentija o RUS 112-113 Z 4
Lavrio o GR 100-101 K 6
Lavrova, buhta ≈ 112-113 O 6
Lavrova, proliv ≈ 84-85 f 2
Lavumisa o SD 220-221 K 3
Lawang o RI 168 I 3
Lawan Gopeng o MAL 162-163 D 2
Lawarai-Pass ▲ PK 138-139 C 2
Lawas o MAL 164-165 D 1
Lawashi River ~ CDN 34-35 P 4
Lawatu o RI 164-165 G 5
Lawford Islands ∧ CDN 30-31 N 2
Lawit, Gunung ▲ RI 162-163 K 4
Lawksawk o MYA 142-143 K 5
Lawn o USA (TX) 264-265 G 6
Lawn Bay ≈ 242-243 N 6
Lawngngaw o MYA 142-143 J 2
Lawngtlai o IND 142-143 H 4
Lawn Hill o AUS 174-175 E 6
Lawnhill o CDN (BC) 228-229 C 3
Lawn Hill National Park ⊥ AUS 174-175 E 6
Lawowa o RI 164-165 H 6
Lawra o GH 202-203 J 4
Lawrence o NZ 182 B 6
Lawrence o USA (KS) 262-263 L 6
Lawrence o USA (MA) 278-279 K 6
Lawrence o USA (NC) 282-283 K 4
Lawrence o USA (NE) 262-263 H 4
Lawrenceburg o USA (KY) 276-277 L 2
Lawrenceburg o USA (TN) 276-277 H 5
Lawrence Station o CDN (NB) 240-241 H 5
Lawrenceville o USA (GA) 284-285 G 3
Lawrenceville o USA (IL) 274-275 L 6
Lawrenceville o USA (VA) 280-281 J 7
Lawrence Wells, Mount ▲ AUS 176-177 F 3
Lawtha o MYA 142-143 H 4
Lawton o USA (ND) 258-259 J 3
Lawton o USA (PA) 280-281 K 2
Lawton o USA (TX) 264-265 F 4
Lawushi Manda National Park ⊥ Z 214-215 F 7

Lay o BF 202-203 K 3
Lay o USA (CO) 254-255 H 3
Laya o RG 202-203 D 5
Laya Dula o RG 202-203 E 5
Layang Layang o MAL 160-161 A 10
Layar, Tanjung ▲ RI 164-165 E 6
Layrat ▲ WSA 188-189 F 7
Laywang Ga o MYA 142-143 K 3
Lay Lake < USA (AL) 284-285 D 3
Layo o PE 70-71 B 4
Layton o USA (FL) 286-287 J 7
Laytonville o CAL 246-247 B 4
Lazarev o RUS 122-123 J 2
Lazarevac o YU 100-101 H 2
Lazareuskoe o RUS 126-127 C 6
Lázaro Cárdenas o MEX 50-51 B 2
Lazdijai o LT 94-95 H 4
Lāze o IR 134-135 E 5
Lazio ☐ I 100-101 D 3
Lazo (ROS) 122-123 E 7
Lazo o RUS (SAH) 110-111 V 6
L. Bistrups Brae ⊏ GRØ 26-27 o 5
Lea o USA (NM) 256-257 M 6
Léach o K 158-159 G 4
Leach Island ∧ CDN (ONT) 236-237 D 5
Leachville o USA (AR) 276-277 E 5
Leacross o CDN (SAS) 232-233 P 3
Lead o USA (SD) 260-261 C 2
Leader o USA (SAS) 232-233 J 5
Lead Hill o USA (AR) 276-277 C 4
Leading Tickles o CDN (NFL) 242-243 N 3
Leadore o USA (ID) 252-253 E 2
Leadpoint o USA (WA) 244-245 H 2
Leadville o USA (CO) 254-255 J 4
Lees Camp o USA (OR) 244-245 B 6
Leaf Bay ≈ 36-37 P 5
Leaf Rapids o CDN 34-35 G 2
Leaf River ~ USA 268-269 L 5
League City o USA 266-269 G 5
Leahy o USA (WA) 244-245 F 3
Leakesville o USA (MS) 268-269 M 5
Leakey o USA (TX) 266-267 H 4
Lea Lea o PNG 183 D 4
Leamington o CDN (ONT) 238-239 C 6
Leamington o USA (UT) 254-255 C 4
Leander o USA (TX) 266-267 K 3
Leander Point ▲ AUS 176-177 C 4
Leandra o ZA 220-221 J 3
Leandro o BR 68-69 F 5
Leandro N. Alem o RA 76-77 K 4
Lea Park o CDN (ALB) 232-233 H 2
Learmonth o AUS 172-173 B 7
Leary o USA (GA) 284-285 F 5
Leasi, Kepulauan ∧ RI 166-167 E 3
Leask o CDN (SAS) 232-233 M 2
Leatherwood o USA (KY) 276-277 M 3
Leaton State Historic Site, Fort ∴ USA (TX) 266-267 C 4
Leavenworth o USA (KS) 262-263 M 5
Leavenworth o USA (WA) 244-245 E 3
Leavenworth, Fort • USA (KS) 262-263 L 5
Leavitt o CDN (ALB) 232-233 F 6
Łeba o PL 92-93 O 1
Lebak o RP 160-161 F 9
Lebam o USA (WA) 244-245 B 4
Lebamba o G 210-211 C 5
Leban Condong, Kampung o MAL 162-163 E 3
Lébango o RCB (Cuv) 210-211 E 3
Lébango ~ RCB 210-211 H 3
Lebanon o IN 274-275 M 4
Lebanon o USA (KS) 262-263 H 5
Lebanon o USA (KY) 276-277 K 3
Lebanon o USA (MO) 276-277 C 3
Lebanon o USA (NE) 262-263 F 5
Lebanon o USA (NH) 278-279 J 5
Lebanon o USA (OH) 280-281 C 4
Lebanon o USA (OR) 244-245 C 6
Lebanon o USA (PA) 280-281 K 3
Lebanon o USA (SD) 260-261 G 1
Lebanon o USA (TN) 276-277 J 4
Lebanon o USA (VA) 280-281 D 7
Lebanon = al-Lubnān ■ RL 128-129 F 5
Lebanon Station o USA (FL) 286-287 G 2
Lebap o TM 136-137 G 4
Lebbeke o B 92-93 H 3
Lebeau o USA (LA) 268-269 J 6
Lebec o USA (CA) 248-249 F 5
Lebed' ~ RUS 114-125 P 2
Lebedjan' o RUS 94-95 Q 5
Lebedyn o UA 102-103 J 2
Lebel-sur-Quévillon o CDN (QUE) 236-237 L 3
Lebida o ZRE 210-211 F 5
Lebiolali o ETH 208-209 H 5
Lébri o G 210-211 D 4
Lebja'ře o KZ 124-125 K 3
Lebja'že o RUS 96-97 F 5
Lebja'žja o RUS 114-115 S 7
Leiden o NL 92-93 H 2
Leifs Ø ∧ GRØ 28-29 W 4
Leigh o USA (NE) 262-263 J 3
Leigh Creek o AUS 178-179 E 6
Leigh Creek South o AUS 178-179 E 6
Leighton o USA (AL) 284-285 C 2
Leigong Shan ▲ VRC 156-157 F 3
Leimebamba o PE 64-65 D 5
Leimus o HN 52-53 B 4
Leinan o USA (SAS) 232-233 L 5
Leine ~ D 92-93 K 2
Leinster o AUS 176-177 F 4
Leiper, Kap ▲ GRØ 26-27 P 4
Leipzig o CDN (SAS) 232-233 K 3
Leipzig o D 92-93 M 3
Leira o N (OPP) 86-87 D 6
Leira ~ N (ROM) 86-87 D 5
Leiria ☆ • P 98-99 C 5
Leirvik o N 86-87 B 7
Leishan o VRC 156-157 F 3
Leisi o EST 94-95 H 2
Leisler, Mount ▲ AUS 176-177 K 1
Leitchfield o USA (KY) 276-277 J 3
Leite, Igarapé do ~ BR 66-67 K 5
Leiter o USA (WY) 252-253 M 2
Leiva o RA 78-79 K 2
Lechuguilla, Bahía ≈ 50-51 L 4
Lĭ8i o LV 94-95 G 3
Le Claire o USA (IA) 274-275 H 3

Lecompte o USA (LA) 268-269 H 5
Łęczyca o • PL 92-93 P 2
Ledang, Gunung ▲ MAL 162-163 E 3
Ledesma o E 98-99 D 4
Ledge o USA (MT) 250-251 J 2
Ledge Point o AUS 176-177 C 5
Ledjanaja o RUS 108-109 b 6
Ledjanaja, gora ▲ RUS 112-113 Q 6
Ledmozero o RUS 88-89 M 4
Ledo o IND 142-143 J 2
Ledong o VRC 156-157 F 7
Leduc o CDN (ALB) 232-233 F 2
Lee o USA (NV) 246-247 K 3
Leka ∧ N 86-87 E 4
Lékana o RCB 210-211 E 5
Leeburn o USA (MN) 270-271 D 3
Leech Lake o USA (MN) 270-271 D 3
Leech Lake Indian Reservation ⋈ USA (MN) 270-271 D 3
Leedale o CDN (ALB) 232-233 D 3
Leeds o GB 90-91 G 5
Leeds o GUY 62-63 F 2
Leeds o USA (ND) 258-259 H 3
Leeds o USA (AL) 284-285 D 3
Leeds, Mount ▲ CDN 26-27 M 4
Leek o GB 90-91 F 5
Leeman o USA 176-177 C 4
Leeman o USA (WI) 270-271 K 6
Leer (Ostfriesland) o D 92-93 J 2
Leer, Pulau ∧ RI 166-167 H 5
Lees o USA (TX) 264-265 H 5
Leesburg o USA (FL) 286-287 H 3
Leesburg o USA (GA) 284-285 F 5
Leesburg o USA (OH) 280-281 C 4
Leesburg o USA (VA) 280-281 J 5
Leeston o NZ 182 D 5
Leesville o USA (LA) 268-269 G 5
Leesville o USA (SC) 284-285 J 3
Leesville o USA (TX) 266-267 K 4
Leeton o AUS 180-181 J 6
Leeudoringstad o ZA 220-221 H 3
Leeu-Gamka o ZA 220-221 E 6
Leeupoort o ZA 220-221 J 4
Leeuwarden o • NL 92-93 H 2
Leeuwin, Cape ▲ AUS 176-177 C 5
Leeuwin-Naturaliste National Park ⊥ AUS 176-177 C 5
Leeuwrivier ~ ZA 220-221 F 6
Lee Vining o USA (CA) 248-249 E 2
Leeward Islands ∧ 56 G 7
Leffelier o CDN (MAN) 234-235 F 5
Léfini ~ RCB 210-211 E 5
Léfini, Réserve de chasse de la ⊥ RCB 210-211 E 5
Lefkáda o GR 100-101 H 5
Lefkáda ∧ GR 100-101 H 5
Lefkónas o GR 100-101 J 4
Lefkosia ★ • CY 128-129 E 5
Lefo, Mont ▲ CAM 204-205 J 6
Lefor o USA (ND) 258-259 E 5
Lefors o USA (TX) 264-265 D 3
Lefroy, Lake o AUS (WA) 176-177 F 5
Lefroy, Lake o AUS (WA) 176-177 G 5
Legal o CDN (ALB) 232-233 E 2
Legape o RB 220-221 G 2
Legend o CDN (ALB) 232-233 G 6
Legendre Island ∧ AUS 172-173 C 6
Leggett o USA (CA) 246-247 B 4
Leggett o USA (TX) 268-269 F 6
Legion Mine o ZW 218-219 E 5
Legionowo o PL 92-93 Q 2
Legkraal o PL 218-219 E 5
Legnica o • PL 92-93 O 3
Legokjawa o RI 168 C 3
Le Grand, Mount ▲ AUS 176-177 G 6
Leguan Island ∧ GUY 62-63 E 2
Legundirua, Pulau ∧ RI 162-163 F 7
Légune o AUS 172-173 J 3
Leh o IND 138-139 F 2
Le Havre o F 90-91 H 7
Lehena o GR 100-101 H 6
Lehi o USA (UT) 254-255 D 4
Lehigh Acres o USA (FL) 286-287 H 5
Lehighton o USA (PA) 280-281 L 3
Lehman Caves ∴ USA (NV) 246-247 L 4
Lehmann o USA (TX) 264-265 B 5
Lehr o USA (MS) 268-269 K 5
Lehr o USA (ND) 258-259 H 5
Lehua Island ∧ USA (HI) 288 E 2
Lehua Landing o USA (HI) 288 E 3
Leiah o PK 138-139 C 4
Leibnitz o A 92-93 N 5
Leicester o GB 90-91 G 5
Leichhardt, Mount ▲ AUS 172-173 L 6
Leichhardt Range ▲ AUS 174-175 J 7
Leichhardt River ~ AUS 174-175 E 5

Leitmeritz = Litoměřice o CZ 92-93 N 3
Leitomischl = Litomyšl o CZ 92-93 O 4
Leitre o PNG 183 A 2
Leiva, Cerro ▲ CO 60-61 D 6
Leiyang o VRC 156-157 H 3
Leizhou Bandao ∪ VRC 156-157 G 6
Leizhou Wan ≈ 156-157 G 6
Lejac o CDN (BC) 228-229 K 2
Lejeune o CDN (QUE) 240-241 G 3
Lejeune Marine Corps Base, Camp ×× USA (NC) 282-283 K 6
Ledong o VRC 154-155 B 3
Lek ~ NL 92-93 H 3
Leka ∧ N 86-87 E 4
Lékana o RCB 210-211 E 5
Lekatero o ZRE 210-211 H 4
Lekeleka o TON 184 IV a 2
Lékéti ~ RCB 210-211 E 5
Lékila o G 210-211 D 4
Lekitobi o RI 164-165 J 4
Lekko ~ RUS 114-115 R 3
Lekoumou □ RCB 210-211 D 5
Lékoni o G 210-211 D 4
Lékoni ~ G 210-211 D 4
Leksand o S 86-87 G 6
Leksozero ~ RUS 88-89 L 5
Lekst, Jbel ▲ MA 188-189 G 6
Leksula o RI 166-167 D 3
Leku o ETH 208-209 D 5
Lela o RI 166-167 B 6
Lelai, Tanjung ▲ RI 164-165 L 3
Lélali ~ RCB 210-211 D 5
Leland o USA (MS) 268-269 K 3
Lefčycy o BY 94-95 L 6
Lelehudi o PNG 183 F 6
Lelépa = Île Lelepa ∧ VAN 184 II b 3
Lelepa, Île = Lelepa ∧ VAN 184 II b 3
Leleque o RA 78-79 D 5
Leling o VRC 154-155 K 3
Lelinguang o RI 166-167 F 5
Lelinta o RI 166-167 F 3
Leljuveem ~ RUS 112-113 Q 2
Lelogama o RI 166-167 B 6
Léliouma o RG 202-203 D 4
Lefvergyrgyn ~ RUS 112-113 M 2
Lema Shilindi o ETH 208-209 F 6
Lematang ~ RI 162-163 F 6
Lembar o RI 168 C 7
Lembé o CAM 204-205 K 6
Lembeh, Pulau ∧ RI 164-165 J 3
Lembeni o EAT 212-213 F 5
Lemberg o CDN (SAS) 232-233 P 5
Lemberg = L'viv ★ UA 102-103 D 3
Lembing, Sungai o MAL 162-163 E 3
Lembo o RI 164-165 H 5
Lemery o RP 160-161 D 6
Lemesos o • CY 128-129 E 5
Lemhi, Fort ∴ USA (ID) 252-253 E 2
Lemhi Pass ∴ USA (MT) 250-251 F 7
Lemhi Range ▲ USA 252-253 E 2
Lemhi River ~ USA 250-251 F 6
Leminx o AUS 20-21 Y 7
Leming o USA (TX) 266-267 J 4
Lemitar o USA (NM) 256-257 J 4
Lem'ju ~ RUS 88-89 X 4
Lem'junskaja vozvyšennost' ▲ RUS 88-89 X 4
Lemmenjoen kansallispuisto ⊥ FIN 88-89 H 2
Lemmon o USA (SD) 260-261 D 1
Lemmon, Mount ▲ USA (AZ) 256-257 F 6
Lemoenshoek o ZA 220-221 E 6
Lemolemo o RI 164-165 L 4
Lemon, Lake o USA (IN) 274-275 M 5
Lemon Creek o CDN (BC) 230-231 M 4
Lemon Grove o USA 248-249 G 7
Le Mont Saint-Michel o ••• F 90-91 G 7
Lemoore o USA (CA) 248-249 E 3
Lemoore Naval Air Station ×× USA (CA) 248-249 E 3
Lemoyne o USA (NE) 262-263 E 3
Lempa, Río ~ ES 52-53 K 5
Lempäälä o FIN 88-89 G 6
Lemprière o CDN (BC) 228-229 P 4
Lemsford o CDN (SAS) 232-233 J 5
Lemsid o WSA 188-189 E 7
Lemtybož o RUS 114-115 D 3
Lemu o WAN 204-205 G 4
Lemukutan, Pulau ∧ RI 162-163 H 4
Lemva ~ RUS 108-109 J 8
Lemvig o DK 86-87 D 8
Lemyethna o MYA 158-159 C 2
Lena o CDN (MAN) 234-235 D 5
Lena ~ RUS 10-11 M 2
Lena o USA (AR) 276-277 B 6
Lena o USA (IL) 274-275 K 3
Lena o USA (MS) 268-269 L 4
Lenakel o VAN 184 II b 4
Lenangguar o RI 168 C 7
Lenapah o USA (OK) 264-265 J 2
Lena River Delta = Lena Delta ∪ RUS 110-111 U 3
Lençóis o BR 72-73 K 2
Lençóis Maranhenses, Parque Nacional dos ⊥ BR 68-69 G 3
Lençóis Paulista o BR 72-73 F 7
Lenda ~ ZRE 212-213 B 3
Lendeh o IR 134-135 D 3

Lendepas o NAM 220-221 D 2
Lendery o RUS 88-89 L 5
Lenexa o USA (KS) 262-263 M 6
Leney o CDN (SAS) 232-233 L 3
Lenge, Bandar-e o IR 134-135 F 5
Lenger o KZ 136-137 L 3
Lenghu o VRC 146-147 L 6
Lengley o CDN (QUE) 240-241 E 3
Lenglong Ling ▲ VRC 154-155 B 3
Lenglong Ling ▲ VRC (GAN) 154-155 C 3
Lengnau o RCA 206-207 E 6
Lengoué ~ RCB 210-211 E 3
Lengshuijiang o VRC 156-157 G 3
Lengshuitan o VRC 156-157 G 3
Leng Su Sin o VRC 156-157 C 5
Lengua de Vaca, Punta ▲ RCH 76-77 B 6
Lengulu o ZRE 210-211 L 2
Lengwe National Park ⊥ MW 218-219 H 3
Lenhovda o S 86-87 G 8
Leninabad = Hudžand o TJ 136-137 L 4
Leninabad = Hudžand o RIM 196-197 D 6
Leninabadskaja oblast □ TJ 136-137 K 5
Leninakan = Gjumri ★ AR 128-129 K 2
Leninoe o UA 102-103 J 3
Leningrad = Sankt-Peterburg ☆ ••• RUS 94-95 M 2
Leningradskaja o RUS (KRD) 102-103 L 4
Leningradskaja ~ RUS 108-109 d 3
Leningradskij o RUS 112-113 U 2
Leningradskij o TJ 136-137 M 5
Leningradskij, lednik ⊏ RUS 108-109 I 2
Leninogor o KZ 124-125 N 3
Leninogorsk o RUS 96-97 H 6
Leninsk o KZ 126-127 P 5
Leninsk o RUS 96-97 D 9
Leninsk o UZ 136-137 N 4
Leninskij o KZ 124-125 L 5
Leninskij o TJ 136-137 L 5
Leninskoe o KS 136-137 N 4
Leninskoe o KZ 126-127 N 4
Leninskoe o RUS 96-97 E 4
Leninskoe o RUS 122-123 E 6
Lenivaja ~ RUS 108-109 X 4
Lenkau o PNG 183 D 4
Lenkivci o UA 102-103 E 2
Lenkoran' = Lankaran o • AZ 128-129 N 3
Lenmalu o RI 166-167 F 2
Lennard ~ AUS 176-177 G 6
Lennox, Isla ∧ RCH 80 G 7
Lennox o USA (SD) 260-261 K 3
Leno-Angarskoe plato ▲ RUS 116-117 L 8
Lenoir o USA (NC) 282-283 F 5
Lenoir City o USA (TN) 282-283 D 5
Lenora o USA (KS) 262-263 G 5
Lenore o CDN (MAN) 234-235 C 5
Lenore Lake o CDN (SAS) 232-233 O 3
Lenox o USA (GA) 284-285 G 5
Lenox o USA (IA) 274-275 D 4
Lens o F 90-91 J 6
Lensk ★ • RUS 118-119 G 5
Lenskie stolby ⋆ RUS 118-119 N 5
Lenswood o CDN (MAN) 234-235 C 2
Lent'evo o RUS 94-95 P 2
Lentiira o FIN 88-89 K 4
Lentini o I 100-101 E 6
Lenwood o USA (CA) 248-249 G 5
Lenya o MYA 158-159 E 5
Léo o BF 202-203 J 4
Leoben o A 92-93 N 5
Leofnard o CDN (SAS) 232-233 N 3
Léogâne o RH 54-55 J 5
Leok o RI 164-165 G 3
Leola o USA (AR) 276-277 C 6
Leola o USA (SD) 260-261 H 1
Leominster o • GB 90-91 F 5
Leominster o USA (MA) 278-279 K 6
León o • E 98-99 E 3
Léon o F 90-91 G 10
León ★ • NIC 52-53 L 7
León o USA (IA) 274-275 E 4
León o USA (OK) 264-265 G 5
León, Cerro ▲ MEX 52-53 F 3
León, Cerro ▲ PY 70-71 G 7
León, De o USA (TX) 264-265 F 6
León, Montes de ▲ E 98-99 D 3
Leona, Punta la ▲ EC 64-65 B 2
Leonard o USA (ND) 258-259 K 5
Leonard o USA (TX) 264-265 H 5
Leonardtown o USA (MD) 280-281 K 5
Leonards o USA (TX) 264-265 H 5
Leonardville o NAM 220-221 D 1
Leonard Wood, Fort ×× USA (MO) 276-277 C 3
Leona River ~ USA 266-267 H 5
Leoncio Prado o PE 64-65 E 3
Leonidas o USA (ID) 250-251 C 7
Leonidas o USA (OK) 272-273 D 5
Leonídio o GR 100-101 J 6
Leonidovka ~ RUS 122-123 K 4
Leonidovo o RUS 122-123 K 4
Leon River ~ USA 264-265 G 6
Leon River ~ USA 266-267 K 2
Leont'eva, ostrov ∧ RUS 112-113 L 1
Leon Viejo ∴ NIC 52-53 L 5
León Downs o AUS 172-173 G 4
Léopold II, Lac = Lac Mai-Ndombe o ZRE 210-211 G 5
Leopoldina o BR 72-73 J 6
Leopold Island o CDN 36-37 S 2
Leopold M'Clintock, Cape ▲ CDN 24-25 N 2

Letsitele o ZA 218-219 F 6
Letsok-Aw Kyun ∧ MYA 158-159 E 5
Letta o CAM 204-205 K 6
Letterkenny o IRL 90-91 D 4
Letts o USA (IN) 274-275 N 5
Letwurung o RI 166-167 E 5
Léuá o ANG 216-217 F 5
Leuanius o SOL 184 I d 1
Leucadia o USA (CA) 248-249 G 6
Leupp o USA (AZ) 256-257 E 3
Leura o AUS 178-179 K 2
Leuser, Gunung ▲ RI 162-163 B 3
Leuser Nature Reserve, Gunung ⊥ RI 162-163 B 3
Leušinskij Tuman, ozero o RUS 114-115 H 5
Leuven o •• B 92-93 H 3
Levack o CDN (ONT) 238-239 D 2
Levanger o RUS 120-121 S 7
Levaja Bojarka ~ RUS 108-109 b 6
Levaja Bureja ~ RUS 122-123 G 3
Levaja Hetta ~ RUS 114-115 L 2
Levaja Kamenka ~ RUS 110-111 d 6
Levaja Lesnaja ~ RUS 120-121 T 4
Levaja Mama ~ RUS 118-119 E 7
Levaja Šapina ~ RUS 120-121 T 6
Levaja Vetv', kanal < RUS 102-103 N 5
Levaja Županova ~ RUS 120-121 S 6
Levan o USA (UT) 254-255 D 4
Levanger o N 86-87 E 5
Levante, Riviera di ∪ I 100-101 B 2
Levantine Basin ≃ 128-129 E 6
Levasi o RUS 126-127 G 6
Levdiev, ostrov ∧ RUS 108-109 M 7
Level, Isla ∧ RCH 80 C 2
Leveland o USA (TX) 264-265 D 5
Leven o GB 90-91 F 3
Leven Bank ≃ 222-223 E 4
Leveque, Cape ▲ AUS 172-173 F 4
Lever, Rio ~ BR 68-69 C 7
Leverett Glacier ⊏ ARK 16 E 0
Leverkusen o D 92-93 J 3
Levick, Mount ▲ ARK 16 F 17
Levidi o GR 100-101 J 6
Levin o NZ 182 E 4
Levinópolis o BR 72-73 H 3
Levis o CDN (QUE) 238-239 O 2
Lévis, Lac o CDN 30-31 L 4
Levisa Fork ~ USA 276-277 N 3
Levittown o USA (PA) 280-281 M 3
Levittown o USA (PR) 54-55 Q 4
Levkadit o GR 100-101 J 5
Levkinskaja o RUS 88-89 V 4
Levroux o F 90-91 H 8
Levski o BG 102-103 D 6
Levuka o FJI 184 III b 2
Levyj Hetagčan ~ RUS 112-113 J 5
Levyj Kedon ~ RUS 112-113 K 4
Levyj Mamakan ~ RUS 118-119 F 7
Léwa o CAM 204-205 K 5
Lewa o RI 168 D 7
Lewallen o USA (TX) 266-267 C 6
Lexa o USA (AR) 276-277 E 6
Lexington o USA (GA) 284-285 G 3
Lexington o USA (KY) 272-273 K 4
Lexington o USA (MI) 272-273 G 4
Lexington o USA (MO) 274-275 E 5
Lexington o USA (MS) 268-269 K 3
Lexington o USA (NC) 282-283 G 5
Lexington o USA (NE) 262-263 G 4
Lexington o USA (OK) 264-265 G 4
Lexington o USA (OR) 244-245 F 5
Lexington o USA (SC) 284-285 J 3
Lexington o USA (TN) 276-277 G 5
Lexington o USA (VA) 280-281 G 6
Lexington Park o USA (MD) 280-281 K 5
Leybourne Islands ∧ CDN 36-37 R 2
Leyburn o AUS 178-179 L 5
Leye o VRC 156-157 E 4
Leyland o CDN (ALB) 228-229 P 4
Leyte ∧ RP 160-161 F 7
Leyte Gulf ≈ 160-161 F 7
Lezama o YV 60-61 H 3
Lezhë o AL 100-101 G 4
Lezhi o VRC 154-155 D 6
ǏGadlaf, Wādī ~ JOR 128-129 J 6
ǏGaut, Wādī ~ SYR 128-129 J 5
LG Deux, Réservoir < CDN 38-39 F 3

L'gotny, mys ● RUS 120-121 H 5
Lgov ○ RUS 102-103 J 2
Lgovski, Dmitriev ○ RUS 94-95 O 5
LG Trois, Réservoir de ◁ CDN 38-39 G 2
I-Hail, Wadi ⋯ SYR 128-129 H 5
Lhari ○ VRC 144-145 J 5
L'Haridon Bight ≈ AUS 176-177 B 3
Lhasa ★ ⋯ VRC 144-145 H 6
Lhasa He ~ VRC 144-145 H 6
Lhazê ○ VRC 144-145 F 6
Lhokseumawe ○ RI 162-163 B 2
Lhoksukon ○ RI 162-163 B 2
Lhorong ○ VRC 144-145 K 5
Lhotse ▲ NEP 144-145 F 7
Lhuntsi ○ BHT 142-143 G 2
Lhünzê ○ VRC 144-145 H 6
Li ○ THA 158-159 E 2
Lia, Río ▲ RI 166-167 D 3
Liambezi, Lake ○ NAM 218-219 C 3
Liang ○ RU 164-165 H 4
Lianga ○ RP 160-161 G 8
Lianga Bay ≈ 160-161 G 8
Liangcheng ○ VRC (NMZ) 154-155 H 1
Liangcheng ○ VRC (SHD) 154-155 L 4
Lianghe ○ VRC (SIC) 156-157 F 2
Lianghe ○ VRC (YUN) 142-143 L 3
Lianghekou ○ VRC 154-155 D 5
Liangping ○ VRC 154-155 E 6
Liangpran, Gunung ▲ RI 164-165 D 3
Liangshan ○ VRC 154-155 K 4
Lianhua ○ VRC 154-155 H 6
Lianhua Shan ▲ VRC 156-157 J 5
Lianjiang ○ VRC (FUJ) 156-157 J 5
Lianjiang ○ VRC (GDG) 156-157 G 6
Lianping ○ VRC 156-157 H 4
Lianshan ○ VRC (GDG) 156-157 H 4
Lianshan ○ VRC (SHD) 154-155 K 4
Lianshan ○ VRC (SIC) 154-155 D 6
Lianshui ○ VRC 154-155 L 5
Liantang ○ VRC 156-157 H 4
Lian Xian ○ VRC 156-157 H 4
Lianyuan ○ VRC 156-157 G 4
Lianyungang ○ VRC 154-155 L 4
Lianyungang (Xinpu) ○ VRC 154-155 L 4
Liaocheng ○ VRC 154-155 J 3
Liao Dao • VRC 144-145 M 2
Liaodong Bandao ⊌ VRC 150-151 D 8
Liaodong Wan ≈ 150-151 C 7
Liaodun ○ VRC 146-147 L 4
Liao He ~ VRC 150-151 C 6
Liaoning □ VRC 150-151 C 6
Liao Shangjingcheng Yizhi ⋰ VRC 148-149 O 6
Liaoyang ○ VRC 150-151 D 7
Liaoyuan ○ VRC 150-151 D 7
Liaozhong ○ VRC 150-151 D 7
Liao Zhongjingcheng Yizhi • VRC 148-149 O 7
Liäquatpur ○ PK 138-139 C 5
Liard Highway ‖ CDN 30-31 H 5
Liard Plateau ▲ CDN 30-31 F 5
Liard River ~ CDN 30-31 H 5
Liat, Pulau ▲ RI 162-163 G 6
Libano ○ CO 60-61 D 5
Libano ○ RA 78-79 J 4
Libao ○ VRC 154-155 M 5
Lihatemo ○ RI 164-165 H 5
Libau ○ CDN (MAN) 234-235 G 4
Libba ○ WAN 204-205 F 3
Libby ○ USA 270-271 E 4
Libby ○ USA (MT) 250-251 D 3
Libenge ○ ZRE 210-211 G 3
Liberal ○ USA (KS) 262-263 F 7
Liberator Lake ○ USA 20-21 L 2
Liberdade, Río ~ BR 68-69 D 3
Liberec ○ CZ 92-93 N 3
Liberia ○ CR 52-53 B 6
Liberia ■ LB 202-203 E 6
Libertad ○ RA 76-77 J 6
Libertad ○ ROU 78-79 L 3
Libertad ○ YV 60-61 G 3
Libertad, La ○ ES 52-53 K 5
Libertad, La ◑ IIN 52-53 L 4
Libertador General San Martin ○ RA (JU) 76-77 E 2
Libertador General San Martin ○ RA (SLU) 78-79 G 2
Liberty ○ CDN (SAS) 232-233 N 4
Liberty ○ USA (IN) 274-275 D 5
Liberty ○ USA (KY) 276-277 D 5
Liberty ○ USA (MS) 268-269 K 5
Liberty ○ USA (NY) 280-281 M 2
Liberty ○ USA (SC) 284-285 D 2
Liberty ○ USA (TX) 276-277 K 4
Liberty ○ USA (TX) 268-269 F 6
Liberty ○ USA (UT) 254-255 D 2
Liberty Hill ○ USA (SC) 284-285 K 2
Liberty Lake ○ USA (WA) 244-245 H 3
Libertytown ○ USA (MD) 280-281 J 4
Libjo ○ RP 160-161 F 7
Libmanan ○ RP 160-161 E 6
Libo, Tanjung ▲ RI 164-165 L 4
Libode ○ ZA 220-221 J 5
Liboi ○ EAK 212-213 H 3
Liboko ○ ZRE 210-211 H 2
Libouma ⊙ G 210-211 D 3
Libourne ○ F 90-91 G 9
Librazhd ★ • AL 100-101 H 4
Libreville ⊛ ⋯ G 210-211 B 3
Librija ○ CO 60-61 E 4
Libro Point ▲ RP 160-161 C 6
Libuganon ~ RP 160-161 F 9
Libyan Desert = Sahrā' al-Libiyā, as- ⊥ LAR 192-193 K 3
Licancabur, Volcán ▲ RCH 76-77 D 2
Licata ● I 100-101 D 6
Lice ○ TR 128-129 J 4
Licenciado Matienzo ○ RA 78-79 K 4
Licheng ○ VRC 154-155 H 3
Lichinga ★ MOC 218-219 H 1
Lichinga, Planalto de ▲ MOC 218-219 H 1

Lichtenburg ○ ZA 220-221 H 3
Lichteneger, Lac ○ CDN 38-39 G 2
Licinio de Almeida ○ BR 72-73 J 3
Liciro ○ MOC 218-219 J 3
Licking ○ USA (MO) 276-277 D 3
Licking River ~ USA 276-277 L 2
Licuare, Río ~ MOC 218-219 J 3
Licungo, Río ~ MOC 218-219 J 3
Lida ○ BY 94-95 J 5
Lidan ~ S 86-87 F 7
Lida Junction ○ USA 248-249 G 2
Liddon Gulf ≈ 24-25 P 3
Liden ○ S 86-87 H 5
Lidgerwood ○ USA (ND) 258-259 K 5
Lidi, Mayo ~ CAM 206-207 B 4
Lidia, Río ~ PE 70-71 B 4
Lidjombo ○ RCA 210-211 F 2
Lidköping ○ S 86-87 F 7
Lido ○ RN 204-205 E 2
Lido di Óstia ○ I 100-101 D 4
Lidzbark Warmiński ○ PL 92-93 Q 1
Liebenthal ○ CDN (SAS) 232-233 J 4
Liebenthal ○ USA (KS) 262-263 G 6
Liebig, Mount ▲ AUS 176-177 L 1
Liechtenstein ■ FL 92-93 K 5
Liège ○ • B 92-93 H 3
Lieksa ○ FIN 88-89 L 5
Liemianzheng ○ VRC 154-155 E 6
Lienz ○ A 92-93 M 5
Liepāja ★ • LV 94-95 G 3
Lier ○ B 92-93 H 3
Lierre = Lier ○ • B 92-93 H 3
Lietnik ○ USA 20-21 F 5
Lièvre, Rivière du ~ CDN 238-239 K 2
Liezen ○ A 92-93 N 5
Lifamatola, Pulau ▲ RI 164-165 K 4
Lifford ★ IRL 90-91 D 4
Li Fiord ≈ (NWT) 26-27 B 3
Lifjell ▲ N 86-87 D 7
Lifuka ▲ TON 184 IV a 1
Lifune ~ ANG 216-217 C 4
Lifupa Lodge ○ MW 218-219 G 1
Ligao ○ RP 160-161 F 6
Ligar ○ TCH 206-207 C 4
Lighfoot Lake ○ AUS 176-177 G 4
Light ○ RP 160-161 F 7
Light, Cape ▲ ARK 16 F 30
Lighthouse (1836) • AUS 180-181 J 7
Lighthouse (1848) • AUS 180-181 G 5
Lighthouse Beach ⊥ • BS 54-55 G 2
Lighthouse Cove ○ CDN (ONT) 238-239 C 6
Lighthouse Point ▲ USA (FL) 286-287 E 2
Lighthouse Reef ▲ BH 52-53 L 3
Lightning Creek ~ USA 252-253 O 2
Lightning Ridge ○ AUS 178-179 J 5
Ligitile ○ USA (ND) 258-259 J 5
Ligonha, Río ~ MOC 218-219 K 2
Ligonier ○ USA (IN) 274-275 N 3
Ligonier ○ USA (PA) 280-281 G 3
Ligowola ~ EAT 214-215 J 6
Ligua, Caleta la ≈ RCH 76-77 B 6
Ligua, La ○ RCH (COQ) 76-77 B 6
Ligua, La ○ RCH (VAL) 78-79 D 2
Ligua, Río la ~ RCH 78-79 D 2
Ligunga ○ EAT 214-215 J 6
Liguria □ I 100-101 B 2
Ligurian Sea = Ligure, Mar ≈ 100-101 B 3
Ligurta ○ USA (AZ) 256-257 A 6
Lihás ○ GR 100-101 J 5
Lihin, al- ○ KSA 130-131 F 5
Lihir Group ▲ PNG 183 G 2
Lihir Island ▲ PNG 183 G 2
Lihuslavl' ○ RUS 94-95 N 3
Lihou Reefs and Cays ▲ AUS 174-175 N 5
Lihovskoj ○ RUS 102-103 M 3
Lihue ○ • USA (HI) 288 F 3
Lihuel Calel, Parque Nacional ⊥ RA 78-79 G 4
Liivi Laht ≈ 94-95 H 2
Lijiang ○ VRC (YUN) 142-143 M 2
Lijiang ○ • VRC (GSU) 156-157 G 4
Lik ~ LAO 156-157 C 7
Lik, Pulau ▲ RI 166-167 K 2
Likala ○ ZRE 210-211 H 3
Likame ~ ZRE 210-211 H 2
Likasi ○ ZRE 214-215 J 6
Likati ~ ZRE (Hau) 210-211 J 2
Likati ~ ZRE 210-211 J 2
Likely ○ CDN (BC) 230-231 L 3
Likely ○ USA (CA) 246-247 E 2
Likete ○ ZRE 210-211 H 4
Likisia = Liquica ○ RI 166-167 C 6
Likoma Islands ▲ MW 214-215 H 7
Likoto ○ ZRE 210-211 J 4
Likouala ○ RCB 210-211 F 2
Likouala ~ RCB 210-211 E 3
Likouala aux Herbes ~ RCB 210-211 F 3
Likum ○ PNG 183 D 2
Likuyu ○ EAT 214-215 J 6
Lilarea ○ AUS 178-179 H 2
Lilbourn ○ USA (MO) 276-277 F 4
Liléani ○ PK 138-139 D 4
Lilikse ○ GH 202-203 J 4
Lilla ○ PK 138-139 D 3
Lille ★ • F 90-91 J 4
Lille Bælt ≈ 86-87 D 9
Lillehammer ★ N 86-87 E 6
Lilleheiskebanke ≈ 28-29 N 4
Lilles, Punta ▲ RCH 78-79 D 2
Lillesand ★ N 86-87 D 7
Lillestrøm ○ CDN (SAS) 232-233 N 5
Lillico Point ▲ CDN 36-37 K 6
Lillie ○ USA (LA) 268-269 H 4
Lillington ○ USA (NC) 284-285 H 2
Lilliwaup ○ USA (WA) 244-245 B 3
Lillooet ○ CDN (BC) 230-231 G 4
Lillooet Lake ○ CDN (BC) 230-231 G 3
Lillooet Range ▲ CDN 230-231 G 3

Lilloet River ~ CDN 230-231 F 3
Lilo ○ ZRE 210-211 K 4
Lilo-an ○ RP 160-161 G 7
Lilongwe ★ • MW 218-219 G 1
Lilovca ○ RA 76-77 F 4
Liloy ○ RP 160-161 E 8
Lily ○ USA (SD) 260-261 J 1
Lily ○ USA (WI) 270-271 K 4
Lilydale ○ AUS 180-181 J 6
Lim ○ RCA 206-207 B 5
Lim ~ YU 100-101 G 3
Lima ○ OM 134-135 G 6
Lima ○ PY 76-77 J 2
Lima ~ USA (MT) 250-251 G 7
Lima ~ USA (OH) 280-281 B 3
Lima, La ○ HN 52-53 L 4
Limache ○ RA 76-77 F 5
Limaduru, La ○ BOL 76-77 E 2
Limal ○ BOL 76-77 E 2
Limão, Igarapé de ~ BR 66-67 K 6
Limão de Curuá ○ BR 62-63 J 5
Limapuluh ○ RI 162-163 C 3
Limar ○ RI 166-167 D 5
Limari, Río ~ RCH 76-77 B 6
Limassawa Island ▲ RP 160-161 F 8
Limassa ○ USA (IN) 276-277 M 4
Limay ○ USA (NJ) 280-281 M 3
Limay ○ USA (TX) 276-277 H 5
Limay, Río ~ RA 78-79 E 5
Limay, Río ~ RA 78-79 F 6
Limbach ○ RP 160-161 E 9
Limbang ○ MAL 164-165 D 1
Limbani ○ PE 70-71 F 4
Limbara ~ ZRE 210-211 K 3
Limbassa ○ ZRE 210-211 J 3
Limbaži ★ • LV 94-95 J 3
Limbdi ○ IND 138-139 C 8
Limbé ○ CAM 204-205 H 6
Limbe ○ MW 218-219 H 2
Limbé ○ RH 54-55 J 5
Limbla ○ AUS 178-179 C 2
Limbo, Pulau ▲ RI 164-165 J 4
Limboto ○ RI 164-165 H 3
Limbunan ○ RP 160-161 E 9
Limbung ○ RI 166-167 E 9
Limbunya ○ AUS 172-173 J 4
Limburg ○ B 92-93 H 3
Limburg an der Lahn ○ • D 92-93 K 3
Lime ○ USA (OR) 244-245 H 6
Lime Acres ○ ZA 220-221 F 4
Limeira ○ BR (MIN) 72-73 H 4
Limeira ○ BR (PAU) 72-73 G 7
Limerick ○ CDN (SAS) 232-233 M 6
Limerick = Luimneach ★ IRL 90-91 C 5
Limestone ○ CDN (NB) 240-241 H 4
Limestone ○ USA 278-279 O 2
Limestone ○ USA (ME) 240-241 J 4
Limestone, Lake ○ USA (TX) 266-267 L 2
Limestone Creek ○ CDN 34-35 J 2
Limestone Peak ▲ USA (AZ) 256-257 F 2
Limestone Rapids ~ CDN 34-35 M 3
Limfjorden ≈ 86-87 D 8
Ligonha, Río ~ MOC 218-219 K 2
Ligonier ○ USA (MN) 274-275 N 3
Limgi ○ VRC 154-155 K 4
Limia, Río ~ E 98-99 D 3
Limingen ○ N 86-87 F 4
Liminka ○ FIN 88-89 H 4
Limmen Bight ≈ AUS 174-175 B 3
Limmen Bight Aboriginal Land ⚒ AUS 174-175 C 4
Limmen Right River ~ AUS 174-175 C 4
Limnos ▲ GR 100-101 K 5
Limnu ~ RUS 120-121 K 6
Limoeiro ○ BR 68-69 L 5
Limoeiro do Ajurú ○ BR 62-63 K 6
Limoeiro do Norte ○ BR 68-69 J 4
Limoges ★ • F 90-91 H 9
Limon ○ USA (CO) 254-255 M 4
Limonar ○ C 54-55 H 4
Limón ★ CR 52-53 C 6
Limoquije ○ BOL 70-71 H 6
Limousin □ F 90-91 H 9
Limoux ○ F 90-91 J 10
Límpio ○ PY 76-77 J 3
Limpopo ○ ZA 218-219 G 6
Limpopo, Río ~ MOC 220-221 L 2
Limpitýfky ~ RUS 114-115 P 2
Limptékan ~ RUS 116-117 M 4
Limuru ○ EAK 212-213 F 4
Limuru ○ KSA 130-131 H 3
Lina ○ KSA 130-131 H 3
Linaäliven ~ S 86-87 K 3
Linahamari ○ RUS 88-89 L 2
Lin'an ○ VRC 154-155 L 6
Linao ○ RP 160-161 D 3
Linao Point ▲ RP 160-161 E 9
Linapacan Island ▲ RP 160-161 C 7
Linapacan Strait ≈ 160-161 C 7
Linares ○ E 98-99 F 5
Linares ○ MEX 50-51 K 5
Linares ○ RA 78-79 D 6
Linas, Monte ▲ I 100-101 B 5
Lincang ○ VRC 142-143 M 4
Linchang ○ VRC 154-155 F 5
Linchuan ○ VRC 156-157 K 3
Lincoln ○ NZ 182 D 5
Lincoln ○ RA 78-79 J 3
Lincoln ★ • GB 90-91 G 5
Lincoln ○ USA (AL) 284-285 D 3
Lincoln ○ USA (AR) 276-277 J 3
Lincoln ○ USA (CA) 246-247 D 5
Lincoln ○ USA (KS) 262-263 H 6
Lincoln ○ USA (ME) 278-279 O 2
Lincoln ○ USA (MO) 274-275 E 5
Lincoln ★ USA (NE) 262-263 J 4
Lincoln ○ USA (NH) 278-279 N 3
Lincoln ○ USA (WV) 280-281 F 4
Lincoln ○ VRC 154-155 L 3
Lincoln Birthplace National Historic Site, Abraham ⋰ USA (KY) 276-277 K 3
Lincoln Boyhood National Memorial • USA (IN) 274-275 M 6
Lincoln Caverns ⋰ USA (PA)
Lincoln City ○ USA (IN) 274-275 L 5
Lincoln City ○ USA (OR) 244-245 A 6
Lincoln Highway ‖ AUS 180-181 D 2

Lincoln National Park ⊥ AUS 180-181 C 3
Lincoln Sea ≈ 26-27 U 2
Lincoln's New Salem • USA (IL) 274-275 L 5
Lincolnton ○ USA (GA) 284-285 H 3
Lincolnton ○ USA (NC) 282-283 F 5
Lind ○ USA (WA) 244-245 G 4
Linda ○ USA (CA) 246-247 D 5
Lindale ○ USA (GA) 284-285 D 2
Lindau (Bodensee) ○ •• D 92-93 K 5
Lindberg, Cape ▲ 26-27 U 4
Lindbrook ○ CDN (ALB) 232-233 H 2
Linde ○ • RUS 110-111 M 6
Linde ~ RUS 110-111 N 7
Linde ~ RUS 110-111 M 6
Lindela ○ MOC 218-219 H 7
Lindeman Group ▲ AUS 174-175 K 7
Linden ○ CDN (ALB) 232-233 H 4
Linden ○ USA (AL) 284-285 C 4
Linden ○ USA (CA) 246-247 D 5
Linden ○ USA (IN) 274-275 M 4
Linden ○ USA (NJ) 280-281 M 3
Linden ○ USA (TX) 276-277 H 5
Lindenow Fjord ≈ 28-29 T 6
Lindesnes ▲ N 86-87 C 8
Lindhard Ø ▲ GRØ 26-27 o 5
Lindi ○ EAU 214-215 J 5
Lindi ★ • EAT (LIN) 214-215 K 5
Lindiang ○ ZRE 210-211 K 3
Lindian ○ VRC 150-151 E 4
Lindi Bay ≈ 214-215 K 5
Lindis Pass ○ NZ 182 B 6
Lindley ○ ZA 220-221 H 3
Lindleysoport ○ ZA 220-221 H 2
Lindos ○ •• GR 100-101 M 6
Lindsay ○ CDN (ONT) 238-239 G 3
Lindsay ○ USA (CA) 248-249 E 3
Lindsay ○ USA (MT) 250-251 O 4
Lindsay ○ USA (OK) 264-265 G 4
Lindsay, Mount ▲ AUS 176-177 J 4
Lindsborg ○ USA (KS) 262-263 J 6
Lindstrom ○ USA (MN) 270-271 F 5
Lindström Peninsula ⊌ 24-25 e 2
Línea de la Concepción, La ○ E 98-99 E 6
Line Islands ▲ KIB 13 M 2
Linejnoe ○ RUS 96-97 F 10
Linéville ○ USA (AL) 284-285 D 3
Lineville ○ USA (IA) 274-275 E 4
Linfen ○ VRC 154-155 G 3
Linganamakki Reservoir ○ IND 140-141 E 3
Lingayen ○ RP 160-161 D 4
Lingayen Gulf ≈ 160-161 D 4
Lingbao ○ VRC 154-155 G 4
Lingbi ○ VRC 154-155 K 4
Lingbm ○ CAM 206-207 B 6
Lingen (Ems) ○ D 92-93 J 2
Lingga ○ MAL 162-163 J 4
Lingga, Kepulauan ▲ RI 162-163 F 5
Lingga, Pulau ▲ RI 162-163 F 5
Lingig ○ RP 160-161 G 8
Lingkeh ○ RI 164-165 G 5
Lingkobu, Tanjung ▲ RI 164-165 K 5
Lingle ○ USA (WY) 252-253 O 4
Lingling ○ VRC 156-157 G 4
Lingngujym, buhta ≈ 112-113 R 6
Lingo ○ USA (NM) 256-257 M 5
Lingomo ○ ZRE (EQU) 210-211 J 3
Lingomo ○ ZRE 210-211 J 4
Lingqi D. • VRC 156-157 J 2
Lingqiu ○ VRC 154-155 H 2
Lingshan ○ VRC 156-157 F 5
Lingshi ○ VRC 154-155 G 3
Lingshui ○ VRC 156-157 G 6
Lingsugür ○ IND 140-141 G 2
Lingtai ○ VRC 154-155 E 4
Lingtou ○ VRC 156-157 F 7
Linguère ★ SN 202-203 C 2
Lingwu ○ VRC 154-155 E 3
Ling Xian ○ VRC 156-157 H 3
Lingxiaoyan • VRC 156-157 G 5
Lingyuan ○ VRC 148-149 O 7
Linh, Ngoc ▲ VN 158-159 J 3
Linhai ○ VRC (HEI) 150-151 C 3
Linhai ○ VRC (ZHE) 156-157 M 2
Linhares ○ BR 72-73 K 5
Linhe ○ VRC 154-155 E 1
Linhem ○ ANG 216-217 D 6
Linjiang ○ VRC 150-151 F 7
Linjiang ○ VRC 154-155 L 3
Linke Lakes ○ AUS 176-177 J 2
Linkiring ○ SN 202-203 D 4
Linköping ★ • S 86-87 G 7
Linkou ○ VRC 150-151 H 5
Linli ○ VRC 156-157 H 5
Linlithgow ○ GB 90-91 D 4
Linn ○ USA (KS) 262-263 J 4
Linn ○ USA (MO) 274-275 F 6
Linn ○ USA (TX) 266-267 J 7
Linn ○ USA (WV) 280-281 F 4
Linneus ○ USA (MO) 274-275 E 5
Linnpeng ○ VRC 156-157 K 3
Linqu ○ VRC 154-155 L 3

Linville Caverns ⋰ USA (NC) 282-283 F 5
Linxi ○ VRC 148-149 O 6
Linxia ○ VRC 154-155 C 4
Lin Xian ○ VRC (HEN) 154-155 H 3
Lin Xian ○ VRC (SHA) 154-155 G 3
Linxiang ○ VRC 156-157 H 2
Linyanti ~ RB 218-219 C 3
Linyanti Swamp ≈ NAM 218-219 B 4
Linyi ○ VRC 154-155 K 3
Linyi ○ VRC (SHD) 154-155 K 3
Linz ★ • A 92-93 N 4
Linzor ○ RCH 76-77 D 2
Lioma ○ MOC 218-219 J 2
Lion, Golfe du ≈ 90-91 J 10
Lion Camp ○ Z 218-219 F 1
Liongsong, Tanjung ▲ RI 168 C 7
Lioni, Caño ~ CO 60-61 G 5
Lion Park ↓ ZA 220-221 H 3
Lions Den ○ ZW 218-219 F 4
Lioppa ○ RI 166-167 C 5
Lios Tuathail = Listowel ○ IRL 90-91 C 5
Lioto ○ VRC 206-207 F 6
Lioua ○ TCH 198-199 G 6
Liouesso ○ RCB 210-211 E 3
Lipa ○ RP 160-161 E 6
Lipale ○ MOC 218-219 J 3
Lipari ○ I 100-101 E 5
Lipari, Isola ▲ I 100-101 E 5
Lipcani ○ MD 102-103 J 3
Lipeck ○ RUS 94-95 Q 5
Lipeo, Río ~ RA 76-77 E 2
Liperi ○ FIN 88-89 K 5
Lipetrén, Sierra ▲ RA 78-79 E 6
Lipetsk = Lipeck ○ RUS 94-95 Q 5
Lipez, Cordillera de ▲ BOL 76-77 D 1
Lipin Bor ○ RUS 94-95 Q 1
Lipis, Kuala ○ MAL 162-163 E 2
Lipiki ○ RUS 94-95 P 5
Lipljan ○ YU 100-101 H 3
Lipno ○ PL 92-93 P 2
Lipno, údolní nádrž ≈ CZ 92-93 N 4
Lipobane, Ponta ▲ MOC 218-219 K 2
Lipova ○ RO 102-103 H 5
Lippe ~ D 92-93 K 3
Lippstadt ○ • D 92-93 K 3
Lipscomb ○ USA (TX) 264-265 D 3
Lipton ○ CDN (SAS) 232-233 P 5
Liptougou ○ BF 202-203 K 2
Liptrap, Cape ▲ AUS 180-181 H 5
Lipu ○ VRC 156-157 G 4
Liquica = Likisia ○ RI 166-167 C 6
Liquíçá ○ RI 166-167 C 6
Lira ○ EAU 212-213 D 2
Liranga ○ RCB 210-211 F 4
Lircay ○ PE 64-65 E 8
Lirung ○ RI 164-165 K 2
Lisakovsk ★ KZ 124-125 G 2
Lisala ○ ZRE 210-211 H 2
Lisboa ★ ⋯ • P 98-99 C 5
Lisbon ○ USA (IL) 274-275 K 3
Lisbon ○ USA (ND) 258-259 K 5
Lisbon ○ USA (OH) 280-281 F 3
Lisbon = Lisboa ★ ⋯ • P 98-99 C 5
Lisbon Falls ○ USA (ME) 278-279 L 4
Lisburn, Cape = Cape Mata'Avea ▲ VAN 184 II a 2
Lisburne, Cape ▲ USA 20-21 G 2
Liscomb ○ CDN (NS) 240-241 N 5
Liscomb Game Sanction ⊥ CDN (NS) 240-241 N 5
Liscomb Island ▲ CDN (NS) 240-241 O 5
Liscomb Mills ○ CDN (NS) 240-241 N 5
Lishan Z.B. ⊥ VRC 154-155 G 4
Lishi ○ VRC (SHA) 154-155 G 3
Lishu ○ VRC 150-151 E 7
Lishui ○ VRC (SIC) 156-157 L 6
Lishui ○ VRC 156-157 L 6
Lisianski Island ▲ USA 14-15 L 5
Lisica ~ RUS 116-117 M 10
Lisica-Pass ○ YU 100-101 J 3
Lisičansk = Lysyčans'k ○ UA 102-103 L 3
Lisieux ○ F 90-91 H 7
Lisinskaja buhta ≈ 120-121 I W 6
Lisja ○ KZ 112-113 K 3
Lisjanskogo, poluostrov ⊌ RUS 120-121 M 4
Liski ○ RUS 102-103 L 2
Lismore ○ AUS (NSW) 178-179 M 5
Lismore ○ CDN (NS) 240-241 N 5
Lismore ○ USA (MN) 270-271 C 7
Lisnaskea ○ GB 90-91 D 4
Lisomu, Tanjung ▲ RI 166-167 C 6
Lissadell ○ AUS 172-173 J 4
Lisse, Pyramids of ⋰ • ET 194-195 E 3
Lister, Mount ▲ ARK 16 F 17
Lister ○ N 86-87 C 7
Lištica = Široki Brijeg ○ BIH 100-101 F 3
Listowel ○ CDN (ONT) 238-239 F 4
Listowel = Lios Tuathail ○ IRL 90-91 C 5
Listvjanka ○ RUS 116-117 M 10
Lit, al- ○ KSA 132-133 E 3
Litang ○ MAL 160-161 C 10
Litang ○ VRC (GXI) 156-157 F 5
Litanó ○ VRC 154-155 B 6
Litáni ~ RL 128-129 F 6
Litani = Itani ~ BR 62-63 G 4
Litchfield ○ USA (CA) 246-247 E 2
Litchfield ○ USA (IL) 274-275 K 6
Litchfield ○ USA (MN) 270-271 D 5
Litchfield ○ USA (NE) 262-263 G 3
Litchfield Beach ⊥ USA (SC) 284-285 L 3

Litchfield Out Station ○ AUS 172-173 K 2
Litchfield Park ⊥ AUS 172-173 K 2
Litchfield Park ○ USA (AZ) 256-257 C 5
Litchville ○ USA (ND) 258-259 J 5
Litgow ○ AUS 180-181 J 7
Lithuania = Lietuva ■ LT 94-95 G 4
Litipära ○ IND 142-143 E 3
Litke ○ RUS (ARH) 108-109 F 5
Litke ○ RUS (HBR) 122-123 J 2
Litke, mys ▲ RUS 112-113 W 1
Litke, poluostrov ⊌ RUS 108-109 J 3
Litoměřice ○ CZ 92-93 N 3
Litomyšl ○ CZ 92-93 O 4
Litovko ○ RUS 122-123 H 2
Littel ○ USA (WA) 244-245 B 4
Little Abitibi Lake ○ CDN 236-237 H 3
Little Abitibi River ~ CDN 236-237 G 2
Little Aden ○ Y 132-133 D 7
Little America ○ USA (WY) 252-253 H 5
Little Andaman ▲ IND 140-141 L 4
Little Arkansas River ~ USA 262-263 J 6
Little Barrier Island ▲ NZ 182 E 2
Little Bay ○ CDN (NFL) 242-243 N 3
Little Bay Beach ⊥ BS 56 D 3
Little Bay de Noc ≈ USA 270-271 L 5
Little Belt Mountains ▲ USA 250-251 H 4
Little Bitterroot River ~ USA 250-251 E 4
Little Black River ~ USA 20-21 T 3
Little Blue River ~ USA 262-263 K 5
Little Bow River ~ CDN 232-233 H 5
Little Buffalo River ~ CDN 30-31 N 5
Little Burnt Bay ○ CDN (NFL) 242-243 N 3
Little Cadotte River ~ CDN 32-33 M 3
Little Cayman ▲ GB 54-55 E 5
Little Chicago ○ CDN 30-31 E 2
Little Churchill River ~ CDN 34-35 J 2
Little Colorado River ~ USA 256-257 E 4
Little Corwallis Island ▲ CDN 24-25 Y 3
Little Creek ○ USA (DE) 280-281 L 4
Little Creek Peak ▲ USA (UT) 254-255 C 6
Little Current ○ CDN (ONT) 238-239 D 3
Little Current River ~ CDN 236-237 D 3
Little Cypress Bayou ~ USA 264-265 G 6
Little Delta River ~ USA 20-21 R 5
Little Desert ⊥ AUS 180-181 E 4
Little Desert National Park ⊥ AUS 180-181 E 4
Little Diomede Island ▲ USA 20-21 F 4
Little Exuma Island ▲ BS 54-55 H 3
Little Falls ○ USA (MN) 270-271 D 5
Little Falls ○ USA (NY) 278-279 G 5
Littlefield ○ USA (AZ) 256-257 B 3
Littlefield ○ USA (TX) 264-265 B 5
Little Fork ○ USA (MN) 270-271 C 2
Little Fork River ~ USA 270-271 C 2
Little Gold River ○ AUS 172-173 J 4
Little Grand Rapids ○ CDN (MAN) 234-235 H 4
Little Harbour ○ BS 54-55 G 2
Little Harbour ○ CDN (NFL) 242-243 L 3
Little Hocking ○ USA (OH) 280-281 E 4
Little Humboldt River ~ USA 246-247 H 2
Little Kanawha River ~ USA 280-281 E 4
Little Karoo = Klein Karoo ⊥ ZA 220-221 E 6
Little Koniuji Island ▲ USA 22-23 S 7
Little Lake ○ USA (CA) 248-249 G 4
Little Lake ○ USA (MI) 270-271 L 4
Little Lost River ~ USA 252-253 G 4
Little Lynches River ~ USA 284-285 K 2
Little Malad River ~ USA 252-253 F 4
Little Mecatina River ~ CDN 38-39 N 2
Little Miami River ~ USA 280-281 B 4
Little Missouri River ~ USA 250-251 P 6
Little Missouri River ~ USA 258-259 E 4
Little Missouri River ~ USA 276-277 B 7
Little Moose Island ▲ CDN (MAN) 234-235 J 3
Little Muddy Creek ~ USA 252-253 H 5
Little Mud River ~ USA 20-21 O 4
Little Mulberry Creek ~ USA 284-285 D 4
Little Nemaha River ~ USA 262-263 L 4
Little Nicobar Island ▲ IND 140-141 L 6
Little Norway ○ USA (CA) 246-247 E 5
Little Osage River ~ USA 274-275 D 6
Little Pee Dee River ~ USA 284-285 L 2
Little Pic ~ CDN 236-237 B 3
Little Quill Lake ○ CDN (SAS) 232-233 O 4
Little Ragged Island ▲ BS 54-55 H 3
Little Rancheria River ~ CDN 30-31 F 4
Little Rapid Creek ~ CDN 30-31 S 6
Little Red Deer River ~ CDN 232-233 G 3
Little Red River ~ USA 276-277 D 5
Little Ridge ○ CDN (MAN) 234-235 E 4
Little River ○ USA (AL) 284-285 D 4
Little River ○ USA (LA) 268-269 H 4
Little River ~ USA 266-267 K 3
Little River ~ USA 276-277 D 6
Little River ~ USA 276-277 A 7
Little River ~ USA 280-281 F 6

Little River ~ USA 282-283 J 5
Little River ~ USA 284-285 D 5
Little River ~ USA 284-285 H 2
Little River ~ USA 284-285 H 3
Little Rock ★ USA (AR) 276-277 C 6
Little Ruaha ~ EAT 214-215 H 5
Little Sable Point ▲ USA (MI) 272-273 L 2
Little Sachigo Lake ○ CDN 34-35 K 3
Little Sahara Recreation Area ⊥ USA (UT) 254-255 C 4
Little Saint Lawrence ○ CDN (NFL) 242-243 N 6
Little Saint Simons Island ▲ USA (GA) 284-285 J 5
Little Salkehatchie River ~ USA 284-285 J 3
Little Salmon Lake ○ CDN 20-21 X 5
Little Salt Lake ○ USA (UT) 254-255 C 6
Little Sandy River ~ USA 276-277 M 2
Little San Salvador Island ▲ BS 54-55 H 2
Little Sauk ○ USA (MN) 270-271 D 5
Little Scarcies of Kaba ~ WAL 202-203 D 5
Little Seal River ~ CDN 30-31 W 6
Little Sevier River ~ USA 254-255 C 6
Little Sioux River ~ USA 274-275 C 2
Little Sitkin Island ▲ USA 22-23 F 7
Little Smoky ○ CDN (ALB) 228-229 R 2
Little Snake River ~ USA 252-253 J 5
Little Tallahatchie ~ USA 268-269 L 2
Little Tallapoosa River ~ USA 284-285 D 3
Little Tanaga Island ▲ USA 22-23 H 7
Little Tennessee River ~ USA 282-283 D 5
Littleton ○ USA (NC) 282-283 K 4
Littleton ○ USA (NH) 278-279 N 3
Little Traverse Bay ≈ 272-273 D 2
Little Valley ○ USA (CA) 246-247 D 3
Little Valley ○ USA (NY) 278-279 C 5
Little Wabash River ~ USA 274-275 K 6
Little White River ~ CDN 238-239 D 3
Little Wichita River ~ USA 264-265 F 5
Little Yellowstone Park ⋰ USA (ND) 258-259 K 5
Littoral □ CAM 204-205 H 6
Lituhi ○ EAT 214-215 H 6
Litunde ○ MOC 218-219 H 1
Litvinova, mys ▲ RUS 108-109 I Y 1
Litvinovo ○ RUS 96-97 F 4
Liu ○ RI 164-165 G 5
Liuba ○ VRC 154-155 E 5
Liúchiu Yü = HU 156-157 M 5
Liucura ○ RCH 78-79 D 5
Liuhe ○ VRC 150-151 E 6
Liuheng Dao ~ VRC 156-157 N 2
Liujiachang ○ VRC 154-155 N 2
Liujiang ○ VRC 156-157 F 4
Liujiaxia SK ○ VRC 154-155 C 4
Liukang ○ VRC 156-157 G 5
Liukanglu, Pulau ▲ RI 164-165 G 6
Liuli ○ EAT 214-215 H 6
Liulin ○ VRC 154-155 G 3
Liupan Shan ▲ VRC 154-155 D 3
Liupanshan Z.B. ⊥ VRC 154-155 E 4
Liupanshui ○ VRC 156-157 E 3
Liúpo ○ MOC 218-219 K 2
Liushai ○ VRC 156-157 E 4
Liushipu ○ VRC 154-155 L 4
Liuwa Plain National Park ⊥ Z 218-219 D 2
Liuxu ○ VRC 156-157 F 4
Liuyang ○ VRC 156-157 H 3
Liuzhao Shan ▲ VRC 156-157 D 5
Liuzhi ○ VRC 156-157 D 3
Liuzhou ○ • VRC 156-157 G 5
Liuzhuang ○ VRC 154-155 M 5
Livádi ○ GR 100-101 K 6
Livadia ○ • GR 100-101 J 5
Livani ○ • LV 94-95 K 3
Livanovka ○ KZ 124-125 C 2
Livelong ○ CDN (SAS) 232-233 K 2
Lively ○ USA (VA) 280-281 K 6
Lively Island ▲ GB 78-79 L 7
Livengood ○ USA 20-21 Q 4
Live Oak ○ USA (CA) 248-249 C 2
Live Oak ○ USA (FL) 286-287 G 1
Livermore ○ USA (CA) 248-249 C 3
Livermore ○ USA (KY) 276-277 H 3
Livermore, Mount ▲ USA (TX) 266-267 C 3
Livermore Falls ○ USA (ME) 278-279 L 4
Liverpool ○ AUS 180-181 L 2
Liverpool ○ CDN (NS) 240-241 L 6
Liverpool ★ • GB 90-91 F 5
Liverpool, Cape ▲ CDN 24-25 h 4
Liverpool Bay ≈ 20-21 Z 2
Liverpool Range ▲ AUS 178-179 K 6
Liviko Pélagos ≈ 100-101 J 7
Livingston ○ USA (AL) 284-285 B 4
Livingston ○ USA (KY) 276-277 L 3
Livingston ○ USA (LA) 268-269 K 6
Livingston ○ USA (MT) 250-251 J 6
Livingston ○ USA (TN) 276-277 K 4
Livingston, Lake ○ USA (TX) 268-269 E 6
Livingstone ★ Z 218-219 C 3
Livingstone Memorial • Z 214-215 F 7
Livingstone Mountains ▲ EAT 214-215 H 6
Livingstonia ○ MW 214-215 H 6
Livingstone's Cave • RB 220-221 G 3
Livno ○ BIH 100-101 F 3
Livny ○ RUS 94-95 P 5
Livonia ○ USA (MI) 272-273 F 5
Livorno ○ I 100-101 C 3
Livradois-Forez, Parc Naturel Régional ⊥ F 90-91 J 9
Livramento do Brumado ○ BR 72-73 K 2

Liwa o **RI** 162-163 F 7
Liwā', al- o **OM** 134-135 G 6
Liwale o **EAT** 214-215 J 5
Liwonde o **MW** 218-219 H 2
Liwonde National Park ⊥ **MW**
  218-219 H 2
Li Xian o **VRC** (GAN) 154-155 F 4
Li Xian o **VRC** (SIC) 154-155 C 6
Lixin o **VRC** 154-155 K 5
Lixus ∴ **MA** 188-189 H 3
Liyang o **VRC** 154-155 L 6
Li Yubu o **SUD** 206-207 H 6
Lizarda o **BR** 68-69 E 6
Lizard Head Peak ▲ **USA** (WY)
  252-253 J 4
Lizard Island ∩ **AUS** 174-175 H 4
Lizard Point ▲ **GB** 90-91 E 7
Lizard Point Indian Reserve ✕ **CDN**
  (MAN) 234-235 C 4
Lizella o **USA** (GA) 284-285 G 3
Lizotte o **CDN** (QUE) 240-241 C 2
Lizton o **USA** (IN) 274-275 M 5
Lizums o **LV** 94-95 K 3
Ljadova ∼ **UA** 102-103 E 3
Ljady o **RUS** 94-95 L 2
Ljahovskie ostrova ∩ **RUS** 110-111 U 2
Ljaki o **AZ** 128-129 M 2
Ljamca o **RUS** 88-89 O 4
Ljamin ∼ **RUS** 114-115 L 4
Ljamin, pervyj ∼ **RUS** 114-115 K 3
Ljamin, vtoroj ∼ **RUS** 114-115 K 3
Ljamskie gory ▲ **RUS** 108-109 Y 7
Ljangar o **TJ** 136-137 N 6
Ljangasovo o **RUS** 96-97 F 4
Ljantorskij o **RUS** 114-115 M 4
Ljapin ∼ **RUS** 114-115 F 3
Ljapiska ∼ **RUS** 118-119 N 3
Ljig o **YU** 100-101 H 2
Ljuban' o **BY** 94-95 L 5
Ljuban' o **RUS** 94-95 M 2
Ljubanskae vadashoviŝča ✦ **BY**
  94-95 L 5
Ljubar o **UA** 102-103 E 3
Ljubercy o **RUS** 94-95 P 4
Ljubertsy = Ljubercy o **RUS** 94-95 P 4
Ljubešiv o **UA** 102-103 D 2
Ljubinskij o **RUS** 114-115 M 7
Ljubljana ★ **SLO** 100-101 E 1
Ljuboml' o **UA** 102-103 D 2
Ljubovija o **YU** 100-101 G 2
Ljubytino o **RUS** 94-95 N 2
Ljugarn o **S** 86-87 J 8
Ljukkum ⊥ **KZ** 124-125 K 5
Ljungan ∼ **S** 86-87 H 5
Ljungby ★ **S** 86-87 F 8
Ljungdalen o **S** 86-87 F 5
Ljusdal o **S** 86-87 H 6
Ljusnan ∼ **S** 86-87 H 6
Ljutoga ∼ **RUS** 122-123 K 5
Lk. Kambera ∼ **RI** 168 E 7
Llaima, Volcán ▲ **RCH** 78-79 D 5
Llallagua o **BOL** 70-71 D 6
Llalli o **PE** 70-71 B 4
Llamara, Salar o **RCH** 76-77 C 1
Llançà o **E** 98-99 J 3
Llancañelo, Laguna y Salina o **RA**
  78-79 E 3
Llanddovery o **GB** 90-91 F 6
Llanes o **E** 98-99 E 3
Llano o **USA** (TX) 266-267 J 3
Llano, El o **PA** 52-53 E 7
Llanobajo o **CO** 60-61 C 6
Llano de la Paciencia ⊥ **RCH** 76-77 C 2
Llano del Quimal ⊥ **RCH** 76-77 C 2
Llano Estacado ✕ **USA** 264-265 A 5
Llano Mariato o **PA** 52-53 D 8
Llano River, North ∼ **USA** 266-267 G 3
Llano River, South ∼ **USA** 266-267 G 3
Llanos, Sierra de los ▲ **RA** 76-77 D 6
Llanos de Aridane, Los o **E**
  188-189 C 6
Llanos de Guarayos ✕ **BOL** 70-71 E 4
Llanos de la Rioja ✕ **RA** 76-77 D 5
Llanquihué o **RCH** 78-79 C 6
Llanquihué, Lago o **RCH** 78-79 C 6
Llao Llao o **RA** 78-79 D 5
Llaylla o **PE** 64-65 E 7
Llay-Llay o **RCH** 78-79 D 2
Lleida o **E** 98-99 H 4
Llera de Canales o **MEX** 50-51 K 6
Llerena o **E** 98-99 D 5
Lleyn Peninsula ✕ **GB** 90-91 E 5
Llica o **BOL** 70-71 C 6
Llico o **RCH** 78-79 C 4
Lliria o **E** 98-99 G 5
Lliscaya, Cerro ▲ **BOL** 70-71 C 6
Lloyd o **USA** (FL) 250-251 K 3
Lloyd Bay ≈ 174-175 G 3
Lloyd Lake o **CDN** 32-33 Q 3
Lloydminster o **CDN** (ALB) 232-233 H 2
Lloyd Rock = The Brothers ∩ **BS**
  54-55 H 3
Lloyd's Camp o **RB** 218-219 C 4
Llullaillaco, Volcán ▲ **RCH** 76-77 C 3
Lluta o **PE** 70-71 A 5
Lluta, Río ∼ **RCH** 70-71 C 6
I-Miyah, Wâdî ∼ **SYR** 128-129 H 5
Lo, Île = Loh ∩ **VAN** 184 II a 1
Loa o **USA** (UT) 254-255 D 5
Loa, Calera o **RCH** 76-77 B 1
Loa, Río ∼ **RCH** 76-77 C 1
Loanda o **ANG** 216-217 D 4
Loanda o **G** 210-211 B 4
Loandji o **ZRE** 210-211 H 6
Loange o **ZRE** 210-211 D 6
Loanja ∼ **Z** 218-219 C 3
Loara o **RI** 164-165 G 5
Loay o **RP** 160-161 F 8
Loban o **RUS** 88-89 S 4
Lobatse o **RB** 220-221 G 3
Lobaye o **RCA** 206-207 C 6
Lobaye o **RCA** 206-207 D 7
Lobaye o **ZRE** 210-211 A 4
Lobé o **CAM** 210-211 C 2
Lobé, Chutes de la = Lobé Falls ∼ **CAM**
  210-211 B 2

Lobecks Pass o **USA** (CA)
  248-249 K 5
Lobé Falls = Chutes de la Lobé ∼ **CAM**
  210-211 B 2
Lobeke o **CAM** 210-211 F 2
Lobería o **RA** 78-79 K 5
Lobez o **PL** 92-93 N 2
Lobira o **SUD** 208-209 A 6
Lobito o **ANG** 216-217 B 6
Lobo o **CAM** 210-211 E 2
Lobo o **RI** 166-167 H 4
Loboko o **RCB** 210-211 D 5
Lobo Lodge o **EAT** 212-213 E 4
Lobos o **RA** 78-79 K 3
Lobos, Caño los ∼ **CO** 64-65 E 1
Lobos, Cayo ∩ **BS** 54-55 G 3
Lobos, Cayo ∩ **MEX** 52-53 L 2
Lobos, Isla ∩ **MEX** 50-51 L 4
Lobos, Islas de ∩ **MEX** 50-51 L 7
Lobos, Punta ▲ **RA** 78-79 E 5
Lobos, Punta ▲ **RCH** (ATA) 76-77 B 5
Lobos, Punta ▲ **RCH** (LIB) 78-79 C 3
Lobos, Punta ▲ **RCH** (TAR) 70-71 B 6
Lobos, Punta ▲ **RCH** (TAR) 76-77 B 1
Lobos, Río Los ∼ **MEX** 50-51 L 4
Lobos de Afuera, Islas ∩ **PE** 64-65 B 5
Lobos de Tierra, Isla ∩ **PE** 64-65 B 5
Lobuja o **RT** 202-203 L 6
Lobu o **RI** 164-165 H 4
Lobuja o **RUS** 112-113 H 3
Lobutcha Creeks ∼ **USA** 268-269 C 4
Lobva o **RUS** 114-115 F 5
Logone o **TCH** 206-207 B 3
Logone, Birni o **CAM** 206-207 B 3
Logone Gana o **TCH** 206-207 B 3
Logone Occidental ∼ **TCH** 206-207 B 4
Logone Occidental o **TCH** 206-207 B 4
Logone Oriental ∼ **TCH** 206-207 B 4
Logone Oriental o **TCH** 206-207 C 4
Logozone o **DY** 204-205 E 5
Logroño o **E** 98-99 F 3
Løgstør o **DK** 86-87 D 8
Loh = Île Lo ∩ **VAN** 184 II a 1
Lohagara o **BD** 142-143 F 4
Lohâghât o **IND** 144-145 C 6
Lohardaga o **IND** 142-143 D 4
Lohârghat o **IND** 142-143 G 3
Lohéac o **F** 90-91 G 8
Lohiniva o **FIN** 88-89 H 3
Lohja o **FIN** 88-89 H 7
Lohjanan o **RI** 164-165 E 4
Loh Liang o **RI** 168 D 7
Loi o **PNG** 183 D 7
Loiborsoit o **EAT** 212-213 F 5
Loi-kaw o **MYA** 142-143 K 6
Loile ∼ **ZRE** 210-211 J 3
Loilo ∼ **ZRE** 210-211 J 3
Loimaa o **FIN** 88-89 G 6
Loima Hills ▲ **EAK** 212-213 E 2
Loir ∼ **F** 90-91 G 8
Loiro Poco o **BR** 66-67 C 2
Loiš ∼ **RUS** 94-95 M 4
Loiš o **UZ** 136-137 K 5
Loi Song ▲ **MYA** 142-143 K 4
Loita Hills ▲ **EAK** 212-213 E 4
Loita Plains ✕ **EAK** 212-213 E 4
Loja ★ **EC** 64-65 C 3
Lojilš o **UZ** 136-137 L 5
Lojmola o **RUS** 88-89 L 6
Lojno o **RUS** 96-97 H 4
Lokalema o **ZRE** 210-211 J 3
Lokandu o **ZRE** 210-211 K 5
Lokan tekojärvi ✦ **FIN** 88-89 J 3
Lokata o **RI** 166-167 F 2
Lokbatan o **AZ** 128-129 N 2
Lokeli o **ZRE** 210-211 K 5
Lokichar o **EAK** (RIF) 212-213 E 2
Lokichar ∼ **EAK** 212-213 E 2
Lokichogio o **EAK** 212-213 B 6
Lokila o **ZRE** 210-211 K 5
Lokitaung o **EAK** 212-213 E 1
Lokja ∼ **RUS** 94-95 M 4
Lokoja o **WAN** 204-205 G 4
Lokolama o **ZRE** 210-211 G 3
Lokolia o **ZRE** 210-211 H 4
Lokolo ∼ **ZRE** 210-211 G 4
Lokomby o **RM** 222-223 E 9
Lokomo o **CAM** 210-211 F 2
Lokomo ∼ **CAM** 210-211 E 2
Lokono o **PNG** 183 D 7
Lokoro ∼ **ZRE** 210-211 G 4
Lokosso o **DY** 204-205 E 5
Lokot o **RUS** 94-95 O 5
Lokoti o **CAM** 206-207 B 5
Lokoundjé ∼ **CAM** 210-211 C 2
Loksiati o **SME** 62-63 G 3
Loks Land ∩ **CDN** 36-37 R 3
Lokutu o **ZRE** 210-211 J 3
Loky ∼ **RM** 222-223 F 4
Lol ∼ **SUD** 206-207 J 5
Lol o **ANG** 216-217 B 7
Lola o **RG** 202-203 F 6
Lola o **ZRE** 210-211 G 5
Lolai o **RI** 164-165 L 3
Lolé ∼ **ZRE** 210-211 K 3
Loléngi o **ZRE** 210-211 H 3
Loleta o **USA** (CA) 246-247 A 3
Lolgorien o **EAK** 212-213 E 4
Lolland ∩ **DK** 86-87 E 9
Lol Lanok o **EAT** 212-213 F 6
Lolo o **USA** (MT) 250-251 E 5
Lolobata o **RI** 164-165 L 3
Lolobau Island ∩ **PNG** 183 F 3
Lolobo o **CI** 202-203 H 6
Loloda Utara, Kepulauan ∩ **RI**
  164-165 L 2
Loloda o **CAM** 210-211 C 2
Lolémé o **RCB** 210-211 D 6
Loeng Nok Tha o **THA** 158-159 H 2
Loeriesfontein o **ZA** 220-221 D 5
Lofa Hills ▲ **LB** 202-203 E 6
Lofé o **SN** 202-203 C 2
Loftahammar o **S** 86-87 H 8
Lofty Range ▲ **AUS** 176-177 E 2

Log o **RUS** 102-103 N 3
Loga o **RN** 204-205 E 2
Loga o **SUD** 206-207 H 6
Logan o **USA** (IA) 274-275 C 3
Logan o **USA** (KS) 262-263 G 5
Logan o **USA** (NM) 256-257 M 3
Logan o **USA** (OH) 280-281 D 6
Logan o **USA** (UT) 254-255 D 2
Logan o **USA** (WV) 280-281 D 6
Logan, Mount ▲ ∼ 20-21 U 6
Loganda ∼ **USA** (NV) 248-249 K 3
Logan Glacier ✦ **USA** 20-21 U 6
Logan Island ∩ **CDN** 234-235 P 4
Logan Lake o **CDN** 230-231 J 4
Logan Martin Lake ✦ **USA** (AL)
  284-285 D 3
Logan Mountains ▲ **CDN** 30-31 E 5
Logan Pass ⋯ **USA** (MT) 250-251 F 3
Logan River ∼ **USA** 254-255 D 2
Logansport o **USA** (IN) 274-275 M 4
Logansport o **USA** (LA) 268-269 G 4
Loganton o **USA** (PA) 280-281 J 2
Loganville o **USA** (GA) 284-285 G 3
Lögar ∼ **AFG** 138-139 B 3
Logas'apan ∼ **RUS** 114-115 J 2
Logaškino o **RUS** 110-111 d 4
Logata ∼ **RUS** 108-109 c 5
Lögdeälven ∼ **S** 86-87 J 5
Loge ∼ **ANG** 216-217 C 7
Logelogle o **EAT** 214-215 K 4
Loggieville o **CDN** (NB) 240-241 K 3
Logobou o **BF** 202-203 K 4
Logoforok o **SUD** 212-213 D 2
Lomaloma o **FJI** 184 III c 2
Lomako ∼ **ZRE** 210-211 H 3
Lomami ∼ **ZRE** (KOR) 210-211 J 4
Lomami o **ZRE** 210-211 K 3
Loma Mountains ▲ **WAL** 202-203 E 5
Lomas, Las o **PE** 64-65 B 4
Lomas Pass o **USA** (MT) 250-251 F 3
Loma San Martín ▲ **RA** 78-79 E 9
Lomas de Arena o **USA** (TX)
  266-267 J 3
Lomas de Vallejos o **RA** 76-77 J 4
Lomas de Zamora o **RA** 78-79 K 3
Lomba ∼ **ANG** 216-217 E 7
Lombadina ✕ **AUS** 172-173 F 4
Lombang o **RI** 164-165 F 5
Lombarda, Serra ▲ **BR** 62-63 J 4
Lombardia o **I** 100-101 B 2
Lombe o **RI** 164-165 H 6
Lomblen (Kawela), Pulau ∩ **RI**
  166-167 B 6
Lombok o **RI** (NBA) 168 C 7
Lombok o **RI** (NBA) 168 C 7
Lombok, Selat ≈ 168 B 7
Lomé ★ **RT** 202-203 L 6
Lomela o **ZRE** 210-211 J 5
Lomela o **ZRE** 210-211 H 4
Lometa o **USA** (TX) 266-267 J 2
Lomgnac o **CDN** (ONT) 236-237 B 3
Long Lake o **CDN** (ONT) 236-237 B 3
Long Lake o **USA** (NY) 278-279 J 5
Long Lake o **USA** (SD) 260-261 G 1
Long Lake o **USA** (WA) 244-245 D 4
Long Lake o **USA** (ND) 258-259 G 5
Long Lake, Indian Reserve ✕ **CDN** (ONT)
  236-237 B 3
Long Lama o **MAL** 164-165 D 2
Long Lellang o **MAL** 164-165 D 2
Long Malinau o **RI** 164-165 E 2
Lomié o **CAM** 210-211 D 2
Loming o **SUD** 206-207 L 6
Lomitas, Las o **RA** 76-77 G 3
Lomond o **CDN** (ALB) 232-233 F 3
Lonahghat o **IND** 144-145 C 6
Lomonosov Ridge ∼ 16 A 25
Lomovoe o **RUS** 88-89 Q 4
Lomphät o **K** 158-159 J 4
Lompobatang, Gunung ▲ **RI**
  164-165 F 6
Lompoc o **USA** (CA) 248-249 D 5
Lompopana, Gunung ▲ **RI** 164-165 F 6
Lompoul o **SN** 202-203 B 2
Lom Sak o **THA** 158-159 F 2
Łomża ★ **PL** 92-93 R 2
Lô'n ∼ **VN** 158-159 K 4
Lona Bay ≈ 36-37 L 2
Lonambo o **EC** 64-65 D 2
Lonar o **IND** 138-139 F 10
Lonâvale o **IND** 138-139 D 10
Lončakovo o **RUS** 122-123 F 5
Longo o **G** 210-211 D 4
Longonjo o **ANG** 216-217 C 6
Longonot ▲ **EAT** 212-213 F 4
Longotea o **PE** 64-65 D 5
Longot'egan ∼ **RUS** 108-109 M 8
Longozabe o **RM** 222-223 F 7
Long Palai o **MAL** 164-165 D 2
Long Pine o **USA** (NE) 262-263 G 2
Long Pine Indian Reservation ✕ **USA**
  (CA) 248-249 F 3
Long Prairie o **USA** (MN) 270-271 D 5
Longquan o **VRC** 156-157 L 2
Long Range Mountains ▲ **CDN**
  242-243 K 5
Longreach o **AUS** 178-179 H 2
Long Seridan o **MAL** 164-165 D 1
Lone Pine o **USA** (CA) 248-249 F 3
Lonepine o **USA** (MT) 250-251 E 4
Lone Rock o **CDN** (SAS) 232-233 J 2
Lone Rock o **USA** (WI) 274-275 H 1
Long Peak ▲ **USA** (CO) 254-255 K 3
Lone Star o **USA** (TX) 268-269 G 4
Longton o **AUS** 174-175 H 7
Longtree o **USA** (WY) 252-253 H 6
Long o **THA** 142-143 L 6
Long o **USA** (SC) 284-285 M 3
Longa o **ANG** (CUA) 216-217 E 7
Longa ∼ **ANG** 216-217 C 5
Longa o **ANG** 216-217 E 8
Longa, proliv ≈ 112-113 T 1
Longá, Río ∼ **BR** 68-69 H 3
Longana o **VAN** 184 II a 2
Long Arroyo ∼ **USA** 256-257 L 5
Longaví, Nevado de ▲ **RCH** 78-79 D 4
Longaví, Río ∼ **RCH** 78-79 D 4
Longbo Z.B. II **VRC** 144-145 L 4
Long Barn o **USA** (CA) 246-247 E 5
Longbawan o **MAL** 164-165 D 2
Long Bay o **RI** 168 D 7
Long Bay ≈ 54-55 G 5
Long Bay ∼ 284-285 M 3
Long Bay Beach o **JA** 54-55 G 5
Longbeach o **CDN** 234-235 P 6
Long Beach o **USA** (CA) 248-249 E 5
Long Beach o **USA** (MS) 268-269 C 4
Long Beach o **USA** (NY) 280-281 N 4
Longbeach o **USA** (WA) 244-245 A 4
Longhua o **VRC** 148-149 N 7
Longhui o **VRC** 156-157 K 2
Longhushan o **VRC** 156-157 L 2
Longido o **EAT** 212-213 F 5
Longikis o **RI** 164-165 E 4
Longiram o **RI** 164-165 E 4
Long Island ∩ **AUS** 178-179 K 2
Long Island ∩ **BS** 54-55 H 3
Long Island ∩ **CDN** (NFL) 242-243 P 4
Long Island ∩ **CDN** (NWT) 36-37 N 7
Long Island ∩ **CDN** (NS) 240-241 J 6
Long Island ∩ **USA** (KS) 262-263 G 5
Long Island ∩ **USA** (NY) 280-281 N 3
Long Island Sound ≈ 36-37 X 7
Long Island Sound ≈ 280-281 O 2
Longitudinal, Valle ✕ **RCH** 78-79 C 4
Longju o **VRC** 150-151 G 6
Longkay o **RI** 164-165 E 4
Long Key ∼ **USA** (FL) 286-287 J 7
Longkou o **VRC** 154-155 M 3
Longlac o **CDN** (ONT) 236-237 B 3
Long Lake ∼ **CDN** 236-237 B 3
Long Nur ✦ **VRC** 146-147 K 5
Lopori ∼ **ZRE** 210-211 H 3
Lopphavet ≈ 86-87 K 1
Lopp Lagoon ≈ 20-21 B 4
Loptjuga ∼ **RUS** 88-89 U 5
Loquilocon o **RP** 160-161 F 7
Lora, Punta o **RCH** 78-79 C 3
Lora, Río ∼ **YV** 60-61 E 3
Lora Creek ∼ **AUS** 178-179 E 5
Lorain o **USA** (OH) 280-281 D 7
Loraine o **USA** (CA) 248-249 F 4
Loraine o **USA** (TX) 264-265 D 6
Loralài o **PK** (BEL) 138-139 B 4
Loralài o **PK** 138-139 B 4
Loranchet o **ANG** 244-245 D 7
Loranstation = Angisoq o **GRØ**
  28-29 S 7
Lordegân o **IR** 134-135 D 3
Lord Howe Island ∩ ⋯ **AUS**
  180-181 N 7
Lord Howe Rise ≈ 13 H 6
Lord Howe Seamounts ≈ 13 H 5
Lord Lindsay River ∼ **CDN** 24-25 Z 5
Lord Loughborough Island ∩ **MYA**
  158-159 D 5
Lord Mayor Bay ≈ 24-25 a 6
Lordsburg o **USA** (NM) 256-257 G 6
Lord's Cove o **CDN** (NFL) 242-243 N 6
Lore o **RI** 166-167 H 4
Lore Lindu National Park ⊥ **RI**
  164-165 G 4
Lorella o **USA** (OR) 244-245 D 8
Loren, Pulau ∩ **RI** 168 E 7
Lorena o **BR** (MAR) 66-67 B 6
Lorena o **BR** (PAU) 72-73 H 7
Lorengau ★ **PNG** 183 D 2
Lorentz ∼ **RI** 166-167 M 6
Lorentz Reserve ⊥ **RI** 166-167 J 4
Lorenzo o **USA** (TX) 264-265 C 5
Lôre Rüd ∼ **AFG** 134-135 M 2
Longsheng o **VRC** 156-157 F 2
Longshou Shan ▲ **VRC** 154-155 B 2
Long Thành o **VN** 158-159 J 9
Longton o **USA** (KS) 262-263 K 6
Longue, Pointe ▲ **CDN** 38-39 E 2
Longueuil o **CDN** (QUE) 238-239 M 3
Long Valley o **CA** 246-247 A 4
Long Valley o **USA** (AZ) 256-257 D 4
Long Valley o **USA** (SD) 260-261 E 3
Long Valley Junction o **USA** (UT)
  254-255 C 6
Longview o **CDN** (ALB) 232-233 D 5
Longview o **USA** (MS) 268-269 M 3
Longview o **USA** (TX) 264-265 K 6
Longview o **USA** (LA) 268-269 G 6
Longville o **USA** (LA) 268-269 G 6
Longwood o **USA** (FL) 286-287 H 4
Longworth o **CDN** (BC) 228-229 N 3
Longxi o **VRC** 154-155 D 4
Long Xian o **VRC** 154-155 D 4
Longxing, Port o **CDN** (ONT) 238-239 F 3
Long Xuyên ★ **VN** 158-159 H 5
Longyao o **VRC** 154-155 J 3
Longyearbyen o **N** 84-85 J 3
Lonquimay o **RCH** 78-79 C 5
Lonkia ∼ **ZRE** 210-211 J 5
Lonkonia ∼ **ZRE** 210-211 J 5
Lono o **USA** (AR) 276-277 D 6
Lonsdale o **USA** (MN) 270-271 E 6
Lons-le-Saunier o **F** 90-91 K 8
Lontar, Pulau ∩ **RI** 166-167 E 4
Lontou o **RMM** 202-203 G 3
Lontra o **BR** 68-69 G 4
Lontra, Ribeirão ∼ **BR** 72-73 D 6
Lontra, Rio ∼ **RCH** 78-79 H 3
Lontué, Rio ∼ **RCH** 78-79 D 4
Lonua ∼ **ZRE** 210-211 J 3
Looc o **RP** (BOH) 160-161 E 8

Lolworth Range ▲ **AUS** 174-175 H 7
Lom o **BG** 102-103 C 6
Lom ∼ **ETH** 208-209 E 1
Lom ∼ **CAM** 204-205 K 6
Lom ★ **N** 86-87 D 6
Loma o **USA** (MT) 250-251 J 4
Loma Alta o **USA** (TX) 266-267 G 4
Loma Bonita o **MEX** 52-53 G 2
Loma de Cabrera o **DOM** 54-55 K 5
Long Cove o **CDN** (NFL) 242-243 P 5
Long Creek o **CDN** (NB) 240-241 J 5
Long Creek o **USA** (OR) 244-245 F 6
Long Creek o **USA** 282-283 D 5
Long Đất o **VN** 158-159 J 5
Longe o **ANG** 216-217 C 3
Longfengyan o **VRC** 156-157 K 3
Long Fjord, De ≈ 26-27 d 2
Longford o **AUS** 180-181 J 6
Longford = An Longfort ★ **IRL**
  90-91 D 5
Longgang Shan ▲ **VRC** 150-151 F 5
Longgang Z.B. ⊥ **VRC** 156-157 E 5
Longgong o **VRC** 156-157 F 3
Longgong D. ∼ **VRC** 156-157 K 2
Look Sembuang o **MAL** 160-161 C 10
Lookout, Cape ▲ **CDN** 34-35 P 3
Lookout, Cape ▲ **USA** 244-245 B 5
Lookout, Cape ▲ **USA** (NC)
  282-283 L 6
Lookout, Mount ▲ **AUS** 174-175 H 6
Lookout Mount ▲ **USA** 20-21 P 3
Lookout Pass o **USA** (ID) 250-251 D 4
Lookout Point ▲ **USA** 20-21 H 4
Lookout Ridge ▲ **USA** 20-21 H 4
Looma o **AUS** 172-173 G 5
Loomis o **CDN** (SAS) 232-233 K 6
Loomis o **USA** 244-245 F 2
Loon o **USA** (WA) 244-245 H 2
Loon Point ▲ **CDN** 38-39 G 2
Loon River ∼ **CDN** 32-33 N 3
Loop o **USA** (TX) 264-265 B 6
Loos o **CDN** (BC) 228-229 O 3
Loosahatchie River ∼ **USA** 276-277 F 5
Loose Creek o **USA** (MO) 274-275 G 6
Loost River o **USA** (AR) 276-277 E 4
Lootsberg Pass o **ZA** 220-221 G 5
Lop o **VRC** 144-145 C 2
Lopary o **RM** 222-223 F 7
Lopatina, gora ▲ **RUS** 122-123 K 5
Lopatino o **RUS** 96-97 D 7
Lopatka, mys ▲ **RUS** 122-123 R 3
Lopatka, poluostrov ▲ **RUS** 110-111 c 4
Lopburi o **THA** 158-159 F 3
Lopča ∼ **RUS** 118-119 L 8
Lopeno o **USA** (TX) 266-267 H 7
Lopevi = Ulveah ∩ **VAN** 184 II b 3
Lopez o **CO** 60-61 C 4
López, Cap ▲ **G** 210-211 B 4
López Mateos, Ciudad o **MEX**
  52-53 G 2
Los o **S** 86-87 G 6
Losai National Reserve ⊥ **EAK**
  212-213 F 3
Los Andes = Sotomayor o **CO**
  64-65 D 1
Los Angeles o • **USA** (CA) 248-249 F 5
Los Angeles Aqueduct ⊲ **USA** (CA)
  248-249 F 4
Losantville o **USA** (IN) 274-275 N 4
Losari o **RI** 168 C 4
Los Cerrillos o **USA** (NM) 256-257 J 4
Los Claros o **YV** 60-61 F 2
Los Coyotes Indian Reservation ✕ **USA**
  (CA) 248-249 H 6
Loseya o **EAT** 212-213 F 5
Los Fresnos o **USA** (TX) 266-267 K 7
Los Haitises, Parque Nacional ⊥ **DOM**
  54-55 L 5
Losier Canyon ∼ **USA** 266-267 F 3
Losier Settlement o **CDN** (NB)
  240-241 L 3
Lošinj ∼ **HR** 100-101 E 2
Los Mochis o **MEX** 50-51 E 5
Loso ∼ **ZRE** 210-211 G 4
Losoni o **RI** 164-165 H 5
Lospatos o **RI** 166-167 D 6
Los Pingüinos, Reserva Faunística ⊥
  RCH 80-81 E 9
Los Pinos River ∼ **USA** 256-257 H 2
Los Reyes Islands ∩ **PNG** 183 E 1
Lossiemouth o **GB** 90-91 F 3
Lossogonoi Plateau ▲ **EAT**
  212-213 F 5
Los Taques o **YV** 60-61 F 2
Lost Creek o **USA** 284-285 D 5
Lost Hills o **USA** (CA) 248-249 E 4
Lost Maples State Natural Area ⊥ • **USA**
  (TX) 266-267 H 4
Lost River ∼ **USA** 280-281 H 4
Lost River Range ▲ **USA** 252-253 G 2
Los Troncos o **BOL** 70-71 F 5
Lost Springs o **USA** (WY) 252-253 O 4
Lost Trail Pass ▲ **USA** (ID) 250-251 F 6
Lostwood o **USA** (ND) 258-259 D 3
Lostwood National Wildlife Refuge ⊥
  USA (ND) 258-259 E 3
Losuia o **PNG** 183 F 5
Los Vilos o **RCH** 76-77 B 6
Lot ∼ **F** 90-91 H 9
Lote 15, Cerro ▲ **RA** 80 E 2
Lotfâbâd o **IR** 136-137 F 6
Lothair o **USA** (MT) 250-251 H 3
Lothal o **IND** 138-139 D 8
Lotia o **IND** 138-139 G 8
Lotikipi Plain ∼ **EAK** 212-213 E 1
Loto o **ZRE** (KOR) 210-211 J 5
Loto o **ZRE** 210-211 J 5
Lotoi ∼ **ZRE** 210-211 G 4
Lotsane ∼ **RB** 218-219 D 6
Lott o **USA** (TX) 266-267 K 2
Lotta ∼ **RUS** 88-89 L 2
Lotuke ▲ **SUD** 208-209 A 6
Lötzen = Giżycko o **PL** 92-93 Q 1
Louangphrabang o **LAO** 156-157 C 7
Loubetsi o **RCB** 210-211 C 5
Loubomo o **RCB** 210-211 C 5
Loubougoula o **RMM** 202-203 H 4
Loudéac o **F** 90-91 F 7
Loudi o **VRC** 156-157 G 3
Loudima o **RCB** (Bou) 210-211 D 6
Loudima ∼ **RCB** 210-211 D 6
Loudonville o **USA** (OH) 280-281 D 7
Loudun o **F** 90-91 H 8
Louessé ∼ **RCB** 210-211 C 5
Louétsi ∼ **G** 210-211 C 5
Louga o **SN** 202-203 B 2
Lougheed Island ∩ **CDN** 24-25 T 4
Loughrea = Baile Locha Riach o **IRL**
  90-91 C 5
Lougou o **DY** 204-205 E 3
Louhi o **RUS** 88-89 M 3
Louingui o **RCB** 210-211 E 6
Louisa o **USA** (KY) 276-277 N 2
Louisa Downs o **AUS** 172-173 H 5
Louisbourg o **CDN** (NS) 240-241 P 5
Louisburg o **USA** (KS) 262-263 M 6
Louisburg o **USA** (NC) 282-283 J 4
Louis Creek o **CDN** (BC) 230-231 J 2
Louisdale o **CDN** (NS) 240-241 O 5
Louise, Lake o **USA** (TX) 266-267 L 4
Louise Island ∩ **CDN** (BC) 228-229 C 4
Louiseville o **CDN** (QUE) 238-239 N 2
Louisiade Archipelago ∩ **PNG** 183 G 6
Louisiana o **USA** (MO) 274-275 G 5
Louisiana ♦ **USA** 268-269 G 5
Lou Island ∩ **PNG** 183 D 2
Louis Trichardt o **ZA** 218-219 E 6
Louisville o **USA** (CO) 254-255 K 4
Louisville o **USA** (GA) 284-285 H 3
Louisville o **USA** (KY) 276-277 K 6
Louisville o **USA** (MS) 268-269 M 3
Louisville o **USA** (NE) 262-263 K 4
Louisville Ridge ≈ 14-15 L 10
Loukoléla o **RCB** 210-211 F 4
Loukouo ∼ **RCB** 210-211 D 5
Loukout Mountain ▲ **USA** 284-285 E 2
Loulan Gucheng ∴ • **VRC** 146-147 J 5
Loulé o **P** 98-99 C 6
Loulouni o **RMM** 202-203 H 4
Lou Lou Park o **AUS** 178-179 J 2
Loumbi o **SN** 196-197 D 7
Loumo, Gati- o **RMM** 202-203 H 2
Loup o **USA** 206-207 L 6
Loupou o **RCB** 210-211 D 5
Loup, Rivière-du- o **CDN** (QUE)
  240-241 J 7
Loup City o **USA** (NE) 262-263 H 3
Loup River ∼ **USA** 262-263 H 3
Loups Marins, Lacs des o **CDN**
  36-37 M 6
Lourdes o **CDN** (NFL) 242-243 M 4
Lourdes o **F** 90-91 G 10
Lourenço o **BR** 62-63 J 4

Lyons River North ~ AUS 176-177 D 2
Lypci o UA 102-103 K 2
Lyra Reef ⌒ PNG 183 G 1
Lysaja, gora ▲ RUS 116-117 F 6
Lysekil ☆ S 86-87 E 7
Lysite o USA (WY) 252-253 L 3
Lyskovo o RUS 96-97 D 5
Lysova, ostrov ⌒ RUS 112-113 L 1
Lys'va ☆ RUS 96-97 K 4
Lysyčans'k o UA 102-103 L 3
Lysychans'k = Lysyčans'k o UA 102-103 L 3
Lysye Gory o RUS 96-97 D 8
Lytle o USA (TX) 266-267 J 4
Lyttelton o NZ 182 D 5
Lytton o CDN (BC) 230-231 H 3
Lyža ~ RUS 88-89 Y 4
Lyža, Ust'- o RUS 88-89 Y 4

M

Ma o CAM 204-205 J 5
Maalaea o USA (HI) 288 J 4
Maalamba o MOC 218-219 G 6
Maamba o Z 218-219 D 3
Ma'an o CAM 210-211 C 2
Ma'ān ☆ JOR 130-131 D 2
Maana'oba = Ngwalulu ⌒ SOL 184 I e 3
Maaninkavaara o FIN 88-89 K 3
Ma'āniya, al- o IRQ 130-131 H 2
Maanselkä ⊥ FIN 88-89 K 3
Ma'anshan o VRC 154-155 L 6
Maan't o MAU (BUL) 148-149 F 3
Maan't o MAU (TÖV) 148-149 H 4
Maardu o EST 94-95 J 2
Maarianhamina = Mariehamn ☆ FIN 88-89 E 6
Maarmorilik o GRØ 26-27 Z 8
Ma'arrat an-Nu'mān o• SYR 128-129 G 5
Maas ~ NL 92-93 J 3
Maasim o RP 160-161 F 10
Masin ☆ RP 160-161 F 7
Maasstroom o ZA 218-219 E 6
Maastricht ☆•• NL 92-93 H 3
Maasupa o SOL 184 I e 3
Maatsuyker Group ⌒ AUS 180-181 J 7
M.A.B., Réserve ⊥ ZRE 214-215 C 6
Maba o RI 164-165 L 3
Mababe Depression ⊥ RB 218-219 C 4
Ma'bad o IR 136-137 D 7
Mabaduam o PNG 183 A 4
Mabaia o ANG 216-217 C 3
Mabana o ZRE 212-213 B 3
Mabanda o BU 212-213 B 6
Mabanda o G 210-211 C 5
Mabanda, Mont ▲ G 210-211 C 5
Mabank o USA (TX) 264-265 H 6
Ma'bar o Y 132-133 D 6
Mabé ~ CAM 204-205 J 5
Mabein o MYA 142-143 K 4
Mabel o USA (MN) 270-271 G 7
Mabel Creek o AUS 178-179 C 5
Mabel Downs o AUS 172-173 J 4
Mabélé o CAM 204-205 K 5
Mabeleapudi o RB 218-219 D 6
Mabel Lake o CDN (BC) 230-231 L 3
Mabel Lake ⊖ CDN (BC) 230-231 L 3
Mabelle o USA (TX) 264-265 E 5
Mabel Range ▲ AUS 170-179 C 4
Mabenge o ZRE 206-207 G 6
Mabest, Lake ⊖ WAL 202-203 E 6
Mabeta o CAM 210-211 B 2
Mabitac o RP 160-161 D 5
Mabo o SN 202-203 C 3
Mabole ~ WAL 202-203 D 5
Mabopane o ZA 220-221 J 2
Mabote o MOC 218-219 H 6
Mabou o CDN (NS) 240-241 O 4
Mabraz, al- o Y 132-133 C 6
Mabrouk o RMM 196-197 K 5
Mabrous o RN 198-199 F 2
Mabrūk o LAR 192-193 G 2
Mabton o USA (WA) 244-245 F 4
Mabu, Monte ▲ MOC 218-219 J 3
Mabuasehube Game Reserve ⊥ RB 220-221 E 2
Mabuiag Island ⌒ AUS 174-175 G 1
Mabuki o EAT 212-213 D 5
Mabula o ZA 220-221 J 2
Mabur ≈ 166-167 K 5
Mabura o GUY 62-63 E 3
Mabuto o WAN 204-205 F 3
Maĉa o RUS 118-119 H 6
Macá, Monte ▲ RCH 80 D 2
Macabi, Isla de ⌒ PE 64-65 C 5
Maçacara o BR 68-69 J 7
Macachín o RA 78-79 H 4
Macaco, Cachoeira do ~ BR 68-69 E 6
Macacos, Ilha dos ⌒ BR 62-63 J 6
Macaé o BR 72-73 K 7
Macaene o MOC 220-221 L 2
Macague, Saut ~ F 62-63 H 4
Maĉah o RUS 110-111 T 6
Macaíba o BR 68-69 L 4
Macajalar Bay ≈ 160-161 F 8
Macajuba o BR 72-73 K 2
Macalister o AUS 174-175 F 6
MacAlpine Lake ⊖ CDN 30-31 S 2
Maçambará o BR 76-77 J 5
Macamic o CDN (QUE) 236-237 J 4
Macan, Kepulauan ⌒ RI 168 E 6
Macanao = Boca de Pozo o YV 60-61 J 2
Macandze o MOC 218-219 G 6
Maçangana, Rio ~ BR 66-67 F 7
Macanillal o YV 60-61 G 4
Macao ◘ P 156-157 H 5
Macao ☆•• P 156-157 H 5
Macao, El o DOM 54-55 L 5
Macapá ☆ BR 62-63 J 5
Macaparana o BR 68-69 L 5
Macapillo o RA 76-77 F 3
Macará o EC 64-65 C 4
Macaracas o PA 52-53 D 8
Maçaranduba, Cachoeira ~ BR 62-63 H 6
Macarani o BR 72-73 K 3
Macarena, Parque Nacional la ⊥ CO 60-61 E 6
Macareo, Caño ~ YV 60-61 L 3
Macari o PE 70-71 B 4
Maçarico, Cachoeira ~ BR 66-67 D 2
Macaroni o AUS 174-175 F 5
Macarretane o MOC 220-221 L 2
Macarthur o AUS 180-181 G 5
Macas o EC 64-65 C 3
Macatanja o MOC 218-219 J 3
Macaú o BR 68-69 K 4
Macau = Macao ☆•• P 156-157 H 5
Macauã, Rio ~ BR 70-71 C 2
Macauari o BR 62-63 E 6
Macaúbas o BR 72-73 J 2
Macaza, Rivière ~ CDN 238-239 L 2
Macbar, Raas ▲ SP 208-209 K 4
Maccles Lake ⊖ CDN (NFL) 242-243 O 4
Mac Cluer Gulf = Teluk Berau ≈ 166-167 G 3
Macculloch, Cape ▲ CDN 24-25 j 4
Mac Cullochs Range ▲ AUS 178-179 G 6
Macdiarmid o CDN (ONT) 234-235 P 5
MacDonald o CDN (MAN) 234-235 E 4
MacDonald, Lake ⊖ AUS 176-177 K 1
MacDonald, Mount ▲ VAN 184 II b 3
Mac Donald Downs o AUS 178-179 C 2
MacDonald Island ⌒ CDN 36-37 N 3
Macdonnell Peninsula ⌣ AUS 180-181 E 3
Macdonnell Ranges ▲• AUS 176-177 L 1
Macdougall Lake ⊖ CDN 30-31 U 2
MacDowall o CDN (SAS) 232-233 N 2
MacDowell Lake ⊖ CDN (ONT) 234-235 L 2
Macedo de Cavaleiros o P 98-99 D 4
Macedonia = Makedonija ■ MK 100-101 H 4
Maceió ☆ BR 68-69 L 6
Macenta o RG 202-203 F 5
Macerata ☆ I 100-101 D 3
Mačevna, buhta ≈ 112-113 Q 6
Macfarlane, Lake ⊖ AUS 178-179 D 6
Macgillycuddy's Reeks ▲ IRL 90-91 C 6
MacGregor o CDN (MAN) 234-235 E 5
MacGregor o USA (TX) 266-267 K 2
Mach o PK 134-135 M 4
Machacamarca o BOL 70-71 D 6
Machachi o EC 64-65 C 2
Machadinho o BR 66-67 F 7
Machadinho, Rio ~ BR 66-67 F 7
Machadinho, Rio ~ BR 66-67 G 7
Machado o BR 72-73 H 6
Machado, Rio ~ BR 70-71 G 2
Machadodorp o ZA 220-221 K 2
Machado ou Ji-Paraná, Rio ~ BR 66-67 F 7
Machagai o RA 76-77 G 4
Machaila o MOC 218-219 G 6
Machakos o EAK 212-213 F 4
Machala ☆ EC 64-65 C 3
Machalilla, Parque Nacional ⊥ EC 64-65 B 2
Machaneng o RB 218-219 D 6
Machang o MAL 162-163 E 2
Machang o VRC 156-157 E 3
Machanga o MOC 218-219 H 5
Machaquilá ∴• GCA 52-53 K 3
Machaquilá, Río ~ GCA 52-53 K 3
Machattie, Lake ⊖ AUS 178-179 E 3
Machawaian Lake ⊖ CDN (ONT) 234-235 P 3
Machecoul o F 90-91 G 8
Macheke o ZW 218-219 F 4
Machemma Ruins ∴• ZA 218-219 E 6
Macheng o VRC 154-155 J 6
Mācherla o IND 140-141 H 2
Machesse o MOC 218-219 H 4
Machias o USA (ME) 278-279 O 4
Machias River ~ USA 278-279 O 4
Machichaco, Cabo ▲ E 98-99 F 3
Machichi River ~ CDN 34-35 L 2
Machile ~ Z 218-219 C 3
Machilipatnam o IND 140-141 J 2
Machina o WAN 198-199 E 6
Machinga o MW 218-219 H 2
Machiques o YV 60-61 E 2
Machmell River ~ CDN 230-231 C 2
Macho, Cienega del ~ USA 256-257 L 5
Macho, El o C 54-55 G 5
Machu Picchu ••• PE 64-65 F 8
Machupo, Río ~ BOL 70-71 E 3
Macia o MOC 220-221 L 2
Maciel o PY 76-77 J 4
Măcin o RO 102-103 F 5
Macintyre River ~ AUS 178-179 K 5
Mack o USA (CO) 254-255 G 4
Maçka ☆ TR 128-129 H 2
MacKay o AUS 178-179 K 1
MacKay o CDN (ALB) 232-233 C 2
MacKay o USA (ID) 252-253 E 3
Mackay, Lake ⊖ AUS 172-173 J 7
Mackay Island National Wildlife Refuge ⊥ USA (NC) 282-283 M 4
MacKay Lake ⊖ CDN 30-31 O 4
Mackay River ~ CDN 32-33 O 3
Mackenzie o CDN 32-33 J 4
Mackenzie o GUY 62-63 E 3
Mackenzie, Kap ▲ GRØ 26-27 p 7
Mackenzie Bay ≈ 20-21 W 2
Mackenzie Bison Sanctuary • CDN 30-31 L 5
Mackenzie Delta ⊥•• CDN 20-21 X 2
Mackenzie Highway II CDN (ALB) 32-33 M 3
Mackenzie Highway II CDN (NWT) 30-31 H 4
Mackenzie King Island ⌒ CDN 24-25 P 2
Mackenzie Mountains ▲ CDN 30-31 C 3
Mackenzie River ~ AUS 178-179 K 2
Mackenzie River ~ CDN 30-31 K 5
Mackinac Bridge II• USA (MI) 272-273 E 2
Mackinac Island ⌒ USA (MI) 272-273 E 2
Mackinac Island State Park • USA (MI) 272-273 E 2
Mackinaw o USA (IL) 274-275 J 4
Mackinaw City o USA (MI) 272-273 E 2
Mackinaw River ~ USA 274-275 K 4
Mackinnon Road o EAK 212-213 G 5
Mackkeys o USA (NC) 282-283 L 5
Macklin o CDN (SAS) 232-233 J 3
Macksburg o USA (IA) 274-275 D 3
Macks Inn o USA (ID) 252-253 G 2
Macksville o AUS 178-179 M 6
Maclaren River ~ USA 20-21 R 5
Maclean o AUS 178-179 M 5
Maclean Strait ≈ 24-25 T 2
Macleantown o ZA 220-221 H 6
Maclear o ZA 220-221 J 5
Maclear, Cape ▲ MW 218-219 H 1
Macleay River ~ AUS 178-179 M 6
Macleod, Fort o CDN (ALB) 232-233 E 6
MacLeod, Lake ⊖ AUS 176-177 B 2
Macmillan Pass ▲ CDN 30-31 E 4
Macmillan Plateau ▲ CDN 20-21 Y 5
Macmillan River ~ CDN 20-21 X 5
MacNutt o CDN (SAS) 232-233 R 4
Maco o RP 160-161 F 9
Maco, Cerro ▲ CO 60-61 D 3
Maçobere o MOC 218-219 G 5
Macocha ▲ CZ 92-93 O 4
Macocola o ANG 216-217 D 3
Macomb o USA (IL) 274-275 H 4
Macomber o USA (WV) 280-281 G 4
Macomér o I 100-101 B 4
Macomia o MOC 214-215 L 7
Mâcon ☆• F 90-91 K 8
Macon o USA (GA) 284-285 G 4
Macon o USA (MO) 274-275 F 5
Macon o USA (MS) 268-269 M 3
Macon o USA (OH) 280-281 C 5
Macondo o ANG (MOX) 214-215 B 7
Macondo ~ ANG 218-219 B 1
Macoppe o RI 164-165 G 6
Macossa o MOC 218-219 G 3
Macoun o CDN (SAS) 232-233 P 6
Macoun Lake ⊖ CDN 34-35 E 2
Macoupin River ~ USA 274-275 H 5
Macouria = Tonate o F 62-63 H 3
Macovane o MOC 218-219 H 5
Macoya o BOL 70-71 C 6
Macpés o CDN (QUE) 240-241 G 2
Macquarie, Lake ⊖ AUS 180-181 L 2
Macquarie Harbour ≈ 180-181 H 7
Macquarie Ridge ≃ 14-15 H 13
Macquarie River ~ AUS 180-181 K 2
MacQuoid Lake ⊖ CDN 30-31 W 4
Macroom = Maigh Chromtha o IRL 90-91 C 6
Macrorie o CDN (SAS) 232-233 L 4
Mac's Corner o USA (SD) 260-261 G 2
Mactan Island ⌒ RP 160-161 E 7
Macucocha, Lago ⊖ PE 64-65 F 9
Macuira, Parque Nacional ⊥ CO 60-61 F 1
Macuma o EC 64-65 D 3
Macumba River ~ AUS 178-179 D 4
Macuna, Raudal ~ CO 66-67 B 3
Macururé o BR 68-69 J 6
Macururé, Rio ~ BR 68-69 J 6
Macusani o PE 70-71 B 4
Macuto o YV 60-61 H 2
Macúzari, Presa ⊖ MEX 50-51 E 4
Macuze o MOC 218-219 J 3
Macwahoc o USA (ME) 278-279 N 3
Mada, River ~ WAN 204-205 H 4
Madabazouma o RCA 206-207 F 6
Madadeni o ZA 220-221 K 3
Madagascar, Arrecife ⌒ MEX 52-53 J 1
Madagascar = Madagasikara ■ RM 222-223 C 7
Madagascar = Madagasikara ⌒ RM 222-223 D 9
Madagascar Basin ≃ 12 D 7
Madagascar Ridge ≃ 9 H 9
Madagli o WAN 204-205 K 3
Madagoi ~ SP 212-213 J 3
Ma Đa Gui o VN 158-159 J 5
Mada'in Salih •• KSA 130-131 E 4
Madakasira o IND 140-141 G 4
Madalena o BR 68-69 J 4
Madama o RN 198-199 F 2
Madamba o RP 160-161 F 9
Madana o TCH 206-207 C 4
Madanapalle o IND 140-141 H 4
Madang ☆• PNG 183 C 3
Madanganj o BD 142-143 G 4
Madaniqa, al- o KSA 132-133 C 5
Madaoua o RN 198-199 B 5
Madara o••• BG 102-103 E 6
Madara Canal < USA (CA) 248-249 E 2
Madarounfa o RN 198-199 C 6
Madau o TM 136-137 D 5
Madau Island ⌒ PNG 183 G 5
Madaun o RUS 120-121 O 3
Madavaram o IND 140-141 J 2
Madawaska o CDN (ONT) 238-239 G 3
Madawaska o USA (ME) 278-279 N 1
Madawaska River ~ CDN 238-239 H 3
Madaya o MYA 142-143 K 4
Madbar o SUD 206-207 K 5
Maddalena, Ísola ⌒ I 100-101 B 4
Maddalena, la o I 100-101 B 4
Madden o CDN (ALB) 232-233 D 4
Maddock o USA (ND) 258-259 H 4
Maddūr o IND 140-141 G 4
Madeir o SUD 206-207 J 5
Madeira o USA (OH) 280-281 B 4
Madeira, Arquipélago da ⌒ P (MAD) 188-189 C 4
Madeira, Rio ~ BOL 70-71 E 2
Madeira, Rio ~ BR 66-67 H 5
Madeira Park o CDN (BC) 230-231 F 4
Madeira Rise ≃ 6-7 H 5
Madeirinha, Rio ~ BR 66-67 G 7
Madelaine, Îles de la ⌒ CDN (QUE) 242-243 G 5
Madeleine, Cap-de-la- o CDN (QUE) 238-239 N 2
Madeleine-Centre o CDN (QUE) 242-243 C 3
Madelia o USA (MN) 270-271 D 6
Madeline o USA (CA) 246-247 E 2
Madeline Island ⌒ USA (WI) 270-271 H 4
Maden ☆ TR 128-129 H 3
Madera o MEX 50-51 E 3
Madera o USA (CA) 248-249 D 3
Madero o SP 212-213 H 4
Mādhavaram o IND 140-141 G 3
Madhira o IND 140-141 J 2
Madhu o CL 140-141 J 6
Madhuban o IND 142-143 D 2
Madhubani o• IND 142-143 E 2
Madhugiri o IND 140-141 G 4
Madhumati ~ BD 142-143 F 4
Madhupur o BD 142-143 G 3
Madhupur o IND 142-143 E 3
Madhya Pradesh ◘ IND 138-139 E 8
Madi, Wādi ~ OM 132-133 H 5
Madiany o EAK 212-213 E 4
Madibira o EAT 214-215 H 5
Madibogo o ZA 220-221 G 3
Madidi, Río ~ BOL 70-71 D 3
Madigan Gulf ⊖ AUS 178-179 D 5
Madihui o VRC 154-155 G 3
Madikeri o• IND 140-141 F 4
Madill o USA (OK) 264-265 H 4
Madimba o ANG 216-217 C 3
Madimba o ZRE 210-211 E 6
Ma'din o SYR 128-129 H 5
Madina o RMM 202-203 F 3
Madina, al- ◘ KSA 130-131 F 5
Madina, al- o Y 132-133 E 6
Madina = Diassa o RMM 202-203 G 4
Madina de Baixo o GNB 202-203 C 4
Madina Junction o WAL 202-203 D 5
Madinani o CI 202-203 G 5
Madina-Oula o RG 202-203 D 5
Madina-Salambandé o RG 202-203 E 4
Madinat al Abyar o LAR 192-193 J 1
Madinat as-Ša'b o Y 132-133 D 7
Madinat as-Sādāt o ET 194-195 E 2
Madinat aš-Širq o Y 132-133 C 6
Madinat at-Ṭaura o SYR 128-129 H 5
Madinat Nāṣir o ET 194-195 F 5
Madinat Šahrā' o ET 194-195 F 6
Madingo-Kayes o RCB 210-211 C 6
Madingou ☆ RCB 210-211 D 6
Madingrin o CAM 206-207 B 4
Madi Opei o EAU 212-213 D 2
Madirovalo o RM 222-223 E 6
Madison o CDN (SAS) 232-233 K 4
Madison o USA (AL) 284-285 D 2
Madison o USA (FL) 286-287 F 1
Madison o USA (GA) 284-285 G 3
Madison o USA (IN) 274-275 N 6
Madison o USA (KS) 262-263 K 6
Madison o USA (ME) 278-279 M 4
Madison o USA (MN) 270-271 B 5
Madison o USA (NC) 282-283 H 4
Madison o USA (NE) 262-263 J 3
Madison o USA (SD) 260-261 J 2
Madison o USA (VA) 280-281 H 5
Madison o USA (WV) 280-281 E 5
Madison o USA (WY) 252-253 H 2
Madison ☆• USA (WI) 274-275 J 1
Madison Bird Refuge ⊥ USA (MT) 250-251 G 7
Madison Canyon Earthquake Area (1959) ∴• USA (MT) 250-251 H 7
Madison River ~ USA 250-251 H 6
Madisonville o USA (KY) 276-277 H 3
Madisonville o USA (LA) 268-269 K 6
Madisonville o USA (TN) 282-283 C 5
Madisonville o USA (TX) 268-269 E 6
Madita, Pr. o RI 168 E 8
Madiun o RI 168 D 3
Madja o RCA 206-207 F 3
Madjingo o G 210-211 E 3
Madley, Mount ▲ AUS 176-177 G 2
Madley Rapids ~ CDN 30-31 Q 3
Mado Derdetu < EAK 212-213 G 3
Mado Gashi o EAK 212-213 G 3
Madoi o VRC 144-145 M 3
Madona ☆•• LV 94-95 K 3
Madooile o SP 212-213 H 2
Madra Dağı ▲ TR 128-129 B 3
Madraka o KSA 130-131 G 6
Madraka, Ra's ▲ OM 132-133 K 4
Madras ☆•• IND 140-141 J 4
Madras o USA (OR) 244-245 D 6
Madre, Laguna ≈ 266-267 K 7
Madre de Chiapas, Sierra ▲ MEX 52-53 H 3
Madre de Deus de Minas o BR 72-73 H 6
Madre de Dios o PE 70-71 B 3
Madre de Dios, Isla ⌒ RCH 80 C 5
Madre de Dios, Río ~ BOL 70-71 D 2
Madre de Dios, Río ~ PE 70-71 C 3
Madre del Sur, Sierra ▲ MEX 52-53 D 3
Madre Occidental, Sierra ▲ MEX 50-51 E 2
Madre Oriental, Sierra ▲ MEX 50-51 H 3
Madrid ☆•• E 98-99 F 4
Madrid o RP 160-161 F 8
Madrid o USA (IA) 274-275 E 3
Madrid o USA (KY) 276-277 J 3
Madrid o USA (NE) 262-263 E 4
Madrid, La o RA 76-77 E 4
Madridejos o E 98-99 F 5
Madrigal o PE 70-71 B 4
Mad River ~ USA 246-247 B 3
Madrona, Sierra ▲ E 98-99 E 5
Maduda o C 54-55 E 3
Madrugada, La o RA 80 G 3
Madsen o CDN (ONT) 234-235 K 3
Madu o SUD 200-201 C 5
Madu, Pulau ⌒ RI 168 E 6
Maduda o ZRE 210-211 D 6
Madula o ZRE 210-211 K 3
Madura, Pulau ⌒ RI 168 E 3
Madura, Selat ≈ 168 E 3
Madurai o•• IND 140-141 H 6
Madura Motel o AUS 176-177 J 5
Madurankuli o CL 140-141 H 7
Madurāntakam o IND 140-141 H 4
Madura Pass • AUS 176-177 J 5
Madyl-Tasa, gora ▲ RUS 110-111 U 4
Madžarovo o BG 102-103 D 7
Madzilobge o RB 218-219 D 5
Madziwadzido o ZW 218-219 E 3
Madziwa Mine o ZW 218-219 F 3
Maebashi ☆ J 152-153 H 6
Mae Chaem o THA 142-143 L 6
Mae Charim o THA 142-143 M 6
Mae Hong Son o THA 142-143 K 6
Mae Khajan o THA 142-143 L 6
Maelang o RI 164-165 H 3
Maele o MOC 220-221 L 2
Mae Nam Khwae Noi ~ THA 158-159 E 3
Maengsan o KOR 150-151 F 8
Mae Pok o THA 158-159 E 2
Mae Sai o THA 142-143 L 5
Mae Sariang o THA 142-143 K 6
Maeser Creek ~ USA 254-255 F 3
Mae Sot o THA 158-159 E 2
Maestra, Sierra ▲ C 54-55 G 4
Maestro de Campo Island ⌒ RP 160-161 D 6
Mae Su o THA 142-143 K 6
Mae Suai o THA 142-143 L 6
Mae Suya o THA 142-143 L 6
Mae Taeng o THA 142-143 L 6
Mae Tub Reservoir ⊖ THA 158-159 E 2
Maevarano ~ RM 222-223 F 5
Maevatanana o RM 222-223 E 6
Maevo o RUS 94-95 L 3
Maewo = Île Aurora ⌒ VAN 184 II b 2
Mafa o RI 164-165 K 3
Mafara, Talata o WAN 198-199 C 6
Mafeking o CDN (MAN) 234-235 B 2
Maféré o CI 202-203 J 7
Mafeteng o LS 220-221 H 4
Maffin o RI 166-167 K 2
Mafia Channel ≈ 214-215 K 4
Mafia Island ⌒ EAT 214-215 K 4
Mafikeng o ZA 220-221 G 2
Mafil o RCH 78-79 C 5
Mafou ~ RG 202-203 E 4
Mafra o BR 74-75 F 6
Mafraq o Y 132-133 C 7
Mafraq, al ☆ JOR 130-131 E 1
Maga o CAM 206-207 B 3
Magadan ☆•• RUS 120-121 O 4
Magadanskij Kava-Čelomdžinskoe lesničestvo, zapovednik ⊥ RUS 120-121 M 3
Magadanskij Ol'skoe lesničestvo, zapovednik ⊥ RUS 120-121 O 4
Magadanskij Sejmčanskoe lesničestvo, zapovednik ⊥ RUS 120-121 P 2
Magadi o EAK 212-213 F 4
Magadi, Lake ⊖ EAK 212-213 F 4
Maġāġa o ET 194-195 E 3
Magaguadavic River ~ CDN 240-241 J 5
Magalakwin ~ ZA 218-219 E 6
Magalhães Barata o BR 68-69 E 2
Magaliesberg Natural Area ⊥ ZA 220-221 H 2
Magallanes, Estrecho de ≈ 80 E 6
Magallanes y Antártica Chilena ◘ RCH 80 F 6
Magamba o RCA 206-207 F 6
Magan o RUS (SAH) 118-119 O 4
Magan ~ RUS 108-109 f 7
Magana, River ~ WAN 204-205 H 4
Magandene o MOC 218-219 G 6
Magangue o CO 60-61 D 3
Maganoy ~ RP 160-161 F 9
Magan-Tas, gora ▲ RUS 110-111 d 5
Magao o TCH 206-207 B 3
Magara o BU 212-213 B 5
Maġāra, Ǧabal ▲ ET 194-195 F 2
Magaras o RUS 118-119 O 4
Maġardal, al- o KSA 132-133 B 4
Magaria o RN 198-199 D 6
Magarida o PNG 183 E 6
Maġārim, al- o Y 132-133 E 6
Magat ~ RP 160-161 D 4
Magaubo o PNG 183 E 6
Magaw o MYA 142-143 K 2
Magazine Mountain ▲ USA (AR) 276-277 B 5
Magba o CAM 204-205 J 6
Magbakele o ZRE 210-211 J 2
Magbuntoso o WAL 202-203 D 5
Magburaka o WAL 202-203 E 5
Magdad o SP 212-213 K 2
Magdagači ☆ RUS (AMR) 118-119 M 9
Magdagači ~ RUS 118-119 M 9
Maġdal 'Anǧar o••• RL 128-129 F 6
Magdalena o BOL 70-71 E 3
Magdalena o MEX 52-53 C 1
Magdalena o RA 78-79 L 3
Magdalena o USA (NM) 256-257 H 4
Magdalena, Bahía ≈ 50-51 C 5
Magdalena, Gunung ▲ MAL 160-161 B 10
Magdalena, Isla ⌒ MEX 50-51 C 5
Magdalena, Isla ⌒ RCH 80 D 2
Magdalena, Punta ▲ CO 60-61 C 6
Magdalena, Río ~ CO 60-61 D 2
Magdalena, Río ~ MEX 50-51 D 2
Magdalena de Kino o MEX 50-51 D 2
Magdalena Tequisistlán o MEX 52-53 G 3
Magda Plateau ▲ CDN 24-25 f 4
Magdeburg ☆• D 92-93 L 2
Magdi o IND 140-141 G 4
Magee o USA (MS) 268-269 L 5
Magej ~ RUS 120-121 F 5
Magelang o RI 168 D 3
Magellan Seamounts ≃ 14-15 J 6
Magens Bay Beach ⊥ USA 286-287 R 2
Magenta, Lake ⊖ AUS 176-177 E 6
Magerøya ⌒ N 86-87 M 1
Magetan o RI 168 D 3
Magga Range ▲ ARK 16 F 35
Maggieville o AUS 174-175 F 5
Maggiore, Lago o I 100-101 B 2
Maghama o RIM 196-197 D 7
Maghnia o DZ 188-189 L 3
Magic City o USA (ID) 252-253 D 3
Magic Hot Springs ∴ USA (ID) 252-253 D 4
Magic Reservoir < USA (ID) 252-253 D 3
Magill, Islas ⌒ RCH 80 D 7
Magindrano o RM 222-223 F 5
Magingo o EAT 214-215 H 6
Magistral'nyj o RUS 116-117 N 7
Mäglie o I 100-101 G 4
Maǧma'a, al- o KSA 130-131 J 5
Magna o USA (UT) 254-255 C 3
Magna Bay o CDN (BC) 230-231 K 3
Magnet o CDN (MAN) 234-235 D 3
Magnet o USA (NE) 262-263 J 2
Magnetawar o CDN (ONT) 238-239 F 3
Magnetawa River ~ CDN 238-239 E 3
Magnetic Island ⌒ AUS 174-175 J 6
Magnetic Point ▲ CDN 28-29 E 3
Magnetity o RUS 88-89 M 2
Magnitogorsk o RUS 96-97 L 7
Magnolia o USA (AR) 276-277 B 7
Magnolia o USA (MS) 268-269 K 5
Magnolia Springs State Park ⊥ USA (GA) 284-285 J 4
Mago ⌒ FJI 184 III c 2
Mago o RUS 122-123 J 2
Màgoé o MOC 218-219 F 2
Magog o CDN (QUE) 238-239 N 3
Magou ~ DY 202-203 L 4
Magoura o DZ 188-189 L 3
Magoye o Z 218-219 D 3
Magpie o CDN (QUE) 242-243 D 2
Magpie, Lac ⊖ CDN 242-243 D 2
Magpie, Rivière ~ CDN 242-243 D 2
Magra ~ BD 142-143 G 3
Magra o DZ 190-191 E 3
Magrath o CDN (ALB) 232-233 F 6
Magrur o SUD 200-201 E 6
Magṭa Laḥjat o RIM 196-197 D 6
Magu, Rio ~ BR 68-69 G 3
Maguan o VRC 156-157 D 5
Maguari o BR 66-67 K 6
Maguari, Cabo ▲ BR 62-63 K 6
Magude o MOC 220-221 L 2
Magui, Lac ⊖ RMM 202-203 E 2
Magumeri o WAN 198-199 F 6
Magunge o ZW 218-219 E 3
Magura o BD 142-143 F 4
Maguse Lake ⊖ CDN 30-31 W 5
Maguse Point ▲ CDN 30-31 X 5
Maguse River ~ CDN 30-31 W 5
Magushan • VRC 156-157 K 3
Magusheni o ZA 220-221 J 5
Magus River ~ CDN 236-237 J 4
Magwe o MYA 142-143 J 5
Magwe o SUD 206-207 L 6
Magyichaung o MYA 142-143 H 5
Maǧz o Y 132-133 C 5
Mahābād o• IR 128-129 L 4
Mahābaleshwar o• IND 140-141 E 2
Mahabe o RM 222-223 D 6
Mahābiša, al- o Y 132-133 C 6
Mahabo o RM (TLA) 222-223 E 9
Mahabo o RM (Tla) 222-223 D 8
Mahačkala ☆ RUS 126-127 G 6
Mahād o IND 138-139 D 10
Mahadday Weeyne o SP 212-213 K 2
Mahafaly ⊥ RM 222-223 C 9
Mahafaly, Tombeau • RM 222-223 D 10
Mahafasa o RM 222-223 E 9
Mahagi o ZRE 212-213 C 2
Mahagi Port o ZRE 212-213 C 2
Mahaicony o GUY 62-63 F 2
Maḥā'il o KSA 132-133 C 4
Mahajamba ~ RM 222-223 E 6
Mahajamba, Helodrano ≈ 222-223 E 5
Mahajanga ◘ RM 222-223 D 7
Mahajanga ☆ RM (Mjg) 222-223 E 5
Mahajanga ~ RM 222-223 D 7
Mahakam ~ RI 164-165 D 3
Mahākik, al- ⊥ KSA 132-133 G 3
Mahal o IND 140-141 H 4
Mahālāni, al- o KSA 130-131 H 4
Mahalapye o RB 218-219 D 6
Mahalchari o BD 142-143 H 4
Mahalevona o RM 222-223 F 5
Mahali Mountains ▲ EAT 214-215 E 4
Maḥalla al-Kubrā, al- o ET 194-195 E 2
Maḥallāt o IR 134-135 D 2
Mahalona o RI 164-165 G 5
Mahalona, Danau ⊖ RI 164-165 G 5
Mahambet ☆ KZ 96-97 G 10
Mahambo o RM 222-223 F 6
Mahameru, Gunung ▲ RI 168 E 4
Mahāmūd-e'Erāqī ☆ AFG 136-137 L 7
Māhān o IR 134-135 G 3
Mahānadi ~ IND 142-143 D 5
Mahānadi Delta ⊥ IND 142-143 E 5
Mahananda ~ IND 142-143 F 3
Mahanay Island ⌒ RP 160-161 F 7
Mahango Game Park ⊥ NAM 216-217 F 9
Mahanoro o RM 222-223 F 7
Maha Oya o CL 140-141 J 7
Mahārājganj o IND 142-143 C 2
Maharashtra ◘ IND 138-139 D 10
Mahārlū, Daryāče-ye ⊖ IR 134-135 E 4
Mahāsamund o IND 142-143 C 5
Maha Sarakham o THA 158-159 G 2
Mahaska o USA (KS) 262-263 J 5
Mahasolo o RM 222-223 E 7
Mahatalaky o RM 222-223 E 10
Mahatsaratsara o RM 222-223 E 8
Maḥaṭṭat 1 o SUD 200-201 E 2
Maḥaṭṭat 2 o SUD 200-201 E 2
Maḥaṭṭat 3 o SUD 200-201 F 2
Maḥaṭṭat 4 o SUD 200-201 F 2
Maḥaṭṭat 5 o SUD 200-201 F 2
Maḥaṭṭat 6 o SUD 200-201 F 2
Maḥaṭṭat 7 o SUD 200-201 F 2
Maḥaṭṭat 8 o SUD 200-201 F 2
Maḥaṭṭat 9 o SUD 200-201 F 3
Maḥaṭṭat 10 o SUD 200-201 F 3
Maḥaṭṭat Ṭalāṭa o ET 194-195 F 2
Mahavanona o RM 222-223 F 4
Mahavavy ~ RM 222-223 E 6
Mahavavy ~ RM 222-223 F 4
Mahavelona o RM (ATN) 222-223 E 7
Mahavelona o RM (TMA) 222-223 F 6
Mahawelatota o CL 140-141 J 7
Mahaweli Ganga ~ CL 140-141 J 7
Mahaxai o LAO 158-159 H 2
Mahayag o RP 160-161 F 8
Mahazoma o RM 222-223 E 6
Maḥbūb o SUD 200-201 D 6
Mahbūbābād o IND 142-143 B 7
Mahbūbnagar o IND 140-141 G 2
Maḥḍa o OM 134-135 F 6
Mahd aḏ-Ḏahab o KSA 130-131 G 6
Mahdia o GUY 62-63 E 3
Mahdia ☆ TN 190-191 H 3
Mahdīšahr o IR 136-137 C 7
Mahe o• IND 140-141 F 5
Mahébourg o• MS 224 C 7
Mahé Island ⌒ SY 224 D 2
Mahendragarh o IND 138-139 F 5
Mahendra Giri ▲ IND 142-143 D 6
Mahenge o EAT 214-215 J 5
Mahesāna o IND 138-139 D 8
Maheshkhali ⌒ BD 142-143 G 5
Maheshpur o IND 142-143 E 3
Maḥfar al-Busayya o IRQ 130-131 K 2
Maḥfar al-Ḥammām o SYR 128-129 H 5
Maḥǧil, al- o Y 132-133 D 5
Mahi ~ IND 138-139 D 8
Mahia Peninsula ⌣ NZ 182 F 3
Māhīdašt o IR 134-135 B 1
Mahila o ZRE 212-213 B 6
Mahilëv o• BY 94-95 M 5
Mahilyow = Mahilëv o• BY 94-95 M 5
Mahimba Kanikolo ⊥ SOL 184 I c 3
Mahin o WAN 204-205 F 5
Mahina o RMM 202-203 E 3
Mahitsy o RM 222-223 E 7
Mahkyetkawng o MYA 142-143 K 3
Mahlabatini o ZA 220-221 K 4
Mahlaing o MYA 142-143 J 5
Mahlake o IR 134-135 E 5
Mahmiya o SUD 200-201 F 4
Mahmoud, Bir o TN 190-191 G 4
Maḥmūdābād o IR 136-137 C 6
Maḥmūdiya, al- ☆ IRQ 128-129 L 6
Mahmud Jig o IR 128-129 M 4
Maḥmūr o IRQ 128-129 K 5
Mahne o IR 134-135 H 1
Māhnešān o IR 128-129 M 4
Mahnja ~ RUS 114-115 O 5
Mahnomen o USA (MN) 270-271 C 3
Maho o CL 140-141 J 7
Mahoba o IND 138-139 G 7
Maho Bay ⊥ NA 56 D 2
Mahomet o USA (IL) 274-275 K 4
Mahone Bay ≈ 38-39 M 6
Mahone Bay ≈ 240-241 L 6
Mahone Bay o CDN (NS) 240-241 L 6
Mahony Lake ⊖ CDN 30-31 G 3
Mahood Falls o CDN (BC) 230-231 J 2
Mahood Lake ⊖ CDN (BC) 230-231 J 2
Mahora o E 98-99 G 5
Mahoua o TCH 206-207 D 3
Mahra, al- ⊥ Y 132-133 G 5
Mahrauni o IND 138-139 G 7
Mahres o TN 190-191 H 3
Mährisch Schönberg = Šumperk o CZ 92-93 O 4
Māhšahr, Bandar-e o IR 134-135 C 3
Mahtowa o USA (MN) 270-271 F 4
Mahūd Budrukh o IND 140-141 F 2
Mahukona o USA (HI) 288 K 4
Mahulu o ZRE 212-213 A 4
Mahuneni o RI 164-165 J 2
Mahur Island ⌒ PNG 183 G 2
Mahuta o WAN 204-205 F 3
Mahuva o IND 138-139 C 9
Maḥwa, al- o KSA 132-133 B 4
Mahwah o IND 138-139 F 6
Mahwit, al- o Y 132-133 C 6
Mahya, Wādi ~ Y 132-133 F 5
Mahzez, Hassi o DZ 188-189 J 6
Mai, Île = Emae ⌒ VAN 184 II b 3
Maiama o PNG 183 D 4
Maiauatá o BR 62-63 K 6
Maibo o TCH 206-207 D 4
Maica, Rivière ~ CDN 38-39 F 4
Maica, Rivière ~ CDN 236-237 M 3
Maicao o CO 60-61 E 2
Maici, Rio ~ BR 66-67 G 6
Maicillar o YV 60-61 G 2
Maicimirim, Rio ~ BR 66-67 F 6
Maicuru, Rio ~ BR 62-63 G 6
Maiden o USA (NC) 282-283 F 5
Maiden, Mount ▲ AUS 176-177 G 3
Maiden Rock o USA (WI) 270-271 F 6
Maidens o USA (VA) 280-281 H 6
Maidens o USA (VA) 280-281 J 6
Maidi o RI 164-165 K 3
Maidi o Y 132-133 C 5
Maidstone o CDN (SAS) 232-233 J 2
Maidstone o GB 90-91 H 6
Maiduguri ☆ WAN 204-205 K 3
Maidūm ∴• ET 194-195 E 3
Maie o ZRE 212-213 C 2
Maiella, la ▲ I 100-101 E 3
Maifa'a o• Y 132-133 E 6
Maigach Mada o SP 212-213 J 2
Maigatari o WAN 198-199 D 6
Maigh Chromtha = Macroom o IRL 90-91 C 6
Maigh Nuad = Maynooth o IRL 90-91 D 5
Maigualida, Sierra de ▲ YV 60-61 J 5
Mai Gudo ▲ ETH 208-209 C 5
Maihar o IND 142-143 B 3
Mainchi o WAN 198-199 C 6
Maijdi o BD 142-143 G 4
Maijia o YV 60-61 K 5
Maijishan Shiku • VRC 154-155 E 4
Maika ~ ZRE 212-213 B 2
Maiko ~ ZRE 210-211 L 4

356 Lyons River North — Maiko

Maiko, Parc National de la ⊥ ZRE 212-213 A 4
Maikonkele o WAN 204-205 G 4
Maikoor, Pulau ∩ RI 166-167 H 5
Mailäni o IND 144-145 C 6
Maillin, Río de ∼ RA 76-77 F 5
Maimana ☆ AFG 136-137 J 7
Maimará o RA 76-77 E 2
Maimilja o RUS 120-121 T 5
Maimón o DOM 54-55 K 5
Maimoon Palace ∴ RI 162-163 C 3
Main ∼ D 92-93 L 3
Main à Dieu o CDN (NS) 240-241 Q 4
Mainau ∼ D 92-93 K 5
Main Brook o CDN (NFL) 242-243 M 1
Main Camp o ZW 218-219 D 4
Main Centre o CDN (SAS) 232-233 L 5
Main Channel ∼ CDN (ONT) 238-239 F 4
Mai-Ndombe, Lac o ZRE 210-211 G 5
Main-Donau-Kanal < D 92-93 L 4
Main Duck Island ∩ CDN (ONT) 238-239 J 5
Maine o USA 278-279 L 4
Maine, Gulf of ≈ 278-279 O 5
Maine TPK II USA (ME) 278-279 L 4
Maing Kwan o MYA 142-143 K 2
Mainistir Fhear Maí = Fermoy ⊥ IRL 90-91 C 5
Mainistir na Búille o IRL 90-91 C 5
Mainistir na Féile = Abbeyfeale o IRL 90-91 C 5
Mainit o RP 160-161 E 8
Mainit o RP (SUN) 160-161 F 8
Mainit, Lake o RP 160-161 F 8
Mainland o CDN (NFL) 242-243 J 4
Mainland o GB 90-91 F 2
Mainling o VRC 144-145 K 6
Mainoru o AUS 174-175 C 4
Main Point o CDN (NFL) 242-243 O 3
Mainpuri o IND 138-139 G 6
Main River ∼ CDN 242-243 L 3
Maintirano o RM 222-223 D 7
Mainz ☆ D 92-93 K 4
Maio, Ilha de ∩ CV 202-203 C 6
Maipo, Río ∼ RCH 78-79 D 2
Maipo, Volcán ▲ RA 78-79 E 3
Maipú o RA 78-79 H 3
Maiquetía o YV 60-61 H 2
Maiquilique o BR 72-73 K 3
Mairana o BOL 70-71 F 6
Mairi o BR 68-69 H 7
Moirinque o BR 72-73 G 7
Mairipotaba o BR 72-73 F 4
Mairi o BR 68-69 H 7
Maïsän II IRQ 128-129 M 7
Maisí o C 54-55 H 4
Maišiagala o LT 94-95 J 4
Maisonnette o CDN (NB) 240-241 K 3
Maitabi, Mount ▲ SOL 184 I e 2
Moitombep o RB 218-219 D 5
Maitén, El o RA 78-79 D 7
Maitland o AUS (NSW) 180-181 L 2
Maitland o AUS (SA) 180-181 D 3
Maitland o CDN (NS) 240-241 M 5
Maitland, Lake o AUS 176-177 H 4
Maitland Range ▲ AUS 172-173 H 3
Maitland River ∼ CDN (ONT) 238-239 D 5
Maitum o RP 160-161 F 9
Maituru o ZRE 212-213 B 2
Maiumo o SUD 200-201 F 6
Maiwa o RI 164-165 F 5
Maiz, Islas del ∩ NIC 52-53 C 5
Maíz Grande, Isla de ∩ NIC 52-53 C 5
Maizho Kunggar o VRC 144-145 H 6
Maíz Pequeña, Isla de ∩ NIC 52-53 C 5
Maizuru o J 152-153 F 7
Maja ∼ RUS 120-121 F 6
Maja ∼ RUS 120-121 G 3
Majačnyj o RUS 96-97 J 7
Majačnyj, mys ▲ RUS 120-121 S 7
Majada o RA 76-77 F 5
Majadas, Las o YV 60-61 J 4
Majagua o C 54-55 F 4
Majahual o MEX 52-53 L 2
Majak o RUS 122-123 G 4
Majalaja o RI 168 B 3
Majalengka o RI 168 C 3
Majda o RUS 88-89 Q 3
Majdanpek o YU 100-101 H 2
Maje o BR 72-73 J 7
Majeicodoteri o YV 60-61 J 6
Majenang o RI 168 C 3
Majene o RI 164-165 E 5
Majestic o CDN (ALB) 232-233 H 5
Majete Game Reserve ⊥ MW 218-219 H 2
Majetú o BOL 70-71 E 3
Majgaon o IND 142-143 C 4
Majgunguna ∼ RUS 116-117 F 4
Majholi o IND 142-143 B 3
Maji o ETH 208-209 B 5
Majiahewan o VRC 154-155 D 3
Majiang o VRC 156-157 E 3
Majirl o RI 164-165 G 5
Majie o VRC 156-157 D 5
Maji Moto o EAT 212-213 E 4
Majla ∼ RUS 120-121 D 3
Majkapcagaj o KZ 124-125 O 5
Majkop ∼ RUS 126-127 C 5
Majli-Saj o KS 136-137 N 4
Majmaga o RUS 118-119 O 4
Majmakan ∼ RUS 120-121 F 5
Majmeča ∼ RUS 108-109 J 6
Majn ∼ RUS 112-113 H 4
Majna ∼ RUS 96-97 F 6
Majnef'tegorn ∼ RUS 112-113 T 5
Majnilnin, Wädí al ∼ LAR 192-193 E 1
Majnskoe ploskogor'e ▲ RUS 112-113 R 4

Major o CDN (SAS) 232-233 J 4
Major Gercino o BR 74-75 F 6
Major Isidoro o BR 68-69 K 4
Major Peak ▲ USA (TX) 266-267 D 3
Majrür, Wádí ∼ SUD 200-201 C 4
Majseevščyna o BY 94-95 L 4
Majskij o USA (AMR) 122-123 C 2
Majskij o RUS (CUK) 112-113 R 2
Majskij o RUS (KAB) 126-127 F 6
Majskij hrebet ▲ RUS 112-113 E 6
Majunga = Mahajanga ☆ RM 222-223 E 6
Majuro ∩ MAI 13 J 2
Maka o LB 202-203 E 6
Maka o SN (FLE) 196-197 B 6
Maka o SN (SO) 202-203 C 3
Maka o SOL 184 I e 3
Makabana o RCB 210-211 D 5
Makacanangano, Pulau ∩ RI 100 D G
Makado o ZW 218-219 E 3
Maka Gouye o SN 202-203 C 3
Makaha o USA (HI) 288 G 3
Makah Indian Reservation ✕ USA (WA) 244-245 A 1
Makak o CAM 204-205 J 5
Makaka o RCB 210-211 D 5
Makalamabedi o RB 218-219 B 5
Makale o EAK 164-165 F 5
Makalondi o RN 202-203 L 3
Makalu ▲ NEP 144-145 F 7
Makamba o BU 212-213 B 6
Makambako o EAT 214-215 H 5
Makanda o RCB 210-211 D 5
Makanza o ZRE 210-211 G 3
Makanza o ZW 218-219 H 1
Makanšy o KZ 124-125 N 5
Makarya o EAT 212-213 E 3
Makapala o USA (HI) 288 K 4
Makapuu Point ▲ USA (HI) 288 H 3
Makar, ostrov ∼ RUS 110-111 W 4
Makarakombu = Mount Popomanaseu ▲ SOL 184 I e 3
Makar'ev o RUS 94-95 S 3
Makarfi o WAN 204-205 G 3
Makari o CAM 198-199 G 6
Makariki o RI 166-167 B 3
Makaroff o CDN (MAN) 234-235 B 3
Makarora o NZ 182 B 6
Makarov o RUS 122-123 K 4
Makarova, ostrov ∼ RUS 108-109 Z 3
Makarov Basin ≃ 16 A 35
Makarov Dvor o RUS 88-89 Q 6
Makarovo o RUS 122-123 Q 4
Makarovo o RUS 116-117 N 7
Makarska o HR 100-101 F 3
Makasa o Z 214-215 F 5
Makasar = Ujung Pandang ☆ RI 164-165 E 6
Makassar = Ujung Pandang ☆ RI 104 100 f 0
Makassar Strait = Makasar, Selat ≈ 164-165 E 5
Makasse ∼ SP 212-213 J 3
Makat o KZ 96-97 H 10
Makawao o USA (HI) 288 J 4
Makay ▲ RM 222-223 D 8
Makedonia = GR 100 100 H 4
Makeevka = Makijivka o UA 102-103 L 3
Makokoda o ZRE 212-213 A 2
Makeni o WAL 202-203 D 4
Makere o EAT 212-213 G 6
Makgadikgadi ∼ RB 218-219 C 5
Makgadikgadi Pans Game Park ⊥ RB 218-219 C 5
Makhaleng ∼ LS 220-221 H 5
Makhdumnagar o IND 142-143 C 2
Makhtal o IND 140-141 G 2
Mokhu o IND 138-139 E 4
Maki o RI 166-167 H 3
Makian, Pulau ∼ RI 164-165 K 3
Makijivka o UA 102-103 L 3
Makira o SOL 184 I e 3
Makinak o CDN (MAN) 234 236 D 4
Maki National Park ⊥ ETH 208-209 C 4
Maklinat Sihan o OM 132-133 H 5
Makinda o EAT 212-213 G 6
Makindu o EAK 212-213 F 5
Makinsk o KZ 124-125 G 2
Makinson Inlet ≈ 24-25 f 2
Makira, Lembalemban'i ▲ RM 222-223 F 5
Makiri, Danau o RI 166-167 G 2
Makijvka = Makijivka o UA 102-103 L 3
Makka ⊡ KSA 132-133 B 3
Makka = Makka ☆ KSA 132-133 A 3
Mak-Klintoka, ostrov ∼ RUS 84-85 a 2
Makkovik o CDN 36-37 U 7
Makkovik Bay ≈ 36-37 U 7
Makmín, al- o IRQ 128-129 K 7
Makó o H 92-93 G 5
Mako o SN 202-203 D 3
Makogai ∼ FJI 184 III b 2
Makokibatan Lake o CDN (ONT) 234-235 Q 3
Makokou ∼ G 210-211 D 3
Makonde Plateau ▲ EAT 214-215 K 6
Makongo o GA 202-203 H 5
Makongolosi o EAT 214-215 G 5
Makoop Lake o CDN 34-35 L 4
Makor o CAM 204-205 K 5
Makoro o ZRE 212-213 B 2
Makosa o ZRE 214-215 E 4
Makotipoko o RCB 210-211 E 4
Makou o ZRE 210-211 D 4
Makoua o TCH 206-207 D 5
Makoubi o RCB 210-211 D 5
Makovo o RUS 96-97 F 10
Makovskaja ∼ RUS 96-97 G 8
Makovskoe, ozero o RUS 108-109 V 8
Makrån Coast Range ▲ PK 134-135 H 6
Maks al-Qiblï, Manzil ∼ ET 194-195 E 5
Maksatiha o RUS 94-95 O 3
Maksimova o RUS 116-117 M 7

Maksimovka o RUS 118-119 E 6
Maksudangarh o IND 138-139 F 7
Maktau o IND 138-139 C 8
Makthar o TN 190-191 G 3
Maklû o IR 128-129 L 3
Makuende o ZRE 214-215 E 4
Makulakubu o ZRE 214-215 C 5
Makunduchi o EAT 214-215 H 6
Makung o RC 156-157 L 5
Makungo o SP 212-213 H 3
Makungo o EAT 214-215 H 5
Makunguwiro o EAT 214-215 H 6
Makuracaki o J 152-153 D 9
Makurdi ☆ WAN 204-205 H 5
Makuru o WAN 184 II b 3
Makushin Bay ≈ 22-23 N 6
Makushin Volcano ▲ USA 22-23 N 6
Makutano o EAK (EAS) 212-213 F 4
Makutano o EAK (RIF) 212-213 F 5
Makuti o ZW 218-219 E 3
Makuyuni o EAT 212-213 F 4
Makwate o RB 218-219 D 6
Makwiro o ZW 218-219 F 3
Mal o IND 142-143 F 2
Mâl o RIM 196-197 O 6
Mala o PE 64-65 D 8
Mala = Mallow ⊥ IRL 90-91 C 5
Mala, Río de ∼ PE 64-65 D 8
Malaba o EAK 212-213 E 3
Malabang o RP 160-161 F 9
Malabar o SY 212-213 J 3
Malabo ★ GQ 210-211 B 2
Malabo o RI 164-165 F 5
Malabrigo, Punta ∼ PE 64-65 C 5
Malabungan o RP 160-161 B 8
Malabwe o Z 218-219 C 3
Malacacheta o BR 72-73 J 4
Malaca o IND 140-141 G 4
Malachi o CDN (ONT) 234-235 J 5
Malacky o SK 92-93 O 4
Malacura o AUS 174-175 G 6
Malad ▲ ER 200-201 J 4
Mala City o USA (ID) 252-253 F 4
Maladzečna o BY 94-95 K 4
Málaga o CO 60-61 E 4
Málaga o E 98-99 E 6
Málaga o USA (NM) 256-257 L 6
Malagarasi o EAT (KIC) 212-213 C 6
Malagarasi ∼ EAT 212-213 C 6
Malagueta, Punta ∼ PE 64-65 C 6
Malah, Chott el ∼ DZ 190-191 E 4
Maláha, al- o KSA 132-133 C 5
Malahajtari ∼ RUS 108-109 g 4
Malahar o RI 168 E 7
Malohot ∼ RUS (WC) 120-221 F 6
Maláhit, al- o Y 132-133 C 5
Malaimbandy o RM 222-223 D 8
Malei o MOC 218-219 J 2
Maleit o SUD 206-207 J 5
Malek o SUD 206-207 K 5
Malekkandi o IR 128-129 M 4
Malélé o RCB 210-211 D 6
Malema o MOC 218-219 J 2
Malé Malé o PNG 183 F 2
Malembo-Nkulu o ZRE 214-215 D 5
Malomba Hodar o SN 202 203 C 2
Malena ∼ RA 70 70 Q 3
Malendo, River ∼ WAN 204-205 H 3
Malendok Island ∼ PNG 183 G 2
Malen'ga o RUS 88-89 O 5
Malonga o ZRE 214-215 D 6
Male polissja ∼ UA 102-103 C 2
Mâlestân o AFG 134-135 M 2
Maleta Lake o CDN 30-31 U 7
Malewâra o IND 142-143 H 4
Malfa o I 100-101 E 5
Malgis o EAK 212-213 F 3
Malgobek o RUS 126-127 F 6
Malgrat de Mar o E 98-99 J 4
Malha o SUD 200-201 C 5
Malhada o BR 72-73 J 3
Malheur Lake o USA (OR) 244-245 D 2
Malheur National Wildlife Refuge ⊥ USA (OR) 244-245 D 2
Malheur River ∼ USA 244-245 D 2
Malí o RA 70-71 J 4
Mali o LB 202-203 F 6
Mali o RG 202-203 D 3
Mali o RMM 202-203 G 2
Mali ★ RMM 202-203 G 2
Mali o ZRE 210-211 L 5
Maliana o RI 166-167 G 6
Maliça o BR 68-69 F 6
Malifut o RI 164-165 K 3
Maligayo o RP 160-161 D 5
Malignant Cove o CDN (NS) 240-241 N 4
Maligne River ∼ CDN 228-229 R 4
Mali K. o MYA 158-159 E 4
Malili o RI 164-165 G 5
Mÿlilla o S 86-87 G 8
Mali Lošinj o HR 100-101 E 2
Malima ∼ FJI 184 III c 2
Malimán de Abajo o RA 76-77 C 5
Malimba o PNG (MAD) 183 C 3
Malán, Rås ▲ PK 134-135 L 6
Malinda o AUS 174-175 H 5
Malingdi o ZRE 210-211 J 6
Malandy Hill ▲ AUS 176-177 D 4
Malin Head ▲ IRL 90-91 D 4
Maline ∼ SN 202-203 D 3
Malino o RI (SLT) 164-165 G 4
Malino o RI (SSE) 164-165 F 6
Malino, Gunung ▲ RI 164-165 G 4
Malinovka o RUS (KMR) 124-125 P 2
Malinovka o RUS 122-123 F 6
Malinyjl o EAT 214-215 J 5
Maliom o PNG 183 D 5
Malipo o VRC 156-157 D 5
Malio o AL 100-101 H 4
Malaran o RA 76-77 D 6
Mali Rajinac ▲ HR 100-101 E 2

Malapatan o RP 160-161 F 10
Malapati Safari Area ⊥ ZW 218-219 F 5
Malappuram o IND 140-141 G 5
Malár o PK 134-135 L 6
Malarba o CAM 204-205 K 5
Malargüe o RA 78-79 E 3
Malargüe, Río ∼ RA 78-79 E 3
Malartic o CDN (QUE) 236-237 K 4
Malartic, Lac o CDN (QUE) 236-237 L 4
Malasait o PNG 183 F 3
Malaso o RI 164-165 F 5
Malaspina Glacier ⊂ USA 20-21 U 7
Malata, Lake o AUS 180-181 C 3
Malatayur, Tanjung ▲ RI 162-163 K 6
Malatya o TR 128-129 H 3
Malaulalo Island ∼ SOL 184 I e 4
Malaut o IND 138-139 E 4
Malavali o IND 140-141 G 4
Malávi o IR 134-135 B 2
Malawali, Pulau ∼ MAL 160-161 B 9
Malawi, Lake o MW 214-215 H 6
Malawi National Park, Lake ⊥ ∴ MW 218-219 H 1
Malay o RP 160-161 E 7
Malay Balay ☆ RP 160-161 F 8
Maláyer o IR 134-135 C 1
Malay Peninsula = Semenanjung Malaysia ⊂ MAL 162-163 E 2
Malaysia ■ MAL 162-163 E 2
Malazgirt o TR 128-129 K 3
Malbaie, La o CDN (QUE) 240-241 E 3
Malbaza o RN 198-199 B 6
Malbhanguwa o NEP 144-145 C 6
Malbon o AUS 178-179 F 1
Malbon Vale o AUS 178-179 E 1
Malboorna o AUS 178-179 C 6
Malbork o PL 92-93 P 1
Malbrán o RA 76-77 F 5
Malcolm o AUS 176-177 F 4
Malcolm o USA (NE) 262-263 K 4
Malcolm River ∼ CDN 20-21 V 2
Malcom, Point ▲ AUS 176-177 G 6
Malden o USA (MO) 276-277 F 4
Maldin o AUS 180-181 H 4
Maldive Islands = Maldives ∩ MV 140-141 B 7
Maldives ∩ MV 140-141 B 6
Maldon o AUS 180-181 H 4
Maldonado o EC 64-65 C 1
Maldonado o ROU 78-79 M 3
Maldonado, Punta ▲ MEX 52-53 E 3
Male ★ MV 140-141 B 5
Male, Lac du o CDN (QUE) 236-237 N 4
Malea, Gunung ▲ RI 162-163 C 4
Maleb o CDN (ALB) 232-233 G 6
Malegaon o IND (MAH) 138-139 E 9
Mâlegaon o IND (MAH) 138-139 F 9
Malei o MOC 218-219 J 2
Maleit o SUD 206-207 J 5
Malole o Z 214-215 G 5
Malolo ∼ FJI 184 III a 2
Malolo o RI 166-167 F 2
Malolotha Nature Reserve ⊥ SD 220-221 K 3
Malom o PNG 183 F 2
Malombe, Lake o MW 218-219 H 2
Malonda o ZRE 214-215 C 5
Malone o USA (NY) 278-279 G 4
Malone o USA (TX) 266-267 L 2
Malone, Lake o USA (KY) 276-277 H 3
Malonga o ZRE 214-215 D 6
Malott o USA (WA) 244-245 D 1
Maloti ∼ RUS 88-89 U 5
Malott ∼ USA (WA) 244 245 D 1
Malozemel'skaja tundra ∼ RUS 88-89 U 3
Malozujka o RUS 88-89 O 5
Malozujka ∼ RUS 88-89 O 5
Malpas Hut o AUS 174-175 G 6
Malpelo, Punta ▲ PE 64-65 B 3
Malpeque o CDN (PEI) 240-241 M 4
Malpeque Bay ≈ 38-39 N 5
Malpica (Malpica de Bergantiños) o E 98-99 C 3
Malprabha ∼ IND 140-141 F 2
Mâlpura o IND 138-139 F 6
Malšúniyah, al- o KSA 130-131 L 5
Malta ▲ LV 94-95 K 3
Malta o M 100-101 E 7
Malta o BR 68-69 K 5
Malta o RI 166-167 G 6
Malta ∼ M 100-101 E 7
Malta o USA (ID) 252-253 F 4
Malta o USA (MT) 250-251 M 3
Maltahöhe o NAM 220-221 C 2
Maltais o CDN (NB) 240-241 J 3
Maltam o CAM 198-199 G 6
Maltan ∼ RUS 120-121 D 3
Maltee o AUS 180-181 B 2
Malton o GB 90-91 G 4
Maluera o MOC 218-219 G 2
Maluku o RI 166-167 H 2
Malúkú ∼ RI 166-167 H 2
Malumfashi o WAN 204-205 G 3
Malunda o RI 164-165 F 5
Malung o S 86-87 F 6
Malungwishi o ZRE 214-215 D 6
Malur o IND 140-141 G 4
Malůt o SUD 206-207 L 3
Maluti Mountains ▲ LS 220-221 H 5
Maluu o SOL 184 I e 3
Mâlvan o IND 140-141 E 2
Malvas ∼ PE 64-65 D 6
Malverick ∼ MW 218-219 G 1
Malvern o USA (AR) 276-277 C 6
Malvern o USA (IA) 262-263 K 4
Malvern o USA (TX) 268-269 E 5
Malvinas, Islas = Falkland Islands ∩ GB 78-79 L 6
Malwal o SUD 206-207 K 4
Malya o EAT 212-213 E 3
Malyinyl o EAT 214-215 J 5
Malyo o RI 166-167 G 6
Malye Čany ozero o RUS 124-125 K 1
Malye Donki ozero o RUS 108-109 a 4
Malygina, proliv ≈ 108-109 O 5

Malita o RP 160-161 F 9
Malitbog o RP 160-161 F 7
Maliva o IND 138-139 C 8
Mÿlwa o IND 138-139 C 8
Maljamar o USA (NM) 256-257 M 6
Malka o PK 134-135 L 6
Malka o RUS 126-127 E 6
Malkangiri o IND 142-143 C 3
Malkapur o IND (MAH) 138-139 F 9
Malkapur o IND 140-141 G 2
Malkara o TR 128-129 B 2
Malkinskij hrebet ▲ RUS 120-121 R 7
Malko Tǎrnovo o BG 102-103 E 7
Malla o IND 140-141 G 2
Mallacoota o AUS 180-181 K 4
Mallacoota Inlet ≈ AUS 180-181 K 4
Mallaig o GB 90-91 E 3
Mallam o NEP 198-199 D 6
Mallapuniyah o AUS 174-175 C 5
Mallawi o ET 194-195 E 4
Mallawiya o SUD 200-201 H 5
Malleco, Río ∼ RCH 78-79 C 5
Mallee Cliffs National Park ⊥ AUS 180-181 G 3
Mallen, laguna ≈ 112-113 S 6
Malleo, Río ∼ RA 78-79 D 6
Mallery Lake o CDN 30-31 U 3
Mallina o AUS 172-173 D 6
Mallin Grande, Cerro ▲ RA 78-79 D 6
Malloch, Cape ▲ CDN 24-25 Q 1
Mallorca ∼ E 98-99 J 5
Mallorytown o CDN (ONT) 238-239 K 4
Mallow = Mala o IRL 90-91 C 5
Malm o N 86-87 E 4
Malmal o PNG 183 D 5
Málmand, Kúh-e ▲ AFG 134-135 K 2
Malmberget o∴ S 86-87 K 3
Malmédy o B 92-93 J 3
Malmesbury o ZA 220-221 C 6
Malmo o CDN (MN) 270-271 E 4
Malmö o∴ S 86-87 F 9
Malmyž o RUS 96-97 G 5
Malo ∼ VAN 184 II e 1
Maloaini o SOL 184 I e 4
Maloarhangel'sk o RUS 94-95 O 6
Maloca Grande o BR 62-63 G 5
Maloca do Gonçalo o BR 66-67 J 6
Maloca Velha o BR 62-63 G 4
Maloconan o RP 160-161 E 8
Malocu Macu o BR 60-61 K 6
Maloe o PE 64-65 D 6
Maloe Hantajskoe, ozero o RUS 108-109 X 7
Maloe Jamnoe ozero o∼ RUS 124-125 L 2
Malojaz o RUS 96-97 L 6
Malokuril'skoe o RUS 122-123 M 7
Malole o FJI 184 III a 2
Malolo o RI 166-167 F 2
Malom o PNG 183 F 2
Malombo o∼ MOC 218-219 H 2
Malombe, Lake o∼ MW 218-219 H 2
Malonda o ZRE 214-215 C 5
Malone o USA (NY) 278-279 G 4
Malou o PNG 183 D 5
Malpica (Malpica de Bergantiños) o E 98-99 C 3
Malpon o AUS 178-179 E 1
Malpeque o CDN (PEI) 240-241 M 4
Malytinskij, zaliv ≈ RUS 120-121 S 6
Malyi Sarykul ozero o RUS 96-97 M 6
Malyj Abakan ∼ RUS 124-125 Q 3
Malyj Abakan ∼ RUS 124-125 Q 3
Malyj Aim ∼ RUS 120-121 E 4
Malyj Amalat ∼ RUS 118-119 F 8
Malyj Ases'egan ∼ RUS 114-115 S 4
Malyj Begičev, ostrov ∼ RUS 110-111 X 2
Malyj Čaun ∼ RUS 112-113 Q 2
Malyj Čaunskij, proliv ≈ 112-113 O 2
Malyj Enisej ∼ RUS 116-117 H 10
Malyj Hamar-Daban, hrebet ▲ RUS 116-117 L 10
Malyj Jugan ∼ RUS 114-115 N 5
Malyj Karmakuly o RUS 108-109 E 5
Malyj Kas ∼ RUS 114-115 O 4
Malyj Kavkaz ▲ GE 126-127 D 7
Malyj Kemčug ∼ RUS 116-117 F 7
Malyj Kemčug ∼ RUS 116-117 F 7
Malyj Ljahovskij, ostrov ∼ RUS 110-111 W 2
Malyj Majn ∼ RUS 112-113 Q 4
Malyj Megtyg'egan ∼ RUS 114-115 Q 4
Malyj Naryn ∼ KS 146-147 C 5
Malyj Nimnyr ∼ RUS (SAH) 118-119 X 9
Malyj Nimnyr ∼ RUS 118-119 M 7
Malyj Ofdoj ∼ RUS 118-119 L 8
Malyj Olër, ozero o RUS 112-113 J 2
Malyj Salym ∼ RUS 114-115 L 4
Malyj Šantar, ostrov ∼ RUS 120-121 G 6
Malyj Sarykul'gorom o RUS 96-97 M 6
Malyj Semljačik, vulkan ▲ RUS 120-121 S 6
Malyj Tagul ∼ RUS 116-117 H 8
Malyj Turtas ∼ RUS 114-115 L 5
Malyj Urkan ∼ RUS 118-119 M 8
Malyj Uzen' ∼ RUS 96-97 G 8
Malyj Uzen' ∼ RUS 96-97 G 8
Malyj Van'kin, mys ▲ RUS 110-111 Y 3
Malyk, ozero o RUS 120-121 M 2
Malyn o UA 102-103 F 3
Malyj Kavkaz = Malyj Kavkaz ▲ GE 126-127 D 7
Mama o RUS (IRK) 118-119 F 6
Mama o RUS 118-119 F 7
Mama, Río ∼ BR 66-67 J 5
Mamadyš o RUS 96-97 G 5
Mombe, Ana o BR 66-67 J 5
Mamaj, kóli ∼ KZ 124-125 G 2
Mamakan o RUS (IRK) 118-119 G 7
Mamakan ∼ RUS 118-119 F 7
Mamallapuram o ∼ IND 140-141 J 4
Maman o PE 64-65 D 6
Mamana Island = Rum Cay ∼ BS 54-55 H 3
Mamanguape o BR 68-69 L 5
Mamanuka Group ∼ FJI 184 III a 2
Mamari o SN 202-203 D 3
Mamasa o RI 164-165 F 5
Mamasiware o RI 166-167 H 3
Mamawi Lake o CDN 30-31 O 6
Mambajao o RP 160-161 F 8
Mambal o CAM 204-205 K 5
Mambaí o BR 72-73 G 3
Mambasa o ZRE 212-213 B 3
Mambeco o MOC 218-219 G 6
Mambenga o ZRE 210-211 G 4
Mamberamo ∼ RI 166-167 J 3
Momberamo-Foja Mountains-Rouffaer Reserves ⊥ RI 166-167 K 3
Mamberano o RI 166-167 J 3
Mambéré ∼ RCA 206-207 C 6
Mambéré-Kadéï ⊡ RCA 206-207 C 6
Mambili ∼ RCB 210-211 E 3
Mambilima Falls o∴ Z 214-215 E 6
Mambonde o ANG 216-217 C 7
Mamboor, Kepulauan ∼ RI 166-167 H 3
Mamborê o BR 74-75 D 5
Mambova Rapids o∼ Z 218-219 C 3
Mambrui o EAK 212-213 H 5
Mamburao o RP 160-161 D 6
Mambwe o Z 214-215 F 5
Mamcai o RI 166-167 H 2
Ma-Me-O-Beach o CDN (ALB) 232-233 E 4
Mamelodi o ZA 220-221 J 2
Mametčinskij, poluostrov ∼ RUS 120-121 S 6
Mametčinskij, zaliv ≈ RUS 120-121 S 6
Mamfé o CAM 204-205 H 5
Mâmi, Ra's ▲ Y 132-133 J 7
Mamiá, Lago o BR 66-67 F 5
Mamiña o RCH 70-71 E 8
Mamit o RI 166-167 H 3
Mamisonski, pereval ∴ GE 126-127 E 6
Mamljutka o KZ 124-125 F 1
Mamma Hawa o CDN (ONT) 236-237 D 2
Mammoth o USA (AZ) 256-257 F 6
Mammoth Cave National Park ⊥ ∴ ∴ USA (KY) 276-277 J 3
Mammoth Hot Springs o USA (WY) 252-253 H 2
Mammoth Spring o USA (AR) 276-277 D 4
Mamoadate, Áreas Indígenas ✕ BR 70-71 B 7
Mamoeiro o BR 66-67 C 7
Mamoiron o RUS 94-95 H 4
Mamonta o RUS 108-109 a 4
Mamonta, poluostrov ∼ RUS 108-109 R 6
Mamonta gora ∴ RUS 120-121 F 2

Mamontovaja ∼ RUS 112-113 U 3
Mamontovo o RUS (ALT) 124-125 M 2
114-115 M 4
Mamoré ∼ BOL 70-71 E 3
Mamori, Lago o BR 66-67 G 4
Mamori, Paraná do ∼ BR 66-67 H 4
Mamoriá o BR 66-67 E 6
Mamoriazinho, Rio ∼ BR 66-67 E 6
Mamou o RG 202-203 D 4
Mamou o USA (LA) 268-269 H 6
Mamoun, Lac o RCA 206-207 F 3
Mampikony o RM 222-223 E 6
Mampong o GH 202-203 K 6
Ma Mrě o VN 158-159 J 5
Mamry, Jezioro o PL 92-93 Q 1
Mamu o RI 164-165 F 4
Mamu o WAN 204-205 E 5
Mamuju o RI 164-165 F 5
Mamûnïye o IR 136-137 F 11
Mamuno o RB 216-217 F 11
Mamure Kalesi ∴ TR 128-129 E 4
Mamuru, Rio ∼ BR 66-67 J 4
Mamutzu o COM 222-223 E 8
Man o CI 202-203 G 6
Man o RCA 206-207 B 7
Man, Río ∼ PE 64-65 F 7
Mana o E 62-63 H 3
Mana ∼ FJI 184 III a 2
Mana ∼ RUS 116-117 F 8
Mana o USA (HI) 288 F 2
Manacacias, Río ∼ CO 60-61 E 6
Manacapurú o BR 66-67 G 4
Manacapurú, Rio ∼ BR 66-67 G 4
Manacas o C 54-55 E 3
Manacor o E 98-99 J 5
Manádir, al- ∴ UAE 132-133 J 2
Manakara o RI 164-165 J 3
Manaffey o COM 222-223 E 8
Managua ★ NIC 52-53 B 4
Managua, Lago de o NIC 52-53 L 5
Manâha o Y 132-133 C 6
Manaia o BR 68-69 F 5
Manajuare o CO 60-61 F 5
Manakana o RM 222-223 E 6
Manakara o RM 222-223 E 7
Manalalondo o RM 222-223 E 7
Manali o IND 138-139 F 3
Manama o UAE 134-135 G 6
Manama o ZW 218-219 E 5
Manáma, al- ★ BRN 134-135 D 6
Mânâmadural o IND 140-141 H 6
Manambaho ∼ RM 222-223 D 6
Manambato o RM 222-223 E 10
Manambolo ∼ RM 222-223 D 7
Mamambulusy o RM 222-223 F 9
Manambondro o RM 222-223 E 9
Manambovo ∼ RM 222-223 D 10
Manamgoora o AUS 174-175 D 5
Manami o RI 166-167 G 6
Manam Isiand o PNG 183 C 3
Manamo, Caño ∼ YV 60-61 K 3
Manamparana ∼ RM 222-223 E 9
Mananá, Cachoeira ∼ BR 62-63 H 4
Mananantanana ∼ RM 222-223 E 8
Mananara ∼ RM 222-223 E 9
Mananara Avaratra o RM 222-223 F 6
Manandona o RM 222-223 E 8
Manangatang o AUS 180-181 G 3
Mananjary o RM (FNS) 222-223 F 8
Mananjary o RM 222-223 E 8
Manankoro o RMM 202-203 G 4
Manantali, Lac de < RMM 202-203 E 3
Manantenina o RM 222-223 E 10
Manantoddy o IND 140-141 G 5
Mana Pass ▲ VRC 144-145 B 5
Mana Pools National Park ⊥ ∴ ∴ ZW 218-219 E 2
Monapoun, Lake o NZ 182 A 6
Manappârai o IND 140-141 H 5
Manar o BR 66-67 G 4
Manaquiri, Lago o BR 66-67 G 4
Manari o PNG 183 D 5
Manariá o BR 66-67 G 4
Manas o PE 64-65 F 4
Manas o VRC 146-147 H 3
Manas, gora ▲ KS 136-137 M 3
Manasarowar = Mapam Yumco o VRC 144-145 C 5
Manas He ∼ VRC 146-147 G 3
Manas Hu o VRC 146-147 H 3
Manaslu ▲ NEP 144-145 E 6
Manassa o USA (CO) 254-255 K 6
Manassas o USA (VA) 280-281 J 5
Manassas National Battlefield Park ∴ USA (VA) 280-281 J 5
Mânăstire Horezu ∴ ∴ RO 102-103 C 5
Manastir Morača ∴ YU 100-101 G 3
Manastir Ostrog ∴ YU 100-101 G 3
Manas Wildlife Sanctuary ∴ ∴ IND 142-143 G 2
Manatee, Lake < USA (FL) 286-287 G 4
Manatee River ∼ USA 286-287 G 4
Manati o C 54-55 F 4
Manati o C 54-55 G 4
Manati o USA (PR) 286-287 P 4
Manatuto o RI 166-167 G 6
Manau o PNG 183 D 5
Man'aung o MYA 142-143 H 6
Man'aung Kyûn ∼ MYA 142-143 H 6
Manaure o CO 60-61 F 2
Manaus ☆ BR 66-67 G 4
Manavgat ★ TR 128-129 D 4
Manawokka, Pulau ∼ RI 166-167 G 9
Mañazo o PE 70-71 E 7
Mânbazâr o IND 142-143 E 4
Manbij ★ SYR 126-129 G 4
Manbirl o RMM 202-203 H 2
Manby, Halvø ∼ GRØ 26-27 U 9
Mancelona o USA (MI) 272-273 O 3
Mancha, La o E 98-99 F 5

Manchao, Sierra de ▲ RA 76-77 D 5
Manchar o IND 138-139 D 10
Manche = English Channel ≈ 90-91 F 6
Mancheng Hanmu ∴ • VRC 154-155 J 2
Mancherāl o IND 138-139 G 10
Manchester o • GB 90-91 F 5
Manchester o USA (CT) 280-281 O 2
Manchester o USA (GA) 284-285 F 4
Manchester o USA (IA) 274-275 G 2
Manchester o USA (KY) 276-277 M 3
Manchester o USA (NH) 278-279 K 6
Manchester o USA (OH) 280-281 C 5
Manchester o USA (TN) 276-277 J 5
Manchester o USA (VT) 278-279 H 5
Manchester o USA (WI) 270-271 J 7
Manchester Lake o CDN 30-31 Q 5
Manchhar Lake o • PK 134-135 M 5
Manchioneal o JA 54-55 G 5
Manchok o WAN 204-205 H 4
Manchuria = Dongbei ⊥ VRC 150-151 E 6
Manciano o I 100-101 C 3
Máncora o PE 64-65 B 4
Mancos o USA (CO) 254-255 G 6
Mancos River ~ USA 254-255 G 6
Mand o PK 134-135 K 5
Mand, Rūd-e ~ IR 134-135 D 4
Manda o EAT (IRI) 214-215 H 6
Manda o EAT (MBE) 214-215 G 4
Manda o ETH 200-201 L 6
Manda o TCH 206-207 D 4
Manda, Parc National de ⊥ TCH 206-207 C 4
Mandabe o RM 222-223 D 8
Mandacaru o BR 68-69 G 3
Mandaguari o BR 72-73 E 7
Mandah = Töhöm o MAU 148-149 J 5
Manda Island ⌒ EAK 212-213 H 5
Mandal ☆ N 86-87 C 7
Mandala, Puncak ▲ RI 166-167 L 4
Mandalay ☆ •• MYA 142-143 K 4
Mandalgov' ☆ MAU 148-149 H 5
Mandalī ☆ IRQ 128-129 L 6
Mandal-Ovoo = Šarhulsan o MAU 148-149 G 5
Mandalselva ~ N 86-87 C 7
Mandan o • USA (ND) 258-259 G 5
Mandaon o RP 160-161 E 6
Mandar, Teluk ≈ 164-165 F 5
Mandara Mountains ▲ WAN 204-205 K 3
Mandarin o USA (FL) 286-287 H 1
Mandas o I 100-101 B 5
Mandasor o IND 138-139 E 7
Mandaue o RP 160-161 E 7
Mandélia o TCH 206-207 B 3
Mandera o EAK 212-213 H 2
Manderson o USA (WY) 252-253 L 2
Mandeville o • JA 54-55 G 5
Mandeville o USA (LA) 268-269 K 6
Mandheera o SP 208-209 G 4
Mandi o • IND 138-139 F 4
Mandi, Raudal ~ CO 66-67 B 2
Mandiakui o RMM 202-203 H 3
Mandiana o RG 202-203 F 4
Mandiangin o RI 162-163 C 5
Mandi Bahāuddin o PK 138-139 D 3
Mandi Burewāla o PK 138-139 D 4
Mandié o MOC 218-219 G 3
Mandi Langwé ▲ CAM 204-205 J 6
Mandimba o MOC 218-219 H 2
Mandingues, Monts ▲ RMM 202-203 F 3
Mandioli, Pulau ⌒ RI 164-165 K 4
Mandioré, Lago o BOL 70-71 J 6
Mandirituba o BR 74-75 F 5
Mandji o G 210-211 C 4
Mandla o IND 142-143 B 4
Mandleshwar o IND 138-139 E 8
Mando o WAN 204-205 G 3
Mandōl o AFG 136-137 M 7
Mandon o RI 166-167 J 2
Mandor o RI 162-163 H 4
Mandora o AUS 172-173 E 5
Mandori o RI 166-167 H 2
Mandoro o ZRE 206-207 J 6
Mandoto o RM 222-223 E 7
Mandoul ~ TCH 206-207 C 4
Mandouri o RT 202-203 L 4
Mandra o PK 138-139 D 3
Mandrare ~ RM 222-223 E 10
Mandrikovo o RUS 112-113 K 3
Mandritsara o RM 222-223 F 5
Mandronarivo o RM 222-223 D 8
Mandrosonoro o RM 222-223 E 8
Mandu o IND 142-143 D 4
Mandul, Pulau ⌒ RI 164-165 E 2
Mandumbua o ANG 216-217 F 7
Mandurah o • AUS 176-177 C 6
Mandúria o I 100-101 F 4
Mandūzāi o AFG 138-139 B 3
Māndvi o IND (GUJ) 138-139 D 9
Māndvi o IND (GUJ) 138-139 B 8
Mandya o IND 140-141 G 4
Mané o BF 202-203 K 3
Maneadero o C 54-55 E 3
Maneadero o MEX 50-51 A 2
Mané Kondjo ~ TCH 206-207 D 3
Manengouba, Massif du ▲ CAM 204-205 H 6
Manerornango o EAT 214-215 K 4
Manes o USA (MO) 276-277 C 3
Manevyči o UA 102-103 D 2
Manfalūt o ET 194-195 E 4
Manflas, Río ~ RCH 76-77 C 5
Manfran o RG 202-203 F 5
Manfred Downs o AUS 174-175 F 7
Manfredónia o I 100-101 E 4
Manfredónia, Golfo di ≈ 100-101 F 4
Manga o BF 202-203 K 4
Manga o BR 72-73 J 3
Manga ▲ CAM 204-205 K 5
Manga o PNG 183 G 3
Manga ⊥ RN 198-199 F 6
Mangabeiras, Chapada das ▲ BR 68-69 E 6
Mangada o ZRE 212-213 A 2
Manga Grande o ANG 216-217 B 3
Mangai o PNG 183 F 2
Mangaïzé o RN 202-203 L 2
Mangalia o • RO 102-103 F 6
Mangalmé o TCH 198-199 J 6
Mangalore o AUS 178-179 J 4
Mangalore o • IND 140-141 F 4
Mangalwedha o IND 140-141 F 2
Mangango o Z 218-219 C 2
Māngaon o IND 138-139 D 10
Mangareva, Île ⌒ F 13 O 5
Mangareva Inseln ⌒ F 13 O 5
Mangas o USA (NM) 256-257 J 4
Mangatupopo o NZ 182 E 3
Mangawan o IND 142-143 B 3
Mangaweka ▲ NZ 182 F 3
Mangbwalu o ZRE 212-213 C 3
Mangdangshan • VRC 154-155 K 4
Măng Đen, Đèo ▲ VN 158-159 K 3
Mange o PNG 183 D 4
Mange o WAL 202-203 D 5
Mangeni, Hamada ⊥ RN 192-193 E 6
Manggar o RI 162-163 H 6
Manggasi o RI 166-167 J 3
Manggawitu o RI 166-167 G 4
Mangguar, Tanjung ▲ RI 166-167 H 3
Mangham o USA (LA) 268-269 J 4
Mangisor, kōli o KZ 124-125 F 1
Mangistau, gory ▲ KZ 126-127 J 5
Mangit ☆ UZ 136-137 G 3
Mangkalihat, Tanjung ▲ RI 164-165 F 3
Mangkok, Tanjung ▲ RI 164-165 E 5
Mangkutana o RI 164-165 G 5
Manglares o CO 60-61 C 5
Manglares, Cabo ▲ CO 64-65 C 1
Manglares, Punta ▲ CO 60-61 C 5
Manglares Churute, Reservat E. ⊥ EC 64-65 C 3
Mangla Reservoir < PK 138-139 D 3
Mangnai o VRC 144-145 H 2
Mangnai Zhen o VRC 146-147 K 6
Mangnuc, Lac o CDN 36-37 L 5
Mango ⌒ TON 184 IV a 2
Mangoaka o RM 222-223 F 4
Mangochi o • MW 218-219 H 2
Mango Creek o BH 52-53 K 3
Mangodara o BF 202-203 H 5
Mangoky ~ RM 222-223 D 8
Mangoky ~ RM 222-223 D 9
Mangole, Pulau ⌒ RI 164-165 J 4
Mangole, Selat ≈ 164-165 J 4
Mangom o CAM 204-205 K 5
Mangombe o ZRE 210-211 L 4
Mangonui o NZ 182 D 1
Mangoro ~ RM 222-223 F 7
Mangowra o AUS 174-175 F 5
Māngrol o IND 138-139 C 9
Mangrullo, Cuchilla de ▲ ROU 74-75 D 9
Mangrūl Pīr o IND 138-139 F 9
Mangshan • VRC 154-155 H 4
Mangu o EAK 212-213 F 4
Manguaurcu o EC 64-65 B 4
Mangūchar o PK 134-135 M 4
Mangue o BR 68-69 F 2
Mangueigne o TCH 206-207 E 3
Mangueira, Lagoa o BR 74-75 D 9
Mangueirinha o BR 74-75 D 5
Manguel Creek o AUS 172-173 F 4
Mangues, Rio dos ~ BR 68-69 D 7
Mangue Seco o BR 68-69 K 7
Mangues Secos, Ponta dos ▲ BR 68-69 G 3
Mangui o VRC 150-151 D 1
Manguito o C 54-55 E 3
Mangum o USA (OK) 264-265 E 4
Mangunça o BR 68-69 F 2
Mangunca, Ilha ⌒ BR 68-69 F 2
Mangungu o ZRE 210-211 F 6
Mangunza o Z 218-219 D 3
Manguohe o VRC 156-157 C 4
Manguredjipa o ZRE 212-213 B 3
Mangut o RUS 118-119 F 11
Mangutiha ~ RUS 114-115 T 3
Mangutiri, Igarapé ~ BR 66-67 D 7
Mang Yang o VN 158-159 K 4
Măng Yang, Đèo ▲ VN 158-159 K 3
Mangyšlak ☆ KZ 126-127 J 5
Mangyšlak o KZ 126-127 J 6
Mangyšlak, plato ▲ KZ 126-127 K 6
Mangyšlakskij zaliv ≈ 126-127 J 5
Mangystau, taulary ▲ KZ 126-127 J 5
Manhan = Tögrög o MAU 146-147 L 2
Manhattan o USA (KS) 262-263 K 5
Manhattan o USA (MT) 250-251 H 6
Manhattan o USA (NV) 246-247 H 5
Manhica o MOC 220-221 L 2
Manhuaçu o BR 72-73 J 6
Manhumirim o BR 72-73 K 6
Mani o CO 60-61 E 5
Mani o TCH 198-199 G 6
Mani o WAN 198-199 C 6
Mani o ZRE 214-215 C 4
Mani, Quebrada de ~ RCH 76-77 C 1
Mania ~ RM 222-223 E 8
Maniaçu o BR 72-73 J 2
Maniamba o MOC 214-215 H 7
Mania-Muna o ZRE 214-215 B 5
Manica o MOC (Man) 218-219 G 4
Manica ◻ MOC 218-219 G 5
Manicaland ◻ ZW 218-219 F 4
Manicani Island ⌒ RP 160-161 F 7
Manicaragua o C 54-55 F 3
Maniche o RH 54-55 J 5
Manicoré o BR 66-67 G 5
Manicoré, Rio ~ BR 66-67 G 6
Manicorézinho, Rio ~ BR 66-67 G 6
Manicouagan, Réservoir < •• CDN 38-39 K 3
Manifold, Cape ▲ AUS 178-179 L 2
Maniganggo o VRC 144-145 M 5
Manigotagan o CDN (MAN) 234-235 G 3
Manihiki Plateau ≃ 13 L 4
Maniitsoq ⌒ GRØ 28-29 O 4
Maniitsoq = Sukkertoppen o GRØ 28-29 O 4
Manika o ZRE 214-215 C 6
Manila ☆ •• RP 160-161 D 5
Manila o USA (AR) 276-277 E 5
Manila o USA (UT) 254-255 F 3
Manila Bay ≈ 160-161 D 5
Manilla o AUS 178-179 L 6
Manily o RUS 112-113 N 5
Manimbaya, Tanjung ▲ RI 164-165 F 4
Maningory ~ RM 222-223 F 6
Maningoza ~ RM 222-223 D 6
Maningrida ⚔ AUS 174-175 C 3
Maninjau o RI 162-163 D 5
Maninjau, Danau o RI 162-163 D 5
Manipa, Pulau ⌒ RI 166-167 D 3
Manipa, Selat ≈ 166-167 D 3
Manipur ◻ IND 142-143 H 3
Manipur ~ IND 142-143 H 3
Maniqui, Río ~ BOL 70-71 D 4
Manisa ☆ • TR 128-129 B 3
Manisaj ~ KZ 126-127 M 4
Manissauá-Miçu, Rio ~ BR 70-71 K 3
Manistee o USA (MI) 272-273 C 3
Manistee River ~ USA 272-273 D 3
Manistique o USA (MI) 270-271 M 5
Manistique Lake ~ USA 270-271 N 4
Manistique River ~ USA 270-271 M 4
Manita pećina •• HR 100-101 E 2
Manito o USA (IL) 274-275 J 4
Manitoba, Lake o CDN (MAN) 234-235 D 3
Manito Lake o CDN (SAS) 232-233 J 3
Manitou o CDN (MAN) 234-235 E 5
Manitou o CDN (QUE) 242-243 C 2
Manitou, Lac o CDN (QUE) 242-243 E 2
Manitou, Rivière ~ CDN 242-243 C 2
Manitou Beach o CDN (SAS) 232-233 N 4
Manitou Falls o CDN (ONT) 234-235 K 4
Manitou Island ⌒ USA (MI) 270-271 L 3
Manitou Islands ⌒ USA (MI) 270-271 M 5
Manitou Lake o CDN (ONT) 238-239 D 3
Manitou Lakes o CDN (ONT) 234-235 L 5
Manitoulin Island ⌒ CDN (ONT) 238-239 C 3
Manitounuk Sound ≈ 36-37 L 7
Manitou Springs o USA (CO) 254-255 L 5
Manitouwadge o CDN (ONT) 236-237 C 3
Manitowaning o CDN (ONT) 238-239 D 3
Manitowoc o USA (WI) 270-271 L 6
Manitsoq ⌒ GRØ 26-27 X 7
Maniwaki o CDN (QUE) 238-239 K 2
Maniwaki Indian Reserve ⚔ CDN (QUE) 238-239 J 2
Maniwori o RI 166-167 H 3
Maniyāchchi o IND 140-141 G 6
Manizales ☆ CO 60-61 D 5
Manja o RM 222-223 D 8
Manjacaze o MOC 220-221 L 2
Manjakandriana o RM 222-223 E 7
Manjakot o PK 138-139 D 2
Manjeri o IND 140-141 G 5
Mānjhand o PK 138-139 B 7
Manjimup o AUS 176-177 D 7
Manjo o CAM 204-205 H 6
Manjou o CAM 204-205 K 6
Manjra ~ IND 138-139 F 10
Mankanza o ZRE 210-211 G 3
Mankargu o GH 202-203 K 4
Mankato o USA (KS) 262-263 H 5
Mankato o USA (MN) 270-271 E 6
Mankayane o SD 220-221 K 3
Mankera o PK 138-139 C 4
Mankessim o GH 202-203 K 7
Manki II o CAM 204-205 J 6
Mankim o CAM 204-205 K 6
Mankins o USA (TX) 264-265 F 5
Mankono ☆ CI 202-203 G 5
Mankota o CDN (SAS) 232-233 L 6
Mankpan o GH 202-203 K 5
Mankranso o GH 202-203 K 6
Mankyclaks, cyganak ≈ 126-127 J 5
Manley Hot Springs o USA 20-21 P 4
Manlius o USA (NY) 278-279 F 6
Manly o USA (IA) 274-275 E 1
Man Na o MYA 142-143 K 4
Manna o RI 162-163 E 7
Mannahill o AUS 180-181 E 2
Manna Hill Gold Field • AUS 180-181 E 2
Mannampitiya o CL 140-141 J 7
Mannar, Gulf of ≈ 140-141 H 6
Mannārgudi o IND 140-141 H 5
Mannar Island ⌒ CL 140-141 H 6
Mannarkkad o IND 140-141 G 5
Manners Creek o AUS 178-179 D 2
Mannheim o • D 92-93 K 4
Manni o VRC 144-145 F 3
Manning o USA (IA) 274-275 C 3
Manning o USA (ND) 258-259 E 4
Manning o USA (SC) 284-285 K 3
Manning, Cape ▲ CDN 24-25 K 3
Manning Park o CDN (BC) 230-231 J 4
Manning Provincial Park ⊥ CDN (BC) 230-231 J 4
Manning Range, Mount ▲ AUS 176-177 E 4
Manning River ~ AUS 178-179 M 6
Manning Strait ≈ 184 I c 2
Mannington o USA (WV) 280-281 F 4
Mann Ranges ▲ AUS 176-177 K 3
Mann River ~ AUS 174-175 C 3
Manns Harbor o USA (NC) 282-283 M 5
Mannville o CDN (ALB) 232-233 G 2
Mano o WAL 202-203 D 5
Manoá Pium, Área Indígena ⚔ BR 62-63 D 4
Mano Junction o WAL 202-203 E 5
Manokwari o RI (IRJ) 166-167 H 2
Manokwari o RI (IRJ) 166-167 H 3
Manolo Fortich o RP 160-161 F 8
Manoma ~ RUS 122-123 G 4
Manombo Atsimo o RM 222-223 C 9
Manometimay o RM 222-223 D 8
Manompana o RM 222-223 F 6
Manonga ~ EAT 212-213 D 5
Manono o ZRE 214-215 D 4
Manonwa o ZRE 210-211 K 6
Manor o CDN (SAS) 232-233 Q 6
Manor o USA (GA) 284-285 H 5
Manor o USA (TX) 266-267 K 3
Mano River o LB (CPM) 202-203 E 6
Mano River ~ LB 202-203 E 6
Manosque o F 90-91 K 10
Manou o RCA 206-207 E 4
Manouane o CDN (QUE) 236-237 O 5
Manouane, Lac o CDN (QUE) 38-39 J 3
Manouane, Lac o CDN (QUE) 236-237 O 5
Manouanis, Lac o CDN 38-39 J 3
Manovo = Tété ~ RCA 206-207 E 4
Manpo o KOR 150-151 F 7
Manresa o E 98-99 H 4
Mānsa o IND 138-139 E 5
Mansa ☆ Z 214-215 E 6
Mansabá o GNB 202-203 C 3
Mansa Konko ☆ • WAG 202-203 C 3
Mansalean o RI 164-165 H 4
Mānsehra o PK 138-139 D 2
Mansel Island ⌒ CDN 36-37 K 3
Mansfield o AUS 180-181 J 4
Mansfield o GB 90-91 G 5
Mansfield o USA (AR) 276-277 A 5
Mansfield o USA (IN) 274-275 L 5
Mansfield o USA (LA) 268-269 G 4
Mansfield o USA (MA) 278-279 K 7
Mansfield o USA (MO) 276-277 C 3
Mansfield o USA (OH) 280-281 D 3
Mansfield o USA (PA) 280-281 J 2
Mansfield o USA (TX) 264-265 G 6
Mansfield o USA (WA) 244-245 F 3
Mansfield, Mount ▲ USA (VT) 278-279 J 4
Mansfield, Port o USA (TX) 266-267 K 7
Mansha ~ Z 214-215 F 6
Mansi o MYA 142-143 J 3
Mansiari o IND 144-145 C 5
Mansidão o BR 68-69 F 7
Mansijsk, Hanty- ☆ RUS 114-115 K 4
Mansilla o E 98-99 F 3
Mansinam, Pulau ⌒ RI 166-167 H 2
Mansle o F 90-91 H 9
Manso, Rio ~ BR 70-71 K 4
Mansôa o GNB 202-203 C 3
Mansôa, Rio ~ GNB 202-203 C 3
Manso au das Mortes, Rio ~ BR 70-71 K 4
Manson o CDN (MAN) 234-235 B 4
Manson o USA (IA) 274-275 D 2
Manson o USA (WA) 244-245 E 3
Manson Creek o CDN 32-33 H 4
Manso-Nkwanta o GH 202-203 K 6
Mansons Landing o CDN (BC) 230-231 D 3
Mansour, El o DZ 188-189 L 7
Mansoura o DZ 190-191 E 2
Mansourah • DZ 188-189 L 3
Mansuar, Pulau ⌒ RI 166-167 F 2
Mansuela o RI 166-167 E 3
Mansuela Reserve ⊥ • RI 166-167 E 3
Mansura o USA (LA) 268-269 H 5
Manṣūrīya, al- o Y 132-133 C 6
Mansurlu o TR 128-129 F 4
Manta o DY 202-203 L 4
Manta o EC 64-65 B 2
Manta, Bahía de ≈ 64-65 B 2
Manta, La o CO 60-61 D 3
Mantaba ~ ZRE 210-211 F 5
Mantador o USA (ND) 258-259 L 5
Mantagao Lake o CDN (MAN) 234-235 F 3
Mantagao River ~ CDN 234-235 F 3
Mantalinga o RI 164-165 G 5
Mantalingajan, Mount ▲ RP 160-161 B 8
Mantanzilla, Quebrada ~ RCH 76-77 B 3
Mantario o CDN (SAS) 232-233 J 4
Mantaro, Río ~ PE 64-65 E 8
Manteca o USA (CA) 248-249 C 2
Mantecal o YV (APU) 60-61 G 4
Mantecal o YV (BOL) 60-61 J 4
Manteco, El o YV 60-61 K 4
Mantehage, Pulau ⌒ RI 164-165 J 3
Mantena o BR 72-73 K 5
Mantenga Falls ~ • SD 220-221 K 3
Manteo o USA (NC) 282-283 M 5
Manthani o IND 138-139 G 10
Manti o USA (AL) 284-285 D 5
Manti o USA (UT) 254-255 D 4
Mantiqueira, Serra da ▲ BR 72-73 G 7
Manto o HN 52-53 L 4
Manton o USA (MI) 272-273 D 3
Manton Knob ▲ AUS 176-177 J 3
Mantova o • I 100-101 C 2
Mantralayam o IND 140-141 G 3
Mäntsälä o FIN 88-89 H 6
Mant's Harbour o CDN (NFL) 242-243 P 4
Mantua o C 54-55 C 3
Mantuan Downs P.O. o AUS 178-179 J 3
Manturovo o RUS 96-97 D 4
Manú o PE 70-71 B 3
Manu o WAN 198-199 B 6
Manú, Parque Nacional ⊥ ••• PE 70-71 B 2
Manu'a Islands ⌒ USA 184 V c 2
Manubepium o RI 166-167 H 2
Manuel o MEX 50-51 K 6
Manuela, La o RA 78-79 H 4
Manuel Alves, Rio ~ BR 68-69 D 7
Manuel Alves Grande, Rio ~ BR 68-69 E 5
Manuel Alves Pequena, Rio ~ BR 68-69 E 6
Manuel Benavides o MEX 50-51 H 3
Manuel Emídio o BR 68-69 G 5
Manuel Lake o CDN 30-31 F 2
Manuel Luís, Recife ⌒ BR 68-69 F 2
Manuel Ribas o BR 74-75 E 5
Manuel Rodríguez, Isla ⌒ RCH 80 D 6
Manuel Tames o C 54-55 H 4
Manuel Urbano o BR 66-67 C 7
Manuel Viana o BR 76-77 K 5
Manuel Vitorino o BR 72-73 K 3
Manūğān o IR 134-135 G 5
Manui, Pulau ⌒ RI 164-165 H 5
Manuk ~ RI 168 C 3
Manuk, Pulau ⌒ RI 166-167 F 4
Manukan o RP 160-161 E 8
Manuk Mankax ⌒ RP 160-161 C 10
Manundi, Tanjung ▲ RI 166-167 H 2
Manupampi, Pulau ⌒ RI 166-167 H 2
Manuran, Pulau ⌒ RI 166-167 F 1
Manurimí, Río ~ BOL 70-71 D 2
Manuripe, Río ~ PE 70-71 C 2
Manuripi, Río ~ BOL 70-71 C 2
Manuripi Heath, Reserve Natural ⊥ BOL 70-71 C 2
Manus Island ⌒ PNG 183 D 1
Manvel o USA (ND) 258-259 K 3
Mānvi o IND 140-141 G 2
Manville o USA (WY) 252-253 O 4
Many o USA (LA) 268-269 G 5
Manyame ~ ZW 218-219 F 3
Manyani o EAK 212-213 G 5
Manyara, Lake o EAT 212-213 E 5
Manyara National Park ⊥ EAT 212-213 E 5
Manyas ☆ TR 128-129 B 2
Manyberries o CDN (ALB) 232-233 H 6
Manyč ~ RUS 102-103 N 5
Manych Depression = Kumo-Manyčskaja vpadina ⌣ RUS 102-103 M 4
Manyémen o CAM 204-205 H 6
Manyinga o Z 218-219 C 1
Many Island Lake o CDN (ALB) 232-233 H 5
Manyoni o EAT 214-215 F 4
Manyoni o EAT 212-213 E 6
Manzai o PK 138-139 C 3
Mānzai o PK 138-139 B 4
Manzanares o CO 60-61 D 5
Manzanares o • E 98-99 F 5
Manzanillo o C 54-55 G 4
Manzanillo o • MEX 52-53 B 2
Manzanillo, Punta ▲ YV 60-61 G 2
Manzanita o USA (OR) 244-245 B 5
Manzanita Indian Reservation ⚔ USA (CA) 248-249 H 7
Manzano o USA (NM) 256-257 J 4
Manzano, El o RCH 78-79 D 3
Manzengele o ZRE 216-217 D 3
Manzhouli o VRC 148-149 N 3
Manzila, Buḥairat al- o ET 194-195 E 2
Manzini o SD 220-221 K 3
Manzurka o RUS (IRK) 116-117 N 9
Manzurka ~ RUS 116-117 N 9
Mao o • DOM 54-55 K 5
Mao ☆ TCH 198-199 G 5
Maogong o VRC 156-157 F 3
Maojing o VRC 154-155 E 3
Maoke, Pegunungan ▲ RI 166-167 J 4
Maolan Z.B. ⊥ • VRC 156-157 E 4
Mao Ling • VRC 154-155 F 4
Maoming o VRC 156-157 G 6
Maonanzu o VRC 156-157 F 4
Maopora, Pulau ⌒ RI 166-167 D 5
Maospati o RI 168 D 3
Maotou Shan ▲ VRC 142-143 M 3
Mao Xian o VRC 154-155 C 6
Mapaga o RI 164-165 F 4
Mapai o MOC 218-219 G 6
Mapam Yumco • VRC 144-145 C 5
Mapamoiwa o PNG 183 F 5
Mapane o RI 164-165 G 4
Mapangu o ZRE 210-211 H 6
Mapari, Rio ~ BR 66-67 D 4
Mapastepec o MEX 52-53 H 4
Mapat, Pulau ⌒ RI 164-165 E 2
Mapes o CDN (BC) 228-229 L 3
Mapharasa o ZW 218-219 E 5
Mapi o RI (IRJ) 166-167 K 5
Mapi ~ RI 166-167 K 5
Mapia, Kepulauan ⌒ RI 166-167 H 1
Mapiá, Rio ~ BR 66-67 H 5
Mapili o RI 164-165 F 5
Mapinhane o MOC 218-219 H 6
Mapire o YV 60-61 J 4
Mapiri o BOL 70-71 C 4
Mapiri, Río ~ BOL 70-71 D 2
Mapiri, Río ~ BOL 70-71 C 4
Mapiripán o CO 60-61 E 6
Maple Bluff o USA (WI) 274-275 J 1
Maple City o USA (MI) 272-273 D 3
Maple Creek o CDN (SAS) 232-233 J 6
Maple Creek ~ CDN 232-233 J 5
Maple Ridge o CDN (BC) 230-231 G 4
Maple Ridge o USA (MI) 272-273 F 3
Maplesville o USA (AL) 284-285 D 4
Mapleton o USA (IA) 274-275 C 2
Mapleton o USA (MI) 272-273 D 3
Mapleton o USA (MN) 270-271 E 7
Mapleton o USA (OR) 244-245 B 6
Maple Valley o USA (WA) 244-245 C 3
Mapmakers Seamount ≃ 14-15 J 5
Mapoon o AUS 174-175 F 3
Mapoon Aboriginal Land ⚔ AUS 174-175 G 2
Mappsville o USA (VA) 280-281 L 6
Maprik o PNG 183 B 2
Māpuca o • IND 140-141 E 3
Mapuera, Rio ~ BR 62-63 E 5
Mapulanguene o MOC 220-221 L 2
Mapunda o ZRE 214-215 C 5
Mapunga o Z 218-219 D 1
Maputi, Pulau ⌒ RI 164-165 F 3
Maputo ◻ MOC 220-221 L 2
Maputo ★ MOC (MAP) 220-221 L 2
Maputo ⊥ MOC 220-221 L 3
Maputo, Baia do ≈ 220-221 L 3
Maputo, Reserva de Elefantes do ⊥ MOC 220-221 L 3
Maputo, Rio ~ MOC 220-221 L 3
Maputsoe o LS 220-221 H 4
Maqāriyūs, Dair ∴ ET 194-195 E 2
Maqên o VRC 154-155 B 4
Maqên Gangri ▲ VRC 144-145 M 3
Maqrat o Y 132-133 G 6
Maqrūn, Al o LAR 192-193 J 2
Maqteïr ⊥ RIM 196-197 E 4
Maqu o VRC 154-155 B 4
Maquan He ~ VRC 144-145 D 5
Maqueda Channel ≈ 160-161 E 6
Maquela do Zombo o ANG 216-217 C 3
Maqueze o MOC 220-221 L 2
Maquía, Río ~ PE 64-65 E 5
Máquina, La o C 54-55 H 4
Maquinchao o RA 78-79 E 6
Maquinista o BOL 70-71 D 2
Maquinista Levet o RA 78-79 F 2
Maquoketa o USA (IA) 274-275 H 2
Maquoketa River ~ USA 274-275 G 2
Mar, La ∴ • MEX 52-53 J 3
Mar, Serra do ▲ BR 72-73 H 7
Mar, Serra do ▲ BR 74-75 F 6
Mara ◻ EAT 212-213 E 4
Mara ~ EAT 212-213 E 4
Mara o GUY 62-63 F 2
Mara o ZA 218-219 E 6
Maraã o BR 66-67 E 3
Marabá o BR 68-69 D 4
Marabadiassa o CI 202-203 H 5
Marabahan o RI 164-165 D 5
Marabatua, Pulau ⌒ RI 164-165 D 6
Marabi, al- o KSA 132-133 C 5
Marabitanas o BR 66-67 D 2
Maracá o BR 62-63 J 4
Maracá, Ilha de ⌒ BR 62-63 J 4
Maracaçumé o BR 68-69 F 3
Maracaçumé, Baía do ≈ 68-69 F 2
Maracaçumé, Rio ~ BR 68-69 F 2
Maracaí o BR 72-73 E 7
Maracaibo ☆ YV 60-61 F 2
Maracaibo, Lago de ≈ 60-61 F 2
Maracá-Jipioca, Estação Ecológica ⊥ BR 62-63 J 4
Maracaju o BR 76-77 K 1
Maracajú, Serra de ▲ BR 76-77 K 1
Maracanã o BR 68-69 E 2
Maracanã, Baía de ≈ 68-69 E 2
Maracanã, Rio ~ BR 66-67 H 7
Maracanai, Cachoeira ~ BR 62-63 H 6
Maracanaquará, Planalto ⊥ BR 62-63 H 5
Maracás o BR 72-73 K 2
Maracas Bay Village o TT 60-61 L 2
Maracay ☆ YV 60-61 H 2
Maracoa o CO 60-61 G 6
Maracó Grande, Valle ⌣ RA 78-79 G 4
Maracuni, Río ~ YV 60-61 J 6
Marādah o LAR 192-193 H 3
Maradankadawala o CL 140-141 J 6
Maradi ◻ RN 198-199 C 5
Maradi ☆ RN (MAR) 198-199 C 6
Maradun o WAN 198-199 C 6
Maraetai o NZ 182 E 2
Marafa o EAK 212-213 G 5
Marag o BR 72-73 L 2
Maragahawewa o CL 140-141 J 6
Marāġe o • IR 128-129 M 4
Maraguay, Punta ▲ YV 60-61 F 2
Marāḥayy o Y 132-133 G 6
Marāhra o IND 138-139 G 6
Marais des Cygnes River ~ USA 274-275 E 6
Marajó, Baía de ≈ 62-63 K 6
Marajó, Ilha de ⌒ BR 62-63 J 6
Marakabei o LS 220-221 J 4
Marakalalo Hills ▲ RB 218-219 D 6
Marakesa o ZRE 210-211 L 3
Maraku o WAN 204-205 H 3
Mara Lake o CDN (BC) 230-231 L 3
Mara Lake o CDN (BC) 230-231 K 3
Maralal o EAK 212-213 F 3
Maralal National Sanctuary ⊥ EAK 212-213 F 3
Maraldy, kōli o KZ 124-125 K 2
Marale o HN 52-53 L 4
Maraleda, Canal ≈ 80 D 2
Marali o RCA 206-207 D 5
Maralinga o AUS 176-177 L 5
Maralinga -Tjarutja Aboriginal Lands ⚔ AUS 176-177 L 4
Maramag o RP 160-161 F 9
Maramasike = Small Malaita ⌒ SOL 184 I e 3
Maramec o USA (OK) 264-265 H 2
Marāmiya, al- o KSA 130-131 E 5
Maramuni o PNG 183 B 3
Maramuni River ~ PNG 183 B 3
Maran o MAL 162-163 E 3
Mārān, Kōh-i- ▲ PK 134-135 M 4
Marana o USA (AZ) 256-257 D 6
Maranchón, Puerto de ▲ E 98-99 F 4
Marand o • IR 128-129 L 3
Marangu o EAT 212-213 F 5
Maranguape o BR 68-69 J 3
Maranhão o BR (AMA) 66-67 J 4
Maranhão ◻ BR 68-69 E 5
Maranhão, Rio ~ BR 72-73 F 3
Maranhoto o BR 66-67 F 4
Maranoa River ~ AUS 178-179 K 4
Marañón, Rio ~ PE 64-65 F 4
Maransabadi, Pulau ⌒ RI 166-167 H 3
Marantale o RI 164-165 G 4
Marantao o RP 160-161 F 9
Maranura o PE 64-65 F 8
Marão o MOC 220-221 M 2
Marahoué ~ CI 202-203 G 6
Maraoué, Parc National de la ⊥ CI 202-203 G 6
Marapa Island ⌒ SOL 184 I e 3
Marapi, Gunung ▲ RI 162-163 D 5
Marapi, Rio ~ BR 62-63 F 5
Marapinim o BR 68-69 E 2
Marapinim, Rio ~ BR 68-69 E 2
Marapiti, Ilha do ⌒ BR 66-67 G 5
Marari, Rio ~ BR 66-67 E 2
Mara River ~ CDN 30-31 P 2
Mara Rosa o BR 72-73 F 2
Maras, Thamad Bū o LAR 192-193 H 3
Mărăşeşti o RO 102-103 E 5
Marāšī, al- o Y 132-133 C 5
Marasimsim o MAL 160-161 B 9
Marassu ~ RUS 124-125 Q 2
Marat o UZ 136-137 J 3
Marat, Ğabal ▲ Y 132-133 G 5
Marata, Ford ≈ 108-109 I c 2
Marateca o P 98-99 C 5
Marathon o AUS 174-175 G 7
Marathon o CDN (ONT) 236-237 B 4
Marathon o USA (FL) 286-287 H 7
Marathon o USA (TX) 266-267 D 3
Maratua, Pulau ⌒ RI 164-165 F 2
Marau o BR 74-75 D 7
Marau o RI 162-163 J 6
Marauiá, Rio ~ BR 66-67 E 2
Marau Island ⌒ SOL 184 I e 4
Maravaam ~ RUS 112-113 U 3
Maravade o IND 140-141 F 2
Maravatío o MEX 52-53 D 2
Marāve Tappe o IR 136-137 D 6
Maravilha o BR 66-67 G 4
Maravilhas o BR 72-73 H 5
Maravilla o BOL 70-71 D 2
Maravillas o MEX 50-51 G 4
Maravillas Creek ~ USA 266-267 D 4
Marāwah o LAR 192-193 J 1
Marawaka o PNG 183 C 4
Marawi = Merowe o • SUD 200-201 E 3
Marawi ☆ RP 160-161 F 9
Marāwi'a, al- o Y 132-133 C 6
Marawiḥ ⌒ UAE 134-135 E 6
Maraxo Patá o BR 62-63 F 5
Marayes o RA 76-77 D 6
Marbella o E 98-99 E 6
Marble o USA (WA) 244-245 H 2
Marble Bar o AUS 172-173 D 6
Marble Canyon o USA (AZ) 256-257 D 2
Marble Canyon ⌣ USA 256-257 D 2
Marble City o USA (OK) 264-265 K 3
Marble Falls o USA (TX) 266-267 J 3
Marble Hall o ZA 220-221 J 2
Marblehead o USA (OH) 280-281 D 2
Marble Hill o USA (MO) 276-277 F 3
Marble Island ⌒ CDN 30-31 Y 4
Marbletop o GB 90-91 H 5
Marbleton o USA (GA) 284-285 F 3
Marble Valley o USA (AL) 284-285 D 3
Marburg (Lahn) o •• D 92-93 K 3
Marcabeli o EC 64-65 C 3
Marcala o HN 52-53 K 4
Marcali o H 92-93 O 5
Marcapata o PE 70-71 B 3
Marcapomacocha o PE 64-65 D 7
Marceau, Lac o CDN 38-39 L 3
Marcel, Lac o CDN 36-37 Q 6
Marcelândia o BR 70-71 K 2
Marcelin o CDN (SAS) 232-233 M 3
Marcelino o BR (AMA) 66-67 D 3
Marcelino o BR (AMA) 66-67 D 2
Marcelino Ramos o BR 74-75 E 6
Marcell o USA (MN) 270-271 E 3
Marcellus o USA (MI) 272-273 D 6
Marcelo o BR 68-69 C 3
Marchajanovskij, ostrov ⌒ RUS 112-113 L 2
Marchand o CDN (MAN) 234-235 G 5
Marche ⊥ F 90-91 H 8
Marche ◻ I 100-101 D 3
Marche-en-Famenne o B 92-93 H 3
Marchena o E 98-99 E 6
Marchena, Isla ⌒ EC 64-65 B 9
Marches Point o CDN (NFL) 242-243 J 4
Marchinbar Island ⌒ AUS 174-175 D 2
Mar Chiquita, Laguna ⌣ RA (BUA) 78-79 J 3
Mar Chiquita, Laguna o RA (BUA) 78-79 L 4
Mar Chiquita, Laguna o RA (COD) 76-77 F 6
Marchwell o CDN (SAS) 232-233 R 5
Marcionílio Sousa o BR 72-73 K 2
Marco o BR 68-69 H 3
Marco o USA (FL) 286-287 H 6
Marcoing, gory ▲ RUS 112-113 Q 2
Marcona o PE 64-65 E 9
Marcos Rondon o BR 70-71 G 3
Marcos Juárez o RA 78-79 H 2
Marcoux o USA (MN) 270-271 B 3
Marcus o USA (IA) 274-275 C 2
Marcus Baker, Mount ▲ USA 20-21 R 6
Marcy, Mount ▲ USA (NY) 278-279 H 4
Marḍ, al- o IRQ 128-129 K 6
Mardakan = Mardakan o • AZ 128-129 O 2
Mardān o PK 138-139 D 2
Mar de Ajó o RA 78-79 L 4
Mar de Espanha o BR 72-73 J 6
Mar del Plata o • RA 78-79 L 4
Mar del Plata Canyon ≃ 78-79 N 4
Mardiān o AFG 136-137 K 6
Mardie o AUS 172-173 B 6
Mardie Island ⌒ AUS 172-173 B 6
Mardin ☆ TR 128-129 J 4
Mardin Dağları ▲ TR 128-129 J 4
Marea del Portillo o • C 54-55 G 5
Marechal Deodoro o • BR 68-69 L 6
Mareeba o AUS 174-175 H 5
Mareeq o SP 208-209 H 7
Marek o RI 164-165 G 6
Maremma ⊥ I 100-101 C 3
Maréna o RMM 202-203 E 2
Marendet o RN 198-199 C 4
Marengāb o IR 134-135 D 1
Marenge o ZRE 212-213 B 6
Marengo o CDN (SAS) 232-233 J 4
Marengo o USA (IA) 274-275 F 3
Marengo o USA (IL) 274-275 K 2
Marenisco o USA (MI) 270-271 J 4
Marennes o F 90-91 G 9
Marerano o RM 222-223 D 8
Mareth o TN 190-191 H 4
Mareton's Harbour o CDN (NFL) 242-243 O 3
Mar'evka o RUS 96-97 F 7
Marevyj o RUS 118-119 M 8
Marfa o USA (TX) 266-267 C 3
Marfa', al- o UAE 134-135 E 6
Marganec = Marhanec' o UA 102-103 J 4

358 Manchao, Sierra de — Marganec

Margaree Forks ○ CDN (NS) 240-241 O 4
Margaree Harbour ○ CDN (NS) 240-241 O 4
Margaree Valley ○ CDN (NS) 240-241 P 4
Margaret, Cape ▲ CDN 24-25 a 5
Margaret, Mount ▲ AUS (SA) 178-179 C 5
Margaret, Mount ▲ AUS (WA) 172-173 C 6
Margaret Creek ~ AUS 178-179 D 5
Margaret Lake ⊖ CDN (ALB) 30-31 M 6
Margaret Lake ⊖ CDN (NWT) 30-31 L 3
Margaret Lake ⊖ CDN (NWT) 30-31 P 4
Margaret River ○ AUS (WA) 176-177 C 6
Margaret River ~ AUS 172-173 H 5
Margaretsville ○ CDN (NS) 240-241 K 5
Margarida, Monte ▲ BR 76-77 J 2
Margarima ○ PNG 183 B 3
Margarita, Isla ⌒ CO 60-61 D 3
Margarita, Isla de ⌒ ·· YV 60-61 J 2
Margarita, La ○ YV 60-61 L 3
Margaritas, Las ○ MEX 52-53 J 3
Margate ○ USA (FL) 286-287 J 5
Marğa'yūn ☆ RL 128-129 F 6
Margeride, Monts de la ▲ F 90-91 J 9
Margeta, Tanjung ▲ RI 166-167 C 6
Marghita ○ RO 102-103 C 4
Margie ○ USA (MN) 270-271 E 2
Margilan ○ UZ 136-137 M 4
Margo ○ CDN (SAS) 232-233 P 4
Margō, Dašt-e ∸ AFG 134-135 K 3
Margos ○ PE 64-65 D 7
Margosatubig ○ RP 160-161 E 9
Margua, Río ~ CO 60-61 E 4
Marguerite ○ CDN (BC) 228-229 M 4
Marguerite, Baie ≈ 16 G 30
Marguerite River ~ CDN 32-33 P 3
Margyang ○ VRC 144-145 G 6
Marha ○ RUS (SAH) 118-119 L 5
Marha ~ RUS 118-119 L 5
Marha ~ RUS 118-119 J 4
Marhačan ~ RUS 118-119 L 5
Marhamat ○ UZ 136-137 N 4
Marhāna • AFG 134-135 M 1
Marhanec' ○ UA 102-103 J 4
Marhara ~ RUS 110-111 J 7
Marhoum ○ DZ 188-189 L 3
Mari ○ BR 68-69 L 5
Mari ○ PNG 183 A 5
Maria ○ BR 62-63 K 6
Maria ○ CDN (QUE) 240-241 K 2
Maria ○ PE 64-65 D 5
María, El ○ PA 52-53 D 7
Maria, Mount ▲ GB 78-79 L 6
María Cleofas, Isla ⌒ MEX 50-51 F 7
Maria da Fé ○ BR 72-73 H 7
María Elena ○ RCH 76-77 C 2
María Eugenia ○ RA 76-77 G 6
María Grande, Arroyo ~ RA 76-77 H 5
María Ignacia ○ RA 78-79 K 4
Maria Island ⌒ AUS (NT) 174-175 C 4
Maria Island ⌒ AUS (TAS) 180-181 J 7
Mariakani ○ EAK 212-213 G 5
Marial ○ USA (OR) 244-245 B 8
María Linda, Río ~ GCA 52-53 J 4
Marialva ○·· P 98-99 D 4
María Madre, Isla ⌒ MEX 50-51 F 7
María Magdalena, Isla ⌒ MEX 50-51 F 7
Marian ○ AUS 178-179 K 1
Mariana ○· BR 72-73 J 6
Mariana, Ilha ⌒ MOC 220-221 L 2
Marianao ○ C 54-55 D 3
Mariana Trench ≃ 14-15 G 6
Mariani ○ IND 142-143 J 2
Marian Lake ⊖ CDN 30-31 L 4
Marianna ○ USA (AR) 276-277 E 6
Marianna ○ USA (FL) 286-287 D 1
Marianne Nunatakker ▲ GRØ 26-27 o 6
Mariano I. Loza ○ RA 76-77 H 5
Marianópolis ○ BR 68-69 F 4
Marian River ~ CDN 30-31 L 4
Mariánské Lázně ○ CZ 92-93 M 4
Mariaou, Adrar ▲ DZ 190-191 G 9
Mariapolis ○ CDN (MAN) 234-235 D 5
Mariaqua, Rio ~ BR 66-67 J 4
Mariarano ○ RM 222-223 E 5
Marías, Islas ⌒ MEX 50-51 F 7
Marias Pass ▲ USA (MT) 250-251 F 3
Marias River ~ USA 250-251 J 3
Maria Teresa ○ ANG 216-217 C 4
María Teresa ○ RA 78-79 J 3
Mariaú, Ponta de ▲ BR 68-69 E 2
Maria van Diemen, Cape ▲ NZ 182 D 1
Mariazell ○ A 92-93 N 5
Ma'rib ○· Y 132-133 D 6
Maribo ○· DK 86-87 E 9
Maribor ○· SLO 100-101 E 1
Marica ~ BG 102-103 E 7
Maricá ○ BR 72-73 J 7
Māri Čāg ○ AFG 136-137 H 7
Maricao ○·· USA (PR) 286-287 P 2
Marico ~ RB 220-221 H 2
Maricopa ○ USA (AZ) 256-257 C 5
Maricopa ○ USA (CA) 248-249 E 4
Maricopa Akchin Indian Reservation ⚔ USA (AZ) 256-257 C 6
Maricunga, Salar de ○ RCH 76-77 C 4
Maridi ○ SUD (SR) 206-207 J 6
Maridi ~ SUD 206-207 J 6
Marie ○ USA (AR) 276-277 E 5
Marié, Rio ~ BR 66-67 D 3
Marie-Galante ⌒ F 56 E 4
Mariehamn ☆ FIN 88-89 E 6
Mariel ○ C 54-55 D 3
Mari-El = Marij Èl, Respublika ▫ RUS 96-97 E 5
Marie Louise Island ⌒ SY 224 C 3
Marie Luise Bank ≃ 160-161 B 7
Marienbad = Mariánské Lázně ○ CZ 92-93 M 4
Marienberg ○ PNG 183 C 2
Mariental ☆ NAM 220-221 C 2
Marienthal ○ CDN (SAS) 232-233 P 6
Mariepauá, Rio ~ BR 66-67 G 5
Marie Shoal ≃ 166-167 E 7
Marie Sophie Gletscher ⊂ GRØ 26-27 g 3
Mariestad ☆ S 86-87 F 7
Marieta ○ YV 60-61 H 5
Marietta ○ USA (GA) 284-285 F 3
Marietta ○ USA (OH) 280-281 E 4
Marietta ○ USA (OK) 264-265 G 5
Marie Valdemar, Kap ▲ GRØ 26-27 q 5
Mariga ○ WAN 204-205 F 3
Mariga, River ~ WAN 204-205 G 3
Marigat ○ EAK 212-213 E 3
Marignane ○ F 90-91 K 10
Marigot ☆ F 56 D 2
Marigot ○ RH 54-55 J 5
Marigot ○ WD 56 E 4
Marihatag ○ RP 160-161 G 8
Marii, mys ▲ RUS 120-121 K 6
Mariinsk ☆ RUS 114-115 T 6
Mariinskoe ○ RUS 122-123 J 3
Marii Prončiščevoj, buhta ≈ 108-109 k 4
Marijampolė ☆·· LT 94-95 H 4
Marikal ○ IND 140-141 G 2
Marilândia do Sul ○ BR 72-73 E 7
Marília ○ BR 72-73 F 7
Marilla ○ CDN (BC) 228-229 J 3
Marimari, Rio ~ BR 66-67 H 5
Marimba ○ ANG 216-217 D 4
Marimbona ~ RM 222-223 F 6
Marimbondo ○ BR 68-69 K 6
Marín ○ E 98-99 C 3
Marín ○ MEX 50-51 J 5
Marin, Le ○ F 56 E 4
Marina ○ USA (AZ) 256-257 A 2
Marina ○ USA (CA) 248-249 C 3
Marina di Léuca ○· I 100-101 G 5
Mar'ina Horka ☆ BY 94-95 L 5
Marina Plains ○ AUS 174-175 G 4
Marinduque Island ⌒ RP 160-161 D 6
Marineland ○ USA (FL) 286-287 H 2
Marineland of Florida ∴ USA (FL) 286-287 H 2
Marine Museum Bath • USA (ME) 278-279 M 5
Marine National Park ⊥ ER 200-201 K 5
Marine National Reserve ⊥ EAK 212-213 H 5
Marine Reserve ⊥• RI (SSE) 168 E 6
Marine Reserve ⊥• RI (STG) 164-165 H 6
Marinette ○ USA (WI) 270-271 L 5
Maringá ○ BR 72-73 E 7
Maringa ~ ZRE 210-211 H 3
Maringouin ○ USA (LA) 268-269 J 6
Maringuè ○ MOC 218-219 H 3
Marinheiros, Ilha dos ⌒ BR 74-75 D 8
Marino Barbareta, Parque Nacional ⊥ HN 52-53 L 3
Marino Guanaja, Parque Nacional ⊥ HN 54-55 C 6
Marino Punta Sal, Parque Nacional ⊥ HN 52-53 L 4
Marinovka ☆ KZ 124-125 F 3
Marion ○ USA (AL) 284-285 C 4
Marion ○ USA (AR) 276-277 E 5
Marion ○ USA (IA) 274-275 G 2
Marion ○ USA (IL) 276-277 G 3
Marion ○ USA (IN) 274-275 N 4
Marion ○ USA (KS) 262-263 J 6
Marion ○ USA (KY) 276-277 G 3
Marion ○ USA (LA) 268-269 H 4
Marion ○ USA (MI) 272-273 D 3
Marion ○ USA (MT) 250-251 E 3
Marion ○ USA (NC) 282-283 E 5
Marion ○ USA (OH) 280-281 C 3
Marion ○ USA (SC) 284-285 L 2
Marion ○ USA (VA) 280-281 E 7
Marion, Lake ⊖ USA (SC) 284-285 K 3
Marion Downs ○ AUS 178-179 E 2
Marion Forks ○ USA (OR) 244-245 D 6
Marion Junction ○ USA (AL) 284-285 C 4
Marion Lake ⊖ USA (KS) 262-263 J 6
Marion Reef ⌒ AUS 174-175 M 6
Maripa ○ GUY 62-63 E 2
Maripasoula ○ F 62-63 G 4
Mariposa ○ USA (CA) 248-249 E 2
Mariposa, Sierra ▲ RCH 76-77 C 2
Mariquita ○ BR 72-73 H 2
Mariquita ○ CO 60-61 D 5
Marisa ○ RI 164-165 G 3
Mariscal Cáceres ○ PE 64-65 E 8
Mariscal de Juárez ○ MEX 52-53 E 3
Mariscal Estigarribia ○ PY 76-77 G 1
Marismas, Las ∸ E 98-99 D 6
Marissa ○ USA (IL) 274-275 J 6
Marita Downs ○ AUS 178-179 G 2
Marite ○ ZA 220-221 K 2
Mariupol' = Maryupol' ○ UA 102-103 K 4
Marivān ○ IR 128-129 M 5
Mariveles ○ RP 160-161 D 5
Märjamaa ○·· EST 94-95 J 2
Mar'janovka ☆ RUS 124-125 H 1
Marjorie Hills ▲ CDN 30-31 U 3
Marjorie Lake ⊖ CDN 30-31 U 3
Marka ☆ SP 212-213 K 3
Markakol ⊖ KZ 124-125 O 4
Markala ○ RMM 202-203 G 3
Markam ○ VRC 144-145 M 6
Markama, proliv ≈ 84-85 d 2
Mārkāpur ○ IND 140-141 H 3
Markara ○ AR 128-129 L 2
Markazi ▫ IR 134-135 C 1
Markdale ○ CDN (ONT) 238-239 E 4
Marked Tree ○ USA (AR) 276-277 E 5
Marken ○ ZA 218-219 E 6
Markey ○ USA (MI) 272-273 E 3
Markham ○ CDN (ONT) 238-239 F 5
Markham ○ USA (MN) 270-271 F 3
Markham ○ USA (WA) 244-245 B 4
Markham, Mount ▲ ARK 16 E 0
Markham Bay ≈ 36-37 N 3
Markham Bay ≈ 183 D 4
Markham Lake ⊖ CDN 30-31 S 4
Markham River ~ PNG 183 D 4
Markinch ○ CDN (SAS) 232-233 O 5
Markit ○ VRC 146-147 C 6
Markivka ○ UA 102-103 L 3
Markle ○ USA (IN) 274-275 N 4
Markleeville ○ USA (CA) 246-247 F 5
Markley, Fort ∴ USA (KS) 262-263 K 5
Markleysburg ○ USA (PA) 280-281 G 4
Markos Paz ○ RA 78-79 K 3
Markounda ○ RCA 206-207 C 5
Markovac ○ YU 100-101 H 2
Markovo ○ RUS (CUK) 112-113 Q 4
Markovo ○ RUS (IRK) 116-117 N 7
Markoy ○ BF 202-203 L 2
Marks ○ RUS 96-97 E 8
Marks ○ USA (MS) 268-269 K 2
Marksville ○ USA (LA) 268-269 H 5
Marktredwitz ○ D 92-93 M 3
Marktredwitz ○ D (BAY) 92-93 M 4
Mark Twain Boyhood Home and Museum • USA (MO) 274-275 G 5
Mark Twain Lake ⊖ USA (MO) 274-275 G 5
Mark Twain National Wildlife Refuge ⊥ USA (IL) 274-275 G 5
Markundi ○ SUD 206-207 F 3
Markūz, al- ○ KSA 130-131 H 2
Markwassie ○ ZA 220-221 H 3
Marla ○ AUS 176-177 M 3
Marlboro ○ CDN (ALB) 232-233 B 2
Marlborough ○ AUS 178-179 K 2
Marlborough ○ GB 90-91 G 6
Marlborough ○ GUY 62-63 E 2
Marlborough ○ USA (MA) 278-279 K 6
Marlborough Sounds ∸ NZ 182 D 4
Marlette ○ USA (MI) 272-273 F 4
Marlin ○ USA (TX) 266-267 L 2
Marlin Coast • AUS 174-175 H 5
Marlinton ○ USA (WV) 280-281 F 5
Marlo ○ AUS 180-181 K 4
Marloth Nature Reserve ⊥ ZA 220-221 E 6
Marlow ○ USA (NH) 278-279 J 5
Marlow ○ USA (OK) 264-265 F 4
Marmagao ○ IND 140-141 E 3
Marmande ○ F 90-91 H 9
Marmara Adası ⌒ TR 128-129 B 2
Marmara Denizi ≈ 128-129 B 2
Marmara Ereğlisi ☆ TR 128-129 B 2
Marmaris ☆·· TR 128-129 C 4
Marmarth ○ USA (ND) 258-259 D 5
Marmelo, Rio ~ BR 66-67 D 7
Marmelos, Rio dos ~ BR 66-67 G 6
Mar Menor ⊖ E 98-99 G 6
Marmion, Lake ⊖ AUS 176-177 F 4
Marmion Lake ⊖ CDN (ONT) 234-235 M 6
Marmites des géants • RM 222-223 E 9
Marmolada ▲ I 100-101 C 1
Marmoles, Parque Nacional Los ⊥ MEX 50-51 K 7
Marmora ○ CDN (ONT) 238-239 H 4
Marmot Bay ≈ 22-23 U 3
Marmot Island ⌒ USA 22-23 V 3
Marmul ○ OM 132-133 J 4
Marne ~ F 90-91 K 7
Marne-au-Rhin, Canal de la < F 90-91 L 7
Marneuli ○ GE 126-127 F 7
Marnoo ○ AUS 180-181 G 4
Maro ○ TCH 206-207 D 4
Maroa ○ YV 60-61 H 6
Maroala ○ RM 222-223 E 5
Maroambihy ○ RM 222-223 F 5
Maroantsetra ○ RM 222-223 F 5
Marofandilia ○ RM 222-223 D 8
Maroharatra ○ RM 222-223 E 8
Marojezy ▲ RM 222-223 F 5
Maroktua ○ RI 162-163 F 5
Marolambo ○ RM 222-223 F 8
Marolinta ○ RM 222-223 D 10
Maromandia ○ RM (MJG) 222-223 F 5
Maromandia ○ RM (TMA) 222-223 G 5
Maromokotro ▲ RM 222-223 F 5
Marondera ○ ZW 218-219 F 4
Marongora ○ ZW 218-219 E 3
Maroni ~ SME 62-63 G 3
Maroochydore-Mooloolaba ○ AUS 178-179 M 4
Maropaika ○ RM 222-223 E 9
Maros ~ H 92-93 Q 5
Maros ○ RI 164-165 F 6
Maroseranana ○ RM 222-223 F 7
Marotandrano ○ RM 222-223 F 6
Marotolana ○ RM 222-223 F 5
Maroua ☆• CAM 206-207 B 3
Marouini ~ F 62-63 H 4
Marova ○ BR 66-67 F 3
Marovato ○ RM (ASA) 222-223 F 4
Marovato ○ RM (MJG) 222-223 F 5
Marovato ○ RM (TLA) 222-223 D 10
Marovoalavo, Lembalemban'i ▲ RM 222-223 F 6
Marovoay ○ RM 222-223 E 6
Marovoay Atsimo ○ RM 222-223 D 6
Marowijnerivier ~ SME 62-63 G 3
Marple Hill ○ USA (NC) 282-283 K 6
Marqab, al- ·· IRQ 128-129 F 5
Marqadā ○ SYR 128-129 J 5
Marqua ○ AUS 178-179 D 2
Marquard ○ ZA 220-221 H 4
Marque, La ○ USA (TX) 268-269 F 7
Marquesas Fracture Zone ≃ 14-15 P 8
Marquesas Islands = Marquises, Îles ⌒ F 13 N 3
Marquesas Keys ⌒ USA (FL) 286-287 G 7
Marquette ○ CDN (MAN) 234-235 F 4
Marquette ○ USA (IA) 274-275 G 1
Marquette ○ USA (MI) 270-271 L 4
Marquette ○ USA (NE) 262-263 H 4
Marquez ○ USA (NM) 256-257 H 3
Marquez ○ USA (TX) 266-267 L 2
Marquis ○ CDN (SAS) 232-233 N 5
Marqūq ○ SUD 206-207 K 4
Marra, Gabal ▲·· SUD 200-201 B 6
Marracua ○ MOC 218-219 J 3
Marracuene ○ MOC 220-221 L 2
Marrakech = Marrākush ☆··· MA 188-189 H 5
Marraket, Hassi ○ DZ 190-191 D 5
Marrākush ☆··· MA 188-189 H 5
Marrān ○ KSA 130-131 G 6
Marrangua, Lagoa ⊖ MOC 220-221 M 2
Marrāt ○ KSA 130-131 J 5
Marrawah ○ AUS 180-181 H 6
Marrecão ○ BR 66-67 D 6
Marree ○ AUS 178-179 E 5
Marrero ○ USA (LA) 268-269 K 7
Marresale ○ RUS 108-109 M 7
Marresal'skie koški ⌒ RUS 108-109 M 7
Marroins, Ilha ⌒ BR 66-67 F 7
Marromeu ○ MOC 218-219 H 4
Marromeu, Reserva de ⊥ MOC 218-219 H 4
Marroonah ○ AUS 176-177 C 1
Marroquí o de Tarifa, Punta ▲ E 98-99 E 6
Marruás ○ BR 68-69 J 5
Marrupa ○ MOC 218-219 J 1
Mars, Le ○ USA (IA) 274-275 B 2
Marsa, La ○ TN 190-191 H 2
Marsá al Burayqah ○ LAR 192-193 H 2
Marsa-Ben-Mehidi ○ DZ 188-189 K 3
Marsabit ○ EAK 212-213 F 2
Marsabit National Reserve ⊥ EAK 212-213 F 2
Marsala ○ I 100-101 D 6
Marsá l-'Alam ○ ET 194-195 G 5
Marsā Maṭrūḥ ☆• ET 194-195 C 2
Marsā Mubārak ○ ET 194-195 G 5
Marsassoum ○ SN 202-203 C 3
Marsden ○ AUS 180-181 J 2
Marsden ○ CDN (SAS) 232-233 J 3
Marsden, Point ▲ AUS 180-181 D 3
Marseille ☆• F 90-91 K 10
Marseilles ○ USA (OH) 280-281 C 3
Marsella ○ CO 60-61 D 5
Māršenān, Kūh-e ▲ IR 134-135 E 2
Marsfjällen ▲ S 86-87 G 4
Marsh, Mount ▲ AUS 172-173 D 7
Marshall ○ CDN (SAS) 232-233 J 2
Marshall ○ LB 202-203 E 6
Marshall ○ USA (AK) 20-21 J 6
Marshall ○ USA (AR) 276-277 C 5
Marshall ○ USA (IL) 274-275 L 5
Marshall ○ USA (MI) 272-273 E 5
Marshall ○ USA (MN) 270-271 C 6
Marshall ○ USA (MO) 274-275 E 5
Marshall ○ USA (ND) 258-259 E 4
Marshall ○ USA (TX) 264-265 K 6
Marshall Islands ⌒ MAI 14-15 J 6
Marshall Lake ⊖ CDN (ONT) 234-235 Q 4
Marshall River ~ AUS 178-179 D 2
Marshall Seamounts ≃ 14-15 J 6
Marshalltown ○ USA (IA) 274-275 E 3
Marshallville ○ USA (GA) 284-285 G 4
Marshburg ○ USA (PA) 280-281 H 2
Marshfield ○ USA (MO) 276-277 C 3
Marshfield ○ USA (WI) 270-271 H 6
Marsh Fork ~ USA 20-21 R 2
Marsh Harbour ○ BS 54-55 G 1
Mars Hill ○ USA (ME) 278-279 O 2
Mars Hill ○ USA (NC) 282-283 E 5
Marsh Island ⌒ USA (LA) 268-269 J 7
Marsh Lake ⊖ CDN 20-21 X 6
Marsh Pass ▲ USA (AZ) 256-257 E 2
Marsh Point ▲ CDN 34-35 K 2
Marshville ○ USA (NC) 282-283 G 6
Marsing ○ USA (ID) 252-253 B 3
Marsiwang ~ RI 166-167 F 3
Marsoui ○ CDN (QUE) 242-243 B 3
Märsta ○ S 86-87 H 7
Mart ○ USA (TX) 266-267 L 2
Martaban ○ MYA 158-159 D 2
Martaban, Gulf of ≈ 158-159 D 2
Martand ○• IND 138-139 E 3
Martap ○ CAM 204-205 K 5
Martapura ○ RI (KSE) 164-165 D 5
Martapura ○ RI (SUS) 162-163 F 7
Marte ○ WAN 198-199 F 6
Marte, Rivière à la ~ CDN 38-39 G 3
Martel ○ CDN (BC) 230-231 H 3
Martell ○ USA (WI) 270-271 F 6
Marten River ○ CDN (ONT) 238-239 F 2
Marten River ~ CDN 30-31 P 5
Martensøya ⌒ N 84-85 M 2
Martensville ○ CDN (SAS) 232-233 M 3
Marthaguy River ~ AUS 178-179 J 6
Martha's Vineyard ⌒ USA (MA) 278-279 L 7
Marti ○ C 54-55 E 3
Martigny ○ CH 92-93 J 5
Martigues ○ F 90-91 K 10
Martil ○ MA 188-189 J 3
Martin ○ SK 92-93 P 4
Martin ○ USA (SC) 284-285 J 3
Martin ○ USA (SD) 260-261 E 3
Martin ○ USA (TN) 276-277 G 4
Martin, Lake < USA (AL) 284-285 E 4
Martinas, Las ○ C 54-55 C 4
Martinborough ○ NZ 182 E 4
Martindale ○ USA (TX) 266-267 K 4
Martineau, Cape ▲ CDN 24-25 e 7
Martinez ○ USA (GA) 284-285 H 3
Martínez de la Torre ○ MEX 52-53 F 1
Martinez Lake ○ USA (AZ) 256-257 A 6
Martinho Campos ○ BR 72-73 H 5
Martin House ○ CDN 20-21 Y 3
Martinique = Oiapoque ○ BR 62-63 J 4
Martinique Passage ≈ 56 E 4
Martin National Wildlife Refuge ⚔ USA (MD) 280-281 K 5
Martinópolis ○ BR 72-73 E 7
Martin Peninsula ⌣ ARK 16 F 25
Martin River ~ CDN 30-31 J 5
Martinsburg ○ USA (IA) 274-275 F 3
Martinsburg ○ USA (WV) 280-281 J 4
Martins Drift ○ RB 218-219 D 6
Martins Ferry ○ USA (OH) 280-281 F 3
Martinsville ○ USA (IN) 274-275 M 5
Martinsville ○ USA (TX) 268-269 F 5
Martinsville ○ USA (VA) 280-281 G 7
Martin Vaz Fracture Zone ≃ 6-7 H 10
Martok ☆ KZ 126-127 M 2
Marton ○ NZ 182 E 4
Martos ○ E 98-99 F 6
Martre, Lac la ⊖ CDN 30-31 K 4
Martti ○ FIN 88-89 K 3
Martuni ○ AR 128-129 L 2
Martynovo ○ KZ 96-97 G 8
Martynovo ○ RUS 124-125 O 2
Maru ○ RI 168 E 7
Maru ○ WAN 198-199 C 6
Maru, Pulau ⌒ RI 166-167 F 5
Maruanum ○ BR 62-63 J 5
Maruchin ∴• MEX 52-53 K 2
Maruda ○ BR 68-69 E 2
Marudá ○ BR 68-69 E 2
Marudi ○ MAL 164-165 D 1
Marudu, Teluk ≈ 160-161 B 9
Ma'rūf ○ AFG 134-135 M 3
Maruhskij, pereval ▲ RUS 126-127 D 6
Marum, Mount ▲ VAN 184 II b 3
Marumbi, Pico ▲ BR 74-75 F 5
Marungu ▲ ZRE 214-215 E 4
Marupa ○ PNG 183 G 3
Marupa, Rio ~ BR 66-67 J 6
Marūqah, Al ○ LAR 192-193 F 4
Māruteru ○ IND 140-141 J 2
Maru'ura ○ SOL 184 I e 3
Marvão ○ P 98-99 D 5
Marvast ○ IR 134-135 F 3
Marv Dašt ○ IR 134-135 E 4
Marve ○ AFG 134-135 K 1
Marvel ○ USA (CO) 254-255 G 6
Marvell ○ USA (AR) 276-277 E 6
Marvine, Mount ▲ USA (UT) 254-255 D 5
Marvyn ○ USA (AL) 284-285 E 4
Marwān ○ KSA 130-131 K 6
Marwayne ○ CDN (ALB) 232-233 H 2
Mary ☆• TM 136-137 G 6
Maryal Bai ○ SUD 206-207 H 4
Mary Anne Group ⌒ AUS 172-173 B 6
Mary Anne Passage ≈ 172-173 B 6
Mary Ann Point ▲ AUS 176-177 F 6
Maryborough ○ AUS (QLD) 178-179 M 3
Maryborough ○ AUS (VIC) 180-181 G 4
Marydale ○ ZA 220-221 F 4
Marydell ○ USA (MS) 268-269 L 4
Maryfield ○ AUS 174-175 B 4
Mary Frances Lake ⊖ CDN 30-31 Q 4
Maryhill ○ USA (WA) 244-245 E 5
Mary Kathleen ∴ AUS 174-175 E 7
Mary Lake ⊖ CDN 30-31 S 4
Maryland ▫ USA 280-281 J 4
Maryneal ○ USA (TX) 264-265 D 6
Mary River ~ AUS 172-173 K 2
Mary River ~ AUS 172-173 H 5
Mary River ~ AUS 178-179 M 3
Marysburg ○ CDN (SAS) 232-233 N 3
Marys Corner ○ USA (WA) 244-245 C 4
Marystown ○ CDN (NFL) 242-243 N 5
Marysvale ○ USA (UT) 254-255 C 5
Marysville ○ CDN (BC) 230-231 N 4
Marysville ○ CDN (ONT) 238-239 J 4
Marysville ○ USA (AR) 276-277 C 7
Marysville ○ USA (CA) 246-247 D 4
Marysville ○ USA (IN) 274-275 N 6
Marysville ○ USA (KS) 262-263 K 5
Marysville ○ USA (OH) 280-281 C 3
Marysville ○ USA (WA) 244-245 C 2
Maryupol' ○ UA 102-103 K 4
Maryvale ○ AUS 174-175 H 6
Maryville ○ USA (MO) 274-275 D 4
Maryville ○ USA (TN) 282-283 D 5
Marzagão ○ BR 72-73 F 4
Marzanābād ○ IR 136-137 B 6
Marzo, 1° de ○ PY 76-77 J 3
Marzo, Punta ▲ CO 60-61 C 4
Marzūq ▫ LAR 192-193 F 5
Marzūq ☆ LAR (MAR) 192-193 E 5
Marzūq, Hamādat ∸ LAR 192-193 E 4
Marzuq, Ṣaḥrā' ∸ LAR 192-193 E 5
Mas, Tanjung ▲ RI 166-167 B 6
Masagaweyn ○ SP 208-209 H 7
Masagua ○ GCA 52-53 J 4
Masaguara ○ HN 52-53 L 4
Masāhim, Kūh-e ▲ IR 134-135 F 3
Masahunga ○ EAT 212-213 D 5
Masai Mara National Reservat ⊥ EAK 212-213 E 4
Masā'iqa, al- ○ OM 132-133 K 2
Masai Steppe ∸ EAT 214-215 J 3
Masaka ☆ EAU 212-213 C 4
Ma'sal ○• KSA 130-131 J 5
Masalembobesar, Pulau ⌒ RI 164-165 D 6
Masalina, Kepulauan ⌒ RI 164-165 E 6
Masally = Masallı ○• AZ 128-129 N 3
Masamba ○ RI 164-165 G 5
Masan ○ ROK 150-151 G 10
Masanga ○ ZRE 210-211 J 4
Maṣāni', al- ○ Y 132-133 D 7
Masapun ○ RI 166-167 D 5
Masār, Gabal ▲ Y 132-133 C 6
Masasi ○ EAT 214-215 K 6
Masatepe ○ NIC 52-53 L 6
Más a Tierra, Isla ⌒ RCH 78-79 C 1
Masavi ○ BOL 70-71 F 6
Masawa ○ RI 164-165 F 5
Masaya ☆• NIC 52-53 L 6
Masbagik ○ RI 168 C 7
Masbate ☆ RP (MAS) 160-161 E 6
Masbate ⌒ RP (MAS) 160-161 E 6
Mascara ☆• DZ 190-191 C 3
Mascarene Basin ≃ 12 D 6
Mascarene Islands ⌒ 224 C 6
Mascarene Plain ≃ 12 O 7
Mascarene Plateau ≃ 12 E 6
Mascasín, Salinas de ○ RA 76-77 D 6
Mascota ○ MEX 52-53 B 1
Mascouche ○ CDN (QUE) 238-239 M 3
Masefield ○ CDN (SAS) 232-233 L 6
Masela, Pulau ⌒ RI 166-167 E 6
Masel'gskaja ○ RUS 88-89 N 5
Måselvfossen ~·· N 86-87 J 2
Maseru ☆ LS 220-221 H 4
Masetleng Pan < RB 220-221 E 1
Mašğed-e Abolfażl ○ IR 134-135 H 4
Mašğed-e Soleimān ○• IR 134-135 C 3
Masha ○ ETH 208-209 B 5
Mašhad ☆·· IR 136-137 F 6
Mashala ○ ZRE 210-211 J 6
Mashan ○ VRC 156-157 F 5
Mashansha, Río ~ PE 64-65 F 7
Mashar ○ SUD 206-207 H 4
Mashava ○ ZW 218-219 F 5
Mashhad = Mašhad ☆·· IR 136-137 F 6
Mashi ○ VRC 156-157 G 2
Mashike ○ J 152-153 J 3
Māshkai ~ PK 134-135 L 5
Māshkel ~ PK 134-135 L 5
Māshkel, Hāmūn-i- ⊖ PK 134-135 K 4
Mashki Chāh ○ PK 134-135 K 4
Mashkode ○ CDN (ONT) 236-237 D 5
Mashonaland Central ▫ ZW 218-219 F 3
Mashonaland East ▫ ZW 218-219 F 3
Mashonaland West ▫ ZW 218-219 E 3
Mashowingrivier ~ ZA 220-221 F 3
Mashra' ar-Raqq ○ SUD 206-207 J 4
Masi ○ N 86-87 L 2
Masia-Mbia ○ ZRE 210-211 F 5
Masian ○ RI 166-167 H 5
Masica, La ○ HN 52-53 L 4
Mašigina, guba ≈ 108-109 G 4
Masila, al- ~ Y 132-133 G 6
Masim, gora ▲ RUS 96-97 K 7
Masi-Manimba ○ ZRE 210-211 F 6
Masi-Masi, Pulau ⌒ RI 166-167 K 3
Masimba, Lake = Sagara, Lake ⊖ EAT 212-213 C 6
Masindi ○ EAU 212-213 C 3
Masindi Port ○ EAU 212-213 D 3
Masinga Reservoir < EAK 212-213 F 4
Masingbi ○ WAL 202-203 E 5
Masinloc ○ RP 160-161 C 5
Maşīra, Gazīrat ⌒ OM 132-133 L 3
Maşīra, Gulf of ≈ 132-133 L 3
Maşīra Channel ≈ 132-133 L 3
Masis ○ AR 128-129 L 2
Masisea ○ PE 64-65 E 6
Masisi ○ ZRE 212-213 B 4
Masiwang, Tanjung ▲ RI 166-167 F 3
Maskanah ○ SYR 128-129 H 4
Maškel, Rūd-e ~ IR 134-135 K 5
Maskelyne Islands ⌒ VAN 184 II a 3
Maskinongé ○ CDN (QUE) 238-239 M 2
Masliya ○ KSA 132-133 C 5
Masljanino ○ RUS 114-115 S 7
Maşna'a, al- ○ OM 132-133 K 2
Masoala, Saikanosy ⌣ RM 222-223 G 5
Masoala, Tanjona ▲ RM 222-223 G 6
Masohi ○ RI 166-167 E 3
Masoko ○ EAT 214-215 G 5
Masoller ○ ROU 76-77 J 6
Masomeloka ○ RM 222-223 F 8
Mason ○ USA (MI) 272-273 E 5
Mason ○ USA (NV) 246-247 F 5
Mason ○ USA (OH) 280-281 B 4
Mason ○ USA (TX) 266-267 H 3
Mason, Lake ⊖ AUS 176-177 E 3
Mason Bay ≈ 182 A 7
Mason City ○ USA (IA) 274-275 E 1
Mason City ○ USA (IL) 274-275 J 4
Masoni, Pulau ⌒ RI 164-165 J 4
Mason River ~ CDN 24-25 H 6
Masontown ○ USA (PA) 280-281 G 4
Maspalomas ○ E 188-189 D 7
Masqa, al- ○ KSA 132-133 C 4
Masqaṭ ★·· OM 132-133 L 2
Massa, Oued ~ MA 188-189 G 6
Massaango ○ ANG 216-217 D 4
Massachusetts ▫ USA 278-279 J 6
Massachusetts, Old Fort ∴ USA (MS) 268-269 M 6
Massachusetts Bay ≈ 278-279 L 6
Massacre Canyon Monument • USA (NE) 262-263 F 4
Massadona ○ USA (CO) 254-255 G 3
Massafra ○· I 100-101 F 4
Massaguet ○ TCH 198-199 G 6
Massajid Cali Guduud ○ SP 208-209 H 7
Massakory ○ TCH 198-199 G 6
Massalassef ○ TCH 206-207 C 3
Massama ○ WAN 198-199 C 6
Massa Marittima ○· I 100-101 C 3
Massangam ○ CAM 204-205 J 6
Massangano ○ ANG 216-217 C 4
Massangena ○ MOC 218-219 G 5
Massangulo ○ MOC 218-219 H 1
Massantola ○ RMM 202-203 G 3
Massapê ○ BR 68-69 H 3
Massaranduba ○ BR 74-75 F 6
Massarole ○ SP 212-213 K 4
Massau ○ ANG 216-217 D 3
Mass City ○ USA (MI) 270-271 J 4
Massena ○ USA (NY) 278-279 G 4
Massenya ○ TCH 206-207 C 3
Masset ○ CDN (BC) 228-229 B 2
Masset Inlet ≈ 228-229 B 3
Massey ○ CDN (ONT) 238-239 C 2
Massey Island ⌒ CDN 24-25 U 3
Massey Sound ≈ 26-27 C 4
Massiac ○ F 90-91 J 9
Massibi ○ ANG 214-215 B 6
Massif Central ▲ F 90-91 J 9
Massigui ○ RMM 202-203 G 4
Massili ~ BF 202-203 K 3
Massillon ○ USA (OH) 280-281 E 3
Massina ○ RMM 202-203 H 3
Massine, Oued ~ DZ 190-191 D 7
Massinga ○ MOC 218-219 H 6
Massingir ○ MOC 218-219 G 6
Massingir, Barragem de < MOC 218-219 F 6
Massira, Barrage al- < MA 188-189 H 4
Masson Island ⌒ ARK 16 G 10
Massosse ○ ANG 216-217 D 7
Maštaga ○ AZ 128-129 O 2
Mastah, ozero ⊖ RUS 118-119 L 3
Mastermans Range ▲ AUS 178-179 L 5
Masterton ○ NZ 182 E 4
Mastic Beach ○ USA (NY) 280-281 O 3
Mastic Point ○ BS 54-55 G 2
Mastodonte, Cerro ▲ RCH 76-77 C 2
Mastūj ~ PK 138-139 D 1
Mastung ○· PK 134-135 M 4
Mastūra ○ KSA 130-131 F 6
Mastūtah, Bi'r al ○ LAR 192-193 F 5
Mas'ūd ○ IRQ 128-129 K 4
Masuda ○ J 152-153 D 7
Masuguru ○ EAT 214-215 K 6
Masuika ○ ZRE 214-215 B 4
Mašuk, gora ▲ RUS 112-113 O 4
Māsur ○ IR 134-135 C 2
Masurai, Gunung ▲ RI 162-163 D 6
Masvingo ▫ ZW 218-219 F 5
Masvingo ☆ ZW (Mvi) 218-219 F 5
Maswaar, Pulau ⌒ RI 166-167 H 3
Maswa Game Reservat ⊥ EAT 212-213 E 5
Maṣyaf ○ SYR 128-129 G 5
Mata ○ ZRE 216-217 F 3
Mata'Avea, Cape = Cape Lisburn ▲ VAN 184 II a 2
Matabeleland North ▫ ZW 218-219 D 4
Matabeleland South ▫ ZW 218-219 E 5
Mata Bia, Gunung ▲ RI 166-167 D 6
Matacawa Levu ⌒ FJI 184 III a 2
Matachel, Río ~ E 98-99 D 5
Matachewan ○ CDN (ONT) 236-237 H 5
Matachic ○ MEX 50-51 F 3
Matacú ○ BOL 70-71 F 5
Matad = Zuunbulag ○ MAU 148-149 M 4
Mata da Corda, Serra da ▲ BR 72-73 G 5
Matadi ☆• ZRE 210-211 D 6
Matador ○ USA (TX) 264-265 D 4
Matagalpa ☆ NIC 52-53 B 5
Matagalpa, Río Grande de ~ NIC 52-53 B 5
Matagami ○ CDN 38-39 F 4
Matagami ○ CDN (QUE) 236-237 L 3
Matagami, Lac ⊖ CDN 38-39 F 4
Matagami, Lac ⊖ CDN (QUE) 236-237 L 3
Matagamon Lake ⊖ USA (ME) 278-279 N 2
Matagorda ○ USA (TX) 266-267 M 5
Matagorda Bay ≈ 266-267 L 5
Matagorda Island ⌒ USA (TX) 266-267 L 5
Matagorda Peninsula ⌣ USA 266-267 L 5
Mataj ~ RUS 122-123 F 5
Matak, Pulau ⌒ RI 162-163 G 3
Matakali ○ RI 164-165 F 5
Matakana Island ⌒ NZ 182 F 2
Matakaoa Point ▲ NZ 182 G 2
Matakawau ○ NZ 182 E 2
Matakil, Chutes de ~·· RCA 206-207 E 4
Matala ○ ANG 216-217 C 7
Matala ○ GR 100-101 K 7
Matāla ○ IND 140-141 G 2
Matala ○ ZRE 210-211 L 5
Matalaque ○ PE 70-71 B 5
Matale ○ CL 140-141 J 7
Matale ○ ZRE 212-213 B 5
Matam ○ SN 202-203 D 2
Maṭāmah, al- ○ Y 132-133 D 5
Mata Mata ○ ZA 220-221 E 2
Matamatá, Cachoeira ~ BR 66-67 G 6
Matamec ○ CDN (QUE) 242-243 B 2
Matamey ○ RN 198-199 D 6
Matamoros ○ MEX (COA) 50-51 H 5
Matamoros ○ MEX (TAM) 50-51 L 5
Matana ○ BU 212-213 B 5
Matana ○ RI 164-165 G 5
Matana, Danau ⊖ RI 164-165 G 5
Matanal Point ▲ RP 160-161 E 9
Ma'tan as Sarah ○ LAR 198-199 K 2
Ma'tan Bisciara ○ LAR 192-193 K 6
Matanda ○ Z 214-215 E 6
Matandu ~ EAT 214-215 K 5
Matane ○ CDN (QUE) 240-241 H 2
Matane, Parc Provincial de ⊥ CDN (QUE) 240-241 H 2
Matanga ○ RI 164-165 H 4
Matanga ○ RM 222-223 E 9
Matankari ○ RN 198-199 B 6
Matantas ○ VAN 184 II a 2
Matanuska River ~ USA 20-21 Q 6
Matanzas ☆ C 54-55 E 3
Matanzas ○ MEX 50-51 J 7
Matanzas ○ YV 60-61 K 3
Matanzilla, Pampa de la ∸ RA 78-79 E 4
Matão ○ BR 72-73 F 6
Mataojo ○ ROU 76-77 J 6
Mataoleo ○ RI 164-165 H 6
Mata Ortiz ○ MEX 50-51 E 2
Matapédia ○ CDN (QUE) 240-241 J 3
Matapédia, Rivière ~ CDN 240-241 H 2
Matapi, Cachoeira ~ BR 66-67 F 2
Matapi, Rio ~ BR 62-63 J 5
Mataquito, Río ~ RCH 78-79 C 3
Matara ○ CL 140-141 J 8
Matara ○· ER 200-201 J 5
Matara ○ PE 64-65 C 5
Matará ○ RA 76-77 F 5
Mataraca ○ BR 68-69 L 5
Mataram ☆ RI 168 C 7
Mataranka ○ AUS 174-175 B 4
Mataró ○ E 98-99 J 4
Mataso ⌒ VAN 184 II b 3
Matatiele ○ ZA 220-221 J 5
Matatindoe Point ▲ RP 160-161 E 8
Mataupa ○ PNG 183 F 5
Matauá, Rio ~ BR 66-67 G 5
Matausu ○ RI 164-165 G 6
Matawai ○ NZ 182 F 3
Matawin, Rivière ~ CDN 238-239 M 2
Matawin Reservoir ⊖ CDN (QUE) 238-239 M 2
Maṭāy ○ ET 194-195 E 3
Matayaya ○ DOM 54-55 K 5
Matechai ○ ANG 216-217 F 5
Matecumbe Key, Lower ⌒ USA (FL) 286-287 J 7
Mategua ○ BOL 70-71 F 3
Matehuala ○ MEX 50-51 J 6
Mateiros ○ BR 68-69 E 7
Matekwe ○ EAT 214-215 K 6

Margaree Forks — Matekwe 359

Matela o LS 220-221 H 4
Matelot o TT 60-61 L 2
Materna o EAT 214-215 H 5
Materna o MOC 218-219 G 2
Matenge o MOC 218-219 G 2
Matera ☆• I 100-101 F 4
Matéri o DY 202-203 L 4
Maternillos, Punta ▲ C 54-55 G 4
Mátészalka o H 92-93 R 5
Matete o ZRE 212-213 A 3
Matetsi o ZW (MAN) 218-219 C 4
Matetsi ~ ZW 218-219 D 4
Mateur o TN 190-191 G 2
Matewar o RI 166-167 K 2
Mather o CDN (MAN) 234-235 D 5
Mātherān o• IND 138-139 D 10
Matheson o CDN (ONT) 236-237 H 4
Matheson Island o CDN (MAN) 234-235 G 3
Matheson Point ▲ CDN 24-25 Y 6
Mathews, Lake o USA (CA) 248-249 G 6
Mathiassen Brook ~ CDN 36-37 H 2
Mathis o USA (TX) 266-267 K 5
Mathiston o USA (MS) 268-269 L 3
Mathoura o AUS 180-181 H 3
Mathura o•• IND 138-139 F 6
Mati ☆ RP 160-161 G 9
Mati ~ RUS 120-121 H 4
Matia ~ EAK 212-213 G 4
Matiacoali o BF 202-203 L 3
Matiāri o PK 138-139 B 7
Matias Cardoso o BR 72-73 J 3
Matias Olímpio o BR 68-69 G 3
Matías Romero o MEX 52-53 G 3
Matibane o MOC 218-219 L 2
Maticora, Río ~ YV 60-61 F 2
Matiguás o NIC 52-53 B 5
Matilde o RA 76-77 G 6
Matilla o RCH 70-71 C 7
Matima o RB 218-219 C 5
Matina o BR 72-73 J 2
Matinenda Lake o CDN (ONT) 238-239 C 2
Matinha o BR 74-75 F 5
Matīši o LV 94-95 J 3
Matjiesfontein o ZA 220-221 E 6
Matlahaw Point ▲ CDN (BC) 230-231 C 4
Mātli o PK 138-139 B 7
Matlock o USA (WA) 244-245 B 3
Matmata o• TN 190-191 G 4
Matnog o RP 160-161 F 6
Mato, El o YV 60-61 J 4
Matochkin Shar, Proliv = Matočkin Šar, proliv ≈ 108-109 F 5
Matočkin Šar o RUS 108-109 G 5
Matočkin Šar, proliv ≈ 108-109 F 5
Matões o BR 68-69 G 4
Mato Grosso o BR 70-71 J 3
Mato Grosso, Planalto do ⌒ BR 70-71 K 4
Mato Grosso do Sul o BR 70-71 J 6
Mato Guarrojo o CO 60-61 F 5
Matola o MOC 220-221 L 2
Matondo o MOC 218-219 H 3
Matong o PNG 183 F 3
Matope o MW 218-219 H 2
Matopo o ZW 218-219 E 5
Matos, Río ~ BOL 70-71 D 4
Matos Costa o BR 74-75 E 6
Matoury o F 62-63 H 3
Mato Verde o BR 72-73 J 3
Matraca o CO 60-61 G 6
Maṭraḥ o• OM 132-133 L 2
Matras Beach • RI 162-163 G 5
Matroosberg o ZA 220-221 D 6
Matru o WAL 202-203 D 6
Matrūbah o LAR 192-193 K 1
Matsalu Riiklik Looduskaitseala ⊥ EST 94-95 H 2
Matsanga o RCB 210-211 D 4
Matsari o CAM 204-205 K 6
Matshumbi o ZRE 212-213 B 4
Matsiatra ~ RM 222-223 E 8
Matsoandakana o RM 222-223 F 5
Matsue o J 152-153 E 7
Matsuka = Achouka o G 210-211 B 4
Matsu Liehtao ⌒ RC 156-157 L 3
Matsumae o J 152-153 J 4
Matsumoto o J 152-153 G 6
Matsu Temple • RC 156-157 M 5
Matsuyama ☆ J 152-153 E 8
Matsuzaka o J 152-153 G 7
Mattagami Lake o CDN (ONT) 236-237 G 5
Mattagami River ~ CDN 236-237 G 3
Mattagami River ~ CDN 236-237 F 2
Mattamuskeet Lake o USA (NC) 282-283 L 5
Mattaponi River ~ USA 280-281 J 6
Mattawa o CDN (ONT) 238-239 G 2
Mattawa o USA (WA) 244-245 F 4
Mattawamkeag o USA (ME) 278-279 N 3
Mattawa River Provincial Park ⊥ CDN (ONT) 238-239 F 2
Mattawishkwia River ~ CDN 236-237 E 3
Mattawitchewan River ~ CDN 236-237 D 3
Matterhorn ▲•• CH 92-93 J 5
Matterhorn ▲ USA (NV) 246-247 K 2
Mattesalja, mys ▲ RUS 108-109 Q 5
Matthews o USA (NC) 282-283 G 5
Matthews Ridge o GUY 62-63 D 2
Matthew Town o BS 54-55 J 4
Mattice o CDN (ONT) 236-237 E 3
Mattili o IND 142-143 C 6
Mattō o J 152-153 G 6
Mattoon o USA (IL) 274-275 K 5
Matty Island ⌒ CDN 24-25 Y 6
Matu o MAL 162-163 J 3
Matua, ostrov ⌒ RUS 122-123 P 4
Matucana o PE 64-65 D 7
Matuda, ozero o RUS 108-109 b 5
Matugama o CL 140-141 J 7
Matukar o PNG 183 C 3
Matuku ⌒ FJI 184 III b 3
Matundu o ZRE 206-207 F 6
Matupi, Igarapé ~ BR 66-67 G 6
Ma'tuq o SUD 200-201 F 5
Maturín ☆ YV 60-61 K 3
Matusadona National Park ⊥ ZW 218-219 E 3
Matuseviča, fiord ≈ 108-109 I b 2
Matveev, ostrov ⌒ RUS 108-109 H 7
Matveevka o RUS (ULN) 96-97 F 6
Matveevka ☆ RUS (ORB) 96-97 H 7
Matveev Kurgan o RUS 102-103 L 4
Maty-Centre o RCB 210-211 E 5
Matykil', ostrov ⌒ RUS 120-121 Q 4
Mau o IND (UTP) 142-143 B 3
Mau o IND (UTP) 142-143 C 3
Mau, Île = Emao ⌒ VAN 184 II b 3
Mauá o BR 72-73 G 7
Maua o EAK 212-213 F 3
Maúa o MOC 218-219 J 1
Mauba, Wādī ~ Y 132-133 G 5
Mauban o RP 160-161 D 5
Maubin o MYA 158-159 C 2
Maubisse o RI 166-167 C 6
Maud o USA (OK) 264-265 H 3
Maud o USA (TX) 264-265 K 5
Maude o AUS 180-181 H 3
Maué o ANG 216-217 E 8
Maués o BR 66-67 J 4
Maués, Rio ~ BR 66-67 J 4
Maués-Mirim, Rio ~ BR 66-67 J 4
Mauganj o IND 142-143 B 3
Maugris o RIM 196-197 C 5
Maui ⌒ USA (HI) 288 J 4
Mauk o RI 168 B 3
Maukeli o RI 168 E 7
Maulamyaing o MYA 158-159 D 2
Maulbronn o••• D 92-93 K 4
Mauldin o USA (SC) 284-285 H 2
Maule, Laguna del o RCH 78-79 D 4
Maule, Río ~ RCH 78-79 C 3
Maule o Pehuenche, Paso ▲ RA 78-79 D 4
Maullín o RCH 78-79 C 6
Maullín, Bahía ≈ 78-79 C 6
Maumee o USA (OH) 280-281 C 2
Maumee River ~ USA 280-281 B 2
Maumela o RI 166-167 C 6
Maumelle, Lake ⊂ USA (AR) 276-277 C 6
Maumere o RI 166-167 B 6
Maun ☆ RB 218-219 B 4
Mauna Kea ▲ USA (HI) 288 K 5
Maunaloa o USA (HI) 288 H 3
Mauna Loa ▲ USA (HI) 288 K 5
Mauneluk River ~ USA 20-21 N 3
Maungmagan Islands ⌒ MYA 158-159 D 3
Maungu o EAK 212-213 G 5
Maunoir, Lac o CDN 30-31 G 2
Maupertuis, Lac o CDN 38-39 J 3
Maupin o USA (OR) 244-245 D 5
Mauqaq o KSA 130-131 G 4
Maur, Wādī ~ Y 132-133 C 6
Mau Rānipur o IND 138-139 G 7
Maure, Col de ▲ F 90-91 L 9
Maurelle Islands Wilderness ⊥ USA 32-33 C 4
Maurepas, Lake o USA (LA) 268-269 K 6
Maurepas, Point ▲ CDN (ONT) 236-237 C 5
Mauri, Río ~ PE 70-71 C 5
Maurice, Lac o CDN (ONT) 236-237 L 5
Maurice, Lake o AUS 176-177 L 4
Maurice Ewing Bank ≃ 6-7 E 14
Mauriceville o USA (TX) 268-269 G 6
Mauricio Batista o BR 76-77 K 5
Maurine o USA (SD) 260-261 D 1
Mauritania = Mauritaniyah ■ RIM 196-197 C 4
Mauritius ■ MS 224 C 7
Mauritius ⌒•• MS 224 C 7
Maury Channel ≈ 24-25 Y 3
Mausolée • RCA 206-207 D 6
Mauston o USA (WI) 270-271 H 7
Mauterndorf o A 92-93 M 5
Mauyama o WAN 204-205 E 2
Mavaca, Río ~ YV 66-67 E 2
Māvelikara o IND 140-141 G 6
Mavengue o ANG 216-217 E 8
Mavila o PE 70-71 C 2
Mavillette o CDN (NS) 240-241 J 6
Mavinga o ANG 216-217 F 7
Mavis Reef ⌒ AUS 172-173 F 3
Mavita o MOC 218-219 G 4
Mavua o Z 218-219 B 2
Mávuè o MOC 218-219 G 5
Mavuji ~ EAT 214-215 K 5
Mavunga ~ ANG 216-217 F 6
Mavuradonha o ZW 218-219 F 3
Mawa o ZRE 210-211 L 2
Mawa-Geti o ZRE 210-211 L 2
Mawai o MAL 162-163 F 4
Mawanella o CL 140-141 J 7
Mawang o VRC 156-157 F 2
Mawanga o ZRE 216-217 D 3
Mawangdui Hanmu ∴ VRC 156-157 H 2
Mawara Island ⌒ PNG 184 I b 2
Mawasangka o RI 164-165 H 6
Māwat o IRQ 128-129 L 5
Mawdin o MYA 158-159 C 3
Mawefan o RI 166-167 H 3
Mawhun o MYA 142-143 K 3
Mawlaik o MYA 142-143 J 4
Maw Point ▲ USA (NC) 282-283 L 5
Mawson o ARK 16 G 7
Max o USA (ND) 258-259 F 4
Maxaans o SP 208-209 H 6
Maxanguape o BR 68-69 L 4
Maxbass o USA (ND) 258-259 F 3
Maxcanú o MEX 52-53 J 1
Maxeys o USA (GA) 284-285 G 3
Maxim o CDN (SAS) 232-233 O 6
Maximeville o CDN (PEI) 240-241 L 4
Máximo Gómez o C 54-55 E 3
Maxixe o MOC 218-219 H 6
Maxstone o CDN (SAS) 232-233 N 6
Maxville o USA (FL) 286-287 G 1
Maxville o USA (MT) 250-251 F 5
Maxwell o USA (CA) 246-247 C 4
Maxwell o USA (NE) 262-263 F 3
Maxwell o USA (NM) 256-257 L 2
Maxwell o USA (TN) 276-277 J 5
Maxwell Bay ≈ 24-25 b 3
Maxwell Fracture Zone ≃ 6-7 F 4
Maxwelton o AUS 174-175 G 7
May o USA (OK) 264-265 E 2
May o USA (TX) 266-267 J 2
May, Kap ▲ GRØ 26-27 Z 2
Maya o• SUD 200-201 F 6
Maya, La o C 54-55 H 4
Maya, Pulau ⌒ RI 162-163 H 5
Mayabander o IND 140-141 L 3
Mayādīn, al- o SYR 128-129 J 5
Mayaguana Island ⌒ BS 54-55 J 3
Mayaguana Passage ≈ 54-55 J 3
Mayagüez o USA (PR) 286-287 O 2
Mayahi o RN 198-199 C 6
Mayala o ZRE 216-217 D 3
Mayama o RCB 210-211 E 5
Mayamaya o EAT 212-213 E 6
Mayamba o ZRE 210-211 F 6
Maya Mountains ▲▲ BH 52-53 K 3
Mayang o VRC 156-157 F 3
Mayanja ~ EAU 212-213 C 3
Mayankwa o Z 218-219 B 2
Mayapan ∴• MEX 52-53 K 1
Mayari o C 54-55 H 4
Mayarí Arriba o C 54-55 H 4
Mayata o RN 198-199 C 5
Maybee o USA (MI) 272-273 F 6
Maybell o USA (CO) 254-255 G 3
Maybelle River ~ CDN 30-31 O 6
Maych'ew o ETH 200-201 J 6
May City o USA (IA) 274-275 C 1
May Dara Shet' ~ ETH 208-209 C 3
Maydena o AUS 180-181 J 7
Maydh o SP (San) 208-209 H 3
Maydh ⌒ SP (San) 208-209 H 3
May Downs o AUS 178-179 K 2
Mayel-Samou ~ SN 202-203 D 3
Mayenne o F 90-91 G 7
Mayenne ~ F 90-91 G 7
Mayer o USA (AZ) 256-257 C 4
Mayerthorpe o CDN (ALB) 232-233 C 2
Mayetta o USA (KS) 262-263 L 5
Mayfair o CDN (SAS) 232-233 L 3
Mayfield o CDN (SAS) 232-233 R 6
Mayfield o USA (ID) 252-253 C 3
Mayfield o USA (KY) 276-277 G 4
Mayfield o USA (UT) 254-255 D 4
Mayflower o USA (AR) 276-277 C 6
Mayhew Lake o USA (MN) 270-271 E 5
Mayhill o USA (NM) 256-257 K 6
May Inlet ≈ 24-25 V 2
Maymont o CDN (SAS) 232-233 L 3
Maymūn, Wādī ~ LAR 190-191 H 5
Maymyo o MYA 142-143 K 4
Maynard o USA (AR) 276-277 E 4
Maynas ⌒ PE 64-65 D 3
Mayne River ~ AUS 178-179 F 2
Mayneside o AUS 178-179 G 2
Māyni o IND 140-141 F 2
Maynooth o CDN (ONT) 238-239 H 3
Maynooth = Maigh Nuad o IRL 90-91 D 5
Mayo o USA (FL) 286-287 F 1
Mayo, 25 de o RA (BUA) 78-79 J 3
Mayo, 25 de o RA (MEN) 78-79 E 3
Mayo, 25 de o ROU 78-79 L 3
Mayo, Río ~ MEX 50-51 E 4
Mayo, Río ~ PE 64-65 D 5
Mayo, Río ~ RA 80 E 2
Mayo Bay ≈ 160-161 G 9
Mayo Belwa o WAN 204-205 K 4
Mayo Butale o WAN 204-205 K 4
Mayo Chehu o WAN 204-205 J 4
Mayo Darle o CAM 204-205 J 5
Mayo Djoi o CAM 206-207 B 4
Mayo Faran o WAN 204-205 K 4
Mayo Jarandi o WAN 204-205 J 5
Mayo-Kebbi □ TCH 206-207 B 3
Mayoko o RCB 210-211 D 5
Mayo Lake o CDN 20-21 X 5
Mayombé ▲▲ G 210-211 C 5
Mayo Ndaga o WAN 204-205 J 5
Mayon Volcano ▲ RP 160-161 E 6
Mayo Oulo o CAM 204-205 K 4
Mayor Buratovich o RA 78-79 H 5
Mayorga o RP 160-161 F 7
Mayor Island ⌒ NZ 182 F 2
Mayor Otano o PY 76-77 K 4
Mayototo o WAL 202-203 E 5
Mayotte ⌒ F 222-223 D 4
Mayoworth o USA (WY) 252-253 M 3
May Pen o JA 54-55 G 6
May Point, Cape ▲ USA (DE) 280-281 M 5
Mayqū' o KSA 130-131 F 3
Mayraira Point ▲ RP 160-161 D 3
Mayran, Desierto de ⌒ MEX 50-51 H 5
May River ~ AUS 172-173 G 4
May River o PNG 183 A 3
Maysel o USA (WV) 280-281 E 5
Mayson Lake o CDN 34-35 C 2
Maysville o USA (KY) 276-277 M 2
Maysville o USA (MO) 274-275 D 5
Maysville o USA (NC) 282-283 K 6
Maysville o USA (OK) 264-265 G 4
Maytown ∴ AUS 174-175 H 5
Mayu ≈ 166-167 K 5
Mayu, Pulau ⌒ RI 164-165 K 3
Mayumba o G 210-211 C 5
Mayumba o ZRE 214-215 E 4
Mayum La ▲ VRC 144-145 D 5
Māyūram o IND 140-141 H 5
May Valley o USA (CO) 254-255 N 5
Mayville o USA (MI) 272-273 F 4
Mayville o USA (ND) 258-259 K 4
Mayville o USA (NY) 278-279 B 6
Maywood o USA (NE) 262-263 F 4
Maza o RA 78-79 H 4
Maza o WAN 204-205 K 3
Mazabuka o Z 218-219 D 2
Mazagão o BR 62-63 J 6
Mazagão Velho o BR 62-63 J 6
Mazagón o E 98-99 D 6
Mazama o USA (WA) 244-245 E 2
Mazamari o PE 64-65 E 7
Mazamet o F 90-91 J 10
Mazan o PE 64-65 F 3
Mazandarān □ IR 136-137 B 6
Mazar o VRC 138-139 F 1
Mazār, Kūh-e ▲ AFG 134-135 L 2
Mazara del Vallo o I 100-101 D 6
Mazār-e Adschaeb •• AFG 136-137 K 6
Mazār-e Šarif ☆ AFG 136-137 K 6
Mazargão o BR 70-71 K 4
Mazar Karasopy • KZ 136-137 K 3
Mazarredo o RA 80 G 3
Mazartag o VRC 146-147 E 6
Mazar Tag ▲ VRC 146-147 D 6
Mazaruni River ~ GUY 62-63 E 3
Mazarwala o VRC 138-139 F 1
Mazatán o MEX (CHI) 52-53 H 4
Mazatán o MEX (SON) 50-51 D 3
Mazatenango ☆ GCA 52-53 J 4
Mazatlán o• MEX 50-51 F 6
Mazatzal Peak ▲ USA (AZ) 256-257 D 4
Mazdaǧān, Rūdhane-ye ~ IR 128-129 N 5
Mažeikiai ☆• LT 94-95 H 3
Mazéla o BF 202-203 G 4
Maze Lake o CDN 30-31 R 4
Mazenod o CDN (SAS) 232-233 M 6
Mazeppa Bay o ZA 220-221 J 6
Mazıdağı ☆ TR 128-129 J 4
Mazimechopes, Rio ~ MOC 220-221 L 2
Mazīnān o IR 136-137 E 6
Mazocahui o MEX 50-51 D 3
Mazoco o MOC 214-215 H 6
Mazo-Cruz o PE 70-71 C 5
Mazoe, Rio ~ MOC 218-219 G 3
Mazomeno o ZRE 212-213 A 6
Mazomora o EAT 214-215 K 4
Mazon o USA (IL) 274-275 K 3
Mazong Shan ▲ VRC 148-149 C 7
Mazorca, Isla ⌒ PE 64-65 D 7
Mazoula o DZ 190-191 F 6
Mazowe o ZW (Mic) 218-219 F 3
Mazowe ~ ZW 218-219 G 3
Mazra'a, al- o JOR 130-131 D 2
Mazra'eh Akhund o IR 134-135 E 3
Mazrūb o SUD 200-201 D 6
Mazsalaca o•• LV 94-95 J 3
Mazu Miao • VRC 156-157 L 4
Mazunga o ZW 218-219 E 5
Mazyr o BY 94-95 L 5
Mazzamitla o MEX 52-53 C 2
Mba o CAM 204-205 J 5
Mbabala o Z 218-219 D 3
Mbabane ★ SD 220-221 K 3
Mbacha o WAN 204-205 H 5
Mbadduna o SOL 184 I c 3
Mbadi o G 210-211 C 5
Mbadjé Akpa o RCA 206-207 E 5
Mbaéré ~ RCA 206-207 C 6
Mbagne o RIM 196-197 D 6
Mbahiakro o CI 202-203 H 6
Mbaiki ☆ RCA 210-211 F 2
Mbakaou o CAM 204-205 K 5
Mbakaou, Barrage de ⊂ CAM 204-205 K 5
Mbakaou, Lac de ⊂ CAM 204-205 K 5
Mbaké o SN 202-203 C 2
Mbako o RCA 206-207 B 6
Mbaku o• Z 214-215 F 5
Mbalabala o ZW 218-219 E 5
Mbalageti ~ EAT 212-213 E 5
Mbalam o CAM 210-211 D 2
Mbalambala o EAK 212-213 G 4
Mbale ☆• EAU 212-213 E 3
Mbali ~ RCA 206-207 C 6
Mbali-Iboma o ZRE 210-211 F 5
Mbalmayo o CAM 210-211 C 2
Mbam ~ CAM 204-205 J 6
Mbam, Massif du ▲ CAM 204-205 J 6
Mbama o CAM 210-211 D 2
Mbama o RCB 210-211 E 4
Mbamba Bay o EAT 214-215 H 6
Mbambanakira o SOL 184 I d 3
Mbam Minkom ▲ CAM 210-211 C 2
Mbandaka ☆ ZRE 210-211 G 3
Mbandjok o CAM 204-205 J 6
Mbandza o G 210-211 E 3
Mbandza-Ndounga o RCB 210-211 E 6
Mbane o SN 196-197 C 6
Mbang o CAM 210-211 E 2
Mbanga o CAM 204-205 H 6
Mbanga o SOL 184 I c 3
Mbangala ~ EAT 214-215 K 6
Mbanika Island ⌒ SOL 184 I d 3
M'banza Congo ☆ ANG 216-217 C 3
Mbanza-Ngungu = Thysville o ZRE 210-211 E 6
Mbar o SN 202-203 C 2
Mbarang'andu o EAT 214-215 J 6
Mbarangandu ~ EAT 214-215 J 6
Mbarara ☆ EAU 212-213 C 4
Mbargué o CAM 204-205 K 6
Mbari ~ RCA 206-207 F 6
Mbarizunga Game Reserve ⊥ SUD 206-207 J 6
Mbaswana o ZA 220-221 L 3
Mbata o RCA 210-211 G 2
Mbati o Z 214-215 F 6
Mbava ⌒ SOL 184 I c 2
Mbe o CAM 204-205 K 5
Mbé o CAM 210-211 E 3
Mbé ~ G 210-211 C 3
Mbé o RCB 210-211 E 5
Mbeiporo o SOL 184 I c 2
Mbéloba o RCA 206-207 E 6
Mbemkuru ~ EAT 214-215 K 5
Mbéna o RCB 210-211 C 6
Mbengué o CI 202-203 H 4
Mbengwi o CAM 204-205 J 5
M'Beni o COM 222-223 C 3
Mbéré ~ CAM 206-207 B 5
Mberengwa o ZW 218-219 E 5
Mbet o CAM 204-205 K 6
Mbéti = Alayo o RCA 206-207 F 6
Mbéwé o CAM 204-205 K 5
Mbeya □ EAT 214-215 G 5
Mbeya ☆ EAT (MBE) 214-215 G 5
Mbeya o Z 214-215 G 6
Mbi ~ RCA 206-207 C 6
Mbiama o WAN 204-205 G 6
Mbié o RCB 210-211 E 4
Mbigou o G 210-211 C 4
Mbinda o RCB 210-211 D 5
Mbinga o EAT 214-215 H 6
Mbini o GQ 210-211 B 3
Mbita o EAK 212-213 E 4
Mbitao o CAM 206-207 B 5
Mbitom o CAM 204-205 K 6
Mbiyi o RCA 206-207 F 5
Mbizi o ZW 218-219 F 5
Mbizi Mountains ▲▲ EAT 214-215 F 4
Mbo o RCA 206-207 D 4
Mboké o CAM 204-205 K 6
Mboki o RCA 206-207 G 6
Mboko o ZRE 212-213 B 5
Mbokonimbeti Island = Sandfly Island ⌒ SOL 184 I d 3
Mbokou ~ RCA 206-207 H 6
Mbolo Island ⌒ SOL 184 I d 3
Mbomo o G 210-211 D 3
Mbomou □ RCA 206-207 F 6
Mbomou ~ RCA 206-207 F 6
Mbon o RCB 210-211 E 5
Mbonge o CAM 204-205 H 6
Mborokua Island ⌒ SOL 184 I d 3
Mboroma o Z 218-219 E 2
Mborong o RI 168 E 7
Mboro-sur-Mer o SN 202-203 B 2
Mbot o CAM 204-205 J 5
Mbouda o CAM 204-205 J 6
Mboula o CAM 204-205 K 5
Mboula o RCA 206-207 C 6
Mbouma o CAM 210-211 D 2
Mboune o SN 202-203 D 2
Mboungou Badouma o G 210-211 D 4
Mbour o SN 202-203 B 2
Mbout o RIM 196-197 D 6
Mboutou ~ RCA 206-207 G 5
Mbozi o EAT 214-215 G 5
Mbozi Meteorit • EAT 214-215 G 5
Mbrés o• RCA 206-207 D 5
Mbu ~ CAM 204-205 H 6
Mbudi o ZRE 210-211 F 6
Mbugwe o EAT 212-213 F 6
Mbuji-Mayi ☆ ZRE (KOR) 214-215 B 4
Mbuji-Mayi ~ ZRE 214-215 B 4
Mbuke Islands ⌒ PNG 183 D 2
Mbulu o EAT 212-213 E 5
Mbuma o SOL 184 I e 3
Mburucuyá o RA 76-77 H 5
Mbuyuni o EAT (KIL) 212-213 F 6
Mbuyuni o EAT (MOR) 214-215 J 4
Mbwamaji o EAT 214-215 K 4
Mbwewe o EAT 214-215 K 4
McAdam National Park ⊥ PNG 183 D 4
McAdoo o USA (TX) 264-265 C 5
McAleese Lake o CDN 30-31 U 5
McAlester o USA (OK) 264-265 J 4
McAlester Army Ammunition Plant xx USA (OK) 264-265 J 4
McAllen o USA (TX) 266-267 J 7
McAllister State Historic Site, Fort • USA (GA) 284-285 J 5
McArthur o USA (OH) 280-281 D 4
McArthur Falls o CDN (MAN) 234-235 G 4
McArthur River ~ AUS 174-175 D 5
McBee o USA (SC) 284-285 K 2
McBeth Fiord ≈ 28-29 F 2
McBeth River ~ CDN 28-29 E 2
McBride o CDN (BC) 228-229 O 3
McCall o USA (ID) 252-253 B 2
McCall Seamount ≃ 288 J 6
McCallum o CDN (NFL) 242-243 M 5
McCamey o USA (TX) 266-267 E 2
McCammon o USA (ID) 252-253 F 4
McCann Lake o CDN 30-31 Q 5
McCarthy o USA 20-21 T 6
McCauley Island ⌒ CDN 228-229 D 3
McCaulley o USA (TX) 264-265 D 6
McCleary o USA (WA) 244-245 B 3
McClellan Creek ~ USA 264-265 D 3
McClellanville o USA (SC) 284-285 L 3
McClenny o USA (FL) 286-287 G 1
McClintock Channel ≈ 24-25 U 4
McClintock Point ▲ CDN 24-25 W 6
McClintock Range ▲▲ AUS 172-173 H 5
McCloud o USA (CA) 246-247 C 2
McCluer Island ⌒ AUS 172-173 L 1
McClure o USA (OH) 280-281 C 2
McClure Strait ≈ 24-25 M 3
McClusky o USA (ND) 258-259 G 4
McClusky Pass ▲ USA (NV) 246-247 J 4
McColl o USA (SC) 284-285 L 2
McComb o USA (MS) 268-269 K 5
McConaughy, Lake C.W. ⊂ USA (NE) 262-263 E 3
McCondy o USA (MS) 268-269 M 3
McConkey Hill ▲ AUS 176-177 F 2
McConnells o USA (SC) 284-285 J 2
McConnellsburg o USA (PA) 280-281 H 4
McConnel Range ▲▲ CDN 30-31 G 3
McConnel River ~ CDN 30-31 W 5
McConnelsville o USA (OH) 280-281 E 4
McCook o USA (NE) 262-263 F 4
McCool o USA (MS) 268-269 L 3
McCool Junction o USA (NE) 262-263 J 4
McCormick o USA (SC) 284-285 H 3
McCoy Creek ~ CDN 232-233 J 6
McCoy Mountains ▲▲ USA 248-249 K 6
McCracken o USA (KS) 262-263 G 6
McCreary o CDN (MAN) 234-235 D 4
McCredie Springs o USA (OR) 244-245 C 7
McCrory o USA (AR) 276-277 D 5
McCulloch o CDN (BC) 230-231 K 4
McCullough Range ▲▲ USA 248-249 J 4
McDavid o USA (FL) 286-287 B 1
McDermitt o USA (NV) 246-247 H 2
McDonald o USA (KS) 262-263 E 5
McDonald Island ⌒ AUS 12 F 10
McDonald Peak ▲ USA (MT) 250-251 F 4
McDonnel, Cape ▲ CDN 30-31 J 2
McDonough o USA (GA) 284-285 F 3
McDouall Peak o AUS 178-179 C 5
McDougal, Lake ⊂ ZW 218-219 F 5
McDougall Sound ≈ 24-25 X 3
McDowell o USA (AZ) 256-257 D 5
McDowell o USA (VA) 280-281 G 5
McDowell Indian Reservation, Fort ✕ USA (AZ) 256-257 D 5
McDowell River ~ CDN 34-35 K 4
McDowell River ~ CDN 234-235 L 2
Mcensk o RUS 94-95 P 5
McEwen o USA (TN) 276-277 H 4
McFaddin o USA (TX) 266-267 K 5
McFarland o USA (CA) 248-249 E 4
McFarlane River ~ CDN 30-31 P 6
McGee o CDN (SAS) 232-233 K 4
McGehee o USA (AR) 276-277 D 7
McGill o USA (NV) 246-247 L 4
McGillivray Bay ≈ 24-25 X 6
McGivney o CDN (NB) 240-241 J 4
McGrath o USA (AK) 20-21 N 5
McGrath o USA (MN) 270-271 E 4
McGregor o USA (MN) 270-271 E 4
McGregor o USA (ND) 258-259 E 3
McGregor, Lake o CDN (ALB) 232-233 F 5
McGregor Range ▲▲ AUS 178-179 G 4
McGregor River ~ CDN 228-229 N 2
McGuire, Mount ▲ USA (ID) 250-251 E 6
McHenry River ~ AUS 174-175 G 2
Mcherrah ⌒ DZ 188-189 J 7
Mcheta o GE 126-127 F 7
Mchinga o EAT 214-215 K 5
Mchinji o MW 218-219 G 1
M'Chouneche o DZ 190-191 F 3
McIlwraith Range ▲▲ AUS 174-175 G 3
McInnes Lake o CDN 34-35 K 4
McInnes Lake o CDN (ONT) 234-235 K 2
McIntosh o USA (SD) 260-261 E 1
McIntyre Bay ≈ 228-229 B 2
McIntyre Bay o CDN (ONT) 234-235 P 5
McIver's o CDN (NFL) 242-243 K 3
McIvor River ~ CDN 30-31 N 6
McKague o CDN (SAS) 232-233 P 3
McKay, Mount ▲ AUS 172-173 E 7
McKay Lake o CDN (NFL) 38-39 M 2
McKay Lake o CDN (ONT) 236-237 B 3
McKay Range ▲▲ AUS 172-173 F 7
McKeand River ~ CDN 36-37 P 2
McKellar o CDN (ONT) 238-239 F 3
McKeller o CDN (ONT) 238-239 F 3
McKenna o USA (WA) 244-245 C 4
McKenzie o USA (AL) 284-285 D 5
McKenzie o USA (TN) 276-277 G 4
McKenzie Bridge o USA (OR) 244-245 C 6
McKenzie Draw ~ USA 264-265 B 6
McKenzie River ~ USA 244-245 C 6
McKinlay o AUS 178-179 F 1
McKinlay River ~ AUS 178-179 F 1
McKinley, Mount ▲•• USA 20-21 P 5
McKinney o USA (TX) 264-265 H 5
McKinney Mountain ▲ USA (TX) 266-267 D 4
McKinnon o USA (WY) 252-253 J 5
McKittrick o USA (CA) 248-249 E 4
McLain o USA (MS) 268-269 M 5
McLaren Creek o AUS 174-175 C 7
McLaren Vale o AUS 180-181 E 3
McLaughlin o USA (SD) 260-261 F 1
McLean o CDN (SAS) 232-233 O 5
McLean o USA (IL) 274-275 J 4
McLean o USA (TX) 264-265 D 3
McLeansboro o USA (IL) 274-275 K 6
McLeary Point ▲ CDN (NWT) 36-37 K 6
McLeese Lake o CDN (BC) 228-229 M 4
McLeod o USA (MT) 250-251 J 6
McLeod o USA (ND) 258-259 K 5
McLeod Bay o CDN 30-31 O 4
McLeod Lake o CDN 32-33 J 4
McLeod River o CDN (ALB) 232-233 B 2
McLeod River ~ CDN 228-229 R 3
McLeod River ~ CDN 232-233 C 2
McLeods Corner o USA (MI) 270-271 N 4
McLeod Valley o CDN (ALB) 232-233 C 2
McLemon, Lake ⌒ AUS 172-173 H 5
M'Clintock o CDN 34-35 J 2
McLoughlin, Mount ▲ USA (OR) 244-245 C 8
McLoughlin Bay ≈ 30-31 U 2
McLure o CDN (BC) 230-231 J 2
McMahon o CDN (SAS) 232-233 L 5
McManaman Lake o CDN 30-31 X 4
McMasterville o CDN (QUE) 238-239 M 3
McMillan o USA (MI) 270-271 N 4
McMillan, Lake o USA (NM) 256-257 L 6
McMinnville o USA (OR) 244-245 B 5
McMinnville o USA (TN) 276-277 K 5
McMorran o CDN (SAS) 232-233 K 4
McMurdo o ARK 16 F 17
McMurdo o CDN (BC) 230-231 N 2
McMurdo Sound ≈ 16 F 17
McMurray o USA (WA) 244-245 C 2
McMurtry, Lake o USA (OK) 264-265 G 2
McNab Cove o CDN (NS) 240-241 P 5
McNary o USA (AZ) 256-257 F 4
McNary o USA (TX) 266-267 B 2
McNaughton Lake ⊂ CDN 30-31 U 2
McNeal o USA (AZ) 256-257 F 7
McNeill o USA (MS) 268-269 L 6
McNeill, Port o CDN (BC) 230-231 B 3
McParlon Lake o CDN (ONT) 236-237 H 2
McPhee Reservoir ⊂ USA (CO) 254-255 G 6
McPherson o USA (KS) 262-263 J 6
McPhersons Pillar ▲ AUS 176-177 H 2
McQuesten River ~ CDN 20-21 W 5
McRae o USA (GA) 284-285 H 4
McRobertson Land ⌒ ARK 16 G 7
McTaggart o CDN (SAS) 232-233 O 6
McTavish o CDN (MAN) 234-235 F 5
McTavish Arm o CDN 30-31 K 2
McVicar Arm o CDN 30-31 J 3
McVille o USA (ND) 258-259 J 4
Mdandu o EAT 214-215 H 5
Mdantsane o ZA 220-221 H 6
Mdina o•• M 100-101 E 7
M'Doukal o DZ 190-191 E 3
M'Drac o VN 158-159 K 4
Meacham o CDN (SAS) 232-233 N 3
Mead o CDN (ONT) 236-237 E 3
Mead o USA (NE) 262-263 K 3
Mead, Lake o USA (NV) 248-249 K 3
Meade o USA (KS) 262-263 F 7
Meade Peak ▲ USA (ID) 252-253 G 4
Meade River ~ USA 20-21 M 2
Meadow o USA (TX) 264-265 B 5
Meadow o USA (UT) 254-255 C 5
Meadowbank o AUS 174-175 H 6
Meadowbank River ~ CDN 30-31 V 3
Meadow Brook Pass ▲ USA (OR) 244-245 G 6
Meadow Creek o CDN (BC) 230-231 M 3
Meadow Creek o USA (ID) 250-251 C 3
Meadowlands o USA (MN) 270-271 F 3
Meadow Portage o CDN (MAN) 234-235 D 3
Meadows o CDN (MAN) 234-235 F 4
Meadow Valley Range ▲▲ USA 248-249 K 2
Meadow Valley Wash ~ USA 248-249 K 3
Meadville o USA (PA) 280-281 F 2
Meaford o CDN (ONT) 238-239 E 4
Meakan-dake ▲ J 152-153 L 3
Mealhada o P 98-99 C 4
Méana o RN 202-203 L 2
Meana o TM 136-137 G 6
Meander River o CDN 30-31 L 6
Mearim, Rio ~ BR 68-69 F 4
Meath Park o CDN (SAS) 232-233 N 2
Meaux o F 90-91 J 7
Mebali o RI 164-165 F 5
Mebane o USA (NC) 282-283 H 4
Mebo, Gunung ▲ RI 166-167 G 2
Mebougou o RMM 202-203 G 4
Mebridege ~ ANG 216-217 B 3
Mecanhelas o MOC 218-219 H 2
Mecatan o MEX 50-51 G 7
Mécatina, Cap ▲ CDN (QUE) 242-243 J 2
Mecaya, Río ~ CO 64-65 E 1
Mecca o USA (CA) 248-249 J 6
Mecca = Makka ☆•• KSA 132-133 A 3
Mecequesse, Rio ~ MOC 218-219 J 2
Mecham, Cape ▲ CDN 24-25 L 3
Mechanicsburg o USA (OH) 280-281 C 3
Mechanicville o USA (NY) 278-279 H 6
Mechāra o ETH 208-209 E 4
Mechelen o• B 92-93 H 3
Mecheria o DZ 188-189 L 4
Méchiméré o TCH 198-199 G 6
Méchins, Les o CDN (QUE) 240-241 J 2
Mechra-Bel-Ksiri o MA 188-189 J 3
Mechra-Benâbbou o MA 188-189 H 4
Mechroha o DZ 190-191 F 2
Mečigmenskij zaliv ≈ 112-113 Y 4
Mecitözü ☆ TR 128-129 F 2
Meckel o USA (KY) 276-277 M 4
Mečkereva ~ RUS 112-113 P 3
Mecklenburger Bucht ≈ 92-93 L 1
Mecklenburg-Vorpommern □ D 92-93 M 2
Meconta o MOC 218-219 K 2
Mecubúri o MOC 218-219 K 2
Mecubúri, Rio ~ MOC 218-219 K 2
Mecúfi o MOC 218-219 L 1
Mecula o MOC 214-215 J 7
Medak o• IND 138-139 G 10
Medan ☆ RI 162-163 C 3
Medan Fair • RI 162-163 C 3
Medang, Pulau ⌒ RI 168 C 7
Medang, Tanjung ▲ RI 162-163 D 3
Medanosa, Punta ▲ RA 80 H 4
Médanos de Coro, Parque Nacional ⊥ YV 60-61 G 2
Medart o USA (FL) 286-287 E 1
Medawachchiya o CL 140-141 J 6
Medd Allah o RMM 202-203 H 2
Médéa ☆ DZ 190-191 D 2
Medeiros o BR 72-73 G 5
Medellín o CO 60-61 D 4
Medelpad ⌒ S 86-87 H 5
Medenine ☆ TN 190-191 H 4
Méderdra o RIM 196-197 C 6
Medford o USA (NJ) 280-281 M 4
Medford o USA (OK) 264-265 G 2
Medford o USA (WI) 270-271 H 5
Medford o• USA (OR) 244-245 C 8
Medgidia o RO 102-103 F 5
Medha o IND 140-141 E 2
Medi o SUD 206-207 K 6
Media Luna o RA 78-79 F 3
Medianeira o BR 76-77 K 3
Mediapolis o USA (IA) 274-275 G 3
Mediaş o• RO 102-103 D 4
Medical Lake o USA (WA) 244-245 H 3
Medical Springs o USA (OR) 244-245 H 5
Medicine Bow o USA (WY) 252-253 M 5
Medicine Bow Mountains ▲▲ USA 252-253 M 5
Medicine Bow Peak ▲ USA (WY) 252-253 M 5
Medicine Creek ~ USA 262-263 F 4

360 Matela — Medicine Creek

Mezón o **BOL** 76-77 E 2
Mežozernyj o **RUS** 96-97 L 6
Mezquita Catedral •• **E** 98-99 E 2
Mezquital o **MEX** (DGO) 50-51 G 6
Mezquital o **MEX** (TAM) 50-51 L 5
Mezquital, Río ~ **MEX** 50-51 G 6
Mfou o **CAM** 210-211 C 2
Mfouati o **RCB** 210-211 D 6
Mfum o **WAN** 204-205 H 6
Mgači o **RUS** 122-123 K 3
Mgangerabeli Plains ⊥ **EAK** 212-213 H 4
Mgbidi o **WAN** 204-205 G 6
Mgende o **EAT** 212-213 C 6
Mgeta o **EAT** 214-215 K 4
Mg.Mu'oh o **VN** 156-157 C 6
Mgneta, Hassi ⁂ **MA** 188-189 K 4
Mgunga o **EAT** 214-215 J 4
Mhamid o **MA** 188-189 J 6
Mhangura o **ZW** 218-219 F 3
Mhasvād o **IND** 140-141 F 2
Mhlatuze ~ **ZA** 220-221 K 4
Miajadas o **E** 98-99 E 5
Mial, Oued ~ **DZ** 190-191 D 6
Miamére o **RCA** 206-207 D 4
Miami o **USA** (AZ) 256-257 E 5
Miami o **USA** (OK) 264-265 K 2
Miami o **USA** (TX) 286-287 J 6
Miami-i ∗ **USA** (FL) 286-287 J 6
Miami, North o **USA** (FL) 286-287 J 6
Miami Beach o **USA** (FL) 286-287 J 6
Miami Canal < **USA** (FL) 286-287 J 5
Miami River ~ **USA** 280-281 B 4
Miami River ~ **USA** 280-281 D 3
Miamo, El o **YV** 62-63 D 2
Mián Channün o **PK** 138-139 D 4
Miandrivazo o **RM** 222-223 D 7
Miangas, Pulau ~ **RI** 164-165 K 1
Miani o **PK** 138-139 D 3
Miani Hor ≈ **PK** 134-135 M 6
Mianmian Shan ▲ **VRC** 156-157 B 2
Mianmin o **PNG** 183 A 3
Mianning o **VRC** 156-157 C 2
Miānwāli o **PK** 138-139 C 3
Mian Xian o **VRC** 154-155 E 5
Mianyang o **VRC** 154-155 D 6
Mianzhu o **VRC** 154-155 D 6
Miao ~ **ZRE** 214-215 B 4
Miaodao Qundao ᴖ **VRC** 150-151 C 8
Miaoergou o **VRC** 146-147 F 3
Miao Li o **RC** 156-157 M 4
Miao Ling ▲ **VRC** 156-157 E 3
Miaozu o **VRC** 156-157 E 3
Miarinarivo o **RM** (ATN) 222-223 E 7
Miarinarivo o **RM** (TMA) 222-223 F 6
Miaru o **PNG** 183 B 5
Miass ∗ **RUS** (CEL) 96-97 M 6
Miass ~ **RUS** 96-97 L 6
Miass ~ **RUS** 114-115 H 7
Miasskoe o **RUS** 96-97 M 6
Miastko o **PL** 92-93 O 1
Miáti o **IND** 138-139 J 4
Mibalaie o **ZRE** 210-211 H 6
Mibenge o **Z** 214-215 E 6
Mibu Island ᴖ **PNG** 183 B 5
Mica o **ZA** 220-221 K 2
Mica Creek o **CDN** (BC) 228-229 Q 4
Micaúne o **MOC** 218-219 J 4
Miccosukee, Lake o **USA** (FL) 286-287 F 1
Michael, Lake o **CDN** 36-37 U 7
Michael, Mount ▲ **PNG** 183 C 4
Michalovce o **SK** 92-93 Q 4
Michel o **CDN** 32-33 Q 3
Michel, Lake o **CDN** (NFL) 242-243 L 2
Michel, Pointe á ▲ **CDN** (QUE) 240-241 G 2
Michelago o **AUS** 180-181 K 3
Michel Peak ▲ **CDN** (BC) 228-229 H 3
Michelsen, Cape ▲ **CDN** 24-25 U 5
Michelson, Mount ▲ **USA** 20-21 S 3
Miches o **DOM** 54-55 L 5
Michichi o **CDN** (ALB) 232-233 F 4
Michie, Lake o **USA** (NC) 282-283 J 4
Michigamme River ~ **USA** 270-271 K 4
Michigan o **USA** 270-271 M 6
Michigan, Lake o **USA** (MI) 272-273 B 5
Michigan Bar o **USA** (CA) 246-247 D 5
Michigan Center o **USA** (MI) 272-273 E 5
Michigan City o **USA** (IN) 274-275 M 3
Michigan City o **USA** (ND) 258-259 J 3
Michigan Potawatomi Indian Reservation ⅄ **USA** (MI) 270-271 L 5
Michilla o **RCH** 76-77 B 2
Michipicoten Bay o **CDN** (ONT) 236-237 G 2
Michipicoten Island ᴖ **CDN** (ONT) 236-237 F 2
Michoacan ▣ **MEX** 52-53 C 2
Michurinsk ∗ Mičurinsk o **RUS** 94-95 R 5
Mico, Río ~ **NIC** 52-53 B 5
Miconge o **ZRE** 210-211 D 6
Micronesia ᴖ **FSM** 13 G 2
Microondas o **MEX** 50-51 O 5
Mičurinsk o **RUS** 94-95 R 5
Midai, Pulau ~ **RI** 162-163 G 4
Midal o **RN** 198-199 B 4
Midale o **CDN** (SAS) 232-233 P 6
Midar o **MA** 188-189 K 3
Midas o **USA** (NV) 246-247 J 2
Midas Şehri ∴ **TR** 128-129 D 3
Mid-Atlantic Ridge ≃ 14 J 5
Mid Baffin o **CDN** 28-29 E 2
Middelburg o **NL** 92-93 G 3
Middelburg o **ZA** (CAP) 220-221 G 4
Middelburg o **ZA** (TRA) 220-221 J 2
Middelpos o **ZA** 220-221 E 5
Middelveld ⊥ **ZA** 220-221 G 3
Middelveld ⊥ **ZA** 220-221 H 2
Middelwit o **ZA** 220-221 H 2

Middendorfa, zaliv ≈ 108-109 Y 4
Middle Alkali Lake o **USA** (CA) 246-247 E 2
Middle Andaman ᴖ **IND** 140-141 J 5
Middlebro o **CDN** (MAN) 234-235 N 4
Middleburg o **USA** (MA) 278-279 L 7
Middleburg o **USA** (NY) 278-279 H 4
Middlecamp o **AUS** 180-181 F 2
Middle Channel ~ **CDN** 20-21 X 2
Middle Creek ~ **USA** 282-283 J 5
Middle Fabius River ~ **USA** 274-275 F 4
Middle Fiord ≈ 26-27 C 4
Middle Fork o **USA** 20-21 T 4
Middle Fork ~ **USA** 276-277 M 3
Middle Fork ~ **USA** 276-277 M 3
Middle Fork Chandalar ~ **USA** 20-21 R 2
Middle Fork John Day River ~ **USA** 244-245 F 3
Middle Fork Koyukuk ~ **USA** 20-21 P 3
Middle Fork Kuskokwim River ~ **USA** 20-21 N 5
Middle Fork Salmon River ~ **USA** 22-23 Q 3
Middle Fork Salt River ~ **USA** 274-275 F 5
Middle Gate o **USA** (NV) 246-247 G 4
Middle Ground o **USA** 54-55 G 2
Middle Hart River ~ **CDN** 20-21 W 4
Middle Island ᴖ **USA** 176-177 G 7
Middle Lake o **CDN** (SAS) 232-233 N 3
Middle Loup River ~ **USA** 262-263 G 3
Middlemount o **AUS** 178-179 K 2
Middle Musquodoboit o **CDN** (NS) 240-241 M 6
Middle Ohio o **CDN** (NS) 240-241 K 7
Middle Park o **AUS** 174-175 G 6
Middle Pease River ~ **USA** 264-265 G 4
Middle Rapids o **CDN** 32-33 O 3
Middle Ridge ▲ **CDN** 242-243 N 4
Middle River o **CDN** 228-229 J 2
Middle River ~ **USA** 270-271 B 2
Middle Sackville o **CDN** (NS) 240-241 M 6
Middle Sand Hills ▲ **CDN** 232-233 H 5
Middlesboro o **USA** (KY) 276-277 M 4
Middlesbrough o **GB** 90-91 G 4
Middleton o **AUS** 178-179 F 2
Middleton o **CDN** (NS) 240-241 K 6
Middleton o **USA** (MI) 272-273 E 4
Middleton o **USA** (TN) 276-277 M 3
Middleton o **USA** (WI) 274-275 J 1
Middleton o **ZA** 220-221 G 6
Middleton, Mount ▲ **CDN** (QUE) 236-237 P 3
Middleton Island ᴖ **USA** 20-21 R 7
Middletown o **USA** (CA) 246-247 C 5
Middletown o **USA** (CT) 280-281 O 2
Middletown o **USA** (DE) 280-281 L 4
Middletown o **USA** (IA) 274-275 G 4
Middletown o **USA** (NY) 280-281 M 2
Middletown o **USA** (OH) 280-281 E 4
Middletown o **USA** (PA) 280-281 J 4
Middletown o **USA** (PA) 280-281 K 3
Middleville o **USA** (MI) 272-273 D 5
Middleville o **USA** (NY) 278-279 G 5
Middlewood o **CDN** (NS) 240-241 K 7
Midfield o **USA** (TX) 266-267 L 5
Midi, Canal du < **F** 90-91 J 10
Midi-Indian Basin ≃ 12 F 5
Mid-Indian Ridge ≃ 12 F 5
Midi-Pyrénées □ **F** 90-91 H 10
Midkiff o **USA** (TX) 266-267 F 2
Midland o **AUS** 176-177 C 5
Midland o **CDN** (ONT) 238-239 F 4
Midland o **USA** (CA) 248-249 K 6
Midland o **USA** (MI) 272-273 E 4
Midland o **USA** (SD) 260-261 F 4
Midland o **USA** (TX) 266-267 E 2
Midlander ▲ **USA** 178-179 H 4
Midlands ▣ **ZW** 218-219 E 4
Midlothian o **USA** (TX) 264-265 G 6
Midnab, al- o **KSA** 130-131 J 5
Midongy ▲ **RM** 222-223 E 9
Midongy Atsimo o **RM** 222-223 E 9
Midouze ~ **F** 90-91 G 10
Mid-Pacific-Seamounts ≃ 14-15 H 5
Midpines o **USA** (CA) 248-249 F 5
Miósandur o **IS** 86-87 c 2
Midsayap o **RP** 160-161 F 9
Midsommerkra o **GRØ** 26-27 g 2
Midu o **VRC** 142-143 M 3
Midvale Summit ▲ **USA** (ID)
Midville o **USA** (GA) 284-285 H 4
Midway o **USA** (AL) 284-285 E 4
Midway o **USA** (AR) 274-275 F 6
Midway o **USA** (MS) 268-269 K 4
Midway o **USA** (TX) 268-269 E 5
Midway Corner o **USA** (AR) 276-277 E 5
Midway Islands ᴖ **USA** 14-15 L 5
Midway Islands ᴖ **USA** 20-21 Q 1
Midway Range ▲ **CDN** 230-231 L 4
Midway Stores o **USA** (SD) 260-261 J 3
Midway Well o **USA** (CA) 248-249 K 6
Midwest o **USA** (WY) 252-253 M 4
Midwest City o **USA** (OK) 264-265 G 3
Midwestern Highway II **AUS** 180-181 H 3
Mië o **ETH** 208-209 E 3
Mile o **VRC** 156-157 C 4
Milepa o **EAT** 214-215 F 5
Miles o **AUS** 178-179 K 5
Miles o **USA** (TX) 266-267 G 2
Miles o **USA** (WA) 244-245 G 3
Miechów o **PL** 92-93 Q 3
Międzyrzec Podlaski o **PL** 92-93 R 3
Międzyrzecz o **PL** 92-93 N 2
Mielec o **PL** 92-93 Q 3
Miélékouka o **RCB** 210-211 D 3
Miembwe o **EAT** 214-215 J 4
Mier o **MEX** 50-51 K 3
Miera o **USA** (NM) 256-257 J 4
Miercurea-Ciuc ∗ **RO** 102-103 D 4

Mieres o **E** 98-99 E 3
Mier y Noriega o **MEX** 50-51 J 6
Mierzeja Wiślana ᴖ **PL** 92-93 P 1
Miette Hot Springs ∴ **CDN** (ALB) 228-229 R 3
Mifflin o **USA** (TN) 276-277 G 5
Migdol o **ZA** 220-221 H 3
Migiónico o **I** 100-101 F 4
Migole o **EAT** 214-215 H 4
Migoli o **EAT** 212-213 H 6
Migori o **EAK** 212-213 D 4
Migration Lake o **CDN** 30-31 P 3
Miguasha, Parc Provencial de ⊥ **CDN** (QUE) 240-241 J 2
Miguel Alemán, Presa < **MEX** 52-53 F 2
Miguel Alves o **BR** 68-69 H 4
Miguel Auza o **MEX** 50-51 H 5
Miguel Calmon o **BR** 68-69 H 7
Miguel Hidalgo, Presa < **MEX** 50-51 G 4
Miguel Leão o **BR** 68-69 J 7
Miguel Pereira o **BR** 72-73 J 7
Miguelopolis o **BR** 72-73 F 6
Migues o **ROU** 78-79 M 3
Mihailov ∗ **RUS** 94-95 Q 4
Mihajlovgrad = Monatana ∗ **BG** 102-103 C 6
Mihajlovka o **KZ** 136-137 M 3
Mihajlovka o **RUS** (BUR) 116-117 M 10
Mihajlovka o **RUS** (ROS) 122-123 D 7
Mihajlovka o **RUS** (SAH) 120-121 E 3
Mihajlovka o **RUS** (VLG) 102-103 N 2
Mihajlovka o **RUS** (VLG) 96-97 N 6
Mihajlovsk o **RUS** 96-97 L 5
Mihalıççık o **TR** 128-129 D 3
Mihalkino o **RUS** 112-113 L 2
Mihama o **J** 152-153 G 7
Mihnevo o **RUS** 94-95 P 4
Miho-wan ≈ 152-153 E 7
Mihrāč, al- o **SUD** 200-201 E 4
Mihuanoyacu o **EC** 64-65 D 7
Mihumo Chini o **EAT** 214-215 K 5
Mijaki, Kirgiz- ∗ **RUS** 96-97 J 7
Mijaly o **KZ** 96-97 H 3
Mijek o **WSA** 196-197 D 3
Mikado o **CDN** (SAS) 232-233 Q 4
Mikasa o **J** 152-153 J 3
Mikaševičy o **BY** 94-95 K 5
Mikawa-wan ≈ 152-153 G 7
Mikčangda ~ **RUS** 108-109 Y 7
Miki o **PNG** 183 B 5
Mikindani o **EAT** 214-215 L 6
Mikkeli ∗ **FIN** 88-89 J 6
Mikkwa River ~ **CDN** 32-33 N 3
Miknás o **MA** 188-189 J 4
Mikojana, zaliv ≈ 108-109 l e 2
Mikonos ᴖ **GR** 100-101 K 6
Mikulkin, mys ▲ **RUS** 88-89 T 3
Mikumi o **EAT** 214-215 J 4
Mikumi Lodge o **EAT** 214-215 J 4
Mikumi National Park ⊥ **EAT** 214-215 J 4
Mikumi-sanmyaku ▲ **J** 152-153 H 6
Mikun' o **RUS** 88-89 V 5
Mikuni o **J** 152-153 G 6
Mikwam River ~ **CDN** 236-237 H 3
Mil ~ **RUS** 120-121 E 3
Mil, Ust'- o **RUS** 120-121 E 4
Mila o **DZ** 190-191 F 2
Milaca o **USA** (MN) 270-271 E 5
Miladummadulu Atoll ᴖ **MV** 140-141 F 4
Milagres o **BR** (BAH) 72-73 L 2
Milagres o **BR** (CEA) 68-69 J 5
Milagro o **EC** 64-65 C 3
Milagro o **USA** (NM) 256-257 K 4
Milagro, El o **MEX** 50-51 H 3
Milagros o **RP** 160-161 E 6
Milait o **GRØ** 28-29 Y 3
Milam o **USA** (TX) 268-269 G 5
Milan o **USA** (GA) 284-285 G 4
Milan o **USA** (KS) 262-263 J 7
Milan o **USA** (MI) 272-273 F 5
Milan o **USA** (MN) 270-271 C 5
Milan o **USA** (MO) 274-275 E 4
Milan o **USA** (NM) 256-257 H 3
Milan = Milano ∗∗∗ **I** 100-101 B 2
Milando o **ANG** 216-217 D 4
Milando, Reserva Especial do ⊥ **ANG** 216-217 D 4
Milang o **AUS** 180-181 E 3
Milange o **MOC** 218-219 H 3
Milange o **ZRE** 212-213 A 5
Milango ~ **RI** 164-165 G 3
Milano ∗∗∗ **I** 100-101 B 2
Milano, Lago o **USA** (TX) 266-267 J 4
Milanoa o **RM** 222-223 F 4
Milas ∗ **TR** 128-129 B 4
Milazzo o **I** 100-101 E 5
Milbank o **USA** (SD) 260-261 K 1
Milbanke Sound ≈ 32-33 F 5
Milbanke Sound ≈ 228-229 F 4
Milbridge o **USA** (ME) 278-279 O 4
Milburn o **USA** (NE) 262-263 G 3
Milden o **CDN** (SAS) 232-233 L 4
Mildet o **MA** 188-189 J 4
Mildred o **USA** (SAS) 232-233 L 2
Mildred o **USA** (MT) 250-251 P 5
Mildura o **AUS** 180-181 F 2
Mildura Gemstone Deposit · **AUS** 176-177 F 5
Mile o **ETH** 208-209 F 3
Mile o **VRC** 156-157 C 4
Milepa o **EAT** 214-215 F 5
Miles o **AUS** 178-179 K 5
Miles o **USA** (TX) 266-267 G 2
Miles o **USA** (WA) 244-245 G 3

Milé Wenz ~ **ETH** 208-209 E 3
Milford o **USA** (CA) 246-247 E 3
Milford o **USA** (CT) 280-281 N 2
Milford o **USA** (DE) 280-281 L 4
Milford o **USA** (IL) 274-275 L 4
Milford o **USA** (MA) 278-279 K 6
Milford o **USA** (MI) 272-273 F 5
Milford o **USA** (NE) 262-263 J 4
Milford o **USA** (NH) 278-279 K 6
Milford o **USA** (PA) 280-281 M 2
Milford o **USA** (UT) 254-255 B 5
Milford o **USA** (VA) 280-281 J 4
Milford Lake o **USA** (KS) 262-263 J 5
Milford Sound ≈ 182 A 6
Milford Sound o **NZ** 182 A 6
Milgarra o **AUS** 174-175 G 2
Milgun o **AUS** 176-177 E 2
Milguveem ~ **RUS** 112-113 R 2
Milhana o **MOC** 218-219 K 2
Mihát o **IRQ** 128-129 L 7
Miliana o **DZ** 190-191 D 2
Milian o **F** 90-91 J 10
Milian o **F** 90-91 J 9
Milibbro o **USA** (VA) 280-281 K 6
Millbrook o **CDN** (ONT) 238-239 G 4
Millbourne o **WY** 252-253 H 5
Mill City o **USA** (OR) 244-245 C 6
Milledgeville o **USA** (GA) 284-285 G 3
Milledgeville o **USA** (IL) 274-275 J 3
Mille Lacs, Lac des o **CDN** (ONT) 234-235 N 4
Mille Lacs Lake o **USA** (MN) 270-271 E 4
Millen o **USA** (GA) 284-285 J 4
Millenbeck o **USA** (VA) 280-281 K 6
Miller o **USA** (NE) 262-263 G 4
Miller o **USA** (OK) 264-265 J 4
Miller o **USA** (SD) 260-261 H 3
Miller o **ZA** 220-221 F 6
Miller, Mount ▲ **USA** 20-21 T 6
Millerdale o **CDN** (SAS) 232-233 K 4
Millerovo o **RUS** 102-103 M 3
Millersburg o **USA** (OH) 280-281 G 3
Millersburg o **USA** (PA) 280-281 K 3
Millers Corners o **USA** (PA) 280-281 H 4
Millers Creek o **USA** 178-179 C 5
Millers Creek Reservoir < **USA** (TX) 264-265 E 5
Millersview o **USA** (TX) 266-267 H 2
Millerton o **BS** 54-55 H 3
Millerton o **CDN** (NB) 240-241 K 4
Millerton o **USA** (NY) 280-281 N 2
Millertown o **CDN** (NFL) 242-243 M 4
Millertown Junction o **CDN** (NFL) 242-243 M 3
Millett o **CDN** (ALB) 232-233 F 3
Millett o **USA** (TX) 266-267 H 5
Millevaches, Plateau de ▲ **F** 90-91 H 9
Millican o **USA** (OR) 244-245 D 7
Millicent o **AUS** 180-181 F 4
Millie o **AUS** 178-179 K 5
Milligan College o **USA** (TN) 282-283 E 4
Milligan Hills ▲ **CDN** 32-33 K 3
Millington o **USA** (TN) 276-277 F 5
Millinocket o **USA** (ME) 278-279 N 3
Millinocket Lake o **USA** (ME) 278-279 N 3
Mill Iron o **USA** (MT) 250-251 P 6
Mill Island ᴖ **ARK** 16 G 11
Millmerran o **AUS** 178-179 L 4
Millport o **USA** (AL) 284-285 B 3
Millrose o **AUS** 176-177 F 3
Millsboro o **USA** (DE) 280-281 L 5
Mills Creek ~ **AUS** 178-179 G 2
Mills Lake o **CDN** 30-31 N 5
Millston o **USA** (WI) 270-271 H 6
Millstream o **AUS** 176-177 D 2
Millstream Chichester National Park ⊥ **AUS** 172-173 C 6
Milltown o **CDN** (NFL) 242-243 N 5
Milltown o **USA** (IN) 274-275 M 6
Millungera o **AUS** 174-175 F 6
Mill Village o **CDN** (NS) 240-241 L 6
Millville o **USA** (NB) 240-241 H 4
Millville o **USA** (NJ) 280-281 M 4
Millwood o **CDN** (MAN) 234-235 B 4
Millwood o **USA** (GA) 284-285 H 5
Millwood o **USA** (OK) 280-281 D 3
Millwood o **USA** (WA) 244-245 H 3
Millwood Lake o **USA** (AR) 276-277 A 7
Millyeewilpa Lake o **AUS** 178-179 D 4
Milly Milly o **AUS** 176-177 D 3
Milne Bay o **PNG** 183 F 6
Milne Inlet ≈ 24-25 g 4
Milne Land ▲ **GRØ** 26-27 m 8
Milner o **CDN** 38-39 L 2
Milnesand o **USA** (NM) 256-257 M 5
Milnthorpe o **GB** 90-91 F 4
Milo o **ETH** 208-209 F 3
Milo o **RG** 196-197 F 4
Milo o **USA** (ME) 278-279 N 3
Milo o **USA** (OK) 264-265 G 4
Milogradovo o **RUS** 122-123 F 7
Milolii o **USA** (HI) 288 K 5
Milos ᴖ **GR** 100-101 K 6
Milos o **GR** 100-101 K 6

Milot o **RH** 54-55 J 5
Milparinka o **AUS** 178-179 F 5
Milpitas o **USA** (CA) 248-249 C 2
Milpitas Wash ~ **USA** 248-249 J 6
Milroy o **USA** (MN) 270-271 D 5
Mil'skaja ravnina ⊥ **AZ** 128-129 M 3
Milton o **CDN** (NFL) 242-243 P 4
Milton o **USA** (DE) 280-281 L 5
Milton o **USA** (FL) 286-287 B 1
Milton o **USA** (IA) 274-275 F 4
Milton o **USA** (ND) 258-259 J 3
Milton o **USA** (OK) 280-281 K 2
Milton o **USA** (PA) 280-281 M 2
Milton o **NZ** 182 B 7
Milton o **USA** (DE) 280-281 L 5
Milton o **USA** (FL) 286-287 B 1
Milton o **USA** (IA) 274-275 F 4
Milton o **USA** (ND) 258-259 J 3
Milton o **USA** (OK) 280-281 K 2
Milton o **USA** (PA) 280-281 M 2
Miltona o **USA** (MN) 270-271 C 4
Milton-Freewater o **USA** (OR) 244-245 G 5
Milton o **USA** (KS) 262-263 J 5
Miltonvale o **USA** (KS) 262-263 J 5
Mittou o **TCH** 206-207 C 3
Miluo o **VRC** 156-157 H 2
Milverton o **CDN** (ONT) 238-239 E 5
Milwaukee o• **USA** (WI) 274-275 L 1
Milwaukie o **USA** (OR) 244-245 C 5
Mimbelly o **RCB** 210-211 F 2
Mimbres River ~ **USA** 256-257 H 6
Mimili (Eyerard Park) o **AUS** 176-177 M 3
Miminiska Lake o **CDN** (ONT) 234-235 P 3
Mi Mi Rocks ᴖ **AUS** 176-177 H 3
Mimizan o **F** 90-91 G 9
Mimongo o **G** 210-211 C 4
Mimoutou o **RCB** 210-211 D 4
Mims o **USA** (FL) 286-287 J 3
Mina o **RI** 166-167 C 7
Mina o **USA** (NV) 246-247 G 5
Mina o **USA** (SD) 260-261 H 1
Miná', al- o **RL** 128-129 F 5
Mina, Salar de la o **RA** 76-77 D 4
Miná' 'Abdallāh o **KWT** 130-131 K 3
Mináb o **IR** 134-135 K 7
Mina Clavero o **RA** 76-77 E 6
Minaçu o **BR** 72-73 F 2
Minahasa Semenao djung ᴖ **RI** 164-165 G 3
Mina Jebel Ali o **UAE** 134-135 F 6
Mina la Casualidad o **RA** 76-77 C 3
Minab o **USA** (NV) 246-247 G 5
Minam o **USA** (OR) 244-245 H 5
Minas o **RI** 162-163 D 4
Minas o **ROU** 78-79 M 3
Minas, Cerro las ▲ **HN** 52-53 K 4
Minas, Sierra de las ▲ **GCA** 52-53 J 4
Minas Basin ≈ 240-241 L 5
Minas de Barroterán o **MEX** 50-51 J 4
Minas de Corrales o **ROU** 76-77 K 6
Minas del Oro ~ **CO** 60-61 E 4
Minas de Matahambre o **C** 54-55 D 3
Minas do Mimoso o **BR** 68-69 H 7
Minas Gerais □ **BR** 72-73 J 4
Minas Novas o **BR** 72-73 J 4
Miná' Šu'uū o **KWT** 130-131 K 3
Minatare o **USA** (NE) 262-263 C 3
Minatitlán o **MEX** (COL) 52-53 B 2
Minatitlán o **MEX** (VER) 52-53 G 3
Minbu o **MYA** 142-143 J 3
Min Buri o **THA** 158-159 F 4
Minburn o **CDN** (ALB) 232-233 G 3
Minch, The ≈ 90-91 E 3
Minch, The Little ≈ 90-91 D 3
Minchika o **WAN** 204-205 K 3
Minchinábad o **PK** 138-139 D 4
Minchinmávida, Volcán ▲ **RCH** 78-79 C 7
Minchumina, Lake o **USA** 20-21 O 5
Minco o **USA** (OK) 264-265 G 3
Mindanao ᴖ **RP** 160-161 G 8
Mindanao Sea ≈ 160-161 E 10
Mindeji Pervyj o **RUS** 116-117 L 7
Mindelo o **CV** 202-203 B 5
Minden o **D** 92-93 K 2
Minden o **USA** (IA) 274-275 E 4
Minden o **USA** (LA) 268-269 G 4
Minden o **USA** (NE) 262-263 H 4
Minderla o **RUS** 116-117 F 7
Mindif o **CAM** 206-207 B 3
Mindif, Dent de ▲ **CAM** 206-207 B 3
Mindik o **PNG** 183 D 4
Mindiptana o **RI** 166-167 L 4
Mindjik o **TCH** 206-207 E 3
Mindo o **EC** 64-65 C 3
Mindon o **MYA** 142-143 J 6
Mindona Lake o **AUS** 180-181 G 2
Mindoro ᴖ **RP** 160-161 D 6
Mindoro Strait ≈ 160-161 D 6
Mindouli o **RCB** 210-211 D 6
Mindourou o **CAM** 210-211 D 2
Minduri o **BR** 72-73 H 6
Mindžívan o **AZ** 128-129 M 3
Mine o **J** (NAG) 152-153 M 3
Mine o **J** (YMG) 152-153 D 7
Mine Centre o **CDN** (ONT) 234-235 L 6
Minehead o **GB** 90-91 F 6
Mineiros o **BR** 72-73 D 4
Mine New Hosco o **CDN** (QUE) 236-237 L 2
Mineola o **USA** (TX) 264-265 J 6
Mineral o **USA** (CA) 246-247 J 6
Mineral, Cerro ▲ **RCH** 80 C 2
Mineral Hot Springs o **USA** (CO) 254-255 K 6
Mineral Point o **USA** (WI) 274-275 H 2

Mineral Springs o **USA** (AR) 276-277 B 7
Mineral Wells o **USA** (TX) 264-265 F 6
Miner River o **USA** 20-21 Z 2
Miners Bird Sanctuary · **CDN** (ONT) 238-239 C 6
Miners Point ▲ **USA** 22-23 U 4
Minersville o **USA** (PA) 280-281 K 3
Minersville o **USA** (UT) 254-255 C 5
Minerva o **USA** (NY) 278-279 H 5
Minerva o **USA** (OH) 280-281 G 3
Minette, Bay o **USA** (AL) 284-285 C 6
Minfeng o **VRC** 144-145 D 2
Minford o **VRC** (OH) 280-281 D 5
Minga o **Z** 218-219 F 2
Minga o **ZRE** 214-215 D 6
Mingala o **RCA** 206-207 G 6
Mingan o **CDN** (QUE) 242-243 J 2
Mingan, Iles de o **CDN** (QUE) 242-243 J 2
Mingan, Rivière ~ **CDN** 242-243 E 2
Minganja o **ZRE** 216-217 F 6
Mingao o **CO** 60-61 H 6
Mingary o **AUS** 180-181 F 2
Mingbulok o **UZ** 136-137 H 3
Mingbulok çukurligi ⊥ **UZ** 136-137 H 3
Mingechevir = Mingaçevir ∗ **AZ** 128-129 M 2
Mingechevirskoe vodohranilišče < **AZ** 128-129 M 2
Mingela o **AUS** 174-175 J 6
Mingenew o **AUS** 176-177 C 4
Minggang o **VRC** 154-155 J 5
Minghoshan = Dunhuang o• **VRC** 146-147 M 5
Mingin o **MYA** 142-143 J 3
Ming Ming o **PNG** 183 B 2
Mingo Lake o **CDN** 36-37 N 2
Mingo National Wildlife Refuge ⊥ **USA** (MO) 276-277 F 3
Mingora o **PK** 138-139 D 2
Mingoyo o **EAT** 214-215 K 6
Minggang o **VRC** 154-155 J 5
Mingshui o **VRC** 150-151 E 4
Mingue o **CAM** 204-205 K 6
Minguri o **MOC** 218-219 L 2
Mingxi o **VRC** 156-157 K 6
Minhe Huizu Tuzu Zizhixian o **VRC** 154-155 C 3
Minh Hòa, Hòn ᴖ **VN** 158-159 H 6
Minh Hpai o **VN** 158-159 H 6
Minhla o **MYA** 142-143 J 6
Minhla o **MYA** 158-159 C 2
Minho, Rio ~ **P** 98-99 C 4
Minichinas Hills ▲ **CDN** 232-233 M 3
Minidoka o **USA** (ID) 252-253 E 4
Minier o **USA** (IL) 274-275 J 4
Minigwal, Lake o **AUS** 176-177 G 4
Minilya o **AUS** 176-177 B 2
Minilya Bridge Roadhouse o **AUS** 176-177 C 1
Minilya River ~ **AUS** 176-177 C 1
Mininian o **CI** 202-203 G 4
Miniota o **CDN** (MAN) 234-235 B 4
Minipi Lake o **CDN** 38-39 O 2
Minisiare, Caño ~ **CO** 60-61 G 4
Mirani o **AUS** 178-179 K 1
Minissa o **BF** 202-203 J 3
Miniss Lake o **CDN** (ONT) 234-235 N 4
Ministro Ramos Mexía o **RA** 78-79 F 6
Minitas, Playa ⊥ **DOM** 54-55 L 5
Minja o **RUS** 118-119 Z 7
Min'jar o **RUS** 96-97 K 6
Min Jiang ~ **VRC** 156-157 D 2
Min Jiang ~ **VRC** 156-157 L 6
Minjilang ⅄ **AUS** 172-173 I 1
Minjip o **PNG** 183 B 3
Miniaton o **AUS** 180-181 D 3
Minle o **VRC** 154-155 C 3
Minlaton o **AUS** 180-181 D 3
Minna ∗ **WAN** 204-205 G 4
Minneapolis o **USA** (KS) 262-263 J 5
Minneapolis o• **USA** (MN) 270-271 E 6
Minnedosa o **CDN** (MAN) 234-235 D 4
Minneola o **USA** (KS) 262-263 F 7
Minneota o **USA** (MN) 270-271 C 6
Minnesota □ **USA** 270-271 B 4
Minnesota River ~ **USA** 270-271 C 6
Minnesott Beach o **USA** (NC) 282-283 L 4
Minnetonka, Lake o **CDN** 232-233 C 4
Minnewaukan o **USA** (ND) 258-259 H 3
Minnie Creek o **AUS** 176-177 C 2
Minnies Out Station o **AUS** 174-175 G 5
Minnipa o **AUS** 180-181 F 2
Minnitaki Lake o **CDN** (ONT) 234-235 M 4
Minnkri o **RMM** 196-197 J 6
Miño, Rio ~ **P** 98-99 C 4
Minong o **USA** (WI) 270-271 G 4
Minonk o **USA** (IL) 274-275 J 4
Minor Hill o **USA** (TN) 276-277 H 5
Minot o **USA** (ND) 258-259 F 3
Minqin o **VRC** 154-155 C 3
Minqing o **VRC** 156-157 L 3
Minquan o **VRC** 154-155 J 4
Min Shan ▲ **VRC** 154-155 C 5
Minsk ∗ **BY** 94-95 K 5
Mińsk Mazowiecki o **PL** 92-93 Q 3
Minster o **CDN** 280-281 B 3
Minstrel Island o **CDN** (BC) 230-231 J 3
Minta o **CAM** 204-205 K 6
Mintabie o **AUS** 176-177 M 3
Mintaqat ash Shu'bah ⊥ **LAR** 192-193 K 2
Mintaqat Umm Khuwayr ⊥ **LAR** 192-193 K 2
Mint Hill o **USA** (NC) 282-283 G 5
Mintirib, al- o• **OM** 132-133 L 2
Minto o **CDN** (MAN) 234-235 D 5
Minto o **CDN** (NB) 240-241 J 4
Minto o **CDN** (YT) 20-21 W 5
Minto o **USA** (ND) 258-259 J 3
Minto, Lac o **CDN** 36-37 M 6
Minto Inlet ≈ 24-25 N 5
Minton o **CDN** (SAS) 232-233 O 6
Minton II o **CAM** 210-211 D 2

Mintonas o **CDN** (MAN) 234-235 B 2
Mintonsville o **USA** (NC) 282-283 L 4
Minturn o **USA** (CO) 254-255 J 4
Minúdašt o **IR** 136-137 D 6
Minvoul o **G** 210-211 D 2
Min Xian o **VRC** 154-155 D 4
Minyá, al- ∗ **ET** 194-195 E 3
Minzawwi, Wādi al- o **OM** 132-133 H 5
Minž'gol ~ **MAU** 148-149 H 3
Mio o **USA** (MI) 272-273 E 3
Miocene o **CDN** (BC) 228-229 N 4
Miosnum, Pulau ᴖ **RI** 166-167 J 3
Miqdādīya, al- ∗ **IRQ** 128-129 L 6
Miquelon o **CDN** 38-39 F 4
Miquelon ᴖ **CDN** (QUE) 236-237 M 3
Miquelon, Cap ▲ **F** (242-243) M 5
Miquihuana o **MEX** 50-51 K 5
Mira o **EC** 64-65 C 1
Mira o **P** 98-99 C 4
Mira, Río ~ **EC** 64-65 C 1
Mirabel o **CDN** (QUE) 238-239 L 3
Mirabela o **BR** 72-73 H 4
Miracema o **BR** 72-73 J 6
Miracema de Tocantins o **BR** 68-69 D 6
Miracosta o **PE** 64-65 C 5
Mirador o **BR** (AMA) 64-65 F 4
Mirador o **BR** (MAR) 68-69 F 5
Mirador, El ∴ **GCA** 52-53 K 3
Mirador, Parque Nacional de ⊥ **BR** 68-69 F 5
Mirador-Dos Lagunas-Río Azul, Parque Nacional ⊥ **GCA** 52-53 K 3
Miradouro o **BR** 72-73 J 6
Miraflores o **BR** 66-67 E 4
Miraflores o **CO** (BOY) 60-61 E 5
Miraflores o **CO** (VAU) 66-67 B 2
Mirage Bay o **CDN** 28-29 E 3
Mirdiglia, Portella della ▲ **I** 100-101 J 5
Miragoâne o **RH** 54-55 J 5
Mira o **IND** 140-141 F 2
Mira Loma o **USA** (CA) 248-249 G 6
Miramar o **BR** 66-67 G 5
Miramar o **RA** 78-79 L 5
Miramichi Bay ≈ 240-241 K 3
Miramichi River ~ **CDN** 240-241 J 4
Miram Shah o **PK** 138-139 C 3
Miran o **PK** 138-139 C 4
Miran o **VRC** 146-147 J 6
Miranda o **BR** (GSU) 70-71 J 7
Miranda o **BR** (MAR) 68-69 F 5
Miranda, Río o **BR** 70-71 J 7
Miranda, Lake o **AUS** 176-177 F 3
Miranda de Douro o **P** 98-99 E 4
Miranda de Ebro o **E** 98-99 F 3
Miranda Downs o **AUS** 174-175 F 5
Mirandela o **BR** 68-69 J 7
Mirandela o **P** 98-99 D 4
Mirandiba o **BR** 68-69 J 6
Mirando City o **USA** (TX) 266-267 H 6
Mirandópolis o **BR** 72-73 E 6
Mirani o **AUS** 178-179 K 1
Miranle da Sura o **BR** 70-71 F 2
Miranorte o **BR** 68-69 D 6
Mirante o **BR** 72-73 J 3
Mirante do Paranapanema o **BR** 72-73 E 7
Mira por vos Cays ᴖ **BS** 54-55 J 3
Mira por vos Passage ≈ 54-55 H 3
Mirassol o **BR** 72-73 E 6
Mirassol d'Oeste o **BR** 70-71 H 4
Miratu, Área Indígena ⅄ **BR** 66-67 E 4
Miratuba, Lago o **BR** 66-67 H 4
Mirbāt o **OM** 132-133 J 5
Mirebalais o **RH** 54-55 J 5
Mirhieft o **MA** 188-189 H 4
Miri o **MAL** 162-163 K 2
Miria o **RN** 198-199 D 6
Mirãlgúda o **IND** 140-141 G 2
Miriam Vale o **AUS** 178-179 L 3
Mirim, Lagoa o **BR** 74-75 F 7
Mirim, Lagoa do o **BR** 74-75 F 7
Mirim do Abufari, Paraná ~ **BR** 66-67 F 5
Mirimire o **YV** 60-61 G 2
Mirina o **GR** 100-101 K 5
Miriñay, Esteros o **RA** 76-77 J 5
Miriñay, Río ~ **RA** 76-77 J 5
Mirinzal o **BR** 68-69 F 3
Miritiparaná, Rio ~ **CO** 66-67 B 3
Miriye, togga ~ **SP** 208-209 G 3
Mirjan o **IND** 140-141 F 3
Mirnoe o **RUS** 114-115 P 6
Mirnyj o **ARK** 16 G 10
Mirnyj ∗ **RUS** 118-119 F 4
Mirobia o **RI** 166-167 K 3
Mirogi o **EAK** 212-213 E 4
Miroki o **UZ** 136-137 L 3
Mirong o **VRC** 156-157 C 5
Mirosławiec o **PL** 92-93 O 2
Mirowai o **PK** 138-139 E 4
Mirpur Batoro o **PK** 138-139 B 7
Mirpur Khās o **PK** 138-139 B 7
Mirpur Mathelo o **PK** 138-139 B 5
Mirpur Sakro o **PK** 134-135 M 6
Mirra Mitta Bore o **AUS** 178-179 E 4
Mirrngadja Village ⅄ **AUS** 174-175 C 3
Mirror o **CDN** (ALB) 232-233 F 3
Mirror River ~ **CDN** 32-33 G 3
Mirrote o **MOC** 218-219 K 1
Mirsale o **SP** 208-209 H 6
Mirtna o **AUS** 178-179 J 1
Mirtóo Pélagos ≈ 100-101 J 6
Miruro o **MOC** 218-219 F 2
Miryang o **ROK** 152-153 G 4
Mirzā 'Arab, Kūh-e ▲ **IR** 134-135 J 2
Mirzapur o **IND** 142-143 C 3
Miryang ∗ **ET** 194-195 C 6
Misaki o **EAT** 212-213 C 4
Misaki o **J** (EHI) 152-153 E 7
Misaki o **J** (OSA) 152-153 F 7

Misantla ○ MEX 52-53 F 2
Misau ○ WAN 204-205 J 3
Misawa ○ J 152-153 J 4
Misaw Lake ○ CDN 30-31 S 6
Miscou Centre ○ CDN (NB) 240-241 L 3
Miscou Island ⌒ CDN (NB) 240-241 L 3
Miscou Point ▲ CDN (NB) 240-241 L 2
Misehkov River ~ CDN 234-235 O 3
Misekumaw Lake ○ CDN 30-31 S 6
Misele ○ ZRE 210-211 F 6
Mishagua, Río ~ PE 64-65 F 7
Mishaleyi ○ VRC 146-147 E 6
Mishamo ○ EAT 212-213 C 6
Mishan ○ VRC 150-151 H 5
Mishanattawa River ~ CDN 34-35 N 3
Mishibishu Lake ○ CDN (ONT) 236-237 C 4
Mishicot ○ USA (WI) 270-271 L 6
Mi-shima ⌒ J 152-153 D 7
Misi ○ FIN 00-09 J 3
Misiki ○ PNG 183 B 4
Misima Island ⌒ PNG 183 G 6
Misión, La ○ MEX 50-51 A 1
Mision de San Fernando ○ MEX 50-51 B 2
Misiones ■ RA 76-77 K 4
Misiones, Sierra de ▲ RA 76-77 K 4
Miski ○ SUD 200-201 B 5
Miškino ☆ RUS (BAS) 96-97 J 6
Miškino ☆ RUS (KRG) 114-115 G 7
Miskitos, Cayos ⌒ NIC 52-53 C 4
Miskolc ○ H 92-93 Q 4
Mismār ○ SUD 200-201 G 3
Mismya, al- ○ SYR 128-129 G 6
Misol-Ha Waterfall ~ • MEX 52-53 H 3
Misool, Pulau ⌒ RI 166-167 F 2
Misouminien ○ CI 202-203 J 6
Miśrāfa, al- ○ Y 132-133 C 6
Misrak Gashemo ○ ETH 208-209 G 4
Misrātah ■ LAR 192-193 F 1
Misrātah ☆ LAR (Mis) 192-193 F 1
Misrikh ○ IND 142-143 B 2
Missanabie ○ CDN (ONT) 236-237 D 4
Misseni ○ RMM 202-203 G 4
Missi Falls ~ CDN 34-35 G 2
Missinaibi Lake ○ CDN (ONT) 236-237 E 4
Missinaibi Lake Provincial Park ⊥ CDN (ONT) 236-237 E 4
Missinaibi River ~ CDN 236-237 F 2
Mission ○ CDN (BC) 230-231 G 4
Mission ○ USA (SD) 260-261 F 3
Mission ○ USA (TX) 266-267 J 7
Mission Beach ○ AUS 174-175 J 5
Misión de San Borja ○ MEX 50-51 C 3
Mission Indian Reservation X USA (CA) 248-249 G 6
Mission Mountains Wilderness Area ⊥ USA (MT) 250-251 F 4
Mission Ridge ○ USA (SD) 260-261 F 2
Mission Valley ○ USA (TX) 266-267 K 5
Mission Viejo ○ USA (CA) 248-249 G 6
Missira ○ SN (SO) 202-203 D 3
Missira ○ SN (SO) 202-203 E 3
Missisagi River ~ CDN 238-239 B 2
Missisa Lake ○ CDN 34-35 O 4
Missisicabi, Rivière ~ CDN 236-237 K 2
Mississagi Provincial Park ⊥ CDN (ONT) 238-239 C 2
Mississagi River Provincial Park ⊥ CDN (ONT) 236-237 F 5
Mississauga ○ CDN (ONT) 238-239 F 5
Mississinewa River ~ USA 274-275 N 4
Mississippi ■ USA 268-269 L 5
Mississippi River ~ CDN 238-239 J 4
Mississippi River ~ USA 4 E 5
Mississippi River Delta ~ USA 268-269 L 7
Mississippi Sound ≈ 268-269 L 6
Missoula ○ USA (MT) 250-251 F 5
Missour ○ MA 188-189 K 4
Missouri ■ USA 274-275 E 6
Missouri Breaks Wild and Scenic River ⊥ USA (MT) 250-251 K 4
Missouri City ○ USA (TX) 268-269 E 7
Missouri Coteau ⊥ CDN 232-233 M 5
Missouri River ~ USA 4 D 4
Missouri Valley ○ USA (IA) 274-275 C 3
Mist ○ USA (OR) 244-245 B 5
Mistake Creek ~ AUS 178-179 G 2
Mistassibi, Rivière ~ CDN 236-237 Q 2
Mistassini ○ CDN (QUE) 236-237 P 2
Mistassini ○ CDN (QUE) 240-241 C 2
Mistassini, Lac ○ CDN (QUE) 236-237 P 2
Mistassini, Rivière ~ CDN 236-237 Q 3
Mistastin Lake ○ CDN (NFL) 36-37 S 7
Mistatim ○ CDN (SAS) 232-233 P 3
Mistawak, Lac ○ CDN (ONT) 236-237 K 3
Mistawak, Rivière ~ CDN 236-237 K 3
Mistawasis Indian Reserve X CDN (SAS) 232-233 M 2
Mistelbach an der Zaya ○ A 92-93 O 4
Misterei ○ SUD 198-199 L 6
Misti, Volcán ▲ PE 70-71 B 5
Mistinibi Lake ○ CDN 36-37 R 7
Mistoles, Laguna los ○ RA 76-77 F 6
Mistra ••• GR 100-101 J 6
Mistuskwia River ~ CDN 236-237 F 2
Misty Fiords National Monument ⊥ • USA 32-33 E 4
Misty Fiords National Monument Wilderness ⊥ • USA 32-33 E 4
Misty Lake ○ CDN 30-31 T 6
Misumba ○ ZRE 210-211 H 6
Misumi ○ J 152-153 D 8
Misvær ○ N 86-87 G 3
Mišwara ○ Y 132-133 D 6
Mita, Punta ▲ MEX 52-53 B 1
Mita Hills Dam < Z 218-219 E 2
Mitaho • RM 222-223 C 10
Mita-Miirim ○ BR 66-67 E 3
Mitande ○ MOC 218-219 J 2
Mitare ○ YV 60-61 F 2
Mitau = Jelgava ○ •• LV 94-95 H 3
Mitchell ○ AUS 178-179 J 4
Mitchell ○ CDN (ONT) 238-239 D 5
Mitchell ○ USA (GA) 284-285 H 3
Mitchell ○ USA (IN) 274-275 M 6
Mitchell ○ USA (NE) 262-263 C 3
Mitchell ○ USA (OR) 244-245 E 6
Mitchell ○ USA (SD) 260-261 H 3
Mitchell, Mount ▲ USA (NC) 282-283 E 5
Mitchell and Alice Rivers National Park ⊥ AUS 174-175 G 4
Mitchell Highway II AUS 178-179 J 6
Mitchell Lake ○ CDN (BC) 228-229 O 4
Mitchell Lake < USA (AL) 284-285 D 4
Mitchell River ○ AUS (WA) 172-173 G 3
Mitchell River ~ AUS 172-173 G 3
Mitchell River ~ AUS 174-175 G 4
Mitchell River National Park ⊥ AUS 180-181 J 4
Mitchell's Bay ○ CDN (ONT) 238-239 C 6
Mitchells Brook ○ CDN (NFL) 242-243 P 5
Mitchelstown = Baile Mhistéala ○ IRL 90-91 C 5
Mitchinamécus, Lac ○ CDN (QUE) 236-237 N 5
Mitchinamecus, Rivière ~ CDN 236-237 O 5
Mitémele, Río ~ GQ 210-211 C 3
Mit Ğamr ○ ET 194-195 E 2
Mithankot ○ PK 138-139 C 5
Mitha Tiwāna ○ PK 138-139 D 3
Mithebah ○ AUS 174-175 D 6
Mithi ○ PK 138-139 B 7
Mithimna ○ GR 100-101 L 5
Miti, Pulau ⌒ RI 164-165 L 3
Mitiamo ○ AUS 180-181 H 4
Mitiaro Island ⌒ NZ 13 M 4
Mitilini ☆ • GR 100-101 L 5
Mitji ~ SN 202-203 D 3
Mitjušiha, guba ≈ 108-109 F 5
Mitla ∴ • MEX 52-53 F 3
Mitla, Laguna ≈ 52-53 D 3
Mitliktavik ○ USA 20-21 K 1
Mito ☆ J 152-153 J 6
Mitoko ○ ZRE 210-211 H 2
Mitole ○ EAT 214-215 K 5
Mitomoni ○ EAT 214-215 H 6
Mitre, Península ~ RA 80 H 7
Mitrofania Island ⌒ USA 22-23 R 5
Mitsamiouli ○ COM 222-223 C 3
Mitsinjo ○ RM 222-223 D 5
Mitsio, Nosy ⌒ RM 222-223 F 4
Mits'iwa ○ • ER 200-201 J 5
Mits'iwa Channel ≈ 200-201 J 5
Mitsuishi ○ J 152-153 K 3
Mitsushima ○ J 152-153 C 7
Mittagong ○ AUS 174-175 G 6
Mitta Mitta ○ AUS 180-181 J 4
Mittlintown ○ USA (PA) 280-281 J 3
Mitu ☆ CO 66-67 B 2
Mitumba, Monts ▲ ZRE 212-213 B 5
Mitunguu ○ EAK 212-213 F 4
Mitwaba ○ ZRE 214-215 D 5
Mityana ○ EAU 212-213 D 3
Mitzic ○ G 210-211 C 3
Miura-hanto ~ J 152-153 H 7
Miwo River ~ PNG 184 I b 2
Mixco ○ • GCA 52-53 J 4
Mixquiahuala ○ MEX 52-53 E 1
Mixteco, Río ~ MEX 52-53 F 2
Mixtlán ○ MEX 52-53 B 1
Miya ○ WAN 204-205 H 3
Miya-gawa ~ J 152-153 G 7
Miyāh, Wādī l- ~ ET 194-195 F 5
Miyake-shima ⌒ J 152-153 H 7
Miyako ○ J 152-153 J 5
Miyakonojō ○ J 152-153 D 9
Miyāndōab ○ • IR 128-129 M 4
Miyāne ○ • IR 128-129 M 4
Miyanoura-dake ▲ J 152-153 D 9
Miya-shima ⌒ •• J 152-153 E 7
Miyazaki ☆ J 152-153 D 9
Miyazu ○ J 152-153 F 7
Miyi ○ VRC 156-157 C 3
Miyoshi ○ J 152-153 E 7
Miyun ○ VRC (BEI) 154-155 K 1
Miyun • VRC (BEI) 154-155 K 1
Mīzānī ○ AFG 134-135 M 2
Mizan Teferi ○ ETH 208-209 B 5
Mizdah ○ LAR 192-193 E 2
Mizen Head ▲ IRL 90-91 C 6
Mizhi ○ VRC 154-155 G 3
Mizil ○ RO 102-103 E 5
Mizo Hills ▲ IND 142-143 H 4
Mizoram ■ IND 142-143 H 4
Mizpah ○ USA (MT) 250-251 O 5
Mizpah Creek ~ USA 250-251 O 5
Mizque ○ BOL 70-71 E 5
Mizque, Río ~ BOL 70-71 E 5
Mizur ○ RUS 126-127 F 6
Mizusawa ○ J 152-153 J 5
Mjadzel ☆ BY 94-95 K 4
Mjagostrov ⌒ RUS 88-89 N 4
Mjakit ○ RUS 120-121 P 3
Mjangad = Bajanhošuu ○ MAU 146-147 K 1
Mjanji ○ EAU 212-213 E 3
Mjatis' ~ RUS 110-111 Z 6
Mjölby ☆ S 86-87 G 7
Mjonga ~ EAT 214-215 J 3
Mjörn ○ S 86-87 F 8
Mjøsa ○ N 86-87 E 6
Mjurjule ~ RUS 110-111 X 7
Mkambati Nature Reserve ⊥ ZA 220-221 J 5
Mkanga ○ EAT 214-215 H 4
Mkata ○ EAT (TAN) 212-213 G 6
Mkata ~ EAT 214-215 J 4
Mkoani ○ EAT 212-213 G 6
Mkokotoni ○ EAT 214-215 K 3
Mkomazi Game Reserve ⊥ EAT 212-213 G 6
Mkondoa ~ EAT 214-215 J 4
Mkondowe ○ MW 214-215 H 6
Mkonjowano ○ EAT 214-215 K 6
Mkowe ○ EAK 212-213 H 5
Mkowela ○ EAT 214-215 K 6
Mkujani ○ EAT 212-213 G 6
Mkunumbi ○ EAK 212-213 H 5
Mkuranga ○ EAT 214-215 K 4
Mkushi ○ Z (CEN) 218-219 E 1
Mkushi ~ Z 218-219 E 2
Mkushi River ○ Z 218-219 E 1
Mkuze ○ ZA (NTL) 220-221 L 3
Mkuze ~ ZA 220-221 K 3
Mkuzi Game Reserve ⊥ ZA 220-221 L 3
Mkwaja ○ EAT 212-213 G 6
Mladá Boleslav ○ •• CZ 92-93 N 3
Mladenovac ○ • YU 100-101 H 2
Mlalo ○ EAT 212-213 G 6
Mlandizi ○ EAT 214-215 K 4
M'lang ○ RP 160-161 F 9
Mława ○ PL 92-93 Q 2
Mlelin ~ RUS 112-113 Q 2
Mlenganapas ▲ ZA 220-221 J 5
Mligasi ~ EAT 212-213 G 6
Mljet ⌒ HR 100-101 F 3
Mljet, Nacionaini park ⊥ HR 100-101 F 3
Mmabatho ☆ ZA 220-221 G 2
Mmadinare ○ RB 218-219 D 5
Mmamabula ○ RB 218-219 D 6
Mmashoro ○ RB 218-219 D 5
Mmathethe ○ RB 220-221 G 2
Mmatshumo ○ RB 218-219 C 5
Mnamuk ○ RI 166-167 D 3
Mnanzi ○ EAT 212-213 G 6
Mnarani ∴ • EAK 212-213 G 5
Mnjoli Dam < SD 220-221 K 3
Mnogoveršinnyj ○ RUS 122-123 H 2
Mo ~ CAM 204-205 H 6
Mo ~ GH 202-203 L 5
Mô ~ RT 202-203 L 5
Moa ○ C 54-55 H 4
Moa ~ WAL 202-203 E 6
Moa, Pulau ⌒ RI 166-167 E 6
Moa, Rio ~ BR 64-65 F 5
Moab ○ USA (UT) 254-255 F 5
Moabi ○ G 210-211 C 5
Moaco, Rio ~ BR 66-67 C 6
Moai •• RCH 78-79 B 2
Moa Island ⌒ AUS 174-175 G 2
Moala ⌒ FJI 184 III b 3
Mo'allemān ○ IR 136-137 D 7
Mo'allem Kalāyeh ○ IR 136-137 B 6
Moamba ○ MOC 220-221 L 2
Moanda ○ G 210-211 D 4
Moanda ~ ZRE 210-211 C 2
Moapa ○ USA (NV) 248-249 K 3
Moapa River Indian Reservation X USA (NV) 248-249 K 3
Möar Bay ≈ 38-39 E 2
Moatize ○ MOC 218-219 G 3
Moba ○ ZRE 214-215 E 4
Mobara ○ J 152-153 J 7
Mobārak, Kūh ○ IR 134-135 G 6
Mobārake ○ IR 134-135 D 2
Mobaye ☆ • RCA 206-207 E 6
Mobayi-Mbongi ○ ZRE 206-207 E 6
Mobdoua ○ RIM 196-197 G 7
Mobeetie ○ USA (TX) 264-265 D 3
Mobena ○ ZRE 210-211 G 3
Moberly ○ USA (MO) 274-275 F 5
Mobert ○ CDN (ONT) 236-237 C 4
Mobile ○ USA (AZ) 256-257 C 5
Mobile ○ • USA (AL) 284-285 B 6
Mobile Bay ≈ 48-49 D 4
Mobile Bay ≈ 284-285 B 6
Mobile River ~ USA 284-285 B 6
Mobridge ○ USA (SD) 260-261 F 1
Moca ☆ DOM 54-55 K 5
Moca ○ GQ 210-211 B 2
Mocajuba ○ BR 68-69 D 3
Moçambicana ⊥ MOC 218-219 H 5
Moçambique ○ MOC 218-219 L 2
Moçambique, Ilha de ⌒ ••• MOC 218-219 L 2
Moccasin ○ USA (AZ) 256-257 C 2
Moccasin ○ USA (MT) 250-251 K 4
Mộc Châu ☆ VN 156-157 D 6
Mocha = al-Muḫā ○ •• Y 132-133 C 7
Mocha, Isla ⌒ RCH 78-79 C 5
Mochara, Cordillera de ▲ BOL 76-77 E 1
Moche Pyramids • PE 64-65 C 6
Mochirma, Parque Nacionale ⊥ YV 60-61 J 2
Mochis, Los ○ MEX 50-51 E 5
Mộc Hóa ○ VN 158-159 H 5
Mochudi ☆ RB 220-221 H 2
Mochumi ○ PE 64-65 C 5
Mocímboa da Praia ○ MOC 214-215 L 6
Mocímboa do Rovuma ○ MOC 214-215 K 6
Mockonema ○ USA (WA) 244-245 H 4
Mocksville ○ USA (NC) 282-283 G 5
Mocó ▲ ANG 216-217 C 6
Mocoa ☆ CO 64-65 D 1
Mocoduene ○ MOC 218-219 H 6
Moções, Rio ~ BR 62-63 K 6
Mocomoco ○ BOL 70-71 C 4
Mocorito ○ MEX 50-51 F 5
Mocotó ○ BR 68-69 E 3
Moctezuma ○ MEX (CHA) 50-51 F 2
Moctezuma ○ MEX (SLP) 50-51 J 6
Moctezuma ○ MEX (SON) 50-51 E 3
Moctezuma, Río ~ MEX 50-51 K 7
Mocuba ○ MOC 218-219 J 3
Mocupe ○ PE 64-65 C 5
Modan ○ RI 166-167 G 3
Modane ○ F 90-91 L 9
Modāsa ○ IND 138-139 D 8
Modderrivier ~ ZA 220-221 G 4
Model ○ USA (CO) 254-255 L 6
Modena ○ I 100-101 C 2
Modena ○ USA (UT) 254-255 B 6
Modesto ○ USA (CA) 248-249 C 2
Modesto Méndez ○ GCA 52-53 K 4
Modjigo ⊥ RN 190-199 F 4
Modoc Point ○ USA (OR) 244-245 D 8
Modoguhe ○ CI 202-203 G 6
Modot ○ MAU 148-149 J 4
Modriča ○ BIH 100-101 G 2
Moebase ○ MOC 218-219 K 3
Moeilijk, Pulau ⌒ RI 164-165 L 4
Moeko ~ ZRE 210-211 G 2
Moen ○ N 86-87 J 2
Moenkopi ○ USA (AZ) 256-257 D 2
Moenkopi Wash ~ USA 256-257 D 2
Moeraki Boulders • NZ 182 C 6
Moerkesung ○ VRC 144-145 E 5
Moero, Lac = Lake Mweru ○ ZRE 214-215 E 5
Moers ○ D 92-93 J 3
Moe-Yallourn ○ AUS 180-181 J 5
Moffat ○ GB 90-91 F 4
Moffat Creek ~ CDN 228-229 N 4
Moffat Secton, Mount ⊥ AUS 178-179 J 3
Moffet, Mount ▲ USA 22-23 H 7
Moffet Point ▲ USA 22-23 P 5
Moffit ○ USA (ND) 258-259 G 5
Mofu ○ Z 214-215 F 6
Moga ~ RUS 116-117 O 5
Moga ○ ZRE 210-211 L 5
Mogadishu = Muqdisho ★ SP 212-213 K 2
Mogadouro ○ P 98-99 D 4
Mogalu ○ ZRE 210-211 G 2
Mogami-gawa ~ J 152-153 J 5
Moganshan • VRC 154-155 L 6
Mogao Ku ••• VRC 146-147 M 5
Mogapinyana ○ RB 218-219 D 6
Mogaung ○ MYA 142-143 K 3
Mogdy ○ RUS (HBR) 122-123 E 3
Mogdy ~ RUS 116-117 N 3
Moğen ○ IR 136-137 G 6
Mogens Heinesens Fjord ≈ 28-29 T 5
Moghrar ○ DZ 188-189 L 4
Mogi Cruzes ○ BR 72-73 G 7
Mogila ▲ EAK 212-213 B 6
Mogilev = Mahilëv ○ • BY 94-95 M 5
Mogilno ○ • PL 92-93 O 2
Mogil'nyj Mys ○ RUS 114-115 R 5
Mogi-Mirim ○ BR 72-73 G 7
Mogincual ○ MOC 218-219 L 2
Mogna ○ RA 76-77 C 6
Mogna, Sierra de ▲ RA 76-77 C 6
Mogoča ☆ RUS 118-119 J 9
Mogoi ○ RI 166-167 G 2
Mogojtuj ☆ RUS 118-119 G 10
Mogok ○ MYA 142-143 K 4
Mogollon Mountains ▲ USA 256-257 G 5
Mogollon Rim ▲ USA 256-257 D 4
Mogotes, Punta ▲ RA 78-79 L 6
Mogotoevo, ozero ○ RUS 110-111 b 3
Mogotón, Cerro ▲ NIC 52-53 L 5
Mogroum ○ TCH 206-207 B 3
Mogui Cheng • VRC 146-147 G 2
Mogūye, Bandar-e ○ IR 134-135 F 5
Mogwase ○ ZA 220-221 H 2
Mogzon ○ RUS 118-119 E 10
Mohács ○ H 92-93 P 5
Mohale's Hoek ○ LS 220-221 H 5
Mohall ○ USA (ND) 258-259 F 3
Mohamed 5., Barrage ⊥ MA 188-189 K 3
Moḥammadābād ○ IR (ESF) 134-135 E 2
Moḥammadābād ○ IR (KER) 134-135 G 4
Moḥammadābād ○ IR (SIS) 134-135 J 3
Moḥammadābād ○ IR (YAZ) 134-135 F 3
Moḥammad Āgā ○ AFG 138-139 B 2
Mohammadia ○ DZ 190-191 C 3
Mohammedia = Al Muhammadiyah ○ MA 188-189 H 4
Mohana ○ IND 142-143 D 6
Mohanganj ○ BD 142-143 G 3
Mohania ○ IND 142-143 C 3
Mohave, Lake ○ USA (NV) 248-249 K 4
Mohawk ○ USA (AZ) 256-257 B 6
Mohawk ○ USA (WI) 270-271 K 3
Mohawk River ~ USA 278-279 G 6
Mohe ○ VRC 150-151 D 1
Mohej ~ RUS 118-119 E 9
Mohenjo Daro ∴ ••• PK 138-139 B 6
Mohican, Cape ▲ USA 20-21 G 6
Moho ○ PE 70-71 C 4
Mohol ○ IND 140-141 F 2
Mohon Peak ▲ USA (AZ) 256-257 B 4
Mohoro ○ EAT 214-215 K 5
Mohovaja ~ RUS 108-109 V 6
Mohovaja, gora ▲ RUS 88-89 S 2
Mohrungen = Morąg ○ PL 92-93 P 2
Mohyliv-Podil's'kyj ☆ UA 102-103 E 3
Moibeen ○ EAK 212-213 E 3
Moila Point ▲ PNG 184 I b 2
Moili ⌒ COM 222-223 C 4
Moimba ○ ANG 216-217 B 8
Moin ○ CR 52-53 C 7
Moincêr ○ VRC 144-145 C 5
Moinerie, Lac la ○ CDN 36-37 Q 6
Moines, Des ○ USA (NM) 256-257 M 2
Moines River, Des ~ USA 274-275 D 2
Moira ○ USA (NY) 278-279 G 4
Mo i Rana ○ N 86-87 G 3
Moirang ○ IND 142-143 H 3
Mõisaküla ○ EST 94-95 J 2
Moiseevskaja ○ RUS 94-95 R 1
Moisie ○ CDN (QUE) 242-243 B 2
Moisie, Rivière ~ CDN 38-39 L 3
Moisie, Rivière ~ CDN 242-243 B 2
Moissac ○ F 90-91 H 9
Moissala ○ TCH 206-207 C 4
Moitaco ○ YV 60-61 J 3
Mojave ○ USA (CA) 248-249 F 4
Mojave Desert ⊥ USA 248-249 G 4
Mojave River ~ USA 248-249 G 5
Mojero ~ RUS 108-109 f 7
Mojerokan ~ RUS 116-117 M 2
Moji Guaçu, Rio ~ BR 72-73 G 6
Mojiquiçaba ○ BR 72-73 L 4
Mojkovac ○ YU 100-101 G 3
Mojo ○ ETH 208-209 D 4
Mojoagung ○ RI 168 E 3
Mojokerto ○ RI 168 E 3
Mojos, Llanos de ⊥ BOL 70-71 D 4
Mojosari ○ RI 168 E 3
Moju, Rio ~ BR 68-69 D 2
Moju dos Campos ○ BR 66-67 K 4
Moj-Urusta ○ RUS 120-121 N 3
Mojyldy ~ KZ 124-125 D 3
Mojynk ⊥ KZ 124-125 G 6
Mojynkūm ⊥ KZ 124-125 D 5
Mojynty ○ KZ 124-125 H 5
Mōka ○ J 152-153 J 6
Mokāma ○ IND 142-143 D 3
Mokambo ○ ZRE 214-215 E 7
Mokau ○ NZ 182 E 3
Mokelumne Aqueduct < USA (CA) 246-247 D 5
Mokelumne Hill ○ USA (CA) 246-247 E 5
Mokgomane ○ RB 220-221 G 2
Mokhotlong ○ LS 220-221 J 4
Mokla ~ RUS 118-119 K 8
Moknine ○ TN 190-191 H 3
Mokoan, Lake ○ AUS 180-181 J 4
Mokobola Pan < RB 218-219 D 5
Mokokchung ○ IND 142-143 J 2
Mokolo ○ CAM 204-205 K 3
Mokolo ~ ZA 220-221 H 2
Mokombe ~ ZRE 210-211 J 4
Mokoreta ○ NZ 182 B 7
Mokoto, Lacs ○ ZRE 212-213 B 4
Mokp'o ○ ROK 150-151 F 10
Mokrous ○ RUS 96-97 E 8
Mokša ~ RUS 94-95 T 5
Mōktama Kwe ≈ 158-159 D 2
Mokwa ○ WAN 204-205 F 4
Mola ~ GH 202-203 K 5
Moladjakit, gora ▲ RUS 116-117 L 3
Molakalmuru ○ IND 140-141 G 3
Molalatau ○ RB 218-219 E 6
Molalē ○ ETH 208-209 D 3
Molalla ○ USA (OR) 244-245 C 5
Molas del Norte, Punta ▲ MEX 52-53 L 1
Molat ⊥ HR 100-101 E 2
Moldary ○ KZ 124-125 L 3
Molde ☆ N 86-87 C 5
Moldova ■ MD 102-103 F 4
Moldova Nouă ○ RO 102-103 B 5
Molegbe ○ ZRE 206-207 E 6
Mole Island ⌒ PNG 183 D 2
Mole Lake Indian Reservation X USA (WI) 270-271 K 5
Mole National Park ⊥ GH 202-203 K 5
Molepolole ☆ RB 220-221 G 2
Moloquo, Morro do ▲ BR 74-75 F 7
Mole River ~ AUS 178-179 L 5
Molétai ○ LT 94-95 J 4
Molfetta ○ I 100-101 F 4
Molibagu ○ RI 164-165 H 3
Molina ○ E 98-99 G 4
Molina ○ RCH 78-79 D 3
Molina de Segura ○ E 98-99 G 5
Moline ○ USA (IL) 274-275 H 3
Moline ○ USA (KS) 262-263 K 7
Moline Mine ○ • AUS 172-173 L 2
Molinggapoto ○ RI 164-165 H 3
Molinillo, Puerto El ▲ E 98-99 F 6
Molino ○ USA (FL) 286-287 B 1
Molinos, Embalse los < RA 76-77 E 6
Molinos, Los ○ USA (CA) 246-247 C 3
Moliro ○ ZRE 214-215 F 5
Molise ■ I 100-101 E 4
Mol'kaj, hrebet ▲ RUS 112-113 J 4
Mollendo ○ PE 70-71 A 5
Mollepata ○ PE 64-65 F 8
Moller, Port ≈ 22-23 Q 5
Mollera, zaliv ≈ 108-109 E 5
Mollerusa = Mollerussa ○ E 98-99 H 4
Mollerussa ○ E 98-99 H 4
Molles, Punta ▲ RCH 78-79 D 2
Molo ○ EAK (RIF) 212-213 E 4
Molo ~ EAK 212-213 E 3
Molo ○ MYA 142-143 K 4
Moločna ~ UA 102-103 J 4
Moločnyj lyman ≈ 102-103 J 4
Molocopote ○ BR 62-63 G 5
Molócuè ~ MOC 218-219 J 2
Molocuè, Rio ~ MOC 218-219 J 2
Molodečno = Maladzečna ☆ BY 94-95 K 4
Molodežnaja ○ ARK 16 G 5
Molodežnyj ☆ KZ 124-125 H 3
Molodëžnyj ○ RUS 120-121 N 2
Molodo ○ RMM 202-203 G 2
Molodo ~ RUS 110-111 O 5
Mologa ~ RUS 94-95 O 2
Molokai ⌒ USA (HI) 288 H 3
Molokai Fracture Zone ≃ 14-15 O 5
Moloma ~ RUS 96-97 E 4
Molona ○ RI 164-165 H 6
Molong ○ AUS 180-181 K 2
Molongda ~ RUS 112-113 L 4
Molongdinskij hrebet ▲ RUS 112-113 L 4
Molopo ~ RB 220-221 E 3
Molopororiver ~ ZA 220-221 G 2
Moloskovicy ○ RUS 94-95 L 2
Moloundou ○ CAM 210-211 E 2
Molsheim ○ • F 90-91 L 7
Molt ○ USA (MT) 250-251 L 6
Molteno ○ ZA 220-221 H 5
Moltenopas ▲ ZA 220-221 F 6
Moltke Nunatak ▲ GRØ 26-27 o 4
Moltyrkan ~ RUS 110-111 V 7
Molu, Pulau ⌒ RI 166-167 F 5
Moluccas = Maluku ■ RI 166-167 D 4
Moluccas = Maluku, Kepulauan ⌒ RI 164-165 K 4
Molucca Sea = Maluku, Laut ≈ 164-165 J 4
Molūkī ○ AFG 136-137 G 7
Molumbo ○ MOC 218-219 J 2
Molume ○ GH 202-203 L 6
Molus River ○ CDN (NB) 240-241 K 4
Molvo ~ RUS 118-119 H 6
Molwe ○ ZRE 214-215 C 6
Moma ○ MOC 218-219 K 3
Moma ~ RUS 110-111 Y 6
Moma ○ ZRE 214-215 B 4
Moma, Ilha de ⌒ MOC 218-219 K 3
Momaligi ○ WAL 202-203 D 6
Momats ~ RI 166-167 K 4
Momba ○ Z 218-219 E 2
Mombaca ○ BR 68-69 J 4
Mombasa ☆ •• EAK 212-213 G 6
Mombasa Marine National Reserve ⊥ EAK 212-213 G 6
Mombenzélé ○ RCB 210-211 F 3
Mombetsu ○ J (HOK) 152-153 K 2
Mombetsu ○ J (HOK) 152-153 K 3
Mombo ~ ANG 216-217 F 5
Mombo ○ EAT 212-213 G 6
Mombongo ○ ZRE (HAU) 210-211 J 3
Mombongo ○ ZRE (HAU) 210-211 K 3
Momboyo ~ ZRE 210-211 G 4
Momburn ○ RI 166-167 K 6
Momfafa, Tanjung ▲ RI 166-167 F 2
Mommon, Tanjung ▲ RI 166-167 G 3
Momo ○ RI 164-165 G 4
Momo-Selennjahskaja vpadina ~ RUS 110-111 W 5
Momote ○ PNG 183 D 2
Momotombo, Volcán ▲ NIC 52-53 L 5
Mompiche, Ensenada de ≈ 64-65 B 1
Mompog Pass ≈ 160-161 E 6
Momponɔ ○ ZRE 210-211 H 3
Mompós ○ ••• CO 60-61 D 3
Momskij hrebet ▲ RUS 110-111 Y 6
Momskiy Khrebet = Momskij hrebet ▲ RUS 110-111 Y 6
Møn ⌒ DK 86-87 F 9
Mon ○ IND 142-143 J 2
Mona ○ USA (UT) 254-255 D 4
Mona, Isla ⌒ USA (PR) 286-287 O 2
Monaco ■ MC 90-91 L 10
Monaco ★ • MC 90-91 L 10
Monaco Deep ≃ 6-7 G 5
Monadotua, Pulau ⌒ RI 164-165 J 3
Monadyr ○ KZ 124-125 G 4
Monaghan = Muineachán ☆ IRL 90-91 D 4
Monahans ○ USA (TX) 266-267 E 2
Monana ○ G 210-211 D 4
Monango ○ USA (ND) 258-259 J 5
Mona Passage ≈ 56 A 2
Monapo ○ MOC 218-219 L 2
Mona Quimbundo ○ ANG 216-217 E 4
Monarch ○ CDN (ALB) 232-233 E 6
Monarch ○ USA (CO) 254-255 J 5
Monarch ○ USA (MT) 250-251 J 4
Monarch Icefield ⊂ CDN (BC) 228-229 H 4
Monarch Mountain ▲ CDN (BC) 230-231 D 2
Monashee Mountains ▲ CDN 228-229 P 4
Monashee Provincial Park ⊥ CDN (BC) 230-231 L 3
Monaši ○ UA 102-103 G 4
Monasterace Marina ○ I 100-101 F 5
Monastery ○ CDN (NS) 240-241 O 5
Monastir ☆ TN 190-191 H 3
Monastyrščina ☆ RUS 94-95 M 4
Monatélé ○ CAM 204-205 J 6
Monati, mys ▲ RUS 120-121 W 6
Monboré ○ CAM 206-207 B 4
Moncão ○ BR 68-69 F 3
Mončegorsk ○ RUS 88-89 M 3
Mönchengladbach ○ D 92-93 J 3
Monchy ○ CDN (SAS) 232-233 L 6
Moncks Corner ○ USA (SC) 284-285 K 3
Monclova ○ MEX 50-51 J 4
Monco Bünnyi ○ VRC 144-145 E 5
Moncton ○ CDN (NB) 240-241 L 4
Mondaí ○ BR 74-75 D 6
Mondamin ○ USA (IA) 274-275 B 3
Mondego, Cabo ▲ P 98-99 C 4
Mondego, Rio ~ P 98-99 C 4
Mondjamboli ○ ZRE 210-211 J 2
Mondjuku ○ ZRE 210-211 H 4
Mondo ○ TCH 198-199 G 6
Mondombe ○ ZRE 210-211 J 4
Mondómo ○ CO 60-61 C 6
Mondoñedo ○ • E 98-99 D 3
Mondono ○ RI 164-165 H 4
Mondovi ○ • I 100-101 A 2
Mondovi ○ USA (WI) 270-271 G 6
Mondragone ○ I 100-101 D 4
Mondrain Island ⌒ AUS 176-177 G 7
Mondubi, Ponta ▲ BR 74-75 G 5
Monduli ○ EAT 212-213 F 5
Monduran Reservoir < AUS 178-179 L 3
Mondy ○ RUS 116-117 K 10
Moné ~ CAM 204-205 H 6
Moneague ○ JA 54-55 G 5
Monemvassía ○ • GR 100-101 J 6
Moneragala ○ CL 140-141 J 7
Moneron, ostrov ⌒ RUS 122-123 J 5
Moneta ○ USA (WY) 252-253 L 3
Monett ○ USA (MO) 276-277 B 4
Monette ○ USA (AR) 276-277 E 5
Money Island = Jinyin Dao ⌒ VRC 158-159 L 2
Monfalcone ○ I 100-101 D 2
Monforte ○ P 98-99 D 5
Monforte de Lemos ○ • E 98-99 D 3
Monga ○ ZRE 206-207 F 6
Mongala ~ ZRE 210-211 H 2
Mongalla ○ SUD 206-207 K 6
Mongar ○ BHT 142-143 G 2
Monge ○ EC 64-65 D 3
Mongemputu ○ ZRE 210-211 H 5
Mongeri ○ WAL 202-203 E 5
Mongers Lake ○ AUS 176-177 D 4
Mongge ○ RI 166-167 G 2
Monggui ○ RI 166-167 H 2
Möng Hpayak ○ MYA 142-143 L 5
Mong Hsan ○ MYA 142-143 K 5
Möng Hsat ○ MYA 142-143 L 5
Mong Ka ○ MYA 142-143 L 5
Möng Küng ○ MYA 142-143 K 5
Mongla ○ BD 142-143 F 4
Möng Mit ○ MYA 142-143 K 4
Möng Nai ○ MYA 142-143 K 5
Mongo ☆ TCH 198-199 J 6
Mongočejaha ~ RUS 108-109 S 5
Mongoj ~ RUS 118-119 F 9
Mongol Altajn Nuruu ▲ MAU 146-147 J 1
Mongol Els ⊥ MAU 146-147 L 2
Mongolia = Mongol Ard Uls ■ MAU 148-149 D 5
Mongomo ○ GQ 210-211 C 3
Möngönmor't = Bulag ○ MAU 148-149 J 4
Mongonu ○ WAN 198-199 F 6
Mongororo ○ TCH 198-199 L 6
Mongotong ○ VRC 144-145 M 6
Mongoumba ○ RCA 210-211 G 2
Möng Pan ○ MYA 142-143 L 5
Möng Ton ○ MYA 142-143 L 5
Mongu ☆ Z 218-219 B 2
Mongua ○ ANG 216-217 C 8
Mongubal, Cachoeira do ~ BR 66-67 J 5
Mongubal Grande, Cachoeira ~ BR 66-67 J 5
Mönguel ○ RIM 196-197 D 6
Möng Yai ○ MYA 142-143 L 4
Möng Yang ○ MYA 142-143 L 5
Möng Yawng ○ MYA 142-143 M 5
Möngyu ○ MYA 142-143 K 4
Mönhbulag ○ MAU 148-149 F 4
Monhegan Island ⌒ USA (ME) 278-279 M 5
Mönhhaan = Bajasgalant ○ MAU 148-149 L 4
Mönh Hajrhan ▲ MAU 146-147 K 2
Moni ○ • RI 168 E 7
Monico ○ USA (WI) 270-271 J 5
Monida ○ USA (MT) 250-251 G 7
Monida Pass ▲ USA (ID) 252-253 F 2
Monimpébougou ○ RMM 202-203 H 2
Moni River ~ PNG 183 E 5
Monito, Isla ⌒ USA (PR) 286-287 O 2
Monitor ○ CDN (ALB) 232-233 H 4
Monitor Pass ▲ USA (CA) 246-247 F 5
Monitor Range ▲ USA 246-247 J 5
Monitos ○ CO 60-61 C 3
Monje ○ RA 78-79 J 2
Monjes, Islas los ⌒ YV 60-61 F 1
Monjolos ○ BR 72-73 H 5
Monkey Bay ○ MW 218-219 H 2
Monkey Mia ○ AUS 176-177 B 2
Mońki ○ PL 92-93 R 2
Monkira ○ AUS 178-179 F 3
Monkman Provincial Park ⊥ CDN (BC) 228-229 N 2
Monkoto ○ ZRE 210-211 H 4
Monkstown ○ CDN (NFL) 242-243 O 5
Monkstown ○ USA (TX) 264-265 J 5
Monmouth ○ USA (IL) 274-275 H 4
Monmouth ○ USA (OR) 244-245 B 6
Monmouth Mountain ▲ CDN (BC) 230-231 F 3
Mono ~ DY 202-203 L 6
Mono, Caño ~ CO 60-61 G 5
Mono, Punta del ▲ NIC 52-53 C 6
Monobamba ○ PE 64-65 E 7
Mono Island ⌒ SOL 184 I b 2
Mono Lake ○ USA (CA) 246-247 G 5
Monólithos ○ GR 100-101 L 6
Monolon ○ AUS 178-179 G 6
Monomoy Point ▲ USA (MA) 278-279 M 7
Monon ○ USA (IN) 274-275 M 4
Monona ○ USA (IA) 274-275 G 1
Monopamba ○ CO 64-65 D 1
Mono Pass ▲ USA (CA) 248-249 F 2
Monos, Los ○ RA 80 F 3
Monou ○ TCH 198-199 L 4
Monowai ○ NZ 182 A 6
Monreal del Campo ○ E 98-99 G 4
Monroe ○ CDN (NFL) 242-243 P 4
Monroe ○ USA (GA) 284-285 G 3
Monroe ○ USA (IA) 274-275 E 3
Monroe ○ USA (MI) 272-273 F 6
Monroe ○ USA (NC) 282-283 G 6
Monroe ○ USA (NY) 280-281 M 2
Monroe ○ USA (OH) 280-281 B 4
Monroe ○ USA (OR) 244-245 B 6
Monroe ○ USA (UT) 254-255 C 5
Monroe ○ USA (WA) 244-245 D 3
Monroe ○ USA (WI) 274-275 J 2
Monroe ○ • USA (LA) 268-269 H 4
Monroe, Lake ○ USA (FL) 286-287 H 3
Monroe City ○ USA (MO) 274-275 G 5
Monroe Lake ~ USA 274-275 M 5
Monroeville ○ USA (AL) 284-285 C 5
Monroeville ○ USA (PA) 280-281 G 3
Monrovia ★ • LB 202-203 E 6
Mons ☆ • B 92-93 G 3
Monsenhor Gil ○ BR 68-69 G 4
Monsenhor Hipolito ○ BR 68-69 H 5
Monserrat, Isla ⌒ MEX 50-51 D 5
Møns Klint ~ • DK 86-87 F 9
Monsombougou ○ RMM 202-203 E 2
Montagne d'Ambre, Parc National de la ⊥ RM 222-223 F 4
Montagne du Pin, Lac de la ○ CDN 38-39 G 2
Montagnes Françaises ▲ F 62-63 G 3
Montagu ○ ZA 220-221 E 6
Montague ○ CDN (PEI) 240-241 N 4
Montague ○ USA (TX) 264-265 G 5
Montague Island ⌒ AUS 180-181 L 4
Montague Island ⌒ USA 20-21 R 6
Montague Sound ≈ 172-173 G 3
Montague Strait ≈ 20-21 Q 7
Montaigu ○ F 90-91 G 8
Montajtas ○ KZ 136-137 L 3
Montalbán ○ E 98-99 G 4
Montalbo ○ E 98-99 F 5
Montalegre ○ ANG 216-217 D 4
Montalegre ○ P 98-99 D 4
Montalto (Monte Cocuzza) ▲ I 100-101 E 5
Montalvânia ○ BR 72-73 H 3
Montalvo ○ EC 64-65 D 3
Montana ☆ BG 102-103 C 6
Montana ■ USA 250-251 H 5
Montaña, La ⊥ PE 64-65 E 5
Montana City ○ USA (MT) 250-251 H 5
Montaña de Yoro, Parque Nacional ⊥ HN 52-53 L 4
Montañas de Onzole ▲ EC 64-65 C 1
Montandón ○ RCH 76-77 C 4
Mont-Apica ○ CDN (QUE) 240-241 D 3

Misantla — Mont-Apica 363

Montargis ○ F 90-91 J 8
Montauban ☆• F 90-91 H 9
Montauk ○ USA (NY) 280-281 P 2
Montauk Point ▲ USA (NY) 280-281 P 2
Montbard ○ F 90-91 K 8
Mont Bata ○ RCA 206-207 B 6
Montbéliard ○• F 90-91 L 8
Mont Blanc ▲•• F 90-91 L 9
Montceau-les-Mines ○ F 90-91 K 8
Montcerf ○ CDN (QUE) 238-239 J 2
Mont-de-Marsan ☆ F 90-91 G 10
Mont-Dore, le ○ F 90-91 J 9
Monte, Laguna del ⊖ RA 78-79 H 4
Monteagle ○ AUS 178-179 J 2
Monteagle ○ USA (TN) 276-277 K 5
Monteagudo ○ BOL 70-71 F 6
Monte Alban ∴•• MEX 52-53 F 3
Monte Alegre ○ BR 62-63 G 6
Monte Alegre de Goiás ○ BR 72-73 G 2
Monte Alegre de Minas ○ BR 72-73 F 5
Monte Alegre de Sergipe ○ BR 68-69 K 7
Monte Aprazível ○ BR 72-73 F 6
Monte Azul ○ BR 72-73 J 3
Montebello ○ CDN (QUE) 238-239 L 3
Montebello Islands ⌒ AUS 172-173 B 6
Monte Belo ○ ANG 216-217 C 6
Monte Bianco = Mont Blanc ▲•• I 100-101 A 2
Monte-Carlo ○ MC 90-91 L 10
Monte Carmelo ○ BR 72-73 G 5
Monte Caseros ○ RA 76-77 J 6
Monte Castelo ○ BR 74-75 E 6
Montecito ○ USA (CA) 248-249 E 5
Monte Comán ○ RA 78-79 F 3
Monte Creek ○ CDN (BC) 230-231 K 3
Monte Cristi ☆ DOM 54-55 K 5
Montecristi ○ EC 64-65 B 2
Monte Cristo ○ BR 66-67 D 5
Monte Cristo ○ USA (WA) 244-245 D 3
Montecristo, Cerro ▲ ES 52-53 K 4
Montecristo, Ísola di ⌒ I 100-101 C 3
Monte Dourado ○ BR 62-63 H 6
Monte Escobedo ○ MEX 50-51 H 6
Montego Bay ○• JA 54-55 G 5
Monte Grande ⊥ BOL 70-71 F 5
Monte Grande ○ NIC 52-53 B 5
Monte Hermoso ○ RA 78-79 J 5
Monteiro ○ BR 68-69 K 5
Monteiro Lobato ○ BR 72-73 H 7
Monte Lake ○ CDN (BC) 230-231 K 3
Monte León, Cerro ▲ RA 80 F 5
Montélimar ○ F 90-91 K 9
Montelimar ○ NIC 52-53 L 6
Monte Lindo, Arroyo ~ RA 76-77 H 3
Monte Lindo, Río ~ PY 76-77 J 2
Monte Lindo Grande, Riacho ~ RA 76-77 H 3
Montello ○ USA (NV) 246-247 L 2
Montello ○ USA (WI) 270-271 J 7
Montemayor, Meseta de ⊥ RA 80 G 2
Montemorelos ○ MEX 50-51 K 5
Montemor-o-Novo ○ P 98-99 C 5
Montenegro ○ BR 74-75 E 7
Montenegro = Crna gora ◘ YU 100-101 G 3
Monte Negro, Quedas de ~ ANG 216-217 B 8
Monte Pascoal, Parque Nacional de ⊥ BR 72-73 L 4
Monte Patria ○ RCH 76-77 B 6
Monte Peruvia • PE 64-65 D 4
Montepescali ○ I 100-101 C 3
Montepío ○ MEX 52-53 G 2
Monte Plata ☆ DOM 54-55 L 5
Montepuez ○ MOC 218-219 K 1
Montepuez, Rio ~ MOC 218-219 K 1
Montepulciano ○• I 100-101 C 3
Monte Quemado ○ RA 76-77 F 3
Monterey ○ USA (TN) 276-277 K 4
Monterey ○ USA (VA) 280-281 G 5
Monterey ○• USA (CA) 248-249 C 3
Montería ☆ CO 60-61 D 3
Montero ○ BOL 70-71 F 5
Monteros ○ RA 76-77 E 4
Monte Rosa ▲ CH 92-93 J 6
Monte Rosa ▲ I 100-101 A 2
Monterrey ☆• MEX 50-51 J 5
Monterrey, Parque Nacional de ⊥ MEX 50-51 J 5
Monterrey Bay ≈ 40-41 D 7
Monterrey Bay ≈ 248-249 C 3
Monterrico ○ GCA 52-53 J 5
Monterrubio ○ CO 60-61 D 2
Montes, Punta ▲ RA 80 F 5
Montes Altos ○ BR 68-69 E 4
Montesano ○ USA (WA) 244-245 B 3
Montesano sulla Marcellana ○ I 100-101 E 4
Monte Sant'Ángelo ○ I 100-101 E 4
Monte Santo ○ BR 68-69 J 7
Monte Santo de Minas ○ BR 72-73 G 6
Montes Claros ○ BR 72-73 J 4
Montes de Oca ○ RA 78-79 H 5
Montesquieu Islands ⌒ AUS 172-173 G 3
Montevallo ○ USA (AL) 284-285 D 3
Montevideo ★• ROU 78-79 L 3
Montevideo ○ USA (MN) 270-271 C 6
Monte Vista ○ USA (CO) 254-255 J 6
Monte Vista National Wildlife Refuge • USA (CO) 254-255 J 6
Montezuma ○ BR 72-73 J 3
Montezuma ○ USA (GA) 284-285 F 4
Montezuma ○ USA (IA) 274-275 F 3
Montezuma ○ USA (IN) 274-275 L 5
Montezuma Castle National Monument ∴ USA (AZ) 256-257 D 4
Montezuma Creek ○ USA (UT) 254-255 F 6
Montezuma Creek ~ USA 254-255 F 6
Montfort ○ USA (WI) 274-275 H 2
Montgomery ○ USA (LA) 268-269 H 5
Montgomery ○ USA (MN) 270-271 E 6
Montgomery ○ USA (WV) 280-281 E 5
Montgomery ☆• USA (AL) 284-285 D 4
Montgomery = Sāhīwāl ○ PK 138-139 D 4
Montgomery City ○ USA (MO) 274-275 G 6
Montgomery Islands ⌒ AUS 172-173 G 3
Monticello ○ USA (AR) 276-277 D 7
Monticello ○ USA (FL) 286-287 F 1
Monticello ○ USA (GA) 284-285 G 3
Monticello ○ USA (IA) 274-275 G 2
Monticello ○ USA (IL) 274-275 K 4
Monticello ○ USA (KY) 276-277 L 4
Monticello ○ USA (MN) 270-271 E 5
Monticello ○ USA (MO) 274-275 G 4
Monticello ○ USA (MS) 268-269 K 5
Monticello ○ USA (NM) 256-257 H 5
Monticello ○ USA (NY) 280-281 M 2
Monticello ○ USA (SC) 284-285 J 2
Monticello ○ USA (UT) 254-255 F 6
Monticello ••• USA (VA) 280-281 H 6
Montijo ○ E 98-99 D 5
Montijo, Golfo de ≈ 52-53 D 8
Montilla ○ E 98-99 E 6
Montima ~ ZRE 210-211 H 2
Montipa ○ ANG 216-217 B 7
Montividiu ○ BR 72-73 E 4
Mont-Louis ○ F 90-91 J 10
Montluçon ○ F 90-91 J 8
Montmagny ○ CDN (QUE) 240-241 E 4
Montmarault ○ F 90-91 J 8
Montmartre ○ CDN (SAS) 232-233 P 5
Mont Nebo ○ CDN (SAS) 232-233 M 2
Monto ○ AUS 178-179 L 3
Montoro ○• E 98-99 E 5
Montoya ○ USA (NM) 256-257 L 3
Montpelier ○ JA 54-55 G 5
Montpelier ○ USA (ID) 252-253 G 4
Montpelier ○ USA (IN) 274-275 N 4
Montpelier ○ USA (ND) 258-259 J 5
Montpelier ○ USA (VA) 280-281 J 6
Montpelier ☆ USA (VT) 278-279 J 4
Montpellier ☆• F 90-91 J 10
Montpensier, Kap ▲ GRØ 26-27 r 5
Montréal ○• CDN (QUE) 238-239 M 3
Montreal Falls ~ CDN 236-237 D 5
Montreal Lake Indian Reserve ⚔ CDN (SAS) 232-233 N 2
Montreal River ○ CDN (ONT) 236-237 D 5
Montreal River ~ CDN 236-237 E 5
Montreal River ~ CDN 236-237 H 5
Montreux ○• CH 92-93 J 5
Montrose ○ CDN (BC) 230-231 M 4
Montrose ○ GB 90-91 F 3
Montrose ○ USA (AR) 276-277 D 7
Montrose ○ USA (CO) 254-255 H 5
Montrose ○ USA (IA) 274-275 G 4
Montrose ○ USA (IL) 274-275 K 5
Montrose ○ USA (PA) 280-281 L 2
Montrose Wildlife Area ⊥ USA (MO) 274-275 D 6
Montrouis ○ RH 54-55 J 5
Monts, Pointe des ▲ CDN (QUE) 242-243 A 3
Mont Saint-Michel, Le ○••• F 90-91 G 7
Mont Sangbé, Parc National du ⊥ CI 202-203 G 5
Mont Selinda ○ ZW 218-219 G 5
Montserrat ◘ GB 56 D 3
Montserrat Island ⌒ GB 56 D 3
Monturaqui ○ RCH 76-77 C 3
Monument ○ USA (CO) 254-255 L 4
Monument ○ USA (NM) 256-257 M 6
Monument ○ USA (OR) 244-245 F 6
Monument Draw ~ USA 264-265 B 6
Monument Hill State Historic Site ∴ USA (TX) 266-267 L 4
Monumento al Soldato Pionero • YV 62-63 D 3
Monumento el Obelisco • YV 60-61 G 2
Monumento Rodrigo Arenas Betancourt • CO 60-61 E 5
Monument Pass ▲ USA (AZ) 256-257 E 2
Monument Rocks ∴ USA (KS) 262-263 F 6
Monument Valley ⌄ USA 254-255 E 6
Monument Valley Navajo Tribal Park ⊥• USA (AZ) 256-257 E 2
Monywa ○ MYA 142-143 J 4
Monza ○• I 100-101 B 2
Monza ○ VRC 144-145 J 4
Monze ○ Z 218-219 D 3
Monzón ○• E 98-99 H 4
Monzon ○ PE 64-65 D 6
Mooat, Danau ⊖ RI 164-165 J 3
Moodiarrup ○ AUS 176-177 D 6
Moody ○ USA (TX) 266-267 K 2
Mooirivier ~ ZA 220-221 H 3
Mooirivier ~ ZA 220-221 K 4
Mooketsi ○ ZA 218-219 F 6
Mooki River ~ AUS 178-179 L 6
Moola, Rio ~ MOC 214-215 H 6
Mooloo Downs ○ AUS 176-177 D 2
Mooloogool ○ AUS 176-177 E 3
Moolooloo Out Station ○ AUS 172-173 K 4
Moomaw, Lake ⊖ USA (VA) 280-281 G 5
Moomba ○ AUS 178-179 F 4
Moomin Creek ~ AUS 178-179 K 5
Moonan Flat ○ AUS 178-179 L 6
Moonaree ○ AUS 178-179 C 6
Moonbeam ○ CDN (ONT) 236-237 F 3
Moonbi Range ▲ AUS 178-179 L 6
Moonda Lake ⊖ AUS 178-179 F 3
Moondarra, Lake ⊖ AUS 174-175 E 7
Moonie ○ AUS 178-179 L 4
Moonie Highway II AUS 178-179 L 4
Moonie River ~ AUS 178-179 K 5
Moonlight Head ▲ AUS 180-181 G 5
Moonta Bay ○ AUS 180-181 D 3
Moonya ○ AUS 178-179 H 2
Moor, Kepulauan ⌒ RI 166-167 H 3
Moora ○ AUS 176-177 D 5
Mooraberree ○ AUS 178-179 F 3
Moorarie ○ AUS 176-177 D 2
Moorari Oil Field • AUS 178-179 F 4
Moorcroft ○ USA (WY) 252-253 O 2
Moordkuil ○ ZA 220-221 D 6
Moore ○ USA (ID) 252-253 E 3
Moore ○ USA (MT) 250-251 K 5
Moore ○ USA (OK) 264-265 G 3
Moore ○ USA (TX) 266-267 H 4
Moore, Lake ⊖ AUS 176-177 D 4
Moore, Mount ▲ AUS 176-177 G 2
Moore Bay ≈ 24-25 N 2
Moorefield ○ USA (WV) 280-281 H 4
Moorefield River ~ USA 280-281 G 5
Moore Haven ○ USA (FL) 286-287 H 5
Moore Home State Historic Site • USA (IL) 274-275 K 5
Mooreland ○ USA (OK) 264-265 E 2
Moore Mountain ▲ USA (ID) 252-253 B 3
Moore Park ○ AUS 178-179 M 3
Moore Park ○ CDN (MAN) 234-235 D 4
Moore River ~ AUS 176-177 C 5
Moore River National Park ⊥ AUS 176-177 C 5
Moores Bridge ○ USA (AL) 284-285 C 3
Moores Creek National Battlefield • USA (NC) 282-283 J 6
Moore's Island ⌒ BS 54-55 G 1
Moorestown ○ USA (MI) 272-273 E 3
Mooresville ○ USA (NC) 282-283 G 5
Mooreton ○ USA (ND) 258-259 L 5
Moorhead ○ USA (MN) 270-271 B 4
Moorhead ○ USA (MS) 268-269 K 3
Mooririvier ○ ZA 220-221 K 4
Moornanyah Lake ⊖ AUS 180-181 G 2
Moorpark ○ USA (CA) 248-249 F 5
Moose ○ USA (WY) 252-253 H 3
Moosehead Lake ⊖ USA (ME) 278-279 M 3
Moose Heights ○ CDN (BC) 228-229 M 3
Moose Hill ○ CDN (ONT) 234-235 O 6
Moosehorn ○ CDN (MAN) 234-235 E 3
Moose Island ⌒ CDN (MAN) 234-235 F 3
Moose Jaw ○ CDN (SAS) 232-233 N 5
Moose Jaw Creek ~ CDN 232-233 O 5
Moose Lake ○ USA (MN) 270-271 F 4
Mooselookmeguntic Lake ⊖ USA (ME) 278-279 L 4
Moose Mount ▲ CDN (SAS) 232-233 Q 6
Moose Mountain Creek ~ CDN 232-233 P 5
Moose Mount Provincial Park ⊥ CDN (SAS) 232-233 Q 6
Moose Pass ○ USA 20-21 Q 6
Moose River ○ CDN (ONT) 236-237 G 2
Moosomin ○ CDN (SAS) 232-233 R 5
Mootwingee Historic Site • AUS 178-179 G 6
Mootwingee National Park ⊥ AUS 178-179 G 6
Mopādu ○ IND 140-141 H 3
Mopán, Río ~ GCA 52-53 K 3
Mopane ○ ZA 218-219 E 6
Mopeia ○ MOC 218-219 H 3
Mopipi ○ RB 218-219 C 5
Mopti ◘ RMM 202-203 H 2
Mopti ☆ RMM (MOP) 202-203 H 2
Moqām, Bandar-e ○ IR 134-135 E 5
Moquegua ☆ PE 70-71 B 5
Moquegua, Río ~ PE 70-71 B 5
Moquehuá ○ RA 78-79 K 3
Mór ○ H 92-93 P 5
Mora ○ CAM 206-207 B 3
Mora ○ E 98-99 F 5
Mora ○ P 98-99 C 5
Mora ○ S 86-87 G 6
Mora ○ USA (MN) 270-271 E 5
Mora ○ USA (NM) 256-257 K 3
Mora, La ○ RA 78-79 F 3
Morab ○ IND 140-141 F 3
Morača ~ YU 100-101 G 3
Moradabad ○ IND 138-139 G 5
Morada Nova ○ BR 68-69 J 4
Morada Nova de Minas ○ BR 72-73 H 5
Morado, Quebrada del ~ RCH 76-77 B 4
Morado I, Cerro ▲ RA 76-77 E 2
Moraes ○ BR 74-75 D 8
Morafeno ○ RM 222-223 E 6
Morafenobe ○ RM 222-223 D 6
Morag ○ PL 92-93 P 2
Morai ○ RI 166-167 H 5
Moraine State Park ⊥ USA (PA) 280-281 F 3
Morais de Almeida ○ BR 66-67 K 6
Morajuana ○ GUY 62-63 E 1
Moralana Creek ~ AUS 178-179 E 6
Moraleda, Canal de ≈ 80 D 2
Moraleja ○ E 98-99 D 4
Moramanga ○ RM 222-223 F 7
Moran ○ USA (KS) 262-263 L 7
Moran ○ USA (MI) 272-273 E 2
Moran ○ USA (TX) 264-265 E 6
Moran ○ USA (WY) 252-253 H 3
Morán, Laguna ⊖ RA 78-79 K 2
Moranbah ○ AUS 178-179 K 2
Moran River ~ AUS 172-173 G 3
Morant Bay ○ JA 54-55 G 6
Morant Cays ⌒ JA 54-55 H 6
Morappur ○ IND 140-141 H 4
Morarano ○ RM (ATN) 222-223 E 7
Morarano ○ RM (Fns) 222-223 E 8
Morarano-Chrome ○ RM 222-223 F 6
Mora River ~ USA 256-257 L 3
Moratalla ○ E 98-99 G 5
Moratuwa ○ CL 140-141 H 7
Moraújo ○ BR 68-69 H 3
Morava ⊥ CZ 92-93 O 4
Morava ~ CZ 92-93 O 4
Moravia ○ USA (IA) 274-275 F 4
Moravia ○ USA (NY) 278-279 E 6
Morávia, Planalto de ▲ MOC 218-219 F 2
Moravian Falls ○ USA (NC) 282-283 F 4
Morawa ○ AUS 176-177 C 4
Moray Downs ○ AUS 178-179 J 1
Moray Firth ≈ 90-91 E 3
Morazán ○ HN 52-53 L 4
Morbanipari, Mount ▲ PNG 183 B 3
Morbi ○ IND 138-139 C 8
Mörbylånga ☆ S 86-87 H 8
Morcego ○ BR 66-67 F 4
Morden ○ CDN (MAN) 234-235 E 5
Mordovo ○ RUS 94-95 R 5
Mordovskij zopovednik ⊥ RUS 94-95 S 4
Mordvinia = Mordovskaja Respublika ◘ RUS 94-95 S 4
Mordvinof, Cape ▲ USA 22-23 O 5
Mordvinova, zaliv ≈ 122-123 K 5
Mordyjaha ~ RUS 108-109 N 6
Mor'e ○ RUS 94-95 M 1
Moreau River ~ USA 260-261 F 1
Morecambe ○ CDN (ALB) 232-233 G 2
Morecambe ○ GB 90-91 F 4
Moree ○ AUS 178-179 K 5
Moreh ○ IND 142-143 J 3
Morehead ○ PNG 183 A 5
Morehead ○ USA (KY) 276-277 M 2
Morehead City ○ USA (NC) 282-283 L 6
Morehead River ~ PNG 183 A 5
Moreira, Arroyo ~ RA 76-77 H 6
More-Ju ~ RUS 108-109 H 8
Morela, Ponta ▲ CV 202-203 C 6
Morelia ○ CO 64-65 E 1
Morelia ☆••• MEX 52-53 D 2
Morell ○ CDN (PEI) 240-241 N 4
Morella ○ AUS 178-179 G 2
Morella ○ E 98-99 G 4
Morelos ○ MEX (COA) 50-51 J 3
Morelos ○ MEX (COA) 50-51 H 3
Morelos ◘ MEX 52-53 E 2
Morembe ○ RM 222-223 C 8
Moremi Wildlife Reserve ⊥ RB 218-219 B 4
Morena ○ IND 138-139 F 6
Morena, Cachoeira ~ BR 66-67 H 4
Morena, Sierra ▲ E 98-99 D 5
Morenci ○ USA (AZ) 256-257 F 5
Morenci ○ USA (MI) 272-273 E 6
Morenero ○ YV 60-61 K 3
Moreno ○ BR 68-69 L 6
Moreno ○ RA 78-79 K 3
Moreno, Bahía ≈ 76-77 B 2
Moreno, Sierra de ▲ RCH 76-77 C 1
Moreno Chillanes ○ EC 64-65 C 2
Moreno Valley ○ USA (CA) 248-249 G 6
Moresby Camp ○ CDN (BC) 228-229 B 3
Moresby Island ⌒ CDN (BC) 228-229 C 4
Mores Creek Summit ▲ USA (ID) 252-253 C 3
Moreton, Cape ▲ AUS 178-179 M 4
Moreton Bay ≈ 178-179 M 4
Moreton Island ⌒ AUS 178-179 M 4
Moreton Post Office ○ AUS 174-175 G 3
Morewood ○ CDN (ONT) 238-239 K 3
Morfou ○ TR 128-129 E 5
Morgāb ○ AFG 136-137 H 7
Morgāb, Daryā-ye ~ AFG 136-137 H 7
Morgābrūd, Daryā-ye ~ AFG 136-137 J 7
Morgan ○ AUS 180-181 E 3
Morgan ○ USA (MN) 270-271 D 6
Morgan ○ USA (TX) 264-265 G 6
Morgan ○ USA (UT) 254-255 D 2
Morgana, proliv ≈ 84-85 h 2
Morgan City ○ USA (AL) 284-285 D 2
Morgan City ○ USA (LA) 268-269 J 7
Morgan Creek ~ USA 250-251 N 3
Morganfield ○ USA (KY) 276-277 H 3
Morgan Hill ○ USA (CA) 248-249 C 2
Morgan Mill ○ USA (TX) 264-265 F 6
Morgan's Corner ○ USA (NC) 282-283 L 4
Morganton ○ USA (NC) 282-283 F 5
Morgantown ○ USA (IN) 274-275 M 5
Morgantown ○ USA (KY) 276-277 J 3
Morgantown ○ USA (WV) 280-281 G 4
Morgan Vale ○ AUS 180-181 F 2
Morgenzon ○ ZA 220-221 J 3
Morgim ○ IND 140-141 E 3
Morhaja ~ RUS 118-119 D 4
Morhiban, Lac de ⊖ CDN 38-39 N 2
Mori ○ J 152-153 J 3
Mori ○ VRC 146-147 K 4
Moriah, Mount ▲ USA (NV) 246-247 L 4
Moriarty ○ USA (NM) 256-257 J 3
Moribaya ○ RG 202-203 F 5
Morice Lake ⊖ CDN (BC) 228-229 G 2
Morice River ~ CDN 228-229 G 2
Moricetown ○ CDN 32-33 G 4
Morichal Largo, Río ~ YV 60-61 K 3
Morichal Viejo ○ CO 60-61 F 6
Morigbadougou ○ RG 202-203 F 5
Morigim ○ IND 140-141 E 3
Morigio Island ⌒ PNG 183 B 4
Morija ○ LS 220-221 H 4
Morijo ○ EAK 212-213 E 4
Moriki ○ WAN 198-199 C 6
Morin Dawa ○ VRC 150-151 E 3
Morin Heights ○ CDN (QUE) 238-239 L 3
Morinville ○ CDN (ALB) 232-233 E 2
Morioka ☆• J 152-153 J 5
Morire ○ MOC 218-219 H 3
Mori River ~ PNG 183 E 5
Morisityj, ostrov ⌒ RUS 126-127 G 5
Morita, La ○ MEX 50-51 G 3
Moriyama ○ J 152-153 F 7
Morjakovskij Zaton ○ RUS 114-115 S 6
Morjen ~ PK 134-135 K 4
Morki ☆ RUS 96-97 F 5
Morkill River ~ CDN 228-229 O 3
Morkoka ~ RUS 116-117 O 2
Morkoka ~ RUS 118-119 G 3
Morlaix ○ F 90-91 F 7
Morland ○ USA (KS) 262-263 F 5
Morley ○ CDN (ALB) 232-233 D 4
Mormanno ○ I 100-101 E 5
Mormon Lake ○ USA (AZ) 256-257 D 4
Mormon Lake ⊖ USA (AZ) 256-257 D 4
Mormon Print Shop • USA (MI) 272-273 D 2
Mormon Range ▲ USA 248-249 K 3
Morne-à-L'eau ○ F 56 E 3
Morne Seychellois National Park ⊥ SY 224 D 2
Morney ○ AUS 178-179 F 3
Morningside ○ CDN (ALB) 232-233 E 3
Morning Star ○ USA (MS) 268-269 K 4
Mornington, Isla ⌒ RCH 80 C 4
Mornington Abyssal Plain ≃ 5 C 10
Mornington Island ⌒ AUS 174-175 E 5
Mornington Island Aboriginal Land Trust ⚔ AUS 174-175 E 5
Moro ○ PE 64-65 C 6
Moro ○ PK 138-139 B 6
Moro ○ USA (OR) 244-245 E 5
Moro, Arroyo el ~ RA 78-79 K 5
Moroak ○ AUS 174-175 B 4
Moro Bay ○ USA (AR) 276-277 C 7
Morobe ○ PNG 183 D 4
Morobo ○ SUD 212-213 C 2
Morocco ○ USA (IN) 274-275 L 4
Morocco = al-Maghrib ■ MA 188-189 H 4
Morococala, Cerro ▲ BOL 70-71 D 6
Moro Creek ~ USA 276-277 C 7
Morodougou ○ RN 202-203 F 4
Morogari ○ SP 208-209 F 6
Morogoro ◘ EAT 214-215 J 5
Morogoro ☆ EAT (MOR) 214-215 J 4
Moro Gulf ≈ 160-161 E 9
Moroiemu ○ RI 166-167 K 5
Morokweng ○ ZA 220-221 F 3
Moromaho, Pulau ⌒ RI 166-167 C 5
Morón ○ C 54-55 F 3
Mörön ☆ MAU 148-149 E 3
Morón ○ RA 78-79 K 3
Moron ○ USA (UT) 254-255 D 4
Morón ○ YV 60-61 G 2
Morona, Río ~ PE 64-65 D 4
Morondava ○ RM 222-223 D 8
Morón de la Frontera ○ E 98-99 E 6
Moroni ○ CI 202-203 G 5
Morongo Indian Reservation ⚔ USA (CA) 248-249 H 5
Moroni ★• COM 222-223 C 3
Moronou ○ CI 202-203 H 6
Morosečnaja ~ RUS 120-121 R 5
Morotai, Pulau ⌒ RI 164-165 L 2
Morotai, Selat ≈ 164-165 K 2
Moroto ☆ EAU 212-213 E 2
Moroto, Mount ▲ EAU 212-213 E 2
Morouba ○ RCA 206-207 E 5
Morowali ○ RI 164-165 G 4
Morowali Reserve ⊥• RI 164-165 G 4
Morozova, mys ▲ RUS 108-109 f 5
Morozovsk ○ RUS 102-103 M 3
Morpará ○ BR 68-69 G 7
Morpeth ○ GB 90-91 G 4
Morreesburg ○ ZA 220-221 D 6
Morretes ○ BR 74-75 F 5
Morrillito, Isla ⌒ USA (PR) 286-287 P 3
Morrilton ○ USA (AR) 276-277 C 5
Morrin ○ CDN (ALB) 232-233 F 4
Morrinhos ○ BR (CEA) 68-69 H 3
Morrinhos ○ BR (GOI) 72-73 F 4
Morrinhos ○ BR (MAR) 68-69 E 6
Morrinhos, Cachoeira ~ BR 66-67 E 7
Morrinsville ○ NZ 182 E 2
Morrión, El ○ MEX 50-51 G 3
Morris ○ CDN (MAN) 234-235 F 5
Morris ○ USA (IL) 274-275 K 3
Morris ○ USA (MN) 270-271 C 5
Morris ○ USA (NY) 278-279 F 6
Morris ○ USA (OK) 264-265 J 3
Morris ○ USA (PA) 280-281 J 2
Morris, Mount ○ AUS 178-179 H 3
Morrisburg ○ CDN (ONT) 238-239 K 3
Morris Jesup, Kap ▲ GRØ 26-27 j 2
Morris Jesup Gletscher ⊂ GRØ 26-27 P 5
Morrison Bay ≈ 158-159 E 5
Morriston ○ USA (FL) 286-287 G 2
Morristown ○ USA (AZ) 256-257 C 5
Morristown ○ USA (NJ) 280-281 M 3
Morristown ○ USA (NY) 278-279 F 4
Morristown ○ USA (SD) 260-261 E 1
Morristown ○ USA (TN) 282-283 D 4
Morrisville ○ USA (NY) 278-279 F 6
Morrisville ○ USA (VT) 278-279 J 4
Morro ○ EC 64-65 B 3
Morro, Canal de ≈ 64-65 B 3
Morro, Punta ▲ MEX 52-53 J 2
Morro, Punta ▲ RCH 76-77 B 4
Morro, Sierra del ▲ RA 78-79 G 2
Morro Agudo ○ BR 72-73 F 6
Morro Bay ○ USA (CA) 248-249 D 4
Morro Chico ○ RCH 80 E 6
Morrocoy, Parque Nacional ⊥ YV 60-61 G 2
Morro de Coco ○ BR 72-73 K 6
Morro do Alvarenga ○ BR 66-67 D 6
Morro do Padre ▲ BR 72-73 G 4
Morro do Pilar ○ BR 72-73 J 5
Morropón ○ PE 64-65 C 4
Morro River ~ WAL 202-203 E 6
Morros ○ BR 68-69 F 3
Morrosquillo, Golfo de ≈ 60-61 D 3
Morrowville ○ USA (KS) 262-263 J 5
Morrumbala ○ MOC 218-219 H 3
Morrumbene ○ MOC 218-219 H 6
Moršank ○ RUS 94-95 R 5
Morse ○ CDN (SAS) 232-233 L 5
Morse ○ USA (TX) 264-265 C 2
Morse Reservoir ⊖ USA (IN) 274-275 M 4
Morsi ○ IND 138-139 G 9
Morskoj, kraj ⌒ KZ 126-127 J 5
Morskoj, ostrov ⌒ KZ 126-127 J 5
Morskoj Birjučok, ostrov ⌒ RUS 126-127 G 5
Morsø ○ DK 86-87 D 8
Morson ○ CDN (ONT) 234-235 J 5
Morstone ○ AUS 174-175 E 6
Mørsvikbotn ○ N 86-87 G 3
Mort, Chutes de la • RM 222-223 F 7
Mortandade, Cachoeira ~ BR 68-69 E 5
Mortara ○ I 100-101 B 2
Morteros ○ RA 76-77 F 6
Mortes, Rio das ~ BR 72-73 E 3
Mortesoro ○ SUD 208-209 B 3
Mortimers ○• BS 54-55 H 3
Mortlach ○ CDN (SAS) 232-233 M 5
Mortlake ○ AUS 180-181 G 5
Morton ○ USA (IL) 274-275 J 4
Morton ○ USA (MN) 270-271 D 6
Morton ○ USA (MS) 268-269 L 4
Morton ○ USA (TX) 264-265 B 5
Morton ○ USA (WA) 244-245 C 4
Morton National Park ⊥ AUS 180-181 L 3
Mort River ~ AUS 178-179 F 1
Mortugaba ○ BR 72-73 J 3
Moruga ○ TT 60-61 L 2
Moruita ○ EAU 212-213 E 3
Morundah ○ AUS 180-181 J 3
Moruppatti ○ IND 140-141 H 5
Moruya ○ AUS 180-181 L 3
Morven ○ AUS 178-179 J 4
Morven ○ USA (GA) 284-285 G 6
Morven ○ USA (NC) 282-283 G 6
Morvongole ▲ EAU 212-213 E 2
Morweena ○ CDN (MAN) 234-235 F 4
Morwell ○ AUS 180-181 J 5
Morzhovoi Bay ≈ 22-23 P 5
Moržovec, ostrov ⌒ RUS 88-89 R 3
Mosa ○ PNG 183 F 3
Moša ~ RUS 88-89 Q 5
Mosby ○ USA (MT) 250-251 M 5
Mosca ○ USA (CO) 254-255 K 6
Moscas, Las ○ RA 78-79 K 2
Mosconi ○ RA 78-79 J 3
Moscow ○ USA (ID) 250-251 C 5
Moscow ○ USA (KS) 262-263 E 7
Moscow ○ USA (TN) 276-277 F 5
Moscow = Moskva ★••• RUS 94-95 P 4
Mosel ~ D 92-93 J 4
Moselebe ~ RB 220-221 F 2
Moselle ~ F 90-91 L 7
Moselle ○ USA (MS) 268-269 L 5
Moselle Swamp ⊖ USA (SC) 284-285 K 3
Mošens'ka dubrava • UA 102-103 G 3
Moser River ○ CDN (NS) 240-241 N 6
Mosers River ○ CDN (NS) 240-241 N 6
Moses ○ USA (NM) 256-257 M 2
Moses, Mount ▲ USA (NV) 246-247 H 3
Moses Lake ○• USA (WA) 244-245 F 3
Moses Point ▲ USA 20-21 J 4
Mosetse ○ RB 218-219 D 5
Mošgān ○ IR 134-135 F 4
Mosgiel ○ NZ 182 C 6
Mosher ○ CDN (ONT) 236-237 D 4
Moshesh's Ford ○ ZA 220-221 H 5
Moshi ☆ EAT 212-213 F 5
Moshi, River ~ WAN 204-205 F 4
Moshi Rest Camp ○ Z 218-219 D 2
Mosi ○ WAN 204-205 E 4
Mosigo ○ PNG 184 I b 2
Mosi-Oa-Tunya National Park ⊥• Z 218-219 C 3
Mosite ○ ZRE 210-211 J 3
Mosjøen ○ N 86-87 F 4
Moskalenki ☆ RUS 124-125 G 1
Moskal'vo ○ RUS 122-123 K 2
Moskenesøya ⌒ N 86-87 F 3
Moskosel ○ S 86-87 J 4
Moškovo ☆ RUS 114-115 R 7
Moskovskij ○ TJ 136-137 L 6
Moskva ★••• RUS (MOS) 94-95 P 4
Moskva ~ RUS 94-95 O 4
Mosley Creek ~ CDN 230-231 D 2
Moso, Île = Verao ⌒ VAN 184 II b 3
Mošok ○ RUS 94-95 R 4
Mosomane ○ RB 220-221 H 2
Mosonmagyaróvár ○ H 92-93 O 5
Mosopa ○ RB 220-221 G 2
Mosque ○• RI 164-165 G 6
Mosque (Gantarang) • RI 168 E 6
Mosqueiro ○ BR (P) 62-63 K 6
Mosqueiro ○ BR (SER) 68-69 K 7
Mosquera ○ CO 60-61 B 6
Mosquero ○ USA (NM) 256-257 M 3
Mosquitia ⊥ HN 54-55 C 7
Mosquito, Río ~ PY 76-77 H 2
Mosquito Bay ≈ 36-37 K 4
Mosquito Creek Reservoir ⊖ USA (OH) 280-281 F 2
Mosquito Fork River ~ USA 20-21 T 5
Mosquito Lagoon ≈ 286-287 J 3
Mosquito Lake ⊖ CDN 30-31 S 4
Mosquitos, Costa de ⌄ NIC 52-53 C 5
Mosquitos, Golfo de los ≈ 52-53 D 7
Moss ☆ N 86-87 E 7
Mossaka ○ RCB 210-211 F 4
Mossbank ○ CDN (SAS) 232-233 N 6
Mossburn ○ NZ 182 B 6
Mosselbaai = Mossel Bay ○ ZA 220-221 F 7
Mossel Bay = Mosselbaai ○ ZA 220-221 F 7
Mossendjo ○ RCB 210-211 D 5
Mosses Hill ○ USA (TX) 268-269 F 6
Mossgiel ○ AUS 180-181 H 2
Mossleigh ○ CDN (ALB) 232-233 E 5
Mossman ○ AUS 174-175 H 5
Mossoró ○ BR 68-69 K 4
Mossoró, Rio ~ BR 68-69 K 4
Moss Point ○ USA (MS) 268-269 M 6
Moss Town ○ BS 54-55 H 2
Mossuril ○ MOC 218-219 L 2
Moss Vale ○ AUS 180-181 L 3
Mossyrock ○ USA (WA) 244-245 C 4
Most ○ CZ 92-93 M 3
Mostaganem ☆ DZ 190-191 C 3
Mostar ○• BIH 100-101 F 3
Mostardas ○ BR 74-75 E 8
Mosteiro de Batalha ••• P 98-99 C 5
Moșteni, Trivalea- ○ RO 102-103 D 5
Møstling Tvillingøen, Kap ▲ GRØ 28-29 U 5
Móstoles ○ E 98-99 F 4
Mostovskoj ○ RUS 126-127 D 5
Mosul = al-Mausil ☆ IRQ 128-129 K 4
Møsvatnet ⊖ N 86-87 D 7
Mot'a ○ ETH 208-209 C 3
Mota ⌒ VAN 184 II a 1
Motaba ~ RCB 210-211 F 2
Motagua, Río ~ GCA 52-53 K 4
Motaha ○ RI 164-165 H 6
Motala ☆• S 86-87 G 7
Mota Lava ⌒ VAN 184 II a 1
Motengpas ▲ LS 220-221 J 4
Motherwell ○ GB 90-91 F 4
Moti, Pulau ⌒ RI 164-165 K 3
Motigu ○ GH 202-203 J 5
Motihari ○ IND 142-143 D 2
Motilla del Palancar ○ E 98-99 G 5
Motiti Island ⌒ NZ 182 F 2
Motley ○ USA (MN) 270-271 D 4
Motloutse ~ RB 218-219 E 6
Motloutse Ruins ∴• RB 218-219 E 6
Motobu ○ J 152-153 B 11
Motorčuna ~ RUS 110-111 N 5
Motor Speedway • USA (IN) 274-275 M 5
Motozintla de Mendoza ○ MEX 52-53 H 4
Motru ○ RO 102-103 C 4
Mott ○ USA (ND) 258-259 E 4
Motueka ○ NZ 182 D 4
Motul ○ MEX 52-53 K 1
Motupe ○ PE 64-65 C 5
Motupena Point ▲ PNG 184 I b 2
Moturiki ⌒ FJI 184 III b 2
Motygino ☆ RUS 116-117 G 6
Motyklej ○ RUS 120-121 N 4
Mouali Gbangba ○ RCB 210-211 F 2
Mouat, Cape ▲ CDN 24-25 h 2
Moubolo, Mont ▲ RN 198-199 E 3
Moubotsi ○ RCB 210-211 D 6
Moucha, Île ⌒ DJI 208-209 F 3
Mouchalagane, Rivière ~ CDN 38-39 K 2
Mouchchene, Ibel ▲ MA 188-189 H 4
Mouchoir Passage ≈ 54-55 K 4
Moudjéria ○ RIM 196-197 D 6
Moúdros ○ GR 100-101 K 5
Mouenda ○ G 210-211 C 5
Mougalaba, Reserve de la ⊥ G 210-211 C 5
Mougamou ○ G 210-211 D 4
Mouila ☆ G 210-211 C 4
Moujia ○ RN 198-199 B 5
Mouka ○ RCA 206-207 E 5
Moukoumbi ○ G 210-211 D 4
Moul ○ RN 198-199 F 5
Moula ~ TCH 206-207 D 4
Moulamein ○ AUS 180-181 H 3
Moulares ○ TN 190-191 G 3
Moulay Bouâzza ○ MA 188-189 H 4
Moulay-Bousselham ○ MA 188-189 H 3
Moulay-Idriss ○•• MA 188-189 J 3
Mould Bay ○ CDN 24-25 M 2
Moulèngui Binza ○ G 210-211 C 5
Moulhoule ○ DJI 208-209 F 2
Moulins ☆• F 90-91 J 8
Mouli Pouli ○ G 210-211 D 4
Moulmein = Maulamyaing ○ MYA 158-159 D 2
Moulmeingyun ○ MYA 158-159 C 2
Mouloud ○ DJI 208-209 F 3
Moulouya, Oued ~ MA 188-189 K 3
Moulouya, Oued ~ MA 188-189 J 4
Moulton ○ USA (AL) 284-285 C 2
Moulton ○ USA (IA) 274-275 F 4
Moulton ○ UGA (TX) 266-267 K 4
Moultrie ○ USA (GA) 284-285 G 5
Moultrie, Lake ⊖ USA (SC) 284-285 K 3
Moulvi Bazar ○ BD 142-143 G 3
Moulvoudaye ○ CAM 206-207 B 3
Mounanko ○ CAM 210-211 B 2
Mound City ○ USA (IL) 276-277 F 3
Mound City ○ USA (KS) 262-263 M 6
Mound City ○ USA (MO) 274-275 C 4
Mound City ○ USA (SD) 260-261 F 1
Mound City Group National Monument ∴ USA (OH) 280-281 D 4
Moundhill Point ▲ USA 22-23 K 6
Moundou ☆ TCH 206-207 C 4
Moundridge ○ USA (KS) 262-263 J 6
Mounds ○ USA (IL) 276-277 F 3
Mound State Monument • USA (AL) 284-285 C 4
Moundsville ○ USA (WV) 280-281 F 4
Moundville ○ USA (AL) 284-285 C 4
Moundville ○ USA (AL) 284-285 C 3
Moungoun-dou-sud ○ RCB 210-211 D 5
Moŭng Roessei ○ K 158-159 G 4
Mounguel ○ CAM 204-205 K 5
Mount Adams Wilderness ⊥ USA (WA) 244-245 D 4
Mountain ○ USA (WI) 270-271 K 5
Mountainair ○ USA (NM) 256-257 J 4
Mountain Brook ○ USA (AL) 284-285 D 3
Mountainburg ○ USA (AR) 276-277 A 5
Mountain City ○ USA (NV) 246-247 K 2
Mountain City ○ USA (TN) 282-283 F 4
Mountain Creek ~ USA 284-285 E 4
Mountain Gate ○ USA (CA) 246-247 C 3
Mountain Grove ○ USA (MO) 276-277 C 3
Mountain Home ○ USA (AR) 276-277 C 4
Mountain Home ○ USA (ID) 252-253 C 3
Mountain Home ○ USA (TX) 266-267 H 3
Mountain Lake ○ CDN 30-31 U 5
Mountain Lake ○ USA (MN) 270-271 D 7
Mountain Lodge ○ EAK 212-213 F 4
Mountain Park ○ CDN (ALB) 228-229 R 4
Mountain Pass ▲ USA (CA) 248-249 J 4
Mountain Pine ○ USA (AR) 276-277 B 6
Mountain Point ○ USA 32-33 E 4

364 Montargis — Mountain Point

Mountain River ~ CDN 30-31 E 3
Mountain Road o CDN (MAN) 234-235 D 4
Mountainside o CDN (MAN) 234-235 C 5
Mountain Springs o USA (NV) 248-249 J 3
Mountain Valley o AUS 174-175 B 4
Mountain View o CDN (ALB) 232-233 E 6
Mountain View o USA (AR) 276-277 C 5
Mountain View o USA (AZ) 256-257 E 6
Mountain View o USA (HI) 288 K 5
Mountain View o USA (MO) 276-277 D 4
Mountain View o USA (WV) 280-281 E 6
Mountain View o USA (WY) 252-253 H 5
Mountain Village o USA 20-21 J 5
Mountain Zebra National Park ⊥ ZA 220-221 G 6
Mount Airy o USA (MD) 280-281 J 4
Mount Airy o USA (NC) 282-283 G 4
Mount Airy o USA (VA) 280-281 G 7
Mount Airy Mesa ▲ USA (NV) 246-247 H 4
Mount Allan o AUS 172-173 L 7
Mount Alto o USA (WV) 280-281 E 5
Mount Amhurst o AUS 172-173 H 5
Mount Aspiring National Park ⊥ NZ 182 B 6
Mount Assiniboine Provincial Park ⊥ CDN (ALB) 232-233 C 4
Mount Augustus o AUS 176-177 D 2
Mount Augustus National Park ⊥ AUS 176-177 D 2
Mount Ayliff o ZA 220-221 J 5
Mount Ayr o USA (IA) 274-275 D 4
Mount Barker o AUS (SA) 180-181 E 3
Mount Barker o AUS (WA) 176-177 D 7
Mount Barnett o AUS 172-173 H 4
Mountbatten Indian Reserve ✗ CDN (ONT) 236-237 F 5
Mount Bayou o USA (MS) 268-269 K 3
Mount Beauty ▲ AUS 180-181 J 4
Mount Belvieu o USA (TX) 268-269 F 7
Mount Brockman o AUS 172-173 C 7
Mount Buffalo National Park ⊥ AUS 180-181 J 4
Mount Bullion o USA (CA) 248-249 D 2
Mount Carleton Provincial Park ⊥ CDN (NB) 240-241 J 3
Mount Carmel o USA (IL) 274-275 L 6
Mount Carmel o USA (ND) 258-259 J 3
Mount Carmel Junction o USA (UT) 254-255 C 6
Mount Carroll o USA (IL) 274-275 J 2
Mount Celia o AUS 176-177 G 4
Mount Charleston o USA (NV) 248-249 J 3
Mount Clemens o USA (MI) 272-273 G 5
Mount Clere o AUS 176-177 D 2
Mount Cook o NZ 182 C 5
Mount Cook National Park ⊥ ·· NZ 182 C 5
Mount Coolon o AUS 178-179 J 1
Mount Croghan o USA (SC) 204-205 K 2
Mount Denison o AUS 172-173 L 7
Mount Desert Island ⌒ USA (ME) 278-279 N 4
Mount Divide o AUS 172-173 E 7
Mount Dora o USA (FL) 286-287 H 3
Mount Dora o USA (NM) 256-257 M 2
Mount Doreen o AUS 172-173 K 7
Mount Douglas o AUS 178-179 J 1
Mount Eba o AUS 178-179 C 6
Mount Ebenezer o AUS 176-177 M 2
Mount Eccles National Park ⊥ AUS 180-181 F 5
Mount Edgar o AUS 172-173 E 6
Mount Edziza Provincial Park ⊥ CDN 32-33 E 3
Mount Elizabeth o AUS 172-173 H 4
Mount Enterprise o USA (TX) 268-269 F 5
Mount Everest ▲ NEP 144-145 F 7
Mount Field National Park ⊥ AUS 180-181 J 7
Mount Fletcher o ZA 220-221 J 5
Mount Florance o AUS 172-173 C 6
Mount Forest o CDN (ONT) 238-239 E 5
Mount Frere o ZA 220-221 J 5
Mount Gambier o AUS 180-181 F 4
Mount Garnet o AUS 174-175 H 5
Mount Gilead o USA (NC) 282-283 H 5
Mount Gilead o USA (OH) 280-281 D 3
Mount Hagen ☆ ·· PNG 183 C 3
Mount Harris Tine Mine Area o AUS 172-173 K 2
Mount Holly o USA (NJ) 280-281 M 3
Mount Holly Springs o USA (PA) 280-281 J 3
Mount Hood o USA (OR) 244-245 D 5
Mount Hope o AUS (NSW) 180-181 H 2
Mount Hope o AUS (SA) 180-181 C 3
Mount Horeb o USA (WI) 274-275 J 1
Mount House o AUS 172-173 G 4
Mount Hutt o NZ 182 C 5
Mount Ida o AUS 176-177 F 4
Mount Ida o USA (AR) 276-277 B 6
Mount Isa o ·· AUS 174-175 E 7
Mount Jackson o AUS 176-177 E 5
Mount Kaichui ▲ SOL 184 I e 3
Mount Kalourat ▲ SOL 184 I e 3
Mount Keith o AUS 176-177 F 3
Mount Lakes Wilderness Area ⊥ USA (OR) 244-245 C 8
Mount Larcom o AUS 178-179 L 2
Mount Lofty Range ▲ AUS 180-181 E 3
Mount Madden Wheat Bin o AUS 176-177 E 6
Mount Magnet o AUS 176-177 D 4
Mount Maitabi ▲ SOL 184 I c 2
Mount Mary o AUS 180-181 E 3
Mount Meigs o USA (AL) 284-285 D 4
Mount Molloy o AUS 174-175 H 5
Mount Montgomery o USA (NV) 248-249 F 2
Mount Morgan o AUS 178-179 L 2
Mount Morris o USA (MI) 272-273 F 4
Mount Morris o USA (WI) 270-271 J 6
Mount Mulgrave o AUS 174-175 G 5
Mount Mulligan o AUS 174-175 H 5
Mount Narryer o AUS 176-177 C 3
Mountnorris Bay ≈ 172-173 L 1
Mount Olive o USA (NC) 282-283 J 5
Mount Padbury o AUS 176-177 E 2
Mount Pearl o CDN (NFL) 242-243 Q 5
Mount Perry o AUS 178-179 L 3
Mount Pleasant o USA (IA) 274-275 G 4
Mount Pleasant o USA (MI) 272-273 E 4
Mount Pleasant o USA (OH) 280-281 D 4
Mount Pleasant o USA (PA) 280-281 G 3
Mount Pleasant o USA (SC) 284-285 L 4
Mount Pleasant o USA (TN) 276-277 H 5
Mount Pleasant o USA (TX) 264-265 K 5
Mount Pleasant o USA (UT) 254-255 D 4
Mount Pocono o USA (PA) 280-281 L 2
Mount Pulaski o USA (IL) 274-275 J 5
Mount Pulog National Park ⊥ RP 160-161 D 4
Mount Rainier National Park ⊥ USA (WA) 244-245 D 4
Mount Remarkable National Park ⊥ AUS 180-181 D 2
Mount Revelstoke National Park ⊥ CDN (BC) 230-231 L 2
Mount Richmond National Park ⊥ AUS 180-181 F 5
Mount Robson o CDN (BC) 228-229 P 3
Mount Robson Provincial Park ⊥ CDN (BC) 228-229 Q 4
Mount Rogers National Recreation Area ⊥ USA (VA) 280-281 E 7
Mount Rupert o ZA 220-221 G 4
Mount Rushmore National Memorial ∴ USA (SD) 260-261 C 3
Mount Sage National Park ⊥ GB 286-287 R 2
Mount Saint Helens National Volcanic Monument ∴ USA (WA) 244-245 D 4
Mount-Sandiman o AUS 176-177 C 2
Mount Sanford o AUS 172-173 K 4
Mount Sasari ▲ SOL 184 I d 3
Mount Seymour Provincial Park ⊥ CDN (BC) 230-231 G 4
Mount Skinner o AUS 178-179 C 2
Mount Somers o NZ 182 C 5
Mount Spokane State Park ⊥ USA (WA) 244-245 H 3
Mount Sterling o USA (IL) 274-275 H 5
Mount Sterling o USA (KY) 276-277 M 2
Mount Sterling o USA (OH) 280-281 C 4
Mount Sterling o USA (WI) 274-275 H 1
Mount Storm Lake o USA (WV) 280-281 G 4
Mount Strzelecki National Park ⊥ AUS 180-181 K 6
Mount Surprise o AUS 174-175 H 6
Mount Swan o AUS 178-179 C 2
Mount Trumbull o USA (AZ) 256-257 B 2
Mount Union o USA (PA) 280-281 J 3
Mount Vernon o AUS 176-177 E 2
Mount Vernon o USA (AL) 284-285 B 5
Mount Vernon o USA (GA) 284-285 H 4
Mount Vernon o USA (IA) 274-275 G 3
Mount Vernon o USA (IL) 274-275 K 6
Mount Vernon o USA (IN) 274-275 L 7
Mount Vernon o USA (KY) 276-277 L 3
Mount Vernon o USA (MO) 276-277 B 3
Mount Vernon o USA (OH) 280-281 D 3
Mount Vernon o USA (OR) 244-245 F 6
Mount Vernon o USA (SD) 260-261 H 3
Mount Vernon o USA (TX) 264-265 J 5
Mount Vernon o USA (WA) 244-245 C 2
Mount Vetters o AUS 176-177 F 5
Mount Walker o AUS 176-177 E 6
Mount Washington o USA (KY) 276-277 K 2
Mount Wedge o AUS (NT) 172-173 L 7
Mount Wedge o AUS (SA) 180-181 C 2
Mount William National Park ⊥ AUS 180-181 K 6
Mount Windsor o AUS 178-179 F 2
Mount Zion o USA (IL) 274-275 K 5
Mount Zion o USA (MD) 280-281 K 5
Mouping o VRC 154-155 D 6
Moura o AUS 178-179 K 3
Moura o BR 62-63 D 6
Moura o ·· P 98-99 D 5
Moura, Cachoeira ~ BR 66-67 H 5
Mourão o P 98-99 D 5
Mouray o TCH 206-207 C 4
Mourdi, Dépression du ⊥ TCH 198-199 K 3
Mourdiah o RMM 202-203 G 2
Mouri Mountains ▲ WAN 204-205 J 4
Mourindi o G 210-211 C 5
Mouroubra o AUS 176-177 D 4
Mouroungoulay o TCH 206-207 C 4
Mouscron o B 92-93 G 3
Mousgougou o TCH 206-207 C 3
Mousðayah o RG 202-203 D 5
Moussa, Hassi < DZ 190-191 C 6
Moussadey o RN 204-205 E 2
Moussafoyo o TCH 206-207 D 4
Moussaya o RG 202-203 E 4
Moussoro o TCH 198-199 H 6
Moustiers-Sainte-Marie o F 90-91 L 10
Moutamba o RCB 210-211 D 5
Mouth of Wilson o USA (VA) 280-281 E 7
Moûtiers o F 90-91 L 9
Moutong o RI 164-165 G 3
Moutouroua o CAM 206-207 B 3
Mouydir, Monts du ▲ DZ 190-191 E 8
Mouyonndzi o RCB 210-211 D 5
Mouzarak o TCH 198-199 G 6
Movila Miresii o RO 102-103 E 5
Moville o USA (IA) 274-275 B 2
Mowanjum ✗ AUS 172-173 F 4
Mowasi o GUY 62-63 E 3
Moweaqua o USA (IL) 274-275 J 5
Mowewe o RI 164-165 G 5
Moxey Town o BS 54-55 G 2
Moxico □ ANG 216-217 E 6
Moxotó, Rio ~ BR 68-69 K 6
Moyagee Gemstone Deposit • AUS 176-177 D 3
Moyahua o MEX 50-51 H 7
Moyale o EAK 212-213 G 2
Moyalé o ETH 208-209 D 7
Moyamba o WAL 202-203 D 5
Moyen Atlas ▲ MA 188-189 H 4
Moyen-Chari □ TCH 206-207 C 4
Moyeni o LS 220-221 H 5
Moyenne Sido o RCA 206-207 D 4
Moyie o CDN (BC) 230-231 O 4
Moyie River ~ CDN 230-231 N 4
Moyie Springs o USA (ID) 250-251 C 3
Moyne, Lac le o CDN 36-37 P 6
Moyo o EAU 212-213 C 2
Moyo ~ RI 168 C 7
Moyo, Pulau ⌒ RI 168 C 7
Moyobamba ☆ PE 64-65 D 5
Moyock o USA (NC) 282-283 L 4
Moyogalpa o NIC 52-53 B 6
Moyo Pulau Reserve ⊥ • RI 168 C 7
Moyowosi ~ EAT 212-213 C 5
Moyssalen ▲ N 86-87 G 2
Moyto o TCH 198-199 H 6
Moyu o VRC 144-145 B 2
Mozaffarābād-e Masileh o IR 134-135 D 1
Možaisk ☆ ·· RUS 94-95 P 4
Mozambique = Moçambique ■ MOC 218-219 G 6
Mozambique Basin ≃ 9 G 8
Mozambique Channel ≈ 218-219 K 6
Mozambique Plateau ≃ 9 G 9
Mozdok o RUS 126-127 F 6
Mozdūrān o IR 136-137 G 6
Možga ☆ RUS 96-97 H 5
Mozyr' = Mazyr o BY 94-95 L 5
Mpoom o GH 202-203 K 6
Mpaka Station o SD 220-221 K 3
Mpala o ZRE 214-215 E 4
Mpama ~ RCB 210-211 E 5
Mpana o GH 202-203 K 5
Mpanda o EAT 214-215 F 4
Mpandamatenga o RB 218-219 C 4
Mpanga o EAT 214-215 K 4
Mpase o ZRE 210-211 H 4
Mpataba o GH 202-203 J 7
Mpatora o EAT 214-215 K 5
Mpem ~ CAM 204-205 J 6
Mpepayi o EAT 214-215 H 6
Mpessuba o RMM 202-203 H 3
Mphaki o LS 220-221 J 5
Mphoengs o ZW 218-219 D 5
Mpiéla o RMM 202-203 G 3
Mpigi o EAU 212-213 D 3
Mpika o Z 214-215 F 6
Mpitimbi o EAT 214-215 H 6
Mpo o ZRE 210-211 G 6
Mpoko ~ RCA 206-207 D 6
Mpoko o ZRE 210-211 G 5
Mponde ~ EAT 212-213 E 6
Mponela o MW 218-219 G 1
Mpongwe o Z 218-219 E 1
Mporaloko o G 210-211 B 4
Mporokoso o Z 214-215 F 5
Mpoukou ~ RCB 210-211 D 5
Mpoumé, Chute ~ • CAM 210-211 C 2
Mpoup ~ CAM 210-211 D 2
Mpouya o RCB 210-211 F 5
Mpraeso o GH 202-203 K 6
Mpui o EAT 214-215 F 5
Mpulungu o Z 214-215 F 5
Mpumalanga o ZA 220-221 K 4
Mpume o ZRE 210-211 G 6
M'Pupa, Rápidos ~ ANG 216-217 F 8
Mpwapwa o EAT 214-215 J 4
Mrakovo ☆ RUS 96-97 K 7
Mrara o DZ 190-191 E 4
Mrassu ~ RUS 124-125 Q 2
Mrčajevci o YU 100-101 H 3
Mrezzig o RMM 196-197 K 5
M'saken o TN 190-191 H 3
Msak Millet ▲ LAR 192-193 D 5
Msandile ~ Z 218-219 G 1
Msangasi ~ EAT 212-213 G 6
Msanzara ~ Z 218-219 F 1
Msata o EAT 214-215 K 4
Msembe o EAT 214-215 H 4
M'Sila ☆ DZ 190-191 E 3
Msima ~ EAT 214-215 F 4
Msinskaja o RUS 94-95 L 2
Msoro o Z 218-219 F 1
Msta ~ RUS 94-95 O 3
Msuna o ZW 218-219 D 4
Mszczonów o PL 92-93 Q 3
Mtakuja o EAT 214-215 F 4
Mtama o EAT 214-215 K 6
Mtambo ~ EAT 214-215 F 4
Mtandikeni o EAT 212-213 G 6
Mtangano Island ⌒ EAT 212-213 D 5
Mtera Dam < EAT 214-215 H 4
Mtina o EAT 214-215 J 6
Mtito Andei o EAK 212-213 G 5
Mto Wa Mbu o EAT 212-213 E 5
Mtubatuba o ZA 220-221 L 4
Mtwara □ EAT 214-215 K 6
Mtwara ☆ EAT (MTW) 214-215 L 6
Muadiala o ZRE 216-217 F 3
Muaguide o MOC 214-215 L 7
Mualádzi o MOC 218-219 G 2
Mualama o MOC 218-219 K 3
Muaná o BR 62-63 K 6
Muanda o ZRE 210-211 D 6
Muangai o ANG 216-217 E 6
Muang Gnômmarat o LAO 158-159 H 2
Muang Hiam o LAO 156-157 C 6
Muang Hôngsa o LAO 156-157 B 7
Muang Houn o LAO 156-157 B 6
Muang Huang o LAO 156-157 C 7
Muang Khammouan o LAO 158-159 H 2
Muang Không o LAO 158-159 H 3
Muang Khôngxédôn o LAO 158-159 H 3
Muang Khoua o LAO 156-157 C 6
Muang May o LAO 158-159 J 3
Muang Namo o LAO 156-157 B 6
Muang Nan o LAO 156-157 B 7
Muang Ou Thai o LAO 156-157 B 5
Muang Pa o LAO 156-157 B 7
Muang Pakbèng o LAO 156-157 B 7
Muang Pak-Cay o LAO 156-157 B 7
Muang Pakxan o LAO 156-157 C 7
Muang Pakxong o LAO 158-159 J 3
Muang Phalan o LAO 158-159 H 2
Muang Phin o LAO 158-159 J 2
Muang Phôn -Hông o LAO 156-157 C 7
Muang Samsip o THA 158-159 H 3
Muang Sing o LAO 156-157 B 6
Muang Souy o LAO 156-157 C 7
Muang Xaignabouri o LAO 156-157 B 7
Muang Xay o LAO 156-157 B 6
Muang Xépôn o LAO 158-159 J 2
Muanza o MOC 218-219 H 4
Muanzanza o ZRE 216-217 F 3
Muar o • MAL 162-163 E 3
Muara o BRU 164-165 D 1
Muara o RI 162-163 D 5
Muaraaman o RI 162-163 E 6
Muaraatap o RI 164-165 E 3
Muarabeliti o RI 162-163 E 6
Muarabengkal o RI 164-165 E 3
Muarabinuangeun o RI 168 A 3
Muarabulian o RI 162-163 E 5
Muarabungo o RI 162-163 E 5
Muaradua o RI 162-163 E 7
Muaraenim o RI 162-163 F 6
Muarahaiung o RI 164-165 D 5
Muarajawa o RI 164-165 E 4
Muara Koman o RI 164-165 D 4
Muaranayan o RI 164-165 E 4
Muarapayang o RI 164-165 D 4
Muarasipit o RI 162-163 E 6
Muarasiberut o RI 162-163 C 5
Muarasimatalu o RI 162-163 C 5
Muarasoma o RI 162-163 C 4
Muaratalang o RI 162-163 E 6
Muaratebo o RI 162-163 E 5
Muaratembesi o RI 162-163 E 5
Muarateweh o RI 164-165 D 4
Muara Tuang o MAL 162-163 J 4
Muarawahau o RI 164-165 E 3
Muari, Pulau ⌒ RI 164-165 K 4
Muâri, Râs ▲ PK 134-135 M 6
Muaro Takus Ruins • RI 162-163 D 4
Muatua o MOC 218-219 K 2
Mubambe o ZRE 214-215 D 6
Mubārak, Ğabal ▲ JOR 130-131 D 2
Mubarek o UZ 136-137 J 5
Mubarraz o KSA 130-131 L 5
Mubayira o ZW 218-219 F 4
Mubende o EAU 212-213 C 3
Mubi o WAN 204-205 K 3
Mubo o VRC 154-155 E 3
Mubrani o RI 166-167 G 2
Mucajaí o BR 62-63 D 4
Mucajaí, Reserva Biológica de ⊥ BR 60-61 K 6
Mucajaí, Rio ~ BR 62-63 D 4
Mucajaí, Serra ▲ BR 60-61 K 6
Mucalic, Rivière ~ CDN 36-37 Q 5
Mucanha ~ MOC 218-219 F 2
Mucari o ANG 216-217 D 4
Muccan o AUS 172-173 E 6
Muchalat Inlet ≈ 230-231 C 4
Muchea o AUS 176-177 C 5
Muchena o MOC 218-219 G 2
Muchinga Escarpment ⊥ Z 218-219 E 2
Muchinga Mountains ▲ Z 214-215 F 7
Muchinka o Z 214-215 F 7
Muchuan o VRC 156-157 C 2
Muchuchu Ruins ∴ • ZW 218-219 F 4
Mucianyu • VRC 154-155 K 1
Muckadilla o AUS 178-179 K 4
Muckaty o AUS 174-175 B 6
Mučnoj, poluostrov ~ RUS 108-109 E 6
Muco, Río ~ CO 60-61 F 5
Mucojo o MOC 214-215 L 7
Muconda o ANG 216-217 F 5
Mucondo o ANG 216-217 C 4
Mucope o ANG 216-217 C 8
Mucubela o MOC 218-219 J 3
Mucucuaú, Rio ~ BR 62-63 D 5
Mucuim, Rio ~ BR 66-67 E 6
Mucujê o BR 72-73 K 2
Mucum o BR 74-75 E 7
Mucumbura o MOC 218-219 F 3
Mucumbura o ZW 218-219 F 3
Mucupia o MOC 218-219 J 4
Mucur ☆ TR 128-129 F 3
Múcura o YV 60-61 J 3
Mucura, Cachoeira da ~ BR 68-69 B 5
Mucuri o BR 72-73 L 5
Mucuri, Rio ~ BR 72-73 L 5
Mucurici o BR 72-73 K 5
Mucuripe, Ponta de ▲ BR 68-69 J 3
Mucuru, Cachoeira ~ BR 62-63 H 5
Mucusso o ANG 216-217 F 8
Mucusso, Acampamento de Caça do o ANG 216-217 F 8
Mucusso, Coutada Pública do ⊥ ANG 216-217 F 8
Mucussueje o ANG 216-217 F 5
Mūd o IR 134-135 H 2
Muḍailif, al- o KSA 132-133 B 4
Muḍairib, al- o • OM 132-133 L 2
Mudaisis o OM 132-133 J 2
Mudanjiang o VRC 150-151 G 5
Mudan Jiang ~ VRC 150-151 G 5
Mudanya ☆ TR 128-129 C 2
Mudarraq o KSA 130-131 H 4
Mudawwa o JOR 130-131 E 3
Muḍayy o OM 132-133 H 5
Mūdbidri o • IND 140-141 F 4
Mud Butte o USA (SD) 260-261 D 2
Mud Creek ~ USA 264-265 G 4
Muddebihāl o IND 140-141 G 2
Mudderbugten ≈ 28-29 P 2
Muddus nationalpark ⊥ • S 86-87 K 3
Muddy Boggy Creek ~ USA 264-265 J 4
Muddy Creek ~ USA 252-253 L 5
Muddy Creek ~ USA 254-255 D 5
Muddy Gap o USA (WY) 252-253 L 4
Muddy Gap ▲ USA (WY) 252-253 L 4
Muddy Pass ▲ USA (CO) 254-255 J 3
Mudgal o IND 140-141 G 2
Mudgee o AUS 180-181 K 2
Mudgeeraba o AUS 178-179 M 6
Mudhol o IND 140-141 F 2
Mudigere o IND 140-141 F 4
Mudigubba o IND 140-141 G 3
Mudimbi o ZRE 210-211 K 5
Mud Island ⌒ CDN (NS) 240-241 J 7
Mudjatik River ~ CDN 34-35 C 2
Mud Lake o USA (ID) 252-253 F 3
Mud Lake o USA (MN) 270-271 C 2
Mudon o MYA 158-159 D 2
Mud River o CDN (ONT) 234-235 P 4
Mud River ~ USA 276-277 J 3
Mudug □ SP 208-209 J 5
Mudujjaha ~ RUS 108-109 S 7
Mudukulattūr o IND 140-141 H 6
Muecate o MOC 218-219 K 2
Mueda o MOC 214-215 K 6
Muelle de los Bueyes o NIC 52-53 B 5
Mueller Range ▲ AUS 172-173 H 5
Muembe o MOC 218-219 H 1
Muende o MOC 218-219 G 2
Muermos, Los o RCH 78-79 C 6
Muerto, Mar ≈ 52-53 G 3
Muerto, Río ~ RA 76-77 F 2
Muertos Trough ≃ 56 A 3
Muezerskij o RUS 88-89 M 5
Mufulira o Z 214-215 E 7
Mufu Shan ▲ VRC 156-157 H 2
Mufu Shan ▲ VRC 156-157 H 2
Muğahhar, Dār o Y 132-133 D 7
Muğaira o KSA 130-131 F 4
Muğal, Wādī ~ SUD 200-201 G 3
Mugang o VRC 156-157 D 5
Mugango o EAT 212-213 D 4
Muganskaja ravnina ⌣ AZ 128-129 N 3
Mugar o IR 134-135 E 2
Muger o ETH 208-209 D 4
Muger Falls ~ ETH 208-209 D 4
Muger Wenz ~ ETH 208-209 D 4
Muggar Kangri ▲ VRC 144-145 F 4
Muggon o AUS 176-177 C 3
Mughal Sarai o IND 142-143 C 3
Mughsail o OM 132-133 H 5
Muğib, Wādī ~ JOR 130-131 D 2
Mugila, Monts ▲ ZRE 214-215 E 4
Mugina o EAT 212-213 B 6
Mugla ☆ TR 128-129 C 4
Muğodžar, tau ▲ KZ 126-127 N 3
Muhabura ▲ EAU 212-213 B 4
Muhāgiria o SUD 206-207 G 3
Muḥaiwir o IRQ 128-129 J 6
Muhala o ZRE 212-213 B 6
Muḥammad, Ra's ▲ ET 194-195 G 4
Muḥammadiya o IRQ 128-129 K 6
Muhammad Qol o SUD 200-201 H 2
Muḥarraq, al- o BRN 134-135 D 5
Muḥāṭ o KSA 132-133 C 5
Muhazi, Lac o RWA 212-213 C 4
Muheit, Wādi ~ SUD 200-201 F 4
Muheza o EAT 212-213 G 6
Muhino o RUS 118-119 N 9
Mühldorf am Inn o D 92-93 M 4
Mühlhausen/ Thüringen o • D 92-93 L 3
Mühlig-Hofmann Mountains = Mühlig-Hofmann-fjella ▲ ARK 16 F 1
Muhorini o EAK 212-213 E 4
Muhor-Konduj o RUS 118-119 F 9
Muhoro o EAK 212-213 E 4
Muhoršibir' o RUS 116-117 N 10
Muhos o FIN 88-89 J 4
Muhu saar ⌒ EST 94-95 H 2
Muhutwe o EAT 212-213 C 4
Muhuwesi ~ EAT 214-215 J 6
Mui o ETH 208-209 B 5
Muico o MOC 218-219 K 1
Muidumbe o MOC 214-215 K 6
Muié o ANG 216-217 F 7
Muine o ANG 216-217 F 8
Muineachán = Monaghan ☆ IRL 90-91 D 4
Muira, Rio ~ MOC 200-201 F 3
Muir Glacier ⊂ USA 20-21 W 7
Muiron Islands ⌒ AUS 172-173 B 6
Muisma ~ RUS 116-117 E 3
Muisne o EC 64-65 B 1
Muite o MOC 218-219 K 2
Muitos Capões o BR 74-75 E 7
Muiuçu ou Puiuçu, Igarapé ~ BR 66-67 H 6
Muizenberg o ZA 220-221 D 7
Muja ~ RUS 118-119 G 7
Mujakan ~ RUS 118-119 F 7
Mujazzam, Sabkhat o LAR 190-191 G 5
Mujeres, Isla ⌒ ·· MEX 52-53 L 1
Mujnak ☆ UZ 136-137 F 3
Mujšin ~ RUS 118-119 G 9
Muju o ROK 150-151 F 9
Mujunkum ⊥ KZ 124-125 H 6
Mukačeve ☆ UA 102-103 C 3
Mukačevo = Mukačeve ☆ UA 102-103 C 3
Mukah o MAL 162-163 K 3
Muka Head ▲ MAL 162-163 D 2
Mukala o ZRE 210-211 F 6
Mukana o ZRE 214-215 D 5
Mukanga o ZRE 216-217 F 3
Mukaryljan ~ RUS 112-113 Q 5
Mukawa o PNG 183 E 5
Mukawa-gawa ~ J 152-153 K 3
Mukawwa', Ğazirat ⌒ SUD 200-201 H 2
Mukdahan o THA 158-159 H 2
Mukden = Shenyang ☆ VRC 150-151 D 7
Mukebo o ZRE 214-215 E 4
Mukeriān o IND 138-139 E 4
Muketei River ~ CDN 234-235 R 2
Muke T'uri o ETH 208-209 D 4
Mukilteo o USA (WA) 244-245 C 3
Mukinbudin o AUS 176-177 E 5
Mukomuko o RI 162-163 D 6
Mukongo o EAU 212-213 D 3
Mu Ko Phi Phi • THA 158-159 E 7
Mukry o TM 136-137 J 6
Muksu ~ TJ 136-137 M 5
Muksuniha ~ RUS 108-109 V 6
Muksunuoha-Tas, gora ▲ RUS 110-111 X 4
Muktsar o IND 138-139 E 4
Mukuku o Z 214-215 E 7
Mukulu, Kayembe- o ZRE 214-215 B 5
Mukulu, Mutombo- o ZRE 214-215 C 5
Mukulushi ~ ZRE 214-215 C 6
Mukunsa o Z 214-215 E 5
Mukupa Kaoma o Z 214-215 F 5
Mukurob • NAM 220-221 D 2
Mūl o IND 138-139 G 9
Mula o E 98-99 G 5
Mula ~ PK 134-135 M 4
Mula, la ▲ I 100-101 E 5
Mulaiih, al- o KSA 130-131 F 5
Mulaku Atoll ⌒ MV 140-141 B 6
Mülali cukurligi ⊥ UZ 136-137 J 4
Mulam ~ RUS 120-121 D 5
Mulamba Gungu, Chute ~ ZRE 214-215 B 5
Mulan o VRC 150-151 G 5
Mulanay o RP 160-161 E 6
Mulanje o MW 218-219 H 2
Mulanje Mountains ▲ MW 218-219 H 2
Mulanweichang • VRC 148-149 N 6
Mulatos o CO 60-61 C 3
Mulawa o PK 138-139 D 3
Mulbāgal o IND 140-141 H 4
Mulberry o USA (AR) 276-277 A 5
Mulberry o USA (FL) 286-287 H 4
Mulberry Creek ~ USA 264-265 C 4
Mulberry Creek ~ USA 284-285 C 4
Mulberry Fork ~ USA 284-285 D 3
Mulberry River ~ USA 276-277 B 5
Mulchatna River ~ USA 20-21 N 6
Mulchen o RCH 78-79 C 4
Mulchole o IND 140-141 G 5
Mulde ~ D 92-93 M 3
Muldrow o USA (OK) 264-265 K 3
Muleba o EAT 212-213 C 4
Mule Creek Junction o USA (WY) 252-253 O 3
Mulegé o • MEX 50-51 D 4
Mulembe o ZRE 212-213 B 5
Muleshoe o USA (TX) 264-265 B 4
Muleta ▲ ETH 208-209 E 4
Muleta ~ RP 160-161 F 9
Mulevala o MOC 218-219 J 3
Mulga Creek ~ AUS 178-179 J 6
Mulgildie o AUS 178-179 L 3
Mulgravo o CDN (NS) 240-241 O 6
Mulgrave Hills ▲ USA 20-21 J 3
Mulgul o AUS 176-177 E 2
Mulhouse o F 90-91 L 8
Mulhurst Bay o CDN (ALB) 232-233 E 2
Muli ≈ 166-167 K 5
Mulia o RI 166-167 J 3
Muli Channel ≈ 166-167 K 5
Mulilansolo o Z 214-215 G 6
Muling o VRC 150-151 H 5
Mulic'ma ~ RUS 118-119 D 6
Mulki o IND 140-141 F 4
Mull ⌒ GB 90-91 D 3
Mullaittivu o CL 140-141 J 6
Mullaley o AUS 178-179 K 6
Mullan o USA (MT) 250-251 D 4
Mullen o USA (NE) 262-263 E 2
Mullens o USA (WV) 280-281 E 6
Müller, Pegunungan ▲ RI 162-163 K 4
Muller Range ▲ PNG 183 B 3
Mullet Key ⌒ USA (FL) 286-287 G 4
Mullett Lake o USA (MI) 272-273 E 2
Mullewa o AUS 176-177 C 4
Mulligan River ~ AUS 178-179 E 3
Mullingar o CDN (SAS) 232-233 L 2
Mullingar = An Muileann -gCearr o IRL 90-91 D 5
Mullins o USA (SC) 284-285 L 2
Mul'muga ~ RUS 118-119 O 8
Mulobezi o Z 218-219 C 3
Mulondo o ANG 216-217 C 7
Mulonga Plain ⊥ Z 218-219 B 3
Mulongo o ZRE 214-215 D 4
Mulongoie ~ ZRE 210-211 L 6
Multai o IND 138-139 G 9
Multan o ·· PK 138-139 C 4
Mulu o ETH 208-209 E 4
Mulu, Gunung ▲ MAL 164-165 D 1
Mulungu ~ ZRE 214-215 B 5
Mulungushi o Z 218-219 E 1
Mulungushi Dam < Z 218-219 E 2
Mūlūr o IND 140-141 F 4
Mulurulu Lake o AUS 180-181 G 2
Mulvihill o CDN (MAN) 234-235 E 4
Mulym'ja ~ RUS 114-115 H 4
Mulyungarie o AUS 178-179 F 6
Muma o ZRE 210-211 J 2
Mumallah o SUD 206-207 G 3
Mumbai = Bombay ☆ IND 138-139 D 10
Mumballup o AUS 176-177 D 6
Mumbeji o Z 218-219 B 1
Mumbleberry Lake o AUS 178-179 E 3
Mumbondo o ANG 216-217 C 5
Mumbué o ANG 216-217 D 6
Mumbwa o Z 218-219 D 2
Mume, Swana- o ZRE 214-215 D 6
Mumena o ZRE 214-215 D 6
Mumeng o PNG 183 D 4
Mumias o EAK 212-213 E 3
Mumoma o ZRE 214-215 B 4
Mumulusan o RI 164-165 H 4
Mun o RI 166-167 G 4
Muna o MEX 52-53 K 1
Muna ~ RUS 110-111 L 6
Muna ~ RUS 110-111 N 5
Muna, Pulau ⌒ RI 164-165 H 6
Muna, Selat ≈ 164-165 H 6
Münajšy o KZ 126-127 K 6
Munakan ~ RUS 110-111 M 6
Munarra o AUS 176-177 E 3
Munaya ~ CAM 204-205 H 6
Muncakabau o RI 162-163 F 7
Munchique, Parque Nacional ⊥ CO 60-61 C 6
Muncho Lake o CDN 30-31 G 6
Muncho Lake Provincial Park ⊥ CDN 30-31 G 6
Muncie o USA (IN) 274-275 N 4
Muncoonie Lake West o AUS 178-179 E 3
Munda o PK 138-139 C 4
Munda o SOL 184 I c 3
Mundabullangana o AUS 172-173 D 6
Mundare o CDN (ALB) 232-233 F 2
Mundaring o AUS 176-177 D 5
Munday o USA (TX) 264-265 E 5
Mundemba o CAM 204-205 H 6
Mundgod o IND 140-141 F 3
Mundico Coelho o BR 66-67 J 6
Mundijong o AUS 176-177 C 6
Mundiwindi o AUS 176-177 F 1
Mundo Novo o BR (BAH) 68-69 H 7
Mundo Novo o BR (GSU) 76-77 K 2
Mundo Nuevo o YV 60-61 J 3
Mundra o IND 138-139 B 8
Mundrabilla o AUS 176-177 J 5
Mundrabilla Motel o AUS 176-177 K 5
Mundubbera o AUS 178-179 L 3
Mundujskoe, ozero o RUS 108-109 X 8
Munduruçânia, Reserva Florestal ⊥ BR (P) 66-67 H 6
Munduruçânia, Reserva Florestal ⊥ BR (P) 66-67 J 6
Mundurúču ~ RUS 118-119 O 5
Mundurucu, Área Indígena ✗ BR 66-67 J 6
Mündwa o IND 138-139 D 6
Munenga o ANG 216-217 C 5
Munera o E 98-99 F 5
Munford o USA (TN) 276-277 F 5
Munfordville o USA (KY) 276-277 K 3
Mungabroom o AUS 174-175 C 5
Mungallala o AUS 178-179 J 4
Mungallala Creek ~ AUS 178-179 J 5
Mungaoli o IND 138-139 G 7
Mungári o MOC 218-219 G 3
Mungbere o ZRE 212-213 B 2
Munger o IND 142-143 E 3
Mungeranie o AUS 178-179 E 5
Munggduresak, Tanjung ▲ RI 162-163 H 4
Mungindi o AUS 178-179 K 5
Munglinup o AUS 176-177 F 6
Mungo o ANG (HBO) 216-217 D 5
Mungo o ANG (LUN) 216-217 F 3
Mungo o SME 62-63 G 3
Mungo National Park ⊥ AUS 180-181 G 2
Mungra Badshahpur o IND 142-143 C 3
Munhango o ANG 216-217 E 6
Munhoz o BR 72-73 G 7
Munich = München ☆ ·· D 92-93 L 4
Muniengashi ~ ZRE 218-219 E 1
Muniesa o E 98-99 G 4
Munikan ~ RUS 122-123 F 2
Munim, Rio ~ BR 68-69 G 3
Munimadugu o IND 140-141 G 3
Munising o USA (MI) 270-271 M 4
Muniungu o ZRE 210-211 F 6
Muniz Freire o BR 72-73 K 6
Munkamba ~ RUS 116-117 N 4
Munkumpu o Z 218-219 D 1
Münly, tau ▲ KZ 124-125 G 5
Munmarlary o AUS 172-173 L 2
Munn, Cape ▲ CDN 36-37 G 2
Munnat o IND 140-141 G 5
Munnikspoort ▲ ZA 220-221 G 6
Muñoz Gamero, Península ⌣ RCH 80 D 6
Munqaṭi', al- o Y 132-133 D 6
Munro, Mount ▲ AUS 180-181 K 6
Munsan o ROK 150-151 F 9
Munse o RI 164-165 H 6
Munson o CDN (ALB) 232-233 F 4
Munson o USA (FL) 286-287 C 1
Münster o • D 92-93 J 3
Münster = Müstair o ·· CH 92-93 L 5
Munte o RI 164-165 F 3
Munteme o EAU 212-213 C 3
Muntgatsi o EAK 212-213 E 3
Muntilan o RI 168 D 3
Muntok o RI 162-163 F 6
Muntu o EAU 212-213 D 3
Muntu o ZRE 210-211 G 5
Munukata o J 152-153 D 8
Munyamadzi ~ Z 218-219 F 1
Munyaroo Conservation Park ⊥ AUS 180-181 D 2
Munyati ~ ZW 218-219 E 3
Munzur Vadisi Milli Parkı ⊥ TR 128-129 H 3
Muoco o MOC 218-219 J 1
Muodoslompolo o S 86-87 L 3
Muohyang San ▲ KOR 150-151 F 7
Mu'ò'ng Cha o VN 156-157 B 6

Mu'ò'ng Lạm ○ **VN** 156-157 D 7
Mu'ò'ng Loi ○ **VN** 156-157 C 6
Mu'ò'ng Mu'o'n ○ **VN** 156-157 C 6
Mu'ò'ng Pồn ○ **VN** 156-157 C 6
Mu'ò'ng Tè ☆ **VN** 156-157 C 5
Muonio ○ **FIN** 88-89 G 3
Muonioälven ~ **S** 86-87 L 3
Muonionjoki ~· **FIN** 88-89 G 3
Muor, Pulau ⌒ **RI** 164-165 L 3
Muostah, mys ▲ **RUS** 110-111 Q 5
Muostah, ostrov ⌒ **RUS** 110-111 S 4
Mupa ○ **ANG** 216-217 C 8
Mupa ~ **MOC** 218-219 H 4
Mupa, Parque Nacional da ⊥ **ANG** 216-217 C 7
Mupamadzi ~ **Z** 218-219 F 1
Mupele, Chute ~ **ZRE** 210-211 K 3
Mupfure ~ **ZW** 218-219 E 3
Muqaddam, Wādī ~ **SUD** 200-201 E 5
Muqakoori ○ **SP** 208-209 H 6
Muqdisho ★ **SP** 212-213 K 2
Muqsim, Ğabal ▲ **ET** 194-195 G 6
Muqšin ○ **OM** 132-133 J 4
Muqui ○ **BR** 72-73 K 6
Muqui, Rio ~ **BR** 70-71 F 2
Muqur ○ **AFG** 134-135 M 2
Mura ○ **BR** 66-67 H 4
Mura ~ **RUS** 116-117 J 7
Muradiye ○ **TR** 128-129 K 3
Murafa ~ **UA** 102-103 F 3
Murair, Ğazīrat ⌒ **ET** 194-195 G 6
Murakami ○ **J** 152-153 H 5
Muralgarra ○ **AUS** 176-177 D 4
Murallón, Cerro ▲ **RCH** 80 D 4
Muramgaon ○ **IND** 142-143 B 5
Muramvya ○ **BU** 212-213 B 5
Muranga ○ **EAK** 212-213 F 4
Murangering ○ **EAK** 212-213 E 2
Muraré, Rio ~ **BR** 62-63 H 5
Muraši ○ **RUS** 96-97 F 4
Murat Çayı ~ **TR** 128-129 K 3
Murat Dağı ▲ **TR** 128-129 C 3
Murat Nehri ~ **TR** 128-129 J 3
Muratus, Pegunungan ▲ **RI** 164-165 D 5
Muravera ○ **I** 100-101 B 5
Murça ○ **P** 98-99 D 4
Mūrče Ḥūrt ○ **IR** 134-135 D 2
Murchinson Range ▲ **AUS** 174-175 C 7
Murchison ○ **AUS** 180-181 H 4
Murchison ○ **NZ** 182 D 4
Murchison, Cape ▲ **CDN** 36-37 R 3
Murchison, Mount ▲ **AUS** 176-177 D 3
Murchison Falls ~ **EAU** 212-213 C 2
Murchison Falls National Park ⊥ **EAU** 212-213 C 2
Murchison Island ⌒ **CDN** (ONT) 234-235 P 4
Murchison River ~ **AUS** 176-177 C 3
Murchison River ~ **CDN** 24-25 a 6
Murchison Settlement Roadhouse ○ **AUS** 176-177 C 3
Murchison Sund ≈ 26-27 P 5
Murchisson, Mount ▲ **WAN** 204-205 H 4
Murcia ○ **E** 98-99 G 6
Murcia ◘ **E** 98-99 G 6
Murder Creek ~ **USA** 284-285 D 5
Murdo ○ **USA** (SD) 260-261 F 3
Murdochville ○ **CDN** (QUE) 240-241 K 2
Murdock ○ **USA** (MN) 270-271 C 5
Murdock ○ **USA** (NE) 262-263 K 4
Murehwa ○ **ZW** 218-219 F 3
Mureji ○ **WAN** 204-205 F 4
Mureş ~ **RO** 102-103 D 4
Muret ○ **F** 90-91 H 10
Murfreesboro ○ **USA** (AR) 276-277 B 6
Murfreesboro ○ **USA** (NC) 282-283 K 4
Murfreesboro ○ **USA** (TN) 276-277 J 5
Murgab ~ **TJ** 136-137 N 5
Murgab ○ **TM** 136-137 H 6
Murgab ~ **TM** 136-137 H 7
Murgal' ~ **RUS** 112-113 O 4
Murgenella X **AUS** 172-173 L 1
Murgenella Wildlife Sanctuary ⊥ **AUS** 172-173 L 1
Murgha Kibzai ○ **PK** 138-139 B 4
Murgho, Hāmūn-i- ⊖ **PK** 134-135 L 5
Murgon ○ **AUS** 178-179 L 4
Murgoo ○ **AUS** 176-177 D 3
Murgud ○ **IND** 140-141 F 2
Muri ○ **VRC** 154-155 B 3
Muriaê ○ **BR** 72-73 J 6
Muriaé, Rio ~ **BR** 72-73 K 6
Murici, Ponta do ▲ **BR** 68-69 F 3
Muricilândia ○ **BR** 68-69 D 5
Muricizal, Rio ~ **BR** 68-69 D 5
Muridke ○ **PK** 138-139 E 4
Muriege ○ **ANG** 216-217 F 4
Murighiol = Indenpenţa ○· **RO** 102-103 F 5
Murillo ○ **CDN** (ONT) 234-235 O 6
Murinja ○ **RUS** 116-117 N 8
Muritiba ○ **BR** 72-73 L 2
Müritz ⊖ **D** 92-93 M 2
Müritz-National-Park ⊥ **D** 92-93 M 2
Muriwai ○ **NZ** 182 F 3
Murizidié Pass ▲ **LAR** 192-193 F 6
Murman, zaliv ≈ 108-109 G 4
Murmanca, buhta ≈ 108-109 N 3
Murmansk ☆ **RUS** 88-89 M 2
Murmanskij bereg ᴗ **RUS** 88-89 M 2
Murmanskiy Bereg = Murmanskij bereg ᴗ **RUS** 88-89 M 2
Murmanskoye Rise ≃ 10-11 C 1
Murmaši ○ **RUS** 88-89 M 2
Muro Lucano ○ **I** 100-101 E 4
Murom ☆ **RUS** 94-95 S 4
Muroran ○ **J** 152-153 J 3
Muros ○ **E** 98-99 C 3
Muroto ○ **J** 152-153 F 8
Muroto-saki ▲ **J** 152-153 F 8
Murphy ○ **USA** (ID) 252-253 B 3
Murphy ○ **USA** (NC) 282-283 C 5
Murphy ○ **USA** (OR) 244-245 B 8
Murphy Head ▲ **CDN** 36-37 S 5
Murphy Hot Springs · **USA** (ID) 252-253 C 4
Murphysboro ○ **USA** (IL) 276-277 F 3
Mūrqūm, Kūh-e ▲ **IR** 134-135 G 2
Murra, al-Buhaira l- < **ET** 194-195 F 2
Murra Murra ○ **AUS** 178-179 J 5
Murray ○ **USA** (IA) 274-275 E 3
Murray ○ **USA** (KY) 276-277 G 4
Murray ○ **USA** (UT) 254-255 D 3
Murray, Cape ▲ **CDN** 24-25 O 2
Murray, Lake ⊖ **PNG** 183 A 4
Murray, Lake < **USA** (OK) 264-265 G 4
Murray, Lake < **USA** (SC) 284-285 J 2
Murray Bridge ○· **AUS** 180-181 E 3
Murray Downs ○ **AUS** 178-179 C 1
Murray Fracture Zone ≃ 14-15 N 4
Murray Harbour ○ **CDN** (NS) 240-241 N 4
Murray Inlet ≈ 24-25 P 3
Murray Islands ⌒ **AUS** 183 C 5
Murray Maxwell Bay ≈ 24-25 f 5
Murray Range ▲ **PNG** 183 B 4
Murray River ~ **AUS** 180-181 E 3
Murray River ~ **CDN** 228-229 N 2
Murray River Basin ∸ **AUS** 180-181 F 2
Murraysburg ○ **ZA** 220-221 F 5
Murray-Sunset National Park ⊥ **AUS** 180-181 F 3
Murray Town ○ **AUS** 180-181 E 2
Murrayville ○ **AUS** 180-181 F 3
Murree ○ **PK** 138-139 D 3
Murrej, mys ▲ **RUS** 84-85 b 2
Murri, Río ~ **CO** 60-61 C 4
Murroa ○ **MOC** 218-219 J 3
Murroe Lake ⊖ **CDN** 30-31 U 6
Murrumbidgee River ~ **AUS** 180-181 H 3
Murrumburrah ○ **AUS** 180-181 K 3
Murrupula ○ **MOC** 218-219 K 2
Murrurundi ○ **AUS** 178-179 L 6
Murrysville ○ **USA** (PA) 280-281 G 3
Murshidābād ○· **IND** 142-143 F 3
Murtajāpur ○ **IND** 138-139 F 9
Murtaugh ○ **USA** (ID) 252-253 D 4
Murtle Lake ⊖ **CDN** (BC) 228-229 P 4
Murtle River ~ **CDN** 228-229 P 4
Murtoa ○ **AUS** 180-181 G 4
Murtovaara ○ **FIN** 88-89 K 4
Muru, Rio ~ **BR** 66-67 B 7
Murua ○ **PNG** 183 C 4
Murua Island = Woodlark Island ⌒ **PNG** 183 G 5
Muruaul, Lake < **USA** (TX) 264-265 K 6
Muruchachi ○ **YV** 60-61 F 3
Murud ○· **IND** 138-139 D 10
Murud, Gunung ▲ **MAL** 164-165 D 2
Muruken ○ **PNG** 183 C 3
Murun, gora ▲ **RUS** 118-119 J 6
Murupara ○ **NZ** 182 F 3
Muruptumatari ~ **RUS** 108-109 h 4
Murupu ○ **BR** 62-63 D 4
Mururé, Igarapé ~ **BR** 68-69 C 6
Mururoa ⌒ **F** 13 O 5
Mururoa Inseln ⌒ **F** 13 O 5
Murwāra ○ **IND** 142-143 B 4
Murwillumbah ○ **AUS** 178-179 M 5
Murygino ○ **RUS** 96-97 F 4
Mürzzuschlag ○ **A** 92-93 N 5
Muş ☆ **TR** 128-129 J 3
Mūsa, 'Ain · **ET** 194-195 F 3
Mūsa, Ğabal ▲ **ET** 194-195 F 3
Mūsā, Ḥōr-e ≈ 134-135 C 3
Mūsa, Wādī ○ **JOR** 130-131 D 2
Musa Ālī Terara ▲ **DJI** 200-201 L 6
Musadi ○ **ZRE** 210-211 J 5
Musaia ○ **WAL** 202-203 E 5
Musai'id ○ **Q** 134-135 D 6
Musaimīr ○ **Y** 132-133 D 7
Mušairib, Ra's ▲ **UAE** 134-135 D 6
Mušairifa, al- ○ **SYR** 128-129 H 4
Mūsa Khel ○ **PK** 138-139 C 3
Mūsa Khel Bāzār ○ **PK** 138-139 B 4
Musala ▲ **BG** 102-103 C 6
Musala, Pulau ⌒ **RI** 162-163 C 4
Muşallā, al- ○ **OM** 132-133 L 2
Musan ○ **KOR** 150-151 G 6
Musandam, Ra's ▲ **OM** 134-135 G 5
Mūsā Qal'e ○ **AFG** 134-135 L 2
Mūsā Qal'e, Rūd-e ~ **AFG** 134-135 L 2
Musa River ~ **PNG** 183 E 5
Musashi ○ **J** 152-153 D 8
Mušattā, Qaşr al- ∴· **JOR** 130-131 E 2
Musawa ○ **WAN** 198-199 C 6
Musawwarat, Temples of · **SUD** 200-201 F 4
Musayyib, al- ☆ **IRQ** 128-129 L 6
Musbat ○ **SUD** 200-201 B 5
Mušbih, Ğabal ▲ **ET** 194-195 G 6
Muscat = Masqaţ ★·· **OM** 132-133 L 2
Muscatatuck River ~ **USA** 274-275 M 6
Muscatine ○ **USA** (IA) 274-275 G 3
Muscoda ○ **USA** (WI) 274-275 H 1
Muse ○ **USA** (OK) 264-265 K 4
Musenge ○ **ZRE** (KIV) 212-213 B 4
Musenge ○ **ZRE** (SHA) 214-215 B 5
Musengezi ~ **ZW** 218-219 F 3
Museo del Oro · **CO** 60-61 D 5
Museum ○· **RI** 164-165 G 6
Musgrave ○ **AUS** 174-175 G 4
Musgrave ○ **CDN** (BC) 230-231 F 5
Musgrave, Port ≈ 174-175 F 3
Musgrave Harbour ○ **CDN** (NFL) 242-243 P 3
Musgrave Ranges ▲ **AUS** 176-177 L 3
Mus-Haja, gora ▲ **RUS** 120-121 J 2
Mushandike Sanctuary ⊥ **ZW** 218-219 F 5
Mushayfāt ○ **SUD** 206-207 K 3
Mushenge ○ **ZRE** 210-211 H 6
Mushie ○ **ZRE** 210-211 F 5
Mushima ○ **Z** 218-219 C 2
Mushipashi ○ **Z** 214-215 F 6
Mushota ○ **Z** 214-215 E 5
Mushu Island ⌒ **PNG** 183 B 2
Músi ~ **IND** 140-141 H 2
Musi ~ **RI** 162-163 F 6
Musidora ○ **CDN** (ALB) 232-233 G 2
Musin ○ **WAN** 204-205 E 5
Musiri ○ **IND** 140-141 H 5
Mūsiyan ○ **IR** 134-135 B 2
Muskeg Lake Indian Reservation X **CDN** (SAS) 232-233 M 3
Muskego ○ **USA** (WI) 274-275 K 2
Muskegon ○ **USA** (MI) 272-273 C 4
Muskegon Heights ○ **USA** (MI) 272-273 C 4
Muskegon River ~ **USA** 272-273 D 4
Muskeg River ○ **CDN** (ALB) 228-229 Q 3
Muskeg River ~ **CDN** 30-31 H 5
Muskingum River ~ **USA** 280-281 E 4
Muskoday Indian Reservation X **CDN** (SAS) 232-233 N 2
Muskogee ○ **USA** (OK) 264-265 J 3
Muskox Lake ⊖ **CDN** 30-31 P 3
Muskratdam Lake ⊖ **CDN** 34-35 L 4
Muskwa ○ **CDN** 30-31 H 6
Muskwa River ~ **CDN** 30-31 H 6
Muskwa River ~ **CDN** 32-33 N 3
Muslimiya ○ **SYR** 128-129 G 4
Musljumovo ☆ **RUS** 96-97 H 6
Musoma ☆ **EAT** 212-213 D 4
Musondweji ~ **Z** 218-219 C 1
Musongoie ○ **ZRE** 214-215 C 5
Mus-Onnjue ~ **RUS** 118-119 O 7
Musoro ○ **Z** 218-219 F 1
Musoshi ○ **ZRE** 214-215 D 6
Musquaro, Lac ⊖ **CDN** (QUE) 242-243 G 2
Musquash ○ **CDN** (NB) 240-241 J 5
Musquodoboit Harbour ○ **CDN** (NS) 240-241 M 6
Mussel Fork ~ **USA** 274-275 F 5
Musselshell ○ **USA** (MT) 250-251 L 5
Musselshell River ~ **USA** 250-251 L 5
Mussende ○ **ANG** 216-217 D 5
Musserra ○ **ANG** 216-217 B 3
Mussolo ○ **ANG** 216-217 D 4
Mussuma ○ **ANG** (MOX) 216-217 F 7
Mussuma ~ **ANG** 216-217 F 7
Mustāfābād ○ **PK** 138-139 D 4
Mustafakemalpaşa ☆ **TR** 128-129 C 2
Mustahil ○ **ETH** 208-209 G 6
Müstair = Münster ○·· **CH** 92-93 L 5
Mustang ○ **NEP** 144-145 D 6
Mustang ~ **USA** 264-265 B 6
Mustang Island ⌒ **USA** (TX) 266-267 K 6
Musters, Lago ⊖ **RA** 80 F 2
Mustique Island ⌒ **WV** 56 E 5
Mustjala ○ **EST** 94-95 H 2
Mustvee ○ **EST** 94-95 K 2
Musu Dan ▲ **KOR** 150-151 G 7
Musún, Cerro ▲ **NIC** 52-53 B 5
Muswellbrook ○ **AUS** 180-181 L 2
Mūţ ○ **ET** 194-195 D 5
Mut ☆ **TR** 128-129 E 4
Mutá, Ponta do ▲ **BR** 72-73 L 2
Mutale ~ **ZA** 218-219 F 6
Mutanda ○ **Z** 214-215 D 7
Muţannā, al ◘ **IRQ** 130-131 J 2
Mutarara ○ **MOC** 218-219 H 3
Mutare ☆· **ZW** 218-219 G 4
Mutarnee ○ **AUS** 174-175 J 6
Muteba, Xá- ○ **ANG** 216-217 D 4
Mutenge ○ **Z** 218-219 E 1
Mutha ○ **EAK** (EAS) 212-213 G 4
Mutha ▲ **EAK** (EAS) 212-213 G 4
Mutici ○ **BR** 68-69 L 6
Mutiene ○ **ZRE** 210-211 E 6
Muting ○ **RI** 166-167 L 5
Mutinglupa ○ **RP** 160-161 D 5
Mutir ○ **EAU** 212-213 C 2
Mutis, Gunung ▲ **RI** 166-167 C 6
Mutki ☆ **TR** 128-129 J 3
Mutni ~ **PK** 134-135 M 6
Mutnyj Materik ○ **RUS** 88-89 X 4
Mutoko ○ **ZW** 218-219 G 3
Mutombo, Bwana- ○ **ZRE** 216-217 E 3
Mutombo-Mukulu ○ **ZRE** 214-215 C 5
Mutomo ○ **EAK** 212-213 G 4
Mutoraj ○ **RUS** 116-117 K 5
Mutorashanga ○ **ZW** 218-219 F 3
Mutoto ○ **ZRE** (KOC) 210-211 J 6
Mutoto ○ **ZRE** (SHA) 214-215 E 4
Mutsamudu ○· **COM** 222-223 D 4
Mutshatsha ○ **ZRE** 214-215 C 6
Mutsu ○ **J** 152-153 J 4
Muttaburra ○ **AUS** 178-179 H 2
Mutton Bay ○ **CDN** (QUE) 242-243 J 2
Mutúali ○ **MOC** 218-219 J 2
Mutukula ○ **EAU** 212-213 C 4
Mutum ○ **BR** (AMA) 66-67 G 6
Mutum ○ **BR** (MIN) 72-73 K 5
Mutum, Cachoeira ~ **BR** 66-67 J 5
Mutum, Ilha do ⌒ **BR** 66-67 F 7
Mutum, Rio ~ **BR** 66-67 C 5
Mutumbi ○ **ZRE** 214-215 E 4
Mutum Biyu ○ **WAN** 204-205 J 4
Mutumbu ○ **ANG** 216-217 D 6
Mutum Daya ○ **WAN** 204-205 J 4
Mutum ou Madeira, Rio ~ **BR** 70-71 K 5
Mutum Paraná ○ **BR** 66-67 E 7
Mutungu-Tari ○ **ZRE** 216-217 D 3
Mutuoca, Ilha da ⌒ **BR** 68-69 F 2
Mutur ○ **CL** 140-141 J 6
Mututi, Ilha ⌒ **BR** 62-63 J 6
Mutu-wan ≈ 152-153 J 4
Mutwanga ○ **ZRE** 212-213 B 3
Muurola ○ **FIN** 88-89 H 3
Mu Us Shamo ∸ **VRC** 154-155 E 2
Mūvattupula ○ **IND** 140-141 G 6
Muwaih, al- ○ **KSA** 130-131 G 6
Muwaiha, Ğabal ▲ **UAE** 134-135 F 6
Muwailih, al- ○ **KSA** 130-131 D 4
Muwassam ○ **KSA** 132-133 C 5
Muwaylih, Bi'r al ○ **LAR** 192-193 H 3
Muwo Island ⌒ **PNG** 183 F 5
Muxima ○ **ANG** 216-217 B 4
Muyinga ○ **BU** 212-213 C 5
Muy Muy ○ **NIC** 52-53 B 5
Muyombe ○ **Z** 214-215 F 6
Muyuka ○ **CAM** 204-205 H 6
Muyumba ○ **ZRE** 214-215 D 4
Muzaffarabad ○ **IND** 138-139 D 2
Muzaffargarh ○ **PK** 138-139 C 4
Muzaffarnagar ○ **IND** 138-139 F 5
Muzaffarpur ○ **IND** 142-143 D 2
Muzāḥimiya, al- ○ **KSA** 130-131 K 5
Muzambinho ○ **BR** 72-73 G 6
Muze ○ **MOC** 218-219 F 2
Muzej narodnoji architektury i pobutu · **UA** 102-103 G 2
Muzej-usad'ba "Tarhany" · **RUS** 94-95 S 5
Muzhen ○ **VRC** 154-155 K 6
Muži ○ **RUS** 114-115 H 2
Muzizi ~ **EAU** 212-213 C 3
Muzkol, hrebet ▲ **TJ** 136-137 N 5
Muzo ○ **CO** 60-61 D 5
Muzon, Cape ▲ **USA** 32-33 D 4
Muztag ▲ **VRC** 144-145 F 2
Muztag ▲ **VRC** 144-145 C 2
Muztagata ▲ **VRC** 146-147 B 6
Mvangan ○ **CAM** 210-211 C 2
Mveng ○ **CAM** 210-211 D 2
Mvengué ○ **CAM** 210-211 C 2
Mvera ○ **MW** 218-219 H 1
Mvolo ○ **SUD** 206-207 J 5
Mvomero ○ **EAT** 214-215 J 4
Mvoung ~ **G** 210-211 D 3
Mvouti ○ **RCB** 210-211 D 6
Mvuha ○ **EAT** 214-215 J 4
Mvuma ○ **ZW** 218-219 F 4
Mvurwi ○ **ZW** 218-219 F 3
Mvuvye ~ **Z** 218-219 F 2
Mwabungu ○ **EAK** 212-213 G 6
Mwadi-Kalumbu ○ **ZRE** 216-217 E 3
Mwadingusha ○ **ZRE** 214-215 D 6
Mwafwe ~ **Z** 218-219 C 1
Mwaga ○ **EAT** 214-215 J 5
Mwala ○ **MW** 218-219 H 3
Mwaleshi ~ **Z** 214-215 F 6
Mwambo ○ **EAT** 214-215 L 6
Mwambwa ~ **Z** 214-215 G 6
Mwami ○ **ZW** 218-219 E 3
Mwana-Ndeke ○ **ZRE** 210-211 L 6
Mwangalala ○ **ZRE** 214-215 D 6
Mwangia, Pania- ○ **ZRE** 214-215 E 4
Mwango ○ **ZRE** 214-215 C 4
Mwanibwaghosu ○ **SOL** 184 I f 4
Mwanisenga ○ **EAT** 212-213 D 6
Mwanza ◘ **EAT** 212-213 D 5
Mwanza ☆· **EAT** (MWA) 212-213 D 5
Mwanza ○ **MW** 218-219 H 2
Mwanza ○ **ZRE** 214-215 D 4
Mwanza Gulf ⊖ **EAT** 212-213 D 5
Mwanzangoma ~ **ZRE** 210-211 J 6
Mwaru ~ **EAT** 212-213 E 6
Mwatasi ○ **EAT** 214-215 J 4
Mwatate ○ **EAK** (COA) 212-213 G 5
Mwatate ~ **EAK** 212-213 G 5
Mwea National Reserve ⊥ **EAK** 212-213 F 4
Mweka ○ **ZRE** 210-211 H 6
Mwembeshi ○ **Z** 218-219 D 2
Mwenda ○ **Z** 214-215 E 6
Mwene-Biji ○ **ZRE** 214-215 B 5
Mwene-Ditu ○ **ZRE** 214-215 B 4
Mwenezi ○ **ZW** (Mvi) 218-219 F 5
Mwenezi ~ **ZW** 218-219 F 5
Mwenga ○ **ZRE** 212-213 B 5
Mweru, Lake = Lac Moero ⊖ **Z** 214-215 E 5
Mweru Wantipa National Park ⊥ **Z** 214-215 E 5
Mwilambwe ○ **ZRE** 214-215 C 5
Mwimbwi ○ **EAT** 214-215 F 5
Mwingi ○ **EAK** 212-213 G 4
Mwinilunga ○ **Z** 214-215 C 6
Mwitika ○ **EAK** 212-213 G 4
Mwitikira ○ **EAT** 214-215 H 4
Mwogo ~ **RWA** 212-213 B 5
Mwombezhi ~ **Z** 218-219 C 1
My ~ **RUS** 122-123 J 2
Mya, Oued ~ **DZ** 190-191 D 6
Myaing ○ **MYA** 142-143 J 5
Myakka City ○ **USA** (FL) 286-287 G 4
Myakka Head ○ **USA** (FL) 286-287 G 4
Myakka River ~ **USA** 286-287 G 4
Myakka River State Park ⊥ **USA** (FL) 286-287 G 4
Myall Lakes National Park ⊥ **AUS** 180-181 M 2
Myanaung ○ **MYA** 142-143 J 6
Myanmar ■ **MYA** 142-143 J 4
Mychajlivka ○ **UA** 102-103 J 4
Mychla ○ **MYA** 142-143 K 6
Mye, Mount ▲ **CDN** 20-21 Y 5
Myerstown ○ **USA** (PA) 280-281 K 3
Myingyan ○ **MYA** 142-143 J 5
Myinmoletkat Taung ▲ **MYA** 158-159 E 4
Myitkyina ○ **MYA** 142-143 K 3
Myitnge ~ **MYA** 142-143 K 5
Myittha ○ **MYA** 142-143 K 5
Mykenai ·· **GR** 100-101 J 6
Mykolajiv ○ **UA** 102-103 G 4
Mykolajivs'ka cerkva · **UA** 102-103 C 3
Mykolayiv = Mykolajiv ○ **UA** 102-103 G 4
Myky, Área Indígena X **BR** 70-71 H 3
Myla ○ **RUS** 88-89 V 4
Myla ~ **RUS** 88-89 V 4
Mylga ~ **RUS** 120-121 N 2
Mylius Erichsen Land ∸ **GRØ** 26-27 m 3
Mylo ○ **USA** (ND) 258-259 H 3
Mymensingh ○ **BD** 142-143 G 3
Mynämäki ○ **FIN** 88-89 F 6
Myndagaj ○ **RUS** 120-121 E 3
Mynfontein ○ **ZA** 220-221 F 5
Mynsualmas ▲ **KZ** 126-127 L 5
Myohaung ○ **MYA** 142-143 J 5
Myoko-san ▲ **J** 152-153 H 6
Myola ○ **AUS** 174-175 F 6
Myola ○ **PNG** 183 D 5
Myotha ○ **MYA** 142-143 J 5
Myra ∴·· **TR** 128-129 D 4
Myre ○ **N** 86-87 d 2
Myrhorod ○ **UA** 102-103 H 3
Myri ○ **IS** 86-87 e 2
Myrnam ○ **CDN** (ALB) 232-233 G 2
Myronivka ☆ **UA** 102-103 G 3
Myrtle ○ **CDN** (ONT) 238-239 G 4
Myrtle Beach ○· **USA** (SC) 284-285 M 3
Myrtle Creek ○ **USA** (OR) 244-245 B 7
Myrtleford ○ **AUS** 180-181 J 4
Myrtle Grove ○ **USA** (LA) 268-269 L 7
Myrtle Point ○ **USA** (OR) 244-245 A 7
Mysen ☆ **N** 86-87 E 7
Mys-Kamennyj ○ **RUS** 108-109 P 7
Myski ○ **RUS** 124-125 P 2
Myškin ☆ **RUS** 94-95 Q 3
Myškino = Myškin ☆ **RUS** 94-95 Q 3
Myślenice ○· **PL** 92-93 P 4
My So'n · **VN** 158-159 K 3
Mysore ○·· **IND** 140-141 G 4
Mystery Caves ∴ **USA** (MN) 270-271 F 7
Mys Želanija ○ **RUS** 108-109 N 3
Myszyniec ○ **PL** 92-93 Q 2
My Tho ☆· **VN** 158-159 J 5
Mytišči ☆ **RUS** 94-95 P 4
Mytishchi = Mytišči ☆ **RUS** 94-95 P 4
Myton ○ **USA** (UT) 254-255 E 3
Mývatn · **IS** 86-87 e 2
Myzeqe ᴗ **AL** 100-101 G 4
M'Zab ∸··· **DZ** 190-191 D 4
M'Zab, Oued ~ **DZ** 190-191 E 4
Mže ~ **CZ** 92-93 M 4
Mzenga ○ **EAT** 214-215 K 4
Mziha ○ **EAT** 212-213 F 6
Mzimba ○ **MW** 214-215 G 6
Mzimkulwana Nature Reserve ⊥ **ZA** 220-221 J 4
Mzuzu ☆ **MW** 214-215 H 6

N

Naab ~ **D** 92-93 M 4
Naala ○ **TCH** 198-199 G 6
Naalehu ○ **USA** (HI) 288 K 5
Na'am ○ **SUD** 206-207 J 4
Na'ām ~ **SUD** 206-207 J 6
Naama ☆ **DZ** 188-189 L 4
Na'ama ○ **ET** 194-195 G 4
Na'ān, an- ○ **KSA** 130-131 K 6
Naantali ○· **FIN** 88-89 G 6
Naas = An Nás ☆ **IRL** 90-91 D 5
Nababeep ○ **ZA** 220-221 C 4
Nabalāt ○ **SUD** 200-201 E 5
Naban SK ⊖ **VRC** 156-157 F 5
Nabar ○ **TCH** 198-199 K 3
Nabarlek ○ **AUS** 174-175 B 3
Nabas ○ **RP** 160-161 E 7
Nabaţīya t-Taḥtā ☆ **RL** 128-129 F 6
Nabavatu ○ **FJI** 184 III b 2
Nabawa ○ **AUS** 176-177 C 4
Nabawan ○ **MAL** 160-161 B 10
Nabberu, Lake ⊖ **AUS** 176-177 F 2
Nabéré, Réserve Partielle de ⊥ **BF** 202-203 J 4
Naberera ○ **EAT** 212-213 F 6
Naberezhnyye Chelny = Nabereżnye Čelny ☆ **RUS** 96-97 H 6
Nabereżnye Čelny ☆ **RUS** 96-97 H 6
Nabesna River ~ **USA** 20-21 T 5
Nabeul ☆ **TN** 190-191 H 2
Nabğa ○ **UAE** 134-135 F 6
Nabgunhe Z.B. ⊥· **VRC** 142-143 L 4
Nabhāniya, an- ○ **KSA** 130-131 H 5
Nabi, Wādī ~ **SUD** 200-201 F 2
Nabil' ~ **RUS** 122-123 K 3
Nabilatuk ○ **EAU** 212-213 E 2
Nabileque, Rio ~ **BR** 70-71 J 7
Nabil'skij, zaliv ≈ 122-123 K 3
Nabingora ○ **EAU** 212-213 C 3
Nabire ○ **RI** 166-167 H 3
Nabisar ○ **PK** 138-139 B 7
Nabi Šu'aib, Ğabal an- ▲ **Y** 132-133 C 6
Nabk, an- ○ **KSA** 130-131 F 2
Nabljudenij, mys ▲ **RUS** 120-121 T 3
Naboga ○ **GH** 202-203 K 5
Naboomspruit ○ **ZA** 220-221 J 2
Nabou ○ **BF** 202-203 J 4
Naboulgou ○ **RT** 202-203 L 4
Nabouwalu ○ **FJI** 184 III b 2
Nabq ○ **ET** 194-195 G 3
Nabukjuak Bay ≈ 36-37 L 2
Nābulus = Shekhem ☆ **WB** 130-131 D 1
Nabuquen, Caño ~ **CO** 60-61 G 6
Nabusamke ○ **EAU** 212-213 D 3
Nabwān ○ **KSA** 130-131 G 4
Nacala ○ **MOC** 218-219 L 2
Načalovo ☆ **RUS** 96-97 F 10
Nacaome ☆ **HN** 52-53 L 5
Nacaroa ○ **MOC** 218-219 K 2
Nacebe ○ **BOL** 70-71 D 2
Naches ○ **USA** (WA) 244-245 E 4
Naches River ~ **USA** 244-245 D 4
Nachicapau, Lac ⊖ **CDN** 36-37 Q 6
Nachingwea ○ **EAT** 214-215 K 6
Nāchna ○ **IND** 138-139 C 6
Nachtigal, Cap ▲ **CAM** 210-211 B 2
Nachtigal, Chutes de ~ **CAM** 204-205 J 6
Nachuge ○ **IND** 140-141 L 4
Nachvak Fiord ≈ 36-37 S 5
Načikinskij, mys ▲ **RUS** 120-121 U 5
Nacimiento Reservoir ⊖ **USA** (CA) 248-249 D 4
Nackara ○ **AUS** 180-181 E 2
Nackawic ○ **CDN** (NB) 240-241 H 4
Nacmine ○ **CDN** (ALB) 232-233 F 4
Naco ○ **CDN** (ALB) 232-233 H 4
Naco ∴ **HN** 52-53 K 4
Nacogdoches ○ **USA** (TX) 268-269 F 5
Nacori Chico ○ **MEX** 50-51 E 3
Nacozari de García ○ **MEX** 50-51 E 2
Nacula ⌒ **FJI** 184 III a 2
Ñacuñán ○ **RA** 78-79 F 3
Ñacuñán, Reserva Ecológica ⊥ **RA** 78-79 E 2
Nacyjanal'ny park Belavežskaja pušča ⊥·· **BY** 94-95 J 5
Nada ○ **USA** (TX) 266-267 L 4
Nadawli ○ **GH** 202-203 J 4
Nād-e 'Alī ☆ **AFG** 134-135 L 3
Nāder Šāh Kōt ○ **AFG** 138-139 C 2
Nadėžnyj, mys ▲ **RUS** 110-111 b 2
Nadi ○ **FJI** 184 III a 2
Nadi ○ **SUD** 200-201 F 3
Nadiād ○ **IND** 138-139 D 8
Nadina River ○ **CDN** (BC) 228-229 H 3
Nadina River ~ **CDN** 228-229 H 3
Nadoba ○ **RT** 202-203 L 4
Nadojaha ~ **RUS** 108-109 N 6
Nador ○ **MA** 188-189 K 3
Nadudoturku ozero ⊖ **RUS** 108-109 U 5
Nadura, Temple of ∴· **ET** 194-195 E 5
Naduri ○ **FJI** 184 III b 2
Nadvirna ☆ **UA** 102-103 D 3
Nadym ○ **RUS** (JAN) 114-115 M 2
Nadym ~ **RUS** 114-115 L 3
Nadymskaja Ob' ≈ 108-109 N 8
Nadzab ○ **PNG** 183 D 4
Nā'ebābād ○ **AFG** 136-137 K 6
Naejangsan National Park ⊥· **ROK** 150-151 F 10
Nærøyfjorden ∸· **N** 86-87 C 6
Næstved ○· **DK** 86-87 E 9
Nafada ○ **WAN** 204-205 J 3
Nafadj, Baté- ○ **RG** 202-203 F 4
Nafadji ○ **SN** 202-203 E 3
Nafaq Aḥmad Ḥamdī (Tunnel) II **ET** 194-195 F 2
Nafi ○ **KSA** 130-131 H 5
Nafiša ○ **ET** 194-195 F 2
Náfpaktos ○ **GR** 100-101 H 5
Nafplio ○· **GR** 100-101 J 6
Naft-e Šāh ○ **IR** 134-135 A 1
Nafūd ad-Daḥī ∸ **KSA** 132-133 D 3
Nafūd al-Kubrā, an- ∸ **KSA** 130-131 G 3
Nafūd al-'Uraik ∸ **KSA** 130-131 H 5
Nafūd as-Sirr ∸ **KSA** 130-131 J 5
Nafūsah, Jabal ▲ **LAR** 192-193 D 2
Nāg ○ **PK** 134-135 L 5
Naga ○ **RP** (CAS) 160-161 E 6
Naga ○ **RP** (CEB) 160-161 E 7
Naǧaf, an- ◘ **IRQ** 128-129 K 7
Naǧaf, an- ☆ **IRQ** (NAG) 128-129 L 7
Naǧafābād ○ **IR** 134-135 D 2
Nagagami Lake ⊖ **CDN** (ONT) 236-237 C 3
Nagagami River ~ **CDN** 236-237 D 3
Nagai Island ⌒ **USA** 22-23 Q 5
Nagaj ○ **IND** 140-141 F 2
Nāgāland ◘ **IND** 142-143 J 2
Naǧ' al-Ma'mariya ○ **ET** 194-195 F 5
Nagamangala ○ **IND** 140-141 G 4
Nagambie ○ **AUS** 180-181 H 4
Nagamisis Provincial Park ⊥ **CDN** (ONT) 236-237 D 3
Nagam River Mission ○ **PNG** 183 B 2
Nagandana ○ **CI** 202-203 H 4
Nagano ○ **J** 152-153 H 6
Naganuma ○ **J** 152-153 J 3
Nagaoka ○ **J** 152-153 H 6
Nagaon ○ **IND** 142-143 H 2
Nagappattinam ○ **IND** 140-141 H 5
Nagara ○ **RMM** 202-203 E 2
Nagare Augū ▲ **MYA** 158-159 C 2
Nagarhole National Park ⊥ **IND** 140-141 G 4
Nagari ○ **IND** 140-141 H 4
Nagarjuna Sāgar ⊖ **IND** 140-141 H 2
Nagar Karnūl ○ **IND** 140-141 H 2
Nagarote ○ **NIC** 52-53 L 5
Nagar Pārkar ○ **PK** 138-139 C 7
Nagarzê ○ **VRC** 144-145 H 6
Nagasaki ☆·· **J** 152-153 C 8
Naga-shima ⌒ **J** 152-153 D 8
Nāgaur ○ **IND** 138-139 D 6
Nagayaman Point ▲ **RP** 160-161 E 3
Nāghbhir ○ **IND** 138-139 G 9
Nagbo ○ **GH** 202-203 K 4
Naǧd ∸ **KSA** 130-131 G 4
Nāgda ○ **IND** 138-139 E 8
Nage ○ **RI** 168 E 7
Nageezi ○ **USA** (NM) 256-257 H 2
Nagercoil ○ **IND** 140-141 G 6
Naǧ 'Hammādī ○ **ET** 194-195 F 4
Nagichot ○ **SUD** 208-209 A 6
Nagina ○ **IND** 138-139 G 5
Naglějngynvaam ~ **RUS** 112-113 O 2
Naglějnyn, gora ▲ **RUS** 112-113 P 2
Naglějnyn, mys ▲ **RUS** 112-113 P 2
Nago ○ **J** 152-153 B 11
Nāgod ○ **IND** 142-143 B 3
Nagor'e ○ **RUS** 94-95 Q 3
Nagorno-Karabahskaja AO ◘ **AZ** 128-129 M 2
Nagorno-Karabakh = Dağlıq Qarabağ Muxtar Vilayati ◘ **AZ** 128-129 M 2
Nagornyj ○ **RUS** (SAH) 118-119 M 8
Nagornyj ☆ **RUS** (KOR) 112-113 U 5
Nagorsk ☆ **RUS** 96-97 G 4
Nagoya ☆· **J** 152-153 G 7
Nāgpur ○· **IND** 138-139 G 9
Nagqu ○ **VRC** 144-145 J 5
Nāgrāl ○ **IND** 140-141 H 2
Naǧrān ◘ **KSA** 132-133 D 4
Naǧrān ☆· **KSA** (NAG) 132-133 D 5
Naǧrān, Wādī ~ **Y** 132-133 D 5
Nagslaran ○ **RP** 160-161 D 5
Nagua ☆ **DOM** 54-55 L 5
Naguabo ○ **USA** (PR) 286-287 Q 2
Nagvaraaluk, Lac ⊖ **CDN** 36-37 O 4
Nagykanizsa ○ **H** 92-93 O 5
Naha ○ **J** 152-153 B 11
Na Haeo ○ **THA** 158-159 F 2
Nāhan ○ **IND** 138-139 F 4
Na Hang ☆ **VN** 156-157 D 5
Nahang, Rūd-e ~ **IR** 134-135 K 5
Nahanni Butte ○ **CDN** 30-31 H 5
Nahanni National Park ⊥·· **CDN** 30-31 G 5
Nahara, Orto- ~ **RUS** 118-119 G 5
Nahatlatch River ~ **CDN** 230-231 G 3
Nahatta ~ **RUS** 110-111 X 6
Naheleg ⌒ **ER** 200-201 K 4
Nahia Lo ☆ **VN** 156-157 D 6
Nāhid, Bi'r ○ **ET** 194-195 D 2
Nahl, Rūd-e ~ **IR** 134-135 H 3
Nahlin ○ **CDN** 32-33 E 2
Nahlin Plateau ▲ **CDN** 32-33 D 2
Nahma Junction ○ **USA** (MI) 270-271 M 5
Nahmint ○ **CDN** (BC) 230-231 E 4
Naho ○ **SOL** 184 I e 3
Nahodka ○ **RUS** (JAN) 108-109 R 8
Nahodka ○ **RUS** (ROS) 122-123 E 7
Nahodka, buhta ≈ 108-109 P 8
Nahodka, ostrov ⌒ **RUS** 112-113 V 1
Nahoi, Cape = Cape Cumberland ▲ **VAN** 184 II a 2
Nahrin ○ **AFG** 136-137 L 6
Nahr Ouessel ~ **DZ** 190-191 C 3
Nahualate, Río ~ **GCA** 52-53 J 4
Nahuatzen ○ **MEX** 52-53 D 2
Nahuélbuta, Cordillera de ▲ **RCH** 78-79 C 5
Nahuélbuta, Parque Nacional ⊥ **RCH** 78-79 C 4
Nahuel Huapi ○ **RA** 78-79 D 6
Nahuel Huapi, Lago ⊖ **RA** 78-79 D 6
Nahuel Huapi, Parque Nacional ⊥ **RA** 78-79 D 6
Nahuel Mapá ○ **RA** 78-79 F 3
Nahum, Hefar ∴· **IL** 130-131 D 1
Nahunta ○ **USA** (GA) 284-285 J 5
Nahuo ○ **VRC** 156-157 G 6
Nahwitti ○ **CDN** (BC) 230-231 A 3
Nā'ī, an- ○ **KSA** 130-131 H 4
Nai, Mũi ▲ **VN** 158-159 H 5
Naiams Fort · **NAM** 220-221 C 3
Naica ○ **MEX** 50-51 G 4
Naicam ○ **CDN** (SAS) 232-233 O 3
Nā'id Abār ○ **KSA** 132-133 C 5
Nā'if al-'Āǧil ○ **IRQ** 128-129 L 7
Naihbawi ○ **IND** 142-143 H 4
Naij Tal ○ **VRC** 144-145 K 3
Naikliu ○ **RI** 166-167 B 6
Naikoon Provincial Park ⊥ **CDN** (BC) 228-229 C 3
Naila ○ **D** 92-93 L 3
Nailaga ○ **FJI** 184 III a 2
Naiman Qi ○ **VRC** 150-151 C 6
Nain ○ **CDN** 36-37 T 6
Nāin ○· **IR** 134-135 E 2
Naini Tāl ○· **IND** 138-139 G 5
Nainpur ○ **IND** 142-143 B 4
Naiopue ○ **MOC** 218-219 J 2
Nairai ⌒ **FJI** 184 III b 2
Nairn ○ **GB** 90-91 F 3
Nairobi ◘ **EAK** 212-213 F 4
Nairobi ★· **EAK** (NAI) 212-213 F 4
Nairobi National Park ⊥·· **EAK** 212-213 F 4
Nairoto ○ **MOC** 214-215 K 7
Naitaba ⌒ **FJI** 184 III c 2
Naivasha ○ **EAK** 212-213 F 4
Naivasha, Lake ⊖ **EAK** 212-213 F 4
Naiwangaa ○ **EAT** 214-215 K 5
Najahan ~ **RUS** 112-113 K 5
Najahanskaja guba ≈ 120-121 S 3
Najahanskij hrebet ▲ **RUS** 112-113 K 5
Najasa ~ **C** 54-55 G 4
Najba ○ **RUS** (SAH) 110-111 S 4
Najba ~ **RUS** 122-123 K 5
Nájera ○·· **E** 98-99 F 3
Najibābād ○ **IND** 138-139 G 5
Najtingejl, proliv ≈ 84-85 a 2
Najverga ~ **RUS** 118-119 G 6
Najzataš, pereval ▲ **TJ** 136-137 N 6
Nakadori-shima ⌒ **J** 152-153 C 8
Na Kae ○ **THA** 158-159 H 2
Nakagawa ○ **J** 152-153 K 2
Naka-gawa ~ **J** 152-153 J 6
Nakamoéka ○ **RCB** 210-211 D 6
Nakamura ○ **J** 152-153 E 8
Nakanai Mountains ▲ **PNG** 183 F 3
Nakanno ○ **RUS** 116-117 O 4
Nakano-shima ⌒ **J** (KGA) 152-153 C 10
Nakano-shima ⌒ **J** (SHM) 152-153 E 6
Nakasato ○ **J** 152-153 J 4
Naka-Shibetsu ○ **J** 152-153 L 3
Nakasongola ○ **EAU** 212-213 D 3
Naka-Tane ○ **J** 152-153 D 9
Nakatsu ○ **J** 152-153 D 8
Nakatsugawa ○ **J** 152-153 G 7
Nakchamik Island ⌒ **USA** 22-23 S 4
Naked Island ⌒ **USA** 20-21 R 6
Nakel = Nakło nad Notecią ○ **PL** 92-93 O 2
Nak'fa ○ **ER** 200-201 J 4
Nakhchyvan = Naxçıvan ☆ **AZ** 128-129 L 3
Nakhon Nayok ○ **THA** 158-159 F 3
Nakhon Pathom ○ **THA** 158-159 F 4
Nakhonphanon ○ **THA** 158-159 H 2
Nakhon Ratchasima ○ **THA** 158-159 G 3
Nakhon Sawan ○ **THA** 158-159 F 3
Nakhon Si Thammarat ○·· **THA** 158-159 E 6
Nakhon Thai ○ **THA** 158-159 F 2
Nakhtarāna ○ **IND** 138-139 B 8
Naki-Est ○ **RT** 202-203 L 4
Nakina ○ **CDN** (ONT) 236-237 B 2
Nakina ○ **USA** (NC) 282-283 J 6
Nakitoma ○ **EAU** 212-213 D 3
Nakivali, Lake ⊖ **EAU** 212-213 C 4
Nakkala ○ **CL** 140-141 J 7
Naknek ○ **USA** 22-23 S 3
Naknek Lake ⊖ **USA** 22-23 S 3
Nako ○ **BF** 202-203 J 4
Nakonde ○ **Z** 214-215 G 5
Nakong-Atinia ○ **GH** 202-203 K 4
Nakop ○ **NAM** 220-221 D 4
Nako-Tombetsu ○ **J** 152-153 K 2
Nakpanduri ○ **GH** 202-203 K 4
Nakpayili ○ **GH** 202-203 L 5
Nakskov ○ **DK** 86-87 E 9
Nakson, gora ▲ **RUS** 116-117 G 3
Naktong Gang ~ **ROK** 150-151 G 10
Nakum ∴ **GCA** 52-53 K 3
Nakuru ☆ **EAK** 212-213 F 4
Nakuru, Lake ⊖ **EAK** 212-213 F 4
Nakusp ○ **CDN** (BC) 230-231 M 3
Nāl ~ **PK** 134-135 L 5
Nalagāmula ○ **IND** 140-141 J 4
Nālāgarh ○ **IND** 138-139 F 4
Nalajh ○ **MAU** 148-149 H 4
Nalatale Ruins ∴· **ZW** 218-219 E 4
Nālatvād ○ **IND** 140-141 G 2
Naláží ○ **MOC** 220-221 L 2
Nalbarra ○ **AUS** 176-177 D 4

366 Mu'ò'ng Lạm — Nalbarra

Nalcayes, Isla ⌒ **RCH** 80 D 3
Nal'čik ☆• **RUS** 104 E 6
Naldrug o **IND** 140-141 G 2
Nalgonda o **IND** 140-141 H 2
Nali o **VRC** 156-157 F 6
Nalim'e, ozero ⊖ **RUS** 108-109 V 8
Nalim-Rassoha ∼ **RUS** 110-111 G 4
Nalimsk o **RUS** 110-111 d 6
Naliya o **IND** 138-139 B 8
Näljänkä o **FIN** 88-89 K 4
Nallıhan ☆ **TR** 128-129 D 2
Nalong o **MYA** 142-143 K 3
Nalusuku Pool < **Z** 218-219 B 3
Nälüt o **LAR** 190-191 H 5
Nama ∼ **NAM** 216-217 F 9
Nama o **RI** 166-167 F 4
Namaa, Tanjung ▲ **RI** 166-167 E 3
Namaacha o **MOC** 220-221 L 2
Namacunde o **ANG** 216-217 C 8
Namacurra o **MOC** 218-219 J 3
Namadgi National Park ⊥ **AUS** 180-181 K 3
Namadī, Daġ-e ⊖ **AFG** 134-135 J 2
Namai o **NEP** 144-145 D 7
Namak, Daryā-ye ⊖ **IR** 134-135 D 1
Namak, Kavir-e ⊖ **IR** 134-135 G 1
Namak, Kūh-e ▲▲ **IR** 134-135 D 4
Namakan ∼ **RUS** 108-109 a 6
Namak-e Sirğān, Kavir-e ⊖ **IR** 134-135 F 4
Namakia o **RM** 222-223 D 5
Nāmakkal o **IND** 140-141 H 5
Namaksār ⊖ **AFG** 134-135 J 2
Namaksar, Kāl-e ⊖ **IR** 134-135 J 1
Namakwaland ∸ **ZA** 220-221 C 4
Namaland ∸ **NAM** 220-221 C 3
Namana ∼ **RUS** 118-119 K 5
Namanga o **EAK** 212-213 F 5
Namangan o **UZ** 136-137 M 4
Namanganskaja oblast' □ **UZ** 136-137 M 4
Namanyere o **EAT** 214-215 F 4
Namao o **CDN** (ALB) 232-233 E 2
Namapa o **MOC** 218-219 K 1
Namaponda o **MOC** 218-219 K 2
Namarrói o **MOC** 218-219 J 2
Namas o **RI** 166-167 L 4
Namasagali o **EAU** 212-213 D 3
Namasale o **EAU** 212-213 D 3
Namassi o **CI** 202-203 J 6
Namatanai o **PNG** 183 G 2
Namatote, Pulau ⌒ **RI** 166-167 G 3
Namba o **ANG** 216-217 C 5
Nambazo o **MW** 218-219 H 2
Nambe Indian Reservation X **USA** (NM) 256-257 K 3
Namber o **RI** 166-167 H 2
Nambi o **AUS** 176-177 F 4
Nambikwara, Área Indígena X **BR** 70-71 H 3
Nambilma, Tanjung ▲ **RI** 166-167 H 4
Nambolaki, Pulau ⌒ **RI** 168 E 6
Namboukaha o **CI** 202-203 H 5
Nambour o **AUS** 178-179 M 4
Nambuangongo o **ANG** 216-217 C 4
Nambucca Heads o **AUS** 178-179 M 6
Nambung National Park ⊥ **AUS** 176-177 C 5
Namche Bazar o **NEP** 144-145 F 7
Nam Chon Reservoir < **THA** 158-159 E 3
Namco o **VRC** 144-145 H 5
Nam Co ⊖ **VRC** (XIZ) 144-145 H 5
Nam Co • **VRC** (XIZ) 144-145 H 5
Namcy ☆• **RUS** 118-119 O 4
Nam ĐDinh o **VN** 156-157 E 6
Nam Du, Quần Đảo ⌒ **VN** 158-159 H 6
Namen = Namur ☆• **B** 92-93 H 3
Namenalala ⌒ **FJI** 184 III b 2
Nametil o **MOC** 218-219 K 2
Namgorab ▲▲ **NAM** 220-221 C 2
Namhae Do ⌒ **ROK** 150-151 F 10
Namhan Gang ∼ **ROK** 150-151 F 9
Nami o **MAL** 162-163 D 1
Namialo o **MOC** 218-219 K 2
Namib Desert = Namibwoestyn ∸ **NAM** 216-217 B 9
Namibe □ **ANG** 216-217 B 7
Namibe ☆• **ANG** (NAM) 216-217 B 7
Namibe, Deserto de ∸ **ANG** 216-217 A 8
Namibe, Reserva de ⊥ **ANG** 216-217 B 7
Namibia ■ **NAM** 216-217 C 10
Namib-Naukluft Park ⊥ **NAM** 220-221 B 2
Namibwoestyn = Namib Desert ∸ **NAM** 216-217 B 9
Namidobe o **MOC** 218-219 J 3
Namie o **J** 152-153 J 6
Namies o **ZA** 220-221 D 4
Namin o **IR** 128-129 N 3
Namina o **MOC** 218-219 K 2
Namioka o **J** 152-153 J 4
Namiquipa o **MEX** 50-51 F 3
Namiroe, Rio ∼ **MOC** 218-219 K 2
Namitete o **MW** 218-219 G 2
Namjagbarwa Feng ▲ **VRC** 144-145 K 6
Namlan o **MYA** 142-143 K 4
Namlea o **RI** 166-167 D 3
Nam Léa, Mount ▲ **K** 158-159 J 4
Namling o **VRC** 144-145 G 6
Nam Ngum Reservoir ⊖ **LAO** 156-157 C 7
Namo o **RI** 164-165 F 4
Namoda, Kaura- o **WAN** 198-199 C 6
Namoi River ∼ **AUS** 178-179 K 6
Namon o **RT** 202-203 L 5
Namor o **BR** 66-67 F 6
Namorona o **RM** 222-223 F 8
Nam Ou ∼ **LAO** 156-157 C 6
Namous, Oued ∼ **DZ** 190-191 D 3
Nampa o **USA** (ID) 252-253 B 3
Nampagan o **MYA** 142-143 J 3
Nampala o **RMM** 202-203 H 2
Nam Pat o **THA** 158-159 F 2
Nampevo o **MOC** 218-219 J 3
Nampo o **KOR** 150-151 E 8
Nam Poon o **THA** 142-143 M 6
Nampuecha o **MOC** 218-219 L 1
Nampula □ **MOC** 218-219 K 2
Nampula ☆ **MOC** (Nam) 218-219 K 2
Namrole o **RI** 166-167 D 3
Namru o **VRC** 144-145 C 5
Namslau = Namysłów o• **PL** 92-93 O 3
Namsos o **N** 86-87 E 4
Namsse La ▲ **VRC** 144-145 D 6
Namsskogan o **N** 86-87 F 4
Namtabung o **RI** 166-167 F 6
Namtha o **MYA** 142-143 J 3
Nam Theun o **LAO** 158-159 H 2
Nam Tok Chat Trakan National Park ⊥ **THA** 158-159 F 2
Nam Trâm, Mũi ▲ **VN** 158-159 K 3
Namtu o **MYA** 142-143 K 4
Namtumbo o **EAT** 214-215 J 6
Namu o **CDN** (BC) 230-231 B 2
Namudi o **PNG** 183 E 5
Namuiranga o **MOC** 214-215 L 6
Namukumbo o **Z** 218-219 D 2
Namuli, Monte ▲ **MOC** 218-219 J 2
Namuno o **MOC** 218-219 K 1
Nam Un Reservoir ⊖ **THA** 158-159 G 2
Namur ☆• **B** 92-93 H 3
Namur o **CDN** (QUE) 238-239 L 3
Namur Lake ⊖ **CDN** 32-33 O 3
Namur Lake Indian Reserve X **CDN** 32-33 O 3
Nāmūs, Wāw an o **LAR** 192-193 G 5
Namutoni o **NAM** 216-217 D 9
Namwaan, Pulau ⌒ **RI** 166-167 F 5
Namwala o **Z** 218-219 D 2
Namwera o **MW** 218-219 H 2
Namwŏn o **ROK** 150-151 F 10
Namy o **RUS** 110-111 T 5
Namyldžylah ∼ **RUS** 118-119 K 5
Namyndykan ∼ **RUS** 112-113 K 4
Namysłów o• **PL** 92-93 O 3
Nan o **THA** 142-143 M 6
Nan, Sa o **THA** 142-143 M 6
Nana o **CAM** 206-207 B 5
Nana ∼ **RCA** 206-207 B 6
Nana Bakassa o **RCA** (OUH) 206-207 C 5
Nana Bakassa ∼ **RCA** 206-207 C 5
Nana Barya ∼ **TCH** 206-207 C 5
Nana Barya, Réserve de la ⊥ **RCA** 206-207 C 5
Nana Candundo o **ANG** 214-215 B 6
Nanae o **J** 152-153 J 4
Nanafalia o **USA** (AL) 284-285 C 4
Nana-Grébizi □ **RCA** 206-207 D 5
Nanaimo o **CDN** (BC) 230-231 F 4
Nanakuli o **USA** (HI) 288 G 3
Nana-Mambéré □ **RCA** 206-207 B 6
Nanambinia o **AUS** 176-177 G 6
Nana Museum of the Arctic • **USA** 20-21 J 3
Nanango o **AUS** 178-179 L 4
Nananu-i-ra ⌒ **FJI** 184 III b 2
Nanao o **J** 152-153 G 6
Nan'ao Dao ⌒ **VRC** 156-157 K 5
Nanase o **PNG** 183 B 4
Nanay, Río ∼ **PE** 64-65 F 3
Nanbu o **VRC** 154-155 E 6
Nancay, Arroyo ∼ **RA** 78-79 K 2
Nance Creek ∼ **USA** 284-285 C 2
Nancha o **VRC** 150-151 G 4
Nanchang ☆• **VRC** 156-157 J 2
Nancheng o **VRC** 156-157 K 3
Nanchital o **MEX** 52-53 G 2
Nanchititla, Parque Natural ⊥ **MEX** 52-53 D 2
Nanchong o **VRC** 154-155 E 6
Nanchuan o **VRC** 156-157 E 2
Nancowry Island ⌒ **IND** 140-141 L 6
Nancy ☆••• **F** 90-91 L 7
Nanda Devi ▲••• **IND** 144-145 B 5
Nandaime o **NIC** 52-53 L 6
Nandalūr o **IND** 140-141 H 3
Nandaly o **AUS** 180-181 G 3
Nandan o **VRC** 156-157 E 4
Nanded o **IND** 138-139 F 10
Nandewar Range ▲▲ **AUS** 178-179 L 6
Nāndghāt o **IND** 142-143 B 5
Nandi o **ZW** 218-219 F 5
Nandigāma o **IND** 140-141 J 2
Nandi Hills o• **IND** 140-141 G 4
Nandikotkūr o **IND** 140-141 H 3
Nanding Hê ∼ **VRC** 142-143 L 4
Nandipadu o **IND** 140-141 H 3
Nandom o **GH** 202-203 J 4
Nandouta o **RT** 202-203 L 5
Nandowrie P.O. o **AUS** 178-179 J 3
Nāndūra o **IND** 138-139 F 9
Nandurbār o **IND** 138-139 E 9
Nandyal o **IND** 140-141 H 3
Nanfeng o **VRC** 156-157 K 3
Nangade o **MOC** 214-215 K 6
Nanga Eboko o **CAM** 204-205 K 6
Nangah Ketungau o **RI** 162-163 J 4
Nangah Pinoh o **RI** 162-163 J 5
Nangah Sokan o **RI** 162-163 J 5
Nangalala X **AUS** 174-175 C 3
Nanganga o **EAT** 214-215 K 6
Nanga Parbat ▲ **PK** 138-139 E 2
Nangarhār □ **AFG** 138-139 C 2
Nangaroro o **RI** 168 E 7
Nanga Tamin o **MAL** 162-163 K 3
Nanga Tayap o **RI** 162-163 J 5
Nangbéto o **RT** 202-203 L 6
Nangbéto, Retenue de < **RT** 202-203 L 6
Nang'egan ∼ **RUS** 114-115 L 3
Nangin o **MYA** 158-159 E 5
Nango o **J** 152-153 D 8
Nangolet o **SUD** 208-209 A 6
Nangomba o **EAT** 214-215 K 6
Nangong o **VRC** 154-155 J 3
Nangqên o **VRC** 144-145 L 4
Nang Rong o **THA** 158-159 G 3
Nānguneri o **IND** 140-141 G 6
Nangurukuru o **EAT** 214-215 K 5
Nanguruwe o **EAT** 214-215 L 6
Nang Xian o **VRC** 144-145 J 6
Nan Hai ≈ 156-157 J 6
Nanhua o **RC** 156-157 M 5
Nanhua o **VRC** 156-157 B 4
Nanhui o **VRC** 154-155 M 6
Nanika Lake ⊖ **CDN** (BC) 228-229 G 3
Nanjangud o• **IND** 140-141 G 4
Nanjian o **VRC** 142-143 M 3
Nanjiang o **VRC** 154-155 E 5
Nanjing ☆• **VRC** 154-155 L 5
Nanjirinji o **EAT** 214-215 K 5
Nankāna Sāhib o **PK** 138-139 D 4
Nankang o **VRC** (GXI) 156-157 F 6
Nankang o **VRC** (JXI) 156-157 J 4
Nanking = Nanjing ☆• **VRC** 154-155 L 5
Nankoku o **J** 152-153 E 8
Nankova o **ANG** 216-217 E 8
Nankunshan • **VRC** 156-157 H 5
Nanle o **VRC** 154-155 J 3
Nanling o **VRC** 154-155 L 6
Nan Ling ▲▲ **VRC** 156-157 G 4
Nanlixa o **MOC** 218-219 J 1
Nannine o **AUS** 176-177 E 3
Nanning ☆ **VRC** 156-157 F 5
Nannup o **AUS** 176-177 C 6
Nano ∼ **DY** 204-205 E 4
Nanoose Bay o **CDN** (BC) 230-231 E 4
Nanoro o **BF** 202-203 J 3
Nanortalik o **GRØ** 28-29 S 6
Nanortalik Banke ≃ 28-29 R 6
Nanosnyj, ostrov ⌒ **RUS** 110-111 X 1
Nanpan Jiang ∼ **VRC** 156-157 D 4
Nanpara o **IND** 142-143 B 2
Nanpeng Liedao ⌒ **VRC** 156-157 K 5
Nanping o **VRC** (FUJ) 156-157 L 3
Nanping o **VRC** (HUN) 156-157 H 2
Nansebo o **ETH** 208-209 D 5
Nansei-shotō ⌒ **J** 152-153 B 11
Nansen, Kap ▲ **GRØ** (ØGR) 26-27 r 4
Nansen, Kap ▲ **GRØ** (ØGR) 28-29 a 2
Nansen, Mount ▲ **CDN** 20-21 W 5
Nansena, ostrov ⌒ **RUS** (ARH) 84-85 d 2
Nansena, ostrov ⌒ **RUS** (TMR) 108-109 Z 3
Nansen Fjord ≈ 28-29 a 2
Nansen Gletscher ⊂ **GRØ** 26-27 V 6
Nansen Land ∸ **GRØ** 26-27 c 2
Nansen Sound ≈ 26-27 E 3
Nanshan Island ⌒ 160-161 A 7
Nanshui SK ⊖ **VRC** 156-157 H 4
Nansio o **EAT** 212-213 D 5
Nantahala Mountains ▲▲ **USA** 282-283 D 5
Nantais, Lac ⊖ **CDN** 36-37 M 4
Nantamba o **PNG** 183 F 3
Nantes ☆• **F** 90-91 G 8
Nanticoke River ∼ **USA** 280-281 L 5
Nanton o **CDN** (ALB) 232-233 E 5
Nanton o **GH** 202-203 K 5
Nantong o **VRC** 154-155 M 5
Nantong (Jinsha) o **VRC** 154-155 M 5
Nantou o **RC** 156-157 M 5
Nantucket o **USA** (MA) 278-279 L 7
Nantucket Island ⌒ **USA** (MA) 278-279 L 7
Nantucket Shoals ≈ 46-47 N 5
Nantucket Shoals ≈ 278-279 L 7
Nantulo o **MOC** 214-215 K 7
Nanuku Passage ≈ 184 III c 2
Nanumea ⌒ **TUV** 13 J 3
Nanuque o **BR** 72-73 K 4
Nanūr o **IR** 128-129 M 5
Nanusa, Kepulauan ⌒ **RI** 164-165 K 1
Nanutarra Roadhouse o **AUS** 172-173 B 7
Nan Xian o **VRC** 156-157 H 2
Nanxiao o **VRC** 156-157 F 5
Nanxijiang • **VRC** 156-157 M 2
Nanxiong o **VRC** 156-157 J 4
Nanxu o **VRC** 156-157 G 4
Nanyamba o **EAT** 214-215 K 6
Nanyang o **VRC** 154-155 H 5
Nanyang Hu ∼ **VRC** 154-155 K 4
Nanyi Hu ⊖ **VRC** 154-155 L 6
Nan-yō o **J** 152-153 J 5
Nanyuki o **EAK** 212-213 F 3
Nanzhai o **VRC** 156-157 F 3
Nanzhang o **VRC** 154-155 G 6
Nanzhao o **VRC** 154-155 H 5
Nanzhila o **Z** (SOU) 218-219 C 3
Nanzhila ∼ **Z** 218-219 D 3
Nao, Cabo de la ▲ **E** 98-99 H 5
Naococane, Lac ⊖ **CDN** 38-39 J 2
Naogaon o **BD** 142-143 F 3
Não-me-Toque o **BR** 74-75 D 7
Náoussa o **GR** 100-101 J 4
Napa o **USA** (CA) 246-247 C 5
Napabale Lagoon ∸•• **RI** 164-165 H 6
Napacao Point ▲ **RP** 160-161 F 8
Napadogan o **CDN** (NB) 240-241 J 4
Napaha o **MOC** 218-219 K 1
Napaiskak o **USA** 20-21 K 6
Napaleofú, Arroyo ∼ **RA** 78-79 K 4
Napanee o **CDN** (ONT) 238-239 J 4
Napanwainami o **RI** 166-167 H 3
Napan-yaur o **RI** 166-167 H 3
Napas o **RUS** 114-115 R 5
Napassorssuaq Fjord ≈ 28-29 T 6
Napatok Bay ≈ 36-37 S 6
Napavine o **USA** (WA) 244-245 B 4
Napeitom o **EAK** 212-213 F 3
Naper o **USA** (NE) 262-263 G 2
Napido o **RI** 166-167 H 2
Napier o **NZ** 182 F 3
Napier o **ZA** 220-221 D 7
Napier, Mount ▲ **AUS** 172-173 J 4
Napier Broome Bay ≈ 172-173 H 3
Napier Downs o **AUS** 172-173 G 4
Napier Mountains ▲▲ **ARK** 16 G 6
Napier Peninsula ∪ **AUS** 174-175 C 3
Napier Range ▲▲ **AUS** 172-173 G 4
Napierville o **CDN** (QUE) 238-239 M 3
Napinka o **CDN** (MAN) 234-235 C 5
Naples o **USA** (FL) 286-287 H 5
Naples o **USA** (ID) 250-251 C 3
Naples o **USA** (NY) 278-279 D 6
Naples o **USA** (SD) 260-261 J 2
Naples o **USA** (TX) 264-265 K 5
Naples = Nápoli ☆••• **I** 100-101 E 4
Napo o **VRC** 156-157 D 5
Napo, Río ∼ **PE** 64-65 F 3
Napoca, Cluj- ☆• **RO** 102-103 C 4
Napoleon o **USA** (IN) 274-275 N 5
Napoleon o **USA** (ND) 258-259 H 5
Napoleon o **USA** (OH) 280-281 B 2
Napoleonville o **USA** (LA) 268-269 J 7
Nápoli ☆••• **I** 100-101 E 4
Nápoli, Golfo di ≈ 100-101 E 4
Napoopoo o **USA** (HI) 288 K 5
Nappa Merrie o **AUS** 178-179 F 4
Napperby o **AUS** 172-173 L 7
Nappernee o **USA** (IN) 274-275 M 3
Naqa, Temples of •• **SUD** 200-201 F 4
Naqāda o **ET** 194-195 F 5
Naqade o• **IR** 128-129 L 4
Naqb, Ra's an- o **JOR** 130-131 D 2
Nār, Umm an- o **UAE** 134-135 F 6
Nara o **AUS** 174-175 G 6
Nara ☆•• **J** 152-153 F 7
Nara o **RMM** 202-203 G 2
Narač o **BY** 94-95 K 4
Nāra Canal < **PK** 138-139 B 6
Naracoorte o **AUS** 180-181 F 4
Naracoorte Caves Conservation Park ⊥ **AUS** 180-181 F 4
Naradhan o **AUS** 180-181 J 2
Naraini o **IND** 142-143 B 3
Nārāinpur o **IND** 142-143 B 6
Nārājankher o **IND** 138-139 F 10
Naramata o **CDN** (BC) 230-231 K 4
Naran o **PK** 138-139 D 2
Naran = Hongor o **MAU** 148-149 L 5
Narandiba o **BR** 72-73 E 7
Naranjal o **EC** 64-65 C 3
Naranjito o **EC** 64-65 C 3
Naranjo ∴• **GCA** 52-53 K 3
Naranjo o **MEX** 50-51 E 5
Naranjos o **MEX** 50-51 L 7
Narao o **J** 152-153 C 8
Narasannapeta o **IND** 142-143 D 6
Narasapuram o **IND** 140-141 J 2
Narasaraopet o **IND** 140-141 J 2
Narasimharajapura o **IND** 140-141 F 4
Narataj o **RUS** 116-117 K 8
Narathiwat ☆ **THA** 158-159 F 7
Nara Visa o **USA** (NM) 256-257 M 3
Naravuka o **FJI** 184 III b 2
Narayangadh o **NEP** 144-145 E 7
Narāyangaon o **IND** 138-139 D 10
Nārāyangarh o **IND** 138-139 E 8
Narbonne o **F** 90-91 J 10
Narcisse o **CDN** (MAN) 234-235 F 4
Narcondan Island ⌒ **IND** 158-159 C 4
Narcosli Creek ∼ **CDN** 228-229 M 4
Narding River ∼ **CDN** 24-25 N 6
Naré o **RA** 76-77 G 6
Nareči, ostrov ⌒ **RUS** 108-109 O 8
Narega Island ⌒ **PNG** 183 E 3
Naregal o **IND** 140-141 F 3
Narembeen o **AUS** 176-177 E 6
Naréna o **RMM** 202-203 F 3
Nares Abyssal Plain ≃ 6-7 C 6
Nares Land ∸ **GRØ** 26-27 b 2
Nares Stræde ≈ 26-27 O 4
Narew o **PL** 92-93 R 2
Narew ∼ **PL** 92-93 Q 2
Nargund o **IND** 140-141 F 3
Nari ∼ **PK** 134-135 M 4
Nāri ∼ **PK** 134-135 M 4
Narib o **NAM** 220-221 C 2
Narijn gol ∼ **MAU** 116-117 F 10
Narijnteel = Cagaan-Ovoo o **MAU** 148-149 E 5
Narimanov ☆ **RUS** 96-97 E 10
Narinda, Helodrano ≈ 222-223 E 5
Narin Nur o **VRC** 154-155 F 2
Narita o• **J** 152-153 J 7
Nar'jan-Mar ☆ **RUS** 88-89 W 3
Narkatiaganj o **IND** 142-143 D 2
Narmada ∼ **IND** 138-139 D 9
Narmajaha ∼ **RUS** 108-109 L 7
Nārnaul o **IND** 138-139 F 5
Narndee o **AUS** 176-177 E 4
Narob ∼ **NAM** 220-221 C 2
Naroda ∼ **RUS** 114-115 F 2
Narodnaja, gora ▲ **RUS** 114-115 F 2
Národní park Šumava ⊥ **CZ** 92-93 M 4
Naro-Fominsk ☆• **RUS** 94-95 P 4
Naro Island ⌒ **RP** 160-161 E 7
Narok o **EAK** 212-213 E 4
Naro Moru o **EAK** 212-213 F 4
Narooma o **AUS** 180-181 L 4
Nārowāl o **PK** 138-139 E 3
Narrabri o **AUS** 178-179 K 6
Narracoota o **AUS** 176-177 E 2
Narragansett Bay ≈ 46-47 N 5
Narragansett Bay ≈ 278-279 K 7
Narrandera o **AUS** 180-181 J 3
Narran Lake ⊖ **AUS** 178-179 J 5
Narran River ∼ **AUS** 178-179 J 5
Narraway River ∼ **CDN** 228-229 O 2
Narrien Range ▲▲ **AUS** 178-179 J 2
Narrogin o **AUS** 176-177 D 6
Narromine o **AUS** 180-181 K 2
Narrow Cape ▲ **USA** 22-23 U 4
Narrows o **USA** (VA) 280-281 F 6
Narrowsburg o **USA** (NY) 280-281 L 2
Narrows Indian Reserve, The X **CDN** (MAN) 234-235 E 3
Narryer, Mount ▲ **AUS** 176-177 D 3
Narsalik o **GRØ** 28-29 Q 6
Narsampet o **IND** 140-141 H 2
Narsaq Kujalleg = Frederiksdal o **GRØ** 28-29 S 6
Narsarsuaq o **GRØ** 28-29 S 6
Narsimhapur o **IND** 138-139 G 8
Narsinghgarh o **IND** 138-139 F 8
Narsipatnam o **IND** 142-143 C 7
Narssaq o **GRØ** 28-29 P 5
Nart o **VRC** 148-149 M 6
Narubis o **NAM** 220-221 D 3
Naru-shima ⌒ **J** 152-153 C 8
Naruto o **J** 152-153 F 7
Narva o• **EST** 94-95 L 2
Narva o **RUS** 116-117 F 8
Narva laht ≈ 94-95 K 2
Narvik o•• **N** 86-87 H 2
Narvskoe vodohranilišče < **RUS** 94-95 L 2
Narwietooma o **AUS** 176-177 M 1
Nary hrebet ▲▲ **RUS** 96-97 K 6
Naryilco o **AUS** 178-179 F 5
Naryn o **KS** 146-147 B 5
Naryn ∼ **KS** 136-137 N 4
Naryn ∼ **KS** 146-147 B 5
Naryn ∼ **KZ** 124-125 J 6
Naryn o **RUS** (TUV) 116-117 G 10
Naryn ∼ **RUS** 116-117 G 10
Naryn-Huduk o **RUS** 126-127 G 5
Naryntau, hrebet ▲▲ **KS** 146-147 C 5
Na'sān, Umm ⌒ **BRN** 134-135 D 5
Nasanabad o **IND** 138-139 G 10
Nasarawa o **WAN** 198-199 B 6
Nasa Test Site xx **USA** (MS) 268-269 L 6
Năsăud o **RO** 102-103 D 4
Naschitti o **USA** (NM) 256-257 G 2
Naselle o **USA** (WA) 244-245 B 4
Nash Harbor o **USA** 20-21 G 6
Nāshik o **IND** 138-139 D 10
Nashino, Río ∼ **EC** 64-65 D 2
Nashū', Wādī an ∼ **LAR** 192-193 E 4
Nashua o **USA** (IA) 274-275 F 2
Nashua o **USA** (MT) 250-251 N 3
Nashua o **USA** (NH) 278-279 K 6
Nashville o **USA** (AR) 276-277 B 7
Nashville o **USA** (GA) 284-285 G 5
Nashville o **USA** (IL) 274-275 J 6
Nashville o **USA** (IN) 274-275 M 5
Nashville o **USA** (KS) 262-263 H 7
Nashville o **USA** (MI) 272-273 D 5
Nashville o **USA** (NC) 282-283 K 5
Nashville ☆• **USA** (TN) 276-277 J 4
Nashville Basin ∪ **USA** 276-277 J 4
Nashwaak o **CDN** (NB) 240-241 J 4
Nashwaak Bridge o **CDN** (NB) 240-241 J 4
Nashwaak River ∼ **CDN** 240-241 J 4
Nashwauk o **USA** (MN) 270-271 E 3
Nasia o **GH** (NOR) 202-203 K 4
Nasia ∼ **GH** 202-203 K 4
Našice o **HR** 100-101 G 2
Näsijärvi ⊖ **FIN** 88-89 G 6
Nasikonis, Tanjung ▲ **RI** 166-167 B 6
Nasipit o **RP** 160-161 F 8
Nāṣir o **SUD** 208-209 A 4
Nāṣir, Buḥairat < **ET** 194-195 F 6
Nasirābād o **IR** 136-137 G 7
Nasirābād o **PK** 134-135 K 5
Nasirābād o **PK** 138-139 B 5
Nāṣirah, Bi'r < **LAR** 192-193 D 2
Nāṣiriya, an- ☆ **IRQ** 128-129 M 7
Nāṣiriya, an- ☆ **IRQ** 130-131 K 2
Naṣiya, Ğabal ▲ **ET** 194-195 F 6
Naskaupi River ∼ **CDN** 36-37 T 7
Nasmah o **LAR** 192-193 E 2
Nasolot National Reservoir ⊥ **EAK** 212-213 E 3
Nasondoye o **ZRE** 214-215 G 6
Nasorolevu ▲ **FJI** 184 III b 2
Nāsriganj o **IND** 142-143 D 3
Naṣriyān o **IR** 134-135 B 2
Nassarawa o **WAN** 204-205 G 4
Nassau ★•• **BS** 54-55 G 2
Nassau, Bahía ≈ 80 G 7
Nassau River ∼ **AUS** 174-175 F 4
Nassau River ∼ **USA** 286-287 H 1
Nassau Sound ≈ 286-287 H 1
Nass Basin ∸ **CDN** 32-33 F 3
Nasser, Lake = Buḥairat Nāṣir < **ET** 194-195 F 6
Nasser, Lake = Nāṣir, Buḥairat < **ET** 194-195 F 6
Nassian o **CI** (BOA) 202-203 J 5
Nassian o **CI** (FER) 202-203 H 5
Nassoukou o **DY** 202-203 L 4
Nass River ∼ **CDN** 32-33 F 4
Nastapoka, Rivière ∼ **CDN** 36-37 L 6
Nastapoka Islands ⌒ **CDN** 36-37 L 6
Nastapoka Sound ≈ 36-37 L 6
Nasugbu o **RP** 160-161 D 5
Nasuraghena o **SOL** 184 I f 4
Nasva o **RUS** 94-95 M 3
Nata o•• **PA** 52-53 D 7
Nata o **RB** (CEN) 218-219 D 5
Nata ∼ **RB** 218-219 D 5
Nataboti o **RI** 166-167 D 3
Natal o **BR** (TOC) 68-69 D 4
Natal ☆ **BR** (RNO) 68-69 L 4
Natal o **CDN** (BC) 230-231 P 4
Natal o **RI** 162-163 C 4
Natal Basin = Mozambique Basin ≃ 9 G 8
Natalia o **USA** (TX) 266-267 J 4
Natalii, buhta ≈ 112-113 R 6
Natal Ridge = Mozambique Plateau ≃ 9 G 9
Natalschwelle ≃ 220-221 M 6
Natal Valley ≃ 9 G 9
Naṭanz o• **IR** 134-135 D 2
Natar o **RI** 162-163 F 7
Natara ∼ **RUS** 110-111 P 5
Nataš, Wādī ∼ **ET** 194-195 F 5
Natashquan o **CDN** (QUE) 242-243 G 2
Natashquan, Pointe de ▲ **CDN** (QUE) 242-243 G 2
Natashquan, Rivière ∼ **CDN** 38-39 O 3
Natashquan River ∼ **CDN** 38-39 N 2
Natchamba o **RT** 202-203 L 5
Natchez o **USA** (MS) 268-269 J 5
Natchez Trace Parkway • **USA** (MS) 268-269 K 4
Natchez Trace Parkway • **USA** (TN) 276-277 H 5
Natchez Trace State Park ⊥ **USA** (TN) 276-277 G 5
Natchitoches o **USA** (LA) 268-269 G 5
Nate o **IND** 140-141 E 2
Natewa Bay ≈ 184 III b 2
Nathahu o **MYA** 158-159 C 2
Nathalia o **AUS** 180-181 H 4
Nathan o **USA** (AR) 276-277 B 6
Nathan River o **AUS** 174-175 C 4
Na Thawi o **THA** 158-159 F 7
Nāthdwāra o **IND** 138-139 D 7
Nathenje o **MW** 218-219 G 2
Nathia Gali o **PK** 138-139 D 2
Nathon o **THA** 158-159 E 6
Nathorst Land ∸ **GRØ** 26-27 m 7
Nathorst Land ∸ **N** 84-85 J 4
Nathrop o **USA** (CO) 254-255 J 5
Natiaboani o **BF** 202-203 L 4
Natingui o **BR** 74-75 E 5
Nation o **USA** 20-21 U 4
National Bison Range ⊥ **USA** (MT) 250-251 E 4
National City o **USA** (CA) 248-249 G 7
National Parachute Test Range • **USA** (CA) 248-249 J 7
National Park o **NZ** 182 E 3
Nationalpark Bayerischer Wald ⊥ **D** 92-93 M 4
Nationalpark Berchtesgaden ⊥ **D** 92-93 M 5
Nationalpark Hochharz ⊥ **D** 92-93 L 3
Nationalpark i Nørdgrønland og Østgrønland ⊥ **GRØ** 26-27 e 5
Nationalpark Niedersächsisches Wattenmeer ⊥ **D** 92-93 J 2
Nationalpark Sächsische Schweiz ⊥ **D** 92-93 N 3
Nationalpark Schleswig-Holsteinisches Wattenmeer ⊥ **D** 92-93 K 1
Nationalpark Vorpommersche Boddenlandschaft ⊥ **D** 92-93 M 1
National Reactor Testing Station xx **USA** (ID) 252-253 F 3
Nation River ∼ **CDN** 32-33 H 4
Natitingou ☆ **DY** 202-203 L 4
Natityay, Ğabal ▲ **ET** 194-195 G 6
Natividade o **BR** 68-69 E 7
Natkusiak Peninsula ∪ **CDN** 24-25 R 4
Natla River ∼ **CDN** 30-31 E 4
Natmauk o **MYA** 142-143 J 5
Natong Kuangqu o **VRC** 156-157 E 2
Nator o **BD** 142-143 F 3
Natovi o **FJI** 184 III b 2
Nat River ∼ **CDN** 236-237 F 4
Natron, Lake ⊖ **EAT** 212-213 F 5
Natrona o **USA** (WY) 252-253 M 3
Naṭrūn, Wādī n- ∼ **ET** 194-195 E 2
Nattam o **IND** 140-141 H 5
Nattavaara station o **S** 86-87 K 3
Natukanaoka Pan ⊖ **NAM** 216-217 C 9
Natuna, Laut ≈ 162-163 G 3
Natuna Besar, Pulau ⌒ **RI** 162-163 H 2
Natural Arch ∴ **USA** (KY) 276-277 L 4
Natural Bridge o **USA** (AL) 284-285 C 2
Natural Bridge ∴ **USA** (AL) 284-285 C 2
Natural Bridge • **USA** (FL) 286-287 E 1
Natural Bridges ∴ **USA** (TN) 276-277 H 5
Natural Bridges National Monument ∴ **USA** (UT) 254-255 F 6
Natural Bridge State Monument • **USA** (MT) 250-251 J 6
Natural Dam Salt Lake ⊖ **USA** (TX) 264-265 C 6
Naturaliste, Cape ▲ **AUS** (TAS) 180-181 K 6
Naturaliste, Cape ▲ **AUS** (WA) 176-177 C 6
Naturaliste Plateau ≃ 176-177 B 6
Naturita o **USA** (CO) 254-255 G 5
Nau o **TJ** 136-137 L 4
Nauabu o **PNG** 183 F 6
Nauarai, Bi'r o **SUD** 200-201 G 2
Nauari o **BR** 62-63 G 5
Naubise o **NEP** 144-145 E 7
Nauchas o **NAM** 220-221 C 1
Naudesberg Pass ▲ **ZA** 220-221 G 6
Naudesnek ▲ **ZA** 220-221 J 5
Nauela o **MOC** 218-219 J 2
Naufal le-Chateau o **IR** 134-135 D 1
Naufrage o **CDN** (NS) 240-241 N 4
Naugarh o **IND** 142-143 C 2
Naujan o **RP** 160-161 D 6
Naujan Lake ⊖ **RP** 160-161 D 6
Naukot o **PK** 138-139 B 7
Naulila o **ANG** 216-217 C 8
Naul'jaha ∼ **RUS** 108-109 H 7
Naumatang o **RI** 166-167 D 5
Naumburg (Saale) o• **D** 92-93 L 3
Nauna Island ⌒ **PNG** 183 E 2
Naungmo o **MYA** 142-143 J 3
Nauru ⌒ **NAU** 13 H 3
Naushahro Firoz o **PK** 138-139 B 6
Nausori o **FJI** 184 III b 3
Nauta o **PE** 64-65 F 4
Nautanwa o **IND** 142-143 C 2
Nautilus, Selat ≈ 166-167 G 4
Nautimuk o **AUS** 180-181 F 4
Nautla o **MEX** 52-53 F 1
Nautsi o **RUS** 88-89 K 2
Nauvoo o **USA** (AL) 284-285 C 3
Nāv o **IR** 128-129 N 4
Nava o **MEX** 50-51 J 3
Nava ∼ **ZRE** 212-213 A 2
Nava de Ricomalillo, La o **E** 98-99 E 5
Navahrudak ☆ **BY** 94-95 J 5
Navahrudskae uzvyšša ▲▲ **BY** 94-95 J 5
Navajo o **USA** (AZ) 256-257 F 3
Navajo o **USA** (NM) 256-257 G 3
Navajo City o **USA** (NM) 256-257 H 2
Navajo Indian Reservation X **USA** (AZ) 256-257 D 2
Navajo Mountain ▲ **USA** (UT) 254-255 E 6
Navajo National Monument ∴ **USA** (AZ) 256-257 E 2
Navajo Reservoir < **USA** (NM) 256-257 H 2
Naval o **RP** 160-161 F 7
Navalmoral de la Mata o **E** 98-99 E 5
Navalmorales, Los o **E** 98-99 E 5
Navan = An Uaimh o **IRL** 90-91 D 5
Navapara o **BD** 142-143 F 4
Navapolack ☆•• **BY** 94-95 L 4
Navapur o **IND** 138-139 D 9
Navarin, mys ▲ **RUS** 112-113 U 5
Navarino, Isla ⌒ **RCH** 80 G 7
Navarino, Pico ▲ **RCH** 80 G 7
Navarra □ **E** 98-99 F 3
Navarre o **AUS** 180-181 G 4
Navarre o **CDN** (ALB) 232-233 E 3
Navarre o **USA** (FL) 286-287 C 1
Navarro o **RA** 78-79 K 3
Navarro o **USA** (CA) 246-247 B 4
Navarro Mills Lake < **USA** (TX) 266-267 L 2
Navas, Las o **RP** 160-161 F 6
Navašino o **RUS** 94-95 S 4
Navasota o **USA** (TX) 266-267 L 3
Navasota River ∼ **USA** 266-267 L 3
Navassa Island ⌒ **USA** 54-55 H 5
Nāve o **AFG** 134-135 M 2
Navere o **RI** 166-167 K 3
Navia o **E** 98-99 D 3
Navidad Bank ≃ 54-55 L 4
Navidad River ∼ **USA** 266-267 L 4
Naviraí o **BR** 76-77 K 2
Naviti ⌒ **FJI** 184 III a 2
Naviu Island ⌒ **PNG** 183 B 5
Navlakhi o **IND** 138-139 C 8
Navlja o **RUS** 94-95 O 5
Năvodari o **RO** 102-103 F 5
Navoi = Navoij ☆ **UZ** 136-137 J 4
Navoij ☆ **UZ** 136-137 J 4
Navojoa o **MEX** 50-51 E 4
Na Vong o **LAO** 156-157 C 6
Nāvor o **AFG** (ĠA) 134-135 M 2
Nāvor ⊖ **AFG** (ĠA) 134-135 M 2
Nāvor, Kōtal-e ▲ **AFG** 134-135 M 1
Navrongo o **GH** 202-203 K 4
Navsāri o **IND** 138-139 D 9
Navua o **FJI** 184 III b 3
Navua River ∼ **FJI** 184 III a 3
Navy Board Inlet ≈ 24-25 f 4
Nāwa o **IND** 138-139 E 6
Nawābshāh o **PK** 138-139 B 6
Nawāda o **IND** 142-143 D 3
Na Wai o **THA** 142-143 L 6
Nawa Kot o **PK** 138-139 C 5
Nawākshūt = Nouakchott ★• **RIM** 196-197 C 5
Nāwalkal o **IND** 140-141 G 2
Nawalpur o **NEP** 144-145 E 7
Nawāpāra o **IND** 142-143 C 5
Nawar o **RT** 202-203 L 5
Nawinda Kuta o **Z** 218-219 C 3
Nawngawn o **MYA** 142-143 L 5
Nawnghkio o **MYA** 142-143 K 4
Nawngleng o **MYA** 142-143 L 4
Nawuni o **GH** 202-203 K 5
Naxçıvan = Naxçıvan Muxtar Respublikası □ **AZ** 128-129 L 3
Náxos o•• **GR** 100-101 K 6
Náxos ⌒ **GR** 100-101 K 6
Naya Chor o **PK** 138-139 B 7
Nāyakanhatti o **IND** 140-141 G 3
Nayar o **MEX** 50-51 G 6
Nayarit □ **MEX** 50-51 G 6
Nayau ⌒ **FJI** 184 III c 2
Nāyband o **IR** 134-135 G 2
Nāyband, Kūh-e ▲ **IR** 134-135 G 2
Nayé o **SN** 202-203 D 2
Nayoro o **J** 152-153 K 2
Nayorunun River ∼ **USA** 22-23 Q 3
Nayouri o **BF** 202-203 L 3
Nayuchi o **MW** 218-219 H 2
Nāyudupeta o **IND** 140-141 H 4
Nazaré o **BR** (APA) 62-63 J 4
Nazaré o **BR** (BAH) 72-73 L 2
Nazaré o **BR** (P) 62-63 K 6
Nazaré o **BR** (TOC) 68-69 E 5
Nazaré o• **P** 98-99 C 5
Nazaré, Cachoeira ∼ **BR** 70-71 G 2
Nazaré da Mata o **BR** 68-69 L 5
Nazaré do Piauí o **BR** 68-69 G 5
Nazareth o **BOL** 70-71 E 4
Nazareth o **CO** 60-61 D 5
Nazareth o **USA** (TX) 264-265 B 4
Nazareth = Naẓerat ☆ **IL** 130-131 D 1
Nazarovo ☆ **RUS** 116-117 E 7
Nazas, Río ∼ **MEX** 50-51 G 5
Nazca o• **PE** 64-65 E 9
Nazca Linea • **PE** 64-65 E 9
Nazca Ridge ≃ 5 C 7
Naze o **J** 152-153 C 10
Naẓerat ☆ **IL** 130-131 D 1
Nazilli ☆ **TR** 128-129 C 4
Nazinskaja ∼ **RUS** 114-115 P 4
Nazirhat o **BD** 142-143 G 4
Nazko o **CDN** (BC) 228-229 L 4
Nazko River ∼ **CDN** 228-229 L 4
Nazombe o **MOC** 214-215 K 6
Nazran ☆ **RUS** 126-127 F 6
Nazrēt o **ETH** 208-209 D 4
Nazwā o• **OM** 132-133 K 2
Nazym ∼ **RUS** 114-115 K 4
Nazyvaevsk ☆ **RUS** 114-115 L 7
Nbâk o **RIM** 196-197 C 6
Nbeïket Dlim o **RIM** 196-197 G 6
Nbeïket el Ahouâch o **RIM** 196-197 H 6
Ncamasere ∼ **RB** 216-217 F 9
Ncanaha o **ZA** 220-221 G 6
Nchalo o **MW** 218-219 H 3
Nchelenge o **Z** 214-215 E 5
Ncojane o **RB** 220-221 E 1
Ncojane Ranches ∸ **RB** 216-217 F 11
Ncora Dam < **ZA** 220-221 H 5
Ncue o **GQ** 210-211 C 2
Ndaki o **RMM** 202-203 K 2
Ndala o **EAT** 212-213 D 6
Ndalambo o **EAT** 214-215 G 5
N'Dalatando ☆ **ANG** 216-217 C 4
Ndali o **DY** 204-205 E 4
Ndanda o **EAT** 214-215 K 6
Ndanda o **RCA** 206-207 F 6
Ndande o **SN** 202-203 B 2
Ndangane o **SN** 202-203 B 2
Ndao, Pulau ⌒ **RI** 166-167 B 7
Ndarapo Swamp ⊖ **EAK** 212-213 G 5
Ndarassa o **RCA** 206-207 F 5
Ndedu o **ZRE** 212-213 B 2
Ndeji o **WAN** 204-205 F 4
Ndekesha o **ZRE** 214-215 B 4
Ndéko ∼ **RCB** 210-211 F 4
Ndélé ☆• **RCA** 206-207 E 4
Ndélélé o **CAM** 206-207 B 6
Ndemba o **CAM** 204-205 K 6
Ndembera ∼ **EAT** 214-215 H 5
Ndendé o **G** 210-211 C 5
Ndeyini < **EAK** 212-213 G 4

Nalcayes, Isla — Ndeyini 367

Ndia ○ SN 202-203 D 2
Ndian ~ CAM 204-205 H 6
Ndiékro ○ CI 202-203 H 6
Ndiguina ○ CAM 206-207 B 3
Ndikiniméki ○ CAM 204-205 J 6
Ndikoko ○ CAM 204-205 J 6
Ndim ○ RCA 206-207 B 5
Ndindi ○ G 210-211 C 5
Ndindi ○ SN 202-203 B 2
Ndioum ○ SN 196-197 C 6
Ndioum Guènt ○ SN 202-203 C 2
Nditam ○ CAM 204-205 J 6
Ndiya ○ WAN 204-205 G 6
N'djaména ★ • TCH 198-199 G 6
Ndji ~ RCA 206-207 F 5
Ndjim ~ CAM 204-205 J 6
Ndjolé ○ CAM 204-205 J 6
Ndjolé ○ G 210-211 C 4
Ndjoundou ○ RCB 210-211 F 4
Ndjwé ~ CAM 210-211 E 2
Ndofane ○ SN 202-203 C 3
Ndogo, Lagune ⊖ G 210-211 B 5
Ndok ○ CAM 206-207 B 5
Ndokama ○ CAM 204-205 J 6
Ndokayo ○ CAM 206-207 B 6
Ndoki ~ RCB 210-211 F 3
Ndola ★ Z 214-215 E 7
Ndom ○ CAM 204-205 J 6
Ndondo ○ SOL 184 I e 3
Ndonga ○ NAM 216-217 F 8
Ndongolo ○ G 210-211 C 3
Ndop ○ CAM 204-205 J 6
Ndora Mountains ▲ WAN 204-205 J 5
Ndorola ○ BF 202-203 H 4
Ndoto Mountains ▲ EAK 212-213 F 3
Ndouci ○ CI 202-203 H 7
Ndoukou ○ RCA 206-207 E 6
Ndoumbou ○ RCA 206-207 C 5
Ndrhamcha, Sebkha ⊖ RIM 196-197 C 5
Ndu ○ CAM 204-205 J 5
Ndu ○ ZRE 206-207 F 6
Nduluku ○ EAK 212-213 F 4
Ndumbwe ○ EAT 214-215 K 6
Ndumo ○ ZA 220-221 L 3
Ndumo Game Reserve ⊥ ZA 220-221 L 3
Ndurumo ~ EAT 212-213 E 6
Ndzouani ⌒ COM 222-223 D 4
Neabul Creek ~ AUS 178-179 J 4
Neagh, Lough ⊖ GB 90-91 D 4
Neah Bay ○ USA (WA) 244-245 A 2
Neakongut Bay ≈ 36-37 K 4
Neale, Lake ⊖ AUS 176-177 K 2
Neale Junction ○ AUS 176-177 H 4
Neales Creek ~ AUS 178-179 C 4
Neales River ~ AUS 178-179 D 5
Néa Moni ∴ GR 100-101 L 5
Néa Moudania ○ GR 100-101 J 4
Neamţ, Piatra- ★ • RO 102-103 E 4
Neápoli ○ GR 100-101 J 6
Neápoli ○ GR 100-101 H 4
Nearchuss Passage ≈ 158-159 D 5
Near Islands ⌒ USA 22-23 C 6
Nebbou ○ BF 202-203 K 4
Nebe ○ RI 166-167 B 6
Nebelat el Hagana ○ SUD 200-201 D 6
Nebine Creek ~ AUS 178-179 J 5
Nebitdag ○ TM 136-137 D 5
Neblina, Cerro de la ▲ YV 66-67 E 2
Neblina, Sierra de la ▲ YV 66-67 E 2
Nebo ○ AUS 178-179 K 1
Nebraska ◘ USA 262-263 D 3
Nebraska City ○ USA (NE) 262-263 L 4
Nebrodi, Monti ▲ I 100-101 E 6
Necanicum Junction ○ USA (OR) 244-245 B 5
Necedah ○ USA (WI) 270-271 H 6
Nečera ~ RUS 118-119 H 6
Nechako Plateau ▲ CDN 228-229 G 2
Nechako Reservoir ⊖ CDN (BC) 228-229 J 3
Nechako River ~ CDN 228-229 K 3
Neche ○ USA (ND) 258-259 K 3
Neches ○ USA (TX) 268-269 E 5
Neches, Port ○ USA (TX) 268-269 G 7
Neches River ~ USA 268-269 F 6
Nechi ○ CO 60-61 D 3
Nechí, Río ~ CO 60-61 D 4
Nechisar National Park ⊥ ETH 208-209 C 5
Neckarboo Range ▲ AUS 180-181 H 2
Necker Island ⌒ USA (HI) 288 I A 1
Necochea ○ RA 78-79 K 5
Necoclí ○ CO 60-61 C 3
Necungas ○ MOC 218-219 H 3
Nédéley ○ TCH 198-199 J 5
Nederland ○ USA (CO) 254-255 K 4
Nederland ○ USA (TX) 268-269 G 7
Nedlouc, Lac ⊖ CDN 36-37 N 6
Nedrata ○ ETH 208-209 D 3
Nedroma ○ DZ 188-189 L 3
Nedryhajliv ○ UA 102-103 H 2
Nedumangad ○ IND 140-141 G 6
Nedunkeni ○ CL 140-141 J 6
N. Edwards ○ USA (CA) 248-249 G 4
Needham, Mount ▲ CDN (BC) 228-229 B 3
Needles ○ CDN (BC) 230-231 L 4
Needles ○ USA (CA) 248-249 K 5
Needmore ○ USA (TX) 264-265 B 4
Needville ○ USA (TX) 268-269 E 7
Neel ○ USA (AL) 284-285 C 2
Neelin ○ CDN (MAN) 234-235 D 5
Neelyville ○ USA (MO) 276-277 E 4
Neenah ○ USA (WI) 270-271 K 6
Neepawa ○ CDN (MAN) 234-235 D 4
Neergaard Lake ⊖ CDN 24-25 g 5
Neerim South ○ AUS 180-181 H 5
Neeses ○ USA (SC) 284-285 J 3
Nefasit ○ ER 200-201 J 5
Nefas Mewch'a ○ ETH 208-209 D 3
Neffatia ○ TN 190-191 H 4
Nefhi Shet' ~ ER 200-201 J 5
Nefta ○ TN 190-191 F 4
Neftchala = Neftçala ○ AZ 128-129 N 3
Neftegorsk ○ RUS (SHL) 122-123 K 2
Neftegorsk ★ RUS (SAM) 96-97 G 7
Neftejugansk ★ RUS 114-115 M 4
Neftekamsk ★ RUS 96-97 J 5
Neftekumsk ★ RUS 126-127 F 5
Nefza ○ TN 190-191 G 2
Negage ○ ANG 216-217 C 3
Négala ○ RMM 202-203 F 3
Negampaha ○ CL 140-141 J 7
Nega Nega ○ Z 218-219 E 2
Néganşi ○ DY 204-205 E 3
Negâr ○ IR 134-135 G 4
Negara ○ RI (KSE) 164-165 D 5
Negara ~ RI 164-165 D 5
Negele ○ ETH 208-209 D 5
Negëlë ○ ETH 208-209 D 6
Negerilama ○ RI 164-165 H 3
Negeri Sembilan ◘ MAL 162-163 E 3
Negev, ha- ⊥ IL 130-131 D 2
Negiralama ○ RI 162-163 D 3
Negjučej ~ RUS 118-119 M 6
Negley ○ USA (TX) 264-265 J 5
Negola ○ ANG 216-217 C 7
Negomane ○ MOC 214-215 K 6
Negombo ○ • CL 140-141 H 7
Negotin ○ • YU 100-101 J 2
Negotino ○ MK 100-101 J 4
Negra, Cordillera ▲ PE 64-65 C 6
Negra, La ○ RA 78-79 K 4
Negra, La ○ RCH 76-77 B 2
Negra, Ponta ▲ BR 68-69 L 4
Negra, Punta ▲ PE 64-65 B 4
Negra, Punta ▲ RA 78-79 K 5
Negril ○ JA 54-55 F 5
Negril Beach ⊥ • JA 54-55 F 5
Negrine ○ DZ 190-191 F 3
Negri River ~ AUS 172-173 J 4
Negrito, El ○ HN 52-53 L 4
Negro, Arroyo ~ ROU 78-79 L 2
Negro, Cerro ▲ PA 52-53 D 7
Negro, Cerro ▲ RA (CHU) 80 F 2
Negro, Cerro ▲ RA (NEU) 78-79 E 5
Negro, Cerro ▲ RCH 76-77 B 4
Negro, Laguna ⊖ ROU 74-75 D 10
Negro, Riacho ~ RA 76-77 H 3
Negro, Río ~ BOL 70-71 F 4
Negro, Río ~ BOL 70-71 E 2
Negro, Río ~ BOL 70-71 D 3
Negro, Río ~ BR 66-67 G 4
Negro, Río ~ BR 70-71 J 6
Negro, Río ~ CO 60-61 H 7
Negro, Río ~ HN 52-53 L 5
Negro, Río ~ PY 76-77 J 3
Negro, Río ~ PY 76-77 J 2
Negro, Río ~ RA 76-77 H 4
Negro, Río ~ RA 78-79 G 5
Negro, Río ~ ROU 78-79 L 2
Negro, Río ~ YV 60-61 E 3
Negros ⌒ RP 160-161 E 8
Negro Urco ○ PE 64-65 F 3
Negru Vodă ○ RO 102-103 F 6
Neguac ○ CDN (NB) 240-241 K 3
Něgus"jah ~ RUS 114-115 N 5
Nehaevskij ○ RUS 102-103 M 2
Nehalem ○ USA (OR) 244-245 B 5
Nehalen River ~ USA 244-245 B 5
Nehāvand ○ • IR 134-135 C 1
Nehbandān ○ IR 134-135 J 3
Nehe ○ VRC 150-151 E 3
Nehoiu ○ RO 102-103 E 5
Nehone ○ ANG 216-217 D 8
Nehuentue ○ RCH 78-79 C 5
Neiafu ○ TON 184 IV b 1
Neiba ★ DOM 54-55 K 5
Neiba, Sierra de ▲ DOM 54-55 K 5
Neiden ○ N 86-87 O 2
Neidenburg = Nidzica ○ • PL 92-93 Q 2
Neidín = Kenmare ○ IRL 90-91 C 6
Neidpath ○ CDN (SAS) 232-233 L 5
Neiges, Piton des ▲ F 224 B 7
Neihart ○ USA (MT) 250-251 J 5
Neijiang ○ VRC 156-157 D 2
Neil Armstrong Air & Space Museum • USA (OH) 280-281 B 3
Neilburg ○ CDN (SAS) 232-233 J 3
Neilersdrif ○ ZA 220-221 E 4
Neils Harbour ○ CDN (NS) 240-241 P 4
Neilton ○ USA (WA) 244-245 B 3
Nei Mongol Gaoyuan ⊥ VRC 148-149 G 7
Neinsberg ▲ NAM 216-217 D 9
Neiriz ○ • IR 134-135 F 4
Neis Beach ○ CDN (SAS) 232-233 N 2
Neiße ~ D 92-93 N 3
Neiva ★ CO 60-61 D 6
Neixiang ○ VRC 154-155 G 5
Neizār ○ IR 134-135 D 1
Neizvestnaja ~ RUS 112-113 V 1
Neja ○ RUS 94-95 S 2
Nejanilin Lake ⊖ CDN 30-31 V 6
Nejime ○ J 152-153 D 9
Nejo ○ ETH 208-209 B 4
Nējtajaha ~ RUS 108-109 Q 6
Nējto, ozero ⊖ RUS 108-109 O 6
Nējto pervoe, ozero ⊖ RUS 108-109 O 6
Nejva ~ RUS 96-97 M 5
Nekā ○ IR 136-137 C 6
Nekékum ~ RUS 110-111 L 4
Nek'emte ★ ETH 208-209 C 4
Nekljudovo ○ RUS 94-95 S 3
Nekob ○ MA 188-189 J 5
Nekongdakon, ozero ⊖ RUS 116-117 L 3
Nekongdokon ~ RUS 116-117 E 3
Nekoosa ○ USA (WI) 270-271 J 6
Neksø ○ DK 86-87 G 9
Neladero, Sierra del ▲ RA 76-77 C 5
Nelamangala ○ IND 140-141 G 4
Nelemnoe ○ RUS 110-111 c 7
Nel'gese ~ RUS 110-111 V 6
Nel'gjuu ~ RUS 118-119 N 7
Nelia ○ AUS 174-175 G 7
Nelidovo ★ RUS 94-95 N 3
Neligh ○ USA (NE) 262-263 H 2
Neligh Mills ∴ USA (NE) 262-263 H 2
Nel'jaty ○ RUS 118-119 G 7
Nel'kan ○ RUS (HBR) 120-121 G 5
Nel'kan ○ RUS (SAH) 110-111 Y 7
Nel'koba ○ RUS 120-121 N 3
Nellie, Mount ▲ AUS 172-173 G 4
Nellikkuppam ○ IND 140-141 H 5
Nellimö ○ FIN 88-89 K 2
Nellis Air Force Range xx USA (NV) 248-249 H 2
Nelliyālam ○ IND 140-141 F 5
Nellore ○ IND 140-141 H 3
Nel'ma ○ RUS 122-123 H 5
Nelma ○ USA (WI) 270-271 K 4
Nèlon ~ RUS 110-111 Q 5
Nelshoogte ▲ ZA 220-221 K 2
Nelson ○ CDN (BC) 230-231 M 4
Nelson ○ NZ 182 D 4
Nelson ○ RA 76-77 G 6
Nelson ○ USA (NE) 262-263 H 4
Nelson ○ USA (NV) 248-249 K 4
Nelson ○ USA (WI) 270-271 G 6
Nelson, Cape ▲ AUS 180-181 F 5
Nelson, Cape ▲ PNG 183 E 5
Nelson, Estrecho ≈ 80 C 5
Nelson, Mount ▲ PNG 183 D 5
Nelson, Port ≈ 34-35 K 2
Nelson Island ⌒ USA 20-21 H 6
Nelson Lakes National Park ⊥ NZ 182 D 5
Nelson-Miramichi ○ CDN (NB) 240-241 K 4
Nelson Museum • KAN 56 D 3
Nelson River ~ CDN 34-35 J 2
Nelsonville ○ USA (OH) 280-281 D 4
Nelspoort ○ ZA 220-221 F 6
Nelspruit ○ • ZA 220-221 K 2
Nelway ○ CDN (BC) 230-231 M 4
Nem ~ RUS 114-115 D 4
Nem, Ust'- ○ RUS 96-97 J 3
Néma ★ RIM 196-197 G 6
Nema ★ RUS 96-97 G 5
Nemah ○ USA (WA) 244-245 B 4
Nemaiah Valley ○ CDN (BC) 230-231 B 2
Něman ~ BY 94-95 K 5
Neman ★ RUS 94-95 H 4
Nembe ○ WAN 204-205 G 6
Nembrala ○ RI 166-167 B 7
Nemenčinė ○ LT 94-95 J 4
Nementcha, Monts des ▲ DZ 190-191 F 3
Némiscau, Lac ⊖ CDN 38-39 F 3
Némiscau, Rivière ~ CDN 38-39 F 3
Nemkučenskij hrebet ▲ RUS 110-111 W 4
Nemnjuga ~ RUS 88-89 S 4
Nemo, vulkan ▲ RUS 122-123 Q 4
Nemours ○ F 90-91 J 7
Nemrut Dağı ∴ TR 128-129 H 4
Nemuj ○ RUS 120-121 G 6
Nemunas ~ LT 94-95 H 4
Nemuro ○ J 152-153 L 3
Nemuro-hantō ⌒ J 152-153 L 3
Nemuro-kaikyō = Kunašírskij proliv ≈ 152-153 L 3
Nemuro-wan ≈ 152-153 L 3
Nemyriv ★ UA 102-103 F 3
Nenagh = An tAonach ○ IRL 90-91 C 5
Nenana ○ USA 20-21 Q 4
Nenasi ○ MAL 162-163 E 3
Nendel'ginskij, hrebet ▲ RUS 110-111 V 6
Nenets Autonomous District = Neneckij avtonomnyj okrug ◘ RUS 88-89 T 3
Nenggiri ~ MAL 162-163 D 2
Nengo ~ ANG 216-217 F 7
Nenjiang ○ VRC 150-151 E 3
Nen Jiang ~ VRC 150-151 D 4
Nenoksa ○ RUS 88-89 P 4
Nens"egan ~ RUS 114-115 K 3
Neo ○ J 152-153 G 7
Neodesha ○ USA (KS) 262-263 L 7
Neola ○ USA (UT) 254-255 E 3
Néo Petritsi ○ GR 100-101 J 4
Neopit ○ USA (WI) 270-271 K 6
Neópolis ○ BR 68-69 K 7
Neosho ○ USA (MO) 276-277 A 4
Neosho River ~ USA 262-263 L 6
Nepa ○ RUS (IRK) 116-117 O 6
Nepa ~ RUS 116-117 N 6
Nepal ■ NEP 144-145 C 6
Nepalganj ○ NEP 144-145 C 6
Nepara ○ NAM 216-217 E 8
Nepean ○ CDN (ONT) 238-239 K 3
Nepean Mine • AUS 176-177 F 5
Nepean Sound ≈ 228-229 E 3
Nepeña ○ PE 64-65 C 6
Nephi ○ USA (UT) 254-255 D 4
Nephin Beg Range ▲ IRL 90-91 C 4
Nepisiguit Bay ≈ 38-39 M 5
Nepisiguit Bay ≈ 240-241 K 3
Nepisiguit River ~ CDN 240-241 J 3
Nepoko ~ ZRE 212-213 A 2
Nepomuceno ○ BR 72-73 J 6
Neponjatnaja ~ RUS 108-109 Y 4
Nèptènnè ~ RUS 116-117 K 4
Neptune Bay ≈ 36-37 R 2
Neptune Beach ○ USA (FL) 286-287 H 1
Neptune Islands ⌒ AUS 180-181 D 3
Nera ~ RUS 110-111 Z 7
Nera, Ust'- ★ • RUS 110-111 Y 7
Nérac ○ F 90-91 H 9
Neragon Island ⌒ USA 20-21 G 6
Nērangda, ozero ⊖ RUS 108-109 c 7
Nerča ~ RUS 118-119 H 9
Nerčinsk ★ RUS 118-119 H 10
Nerčugan ~ RUS 118-119 H 9
Nerehta ★ • RUS 94-95 R 3
Nereta ○ • LV 94-95 J 3
Neretva ~ HR 100-101 F 3
Neria ≈ 28-29 Q 6
Neria ⌒ GRØ 28-29 Q 6
Nerica ~ RUS 88-89 W 4
Neriquinha ○ ANG 216-217 F 7
Neris (Vilija) ~ LT 94-95 J 4
Nerjuktajinsk (Pervyj) ○ RUS 118-119 J 5
Nerjungri ★ • RUS 118-119 M 7
Nerka, Lake ⊖ USA 22-23 R 3
Ner' ~ RUS 94-95 P 3
Nerla ○ IND 140-141 F 2
Nero, ozero ⊖ RUS 94-95 Q 3
Nerohi ○ RUS 114-115 F 3
Nerojka, gora ▲ RUS 114-115 E 2
Nerong, Selat ≈ 166-167 G 4
Nerópolis ○ BR 72-73 F 4
Nerpič'e ○ RUS 122-123 L 4
Nerpič'e, ozero ⊖ RUS (KMC) 120-121 U 5
Nerpič'e, ozero ⊖ RUS (SAH) 112-113 L 2
Nerpičij, mys ▲ RUS 110-111 Y 2
Nerpo ○ RUS 118-119 G 7
Nerren Nerren ○ AUS 176-177 C 3
Nerrima ○ AUS 172-173 G 5
Nerskoe ploskogor'e ▲ RUS 110-111 Z 7
Neruta ~ RUS 88-89 X 3
Nerutajaha ~ RUS 108-109 N 7
Nes ○ N 86-87 D 6
Nes' ○ RUS 88-89 S 3
Nes' ~ RUS 88-89 S 3
Nešāpūr ○ • IR 136-137 F 6
Nesbitt ○ CDN (MAN) 234-235 D 5
Nesebăr ○ ∴ BG 102-103 E 6
Nes'egan ~ RUS 114-115 G 2
Nesgo ○ PNG 183 F 2
Neškan ○ RUS 112-113 Y 3
Neskaupstaður ○ IS 86-87 g 2
Nèskènpil'gyn, laguna ≈ 112-113 Y 3
Nesna ○ N 86-87 F 3
Nesøya ⌒ N 86-87 F 3
Nespelem ○ USA (WA) 244-245 G 2
Ness City ○ USA (KS) 262-263 G 6
Nessona ○ MOC 218-219 H 4
Nestaocano, Rivière ~ CDN 236-237 P 2
Nesterov = Žovkva ★ UA 102-103 C 2
Nesterovo ○ RUS 116-117 N 9
Nestiary ○ RUS 96-97 D 5
Nestorville ○ USA (WV) 280-281 G 4
Nët ~ RUS 120-121 H 4
Netaar ○ RI 166-167 L 3
Netanya ★ IL 130-131 D 1
Netarhāt ○ IND 142-143 D 4
Netarts ○ USA (OR) 244-245 B 5
Netawaka ○ USA (KS) 262-263 L 5
Netcong ○ USA (NJ) 280-281 M 3
Netherhill ○ CDN (SAS) 232-233 K 4
Netherlands = Nederland ■ NL 92-93 G 2
Netherlands Antilles = Nederlandse Antillen ◘ NA 60-61 G 1
Netia ○ MOC 218-219 K 2
Neto ~ I 100-101 F 5
Netrakona ○ BD 142-143 G 3
Netsilik Lake ⊖ CDN 24-25 a 6
Nettilling Lake ⊖ CDN 28-29 E 3
Nett Lake ○ USA (MN) 270-271 E 2
Nett Lake ⊖ USA (MN) 270-271 E 2
Nett Lake Indian Reservation ✗ USA 270-271 E 2
Nettleton ○ USA (MS) 268-269 M 2
Nettling Fjord ≈ 28-29 F 3
Nettogami Lake ⊖ CDN (ONT) 236-237 H 2
Nettogami River ~ CDN 236-237 H 2
Neubrandenburg ○ D 92-93 M 2
Neuchâtel ★ • CH 92-93 J 5
Neuchâtel, Lac de ⊖ CH 92-93 J 5
Neudač, buhta ≈ 108-109 I f 2
Neudorf ○ CDN (SAS) 232-233 P 5
Neuenahr-Ahrweiler, Bad ○ • D 92-93 J 3
Neuenburg = Neuchâtel ★ • CH 92-93 J 5
Neuenburger See = Lac de Neuchâtel ⊖ CH 92-93 J 5
Neufchâteau ○ B 92-93 H 4
Neufchâteau ○ F 90-91 K 7
Neufchâtel-en-Bray ○ F 90-91 H 7
Neuhaus = Jindřichův Hradec ○ CZ 92-93 N 4
Neumarkt in der Oberpfalz ○ D 92-93 L 4
Neumünster ○ D 92-93 K 1
Neunkirchen ○ A 92-93 O 5
Neunkirchen ○ D 92-93 J 4
Neupokoeva, mys ▲ RUS 108-109 c 3
Neupokoeva, ostrov ⌒ RUS 108-109 R 5
Neuquén ◘ RA 78-79 D 5
Neuquén ★ RA (NEU) 78-79 E 5
Neuquén, Río ~ RA 78-79 E 4
Neuruppin ○ • D 92-93 M 2
Neu Sandez = Nowy Sącz ★ • PL 92-93 Q 4
Neuschwanstein •• D 92-93 L 5
Neuse River ~ USA 282-283 L 6
Neusiedler See ⊖ A 92-93 O 5
Neusohl = Banská Bystrica ○ SK 92-93 P 4
Neustadt (Orla) ○ D 92-93 L 3
Neustadt an der Aisch ○ D 92-93 L 4
Neustrelitz ○ • D 92-93 M 2
Neutenskij hrebet ▲ RUS 112-113 N 4
Neu-Titschein = Nový Jičín ○ CZ 92-93 P 4
Neutral Hills ○ CDN (ALB) 232-233 H 3
Neutral Junction ○ AUS 178-179 C 1
Neuwied ○ D 92-93 J 3
Neva ~ RUS 94-95 M 2
Nevada ○ USA (IA) 274-275 E 2
Nevada ○ USA (MO) 276-277 A 3
Nevada ◘ USA 246-247 G 4
Nevada, Sierra ▲ RA 78-79 E 7
Nevada Scheelite Mine ○ USA (NV) 246-247 G 4
Nevada Test Site xx USA (NV) 248-249 H 2
Nevadita, La ○ CO 60-61 E 2
Nevado, Cerro ▲ RCH 78-79 C 7
Nevado, Cerro el ▲ RA 78-79 E 3
Nevado, Sierra del ▲ RA 78-79 E 3
Nevado Cóndor ▲ RCH 80 D 2
Nevado de Chañi ▲ RA 76-77 E 3
Nevado de Colima ▲ MEX 52-53 C 2
Nevado del Huila, Parque Nacional ⊥ CO 60-61 D 6
Nevado de los Palos ▲ RCH 80 D 2
Nevado del Ruiz ▲ CO 60-61 D 5
Nevado del Tolima ▲ CO 60-61 D 5
Nevado de Toluca, Parque Nacional ⊥ MEX 52-53 E 2
Nevados, Parque Nacional los ⊥ CO 60-61 D 5
Neve, Serra do ▲ ANG 216-217 B 6
Nevel' ★ RUS 94-95 L 3
Nevel'sk ○ RUS 122-123 J 5
Nevel'skogo, proliv ≈ 122-123 J 3
Never ○ RUS 118-119 M 8
Nevers ★ • F 90-91 J 8
Neversink River ~ USA 280-281 M 2
Nevertire ○ AUS 178-179 J 6
Neves, Rio ~ BR 68-69 F 5
Nevesinje ○ BIH 100-101 G 3
Neville ○ CDN (SAS) 232-233 L 6
Nevinnomyssk ○ RUS 104 C 4
Nevis ○ CDN (ALB) 232-233 E 3
Nevis Island ⌒ KAN 56 D 3
Nev'jansk ★ RUS 96-97 M 5
Nevşehir ★ • TR 128-129 F 3
Nevskoe, ozero ⊖ RUS 122-123 K 4
New Aiyansh ○ CDN 32-33 F 4
Newala ○ EAT 214-215 K 6
New Albany ○ USA (IN) 274-275 N 6
New Albany ○ USA (MS) 268-269 L 2
New Albin ○ USA (IA) 274-275 G 1
New Alton Downs ○ AUS 178-179 E 4
New Amsterdam ○ GUY 62-63 F 2
Newark ○ USA (AR) 276-277 D 5
Newark ○ USA (DE) 280-281 L 4
Newark ○ USA (NJ) 280-281 M 3
Newark ○ USA (NY) 278-279 D 5
Newark ○ USA (OH) 280-281 D 3
Newark on Trent ○ • GB 90-91 G 5
New Athens ○ USA (IL) 274-275 J 6
New Athens ○ USA (OH) 280-281 E 3
New Augusta ○ USA (MS) 268-269 L 5
Newaygo ○ USA (MI) 272-273 D 4
New Baltimore ○ USA (MI) 272-273 G 5
New Bedford ○ USA (MA) 278-279 L 7
New Bercthal ○ CDN (MAN) 234-235 F 5
Newberg ○ USA (OR) 244-245 C 5
New Berlin ○ USA (NY) 278-279 F 6
New Bern ○ USA (NC) 282-283 K 5
Newbern ○ USA (TN) 276-277 F 4
Newberry ○ USA (FL) 286-287 G 2
Newberry ○ USA (MI) 270-271 N 4
Newberry ○ USA (SC) 284-285 J 2
New Bethlehem ○ USA (PA) 280-281 G 2
New Bight ○ BS 54-55 H 2
New Bonaventure ○ CDN (NFL) 242-243 P 4
New Boston ○ USA (IL) 274-275 H 3
New Boston ○ USA (IN) 274-275 M 6
New Boston ○ USA (MO) 274-275 F 5
New Boston ○ USA (OH) 280-281 D 5
New Boston ○ USA (TX) 264-265 K 5
New Bothwell ○ CDN (MAN) 234-235 G 5
New Braunfels ○ USA (TX) 266-267 J 4
New Brigden ○ CDN (ALB) 232-233 H 4
New Britain ⌒ PNG 183 E 4
New Britain ○ USA (CT) 280-281 O 2
New Britain Trench ≃ 183 E 4
New Brockton ○ USA (AL) 284-285 E 5
New Brunswick ◘ CDN 240-241 J 3
New Brunswick ○ USA (NJ) 280-281 M 3
New Buffalo ○ USA (MI) 272-273 C 6
Newburgh ○ USA (NY) 280-281 M 2
New Burnside ○ USA (IL) 276-277 G 3
Newbury ○ GB 90-91 G 6
Newburyport ○ USA (MA) 278-279 L 6
New Bussa ○ WAN 204-205 F 4
Newby River ~ CDN 32-33 P 3
New Caledonia = Nouvelle-Calédonie ⌒ F 13 H 5
New Caledonia Basin ≃ 13 H 5
New Canaan ○ CDN (NB) 240-241 K 4
New Carlisle ○ CDN (QUE) 240-241 K 2
New Carlisle ○ USA (OH) 280-281 B 4
Newcastle ○ AUS 180-181 L 2
Newcastle ○ CDN (NB) 240-241 K 3
Newcastle ○ CDN (ONT) 238-239 G 5
Newcastle ○ GB 90-91 E 4
Newcastle ○ USA (CA) 246-247 D 5
New Castle ○ USA (IN) 274-275 N 5
Newcastle ○ USA (NE) 262-263 K 2
New Castle ○ USA (PA) 280-281 F 2
Newcastle ○ USA (TX) 264-265 E 5
Newcastle ○ USA (UT) 254-255 B 6
New Castle ○ USA (VA) 280-281 F 6
Newcastle ○ USA (WY) 252-253 O 3
Newcastle ○ ZA 220-221 J 3
Newcastle Creek ~ AUS 174-175 C 5
Newcastle upon Tyne ★ GB 90-91 G 4
Newcastle Waters ○ AUS 174-175 B 5
Newcastle West = An Caisleán Nua ○ IRL 90-91 C 5
New Centreville ○ USA (PA) 280-281 G 4
New Cleeves ○ CDN (SAS) 232-233 J 2
New Cornwall ○ CDN (NS) 240-241 L 6
New Cumberland ○ USA (PA) 280-281 K 3
Newdale ○ CDN (MAN) 234-235 C 4
Newdale ○ USA (ID) 252-253 G 3
New Dayton ○ CDN (ALB) 232-233 F 6
New Deal ○ USA (TX) 264-265 C 5
New Delamere ○ AUS 172-173 K 3
New Delhi ★ • IND 138-139 F 5
New Denver ○ CDN (BC) 230-231 M 4
New Dixie ○ AUS 174-175 G 4
Newell ○ USA (SD) 260-261 C 2
Newell, Lake ⊖ AUS 176-177 J 2
Newell, Lake ⊖ CDN (ALB) 232-233 G 5
New Ellenton ○ USA (SC) 284-285 J 3
Newell Highway II AUS 178-179 K 6
Newellton ○ USA (LA) 268-269 J 4
New England ○ USA (ND) 258-259 E 5
New England Highway II AUS 178-179 L 6
New England National Park ⊥ AUS 178-179 M 6
New England Range ▲ AUS 178-179 L 6
New England Seamounts ≃ 6-7 C 5
Newenham, Cape ▲ USA 22-23 P 3
New Era ○ USA (MI) 272-273 C 4
New Featherstone ○ ZW 218-219 F 4
Newfolden ○ USA (MN) 270-271 B 2
Newfound Gap ▲ USA (NC) 282-283 D 5
Newfoundland ◘ CDN 38-39 N 2
Newfoundland, Grand Banks of ≃ 6-7 D 4
Newfoundland, Island of ⌒ CDN (NFL) 242-243 L 4
Newfoundland Evaporation Basin ⊥ USA 254-255 B 2
New Gabloi ○ LB 202-203 F 6
New Galloway ○ GB 90-91 E 4
Newgate ○ CDN (BC) 230-231 O 4
New Georgia ⌒ SOL 184 I c 3
New Georgia Group ⌒ SOL 183 c 3
New Georgia Sound = The Slot ≈ 183 c 2
New Germany ○ CDN (NS) 240-241 L 6
New Glarus ○ USA (WI) 274-275 J 2
New Glasgow ○ CDN (NS) 240-241 N 5
New Grand Chain ○ USA (IL) 276-277 F 3
New Greenleaf ○ USA (MI) 272-273 F 4
New Guinea ⌒ RI 166-167 J 3
New Guinea = New Guinea ⌒ RI 166-167 J 3
New Guinea Trench ≃ 166-167 J 2
Newgulf ○ USA (TX) 268-269 E 7
Newhalem ○ USA (WA) 244-245 D 2
Newhalen ○ USA 22-23 T 3
Newhalen River ~ USA 22-23 T 3
New Halfa ○ SUD 200-201 G 5
Newhall ○ USA (CA) 248-249 F 5
New Hamilton ○ USA 20-21 K 5
New Hampshire ◘ USA 278-279 K 5
New Hampton ○ USA (IA) 274-275 F 1
New Hanover ⌒ PNG 183 F 2
New Hanover ○ ZA 220-221 J 4
New Harbor ○ USA (ME) 278-279 M 5
New Harmony ○ USA (IN) 274-275 L 6
Newhaven ○ AUS 172-173 K 7
Newhaven ○ GB 90-91 H 6
New Haven ○ USA (IN) 274-275 N 3
New Haven ○ USA (KY) 276-277 K 3
New Haven ○ • USA (CT) 280-281 O 2
New Hazelton ○ CDN 32-33 G 4
New Hebrides = Nouvelles Hébrides ⌒ VAN 184 II a 1
New Hope ○ USA (AL) 284-285 D 2
New Hope ○ USA (PA) 280-281 M 3
New Iberia ○ USA (LA) 268-269 J 6
New Ireland ⌒ PNG 183 F 2
New Jersey ◘ USA 280-281 M 4
New Jersey Turnpike ○ USA (NJ) 280-281 M 3
Newkirk ○ USA (NM) 256-257 L 3
Newkirk ○ USA (OK) 264-265 G 2
New Knockhock ○ USA 20-21 H 5
Newlands ○ CDN (BC) 228-229 M 2
New Lebanon ○ USA (NY) 278-279 H 6
New Leipzig ○ USA (ND) 258-259 F 5
New Lexington ○ USA (AL) 284-285 C 3
New Lexington ○ USA (OH) 280-281 D 4
Newlin ○ USA (TX) 264-265 D 4
New Lisbon ○ USA (WI) 270-271 H 7
New Liskeard ○ CDN (ONT) 236-237 J 5
New London ○ CDN (PEI) 240-241 M 4
New London ○ USA (IA) 274-275 G 4
New London ○ USA (MN) 270-271 D 5
New London ○ USA (MO) 274-275 G 5
New London ○ USA (WA) 244-245 B 3
New London ○ USA (WI) 270-271 K 6
New London ○ • USA (CT) 280-281 O 2
New Madrid ○ USA (MO) 276-277 F 4
Newman ○ AUS 172-173 D 7
Newman ○ USA (CA) 248-249 C 2
Newman ○ USA (IL) 274-275 L 5
Newman ○ USA (NM) 256-257 J 6
Newman Bugt ≈ 26-27 V 3
Newmarket ○ CDN (ONT) 238-239 F 4
Newmarket ○ • GB 90-91 H 5
New Market ○ USA (TN) 282-283 D 4
New Market ○ USA (VA) 280-281 H 5
New Martinsville ○ USA (WV) 280-281 F 4
New Matamoras ○ USA (OH) 280-281 E 4
New Meadows ○ USA (ID) 252-253 B 2
New Mexico ◘ USA 256-257 J 4
New Milford ○ USA (CT) 280-281 N 2
New Milford ○ USA (PA) 280-281 L 2
New Mirpur ○ IND 138-139 D 3
New Moore ○ USA (TX) 264-265 B 5
Newnan ○ USA (GA) 284-285 F 3
Newnes ∴ AUS 180-181 L 2
New Norfolk ○ AUS 180-181 J 7
New Norway ○ CDN (ALB) 232-233 F 3
New Orleans ○ USA (LA) 268-269 K 7
New Osgoode ○ CDN (SAS) 232-233 P 2
New Osnaburgh ○ CDN (ONT) 234-235 N 3
New Paltz ○ USA (NY) 280-281 M 2
New Pekin ○ USA (IN) 274-275 M 6
New Perlican ○ CDN (NFL) 242-243 P 5
New Philadelphia ○ USA (OH) 280-281 E 3
New Pine Creek ○ USA (OR) 244-245 E 8
New Plymouth ○ NZ 182 E 3
New Plymouth ○ USA (ID) 252-253 B 3
Newport ○ CDN (NS) 240-241 L 6
Newport ○ CDN (QUE) 240-241 L 2
Newport ○ GB (ENG) 90-91 G 6
Newport ○ GB (WAL) 90-91 F 6
Newport ○ USA (AR) 276-277 D 5
Newport ○ USA (FL) 286-287 E 1
Newport ○ USA (KY) 276-277 L 1
Newport ○ USA (NC) 282-283 L 6
Newport ○ USA (NE) 262-263 G 2
Newport ○ USA (NH) 278-279 J 5
Newport ○ USA (OH) 280-281 B 3
Newport ○ USA (OR) 244-245 A 6
Newport ○ USA (TN) 282-283 D 5
Newport ○ USA (TX) 264-265 F 5
Newport ○ USA (VA) 280-281 F 6
Newport ○ USA (VT) 278-279 J 4
Newport ○ USA (WA) 244-245 H 2
Newport ○ • USA (RI) 278-279 K 7
Newport Beach ○ USA (CA) 248-249 G 6
Newport News ○ USA (VA) 280-281 K 7
New Port Richey ○ USA (FL) 286-287 G 3
New Prague ○ USA (MN) 270-271 E 6
New Princeton ○ USA (OR) 244-245 G 7
New Providence ⌒ BS 54-55 G 2
Newquay ○ • GB 90-91 E 6
New Raymer ○ USA (CO) 254-255 M 3
New Richland ○ USA (MN) 270-271 E 7
New Richmond ○ CDN (QUE) 240-241 K 2
New Richmond ○ USA (WI) 270-271 F 5
New Ringold ○ USA (OK) 264-265 J 4
New River ~ GUY 62-63 F 4
New River ○ USA (AZ) 256-257 C 5
New River ~ USA 280-281 F 7
New River ~ USA 282-283 K 6
New River ~ USA 282-283 F 4
New River ~ USA 284-285 G 5
New River ~ USA 286-287 E 1
New Roads ○ USA (LA) 268-269 J 6
New Rochelle ○ USA (NY) 280-281 N 3
New Rockford ○ USA (ND) 258-259 H 4
New Ross ○ CDN (NS) 240-241 L 6
New Ross = Ros Mhic Thriúin ○ IRL 90-91 D 5
Newry ○ AUS 172-173 J 4
Newry ○ USA (ME) 278-279 L 4
Newry Island ⌒ AUS 174-175 K 7
New Salem ○ USA (ND) 258-259 F 5
New Schwabenland ⊥ ARK 16 F 36
New Sharon ○ USA (IA) 274-275 F 3
New Siberian Islands = Novosibirskie ostrova ⌒ RUS 110-111 Z 3
New Site ○ USA (AL) 284-285 E 3
New Smyrna Beach ○ USA (FL) 286-287 J 2
Newsome ○ USA (TX) 264-265 J 6
New South Wales ◘ AUS 180-181 G 2
New Springs ○ AUS 176-177 F 2
New Stanton ○ USA (PA) 280-281 G 3
Newstead ○ CDN (NFL) 242-243 O 3
New Stuyahok ○ USA 22-23 S 3
New Summerfield ○ USA (TX) 268-269 E 5
Newton ○ USA (GA) 284-285 F 5
Newton ○ USA (IA) 274-275 E 3
Newton ○ USA (IL) 274-275 K 6
Newton ○ USA (KS) 262-263 J 6
Newton ○ USA (MS) 268-269 L 4
Newton ○ USA (NC) 282-283 F 5
Newton ○ USA (NJ) 280-281 M 2
Newton ○ USA (TX) 268-269 G 6
Newton Grove ○ USA (NC) 282-283 J 5
Newton Lake < USA (IL) 274-275 K 6
Newton Mills ○ CDN (NS) 240-241 N 5
Newtontoppen ▲ N 84-85 K 3
Newtown ○ CDN (NFL) 242-243 P 3
New Town ○ USA (ND) 258-259 E 4
Newtownabbey ○ GB 90-91 E 4
Newtown Steward ○ GB 90-91 D 4
New Ulm ○ USA (MN) 270-271 D 6
New Vienna ○ USA (OH) 280-281 C 4
New Waterford ○ CDN (NS) 240-241 P 4
New Waverly ○ USA (TX) 268-269 E 6
New Westminster ○ CDN (BC) 230-231 G 4
New World Island ⌒ CDN (NFL) 242-243 O 3
New York ○ • USA (NY) 280-281 N 3
New York ◘ USA 278-279 C 6
New York Mountains ▲ USA 248-249 J 4
New York State Thruway II USA (NY) 280-281 M 2
New Zealand ■ NZ 182 D 6
New Zealand ⌒ NZ 182 D 6
Nexapa, Río ~ MEX 52-53 E 2
Nexpa, Río ~ MEX 52-53 C 2
Neyyāttinkara ○ IND 140-141 G 6
Nezahualcóyotl, Ciudad ○ MEX 52-53 E 2
Nezahualcóyotl, Presa < MEX 52-53 H 3
Neždaninskoe ○ RUS 120-121 H 2
Nežin = Nižyn ○ UA 102-103 G 2
Neznaemyj, zaliv ≈ 108-109 G 5
Neznanovo ○ RUS 94-95 R 4
Nezperce ○ USA (ID) 250-251 C 5
Nez Perce Indian Reservation ✗ USA (ID) 250-251 C 5
Nez Perce National Historic Park • USA (ID) 250-251 C 5
Nez Perce Pass ▲ USA (ID) 250-251 E 6
Nezpique, Bayou ~ USA 268-269 H 6
Nfiss, Oued ~ MA 188-189 G 5
Ngabang ○ RI 162-163 H 4
Ngabé ○ RCB 210-211 F 5
Ngabordamlu, Tanjung ▲ RI 166-167 H 5
Ngabu ○ MW 218-219 H 3
Ngabwe ○ Z 218-219 D 1
Ngadda, River ~ WAN 204-205 K 2
Ngadiluwih ○ RI 168 E 3
Ngadza ○ RCA 206-207 E 6
Ngala ○ WAN 198-199 G 6
Ngali ○ ZRE 210-211 G 5
Ngalo ○ ZRE 206-207 F 6
Ngalu ○ • RI 168 E 8
Ngam ○ CAM 206-207 B 5
Ngam ○ TCH 206-207 C 3

368 Ndia — Ngam

Ntambu o Z 214-215 C 7
Ntandembele o ZRE 210-211 F 5
Ntatrat o RIM 196-197 C 6
Ntcheu o MW 218-219 H 2
Ntchisi o MW 218-219 G 1
Nteko o Z 214-215 G 5
Ntem ~ CAM 210-211 C 2
Ntemwa o Z 218-219 D 2
Nterguent o RIM 196-197 D 5
Nthalire o MW 214-215 G 6
Nthunga o MW 214-215 H 7
Ntibane o ZA 220-221 J 5
Ntimaru o EAK 212-213 E 4
Ntiona o TCH 198-199 G 5
Ntokou o G 210-211 E 3
Ntomba, Lac ⊖• ZRE 210-211 F 4
Ntoum o G 210-211 B 3
Ntsel, Hassi < DZ 190-191 F 7
Ntsou o RCB 210-211 E 4
Ntui o CAM 204-205 J 6
Ntungamo o EAU 212-213 C 4
Ntusi o EAU 212-213 C 3
Ntwetwe Pan ⊖ RB 218-219 C 5
Nu'airiya, an- o KSA 130-131 L 4
Nuakata Island ⌒ PNG 183 F 6
Nuaneteze, Rio ~ MOC 218-219 F 6
Nuangan o RI 164-165 J 3
Nuangola o USA (PA) 280-281 L 2
Nūba, Buhairat ⊖ SUD 200-201 E 2
Nubarašen o AR 128-129 L 2
Nubeena o AUS 180-181 J 7
Nubia = Nūba, an- ∸ SUD 200-201 D 3
Nubian Desert = Nūba, Ṣaḥrā' an- ∸ SUD 200-201 E 2
Nubieber o USA (CA) 246-247 D 2
Ñuble, Río ~ RCH 78-79 C 4
Nuboai o RI 166-167 J 3
Nučča ~ RUS 110-111 W 4
Nucla o USA (CO) 254-255 G 5
Nucuray, Río ~ PE 64-65 D 4
Nudlung Fiord ≈ 28-29 G 2
Nudo Aricoma ▲ PE 70-71 B 4
Nudo Chicllaraza ▲ PE 64-65 E 8
Nudo de Apolobamba ▲ PE 70-71 C 4
Nudo de Sunipani ▲ PE 70-71 B 4
Nudymi ~ RUS 120-121 H 4
Nueces River ~ USA 266-267 H 5
Nueces River, East ~ USA 266-267 G 4
Nueces River, West ~ USA 266-267 G 4
Nueltin Lake ⊖ CDN 30-31 U 5
Nuestra Señora del Rosario de Caá Catí o RA 76-77 J 4
Nueva, Isla ⌒ RCH 80 G 7
Nueva, La o EC 64-65 D 1
Nueva Alejandría o PE 64-65 F 4
Nueva Arcadia o HN 52-53 K 4
Nueva Ciudad Guerrero o MEX 50-51 K 4
Nueva Coahuila o MEX 52-53 J 2
Nueva Constitución o RA 78-79 F 3
Nueva Era o RP 160-161 D 4
Nueva Esperanza o RA (SAE) 76-77 F 4
Nueva Esperanza o RA (SAE) 76-77 E 4
Nueva Florida o YV 60-61 G 3
Nueva Galia o RA 78-79 G 3
Nueva Gerona ☆ C 54-55 D 4
Nueva Granada o CO 60-61 D 3
Nueva Guinea o NIC 52-53 B 6
Nueva Imperial o RCH 78-79 C 5
Nueva Italia o PY 76-77 J 3
Nueva Italia o RA 76-77 G 5
Nueva Italia de Ruíz o MEX 52-53 C 2
Nueva Lubecka o RA 80 E 2
Nueva Ocotepeque ☆ HN 52-53 K 4
Nueva Palmira o ROU 78-79 K 2
Nueva Pompeya o RA 76-77 G 3
Nueva Rosita o MEX 50-51 J 4
Nueva San Salvador ☆ ES 52-53 K 5
Nuevitas o C 54-55 G 4
Nuevo, Cayo ⌒ MEX 52-53 H 1
Nuevo, Golfo ≈ 78-79 G 7
Nuevo Andoas o PE 64-65 D 3
Nuevo Campechito o MEX 52-53 H 2
Nuevo Casas Grandes o MEX 50-51 F 2
Nuevo Esperanza o PE 64-65 E 2
Nuevo Laredo o MEX 50-51 K 4
Nuevo Leon ▫ MEX 50-51 J 4
Nuevo Mundo o CO 60-61 F 5
Nuevo Mundo, Cerro ▲ BOL 76-77 D 1
Nuevo Padilla o MEX 50-51 K 5
Nuevo Riaño o E 98-99 E 3
Nuevo Rocafuerte o EC 64-65 E 2
Nuevo Turino o RA 76-77 G 6
Nugaal ▫ SP 208-209 H 4
Nugaal, togga ~ SP 208-209 J 4
Nuga Nuga, Lake ⊖ AUS 178-179 K 3
Nugents Corner o USA (WA) 244-245 C 2
Nugong, Mount ▲ AUS 180-181 J 4
Nugtat Bülis al Habiliyah o LAR 192-193 D 1
Nuguaçu o BR 68-69 H 7
Nuguškoe vodohranilišče < RUS 96-97 K 7
Nuḥaib o IRQ 128-129 K 6
Nuhaida o OM 132-133 K 2
Nuhaka o NZ 182 F 3
Nuiqsut o USA 20-21 P 1
Nùi Thành o VN 158-159 K 3
Nuja = Karksi-Nuja o• EST 94-95 J 2
Nüjiang ~ VRC 144-145 B 4
Nu Jiang ~ VRC 142-143 L 3
Nükābād o IR 134-135 J 4
Nuku Bay ≈ 22-23 V 3
Nuka Island ⌒ USA 22-23 V 3
Nuka River ~ USA 20-21 L 2
Nukhaylah (Merga) o SUD 200-201 C 3
Nukiki o SOL 184 I c 2
Nukko Lake o CDN (BC) 228-229 L 2
Nukshak, Cape ▲ USA 22-23 U 3
Nuku o PNG 183 B 2
Nuku'alofa ★• TON 184 IV a 2
Nukubasaga ⌒ FJI 184 III c 2
Nuku-Hiva ⌒ F 13 N 3
Nukuhu o PNG 183 E 3
Nukulaelae Atoll ⌒ TUV 13 J 3
Nukus ☆ UZ 136-137 F 3
Nulato o USA 20-21 L 4
Nulato River ~ USA 20-21 L 4
Nuli o ZW 218-219 F 6
Nullagine o AUS 172-173 E 6
Nullagine River ~ AUS 172-173 E 6
Nulla Nulla o AUS 174-175 H 6
Nullarbor National Park ⊥ AUS 176-177 K 5
Nullarbor Plain ∸ AUS 176-177 J 5
Nullarbor Regional Reserve ⊥ AUS 176-177 K 5
Nullarbor Roadhouse o AUS 176-177 L 5
Nuluk River ~ USA 20-21 G 4
Num o NEP 144-145 F 7
Num, Pulau ⌒ RI 166-167 H 2
Numaligarh o IND 142-143 H 2
Numalla, Lake ⊖ AUS 178-179 H 5
Numan o WAN 204-205 K 4
Nu'mān, Ğazīrat an- ⌒ KSA 130-131 D 4
Nū'mān, Ma'arrat an- o• SYR 128-129 G 5
Numancia (Ruinas celtibércas y romanas) ∴• E 98-99 F 4
Nu'māniya, an- ☆ IRQ 128-129 L 6
Numata o J (GUM) 152-153 H 6
Numata o J (HOK) 152-153 J 3
Numatinna ~ SUD 206-207 H 5
Numazu o J 152-153 H 7
Number 24 Well o AUS 172-173 F 7
Number 35 Well < AUS 172-173 G 7
Numbi o ZRE 212-213 B 4
Numbulwar ✕ AUS 174-175 C 4
Numedal ∸ N 86-87 D 6
Numfor, Pulau ⌒ RI 166-167 H 2
Numil Downs o AUS 174-175 F 6
Numto o RUS 114-115 L 3
Numto, ozero ⊖ RUS 114-115 L 3
Numto, uval ▲ RUS 114-115 K 3
Numurkah o AUS 180-181 H 4
Nunalla (abandoned) o CDN 30-31 W 6
Nunarsuaq ⌒ GRØ 28-29 U 5
Nunarsuit ⌒ GRØ 28-29 Q 6
Nunataarssuk ▲ GRØ 28-29 Q 4
Nunavakanuk Lake ⊖ USA 20-21 H 5
Nunavakpak Lake ⊖ USA 20-21 J 6
Nunavaugaluk, Lake ⊖ USA 22-23 R 3
Nunavik ⌄ GRØ 26-27 X 8
Nunda o USA (NY) 278-279 D 6
Nunda o USA (SD) 260-261 J 2
Nundle o AUS 178-179 L 6
Nundroo o AUS 176-177 M 5
Nuneca o USA (MI) 272-273 C 4
Núñez, Isla ⌒ RCH 80 D 6
Nungesser Lake ⊖ CDN (ONT) 234-235 K 3
Nungo o MOC 218-219 J 1
Nungwaia o PNG 183 B 2
Nungwe Bay ≈ EAT 212-213 D 5
Nunim Lake ⊖ CDN 30-31 S 6
Nunivak Island ⌒ USA 20-21 G 0
Nunjamo o RUS 112-113 Z 4
Nunjamovaam ~ RUS 112-113 X 4
Nunligran o RUS (CUK) 112-113 X 4
Nunligran o RUS (CUK) 112-113 T 3
Nunn o USA (CO) 254-255 L 3
Ñuñoa o PE 70-71 B 4
Nun River ~ WAN 204-205 G 6
Nunukan Timur, Pulau ⌒ RI 164-165 E 1
Nuora ~ RUS 118-119 O 3
Nuoraldžyma ~ RUS 118-119 M 4
Nuoro o I 100-101 B 4
Nuporanga o BR 72-73 G 6
Nuqay, Jabal ▲ LAR 192-193 H 6
Nuqra, an- o KSA 130-131 G 5
Nuqruş, Ğabal ▲ ET 194-195 G 5
Nuqūb o Y 132-133 D 6
Nuqum, Ğabal ▲ Y 132-133 D 6
Nūr o IR 136-137 B 6
Nura o KZ (AKT) 126-127 P 3
Nūra ~ KZ 124-125 F 3
Nūrābād o• IR (FAR) 134-135 D 3
Nūrābād o• IR (LOR) 134-135 B 1
Nurata ☆ UZ 136-137 J 4
Nuratalıdy o KZ 124-125 H 4
Nurato tog tizmasi ▲ UZ 136-137 J 4
Nur Dağları ▲ TR 128-129 G 4
Nurei o SUD 198-199 L 6
Nurek o TJ 136-137 L 5
Nuremberg = Nürnberg o D 92-93 L 4
Nūrestān o• AFG 138-139 C 2
Nūr Gāma o PK 134-135 M 4
Nurhak ☆ TR 128-129 G 4
Nurhak Dağı ▲ TR 128-129 G 3
Nuri o MEX 50-51 E 3
Nuri •• SUD 200-201 E 3
Nuri, Teluk ≈ 162-163 H 5
Nuriootpa o AUS 180-181 E 3
Nurkaat o RI 166-167 F 5
Nurlat ☆ RUS 96-97 G 6
Nurmes o FIN 88-89 K 5
Nurmijärvi o FIN 88-89 K 5
Nürnberg o D 92-93 L 4
Nurobod ☆ UZ 136-137 K 5
Nurota sovhozi o UZ 136-137 K 4
Nūrpur o PK 138-139 C 4
Nursery o USA (TX) 266-267 K 5
Nusa Barung, Pulau ⌒ RI 168 E 4
Nusa Dua o RI 168 B 7
Nusa Kambangan ⌒ RI 168 C 3
Nusa Laut, Pulau ⌒ RI 166-167 E 3
Nusa Tenggara Barat ▫ RI 168 C 6
Nusa Tenggara Timur ▫ RI 166-167 B 6
Nusawulan o RI 166-167 G 4
Nusaybin ☆ TR 128-129 J 4
Nusela, Kepulauan ⌒ RI 166-167 F 2
Nushagak Bay ≈ 22-23 R 3
Nushagak Peninsula ⌄ USA 22-23 R 3
Nushagak River ~ USA 22-23 S 3
Nu Shan ▲ VRC 142-143 L 2
Nushki o PK 134-135 L 4
Nutaarmiut ⌒ GRØ 26-27 X 7
Nutak o CDN 36-37 T 6
Nutaugé, laguna ≈ 112-113 W 3
Nut Mountain o CDN (SAS) 232-233 P 3
Nutrias, Las o RA 78-79 K 5
Nutrioso o USA (AZ) 256-257 F 5
Nuttal o PK 138-139 B 5
Nutuvukti Lake ⊖ USA 20-21 N 3
Nutwood Downs o AUS 174-175 C 4
Nuu o EAK 212-213 G 4
Nuugaatsiaq o GRØ 26-27 Y 8
Nuuk = Godthåb ☆ GRØ 28-29 P 4
Nuuk Kangerluaq ≈ 28-29 P 4
Nuurst o MAU 148-149 J 4
Nuussuaq Halvø ⌄ GRØ 28-29 O 1
Nuvuk Point ▲ CDN 36-37 R 2
Nuwaibi' al-Muzayyina o ET 194-195 G 3
Nuwaisib, al- o KWT 130-131 L 3
Nuwara Eliya o•• CL 140-141 J 7
Nuwefontein o NAM 220-221 D 3
Nuweh o RI 166-167 K 5
Nuwekloof ▲ ZA 220-221 F 6
Nuwerus o ZA 220-221 D 5
Nuweveldberge ▲ ZA 220-221 E 6
Nuy o ZA 220-221 D 6
Nuyakuk Lake ⊖ USA 22-23 R 3
Nuyts Archipelago ⌒ AUS 180-181 B 2
Nuyts Reefs ⌒ AUS 180-181 B 2
Nūzvīd o IND 140-141 J 2
Nwa o CAM 204-205 J 5
Nwanetsi o ZA 220-221 L 2
N.W. Crocodile Island ⌒ AUS 174-175 C 2
Nxai Pan ⊖ RB 218-219 C 4
Nxai Pan National Park ⊥ RB 218-219 C 4
Nya ~ TCH 206-207 B 4
Nyabarongo ~ RWA 212-213 B 4
Nyabisindu o RWA 212-213 B 5
Nyadire ~ ZW 218-219 G 3
Nyagassola o RG 202-203 F 3
Nya-Ghezi o ZRE 212-213 B 5
Nyahanga o EAT 212-213 D 5
Nyahua ~ EAT 212-213 D 6
Nyahururu o EAK 212-213 F 3
Nyah West o AUS 180-181 G 3
Nyainqêntanglha Feng ▲ VRC 144-145 H 5
Nyainqêntanglha Shan ▲ VRC 144-145 G 6
Nyainrong o VRC 144-145 J 4
Nyakahura o EAT 212-213 C 5
Nyakanazi o EAT 212-213 C 5
Nyak Co ⊖ VRC 144-145 B 4
Nyalà o SUD 200-201 B 6
Nyalam o VRC 144-145 E 6
Ny Ålesund o N 84-85 G 3
Nyali o G 210-211 C 5
Nyalikungu o EAT 212-213 D 5
Nyamandhlovu o ZW 218-219 E 4
Nyamapanda o ZW 218-219 G 3
Nyamassila o RT 202-203 L 6
Nyāmati o IND 140-141 F 3
Nyamirembe o EAT 212-213 D 5
Nyamlell o SUD 206-207 H 4
Nyamoko o CAM 204-205 J 6
Nyamuswa o EAT 212-213 E 5
Nyanding, Khor ~ SUD 206-207 L 4
Nyanga ~ G 210-211 C 5
Nyanga o RCB 210-211 C 5
Nyanga o• ZW 218-219 G 4
Nyangamara o EAT 214-215 K 6
Nyanza ▫ EAK 212-213 E 4
Nyanza Lac o BU 212-213 B 6
Nyarling River ~ CDN 30-31 M 5
Nyaru o EAK 212-213 E 3
Nyasa o ZRE 210-211 L 6
Nyasa, Lake ⊖ EAT 214-215 H 6
Nyassar o CAM 206-207 B 5
Nyaungkhashe o MYA 158-159 D 2
Nyaunglebin o MYA 158-159 D 2
Nyaung U o MYA 142-143 J 5
Nyazura o ZW 218-219 G 4
Nyazwidzi ~ ZW 218-219 F 4
Nybergsund o N 86-87 F 6
Nyborg o N 86-87 F 9
Nyhorg o• DK 86-87 E 9
Nybro ☆ S 86-87 G 8
Nyčalah o RUS 110-111 a 5
Nyda o RUS (JAN) 108-109 P 8
Nyda ~ RUS 108-109 Q 8
Nyé ~ G 210-211 C 2
Nye o USA (OR) 244-245 G 5
Nyeboe Land ∸ GRØ 26-27 W 3
Nyegezi o EAT 212-213 D 5
Nyenase o GH 202-203 K 7
Nyensung o GH 202-203 K 5
Nyeri ☆ EAK 212-213 F 4
Nyeri ▲ EAU 212-213 C 2
Ny-Friesland ⌄ N 84-85 K 3
Nygčekveem ~ RUS 112-113 T 5
Nygčigen, mys ▲ RUS 112-113 Y 4
Nyibiam o WAN 204-205 H 4
Nyiel o SUD 206-207 K 5
Nyika o ZW 218-219 F 4
Nyikine o SN 202-203 B 3
Nyima o VRC 144-145 F 5
Nyimba o Z 218-219 F 2
Nyiminiama o RMM 202-203 J 2
Nyingchi o VRC 144-145 K 6
Nyiragongo ▲ ZRE 212-213 B 4
Nyírbátor o H 92-93 R 5
Nyíregyháza o H 92-93 Q 5
Nyiri Desert ∸ EAK 212-213 F 5
Nyiru Range ▲ EAK 212-213 F 2
Nyjskij, zaliv ≈ 122-123 K 3
Nykarleby o FIN 88-89 G 5
Nykia National Park ⊥ MW 214-215 G 6
Nykia Plateau ▲• MW 214-215 G 6
Nykøbing Falster o DK 86-87 E 9
Nykøbing Mors o DK 86-87 D 8
Nyköping o S 86-87 H 7
Nyland = Uusima ∸ FIN 88-89 H 6
Nylrivier ~ ZA 220-221 J 2
Nylstroom o ZA 220-221 J 2
Nymagee o AUS 180-181 J 2
Nymburk o• CZ 92-93 N 3
Nymphe Bank ≈ 90-91 D 6
Nynäshamn ☆ S 86-87 H 7
Nyngan o AUS 178-179 J 6
Nyoma Rap o IND 138-139 G 3
Nyong ~ CAM 210-211 C 2
Nyons o F 90-91 K 9
Nyos, Lac ⊖ CAM 204-205 J 5
Nyrud o RUS 88-89 K 2
Nyš o RUS (SHL) 122-123 K 3
Nyš ~ RUS 122-123 K 3
Nysa o• PL 92-93 O 3
Nysa Kłodzka ~ PL 92-93 O 3
Nysa Łużycka ~ PL 92-93 N 3
Nyssa o USA (OR) 244-245 H 7
Nytva ☆ RUS 96-97 J 5
Nyudō-saki ▲ J 152-153 H 4
Nyumba ya Mungu Reservoir < EAT 212-213 F 5
Nyunzu o ZRE 212-213 B 6
Nyvrovo o RUS 120-121 K 6
Nyžni Sirohozy o UA 102-103 J 4
Nyžni Torhaji o UA 102-103 J 4
Nyžn'ohirs'kyj ☆ UA 102-103 J 5
Nzako o RCA (Mbo) 206-207 F 6
Nzako ~ RCA 206-207 F 6
Nzambi o RCB 210-211 C 5
Nzara o SUD 206-207 J 6
Nzassi o RCB 210-211 D 6
Nzébéla o RG 202-203 F 5
Nzega o EAT 212-213 D 6
Nzérékoré ▫ RG 202-203 F 5
Nzérékoré ☆ RG 202-203 F 6
N'Zeto o ANG 216-217 B 3
Nzi ~ CI 202-203 H 6
Nzili, Bahr ~ RCA 206-207 F 3
Nzilo, Lac < ZRE 214-215 C 6
Nzima o EAT 212-213 D 5
Nzo ~ CI 202-203 G 6
Nzo o RG 202-203 F 6
N'zo, Réserve de faune du ⊥ CI 202-203 G 6
Nzoia ~ EAK 212-213 E 3
Nzoro o RCA 206-207 B 5
Nzoro ~ ZRE 212-213 C 2

O

Oā', Wādi al- ~ KSA 130-131 F 4
Oahe, Lake ⊖ USA (SD) 260-261 F 2
Oahu ⌒ USA (HI) 288 H 3
Oakbank o AUS 180-181 F 2
Oak Bay o CDN (BC) 230-231 F 5
Oak Bluff o CDN (MAN) 234-235 F 5
Oak Bluffs o USA (MA) 278-279 L 7
Oakburn o CDN (MAN) 234-235 C 4
Oak City o USA (NC) 282-283 K 5
Oak City o USA (UT) 254-255 C 4
Oak Creek o USA (CO) 254-255 J 3
Oak Creek o USA (WI) 274-275 L 2
Oakdale o USA (CA) 248-249 D 2
Oakdale o USA (LA) 268-269 H 6
Oakes o USA (ND) 258-259 J 5
Oakey o AUS 178-179 L 4
Oakey Creek ~ AUS 178-179 L 4
Oak Grove o USA (LA) 268-269 J 4
Oak Harbor o USA (OH) 280-281 C 2
Oak Harbor o USA (WA) 244-245 C 2
Oak Hill o USA (AL) 284-285 C 5
Oak Hill o USA (FL) 286-287 J 3
Oak Hill o USA (OH) 280-281 D 5
Oak Hill o USA (WV) 280-281 E 6
Oak Hills o AUS 174-175 H 6
Oakhurst o USA (CA) 248-249 E 2
Oak Lake o CDN (MAN) 234-235 C 5
Oak Lake ⊖ CDN (MAN) 234-235 C 5
Oakland o CDN (MAN) 234-235 E 4
Oakland o USA (CA) 248-249 B 2
Oakland o USA (IA) 274-275 C 3
Oakland o USA (IL) 274-275 K 5
Oakland o USA (MD) 280-281 G 4
Oakland o USA (MS) 268-269 L 2
Oakland o USA (NE) 262-263 K 3
Oakland City o USA (IN) 274-275 L 6
Oakland Park o USA (FL) 286-287 J 5
Oaklands o AUS 180-181 J 3
Oak Lawn o USA (IL) 274-275 L 3
Oak Level o USA (AL) 284-285 E 3
Oakley o USA (ID) 252-253 E 4
Oakley o USA (KS) 262-263 F 5
Oakover River ~ AUS 172-173 E 6
Oak Park o USA (GA) 284-285 H 4
Oak Point o CDN (MAN) 234-235 F 4
Oak Ridge o USA (LA) 268-269 J 4
Oakridge o USA (OR) 244-245 C 7
Oak Ridge o USA (TN) 282-283 C 4
Oak Ridge o USA (TX) 268-269 E 6
Oak River o CDN (MAN) 234-235 C 4
Oakshela o CDN (SAS) 232-233 Q 5
Oakview o CDN (MAN) 234-235 E 3
Oak View o USA (CA) 248-249 E 5
Oakville o CDN (MAN) 234-235 E 5
Oakville o CDN (ONT) 238-239 F 5
Oakville o USA (TX) 266-267 J 5
Oakville o USA (WA) 244-245 B 4
Oakwood o USA (IL) 274-275 L 4
Oakwood o USA (OK) 264-265 F 3
Oakwood o USA (TN) 276-277 H 4
Oakwood o USA (TX) 268-269 E 5
Oaky Creek o AUS 178-179 K 2
Oamaru o NZ 182 C 6
Oan o RI 164-165 G 3
Oasis o USA (CA) 248-249 G 2
Oasis o USA (NM) 256-257 L 5
Oasis o USA (NV) 246-247 L 2
Oates Land ∸ ARK 16 F 17
Oatlands o AUS 180-181 J 7
Oatman o USA (AZ) 256-257 A 3
Oaxaca ▫ MEX 52-53 F 3
Oaxaca de Juárez ☆ ••• MEX 52-53 F 3
Ob' o RUS (NVS) 114-115 R 7
Ob' ~ RUS 10-11 G 2
Oba o CDN (ONT) 236-237 D 3
Oba o WAN 204-205 F 5
Obaa o RI 166-167 K 5
Obaba o RCB 210-211 F 4
Obagan ~ KZ 124-125 D 2
Obaha o PNG 183 E 5
Obakamiga Lake ⊖ CDN (ONT) 236-237 C 3
Obala o CAM 204-205 J 6
Obalapuram o IND 140-141 G 3
Obama o J 152-153 F 7
Obamska, Rivière ~ CDN 38-39 E 3
Oban o AUS 178-179 E 1
Oban o CDN (SAS) 232-233 K 3
Oban o GB 90-91 E 3
Oban o RCB 210-211 E 4
Oban o WAN 204-205 H 6
Obanazawa o J 152-153 J 5
Oban Hills ▲ WAN 204-205 H 6
Obanska, Rivière ~ CDN 236-237 K 2
Obatanga Provincial Park ⊥ CDN (ONT) 236-237 C 4
Öbe o• AFG 134-135 K 1
Obe = Île Aoba ⌒ VAN 184 II a 2
Obed o CDN (ALB) 228-229 R 3
Obed River ~ USA 282-283 C 4
Obehie o WAN 204-205 G 6
Obeiz, hrebet ▲ RUS 114-115 E 2
Obele o WAN 204-205 G 5
Obelial o LT 94-95 J 4
Obel-prolaz ▲ MK 100-101 J 4
Obera o• RA 76-77 K 4
Oberlin o USA (KS) 262-263 F 5
Oberlin o USA (LA) 268-269 H 6
Oberon o AUS 180-181 K 2
Oberon o CDN (MAN) 234-235 D 4
Oberösterreich ▫ A 92-93 M 4
Oberpfälzer Wald ∸ D 92-93 M 4
Oberstdorf o• D 92-93 L 5
Oberstein, Idar- o D 92-93 J 4
Obhur o KSA 132-133 A 3
Obi o WAN 204-205 H 4
Obi, Pulau ⌒ RI 164-165 K 4
Obi, Selat ≈ 164-165 K 4
Obiaruku o WAN 204-205 G 6
Óbidos o BR 62-63 G 6
Óbidos o•• P 98-99 C 5
Obigarm o TJ 136-137 L 5
Obihingou ~ TJ 136-137 M 5
Obihiro o J 152-153 K 3
Obilatu, Pulau ⌒ RI 164-165 K 4
Obion o USA (TN) 276-277 F 4
Obispo Trejo o RA 76-77 F 6
Obitočna kosa ⌄ UA 102-103 K 4
Oblačnaja, gora ▲ RUS 122-123 F 7
Oblačnyj Golec, gora ▲ RUS 120-121 F 5
Oblong o USA (IL) 274-275 L 6
Obluč'e o RUS 122-123 D 4
Oblukovina ~ RUS 120-121 R 6
Obninsk o RUS 94-95 P 4
Obo ☆ RCA 206-207 H 6
Obo o VRC 154-155 B 3
Oboa ▲ EAU 212-213 E 3
Obock o DJI 200-201 L 6
Obogu o GH 202-203 K 6
Obojan o RUS 102-103 K 2
Obokote o ZRE 210-211 L 4
Oboli o RCB 210-211 E 4
Obolo o WAN 204-205 G 5
Obonga Lake ⊖ CDN (ONT) 234-235 O 4
Obout o CAM 210-211 C 2
Obouya o RCB 210-211 E 4
Obozerskij o RUS 88-89 Q 5
Obra ~ PL 92-93 N 2
Obregón, Ciudad o MEX 50-51 E 4
Obrenovac o YU 100-101 H 2
O'Brien o USA (OR) 244-245 B 8
O'Brien Creek ~ USA 250-251 J 3
Obrovac o HR 100-101 E 2
Obručevo, vozvyšennost' ▲ RUS 120-121 V 7
Obruchev Rise ≃ 14-15 J 2
Obruk Yaylâsı ▲ TR 128-129 E 3
Obryvistaja, gora ▲ RUS 112-113 S 3
Obryvistyj, mys ▲ RUS (KOR) 112-113 M 5
Obryvistyj, mys ▲ RUS (TMR) 108-109 I c 2
Obščij syrt ▲ RUS 96-97 F 8
Observatório Astronómico • RA 76-77 C 6
Observatory Hill ▲ AUS 176-177 M 4
Observatory Inlet ≈ 32-33 F 4
Obskaja guba ≈ 108-109 P 8
Obskaya Guba = Obskaja guba ≈ 108-109 P 8
Obuasi o CI 202-203 K 6
Obubra o WAN 204-205 H 5
Obuchiv o UA 102-103 G 2
Obudu o WAN 204-205 H 5
Obudu Cattle Ranch o• WAN 204-205 H 5
Obusa o RUS (UST) 116-117 L 9
Obusa ~ RUS 116-117 M 9
Obytočna zatoka ≈ 102-103 J 4
Očakiv o UA 102-103 G 4
Ocala o USA (FL) 286-287 G 2
Ocalli o PE 64-65 C 5
Očamčira o GE 126-127 D 6
Ocampo o MEX (COA) 50-51 H 4
Ocampo o MEX (TAM) 50-51 K 6
Ocaña o CO 60-61 E 3
Ocaña o E 98-99 F 5
Ocapi, Parc National de la ⊥ ZRE 212-213 A 3
Ocaso o CO 64-65 F 1
Ocate o USA (NM) 256-257 K 2
Occidente o CO 64-65 F 2
Ocean City o USA (MD) 280-281 L 5
Ocean City o USA (NJ) 280-281 M 4
Ocean City o USA (WA) 244-245 A 3
Ocean Falls o CDN (BC) 228-229 G 4
Ocean Grove-Barwon Heads o AUS 180-181 H 5
Oceanographer Fracture Zone ≃ 6-7 E 5
Ocean Shores o USA (WA) 244-245 A 4
Oceanside o USA (CA) 248-249 G 6
Ocean Springs o USA (MS) 268-269 M 6
Ocean View o USA (NJ) 280-281 M 4
Očenyrd, gora ▲ RUS 108-109 L 7
Očer ☆ RUS 96-97 J 5
Ochiai o J 152-153 E 7
O'Chiese Indian Reserve ✕ CDN (ALB) 232-233 C 3
Ochito ~ PK 134-135 M 6
Ochlockonee River ~ USA 286-287 E 1
Ochoa, La o MEX 50-51 H 5
Ochobo o WAN 204-205 G 5
Ochopee o USA (FL) 286-287 H 6
Ocho Rios o• JA 54-55 G 5
Ochre River o CDN (MAN) 234-235 D 3
Ochtyrka o UA 102-103 J 2
Ocilla o USA (GA) 284-285 G 5
Ockelbo o S 86-87 H 6
Ocmulgee National Monument • USA (GA) 284-285 G 4
Ocmulgee River ~ USA 284-285 H 5
Ocoa, Bahía de ≈ 54-55 K 5
Ocoa, Sierra de ▲ DOM 54-55 K 5
Ocoee o USA (TN) 282-283 C 5
Ocoee, Lake ⊖ USA (TN) 282-283 C 5
Ocoña o PE 70-71 A 5
Ocoña, Río de ~ PE 70-71 A 5
Oconee, Lake < USA (GA) 284-285 G 3
Oconee River ~ USA 284-285 H 4
Oconee River, North ~ USA 284-285 G 2
Ocongate o PE 70-71 B 3
O'Connor, Port o USA (TX) 266-267 L 5
Oconomowoc o USA (WI) 274-275 K 1
Oconto o USA (NE) 262-263 G 3
Oconto o USA (WI) 270-271 L 6
Oconto River ~ USA 270-271 K 6
Ocoruro o PE 70-71 B 4
Ocós o GCA 52-53 H 4
Ocosingo o MEX 52-53 H 3
Ocotal ☆ NIC 52-53 L 5
Ocotillo Wells o USA (CA) 248-249 H 6
Ocotito, El o MEX 52-53 E 3
Ocotlán o MEX (JAL) 52-53 C 1
Ocotlán o• MEX (OAX) 52-53 F 3
Ocozocoautla o MEX 52-53 H 3
Ocracoke Island ⌒ USA (NC) 282-283 M 5
Ocracoke o USA (NC) 282-283 M 5
Ocreza, Ribeiro do ~ P 98-99 D 5
Ocros o PE (ANC) 64-65 D 7
Ocros o PE (AYA) 64-65 F 8
Octavia o USA (NE) 262-263 J 3
Octotillo o USA (CA) 248-249 H 7
Octy, Mount ▲ AUS 178-179 C 1
Ocú o• PA 52-53 D 8
Ocua o MOC 218-219 K 1
Očugui-Botuobuja ~ RUS 118-119 G 4
Ocujal o C 54-55 G 5
Ocumare del Tuy o YV 60-61 H 2
Ocuri o BOL 70-71 E 6
Oda o GH 202-203 K 7
Ódáðahraun ▲ IS 86-87 e 2
Odaejin o KOR 150-151 G 7
Odaesan National Park ⊥• ROK 150-151 G 9
Odammun ~ RI 166-167 K 5
Ödate o J 152-153 J 4
Odawara o J 152-153 H 7
Odda, Oke- o WAN 204-205 F 4
Odebolt o USA (IA) 274-275 C 2
Odei River ~ CDN 34-35 G 2
Odell o USA (IN) 274-275 L 4
Odell o USA (NE) 262-263 K 4
Odell o USA (TX) 264-265 E 4
Odem o USA (TX) 266-267 K 6
Odemira o P 98-99 C 6
Ödemiş ☆ TR 128-129 B 3
Odendaalsrus o ZA 220-221 H 3
Odense o• DK 86-87 E 9
Odenton o USA (MD) 280-281 K 4
Oder ~ D 92-93 N 2
Oderbruch ∸ D 92-93 N 2
Odesa ☆•• UA 102-103 G 4
Odesa o USA (NJ) 280-281 L 4
Odessa o CDN (SAS) 232-233 P 5
Odessa o USA (MO) 274-275 E 6
Odessa o USA (TX) 266-267 E 2
Odessa o USA (WA) 244-245 G 3
Odessa = Odesa ☆•• UA 102-103 G 4
Odienné ☆• CI 202-203 G 5
Odighi o WAN 204-205 F 5
Odincovo ☆ RUS 94-95 P 4
Odiongan o RP 160-161 D 6
Odjala o G 210-211 D 4
Odjan, zaliv ≈ 120-121 O 4
Odoev ☆ RUS 94-95 P 5
Odomlja ☆ RUS 94-95 O 3
Odon o USA (IN) 274-275 M 6
Ödöngk o K 158-159 H 5
Odonkawkrom o GH 202-203 K 6
O'Donnell o USA (TX) 264-265 C 6
O'Donnell River ~ AUS 172-173 H 5
Odorheiu Secuiesc o RO 102-103 D 4
Odra ~ PL 92-93 N 2
Odrus ~ SUD 200-201 H 3
Odum o USA (GA) 284-285 H 5
Odupónkpehe o GH 202-203 K 7
Odžaci o YU 100-101 G 2
Odzala, Parc National d' ⊥ RCB 210-211 E 3
Odzema o RCB 210-211 F 4
Odzi o ZW (Mcl) 218-219 G 4
Odzi ~ ZW 218-219 G 4
Odziba o RCB 210-211 E 5
Oeiras o BR 68-69 G 5
Oeiras do Para o BR 62-63 K 6
Oekussi o RI 166-167 C 6
Oelrichs o USA (SD) 260-261 C 3
Oelwein o USA (IA) 274-275 G 2
Oenpelli ✕ AUS 174-175 B 3
Oesilo o RI 166-167 C 6
Oever, Den o NL 92-93 H 2
Of ☆ TR 128-129 J 2
Ofa o WAN 204-205 F 4
Ófærufoss •• IS 86-87 d 3
O'Fallon Creek ~ USA 250-251 O 5
Ofanto ~ I 100-101 E 4
Ofaqin o JOR 130-131 D 2
Ofcolaco o ZA 220-221 K 2
Ofe, River ~ WAN 204-205 F 4
Ofelia, La o RA 78-79 D 5
Ofere o WAN 204-205 G 4
Offenbach am Main o D 92-93 K 3
Offenburg o D 92-93 J 4
Offerle o USA (KS) 262-263 G 7
Officer Creek ~ AUS 176-177 M 3
Offoué ~ G 210-211 C 4
Offoue, Réserve de l' ⊥ G 210-211 C 4
Offumpo o CI 202-203 H 7
Ofhidro, Isla ⌒ RCH 80 C 4
Oficinna Victoria o RCH 70-71 C 7
Ofinso o GH 202-203 K 6
Ofizina Alemania o RCH 76-77 C 3
Ofjord ≈ 26-27 m 8
Ofoase o GH 202-203 K 6
Ofolanga ⌒ TON 184 IV a 1
Ofotfjorden ≈ 86-87 H 2
Ofu o USA 184 V c 2
Ofugo o WAN 204-205 G 5
Ofu Island ⌒ USA 184 V c 2
Ōfunato o J 152-153 J 5
Oga o J 152-153 H 5
Oga, zaliv ≈ 108-109 H 4
Ogaden ∸ ETH 208-209 F 5
Oga-hanto ⌄ J 152-153 H 5
Ōgaki o J 152-153 G 7
Ogaki-Hachim-Shrine • J 152-153 J 5
Ogallala o USA (NE) 262-263 E 3
Ogan ~ RI 162-163 F 6
Oganda, Parc National de l' ⊥ G 210-211 C 4
Oganda, Portes de l' • G 210-211 C 4
Ogani o WAN 204-205 G 6
Ogar, Pulau ⌒ RI 166-167 G 3
Ogascana, Lac ⊖ CDN (QUE) 236-237 K 5
Ogba o WAN 204-205 F 5
Ogbia o WAN 204-205 G 6
Ogbomoso o WAN 204-205 F 4
Ogden o CDN (NS) 240-241 O 5
Ogden o USA (AR) 276-277 A 7
Ogden o USA (IA) 274-275 D 2
Ogden o USA (UT) 254-255 D 2
Ogden Center o USA (MI) 272-273 F 6
Ogdensburg o USA (NY) 278-279 F 4
Ogeechee River ~ USA 284-285 J 4
Ogeechee River ~ USA 284-285 H 3
Ogema o CDN (SAS) 232-233 O 6
Ogema o USA (MN) 270-271 C 3
Ogema o USA (WI) 270-271 H 5
Ogembo o EAK 212-213 E 4
Oger = Ogre ☆•• LV 94-95 J 3
Ogi o J 152-153 H 6
Ogies o ZA 220-221 J 3
Ogiinuur = Zögstej o MAU 148-149 F 4
Ogilvie o AUS 176-177 C 4
Ogilvie o CDN 20-21 V 4
Ogilvie Mountains ▲ CDN 20-21 U 3
Ogilvie River ~ CDN 20-21 V 4
Oglala o USA (SD) 260-261 D 3
Oglala Pass ≈ 22-23 F 7
Oglanly o TM 136-137 D 5
Oglat Beraber o MA 188-189 K 5
Oglat el Faci o DZ (TIN) 188-189 L 7
Oglat el Faci o DZ (TIN) 188-189 J 7
Oglat el Khnâchîch o RMM 196-197 J 4
Oglat Marhboura o DZ 188-189 L 4
Ogle Point ▲ CDN 24-25 Y 6
Oglethorpe o USA (GA) 284-285 F 4
Oglinga Island ⌒ USA 22-23 G 7
Ogmore o AUS 178-179 K 2
Ognon ~ F 90-91 L 8
Ogodža o RUS 122-123 E 2
Ogoja o WAN 204-205 H 5
Ogoki Lake ⊖ CDN (ONT) 234-235 Q 4
Ogoki Reservoir ⊖ CDN (ONT) 234-235 P 4
Ogoki River ~ CDN 234-235 P 4
Ogoki River ~ CDN 234-235 R 3
Ogooué ~ G 210-211 C 4
Ogorodtah o RUS 118-119 P 4
Ogoron o RUS 118-119 O 8
Ogou ~ RT 202-203 L 5
Ogoulou ~ G 210-211 C 4
Ogr o SUD 200-201 C 6
Ogre ☆• LV 94-95 J 3
Ogulin o HR 100-101 E 2
Ogun o WAN (OYO) 204-205 F 4
Ogun ▫ WAN 204-205 E 5
Ogun, River ~ WAN 204-205 E 5
Ogurčinskij, ostrov ⌒ TM 136-137 C 5
Ogurugu o WAN 204-205 G 5
Oguta o WAN 204-205 G 6
Ogwashi-Uku o WAN 204-205 G 5
Oha ☆• RUS 122-123 K 2
Ohafia o WAN 204-205 G 6
Ohai o NZ 182 A 6
Ohanapecosh o USA (WA) 244-245 D 4
Ohansk ☆ RUS 96-97 J 5
Ohanskaja vozvyšennost' ▲ RUS 96-97 J 5
Ōhata o J 152-153 J 4
Ohaton o CDN (ALB) 232-233 F 3
Ohau, Lake ⊖ NZ 182 B 6
Ohi ▲ GR 100-101 K 5
O'Higgins, Lago ⊖ RCH 80 D 4
Ohinskij perešeek ⌄ RUS 122-123 K 2
Ohio ▫ USA 280-281 C 3
Ohiopyle o USA (PA) 280-281 G 4
Ohiopyle State Park ⊥ USA (PA) 280-281 G 4
Ohio River ~ USA 276-277 G 3
Ohogamuit o USA 20-21 K 6
Ohogrigol ~ RUS 114-115 P 3
Ohonua o TON 184 IV a 2
Ohoopee River ~ USA 284-285 H 4
Ohota ~ RUS 120-121 K 4
Ohotsk ☆• RUS 120-121 K 4
Ohotskij Perevoz o RUS 120-121 F 3
Ohotskoe o RUS 122-123 K 5
Ohře ~ CZ 92-93 M 3
Ohrid o••• MK 100-101 H 4
Ohridsko Ezero ⊖ MK 100-101 H 4
Ohrigstad o ZA 220-221 K 2
Ohrit, Liqueni i ⊖ AL 100-101 H 4
Ohura o NZ 182 E 3
Oiapoque ~ BR 62-63 H 4
Oiapoque = Martinique o BR 62-63 J 4
Oiapoque, Reserva Biológica de ⊥ BR 62-63 H 4
Oies, Ile aux ⌒ CDN (QUE) 240-241 E 3
Ōi-gawa ~ J 152-153 H 7
Oijärvi o FIN 88-89 H 4
Oil City o USA (LA) 268-269 G 4
Oil City o USA (PA) 280-281 G 2

Ntambu — Oil City 371

Oil Creek State Park ⊥ USA (PA) 280-281 G 2
Oildale ○ USA (CA) 248-249 E 4
Oil Gathering Station ○ LAR 192-193 G 3
Oilmont ○ USA (MT) 250-251 H 3
Oil Springs ○ CDN (ONT) 238-239 C 6
Oil Through ○ USA (AR) 276-277 D 5
Oilton ○ USA (TX) 266-267 J 6
Oise ~ F 90-91 J 7
Ōita ☆ J 152-153 D 8
Oja ~ RUS 116-117 F 9
Ojai ○ USA (CA) 248-249 E 5
Ojašinskij, Stancionno- ○ RUS 114-115 R 7
Oje ○ WAN 204-205 G 5
Ojibwa ○ USA (WI) 270-271 G 5
Ojinaga ○ MEX 50-51 G 3
Ojiya ○ J 152-153 H 6
Ojmauyt ○ KZ 126-127 L 4
Ojmjakon ○ RUS 120-121 K 2
Ojmjakonskoe nagor'e ▲ RUS 120-121 J 2
Ojmur ○ RUS 116-117 N 9
Ojnaa ○ RUS 116-117 H 10
Ojobo ○ WAN 204-205 F 6
Ojo Caliente ○ MEX 50-51 H 6
Ojo Caliente ○ USA (NM) 256-257 J 2
Ojo de Carrizo ○ MEX 50-51 G 3
Ojo de Liebre, Laguna ≈ 50-51 B 4
Ojo Feliz ○ USA (NM) 256-257 K 2
Ojokkuduk ○ UZ 136-137 J 4
Ojos del Salado, Nevado ▲ RCH 76-77 C 4
Ojos Negros ○ MEX 50-51 A 2
Ojotung ○ RUS 110-111 b 4
Ojsylkara ~ KZ 126-127 N 3
Oj-Tal ○ KS 146-147 B 5
Oj-Tal ~ KS 136-137 N 4
Ojtal ○ KZ 136-137 N 3
Oju ○ WAN 204-205 H 5
Ojuelos de Jalisco ○ MEX 50-51 J 7
Ojusardah ○ RUS 112-113 H 2
Ojusut ○ RUS 118-119 G 4
Oka ○ CDN (QUE) 238-239 L 3
Oka ○ RCB 210-211 E 5
Oka ~ RUS 94-95 P 4
Oka ~ RUS 116-117 K 8
Oka ○ WAN 204-205 F 5
Okaba ○ RI 166-167 K 6
Okahandja ☆ NAM 216-217 D 10
Okakarara ○ NAM 216-217 D 10
Okak Island ⌒ CDN 36-37 T 6
Okali ○ RCB 210-211 E 4
Okaliktok Islands ⌒ CDN 36-37 U 7
Okanagan Centre ○ CDN (BC) 230-231 K 3
Okanagan Falls ○ CDN (BC) 230-231 K 4
Okanagan Indian Reserve X CDN (BC) 230-231 K 3
Okanagan Lake ⊖ CDN (BC) 230-231 K 4
Okanagan Landing ○ CDN (BC) 230-231 K 3
Okanagan Range ▲ CDN 230-231 J 4
Okanagan Valley ⌣ CDN 230-231 K 4
Okangoho ○ NAM 216-217 D 10
Okankolo ○ NAM 216-217 D 8
Okano ~ G 210-211 C 3
Okanogan ○ USA (WA) 244-245 F 2
Okanogan Range ▲ 244-245 E 1
Okanogan River ~ USA (WA) 244-245 F 2
Okanono ○ NAM 216-217 C 10
Okapa ○ PNG 183 C 4
Okapilco Creek ~ USA 284-285 G 5
Okāra ○ PK 138-139 D 4
Okarche ○ USA (OK) 264-265 G 3
Okarem = Ekerem ○ TM 136-137 C 5
Okata ○ WAN 204-205 E 4
Okatibbee Lake < USA (MS) 268-269 M 4
Okatjoruu ○ NAM 216-217 E 9
Okatjuru ○ NAM 216-217 C 9
Okato ○ NZ 182 D 3
Okatoma Creek ~ USA 268-269 L 5
Okaukuejo ○ NAM 216-217 C 9
Okavango ~ NAM 216-217 F 8
Okavango Delta ⁘ RB 218-219 B 4
Okavango River Lodge ○ RB 218-219 B 4
Okave ○ NAM 216-217 D 10
Okaya ○ J 152-153 H 6
Okayama ○ J 152-153 E 7
Okazaki ○ J 152-153 G 7
Okazize ○ NAM 216-217 D 10
Okdarjo ~ UZ 136-137 K 5
Okeechobee ○ USA (FL) 286-287 J 4
Okeechobee, Lake ⊖ USA (FL) 286-287 J 5
Okeene ○ USA (OK) 264-265 F 2
Okefenokee National Wildlife Refuge ⊥ USA (GA) 284-285 H 6
Okefenokee Swamp ⊖ USA (GA) 284-285 H 6
Oke-Iho ○ WAN 204-205 E 4
Okélataka ○ RCB 210-211 E 4
Okemah ○ USA (OK) 264-265 H 3
Okemasis Indian Reservation X CDN (SAS) 232-233 M 3
Okene ○ WAN 204-205 G 5
Oke-Odde ○ WAN 204-205 F 4
Oké Owo ○ DY 204-205 E 4
Oketsew ○ GH 202-203 K 7
Okha ○ IND 138-139 B 8
Okha Māthi ○ IND 138-139 B 8
Okhotsk, Sea of = Ohotskoe more ≈ 10-11 O 3
Oki ○ RI 166-167 D 3
Okiep ○ ZA 220-221 C 4
Okigwe ○ WAN 204-205 G 6
Oki-kaikyō ≈ 152-153 E 7
Okinawa ☆ J 152-153 B 11
Okinawa-shima ⌒ J 152-153 C 11
Okinawa-shotō ⌒ J 152-153 B 11
Okinoerabu-shima ⌒ J 152-153 C 11
Okino-shima ⌒ J 152-153 E 8
Oki-shotō ⌒ J 152-153 E 6
Oki-tai ≃ 152-153 F 6
Okitipupa ○ WAN 204-205 F 5
Okkan ○ MYA 158-159 C 2
Okkurgan ☆ UZ 136-137 L 4
Okkyn"egan ~ RUS 114-115 R 3
Okla ○ CDN (SAS) 232-233 P 3
Oklahoma ■ USA 264-265 F 3
Oklahoma City ☆ USA (OK) 264-265 G 3
Oklan ○ RUS (KOR) 112-113 O 5
Oklan ~ RUS 112-113 N 5
Oklanskoe plato ▲ RUS 112-113 N 5
Oklawaha, Lake < USA (FL) 286-287 H 2
Oklawaha River ~ USA 286-287 H 2
Okmulgee ○ USA (OK) 264-265 J 3
Oko ○ WAN 204-205 F 5
Oko, Wādi ~ SUD 200-201 G 2
Okoboji ○ USA (IA) 274-275 C 1
Ok Ohm River ~ PNG 183 B 3
Okok ~ EAU 212-213 D 2
Okokmilaga River ~ USA 20-21 O 2
Okola ○ CAM 204-205 J 6
Okolli Island ⌒ CDN 36-37 L 2
Okollo ○ EAU 212-213 C 2
Okolona ○ USA (MS) 268-269 M 2
Okondja ○ G 210-211 D 4
Okondjatu ○ NAM 216-217 E 10
Okongo ○ NAM 216-217 D 8
Okongomba ○ NAM 216-217 B 9
Okoppe ○ J 152-153 K 2
Okoppe, Nishi- ○ J 152-153 K 2
Okora, Mount ▲ WAN 204-205 G 5
Okoruro ○ BOL 70-71 C 5
Okotoks ○ CDN (ALB) 232-233 E 5
Okotusu < NAM 216-217 A 8
Okoyo ○ RCB 210-211 E 4
Okpala-Ngwa ○ WAN 204-205 G 6
Okpara ~ DY 204-205 E 4
Okpo ○ MYA 142-143 J 6
Okrika ○ WAN 204-205 G 6
Okrouyo ○ CI 202-203 G 7
Oksaj, gory ▲ TJ 146-147 B 7
Oksapmin ○ PNG 183 B 3
Øksfjord ○ N 86-87 L 1
Øksfjordjøkelen ▲ • N 86-87 L 1
Oksibil ○ RI 166-167 L 4
Oksino ○ RUS 88-89 W 3
Okskij Gosudarstevennyj zapovednik ⊥ RUS 94-95 R 4
Oksovskij ○ RUS 88-89 P 5
Okstindan ▲ N 86-87 G 4
Okstindane ▲ N 84-85 J 3
Oksu ~ AFG 146-147 B 7
Oksym ~ RUS 114-115 U 4
Oktemberjan ○ AR 128-129 L 2
Oktjabrina ○ RUS 112-113 J 5
Oktjabr'sk ☆ KZ 126-127 M 3
Oktjabr'sk ○ RUS 96-97 F 7
Oktjabr'skaja, gora ▲ RUS 108-109 f 3
Oktjabr'skij ○ RUS (AMR) 122-123 C 2
Oktjabr'skij ○ RUS (ARH) 88-89 R 6
Oktjabr'skij ○ RUS (BAS) 96-97 H 6
Oktjabr'skij ○ RUS (IRK) 116-117 J 7
Oktjabr'skij ○ RUS (KMC) 122-123 R 2
Oktjabr'skij ○ RUS (MUR) 88-89 N 3
Oktjabr'skij ○ RUS (ULN) 96-97 F 6
Oktjabr'skij ○ RUS (VOL) 88-89 O 6
Oktjabr'skij ☆ RUS (PRM) 96-97 K 5
Oktjabr'skoe ☆ RUS 96-97 J 7
Oktjabr'skoje ☆ RUS 114-115 G 7
Oktjabr'skoj Revoljucii, ostrov ⌒ RUS 108-109 I a 2
Oktoš ☆ UZ 136-137 J 5
Oktumkum ⁘ TM 136-137 C 4
Oktwin ○ MYA 142-143 K 6
Oktyabr'skiy = Oktjabr'skij ○ RUS 96-97 H 6
Oku ○ CAM 204-205 J 5
Oku ○ J 152-153 C 11
Oku ~ ZRE 210-211 L 4
Oku, Mont ▲ CAM 204-205 J 5
Okubie ○ WAN 204-205 F 6
Ōkuchi ○ J 152-153 D 8
Okulovka ☆ RUS 94-95 N 2
Okunajka ~ RUS 118-119 D 7
Okundi ○ WAN 204-205 H 5
Okushiri ○ J 152-153 H 3
Okushiri-tō ⌒ J 152-153 H 3
Okuta ○ WAN 204-205 E 4
Okwa ~ RB 216-217 F 11
Okwa, River ~ WAN 204-205 G 4
Olá ○ PA 52-53 D 7
Ola ☆ • RUS (MAG) 120-121 O 4
Ola ~ RUS 120-121 O 4
Ola ○ USA (AR) 276-277 B 5
Ola ○ USA (ID) 252-253 B 2
Ola, Joškar- ○ RUS 96-97 E 5
Olaf Prydz bukt ≈ 16 G 8
Ólafsfjörður ○ IS 86-87 d 1
Ólafsvík ○ IS 86-87 b 2
Olancha ○ USA (CA) 248-249 G 3
Olanchito ○ HN 52-53 L 4
Öland ⌒ • S 86-87 H 8
Olanga ~ RUS 88-89 L 3
Olanta ○ USA (SC) 284-285 L 3
Olary ○ AUS 180-181 F 2
Olathe ○ USA (CO) 254-255 H 5
Olathe ○ USA (KS) 262-263 M 6
Olavarria ○ RA 78-79 J 4
Olav V Land ⁘ N 84-85 L 3
Olbernhau ○ D 92-93 M 3
Ólbia ○ I 100-101 B 4
Ol'čan ○ RUS 110-111 Y 7
Olcott ○ USA (NY) 278-279 C 5
Old Andado ∴ AUS 178-179 C 3
Old Bohemia Church • USA (MD) 280-281 L 4
Old Brahmaputra ~ BD 142-143 G 3
Old Celebration Mine • AUS 176-177 F 5
Old Coralie (Ruins) ○ AUS 174-175 F 6
Old Cork ○ AUS 178-179 F 2
Old Crow ○ CDN 20-21 V 3
Old Crow Mount ▲ CDN 20-21 U 3
Old Crow River ~ CDN 20-21 V 3
Old Delamere ○ AUS 172-173 K 3
Old Dime ○ USA (TX) 266-267 L 3
Old Dongola • SUD 200-201 E 3
Old Dutch Capital of Biak ⊥ • RI 166-167 J 2
Oldë ~ RUS 110-111 V 5
Oldeani ○ EAT (ARV) 212-213 E 5
Oldeani ▲ EAT (ARU) 212-213 E 5
Olden ○ USA (MO) 276-277 D 4
Oldenburg ○ D 92-93 K 2
Oldenburg (Holstein) ○ D 92-93 L 1
Olderdalen ○ N 86-87 K 2
Olderfjord ○ N 86-87 M 1
Oldest Christian Mission Site • CDN (QUE) 240-241 F 2
Old Factory Bay ≈ 38-39 E 2
Old Faithful ○ USA (WY) 252-253 H 2
Old Faithful Geyser ∴ USA (WY) 252-253 H 2
Oldfield River ~ AUS 176-177 F 6
Old Ford ○ USA (NC) 282-283 K 5
Old Forge ○ USA (NY) 278-279 G 5
Old Fort Benton • USA (MT) 250-251 J 4
Old Fort Dodge ∴ USA (KS) 262-263 G 7
Old Fort Hays • USA (KS) 262-263 G 6
Old Fort Henry • CDN (ONT) 238-239 J 4
Old Fort Massachusetts • USA (MS) 268-269 M 6
Old Fort Parker State Historic Site ∴ USA (TX) 266-267 L 2
Old Fort River ~ CDN 30-31 O 6
Old Ghan Route, The II • AUS 178-179 C 3
Old Glory ○ USA (TX) 264-265 D 5
Oldham ○ GB 90-91 F 5
Oldham ○ USA (SD) 260-261 J 2
Old Harbor ○ USA 22-23 U 4
Old Herbert Vale ○ AUS 174-175 E 6
Old Hickory Reservoir < USA (TN) 276-277 J 4
Old Horse Springs ○ USA (NM) 256-257 G 5
Old Houlka ○ USA (MS) 268-269 M 2
Old Irontown Ruins • USA (UT) 254-255 B 6
Old Ivy Mine ○ AUS 172-173 L 6
Old Limbunya ○ AUS 172-173 J 4
Oldman Creek ~ CDN 228-229 R 3
Oldman River ~ CDN 232-233 D 6
Old Minto ○ USA 20-21 Q 4
Old Mkushi ○ Z 218-219 E 2
Old Numery ○ AUS 178-179 C 2
Oldoiniyo Orok ▲ EAK 212-213 F 5
Ol Doinyo Lengai ▲ EAT 212-213 E 5
Ol Doinyo Lenkiyio ▲ EAK 212-213 F 3
Ol-Doinyo Sabuk National Park ⊥ • EAK 212-213 F 4
Ol'doj ~ RUS 118-119 L 9
Oldon ~ RUS 118-119 F 5
Old Orchard Beach ○ USA (ME) 278-279 L 5
Old Oyo Game Reserve ⊥ WAN 204-205 F 4
Old Parakylia ○ AUS 178-179 D 6
Old Perlican ○ CDN (NFL) 242-243 Q 4
Old Rampart ○ USA 20-21 U 3
Old River ○ USA (CA) 248-249 E 4
Old River Lake ⊖ USA (MS) 268-269 J 5
Oldsíjt gol ~ MAU 148-149 D 4
Old Sitka ○ USA 32-33 C 3
Old Station ○ USA (CA) 246-247 D 3
Old Stock Exchange • ZA 220-221 K 2
Old Town ○ USA (FL) 286-287 G 2
Old Town ○ USA (ME) 278-279 N 4
Old Trap ○ USA (NC) 282-283 L 4
Olduvai Gorge • EAT 212-213 E 5
Old Village ○ USA 20-21 N 6
Old Wives Lake ⊖ CDN (SAS) 232-233 M 5
Old Woman Mountains ▲ USA 248-249 J 5
Old Woman River ~ USA 20-21 L 5
Olean ○ USA (NY) 278-279 C 6
O'Leary ○ CDN (PEI) 240-241 L 4
Oleb ○ SUD 200-201 H 4
Olecko ○ PL 92-93 R 1
Oleiros ○ P 98-99 D 5
Olëkma ○ RUS (AMR) 118-119 K 7
Olëkma ~ RUS 118-119 K 5
Olëkminsk ☆ • RUS 118-119 K 5
Olëkminskij stanovik ▲ RUS 118-119 H 9
Olëkminskij zapovednik ⊥ RUS 118-119 L 6
Olëkmo-Čarskoe nagor'e ▲ RUS 118-119 J 6
Oleksandrivka ○ UA 102-103 H 3
Ølendi ~ KZ 96-97 H 8
Olenegorsk ○ RUS 110-111 a 5
Olenëk ○ RUS (SAH) 110-111 J 5
Olenëk ~ RUS 110-111 O 3
Olenëk, Ust'- ○ RUS 110-111 M 3
Olenëkskaja, protoka ~ RUS 110-111 O 3
Olenëkskij zaliv ≈ 110-111 M 3
Olenguj ~ RUS 118-119 F 10
Olenguruone ○ EAK 212-213 E 4
Olenica ○ RUS 88-89 N 3
Olenij, mys ▲ RUS 108-109 R 5
Olenij, ostrov ⌒ RUS (JAN) 108-109 R 5
Olenij, ostrov ⌒ RUS (KAR) 88-89 N 4
Olenij, ostrov ⌒ RUS (TMR) 108-109 V 4
Olenij, proliv ≈ 108-109 S 5
Olenino ○ RUS 94-95 N 3
Olen'ja ~ RUS 122-123 K 4
Olenogorsk ○ RUS 88-89 M 2
Olentangy River ~ USA 280-281 C 3
Ølenti ~ KZ 124-125 J 2
Olër ~ RUS 112-113 J 2
Ole Rømer Land ⁘ GRØ 26-27 n 6
Oléron, Île d' ⌒ F 90-91 G 9
Olesskyj zamok • UA 102-103 D 2
Oletha ○ USA (TX) 266-267 L 2
Olevs'k ○ UA 102-103 E 2
Olex ○ USA (OR) 244-245 E 5
Ølfjellet ▲ N 86-87 G 3
Ol'ga ○ RUS (ROS) 122-123 F 7
Ol'ga ~ RUS 118-119 N 9
Olga, Lac ⊖ CDN 38-39 F 4
Olga, Mount = Kata Tjuta ▲ AUS 176-177 L 2
Ol'ga, mys ▲ RUS 120-121 T 6
Olgastretet ≈ 84-85 N 3
Ölgij ○ MAU 146-147 J 1
Ölgij = Har-Us ○ MAU 116-117 F 11
Ol'ginsk ○ RUS 122-123 E 2
Olgujdah ○ RUS (SAH) 118-119 F 4
Olgujdah ~ RUS 118-119 F 3
Olha ○ CDN (MAN) 234-235 C 4
Olhão ○ P 98-99 D 6
Olho d'Água do Casado ○ BR 68-69 K 6
Ol'hon, ostrov ⌒ RUS 116-117 N 9
Ol'hovka ○ RUS 96-97 D 9
Oli ~ DY 204-205 E 3
Oli ○ WAN 204-205 F 4
Olib ⌒ HR 100-101 E 2
Olifants ~ NAM 220-221 C 1
Olifants ○ ZA 218-219 F 6
Olifantshoek ○ ZA 220-221 F 3
Olifantsrivier ~ ZA 220-221 J 2
Olifantsrivier ~ ZA 220-221 D 6
Olifantsrivier ~ ZA 220-221 E 6
Oliktok Point ▲ USA 20-21 Q 1
Oli Kültyk, sor ⁘ KZ 126-127 K 5
Olimarao ⌒ FSM 13 F 2
Olimar Chico, Río ~ ROU 78-79 M 2
Olimbia ○ GR 100-101 H 6
Olimpia ○ BR 72-73 F 6
Ólimpos ▲ GR 100-101 J 4
Olin ○ USA (TX) 266-267 J 2
Olinalá ○ MEX 52-53 E 3
Olinda ○ ••• BR 68-69 L 5
Olindina ○ BR 68-69 J 7
Olinga ○ MOC 218-219 J 3
Olio ○ AUS 178-179 G 1
Oliva ○ E 98-99 G 5
Oliva ○ RA 78-79 H 2
Oliva de la Frontera ○ E 98-99 D 5
Olivares, Cordillera de ▲ RA 76-77 C 6
Olive ○ USA (MT) 250-251 O 6
Olive Branch ○ USA (MS) 268-269 L 2
Olivedos ○ BR 68-69 K 5
Olive Hill ○ USA (KY) 276-277 M 2
Olivehill ○ USA (TN) 276-277 G 5
Oliveira ○ BR 72-73 H 6
Oliveira dos Brejinhos ○ BR 72-73 J 2
Olivença-a-Nova ○ ANG 216-217 B 7
Olivenza ○ E 98-99 D 5
Oliver ○ CDN (BC) 230-231 K 4
Oliver ○ USA (GA) 284-285 J 4
Oliver Creek ~ CDN 230-231 K 2
Oliver Lake ⊖ CDN 34-35 E 2
Oliver Sound ≈ 24-25 h 4
Oliver Springs ○ USA (TN) 282-283 C 4
Olivet ○ USA (SD) 260-261 J 3
Olivia ○ USA (MN) 270-271 D 6
Olivier Islands ⌒ CDN 20-21 X 2
Ol Joro Orok ○ EAK 212-213 F 4
Oljoro Wells ○ EAT 212-213 F 6
Oljutorskij, mys ▲ RUS 112-113 Q 7
Oljutorskij hrebet ▲ RUS 112-113 Q 6
Oljutorskij poluostrov ⌣ RUS 112-113 Q 6
Oljutorskij zaliv ≈ 112-113 O 6
Ol Kejju Ado ~ EAK 212-213 F 5
Olla ○ USA (LA) 268-269 H 5
Ollagüe ○ RCH 76-77 C 1
Ollagüe, Volcán ▲ BOL 76-77 C 1
Ollita, Cordillera de ▲ RA 76-77 B 6
Ollmazor ○ UZ 136-137 K 4
Olmedo ○ E 98-99 E 4
Olmesutye ○ EAK 212-213 E 4
Olmito ○ USA (TX) 266-267 K 7
Olmos ○ PE 64-65 C 4
Olmos Creek, Los ~ USA 266-267 J 6
Olmütz = Olomouc ○ CZ 92-93 O 4
Olney ○ USA (IL) 274-275 K 6
Olney ○ USA (MD) 280-281 J 4
Olney ○ USA (MT) 250-251 E 3
Olney ○ USA (TX) 264-265 F 5
Oloči ○ RUS 118-119 J 10
Olodio ○ CI 202-203 G 7
Olofström ☆ S 86-87 G 8
Ologbo Game Reserve ⊥ WAN 204-205 F 5
Ologo, Čapo- ○ RUS 118-119 J 7
Oloibiri ○ WAN 204-205 G 6
Oloiserri ○ EAK 212-213 F 5
Oloitokitok ○ EAK 212-213 F 5
Oloj ~ RUS 112-113 L 4
Olojčan ~ RUS 112-113 L 3
Olojskij hrebet ▲ RUS 112-113 K 3
Ololdou ○ SN 202-203 D 2
Olom ○ RUS 118-119 J 5
Olomane, Rivière ~ CDN 242-243 H 2
Olomburi ○ SOL 184 I e 3
Olomouc ○ CZ 92-93 O 4
Olonec ○ RUS 94-95 N 1
Olongapo ○ RP 160-161 D 5
Olonki ○ RUS 116-117 L 9
Olorgasailie National Monument • EAK 212-213 F 4
Oloron-Sainte-Marie ○ • F 90-91 G 10
Olosega Island ⌒ USA 184 V c 2
Olov, gora ▲ RUS 88-89 O 5
Olovjannaja ○ RUS 118-119 G 10
Olowalu ○ USA (HI) 288 J 4
Olrik Fjord ≈ 26-27 Q 5
Ol'ša ○ RUS 94-95 M 4
Olsztyn ☆ • PL 92-93 Q 2
Olsztynek ○ PL 92-93 Q 2
Olt ~ RO 102-103 D 5
Olt, Drăgănești ○ RO 102-103 D 5
Olta ○ RA 76-77 D 6
Olten ○ CH 92-93 J 5
Oltenița ○ • RO 102-103 E 5
Oltepesi ○ EAK 212-213 F 4
Oltinkŭl ○ UZ 136-137 F 3
Ol'tjan ~ RUS 112-113 H 4
Olton ○ USA (TX) 264-265 B 4
Oltu ☆ TR 128-129 J 2
Oltu Çayı ~ TR 128-129 J 2
Ol Tukai ○ EAK 212-213 F 5
Oluanpi ○ RC 156-157 M 6
Oluanpi ▲ RC 156-157 M 6
Oluku ○ WAN 204-205 F 5
Olu Malua = Three Sisters Islands ⌒ SOL 184 I f 4
Olur ☆ TR 128-129 K 2
Olustee ○ USA (OK) 264-265 E 4
Olustee Creek ~ USA 286-287 G 1
Olutange ○ RP 160-161 E 9
Olutange Island ⌒ RP 160-161 E 9
Olvido, El ○ CO 60-61 F 6
Ol'vinskij Kamen', gora ▲ RUS 114-115 E 5
Olymp = Ólimpos ▲ GR 100-101 J 4
Olympia ••• GR 100-101 H 6
Olympia ☆ USA (WA) 244-245 C 3
Olympic Dam ○ AUS 178-179 D 6
Olympic Mountains ▲ USA 244-245 B 3
Olympic National Park ⊥ ••• USA (WA) 244-245 B 3
Olympic National Park ⊥ ••• USA (WA) 244-245 A 2
Olympos ▲ CY 128-129 E 5
Olympus, Mount ▲ USA (WA) 244-245 B 3
Olynthos • GR 100-101 J 4
Ölzijm ○ MAU 148-149 E 3
Om' ~ RUS 114-115 N 7
Ōma ○ J 152-153 J 4
Oma ○ RUS 88-89 T 3
Oma ~ RUS 88-89 T 3
Oma ○ USA (MS) 268-269 K 5
Oma ○ VRC 144-145 D 4
Ōmachi ○ J 152-153 G 6
Ōmae-saki ▲ J 152-153 H 7
Ōmagari ○ J 152-153 J 5
Omagh ☆ • GB 90-91 D 4
Omaha ○ USA (AL) 284-285 E 3
Omaha ○ USA (AL) 284-285 E 4
Omaha ○ USA (AR) 276-277 B 4
Omaha ○ USA (NE) 262-263 L 3
Omaha Indian Reservation X USA (NE) 262-263 K 2
Omak ○ USA (WA) 244-245 F 2
Omakau ○ NZ 182 B 6
Omakwia ○ GUY 62-63 E 3
Omal ~ RUS 122-123 G 2
Oman, Gulf of ≈ 134-135 H 6
Oman = 'Umān, Salṭanat ■ OM 132-133 J 4
Oman Lake ⊖ CDN (NWT) 30-31 S 4
Oman Lake ⊖ CDN (SAS) 30-31 Q 6
Omapere ○ NZ 182 D 1
Omarama ○ NZ 182 B 6
Omar Combon ○ SP 212-213 K 2
Omarolluk Sound ≈ 36-37 K 7
Omaruru ☆ NAM (OMA) 216-217 C 10
Omaruru ~ NAM 216-217 D 10
Omas ○ PE 64-65 D 8
Oma-saki ▲ J 152-153 J 4
Omatako ▲ NAM (OKA) 216-217 D 10
Omatako ~ NAM 216-217 F 9
Omate ○ PE 70-71 B 5
Omati ○ PNG 183 B 4
Omati River ~ PNG 183 B 4
Omawewozonyanda ○ NAM 216-217 E 10
Ombabika Bay ○ CDN (ONT) 234-235 P 4
Ombai = Pulau Alor ⌒ RI 166-167 C 6
Ombai, Selat ≈ 166-167 C 6
Ombalantu ○ NAM 216-217 C 8
Ombella ~ RCA 206-207 D 6
Ombella-Mpoko ■ RCA 206-207 C 6
Ombos • ET 194-195 F 5
Ombotozu ▲ NAM 216-217 D 10
Omboué ○ G 210-211 B 4
Ombrone ~ I 100-101 C 3
Ombu ○ RA 76-77 G 6
Ombues de Lavalle ○ ROU 78-79 L 2
Ombuku ~ NAM 216-217 B 8
Omčak ○ RUS 120-121 M 3
Omchi ○ TCH 198-199 H 2
Omčikandja ○ RUS 110-111 X 5
Omčug, Ust'- ☆ RUS 120-121 N 3
Omdurman = Umm Durmān ○ • SUD (Har) 200-201 F 5
Ōme ○ J 152-153 H 7
Omega ○ USA (NM) 256-257 G 4
Omel'dinskij hrebet ▲ RUS 122-123 G 2
Omelič ~ RUS 114-115 Q 5
Omeo ○ AUS 180-181 J 4
Omer ○ USA (MI) 272-273 F 3
Ometepe, Isla de ⌒ NIC 52-53 B 6
Ometepec ○ • MEX 52-53 E 3
Omgon, mys ▲ RUS 120-121 R 5
Omi, Río ~ BOL 70-71 E 3
Ōmi-Hachiman ○ J 152-153 G 7
Omineca Mountains ▲ CDN 32-33 G 3
Omineca River ~ CDN 32-33 H 4
Ominzatov togiari ▲ UZ 136-137 H 4
Omiš ○ • HR 100-101 F 3
Ōmi-shima ⌒ J 152-153 E 7
Omitara ○ NAM 216-217 E 11
Ōmiya ○ J 152-153 H 7
Ommaney, Cape ▲ USA 32-33 C 3
Ommanney Bay ≈ 24-25 V 4
Omnial ○ RI 166-167 E 2
Omnja ~ RUS 120-121 F 4
Ömnögov' ■ MAU 148-149 F 6
Omoa ○ • HN 52-53 K 4
Omoku ○ WAN 204-205 G 6
Omoloj ~ RUS 110-111 T 4
Omolon ~ RUS 112-113 K 2
Omo Nada ○ ETH 208-209 C 5
Omo National Park ⊥ ETH 208-209 B 5
Omono-gawa ~ J 152-153 J 5
Omoto-gawa ~ J 152-153 J 5
Omo Wenz ~ ETH 208-209 C 6
Ompah ○ CDN (ONT) 238-239 J 3
Ompupa ○ ANG 216-217 B 8
Omrel'kaj ~ RUS 112-113 Q 2
Omsk ☆ • RUS 124-125 H 1
Omskij ○ RUS 116-117 L 8
Omsukčan ☆ RUS 112-113 H 5
Omsukčanskij hrebet ▲ RUS 112-113 H 4
Ōmu ○ J 152-153 K 2
Omu-Aran ○ WAN 204-205 F 4
Omulevka ~ RUS 110-111 c 7
Omulevka ~ RUS 120-121 M 2
Omulljahskaja guba ≈ 110-111 Z 3
Omuo ○ WAN 204-205 F 5
Omuramba Ovambo ~ NAM 216-217 D 9
Ōmura-wan ≈ 152-153 C 8
Omurtag ○ BG 102-103 E 6
Ōmuta ○ J 152-153 D 8
Omutinskij ☆ RUS 114-115 J 6
Omutninsk ☆ RUS 96-97 H 4
Oña ○ E 98-99 F 3
Oña ○ EC 64-65 C 3
Ona ~ RUS 118-119 D 9
Ona ~ RUS 124-125 Q 3
Ona Basin ≃ 6-7 D 14
Onakawana ○ CDN (ONT) 236-237 G 2
Onakawana River ~ CDN 236-237 G 2
Onaman Lake ⊖ CDN (ONT) 234-235 Q 4
Onamia ○ USA (MN) 270-271 E 4
Onancock ○ USA (VA) 280-281 L 6
Onandaga Cave State Park ⊥ USA (MO) 274-275 G 6
Onang ○ RI 164-165 F 5
Onanga ○ USA (IL) 274-275 K 4
Onanganjang ○ RI 162-163 C 4
Onangué, Lac ⊖ G 210-211 C 4
Onanhasang ○ RI 162-163 C 4
Onaping Lake ⊖ CDN (ONT) 238-239 D 2
Onawa ○ USA (IA) 274-275 B 2
Onaway ○ USA (MI) 272-273 E 2
Onça, Cachoeira da ~ BR 62-63 G 6
Onça, Corredeira ~ BR 66-67 H 6
Onça, Travessia da ~ BR 68-69 B 4
Onças, Lago das ⊖ BR 70-71 J 5
Oncativo ○ RA 76-77 F 6
Oncócua ○ ANG 216-217 B 8
Onda ○ E 98-99 G 5
Onda ~ RUS 88-89 M 5
Ondangwa ☆ NAM 216-217 C 8
Ondas, Rio das ~ BR 72-73 H 2
Ondaw ○ MYA 142-143 J 4
Ondo ○ WAN (OND) 204-205 F 5
Ondo ■ WAN 204-205 F 5
Ondores ○ PE 64-65 D 7
Öndörhaan ☆ MAU 148-149 K 4
Ondozero ○ RUS (KAR) 88-89 M 5
Ondozero ○ RUS (KAR) 88-89 M 5
Onega ○ RUS 88-89 P 5
Onega ~ RUS 88-89 P 5
Önege ○ KZ 96-97 E 9
One Hundred and Fifty Mile House ○ CDN (BC) 228-229 N 4
One Hundred Mile House ○ CDN (BC) 230-231 H 2
Oneida ○ USA (NY) 278-279 F 5
Oneida ○ USA (TN) 282-283 C 4
Oneida Indian Reservation X CDN (ONT) 238-239 D 6
Oneida Indian Reservation X USA (WI) 270-271 K 6
Oneida Lake ⊖ USA (NY) 278-279 F 5
O'Neill ○ USA (NE) 262-263 H 2
Oneko, ozero ⊖ RUS 116-117 E 3
Onekotan, ostrov ⌒ RUS 122-123 Q 4
Onema-Okolo ○ ZRE 210-211 J 5
Onema Ututu ○ ZRE 210-211 J 5
Onemen, zaliv ≈ 112-113 T 4
Oneonta ○ USA (AL) 284-285 D 3
Oneonta ○ USA (NY) 278-279 F 6
Onești ○ RO 102-103 E 4
Onezhskaya Guba = Onežskaja guba ≈ 88-89 N 4
Onežskaja guba ≈ 88-89 N 4
Onežskij poluostrov ⌣ RUS 88-89 N 4
Onežskoe ozero ⊖ RUS 88-89 N 6
Onga ○ G 210-211 E 4
Ongandjera ○ NAM 216-217 C 8
Ông Cô, Đèo ▲ VN 158-159 K 5
Ongeri ○ ZRE 210-211 K 6
Ongersrivier ~ ZA 220-221 F 5
Ongi ○ MAU 148-149 F 5
Ongi gol ~ MAU 148-149 F 4
Ongjin ○ KOR 150-151 E 9
Ongka ○ RI 164-165 G 3
Ongkaw ○ RI 164-165 J 3
Ongkharak ○ THA 158-159 F 3
Ongniud Qi ○ VRC 148-149 O 6
Ongoka ○ ZRE 210-211 L 4
Ongole ○ IND 140-141 J 3
Ongon ○ PE 64-65 D 6
Ongon = Havirga ○ MAU 148-149 L 5
Ongongoro ○ NAM 216-217 E 10
Ongonyi ○ RCB 210-211 F 4
Ongoro Gotjari ○ NAM 216-217 D 11
Onhne ○ MYA 158-159 D 2
Oni ○ GE 126-127 E 6
Oni, River ~ WAN 204-205 F 5
Onibe ~ RM 222-223 F 6
Onida ○ USA (SD) 260-261 F 2
Onie ú Olin, Río ~ RA 80 E 3
Onilahy ~ RM 222-223 D 9
Onin (Fakfak) Peninsula ⌣ RI 166-167 F 3
Onioni ○ PNG 183 E 6
Onion Lake ○ CDN (SAS) 232-233 J 2
Onitsha ☆ WAN 204-205 G 5
Onive ~ RM 222-223 E 7
Onkamo ○ FIN 88-89 L 5
Onkivesi ⊖ FIN 88-89 J 5
Onnekon ~ RUS 118-119 O 6
Onnës ○ RUS 120-121 E 3
Onnë-Siligir ~ RUS 110-111 J 6
Ono ⌒ FJI 184 III b 3
Ōno ○ J 152-153 G 7
Onoko ○ TCH 206-207 B 3
Onomichi ○ J 152-153 E 7
Onon ~ RUS 118-119 G 10
Onon gol ~ MAU 148-149 K 3
Onor ○ RUS (SHL) 122-123 K 3
Onor ~ RUS 122-123 K 3
Onor, gora ▲ RUS 122-123 K 3
Onotoa ⌒ KIR 13 J 3
Onoto ○ YV 60-61 J 3
Onoway ○ CDN (ALB) 232-233 D 2
Onseepkans ○ ZA 220-221 D 4
Onslow ○ AUS 172-173 B 6
Onslow Bay ≈ 48-49 K 2
Onslow Bay ≈ 282-283 K 6
Ontake-san ▲ J 152-153 G 7
Ontar ○ VAN 184 II a 2
Ontaratue River ~ CDN 20-21 Z 3
Ontario ■ CDN 234-235 K 4
Ontario ○ USA (CA) 248-249 G 5
Ontario ○ USA (OR) 244-245 H 6
Ontario ○ USA (WI) 270-271 H 7
Ontario, Lake ⊖ 46-47 J 4
Ontario, Lake ⊖ 278-279 C 5
Ontario Peninsula ⌣ CDN 238-239 D 5
Ontmoeting ○ ZA 220-221 E 3
Ontonagon ○ USA (MI) 270-271 J 4
Ontonagon River ~ USA 270-271 J 4
Ontong Java ⌒ SOL 184 I d 1
Ōnuma Quasi National Park ⊥ J 152-153 J 4
Onverwacht ☆ SME 62-63 G 3
Onwul River ~ WAN 204-205 H 5
Onyx ○ USA (CA) 248-249 F 4
Onyx Cave ∴ USA (AR) 276-277 B 4
Oobagooma ○ AUS 172-173 G 4
Oodnadatta ○ AUS 178-179 C 4
Oodnadatta Track II AUS 178-179 C 5
Oodonggo ○ RI 168 D 7
Oodweyne ○ SP 208-209 G 4
Ookala ○ USA (HI) 288 K 4
Ooldea Range ▲ AUS 176-177 L 5
Oolloo ○ AUS 172-173 K 2
Oologah Lake ⊖ USA (OK) 264-265 J 2
Oona River ○ CDN (BC) 228-229 D 3
Ooratippra ○ AUS 178-179 D 1
Oorindi ○ AUS 174-175 F 7
Oos-Londen = East London ☆ • ZA 220-221 H 6
Ooste Lake ⊖ CDN (BC) 228-229 H 3
Oostende ○ • B 92-93 G 3
Oostermoed ○ ZA 220-221 H 2
Oosterschelde ≈ 92-93 G 3
Ootsa Lake ⊖ CDN (BC) 228-229 J 3
Opachuanau Lake ⊖ CDN 34-35 G 2
Opaka ○ BG 102-103 E 6
Opal ○ CDN (ALB) 232-233 E 2
Opal ○ USA (WY) 252-253 H 5
Opala ~ RUS 122-123 R 2
Opala ○ ZRE 210-211 K 4
Opalocka ○ USA (FL) 286-287 J 6
Opang ○ RI 164-165 K 4
Opari ○ SUD 212-213 D 2
Oparino ○ RUS 96-97 F 4
Opasatika ○ CDN (ONT) 236-237 F 3
Opasatika Lake ⊖ CDN 236-237 E 3
Opasatika River ~ CDN 236-237 F 2
Opasnyj, mys ▲ RUS (KMC) 120-121 S 7
Opasnyj, mys ▲ RUS (KOR) 120-121 U 3
Opataca, Lac ⊖ CDN (QUE) 236-237 O 2
Opatija ○ HR 100-101 E 2
Opava ○ CZ 92-93 O 4
Opawica, Lac ⊖ CDN (QUE) 236-237 N 3
Opelika ○ USA (AL) 284-285 E 4
Opelousas ○ USA (LA) 268-269 H 6
Opémisca, Lac ⊖ CDN 236-237 O 3
Opémiska, Mount ▲ CDN 236-237 O 3
Open Bay ≈ 183 F 3
Open Bay ○ PNG (ENB) 183 F 3
Openshaw ○ CDN (SAS) 232-233 Q 6
Opeongo Lake ⊖ CDN (ONT) 238-239 G 3
Opeta, Lake ⊖ EAU 212-213 E 3
Opheim ○ USA (MT) 250-251 N 3
Ophir ○ CDN (ONT) 238-239 B 2
Ophir ○ USA 20-21 M 5
Ophir, Gunung ▲ RI 162-163 C 4
Ophthalmia Range ▲ AUS 172-173 D 7
Opi ○ WAN 204-205 G 5
Opichén ○ MEX 52-53 K 1
Opienge ○ ZRE 212-213 A 3
Opihikao ○ USA (HI) 288 L 5
Opikeigen Lake ⊖ CDN (ONT) 234-235 P 3
Opilja ▲ UA 102-103 D 3
Opinaca, Réservoir < CDN 38-39 F 2
Opinaca, Rivière ~ CDN 38-39 G 2
Opinnagau Lake ⊖ CDN 34-35 O 4
Opinnagau River ~ CDN 34-35 P 3
Opiscotéo, Lac ⊖ CDN 38-39 K 2
Opiscotiche, Lac ⊖ CDN 38-39 L 2
Opišn'a ○ UA 102-103 J 3
Opitsat ○ CDN (BC) 230-231 D 4
Opobo ○ WAN 204-205 G 6
Opočka ☆ RUS 94-95 L 3
Opocopa, Lac ⊖ CDN 38-39 L 2
Opoczno ○ PL 92-93 Q 3
Opole ☆ • PL 92-93 O 3
Opopeo ○ MEX 52-53 D 2
Opornyj ○ KZ 96-97 J 10
Opotiki ○ NZ 182 F 3
Opp ○ USA (AL) 284-285 D 5
Oppa-wan ≈ 152-153 J 5
Oppdal ☆ N 86-87 D 5
Opportunity ○ USA (MT) 250-251 G 5
Opportunity ○ USA (WA) 244-245 H 3
Opposite Island ⌒ CDN 36-37 H 2
Oppstryn ○ N 86-87 C 6
Optima ○ USA (OK) 264-265 C 2
Optima National Wildlife Refuge ⊥ USA (OK) 264-265 C 2
Optima Reservoir ⊖ USA (OK) 264-265 C 2
Opuka ~ RUS 112-113 R 5
Opuka, laguna ≈ 112-113 S 6
Opunake ○ NZ 182 D 3
Opuntia Lake ⊖ CDN (SAS) 232-233 K 4
Opuwo ☆ NAM 216-217 B 9
Oquawka ○ USA (IL) 274-275 H 4
Oquossoc ○ USA (ME) 278-279 L 4
Ör ~ KZ 126-127 N 3
Or' ~ RUS 96-97 L 8
Or, Cape d' ▲ CDN (NS) 240-241 L 5
Ora ○ PNG 183 F 3
Ora ~ VAN 184 II a 2
Oraba ○ EAU 212-213 C 2
Oracle ○ USA (AZ) 256-257 E 6

372 Oil Creek State Park — Oracle

Oracle Junction ○ USA (AZ) 256-257 E 6
Oradea ☆• RO 102-103 B 4
Öræfajökull ▲ IS 86-87 e 2
Orah ○ WAN 204-205 F 5
Orai ○ IND 138-139 G 7
Oraibi Wash ~ USA 256-257 E 3
Oral ☆ KZ 96-97 G 8
Oral ~ KZ 96-97 G 9
Ora Loma ○ USA (CA) 248-249 D 3
Oral üstirti ▲ RUS 124-125 B 2
Orami ○ PNG 184 I b 2
Oran = Wahrân ☆• DZ 188-189 L 3
Oranapai ○ GUY 62-63 E 2
Orange ○ AUS 180-181 K 2
Orange ○• F 90-91 K 9
Orange ○ USA (TX) 268-269 G 6
Orange ○ USA (VA) 280-281 H 5
Orange ~ ZA 220-221 D 4
Orange, Cap ▲ F 62-63 J 3
Orange, Port ○ USA (FL) 286-287 J 2
Orange Bay ≈ 242-243 M 2
Orangeburg ○ USA (SC) 284-285 K 3
Orange Cay ∴ BS 54-55 F 2
Orange Cove ○ USA (CA) 248-249 E 3
Orangedale ○ CDN (NS) 240-241 O 5
Orange Fan ≃ 6-7 L 12
Orange Free State = Oranje Vrystaat ◘ ZA 220-221 G 4
Orange Grove ○ USA (TX) 266-267 K 6
Orange Lake ○ USA (FL) 286-287 G 2
Orange Park ○ USA (FL) 286-287 H 1
Orangerie Bay ≈ 183 E 6
Orangeville ○ CDN (ONT) 238-239 E 5
Orangeville ○ USA (IL) 274-275 J 2
Orangeville ○ USA (MI) 272-273 D 5
Orange Walk ○ BH 52-53 K 2
Orangi ~ EAT 212-213 E 5
Orango, Ilha de ∴ GNB 202-203 B 4
Orangozinho, Ilha de ∴ GNB 202-203 C 4
Orangutang, mys ▲ RUS 112-113 R 6
Orania ○ ZA 220-221 G 4
Oranjefontein ○ ZA 218-219 D 6
Oranje Gebergte ▲ SME 62-63 G 4
Oranjemund ○ NAM 220-221 C 4
Oranjerivier ~ ZA 220-221 F 4
Oranjestad ☆ ARU 60-61 F 1
Oranjestad ☆• NA 56 D 3
Oranjeville ○ ZA 220-221 J 3
Oranje Vrystaat ◘ ZA 220-221 G 4
Oransbari ○ RI 166-167 H 2
Oranžeri ○ RUS 126-127 G 5
Orapa ○ RB 218-219 C 5
Oras ○ RP 160-161 F 6
Oratia, Mount ▲ USA 22-23 Q 3
Oratorio ○ RA 76-77 D 2
Orattanādu ○ IND 140-141 H 5
Orava ○ PNG 184 I b 2
Oravița ○ RO 102-103 B 5
Orb ~ F 90-91 J 10
Orbata, Jebel ▲ TN 190-191 G 3
Orbetello ○ I 100-101 C 3
Órbigo, Río ~ E 98-99 E 3
Orbost ○ AUS 180-181 K 4
Orcadas ○ ARK 16 G 32
Orchard ○ USA (NE) 262-263 H 2
Orchard City ○ USA (CO) 254-255 H 5
Orchards ○ USA (WA) 244-245 C 5
Orchard Valley ○ USA (WY) 252-253 O 5
Orchardville ○ USA (IL) 274-275 K 6
Orchila, Isla ∴ YV 60-61 H 2
Orco ~ I 100-101 A 2
Orcococha, Lago ○ PE 64-65 E 8
Orcopampa ○ PE 64-65 F 9
Ord ○ USA (NE) 262-263 H 3
Ord, Mount ▲ AUS 172-173 G 4
Orda ☆ RUS 96-97 K 5
Orda ⊂ TCH 198-199 H 2
Ordale ○ CDN (SAS) 232-233 M 2
Ordenikidze ☆ KZ 124-125 B 2
Orderville ○ USA (UT) 254-255 C 6
Ordes ○• E 98-99 C 3
Ord Mountain ▲ USA (CA) 248-249 H 5
Ordoqui ○ RA 78-79 J 3
Ordos = Mu Us Shamo ⊥ VRC 154-155 E 2
Ord Regeneration Depot ○ AUS 172-173 J 4
Ord River ~ AUS 172-173 J 4
Ordu ☆ TR 128-129 G 2
Ordubad ○ AZ 128-129 M 3
Ordway ○ USA (CO) 254-255 M 5
Ordynskoe ☆ RUS 124-125 M 1
Ordžonikidze ○ UA 102-103 J 4
Ordžonikidzeabad = Kofarnihon ○ TJ 136-137 L 5
Ore ○ WAN 204-205 F 5
Örebro ☆• S 86-87 G 7
Ore City ○ USA (TX) 264-265 K 6
Oredež ○ RUS 94-95 M 2
Oregon ○ USA (MO) 274-275 C 5
Oregon ○ USA (OH) 280-281 C 2
Oregon ○ USA (WI) 274-275 J 2
Oregon ◘ USA 244-245 B 7
Oregon Caves National Monument ∴ USA (OR) 244-245 B 8
Oregon City ○ USA (OR) 244-245 C 5
Oregon Dunes ⊥ USA (OR) 244-245 A 7
Oregon Inlet ≈ 282-283 M 5
Orehovo-Zuevo ☆ RUS 94-95 Q 4
Orekhovo-Zuyevo = Orehovo-Zuevo ☆ RUS 94-95 Q 4
Orel ○ RUS 94-95 P 5
Orel' ~ UA 102-103 J 3
Orel', ozero ○ RUS 122-123 H 2
Orellana ○ PE (AMA) 64-65 C 4
Orellana ○ PE (LOR) 64-65 E 5
Orellana la Vieja ○ E 98-99 E 5
Orem ○ USA (UT) 254-255 D 3
Ören ○ TR 128-129 B 4
Orenburg ☆ RUS 96-97 J 8
Oreng ○ RI 162-163 B 2
Orense = Ourense ○ E 98-99 D 3
Orerokpe ○ WAN 204-205 F 6
Øresund ≈ 86-87 F 9
Oretown ○ USA (OR) 244-245 B 5
Orewa ○ NZ 182 E 2
Orford, Port ○ USA (OR) 244-245 A 8
Organ ○ USA (NM) 256-257 J 6
Organabo ○ F 62-63 H 3
Organ Pipe Cactus National Monument ∴ USA (AZ) 256-257 C 6
Orgeev = Orhei ☆ MD 102-103 F 4
Orgūn ○ AFG 138-139 B 3
Orhaneli ☆ TR 128-129 C 3
Orhangazi ○ TR 128-129 C 2
Orhei ☆ MD 102-103 F 4
Orhej = Orhei ☆ MD 102-103 F 4
Orhon ○ MAU 148-149 G 3
Orhon gol ~ MAU 148-149 F 3
Ori ~ RT 202-203 L 5
Orianda, laguna ○ RUS 112-113 U 5
Orica ○ HN 52-53 L 4
Orichiv ○ UA 102-103 J 4
Orick ○ USA (CA) 246-247 A 2
Orient ○ USA (SD) 260-261 G 2
Orient ○ USA (WA) 244-245 G 2
Oriental, Cordillera ▲ DOM 54-55 L 5
Oriental, Llanura ▲ DOM 54-55 L 5
Orient Bay ○ CDN (ONT) 234-235 P 5
Oriente ○ RA 78-79 J 5
Oriente, Cachoeira do ~ BR 66-67 E 7
Orient Point ○ USA (NY) 280-281 O 2
Orihuela ○ E 98-99 G 5
Orillia ○ CDN (ONT) 238-239 F 4
Orin ○ USA (WY) 252-253 N 4
Orinduik ○ GUY 62-63 D 3
Orinoca ○ BOL 70-71 D 6
Orinoco, Delta del ≈ 60-61 L 3
Orinoco, Llanos del ⊥ 60-61 F 6
Orinoco, Río ~ YV 60-61 J 6
Oriomo ○ PNG 183 B 5
Orion ○ CDN (ALB) 232-233 H 6
Orion ○ USA (AL) 284-285 E 5
Orion ○ USA (AR) 276-277 C 6
Oriska ○ USA (ND) 258-259 K 5
Orissa ◘ IND 142-143 C 5
Orissaare ○ EST 94-95 H 2
Oristano ○• I 100-101 B 5
Orito ○ CO 64-65 D 1
Orituco ○ YV 60-61 H 3
Orituco, Río ~ YV 60-61 H 3
Oritupano, Río ~ YV 60-61 K 3
Orivesi ○ FIN 88-89 H 6
Oriximiná ○ BR 62-63 G 6
Orizaba ○• MEX 52-53 F 2
Orizaba, Pico de ▲ MEX 52-53 F 2
Orjahovo ○ BG 102-103 C 6
Orjen ▲ YU 100-101 G 3
Orjen, Nacionalni park ⊥ YU 100-101 G 3
Orjus-Miele ~ RUS 118-119 K 7
Orkadiéré ○ SN 202-203 D 2
Orkanger ○ N 86-87 D 5
Örkelljunga ○ S 86-87 F 8
Orkjuile, mys ▲ RUS 110-111 3 4
Orkla ○ N 86-87 D 5
Orkney ○ CDN (SAS) 232-233 L 6
Orkney ○ ZA 220-221 H 3
Orkney Islands ∴ GB 90-91 F 2
Orla ○ USA (TX) 266-267 D 2
Orlameš ○ AFG 136-137 K 6
Orland ○ USA (CA) 246-247 C 4
Orlândia ○ BR 72-73 G 6
Orlando ○• USA (FL) 286-287 H 3
Orlo̧ăo ○ BR 74-75 F 7
Orléanais ∴ F 90-91 H 8
Orléans ○ F 90-91 H 8
Orleans ○ USA (IN) 274-275 M 6
Orleans ○ USA (MA) 278-279 M 7
Orleans ○ USA (NE) 262-263 G 4
Orléans, Île d' ∴ CDN (QUE) 240-241 E 4
Orleans Farms ○ AUS 176-177 G 6
Orle River Game Reserve ⊥ WAN 204-205 G 5
Orlik ☆ RUS 116-117 J 9
Orlinaja gora ▲ RUS 112-113 U 5
Orlinga ○ RUS (IRK) 116-117 M 7
Orlinga ~ RUS 116-117 N 8
Orlov Gaj ○ RUS 96-97 F 8
Orlovka ○ RUS (NVS) 114-115 O 6
Orlovka ~ RUS 112-113 N 3
Orlovka ~ RUS 112-113 P 4
Orlovka ~ RUS 114-115 T 5
Orlovka ~ RUS 122-123 C 2
Orlovskij ○ RUS 102-103 N 4
Orlovskij, mys ▲ RUS 88-89 Q 3
Orlovskij hrebet ▲ RUS 112-113 N 3
Orlovskij zaliv ≈ 88-89 Q 3
Orlu ○ WAN 204-205 G 6
Orman Reef ∴ AUS 183 B 5
Ormāra ○ PK 134-135 L 6
Ormāra, Rās ▲ PK 134-135 L 6
Ormea ○• I 100-101 A 2
Ormiston ○ CDN (SAS) 232-233 N 6
Ormiston Gorge National Park ⊥ AUS 176-177 M 1
Ormoc ○ RP 160-161 F 7
Ormond Beach ○ USA (FL) 286-287 H 2
Ormonde Island ∴ CDN 24-25 e 6
Ormos Almirou ≈ 100-101 K 7
Ormsby ○ USA (MN) 270-271 D 7
Ormstown ○ CDN (QUE) 238-239 M 3
Ormtjern nasjonalpark ⊥ N 86-87 D 6
Orne ~ F 90-91 G 7
Ørnes ○ N 86-87 F 3
Örnsköldsvik ○ S 86-87 J 5
Oro, Lac ○ RMM 196-197 J 6
Oro, Mesa del ▲ USA 256-257 H 4
Oro, Río de ~ RA 76-77 H 4
Oro, Río del ~ MEX 50-51 G 5
Orobayaya ○ BOL 70-71 F 3
Oro Blanco ○ USA (AZ) 256-257 D 7
Orocó ○ BR 68-69 J 6
Orocue ○ CO 60-61 F 5
Orodara ○ BF 202-203 H 4
Orodel ○• RO 102-103 C 5
Oroek ○ RUS 110-111 d 7
Orofino ○ USA (ID) 250-251 C 5
Orog nuur ○ MAU 148-149 E 5
Orogrande ○ USA (NM) 256-257 J 6
Orol dengizi = Aral tengizi ○ 126-127 N 5
Orom ○ EAU 212-213 D 2
Oromocto ○ CDN (NB) 240-241 J 5
Oromocto Lake ○ CDN (NB) 240-241 J 5
Oron ○ RUS 118-119 H 7
Oron ○ WAN 204-205 H 6
Orondo ○ USA (WA) 244-245 E 3
Oroners Out Station ○ AUS 174-175 G 4
Oronga ○ PNG 183 C 3
Orono ○ USA (ME) 278-279 N 4
Orono ○ USA (MN) 270-271 E 6
Oronoquerivier ~ GUY 62-63 F 4
Orope ○ YV 60-61 E 3
Oropesa ○• E 98-99 E 5
Oropesa, Río ~ PE 64-65 F 8
Oroqen Zizhiqi ○ VRC 150-151 D 2
Oroquieta ☆ RP 160-161 E 8
Orós ○ BR 68-69 J 5
Orós, Açude ⊂ BR 68-69 J 5
Orosei ○ I 100-101 B 4
Orosháza ○ H 92-93 Q 5
Orosi ○ USA (CA) 248-249 E 3
Orosmayo, Río de ~ RA 76-77 D 2
Orotina ○ CR 52-53 B 7
Orotko, ozero ○ RUS 110-111 W 4
Orotuk ○ RUS 120-121 N 2
Orotukan ○ RUS (MAG) 120-121 O 2
Orotukan ~ RUS 120-121 O 2
Orovada ○ USA (NV) 246-247 H 2
Oro Valley ○ USA (AZ) 256-257 E 6
Oroville ○ USA (WA) 244-245 F 2
Oroville ○• USA (CA) 246-247 D 4
Oroville Reservoir ⊂ USA (CA) 246-247 D 4
Oroya, La ○ PE 64-65 E 7
Orpheus Lake ○ CDN 30-31 Q 5
Orquideas, Parque Nacional las ⊥ CO 60-61 C 4
Orr ○ USA (MN) 270-271 F 2
Orroroo ○ AUS 180-181 E 2
Orrville ○ USA (AL) 284-285 C 4
Orša ☆ BY 94-95 M 4
Orsa ○ S 86-87 G 6
Orsha = Orša ☆ BY 94-95 M 4
Orsk ○ RUS 96-97 L 8
Ørstavik ☆ N 86-87 C 5
Ortaca ☆ TR 128-129 C 4
Ortaköy ○ TR 128-129 F 3
Ortasu ~ KZ 124-125 J 5
Orte ○ I 100-101 D 3
Ortega ○ CO 60-61 D 6
Ortegal, Cabo ▲ E 98-99 D 3
Ortegueza, Río ~ CO 64-65 E 1
Orthez ○ F 90-91 G 10
Ortho, Río ~ BOL 70-71 D 2
Ortigueira ○ BR 74-75 E 5
Ortigueira ○ E 98-99 D 3
Orting ○ USA (WA) 244-245 C 3
Ortit ○ GRØ 28-29 V 4
Ortiz ○ MEX 50-51 D 3
Ortiz ○ YV 60-61 H 3
Ort'jagun ~ RUS 114-115 N 4
Ortler = Ortles ▲ I 100-101 C 1
Ortona ○ I 100-101 E 3
Orto-Nahara ○ RUS 118-119 G 5
Ortonville ○ USA (MI) 272-273 F 5
Ortonville ○ USA (MN) 270-271 B 5
Orto-Surt ○ RUS 118-119 M 4
Oruro ○ CO 60-61 E 3
Oruhito ○ NAM 216-217 B 9
Orulgan, hrebet ▲ RUS 110-111 H 5
Orūmīyeh ☆ IR 128-129 L 4
Orūmīye, Daryāče-ye ○ IR 128-129 L 3
Oruro ☆ BOL 70-71 D 6
Orust ∴ S 86-87 E 7
Orūzgān ○ AFG (OR) 134-135 M 2
Orūzgān ◘ AFG 134-135 L 2
Orvieto ○• I 100-101 D 3
Orville Escarpment ▲ ARK 16 F 30
Orwell ○ USA (OH) 280-281 F 2
Orzüye ○ IR 134-135 G 4
Oržycja ~ UA 102-103 H 3
Orzysz ○• PL 92-93 Q 2
Oš ☆ KS 136-137 N 4
Os ☆ N 86-87 E 5
Osa ☆ RUS (PRM) 96-97 J 5
Osa ☆ RUS (UST) 116-117 L 9
Oša ~ RUS 114-115 M 6
Osa ~ RUS 116-117 M 9
Osa, Peninsula de ∪ CR 52-53 C 7
Osage ○ CDN (SAS) 232-233 P 6
Osage ○ USA (AR) 276-277 B 4
Osage ○ USA (IA) 274-275 F 1
Osage Beach ○ USA (MO) 274-275 F 6
Osage City ○ USA (KS) 262-263 L 6
Osage Fork ~ USA 276-277 C 3
Osage River ~ USA 274-275 F 6
Osage River ~ USA 276-277 A 3
Ōsaka ☆• J 152-153 F 7
Osakarovka = Askarly ☆ KZ 124-125 H 3
Ōsaka-wan ≈ 152-153 F 7
Osakis ○ USA (MN) 270-271 C 5
Osasco ○ BR 72-73 G 7
Osawatomie ○ USA (KS) 262-263 M 6
Osborne ○ CDN (MAN) 234-235 F 5
Osborne ○ USA (KS) 262-263 H 5
Osburn ○ USA (ID) 250-251 C 4
Osby ○ S 86-87 F 8
Osca, Río ~ BOL 70-71 E 5
Oscar ○ F 62-63 H 4
Oscar II land ⊥ N 84-85 H 3
Oscar Soto Máynes ○ MEX 50-51 F 3
Osceola ○ USA (AR) 276-277 F 5
Osceola ○ USA (IA) 274-275 E 3
Osceola ○ USA (MO) 274-275 E 6
Osceola ○ USA (NE) 262-263 J 3
Osceola ○ USA (SD) 260-261 J 2
Osceola ○ USA (WI) 270-271 F 5
Oschiri ○ I 100-101 B 4
Oscoda ○ USA (MI) 272-273 F 3
Oscura ○ USA (NM) 256-257 J 5
Oscura, Punta ▲ GQ 210-211 B 2
Oscura Peak ▲ USA (NM) 256-257 J 5
Osetr ~ RUS 94-95 Q 4
Osgood ○ USA (IN) 274-275 N 5
Osh = Oš ☆ KS 136-137 N 4
Oshakati ○ NAM 216-217 C 8
Oshamambe ○ J 152-153 J 3
Oshawa ○ CDN (ONT) 238-239 G 5
Oshetna River ~ USA 20-21 R 5
Oshika-hanto ∪ J 152-153 J 5
Oshikango ○ NAM 216-217 C 8
Oshikuku ○ NAM 216-217 C 8
Ōshima ○ J (TOK) 152-153 H 7
Ō-shima ∴ J (KGA) 152-153 C 10
Ōshima ∴ J (TOK) 152-153 H 7
Ō-shima ∴ J (YMG) 152-153 E 8
Oshima-hantō ∪ J 152-153 J 3
Oshivelo ○ NAM 216-217 D 9
Oshkosh ○ USA (NE) 262-263 D 3
Oshkosh ○ USA (WI) 270-271 K 6
Oshun, River ~ WAN 204-205 F 5
Oshwe ○ ZRE 210-211 G 5
Osiān ○ IND 138-139 D 6
Osijek ☆• HR 100-101 G 2
Osilinka River ~ CDN 32-33 H 3
Osinniki ☆ RUS 124-125 P 2
Osinovaja, Bol'šaja ~ RUS 112-113 R 3
Osinovka ○ RUS 116-117 K 7
Osinovo ○ RUS 88-89 R 5
Osinovoe Pleso ○ RUS 114-115 T 7
Osinovskij hrebet ▲ RUS 112-113 S 3
Osinovskij porog •• RUS 114-115 U 4
Oskaloosa ○ USA (IA) 274-275 F 3
Oskaloosa ○ USA (KS) 262-263 L 5
Oskarshamn ☆ S 86-87 H 8
Oskélanéo ○ CDN (QUE) 236-237 N 4
Öskemen ○ KZ 124-125 N 4
Os'kino ○ RUS 102-103 L 2
Os'kino ○ RUS 116-117 N 5
Oskoba ~ RUS 116-117 K 6
Oškoto, ozero ○ RUS 88-89 Y 3
Oskū ○ IR 128-129 M 4
Osland ○ CDN (BC) 228-229 D 2
Osler ○ CDN (SAS) 232-233 M 3
Osljanka, gora ▲ RUS 114-115 E 5
Oslo ★• N 86-87 E 7
Oslo ○ USA (MN) 270-271 A 2
Oslofjorden ≈ 86-87 E 7
Osmānābād ○ IND 138-139 F 10
Osmancık ☆ TR 128-129 F 2
Osmaneli ☆ TR 128-129 D 2
Osmaniye ☆ TR 128-129 G 4
Osmānnagar ○ IND 138-139 G 10
Os'mino ○ RUS 94-95 L 2
Ösmo ○ S 86-87 H 7
Osnabrück ○• D 92-93 K 2
Osnaburgh House ○ CDN (ONT) 234-235 N 3
Ošnūye ○• IR 128-129 L 4
Oso ○ USA (WA) 244-245 D 2
Oso ~ ZRE 212-213 A 4
Oso, El ○ YV 60-61 J 5
Osogbo ○• WAN 204-205 F 5
Osogovski pl. ▲ MK 100-101 J 3
Osório ○ BR 74-75 E 7
Osório da Fonseca ○ BR 66-67 H 4
Osorno ○ E 98-99 E 3
Osorno ○ RCH 78-79 C 6
Osorno, Volcán ▲ RCH 78-79 C 6
Osoro ○ WAN 204-205 G 5
Osoyoos ○ CDN (BC) 230-231 K 4
Osoyoos Indian Reserve ⚔ CDN (BC) 230-231 K 4
Osøyra ○ N 86-87 B 6
Ospasquia Provincial Park ⊥ CDN 34-35 K 4
Ospika River ~ CDN 32-33 H 3
Ospino ○ YV 60-61 G 3
Osprey ○ USA (FL) 286-287 G 4
Osprey Reef ∴ AUS 174-175 J 3
Ossa ▲ P 98-99 D 5
Ossa, Mount ▲ AUS 180-181 J 6
Ossabaw Island ∴ USA (GA) 284-285 J 5
Ossabaw Sound ≈ 284-285 J 5
Ossa de Montiel ○ E 98-99 F 5
Ossalinskij kraž ▲ RUS 110-111 c 7
Osse, River ~ WAN 204-205 F 5
Ossélé ○ RCB 210-211 E 4
Osseo ○ USA (MN) 270-271 E 5
Osseo ○ USA (WI) 270-271 G 6
Ossima ○ PNG 183 A 2
Ossineke ○ USA (MI) 272-273 F 3
Ossining ○ USA (NY) 280-281 N 2
Ossokmanuan Lake ○ CDN 38-39 M 2
Ossora ☆ RUS 120-121 U 4
Ossora, buhta ≈ 120-121 U 4
Ostaškin, kamen' • RUS 114-115 T 7
Ostaškov ☆ RUS 94-95 N 3
Östavall ○ S 86-87 G 5
Østby ○ N 86-87 E 6
Oste ~ D 92-93 K 2
Ostenfeld ○ CDN (MAN) 234-235 G 5
Oster ~ RUS 94-95 N 5
Österbotten = Pohjanmaa ⊥ FIN 88-89 G 5
Österbybruk ○ S 86-87 H 6
Østerdalen ∪ N 86-87 E 6
Östergötland ⊥ S 86-87 G 7
Østerø = Eysturoy ∴ FR 90-91 D 1
Östersund ☆• S 86-87 G 5
Osterwick ○ CDN (MAN) 234-235 E 5
Østgrønland = Tunu ◘ GRØ 26-27 d 8
Östhammar ○ S 86-87 J 6
Oštinskij Pogost ○ RUS 94-95 O 1
Ostorinān ○ IR 134-135 C 1
Ostraja, gora ▲ RUS (KOR) 112-113 P 5
Ostraja, gora ▲ RUS (KOR) 120-121 T 4
Ostraja, gora ▲ RUS (ROS) 122-123 E 6
Ostrau = Ostrava ○ CZ 92-93 P 4
Ostrau = Ostrov nad Oslavou ○ CZ 92-93 N 4
Ostrava ○ CZ 92-93 P 4
Ostrjak, gora ▲ RUS 112-113 Q 4
Ostróda ○• PL 92-93 P 2
Ostrogožsk ○ RUS 102-103 L 2
Ostrołęka ☆• PL 92-93 Q 2
Ostrov ○ RO 102-103 E 5
Ostrov ☆ RUS 94-95 L 3
Ostroveršinnyj hrebet ▲ RUS 112-113 N 4
Ostrovnoe ○ RUS (CUK) 112-113 N 2
Ostrovnoe ○ RUS (ORB) 96-97 K 8
Ostrovnoj, mys ▲ RUS 114-115 M 2
Ostrovnoj, zaliv ≈ 120-121 Q 3
Ostrovskoe ○ RUS 94-95 S 3
Ostrowiec Świętokrzyski ○ PL 92-93 Q 3
Ostrów Mazowiecka ○ PL 92-93 Q 2
Ostrów Wielkopolski ☆• PL 92-93 O 3
Osttirol ◘ A 92-93 M 5
Ostuni ○ I 100-101 F 4
Ošturān, Kūh-e ▲ IR 134-135 C 2
Öşt Vank • TR 128-129 J 2
O'Sullivan Lake ○ CDN (ONT) 234-235 Q 4
Ōsumi-hantō ∪ J 152-153 D 9
Ōsumi-kaikyō ≈ 152-153 D 9
Ōsumi-shotō ∴ J 152-153 D 9
Osuna ○ E 98-99 E 6
Oswegatchie River ~ USA 278-279 F 4
Oswego ○ USA (KS) 262-263 L 7
Oswego ○ USA (NY) 278-279 E 5
Oswego River ~ USA 278-279 E 5
Oświęcim ○•• PL 92-93 P 3
Ōta ○ J 152-153 E 7
Otacílio Costa ○ BR 74-75 E 6
Ōta-gawa ~ J 152-153 E 7
Otago Peninsula ∪•• NZ 182 C 6
Otajkačanskij hrebet ▲ RUS 112-113 S 3
Otaki ○ NZ 182 E 4
Otakwa ○ RI (IRJ) 166-167 J 4
Otakwa ~ RI 166-167 J 4
Otaru ○ J 152-153 J 3
Otasawian River ~ CDN 236-237 D 2
Otatal, Cerro ▲ MEX 50-51 D 3
Otavalo ○• EC 64-65 C 1
Otavi ○ NAM 216-217 D 9
Otchinjau ○ ANG 216-217 B 8
OTC International Satellite Earth Station • AUS 176-177 M 5
O.T.Downs ○ AUS 174-175 C 5
Otelnuk, Lac ○ CDN 36-37 P 6
Oterkpolu ○ GH 202-203 K 6
Otgon Tėngėr ▲ MAU 148-149 C 4
O'the Cherokees, Lake ○ USA (OK) 264-265 K 2
Othello ○ USA (WA) 244-245 F 4
O'the Pines, Lake ○ USA (TX) 264-265 K 6
Otherside River ~ CDN 30-31 Q 6
Oti ~ GH 202-203 L 5
Oti ○ RI 164-165 F 4
Oti, Réserve de l' ⊥ RT 202-203 L 4
Otinolândia ○ BR 72-73 J 3
Otis ○ USA (NM) 256-257 L 6
Otish, Monts ▲ CDN 38-39 J 2
Otjikondo ○ NAM 216-217 C 9
Otjikoto Lake • NAM 216-217 D 9
Otjimbingwe ○• NAM 216-217 D 11
Otjinene ○ NAM 216-217 E 10
Otjinhungwa ○ NAM 216-217 B 8
Otjisemba ○ NAM 216-217 D 10
Otjitanda ○ NAM 216-217 B 8
Otjiwarongo ☆ NAM 216-217 D 10
Otjosondjou ~ NAM 216-217 E 10
Otjosondu ○ NAM 216-217 D 10
Otmėk, pereval ▲ KS 136-137 N 3
Otoca ○ PE 64-65 E 9
Otog Qi ○ VRC 154-155 E 2
Otog Qian Qi ○ VRC 154-155 E 2
Otoineppu ○ J 152-153 K 2
Otola ○ DY 202-203 L 5
Otorohanga ○ NZ 182 E 3
Otoskwin River ~ CDN 234-235 O 3
Otosquen ○ CDN (SAS) 232-233 R 2
Otoyo ○ J 152-153 E 8
Otra ~ N 86-87 C 7
Otradnaja ○ RUS 126-127 D 5
Otradnyj ○ RUS 96-97 G 7
Otranto ○ I 100-101 G 4
Otranto, Canale d' ≈ 100-101 G 4
Otrožnyj ○ RUS 112-113 R 4
Otsego ○ USA (OH) 280-281 E 3
Otsego Lake ○ USA (NY) 278-279 G 6
Otselic ○ USA (NY) 278-279 F 6
Ōtsu ☆ J 152-153 F 7
Ōtsuki ○ J 152-153 H 7
Otta ~ N 86-87 C 5
Ottappidāram ○ IND 140-141 H 6
Ottawa ★• CDN (ONT) 238-239 K 3
Ottawa ○ USA (IL) 274-275 K 3
Ottawa ○ USA (KS) 262-263 L 6
Ottawa ○ USA (OH) 280-281 B 2
Ottawa River ~ CDN 238-239 F 2
Otte Krupens Fjord ≈ 28-29 U 5
Ottenby ○ S 86-87 H 8
Otter ○ CDN (QUE) 242-243 E 3
Otter ○ USA (MT) 250-251 N 6
Otter, Peaks of ▲ USA (VA) 280-281 G 6
Otterburne ○ CDN (MAN) 234-235 G 5
Otter Creek ○ USA (FL) 286-287 G 2
Otter Creek ~ USA 254-255 D 5
Otter Creek ~ USA 278-279 H 5
Otter Creek Reserve ○ USA (UT) 254-255 D 5
Otter Head ▲ CDN (ONT) 236-237 B 4
Otter Island ∴ CDN (ONT) 236-237 B 4
Otter Island ∴ USA 22-23 L 4
Otter Lake ○ CDN (QUE) 238-239 J 3
Otter Lake ○ USA (MI) 272-273 F 4
Otter Lake ○ USA (IL) 274-275 J 5
Otterøyane, Von ∴ N 84-85 M 3
Otter Point ▲ USA 22-23 P 5
Otter Rapids ○ CDN (ONT) 236-237 G 2
Otter River ~ CDN 34-35 M 4
Otter Rock ○ USA (OR) 244-245 A 6
Ottertail ○ USA (MN) 270-271 C 4
Otthon ○ CDN (SAS) 232-233 Q 4
Otto Fiord ≈ 26-27 F 3
Otto-Sala ~ RUS 110-111 S 7
Ottosdal ○ ZA 220-221 G 3
Ottoshoop ○ ZA 220-221 G 2
Ottuk ○ KS 146-147 C 4
Ottumwa ○ USA (IA) 274-275 F 3
Otu ○ CAM 204-205 H 6
Otukamamoan Lake ○ CDN (ONT) 234-235 L 6
Otukpa ○ WAN 204-205 G 5
Otumpa ○ RA 76-77 F 4
Otuquis, Bañados de ○ BOL 70-71 H 6
Otuquis, Río ~ BOL 70-71 H 6
Oturkpo ○ WAN 204-205 H 5
Otu Tolu Group ∴ TON 184 IV a 2
Otuzco ○ PE 64-65 C 5
Otway ○ USA (OH) 280-281 C 5
Otway, Cape ▲ AUS 180-181 G 5
Otway, Seno ≈ 80 E 6
Otway National Park ⊥ AUS 180-181 G 5
Otwell ○ USA (AR) 276-277 E 5
Oua ~ G 210-211 D 3
Ouachita, Lake ○ USA (AR) 276-277 B 6
Ouachita Mountains ▲ USA 264-265 J 4
Ouachita River ~ USA 268-269 J 4
Ouachita River ~ USA 276-277 C 7
Ouadda ○ RCA 206-207 F 4
Ouaddaï ◘ TCH 198-199 K 6
Ouadey, El ~ TCH 198-199 J 6
Ouâd Nâga ○ RIM 196-197 C 6
Ouadou ~ RIM 196-197 E 7
Ouagadougou ★• BF 202-203 K 3
Ouagar, I-n- ○ RN 198-199 C 4
Ouahabou ○ BF 202-203 J 4
Ouahigouya ☆ BF 202-203 J 3
Ouaka ◘ RCA 206-207 E 5
Ouaka ~ RCA 206-207 E 6
Ouaké ○ DY 202-203 L 5
Oualâta ○ RIM 196-197 G 6
Oualia ○ RMM 202-203 E 3
Oualla ▲ RG 202-203 E 4
Ouallam ○ RN 204-205 E 1
Ouana = Wagny ~ G 210-211 D 4
Ouanary ○ F 62-63 J 3
Ouanazein ○ TCH 198-199 H 4
Ouanda Djallé ○• RCA 206-207 F 4
Ouandago ○ RCA 206-207 D 5
Ouandja ○ RCA (Kot) 206-207 F 4
Ouandja ○ RCA (Vak) 206-207 F 4
Ouandja ~ RCA 206-207 F 4
Ouandja-Vakaga, Réserve de faune de la ⊥ RCA 206-207 F 4
Ouando ○ RCA 206-207 G 6
Ouango ○ RCA 206-207 F 6
Ouangolodougou ○ CI 202-203 H 5
Ouaninou ○• CI 202-203 G 5
Ouar, Erg el ⊥ DZ 190-191 F 6
Ouara ~ RCA 206-207 G 6
Ouarak ○ SN 202-203 B 2
Ouarâne ⊥ RIM 196-197 E 4
Ouareau, Rivière ~ CDN 238-239 M 2
Ouargaye ○ BF 202-203 L 4
Ouargla ☆• DZ 190-191 E 5
Ouaritoufoulout ○ RMM 196-197 M 6
Ouarkla ○ CAM 206-207 B 4
Ouarkziz, Jbel ⊥ MA 188-189 F 6
Ouarsenis, Massif de l' ▲ DZ 190-191 C 3
Ouarzazate ☆ MA 188-189 H 5
Ouassa Bamvélé ○ CAM 204-205 K 6
Ouatagouna ○ RMM 202-203 L 2
Ouatcha ○ RN 198-199 D 6
Ouatéré Galafondo ○ RCA 206-207 D 6
Oubangui ~ RCB 210-211 F 4
Ouchi ○ VRC 156-157 H 2
Oudâne ○• RIM 196-197 E 4
Ouday ~ WSA 196-197 C 4
Oudenaarde ○• B 92-93 G 3
Oudingueur, Gorges de l' • TCH 198-199 H 2
Oudjilla ○• CAM 206-207 B 3
Oudna • TN 190-191 H 2
Oudtshoorn ○ ZA 220-221 F 6
Oué'a ○ DJI 208-209 F 3
Oued el Abiod ○ RIM 196-197 D 6
Oued el Hajar ○ RMM 196-197 J 5
Oueden en Nsa ~ DZ 190-191 D 4
Oued Mimoun ☆ DZ 188-189 L 3
Oued Rhiou ○ DZ 190-191 C 3
Oued Rhir ⊥ DZ 190-191 F 4
Oued Tlélat ○ DZ 188-189 L 3
Oued-Zem ○ MA 188-189 H 4
Oued Zenati ○ DZ 190-191 F 2
Ouéléssébougou ○ RMM 202-203 G 4
Ouéllé ○ CI 202-203 H 6
Ouémé ~ DY 204-205 E 5
Ouémé = Affon ~ DY 202-203 L 5
Ouenkoro ○ RMM 202-203 J 3
Ouénou ○ DY 204-205 E 4
Ouenza ○ DZ 190-191 G 3
Oué-Oué ○ DY 204-205 E 4
Ouerrha, Oued ~ MA 188-189 J 3
Ouessa ○ BF 202-203 J 4
Ouessant ∴ F 90-91 E 7
Ouèssè ○ DY 204-205 E 4
Ouest, Pointe de l' ▲ CDN (QUE) 242-243 D 3
Ouest = West ◘ CAM 204-205 J 6
Ouezzane ○ MA 188-189 J 3
Oufrane ○ DZ 190-191 C 6
Ougarou ○ BF 202-203 L 3
Oughterard = Uachtar Ard ○ IRL 90-91 C 5
Ougooué ~ RCB 210-211 D 5
Ouham ◘ RCA 206-207 C 5
Ouham ~ TCH 206-207 C 4
Ouham-Pendé ◘ RCA 206-207 B 5
Ouidah ○• DY 204-205 E 5
Ouidi ○ RN 198-199 F 5
Ouinardène ○ RMM 196-197 K 6
Ouinhi ○ DY 204-205 E 5
Oujâf ○ RIM 196-197 G 6
Oujda = Ujdah ☆ MA (Ojd) 188-189 L 3
Oujeft ○ RIM 196-197 D 4
Ou Jiang ~ VRC 156-157 M 2
Ouka ~ RCA 206-207 E 5
Oukaimeden ○ MA 188-189 H 5
Oukal ○ AFG 134-135 J 2
Oukraal ○ ZA 220-221 D 7
Oukré ○ RIM 196-197 E 6
Oula, Madina- ○ RG 202-203 D 5
Oulad-Teïma ○ MA 188-189 G 5
Oulainen ○ FIN 88-89 H 4
Ould Yenjé ○ RIM 196-197 E 7
Ouled Allenda ○ DZ 190-191 F 4
Ouled Djellal ○ DZ 190-191 E 3
Ouled Naïl, Monts de ▲ DZ 190-191 D 3
Ouli ○ CAM 206-207 B 6
Oulmes ○ MA 188-189 J 4
Oulnina Hill ▲ AUS 180-181 E 2
Oulo, Mayo ~ CAM 204-205 K 4
Oulu ☆ FIN 88-89 H 4
Oulu, Bahr ~ RCA 206-207 F 3
Oulujärvi ○ FIN 88-89 J 4
Oulujoki ~ FIN 88-89 H 4
Oum, Bir ○ TN 190-191 F 4
Oumache ○ DZ 190-191 E 3
Oumba ~ G 210-211 C 4
Oum-Chalouba ○ TCH 198-199 K 5
Oumcheggag ○ WSA 188-189 E 7
Oum Djerane ○ DZ 190-191 C 3
Oumé ☆ CI 202-203 H 6
Oum el Achar ○ DZ 188-189 G 6
Oum el Bouaghi ☆ DZ 190-191 F 3
Oum er Rbia, Oued ~ MA 188-189 J 4
Oum-Hadjer ○ TCH 198-199 J 6
Oumm Debua, Sebkha ○ WSA 188-189 E 7
Oumm ed Droûs Guebli, Sebkhet ○ RIM 196-197 E 2
Oumm ed Droûs Telli, Sebkhet ○ RIM 196-197 E 2
Oumm el Khezz ○ RIM 196-197 E 6
Ounâne, Bir ○ RMM 196-197 J 4
Ounane, Djebel ▲ DZ 190-191 F 8
Ounara ○ MA 188-189 G 5
Ounasjoki ~ FIN 88-89 H 3
Ounay, Kōtal-e ▲ AFG 138-139 B 2
Oundou ~ RG 202-203 E 4
Oungre ○ CDN (SAS) 232-233 P 6
Ounianga Kébir ○ TCH 198-199 K 3
Ounianga Sérir ○ TCH 198-199 K 3
Ountivou ○ RT 202-203 L 6
Ouo ○ RMM 202-203 J 2
Ouogo ○ RCA 206-207 C 5
Ouray ○ USA (CO) 254-255 H 5
Ouray ○ USA (UT) 254-255 F 3
Oureï ○ RIM 196-197 G 6
Ouré-Kaba ○ RG 202-203 E 4
Ourém ○ BR 68-69 E 2
Ourense (Orense) ○ E 98-99 D 3
Ouret, Oued ~ DZ 190-191 G 8
Ouricana, Serra do ▲ BR 72-73 K 3
Ouricuri ○ BR 68-69 H 5
Ourikéla ○ RMM 202-203 H 3
Ourilândia ○ BR 68-69 C 5
Ourinhos ○ BR 72-73 F 7
Ourini ○ TCH 198-199 L 4
Ourique ○ P 98-99 C 6
Ourlal ○ DZ 190-191 E 3
Ouro, Rio do ~ BR 72-73 F 2
Ouro Amat ○ SN 202-203 D 2
Ouro Branco ○ BR 68-69 H 7
Ourofane ○ RN 198-199 D 5
Ouro Fino ○ BR 72-73 G 7
Ouro Prêto ○•• BR 72-73 J 6
Ouro Preto, Rio ~ BR 70-71 E 2
Ouro Preto d'Oeste ○ BR 70-71 F 2
Ouro Sawabé ○ RN 202-203 L 3
Ouro Sogui ○ SN 202-203 D 2
Ouroun Rapids ~ WAN 204-205 F 4
Ouro Velho ○ BR 68-69 K 5
Oursi ○ BF 202-203 K 2
Oursi, Mare de ○ BF 202-203 K 2
Ous ○ RUS 114-115 F 4
Ou-sanmyaku ▲ J 152-153 J 5
Ouse ~ GB 90-91 G 5
Oushutou ○ VRC 154-155 L 4
Oussemial, Jemâa-Ida ○ MA 188-189 G 6
Oussouye ○ SN 202-203 B 3
Oust, Djebel ▲ DZ 188-189 L 4
Outamba-Kilimbi National Park ⊥ WAL 202-203 D 5
Outaouais ▲ CDN 238-239 H 2
Outaouais, River ~ CDN 238-239 K 3
Outaouais, Rivière des ~ CDN 236-237 K 5
Outaouais, Rivière des ~ CDN 236-237 M 5
Outaouais, Rivière des ~ CDN 238-239 G 2
Outardes, Rivière aux ~ CDN 38-39 K 3
Outat-Oulad-El-Hajj ○ MA 188-189 K 4
Outeid Arkass ○ RMM 196-197 H 6
Outeniekwaberge ▲ ZA 220-221 E 6
Outer Bill Bailey Bank = Outer Bailey Bank ≃ 90-91 A 1
Outer Hebrides ∴ GB 90-91 D 3
Outer Island ∴ USA (WI) 270-271 H 3
Outfene ○ RIM 196-197 F 6
Outing ○ USA (MN) 270-271 E 4
Outjo ☆ NAM 216-217 D 10
Outlet Bay ○ CDN 30-31 T 4
Outlook ○ CDN (SAS) 232-233 L 4
Outlook ○ USA (MT) 250-251 P 3
Outokumpu ○ FIN 88-89 K 5
Outoul ○ DZ 190-191 E 9
Ouyen ○ AUS 180-181 G 3
Ouzibi ~ G 210-211 C 5
Ouzoud, Cascades d' ~• MA 188-189 H 4
Ouzzeine, Adrar- ⊥ RMM 196-197 L 5
Ovalau ∴ FJI 184 III b 2
Ovalle ○ RCH 76-77 B 6
Ovamboland ⊥ NAM 216-217 C 9
Ovan ○ G 210-211 D 3
Ovana, Cerro ▲ YV 60-61 H 5
Ovando ○ USA (MT) 250-251 F 4
Ovar ○ P 98-99 C 4
Ovau Island ∴ SOL 184 I c 2
Ovcyna, proliv ≈ 108-109 S 5
Ovejas, Cerro de las ▲ RA 78-79 G 2
Ovejería ○ RA 78-79 F 3
Oveng ○ CAM 210-211 D 2
Ovens, The ∴ CDN (NS) 240-241 L 6
Ovens Natural Park ⊥ CDN (NS) 240-241 L 6
Ovens River ~ AUS 180-181 J 4
Overflowing River ~ CDN 232-233 R 2
Overgaard ○ USA (AZ) 256-257 E 4
Övergård ○ N 86-87 J 2
Överkalix ○ S 86-87 L 3
Overlander Roadhouse ○ AUS 176-177 C 3
Overland Park ○ USA (KS) 262-263 M 6
Overton ○ USA (NV) 248-249 K 3
Overton ○ USA (TX) 264-265 K 6
Övertorneå ○• S 86-87 L 3

Oracle Junction — Övertorneå 373

Panamint Valley ⌣ USA 248-249 G 3
Panamo o YV 60-61 K 4
Pan'an o VRC 156-157 M 2
Panao o PE 64-65 E 6
Panaon Island ⌒ RP 160-161 F 7
Panarea, Ísola ⌒ I 100-101 E 5
Panarik o RI 162-163 H 3
Panaro ~ I 100-101 C 2
Panarukan o RI 168 E 3
Panay ⌒ RP 160-161 D 7
Panay ~ RP 160-161 E 7
Panay Gulf ≈ 160-161 E 7
Panban o AUS 180-181 G 2
Pancada, Cachoeira ~ BR 60-61 K 6
Pancake Rocks and Blowholes •• NZ 182 C 5
Pancas, Rio ~ BR 72-73 K 5
Pančevo o• YU 100-101 H 2
Panchane o MOC 220-221 L 2
Panchari Bazar o BD 142-143 G 4
Pancho Negro o EC 64-65 C 3
Pončicev vrh ▲ YU 100 101 H 3
Pançudo o BR 62-63 J 6
Pancungapang, Gunung ▲ RI 164-165 D 3
Panda o MOC 218-219 H 7
Pandaidori, Kepulauan ⌒ RI 166-167 J 2
Pandale o USA (TX) 266-267 F 3
Pandalkudi o IND 140-141 H 6
Pandan o RP (ANT) 160-161 E 7
Pandan o RP (CAT) 160-161 F 5
Pandanan Island ⌒ RP 160-161 B 8
Pandan Bay ≈ 160-161 D 7
Pandang Endau o MAL 162-163 E 3
Pandanus o AUS 174-175 H 6
Pandattarippu o CL 140-141 H 6
Pāndavapura o IND 140-141 G 4
Pan de Azúcar, Cerro ▲ RA 80 F 4
Pan de Azúcar, Parque Nacional ⊥ RCH 76-77 B 4
Pan de Azúcar, Quebrada ~ RCH 76-77 B 4
Pandegelang o RI 168 B 3
Pandeiros, Riachão ~ BR 72-73 H 3
Pandėlys o•• LT 94-95 J 3
Pandhāna o IND 138-139 F 9
Pandharpur o• IND 140-141 F 2
Pandi o CO 60-61 D 5
Pandiri o RI 164-165 G 4
Pandivalasai o IND 140-141 H 6
Pando o ROU 78-79 M 3
Pondogari o WAN 204 205 G 3
Pandu o ZRE 206-207 D 6
Pañe, Lago o PE 70-71 B 4
Panelão, Paraná do ~ BR 66-67 F 5
Panelas o BR (MAT) 66-67 G 7
Panelas o BR (PER) 68-69 K 6
Panevėžys o•• LT 94-95 J 4
Panfilov = Zharkent o KZ 124-125 M 6
Panfilovcev, zaliv ≈ 108-109 Z 2
Panğ, Daryā-ye ~ AFG 136-137 M 6
Panga o ZRE 210-211 L 3
Pangāb o AFG 134-135 M 1
Pangai o TON 184 IV a 1
Pangaimotu ⌒ TON 184 IV b 1
Pangala o RCB 210-211 E 5
Pangandaran o RI 168 C 3
Pangani o EAT (TAN) 212-213 G 6
Pangani ~ EAT 212-213 F 5
Pangar ~ CAM 204-205 K 6
Pangar Djerem, Réserve ⊥ CAM 204-205 K 5
Pangburn o USA (AR) 276-277 D 5
Pangelah o RI 164-165 D 5
Pangeo o RI 164-165 L 2
Pangertot Peninsula ⌣ CDN 30-31 X 4
Pangga, Tanjung ▲ RI 168 C 7
Panggoe o SOL 184 I c 2
Panggul o RI 168 D 4
Pangi o ZRE 210-211 L 5
Pangia o PNG 183 C 4
Pangian o RI 164-165 F 4
Pangin o IND 142-143 J 1
Pang Kae o THA 158-159 F 3
Pangkah, Tanjung ▲ RI 168 E 3
Pangkajene o RI (SSE) 164-165 F 5
Pangkajene o RI (SSE) 164-165 F 6
Pangkalanbrandan o RI 162-163 C 2
Pangkalanbuun o RI 162-163 J 6
Pangkalandurian o RI 162-163 E 5
Pangkalanpanduk o RI 162-163 E 4
Pangkalansusu o RI 162-163 C 2
Pangkalaseang o RI 164-165 H 4
Pangkalpinang o RI 162-163 G 6
Pangkor, Pulau ⌒ MAL 162-163 D 2
Pang La o THA 142-143 L 6
Panglao o RP 160-161 E 8
Panglao Island ⌒ RP 160-161 E 8
Pangman o CDN (SAS) 232-233 O 6
Pangnirtung o CDN 28-29 H 3
Pango o PNG 183 G 2
Pangoa o PNG 183 A 4
Pango Aluquem o ANG 216-217 C 4
Pangonda o RCA 206-207 E 5
Pangquangou Z.B. ⊥ VRC 154-155 G 3
Pangu o VRC 150-151 D 1
Pangu, Chutes ~ ZRE 210-211 L 2
Panguipulli o RCH 78-79 C 5
Panguipulli, Lago o RCH 78-79 C 5
Panguitch o USA (UT) 254-255 C 6
Panguma o WAL 202-203 E 5
Panguruan o RI 162-163 C 3
Pangutaran Group ⌒ RP 160 161 D 9
Pangutaran Island ⌒ RP 160-161 D 9
Pangzula o VRC 144-145 M 6
Panhame, Rio ~ MOC 218-219 F 2
Panhandle o USA (TX) 264-265 C 3
Paniai, Danau o RI 166-167 J 3
Pania-Mwanga o ZRE 214-215 E 4
Panio Mutombo o ZRE 210-211 J 6
Panipat o IND 138-139 F 5
Panitan o RP 160-161 C 8
Panja ~ RUS 114-115 P 5
Panjang o RI 162-163 F 7
Panjang, Pulau ⌒ RI (JBA) 168 B 2
Panjang, Pulau ⌒ RI (MAL) 166-167 F 4
Panjang, Selat ≈ 162-163 E 4
Panjang, Tanjung ▲ RI 164-165 G 3
Panjgūr o PK 134-135 L 5
Panjin o VRC 150-151 D 7
Panjnad ~ PK 138-139 C 5
Panjpāi o PK 134-135 M 4
Pankof, Cape ▲ USA 22-23 P 5
Pankrat'eva, ostrov ⌒ RUS 108-109 J 3
Pankshin o WAN 204-205 H 4
Panlong o VRC 154-155 E 6
P'anmunjŏm o KOR 150-151 F 9
Panna o IND 142-143 B 3
Pannawonica o AUS 172-173 C 6
Panne, De o B 92-93 G 3
Panngi o VAN 184 II b 2
Panny River ~ CDN 32-33 N 3
Panora o USA (IA) 274-275 D 3
Panorama o BR 72-73 E 6
Panshan • VRC 154-155 K 1
Panshanu-Pass ▲ WAN 204-205 H 3
Panshi o VRC 150-151 F 6
Panshi Ju ⌒ VRC 158-159 L 2
Pansian o RP 160-161 D 3
Pānskura o IND 142-143 E 4
Pantai o RI 164-165 E 5
Pantai Remis o MAL 162-163 D 2
Pantanal, Igarapé ~ BR 66-67 J 6
Pantanal de Nabileque o BR 70-71 J 7
Pantanal do São Lourenço ~ BR 70-71 J 6
Pantanal Matogrossense ~ BR 70-71 J 5
Pantanal Matogrossense, Parque Nacional do ⊥ BR 70-71 J 5
Pântano do Sul o BR 74-75 F 6
Pântano Grande o BR 74-75 D 8
Pantasma o NIC 52-53 B 5
Pantekra o RI 162-163 B 2
Pantelleria o I 100-101 C 6
Pantelleria, Ísola di ⌒ I 100-101 D 6
Pantemakassar o RI 166-167 C 6
Panteraja o RI 162-163 B 2
Pantha o MYA 142-143 J 4
Panti o RI (SUB) 162-163 D 4
Panti ∸• RI 166-167 E 4
Pantoja o PE 64-65 E 2
Pantonbili o RI 162-163 B 2
Pantu o MAL 162-163 J 4
Pantukan o RP 160-161 F 9
Panu o ZRE 210-211 G 5
Pánuco o MEX 50-51 K 6
Pánuco, Río ~ MEX 50-51 K 7
Pan Xian o VRC 156-157 D 4
Panyabungan o RI 162-163 C 4
Panyam o WAN 204-205 H 4
Panyčevo o RUS 114-115 Q 6
Panyikleang, Pulau ⌒ RI 164-165 F 5
Panzakent ☆• TJ 136-137 K 5
Panzarani o CI 202-203 J 5
Panzhihua o VRC 156-157 B 3
Panzi o ZRE 216-217 D 3
Panzós o GCA 52-53 K 4
Pao, El o YV 60-61 K 3
Pao, Río ~ YV 60-61 G 3
Pão de Açucar o BR 68-69 K 6
Pao de La Fortuna, El o YV 60-61 K 4
Páola o I 100-101 F 5
Paola o USA (KS) 262-263 M 6
Paoli o USA (IN) 274-275 M 6
Paoli o USA (OK) 264-265 G 4
Paoni o RI 166-167 E 3
Paonia o USA (CO) 254-255 H 5
Paoua o RCA 206-207 C 5
Paouignan o DY 204-205 E 5
Pap o UZ 136-137 M 4
Pápa o H 92-93 O 5
Papa o USA (HI) 288 K 5
Papadiánika o GR 100-101 J 6
Papagaio o BR 68-69 F 5
Papagaio, Rio ~ BR 66-67 K 6
Papagaios o BR 72-73 H 5
Papagayo, Golfo de ≈ 52-53 B 6
Papagayo, Río ~ MEX 52-53 E 3
Pāpāgni ~ IND 140-141 H 3
Pāpāgni ~ IND 140-141 G 4
Papago Indian Reservation ⚔ USA (AZ) 256-257 C 6
Papaikou o USA (HI) 288 K 5
Papakura o NZ 182 E 2
Papalote o USA (TX) 266-267 K 5
Papantla de Olarte o MEX 52-53 F 1
Papar o MAL 160-161 A 10
Paparoa National Park ⊥• NZ 182 C 5
Papeete ☆ F 13 N 4
Papel, Embalse < RCH 78-79 D 2
Papela o RI 166-167 B 7
Papera o BR 66-67 E 3
Papey ⌒ IS 86-87 f 2
Papialou Island ⌒ PNG 183 D 2
Papigochic, Río ~ MEX 50-51 E 3
Papillion o USA (NE) 262-263 K 3
Papisoi, Tanjung ▲ RI 166-167 G 4
Paporotno o RUS 94-95 M 2
Paposa o RCH 76-77 B 3
Pappadahandi o IND 142-143 C 6
Papua, Gulf of ≈ 183 C 5
Papua New Guinea ■ PNG 183 B 4
Papuk ▲ HR 100-101 F 2
Papun o MYA 142-143 K 6
Papunáua, Rio ~ CO 60-61 F 7
Papunya o AUS 176-177 L 1
Papurí o CO 66-67 C 2
Paqiu o SUD 206-207 K 5
Paquera o CR 52-53 B 7
Paquetville o CDN (NB) 240-241 K 3
Paquica, Cabo ▲ RCH 76-77 B 1
Paquiçama o BR 68-69 C 3
Paquisha o EC 64-65 C 3
Pará ◻ BR 66-67 J 6
Pará, Ilha do ⌒ BR 62-63 J 6
Pará, Rio ~ BR 62-63 K 6
Para, Rio ~ BR 72-73 H 6
Para, Rio ~ BR 72-73 H 5
Parabeľ o RUS (TOM) 114-115 Q 5
Parabeľ ~ RUS 114-115 Q 5
Parabuburo, Área Indígena ⚔ BR 72-73 D 3
Paraburdoo o AUS 172-173 C 7
Paracale o RP 160-161 E 5
Paracambi o BR 72-73 J 7
Paracanã, Área Indígena ⚔ BR 68-69 C 4
Paracas o PE 64-65 D 8
Paracas, Bahía de ≈ 64-65 D 8
Paracas, Península de ⌣ PE 64-65 D 8
Paracas, Punta ▲ PE 64-65 D 8
Paracas, Reserva Nacional ⊥ PE 64-65 D 9
Paracatu o BR 72-73 G 4
Paracatu, Rio ~ BR 72-73 H 4
Paracauti, Rio ~ BR 62-63 K 6
Paracel Islands = Xishaqundao ⌒ VRC 158-159 L 2
Parachilna o AUS 178-179 E 6
Pārachinār o PK 138-139 C 3
Parachute o USA (CO) 254-255 G 4
Paraćin o YU 100-101 H 3
Paraconi, Rio ~ BR 66-67 H 4
Paracuaro o MEX 52-53 C 2
Paracuru o BR 68-69 J 3
Parada o BR 68-69 C 3
Parade o USA (SD) 260-261 E 1
Pará de Minas o BR 72-73 H 5
Paradero o YV (ANZ) 60-61 J 3
Paradero o YV (SUC) 60-61 K 2
Paradise o CDN (NFL) 242-243 P 4
Paradise o USA (CA) 246-247 D 4
Paradise o USA (KS) 262-263 H 5
Paradise o USA (MI) 270-271 N 4
Paradise o USA (NV) 248-249 J 3
Paradise o USA (UT) 254-255 D 2
Paradise Hill o CDN (SAS) 232-233 J 2
Paradise Hill Pass ▲ USA (NV) 246-247 H 2
Paradise Island ⌒ BS 54-55 G 2
Paradise Valley o USA (NV) 246-247 H 2
Parado o RI 168 D 7
Parado, Rio ~ BR 70-71 K 2
Pará do Uruará ~ BR 68-69 B 3
Paradox o USA (CO) 254-255 G 5
Paradwip o IND 142-143 E 5
Paragominas o BR 68-69 E 3
Paragould o USA (AR) 276-277 E 4
Paragua, La o YV 60-61 K 4
Paragua, Reserva Forestal La ⊥ YV 60-61 K 4
Paraguá, Río ~ BOL 70-71 G 4
Paragua, Río ~ YV 60-61 K 5
Paraguaçu, Rio ~ BR 72-73 K 2
Paraguaçu Paulista o BR 72-73 E 7
Paraguai, Rio ~ BR 70-71 J 5
Paraguaipoa o YV 60-61 F 2
Paraguana, Península de ⌣ YV 60-61 F 1
Paraguarí o PY 76-77 J 3
Paraguassú, Área Indígena ⚔ BR 72-73 L 3
Paraguay ■ PY 76-77 G 2
Paraguay, Río ~ RA 76-77 H 4
Paraíba ◻ BR 68-69 J 5
Paraíba, Rio ~ BR 68-69 L 5
Paraibuna o BR 72-73 H 7
Paraibuna, Represa < BR 72-73 H 7
Parainen o FIN 88-89 G 6
Paraíso o BR (AMA) 66-67 D 5
Paraíso o BR (AMA) 66-67 H 6
Paraíso o BR (GSU) 72-73 D 5
Paraíso o BR (RSU) 76-77 K 6
Paraíso o CR 52-53 C 7
Paraíso o• MEX 52-53 H 2
Paraíso, El o BOL 70-71 G 4
Paraíso, El o CO 60-61 E 3
Paraíso, El o HN 52-53 L 5
Paraíso, Ilhas do ⌒ MOC 218-219 H 5
Paraíso, Río ~ BOL 70-71 G 4
Paraíso do Leste o BR 70-71 K 5
Paraíso do Norte o BR 72-73 D 7
Paraíso do Tocantins o BR 68-69 D 7
Paraisópolis o BR 72-73 H 7
Pārak o IR 134-135 J 6
Parakan o RI 168 D 3
Parakao o NZ 182 D 1
Parakou ☆ DY 204-205 E 4
Paralia o GR 100-101 J 6
Paratinga, Rio ~ BR 72-73 H 7
Parama Island ⌒ PNG 183 B 5
Paramakkudi o IND 140-141 H 6
Paramaribo ★• SME 62-63 G 3
Parambu o BR 68-69 H 5
Parambul o IND 140-141 F 4
Paramillo, Nudo de ▲ CO 60-61 D 4
Paramillo, Parque Nacional ⊥ CO 60-61 C 4
Paramirim o BR 72-73 J 2
Paramirim, Rio ~ BR 68-69 G 7
Páramo Frontino ▲ CO 60-61 C 4
Paramonga • PE 64-65 D 7
Paramušir, ostrov ⌒ RUS 122-123 Q 3
Paran o RI 164-165 D 5
Paran, Nāal ~ IL 130-131 D 2
Paraná o BR 72-73 G 2
Paraná ◻ BR 74-75 D 5
Paraná ☆• RA 76-77 G 6
Paraná, Delta del ~ RA 78-79 K 3
Paraná, Rio ~ BR 68-69 F 3
Paraná, Rio ~ BR 72-73 G 2
Paraná, Rio ~ RA 76-77 G 6
Paraná, Río ~ RA 78-79 K 2
Paraná Bravo, Río ~ RA 78-79 K 2
Paranacito, Río ~ RA 78-79 K 2
Paraná de Jacumpa ~ BR 66-67 C 4
Paraná do Ouro ~ BR 66-67 B 7
Paraná do Ramos ~ BR 66-67 J 4
Paranaguá o BR 74-75 F 5
Paranaguá, Baía de ≈ 74-75 F 5
Paraná Guazu, Río ~ RA 78-79 K 2
Paranaíba o BR 72-73 E 5
Paranaíba, Rio ~ BR 68-69 B 7
Paranaíba, Rio ~ BR 72-73 E 5
Paranaíba, Rio ~ BR 72-73 G 5
Paraná Ibicuy, Río ~ RA 78-79 K 2
Paranaiguara o BR 72-73 E 5
Paranaíta o BR 66-67 J 7
Paraná Juca o BR 66-67 C 2
Paranal o RCH 76-77 B 3
Paranam o SME 62-63 G 3
Paraná Mini, Río ~ RA 76-77 H 5
Paraná Panapuã ~ BR 66-67 E 4
Paranapanema, Rio ~ BR 72-73 D 7
Paranapebas o BR 68-69 D 5
Paraná Piacaba, Serra ▲ BR 74-75 F 5
Paranaquara, Serra ▲ BR 62-63 H 6
Paranatinga o BR 70-71 K 4
Paranatinga, Rio ~ BR 70-71 K 4
Paranavaí o BR 72-73 D 7
Parandak o IR 136-137 B 7
Parang o RP (MAG) 160-161 F 9
Parang o RP (SUL) 160-161 D 10
Parang, Pulau ⌒ RI 166-167 F 3
Paranga o EAU 212-213 D 2
Paran'ga ☆ RUS 96-97 F 5
Parantan o CL 140-141 J 6
Parapeba o BR 72-73 H 5
Paraopeba, Rio ~ BR 72-73 H 5
Paraparaumu o NZ 182 E 4
Parapeti, Río ~ BOL 70-71 F 6
Parapol'skij Dol, ravnina ⌣ RUS 120-121 U 3
Parapuã o BR 72-73 E 6
Parara = Vonavona ⌒ SOL 184 I c 3
Pará Ridge ≃ 62-63 K 3
Parás o MEX 50-51 K 4
Parás o PE 64-65 E 8
Parasi o NEP 144-145 D 7
Paraso o SOL 184 I c 2
Parata, Pointe de la ▲ F 98-99 M 4
Paratebueno o CO 60-61 E 5
Parateca o BR 72-73 J 2
Parati o•• BR 72-73 H 7
Paratinga o BR 72-73 J 2
Paratoo o AUS 180-181 E 2
Paratunka o RUS 120-121 S 7
Parauapebas, Rio ~ BR 68-69 C 5
Parauari, Rio ~ BR 66-67 J 5
Paraúna o BR 72-73 E 4
Paravur o IND 140-141 G 6
Paray-le-Monial o• F 90-91 K 8
Paray Tepuy o YV 62-63 D 3
Parazinho o BR 68-69 L 4
Pārbati ~ IND 138-139 F 7
Parbhani o IND 138-139 F 10
Parbig ~ RUS 114-115 Q 6
Parc du Mont Tremblant ⊥ CDN (QUE) 238-239 L 2
Parc Gatineau ⊥ CDN (QUE) 238-239 J 3
Parc National de la Mauricie ⊥ CDN (QUE) 238-239 M 2
Parc Naturel Régional d'Armorique ⊥ F 90-91 F 7
Parc Naturel Régional de Brière ⊥ F 90-91 F 8
Parc Naturel Régional de Brotonne ⊥ F 90-91 H 7
Parc Naturel Régional de Camargue ⊥• F 90-91 K 10
Parc Naturel Régional de la Corse ⊥ F 98-99 M 3
Parc Naturel Régional du Marais Poitevin Val de Sèvre et ⊥ F 90-91 G 8
Parcoy o PE 64-65 D 5
Parc Provincial de Mistassini ⊥ CDN 38-39 H 3
Parc Provincial de Port Cartier Sept-Îles ⊥ CDN (QUE) 242-243 B 2
Parc Provincial des Laurentides ⊥ CDN (QUE) 240-241 D 3
Parc Provincial du Frontenau ⊥ CDN (QUE) 238-239 O 3
Parc Régional des Landes de Gascogne ⊥ F 90-91 G 9
Parc Régional des Volcans d'Auvergne ⊥ F 90-91 J 9
Parc Régional du Luberon ⊥ F 90-91 K 10
Parc Régional du Morvan ⊥ F 90-91 J 8
Parc Régional du Vercors ⊥ F 90-91 K 9
Parczew o PL 92-93 R 3
Pardi o IND 138-139 D 9
Pardillal o YV (ANZ) 60-61 J 3
Pardillal o YV (ARA) 60-61 H 3
Pardo, Rio ~ BR 64-65 F 4
Pardo, Rio ~ BR 68-69 B 4
Pardo, Rio ~ BR 70-71 F 2
Pardo, Rio ~ BR 72-73 D 6
Pardo, Rio ~ BR 72-73 K 3
Pardo, Rio ~ BR 72-73 F 6
Pardoo Roadhouse o AUS 172-173 D 6
Pardubice o CZ 92-93 N 3
Pardubitz = Pardubice o• CZ 92-93 N 3
Pare o RI 168 E 3
Parece Vela Basin ≃ 14-15 F 6
Parecis o BR 70-71 J 4
Parecis, Chapada dos ▲ BR 70-71 F 2
Parecis, Rio ~ BR 70-71 J 3
Paredão de Minas o BR 72-73 H 4
Paredítas o RA 78-79 E 3
Paredón o• MEX 52-53 H 3
Paren' o RUS (KOR) 112-113 M 5
Paren' ~ RUS 112-113 L 5
Paren' ~ RUS 112-113 M 5
Paren', Verhnij o RUS 112-113 M 5
Parenda o IND 138-139 E 10
Parengo o IND 142-143 J 1
Paren'skoe, ozero o RUS 112-113 M 5
Parent o CDN (QUE) 236-237 O 5
Parent, Lac o CDN (QUE) 236-237 L 4
Parepare o RI 164-165 F 6
Paresi, Área Indígena ⚔ BR 70-71 H 4
Paresi do Rio Formoso, Área Indígena ⚔ BR 70-71 H 4
Párga o GR 100-101 H 5
Pargaon Sudrik o IND 138-139 E 10
Pargas = Parainen o FIN 88-89 G 6
Pargua o RCH 78-79 C 6
Parguaza, Río ~ YV 60-61 H 5
Parguaza, Serranía de ▲ YV 60-61 H 5
Parguera ∸ USA 286-287 O 3
Parhar o TJ 136-137 L 6
Paria o BOL 70-71 D 5
Paria, Golfo de ≈ 60-61 K 2
Paria, Península de ⌣ YV 60-61 K 2
Pariacoto o PE 64-65 D 6
Pariaguán o YV 60-61 J 3
Pariaman o RI 162-163 D 5
Paria River ~ USA 254-255 D 6
Paricatuba o BR 66-67 G 5
Paricutín, Volcán ▲ MEX 52-53 C 2
Parika o GUY 62-63 E 2
Parima, Serra ▲ BR 60-61 J 6
Parinacochas, Lago o PE 64-65 F 9
Parinari o PE 64-65 E 4
Pariñas, Punta ▲ PE 64-65 B 4
Parintins o BR 66-67 J 4
Paripiranga o BR 68-69 K 7
Paririque Grande o RA 76-77 D 2
Paris o CDN (ONT) 238-239 E 5
Paris ★••• F 92-93 G 4
Paris o USA (AR) 276-277 B 5
Paris o USA (ID) 252-253 G 4
Paris o USA (IL) 274-275 L 5
Paris o USA (KY) 276-277 L 2
Paris o USA (MO) 274-275 G 5
Paris o USA (TN) 276-277 G 4
Paris o USA (TX) 264-265 J 5
Pariserømme ⌒ GRØ 26-27 q 4
Parish Glacier ⊂ CDN 26-27 M 4
Paris Mountain State Park ⊥ USA (SC) 284-285 H 2
Pārispea o EST 94-95 J 2
Parit o MAL 162-163 D 2
Parit o RI 162-163 D 4
Parita o PA 52-53 D 7
Parita, Golfo de ≈ 52-53 D 7
Parittanjungmelayu o RI 162-163 E 5
Pāriz o IR 134-135 F 4
Parkāl o IND 138-139 G 10
Parkano o FIN 88-89 G 5
Parkbeg o CDN (SAS) 232-233 M 5
Park City o USA (KY) 276-277 J 3
Park City o USA (UT) 254-255 D 3
Parkent o UZ 136-137 L 4
Parker o USA (AZ) 256-257 A 4
Parker o USA (SD) 260-261 J 3
Parker, Mount ▲ AUS 172-173 J 4
Parker Dam o USA (CA) 248-249 K 5
Parker Lake o CDN 30-31 W 4
Parkersburg o USA (IA) 274-275 F 2
Parkersburg o USA (WV) 280-281 E 4
Parkers Prairie o USA (MN) 270-271 C 4
Parkerview o CDN (SAS) 232-233 P 4
Parkes o AUS 180-181 K 2
Park Falls o USA (WI) 270-271 H 5
Parkfield o USA (CA) 248-249 D 4
Parkhill o CDN (ONT) 238-239 D 5
Parkin o USA (AR) 276-277 E 5
Parkman o CDN (SAS) 232-233 R 6
Parkman o USA (OH) 280-281 E 2
Parkman o USA (WY) 252-253 L 2
Park Range ▲ USA 254-255 J 3
Park Rapids o USA (MN) 270-271 C 4
Park Rapids o USA (WA) 244-245 H 2
Park River o USA (ND) 258-259 K 3
Park River ~ USA 258-259 K 3
Park Rynie o ZA 220-221 K 5
Parkside o CDN (SAS) 232-233 M 2
Parkston o USA (SD) 260-261 J 3
Parksville o CDN (BC) 230-231 E 4
Parlākimidi o IND 142-143 D 6
Parli o IND 138-139 F 10
Parma o•• I 100-101 C 2
Parma o USA (ID) 252-253 B 3
Parma o USA (OH) 280-281 E 2
Parmana o YV 60-61 J 4
Parnaguá o BR 68-69 F 7
Parnaíba o BR 68-69 H 3
Parnaíba, Rio ~ BR 68-69 G 3
Parnaíba, Serra da ▲ BR 68-69 E 6
Parnamirim o BR 68-69 J 6
Parnarama o BR 68-69 G 4
Parnassus o NZ 182 D 5
Parndana o AUS 180-181 D 3
Pärnu ☆•• EST 94-95 J 2
Pärnu-Jaagupi o•• EST 94-95 J 2
Paro o BHT 142-143 F 2
Paromang o RI 168 E 6
Paron o USA (AR) 276-277 C 6
Paroo o AUS 176-177 E 3
Paroo River ~ AUS 178-179 H 4
Pároo o GR 100-101 K 6
Páros ⌒ GR 100-101 K 6
Parou, Kūh-e ▲ IR 134-135 B 1
Parow o ZA 220-221 D 6
Parowan o USA (UT) 254-255 C 6
Par Pond < USA (SC) 284-285 J 3
Parraburdoo Mining Area • AUS 172-173 C 7
Parral o RCH 78-79 D 4
Parramatta o AUS 180-181 L 2
Parramore Island ⌒ USA (VA) 280-281 L 6
Parras de la Fuente o MEX 50-51 H 5
Parrish o USA (WI) 270-271 J 5
Parrita o CR 52-53 B 7
Parrott o USA (GA) 284-285 F 5
Parrsboro o CDN (NS) 240-241 L 5
Parrs Halt o ZA 218-219 D 6
Parry o CDN (SAS) 232-233 O 6
Parry, Cape ▲ CDN 24-25 K 5
Parry, Kap ▲ GRØ (NGR) 26-27 P 5
Parry, Kap ▲ GRØ (ØGR) 26-27 p 7
Parry, Lac o CDN 36-37 M 5
Parry Bay ≈ 24-25 f 6
Parry Beach o AUS 176-177 D 7
Parry Falls ~ CDN 30-31 P 4
Parry Island ⌒ CDN (ONT) 238-239 E 3
Parry Island Indian Reservation ⚔ CDN (ONT) 238-239 E 3
Parry Islands ⌒ CDN 24-25 P 3
Parryøya ⌒ N 84-85 M 2
Parry Peninsula ⌣ CDN 24-25 K 6
Parry Sound o CDN (ONT) 238-239 E 3
Pārsābād o IR 128-129 M 3
Parseierspitze ▲ A 92-93 L 5
Parshall o USA (ND) 258-259 E 4
Parsnip River ~ CDN 228-229 M 2
Parsoburan o RI 162-163 C 3
Parsons o USA (KS) 262-263 L 7
Parsons o USA (TN) 276-277 G 5
Parsons, Mount ▲ AUS 174-175 C 3
Parsons Lake o CDN 20-21 Y 2
Parson's Pond o CDN (NFL) 242-243 L 2
Parson's Pond o CDN (NFL) 242-243 L 3
Parsons Range ▲ AUS 174-175 C 3
Partābpur o IND 142-143 C 4
Partago o DY 202-203 L 5
Partāwal o IND 142-143 C 2
Pårtefjällen ▲ S 86-87 H 3
Partenkirchen, Garmisch- o• D 92-93 L 5
Parthenay o F 90-91 G 8
Pārtibanūr o IND 140-141 H 6
Partizanka o KZ 124-125 G 2
Partizansk o RUS (KRN) 116-117 G 6
Partizansk o RUS (ROS) 122-123 E 7
Partoun o USA (UT) 254-255 B 4
Partridge Island ⌒ CDN 34-35 N 2
Partūr o IND 138-139 F 10
Paru, Ilha ⌒ BR 62-63 G 6
Paru, Rio ~ BR 62-63 H 5
Paru, Rio ~ YV 60-61 J 5
Paruá o BR 68-69 F 3
Paru de Este, Área Indígena ⚔ BR 62-63 G 5
Paru de Este, Rio ~ BR 62-63 G 5
Paruna o AUS 180-181 F 3
Parur o IND 140-141 G 5
Paruro o PE 70-71 B 3
Parusovaja ~ RUS 108-109 U 8
Parvān ◻ AFG 138-139 B 2
Pārvatīpuram o IND 142-143 C 6
Parvatsar o IND 138-139 E 6
Paryang o VRC 144-145 D 5
Parys o ZA 220-221 H 3
Pas, Rivière de ~ CDN 36-37 R 7
Paša o RUS 94-95 N 1
Pasāband o AFG 134-135 L 2
Pasadena o CDN (NFL) 242-243 L 3
Pasadena o USA (CA) 248-249 F 5
Pasadena o USA (TX) 268-269 E 7
Pasaje o EC 64-65 C 3
Pasaje o Juramento, Río ~ RA 76-77 E 3
Pasān o IND 142-143 C 4
Pasangkayu o RI 164-165 F 4
Pasapuat o RI 162-163 D 6
Pasaquina o ES 52-53 L 5
Pasarae o SOL 184 I c 2
Pasarbantal o RI 162-163 D 6
Pasarbembah o RI 162-163 E 6
Pāsārgād o•• IR 134-135 E 3
Pasarsibuhuan o RI 162-163 C 4
Pasarsorkam = Sorkam o RI 162-163 C 4
Pasartalo o RI 162-163 E 7
Pasarwajo o RI 164-165 H 6
Pasawng o MYA 142-143 K 6
Pasayten Wilderness ⊥ USA (WA) 244-245 E 2
Pascagoula o USA (MC) 268 269 M 6
Pascagoula River ~ USA 268-269 M 6
Pascal o CDN (SAS) 232-233 L 2
Pașcani o RO 102-103 E 4
Pasco o USA (WA) 244-245 F 4
Pascoe, Mount ▲ AUS 176-177 F 3
Pasco Island ⌒ AUS 172-173 B 6
Pasewalk o• D 92-93 M 2
Pasfield Lake o CDN 30-31 R 6
Pasi, Pulau ⌒ RI 168 E 6
Pasiene o•• LV 94-95 L 3
Pasig ☆ RP 160-161 D 5
Pa'sina o RUS 116-117 J 6
Pasinler ☆ TR 128-129 J 3
Paširo o RUS 114-115 R 7
Pasión, Río de la ~ GCA 52-53 J 3
Pasir, Tanjung ▲ MAL 162-163 J 3
Pasir, Tanjung ▲ RI 162-163 H 5
Pasir Panjang o MAL 162-163 D 3
Pasirpengarayan o RI 162-163 D 4
Pasir Puteh o MAL 162-163 E 2
Pasirputih o RI 166-167 C 6
Pasitelu, Kepulauan ⌒ RI 168 E 6
Påskallavik o S 86-87 H 8
Paskenta o USA (CA) 246-247 C 4
Pasłęk o• PL 92-93 P 1
Pasley, Cape ▲ AUS 176-177 G 6
Pasley Bay ≈ 24-25 Y 5
Pašman ⌒ HR 100-101 E 3
Pasmore River ~ AUS 178-179 E 6
Pasni o PK 134-135 K 6
Paso o RI 166-167 E 3
Paso, El o USA (IL) 274-275 J 4
Paso, El o• USA (TX) 266-267 A 2
Paso de Barahona ▲ RA 76-77 B 6
Paso de Indios o RA 78-79 E 7
Paso del Agua Negra ▲ RA 76-77 C 6
Paso de la Guardia ▲ RA 76-77 B 6
Paso de la Laguna o RA 76-77 H 6
Paso de las Piedras, Embalse < RA 78-79 J 5
Paso de Lesca o C 54-55 G 4
Paso del Indio ≈ 80 C 4
Paso de los Algarrobos o RA 78-79 F 4
Paso de los Indios o RA 78-79 E 5
Paso de los Libres o RA 76-77 J 5
Paso de los Toros o ROU 78-79 L 2
Paso del Rey o RA 78-79 F 2
Paso del Sapo o RA 78-79 E 7
Paso del Toro o MEX 52-53 F 2
Paso de Ovejas o MEX 52-53 F 2
Paso de Patria o PY 76-77 H 4
Paso de San Francisco ▲ RA 76-77 C 4
Paso de Vacas Helados ▲ RA 76-77 C 5
Paso Flores o RA 78-79 D 6
Paso Nacional o MEX 50-51 H 5
Paso Nuevo o YV 60-61 K 3
Paso Pichereguas ▲ RA 76-77 C 6
Paso Real de Macaira o YV 60-61 H 3
Paso Real de San Diego o C 54-55 D 3
Paso Robles o USA (CA) 248-249 D 4
Paso Rodolfo Roballos o RA 80 E 3
Paspébiac o CDN (QUE) 240-241 K 2
Pasqua o CDN (SAS) 232-233 N 5
Pasquatchai River ~ CDN 34-35 L 3
Pasquia Hills ▲ CDN 232-233 P 3
Pasrur o PK 138-139 E 3
Passa ~ G 210-211 E 4
Passa e Fica o BR 68-69 L 5
Passagem o BR 68-69 L 5
Passagem Franca o BR 68-69 G 5
Passage Point ▲ CDN 24-25 O 4
Passamaquoddy Bay ≈ 240-241 H 5
Passau o D 92-93 M 4
Passayten Wilderness Area ⊥ USA (WA) 244-245 E 2
Pass Christian o USA (MS) 268-269 L 6
Passi o RP 160-161 E 7
Passi o SN 202-203 B 3
Passira o BR 68-69 L 5
Pass Island o CDN (NFL) 242-243 M 5
Pass Lake o CDN (ONT) 234-235 P 6
Passmore o CDN (BC) 230-231 M 4
Passo da Guarda o BR 76-77 J 6
Passo Fundo o BR 74-75 D 7
Passo Fundo, Represa de < BR 74-75 D 6
Passo Real, Represa de < BR 74-75 D 7
Passos o BR 72-73 G 6
Passu Keah = Panshi Ju ⌒ VRC 158-159 L 2
Pastaza, Río ~ PE 64-65 D 3
Pasteur o RA 78-79 H 3
Pasto ☆ CO 64-65 D 1
Pastol Bay ≈ 20-21 J 5
Pastor, El o MEX 50-51 G 3
Pastos Bons o BR 68-69 F 5
Pastos Chicos, Río ~ RA 76-77 D 2
Pastos Grandes, Sierra de los ▲ RA 76-77 D 3
Pastrana o E 98-99 F 4
Pastura o USA (NM) 256-257 L 4
Pasuruan o RI 168 E 3
Pasvalys ☆ LT 94-95 J 3
Pasvikelva ~ N 86-87 O 2
Pata o BOL 70-71 C 4
Pata o CO 66-67 B 3
Pata o RCA 206-207 E 4
Pata o SN 202-203 C 3
Patacamaya o BOL 70-71 D 5
Patache, Punta ▲ RCH 70-71 B 7
Patadkal o••• IND 140-141 F 3
Patagonia o USA (AZ) 256-257 E 7
Patagonia = Patagónia ∸ 80 E 5
Patagonian Shelf ≈ 5 E 10
Patagónica, Cordillera ▲ RCH 80 D 5
Pata Island ⌒ RP 160-161 D 10
Pataiya o IND 140-141 G 5
Patalasang o RI 164-165 F 6
Patambalu o ZRE 210-211 G 5
Patambuco o PE 70-71 C 4
Patamuté o BR 68-69 J 6
Pātan o IND (GUJ) 138-139 D 8
Pātan o IND (MAH) 140-141 E 2
Patani o RI 164-165 L 3
Patani o WAN 204-205 G 6
Patas o IND 138-139 E 10
Pata Temple • VRC 164 166 H 4
Patauá, Cachoeira do ~ BR 66-67 G 7
Patauá Creek ~ USA 284-285 F 5
Patay Rondos o PE 64-65 D 6
Patchepawapoko River ~ CDN 34-35 P 4
Patchogue o USA (NY) 280-281 N 3
Patea o NZ 182 E 3
Pategi o WAN 204-205 F 4
Pate Island ⌒ EAK 212-213 H 5
Patelão, Rio ~ BR 70-71 J 2
Patensie o ZA 220-221 G 6
Paternó o I 100-101 E 6
Paternoster o ZA 220-221 C 6
Pateros o USA (WA) 244-245 F 2
Paterson o USA (NJ) 280-281 M 3
Paterson o USA (WA) 244-245 F 5
Paterson o ZA 220-221 G 6
Paterson Inlet ≈ 182 B 7
Paterson Range ▲ AUS 172-173 F 6
Pathalala o NEP 144-145 E 7
Pathalgaon o IND 142-143 C 4
Pathānkot o IND 138-139 E 3
Patharkot o NEP 144-145 E 7
Pathfinder Reservoir o USA (WY) 252-253 M 4
Pathin o THA 158-159 E 5
Pathlow o CDN (SAS) 232-233 O 3
Pāthri o IND 138-139 F 10
Pāthrud o IND 138-139 E 10
Pathum Thani o THA 158-159 F 3
Pati o RI 168 D 3
Patia = El Bordo o CO 60-61 C 6
Patía, Río ~ CO 60-61 B 7
Patiala o IND 138-139 F 4
Patillas o•• USA (PR) 286-287 P 2
Patinti, Selat ≈ 164-165 K 4
Patio Chiquito o CO 60-61 F 5
Patiroriolo o RI 164-165 G 6
Pativilca o PE 64-65 D 7
Pātkai Bum ▲ IND 142-143 J 2
Patman, Lake o USA (TX) 264-265 K 5
Pat Mayse Lake < USA (TX) 264-265 J 5
Pátmos ⌒ GR 100-101 L 6
Patna ☆ IND 142-143 D 3
Patnanungan Island ⌒ RP 160-161 E 5
Patnitola o BD 142-143 F 3
Patnos ☆ TR 128-129 K 3
Pato, Cachoeira do ~ BR 62-63 E 6
Pato Branco o BR 74-75 D 6
Patoka o USA (IL) 274-275 J 6
Patoka Lake o USA (IN) 274-275 M 6
Patoka River ~ USA 274-275 L 6
Patom, Bol'šoj ~ RUS 118-119 G 5
Patomskoe, nagor'e ∸ RUS 118-119 F 6
Patonga o AUS 172-173 L 2
Patonga o EAU 212-213 D 2
Patopsco Reservoir o USA (MD) 280-281 K 4
Patos o BR (CEA) 68-69 H 3
Patos o BR (PA) 68-69 K 5
Patos, Cachoeira dos ~ BR 70-71 H 2
Patos, Lagoa dos ~ BR 74-75 E 8
Patos, Río de los ~ RA 78-79 E 2
Patos de Minas o BR 72-73 G 5
Patos ou São José, Rio dos ~ BR 70-71 J 3
Patquia o RA 76-77 D 6
Pátra ☆• GR 100-101 H 5

Panamint Valley — Pátra 375

Patraikos Kólpos ≈ 100-101 H 5
Patrakeevka ○ **RUS** 88-89 Q 4
Patreksfjörður ☆ **IS** 86-87 b 2
Patricia ○ **CDN** (ALB) 232-233 G 5
Patricia ○ **USA** (TX) 264-265 B 6
Patricios, Los ○ **CO** 66-67 B 3
Patrick ○ **USA** (SC) 284-285 K 2
Patrimonjo ○ **BR** 72-73 F 5
Patrocínio ○ **BR** 72-73 G 5
Pattamada ○ **IND** 140-141 G 6
Pattani ☆ **THA** 158-159 F 7
Pattaya ○•• **THA** 158-159 F 4
Patten River ~ **CDN** 236-237 J 3
Patterson ≈ 172-173 K 2
Patterson ○ **USA** (CA) 248-249 C 2
Patterson ○ **USA** (GA) 284-285 H 5
Patterson ○ **USA** (ID) 252-253 E 2
Patterson ○ **USA** (LA) 268-269 J 7
Patterson, Mount ▲ **AUS** 176-177 F 2
Patterson, Mount ▲ **CDN** 20-21 X 4
Patterson Pass ▲ **USA** (NV) 246-247 L 5
Patti ○ **I** 100-101 E 5
Pattison ○ **USA** (MS) 268-269 K 5
Pattoki ○ **PK** 138-139 D 4
Patton ○ **USA** (MO) 276-277 E 3
Pattonsburg ○ **USA** (MO) 274-275 D 4
Pattukkottai ○ **IND** 140-141 H 5
Patu ○ **BR** 68-69 K 5
Patuakhali ○ **BD** 142-143 G 4
Patuca, Punta ▲ **HN** 54-55 C 7
Patuca, Río ~ **HN** 54-55 C 7
Patugu ○ **RI** 168 E 6
Patullo, Mount ▲ **CDN** 32-33 F 3
Patungan ○ **RP** 160-161 D 5
Paturau River ○ **NZ** 182 D 4
Patuxent River ~ **USA** 280-281 K 5
Patvinsuom kansallispuisto ⊥ **FIN** 88-89 L 5
Pátzcuaro ○•• **MEX** 52-53 D 2
Patzimaro ○ **MEX** 52-53 C 1
Pau ☆• **F** 90-91 G 10
Pau, Tanjung ▲ **RI** 166-167 B 6
Pau Alto, Rio ~ **BR** 72-73 L 4
Paucarbamba ○ **PE** 64-65 E 8
Paucarcolla ○ **PE** 70-71 B 4
Paucartambo ○ **PE** 70-71 B 3
Paucartambo, Río ~ **PE** 64-65 E 7
Pau d'Arco, Rio ~ **BR** 68-69 C 5
Pau de Ferros ○ **BR** 68-69 J 5
Pauh ○ **RI** 162-163 E 6
Pauini ○ **BR** 66-67 D 6
Pauini, Rio ~ **BR** 66-67 F 3
Pauini, Rio ~ **BR** 66-67 D 6
Pauk ○ **MYA** 142-143 J 5
Paukkaung ○ **MYA** 142-143 J 6
Paulatuk ○ **CDN** 24-25 K 6
Paulaya, Río ~ **HN** 54-55 C 7
Paul B. Johnson State Park ⊥ **USA** (MS) 268-269 L 5
Paul Bunyan & Blue Ox Statue • **USA** (MN) 270-271 D 3
Paulden ○ **USA** (AZ) 256-257 C 4
Paulding ○ **USA** (OH) 280-281 B 2
Paulina ○ **USA** (OR) 244-245 F 6
Paulina Peak ▲ **USA** (OR) 244-245 D 7
Pauline ○ **USA** (ID) 252-253 F 4
Paul Island ⌒ **CDN** 36-37 T 6
Paul Island ⌒ **USA** 22-23 R 5
Paulista ○ **BR** 68-69 L 5
Paulistana ○ **BR** 68-69 H 6
Paullina ○ **USA** (IA) 274-275 C 2
Paulo Afonso ○• **BR** 68-69 J 6
Paulo Afonso, Parque Nacional ⊥ **BR** 68-69 J 6
Paulo de Faria ○ **BR** 72-73 F 6
Paulo Ramos ○ **BR** 68-69 F 4
Paulpietersburg ○ **ZA** 220-221 K 3
Paul Roux ○ **ZA** 220-221 H 4
Paul Sauer Dam < **ZA** 220-221 G 6
Paul Spur ○ **USA** (AZ) 256-257 F 7
Pauls Valley ○ **USA** (OK) 264-265 G 4
Paungdawthi ○ **MYA** 158-159 D 2
Paungde ○ **MYA** 142-143 J 6
Pauni ○ **IND** 138-139 G 9
Paup ○ **PNG** 183 B 2
Pauri ○ **IND** 138-139 F 7
Pausa ○ **PE** 64-65 F 9
Paute ○ **EC** 64-65 C 3
Pauto, Río ~ **CO** 60-61 F 5
Pau Uma, Île = Paama ⌒ **VAN** 184 II b 3
Pauwasi ~ **RI** 166-167 L 3
Pauwela ○ **USA** (HI) 288 J 4
Pāvagada ○ **IND** 140-141 G 3
Pavant Range ▲ **USA** 254-255 C 5
Pavão ○ **BR** 72-73 K 4
Pāve ○ **IR** 128-129 M 5
Pavia ☆• **I** 100-101 B 2
Pavilion ○ **CDN** (BC) 230-231 H 3
Pavilion ○ **USA** (NY) 278-279 C 6
Pavillion ○ **USA** (WY) 252-253 K 3
Pāvilosta ○ **LV** 94-95 G 3
Pavlikeni ○ **BG** 102-103 D 6
Pavlodar ☆• **KZ** 124-125 K 2
Pavlof Bay ≈ 22-23 Q 5
Pavlof Islands ⌒ **USA** 22-23 Q 5
Pavlof Volcano ▲ **USA** 22-23 Q 5
Pavlograd = Pavlohrad ○ **UA** 102-103 J 3
Pavlogradka ☆ **RUS** 124-125 H 1
Pavlohrad ○ **UA** 102-103 J 3
Pavlovac ○ **HR** 100-101 F 2
Pavlovič, Erofej ○ **RUS** 118-119 L 8
Pavlovka ○ **RUS** 96-97 E 7
Pavlovo ☆ **RUS** 94-95 S 4
Pavlovsk ○ **RUS** 102-103 M 2
Pavlovsk ○•• **RUS** (LEN) 94-95 M 2
Pavlovsk ☆ **RUS** 124-125 N 2
Pavlovskij Posad ☆ **RUS** 94-95 Q 4
Pavlovskoe vodohranilišče < **RUS** 96-97 K 6
Pavlyš ○ **UA** 102-103 H 3
Pavo ○ **USA** (GA) 284-285 G 6
Pavon, Arroyo ~ **RA** 78-79 J 2
Pavullo nel Frignano ○ **I** 100-101 C 2
Pavuvu Island ⌒ **SOL** 184 I d 3
Pavylon, ozero ⊖ **RUS** 110-111 d 5
Pawaia ○ **PNG** 183 C 4
Pawan ~ **RI** 162-163 J 5
Pawāyān ○ **IND** 144-145 C 6
Pawé ▲ **CAM** 204-205 J 6
Pawhuska ○ **USA** (OK) 264-265 H 2
Pawleys Island ○ **USA** (SC) 284-285 L 3
Pawnee ○ **USA** (OK) 264-265 H 2
Pawnee Bill Museum • **USA** (OK) 264-265 H 2
Pawnee City ○ **USA** (NE) 262-263 K 4
Pawnee Indian Village ∴ **USA** (KS) 262-263 J 5
Pawnee River ~ **USA** 262-263 G 6
Pawnee Rock ○ **USA** (KS) 262-263 H 6
Pawnee Rock State Monument • **USA** (KS) 262-263 H 6
Paw Paw ○ **USA** (MI) 272-273 D 5
Pawtucket ○ **USA** (RI) 278-279 K 7
Pawut ○ **MYA** 158-159 E 4
Paxí ⌒ **GR** 100-101 H 5
Paxiúba, Rio ~ **BR** 66-67 G 7
Paxson ○ **USA** 20-21 S 5
Paxton ○ **USA** (IL) 274-275 K 4
Paxton ○ **USA** (NE) 262-263 E 3
Paxville ○ **USA** (SC) 284-285 K 3
Paya, Parque Nacional la ⊥ **CO** 64-65 E 1
Payagyi ○ **MYA** 158-159 D 2
Payahe ○ **RI** 164-165 K 3
Payakumbuh ○ **RI** 162-163 D 5
Payang, Gunung ▲ **RI** 164-165 D 3
Payar ○ **SN** 202-203 C 2
Payas, Cerro ▲ **HN** 54-55 C 7
Payer, Kap ▲ **GRØ** 26-27 b 2
Payer Land ∸ **GRØ** 26-27 o 6
Payero, Río ~ **CO** 60-61 E 5
Payette ○ **USA** (ID) 252-253 B 2
Payette River ~ **USA** 252-253 B 3
Payne, Lac ⊖ **CDN** 36-37 M 5
Payne Bay ≈ 36-37 P 4
Paynes Creek ○ **USA** (CA) 246-247 D 3
Paynes Find ○ **AUS** 176-177 D 4
Paynesville ○ **AUS** 180-181 J 4
Paynesville ○ **USA** (MN) 270-271 D 5
Paynton ○ **CDN** (SAS) 232-233 K 2
Payogasta ○ **RA** 76-77 D 3
Payong, Tanjung ▲ **MAL** 162-163 K 3
Paysandú ☆ **ROU** 78-79 K 2
Pays de la Loire □ **F** 90-91 G 8
Payson ○ **USA** (AZ) 256-257 D 4
Payson ○ **USA** (UT) 254-255 D 3
Payún, Altiplanicie del ▲ **RA** 78-79 E 4
Payún, Cerro ▲ **RA** 78-79 E 4
Payung ○ **RI** 162-163 G 6
Pa Yup ○ **THA** 158-159 F 4
Payyannūr ○ **IND** 140-141 F 4
Paz, Corredeira da ~ **BR** 68-69 B 6
Paz, La ○ **CO** 60-61 E 2
Paz, La ☆ **HN** 52-53 L 4
Paz, La ☆• **MEX** 50-51 D 5
Paz, La ○ **RA** (COD) 78-79 G 2
Paz, La ○ **RA** (ERI) 76-77 H 6
Paz, La ○ **RA** (MEN) 78-79 F 2
Paz, La ○ **ROU** 78-79 L 3
Paz, Ribeiro da ~ **BR** 68-69 C 6
Paz, Río de la ~ **BOL** 70-71 D 5
Pazar ☆ **TR** 128-129 J 2
Pazarbaşı Burnu ▲ **TR** 128-129 D 2
Pazarcık ○ **TR** 128-129 G 4
Pazardžik ○• **BG** 102-103 D 6
Paz Centro, La ○ **NIC** 52-53 L 5
Paz del Río ○ **CO** 60-61 E 4
Pazha ○ **PK** 138-139 B 5
Pazos Kanki ○ **RA** 78-79 H 3
Pcič ~ **BY** 94-95 K 5
Pčinja ~ **MK** 100-101 H 4
Pe ○ **MYA** 158-159 E 4
Peabody ○ **USA** (KS) 262-263 J 6
Peabody Bugt ≈ 26-27 R 4
Peace Point ○ **CDN** 30-31 N 6
Peace River ○ **CDN** (ALB) 32-33 M 3
Peace River ~ **CDN** 30-31 L 6
Peace River ~ **CDN** 32-33 J 3
Peace River ~ **USA** 286-287 H 4
Peach Creek ~ **USA** 266-267 K 4
Peachland ○ **CDN** (BC) 230-231 K 4
Peach Springs ○ **USA** (AZ) 256-257 B 3
Peachtree City ○ **USA** (GA) 284-285 F 3
Peacock Bay ≈ 16 F 26
Peacock Hills ▲ **CDN** 30-31 O 3
Pea Island National Wildlife Refuge ⊥ **USA** (NC) 282-283 M 5
Peak Charles National Park ⊥ **AUS** 176-177 F 6
Peak District National Park ⊥ **GB** 90-91 G 5
Peak Downs Mine • **AUS** 178-179 K 2
Peake ○ **AUS** 180-181 E 3
Peake Creek ~ **AUS** 178-179 C 5
Peaked Point ▲ **RP** 160-161 C 7
Peak Hill ○ **AUS** (NSW) 180-181 K 2
Peak Hill ○ **AUS** (WA) 176-177 E 2
Peak Mountain ▲ **USA** (CA) 248-249 E 5
Peale, Mount ▲ **USA** (UT) 254-255 F 5
Pearblossom ○ **USA** (CA) 248-249 G 5
Pearce ○ **CDN** (ALB) 232-233 E 6
Pearce ○ **USA** (AZ) 256-257 F 7
Pearce Point ▲ **AUS** 172-173 J 3
Pearcy ○ **USA** (AR) 276-277 B 6
Peard Bay ≈ 20-21 L 1
Pea Ridge National Military Park • **USA** (AR) 276-277 A 4
Pearisburg ○ **USA** (VA) 280-281 F 6
Pea River ~ **USA** 284-285 D 5
Pea River ~ **USA** 284-285 E 5
Pearl ○ **USA** (MS) 268-269 K 4
Pearland ○ **USA** (TX) 268-269 E 7
Pearl City ○ **USA** (HI) 288 H 3
Pearl Harbor ≈• 288 G 3
Pearl River ○ **USA** (LA) 268-269 L 6
Pearl River ~ **USA** 268-269 L 5
Pearsall ○ **USA** (TX) 266-267 H 5
Pearse Island ⌒ **CDN** (BC) 228-229 D 2
Pearson ○ **USA** (AL) 284-285 C 3
Pearson ○ **USA** (GA) 284-285 H 5
Pearston ○ **ZA** 220-221 G 6
Peary Channel ≈ 24-25 U 1
Peary Gletscher ⊂ **GRØ** 26-27 U 5
Peary Land ∸ **GRØ** 26-27 f 2
Pease River ~ **USA** 264-265 E 4
Peawanuck ○ **CDN** 34-35 O 3
Peba, Rio ~ **BR** 68-69 D 5
Pebane ○ **MOC** 218-219 K 3
Pebas ○ **PE** 66-67 B 4
Pebble Island ⌒ **GB** 78-79 L 6
Pěč ○ **AFG** 138-139 C 2
Peć ○• **YU** 100-101 H 3
Pečal'ky ~ **RUS** 114-115 R 2
Pecangakan ○ **RI** 168 D 3
Peçanha ○ **BR** 72-73 J 5
Pecan Island ○ **USA** (LA) 268-269 H 7
Peças, Ilha das ⌒ **BR** 74-75 F 5
Pecatonica River ~ **USA** 274-275 J 2
Pečenežske vodoschovyšče < **UA** 102-103 K 2
Pečenga ○ **RUS** 88-89 L 2
Pechanga Indian Reservation ✕ **USA** (CA) 248-249 G 6
Peche-Merle, Grotte du • **F** 90-91 H 9
Pechora = Pečora ~ **RUS** 88-89 W 3
Pechorskaya Guba = Pečorskaja guba ≈ 88-89 X 2
Pechorskoye More = Pečorskoe more ≈ 88-89 V 2
Pecixe, Ilha de ⌒ **GNB** 202-203 B 4
Peckerwood Lake < **USA** (AR) 276-277 D 6
Peck Lake, Fort ⊖ **USA** (MT) 250-251 N 4
Pecnoj tubek ~ **KZ** 96-97 G 10
Pečora ☆ **RUS** (KOM) 88-89 Y 4
Pečora ~ **RUS** 88-89 W 3
Pečoro-Ilyčskij, zapovednik ⊥ **RUS** 114-115 E 3
Pečorsk, Troicko- ☆ **RUS** 114-115 D 3
Pečorskaja grjada ▲ **RUS** 88-89 X 3
Pečorskaja guba ≈ 88-89 X 2
Pečorskoe More ≈ 88-89 V 2
Pecos ○ **USA** (NM) 256-257 K 3
Pecos ○ **USA** (TX) 266-267 D 2
Pecos National Historic Park ∴ **USA** (NM) 256-257 K 3
Pecos Plains ∸ **USA** 256-257 L 5
Pecos River ~ **USA** 256-257 L 4
Pecos River ~ **USA** 266-267 F 3
Pécs ○•• **H** 92-93 P 5
Pedasi ○ **PA** 52-53 D 8
Pedda Ahobilam ○ **IND** 140-141 H 3
Pedda Arikatla ○ **IND** 140-141 H 3
Peddapalli ○ **IND** 138-139 G 10
Pedder, Lake ⊖ **AUS** 180-181 J 7
Peddie ○ **ZA** 220-221 H 6
Pedergosa Mountains ▲ **USA** 256-257 F 7
Pedernales ☆ **DOM** 54-55 K 6
Pedernales ○ **RCH** 76-77 C 4
Pedernales ○ **YV** 60-61 K 3
Pedernales, Punta ▲ **EC** 64-65 B 1
Pedernales, Salar de ⊖ **RCH** 76-77 C 4
Pedernales River ~ **USA** 266-267 J 3
Pederneira, Cachoeira ~ **BR** 66-67 E 7
Pederneiras ○ **BR** 72-73 F 7
Pé de Serra ○ **BR** 68-69 J 7
Pedirka ○ **AUS** 178-179 C 4
Pediwang ○ **RI** 164-165 K 3
Pedra Alta, Cachoeira ~ **BR** 68-69 C 3
Pedra Azul ○ **BR** 72-73 K 3
Pedra Azul, Pico ▲ **BR** 72-73 K 6
Pedra Badejo ○ **CV** 202-203 C 6
Pedra Branca ○ **BR** 68-69 J 4
Pedra Corrida ○ **BR** 72-73 J 5
Pedra de Amolar, Rio ~ **BR** 68-69 E 6
Pedra do Feitiço ○ **ANG** 216-217 B 2
Pedra-Furada, Riachão ~ **BR** 68-69 E 6
Pedra Grande ○ **BR** 72-73 K 3
Pedra Lavrada ○ **BR** 68-69 K 5
Pedra Lume ○ **CV** 202-203 C 5
Pedra Preta ○ **BR** 70-71 K 5
Pedra Preta, Corredeira da ~ **BR** 68-69 C 5
Pedras, Cachoeira ~ **BR** 68-69 D 7
Pedras Descobertas ~ **BR** 70-71 J 3
Pedras Grandes ○ **BR** 74-75 F 7
Pedras Negras • **ANG** 216-217 C 4
Pedras Negras ○ **BR** 70-71 F 3
Pedras Tinhosas ⌒ **STP** 210-211 b 2
Pedregal ○ **BR** 76-77 K 6
Pedregal ○ **YV** 60-61 F 2
Pedregal, Río ~ **MEX** 52-53 H 3
Pedregal, Río ~ **YV** 60-61 F 2
Pedregulho ○ **BR** 72-73 G 6
Pedreira, Rio ~ **BR** 62-63 J 5
Pedreiras ○ **BR** (MAR) 68-69 F 4
Pedreiras ○ **BR** (P) 66-67 K 5
Pedreiras ○ **BR** (RSU) 74-75 D 9
Pedrera, La ○ **CO** 66-67 C 3
Pedrero, Cerro el ▲ **RA** 80 E 2
Pedriceña ○ **MEX** 50-51 H 5
Pedrinhas ○ **BR** 68-69 K 7
Pedro Afonso ○ **BR** 68-69 D 6
Pedro Alexandre ○ **BR** 68-69 K 6
Pedro Antunes ○ **BR** 74-75 D 8
Pedro Avelino ○ **BR** 68-69 K 4
Pedro Barros ○ **BR** 74-75 G 5
Pedro Betancourt ○ **C** 54-55 E 3
Pedro Canário ○ **BR** 72-73 L 5
Pedro Carbo ○ **EC** 64-65 B 2
Pedro Cays ⌒ **JA** 54-55 F 6
Pedro de Valdivia ○ **RCH** 76-77 C 2
Pedro Gomes ○ **BR** 70-71 K 6
Pedro II ○ **BR** 68-69 H 4
Pedro J. Montero ○ **EC** 64-65 C 3
Pedro Juan Caballero ☆ **PY** 76-77 K 2
Pedro Luro ○ **RA** 78-79 H 5
Pedro Montoya ○ **MEX** 50-51 K 7
Pedroñeras, Las ○ **E** 98-99 F 5
Pedro Osório ○ **BR** 74-75 D 8
Pedro Vega ∴• **MEX** 52-53 J 3
Peebinga ○ **AUS** 180-181 F 3
Peebles ○ **CDN** (SAS) 232-233 Q 5
Peebles ○ **GB** 90-91 F 4
Peebles ○ **USA** (OH) 280-281 C 5
Peedamulla ○ **AUS** 172-173 B 6
Pee Dee National Wildlife Refuge ⊥ **USA** (NC) 282-283 G 5
Pee Dee River ~ **USA** 284-285 L 2
Peekskill ○ **USA** (NY) 280-281 N 2
Peel ○• **GBM** 90-91 E 4
Peel Channel ~ **CDN** 20-21 X 2
Pe Ell ○ **USA** (WA) 244-245 B 4
Peel Plateau ▲ **CDN** 20-21 Y 3
Peel Point ▲ **CDN** 24-25 P 4
Peel River ~ **AUS** 178-179 L 6
Peel River ~ **CDN** 20-21 W 4
Peel River Game Reserve ⊥ **CDN** 20-21 Y 3
Peel Sound ≈ 24-25 Y 4
Peene ~ **D** 92-93 M 2
Peeples Valley ○ **USA** (AZ) 256-257 C 4
Peeramudlayeppa Lake ⊖ **AUS** 178-179 D 4
Peera Peera Poolanna Lake ⊖ **AUS** 178-179 D 4
Peerless ○ **USA** (MT) 250-251 O 3
Peerless Lake ⊖ **CDN** 32-33 N 3
Peers ○ **CDN** (ALB) 232-233 C 2
Peesane ○ **CDN** (SAS) 232-233 P 3
Peetz ○ **USA** (CO) 254-255 M 3
Pegasus Bay ≈ 182 D 5
Pegatan ○ **RI** 162-163 K 6
Peggys Cove ○• **CDN** (NS) 240-241 M 6
Peg. Müller ▲ **RI** 162-163 K 4
Pego ○ **E** 98-99 G 5
Pego ○ **P** 98-99 C 5
Pegram ○ **USA** (TN) 276-277 H 4
Pegtymel' ~ **RUS** 112-113 R 2
Pegtymel'skij hrebet ▲ **RUS** 112-113 S 2
Pegu ○ **MYA** 158-159 D 2
Peguis Indian Reserve ✕ **CDN** (MAN) 234-235 F 3
Pegunungan Barisan ▲ **RI** 162-163 D 5
Pegyš ○ **RUS** 88-89 V 5
Péhonko ○ **DY** 202-203 L 4
Pehuajó ○ **RA** 78-79 J 3
Pehuén-Co ○ **RA** 78-79 J 5
Peigan Indian Reserve ✕ **CDN** (ALB) 232-233 E 6
Peili ○ **SUD** 206-207 H 5
Peinata, Cerro ▲ **RA** 80 D 5
Peipsi Järv ⊖ **EST** 94-95 K 2
Peipus, Lake = Peipsi Järv ⊖ **EST** 94-95 K 2
Peixe ○ **BR** 72-73 F 2
Peixe, Lagoa do ⊖ **BR** 74-75 E 8
Peixe, Rio ~ **BR** 72-73 D 4
Peixe, Rio do ~ **BR** 72-73 F 4
Peixe, Rio do ~ **BR** 72-73 F 3
Peixe, Rio do ~ **BR** 72-73 E 3
Peixeboi ○ **BR** 68-69 E 2
Peixe Couro ou Aquinabo, Rio ~ **BR** 70-71 K 5
Peixes ou de São Francisco, Rio dos ~ **BR** 70-71 J 2
Pei Xian ○ **VRC** 154-155 K 4
Peixoto, Represa < **BR** 72-73 G 6
Peixoto de Azevedo ○ **BR** 70-71 K 2
Peixoto de Azevedo, Rio ~ **BR** 70-71 K 2
Pejantan, Pulau ⌒ **RI** 162-163 G 4
Pekabata ○ **RI** 164-165 F 5
Pekalongan ○ **RI** 168 C 3
Pekan ○• **MAL** 162-163 E 3
Pekanbaru ☆ **RI** 162-163 D 4
Pekin ○ **USA** (IL) 274-275 J 4
Pekin ○ **USA** (ND) 258-259 J 4
Pekin, Pulau ⌒ **RI** 164-165 E 2
Peking = Beijing ★••• **VRC** 154-155 K 2
Pekinga ○ **DY** 204-205 E 2
Peklino ○ **RUS** 94-95 N 5
Peko, Mont ▲ **CI** 202-203 G 6
Peko, Parc National du Mont ⊥ **CI** 202-203 G 6
Peko Mine • **AUS** 174-175 C 6
Pekul'nej, hrebet ▲ **RUS** 112-113 S 4
Pékyl'nejskoe, ozero ⊖ **RUS** 112-113 T 5
Péla ○ **RG** 202-203 F 6
Pelabuhanratu ○ **RI** 168 B 3
Pelabuhan Ratu, Teluk ≈ 168 B 3
Pelada, Pampa ∸ **RA** 80 F 2
Pelahatchie ○ **USA** (MS) 268-269 L 4
Pelaihari ○ **RI** 164-165 D 5
Pelau ⌒ **SOL** 184 I d 1
Pelé, Mont ▲ **G** 210-211 C 5
Pélébina ○ **DY** 202-203 L 5
Pelechuco ○ **BOL** 70-71 C 4
Peleduj ~ **RUS** 118-119 F 6
Pelée, Mont ▲ **F** 56 E 4
Pelee, Point ▲ **CDN** (ONT) 238-239 C 7
Pelee Island ⌒ **CDN** (ONT) 238-239 C 7
Pelei ○ **RI** 164-165 H 4
Pelejo ○ **PE** 64-65 E 5
Pelekech ▲ **EAK** 212-213 E 2
Pelencho ○ **YV** 60-61 L 3
Peleng, Pulau ⌒ **RI** 164-165 H 4
Peleng, Selat ≈ 164-165 H 4
Pélézi ○ **CI** 202-203 G 6
Pelham ○ **AUS** 174-175 G 6
Pelham ○ **USA** (AL) 284-285 D 3
Pelhřimov ○ **CZ** 92-93 N 4
Pelican ○ **USA** 32-33 B 3
Pelican, Lac ⊖ **CDN** 36-37 N 5
Pelican Lake ⊖ **CDN** (MAN) 234-235 C 2
Pelicano, Quebrada del ~ **RCH** 76-77 B 5
Pelican Point (Beach) • **AUS** 176-177 B 2
Pelican Rapids ○ **CDN** (MAN) 234-235 C 2
Pelikan Lake ⊖ **USA** (MN) 270-271 F 2
Pelikan Rapids ○ **USA** (MN) 270-271 B 4
Pelileo ○ **EC** 64-65 C 2
Pelindã, Ponta ▲ **GNB** 202-203 B 4
Pelion ○ **USA** (SC) 284-285 J 3
Pelkie ○ **USA** (MI) 270-271 K 4
Pelkosenniemi ○ **FIN** 88-89 J 3
Pella ○ **USA** (IA) 274-275 F 3
Pelland ○ **USA** (MN) 270-271 E 2
Pellatt Lake ⊖ **CDN** 30-31 P 3
Pell City ○ **USA** (AL) 284-285 D 3
Pellegrini ○ **RA** 78-79 H 4
Pellegrini, Lago ⊖ **RA** 78-79 F 5
Pelletier ○ **CDN** (QUE) 240-241 F 3
Pell Inlet ≈ 24-25 U 3
Pello ○ **FIN** 88-89 G 3
Pellston ○ **USA** (MI) 272-273 E 2
Pellworm ⌒ **D** 92-93 K 1
Pelly ○ **CDN** (SAS) 232-233 R 4
Pelly Bay ≈ 24-25 b 6
Pelly Bay ○ **CDN** 24-25 b 6
Pelly Island ⌒ **CDN** 20-21 X 2
Pelly Lake ⊖ **CDN** 30-31 T 3
Pelly Mountains ▲ **CDN** 20-21 Y 6
Pelly Plateau ▲ **CDN** 20-21 Z 5
Pelly Point ▲ **CDN** 24-25 W 5
Pelly River ~ **CDN** 20-21 W 5
Pelmadulla ○ **CL** 140-141 J 7
Pelokang, Pulau ⌒ **RI** 168 D 6
Pelona Mountain ▲ **USA** (NM) 256-257 G 5
Pelopónissos □ **GR** 100-101 J 6
Pelopónnissos ~ **GR** 100-101 H 6
Peloritani, Monti ▲ **I** 100-101 E 5
Pelotas ○ **BR** 74-75 D 8
Pelsart Group ⌒ **AUS** 176-177 C 4
Pelulutepu ○ **SME** 62-63 G 4
Pelus ~ **MAL** 162-163 D 2
Pelusium ∴• **ET** 194-195 F 2
Pelym ~ **RUS** 114-115 F 4
Pelymskij Tuman, ozero ⊖ **RUS** 114-115 G 4
Pemadumcook Lake ⊖ **USA** (ME) 278-279 M 3
Pemalang ○ **RI** 168 C 3
Pemali, Tanjung ▲ **RI** (SLT) 164-165 H 4
Pemali, Tanjung ▲ **RI** (STG) 164-165 H 6
Pemangil, Pulau ⌒ **MAL** 162-163 F 3
Pemangkat ○ **RI** 162-163 H 4
Pemarung, Tanjung ▲ **RI** 164-165 E 4
Pematang Purba ○ **RI** 162-163 C 3
Pematangsiantar ○ **RI** 162-163 C 3
Pematangtanabjawa ○ **RI** 162-163 C 3
Pemba ☆ **MOC** 214-215 L 7
Pemba ○ **Z** 218-219 D 3
Pemba Channel ≈ 212-213 G 6
Pemba Island ⌒ **EAT** 212-213 G 6
Pembe ○ **MOC** 218-219 H 6
Pemberton ○• **AUS** 176-177 D 7
Pemberton ○ **CDN** (BC) 230-231 G 3
Pemberton ○ **USA** (MN) 270-271 E 6
Pemberton Icefield ⊂ **CDN** (BC) 230-231 F 3
Pemberton Meadows ○ **CDN** (BC) 230-231 F 3
Pembina River ~ **CDN** 232-233 B 2
Pembina River ~ **CDN** 234-235 D 5
Pembine ○ **USA** (WI) 270-271 K 5
Pembre ○ **RI** 166-167 J 5
Pembridge ○ **CDN** (ALB) 232-233 D 2
Pembroke ○ **CDN** (ONT) 238-239 H 3
Pembroke ○• **GB** 90-91 E 6
Pembroke ○ **USA** (GA) 284-285 J 4
Pembroke ○ **USA** (NC) 282-283 H 6
Pembroke Castle •• **GB** 90-91 E 6
Pembrokeshire Coast National Park ⊥ **GB** 90-91 E 6
Pemuco ○ **RCH** 78-79 C 4
Pen ○ **IND** 138-139 D 10
Peña Blanco ○ **RCH** 76-77 B 4
Peñadoto, ozero ⊖ **RUS** 108-109 P 7
Peñafiel ○ **E** 98-99 E 4
Penafiel ○ **P** 98-99 C 4
Peñaflor ○ **RCH** 78-79 D 2
Penalva ○ **BR** 68-69 F 3
Penambulai, Pulau ⌒ **RI** 166-167 H 5
Penampang ○ **MAL** 160-161 B 10
Peña Nevada, Cerro ▲ **MEX** 50-51 K 6
Penang □ **MAL** 162-163 D 2
Penang, Pulau ⌒•• **MAL** 162-163 D 2
Penanjung Game Park ⊥ **RI** 168 C 3
Penápolis ○ **BR** 72-73 E 6
Penarak, Kampung ○ **MAL** 162-163 E 2
Peñaranda de Bracamonte ○ **E** 98-99 E 4
Peñarroya ▲ **E** 98-99 G 4
Peñarroya-Pueblonueva ○ **E** 98-99 E 5
Peñas, Cabo ▲ **RA** 80 G 6
Peñas, Golfo de ≈ 80 C 3
Peñas, Las ○ **RA** 76-77 D 5
Peñas, Sierra de las ▲ **RA** 78-79 G 2
Peñas Blancas ○ **NIC** 52-53 B 6
Peñasco, Rio ~ **USA** 256-257 L 6
Peñas Negras ○ **YV** 60-61 J 4
Pench National Park ⊥ **IND** 138-139 G 9
Penck, Cape ▲ **ARK** 16 G 9
Pendarves ○ **NZ** 182 C 5
Pendé ○ **RCA** (OUP) 206-207 C 5
Pendé ~ **RCA** 206-207 B 5
Pendelton Bay ○ **CDN** (BC) 228-229 J 2
Pendembu ○ **WAL** (EAS) 202-203 E 5
Pendembu ○ **WAL** (NOR) 202-203 D 5
Pendeng ○ **RI** 162-163 B 2
Pender ○ **USA** (NE) 262-263 K 2
Pender Bay ≈ 172-173 F 4
Pender Island ○ **CDN** (BC) 230-231 F 5
Pendjari ~ **DY** 202-203 L 4
Pendjari, Parc National de la ⊥ **DY** 202-203 L 4
Pendjari, Zone Cynégétique de la ⊥ **DY** 202-203 L 4
Pendjua ○ **ZRE** 210-211 G 4
Pendleton ○ **USA** (IN) 274-275 N 5
Pendleton ○ **USA** (OR) 244-245 G 5
Pendopo ○ **RI** 162-163 E 6
Pend Oreille, Mount ▲ **USA** (ID) 250-251 C 3
Pend Oreille Lake ⊖ **USA** (ID) 250-251 C 3
Pend Oreille River ~ **USA** 244-245 H 2
Pendroy ○ **USA** (MT) 250-251 G 3
Pendryl ○ **CDN** (ALB) 232-233 D 3
Pendulium Øer ⌒ **GRØ** 26-27 q 6
Penebangan, Pulau ⌒ **RI** 162-163 H 5
Penebel ○ **RI** 168 B 7
Peneda ▲ **P** 98-99 C 4
Penedo ○ **BR** 68-69 K 7
Pene-Katamba ○ **ZRE** 210-211 K 4
Penela ○ **P** 98-99 C 4
Pene-Mende ○ **ZRE** 212-213 B 6
Pénessoulou ○ **DY** 202-203 L 5
Penet, Tanjung ▲ **RI** 162-163 F 7
Penetanguishene ○ **CDN** (ONT) 238-239 F 4
Penfro = Pembroke ○ **GB** 90-91 E 6
Pengalengan ○ **RI** 168 B 3
Peng'an ○ **VRC** 154-155 E 6
Penganga ~ **IND** 138-139 G 10
Pengastulan ○ **RI** 168 B 7
Pengchia Yü ⌒ **RC** 156-157 N 4
Penge ○ **ZRE** (HAU) 212-213 A 2
Penge ○ **ZRE** (KOR) 210-211 K 6
Penge, Chute ~ **ZRE** 212-213 B 3
Penghu Islands ⌒ **RC** 156-157 L 5
Pengjie ○ **VRC** 154-155 F 6
Pengkalan Kubor, Kampung ○ **MAL** 162-163 E 2
Pengkou ○ **VRC** 156-157 K 4
Penglai ○ **VRC** 154-155 M 3
Penglai ○ **VRC** 156-157 G 7
Penglai Ge • **VRC** 154-155 M 3
Pengshan ○ **VRC** 154-155 C 6
Pengshui ○ **VRC** 156-157 F 2
Penguin ○ **AUS** 180-181 J 6
Penguin Bank ≃ 288 H 4
Penguin Island ⌒ **CDN** (NFL) 242-243 M 5
Penguin Shoal ⌒ **AUS** 172-173 G 2
Pengxi ○ **VRC** 154-155 D 6
Penhalonga ○ **ZW** 218-219 G 4
Penhoek Pass ▲ **ZA** 220-221 H 5
Péni ○ **BF** 202-203 H 4
Peniche ○• **P** 98-99 C 5
Penida, Nusa ⌒ **RI** 168 B 7
Peninga ○ **RUS** 88-89 M 5
Penington ○ **USA** (AL) 284-285 B 4
Peninsular Development Road II **AUS** 174-175 G 4
Peninsular Lake ⊖ **CDN** (ONT) 234-235 P 3
Penitente, Serra do ▲ **BR** 68-69 E 6
Pénjamo ○ **MEX** 52-53 D 1
Penmarc'h ○• **F** 90-91 E 8
Penmarc'h, Pointe de ▲• **F** 90-91 E 8
Pennādam ○ **IND** 140-141 H 5
Pennant ○ **CDN** (SAS) 232-233 K 5
Pennant Point ▲ **CDN** (NS) 240-241 M 6
Penner ~ **IND** 140-141 H 3
Penneshaw ○ **AUS** 180-181 D 3
Penn Hills ○ **USA** (PA) 280-281 G 3
Pennines, The ▲ **GB** 90-91 F 4
Pennsboro ○ **USA** (WV) 280-281 F 4
Pennsville ○ **USA** (NJ) 280-281 L 4
Pennsylvania □ **USA** 280-281 G 2
Pennsylvania TPK II **USA** (PA) 280-281 K 3
Penny ○ **CDN** (BC) 228-229 N 3
Penn Yan ○ **USA** (NY) 278-279 D 6
Penny Farms ○ **USA** (FL) 286-287 H 2
Penny Highlands ▲ **CDN** 28-29 G 3
Penny Ice Cap ⊂ **CDN** 28-29 G 3
Pennyroyal Plateau ▲ **USA** 276-277 J 4
Penny Strait ≈ 24-25 X 2
Peno ☆ **RUS** 94-95 N 3
Penobscot Bay ≈ 278-279 N 4
Penobscot River ~ **USA** 278-279 N 3
Penoka ○ **LB** 202-203 G 7
Penola ○ **AUS** 180-181 F 4
Peñón Blanco ○ **MEX** 50-51 H 5
Peñón del Rosario, Cerro ▲ **MEX** 52-53 E 2
Penong ○ **AUS** 176-177 M 5
Peñón Nevada del Falso Azufre ▲ **RCH** 76-77 C 4
Peñón Nevado del Falso Azufre ▲ **RA** 76-77 C 4
Penonomé ☆•• **PA** 52-53 D 7
Penot, Mount ▲ **VAN** 184 II a 3
Penrhyn, Cape ▲ **CDN** 24-25 f 7
Penrhyn Basin ≃ 13 M 3
Penrith ○ **GB** 90-91 F 4
Penrose ○ **USA** (CO) 254-255 K 5
Pensa ○ **BF** 202-203 K 3
Pensacola ○ **USA** (FL) 286-287 B 1
Pensacola Bay ≈ 286-287 B 1
Pensacola Mountains ▲ **ARK** 16 E 0
Pensamiento, El ○ **BOL** 70-71 G 4
Pense ○ **CDN** (SAS) 232-233 O 5
Pensepeľ, mys ▲ **RUS** 120-121 T 4
Penshurst ○ **AUS** 180-181 G 4
Pensilvania ○ **CO** 60-61 D 5
Pentálofos ○ **GR** 100-101 H 4
Pentecost □ **VAN** 184 II b 2
Pentecost Downs ○ **AUS** 172-173 H 4
Pentecostes ○ **BR** 68-69 J 3
Pentecost Island = Île Pentecôte ⌒ **VAN** 184 II b 2
Pentecost Range ▲ **AUS** 172-173 H 3
Pentecost River ~ **AUS** 172-173 H 3
Pentecôte, Île = Pentecost Island ⌒ **VAN** 184 II b 2
Pentecôte, Rivière ○ **CDN** (QUE) 242-243 A 3
Pentenga ○ **BF** 202-203 L 4
Penticton ○ **CDN** (BC) 230-231 K 4
Penticton Indian Reserve ✕ **CDN** (BC) 230-231 K 4
Pentland ○ **AUS** 174-175 H 7
Pentland Firth ≈ 90-91 F 2
Pentwater ○ **USA** (MI) 272-273 C 4
Penu ○ **RI** 164-165 J 4
Penuin, Fiordo ≈ 80 C 4
Penukonda ○• **IND** 140-141 G 3
Penwegon ○ **MYA** 142-143 K 6
Penwell ○ **USA** (TX) 266-267 E 2
Penylan Lake ⊖ **CDN** 30-31 Q 5
Penyu, Kepulauan ⌒ **RI** 166-167 D 4
Penyu, Teluk ≈ 168 C 3
Penza ☆ **RUS** 96-97 D 7
Penzance ○ **GB** 90-91 E 6
Penzance Lake ⊖ **CDN** 30-31 Q 5
Penze ○ **VRC** 156-157 J 2
Penzele ○ **ZRE** 210-211 G 4
Penžina ~ **RUS** 112-113 O 5
Penžinskaja guba ≈ 112-113 L 6
Penžinskij hrebet ▲ **RUS** 120-121 V 3
Peoria ○ **USA** (AZ) 256-257 C 5
Peoria ○ **USA** (IL) 274-275 J 4
Pep ○ **USA** (NM) 256-257 M 5
Pepa ○ **ZRE** 214-215 E 4
Pepacton Reservoir ⊖ **USA** (NY) 278-279 G 6
Pepani ~ **ZA** 220-221 F 3
Pepeekeo ○ **USA** (HI) 288 K 5
Pepita ou Porte Alegre, Rio ~ **BR** 68-69 B 6
Peque ○ **CO** 60-61 D 4
Pequena, Cachoeira ~ **BR** 68-69 C 3
Pequeri, Rio ~ **BR** 70-71 K 5
Pequop Summit ▲ **USA** (NV) 246-247 L 2
Pequot Lakes ○ **USA** (MN) 270-271 D 4
Pera, Bol'šaja ~ **RUS** 122-123 C 3
Perabumulih ○ **RI** 162-163 F 6
Pérade, La ○ **CDN** (QUE) 238-239 N 2
Peraguaizinho, Rio ~ **BR** 70-71 J 4
Peraiyur ○ **IND** 140-141 G 6
Perak □ **MAL** 162-163 D 2
Perak ○ **RI** 168 E 3
Perambalūr ○ **IND** 140-141 H 5
Perämeri ≈ 88-89 G 4
Perapat, Tanjung ▲ **MAL** 164-165 D 1
Peras-2 ▲ **MEX** 50-51 G 5
Perbaugan ○ **RI** 162-163 C 3
Perbulan ○ **RI** 162-163 C 3
Percé ○ **CDN** (QUE) 240-241 L 2
Percival ○ **CDN** (SAS) 232-233 Q 5
Percival Lakes ⊖ **AUS** 172-173 G 6
Percy, Mount ▲ **AUS** 172-173 G 4
Percy Isles ⌒ **AUS** 178-179 L 1
Percy Priest Lake, J. ⊖ **USA** (TN) 276-277 J 4
Percy Quin State Park ⊥ **USA** (MS) 268-269 K 5
Perdekop ○ **ZA** 220-221 J 3
Perdida, Rio ~ **BR** 68-69 E 6
Perdido, Arroyo ~ **RA** 78-79 F 7
Perdido Bay ≈ 286-287 B 1
Perdido River ~ **USA** 286-287 B 1
Perdidos, Cachoeira dos ~ **BR** 70-71 H 2
Perdizes ○ **BR** 72-73 G 5
Perdões ○ **BR** 72-73 H 6
Perdón, Puerto del ▲ **E** 98-99 G 3
Perdue ○ **CDN** (SAS) 232-233 L 3
Perehins'ke ○ **UA** 102-103 D 3
Pereira ☆ **CO** 60-61 D 5
Pereira, Cachoeira ~ **BR** 66-67 J 5
Pereira Barreto ○ **BR** 72-73 E 6
Pereirinha ○ **BR** 66-67 J 7
Perejaslav-Chmel'nyc'kyj ○ **UA** 102-103 G 2
Perejaslavka ○ **RUS** 122-123 F 5
Pereljub ☆ **RUS** 96-97 G 8
Pereljubovka ○ **KZ** 126-127 M 3
Peremetnoe ☆ **KZ** 96-97 G 8
Peremul Par ∸ **IND** 140-141 B 2
Perené, Río ~ **PE** 64-65 E 7
Perenjori ○ **AUS** 176-177 D 4
Pèrèrè ○ **DY** 204-205 E 4
Pereščepyne ○ **UA** 102-103 J 3
Pereslavl'-Zalesskij ○• **RUS** 94-95 Q 3
Perevolockij ☆ **RUS** 96-97 J 8
Perevoz ○ **RUS** (GOR) 96-97 D 6
Perevoz ○ **RUS** (IRK) 118-119 H 6
Perevoznaja, guba ≈ 108-109 H 7
Perez ○ **RA** 78-79 J 2
Perez ○ **USA** (CA) 246-247 D 2
Pergamino ○ **RA** 78-79 J 2
Pergamon ∴•• **TR** 128-129 B 3
Perge ∴•• **TR** 128-129 D 4
Pérgola ○ **I** 100-101 D 3
Perham ○ **USA** (MN) 270-271 C 4
Perhentian Besar, Pulau ⌒ **MAL** 162-163 E 2
Perho ○ **FIN** 88-89 H 5
Perhonjoki ~ **FIN** 88-89 G 5
Periá, Rio ~ **BR** 68-69 G 3
Peribán de Ramos ○ **MEX** 52-53 C 2
Péribonca, Lac ⊖ **CDN** 38-39 J 3
Péribonca, Rivière ~ **CDN** 38-39 J 3
Péribonka ○ **CDN** (QUE) 240-241 C 2
Peribonka ○ **CDN** (QUE) 240-241 C 2
Perico ○ **C** 54-55 E 3
Perico ○ **USA** (TX) 264-265 B 2
Perico Creek ~ **USA** 264-265 B 2
Pericos ○ **MEX** 50-51 F 5
Peridot ○ **USA** (AZ) 256-257 E 5
Périgban ○ **BF** 202-203 J 4
Perigord ○ **CDN** (SAS) 232-233 P 3
Perigosa, Cachoeira ~ **BR** 70-71 H 2
Perigoso, Canal ~ **BR** 62-63 K 6
Périgueux ☆•• **F** 90-91 H 9
Perijá, Parque Nacional ⊥ **YV** 60-61 E 3
Perijá, Sierra de ▲ **YV** 60-61 E 3
Peri Lake ⊖ **AUS** 178-179 G 6
Peril Strait ≈ 32-33 C 3
Perim = Barīm, Ǧazīrat ⌒ **Y** 132-133 C 7
Peringat ○ **MAL** 162-163 E 1
Periptaveto, ozero ~ **RUS** 108-109 S 6
Periquen ○ **YV** 62-63 D 3
Periquito, Cachoeira ~ **BR** 66-67 K 6
Periquito, Cachoeira do ~ **BR** 66-67 G 6
Peristrema • **TR** 128-129 F 3
Peri Suyu ~ **TR** 128-129 H 3
Perito Moreno ○ **RA** 80 E 3
Peritoro ○ **BR** 68-69 F 4
Periyar Lake ⊖ **IND** 140-141 G 6
Perkat, Tanjung ▲ **RI** 162-163 F 5
Perkins ○ **USA** (MI) 270-271 L 5
Perkins ○ **USA** (OK) 264-265 G 3
Perkinstown ○ **USA** (WI) 270-271 H 5
Perkiston ○ **USA** (MS) 268-269 L 6
Perla, La ○ **MEX** 50-51 G 3
Perlah ▲ **MAL** 162-163 E 3
Perlas, Archipiélago de las ⌒ **PA** 52-53 E 7
Perlas, Cayos de ⌒ **NIC** 52-53 C 5
Perlas, Laguna de ⊖ **NIC** 52-53 C 5

376 Patraikos Kólpos — Perlas, Laguna de

Perlas, Punta de ▲ NIC 52-53 C 5
Perleporten o N 84-85 L 5
Perley o USA (MN) 270-271 B 3
Perlis ◘ MAL 162-163 D 1
Perlis, Kuala o MAL 162-163 D 1
Perm' ☆ RUS 96-97 K 4
Perma o DY 202-203 L 4
Perma o USA (MT) 250-251 E 4
Përmet ☆ AL 100-101 H 4
Permin Land ⩢ GRØ 26-27 Z 3
Pernambuco ◘ BR 68-69 J 6
Pernambuco Abyssal Plain ≃ 6-7 G 9
Pernambut o IND 140-141 H 4
Pernatty Lagoon ⊖ AUS 178-179 D 6
Pernehué, Cordillera de ▲ RCH 78-79 D 4
Pernik o BG 102-103 C 6
Perniö o FIN 88-89 G 6
Pernštejn • CZ 92-93 O 4
Perola o BR 72-73 D 7
Peron North, Cape ▲ AUS 176-177 B 2
Peron Peninsula ⌣ AUS 176-177 B 2
Perote o MEX 52-53 F 2
Perote o USA (AL) 284-285 E 5
Peroto o BOL 70-71 E 4
Perouse Strait, La = Laperuza, proliv ≈ 122-123 J 6
Perow o CDN (BC) 228-229 H 2
Perpignan ☆ • F 90-91 J 10
Perquilauquén, Río ~ RCH 78-79 D 4
Perrault Falls o CDN (ONT) 234-235 K 4
Perret, Punta ▲ YV 60-61 F 2
Perrin o USA (TX) 264-265 F 5
Perrine o USA (FL) 286-287 J 6
Perrin Vale o AUS 176-177 F 4
Perris o USA (CA) 248-249 G 6
Perrivale o AUS 174-175 G 6
Perro, Laguna del ⊖ USA (NM) 256-257 K 4
Perry o CDN (ONT) 236-237 D 5
Perry o USA (FL) 286-287 F 1
Perry o USA (GA) 284-285 G 4
Perry o USA (IA) 274-275 D 3
Perry o USA (MI) 272-273 E 5
Perry o USA (MO) 274-275 G 5
Perry o USA (OK) 264-265 G 2
Perry o USA (TX) 266-267 L 2
Perry Island ⌒ USA 20-21 R 6
Perry Lake ⊖ USA (KS) 262-263 L 5
Perry River ~ CDN 30-31 T 2
Perry River ~ CDN 230-231 L 2
Perryton o USA (TX) 264-265 D 2
Perryville o USA (AK) 22-23 R 5
Perryville o USA (AR) 276-277 C 5
Perryville o USA (MO) 276-277 F 3
Persepolis ∴ ••• IR 134-135 E 4
Perseverança o BR 66-67 E 3
Perseverancia o BOL 70-71 F 4
Perseverança o BR 68-69 F 2
Persian Gulf ≈ 134-135 C 4
Pertek ☆ TR 128-129 H 3
Perth o AUS (TAS) 180-181 J 6
Perth ☆ • AUS (WA) 176-177 C 5
Perth o CDN (ONT) 238-239 J 4
Perth o GB 90-91 F 3
Perth Amboy o USA (NJ) 280-281 M 3
Perth-Andover o CDN (NB) 240-241 H 4
Perth Basin ≃ 13 B 5
Perth Road o CDN (ONT) 238-239 J 4
Pertominsk o RUS 88-89 P 4
Pertuis Breton ≈ 90-91 G 8
Pertuis d'Antioche ≈ 90-91 G 8
Pertusato, Capo ▲ F 98-99 M 4
Perú o BOL 70-71 D 3
Peru ■ PE 64-65 D 4
Peru o USA (IL) 274-275 J 3
Peru o USA (IN) 274-275 M 4
Peru o USA (NE) 262-263 L 4
Peru, El o YV 62-63 D 2
Peru Basin ≃ 5 C 6
Peru-Chile Trench ≃ 64-65 B 5
Perugia ☆ • I 100-101 D 3
Perugorria o RA 76-77 H 5
Peruhumpenai Mountains Reserve ⊥ • RI 164-165 G 5
Peruibe o BR 74-75 G 5
Peruipe, Rio ~ BR 72-73 L 4
Perumpāvūr o IND 140-141 G 5
Perundurai o IND 140-141 G 5
Perung o RI 168 C 7
Perupuk, Tanjung ▲ RI 164-165 F 3
Pervari ☆ TR 128-129 K 4
Perves, Alt de ▲ E 98-99 H 3
Pervomaevka o RUS 116-117 O 9
Pervomaiskyj o UA 102-103 K 3
Pervomajs'k o UA (LUG) 102-103 L 3
Pervomajs'k ☆ UA (NIK) 102-103 G 3
Pervomajsk = Pervomajs'k ☆ UA 102-103 G 3
Pervomajs'ke ☆ UA 102-103 H 5
Pervomajskij o KZ 124-125 N 3
Pervomajskij o RUS 94-95 R 5
Pervomajskij o RUS 118-119 G 10
Pervomajskij o RUS (CEL) 96-97 M 6
Pervomajskij ☆ RUS (ORB) 96-97 G 8
Pervomajskoe o RUS (LEN) 94-95 L 1
Pervomajskoe o RUS (SHL) 122-123 K 4
Pervosovetsk ☆ KZ 96-97 G 8
Pervoural'sk ☆ RUS 96-97 L 5
Pervyj Kuril'skij proliv ≈ 122-123 R 3
Peša ~ RUS 88-89 T 3
Pesalai o CL 140-141 H 6
Pesaro o I 100-101 D 3
Pesca, La o MEX 50-51 L 6
Pesca, Punta ▲ RCH 78-79 C 4
Pescada, Ponta da ▲ BR 62-63 J 4
Pescadero o USA (CA) 248-249 B 2
Pescado Castigado, Arroyo el ~ RA 78-79 K 4
Pescadores = Penghu Islands ⌒ RC 156-157 L 5
Pesčanaja ~ RUS 124-125 O 2
Pesčanka ~ RUS 88-89 U 2
Pesčanoe o RUS 88-89 N 5
Pesčanoe, ozero ⊖ RUS 88-89 W 2
Pesčanoe ozero ⊖ RUS 124-125 L 2
Pesčanokopskoe o RUS 102-103 M 4
Pesčany, mys ▲ KZ 126-127 J 6
Pesčanyj, mys ▲ RUS 108-109 I e 2
Pescara ☆ • I 100-101 E 3
Pescara Cassiano o MOC 218-219 H 2
Peščera Kristaličeska •• UA 102-103 E 3
Pescodo, Río ~ RA 76-77 E 2
Pescovaja, buhta ≈ 112-113 U 1
Peshāwar ☆ •• PK 138-139 C 3
Peshkopi ☆ •• AL 100-101 H 4
Peshtigo o USA (WI) 270-271 L 5
Peshtigo River ~ USA 270-271 K 5
Pesjakov, ostrov ⌒ RUS 88-89 Y 2
Peski Sëjunagsak ⩢ TM 136-137 D 5
Peškovka ☆ KZ 124-125 C 2
Pesqueira o BR 68-69 K 6
Pesquería, Río ~ MEX 50-51 J 4
Peštera o BG 102-103 D 6
Pestovo o RUS 94-95 O 2
Pestravka ☆ RUS 96-97 F 7
Petah Tiqwa ☆ IL 130-131 D 1
Petäjävesi o FIN 88-89 H 5
Petak, Tanjung ▲ RI 164-165 L 3
Petal o USA (MS) 268-269 L 5
Petaling Jaya o MAL 162-163 D 3
Petaluma o USA (CA) 246-247 C 5
Petani, Sungai o MAL 162-163 D 2
Petaquillas o MEX 52-53 E 3
Petarbar o IND 142-143 D 4
Petare o YV 60-61 H 2
Petas, Río Las ~ BOL 70-71 H 5
Petatlán o MEX 52-53 D 3
Petauke o Z 218-219 F 2
Petawanga Lake ⊖ CDN (ONT) 234-235 P 3
Petawawa o CDN (ONT) 238-239 H 3
Petcacab o MEX 52-53 K 2
Petchaburi o THA 158-159 E 4
Pété o CAM 206-207 B 3
Pétel, Djoutou- o RG 202-203 D 4
Petén Itzá, Lago ⊖ GCA 52-53 K 3
Petenwell Lake < USA (WI) 270-271 J 6
Peterbell o CDN (ONT) 236-237 E 4
Peterborough o AUS (SA) 180-181 E 2
Peterborough o AUS (VIC) 180-181 G 5
Peterborough o • CDN (ONT) 238-239 G 4
Peter Borough o • CDN (ONT) 238-239 G 4
Peterborough o • GB 90-91 G 5
Peterborough o USA (NH) 278-279 K 6
Peterhead o GB 90-91 G 3
Peter Island ⌒ GB 286-287 R 2
Peter Lake ⊖ CDN 30-31 X 4
Peter Lougheed Provincial Park ⊥ CDN (ALB) 232-233 C 5
Petermann Aboriginal Land ⵅ AUS 176-177 K 2
Petermann Bjerg ▲ GRØ 26-27 I 7
Petermann Fjord ≈ 26-27 U 3
Petermann Gletscher ⊂ GRØ 26-27 U 3
Petermann Ranges ▲ AUS 176-177 K 2
Peteroa, Volcán ▲ RA 78-79 D 3
Peter Pond Lake ⊖ CDN 32-33 Q 3
Peter Richards, Cape ▲ CDN 24-25 M 5
Petersburg o USA (AK) 32-33 D 3
Petersburg o USA (IL) 274-275 J 4
Petersburg o USA (IN) 274-275 L 6
Petersburg o USA (ND) 258-259 K 3
Petersburg o USA (NE) 262-263 H 3
Petersburg o USA (NY) 278-279 H 6
Petersburg o USA (OK) 264-265 G 5
Petersburg o USA (TN) 276-277 J 5
Petersburg o USA (TX) 264-265 C 5
Petersburg o USA (VA) 280-281 J 6
Petersburg o USA (WV) 280-281 G 4
Petersburg Creek-Duncan Salt Chuck Wilderness ⊥ USA 32-33 D 3
Petersburg National Battlefield • USA (VA) 280-281 J 6
Peter's Mine o GUY 62-63 E 2
Peterson o CDN (SAS) 232-233 N 3
Peterson o USA (IA) 274-275 C 2
Peterson, ostrov ⌒ RUS 108-109 b 3
Peterstown o USA (WV) 280-281 F 6
Petersville o USA 20-21 P 5
Pethel Peninsula ⌣ CDN 30-31 O 4
Petifu Junction o WAL 202-203 D 5
Petín o E 98-99 D 3
Pétionville o • RH 54-55 J 5
Petit-Bourg o F 56 E 3
Petit-Cap o CDN (QUE) 242-243 D 3
Petitcodiac o CDN (NB) 240-241 K 5
Petitcodiac River ~ CDN 240-241 K 5
Petite Bois Island ⌒ USA (MS) 268-269 M 6
Petite Forte o CDN (NFL) 242-243 O 5
Petite Kabylie ⩢ DZ 190-191 E 2
Petite-Rivière-de-Île o CDN (NB) 240-241 L 3
Petite Rivière de la Baleine ~ CDN 36-37 L 7
Petite Rivière de Povungnituk ~ CDN 36-37 M 4
Petites-Bergeronnes o CDN (QUE) 240-241 F 2
Petit Étang o CDN (NS) 240-241 P 4
Petite-Vallée o CDN (QUE) 242-243 C 3
Petit Goâve o RH 54-55 J 5
Petit Jardin o CDN (NFL) 242-243 J 4
Petit Jean Mountain ▲ USA 276-277 B 6
Petit Jean State Park ⊥ USA (AR) 276-277 C 5
Petit Lac des Loups Marins ⊖ CDN 36-37 N 6
Petit Lac Manicouagan ⊖ CDN 38-39 L 3
Petit Lac Opinaca ⊖ CDN 38-39 F 2
Petit Loango, Parc National du ⊥ G 210-211 B 5
Petit Mécatina, Île du ⌒ CDN (QUE) 242-243 J 2
Petit Mécatina, Rivière du ~ CDN 38-39 O 3
Petit Mont Cameroun ▲ CAM 204-205 H 6
Petitot River ~ CDN 30-31 J 6
Petit Point ▲ AUS 176-177 B 2
Petit-Rocher o CDN (NB) 240-241 K 3
Petit-Saguenay o CDN (QUE) 240-241 E 2
Petits-Escoumins o CDN (QUE) 240-241 F 2
Petitsikapau Lake ⊖ CDN 36-37 Q 7
Petläd o IND 138-139 D 8
Peto o MEX 52-53 K 1
Petoh o MAL 162-163 E 3
Petorca, Río ~ RCH 78-79 D 2
Petoskey o USA (MI) 272-273 E 2
Petra ∴ ••• JOR 130-131 D 2
Petra, ostrova ⌒ RUS 108-109 k 3
Petra I, ostrov ⌒ ARK 16 G 27
Petrel Bank ≃ 22-23 F 6
Petrič o BG 102-103 C 7
Petrified Forest • USA (MS) 268-269 K 4
Petrified Forest National Park ∴ USA (AZ) 256-257 F 4
Petrified Wood Park ∴ USA (SD) 260-261 D 1
Petrinja o HR 100-101 F 2
Petriščevo o RUS 94-95 N 4
Petrivs'ka forteč'a • UA 102-103 K 4
Petro o PK 138-139 C 6
Petrodvorec o RUS 94-95 L 2
Petroglyphs • USA (HI) 288 J 4
Petroglyphs National Park • CDN (ONT) 238-239 G 4
Petrohué o RCH 78-79 C 6
Petrokrepost' = Šlisselburg o RUS 94-95 M 2
Petrolândia o BR 68-69 J 6
Petrolia o USA (CA) 246-247 A 3
Petrolia o USA (TX) 264-265 F 5
Petrolina o BR 68-69 H 6
Petrolina de Goiás o BR 72-73 F 4
Petropavl ☆ • KZ 124-125 F 1
Petropavlivka o UA 102-103 K 3
Petropavlovka o KZ 126-127 M 2
Petropavlovka o RUS (BUR) 116-117 M 10
Petropavlovka o RUS (IRK) 116-117 J 7
Petropavlovsk o RUS 116-117 O 6
Petropavlovsk-Kamčatskij ☆ • RUS 120-121 S 7
Petropavlovsk Kamchatskiy = Petropavlovsk-Kamčatskij ☆ • RUS 120-121 S 7
Petropavlovskoe, ozero ⊖ RUS 122-123 F 4
Petrópolis o BR 72-73 J 7
Petróquimica o RA 80 G 2
Petroşani o RO 102-103 C 5
Petrovac o YU 100-101 H 3
Petrovka o RUS 124-125 O 2
Petrovsk o RUS 96-97 D 7
Petrovsk-Zabajkal'skij o RUS 116-117 O 10
Petrov Val o RUS 96-97 D 8
Petrozavodsk ☆ RUS 88-89 N 6
Petrusburg o ZA 220-221 G 4
Petrusdal o NAM 220-221 C 1
Petrus Steyn o ZA 220-221 J 3
Petrusville o ZA 220-221 G 5
Petrykav o BY 94-95 L 5
Pettigrew o USA (AR) 276-277 B 5
Pettus o USA (TX) 266-267 K 5
Petty Harbour o CDN (NFL) 242-243 Q 5
Petuhovo ☆ RUS 114-115 J 7
Petuški o RUS (SAH) 112-113 L 2
Petuški ☆ RUS (VL) 94-95 Q 4
Peulik, Mount ▲ USA 22-23 S 4
Peulla o RCH 78-79 C 6
Peumo o RCH 78-79 D 3
Peunto, ozero ⊖ RUS 108-109 O 7
Pereula ~ RI 162-163 B 2
Peureula, Tanjung ▲ RI 162-163 B 2
Peureulak o RI 162-163 B 2
Peusangan ~ RI 162-163 B 2
Pevek o RUS 112-113 Q 2
Peyuami, Sierra ▲ YV 60-61 K 5
Peza ~ RUS 88-89 S 4
Pezas o RUS 114-115 T 7
Pézenas o F 90-91 J 10
Peženka ~ RUS 112-113 M 3
Pežostrov ⌒ RUS 88-89 M 3
Pezu o PK 138-139 C 3
Pfarrkirchen o D 92-93 M 4
Pfizner, Mount ▲ AUS 178-179 C 2
Pforzheim o D 92-93 K 4
Phāgi o IND 138-139 E 6
Phaileng o IND 142-143 H 4
Phalaborwa o ZA 218-219 F 6
Phalodi o IND 138-139 D 6
Phalombe o MW 218-219 H 2
Phāltan o IND 140-141 F 2
Phan o THA 142-143 L 6
Phang Khon o THA 158-159 G 2
Phangnga o THA 158-159 E 6
Phanom o THA 158-159 E 6
Phanom Dong Rak ▲ THA 158-159 G 3
Phanom Sarakham o THA 158-159 F 4
Phan Rang Tháp Chàm o VN 158-159 K 5
Phan Thiêt ☆ VN 158-159 K 5
Phantoms Cave = Trou des Fantomes • CAM 210-211 C 2
Pharenda o IND 142-143 C 2
Pharr o USA (TX) 266-267 J 7
Phaselis ∴ •• TR 128-129 D 4
Phatthalung o THA 158-159 F 7
Phayakhapun Phiasi o THA 158-159 G 3
Phayao o THA 142-143 L 6
Phayuha Khiri o THA 158-159 F 3
Phedra o SME 62-63 G 3
Phelp River ~ AUS 174-175 C 3
Phelps Lake ⊖ CDN 30-31 S 6
Phelps Lake ⊖ USA (NC) 282-283 L 5
Phenix City o USA (AL) 284-285 E 4
Phetchabun o THA 158-159 F 2
Phibun Mangsahan o THA 158-159 H 3
Phichit o THA 158-159 F 2
Phikwe, Selebi- o RB 218-219 D 6
Philadelphia o USA (MS) 268-269 L 4
Philadelphia o • USA (PA) 280-281 L 4
Philae ∴ ••• ET 194-195 F 6
Phil Campbell o USA (AL) 284-285 C 2
Phil Campbell o USA (AL) 284-285 B 2
Philip o USA (SD) 260-261 E 2
Philip Broke, Kap ▲ GRØ 26-27 r 6
Philipp o USA (MS) 268-269 K 3
Philippeville o B 92-93 H 3
Philippi o USA (WV) 280-281 F 4
Philippi, Lake ⊖ AUS 178-179 E 3
Philippi, Monte ▲ RA 80 E 5
Philippine Basin ≃ 14-15 M 6
Philippines = Pilipinas ■ RP 160-161 C 4
Philippines = Pilipinas ⌒ RP 160-161 C 4
Philippine Sea ≈ 160-161 F 4
Philippine Trench ≃ 160-161 G 6
Philippolis o ZA 220-221 G 5
Philipsburg ☆ NA 56 D 2
Philipsburg o USA (MT) 250-251 F 5
Philipsburg o USA (PA) 280-281 H 3
Philip Smith Mountains ▲ USA 20-21 Q 2
Philipstown o ZA 220-221 G 5
Phil Kearny, Fort • USA (WY) 252-253 M 2
Phillip Bay, Port ≈ 180-181 H 5
Phillip Creek o AUS 174-175 C 6
Phillip Creek Station o AUS 174-175 C 6
Phillip Gap ▲ USA (NC) 282-283 F 4
Phillip Island ⌣ AUS 180-181 H 5
Phillips o USA (ME) 278-279 L 4
Phillips o USA (WI) 270-271 H 5
Phillips Arm o CDN (BC) 230-231 D 3
Phillipsburg o USA (KS) 262-263 G 5
Phillipsburg o USA (MO) 276-277 C 3
Phillipsburg o USA (NJ) 280-281 L 3
Phillips Mountains ▲ ARK 16 F 23
Phillips Point ▲ CDN 24-25 h 2
Phillips Range ▲ AUS 172-173 G 4
Philo o USA (CA) 246-247 B 4
Philomath o USA (OR) 244-245 B 6
Philpots Island ⌒ CDN 24-25 g 3
Philpott Lake ⊖ USA (VA) 280-281 F 7
Phippen o CDN (SAS) 232-233 K 3
Phippsøya ⌒ N 84-85 M 2
Phitsanulok o THA 158-159 F 2
Phitshane o RB 220-221 G 2
Phnom Penh = Phnum Pénh ★ • K 158-159 H 5
Phnum Pénh ★ • K 158-159 H 5
Phoenix o USA (MI) 270-271 K 3
Phoenix ☆ • USA (AZ) 256-257 C 5
Phoenix Islands ⌒ KIB 13 K 3
Phoenixville o USA (CT) 278-279 J 7
Phoenixville o USA (PA) 280-281 L 3
Phon o THA 158-159 G 3
Phon o THA 158-159 H 2
Phoncharoen o THA 158-159 G 2
Phonda o IND 140-141 E 2
Phôngsali o LAO 156-157 C 6
Phong Tho o VN 156-157 C 5
Phong Thong o THA 158-159 G 2
Phôn Sa Van o LAO 156-157 C 7
Phoque, Rivière au ~ CDN 36-37 K 7
Phou Khoun o LAO 156-157 C 7
Phrae o THA 142-143 M 6
Phra Mae Ya Shrine • THA 158-159 E 2
Phranakhon Si Ayutthaya = Ayutthaya o ••• THA 158-159 F 3
Phran Kratai o THA 158-159 E 2
Phra Pathom Chedi •• THA 158-159 E 4
Phú Bài o VN 158-159 J 2
Phù Cát o VN 158-159 K 3
Phu Đen Đin ▲ VN 156-157 C 5
Phù Hung o VN 158-159 J 5
Phuket o • THA 158-159 E 7
Phu Khieo o THA 158-159 G 2
Phukradung o THA 158-159 F 2
Phulbari o BD 142-143 F 3
Phuldu o IND 142-143 H 4
Phú Lộc ☆ VN 158-159 J 2
Phumī Āntoät o K 158-159 G 5
Phumī Bahm o K 158-159 H 4
Phumī Bā Kêv o K 158-159 J 4
Phumī Boeng Préav o K 158-159 G 5
Phumī Bung Lung o K 158-159 J 4
Phumī Chhlong o K 158-159 H 4
Phumī Choām Sla o K 158-159 G 5
Phumī Chŏng Kai o K 158-159 G 4
Phumī Chuk o K 158-159 H 5
Phumī Damnak o K 158-159 H 5
Phumī Dei Lo o K 158-159 H 5
Phumī Kâmpóng Strălaun o K 158-159 H 3
Phumī Kâmpóng Trâbêk o K 158-159 H 4
Phumī Kdŏl Kraŏm o K 158-159 G 4
Phumī Khley o K 158-159 H 4
Phumī Khna o K 158-159 H 5
Phumī Klāng Khval o K 158-159 J 4
Phumī Krêk o K 158-159 H 5
Phumī Labang Siĕk o K 158-159 J 4
Phumī Leu o K 158-159 J 4
Phumī Mlu Prey o K 158-159 H 4
Phumī o Snguŏt o K 158-159 G 4
Phumiphon Reservoir ⊖ THA 158-159 E 2
Phumī Phsa Rôméas o K 158-159 H 4
Phumī Prêk Khsay o K 158-159 H 5
Phumī Prêk Thmei o K 158-159 H 5
Phumī Pring o K 158-159 H 4
Phumī Sala Vichey o K 158-159 H 4
Phumī Sâmraŏng o K 158-159 G 3
Phumī Spoe Tbong o K 158-159 H 4
Phumī Taek Sŏk o K 158-159 G 4
Phumī Thkov o K 158-159 G 4
Phumī Thmâ Pók o K 158-159 G 4
Phumī Véal Rénh o K 158-159 G 5
Phú My o VN 158-159 K 3
Phú My o VN 158-159 J 5
Phú Nhon o VN 158-159 K 3
Phunphin o THA 158-159 E 6
Phuntsholing o BHT 142-143 F 2
Phu'ó'c Long o VN 158-159 H 6
Phu'ó'c So'n o VN 158-159 J 3
Phú Quốc, Đảo ⌒ VN 158-159 G 5
Phù Qúy = Cù Lao Thu ⌒ VN 158-159 K 5
Phurkia o IND 138-139 G 4
Phu Tho ☆ VN 156-157 D 6
Phutnaditjhaba o ZA 220-221 J 4
Phutthaisong o THA 158-159 G 3
Phu Yen ▲ THA 158-159 F 2
Piaçabuçu o BR 68-69 K 7
Piaca dos Mineiros o BR 72-73 D 5
Piacenza ☆ • I 100-101 B 2
Piamonte o CO 60-61 D 4
Pianag o RP 160-161 D 6
Pianco o BR 68-69 K 5
Piancó, Rio ~ BR 68-69 J 5
Pian Creek ~ AUS 178-179 K 5
Piandang, Tanjung o MAL 162-163 D 2
Piangil o AUS 180-181 G 3
Pianguan o VRC 154-155 G 2
Piankana o ZRE 210-211 G 5
Pianosa, Ísola ⌒ I 100-101 C 3
Piapot o CDN (SAS) 232-233 J 5
Piapot Indian Reservation ⵅ CDN (SAS) 232-233 O 5
Piaseczno o PL 92-93 Q 2
Piaski o PL 92-93 R 3
Piatra-Neamţ ☆ • RO 102-103 E 4
Piauí ◘ BR 68-69 F 5
Piauí, Rio ~ BR 68-69 K 7
Piauí, Rio ~ BR 68-69 G 5
Piave ~ I 100-101 D 1
Piaxtla, Punta ▲ MEX 50-51 F 6
Piaxtla, Río ~ MEX 50-51 F 6
Pibor ~ SUD 208-209 A 5
Pibor Post o SUD 208-209 A 5
Pibrans = Příbram o CZ 92-93 N 4
Pica o RCH 70-71 C 7
Pica, La o YV 60-61 J 3
Picacho o USA (AZ) 256-257 D 6
Picacho o USA (CA) 248-249 K 6
Picacho o USA (NM) 256-257 K 5
Picacho de la Laguna ▲ MEX 50-51 E 6
Picada o BR 70-71 K 5
Pičaevo o RUS 94-95 S 5
Picão, Ponta do ▲ BR 72-73 J 7
Pica-Pau, Cachoeira ~ BR 62-63 E 6
Picard ⌒ SY 222-223 E 2
Picardie ◘ F 90-91 H 6
Picayune o USA (MS) 268-269 L 6
Picentini, Monti ▲ I 100-101 E 4
Pich o MEX 52-53 J 2
Pichalo, Punta ▲ RCH 70-71 B 6
Pichaman o RCH 78-79 C 3
Pichana, Río ~ RA 76-77 E 6
Pichanal o RA 76-77 E 2
Picher o USA (OK) 264-265 K 2
Pichilemu o RCH 78-79 D 3
Pichileufu, Cerro ▲ RA 78-79 D 6
Pichilingue o MEX 50-51 D 5
Pichi Mahuida o RA 78-79 G 5
Pichincha, Volcán ▲ EC 64-65 C 2
Pichi Richi Railway • AUS 180-181 D 2
Pichis, Río ~ PE 64-65 E 7
Pichor o IND 138-139 G 7
Pichucalco o MEX 52-53 H 3
Pichupichu, Volcán ▲ PE 70-71 B 5
Pic Island ⌒ CDN (ONT) 236-237 B 4
Pickens o USA (MS) 268-269 L 4
Pickens o USA (OK) 264-265 J 4
Pickens o USA (SC) 284-285 H 2
Pickens, Fort • USA (FL) 286-287 B 1
Pickerel Lake ⊖ CDN (ONT) 234-235 M 6
Pickerel River ~ CDN 238-239 E 3
Pickering o USA (LA) 268-269 G 5
Pickertaramoor ⵅ AUS 172-173 K 1
Pickford o USA (MI) 270-271 O 4
Pickneyville o USA (IL) 274-275 J 6
Pickstown o USA (SD) 260-261 H 3
Pickwick Landing State Park ⊥ USA (TN) 276-277 G 5
Pico, Ilha do ⌒ P 9 A 2
Pico da Neblina, Parque Nacional do ⊥ BR 66-67 D 2
Pico de Orizaba, Parque Nacional ⊥ MEX 52-53 F 2
Pico de Salamanca o RA 80 G 2
Pico de Teide ▲ •• E 188-189 C 6
Pico Fracture Zone ≃ 6-7 F 5
Pico Negro, Cerro ▲ RCH 70-71 C 6
Picos o BR 68-69 H 5
Picos, Los o MEX 50-51 H 3
Picota o PE 64-65 D 5
Pico Truncado o RA 80 G 3
Pic River ~ CDN 236-237 B 3
Picton o • AUS 180-181 L 3
Picton o CDN (ONT) 238-239 H 4
Picton o NZ 182 E 4
Picton, Isla ⌒ RCH 80 G 7
Pictou o CDN (NS) 240-241 N 5
Pictou Island o CDN (NS) 240-241 N 5
Pictou Island ⌒ CDN (NS) 240-241 N 5
Picture Butte o CDN (ALB) 232-233 F 6
Pictured Rocks National Lakeshore ⊥ USA (MI) 270-271 M 4
Picturesque Site ∴ • RI 166-167 H 2
Picudo, Cerro ▲ RA 80 F 3
Picuí o BR 68-69 K 5
Picunda o • GE 126-127 D 6
Picunda, mys ▲ GE 126-127 D 6
Picún Leufú o RA 78-79 E 5
Picún Leufú, Arroyo ~ RA 78-79 E 5
Picúnleufú, Cerro ▲ RA 78-79 D 5
Picuris Indian Reservation ⵅ USA (NM) 256-257 K 2
Pidando ⌒ KOR 150-151 E 8
Pidarak o PK 134-135 K 6
Pidie, Ujung ▲ RI 162-163 A 2
Pidurutalagala ▲ CL 140-141 J 7
Piebli o CI 202-203 G 6
Piedad de Cavadas, La o MEX 52-53 C 1
Piedade o BR 72-73 G 7
Pié de Palo, Sierra ▲ RA 76-77 C 6
Piedmont o USA (AL) 284-285 E 3
Piedmont o USA (MO) 276-277 E 3
Piedmont o USA (SD) 260-261 C 2
Piedmont Lake < USA (OH) 280-281 E 3
Piedmont National Wildlife Refuge ⊥ USA (GA) 284-285 G 3
Piedra, Cerro ▲ RCH 78-79 C 4
Piedrabuena o E 98-99 E 5
Piedra del Águila o RA 78-79 D 6
Piedra de la Virgen • YV 62-63 D 3
Piedra de Olla, Cerro ▲ MEX 52-53 F 3
Piedra Echada o RA 78-79 H 5
Piedrahita o E 98-99 E 4
Piedra River ~ USA 254-255 H 6
Piedras, Las o PE 70-71 C 3
Piedras, Las o ROU 78-79 L 3
Piedras, Punta ▲ RA 78-79 L 3
Piedras Altas o BR 74-75 D 8
Piedras Blancas o CR 52-53 C 7
Piedras Negras ∴ • GCA 52-53 J 3
Piedras Negras o MEX 50-51 J 3
Piedra Sola o ROU 78-79 L 2
Piedras Point ▲ RP 160-161 C 7
Piedritas o MEX 50-51 H 3
Piedritas o RA 78-79 H 3
Pie Island ⌒ CDN (ONT) 234-235 O 6
Piekenaarskloof ▲ ZA 220-221 D 6
Pieksämäki o FIN 88-89 J 5
Piéla o BF 202-203 K 3
Pielavesi o FIN 88-89 J 5
Pielinen ⊖ FIN 88-89 K 5
Pieljekaise nationalpark ⊥ S 86-87 H 3
Pieman River ~ AUS 180-181 H 6
Piemonte ◘ I 100-101 A 2
Pienaarsrivier o ZA 220-221 J 2
Piendamo o CO 60-61 C 6
Pieniężno o • PL 92-93 Q 1
Pienza o • I 100-101 C 3
Pierce o USA (ID) 250-251 D 5
Pierce o USA (NE) 262-263 J 2
Pierce Inlet, Fort ≈ 286-287 J 4
Pierce Lake ⊖ CDN 34-35 K 3
Pierceville o USA (KS) 262-263 F 7
Pieres o RA 78-79 K 5
Pierowall o GB 90-91 F 2
Pierre ☆ USA (SD) 260-261 F 2
Pierre Hoho o F 62-63 H 4
Pierre Lake ⊖ CDN (ONT) 236-237 H 3
Pierrette o F 62-63 H 3
Pierre Verendrye Monument, Fort • USA (SD) 260-261 F 2
Pierreville o CDN (QUE) 238-239 N 2
Pierreville o TT 60-61 L 2
Pierson o CDN (MAN) 234-235 B 5
Pierson o USA (FL) 286-287 H 2
Pierz o USA (MN) 270-271 D 5
Piešťany o SK 92-93 O 4
Pietarsaari = Jakobstad o FIN 88-89 G 5
Pietermaritzburg ☆ •• ZA 220-221 K 4
Pietersburg o ZA 218-219 E 6
Pietlo o LB 202-203 F 7
Pie Town o USA (NM) 256-257 G 4
Piet Plessis o ZA 220-221 G 3
Piet Retief o • ZA 220-221 K 3
Pietroşani o RO 102-103 D 6
Pifo o EC 64-65 C 2
Pigeon Creek ~ USA 284-285 D 5
Pigeon Forge o USA (NC) 282-283 D 5
Pigeon Hill o CDN (NB) 240-241 L 3
Pigeon Hole o AUS 172-173 K 4
Pigeon Lake ⊖ CDN (ALB) 232-233 D 2
Pigeon River ~ USA 274-275 N 3
Piggott o USA (AR) 276-277 E 4
Piggs Peak o SD 220-221 K 2
Pignon o RH 54-55 J 5
Pigu o GH 202-203 K 5
Pigüé o RA 78-79 H 4
Pigüé, Arroyo ~ RA 78-79 H 4
Pigum Do ⌒ ROK 150-151 E 10
Pihtipudas o FIN 88-89 H 5
Pihtovyj grebon', gora ▲ RUS 114-115 S 7
Pijijiapan o • MEX 52-53 H 4
Pikalevo o RUS 94-95 O 2
Pikangikum o CDN (ONT) 234-235 K 3
Pikangikum Lake ⊖ CDN (ONT) 234-235 J 3
Pikas', hrebet ▲ RUS 112-113 Q 5
Pikasilla o EST 94-95 K 2
Pikas'vajat ~ RUS 112-113 R 5
Pike o USA (NY) 278-279 C 6
Pike Island ⌒ CDN 36-37 P 3
Pike Lake o CDN (SAS) 232-233 M 4
Pikes Peak ▲ USA (CO) 254-255 K 5
Piketberg o ZA 220-221 D 6
Piketon o USA (OH) 280-281 C 4
Pikeville o USA (KY) 276-277 N 3
Pikeville o USA (TN) 276-277 K 5
Pikin Rio ~ SME 62-63 G 4
Pikiutdleq = Køge Bugt ≈ 28-29 U 4
Pikmiktalik o USA 20-21 J 5
Pikounda o RCB 210-211 F 3
Pikovka, Bol'šaja ~ RUS 114-115 R 5
Piła ☆ • PL 92-93 O 2
Pila o RA 78-79 K 4
Pila, La o MEX 50-51 J 6
Pilaga, Riacho ~ RA 76-77 H 3
Pilah, Kuala o MAL 162-163 E 3
Pila Kyun ⌒ MYA 158-159 D 5
Pilane o RB 220-221 H 2
Pilanesberg ▲ ZA 220-221 H 2
Pilanesberg National Park ⊥ ZA 220-221 H 2
Pilang o RI 164-165 D 5
Pilani o IND 138-139 E 5
Pilão Arcado o BR 68-69 G 6
Pilar o • IND 140-141 F 3
Pilar ☆ PY 76-77 H 4
Pilar o RA (BUA) 78-79 K 3
Pilar o RA (COD) 76-77 F 6
Pilar o RP 160-161 G 8
Pilar de Goiás o BR 72-73 F 3
Pilas Group ⌒ RP 160-161 D 9
Pilas Island ⌒ RP 160-161 D 9
Pilaya, Río ~ BOL 76-77 E 1
Pilbara ⩢ AUS 172-173 C 7
Pilcaniyeu o RA 78-79 D 6
Pilcomayo, Río ~ PY 76-77 G 2
Pilcopata o PE 70-71 B 3
Pil'da ~ RUS 122-123 H 3
Pile Bay Village o USA 22-23 U 3
Pileru o IND 140-141 H 4
Pilger o CDN (SAS) 232-233 N 3
Pilgrams = Pelhřimov o CZ 92-93 N 4
Pilgrim Springs o USA 20-21 H 4
Pilgrim's Rest o • ZA 220-221 K 2
Pilibhit ☆ IND 138-139 G 5
Piling Lake ⊖ CDN 28-29 C 2
Pilka ~ RUS 118-119 F 6
Pilliga o AUS 178-179 K 6
Pillinger o AUS 180-181 H 7
Pillo, Isla del ⌒ RA 78-79 J 2
Pillsbury o USA (ND) 258-259 K 4
Pilluana o PE 64-65 D 5
Pil'nja, ozero ⊖ RUS 108-109 H 7
Pilões o BR (MIN) 72-73 H 3
Pilões o BR (PA) 68-69 L 5
Pilón o C 54-55 G 5
Pilón, El o PA 52-53 D 8
Pilón, Río ~ MEX 50-51 J 5
Pilos o GR 100-101 H 6
Pilot, The ▲ AUS 180-181 K 4
Pilota Mohotkina, ostrov ⌒ RUS 108-109 b 3
Pilot Knob ▲ USA (ID) 250-251 D 6
Pilot Mound o CDN (MAN) 234-235 E 5
Pilot Mountain o USA (NC) 282-283 G 4
Pilot Peak ▲ USA (NV) 246-247 H 5
Pilot Point o USA 22-23 S 4
Pilot Point o USA (TX) 264-265 H 5
Pilot Rock o USA (OR) 244-245 G 5
Pilot Station o USA 20-21 J 6
Pilowo o RI 164-165 G 5
Piquen, Cerro ▲ RCH 78-79 C 4
Pilsen = Plzeň o CZ 92-93 M 4
Pil'tanlor, ozero ⊖ RUS 114-115 M 4
Pil'tun, zaliv ≈ 122-123 K 2
Pil'vo o RUS 122-123 K 3
Pim ~ RUS 114-115 L 4
Pima o USA (AZ) 256-257 F 6
Pimba o AUS 178-179 D 6
Pimbee o AUS 176-177 C 2
Pimenta Bueno o BR 70-71 G 2
Pimenteiras o BR (PIA) 68-69 H 5
Pimenteiras o BR (RON) 70-71 G 3
Pimentel o PE 64-65 C 5
Pimentel Barbosa, Área Indígena ⵅ BR 72-73 E 2
Pim Island ⌒ CDN 26-27 N 4
Pimpalgaon Basvant o IND 138-139 E 9
Pina o GH 202-203 K 4
Piña o PA 52-53 D 7
Piña, Cerro ▲ PA 52-53 E 8
Pinabasan, Pulau ⌒ RI 164-165 E 2
Pinacate, Cerro del ▲ MEX 50-51 C 2
Pináculo, Cerro ▲ RA 80 D 5
Pinagsabangan o RP 160-161 D 6
Piñal, El o CO 60-61 D 3
Pinaleno Mountains ▲ USA 256-257 E 6
Piñalito o CO 60-61 E 6
Pinamalayan o RP 160-161 D 6
Pinamar o RA 78-79 L 4
Pinamula o RI 164-165 G 3
Pinang o RI 162-163 H 4
Pinanga o ZRE 210-211 G 5
Pinangah o MAL 160-161 B 10
Pinantan o CDN (BC) 230-231 J 3
Pinarbaşı ☆ TR 128-129 G 3
Pinar del Río ☆ C 54-55 D 3
Pinaré o BR 74-75 E 5
Pinarhisar ☆ TR 128-129 B 2
Pinatubo, Mount ▲ RP 160-161 D 5
Pinawa o CDN (MAN) 234-235 H 4
Pincher o CDN (ALB) 232-233 E 6
Pincher Creek o CDN (ALB) 232-233 E 6
Pinchi o CDN (BC) 228-229 K 2
Pinçon, Mont ▲ F 90-91 G 7
Pincón de Boygorri, Represa < ROU 78-79 L 2
Pinconning o USA (MI) 272-273 F 4
Pińczów o • PL 92-93 Q 3
Pinda o MOC 218-219 H 3
Pindaí o BR 72-73 J 3
Pindaíba, Rio ~ BR 72-73 D 3
Pindal o EC 64-65 B 4
Pindar o AUS 176-177 C 4
Pindarama do Tocantins o BR 68-69 F 7
Pindaré, Rio ~ BR 68-69 E 4
Pind Dādan Khān o PK 138-139 D 3
Pindi Bhattiān o PK 138-139 D 4
Pindi Gheb o PK 138-139 D 3
Pindiu o PNG 183 D 4
Pindolo o RI 164-165 G 5
Pindos Oros ▲ GR 100-101 H 5
Pinduši o RUS 88-89 N 5
Pine o USA (AZ) 256-257 D 4
Pine Apple o USA (AL) 284-285 D 5
Pine Barren Creek ~ USA 284-285 D 5
Pine Bluff o USA (AR) 276-277 C 6
Pine Bluffs o USA (WY) 252-253 O 5
Pine City o USA (MN) 270-271 F 5
Pine City o USA (OR) 244-245 F 5
Pine Creek o • AUS 172-173 K 2
Pine Creek ~ CDN 30-31 K 4
Pinecreek o USA (MN) 270-271 C 2
Pine Creek o USA (MT) 250-251 J 6
Pine Creek ~ USA 280-281 J 2
Pine Creek Gorge ∴ USA (PA) 280-281 J 2
Pine Creek Indian Reserve ⵅ CDN (MAN) 234-235 C 2
Pine Creek Lake < USA (OK) 264-265 J 4
Pinedale o USA (WY) 252-253 J 4
Pine Dock o CDN (MAN) 234-235 G 3
Pine Falls o CDN (MAN) 234-235 G 4
Pinefield o BS 54-55 J 3
Pine Flat o USA (CA) 248-249 F 4
Pine Flat Reservoir ⊖ USA (CA) 248-249 E 3
Pinega o RUS 88-89 R 4
Pinega ~ RUS 88-89 S 5
Pinegrove o AUS 176-177 C 3
Pine Grove o USA (OR) 244-245 D 5

Perlas, Punta de — Pine Grove 377

Pine Hill ○ AUS 178-179 B 2
Pine Hill ○ CDN (QUE) 238-239 L 3
Pine Hill ○ USA (AL) 284-285 C 5
Pinehurst ○ USA (CA) 248-249 E 3
Pinehurst ○ USA (NC) 282-283 H 5
Pineimuta River ~ CDN 34-35 M 4
Pineimuta River ~ CDN 234-235 O 2
Pine Island ○ USA (LA) 268-269 H 6
Pine Island ○ USA (MN) 270-271 F 6
Pine Island ⌒ USA (FL) 286-287 G 5
Pine Island Bay ≈ 16 F 26
Pine Island Bayou ~ USA 268-269 F 6
Pine Islands ⌒ USA (FL) 286-287 H 7
Pine Island Sound ≈ 286-287 G 5
Pine Lake ○ CDN (ALB) 232-233 E 3
Pineland ○ USA (SC) 284-285 J 4
Pineland ○ USA (TX) 268-269 G 5
Pine Level ○ USA (AL) 284-285 D 4
Pinellas Park ○ USA (FL) 286-287 G 4
Pine Lodge ○ USA (NM) 256-257 K 5
Pine Mountain ○ USA (GA) 284-285 F 4
Pine Mountain ▲ USA 284-285 F 4
Pine Mountain Summit ▲ USA (CA) 248-249 E 5
Pinemuta River ~ CDN 234-235 N 2
Pine Point ▲ CDN (NWT) 30-31 M 5
Pine Portage ○ CDN (ONT) 234-235 P 5
Piñera ○ ROU 78-79 L 2
Pine Ridge ○ USA (CA) 248-249 E 2
Pine Ridge ○ USA (SD) 260-261 D 3
Pine Ridge Indian Reservation ✕ USA (SD) 260-261 D 3
Pine River ○ CDN (MAN) 234-235 C 3
Pine River ~ CDN 30-31 Q 6
Pine River ~ CDN 32-33 J 4
Pine River ○ USA (MN) 270-271 D 4
Pinerolo ○ I 100-101 A 2
Pines, Point of ○ USA (AZ) 256-257 F 5
Pine Springs ○ USA (TX) 266-267 C 2
Pineto ○ I 100-101 E 3
Pinetop-Lakeside ○ USA (AZ) 256-257 F 4
Pinetops ○ USA (NC) 282-283 K 5
Pinetown ○ ZA 220-221 K 4
Pinetta ○ USA (FL) 286-287 F 1
Pine Valley ○ USA (UT) 254-255 B 6
Pineview ○ USA (GA) 284-285 G 4
Pineview ○ USA (UT) 254-255 D 3
Pine Village ○ USA (IN) 274-275 L 4
Pineville ○ USA (KY) 276-277 M 4
Pineville ○ USA (LA) 268-269 H 5
Pineville ○ USA (MO) 276-277 A 4
Pineville ○ USA (WV) 280-281 E 6
Pine Woods ○ USA (MS) 268-269 L 4
Piney ○ CDN (MAN) 234-235 H 5
Piney Buttes ⩡ USA 250-251 M 4
Piney Creek ~ USA 276-277 B 5
Piney Island ⌒ USA (FL) 286-287 E 1
Pingal ○ IND 138-139 D 1
Ping'an ○ VRC 156-157 C 3
Pingaring ○ AUS 176-177 E 6
Pingba ○ VRC 156-157 E 3
Pingchang ○ VRC 154-155 E 6
Pingchao ○ VRC 154-155 M 5
Pingdingshan ○ VRC 154-155 H 5
Pingding Shan ▲ VRC 150-151 G 4
Pingdu ○ VRC 154-155 L 3
Pingelly ○ AUS 176-177 D 6
Pinger Point ▲ CDN 24-25 f 6
Pingguo ○ VRC 156-157 E 5
Pinghe ○ VRC 156-157 K 4
Pinghu ○ VRC 154-155 M 6
Pingjiang ○ VRC (GZH) 156-157 F 4
Pingjiang ○ VRC (HUN) 156-157 H 2
Pingle ○ VRC 156-157 G 4
Pingli ○ VRC 154-155 F 5
Pingliang ○ VRC 154-155 E 4
Pingling ○ VRC 156-157 J 5
Pinglu ○ VRC 154-155 H 2
Pinglu ○ VRC 156-157 F 5
Pingluo ○ VRC 154-155 E 2
Pingnan ○ VRC (FUJ) 156-157 L 3
Pingnan ○ VRC (GXI) 156-157 G 5
Pingo, El ○ RA 76-77 H 6
Pingo Pingo, Cerro ▲ RCH 76-77 C 2
Pingquan ○ VRC 148-149 O 7
Pingree ○ USA (ND) 258-259 J 4
Pingrup ○ AUS 176-177 E 6
Pingshan ○ VRC (HEB) 154-155 J 2
Pingshan ○ VRC (HEI) 150-151 F 5
Pingshi ○ VRC 156-157 H 4
Pingtang ○ VRC 156-157 E 4
Pingtung ○ RC 156-157 M 5
Pingua Hills ▲ CDN 28-29 D 3
Pingüicas, Cerro ▲ MEX 50-51 K 7
Pingurbek Island ⌒ USA 22-23 O 3
Pingwang ○ VRC 154-155 M 6
Pingwu ○ VRC 154-155 D 5
Pingxiang ○ VRC (GXI) 156-157 E 5
Pingxiang ○ VRC (JXI) 156-157 H 3
Pingyang ○ VRC 156-157 M 3
Pingyao ○ VRC 154-155 H 3
Pingyi ○ VRC 154-155 K 4
Pingyin ○ VRC 154-155 K 3
Pingyu ○ VRC 154-155 J 5
Pingyuan ○ VRC 156-157 J 4
Pingyuanjie ○ VRC 156-157 C 5
Pinhal ○ BR 74-75 E 8
Pinhalzinho ○ BR 74-75 D 6
Pinhão ○ BR 74-75 E 5
Pinheiro ○ BR 68-69 F 3
Pinheiro Machado ○ BR 74-75 D 8
Pinheiros ○ BR 72-73 K 5
Pinhél ○ BR 66-67 K 4
Pinhuã, Rio ~ BR 66-67 E 6
Pini, Pulau ⌒ RI 162-163 C 4
Pinillos ○ CO 60-61 D 3
Pinjarra ○· AUS 176-177 C 6
Pinjug ○ RUS 96-97 E 3
Pinkawillinie Conservation Park ⊥ AUS 180-181 C 2
Pinkha ○ MYA 142-143 J 3
Pink Hill ○ USA (NC) 282-283 K 5
Pink Mountain ○ CDN 32-33 J 3
Pink River ~ CDN 34-35 D 2
Pinland ○ USA (FL) 286-287 F 2
Pinlebu ○ MYA 142-143 J 3
Pinnacles ○ AUS 176-177 F 4
Pinnacles, The ·· AUS 176-177 C 5
Pinnacles National Monument ∴ USA (CA) 248-249 C 3
Pinnaroo ○ AUS 180-181 F 3
Pinogu ○ RI 164-165 H 3
Pinoh ~ RI 162-163 J 5
Pino Hachado, Paso de ▲ RA 78-79 D 5
Pinola ○ USA (MS) 268-269 L 5
Piñon ○ USA (AZ) 256-257 E 2
Pinon ○ USA (NM) 256-257 K 6
Pinon Canyon ○ USA (CO) 254-255 M 6
Piñon Hills ○ USA (CA) 248-249 G 5
Pinos ○ MEX 50-51 J 6
Pinos, Mount ▲ USA (CA) 248-249 E 5
Pinos Altos ○ USA (NM) 256-257 G 6
Pinotepa Nacional ○· MEX 52-53 E 3
Pinrang ○ RI 164-165 F 5
Pins, Pointe aux ▲ CDN (ONT) 238-239 D 6
Pinsk ○ BY 94-95 K 5
Pinski bolota ⩡ UA 102-103 D 2
Pinta, Isla ⌒ EC 64-65 B 9
Pintada, La ○ PA 52-53 D 7
Pintada, Sierra ▲ MEX 50-51 B 4
Pintadas ○ BR 68-69 J 7
Pintado ○ BR 68-69 G 6
Pintado, Cerro ▲ RA 80 D 4
Pintado, Rio ~ BR 72-73 E 2
Pintados ○ RCH 70-71 C 7
Pintados, Salar de ○ RCH 70-71 C 7
Pintatu ○ RI 164-165 K 3
Pinto ○ RA 76-77 F 5
Pinto Creek ~ CDN 228-229 R 3
Pinto Creek ~ CDN 228-229 P 2
Pinto Creek ~ CDN 232-233 L 6
Pinto Summit ▲ USA (NV) 246-247 K 4
Pintoyacu, Río ~ EC 64-65 D 2
Pinturas, Río ~ RA 80 E 3
Pintuyan ○ RP 160-161 F 8
Pintwater Range ▲ USA 248-249 J 3
Piñuelas ○ CO 60-61 D 2
Piñuña Negra ○ CO 64-65 D 1
Pinware ○ CDN (NFL) 242-243 M 1
Pinware River ~ CDN 38-39 Q 3
Pinware River Provincial Park ⊥ CDN (NFL) 242-243 M 1
Pinzon, Canal de ≈ 64-65 B 10
Pinzon, Isla ⌒ EC 64-65 B 10
Pioche ○ USA (NV) 248-249 K 2
Piodi ○ ZRE 214-215 C 4
Pio IX ○ BR 68-69 H 5
Pioka ○ ZRE 210-211 E 6
Piombino ○ I 100-101 C 3
Pioneer ○ USA (AZ) 256-257 B 5
Pioneer ○ USA (CA) 246-247 E 5
Pioneer Fracture Zone ≃ 14-15 O 4
Pioneer Huron City · USA (MI) 272-273 G 3
Pioneer Mountains ▲ USA 250-251 F 6
Pioneer Mountains ▲ USA 252-253 D 3
Pioneer Woman Monument ∴ USA (OK) 264-265 G 2
Pioneiros d'Oeste ○ BR 72-73 D 3
Pioner ○ RUS 122-123 M 6
Pioner, ostrov ⌒ RUS 108-109 I Y 2
Piore River ~ PNG 183 A 2
Piorini ○ BR 66-67 F 4
Piorini, Lago ○ BR 66-67 F 4
Piotrków Trybunalski ☆ PL 92-93 P 3
Pio XII. ○ BR 68-69 F 3
Pipa, Cerro ▲ RA 78-79 E 6
Pipalyatjara ○ AUS 176-177 K 3
Pipanaco, Salar de ○ RA 76-77 D 5
Piparia ○ IND 138-139 G 8
Pipe Spring National Monument · USA (AZ) 256-257 C 2
Pipestone ○ CDN (ALB) 232-233 E 2
Pipestone ○ CDN (MAN) 234-235 C 5
Pipestone ○ USA (MN) 270-271 B 7
Pipestone Creek ~ CDN 232-233 Q 5
Pipestone National Monument ∴· USA (MN) 270-271 B 6
Pipestone Pass ▲ USA (MT) 250-251 G 6
Pipestone River ~ CDN 30-31 Q 6
Pipestone River ~ CDN 234-235 N 2
Pipi ~ RCA 206-207 F 4
Pipi, Gorges de la ·· RCA 206-207 F 4
Pipili ○ IND 142-143 D 5
Pipinas ○ RA 78-79 L 3
Pipiriki ○ NZ 182 E 3
Piplān ○ PK 138-139 C 3
Piplod ○ IND 138-139 D 8
Pipmuacan, Réservoir < CDN 38-39 J 4
Pipon Island ⌒ AUS 174-175 H 4
Pipri ○ IND 142-143 C 3
Piprod ○ IND 142-143 B 4
Piqua ○ USA (OH) 280-281 B 3
Piqua Historic Area · USA (OH) 280-281 B 3
Piquenes, Paso de los ▲ RA 78-79 E 2
Piqueras, Puerto de ▲ E 98-99 F 3
Piquet Carneiro ○ BR 68-69 J 4
Piquete ○ BR 72-73 H 7
Piqui ○ BR 76-77 K 1
Piquiri, Rio ~ BR 74-75 D 5
Pir ○ IR 134-135 B 2
Pira ○ DY 202-203 L 5
Pirabeiraba ○ BR 74-75 F 6
Piraca, Rio ~ BR 72-73 F 4
Piracaia ○ BR 72-73 G 7
Piracanjuba ○ BR 72-73 F 4
Piracanjuba, Rio ~ BR 70-71 J 4
Piracicaba ○ BR 72-73 G 7
Piracuruca ○ BR 68-69 H 3
Piracuruca, Rio ~ BR 68-69 H 4
Pirada ○ GNB 202-203 C 3
Pirada Km. 101 ○ RA 76-77 E 5
Pirahã, Área Indígena ✕ BR 66-67 F 6
Piraí ○ BR 66-67 J 4
Piraí do Sul ○ BR 74-75 F 5
Pirajiba ○ BR 72-73 J 2
Piraju ○ BR 72-73 F 7
Pirajuí ○ BR 72-73 F 7
Pirambu ○ BR 68-69 K 7
Piramidal'nyj, pik ▲ KS 136-137 M 5
Pirámide, Cerro ▲ RCH 80 D 4
Pirané ○ RA 76-77 H 3
Piranga ○ BR 72-73 J 6
Piranga, Rio ~ BR 72-73 J 6
Pirangi, Rio ~ BR 68-69 J 4
Piranguinho ○ BR 72-73 H 7
Piranha, Rio ~ BR 66-67 D 6
Piranhaquara, Igarapé ~ BR 68-69 B 4
Piranhas ○ BR (ALA) 68-69 K 6
Piranhas ○ BR (GOI) 72-73 E 4
Piranhas, Rio ~ BR 66-67 J 6
Piranhas, Rio ~ BR 68-69 D 6
Piranhas, Rio ~ BR 68-69 K 5
Piranhas, Rio ~ BR 72-73 E 4
Pīrānšahr ○ IR 128-129 L 4
Piranteira, Cachoeira ~ BR 66-67 F 2
Pira Paraná, Rio ~ CO 66-67 B 3
Pirapemas ○ BR 68-69 F 3
Pirapó, Rio ~ BR 72-73 D 7
Pirapó, Rio ~ PY 76-77 J 4
Pirapó, Serra do ▲ BR 76-77 K 5
Pirapora ○ BR 72-73 H 4
Pirapozinho ○ BR 72-73 E 7
Piraquara ○ BR 74-75 F 5
Pirarajá ○ ROU 78-79 M 2
Pirassununga ○ BR 72-73 G 6
Piratinga, Rio ~ BR 72-73 G 3
Piray, Río ~ BOL 70-71 F 6
Pircas, Cerro ▲ RA 76-77 C 6
Pirda ~ RUS 116-117 M 3
Pireás ○ GR 100-101 J 6
Pirehueico, Lago ○ RCH 78-79 D 5
Pirenópolis ○ BR 72-73 F 3
Pires do Rio ○ BR 72-73 F 4
Pirgí ○ GR 100-101 K 5
Pirgos ○ GR 100-101 H 6
Pirgos ○ GR 100-101 K 7
Piriá, Rio ~ BR 68-69 E 2
Piriápolis ○ ROU 78-79 M 3
Pirica, Río ~ RA 76-77 D 4
Pirie, Lac ○ CDN (ONT) 236-237 L 2
Piri Grande ○ BR 62-63 J 5
Pirin, Naroden Park ⊥··· BG 102-103 C 7
Pirinem ○ RUS 88-89 S 4
Pirineos ▲ E 98-99 G 3
Piripá ○ BR 72-73 K 3
Piripiri ○ BR 68-69 H 4
Piritiba ○ BR 68-69 H 7
Piriyāpatna ○ IND 140-141 F 4
Pirjo Goth ○ PK 138-139 B 6
Pir Mangho ○· PK 134-135 M 6
Pirmasens ○ D 92-93 J 4
Pirna ○· D 92-93 M 3
Piro ○ MOC 218-219 H 4
Pirojpur ○ BD 142-143 G 4
Piros, Cerro los ▲ RCH 78-79 C 4
Pirot ○· YU 100-101 J 3
Pirovac ○ HR 100-101 E 3
Pirožnikova ~ RUS 120-121 S 5
Pirpainti ○ IND 142-143 E 3
Pir Panchal Range ▲ IND 138-139 E 2
Pirré, Cerro ▲ PA 52-53 F 8
Pirsagat ~ AZ 128-129 N 2
Pirtleville ○ USA (AZ) 256-257 F 7
Pirttikoski ○ FIN 88-89 J 3
Piru ○ RI 166-167 E 3
Piru ○ USA (CA) 248-249 F 5
Piru, Teluk ≈ 166-167 E 3
Piruru ○ GUY 62-63 F 3
Pisa ○··· I 100-101 C 3
Pisac ○ PE 70-71 B 3
Pisacoma ○ PE 70-71 C 5
Pisagua ○ RCH 70-71 B 6
Pisanda ○ CO 64-65 D 1
Pisandaungsaung ○ MYA 158-159 E 5
Pisang, Kepulauan ⌒ RI 166-167 G 3
Pisau, Tanjung ▲ MAL 160-161 C 9
Pisba, Parque Nacional ⊥ CO 60-61 E 5
Pišča ○ UA 102-103 C 2
Pisco ○ PE 64-65 D 8
Pisco Elquí ○ RCH 76-77 B 6
Piscovo ○· RUS 94-95 R 3
Písek ○ CZ 92-93 N 4
Pisek ○ USA (ND) 258-259 K 3
Písek = Písek ○ CZ 92-93 N 4
Pisgah ○ USA (IA) 274-275 C 3
Pisgah ○ USA (NC) 282-283 H 5
Pisgah Crater · USA (CA) 248-249 H 5
Pishan ○ VRC 144-145 B 2
Pishin ○ PK 134-135 M 3
Pishin Lora ~ PK 134-135 L 4
Pishin Lora ~ PK 134-135 M 3
Pišin ○ IR 134-135 J 5
Pisinimo ○ USA (AZ) 256-257 C 6
Pismo Beach ○ USA (CA) 248-249 D 4
Pismo Beach · USA (CA) 248-249 D 4
Piso, Lake ○ LB 202-203 E 6
Piso Firme ○ BOL 70-71 G 3
Pisqui, Río ~ PE 64-65 E 5
Pissila ○ BF 202-203 K 3
Piste ○ MEX 52-53 K 1
Pisticci ○ I 100-101 F 4
Pistóia ○ I 100-101 C 3
Pistolet Bay ≈ 38-39 R 3
Pistolet Bay ≈ 242-243 N 1
Pistol River ○ USA (OR) 244-245 A 8
Pisuerga, Río ~ E 98-99 E 3
Pisz ○· PL 92-93 Q 2
Pit ○ RI 166-167 K 3
Pit, Bol'šoj ~ RUS 116-117 F 6
Pita ○ RG 202-203 D 4
Pita, La ∴ PA 52-53 D 7
Pitaga ○ CDN 38-39 M 2
Pital ○ CO 60-61 D 6
Pitalito ○ CO 60-61 C 7
Pitanga ○ BR 74-75 E 5
Pitangui ○ BR 72-73 H 5
Pitarpunga Lake ○ AUS 180-181 G 3
Pitas ○ MAL 160-161 B 9
Pītāv ○ AFG 136-137 M 6
Pitcairn Island ⌒ GB 13 O 5
Pitche ○ GNB 202-203 D 3
Pitch Lake · TT 60-61 L 2
Pite ○ S 86-87 K 4
Piteälven ~ S 86-87 J 4
Pitești ☆· RO 102-103 D 5
Pit-Gorodok ○ RUS 116-117 E 6
Pithāpuram ○ IND 142-143 C 7
Pithara ○ AUS 176-177 D 5
Pithiviers ○ F 90-91 J 7
Piti ~ EAT 214-215 G 4
Piti, Lagoa ○ MOC 220-221 L 3
Pitigala ○ CL 140-141 J 7
Pitinga, Rio ~ BR 62-63 E 6
Pitjantjatjara Aboriginal Land ✕ AUS 176-177 L 3
Pitkas Point ○ USA 20-21 J 5
Pitkin ○ USA (CO) 254-255 J 5
Pitkin ○ USA (LA) 268-269 H 6
Pitkjaranta ☆ RUS 88-89 L 6
Pitljar ~ RUS 114-115 J 2
Pitman ○ CDN (SAS) 232-233 N 5
Pitmegea River ~ USA 20-21 H 2
Pitoa ○ CAM 204-205 K 4
Pitok River ~ CDN 30-31 T 2
Pit River ~ USA 246-247 D 2
Pitrufquen ○ RCH 78-79 C 5
Pitt, Canal ≈ 80 C 5
Pitt Island ⌒ CDN (BC) 228-229 D 3
Pitt Lake ○ CDN (BC) 230-231 G 4
Pitt Meadows ○ CDN (BC) 230-231 G 4
Pittsboro ○ USA (NC) 282-283 H 5
Pittsburg ○ USA (KS) 262-263 M 7
Pittsburg ○ USA (KY) 276-277 L 3
Pittsburg ○ USA (TX) 264-265 K 6
Pittsburgh ○ USA (CA) 246-247 D 5
Pittsburgh ○ USA (PA) 280-281 G 3
Pittsfield ○ USA (IL) 274-275 H 5
Pittsfield ○ USA (MA) 278-279 H 6
Pittsfield ○ USA (ME) 278-279 M 4
Pittsfield ○ USA (PA) 280-281 G 2
Pittston ○ USA (PA) 280-281 L 2
Pittston Farm ○ USA (ME) 278-279 M 3
Pitts Town ○ BS 54-55 J 3
Pittsview ○ USA (AL) 284-285 E 4
Pittsville ○ USA (MD) 280-281 L 5
Pittsville ○ USA (WI) 270-271 H 6
Pittsworth ○ AUS 178-179 L 4
Pitu ~ EAT 214-215 H 5
Pituffik Gletscher ⊂ GRØ 26-27 Q 5
Pituil ○ RA 76-77 D 5
Pituil, Río ~ RA 76-77 D 5
Pituri Creek ~ AUS 178-179 E 2
Pitz Lake ○ CDN 30-31 V 4
Piu ○ PNG 183 D 4
Piũí ○ BR 72-73 H 6
Piulip Nunaa ⩡ GRØ 26-27 Q 5
Pium ○ BR 68-69 D 7
Pium, Rio ~ BR 68-69 D 7
Piúma ○ BR 72-73 K 6
Piuna ○ BOL 70-71 C 4
Piura ○ PE 64-65 B 4
Piura, Río ~ PE 64-65 B 4
Piva ~ YU 100-101 G 3
Pivabiska Lake ○ CDN (ONT) 236-237 E 3
Pivdennyj Buh ~ UA 102-103 G 4
Pivnično-Kryms'kyj, kanal < UA 102-103 J 5
Pivot ○ CDN (ALB) 232-233 H 5
Pivski manastir · YU 100-101 G 3
Pixa ○ VRC 144-145 B 2
Pi Xian ○ VRC (JIA) 154-155 K 4
Pi Xian ○ VRC (SIC) 154-155 C 6
Pixley ○ USA (CA) 248-249 E 4
Pixley National Wildlife Refuge ⊥· USA (CA) 248-249 E 4
Pixoyal ○ MEX 52-53 J 2
Pixtun ○ MEX 52-53 J 2
Pīž ~ RUS 96-97 J 5
Pizhi ○ WAN 204-205 F 4
Pižma ~ RUS 88-89 V 4
Pizzo ○ I 100-101 F 5
Pjadungina ~ RUS 114-115 Q 5
Pjagina, poluostrov ⌒ RUS 120-121 Q 4
Pjakupur ~ RUS 114-115 N 3
Pjakuto, ozero ○ RUS 114-115 M 3
Pjandž ○ TJ 136-137 L 6
Pjandž ~ TJ 136-137 M 5
Pjaozero ○ RUS 88-89 L 3
Pjasedajaha ~ RUS 108-109 N 6
Pjasina ~ RUS 108-109 W 5
Pjasino, ozero ○ RUS 108-109 W 7
Pjasinskij zaliv ≈ 108-109 V 4
Pjatibratskij, mys ▲ RUS 120-121 S 4
Pjatigorsk ○· RUS 104 D 4
Pjat'-Jah ○ RUS 114-115 M 4
Pjatychatky ○ UA 102-103 H 3
Pjŏngjang = Pyongyang ★ KOR 150-151 E 8
Pjul'ky ~ RUS 114-115 S 2
P.K. le Rouxdam < ZA 220-221 G 5
P.K. Rouge ○ RCB 210-211 E 5
Plá ○ RA 78-79 J 3
Place, La ○ USA (LA) 268-269 K 6
Placentia ○ CDN (NFL) 242-243 P 5
Placentia Bay ≈ 38-39 R 5
Placentia Bay ≈ 242-243 O 5
Placer ○ RP 160-161 E 7
Placerville ○ USA (CA) 246-247 E 5
Placerville ○ USA (CO) 254-255 G 5
Placetas ○ C 54-55 F 3
Placeton, Cerro del ▲ RCH 76-77 B 5
Placid, Lake ○ USA (FL) 286-287 H 4
Placido de Castro ○ BR 70-71 D 2
Placita ○ USA (NM) 256-257 H 5
Placitas ○ USA (NM) 256-257 K 2
Placongo ○ RCB 210-211 D 5
Plain ○ USA (WA) 244-245 E 3
Plain City ○ USA (OH) 280-281 C 3
Plain City ○ USA (UT) 254-255 C 2
Plain Dealing ○ USA (LA) 268-269 G 4
Plainfield ○ USA (IA) 274-275 F 2
Plainfield ○ USA (WI) 270-271 J 6
Plains ○ USA (GA) 284-285 F 4
Plains ○ USA (KS) 262-263 F 7
Plains ○ USA (MT) 250-251 E 4
Plains ○ USA (TX) 264-265 B 5
Plainview ○ USA (MN) 270-271 F 6
Plainview ○ USA (NE) 262-263 J 2
Plainview ○ USA (TX) 264-265 C 4
Plainville ○ USA (KS) 262-263 G 5
Plainwell ○ USA (MI) 272-273 D 5
Plaju ○ RI 162-163 F 6
Plampang ○ RI 168 C 7
Plana Cays ⌒ BS 54-55 J 3
Planada ○ USA (CA) 248-249 D 2
Planadas ○ CO 60-61 D 6
Planaltina ○ BR (FED) 72-73 G 3
Planaltina ○· BR (GOI) 72-73 G 3
Planaltina do Paraná ○ BR 72-73 D 7
Planalto ○ BR (BAH) 72-73 K 3
Planalto ○ BR (PAR) 74-75 D 5
Planalto ○ BR (RSU) 74-75 D 6
Planas, Río ~ CO 60-61 F 5
Planchón, El ∴· MEX 52-53 J 3
Planchon, Paso del ▲ RCH 78-79 D 3
Plandi ~ BF 202-203 H 4
Planeta Rica ○ CO 60-61 D 3
Planet Creek ~ AUS 178-179 K 3
Planet Downs ○ AUS 174-175 E 6
Plankinton ○ USA (SD) 260-261 H 3
Plano ○ USA (TX) 264-265 H 5
Plano Alto ○ BR 76-77 J 5
Plant, La ○ USA (SD) 260-261 F 1
Planta de Azufre ○ RA 78-79 D 3
Planta Esmeralda ○ RCH 76-77 B 3
Plantation Key ⌒ USA (FL) 286-287 J 7
Plant City ○ USA (FL) 286-287 G 3
Planura ○ BR 72-73 F 6
Plaquemine ○ USA (LA) 268-269 J 6
Plaridel ○ RP 160-161 E 8
Plasë ○ AL 100-101 H 4
Plasencia ○ E 98-99 D 4
Plast ○ RUS 96-97 M 6
Plaster City ○ USA (CA) 248-249 J 7
Plaster Rock ○ CDN (NB) 240-241 H 4
Plastun ○ RUS 122-123 G 6
Plata, Isla de la ⌒ EC 64-65 B 2
Plata, La ☆· RA 78-79 L 3
Plata, La ○ USA (MO) 274-275 F 4
Plata, Lago la ○ RA 80 E 2
Plata, Minas de ○··· MEX 50-51 H 6
Plata, Río de la ~ RA 78-79 K 3
Plata, Río de la ~ USA 286-287 P 2
Platanal = Majeicodoteri ○ YV 60-61 J 6
Platbakkies ○ ZA 220-221 D 5
Plate, Île ⌒ SY 224 C 6
Plateau ◘ WAN 204-205 G 4
Plateaux ◘ RCB 210-211 E 5
Plateforme, La ○ RH 54-55 J 5
Platen, Kapp ▲ N 84-85 N 2
Plateros ○ MEX 50-51 H 6
Platina ○ USA (CA) 246-247 C 3
Platinum ○ USA 22-23 Q 3
Plato ○ CDN (SAS) 232-233 K 4
Plato ○ CO 60-61 D 3
Plato de Sopa ○ RCH 76-77 C 3
Platón Sánchez ○ MEX 50-51 K 7
Platoro ○ USA (CO) 254-255 J 6
Platt Bank ≃ 278-279 M 5
Platte ○ USA (SD) 260-261 H 3
Platte City ○ USA (MO) 274-275 D 5
Platten ○ USA (ME) 278-279 M 2
Platte River ~ USA 262-263 H 4
Platte River ~ USA 274-275 D 4
Platteville ○ USA (CO) 254-255 L 3
Platteville ○ USA (WI) 274-275 H 2
Plattsburg ○ USA (MO) 274-275 D 5
Plattsburgh ○ USA (NY) 278-279 H 4
Plattsmouth ○ USA (NE) 262-263 L 4
Platveld ○ NAM 216-217 D 9
Plauen ○ D 92-93 M 3
Plavinas ○ LV 94-95 J 3
Plavnikovye, ostrova ⌒ RUS 108-109 V 4
Plavsk ☆· RUS 94-95 P 5
Playa Blanca ○ E 188-189 E 6
Playa Bonita ○ YV 60-61 E 2
Playa Dayaniguas ○ C 54-55 D 3
Playa de Florida ○ C 54-55 F 4
Playa del Carmen ○· MEX 52-53 L 1
Playa Lauro Villar ○ MEX 50-51 L 5
Playa Los Corchos ○ MEX 50-51 G 7
Playa Noriega, Laguna ○ MEX 50-51 D 3
Playa Rosario ○· C 54-55 D 3
Playas ○ EC 64-65 B 3
Playa Vicente ○ MEX 52-53 G 3
Plây Ku ☆ VN 158-159 K 4
Plaza ○ USA (ND) 258-259 F 3
Plaza Huincul ○ RA 78-79 E 5
Pleasant ○ USA (IN) 274-275 N 6
Pleasant, Lake ○ USA (AZ) 256-257 C 5
Pleasant Bay ○ CDN (NS) 240-241 P 4
Pleasant Grove ○ USA (AL) 284-285 D 3
Pleasant Grove ○ USA (AL) 284-285 C 3
Pleasant Grove ○ USA (NC) 282-283 L 5
Pleasant Hill ○ USA (IL) 274-275 H 5
Pleasant Hill ○ USA (LA) 268-269 G 5
Pleasant Hill ○ USA (MO) 274-275 D 6
Pleasant Hill ○ USA (SC) 284-285 K 2
Pleasant Lake ○ USA (ND) 258-259 H 3
Pleasanton ○ USA (KS) 262-263 M 6
Pleasant Plains ○ USA (AR) 276-277 C 5
Pleasant Valley ○ USA (OR) 244-245 H 6
Pleasant View ○ USA (CO) 254-255 G 6
Pleasanton ○ USA (TX) 266-267 J 4
Pledger Lake ○ CDN (ONT) 236-237 E 2
Plenty ○ CDN (SAS) 232-233 K 4
Plenty, Bay of ≈ 182 F 2
Plenty Downs ∴ AUS 178-179 D 2
Plenty Highway II AUS 178-179 D 2
Plenty River ~ AUS 178-179 C 2
Plentywood ○ USA (MT) 250-251 P 3
Plered ○ RI 168 B 3
Plešanovo ☆ RUS 96-97 H 7
Plesant, Mount ▲ USA (VA) 280-281 G 6
Pleščanicy ○ BY 94-95 K 4
Pleseck ☆ RUS 88-89 Q 5
Pleskau = Pskov ☆·· RUS 94-95 L 3
Pleskauer See = Pskovskoe ozero ○ RUS 94-95 K 2
Pleso, Osinovoe ○ RUS 114-115 T 7
Plessisville ○ CDN (QUE) 238-239 O 2
Pleszew ○ PL 92-93 O 3
Plétipi, Lac ○ CDN 38-39 J 3
Plettenbergbaai ○· ZA 220-221 F 7
Plettenberg Bay = Plettenbergbaai ○· ZA 220-221 F 7
Pleven ○ BG 102-103 D 6
Plevna ○ USA (MT) 250-251 P 5
Plevna Downs ○ AUS 178-179 G 4
Pliny ○ USA (MN) 270-271 E 4
Plitvica ○ HR 100-101 E 2
Plitvička Jezera, Nacionalni park ⊥··· HR 100-101 E 2
Pljevlja ○· YU 100-101 G 3
Ploaghe ○ I 100-101 B 4
Ploče ○ HR 100-101 F 3
Płock ☆·· PL 92-93 P 2
Ploërmel ○ F 90-91 F 8
Ploiești ☆· RO 102-103 E 5
Płońsk ○ PL 92-93 Q 2
Ploskij, mys ▲ RUS 110-111 b 2
Ploskoš' ○ RUS 94-95 M 3
Ploso ○ RI 168 E 3
Plotava ○ RUS 124-125 M 2
Plotnikova ~ RUS 122-123 R 2
Plotnikovo ○ RUS 114-115 R 6
Plouézec ○ F 90-91 F 7
Plouguer, Carhaix- ○ F 90-91 F 7
Plovdiv ☆ BG 102-103 D 6
Plover ○ USA (WI) 270-271 J 6
Plover Islands ⌒ USA 20-21 N 1
Plumas ○ CDN (MAN) 234-235 D 4
Plum Coulee ○ CDN (MAN) 234-235 F 5
Plum Creek ~ USA 266-267 K 4
Plummer ○ USA (ID) 250-251 C 4
Plummer ○ USA (MN) 270-271 B 3
Plummer, Mount ▲ USA 20-21 L 6
Plumridge Lakes ○ AUS 176-177 H 4
Plumtree ○ ZW 218-219 D 5
Plungė ☆·· LT 94-95 G 4
Plunkett ○ CDN (SAS) 232-233 N 4
Plush ○ USA (OR) 244-245 F 8
Plutarco Elías Calles, Presa < MEX 50-51 E 3
Plymouth ○ GB 90-91 E 6
Plymouth ○· GB 56 D 3
Plymouth ○ TT 60-61 L 2
Plymouth ○ USA (CA) 246-247 E 5
Plymouth ○ USA (IN) 274-275 M 3
Plymouth ○ USA (MI) 272-273 F 5
Plymouth ○ USA (NC) 282-283 L 5
Plymouth ○ USA (NE) 262-263 K 4
Plymouth ○ USA (NH) 278-279 K 5
Plymouth ○ USA (PA) 280-281 L 2
Plymouth ○ USA (RI) 278-279 L 7
Plymouth ○ USA (WA) 244-245 F 5
Plymouth ○ USA (WI) 270-271 K 1
Plzeň ○ CZ 92-93 M 4
Pniewy ○ PL 92-93 O 2
Pô ○ BF 202-203 K 4
Po ~ I 100-101 C 2
Pô, Parc National de ⊥ BF 202-203 K 4
Poan High Knob ▲ USA (NC) 282-283 E 4
Poano ○ CI 202-203 K 6
Poat, Pulau ⌒ RI 164-165 H 3
Poatina ○ AUS 180-181 J 6
Pobè ○ DY 204-205 E 5
Pobeda ○ TM (ASH) 136-137 G 6
Pobeda ○ TM (MAR) 136-137 H 6
Pobeda, gora ▲ RUS 110-111 a 7
Pobé Mengao ○ BF 202-203 K 3
Población ○ RCH 78-79 D 3
Pobla de Segur, la ○ E 98-99 H 3
Poblet, Reial Monestir de ··· E 98-99 H 4
Poča ○ RUS 88-89 P 5
Pocahontas ○ CDN (ALB) 228-229 R 3
Pocahontas ○ USA (AR) 276-277 E 4
Pocahontas ○ USA (IA) 274-275 D 2
Pocahontas ○ USA (IL) 274-275 J 6
Pocatello ○ USA (ID) 252-253 F 4
Pocatière, La ○ CDN (QUE) 240-241 E 3
Poccha, Río ~ PE 64-65 D 6
Počep ○ RUS 94-95 N 5
Pocetas ○ YV 60-61 F 4
Pochotitán ○ MEX 50-51 G 7
Pocinhos ○ BR 68-69 K 5
Počinok ☆ RUS 94-95 N 4
Počitelj · BIH 100-101 F 3
Pocito, El ○ BOL 70-71 F 4
Pocitos, Salar ○ RA 76-77 D 3
Pocoata ○ BOL 70-71 D 6
Poço de Fora ○ BR 68-69 J 6
Poções ○ BR 72-73 K 3
Poções ○ BR 68-69 H 5
Pocomoke City ○ USA (MD) 280-281 L 5
Pocomoke River ~ USA 280-281 L 5
Pocomoke Sound ≈ 280-281 L 6
Pocone ○ BR 70-71 J 5
Poço Redondo ○ BR 68-69 K 6
Poços de Caldas ○ BR 72-73 G 6
Poço Verde ○ BR 68-69 J 7
Pocrane ○ BR 72-73 K 5
Podberez'e ○ RUS (NVG) 94-95 M 2
Podberez'e ○ RUS (PSK) 94-95 M 3
Podbořany ○ CZ 92-93 M 3
Podborov'e ○ RUS 94-95 L 3
Podčer'e ○ RUS (KOM) 114-115 D 3
Podčer'e ~ RUS 114-115 E 3
Poddor'e ○ RUS 94-95 M 3
Podelga ~ RUS 114-115 R 4
Podena, Kepulauan ⌒ RI 166-167 K 3
Podgorenskij ○ RUS 102-103 L 2
Podgorica ☆ YU 100-101 G 3
Podgornyj, aral ⌒ KZ 126-127 J 5
Podile ○ IND 140-141 H 3
Podil's'ka vysočyna ▲ UA 102-103 D 3
Podkagernaja, buhta ≈ 120-121 T 3
Podkamennaja ~ RUS 110-111 G 2
Podkamennaja Tunguska ~ RUS 116-117 E 5
Podkamennaja Tunguska = Podkamennaja Tunguska ~ RUS 116-117 E 5
Podkova ○ BG 102-103 D 7
Podkova, ostrov ⌒ RUS 108-109 V 4
Podlomka ~ RUS 88-89 O 5
Podocarpus, Parque Nacional ⊥ EC 64-65 C 4
Podol'sk ☆· RUS 94-95 P 4
Podor ○ SN 196-197 C 6
Podora ○ RUS 88-89 X 5
Podporož'e ○ RUS 94-95 O 1
Podravska Slatina ○ HR 100-101 F 2
Podupalskij Ústirti ▲ KZ 126-127 M 3
Podyem-Mihajlovka ○ RUS 96-97 G 7
Poe Bank ≃ 158-159 D 6
Poechos, Embalse < PE 64-65 B 4
Poelela, Lagoa ○ MOC 218-219 H 7
Poeppel Corner · AUS 178-179 D 3
Pofadder ○ ZA 220-221 D 4
Pogge II, Chute ~· ZRE 216-217 F 3
Poggibonsi ○ I 100-101 C 3
Pogibi ○ RUS 122-123 J 2
Pognoa ○ BF 202-203 L 4
Pogo ○ CI 202-203 H 4
Pogoanele ○ RO 102-103 E 5
Pogorelec ○ RUS 88-89 S 4
Pogost ○ RUS 88-89 Q 5
Pogradec ☆·· AL 100-101 H 4
Pograničnyi ○ BY 94-95 J 5
Pograničnyj ○ RUS 122-123 D 6
Pogromni Volcano ▲ USA 22-23 O 5
Poguba, Rio ~ BR 70-71 K 5
Pogynden ~ RUS 112-113 M 2
Pogyndino ○ RUS 112-113 N 2
Poh ○ RI 164-165 H 4
P'ohang ○ ROK 150-151 G 9
Pohénégamook ○ CDN (QUE) 240-241 F 3
Pohiois-li ○ FIN 88-89 H 4
Pohjanlahti ≈ 86-87 K 5
Pohjanmaa ⩡ FIN 88-89 G 5
Pohodsk ○ RUS 112-113 L 2
Pohvistnevo ☆ RUS 96-97 H 7
Poie ○ ZRE 210-211 J 5
Poi Island ⌒ SOL 184 I e 4
Poile, La ○ CDN (NFL) 242-243 K 5
Poinsett, Lake ○ USA (SD) 260-261 J 2
Point, Cap ▲ WL 56 E 4
Point "A" Lake < USA (AL) 284-285 D 5
Point au Fer ▲ USA (LA) 268-269 J 7
Point au Mal ○ CDN (NFL) 242-243 K 4
Point Austin ▲ AUS 174-175 F 5
Point Baker ○ USA 32-33 D 3
Point Bickerton ○ CDN (NS) 240-241 O 5
Pointblank ○ USA (TX) 268-269 E 6
Point Bridget State Park ⊥ USA 32-33 C 2
Point Dume Beach · USA (CA) 248-249 F 5
Pointe-à-la-Garde ○ CDN (QUE) 240-241 J 2
Pointe-à-Pitre ○ F 56 E 3
Pointe-au-Père ○ CDN (QUE) 240-241 G 2
Pointe-aux-Anglais ○ CDN (QUE) 242-243 A 3
Pointe-Carleton ○ CDN (QUE) 242-243 E 3
Pointe des Lataniers ○ RH 54-55 J 5
Pointe du Bois ○ CDN (MAN) 234-235 H 4
Pointe-Mistassini ○ CDN (QUE) 242-243 A 3
Pointe Noire ○ F 56 E 3
Pointe-Noire ☆ RCB 210-211 C 6
Pointe Ouest ▲ RH 54-55 J 4
Pointe Parent ○ CDN (QUE) 242-243 G 2
Pointe Rivière de l'Artibonite ○ RH 54-55 J 5
Point Gamble ○ USA (WA) 244-245 C 3
Point Grondine Indian Reservation ✕ CDN (ONT) 238-239 D 3
Point Harbor ○ USA (NC) 282-283 M 4
Point Hope ○ USA 20-21 G 2
Point Judith ○ USA (RI) 278-279 K 7
Point Lake ○ CDN 30-31 N 3
Point Lay ○ USA 20-21 J 2
Point Leamington ○ CDN (NFL) 242-243 N 3
Point Lookout ○ USA (MD) 280-281 K 5
Point Lookout ▲ USA (MD) 280-281 K 5
Point Marion ○ USA (PA) 280-281 G 4
Point May ○ CDN (NFL) 242-243 N 6
Point Mc Leay ○ AUS 180-181 E 3
Point Michaud ○ CDN (NS) 240-241 P 5
Point of Rocks ○ USA (MD) 280-281 J 4
Point of Rocks ○ USA (WY) 252-253 K 5
Point Pedro ○ CL 140-141 J 6
Point Pelee National Park ⊥ CDN (ONT) 238-239 C 7
Point Pleasant ○ USA (NJ) 280-281 M 3
Point Pleasant ○ USA (WV) 280-281 D 5
Point Pleasant State Historic Monument · USA (WV) 280-281 D 5
Point Renfrew ○ CDN (BC) 230-231 E 5
Point Reyes National Seashore ⊥ USA (CA) 246-247 B 5
Point Salvation Aboriginal Land ✕ AUS 176-177 H 4
Point Samson ○ AUS 172-173 C 6
Point Stuart ∴ AUS 172-173 K 2
Point Washington ○ USA (FL) 286-287 C 1
Poisson-Blanc ○ CDN (QUE) 236-237 P 3
Poissonnier Point ▲ AUS 172-173 D 5
Poitiers ☆· F 90-91 H 8
Poitou ⩡ F 90-91 G 8
Poitou-Charentes ◘ F 90-91 G 8
Poivre Atoll ⌒ SY 224 C 2
Poix-de-Picardie ○ F 90-91 H 7
Pojarkovo ☆ RUS 122-123 C 4

378 Pine Hill — Pojarkovo

Pojasovyj kamen' hrebet ▲ RUS 114-115 E 4
Pojezierze Mazurskie ⊥ PL 92-93 P 2
Pojezierze Pomorskie ⊥ PL 92-93 O 2
Pojkovskij ○ RUS 114-115 L 4
Pojlovajaha ~ RUS 108-109 R 7
Pojlovajaha, Arka- ~ RUS 108-109 Q 8
Pojlu ○ AZ 128-129 M 2
Pojma ~ RUS 116-117 H 7
Pojmyga ~ RUS 116-117 N 6
Pojo, Río de ~ BOL 70-71 E 5
Pojuca ○ BR 72-73 L 2
Pojuca, Rio ~ BR 72-73 L 2
Pojuščie peski •• RUS 118-119 D 9
Pokanaevka ○ RUS 116-117 H 7
Pokaran ○ IND 138-139 C 6
Pokataroo ○ AUS 178-179 K 5
Pokemouche ○ CDN (NB) 240-241 L 3
Pokhara ○• NEP 144-145 E 6
Pokigron ○ SME 62-63 G 3
Po-kil Do ⌒ ROK 150-151 F 10
Pokka ○ FIN 88-89 H 2
Poko ○ ZRE 210-211 L 2
Pokojnickaja ~ RUS 108-109 U 8
Pokok Sena ○ MAL 162-163 D 1
Pokofka ~ RUS 114-115 R 3
Pokrovka ○ KS 146-147 C 4
Pokrovka ○ KZ 126-127 M 3
Pokrovka ○ RUS 114-115 O 7
Pokrovsk ○ RUS (IRK) 116-117 H 8
Pokrovsk ☆ RUS (SAH) 118-119 O 5
Pokrovs'ke ○ UA 102-103 K 4
Pokšen'ga ~ RUS 88-89 R 5
Pokuma ○ Z 218-219 D 3
Pokur ○ RUS 114-115 N 4
Pola ○ RP 160-161 D 6
Pola, La ○•• E 98-99 E 3
Polacca ○ USA (AZ) 256-257 E 3
Polacca Wash ~ USA 256-257 E 3
Polače ○• HR 100-101 F 3
Polack ☆•• BY 94-95 L 4
Pola de Laviana ○ E 98-99 E 3
Pola de Lena ○ E 98-99 E 3
Poladpur ○ IND 140-141 E 2
Polān ○ IR 134-135 J 6
Polanco ○ ROU 78-79 M 2
Polanco ○ RP 160-161 E 8
Poland = Polska ■ PL 92-93 O 3
Polar Bear Provincial Park ⊥ CDN 34-35 N 3
Polaris ○ USA (MT) 250-251 F 6
Polaris Forland ⊥ GRØ 26-27 U 3
Polar Plateau ▲ ANK 16 E 31
Polatlı ○ TR 128-129 E 3
Polavaram ○ IND 142-143 B 7
Polazna ○ RUS 96-97 K 4
Polcura, Río ~ RCH 78-79 D 4
Pole Abyssal Plain ≈ 16 A 14
Pol-e 'Alam ☆ AFG 138-139 B 2
Polcang ⌒ RI 164-165 G 6
Polebridge ○ USA (MT) 250-251 E 3
Pol-e Fasā ○ IR 134-135 E 4
Pol-e Ḫomrī ○ AFG 136-137 L 7
Pol-e Ḫomrī, Darryā-ye ~ AFG 136-137 L 7
Pol-e Loušān ○ IR 128-129 N 4
Pol-e Safid ○ IR 136-137 C 6
Polessk ☆ RUS 94-95 G 4
Polevskoj ☆ RUS 96-97 M 5
Polewali ○ RI 164-165 F 5
Polgahawela ○ CL 140-141 J 7
Poli ○ CAM 204-205 K 4
Poli ○ CY 128-129 E 5
Policastro, Golfo di ≈ 100-101 E 5
Police, Pointe ▲ SY 224 D 2
Policemans Point ○ AUS 180-181 E 4
Policoro ○ I 100-101 F 4
Poligiros ○ GR 100-101 J 4
Polihnitos ○ GR 100-101 L 5
Polikastro ○ GR 100-101 J 4
Poliny Osipenko, imeni ☆ RUS 122-123 G 2
Polis'ke ○ UA 102-103 F 2
Politovo ○ RUS 88-89 U 4
Pulíva ~ RUS 116-117 L 6
Polja ~ RUS 94-95 Q 4
Poljakovskij ○ RUS 118-119 N 9
Poljana ○ UA 102-103 C 3
Poljamoe ○ RUS 110-111 b 4
Poljarnyj ○ RUS (CUK) 112-113 U 2
Poljarnyj ○ RUS (MUR) 88-89 M 2
Poljarnyj ○ RUS (SAH) 110-111 H 6
Poljarnyj hrebet ▲ RUS 120-121 O 2
Poljarnyj Ural ▲ RUS 108-109 J 9
Polk ○ USA (AL) 284-285 D 4
Polk, Fort ✕✕ USA (LA) 268-269 G 5
Pollāchi ○ IND 140-141 G 5
Pollença ○ E 98-99 J 5
Pollilo ○ RP 160-161 D 5
Pollilo Island ⌒ RP 160-161 D 5
Pollilo Islands ⌒ RP 160-161 E 5
Pollilo Strait ≈ 160-161 D 5
Pollino, Parco del ⊥ I 100-101 F 5
Pollock ○ USA (ID) 250-251 C 6
Pollock ○ USA (LA) 268-269 H 5
Pollock Hills ▲ AUS 172-173 H 7
Pollockville ○ CDN (ALB) 232-233 G 4
Poľnoj Voronež ~ RUS 94-95 R 5
Polo ○ USA (IL) 274-275 J 3
Polobaya Grande ○ PE 70-71 B 5
Polochic, Río ~ GCA 52-53 K 4
Polock = Polack ☆•• BY 94-95 L 4
Pologij-Sergeeva, ostrov ⌒ RUS 108-109 T 4
Pologoe Zajmišče ○ RUS 96-97 E 9
Polohy ○ UA 102-103 K 4
Polom ○ RUS 96-97 G 4
Polomolok ○ RP 160-161 F 9
Polonina-Runa hora ▲ UA 102-103 C 3
Polonnaruwa ○••• CL 140-141 J 7
Polousnyj krjaž ▲ RUS 110-111 X 5
Polovinnoe, ozero ○ RUS 108-109 W 6
Polson ○ USA (MT) 250-251 E 4
Poltava ☆ UA 102-103 J 3
Poltavka ☆ RUS 124-125 G 1
Põltsamaa ○•• EST 94-95 J 2
Poluj ~ RUS 108-109 M 8
Poluj ~ RUS 114-115 K 2
Polujskaja vozvyšennost' ▲ RUS 114-115 J 2
Polūr ○ IND 140-141 H 4
Põlva ☆ EST 94-95 K 2
Polvadera Peak ▲ USA (NM) 256-257 J 2
Polvār, Rūd-e ~ IR 134-135 E 3
Polvaredas ○ RA 78-79 K 3
Polvora ○ PE 64-65 D 5
Polwarth ○ CDN (SAS) 232-233 M 2
Põlwe = Põlva ☆ EST 94-95 K 2
Polyarnyy Ural = Poljarnyj Ural ▲ RUS 108-109 J 9
Polynesia ⌒ 13 L 2
Polyuc ○ MEX 52-53 K 2
Poma ○ ZRE 210-211 K 4
Pomabamba ○ PE 64-65 D 6
Pomacanchi ○ PE 70-71 B 3
Pomahuaca ○ PE 64-65 C 4
Pomarkku ○ FIN 88-89 F 6
Pomasi, Cerro de ▲ PE 70-71 B 4
Pombal ○ BR (PA) 68-69 K 5
Pombal ○ BR (RON) 70-71 F 2
Pombal ○ P 98-99 C 5
Pombal, Igarapé do ~ BR 68-69 B 5
Pombangi ○ RI 164-165 G 5
Pombas ○ BR 66-67 F 3
Pombas, Rio das ~ BR 66-67 G 6
Pombuige ~ ANG 216-217 C 5
Pomene ○ MOC 218-219 H 6
Pomerene ○ USA (AZ) 256-257 E 6
Pomeroy ○ USA (OH) 280-281 D 4
Pomeroy ○ USA (WA) 244-245 H 4
Pomeroy ○ ZA 220-221 K 4
Pomfret ○ ZA 220-221 F 2
Pomio ○ PNG 183 F 3
Pomme de Terre Lake ○ USA (MO) 276-277 B 3
Pomona ○ RA 78-79 G 5
Pomona ○ USA (CA) 248-249 G 5
Pomona ○ USA (KS) 262-263 L 6
Pomona Lake ○ USA (KS) 262-263 L 6
Pomorska, Zatoka ≈ 92-93 N 1
Pomorskij proliv ≈ 88-89 U 2
Pomorskoe ○ RUS 108-109 E 5
Pomos ○ CY 128-129 E 5
Pompano Beach ○ USA (FL) 286-287 J 5
Pompei •• I 100-101 E 4
Pompéia ○ BR 72-73 E 7
Pompeu ○ BR 72-73 H 5
Pompeys Pillar ○ USA (MT) 250-251 M 6
Pompeys Pillar • USA (MT) 250-251 M 5
Pom Phra Chunlachomklao ○ THA 158-159 F 4
Pompton Lakes ○ USA (NJ) 280-281 M 3
Pompué, Rio ~ MOC 200-201 F 3
Pomr', zaliv ≈ 122-123 K 2
Pomut ~ RUS 114-115 K 3
Ponape ⌒ FSM 13 G 2
Ponass Lake ○ CDN (SAS) 232-233 O 3
Ponazyrevo ○ RUS 96-97 E 4
Ponca ○ USA (NE) 262-263 K 2
Ponca City ○ USA (OK) 264-265 G 2
Ponce ○ USA (PR) 286-287 P 2
Ponce de Leon ○ USA (FL) 286-287 D 1
Poncha Springs ○ USA (CO) 254-255 J 5
Ponchatoula ○ USA (LA) 268-269 K 6
Poncheville, Lac ○ CDN 38-39 F 3
Poncheville, Lac ○ CDN (QUE) 236-237 M 2
Pond ○ USA (CA) 248-249 F 4
Pond Creek ○ USA (OK) 264-265 G 2
Pondera Coulee ~ USA 250-251 H 3
Ponderosa ○ USA (CA) 248-249 F 3
Pond Fork ~ USA 280-281 E 6
Pondicherry ■ IND 140-141 H 5
Pondicherry ☆•• IND 140-141 H 5
Pond Inlet ≈ 24-25 h 4
Pond Inlet ○ CDN 24-25 h 4
Pondosa ○ USA (CA) 246-247 D 2
Pond River ~ USA 276-277 H 3
Ponds, Isle of ⌒ CDN 38-39 R 2
Ponds Lake, River of ○ CDN (NFL) 242-243 L 2
Pondung Lamanggang ○ RI 162-163 D 6
Poneloya ○ NIC 52-53 L 5
Ponente, Riviera di ⌣ I 100-101 A 3
Ponerečnyj Algan ~ RUS 112-113 R 4
Ponferrada ○• E 98-99 D 3
Pônfi ~ MOC 218-219 G 2
Pongaí ○ BR 72-73 F 6
Pongara, Pointe ▲ G 210-211 B 3
Pong Chi ○ THA 158-159 F 2
Pong Nam Ron ○ THA 158-159 G 4
Pongo ~ SUD 206-207 H 5
Pongo de Cumbinama ~ PE 64-65 C 4
Pongo de Paquipachango ~ PE 64-65 E 7
Pongola ○ ZA (TRA) 220-221 K 3
Pongola ~ ZA 220-221 K 3
Pongolapoortdam < ZA 220-221 L 3
Pongore ○ ZW 218-219 D 4
Poni ~ BF 202-203 J 4
Ponindilisa, Tanjung ▲ RI 164-165 G 4
Ponio ○ RT 202-203 L 4
Ponio, Río ~ RCH 76-77 B 6
Ponna ○ MYA 142-143 J 5
Ponnaiyar ~ IND 140-141 H 4
Ponnāni ○ IND 140-141 F 5
Ponneri ○ IND 140-141 J 4
Ponnūru Nidubrolu ○ IND 140-141 J 2
Ponoj ○ RUS 88-89 Q 3
Ponoj ~ RUS 88-89 N 3
Ponoka ○ CDN (ALB) 232-233 E 3
Ponomarevka ○ RUS (NVS) 114-115 R 6
Ponomarevka ☆ RUS (ORB) 96-97 J 7
Ponondougou ○ CI 202-203 G 5
Ponorogo ○ RI 168 D 3
Ponrang ○ RI 164-165 G 5
Ponson Island ⌒ RP 160-161 F 7
Ponta ○ BR 66-67 E 3
Ponta Delgada ☆ P 6-7 G 5
Ponta de Mata ○ YV 60-61 K 3
Ponta de Pedras ○ BR 62-63 K 6
Ponta dos Indios ○ BR 62-63 J 3
Ponta do Sol ○ CV 202-203 B 5
Ponta do Zumbi ○ BR 68-69 F 2
Ponta Freitas Morna ○ ANG 216-217 B 3
Ponta Grossa ○ BR 74-75 E 5
Pontal ○ BR 72-73 F 6
Pontal, Rio do ~ BR 68-69 H 6
Pontalina ○ BR 72-73 F 4
Pontan River ~ CDN 30-31 L 6
Ponta Porã ○ BR 76-77 K 2
Pontarlier ○• F 90-91 L 8
Pontas de Pedras ○ BR 68-69 L 5
Pont-Audemer ○ F 90-91 H 7
Pontchartrain, Lake ○ USA (LA) 268-269 K 6
Pontchâteau ○ F 90-91 F 8
Pont do Suort, el ○ E 98-99 H 3
Pont du Gard ••• F 90-91 K 10
Ponte Alta, Rio ~ BR 68-69 E 7
Ponte Alta do Tocantins ○ BR 68-69 E 7
Ponteareas ○ E 98-99 C 3
Ponte Branca ○ BR 72-73 D 4
Ponte da Barca ○ P 98-99 C 4
Ponte de Itabapoana ○ BR 72-73 K 6
Ponte de Sor ○ P 98-99 C 5
Ponte Firme ○ BR 72-73 G 5
Ponteix ○ CDN (SAS) 232-233 L 6
Ponte Nova ○ BR 72-73 J 6
Ponte Ribeiro, Lago ○ BR 70-71 H 4
Pontes e Lacerda ○ BR 70-71 H 4
Ponte Serrada ○ BR 74-75 D 6
Pontevedra ○ E 98-99 C 3
Pontiac ○ USA (IL) 274-275 K 4
Pontiac ○ USA (MI) 272-273 F 5
Pontianak ☆ RI 162-163 H 5
Pontian Kecil ○ MAL 162-163 E 4
Pontic Mountains = Kuzey Anadolu Dağları ▲ TR 128-129 E 2
Pontivy ○ F 90-91 F 7
Ponto Arari ○ BR 62-63 J 5
Ponto Busch ○ BOL 70-71 J 6
Pontoise ☆ F 90-91 J 7
Pontokerasia ○ GR 100-101 J 4
Ponton Creek ~ AUS 176-177 G 5
Pontorson ○ F 90-91 G 7
Pontotoc ○ USA (MS) 268-269 L 2
Pontotoc ○ USA (TX) 266-267 J 3
Pontrémoli ○• I 100-101 B 2
Pontrilas ○ CDN (SAS) 232-233 O 2
Pont-Rouge ○ CDN (QUE) 238-239 O 2
Ponts ○ E 98-99 H 4
Pontypool ○ CDN (ONT) 238-239 G 4
Ponuga ○ PA 52-53 D 8
Pony Express Station ∴ USA (KS) 262-263 K 5
Ponza ○ I 100-101 D 4
Ponziane, Ísole ⌒ I 100-101 D 4
Poochera ○ AUS 180-181 C 2
Pool ■ RCB 210-211 E 5
Poole ○ GB 90-91 G 6
Poole's Monument • AUS 178-179 F 5
Poolesville ○ USA (MD) 280-281 J 4
Pooley Island ⌒ CDN (BC) 228-229 F 4
Pool Malebo ○ ZRE 210-211 E 6
Poolowanna Lake ○ AUS 170-179 D 4
Pools Cove ○ CDN (NFL) 242-243 N 5
Poolville ○ USA (TX) 264-265 G 6
Poonamallee ○ IND 140-141 J 4
Pooncarie ○ AUS 180-181 G 2
Pooneryn ○ CL 140-141 J 6
Poopó ○ BOL 70-71 D 6
Poopó, Lago de ○ BOL 70-71 D 6
Pooppelloe Lake ○ AUS 178-179 G 6
Poorman ○ USA 20-21 N 4
Poor Man Indian Reserve ✕ CDN (SAS) 232-233 O 4
Popa Falls ~• NAM 216-217 F 9
Popayan ☆•• CO 60-61 C 6
Popča ○ RUS 88-89 W 5
Pope ○• LV 94-95 G 3
Popenguine ○• SN 202-203 B 2
Poperechnoi Island ⌒ USA 22-23 Q 5
Poperinge ○ B 92-93 G 3
Popham Bay ≈ 36-37 R 2
Popham Beach ○ USA (ME) 278-279 M 5
Popigaj ○ RUS (TMR) 110-111 H 4
Popigaj ~ RUS 110-111 H 4
Popigaj ~ RUS 110-111 F 3
Popilta Lake ○ AUS 180-181 F 2
Poplar ○ USA (CA) 248-249 E 3
Poplar ○ USA (MN) 270-271 D 4
Poplar ○ USA (MT) 250-251 O 3
Poplar ○ USA (WI) 270-271 G 4
Poplar Bay ○ CDN (ALB) 232-233 D 2
Poplar Bluff ○ USA (MO) 276-277 E 4
Poplarfield ○ CDN (MAN) 234-235 F 4
Poplar Hill ○ CDN (ONT) 234-235 J 2
Poplar Hill ○ USA (VA) 280-281 F 6
Poplar Point ○ CDN (MAN) 234-235 F 4
Poplar Rapids River ~ CDN 236-237 G 3
Poplar River ~ CDN 30-31 J 5
Poplar River ~ CDN 232-233 N 6
Poplar River ~ CDN 234-235 F 2
Poplar River ~ CDN 234-235 G 2
Poplarville ○ USA (MS) 268-269 L 6
Popocatepetl, Volcán ▲•• MEX 52-53 E 2
Popof Island ⌒ USA 22-23 Q 5
Popoh ○ RI 168 D 4
Popokabaka ○ ZRE 210-211 F 6
Pópoli ○ I 100-101 D 3
Popomanaseu, Mount = Makarakombu ▲ SOL 184 I e 3
Popondetta ☆ PNG 183 E 5
Popovka ○ RUS (ROS) 102-103 M 3
Popovka ~ RUS 110-111 c 7
Popovka ~ RUS 120-121 P 2
Popovo ○ BG 102-103 E 6
Popov Porog ○ RUS 88-89 N 5
Poprad ○ SK 92-93 Q 4
Poptún ○ GCA 52-53 K 3
Poquoson ○ USA (VA) 280-281 K 6
Porāli ~ PK 134-135 M 6
Porangatu ○ BR 72-73 F 2
Porbandar ○• IND 138-139 B 9
Porčaman ○ AFG 134-135 K 2
Porção, Cachoeira do ~ BR 68-69 B 3
Porcher Island ⌒ CDN (BC) 228-229 D 3
Porciúngula ○ BR 72-73 J 6
Porcos, Riacho dos ~ BR 68-69 J 5
Porcos, Rio dos ~ BR 72-73 H 2
Porcupine ○ USA 20-21 W 7
Porcupine, Cape ▲ CDN 38-39 Q 2
Porcupine Abyssal Plain ≃ 6-7 H 3
Porcupine Forest Reserve ⊥ CDN (MAN) 234-235 B 2
Porcupine Gorge National Park ⊥ AUS 174-175 H 7
Porcupine Plain ○ CDN (SAS) 232-233 P 3
Porcupine Plain ⊥ CDN 20-21 V 2
Porcupine Plateau ▲ CDN 20-21 U 3
Porcupine River ~ CDN 30-31 R 6
Porcupine River ~ USA 20-21 U 3
Porcupine State Park ⊥ USA (MI) 270-271 J 4
Pordenone ☆• I 100-101 D 2
Pore ○ CO 60-61 F 5
Porebada ○ PNG 183 D 5
Porecatu ○ BR 72-73 E 7
Poreckoe ○ RUS 96-97 E 6
Porédaka ○ RG 202-203 D 4
Porekautimbu, Gunung ▲ RI 164-165 G 4
Porga ○ DY 202-203 L 4
Porgera ○ PNG 183 B 3
Porhov ☆ RUS 94-95 L 3
Pori ○ FIN 88-89 F 6
Porirua ○ NZ 182 E 4
Porjus ○ S 86-87 J 3
Pork Peninsula ⌣ CDN 30-31 X 4
Porlakshöfn ○ IS 86-87 c 3
Porlamar ○ YV 60-61 K 2
Porog ○ RUS 88-89 P 5
Poro Island ⌒ RP 160-161 F 7
Poro Island ⌒ SOL 184 I c 2
Poroma ○ PNG 183 B 4
Poronaj ~ RUS 122-123 K 4
Poronajsk ○ RUS 122-123 K 4
Porong ○ RI 168 E 3
Póros ○ GR 100-101 H 5
Porosozero ○ RUS 88-89 M 5
Porotos, Punta ▲ RCH 76-77 B 5
Porožsk ○ RUS 88-89 W 5
Porpoise Bay ≈ 16 G 13
Porquis Junction ○ CDN (ONT) 236-237 H 4
Porsangen ≈ 86-87 M 1
Porsangerhalvøya ⌣ N 86-87 M 1
Porsea ○ RI 162-163 C 3
Porsgrunn ☆ N 86-87 D 7
Porsild Mountains ▲ CDN 36-37 H 2
Porsuk Çayı ~ TR 128-129 D 3
Port, Le ○ F 224 B 7
Porta, Rio da ~ BR 68-69 C 5
Port Adelaide ○ AUS 180-181 E 3
Portage ○ CDN (PEI) 240-241 L 4
Portage ○ USA (AK) 20-21 Q 6
Portage ○ USA (UT) 254-255 C 2
Portage ○ USA (WI) 270-271 J 7
Portage Bay ≈ 22-23 T 4
Portage Bay ○ CDN (MAN) 234-235 E 3
Portage la Prairie ○ CDN (MAN) 234-235 E 5
Portageville ○ USA (MO) 276-277 F 4
Portal ○ USA (ND) 258-259 E 3
Port Alberni ○ CDN (BC) 230-231 E 4
Port Albert ○• AUS 180-181 J 5
Port Albion ○ CDN (BC) 230-231 D 5
Portalegre ○• P 98-99 D 5
Portales ○ USA (NM) 256-257 M 4
Port Alexander ○ USA 32-33 C 3
Port Alfred ○ ZA 220-221 H 6
Port Alice ○ CDN (BC) 230-231 B 3
Port Allegany ○ USA (PA) 280-281 H 2
Port Allen ○ USA (HI) 288 F 3
Port Allen ○ USA (LA) 268-269 J 6
Port Alma ○ AUS 178-179 L 2
Port Andrew ○ USA (WI) 274-275 H 1
Port Antonio ○• JA 54-55 G 5
Portão de Baixo, Cachoeira ~ BR 66-67 K 5
Port Arthur ○• AUS 180-181 J 7
Port Arthur ○ USA (TX) 268-269 G 7
Port Arthur = Lüshun ○ VRC 150-151 C 8
Port Askaig ○ GB 90-91 D 4
Port au Choix ○ CDN (NFL) 242-243 L 2
Port Augusta ○ AUS 180-181 D 2
Port au Port Bay ≈ 242-243 K 4
Port au Port Peninsula ⌣ CDN 242-243 J 4
Port-au-Prince ★• RH 54-55 J 5
Port Austin ○ USA (MI) 272-273 G 3
Port aux Choix National Historic Park • CDN (NFL) 242-243 L 2
Port Bay, Port au ≈ 38-39 P 4
Port Bell ○ EAU 212-213 D 3
Port-Bergé = Boriziny ○ RM 222-223 E 5
Port Blair ☆ IND 140-141 L 4
Port Blandford ○ CDN (NFL) 242-243 O 4
Port Bolivar ○ USA (TX) 268-269 F 7
Port Broughton ○ AUS 180-181 D 2
Port Bruce ○ CDN (ONT) 238-239 D 6
Port Burwell ○ CDN (ONT) 238-239 E 6
Port Campbell ○ AUS 180-181 G 5
Port Campbell National Park ⊥ AUS 180-181 G 5
Port Charlotte ○ USA (FL) 286-287 G 4
Port Chester ○ USA (NY) 280-281 N 3
Port Chilkoot ○ USA 20-21 X 7
Port Clements ○ CDN (BC) 228-229 B 3
Port Clinton ○ USA (OH) 280-281 D 2
Port Clyde ○ USA (ME) 278-279 M 5
Port Coquitlam ○ CDN (BC) 230-231 G 4
Port-Daniel ○ CDN (QUE) 240-241 L 2
Port-Daniel, Réserve faunique de ⊥ CDN (QUE) 240-241 L 2
Port-de-Paix ☆ RH 54-55 J 5
Port Dickson ○• MAL 162-163 D 3
Port Douglas ○ AUS 174-175 H 5
Port Dover ○ CDN (ONT) 238-239 E 6
Port Dufferin ○ CDN (NS) 240-241 N 6
Porte, La ○ USA (IN) 274-275 M 3
Porte, La ○ USA (TX) 268-269 E 7
Port Edward ○ CDN (BC) 228-229 D 2
Port Edward ○ ZA 220-221 K 5
Porteira, Cachoeira da ~ BR 66-67 H 7
Porteiras ○ BR 62-63 F 6
Porteirinha ○ BR 72-73 J 3
Portél ○ BR 62-63 J 6
Portel ○ P 98-99 D 5
Portelândia ○ BR 72-73 D 4
Port Elgin ○ CDN (NB) 240-241 L 4
Port Elgin ○ CDN (ONT) 238-239 D 4
Port Elizabeth ○ ZA 220-221 G 6
Port Ellen ○ GB 90-91 D 4
Porteno, Río ~ RA 76-77 H 3
Porter ○ CDN (SAS) 232-233 K 3
Porter ○ USA (WA) 244-245 B 4
Porters Corner ○ USA (MT) 250-251 F 5
Porterville ○ USA (CA) 248-249 E 3
Porterville ○ ZA 220-221 D 6
Portes de l'Enfer ~•• ZRE 212-213 A 6
Port Essington ○ CDN (BC) 228-229 E 2
Portezuela ▲ BOL 76-77 C 1
Portezuela del Huaytiquina ▲ RCH 76-77 D 2
Portezuela Llullaillaco Norte ▲ RCH 76-77 C 3
Portezuela Pasto Ventura ▲ RA 76-77 D 4
Portezuelo ○ RCH 78-79 C 4
Portezuelo, El ○ RA 76-77 E 5
Port Fitzroy ○ NZ 182 E 2
Port Fourchon ○ USA (LA) 268-269 K 7
Port-Gentil ☆ G 210-211 B 4
Port Germein ○ AUS 180-181 D 2
Port Gibson ○ USA (MS) 268-269 J 5
Port Grosvenor ○ ZA 220-221 J 5
Port-Harcourt ☆ WAN 204-205 G 6
Port Hardy ○ CDN (BC) 230-231 B 3
Port Harrison = Inukjuak ○ CDN 36-37 K 5
Port Hawkesbury ○ CDN (NS) 240-241 O 5
Port Hedland ○ AUS 172-173 D 6
Port Heiden ○ USA 22-23 R 4
Port Henry ○ USA (NY) 278-279 H 4
Porthill ○ USA (ID) 250-251 C 3
Port Hilford ○ CDN (NS) 240-241 O 5
Port Hood ○ CDN (NS) 240-241 O 4
Port Hope ○ CDN (ONT) 238-239 G 5
Port Hope ○ USA (MI) 272-273 G 4
Port Hope Simpson ○ CDN 38-39 Q 2
Port Howard ○ GB 78-79 L 6
Port Howe ○ BS 54-55 H 2
Port Hueneme ○ USA (CA) 248-249 E 5
Port Huron ○ USA (MI) 272-273 G 5
Portimão ○ P 98-99 C 6
Portimo ○ FIN 88-89 J 3
Portis ○ USA (KS) 262-263 H 5
Port Isabel ○ USA (TX) 266-267 K 7
Port Isabel Lighthouse State Historic Site ∴ USA (TX) 266-267 K 7
Port Jackson ○ NZ 182 E 2
Port Jefferson ○ USA (NY) 280-281 M 3
Port Jervis ○ USA (NY) 280-281 M 2
Port Kenny ○ AUS 180-181 C 2
Port Kent ○ USA (NY) 278-279 H 4
Port Lairge = Waterford ○• IRL 90-91 D 5
Portland ○ AUS 180-181 F 5
Portland ○ USA (IN) 274-275 O 4
Portland ○ USA (ME) 278-279 L 5
Portland ○ USA (MI) 272-273 E 5
Portland ○ USA (OR) 244-245 C 5
Portland ○ USA (TN) 276-277 J 4
Portland ○ USA (TX) 266-267 K 6
Portland, Cape ▲ AUS 180-181 J 6
Portland Bay ≈ 180-181 F 5
Portland Bight ≈ 54-55 G 6
Portland Canal ≈ 32-33 E 4
Portland Creek ○ CDN (NFL) 242-243 L 2
Portland Creek Pond ○ CDN (NFL) 242-243 L 2
Portland Inlet ≈ 228-229 D 2
Portland Island ⌒ NZ 182 F 4
Portland Point ▲ JA 54-55 G 6
Port Langdo ≈ 174-175 D 3
Port Laoise ○ IRL 90-91 D 5
Port Lincoln ○•• AUS 180-181 C 3
Port Lions ○ USA 22-23 U 4
Portlock Reefs ⌒ PNG 183 C 5
Port Loko ○ WAL 202-203 D 5
Port-Louis ○ F 56 E 3
Port Louis ★• MS 224 C 7
Port Mac Donnell ○ AUS 180-181 F 5
Port Macquarie ○ AUS 178-179 M 6
Port Maitland ○ CDN (NS) 240-241 J 7
Port Mansfield ○ USA (TX) 266-267 K 7
Port Maria ○ JA 54-55 G 5
Port Mathurin ○ MS 224 F 6
Port Maurant ○ GUY 62-63 F 2
Port Mayaca ○ USA (FL) 286-287 J 4
Port Mc Arthur ≈ 174-175 D 4
Port Mellon ○ CDN (BC) 230-231 F 4
Port Menier ○ CDN (QUE) 242-243 D 3
Port Moller ○ USA 22-23 Q 5
Port Moody ○ CDN (BC) 230-231 G 4
Portmore ○ JA 54-55 G 6
Port Moresby ★• PNG 183 D 5
Port Morien ○ CDN (NS) 240-241 Q 4
Port Neill ○ AUS 180-181 D 3
Port Nelson ○ BS 54-55 H 3
Port Nelson (abandoned) ○ CDN 34-35 K 2
Portneuf, Rivière ~ CDN 240-241 F 2
Port Neville ○ CDN (BC) 230-231 C 3
Portnjagino, ozero ○ RUS 110-111 F 2
Port Nolloth ○ ZA 220-221 C 4
Port Norris ○ USA (NJ) 280-281 L 4
Port-Nouveau-Québec ○ CDN 36-37 R 5
Porto ○ BR 68-69 G 3
Porto ○ F 98-99 M 3
Porto ☆•• P 98-99 C 4
Pôrto Acre ○ BR 66-67 D 7
Pôrto Alegre ○ BR 70-71 J 5
Porto Alegre ○ BR (BAH) 72-73 K 2
Porto Alegre ○ BR (P) 66-67 J 5
Porto Alegre ☆ BR (RSU) 74-75 E 8
Porto-Alegre ○ STP 210-211 b 2
Porto Alegre do Norte ○ BR 68-69 C 7
Porto Amazonas ○ BR 74-75 F 5
Porto Amboim ○ ANG 216-217 B 5
Porto Antunes ○ BR 66-67 D 4
Porto Azzurro ○ I 100-101 C 3
Portobelo ○•• PA 52-53 E 7
Porto Belo, Baía de ≈ 74-75 F 6
Porto Belo, Ponta do ▲ BR 74-75 F 6
Porto Bicentenário ○ BR 70-71 F 2
Porto Braga ○ BR (AMA) 66-67 E 4
Porto Braga ○ BR (GSU) 70-71 J 7
Porto Camargo ○ BR 72-73 D 7
Porto Cristo ○ E 98-99 J 5
Porto da Soledade ○ BR 72-73 G 4
Porto de Fora ○ BR 70-71 K 5
Porto de Pedras ○ BR 68-69 L 6
Porto do Caititu ○ BR 68-69 F 4
Porto do Mangue ○ BR 68-69 K 4
Porto do Moz ○ BR 62-63 H 6
Porto dos Gaúchos ○ BR 70-71 J 2
Porto dos Mosteiros ○ CV 202-203 B 6
Porto Esperanza ○ RA 76-77 K 4
Porto Esperidião ○ BR 70-71 H 4
Porto Estrela ○ BR 70-71 J 4
Porto Euchides da Cunha ○ BR 72-73 D 7
Portoferráio ○ I 100-101 C 3
Porto Ferreira ○ BR 72-73 G 6
Port of Ness ○ GB 90-91 D 2
Porto Franco ○ BR 68-69 E 5
Port of Spain ★ TT 60-61 L 2
Porto Gen. Nac. el Portillo ▲ RA 78-79 E 2
Porto Grande ○ BR 62-63 J 5
Portogruaro ○• I 100-101 D 2
Porto Henrique ○ MOC 220-221 L 3
Pôrto Jofre ○ BR 70-71 J 5
Portola ○ USA (CA) 246-247 E 4
Porto Levante ○ I 100-101 E 5
Pôrto Lucena ○ BR 76-77 K 4
Port-Olry ○ VAN 184 II a 2
Port Omna = Portumna ○ IRL 90-91 C 5
Porto Moniz ○ P 188-189 C 4
Porto Mosquito ○ CV 202-203 C 6
Pôrto Murtinho ○ BR 76-77 J 1
Porto Nacional ○ BR 68-69 D 7
Porto Novo ○ BR 72-73 J 2
Porto-Novo ★• DY 204-205 E 5
Portonovo ○ IND 140-141 H 5
Porto Novo, Vila de ○ CV 202-203 B 5
Porto Quebra ○ BR 66-67 F 4
Port Orchard ○ USA (WA) 244-245 C 3
Porto Reis ○ BR 66-67 E 4
Pôrto Rico ○ BR 70-71 D 2
Porto Rolha ○ BR 70-71 E 2
Porto Santo ⌒ P (MA) 188-189 C 4
Porto Santo ⌒ P (MAD) 188-189 C 4
Pôrto São José ○ BR 72-73 D 7
Portoscuso ○ I 100-101 B 5
Porto Seguro ○• BR 72-73 L 4
Porto Seguro, Corredeira ~ BR 68-69 B 5
Porto Tolle ○ I 100-101 D 2
Porto Tórres ○ I 100-101 B 4
Pôrto União ○ BR 74-75 E 6
Pôrto Valter ○ BR 64-65 F 6
Porto-Vecchio ○ F 98-99 M 4
Porto Velho ☆ BR 66-67 F 7
Portoviejo ○ EC 64-65 C 3
Portoviejo ☆ EC 64-65 B 2
Portpatrick ○ GB 90-91 E 4
Port Perry ○ CDN (ONT) 238-239 G 4
Port Philip ○ CDN (NS) 240-241 M 5
Port Pirie ○ AUS 180-181 D 2
Port Radium ○ CDN 30-31 L 2
Portree ○ GB 90-91 D 3
Port Rowan ○ CDN (ONT) 238-239 E 6
Port Royal ○ USA (VA) 280-281 J 5
Port Royal National Historic Park • CDN (NS) 240-241 K 6
Port Royal Sound ≈ 284-285 K 4
Port Said = Būr Sa'īd ☆ ET (BUR) 194-195 F 2
Port Saint Joe ○ USA (FL) 286-287 D 2
Port Saint Johns ○ ZA 220-221 J 5
Port-Saint-Louis-du-Rhône ○ F 90-91 K 10
Port Saint Lucie ○ USA (FL) 286-287 J 4
Portsalon ○ IRL 90-91 D 4
Port Salut ○ RH 54-55 J 5
Port Salut, Plage ⊥• RH 54-55 H 5
Port Sanilac ○ USA (MI) 272-273 G 4
Port Saunders ○ CDN (NFL) 242-243 L 2
Port Shepstone ○ ZA 220-221 K 5
Port Simpson ○ CDN (BC) 228-229 D 2
Portsmouth ○ GB 90-91 G 6
Portsmouth ○ USA (IA) 274-275 C 3
Portsmouth ○ USA (NH) 278-279 L 5
Portsmouth ○ USA (OH) 280-281 D 5
Portsmouth ○ USA (VA) 280-281 K 7
Portsmouth ○ WD 56 E 4
Portsmouth Island ⌒ USA (NC) 282-283 L 5
Port Stephens ○ GB 78-79 K 7
Port Sudan = Būr Sūdān ☆• SUD 200-201 H 3
Port Sulphur ○ USA (LA) 268-269 L 7
Port Talbot ○ CDN (ONT) 238-239 D 6
Porttipahdan tekojärvi ○ FIN 88-89 J 2
Port Townsend ○• USA (WA) 244-245 C 2
Portugais, Grotte des = Tenika • RM 222-223 D 9
Portugal ■ P 98-99 B 4
Portugal, Cachoeira ~ BR 66-67 E 7
Portugal Cove ○ CDN (NFL) 242-243 Q 5
Portugal Cove South ○ CDN (NFL) 242-243 P 6
Portuguesa, Río ~ YV 60-61 H 3
Portuguese Cove ○ CDN (NS) 240-241 M 6
Portumna = Port Omna ○ IRL 90-91 C 5
Port-Vato ○ VAN 184 II b 3
Port-Vendres ○ F 90-91 J 10
Port Victoria ○ AUS 180-181 D 3
Port Victoria ○ EAK 212-213 D 3
Port-Vila ★• VAN 184 II b 3
Port Vincent ○ AUS 180-181 D 3
Port Wakefield ○ AUS 180-181 E 3
Port Washington ○ USA (WI) 274-275 L 1
Port Welshpool ○ AUS 180-181 J 5
Port Wing ○ USA (WI) 270-271 G 4
Porvij, mys ▲ RUS 108-109 P 6
Poruk Çayı ~ TR 128-129 D 3
Porumamilla ○ IND 140-141 H 3
Porvenir ○ 64-65 B 10
Porvenir ○ BOL 70-71 C 2
Porvenir ○ PE 64-65 D 3
Porvenir ○ RCH 80 E 6
Porvenir, El ○ MEX 50-51 G 2
Porvenir, El ☆ PA 52-53 E 7
Porvenir, El ○ YV (APU) 60-61 G 4
Porvenir, El ○ YV (BAR) 60-61 F 4
Posadas ☆ RA 76-77 K 4
Pošegda ○ RUS 88-89 R 5
Pošehon'e ○ RUS 94-95 Q 2
Pošehon'e-Volodarsk = Pošehon'e ○ RUS 94-95 Q 2
Poseidon, Temple of •• GR 100-101 K 6
Posen ○ USA (MI) 272-273 F 2
Posesión, Bahía ≈ 80 F 6
Posevnaja ○ RUS 124-125 N 1
Poshkokagan River ~ CDN 234-235 O 5
Posik, Pulau ⌒ RI 162-163 F 5
Posio ○ FIN 88-89 K 3
Posiposi ○ RI 164-165 L 2
Posito, El ∴• BH 52-53 K 3
Poso ○ RI 164-165 G 4
Poso, Danau ○ RI 164-165 G 4
Posof ☆ TR 128-129 K 2
Posŏng ○ ROK 150-151 F 10
Posorja ○ EC 64-65 B 3
Pospeliha ○ RUS 124-125 M 3
Posse ○ BR 72-73 G 3
Possel ○ RCA 206-207 D 6
Possession, Point ▲ USA 20-21 P 6
Possessioneiland ⌒ NAM 220-221 B 3
Possoš' ○ RUS 102-103 L 2
Possum Kingdom Lake ○ USA (TX) 264-265 F 6
Post ○ USA (OR) 244-245 E 6
Post ○ USA (TX) 264-265 C 5
Posta Cambio a Zalazar ○ RA 76-77 G 3
Posta Km. 45 ○ RA 76-77 G 3
Posta Lencina ○ RA 76-77 G 3
Post Arinda ○ GUY 62-63 E 3
Poste-de-la-Baleine ○ CDN 36-37 L 7
Post Falls ○ USA (ID) 250-251 C 4
Postmasburg ○ ZA 220-221 F 4
Posto Ajuricaba ○ BR 66-67 F 2
Postoak ○ USA (MO) 274-275 E 6
Posto Cocraimore ○ BR 68-69 B 6
Post Office Tree • ZA 220-221 F 7
Posto Funai ○ BR 62-63 D 6
Posto Funai ○ BR (AMA) 62-63 E 6
Posto Funai ○ BR (AMA) 62-63 D 6
Posto Funai ○ BR (AMA) 64-65 F 4
Posto Funai ○ BR (APA) 62-63 J 4
Postojna ○ SLO 100-101 E 2
Postojnska jama •• SLO 100-101 E 2
Posto Uaçá ○ BR 62-63 J 4
Postrervalle ○ BOL 70-71 F 6
Postville ○ USA (IA) 274-275 G 1
Pota ○ RI 168 E 7
Potato Creek ~ USA 284-285 F 4
Potawatomi Indian Reservation ✕ USA (KS) 262-263 L 5
Potchefstroom ○ ZA 220-221 H 3
Potčurk, gora ▲ RUS 88-89 W 5
Poté ○ BR 72-73 K 4
Poteau ○ USA (OK) 264-265 K 3
Poteau Mountain ▲ USA 276-277 A 6
Poteau River ~ USA 264-265 K 3
Poteet ○ USA (TX) 266-267 J 4
Potengi ○ BR 68-69 H 5
Potenji, Rio ~ BR 68-69 K 4
Potenza ☆• I 100-101 E 4
Potfontein ○ ZA 220-221 G 5
Potgietersrus ○ ZA 220-221 J 2
Poth ○ USA (TX) 266-267 J 4
Potherie, Lac la ○ CDN 36-37 N 5
Potholes Reservoir ○ USA (WA) 244-245 F 3
Poti ○• GE 126-127 D 6
Poti, Rio ~ BR 68-69 G 4
Potidaia • GR 100-101 J 4
Potiguara, Área Indígena ✕ BR 68-69 L 5
Potimalal, Río ~ RA 78-79 D 4
Potin ○ IND 142-143 H 2
Potiragua ○ BR 72-73 L 3
Potiskum ○ WAN 204-205 J 3
Pot Jostler Creek ~ AUS 178-179 F 2
Potlatch ○ USA (ID) 250-251 C 5
Pot Mountain ▲ USA (ID) 250-251 D 5
Potol Point ▲ RP 160-161 D 7
Potomac River ~ USA 280-281 J 4
Potomac River ~ USA 280-281 K 5
Potoru ○ WAL 202-203 D 6
Potosí ☆ BOL 70-71 E 6
Potosí ○ NIC 52-53 L 5
Potosi ○ USA (MO) 276-277 E 3
Potosi, Río ~ MEX 50-51 K 5
Pototan ○ RP 160-161 E 7
Potrerillos ○ RA 78-79 E 2
Potrerillos, Río ~ RCH 76-77 B 5
Potrero ○ USA (CA) 248-249 H 7
Potrero de Gallegos ○ MEX 50-51 H 6
Potrero del Llano ○ MEX 50-51 G 3

Pojasovyj kamen' hrebet — Potrero del Llano 379

Puerto Sandino ○ NIC 52-53 L 5
Puerto San Julián ○ RA 80 G 4
Puerto San Martín ○ PE 64-65 D 8
Puerto Santa Cruz ○ RA 80 F 5
Puerto Saucedo ○ BOL 70-71 F 3
Puerto Siles ○ BOL 70-71 E 3
Puerto Silvania ○ CO 66-67 B 2
Puerto Suarez ○ BOL 70-71 J 6
Puerto Tacurú Pytá ○ PY 76-77 J 2
Puerto Tamborapa ○ PE 64-65 C 4
Puerto Tejada ○ CO 60-61 C 6
Puerto Tumaco = Sabaloyaco ○ EC 64-65 F 3
Puerto Turumbán ○ GUY 62-63 D 2
Puerto Valencia ○ CO 60-61 G 6
Puerto Vallarta ○• MEX 52-53 B 1
Puerto Varas ○ RCH 78-79 C 6
Puerto Victoria ○ PE 64-65 E 6
Puerto Viejo ○ CR (Car) 52-53 C 7
Puerto Viejo ○ CR (HER) 52-53 B 6
Puerto Villamil ○ EC 64-65 B 10
Puerto Visser ○ RA 80 G 2
Puerto Weber ○ RCH 80 D 5
Puerto Williams ○ RCH 80 G 7
Puerto Yahape ○ RA 76-77 J 4
Puerto Yungay ○ RCH 80 D 3
Puesto Avanzado ○ PE 64-65 D 3
Puesto Esperanza ○ PY 76-77 H 2
Pueyrredón, Lago ○ RA 80 E 3
Pugačev ☆ RUS 96-97 F 7
Pugačevo ○ RUS 122-123 K 4
Pugačev muzej uji • KZ 96-97 G 8
Puge ○ VRC 156-157 C 3
Puger ○ RI 168 E 4
Puget Sound ≈ 244-245 C 3
Pugima ○ RI 166-167 K 4
Puglia ▫ I 100-101 E 4
Pugwash ○ CDN (NS) 240-241 M 5
Puhal-e Hamir, Kūh-e ▲ IR 134-135 F 5
Puhos ○ FIN 88-89 K 5
Puiatoq ≈ 28-29 T 6
Puig ○ SUD 206-207 J 4
Puig Major ▲ E 98-99 J 5
Puinahua, Canal de < PE 64-65 E 4
Puir ○ RUS 122-123 J 2
Puissortoq Gletscher ⊂ GRØ 28-29 T 5
Pujehun ○ WAL 202-203 E 6
Pujiang ○ VRC (SIC) 154-155 C 6
Pujiang ○ VRC (ZHE) 156-157 L 2
Pujonryong Sanmaek ▲ KOR 150-151 F 7
Pukaki, Lake ○ NZ 182 C 5
Pukalani ○ USA (HI) 288 J 4
Puk'ansan National Park ⊥ • KOR 150-151 F 9
Pukaskwa National Park ⊥ • CDN (ONT) 236-237 B 4
Pukchong ○ KOR 150-151 G 7
Pukë ☆ • AL 100-101 G 3
Pukekohe ○ NZ 182 E 2
Pukota ○ Z 218-219 E 1
Pukšen'ga ~ RUS 88-89 Q 5
Puksubaek San ▲ KOR 150-151 F 7
Pukuanratu ○ RI 162-163 F 7
Pukuatu, Tanjung ▲ RI 166-167 B 7
Pula ○ HR 100-101 D 2
Pula ○ I 100-101 B 5
Pula, Goi- ○ ZRE 214-215 D 4
Pulai ○ RI 164-165 F 3
Pulaksama ○ RI 102-103 D 3
Pulanduta Point ▲ RP 160-161 E 7
Pulangi ~ RP 160-161 F 9
Pulangpisau ○ RI 164-165 D 5
Pular, Cerro ▲ RCH 76-77 C 3
Pularumpi ☆ AUS 172-173 K 1
Pulasi, Pulau ∩ RI 168 E 6
Pulaski ○ USA (NY) 278-279 E 5
Pulaski ○ USA (TN) 276-277 H 5
Pulaski ○ USA (VA) 280-281 F 6
Pulaski National Monument, Fort • USA (GA) 284-285 K 4
Pulau ○ RI (IRN) 162-163 D 6
Pulau ~ RI 166-167 K 4
Pulau Banding ○ MAL 162-163 D 2
Pulauberingin ○ RI 162-163 E 7
Pulausekopong, Tanjung ▲ RI 162-163 F 7
Pulau Tiga Park ⊥ MAL 160-161 A 10
Puławy ○• PL 92-93 Q 3
Puleowine = Apetina ○ SME 62-63 G 4
Pulguk Sa • ROK 150-151 G 10
Pulicat ○ IND 140-141 J 4
Pulicat Lake ○ IND 140-141 J 4
Pulie River ~ PNG 183 E 3
Pulingom ○ IND 140-141 F 4
Pulisan, Tanjung ▲ RI 164-165 J 3
Pulivendla ○ IND 140-141 H 3
Puliyangudi ○ IND 140-141 G 6
Pulkkila ○ FIN 88-89 H 4
Pullman ○ USA (WA) 244-245 H 4
Pullo ○ PE 64-65 F 9
Pulmoddai ○ CL 140-141 J 6
Pulo Buda ∩ MYA 158-159 E 5
Pulog, Mount ▲ RP 160-161 D 4
Pulozero ○ RUS 88-89 M 2
Pulpit Harbor ○ USA (ME) 278-279 N 4
Pulp River ○ CDN (MAN) 234-235 C 3
Pulpul ○ PNG 183 F 3
Pułtusk ○• PL 92-93 Q 2
Pulu ○ VRC 144-145 C 2
Pülümür ☆ TR 128-129 H 3
Pulupandan ○ RI 164-165 H 5
Puluqui, Isla ∩ RCH 78-79 C 6
Pulwama ○ IND 138-139 E 3
Puma ○ EAT 212-213 E 6
Puma Yumco ○ VRC 144-145 H 6
Pumpville ○ USA (TX) 266-267 F 4
Puna ○ EC 64-65 C 3
Puna, Isla ∩ EC 64-65 B 3
Puna de Argentina ⊥ RA 76-77 D 3
Punakaiki ○ NZ 182 C 5
Punakha ○ BHT 142-143 F 2
Punalür ○ IND 140-141 G 6
Punang ○ MAL 164-165 D 1
Punarupka ○ PNG 183 F 3
Punāsa ○ IND 138-139 F 8
Punata ○ BOL 70-71 E 5
Punch ○ IND 138-139 E 3
Punch ○ IND 138-139 E 3
Punchaw ○ CDN (BC) 228-229 L 3
Punda Hamlets ○ PNG 183 A 2
Punda Maria ○ ZA 218-219 F 6
Pundanhar ○ MOC 214-215 L 6
Pune ○• IND 138-139 D 10
Punei, Tanjung ▲ RI 162-163 F 6
Pungai, Kampung ○ MAL 162-163 F 4
Pungali ~ RUS 112-113 H 4
Pungalina ○ AUS 174-175 D 5
Punganuru ○ IND 140-141 H 4
Punggaluku ○ RI 164-165 H 6
Pungo Andongo ○ ANG 216-217 C 4
Púngoe ~ MOC 218-219 G 4
Púngoè, Rio ~ MOC 218-219 G 4
Pungo National Wildlife Refuge ⊥ USA (NC) 282-283 L 5
Pungo River ~ USA 282-283 L 5
Pungwe Falls ~ • ZW 218-219 G 4
Punia ○ ZRE 210-211 L 4
Punilla, La ○ RCH 78-79 D 4
Punilla, Sierra de la ▲ RA 76-77 C 5
Puning ○ VRC 156-157 K 5
Punja ○ RUS 116-117 J 6
Punjab ▫ PK 138-139 C 4
Punkaharju ○ FIN 88-89 K 6
Punkalaidun ○ FIN 88-89 G 6
Punkasalmi = Punkaharju ○ FIN 88-89 K 6
Punkin Center ○ USA (CO) 254-255 M 5
Puno ☆ • PE 70-71 B 4
Punos ○ PE 64-65 D 6
Punrun, Lago ○ PE 64-65 D 7
Punta, La ○ RA 76-77 E 5
Punta Alegre ○ C 54-55 F 3
Punta Allen ○ MEX 52-53 L 2
Punta Alta ○ RA 78-79 H 5
Punta Arenas ☆ RCH 80 E 6
Punta Arenas, Caleta ≈ 76-77 B 1
Punta Cana ○ DOM 54-55 L 5
Punta Cardón ○ YV 60-61 F 2
Punta Chame ○ PA 52-53 E 7
Punta Corral ○ RA 76-77 F 5
Punta de Balosto ○ RA 76-77 D 4
Punta de Bombon ○ PE 70-71 B 5
Punta de Díaz ○ RCH 76-77 B 5
Punta del Agua ○ RA 78-79 E 3
Punta del Este ○ C 54-55 D 4
Punta Delgada ○ RA 78-79 H 7
Punta Delgada ○ RCH 80 F 6
Punta de los Llanos ○ RA 76-77 D 6
Punta del Viento ○ RCH 76-77 B 5
Punta Eugenia ○ MEX 50-51 B 4
Punta Gorda ○ BH 52-53 K 3
Punta Gorda ○ USA (FL) 286-287 G 5
Punta Gorda, Playa ⊥ • DOM 54-55 L 5
Punta Negra, Salar ○ RCH 76-77 C 3
Punta Norte ○ RA 78-79 H 7
Punta Nueva ○ YV 60-61 K 4
Punta Piaroa ○ YV 60-61 J 6
Puntarenas ☆ • CR 52-53 B 7
Puntas Negras, Cordon de ▲ RCH 76-77 D 2
Punta Sur del Cabo San Antonio ▲ RA 78-79 L 4
Puntawolana, Lake ○ AUS 178-179 E 5
Punto Alegre ○ BR 62-63 J 6
Punto Catatumbo ○ YV 60-61 E 3
Punto da Barca ○ BR 62-63 K 6
Punto Fijo ○ YV 60-61 F 2
Punto M.O.P. ○ YV 60-61 K 6
Punxsutawney ○ USA (PA) 280-281 H 3
Puolanka ○ FIN 88-89 J 4
Puponga ○ NZ 182 D 4
Puprl ○ IND 142-143 D 2
Puquan ○ RI 168 B 7
Pupunhas, Ilha ∩ BR 66-67 F 6
Pupū Pu'e National Parc ⊥ WS 184 V b 1
Pupyr, mys ▲ RUS 112-113 M 5
Puqi ○ VRC 156-157 H 2
Puquina ○ PE 70-71 B 5
Puquio ○ PE 64-65 E 9
Pur ~ RUS 108-109 S 8
Pur ~ RUS 114-115 O 2
Pura ~ RUS 108-109 W 5
Puraca, Cachoeira da ~ BR 66-67 H 6
Puracé, Parque Nacional ⊥ CO 60-61 C 6
Puracé, Volcán ▲ CO 60-61 C 6
Purándiro ○ MEX 52-53 D 1
Purangarh ○ IND 140-141 E 2
Puranpur ○ IND 144-145 C 6
Puraquê Ponta ○ BR 66-67 C 2
Purari River ~ PNG 183 C 4
Purbalingga ○ RI 168 C 3
Purcell ○ USA (OK) 264-265 G 3
Purcell Mountains ▲ CDN 230-231 M 2
Purcell Wilderness Conservancy ⊥ • CDN (BC) 230-231 N 3
Purchase Bay ≈ 24-25 N 3
Purchena ○ E 98-99 F 6
Purdum ○ USA (NE) 262-263 F 2
Purdy Islands ∩ PNG 183 D 2
Pure, Rio ~ EC 66-67 C 4
Pureba Conservation Reserve ⊥ AUS 180-181 C 2
Pureh ○ RUS 94-95 S 3
Purepero ○ MEX 52-53 C 2
Puretê ou Purata, Rio ~ BR 66-67 C 4
Purgatoire River ~ USA 254-255 M 6
Purgatorio ○ YV 62-63 D 2
Puri ○ ANG 216-217 C 3
Puri ○•• IND 142-143 D 6
Puricaure ○ YV 60-61 F 2
Purificacion ○ CO 60-61 D 6
Purificación ○ MEX 52-53 B 2
Purificacion, Rio ~ MEX 52-53 B 2
Puring ○ RI 168 C 3
Purinskoe vtoroe, ozero ○ RUS 108-109 X 6
Purísima, La ○ MEX 50-51 C 4
Purma ○ EC 64-65 F 3
Purmamarca ○ RA 76-77 E 2
Purna ○ IND (MAH) 138-139 F 10
Pūrna ~ IND 138-139 F 9
Purnač ~ RUS 88-89 P 3
Pūrnia ○ IND 142-143 E 3
Purnong ○ AUS 180-181 E 3
Purpe ○ RUS (JAN) 114-115 O 2
Purpe ~ RUS 114-115 N 2
Purple Springs ○ CDN (ALB) 232-233 G 6
Purranque ○ RCH 78-79 C 6
Purros ○ NAM 216-217 B 9
Puruarán ○ MEX 52-53 D 2
Puruí, Rio ~ BR 66-67 C 3
Purukcahu ○ RI 164-165 D 4
Puruliya ○ IND 142-143 E 4
Purureche ○ YV 60-61 F 2
Purus, Rio ~ BR 66-67 E 5
Purutu Island ∩ PNG 183 B 5
Pürvāchal ⊥ IND 142-143 H 4
Purvis ○ USA (MS) 268-269 L 5
Purwakarta ○ RI 168 B 3
Purwo, Tanjung ▲ RI 168 B 7
Purwodadi ○ RI 168 D 3
Purwodari ○ RI 168 D 3
Purwokerto ○ RI 168 C 3
Purworejo ○ RI 168 D 3
Puryong ○ KOR 150-151 G 6
Purzell Mount ▲ USA 20-21 M 3
Pusa ○ MAL 162-163 J 4
Pusan ○ ROK 150-151 G 10
Pusat Gajo, Pegunungan ▲ RI 162-163 B 2
Pusegaon ○ IND 140-141 F 2
Pusesāvli ○ IND 140-141 F 2
Pushkar ○ IND 138-139 E 6
Pusisama ○ SOL 184 I c 2
Puškarëva, ostrov ∩ RUS 112-113 L 1
Puškin ○•• RUS 94-95 M 2
Puškino ○ RUS 96-97 E 8
Puškino = Biljasuvar ○ AZ 128-129 N 3
Puskwaskau River ~ CDN 32-33 M 4
Pušlahta ○ RUS 88-89 O 4
Pušma ☆ RUS 114-115 G 6
Pušnoj ○ RUS 88-89 N 4
Pusok Sa • ROK 150-151 G 9
Püspökladány ○ H 92-93 Q 5
Pustaja ~ RUS 120-121 U 3
Pusticamicca, Lac ○ CDN 38-39 F 4
Pusticamicca, Lac ○ CDN (QUE) 236-237 M 3
Pustoška ☆ RUS 94-95 L 3
Pustunich ∴• MEX 52-53 J 2
Pusuga ○ GH 202-203 K 5
Putahow Lake ○ CDN 30-31 T 6
Putahow River ~ CDN 30-31 T 5
Putai ○ RC 156-157 M 5
Putao ○ MYA 142-143 K 2
Puteran, Pulau ∩ RI 168 B 6
Puthein (Bassein) ○ MYA 158-159 C 2
Puthukkudiyiruppu ○ CL 140-141 J 6
Putia ○ RI 166-167 D 3
Putian ○ VRC 156-157 L 4
Putina ○ PE 70-71 C 4
Putina, Rio ~ PE 70-71 C 4
Putineiu ○ RO 102-103 D 6
Puting, Tanjung ▲ RI 162-163 J 6
Putnam ○ USA (CT) 278-279 K 7
Putnam ○ USA (OK) 264-265 F 3
Putnam ○ USA (TX) 264-265 E 6
Putončany ○ RUS 116-117 F 3
Putorana, plato ▲ RUS 108-109 Z 7
Putoranskij zapovednik ⊥ RUS 108-109 a 7
Putre ○ RCH 70-71 C 6
Putre, Nevado de ▲ RCH 70-71 C 6
Putsonderwater ○ ZA 220-221 E 4
Puttalam ○ CL 140-141 H 6
Puttalam Lagoon ≈ 140-141 H 6
Puttgarden ○ D 92-93 L 1
Puttur ○ IND (ANP) 140-141 H 4
Puttur ○ IND (KAR) 140-141 F 4
Putty ○ AUS 180-181 L 2
Putumayo, Río ~ PE 64-65 G 3
Putuoshan • VRC 154-155 N 6
Putus, Tanjung ▲ RI 162-163 H 5
Putusibau ○ RI 162-163 K 4
Putyvl' ○ UA 102-103 H 2
Puuanahulu ○ USA (HI) 288 K 5
Puuhonua o Honaunau National Historical Park ⊥ • USA (HI) 288 K 5
Puukohola Heiau National Historical Park ⊥ • USA (HI) 288 K 5
Puula ○ FIN 88-89 J 6
Puumala ○ FIN 88-89 K 6
Puu Ulaula ▲ USA (HI) 288 J 4
Puuwai ○ USA (HI) 288 E 3
Pu Xian ○ VRC 154-155 G 3
Puxico ○ USA (MO) 276-277 E 4
Puyallup ○ USA (WA) 244-245 C 3
Puyang ○ VRC 154-155 J 4
Puyehue ○ RCH 78-79 C 6
Puyehue, Lago ○ RCH 78-79 C 6
Puyehue, Parque Nacional ⊥ RCH 78-79 C 6
Puyehue, Volcán ▲ RCH 78-79 C 6
Puy-en-Velay, le ☆ • F 90-91 J 9
Puymorens, Col de ▲ F 90-91 H 10
Puyo ☆ EC 64-65 D 2
Puyuguapi, Canal ≈ 80 D 2
Pūzak, Hāmūn-e ○ AFG 134-135 J 3
Puzino ○ RUS 122-123 D 5
Pwalugu ○ GH 202-203 K 4
Pwani ▫ EAT 214-215 K 4
Pweto ○ ZRE 214-215 E 5
Pwllheli ○ GB 90-91 E 5
PWV = Pretoria Witwatersrand Vereeniging ▫ ZA 220-221 H 2
Pyachnung ○ MYA 142-143 J 5
Pyanangazu ○ MYA 142-143 K 5
Pyawbwe ○ MYA 142-143 K 5
Pyechin ○ MYA 142-143 H 6
Pye Islands ∩ USA 20-21 V 3
Pyhäjärvi ○ FIN 88-89 H 5
Pyhäjoki ○ FIN 88-89 H 4
Pyhäjoki ~ FIN 88-89 H 4
Pyhäntä ○ FIN 88-89 J 4
Pyhäselkä ○ FIN 88-89 K 5
Pyhätunturi ▲ FIN 88-89 J 3
Pyingaing ○ MYA 142-143 J 4
Pyinmana ○ MYA 142-143 K 6
Pyjakojajaha ~ RUS 108-109 N 6
Pylema ○ RUS 88-89 S 4
Pylginskij hrebet ▲ RUS 112-113 O 7
Pylgovajam ~ RUS 112-113 O 6
Pymatuning Reservoir ○ USA (PA) 280-281 F 2
Pymatuning State Park ⊥ USA (PA) 280-281 F 2
Pyngan ○ UZ 136-137 M 4
Pyonggang ○ KOR 150-151 F 8
Pyongsan ○ KOR 150-151 F 8
Pyongsong ○ KOR 150-151 E 8
Pyŏngt'aek ○ ROK 150-151 F 9
Pyongyang ★ KOR 150-151 E 8
Pyote ○ USA (TX) 266-267 D 2
Pyramid ○ RI 166-167 K 3
Pyramiden ○ N 84-85 K 3
Pyramid Hill ○ AUS 180-181 H 4
Pyramid Lake ○ AUS 176-177 F 6
Pyramid Lake ○ USA (NV) 246-247 F 3
Pyramid Lake Indian Reservation ⚔ USA (NV) 246-247 F 3
Pyramids Mountains ▲ USA 256-257 G 6
Pyrénées, Parc National des ⊥ • F 90-91 G 10
Pyrenees = Pyrénées ▲ F 98-99 G 3
Pyre Peak ▲ USA 22-23 K 6
Pyrjatyn ○ UA 102-103 H 2
Pyrkanaj ▲ RUS 112-113 N 2
Pyrzyce ○• PL 92-93 N 2
Pyščyg ○ RUS 96-97 D 4
Pyšma ~ RUS 96-97 M 5
Pyšma ~ RUS 114-115 J 6
Pyssa ~ RUS 88-89 U 4
Pytalovo = Abrene ☆ RUS 94-95 K 3
Pythonga, Lac ○ CDN (QUE) 238-239 J 2
Pyt'-Jah = Pjat'-Jah ○ RUS 114-115 M 4
Pyttegga ▲ N 86-87 C 5
Pyu ○ MYA 142-143 K 6
Pyžina ~ RUS 114-115 R 5

Q

Qa'āmiyāt, al- ⊥ KSA 132-133 E 5
Qaanaaq = Thule ☆ GRØ 26-27 Q 5
Qaarsut ○ GRØ 28-29 O 1
Qab ○ VRC 154-155 E 2
Qabane ○ LS 220-221 J 4
Qabr Hūd ○ Y 132-133 F 5
Qacha's Nek ○ LS 220-221 J 5
Qadom ○ SUD 200-201 D 6
Qadamgāh ○ IR 136-137 F 6
Qadarif, al- ○ SUD 200-201 G 5
Qādes ○ AFG 134-135 K 1
Qadir Purrān ○ PK 138-139 C 4
Qādisīya, al- ▫ IRQ 128-129 L 7
Qādisīya, al- ∴• IRQ 128-129 K 5
Qafa ○ OM 132-133 H 5
Qaffāy, al- ∩ UAE 134-135 D 6
Qagan Nur ○ VRC (NMZ) 154-155 F 2
Qagan Nur ○ VRC (JIL) 150-151 E 5
Qagan Nur ○ VRC (NMZ) 148-149 M 6
Qagcaka ○ VRC 144-145 C 4
Qagdlumiut ○ GRØ 28-29 S 6
Qahar Youyi Houqi ○ VRC 148-149 L 7
Qahar Youyi Zhongqi ○ VRC 148-149 L 7
Qahavand ○ IR 134-135 C 1
Qahb, Ġabal al- ▲ KSA 130-131 J 5
Qāhira, al- ★ ••• ET 194-195 E 2
Qahmah, al- ○ KSA 132-133 B 4
Qa'īd, Abū al- ○ KSA 132-133 C 5
Qaidam He ~ VRC 144-145 L 2
Qaidam Pendi ⊥ VRC 146-147 L 6
Qāimšahr ○ IR 136-137 C 6
Qaisār ○ AFG 136-137 J 7
Qaiwain, Umm al- ○ UAE 134-135 F 6
Qā'iya, al- ○ KSA 130-131 H 5
Qala'a, Al ○ LAR 192-193 F 2
Qala'an-Nahl ○ SUD 200-201 G 6
Qalamat Nadqan ○ KSA 132-133 G 2
Qalana ○ Y 132-133 G 6
Qalansiya ○ Y 132-133 H 7
Qalat ○ AFG 134-135 M 2
Qalat al-Hafirah • KSA 130-131 F 5
Qal'at al-Hiṣn ∴ SYR 128-129 G 5
Qal'at al-Mu'azzam ○ KSA 130-131 E 4
Qal'at ar-Rabaḍ ∴• JOR 130-131 D 1
Qalat az Zubaidiyah • KSA 130-131 F 5
Qal'at Ġābir • SYR 128-129 H 5
Qal'at Hamidi ○ IRQ 128-129 L 6
Qal'at Ṣalāhaddin ∴• SYR 128-129 G 5
Qal'at Sālih ☆ IRQ 128-129 M 7
Qal'at Sam'ān •• SYR 128-129 G 4
Qal'at Sukkar ☆ IRQ 128-129 M 7
Qal'a-ye Nau ☆ AFG 136-137 H 7
Qal'e Dize ☆ IRQ 128-129 L 4
Qal'e Ra'isi ○ IR 134-135 D 3
Qal'e-ye Kāh ○ AFG 134-135 J 2
Qal'e-ye Mīr Dāvūd ○ AFG 134-135 K 1
Qal'e-ye Panğe ○ AFG 136-137 N 6
Qalhāt ○ OM 132-133 L 2
Qalība, al- ○ KSA 130-131 E 3
Qalluviartuuq, Lac ○ CDN 36-37 M 5
Qalti al-Adusa ○ SUD 200-201 C 4
Qalti al-Khudaira ○ SUD 200-201 C 4
Qalti Immaseri ○ SUD 200-201 B 5
Qalyūb ○ ET 194-195 E 2
Qambar ○ PK 134-135 M 5
Qamdo ○ VRC 144-145 L 5
Qamea ∩ FJI 184 III c 2
Qaminis ○•• LAR 192-193 J 2
Qāmišli, al- ☆ SYR 128-129 J 4
Qamsar ○ IR 134-135 D 2
Qanā ○ KSA 130-131 G 4
Qandahār ▫ AFG 134-135 L 3
Qandahār ☆• AFG (QA) 134-135 L 3
Qandala ○ SP 208-209 J 3
Qaqortoq = Julianehab ○ GRØ 28-29 R 6
Qāra ○ ET 194-195 C 3
Qāra ○ KSA 130-131 G 3
Qarā', Ġabal al- ▲ OM 132-133 H 5
Qara Āġaǰ, Rūdḫāne-ye ~ IR 134-135 E 4
Qarabāġ ○ AFG (ĠA) 138-139 B 3
Qarabāġ ○ AFG (HE) 134-135 J 1
Qarabāġ ○ AFG (KB) 138-139 B 2
Qara Čāy ~ IR 128-129 N 5
Qara Dāġ ▲ IR 128-129 M 3
Qara Dāġ ▲ IRQ 128-129 L 5
Qaraghandy = Karaġandy ☆ KZ 124-125 H 4
Qarah Dāġ ▲ IRQ 128-129 K 4
Qarajaqs Isfjord ≈ 28-29 P 1
Qaramqol ○ AFG 136-137 J 6
Qarānqū, Rūd-e ~ IR 128-129 M 4
Qara Qash ~ IND 138-139 G 2
Qarārat al Hayyirah ~ LAR 192-193 F 4
Qarārat an Nā'ikah ○ LAR 192-193 H 4
Qara Sū ~ IR 134-135 B 1
Qar'āt ad Dibah, Bi'r < LAR 190-191 G 6
Qardabah, Al ○ LAR 192-193 K 1
Qardho ○ SP 208-209 J 4
Qardlit Ikerat ≈ 28-29 V 4
Qare Āġāj ○ IR 128-129 M 4
Qare Sū ~ IR 136-137 E 6
Qare Ẓiyā'od-Dīn ○ IR 128-129 L 3
Qarhan ○ VRC 144-145 K 2
Qārloq ○ IR 136-137 E 6
Qarqāi ○ AFG 138-139 C 2
Qarqan He ~ VRC 146-147 H 6
Qarqaraut, Wādī ~ Y 132-133 G 6
Qārūn, Birkat ○ ET 194-195 E 3
Qaryah ash Sharqiyah, Al ○ LAR 192-193 E 2
Qaryās, Bi'r ○ LAR 192-193 G 3
Qaryat Abū Nujaym ○ LAR 192-193 F 2
Qaryat Abū Qurays ○ LAR 192-193 F 2
Qaryatain, al- ○ SYR 128-129 G 5
Qaryat al Fā'idiyah ○ LAR 192-193 J 1
Qaryat al-'Ulyā ○ KSA 130-131 K 4
Qaryat az Zuwaytīnah ○ LAR 192-193 J 2
Qaryat Shumaykh ○ LAR 192-193 E 2
Qarzah, Wādī ~ LAR 192-193 E 2
Qaṣab, Wādī ~ IRQ 128-129 K 5
Qaṣabāt, Al ○ LAR 192-193 F 1
Qaṣabe ▲ IR 128-129 M 3
Qasi bu Hadi ○ LAR 192-193 G 2
Qasigiannguit = Christianshåb ○ GRØ 28-29 P 2
Qasir, Sabhat al- ○ SYR 128-129 J 5
Qaṣr al-Farāfira ○ ET 194-195 C 4
Qaṣr al-Ḥair • SYR 128-129 H 5
Qaṣr al-Ḥair al-Ġarbī ∴• SYR 128-129 G 5
Qaṣr al-Harāna ∴• JOR 130-131 E 2
Qaṣr al Jady ○ LAR 192-193 L 2
Qaṣr al Khamrah ○ LAR 192-193 J 1
Qaṣr al-Mušattā ∴• JOR 130-131 E 2
Qaṣr al Qarn ○ LAR 192-193 L 2
Qaṣr 'Amīq ○ IRQ 128-129 J 6
Qaṣr ash Shaqqah ○ LAR 192-193 L 2
Qaṣr at-Tūbā ∴• JOR 130-131 E 2
Qaṣr-e Qand ○ IR 134-135 J 5
Qaṣr-e Šīrīn ○• IR 134-135 A 1
Qaṣr Ibn Rashid Palace • KSA 130-131 G 4
Qaṣrik ○ IR 128-129 L 3
Qaṣr Šaqra ∴• IRQ 130-131 K 2
Qassiarsuk ○ GRØ 28-29 S 6
Qassim, al- ▫ KSA 130-131 H 5
Qāt, Bi'r al ○ LAR 192-193 F 3
Qa'taba ○ Y 132-133 D 7
Qaṭanā ○ SYR 128-129 G 6
Qatar = Qaṭar ■ Q 134-135 D 6
Qaṭīf, al- ○ KSA 134-135 D 5
Qaṭīf, Bi'r al ○ LAR 192-193 E 3
Qatlīš ○ IR 136-137 E 6
Qaṭn, al- ○ KSA 130-131 K 6
Qaṭn, al- ○ Y 132-133 F 6
Qaṭrāna, al- ○ JOR 130-131 E 2
Qaṭrānī, Ġabal ▲ ET 194-195 E 3
Qaṭrūn, Al ○ LAR 192-193 F 5
Qaṭrūye ○ IR 134-135 F 4
Qaṭṭār, Ġabal ▲ ET 194-195 F 4
Qattara Depression = Qaṭṭāra, Munhafad al ⊥ ET 194-195 C 3
Qaṭṭūsah, Sarīr al ⊥ LAR 192-193 F 4
Qawām al-Ḥamza ○ IRQ 128-129 L 7
Qawz Rajab ○ SUD 200-201 G 4
Qāyen ○• IR 134-135 H 2
Qaysan ○ SUD 208-209 B 3
Qayyāra ○ IRQ 128-129 K 5
Qazvīn ○• IR 128-129 N 4
Qeersorfik = Ikamiut ○ GRØ 28-29 P 2
Qelelevu ∩ FJI 184 III c 2
Qeqertaq ○ GRØ (VGR) 28-29 P 1
Qeqertaq ∩ GRØ (VGR) 26-27 X 8
Qeqertarssuaq ∩ GRØ (VGR) 26-27 Y 8
Qeqertarssuaq ∩ GRØ (VGR) 26-27 X 7
Qeqertarsuaq = Godhavn ○ GRØ 28-29 O 2
Qeqertarsuatsiaat = Fiskenæsset ○ GRØ 28-29 P 5
Qeqertat ○ GRØ 26-27 R 5
Qerri ○ SUD 200-201 F 4
Qešm ○• IR 134-135 G 5
Qešm, Ğazīre-ye ∩ IR 134-135 G 5
Qezaltepeque ○ ES 52-53 K 5
Qezel ○ AFG 134-135 M 1
Qezel Ūzan, Rūd-e ~ IR 128-129 M 4
Qezel Ūzan Qoli, Čam-e ~ IR 128-129 M 5
Qian'an ○ VRC 150-151 E 5
Qianarteq ∩ GRØ 28-29 W 4
Qiandaohu • VRC 156-157 L 2
Qianfoshan • VRC 154-155 K 3
Qianfo Yan • VRC 154-155 D 5
Qianheshangyuan ○ VRC 154-155 F 3
Qianjiang ○ VRC (HUB) 154-155 H 6
Qianjiang ○ VRC (SIC) 156-157 F 2
Qianjin ○ VRC 150-151 J 4
Qian Ling ∴• VRC 154-155 F 4
Qianshan ○ VRC (ANH) 154-155 K 6
Qianshan ○ VRC (GDG) 156-157 J 5
Qian Shan ▲ VRC 150-151 D 7
Qianshan • VRC (LIA) 150-151 D 7
Qianwei ○ VRC 156-157 C 2
Qianxi ○ VRC 156-157 E 3
Qian Xian ○ VRC 154-155 F 4
Qianyang ○ VRC (HUN) 156-157 G 3
Qianyang ○ VRC (SXI) 154-155 E 4
Qiaochuan ○ VRC 154-155 E 3
Qiaojiang ○ VRC 156-157 E 5
Qiaojia ○ VRC 156-157 C 3
Qiaojian ○ VRC 156-157 E 5
Qiaowan ○ VRC 148-149 C 7
Qiaozhen ○ VRC 154-155 F 3
Qichoi ○ VRC 156-157 F 6
Qichun ○ VRC 154-155 J 6
Qidong ○ VRC 154-155 M 6
Qidugou ○ VRC 144-145 K 3
Qiemo ○ VRC 146-147 G 6
Qift ○ ET 194-195 F 5
Qijiang ○ VRC 156-157 E 2
Qijiaojing ○ VRC 146-147 K 4
Qila Didār Singh ○ PK 138-139 E 3
Qila Lādgasht ○ PK 134-135 K 5
Qilaotu Shan ▲ VRC 148-149 O 6
Qila Saifullāh ○ PK 138-139 B 4
Qilian ○ VRC 154-155 B 2
Qilian Shan ▲ VRC 146-147 N 6
Qilian Shan ▲ VRC (GAN) 146-147 O 6
Qilwa ○ KSA 132-133 B 4
Qimen ○ VRC 156-157 K 2
Qina ☆ ET 194-195 F 4
Qinā, Wādī ~ ET 194-195 F 4
Qin'an ○ VRC 154-155 D 4
Qin Binmayong ∴••• VRC 154-155 F 4
Qing'an ○ VRC 150-151 F 4
Qingdao ☆ VRC 154-155 M 3
Qing Donling • VRC 154-155 K 1
Qinggang ○ VRC 150-151 F 4
Qinghai ▫ VRC 144-145 J 2
Qinghai Hu ○ VRC 144-145 M 2
Qinghai Nanshan ▲ VRC 144-145 M 2
Qinghe ○ VRC (HEB) 154-155 J 3
Qinghe ○ VRC (XUZ) 146-147 K 2
Qingjian ○ VRC 154-155 G 3
Qing Jiang ~ VRC 154-155 G 6
Qingkou ○ VRC 156-157 E 3
Qinglan • VRC 156-157 G 7
Qinglong ○ VRC 154-155 L 1
Qinglong D. • VRC 156-157 F 3
Qingping ○ VRC 156-157 F 6
Qingpu ○ VRC 154-155 M 6
Qingshan ○ VRC 154-155 J 6
Qingshizoi ○ VRC 154-155 B 3
Qingshui ○ VRC 154-155 E 4
Qingshuihe ○ VRC (NMZ) 154-155 G 2
Qingshuihe ○ VRC (QIN) 144-145 L 4
Qingshui He ~ VRC 154-155 E 3
Qingtang ○ VRC 156-157 H 4
Qingtian ○ VRC 156-157 M 2
Qingtongxia ○ VRC 154-155 E 2
Qing Xiling • VRC 154-155 J 2
Qingxu ○ VRC 154-155 H 3
Qingyang ○ VRC (ANH) 154-155 K 6
Qingyang ○ VRC (GAN) 154-155 E 3
Qingyuan ○ VRC (GDG) 156-157 H 5
Qingyuan ○ VRC (LIA) 150-151 E 6
Qingyuanshan • VRC 156-157 L 3
Qingyun Huaxuechang • VRC 150-151 G 5
Qingzhang Gaoyuan ⊂ VRC 144-145 D 4
Qingzhen ○ VRC 156-157 E 3
Qingzhou ○ VRC 154-155 L 3
Qinhuangdao ○ VRC 154-155 L 2
Qin Ling ▲ VRC 154-155 E 5
Qintang ○ VRC 156-157 F 5
Qinwangiao Shan ▲ VRC 156-157 E 4
Qin Xian ○ VRC 154-155 H 3
Qinyang ○ VRC 154-155 H 4
Qinzhou ○ VRC 156-157 F 6
Qinzhou Wan ≈ 156-157 F 6
Qionghai ○ VRC 156-157 G 7
Qionglai ○ VRC 154-155 C 6
Qionglai Shan ▲ VRC 154-155 C 6
Qiongzhong ○ VRC 156-157 F 7
Qiongzhou Haixia ≈ 156-157 F 6
Qiqian ○ VRC 150-151 C 1
Qiqihar ○ VRC 150-151 D 4
Qiqushan Damiao • VRC 154-155 D 6
Qīr ○ IR 134-135 E 4
Qira ○ VRC 144-145 C 2
Qīsba, Ra's ▲ KSA 130-131 D 3
Qisha ○ VRC 156-157 F 6
Qishu ○ VRC 156-157 F 5
Qīšla, al- ○ IRQ 130-131 L 3
Qišn ○ Y 132-133 G 6
Qitai ○ VRC 146-147 J 4
Qitaihe ○ VRC 150-151 H 5
Qitbīt, Wādī ~ OM 132-133 J 4
Qitian Ling ▲ VRC 156-157 H 4
Qiubei ○ VRC 156-157 D 4
Qiujin ○ VRC 156-157 J 2
Qixia ○ VRC 154-155 M 3
Qiyang ○ VRC 156-157 G 3
Qiyuanshan • VRC 156-157 L 2
Qizhou Liedao ∩ VRC 156-157 G 7
Qogir Feng = K2 ▲ VRC 138-139 F 2
Qoğūr ○ IR 128-129 M 4
Qohrūd, Kūhhā-ye ▲ IR 134-135 D 1
Qoltag ▲ VRC 146-147 J 4
Qom ○•• IR 134-135 D 1
Qom, Rūd-e ~ IR 134-135 D 1
Qomolangma Feng = Mount Everest ▲ VRC 144-145 F 7
Qomše ○• IR 134-135 D 2
Qonggyai ○ VRC 144-145 H 6
Qongkol ○ VRC 146-147 H 5
Qooriga Neegro ≈ 208-209 J 5
Qorqi ○ IR 136-137 F 6
Qōrsungnitsoq ∩ GRØ 28-29 P 2
Qorve ○ IR (HAM) 128-129 N 5
Qorve ○ IR (KOR) 128-129 M 5
Qoryooley ○ SP 212-213 K 3
Qostanay = Kostanaj ☆ KZ 124-125 C 2
Qotābād ○ IR 134-135 E 4
Qotūr ○ IR 128-129 L 3
Qotūr Čāy ~ IR 128-129 L 3
Quabbin Reservoir ○ USA (MA) 278-279 J 6
Quadeville ○ CDN (ONT) 238-239 H 3
Quadra Island ∩ CDN (BC) 230-231 D 3
Quadros, Lagoa dos ○ BR 74-75 E 7
Quaidabad ○ PK 138-139 C 3
Quail ○ USA (TX) 264-265 D 4
Quairading ○ AUS 176-177 D 6
Quakertown ○ USA (PA) 280-281 L 3
Qualicum Beach ○ CDN (BC) 230-231 E 4
Quallene ○ DZ 190-191 C 8
Quambone ○ AUS 178-179 J 6
Quamby ○ AUS 174-175 F 7
Quanah ○ USA (TX) 264-265 E 4
Quân Dao Nam Du ∩ VN 158-159 H 6
Quảng Ngãi ○•• VN 158-159 K 3
Quan Hóa ○ VN 156-157 D 6
Quantico Marine Corps ✕✕ USA (VA) 280-281 J 5
Quanzerbé ○ RN 202-203 L 2
Quanzhou ○ VRC (GXI) 156-157 G 4
Quanzhou ○• VRC (FUJ) 156-157 L 4
Quapaw ○ USA (OK) 264-265 K 2
Qu'Appelle ○ CDN (SAS) 232-233 P 5
Qu'Appelle River ~ CDN 232-233 N 5
Quaqtaq ○ CDN 36-37 P 4
Quaraí ○ BR 76-77 J 6
Quarkoye ○ BF 202-203 J 3
Quarryville ○ USA (PA) 280-281 K 4
Quartier Militaire ○ MS 224 C 7
Quartu Sant'Elena ○ I 100-101 B 5
Quartzite Lake ○ CDN 30-31 W 4
Quartzite Mountain ▲ USA (NV) 248-249 H 2
Quartz Lake ○ CDN (NWT) 24-25 f 5
Quartz Mountain ○ USA (OR) 244-245 E 8
Quartz Mountain State Park ⊥ • USA (OK) 264-265 E 4
Quartzsite ○ USA (AZ) 256-257 A 5
Quathiaski Cove ○ CDN (BC) 230-231 D 3
Quatipuru, Ponta de ▲ BR 68-69 E 2
Quatorze de Abril, Cachoeira ~ BR 62-63 G 5
Quatorze de Abril, Rio ~ BR 70-71 G 2
Quatre Cantons, Lac de = Vierwaldstädtersee ○ CH 92-93 K 5
Quatsino Sound ≈ 32-33 F 6
Quatsino Sound ≈ 230-231 A 3
Quay ○ USA (NM) 256-257 M 4
Qubayyat, al- ○ RL 128-129 G 5
Qubbah, Al ○• LAR 192-193 K 1
Qūčān ○• IR 136-137 F 6
Qudaih ○ KSA 134-135 D 5
Quds, al- = Yerushalayim ★••• IL 130-131 D 2
Qué ~ ANG 216-217 C 7
Queanbeyan ○ AUS 180-181 K 3
Québec ▫ CDN 38-39 F 3
Québec ★ ••• CDN (QUE) 238-239 O 2
Quebo ○ GNB 202-203 C 4
Quebra-Anzol, Rio ~ BR 72-73 G 5
Quebracho ○ ROU 76-77 J 6
Quebrada Arriba ○ YV 60-61 F 2
Quebrada de los Cuervos • ROU 78-79 M 2
Quebrada Honda ○ CR 52-53 B 6
Quedas ○ MOC 218-219 G 4
Quedas do Iguaçu ○ BR 74-75 D 5
Quedas do Lúrio ~• MOC 218-219 L 1
Quedlinburg ○•• D 92-93 L 3
Queen, De ○ USA (AR) 276-277 A 6
Queen Alexandra Range ▲ ARK 16 E 0
Queen Bess, Mount ▲ CDN (BC) 230-231 E 2
Queen Charlotte Bay ≈ 78-79 K 6
Queen Charlotte City ○ CDN (BC) 228-229 B 3
Queen Charlotte Islands ∩ CDN (BC) 228-229 C 4
Queen Charlotte Islands ∩ CDN (BC) 228-229 A 3
Queen Charlotte Islands Museum • CDN (BC) 228-229 C 3
Queen Charlotte Mountains ▲ CDN 228-229 B 4
Queen Charlotte Sound ≈ 228-229 D 5
Queen Charlotte Strait ≈ 32-33 G 6
Queen Charlotte Strait ≈ 230-231 B 2
Queen City ○ USA (MO) 274-275 F 4
Queen Elizabeth Islands ∩ CDN 16 B 30
Queen Elizabeth National Park ⊥ EAU 212-213 B 4
Queen Lake, De ~ USA 276-277 A 6
Queen Mary Land ⊥ ARK 16 G 10
Queen Maud Gulf ≈ 24-25 U 6
Queens Bay ○ CDN (BC) 230-231 N 4
Queens Cape ▲ CDN 36-37 R 2
Queens Channel ≈ 24-25 X 2
Queens Channel ≈ 172-173 J 3
Queenscliff ○ AUS 180-181 H 5
Queensferry ○• GB 90-91 F 4
Queensland ▫ AUS 174-175 E 6
Queenslander II AUS 174-175 K 7
Queensland Plateau ≃ 13 F 4
Queensport ○ CDN (NS) 240-241 O 5
Queens Sound ≈ 230-231 A 2
Queenstown ○ AUS 180-181 H 7
Queenstown ○ CDN (ALB) 232-233 F 5
Queenstown ○ NZ 182 B 6
Queenstown ○ ZA 220-221 H 5
Queen Victoria Rock ▲ AUS 176-177 F 5
Que'ergou ○ VRC 146-147 H 4
Queets ○ USA (WA) 244-245 A 3
Queguay Grande, Río ~ ROU 78-79 L 2
Quehue ○ PE 70-71 B 4
Quehué ○ RA 78-79 G 4
Quehué, Valle de ~ RA 78-79 G 4
Queidār ○ IR 128-129 N 4
Queilén ○ RCH 78-79 C 7
Queimadas ○ BR (BAH) 68-69 J 7
Queimadas ○ BR (PA) 68-69 L 5
Queirós ○ BR 72-73 E 6
Queiros, Cape ▲ VAN 184 II a 2
Quela ○ ANG 216-217 D 4
Quélé ○ CI 202-203 G 4
Quelele ○ ANG 216-217 E 4
Quelimane ☆ MOC 218-219 J 3
Quellón ○ RCH 78-79 C 7
Quellouno ○ PE 64-65 F 8
Quelo ○ ANG 216-217 B 3
Queluz ○ BR 72-73 H 7
Quemado ○ USA (NM) 256-257 G 4
Quemado ○ USA (TX) 266-267 G 5
Quemado, Cerro ▲ CO 60-61 D 2

Puerto Sandino — Quemado, Cerro 381

Quemado de Güines o C 54-55 E 3
Quemados, Punta de ▲ C 54-55 H 4
Quembo ~ ANG 216-217 E 7
Quemchi o RCH 78-79 C 7
Quemu Quemu o RA 78-79 H 4
Quenco, Cerro ▲ BOL 76-77 E 1
Queñoal, Río ~ BOL 76-77 D 2
Quénonisca, Lac o CDN (ONT) 236-237 M 2
Quepe, Río ~ RCH 78-79 C 5
Quê Phong ☆ VN 156-157 D 7
Quepos o CR 52-53 B 7
Quepos, Punta ▲ CR 52-53 B 7
Quequén o RA 78-79 K 5
Quequén Grande, Río ~ RA 78-79 K 5
Quequén Salado, Río ~ RA 78-79 J 5
Querari o CO 66-67 C 2
Querari, Río ~ CO 66-67 B 2
Querco o PE 64-65 E 8
Querência do Norte o BR 72-73 D 7
Querendaro o MEX 52-53 D 2
Querétaro ▫ MEX 52-53 D 1
Quero o EC 64-65 C 2
Querobamba o PE 64-65 F 8
Querocotillo o PE 64-65 C 5
Quesnel o CDN (BC) 228-229 M 4
Quesnel Lake o CDN (BC) 228-229 N 4
Quesnel River ~ CDN 228-229 M 4
Quesso ☆ RCB 210-211 F 3
Questa o USA (NM) 256-257 K 2
Quetico o CDN (ONT) 234-235 N 6
Quetico Lake o CDN (ONT) 234-235 M 6
Quetico Provincial Park ⊥ CDN (ONT) 234-235 M 6
Quetico Provincial Park ⊥ USA (MN) 270-271 G 2
Quetta ☆ • PK 134-135 M 3
Queue de Turtue, Bayou ~ USA 268-269 H 6
Queulat, Parque Nacional ⊥ RCH 80 D 2
Queva, Nevado ▲ RA 76-77 D 3
Queve ~ ANG 216-217 C 5
Quevedo o EC 64-65 C 2
Quevedo, Río ~ EC 64-65 C 2
Quévillon, Lac o CDN (QUE) 236-237 M 3
Quezaltenango ☆ • GCA 52-53 J 4
Quezon o RP 160-161 C 8
Quezon City o RP 160-161 D 5
Quezzam, In- o DZ 198-199 B 3
Qufu o ••• VRC 154-155 K 4
Quiabaya o BOL 70-71 C 4
Quiaca, La o RA 76-77 E 2
Quiahniztlan • MEX 52-53 F 2
Quiba o ZA 220-221 H 5
Quibala o ANG (CZS) 216-217 C 5
Quibala o ANG (ZAI) 216-217 B 3
Quibaxe o ANG 216-217 C 4
Quibdó ☆ CO 60-61 C 5
Quibell o CDN (ONT) 234-235 K 5
Quiberon o F 90-91 F 8
Quibor o YV 60-61 G 3
Quicabo o ANG 216-217 B 4
Quicacha o PE 64-65 F 9
Quiçama, Parque Nacional do ⊥ ANG 216-217 B 4
Quichaura, Cerro ▲ RA 78-79 D 7
Quicksand o USA (KY) 276-277 M 3
Quiculungo o ANG 216-217 C 4
Quidico o RCH 78-79 C 5
Quidong o VRC 166 167 H 3
Quiet Lake o CDN 20-21 Y 6
Quijadas, Sierra las ▲ RA 78-79 F 2
Quijingue o BR 68-69 J 7
Quijotoa o USA (AZ) 256-257 C 6
Quijoux, Col ▲ RCA 206-207 F 4
Quila o MEX 50-51 F 5
Quilán, Cabo ▲ RCH 78-79 B 7
Quilandi o IND 140-141 F 5
Quilca o PE (ARE) 70-71 A 5
Quilca o PE (LIM) 64-65 D 7
Quilcene o USA (WA) 244-245 C 3
Quilchena o CDN (BC) 230-231 J 3
Quilemba o ANG 216-217 B 7
Quilenda o ANG 216-217 C 5
Quilengues o ANG 216-217 C 7
Quillacollo o BOL 70-71 D 5
Quillagua o RCH 76-77 C 1
Quillan o F 90-91 J 10
Quillayute Indian Reservation X USA (WA) 244-245 A 3
Quillen, Río ~ RCH 78-79 C 5
Quill Lake o CDN (SAS) 232-233 O 3
Quill Lakes o CDN (SAS) 232-233 O 4
Quilmes o RA 78-79 K 3
Quilombo dos Dembos o ANG 216-217 C 4
Quilon o • IND 140-141 G 6
Quilpie o AUS 178-179 H 4
Quilpue o RCH 78-79 D 2
Quilua o MOC 218-219 K 3
Quilu Hu o VRC 156-157 C 4
Quimantag ▲ VRC 144-145 H 2
Quimbala o ANG 216-217 C 2
Quimbaya o CO 60-61 D 5
Quimbele o ANG 216-217 D 3
Quimet o CDN (ONT) 234-235 P 6
Quimili o RA 76-77 F 4
Quimome, Río ~ BOL 70-71 G 6
Quimper ☆ • F 90-91 E 8
Quinabucasan Point ▲ RP 160-161 E 5
Quinapondan o RP 160-161 F 7
Quinault o USA (WA) 244-245 B 3
Quinault Indian Reservation X USA (WA) 244-245 A 3
Quinault River ~ USA 244-245 B 3
Quince Mil o PE 70-71 B 3
Quinchao, Isla ⌂ RCH 78-79 C 7
Quinché, Raudal ~ CO 66-67 B 3
Quincy o USA (FL) 286-287 E 1
Quincy o USA (IL) 274-275 G 5
Quincy o USA (MA) 278-279 L 6
Quincy o USA (WA) 244-245 F 3
Quincy, De o USA (LA) 268-269 G 6
Quincy Hills ▲ USA 274-275 G 5
Quines o RA 78-79 G 2
Quinga o MOC 218-219 L 2
Quingenge o ANG 216-217 C 6
Quinhagak o USA 22-23 Q 3
Quinhámel o GNB 202-203 C 4
Quiniluban Group ⌂ RP 160-161 D 7
Quinjalca o PE 64-65 D 5
Quinkan Nature Reserve ⊥ AUS 174-175 H 4
Quinlan o USA (TX) 264-265 H 6
Quinn River ~ USA 246-247 G 2
Quinns Rocks o AUS 176-177 C 5
Quinota o PE 64-65 F 9
Quintana de la Serena o E 98-99 E 5
Quintana Roo ▫ MEX 52-53 K 2
Quintana Roo, Parque Nacional de ⊥ MEX 52-53 L 1
Quinter o USA (KS) 262-263 F 5
Quintero o RCH 78-79 D 2
Quintero, Bahía ≈ 78-79 D 2
Quintín Banderas o C 54-55 E 3
Quinto, Río ~ RA 78-79 G 2
Quinton o CDN (SAS) 232-233 O 4
Quinton o USA (OK) 264-265 J 3
Quinzala o ANG 216-217 C 3
Quinzau o ANG 216-217 B 3
Quionga o MOC 214-215 L 6
Quiongua o ANG 216-217 C 4
Quiotepec o MEX 52-53 F 3
Quipapa o BR 68-69 K 6
Quipeio o ANG 216-217 C 6
Quipungo o ANG 216-217 C 7
Quiriguá ∴••• GCA 52-53 K 4
Quirihué o RCH 78-79 C 4
Quirima o ANG 216-217 E 5
Quirindi o AUS 178-179 L 6
Quiriñeo, Cerro ▲ RCH 78-79 D 3
Quirinópolis o BR 72-73 E 5
Quiriquire o YV 60-61 K 3
Quiroga o BOL 70-71 E 6
Quiroga o MEX 52-53 D 2
Quiroga o RA 78-79 J 3
Quiroga, Punta ▲ RA 78-79 G 7
Quiros o YV 60-61 F 2
Quirpon o CDN (NFL) 242-243 N 1
Quiruvilca o PE 64-65 C 5
Quisquiro, Salar de o RCH 76-77 D 2
Quissanga o MOC 214-215 L 7
Quissico o MOC 220-221 M 2
Quitandinha o BR 74-75 F 5
Quitapa o ANG 216-217 E 5
Quitaque o USA (TX) 264-265 C 4
Quiterajo o MOC 214-215 L 6
Quitéria, Rio ~ BR 72-73 E 5
Quiteve o ANG 216-217 C 8
Quitexe o ANG 216-217 C 3
Quitilipi o RA 76-77 G 4
Quitman o USA (AR) 276-277 C 5
Quitman o USA (GA) 284-285 G 6
Quitman o USA (LA) 268-269 H 4
Quitman o USA (MS) 268-269 M 4
Quitman o USA (TX) 264-265 J 6
Quitman Ruins, Fort • USA (TX) 266-267 B 2
Quito ☆ ••• EC 64-65 C 2
Quivira National Wildlife Refuge ⊥ USA (KS) 262-263 H 6
Quivolgo o RCH 78-79 C 3
Quixadá o BR 66-67 D 7
Quixada o BR 68-69 J 4
Quixaxe o MOC 218-219 L 2
Quixeramobim o BR 68-69 J 4
Quizenga o ANG 216-217 C 4
Qujiang o VRC 156-157 H 4
Qujing o VRC 156-157 C 4
Qulin o USA (MO) 276-277 E 4
Qulita, Umm o Y 132-133 E 7
Qumar He ~ VRC 144-145 J 3
Qumar Heyan o VRC 144-145 J 3
Qumarlêb o VRC 144-145 K 3
Qummāh, Ğazīrat ⌂ KSA 132-133 B 5
Qunaiṭira, al- ☆ SYR 128-129 F 6
Qunfuḏa, al- o KSA 132-133 B 4
Quobba o AUS 176-177 B 2
Quobba, Point ▲ AUS 176-177 B 2
Quoich River ~ CDN 30-31 W 2
Quoin, Du o USA (IL) 274-275 J 6
Quoin Head ▲ AUS 176-177 B 2
Quoin Island ⌂ AUS 172-173 J 3
Quoy, Pulau ⌂ RI 166-167 F 1
Qurayd o SUD 206-207 K 3
Qurayyāt o • OM 132-133 L 2
Qurayyāt, al- ▫ KSA 130-131 E 3
Qurayyāt, al- ☆ • KSA (QUR) 130-131 E 2
Qurdūd o SUD 206-207 J 3
Qureida o SUD 206-207 G 3
Qurna, al- ☆ IRQ 128-129 M 7
Qurnat as-Saudā' ▲ RL 128-129 G 5
Qurrāsah o SUD 200-201 F 5
Qūs o • ET 194-195 F 5
Quṣaiba o IRQ 128-129 J 5
Quṣair, al- o IRQ 130-131 J 2
Quṣair, al- ☆ SYR 128-129 G 5
Qusair 'Amra ∴••• JOR 130-131 E 2
Qusay'ir o Y 132-133 G 6
Qusum o VRC 144-145 J 6
Qutaifa, al- ☆ SYR 128-129 G 6
Qutau ▲ KZ 124-125 K 4
Qutdligssat o GRØ 28-29 O 1
Qutdlikorssuit ⌂ GRØ 26-27 W 7
Quthing = Moyeni o LS 220-221 H 5
Qutsigsormiut ⌂ GRØ 28-29 U 5
Quṭū', Ğazīrat ⌂ KSA 132-133 B 4
Quṭūf o UAE 132-133 H 2
Quwair, al- o IRQ 128-129 K 4
Quwāra, al- o KSA 130-131 H 4
Quwu Shan ▲ VRC 154-155 D 3
Qu Xian o VRC 154-155 E 6
Qüxü o VRC 144-145 H 6
Quyāğū o IRQ 128-129 L 5
Quyang o VRC 154-155 J 2
Quyanghai SK o VRC 156-157 H 4
Quynh Lu'u o VN 156-157 D 7
Quy Nho'n ☆ • VN 158-159 K 4
Qūz, al- o KSA 132-133 B 4
Qūz, al- o Y 132-133 G 6
Quza, al- o Y 132-133 F 6
Quzhou o VRC 156-157 L 2
Qwa Qwa (former Homeland, now part of Oranje Vrystaat) ▫ ZA 220-221 G 4
Qyzylorda = Kyzylorda ☆ KZ 124-125 D 6

R

Raab ~ A 92-93 N 5
Raahe o FIN 88-89 H 4
Raanes Peninsula ⌂ CDN 26-27 G 4
Raanujärvi o FIN 88-89 H 3
Raas, Pulau ⌂ RI 168 B 6
Raattama o FIN 88-89 H 2
Rab o • HR 100-101 E 2
Rab ⌂ •• HR 100-101 E 2
Raba o • RI 168 D 7
Rabaable o SP 208-209 J 4
Rabad, Qal'at ar- ∴ • JOR 130-131 D 1
Rabah o WAN 198-199 B 6
Rabak o SUD 200-201 F 6
Rabal o RI 166-167 H 5
Rabang o VRC 144-145 C 4
Rabaraba o PNG 183 E 5
Rabārika o IND 138-139 C 9
Rabat o M 100-101 E 7
Rabat = Ar-Ribāṭ ☆ •• MA 188-189 H 4
Rabat = Victoria o M 100-101 E 6
Rabaul ☆ • PNG 183 G 3
Rabba o WAN 204-205 F 4
Rabbād, ar- ⊥ UAE 132-133 J 2
Rabbit Ears Pass ▲ USA (CO) 254-255 J 3
Rabbit Flat Store o AUS 172-173 K 6
Rabbit Lake o CDN (SAS) 232-233 L 2
Rabbit River ~ CDN 30-31 F 6
Rabbitskin River ~ CDN 30-31 J 5
Raber o USA (MI) 270-271 O 4
Rabi ⌂ FJI 184 III c 2
Rabī'a o IRQ 128-129 K 4
Rabia o RI 166-167 F 2
Rābiğ o KSA 130-131 F 6
Rabka o PL 92-93 P 4
Rabkavi Banhatti o IND 140-141 F 2
Raboĉeostrovsk o RUS 88-89 N 4
Rabo da Onça o BR 66-67 E 3
Rābor o IR 134-135 G 4
Raboti Malik, korvonsaroj • UZ 136-137 J 5
Rabt Sbayta ⊥ WSA 196-197 C 3
Rabun Bald ▲ USA (GA) 284-285 G 2
Rabwah o PK 138-139 D 4
Rabyanah o LAR 192-193 K 5
Raccon Cay ⌂ BS 54-55 H 3
Raccoon Creek ~ USA 280-281 D 5
Raccoon Creek State Park ⊥ USA (PA) 280-281 F 3
Raceland o USA (LA) 268-269 K 7
Race Pond o USA (GA) 284-285 H 6
Rachal o USA (TX) 266-267 J 7
Rachel o USA (NV) 248-249 J 2
Rạch Giá ☆ • VN 158-159 H 5
Rachid o RIM 196-197 E 5
Rachiv ☆ UA 102-103 D 3
Racibórz o PL 92-93 P 3
Racine o USA (OH) 280-281 E 5
Racine o USA (WI) 274-275 L 2
Racing River ~ CDN 30-31 G 6
Rackham o CDN (MAN) 234-235 C 4
Rackla Range ▲ CDN 20-21 X 4
Radā' o Y 132-133 D 6
Radama, Nosy ⌂ RM 222-223 E 4
Rădăuţi o RO 102-103 D 4
Radcliff o USA (KY) 276-277 K 3
Radde o RUS 122-123 D 4
Radechiv o UA 102-103 D 2
Radford o USA (AL) 284-285 C 4
Radford o USA (VA) 280-281 F 6
Radford Lake o CDN 30-31 R 4
Radford River ~ CDN 30-31 R 4
Rādhan o PK 134-135 M 5
Rādhānagari o • IND 140-141 E 2
Rādhanpur o IND 138-139 C 8
Radial'naja, gora ▲ RUS 112-113 Q 3
Radimlja • BIH 100-101 F 3
Radio Australia • AUS 172-173 K 2
Radio Australia Station • AUS 176-177 B 2
Radio Telescope • AUS 180-181 K 2
Radioville o USA (IN) 274-275 M 3
Radisson o CDN (QUE) 38-39 F 2
Radisson o CDN (SAS) 232-233 L 3
Radisson, Pointe ▲ CDN 36-37 N 3
Radium Hot Springs o CDN (BC) 230-231 O 3
Radium Springs o USA (NM) 256-257 J 6
Rādkān o IR 136-137 F 6
Radom ☆ PL 92-93 Q 3
Radom o SUD 206-207 G 4
Radomsko o PL 92-93 P 3
Radoviš o MK 100-101 J 4
Radstadt o • A 92-93 M 5
Radužnyj o RUS 114-115 O 3
Radviliškis ☆ •• LT 94-95 H 4
Radville o CDN (SAS) 232-233 O 6
Radwan o KSA 130-131 G 6
Radzyń Podlaski o PL 92-93 R 3
Rae o CDN 30-31 L 4
Rāe Bareli o IND 142-143 B 2
Raeford o USA (NC) 282-283 H 6
Rae Isthmus ⌣ CDN 24-25 c 7
Rae Lake o CDN 30-31 L 3
Rae River ~ CDN 24-25 M 6
Raeside, Lake o AUS 176-177 F 4
Raes Junction o NZ 182 B 6
Rae Strait ≈ 24-25 Y 6
Raetihi o NZ 182 E 3
Raevskij ☆ RUS 96-97 J 6
Rafaela o RA 76-77 G 6
Rafael Freyre o C 54-55 G 4
Rafah o AUT 130-131 D 2
Rafai o RCA 206-207 F 6
Raffingora o ZW 218-219 F 3
Raffin-Kada o WAN 204-205 H 5
Rafhā' o KSA 130-131 H 3
Rafin-Cabas o WAN 204-205 H 4
Rāfit, Ğabal ▲ SUD 200-201 F 2
Rafsai o MA 188-189 J 3
Rafsanğān o • IR 134-135 G 3
Raft River ~ CDN 230-231 K 2
Raft River ~ USA 252-253 E 4
Raft River Mountains ▲ USA 254-255 B 2
Raga o SUD (SR) 206-207 G 4
Raga ~ SUD 206-207 G 4
Ragaing Yōma ▲ MYA 142-143 J 6
Ragama o CL 140-141 H 7
Ragang, Mount ▲ RP 160-161 F 9
Ragay Gulf ≈ 160-161 E 6
Ragged Island ⌂ CDN 36-37 U 7
Ragged Island ⌂ USA (ME) 278-279 N 5
Ragged Island Range ⌂ BS 54-55 H 3
Raghwan o KSA 132-133 A 3
Raglan o NZ 182 E 2
Ragland o USA (NM) 256-257 M 4
Ragley o USA (LA) 268-269 G 6
Rago o USA (KS) 262-263 H 7
Rago nasjonalpark ⊥ N 86-87 G 3
Ragozina, mys ▲ RUS 108-109 N 5
Ragusa o I 100-101 E 6
Raha o RI 164-165 H 6
Rahad ~ ETH 200-201 H 6
Rahad al-Bardī o SUD 206-207 F 3
Rahama o WAN 204-205 H 3
Rāhatgarh o IND 138-139 G 8
Rahhāliya, ar- o IRQ 128-129 K 6
Rahib o SUD 200-201 C 4
Rahibat, Al o LAR 192-193 D 2
Rāhida, ar- o Y 132-133 D 7
Rahim ki Bāzār o PK 138-139 B 7
Rahimyār Khān o PK 138-139 C 5
Rahmanov bŭlaktary o KZ 124-125 P 4
Rahmanovka o RUS 96-97 F 8
Rahmat, Ra's ▲ ER 200-201 L 6
Rahmet o KZ 124-125 D 4
Rahole National Reserve ⊥ EAK 212-213 G 3
Råholt o N 86-87 E 6
Rahouia o DZ 190-191 C 3
Rahué o RA 78-79 D 5
Rahue, Río ~ RCH 78-79 C 6
Raiatea, Île ⌂ F 13 M 4
Rāichūr o • IND 140-141 G 2
Raida o Y 132-133 D 6
Raiford o USA (FL) 286-287 G 1
Raiganj o IND 142-143 F 3
Raigarh o IND 142-143 C 5
Raijua, Pulau ⌂ RI 168 E 8
Raikal o IND 138-139 G 10
Railroad Pass ▲ USA (NV) 246-247 H 4
Railroad Valley ⌣ USA 246-247 K 5
Raima, Wādī ~ Y 132-133 C 6
Rain, ar- o KSA 130-131 J 6
Raina Adelaida, Archipiélago ⌂ RCH 80 C 6
Rainbow o USA 20-21 Q 6
Rainbow o USA (OR) 244-245 C 6
Rainbow Beach o AUS 178-179 M 3
Rainbow Bridge National Monument ∴ USA (UT) 254-255 E 6
Rainbow City o USA (AL) 284-285 D 3
Rainbow Falls ~ • USA 288 K 5
Rainbow Lake o CDN 30-31 K 6
Rainier o CDN (ALB) 232-233 F 5
Rainier o USA (OR) 244-245 C 4
Rainier, Mount ▲ USA (WA) 244-245 D 4
Rainpura o IND 140-141 G 3
Rainsville o USA (AL) 284-285 E 2
Rainy Lake o CDN (ONT) 234-235 K 6
Rainy River o CDN (ONT) 234-235 J 6
Rainy River ~ USA 270-271 E 2
Raipur o IND (MAP) 142-143 B 5
Raipur o IND (MAP) 142-143 B 3
Raisüt o OM 132-133 J 5
Raith o CDN (ONT) 234-235 O 6
Rai Valley o NZ 182 D 4
Raivavae, Îles ⌂ F 13 N 5
Rāiwind o PK 138-139 E 4
Raja, Pulau ⌂ RI 168 E 3
Raja Ampat, Kepulauan ⌂ RI 166-167 E 2
Rajada o BR 68-69 H 6
Rājahmundry o IND 142-143 B 7
Rājākhera o IND 138-139 G 6
Rajampet o IND 140-141 H 3
Rajang o MAL (SAR) 162-163 J 3
Rajang ~ MAL 162-163 K 3
Rājanpur o PK 138-139 C 5
Rājāpalaiyam o IND 140-141 G 6
Rājapur o IND 140-141 E 2
Rajasthan ▫ IND 138-139 C 6
Rajčihinsk o RUS 122-123 C 4
Rajga ~ RUS 114-115 S 5
Rājgarh o IND (RAJ) 138-139 E 5
Rājgarh o IND (RAJ) 138-139 F 6
Rajin o KOR 150-151 H 6
Rajkoke, ostrov ⌂ RUS 122-123 P 4
Rājkot o IND 138-139 C 8
Rājmahāl o IND 142-143 E 3
Rājmahal Hills ▲ IND 142-143 E 3
Rāj-Nāndgaon o IND 142-143 B 5
Rajnera, ostrov ⌂ RUS 84-85 f 2
Rājpipla o IND 138-139 D 9
Raj Samund o IND 138-139 D 7
Rajshahi o BD 142-143 F 3
Raka o VRC 144-145 E 6
Rakan, Ra's ▲ Q 134-135 D 5
Rakaposhi ▲ IND 138-139 E 1
Rakata, Pulau ⌂ •• RI 168 A 3
Rakaye o BF 202-203 K 4
Rakhni o PK (BEL) 138-139 B 4
Rakhni ~ PK 138-139 B 5
Rakhshān ~ PK 134-135 K 5
Rakiraki o FJI 184 III b 2
Rakit, Pulau ⌂ RI 168 C 2
Rakitnoe o RUS 122-123 F 6
Rakom o THA 158-159 G 4
Rakonitz = Rakovník o CZ 92-93 M 3
Rakops o RB 218-219 C 5
Rako Raaxo o SP 208-209 J 4
Rakovník o CZ 92-93 M 3
Rakovskaja o RUS 88-89 Q 5
Rakuŝeĉnyj, mys ▲ KZ 126-127 J 6
Rakvere ☆ •• EST 94-95 K 2
Rakwa o RI 166-167 H 3
Ralco o RCH 78-79 D 4
Rālegaon o IND 138-139 G 9
Raleigh o CDN (NFL) 242-243 N 1
Raleigh o USA (MS) 268-269 L 4
Raleigh ☆ USA (NC) 282-283 J 5
Raleigh Bay ≈ 282-283 L 6
Raleigh National Historic Site, Fort • USA (NC) 282-283 M 5
Raleighvallen ~ SME 62-63 F 3
Raleighvallen Voltzberg, National Reservaat ⊥ SME 62-63 F 3
Raley o CDN (ALB) 232-233 E 6
Ralls o USA (TX) 264-265 C 5
Ralph o CDN (SAS) 232-233 P 6
Ralston o USA (NE) 262-263 K 3
Ralston o USA (WA) 244-245 G 4
Ralston o USA (WY) 252-253 K 2
Rama o CDN (SAS) 232-233 P 4
Rama o NIC 52-53 B 5
Rāmabhadrapuram o IND 142-143 C 6
Rama Calda o RA 78-79 E 3
Rāmachandrapuram o IND 140-141 K 2
Ramad, Hassi < DZ 190-191 F 6
Ramada, La o RA 76-77 E 4
Ramadas, Las o RCH 76-77 B 6
Ramādī, ar- ☆ IRQ 128-129 K 6
Ramadillas o RCH 76-77 C 1
Ramagiri o IND 140-141 G 3
Ramah o USA (NM) 256-257 G 3
Ramah Navajo Indian Reservation X USA (NM) 256-257 G 4
Rāmak o AFG 138-139 B 3
Ramalho, Serra do ▲ BR 72-73 H 2
Ramallāh ☆ WB 130-131 D 2
Ramallo o RA 78-79 J 2
Rāmanāthapuram o IND 140-141 H 6
Rāmānuj Ganj o IND 142-143 C 4
Ramardori o RI 166-167 H 2
Rāmasamudram o IND 140-141 G 5
Ramatlabama o ZA 220-221 G 2
Ramayampet o IND 138-139 G 10
Rāmāypatnam o IND 140-141 J 3
Rambipuji o RI 168 E 4
Rambouillet o F 90-91 H 7
Rambrè o MYA 142-143 H 6
Rambrè ⌂ MYA 142-143 H 6
Rambutyo Island ⌂ PNG 183 D 2
Ramea o CDN (NFL) 242-243 L 5
Ramea Island ⌂ CDN (NFL) 242-243 L 5
Rameau o CDN (QUE) 240-241 L 2
Rame Head ▲ AUS 180-181 K 4
Ramena o RM 222-223 F 4
Rameški ☆ RUS 94-95 P 3
Rāmeswaram o •• IND 140-141 H 6
Ramey o USA (MN) 270-271 E 5
Ramezān Kalak o IR 134-135 J 5
Ramgarh o BD 142-143 G 4
Ramgarh o IND (BIH) 142-143 D 4
Rāmgarh o IND (MAP) 142-143 C 4
Rāmgarh o IND (MAP) 142-143 C 4
Rāmgarh o IND (RAJ) 138-139 C 6
Rāmhormoz o IR 134-135 C 3
Ramhurst o USA (GA) 284-285 F 2
Ramingining X AUS 174-175 C 3
Ramis Shet' ~ ETH 208-209 E 4
Ramkan o • IR 134-135 G 5
Ramkhamhaeng National Park ⊥ THA 158-159 E 2
Raml o IRQ 128-129 K 5
Ramla ☆ IL 130-131 D 2
Ramlat al-Ğāfa ⊥ OM 132-133 J 3
Ramlat al-Wahība ⊥ OM 132-133 L 2
Ramlat as-Sab'atain ⊥ Y 132-133 D 6
Ramlat Rabyanah ⊥ LAR 192-193 J 5
Ramlu ▲ ER 200-201 K 6
Ramnaga o IND 142-143 B 2
Rāmnagar o IND 138-139 B 3
Rāmnagar o IND 138-139 G 5
Rāmnagar o IND 142-143 B 3
Ramo o ETH 208-209 E 5
Ramon o USA (NM) 256-257 L 4
Ramon, Mitzpé o IL 130-131 D 2
Ramona o USA (CA) 248-249 H 6
Ramonal ∴ • MEX 52-53 K 2
Ramones, Los o MEX 50-51 K 5
Ramon Grande, Laguna o PE 64-65 B 4
Ramore o CDN (ONT) 236-237 H 4
Ramos o BR 62-63 H 6
Ramos, Cachoeira ~ BR 70-71 G 2
Ramos, Río de ~ MEX 50-51 G 5
Ramos Arizpe o MEX 50-51 J 5
Ramos Island ⌂ RP 160-161 B 8
Ramos Otero o RA 78-79 K 4
Ramotswa o RB 220-221 G 2
Rampa o ANG 216-217 C 4
Rampart o USA 20-21 P 4
Ramparts River ~ CDN 30-31 D 3
Rāmpur o IND (GUJ) 138-139 D 8
Rāmpur o IND (HIP) 138-139 F 4
Rāmpur o IND (MAP) 142-143 B 4
Rāmpur o IND (ORI) 142-143 D 5
Rāmpur o IND (UTP) 138-139 G 5
Rāmpura o IND 138-139 E 7
Rampur Hāt o IND 142-143 E 3
Ramree = Rambrè o MYA 142-143 H 6
Ramree Island = Rambrè ⌂ MYA 142-143 H 6
Ram River ~ CDN 30-31 H 5
Ram River ~ CDN 232-233 C 3
Rams o UAE 134-135 F 6
Rāmsar o • IR 136-137 B 6
Ramsay, Mount ▲ AUS 172-173 H 5
Ramsay Lake o CDN (ONT) 236-237 F 5
Rāmše o IR 134-135 E 3
Ramsele o S 86-87 H 5
Ramseur o USA (NC) 282-283 H 5
Ramsey o CDN (ONT) 236-237 F 5
Ramsey o USA (IL) 274-275 J 5
Ramsey o USA (NC) 282-283 F 5
Ramsgate o • GB 90-91 H 6
Ramsgate o ZA 220-221 K 5
Ramsing o IND 142-143 J 1
Rāmšīr o IR 134-135 C 3
Ramsjö o S 86-87 G 5
Ramta, ar ☆ JOR 130-131 E 1
Rāmtek o IND 138-139 G 9
Ramu o BD 142-143 H 5
Ramu o EAK 212-213 H 2
Ramu National Park ⊥ PNG 183 C 3
Ramundberget o S 86-87 F 5
Ramu River ~ PNG 183 C 3
Ramusio, Lac o CDN 36-37 S 7
Ramvik o S 86-87 H 5
Ramygala o •• LT 94-95 J 4
Ran o WAN 198-199 G 6
Rana, Danau o RI 166-167 D 3
Rana, La o C 54-55 F 3
Rānahu o PK 138-139 B 7
Ranai o RI 162-163 H 3
Ranakah, Gunung ▲ RI 168 E 7
Rana Pratap Sāgar o IND 138-139 E 7
Ranarmoye ~ RI 166-167 F 5
Ranau o MAL 160-161 B 10
Ranau, Danau o RI 162-163 E 7
Ranbausawa, Tanjung ▲ RI 166-167 J 3
Ranburne o USA (AL) 284-285 E 3
Rancagua ☆ RCH 78-79 D 3
Rancahué, Cerro ▲ RA 78-79 D 5
Rancharia o BR 72-73 E 7
Rancheria, Río ~ CO 60-61 E 2
Rancheria River ~ CDN 30-31 E 5
Ranchester o USA (WY) 252-253 L 2
Rānchi o •• IND 142-143 D 4
Rānchi Plateau ▲ IND 142-143 D 4
Rancho California o USA (CA) 248-249 G 6
Rancho Cordova o USA (CA) 246-247 D 5
Rancho Queimado o BR 74-75 F 6
Ranchos o RA 78-79 K 3
Rancho Velho o BR 74-75 E 8
Rancho Viejo o MEX 52-53 E 3
Ranchuelo o C 54-55 E 3
Ranco, Lago o RCH 78-79 C 6
Rand o USA (CO) 254-255 J 3
Randa o DJI 208-209 F 3
Randado o USA (TX) 266-267 J 6
Randale ~ DJI 200-201 L 6
Randall Dam, Fort • USA (SD) 260-261 H 3
Randangan-Panua Reserves ⊥ • RI 164-165 G 3
Randazzo o I 100-101 E 6
Randberge ▲ ZA 220-221 K 3
Randeggi o WAN 204-205 G 3
Randers o DK 86-87 E 8
Randfontein o ZA 220-221 H 3
Randijaure o S 86-87 J 3
Randle o USA (WA) 244-245 D 4
Randlett o USA (OK) 264-265 F 4
Randolph o USA (KS) 262-263 K 5
Randolph o USA (NE) 262-263 J 2
Randolph o USA (TN) 276-277 F 5
Randolph o USA (UT) 254-255 D 2
Randolph o USA (VT) 278-279 J 5
Random Island ⌂ CDN (NFL) 242-243 P 4
Randowaya o RI 166-167 J 2
Randsburg o USA (CA) 248-249 G 4
Randsfjorden o N 86-87 E 6
Randudongkal o RI 168 C 3
Rånealven ~ S 86-87 K 3
Ranemsletta o N 86-87 E 4
Ranérou o SN 202-203 D 2
Ranfurly o CDN (ALB) 232-233 G 2
Rang o K 158-159 J 4
Rangaranga o RI 164-165 H 4
Rangasa, Tanjung ▲ RI 164-165 F 5
Range o USA (AL) 284-285 C 5
Rangeley o USA (ME) 278-279 L 4
Rangely o USA (CO) 254-255 G 3
Ranger o CDN (SAS) 232-233 L 2
Ranger o USA (TX) 264-265 F 6
Rangers Valley o AUS 178-179 H 2
Ranger Uranium Mine o • AUS 172-173 L 2
Ranges Valley o AUS 178-179 F 1
Rangia o IND 142-143 G 2
Rangiora o NZ 182 D 5
Rangkasbitung o RI 168 B 3
Rangnim o KOR 150-151 F 7
Rangnim Sanmaek ▲ KOR 150-151 F 7
Rangoon = Yangon ☆ •• MYA 158-159 D 2
Rangpur o BD 142-143 F 3
Rangpur Canal < PK 138-139 C 4
Rangsang, Pulau ⌂ RI 162-163 E 4
Ranguana Cay ⌂ BH 52-53 K 3
Ranhal o PK 138-139 C 5
Rānibennur o IND 140-141 F 3
Rāniganj o IND 142-143 E 2
Rāniganj o IND 142-143 E 4
Rānikhet o • IND 138-139 G 5
Ranikot ∴ • PK 138-139 B 7
Rānipettai o IND 140-141 H 4
Rānipur o PK 138-139 B 6
Rāniya ☆ IRQ 128-129 L 4
Ranken Store o AUS 174-175 D 6
Rankin o USA (IL) 274-275 L 4
Rankin o USA (OK) 264-265 E 3
Rankin o USA (TX) 266-267 F 2
Rankin Inlet ≈ 30-31 X 4
Rankin Inlet o CDN 30-31 X 4
Rankin's Pass ▲ ZA 220-221 H 2
Rankins Springs o AUS 180-181 J 2
Rankoshi o J 152-153 J 3
Rannee o RUS 96-97 H 8
Rannes o AUS 178-179 L 3
Rann of Kachchh ⊥ IND 138-139 B 7
Rano o WAN 204-205 H 3
Ranobe ~ RM 222-223 D 6
Ranohira o RM 222-223 D 9
Ranoke o CDN (ONT) 236-237 G 2
Ranoketang o RI 164-165 J 3
Ranomafana o RI 164-165 H 6
Ranomafana o RM (FNS) 222-223 E 8
Ranomafana o RM (TMA) 222-223 E 10
Ranomafana o RM (TMA) 222-223 F 7
Ranomena o RM 222-223 E 9
Ranong o THA 158-159 E 6
Ranongga ⌂ SOL 184 I c 3
Ranopiso o RM 222-223 E 10
Ranot o THA 158-159 F 7
Ranotsara Avaratra o RM 222-223 E 9
Ranquil, Caleta ≈ 78-79 C 4
Ranquil-Có o RA 78-79 E 4
Ranquil Norte o RA 78-79 E 4
Ransiki o RI 166-167 H 2
Ransom o USA (KS) 262-263 G 6
Ransom o USA (MI) 272-273 E 6
Rantabe o RM (TMA) 222-223 F 5
Rantabe ~ RM 222-223 F 5
Rantau o RI 164-165 D 5
Rantau (Tebingtinggi), Pulau ⌂ RI 162-163 E 4
Rantaubalai o RI 164-165 D 5
Rantaupanjang o RI 162-163 E 5
Rantauparangin o RI 162-163 D 4
Rantauprapat o RI 162-163 C 3
Rantaupulut o RI 162-163 K 5
Rantberge ▲ NAM 220-221 C 1
Rantemario, Gunung ▲ RI 164-165 G 5
Rantepao o RI 164-165 F 5
Rantoul o USA (IL) 274-275 K 4
Rantyirrity Point ▲ AUS 174-175 C 4
Ranua o FIN 88-89 J 4
Ranya o KSA 132-133 C 3
Ranya, Wādī ~ KSA 132-133 C 3
Rao o SN 196-197 B 7
Raohe o VRC 150-151 J 4
Raoping o VRC 156-157 K 5
Rapa ⌂ F 13 N 5
Rapa, Ponta do ▲ BR 74-75 F 6
Rapallo o I 100-101 B 2
Rapa Nui = Isla de Pascua ⌂ RCH 78-79 B 2
Rāpar o IND 138-139 C 8
Rapel, Río ~ RCH 78-79 D 2
Rapelje o USA (MT) 250-251 K 6
Raper, Cabo ▲ RCH 80 C 3
Raper, Cape ▲ CDN 28-29 G 2
Rapidan River ~ USA 280-281 H 5
Rapid City o CDN (MAN) 234-235 C 4
Rapid City o USA (MI) 272-273 D 3
Rapid City o USA (SD) 260-261 C 2
Rapide-Blanc o CDN (QUE) 236-237 P 5
Rapide-Deux o CDN (QUE) 236-237 K 5
Rapide-Sept o CDN (QUE) 236-237 K 5
Rapid of the Drowned ~ CDN 30-31 G 6
Rapidos Coemani ~ CO 64-65 F 2
Rapid River ~ CDN 30-31 E 6
Rapid River o USA (MI) 270-271 M 5
Rapid River ~ USA 270-271 D 2
Rapids o USA 20-21 S 5
Rapids City o USA (IL) 274-275 H 3
Rāpina o EST 94-95 K 2
Rapla o •• EST 94-95 J 2
Raposa o BR 68-69 F 3
Raposa Serra do Sol, Área Indígena X BR 62-63 D 3
Rappang o RI 164-165 F 5
Rapti ~ NEP 142-143 C 2
Rapulo, Río ~ BOL 70-71 D 4
Rapur o IND 140-141 H 3
Rapu-Rapu Island ⌂ RP 160-161 F 6
Raqdalin o LAR 192-193 D 1
Raqqa, ar- ☆ SYR 128-129 H 5
Râqûbah, Ar o LAR 192-193 H 3
Raquette River ~ USA 278-279 G 4
Raragala Island ⌂ AUS 174-175 D 2
Rare ~ EAK 212-213 G 5
Rarotonga Island ⌂ NZ 13 M 5
Rašaant o MAU 146-147 K 2
Rašaant = Ulaanšivèèt o MAU 148-149 F 4
Rasa Island ⌂ RP 160-161 C 8
Rašakān o IR 128-129 L 4
Ra's al-'Ain ☆ SYR 128-129 J 4
Ra's al-Barr o ET 194-195 E 2
Ra's al-Ḫafğī o KSA 130-131 L 3
Ra's al Hilāl o LAR 192-193 K 1
Rasātin, ar- ▲ JOR 130-131 F 1
Ras Attabil o LAR 192-193 E 2
Rasawi o RI 166-167 H 3
Rasĉenënnyj hrebet ▲ RUS 112-113 S 5
Ras Dashen Terara ▲ ETH 200-201 J 6
Raseiniai ☆ •• LT 94-95 H 4
Ras el Erg, Hassi o DZ 190-191 D 6
Râs El Ma o DZ 188-189 L 3
Râs el Mâ o RMM 196-197 H 6
Rasgado o BR 66-67 D 5
Ra's Ġārib o ET 194-195 F 3
Rasha o VRC 144-145 M 5
Rashād o SUD 206-207 K 3
Rāsib, Ra's ▲ KSA 132-133 B 5
Ra's Ibn Hāni' ▲ SYR 128-129 F 5
Rašīd o • ET 194-195 E 2
Rašīd o SUD 200-201 G 6
Rašīd, Ğabal ▲ SYR 128-129 G 5
Rašīd, Maṣabb ~ ET 194-195 E 2
Rašīdiya o SYR 128-129 J 4
Rāsipuram o IND 140-141 H 5
Rasirik o PNG 183 G 2
Rasi Salai o THA 158-159 H 3
Rāsk o IR 134-135 J 5
Raška o YU 100-101 H 3
Rās Kōh ▲ PK 134-135 L 4
Raskovoj, imeni o RUS 120-121 M 2
Ras Lanuf o LAR 192-193 H 3
Ra's Madhar, Ğabal ▲ KSA 130-131 E 5
Rasm al-Arwām, Sabḫat o SYR 128-129 G 5
Ra's Muhammad National Park ⊥ ET 194-195 G 4
Rasmussen Basin ≈ 24-25 Y 6
Raso, Ilhéu ⌂ CV 202-203 B 5
Rasoabe, Farihy o RM 222-223 F 7
Raso da Caterina ▲ BR 68-69 J 6
Rason Lake o AUS 176-177 H 4
Ra's oš-Saṭṭ ▲ IR 134-135 D 4
Raspberry Island ⌂ USA 22-23 U 3
Rasra o IND 142-143 C 3
Rass, ar- o KSA 130-131 H 5
Rašša o Y 132-133 E 6
Rass Ajdir o TN 192-193 D 1
Rasskazovo o RUS 94-95 R 5
Rassoha ~ RUS 108-109 b 6
Rassoha ~ RUS 110-111 b 7
Rassoha ~ RUS 110-111 d 5

382 Quemado de Güines — Rassoha

Rassoha ~ RUS 110-111 G 4
Rassošina ~ RUS 120-121 R 6
Rassošina ~ RUS 120-121 S 5
Rasšua, ostrov ⌒ RUS 122-123 P 5
Rašt ☆• IR 128-129 N 4
Rastān, ar- ☆ SYR 128-129 G 5
Rastatt o• D 92-93 K 4
Raštḫvār o IR 134-135 H 1
Răstoci o RO 102-103 C 4
Rastorgueva, ostrov ⌒ RUS 108-109 V 4
Rastro ▲ MEX 50-51 K 5
Rasu, Monte ▲ I 100-101 B 4
Rasūlnagar o PK 138-139 D 3
Ratangarh o IND 138-139 E 5
Rätansbyn o S 86-87 G 5
Ratcatchers Lake ⊕ AUS 180-181 G 2
Ratcha Buri o THA 158-159 E 4
Ratchford Creek ~ CDN 230-231 L 2
Ratcliff o USA (TX) 268-269 E 5
Ratcliff City o USA (OK) 264-265 G 4
Rat Creek ~ CDN 232-233 C 2
Ratewo, Pulau ⌒ RI 166-167 H 3
Rāth o IND 138-139 G 7
Rathbon Ø ⌒ GRØ 26-27 p 8
Rathbun Lake ⊕ USA (IA) 274-275 E 4
Rathdrum o USA (ID) 250-251 C 4
Rathedaung o MYA 142-143 H 5
Rathenow o D 92-93 M 2
Rathtrevor Beach ⊥• CDN 230-231 E 4
Rathwell o CDN (MAN) 234-235 E 5
Ratibor = Racibórz o PL 92-93 P 3
Rätische Alpen ▲▲ CH 92-93 K 5
Rat Island ⌒ USA 22-23 F 7
Rat Islands ⌒ USA 22-23 D 6
Rat Lake ⊕ CDN 34-35 G 2
Ratlām o IND 138-139 E 8
Ratmanova, ostrov ⌒ RUS 112-113 Q 4
Ratnachuli ▲ NEP 144-145 E 6
Ratnapura o CL 140-141 J 7
Ratne o UA 102-103 D 2
Rato, Igarapé do ~ BR 66-67 J 5
Ratodero o PK 138-139 B 6
Raton o USA (NM) 256-257 L 2
Raton Pass ▲ USA (CO) 254-255 L 6
Rat River ~ CDN 20-21 W 3
Ratta o RUS (JAN) 114-115 R 3
Ratta ~ RUS 114-115 S 3
Rattan o USA (OK) 264-265 J 4
Rattaphum o THA 158-159 F 7
Rattlesnake Creek ~ USA 262-263 G 7
Rattling Brook o CDN (NFL) 242-243 M 3
Rättvik o S 86-87 G 6
Ratz, Mount ▲ CDN 32-33 D 3
Ratzeburg o• D 92-93 L 2
Rau o RI 162-163 C 4
Rau, Pulau ⌒ RI 164-165 L 2
Raub o MAL 162-163 D 3
Rauch o RA 78-79 K 4
Raučua ~ RUS 112-113 O 2
Raučuanskij hrebet ▲▲ RUS 112-113 O 2
Rauda, ar- o KSA 130-131 J 5
Rauda, ar- o Y 132-133 D 6
Rauda, ar- o Y 132-133 E 6
Raudales de Malpaso o MEX 52-53 H 3
Raudatain, ar- o KWT 130-131 K 3
Raudat Habbās o KSA 130-131 J 3
Raufarhöfn o IS 86-87 f 1
Raukumara Plain ≃ 182 F 1
Raukumara Range ▲▲ NZ 182 F 3
Raul, ar- o UAE 134-135 G 6
Raul Pialo o BR 76-77 K 6
Raul Soares o BR 72-73 J 6
Rauma o••• FIN 88-89 F 6
Rauma ~ N 86-87 C 5
Raung, Gunung ▲ RI 168 B 7
Raunsepna o PNG 183 F 3
Raurkela o• IND 142-143 D 4
Rausu o J 152-153 L 2
Rausu-d. ▲ J 152-153 L 2
Rāut ~ MD 102-103 F 4
Rautavaara o FIN 88-89 K 5
Ravalli o USA (MT) 250-251 E 4
Ravānd o IR 134-135 D 1
Rāvand, Čam-e ~ IR 134-135 B 1
Ravanel o USA (SC) 284-285 K 4
Ravānsar o IR 134-135 B 1
Rāvar o IR 134-135 G 3
Rava-Rus'ka o UA 102-103 C 2
Ravat o KS 136-137 M 5
Ravendale o CDN (SAS) 232-233 P 2
Ravendale o USA (CA) 246-247 E 3
Ravenna ☆•• I 100-101 D 2
Ravenna o USA (NE) 262-263 H 3
Ravenna o USA (OH) 280-281 E 2
Ravensborne Creek ~ AUS 178-179 H 3
Ravensburg o• D 92-93 K 5
Ravenscrag o CDN (SAS) 232-233 J 6
Ravenshoe o AUS 174-175 H 5
Ravensthorpe o AUS 176-177 F 6
Ravenswood ∴ AUS 174-175 J 7
Ravenswood o USA (WV) 280-281 E 5
Rāvi ~ IND 138-139 E 3
Rāvi ~ PK 138-139 D 4
Ravn, Kap ▲ GRØ 28-29 a 2
Ravnina o TM 136-137 H 6
Ravo ~ SOL 184 I e 4
Rāvuludiki o IND 140-141 G 3
Rāwa o IRQ 128-129 J 5
Rawa Aopa/ Watumohae National Park ⊥ RI 164-165 G 6
Rawalak o PK 138-139 D 3
Rāwalpindi o PK 138-139 D 3
Rawalpindi Lake ⊕ CDN 30-31 M 3
Rawa Mazowiecka o PL 92-93 Q 3
Rāwandūz ☆ IRQ 128-129 L 4
Rawang o MAL 162-163 D 3
Rawarra ~ RI 166-167 G 2
Rawas o RI (IRJ) 166-167 G 2
Rawas ~ RI 162-163 E 6
Rawāwais, Wādī ~ LAR 192-193 F 2
Rawicz o• PL 92-93 O 3
Rawlinna o AUS 176-177 H 5
Rawlins o USA (WY) 252-253 L 5
Rawlinson, Mount ▲ AUS 176-177 J 2
Rawlinson Range ▲▲ AUS 176-177 J 2
Rawson ☆ RA 78-79 G 7
Rawu o VRC 144-145 L 6
Rawua o RI 164-165 H 5
Rāwuk, ar- o Y 132-133 F 6
Ray o USA (MN) 270-271 E 2
Ray o USA (ND) 258-259 D 3
Ray, Cape ▲ CDN (NFL) 242-243 J 5
Raya, Am o TCH 198-199 H 4
Raya, Gunung ▲ RI 162-163 K 5
Raya, Tanjung ▲ RI (ACE) 162-163 B 3
Raya, Tanjung ▲ RI (SUS) 162-163 G 5
Rāyachoti o IND 140-141 H 3
Rāyadrug o IND 140-141 G 3
Rāyagada o IND 142-143 C 6
Rayakottai o IND 140-141 H 4
Rayao, Raudal de ~ CO 60-61 G 6
Rāyāt o IRQ 128-129 L 4
Raybiraj o NEP 144-145 F 7
Rayborn o USA (TX) 268-269 F 6
Rāyin o IR 134-135 G 4
Raymond o CDN (ALB) 232-233 F 6
Raymond o USA (IL) 274-275 J 5
Raymond o USA (ME) 278-279 L 5
Raymond o USA (MS) 268-269 K 4
Raymond o USA (MT) 250-251 P 3
Raymond o USA (WA) 244-245 B 4
Raymond Terrace o AUS 180-181 L 2
Raymondville o USA (TX) 266-267 K 7
Raymore o CDN (SAS) 232-233 O 4
Ray Mountains ▲▲ USA 20-21 O 4
Rayne o USA (LA) 268-269 H 6
Raynesford o USA (MT) 250-251 J 4
Rayo ▲ MEX 50-51 G 5
Rayo Cortado o RA 76-77 F 6
Rayón o MEX (CHI) 52-53 H 3
Rayón o MEX (SLP) 50-51 K 7
Rayón o MEX (SON) 50-51 D 3
Rayong o THA 158-159 F 4
Raypatan o IND 140-141 E 2
Ray Roberts, Lake ⊕ USA (TX) 264-265 G 5
Raytown o USA (MO) 274-275 D 6
Rayville o USA (LA) 268-269 J 4
Rayyān, ar- o Q 134-135 D 6
Rāz o IR 136-137 E 6
Raz, Pointe du ⌣ F 90-91 E 7
Razan o IR 128-129 N 5
Razdan o AR 128-129 L 2
Razdol'naja ~ RUS 122-123 D 6
Razdol'noe o RUS 122-123 D 7
Rāzeqān o IR 128-129 N 5
Razgort o RUS 88-89 U 5
Razgrad ☆ BG 102-103 E 6
Rāzī o• IR 136-137 D 6
Razim, Lacul ⊕ RO 102-103 F 5
Razlog o BG 102-103 C 7
Razmak o PK 138-139 B 3
Ré, Île de ⌒ F 90-91 G 8
Reading o GB 90-91 G 6
Reading o USA (IL) 274-275 K 3
Reading o USA (OH) 280-281 B 4
Reading o• USA (PA) 280-281 L 3
Readstown o USA (WI) 274-275 H 1
Reagan o USA (TX) 266-267 L 2
Real, Cordillera ▲▲ BOL 70-71 C 4
Real, Cordillera ▲▲ EC 64-65 C 3
Real, Estero ~ NIC 52-53 L 5
Real, Rio ~ BR 68-69 K 7
Real de Santa Maria, El o PA 52-53 F 7
Realeza o BR 72-73 J 6
Realico o RA 78-79 G 3
Realitos o USA (TX) 266-267 J 6
Reardan o USA (WA) 244-245 H 3
Rebalse, El o MEX 50-51 G 3
Rebbenesøy ⌒ N 86-87 J 1
Rebecca, Lake ⊕ AUS 176-177 G 5
Rebecca, Mount ▲ AUS 176-177 C 3
Reboly o RUS 88-89 L 5
Rebordelo, Ponta ▲ BR 62-63 K 5
Rebro, mys ▲ RUS 120-121 U 3
Rebun o J 152-153 J 2
Rebun-suido ≈ 152-153 J 2
Rebun-tō ⌒ J 152-153 J 2
Recalde o RA 78-79 J 4
Rečane o RUS 94-95 M 3
Hecheachic o MEX 50-51 F 4
Recherche, Archipelago of the ⌒ AUS 176-177 G 7
Rečica = Rèčyca o BY 94-95 M 5
Recife o BR (AMA) 66-67 B 6
Recife ☆ BR (PER) 68-69 L 6
Recife, Kaap ▲ ZA 220-221 G 7
Recife Grande, Cachoeira ~ BR 70-71 H 2
Récifs, Îles = Reef Islands ⌒ VAN 184 II a 1
Rečka, Bol'šaja ~ RUS 124-125 O 2
Recknitz ~ D 92-93 M 1
Reco o CDN (ALB) 232-233 B 2
Reconquista o RA 76-77 H 5
Recreio o BR 72-73 J 6
Recreo o RA 76-77 E 5
Rector o USA (AR) 276-277 E 4
Recuay o PE 64-65 D 6
Rèčyca o BY 94-95 M 5
Recz o PL 92-93 N 2
Redang, Pulau ⌒ MAL 162-163 E 2
Redbank o AUS 180-181 G 4
Red Bank o CDN (NB) 240-241 K 4
Red Bank o USA (NJ) 280-281 M 3
Red Bank o USA (TN) 276-277 K 5
Red Bank 4 Indian Reserve ⅄• CDN (NB) 240-241 K 4
Red Basin = Sichuan Pendi ≃ VRC 156-157 D 2
Red Bay o CDN (NFL) 242-243 M 1
Red Bay o USA (AL) 284-285 B 2
Redberry Lake ⊕ CDN (SAS) 232-233 L 3
Red Bird o USA (WY) 252-253 O 3
Red Bluff o USA (CA) 246-247 C 3
Red Bluff Lake ⊂ USA (TX) 266-267 D 2
Red Boiling Springs o USA (TN) 276-277 K 4
Redbridge o CDN (ONT) 238-239 F 2
Red Bud o USA (IL) 274-275 J 6
Redbush o USA (KY) 276-277 N 3
Red Butte ▲ USA (AZ) 256-257 C 3
Redby o USA (MN) 270-271 D 3
Red Cliff ▲ AUS 178-179 C 2
Redcliff o CDN (ALB) 232-233 H 5
Redcliff o ZW 218-219 E 4
Redcliffe, Mount ▲ AUS 176-177 F 4
Red Cliff Indian Reservation ⅄ USA (WI) 270-271 G 4
Red Cliffs o AUS 180-181 G 3
Red Cloud o USA (NE) 262-263 H 4
Red Creek ~ USA 268-269 L 6
Red Deer o CDN (ALB) 232-233 E 3
Red Deer Creek ~ CDN 228-229 O 2
Red Deer Hill o CDN (SAS) 232-233 N 2
Red Deer River ~ CDN 232-233 E 3
Red Deer River ~ CDN 232-233 Q 3
Red Deer Valley Badlands ≃ CDN 232-233 F 4
Reddersburg o ZA 220-221 H 4
Reddick o USA (IL) 274-275 K 3
Redding o USA (CA) 246-247 C 3
Redding Creek ~ CDN 230-231 N 4
Reddit o CDN (ONT) 234-235 J 5
Redditch o GB 90-91 G 5
Redditt o CDN (ONT) 234-235 J 5
Red Earth o CDN (SAS) 232-233 P 2
Redearth Creek ~ CDN 32-33 N 3
Redenção o BR (CEA) 68-69 J 4
Redenção o BR (P) 68-69 D 5
Redenção do Gurguéira o BR 68-69 F 6
Redentora o BR 74-75 D 6
Redeyef o TN 190-191 G 3
Red Feather Lakes o USA (CO) 254-255 K 3
Redfield o CDN (SAS) 232-233 L 3
Redfield o USA (AR) 276-277 C 6
Redfield o USA (NY) 278-279 F 5
Redfield o USA (SD) 260-261 H 2
Redford o USA (TX) 266-267 C 4
Red Harbour o CDN (NFL) 242-243 N 5
Red Hill o AUS 172-173 C 7
Red Hills ▲▲ USA 262-263 G 7
Red Hook o USA (NY) 280-281 N 2
Red House o USA (VA) 280-281 H 6
Rédics o H 92-93 O 5
Redig o USA (SD) 260-261 C 1
Red Indian Lake ~ CDN 242-243 L 4
Redington o USA (AZ) 256-257 E 6
Red Jacket o CDN (SAS) 232-233 R 5
Redkey o USA (IN) 274-275 N 4
Redkino o RUS 94-95 P 3
Redknife River ~ CDN 30-31 K 5
Red Lake o CDN (BC) 230-231 J 3
Red Lake o CDN (ONT) 234-235 K 3
Red Lake ⊕ CDN (ONT) 234-235 J 3
Red Lake o USA (AZ) 256-257 E 2
Red Lake ⊕ USA (AZ) 256-257 C 3
Red Lake ⊕ USA (AZ) 256-257 A 3
Red Lake Falls o USA (MN) 270-271 B 3
Red Lake Indian Reservation ⅄ USA (MN) 270-271 C 1
Red Lake River ~ USA 270-271 C 2
Red Lake Road o CDN (ONT) 234-235 K 5
Red Lake State Management Area ⊥ USA (MN) 270-271 C 2
Redlands o USA (CA) 248-249 G 5
Red Lion o USA (PA) 280-281 K 4
Red Lodge o USA (MT) 250-251 K 6
Redmond o AUS 176-177 D 7
Redmond o USA (OR) 244-245 D 6
Redmond o USA (WA) 244-245 C 3
Red Mountain o USA (CA) 248-249 G 4
Red Mountain ▲ USA (MT) 250-251 G 4
Red Mountain Pass ▲ USA (CO) 254-255 H 6
Red Oak o USA (IA) 274-275 C 3
Redoak o USA (OH) 280-281 C 5
Redon o F 90-91 F 8
Redonda ⌒ AG 56 D 3
Redonda, Isla ⌒ YV 60-61 L 3
Redonda Bay o CDN (BC) 230-231 E 3
Redonda Island ⌒ CDN (BC) 230-231 E 3
Redondela, La o E 98-99 C 3
Redondo o P 98-99 D 5
Redoubt Volcano ▲ USA 20-21 O 6
Redoute Flatters • RN 198-199 C 2
Red Owl o USA (SD) 260-261 D 2
Red Pass o CDN (BC) 228-229 Q 3
Red Pheasant o CDN (SAS) 232-233 K 3
Red River ~ AUS 174-175 G 5
Red River ~ CDN 30-31 E 6
Red River ~ USA 264-265 G 5
Red River ~ USA 264-265 F 6
Red River ~ USA 268-269 H 5
Red River ~ USA 276-277 M 3
Red River ~ USA 276-277 H 4
Red River of the North ~ USA 270-271 A 2
Red Rock o CDN (ONT) 234-235 P 6
Red Rock o USA (AZ) 256-257 F 2
Red Rock o USA (AZ) 256-257 D 6
Red Rock o USA (OK) 264-265 G 2
Red Rock o USA (PA) 280-281 K 2
Red Rock o USA (TX) 266-267 K 4
Redrock Coulee ~ USA 250-251 K 3
Red Rock Creek ~ USA 264-265 G 2
Redrock Lake ⊕ CDN 30-31 M 3
Red Rock Pass ▲ USA (ID) 252-253 G 2
Red Rock Pass ▲ USA (NV) 246-247 K 4
Red Rock Reservoir ⊂ USA (IA) 274-275 E 3
Red Rock River ~ USA 250-251 G 7
Red Rose o CDN (MAN) 234-235 F 3
Redscar Bay ≈ 183 D 5
Red Sea ≈ 10-11 C 6
Red Shirt o USA (SD) 260-261 D 3
Red Spring o USA (MO) 276-277 B 4
Red Springs o USA (NC) 282-283 H 6
Redstone o CDN (BC) 228-229 L 4
Redstone o USA (MT) 272-273 E 4
Redstone Arsenal ✕✕ USA (AL) 284-285 D 2
Redstone River ~ CDN 30-31 F 4
Red Sucker Lake ⊕ CDN 34-35 K 3
Red Sucker River ~ CDN 34-35 K 3
Redsucker River ~ CDN 236-237 G 3
Redut o KZ 96-97 H 10
Redvers o CDN (SAS) 232-233 R 6
Redwater o CDN (ALB) 232-233 E 2
Redwater Creek ~ USA 250-251 O 4
Red Willow o CDN (ALB) 232-233 F 3
Red Willow Creek ~ USA 262-263 F 4
Redwillow Rapids ~ CDN 30-31 S 6
Redwillow River ~ CDN 32-33 L 4
Red Wing o USA (MN) 270-271 F 6
Redwood o USA (MS) 268-269 K 4
Redwood City o USA (CA) 248-249 B 2
Redwood Empire ≃ USA 246-247 B 2
Redwood Falls o USA (MN) 270-271 C 6
Redwood National Park ⊥••• USA (CA) 246-247 A 2
Redwood Valley o USA (CA) 246-247 B 4
Ree, Lough ⊕ IRL 90-91 D 5
Reed o USA (OK) 264-265 E 4
Reed Bank ≃ 160-161 B 7
Reed City o USA (MI) 272-273 D 4
Reeder o USA (ND) 258-259 E 5
Reedley o USA (CA) 248-249 E 3
Reedpoint o USA (MT) 250-251 K 6
Reedsburg o USA (WI) 274-275 H 1
Reedsport o USA (OR) 244-245 A 7
Reedville o USA (VA) 280-281 K 6
Reedy Creek ~ AUS 180-181 K 4
Reedy Creek ~ USA 286-287 H 3
Reedy River ~ USA 284-285 H 2
Reedy Springs o AUS 174-175 H 6
Reef Icefield ⊂ CDN (BC) 228-229 Q 3
Reef Islands = Îles Récifs ⌒ VAN 184 II a 1
Reefton o NZ 182 C 5
Reelfoot Lake ⊕ USA (TN) 276-277 F 4
Reese o USA (MI) 272-273 F 4
Reese River ~ USA 246-247 H 4
Reeves o USA (LA) 268-269 G 6
Refahiye ☆ TR 128-129 H 3
Reform o USA (AL) 284-285 B 3
Reforma, La o C 54-55 D 4
Reforma, La o RA 78-79 K 3
Reforma, La o YV 62-63 D 2
Reforma, Rio ~ MEX 50-51 E 4
Reftinskij o RUS 96-97 M 5
Refuge Cove o CDN (BC) 230-231 E 3
Refuge Headquarters o USA (OR) 244-245 F 8
Refugio o RCH 78-79 D 5
Refugio o USA (TX) 266-267 K 5
Refugio, El o MEX 50-51 J 5
Refugio, Isla ⌒ RCH 78-79 C 7
Refugio, Punta ▲ MEX 50-51 C 3
Refugio Beach • USA (CA) 248-249 D 5
Refugio la Faja o RA 78-79 E 3
Rega ~ PL 92-93 N 2
Regaïa o MA 188-189 H 4
Regalo o BR 68-69 F 6
Regalo, El o YV 60-61 G 3
Regen o D (BAY) 92-93 M 4
Regen ~ D 92-93 M 4
Regência o BR 72-73 L 5
Regência, Ponta de ▲ BR 72-73 L 5
Regeneração o BR 68-69 G 5
Regensburg o D 92-93 M 4
Regent o CDN (MAN) 234-235 C 5
Regent o USA (ND) 258-259 F 5
Regente Feijó o BR 72-73 E 7
Régestān ≃ AFG 134-135 L 3
Reggane o DZ 190-191 C 7
Reggio o USA (LA) 268-269 L 7
Réggio di Calábria o I 100-101 E 5
Réggio nell'Emilia ☆ I 100-101 C 2
Reggou o MA 188-189 K 4
Reghin o RO 102-103 D 4
Regina ☆ CDN (SAS) 232-233 O 5
Régina o F 62-63 H 3
Regina Beach o CDN (SAS) 232-233 O 5
Registro o BR 74-75 G 5
Regocijo o MEX 50-51 G 6
Regola o RI 166-167 E 6
Regone o MOC 218-219 K 3
Regresso, Cachoeira do ~ BR 62-63 G 6
Reguengos de Monsaraz o P 98-99 D 5
Regway o CDN (SAS) 232-233 O 6
Rehli o IND 138-139 G 8
Rehoboth o NAM 220-221 C 1
Rehoboth Bay ≈ 280-281 L 5
Rehovot ☆ IL 130-131 D 2
Reichenberg = Liberec o• CZ 92-93 N 3
Reid Lake o CDN (BC) 228-229 L 3
Reidsville o USA (GA) 284-285 H 4
Reidsville o USA (NC) 282-283 H 4
Reigate o GB 90-91 G 6
Reims ☆••• F 90-91 K 7
Reindeer Depot o CDN 20-21 Y 2
Reindeer Island ⌒ CDN (MAN) 234-235 E 2
Reindeer Lake ⊕ CDN 34-35 E 2
Reindeer Station o USA 20-21 K 3
Reine o N 86-87 F 3
Reine, La o CDN (QUE) 236-237 J 4
Reinga, Cape ▲ NZ 182 D 1
Reinosa o• E 98-99 E 3
Reinsdyrflya ⌣ N 84-85 H 3
Reisaelva ~ N 86-87 K 2
Reisa nasjonalpark ⊥ N 86-87 K 2
Reisjärvi o FIN 88-89 H 5
Reisterstown o USA (MD) 280-281 K 4
Reitoca o HN 52-53 L 5
Reitz o ZA 220-221 J 3
Reivilo o ZA 220-221 G 3
Rejaf o SUD 206-207 K 6
Rejdovo o RUS 122-123 N 6
Rekinniskaja guba ≈ 120-121 U 3
Rekkam, Plateau du ▲▲ MA 188-189 K 4
Relem, Cerro ▲ RA 78-79 D 5
Reliance o CDN 30-31 P 4
Reliance o USA (SD) 260-261 G 3
Reliance o USA (WY) 252-253 J 5
Relizane o DZ 190-191 C 3
Rellano o MEX 50-51 G 4
Relógio o BR 74-75 E 5
Relok, Kampung o MAL 162-163 E 2
Reloncaví, Seno de ≈ 78-79 C 6
Remada o TN 190-191 H 4
Remanso o BR (AMA) 66-67 C 6
Remanso o BR (BAH) 68-69 G 6
Remarkable, Mount ▲ AUS (QLD) 174-175 E 7
Remarkable, Mount ▲ AUS (SA) 180-181 E 2
Remarkable, Mount ▲ AUS (WA) 172-173 H 4
Rembang o RI 168 D 3
Rembang, Teluk ≈ 168 D 3
Remboken o• RI 164-165 J 3
Remedios o C 54-55 F 3
Remedios o PA 52-53 D 7
Remedios, Río Los ~ MEX 50-51 F 5
Remel El Abiod ▲ TN 190-191 G 5
Remennikovo o RUS 94-95 L 3
Remer o USA (MN) 270-271 E 3
Remešk o IR 134-135 H 5
Remígio o BR 68-69 L 5
Remington o USA (IN) 274-275 L 4
Rémire o F 62-63 H 3
Remiremont o F 90-91 L 7
Remolino, El o MEX 50-51 J 3
Remolino, Puerto o RA 80 G 7
Rena ☆ N 86-87 E 6
Renaico, Río ~ RCH 78-79 C 4
Renard, Rivière-au- o CDN (QUE) 240-241 L 2
Renard Island ⌒ PNG 183 G 6
Renata o CDN (BC) 230-231 L 4
Renca o RA 78-79 G 2
Renčeni o LV 94-95 J 3
Renčin humbe = Zöölön o MAU 148-149 E 2
Rencontre East o CDN (NFL) 242-243 N 5
Rencoret o RCH 76-77 C 2
Rende o• RI 168 E 7
Rend Lake ⊕ USA (IL) 274-275 J 6
Rendo o ETH 208-209 F 5
Rendova ⌒ SOL 184 I c 3
Rendsburg o• D 92-93 K 1
René Brunell Provincial Park ⊥ CDN (ONT) 236-237 F 3
Renews o CDN (NFL) 242-243 Q 6
Renfrew o CDN (ONT) 238-239 J 3
Rengas, Tanjung ▲ RI 164-165 F 5
Rengat o RI 162-163 E 5
Rengel o RI 168 E 3
Rengleng River ~ CDN 20-21 Y 3
Rengo o RCH 78-79 D 3
Renhe o VRC 154-155 E 6
Renhua o VRC 156-157 H 4
Renhuai o VRC 156-157 E 3
Reni ☆ UA 102-103 F 5
Reni, Pulau ⌒ RI 166-167 F 1
Renigunta o IND 140-141 H 4
Reñihue, Fiordo ≈ 78-79 C 7
Reninjauan o RI 162-163 D 4
Renland ≃ GRØ 26-27 m 8
Renmark o AUS 180-181 F 3
Renmei o VRC 154-155 B 6
Rennell, Islas ⌒ RCH 80 C 5
Rennell Sound ≈ 228-229 B 3
Renner Springs o AUS 174-175 B 6
Rennes ☆• F 90-91 G 7
Rennick Glacier ⊂ ARK 16 F 17
Rennie o CDN (MAN) 234-235 H 5
Rennie Lake ⊕ CDN 30-31 R 5
Reno o USA (MN) 270-271 G 7
Reno o• USA (NV) 246-247 F 4
Reno, El o USA (OK) 264-265 G 3
Renosterrivier ~ ZA 220-221 E 5
Renosterrivier ~ ZA 220-221 H 3
Renous o CDN (NB) 240-241 K 4
Renovo o USA (PA) 280-281 J 2
Renqiu o VRC 154-155 K 2
Rens Fiord ≈ 26-27 C 3
Renshi o VRC 156-157 E 5
Rensselaer o USA (IN) 274-275 L 4
Renton o USA (WA) 244-245 C 3
Rentoul River ~ PNG 183 B 4
Renville o USA (MN) 270-271 C 6
Renwick o USA (IA) 274-275 E 2
Reo o• BF 202-203 J 3
Reo o RI 168 E 7
Reodhar o IND 138-139 D 7
Réole, la o F 90-91 G 9
Repalle o IND 140-141 J 2
Repartimento o BR (AMA) 66-67 G 4
Repartimento o BR (AMA) 66-67 J 4
Repartimento, Corredeira do ~ BR 68-69 C 5
Repentigny o CDN (QUE) 238-239 M 3
Repetekskij zapovednik ⊥ TM 136-137 H 5
Republic o USA (MI) 270-271 L 4
Republic o USA (MO) 276-277 B 3
Republic o USA (WA) 244-245 G 2
Republican River ~ USA 262-263 H 4
Repulse Bay ≈ 24-25 c 7
Repulse Bay o CDN 24-25 c 7
Repununi River ~ GUY 62-63 E 4
Reque o PE 64-65 C 5
Requena o E 98-99 G 5
Requena o PE 64-65 F 4
Requena o YV 60-61 J 3
Rera o BR 62-63 D 3
Rerhoch, Tin o DZ 198-199 B 2
Reriutaba o BR 68-69 H 4
Reşadiye o TR 128-129 G 4
Reşadiye ☆ TR 128-129 G 2
Reşadiye Yarımadası ⌣ TR 128-129 B 4
Reschenpass = Passo di Rèsia ▲ I 100-101 C 1
Reseida, Wādī ~ SUD 200-201 F 2
Resen o MK 100-101 H 4
Resende o BR 72-73 H 7
Reserva o BR 74-75 E 5
Reserva o CO 64-65 F 2
Reserva Natural de Ría Formosa ⊥ P 98-99 D 6
Reserva Natural do Estuário do Sado ⊥ P 98-99 C 5
Reserve o CDN (SAS) 232-233 Q 3
Reserve o USA (KS) 262-263 L 5
Reserve o USA (MT) 250-251 P 3
Reserve o USA (NM) 256-257 G 5
Réserve d'Ashuapmushuan ⊥ CDN 38-39 H 4
Réserve d'Ashuapmushuan ⊥ CDN (QUE) 236-237 P 3
Réserve de Assinica, La ⊥ CDN 38-39 G 3
Réserve Faunique de Pipineau Labelle ⊥ CDN (QUE) 238-239 K 2
Réserve Faunique Mastigouche ⊥ CDN (QUE) 238-239 M 2
Réserve Faunique Rouge-Matawin ⊥ CDN (QUE) 238-239 L 2
Reserve Mines o CDN (NS) 240-241 P 4
Réservoir Baskatong ⊂ CDN (QUE) 238-239 K 2
Réservoir Manicouagan ⊥•• CDN 38-39 K 3
Rèsia, Passo di = Reschenpass ▲ I 100-101 C 1
Resistencia ☆ RA 76-77 H 4
Reşita ☆ RO 102-103 B 5
Resolute o CDN 24-25 Y 3
Resolution Island ⌒ CDN (NWT) 36-37 R 4
Resolution Island ⌒ NZ 182 A 6
Resource o CDN (SAS) 232-233 O 3
Resplendor o BR 72-73 K 5
Restauração o BR 62-63 D 5
Restauración o DOM 54-55 K 5
Resthaven Icefield ⊂ CDN (ALB) 228-229 P 3
Restigouche o CDN (QUE) 240-241 J 2
Restigouche Indian Reserve ⅄• CDN (QUE) 240-241 H 2
Restigouche River ~ CDN 240-241 H 3
Restin, Punta ▲ PE 64-65 B 4
Restinga de Marambaia ⌣ BR 72-73 J 7
Restinga Seca o BR 74-75 D 7
Reston o CDN (MAN) 234-235 B 5
Restored Village • USA (IA) 274-275 G 4
Restoule o CDN (ONT) 238-239 F 2
Resurrection, Cape ▲ USA 20-21 Q 7
Retalhuleu ☆ GCA 52-53 J 4
Retallack o CDN (BC) 230-231 M 3
Retamo, El o RA 78-79 F 2
Retchel Head ▲ CDN 36-37 S 5
Retem, Oued ~ DZ 190-191 E 4
Retén Atalaya o RCH 78-79 D 2
Reten Laguna o RA 78-79 D 4
Rethel o F 90-91 K 7
Réthimno o GR 100-101 K 7
Reting • VRC 144-145 H 5
Retiro o BR (AMA) 66-67 D 4
Retiro o BR (MAT) 72-73 D 3
Retiro, El o YV 60-61 H 3
Retiro Baia Grande o BR 70-71 K 5
Retiro São Benedito o BR 70-71 J 5
Retlaw o CDN (ALB) 232-233 F 5
Retra o PK 138-139 C 4
Retreat o AUS 178-179 G 3
Return Islands ⌒ USA 20-21 Q 1
Réunion ⌒•• F 224 B 7
Reus o E 98-99 H 4
Reutlingen o• D 92-93 K 4
Reva o USA (SD) 260-261 C 1
Reval = Tallinn ☆•• EST 94-95 J 2
Revda ☆ RUS 96-97 L 5
Reveca o RCH 76-77 B 2
Reveille Peak ▲ USA (NV) 248-249 H 2
Revello Channel ≈ 140-141 L 6
Revelstoke o CDN (BC) 230-231 L 3
Revelstoke, Lake ⊕ CDN (BC) 230-231 L 2
Reventon, El o MEX 50-51 J 6
Revenue o CDN (SAS) 232-233 K 3
Revés, El o MEX 50-51 H 4
Révia o MOC 218-219 J 1
Revilla Gigedo, Islas ⌒ MEX 50-51 A 7
Revillagigedo Channel ≈ 32-33 E 4
Revillagigedo Island ⌒ USA 32-33 E 4
Revillo o USA (SD) 260-261 K 1
Revoljucii, pik ▲ TJ 136-137 N 5
Revue ~ MOC 218-219 G 4
Rewa o IND 142-143 B 3
Reward o CDN (SAS) 232-233 J 3
Rewari o IND 138-139 F 5
Rewa River ~ FJI 184 III b 2
Rex, Mount ▲ ARK 16 F 29
Rexburg o USA (ID) 252-253 G 3
Rexford o USA (KS) 262-263 F 5
Rexford o USA (MT) 250-251 D 3
Rexton o CDN (NB) 240-241 L 4
Rey, Arroyo del ~ RA 76-77 H 5
Rey, El o RA 76-77 E 3
Rey, Isla de ⌒ PA 52-53 E 7
Rey, Laguna del o MEX 50-51 H 4
Rey, Mayo ~ CAM 206-207 B 4
Reyābād o IR 136-137 D 6
Rey Bouba o CAM 206-207 B 4
Reydon o USA (OK) 264-265 E 3
Reyes o BOL 70-71 D 4
Reyes, Point ▲ USA (CA) 246-247 B 5
Reyes, Point ▲ USA (CA) 248-249 A 2
Reyes, Punta ▲ CO 60-61 B 6
Reyes, Punta das ▲ RCH 70-77 B 3
Reyes Creek ▲ USA (CA) 248-249 E 5
Reyes Salgado, Los o MEX 52-53 C 2
Reyhanlı ☆ TR 128-129 G 4
Reykjanes Ridge ≃ 6-7 F 3
Reykjanestá ▲ IS 86-87 b 3
Reykjavík o CDN (MAN) 234-235 E 3
Reykjavík ☆• IS 86-87 c 2
Reynaud o CDN (SAS) 232-233 N 3
Reynolds o USA (GA) 284-285 F 4
Reynolds o USA (ID) 252-253 B 3
Reynolds o USA (IN) 274-275 M 4
Reynolds o USA (ND) 258-259 K 4
Reynoldsburg o USA (OH) 280-281 D 4
Reynolds Range ▲▲ AUS 172-173 L 7
Reynosa o MEX 50-51 K 4
Reyy o• IR 136-137 B 7
Rež ☆ RUS 96-97 M 5
Reza, gora ▲ TM 136-137 F 6
Rēzekne ☆•• LV 94-95 K 3
Rezina ☆ MD 102-103 F 4
Rēznas ezers ⊕• LV 94-95 K 3
Rezovo o BG 102-103 E 6
Režvān Šahr o IR 128-129 N 4
Rhame o USA (ND) 258-259 D 5
Rharb ≃ MA 188-189 H 3
Rharous o RMM 196-197 L 5
Rhea o USA (OK) 264-265 E 3
Rhein o CDN (SAS) 232-233 Q 4
Rhein ~ D 8 D 3
Rheine o D 92-93 J 2
Rheinfall ~•• CH 92-93 K 5
Rheinland-Pfalz □ D 92-93 J 3
Rheinwaldhorn ▲ CH 92-93 K 5
Rhemilès o DZ 188-189 J 6
Rhems o USA (SC) 284-285 L 3
Rheris, Oued ~ MA 188-189 J 5
Rhine o USA (GA) 284-285 G 5
Rhine = Rhein ~ D 8 D 3
Rhinelander o USA (WI) 270-271 J 5
Rhino Camp o EAU 212-213 C 2
Rhiou, Oued ~ DZ 190-191 C 3
Rhir, Cap ▲ MA 188-189 G 5
Rhode Island □ USA 278-279 K 7
Rhode Island ⌒ USA (RI) 278-279 K 7
Rhodes Inyangani National Park ⊥ ZW 218-219 G 4
Rhodes Matopos National Park ⊥ ZW 218-219 E 5
Rhododendron o USA (OR) 244-245 D 5
Rhodope Mountains = Rodopi ▲▲ BG 102-103 C 7
Rhome o USA (TX) 264-265 G 5
Rhön ▲▲ D 92-93 K 3
Rhondda o GB 90-91 F 6
Rhône ~ CH 92-93 J 5
Rhône ~ F 90-91 K 10
Rhône-Alpes □ F 90-91 K 9
Rhoraffa, Bir o DZ 190-191 G 5
Rhoufi o• DZ 190-191 F 3
Rhourd El Baguel o DZ 190-191 F 5
Rhum ⌒ GB 90-91 D 3
Rhumel, Oued ~ DZ 190-191 F 2
Rhyolite Ghost Town ∴• USA (NV) 248-249 H 3
Riaba o GQ 210-211 B 2
Ría Celestún Parque Natural ⊥ MEX 52-53 J 1
Riachão o BR 68-69 E 5
Riachão, Rio ~ BR 68-69 G 5
Riachão das Neves o BR 68-69 F 7
Riachão do Banabuiú o BR 68-69 J 4
Riachão do Jacuípe o BR 68-69 J 7
Riacho Alegre ~ PY 76-77 H 1
Riacho Carpincho ~ PY 76-77 H 2
Riacho de Santana o BR 72-73 J 2
Riacho do Sal o BR 68-69 J 6
Riacho dos Machados o BR 72-73 J 3
Riacho Obilebit ~ PY 76-77 H 1
Riacho Paraguay ~ PY 76-77 H 2
Riachos, Isla de los ⌒ RA 78-79 H 6
Riacho Seco o BR 68-69 J 6
Riacho Yacaré Norte ~ PY 76-77 H 2
Riákia o GR 100-101 J 4
Riamkanan, Danau ⊕ RI 164-165 D 5
Rianápolis o BR 72-73 F 3
Riangnom o SUD 206-207 K 4
Riaño, Embalse de ⊂ E 98-99 E 3
Riau □ RI 162-163 D 5
Riau, Kepulauan ⌒ RI 162-163 F 4
Ribadavia o• E 98-99 C 3
Ribadeo o E 98-99 D 3
Ribadesella o E 98-99 E 3
Ribah o WAN 204-205 F 3
Riban'i Manamby ▲▲ RM 222-223 D 9
Ribariće o YU 100-101 H 3
Ribas do Rio Pardo o BR 72-73 D 6
Ribāṭ, ar- o IRQ 120-129 J 5
Ribatejo ≃ P 98-99 C 5
Ribāṭ Qila o PK 134-135 J 4
Ribáuè o MOC 218-219 K 2
Ribe o•• DK 86-87 D 9
Ribeira Brava, Vila de o CV 202-203 B 5
Ribeira do Pombal o BR 68-69 J 7
Ribeira do Pombal, Rio ~ BR 68-69 J 7
Ribeirão o BR 68-69 L 6
Ribeirão, Área Indígena ⅄ BR 70-71 E 2
Ribeirão, Rio ~ BR 70-71 E 2
Ribeirão das Néves o BR 72-73 H 5
Ribeirão do Pinhal o BR 72-73 E 7
Ribeirão Preto o BR 72-73 G 6
Ribeiro Gonçalves o BR 68-69 F 5
Ribera o I 100-101 D 6
Ribera o USA (NM) 256-257 K 3
Ribérac o F 90-91 H 9
Riberalta o BOL 70-71 D 2
Ribnița ☆ MD 102-103 F 4
Ribnitz-Damgarten o D 92-93 M 1
Ribo Escale o SN 202-203 C 2
Ribstone o CDN (ALB) 232-233 H 3
Ribstone Creek ~ CDN 232-233 G 3
Ricardo o USA (TX) 266-267 K 6
Ricardo Flores Magón o MEX 50-51 F 3
Ricaute o CO 60-61 D 6
Rice o USA (CA) 248-249 K 5
Rice o USA (TX) 266-267 L 2
Rice o USA (WA) 244-245 G 2
Riceboro o USA (GA) 284-285 J 5
Rice Hill o USA (OR) 244-245 B 7
Rice Historic Site, Fort • USA (ND) 258-259 G 5
Rice Lake ⊕ CDN (ONT) 238-239 G 4
Rice Lake o USA (WI) 270-271 G 5
Rice Terraces ••• RP 160-161 D 4
Riceton o CDN (SAS) 232-233 O 5
Riceville o USA (PA) 280-281 G 2
Rich o MA 188-189 J 4
Richan o CDN (ONT) 234-235 L 5
Richão do Dantas o BR 68-69 K 7
Richão dos Paulos o BR 68-69 F 6
Richard Collinson Inlet ≈ 24-25 P 4
Richardsbaai = Richards Bay o ZA 220-221 L 4

Rassoha — Richardsbaai 383

Richards Bay = Richardsbaai o **ZA** 220-221 L 4
Richards Island ⌒ **CDN** 20-21 Y 2
Richardson o **USA** (OR) 244-245 B 7
Richardson o **USA** (TX) 264-265 H 6
Richardson, Cape ▲ **CDN** 24-25 d 6
Richardson Bay ≈ 30-31 M 2
Richardson Island ⌒ **CDN** 30-31 L 3
Richardson Islands ⌒ **CDN** 24-25 R 6
Richardson Lake ⊖ **CDN** 30-31 O 6
Richardson Mountains ▲ **CDN** 20-21 W 2
Richardson Point ▲ **AUS** 180-181 H 6
Richardson River ~ **CDN** 30-31 L 2
Richardson River ~ **CDN** 32-33 P 3
Richards Trench ≃ 76-77 B 4
Richard Toll o **SN** 196-197 C 6
Richardton o **USA** (ND) 258-259 E 5
Richburg o **USA** (SC) 284-285 J 2
Riche, Cape ▲ **AUS** 176-177 E 7
Richelieu, Rivière ~ **CDN** 238-239 M 3
Richer o **CDN** (MAN) 234-235 G 5
Richey o **USA** (MT) 250-251 O 4
Richfield o **USA** (ID) 252-253 D 3
Richfield o **USA** (KS) 262-263 E 7
Richfield o **USA** (NC) 282-283 G 5
Richfield o **USA** (UT) 254-255 C 5
Richfield Springs o **USA** (NY) 278-279 G 6
Richford o **USA** (NY) 278-279 E 6
Richford o **USA** (VT) 278-279 J 4
Richgrove o **USA** (CA) 248-249 E 4
Rich Hill o **USA** (MO) 274-275 D 6
Richibucto o **CDN** (NB) 240-241 L 4
Richibucto 15 Indian Reserve X · **CDN** (NB) 240-241 L 4
Richibucto-Village o **CDN** (NB) 240-241 L 4
Richland o **USA** (GA) 284-285 F 4
Richland o **USA** (MO) 276-277 C 3
Richland o **USA** (OR) 244-245 H 6
Richland o **USA** (TX) 266-267 L 2
Richland o **USA** (WA) 244-245 F 4
Richland Balsam ▲ **USA** (NC) 282-283 E 5
Richland Center o **USA** (WI) 274-275 H 1
Richland Creek ~ **USA** 266-267 L 2
Richland Creek Reservoir ⊖ **USA** (TX) 264-265 H 6
Richlands o **USA** (VA) 280-281 E 6
Richlands Springs o **USA** (TX) 266-267 J 2
Richmomd o **USA** (MI) 272-273 G 5
Richmond o **AUS** 174-175 G 7
Richmond o **CDN** (BC) 230-231 F 4
Richmond o **CDN** (ONT) 238-239 K 3
Richmond o **CDN** (QUE) 238-239 N 3
Richmond o **NZ** 182 D 4
Richmond o **USA** (CA) 248-249 B 2
Richmond o **USA** (IL) 274-275 K 2
Richmond o **USA** (IN) 274-275 O 5
Richmond o **USA** (KS) 262-263 L 6
Richmond o **USA** (KY) 276-277 L 3
Richmond o **USA** (MO) 274-275 E 5
Richmond o **USA** (OH) 280-281 F 3
Richmond o **USA** (TX) 268-269 E 7
Richmond ☆ **USA** (VA) 280-281 J 6
Richmond o **ZA** (CAP) 220-221 F 5
Richmond o **ZA** (NTL) 220-221 K 4
Richmond Dale o **USA** (OH) 280-281 D 4
Richmond Hill o **CDN** (ONT) 238-239 F 6
Richmond Hill o **USA** (GA) 284-285 J 5
Richmond Hills o **AUS** 178-179 H 2
Richmond River ~ **AUS** 178-179 M 5
Richmound o **CDN** (SAS) 232-233 J 5
Rich Mountain ▲ **USA** (AR) 276-277 A 6
Rich Square o **USA** (NC) 282-283 K 4
Richtersveld National Park ⊥ **ZA** 220-221 C 4
Richthofen, Mount ▲ **AUS** 172-173 C 6
Richton o **USA** (MS) 268-269 M 5
Rich Valley o **CDN** (ALB) 232-233 D 2
Richwood o **USA** (WV) 280-281 F 5
Ricinus o **CDN** (ALB) 232-233 D 3
Ricketts, Cape ▲ **CDN** 24-25 a 3
Rickman o **USA** (TN) 276-277 K 4
Rickwood Caverns · **USA** (AL) 284-285 D 3
Rico o **USA** (CO) 254-255 G 6
Ricrah o **PE** 64-65 E 7
Ridder, De o **USA** (LA) 268-269 G 6
Riddersprangeт · **N** 86-87 D 6
Riddle o **USA** (ID) 252-253 B 4
Riddle o **USA** (OR) 244-245 B 8
Rideau Hills ▲ **CDN** 238-239 H 4
Rideau Lake ⊖ **CDN** (ONT) 238-239 J 4
Ridge o **USA** (TX) 266-267 L 2
Ridgecrest o **USA** (CA) 248-249 G 4
Ridgedale o **CDN** (SAS) 232-233 O 2
Ridgefield o **USA** (WA) 244-245 C 5
Ridgeland o **USA** (MS) 268-269 K 4
Ridgeland o **USA** (SC) 284-285 K 4
Ridgely o **USA** (TN) 276-277 F 4
Ridge River ~ **CDN** 236-237 D 2
Ridgetown o **CDN** (ONT) 238-239 D 6
Ridgeville o **CDN** (MAN) 234-235 F 5
Ridgeville o **USA** (IN) 274-275 N 4
Ridgeway o **USA** (SC) 284-285 K 2
Ridgewood Summit ▲ **USA** (CA) 246-247 B 4
Ridgway o **USA** (CO) 254-255 H 5
Ridgway o **USA** (PA) 280-281 H 2
Riding Mountain ▲ **CDN** 234-235 C 4
Riding Mountain National Park ⊥ **CDN** (MAN) 234-235 C 4
Riebeck Bay ≈ 183 E 3
Riebeek Kasteel o **ZA** 220-221 D 6
Riebeek-Oos o **ZA** 220-221 H 6
Riebeekstaad o **ZA** 220-221 H 3
Riecito o **YV** 60-61 G 2
Riecito, Río ~ **YV** 60-61 G 4
Rieppe ▲ **N** 86-87 K 2
Riesa o **D** 92-93 M 3
Riesco, Isla ⌒ **RCH** 80 D 6
Rietavas o **LT** 94-95 G 4
Rietbron o **ZA** 220-221 F 6
Rietfontein o **NAM** 216-217 F 10
Rietfontein ~ **NAM** 216-217 F 10
Rietfontein o **ZA** 220-221 E 3
Rieti ☆ **I** 100-101 D 3
Rietrivier ~ **ZA** 220-221 G 4
Rietse Vloer ⊖ **ZA** 220-221 E 5
Rietvlei o **ZA** 220-221 K 4
Rievaulx Abbey ·· **GB** 90-91 G 4
Rifāʿi, ar- ☆ **IRQ** 128-129 M 7
Rifaina o **BR** 72-73 G 6
Riffe Lake ⊖ **USA** (WA) 244-245 C 4
Rifle o **USA** (CO) 254-255 H 4
Rifleman Bank ≃ 158-159 L 7
Rift Valley □ **EAK** 212-213 F 2
Rift Valley ∸ ·· **EAK** 212-213 F 4
Rift Valley National Park ⊥ **ETH** 208-209 D 5
Rig, Bandar-e o **IR** 134-135 D 4
Riga ★ ·· **LV** 94-95 J 3
Riga, Gulf of = Rīgas Jūras Līcis ≈ 94-95 H 3
Riga = Rīga ★ ·· **LV** 94-95 J 3
Riğā', Umm o **Y** 132-133 D 7
Rigacikun o **WAN** 204-205 G 3
Riğal Alma' o **KSA** 132-133 C 4
Rīgas Jūras Līcis ≈ 94-95 H 3
Rigaud o **CDN** (QUE) 238-239 L 3
Rigby o **USA** (ID) 252-253 G 3
Riggins o **USA** (ID) 250-251 C 6
Rigolet o **CDN** 36-37 U 7
Rig Rig o **TCH** 198-199 G 5
Rigsdagen, Kap ▲ **GRØ** 26-27 o 2
Riguldi o **EST** 94-95 H 2
Riḥab, ar- ∸ **IRQ** 128-129 L 7
Riihimäki o **FIN** 88-89 H 6
Riiser-Larsen halvØy ∸ **ARK** 16 G 4
Riisitunturin kansallispuisto ⊥ **FIN** 88-89 K 3
Riistina o **FIN** 88-89 J 6
Rijau o **WAN** 204-205 F 3
Rijeka o **HR** 100-101 E 2
Rijpfjorden ≈ 84-85 N 2
Rikām Panchū, Gardaneh-ye ▲ **IR** 134-135 J 5
Rikbaktsa, Área Indígena X **BR** 70-71 H 2
Rikorda, mys ▲ **RUS** 122-123 M 6
Rikorda, proliv ≈ 122-123 P 5
Rikuchū-Kaigan National Park ⊥ **J** 152-153 K 5
Rikumbetsu o **J** 152-153 K 3
Rila o · **BG** 102-103 C 6
Rila ▲ **BG** 102-103 C 6
Riley o **USA** (KS) 262-263 K 5
Riley o **USA** (OR) 244-245 F 7
Riley, Fort · **USA** (KS) 262-263 K 5
Rileyville o **USA** (PA) 280-281 L 2
Rillito o **USA** (AZ) 256-257 D 6
Rilski Manastir ··· **BG** 102-103 C 6
Rima ~ **WAN** 198-199 B 6
Rima, Wādī ar- ~ **KSA** 130-131 H 5
Rimac, Río ~ **PE** 64-65 D 8
Rimbey o **CDN** (ALB) 232-233 D 3
Rime ~ **TCH** 198-199 J 5
Rimé, Ouadi ~ **TCH** 198-199 J 6
Rimel o **USA** (WV) 280-281 F 5
Rímini o **I** 100-101 D 2
Rîmnicu Sărat o **RO** 102-103 E 5
Rîmnicu Vîlcea ☆ · **RO** 102-103 D 5
Rimouski o **CDN** (QUE) 240-241 G 2
Rimouski, Réserve de ⊥ **CDN** (QUE) 240-241 G 2
Rimrock o **USA** (WA) 244-245 D 4
Rimsko-Korsakovka o **RUS** 96-97 F 8
Rim Village o **USA** (OR) 244-245 C 8
Rinaré o **BR** 68-69 J 4
Rinca, Pulau ⌒ **RI** 168 D 7
Rincão o **BR** 72-73 F 6
Rincón o **CR** 52-53 C 7
Rincón o **DOM** 54-55 K 5
Rincon o **USA** (NM) 256-257 H 6
Rincón o · **USA** (PR) 286-287 O 2
Rincon, Cerro ▲ **RA** 76-77 D 3
Rincón, Salina del ⊖ **RA** 76-77 D 3
Rinconada o **RA** 76-77 D 2
Rinconada o **USA** (NM) 256-257 K 2
Rincón de la Vieja, Parque Nacional ⊥ **CR** 52-53 B 6
Rincón de la Vieja, Volcán ▲ **CR** 52-53 B 6
Rincón del Guanal o **C** 54-55 D 4
Rincon de Palometas o **BOL** 70-71 F 5
Rincos de Romos o **MEX** 50-51 H 6
Rind ~ **IND** 142-143 B 2
Rindal ☆ **N** 86-87 D 5
Ringba o **VRC** 154-155 H 6
Ringgi o **SOL** 184 I c 3
Ringgold o **USA** (LA) 268-269 G 4
Ringgold o **USA** (TX) 264-265 G 5
Ringgold Isles ⌒ **FJI** 184 III c 2
Ringim o **WAN** 198-199 D 6
Ringkøbing o **DK** 86-87 D 8
Ringkøbing Fjord ⊖ **DK** 86-87 D 8
Ringling o **USA** (MT) 250-251 J 5
Ringling o **USA** (OK) 264-265 G 4
Ring of Kerry · **IRL** 90-91 B 6
Ringoma o **ANG** 216-217 D 6
Ringvassøy ⌒ **N** 86-87 J 2
Ringwood o **AUS** 178-179 C 2
Ringwood o **USA** (OK) 264-265 F 2
Riñihue, Lago ⊖ **RCH** 78-79 C 5
Riñinahue o **RCH** 78-79 C 6
Riniquiarí o **CO** 60-61 F 6
Rinjani, Gunung ▲ **RI** 168 C 7
Rintala o **RUS** 88-89 K 6
Río o **GR** 100-101 H 5
Rio, El o **DOM** 54-55 K 5
Río Abiseo, Parque Nacional ⊥ ··· **PE** 64-65 D 5
Rio Acre, Estação Ecologica ⊥ **BR** 70-71 B 2
Rio Amazonas, Estuário do ~ **BR** 62-63 K 5
Rio Ariapo o **BR** 66-67 E 2
Río Ariguaisa o **YV** 60-61 E 3
Río Azul ∴ · **GCA** 52-53 K 3
Riobamba o **EC** 64-65 C 2
Rio Bananal o **BR** 72-73 K 5
Rio-Biá, Áreas Indígenas X **BR** 66-67 D 5
Río Blanco o **CO** 60-61 C 6
Ríoblanco o **CO** 60-61 D 6
Rio Blanco o **USA** (CO) 254-255 H 4
Rio Bonito o **BR** (PAR) 74-75 E 5
Rio Bonito o **BR** (RIO) 72-73 J 7
Rio Branco o **BR** (ACR) 64-65 F 6
Rio Branco o **BR** (MAT) 70-71 H 4
Rio Branco ☆ **BR** (ACR) 66-67 D 7
Río Branco o **ROU** 74-75 D 9
Rio Branco, Área Indígena X **BR** 70-71 F 3
Rio Branco, Parque Nacional do ⊥ **BR** 66-67 F 2
Rio Branco do Sul o **BR** 74-75 F 5
Río Bravo o **GCA** 52-53 J 4
Río Bravo o **MEX** 50-51 K 5
Río Bravo, Parque Internacional del ⊥ **MEX** 50-51 H 3
Rio Brilhante o **BR** 76-77 K 1
Rio Bueno o **JA** 54-55 G 5
Río Bueno o **RCH** 78-79 C 6
Río Caribe o **YV** 60-61 K 2
Rio Casca o **BR** 72-73 J 6
Río Cauto o **C** 54-55 G 4
Río Ceballos o **RA** 76-77 E 6
Río Chico o **YV** 60-61 J 2
Río Chiquito o **HN** 54-55 C 7
Río Clarillo, Parque Nacional ⊥ **RCH** 78-79 D 2
Rio Claro o **BR** 72-73 G 7
Rio Claro o **TT** 60-61 L 2
Río Colorado o **RA** 78-79 G 5
Rio Conchas o **BR** 70-71 K 4
Río Cuarto o **RA** 78-79 G 2
Rio das Pedras o **MOC** 218-219 H 6
Rio de Janeiro □ **BR** 72-73 J 7
Rio de Janeiro ☆ ·· **BR** (RIO) 72-73 J 7
Rio de Janeiro, Serra do ▲ **BR** 72-73 H 4
Río de la Plata ≈ 78-79 L 3
Rio Dell o **USA** (CA) 246-247 A 3
Rio do Pires o **BR** 72-73 J 2
Rio do Prado o **BR** 72-73 K 4
Rio do Sul o **BR** 74-75 F 6
Río Dulce, Parque Nacional ⊥ **GCA** 52-53 K 4
Río Gallegos ☆ **RA** 80 F 5
Río Grande o **BOL** 70-71 D 7
Rio Grande o **BR** 74-75 D 9
Río Grande o **MEX** 50-51 H 6
Río Grande o **RA** 80 G 6
Rio Grande o **USA** (NJ) 280-281 M 4
Rio Grande ~ **USA** 254-255 J 6
Rio Grande ~ **USA** 256-257 J 4
Rio Grande ~ **USA** 266-267 G 5
Río Grande, Ciudad de = Río Grande o **MEX** 50-51 H 6
Río Grande, Salar de ⊖ **RA** 76-77 C 3
Rio Grande City o **USA** (TX) 266-267 J 7
Rio Grande de Buba ~ **GNB** 202-203 C 4
Rio Grande do Norte □ **BR** 68-69 K 4
Rio Grande do Sul □ **BR** 76-77 K 5
Rio Grande Fracture Zone ≃ 6-7 H 11
Rio Grande Plateau ≃ 6-7 F 12
Rio Gregorio, Área Indígena X **BR** 66-67 B 7
Rio Guaporé, Área Indígena X **BR** 70-71 E 2
Río Guengue o **RA** 80 E 2
Riohacha ☆ **CO** 60-61 E 2
Rio Hato o **PA** 52-53 D 7
Río Hondo o **GCA** 52-53 K 4
Río Hondo, Embalse < **RA** 76-77 E 4
Río Hondo, Termas de o · **RA** 76-77 E 4
Río Ichilo o **BOL** 70-71 E 5
Rioja o **PE** 64-65 D 5
Rioja, La □ **E** 98-99 F 3
Rioja, La □ **RA** 76-77 C 5
Rioja, La ☆ · **RA** (LAR) 76-77 D 5
Río Lagartos o · **MEX** 52-53 K 1
Río Lagartos, Parque Natural ⊥ **MEX** 52-53 L 1
Rio Largo o **BR** 68-69 L 6
Riom o **F** 90-91 J 9
Rio Maior o **P** 98-99 C 5
Río Malo o **RCH** 78-79 D 3
Río Mayo o **RA** 80 E 2
Rio Mequens, Área Indígena X **BR** 70-71 G 3
Río Mulatos o **BOL** 70-71 D 6
Riondel o **CDN** (BC) 230-231 N 4
Rio Negrinho o **BR** 74-75 F 6
Rio Negro o **BR** (GSU) 70-71 J 6
Rio Negro o **BR** (GSU) 70-71 K 6
Rio Negro o **BR** (PAR) 74-75 F 6
Ríonegro o **CO** 60-61 E 4
Río Negro □ **RA** 78-79 E 6
Río Negro o **RCH** 78-79 C 6
Rio Negro, Pantanal do ⊖ **BR** 70-71 J 6
Río Negro, Represa del < **ROU** 78-79 L 2
Rio Negro, Reserva Florestal do ⊥ **BR** 66-67 C 2
Rio Negro Ocalai, Área Indígena X **BR** 70-71 E 2
Rioni ~ **GE** 126-127 E 5
Rio Pardo o **BR** 74-75 D 7
Rio Pardo de Minas o **BR** 72-73 J 3
Río Pilcomayo, Parque Nacional ⊥ **RA** 76-77 H 3
Río Plátano, Parque Nacional ⊥ ··· **HN** 54-55 C 7
Rio Pomba o **BR** 72-73 J 6
Rio Preto o **BR** 72-73 J 7
Rio Prêto, Serra do ▲ **BR** 72-73 G 4
Rio Preto da Eva o **BR** 66-67 H 4
Río Primero o **RA** 76-77 F 6
Rio Quente · **BR** 72-73 F 4
Rio San Juan o **DOM** 54-55 K 5
Río Seco o **RA** 76-77 E 2
Río Seco o **YV** 60-61 F 2
Río Segundo o **RA** 76-77 F 6
Río Simpson, Parque Nacional ⊥ **RCH** 80 D 2
Rio Sono o **BR** 68-69 E 6
Río Sucio o **CO** 60-61 D 4
Ríosucio o **CO** (CAL) 60-61 D 5
Ríosucio o **CO** (CHO) 60-61 C 4
Rio Telha o **BR** 74-75 E 7
Río Tercero, Embalse del < **RA** 78-79 G 2
Rio Tinto o **BR** 68-69 L 5
Río Tocuyo o **YV** 60-61 G 2
Rio Trombetas, Reserva Biológica do ⊥ **BR** 62-63 F 6
Riou, Point ▲ **USA** 20-21 U 7
Rioug o **RIM** 196-197 E 6
Riou Lake ⊖ **CDN** 30-31 Q 6
Rio Verde o **BR** 72-73 E 4
Río Verde o **MEX** 50-51 K 7
Río Verde o **YV** 60-61 H 3
Rio Verde de Mato Grosso o **BR** 70-71 K 6
Rio Vermelho o **BR** 72-73 J 5
Río Villegas o **RA** 78-79 D 6
Rio Vista o **USA** (CA) 246-247 D 5
Rio Vista o **USA** (TX) 264-265 G 6
Riozinho ~ **BR** 66-67 D 6
Riozinho ~ **BR** 68-69 F 6
Riozinho, Rio ~ **BR** 66-67 D 4
Riozinho, Rio ~ **BR** 68-69 B 5
Riozinho do Anfrísio ~ **BR** 66-67 K 5
Riozinho ou Rio Verde, Rio ~ **BR** 72-73 E 2
Ripky o **UA** 102-103 G 2
Ripley o **USA** (CA) 248-249 K 6
Ripley o **USA** (KY) 276-277 M 2
Ripley o **USA** (MS) 268-269 M 2
Ripley o **USA** (TN) 276-277 F 5
Ripley o **USA** (WV) 280-281 E 5
Ripoll o · **E** 98-99 J 3
Ripon o **USA** (WI) 270-271 K 7
Ririe o **USA** (ID) 252-253 G 3
Rišā', Wādī ar- ~ **KSA** 130-131 J 5
Risālpur o **PK** 138-139 D 2
Risasa o **ZRE** 210-211 K 4
Rishikesh o **IND** 138-139 G 4
Rishiri o **J** 152-153 J 2
Rishirifuji o **J** 152-153 J 2
Rishiri-Rebun National Park ⊥ **J** 152-153 J 2
Rishiri-suido ≈ 152-153 J 2
Rishiri-tō ⌒ **J** 152-153 J 2
Rishon le Ẕiyyon ☆ **IL** 130-131 D 2
Rising Star o **USA** (TX) 264-265 F 6
Rising Sun o **USA** (IN) 274-275 O 6
Rison o **USA** (AR) 276-277 C 7
Risør ☆ · **N** 86-87 D 7
Risøyhamn o **N** 86-87 G 2
Rissa o **N** 86-87 E 5
Rissani o **MA** 188-189 J 5
Rištan o **UZ** 136-137 M 4
Risti o **EST** 94-95 J 2
Ritchie o **ZA** 220-221 G 4
Ritch Island ⌒ **CDN** 30-31 K 2
Rīthi o **IND** 142-143 B 4
Rito o **ANG** 216-217 E 8
Rito, El o **USA** (NM) 256-257 J 2
Ritta Island ⌒ **USA** (FL) 286-287 J 5
Ritter o **USA** (OR) 244-245 F 6
Ritter, Mount ▲ **USA** (CA) 248-249 E 2
Ritzville o **USA** (WA) 244-245 G 3
Riv ~ **UA** 102-103 F 3
Rivadavia o **RA** (BUA) 78-79 J 3
Rivadavia o **RA** (MEN) 78-79 E 2
Rivadavia o **RA** (SAJ) 76-77 C 6
Rivadavia o **RA** (SAL) 76-77 F 3
Rivadavia o **RCH** 76-77 B 5
Riva del Garda o **I** 100-101 C 2
Rivalensundet ≈ 84-85 P 3
Rīvaš o **IR** 136-137 F 7
Rivas ☆ **NIC** 52-53 B 6
Rivera o **EC** 64-65 C 3
Rivera o **RA** 78-79 H 4
Rivera ☆ **ROU** 76-77 K 6
Riverbank o **USA** (CA) 248-249 D 2
Riverboat Cruise · **AUS** (NSW) 180-181 H 3
Riverboat Cruise · **AUS** (SA) 180-181 E 3
River Cess o **LB** 202-203 F 7
Rivercourse o **CDN** (ALB) 232-233 H 2
Riverdale o **USA** (CA) 248-249 E 3
Riverdale o **USA** (ND) 258-259 F 4
River Falls o **USA** (WI) 270-271 F 6
Riverhead o **USA** (NY) 280-281 O 3
River Hebert o **CDN** (NS) 240-241 L 5
River Hills o **CDN** (MAN) 234-235 H 4
Riverhurst o **CDN** (SAS) 232-233 M 5
Riverina ⌣ **AUS** 180-181 H 3
River John o **CDN** (NS) 240-241 M 5
Rivero, Isla ⌒ **RCH** 80 C 2
River of No Return Wilderness ⊥ **USA** (ID) 250-251 D 6
River of Ponds o **CDN** (NFL) 242-243 L 2
Rivers o **CDN** (MAN) 234-235 C 4
Rivers □ **WAN** 204-205 G 6
Rivers, Lake of the ⊖ **CDN** (SAS) 232-233 N 6
Riversdal = Riversdale o **ZA** 220-221 E 7
Riversdale o **BH** 52-53 K 3
Riversdale o **CDN** (ONT) 238-239 D 4
Riversdale = Riversdal o **ZA** 220-221 E 7
Riversdale Beach o **NZ** 182 F 4
Riverside o **AUS** 178-179 K 1
Riverside o **USA** (CA) 248-249 G 6
Riverside o **USA** (IA) 274-275 G 3
Riverside o **USA** (ID) 252-253 F 3
Riverside o **USA** (MD) 280-281 J 5
Riverside o **USA** (OR) 244-245 G 7
Riverside o **USA** (WA) 244-245 F 2
Riverside o **USA** (WY) 252-253 M 5
Rivers Inlet ≈ 230-231 B 2
Riverslea Oil Field · **AUS** 178-179 K 4
Riversleigh o **AUS** 174-175 E 6
Riverton o **CDN** (MAN) 234-235 G 4
Riverton o **NZ** 182 B 7
Riverton o **USA** (IL) 274-275 J 5
Riverton o **USA** (WY) 252-253 K 3
River Valley o **CDN** (ONT) 238-239 E 2
Riverview o **CDN** (NB) 240-241 L 4
Rivesaltes o **F** 90-91 J 10
Riviera o **USA** (TX) 266-267 K 6
Riviera Beach o **USA** (FL) 286-287 J 5
Riviera Beach o **USA** (TX) 266-267 K 6
Rivière, George ~ **CDN** 36-37 Q 5
Rivière-a-Pierre o **CDN** (QUE) 238-239 N 2
Rivière-au-Tonnere o **CDN** (QUE) 242-243 D 2
Rivière-aux-Saumons o **CDN** (QUE) 242-243 F 3
Rivière-Bleue o **CDN** (QUE) 240-241 F 3
Rivière-Boisvert o **CDN** (QUE) 236-237 O 3
Rivière-de-la-Chaloupe o **CDN** (QUE) 242-243 F 3
Rivière-Éperlan o **CDN** (QUE) 240-241 F 2
Rivière-Éternité o **CDN** (QUE) 240-241 E 2
Rivière-Pigou o **CDN** (QUE) 242-243 C 2
Rivière Qui Barre o **CDN** (ALB) 232-233 E 2
Rivière Veuve o **CDN** (ONT) 238-239 E 2
Riviersonderend o **ZA** 220-221 D 7
Rivne o **UA** 102-103 E 2
Rivoli o **I** 100-101 A 2
Rivungo o **ANG** 218-219 B 3
Riwat o **PK** 138-139 D 3
Riwoqê o **VRC** 144-145 L 5
Riyāḍ, ar- □ **KSA** 130-131 J 6
Riyāḍ al-Ḫabra o **KSA** 130-131 H 4
Riyadh = Ar-Riyāḍ ★ ·· **KSA** 130-131 K 5
Rize ☆ **TR** 128-129 J 2
Rizhao o **VRC** 154-155 L 4
Rizokarpaso o **TR** 128-129 F 5
Rizzuto, Capo ▲ **I** 100-101 F 5
Rjabovskij o **RUS** 102-103 M 2
Rjazan' ☆ ·· **RUS** 94-95 Q 4
Rjažsk ☆ · **RUS** 94-95 R 5
Rjukan ☆ **N** 86-87 D 7
Rkîz o **RIM** 196-197 C 6
Rkîz, Lac ⊖ **RIM** 196-197 C 6
Roadhouse o **AUS** 174-175 B 5
Road River ~ **CDN** 20-21 X 3
Road Town ☆ ·· **GB** 286-287 R 2
Roan Cliffs ▲ **USA** 254-255 F 4
Roan Mountain o **USA** (TN) 282-283 E 4
Roanne o **F** 90-91 K 8
Roanoke o **USA** (AL) 284-285 E 3
Roanoke o **USA** (TX) 264-265 G 5
Roanoke o **USA** (VA) 280-281 G 6
Roanoke Island ⌒ **USA** (NC) 282-283 M 5
Roanoke Rapids o **USA** (NC) 282-283 K 4
Roanoke Rapids Lake ⊖ **USA** (NC) 282-283 K 4
Roanoke River ~ **USA** 280-281 G 6
Roanoke River ~ **USA** 282-283 K 4
Roaring Springs o **USA** (TX) 264-265 D 5
Roaring Springs Ranch o **USA** (OR) 244-245 G 8
Roatán ☆ **HN** 52-53 L 3
Roatán, Isla de ⌒ **HN** 52-53 L 3
Robalo, Cachoeira do ~ **BR** 70-71 K 6
Roban o **MAL** 162-163 J 4
Robanda o **EAT** 212-213 E 5
Robāṭak o **AFG** 136-137 L 6
Robāṭ-e Ğa'lī o **AFG** 134-135 J 4
Robāṭ-e Ḫān o **IR** 134-135 G 2
Robāṭe Ḫošāb o **IR** 134-135 G 2
Robāṭ-e Ḫošk o **AFG** 134-135 K 2
Robāṭ-e-Mīrzā, Kōtal-e ▲ **AFG** 134-135 K 1
Robāṭ-e Pošt Badām o **IR** 134-135 F 2
Robāṭ-e Sang o **IR** 136-137 F 7
Robāṭ-e Sangī-ye Pāin o **AFG** 134-135 K 1
Robāṭkarīm o **IR** 136-137 B 7
Robb o **CDN** (ALB) 232-233 B 2
Robbeneiland ⌒ **ZA** 220-221 D 6
Robbies Pass ▲ **NAM** 216-217 B 9
Robbins o **USA** (NC) 282-283 H 5
Robbins Island ⌒ **AUS** 180-181 H 6
Robbinsville o **USA** (NC) 282-283 D 5
Robe o **AUS** 180-181 E 4
Robē o **ETH** (Ars) 208-209 D 5
Robē o **ETH** (Bal) 208-209 E 5
Robe, Mount ▲ **AUS** 178-179 F 6
Robeline o **USA** (LA) 268-269 G 5
Robe River ~ **AUS** 172-173 B 6
Robersonville o **USA** (NC) 282-283 K 5
Robert, Le o **F** 56 E 4
Roberta o **USA** (GA) 284-285 F 4
Robert Lee o **USA** (TX) 266-267 G 2
Roberts o **USA** (IL) 274-275 K 4
Robert's Arm o **CDN** (NFL) 242-243 N 3
Roberts Creek o **CDN** (BC) 230-231 F 4
Roberts Creek Montain ▲ **USA** (NV) 246-247 J 4
Robertsdale o **USA** (AL) 284-285 C 6
Robertsganj o **IND** 142-143 C 3
Robertson o **USA** (WY) 252-253 H 5
Robertson o **ZA** 220-221 D 6
Robertson, Kap ▲ **GRØ** 26-27 O 5
Robertson, Lac ⊖ **CDN** (QUE) 242-243 J 2
Robertson, Lake < **ZW** 218-219 F 3
Robertson Bay ≈ 16 F 18
Robertson Bay ≈ 36-37 K 7
Robertson Fjord ≈ 26-27 P 5
Robertson Range ▲ **AUS** 172-173 E 7
Robertson River ~ **CDN** 24-25 e 5
Robertsons Øy ⌒ **ARK** 16 G 31
Roberts Port ☆ **LB** 202-203 E 6
Robertville o **CDN** (NB) 240-241 K 3
Roberval o **CDN** (QUE) 240-241 C 2
Robī o **ETH** 208-209 D 4
Robin Falls · **AUS** 172-173 K 2
Robinhood o **CDN** (SAS) 232-233 J 2
Robins Camp o **ZW** 218-219 C 4
Robinson o **USA** (IL) 274-275 L 5
Robinson o **USA** (ND) 258-259 H 4
Robinson o **USA** (TX) 266-267 K 2
Robinson, Mount ▲ **AUS** 172-173 D 7
Robinson Island ⌒ **ARK** 16 G 30
Robinson Pass ▲ **ZA** 220-221 F 6
Robinson Range ▲ **AUS** 176-177 E 2
Robinson River o **AUS** (NT) 174-175 D 5
Robinson River ~ **AUS** 174-175 D 5
Robinson River o **PNG** 183 E 6
Robinson Sound ≈ 36-37 R 3
Robinsons River ~ **CDN** 242-243 K 4
Robinson Summit ▲ **USA** (NV) 246-247 K 4
Robinsonville o **CDN** (NB) 240-241 H 3
Robinvale o **AUS** 180-181 G 3
Robious o **USA** (VA) 280-281 J 6
Robla, La o **E** 98-99 E 3
Roble Alto, Cerro ▲ **RCH** 78-79 D 2
Robles Junction o **USA** (AZ) 256-257 D 6
Roblin o **CDN** (MAN) 234-235 B 3
Roblin o **CDN** (ONT) 238-239 H 4
Robooksibia o **RI** 166-167 H 2
Rob Roy Island ⌒ **SOL** 184 I c 2
Robsart o **CDN** (SAS) 232-233 J 6
Robson o **CDN** (BC) 230-231 M 4
Robson, Mount ▲ **CDN** (BC) 228-229 P 3
Robstown o **USA** (TX) 266-267 K 6
Roby o **USA** (MO) 276-277 C 3
Roby o **USA** (TX) 264-265 D 6
Roca, Cabo da ▲ ·· **P** 98-99 C 5
Roca, Península ⌣ **RCH** 80 D 5
Roça de Bruno o **BR** 68-69 E 2
Roca de la Sierra, La o **E** 98-99 D 5
Rocafuerte o **EC** 64-65 B 2
Rocanville o **CDN** (SAS) 232-233 R 5
Roca Partida, Isla ⌒ **MEX** 50-51 B 7
Rocas, Atol das ⌒ **BR** 68-69 L 1
Rocas Alijos ⌒ **MEX** 50-51 B 5
Roça Tapirapé o **BR** 68-69 C 6
Rocha ☆ **ROU** 78-79 M 3
Rocha, Laguna de ⊖ **ROU** 78-79 M 3
Rochebaucourt o **CDN** (QUE) 236-237 L 4
Roche Cabrit o **F** 62-63 H 3
Rochedo o **BR** 70-71 K 6
Rochefort o **F** 90-91 G 9
Rochelle o **USA** (GA) 284-285 G 5
Rochelle o **USA** (IL) 274-275 J 3
Rochelle o **USA** (TX) 266-267 H 2
Rochelle, la o **CDN** (MAN) 234-235 G 5
Rochelle, la ☆ · **F** 90-91 G 8
Roche River, La ~ **CDN** 30-31 O 5
Rocher River o **CDN** 30-31 N 5
Roches Point o **CDN** (ONT) 238-239 F 4
Rochester o **AUS** 180-181 H 4
Rochester o **USA** (IN) 274-275 M 3
Rochester o **USA** (KY) 276-277 J 3
Rochester o **USA** (MI) 272-273 F 5
Rochester o **USA** (NH) 278-279 L 5
Rochester o **USA** (NY) 278-279 D 5
Rochester o **USA** (TX) 264-265 E 5
Rochester o **USA** (VT) 278-279 J 5
Rochester o **USA** (WA) 244-245 B 4
Rochester o · **USA** (MN) 270-271 F 6
Roche-sur-Yon, la ☆ · **F** 90-91 G 8
Rochon Sands o **CDN** (ALB) 232-233 F 3
Rock o **USA** (MI) 270-271 L 4
Rockall Plateau ≃ 6-7 H 3
Rockall Trough ≃ 6-7 H 3
Rock Bay o **CDN** (BC) 230-231 D 3
Rock Camp o **USA** (WV) 280-281 F 6
Rock Cave o **USA** (WV) 280-281 F 5
Rock Creek o **CDN** (BC) 230-231 K 4
Rock Creek ~ **USA** 254-255 E 3
Rockdale o **USA** (TX) 266-267 L 3
Rockefeller National Wildlife Refuge ⊥ **USA** (LA) 268-269 H 7
Rockefeller Plateau ▲ **ARK** 16 F 24
Rock Engravings Music Stones · **NAM** 220-221 C 3
Rock Falls o **USA** (IL) 274-275 J 3
Rockford o **USA** (AL) 284-285 D 4
Rockford o **USA** (IL) 274-275 J 2
Rockford o **USA** (OH) 280-281 B 3
Rockford o **USA** (WA) 244-245 H 3
Rockglen o **CDN** (SAS) 232-233 N 6
Rock Hall o **USA** (MD) 280-281 K 4
Rockhampton o · **AUS** 178-179 L 2
Rockhampton Downs o **AUS** 174-175 C 6
Rockhaven o **CDN** (SAS) 232-233 K 3
Rock Hill o **USA** (SC) 284-285 J 2
Rockingham o **USA** (NC) 282-283 H 6
Rockingham Bay ≈ 174-175 J 6
Rock Island o **CDN** (QUE) 238-239 N 3
Rock Island ⌒ **USA** (WI) 270-271 M 5
Rocklake o **USA** (ND) 258-259 H 3
Rock Lake ⊖ **USA** (WA) 244-245 H 3
Rockland o **CDN** (ONT) 238-239 K 3
Rockland o **USA** (ID) 252-253 F 4
Rockland o **USA** (ME) 278-279 M 4
Rocklands Reservoir < **AUS** 180-181 G 4
Rocklea o **AUS** 172-173 C 7
Rockledge o **USA** (FL) 286-287 J 3
Rockmart o **USA** (GA) 284-285 E 2
Rock of Cashel ·· **IRL** 90-91 D 5
Rock Point o **USA** (MD) 280-281 K 5
Rockport o **USA** (IN) 274-275 L 7
Rock Port o **USA** (MO) 274-275 C 4
Rockport o **USA** (TX) 266-267 K 5
Rockport o **USA** (WA) 244-245 D 2
Rock Rapids o **USA** (IA) 274-275 B 1
Rock River ~ **CDN** 20-21 X 3
Rock River ~ **CDN** 30-31 F 5
Rock River o **USA** (WY) 252-253 N 5
Rock River ~ **USA** 270-271 B 7
Rock River ~ **USA** 274-275 J 3
Rock Sound o · **BS** 54-55 G 2
Rock Springs o **USA** (AZ) 256-257 C 4
Rock Springs o **USA** (MT) 250-251 N 5
Rocksprings o **USA** (TX) 266-267 G 3
Rock Springs o **USA** (WY) 252-253 J 5
Rockstone o **GUY** 62-63 E 2
Rockton o **AUS** 180-181 K 4
Rockville o **USA** (IN) 274-275 L 5
Rockville o **USA** (MD) 280-281 J 4
Rockville o **USA** (NE) 262-263 H 3
Rockville o **USA** (UT) 254-255 B 6
Rockwall o **USA** (TX) 264-265 H 6
Rockwell City o **USA** (IA) 274-275 D 2
Rockwood o **USA** (ME) 278-279 M 3
Rockwood o **USA** (TN) 282-283 C 5
Rockwood o **USA** (TX) 266-267 H 2
Rocky o **USA** (OK) 264-265 E 3
Rocky Arroyo ~ **USA** 256-257 L 6
Rocky Boy o **USA** (MT) 250-251 K 3
Rocky Boys Indian Reservation X **USA** (MT) 250-251 K 3
Rocky Ford o **USA** (CO) 254-255 M 5
Rocky Fork Lake < **USA** (OH) 280-281 C 4
Rocky Gap o **USA** (VA) 280-281 E 6
Rocky Gully o **AUS** 176-177 D 7
Rocky Harbour o **CDN** (NFL) 242-243 L 3
Rocky Island Lake ⊖ **CDN** (ONT) 238-239 C 2
Rocky Mount o **USA** (NC) 282-283 K 5
Rocky Mount o **USA** (VA) 280-281 G 6
Rocky Mountain House o **CDN** (ALB) 232-233 D 3
Rocky Mountain House National Historic Park · **CDN** (ALB) 232-233 D 3
Rocky Mountain National Park ⊥ **USA** (CO) 254-255 K 3
Rocky Mountains ▲ 4 B 3
Rocky Mountains Forest Reserve ⊥ **CDN** (ALB) 232-233 D 6
Rocky Mountains Forest Reserve ⊥ **CDN** (ALB) 232-233 B 3
Rocky Point o **CDN** (PEI) 240-241 M 4
Rocky Point ▲ **NAM** 216-217 B 9
Rockypoint o **USA** (WY) 252-253 N 2
Rocky Point ▲ **USA** 20-21 J 4
Rocky Rapids o **CDN** (ALB) 232-233 D 2
Rocky River ~ **CDN** 228-229 R 3
Rocky River ~ **USA** 282-283 G 5
Rocky River ~ **USA** 282-283 H 5
Roda, La o **E** 98-99 F 5
Roda Velha o **BR** 72-73 H 2
Rōdbār o **AFG** 134-135 K 3
Rødberg o **N** 86-87 D 6
Rødbyhavn o **DK** 86-87 E 9
Roddickton o **CDN** (NFL) 242-243 M 2
Rodds Bay ≈ 178-179 L 2
Røde Fjord ≈ 26-27 I 8
Rodel o **GB** 90-91 D 3
Rodelas o **BR** 68-69 J 6
Rodeo o **USA** (NM) 256-257 G 7
Rodeo Viejo o **PA** 52-53 D 7
Roderick Island ⌒ **CDN** (BC) 228-229 F 4
Rodez ☆ · **F** 90-91 J 9
Rodgers Bank ≃ 72-73 M 4
Rodi, Tanjung ▲ **RI** 166-167 B 7
Rodino ☆ **RUS** 124-125 M 2
Rodnei, Munții ▲ **RO** 102-103 D 4
Rodney o **USA** (MS) 268-269 J 5
Rodney, Cape ▲ **NZ** 182 E 2
Rodniki o **RUS** 94-95 R 3
Rodnikovskoe o **KZ** 124-125 H 3
Rododero-Playa, El · **CO** 60-61 D 2
Ródos ☆ ·· **GR** 100-101 M 6
Ródos ⌒ **GR** 100-101 M 6
Rodrigues, Île ⌒ **MS** 224 F 6
Rodrigues Ridge ≃ 224 E 6
Rodríguez, Los o **MEX** 50-51 J 4
Rodžers, buhta ≈ 112-113 V 1
Roe, Lake ⊖ **AUS** 176-177 G 5
Roebourne o **AUS** 172-173 C 6
Roebuck Bay ≈ 172-173 F 5
Roebuck Roadhouse o **AUS** 172-173 F 4
Roedtan o **ZA** 220-221 J 2
Roe River ~ **AUS** 172-173 G 3
Roermond o **NL** 92-93 J 3
Roeselare o **B** 92-93 G 3
Roff o **USA** (OK) 264-265 H 4
Rofia o **WAN** 204-205 F 3
Rogačeva ~ **RUS** 108-109 E 6
Rogačevka o **RUS** 102-103 L 2
Rogačevo o **RUS** 94-95 P 3
Rogagua, Lago ⊖ **BOL** 70-71 D 3
Rogaguado o **BOL** 70-71 E 3
Rogasen = Rogoźno o **PL** 92-93 O 2
Rogatica o **BIH** 100-101 G 3
Rogberi o **WAL** 202-203 D 5
Rogeia Island ⌒ **PNG** 183 F 6
Rogers o **USA** (AR) 276-277 A 4
Rogers o **USA** (ND) 258-259 J 4
Rogers o **USA** (TX) 266-267 K 3
Rogers, Mount ▲ **USA** (VA) 280-281 E 7
Rogers City o **USA** (MI) 272-273 F 2
Rogers Lake ⊖ **USA** (CA) 248-249 G 5
Rogerson o **USA** (ID) 252-253 D 4
Rogers Pass o **CDN** (BC) 230-231 M 2
Rogers Pass ▲ **CDN** (BC) 230-231 M 2
Rogers Pass ▲ **USA** (MT) 250-251 G 4
Rogersville o **CDN** (NB) 240-241 K 4
Rogersville o **USA** (AL) 284-285 C 2
Rogersville o **USA** (TN) 282-283 D 4
Roggeveen Basin ≃ 5 B 8
Roggeveldberge ▲ **ZA** 220-221 E 5
Rognan o **N** 86-87 G 3
Rogo o **WAN** 204-205 G 3
Rogoaguado, Lago ⊖ **BOL** 70-71 E 3
Rogovaja, Bol'šaja ~ **RUS** 108-109 J 8
Rogoźno o **PL** 92-93 O 2
Rogue River ~ **USA** 244-245 A 8
Rogun o **WAN** 204-205 F 4
Roha o **IND** 138-139 D 10
Rohat o **IND** 138-139 D 7
Rohatyn ☆ **UA** 102-103 D 3
Rohault, Lac ⊖ **CDN** 38-39 G 4
Rohault, Lac ⊖ **CDN** (QUE) 236-237 O 3
Rohmojva, gora ▲ **RUS** 88-89 K 3
Rohri o **PK** 138-139 B 6

384 Richards Bay — Rohri

Rohri Canal < PK 138-139 B 6
Rohru o IND 138-139 F 4
Rohtak o IND 138-139 F 5
Rohtak, Rūdḫāne-ye ~ IR 134-135 K 5
Rohtas Fort • PK 138-139 D 3
Rohuküla o EST 94-95 H 2
Rohwer o USA (AR) 276-277 D 7
Roi Et o THA 158-159 G 2
Roja o•• LV 94-95 H 3
Roja, Punta ▲ RA 80 H 2
Rojas o RA 78-79 J 3
Rojhān o PK 138-139 B 5
Rojo, Cabo ▲ MEX 50-51 L 7
Rojo, Cabo ▲ USA (PR) 286-287 O 3
Rokan o RI 162-163 D 4
Rokan-Kanan ~ RI 162-163 D 4
Rokan-Kiri ~ RI 162-163 D 4
Rokeby o AUS 174-175 G 3
Rokeby o CDN (SAS) 232-233 Q 4
Rokeby-Croll Creek National Park ⊥ AUS 174-175 G 3
Rokiškis ☆•• LT 94-95 J 4
Rokkasho o J 152-153 J 4
Rokom o SUD 206-207 K 6
Rokskij, pereval ▲ RUS 126-127 F 6
Roland o CDN (MAN) 234-235 F 5
Rolândia o BR 72-73 E 7
Røldal o N 86-87 C 7
Roldán o RA 78-79 J 2
Rolette o USA (ND) 258-259 H 3
Rolim de Moura o BR (RON) 70-71 G 2
Rolim de Moura o BR (RON) 70-71 F 3
Roll o USA (AZ) 256-257 B 6
Roll o USA (OK) 264-265 E 3
Rolla ⌒ N 86-87 H 2
Rolla o USA (KS) 262-263 E 7
Rolla o USA (MO) 276-277 D 3
Rolla o USA (ND) 258-259 H 3
Rollapenta o IND 140-141 H 3
Rolleston o AUS 178-179 K 3
Rolleston o NZ 182 D 5
Rollet o CDN (QUE) 236-237 J 5
Rolleville o• BS 54-55 H 3
Rolling Fork o USA (MS) 268-269 K 4
Rolling Fork ~ USA 276-277 K 3
Rolling Hills o CDN (ALB) 232-233 G 5
Rolling River Indian Reserve ⅄ CDN (MAN) 234-235 D 4
Rollins o USA (MN) 270-271 G 3
Rollins o USA (MT) 250-251 E 4
Rolvsøya ⌒ N 86-87 M 1
Roma o AUS 178-179 K 4
Roma ★••• I 100-101 D 4
Roma o LS 220-221 H 4
Roma o S 86-87 J 8
Roma o USA (TX) 266-267 J 7
Roma, Pulau ⌒ RI 166-167 D 5
Romain, Cape ▲ USA (SC) 284-285 L 4
Romaine o CDN (QUE) 242-243 H 2
Romaine, Rivière ~ CDN 38-39 N 3
Romain o BG 102-103 C 6
Roman o• RO 102-103 E 4
Romana, La ☆ DOM 54-55 L 5
Romanche Fracture Zone ≃ 6-7 G 9
Romancoke o USA (MD) 280-281 K 5
Romanek, Lac o CDN 36-37 Q 6
Romang, Selat ≈ 166-167 D 5
Romania = România ■ RO 102-103 C 5
Romanina, Bol'šaja ~ RUS 108-109 c 6
Roman-Koš, hora ▲ UA 102-103 J 5
Romano, Cape ▲ USA (FL) 286-287 H 6
Romano, Cayo ⌒ C 54-55 F 3
Romanovka o RUS 118-119 F 9
Romans-sur-Isère o F 90-91 K 9
Romanzof, Cape ▲ USA 20-21 G 6
Romanzof Mountains ▲ USA 20-21 S 2
Romblon ☆ RP 160-161 E 6
Romblon Island ⌒ RP 160-161 E 6
Romblon Strait ≈ 160-161 E 6
Rome o USA (AL) 284-285 D 5
Rome o USA (GA) 284-285 E 2
Rome o USA (NY) 278-279 F 5
Rome o USA (OH) 280-281 F 2
Rome o USA (OR) 244-245 H 8
Rome o USA (TN) 276-277 J 4
Rome = Roma ★••• I 100-101 D 4
Romeo o USA (MI) 272-273 F 5
Romeoville o USA (IL) 274-275 K 3
Romero o USA (TX) 264-265 B 3
Romero, Isla ⌒ RCH 80 C 2
Romer Sø o GRØ 26-27 q 3
Romita o MEX 52-53 D 1
Rommani o MA 188-189 H 4
Romney o USA (IN) 274-275 M 4
Romney o USA (WV) 280-281 H 4
Romny o RUS 122-123 C 3
Romny o UA 102-103 H 2
Rømø ⌒ DK 86-87 D 9
Romodan o UA 102-103 H 2
Romorantin-Lanthenay o F 90-91 H 8
Rompía o YV 60-61 H 4
Rompin ~ MAL 162-163 E 3
Romsdalen ⌣ N 86-87 C 5
Ronan o USA (MT) 250-251 E 4
Roncador o BR 74-75 D 5
Roncador, Serra do ▲ BR 72-73 E 2
Roncador Reef ⌒ SOL 184 I d 2
Roncesvalles o• E 98-99 G 3
Roncière Falls, La ~ CDN 24-25 L 6
Ronda o E 98-99 E 6
Ronda, Serranía de ▲ E 98-99 E 6
Rønde o DK 86-87 E 8
Ronde, Rivière la ~ CDN 38-39 L 2
Ronde Island ⌒ WG 56 E 5
Rondon o BR 72-73 D 7
Rondon, Pico ▲ BR 66-67 F 2
Rondon Dopara o BR 68-69 D 4
Rondônia ■ BR 70-71 F 2
Rondonópolis o BR 70-71 K 5
Rond-Point de Gaulle ▲ TCH 198-199 H 3
Rondslottet ▲ N 86-87 D 6
Rondu o IND 138-139 E 2
Rong'an o VRC 156-157 F 4
Rongbuk o VRC 144-145 F 6
Rongchang o VRC 156-157 D 2
Rongcheng o VRC 154-155 N 3
Rongjiang o VRC 156-157 F 4
Rongkong ~ RI 164-165 G 5
Rong Kwang o THA 142-143 M 6
Rongo o EAK 212-213 E 4
Rô'ng Quèn, Mũi ▲ VN 156-157 D 7
Rongshui o VRC 156-157 F 4
Rõngu o EST 94-95 K 2
Rong Xian o VRC (GXI) 156-157 G 5
Rong Xian o VRC (SIC) 156-157 D 2
Rønne o DK 86-87 G 9
Ronne Bay ≈ 16 F 29
Ronneby ☆ S 86-87 G 8
Rönnöfors o S 86-87 F 5
Ron Phibun o THA 158-159 E 6
Ronsard, Cape ▲ AUS 176-177 B 2
Ronuro, Rio ~ BR 70-71 K 3
Roodepoort o ZA 220-221 H 3
Roof Butte ▲ USA (AZ) 256-257 F 2
Rooiberge ▲ ZA 220-221 J 4
Rooibokkraal o ZA 220-221 H 2
Rooikloof ▲ ZA 220-221 E 6
Rooikop o NAM 216-217 C 11
Rooikraal o ZA 220-221 J 2
Rooirand ▲ NAM 220-221 C 2
Room, Pulau ⌒ RI 166-167 H 3
Rooney Point ▲ AUS 178-179 M 3
Roopville o USA (GA) 284-285 E 3
Roosevelt o USA (AZ) 256-257 D 5
Roosevelt o USA (OK) 264-265 E 4
Roosevelt o USA (TX) 266-267 G 3
Roosevelt o USA (UT) 254-255 E 3
Roosevelt o USA (WA) 244-245 E 5
Roosevelt, Área Indígena ⅄ BR 70-71 G 2
Roosevelt, Mount ▲ CDN 30-31 G 6
Roosevelt, Rio ~ BR 66-67 G 7
Roosevelt Beach o USA (OR) 244-245 A 6
Roosevelt Campobello International Park ∴ CDN (NB) 240-241 J 6
Roosevelt Fjelde ▲ GRØ 26-27 g 2
Roosevelt Island ⌒ ARK 16 F 21
Roossenekal o ZA 220-221 J 2
Roosville o CDN (BC) 230-231 O 4
Rootok Island ⌒ USA 22-23 O 5
Root River ~ CDN 30-31 G 4
Root River ~ USA 270-271 G 7
Roper Bar o AUS 174-175 C 4
Roper River ~ AUS 174-175 C 4
Roper Valley o AUS 174-175 C 4
Ropesville o USA (TX) 264-265 B 6
Roquefort o F 90-91 G 9
Roques, Islas los ⌒ YV 60-61 H 2
Roques, Los o YV 60-61 H 2
Roraima ■ BR 62-63 D 5
Roraima, Mount ▲ GUY 62-63 D 3
Roraya ~ RI 164-165 H 6
Rorey Lake o CDN 30-31 F 2
Rori o RI 166-167 J 2
Rorketon o CDN (MAN) 234-235 D 3
Røros ☆•• N 86-87 E 5
Rørvik o N 86-87 E 4
Ros' ~ UA 102-103 G 3
Rosa o CDN (MAN) 234-235 G 5
Rosa, La o YV 60-61 G 3
Rosa, Lake o BS 54-55 J 4
Rosa, Río Santa ~ BOL 70-71 D 5
Rosal o BR 72-73 K 6
Rosal' o RUS 94-95 Q 4
Rosal, El o CO 60-61 D 5
Rosal de la Frontera o E 98-99 D 6
Rosalia o USA (WA) 244-245 H 3
Rosalind o CDN (ALB) 232-233 F 3
Rosamond o USA (CA) 248-249 F 5
Rosamoraga o MEX 50-51 G 6
Rosana o BR 72-73 D 7
Rosário o BR 68-69 F 3
Rosario o DOM 54-55 K 5
Rosario o MEX 50-51 E 4
Rosario o PE 70-71 B 4
Rosario o PY 76-77 J 3
Rosario o RA (JU) 76-77 D 2
Rosario o• RA (SAF) 78-79 J 2
Rosario o ROU 78-77 D 4
Rosario o RP (BTG) 160-161 D 6
Rosario o RP (LUN) 160-161 D 4
Rosario, Cayo del ⌒ C 54-55 E 4
Rosario, El o MEX (BCN) 50-51 B 2
Rosario, El o MEX (SIN) 50-51 G 6
Rosario, El o YV 60-61 J 4
Rosario, Río ~ RA 76-77 E 3
Rosario, Río ~ RA 76-77 D 2
Rosario de la Frontera o• RA 76-77 E 3
Rosario de Lerma o RA 76-77 E 3
Rosario del Ingre o BOL 70-71 F 7
Rosario del Tala o RA 78-79 K 2
Rosário do Catete o BR 68-69 K 7
Rosário do Sul o BR 76-77 K 6
Rosário Oeste o BR 70-71 J 4
Rosario Strait ≈ 244-245 C 2
Rosarito o MEX (BCN) 50-51 B 3
Rosarito o MEX (BCS) 50-51 D 4
Rosarito o• MEX (BCN) 50-51 A 1
Rosas o CO 60-61 C 6
Rosas, Las o MEX 52-53 H 3
Rosas, Las o RA 78-79 J 2
Rosaspata o PE 70-71 C 4
Rosa Zárate o EC 64-65 C 1
Rosburg o USA (WA) 244-245 B 4
Roscoe o USA (NY) 280-281 M 2
Roscoe o USA (SD) 260-261 G 1
Roscoe o USA (TX) 264-265 D 6
Roscoe River ~ CDN 24-25 M 6
Roscoff o F 90-91 F 7
Ros Comáin = Roscommon ☆ IRL 90-91 C 5
Roscommon o USA (MI) 272-273 E 3
Roscommon = Ros Comáin ☆ IRL 90-91 C 5
Ros Cré = Roscrea o IRL 90-91 D 5
Roscrea = Ros Cré o IRL 90-91 D 5
Roseau o USA (MN) 270-271 C 2
Roseau ★ WD 56 E 4
Roseau River ~ USA 270-271 B 2
Roseau River Wildlife Refuge ⊥ USA (MN) 270-271 B 2
Roseaux o RH 54-55 H 5
Rosebank o CDN (MAN) 234-235 E 5
Rose Belle o MS 224 C 7
Rosebery o AUS 180-181 H 6
Roseblade Lake o CDN 30-31 V 5
Rose Blanche o CDN (NFL) 242-243 K 5
Roseboro o USA (NC) 282-283 J 6
Rosebud o CDN (ALB) 232-233 F 4
Rose Bud o USA (AR) 276-277 C 5
Rosebud o USA (SD) 260-261 F 3
Rosebud o USA (TX) 266-267 L 2
Rosebud Creek ~ USA 250-251 N 6
Rosebud Indian Reservation ⅄ USA (SD) 260-261 F 3
Rosebud River ~ CDN 232-233 E 4
Roseburg o USA (OR) 244-245 B 7
Rose City o USA (MI) 272-273 E 3
Rose Creek ~ CDN 232-233 D 3
Rosedale o AUS 178-179 J 2
Rosedale o CDN (ALB) 232-233 F 4
Rosedale o CDN (BC) 230-231 H 4
Rosedale o USA (IN) 274-275 L 5
Rosedale o USA (MS) 268-269 J 3
Rosefield o USA (LA) 268-269 H 5
Roseglen o USA (ND) 258-259 F 4
Rose Harbour o CDN (BC) 228-229 C 4
Rose Hill o MS 224 C 7
Rose Hill o USA (MS) 268-269 L 4
Rose Hill o USA (NC) 282-283 J 6
Roseisle o CDN (MAN) 234-235 E 5
Rose Lake o CDN (BC) 228-229 H 2
Rose Lake o USA (ID) 250-251 C 4
Roseland o USA (LA) 268-269 K 6
Roselle o USA (IL) 274-275 K 3
Rosemount o USA (MN) 270-271 E 6
Rosenberg o USA (TX) 268-269 E 7
Rosenberg = Ružomberok o SK 92-93 P 4
Rosenberg, Sulzbach- o D 92-93 L 4
Rosenburg o CDN (MAN) 234-235 F 3
Rosendal ☆ N 86-87 C 7
Rosendal o ZA 220-221 H 4
Rosenfeld o USA (TX) 266-267 E 3
Rosenheim o• D 92-93 M 5
Rosenort o CDN (MAN) 234-235 F 5
Rose Point ▲ CDN (BC) 228-229 C 2
Rose Prairie o CDN 32-33 K 3
Rose River ~ AUS 174-175 C 3
Roses o USA (PA) 280-281 G 2
Rosetilla o MEX 50-51 G 3
Rosetown o CDN (SAS) 232-233 L 4
Rosetta = Rašīd o• ET 194-195 E 2
Rosette o USA (UT) 254-255 B 2
Rose Valley o CDN (SAS) 232-233 P 3
Roseveor o CDN (ALB) 232-233 B 2
Roseveltpiek ▲ SME 62-63 G 4
Roseville o USA (IL) 274-275 H 4
Roseville Rio o USA (CA) 246-247 D 5
Rosewood o AUS 172-173 J 4
Rosharon o USA (TX) 268-269 E 7
Rosh Pinah o NAM 220-221 C 3
Rosie Creek o AUS 174-175 C 4
Rosiers, Cap-des- o CDN (QUE) 240-241 L 2
Rosignano Marittima o I 100-101 C 3
Rosignol o GUY 62-63 F 2
Roșiori de Vede o RO 102-103 D 5
Rosita, La o CO 60-61 F 5
Rosita, La o NIC 52-53 B 5
Roskilde o•• DK 86-87 F 9
Roslavl' o RUS 94-95 N 5
Roslin o CDN (ONT) 238-239 H 4
Roslyn Lake o CDN (ONT) 234-235 Q 5
Rosman o USA (NC) 282-283 E 5
Rosmead o ZA 220-221 G 5
Ros Mhic Thriúin = New Ross o IRL 90-91 D 5
Ross, Cape ▲ RP 160-161 C 7
Rossano o I 100-101 F 5
Ross Barnett Reservoir < USA (MS) 268-269 L 4
Ross Bay ≈ 24-25 d 7
Ross Bay Junction o CDN 38-39 L 2
Ross-Béthio o SN 196-197 B 6
Rossburn o CDN (MAN) 234-235 C 4
Ross City o USA (TX) 264-265 C 6
Rosseau o CDN (ONT) 238-239 F 3
Rosseau, Lake o CDN (ONT) 238-239 F 3
Rosser o CDN (MAN) 234-235 F 4
Ross Ice Shelf ⊂ ARK 16 E 0
Rossignol, Lac o CDN 38-39 H 2
Rossignol, Lake o CDN (NS) 240-241 K 6
Rössing o NAM 216-217 C 11
Ross Inlet ≈ 24-25 c 7
Ross Island ⌒ ARK 16 F 17
Ross Island ⌒ ARK 16 G 31
Ross Lake o USA (WA) 244-245 E 2
Rossland o CDN (BC) 230-231 M 4
Rosslare = Ros Láir o IRL 90-91 D 5
Rosso ☆ RIM 196-197 C 6
Rossomaha ~ RUS 114-115 T 5
Rossošino o RUS 118-119 G 8
Rossouw o ZA 220-221 H 5
Rossport o CDN (ONT) 234-235 Q 6
Ross River o AUS 178-179 C 2
Ross River o CDN (NWT) 20-21 Y 6
Ross River ~ CDN 20-21 Z 5
Ross Sea ≈ 16 F 19
Rosston o USA (AR) 276-277 B 7
Rosston o USA (OK) 264-265 E 2
Røssvatnet o N 86-87 F 4
Rossville o AUS 174-175 H 4
Rosswood o CDN (BC) 228-229 F 2
Røst o N 86-87 F 3
Rostāq o AFG 136-137 L 6
Rostāq o IR 134-135 E 5
Rosthern o CDN (SAS) 232-233 M 3
Rostock o•• D 92-93 M 1
Rostov ☆•• RUS 94-95 Q 3
Rostov-na-Donu ☆ RUS 102-103 L 4
Rostraver o USA (PA) 280-281 G 3
Rostrenen o F 90-91 F 7
Roswell o USA (GA) 284-285 F 2
Roswell o USA (NM) 256-257 L 5
Roswell o USA (SD) 260-261 J 2
Rosyth o CDN (ALB) 232-233 G 3
Rotan o USA (TX) 264-265 D 6
Rote = Pulau Roti ⌒ RI 166-167 B 7
Rothenburg ob der Tauber o•• D 92-93 L 4
Rotherham o GB 90-91 G 5
Rothesay o• GB 90-91 E 4
Rothsay o USA (MN) 270-271 B 4
Rothschild o USA (WI) 270-271 J 6
Roti o RI 166-167 B 7
Roti, Pulau ⌒ RI 166-167 B 7
Roti, Selat ≈ 166-167 B 7
Rotifunk o WAL 202-203 D 5
Roto o AUS 180-181 H 2
Rotonda West o USA (FL) 286-287 G 5
Rotondo, Monte ▲ F 98-99 M 3
Rotorua o•• NZ 182 F 3
Rotterdam o• NL 92-93 H 3
Rottnest Island o• AUS (WA) 176-177 C 6
Rottnest Island ⌒ AUS (WA) 176-177 C 6
Rottweil o• D 92-93 K 4
Roualist Bank ≃ 158-159 H 6
Roubaix o F 90-91 J 6
Rouen ☆• F 90-91 H 7
Rouge, Rivière ~ CDN 238-239 L 3
Rouge, Rivière ~ CDN 238-239 L 2
Rough River ~ USA 276-277 J 3
Rough River Reservoir < USA (KY) 276-277 J 3
Rough Rock o USA (AZ) 256-257 F 2
Rouhia o TN 190-191 G 3
Rouleau o CDN (SAS) 232-233 O 5
Roumsiki o• CAM 204-205 K 3
Roundeyed, Lac o CDN 38-39 J 2
Roundhead o USA (OH) 280-281 C 3
Round Hill o CDN (ALB) 232-233 F 2
Round Hill o USA (KY) 276-277 J 3
Round House ▲ USA (KS) 262-263 G 6
Round Lake o CDN (ONT) 238-239 H 3
Round Mountain ▲ AUS 178-179 M 6
Round Mountain o USA (CA) 246-247 D 3
Round Mountain o USA (NV) 246-247 H 5
Round Pond o CDN (NFL) 242-243 N 4
Round Rock o USA (AZ) 256-257 F 2
Round Rock o USA (TX) 266-267 K 3
Round Spring o USA (MO) 276-277 D 3
Round Spring Cave • USA (MO) 276-277 D 3
Round Top o USA (TX) 266-267 L 3
Roundup o USA (MT) 250-251 L 5
Round Valley Indian Reservation ⅄ USA (CA) 246-247 B 4
Rounthwaite o CDN (MAN) 234-235 D 5
Roura o F 62-63 H 3
Rouses Point o USA (NY) 278-279 H 4
Route des Kasbahs • MA 188-189 H 5
Routhierville o CDN (QUE) 240-241 H 2
Rouxville o ZA 220-221 H 5
Rouyn-Noranda o CDN (QUE) 236-237 J 4
Rovdino o RUS 88-89 R 6
Roven'ky o UA 102-103 L 3
Rover o USA (AR) 276-277 B 6
Rover, Mount ▲ CDN 20-21 U 3
Rovereto o• I 100-101 C 2
Rovemi o RA 76-77 G 4
Rovigo ☆ I 100-101 C 2
Rovinari o RO 102-103 C 5
Rovinj o• HR 100-101 D 2
Rovno = Rivne o UA 102-103 E 2
Rovnoe o RUS 96-97 E 8
Rovnyj, mys ▲ RUS 120-121 V 4
Rovnyj, ostrov ⌒ RUS 120-121 U 3
Rovubo ~ EAT 212-213 C 6
Rovuma, Rio = Ruvuma ~ MOC 214-215 K 6
Rowala Kot o IND 138-139 D 3
Rowan, Port o CDN (ONT) 238-239 E 6
Rowatt o CDN (SAS) 232-233 O 5
Rowden o USA (TX) 264-265 E 6
Rowdy o USA (KY) 276-277 M 3
Rowena o USA (TX) 266-267 G 2
Rowland o USA (NC) 282-283 H 6
Rowletta o CDN (SAS) 232-233 N 5
Rowley o CDN 24-25 g 6
Rowley Island ⌒ CDN 24-25 h 6
Rowley Lake o CDN 30-31 R 5
Rowley River ~ CDN 24-25 j 5
Rowley Shelf ≃ 172-173 C 5
Rowley Shoals ⌒ AUS 172-173 D 4
Roxa, Ilha ⌒ GNB 202-203 C 4
Roxas o RP (ISA) 160-161 D 4
Roxas o RP (MIO) 160-161 D 6
Roxas o RP (PAL) 160-161 C 7
Roxas ☆ RP (CAP) 160-161 E 7
Roxboro o USA (NC) 282-283 J 4
Roxborough Downs o AUS 178-179 E 2
Roxby Downs o AUS 178-179 D 6
Roxie o USA (MS) 268-269 J 5
Roxo, Cap ▲ GNB 202-203 B 3
Roxton o USA (TX) 264-265 J 5
Roxton Falls o CDN (QUE) 238-239 N 3
Roy o USA (MT) 250-251 L 4
Roy o USA (NM) 256-257 L 3
Roy o USA (TX) 264-265 B 4
Roy o USA (UT) 254-255 C 2
Roy, Lac le o CDN 36-37 M 5
Royal, Mount ▲ CDN (ONT) 234-235 P 5
Royal Center o USA (IN) 274-275 M 4
Royal Charlotte, Bank ≃ 72-73 L 4
Royal Chitawan National Park ⊥••• NEP 144-145 E 7
Royal City o USA (WA) 244-245 F 4
Royale, Isle ⌒ USA (MI) 270-271 J 3
Royal Geographical Society Islands ⌒ CDN 24-25 W 6
Royal Gorge • USA (CO) 254-255 K 5
Royal Island ⌒ BS 54-55 G 2
Royal Natal National Park ⊥ ZA 220-221 J 4
Royal National Park ⊥ AUS 180-181 L 3
Royal Palace o• RI 168 D 7
Royal Palm Hammock o USA (FL) 286-287 H 6
Royal Park o CDN (ALB) 232-233 F 2
Royal Society Range ▲ ARK 16 F 16
Royal Sound, Port ≈ 48-49 H 3
Royalties o CDN (ALB) 232-233 D 5
Royalton o USA (MN) 270-271 D 5
Royalton o USA (VT) 278-279 J 5
Royan o• F 90-91 G 9
Roye o F 90-91 J 7
Roy Hill o AUS (WA) 172-173 D 7
Roy Hill ▲ AUS (WA) 172-173 D 7
Røyrvik o N 86-87 F 4
Royston o USA (GA) 284-285 G 2
Rožaje o• YU 100-101 H 3
Różan o PL 92-93 Q 2
Rozdol'ne ☆ UA 102-103 H 5
Rozel o USA (KS) 262-263 G 6
Rozet o USA (WY) 252-253 N 2
Rozivka o UA 102-103 K 4
Rožňava o SK 92-93 Q 4
Rozy Ljuksemburg, mys ⌣ RUS 108-109 I c 1
r-Raṭqa, Wādī ~ IRQ 128-129 J 6
Rtiščevo o RUS 94-95 S 5
Ruacana o NAM 216-217 C 8
Ruacaná, Quedas do ~•• ANG 216-217 C 8
Ruacana Falls ~•• NAM 216-217 C 8
Ruaha National Park ⊥ EAT 214-215 H 4
Ruahine Range ▲ NZ 182 F 3
Ru'ais o UAE 134-135 E 6
Ruangwa o EAT 214-215 K 6
Ruapehu, Mount ▲ NZ 182 E 3
Ruapuke Island ⌒ NZ 182 B 7
Ruarwe o MW 214-215 H 6
Ruatahuna o NZ 182 F 3
Ruatoria o NZ 182 G 2
Ruawai o NZ 182 E 2
Ru'ays, Wādī ar ~ LAR 192-193 G 4
Rubafu o EAT 212-213 C 4
Rubai'īya, ar- o KSA 130-131 J 4
Rub' al-Ḫālī, ar- ⊥ KSA 132-133 D 4
Rubcovsk o RUS 124-125 M 3
Rubeho Mountains ▲ EAT 214-215 J 4
Rubens, Río ~ RCH 80 D 6
Rubeshibe o J 152-153 K 3
Rubi o ZRE (HAU) 210-211 K 2
Rubi ~ ZRE 210-211 K 2
Rubiataba o BR 72-73 F 3
Rubicon River ~ USA 246-247 E 5
Rubikon, mys ▲ RUS 112-113 S 6
Rubim o BR 72-73 K 4
Rubinéia o BR 72-73 E 6
Rubio o YV 60-61 E 4
Ruble o USA (IA) 274-275 B 2
Rubondo Island ⌒ EAT 212-213 C 5
Rubondo National Park ⊥ EAT 212-213 C 5
Ruby o USA 20-21 N 4
Ruby o USA (AZ) 256-257 D 7
Ruby Dome ▲ USA (NV) 246-247 K 3
Ruby Lake o CDN (SAS) 232-233 Q 2
Ruby Lake o USA (NV) 246-247 K 3
Ruby Mountains ▲ USA 246-247 K 3
Ruby Plains o AUS 172-173 H 5
Ruby Range ▲ CDN 20-21 V 6
Ruby River ~ USA 250-251 G 6
Rubys Inn o USA (UT) 254-255 C 6
Rubyvale o AUS 178-179 J 2
Ruby Valley o USA (NV) 246-247 K 3
Rucachoroi, Cerro ▲ RA 78-79 D 5
Rucava o LV 94-95 G 3
Ruch o USA (OR) 244-245 B 8
Ruči o RUS 88-89 Q 3
Rucio, El o MEX 50-51 H 6
Ruckersville o USA (VA) 280-281 H 5
Rud o IR 134-135 J 1
Rudal o AUS 180-181 D 2
Rudall River National Park ⊥ AUS 172-173 F 7
Rūdbar o• IR 128-129 N 4
Ruddell o CDN (SAS) 232-233 L 3
Ruddera, buhta ≈ 112-113 W 4
Rūd-e Čālus ~ IR 136-137 B 6
Rūd-e Helle ~ IR 134-135 D 4
Rūdehen o IR 136-137 B 7
Rūd-e Mārūn ~ IR 134-135 C 3
Rudewa o EAT 214-215 H 6
Rūdḫāne-ye 'Alīābād ~ IR 134-135 J 3
Rūdḫāne-ye Ġarrāhī ~ IR 134-135 C 3
Rūdḫāne-ye Nekā ~ IR 136-137 C 6
Rudkøbing o• DK 86-87 E 9
Rudnaja Pristan' o RUS 122-123 F 6
Rudnik ▲• YU 100-101 H 2
Rudnja ☆ RUS 94-95 M 4
Rudnyj o KZ 124-125 C 2
Rudnyy = Rudnyj o KZ 124-125 C 2
Rud Ø ⌒ GRØ 28-29 T 5
Rudolf, Lake = Turkana, Lake o EAK 212-213 F 1
Rudol'fa o RUS 84-85 e 2
Rudol'fa, ostrov ⌒ RUS 84-85 f 2
Rudong o VRC 154-155 M 5
Rūdsar o IR 136-137 B 6
Rudyard o USA (MI) 270-271 O 4
Rudyard o USA (MT) 250-251 J 3
Rue, La o USA (TX) 264-265 J 6
Ruente Nacional o CO 60-61 E 5
Ruenya ~ ZW 218-219 G 3
Rufā'ah o SUD 200-201 F 5
Ruff Creek o USA (PA) 280-281 F 4
Ruffin o USA (SC) 284-285 K 3
Rufiji ~ EAT 214-215 J 5
Rufino o BR 62-63 F 6
Rufino o RA 78-79 H 3
Rufisque o SN 202-203 B 2
Rufrufua o RI 166-167 G 3
Rufunsa o Z (Lus) 218-219 E 2
Rufunsa ~ Z 218-219 E 2
Rufus o USA (OR) 244-245 E 5
Rufus Lake o CDN 20-21 Z 2
Rugāji o LV 94-95 K 3
Rugao o VRC 154-155 M 5
Rugby o USA (ND) 258-259 G 3
Rügen ⌒ D 92-93 M 1
Rügenwalde = Darłowo o• PL 92-93 O 1
Rugged Island ⌒ USA 20-21 Q 7
Rugheiwa o SUD 200-201 E 4
Rugufu ~ EAT 212-213 C 6
Ruhayyah, Ġabal ar- ▲ KSA 130-131 L 4
Ruhengeri o RWA 212-213 B 4
Ruhnu saar ⌒• EST 94-95 H 3
Ruhudji ~ EAT 214-215 H 5
Ruhuhu ~ EAT 214-215 H 6
Rui'an o VRC 156-157 M 3
Rui Barbosa o BR 72-73 K 2
Ruichang o VRC 156-157 J 2
Ruicheng o VRC 154-155 G 4
Ruidosa o USA (TX) 266-267 C 3
Ruidoso o USA (NM) 256-257 K 5
Ruidoso Downs o USA (NM) 256-257 K 5
Ruijin o VRC 156-157 J 4
Ruiki ~ ZRE 210-211 K 4
Ruili o VRC 142-143 K 3
Ruimte o NAM 220-221 B 1
Ruinas Cayastá • RA 76-77 G 6
Ruinas Indígenas de Quilmes • RA 76-77 D 4
Ruins of Sambor • K 158-159 H 4
Ruins of Sampanago • MYA 142-143 K 3
Ruipa o EAT 214-215 J 5
Ruiru o EAK 212-213 F 4
Ruisseau-à-Rebours o CDN (QUE) 242-243 C 3
Ruitersbos o ZA 220-221 F 6
Ruiz, Nevado del ▲ CO 60-61 D 5
Rūjiena o•• LV 94-95 J 3
Ruka o FIN 88-89 K 3
Rukanga o EAK 212-213 G 5
Rukarara ~ RWA 212-213 B 5
Ruki ~ ZRE 210-211 G 4
Rukua o RI 164-165 J 6
Rukutama ~ RUS 122-123 K 4
Rukwa ■ EAT 214-215 F 4
Rukwa, Lake o EAT 214-215 F 4
Rule o USA (TX) 264-265 E 5
Rulenge o EAT 212-213 C 5
Ruleville o USA (MS) 268-269 K 3
Ruma o WAN 198-199 C 6
Ruma o YU 100-101 G 2
Rumāḥ o KSA 130-131 K 5
Rumahbaru o RI 162-163 B 2
Rumahkai o RI 166-167 E 3
Rumah Kulit o MAL 164-165 D 2
Rumahtinggih o RI 166-167 I 5
Rumaila o IRQ 130-131 K 2
Ruma National Park ⊥ EAK 212-213 E 4
Rumbek o SUD 206-207 J 5
Rumberpon, Pulau ⌒ RI 166-167 H 2
Rumble Beach o CDN (BC) 230-231 D 3
Rum Cay = Mamana Island ⌒ BS 54-55 H 3
Rumeila o SUD 200-201 G 6
Rum Jungle o AUS 172-173 K 2
Rummāna o ET 194-195 F 2
Rumo o BR 68-69 F 2
Rumoi o J 152-153 J 3
Rumonge o BU 212-213 B 5
Rumorosa, La o• MEX 50-51 A 1
Rumphi o MW 214-215 G 6
Rumpi Hills ▲ CAM 204-205 H 6
Rum River ~ USA 270-271 E 5
Rumsey o CDN (ALB) 232-233 F 4
Rumuruti o EAK 212-213 F 3
Run, Pulau ⌒ RI 166-167 E 4
Runan o VRC 154-155 J 5
Runaway, Cape ▲ NZ 182 F 2
Runaway Bay o JA 54-55 G 5
Runazi o EAT 212-213 C 5
Runde ~ ZW 218-219 G 5
Rundeng o RI 162-163 B 3
Rundu ☆ NAM 216-217 E 8
Runduma, Pulau ⌒ RI 164-165 J 6
Runge o USA (TX) 266-267 K 5
Rungu o ZRE 212-213 A 2
Rungwa o EAT (RUK) 214-215 F 4
Rungwa o EAT (SIN) 214-215 G 4
Rungwa ~ EAT 214-215 G 4
Rungwa Game Reserve ⊥ EAT 214-215 G 4
Runmarö ⌒ S 86-87 J 7
Running Springs o USA (CA) 248-249 G 5
Running Water Draw ~ USA 264-265 B 4
Runnymede o AUS 174-175 G 7
Runnymede o CDN (SAS) 232-233 R 4
Runton Range ▲ AUS 172-173 F 7
Ruokolahti o FIN 88-89 K 6
Ruoqiang o VRC 146-147 J 6
Ruo Shui ~ VRC 148-149 D 7
Ruo Shui ~ VRC 154-155 B 2
Ruovesi o FIN 88-89 H 6
Rupanco, Lago o RCH 78-79 C 6
Rupanyup o AUS 180-181 G 4
Rupat, Pulau ⌒ RI 162-163 D 4
Rupat, Selat ≈ 162-163 D 4
Rupert o USA (AR) 276-277 C 5
Rupert o USA (ID) 252-253 E 4
Rupert o USA (WV) 280-281 F 6
Rupert, Fort o CDN 38-39 E 3
Rupert, Rivière de ~ CDN 38-39 E 3
Rupisi o ZW 218-219 G 5
Ruponda o EAT 214-215 K 6
Ruppert Coast ⌣ ARK 16 F 22
Ruqai', ar- o KSA 130-131 K 3
Ruqayba o SUD 200-201 E 5
Rural Hall o USA (NC) 282-283 G 4
Rurópolis Presidente Médici o BR 66-67 K 5
Rurutu, Île ⌒ F 13 M 5
Ruṣāfa, ar- o•• SYR 128-129 H 5
Rušan o TJ 136-137 M 6
Rusanova, lednik ⊂ RUS 108-109 I b 2
Rusanova, zaliv ≈ 108-109 J 4
Rusanovo o RUS 108-109 G 6
Rusape o ZW 218-219 G 4
Ruṣayriṣ Dam < SUD 208-209 B 3
Ruse o BG 102-103 D 6
Rushan o VRC 154-155 M 3
Rush Center o USA (KS) 262-263 G 6
Rush City o USA (MN) 270-271 F 5
Rush Creek ~ USA 254-255 M 5
Rush Creek ~ USA 264-265 G 4
Rushfort o USA (MN) 270-271 G 7
Rush Lake o CDN (SAS) 232-233 L 5
Rush Springs o USA (OK) 264-265 G 4
Rushville o USA (IL) 274-275 H 4
Rushville o USA (IN) 274-275 N 5
Rushville o USA (NE) 262-263 D 2
Rushworth o AUS 180-181 H 4
Rusizi ~ BU 212-213 B 5
Rusk o USA (TX) 268-269 E 5
Rus'ka o UA 102-103 D 4
Rus'ka, Rava- o UA 102-103 C 2
Ruskin o USA (FL) 286-287 G 4
Ruskin o USA (NE) 262-263 J 4
Ruskele o S 86-87 J 4
Rusnė o•• LT 94-95 G 4
Ruso o USA (ND) 258-259 G 4
Rus Rus o HN 52-53 B 4
Russas o BR 68-69 K 4
Russel o CDN (MAN) 234-235 B 4
Russel o USA (MN) 270-271 C 6
Russell o USA (KS) 262-263 H 6
Russell o USA (ND) 258-259 G 3
Russell o USA (NY) 278-279 F 4
Russell, Cape ▲ CDN 24-25 N 3
Russell, Kap ▲ GRØ 26-27 Q 4
Russell, Mount ▲ AUS 172-173 K 7
Russell, Mount ▲ USA 20-21 P 5
Russel Lake o CDN 30-31 M 4
Russell Fiord ≈ 20-21 V 7
Russell Fiord Wilderness ⊥ USA 20-21 V 7
Russell Gletscher ⊂ GRØ 28-29 P 3
Russell Inlet ≈ 20-21 Z 2
Russell Island ⌒ CDN 24-25 W 4
Russell Islands ⌒ SOL 184 I d 3
Russell Lake o CDN 34-35 F 2
Russell Lake < USA (GA) 284-285 H 2
Russellville o USA (AL) 284-285 C 2
Russellville o USA (AR) 276-277 B 5
Russellville o USA (KY) 276-277 J 4
Russel Springs o USA (KS) 262-263 E 6
Russia = Rossija ■ RUS 94-95 O 5
Russian River ~ USA 246-247 B 4
Russiaville o USA (IN) 274-275 M 4
Russkaja Gavan', zaliv ≈ 108-109 K 3
Russkaja Lučajaha ~ RUS 108-109 T 8
Russkaja Rečka o RUS 118-119 K 5
Russkaja Tavra o RUS 96-97 K 5
Russkie gory ▲ RUS 112-113 P 4
Russkij, ostrov ⌒ RUS 108-109 b 3
Russkij Žavorot, poluostrov ⌣ RUS 88-89 W 2
Rustāq, ar- o OM 132-133 K 2
Rustavi o GE 126-127 F 7
Rustburg o USA (VA) 280-281 G 6
Rust de Winter o ZA 220-221 J 2
Rust de Winterdam < ZA 220-221 J 2
Rustefjelbma o N 86-87 O 1
Rustenburg o ZA 220-221 H 2
Rustfontein Dam < ZA 220-221 H 4
Rustic o USA (CO) 254-255 K 3
Ruston o USA (LA) 268-269 H 4
Rusumo Falls ~• EAT 212-213 C 5
Ruta o RI 164-165 K 4
Rutaimi, ar- o IRQ 128-129 J 5
Rutan o CDN (SAS) 232-233 N 3
Rutana o BU 212-213 C 5
Rutba, ar- o IRQ 128-129 J 6
Ruten ▲ N (OPP) 86-87 D 6
Ruten ▲ N (STR) 86-87 D 5
Ruteng o• RI 168 E 7
Rutenga o ZW 218-219 F 5
Ruth o USA (NC) 282-283 F 5
Ruth o USA (NV) 246-247 L 4
Rutherford Fork ~ USA 276-277 G 4
Rutherglen o AUS 180-181 J 4
Ruthilda o CDN (SAS) 232-233 K 4
Ruthville o USA (ND) 258-259 F 3
Ruti o PNG 183 C 3
Rutland o CDN (BC) 230-231 K 4
Rutland o CDN (SAS) 232-233 J 3
Rutland o USA (VT) 278-279 J 5
Rutland Island ⌒ IND 140-141 L 4
Rutland Plains o AUS 174-175 F 4
Rutledge o USA (TN) 282-283 D 4
Rutledge Lake o CDN 30-31 O 5
Rutledge River ~ CDN 30-31 O 5
Rutog o VRC 144-145 B 4
Rutshuru o ZRE 212-213 B 4
Rutukira ~ EAT 214-215 H 6
Rutul o RUS 126-127 G 7
Ru'us al-Ǧibāl ▲ OM 134-135 G 6
Ruvu ~ EAT 214-215 K 4
Ruvubu, Parc National de la ⊥ BU 212-213 C 5
Ruvuma ■ EAT 214-215 H 6
Ruvuma = Rio Rovuma ~ EAT 214-215 K 6
Ruwaiḍa, ar- o KSA (RIY) 130-131 J 6
Ruwaiḍa, ar- o KSA (RIY) 130-131 J 5
Ruwais, ar- o Q 134-135 D 5
Ruwaišid, Wādī r- ~ JOR 130-131 F 1
Ruwāq, Ǧabal ar- ▲ SYR 128-129 G 5
Ruwenzori ▲ ZRE 212-213 B 3
Ruwī o OM 132-133 L 2
Ruya ~ ZW 218-219 F 3
Ruyang o VRC 154-155 H 4
Rū-ye Dōāb o AFG 136-137 K 7
Ruyigi o BU 212-213 C 5
Ruyuan o VRC 156-157 H 4
Ruza ☆ RUS 94-95 P 4
Ruzaevka o RUS 96-97 D 6
Ružany o BY 94-95 J 5
Ruzhou o VRC 154-155 H 4
Ružomberok o SK 92-93 P 4
Rwamagana o RWA 212-213 C 4
Rwanda ■ RWA 212-213 B 5
Rwashamaire o EAU 212-213 C 4
Rweru, Lac o BU 212-213 C 5
Ryan o USA (OK) 264-265 G 4
Ryan, Mount ▲ AUS (NSW) 180-181 K 2
Ryan, Mount ▲ AUS (QLD) 174-175 G 4

Rohri Canal — Ryan, Mount 385

Salvador, Lake ○ **USA** (LA) 268-269 K 7
Salvador, Passe de ▲ **RN** 192-193 E 6
Salvador do Sul o **BR** 74-75 E 7
Salvage o **CDN** (NFL) 242-243 P 4
Salvaterra o **BR** 62-63 K 6
Salvaterra o **E** 98-99 C 3
Salvatierra o **MEX** 52-53 D 1
Salvation, Point ▲ **AUS** 176-177 G 4
Salvator Rosa Section ⊥ **AUS** 178-179 J 3
Salve Ø ⌒ **GRØ** 26-27 R 5
Salve River ~ **CDN** 30-31 O 6
Salvo o **USA** (NC) 282-283 M 5
Salvus o **CDN** (BC) 228-229 E 2
Salwā, as- o **KSA** 134-135 D 6
Salwā Baḥrī o **ET** 194-195 F 5
Salween = Thanlwin Myit ~ **MYA** 142-143 K 6
Salyan o **AZ** 128-129 N 3
Salyersville o **USA** (KY) 276-277 M 3
Šalyhyne o **UA** 102-103 J 2
Salzberger Bay ≈ 16 F 22
Salzburg □ **A** 92-93 M 5
Salzburg ☆·· **A** 92-93 M 5
Salzgitter o **D** 92-93 L 2
Salzwedel o· **D** 92-93 L 2
Sam o **G** 210-211 C 3
Ša'm, aš o **UAE** 134-135 G 5
Sam, kum ∸ **KZ** 126-127 L 5
Sama o **PE** 70-71 B 5
Sama, Río ~ **PE** 70-71 B 5
Samachique o **MEX** 50-51 F 4
Samachvalavičy o **BY** 94-95 K 5
Samadābād o **IR** 134-135 H 2
Samagaltaj ☆ **RUS** 116-117 G 10
Samah ~ **MYA** 142-143 K 5
Samā'il o **OM** 132-133 L 2
Samaipata · **BOL** 70-71 F 6
Samak, Tanjung ▲ **RI** 162-163 F 5
Samakona o **CI** 202-203 G 5
Samakoulou o **RMM** 202-203 F 3
Samal o **RP** 160-161 F 9
Samal, Tanjung ▲ **RI** 166-167 E 3
Samalá, Río ~ **GCA** 52-53 J 4
Samalayuca o **MEX** 50-51 F 2
Samales Group ⌒ **RP** 160-161 D 9
Samalga Island ⌒ **USA** 22-23 M 6
Samalga Pass ≈ 22-23 M 6
Samal Island ⌒ **RP** 160-161 F 9
Sāmalkot o **IND** 142-143 C 7
Samalusi o **LAR** 192-193 J 1
Samālūṭ o **ET** 194-195 E 3
Šamalzāi o **AFG** 134-135 M 3
Samambaia, Rio ~ **BR** 72-73 D 7
Šaman, gora · **RUS** 122-123 H 3
Sam'ān, Qal'at ·· **SYR** 128-129 G 4
Samaná ☆·· **DOM** 54-55 L 5
Samaná, Bahía de ≈ 54-55 L 5
Samaná, Cabo ▲ **DOM** 54-55 L 5
Samaná, Península ⌣ **DOM** 54-55 L 5
Samana Cay ⌒ **BS** 54-55 J 3
Samanco o **PE** 64-65 C 6
Samandağ ☆ **TR** 128-129 F 4
Samandré Lake ○ **CDN** 30-31 M 2
Samanga o **EAT** 214-215 K 5
Samangān o **AFG** (SAM) 136-137 L 6
Samangān □ **AFG** 136-137 K 6
Samangan, Rūd-e ~ **AFG** 136-137 K 7
Šamaniha ~ **RUS** 110-111 d 7
Šamanij kamen' · **RUS** 116-117 M 8
Šamanka ~ **RUS** 120-121 T 4
Samanturai o **CL** 140-141 J 7
Samaqua, Rivière ~ **CDN** 236-237 O 3
Samar ⌒ **RP** 160-161 F 7
Samara ☆ **RUS** 96-97 G 7
Samara ~ **RUS** 96-97 H 7
Samara ~ **UA** 102-103 J 3
Samara ~ **UA** 102-103 K 3
Samarai o **PNG** 183 F 6
Samarang, Tanjung ▲ **MAL** 160-161 B 9
Samarga o **RUS** (HRB) 122-123 H 5
Samarga ~ **RUS** 122-123 H 5
Samari o **PNG** 183 B 5
Samariapo o **YV** 60-61 H 5
Samarinda ☆· **RI** 164-165 E 4
Samarkand ☆·· **UZ** 136-137 K 5
Samarkand = Samarkand ☆·· **UZ** 136-137 K 5
Samarkandskaja oblast' □ **UZ** 136-137 H 3
Samarqand = Samarkand ☆·· **UZ** 136-137 K 5
Sāmarrā' ☆· **IRQ** 128-129 K 5
Samar Sea ≈ 160-161 F 6
Samarskoe o **KZ** 124-125 N 4
Samarskoe vodohranilišče < **RUS** 96-97 F 7
Samaru o **WAN** 204-205 G 3
Samastipur o **IND** 142-143 D 3
Samate o **RI** 166-167 F 2
Samatiguila o· **CI** 202-203 G 5
Sāmatra o **IND** 138-139 B 8
Samaúma o **BR** 66-67 F 3
Samāwa, as- ☆ **IRQ** 128-129 L 7
Samaysa Dheer o **SP** 208-209 J 4
Samba o **BF** 202-203 J 3
Samba o **IND** 138-139 E 3
Samba o **RCA** 206-207 C 6
Samba ~ **RI** 162-163 K 5
Samba o **ZRE** (EQU) 210-211 H 3
Samba o **ZRE** (KIV) 210-211 L 6
Samba Caju o **ANG** 216-217 C 4
Sambailo o **RG** 202-203 D 3
Sambalgou o **BF** 202-203 L 3
Sambaliung Pegunungan ▲ **RI** 164-165 E 3
Sambalpur o **IND** 142-143 C 5
Sambao ~ **RM** 222-223 D 6
Sambar, Tanjung ▲ **RI** 162-163 J 6
Sambas o **RI** (KBA) 162-163 H 4
Sambas ~ **RI** 162-163 H 4
Sambau o **RI** 162-163 F 5
Sambava o **RM** 222-223 G 5
Sambazô, Rio ~ **MOC** 218-219 H 4
Samberi o **RI** 166-167 H 2
Sambhal o **IND** 138-139 G 5
Sambialgou o **BF** 202-203 L 3
Sambir ☆ **UA** 102-103 C 3
Sambirano ~ **RM** 222-223 F 4
Sambisumbi o **SOL** 184 I c 2
Sambito, Rio ~ **BR** 68-69 H 5
Sambo o **ANG** 216-217 D 6
Sambo o **RI** 164-165 F 5
Samboja o **RI** 164-165 E 4
Samborombón, Bahía ≈ 78-79 L 3
Samborombón, Río ~ **RA** 78-79 L 3
Samborondón o **EC** 64-65 C 2
Sāmbrāni o **IND** 140-141 F 3
Sambriāl o **PK** 138-139 E 3
Sambro o **CDN** (NS) 240-241 M 6
Samburg o **RUS** 108-109 S 8
Samburu o **EAK** 212-213 G 5
Samburu National Reserve ⊥ **EAK** 212-213 F 3
Sambusu o **NAM** 216-217 E 8
Samch'ŏk o **ROK** 150-151 G 9
Samch'ŏnp'o o **ROK** 150-151 G 10
Samdrup Jonkhar o **BHT** 142-143 G 2
Same o **EAT** 212-213 F 6
Samene, Oued ~ **DZ** 190-191 F 7
Sam Ford Fiord ≈ 26-27 P 8
Samfya o **Z** 214-215 E 6
Samḥa ⌒ **Y** 132-133 H 7
Samha, al- o **UAE** 134-135 F 6
Šamhor = Šamkir o· **AZ** 128-129 L 2
Sámi o **GR** 100-101 H 5
Sami o **IND** 138-139 C 8
Samia o **RN** 198-199 D 5
Samia, Tanjung ▲ **RI** 164-165 H 3
Sāmi ji Veri o **PK** 138-139 C 7
Šāmilī, aš- o **KSA** 130-131 G 4
Samīm, Umm as- ∸ **OM** 132-133 J 3
Samīrā' o **KSA** 130-131 H 4
Samiria, Río ~ **PE** 64-65 E 4
Samiṭa o **KSA** 132-133 C 5
Šāmiya, aš- ∸ **IRQ** 130-131 K 2
Samjiyon o **KOR** 150-151 G 7
Samka o **MYA** 142-143 K 5
Šamkir = Şamkir o· **AZ** 128-129 L 2
Šammar, Ǧabal ▲ **KSA** 130-131 F 4
Sám Nám o **VN** 156-157 C 6
Samnū o **LAR** 192-193 F 4
Samo o **CI** 202-203 J 7
Samo o **PNG** 183 G 2
Samoa o **ANG** 216-217 F 4
Samoa Basin ≃ 13 L 4
Samoa-i-Sisifo ■ **WS** 184 V a 1
Samoa Islands ⌒ **WS** 184 V a 1
Samoded o **RUS** 88-89 Q 5
Samoé o **RG** 202-203 F 6
Samoedskaja Rečka ~ **RUS** 108-109 Y 6
Samojlovka o **RUS** 102-103 N 2
Samokov o **BG** 102-103 C 6
Samoleta, ostrov ⌒ **RUS** 110-111 N 3
Samorogouan o **BF** 202-203 H 4
Sámos ☆· **GR** 100-101 L 6
Sámos ⌒ **GR** 100-101 L 6
Samosir, Pulau ⌒ **RI** 162-163 C 3
Samothráki o **GR** 100-101 K 4
Samothráki ⌒ **GR** 100-101 K 4
Samotlor, ozero ○ **RUS** 114-115 O 4
Sampa o **GH** 202-203 J 6
Sampacho o **RA** 78-79 G 2
Sampadi o **MAL** 162-163 H 4
Sampaga o **RI** 164-165 F 5
Sampaio o **BR** 68-69 E 4
Sampang o **RI** 168 E 3
Sampara ~ **RI** 164-165 H 5
Sampelga o **BF** 202-203 L 3
Sampit o **RI** (KTE) 162-163 K 6
Sampit ~ **RI** 162-163 K 6
Sampit Teluk ≈ 162-163 K 6
Sampolawa o **RI** 164-165 H 6
Sampsel o **USA** (MO) 274-275 E 5
Sampun o **PNG** 183 G 3
Sampwe o **ZRE** 214-215 D 5
Sam Rayburn Lake < **USA** (TX) 268-269 F 5
Samrē o **ETH** 200-201 J 6
Samreboe o **GH** 202-203 J 7
Sams o **USA** (CO) 254-255 H 5
Samsam o **SUD** 200-201 G 6
Samsang o **VRC** 144-145 D 5
Samsherpur o **IND** 138-139 D 10
Šamsiya, aš- o **KSA** 130-131 J 4
Samsø ⌒ **DK** 86-87 E 9
Samson o **USA** (AL) 284-285 D 5
Sām So'n o **VN** 156-157 D 7
Samson Indian Reserve X **CDN** (ALB) 232-233 E 3
Samsudin Noor · **RI** 164-165 D 5
Samsun ☆· **TR** 128-129 G 2
Samtredia o **GE** 126-127 E 6
Samucumbi o **ANG** 216-217 E 6
Samuel, Represa de < **BR** 66-67 F 7
Samuels o **USA** (ID) 250-251 C 3
Samuhú o **RA** 76-77 G 4
Samulondo o **ZRE** 214-215 B 5
Samundri o **PK** 138-139 D 4
Samur ~ **AZ** 128-129 N 2
Samur-Apšceronskij kanal < **AZ** 128-129 N 2
Samuro, Raudal ~ **CO** 60-61 G 6
Samut Prakan o **THA** 158-159 F 4
Samut Sakhon o **THA** 158-159 F 4
Samut Songkhram o **THA** 158-159 E 4
San ~ **K** 158-159 J 3
San ~ **PL** 92-93 R 4
San o **RMM** 202-203 H 3
Saña o **PE** 64-65 C 5
Sanā o **Y** 132-133 F 5
Ṣan'ā' ★··· **Y** 132-133 D 6
Sanā, Wādī ~ **Y** 132-133 F 6
Sanaa = Ṣan'ā' ★··· **Y** 132-133 D 6
Sanaag □ **SP** 208-209 H 3
Sanaba o **BF** 202-203 J 3
Sanaba ~ **RMM** 202-203 F 2
Sanabria o **CO** 60-61 C 6
Sanae o **ARK** 16 F 36
Sanāfir, Ǧazīrat ⌒ **KSA** 130-131 D 4
Sanaga ~ **CAM** 216-217 C 2
San Agusin o **YV** 60-61 H 4
San Agustín, Arroyo ~ **BOL** 70-71 D 3
San Agustin, Cape ▲ **RP** 160-161 G 9
San Agustín, Parque Arqueológico ··· **CO** 60-61 C 7
San Agustín de Valle Fértil o **RA** 76-77 D 6
Sanak o **USA** 22-23 P 5
Sanak Island ⌒ **USA** 22-23 P 5
Sanak Islands ⌒ **USA** 22-23 P 5
San Alberto o **CO** 60-61 E 4
San Alejandro o **PE** 64-65 E 6
Sanām, as- ∸ **KSA** 132-133 G 3
Şanamain, aš- o **SYR** 128-129 G 6
San Ana o **BR** 66-67 C 2
Sanana o **RI** 164-165 J 5
Sanana, Pulau ⌒ **RI** 164-165 J 5
Sanandağ ☆· **IR** 128-129 M 5
Sanando o **RMM** 202-203 G 3
San Andreas o **USA** (CA) 246-247 E 5
San Andrés o **C** 54-55 G 4
San Andres o **CO** 60-61 D 4
San Andres o **RP** 160-161 F 6
San Andres, Quebrada de ~ **RCH** 76-77 C 4
San Andrés de Giles o **RA** 78-79 K 3
San Andres de Sotavento o **CO** 60-61 D 3
San Andres Mountains ▲ **USA** 256-257 J 6
San Andres National Wildlife Refuge · **USA** (NM) 256-257 J 6
San Andres Point ▲ **RP** 160-161 D 6
San Andrés y Sauces o **E** 188-189 C 6
San Andros o **BS** 54-55 F 2
Sananduva o **BR** 74-75 E 6
Sanane Besar, Pulau ⌒ **RI** 168 D 6
Sananferedougou o **CI** 202-203 G 4
San Angelo o **USA** (TX) 266-267 G 2
Sanankoroba o **RMM** 202-203 G 3
San Anselmo o **USA** (CA) 248-249 B 2
San Anton o **PE** 70-71 B 4
San Antonio o **BH** 52-53 K 3
San Antônio o **BR** 62-63 J 5
San Antonio o **CO** 60-61 B 7
San Antonio o **MEX** 50-51 D 6
San Antonio o **RA** 78-79 F 2
San Antonio o **RCH** 78-79 D 2
San Antonio o **USA** (NM) 256-257 J 5
San Antonio o· **USA** (TX) 266-267 J 4
San Antonio o **YV** 60-61 H 6
San Antonio, Cabo ⌣ **RA** 78-79 L 4
San Antonio, Cabo de ▲ **C** 54-55 C 4
San Antônio, Cachoeira de o **BR** 62-63 H 6
San Antonio, Río ~ **BOL** 76-77 D 1
San Antonio, Sierra de ▲ **MEX** 50-51 D 2
San Antonio Bay ≈ 160-161 B 8
San Antonio Bay ≈ 266-267 L 5
San Antonio da Tabasca o **YV** 60-61 K 3
San Antonio de Areco o **RA** 78-79 K 3
San Antonio de Esmoraca o **BOL** 76-77 D 1
San Antonio de Esquilache o **PE** 70-71 B 5
San Antonio de Getucha o **CO** 64-65 E 1
San Antonio de Golfo o **YV** 60-61 K 2
San Antonio de los Baños o **C** 54-55 D 3
San Antonio de los Cobres o **RA** 76-77 D 3
San Antonio del Sur o **C** 54-55 H 4
San Antonio de Tamanaco o **YV** 60-61 H 3
San Antonio El Grande o **MEX** 50-51 G 3
San Antonio Huitepec o **MEX** 52-53 F 3
San Antonio Mountain ▲ **USA** (NM) 256-257 K 6
San Antonio Oeste o **RA** 78-79 G 6
San Antonio River ~ **USA** 266-267 K 5
San Antonio Villalongín o **MEX** 52-53 D 2
San Antonio y Torcuga, Canal < **RA** 78-79 H 2
San Ardo o **USA** (CA) 248-249 D 3
Sanaroa Island ⌒ **PNG** 183 F 5
San Augustín o **CO** 60-61 C 6
San Augustín o **MEX** 50-51 B 3
San Augustin o **RP** 160-161 E 6
San Augustine o **USA** (TX) 268-269 F 5
Sanāw o **Y** 132-133 G 5
Sanāwad o **IND** 138-139 F 8
Sanba o **VRC** 144-145 M 6
San Bartolo o **BOL** 70-71 D 4
San Bartolo o **PE** 64-65 D 8
San Bartolomé de Tirajana o **E** 188-189 D 7
Sanbei Yangchang o **VRC** 154-155 E 2
San Benedetto del Tronto o **I** 100-101 D 3
San Benedicto, Isla ⌒ **MEX** 50-51 C 7
San Benito o **GCA** 52-53 K 3
San Benito o **NIC** 52-53 L 5
San Benito o **USA** (TX) 266-267 K 7
San Benito Abad o **CO** 60-61 D 3
San Benito Mountain ▲ **USA** (CA) 248-249 D 3
San Bernardino o **USA** (CA) 248-249 G 5
San Bernardino Strait ≈ 160-161 F 6
San Bernard National Wildlife Refuge ⊥ **USA** (TX) 266-267 M 5
San Bernardo o **RA** (BUA) 78-79 J 4
San Bernardo o **RA** (SAF) 76-77 G 5
San Bernardo o **RCH** 78-79 D 2
San Bernardo, Islas de ⌒ **CO** 60-61 C 3
San Bernardo, Punta ▲ **CO** 60-61 C 3
San Bernardo del Viento o **CO** 60-61 D 3
San Bernhard River ~ **USA** 268-269 E 7
San Blas o **MEX** (COA) 50-51 J 4
San Blas o **MEX** (SIN) 50-51 E 4
San Blas o· **MEX** (NAY) 50-51 G 7
San Blas, Archipiélago de ⌒·· **PA** 52-53 E 7
San Blas, Cape ▲ **USA** (FL) 286-287 D 2
San Blas, Cordillera de ▲ **PA** 52-53 E 7
San Borja o **BOL** 70-71 D 4
San Borja, Sierra de ▲ **MEX** 50-51 C 3
Sanborn o **USA** (MN) 270-271 C 6
Sanbornville o **USA** (NH) 278-279 K 5
San Buenaventura o **BOL** 70-71 D 4
San Buenaventura o **MEX** 50-51 J 4
San Buenaventura, Cordillera de ▲ **RA** 76-77 C 4
Sanca o **CDN** (BC) 230-231 N 4
Sança o **MOC** 218-219 H 3
San Carlos o **MEX** (BCS) 50-51 C 5
San Carlos o **MEX** (COA) 50-51 J 3
San Carlos o **MEX** (TAM) 50-51 K 5
San Carlos ☆ **NIC** 52-53 B 6
San Carlos o· **PA** 52-53 E 7
San Carlos o **RA** (MEN) 78-79 E 2
San Carlos o **RA** (SAE) 76-77 F 5
San Carlos o **RCH** 78-79 D 4
San Carlos o **ROU** 78-79 M 3
San Carlos o **RP** (NED) 160-161 E 7
San Carlos o **RP** (PAN) 160-161 D 5
San Carlos o **USA** (AZ) 256-257 E 5
San Carlos ☆ **YV** 60-61 G 3
San Carlos, Arroyo ~ **RA** 78-79 E 3
San Carlos, Caldera de ▲ **GQ** 210-211 B 2
San Carlos = Ciudad Quesada o **CR** 52-53 B 6
San Carlos, Punta ▲ **MEX** 50-51 C 4
San Carlos, Río ~ **CR** 52-53 B 6
San Carlos, Río ~ **PY** 76-77 H 2
San Carlos Bay ≈ 286-287 G 5
San Carlos de Bariloche o· **RA** 78-79 D 6
San Carlos de Bolívar o **RA** 78-79 J 4
San Carlos de Guaroa o **CO** 60-61 E 6
San Carlos del Meta o **YV** 60-61 H 4
San Carlos del Zulia o **YV** 60-61 F 3
San Carlos de Río Negro o **YV** 66-67 D 2
San Carlos Indian Reservation X **USA** (AZ) 256-257 E 5
San Carlos Lake ○ **USA** (AZ) 256-257 E 5
San Carlos Yautepec o **MEX** 52-53 F 3
San Cayetano o **CO** 60-61 D 5
San Cayetano o **RA** 78-79 K 5
Sancha o **VRC** (GXI) 156-157 F 4
Sancha o **VRC** (SHA) 154-155 G 2
Sanchakou o **VRC** 146-147 D 6
Sánchez o **DOM** 54-55 L 5
Sánchez, Cerro ▲ **RA** 80 F 5
Sánchez Magallanes o· **MEX** 52-53 H 2
Sanchi o··· **IND** 138-139 F 8
Sanchi River ~ **PNG** 183 B 2
Sānchor o **IND** 138-139 C 7
San Christóbal, Quebrada ~ **RCH** 76-77 C 2
San Cirilo, Cerro ▲ **PE** 64-65 C 5
San Clara o **CDN** (MAN) 234-235 B 3
San Clemente o **E** 98-99 F 5
San Clemente o **RCH** 78-79 D 3
San Clemente o **USA** (CA) 248-249 G 6
San Clemente del Tuyú o **RA** 78-79 L 4
San Clemente Island ⌒ **USA** (CA) 248-249 F 7
San Clemente o San Valentin, Cerro ▲ **RCH** 80 D 3
Sanclerlândia o **BR** 72-73 E 4
Sanco o **USA** (TX) 264-265 D 6
Sancos o **PE** 64-65 F 9
San Cosme y Damián o··· **PY** 76-77 J 4
San Cristóbal o **BOL** 76-77 D 1
San Cristóbal o **C** 54-55 D 3
San Cristóbal ☆· **DOM** 54-55 K 5
San Cristóbal o **PA** 52-53 D 7
San Cristobal o **RA** 76-77 G 6
San Cristóbal o **RCH** 76-77 C 2
San Cristobal ⌒ **SOL** 184 I e 4
San Cristóbal ☆ **YV** 60-61 E 4
San Cristóbal, Isla ⌒ **EC** 64-65 C 10
San Cristobal, Volcán ▲ **NIC** 52-53 L 5
San Cristóbal de las Casas o·· **MEX** 52-53 H 3
San Cristobal Wash ~ **USA** 256-257 B 6
Sancti Spíritu o **RA** 78-79 H 3
Sancti Spíritus ☆·· **C** 54-55 F 4
Sanctuary o **CDN** (SAS) 232-233 K 5
Sančursk o **RUS** 96-97 E 5
Sancy, Puy de ▲·· **F** 90-91 J 9
Sand ☆ **N** 86-87 C 7
Sand ~ **ZA** 218-219 E 6
Sandafa al-Far o **ET** 194-195 E 3
Sandakan o **MAL** 160-161 C 10
Sandakan, Teluk ≈ 160-161 B 10
Šāndak Bālā ~ **IR** 134-135 H 4
Sandal, ozero ○ **RUS** 88-89 M 5
Sandama o **RG** 202-203 F 3
Sandando o **ANG** 216-217 F 5
Sandane ☆ **N** 86-87 C 6
Sandanski o **BG** 102-103 C 7
Sandaré o **RMM** 202-203 E 2
Sand Arroyo River ~ **USA** 254-255 N 6
Sanday ⌒ **GB** 90-91 F 2
Sandberg o **ZA** 220-221 D 6
Sandburg Home National Historic Site, Carl · **USA** (NC) 282-283 E 5
Sand Creek ~ **USA** 254-255 M 4
Sandefjord ☆ **N** 86-87 E 7
Sandégué o **CI** 202-203 J 6
Sandema o **GH** 202-203 K 4
Sānderão o **IND** 138-139 D 7
Sanders o **USA** (AZ) 256-257 F 3
Sanderson o **USA** (TX) 266-267 E 3
Sanderson Canyon ~ **USA** 266-267 E 4
Sanderson Lake ○ **CDN** 30-31 R 5
Sandersville o **USA** (GA) 284-285 H 3
Sandfire Flat Roadhouse o **AUS** 172-173 E 5
Sandfloeggi ▲ **N** 86-87 C 7
Sandfly Island = Mbokonimbeti Island ⌒ **SOL** 184 I d 3
Sandford Lake ○ **CDN** (ONT) 234-235 M 5
Sandhill o **CDN** (ONT) 238-239 F 5
Sandhill o **USA** (MS) 268-269 L 4
Sand Hill o **USA** (MS) 268-269 M 5
Sand Hill River ~ **CDN** 38-39 Q 2
Sand Hill River ~ **USA** 270-271 B 3
Sand Hills ▲ **USA** 262-263 E 2
Sandhornøy ⌒ **N** 86-87 G 3
Šandī o **SUD** 200-201 F 4
Sandia o **PE** 70-71 C 4
Sandia Crest ▲ **USA** (NM) 256-257 J 3
Sandian He ~ **VRC** 148-149 M 7
San Diego o **USA** (TX) 266-267 J 6
San Diego o· **USA** (CA) 248-249 G 7
San Diego, Cabo ▲ **RA** 80 H 7
San Diego de Alcala · **USA** (CA) 248-249 G 7
San Diego de la Unión o **MEX** 50-51 J 7
Sandies Creek ~ **USA** 266-267 K 4
Sandıklı ☆ **TR** 128-129 D 3
Sandila o **IND** 142-143 B 2
Sandilands Forest Reserve ⊥ **CDN** (MAN) 234-235 G 5
Sanding, Pulau ⌒ **RI** 162-163 D 6
Sanding, Selat ≈ 162-163 D 6
Sandino o **C** 54-55 C 3
San Dionisio del Mar o **MEX** 52-53 G 3
Sand Islands ⌒ **USA** 20-21 G 5
Sand Lake o **CDN** (ONT) 236-237 D 5
Sand Lake o **CDN** (ONT) 238-239 F 3
Sand Lake ○ **CDN** (NWT) 30-31 U 3
Sand Lake ○ **CDN** (ONT) 234-235 J 4
Sandlake o **USA** (OR) 244-245 B 5
Sand Lake ○ **USA** (OK) 264-265 H 2
Sand Mountains ▲ **USA** 284-285 D 2
Sandnes ☆ **N** 86-87 B 7
Sandnessjøen o **N** 86-87 F 3
Sandoa o **ZRE** 214-215 B 5
Sandomierska, Kotlina ⌣ **PL** 92-93 Q 3
Sandomierz o·· **PL** 92-93 Q 3
Sandougou o **CI** 202-203 H 6
Sandougou ~ **SN** 202-203 C 3
Sandoval o **USA** (IL) 274-275 J 6
Sandover Highway II **AUS** 178-179 D 1
Sandover River ~ **AUS** 178-179 C 1
Sandovo o **RUS** 94-95 P 2
Sandoway o **MYA** 142-143 J 6
Sand Pass ▲ **USA** (UT) 254-255 B 4
Sand Point o **CDN** (NS) 240-241 O 5
Sand Point o **USA** 22-23 Q 5
Sandpoint o **USA** (ID) 250-251 C 3
Sandrakatsy o **RM** 222-223 F 6
Sandrakota ~ **RM** 222-223 F 5
Sandratsino ~ **RM** 222-223 F 6
Sandridge o **CDN** (MAN) 234-235 F 4
Šandrin ~ **RUS** 110-111 c 4
Sand River ~ **PNG** 183 A 2
Sandrivier ~ **ZA** 220-221 H 4
Sandrun ~ **RUS** 110-111 d 4
Sandspit o **CDN** (BC) 228-229 C 3
Sand Springs o **USA** (MT) 250-251 M 4
Sand Springs o **USA** (OK) 264-265 H 2
Sandstad o **N** 86-87 D 5
Sandstone o **AUS** 176-177 E 4
Sandstone o **USA** (MN) 270-271 F 4
Sandur o **IND** 140-141 G 3
Sandusky o **USA** (MI) 272-273 G 4
Sandusky o **USA** (OH) 280-281 D 2
Sandusky River ~ **USA** 280-281 C 3
Sandveld Nature Reserve ⊥ **ZA** 220-221 G 3
Sandvig o **DK** 86-87 G 9
Sandvika o **S** 86-87 F 5
Sandviken ☆ **S** 86-87 H 6
Sandvisbaai ≈ 220-221 B 1
Sandwich o **USA** (IL) 274-275 K 3
Sandwich, Cape ▲ **AUS** 174-175 J 6
Sandwich Bay ○ **CDN** 38-39 Q 2
Sandwich Harbour o **NAM** 220-221 B 1
Sandwip o **BD** (CTG) 142-143 G 4
Sandwip ~ **BD** 142-143 G 4
Sandwith o **CDN** (SAS) 232-233 K 2
Sandy o **USA** (OR) 244-245 C 5
Sandy o **USA** (UT) 254-255 D 3
Sandy Bar ▲ **CDN** (MAN) 234-235 F 2
Sandy Bay Indian Reserve X **CDN** (MAN) 234-235 E 4
Sandy Beach o **CDN** (ALB) 232-233 D 2
Sandy Bight ≈ 176-177 G 6
Sandy Cape ▲ **AUS** 178-179 M 3
Sandy Cove o **CDN** (NS) 240-241 J 6
Sandy Creek ~ **AUS** 178-179 J 2
Sandy Creek ~ **AUS** 178-179 H 2
Sandy Creek ~ **AUS** 180-181 H 2
Sandy Creek ~ **USA** 252-253 J 4
Sandy Creek ~ **USA** 262-263 J 4
Sandy Desert ∸ **PK** 134-135 K 4
Sandy Harbor Beach o **USA** (NY) 278-279 D 5
Sandy Hills ▲ **USA** 264-265 J 6
Sandy Hook o **USA** (KY) 276-277 M 2
Sandy Hook o **USA** (MS) 268-269 L 5
Sandykači o **TM** 136-137 H 6
Sandy Lake o **CDN** (MAN) 234-235 C 4
Sandy Lake o **CDN** (ONT) 34-35 K 4
Sandy Lake ○ **CDN** (NFL) 242-243 M 3
Sandy Lake ○ **CDN** (NWT) 20-21 Z 3
Sandy Lake ○ **CDN** (ONT) 234-235 K 2
Sandy Lake o **USA** (PA) 280-281 F 2
Sandy Lake Indian Reserve X **CDN** 34-35 K 4
Sandy Point o **BS** 54-55 G 1
Sandy Point ▲ **IND** 140-141 L 4
Sandy Ridge o **USA** (NC) 282-283 G 4
Sandy River ~ **CDN** 36-37 P 7
Sandy River ~ **USA** 276-277 G 4
Sandy Springs o **USA** (OH) 280-281 C 5
San Estanislao o **CO** 60-61 D 2
San Estanislao o **PY** 76-77 J 3
San Esteban o **HN** 54-55 C 7
San Esteban o **MEX** 50-51 C 4
San Estéban, Golfo ≈ 80 C 3
San Esteban, Isla ⌒ **MEX** 50-51 C 3
San Felipe o **MEX** (GTO) 50-51 J 7
San Felipe o **MEX** (YUC) 52-53 K 1
San Felipe o· **MEX** (BCN) 50-51 B 2
San Felipe o **RCH** 78-79 D 2
San Felipe ☆ **YV** 60-61 G 2
San Felipe, Bahía ≈ 80 F 6
San Felipe, Castillo de · **GCA** 52-53 K 4
San Felipe, Cayos de ⌒ **C** 54-55 D 4
San Felipe, Parque Natural ⊥ **MEX** 52-53 K 1
San Felipe de Vichayal o **PE** 64-65 B 4
San Felipe Nuevo Mercurio o **MEX** 50-51 H 5
San Felipe Pueblo o **USA** (NM) 256-257 J 3
San Félix o **YV** 60-61 F 2
San Fernando o **E** 98-99 D 6
San Fernando o **MEX** 50-51 K 5
San Fernando o **RA** 76-77 D 4
San Fernando o **RCH** 78-79 D 3
San Fernando ☆ **RP** (LUN) 160-161 D 4
San Fernando ☆ **RP** (PAM) 160-161 D 5
San Fernando o **TT** 60-61 L 2
San Fernando o **USA** (CA) 248-249 F 5
San Fernando, Río ~ **BOL** 70-71 H 5
San Fernando, Río ~ **MEX** 50-51 K 5
San Fernando de Apure ☆ **YV** 60-61 H 4
San Fernando de Atabapo o **YV** 60-61 H 5
San Fernando del Valle de Catamarca ☆· **RA** 76-77 E 5
Sånfjället nationalpark ⊥ **S** 86-87 F 5
Sanford o **CDN** (MAN) 234-235 F 5
Sanford o **USA** (FL) 286-287 H 3
Sanford o **USA** (ME) 278-279 L 5
Sanford o **USA** (NC) 282-283 H 5
Sanford, Mount ▲ **USA** 20-21 S 5
Sanford River ~ **AUS** 176-177 D 3
San Francisco o **BOL** 70-71 E 5
San Francisco o **BOL** 70-71 E 4
San Francisco ☆ **ES** 52-53 K 5
San Francisco o **PE** 64-65 F 8
San Francisco o **RA** 76-77 F 6
San Francisco o **RP** 160-161 F 8
San Francisco o·· **USA** (CA) 248-249 B 2
San Francisco o **YV** 60-61 F 2
San Francisco, Cabo de ▲ **EC** 64-65 B 1
San Francisco, Igarapé ~ **BR** 66-67 C 7
San Francisco, Río ~ **RA** 76-77 C 6
San Francisco, Sierra de ▲··· **MEX** 50-51 C 4
San Francisco Bay ≈ 40-41 C 7
San Francisco Bay ≈ 248-249 B 2
San Francisco Creek ~ **USA** 266-267 E 4
San Francisco de Becerra o **HN** 52-53 L 4
San Francisco de Bellocq o **RA** 78-79 J 5
San Francisco de Borja o **MEX** 50-51 F 4
San Francisco de Horizonte o **MEX** 50-51 H 5
San Francisco de Laishi o **RA** 76-77 H 4
San Francisco de la Paz o **HN** 52-53 L 4
San Francisco del Chañar o **RA** 76-77 F 5
San Francisco del Oro o **MEX** 50-51 G 4
San Francisco del Rincón o **MEX** 52-53 D 1
San Francisco de Macoris ☆ **DOM** 54-55 K 5
San Francisco de Mostazal o **RCH** 78-79 D 2
San Francisco Ixhuatán o **MEX** 52-53 G 3
San Francisco River ~ **USA** 256-257 F 5
San Francisco River ~ **USA** 256-257 G 5
San Francisco Wash ~ **USA** 256-257 D 3
San Francisquito o **MEX** 50-51 C 3
Sang o **GH** 202-203 K 5
Sanga o **ANG** 216-217 C 5
Sanga o **BF** 202-203 L 4
Sanga o **EAU** 212-213 C 4
Sanga o **MOC** 214-215 H 7
Sanga o· **RMM** 202-203 J 2
San Gabriel o **EC** 64-65 D 1
San Gabriel da Cachoeira o **BR** 66-67 D 3
San Gabriel Mixtepec o **MEX** 52-53 F 3
San Gabriel Mountains ▲ **USA** 248-249 F 5
San Gabriel River ~ **USA** 266-267 K 3
Sangagüey, Volcán ▲ **MEX** 50-51 G 7
Sanga-Jurjah ~ **RUS** 110-111 X 3
Sangala o **RI** 164-165 G 5
San Galgano · **I** 100-101 C 3
San Gallan, Isla ⌒ **PE** 64-65 D 8
Sangama o **EAT** 214-215 G 5
Sangameshwar o **IND** 140-141 E 2
Sangamner o **IND** 138-139 E 10
Sangamon River ~ **USA** 274-275 J 4
Sangān o **IR** 134-135 J 1
Sanganer o **IND** 138-139 E 6
Sangar ☆ **RUS** 118-119 N 4
Sangardo o **RG** 202-203 E 5
Sangarh ~ **PK** 138-139 C 4
Sangata o **RI** 164-165 E 3
Sangau, Tanjung ▲ **RI** 162-163 F 5
Sangāv o **IRQ** 128-129 L 5
Sangay, Parque Nacional de ⊥··· **EC** 64-65 C 2
Sangay, Volcán ▲ **EC** 64-65 C 3
Sangayam o **RI** 164-165 D 5
Sangbast o **IR** 136-137 F 7
Sangbé o **CAM** 204-205 K 5
Sangbor o **AFG** 136-137 H 7
Sang Čārak o **AFG** 136-137 K 7
Sangchris Lake ○ **USA** (IL) 274-275 J 5
Sange o **ZRE** 214-215 E 4
Sangeang, Pulau ⌒ **RI** 168 D 7
San Genaro o **RA** 78-79 J 2
Sanger o **USA** (CA) 248-249 E 3
Sanger o **USA** (TX) 264-265 G 5
San Germán o· **USA** (PR) 286-287 O 2
Sanggan He ~ **VRC** 154-155 J 1
Sanggau o **RI** 162-163 J 4
Sangha □ **RCA** 210-211 E 2
Sangha □ **RCB** 210-211 E 3
Sangha ~ **RCB** 210-211 F 3
Sānghar o **PK** 138-139 B 6
Sangiang, Pulau ⌒ **RI** 162-163 F 7
Sangihe, Kepulauan ⌒ **RI** 164-165 J 2
Sangijn Dalaj o **MAU** 148-149 G 4
Sangijn Dalaj nuur ○ **MAU** 148-149 D 3
San Gil o **CO** 60-61 E 4
Sangil'ka ~ **RUS** 114-115 Q 4
San Gimignano o··· **I** 100-101 C 3
Sangīn o **AFG** 134-135 L 2
Šangina ~ **RUS** 110-111 b 5
Sanginkylä o **FIN** 88-89 J 4
San Giovanni in Fiore o **I** 100-101 F 5
Sangir, Kepulauan ⌒ **RI** 164-165 J 2
Sangir, Pulau ⌒ **RI** 164-165 J 2
Sangkha Buri o **THA** 158-159 E 3
Sangkulirang o **RI** 164-165 E 3
Sângkŭm Ândet o **K** 158-159 J 4
Sāngla Hill o **PK** 138-139 D 4
Sāngli o· **IND** 140-141 F 2
Sanglia Dol (traditional Village) · **RI** 166-167 F 5
Sangmelima o· **CAM** 210-211 D 2
Sango o **ZW** 218-219 F 6
Sangola o **IND** 140-141 F 2
Sangolquí o **EC** 64-65 C 2
Sangonera, Río ~ **E** 98-99 G 6
Sangoshe o **RB** 218-219 B 4
San Gottardo, Passo del ▲ **CH** 92-93 K 5
Sangouani o **CI** 202-203 G 5
Sangouiné o **CI** 202-203 G 6
Sangowo o **RI** 164-165 L 2
Sangradouro, Área Indígena X **BR** 72-73 D 3
Sangraduoro, Rio ~ **BR** 70-71 J 5
Sangrafa o **RIM** 196-197 D 6
Sangre de Cristo Mountains ▲ **USA** 254-255 K 6
San Gregorio o **MEX** 52-53 J 4
San Gregorio o **PE** 64-65 F 6
San Gregorio o **USA** (CA) 248-249 B 2
San Gregorio Carrio o **ROU** 78-79 L 2
Sangre Grande o **TT** 60-61 L 2
Sangrūr o **IND** 138-139 E 4
Sangsang o **VRC** 144-145 F 6
Sangudo o **CDN** (ALB) 232-233 D 2
Sangue, Rio do ~ **BR** 70-71 H 2
Sanguéya o **RG** 202-203 C 4
Sanguiana o **RG** 202-203 E 4
San Guillermo o **RP** 160-161 D 4
Sangutane, Rio ~ **MOC** 218-219 G 6
Sangwali o **NAM** 218-219 B 4
Sangzhi o **VRC** 156-157 G 2
Sanhala o **CI** 202-203 G 4
Šanhar o **RUS** 116-117 K 9
San Hilario o **RA** 76-77 H 4
Sâni o **RIM** 196-197 E 6
Sanibel o **USA** (FL) 286-287 G 5
Sanibel Island ⌒ **USA** (FL) 286-287 G 5
San Ignacio o **CR** 52-53 B 7
San Ignacio o **MEX** (SIN) 50-51 F 6
San Ignacio o· **MEX** (BCS) 50-51 C 4
San Ignacio o **PE** 64-65 C 4
San Ignacio o **PY** 76-77 J 4
San Ignacio o **YV** 62-63 D 3
San Ignacio, Isla de ⌒ **MEX** 50-51 F 5
San Ignacio de Velasco o **BOL** 70-71 G 5
San Ignacio Miní o··· **RA** 76-77 K 4
San Ignazio o **BH** 52-53 K 3
San Ildefonso, Cape ▲ **RP** 160-161 E 4
Sanipas ▲ **LS** 220-221 J 4
Sanire o **PE** 70-71 B 3
San Isidro o **NIC** 52-53 L 5
San Isidro o **RA** 78-79 K 3
San Isidro o **USA** (TX) 266-267 J 7
San Isidro o **YV** 62-63 D 2
San Isidro de El General o **CR** 52-53 C 7
San Jacinto o **PE** 64-65 B 4
San Jacinto o **RP** 160-161 E 6
San Jacinto, East Fork ~ **USA** 268-269 E 6
San Jacinto, Mount ▲ **USA** (CA) 248-249 H 6
San Jacinto, West Fork ~ **USA** 268-269 E 6
San Jaime o **RA** 76-77 H 6
San Janvier o **E** 98-99 G 6
San Javier o **BOL** 70-71 E 4
San Javier o **MEX** 50-51 D 5
San Javier o **RA** (COD) 78-79 G 2
San Javier o **RA** (SAF) 76-77 H 6
San Javier, Río ~ **RA** 76-77 H 5
San Javier de Loncomilla o **RCH** 78-79 D 3
Sanje o **EAU** 212-213 C 4
San Jeronimo, Isla ⌒ **RA** 76-77 H 5
Sanjia o **VRC** 156-157 G 5
Sanjiang o **VRC** 156-157 F 4
Sanjiaotang o **VRC** 156-157 M 2
Sanjō o **J** 152-153 H 6
San Joaquim o **BR** 62-63 K 6
San Joaquín o **MEX** 52-53 E 1
San Joaquín o **RA** 78-79 H 3
San Joaquín o **YV** 60-61 H 2
San Joaquin o **YV** 60-61 J 3
San Joaquin, Cerro ▲ **EC** 64-65 C 10
San Joaquín, Río ~ **BOL** 70-71 F 3
San Joaquin River ~ **USA** 248-249 D 2
San Joaquin Valley ⌣ **USA** 248-249 C 2
San Jon o **USA** (NM) 256-257 M 3
San Jorge o **CO** 60-61 G 4
San Jorge o **RA** 76-77 G 6
San Jorge o **ROU** 78-79 M 2
San Jorge, Bahía ≈ 50-51 C 2
San Jorge, Golfo ≈ 80 G 2
San Jorge, Río ~ **CO** 60-61 D 3
San Jorge Island ⌒ **SOL** 184 I d 3
San José o **CO** 64-65 D 1
San José ★· **CR** 52-53 B 7

388 Salvador, Lake — San José

San José ○ E 98-99 F 6
San José ○ HN 52-53 L 4
San José ○ MEX 50-51 D 4
San José ∼ MEX 50-51 E 6
San José ○ PY 76-77 J 3
San José ○ RA (CAT) 76-77 D 4
San José ○ RA (MIS) 76-77 K 4
San Jose ○ RP (MID) 160-161 D 6
San Jose ○ RP (NEC) 160-161 D 5
San Jose ☆ RP (ANT) 160-161 D 7
San Jose ○ USA (CA) 248-249 C 2
San Jose ○ USA (IL) 274-275 J 4
San José ○ YV 60-61 E 2
San José, Golfo ≈ 78-79 G 7
San José, Isla ⌒ MEX 50-51 D 5
San José, Isla ⌒ PA 52-53 E 7
San José, Río ∼ RCH 78-79 C 5
San Jose, Rio ∼ USA 256-257 H 4
San José, Volcán ▲ RA 78-79 E 2
San José de Amacuro ○ YV 62-63 D 1
San José de Buja ○ YV 60-61 K 3
San José de Chimbo ○ EC 64-65 C 2
San José de Chiquitos ○••• BOL 70-71 G 5
San José de Dimas ○ MEX 50-51 D 3
San José de Feliciano ○ RA 76-77 H 6
San José de Gracia ○ MEX 50-51 F 4
San José de Guanipa ○ YV 60-61 J 3
San José de Guaribe ○ YV 60-61 J 3
San José de Jáchal ○ RA 76-77 C 6
San José de la Dormida ○ RA 76-77 F 6
San Jose del Alto ○ PE 64-65 C 4
San José de la Mariquina ○ RCH 78-79 C 5
San José de las Lajas ○ C 54-55 D 3
San José del Cabo ○• MEX 50-51 E 6
San José del Guaviare ○ CO 60-61 E 6
San José del Monte ○ RP 160-161 D 5
San José del Morro ○ RA 78-79 G 2
San José del Palmar ○ CO 60-61 C 5
San José del Progreso ○ MEX 52-53 F 3
San José de Maipo ○ RCH 78-79 D 2
San José de Mayo ☆ ROU 78-79 L 3
San José de Ocoa ○ DOM 54-55 K 5
San Jose de Quero ○ PE 64-65 E 8
San José de Raices ○ MEX 50-51 J 5
San Jose Island ⌒ USA (TX) 266-267 L 6
San José Iturbide ○ MEX 50-51 J 7
San Jose River ∼ CDN 230-231 H 2
Sanju ○ VRC 144-145 B 2
San Juan ○ BOL 70-71 G 6
San Juán ○ BOL 70-71 D 7
San Juan ☆ DOM 54-55 K 5
San Juan ○ PE (ICA) 64-65 E 9
San Juan ○ PE (LOR) 66-67 B 5
San Juan □ RA 76-77 C 6
San Juan ☆• RA (SAJ) 76-77 C 6
San Juán ○ RCH 76-77 C 2
San Juan ○ RP 160-161 F 7
San Juan ○ USA (AK) 20-21 Q 6
San Juan ☆••• USA (PR) 286-287 P 2
San Juan, Bahía ≈ 64-65 E 9
San Juan, Cabo ▲ GQ 210-211 D 3
San Juan, Cabo ▲ RA 80 J 7
San Juan, Punta ▲ PE 64-65 E 9
San Juan, Quebrada ∼ RCH 76-77 B 5
San Juan, Río ∼ BOL 70-71 D 6
San Juan, Río ∼ BOL 76-77 E 1
San Juan, Río ∼ CO 60-61 C 5
San Juan, Río ∼ DOM 54-55 K 5
San Juan, Río ∼ MEX 50-51 G 5
San Juan, Río ∼ NIC 52-53 B 6
San Juan, Río ∼ PY 76-77 H 2
San Juan, Río ∼ RA 78-79 E 2
San Juan, Río ∼ ROU 78-79 L 3
San Juan, Río ∼ YV 60-61 K 2
San Juan Bautista ☆ PY 76-77 J 4
San Juan Bautista ○ RCH 78-79 C 1
San Juan Bautista ○ YV 60-61 K 2
San Juan Capistrano ○ USA (CA) 248-249 G 6
San Juan Chiquihuitlán ○ MEX 52-53 F 3
San Juan de Alacant ○ E 98-99 G 5
San Juan de Alicante = San Juan de Alacant ○ E 98-99 G 5
San Juan de Arama ○ CO 60-61 E 6
San Juan de Colon ○ YV 60-61 E 3
San Juán de Flores ○ HN 52-53 L 4
San Juan de Guadalupe ○ MEX 50-51 H 5
San Juan de Guia, Cabo ▲ CO 60-61 D 2
San Juan de la Costa ○ MEX 50-51 D 5
San Juán del Caite ○ HN 52-53 K 4
San Juan del César ○ CO 60-61 E 2
San Juan de Lima, Punta ▲ MEX 52-53 C 2
San Juán de Limay ○ NIC 52-53 L 5
San Juán del Norte, Bahía de ≈ 52-53 C 6
San Juan de los Cayos ○ YV 60-61 G 2
San Juan de los Galdonas ○ YV 60-61 K 2
San Juan de los Lagos ○ MEX 50-51 H 7
San Juan de los Morros ☆ YV 60-61 H 3
San Juan de los Planes ○• MEX 50-51 E 6
San Juan del Río ○ MEX (DGO) 50-51 G 5
San Juan del Río ○ MEX (QRO) 52-53 E 1
San Juán del Sur ○ NIC 52-53 B 6
San Juan de Manpiare ○ YV 60-61 H 5
San Juan de Pastocalle ○ EC 64-65 C 2
San Juan de Sabinas ○ MEX 50-51 J 4
San Juan de Tocoma ○ YV 60-61 K 4
San Juan de Yanac ○ PE 64-65 E 8
San Juan Evangelista ○ MEX 52-53 G 3
San Juan Indian Reservation ✕ USA (NM) 256-257 J 2
San Juan Islands ⌒ USA (WA) 244-245 C 2
San Juanito ○ MEX 50-51 F 4
San Juanito, Isla ⌒ MEX 50-51 F 7
San Juan Ixcaquixtla ○ MEX 52-53 F 2
San Juan Mountains ▲ USA 254-255 H 6
San Juan National Historic Park ⊥ USA 244-245 B 2
San Juan River ∼ USA 248-249 D 4
San Juan River ∼ USA 254-255 E 6
San Juan Seamount ≃ 248-249 D 6
San Juan y Martínez ○ C 54-55 D 3
San Just, Puerto de ▲ E 98-99 G 4
San Justo ○ RA 76-77 G 6
Sankadiakro ○ CI 202-203 J 6
Sankarani ∼ RG 202-203 F 4
Sankarankovil ○ IND 140-141 G 6
Sankari Drug ○ IND 140-141 G 5
Sankha ○ THA 158-159 G 3
Sankosh ∼ BHT 142-143 F 2
Sankt Gallen ☆••• CH 92-93 K 5
Sankt Gotthardpass = Passo del San Gottardo ▲ CH 92-93 K 5
Sankt Joachimsthal = Jáchymov ○ CZ 92-93 M 3
Sankt Moritz ○• CH 92-93 K 5
Sankt-Peterburg ☆••• RUS 94-95 M 2
Sankt Peter-Ording ○ D 92-93 K 1
Sankt Pölten ☆ A 92-93 N 4
Sankulirang, Teluk ≈ 164-165 F 3
Sankuru ∼ ZRE 210-211 J 6
San Leonardo de Yagüe ○ E 98-99 F 4
Sanlifan ○ VRC 154-155 J 6
Şanlı Urfa ☆• TR 128-129 H 4
San Lorenzo ○ BOL 70-71 H 5
San Lorenzo ○ CO 60-61 F 4
San Lorenzo ○ EC (ESM) 64-65 C 1
San Lorenzo ○ EC (MAN) 64-65 B 2
San Lorenzo ○ HN 52-53 L 5
San Lorenzo ○ PE 70-71 C 2
San Lorenzo ○ RA (CO) 76-77 H 5
San Lorenzo ○• RA (SAF) 78-79 J 2
San Lorenzo ○ RP 160-161 E 5
San Lorenzo ○ USA (NM) 256-257 H 6
San Lorenzo ○ USA (PR) 286-287 Q 2
San Lorenzo, Cabo ▲ EC 64-65 B 2
San Lorenzo, Cerro ▲ PE 64-65 C 5
San Lorenzo, Isla ⌒ MEX 50-51 C 3
San Lorenzo, Isla ⌒ PE 64-65 D 8
San Lorenzo, Río ∼ MEX 50-51 K 5
San Lorenzo, Río ∼ MEX 50-51 F 5
San Lorenzo, Sierra de ▲ E 98-99 F 3
San Louis Pass ≈ 268-269 E 7
San Lourdes ○ BOL 70-71 C 2
Sanlúcar de Barrameda ○ E 98-99 D 6
Sanlúcar la Mayor ○ E 98-99 D 6
San Lucas ○ USA (CA) 248-249 C 3
San Lucas, Cabo ▲•• MEX 50-51 E 6
San Luís ○ C 54-55 H 4
San Luis ○ CO 60-61 D 4
San Luís ○ GCA 52-53 K 3
San Luis ○ MEX 50-51 B 3
San Luis □ RA 78-79 F 2
San Luis ☆ RA (SLU) 78-79 F 2
San Luis ○ RCH 76-77 C 4
San Luis ○ ROU 74-75 D 9
San Luis ○ RP 160-161 F 7
San Luis ○ USA (AZ) 256-257 D 6
San Luis ○ USA (CO) 254-255 K 6
San Luis ○ YV 60-61 G 2
San Luis, Lago de ⬭ BOL 70-71 E 3
San Luis, Sierra de ▲ RA 78-79 F 2
San Luis Acatlán ○ MEX 52-53 E 3
San Luis Canal ⟨ USA (CA) 248-249 D 3
San Luis Creek ∼ USA 254-255 K 5
San Luis del Cordero ○ MEX 50-51 G 5
San Luis del Palmar ○• RA 76-77 H 4
San Luis de Shuaro ○ PE 64-65 F 7
San Luis Obispo ○ USA (CA) 248-249 D 4
San Luis Potosí □ MEX 50-51 H 6
San Luis Reservoir ⬭ USA (CA) 248-249 C 2
San Luis Rey de Francia • USA (CA) 248-249 G 6
San Luis Río Colorado ○• MEX 50-51 B 1
San Luis San Pedro ○ MEX 52-53 D 3
San Luis Valley ⌣ USA 254-255 K 6
San Luiz de la Paz ○ MEX 50-51 J 7
Sanluri ○ I 100-101 B 5
San Manuel ○ C 54-55 G 4
San Manuel ○ USA (AZ) 256-257 E 6
San Marcial ○ USA (NM) 256-257 J 5
San Marco, Capo ▲ I 100-101 B 5
San Marco, Capo ▲ I 100-101 D 6
San Marcos ○ BR 62-63 K 6
San Marcos ☆ GCA 52-53 J 4
San Marcos ○ MEX 52-53 E 3
San Marcos ○ USA (TX) 266-267 K 4
San Marcos, Isla ⌒ MEX 50-51 C 4
San Marcos, Laguna ≈ 52-53 E 3
San Marcos de Colón ○ HN 52-53 L 5
San Marcos River ∼ USA 266-267 K 4
San Marcus Pass ▲ USA (CA) 248-249 E 5
San Mariano ○ RP 160-161 E 4
San Marino ○ AUS 178-179 C 5
San Marino ■ RSM 100-101 C 3
San Marino ★• RSM 100-101 D 3
San Martín ○ CO 60-61 E 6
San Martín ○ RA 76-77 E 5
San Martín, Lago ⬭ RA 80 D 4
San Martín, Península ⌣ RCH 80 C 4
San Martín, Río ∼ BOL 70-71 F 3
San Martín Chalchicuautla ○ MEX 50-51 K 7
San Martín de los Andes ○ RA 78-79 D 6
San Mateo ○ USA (CA) 248-249 B 2
San Mateo ○ USA (NM) 256-257 H 3
San Mateo ○ YV 60-61 J 3
San Mateo Ixtatán ○ GCA 52-53 J 4
San Mateo Matengo ○ MEX 52-53 E 2
San Mateo Peak ▲ USA (NM) 256-257 H 5
San Matías ○ BOL 70-71 H 5
San Matías, Golfo ≈ 78-79 G 6
Sanmaur ○ CDN (QUE) 236-237 P 5
Sanmen ○ VRC 156-157 M 2
Sanmen Wan ≈ 156-157 M 2
Sanmenxia ○• VRC 154-155 G 4
San Miguel ○ CO 66-67 B 2
San Miguel ○ E 188-189 C 6
San Miguel ○ EC (BOL) 64-65 C 2
San Miguel ○ EC (ESM) 64-65 C 1
San Miguel ☆ ES 52-53 K 5
San Miguel ○ PA 52-53 E 7
San Miguel ○ PE 64-65 F 8
San Miguel ○ RA (BUA) 78-79 K 3
San Miguel ○ RA (COR) 76-77 J 4
San Miguel ○ RP 160-161 E 9
San Miguel ○ USA (AZ) 256-257 D 7
San Miguel ○ USA (CA) 248-249 D 4
San Miguel ⌒ USA (CA) 248-249 D 5
San Miguel ○ YV 60-61 J 3
San Miguel, Cerro ▲ BOL 70-71 G 6
San Miguel, Río ∼ BOL 70-71 G 5
San Miguel, Río ∼ CO 64-65 D 1
San Miguel, Río ∼ MEX 50-51 F 4
San Miguel, Río ∼ MEX 50-51 D 3
San Miguel, Sierra ▲ RCH 76-77 C 4
San Miguel, Volcán ▲ ES 52-53 K 5
San Miguel Aloapan ○ MEX 52-53 F 3
San Miguel Bay ≈ 160-161 E 6
San Miguel Creek ∼ USA 266-267 J 5
San Miguel de Allende ○• MEX 52-53 D 1
San Miguel de Baga ○ C 54-55 G 4
San Miguel de Huachi ○ BOL 70-71 D 4
San Miguel del Monte ○ RA 78-79 K 3
San Miguel de Pallaques ○ PE 64-65 C 5
San Miguel de Salcedo ○ EC 64-65 C 2
San Miguel de Tucumán ☆• RA 76-77 E 4
San Miguelito ○ BOL 70-71 C 2
San Miguelito ○ MEX 50-51 E 2
San Miguelito ○ NIC 52-53 B 6
San Miguel River ∼ USA 254-255 G 5
San Miguel Sola de Vega ○ MEX 52-53 F 3
San Miguel Suchixtepec ○ MEX 52-53 F 3
San Miguel Tulancingo ○• MEX 52-53 F 3
Sanming ○ VRC 156-157 K 3
San Narcisco ○ RP 160-161 D 5
Sannaspos ○ ZA 220-221 H 4
San Nicolas ○ BOL 70-71 E 4
San Nicolás ○ MEX 50-51 E 3
San Nicolás, Bahía ≈ 64-65 E 9
San Nicolas de los Arroyos ○ RA 78-79 J 2
San Nicolas de los Garzas ○ MEX 50-51 J 5
San Nicolás de Tolentino ○ E 188-189 D 7
San Nicolas Island ⌒ USA (CA) 248-249 E 6
San Nicolás Tolentino ○ MEX 50-51 J 6
Sannieshof ○ ZA 220-221 G 3
Sannikova ○ RUS 110-111 W 2
Sannikova, proliv ≈ 110-111 W 2
Sanniquellie ☆ LB 202-203 F 6
Sannohe ○ J 152-153 J 4
Sanogasta, Sierra de ▲ RA 76-77 D 5
Sanok ○• PL 92-93 R 4
San Onofre ○ CO 60-61 D 3
Sanostee ○ USA (NM) 256-257 G 2
Sanoyie ○ LB 202-203 F 6
San Pablo ○ BOL 70-77 D 1
San Pablo ○ C 54-55 F 4
San Pablo ○ CO (BOL) 60-61 E 4
San Pablo ○ CO (NAR) 64-65 D 1
San Pablo ○ PE 64-65 C 5
San Pablo ○ RCH 78-79 C 6
San Pablo ○ RP 160-161 D 5
San Pablo ○ YV (ANZ) 60-61 J 3
San Pablo ○ YV (BOL) 60-61 H 4
San Pablo ○ YV (BOL) 60-61 K 4
San Pablo, Punta ▲ MEX 50-51 B 4
San Pablo, Río ∼ BOL 70-71 F 4
San Pablo, Río ∼ PE 64-65 C 4
San Pablo Balleza ○ MEX 50-51 F 4
San Pablo Bay ≈ 246-247 C 5
San Pablo de Balzar, Cordillera de ▲ EC 64-65 B 2
Sanpaka ○ RMM 202-203 F 2
San Pascual ○ RP 160-161 E 6
San Pasqual Indian Reservation ✕ USA (CA) 248-249 H 6
San Pedro ○ BOL 70-71 F 5
San Pedro ∼ C 54-55 F 4
San Pédro ○ CI 202-203 G 7
San Pedro ○ CO 60-61 D 4
San Pedro ○ MEX (BCS) 50-51 D 6
San Pedro ○ MEX (CHA) 50-51 G 3
San Pedro ○ MEX (SON) 50-51 D 3
San Pedro ○ MEX (SON) 50-51 C 2
San Pedro ○ PE 70-71 B 2
San Pedro ☆ PY 76-77 J 3
San Pedro ○ RA (BUA) 78-79 K 2
San Pedro ○ RA (JU) 76-77 E 3
San Pedro ○ RA (MIS) 76-77 K 4
San Pedro ○ RA (SAE) 76-77 E 4
San Pedro ○ RCH (ANT) 76-77 C 1
San Pedro ○ RCH (BIO) 78-79 C 4
San Pedro ○ RP 160-161 E 6
San Pedro ○ YV 60-61 K 2
San Pedro, Isla ⌒ RCH 78-79 C 7
San Pedro, Observatorio de • MEX 50-51 B 2
San Pedro, Punta ▲ RCH 76-77 B 3
San Pedro, Río ∼ BOL 70-71 C 2
San Pedro, Río ∼ BOL 76-77 D 1
San Pedro, Río ∼ GCA 52-53 J 3
San Pedro, Río ∼ MEX 50-51 F 4
San Pedro, Río ∼ MEX 50-51 G 6
San Pedro, Río ∼ MEX 52-53 B 2
San Pedro, Río ∼ RCH 76-77 C 2
San Pedro, Sierra de ▲ E 98-99 D 5
San Pedro, Volcán ▲ RCH 76-77 C 1
San Pedro Channel ≈ 248-249 F 6
San Pedro de Atacama ○• RCH 76-77 C 2
San Pedro de Buena Vista ○ BOL 70-71 E 6
San Pedro de Cachi ○ PE 64-65 E 8
San Pedro de Colalao ○ RA 76-77 E 4
San Pedro de Coris ○ PE 64-65 E 8
San Pedro de Curahuara ○ BOL 70-71 C 5
San Pedro de la Cueva ○ MEX 50-51 E 3
San Pedro de Las Bocas ○ YV 60-61 K 4
San Pedro de las Colonias ○ MEX 50-51 H 5
San Pedro de Lloc ○ PE 64-65 C 5
San Pedro del Norte ○ NIC 52-53 B 5
San Pedro del Paraná ○ PY 76-77 J 4
San Pedro de Macorís ☆ DOM 54-55 L 5
San Pedro de Quemes ○ BOL 70-71 C 7
San Pedro de Urabá ○ CO 60-61 C 3
San Pedro el Alto ○ MEX 52-53 F 3
San Pedro Huamelula ○ MEX 52-53 G 3
San Pedro Lagunillas ○ MEX 50-51 G 7
San Pedro Mártir, Sierra de ▲ MEX 50-51 B 2
San Pedro Nolasco, Isla ⌒ MEX 50-51 D 4
San Pedro Norte ○ RA 76-77 E 6
San Pedro Peak ▲ USA (NM) 256-257 J 2
San Pedro River ∼ USA 256-257 E 6
San Pedro Sacatepéquez ○ GCA 52-53 J 4
San Pedro Sula ☆ HN 52-53 K 4
San Pedro Tapanatepec ○ MEX 52-53 G 3
San Pietro, Ísola di ⌒ I 100-101 B 5
Sanpoil River ∼ USA 244-245 G 2
Sanpoku ○ J 152-153 H 5
Sanqingshan • VRC 156-157 L 2
Sanquianga, Parque Nacional ⊥ CO 60-61 B 6
San Quintín ○ MEX 50-51 B 2
San Quintín, Cabo ▲ MEX 50-51 B 2
San Rafael ○ BOL (COC) 70-71 E 5
San Rafael ○ BOL (PAZ) 70-71 C 4
San Rafael ○ BOL (SAC) 70-71 G 5
San Rafael ○ CO 66-67 D 2
San Rafael ○ CR 52-53 B 6
San Rafael ○ MEX (DGO) 50-51 G 5
San Rafael ○ MEX (NL) 50-51 J 5
San Rafael ○ PE 64-65 D 7
San Rafael ○ RA 78-79 E 3
San Rafael ○ YV 60-61 F 2
San Rafael, Cabo ▲ DOM 54-55 L 5
San Rafael, Glaciar ⊂ RCH 80 D 3
San Rafael, Río ∼ BOL 70-71 H 6
San Rafael, Río ∼ MEX 50-51 K 6
San Rafael de Curiapo ○ YV 60-61 L 3
San Rafael de Imataca ○ YV 62-63 D 2
San Rafael de Onoto ○ YV 60-61 G 3
San Rafael Knob ▲ USA (UT) 254-255 E 5
San Rafael Mountains ▲ USA 248-249 D 5
San Rafael River ∼ USA 254-255 E 4
San Ramon ○ BOL (BEN) 70-71 E 3
San Ramon ○ BOL (SAC) 70-71 F 4
San Ramón ○ C 54-55 G 4
San Ramón ○ CR 52-53 B 6
San Ramon ○ PE 64-65 E 7
San Ramón ○ PE 64-65 D 4
San Ramón ○ RA 76-77 D 6
San Ramón ○ RCH 76-77 B 4
San Ramon ○ ROU 78-79 M 3
San Ramon ○ RP 160-161 D 9
San Ramón, Río ∼ BOL 70-71 G 4
San Ramón de la Nueva Oran ○ RA 76-77 E 2
San Remo ○ I 100-101 A 3
San Roberto ○ MEX 50-51 J 5
San Roque ○ CO 60-61 E 3
San Roque ○ E 98-99 E 6
San Roque ○ MEX 50-51 B 4
San Roque ○ RP 160-161 F 7
San Roque ○ RP 160-161 D 5
San Roque ○ RP (NSA) 160-161 F 6
San Saba ○ USA (TX) 266-267 J 2
San Saba River ∼ USA 266-267 H 3
San Salvador ⌒ BS 54-55 H 2
San Salvador ★• ES 52-53 K 5
San Salvador ○ PE 66-67 B 4
San Salvador ○ RA (CO) 76-77 J 5
San Salvador ○ RA (ERI) 76-77 H 6
San Salvador, Canal de ≈ 64-65 B 10
San Salvador = Guanahani Island ⌒ BS 54-55 H 2
San Salvador, Isla ⌒ EC 64-65 B 10
San Salvador, Río ∼ ROU 78-79 L 2
San Salvador de Jujuy ☆ RA 76-77 E 3
San Salvador el Seco ○ MEX 52-53 F 2
Sansanding ○ RMM 202-203 H 3
San Sandrés, Laguna de ⬭ MEX 50-51 L 6
Sansanné-Mango ○ RT 202-203 L 4
Sansárpur ○ IND 144-145 C 6
Sans Bois Creek ∼ USA 264-265 J 3
San Sebastian ○ MEX 52-53 B 1
San Sebastián ○ RA 80 F 6
San Sebastian ○ USA (PR) 286-287 P 2
San Sebastián, Bahía ≈ 80 F 6
San Sebastián de Buenavista ○ CO 60-61 D 3
San Sebastián de la Gomera ○ E 188-189 C 6
San Sebastián de los Reyes ○ E 98-99 F 4
San Sebastião do Uatuma ○ BR 66-67 J 4
Sansepolcro ○ I 100-101 D 3
San Severo ○ I 100-101 E 4
Sansha Wan ≈ 156-157 L 3
Sanshui ○ VRC 156-157 H 5
San Silvestre ○ BOL 70-71 C 2
San Silvestre ○ YV 60-61 F 3
San Simeon ○ USA (CA) 248-249 C 4
San Simon ○ USA (AZ) 256-257 F 6
San Simón, Río ∼ BOL 70-71 F 3
San Simon River ∼ USA 256-257 E 6
Sanso ○ RMM 202-203 G 4
Sans Sault Rapids ∼ CDN 30-31 E 3
Sans Souci ○ USA (MI) 272-273 G 5
Sansui ○ VRC 156-157 F 3
Sansundi ○ RI 166-167 H 2
Sansu-ri ○ KOR 150-151 F 7
Sansynakac žyrasy ▲ KZ 126-127 O 2
Santa ○ PE 64-65 C 6
Santa ○ USA (ID) 250-251 C 4
Santa, Isla ⌒ PE 64-65 C 6
Santa, Río ∼ PE 64-65 D 6
Santa Ana ○ BOL (BEN) 70-71 E 3
Santa Ana ○ BOL (SAC) 70-71 H 6
Santa Ana ○ C 54-55 D 3
Santa Ana ○ CO 60-61 D 3
Santa Ana ○ EC 64-65 B 2
Santa Ana ☆ ES 52-53 K 5
Santa Ana ○ HN 52-53 L 5
Santa Ana ○ MEX (SON) 50-51 D 2
Santa Ana ○ MEX (TAB) 52-53 H 2
Santa Ana ○ PE 64-65 E 9
Santa Ana ○ RA 76-77 K 4
Santa Ana ○ RP 160-161 E 3
Santa Ana ○ USA (CA) 248-249 G 6
Santa Ana ○ YV 60-61 J 3
Santa Ana, Bahía ≈ 50-51 C 4
Santa Ana, Río ∼ YV 60-61 E 3
Santa Ana Island ⌒ SOL 184 I f 4
Santa Ana Maya ○ MEX 52-53 D 1
Santa Anna ○ USA (TX) 266-267 H 2
Santa Bárbara ○ BR (AMA) 66-67 D 5
Santa Bárbara ○ BR (MIN) 72-73 J 5
Santa Bárbara ○ CO 60-61 D 5
Santa Bárbara ☆ HN 52-53 K 4
Santa Bárbara ○ MEX 50-51 G 4
Santa Bárbara ○ RCH 78-79 C 4
Santa Barbara ○• USA (CA) 248-249 E 5
Santa Bárbara ○ YV (AMA) 60-61 H 6
Santa Bárbara ○ YV (ANZ) 60-61 K 3
Santa Bárbara ○ YV (BAR) 60-61 F 4
Santa Bárbara ○ YV (BOL) 60-61 K 4
Santa Bárbara ○ YV (GUA) 60-61 J 3
Santa Bárbara, Parque Nacional ⊥ HN 52-53 K 4
Santa Bárbara, Río ∼ BOL 70-71 G 5
Santa Bárbara, Serra de ▲ BR 70-71 H 4
Santa Barbara, Sierra de ▲ RA 76-77 E 3
Santa Barbara Channel ≈ 248-249 D 5
Santa Bárbara do Sul ○ BR 74-75 D 7
Santa Barbara Island ⌒ USA (CA) 248-249 E 6
Santa Brígida ○ BR 68-69 J 6
Santa Casilda ○ MEX 52-53 D 2
Santa Catalina ○ RA 76-77 E 5
Santa Catalina ○ RP 160-161 E 8
Santa Catalina, Arroyo ∼ RA 78-79 G 2
Santa Catalina, Gulf of ≈ 40-41 E 9
Santa Catalina, Gulf of ≈ 248-249 F 6
Santa Catalina, Isla ⌒ MEX 50-51 D 5
Santa Catalina Island ⌒ USA (CA) 248-249 F 6
Santa Catalina Island = Owa Riki ⌒ SOL 184 I f 4
Santa Catarina □ BR 74-75 D 6
Santa Catarina ○ CV 202-203 C 6
Santa Catarina ○ MEX 50-51 J 5
Santa Catarina, Ilha de ⌒ BR 74-75 F 6
Santa Catarina, Río ∼ MEX 52-53 E 3
Santa Cecília ○ BR 74-75 E 6
Santa Clara ○ BR 62-63 J 6
Santa Clara ☆•• C 54-55 F 3
Santa Clara ○ RA 76-77 E 3
Santa Clara ○ USA (UT) 254-255 B 6
Santa Clara ○ YV 60-61 J 3
Santa Clara, Bahía de ≈ 54-55 E 3
Santa Clara, Isla ⌒ RCH 78-79 C 1
Santa Clara, Río ∼ MEX 50-51 F 3
Santa Clara, Sierra de ▲ MEX 50-51 C 4
Santa Clara Indian Reservation ✕ USA (NM) 256-257 J 3
Santa Clotilde ○ PE 64-65 F 3
Santa Comba Dão ○ P 98-99 C 4
Santa Cruz ○ BOL 70-71 C 4
Santa Cruz ○ BR (BAH) 68-69 H 6
Santa Cruz ○ BR (GSU) 70-71 J 7
Santa Cruz ○ BR (P) 66-67 J 4
Santa Cruz ○ BR (P) 68-69 B 3
Santa Cruz ○ BR (PAU) 72-73 G 6
Santa Cruz ○ BR (RNO) 68-69 K 5
Santa Cruz ○ BR (RON) 66-67 F 7
Santa Cruz ○ CR 52-53 B 6
Santa Cruz ∼ MEX 50-51 D 5
Santa Cruz ○ PE (LIM) 64-65 D 7
Santa Cruz ○ PE (LOR) 64-65 E 4
Santa Cruz □ RA 80 E 3
Santa Cruz ○ RCH 78-79 D 3
Santa Cruz ○ RP (DAS) 160-161 F 9
Santa Cruz ○ RP (MAR) 160-161 E 6
Santa Cruz ○ RP (ZAM) 160-161 C 5
Santa Cruz ☆ RP (LAG) 160-161 D 5
Santa Cruz ○ USA (AZ) 256-257 C 7
Santa Cruz ○• USA (CA) 248-249 B 3
Santa-Cruz ○ YV 62-63 D 2
Santa Cruz ○ YV (APU) 60-61 G 4
Santa Cruz ○ YV (BOL) 60-61 K 4
Santa Cruz, Isla ⌒ EC 64-65 B 10
Santa Cruz, Río ∼ MEX 76-77 E 2
Santa Cruz, Río ∼ RA 80 E 5
Santa Cruz, Río ∼ RA 80 F 5
Santa Cruz Cabrália ○ BR 72-73 L 4
Santa Cruz de Bucaral ○ YV 60-61 G 2
Santa Cruz de Campezo = Santi Kurutze Kanpezu ○ E 98-99 F 3
Santa Cruz de la Palma ○ E 188-189 C 6
Santa Cruz de la Sierra ☆ BOL 70-71 F 5
Santa Cruz del Norte ○ C 54-55 E 3
Santa Cruz del Quiché ☆ GCA 52-53 J 4
Santa Cruz del Sur ○ C 54-55 G 4
Santa Cruz de Mudela ○ E 98-99 F 5
Santa Cruz de Tenerife ☆ E 188-189 C 6
Santa Cruz do Arari ○ BR 62-63 K 6
Santa Cruz do Capibaribe ○ BR 68-69 K 5
Santa Cruz do Sul ○ BR 74-75 D 7
Santa Cruz Island ⌒ USA (CA) 248-249 E 5
Santa Cruz Verapaz ○ GCA 52-53 J 4
Santa de Ayes Laguna Colorada, Parque Nacional ⊥ BOL 76-77 D 2
Santa Doménica Talão ○ I 100-101 E 5
Santa Elena ○ EC 64-65 B 3
Santa Elena ○ MEX 50-51 H 4
Santa Elena ○ RA 76-77 H 6
Santa Elena ○ YV 60-61 K 3
Santa Elena, Bahía de ≈ 52-53 B 6
Santa Elena, Bahía de ≈ 64-65 B 3
Santa Elena, Cabo ▲ CR 52-53 B 6
Santa Elena, Cerro ▲ RA 80 H 2
Santa Elena de Arenales ○ YV 60-61 F 3
Santa Elena de Uairén ○ YV 62-63 D 3
Santa Eleodora ○ RA 78-79 H 3
Santa Eugenia (Ribeira) ○ E 98-99 C 3
Santa Eulalia ○ MEX 50-51 J 3
Santa Fé ○ BR 68-69 J 5
Santa Fé ○ C 54-55 D 3
Santa Fe ○ CO 60-61 F 4
Santa Fé ○ E 98-99 F 6
Santa Fé ○ PA (Dar) 52-53 E 7
Santa Fé ○ PA (Ver) 52-53 D 7
Santa Fé ○ PE 64-65 F 4
Santa Fé □ RA 76-77 G 5
Santa Fé ☆ RA (SAF) 76-77 G 6
Santa Fe ○ RP 160-161 E 9
Santa Fe ○ RP 160-161 D 5
Santa Fe ○ USA (TX) 268-269 E 7
Santa Fe ☆• USA (NM) 256-257 K 3
Santa Fe, Isla ⌒ EC 64-65 B 10
Santa Fé de Minas ○ BR 72-73 H 4
Santa Fé do Sul ○ BR 72-73 E 6
Santa Fe River ∼ USA 286-287 G 2
Santa Filomena ○ BR 68-69 F 6
Santa Helena ○ BR (MAR) 68-69 F 3
Santa Helena ○ BR (PAR) 76-77 K 3
Santa Helena ○ CO 60-61 E 6
Santa Helena de Cusima ○ CO 60-61 F 5
Santa Helena de Goiás ○ BR 72-73 E 4
Santai ○ VRC 154-155 D 6
Santa Inês ○ BR (BAH) 72-73 L 2
Santa Inês ○ BR (MAR) 68-69 F 3
Santa Inés ○ YV 60-61 G 2
Santa Ines ○ YV 60-61 J 3
Santa Ines, Bahía ≈ 50-51 D 4
Santa Inés, Isla ⌒ RCH 80 D 6
Santa Isabel ○ MEX 52-53 H 3
Santa Isabel ○ PA 52-53 E 7
Santa Isabel ○ PE 64-65 E 4
Santa Isabel ○ RA 78-79 F 4
Santa Isabel ⌒ SOL 184 I d 2
Santa Isabel ○ USA (PR) 286-287 P 3
Santa Isabel, Cachoeira ∼ BR 68-69 D 5
Santa Isabel, Río ∼ GCA 52-53 K 4
Santa Isabel do Araguaia ○ BR 68-69 D 5
Santa Isabel d'Oeste ○ BR 74-75 D 5
Santa Isabel do Pará ○ BR 62-63 K 6
Santa Isabel do Preto ○ BR 72-73 H 7
Santa Isabel do Rio Negro ○ BR 66-67 E 3
Santa Júlia ○ BR 66-67 G 6
Santa Lucia ○ C 54-55 D 3
Santa Lucía ○ EC 64-65 C 2
Santa Lucia ○ PE 70-71 B 4
Santa Lucía ○ RA (CO) 76-77 H 5
Santa Lucía ○ RA (SAJ) 76-77 C 6
Santa Lucía ○ ROU 78-79 L 3
Santa Lucía, Río ∼ RA 76-77 H 5
Santa Lucía, Río ∼ ROU 78-79 L 3
Santa Lucía, Sierra de ▲ MEX 50-51 C 4
Santa Lucia Bank ≃ 248-249 C 5
Santa Lucia la Reforma ○ GCA 52-53 J 4
Santa Lucia Range ▲ USA 248-249 C 3
Santa Lugarda, Punta ▲ MEX 50-51 E 4
Santa Luisa ○ RCH 76-77 B 3
Santa Luz ○ BR (BAH) 68-69 J 7
Santa Luz ○ BR (PIA) 68-69 F 6
Santa Luzia ○ BR (BAH) 72-73 L 3
Santa Luzia ○ BR (MAR) 68-69 F 3
Santa Luzia ○ BR (MIN) 72-73 J 5
Santa Luzia ○ BR (PA) 68-69 K 5
Santa Luzia ○ BR (ROR) 62-63 D 5
Santa Luzia, Ilha de ⌒ CV 202-203 B 5
Santa Luzia do Pacuí ○ BR 62-63 J 5
Santa Magdalena ○ RA 78-79 H 3
Santa Margarita, Isla ⌒ MEX 50-51 D 5
Santa Maria ○ ANG 216-217 B 6
Santa Maria ○ BR (AMA) 66-67 H 5
Santa Maria ○ BR (P) 62-63 J 6
Santa Maria ○ BR (RSU) 74-75 D 7
Santa Maria ○ CO 60-61 E 5
Santa Maria ○ CR 52-53 C 7
Santa Maria ○ CV 202-203 C 5
Santa Maria ○ HN 52-53 L 4
Santa Maria ○ PA 52-53 D 7
Santa Maria ○ RA 76-77 F 2
Santa Maria ○ RP 160-161 F 9
Santa Maria ○ USA (CA) 248-249 D 5
Santa Maria ○ YV 60-61 F 3
Santa Maria ○ YV (APU) 60-61 H 4
Santa Maria ○ YV (SUC) 60-61 K 2
Santa Maria, Bahía ≈ 50-51 B 2
Santa Maria, Boca ≈ 50-51 L 5
Santa Maria, Cabo de ▲ P 98-99 D 6
Santa Maria, Cape ▲ BS 54-55 H 3
Santa Maria, Corredeira ∼ BR 66-67 H 6
Santa Maria, Isla ⌒ EC 64-65 B 10
Santa Maria, Isla ⌒ RCH 78-79 C 4
Santa Maria, Laguna de ⬭ MEX 50-51 F 2
Santa Maria, Punta ▲ ROU 78-79 M 3
Santa Maria, Ribeiro ∼ BR 68-69 D 5
Santa Maria, Rio ∼ BR 72-73 G 3
Santa Maria, Río ∼ MEX 50-51 F 2
Santa Maria, Río ∼ MEX 50-51 J 7
Santa Maria, Río ∼ RA 76-77 E 4
Santa Maria da Vitória ○ BR 72-73 H 2
Santa Maria da Vitória, Mosteiro de •• P 98-99 C 5
Santa Maria de Ipire ○ YV 60-61 J 3
Santa Maria de Itabira ○ BR 72-73 J 5
Santa Maria de Jebitá ○ BR 72-73 K 6
Santa Maria del Camí ○ E 98-99 J 5
Santa Maria del Oro ○ MEX 50-51 G 5
Santa Maria de Los Guaicas ○ YV 60-61 J 6
Santa Maria del Río ○ MEX 50-51 J 7
Santa Maria del Valle ○ PE 64-65 D 6
Santa Maria de Nanay ○ PE 64-65 F 3
Santa Maria de Nieva ○ PE 64-65 D 4
Santa Maria di Léuca, Capo ▲ I 100-101 G 5
Santa Maria do Para ○ BR 68-69 E 2
Santa Maria do Suaçuí ○ BR 72-73 J 5
Santa Maria Ecatepec ○ MEX 52-53 G 3
Santa Maria Eterna ○ BR 72-73 L 3
Santa Maria Island = Île Gaua ⌒ VAN 184 II a 2
Santa María Zacatepec ○ MEX 52-53 F 3
Santa María Zoquitlán ○ MEX 52-53 F 3
Santa Marta ○ ANG 216-217 B 6
Santa Marta ○ C 54-55 E 3
Santa Marta ☆• CO 60-61 D 2
Santa Marta, Cabo de ▲ BR 74-75 F 7
Santa Monica ○ USA (CA) 248-249 F 5
Santa Monica Mountains National Recreation Area • USA (CA) 248-249 E 5
Santan ○ RI 164-165 E 4
Santan, Tanjung ▲ RI 164-165 E 3
Santana ○ BR (AMA) 66-67 F 3
Santana ○ BR (APA) 62-63 J 6
Santana ○ BR (BAH) 72-73 H 2
Santana ○ BR (P) 68-69 E 3
Santana ○ CO (MET) 60-61 D 6
Santana ○ CO (SAN) 60-61 E 4
Santana ○ P 188-189 C 4
Santana, Área Indígena ✕ BR 70-71 K 4
Santana, Cachoeira ∼ BR 72-73 F 3
Santana, Ilha ⌒ BR 68-69 G 3
Santana, Ribeiro ∼ BR 68-69 C 6
Santana, Rio ∼ BR 68-69 G 6
Santana da Boa Vista ○ BR 74-75 D 8
Santana da Vargem ○ BR 72-73 H 6
Santana de Pirapama ○ BR 72-73 H 5
Santana do Acaraú ○ BR 68-69 H 3
Santana do Araguaia ○ BR 68-69 C 6
Santana do Garambeu ○ BR 72-73 H 6
Santana do Ipanema ○ BR 68-69 K 6
Santana do Itararé ○ BR 72-73 F 7
Santana do Livramento ○ BR 76-77 K 6
Santana do Manhuaçu ○ BR 72-73 K 6
Santana do Matos ○ BR 68-69 K 4
Santander ○• E 98-99 F 3
Santander ○ RP 160-161 E 8
Santander Jiménez ○ MEX 50-51 K 5
Santanilla, Islas = Islas del Cisne ⌒ HN 54-55 D 6
Sant'Antíoco ○ I 100-101 B 5
Sant'Antíoco, Ísola di ⌒ I 100-101 B 5
Santa Olalla del Cala ○ E 98-99 D 6
Santa Paula ○ USA (CA) 248-249 E 5
Santa Pola ○ E 98-99 G 5
Santaquin ○ USA (UT) 254-255 D 4
Santa Quitéria ○ BR 68-69 H 4
Santa Quitéria do Maranhão ○ BR 68-69 G 3
Sant'Arcángelo ○ I 100-101 F 4
Santarém ○ BR 66-67 K 4
Santarém ○• P 98-99 C 5
Santarém, Ponta de ▲ BR 62-63 J 5
Santarém Novo ○ BR 68-69 E 2
Santaren Channel ≈ 54-55 F 2
Santa Rita ∴• BH 52-53 K 2
Santa Rita ○ BR (AMA) 66-67 C 4
Santa Rita ○ BR (PA) 68-69 L 5
Santa Rita ○ CO (CA) 64-65 F 1
Santa Rita ○ CO (VIC) 60-61 G 5
Santa Rita ○ HN 52-53 L 4
Santa Rita ○ MEX 50-51 D 5
Santa Rita ○ PA 52-53 D 7
Santa Rita ○ YV (BOL) 60-61 K 3
Santa Rita ○ YV (GUA) 60-61 H 3
Santa Rita ○ YV (ZUL) 60-61 F 2
Santa Rita, Ilha de ⌒ BR 62-63 F 6
Santa Rita de Caldas ○ BR 72-73 G 7
Santa Rita de Cássia ○ BR 68-69 F 7
Santa Rita do Araguaia ○ BR 72-73 D 4
Santa Rita do Sul ○ BR 74-75 E 8
Santa Rosa ○ BOL (BEN) 70-71 D 4
Santa Rosa ○ BOL (PAN) 70-71 D 2
Santa Rosa ○ BR (CAT) 74-75 F 7
Santa Rosa ○ BR (RON) 70-71 G 3
Santa Rosa ○ BR (ROR) 60-61 K 6
Santa Rosa ○ BR (RSU) 76-77 K 4
Santa Rosa ○ BR (TOC) 68-69 D 7
Santa Rosa ○ CO (CAU) 64-65 D 1
Santa Rosa ○ CO (GU) 60-61 G 6
Santa Rosa ○ CO (VAU) 66-67 B 2
Santa Rosa ○ EC (ELO) 64-65 C 3
Santa Rosa ○ EC (PAS) 64-65 D 3
Santa Rosa ○ MEX (BCS) 50-51 E 6
Santa Rosa ○ MEX (QR) 52-53 K 2
Santa Rosa ○ PE (LOR) 64-65 F 3
Santa Rosa ○ PE (PUN) 70-71 B 4
Santa Rosa ○ RA (CO) 76-77 H 5
Santa Rosa ☆ RA (LAP) 78-79 G 4
Santa Rosa ○ USA (CA) 246-247 C 5
Santa Rosa ○ USA (NM) 256-257 L 4
Santa Rosa ○ YV (ANZ) 60-61 J 3
Santa Rosa ○ YV (APU) 60-61 G 4
Santa Rosa ○ YV (BOL) 60-61 K 4
Santa Rosa, Bajo de ≈ 62-63 K 5
Santa Rosa, Cordillera de ▲ RA 76-77 C 5
Santa Rosa, Isla ⌒ EC 64-65 C 1
Santa Rosa, Lago ⬭ BOL 70-71 H 6
Santa Rosa Aboriginal Land ✕ AUS 178-179 C 2
Santa Rosa de Amonadona ○ YV 66-67 D 2
Santa Rosa de Copán ☆ HN 52-53 K 4
Santa Rosa de Cusubamba ○ EC 64-65 C 2
Santa Rosa del Conlara ○ RA 78-79 G 2

San José — Santa Rosa del Conlara 389

Santa Rosa de los Pastos Grandes ○ **RA** 76-77 D 3
Santa Rosa de Ocopa • **PE** 64-65 E 7
Santa Rosa de Quijos ○ **EC** 64-65 D 2
Santa Rosa de Sucumbis ○ **EC** 64-65 D 1
Santa Rosa de Viterbo ○ **BR** 72-73 G 6
Santa Rosa dos Dourados ○ **BR** 72-73 G 5
Santa Rosa Indian Reservation ✕ **USA** (CA) 248-249 H 6
Santa Rosa Island ⌒ **USA** (CA) 248-249 D 6
Santa Rosa Island ⌒ **USA** (FL) 286-287 C 1
Santa Rosa Lake < **USA** (NM) 256-257 L 3
Santa Rosalía ○• **MEX** 50-51 C 4
Santa Rosalia ○ **YV** 60-61 J 4
Santa Rosa Range ⛰ **USA** 246-247 H 2
Santa Rosa Wash ~ **USA** 256-257 D 6
Šantarskie, ostrova ⌒ **RUS** 120-121 G 6
Šantarskoe more ≈ 120-121 G 6
Santa Si • **VRC** 142-143 M 3
Santa Sylvina ○ **RA** 76-77 G 4
Santa Tecla = Nueva San Salvador ○ **ES** 52-53 K 5
Santa Teresa ✕ **AUS** 178-179 C 3
Santa Teresa ○ **MEX** 50-51 L 5
Santa Teresa ○ **RA** 78-79 J 2
Santa Teresa ○ **YV** 60-61 H 2
Santa Teresa, Parque Nacional de ⊥ **ROU** 74-75 D 10
Santa Teresa, Punta ▲ **MEX** 50-51 D 4
Santa Teresa, Rio ~ **BR** 72-73 F 2
Santa Teresa de Goiás ○ **BR** 72-73 F 2
Santa Teresa di Gallura ○ **I** 100-101 B 4
Santa Teresinha de Goiás ○ **BR** 72-73 F 3
Santa Teresita ○ **RA** 78-79 L 4
Santa Terezinha ○ **BR** 68-69 C 7
Santa Ursula, Cachoeira ~ **BR** 66-67 H 7
Sant' Auta ○ **BR** 74-75 E 8
Santa Victoria ○ **RA** 76-77 E 2
Santa Victoria, Río ~ **RA** 76-77 E 2
Santa Victoria, Sierra ⛰ **RA** 76-77 E 2
Santa Vitória do Palmar ○ **BR** 74-75 D 9
San-ta-Wani Safari Lodge ○ **RB** 218-219 B 4
Santa Ynez ○ **USA** (CA) 248-249 D 5
Santa Ynez Mountains ⛰ **USA** 248-249 D 5
Santa Ysabel ○ **USA** (CA) 248-249 H 6
Sant Carles de la Ràpita ○ **E** 98-99 H 4
Sant Celoni ○ **E** 98-99 J 4
Santchou ○ **CAM** 204-205 H 6
Santee ○ **USA** (CA) 248-249 H 7
Santee ○ **USA** (NE) 262-263 J 2
Santee Indian Reservation ✕ **USA** (NE) 262-263 J 2
Santee National Wildlife Refuge ⊥ **USA** (SC) 284-285 K 3
Santee River ~ **USA** 284-285 L 3
Sante Marie Among the Hurons Historic Park • **CDN** (ONT) 238-239 F 4
San Tempo, Sierra de ⛰ **BOL** 76-77 E 2
Sant Feliu de Guíxols ○ **E** 98-99 J 4
Sant Francesc de Formentera ○ **E** 98-99 H 5
Santhe ○ **MW** 218-219 G 1
Santiago ○ **BOL** 70-71 H 6
Santiago ○ **BR** 76-77 K 5
Santiago ○ **CO** 60-61 E 4
Santiago ○ **EC** 64-65 C 3
Santiago ○ **MEX** (BCS) 50-51 E 6
Santiago ○ **MEX** (NL) 50-51 J 5
Santiago ☆ **PA** 52-53 D 7
Santiago ★•• **RCH** 78-79 D 2
Santiago ○ **RP** 160-161 D 4
Santiago, Cabo ▲ **RCH** 80 C 5
Santiago, Cerro ▲ **PA** 52-53 D 7
Santiago, Ilha de = Ilha de São Tiago ⌒ **CV** 202-203 C 6
Santiago, Punta ▲ **GQ** 210-211 B 2
Santiago, Río ~ **PE** 64-65 D 3
Santiago, Río de ~ **MEX** 50-51 H 5
Santiago Atitlán ○ **GCA** 52-53 J 4
Santiago Chazumba ○ **MEX** 52-53 F 2
Santiago de Cao ○ **PE** 64-65 C 5
Santiago de Choeorvos ○ **PE** 64-65 E 8
Santiago de Chuco ○ **PE** 64-65 C 6
Santiago de Compostela ○••• **E** 98-99 C 3
Santiago de Cuba ☆•• **C** 54-55 H 4
Santiago de Cuba, Bahía de ≈ 54-55 G 5
Santiago del Estero □ **RA** 76-77 E 4
Santiago del Estero ☆ **RA** (SAE) 76-77 E 4
Santiago de Los Caballeros ○ **MEX** 50-51 F 5
Santiago de los Cabelloros ☆• **DOM** 54-55 K 5
Santiago de Machaca ○ **BOL** 70-71 C 5
Santiago de Pacaguaras ○ **BOL** 70-71 C 3
Santiago Ixcuintla ○ **MEX** 50-51 G 7
Santiago Jamiltepec ○ **MEX** 52-53 F 3
Santiago Maravatío ○ **MEX** 52-53 D 1
Santiago Mountains ⛰ **USA** 266-267 D 3
Santiago Papasquiaro ○ **MEX** 50-51 G 5
Santiago Papasquiaro, Río ~ **MEX** 50-51 G 5
Santiago Peak ▲ **USA** (TX) 266-267 D 4
Santiago Tamazola ○ **MEX** 52-53 E 3
Santiago Tuxtla ○• **MEX** 52-53 G 2
Santiago Yosondúa ○ **MEX** 52-53 F 3
Santiam Junction ○ **USA** (OR) 244-245 D 6
San Tiburcio ○ **MEX** 50-51 J 5
Santigi ○ **RI** 164-165 G 3
Santigi, Tanjung ▲ **RI** (SLT) 164-165 G 3
Santigi, Tanjung ▲ **RI** (SLT) 164-165 H 4
Santiguila ○ **RMM** 202-203 G 3
Santipur ○ **IND** 142-143 B 5
Säntis ▲ **CH** 92-93 K 5
Santissima Trinità di Saccàrgia • **I** 100-101 B 4
Sant Joan de Labritja ○ **E** 98-99 H 5
Sant Jordi, Golf de ≈ 98-99 H 4
Santo ○ **USA** (TX) 264-265 F 6
Santo/ Malo □ **VAN** 184 II a 2
Santo Agostinho ○ **BR** 72-73 K 5
Santo Amaro ○ **BR** 66-67 B 6
Santo Amore, Ilha de ⌒ **BR** 72-73 H 7
Santo André ○ **ANG** 216-217 C 6
Santo André ○ **BR** (P) 62-63 K 6
Santo André ○ **BR** (PAU) 72-73 G 7
Santo Ângelo ○• **BR** 76-77 K 5
Santo Antão, Ilha de ⌒• **CV** 202-203 B 5
Santo António ○ **BR** 62-63 F 6
Santo Antonio ○ **BR** 66-67 G 4
Santo Antônio ○ **BR** 68-69 L 5
Santo António ○ **CV** 202-203 C 6
Santo Antonio ○ **STP** 210-211 b 2
Santo Antônio, Ponta de ▲ **BR** 68-69 L 5
Santo Antonio, Rio ~ **BR** 68-69 D 7
Santo Antônio da Patrulha ○ **BR** 74-75 E 7
Santo Antonio de Leverger ○ **BR** 70-71 J 4
Santo Antônio de Lisboa ○ **BR** 68-69 H 5
Santo Antonio Desejado ○ **BR** 66-67 D 7
Santo Antônio do Içá ○ **BR** 66-67 D 4
Santo Antônio do Monte ○ **BR** 72-73 H 6
Santo Antônio dos Lopes ○ **BR** 68-69 F 4
Santo Antônio do Sudoeste ○ **BR** 74-75 D 6
Santo Corazón ○ **BOL** 70-71 H 5
Santo Domingo ○ **C** 54-55 E 3
Santo Domingo ○ **CO** 60-61 D 4
Santo Domingo ★••• **DOM** 54-55 L 5
Santo Domingo ○ **MEX** (BCS) 50-51 D 5
Santo Domingo ○ **MEX** (JAL) 50-51 G 7
Santo Domingo ○ **MEX** (SLP) 50-51 J 6
Santo Domingo ○ **NIC** 52-53 B 5
Santo Domingo ○ **RA** 76-77 F 3
Santo Domingo, Cay ⌒ **BS** 54-55 H 4
Santo Domingo, Río ~ **MEX** 52-53 J 3
Santo Domingo, Río ~ **MEX** 52-53 F 3
Santo Domingo, Río ~ **MEX** 52-53 H 3
Santo Domingo, Río ~ **YV** 60-61 F 3
Santo Domingo de Acobamba ○ **PE** 64-65 E 7
Santo Domingo de los Colerados ○ **EC** 64-65 C 2
Santo Domingo Indian Reservation ✕ **USA** (NM) 256-257 J 3
Santo Domingo Pueblo ○ **USA** (NM) 256-257 J 3
Santo Domingo Tehuantepec ○• **MEX** 52-53 G 3
Santo Inácio do Piauí ○ **BR** 68-69 H 5
San Tomé ○ **YV** 60-61 J 3
Santoméri ○ **GR** 100-101 H 6
Santoña ○ **E** 98-99 F 3
Santonia ○ **F** 62-63 G 3
Santop ▲ **VAN** 184 II b 4
Santópolis do Aguapeí ○ **BR** 72-73 E 6
Santoríni = Thíra ⌒•• **GR** 100-101 K 6
Santos ○ **AUS** 178-179 F 5
Santos ○ **BR** 72-73 G 7
Santos, Baía de ≈ 72-73 G 7
Santos, El ○ **C** 54-55 F 3
Santos, General ☆ **RP** 160-161 F 9
Santos, Los ○•• **PA** 52-53 D 8
Santos Dumont ○ **BR** 72-73 J 6
Santos Lugares ○ **RA** 76-77 F 4
Santos Mercado ○ **BOL** 66-67 D 7
Santos Plateau ≃ 6-7 E 11
Santo Tirso ○ **P** 98-99 C 4
Santo Tomás ○ **MEX** 50-51 F 3
Santo Tomás ○ **MEX** 50-51 A 2
Santo Tomás ○ **NIC** 52-53 B 5
Santo Tomas ○ **PA** 52-53 C 7
Santo Tomas ○ **RP** 160-161 F 9
Santo Tomás, Punta ▲ **MEX** 50-51 A 2
Santo Tomas, Río ~ **PE** 64-65 F 9
Santo Tomás, Volcán ▲ **GCA** 52-53 J 4
Santo Tomé ○ **RA** (CO) 76-77 J 5
Santo Tomé ○ **RA** (SAF) 76-77 G 6
Santu Antine, Nuraghe • **I** 100-101 B 4
Santuaria Nacional de Ampay ⊥ **PE** 64-65 F 8
Santuario de Flora y Fauna Arauca ⊥ **CO** 60-61 F 4
Santuario de la Coromoto ○• **YV** 60-61 G 3
Santuario del Cisne • **EC** 64-65 C 3
Santuario Nacional Huayllay ⊥ **PE** 64-65 D 7
Santuario Virgen de las Lajas • **CO** 64-65 D 1
Santubong ○ **MAL** 162-163 J 4
Santu Lussùrgiu ○ **I** 100-101 B 4
Sanup Plateau ⛰ **USA** 256-257 B 3
San Vicente ○ **BOL** 76-77 D 1
San Vicente ☆ **ES** 52-53 K 5
San Vicente ○ **RA** 76-77 K 4
San Vicente ○ **YV** (AMA) 60-61 H 5
San Vicente ○ **YV** (ANZ) 60-61 J 3
San Vicente ○ **YV** (SUC) 60-61 K 2
San Vicente, Bahía ≈ 78-79 C 4
San Vicente de Tagua ○ **RCH** 78-79 D 3
San Vicente Tancuayalab ○ **MEX** 50-51 K 7
San Victor ○ **GUY** 62-63 D 2
San Víctor ○ **RA** 76-77 H 6
San Vincente de Caguan ○ **CO** 60-61 D 6
San Vincente de Cañete ○ **PE** 64-65 D 8
San Vito ○ **CR** 52-53 C 7
San Vito, Capo ▲ **I** 100-101 D 5
San Vito, Capo ▲ **I** 100-101 F 4
San Xavier Indian Reservation ✕ **USA** (AZ) 256-257 D 6
Sanya ○• **VRC** 156-157 F 7
Sanya Juu ○ **EAT** 212-213 F 5
Sanyang ○ **VRC** 156-157 L 2
Sanyat ad Daffah ○ **LAR** 192-193 L 2
Sanyati ○ **ZW** (Mlw) 218-219 E 3
Sanyati ~ **ZW** 218-219 E 3
Sanying ○ **VRC** 154-155 E 3
San Ysidro ○ **USA** (NM) 256-257 J 3
Sanyuan ○ **VRC** 154-155 F 4
Sanza Pombo ○ **ANG** 216-217 C 3
São Agostinho, Cabo de ▲ **BR** 68-69 L 6
São Amaro ○• **BR** 72-73 L 2
São André, Ribeiro ~ **BR** 72-73 G 4
São Antônia ○ **BR** 62-63 D 4
São Antonio ○ **BR** 66-67 K 6
São Antônio, Cachoeira ~ **BR** 66-67 E 7
São Antônio, Rio ~ **BR** 72-73 K 2
São Antônio, Rio ~ **BR** 72-73 J 5
São Antônio da Abunari ○ **BR** 62-63 D 6
São Antônio da Platina ○ **BR** 72-73 E 7
São Antônio das Missões ○ **BR** 76-77 K 5
São Antônio de Jesus ○ **BR** 72-73 L 2
São Antônio de Pádua ○ **BR** 72-73 J 6
São Antônio de Posse ○ **BR** 72-73 G 7
São Antônio do Amparo ○ **BR** 72-73 H 6
São Antônio do Jacinto ○ **BR** 72-73 K 4
São Bartolomeu, Rio ~ **BR** 72-73 G 4
São Benedito, Rio ~ **BR** 66-67 J 7
São Bento ○ **BR** (GSU) 70-71 J 6
São Bento ○ **BR** (MAR) 68-69 F 3
São Bento ○ **BR** (P) 68-69 E 3
São Bento do Norte ○ **BR** 68-69 K 4
São Bento do Sul ○ **BR** 74-75 F 6
São Bento do Una ○ **BR** 68-69 K 6
São Bernardo ○ **BR** (MAR) 68-69 G 3
São Bernardo ○ **BR** (RSU) 76-77 K 5
São Borja ○ **BR** 76-77 K 5
São Caetano de Odivelas ○ **BR** 62-63 K 6
São Caitano ○ **BR** 68-69 K 6
São Canuto ○ **BR** 76-77 K 5
São Carlos ○ **BR** (CAT) 74-75 D 6
São Carlos ○ **BR** (PAU) 72-73 G 7
São Carlos ○ **BR** (RON) 70-71 E 2
São Cosme ○ **BR** 62-63 J 6
São Cristóvão ○ **ANG** 216-217 B 6
São Cristóvão ○• **BR** 68-69 K 7
São Cruz, Ribeiro de ~ **BR** 72-73 G 4
São Desidério ○ **BR** 72-73 H 2
São Domingos ○ **BR** (AMA) 66-67 F 6
São Domingos ○ **BR** (GOI) 72-73 G 2
São Domingos ~ **BR** 70-71 F 3
São Domingos ○ **GNB** 202-203 B 3
São Domingos, Rio ~ **BR** 72-73 G 2
São Domingos, Serra de ⛰ **BR** 72-73 G 3
São Domingos da Maranhão ○ **BR** 68-69 F 4
São Domingos da Prata ○ **BR** 72-73 J 5
São Domingos do Azeitão ○ **BR** 68-69 F 5
São Domingos do Capim ○ **BR** 68-69 E 2
São Efigênia de Minas ○ **BR** 72-73 J 5
São Estêvão ○ **BR** 72-73 L 2
São Felício ○ **BR** 62-63 H 5
São Felix de Balsas ○ **BR** 68-69 F 5
São Felix do Araguaia ○ **BR** 68-69 C 7
São Félix do Piauí ○ **BR** 68-69 G 4
São Felix do Xingu ○ **BR** 68-69 C 5
São Fidélis ○ **BR** 72-73 K 6
São Filipe ○ **CV** 202-203 B 6
São Florêncio, Cachoeira ~ **BR** 66-67 H 7
São Francisco ○ **BR** (GSU) 70-71 J 6
São Francisco ○ **BR** (MIN) 72-73 H 3
São Francisco ○ **BR** (P) 68-69 E 3
São Francisco, Cachoeira ~ **BR** 66-67 K 5
São Francisco, Ilha de ⌒ **BR** 74-75 F 6
São Francisco, Rio ~ **BR** 66-67 E 7
São Francisco, Rio ~ **BR** 68-69 K 6
São Francisco, Rio ~ **BR** 72-73 K 3
São Francisco, Serra de ⛰ **BR** 74-75 D 5
São Francisco das Chagas ○ **BR** 62-63 F 6
São Francisco de Assis ○ **BR** 76-77 K 5
São Francisco de Paula ○ **BR** 74-75 E 7
São Francisco do Maranhão ○ **BR** 68-69 G 5
São Francisco do Sul ○ **BR** 74-75 F 6
São Gabriel ○ **BR** (CAT) 74-75 F 6
São Gabriel ○ **BR** (RSU) 76-77 K 6
São Gabriel da Palha ○ **BR** 72-73 K 5
São Geraldo do Araguaia ○ **BR** 68-69 D 5
São Gonçalo ○ **BR** 72-73 J 7
São Gonçalo do Abaeté ○ **BR** 72-73 H 5
São Gonçalo do Amarante ○ **BR** 68-69 J 3
São Gonçalo do Para ○ **BR** 72-73 H 5
São Gonçalo do Rio ○ **BR** 72-73 J 5
São Gonçalo do Sapucaí ○ **BR** 72-73 H 6
São Gotardo ○ **BR** 72-73 G 5
Sao Hill ○ **EAT** 214-215 H 5
São Inácio ○ **BR** 72-73 E 7
São Jerônimo ○ **BR** 74-75 E 7
São Jerônimo, Serra de ⛰ **BR** 70-71 K 5
São João ○ **BR** 66-67 G 5
São João, Ilha de ⌒ **BR** 68-69 F 2
São João, Ribeiro ~ **BR** 72-73 K 4
São João, Rio ~ **BR** 72-73 E 2
São João, Serra de ⛰ **BR** 74-75 E 5
São João Batista ○ **BR** 68-69 F 3
São João Batista do Gloria ○ **BR** 72-73 G 6
São João da Alicança ○ **BR** 72-73 G 3
São João da Barra ○ **BR** 72-73 K 6
São João da Barra, Cachoeira ~ **BR** 66-67 H 7
São João da Barra, Rio ~ **BR** 66-67 H 7
São João da Ponte ○ **BR** 72-73 H 3
São João da Pracajuba ○ **BR** 62-63 J 6
São João de Cortes ○ **BR** 68-69 F 3
São João del Rei ○• **BR** 72-73 H 6
São João de Meriti ○ **BR** 72-73 J 7
São João do Araguaia ○ **BR** 68-69 D 4
São João do Branco, Igarapé ~ **BR** 70-71 F 2
São João do Caiuá ○ **BR** 72-73 D 7
São João do Paraiso ○ **BR** 72-73 J 3
São João do Paraná ○ **BR** 66-67 J 7
São João do Piaui ○ **BR** 68-69 G 6
São João do Sabuji ○ **BR** 68-69 K 5
São João do Tigre ○ **BR** 68-69 K 6
São João Evangelista ○ **BR** 72-73 J 5
São Joaquim ○ **BR** (AMA) 66-67 D 2
São Joaquim ○ **BR** (CAT) 74-75 F 7
São Joaquim, Parque Nacional de ⊥ **BR** 74-75 F 7
São Joaquim da Barra ○ **BR** 72-73 G 6
São Jorge, Ilha ⌒ **BR** 68-69 F 2
São Jorge do Jvaí ○ **BR** 72-73 D 7
São José ○ **BR** (ACR) 66-67 C 7
São José ○ **BR** (CAT) 74-75 F 6
São José ○ **BR** (P) 68-69 D 3
São Jóse, Baía ≈ 68-69 G 3
São José, Igarapé ~ **BR** 68-69 B 4
São José de Piranhas ○ **BR** 68-69 J 5
São José de Ribamar ○ **BR** 68-69 F 3
São José di Mipibu ○ **BR** 68-69 L 5
São José do Anauá ○ **BR** 62-63 D 5
São José do Barreiro ○ **BR** 72-73 H 7
São José do Belmonte ○ **BR** 68-69 J 5
São José do Caciporé ○ **BR** 62-63 J 4
São José do Calcado ○ **BR** 72-73 K 6
São José do Cedro ○ **BR** 74-75 D 6
São José do Cerrito ○ **BR** 74-75 E 6
São José do Egito ○ **BR** 68-69 K 5
São José do Norte ○ **BR** 74-75 D 9
São José do Peixe ○ **BR** 68-69 G 5
São José do Prado ○ **BR** 72-73 L 4
São José do Rio Claro ○ **BR** 70-71 J 3
São José do Rio Preto ○ **BR** 72-73 F 6
São José dos Campos ○ **BR** 72-73 H 7
São José dos Cordeiros ○ **BR** 68-69 K 5
São José dos Dourados, Rio ~ **BR** 72-73 E 6
São José dos Martírios ○ **BR** 68-69 D 5
São José dos Pinhais ○ **BR** 74-75 F 5
São José do Xingu ○ **BR** 68-69 B 7
São Julia do Jurupari ○ **BR** 62-63 J 5
São Juliana ○ **BR** 72-73 G 5
Saoleil Ashraf ○ **SUD** 200-201 G 6
São Lourenço, Riachão ~ **BR** 68-69 G 6
São Lourenço, Rio ~ **BR** 70-71 K 5
São Lourenço do Sul ○ **BR** 74-75 E 8
São Lucas ○ **ANG** 216-217 D 5
São Lucas, Cachoeira ~ **BR** 66-67 H 7
São Luís ○ **BR** (AMA) 66-67 E 3
São Luís ○ **BR** (AMA) 66-67 G 4
São Luís ☆• **BR** (MAR) 68-69 F 3
São Luis, Cachoeira ~ **BR** 66-67 H 7
São Luís, Ilha de ⌒ **BR** 68-69 F 3
São Luis de Montes Belos ○ **BR** 72-73 E 4
São Luís do Curu ○ **BR** 68-69 J 3
São Luis do Paraitinga ○ **BR** 72-73 H 7
São Luis do Purunã ○ **BR** 74-75 F 5
São Luis do Quitunde ○ **BR** 68-69 L 6
São Luís do Tapajós ○ **BR** 66-67 J 5
São Luis Gonzaga ○ **BR** 76-77 K 5
São Luis Gonzaga do Maranhão ○ **BR** 68-69 F 4
São Manuel ○ **BR** (MAT) 70-71 K 4
São Manuel ○ **BR** (PAU) 72-73 F 7
São Manuel ou Teles Pires, Rio ~ **BR** 66-67 J 7
São Marcos, Área Indígena ✕ **BR** (MAT) 72-73 D 3
São Marcos, Área Indígena ✕ **BR** (ROR) 62-63 D 3
São Marcos, Baía de ≈ 68-69 F 3
São Marcos, Rio ~ **BR** 72-73 G 4
São Martinho ○ **BR** 74-75 F 7
São Mateus ○ **BR** 72-73 L 5
São Mateus, Pico ▲ **BR** 72-73 K 6
São Mateus do Sul ○ **BR** 74-75 E 5
São Miguel ○ **BR** (APA) 62-63 J 5
São Miguel ○ **BR** (MAT) 72-73 D 2
São Miguel ○ **BR** (RNO) 68-69 J 5
São Miguel, Ilha de ⌒ **P** 6-7 G 5
São Miguel, Rio ~ **BR** 70-71 J 3
São Miguel, Rio ~ **BR** 70-71 F 3
São Miguel Arcanjo ○ **BR** 72-73 G 7
São Miguel das Missões ○••• **BR** 76-77 K 5
São Miguel do Araguaia ○ **BR** 72-73 E 2
São Miguel d'Oeste ○ **BR** 74-75 D 6
São Miguél do Guama ○ **BR** 68-69 E 2
São Miguel do Iguaçu ○ **BR** 76-77 K 3
São Miguel dos Campos ○ **BR** 68-69 K 6
São Miguel dos Macacos ○ **BR** 62-63 J 6
São Miguel do Tapuio ○ **BR** 68-69 H 4
Saona, Isla ⌒ **DOM** 54-55 L 5
Saône ~ **F** 90-91 L 7
São Nicolau ○ **ANG** 216-217 B 7
São Nicolau ○ **BR** 76-77 K 5
São Nicolau, Ilha de ⌒ **CV** 202-203 B 5
São Nicolau, Rio ~ **BR** 68-69 H 4
São Onofre, Rio ~ **BR** 72-73 J 2
São Paulo □ **BR** 72-73 E 6
São Paulo ☆• **BR** (PAU) 72-73 G 7
São Paulo de Olivença ○ **BR** 66-67 C 4
São Pedro ○ **BR** (AMA) 66-67 D 3
São Pedro ○ **BR** (MIN) 72-73 K 4
São Pedro ○ **BR** (P) 68-69 C 3
São Pedro ○ **BR** (PAU) 72-73 G 7
São Pedro ○ **BR** (RNO) 68-69 L 4
São Pedro ○ **CV** 202-203 B 5
São Pedro, Ribeiro ~ **BR** 72-73 G 4
São Pedro, Rio ~ **BR** 70-71 G 2
São Pedro, Rio de ~ **BR** 68-69 H 5
São Pedro da Aldeia ○ **BR** 72-73 J 7
São Pedro da Garça ○ **BR** 72-73 J 4
São Pedro da Quilemba ○ **ANG** 216-217 C 4
São Pedro do Butiá ○ **BR** 76-77 K 5
São Pedro do Icó ○ **BR** 66-67 C 7
São Pedro do Paraná ○ **BR** 72-73 D 7
São Pedro do Piauí ○ **BR** 68-69 G 4
São Pedro dos Crentes ○ **BR** 68-69 E 5
São Pedro do Sul ○ **BR** 76-77 K 5
São Raimundo das Mangabeiras ○ **BR** 68-69 F 5
São Raimundo Nonato ○ **BR** 68-69 G 6
São Ramão ○ **BR** 72-73 H 4
São Romão ○ **BR** 66-67 D 5
São Roque, Cachoeira ~ **BR** 70-71 F 2
São Sebastião ○ **BR** 72-73 H 7
São Sebastião, Ilha de ⌒ **BR** 72-73 H 7
São Sebastião, Ponta ▲ **MOC** 218-219 H 6
São Sebastião da Amoreira ○ **BR** 72-73 E 7
São Sebastião da Boa Vista ○ **BR** 62-63 K 6
São Sebastião da Gama ○ **BR** 72-73 G 6
São Sebastião do Caí ○ **BR** 74-75 E 7
São Sebastião do Maranhão ○ **BR** 72-73 J 5
São Sebastião do Paraíso ○ **BR** 72-73 G 6
São Sebastião do Rio Verde ○ **BR** 72-73 H 7
São Sebastião dos Poções ○ **BR** 72-73 H 3
São Sebastião do Tocantins ○ **BR** 68-69 D 4
São Sepé ○ **BR** 74-75 D 8
São Simão, Cachoeira ~ **BR** 66-67 H 7
São Simão, Ponta ▲ **BR** 74-75 E 8
São Simão ou Branco, Rio ~ **BR** 70-71 F 3
São Teotónio ○ **P** 98-99 C 6
São Tiago, Ilha de = Ilha de Santiago ⌒ **CV** 202-203 C 6
São Timóteo ○ **BR** 72-73 J 2
São Tomé ○ **BR** (APA) 62-63 J 6
São Tomé ○ **BR** (RIO) 72-73 K 7
São Tomé ★ **STP** 210-211 B 5
São Tomé ⌒ **STP** 210-211 b 2
São Tomé, Cabo de ▲ **BR** 72-73 K 6
São Tomé and Príncipe = São Tomé e Príncipe ■ **STP** 210-211 B 5
Saoura, Oued ~ **DZ** 188-189 L 6
São Valentim ○ **BR** 74-75 D 6
São Vendelino ○ **BR** 74-75 E 7
São Vice ○ **BR** 76-77 K 5
São Vicente ○ **BR** (ACR) 66-67 B 6
São Vicente ○ **BR** (GOI) 72-73 G 2
São Vicente ○ **BR** (GSU) 70-71 J 6
São Vicente ○ **BR** (MAT) 70-71 K 4
São Vicente ○ **BR** (P) 62-63 J 6
São Vicente ○ **BR** (PAU) 72-73 G 7
São Vicente, Cabo de ▲ **P** 98-99 C 6
São Vicente, Ilha de ⌒ **CV** 202-203 B 5
São Vicente, Rio ~ **BR** 68-69 G 5
São Vicente Ferrer ○ **BR** 68-69 F 3
Sapang ○ **MAL** 160-161 C 10
Sapão, Rio ~ **BR** 68-69 F 7
Saparua ○ **RI** 166-167 E 3
Saparua, Pulau ⌒ **RI** 166-167 E 3
Sapé ○ **BR** 68-69 L 5
Sape ○ **RI** 168 D 7
Sape, Selat ≈ 168 D 7
Sapeaçu ○ **BR** 72-73 L 2
Sapele ○ **WAN** 204-205 F 6
Sapello ○ **USA** (NM) 256-257 K 3
Sapelo Island ⌒ **USA** (GA) 284-285 J 5
Sapelo Sound ≈ 284-285 J 5
Sapërnoe ○ **RUS** 94-95 L 1
Sápes ○ **GR** 100-101 K 4
Şaphane Dağı ▲ **TR** 128-129 C 3
Šapina ~ **RUS** 120-121 S 6
Sapinero ○ **USA** (CO) 254-255 H 5
Sapiranga ○ **BR** 74-75 E 7
Sapiranga do Sul ○ **BR** 74-75 E 7
Sapi Safari Area ⊥ **ZW** 218-219 E 2
Šapki ○ **RUS** 94-95 M 2
Šapkina ~ **RUS** 88-89 X 3
Sap Malua ○ **THA** 158-159 G 3
Sapo, Serrania del ⛰ **PA** 52-53 E 8
Sapoba ○ **WAN** 204-205 F 5
Sapočani ••• **YU** 100-101 H 3
Sapocoy, Mount ▲ **RP** 160-161 D 4
Sapodilla Cays ⌒ **BH** 52-53 K 3
Saponac ○ **USA** (ME) 278-279 N 3
Saponé ○ **BF** 202-203 K 3
Sapo Sapo ○ **ZRE** 210-211 J 6
Saposoa ○ **PE** 64-65 D 5
Sapouy ○ **BF** 202-203 K 4
Sappa Creek ~ **USA** 262-263 F 5
Sapphire Mountains ⛰ **USA** 250-251 F 5
Sappho ○ **USA** (WA) 244-245 A 2
Sapporo ☆ **J** 152-153 J 3
Sapri ○ **I** 100-101 E 4
Šapšal'skij hrebet ⛰ **RUS** 124-125 Q 3
Sapucaí, Rio ~ **BR** 72-73 F 6
Sapucaia ○ **BR** (AMA) 66-67 J 4
Sapucaia ○ **BR** (MIN) 72-73 J 6
Sapucaia ○ **BR** (RIO) 72-73 J 7
Sapudi, Pulau ⌒ **RI** 168 B 6
Sapuka-Besar, Pulau ⌒ **RI** 168 D 6
Sapulpa ○ **USA** (OK) 264-265 H 2
Sapulu ○ **RI** 168 E 3
Sapulut ○ **MAL** 160-161 B 10
Saputing Lake ⊖ **CDN** 24-25 d 5
Saqadi ○ **SUD** 200-201 F 6
Sāqain ○ **Y** 132-133 C 5
Sāqiya ○ **IRQ** 128-129 K 5
Šaqlāwa ☆ **IRQ** 128-129 L 4
Saqqaq ○ **GRØ** 28-29 P 1
Şaqqāra ○ **ET** 194-195 E 3
Saqqara, Pyramids of ∴••• **ET** 194-195 E 3
Šaqqat al-Ḩarita ∸ **KSA** 132-133 D 5
Saqqez ○ **IR** 128-129 M 4
Şaqr ○ **Y** 132-133 G 6
Šaqrā' ○ **KSA** 130-131 J 5
Šaqrā' ○ **Y** 132-133 D 7
Šaqū ○ **IR** 134-135 G 5
Šar ○ **KZ** 124-125 M 4
Šar ~ **KZ** 124-125 M 4
Ša'r', aš ○ **KSA** 130-131 J 4
Sara ○ **BF** 202-203 J 4
Sara ○ **RI** 166-167 G 3
Sara ○ **RP** 160-161 E 7
Ša'rā', aš- ○ **KSA** 132-133 B 3
Sara, Col de ▲ **RN** 198-199 F 2
Saraar, Bannaanka ∸ **SP** 208-209 G 4
Sarāb ○ **IR** 128-129 M 4
Sarāb Dōre ○ **IR** 134-135 C 2
Saraburi ○ **THA** 158-159 F 3
Šaraf al-Ba'l ○ **KSA** 130-131 D 3
Sarafara ~ **SUD** 206-207 K 3
Saraf Doungous ○ **TCH** 198-199 J 6
Saraféré ○ **RMM** 202-203 J 2
Sarafğegān ○ **IR** 134-135 D 1
Šarafḫāne ○ **IR** 128-129 L 3
Šarafiya, aš- ○ **KSA** 132-133 B 3
Saragosa ○ **USA** (TX) 266-267 D 2
Saraguro ○ **EC** 64-65 C 3
Sarah Lake ⊖ **CDN** 30-31 L 4
Saraḫs ○ **IR** 136-137 G 6
Sarahsville ○ **USA** (OH) 280-281 E 4
Sarai ○ **RUS** 94-95 R 5
Šarā'i', aš- ○ **KSA** 132-133 A 3
Sarai Gambila ○ **PK** 138-139 C 3
Saraipāli ○ **IND** 142-143 C 5
Sarajevo ★ **BIH** 100-101 G 3
Saraj-Ordasy ansambli • **KZ** 136-137 L 3
Sara-Kawa ○ **RT** 202-203 L 5
Saraktaš ☆ **RUS** 96-97 K 8
Sarala ○ **CI** 202-203 G 5
Saraland ○ **USA** (AL) 284-285 B 6
Saramaccarivier ~ **SME** 62-63 G 3
Saran' ○ **KZ** 124-125 H 4
Šaran ☆ **RUS** 96-97 J 6
Saran, Gunung ▲ **RI** 162-163 J 5
Saranac Lake ○ **USA** (NY) 278-279 G 4
Saranac River ~ **USA** 278-279 H 4
Saranda ○ **EAT** 212-213 E 6
Sarandë ☆•• **AL** 100-101 H 5
Sarandi ○ **BR** 74-75 D 6
Sarandi, Arroyo ~ **RA** 76-77 H 6
Sarandi del Yí ○ **ROU** 78-79 M 2
Sarandi de Navarro ○ **ROU** 78-79 L 2
Sarandi Grande ○ **ROU** 78-79 L 2
Sarang ○ **IND** 142-143 J 2
Šaranga ○ **RUS** 96-97 E 5
Sarangani Bay ≈ 160-161 F 10
Sarangani Island ⌒ **RP** 160-161 F 10
Saranglayang, Tanjung ▲ **RI** 162-163 G 6
Sārangpur ○ **IND** 138-139 F 8
Sarannoe, ozero ⊖ **RUS** 120-121 I W 6
Saranpaul' ○ **RUS** 114-115 F 2
Saransk ○ **RUS** 96-97 D 6
Saranzal ○ **BR** 68-69 D 4
Šarapov Šar, zaliv ≈ 108-109 M 6
Šarapovy koški, ostrova ⌒ **RUS** 108-109 M 6
Sarapul ☆ **RUS** 96-97 H 5
Sarapul'skaja vozvyšennost' ⛰ **RUS** 96-97 H 5
Šaraqraq ○ **SYR** 128-129 H 4
Sarār ○ **Y** 132-133 G 6
Sarare, Área Indígena ✕ **BR** 70-71 H 4
Sarare, Rio ~ **BR** 70-71 H 4
Sarare, Río ~ **YV** 60-61 F 4
Sarasota ○ **USA** (FL) 286-287 G 4
Sarasota Bay ≈ 286-287 G 4
Sarata ~ **UA** 102-103 F 4
Saratoga ○ **USA** (AR) 276-277 B 7
Saratoga ○ **USA** (CA) 248-249 B 2
Saratoga ○ **USA** (NC) 282-283 K 5
Saratoga ○ **USA** (WY) 252-253 M 5
Saratoga Hot Springs ∴ **USA** (WY) 252-253 M 5
Saratoga National Historic Park • **USA** (NY) 278-279 H 5
Saratoga Springs ○ **USA** (NY) 278-279 H 5
Saratok ○ **MAL** 162-163 J 4
Saratov ☆ **RUS** 96-97 E 8
Saratovskoe vodohranilišče < **RUS** 96-97 F 7
Saratovskoye Vodokhranilishche = Saratovskoe vodohraniliŝč < **RUS** 96-97 F 7
Šaraura, aš- ○ **KSA** 132-133 E 5
Sarāvān ○ **IR** 134-135 K 5
Saravan ○ **LAO** 158-159 J 3
Sarawak □ **MAL** 162-163 J 3
Saray ☆ **TR** 128-129 B 2
Saraya ○ **SN** 202-203 E 3
Sarāyān ○ **IR** 134-135 H 2
Sarayköy ☆ **TR** 128-129 C 4
Šarbakty ○ **KZ** 124-125 L 3
Sar Bandar ○ **IR** 134-135 C 3
Sarbāz ○ **IR** (SIS) 134-135 J 5
Sarbāz ∸ **IR** 134-135 J 5
Sarbāz, Rūdḫāne-ye ~ **IR** 134-135 J 5
Sarbiše ○ **IR** 134-135 H 2
Šarbitāt ○ **OM** 132-133 K 5
Šarbitāt, Ra's ▲ **OM** 132-133 K 5
Sarbulak ○ **VRC** 146-147 J 2
Sarcee Indian Reservation ✕ **CDN** (ALB) 232-233 D 5
Sarco ○ **RCH** 76-77 B 5
Sarcoxie ○ **USA** (MO) 276-277 A 3
Sarda ~ **NEP** 144-145 C 6
Sardanga ○ **RUS** 118-119 H 4
Šardara ☆ **KZ** 136-137 L 4
Šardara, kūm ∸ **KZ** 136-137 K 4
Šardara sukojmasy < **KZ** 136-137 L 4
Sardārshahr ○ **IND** 138-139 E 5
Sardašt ○ **IR** (AZG) 128-129 L 4
Sardašt ○ **IR** (HUZ) 134-135 D 3
Sarde Band < **AFG** 138-139 B 3
Sardegna, Mar di ≃ 98-99 L 4
Sardegna, Punta ⌒ **I** 100-101 B 4
Sardes ∴•• **TR** 128-129 C 3
Sardinas ○ **EC** 64-65 D 2
Sardinata ○ **CO** 60-61 E 3
Sardinia ○ **USA** (IN) 274-275 N 5
Sardinia = Sardegna □ **I** 100-101 B 4
Sardinia = Sardegna ⌒ **I** 100-101 A 4
Sardis ○ **CDN** (BC) 230-231 H 4
Sardis ○ **USA** (GA) 284-285 J 4
Sardis ○ **USA** (MS) 268-269 L 2
Sardis Lake ⊖ **USA** (MS) 268-269 L 2
Sardis Lake ⊖ **USA** (OK) 264-265 J 4
Šardonem' ○ **RUS** 88-89 S 5
Sare, Rumah ○ **MAL** 164-165 D 1
Sarege, Pulau ⌒ **RI** 168 D 6
Sar'ein ○• **IR** 128-129 N 3
Saré Kali ○ **RG** 202-203 D 4
Sareks nationalpark ⊥ **S** 86-87 H 3
Saré Ndiaye ○ **SN** 202-203 C 3
Sar-e Pol ○ **AFG** 136-137 J 6
Sar-e Pol, Daryā-ye ~ **AFG** 136-137 J 6
Sar-e Pol-e Ẕahāb ○• **IR** 134-135 A 1
Sarepta ○ **USA** (MS) 268-269 L 2
Saréyamou ○ **RMM** 196-197 J 6
Sarezckoe, ozero ⊖ **TJ** 136-137 N 5
Sarfannguaq ○ **GRØ** 28-29 O 3
Šarga ○ **MAU** 146-147 M 2
Šarga ○ **MAU** 148-149 D 3
Šargalant ○ **MAU** 146-147 K 2
Sargapur ○ **IND** 140-141 G 2
Sargasso Sea ≈ 6-7 B 5
Sargent ○ **USA** (NE) 262-263 G 3
Sargent ○ **USA** (TX) 266-267 M 5
Sargent Icefield ⊂ **USA** 20-21 Q 6
Sargento, Bahía ≈ 50-51 C 3
Sargento Ayte Víctor Sanabria ○ **RA** 76-77 G 3
Sargents ○ **AUS** 172-173 K 2
Sargodha ○ **PK** 138-139 D 3
Sargul', ozero ⊖ **RUS** 124-125 L 1
Sarh ☆ **TCH** 206-207 D 4
Sarḥād ∸ **IR** 134-135 J 4
Sarhro, Jbel ⛰ **MA** 188-189 H 5
Šarhulsan ○ **MAU** 148-149 G 5
Sārī ☆• **IR** 136-137 C 6
Šari ○ **KSA** 130-131 H 4
Šārī, Buḥairat < **IRQ** 128-129 L 5
Saria ⌒ **GR** 100-101 L 7
Saria ○ **IND** 138-139 E 3
Sariā, Rio ~ **BR** 66-67 E 6
Sariba Island ⌒ **PNG** 183 F 6
Saribi, Tanjung ▲ **RI** 166-167 H 2
Saric ○ **MEX** 50-51 D 2
Sarichef, Cape ▲ **USA** 22-23 O 5
Şarif ○ **Y** 132-133 G 5
Šarīfa, Ğazīrat ⌒ **KSA** 132-133 B 3
Sariga, Kepulauan ⌒ **RI** 166-167 G 3
Sarıgöl ☆ **TR** 128-129 C 3
Sarıkamış ☆ **TR** 128-129 K 2
Sarıkaya ☆ **TR** 128-129 F 3
Sarikei ○ **MAL** 162-163 J 3
Sarina ○ **AUS** 178-179 K 1
Sarina Beach ○ **AUS** 178-179 K 1
Sariñena ○ **E** 98-99 G 4
Saripai ○ **RI** 164-165 D 4
Sar-i-Parom ○ **PK** 134-135 K 5
Šāriqa, aš- ○ **UAE** 134-135 F 6
Sariri ○ **PNG** 183 E 5
Sarīr Kalanshiyū ∸ **LAR** 192-193 J 4
Sarita ○ **CDN** (BC) 230-231 D 5
Sarita ○ **USA** (TX) 266-267 K 6
Sariwon ○ **KOR** 150-151 E 8
Šar'ja ○ **RUS** 96-97 D 4
Sark ⌒ **GBG** 90-91 F 7
Šarkan ☆ **RUS** 96-97 H 5
Sarķant ○ **KZ** 124-125 L 6
Sarkari Tala ○ **IND** 138-139 C 6
Šarkavščyna ☆ **BY** 94-95 K 4
Şarkîkaraağaç ☆ **TR** 128-129 D 3
Šarkin ○ **KZ** 96-97 G 9
Sarkin Kudin ○ **WAN** 204-205 H 4
Şarkışla ☆ **TR** 128-129 G 3
Şarköy ☆ **TR** 128-129 B 2
Sarlat Ghar ⛰ **PK** 134-135 M 4
Sarlat-la-Canéda ○ **F** 90-91 H 9
Šarlauk = Šarlavuk ○ **TM** 136-137 D 5
Šarlavuk = Šarlauk ○ **TM** 136-137 D 5
Sarles ○ **USA** (ND) 258-259 J 3
Šarlyk ☆ **RUS** 96-97 J 7
Šarma ○ **KSA** 130-131 D 3
Sarmanovo ☆ **RUS** 96-97 H 6
Sărmăşel Gară ○ **RO** 102-103 D 4
Šarm aš-Šaiḫ ○• **ET** 194-195 G 4
Sarmette ○ **VAN** 184 II a 3
Sarmi ○ **RI** 166-167 K 2
Sarmiento ○ **RA** (CHU) 80 F 2
Sarmiento ○ **RA** (COD) 76-77 E 6
Sarmiento, Monte ▲ **RCH** 80 E 7
Sarmsabun ~ **RUS** 114-115 Q 3
Šarmuḫiya ○ **IRQ** 128-129 M 7
Särna ○ **S** 86-87 F 6
Sarnako ○ **RI** 164-165 G 5
Sarnia ○ **CDN** (ONT) 238-239 C 6
Sarny ○ **UA** 102-103 E 2
Sarōbi ○• **AFG** 138-139 B 2
Sarolangun ○ **RI** 162-163 E 6
Saroma ○ **J** 152-153 K 2
Saroma-ko ⊖ **J** 152-153 K 2
Šaromy ○ **RUS** 120-121 S 6
Sarona ○ **USA** (WI) 270-271 G 5
Saronikós Kólpos ≈ 100-101 J 6
Sarore ○ **RI** 166-167 L 6
Saros Körfezi ≈ 128-129 B 2
Šarovce ○ **SK** 92-93 P 4
Sarpinskie ozera ⊖ **RUS** 96-97 D 9
Sarpsborg ☆ **N** 86-87 E 7
Sarqardliit ⌒ **GRØ** 28-29 O 2
Şarrār, aş ○ **KSA** 130-131 L 4
Sarre ~ **F** 90-91 L 7
Sarre, La ○ **CDN** (QUE) 236-237 J 4
Sarrebourg ○ **F** 90-91 L 7
Sarria ○ **E** 98-99 D 3
Sarro ○ **RMM** 202-203 H 3
Sarstoon River ~ **BH** 52-53 K 4
Sartang ~ **RUS** 110-111 T 6
Sartell ○ **USA** (MN) 270-271 D 5
Sartène ○• **F** 98-99 M 4
Sarthe ~ **F** 90-91 G 8
Sartinville ○ **USA** (MS) 268-269 K 5
Sartlan, ozero ⊖ **RUS** 114-115 P 7
Saru, Kaffin- ○ **WAN** 204-205 G 4
Sarubetsu ○ **J** 152-153 K 3
Sarufutsu ○ **J** 152-153 K 2
Saru-gawa ~ **J** 152-153 K 3
Šar-Us gol ~ **MAU** 148-149 C 4
Saruwaged Range ⛰ **PNG** 183 D 4

390 Santa Rosa de los Pastos Grandes — Saruwaged Range

Sárvár o **H** 92-93 O 5
Sarvestán o **IR** 134-135 E 4
Šarwain, Ra's ▲ **Y** 132-133 G 6
Saryagaš o **KZ** 136-137 L 4
Sary-Bulak o **KS** 146-147 B 5
Sarybylak o **KS** 136-137 M 3
Saryčevo o **RUS** 122-123 P 4
Sary-Džaz ~ **KS** 146-147 D 4
Saryesik Atyrau o **KZ** 124-125 J 6
Saryg-Sep o **RUS** 116-117 G 10
Sary Hobda ~ **KZ** 126-127 M 3
Saryjazinskoe vodohranilišče ◁ **TM** 136-137 H 4
Sarykamysskaja kotlorina ◡ **UZ** 136-137 E 3
Sarykamysskoe ozero o **UZ** 136-137 E 3
Sarykamysskoe ozero = Sarygamyš köli o **TM** 136-137 E 4
Saryköl o **KZ** 124-125 D 2
Sarykopa, köli o **KZ** 124-125 D 3
Sarykudyk o **KZ** 96-97 F 9
Sarykul' o **UZ** 136-137 K 5
Sarylah o **RUS** 110-111 Y 7
Sarymojyn, köli o **KZ** 124-125 J 7
Saryözek o **KZ** 124-125 K 6
Saryozen ~ **KZ** 124-125 D 3
Sarypovo o **RUS** 114-115 U 7
Saryšagan o **KZ** 124-125 H 5
Sarysu ~ **KZ** 124-125 F 4
Sary syganak köli o **KZ** 96-97 F 9
Sary-Taš o **KS** 136-137 N 5
Sary-Torgaj ~ **KZ** 124-125 E 4
Sarzal o **KZ** 124-125 L 4
Saržo, kuduk o **UZ** 136-137 E 3
Sasa o **PNG** 183 G 2
Sasabe o **USA** (AZ) 256-257 D 7
Sasabeneh o **ETH** 208-209 F 4
Sasar, Tanjung ▲ **RI** 168 D 7
Sasaräm o **IND** 142-143 D 3
Sasebo o **J** 152-153 C 8
Šašgäv, Kötal-e ▲ **AFG** 138-139 B 3
Saskaľ o **RUS** 122-123 B 8
Saskatchewan, Fort o **CDN** (ALB) 232-233 E 2
Saskatchewan Landing Provincial Park ⊥ **CDN** (SAS) 232-233 L 5
Saskatchewan River ~ **CDN** 232-233 P 2
Saskatchewan River Crossing o **CDN** (ALB) 232-233 B 4
Saskatoon o **CDN** (SAS) 232-233 M 3
Saskylah o **RUS** 110-111 K 4
Saslaya, Cerro ▲ **NIC** 52-53 B 5
Saslaya, Parque Nacional ⊥ **NIC** 52-53 B 5
Sasmik, Cape ▲ **USA** 22-23 H 7
Šasolburg o **J** 152-153 C 8
Sasoma o **IND** 138-139 F 2
Sasovo o **RUS** 94-95 N 4
Sassafras Mountain ▲ **USA** (NC) 282-283 D 5
Sassandra ☆ **CI** (SAS) 202-203 G 7
Sassandra ~ **CI** 202-203 G 7
Sāssari ☆ **I** 100-101 B 4
Sasselé o **RCA** 206-207 C 6
Sasser o **USA** (GA) 284-285 F 3
Sassi o **I** 100-101 C 2
Sassi di Matera ∴ **I** 100-101 C 2
Sassié Island ▲ **AUS** 174-175 G 1
Sassnitz o **D** 92-93 M 1
Saßnitz = Sassnitz o **D** 92-93 M 1
Sassoumbourouom o **RN** 198-199 D 6
Sass River o **CDN** 30-31 N 5
Sass Town o **LB** 202-203 F 7
Sastre o **RA** 76-77 G 6
Sastyg-Hem o **RUS** 116-117 G 9
Sasvad o **IND** 138-139 F 10
Sasykkol o **KZ** 124-125 M 5
Sogykköl o **KZ** (KST) 124-125 B 2
Sasyk ozero o **UA** 102-103 H 5
Saşyr o **RUS** 110-111 a 7
Šeta o **J** 152-153 C 9
Satadougou-Tintiba o **RMM** 202-203 E 3
Sataga o **RUS** 118-119 L 3
Satama-Sokoro o **CI** 202-203 H 6
Satama-Sokoura o **CI** 202-203 H 6
Sata misaki ▲ **J** 152-153 D 9
Satäna o **IND** 138-139 E 9
Satanta o **USA** (KS) 262-263 F 7
Sätära o **IND** 140-141 E 2
Satara o **ZA** 220-221 K 2
Satartia o **USA** (MS) 268-269 K 4
Satellite Bay o **CDN** 24-25 N 2
Satellite Beach o **USA** (FL) 286-287 J 3
Satéma o **RCA** 206-207 E 6
Satengar, Kepulauan ▲ **RI** 168 C 6
Satengar, Pulau ▲ **RI** 168 C 6
Sathing Phra o **THA** 158-159 F 5
Satilla River ~ **USA** 284-285 J 5
Satilla River ~ **USA** 284-285 H 5
Satilpa Creek ~ **USA** 284-285 C 5
Satipo o **PE** 64-65 E 7
Satiri o **BF** 202-203 H 4
Satiwäla o **PK** 138-139 D 4
Satka ☆ **RUS** 96-97 L 6
Satjuj ~ **IND** 138-139 E 4
Satluj ~ **IND** 138-139 E 4
Satna o **IND** 142-143 B 3
Sato o **J** 152-153 C 9
Sátoraljaújhely o **H** 92-93 Q 4
Sätpura Range ▲ **IND** 138-139 E 9
Šatra, aš- o **IRQ** 128-129 M 7
Satrokala o **RM** 222-223 D 9
Šatrovo o **RUS** 114-115 H 6
Satsuma-hantō ◡ **J** 152-153 D 9
Sattahip o **THA** 158-159 F 4
Šatt al-'Arab ~ **IRQ** 128-129 N 7
Šatt al-Hilla ~ **IRQ** 128-129 L 6
Sattenapalle o **IND** 140-141 J 2
Šatt-e Šūr ~ **IR** 134-135 E 1
Satti o **IND** 138-139 F 2
Satū, Kôtal-e ▲ **AFG** 134-135 M 1
Sätuimaluflluf o **WS** 184 V a 1
Satuk o **THA** 158-159 G 3
Satu Mare o **RO** 102-103 C 4
Satun o **THA** 158-159 F 7

Satunan-shotō ⊥ **J** 152-153 C 11
Šatura o **RUS** 94-95 Q 4
Saturna o **CDN** (BC) 230-231 F 5
Satus Pass ▲ **USA** (WA) 244-245 E 4
Saty o **KZ** 146-147 D 4
Satymangalam o **IND** 140-141 G 5
Saúbak o **JOR** 130-131 D 2
Sauble Falls o **CDN** (ONT) 238-239 D 4
Sauce, El o **NIC** 52-53 L 5
Sauce Blanco o **RA** 78-79 H 6
Sauce Chico, Río ~ **RA** 78-79 H 6
Sauce Corto, Arroyo ~ **RA** 78-79 J 4
Sauces, Los o **RCH** 78-79 C 4
Saucillo o **MEX** (MS) 268-269 L 6
Sauda ~ **N** 86-87 C 7
Saudä', as- ~ **Y** 132-133 J 5
Saudade o **BR** 66-67 E 5
Saudade, Cachoeira de ▲ **BR** 72-73 D 3
Saudade, Serra da ▲ **BR** 72-73 H 5
Saudärkrkur o **IS** 86-87 d 2
Saudavel o **BR** 72-73 J 2
Saúde o **BR** 68-69 H 7
Saudi Arabia = al-Mamlaka al-'Arabiya as-Sa'ūdiya o **KSA** 130-131 F 3
Saueninä, Rio ~ **BR** 70-71 H 3
Sauer o **ZA** 220-221 D 6
Saüerüinä ou Papagaio, Rio ~ **BR** 70-71 H 4
Saugatuck o **USA** (MI) 272-273 C 5
Saugeen River o **CDN** 238-239 D 4
Saugstad, Mount ▲ **CDN** (BC) 228-229 H 4
Šauildir ▲ **KZ** 136-137 L 3
Saujil o **RA** 76-77 D 5
Sauk Centre o **USA** (MN) 270-271 C 5
Sauk City o **USA** (WI) 274-275 J 1
Saukorem o **RI** 166-167 G 2
Sauk Rapids o **USA** (MN) 270-271 D 5
Saül o **F** 62-63 H 4
Sauldre ~ **F** 90-91 J 8
Saulieu o **F** 90-91 K 8
Saulkrasti o **LV** 94-95 J 3
Sault-au-Mouton o **CDN** (QUE) 240-241 F 2
Saulteaux Indian Reservation ⋊ **CDN** (SAS) 232-233 K 2
Sault Sainte Marie o **CDN** (ONT) 236-237 D 4
Sault Sainte Marie o **USA** (MI) 270-271 O 4
Saum o **USA** (MN) 270-271 D 3
Saum, as- o **Y** 132-133 F 5
Saumarez Reef ▲ **AUS** 174-175 M 1
Saumlakki o **RI** 166-167 K 5
Saumur o **F** 90-91 H 8
Saundatti o **IND** 140-141 F 3
Saunders o **USA** (MN) 270-271 D 3
Saunders o **CDN** (ALB) 232-233 D 3
Saunders Point ▲ **AUS** 176-177 G 5
Saunders Ø ▲ **GRØ** 26-27 P 5
Saunemin o **USA** (IL) 274-275 K 4
Saunyi o **EAT** 212-213 F 6
Sauqira o **OM** 132-133 L 4
Sauqira Bay ≈ **OM** 132-133 K 4
Sauren o **PNG** 183 E 3
Sauri Hill ▲ **WAN** 204-205 G 3
Saurimo o **ANG** 216-217 E 4
Saurìwaunawa o **GUY** 62-63 E 4
Sausalito o **USA** (CA) 248-249 R 2
Sausu o **RI** 164-165 G 4
Sautar o **ANG** 216-217 E 5
Sautátá o **CO** 60-61 C 4
Sauvage, Lac du o **CDN** 30-31 P 3
Sauvolles, Lac o **CDN** 38-39 H 2
Sauz, El o **MEX** 50-51 F 3
Sauzal o **RCH** 78-79 C 3
Sávã o **IND** 130-131 J 5
Sava ~ **HN** 52-53 L 4
Sava ~ **HR** 100-101 F 2
Sázova ~ **CZ** 92-93 N 4
Sazln o **PK** 138-139 D 2
Sazonovo o **RUS** 94-95 O 2
Saztöbe o **KZ** 136-137 M 3
Suzykuľ, ozero ~ **KZ** 114-115 J 7
Sbaa o **DZ** 188-189 L 6
Sbeïtla o **TN** 190-191 G 3
Scaër o **F** 90-91 F 7
Scafell Pike ▲ **GB** 90-91 F 4
Scales Mound o **USA** (IL) 274-275 H 2
Scammon Bay ≈ 20-21 G 6
Scammon Bay o **USA** (AK) 20-21 G 6
Scamp Hill ▲ **AUS** 176-177 J 2
Scandia o **CDN** (ALB) 232-233 E 3
Scandia o **USA** (KS) 262-263 J 5
Scandola, La ∴ **F** 98-99 M 3
Scapa o **CDN** (ALB) 232-233 G 4
Scapegoat Wilderness Area ⊥ **USA** (MT) 250-251 G 4
Scappoose o **USA** (OR) 244-245 C 5
Ščara ~ **BY** 94-95 J 5
Scarborough o **GB** 90-91 G 4
Scarborough o **TT** 60-61 L 2
Scarborough Shoal ▲ 160-161 B 5
Scarth o **CDN** (MAN) 234-235 C 5
Ščastja, zaliv ≈ 122-123 J 2
Scawfell Bank ▲ 158-159 J 7
Scawfell Island ▲ **AUS** 174-175 K 7
Sceccai Reba ▲ **ER** 200-201 H 4
Ščekino o **RUS** 94-95 N 5
Ščelbožď o **RUS** 88-89 W 3
Ščeljajur o **RUS** 88-89 W 4
Ščelkovo o **RUS** 94-95 P 4
Scenic o **USA** (SD) 260-261 D 3
Scenic Narrow Gauge Steam Railroad • **USA** (CO) 254-255 H 4
Ščerbakovo o **KZ** 124-125 O 3
Schaffhausen o **CH** 92-93 K 5
Schakalskuppe o **NAM** 220-221 D 4
Schefferville o **CDN** 36-37 O 7
Scheibenberg o **D** 92-93 G 3
Schei Peninsula ◡ **CDN** 26-27 F 3
Schelde ~ **B** 92-93 G 3
Schell Creek Range ▲ **USA** 246-247 L 5
Schemnitz = Banská Štiavnica o **SK** 92-93 P 4
Schenectady o **USA** (NY) 278-279 H 6
Scheveningen o **NL** 92-93 H 2
Schidni Karpaty ▲ **UA** 92-93 R 4

Savona ☆ **I** 100-101 B 2
Savonlinna o **FIN** 88-89 K 6
Savoonga o **USA** (AK) 20-21 E 5
Savory River ~ **AUS** 172-173 E 7
Savot o **USA** 136-137 G 4
Savu = Pulau Sawu o **RI** 168 E 8
Savu o **IND** 130-131 D 2
Savukoski o **FIN** 88-89 K 3
Savusavu o **FJI** 184 III b 2
Savusavu Bay ≈ **184** III b 2
Savu Sea = Sawu, Laut ≈ 166-167 A 6
Savute o **RB** 218-219 B 4
Schoharie Creek ~ **USA** 278-279 G 6
Schokland ∴•••• **NL** 92-93 H 2
Schoodic Lake o **USA** (ME) 278-279 N 3
Schoodic Point ▲ **USA** (ME) 278-279 N 4
Schoolcraft o **USA** (MI) 272-273 D 5
Schoombee o **ZA** 220-221 G 5
Schoonrewoerd, Lake o **AUS** 180-181 J 7
Schouten Islands ▲ **PNG** 183 C 2
Schouwen ∴ **NL** 92-93 G 3
Schrader Range ▲ **PNG** 183 C 2
Schreiber o **CDN** (ONT) 234-235 Q 6
Schrobenhausen o **D** 92-93 L 4
Schroda = Środa Wielkopolska o **PL** 92-93 O 2
Schroeder o **USA** (MN) 270-271 H 3
Schroffenstein ▲ **NAM** 220-221 C 5
Schuchert Flod ≈ 26-27 n 8
Schuckmansburg o **NAM** 218-219 C 3
Schulenburg o **USA** (TX) 266-267 L 4
Schuler o **CDN** (ALB) 232-233 H 5
Schulls, Scuols/ o **CH** 92-93 L 5
Schultz Lake o **CDN** 30-31 V 3
Schurz o **USA** (NV) 246-247 G 5
Schuyler o **USA** (NE) 262-263 J 3
Schuylkill River ~ **USA** 280-281 L 3
Schwabach o **D** 92-93 L 4
Schwäbische Alb ▲ **D** 92-93 K 4
Schwäbisch Gmünd o • **D** 92-93 K 4
Schwäbisch Hall o **D** 92-93 K 4
Schwandorf o **D** 92-93 M 4
Schwaner, Pegunungan ▲ **RI** 164-165 B 4
Schwarzrand ▲ **NAM** 220-221 C 2
Schwarzwald ▲ **D** 92-93 K 4
Schwatka Mountains ▲ **USA** 20-21 M 3
Schwedt o **D** 92-93 N 2
Schweinfurt o **D** 92-93 L 3
Schweizergletscher ▲ **ARK** 16 F 33
Schweizer Jura ▲ **CH** 92-93 J 5
Schweizerland ▲ **GRØ** 28-29 W 3
Schweizer Reneke o **ZA** 220-221 G 3
Schwerin o **D** 92-93 L 2
Schwerin Mural Crescent ▲ **AUS** 176-177 K 2
Schwyz ☆ **CH** 92-93 K 5
Sciacca o **I** 100-101 F 6
Scigliano ☆ **RU3** 102-100 K 2
Scie, La o **CDN** (NFL) 242-243 N 3
Scigny o **RU3** 102-100 K 2
Scioto River ~ **USA** 280-281 C 4
Scipio o **USA** (UT) 254-255 C 4
Scobey o **USA** (MT) 250-251 O 3
Scoresby Land ⊥ **GRØ** 26-27 n 8
Scoresbysund = Ittoqqortoormiit o **GRØ** 26-27 p 8
Scotch Creek o **CDN** 230-231 K 2
Scotia o **CDN** (ALB) 232-233 G 3
Scotia o **USA** (CA) 248-249 A 3
Scotia o **USA** (NE) 262-263 H 4
Scotia Bay o **CDN** 20-21 Y 7
Scotia Sea ≈ 6-7 D 14
Scotland o **CDN** (NFL) 242-243 N 3
Scotland o **GB** 90-91 E 3
Scotland o **USA** (SD) 260-261 J 3
Scotland Neck o **USA** (NC) 282-283 N 4
Scotsburn o **CDN** 240-241 N 5
Scotsguard o **CDN** (SAS) 232-233 M 3
Scotstown o **CDN** (QUE) 238-239 O 3
Scottsville o **CDN** (NS) 240-241 O 4
Scott o **ARK** 16 F 17
Scott o **CDN** (SAS) 232-233 K 3
Scott, Cape ▲ **AUS** 172-173 J 2
Scott, Cape ▲ **CDN** (NWT) 24-25 O 2
Scott, Mount ▲ **USA** (OR) 244-245 K 1
Scott Channel ≈ 32-33 F 6
Scott Channel ≈ 230-231 A 3
Scott City o **USA** (KS) 262-263 F 6
Scott City o **USA** (MO) 276-277 F 3
Scott Glacier ⊂ **ARK** 16 G 11
Scott Glacier ⊂ **ARK** 16 E 0
Scott Inlet ≈ 26-27 P 8
Scott Islands ▲ **CDN** (BC) 230-231 A 3
Scott Lake o **CDN** (SAS) 232-233 N 2
Scott National Historic Site, Fort ∴ **USA** (KS) 262-263 M 7
Scott Point ▲ **AUS** 174-175 G 3
Scott Reef ▲ **AUS** 172-173 F 2
Scotts Bay o **CDN** (NS) 240-241 L 5
Scottsbluff o **USA** (NE) 262-263 C 3
Scotts Bluff National Monument ∴ **USA** (NE) 262-263 C 3
Scottsboro o **USA** (AL) 284-285 D 2
Scottsburg o **USA** (IN) 274-275 N 6
Scottsdale o **AUS** 180-181 J 6
Scottsville o **USA** (KY) 276-277 J 4
Scottville o **USA** (MI) 272-273 C 4
Scotty's Castle • **USA** (CA) 248-249 G 2
Scotty's Junction o **USA** (NV) 248-249 G 2
Scout Lake o **CDN** (SAS) 232-233 N 3
Scranton o **CDN** (NS) 240-241 O 5
Scranton o **USA** (NC) 282-283 L 5
Scranton o **USA** (PA) 280-281 L 2

Screven o **USA** (GA) 284-285 H 5
Scribner o **USA** (NE) 262-263 K 3
Scuba diving o **RI** 164-165 J 3
Scuol/ Schuls o **CH** 92-93 L 5
Ščuč 'e o **RUS** (JAN) 108-109 N 8
Ščuč'e o **RUS** (KRG) 114-115 G 7
Ščuč'e, ozero o **RUS** 92-93 H 6
Ščučij hrebet ▲ **RUS** 112-113 P 4
Ščučinsk o **KZ** 114-115 H 7
Ščuč'ja ~ **RUS** 108-109 M 8
Ščuč'yn o **BY** 94-95 J 5
Seal o **LT** 94-95 H 3
Sedalia o **USA** (MO) 274-275 D 3
Sedan o **AUS** (QLD) 178-179 G 3
Sedan o **AUS** (SA) 180-181 G 3
Sedan o **F** 90-91 K 7
Sedan o **USA** (KS) 262-263 K 7
Sedan o **USA** (NM) 256-257 D 6
Sedanka o **RUS** (KOR) 120-121 S 5
Sedati o **RI** 168 J 6
Seddon, Kap ▲ **GRØ** 26-27 V 6
Seddons Corner o **CDN** (MAN) 234-235 G 4
Seddonville o **NZ** 182 C 4
Sedede o **NZ** 182 A 6
Sederberg ▲ **ZA** 220-221 D 6
Sedgefield o **ZA** 220-221 F 7
Sedgewick o **CDN** (ALB) 232-233 G 3
Sedgwick o **USA** (CO) 254-255 N 3
Sedgwick o **USA** (KS) 262-263 J 7
Sédhiou o **SN** 202-203 C 3
Sedié o **IR** 134-135 H 6
Sedič, Rüdhäne-ye ~ **IR** 134-135 H 6
Sedju ~ **RUS** 88-89 W 5
Sedley o **CDN** (SAS) 232-233 O 5
Sedoa o **RI** 164-165 G 4
Sedom o • **IL** 130-131 D 2
Sedona o **USA** (AZ) 256-257 D 4
Sedova, pik ▲ **RUS** 108-109 F 5
Sedova, zaliv ≈ 108-109 H 4
Sedrata o **DZ** 190-191 G 2
Sedro Woolley o **USA** (WA) 244-245 C 2
Seduva o **LT** 94-95 H 3
Seebe o **CDN** (ALB) 232-233 C 4
Seeber o **RA** 76-77 G 6
Seedskadee National Wildlife Refuge ⊥ **USA** (WY) 252-253 J 3
Seeheim o **NAM** 220-221 D 4
Seeis o **NAM** (WIN) 216-217 D 11
Seeis ~ **NAM** 216-217 D 11
Seekaskootch Indian Reserve ⋊ **CDN** (SAS) 232-233 J 2
Seekoegat o **ZA** 220-221 F 6
Seekoerivier ~ **ZA** 220-221 G 5
Seeley Lake o **USA** (MT) 250-251 F 4
Seely o **USA** (WY) 252-253 O 2
Seelyville o **USA** (IN) 274-275 L 5
Seemore Downs o **AUS** 176-177 H 5
Seeuva o **LS** 220-221 H 5
Seba o **RI** 168 E 8
Sébaco o **NIC** 52-53 L 5
Sebago Lake o **USA** (ME) 278-279 L 5
Sebakor, Teluk ≈ 166-167 G 3
Sebalino o **RUS** 124-125 O 3
Sebamban o **RI** 164-165 D 5
Sebangan Teluk ≈ 162-163 K 6
Sebangka, Pulau ▲ **RI** 162-163 F 4
Sebaqatu o **LS** 220-221 H 5
Sebarak o **RI** 166-167 G 3
Sebastian o **USA** (FL) 286-287 J 4
Sebastian Vizcaíno, Bahía de ≈ 50-51 B 3
Sebatik, Pulau ▲ **RI** 164-165 E 1
Sebauh o **MAL** 162-163 L 4
Sebayan, Gunung ▲ **RI** 162-163 J 5
Sebba o **BF** 202-203 K 3
Sebderat o **ER** 200-201 H 5
Sebdou o **DZ** 188-189 L 3
Sébé ~ **G** 210-211 D 4
Sébec Lake o **USA** (ME) 278-279 M 3
Sebekino o **RUS** 102-103 K 2
Sébékoro o **RMM** 202-203 F 3
Sebesi, Pulau ▲ **RI** 162-163 F 7
Sebeta o **ETH** 208-209 D 4
Sebewaing o **USA** (MI) 272-273 F 4
Sebez o **RUS** 94-95 L 3
Šebinkarahisar ☆ **TR** 128-129 H 2
Sebino = Lago d'Iseo o **I** 100-101 C 2
Sebiy o **RO** 102-103 C 4
Sebit o **EAK** 212-213 E 4
Sebjabu, Pulau ▲ **RI** 164-165 E 1
Sebjaüu o **MAL** 162-163 J 4
Sebnitz o **D** 92-93 N 3
Sebou ~ **MA** 188-189 J 4
Seboyeta o **USA** (NM) 256-257 H 3
Sebree o **USA** (KY) 276-277 H 3
Sebring o **USA** (FL) 286-287 H 4
Sebta = Ceuta o **E** 98-99 E 7
Sebuku, Pulau ▲ **RI** 164-165 E 2
Sebuku, Teluk ≈ 164-165 E 2
Sebunino o **RUS** 122-123 J 5
Sebuyau o **MAL** 162-163 J 4
Sebyar ~ **RI** 166-167 G 2
Seby' ~ **RUS** 88-89 W 4
Seçanca o **RA** 76-77 K 6
Seca, Cachoeira ▲ **BR** 66-67 K 5
Seca, Pampa o **RA** 78-79 F 5
Secacang o **RI** 168 D 3
Secca Abü el-cosu o **ER** 200-201 K 5
Sechelt o **CDN** (BC) 230-231 F 4
Sechura o **PE** 64-65 B 4
Sechura, Bahía de ≈ 64-65 B 4
Sechura, Desierto de ⊥ **PE** 64-65 B 4
Seco, Río ~ **RA** 76-77 G 4
Seia o **P** 98-99 D 4

Seco de las Peñas, Río ~ **RA** 78-79 E 3
Seco ó Yaminué, Arroyo ~ **RA** 78-79 F 4
Secos ou do Rombo, Ilheus ~ **CV** 202-203 B 6
Secretary Island ▲ **NZ** 182 A 6
Secunderábád o **IND** 140-141 G 1
Sécure, Río ~ **BOL** 70-71 E 4
Security-Widefield o **USA** (CO) 254-255 L 5
Seda o **LT** 94-95 H 3
Sedalia o **USA** (MO) 274-275 D 3
Seibert o **USA** (CO) 254-255 N 4
Seibo, El o **DOM** 54-55 L 5
Seigals Creek o **AUS** 174-175 D 5
Seih 'Ali o **AFG** 138-139 B 2
Seikan Tunnel •/ **J** 152-153 J 4
Seikpyu o **MYA** 142-143 J 5
Seiland ▲ **N** 86-87 L 1
Seiling o **USA** (OK) 264-265 F 2
Seille ~ **F** 90-91 K 8
Seinäjoki o **FIN** 88-89 G 5
Seine ~ **F** 90-91 H 7
Seine, Baie de la ≈ 90-91 G 7
Seine River ~ **CDN** 234-235 L 6
Seine Seamount ≃ 188-189 D 4
Seinma o **RI** 166-167 K 4
Seira o **ETH** 208-209 C 5
Seis de Julho, Cachoeira ~ **BR** 66-67 F 7
Seival o **BR** 74-75 D 8
Šelju ☆ **RUS** 118-119 H 4
Sejaha o **RUS** (JAN) 108-109 P 6
Sejaha ~ **RUS** 108-109 O 7
Sejaha ~ **RUS** 108-109 N 6
Sejaka o **RI** 164-165 E 5
Sejenane o **TN** 190-191 G 2
Sejm ~ **RUS** 102-103 K 2
Sejm ~ **UA** 102-103 J 2
Sejm ~ **UA** 102-103 J 2
Sejmčan ☆• **RUS** (MAG) 120-121 P 2
Sejmčan ~ **RUS** 120-121 O 2
Sejmdže o **RUS** 118-119 N 7
Sejmkan ~ **RUS** 120-121 N 3
Sejorong o **RI** 168 C 7
Seka o **ETH** 208-209 C 5
Seka Banza o **ZRE** 210-211 D 6
Sekak o **RI** 166-167 G 2
Sekampung ~ **RI** 162-163 F 7
Sekatak Teluk o **RI** 164-165 E 2
Sekenke o **EAT** 212-213 E 6
Seki o **J** 152-153 D 7
Sekigahara-Oro Quasi National Park ⊥ **J** 152-153 D 7
Sekinchan, Kampung o **MAL** 162-163 D 3
Sekoma o **RB** 220-221 F 2
Sekondi ★ **GH** 202-203 K 7
Sek'ot'a o **ETH** 200-201 K 7
Šeksna o **RUS** 94-95 O 3
Sela Dingay o **ETH** 208-209 D 4
Selagskij, mys ▲ **RUS** 112-113 Q 1
Selah o **USA** (WA) 244-245 E 4
Šelälè ☆ **TR** 128-129 D 4
Salama o **RMM** 202-203 K 1
Selangor □ **MAL** 162-163 D 3
Selangor, Kuala o **MAL** 162-163 D 3
Selaphum o **THA** 158-159 G 3
Selapiu Island ▲ **PNG** 183 F 2
Šelaru, Pulau ▲ **RI** 166-167 K 5
Šelaša o **RUS** 88-89 W 4
Selatan, Tanjung ▲ **RI** 164-165 D 6
Selatan Natuna Kepulauan ▲ 162-163 H 3
Selatpanjang o **RI** 162-163 E 4
Selawik o **USA** 20-21 K 3
Selawik Lake o **USA** 20-21 K 3
Selawik River ~ **USA** 20-21 L 3
Selayar = Benteng o **RI** 168 E 6
Selayar, Pulau ▲ (JAM) 162-163 F 5
Selayar, Pulau ▲ **RI** (SSE) 168 E 5
Selayar, Selat ≈ 164-165 G 6
Selba o **BF** 202-203 K 4
Selbu o **N** 86-87 E 5
Selby o **USA** (SD) 260-261 F 1
Selbyville o **USA** (DE) 280-281 L 5
Selçuk ☆ **TR** 128-129 B 4
Seldən o **USA** (KS) 262-263 F 5
Seldja, Gorges du • **TN** 190-191 G 3
Soldovia o **USA** 22-23 V 3
Sele, Tanjung ▲ **RI** 166-167 G 2
Šeleèje o **RUS** 114-115 R 6
Šelehov o **RUS** 116-117 L 9
Selemadeg o **RI** 168 B 7
Seleng Wenz ~ **ETH** 208-209 C 6
Segera o **EAT** 212-213 G 6
Segeri o **RI** 164-165 F 6
Seget o **RI** 166-167 F 2
Segeža ☆ **RUS** 88-89 N 5
Segjan-Kjuël o **RUS** 118-119 P 4
Šegmas o **RUS** 88-89 V 4
Segnán o **AFG** 136-137 M 6
Segno o **USA** (TX) 266-267 K 4
Segoch, Küh-e ▲ **IR** 134-135 G 3
Segogohorang o **RI** 168 J 5
Segomat o **MAL** 162-163 E 3
Segora Anaken ≈ 168 C 3
Segorbe o **E** 98-99 G 4
Segou ☆ **RMM** 202-203 G 3
Ségou ★ **RMM** (SÉ) 202-203 G 3
Ségou ~ **RMM** 202-203 G 2
Segovia o **CO** 60-61 D 4
Segovia o • **E** 98-99 E 4
Segozero o **RUS** 88-89 N 5
Segré o **F** 90-91 G 8
Segre, el ~ **E** 98-99 H 4
Séguam Island ▲ **USA** 22-23 A 3
Séguam Pass ≈ 22-23 K 6
Séguédine o **RN** 198-199 F 2
Séguéla ☆ **CI** 202-203 G 6
Séguéla ~ **RMM** 202-203 G 3
Séguénéga o **BF** 202-203 K 3
Séguéla o **RMM** 202-203 G 3
Seguin o **USA** (TX) 266-267 K 4
Seguin River o **CDN** 238-239 F 3
Segula Island ▲ **USA** 22-23 G 6
Segunda, Río ~ **RA** 76-77 F 6
Segura ~ **E** 98-99 F 6
Segura, Sierra de ▲ **E** 98-99 F 6
Seguro o **BR** 88-89 M 5
Sehestedts Fjord ≈ 28-29 T 3
Sehithwa o **RB** 218-219 B 4
Sehkwehn River ~ **LB** 202-203 F 6
Seho, Pulau ▲ **RI** 164-165 J 4
Sehonghong o **LS** 220-221 J 4
Sehore o **IND** 138-139 F 8
Sehwän o • **PK** 134-135 M 5
Seia o **P** 98-99 D 4
Seibert o **USA** (CO) 254-255 N 4
Seibo, El o **DOM** 54-55 L 5
Seilbert o **USA** (CO) 254-255 N 4
Selendi ☆ **TR** 128-129 C 3
Selenga ~ **RUS** 116-117 H 9
Sèlèngè o **MAU** 148-149 G 3
Sèlèngè o **MAU** 148-149 G 3
Selengei o **EAK** 212-213 F 7
Sélèngé mörön ~ **MAU** 148-149 G 3
Selenginsk o **RUS** 116-117 J 9
Selennahskij hrebet ▲ **RUS** 110-111 V 4
Selennjah ~ **RUS** 110-111 Y 6
Sele Pele, Tanjung ▲ **RI** 166-167 F 2
Sélestat o **F** 90-91 L 7
Séléti o **SN** 202-203 J 3
Selfoss o **IS** 86-87 c 3
Selfridge o **USA** (ND) 258-259 G 5
Sel'gi o **RUS** 88-89 N 5
Selib o **RUS** 88-89 U 5
Sélibabi o **RIM** 202-203 D 3
Seliger, ozero o **RUS** 88-89 N 3
Seligman o **USA** (AZ) 256-257 C 4
Seligman o **USA** (MO) 276-277 D 4
Selihino o **RUS** 122-123 G 3
Šelihova, zaliv ≈ 120-121 R 3
Sélim o **RCA** 206-207 H 5
Seling o **IND** 142-143 H 4
Sélingue, Lac de ⊂ **RMM** 202-203 F 4
Selinnkegni o **RMM** 202-203 F 3
Selinsgrove o **USA** (PA) 280-281 K 3
Selitkan ~ **RUS** 122-123 F 2
Seljansckaja guba ≈ 110-111 W 4
Seljelvnes o **N** 86-87 G 3
Selkämeri ~ 88-89 E 6
Selkirk o **CDN** (MAN) 234-235 G 4
Selkirk o **CDN** (ONT) 238-239 F 6
Selkirk Mountains ▲ **CDN** 230-231 M 2
Selkirk Mountains ▲ **USA** 250-251 C 3

Selle, Massif de la ▲ RH 54-55 J 5
Selleck ○ USA (WA) 244-245 D 3
Sellers ○ USA (AL) 284-285 D 4
Sellers ○ USA (MS) 268-269 L 6
Sellersburg ○ USA (IN) 274-275 M 6
Selles-sur-Cher ○ F 90-91 H 8
Sellljah ~ RUS 110-111 X 4
Sello, Lago del ○ RA 80 E 3
Sells ○ USA (AZ) 256-257 D 7
Selma ○ USA (AL) 284-285 C 4
Selma ○ USA (CA) 248-249 E 3
Selmer ○ USA (TN) 276-277 G 5
Selokan, Tanjung ▲ RI 162-163 F 6
Sélo Kouré ○ RG 202-203 E 4
Selong ○ RI 168 C 7
Šelonskie ostrova ⌒ RUS 110-111 W 4
Šelopugino ☆ RUS 118-119 H 10
Selouane ○ MA 188-189 K 3
Selous ○ ZW 218-219 F 4
Selous, Mount ▲ CDN 20-21 Y 5
Selous Game Reserve ⊥ ••• EAT 214-215 J 5
Selsele-ye Pir-e Šūrān ▲ IR 134-135 J 4
Selter Island ⌒ CDN (ONT) 234-235 Q 6
Šel'tinga ○ RUS 120-121 M 4
Šel'tinga, zaliv ≈ 120-121 N 4
Selty ☆ RUS 96-97 H 5
Selu ○ IND 138-139 F 10
Selu, Pulau ⌒ RI 166-167 F 5
Selva Alegre ○ EC 64-65 C 1
Selvagens, Ilhas ⌒ P 188-189 D 5
Selvas ⊥ BR 66-67 D 5
Selvíria ○ BR 72-73 E 6
Selway-Bitterroot Wilderness ⊥ USA (ID) 250-251 D 5
Selway Falls ~ USA 250-251 D 5
Selway River ~ USA 250-251 D 5
Selwyn, Détroit de ≈ 184 II b 3
Selwyn Lake ○ CDN 30-31 R 5
Selwyn Mountains ▲ CDN 20-21 X 4
Selwyn Post Office ○ AUS 178-179 F 1
Selwyn Range ▲ AUS 178-179 F 1
Semajang, Danau ○ RI 164-165 E 4
Semamung ○ RI 168 C 7
Semangka ~ RI 162-163 F 7
Semangka, Teluk ≈ 162-163 F 7
Semans ○ CDN (SAS) 232-233 O 4
Semanu ○ RI 164-165 E 2
Semarang ☆ RI 168 D 3
Semaras ○ RI 164-165 E 5
Sematan ○ MAL 162-163 H 4
Semau, Pulau ⌒ RI 166-167 B 7
Sembabule ○ EAU 212-213 C 4
Sembakung ~ RI 164-165 E 2
Sembatti ○ IND 140-141 G 5
Sembe ○ LB 202-203 E 6
Sembé ○ RCB 210-211 E 3
Sembehon ○ WAL 202-203 E 6
Sembehun ○ WAL 202-203 D 6
Semberang ○ RI 164-165 F 3
Semberong ~ MAL 162-163 E 3
Sembilan, P. ▲ RI 162-163 D 2
Şemdinli ☆ TR 128-129 L 4
Sémé ○ CI 202-203 G 4
Semeih ○ SUD 200-201 E 6
Semej ○ KZ 124-125 M 3
Semejka, gora ▲ RUS 110-111 V 5
Sèmè-Kpodji ○ DY 204-205 E 5
Semenanjung Blambangan Game Park ⊥ RI 168 B 7
Semenov ○ RUS 96-97 D 5
Semënovka ○ RUS 122-123 B 3
Semera ○ MAL 162-163 J 4
Semeteh ○ RI 162-163 E 6
Semiahmoo Bay ≈ 244-245 C 2
Semiai, Pulau ⌒ RI 166-167 G 3
Semichi Islands ⌒ USA 22-23 C 6
Semi Desert ⊥ AUS 174-175 C 7
Semidi Islands ⌒ USA 22-23 S 4
Sémien ○ CI 202-203 G 6
Semikarakorsk ○ RUS 102-103 M 4
Semillero ○ GCA 52-53 J 4
Semiluki ○ RUS 102-103 L 2
Seminoe Dam ○ USA (WY) 252-253 M 4
Seminoe Reservoir ○ USA (WY) 252-253 M 4
Seminole ○ USA (OK) 264-265 H 3
Seminole ○ USA (TX) 264-265 B 6
Seminole, Lake < USA (GA) 284-285 F 6
Seminole Draw ~ USA 264-265 B 6
Seminskij, pereval ▲ RUS 124-125 O 3
Semiozernoe ☆ KZ 124-125 D 2
Semipalatinsk = Semey ○ KZ 124-125 M 3
Semirara Island ⌒ RP 160-161 D 6
Semirom ○ IR 134-135 D 3
Semisopochnoi Island ⌒ USA 22-23 F 7
Semitau ○ RI 162-163 J 4
Semliki ~ ZRE 212-213 B 3
Semna ○ SUD 200-201 E 2
Semnān ▫ IR 134-135 E 1
Semnān ☆ • IR 136-137 C 7
Semolale ○ RB 218-219 E 5
Šemonaiha ○ KZ 124-125 M 3
Semongkat ○ RI 168 C 7
Sempang Mangayan, Tanjung ▲ MAL 160-161 B 9
Sempol ○ • RI 168 B 7
Semporna ○ MAL 160-161 C 10
Sempu, Pulau ⌒ RI 168 E 4
Šemšak ○ • IR 136-137 B 7
Sem-Tripa, Cachoeira ~ BR 66-67 K 5
Semu ~ EAT 212-213 E 5
Semuntai, Tanjung ▲ RI 164-165 F 3
Sèmža ○ RUS 88-89 S 3
Sen' ~ RUS 118-119 H 7
Sena ○ BOL 70-71 D 2
Sena, Río ~ BOL 70-71 D 2
Senachwine Lake ○ USA (IL) 274-275 J 3
Senador ○ BR 68-69 H 3
Senador José Porfírio ○ BR 68-69 C 3
Senador Pompeu ○ BR 68-69 J 4
Sen'afē ○ ER 200-201 J 5
Senaki ○ • GE 126-127 E 6
Señal Canoas ▲ PE 64-65 D 7
Señal Huascarán ▲ PE 64-65 D 6
Señal Mongon ▲ PE 64-65 C 6
Señal Nevado Champará ▲ PE 64-65 D 6
Sena Madureira ○ BR 66-67 C 7
Senanga ○ Z 218-219 B 3
Šenāš, Ra's-e ▲ IR 134-135 F 5
Senate ○ CDN (SAS) 232-233 J 6
Senath ○ USA (MO) 276-277 E 4
Senatobia ○ USA (MS) 268-269 L 2
Senaton, Teluk ≈ 162-163 A 3
Sendafa ○ ETH 208-209 D 4
Sendai ○ J (KGA) 152-153 D 9
Sendai ☆ • J (MIY) 152-153 J 5
Sendai-wan ≈ 152-153 J 5
Sendān Dāğ, Kūh-e ▲ IR 128-129 N 4
Sendelingsfontein ○ ZA 220-221 H 3
Sendhwa ○ IND 138-139 E 9
Senebui, Tanjung ▲ RI 162-163 D 3
Seneca ○ USA (AZ) 256-257 E 5
Seneca ○ USA (IL) 274-275 K 3
Seneca ○ USA (KS) 262-263 K 5
Seneca ○ USA (MO) 276-277 A 4
Seneca ○ USA (NE) 262-263 F 3
Seneca ○ USA (OR) 244-245 G 6
Seneca ○ USA (SC) 284-285 H 2
Seneca ○ USA (SD) 260-261 G 1
Seneca Caverns ∴ USA (WV) 280-281 G 5
Seneca Falls ○ USA (NY) 278-279 E 6
Seneca Lake ○ USA (NY) 278-279 E 6
Seneca Rocks ○ USA (WV) 280-281 G 5
Seneca Rocks National Recreation Area ⊥ USA (WV) 280-281 G 5
Senecaville Lake ○ USA (OH) 280-281 E 4
Sénégal ~ SN 196-197 C 6
Senegal = Sénégal ■ SN 202-203 C 2
Senekal ○ ZA 220-221 H 4
Senero, Río ~ BOL 70-71 E 4
Seney ○ USA (MI) 270-271 N 4
Seney National Wildlife Refuge ⊥ USA (MI) 270-271 M 4
Senga ○ MW 218-219 H 1
Sengan ○ WAN 204-205 F 6
Sengbo ○ RI 166-167 K 3
Senge ○ ZRE 212-213 B 5
Sengejskij, ostrov ⌒ RUS 88-89 V 2
Sênggê Zangbo ~ VRC 144-145 C 4
Senggigi ○ • RI 168 C 7
Sengilen, hrebet ▲ RUS 116-117 G 10
Sengkiju ~ RUS 110-111 J 5
Senguer, Río ~ RA 80 F 2
Sengwa ~ ZW 218-219 E 3
Senhora do Porto ○ BR 72-73 J 5
Senhor do Bonfim ○ BR 68-69 H 7
Senia, Bir ○ DZ 190-191 B 4
Senigallia ○ I 100-101 D 3
Senindara ○ RI 166-167 G 3
Senirkent ☆ TR 128-129 D 3
Senj ○ HR 100-101 E 2
Senja ⌒ N 86-87 H 2
Senjavina, proliv ≈ 112-113 Y 4
Senkanse ○ BF 202-203 L 4
Şenkaya ☆ TR 128-129 K 2
Senkobo ○ Z 218-219 C 3
Şenkursk ○ RUS 88-89 R 5
Senmonorom ○ K 158-159 J 4
Senmuto, ozero ○ RUS 114-115 P 2
Sennār ☆ • SUD 200-201 F 6
Sennār Dam < SUD 200-201 F 6
Senneterre ○ CDN (QUE) 236-237 L 4
Sennoj ○ RUS 96-97 E 7
Sénoba ○ SN 202-203 C 3
Senoia ○ USA (GA) 284-285 F 3
Senorbì ○ I 100-101 B 5
Sénoudébou ○ • SN 202-203 D 2
Senqunyana ~ LS 220-221 J 4
Sens ○ F 90-91 J 7
Senta ○ YU 100-101 H 2
Šentala ☆ RUS 96-97 G 6
Sentani, Danau ○ RI 166-167 L 3
Sentarum, Danau ○ RI 162-163 K 4
Sentinel ○ USA (AZ) 256-257 B 6
Sentinel ○ USA (OK) 264-265 E 3
Sentinel Peak ▲ CDN (BC) 228-229 N 2
Sentinel Range ▲ ARK 16 F 28
Sentolo ○ RI 168 D 3
Sento Sé ○ BR 68-69 H 6
Sentrum ○ ZA 220-221 H 2
Senuda ○ RI 162-163 K 6
Senye ○ GQ 210-211 B 3
Seonath ~ IND 142-143 B 5
Seoni ○ IND 138-139 G 8
Seoni Mālwa ○ IND 138-139 F 8
Seorinārāyan ○ IND 142-143 C 5
Seoul = Sŏul ★ ROK 150-151 F 9
Sepa ○ RI 166-167 E 3
Sepakat, Tanjung ▲ RI 164-165 E 2
Sepang ○ RI 168 E 7
Sepanjang, Pulau ⌒ RI 168 B 6
Separ ○ USA (NM) 256-257 G 6
Separation Point ○ CDN 38-39 Q 2
Separation Point ▲ NZ 182 D 4
Sepasu ○ RI 164-165 E 3
Sepatini, Rio ~ BR 66-67 E 6
Sepeteri ○ WAN 204-205 E 4
Šepetivka ☆ UA 102-103 E 2
Sepiddašt ○ IR 134-135 C 2
Sepik River ~ PNG 183 C 3
Sepilok Sanctuary ⊥ MAL 160-161 B 10
Šepit ○ UA 102-103 D 4
Sepo ○ KOR 150-151 F 8
Sepo ○ RI 164-165 L 3
Sepólno Krajeńskie ○ PL 92-93 O 2
Sepon ○ IND 142-143 J 2
Sepoti, Rio ~ BR 66-67 G 6
Sepotuba, Rio ~ BR 70-71 J 4
Sept-des-Gzoula ○ MA 188-189 G 4
Septembre, Embalse de 15 < ES 52-53 K 5
Septentrional, Cordillera ▲ DOM 54-55 K 5
Sept-Îles ○ CDN (QUE) 242-243 B 2
Sept-Îles, Baie des ≈ 242-243 B 2
Sepupa ○ RB 218-219 B 4
Seputih ~ RI 162-163 F 7
Sequatchie River ~ USA 276-277 K 5
Sequim ○ USA (WA) 244-245 C 2
Sequoia National Park ⊥ USA (CA) 248-249 F 3
Sequoyah National Wildlife Refuge ⊥ USA (OK) 264-265 J 3
Sequoyah's Cabin ∴ USA (OK) 264-265 K 3
Šerabad ~ UZ 136-137 K 6
Şerafettin Dağları ▲ TR 128-129 J 3
Serafimovič ○ RUS 102-103 N 3
Serafina ○ USA (NM) 256-257 K 3
Šeragul ○ RUS 116-117 K 8
Serahs ○ TM 136-137 G 6
Seraij ○ RI 164-165 J 3
Seraja gora ▲ RUS 112-113 O 4
Seram ○ IND 140-141 G 2
Seram, Pulau ⌒ RI 166-167 E 3
Seram Laut, Pulau ⌒ RI 166-167 F 3
Serang ○ RI (JBA) 168 B 3
Serang ~ RI 168 D 3
Seraran ○ RI 166-167 G 3
Sérarou ○ DY 204-205 E 4
Serasan, Pulau ⌒ RI 162-163 H 3
Serasan, Selat ≈ 162-163 H 3
Šerbakty ☆ KZ 124-125 L 2
Serbewel ~ CAM 198-199 G 6
Serbia = Srbija ▫ YU 100-101 G 2
Serca ○ VRC 144-145 K 5
Serčeja ~ RUS 88-89 X 3
Serdce-Kamen', mys ▲ RUS 112-113 Z 3
Serdo ○ ETH 208-209 E 3
Serdobsk ○ RUS 96-97 D 7
Sérébou ○ CI 202-203 J 6
Serebrjansk ○ KZ 124-125 N 4
Seredka ○ RUS 94-95 L 2
Sérédou ○ RG 202-203 F 5
Şereflikoçhisar ☆ TR 128-129 E 3
Serein ~ F 90-91 K 8
Serekunda ○ WAG 202-203 B 3
Seremban ☆ • MAL 162-163 D 3
Serena, La ☆ • RCH 76-77 B 5
Serengeti National Park ⊥ ••• EAT 212-213 E 5
Serengeti Plain ~ EAT 212-213 E 5
Serengeti Plains ⊥ EAK 212-213 F 5
Serenje ○ Z 218-219 F 1
Sereno, Rio ~ BR 68-69 E 5
Séres ○ GR 100-101 J 4
Seret ~ UA 102-103 D 3
Serež ~ RUS 114-115 U 7
Sergač ○ RUS 96-97 D 6
Sergeevka ○ RUS 122-123 E 7
Sergeevsk ☆ RUS 96-97 G 7
Sergeevskoe sukojmasy < KZ 124-125 E 2
Sergeja Kirova, ostrova ⌒ RUS 108-109 X 3
Sèrgèlèn ○ MAU 148-149 K 4
Sergeljah ~ RUS 118-119 J 5
Sergeulangit, Pegunungan ▲ RI 162-163 B 3
Sergiev Posad ☆ ••• RUS 94-95 Q 3
Sergino ○ RUS 116-117 N 9
Sergipe ▫ BR 68-69 K 7
Sergipe, Rio ~ BR 68-69 K 7
Sergiyev Posad = Sergiev-Posad ☆ ••• RUS 94-95 Q 3
Sergozero ○ RUS 88-89 O 3
Seria ○ BRU 164-165 D 1
Serian ○ MAL 162-163 J 4
Sériba ○ RG 202-203 D 4
Seribu, Kepulauan ⌒ RI 168 B 2
Seribudolok ○ RI 162-163 C 3
Sericita ○ BR 72-73 J 6
Sérifos ⌒ GR 100-101 K 6
Serik ☆ TR 128-129 D 4
Serikkembelo ○ RI 166-167 D 3
Seringal Jaboti ○ BR 70-71 F 2
Seringal Santa Maria ○ BR 66-67 E 6
Seringal São Pedro ○ BR 70-71 F 2
Seringal Torrões ○ BR 66-67 D 6
Seringapatam Reef ⌒ AUS 172-173 F 2
Serinhisar ☆ TR 128-129 C 4
Serki ~ RUS 110-111 N 6
Serkout ▲ DZ 190-191 F 9
Šerlovaja Gora ○ RUS 118-119 H 10
Sermata, Kepulauan ⌒ RI 166-167 E 6
Sermata, Pulau ⌒ RI 166-167 E 6
Sermersooq ⌒ GRØ 28-29 S 6
Sermersûq ▲ GRØ 28-29 S 6
Sermiligaaq ≈ 28-29 W 3
Sermiligaarsuk ≈ 28-29 Q 6
Sermilik ≈ 28-29 S 6
Sermilik ≈ 28-29 Q 6
Sermilik ≈ 28-29 W 3
Sermowai ~ RI 166-167 L 3
Sernovodsk ○ RUS 122-123 L 7
Seroglazka ○ RUS 96-97 E 10
Seronera Lodge ○ EAT 212-213 E 5
Seronga ○ RB 218-219 B 4
Serou ○ IR 128-129 L 4
Serouenout, Hassi < DZ 190-191 F 8
Serov ☆ RUS 114-115 F 5
Sorowo ☆ RB 218 219 D 6
Serpa ○ P 98-99 D 6
Serpentine Hot Springs ○ USA 20-21 H 4
Serpentine River ~ USA 20-21 H 3
Serpent Mound State Memorial • USA (OH) 280-281 C 4
Serpent River ○ CDN (ONT) 238-239 C 2
Serpents, Île aux ⌒ MS 224 C 6
Serpuhov ☆ • RUS 94-95 P 4
Serpukhov = Serpuhov ☆ • RUS 94-95 P 4
Serra ○ BR 72-73 K 6
Serra Bonita ○ BR 72-73 G 3
Serra Branca ○ BR 68-69 K 5
Serra da Bocaina, Parque Nacional da ⊥ BR 72-73 H 7
Serra da Canastra, Parque Nacional da ⊥ BR 72-73 G 6
Serra da Capivara, Parque Nacional da ⊥ ••• BR 68-69 G 6
Serra das Araras ○ BR 72-73 H 3
Serra do Divisor, Parque Nacional da ⊥ BR 64-65 F 6
Serra do Moa ○ BR 64-65 F 5
Serra do Navio ○ BR 62-63 H 5
Serra do Salitre ○ BR 72-73 G 5
Serra Dourada ○ BR (BAH) 72-73 J 2
Serra Dourada ○ BR (MAT) 72-73 D 2
Serra Encantada, Igarapé ~ BR 68-69 B 5
Serra Hills ▲ PNG 183 A 2
Serra Mecula ▲ MOC 218-219 J 1
Serra Morena, Área Indígena ✗ BR 70-71 H 2
Serrana ○ BR 72-73 G 6
Serra Negra, Reserva Biológica da ⊥ BR 68-69 J 6
Serrania, La ⊥ CO 60-61 E 6
Serranía de Ayapel ▲ CO 60-61 D 4
Serranía de Baudó ▲ CO 60-61 C 4
Serranía de Caiza ▲ BOL 76-77 F 1
Serranía de Ibobobo ▲ BOL 76-77 F 1
Serranía de la Macarena ▲ CO 60-61 E 6
Serranía de la Neblina, Parque Nacional ⊥ YV 66-67 D 2
Serranía del Beu ▲ BOL 70-71 C 4
Serranía de Mapichi ▲ YV 60-61 H 5
Serranía de Naquen ▲ CO 60-61 G 6
Serranía de Sicasica ▲ BOL 70-71 D 5
Serranía de Zuriara ▲ RA 76-77 D 4
Serranilla, Banco de ≃ 54-55 F 7
Serrano, Isla ⌒ RCH 80 C 4
Serranópolis ○ BR 72-73 D 5
Serra Preta ○ BR 72-73 L 2
Serraria ○ BR 68-69 E 3
Serraria, Ilha da ⌒ BR 62-63 J 6
Serra San Bruno ○ I 100-101 F 5
Serrat, Cap ▲ TN 190-191 G 2
Serra Talhada ○ BR 68-69 J 5
Serres ○ F 90-91 K 9
Serrinha ○ BR 68-69 J 7
Serro ○ BR 72-73 J 5
Serrolândia ○ BR (BAH) 68-69 H 7
Serrolândia ○ BR (PER) 68-69 H 5
Sersou, Plateau du ▲ DZ 190-191 C 3
Sertā ○ P 98-99 C 5
Serta ~ RUS 114-115 U 7
Sertânia ○ BR 68-69 K 6
Sertanópolis ○ BR 72-73 E 7
Sertão ⊥ BR 68-69 E 5
Sertão de Camapuã ⊥ BR 72-73 D 5
Sertãozinho ○ BR 72-73 G 6
Sêrtar ○ VRC 154-155 B 5
Serti ○ WAN 204-205 J 5
Sertung, Pulau ⌒ RI 168 A 3
Sēru ○ ETH 208-209 E 5
Serua, Pulau ⌒ RI 166-167 F 5
Serui ○ RI 166-167 J 2
Seruini, Rio ~ BR 66-67 D 7
Serule ○ RB 218-219 D 5
Serutu, Pulau ⌒ RI 162-163 H 5
Seruyan ~ RI 162-163 K 6
Servi ○ TR 128-129 J 3
Sérvia ○ GR 100-101 J 4
Service Creek ○ USA (OR) 244-245 E 6
Sêrxü ○ VRC 144-145 M 4
Seryh Gusej, ostrova ⌒ RUS 112-113 X 3
Seryševo ○ RUS 122-123 C 3
Sesayap ○ RI (KTI) 164-165 E 2
Sesayap ~ RI 164-165 E 2
Šeš Borğe ○ AFG 134-135 M 2
Şeşe ○ ZRE 210-211 K 2
Seseganaga Lake ○ CDN (ONT) 234-235 N 4
Sese Islands ⌒ EAU 212-213 D 4
Sesenge ○ ZRE 212-213 B 2
Sesenta, El ○ CO 60-61 E 3
Sesepe ○ RI 164-165 K 4
Sesfontein ○ NAM 216-217 B 9
Seshego ○ ZA 218-219 E 6
Sesheke ○ Z 218-219 C 3
Sesibi, Temple of • SUD 200-201 E 2
Sesimbra ○ • P 98-99 C 5
Seskarö ○ S 86-87 L 4
Šešma ~ RUS 96-97 G 6
Sespamco ○ USA (TX) 266-267 J 4
Sesriem ○ NAM 220-221 B 2
Sessa ○ ANG 216-217 E 6
Sesser ○ USA (IL) 274-275 J 6
Šeštamad ○ IR 136-137 E 7
Sesuntepeque ☆ ES 52-53 K 5
Šet-Bakanas ~ KZ 124-125 J 6
Sète ○ F 90-91 J 10
Sete de Setembro, Área Indígena ✗ BR 70-71 G 2
Sete de Setembro, Rio ~ BR 72-73 D 2
Sete Lagoas ○ BR 72-73 H 5
Setenta, Pampa del ⊥ RA 80 F 3
Sete Quedas, Ilha das ⌒ BR 72-73 D 7
Sete Quedas, Salto das ~ BR 66-67 J 7
Setermoen ○ N 86-87 J 2
Setesdal ⌣ N 86-87 C 7
Sethkokna River ~ USA 20-21 O 4
Seti ~ NEP 144-145 C 6
Sétif ☆ DZ 190-191 E 2
Sotit ~ SUD 200 201 H 6
Setlagole ○ ZA 220-221 G 3
Seto-naikai ≈ 152-153 E 7
Seto-Naikai National Park ⊥ J 152-153 D 8
Setouchi ○ J 152-153 C 10
Šetre ☆ KZ 126-127 K 5
Settat, Djebel ▲ DZ 190-191 D 7
Settat ☆ MA 188-189 H 4
Setté Cama ○ G 210-211 B 5
Sette-Daban, hrebet ▲ RUS 120-121 G 2
Setters ○ USA (ID) 250-251 C 4
Settiya ○ IND 140-141 H 5
Settlement, The ○ GB 286-287 R 2
Settlers ○ ZA 220-221 J 2
Setto ○ DY 204-205 E 5
Setúbal ○ P 98-99 C 5
Setúbal, Baía de ≈ 98-99 C 5
Setubinha ○ BR 72-73 J 4
Šet-Yrgyz ~ KZ 126-127 N 3
Seu d'Urgell, la ○ • E 98-99 H 3
Seul' ~ RUS 114-115 J 4
Seul, Lac ○ CDN (ONT) 234-235 L 4
Seulimeum ○ RI 162-163 A 2
Seuté, Hosséré ▲ CAM 204-205 K 5
Sevan ○ AR 128-129 L 2
Sevan, ozero ○ AR 128-129 L 2
Sévaré ○ RMM 202-203 H 2
Sevaruyo ○ BOL 70-71 D 6
Sevastopol' ○ •• UA 102-103 H 5
Ševčenko = Aktau ☆ KZ 126-127 J 6
Ševčenko, Fort- ○ KZ 126-127 J 5
Seven Emu ○ AUS 174-175 D 5
Seven Islands Bay ≈ 36-37 S 5
Seven Lakes ○ USA (NM) 256-257 H 3
Seven Mile Beach ⊥ AUS 176-177 C 4
Seven Persons ○ CDN (ALB) 232-233 H 6
Seven Persons Creek ~ CDN 232-233 H 6
Seven Springs ○ USA (AZ) 256-257 D 5
Seventeen Mile Ranch ○ USA (AZ) 256-257 B 4
Seventy Five Mile Beach ⊥ • AUS 178-179 M 3
Seventy Mile House ○ CDN (BC) 230-231 H 2
Severgina, proliv ≈ 122-123 Q 4
Severgino ○ RUS 122-123 Q 4
Severn ~ GB 90-91 F 6
Severn ○ ZA 220-221 F 3
Severnaja ~ RUS 108-109 j 4
Severnaja ~ RUS 108-109 X 8
Severnaja ~ RUS 110-111 M 6
Severnaja Čunja ~ RUS 116-117 M 5
Severnaja Dvina ~ RUS 88-89 Q 5
Severnaja grjada ▲ RUS 108-109 d 4
Severnaja Kel'tma ~ RUS 96-97 J 3
Severnaja Mylva ~ RUS 114-115 D 3
Severnaja Sos'va ~ RUS 114-115 F 3
Severnaja Sos'va ~ RUS 114-115 G 3
Severnaja Sul'meneva, guba ≈ 108-109 F 4
Severnaja Tajmura ~ RUS 116-117 L 4
Severnaja Zemlja ⌒ RUS 108-109 I c 1
Severnaya Dvina = Severnaja Dvina ~ RUS 88-89 Q 5
Severn Falls ○ CDN (ONT) 238-239 F 4
Severn Lake ○ CDN 34-35 L 4
Severnoe ○ RUS (NVS) 114-115 P 6
Severnoe ☆ RUS (ORB) 96-97 H 6
Severnoe, ozero ○ RUS 116-117 F 2
Severn River ~ AUS 178-179 L 5
Severn River ~ CDN 34-35 M 3
Severn River ~ CDN 234-235 L 2
Severnye uvaly ▲ RUS 96-97 J 4
Severnyj ○ RUS (KAR) 88-89 M 4
Severnyj ○ RUS (KOM) 108-109 L 8
Severnyj ○ RUS (SAH) 110-111 U 4
Severnyj, mys ▲ RUS (SAH) 110-111 U 2
Severnyj, mys ▲ RUS (TMR) 108-109 S 5
Severnyj, ostrov ⌒ RUS (TMR) 108-109 k 3
Severnyj, ostrov ⌒ RUS (TMR) 108-109 Y 3
Severnyj, proliv ≈ 110-111 H 2
Severnyj, zaliv ≈ 120-121 K 6
Severnyj Kamen' ⌒ RUS 108-109 X 8
Severnyj liman ≈ 112-113 Q 6
Severnyj Pèkul'nejveem ~ RUS 112-113 R 4
Severnyj proliv ≈ 120-121 G 6
Severnyj Uj ~ RUS 120-121 G 5
Severnyj Ural ▲ RUS 114-115 E 5
Severnyy Ural = Severnyj Ural ▲ RUS 114-115 E 5
Severobajkal'sk ☆ RUS 118-119 D 8
Severo-Bajkal'skoe, nagor'e ▲ RUS 118-119 E 7
Severodonec'k ○ UA 102-103 L 3
Severodvinsk ○ RUS 88-89 P 4
Severo-Enisejsk ☆ RUS 116-117 F 5
Severo-Kuril'sk ○ RUS 122-123 R 3
Severomorsk ○ RUS 88-89 M 2
Severo-Sahalinskaja ravnina ⌣ RUS 122-123 J 3
Severo sos'vinskaja vozvyšennost' ▲ RUS 114-115 G 4
Severoural'sk ○ RUS 114-115 F 4
Severo-Vostočnyj, proliv ≈ 84-85 f 2
Severo-Vostočnyj proliv ≈ 120-121 G 6
Severo-Zadonsk ○ RUS 94-95 Q 4
Severo-Zapadnyj, mys ▲ RUS 120-121 I V 6
Severskij Donec ~ RUS 102-103 L 3
Severskij Donec ~ RUS 102-103 M 3
Severy ○ USA (KS) 262-263 K 7
Sevettijärvi ○ FIN 88-89 K 2
Sevey ○ USA (NY) 278-279 G 4
Sevier ○ USA (UT) 254-255 C 5
Sevier Bridge Reservoir < USA (UT) 254-255 D 4
Sevier Desert ⊥ USA 254-255 C 4
Sevier Lake ○ USA (UT) 254-255 B 5
Sevier River ~ USA 254-255 C 4
Sevierville ○ USA (TN) 282 283 D 5
Sevigny Point ▲ CDN 24-25 f 6
Sevilla ○ CO 60-61 D 5
Sevilla ○ ••• E 98-99 E 6
Seville ○ USA (FL) 286-287 H 2
Seville ○ USA (GA) 284-285 G 5
Ševli ~ RUS 122-123 E 2
Sevlievo ○ BG 102-103 D 6
Sevrej = Sajnšand ○ MAU 148-149 F 6
Sèvre Niortaise ~ F 90-91 G 8
Sevsk ○ RUS 94-95 O 5
Sevštari ○ • BG 102-103 E 6
Sewa ~ WAL 202-203 D 6
Sewall ○ CDN (BC) 228-229 B 3
Sewanee ○ USA (TN) 276-277 K 5
Seward ○ USA (AK) 20-21 Q 6
Seward ○ USA (NE) 262-263 J 4
Seward Glacier ⊂ CDN 20-21 U 6
Seward Peninsula ⌣ USA 20-21 G 4
Sewell ○ RCH 78-79 D 3
Sewell Inlet ○ CDN (BC) 228-229 B 4
Sewerimabu ○ PNG 183 B 5
Sexsmith ○ CDN 32-33 L 4
Sey ○ RA 76-77 D 2
Seyahū ○ IR 134-135 G 5
Seybouse, Oued ~ DZ 190-191 F 2
Seychelles ■ SY 224 A 5
Seychelles ⌒ SY 224 A 5
Seychelles Bank ≃ 224 D 2
Seydişehir ☆ TR 128-129 D 4
Seyðisfjörður ☆ IS 86-87 f 2
Seyhan Baraji < TR 128-129 F 4
Seyhan N. ~ TR 128-129 F 4
Seyhan Nehri ~ TR 128-129 F 4
Seyitgazi ☆ TR 128-129 D 3
Seymour ○ AUS 180-181 H 4
Seymour ○ USA (IA) 274-275 E 4
Seymour ○ USA (IN) 274-275 N 6
Seymour ○ USA (MO) 276-277 C 3
Seymour ○ USA (TX) 264-265 E 5
Seymour ○ ZA 220-221 H 6
Seymour Arm ○ CDN (BC) 230-231 K 2
Seymour Canal ≈ 32-33 C 3
Seymour Inlet ≈ 230-231 B 2
Seymour River ~ CDN 230-231 L 2
Seymourville ○ CDN (MAN) 234-235 G 3
Seymourville ○ USA (LA) 268-269 J 6
Seyyedābād ○ AFG 138-139 B 2
Seyyedābād ○ IR (HOR) 136-137 F 6
Seyyedābād ○ IR (MAZ) 136-137 E 6
Seyyedān ○ IR 128-129 M 5
Seyyed Karam ○ AFG 138-139 B 3
Sézanne ○ F 90-91 J 7
Sezela ○ ZA 220-221 K 5
Sezin ○ MYA 142-143 K 3
Sfakia ○ GR 100-101 K 7
Sfax ☆ TN 190-191 H 3
Sfînári ○ GR 100-101 J 7
Sfîntu Gheorghe ☆ • RO 102-103 D 5
Sfissifa ○ DZ 188-189 L 4
Sfizef ○ DZ 188-189 L 3
's-Gravenhage = Den Haag ○ •• NL 92-93 H 2
Sgurr Mór ▲ GB 90-91 E 3
Shaanxi ▫ VRC 154-155 E 5
Shaba ▫ ZRE 214-215 C 5
Shaba National Reserve ⊥ EAK 212-213 F 3
Shabaqua Corners ○ CDN (ONT) 234-235 O 6
Shabasha ○ SUD 200-201 F 5
Shabaskwia Lake ○ CDN (ONT) 234-235 O 3
Shabeellaha Dhexe ▫ SP 212-213 K 2
Shabeellaha Hoose ▫ SP 212-213 J 3
Shabeelle, Webi ~ SP 212-213 J 3
Shabogamo Lake ○ CDN 38-39 L 2
Shabqadar ○ PK 138-139 C 2
Shabunda ○ ZRE 212-213 A 5
Shabuskwia Lake ○ CDN (ONT) 234-235 P 3
Shache ○ VRC 146-147 C 6
Shackleton ○ CDN (SAS) 232-233 K 5
Shackleton Ice Shelf ⊂ ARK 16 G 10
Shackleton Inlet ≈ 16 E 0
Shackleton Range ▲ ARK 16 E 0
Shādan Lund ○ PK 138-139 C 4
Shadao ○ VRC 156-157 F 2
Shādara ○ PK 138-139 E 4
Shade Gap ○ USA (PA) 280-281 J 3
Shadehill ○ USA (SD) 260-261 D 1
Shadehill Reservoir ○ USA (SD) 260-261 D 1
Shadiwāl ○ PK 138-139 E 3
Shadon Downs ○ AUS 174-175 C 5
Shady Cove ○ USA (OR) 244-245 C 8
Shady Dale ○ USA (GA) 284-285 G 3
Shaerer Dale ○ CDN 32-33 K 3
Shafter ○ USA (CA) 248-249 E 4
Shafter ○ USA (NV) 246-247 L 3
Shafter ○ USA (TX) 266-267 C 4
Shafter Lake ○ USA (TX) 264-265 B 6
Shagamu River ~ CDN 34-35 N 3
Shagari ○ WAN 198-199 B 6
Shagein ▲ EAT 212-213 G 6
Shageluk ○ USA 20-21 L 5
Shag Harbour ○ CDN (NS) 240-241 K 7
Shagoujie ○ VRC 154-155 F 5
Shagunnu ○ WAN 204-205 F 3
Shagwa ○ WAN 204-205 F 3
Shāhāda ○ IND 138-139 E 9
Shah Alam ○ MAL 162-163 D 3
Shāhāpur ○ IND 138-139 D 10
Shahar Sultān ○ PK 138-139 C 5
Shāhbandar ○ PK 134-135 M 6
Shāhbāz Kalāt ○ PK 134-135 K 5
Shahbazpur ~ BD 142-143 G 4
Shahda Bohotleh ○ SP 208-209 H 4
Shāhdādkot ○ PK 134-135 M 5
Shāhdādpur ○ PK 138-139 B 7
Shahdol ○ IND 142-143 B 4
Shahe ○ VRC (HEB) 154-155 J 3
Shahe ○ VRC (SHD) 154-155 L 3
Shāhganj ○ IND 142-143 C 2
Shāh Hasan ○ PK 134-135 M 5
Shahhāt ∴ •• LAR 192-193 J 1
Shahistagani ○ BD 142-143 G 3
Shahjahānpur ○ IND 138-139 G 6
Shāh Kot ○ PK 138 130 D 4
Shāhpur ○ IND (KAR) 140-141 G 2
Shāhpur ○ IND (RAJ) 138-139 E 6
Shāhpur ○ PK 138-139 D 3
Shahwī, Bi'r ash ○ LAR 192-193 F 2
Shaighālū ○ PK 138-139 B 4
Shai Hills Game Reserve ⊥ GH 202-203 L 7
Shaikhpura ○ IND 142-143 D 3
Shaka, Ras ▲ EAK 212-213 H 5
Shakani ☆ • EAK 212-213 H 4
Shakargarh ○ PK 138-139 E 3
Shakaskraal ○ ZA 220-221 K 4
Shakawe ○ RB 216-217 F 9
Shakertown ∴ USA (KY) 276-277 K 3
Shakespeare Ghost Town • USA (NM) 256-257 G 6
Shakespeare Island ⌒ CDN 234-235 P 5
Shakiso ○ ETH 208-209 D 6
Shakleford Banks ≃ 282-283 L 6
Shakotan-misaki ▲ J 152-153 J 3
Shākshūk ○ LAR 192-193 D 1
Shaktoolik ○ USA 20-21 K 4
Shaktoolik River ~ USA 20-21 K 4
Shalaanbood ○ SP 212-213 K 3
Shala Hāyk' ○ ETH 208-209 D 5
Shalalth ○ CDN (BC) 230-231 G 3
Shaler Mountains ▲ CDN 24-25 Q 5
Shāli al-Fīl ○ SUD 208-209 B 3
Shallotte ○ USA (NC) 282-283 J 7
Shallow Bay ≈ 20-21 X 2
Shallow Lake ○ AUS 178-179 F 3
Shallow Water ○ USA (KS) 262-263 F 6
Shaluli Shan ▲ VRC 144-145 M 5
Shama ~ EAT 214-215 G 4
Shamakhy = Samax ○ AZ 128-129 N 2
Shamattawa River ~ CDN 34-35 O 3
Shambe ○ SUD 206-207 K 5
Shamboyacu ○ PE 64-65 D 5
Shambu ○ ETH 208-209 C 4
Shames ○ CDN (BC) 228-229 F 2
Shamganj ○ BD 142-143 G 3
Shamli ○ IND 138-139 F 5
Shamman ○ SUD 200-201 G 6
Shamokin ○ USA (PA) 280-281 K 3
Shamputa ○ Z 218-219 D 2
Shamrock ○ CDN (SAS) 232-233 M 5
Shamrock ○ USA (TX) 264-265 D 3
Shamsābād ○ IND 140-141 H 2
Shamshergani ○ NEP 144-145 C 6
Shamva ○ ZW 218-219 F 3
Shanbahe ○ VRC 154-155 J 6
Shandaken ○ USA (NY) 278-279 G 6
Shandan ○ VRC 154-155 B 2
Shandon ○ USA (CA) 248-249 D 4
Shandong ▫ VRC 154-155 K 3
Shandong Bandao ⌣ VRC 154-155 K 3
Shangani ○ ZW 218-219 E 4
Shangcai ○ VRC 154-155 J 5
Shangcheng ○ VRC 154-155 J 6
Shangchuan Dao ⌒ VRC 156-157 H 6
Shangdu ○ VRC 148-149 L 7
Shangev-Tiev ○ WAN 204-205 H 5
Shanggao ○ VRC 156-157 J 2
Shang Gongma ○ VRC 144-145 M 4
Shanghai ☆ •• VRC 154-155 M 6
Shanghai Shi ▫ VRC 154-155 M 6
Shanghang ○ VRC 156-157 K 4
Shanghe ○ VRC 154-155 K 3
Shangla Pass ▲ PK 138-139 D 2
Shanglin ○ VRC 156-157 F 5
Shangman ○ VRC 154-155 G 5
Shangombo ○ Z 218-219 B 3
Shangqiu ○ VRC 154-155 J 4
Shangrao ○ VRC 156-157 K 2
Shangtu ○ VRC 156-157 J 2
Shangying ○ VRC 156-157 E 5
Shangyou Yichang ○ VRC 146-147 E 5
Shangyu ○ VRC 154-155 M 6
Shangzhi ○ VRC 150-151 F 5
Shangzhou ○ VRC 154-155 F 5
Shanhaiguan ○ VRC (HEB) 154-155 L 1
Shanhaiguan • VRC (HEB) 154-155 L 1
Shanhetun ○ VRC 150-151 F 5
Shani ○ WAN 204-205 K 3
Shaniko ○ USA (OR) 244-245 E 6
Shanjuan D. • VRC 154-155 L 6
Shankou ○ VRC (GXI) 156-157 F 6
Shankou ○ VRC (HUN) 156-157 G 2
Shannon ○ AUS 176-177 D 7
Shannon ~ IRL 90-91 C 5
Shannon ○ USA (MS) 268-269 M 2
Shannon = Sionainn ○ IRL 90-91 C 5
Shannon Bay ○ CDN (BC) 228-229 B 3
Shannon Ø ⌒ GRØ 26-27 q 6
Shannon Sund ≈ 26-27 q 6
Shanshan ○ VRC 146-147 K 4
Shantarskiye Ostrova = Šantarskie, ostrova ⌒ RUS 120-121 G 6
Shantou ○ VRC 156-157 K 5
Shantung Peninsula = Shandong Bandao ⌣ VRC 154-155 K 3
Shanusi ○ PE 64-65 D 5
Shanwei ○ VRC 156-157 J 5
Shanxi ▫ VRC 154-155 G 2
Shan Xian ○ VRC 154-155 K 4
Shanyang ○ VRC 154-155 F 5
Shanyin ○ VRC 154-155 H 2
Shaodong ○ VRC 156-157 G 3
Shaoguan ○ • VRC 156-157 H 4
Shaolin Si • VRC 154-155 H 4
Shaoshan ○ VRC 156-157 H 3
Shaowu ○ VRC 156-157 K 3
Shaoxing ○ VRC 154-155 M 6
Shaoyang ○ VRC 156-157 G 3
Shaoyang (Tangdukou) ○ VRC 156-157 G 3
Shapembe ○ ZRE 210-211 H 6
Shaping ○ VRC 156-157 F 5
Shapotou • VRC 154-155 D 3
Shāpur Chākar ○ PK 138-139 B 6
Shaquanzi ○ VRC 146-147 F 3
Sharan Jogizai ○ PK 138-139 B 4
Shara Tohay ○ VRC 144-145 L 2
Sharbot Lake ○ CDN (ONT) 238-239 J 4
Share ○ WAN 204-205 F 4
Shargalle ○ WAN 198-199 D 6
Shari ○ J 152 153 L 3
Shari ~ ZRE 212-213 C 2
Sharjah = aš-Šariqa ○ UAE 134-135 F 6
Shark Bank ≃ 100-101 C 6
Shark Bay ⊥ ••• AUS 176-177 B 2
Shark Bay ○ VAN 184 II a 2
Sharon ○ USA (PA) 280-281 F 2
Sharon Springs ○ USA (KS) 262-263 E 6
Sharpe, Lake ○ AUS 176-177 F 6
Sharpe Lake ○ CDN 34-35 K 3
Sharp Mount ▲ CDN 20-21 V 3
Sharpsburg ○ USA (KY) 276-277 M 2
Sharqpur ○ PK 138-139 E 4
Sharwangai ○ PK 138-139 C 3
Shasha ○ ETH 208-209 B 5
Shasha ~ WAN 204-205 F 5
Shashani ~ ZW 218-219 E 5
Shashe ○ RB 218-219 D 5
Shashe ~ ZW 218-219 E 5
Shashemenē ○ ETH 208-209 D 5
Shashi ○ VRC 154-155 H 6

392 Selle, Massif de la — Shashi

Sill, Fort ✕✕ USA (OK) 264-265 F 4
Silla o E 98-99 G 5
Sillänwäli o PK 138-139 D 4
Sillein = Žilina o SK 92-93 P 4
Silli o BF 202-203 J 4
Sillod o IND 138-139 D 4
Silmi o ETH 208-209 H 4
Śiřnaja Balka o KZ 96-97 F 8
Sil Nakya o USA (AZ) 256-257 D 6
Siloam Springs o USA (AR)
   276-277 A 4
Silobela o ZW 218-219 E 4
Silom o PNG 183 G 2
Silong o VRC 156-157 F 5
Silopi o TR 128-129 K 4
Silovajaha ∿ RUS 108-109 K 7
Silovo o RUS 94-95 R 4
Silowana Plains ⊥ Z 218-219 B 3
Silsand o N 86-87 H 2
Silsbee o USA (TX) 268-269 F 6
Silton o CDN (SAS) 232-233 O 5
Siltou o TCH 198-199 G 4
Siluas o WAN 204-205 F 5
Siluko, River ∿ WAN 204-205 F 5
Silutė o • LT 94-95 G 4
Silutshana o ZA 220-221 K 4
Silva o USA (NE) 262-263 J 3
Silva, Recife do ∿ BR 68-69 F 2
Silva, Ribeiro da ∿ BR 72-73 E 2
Silvan o TR 128-129 J 3
Silvan Baraji < TR 128-129 J 3
Silvâne o IR 128-129 L 4
Silvânia o BR 72-73 F 4
Silva Porto Gare o ANG 216-217 D 6
Silvassa o IND 138-139 D 9
Silver o CDN (MAN) 234-235 F 4
Silver Bank ≃ 54-55 L 4
Silver Bank Passage ≃ 54-55 K 4
Silver Bay o USA (MN) 270-271 G 3
Silver Beach o USA (VA) 280-281 L 6
Silver City o USA (IA) 274-275 C 3
Silver City o USA (NM) 256-257 Q 6
Silver City o USA (TX) 266-267 L 2
Silver City o • USA (ID) 252-253 B 3
Silver City Highway II AUS 180-181 F 6
Silver Creek o USA (NE) 262-263 J 3
Silver Creek o USA (NY) 278-279 B 6
Silver Creek o USA 244-245 F 7
Silverdale o USA (WA) 244-245 C 4
Silverdale o USA (WA) 244-245 C 4
Silver Dollar o CDN (ONT) 234-235 M 5
Silver Gate o USA (MT) 250-251 K 6
Silver Islet o CDN (ONT) 234-235 L 7
Silver Lake o USA (OR) 244-245 D 7
Silver Lake o USA (CA) 248-249 H 4
Silver Park o CDN (SAS) 232-233 O 3
Silverpeak o USA (NV) 248-249 G 2
Silver Plains o AUS 174-175 G 4
Silversand o NAM 216-217 D 11
Silver Springs o • USA (FL)
   286-287 G 2
Silver Star Mine o USA 174-175 E 6
Silver Star Provincial Recreation Area ⊥
   CDN (BC) 230-231 L 3
Silverthorne o USA (CO) 254-255 J 4
Silverthrone Glacier ⊂ CDN (BC)
   230-231 C 2
Silverthrone Mountain ▲ CDN (BC)
   230-231 C 2
Silverton o AUS 178-179 F 6
Silverton o CDN (MAN) 234-235 D 4
Silverton o USA (CO) 254-255 H 6
Silverton o USA (OR) 244-245 C 5
Silverton o USA (TX) 264-265 C 4
Silver Zone Pass ⩙ USA (NV)
   246-247 L 3
Silves o BR 66-67 H 4
Silves o • P 98-99 C 6
Silvia o CO 60-61 C 6
Silvies River ∿ USA 244-245 F 7
Silvituc o MEX 52-53 J 2
Silvrettagruppe ▲ CH 92-93 K 5
Sim ★ RUS 96-97 K 6
Sim ∿ RUS 96-97 K 6
Sima o COM 222-223 D 4
Sima o USA (CO) 254-255 L 4
Simakalo o RI 162-163 D 6
Simalugiri o IND 142-143 J 2
Simamba o Z 218-219 C 3
Simanindo o • RI 162-163 C 3
Śimanovsk o RUS 122-123 B 3
Simao o VRC 156-157 B 5
Simão Dias o BR 68-69 K 7
Simão Pereira o BR 72-73 J 6
Simara Island ∿ RP 160-161 E 6
Simard, Lac o CDN (QUE) 236-237 K 5
Simatang, Pulau ∿ RI 164-165 G 3
Simav ★ TR 128-129 C 3
Simav Çayı ∿ TR 128-129 C 3
Simba o ZRE 210-211 J 3
Simbai o PNG 183 C 3
Simberi Island ∿ PNG 183 G 2
Simbi o RMM 202-203 D 3
Simbirsk = RUS 96-97 F 6
Simbo o EAT 212-213 B 6
Simbo o MYA 142-143 K 3
Simbo ∿ SOL 184 I c 3
Simcoe o CDN (ONT) 238-239 E 6
Simcoe, Lake o CDN (ONT)
   238-239 F 4
Simdega o IND 142-143 H 4
Simën ▲ ETH 200-201 J 6
Simën National Park ⊥ ••• ETH
   208-209 D 2
Simenti o SN 202-203 D 3
Simeonof Island ∿ USA 22-23 H 5
Simeto ∿ I 100-101 E 6
Simeulue, Pulau ∿ RI 162-163 B 3
Simferopol ☆ • UA 102-103 J 5
Simga o IND 142-143 H 5
Simhadripuram o IND 140-141 H 3
Simhân, Ǧabal ▲ OM 132-133 J 5
Simi ★ GR 100-101 L 6
Simianorva ∿ RM 222-223 F 6
Simiegan ∿ RUS 114-115 M 3

Simikot o NEP 144-145 C 6
Similigurha o IND 142-143 H 6
Similkameen River ∿ CDN 230-231 J 4
Simindou o RCA 206-207 J 3
Simine Rūd ∿ IR 128-129 L 4
Siminiout o RZ 62-63 H 4
Simiri o RN 204-205 F 3
Simirinundu o GUY 62-63 H 2
Simiš, Rūd-e ∿ IR 134-135 J 5
Simitli o BG 102-103 C 7
Simiutaq ∿ GRØ 28-29 O 3
Simi Valley o USA (CA) 248-249 F 3
Simiyu ∿ EAT 212-213 E 3
Simla ★ IND 138-139 F 4
Similpal National Park ⊥ IND
   142-143 J 5
Simmesport o USA (LA) 268-269 J 6
Simmie o CDN (SAS) 232-233 K 6
Simmler o USA (CA) 248-249 E 4
Simmons's Peninsula ∿ CDN 24-25 b 2
Simms o BS 54-55 H 3
Simms o USA (MT) 250-251 H 4
Simo ∿ FIN 88-89 H 4
Simões o BR 68-69 H 5
Simões Filho o BR 72-73 L 2
Simojärvi o FIN 88-89 J 3
Simojovel de Allende o MEX 52-53 H 3
Simon, Lac o CDN (QUE) 238-239 K 3
Simona o BOL 70-71 G 4
Simonette River ∿ CDN 228-229 R 2
Simoni o Z 214-215 B 4
Simonstad = Simon's Town o ZA
   220-221 D 7
Simon's Town = Simonstad o ZA
   220-221 D 7
Simoom Harbour o CDN (BC)
   230-231 C 3
Simoon Sound o CDN (BC)
   230-231 C 3
Simpang o RI 162-163 F 5
Simpang Ampat Rungkup o MAL
   162-163 D 3
Simpang-Kanan ∿ RI 162-163 C 3
Simpangkawat o RI 162-163 C 3
Simpang Kiri ∿ RI 162-163 B 3
Simpangsukarame o RI 162-163 F 7
Simpatia o BR 66-67 B 7
Simplicio Mendes o BR 68-69 H 5
Simplonpass ⩙ CH 92-93 K 5
Simpson, Rio ∿ RCH 80 D 2
Simpson o CDN (SAS) 232-233 N 4
Simpson o USA (LA) 268-269 H 5
Simpson o USA (MT) 250-251 J 3
Simpson, Cape ∿ USA 20-21 N 1
Simpson, Mount ▲ PNG 183 E 6
Simpson, Port o CDN (BC) 228-229 D 2
Simpson Bay ≈ 24-25 P 6
Simpson Desert ⫛ AUS 178-179 D 4
Simpson Desert Conservation Park ⊥
   AUS 178-179 D 4
Simpson Desert National Park ⊥ AUS
   178-179 E 4
Simpson Island o CDN (ONT)
   234-235 Q 6
Simpson Islands ∿ CDN 30-31 N 5
Simpson Lake o CDN 24-25 J 6
Simpson Peninsula ⫛ CDN 24-25 b 6
Simpson Regional Reserve ⊥ AUS
   178-179 D 4
Simpson River ∿ CDN 30-31 U 2
Simpsons Gap National Park ⊥ AUS
   178-179 D 2
Simpson Strait ≈ 24-25 X 6
Simpsonville o USA (SC) 284-285 H 2
Simrishamn o S 86-87 F 9
Simsk o RUS 94-95 M 2
Sims Lake o CDN 36-37 Q 7
Simsom, Isla ∿ RCH 80 D 2
Simtustus, Lake o USA (OR)
   244-245 D 6
Simuk, Pulau ∿ RI 162-163 B 5
Simunjan o MAL 162-163 J 4
Simunul Island ∿ RP 160-161 C 10
Simušir, ostrov ∿ RUS 122-123 P 5
Sinâ' ∿ ET 194-195 F 3
Sina o PE 70-71 G 7
Sinabang o RI 162-163 B 3
Sina Dagha o SP 208-209 H 6
Sinadipan o RP 160-161 D 4
Šinăfiya, as- o IRQ 128-129 L 7
Sinagoga, Ponta da o CV 202-203 B 5
Sinai, Mount = Ǧabal Mūsa ▲ ET
   194-195 F 3
Sinai = Sinâ' ∿ ET 194-195 F 3
Sinaia o • RO 102-103 D 5
Sinaloa ▣ MEX 50-51 E 4
Sinaloa, Rio ∿ MEX 50-51 E 5
Sinaloa de Leyva o MEX 50-51 E 5
Sinamaico o YV 60-61 G 2
Sinamatella Camp o ZW 218-219 D 4
Sinan o VRC 156-157 F 3
Sinanpaşa ★ TR 128-129 D 3
Šinâş o OM 134-135 G 6
Sinau o WAN 204-205 E 4
Sinăwin o LAR 190-191 H 5
Sinawongourou o DY 204-205 E 3
Sinazongwe o Z 218-219 D 3
Sinbaungwe o MYA 142-143 J 6
Sinbyugyun o MYA 142-143 J 5
Sincan o TR 128-129 G 3
Since o CO 60-61 D 3
Sincelejo o CO 60-61 D 3
Sincerin o CO 60-61 D 2
Sinchangbyin o MYA 142-143 H 5
Sinclair o CDN (MAN) 234-235 D 5
Sinclair o USA (WY) 252-253 L 3
Sinclair, Lake o USA (GA) 284-285 G 3
Sinclair Mills o CDN (BC) 228-229 N 2
Sincorá, Serra do ∿ BR 72-73 K 2
Sincos o BR 64-65 E 7
Sind ∿ IND 138-139 G 6
Sind = Indus ∿ IND 138-139 F 2
Sind o PK 134-135 K 3
Šindand o AFG 134-135 K 2
Šindand, Rūd-e ∿ AFG 134-135 K 2
Sindangan o RP 160-161 E 7
Sindangan Bay ≈ 160-161 E 8
Sindangbarang o RI 168 B 3

Sindanglaut o RI 168 C 3
Sindari o IND 138-139 C 7
Sindia o SN 202-203 B 2
Simine Rūd ∿ IR 194-195 H 6
Sindou o BF 202-203 H 4
Sine ∿ SN 202-203 B 2
Sinee morco cyganaky ≈ 96-97 H 1
Sinegor'e o USA 120-121 O 2
Sinegorsk o RUS 122-123 K 5
Sinegorskij o RUS 102-103 M 3
Sinei o RI 168 B 7
Sines o P 98-99 C 6
Sines, Cabo de ∿ P 98-99 C 6
Siné-Saloum, Parc National du ⊥ SN
   202-203 B 2
Sinetta o FIN 88-89 H 3
Šinežinsk = Zalaa o MAU 148-149 D 5
Sinfra o SUD 200-201 F 6
Singa o SUD 200-201 F 6
Singako o TCH 206-207 J 4
Singapore ☆ SGP 162-163 E 4
Singapore o SGP 162-163 E 4
Singapore, Selat ≈ 162-163 E 4
Singâr, Balad o IRQ 128-129 J 4
Singâr, Ǧabal ▲ IRQ 128-129 J 4
Singaraja o RI 168 B 7
Singaung o MYA 142-143 J 5
Sing Buri o THA 158-159 F 3
Singer o USA (LA) 268-269 G 6
Singhampton o CDN (ONT)
   238-239 E 4
Singida o EAT 214-215 H 4
Singida o EAT (SIN) 212-213 E 6
Singida ▣ EAT 212-213 E 6
Singirin o RI 164-165 G 6
Singkangon o RI 164-165 G 6
Singkarak o RI 162-163 C 3
Singkarak, Danau o RI 162-163 D 5
Singkawang o RI 162-163 H 4
Singkep, Pulau ∿ RI 162-163 F 5
Singkil = Singkilbaru o RI 162-163 B 3
Singkilbaru o RI 162-163 B 3
Singleton o AUS 180-181 L 2
Singleton, Mount ▲ AUS (NT)
   172-173 K 7
Singleton, Mount ▲ AUS (WA)
   176-177 D 4
Singorokai o PNG 183 D 3
Singosari o RI 168 E 3
Singou ∿ BF 202-203 L 4
Singou, Réserve du ⊥ BF 202-203 L 4
Sirasso o CI 202-203 G 4
Singuédeze, Rio ∿ MOC 218-219 F 3
Singye o KOR 150-151 F 7
Sinharagama o CL 140-141 J 6
Sinharaja Forest Reserve ⊥ ••• CL
   140-141 J 7
Sirdan o IR 128-129 L 5
Sirdar o CDN (BC) 230-231 N 4
Sinie Lipjagi o RUS 102-103 L 5
Sinij, hrebet ▲ RUS 122-123 E 6
Sinisciola o I 100-101 B 4
Sinj o HR 100-101 F 3
Sinjai o RI 164-165 G 6
Sinjajala ∿ RUS 118-119 N 5
Sinjembela o Z 218-219 B 3
Sinjuga o RUS 118-119 G 7
Sinkát o SUD 200-201 J 5
Sinkiang = Xinjiang Uygur Zizhiqu ▣ VRC
   146-147 D 5
Sinko o RG 202-203 F 5
Sinmido o KOR 150-151 E 8
Sinnamary o F 62-63 H 3
Sinnamary ∿ F 62-63 H 3
Sinnar o IND 138-139 E 10
Sinnett o CDN (SAS) 232-233 O 4
Sinnicolau Mare o RO 102-103 B 4
Sin Nombre, Cerro ▲ RCH 80 D 3
Sinnūris o ET 194-195 E 3
Sinop o BR 70-71 K 2
Sinop ★ TR 128-129 F 1
Sinop o TR 128-129 F 1
Sinque ∿ LS 220-221 J 5
Sinšâr o SYR 128-129 G 5
Sinsicap o PE 64-65 C 5
Sinsk o RUS 118-119 N 5
Sintaluta o CDN (SAS) 232-233 P 5
Sintang o RI 162-163 J 4
Sint Eustatius ∿ NA 56 D 3
Sint Maarten ∿ NA 56 D 2
Sint Nicolaas o ARU 60-61 G 1
Sint-Niklaas o B 92-93 H 3
Sinton o USA (TX) 266-267 K 4
Sintong o RI 162-163 D 4
Sintra o • • P 98-99 C 5
Sinú, Rio ∿ CO 60-61 D 3
Sinuiju o KOR 150-151 E 7
Sinujiif o SP 208-209 J 4
Sinuk o USA 20-21 G 4
Sinuk River ∿ USA 20-21 H 4
Sinungu o Z 218-219 D 2
Siodjuru o SOL 184 I e 3
Siófok o H 92-93 P 5
Sioma o Z 218-219 B 3
Sioma Ngwezi National Park ⊥ Z
   218-219 B 3
Sion = CH 92-93 J 5
Sionainn = Shannon o IRL 90-91 C 5
Siorapaluk o GRØ 26-27 P 5
Siorarsuk Peninsula ∿ CDN 24-25 f 5
Siota o RI 166-167 D 6
Siota o SOL 184 I e 3
Sioux Center o USA (IA) 274-275 B 1
Sioux City o USA (IA) 274-275 B 2
Sioux Falls o • USA (SD) 260-261 K 3
Sioux Indian Museum • USA (SD)
   260-261 F 3
Sioux Lookout o CDN (ONT)
   234-235 M 4
Sioux Narrows o CDN (ONT)
   234-235 L 5
Sioux Rapids o USA (IA) 274-275 C 2
Sioux Valley o USA (MN) 270-271 C 7
Sipacate o GCA 52-53 G 3
Sipahutar o RI 162-163 C 3
Sipai o PNG 184 I b 1
Sindangan Bay ∿ RI 168 B 3

Sipalwini ∿ SME 62-63 F 4
Sipán o PE 64-65 C 5
Sipang, Tanjung ∿ MAL 162-163 J 4
Sipao o YV 60-61 J 4
Sipapo, Reserva Florestal ⊥ YV
   60-61 H 5
Sipi o CO 60-61 C 5
Sipicyno o RUS 88-89 T 6
Sipilou o CI 202-203 F 6
Siping o VRC 150-151 E 7
Sipiongot o RI 162-163 C 4
Sipirok o RI 162-163 C 3
Sipitang o MAL 160-161 A 10
Sipiwesk o CDN 34-35 C 2
Siple, Mount ▲ ARK 16 F 24
Sipora, Selat ≈ 162-163 C 5
Sipovles o RUS 102-103 M 2
Sippar o ••• IRQ 128-129 L 6
Siwâ o • Y 132-133 D 6
Sirykrabet ∴ KZ 126-127 P 5
Sis o IR 128-129 L 5
Šiš ∿ RUS 114-115 N 6
Sisa o PE 64-65 D 5
Sisa, Mount ▲ PNG 183 B 4
Sisak o HR 100-101 F 3
Si Sa Ket o THA 158-159 H 3
Sisal o MEX 52-53 J 1
Sisal, Arrecife ∿ MEX 52-53 J 1
Sisaia, Rio ∿ NIC 52-53 B 5
Siska o IR 128-129 L 5
Si Satchanalai o THA 158-159 E 2
Si Satchanalai National Park ⊥ THA
   158-159 E 2
Si Sawat o THA 158-159 E 3
Sisember o RI 166-167 H 2
Šišhëd gol ∿ MAU 148-149 D 2
Sishen o ZA 220-221 F 4
Sishiliang o VRC 154-155 F 2
Sishui o VRC 154-155 K 4
Sisian o AR 128-129 L 3
Sisi Bargaon o IND 142-143 J 2
Sisim ∿ RUS 116-117 F 8
Sisimiut = Holsteinsborg o GRØ
   28-29 O 3
Siskiwit Bay ≈ 270-271 K 3
Siskiyou o USA (OR) 244-245 C 8
Siskiyou Mountains ▲ USA
   246-247 B 2
Si Songkhram o THA 158-159 H 2
Sisôphôn o K 158-159 G 4
Sisquelan, Península ∿ RCH 80 D 3
Sisquoc o USA (CA) 248-249 D 5
Sisquoc River ∿ USA 248-249 E 5
Sissano o PNG 183 B 1
Sisseton o USA (SD) 260-261 J 1
Sisseton Indian Reservation ⟓ USA (SD)
   260-261 J 1
Sissonville o USA (WV) 280-281 E 5
Sistán o IR 134-135 J 3
Sistán, Daryace-ye o IR 134-135 J 3
Sistán-ő-Bálúcěstán ▣ IR 134-135 J 3
Sister Bay o USA (WI) 270-271 L 5
Sisterdale o USA (TX) 266-267 J 4
Sisteron o F 90-91 M 7
Sisters o USA (OR) 244-245 D 6
Sistonens Crs. o CDN (ONT)
   234-235 O 6
Sitakili o RMM 202-203 E 3
Sitalike o EAT 214-215 F 4
Sitamarhi o IND 142-143 H 2
Sitang o VRC 154-155 B 3
Sitápur o IND 142-143 B 2
Sitasjaure o S 86-87 H 2
Sithobela o SD 220-221 K 3
Sithonía ⫛ GR 100-101 J 4
Sitía o GR 100-101 L 7
Sitia o GR 100-101 L 7
Sitidgi Lake o CDN 20-21 Z 2
Sitiecito o C 54-55 E 3
Sitila o MOC 218-219 H 6
Sitio da Abadia o BR 72-73 G 3
Sítio do Mato o BR 72-73 J 2
Sitio Novo o BR 68-69 G 4
Sitio Nôvo do Tocantins o BR 68-69 D 4
Sitionuevo o CO 60-61 D 2
Sitka o USA (KS) 262-263 G 7
Sitka o • USA (AK) 32-33 C 3
Sitkalidak Island ∿ USA 22-23 H 4
Sitkinak, Cape ∿ USA 22-23 U 4
Sitkinak Island ∿ USA 22-23 U 4
Sitkinak Strait ≈ 22-23 T 4
Sitkino o RUS 116-117 J 7
Sitkum o USA (OR) 244-245 B 7
Sitnica ∿ YU 100-101 H 3
Sitona o BR 200-201 J 5
Sitoti o Z 218-219 B 3
Sitra o RUS (SAH) 118-119 O 4
Sitte o RUS 118-119 N 4
Sitten = Sion o CH 92-93 J 5
Šitrnak ★ TR 128-129 K 4
Sitrohl o IR 138-139 D 7
Sirokaja gora ▲ RUS 96-97 L 5
Široki Brijeg o BIH 100-101 F 3
Sirokij, kanal ∿ RUS 126-127 E 5
Širokostan, poluostrov ∿ RUS
   110-111 W 3
Širokovo o RUS 116-117 J 8
Sirombu o RI 162-163 B 4
Sironcha o IND 138-139 G 10
Sirong o RI 164-165 H 4
Sirong o VRC 156-157 F 4
Sironj o IND 138-139 F 7
Siros o GR 100-101 J 5
Siroua, Jbel ▲ MA 188-189 H 5
Sirri, Ǧazire-ye o IR 134-135 H 5
Sir Robert Campbell Island ∿ MYA
   158-159 F 5
Sir R. Squires Memorial Provincial Park ⊥
   CDN (NFL) 242-243 L 3
Sirsa o IND 138-139 E 5
Sirsăla o IND 138-139 F 10
Sirsi o IND 140-141 F 3

Sirsilla o IND 138-139 G 10
Sirsir o SUD 206-207 K 6
Širšov, Mount ▲ USA 176-177 K 3
Siruguppa o IND 140-141 G 3
Siru'iye o IR 134-135 G 4
Sivrihisar ★ TR 128-129 D 3
Sirûr o IND 138-139 E 10
Sirusábâd o IR 134-135 F 3
Širvan o IR 136-137 E 6
Širvan, Âb-e o IR 128-129 L 4
Širvän e Mäzin o IRQ 128-129 L 4
Sirvankaja ∴ TM 136-137 F 3
Sirvanskaja ravnina ∴ AZ 128-129 M 2
Širvanskij zapovednik ⊥ AZ
   128-129 N 3
Širvintos o LT 94-95 J 4
Siwâ o • Y 132-133 D 6
Sirykrabet ∴ KZ 126-127 P 5
Sis o IR 128-129 L 5
Šiš ∿ RUS 114-115 N 6
Sisa o PE 64-65 D 5
Sis Mountain ▲ PNG 183 B 4
Sisak o IR 128-129 L 5
Si Sa Ket o THA 158-159 H 3
Sisal o MEX 52-53 J 1
Si Thát o THA 158-159 G 2
Sivaganga o IND 140-141 H 5
Sivakasi o RUS 118-119 N 9
Sivakka o RUS 88-89 K 5
Sivas ★ TR 128-129 H 2
Sivé o RIM 196-197 D 7
Śvelučj, vulkan ▲ RUS 120-121 T 5
Siver ∿ RUS 112-113 J 3
Siverek ★ TR 128-129 H 4

Siverga, ozero o RUS 114-115 K 7
Siverskij hrebet ▲ RUS 112-113 K 3
Sivers'kyj Donec' ∿ UA 102-103 K 3
Sivolodnda o RUS 108-109 K 8
Sivomaskinskij o RUS 108-109 K 8
Sivrice o TR 128-129 H 3
Sivučij, mys ▲ RUS (KMC) 120-121 U 5
Sivučij, mys ▲ RUS (KMC) 122-123 R 3
Siwa o ET 192-193 B 4
Siwa, al-Wähät ∴ ET 192-193 B 4
Siwan o IND 142-143 D 2
Sixaola o CR 52-53 C 7
Si Xian o VRC 154-155 K 4
Sixaola o PA 52-53 C 7
Six Lakes o USA (MI) 272-273 D 4
Six Nations Indian Reservation ⟓ CDN
   (ONT) 238-239 E 5
Siyabuswa o ZA 220-221 J 2
Siyäh, Kūh-e ▲ IR 134-135 D 4
Siyäh Kūh, Selsele-ye ▲ IR 134-135 L 2
Siyäl, Ǧazä'ir ∿ ET 194-195 H 6
Siyän Češme o IR 128-129 L 3
Siyang o VRC 154-155 L 5
Siyang o VRC 156-157 E 5
Siyeteb o SUD 200-201 J 5
Siziwang Qi o VRC 148-149 K 7
Sizun o F 90-91 E 7
Sjælland ∴ DK 86-87 E 9
Sjain o RUS 122-123 F 5
Sjakutajaha ∿ RUS 108-109 R 6
Sjamža o RUS 94-95 R 1
Sjan ∿ RUS 116-117 O 3
Sjanno o BY 94-95 L 4
Sjapjakine ∿ RUS 110-111 d 7
Sjarednelimanskaja nizina ∴ 94-95 J 5
Sjas'stroj o RUS 94-95 N 1
Sjavtaso o RUS 108-109 O 7
Sjavtato, ozero o RUS 108-109 O 7
Sjenica o YU 100-101 H 3
Sjöbo o S 86-87 F 9
Sjøholt o N 86-87 C 5
Sjøvegan o N 86-87 H 2
Sjubreken o S 84-85 F 3
Sjugdžer, ozero o RUS 118-119 G 3
Sjul'ban o RUS 118-119 F 4
Sjul'djukar o RUS 118-119 F 4
Sjumsi o RUS 96-97 G 5
Sjun' ∿ RUS 96-97 H 5
Sjun'egan ∿ RUS 114-115 K 3
Sjungjude o RUS 110-111 N 5
Sjuøyane ∿ N 84-85 M 2
Sjurjah-Džangy, krjaž ▲ RUS
   110-111 K 3
Sjurjuktjah ∿ RUS 110-111 X 6
Sjurjuktjah ∿ RUS 110-111 X 4
Sjurkum o RUS 122-123 J 3
Sjurkum, mys ▲ RUS 122-123 J 3
Skaap o NAM 220-221 C 1
Skadarsko jezero o YU 100-101 G 3
Skadovs'k o UA 102-103 H 4
Skærfjorden ≈ 26-27 q 5
Skagastølind = Höfdakaupstadur o IS
   86-87 c 2
Skagen o DK 86-87 E 8
Skagern o S 86-87 D 8
Skagerrak ≈ 86-87 D 8
Skagit Provincial Park o CDN (BC)
   230-231 H 4
Skagit River ∿ USA 244-245 D 2
Skagsharnn o S 86-87 H 5
Skagway o • USA 20-21 X 7
Skåla o GR 100-101 J 6
Skålevik o S 86-87 C 7
Skálholt o IS 86-87 d 2
Skalistaja, gora ▲ RUS 120-121 U 5
Skalistyj Golec, gora ▲ RUS
   118-119 J 7
Skalistyj ∴ RUS 126-127 D 5
Skalistyj, hrebet ▲ RUS 120-121 G 2
Skalistyj, mys ▲ RUS 110-111 U 2
Skalkaho Pass ⩙ USA (MT)
   250-251 F 5
Skanderborg o DK 86-87 D 8
Skandinavia ∴ 8 E 2
Skane ∴ S 86-87 E 9
Skånevik o N 86-87 B 7
Skara o S 86-87 D 7
Skärgårdshavets nationalpark ⊥ FIN
   88-89 F 7
Skarsvåg o N 86-87 M 1
Skarżysko-Kamienna o PL 92-93 S 3
Skaudvilė o LT 94-95 H 4
Skaymat o WSA 196-197 C 2
Skead o CDN (ONT) 238-239 D 4
Skeena o CDN (BC) 228-229 E 2
Skeena Mountains ▲ CDN 32-33 O 3
Skeena River ∿ CDN 228-229 D 2
Skegness o GB 90-91 G 5
Skeidðrársandur ∴ IS 86-87 e 3
Skeldon o GUY 62-63 H 3
Skeleton Coast Park ⊥ NAM
   216-217 B 8
Skellefteå o • S 86-87 K 4
Skelleftehamn o S 86-87 J 4
Skene Bay ≈ 24-25 S 3
Skerki Bank ≃ 100-101 C 6
Skhira o TN 190-191 H 3
Skhirat o MA 188-189 H 4
Skhour-des-Rehamna o MA
   188-189 H 4
Ski ★ N 86-87 E 7
Skiathos o GR 100-101 J 5
Skiatook o USA (OK) 264-265 H 2
Skiatook Lake o USA (OK)
   264-265 H 2
Skiboten o N 86-87 K 2
Skidegate o CDN (BC) 228-229 B 3
Skidegate Channel ∿ CDN 228-229 B 3
Skidegate Inlet ≈ 228-229 C 3
Skidmore o USA (TX) 266-267 K 5

Skien ★ N 86-87 D 7
Skiff o CDN (ALB) 232-233 G 6
Skihist Mountain ▲ CDN (BC)
   230-231 H 3
Skikda o DZ 190-191 F 2
Skilak Lake o USA 20-21 P 6
Skiller Fork River ∿ USA 274-275 K 6
Skipperville o USA (AL) 284-285 D 5
Skipskog o ZA 220-221 E 7
Skipton o AUS 180-181 G 4
Skipton o GB 90-91 F 5
Skiros o GR 100-101 K 5
Skirring, Cap ▲ SN 202-203 B 3
Skive o DK 86-87 D 8
Skjálfandafljót ∿ IS 86-87 e 2
Skjern o DK 86-87 K 1
Skjervøy o N 86-87 K 1
Skjolden o N 86-87 C 6
Skjoldungen o GRØ 28-29 U 5
Skjoldungen ∿ GRØ 28-29 U 5
Sklad o RUS 110-111 O 4
Sklov o BY 94-95 M 4
Škocjanske jame o ••• SLO 100-101 J 2
Skógafoss ∿ IS 86-87 d 3
Skokie o USA (IL) 274-275 J 3
Sköllersta o S 86-87 G 7
Skön o K 158-159 H 4
Skookumchuck o CDN (BC)
   230-231 O 4
Skookumchuck Creek ∿ CDN
   230-231 N 4
Skópelos o GR 100-101 J 5
Skopin o RUS 102-103 L 2
Skopje ★ MK 100-101 H 3
Skorodnoe o RUS 102-103 J 2
Skosai o RI 166-167 L 4
Skotterud o N 86-87 F 7
Skoura o MA 188-189 H 5
Skovde o S 86-87 F 7
Skovorodino o RUS 118-119 L 9
Skowhegan o USA (ME) 278-279 M 4
Skownan o CDN (MAN) 234-235 D 3
Skrimfjella ▲ N 86-87 D 7
Skriveri o • LV 94-95 J 3
Skruis Point o CDN 24-25 b 3
Skrunda o LV 94-95 H 3
Skudeneshavn o N 86-87 B 7
Skukuza o ZA 220-221 K 2
Skuljabiha o RUS 96-97 D 5
Skull Mountain ▲ USA (NV)
   248-249 H 3
Skull Rock Pass ⩙ USA (UT)
   254-255 B 4
Skull Valley Indian Reservation ⟓ USA
   (UT) 254-255 C 4
Skuna River ∿ USA 268-269 L 3
Skunk River ∿ USA 274-275 F 3
Skuodas o LT 94-95 G 4
Skuratova, mys ▲ RUS 108-109 N 5
Skuratovskij o RUS 94-95 P 4
Skutvik o N 86-87 G 2
Skvyra o UA 102-103 F 3
Skwentna River ∿ USA 20-21 O 6
Skwierzyna o PL 92-93 N 2
Skye ∿ GB 90-91 D 3
Skykomish o USA (WA) 244-245 D 3
Skykomish River ∿ USA 244-245 D 3
Sky Lake Wilderness Area ⊥ USA (OR)
   244-245 C 8
Skyline Caverns ∿ USA (VA)
   280-281 H 5
Skyline Drive II USA (VA) 280-281 H 5
Skyring, Monte ▲ RCH 80 D 7
Skyring, Peninsula ∿ RCH 80 C 2
Skyriŋ, Seno ≈ 80 D 6
Slå o MA 188-189 H 4
Slade Point ▲ AUS 174-175 G 2
Slagelse o DK 86-87 E 9
Slamet, Gunung ▲ RI 168 C 3
Slancy ★ RUS 94-95 L 2
Slapout o USA (OK) 264-265 D 2
Śląsk o PL 92-93 N 3
Śląska, Nizina ∴ PL 92-93 N 3
Slate Islands ∿ CDN (ONT)
   236-237 B 4
Slater o USA (MO) 274-275 E 4
Slatina o RO 102-103 D 5
Slaton o USA (TX) 264-265 C 5
Slaughterville o USA (OK) 264-265 G 3
Slautnoe o RUS 112-113 P 5
Slave Coast ∿ 204-205 D 4
Slave Lake o CDN 30-31 M 5
Slave Point ▲ CDN 30-31 M 5
Slave River ∿ CDN 30-31 N 5
Slavgorod o RUS 124-125 L 2
Slavharad ★ BY 94-95 M 5
Slavjanka o RUS (ROS) 122-123 C 4
Slavjanka o RUS (ROS) 122-123 D 7
Slavjansk = Slovjans'k o UA
   102-103 K 3
Slavjansk-na-Kubani o RUS 102-103 L 5
Slavkoviči o RUS 94-95 L 3
Slavkov u Brna o CZ 92-93 O 4
Slavnoe o RUS 122-123 N 6
Slavonice o CZ 92-93 N 4
Slawi o RI 168 C 3
Slawno o PL 92-93 O 1
Slayton o USA (MN) 270-271 C 7
Sleeman o CDN (ONT) 234-235 J 6
Sleeper Islands ∿ CDN 36-37 N 4
Sleeping Bear Dunes National Lakeshore
   • USA (MI) 272-273 C 2
Sleeping Giant Provincial Park ⊥ CDN
   (ONT) 234-235 P 6
Sleepy Eye o USA (MN) 270-271 D 6
Sleisbeck Mine o • AUS 172-173 L 2
Sletten = Ammassivik o GRØ 28-29 S 6
Slidell o USA (LA) 268-269 L 6
Slidell o USA (TX) 264-265 G 5
Slide Mountain ▲ USA (NY)
   280-281 M 2
Slieve League ▲ IRL 90-91 C 4
Sligeach = Sligo o IRL 90-91 C 4
Sligo = Sligeach o IRL 90-91 C 4
Slim o DZ 190-191 D 3
Slim Creek o CDN (BC) 228-229 N 3
Slim River o MAL 162-163 D 3
Šlissel'burg o RUS 94-95 M 2

Slite ○ S 86-87 J 8
Sliven ○ BG 102-103 E 6
Sljeme ▲ HR 100-101 E 2
Sljudjanka ☆ RUS 116-117 L 10
Šljupočnyj, mys ▲ RUS 112-113 Q 6
Sloan ○ USA (IA) 274-275 B 2
Sloan River ~ CDN 30-31 M 2
S'loboda Bol'šaja Martynovka ○ RUS 102-103 M 4
Slobodskoj ☆ RUS 96-97 G 4
Slobozia ☆ RO 102-103 E 5
Slocan ○ CDN (BC) 230-231 M 4
Slocan Park ○ CDN (BC) 230-231 M 4
Slocan River ~ CDN 230-231 M 4
Slogen ▲ N 86-87 C 5
Slonim ○ BY 94-95 J 5
Sloping Point ▲ AUS 172-173 C 6
Slovak ○ USA (AR) 276-277 D 6
Slovakia = Slovenská Republika ■ SK 92-93 O 4
Slovenia = Slovenija ■ SLO 100-101 D 2
Slovenské rudohorie ▲ SK 92-93 P 4
Slovjans'k ○ UA 102-103 K 3
Slov'yans'k = Slovjans'k ○ UA 102-103 K 3
Słowiński Park Narodowy ⊥ PL 92-93 O 1
Složnyj, ostrov ⌒ RUS 108-109 X 3
Sluč ~ UA 102-103 E 3
Sluck ○ BY 94-95 K 5
Sluderno = Schluderns ○ I 100-101 C 1
Slunj ○ HR 100-101 E 2
Słupsk ☆• PL 92-93 O 1
Slurry ○ ZA 220-221 G 2
Smackover ○ USA (AR) 276-277 C 7
Småland ⊥ S 86-87 F 8
Smålandsstenar ○ S 86-87 F 8
Smaljany ○ BY 94-95 M 4
Small ○ USA (ID) 252-253 F 2
Small Malaita = Maramasike ⌒ SOL 184 I e 3
Small Point ▲ USA (ME) 278-279 M 5
Smalltree Lake ○ CDN 30-31 R 5
Smallwood Reservoir < CDN 36-37 R 7
Smara ○ WSA 188-189 F 7
Smarhon' ☆ BY 94-95 K 4
Smart Syndicate Dam < ZA 220-221 F 5
Smeaton ○ CDN (SAS) 232-233 O 2
Smederevo ○•• YU 100-101 H 2
Smela = Smila ○ UA 102-103 G 3
Smet, De ○ USA (SD) 260-261 J 2
Smethport ○ USA (PA) 280-281 H 2
Smidovič ○ RUS (ARH) 108-109 G 4
Smidovič ○ RUS (ROS) 122-123 E 4
Šmidta, grjada ▲ RUS 110-111 W 1
Šmidta, Mys ○ RUS 112-113 V 2
Šmidta, mys ▲ RUS 112-113 V 2
Šmidta, poluostrov ~ RUS 120-121 K 6
Smila ○ UA 102-103 G 3
Smiley ○ CDN (SAS) 232-233 J 4
Smiltene ○•• LV 94-95 J 3
Smirnenski ○ BG 102-103 E 6
Smirnyh ○ RUS 122-123 K 4
Smir-Restinga ○ MA 188-189 J 3
Smith ○ CDN 32-33 N 4
Smith, Cape ▲ CDN 36-37 K 4
Smith Arm ○ CDN 30-31 H 2
Smith Bay ≈ 20-21 N 1
Smith Bay ≈ 24-25 g 2
Smith Center ○ USA (KS) 262-263 H 5
Smithdale ○ USA (MS) 268-269 K 5
Smithers ○ CDN (BC) 228-229 G 2
Smithfield ○ USA (NC) 282-283 J 5
Smithfield ○ USA (UT) 254-255 D 2
Smithfield ○ USA (VA) 280-281 K 6
Smith Field ○ USA (WV) 280-281 F 4
Smithfield ○ ZA 220-221 H 5
Smith Inlet ≈ 230-231 B 2
Smith Island ⌒ CDN (NWT) 24-25 f 2
Smith Island ⌒ CDN (NWT) 36-37 K 4
Smith Island ⌒ IND 140-141 L 3
Smith Island ⌒ USA (MD) 280-281 K 5
Smithland ○ USA (IA) 274-275 C 2
Smithland ○ USA (TX) 264-265 K 6
Smith Mountain Lake ○ USA (VA) 280-281 G 6
Smith Peak ▲ USA (ID) 250-251 C 3
Smith Point ▲ AUS 172-173 L 1
Smith Point ○ USA (TX) 268-269 F 7
Smith River ○ USA (CA) 246-247 A 2
Smith River ~ USA 250-251 H 4
Smiths Corner ○ CDN (NB) 240-241 K 4
Smiths Falls ○ CDN (ONT) 238-239 J 4
Smiths Ferry ○ USA (ID) 252-253 B 2
Smiths Grove ○ USA (KY) 276-277 J 3
Smithton ○ AUS 180-181 H 6
Smithville ○ CDN (ONT) 238-239 F 5
Smithville ○ USA (GA) 284-285 F 5
Smithville ○ USA (OK) 264-265 K 4
Smithville ○ USA (TN) 276-277 K 5
Smithville ○ USA (TX) 266-267 K 4
Smithville ○ USA (WV) 280-281 E 4
Smithville Reservoir ○ USA (MO) 274-275 D 5
Smjadovo ○ BG 102-103 E 6
S. M. Jørgensen, Kap ▲ GRØ 28-29 Y 3
Smoke Creek Desert ⊥ USA 246-247 F 3
Smoke Hole Caverns • USA (WV) 280-281 G 4
Smoke River ~ CDN 20-21 a 2
Smokey Hill Air National Guard Range • USA (KS) 262-263 J 6
Smoking Tent ○ CDN (SAS) 232-233 Q 3
Smoky Bay ≈ 180-181 B 2
Smoky Bay ○ AUS (SA) 180-181 B 2
Smoky Cape ▲ AUS 178-179 M 6
Smoky Falls ○ CDN (ONT) 236-237 F 2
Smoky Falls ~ CDN 236-237 F 2
Smoky Hill River ~ USA 254-255 N 5
Smoky Hill River ~ USA 262-263 F 6
Smoky Hills ▲ USA (KS) 262-263 G 5
Smoky Mountains ▲ USA 252-253 D 3
Smoky River ~ CDN 228-229 P 3
Smøla ⌒ N 86-87 C 5
Smolensk ☆• RUS 94-95 N 4
Smolensko-Moskovskaja vozvyšennost' ▲ RUS 94-95 N 4
Smolevići ○ BY 94-95 L 4
Smólikas ▲ GR 100-101 H 4
Smoljan ○ BG 102-103 D 7
Smoljaninovo ○ RUS 122-123 E 7
Smoot ○ USA (WY) 252-253 H 4
Smooth Rock Falls ○ CDN (ONT) 236-237 G 3
Smoothrock Lake ○ CDN (ONT) 234-235 O 4
Smörfjöll ▲ IS 86-87 f 2
Smuts ○ CDN (SAS) 232-233 M 3
Smyer ○ USA (TX) 264-265 B 5
Smyrna ○ USA (DE) 280-281 L 4
Smyrna ○ USA (GA) 284-285 F 3
Smyrna ○ USA (OH) 280-281 E 3
Smyrna ○ USA (TN) 276-277 J 5
Smyčljaevek ○ RUS 96-97 G 7
Smyth, Canal ≈ 80 C 5
Snabai ○ RI 166-167 H 2
Snaefell ▲•• GBM 90-91 E 4
Snake and Manjang Caverns • ROK 150-151 F 11
Snake Falls ○ CDN (ONT) 234-235 K 4
Snake Indian River ~ CDN 228-229 Q 3
Snake Island ⌒ AUS 180-181 J 5
Snake River ~ CDN 20-21 Y 4
Snake River ~ USA 244-245 G 4
Snake River ~ USA 252-253 B 3
Snake River Canyon ∴ USA (WA) 244-245 H 4
Snake River Plains ~ USA 252-253 E 4
Snape Island ⌒ CDN 36-37 K 7
Snare Lake ○ CDN 30-31 M 3
Snare River ~ CDN 30-31 L 4
Snåsa ○ N 86-87 F 4
Snåsvatnet ○ N 86-87 E 4
Snead ○ USA (AL) 284-285 D 2
Sneedville ○ USA (TN) 282-283 D 4
Sneek ○• NL 92-93 H 2
Sneeuberg ▲ ZA 220-221 G 5
Snelling ○ USA (CA) 248-249 D 2
Snellman ○ USA (MN) 270-271 C 4
Snellville ○ USA (GA) 284-285 G 3
Sněžka ▲• CZ 92-93 N 3
Snežnaja ~ RUS 116-117 L 10
Snežnaja, gora ▲ KS 136-137 N 4
Snežnaja, gora ▲ RUS 112-113 N 4
Snežnoe ○ RUS 112-113 R 4
Snežnogorsk ○ RUS 108-109 W 7
Snežnogorskij ○ RUS 118-119 O 8
Śniardwy, Jezioro ○ PL 92-93 Q 2
Śnieżka ▲•• PL 92-93 N 3
Snihurivka ○ UA 102-103 H 4
Snipe Lake ○ CDN (SAS) 232-233 K 4
Snipe Lake ○ CDN 32-33 M 4
Snižne ○ UA 102-103 L 3
Snøhetta ▲ N 86-87 D 5
Snohomish ○ USA (WA) 244-245 C 3
Snønuten ▲ N 86-87 C 7
Snooks Arm ○ CDN (NFL) 242-243 N 3
Snopa ~ RUS 88-89 T 3
Snoqualmie Pass ▲ USA 244-245 D 3
Snota ▲ N 86-87 D 5
Snøtinden ▲•• N 86-87 F 3
Snøtoppen ▲ N 84-85 L 2
Snowbank River ~ CDN 24-25 c 7
Snowbird Lake ○ CDN 30-31 S 5
Snowbird Mountains ▲ USA 282-283 D 5
Snowcrest Mountain ▲ CDN (BC) 230-231 N 4
Snowden ○ CDN (SAS) 232-233 O 2
Snowdon ▲ GB 90-91 E 5
Snowdrift ○ CDN 30-31 O 4
Snowdrift River ~ CDN 30-31 P 4
Snowflake ○ CDN (MAN) 234-235 E 5
Snowflake ○ USA (AZ) 256-257 E 4
Snow Hill ○ USA (MD) 280-281 L 5
Snow Hill ○ USA (NC) 282-283 K 5
Snow Hill Island ⌒ ARK 16 G 31
Snow Lake ○ USA (AR) 276-277 D 6
Snow Mount ▲ USA (CA) 246-247 C 4
Snowshoe Peak ▲ USA (MT) 250-251 D 3
Snowtown ○ AUS 180-181 E 2
Snowville ○ USA (UT) 254-255 C 2
Snow Water Lake ○ USA (NV) 246-247 L 3
Snowy Mountains ▲ AUS 180-181 K 4
Snowy River ~ AUS 180-181 K 4
Snowy River National Park ⊥ AUS 180-181 K 4
Snug Corner ○ BS 54-55 J 3
Snuöl ○ K 158-159 J 4
Snyde Bay ≈ 36-37 T 6
Snyder ○ USA (AR) 276-277 D 7
Snyder ○ USA (NE) 262-263 K 3
Snyder ○ USA (OK) 264-265 F 4
Soabuwe ○ RI 166-167 E 3
Soacha ○ CO 60-61 D 5
Soalala ○ RM 222-223 D 6
Soamanonga ○ RM 222-223 D 9
Soån ~ PK 138-139 C 3
Soanierana-Ivongo ○ RM 222-223 F 6
Soanindrariny ○ RM 222-223 E 7
Soan River ~ PNG 183 B 4
Soap Lake ○ USA (WA) 244-245 F 3
Soa-Siu ○ RI 164-165 K 3
Soata ○ CO 60-61 E 4
Soavina ○ RM (FNS) 222-223 F 8
Soavina ○ RM (Fns) 222-223 E 8
Soavinandriana ○ RM 222-223 E 7
Sob' ○ RUS (JAN) 108-109 L 8
Sob' ~ RUS 108-109 L 8
Sob ~ UA 102-103 F 3
Soba ○ WAN 204-205 H 3
Sobaecksan National Park ⊥• ROK 150-151 G 9
Sobaek Sanmaek ▲ ROK 150-151 F 10
Sobangouma ○ RMM 202-203 J 2
Sobāt ~ SUD 206-207 L 4
Soberbio, El ○ RA 76-77 K 4
Sober Island ⌒ CDN (NS) 240-241 N 6
Sobger ~ RI 166-167 L 3
Sobinka ☆ RUS 94-95 R 4
Sobni ▲ ETH 200-201 J 5
Sobo-Katamuki Quasi National Park ⊥ J 152-153 D 8
Sobolevka, Ust'- ○ RUS 122-123 H 5
Sobolevo ☆ RUS 120-121 Q 6
Soboloh ○ RUS 110-111 Y 6
Soboloh-Majan ~ RUS 110-111 P 6
Sobopol ~ RUS 110-111 R 6
Sobor, skala • RUS 122-123 D 3
Sobo-Sise, ostrov ⌒ RUS 110-111 R 3
Sobradinho ○ BR (FED) 72-73 G 3
Sobradinho ○ BR (MAR) 68-69 G 5
Sobradinho ○ BR (RSU) 74-75 D 7
Sobradinho, Represa de < BR 68-69 G 7
Sobrado, Rio ~ BR 72-73 G 2
Sobral ○ BR (ACR) 66-67 B 7
Sobral ○ BR (CEA) 68-69 H 3
Sobtyegan ~ RUS 114-115 J 2
Socavão ○ BR 74-75 F 5
Sochaczew ○ PL 92-93 Q 2
Sochora, Rio ~ BOL 76-77 E 1
Soči ○•• RUS 126-127 C 6
Social Circle ○ USA (GA) 284-285 G 3
Society Hill ○ USA (SC) 284-285 L 2
Society Islands = Société, Îles de la ⌒ F 13 M 4
Socompa ○ RA 76-77 C 3
Socorra, Isla ⌒ MEX 50-51 C 7
Socorro ○ BR 72-73 G 7
Socorro ○ CO 60-61 E 4
Socorro ○ USA (NM) 256-257 J 4
Socorro ○ USA (TX) 266-267 A 2
Socorro, El ○ CO 60-61 F 4
Socorro do Piauí ○ BR 68-69 G 5
Socota ○ CO 60-61 E 4
Socota ○ PE 64-65 C 5
Socotra = Suquṭrā ⌒ Y 132-133 J 7
Sóc Trăng ○ VN 158-159 H 6
Sočur ~ RUS 114-115 U 5
Soda Creek ○ CDN (BC) 228-229 M 4
Soda Lake ○ USA (CA) 248-249 J 4
Soda Lake ○ USA (CA) 248-249 E 4
Sodankylä ○ FIN 88-89 J 3
Soda Springs ○ USA (ID) 252-253 G 4
Soddle Lake ○ CDN 30-31 L 4
Soddy-Daisy ○ USA (TN) 276-277 K 5
Soder, Mount ▲ AUS 176-177 M 1
Sodere ○• ETH 208-209 D 4
Söderfors ○ S 86-87 H 6
Söderhamn ○ S 86-87 H 6
Söderköping ○• S 86-87 H 7
Södertälje ☆ S 86-87 H 7
Sodiri ○ SUD 200-201 D 5
Sodium ○ ZA 220-221 F 5
Sodo ○ ETH 208-209 C 5
Södra Möckleby ○ S 86-87 H 8
Södra Vallgrund ○ FIN 88-89 F 5
Soe ○ RI 166-167 C 6
Soekmekaar ○ ZA 218-219 E 6
Soeng Sàn ○ THA 158-159 G 3
Soetendalsvlei ○ ZA 220-221 D 7
Sofala ○ MOC (Sof) 218-219 H 5
Sofala ■ MOC 218-219 H 4
Sofara ○ RMM 202-203 H 2
Sofia ~ RM 222-223 E 5
Sofia = Sofija ★••• BG 100-101 J 3
Sofija ★••• BG 100-101 J 3
Sofijsk ○ RUS (HBR) 122-123 F 2
Sofijsk ○ RUS (HBR) 122-123 H 3
Sof Omar caves • ETH 208-209 D 5
Sofporog ○ RUS 88-89 L 4
Soğā'abād ○ IR 134-135 D 2
Sogakofe ○ GH 202-203 L 6
Sogamoso ○ CO 60-61 E 5
Sogamoso, Río ~ CO 60-61 E 4
Soğanlı Çayı ~ TR 128-129 E 2
Sogda ○ RUS 122-123 E 3
Sogeram River ~ PNG 183 C 3
Sogeri ○ PNG 183 D 5
Sognal ≈ N 86-87 B 6
Søgne ☆ N 86-87 C 7
Sognefjorden ≈ 86-87 B 6
Sognesjøen ≈ 86-87 B 6
Sogod ○ RP 160-161 F 7
Sogolle ○ TCH 198-199 G 5
Sogoot ○ MAU 148-149 D 3
Sogoubéni ○ RG 202-203 F 5
Sogra ○ RUS 88-89 T 5
Sŏgüip'o ○ ROK 150-151 F 11
Söğüt ○ TR 128-129 C 4
Söğütlü Çayı ~ TR 128-129 G 3
Sog Xian ○ VRC 144-145 J 5
Soh ○ UZ 136-137 M 5
Sohagi ○ IND 142-143 B 3
Soheil ○ IR 134-135 E 2
Sohela ○ IND 142-143 C 5
Sohonto, ozero ○ RUS 108-109 O 7
Sohor, gora ▲ RUS 116-117 M 10
Sohós ○ GR 100-101 J 4
Sohŭksan Do ⌒ ROK 150-151 E 10
Soin ○ BF 202-203 J 3
Sointula ○ CDN (BC) 230-231 C 3
Soi Rap, Cửa ≈ 158-159 J 5
Sōja ○ J 152-153 E 7
Sojana ○ RUS 88-89 R 4
Sojat ○ IND 138-139 D 7
Sojda ~ RUS 88-89 O 6
Sojma ~ RUS 88-89 V 3
Sojna ○ RUS 88-89 S 3
Sŏjošon Man ≈ 150-151 E 8
Sojoton Point ▲ RP 160-161 E 8
Sojuznoe ○ KZ 126-127 O 2
Sojva ~ RUS 88-89 X 5
Sok ~ RUS 96-97 G 7
Šokaj-Datka mazar • KZ 136-137 L 3
Šokal'skogo, mys ▲ RUS 108-109 Q 5
Šokal'skogo, proliv ≈ 108-109 I d 2
Sokch'o ○ ROK 150-151 G 8
Söke ☆ TR 128-129 B 4
Sokele ○ ZRE 214-215 C 5
Sokhumi = Suchumi ☆ GE 126-127 D 6
Soko ○ CI 202-203 J 6
Soko Banja ○•• YU 100-101 H 3
Sokodé ☆ RT 202-203 L 5
Sokode Etoe ○ GH 202-203 L 6
Sokol ○ RUS 94-95 R 2
Sokol ○ RUS 122-123 K 5
Sokol ○ RUS (MAG) 120-121 O 4
Sokółka ○ PL 92-93 R 2
Sokolo ○ RMM 202-203 G 2
Sokołów Podlaski ○ PL 92-93 R 2
Sokone ○ SN 202-203 B 3
Søkongen Ø ⌒ GRØ 28-29 a 2
Sokoro, Satama- ○ CI 202-203 H 6
Sokosti ▲ FIN 88-89 K 2
Sokotindji ○ DY 204-205 E 3
Sokoto ■ WAN 204-205 F 3
Sokoto ☆ WAN (SOK) 204-205 F 2
Sokoto, River ~ WAN 204-205 F 3
Sokoura ○ RMM 202-203 J 3
Sokoura, Satama- ○ CI 202-203 H 6
Šokša ○ RUS 88-89 N 6
Sola ○ C 54-55 G 4
Sola ○ VAN 184 II a 1
Sola, Baga ○ TCH 198-199 G 6
Solan ○ IND 138-139 F 4
Solana Beach ○ USA (CA) 248-249 G 7
Solana del Pino ○ E 98-99 E 5
Solander Island ⌒ NZ 182 A 7
Solano ○ YV 66-67 D 2
Solano, Bahía ≈ 80 G 2
Solano, Punta San Francisco ▲ CO 60-61 C 4
Solāpur ○• IND 140-141 F 2
Solar Observatory • AUS 178-179 K 6
Solarte, Raudal ~ CO 66-67 B 3
Solat, Gunung ▲ RI 164-165 K 3
Solberg ○ S 86-87 H 5
Soldado Monge ○ EC 64-65 D 3
Soldatskaja Tašla ○ RUS 96-97 F 7
Soldau = Działdowo ○• PL 92-93 Q 2
Sol de Julio ○ RA 76-77 F 5
Soldier Creek ~ USA 262-263 L 5
Soldier Point ▲ AUS 172-173 K 1
Soldier Summit ○ USA (UT) 254-255 D 4
Soldotna ○ USA 20-21 P 6
Soledad ○ CO 60-61 D 2
Soledad ○ USA (CA) 248-249 C 3
Soledad ○ YV 60-61 K 3
Soledad, Isla ⌒ CO 60-61 C 6
Soledad, La ○ CO 60-61 F 5
Soledad, La ○ MEX (COA) 50-51 J 4
Soledad, La ○ MEX (DGO) 50-51 G 5
Soledad de Doblado ○ MEX 52-53 F 2
Soledad Diéz Gutiérrez ○ MEX 50-51 J 6
Soledade ○ BR (PA) 68-69 K 5
Soledade ○ BR (RSU) 74-75 D 7
Soledade, Cachoeira ~ BR 68-69 B 4
Soledar ○ UA 102-103 L 3
Sølen ▲ N 86-87 E 6
Solënaja ~ RUG 108 100 U 7
Solenoe, ozero ○ RUS 114-115 L 7
Solentiname, Archipiélago de ⌒ NIC 52-53 B 6
Solënyj ○ RUS 96-97 E 10
Solenzara ○ F 98-99 M 4
Solenzo ○ BF 202-203 H 3
Soleure = Solothurn ☆ CH 92-93 J 5
Solgara ○ AFG 136-137 K 6
Solgonskij krjaž ⊥ RUS 116-117 E 8
Solhābād ○ IR 136-137 E 7
Solhan ☆ TR 128-129 J 3
Soligalič ○ RUS 94-95 S 2
Soligorsk = Salihorsk ○ BY 94-95 K 5
Solikamsk ☆ RUS 114-115 D 5
Sol'-Ileck ☆ RUS 96-97 J 8
Solimões, Rio ~ BR 66-67 F 4
Solingen ○ D 92-93 J 3
Solita ○ CO 64-65 E 1
Solitaire ○ NAM 220-221 C 1
Soljanka ☆ KZ 96-97 G 8
Soljanka ○ RUS (SAH) 118-119 K 5
Soljanka ○ RUS (SAR) 96-97 G 8
Solleftea ○ S 86-87 H 5
Sóller ○ E 98-99 J 5
Solna ○ BF 202-203 L 3
Solnečnogorsk ☆ RUS 94-95 P 3
Solnečnyj ○ RUS (SAH) 120-121 G 3
Solnečnyj ☆ RUS (HBR) 122-123 G 3
Solo ○ RI 164-165 G 6
Solodniki ○ RUS 96-97 D 9
Šolohovskij ○ RUS 102-103 M 3
Solok ○• RI 162-163 D 5
Sololá ☆ GCA 52-53 J 4
Sololo ○ EAK 212-213 G 2
Soloma ○ GCA 52-53 J 4
Solomon ○ USA (AZ) 256-257 F 6
Solomon ○ USA (KS) 262-263 J 6
Solomon Islands ⌒ 184 I b 2
Solomon Islands ■ SOL 184 I c 2
Solomon River ~ USA 262-263 H 5
Solomons ○ USA (MD) 280-281 K 5
Solomon Sea ≈ 183 E 4
Solon ○ VRC 150-151 C 4
Soloncy ○ RUS (HBR) 122-123 J 2
Soloncy ○ RUS (IRK) 116-117 J 8
Solonešnoe ○ RUS 124-125 O 3
Solongotyn davaa ▲ MAU 148-149 D 3
Solonópole ○ BR 68-69 J 4
Solon Springs ○ USA (WI) 270-271 G 4
Solor, Kepulauan ⌒ RI 166-167 B 6
Solor, Pulau ⌒ RI 162-163 G 2
Solor, Pulau ⌒ RI (NTI) 166-167 B 6
Solothurn ☆•• CH 92-93 J 5
Solovecki ○ RUS 88-89 N 4
Soloveckie ostrova ⌒••• RUS 88-89 N 4
Solov'ëvsk ○ RUS (AMR) 118-119 M 9
Solov'ëvsk ○ RUS (CTN) 118-119 G 11
Solsgirth ○ CDN (MAN) 234-235 C 4
Solsona ○• E 98-99 H 4
Solsona ○ RP 160-161 D 3
Solsqua ○ CDN (BC) 230-231 K 3
Soltānābād ○ IR 136-137 F 6
Soltān Bakvā ○ AFG 134-135 K 2
Soltane, Bir ○ TN 190-191 G 4
Soltāniye ○• IR 128-129 N 4
Soltau ○ D 92-93 K 2
Soltau, tau ▲ KZ 126-127 K 5
Soltanah, ozero ○ RUS 110-111 Y 4
Solusi ○ ZW 218-219 E 5
Solvang ○• USA (CA) 248-249 D 5
Sölvesborg ☆ S 86-87 G 8
Solway ○ USA (MN) 270-271 C 3
Solway Firth ○ GB 90-91 F 4
Solwezi ☆ Z 214-215 D 7
Sol'zavod ○ RUS 116-117 K 5
Sōma ○ J 152-153 J 6
Soma ☆ TR 128-129 B 3
Somabhula ○ ZW 218-219 E 4
Somadougou ○ RMM 202-203 H 2
Somalia = Soomaaliya ■ SP 212-213 J 2
Somali Basin ▲ 12 D 4
Somalomo ○ CAM 210-211 D 2
Sombo ○ ANG (LUS) 216-217 F 4
Sombo ~ ANG 216-217 F 4
Sombor ○• YU 100-101 G 2
Sombrerete ○ MEX 50-51 H 6
Sombrero ⌒ KAN 56 D 2
Sombrero ○ RCH 80 F 6
Sombrero, El ○ RA 80 F 2
Sombrero, El ○ YV 60-61 H 3
Sombrero Channel ≈ 140-141 L 6
Sombrio, Lagoa ○ BR 74-75 F 7
Som Det ○ THA 158-159 G 2
Somerdale ○ USA (NJ) 280-281 M 4
Somerdale ○ USA (NJ) 280-281 L 4
Somero ○ FIN 88-89 G 6
Somers ○ USA (MT) 250-251 E 3
Somerset ○ AUS 174-175 G 2
Somerset ○ CDN (MAN) 234-235 E 5
Somerset ○ USA (CA) 246-247 E 5
Somerset ○ USA (CO) 254-255 H 5
Somerset ○ USA (KY) 276-277 L 3
Somerset ○ USA (MI) 272-273 E 5
Somerset ○ USA (OH) 280-281 D 4
Somerset ○ USA (PA) 280-281 G 3
Somerset Aboriginal Land ⚔ AUS 174-175 G 2
Somerset East = Somerset-Oos ○• ZA 220-221 G 6
Somerset Island ⌒ CDN 24-25 Z 4
Somerset-Oos ○• ZA 220-221 G 6
Somersetwes ○ ZA 220-221 D 7
Somersville ○ USA (OH) 280-281 C 3
Somerville ○ USA (PA) 280-281 M 3
Somerville ○ USA (TN) 276-277 F 5
Somerville ○ USA (TX) 266-267 L 3
Somerville Lake < USA (TX) 266-267 L 3
Somes Bar ○ USA (CA) 246-247 B 2
Somil ○ ANG 216-217 F 7
Somme ~ F 90-91 H 6
Sommen ○ S 86-87 G 7
Sommerberry ○ CDN (SAS) 232-233 P 5
Sommerton ○ USA (AZ) 256-257 A 6
Somnia ⌒ N 86-87 F 4
Somnenija, buhta ≈ 112-113 O 6
Somnja ~ RUS 122-123 H 2
Somokoro ○ CI 202-203 H 5
Somosomo ○ FJI 184 III c 2
Somosomo Strait ≈ 184 III b 2
Somotillo ○ NIC 52-53 L 5
Somoto ☆ NIC 52-53 L 5
Sompeta ○ IND 142-143 D 6
Som Poi ○ THA 158-159 G 3
Somra ○ MYA 142-143 J 3
Son ~ IND 142-143 D 3
Soná ○ PA 52-53 D 7
Sonaco ○ GNB 202-203 C 3
Sonaimur ○ BD 142-143 G 4
Sonanga ○ RMM 202-203 G 3
Sonapur ○ IND (ASS) 142-143 G 2
Sonapur ○ IND (ORI) 142-143 C 5
Sonār ~ IND 138-139 G 7
Sonbong ○ KOR 150-151 H 6
Sonchon ○ KOR 150-151 E 8
Soncillo ○ E 98-99 F 3
Sondagrivier ~ ZA 220-221 G 6
Sønderborg ○ DK 86-87 D 9
Sondershausen ○ D 92-93 L 3
So'n Đọng ☆ VN 156-157 F 6
Sondre Isortoq ≈ 28-29 O 4
Søndrestrømfjord = Kangerlussuaq ○ GRØ 28-29 P 3
Søndre Upernavik = Upernavik Kujalleq ○ GRØ 26-27 X 7
Sondrio ☆ I 100-101 B 1
Sondu ○ EAK 212-213 E 4
Sonepat ○ IND 138-139 F 5
Song ○ MAL 162-163 K 3
Song ○ WAN 204-205 K 4
Songa ○ RI 164-165 K 4
Songa ○ ZRE 214-215 C 5
Songaw Lagoon ○ GH 202-203 L 7
Sông Ba ~ VN 158-159 K 4
Sông Câu ○ VN 158-159 K 4
Sông Cô Chiên ~ VN 158-159 J 5
Sông Cua Dai ~ VN 158-159 J 5
Sông Đa ~ VN 156-157 D 6
Sông Đồng Nai ~ VN 158-159 J 5
Songea ☆ EAT 214-215 H 6
Songgato ~ RI 166-167 L 3
Sông Hâu ~ VN 158-159 H 5
Sông Hồng ~ VN 156-157 D 5
Songhua Hu ○ VRC (JIL) 150-151 F 6
Songhua Hu • VRC (JIL) 150-151 F 6
Songhua Jiang ~ VRC 150-151 E 5
Songino = Cavdan ○ MAU 148-149 C 3
Songir ○ IND 138-139 E 9
Songjiang ○ VRC (JIL) 150-151 G 6
Songjiang ○ VRC (SGH) 154-155 M 6
Songkhla ☆ THA 158-159 F 7
Songkou ○ VRC 156-157 L 4
Song Ling ▲ VRC 154-155 L 1
Sông Lũy ○ VN 158-159 K 5
Songming ○ VRC 156-157 C 4
Songnam ○ ROK 150-151 F 9
Songnim ○ KOR 150-151 E 8
Songnisan National Park ⊥• ROK 150-151 F 9
Songo ○ ANG 216-217 C 3
Songo ○ MOC 218-219 G 2
Songo ○ SUD 206-207 G 4
Songololo ○ ZRE 210-211 E 6
Songo Mnara ∴•• EAT 214-215 K 5
Songpan ○ VRC 154-155 C 5
Song Phinong ○ THA 158-159 E 3
Songsang ○ IND 142-143 H 3
Songsha ○ VRC 144-145 C 5
Song Shan ▲ VRC 154-155 H 4
Songshang • VRC 154-155 H 4
Songshan Z.B. ⊥ • VRC 154-155 J 1
Sông Tiền ~ VN 158-159 H 5
Songwe ~ EAT 214-215 G 5
Song Xian ○ VRC 154-155 H 4
Songyang ○ VRC 156-157 L 2
Songyu Cave • ROK 150-151 G 9
Songzi ○ VRC 154-155 G 6
So'n Hiệp ○ VN 158-159 K 5
Sonid Youqi ○ VRC 148-149 L 6
Sonid Zuoqi ○ VRC 148-149 L 6
Soniquera, Cerro ▲ BOL 76-77 D 2
Sonitė, Bol'šaja ~ RUS 108-109 Z 6
Sonjo ○ EAT 212-213 E 5
Sonjol, Gunung ▲ RI 164-165 G 3
Sonkwale Mountains ▲ WAN 204-205 H 5
So'n La ☆ VN 156-157 C 6
Son Mbong ○ CAM 210-211 C 2
Sonmiāni Bay ≈ 134-135 M 6
Sonneberg ○ D 92-93 L 3
Sonningdale ○ CDN (SAS) 232-233 L 3
Sono, Rio do ~ BR 68-69 E 6
Sono, Rio do ~ BR 72-73 H 4
Sonoita ○ USA (AZ) 256-257 E 7
Sonoma ○ USA (CA) 246-247 C 5
Sonoma Range ▲ USA 246-247 H 3
Sonora ○ MEX 50-51 B 1
Sonora ■ MEX 50-51 D 3
Sonora ○ USA (CA) 248-249 D 2
Sonora ○ USA (TX) 266-267 G 3
Sonora, Río ~ MEX 50-51 D 3
Sonora Island ⌒ CDN (BC) 230-231 D 3
Sonora Junction ○ USA (CA) 246-247 F 5
Sonoran Desert ⊥ USA 248-249 K 6
Sonoumon ○ DY 204-205 E 4
Sonoyta ○ MEX 50-51 C 2
Sonqor ○ IR 134-135 B 1
Sonskij ○ RUS 116-117 E 8
Sonsón ○ CO 60-61 D 5
Sonsonate ☆ ES 52-53 K 5
Sonstraal ○ ZA 220-221 F 3
Sonta ○ ZRE 214-215 E 6
So'n Tây, Thị Xã ☆ VN 156-157 D 6
Sooke ○ CDN (BC) 230-231 F 5
Sooner Lake ○ USA (OK) 264-265 G 2
Soos, Tanjung ▲ RI 166-167 E 2
Sooyac ○ SP 212-213 J 3
Sopachuy ○ BOL 70-71 E 6
Sopau ○ PNG 183 G 2
Sopčaju ~ RUS 108-109 K 7
Sopchoppi ○ USA (FL) 286-287 E 1
Soperton ○ USA (GA) 284-285 H 4
Soperton ○ USA (WI) 270-271 K 5
Sŏp Hao ○ LAO 156-157 D 6
Sop Huai ○ THA 142-143 L 6
Sopi ○ RI 164-165 L 2
Sopi, Tanjung ▲ RI 164-165 L 2
Sopinusa ○ RI 166-167 G 3
Sop Moei ○ THA 158-159 D 2
Sopo ~ SUD 206-207 H 4
Sopočnaja ~ RUS 120-121 Q 5
Sopore ○ IND 138-139 E 2
Sopot ○•• PL 92-93 P 1
Sop Prap ○ THA 158-159 E 2
Sopron ○•• H 92-93 O 5
Sop's Arm ○ CDN (NFL) 242-243 M 3
Sopsoum ○ LAO 156-157 D 6
Soquee River ~ USA 284-285 G 2
Sôr, Ribeira de ~ P 98-99 D 5
Sora ○ I 100-101 D 4
Sora, Río de ~ RA 76-77 E 2
Sorab ○ IND 140-141 F 3
Soracaba, Rio ~ BR 72-73 G 7
Sorāh ○ PK 138-139 B 6
Sŏraksan ▲ ROK 150-151 G 8
Sŏraksan National Park ⊥• ROK 150-151 G 8
Sora Mboum ○ CAM 206-207 B 5
Sorapa ○ PE 70-71 C 5
Soras, Río ~ PE 64-65 F 9
Sorata ○ BOL 70-71 C 4
Sŏrath ~ IND 138-139 B 9
Sorati-gawa ~ J 152-153 K 3
Sorau ○ WAN 204-205 K 4
Søraust-spitsbergen nat-res ⊥ N 84-85 M 3
Sorbas ○ E 98-99 F 6
Sore ○ F 90-91 G 9
Sorel ○ CDN (QUE) 238-239 M 2
Sorell-Midway Point ○ AUS 180-181 J 7
Sorere ○ EAU 212-213 D 3
Sør-Flatanger ○ N 86-87 E 4
Sorfta ○ ETH 208-209 D 5
Sorgun ☆ TR 128-129 F 3
Sorḥ, Kōtal-e ▲ AFG 134-135 L 1
Sorḥ, Kūh-e ▲ IR 134-135 F 2
Sorḥ, Kūh-e ▲ IR 136-137 E 7
Sorḥ-ŏ-Pārsā ○ AFG 138-139 B 2
Sori ○ DY 204-205 E 3
Soria ○• E 98-99 F 4
Sorido ○ RI 166-167 J 2
Sorkam ○ RI 162-163 C 3
Sørkapp ▲ N 26-27 v 8
Sørkapp Land ⊥ N 84-85 K 4
Sørkappøya ⌒ N 84-85 K 4
Sørli ○ N 86-87 F 4
Sormiento, Canal ≈ 80 C 5
Soro ○ IND 142-143 E 5
Soro ○ PK 134-135 M 3
Soro = Bahr el Ghazal ~ TCH 198-199 H 5
Soroa, Maïné- ○ RN 198-199 F 6
Sorobango ○ CI 202-203 J 5
Soroca ☆ MD 102-103 F 3
Sorocaba ○ BR 72-73 G 7
Soročinsk ☆ RUS 96-97 H 7
Soroki = Soroca ☆ MD 102-103 F 3
Sorokino ○ RUS 94-95 L 3
Sorokskaja guba ≈ 88-89 N 4
Sorombéo ○ CAM 206-207 B 4
Sorondideri ○ RI 166-167 H 2
Sorong ○ RI 166-167 F 2
Sororó, Rio ~ BR 68-69 D 4
Soroti ○ EAU 212-213 D 3
Sørøya ⌒ N 86-87 L 1
Sørøysundet ≈ 86-87 L 1
Sorraia, Rio ~ P 98-99 C 5
Sorrento ○ CDN (BC) 230-231 K 3
Sorrento ○• I 100-101 E 4
Sorrento ○ USA (LA) 268-269 K 6
Sorriso ○ BR 70-71 K 3
Sør-Rondane ▲ ARK 16 F 3
Sorsele ○ S 86-87 H 4
Sorsk ○ RUS 116-117 E 8
Sorsogon ☆ RP 160-161 E 6
Sørspitsbergen nasjonalpark ⊥ N 84-85 J 4
Sørstraumen ○ N 86-87 K 2
Sort ○ E 98-99 H 3
Šortandy ☆ KZ 124-125 G 3
Sortavala ○ RUS 88-89 L 6
Sortebræ ⊏ GRØ 28-29 b 2
Sortehest ▲ GRØ 26-27 l 7
Sortija, La ○ RA 78-79 J 5
Sortland ○ N 86-87 G 2
Sorūbi ○ AFG 138-139 B 3
Sorūd, Rūdḫāne-ye ~ IR 136-137 B 7
Sorum ~ RUS 114-115 K 2
Sørvær ○ N 86-87 F 3
Sørvågen ○ N 86-87 F 3
Sørvágur ○ FR 90-91 D 1
Sorvenok ○ KZ 124-125 P 4
Sørvika ○ N 86-87 E 5
Sŏsan ○ ROK 150-151 F 9
Sŏsan Haean National Park ⊥• ROK 150-151 E 9
Soscumica, Lac ○ CDN (QUE) 236-237 L 2
Soskie jary ▲ RUS 96-97 G 7
Sosneado, El ○ RA 78-79 E 3
Sosnogorsk ○ RUS 88-89 W 5
Sosnove ○ UA 102-103 E 2
Sosnovec, ostrov ⌒ RUS 88-89 Q 3
Sosnovka ○ RUS (BUR) 118-119 D 8
Sosnovka ○ RUS (KIR) 96-97 G 5
Sosnovka ○ RUS (MUR) 88-89 Q 3
Sosnovo-Ozërskoe ☆ RUS 118-119 E 9
Sosnovyj ○ RUS 88-89 M 3
Sosnovyj Bor ○ RUS (HMN) 114-115 Q 4
Sosnovyj Bor ○ RUS (LEN) 94-95 L 2
Sosnowiec ○ PL 92-93 P 3
Soso Bay ≈ 184 III b 3
Sosogoh ○ MAL 160-161 B 10
Sosok ○ RI 162-163 J 4
Sosso ○ RCA 210-211 E 2
Sosso, Cascades de ~• DY 204-205 E 3
Sossusvlei ○• NAM 220-221 B 2
Šostka ○ UA 102-103 H 2
Sosúa ○• DOM 54-55 K 5
Sos'va ☆ RUS (SVR) 114-115 F 5
Sos'va ~ RUS 114-115 G 5
Sot' ~ RUS 94-95 R 2
Sota ~ DY 204-205 E 3
Sotará, Volcán ▲ CO 60-61 C 6
Sotavento, Ilhas de ⌒ CV 202-203 B 6
Sotério, Rio ~ BR 70-71 E 2
Sotian ○ RMM 202-203 G 4
Sotik ○ EAK 212-213 E 4
Sotkamo ○ FIN 88-89 K 4
Soto ○ RA 76-77 E 6
Soto, De ○ USA (MO) 274-275 H 6
Soto, De ○ USA (WI) 274-275 G 1
Soto, Isla ⌒ PE 70-71 C 4
Soto la Marina ○ MEX 50-51 K 6
Sotomayo, Quebrada ~ BOL 76-77 D 1
Sotomayor = Los Andes ○ CO 64-65 D 1
Šotorḫūn, Kōtal-e ▲ AFG 134-135 L 1
Sotouboua ○ RT 202-203 L 5
Sotuta ○ MEX 52-53 K 1
Souanké ○ RCB 210-211 E 2
Soubakaniédougou ○ BF 202-203 H 4
Soubakpérou ▲ DY 204-205 E 4
Soubala ○ RMM 202-203 C 4
Soubané ○ RG 202-203 C 4
Soubéira ○ BF 202-203 K 3
Soubré ☆ CI 202-203 G 7
Soudan ○ AUS 174-175 D 7
Soudan Bank ≃ 224 D 6
Soudougui ○ BF 202-203 L 4
Souellaba, Pointe de ▲ CAM 210-211 B 2
Souf ⊥ DZ 190-191 F 4
Souf, Oued ~ DZ 190-191 D 7
Soufa, Passe de ▲ RIM 196-197 E 7
Soufflets River ~ CDN 242-243 M 2
Soufrière ☆ WL 56 E 5
Soufrière ▲ WV 56 E 5
Soufrière, La ▲ F 56 E 3
Sougueur ○ DZ 190-191 C 3
Souillac ○ MS 224 C 7
Souk Ahras ☆ DZ 190-191 F 2
Souk-el-Arab-des-Beni-Hassan ○ MA 188-189 J 3
Souk-el-Arab-du-Rharb ○ MA 188-189 H 3
Souk-el-Kella ○ MA 188-189 J 3
Souk-Jemaâ-des-Oulad-Abbou ○ MA 188-189 H 4
Soukoukoutane ○ RN 204-205 E 1
Souk-Tleta-des-Akhasass ○ MA 188-189 G 6
Sŏul ★ ROK 150-151 F 9
Soulabali ○ SN 202-203 C 3
Soulis Pond ○ CDN (NFL) 242-243 O 4
Šouma'e Sarā ○ IR 128-129 N 4
Soummam, Oued ~ DZ 190-191 E 2
Sounders River ~ CDN 36-37 L 2
Sound Hill Cove ≈ 38-39 Q 2
Sounding Creek ~ CDN 232-233 H 4
Sounding Lake ○ CDN (ALB) 232-233 H 3
Sounga ○ G 210-211 B 5
Soungrougrou ~ SN 202-203 C 3
Sources, Mont aux ▲•• LS 220-221 J 4
Souris ○ CDN (MAN) 234-235 C 5
Souris ○ CDN (PEI) 240-241 N 4
Souris ○ USA (ND) 258-259 G 3
Souris River ~ CDN 232-233 P 6
Souris River ~ CDN 234-235 C 5
Souris River ~ USA 258-259 F 3
Sour Lake ○ USA (TX) 268-269 F 6
Sourou ~ RMM 202-203 J 3
Souroukaha ○ CI 202-203 H 5
Sous, Oued ~ MA 188-189 G 5
Sousa ○ BR 68-69 J 5
Sousel ○ P 98-99 D 5

Slite — Sousel 395

Sousse ☆••• TN 190-191 H 3
Souterraine, la o F 90-91 H 8
South = Sud ■ CAM 210-211 C 2
South, Tanjung ▲ RI 164-165 D 6
South Africa = Suid-Afrika ■ ZA 220-221 E 5
South Alligator River ~ AUS 172-173 L 2
Southampton o CDN (NS) 240-241 L 5
Southampton o CDN (ONT) 238-239 D 4
Southampton o• GB 90-91 G 6
Southampton o USA (NY) 280-281 O 3
Southampton Island ⌒ CDN 36-37 G 2
South Andaman ⌒ IND 140-141 L 4
South Andros Island ⌒ BS 54-55 G 3
South Aulatsivik Island ⌒ CDN 36-37 T 6
South Australia ■ AUS 178-179 C 4
South Australia Basin ≃ 13 D 6
Southaven o USA (MS) 268-269 L 2
South Baldy ▲ USA (NM) 256-257 H 4
South Banda Basin ≃ 166-167 D 5
Southbank o CDN (BC) 228-229 J 2
South Baranof Island Wilderness ⊥ USA 32-33 C 3
South Bay ≈ 36-37 H 2
South Bay o CDN (ONT) 234-235 L 3
South Baymouth o CDN (ONT) 238-239 C 3
South Beloit o USA (IL) 274-275 J 2
South Bend o USA (IN) 274-275 M 3
South Bend o USA (TX) 264-265 F 5
South Bend o USA (WA) 244-245 B 4
South Bentinck Arm ~ CDN 228-229 H 4
South Bimini ⌒ BS 54-55 F 2
South-Bolton o CDN (QUE) 238-239 N 3
South Boston o USA (VA) 280-281 H 7
South Branch o CDN (NFL) 242-243 J 5
South Branch Potomac River ~ USA 280-281 H 4
South Brook o CDN (NFL) 242-243 M 3
South Brook ~ CDN 242-243 M 3
South Brookfield o CDN (NS) 240-241 L 6
South Buganda ■ EAU 212-213 C 4
South Caicos ⌒ GB 54-55 K 4
South Cape ▲ CDN 24-25 d 2
South Cape ▲ USA 22-23 T 5
South Cape Seamount ≃ 288 K 6
South Carolina ■ USA 284-285 J 2
South Charleston o USA (OH) 280-281 C 4
South Charleston o USA (WV) 280-281 E 5
South China o USA (ME) 278-279 M 4
South China Basin ≃ 160-161 A 5
South China Sea ≈ 10-11 L 7
South Coast Range ▲ AUS 180-181 K 4
South Cooking Lake o CDN (ALB) 232-233 E 2
South Cove o USA (AZ) 256-257 A 2
South Dakota ■ USA 260-261 E 1
South East ■ RB 220-221 G 2
South East Aru Marine Reserve ⊥• RI 166-167 H 5
South East Bight o CDN (NFL) 242-243 O 5
South East Cape ▲ AUS 180-181 J 7
Southeast Cape ▲ USA 20-21 F 5
Southeast Indian Ridge ≃ 12 F 8
South East Islands ⌒ AUS 176-177 G 7
South East Point ▲ AUS 180-181 J 5
Southeast Point ▲ BS 54-55 J 4
South End ▲ AUS 172-173 B 6
Southend o CDN 34-35 E 2
Southend-on-Sea o GB 90-91 H 6
Southern ■ EAU 212-213 C 4
Southern ■ MW 218-219 H 2
Southern ■ RB 220-221 F 2
Southern ■ Z 218-219 C 3
Southern Alps ▲ NZ 182 B 6
Southern Cross o AUS 176-177 E 5
Southern Cross Club o GB 54-55 E 5
Southern Harbour o CDN (NFL) 242-243 P 5
Southern Indian Lake o CDN 34-35 G 2
Southern Kashiji ~ Z 218-219 B 2
Southern Long Cays ⌒ BH 52-53 K 3
Southern Lueti ~ Z 218-219 B 2
Southern National Park ⊥ SUD 206-207 J 5
Southern Pines o USA (NC) 282-283 H 5
Southern Region ■ SUD 206-207 H 5
Southern Uplands ▲ GB 90-91 E 4
Southern Ute Indian Reservation ✕ USA (CO) 254-255 H 6
Southesk River ~ CDN 228-229 R 4
Southesk Tablelands ▲ AUS 172-173 H 6
Southey o CDN (SAS) 232-233 O 5
South Fabius River ~ USA 274-275 F 4
South Fiji Basin ≃ 13 J 5
South Fork o CDN (SAS) 232-233 K 6
South Fork o USA (CO) 254-255 J 6
South Fork ~ USA 276-277 F 5
South Fork ~ USA 276-277 G 4
South Fork ~ USA 280-281 E 7
South Fork Cumberland River ~ USA 282-283 C 4
South Fork John Day River ~ USA 244-245 F 6
South Fork Koyukuk ~ USA 20-21 P 3
South Fork Kuskokwim River ~ USA 20-21 N 5
South Fork Licking River ~ USA 276-277 L 2
South Fork Owyhee River ~ USA 252-253 B 4
South Fork Republican River ~ USA 254-255 N 4
South Fork River ~ USA 280-281 E 4
South Fork Salmon River ~ USA 252-253 C 2
South Fork Salt River ~ USA 274-275 G 5
South Fork Shenandoah River ~ USA 280-281 H 5
South Fork Solomon River ~ USA 262-263 F 5
South Fork Trinity River ~ USA 246-247 B 3
South Fork White River ~ USA 260-261 E 3
South Galway o AUS 178-179 G 3
Southgate River ~ CDN 230-231 E 3
South Georgia ⌒ GB 78-79 O 7
South Grand River ~ USA 274-275 D 6
South Gut Saint Ann's o CDN (NS) 240-241 P 4
South Harbour o CDN (NS) 240-241 P 4
South Haven o USA (KS) 262-263 J 7
South Haven o USA (MI) 272-273 C 5
South Head o AUS 174-175 G 6
South Heart o USA (ND) 258-259 E 5
South Heart River ~ CDN 32-33 M 4
South Henik Lake o CDN 30-31 V 5
South Hill o USA (VA) 280-281 H 7
South Horr o EAK 212-213 F 2
South Indian Lake o CDN 34-35 G 2
South Island ⌒ EAK 212-213 F 2
South Island ⌒ NZ 182 B 5
South Junction o CDN (MAN) 234-235 H 5
South Junction o USA (OR) 244-245 D 6
South Kitui National Reserve ⊥ EAK 212-213 G 4
South Knife River ~ CDN 30-31 V 6
South Korea = Taehan-Min'guk ■ ROK 150-151 G 9
South Lake Tahoe o USA (CA) 246-247 F 5
Southland o USA (TX) 264-265 C 5
South Loup River ~ USA 262-263 G 3
South Luangwa National Park ⊥•• Z 214-215 F 7
South Luconia Shoals ≃ 162-163 K 2
South Lyon o USA (MI) 272-273 F 5
South Male Atoll ⌒ MV 140-141 B 6
South Malosmadulu Atoll ⌒ MV 140-141 B 5
South Milford o CDN (NS) 240-241 K 6
South Milwaukee o USA (WI) 274-275 L 2
South Moresby Gwaii Haanas National Park Reserve ⊥ CDN (BC) 228-229 C 4
South Moresby Gwaii Haanas National Provincial Reserve ⊥•• CDN (BC) 228-229 C 4
South Moresby National Park Reserve ⊥•• CDN (BC) 228-229 C 4
South Mountain o CDN (ONT) 238-239 K 4
South Mountain ▲ USA (ID) 252-253 B 4
South Nahanni River ~ CDN 30-31 E 4
South Nation River ~ CDN 238-239 K 3
South Negril Point ▲ JA 54-55 F 5
South Nilandu Atoll ⌒ MV 140-141 B 6
South Ogden o USA (UT) 254-255 D 2
South Orkneys ▲ GB 16 G 32
South Ossetia = Jugo-Osetinskaja Avtonomnaja Respublika ■ GE 126-127 F 6
South Pacific Ocean ≈ 14-15 N 11
South Pare Mountains ▲ EAT 212-213 F 6
South Paris o USA (ME) 278-279 L 4
South Pass ▲ USA (CA) 248-249 K 5
South Pass ▲ USA (WY) 252-253 K 4
South Pass City o USA (WY) 252-253 K 4
South Pease River ~ USA 264-265 D 5
South Pender o CDN (BC) 230-231 F 5
South Peron Island ⌒ AUS 172-173 K 2
South Pittsburg o USA (TN) 276-277 K 5
South Plains o USA (TX) 264-265 C 4
South Platte River ~ USA 254-255 M 3
South Point ▲ BS 54-55 H 3
South Pole ARK 16 E 0
South Porcupine o CDN (ONT) 236-237 G 4
Southport o AUS (QLD) 178-179 M 4
Southport o AUS (TAS) 180-181 J 7
Southport o CDN (NFL) 242-243 P 4
Southport o• GB 90-91 F 5
Southport o USA (FL) 286-287 D 1
Southport o USA (NC) 282-283 J 7
South Prince of Wales Wilderness ⊥• USA 32-33 D 4
South Racoon River ~ USA 274-275 D 3
South Redstone River ~ CDN 30-31 F 4
South River o CDN (ONT) 238-239 F 3
South River ~ CDN 238-239 F 3
South River ~ USA 282-283 J 6
South Rukuru ~ MW 214-215 G 6
South Sandwich Trench ≃ 6-7 G 14
South Saskatchewan River ~ CDN 232-233 L 4
South Seal River ~ CDN 34-35 G 2
South Shetlands ▲ GB 16 G 30
South Shields o GB 90-91 G 4
South Shore o USA (KY) 276-277 N 2
South Shore o USA (SD) 260-261 K 1
South Sioux City o USA (NE) 262-263 K 2
South Six City o USA (IA) 274-275 B 2
South Slocan o CDN (BC) 230-231 M 4
South Solitary Island ⌒ AUS 178-179 M 6
South Spicer Island ⌒ CDN 24-25 h 6
South Stradbroke Island ⌒ AUS 178-179 M 4
South Sulphur River ~ USA 264-265 J 5
South Sunday Creek ~ USA 250-251 N 5
South Taranaki Bight ≈ 182 E 4
South Tasman Rise ≃ 13 F 7
South Tetagouche o CDN (NB) 240-241 K 3
South Teton Wilderness Area ⊥ USA (WY) 252-253 H 3
South Thompson River ~ CDN 230-231 K 3
South Tucson o USA (AZ) 256-257 E 6
South Turkana National Reservoir ⊥ EAK 212-213 E 3
South Tweedsmuir Island ⌒ CDN 28-29 C 2
South Twin Island ⌒ CDN 38-39 E 2
South Twin Lake o CDN (NFL) 242-243 N 3
South Uist ⌒ GB 90-91 D 3
South Wellesley Islands ⌒ AUS 174-175 E 5
South-West = Sud Ouest ■ CAM 204-205 H 6
South West Cape ▲ AUS 180-181 J 7
Southwest Cape ▲ NZ 182 A 7
South Western Highway II AUS 176-177 C 6
Southwest Gander River ~ CDN 242-243 N 4
South West Harbor o USA (ME) 278-279 N 4
Southwest Indian Ridge ≃ 12 B 9
South West Island ⌒ AUS 174-175 K 5
Southwest Miramichi River ~ CDN 240-241 J 4
South West National Park ⊥ AUS 180-181 J 7
Southwest Pacific Basin ≃ 14-15 N 11
Southwest Passage ≈ 268-269 H 7
Southwest Point ▲ BS 54-55 J 4
Southwest Point ▲ BS 54-55 H 3
Southwest Point ▲ BS 54-55 G 2
South West Rocks o AUS 178-179 M 6
Southworth o USA (WA) 244-245 C 3
Souto Soares o BR 72-73 K 2
Soutpan o ZA 220-221 H 4
Soutpansberg ▲ ZA 218-219 E 6
Soutpansnek ▲ ZA 220-221 G 6
Soutrivier ~ ZA 220-221 D 5
Soutrivier ~ ZA 220-221 E 4
Soverato o I 100-101 F 5
Sovereign o CDN (SAS) 232-233 L 4
Sovereign Hill • AUS 180-181 G 4
Sovetabad o UZ 136-137 N 4
Sovetašen = Nubarašen o AR 128-129 L 2
Sovetsk o RUS (KIR) 96-97 F 5
Sovetsk o• RUS (RF) 94-95 G 4
Sovetskaja o RUS (KRA) 126-127 D 5
Sovetskaja o RUS (STA) 126-127 F 6
Sovetskaja gora ▲ RUS 112-113 V 1
Sovetskaja Gavan' o RUS 122-123 J 4
Sovetskij o RUS (MAR) 96-97 F 5
Sovetskij ☆ RUS (HMN) 114-115 G 4
Sovetskoe, ozero o RUS 108-109 U 8
Sovhoz, Bol'šereckij o RUS 122-123 R 2
Sovpol'e o RUS 88-89 S 4
Sowa Pan o RB 218-219 C 5
Soweto o ZA 220-221 H 3
Soy o EAK 212-213 E 3
Sōya-kaikyō ≈ 152-153 J 2
Soyaló o MEX 52-53 H 3
Sōya-misaki ▲ J 152-153 J 2
Soyo o ANG 216-217 B 3
Sož ~ BY 94-95 M 5
Sozak o KZ 124-125 F 6
Sozva ~ RUS 88-89 W 3
Spa o• B 92-93 H 3
Spade o USA (TX) 264-265 B 5
Spafar'eva, ostrov ⌒ RUS 120-121 N 4
Spain = España ■ E 98-99 D 4
Spalding o AUS 180-181 E 2
Spalding o CDN (SAS) 232-233 O 3
Spalding o USA (NE) 262-263 H 3
Spaldings o JA 54-55 G 5
Spanberga, proliv ≈ 122-123 M 7
Spanda, Akra ▲ GR 100-101 J 7
Spangle o USA (WA) 244-245 H 3
Spaniard's Bay o CDN (NFL) 242-243 P 5
Spanish o CDN (ONT) 238-239 C 2
Spanish Fork o USA (UT) 254-255 D 3
Spanish Peak ▲ USA (OR) 244-245 F 6
Spanish Point ▲ AG 56 E 3
Spanish River ~ CDN 238-239 D 2
Spanish River Indian Reserve ✕ CDN (ONT) 238-239 C 2
Spanish Town o GB 286-287 R 2
Spanish Town o•• JA 54-55 G 6
Spanish Wells o BS 54-55 G 2
Sparbo, Cape ▲ CDN 24-25 e 3
Sparbu o N 86-87 E 5
Sparke Range ▲ AUS 172-173 H 5
Sparkman o USA (AR) 276-277 C 7
Sparks o USA (NV) 246-247 F 4
Sparrows Point o USA (MD) 280-281 K 4
Sparta o CDN (ONT) 238-239 D 6
Sparta o USA (GA) 284-285 H 3
Sparta o USA (NC) 282-283 F 4
Sparta o USA (TN) 276-277 K 5
Sparta o USA (WI) 270-271 H 7
Spartanburg o USA (SC) 284-285 J 2
Spartel, Cap ▲ MA 188-189 J 3
Spárti o• GR 100-101 J 6
Sparwood o CDN (BC) 230-231 P 4
Spas-Demensk o RUS 94-95 O 4
Spas-Klepiki ☆ RUS 94-95 R 4
Spasskaja Guba o RUS 88-89 M 5
Spassk-Dal'nij o RUS 122-123 E 6
Spassk-Rjazanskij o• RUS 94-95 R 4
Spath Plateau ▲ GRØ 26-27 p 7
Spatsizi Plateau ▲ CDN 32-33 F 3
Spatsizi Plateau Wilderness Provincial Park ⊥ CDN (BC) 32-33 F 3
Spatsizi River ~ CDN 32-33 F 3
Spavinaw Creek ~ USA 264-265 K 2
Speaks o USA (TX) 266-267 L 4
Spearfish o USA (SD) 260-261 C 2
Spearhole Creek ~ AUS 172-173 D 7
Spearman o USA (TX) 264-265 C 2
Specimen Hill ▲ AUS 178-179 L 3
Speculator o USA (NY) 278-279 G 5
Speed o USA (WV) 280-281 E 5
Speedwell Island ⌒ GB 78-79 L 7
Speers o CDN (SAS) 232-233 L 3
Speery Island ⌒ GB 202-203 C 8
Speightstown o BDS 56 F 5
Speke Gulf o EAT 212-213 D 5
Spence Bay ≈ 24-25 Z 6
Spence Bay o CDN 24-25 Z 6
Spencer o USA (IA) 274-275 C 1
Spencer o USA (ID) 252-253 F 2
Spencer o USA (IN) 274-275 M 5
Spencer o USA (NE) 262-263 H 2
Spencer o USA (TN) 276-277 K 5
Spencer o USA (WV) 280-281 E 5
Spencer, Cape ▲ AUS 180-181 D 3
Spencer, Cape ▲ CDN (NB) 240-241 K 5
Spencer, Cape ▲ USA 32-33 B 2
Spencer, Point ▲ USA 20-21 G 4
Spencer Gulf ≈ 180-181 D 3
Spencerville o CDN (ONT) 238-239 K 4
Spencerville o USA (OH) 280-281 B 3
Spences Bridge o CDN (BC) 230-231 H 3
Spěra o AFG 138-139 B 3
Sperling o CDN (MAN) 234-235 F 5
Sperryville o USA (VA) 280-281 H 5
Spessart ▲ D 92-93 K 4
Spetch o CDN (BC) 230-231 G 3
Spey ~ GB 90-91 F 3
Speyer o• D 92-93 K 4
Spezzano Albanese o I 100-101 F 5
Spicewood o USA (TX) 266-267 J 3
Spickard o USA (MO) 274-275 E 4
Spiekeroog ⌒ D 92-93 J 2
Spiller Channel ~ CDN 228-229 F 4
Spillimacheen o CDN (BC) 230-231 N 3
Špil'-Tarbagannah, gora ▲ RUS 120-121 H 3
Spinazzola o I 100-101 F 4
Spin Bōldak o AFG 134-135 M 3
Spink o USA (SD) 260-261 K 4
Spirit Falls o USA (WI) 270-271 J 5
Spirit Lake o USA (IA) 274-275 C 1
Spiritwood o CDN (SAS) 232-233 L 2
Spiritwood Lake o USA (ND) 258-259 J 4
Spirka ~ RUS 110-111 U 4
Spiro o USA (OK) 264-265 K 3
Spišský hrad ••• SK 92-93 Q 4
Spitak o AR 128-129 L 2
Spit Point ▲ AUS 172-173 D 6
Spitskopvlei o ZA 220-221 G 5
Spittal an der Drau o A 92-93 M 5
Spitzkoppe ▲• NAM 216-217 C 10
Split o••• HR 100-101 F 3
Split, Cape ▲ CDN (NS) 240-241 L 5
Split Island ⌒ CDN 36-37 K 6
Split Lake o CDN (MAN) 34-35 H 2
Split Lake Indian Reserve ✕ CDN 34-35 J 2
Split Rock Dam < AUS 178-179 L 6
Spofford o USA (TX) 266-267 G 4
Špogi o LV 94-95 K 3
Spokane o USA (MO) 276-277 B 4
Spokane o• USA (WA) 244-245 H 3
Spokane House • USA (WA) 244-245 H 3
Spokane Indian Reservation ✕ USA (WA) 244-245 H 3
Spokane River ~ USA 244-245 G 3
Špola o UA 102-103 G 3
Spoleto o• I 100-101 D 3
Spondin o CDN (ALB) 232-233 G 4
Spooner o USA (WI) 270-271 G 5
Spoon River ~ USA 274-275 H 4
Sporades = Sporádes, Notioi ⌒ GR 100-101 K 6
Sporádes, Vóries ⌒ GR 100-101 J 5
Sporavskoe, vozero o BY 94-95 J 5
Spornoe o RUS 120-121 O 2
Sporyj Navolok, mys ▲ RUS 108-109 N 3
Spotted House o USA (WY) 252-253 N 2
Spotted Island ⌒ CDN (NFL) 38-39 R 2
Spotted Range ▲ USA 248-249 J 3
Sprague o CDN (MAN) 234-235 H 5
Sprague o USA (WA) 244-245 H 3
Sprague River ~ USA 244-245 D 8
Spray o USA (OR) 244-245 F 6
Spree ~ D 92-93 M 2
Sprenger, Lake o AUS 176-177 H 2
Sprengisandur ▲ IS 86-87 d 2
Spring Bay ≈ 24-25 Z 6
Springbok o ZA 220-221 C 4
Springbrook o USA (WI) 270-271 G 5
Spring City o USA (TN) 282-283 C 5
Spring Coulee o CDN (ALB) 232-233 E 6
Spring Creek o AUS (QLD) 174-175 H 6
Spring Creek ~ AUS 178-179 F 2
Spring Creek ~ USA 266-267 G 2
Spring Creek ~ USA 268-269 E 6
Springdale o CDN (NFL) 242-243 M 3
Springdale o USA (AR) 276-277 A 4
Springdale o USA (WA) 244-245 H 2
Springer o USA (NM) 256-257 L 2
Springer o USA (OK) 264-265 G 4
Springer Mountain ▲ USA (GA) 284-285 F 2
Springerville o USA (AZ) 256-257 F 4
Springfield o CDN (NB) 240-241 K 5
Springfield o USA (CO) 254-255 N 6
Springfield o USA (FL) 286-287 D 1
Springfield o USA (GA) 284-285 J 4
Springfield o USA (ID) 252-253 F 3
Springfield o USA (IL) 274-275 J 5
Springfield o USA (KY) 276-277 K 3
Springfield o USA (MA) 278-279 J 6
Springfield o USA (ME) 278-279 N 3
Springfield o USA (MN) 270-271 D 6
Springfield o USA (MO) 276-277 B 3
Springfield o USA (OH) 280-281 C 4
Springfield o USA (OR) 244-245 B 6
Springfield o USA (SD) 260-261 J 4
Springfield o USA (TN) 276-277 J 4
Springfield o USA (VA) 280-281 J 5
Springfield o USA (VT) 278-279 J 5
Springfield, Lake o USA (IL) 274-275 J 5
Springfield Plateau ▲ USA 276-277 B 3
Springfontein o ZA 220-221 G 5
Spring Garden o GUY 62-63 E 2
Spring Green o USA (WI) 274-275 H 1
Spring Grove o USA (VA) 280-281 K 6
Springhill o CDN (NS) 240-241 L 5
Spring Hill o USA (FL) 286-287 G 3
Spring Hill o USA (KS) 262-263 M 6
Springhill o USA (LA) 268-269 G 4
Spring Hill o USA (TN) 276-277 J 5
Springhouse o CDN (BC) 230-231 G 2
Spring Lake o USA (NC) 282-283 J 5
Springlake o USA (TX) 264-265 B 4
Spring Mill State Park • USA (IN) 274-275 M 6
Spring Mountain Ranch State Park ⊥• USA (NV) 248-249 J 3
Spring Mountains ▲ USA 248-249 J 3
Springrale o AUS 178-179 F 2
Spring River ~ USA 264-265 K 2
Spring River ~ USA 276-277 A 3
Spring River ~ USA 276-277 D 4
Springs o ZA 220-221 J 3
Springside o CDN (SAS) 232-233 Q 4
Springs Junction o NZ 182 D 5
Springsure o AUS 178-179 K 3
Springtown o USA (TX) 264-265 G 6
Springvale o AUS 172-173 H 4
Spring Vale o AUS 174-175 D 6
Springvale o USA (ME) 278-279 L 5
Springvale Homestead o AUS 172-173 L 3
Spring Valley o CDN (SAS) 232-233 N 6
Spring Valley o USA (CA) 248-249 G 7
Spring Valley o USA (IL) 274-275 J 3
Spring Valley o USA (MN) 270-271 F 7
Spring Valley o ZA 220-221 H 6
Springview o USA (NE) 262-263 G 2
Springville o USA (AL) 284-285 D 3
Springville o USA (CA) 248-249 F 3
Springville o USA (NY) 278-279 C 6
Springville o USA (UT) 254-255 D 3
Springwater o CDN (SAS) 232-233 K 4
Sproat Lake o CDN (BC) 230-231 E 4
Sprouses Corner o USA (VA) 280-281 H 6
Sprova o N 86-87 E 4
Spruce Brook o CDN (NFL) 242-243 K 4
Sprucedale o CDN (ONT) 238-239 F 3
Spruce Grove o CDN (ALB) 232-233 E 2
Spruce Home o CDN (SAS) 232-233 N 2
Spruce Island ⌒ USA 22-23 U 4
Spruce Knob ▲ USA (WV) 280-281 G 5
Spruce Knob National Recreation Area ⊥ USA (WV) 280-281 G 5
Spruce Lake o CDN (SAS) 232-233 K 2
Spruce Mountain ▲ USA (NV) 246-247 L 3
Spruce Pine o USA (NC) 282-283 E 5
Spruce River ~ CDN 30-31 V 6
Spruce View o CDN (ALB) 232-233 D 3
Spruce Woods Forest Reserve ⊥ CDN (MAN) 234-235 D 5
Spruce Woods Provincial Park ⊥ CDN (MAN) 234-235 D 5
Spur o USA (TX) 264-265 D 5
Spurger o USA (TX) 268-269 F 6
Spurn Head ▲ GB 90-91 H 5
Sputinow o CDN (ALB) 232-233 H 2
Squamish o CDN (BC) 230-231 F 4
Squapan Lake o USA (ME) 278-279 N 2
Square Hill ▲ AUS 176-177 H 3
Square Ilands o CDN 38-39 R 2
Square Lake o USA (ME) 278-279 N 1
Squamish River ~ CDN 230-231 F 3
Squatec o CDN (QUE) 240-241 G 3
Squaw Creek National Wildlife Refuge ⊥ USA (MO) 274-275 C 4
Squaw Lake o USA (MN) 270-271 D 3
Squaw River ~ CDN 236-237 B 2
Squilax o CDN (BC) 230-231 K 3
Squillace, Golfo di ≈ 100-101 F 5
Squires, Mount ▲ AUS 176-177 J 3
Squirrel River ~ CDN 236-237 D 2
Squirrel River ~ USA 20-21 K 3
Sragen o RI 168 D 3
Srbica o YU 100-101 H 3
Srbobran o YU 100-101 G 2
Srebărna, Naroden Park ⊥••• BG 102-103 E 5
Sredec o BG 102-103 E 6
Sredinnyj hrebet ▲ RUS 120-121 R 7
Srednebelaja o RUS 122-123 C 3
Srednee Kujto, ozero o RUS 88-89 L 4
Srednekan, Ust'- o RUS 120-121 P 2
Srednekolymsk o RUS 110-111 d 6
Sredneobskaja nizmennost' ~ RUS 114-115 L 3
Srednerusskaâ vozvyšennost' ▲ RUS 8 G 3
Sredne russkaja vozvyšennost' ▲ RUS 94-95 Q 5
Srednij, ostrov ⌒ RUS 108-109 Y 3
Srednij, proliv ≈ 112-113 P 2
Srednij Ikorec o RUS 102-103 L 2
Srednij Kalar o RUS 118-119 H 8
Srednij Mamakan ~ RUS 118-119 G 7
Srednij Ural ▲ RUS 114-115 E 5
Srednij Vilijuikan ~ RUS 116-117 N 3
Srednij zaliv ≈ 120-121 S 3
Sredniy Ural = Srednij Ural ▲ RUS 114-115 E 5
Srednjaja ~ RUS 110-111 K 3
Srednjaja, gora ▲ RUS 108-109 a 4
Srednjaja Kočoma ~ RUS 116-117 N 4
Srednjaja Mokla ~ RUS 118-119 J 8
Srednjaja Olëkma o RUS 118-119 K 8
Srednogorie = Pirdop + Zlatica o BG 102-103 D 6
Šrenk ~ RUS 108-109 c 4
Srê Noy o K 158-159 H 4
Srê Sbov o K 158-159 J 4
Sretensk ☆ RUS 118-119 H 9
Sribne o UA 102-103 H 2
Sri Dungargarh o IND 138-139 E 5
Srikākulam o IND 142-143 C 6
Sri Kālahasti o• IND 140-141 H 4
Sri Lanka ■ CL 140-141 J 6
Srinagar ☆• IND 138-139 E 2
Srinakarin National Park ⊥• THA 158-159 E 3
Srinakarin Reservoir < THA 158-159 E 3
Sringeri o IND 140-141 F 4
Srinivāspur o IND 140-141 H 4
Sriparumbudur o IND 140-141 H 4
Srirāmapura o IND 140-141 G 4
Srirāmpur o IND 138-139 E 10
Srirangam o• IND 140-141 H 5
Srirangapatnam o• IND 140-141 G 4
Srīrangarājupuram o IND 140-141 H 3
Srisailam o IND 140-141 H 2
Sri Toi o PK 138-139 B 4
Srivaikuntam o IND 140-141 G 6
Srivardhan o IND 138-139 D 10
Srivilliputtūr o• IND 140-141 G 6
Środa Wielkopolska o PL 92-93 O 2
Srostki o RUS 124-125 O 2
Srungavarapukota o IND 142-143 C 6
ş-Şawāb, Wādī ~ SYR 128-129 J 5
Staaten River ~ AUS 174-175 G 5
Staaten River National Park ⊥ AUS 174-175 G 5
Stabbursdalen nasjonalpark ⊥ N 86-87 M 1
Stabkirche Urnes ••• N 86-87 C 6
Stackpool o CDN (ONT) 236-237 G 5
Stack Skerry ⌒ GB 90-91 E 2
Stacyville o USA (IA) 274-275 F 1
Stade o• D 92-93 K 2
Staduhino o RUS 112-113 O 3
Staffell o USA (AR) 276-277 D 5
Stafford ☆ GB 90-91 F 5
Stafford o USA (KS) 262-263 H 7
Stafford Springs o USA (CT) 280-281 O 2
Stahanov = Kadijivka o UA 102-103 L 3
Staines, Península ⌣ RCH 80 D 5
Staked Plain = Llano Estacado ⌣ USA 264-265 A 5
Stalingrad = Zarizyn ☆• RUS 96-97 D 9
Stalwart o CDN (SAS) 232-233 N 4
Stamberg, gora ▲ RUS 122-123 K 5
Stamford o AUS 178-179 G 1
Stamford o GB 90-91 G 5
Stamford o USA (CT) 280-281 N 2
Stamford o USA (NY) 278-279 G 6
Stamford o USA (TX) 264-265 E 6
Stamford, Lake < USA (TX) 264-265 E 5
Stamping Ground o USA (KY) 276-277 L 2
Stampriet o NAM 220-221 D 2
Stamps o USA (AR) 276-277 B 7
Stamsund o N 86-87 F 2
Stanberry o USA (MO) 274-275 D 4
Stancionno-Ojašinskij o RUS 114-115 R 7
Standard o CDN (ALB) 232-233 F 4
Standerton o ZA 220-221 J 3
Standing Rock Indian Reservation ✕ USA (SD) 260-261 E 1
Standing Stone State Park ⊥ USA (TN) 276-277 K 4
Standish o USA (MI) 272-273 F 4
Stand Off o CDN (ALB) 232-233 E 6
Stand Rock • USA (WI) 270-271 J 7
Stanfield o USA (AZ) 256-257 D 6
Stanfield o USA (OR) 244-245 F 5
Stanford o USA (KY) 276-277 L 3
Stanford o USA (MT) 250-251 J 4
Stang, Cape ▲ CDN 24-25 U 5
Stanger o ZA 220-221 K 4
Stanhope o AUS 180-181 H 4
Stanhope o CDN (PEI) 240-241 M 4
Stanhope o GB 90-91 F 4
Staniard Creek o BS 54-55 G 2
stanica Bagaevskaja o RUS 102-103 M 4
Staniel Cay Beach ▲• BS 54-55 G 2
Stanislaus River ~ USA 246-247 E 5
Stanke Dimitrov = Dupnica o BG 102-103 C 6
Stanley o AUS 180-181 H 6
Stanley o CDN (NB) 240-241 J 4
Stanley ☆ GB 78-79 M 6
Stanley o USA (ID) 252-253 D 2
Stanley o USA (ND) 258-259 E 3
Stanley o USA (NM) 256-257 K 3
Stanley, Mount ▲ ZRE 212-213 B 3
Stanley, Port o CDN (ONT) 238-239 D 6
Stanley Pool o ZRE 210-211 E 6
Stanley Reservoir o IND 140-141 G 5
Stanleyville = Kisangani ☆ ZRE 210-211 K 3
Stanmore o CDN (ALB) 232-233 G 4
Stanmore o ZW 218-219 E 5
Stannard Rock ⌒ USA (MI) 270-271 L 3
Stanovik, hrebet ▲ RUS 118-119 F 11
Stanovoe kölí o KZ 124-125 F 1
Stanovoe nagor'e ▲ RUS 118-119 E 7
Stanovoj hrebet ▲ RUS 118-119 L 7
Stanovoye Nagor'ye = Stanovoe nagor'e ▲ RUS 118-119 E 7
Stanovoy Khrebet = Stanovoj hrebet ▲ RUS 118-119 L 7
Stansmore Range ▲ AUS 172-173 H 6
Stanthorpe o AUS 178-179 L 5
Stanton o USA (MI) 272-273 D 4
Stanton o USA (ND) 258-259 F 4
Stanton o USA (NE) 262-263 J 3
Stanton o USA (TN) 276-277 F 5
Stanton o USA (TX) 264-265 C 6
Stanwell o AUS 178-179 L 2
Stanwell Fletcher Lake o CDN 24-25 Y 4
Stanwix National Monument, Fort • USA (NY) 278-279 F 5
Stanwood o USA (MI) 272-273 D 4
Stanwood o USA (WA) 244-245 C 2
Stanyčno-Luhans'ke o UA 102-103 L 3
Stapleford o ZW 218-219 G 4
Staples o CDN (ONT) 238-239 C 6
Staples o USA (MN) 270-271 D 4
Stapleton o USA (NE) 262-263 F 3
Stapylton Bay ≈ 24-25 O 6
Star o CDN (ALB) 232-233 F 2
Star o USA (MS) 268-269 K 4
Staraja Kulatka ☆ RUS 96-97 E 7
Staraja Majna ☆ RUS 96-97 F 6
Staraja Poltavka ☆ RUS 96-97 E 8
Staraja Russa ☆ RUS 94-95 M 3
Staraja Toropa o RUS 94-95 M 3
Stará Ľubovňa o SK 92-93 Q 4
Staravina o MK 100-101 H 4
Stara Zagora o BG 102-103 D 6
Starboard o USA (ME) 278-279 O 4
Starbuck o CDN (MAN) 234-235 F 5
Starbuck o USA (MN) 270-271 C 5
Starbuck Island ⌒ KIB 13 M 3
Star City o CDN (SAS) 232-233 O 3
Star City o USA (AR) 276-277 D 7
Starcke o AUS 174-175 H 4
Starcke National Park ⊥ AUS 174-175 H 4
Stargard Szczeciński o PL 92-93 N 2
Starica o RUS (AST) 96-97 D 9
Starica o RUS (TVR) 94-95 O 3
Starigrad-Paklenica o HR 100-101 E 2
Stari Nadym o RUS 114-115 M 2
Stark o USA (KS) 262-263 L 7
Starke o USA (FL) 286-287 G 2
Stark Lake o CDN 30-31 O 4
Starks o USA (LA) 268-269 G 6
Starkville o USA (CO) 254-255 L 6
Starkville o USA (MS) 268-269 M 3
Starkweather o USA (ND) 258-259 J 3
Starnberg o D 92-93 L 4
Starnberger See o D 92-93 L 5
Starobaltačevo ☆ RUS 96-97 J 5
Starobeševe o UA 102-103 L 4
Starobil's'k o UA 102-103 L 3
Starokostjantyniv ☆ UA 102-103 E 3
Starominskaja o RUS 102-103 L 4
Staro Orjahovo o BG 102-103 E 6
Staroščerbinovskaja o RUS 102-103 L 4
Starosubhangulovo o RUS 96-97 K 7
Starting Point to Baliem Valley • RI 166-167 K 4
Start Point ▲ GB 90-91 F 6
Startup o USA (WA) 244-245 D 3
Staryj Oskol o RUS 102-103 K 2
Starya Darohi o BY 94-95 L 5
State Bridge o USA (CO) 254-255 J 4
State College o USA (PA) 280-281 J 3
State Line o USA (MS) 268-269 M 5
Stateline o USA (NV) 248-249 J 4
Staten Island ⌒ USA (NY) 280-281 M 3
Statenville o USA (GA) 284-285 G 6
Statesboro o USA (GA) 284-285 J 4
Statesville o USA (AL) 284-285 D 5
Statesville o USA (NC) 282-283 G 5
Statham o USA (GA) 284-285 G 3
Station Nord o GRØ 26-27 r 3
Statue of Liberty ••• USA (NY) 280-281 N 3
Stauffer o CDN (ALB) 232-233 D 3
Stauing Alper ▲ GRØ 26-27 n 7
Staunton o USA (IL) 274-275 J 6
Staunton o USA (VA) 280-281 G 5
Stavanger ☆• N 86-87 B 7
Stave Lake o CDN (BC) 230-231 G 4
Stavely o CDN (ALB) 232-233 E 5
Stavropol' ☆ RUS 102-103 M 5
Stavropol'skij kraj ■ RUS 126-127 E 5
Stawell o AUS 180-181 G 4
Stayner o CDN (ONT) 238-239 E 4
Stayton o USA (OR) 244-245 C 6
Steady Brook o CDN (NFL) 242-243 L 4
Steamboat o USA (OR) 244-245 C 7
Steamboat Springs o USA (CO) 254-255 J 3
Steamboat Trading Post o USA (AZ) 256-257 F 3
Stebbins o USA 20-21 J 5
Steedman o USA (MO) 274-275 G 6
Steele o USA (AL) 284-285 D 3
Steele o USA (MO) 276-277 F 4
Steele o USA (ND) 258-259 H 5
Steele, Fort o CDN (BC) 230-231 O 4
Steele, Mount ▲ CDN 20-21 U 6
Steele Bayou ~ USA 268-269 J 4
Steele Island ⌒ ARK 16 F 30
Steelman o CDN (SAS) 232-233 Q 6
Steelpoortrivier ~ ZA 220-221 J 2
Steel River ~ CDN 236-237 B 3
Steels Harbor Island ⌒ USA (ME) 278-279 O 4
Steelville o USA (MO) 276-277 D 3
Steenkampsberge ▲ ZA 220-221 J 2
Steen River ~ CDN 30-31 L 6
Steensby Gletscher ⊂ GRØ 26-27 Y 3
Steensby Inlet ≈ 24-25 h 4
Steensby Land ▲ GRØ 26-27 P 5
Steensby Peninsula ⌣ CDN 24-25 d 4
Steens Mountain ▲ USA 244-245 G 8
Steenstrup Gletscher ⊂ GRØ 26-27 V 6
Steenwijk o NL 92-93 J 2
Steep Bank River ~ CDN 32-33 P 3
Steep Cape ▲ USA 22-23 U 3
Steep Point ▲ AUS 176-177 B 3
Steep Rock o CDN (MAN) 234-235 E 3
Steeprock o CDN (MAN) 234-235 E 3
Steese Highway II USA 20-21 R 4
Stefansson Island ⌒ CDN 24-25 T 4
Steffen, Cerro ▲ RA 80 E 2
Ştei o RO 102-103 C 4
Steiermark ■ A 92-93 N 5
Steilloopsbrug o ZA 218-219 E 6
Steilrand o ZA 220-221 K 3
Steilrandberge ▲ NAM 216-217 B 8
Stein am Rhein o CH 92-93 K 5
Steinbach o CDN (MAN) 234-235 G 5
Steine o N 86-87 G 2

Steinen, Rio ~ BR 70-71 K 3
Steinhagen Lake, B.A. < USA (TX) 268-269 F 6
Steinhatchee o USA (FL) 286-287 F 2
Steinhausen o NAM 216-217 E 10
Steinkjer ☆ N 86-87 E 4
Steinkopf o ZA 220-221 C 4
Steins o USA (NM) 256-257 G 6
Steins Ghost Town • USA (NM) 256-257 G 6
Steinsland o N 86-87 H 2
Stella o ZA 220-221 G 3
Stellarton o CDN (NS) 240-241 N 5
Stellenbosch o• ZA 220-221 D 6
Stellera, gora ▲ RUS 120-121 I W 6
Stèlvio, Parco Nazionale d. = Nationalpark Stilfser Joch ⊥ I 100-101 C 1
Stendal o• D 92-93 L 2
Stenoby o S 86-87 F 7
Stenen o CDN (SAS) 232-233 Q 4
Stenón Elafonissou ≈ 100-101 J 6
Stenón Kásu ≈ 100-101 L 7
Stenón Kimolou Sífnou ≈ 100-101 K 6
Stenón Kithéron ≈ 100-101 J 6
Stenón Kíthnou ≈ 100-101 K 6
Stenón Serífou ≈ 100-101 K 6
Stenón Sífnou ≈ 100-101 K 6
Stenungsund ☆ S 86-87 E 7
Stepanakert = Khankendi ☆ AZ 128-129 M 3
Stepanavan o AR 128-129 L 2
Stepan Razin o AZ 128-129 O 2
Stephanie Wildlife Reserve ⊥ ETH 208-209 C 6
Stephan Strait ≈ 183 C 3
Stephen o USA (MN) 270-271 B 2
Stephens o USA (AR) 276-277 B 7
Stephens, Cape ▲ NZ 182 D 4
Stephens City o USA (VA) 280-281 H 4
Stephens Creek ~ AUS 180-181 F 2
Stephens Island ⌒ CDN (BC) 228-229 C 2
Stephenson o USA (MI) 270-271 L 5
Stephenson Ø ⌒ GRØ 26-27 a 2
Stephens Passage ≈ 32-33 C 2
Stephenville o CDN (NFL) 242-243 K 4
Stephenville o USA (TX) 264-265 F 6
Stephenville Crossing o CDN (NFL) 242-243 K 4
Stepnoe o RUS (CEL) 96-97 M 6
Stepnoe ☆ RUS (SAR) 96-97 E 8
Stepovak Bay ≈ 22-23 R 5
Steppe, The = Kazahskij melkosopočnik ⩤ KZ 124-125 F 3
Steptoe o USA (WA) 244-245 H 3
Sterkfontein dam < ZA 220-221 J 4
Sterkspruit o ZA 220-221 H 5
Sterkstroom o ZA 220-221 H 5
Sterlibaševo ☆ RUS 96-97 J 7
Sterling o USA (CO) 254-255 M 3
Sterling o USA (KS) 262-263 H 6
Sterling o USA (ND) 258-259 G 5
Sterling o USA (OK) 264-265 F 4
Sterling o ZA 220-221 E 5
Sterling City o USA (TX) 266-267 G 2
Sterling Heights o USA (MI) 272-273 F 5
Sterling Highway II USA 22-23 V 3
Sterling Landing o USA 20-21 N 5
Sterlington o USA (LA) 268-269 H 4
Sterlitamak ☆ RUS 96-97 J 7
Stérnes o GR 100-101 K 7
Steroh o Y 132-133 H 7
Stettin Bay ≈ 183 F 3
Stettiner Haff ⊂ D 92-93 N 2
Stettler o CDN (ALB) 232-233 F 3
Steuben o USA (MI) 270-271 M 4
Steubenville o USA (OH) 280-281 F 3
Stevenage o GB 90-91 G 6
Stevenson o USA (AL) 284-285 E 2
Stevenson o USA (WA) 244-245 D 5
Stevenson, Mount ▲ CDN (BC) 228-229 N 4
Stevenson Creek ~ AUS 178-179 C 4
Stevenson Mountain ▲ USA (OR) 244-245 E 6
Stevensons Peak ▲ AUS 176-177 L 2
Stevens Pass ▲ USA (WA) 244-245 D 3
Stevens Point o USA (WI) 270-271 J 6
Stevens Village o USA 20-21 Q 3
Stevensville o USA (MI) 272-273 C 5
Stevensville o USA (MT) 250-251 E 5
Stevinson o USA (CA) 248-249 D 2
Steward Ø ⌒ GRØ 26-27 o 9
Stewardson Inlet o CDN (BC) 230-231 C 4
Stewart o CDN 32-33 F 4
Stewart o USA (MN) 270-271 D 6
Stewart, Cape ▲ AUS 174-175 C 2
Stewart, Isla ⌒ RCH 80 E 7
Stewart, Monte ▲ RCH 80 E 7
Stewart, Mount ▲ AUS 174-175 H 7
Stewart, Mount ▲ CDN 20-21 V 5
Stewart Crossing o CDN 20-21 W 5
Stewart Island ⌒ NZ 182 A 7
Stewart Islands ⌒ SOL 184 I f 3
Stewart Lake o CDN 30-31 Z 2
Stewart Plateau ▲ CDN 20-21 W 4
Stewart River ~ CDN 20-21 V 5
Stewarts Point o USA (CA) 246-247 B 5
Stewartstown o USA (NH) 278-279 K 4
Stewart Valley o CDN (SAS) 232-233 L 5
Stewartville o USA (MN) 270-271 F 7
Stewiacke o CDN (NS) 240-241 M 5
Stewiacke River ~ CDN 240-241 M 5
Steynsburg o ZA 220-221 G 5
Steynsrus o ZA 220-221 H 3
Steyr o• A 92-93 N 4
Steytlerville o ZA 220-221 G 6
Stickney o USA (SD) 260-261 H 3
Stickney Corner o USA (ME) 278-279 M 4
Stiegler's Gorge • EAT 214-215 K 4
Stigler o USA (OK) 264-265 J 3
Stikine-Leconte Wilderness ⊥ • USA 32-33 D 3
Stikine Plateau ▲ CDN 32-33 D 2
Stikine Ranges ▲ CDN 20-21 Z 7
Stikine River ~ CDN 32-33 F 3
Stikine Strait ≈ 32-33 D 3
Stile o DZ 190-191 E 3
Stiles o USA (TX) 266-267 F 2
Stiles Junction o USA (WI) 270-271 K 6
Stilfontein o ZA 220-221 H 3
Stilfser Joch = Passo dello Stèlvio ▲ I 100-101 C 1
Stillhouse Hollow Lake < USA (TX) 266-267 K 3
Stillons o USA (AR) 276-277 C 7
Stillwater o USA (MN) 270-271 F 5
Stillwater o USA (NV) 246-247 G 4
Stillwater o USA (OK) 264-265 G 2
Stillwater Mountains ▲ USA 246-247 G 4
Stillwater River ~ USA 250-251 K 6
Stilo o I 100-101 F 5
Stilo, Punta ▲ I 100-101 F 5
Stilwell o USA (OK) 264-265 K 3
Stinear Nunataks ▲ ARK 16 F 7
Stinkingwater Pass ▲ USA (OR) 244-245 G 7
Stinnett o USA (TX) 264-265 C 3
Stintino o I 100-101 B 4
Štip o MK 100-101 J 4
Stirling o AUS (NT) 172-173 L 6
Stirling o AUS (QLD) 174-175 F 5
Stirling o CDN (ALB) 232-233 F 6
Stirling o CDN (ONT) 238-239 H 4
Stirling o• GB 90-91 F 3
Stirling Creek ~ AUS 172-173 J 4
Stirling North o AUS 180-181 D 2
Stirling Range National Park ⊥ AUS 176-177 D 7
Stjørdalshalsen o N 86-87 E 5
Stockach o D 92-93 K 5
Stockbridge o USA (GA) 284-285 F 3
Stockbridge o USA (MI) 272-273 E 5
Stockbridge Indian Reservation ⚔ USA (WI) 270-271 J 6
Stockdale o USA (TX) 266-267 K 4
Stockerau o A 92-93 O 4
Stockers Hill ▲ CDN (NFL) 242-243 M 1
Stockett o USA (MT) 250-251 H 4
Stockholm o CDN (SAS) 232-233 Q 5
Stockholm ★•• S 86-87 J 7
Stockman's Hall of Fame • AUS 178-179 H 2
Stockport o AUS 178-179 E 2
Stockport o GB 90-91 F 5
Stockton o USA (CA) 248-249 C 2
Stockton o USA (FL) 286-287 G 1
Stockton o USA (IL) 274-275 H 2
Stockton o USA (KS) 262-263 G 5
Stockton o USA (MO) 276-277 B 3
Stockton Island ⌒ USA (WI) 270-271 H 4
Stockton Islands ⌒ USA 20-21 R 1
Stockton Lake ⊂ USA (MO) 276-277 B 3
Stockton Plateau ▲ USA 266-267 D 3
Stockville o USA (NE) 262-263 F 4
Stöde o S 86-87 H 5
Stœ̆ng Trêng o K 158-159 H 4
Stoffberg o ZA 220-221 J 2
Stohid ~ UA 102-103 D 2
Stojba o RUS 122-123 D 2
Stokan, gora ▲ RUS 122-123 M 6
Stoke-on-Trent o GB 90-91 F 5
Stokes, Bahía ≈ 80 D 7
Stokesdale o USA (PA) 280-281 J 2
Stokes Point ▲ AUS 180-181 G 6
Stokes Range ▲ AUS 172-173 K 3
Stokkvågen o N 86-87 F 3
Stokmarknes o N 86-87 G 2
Stolac o BIH 100-101 F 3
Stolbovaja ~ RUS 116-117 E 4
Stolbovoe, ozero ⊂ RUS 120-121 U 5
Stolbovoj, mys ▲ RUS 120-121 U 5
Stolbovoj, ostrov ⌒ RUS 110-111 V 2
Stolby o RUS 110-111 U 6
Stolby, zapovednik ⊥ RUS 116-117 F 8
Stole, Mountain ▲ PNG 183 A 3
Stolin o BY 94-95 K 6
Stompneuspunt ▲ ZA 220-221 C 6
Ston o HR 100-101 F 3
Stonecircles • WAG 202-203 C 3
Stonecliffe o CDN (ONT) 238-239 H 2
Stone Forest •• VRC 156-157 C 4
Stone Gabin o USA (AZ) 256-257 A 5
Stoneham o USA (CO) 254-255 M 3
Stone Harbor o USA (NJ) 280-281 M 4
Stonehaven o GB 90-91 F 3
Stonehenge o AUS 178-179 G 3
Stonehenge ••• GB 90-91 G 6
Stone House o USA (PA) 280-281 G 2
Stone Indian Reserve ⚔ CDN (BC) 230-231 F 2
Stone Lake ⊂ CDN (ONT) 234-235 Q 4
Stone Lake o USA (WI) 270-271 G 5
Stonepynten ▲ N 84-85 O 4
Stoner o CDN (BC) 228-229 M 3
Stone Rondavel • NAM 220-221 D 3
Stones River National Battlefield ∴ • USA (TN) 276-277 J 5
Stonewall o CDN (MAN) 234-235 F 4
Stonewall o USA (MS) 268-269 M 4
Stonewall o USA (TX) 266-267 J 3
Stoney Point ▲ AUS 178-179 F 4
Stonington o ARK 16 G 30
Stonington o USA (ME) 278-279 N 4
Stony, Pointe ▲ CDN 36-37 P 5
Stony Beach o CDN (SAS) 232-233 N 5
Stony Creek o USA (VA) 280-281 J 7
Stony Creek Indian Reserve ⚔ CDN (BC) 228-229 K 3
Stonyford o USA (CA) 246-247 C 4
Stony Indian Reserve ⚔ CDN (ALB) 232-233 D 4
Stony Island ⌒ CDN 38-39 R 2
Stony Island ⌒ USA (NY) 278-279 E 5
Stony Lake o CDN 30-31 U 6
Stony Lake ⊂ CDN (ONT) 238-239 G 4
Stony Lake o USA (MI) 272-273 C 4
Stony Mountain o CDN (MAN) 234-235 F 4
Stony Plain o CDN (ALB) 232-233 D 2
Stony Point ▲ CDN (MAN) 234-235 F 3
Stony Point ▲ USA (NY) 278-279 E 5
Stony Rapids o CDN 30-31 R 6
Stonyridge o CDN (ONT) 238-239 G 4
Stony River o USA 20-21 M 6
Stony River ~ USA 20-21 N 6
Stopem Blockem Range ▲ AUS 174-175 H 6
Storå ~ DK 86-87 D 8
Stora Blåsjön o S 86-87 G 4
Stora Lulevatten ⊂ S 86-87 J 3
Stora Sjöfallets nationalpark ⊥•• S 86-87 H 3
Storavan ⊂ S 86-87 J 4
Storby o FIN 88-89 E 6
Stord ⌒ N 86-87 B 7
Store Bælt ≈ 86-87 E 9
Store Hellefiskebanke ⩤ 28-29 N 3
Store Koldewey ⌒ GRØ 26-27 q 5
Støren ☆ N 86-87 E 5
Store Sotra ⌒ N 86-87 B 6
Storfjordbanken ⩤ 84-85 M 4
Storfjorden ≈ 84-85 L 4
Storfjordrenna ⩤ 84-85 K 4
Storfors ☆ S 86-87 G 7
Storforsen ~•• S 86-87 K 4
Storforshei o N 86-87 G 3
Storis Passage ≈ 24-25 W 6
Storjord o N 86-87 G 3
Storkerson, Cape ▲ CDN 24-25 T 4
Storkerson Bay ≈ 24-25 J 4
Storkerson Peninsula ⌣ CDN 24-25 S 4
Storlien o S 86-87 F 5
Storm Bay ≈ 180-181 J 7
Stormberg o ZA (CAP) 220-221 H 5
Stormberg ▲ ZA 220-221 H 5
Storm Lake o USA (IA) 274-275 C 2
Stormrivier o ZA 220-221 F 6
Stormsvlei o ZA 220-221 E 7
Stornoway o CDN (QUE) 238-239 O 3
Stornoway o GB 90-91 D 2
Støt Ø ⌒ GRØ 26-27 m 8
Storø ⌒ GRØ 28-29 X 3
Storøen ⌒ GRØ 26-27 q 4
Storøya ⌒ N 84-85 Q 2
Storož ~ RUS 120-121 T 6
Storoževoj, mys ▲ RUS 120-121 S 3
Storoževsk o RUS 88-89 W 5
Storsätern o S 86-87 F 5
Storsjö o S 86-87 F 5
Storsjön ⊂• S 86-87 G 5
Storsjøen ~ N 86-87 E 6
Storsjön ⊂ S 86-87 G 4
Storsteinhalvøya ⌣ N 84-85 L 2
Storstrømmen ≈ 26-27 o 5
Storthoaks o CDN (SAS) 232-233 R 6
Stortoppen ▲ S 86-87 H 3
Storuman o S (AC) 86-87 H 4
Storuman ⊂ S (AC) 86-87 H 4
Storvik o S 86-87 H 6
Story o USA (WY) 252-253 M 2
Story City o USA (IA) 274-275 E 2
Stöttingfjället ▲ S 86-87 H 4
Stouffville o CDN (ONT) 238-239 F 5
Stoughton o CDN (SAS) 232-233 P 6
Stoughton o USA (WI) 274-275 J 2
Stoŭng o K 158-159 H 4
Stout Lake ⊂ CDN 34-35 J 4
Stout Lake ⊂ CDN (ONT) 234-235 J 2
Stowe o USA (VT) 278-279 J 4
Strabane o GB 90-91 D 4
Strachan o CDN (ALB) 232-233 C 3
Strahan o AUS 180-181 H 7
Straight Lake ⊂ CDN 34-35 N 4
Strait of Malacca = Melaka, Selat ≈ 162-163 C 2
Straits of Mackinac ≈ 272-273 D 2
Strakonice o CZ 92-93 M 4
Strakonitz = Strakonice o CZ 92-93 M 4
Stralki o BY 94-95 L 4
Stralsund o•• D 92-93 M 1
Strand o ZA 220-221 D 7
Strandfontein o ZA 220-221 D 5
Strang o USA (NE) 262-263 J 4
Stranger River ~ USA 262-263 L 5
Strangford o• GB 90-91 E 4
Stranraer o CDN (SAS) 232-233 K 4
Stranraer o GB 90-91 E 4
Strasbourg o CDN (SAS) 232-233 O 4
Strasbourg ☆••• F 90-91 L 7
Strasburg o USA (CO) 254-255 L 4
Strasburg o USA (ND) 258-259 G 5
Strasburg o USA (VA) 280-281 H 5
Stratford o CDN (ONT) 238-239 E 5
Stratford o NZ 182 E 3
Stratford o USA (CA) 248-249 E 3
Stratford o USA (OK) 264-265 H 4
Stratford o USA (TX) 264-265 B 2
Stratford o USA (WI) 270-271 H 6
Stratford-upon-Avon o• GB 90-91 G 5
Strathburn o AUS 174-175 G 4
Strathclair o CDN (MAN) 234-235 C 4
Strathcona Provincial Park ⊥ CDN (BC) 230-231 D 4
Strathcona o USA (MN) 270-271 B 2
Strathcona Sound ≈ 24-25 d 4
Strathfillan o AUS 178-179 G 2
Strathgordon o AUS (QLD) 174-175 G 4
Strathgordon o AUS (TAS) 180-181 J 7
Strathhaven o AUS 174-175 G 4
Strathleven o AUS 174-175 G 4
Strathlorne o CDN (NS) 240-241 O 4
Strathmore o AUS (QLD) 174-175 G 5
Strathmore o AUS (QLD) 174-175 J 7
Strathmore o CDN (ALB) 232-233 E 4
Strathnaver o CDN (BC) 228-229 M 3
Strathroy o CDN (ONT) 238-239 D 6
Stratóni o GR 100-101 J 4
Stratton o CDN (ONT) 234-235 J 6
Stratton o USA (CO) 254-255 N 4
Stratton o USA (ME) 278-279 L 3
Stratton o USA (NE) 262-263 E 4
Stratton Mountain ▲ USA (VT) 278-279 J 5
Straubing o D 92-93 M 4
Straubville o USA (ND) 258-259 K 5
Straughn o USA (IN) 274-275 N 5
Stravropol'-na-Volgi ☆ RUS 96-97 F 7
Strawberry o USA (CA) 246-247 E 5
Strawberry, Cape ▲ CDN 36-37 U 7
Strawberry Point o USA (IA) 274-275 G 2
Strawberry Reservoir < USA (UT) 254-255 D 3
Strawberry River ~ USA 254-255 E 3
Strawberry River ~ USA 276-277 D 4
Strawn o USA (TX) 264-265 F 6
Streaky Bay ≈ 180-181 C 2
Streaky Bay o AUS (SA) 180-181 C 2
Streamstown o CDN (ALB) 232-233 H 2
Streatfield Lake ⊂ CDN 34-35 O 4
Streatham o AUS 180-181 G 4
Streator o USA (IL) 274-275 K 3
Street o GB 90-91 F 6
Streeter o USA (ND) 258-259 H 5
Streetman o USA (TX) 266-267 L 2
Strehaia o RO 102-103 C 5
Streich Mound ▲ AUS 176-177 G 5
Strelka o RUS (KRN) 116-117 F 6
Strelka o RUS (MAG) 120-121 P 3
Strelka-Čunja o RUS 116-117 L 5
Strelley o AUS 172-173 D 6
Strel'na o RUS (MUR) 88-89 P 3
Strel'na ~ RUS 88-89 P 3
Strenči o LV 94-95 J 3
Stresa o• I 100-101 B 2
Stretch Range ▲ AUS 172-173 H 6
Strevell o USA (ID) 252-253 E 4
Streymoy ⌒ FR 90-91 D 1
Strezelecki Track • AUS 178-179 E 6
Streževoj o RUS 114-115 O 4
Strickland River ~ PNG 183 B 3
Strickler o USA (AR) 276-277 A 5
Striding River ~ CDN 30-31 S 5
Strindberg Land ⩤ GRØ 26-27 n 6
Stringtown o USA (OK) 264-265 H 4
Strizament, gora ▲ RUS 126-127 E 5
Strobel, Lago ⊂ RA 80 E 4
Stroeder o RA 78-79 H 6
Strofiliá o GR 100-101 J 5
Strogonof Point ▲ USA 22-23 R 4
Strokkurgeysir •• IS 86-87 c 2
Strómboli, Ísola ⌒~ I 100-101 E 5
Strome o CDN (ALB) 232-233 F 3
Stromness o GB 90-91 F 2
Strømø = Streymoy ⌒ FR 90-91 D 1
Stromsburg o USA (NE) 262-263 J 3
Strömstad ☆ S 86-87 E 7
Strömsund o S 86-87 G 5
Ströms vattudal ⩤ S 86-87 G 4
Strong o USA (AR) 276-277 C 7
Strong o USA (MS) 268-269 M 3
Strong, Mount ▲ PNG 183 D 4
Strong City o USA (KS) 262-263 K 6
Strongfield o CDN (SAS) 232-233 M 4
Stronghurst o USA (IL) 274-275 H 4
Strong River ~ USA 268-269 L 4
Strongsville o USA (OH) 280-281 E 2
Stronsay ⌒ GB 90-91 F 2
Stroud o AUS 180-181 L 2
Stroud o USA (OK) 264-265 H 3
Stroudsburg o USA (PA) 280-281 L 2
Struan o CDN (SAS) 232-233 L 3
Struer o DK 86-87 D 8
Struga o• MK 100-101 H 4
Struisbaai ≈ 220-221 E 7
Strumešnica ~ MK 100-101 J 4
Strumica o• MK 100-101 J 4
Strydenburg o ZA 220-221 F 4
Strydpoortberge ▲ ZA 220-221 J 2
Stryj ☆ UA 102-103 C 3
Stryj ~ UA 102-103 C 3
Stryker o USA (MT) 250-251 E 3
Strymón ~ GR 100-101 J 4
Strypa ~ UA 102-103 D 3
Strzelce Krajeńskie o PL 92-93 N 2
Strzelecki Creek ~ AUS 178-179 F 5
Strzelecki Regional Reserve ⊥ AUS 178-179 F 5
Stuart o USA (FL) 286-287 J 4
Stuart o USA (IA) 274-275 D 3
Stuart o USA (NE) 262-263 G 2
Stuart o USA (OK) 264-265 H 4
Stuart o USA (VA) 280-281 F 7
Stuart, Mount ▲ AUS 172-173 C 7
Stuart Bluff Range ▲ AUS 172-173 L 7
Stuartburn o CDN (MAN) 234-235 G 5
Stuart Highway II AUS 172-173 L 3
Stuart Island o CDN (BC) 230-231 D 3
Stuart Island ⌒ USA 20-21 J 5
Stuart Lake ⊂ CDN (BC) 228-229 K 2
Stuart Memorial • AUS 174-175 C 6
Stuart Ranges ▲ AUS 178-179 C 5
Stuart River ~ CDN 228-229 L 2
Stubbenkammer ▲• D 92-93 M 1
Studenčeskoe o KZ 126-127 M 2
Studenica o••• YU 100-101 H 3
Studina o RO 102-103 D 6
Stugun o S 86-87 G 5
Stuie o CDN (BC) 228-229 H 4
Stull Lake ⊂ CDN 34-35 K 3
Stump Lake o CDN (BC) 230-231 J 3
Stupino ☆ RUS 94-95 Q 4
Sturgeon o CDN (QUE) 236-237 N 5
Sturgeon Bay ⊂ CDN (MAN) 234-235 E 2
Sturgeon Bay o USA (WI) 270-271 L 6
Sturgeon Falls o CDN (ONT) 238-239 F 2
Sturgeon Lake ⊂ CDN (ALB) 32-33 M 4
Sturgeon Lake ⊂ CDN (ONT) 234-235 N 5
Sturgeon Lake ⊂ CDN (ONT) 238-239 G 4
Sturgeon Lake Indian Reserve ⚔ CDN 32-33 M 4
Sturgeon River ~ CDN 34-35 L 3
Sturgeon River ~ CDN 232-233 M 2
Sturgeon River ~ CDN 236-237 H 5
Sturgeon River ~ USA 270-271 K 4
Stures Islands ⌒ CDN 24-25 e 7
Sturgis o CDN (SAS) 232-233 Q 4
Sturgis o USA (MI) 272-273 D 6
Sturgis o USA (MS) 268-269 L 3
Sturgis o USA (SD) 260-261 C 2
Šturmovoj o RUS 120-121 N 2
Štúrovo o SK 92-93 P 5
Sturt, Mount ▲ AUS 178-179 F 5
Sturt Bay ≈ 180-181 D 3
Sturt Creek o AUS (WA) 172-173 J 5
Sturt Creek ~ AUS 172-173 J 5
Sturt Highway II AUS 180-181 H 3
Sturt National Park ⊥ AUS 178-179 F 5
Sturt Stony Desert ⌣ AUS 178-179 E 4
Stutterheim o ZA 220-221 H 6
Stuttgart ☆• D 92-93 K 4
Stuttgart o USA (AR) 276-277 D 6
Stuyahok o USA 20-21 K 5
Styal o CDN (ALB) 232-233 C 2
Stygge Glacier ⊂ CDN 26-27 L 4
Stykkishólmsbær ☆ IS 86-87 b 2
Styr ~ UA 102-103 D 2
Styx River ~ USA 286-287 B 1
Šu ~ KZ 124-125 G 6
Suai o MAL 162-163 K 3
Suai o RI 166-167 C 6
Su'aiba, aš- o KSA 130-131 H 4
Suain o PNG 183 B 2
Suakin o• SUD 200-201 H 3
Suakin Archipelago ⌒ SUD 200-201 J 3
Suakoko o LB 202-203 F 6
Suam ~ EAK 212-213 E 3
Suana o ZRE 216-217 F 3
Suao o RC 156-157 M 4
Sua Phung o THA 158-159 E 4
Suapi o BOL 70-71 D 4
Suapure, Río ~ YV 60-61 H 4
Suaruru, Cordillera de ▲ BOL 76-77 E 1
Suasúa o YV 62-63 D 2
Suavanao o SOL 184 I d 2
Suay Rièng o K 158-159 H 5
Šu'b, Ra's ▲ Y 132-133 H 7
Šu'ba, aš- o KSA 130-131 J 3
Šubaiḥi, aš- ⩤ Y 132-133 C 7
Šubaikiya, aš- o KSA 130-131 H 5
Subang o RI 168 B 3
Suban Point ▲ RP 160-161 E 6
Suban Siri ~ IND 142-143 H 2
Šubarkŭdyk ☆ KZ 126-127 M 3
Šubaršy o KZ 126-127 M 3
Subate o• LV 94-95 J 3
Subei o VRC 146-147 M 6
Šuberta, mys ▲ RUS 108-109 O 5
Šuberta, zaliv ≈ 108-109 F 5
Subi Besar, Pulau ⌒ RI 162-163 H 3
Šubiya, aš- o KWT 130-131 L 3
Sublett o USA (ID) 252-253 E 4
Sublette o USA (KS) 262-263 F 7
Subotica ☆• YU 100-101 G 1
Šubrā al-Ḫaima o ET 194-195 E 2
Subrahmanya o IND 140-141 F 4
Subway Caves ∴ USA (CA) 246-247 D 3
Sucatinga o BR 68-69 J 4
Success o CDN (SAS) 232-233 K 5
Suceava ☆ RO 102-103 E 4
Suches o USA (GA) 284-285 F 2
Suches, Lago ⊂ PE 70-71 B 5
Suches, Río ~ PE 70-71 C 4
Suchiapa, Río ~ MEX 52-53 H 3
Suchil o MEX 50-51 H 6
Suchumi ☆ GE 126-127 D 6
Sucio, Río ~ CO 60-61 C 4
Suckling, Mount ▲ PNG 183 E 5
Sucre ☆••• BOL 70-71 E 6
Sucre o CO 60-61 D 3
Sucre o EC 64-65 B 2
Sucúa o EC 64-65 C 3
Suçuarana o BR 72-73 K 3
Suçuarana, Serra do ▲ BR 72-73 H 3
Sucunduri, Rio ~ BR 66-67 H 6
Sucupira do Norte o BR 68-69 F 5
Sucuriju o BR 62-63 K 5
Sucuriú, Cachoeira ~ BR 68-69 E 5
Sucuriú, Rio ~ BR 72-73 D 6
Sud = South ⊡ CAM 210-211 C 2
Suda ~ RUS 94-95 P 2
Sudaira, as- o KSA 132-133 B 3
Sudak ☆• UA 102-103 J 5
Sudan ⩤ 9 D 4
Sudan o USA (TX) 264-265 B 4
Sudan = As-Sūdān ■ SUD 200-201 D 4
Sudbury o• CDN (ONT) 238-239 E 2
Sud-Camerounais, Plateau ▲ CAM 204-205 K 6
Sudd ⩤ SUD 206-207 K 4
Suddie o GUY 62-63 E 2
Sudety ⩤ CZ 92-93 N 3
Sūd Gān o IR 134-135 D 2
Sudirman, Pegunungan ▲ RI 166-167 J 3
Sudislavl' o RUS 94-95 R 3
Sud ou de la Hotte, Massif du ▲ RH 54-55 H 5
Sud-Ouest = South-West ⊡ CAM 204-205 H 6
Sudskoe, Borisovo- o RUS 94-95 P 2
Suduci, kūli ⊂ UZ 136-137 F 3
Suðureyri o IS 86-87 b 1
Sudwala Caves • ZA 220-221 K 2
Sudža o RUS 102-103 J 2
Sudženskoe, Anžero- o RUS 114-115 T 6
Sue ~ SUD 206-207 J 5
Sueca o E 98-99 G 5
Sueco, El o MEX 50-51 F 3
Suehn, Big o LB 202-203 F 7
Suemez Island ⌒ USA 32-33 D 4
Suess Land ⩤ GRØ 26-27 m 7
Sueur, Le o USA (MN) 270-271 E 6
Suez = as-Suwais ☆ ET (SUW) 194-195 F 3
Suez, Gulf of = as-Suwais, Ḫalīğ ≈ 194-195 F 3
Suez Canal = Suwais, Qanāt as- < ET 194-195 F 2
Sūf, Darre-ye ~ AFG 136-137 K 7
Sufetula • TN 190-191 G 3
Suffern o USA (NY) 280-281 M 2
Suffield o CDN (ALB) 232-233 G 5
Suffolk o USA (VA) 280-281 K 7
Sūfījon mašiti • UZ 136-137 J 4
Šūfiyān o IR 128-129 L 3
Šuga ~ RUS 108-109 O 8
Sugaing o• MYA 142-143 J 5
Sugal o RP 160-161 F 10
Sūg al Khamīs o LAR 192-193 E 1
Sugar Creek ~ USA 274-275 L 5
Sugar Grove o USA (VA) 280-281 E 7
Sugar Land o USA (TX) 268-269 E 7
Sugarloaf Mountain ▲ USA (ME) 278-279 L 3
Sugarloaf Mountain ▲ AUS 180-181 K 2
Sugarloaf Mountain ▲ USA 22-23 S 3
Sugar River ~ USA 274-275 J 2
Sugar Town • AUS 174-175 J 5
Sugarville o USA (UT) 254-255 C 4
Sugbongkogon o RP 160-161 F 8
Suge La ▲ VRC 144-145 H 6
Suggan Buggan o AUS 180-181 K 4
Sugi, Pulau ⌒ RI 162-163 E 4
Sugihwaras o RI 162-163 E 7
Suğla Gölü ⊂ TR 128-129 E 4
Sugluk Inlet ≈ 36-37 M 3
Sugmutun"egan ~ RUS 114-115 R 4
Sugoj ~ RUS 112-113 H 4
Sugu o WAN 204-205 K 4
Sugun o VRC 146-147 C 6
Šugur o RUS 114-115 J 4
Sugut, Tanjung ▲ MAL 160-161 B 9
Suguta ~ EAK 212-213 F 3
Sugža ~ RUS 120-121 G 2
Sūhāǧ ☆• ET 194-195 E 4
Šuḥair, Abū ☆ IRQ 128-129 L 7
Šuḥair, aš- o Y 132-133 F 6
Suhait o VRC 154-155 D 2
Suhaja Bahta ~ RUS 114-115 U 3
Suhaja Tunguska ~ RUS 114-115 U 2
Šuḥār o• OM 132-133 K 1
Suhariha ~ RUS 108-109 W 8
Suharnyj, ostrov ⌒ RUS 112-113 L 2
Suhbaatar ⊡ MAU 148-149 L 4
Suheli Par ⩤ IND 140-141 E 5
Suhiniči o RUS 94-95 O 4
Suhl o D 92-93 L 3
Suhmiten"jah ~ RUS 114-115 M 5
Suḫna, as- o SYR 128-129 H 5
Suḫna, as- o Y 132-133 C 6
Suhodol o RUS 96-97 G 7
Suhoj Log ☆ RUS 96-97 M 5
Suhoj Nos, mys ▲ RUS 108-109 E 5
Suhoj Pit ~ RUS 116-117 F 6
Suhoj Poluj ~ RUS 114-115 K 2
Suhona ~ RUS 94-95 S 1
Suhum o GH 202-203 K 6
Şuhut ☆ TR 128-129 D 3
Sui ~ DY 204-205 E 4
Sūi o PK 138-139 B 5
Sui o PNG 183 B 5
Suiá-Miçu, Rio ~ BR 68-69 D 7
Suiá Missu, Rio ~ BR 72-73 D 2
Suibin o VRC 150-151 H 4
Suichang o VRC 156-157 L 2
Suichuan o VRC 156-157 J 3
Suide o VRC 154-155 G 3
Suifenhe o VRC 150-151 H 5
Suigam o IND 138-139 C 7
Suihua o VRC 150-151 F 4
Suijiang o VRC 156-157 C 2
Suileng o VRC 150-151 F 4
Suining o VRC (HUN) 156-157 G 3
Suining o VRC (JIA) 154-155 K 5
Suining o VRC (SIC) 154-155 D 6
Suir ~ IRL 90-91 D 5
Suixi o VRC 156-157 G 6
Sui Xian o VRC 154-155 J 4
Suiyang o VRC (GZH) 156-157 E 3
Suiyang o VRC (HEI) 150-151 H 5
Suizhou o VRC 154-155 H 6
Šuja ☆ RUS 94-95 R 3
Šuja ~ RUS 88-89 M 6
Sujālpur o IND 138-139 F 8
Sujāwal o PK 138-139 B 7
Šujostrov ⌒ RUS 88-89 N 4
Sujutkina Kosa, mys ▲ RUS 126-127 G 5
Šukābād o IR 134-135 C 2
Sukabumi o RI 168 B 3
Sukadana o RI (KBA) 162-163 H 5
Sukadana o RI (LAM) 162-163 F 7
Sukadana Teluk ≈ 162-163 H 5
Sukagawa o J 152-153 J 6
Sukamenang o RI 162-163 E 6
Sukaraja o RI (JTE) 168 C 3
Sukaraja o RI (KBA) 162-163 J 6
Sukauegara o RI 168 B 3
Sukeva o FIN 88-89 J 5
Sukhothai o••• THA 158-159 E 2
Suki o PNG 183 A 5
Sukkar, as- o SYR 128-129 J 5
Sukkar, Qal'at ☆ IRQ 128-129 M 7
Sukkertoppen = Maniitsoq o GRØ 28-29 O 4
Sukkertoppen Isflade ⊂ GRØ 28-29 O 3
Sukkozero o RUS 88-89 M 5
Sukkur o•• PK 138-139 B 6
Sukkwan Island ⌒ USA 32-33 D 4
Sukodadi o RI 168 E 3
Sukoharjo o RI 168 D 3
Sukopuro o RI 168 E 3
Sukorejo o RI 168 D 3
Sukpai ~ RUS 122-123 G 5
Sukses o NAM 216-217 D 10
Suksun ☆ RUS 96-97 K 5
Sukumo o J 152-153 E 8
Sukunka River ~ CDN 32-33 J 4
Sul, Canal do ~ BR 62-63 K 6
Sula ⌒ N 86-87 B 6
Sula ~ RUS 88-89 U 3
Sula ~ RUS 88-89 U 4
Sula ~ UA 102-103 H 3
Sula o USA 250-251 F 6
Sula, Kepulauan ⌒ RI 164-165 J 4
Sūlagiri o IND 140-141 H 4
Sulaib aṭ-Tarfā' ⩤ KSA 130-131 G 3
Sulaimāniya, as- ☆ IRQ 128-129 L 5
Sulaimānīya, as- ☆ IRQ 128-129 L 5
Sulaiman Range ▲ PK 138-139 B 5
Sulak ~ RUS 126-127 G 6
Sulakkan ~ RUS 110-111 a 6
Sulakyurt ☆ TR 128-129 E 2
Sulamu o RI 166-167 B 7
Sulat ~ RP 160-161 F 7
Sulatna River ~ USA 20-21 N 4
Sulawesi ⌒ RI 164-165 F 5
Sulawesi, Laut ≈ 164-165 F 2
Sulawesi Selatan ⊡ RI 164-165 F 5
Sulawesi Tengah ⊡ RI 164-165 F 4
Sulawesi Tenggara ⊡ RI 164-165 G 5
Sulawesi Utara ⊡ RI 164-165 J 3
Sulayyil, as- o KSA 132-133 D 3
Şulb, aş- ▲ KSA 130-131 K 4
Sulb, Temple of • SUD 200-201 E 2
Sulby Creek ~ CDN 232-233 K 2
Sulechów o• PL 92-93 N 2
Suleja o WAN 204-205 G 4
Sulejów o• PL 92-93 P 3
Sulen, Mount ▲ PNG 183 B 2
Sule Skerry ⌒ GB 90-91 E 2
Šul'gan-Taš zapovednik ⊥ RUS 96-97 K 7
Sūlīč o AFG 136-137 K 7
Suliki o RI 162-163 D 5
Sulima o WAL 202-203 E 6
Sulina o• RO 102-103 F 5
Sulina, Braţul ~ RO 102-103 F 5
Sulitelma ▲ S 86-87 H 3
Sulitjelma o N 86-87 H 3
Suljukta o KS 136-137 L 5
Sulkovskogo, mys ▲ RUS 120-121 I W 6
Sullana ☆ PE 64-65 B 4
Sulligent o USA (AL) 284-285 B 3
Sullivan o USA (IL) 274-275 K 5
Sullivan o USA (IN) 274-275 L 5
Sullivan o USA (MO) 274-275 G 6
Sullivan Lake o CDN (ALB) 232-233 G 3
Sullivan Lake ⊂ CDN (ALB) 232-233 G 4
Sullivan River ~ CDN 230-231 M 2
Sullorsuaq Vaigat ≈ 28-29 N 1
Sully o USA (IA) 274-275 F 3
Sully-sur-Loire o F 90-91 J 8
Sulmona o I 100-101 D 3
Sulop o RP 160-161 F 9
Sulphur o USA (LA) 268-269 G 6
Sulphur o USA (NV) 246-247 G 3
Sulphur o USA (OK) 264-265 H 4
Sulphur Bank ⩤ 72-73 M 4
Sulphur Bluff o USA (TX) 264-265 J 5
Sulphur River ~ USA 264-265 K 5
Sulphur River ~ USA 276-277 B 7
Sulphur Springs o USA (TX) 264-265 J 5
Sulphur Springs Draw ~ USA 264-265 B 5
Sultan o CDN (ONT) 236-237 F 5
Sultān o IRQ 128-129 L 6
Sultandağı ☆ TR 128-129 D 3
Sultan Dağları ▲ TR 128-129 D 3
Sultan Hamud o EAK 212-213 F 5
Sultanhanı o TR 128-129 E 3
Sultan Kudarat o RP 160-161 F 9
Sultānpur o IND 142-143 C 2
Sultānpur = Kulu o•• IND 138-139 F 4
Sultan-Ubajs ▲ UZ 136-137 G 3
Sultepec, Río ~ MEX 52-53 D 2
Sulu o ZRE 210-211 K 6
Sulu, Laut = Sulu Sea ≈ 160-161 C 8
Suluan Island ⌒ RP 160-161 F 7
Sulu Archipelago ⌒ RP 160-161 D 10
Suluistyk ~ TJ 146-147 B 7
Suluk ~ RUS 122-123 F 3
Sulukaska, togi ▲ KZ 136-137 G 3
Sülüklü o TR 128-129 E 3
Suluita o ETH 208-209 D 4
Sulumei River ~ PNG 183 B 3
Suluntah o LAR 192-193 J 1
Sulūq o LAR 192-193 J 2
Sūlūru o IND 140-141 H 4
Sulusaray o TR 128-129 G 2
Sulu Sea ≈ 160-161 C 8
Sülütöbe o KZ 124-125 E 6
Sulzbach-Rosenberg o D 92-93 L 4
Sumaco o EC 64-65 D 2
Sumaco, Volcán ▲ EC 64-65 D 2
Sumahode o RI 164-165 K 3
Sumaianyar o RI 164-165 E 5
Sumair, Ġazīrat ⌒ KSA 132-133 C 5
Šumanaj o UZ 136-137 F 3
Šūmār o IR 134-135 A 2
Sumara, Naqīl ▲ Y 132-133 D 6
Sumaroto o RI 168 D 3
Sumas o USA (WA) 244-245 C 2
Sumatera Barat ⊡ RI 162-163 C 5
Sumatera Selatan ⊡ RI 162-163 E 6
Sumatera Utara ⊡ RI 162-163 B 4
Sumatra o USA (FL) 286-287 E 1
Sumatra o USA (MT) 250-251 M 5
Sumatra = Sumatera ⌒ RI 162-163 B 2
Sumaúma o BR 66-67 G 6
Šumava ▲ CZ 92-93 M 4
Sumba o ANG 216-217 B 3
Sumba ⌒ RI 168 E 7
Sumba, Île ⌒ ZRE 210-211 G 3
Sumba, Selat ≈ 168 D 7
Šumbar ~ TM 136-137 E 5
Sumbawa ⌒ RI 168 C 7
Sumbawa Besar o RI 168 C 7
Sumbawanga ☆ EAT 214-215 F 4
Sumbe ☆ ANG 216-217 B 5
Sumbe o KZ 146-147 E 4
Sumbèr = Čojr o MAU 148-149 J 4
Sumbi o ZRE 210-211 D 6
Sumbu o Z 214-215 F 5
Sumbu National Park ⊥ Z 214-215 F 5
Sumburgh o GB 90-91 G 2
Sumbuya o WAL 202-203 E 6
Sumé o BR 68-69 K 5
Sumedang o RI 168 B 3
Sumelas • TR 128-129 H 2
Šumen o BG 102-103 E 6
Sumenep o RI 168 E 3
Šumerlja o RUS 96-97 E 6
Sumgayıt = Sumqayıt o• AZ 128-129 N 2
Sumidouro Grande, Rio ~ BR 70-71 J 4
Šumiha ☆ RUS 114-115 G 7
Šumilina ☆ BY 94-95 L 4

Steinen, Rio — Šumilina 397

Tehuantepec, Río ~ MEX 52-53 G 3
Tehuantepec Ridge ≃ 4 E 7
Tehumardi o EST 94-95 H 2
Teide, Parque Nacional del ⊥ E 188-189 C 6
Teide, Pico del ▲•• E 188-189 C 6
Telma, Oulad- o MA 188-189 G 5
Teiskot o RMM 196-197 L 6
Teiti o SUD 200-201 E 3
Teixeira o BR 68-69 K 5
Teixeira de Freitas o BR 72-73 L 4
Teixeira Soares o BR 74-75 E 5
Teja ~ RUS 116-117 F 5
Tejakula o RI 168 B 7
Tejar, El o RA 78-79 J 3
Tejira o RN 198-199 D 5
Tejkovo ☆ RUS 94-95 R 3
Tejo, Rio ~ BR 64-65 F 6
Tejo, Rio ~ P 98-99 C 5
Tejon Pass ▲ USA (CA) 248-249 F 5
Tejupilco de Hidalgo o MEX 52-53 D 2
Tekadu o PNG 183 D 4
Te Kaha o NZ 182 F 2
Tekamah o USA (NE) 262-263 K 3
Tékane o RIM 196-197 C 6
Tekapo, Lake o NZ 182 C 5
Tekax de Álvaro Obregón o MEX 52-53 K 1
Teke, köli o KZ 124-125 H 2
Tekeim o SUD 206-207 K 3
Tekek, Kampung o• MAL 162-163 F 3
Tekeli o KZ 124-125 L 6
Tekes o VRC 146-147 E 4
Tekes He ~ VRC 146-147 E 4
Teketau ▲ KZ 126-127 P 2
Tekezē Wenz ~ ETH 200-201 H 5
Tekhammalt, Oued ~ DZ 190-191 D 9
Tekhammat, Oued ~ DZ 190-191 G 7
Tekirdağ ☆ TR 128-129 B 2
Tekit o MEX 52-53 K 1
Tekkali o IND 142-143 D 6
Teklatnika River ~ USA 20-21 Q 4
Tekman ☆ TR 128-129 J 3
Teknaf o BD 142-143 H 5
Tekoa o USA (WA) 244-245 H 3
Tèkodeľka ~ RUS 114-115 Q 2
Tekom o MEX 52-53 K 1
Tekouiat, Oued ~ DZ 190-191 D 9
Tékro o TCH 198-199 K 3
Teku o RI 164-165 H 4
Te Kuiti o NZ 182 E 3
Tela o HN 52-53 L 4
Tela o ZRE 214-215 E 7
Telaga o RI 168 C 3
Telagapulang o RI 162-163 K 6
Telagh o DZ 188-189 L 3
Telan, ostrov ⌒ RUS 120-121 S 3
Telanaipura = Jambi ☆ RI 162-163 E 5
Telanskij, mys ▲ RUS 120-121 S 3
Telaqua Lake o USA 20-21 N 6
Telarah o AUS 178-179 J 2
Telares o RA 76-77 F 5
Tel Ashqelon ∴• IL 130-131 D 2
Télatai o RMM 196-197 L 6
Telavi o GE 126-127 F 7
Tel Aviv-Yafo ☆ IL 130-131 D 1
Telč o••• CZ 92-93 N 4
Telchac o MEX 52-53 K 1
Telde o E 188-189 D 7
Tele ~ ZRE 210-211 K 2
Télé, Lac o RMM 196-197 J 6
Teleckoe, ozero o•• RUS 124-125 P 3
Telefomin o PNG 183 A 3
Telegootherra, Mount ▲ AUS 176-177 D 3
Telegraph o USA (TX) 266-267 H 3
Telegraph Creek o CDN 32-33 E 3
Telegraph Range ▲ CDN 228-229 L 3
Telekitonga ⌒ TON 184 IV a 2
Teleköl o KZ 124-125 E 6
Teleköl kanal < KZ 124-125 E 6
Telêmaco Borba o BR 74-75 E 5
Télemsès o RN 198-199 B 5
Telemzane o DZ 190-191 E 4
Telen ~ RI 164-165 E 3
Teleneşti = Teleneşti ☆ MD 102-103 F 4
Teleneşti ☆ MD 102-103 F 4
Telenešty = Teleneşti ☆ MD 102-103 F 4
Teleorman ~ RO 102-103 D 5
Telerghma o DZ 190-191 F 2
Telerhteba, Djebel ▲ DZ 190-191 F 8
Teles Pires ou São Manuel, Rio ~ BR 70-71 K 3
Telfer o• AUS 172-173 F 6
Telfordville o CDN (ALB) 232-233 D 2
Télimélé o RG 202-203 D 4
Teljo, Ğabal ▲ SUD 200-201 B 5
Telkwa o CDN (BC) 228-229 G 2
Telkwa River ~ CDN 228-229 G 2
Tell o USA (TX) 264-265 D 4
Tell Atlas = Tellien, Atlas ▲ DZ 188-189 L 3
Tell City o USA (IN) 274-275 M 7
Tell el-Amarna ∴• ET 194-195 E 4
Teller o USA 20-21 G 4
Tellico Lake < USA (TN) 282-283 C 5
Tellis o TCH 198-199 H 5
Tello, Chute du ~• CAM 204-205 K 5
Telloh ∴• IRQ 128-129 M 7
Telluride o USA (CO) 254-255 H 6
Telmen = Övögdij o MAU 148-149 C 3
Telmèn nuur o MAU 148-149 C 3
Telmet, Col de ▲ DZ 190-191 F 3
Telogia Creek ~ USA 286-287 E 1
Teloloapan o MEX 52-53 E 2
Telouèt o• MA 188-189 H 5
Telpani o NEP 144-145 C 6
Telpoziz, gora ▲ RUS 114-115 E 3
Telsang o IND 140-141 F 2
Telsen o RA 78-79 F 7
Telšiai ☆•• LT 94-95 H 4
Telteié o ETH 208-209 C 6
Teltsch = Telč o CZ 92-93 N 4
Telukan o RI 168 C 7
Telukbatang o RI 162-163 H 5
Telukbayur o RI (KTI) 164-165 E 2
Telukbayur o RI (SUB) 162-163 D 5
Telukbetung = Bandar Lampung ☆ RI 162-163 F 7
Telukbutun o RI 162-163 H 2
Telukdalam o RI 162-163 B 4
Teluk Intan o• MAL 162-163 D 2
Teluk Kumbar o MAL 162-163 D 2
Teluklembu, Ujung ▲ RI 162-163 D 5
Teluknibung o RI 162-163 C 3
Teluk Penarik ≈ 162-163 G 3
Telukpulaidalem o RI 162-163 C 3
Teluk Sinabang ≈ 162-163 B 3
Teluku o RI 164-165 H 5
Tely ~ ZRE 212-213 A 2
Tem o RN 202-203 L 2
Téma o BF 202-203 K 3
Téma o• GH 202-203 K 7
Temacine o DZ 190-191 F 4
Temagami o CDN (ONT) 236-237 J 5
Temagami, Lake o CDN (ONT) 238-239 E 2
Temanggung o RI 168 D 3
Temascal, El o MEX 50-51 K 5
Temascaltepec o MEX 52-53 D 2
Temax o MEX 52-53 K 1
Temazcal o MEX 52-53 F 2
Temazcaltepec o MEX 52-53 F 3
Temba o ZA 220-221 J 2
Tembagapura o RI 166-167 J 4
Tembe Elefant Reserve ⊥ ZA 220-221 L 3
Tembeling o• MAL 162-163 E 2
Tembenči ~ RUS 116-117 J 3
Tembenči, ozero o RUS 116-117 G 2
Tembesi ~ RI 162-163 E 6
Tembilahan o RI 162-163 E 5
Tembito o RI 164-165 G 3
Tembladera o PE 64-65 C 5
Temblador o YV 60-61 K 3
Tembladoras, Laguna ≈ 52-53 H 4
Temblor Range ▲ USA 248-249 D 4
Tembo o ZRE 216-217 D 3
Tembo, Chutes ~ ZRE 216-217 D 3
Tembo Aluma o ANG 216-217 D 3
Tembwe o Z 214-215 G 6
Temcha ~ ETH 208-209 C 3
Temelon o GQ 210-211 C 3
Téméra o RMM 196-197 K 6
Temerloh o• MAL 162-163 E 3
Teminabuan o RI 166-167 F 2
Temir ~ KZ 126-127 M 3
Temirlan ☆ KZ 136-137 L 3
Temirovka o KS 146-147 C 4
Temírtau o KZ 124-125 H 3
Temirtau = Temírtau o KZ 124-125 H 3
Témiscamie, Rivière ~ CDN 38-39 H 3
Témiscaming o CDN (QUE) 238-239 F 2
Témiscamingue, Lac o CDN (QUE) 236-237 J 5
Témiscouata, Lac o CDN (QUE) 240-241 G 3
Temki o TCH 206-207 D 3
Temnik ~ RUS 116-117 M 10
Temnikov o RUS 94-95 S 4
Tëmnyj, mys ▲ RUS 112-113 Q 6
Temo o MEX 52-53 H 3
Temon o RI 168 D 3
Temora o AUS 180-181 J 3
Témoris o MEX 50-51 E 4
Tempe o USA (AZ) 256-257 D 5
Tempe, Danau o RI 164-165 F 6
Tempeh o RI 168 E 4
Temperance o USA (MI) 272-273 F 6
Tempestad o PE 64-65 E 2
Témpio Pausánia o I 100-101 B 4
Templadera del Derrumbe, La o MEX 50-51 F 5
Temple o USA (OK) 264-265 F 4
Temple o USA (TX) 266-267 K 2
Temple Bay ≈ 174-175 G 3
Templeman o USA (VA) 280-281 K 5
Templer Bank ≃ 160-161 B 7
Temple Terrace o USA (FL) 286-287 G 3
Templeton o USA (CA) 248-249 D 4
Templo de Viracocha • PE 70-71 B 4
Tempoal de Sánchez o MEX 50-51 K 7
Tempué o ANG 216-217 E 6
Temrjuk o RUS 102-103 K 5
Temrjukskij zaliv ≈ 102-103 K 5
Temuco ☆ RCH 78-79 C 5
Temuka o NZ 182 C 6
Ten o CO 60-61 E 5
Tena ☆ EC 64-65 D 2
Tenabó o MEX 52-53 J 1
Ténado o BF 202-203 J 3
Tenaghau = Aola o SOL 184 I e 3
Tenaha o USA (TX) 268-269 F 5
Tenakee Springs o USA 32-33 C 3
Tenaker Inlet ≈ 32-33 C 3
Tenāli o IND 140-141 J 2
Tenamatua, Gunung ▲ RI 164-165 G 4
Tenancingo o MEX 52-53 E 2
Tenasserim = Tanintharí o MYA 158-159 E 4
Tenasserim Island ⌒ MYA 158-159 D 4
Tenassorim = Tanintharí ~ MYA 158-159 E 4
Tenau o RI 166-167 B 7
Tenaún o RCH 78-79 C 7
Tenby o• GB 90-91 E 6
Tendaba o WAG 202-203 C 3
Tendaho o ETH 208-209 E 3
Ten Degree Channel ≈ 140-141 L 4
Tendik o KZ 124-125 J 3
Tendjedj ▲ DZ 190-191 F 9
Tendō o J 152-153 J 5
Tendouk o SN 202-203 B 3
Tendoy o USA (ID) 252-253 E 2
Tendrara o MA 188-189 K 4
Tendrivs'ka Kosa ∸ UA 102-103 G 4
Tendūkheda o IND 138-139 G 8
Téné o RMM 202-203 H 3
Tenemejal, Tanjung ▲ RI 164-165 G 5
Ténenkou o RMM 202-203 H 2
Tenente Marques, Rio ~ BR 70-71 G 2
Ténentou o RMM 202-203 G 4
Ténéré ∸ RN 198-199 E 4
Ténéré, Erg du ∸ RN 198-199 E 4
Ténéré du Tafassasset ∸ RN 198-199 E 2
Tenerife ⌒ E 188-189 C 6
Ténès o DZ 190-191 C 2
Tengah, Kampung o MAL 162-163 F 4
Tengah, Kepulauan ⌒ RI 168 C 6
Tengahdai o RI 166-167 B 6
Tengchong o VRC 142-143 L 3
Tenggara, Kepulauan ⌒ RI 166-167 F 5
Tenggarong o• RI 164-165 E 4
Tengger Shamo ∸ VRC 154-155 D 2
Tenggol, Pulau ⌒ MAL 162-163 E 2
Tengiz-Kürgalža ojpaty ∸ KZ 124-125 F 3
Teng Kangpoche ▲ NEP 144-145 F 7
Tengréla ☆ CI 202-203 G 4
Teng Xian o VRC 156-157 G 5
Tengzhou o VRC 154-155 K 4
Tenharim/ Igarapé Prêto, Área Indígena X BR 66-67 G 7
Tenharim/ Transamazônica, Área Indígena X BR 66-67 F 7
Teniente 1° Alfredo Stroessner o PY 76-77 G 2
Teniente Enciso, Parque Nacional ⊥ PY 76-77 G 2
Teniente General J.C. Sánchez o RA 76-77 H 3
Teniente Matienzo o ARK 16 G 31
Tenika • RM 222-223 D 9
Tenille o USA (FL) 286-287 F 2
Tenindewa o AUS 176-177 C 4
Tenino o USA (WA) 244-245 C 4
Tenis, ozero o RUS 114-115 M 6
Teniz, köli o KZ 124-125 D 1
Teniz köli o KZ 124-125 F 3
Tenja Seda, gora ▲ RUS 88-89 V 2
Tenkanyj, hrebet ▲ RUS 112-113 Y 3
Tenkási o IND 140-141 G 6
Tenke o ZRE 214-215 D 6
Tenkeli o RUS 110-111 X 4
Tènkèrgynpil'gyn, laguna ≈ 112-113 V 2
Tènki ~ RUS 110-111 T 5
Tenkiller Lake o USA (OK) 264-265 K 3
Tenkodogo ☆• BF 202-203 K 4
Tenläu o IND 140-141 L 6
Tenmile Creek ~ USA 268-269 H 6
Ten Mile Lake o CDN (NFL) 242-243 M 1
Ten Mile Pond o CDN (NFL) 242-243 P 3
Tennant Creek o• AUS 174-175 C 6
Tennent Islands ⌒ CDN 24-25 Y 6
Tennessee o USA (TX) 268-269 E 5
Tennessee ◘ USA 276-277 F 5
Tennessee Ridge o USA (TN) 276-277 H 4
Tennessee River ~ USA 276-277 H 5
Tennessee River ~ USA 282-283 C 5
Tennille o USA (GA) 284-285 H 4
Tennyson o USA (TX) 266-267 G 2
Teno ~ FIN 88-89 J 2
Teno, Río ~ RCH 78-79 D 3
Tenochtitlán o MEX 52-53 G 3
Tenom o MAL 160-161 A 10
Tenosique de Pino Suárez o MEX 52-53 J 3
Tenouchfi, Djebel ▲ DZ 188-189 L 3
Tenoûmer ▲ RIM 196-197 E 3
Tenryu-gawa ~ J 152-153 G 7
Tensas River ~ USA 268-269 J 4
Tensas River National Wildlife Refuge ⊥ USA (LA) 268-269 J 4
Tensaw River ~ USA 284-285 C 6
Tensed o USA (ID) 250-251 C 4
Tensift, Oued ~ MA 188-189 G 5
Ten Sleep o USA (WY) 252-253 L 2
Tenstrike o USA (MN) 270-271 D 3
T'enta o ETH 208-209 D 3
Tente o RI 168 D 7
Tentek ~ KZ 124-125 M 6
Tenteksor ∸ KZ 96-97 H 10
Tenteksor köl o KZ 124-125 C 2
Tentena o RI 164-165 G 4
Tenterfield o AUS 178-179 M 5
Ten Thousand Islands ⌒ USA (FL) 286-287 H 6
Tentolotianan, Gunung ▲ RI 164-165 G 3
Tentugal o BR 68-69 E 2
Tenuchchad, Oued ~ WSA 188-189 G 7
Teo-Ašuu, pereval ▲ KS 136-137 N 3
Teocaltiche o MEX 50-51 H 7
Teocuitatlán de Corona o MEX 52-53 C 1
Teodoro Sampaio o BR (BAH) 72-73 L 2
Teodoro Sampaio o BR (PAU) 72-73 D 7
Teodoro Schmidt o RCH 78-79 C 5
Teofilândia o BR 68-69 J 7
Teófilo Otoni o BR 72-73 K 4
Teofipol' ☆ UA 102-103 E 3
Teos • TR 128-129 B 3
Teotepec, Cerro ▲ MEX 52-53 D 3
Teotihuacán ∴••• MEX 52-53 E 2
Teotitlán del Camino o MEX 52-53 F 2
Tepa o GH 202-203 J 6
Tepalcatepec o MEX 52-53 C 2
Tepatitlán o MEX 52-53 C 1
Tepeaca o MEX 52-53 F 2
Tepechitlán o MEX 50-51 H 7
Tepecoacuilco o MEX 52-53 E 2
Tepehuanes o MEX 50-51 G 5
Tepehuanes, Río los ~ MEX 50-51 F 5
Tepeji del Río o MEX 52-53 E 2
Tepelenë ☆•• AL 100-101 H 4
Tepere o MOC 218-219 K 1
Tepetzintla o MEX 50-51 L 7
Tépi o ETH 208-209 B 5
Tepic ☆ MEX 50-51 G 7
Tepich o MEX 52-53 K 1
Teplice o CZ 92-93 M 3
Teplitz = Teplice o CZ 92-93 M 3
Teploe ☆ RUS 94-95 P 5
Teploključenka o KS 146-147 D 4
Teplyj Ključ o RUS 120-121 G 2
Tepoca, Bahía de ≈ 50-51 C 2
Tepoca, Cabo ▲ MEX 50-51 C 3
Teptep o PNG 183 D 3
Tepuxtla o MEX 50-51 F 6
Tequeje, Río ~ BOL 70-71 D 3
Teques, Los ☆ YV 60-61 H 2
Tequesquite Creek ~ USA 256-257 M 3
Tequila o• MEX 52-53 C 1
Tequisquiapan o MEX 52-53 E 1
Téra o RN 202-203 L 2
Tera, Río ~ E 98-99 E 4
Teradomari o J 152-153 H 6
Terakeka o SUD 206-207 K 6
Téramo ☆ I 100-101 D 3
Terán o CO 64-65 C 1
Terang o AUS 180-181 G 5
Terapo o PNG 183 D 5
Teratani ~ PK 138-139 B 5
Terbanggibesar o RI 162-163 F 7
Terbang Selatan, Pulau ⌒ RI 166-167 E 5
Terbjas o RUS 118-119 K 3
Tercan ☆ TR 128-129 J 3
Terceira, Ilha ⌒ P 6-7 G 5
Terceiro Acampamento o BR 62-63 H 5
Tercero, Río ~ RA 78-79 H 2
Terchicherin, Erg in ∸ RMM 196-197 K 4
Tere ~ RUS 116-117 G 4
Terebija ~ UA 102-103 C 3
Terebo o PNG 183 B 2
Terebovlja ☆ UA 102-103 D 3
Terek o RUS 126-127 F 6
Terek ~ RUS 126-127 F 6
Terekhol o IND 140-141 E 3
Terekli-Mekteb o RUS 126-127 F 5
Terékolé ~ RMM 202-203 F 2
Terekti o KZ 124-125 F 4
Terëlž o MAU 148-149 J 4
Terence Bay o CDN (NS) 240-241 M 6
Teren'ga ☆ RUS 96-97 F 7
Terengganu ◘ MAL 162-163 E 2
Terengganu, Kuala ☆• MAL 162-163 E 2
Terenni ∴• RIM 196-197 F 6
Terenos o BR 70-71 K 7
Terepaima, Parque Nacional ⊥ YV 60-61 G 3
Teresén o YV 60-61 K 2
Teresina ☆ BR 68-69 G 4
Tereška ~ RUS 96-97 E 7
Teresópolis o BR 72-73 J 7
Terezinha de Goiás o BR 72-73 G 2
Terezy Klavenes, zaliv ≈ 108-109 f 3
Teriberka o RUS 88-89 N 2
Teriberka ~ RUS 88-89 N 2
Teridgerie Creek ~ AUS 178-179 K 6
Terina ~ RUS 116-117 J 6
Terin Kōt ☆ AFG 134-135 L 2
Terisakkan ~ KZ 124-125 E 3
Terlingua o USA (TX) 266-267 D 4
Terlingua Creek ~ USA 266-267 D 4
Terma, Ra's ▲ ER 200-201 L 6
Terma do Quilombo • BR 72-73 F 7
Termas de Chillán o RCH 78-79 D 4
Termas de Guaviyu • ROU 76-77 J 6
Termas de Jurema • BR 74-75 D 5
Termas del Daymán • ROU 76-77 J 6
Termas del Flaco o RCH 78-79 D 3
Termas de Pemehue o RCH 78-79 D 5
Termas do Gravatal • BR 74-75 F 7
Termas Talacasto • RA 76-77 C 6
Terme ☆ TR 128-129 G 2
Termessé o RG 202-203 D 3
Termez ☆• UZ 136-137 K 6
Termiang, Pulau ⌒ RI 162-163 F 4
Términi Imerese o I 100-101 D 6
Términi Imerese, Golfo di ≈ 100-101 D 5
Terminillo, Monte ▲•• I 100-101 D 3
Términos, Laguna de ≈ 52-53 J 2
Termit o RN 198-199 E 4
Termit, Massif de ▲ RN 198-199 E 4
Térmoli o I 100-101 E 3
Term Point ▲ CDN 30-31 X 4
Ternate o• RI 164-165 K 3
Ternay, Lac o CDN 38-39 K 2
Ternej o RUS 122-123 G 6
Terni ☆ I 100-101 D 3
Ternopil' ☆ UA 102-103 D 3
Ternopol' = Ternopil' ☆ UA 102-103 D 3
Terolak, Kampung o MAL 162-163 D 2
Terou ~ DY 202-203 L 5
Terowie o AUS 180-181 E 2
Terpenija, mys ▲ RUS 122-123 L 4
Terpenija, poluostrov ⌣ RUS 122-123 L 4
Terpenija, zaliv ≈ 122-123 K 4
Terpjaj-Tumsa, poluostrov ⌣ RUS 110-111 M 3
Terra Alta o BR 68-69 E 2
Terra Bella o USA (CA) 248-249 E 4
Terra Boa o BR 72-73 D 7
Terra Branca o BR 72-73 J 4
Terrace o CDN (BC) 228-229 F 2
Terracebaai o NAM 216-217 B 9
Terrace Bay o CDN (ONT) 234-235 Q 6
Terrace Mountain ▲ USA (UT) 254-255 B 2
Terraces, The ▲ AUS 176-177 F 4
Terracina o I 100-101 D 4
Terra de Areia o BR 74-75 E 7
Terra Firma o ZA 220-221 F 2
Terrāk o N 86-87 F 4
Terral o USA (OK) 264-265 G 5
Terralba o I 100-101 B 5
Terra Nivea ▲ CDN 36-37 Q 3
Terra Nova o BR (ACR) 66-67 C 7
Terra Nova o BR (PER) 68-69 J 6
Terra Nova o CDN (NFL) 242-243 O 4
Terra Nova do Norte o BR 70-71 K 2
Terra Nova National Park ⊥ CDN (NFL) 242-243 O 4
Terra Preta o BR 66-67 H 6
Terra Preta, Igarapé ~ BR 66-67 H 5
Terra Vermelha o BR 76-77 J 1
Terrebonne o CDN (QUE) 238-239 M 3
Terrebonne o USA (OR) 244-245 D 6
Terrebonne Bay ≈ 268-269 K 7
Terre Haute o USA (IN) 274-275 L 5
Terrell o USA (TX) 264-265 H 6
Terrenate o MEX 52-53 F 2
Terrenceville o CDN (NFL) 242-243 O 5
Terre Noire Creek ~ USA 276-277 B 6
Terreton o USA (ID) 252-253 F 3
Terrier Rouge o RH 54-55 K 5
Terril o USA (IA) 274-275 D 1
Terry o USA (MT) 250-251 O 5
Terry Hie Hie o AUS 178-179 L 5
Tersakan Gölü o TR 128-129 E 3
Tersakkan ~ KZ 124-125 E 4
Terschelling ⌒ NL 92-93 H 2
Tersef o TCH 198-199 H 6
Terskenespe ~ KZ 124-125 E 5
Terskij bereg ⌣ RUS 88-89 O 3
Tersko-Kumskij kanal < RUS 126-127 F 5
Terter ~ AZ 128-129 M 2
Terter = Tartar o AZ 128-129 M 2
Tertež o RUS 116-117 F 8
Teruel o CO 60-61 D 6
Teruel o••• E 98-99 G 4
Terujak o RI 162-163 B 2
Tervel o BG 102-103 E 6
Tervo o FIN 88-89 J 5
Tervola o FIN 88-89 H 3
Tes' o RUS 116-117 E 8
Tes, Lake = Letas, Lac o VAN 184 II a 2
Tes = Zur o MAU 116-117 G 11
Tesalia o CO 60-61 D 6
Teschen = Český Těšín o CZ 92-93 P 4
Tescott o USA (KS) 262-263 J 5
Tésécau, Lac o CDN 38-39 G 3
Teselima o GH 202-203 J 5
Teseny o ER 200-201 H 5
Tes gol ~ MAU 116-117 F 10
Tes gol ~ MAU 148-149 C 3
Teshekpuk Lake o USA 20-21 O 1
Tes-Hem ~ RUS 116-117 G 10
Teshikaga o J 152-153 L 3
Teshio-santi ▲ J 152-153 J 3
Teslin o CDN 20-21 Y 6
Teslin Lake o CDN 20-21 Y 7
Teslin River ~ CDN 20-21 X 6
Tesouras, Rio ~ BR 72-73 E 3
Tessalit o RMM 196-197 L 4
Tessaoua o RN 198-199 D 6
Tessaout, Oued ~ MA 188-189 H 5
Tesselamane o RMM 196-197 M 6
Tessema ~ RUS 108-109 e 3
Tesseralik o CDN 36-37 R 2
Tesséroukane o RN 198-199 C 3
Tessier, Lac o CDN (QUE) 236-237 N 4
Tessik Lake o CDN 36-37 M 2
Tessiner Alpen = Alpi Ticinese ▲ CH 92-93 K 5
Tessit o RMM 202-203 L 2
Tessoum, Tegguidda-n- o RN 198-199 C 4
Tessounfat o RMM 196-197 L 4
Test, Tizi-n ▲ MA 188-189 G 5
Teste, la o F 90-91 G 9
Testerazo, El o MEX 50-51 A 1
Testigos, Islas Los ⌒ YV 60-61 K 2
Testour o TN 190-191 G 2
Tesuque Indian Reservation X USA (NM) 256-257 K 3
Têt ~ F 90-91 J 10
Tetachuck Lake o CDN (BC) 228-229 J 3
Tètanto, ozero o RUS 108-109 O 7
Tetas, Punta ▲ RCH 76-77 B 2
Tetcela River ~ CDN 30-31 H 5
Tete ◘ MOC 218-219 F 2
Tete ☆ MOC (Tet) 218-219 G 3
Tété = Manovo ~ RCA 206-207 E 4
Tetebatu o•• RI 168 C 7
Tête d'Ours, Lac o CDN 30-31 O 4
Tetehui o PNG 183 C 4
Teteja ~ RUS 116-117 N 5
Tête Jaune Cache o CDN (BC) 228-229 P 4
Tetepare ⌒ SOL 184 I c 3
Tetere ~ RUS 116-117 L 5
Te Te Re o SOL 184 I e 4
Teteriv ~ UA 102-103 G 2
Teterow o• D 92-93 M 2
Teteven o BG 102-103 D 6
Tethul River ~ CDN 30-31 O 5
Tetijiv ☆ UA 102-103 F 3
Tétini ▲ RG 202-203 F 5
Tetjuši ☆ RUS 96-97 F 6
Tetlin Junction o USA 20-21 T 5
Tetlin Lake o USA 20-21 T 5
Tetlin River ~ USA 20-21 T 5
Tetonia o USA (ID) 252-253 G 3
Teton River ~ USA 250-251 H 4
Teton Village o USA (WY) 252-253 H 3
Tetouan = Titwân ☆• MA 188-189 J 3
Tétouan = Titwân ☆• MA 188-189 J 3
Tetovo o• MK 100-101 H 3
Tetris, Monte ▲ RA 80 D 4
Tetulia ~ BD 142-143 G 4
Teturi o ZRE 212-213 B 3
Teuco, Río ~ RA 76-77 F 2
Teulada o I 100-101 B 5
Teulada, Capo ▲ I 100-101 B 5
Teulon o CDN (MAN) 234-235 F 4
Teun, Pulau ⌒ RI 166-167 E 5
Teuri-tō ⌣ J 152-153 J 2
Teutoburger Wald ▲ D 92-93 J 2
Teutônia o BR 74-75 E 7
Teutonic Mining Centre o AUS 176-177 F 4
Tévere ~ I 100-101 D 3
Teverya ☆ IL 130-131 D 1
Tevi, mys ▲ RUS 120-121 T 4
Tevriz ☆ RUS 114-115 M 6
Te Waewae Bay ≈ NZ 182 A 7
Tewah o RI 162-163 K 5
Tewantin o AUS 178-179 M 4
Tëwo o VRC 154-155 C 4
Tewure o WAN 204-205 F 4
Texada Island ⌒ CDN (BC) 230-231 E 4
Texana, Lake < USA (TX) 266-267 L 5
Texarkana o USA (AR) 276-277 B 7
Texas o AUS 178-179 L 5
Texas ◘ USA 266-267 D 3
Texas City o USA (TX) 268-269 F 7
Texas Downs o AUS 172-173 J 4
Texas Point ▲ USA (TX) 268-269 G 7
Texcoco o MEX 52-53 E 2
Texel ⌒ NL 92-93 H 2
Texhoma o USA (TX) 264-265 C 2
Texiguat o HN 52-53 L 5
Texline o USA (TX) 264-265 A 2
Texola o USA (OK) 264-265 E 3
Texoma, Lake o USA (OK) 264-265 H 5
Texon o USA (TX) 266-267 F 2
Teyateyaneng o LS 220-221 H 4
Teymurlu o IR 128-129 L 4
Tezejol o TM 136-137 G 6
Teziutlán o MEX 52-53 F 2
Tezpur o• IND 142-143 H 2
Tezzeron Creek ~ CDN 228-229 K 2
Tezzeron Lake o CDN (BC) 228-229 K 2
Tfaritiy o WSA 188-189 F 7
Tha-Anne River ~ CDN 30-31 V 5
Thabana Ntlenyana ▲ LS 220-221 J 4
Thaba Nchu o ZA 220-221 H 4
Thaba Putsoa ▲ LS 220-221 H 5
Thaba Tseka o LS 220-221 J 4
Thabazimbi o ZA 220-221 H 2
Thabeikkyin o MYA 142-143 J 4
Tha Bo o THA 158-159 G 2
Tha Champa o THA 158-159 H 2
Thach An o VN 156-157 E 5
Tha Chana o THA 158-159 E 6
Thạch Bi o VN 158-159 K 3
Thạch Trụ o VN 158-159 K 3
Thackaringa ∴ AUS 180-181 F 2
Thādiq o KSA 130-131 J 5
Thafmakó o GR 100-101 J 5
Thagaya o MYA 142-143 K 6
Thái Bình ☆ VN 156-157 E 6
Thái Hòa ☆ VN 156-157 D 7
Thailand, Gulf of ≈ 158-159 F 5
Thailand = Muang Thai ◘ THA 158-159 E 2
Thái Nguyên ☆ VN 156-157 D 6
Thakadu o RB 218-219 D 5
Thakaundrove Peninsula ⌣ FJI 184 III b 2
Thakurgaon o BD 142-143 F 2
Thal o PK 138-139 C 3
Thala o TN 190-191 G 3
Thalang o THA 158-159 E 6
Thalberg o CDN (MAN) 234-235 G 4
Thalbitzer, Cape ▲ CDN 24-25 h 6
Thal Canal < PK 138-139 C 4
Thale Luang ≈ 158-159 F 7
Thalia o USA (TX) 264-265 E 5
Thallon o AUS 178-179 K 5
Thalpar o IND 138-139 E 2
Thamad al Qaṭṭār o LAR 192-193 F 3
Thamad Bū Hashīshah o LAR 192-193 H 4
Thamad Qabr Ṣāliḥ < LAR 192-193 D 2
Thamaga o RB 220-221 G 2
Tha Mai o THA 158-159 G 4
Thames ~ GB 90-91 G 6
Thames River ~ CDN 238-239 D 6
Thames River ~ USA 280-281 O 2
Thamesville o CDN (ONT) 238-239 D 6
Tham Than National Park ⊥ THA 158-159 E 3
Thana o IND 138-139 D 10
Thanatpin o MYA 158-159 D 2
Thanbyuzayat o MYA 158-159 D 3
Thăng Bình o VN 158-159 K 3
Thangoo o AUS 172-173 F 5
Thanh Hòa o VN 158-159 J 5
Thanh Hóa ☆ VN 156-157 D 7
Thành Phố Hồ Chí Minh ☆•• VN 158-159 J 5
Thanh Sơn ☆ VN 156-157 D 6
Thanjavur o••• IND 140-141 H 5
Thankot o NEP 144-145 E 7
Than Kyun ⌒ MYA 158-159 E 6
Thanlwin Myit ~ MYA 142-143 K 6
Thāno Būla Khān o PK 134-135 M 6
Than Uyên ☆ VN 156-157 C 6
Thanyit o MYA 142-143 J 3
Thanze o MYA 158-159 C 2
Thaoge ~ RB 218-219 B 4
Thaolintoa Lake o CDN 30-31 V 5
Thảo Phi Tung o VN 156-157 D 5
Tha Pla o THA 158-159 F 2
Thap Put o THA 158-159 E 6
Thap Sakae o THA 158-159 E 5
Thap Than o THA 158-159 E 3
Thar ∸ IND 138-139 C 6
Tharād o IND 138-139 C 7
Tharaka o EAK 212-213 G 4
Tharb o KSA 130-131 G 5
Thar Desert ∸ PK 138-139 B 6
Thargomindah o AUS 178-179 G 5
Tharp Fracture Zone ≃ 14-15 O 13
Thárros • I 100-101 B 5
Tharsis o E 98-99 D 6
Tha Sae o THA 158-159 E 5
Tha Sala o THA 158-159 E 6
Tha Song Yang o THA 158-159 E 2
Thássos o GR 100-101 K 4
Thássos ⌒ GR 100-101 K 4
Thatcher o USA (AZ) 256-257 F 6
Thatcher o USA (CO) 254-255 L 6
Thất Khê ☆ VN 156-157 E 5
Thaton o MYA 158-159 D 2
That Phanom o THA 158-159 H 2
Thatta o••• PK 134-135 M 6
Tha Tum o THA 158-159 G 3
Thaungdut o MYA 142-143 J 3
Tha Uthen o THA 158-159 H 2
Tha Wang Pha o THA 142-143 M 6
Thayawthadangyi Kyun ⌒ MYA 158-159 D 4
Thayer o USA (KS) 262-263 L 7
Thayer o USA (MO) 276-277 D 4
Thayetmyo o MYA 142-143 J 6
Thayne o USA (WY) 252-253 H 4
The Alps ▲ AUS 178-179 K 2
Theba o USA (AZ) 256-257 C 6
The Beaches o CDN (NFL) 242-243 M 3
The Berkshire ▲ USA 278-279 H 6
Thebes ∴••• ET 194-195 F 5
The Brothers = Lloyd Rock ⌒ BS 54-55 H 3
The Caves o AUS 178-179 L 2
The Current o BS 54-55 G 2
Thedford o USA (NE) 262-263 F 3
The English Company's Islands ⌒ AUS 174-175 D 3
Theewaterskloof Dam < ZA 220-221 D 7
The Forks o USA (ME) 278-279 M 3
The Four Archers • AUS 174-175 C 4
The Gap o USA (AZ) 256-257 D 2
The Gums o AUS 178-179 L 4
The Haven o ZA 220-221 J 6
Theinkun o MYA 158-159 E 5
Thekkadi o IND 140-141 G 6
Thekulthili Lake o CDN 30-31 P 5
The Lakes National Park ⊥ AUS 180-181 J 4
Thelon River ~ CDN 30-31 R 4
The Lynd Junction o AUS 174-175 H 6
The Monument o AUS 178-179 E 1
Thenia o DZ 190-191 D 2
Theniet El Had o DZ 190-191 D 3
Thenzawl o IND 142-143 H 4
Theo, Mount ▲ AUS 172-173 K 6
The Oaks o USA (CA) 248-249 F 5
Theodore o AUS 178-179 L 3
Theodore o CDN (SAS) 232-233 Q 4
Theodore o USA (AL) 284-285 B 6
Theodore Roosevelt Lake < USA (AZ) 256-257 D 5
Theodore Roosevelt National Park North Unit ⊥ USA (ND) 258-259 D 4
Theodore Roosevelt National Park South Unit ⊥ USA (ND) 258-259 D 5
Theodosia o USA (MO) 276-277 C 4
Thep Sa Thit o THA 158-159 F 3
Therhi o PK 138-139 B 6
Thermaïkós Kólpos ≈ 100-101 J 4
Thermal City o USA (NC) 282-283 F 5
Thermopolis o USA (WY) 252-253 K 3
The Rock o AUS 180-181 J 3
Theron Range ▲ ARK 16 E 0
The Settlement o GB 286-287 R 2
The Shoals Provincial Park ⊥ CDN (ONT) 236-237 E 5
Thesiger Bay ≈ 24-25 K 5
The Slot = New Georgia Sound ≈ 184 I c 2
Thessalía ⌣ GR 100-101 H 5
Thessalía ◘ GR 100-101 H 5
Thessalon o CDN (ONT) 238-239 B 2
Thessaloníki ☆••• GR 100-101 J 4
Thetford o GB 90-91 H 5
Thetford Mines o CDN (QUE) 238-239 O 2
The Three Sisters ⌒ AUS 174-175 G 2
Thetis Island o CDN (BC) 230-231 F 5
The Twelve Apostles •• AUS 180-181 G 5
Theunissen o ZA 220-221 H 4
Thevenard Island ⌒ AUS 172-173 B 6
The Village o USA (OK) 264-265 G 3
The Village of Soya Atas (Victoria Fort) ∴• RI 166-167 E 3
The Wash ≈ GB 90-91 H 5
Thíamis ~ GR 100-101 H 5
Thibodaux o USA (LA) 268-269 K 7
Thickwood Hills ▲ CDN 232-233 L 2
Thief Lake Wildlife Refuge ⊥ USA (MN) 270-271 C 2
Thief River Falls o USA (MN) 270-271 B 2
Thiel Mountains ▲ ARK 16 E 0
Thiès ☆• SN 202-203 B 2
Thika o EAK 212-213 F 4
Thikri o IND 138-139 E 8
Thillé Boubakar o SN 196-197 C 6
Thilogne o SN 196-197 D 7
Thimphu ☆• BHT 142-143 F 2
Thingsat o IND 142-143 H 3
Þingvallavatn o IS 86-87 c 2
Þingvellir o• IS 86-87 c 2
Thionville o F 90-91 L 7
Thira o GR 100-101 K 6
Thira ⌒•• GR 100-101 K 6
Thirsk o GB 90-91 G 4
Thirsty, Mount ▲ AUS 176-177 F 6
Thirtymile Creek ~ USA 250-251 L 3
Thirty Mile Lake o CDN 30-31 V 4
Thirunallar Temple • IND 140-141 H 5
Thiruvarur o IND 140-141 H 5
Thisbi o GR 100-101 J 5
Thisted o DK 86-87 D 8
Thistle Island ⌒ AUS 180-181 D 3
Thitani o EAK 212-213 F 4
Thiva o GR 100-101 J 5
Thị Xã Sơn Tây ☆ VN 156-157 D 6
Þjóðgarður Skaftafell ⊥ IS 86-87 e 2
Þjórsá ~ IS 86-87 d 2
Þjórsá ~ IS 86-87 c 3
Thlewiaza River ~ CDN 30-31 V 5
Thoa River ~ CDN 30-31 Q 5
Thổ Chu, Hòn ⌒ VN 158-159 G 6
Thoen o THA 158-159 E 2
Thoeng o THA 142-143 M 6
Thohoyandou ☆ ZA 218-219 F 6
Thomas o USA (OK) 264-265 F 3
Thomas o USA (SD) 260-261 J 2
Thomas o USA (WV) 280-281 G 4
Thomas Hill Reservoir o USA (MO) 274-275 F 5
Thomas Hubbard, Cape ▲ CDN 26-27 C 3
Thomas Lake, J.B. o USA (TX) 264-265 C 6
Thomas-Müntzer-Stadt Mühlhausen = Mühlhausen o• D 92-93 L 3
Thomas Pass ▲ USA (UT) 254-255 B 4
Thomas River ~ AUS 176-177 D 2
Thomassique o USA (GA) 286-287 F 1
Thomaston o USA (AL) 284-285 C 4
Thomaston o USA (GA) 284-285 F 4
Thomaston Corner o CDN (NB) 240-241 H 5

Tehuantepec, Río — Thomaston Corner 401

Toad River ∼ CDN 30-31 G 6
Toak o VAN 184 II b 3
Toamasina ◘ RM 222-223 F 6
Toamasina ☆ RM (TMA) 222-223 F 7
Toano o USA (VA) 280-281 K 6
Toari o BR 66-67 D 6
Toaupulai o IND 140-141 G 6
Toaya o RI 164-165 F 4
Toba o CDN (BC) 230-231 E 3
Toba o J 152-153 G 7
Toba o VRC 144-145 L 5
Toba, Isla ⌒ RA 80 H 2
Tobacco Range ⌒ BH 52-53 K 3
Tobago ⌒ TT 60-61 L 2
Toba Inlet ≈ 32-33 H 6
Toba Inlet ≈ 230-231 E 3
Toba Kākar Range ▲ PK 134-135 M 3
Tobalai, Pulau ⌒ RI 164-165 L 4
Tobalai, Selat ≈ 164-165 L 4
Tobamawu o RI 164-165 G 4
Toba River ∼ CDN 230-231 E 3
Tobarra o E 98-99 G 5
Toba Tek Singh o PK 138-139 D 4
Tobe o USA (CO) 254-255 M 6
Tobeatic Game Sanctuary ⊥ CDN (NS) 240-241 K 6
Tobejuba, Isla ⌒ YV 60-61 L 3
Tobelo o RI 164-165 K 3
Tobelombang o RI 164-165 G 4
Tobermorey o AUS 178-179 D 2
Tobermory o• CDN (ONT) 238-239 D 3
Tobermory o GB 90-91 D 3
Tobias Barreto o BR 68-69 J 7
Tobin, Kap = Uunarteq o GRØ 26-27 p 8
Tobin, Mount ▲ USA (NV) 246-247 H 3
Tobin Lake o AUS 172-173 G 6
Tobin Lake o CDN (SAS) 232-233 P 2
Tobin Lake o CDN (SAS) 232-233 P 2
Tobique 20 Indian Reserve X • CDN (NB) 240-241 H 4
Tobique River ∼ CDN 240-241 H 3
Tobishima ⌒ J 152-153 H 5
Toboali o RI 162-163 G 6
Tobol ∼ RUS 114-115 H 7
Tobol ∼ RUS 114-115 J 6
Tobol ∼ RUS 124-125 B 3
Toboli o RI 164-165 G 4
Tobol'sk ☆• RUS 114-115 K 5
Tobol'skij materik, vozvyšennost' ▲ RUS 114-115 K 5
Tobré o DY 204-205 E 3
Tobseda o RUS 88-89 W 2
Toby = Morarano o RM 222-223 E 8
Tobyčan ∼ RUS 110-111 X 7
Tobyl o KZ (KST) 124-125 C 2
Tobyl ∼ KZ 124-125 C 2
Tobys' ∼ RUS 88-89 W 5
Tobyš ∼ RUS 88-89 V 4
Tobyšskaja vozvyšennost' ▲ RUS 88-89 V 3
Toca o CO 60-61 E 5
Tocache Nuevo o PE 64-65 D 6
Tocaima o CO 60-61 D 5
Tocancipa o CO 60-61 E 5
Tocantinia o BR 68-69 D 6
Tocantinópolis o BR 68-69 E 5
Tocantins ◘ BR 68-69 D 7
Tocantins, Rio ∼ BR 62-63 K 6
Tocantins, Rio ∼ BR 68-69 E 5
Toccoa o USA (GA) 284-285 G 2
Točes ∼ RUS 114-115 U 4
Tochatwi Bay o CDN 30-31 O 4
Tochcha Lake o CDN (BC) 228-229 J 2
Tochi ∼ PK 138-139 B 3
Toch'o Do ⌒ ROK 150-151 E 10
Toco o ANG 216-217 B 7
Toco o RCH 76-77 C 2
Toco o TT 60-61 L 2
Tocoa River ∼ USA 284-285 F 2
Toconquis, Cerros de ▲ RA 76-77 D 3
Tocopilla o RCH 76-77 B 2
Tocopuri, Cerros de ▲ BOL 76-77 D 2
Tocota o RA 76-77 C 6
Tocumwal o AUS 180-181 H 3
Tocuyito o YV 60-61 G 2
Tocuyo, El o YV 60-61 G 3
Tocuyo, Río ∼ YV 60-61 G 2
Toda-saki ▲ J 152-153 K 5
Todd River ∼ AUS 178-179 C 3
Todeli o RI 164-165 J 4
Todenyang o EAK 212-213 B 6
Tödi ▲ CH 92-93 K 5
Todi o• I 100-101 D 3
Todin o BF 202-203 J 3
Todlo o RI 166-167 F 2
Todmorden o AUS 178-179 C 4
Todos los Santos, Lago o RCH 78-79 C 6
Todos os Santos, Baía de ≈ 72-73 L 2
Todos os Santos, Rio ∼ BR 72-73 K 4
Todos Santos o BOL 70-71 E 5
Todos Santos o MEX 50-51 D 6
Todra, Gorges du • MA 188-189 J 5
Todža, ozero = Azas, ozero o RUS 116-117 H 9
Todžinskaja kotlovina ⊥ RUS 116-117 H 9
Toéguin o BF 202-203 K 3
Toekomstig-stuwmeer o SME 62-63 F 3
Toéni o BF 202-203 J 3
Toéssé o BF 202-203 K 4
Toez o CO 60-61 C 6
Toffo o DY 204-205 E 5
Tofield o CDN (ALB) 232-233 F 2
Tofino o CDN (BC) 230-231 D 4
Töfsingdalens nationalpark ⊥ S 86-87 F 5
Tofua ⌒ TON 184 IV a 1
Toga, Île = Toga ⌒ VAN 184 II a 1
Toga = Île Toga ⌒ VAN 184 II a 1
Togafo o RI 164-165 K 3
Toganaly o AZ 128-129 M 2
Tōgane o J 152-153 J 7
Togba o RIM 196-197 E 6
Togdheer ◘ SP 208-209 G 4
Tog Dheer, togga ∼ SP 208-209 H 4
Togi o J 152-153 G 6
Togiak o USA 22-23 Q 3
Togiak Bay ≈ 22-23 Q 3
Togian, Kepulauan ⌒ RI 164-165 G 4
Togian, Pulau ⌒ RI 164-165 G 4
Togni o SUD 200-201 G 3
Togo o CDN (SAS) 232-233 R 4
Togo o PNG 183 B 5
Togo ■ RT 204-205 D 4
Togo o USA (MN) 270-271 E 3
Togo, Lac o RT 202-203 L 6
Togoba o PNG 183 C 3
Togobala o CI 202-203 G 5
Togo Hills ▲ GH 202-203 L 6
Togolika ∼ RUS 114-115 T 5
Togoromá o CO 60-61 C 5
Togou o RMM 202-203 H 3
Tögrög o MAU 146-147 L 2
Togtoh o VRC 154-155 G 1
Toguchin ☆ RUS 114-115 S 7
Togueré-Koumbé o RMM 202-203 H 2
Togul ☆ RUS 124-125 P 2
Tog Wajaale o SP 208-209 F 4
Togwotee Pass ▲ USA (WY) 252-253 H 3
Toğyzak ∼ KZ 124-125 C 2
Tohāna o IND 138-139 E 5
Tohareu, poluostrov ⌒ RUS 122-123 H 2
Tohatchi o USA (NM) 256-257 G 3
Tohiatoš o UZ 136-137 F 3
Tohma Çayı ∼ TR 128-129 H 3
Tōhoku o J 152-153 J 4
Töhöm o MAU 148-149 J 5
Tohomo ∼ RUS 116-117 G 5
Tohopekaliga, Lake o USA (FL) 286-287 H 3
Tohoun o RT 202-203 L 6
Toibalewe o IND 140-141 L 4
Toili o RI 164-165 H 4
Toineke o RI 166-167 C 7
Toison, La o RH 54-55 K 5
Toivala o FIN 88-89 J 5
Tojo o J 152-153 E 7
Tojoku o RUS 118-119 K 4
Tojtepa o UZ 136-137 L 4
Tok ∼ RUS 96-97 H 7
Tok ∼ RUS 118-119 O 8
Toka o GUY 62-63 E 4
Tokachi-dake ▲ J 152-153 K 3
Tokachi-gawa ∼ J 152-153 K 3
Tokamachi o J 152-153 H 6
Tokapalle o IND 140-141 H 3
Tōkar o SUD 200-201 H 3
Tokara-kaikyō ≈ 152-153 C 9
Tokara-rettō ⌒ J 152-153 C 10
Tokat ☆• TR 128-129 G 2
Tŏkchŏkto ⌒ ROK 150-151 E 9
Tokchon o KOR 150-151 F 8
Tok Do ⌒ ROK 150-151 H 9
Tokeland o USA (OR) 244-245 A 4
Tokelau Islands ⌒ NZ 13 K 3
Toki o TCH 206-207 C 4
Tokio o BOL 70-71 C 2
Tokio o USA (TX) 264-265 B 5
Tok Junction o USA 20-21 T 5
Tokko o RUS (SAH) 118-119 J 6
Tokko ∼ RUS 118-119 J 6
Tokko ∼ RUS 118-119 J 7
Toklat River ∼ USA 20-21 P 4
Tokma o RUS 116-117 M 6
Tokmak o UA 102-103 J 4
Tokoro o J 152-153 L 2
Tokoroa o NZ 182 E 3
Tokounou o RG 202-203 F 5
Toksovo o RUS 94-95 M 1
Toksum o VRC 146-147 J 4
Toktogul o KS 136-137 N 4
Toktogul'skoje vodohranilišče < KS 136-137 N 4
Tokuma o RUS 110-111 U 6
Tokunoshima o J 152-153 C 11
Tokuno-shima ⌒ J 152-153 C 11
Tokur-Jurjah ∼ RUS 112-113 J 4
Tokushima ☆ J 152-153 F 7
Tokuyama o J 152-153 D 7
Tokwe ∼ ZW 218-219 F 5
Toky, Chute ∼ ZRE 212-213 B 3
Tōkyō ☆• J 152-153 H 7
Tōkyō-wan ≈ 152-153 H 7
Tŏkyusan National Park ⊥ • ROK 150-151 F 10
Tol o PNG 183 G 3
Tola, La o EC 64-65 C 1
Tolabit o RI 164-165 K 3
Tolaga Bay o NZ 182 G 3
Tolala o RI 164-165 G 5
To' Lan o VN 158-159 K 5
Tōlanaro o• RM 222-223 E 10
Tolapalca, Río ∼ BOL 70-71 D 6
Tolar o USA (NM) 256-257 M 4
Tolar, Cerro ▲ RCH 76-77 B 1
Tolbazy ☆ RUS 96-97 J 6
Tolbo o MAU 146-147 K 1
Tolbo nuur o MAU 146-147 J 1
Tolbuhin = Dobrič o BG 102-103 E 6
Tolbuzino o RUS 118-119 M 9
Toldi o GH 202-203 K 5
Tolé o PA 52-53 D 7
Tolé o RCA 206-207 B 5
Toledo o BOL 70-71 D 6
Toledo o BR 74-75 D 5
Toledo o CDN (ONT) 238-239 K 4
Toledo o••• E 98-99 E 5
Toledo o USA (OH) 280-281 C 2
Toledo o USA (OR) 244-245 B 6
Toledo, Montes de ▲ E 98-99 E 5
Toledo Bend Reservoir < USA (TX) 268-269 G 5
Toledo City o RP 160-161 E 7
Tolga o DZ 190-191 E 3
Tolhuaca, Parque Nacional ⊥ RCH 78-79 D 5
Tolhuin o RA 80 G 7
Toli o VRC 146-147 F 3
Toliara ◘ RM 222-223 C 9
Toliara ☆• RM (Tla) 222-223 C 9
Tolima A o CO 64-65 F 2
Tolimán o MEX 52-53 E 1
Tolitoli o RI 164-165 G 3
Tol'jatti = Stavropol'-na-Volgi ☆ RUS 96-97 F 7
Tol'ka ∼ RUS 114-115 Q 3
Tolland o CDN (ALB) 232-233 H 2
Tolleson o USA (AZ) 256-257 C 5
Tolley o USA (ND) 258-259 F 3
Tollhouse o USA (CA) 248-249 E 2
Tol'ja, zaliv ≈ 108-109 d 3
Tolmačovo o RUS 94-95 L 2
Tolo o ZRE 210-211 G 5
Tolo, Teluk ≈ 164-165 G 5
Tolode o LB 202-203 F 6
Tolofu o RI 164-165 K 3
Tolokiwa Island ⌒ PNG 183 D 3
Tololalai (Muslim Tombs) o • RI 168 D 7
Tolon o• RUS 120-121 E 3
Tolongoina o RM 222-223 E 8
Tolono o USA (IL) 274-275 K 5
Tolonuu, Pulau ⌒ RI 164-165 L 3
Tolosa o E 98-99 F 3
Tolovana River ∼ USA 20-21 Q 4
Tolsan Do ⌒ ROK 150-151 F 10
Tolstoi o CDN (MAN) 234-235 G 5
Tolstova, mys ▲ RUS 110-111 V 2
Tolstyj, mys ▲ RUS 120-121 W 6
Toltén o RCH 78-79 C 5
Toltén, Río ∼ RCH 78-79 C 5
Tolu o CO 60-61 D 3
Toluca ☆• MEX 52-53 E 2
Toluca de Lerdo = Toluca ☆• MEX 52-53 E 2
Toluk o KS 136-137 N 4
Toluviejo o CO 60-61 D 3
Tolwe o ZA 218-219 E 6
Tol'yatti = Stavropol'-na-Volgi ☆ RUS 96-97 F 7
Tölz, Bad o D 92-93 L 5
Tom' ∼ RUS 114-115 S 6
Tom' ∼ RUS 122-123 C 3
Tom o USA (OK) 264-265 K 5
Tom o UZ 136-137 J 5
Toma o BF 202-203 J 3
Toma, La o RA 78-79 G 2
Toma, Río la ∼ RA 76-77 D 4
Tomah o USA (WI) 270-271 H 7
Tomahawk o USA (WI) 270-271 J 5
Tomakomai o J 152-153 J 3
Tomales Bay ≈ 246-247 B 5
Tomali o RI 164-165 G 4
Tomani o MAL 160-161 A 10
Tomanivi ▲ FJI 184 III b 2
Tomar o BR 66-67 F 3
Tomar o••• P 98-99 C 5
Tomari, Talahini- o CI 202-203 J 5
Tomari o RUS 122-123 K 5
Tomarovka o RUS 102-103 K 2
Tomarza ☆ TR 128-129 F 3
Tomas o PE 64-65 E 8
Tomás Garrido o MEX 52-53 K 2
Tomásia o BR 68-69 E 6
Tomaszów Lubelski o PL 92-93 R 3
Tomaszów Mazowiecki o PL 92-93 P 3
Tomat o SUD (Kas) 200-201 G 5
Tomat o SUD (NR) 206-207 H 3
Tomatán o MEX 50-51 B 3
Tomatlán o MEX 52-53 B 2
Tombador, Serra do ▲ BR 70-71 J 2
Tombali, Rio ∼ GNB 202-203 C 4
Tomball o USA (TX) 268-269 E 6
Tombe o ANG 216-217 D 6
Tombeaux • TCH 198-199 H 2
Tombe du Camerounais ▲ TCH 198-199 H 3
Tombel o CAM 204-205 H 6
Tombetsu, Hama- o J 152-153 K 2
Tombetsu, Nako- o J 152-153 K 2
Tombetsu, Shō- o J 152-153 K 2
Tombigbee River ∼ USA 284-285 B 5
Tombo, Punta ▲• RA 80 H 2
Tomboco o ANG 216-217 B 3
Tombokro o CI 202-203 H 6
Tombolo o RI 164-165 F 6
Tombouctou o••• RMM 196-197 J 6
Tombstone o USA (AZ) 256-257 E 7
Tombua o ANG 216-217 A 7
Tomé o RCH 78-79 C 4
Tome o USA (NM) 256-257 J 4
Tomea, Pulau ⌒ RI 164-165 H 6
Tomé-Açu o BR 68-69 D 3
Tomelloso o E 98-99 F 5
Tomi ∼ RCA 206-207 D 6
Tomichi Creek ∼ USA 254-255 J 5
Tomiko o CDN (ONT) 238-239 F 2
Tomina, Río ∼ BOL 70-71 E 6
Tominé ∼ RG 202-203 D 4
Tomingley o AUS 180-181 K 2
Tomini o RI 164-165 G 3
Tomini, Teluk ≈ 164-165 G 4
Tominián o RMM 202-203 H 3
Tomioka o J 152-153 H 6
Tomkinson Ranges ▲ AUS 176-177 K 3
Tomma ⌒ N 86-87 F 3
Tommot o RUS 118-119 N 6
Tommotskij massiv ▲ RUS 110-111 W 5
Tomo, Río ∼ CO 60-61 G 5
Tomochic o MEX 50-51 F 3
Tomohon o RI 164-165 J 3
Tomori o RCA 210-211 E 2
Tomorrit, Mali i ▲ AL 100-101 H 4
Tompira o RI 164-165 G 5
Tompi Seleka o ZA 220-221 J 2
Tompkins o CDN (SAS) 232-233 K 5
Tompkinsville o USA (KY) 276-277 K 4
Tompo o RI 164-165 G 3
Tompo o RUS (SAH) 120-121 F 2
Tompo ∼ RUS 120-121 F 2
Tom Price o AUS 172-173 C 7
Tom Price, Mount ▲ AUS 172-173 C 7
Tompuda ∼ RUS 118-119 E 8
Tomsk ☆• RUS 114-115 S 6
Toms River o USA (NJ) 280-281 M 4
Tom Steed o USA (OK) 264-265 E 4
Tomtor o RUS (SAH) 110-111 T 6
Tomtor o RUS (SAH) 120-121 E 2
Tomu o RI 166-167 G 3
Tomur Feng ▲ VRC 146-147 E 4
Tomu River ∼ PNG 183 B 4
Tom White, Mount ▲ USA 20-21 T 6
Tonalá o MEX (JAL) 52-53 C 1
Tonalá o• MEX (CHI) 52-53 H 3
Tonami o J 152-153 G 6
Tonantins o BR 66-67 D 4
Tonasket o USA (WA) 244-245 F 2
Tonate o F 62-63 H 3
Tonawanda Indian Reservation X USA (NY) 278-279 C 5
Tonb-e Bozorg, Ğazire-ye ⌒ IR 134-135 F 5
Tonb-e Kuček, Ğazire-ye ⌒ IR 134-135 F 5
Tonda o PNG 183 A 5
Tondano o RI 164-165 J 3
Tondano, Danau o RI 164-165 J 3
Tonde o Z 218-219 E 1
Tønder o• DK 86-87 D 9
Tondi o IND 140-141 H 6
Tondibi o RMM 196-197 K 6
Tondidji o RMM 202-203 E 3
Tondigamé Goulbi ∼ RN 204-205 E 2
Tondi Kiwidi o RN 204-205 E 1
Tondon o RG 202-203 D 4
Tondong o RI 164-165 F 5
Toné o BF 202-203 J 4
Tone-gawa ∼ J 152-153 H 6
Tonekābon o IR 136-137 B 6
Tong o SUD (SR) 206-207 J 5
Tong ∼ SUD 206-207 J 5
Tonga o CAM 204-205 J 6
Tonga o SUD 206-207 K 4
Tonga ■ TON 184 IV a 1
Tongaat o ZA 220-221 K 4
Tonga Islands ⌒ TON 184 IV a 2
Tongaland ⌒ ZA 220-221 L 3
Tong'an o VRC 156-157 L 4
Tonga Ridge ≃ 184 IV a 2
Tongariki ⌒ VAN 184 II b 3
Tongariro National Park ⊥••• NZ 182 E 3
Tongatapu ⌒ TON 184 IV a 2
Tongatapu Group ⌒ TON 184 IV a 2
Tonga Trench ≃ 13 K 4
Tongbai o VRC 154-155 H 5
Tongbai Shan ▲ VRC 154-155 H 5
Tongcheng o VRC (ANH) 154-155 K 6
Tongcheng o VRC (HUB) 156-157 H 2
Tongchon o KOR 150-151 F 8
Tongchuan o VRC 154-155 F 4
Tongdao o VRC 156-157 F 3
Tongde o VRC 154-155 B 4
T'ongdo Sa • ROK 150-151 G 10
Tongehatan Point ▲ RP 160-161 D 10
Tongerai, Tanjung ▲ RI 166-167 G 3
Tonggu o VRC 156-157 J 2
Tongguan o VRC 154-155 G 4
Tongguzbasti o VRC 146-147 E 6
Tonggu Zhang ▲ VRC 156-157 K 4
Tonghae o ROK 150-151 G 9
Tonghai o VRC 156-157 C 4
Tonghaiko o VRC 154-155 H 6
Tonghe o VRC 150-151 G 5
Tonghua o VRC 150-151 E 7
Tong Island ⌒ PNG 183 D 2
Tongjiang o VRC (HEI) 150-151 J 4
Tongjiang o VRC (SIC) 154-155 E 6
Tongjosŏn Man ≈ 150-151 F 8
Tongkomanino o RI 164-165 G 5
Tongku o RI 164-165 G 4
Tongliang o VRC 156-157 E 2
Tongliao o VRC 150-151 D 6
Tongling o VRC 154-155 K 6
Tonglu o VRC 156-157 L 2
Tongmu o VRC 156-157 H 3
Tongnan o VRC 154-155 D 6
Tongo o RCB 210-211 F 4
Tongoa ⌒ VAN 184 II b 3
Tongobory o RM 222-223 D 9
Tongomayel o BF 202-203 K 2
Tongren o VRC (GZH) 156-157 F 3
Tongren o VRC (QIN) 154-155 B 4
Tongsa o BHT 142-143 G 2
Tongshan o VRC 156-157 J 2
Tongshi o• VRC 156-157 F 7
Tongtian He ∼ VRC 144-145 K 3
Tongue o• GB 90-91 E 2
Tongue River ∼ USA 250-251 N 6
Tonguo ∼ RUS 118-119 K 4
Tonguro, Rio ∼ BR 72-73 D 2
Tongxiang o VRC 154-155 M 6
Tongxin o VRC 154-155 D 3
Tongyu o VRC (JIL) 150-151 D 5
Tongyu o VRC (SHA) 154-155 H 3
Tongzi o VRC 156-157 E 2
Tonhil = Zujl o MAU 146-147 L 2
Tonichi o MEX 50-51 E 3
Tonila o MEX 52-53 C 2
Tonimuca, Raudal ∼ CO 66-67 B 3
Tonina o CO 60-61 H 6
Toniná ∴• MEX 52-53 H 3
Tonk o IND 138-139 E 6
Tonka o RMM 196-197 J 6
Tonkawa o USA (OK) 264-265 G 2
Tonkensval ∼ SME 62-63 F 3
Tonki Cape ▲ USA 22-23 V 3
Tonkin o CDN (SAS) 232-233 Q 4
Tonkin, Gulf of ≈ 156-157 E 6
Tonkui, Mont ▲ CI 202-203 G 6
Tonlé Sab o K 158-159 H 4
Tonnerre o F 90-91 J 8
Tōno o J 152-153 J 5
Tonoda ∼ RUS 118-119 G 6
Tonono o RA 76-77 F 2
Tonopah o USA (AZ) 256-257 C 5
Tonopah o USA (NV) 246-247 H 5
Tonopah Test Range Atomic Energy Commission xx USA (NV) 248-249 H 2
Tonoro o YV 60-61 K 3
Tonosi o PA 52-53 D 8
Tonosyō o J 152-153 F 7
Tonotha o RB 218-219 D 5
Tonozero o RUS 88-89 M 4
Tonquil Island ⌒ RP 160-161 D 10
Ton Sai o THA 158-159 F 7
Tønsberg ☆ N 86-87 E 7
Tonsina o USA 20-21 S 6
Tonstad ☆ N 86-87 C 7
Tontado, Caleta ≈ 76-77 B 5
Tontal, Sierra del ▲ RA 76-77 C 6
Tontelbos o ZA 220-221 E 5
Tonto, Río ∼ MEX 52-53 F 2
Tonto Basin o USA (AZ) 256-257 D 5
Tonto National Monument • USA (AZ) 256-257 D 5
Tonumea ⌒ TON 184 IV a 2
Tonya ☆ TR 128-129 H 2
Tony Creek ∼ CDN 228-229 R 2
Tonzona River ∼ USA 20-21 O 5
Toobanna o AUS 174-175 J 6
Toobli o LB 202-203 F 6
Toodyay o AUS 176-177 D 5
Tooele o USA (UT) 254-255 C 3
To Okena o PNG 183 D 4
Toolebuc o AUS 178-179 F 2
Toolik River ∼ USA 20-21 Q 2
Toolondo o AUS 180-181 F 4
Tooloombilla o AUS 178-179 K 3
Toompine o AUS 178-179 H 4
Toomula o AUS 174-175 J 6
Tooncatchyin Creek ∼ AUS 178-179 E 5
Toora-Hem o RUS 116-117 H 9
Toormt o MAU 116-117 F 10
Toornaarsuk ⌒ GRØ 28-29 Q 6
Toowoomba o AUS 178-179 L 4
Top, Ozero = Topozero o RUS 88-89 M 4
Topagoruk River ∼ USA 20-21 N 1
Topanga o USA (CA) 248-249 F 5
Topar o KZ 124-125 J 6
Topasovèj, ostrov ⌒ RUS 108-109 M 7
Topawa o USA (AZ) 256-257 D 7
Topaz o USA (CA) 246-247 F 5
Topaz Lake o USA (NV) 246-247 F 5
Topeka ☆ USA (KS) 262-263 L 5
Topia o MEX 50-51 F 5
Topia ∼ RCA 206-207 C 6
Topia, Quebrada ∼ MEX 50-51 F 5
Topko, gora ▲ RUS 120-121 G 5
Topley o CDN (BC) 228-229 H 2
Topley Landing o CDN (BC) 228-229 H 2
Toplita o• RO 102-103 D 4
Topocalma, Punta ▲ RCH 78-79 C 3
Topock o USA (AZ) 256-257 A 4
Top of the World Provincial Park ⊥ CDN (BC) 230-231 O 4
Topografičeskaja, grjada ▲ RUS 108-109 Z 4
Topol o RUS 116-117 G 7
Topola o• YU 100-101 H 2
Topoli o ZRE 212-213 A 2
Topolinoe o RUS 120-121 F 1
Topolobampo o MEX 50-51 E 5
Topolovgrad o BG 102-103 E 6
Topolovka o RUS 120-121 T 3
Topozero o RUS 88-89 M 4
Toppenish o USA (WA) 244-245 E 4
Toppi-misaki ▲ J 152-153 J 4
Toprakkale ∴• TR 128-129 K 3
Tops, Mount ▲ AUS 172-173 L 6
Topsfield o USA (ME) 278-279 O 3
Top Springs o AUS (NT) 172-173 K 4
Top Springs ∴ AUS (NT) 174-175 C 5
Topura o PNG 183 F 6
Topyrakkala • UZ 136-137 G 4
Toquerville o USA (UT) 254-255 B 6
Tor o ETH 208-209 A 5
Torajan Villages, Typical X • RI 164-165 F 5
Toramarkog o VRC 144-145 L 4
Torata o PE 70-71 B 5
Torbanlea o AUS 178-179 M 3
Torbat-e Ğām o• IR 136-137 G 7
Torbat-e Heidarīye o• IR 136-137 F 7
Tor Day ≈ 240-241 O 5
Torbay o AUS 176-177 D 7
Torbay o CDN (NFL) 242-243 Q 5
Torbay o GB 90-91 F 6
Torboy o USA (WA) 244-245 G 2
Torch River ∼ CDN 232-233 P 2
Tordenskjøld, Kap ▲ GRØ 28-29 T 6
Tordesillas o E 98-99 E 4
Töre o S 86-87 L 4
Torej, Zun, ozero o RUS 118-119 H 10
Torell Land ⊥ N 84-85 K 4
Torello o E 98-99 J 3
Torenur o IND 140-141 F 4
Toreo Bugis o RI 164-165 H 5
Torğaj o KZ (KST) 126-127 P 3
Torğaj ∼ KZ 124-125 C 4
Torğaj ∼ KZ 126-127 P 3
Torğaj kolaty ∪ KZ 126-127 P 3
Torğaj üstirti ▲ KZ 124-125 B 3
Torgau o• D 92-93 M 3
Torgun ∼ RUS 96-97 E 8
Torhout o B 92-93 G 3
Tori o RMM 202-203 J 3
Toribio o CO 60-61 C 6
Tori-Bossito o DY 204-205 E 5
Torino ☆• I 100-101 A 2
Torino, Cachoeira do ∼ BR 62-63 F 6
Tori-shima ⌒ J 152-153 C 11
Torit o SUD 206-207 L 6
Toritama o BR 68-69 K 6
Toriu o PNG 183 F 3
Toriud o IR 136-137 D 7
Torje, Barun, ozero o RUS 118-119 G 10
Torkamān o IR 128-129 M 4
Torkemān, Bandar-e o IR 136-137 D 6
Torlu River ∼ PNG 183 F 3
Tormèmtor, ozero o RUS 114-115 P 4
Torment, Point ▲ AUS 172-173 F 4
Tormes, Río ∼ E 98-99 E 4
Tormosin o RUS 102-103 N 3
Tornado Mountain ▲ CDN (BC) 230-231 P 4
Torneälven ∼ S 86-87 L 3
Torneträsk o• S 86-87 J 2
Torngat Mountains ▲ CDN 36-37 R 5
Tornik ▲ YU 100-101 G 3
Tornio o FIN 88-89 H 4
Tornionjoki ∼ FIN 88-89 G 3
Tornquist o RA 78-79 H 5
Toro o E 98-99 E 4
Toro o EAU 212-213 C 3
Toro, Cerro del ▲ RA 76-77 C 5
Toro, Isla del ⌒ MEX 50-51 L 7
Toro, Lago del o RCH 80 D 5
Toro, Punta ▲ RCH 78-79 D 2
Torobuku o RI 164-165 H 6
Torodi o RN 202-203 L 3
Toro Doum o TCH 198-199 H 4
Toro Game Reservat ⊥ EAU 212-213 C 3
Torokina o PNG 184 I b 2
Toro Kinkéné o CI 202-203 H 5
Torokoroba o RMM 202-203 G 3
Törökszentmiklós o H 92-93 Q 5
Torola, Río ∼ ES 52-53 K 5
Torom o RUS (HBR) 120-121 F 6
Torom ∼ RUS 120-121 F 6
Toro Negro, Sierra del ▲ RA 76-77 C 5
Toronto ☆• CDN (ONT) 238-239 F 5
Toronto o USA (KS) 262-263 L 7
Toronto Lake o USA (KS) 262-263 L 7
Toropec ☆ RUS 94-95 M 3
Toroq o IR 136-137 F 6
Tororo o EAU 212-213 E 3
Torqabe o IR 136-137 F 6
Torquato Severo o BR 76-77 K 6
Torquay o CDN (SAS) 232-233 P 6
Torquinie, Lake o AUS 178-179 E 3
Torrabaai o NAM 216-217 B 10
Torrance o USA (CA) 248-249 F 6
Torrão o P 98-99 C 5
Torrealba o YV 60-61 J 3
Torre del Greco o I 100-101 E 4
Torre de Moncorvo o P 98-99 D 4
Torrelaguna o E 98-99 F 4
Torrelavega o E 98-99 E 3
Torremolinos o E 98-99 E 6
Torrens, Cape ▲ CDN 24-25 a 2
Torrens, Lake o AUS 178-179 D 6
Torrens Creek o AUS (QLD) 174-175 H 7
Torrens Creek ∼ AUS 178-179 H 2
Torrens River ∼ CDN 228-229 P 2
Torreón o MEX 50-51 H 5
Torreon o USA (NM) 256-257 H 3
Torre-Pacheco o E 98-99 G 6
Torres o• BR 74-75 F 7
Torres, Îles = Torres Islands ⌒ VAN 184 II a 1
Torres del Paine o RCH 80 D 5
Torres del Paine, Parque Nacional ⊥•• RCH 80 D 5
Torres Islands = Îles Torres ⌒ VAN 184 II a 1
Torres Martinez Indian Reservation X USA (CA) 248-249 H 6
Torres Novas o P 98-99 C 5
Torres Strait ≈ 174-175 F 1
Torres Vedras o P 98-99 C 5
Torrevieja o E 98-99 G 6
Torrey o USA (UT) 254-255 D 5
Torricelli Mountains ▲ PNG 183 B 2
Torrijos o E 98-99 E 5
Torrington o CDN (ALB) 232-233 E 4
Torrington o USA (CT) 280-281 N 2
Torrington o USA (WY) 252-253 O 4
Tor Rock ▲ AUS 174-175 B 2
Torrock o TCH 206-207 B 4
Torrön o S 86-87 F 5
Torsås ☆ S 86-87 H 8
Torsby ☆• S 86-87 F 6
Torset, Oued ∼ DZ 190-191 G 8
Tórshavn ☆ FR 90-91 D 1
Torsö ⌒ S 86-87 F 7
Torssuqatak ≈ 28-29 P 2
Tortas, Cachoeira das ∼ BR 70-71 J 4
Tortel o RCH 80 D 3
Tortiya o• CI 202-203 H 5
Törtköl o KZ 136-137 L 3
Tortola ⌒ GB 56 C 2
Tortola ⌒ GB 286-287 R 2
Tórtoles de Ésgueva o E 98-99 E 4
Tortona o I 100-101 B 2
Tortosa o E 98-99 H 4
Tortosa, Cabo de ▲ E 98-99 H 4
Tortue, Île de la ⌒ RH 54-55 J 4
Tortuga, Isla ⌒ MEX 50-51 D 4
Tortuga, Isla La ⌒ YV 60-61 J 2
Tortuguero, Parque Nacional ⊥ CR 52-53 C 6
Tortuguilla o C 54-55 H 5
Tortum ☆ TR 128-129 J 2
Torue o RI 164-165 G 4
Torugart o VRC 146-147 B 5
Torul ☆ TR 128-129 H 2
Toruń ☆•• PL 92-93 P 2
Torup o S 86-87 F 8
Tõrva o•• EST 94-95 J 2
Torwood o AUS 174-175 G 5
Tory o RUS 116-117 L 10
Tory Hill o CDN (ONT) 238-239 G 4
Toržkovskaja grjada ▲ RUS 94-95 O 3
Toržok ☆ RUS 94-95 O 3
Torzym o PL 92-93 N 2
Tosagua o EC 64-65 B 2
Tosari o RI 168 E 3
Tosa-shimizu o J 152-153 E 8
Tosa-wan ≈ 152-153 E 8
Tosca o ZA 220-221 F 2
Toscana ◘ I 100-101 C 3
Toscas, Las o RA (BUA) 78-79 J 3
Toscas, Las o RA (SAF) 76-77 H 5
Toscas, Las o ROU 78-79 M 2
Toshām o IND 138-139 E 5
Toshima ⌒ J 152-153 H 7
Toshino-Kumano National Park ⊥ J 152-153 G 7
Tosi o SUD 206-207 K 3
Toškent ☆•• UZ 136-137 L 4
Toškuduk, kumlik ∴ UZ 136-137 G 3
Toškŭrgon o UZ 136-137 K 5
Tosno ☆ RUS 94-95 M 2
Tosoncengel o MAU 148-149 D 3
Toson Hu o VRC 144-145 L 2
Tostado o RA 76-77 G 5
Tõstamaa o EST 94-95 H 2
Toston o USA (MT) 250-251 H 5
Tošviska o RUS 88-89 W 3
Tosya ☆ TR 128-129 F 2
Tot o EAK 212-213 E 3
Totaranui o NZ 182 D 4
Toteng o RB 218-219 B 5
Tôtes o F 90-91 H 7
Totias o SP 212-213 J 2
Tot'ma o RUS 94-95 S 2
Totnes o CDN (SAS) 232-233 K 4
Totnes Fiord ≈ 28-29 J 3
Totness ☆ SME 62-63 F 3
Toto o ANG 216-217 C 3
Toto o WAN 204-205 G 4
Totogan Creek ∼ CDN 234-235 O 2
Totogan Lake o CDN (ONT) 234-235 O 2
Totoglag o VAN 184 II a 1
Totok o RI 164-165 J 3
Totolán o MEX 52-53 C 1
Totolapan o MEX 52-53 F 3
Totomai, Monts ▲ RN 198-199 G 2
Totonicapán ☆• GCA 52-53 J 4
Totora o BOL (COC) 70-71 E 5
Totora o BOL (ORU) 70-71 C 5
Totoral o RCH 76-77 B 4
Totoral, Quebrada del ∼ RCH 76-77 B 4
Totoralejos o RA 76-77 E 5
Totoralito, Fort • RA 76-77 G 4
Totoras o RA 78-79 J 2
Totota o LB 202-203 F 6
Totoya ⌒ FJI 184 III c 3
Totta ∼ RUS 120-121 G 5
Tottan Range ▲ ARK 16 F 35
Totten Glacier ⊂ ARK 16 G 12
Tottenham o AUS 180-181 J 2
Tottenham o CDN (ONT) 238-239 F 4
Tottori ☆ J 152-153 F 7
Totumito o YV 60-61 F 4
Totydèottajaha, Bol'šaja ∼ RUS 108-109 T 8
Touâjîl o RIM 196-197 D 3
Touak Fiord ≈ 36-37 S 2
Touâret o RN 198-199 C 2
Touaris, Djebel ▲ DZ 188-189 K 6
Touat ∴ DZ 188-189 L 7
Touba o CI 202-203 G 5
Touba o• SN 202-203 C 2
Toubacouta o SN 202-203 B 3
Toubéré Bafal o SN 202-203 D 2
Toubkal, Jbel ▲ MA 188-189 H 5
Touboro o CAM 206-207 B 5
Touboutou, Chutes de ∼• RCA 206-207 B 6
Toucha, Djebel ▲ DZ 188-189 L 5
Touchet o USA (WA) 244-245 G 4
Toucy o F 90-91 J 8
Toueyyirât o RMM 196-197 J 5
Tougan o BF 202-203 J 3
Tougbé o RG 202-203 E 4
Touggourt o• DZ 190-191 F 4
Tougnifili o RG 202-203 C 4
Tougouri o BF 202-203 K 3
Tougoutaou o RN 198-199 C 5
Touijinet o RIM 196-197 F 5
Touila, Bir o TN 190-191 G 4
Toujil o RIM 196-197 F 5
Toukoto o RMM 202-203 F 3
Toukountouna o DY 202-203 L 4
Toul o• F 90-91 K 7
Toulépleu o CI 202-203 F 6
Touliu o RC 156-157 M 5
Toulon ☆ F 90-91 K 10
Toulon o USA (IL) 274-275 J 3
Toulou, Abri des • RCA 206-207 E 4
Touloukonga o TCH 206-207 D 3
Toulouse ☆•• F 90-91 H 10
Toumbélaga o RN 198-199 C 5
Toumma, Tin ∴ RN 198-199 F 4
Toumodi o CI 202-203 H 6
Toumoundjila o RN 202-203 F 4
Tounassine, Hamada ∴ DZ 188-189 H 6
Tounfafi o RN 198-199 B 5
Toungo o WAN 204-205 K 4
Toungoo o MYA 142-143 K 6
Toungour o TCH 198-199 J 4
Toura ∼ BF 202-203 K 3
Toura o DY 204-205 E 3
Touragondi o AFG 136-137 H 7
Tourassinne o RIM 196-197 E 2
Tourba o TCH 198-199 G 6
Tourcoing o F 90-91 J 6
Touré Kounda o SN 202-203 D 3
Tour Ham o AFG 138-139 C 2
Touriñán, Cabo ▲ E 98-99 C 3
Tourine o RIM 196-197 E 3
Tournai o• B 92-93 G 3
Tournavista o PE 64-65 E 6
Tourndé, Oued ∼ DZ 190-191 H 9
Tourni o BF 202-203 H 4
Tournus o F 90-91 K 8
Touros o BR 68-69 L 4
Tourou ▲ CAM 204-205 K 3
Touroua o CAM 204-205 K 4
Touroug o MA 188-189 J 5
Tourougoumbé o RMM 202-203 F 2
Touroukoro o BF 202-203 H 4
Tours o F 90-91 H 8
Tour Village, De o USA (MI) 272-273 F 2
Touside, Pic ▲ TCH 198-199 H 2
Toussoro, Mont ▲ RCA 206-207 F 4
Toutes Aides o CDN (MAN) 234-235 D 3
Toutoukro o CI 202-203 H 6
Touwsrivier o ZA (CAP) 220-221 E 6
Touwsrivier ∼ ZA 220-221 E 6
Töv ◘ MAU 148-149 G 4
Tovar o YV 60-61 F 3
Tovar Donoso o EC 64-65 C 1
Tovarkovskij o RUS 94-95 Q 5
Tovdalselva ∼ N 86-87 D 7
Tovuz o AZ 128-129 L 2
Tow o USA (TX) 266-267 J 3
Towada o J 152-153 J 4
Towada Hachimantai National Park ⊥ J 152-153 J 5
Towada-ko • J 152-153 J 4

Toad River — Towada-ko 403

Towakaima o **GUY** 62-63 D 2
Towanda o **USA** (KS) 262-263 K 7
Towanda o **USA** (PA) 280-281 L 2
Towaoc o **USA** (CO) 254-255 G 6
Towari o **RI** 164-165 G 6
Towe o **LB** 202-203 F 6
Tower o **USA** (MN) 270-271 F 3
Towera o **AUS** 172-173 B 7
Towerhill Creek ~ **AUS** 178-179 H 1
Tower Peak ▲ **AUS** 176-177 H 4
Tower-Roosevelt o **USA** (WY) 252-253 H 2
Towla o **ZW** 218-219 E 5
Town Creek o **USA** (AL) 284-285 C 2
Town Creek ~ **USA** 284-285 C 2
Town Creek ~ **USA** 284-285 D 2
Town Creek Indian Mound • **USA** (NC) 282-283 H 5
Towne Pass ▲ **USA** (CA) 248-249 G 3
Towner o **USA** (CO) 254-255 N 5
Towner o **USA** (ND) 258-259 G 2
Townley o **USA** (AL) 284-285 C 3
Townsend o **USA** (GA) 284-285 J 5
Townsend o **USA** (MT) 250-251 H 5
Townsend o **USA** (MT) 270-271 K 5
Townsend Lake o **CDN** 30-31 W 4
Townsend Ridges ▲▲ **AUS** 176-177 J 3
Townsend Peak ▲ **USA** (VT) 278-279 J 5
Townshend Island ▲ **AUS** 178-179 L 2
Towns River ~ **AUS** 174-175 C 4
Townsville o •• **AUS** 174-175 J 4
Towot o **SUD** 208-209 B 5
Towson o **USA** (MD) 280-281 K 4
Towuti, Danau o **RI** 164-165 G 5
Toxkan He ~ **VRC** 146-147 D 5
Toyah o **USA** (TX) 266-267 D 2
Toyah, Lake o **USA** (TX) 266-267 D 2
Toyah Creek ~ **USA** 266-267 D 2
Toyahvale o **USA** (TX) 266-267 D 2
Tōya-ko o **J** 152-153 J 3
Toyama o **J** 152-153 J 5
Toyama-wan o **J** 152-153 G 6
Toyo o **J** 152-153 F 8
Toyohashi o **J** 152-153 G 7
Toyokawa o **J** 152-153 G 7
Toyooka o **J** 152-153 F 7
Toyota o **J** 152-153 G 7
Toyotomi o **J** 152-153 J 2
Tozer, Mount ▲ **AUS** 174-175 G 3
Tozeur ☆ • **TN** 190-191 G 4
Tozitna River ~ **USA** 20-21 O 4
Trabária, Bocca ▲ **I** 100-101 D 3
Trà Bồng o **VN** 158-159 K 3
Trabzon ☆ •• **TR** 128-129 H 2
Tracadie o **CDN** (NB) 240-241 L 3
Tracadie o **CDN** (PEI) 240-241 O 4
Trácino o **I** 100-101 D 6
Tracy o **CDN** (NB) 240-241 J 5
Tracy o **USA** (AZ) 256-257 C 6
Tracy o **USA** (CA) 248-249 C 2
Tracy o **USA** (MN) 270-271 C 6
Tracy Arm Fords Terror Wilderness ⊥• **USA** 32-33 H 3
Tracy City o **USA** (TN) 276-277 K 5
Tradewater River ~ **USA** 276-277 H 3
Trading River ~ **CDN** 234-235 O 3
Traela, Punta de ▲ **RA** 78-79 D 2
Trænstaven ~ **N** 86-87 E 3
Traer o **USA** (IA) 274-275 F 2
Tragacete o **E** 98-99 G 4
Traiguén o **RCH** 78-79 C 5
Traiguen, Isla ▲ **RCH** 80 D 2
Trail o **CDN** (BC) 230-231 M 4
Trail o **USA** (MN) 270-271 C 3
Trail o **USA** (OR) 244-245 C 8
Trail City o **USA** (SD) 260-261 F 1
Traill Ø ▲ **GRØ** 26-27 o 7
Traine River ~ **AUS** 172-173 H 4
Traipu o **BR** 68-69 K 6
Traíra, Serra do ▲ **BR** 66-67 C 3
Trairão, Rio ~ **BR** 68-69 C 5
Trairi o **BR** 68-69 J 3
Trajgorodskaja ~ **RUS** 114-115 P 4
Trakai ★ **LT** 94-95 J 4
Trakan Phut Phon o **THA** 158-159 H 3
Trakošćan • **HR** 100-101 E 1
Trakt o **RUS** 88-89 V 5
Tralee = Trá Lí ★ **IRL** 90-91 C 5
Trá Lí = Tralee o **IRL** 90-91 C 5
Trällwing = Welshpool o **GB** 90-91 F 5
Tramandaí o **BR** 74-75 E 7
Tramanu ~ **RI** 166-167 D 6
Trammel Fork ~ **USA** 276-277 J 4
Trampa, La o **PE** 64-65 B 5
Tramping Lake o **CDN** (SAS) 232-233 K 3
Tramping Lake ~ **CDN** (SAS) 232-233 K 3
Trà My o **VN** 158-159 K 3
Trần o **BG** 102-103 C 6
Tranås ★ **S** 86-87 G 7
Tranche-sur-Mer, la o **F** 90-91 G 8
Trang o **THA** 158-159 E 7
Trangan, Pulau ▲ **RI** 166-167 H 5
Trangie o **AUS** 180-181 J 2
Tranomaro o **RM** 222-223 E 10
Tranoroa o **RM** 222-223 D 10
Tranqui, Isla ▲ **RCH** 78-79 C 7
Tranquille o **CDN** (BC) 230-231 J 3
Trans Africa Route = Route transafricaine II **WAN** 204-205 G 5
Transăh o **IR** 128-129 M 4
Trans-Amazon Highway = Transamazônica II **BR** 66-67 H 6
Trans-Australian-Railway II **AUS** 176-177 K 5
Trans-Canada-Highway • **CDN** 230-231 H 3
Transhimalaya = Gangdisê Shan ▲▲ 144-145 C 5
Transkei (former Homeland, now part of East-Cape) ~ **ZA** 220-221 H 7
Transsua o **CI** 202-203 J 6
Transylvania = Transilvani, Podişul ~ **RO** 102-103 C 4
Transylvanian Alps = Carpaţii Meridionali ▲▲ **RO** 102-103 C 5
Tranum o **MAL** 162-163 D 3
Tranzitnyj o **RUS** 112-113 V 3

Trà Ôn o **VN** 158-159 H 6
Trapalco, Cerro ▲ **RA** 78-79 E 6
Trapalcó, Salinas ~ **RA** 78-79 F 5
Trápani o **I** 100-101 D 5
Traralgon o **AUS** 180-181 J 5
Trarza ~ **RIM** 196-197 C 5
Trârza ☲ **RIM** 196-197 C 6
Trasimeno, Lago o **I** 100-101 D 3
Traskwood o **USA** (AR) 276-277 C 6
Trás os Montes e Alto Douro ~ **P** 98-99 D 4
Trat o **THA** 158-159 G 4
Trautenau = Trutnov o **CZ** 92-93 N 3
Trautfetter ~ **RUS** 108-109 d 4
Travaillant Lake o **CDN** 20-21 Z 3
Travelers Rest o **USA** (SC) 284-285 F 2
Traveler's Rest State Historic Site • **USA** (GA) 284-285 G 2
Travellers Lake o **AUS** 180-181 F 2
Travellers Rest ~ **USA** 250-251 E 5
Travemünde o **D** 92-93 L 2
Traverse, Lake o **USA** (SD) 260-261 K 1
Traverse City o **USA** (MI) 272-273 D 3
Traverse Peak ▲ **USA** 20-21 L 4
Travers Reservoir o **CDN** (ALB) 232-233 F 5
Travesía del Tunuyán ☲ **RA** 78-79 E 2
Travesía Puntana ~ **RA** 78-79 F 3
Travessia de Caju ~ **BR** 68-69 D 5
Travessia do Jacuzao ~ **BR** 68-69 D 5
Trà Vinh o **VN** 158-159 J 6
Travellín o **RA** 78-79 D 7
Trevíglio o **I** 100-101 B 2
Treviso o **BR** 74-75 F 7
Treviso ☆ **I** 100-101 D 2
Trevlac o **USA** (IN) 274-275 M 5
Trewdate o **CDN** (SAS) 232-233 M 5
Thäza ☲• **RMM** 196-197 H 3
Triabunna o **AUS** 180-181 J 7
Triang o **MAL** 162-163 E 3
Triangle o **CDN** 32-33 M 4
Triangle o **USA** (NC) 282-283 F 5
Triangle o **ZW** 218-219 F 5
Triângulos, Arrecifes ▲ **MEX** 52-53 H 1
Trianon o **RH** 54-55 J 5
Tribugá o **CO** 60-61 C 5
Tribugá, Golfo de ≈ 60-61 C 5
Tribulation National Park, Cape ⊥ **AUS** 174-175 H 5
Tribune o **CDN** (SAS) 232-233 P 6
Tribune o **USA** (KS) 262-263 E 6
Tricase o **I** 100-101 G 5
Trici o **IND** 140-141 G 5
Trici o **BR** 68-69 H 4
Tri City o **USA** (TX) 276-277 G 4
Trida o **AUS** 180-181 H 2
Tridell o **USA** (UT) 254-255 F 3
Trident o **USA** (MT) 250-251 H 5
Trident Peak ▲ **USA** (NV) 246-247 G 2
Trier o **D** 92-93 J 4
Trieste ☆ • **I** 100-101 D 2
Trieste, Golfo di = Trieste, Gulf of ≈ 100-101 D 2
Trieste, Gulf of = Trieste, Golfo di ≈ 100-101 D 2
Triglav ▲ **SLO** 100-101 D 1
Triglavski Narodni Park ⊥ **SLO** 100-101 D 1
Trigo, El o **RA** 78-79 K 3
Trigonon o **GR** 100-101 H 4
Trikala o **GR** 100-101 H 5
Trikkandiyur o **IND** 140-141 F 5
Trikonamadu o **CL** 140-141 H 4
Trikora, Puncak ▲ **RI** 166-167 K 4
Trilbar o **AUS** 176-177 D 2
Trilsbeck Lake o **CDN** (ONT) 236-237 F 4
Trim = Baile Átha Troim ☆ • **IRL** 90-91 D 5
Trimble o **USA** (MO) 274-275 D 5
Trincheras, Las o **YV** 60-61 J 4
Trincomalee o • **CL** 140-141 J 6
Trindade o **BR** (GO) 72-73 F 4
Trindade o **BR** (PER) 68-69 H 5
Trindade o **BR** (ROR) 62-63 D 5
Tring o **PNG** 183 B 2
Trinidad o **BOL** 70-71 E 4
Trinidad o • **C** 54-55 F 4
Trinidad o **CO** 60-61 F 5
Trinidad o **PY** 76-77 K 4
Trinidad ▲ **ROU** 78-79 L 2
Trinidad ☲ **TT** 60-61 L 2
Trinidad o **USA** (CA) 244-245 A 6
Trinidad o **USA** (CO) 254-255 L 6
Trinidad o **USA** (NE) 262-263 E 4
Trinidad o **USA** (TN) 276-277 G 5
Trinidad o **USA** (NJ) 280-281 M 3
Trinidad and Tobago ■ **TT** 60-61 L 2
Trinidad de Arauca, La o **YV** 60-61 G 4
Trinidade o **BR** 68-69 D 3
Trinidade, Ilha da ▲ **BR** 66-67 H 4
Trinitaria, La o **MEX** 52-53 H 3
Trinity o **CDN** (NFL) 242-243 P 4
Trinity o **USA** (TN) 274-275 M 7
Trinity o **USA** (TX) 268-269 E 6
Trinity Bay ≈ 38-39 S 5
Trinity Bay ≈ 242-243 P 5
Trinity Center o **USA** (CA) 246-247 C 3
Trinity East o **CDN** (NFL) 242-243 P 4
Trinity Islands ▲ **USA** 22-23 T 4
Trinity Range ▲▲ **USA** 246-247 F 4
Trinity River ~ **USA** 246-247 B 3
Trinity River ~ **USA** 266-267 L 2
Trinity River ~ **USA** 268-269 F 6
Trinity Site • **USA** (NM) 256-257 J 5
Trinkat Island ▲ **IND** 140-141 L 5
Triolet o **MS** 224 C 7
Trion o **USA** (GA) 284-285 E 2
Tríos o **BR** 62-63 G 4
Trípoli o **GR** 100-101 J 5
Trípoli = Tarābulus ★ • **LAR** 192-193 J 1
Tripolis = Tarābulus ★ • **LAR** 192-193 J 1
Tripolitania = Tarābulus ~ **LAR** 192-193 J 2
Tripp o **USA** (SD) 260-261 J 3
Tripton o **USA** (UT) 254-255 D 5
Tripura ☲ **IND** 142-143 F 3
Tristan da Cunha Fracture Zone ≃ 6-7 G 12

Três Marias, Represa < **BR** 72-73 H 5
Três Mojones o **RA** 76-77 G 4
Três Montes, Cabo ▲ **RCH** 80 C 3
Três Montes, Peninsula ~ **RCH** 80 C 3
Três Palmas o **CO** 60-61 D 3
Três Palmeiras o **BR** 74-75 D 6
Três Palos, Laguna o **MEX** 52-53 E 3
Três Passos o **BR** 74-75 D 6
Três Picos, Cerro ▲ **RA** 78-79 J 5
Três Piedras o **USA** (NM) 256-257 K 2
Três Praias o **BR** 66-67 D 7
Três Puntas ▲ **GCA** 52-53 K 4
Três Puntas, Cabo ▲ **RA** 80 H 3
Três Ranchos o **BR** 72-73 G 5
Três Ríos o **BR** 72-73 J 7
Três Valles o **MEX** 52-53 F 2
Três Vendas o **BR** 76-77 K 6
Três Vírgenes, Volcán de las ▲ **MEX** 50-51 C 4
Três Zapotes ∴• **MEX** 52-53 G 2
Tretes o **RI** 168 E 3
Tretij, ostrov ▲ **RUS** 120-121 U 3
Tret'jakovo o **RUS** 124-125 M 3
Treuburg = Olecko o **PL** 92-93 R 1
Treuenbrietzen o **D** 92-93 M 2
Treuer Range ▲▲ **AUS** 172-173 K 7
Trêve, Lac la o **CDN** (ONT) 236-237 N 4
Trevelin o **RA** 78-79 D 7
Trewin o **N** 86-87 F 4
Trogir o •• **HR** 100-101 F 3
Troick o **RUS** (KRN) 116-117 O 7
Troick ★ **RUS** (MR) 96-97 M 6
Troickij o **RUS** 114-115 G 6
Troicko-Pečorsk o **RUS** 114-115 D 3
Trois Fourches, Cap des ▲ **MA** 188-189 K 3
Trois-Îlets, Les o **F** 56 E 4
Trois-Pistoles o **CDN** (QUE) 240-241 F 2
Trois-Rivières o **CDN** (QUE) 238-239 N 2
Trois Rivières, Les o **RH** 54-55 J 5
Trois Sauts o **F** 62-63 H 4
Trojan o **BG** 102-103 D 6
Trojes, Las o **HN** 52-53 K 8
Trojnoj, ostrov ▲ **RUS** 108-109 U 4
Trolla o **TCH** 198-199 G 5
Trollättan o **S** 86-87 F 7
Trollindalen ~ **N** 86-87 C 5
Tromai, Baía do o **BR** 68-69 F 2
Tromai, Rio ~ **BR** 68-69 F 2
Trombetas, Rio ~ **BR** 62-63 F 5
Trom°egan ~ **RUS** 114-115 M 3
Tromelin, Île ▲ **F** 12 H 4
Trompsburg o **ZA** 220-221 G 5
Tromsø ☆ • **N** 86-87 J 2
Trona o **USA** (CA) 248-249 G 4
Tronador, Cerro ▲ **RCH** 78-79 C 6
Troncal, La o **EC** 64-65 C 3
Troncoso o **MEX** 50-51 H 6
Trondheim ☆ • **N** 86-87 D 5
Trondheimsfjorden ≈ **N** 86-87 D 5
Troodos ▲ **CY** 128-129 E 5
Troodos, Kirchen von = Ekklisia •••• **CY** 128-129 E 5
Tropas, Río das ~ **BR** 66-67 F 5
Tropea o **I** 100-101 F 6
Tropêco Grande, Cachoeira do ~ **BR** 72-73 F 2
Tropia, Ponta ▲ **BR** 68-69 H 3
Tropico, El o **C** 54-55 E 3
Tropic of Cancer 6-7 X 5
Tropic of Cancer Monument • **MEX** 50-51 E 6
Tropic of Capricorn 6-7 B 10
Tropojë o **AL** 100-101 H 3
Troppau = Opava o **CZ** 92-93 O 4
Trosna o **RUS** 94-95 O 5
Trostjanec' o **UA** 102-103 J 2
Trotters o **USA** (ND) 258-259 D 4
Troubador Shoal o 166-167 B 6
Trou du Nord o **RH** 54-55 J 5
Troughton Island o **AUS** 172-173 H 2
Trouin o **RH** 54-55 J 5
Troup o **USA** (TX) 264-265 J 6
Trousdale o **USA** (TN) 276-277 K 5
Troutbeck o **ZW** 218-219 G 4
Trout Creek o **CDN** (ONT) 238-239 F 3
Trout Creek o **USA** 250-251 G 5
Trout Creek ~ **USA** 256-257 B 3
Trout Lake o **CDN** (BC) 230-231 M 3
Trout Lake o **CDN** (NWT) 30-31 N 4
Trout Lake o **CDN** (ONT) 234-235 K 3
Trout Lake o **USA** (MI) 270-271 N 4
Trout Lake o **USA** (WA) 244-245 D 5
Trout River o **CDN** (NFL) 242-243 K 3
Trout River ~ **CDN** 30-31 J 5
Trout River ~ **CDN** 30-31 N 3
Trout River ~ **USA** 20-21 V 3
Troux aux Cerfs • **MS** 224 C 7
Trovoada, Cachoeira da ~ **BR** 66-67 K 5
Trowulan o **RI** 168 E 3
Troy o **USA** (AL) 284-285 D 5
Troy o **USA** (ID) 250-251 C 5
Troy o **USA** (IN) 274-275 M 7
Troy o **USA** (KS) 262-263 L 5
Troy o **USA** (MT) 274-275 H 6
Troy o **USA** (MT) 250-251 D 3
Troy o **USA** (NC) 282-283 H 5
Troy o **USA** (NY) 278-279 H 6
Troy o **USA** (OH) 280-281 B 3
Troy o **USA** (OR) 244-245 H 5
Troy o **USA** (PA) 280-281 K 2
Troya, Río de la ~ **RA** 76-77 C 5
Troya, Río la ~ **RA** 76-77 C 4
Troyes ☆ • **F** 90-91 K 7
Troy Peak ▲ **USA** (NV) 246-247 K 5
Trpanj o **HR** 100-101 F 3
Trstenik o **YU** 100-101 H 3
Trpang Bàng o **VN** 158-159 H 5
Truandó, Río ~ **CO** 60-61 C 4
Truant Island ▲ **AUS** 172-173 K 2
Trubčevsk o **RUS** 94-95 N 5
Truchas o **USA** (NM) 256-257 K 2
Truck Island ▲ **FSM** 13 G 2
Trucu o **BR** 68-69 J 5
Trucu, Cape ▲ **CDN** 36-37 R 3
Truesdale o **USA** (MO) 274-275 G 6
Trufanova o **RUS** 88-89 S 4

Truite, Lac-à-la- o **CDN** (QUE) 236-237 K 5
Tristao, Îles ▲ **RG** 202-203 C 4
Triste, Golfo ≈ 60-61 H 2
Triste, Monte ▲ **RA** 78-79 G 7
Trisul ▲ **IND** 138-139 G 4
Trisuli Bazar o **NEP** 144-145 E 7
Tri Tôn o **VN** 158-159 H 5
Triton, Teluk ≈ 166-167 H 3
Triton Island = Zhongjian Dao ▲ **VRC** 158-159 L 2
Triune o **USA** (TN) 276-277 J 5
Triunfo o **BR** 74-75 E 7
Triunfo, El o **MEX** 50-51 D 6
Triunfo, Igarapé ~ **BR** 68-69 B 5
Triunvirato o **RA** 78-79 J 4
Trivales-Moşteni o **RO** 102-103 D 5
Trivandrum ★ **IND** 140-141 G 6
Trnava o **SK** 92-93 O 4
Trocana, Ilha ▲ **BR** 66-67 H 5
Trocatá, Área Indígena ▲ **BR** 68-69 D 3
Trochu o **CDN** (ALB) 232-233 E 4
Trocoman, Río ~ **RA** 78-79 D 4
Troebratskij o **KZ** 124-125 E 1

Trujillo o **HN** 54-55 C 7
Trujillo o • **PE** 64-65 B 5
Trujillo o **USA** (NM) 256-257 L 3
Trujillo ☆ **YV** 60-61 F 3
Truman o **USA** (AR) 276-277 E 5
Truman o **USA** (MN) 270-271 D 7
Truman National Historic Site, Harry S. • **USA** (MO) 274-275 D 5
Trumann o **USA** (AR) 276-277 E 5
Trumbull, Mount ▲ **USA** (AZ) 256-257 B 4
Trumon o **RI** 162-163 B 3
Trung Khánh o **VN** 156-157 J 3
Trung Liên o **VN** 156-157 C 5
Trừ'ng Lớn, Hòn ▲ **VN** 158-159 J 6
Trunkey Creek o **AUS** 180-181 K 2
Truro o **CDN** (NS) 240-241 M 4
Truro o **USA** (IA) 274-275 D 3
Trus Madi, Gunung ▲ **MAL** 160-161 J 3
Trutch o **CDN** 32-33 J 3
Truth or Consequences o **USA** (NM) 256-257 H 5
Trutnov o **CZ** 92-93 N 3
Truva (Troja) ∴•• **TR** 128-129 B 3
Truxno o **USA** (LA) 268-269 H 4
Truxton o **USA** (AZ) 256-257 B 3
Tryon o **USA** (NE) 262-263 F 3
Tryon Island ▲ **AUS** 178-179 L 2
Tryphena o **NZ** 182 E 2
Trzebnica o • **PL** 92-93 O 2
Trzemeszno o **PL** 92-93 O 2
Tsacha Lake o **CDN** (BC) 228-229 K 3
Tsadumu o **IND** 140-141 K 4
Tsagaan ▲ **MAU** 148-149 E 2
Tsala Apopka Lake o **USA** (FL) 286-287 G 3
Tsalwor Lake o **CDN** 30-31 P 6
Tsama I o **RCB** 210-211 E 4
Tsamai o **WAN** 198-199 B 6
Tsandi o **NAM** 216-217 C 8
Tsanyawa o **WAN** 198-199 C 6
Tsaramandroso o **RM** 222-223 E 6
Tsaranonenana o **RM** 222-223 F 5
Tsaratanana o **RM** (MJG) 222-223 E 5
Tsaratanana ▲ **RM** 222-223 F 4
Tsarisberge ▲▲ **NAM** 220-221 C 4
Tsarishoogte Pass ▲ **NAM** 220-221 C 2
Tsau o **RB** 218-219 B 5
Tsauchab ~ **NAM** 220-221 B 2
Tsavo o **EAK** 212-213 G 5
Tsavo ~ **EAK** 212-213 G 5
Tsavo East National Park ⊥ **EAK** 212-213 G 5
Tsavo Safari Camp o **EAK** 212-213 G 5
Tsavo West National Park ⊥ **EAK** 212-213 F 5
Tsawah o **LAR** 192-193 E 4
Tsawwassen o **CDN** (BC) 230-231 F 4
Tsazar o **IND** 138-139 F 3
Tschida, Lake o **USA** (ND) 258-259 F 5
Tseikuru o **EAK** 212-213 G 4
Tselinograd = Akmola o **KZ** 124-125 G 3
Tsembo o **RCB** 210-211 D 5
Tseminyu o **IND** 142-143 J 3
Tses o **NAM** 220-221 D 2
Tsévié o **RT** 202-203 L 6
Tshabong ★ **RB** 220-221 F 3
Tshako o **ZRE** 214-215 B 5
Tshane o **RB** 220-221 E 2
Tshela o **ZRE** 210-211 D 6
Tshenga-Oshwe o **ZRE** 210-211 J 5
Tshesebe o **RB** 218-219 D 5
Tshibala o **ZRE** 216-217 F 7
Tshibeke o **ZRE** 214-215 B 5
Tshibuka o **ZRE** 216-217 F 7
Tshibwika o **ZRE** 216-217 H 4
Tshidilamolomo o **ZA** 220-221 G 2
Tshie o **ZRE** 214-215 B 5
Tshikapa o **ZRE** (KOC) 216-217 F 3
Tshikapa o **ZRE** 216-217 F 3
Tshikula o **ZRE** 214-215 B 5
Tshilenge o **ZRE** 214-215 B 4
Tshimbalanga o **ZRE** 214-215 B 6
Tshimboko o **ZRE** 214-215 B 4
Tshimbulu o **ZRE** 214-215 B 4
Tshimbungu o **ZRE** 214-215 B 5
Tshintshanku o **ZRE** 214-215 B 4
Tshipise o **ZA** 218-219 F 6
Tshisenda o **ZRE** 214-215 D 7
Tshisenge o **ZRE** 216-217 F 3
Tshisonge o **ZRE** 214-215 B 7
Tshitadi o **ZRE** 216-217 F 3
Tshitanzu o **ZRE** 214-215 B 5
Tshkheenickh River ~ **CDN** 228-229 F 2
Tshofa o **ZRE** (EQ) 214-215 C 6
Tshokwane o **ZA** 220-221 K 2
Tsholotsho o **ZW** 218-219 D 4
Tshongwe o **ZA** 214-215 C 4
Tshootsha = Kalkfontein o **RB** 216-217 F 1
Tshopo ~ **ZRE** 210-211 L 3
Tshuapa ~ **ZRE** 210-211 H 4
Tshunga, Chutes ~ **ZRE** 210-211 K 3
Tsiafajavona ▲ **RM** 222-223 E 7
Tsiaki o **RCB** 210-211 D 5
Tsianaloka o **RM** 222-223 D 8
Tsiazompaniry o **RM** 222-223 E 7
Tsimafana o **RM** 222-223 C 7
Tsimanampetsotsa, Farihy o **RM** 222-223 C 10
Tsimazava o **RM** 222-223 D 8
Tsimlyanskoye Vodokhranilishche = Cimljanskoe vodohranilišč < **RUS** 102-103 N 4
Tsindia ▲ **RM** 222-223 E 7
Tsinaloka o **RM** 222-223 D 8

Tsingtao = Qingdao ☆ **VRC** 154-155 M 3
Tsingy de Bamaraha Strict Nature Reserve ⊥•• **RM** 222-223 D 7
Tsininigia o **RM** 222-223 E 5
Tsinjoarivo o **RM** 222-223 E 7
Tsinjomitondraka o **RM** 222-223 E 5
Tsinjomorona o **RM** 222-223 F 5
Tsintsabis o **NAM** 216-217 D 9
Tsiombe o **RM** 222-223 E 10
Tsiribihina ~ **RM** 222-223 D 7
Tsiroanomandidy o **RM** 222-223 E 6
Tsiroanomandidy o **RM** 222-223 E 6
Tsitoandroina o **RM** 222-223 E 8
Tsitsikamma National Park ⊥ **ZA** 220-221 F 7
Tsitsutl Peak ▲ **CDN** (BC) 228-229 J 4
Tsivory o **RM** 222-223 E 10
Tsoe o **RB** 218-219 C 5
Tsogstsalu o **IND** 138-139 G 2
Tsolo o **ZA** 220-221 J 5
Tsomo o **ZA** (CAP) 220-221 H 6
Tsomo ~ **ZA** 220-221 H 5
Tso Morari o **IND** 138-139 G 3
Tsu o **J** 152-153 G 7
Tsubata o **J** 152-153 G 6
Tsuchiura o **J** 152-153 J 6
Tsugaru Quasi National Park ⊥ **J** 152-153 J 4
Tsugaru Strait = Tsugaru-kaikyō **J** 152-153 H 4
Tsu Lake o **CDN** 30-31 N 5
Tsuli o **RB** 218-219 D 4
Tsumbiri o **ZRE** 210-211 F 5
Tsumeb ★ **NAM** 216-217 F 9
Tsumkwe ★ **NAM** 216-217 F 9
Tsuruga o **J** 152-153 F 8
Tsurugi-san ▲ **J** 152-153 F 8
Tsurui o **J** 152-153 L 3
Tsuruoka o **J** 152-153 H 5
Tsushima ▲ **J** 152-153 C 7
Tsuyama o **J** 152-153 E 7
Tswaane o **RB** (GHA) 216-217 F 11
Tswaane o **RB** (KWE) 218-219 B 6
Ttati, Laguna ▲ **RA** 76-77 H 5
t-Tawil, Wādi ~ **IRQ** 128-129 K 5
t-Tūbal, Wādi ~ **IRQ** 128-129 K 6
Tu ~ **RUS** 118-119 N 9
Tua, Tanjung ▲ **RI** 162-163 F 7
Tuaim = Tuam o **IRL** 90-91 C 5
Tual o **RI** 166-167 G 4
Tuam = Tuaim o **IRL** 90-91 C 5
Tuambli o **CI** 202-203 F 6
Tuameseh, Tanjung ▲ **RI** 166-167 C 6
Tuam Island ▲ **PNG** 183 E 3
Tuamotu Archipelago = Tuamotu, Îles o **F** 13 N 4
Tuapse o **RUS** 126-127 C 5
Tuaran o **MAL** 160-161 J 2
Tuare o **RI** 164-165 G 4
Tua River ~ **PNG** 183 C 4
Tuba ~ **RUS** 116-117 F 9
Tūbā, Qaṣr at- ∴•• **JOR** 130-131 E 2
Tubac o **USA** (AZ) 256-257 D 7
Tuba City o **USA** (AZ) 256-257 D 2
Tubaiq, Ǧabal at- ▲▲ **KSA** 130-131 E 3
Tuban o **RI** 168 E 3
Tubarão o **BR** 74-75 F 7
Tubarão Latunde, Área Indígena ▲ **BR** 70-71 G 3
Tŭjhās o **WR** 130-131 D 1
Tubau o **MAL** 162-163 K 3
Tubeir Bûzačy ~ **KZ** 126-127 J 5
Tubek Tub-Karagan ~ **KZ** 126-127 J 5
Tubeya o **ZRE** 214-215 B 5
Tubili Point ▲ **RP** 160-161 D 6
Tübingen o • **D** 92-93 K 4
Tubisyimita o **RI** 166-167 G 2
Tubkaragan, mujisi ▲ **KZ** 126-127 J 5
Tubmanburg o **LB** 202-203 E 6
Tubo, River o **WAN** 204-205 G 3
Tuborg Fondets Land ~ **GRØ** 26-27 o 4
Tubruq o **LAR** 192-193 K 2
Tubruq ☆ **LAR** (TUB) 192-193 K 1
Tubuai-Inseln o **F** 13 M 5
Tuburan o **RP** 160-161 E 7
Tucacas o **YV** 60-61 G 2
Tucano o **BR** 68-69 J 7
Tucapel, Punta ▲ **RCH** 78-79 C 4
Tucavaca, Río o **BOL** 70-71 H 4
Tucha River ~ **VRC** 156-157 D 3
Tucheng o **CDN** 30-31 S 5
Tuchitua o **CDN** 30-31 S 5
Tuchola o **PL** 92-93 O 2
Tucholka o **UA** 102-103 C 3
Tuckanarra o **AUS** 176-177 D 3
Tucker o **USA** (AR) 276-277 D 6
Tucker o **USA** (TX) 268-269 E 5
Tucker Bay ≈ 16 F 18
Tuckerman o **USA** (AR) 276-277 D 5
Tuckerton o **USA** (NJ) 280-281 M 4
Tuckfield, Mount ▲ **AUS** 172-173 G 5
Tucson o **USA** (AZ) 256-257 D 6
Tucucu, Río ~ **YV** 60-61 K 3
Tucum, Corredeira do ~ **BR** 70-71 J 4
Tucumã o **BR** 66-67 H 6
Tucumán ▲ **RA** 76-77 E 4
Tucumcari o **USA** (NM) 256-257 M 3
Tucuña o **CO** 60-61 G 6
Tucunare, Raudal ~ **CO** 66-67 J 3
Tucupido o **YV** 60-61 H 3
Tucuriba o **BR** 66-67 H 5
Tucuriba, Corredeira ~ **BR** 66-67 H 5
Tucurui o **BR** 68-69 D 4
Tucurui, Represa de < **BR** 68-69 D 4
Tucutibapo o **CO** 66-67 D 2
Tucu Tucu, Estancia o **RA** 80 E 4
Tüdakül, külî o **UZ** 136-137 J 5
Tudela o **E** 98-99 G 3
Tudela o **RP** 160-161 E 8
Tudela o **EST** 94-95 K 2
Tudu o **EST** 94-95 K 2

Tudun Wada o **WAN** 204-205 H 3
Tuekta o **RUS** 124-125 O 3
Tuena o **AUS** 180-181 K 3
Tueré, Río ~ **BR** 68-69 C 4
Tuetue o **RI** 164-165 H 6
Tufanbeyli o **TR** 128-129 G 3
Tuffnell o **CDN** (SAS) 232-233 P 4
Tufi o **PNG** 183 E 4
Tugaloo Lake o **USA** (GA) 284-285 G 2
Tugaloo River ~ **USA** 284-285 G 2
Tugaske o **CDN** (SAS) 232-233 M 5
Tugela ~ **ZA** 220-221 K 4
Tugela Ferry o **ZA** 220-221 K 4
Tug Fork ~ **USA** 280-281 E 6
Tug Hill ▲ **USA** (NY) 278-279 F 5
Tugidak Island ▲ **USA** 22-23 T 4
Tugtorqurtôq ~ **GRØ** 26-27 W 7
Tugtuilik o **GRØ** 28-29 O 2
Tugu o **GH** 202-203 K 5
Tuguegarao o **RP** 160-161 D 4
Tugulym o **RUS** 114-115 H 6
Tugur o **RUS** (HBR) 122-123 G 2
Tugur ~ **RUS** 122-123 G 2
Tugurskij poluostrov ~ **RUS** 122-123 G 2
Tugurskij zaliv ≈ 122-123 G 2
Tuguttur ~ **RUS** 110-111 F 4
Tugyi o **MYA** 158-159 C 2
Tuhan, Wâdî ~ **Y** 132-133 D 7
Tuhsiqat ~ **RUS** 114-115 O 5
Tui o • **E** 98-99 C 3
Tuichi, Río ~ **BOL** 70-71 C 4
Tuina o **RCH** 76-77 C 2
Tuineje o **E** 188-189 D 6
Tuisen o **IND** 142-143 H 4
Tuitán o **MEX** 50-51 G 5
Tuiué o **BR** 66-67 F 5
Tuj ~ **RUS** 114-115 M 6
Tujau, Tanjung ▲ **RI** 166-167 D 5
Tujmazy ★ **RUS** 96-97 H 6
Tujin gol ~ **MAU** 148-149 L 5
Tujun ~ **RUS** 122-123 E 3
Tukalan ~ **RUS** 108-109 e 7
Tukan ~ **RUS** 114-115 M 9
Tukangbesi, Kepulauan ▲ **RI** 164-165 H 6
Tukarak Island ▲ **CDN** 36-37 K 6
Tuki o **SOL** 184 I 2
Tukola Tolha o **VRC** 144-145 K 3
Tukosmera ▲ **VAN** 184 II b 4
Tükrah o **LAR** 192-193 J 1
Tuktoyaktuk o **CDN** 20-21 Y 2
Tukulan ~ **RUS** 120-121 L 2
Tukums o • **LV** 94-95 H 5
Tukuringra, hrebet ▲▲ **RUS** 118-119 M 8
Tukuyu o **EAT** 214-215 G 5
Tula o **EAK** (COA) 212-213 G 4
Tula ~ **EAK** 212-213 G 4
Tula o **MEX** 50-51 K 6
Tula ~ **RUS** 94-95 P 4
Tula o **Y** 132-133 C 6
Tulá ~ **Y** 132-133 C 6
Tula de Allende o • **MEX** 52-53 E 1
Tuladenggi o **RI** 164-165 G 3
Tula Hill ▲ **WAN** 204-205 J 4
Tūlak o • **AFG** 134-135 K 2
Tulalip Indian Reservation ▲ **USA** (WA) 244-245 C 2
Tulameen o **CDN** (BC) 230-231 J 4
Tulameen River ~ **CDN** 230-231 J 4
Tulancingo o **MEX** 52-53 E 1
Tulare o **USA** (CA) 248-249 E 3
Tulare o **USA** (SD) 260-261 H 2
Tulare Lake o **USA** (CA) 248-249 E 4
Tularosa o **USA** (NM) 256-257 J 5
Tularosa River ~ **USA** 256-257 G 5
Tulate o **GCA** 52-53 J 4
Tula Yiri o **WAN** 204-205 J 4
Tulbagh o • **ZA** 220-221 D 6
Tulcan o **EC** 64-65 D 1
Tulcea o • **RO** 102-103 F 5
Tuľčyn o **UA** 102-103 E 4
Tule, El o **MEX** 50-51 J 3
Tule, Estero del ~ **MEX** 50-51 F 5
Tuléar = Toliara ★ **RM** (Tla) 222-223 C 9
Tulebaevo o **KZ** 124-125 J 1
Tulehu o **RI** 166-167 E 3
Tulelake o **USA** (CA) 246-247 D 2
Tule Lake o **USA** (CA) 246-247 D 2
Tule Lake National Wildlife Refuge ⊥ **USA** (CA) 246-247 D 2
Tulema Lake o **CDN** 30-31 U 4
Tulen' o **RUS** 116-117 H 7
Tule River Indian Reservation ▲ **USA** (CA) 248-249 F 3
Tuleta o **USA** (TX) 266-267 K 5
Tulia o **USA** (TX) 264-265 C 4
Tuli Block Farms ▲ **RB** 218-219 D 6
Tulipan o **MEX** 52-53 E 3
Tülāpur o **IND** 140-141 G 2
Tullah, At o **LAR** 192-193 K 5
Tullahoma o **USA** (TN) 276-277 J 5
Tullamore o **AUS** 180-181 J 2
Tullamore = Tulach Mhór o **IRL** 90-91 D 5
Tulle o • **F** 90-91 H 9
Tullibigeal o **AUS** 180-181 J 2
Tullos o **USA** (LA) 268-269 H 5
Tullulah Falls o **USA** (GA) 284-285 G 2
Tullus o **SUD** 206-207 D 3
Tully o **AUS** 174-175 H 5
Tully Range ▲▲ **AUS** 178-179 G 2
Tuloma o **RUS** 88-89 M 2
Tuloppio o **FIN** 88-89 N 3
Tulsa o **USA** (OK) 264-265 J 2
Tulsequah o **CDN** 32-33 D 2
Tulsipur o **IND** 142-143 C 2
Tulu o **BOL** 183 D 1
Tulua o **CO** 60-61 C 5
Tulu Amara Terara ▲ **ETH** 208-209 C 4
Tulu Bolo o **ETH** 208-209 D 4
Tuluksak o **USA** 20-21 K 6

Tūlūl al-Ašaqif ▲ JOR 130-131 E 1
Tulúm ○ MEX 52-53 L 1
Tulumayo, Río ~ PE 64-65 E 7
Tulume ○ ZRE 214-215 B 4
Tulun ☆ RUS 116-117 K 8
Tulungagung ○ RI 168 D 4
Tulungselapan ○ RI 162-163 F 6
Tulu Welel ▲ ETH 208-209 B 4
Tulvinskaja vozvyšennost' ▲ RUS 96-97 K 5
Tuma ○ RUS 94-95 R 4
Tuma, Río ~ NIC 52-53 B 5
Ṯuma, Wādī ~ IRQ 128-129 K 6
Tumacacori National Monument • USA (AZ) 256-257 D 7
Tumaco ○ CO 60-61 B 7
Tumagabok ○ RP 160-161 D 6
Tumair ○ KSA 130-131 J 5
Tuma Island ⌒ PNG 183 F 5
Tumalin ○ RP 160-161 D 5
Tumalo ○ USA (OR) 244-245 D 6
Tuman Gang ~ KOR 150-151 G 6
Tumannyj ○ RUS 88-89 N 2
Tumanšet ~ RUS 116-117 H 8
Tumanskij hrebet ▲ RUS 120-121 Q 3
Tumara ~ RUS 118-119 P 3
Tumat ○ RUS 110-111 W 4
Tumat, Khor ~ SUD 208-209 B 3
Tumatskaja, protoka Bol'šaja ~ RUS 110-111 Q 3
Tumba ☆ S 86-87 H 7
Tumba ○ ZRE 210-211 J 5
Tumbanglahung ○ RI 164-165 D 4
Tumbarumba ○ AUS 180-181 J 3
Tumbengu ~ ZRE 210-211 J 4
Tumbes ☆ PE 64-65 B 3
Tumbes, Bahía de ≈ 64-65 B 3
Tumbes, Península de ⌣ RCH 78-79 C 4
Tumbes, Punta ▲ RCH 78-79 C 4
Tumbler Ridge ○ CDN 32-33 K 4
Tumbu ○ RI 164-165 F 5
Tumbwe ○ ZRE 214-215 D 6
Tumby Bay ○ AUS 180-181 D 3
Tumd Youqi ○ VRC 154-155 G 1
Tumd Zuoqi ○ VRC 154-155 G 1
Tumen ○ VRC 150-151 G 6
Tumèncogt = Hanhöhij ○ MAU 148-149 L 4
Tumen Jiang ~ VRC 150-151 G 6
Tumeremo ○ YV 62-63 D 2
Tumgaon ○ IND 142-143 C 5
Tumindao Island ⌒ RP 160-161 C 10
Tumkūr ○ IND 140-141 G 4
Tumlingtar ○ NEP 144-145 F 7
Tumnin ~ RUS 122-123 H 4
Tumoiscatío del Ruíz ○ MEX 52-53 C 2
Tumpang ○• RI 168 E 4
Tumpu, Gunung ▲ RI 164-165 H 4
Tumputiga, Gunung ▲ RI 164-165 H 4
Tumrok, hrebet ▲ RUS 120-121 S 6
Tumsar ○ IND 138-139 G 9
Tumu ○ GH 202-203 K 4
Tumucumaque, Parque Indígena do ⵅ BR 62-63 G 4
Tumucumaque, Serra do ▲ BR 62-63 G 4
Tumul ○ RUS 118-119 P 4
Tumupasa ○ BOL 70-71 D 4
Tumureng ○ GUY 62-63 D 2
Tumut ○ AUS 180-181 K 3
Tumwater ○ USA (WA) 244-245 C 3
Tuna ○ GH 202-203 J 5
Tu Na, Đèo ▲ VN 158-159 K 4
Tuna Gain ○ RI 166-167 G 3
Tunago Lake ○ CDN 30-31 G 2
Tunaida ○ ET 194-195 D 5
Tunaiča, ozero ○ RUS 122-123 K 5
Tūnalī Sālang • AFG 136-137 L 7
Tunapa, Cerro ▲ BOL 70-71 D 6
Tunapuna ○ TT 60-61 L 2
Tunas, Las ☆ C 54-55 G 4
Tunas, Sierra de las ▲ RA 78-79 J 4
Tunas de Zaza ○ C 54-55 F 4
Tunas Grandes, Lagunas las ○ RA 78-79 H 3
Tunaydibah ○ SUD 200-201 G 6
Tunceli ☆ TR 128-129 H 3
Tunchang ○ VRC 156-157 G 7
Tuncurry ○ AUS 180-181 M 2
Tunda, Pulau ⌒ RI 168 B 2
Tundak ~ RUS 118-119 H 8
Tund las Raíces • RCH 78-79 D 5
Tundulu ○ Z 214-215 E 5
Tunduma ○ EAT 214-215 G 5
Tunduru ○ EAT 214-215 J 6
Tundyk ~ KZ 124-125 K 3
Tundža ~ BG 102-103 E 6
Tunertooq ⌒ GRØ 28-29 P 2
Tunga ○ WAN 204-205 H 4
Tungabhadra ~ IND 140-141 G 3
Tungabhadra Reservoir ○ IND 140-141 G 3
Tungaru ○ SUD 206-207 K 3
Tungawan ○ RP 160-161 E 9
Tungaztarim ○ VRC 144-145 D 2
Tungho ○ RC 156-157 M 5
Tungi ○ BD 142-143 G 4
Tungir ~ RUS 118-119 K 8
Tungirskij, hrebet ▲ RUS 118-119 J 8
Tungkaranasam ○ RI 164-165 E 5
Tungku ○ MAL (SAB) 160-161 C 10
Tungku ○ MAL (SAR) 162-163 K 3
Tungokočen ○ RUS 118-119 G 9
Tungor ○ RUS 122-123 K 2
Tungshih ○ RC 156-157 M 4
Tungsten ○ CDN 30-31 E 5
Tungurahua, Volcán ▲ EC 64-65 C 2
Tungurča ~ RUS 118-119 K 7
Tunguru ○ EAT 212-213 D 5
Tunguskaja vozvyšennost' ▲ RUS 88-89 M 4
Tungusskoe-Central'no, plato ⊥ RUS 116-117 K 5
Tungusskogo meteorita, mesto padenija • RUS 116-117 L 5
Tunguwatu ○ RI 166-167 H 4
Tunhel ○ MAU 148-149 H 3
Tuni ○ IND 142-143 C 7
Tunia, La ○ CO 64-65 F 1
Tunica ○ USA (MS) 268-269 K 2
Tunis ★••• TN 190-191 H 2
Tunis ○ USA (TX) 266-267 L 3
Tunis, Golfe de ≈ 190-191 H 2
Tunisia = Tunisiyah ■ TN 190-191 G 4
Tunja ☆ CO 60-61 E 5
Tunkal ~ RI 162-163 E 5
Tunkhannock ○ USA (PA) 280-281 L 2
Tunku Abdul Rahman National Park ⊥ MAL 160-161 A 9
Tunnel Creek National Park ⊥ AUS 172-173 G 4
Tunnel du Legionnaire • MA 188-189 J 4
Tunnsjøen ○ N 86-87 F 4
Tunqiu ○ VRC 156-157 F 4
Tuntum ○ BR 68-69 F 4
Tuntutuliak ○ USA 20-21 J 6
Tunu = Østgrønland ◘ GRØ 26-27 d 8
Tunuí, Cachoeira ~ BR 66-67 C 2
Tunulic, Rivière ~ CDN 36-37 Q 5
Tunulliarfik ≈ 28-29 R 6
Tununak ○ USA 20-21 H 6
Tunungayualok Island ⌒ CDN 36-37 T 6
Tununuk ○ CDN 20-21 Y 2
Tunuyan ○ RA 78-79 E 2
Tunuyán, Río ~ RA 78-79 F 2
Tunuyan, Sierra de ▲ RA 78-79 E 2
Tunuyánviejo, Río ~ RA 78-79 F 2
Tuoa Creek ~ PNG 183 C 4
Tuobuja ○ RUS 118-119 L 4
Tuo Jiang ~ VRC 156-157 D 2
Tuolba ~ RUS 118-119 L 5
Tuolbačan ~ RUS 118-119 L 5
Tuoi Kručs ○ K 158-159 G 4
Tuolumne ○ USA (CA) 248-249 D 2
Tuolumne River ~ USA 248-249 D 2
Tu'o'ng Du'o'ng ☆ VN 156-157 D 7
Tuora ~ RUS 118-119 M 6
Tuora-Sis, hrebet ▲ RUS 110-111 Q 4
Tuostah ~ RUS 110-111 V 6
Tuotuo He ~ VRC 144-145 H 3
Tuotuo Heyan ○ VRC 144-145 J 3
Tupā ○ BR 72-73 E 6
Tupaciguara ○ BR 72-73 F 5
Tupambaé ○ ROU 78-79 M 2
Tupana, Rio ~ BR 66-67 G 5
Tupanaci ○ BR 68-69 J 6
Tupanatinga ○ BR 68-69 K 6
Tupanciretã ○ BR 74-75 D 7
Tuparro, Caño ~ CO 60-61 G 5
Tuparrito, Caño ~ CO 60-61 G 5
Tuparro, Río ~ CO 60-61 G 5
Tupé II ○ BR 66-67 D 2
Tupelo ○ USA (AR) 276-277 D 5
Tupelo ○ USA (MS) 268-269 M 2
Tupelo ○ USA (OK) 264-265 H 4
Tupelo National Battlefield ∴ USA (MS) 268-269 M 2
Tupik ☆ RUS 118-119 J 8
Tupilco ○ MEX 52-53 H 2
Tupim, Rio ~ BR 72-73 K 2
Tupinambarana, Ilha ⌒ BR 66-67 H 4
Tupinier, Kap ▲ GRØ 28-29 b 2
Tupiratins ○ BR 68-69 D 6
Tupitina ○ MEX 52-53 C 2
Tupiza ○ BOL 76-77 E 1
Tupiza, Río ~ BOL 76-77 E 1
Tupper ○ CDN 32-33 K 4
Tupper Lake ○ USA (NY) 278-279 G 4
Tupran ○ IND 140-141 H 2
Tupungato ○ RA 78-79 F 2
Tupungato, Cerro ▲ RA 78-79 E 2
Tupure ○ YV 60-61 F 2
Tuquan ○ VRC 150-151 C 5
Tuque, La ○ CDN (QUE) 240-241 C 3
Tuquerres ○ CO 64-65 D 1
Tuqu Gang ≈ 156-157 F 7
Tūr, at- ○ Y 132-133 C 6
Tura ○ IND 142-143 G 3
Tura ~ PA 52-53 E 8
Tura ☆ RUS (EVN) 116-117 K 3
Tura ~ RUS 96-97 L 4
Tura ~ RUS 114-115 H 6
Tura ~ RUS 114-115 J 6
Tura ~ RUS 118-119 F 10
Tura ○ VRC 144-145 F 2
Turaba ○ KSA (HA) 130-131 F 4
Turaba ○ KSA (MAK) 132-133 B 3
Turagua, Cerro ▲ YV 60-61 J 4
Turagua, Serranía ▲ YV 60-61 J 4
Turaif ○ KSA 130-131 F 2
Turaif ○ SYR 128-129 H 5
Turakurgan ○ UZ 136-137 M 4
Turama ~ RUS 116-117 H 5
Turama River ~ PNG 183 B 4
Turan ☆ RUS 116-117 F 9
Turangi ○ NZ 182 E 3
Turan Lowland = Turan persligi ⌣ 136-137 F 5
Turan Lowland = Turanskaja nizmennost' ⌣ 136-137 F 5
Turāq al-'Ilab ▲ SYR 128-129 H 6
Turba ○ EST 94-95 J 2
Turba, at- ○ Y 132-133 C 7
Turba, at- ○ Y 132-133 D 7
Turbaco ○ CO 60-61 D 2
Turbat ○ PK 134-135 K 6
Turbeville ○ USA (SC) 284-285 K 3
Turbihal ○ IND 140-141 G 3
Turbio, El ○ RA 80 D 5
Turbio, Río ~ RA 80 E 5
Turbio, Río ~ RCH 76-77 C 4
Turbio, Río ~ RCH 76-77 B 5
Turbo ○ CO 60-61 C 3
Turbón, Raudal el ~ CO 66-67 B 2
Turco ○ BOL 70-71 C 6
Turco, Río ~ BOL 70-71 C 6
Turda ○ RO 102-103 C 4
Turda ○ SUD 206-207 J 3
Turee Creek ○ AUS (WA) 176-177 E 1
Turee Creek ~ AUS 176-177 D 1
Turek ○ PL 92-93 P 2
Turen ○ RI 168 E 4
Turgen ~ KZ 146-147 C 4
Türgen ▲ MAU 116-117 E 11
Turgeon, Rivière ~ CDN 236-237 J 3
Turgut ○ TR 128-129 D 3
Turgutlu ☆ TR 128-129 B 3
Turhal ☆• TR 128-129 G 2
Türi ○ EST 94-95 J 2
Turi, Igarapé ~ BR 66-67 D 3
Turia, Río ~ E 98-99 G 4
Turiaçu ○ BR 68-69 F 2
Turiaçu, Baía de ≈ 68-69 F 2
Turiaçu, Rio ~ BR 68-69 F 3
Turiamo ○ YV 60-61 H 2
Turiančaj ~ AZ 128-129 M 2
Turiani ○ EAT 214-215 J 4
Túriba ○ YV 60-61 H 4
Turimaquire, Cerro ▲ YV 60-61 K 2
Turin ○ CDN (ALB) 232-233 F 6
Turin ○ USA (IA) 274-275 C 2
Turin = Torino ☆• I 100-101 A 2
Turinsk ☆ RUS 114-115 G 5
Turinskaja ravnina ⌣ RUS 114-115 G 6
Turinskaja Sloboda ☆ RUS 114-115 H 6
Tur'ja ○ RUS 88-89 V 5
Turka ○ RUS 116-117 O 9
Turka ☆ UA 102-103 C 3
Turkana ⊥ EAK 212-213 E 2
Turkana, Lake ○ EAK 212-213 F 1
Turkestan ○ KZ 136-137 L 3
Turkestanskij hrebet ▲ UZ 136-137 K 5
Turkestanskij kanal < KZ 136-137 L 3
Turkey ○ USA (TX) 264-265 D 4
Turkey = Türkiye ■ TR 128-129 C 3
Turkey Creek ○ AUS 172-173 J 4
Turkey Creek ○ USA (LA) 268-269 H 6
Turkey Creek ~ USA 262-263 J 4
Turkey Creek ~ USA 264-265 G 2
Turkey Creek ~ USA 284-285 J 2
Turkey Flat ○ USA (AZ) 256-257 F 6
Turkey Mountain ▲ AUS 178-179 L 4
Turkey Point ○ CDN (ONT) 238-239 E 6
Turkey River ~ USA 274-275 G 2
Turkistan ☆ KZ 136-137 L 3
Türkmen Dağı ▲ TR 128-129 D 3
Turkmenistan = Türkmenistan ■ TM 136-137 D 5
Turkmen-Kala ○ TM 136-137 H 6
Turkmenskij zaliv ≈ 136-137 C 5
Türkoğlu ☆ TR 128-129 G 4
Turks Island Passage ≈ 54-55 K 4
Turks Islands ⌒ GB 54-55 K 4
Turku = Åbo ☆• FIN 88-89 G 6
Turkwel ~ EAK 212-213 E 2
Turkwel Gorge Reservoir < EAK 212-213 E 3
Turlock ○ USA (CA) 248-249 D 2
Turmalina ○ BR 72-73 J 4
Turmantas ○ LT 94-95 K 4
Turn ○ USA (NM) 256-257 J 4
Turnagain, Cape ▲ NZ 182 F 4
Turnagain Arm ≈ 20-21 P 6
Turnagain Island ⌒ AUS 174-175 G 1
Turnagain Point ▲ CDN 24-25 R 6
Turnagain River ~ CDN 30-31 E 6
Turneffe Islands ⌒ BH 52-53 L 3
Turner ○ USA (ME) 278-279 L 4
Turner ○ USA (MT) 250-251 L 3
Turner ○ USA (OR) 244-245 C 6
Turner Lake ○ CDN 32-33 Q 3
Turner Ø ⌒ GRØ 28-29 d 2
Turner River ~ AUS 172-173 D 6
Turners Peninsula ⌣ WAL 202-203 D 6
Turnersville ○ USA (TX) 266-267 K 2
Turner Turnpike II USA (OK) 264-265 G 3
Turner Valley ○ CDN (ALB) 232-233 D 5
Turnerville ○ USA (SD) 260-261 K 2
Turnhout ○ B 92-93 H 3
Turnpike Creek ~ USA 284-285 H 5
Turnu Măgurele ○ RO 102-103 D 6
Turočak ☆ RUS 124-125 P 2
Turon ○ USA (KS) 262-263 H 7
Turpan ○ VRC 146-147 J 4
Turpan Pendi ⊥ VRC 146-147 J 4
Turpin ○ USA (OK) 264-265 D 2
Turpsal = Järve ○ EST 94-95 K 2
Turra • SUD 200-201 B 6
Turrell ○ USA (AR) 276-277 E 5
Turrialba ○ CR 52-53 C 7
Tursāq ○ IRQ 128-129 L 6
Tursuntskij Tuman, ozero ○ RUS 114-115 G 4
Tursunzade ○ TJ 136-137 L 5
Turt ○ MAU 148-149 E 2
Turt (Hanh) ○ MAU 148-149 E 2
Turtas ~ RUS 114-115 K 5
Türtkül ☆ UZ 136-137 G 4
Turtle Creek Reservoir ○ USA (IN) 274-275 L 5
Turtle Farm • GB 54-55 E 5
Turtleford ○ CDN (SAS) 232-233 K 2
Turtle Head Island ⌒ AUS 183 B 6
Turtle Islands ⌒ RP 160-161 C 9
Turtle Islands Marine Park ⊥ MAL 160-161 C 9
Turtle Lake ○ CDN (SAS) 232-233 K 2
Turtle Lake ○ USA (ND) 258-259 G 4
Turtle Lake ○ USA (WI) 270-271 F 5
Turtle Mountain ▲ CDN 234-235 C 5
Turtle Mountain Indian Reservation ⵅ USA (ND) 258-259 H 3
Turton Lake ○ CDN 30-31 G 3
Turu ~ RUS 116-117 L 3
Turu, Wangasi- ○ GH 202-203 K 5
Turu Cay Island ⌒ AUS 183 A 5
Turuchipa, Río ~ BOL 70-71 E 6
Turuhan ~ RUS 108-109 V 8
Turuhan ~ RUS 114-115 T 2
Turuhansk ○ RUS 114-115 T 2
Turuhanskaja nizmennost' ⌣ RUS 114-115 T 2
Turuktah, mys ▲ RUS 110-111 W 4
Turuna, Rio ~ BR 62-63 F 5
Turuntaevo ○ RUS (TOM) 114-115 T 6
Turuntaevo ☆ RUS (BUR) 116-117 N 9
Turvânia ○ BR 72-73 E 4
Turvo, Rio ~ BR 72-73 E 4
Turvo, Rio ~ BR 72-73 F 6
Turvolândia ○ BR 72-73 H 6
Turwi ~ ZW 218-219 F 5
Tūs ○ IR 136-137 F 6
Tušama ~ RUS 116-117 K 7
Tuscaloosa ○ USA (AL) 284-285 C 3
Tuscaloosa, Lake < USA (AL) 284-285 C 3
Tuscánia ○• I 100-101 C 3
Tuscarora ○ USA (NV) 246-247 J 2
Tuscola ○ USA (IL) 274-275 K 5
Tuscola ○ USA (TX) 264-265 E 6
Tusculum ○ USA (TN) 282-283 E 4
Tuscumbia ○ USA (AL) 284-285 B 2
Tuscumbia ○ USA (MO) 274-275 F 6
Tusenøyane ⌒ N 84-85 M 4
Tushar Mountains ▲ USA 254-255 C 5
Tušig=Zèltèr ○ MAU 148-149 G 2
Tuskegee ○• USA (AL) 284-285 E 4
Tuskegee Institute National Historic Site • USA (AL) 284-285 E 4
Tustumena Lake ○ USA 20-21 P 6
Tutaev ☆•• RUS 94-95 Q 3
Tutak ☆ TR 128-129 K 3
Tuticorin ○ IND 140-141 H 6
Tutóia ○ BR 68-69 G 3
Tutoko, Mount ▲ NZ 182 B 6
Tutončana ~ RUS 116-117 F 3
Tutong ○ BRU 164-165 D 1
Tutrakan ○ BG 102-103 E 5
Tuttle ○ USA (ND) 258-259 H 4
Tuttle ○ USA (OK) 264-265 G 3
Tuttle Creek Lake ○ USA (KS) 262-263 K 5
Tuttle Town ○ USA (CA) 246-247 E 5
Tuttosoni, Nuraghe • I 100-101 B 4
Tutuaca ○ MEX 50-51 F 3
Tutuala ○ RI 166-167 D 6
Tutuba ⌒ VAN 184 II a 2
Tutuila Island ⌒ USA 184 V b 2
Tutukpene ○ GH 202-203 L 5
Tutume ○ RB 218-219 D 5
Tutup, Tanjung ▲ MAL 160-161 C 10
Tutupa ○ RI 164-165 K 4
Tutura ○ RUS (IRK) 116-117 M 8
Tutura ~ RUS 116-117 M 8
Tutwiler ○ USA (MS) 268-269 K 3
Tuul gol ~ MAU 148-149 G 4
Tuusniemi ○ FIN 88-89 K 5
Tuva = Tuva, Respublika ◘ RUS 116-117 F 10
Tuvšinširèè = Sèrgèlèn ○ MAU 148-149 K 4
Tuwaiq, Ǧabal ▲ KSA 132-133 D 3
Tūwal ○ KSA 130-131 F 6
Tuxcueca ○ MEX 52-53 C 1
Tuxedni Bay ≈ 20-21 O 6
Tuxford ○ CDN (SAS) 232-233 N 5
Tuxpan ○ MEX (NAY) 50-51 G 7
Tuxpan ○• MEX (JAL) 52-53 C 2
Tuxpan, Río ~ MEX 52-53 F 1
Tuxpan de Rodriguez Cano ○ MEX 52-53 F 1
Tuxtla, Sierra de los ▲ MEX 52-53 G 2
Tuxtla Gutiérrez ☆• MEX 52-53 H 3
Tuy, Río ~ YV 60-61 H 2
Tuya River ~ CDN 32-33 E 2
Tuyên Quang ☆ VN 156-157 D 6
Tuy Hòa ○ VN 158-159 K 4
Tuy Phong ○ VN 158-159 K 5
Tuyserkān ○• IR 134-135 C 1
Tūzdykól ○ KZ 136-137 M 3
Tuz Gölü ○ TR 128-129 E 3
Tūz Ḫurmātū ☆ IRQ 128-129 L 5
Tuzigoot National Monument • USA (AZ) 256-257 D 4
Tuzla ○• BIH 100-101 G 2
Tuzla Çayı ~ TR 128-129 J 3
Tuzlov ~ RUS 102-103 L 4
Tuzluca ☆ TR 128-129 K 2
Tuzule ○ ZRE 214-215 B 4
Tvøroyri ○ FR 90-91 D 1
Tvelitsund ○ N 86-87 D 7
Tver' ☆•• RUS 94-95 P 3
Tverrfjelli ⌣ N 86-87 D 5
TV Tower • USA (MN) 270-271 A 3
Tweed ○ CDN (ONT) 238-239 H 4
Tweed ~ GB 90-91 F 4
Tweed Heads ○ AUS 178-179 M 5
Tweedsmuir Provincial Park ⊥ CDN (BC) 228-229 H 3
Tweefontein ○ ZA 220-221 D 6
Tweeling ○ ZA 220-221 J 3
Twee Rivier ○ NAM 220-221 D 2
Twee Rivieren ○ ZA 220-221 E 3
Tweespruit ○ ZA 220-221 H 4
Twentynine Palms ○ USA (CA) 248-249 H 5
Twentynine Palms Indian Reservation ⵅ USA (CA) 248-249 H 5
Twentynine Palms Marine Corps Base xx USA (CA) 248-249 H 5
Twilight Cove ≈ 176-177 H 6
Twillingate ○ CDN (NFL) 242-243 O 3
Twin Bridges ○ USA (MT) 250-251 G 6
Twin Butte ○ CDN (ALB) 232-233 E 6
Twin Buttes Reservoir < USA (TX) 266-267 G 2
Twin City ○ CDN (ONT) 234-235 O 6
Twin City ○ USA (GA) 284-285 H 4
Twin Falls ○ USA (ID) 252-253 D 4
Twingge ○ MYA 142-143 K 4
Twingi ○ Z 214-215 E 6
Twin Mount ▲ USA 20-21 T 4
Twin Mountain ○ USA (NH) 278-279 K 4
Twin Oaks Reservoir ○ USA (TX) 266-267 L 2
Twin Peaks ○ AUS 176-177 C 3
Twin Sisters ○ USA (TX) 266-267 J 3
Twin Summit ▲ USA (NV) 246-247 J 3
Twin Valley ○ USA (MN) 270-271 C 3
Twisp ○ USA (WA) 244-245 E 2
Twitty ○ USA (TX) 264-265 D 3
Twitya River ~ CDN 30-31 E 4
Twizel ○ NZ 182 C 6
Two Buttes ○ USA (CO) 254-255 N 6
Two Buttes Creek ~ USA 254-255 N 6
Two Creeks ○ CDN (MAN) 234-235 B 4
Two Creeks ○ USA (WI) 270-271 L 6
Twodot ○ USA (MT) 250-251 J 5
Twofold Bay ≈ 180-181 K 4
Two Harbors ○ USA (MN) 270-271 G 3
Two Headed Island ⌒ USA 22-23 U 4
Two Hills ○ CDN (ALB) 232-233 G 2
Two Inlets ○ USA (MN) 270-271 C 3
Two Medicine River ~ USA 250-251 F 3
Twopete Mountain ▲ CDN 20-21 Y 5
Two Rivers ○ USA (WI) 270-271 L 6
Two Rocks ○ AUS 176-177 C 5
Twyfelfontein • NAM 216-217 C 10
Tyara, Cayo ⌒ NIC 52-53 C 5
Tybee Island ○ USA (GA) 284-285 K 4
Tyčany ~ RUS 116-117 J 5
Tychy ○ PL 92-93 P 3
Tydyotta ~ RUS 114-115 O 2
Tye ○ CDN (BC) 230-231 N 4
Tyélé ○ RMM 202-203 G 3
Tygart Lake ○ USA (WV) 280-281 F 4
Tygart River ~ USA 280-281 F 4
Tygarts Creek ~ USA 276-277 M 2
Tygda ○ RUS (AMR) 118-119 N 9
Tygda ~ RUS 118-119 N 9
Tyger River ~ USA 284-285 J 2
Tygh Valley ○ USA (OR) 244-245 D 5
Tyiebas, cyganak ≈ 126-127 N 4
Tyl' ~ RUS 120-121 F 6
Tylawa ○ PL 92-93 Q 4
Tyler ○ USA (TX) 264-265 J 6
Tyler ○ USA (WA) 244-245 H 3
Tyler ○ USA (WV) 280-281 F 4
Tylertown ○ USA (MS) 268-269 K 5
Tylgovajam ~ RUS 112-113 O 6
Tylihul ~ UA 102-103 F 4
Tylihul's'kyj lyman ≈ 102-103 G 4
Tylnoj ~ RUS 112-113 M 5
Tym ~ RUS 114-115 T 4
Tym ~ RUS 114-115 Q 5
Tym' ~ RUS 122-123 K 3
Tym, Ust'- ○ RUS 114-115 Q 5
Tymerokan ~ RUS 116-117 F 2
Tymlat ☆ RUS 120-121 U 4
Tymna ~ RUS 118-119 O 8
Tymna, laguna ≈ 112-113 U 4
Tymovskoe ☆ RUS 122-123 K 3
Tympyčan, Uèl' ~ RUS 118-119 E 5
Tympylykan ~ RUS 118-119 L 3
Tymtej ~ RUS 120-121 L 2
Tynda ☆ RUS (AMR) 118-119 M 8
Tynda ~ RUS 118-119 M 8
Tyndall ○ CDN (MAN) 234-235 G 4
Tyndall ○ USA (SD) 260-261 J 4
Tyndall Air Force Base xx USA (FL) 286-287 D 1
Tyndik ~ KZ 124-125 K 3
Tyndrum ○ GB 90-91 E 3
Tyne ~ GB 90-91 G 4
Tynep ~ RUS 114-115 U 3
Tyner ○ USA (KY) 276-277 M 3
Tyne Valley ○ CDN (PEI) 240-241 M 4
Tynset ☆ N 86-87 E 5
Typtygir, köli ○ KZ 124-125 D 2
Tyr ∴••• RL 120-121 D 4
Tyrifjorden ○ N 86-87 E 6
Tyrkan ~ RUS 120-121 E 5
Tyrma ○ RUS (HBR) 122-123 E 3
Tyrma ~ RUS 122-123 E 3
Tyrnyauz ○ RUS 126-127 E 6
Tyro ○ USA (AR) 276-277 D 7
Tyrone ○ USA (GA) 284-285 H 3
Tyrone ○ USA (NM) 256-257 G 6
Tyrone ○ USA (OK) 264-265 C 2
Tyrone ○ USA (PA) 280-281 H 3
Tyrrell Lake ○ AUS 180-181 G 3
Tyrrell Lake ○ CDN 30-31 R 4
Tyrrhenian Basin ≈ 100-101 C 5
Tyrrhenian Sea ≈ 100-101 C 5
Tyrs Bjerge ▲ GRØ 28-29 U 5
Tyrtova, ostrov ⌒ RUS 108-109 b 3
Tyry ~ RUS 120-121 G 2
Tyškanbaj ○ KZ 126-127 P 2
Tysnesøy ~ N 86-87 B 6
Tytyl', ozero ○ RUS 112-113 P 3
Tyumen' = Tjumen' ☆ RUS 114-115 H 6
Tzaneen ○ ZA 218-219 F 6
Tzinteel ○ MEX 52-53 H 3
Tziscao ○ MEX 52-53 J 3
Tzonconejo, Río ~ MEX 52-53 J 3
Tzucacab ○ MEX 52-53 K 1

U

Uaçá, Área Indígena ⵅ BR 62-63 J 4
Uacaca, Cachoeira ~ CO 66-67 C 2
Uachtar Ard = Oughterard ○ IRL 90-91 C 5
Uaco Cungo ○ ANG 216-217 C 5
Uacuru, Cachoeira ~ BR 70-71 G 2
Ua'ili, Wādi al- ~ KSA 130-131 F 2
Uala, zaliv ≈ 120-121 U 3
Uamba ○ ANG 216-217 D 3
Uanda ○ AUS 178-179 H 1
Uanga ~ RUS 122-123 K 2
Uangando ~ ANG 216-217 D 8
Uape ○ MOC 218-219 K 3
Uapuí, Cachoeira ~ BR 66-67 C 2
Uarges ▲ EAK 212-213 F 3
Uar Igarore < SP 212-213 J 3
Uarini ○ BR 66-67 E 4
Uarini, Rio ~ BR 66-67 D 5
Uaroo ○ AUS 172-173 B 7
Uati-Paraná, Área Indígena ⵅ BR 66-67 D 4
Uatuma, Rio ~ BR 66-67 H 4
Uauá ○ BR 68-69 J 6
Uauaretê ○ BR 66-67 C 2
Uaupés, Rio ~ BR 66-67 D 2
Uaus, Ra's ▲ OM 132-133 J 5
Uavala ~ ANG 216-217 D 8
Uaxactún ∴ GCA 52-53 K 3
Uaza ▲ ETH 200-201 J 6
Ub ○ YU 100-101 H 2
Ubá ○ BR 72-73 J 6
Uba ~ KZ 124-125 N 3
Uba ○ WAN 204-205 K 3
Ubai ○ BR 72-73 H 4
Ubai ○ PNG 183 F 3
'Ubaid ○ SUD 200-201 B 6
Ubaila ○ IRQ 128-129 J 6
'Ubaila, al- ○ KSA 132-133 G 2
Ubaitaba ○ BR 72-73 L 3
Ubajay ○ RA 76-77 H 6
Ubaldino Taques ○ BR 74-75 E 6
Ubangi ~ ZRE 210-211 F 3
Ubangui ~ ZRE 210-211 G 1
Ubaporanga ○ BR 72-73 J 5
Ubar ∴• OM 132-133 H 4
Ubarc' ~ BY 94-95 K 6
Ubatã ○ BR 72-73 L 3
Ubate ○ CO 60-61 E 5
Ubatuba ○ BR 72-73 H 7
Ubauro ○ PK 138-139 B 5
'Ubayyiḍ, Wādī l- ~ IRQ 128-129 J 7
Ube ○ J 152-153 D 8
Úbeda ○ E 98-99 F 5
Ubehebe Crater • USA (CA) 248-249 G 3
Ubekendt Ejland ⌒ GRØ 26-27 Y 8
Uberaba ○ BR 72-73 G 5
Uberaba, Lago ○ BR 70-71 J 5
Uberaba, Rio ~ BR 72-73 F 5
Uberlândia ○ BR (MIN) 72-73 F 5
Uberlândia ○ BR (ROR) 62-63 E 5
Ubia, Gunung (Gunung Leonard Darwin) ▲ RI 166-167 J 4
Ubiaja ○ WAN 204-205 G 5
Ubina ○ BOL 70-71 D 7
Ubinskoe ○ RUS 114-115 P 7
Ubinskoe, ozero ○ RUS 114-115 P 7
Ubirajara ○ BR 72-73 F 7
Ubirr ○ AUS 172-173 L 2
Ubojnaja ~ RUS 108-109 U 5
Ubol Rat Reservoir ○ THA 158-159 G 2
Ubombo ▲ ZA 220-221 L 3
Ubon Ratchathani ○ THA 158-159 H 3
Ubovka ○ RUS 122-123 F 6
Ubundu ○ ZRE 210-211 K 4
Uč-Adži ○ TM 136-137 H 5
Učaly ☆ RUS 96-97 L 6
Učami ~ RUS 116-117 H 4
Ucapinima ○ CO 66-67 C 2
Ucayali, Río ~ PE 64-65 F 4
Učdepe ○ TM 136-137 H 6
Uch ○•• PK 138-139 C 5
Ucharonidge ○ AUS 174-175 C 5
Uchee Creek ~ USA 284-285 E 4
Uchiura-wan ≈ 152-153 J 3
Uchiza ○ PE 64-65 D 6
Učkeken ○ RUS 126-127 E 6
Učkuduk ☆ UZ 136-137 H 3
Učkurgan ○ UZ 136-137 N 4
Ucluelet ○ CDN (BC) 230-231 D 5
Učničiija ~ RUS 112-113 P 5
Ucross ○ USA (WY) 252-253 M 2
Učsaj ○ UZ 136-137 F 3
Uctagankum ⊥ TM 136-137 E 4
Ucua ○ ANG 216-217 C 4
Učur ~ RUS 120-121 D 4
Uda ~ RUS 116-117 J 8
Uda ~ RUS 116-117 O 10
Uda ~ RUS 120-121 F 6
Udačnyj ○ RUS 110-111 J 6
Udagamandalam ○ IND 140-141 G 5
Udaia ○ IND 142-143 E 5
'Udaib, al- ○ KSA 130-131 E 4
'Udaiba, 'Uqlat al- ○ IRQ 130-131 K 3
'Udaid, al- ○ UAE 134-135 D 6
Udaipur ○ IND (RAJ) 142-143 G 4
Udaipur ○ IND (RAJ) 138-139 D 7
Udaiyarpalaiyam ○ IND 140-141 H 5
Udaquiola ○ RA 78-79 K 4
Udayagiri ○ IND 140-141 H 3
Udbina ○ HR 100-101 E 2
Uddeholm ○• S 86-87 F 6
Uddevalla ☆ S 86-87 E 7
Uddjaure ○ S 86-87 H 4
Udegi ○ WAN 204-205 G 4
Udgir ○ IND 138-139 F 10
Udhampur ○ IND 138-139 E 3
Udi ○ WAN 204-205 G 5
Udine ☆• I 100-101 D 1
Udinsk ○ RUS 122-123 H 2
Udintsev Fracture Zone ≃ 14-15 N 13
Udispattu ○ CL 140-141 J 7
Udja ~ RUS 110-111 K 4
Udmurtia = Udmurtskaja Respublika ◘ RUS 96-97 H 5
Udobnaja ○ RUS 126-127 D 5
Udobnaja, buhta ≈ 108-109 I b 2
Udokan, hrebet ▲ RUS 118-119 J 7
Udon Thani ○ THA 158-159 G 2
Udova ~ RUS 120-121 R 6
Udpūdi ○ IND 140-141 F 2
Udskaja guba ≈ 120-121 F 6
Udskoe ○ RUS 120-121 F 6
Udubaddawa ○ CL 140-141 H 7
Udumalaippettai ○ IND 140-141 G 5
Udupi ○ IND 140-141 F 4
Udu Point ▲ FJI 184 III c 2
Udy ~ RUS 102-103 K 2
Udyhyn ~ RUS 120-121 D 6
Udyl', ozero ○ RUS 122-123 H 2
Udzhar = Ucar ○ AZ 128-129 M 2
Uebonti ○ RI 164-165 G 4
Ueca ▲ ETH 208-209 C 4
Ueda ○ J 152-153 H 6
Uedinenija, ostrov ⌒ RUS 108-109 U 3
Uekuli ○ RI 164-165 G 4
Uèle ~ RUS 110-111 K 3
Uele ~ ZRE 210-211 J 2
Uèlen ○• RUS 112-113 a 3
Uèlgi, ozero ○ RUS 96-97 M 6
Uèl'-Siktjah ~ RUS 110-111 P 5
Uèl'-Tympyčan ~ RUS 118-119 E 5
Uelzen ○ D 92-93 L 2
Uembje, Lagoa ○ MOC 220-221 L 2
Ueno ○ J 152-153 G 7
Uere ~ ZRE 206-207 H 6
Ueré, Rio ~ BR 66-67 D 5
Ufa ☆ RUS 96-97 J 6
Ufa ~ RUS 96-97 K 5
Ufeyn ○ SP 208-209 J 3
Ufimskoe plato ▲ RUS 96-97 K 6
Uftjuga ~ RUS 88-89 T 6
Ugab ~ NAM 216-217 D 9
Ugahan ○ RUS 118-119 G 6
Ugak Island ⌒ USA 22-23 U 4
Ugāle ○ LV 94-95 H 3
Ugalla ○ EAT (RUK) 212-213 C 6
Ugalla ~ EAT 212-213 C 6
Ugalla River Game Reserve ⊥ EAT 212-213 C 6
Ugamak Island ⌒ USA 22-23 O 5
Uganda ■ EAU 212-213 C 2
Uganik Island ⌒ USA 22-23 U 4
Ugarit ∴•• SYR 128-129 F 5
Ugashik Bay ≈ 22-23 R 4
Ugashik Lake ○ USA 22-23 S 4
Ugatkyn ~ RUS 112-113 Q 3
Ugayb, Wādī al < LAR 192-193 G 3
Ugba ○ WAN 204-205 H 5
Ugbala ○ WAN 204-205 H 5
Ugbenu ○ WAN 204-205 F 5
Ugep ○ WAN 204-205 H 6
Ughelli ○ WAN 204-205 F 6
Ugie ○ ZA 220-221 J 5
Ugjokfok Bay ≈ 36-37 T 7
Uglegorsk ○ RUS 122-123 K 4
Ugleural'skij ○ RUS 96-97 K 4
Uglič ☆•• RUS 94-95 Q 3
Uglovoe ○ RUS 122-123 C 3
Uglovoe, ozero ○ RUS 108-109 I Z 1
Ugo ○ WAN 204-205 G 5
Ugojan ○ RUS 118-119 M 6
Ugol'naja ~ RUS 108-109 c 4
Ugol'naja, buhta ≈ 112-113 U 5
Ugol'noe ○ RUS 110-111 b 7
Ugol'nye Kopi ○ RUS 112-113 T 4
Ugol'nyj ○ RUS 118-119 M 7
Ugol'nyj, mys ▲ RUS 120-121 U 3
Ugra ○ RUS 94-95 O 4
Ugssugtussoq ≈ 28-29 V 4
Uḫaidir ∴• IRQ 128-129 K 6
Uhen ○ WAN 204-205 F 5
Uherské Hradiště ○ CZ 92-93 O 4
Uhi ○ WAN 204-205 G 5
Uhiere ○ WAN 204-205 F 5
Uhlava ~ CZ 92-93 M 4
Uhlenhorst ○ NAM 220-221 C 1
Uhma ~ RUS 88-89 W 5
Uhlovo ☆ RUS 94-95 R 5
Uhrichsville ○ USA (OH) 280-281 E 3
Uhta ○ RUS 88-89 W 5
Uhta ~ RUS 88-89 W 5
Uhuru Peak ▲ EAT 212-213 F 5
Uib ○ NAM 216-217 D 9
Uíge ◘ ANG 216-217 C 3
Uíge ☆ ANG (UIG) 216-217 C 3
Uiha ⌒ TON 184 IV a 1
Ŭijŏngbu ○ ROK 150-151 F 9
Ŭiju ○ KOR 150-151 E 7
Uinskoe ☆ RUS 96-97 K 5
Uintah and Ouray Indian Reservation ⵅ USA (UT) 254-255 E 3
Uinta Mountains ▲ USA 254-255 E 3
Uinta River ~ USA 254-255 E 3
Uirapuru ○ BR 70-71 H 4
Uiraúna ○ BR 68-69 J 5
Uis Myn ○ NAM 216-217 C 10
Ŭisŏng ○ ROK 150-151 G 9
Uitenhage ○ ZA 220-221 G 6
Uivak, Cape ▲ CDN 36-37 S 5
Uivaq ⌒ GRØ 28-29 U 5
Uižèn ○ MAU 148-149 H 5
Uj ~ RUS 96-97 L 6
Uj ~ RUS 114-115 G 7
Uj ~ RUS 114-115 N 6
Ujali ○ WAN 204-205 G 5
Ujaly ○ KZ (KZL) 126-127 O 6
Ujaly ○ KZ (MNG) 126-127 L 5
Ujaly ○ TJ 136-137 L 5
Ujan ~ RUS 120-121 E 5
Ujana ~ RUS 120-121 F 2
Ujandina ~ RUS 110-111 Z 6
Ujar ☆ RUS 116-117 G 8
Ujdah ☆ MA 188-189 L 3
Ujelang ⌒ MAI 13 H 2
Uji ○ J 152-153 F 7
Uji-guntō ⌒ J 152-153 C 9
Ujiji ○• EAT 212-213 B 6
Ujil ~ KZ 96-97 H 9
Ujil ~ KZ 126-127 L 3
Ujir, Pulau ⌒ RI 166-167 H 4
Ujjain ○ IND 138-139 E 8
Ujmen' ☆ RUS 124-125 P 3
Ujohbilang ○ RI 164-165 D 3
Ujskoe ○ RUS 96-97 M 6
Ujuk ○ KZ 136-137 M 3
Ujuk ~ RUS 116-117 F 10
Ujukskij, hrebet ▲ RUS 116-117 F 10
Ujungbatu ○ RI 162-163 D 4
Ujungberung ○ RI 168 B 3
Ujung Kulon Game Park ⊥ RI 168 A 3
Ujung Kulon National Park ⊥••• RI 168 A 3
Ujunglamuru ○ RI 164-165 F 6
Ujung Pandang ☆ RI 164-165 F 6
Ujvinvyvajam ~ RUS 120-121 V 3
Ujyk ○ KZ 136-137 M 3
Uka ~ RUS 120-121 T 5
Ukara Island ⌒ EAT 212-213 D 4
'Ukāš, Tulūl al- ▲ IRQ 128-129 K 7
Ukata ○ WAN 204-205 F 3
Ukatnyj, ostrov ⌒ RUS 126-127 H 5
Ukehe ○ WAN 204-205 G 5
Ukèlajat ~ RUS 112-113 R 6
Ukèlajat, hrebet ▲ RUS 112-113 Q 6
Ukerewe Island ⌒ EAT 212-213 D 5
Ukhrul ○ IND 142-143 J 3
Ukhta = Uhta ○ RUS 88-89 W 5
Ukiah ○ USA (CA) 246-247 B 4
Ukiah ○ USA (OR) 244-245 G 5
Uki Ni Masi Island ⌒ SOL 184 I e 4
Ukinskaja guba ≈ 120-121 U 5
Ukkusissat ○ GRØ 26-27 Z 8
Ukläna ○ IND 138-139 E 5
Ukmergė ∴•• LT 94-95 J 4
Ukolnoi Island ⌒ USA 22-23 Q 5
Ukraina ○ CDN (MAN) 234-235 C 3
Ukraine = Ukrajina ■ UA 102-103 E 3
Ukšum ~ RUS 118-119 G 8
Uktym ~ RUS 88-89 U 5
Ukukit ~ RUS 110-111 L 5
Uku-shima ⌒ J 152-153 C 8
Ukwatutu ○ ZRE 206-207 H 6

Tūlūl al-Ašaqif — Ukwatutu 405

Ul ~ **RUS** 122-123 H 2
Ula ☆ **TR** 128-129 C 4
'Ulā, al- o·· **KSA** 130-131 E 4
Ulaanbaatar ★ **MAU** 148-149 H 4
Ulaan-Èrèg o **MAU** 148-149 J 4
Ulaangom ☆ **MAU** 116-117 F 11
Ulaanhudag o **MAU** 148-149 G 4
Ulaan nuur o **MAU** 148-149 F 5
Ulaanšivèèt o **MAU** 148-149 F 4
Ulaan Tajga ∸ **MAU** 148-149 D 2
Ulagan, Ust'- ☆ **RUS** 124-125 Q 3
Ulah-An o **RUS** 118-119 O 5
Ulahan-Bom, hrebet ▲ **RUS** 120-121 G 2
Ulahan-Botuobuja ~ **RUS** 118-119 F 4
Ulahan-Jurjah ~ **RUS** 110-111 O 3
Ulahan-Kjuëgjuljur ~ **RUS** 110-111 T 4
Ulahan-Kjuël' o **RUS** (SAH) 110-111 V 6
Ulahan-Kjuël' • **RUS** (SAH) 110-111 a 7
Ulahan-Murbajy ~ **RUS** 118-119 F 5
Ulahan-Siligile ~ **RUS** 120-121 D 4
Ulahan-Sis, hrebet ▲ **RUS** 110-111 b 5
Ulahan Taryn • **RUS** 110-111 Z 7
Ulahan-Taryn-Jurjah ~ **RUS** 110-111 Y 7
Ulahan-Tirentjah ~ **RUS** 110-111 P 5
Ulahan-Vava ~ **RUS** 116-117 N 3
Ulah-Tas, gora ▲ **RUS** 110-111 d 4
'Ulaim az-Zama ▲ **KSA** 130-131 G 3
Ulak Island ⌒ **USA** 22-23 G 7
Ulamona o **PNG** 183 F 3
Ulan o **VRC** 144-145 M 2
Ulan Bator = Ulaanbaatar ★ **MAU** 148-149 H 4
Ūlanbel o **KZ** 124-125 G 6
Ulan-Burgasy, hrebet ▲ **RUS** 116-117 O 9
Ūlang, Daryā-ye ~ **AFG** 134-135 K 2
Ulanhot o **VRC** 150-151 D 4
Ulanlinggi o **VRC** 146-147 H 4
Ulansuhai Nur o **VRC** 154-155 F 1
Ulan Tohoi o **VRC** 148-149 E 7
Ulan-Udè ☆• **RUS** 116-117 N 10
Ulan Ude = Ulan-Udè ☆• **RUS** 116-117 N 10
Ulan Ul Hu o **VRC** 144-145 H 3
Ulapara o **BD** 142-143 F 3
Ulapes, Sierra de ▲ **RA** 76-77 D 6
Ularbemban o **RI** 162-163 E 4
Ulaş ☆ **TR** 128-129 G 3
Ulawa Island ⌒ **SOL** 184 I e 3
Ulawun, Mount ▲ **PNG** 183 F 3
Ulaya o **EAT** 214-215 J 4
Ulbanep, Mount ▲ **PNG** 183 B 2
Ul'banskij zaliv ≈ 122-123 G 2
Ulbeja ~ **RUS** 120-121 L 4
Ul'beja ~ **RUS** 120-121 K 3
Ulcinj o **YU** 100-101 G 4
Ulco o **ZA** 220-221 G 4
Ul'durga ~ **RUS** 118-119 G 9
Uleâborg ☆ **FIN** 88-89 H 4
Ulefoss ☆ **N** 86-87 D 7
Ulemaririvier ~ **SME** 62-63 G 4
Ülen Vladimirovka o **KZ** 124-125 L 3
Ulete o **EAT** 214-215 H 5
Uliaga Island ⌒ **USA** 22-23 M 6
Uliastaj ☆ **MAU** 148-149 C 4
Uliga = Dalap-Uliga-Darrit ★ **MAI** 13 J 2
Ulindi ~ **ZRE** 210-211 L 4
Ulindi ~ **ZRE** 212-213 B 5
Ul'inskij hrebet ▲ **RUS** 120-121 H 5
Ul'ja o **RUS** (HBR) 120-121 J 4
Ul'ja ~ **RUS** 120-121 J 4
Uljagan ~ **RUS** 112-113 L 4
Uljanivka ☆ **UA** 102-103 G 3
Ul'janovka o **RUS** 94-95 M 2
Ul'janovo o **RUS** 94-95 H 4
Ul'janovo o **UZ** 136-137 L 4
Ul'janovsk = Simbirsk ☆ **RUS** 96-97 F 6
Ul'janovskij ☆ **KZ** 124-125 H 3
Uljatuj o **RUS** 118-119 H 10
Uljin o **ROK** 150-151 G 9
Uljuveem ~ **RUS** 112-113 X 3
Uljuveemskaja vpadina ∸ **RUS** 112-113 X 3
Ulkajyk ~ **KZ** 126-127 P 2
Ūlkajyk ~ **KZ** 126-127 P 3
Ul'kan ~ **RUS** 116-117 N 8
Ulkan ~ **RUS** 120-121 H 5
Ülken Acbolat, köli o **KZ** 124-125 K 2
Ülken-Aktau, tau ▲ **KZ** 136-137 L 3
Ulken Borsyk, kūm ∸ **KZ** 126-127 N 4
Ülken Cobda ~ **KZ** 126-127 L 2
Ulken-Karoj, köli o **KZ** 124-125 G 2
Ülken Özen ~ **KZ** 96-97 F 9
Ülken Šagan o **KZ** 96-97 G 8
Ülken sor ∸ **KZ** 126-127 J 5
Ulla, Río ~ **E** 98-99 C 3
Ulladulla o **AUS** 180-181 L 3
Ullahan-Kjuel', ozero o **RUS** 110-111 P 6
Ullāl o **IND** 140-141 F 4
Ullånger o **S** 86-87 J 5
Ullapool o• **GB** 90-91 E 3
Ulla Ulla o **BOL** 70-71 C 4
Ulla Ulla, Reserva Faunistica ⊥ **BOL** 70-71 C 4
Ullawarra o **AUS** 176-177 D 1
Ulloma o **BOL** 70-71 C 5
Ullsfjorden ≈ 86-87 J 2
Ullüng o **ROK** 150-151 H 9
Ullüng Do ⌒ **ROK** 150-151 H 9
Ulm o• **D** 92-93 K 4
Ulm o **USA** (AR) 276-277 D 6
Ulm o **USA** (MT) 250-251 H 4
Ulm o **USA** (WY) 252-253 M 2
Ul'ma ~ **RUS** 122-123 D 3
Ulmer o **USA** (SC) 284-285 J 3
Ulongwé o **MOC** 218-219 H 2
Uloowaranie, Lake o **AUS** 178-179 E 4
Ulricehamn ☆ **S** 86-87 F 8
Ulsan o **ROK** 150-151 G 10
Ultima o **AUS** 180-181 G 3
Ulu o **MYA** 158-159 E 5
Ulu o **RI** 164-165 J 2
Ulu o **RUS** (SAH) 118-119 N 5
Ulu ~ **RUS** 118-119 N 5
Ulu o **SUD** 208-209 A 3
Ulúa, Río ~ **HN** 52-53 K 4
Uluaa ⌒ **GRØ** 26-27 X 7
Ulubat Gölü o **TR** 128-129 C 2
Uluçınar o **TR** 128-129 F 4
Uludağ ▲ **TR** 128-129 C 2
Uludere ☆ **TR** 128-129 K 4
Uludoruk Tepe ▲ **TR** 128-129 K 4
Ulugqat o **VRC** 146-147 B 6
Uluguru Mountains ▲ **EAT** 214-215 J 4
Ului Island ⌒ **AUS** 183 B 6
Uluinggalau ▲ **FJI** 184 III b 2
Ulujami o **RI** 168 C 3
Ulujul ~ **RUS** 114-115 T 6
Uluksan Peninsula ⌣ **CDN** 24-25 d 4
Ulungur He ~ **VRC** 146-147 H 2
Ulungur Hu o **VRC** 146-147 H 2
Ulupalakua Ranch o **USA** (HI) 288 J 4
Uluputur o **PNG** 183 G 2
Uluru National Park ⊥ ··· **AUS** 176-177 L 2
Ulut ~ **RP** 160-161 F 7
Ulu Tiram o **MAL** 162-163 E 4
Ulva o **AUS** 178-179 H 1
Ulveah = Lopevi ⌒ **VAN** 184 II b 3
Ulverstone o **AUS** 180-181 J 6
'Ulyā, Wādī l- o **OM** 132-133 K 2
Ulysses o **USA** (KS) 262-263 E 7
Ulysses o **USA** (NE) 262-263 J 3
Ūly-Taldyk ~ **KZ** 126-127 N 3
Ūlytau tauy ▲ **KZ** 124-125 E 5
Ūly-Žylancak ~ **KZ** 124-125 D 4
Ulz gol ~ **MAU** 148-149 L 3
Uma ~ **ZRE** 210-211 L 3
Umadam o **SUD** 200-201 H 4
Umair o **KSA** 132-133 C 5
Umaish o **WAN** 204-205 G 4
Umaki o **CO** 60-61 F 2
Umak Island ⌒ **USA** 22-23 J 7
Umala o **BOL** 70-71 C 5
Umal'ta, Ust'- o **RUS** 122-123 E 3
Umán o **MEX** 52-53 K 1
Uman' ☆ **UA** 102-103 G 3
Umanak = Uummannaq o **GRØ** 28-29 O 1
Umanak Fjord ≈ 26-27 Y 8
Umanaq o **GRØ** 28-29 P 4
Umangcinang, Tanjung ▲ **RI** 164-165 E 5
Umarga o **IND** 140-141 G 2
Umari, Rio ~ **BR** 66-67 E 7
Umaria o **IND** 142-143 B 4
Umarkhed o **IND** 138-139 F 10
Umarkot o **PK** 138-139 B 7
Umarkote o **IND** 142-143 C 6
Umaroona Lake o **AUS** 178-179 D 4
Umatilla o **USA** (FL) 286-287 H 3
Umatilla o **USA** (OR) 244-245 F 5
Umatilla Indian Reservation X **USA** (OR) 244-245 G 5
Umatilla River ~ **USA** 244-245 F 5
Umba ~ **EAT** 212-213 G 6
Umba o **RUS** 88-89 N 3
Umbakumba X **AUS** 174-175 D 3
Umbarger o **USA** (TX) 264-265 B 4
Umbe o **PE** 64-65 D 6
Umbeb Bay ≈ 184 II a 3
Umbelasha ~ **SUD** 206-207 F 4
Umboi Island ⌒ **PNG** 183 D 3
Umbozero o **RUS** 88-89 N 3
Umbraj o **IND** 140-141 F 2
Umbria ▫ **I** 100-101 C 3
Umbukul o **PNG** 183 E 2
Umbulan Gayohpecoh o **RI** 162-163 F 6
Umbuluzi ~ **MOC** 220-221 L 3
Umbumbulu o **ZA** 220-221 K 5
Umburanas o **BR** 68-69 H 7
Umbuzeiro o **BR** 68-69 L 5
Ume ~ **ZW** 218-219 E 3
Umeå ☆• **S** 86-87 K 5
Umeälven ~ **S** 86-87 J 4
Umfolozi Game Reserve ⊥ **ZA** 220-221 K 4
Umiat o **USA** 20-21 O 2
Umiivik Bugt ≈ 28-29 U 4
Umirim o **BR** 68-69 J 3
Umitker o **KZ** 124-125 J 3
Umkomaas o **ZA** (NTL) 220-221 K 5
Umkomaas ~ **ZA** 220-221 K 5
Umlekan o **RUS** 118-119 N 9
Umm al Aranib o **LAR** 192-193 F 4
Umm al-Ǧimāl .:.• **JOR** 130-131 E 1
Umm al-Ḥait, Wādī = Ibn Ḥauṭar, Wādī ~ **OM** 132-133 J 4
Umm al 'Izām, Sabkhat o **LAR** 192-193 F 2
Ummannanarsuaq = Kap Farvel ▲ **GRØ** 28-29 T 7
Umm ar Rizam o **LAR** 192-193 K 1
Umm Ašar Aš-Šarqiyā o **KSA** 130-131 J 4
Umm Ba'ānib, Ǧabal ▲ **ET** 194-195 F 4
Umm Badr o **SUD** 200-201 C 5
Umm Barbit o **SUD** 206-207 L 3
Umm Bel o **SUD** 200-201 D 6
Umm Buru o **SUD** 198-199 L 5
Umm Būshah o **SUD** 200-201 E 6
Umm Dafag o **SUD** 206-207 F 3
Umm Dam o **SUD** 200-201 E 6
Umm Defeis o **SUD** 200-201 D 6
Umm Digulgulaya o **SUD** 206-207 G 3
Umm Dubban o **SUD** 200-201 D 5
Umm Durmān o·· **SUD** 200-201 F 5
Umm Gamāla o **SUD** 206-207 J 3
Umm Gederri o **SUD** 206-207 F 3
Umm Ḥarāz o **SUD** 206-207 F 3
Umm Ḥawsh o **SUD** 200-201 C 6
Umm Ḥibāl, Bi'r o **ET** 194-195 F 6
Umm Hitan o **SUD** 206-207 K 3
Ummī, Godār-e ▲ **IR** 134-135 H 1
Umm 'Illah, Sarīr ∸ **LAR** 192-193 F 4
Umm Inderaba o **SUD** 200-201 E 5
Umm Kaddādah o **SUD** 200-201 C 6
Umm Marahik o **SUD** 200-201 B 6
Umm Mirdi o **SUD** 200-201 F 3
Umm Naqqāt, Ǧabal ▲ **ET** 194-195 G 5
Umm Qaṣr o **IRQ** 130-131 K 2
Umm Qozein o **SUD** 200-201 C 5
Umm Qurein o **SUD** 200-201 D 4
Umm Raḥaw o **SUD** 200-201 F 3
Umm Rumetla o **SUD** 200-201 E 4
Umm Ruwābah o **SUD** 200-201 E 6
Umm Sa'ad o **LAR** 192-193 L 2
Umm Sagura o **SUD** 206-207 J 4
Umm Sa'īd = Musai'īd o **Q** 134-135 D 6
Umm Sayyālah o **SUD** 200-201 E 5
Umm Segelti o **SUD** 200-201 E 6
Umnak o **USA** 22-23 M 6
Umnak Island ⌒ **USA** 22-23 M 6
Umnak Pass ≈ 22-23 N 6
Umniati o **ZW** 218-219 E 4
Umpaqua River ~ **USA** 244-245 B 7
Um Phang o **THA** 158-159 E 3
Umpuhua o **MOC** 218-219 K 2
Umran o **KSA** 130-131 L 5
Umrer o **IND** 138-139 G 9
Umsini, Gunung ▲ **RI** 166-167 G 2
Umtata ☆ **ZA** 220-221 J 5
Umtentu o **ZA** 220-221 K 5
Umuahia o **WAN** 204-205 G 6
Umuarama o **BR** 72-73 D 7
Umuda Island ⌒ **PNG** 183 B 5
Umu-Duru o **WAN** 204-205 G 6
Umunede o **WAN** 204-205 G 5
Umutina, Área Indígena X **BR** 70-71 J 4
Umutu o **WAN** 204-205 G 6
Umvukwe Range ▲ **ZW** 218-219 F 3
Umvurudzi Safari Area ⊥ **ZW** 218-219 F 3
Umzimkulu o **ZA** (NTL) 220-221 J 5
Umzimkulu ~ **ZA** 220-221 K 5
Umzimvubu ~ **ZA** 220-221 J 5
Umzingwani ~ **ZW** 218-219 E 5
Umzinto o **ZA** 220-221 K 5
Una o **BR** 72-73 L 3
Una o **IND** 138-139 F 4
Una o **RUS** 88-89 P 4
Una o **USA** (AR) 276-277 D 5
Una, Reserva Biológica de ⊥ **BR** 72-73 L 3
Una, Rio ~ **BR** 68-69 K 6
Unadilla o **USA** (GA) 284-285 G 4
Unaha ~ **RUS** 118-119 N 8
Unaí o **BR** 72-73 G 4
Unaiza o **JOR** 130-131 D 2
'Unaiza o **KSA** 130-131 J 4
Unalakleet o **USA** 20-21 K 5
Unalakleet River ~ **USA** 20-21 K 5
Unalaska o **USA** 22-23 N 6
Unalaska Bay ≈ 22-23 N 6
Unalaska Island ⌒ **USA** 22-23 N 6
Unalga Island ⌒ **USA** 22-23 N 6
Unango o **MOC** 214-215 H 7
Unare, Río ~ **YV** 60-61 J 3
Unari, Corredeira ~ **BR** 66-67 C 2
Unauna o **RI** 164-165 G 4
Unauna, Pulau ⌒ **RI** 164-165 G 4
Unawari o **RI** 166-167 H 3
Unbunmaroo, Mount ▲ **AUS** 178-179 F 2
Uncas o **CDN** (ALB) 232-233 E 2
Unčen' = Ungheni ☆ **MD** 102-103 E 4
Unčeny = Ungheni ☆ **MD** 102-103 E 4
Uncompahgre Peak ▲ **USA** (CO) 254-255 H 5
Uncompahgre Plateau ▲ **USA** 254-255 G 5
Uncompahgre River ~ **USA** 254-255 H 5
Unda ~ **RUS** 118-119 H 10
Undandita o **AUS** 176-177 M 1
Underberg o **ZA** 220-221 J 4
Underbool o **AUS** 180-181 F 3
Underground River • **RP** 160-161 C 7
Underwood o **USA** (ND) 258-259 F 4
Underwood o **USA** (WA) 244-245 D 5
Undjuljung ~ **RUS** 110-111 P 6
Undozero, ozero o **RUS** 88-89 P 5
Undu, Tanjung ▲ **RI** 168 E 8
Unduma, Río ~ **BOL** 70-71 D 3
Undur o **RI** 166-167 F 3
Unea Island ⌒ **PNG** 183 E 3
Uneča o **RUS** 94-95 N 5
Uneí, Igarapé ~ **BR** 66-67 D 3
Uneiuxi, Área Indígena X **BR** 66-67 D 3
Uneiuxi, Rio ~ **BR** 66-67 D 3
Uneiuxi, Serra de ▲ **BR** 66-67 D 3
Unga Island ⌒ **USA** 22-23 Q 5
Ungalik o **USA** 20-21 K 4
Ungalik River ~ **USA** 20-21 K 4
Ungarie o **AUS** 180-181 J 2
Ungarra o **AUS** 180-181 D 3
Unga Strait ≈ 22-23 Q 5
Ungava, Péninsule d' ⌣ **CDN** 36-37 L 4
Ungava Bay ≈ 36-37 P 5
Ungerem o **PNG** 183 A 4
Ungheni ☆ **MD** 102-103 E 4
Ungjuèle ~ **RUS** 118-119 O 6
Ungo ~ **RUS** 118-119 D 10
Ungra ~ **RUS** 118-119 L 7
Unguz ∸ **TM** 136-137 F 5
Ungwana Bay ≈ 212-213 H 5
Unhe o **ANG** 216-217 F 8
Uni ☆ **RUS** 96-97 G 5
Unia, Lac o **ZRE** 210-211 K 5
Uniab ~ **NAM** 216-217 B 9
União o **BR** (AMA) 66-67 B 6
União o **BR** (AMA) 66-67 C 4
União o **BR** (GSU) 70-71 K 5
União o **BR** (MAR) 68-69 F 2
União o **BR** (PIA) 68-69 G 4
União da Vitória o **BR** 74-75 E 6
União dos Palmares o **BR** 68-69 K 6
Unicoi Mountains ▲ **USA** 282-283 C 5
Unimak o **USA** 22-23 O 5
Unimak Bigh ≈ 22-23 O 5
Unimak Island ⌒ **USA** 22-23 O 5
Unimak Pass ≈ 22-23 O 5
Unini, Rio ~ **BR** 66-67 F 3
Unión o **RA** 78-79 G 3
Union o **USA** (MI) 272-273 D 6
Union o **USA** (MO) 274-275 G 6
Union o **USA** (MS) 268-269 L 4
Union o **USA** (OH) 280-281 B 4
Union o **USA** (OR) 244-245 H 5
Union o **USA** (SC) 284-285 J 2
Union o **USA** (TX) 264-265 D 6
Union o **USA** (WV) 280-281 F 6
Unión, Bahía ≈ 78-79 H 5
Unión, La o **E** 98-99 G 6
Unión, La ☆ **ES** 52-53 L 5
Unión, La o **HN** 52-53 L 4
Unión, La o **MEX** 52-53 K 3
Union, La o **MEX** 52-53 D 3
Unión, La o **RCH** 78-79 C 6
Union, Mount ▲ **USA** (AZ) 256-257 C 4
Unión, Río La ~ **MEX** 52-53 D 2
Union Bay o **CDN** (BC) 230-231 E 4
Union Church o **USA** (MS) 268-269 K 5
Union City o **USA** (CA) 248-249 C 2
Union City o **USA** (IN) 274-275 O 4
Union City o **USA** (MI) 272-273 D 5
Union City o **USA** (PA) 280-281 G 2
Union City o **USA** (TN) 276-277 F 4
Union Creek o **USA** (OR) 244-245 C 8
Uniondale o **ZA** 220-221 F 6
Unión de Tula o **MEX** 52-53 B 2
Union Gap o **USA** (WA) 244-245 E 4
Unión Hidalgo o **MEX** 52-53 G 3
Union Island ⌒ **WV** 56 E 5
Unión Juárez o **MEX** 52-53 H 4
Union National Monument, Fort • **USA** (NM) 256-257 K 3
Union Pass ▲ **USA** (AZ) 256-257 A 3
Union Point o **USA** (GA) 284-285 G 3
Union Springs o **USA** (AL) 284-285 E 4
Uniontown o **USA** (AL) 284-285 C 4
Uniontown o **USA** (PA) 280-281 G 4
Unionville o **USA** (IL) 274-275 J 3
Unionville o **USA** (MO) 274-275 E 4
Unionville o **USA** (NV) 246-247 G 3
Unipouheos Indian Reserve X **CDN** (ALB) 232-233 H 2
Unita o **PE** 64-65 D 3
United Arab Emirates = Daulat al-Imārāt al-'Arabiya Al-Mu ■ **UAE** 132-133 H 2
United Kingdom ■ **GB** 90-91 H 4
United States Air Force Academy xx **USA** (CO) 254-255 L 5
United States Atomic Energy Reserve xx **USA** (CO) 254-255 G 5
United States Military Academy • **USA** (NY) 280-281 M 2
United States Naval Ammunition Depot (Crane) xx **USA** (IN) 274-275 M 6
United States of America ■ **USA** 244-245 C 5
United States Range ▲ **CDN** 26-27 J 3
Unity o **CDN** (SAS) 232-233 J 3
Unity o **USA** (ME) 278-279 M 4
Unity o **USA** (OR) 244-245 G 6
Universal City o **USA** (TX) 266-267 J 4
Universitetskij, lednik ⊂ **RUS** 108-109 I c 2
University City o **USA** (MO) 274-275 H 6
University of Virginia ··· **USA** (VA) 280-281 H 6
University Park o **USA** (NM) 256-257 J 6
Unmet o **VAN** 184 II a 3
Unnão o **IND** 142-143 B 2
Unnejvajam ~ **RUS** 112-113 O 6
Uno o **GNB** 202-203 B 4
Uno, Ilha de ⌒ **GNB** 202-203 B 4
Unpongkor o **VAN** 184 II b 4
Unsan o **KOR** 150-151 E 7
Unskaja guba ≈ 88-89 P 4
Untor, ozero o **RUS** 114-115 H 3
Unturán, Sierra de ▲ **YV** 66-67 E 2
Unuk River ~ **CDN** 32-33 E 3
Unwin o **CDN** (SAS) 232-233 J 3
Ünye ☆ **TR** 128-129 G 2
Unža ~ **RUS** 94-95 S 3
Unža ~ **RUS** 96-97 D 4
Unzen Amakusa National Park ⊥ **J** 152-153 D 8
Uojan, Novyj o **RUS** 118-119 E 7
Uol'can ~ **RUS** 110-111 Y 7
Uông Bí ☆ **VN** 156-157 E 6
Uoro o Mbini, Rio ~ **GQ** 210-211 B 3
Uozo o **J** 152-153 G 6
Upala o **CR** 52-53 B 6
Upata o **YV** 60-61 K 3
Upatoi River ~ **USA** 284-285 F 4
Upemba, Lac o **ZRE** 214-215 D 5
Upemba, Parc National de l' ⊥ **ZRE** 214-215 D 5
Upernagssivik ⌒ **GRØ** 28-29 U 4
Upernavik o **GRØ** (VGR) 26-27 W 7
Upernavik ⌒ **GRØ** (VGR) 26-27 Y 8
Upernavik Kujalleq = Søndre Upernavik o **GRØ** 26-27 X 7
Uphan o **USA** (ND) 258-259 G 3
Upi o **RP** 160-161 F 9
Upington o **ZA** 220-221 E 4
Upolokša o **RUS** 88-89 L 3
'Upolu Island ⌒ **WS** 184 V b 1
Upolu Point ▲ **USA** (HI) 288 K 4
Uporovo ☆ **RUS** 114-115 J 6
Upper Arrow Lake o **CDN** (BC) 230-231 M 3
Upper Canada Village • **CDN** (ONT) 238-239 K 4
Upper East Region ▫ **GH** 202-203 K 4
Upper Ferry o **CDN** (NFL) 242-243 J 5
Upper Forster Lake o **CDN** 34-35 D 2
Upper Fraser o **CDN** (BC) 228-229 N 2
Upper Guinea ∸ 9 B 5
Upper Hat Creek o **CDN** (BC) 230-231 H 3
Upper Humber River ~ **CDN** 242-243 L 3
Upper Indian Pond o **CDN** (NFL) 242-243 M 3
Upper Karoo = Hoë Karoo ∸ **ZA** 220-221 D 5
Upper Klamath Lake o **USA** (OR) 244-245 D 8
Upper Lake o **USA** (CA) 246-247 C 4
Upper Lake o **USA** (CA) 246-247 E 2
Upper May ~ **PNG** 183 A 3
Upper Musquodoboit o **CDN** (NS) 240-241 N 5
Upper Ouachita National Wildlife Refuge ⊥ **USA** (LA) 268-269 H 4
Upper Peninsula ⌣ **USA** 270-271 M 4
Upper Rawdor o **CDN** (NS) 240-241 M 5
Upper Red Lake o **USA** (MN) 270-271 D 2
Upper Sandusky o **USA** (OH) 280-281 C 3
Upper Sioux Indian Reservation X **USA** (MN) 270-271 C 6
Upper Souris National Wildlife Refuge ⊥ **USA** (ND) 258-259 F 3
Upper Three Runs Creek ~ **USA** 284-285 J 3
Upper Twin Lake o **CDN** (ONT) 236-237 B 2
Upper West Region ▫ **GH** 202-203 J 4
Uppland ∸ **S** 86-87 H 7
Uppsala o·· **S** 86-87 H 7
Upright, Cape ▲ **USA** 48-49 Y 6
Upright, Cape ▲ **USA** 112-113 Y 6
Upsala o **CDN** (ONT) 234-235 N 5
Upsalquitch River ~ **CDN** 240-241 J 3
Upshi o **IND** 138-139 F 3
Upstart, Cape ▲ **AUS** 174-175 J 6
Upstart Bay ≈ 174-175 J 6
Upton o **USA** (KY) 276-277 K 3
Upton o **USA** (WY) 252-253 O 2
Upuí, Corredeira ~ **BR** 66-67 H 6
'Uqair, al- o **KSA** 134-135 D 6
'Uqaylah, Al o **LAR** 192-193 H 2
'Uqlat aṣ-Ṣuqūr o **KSA** 130-131 H 5
'Uqlat Ibn Ǧabrain o **KSA** 130-131 G 4
Ur .:.• **IRQ** 130-131 K 2
Ura ~ **RUS** 118-119 H 5
Urabá, Golfo de ≈ 60-61 C 3
Uracoa o **YV** 60-61 K 3
Urad Houqi o **VRC** 148-149 H 7
Urad Qianqi o **VRC** 154-155 F 1
Urad Zhongqi o **VRC** 148-149 J 7
Uraguba o **RUS** 88-89 M 2
Urahoro o **J** 152-153 K 3
Uraim, Rio ~ **BR** 68-69 E 3
Uraj o **RUS** 114-115 H 4
Urak ~ **RUS** 120-121 K 4
Urakawa o **J** 152-153 K 3
Urakskoe plato ▲ **RUS** 120-121 J 4
Ural ~ **RUS** 96-97 L 7
Uralla o **AUS** 178-179 L 6
Ural Mountains = Ural'skij hrebet ▲ **RUS** 96-97 M 2
Ural'skij, Kamensk- ☆ **RUS** 96-97 M 5
Ural-Tau hrebet ▲ **RUS** 96-97 K 7
Ural üstirti ▲ **KZ** 124-125 B 2
Urama o **YV** 60-61 G 2
Uran o **IND** 138-139 D 10
Urana o **AUS** 180-181 J 3
Urana, Lake o **AUS** 180-181 J 3
Urandangi o **AUS** 178-179 E 1
Urandi o **BR** 72-73 J 3
Uranie, Pulau ⌒ **RI** 166-167 F 1
Uranium City o **CDN** 30-31 P 6
'Uraq o **SUD** 200-201 F 5
Urariá, Paraná ~ **BR** 66-67 H 4
Uraricuera, Rio ~ **BR** 62-63 D 4
Ura-Tjube o• **TJ** 136-137 L 5
Uravakonda o **IND** 140-141 G 3
Urawa ☆ **J** 152-153 H 7
'Urayyiḍa, Bi'r o **ET** 194-195 E 3
Urbana o **USA** (IL) 274-275 K 4
Urbana o **USA** (OH) 280-281 C 3
Urbandale o **USA** (IA) 274-275 E 3
Urbank o **USA** (MN) 270-271 C 4
Urbano Noris o **C** 54-55 G 4
Urbano Santos o **BR** 68-69 G 3
Urbi o **SUD** 200-201 E 3
Urbinasopon o **RI** 166-167 F 2
Urbino o **I** 100-101 D 3
Urcos o **PE** 70-71 B 3
Urcubamba, Río ~ **PE** 64-65 C 4
Urdaneta o **RP** 160-161 D 5
Urd gol o **MAU** 146-147 L 2
Urdinarrain o **RA** 78-79 K 2
Urdjužskoe, ozero o **RUS** 88-89 V 3
Urd Tamir gol ~ **MAU** 148-149 E 4
Ure o **WAN** 204-205 G 4
Ureca o **GQ** 210-211 B 2
Ureliki o **RUS** 112-113 Y 4
Urema ~ **RI** 166-167 H 3
Uren o **CDN** (SAS) 232-233 M 5
Uren' o **RUS** 96-97 D 5
Urenga hrebet ▲ **RUS** 96-97 L 6
Urengoj o **RUS** 114-115 P 2
Ureparapara ⌒ **VAN** 184 II a 1
Urer'jaha ~ **RUS** 88-89 Y 3
Ures o **MEX** 50-51 D 3
Urewera National Park ⊥ **NZ** 182 F 3
Urfa = Şanlı Urfa ☆• **TR** 128-129 H 4
Urfa Yaylâsı ▲ **TR** 128-129 H 4
Urgal o **RUS** (HBR) 122-123 E 3
Urgal ~ **RUS** 122-123 E 3
Urgamal = Hungij o **MAU** 146-147 M 1
Urganč ☆ **UZ** 136-137 G 4
Urganch = Urganč ☆ **UZ** 136-137 G 4
Urgenć = Urganč ☆ **UZ** 136-137 G 4
Ürgüp ☆·· **TR** 128-129 F 3
Urgut ☆ **UZ** 136-137 K 5
Urho o **VRC** 146-147 G 2
Urho Kekkosen kansallispuisto ⊥ **FIN** 88-89 J 2
Uri o **IND** 138-139 E 2
Uri o **TCH** 198-199 J 2
Uriah o **USA** (AL) 284-285 C 5
Uriangato o **MEX** 52-53 D 1
Uribante, Río ~ **YV** 60-61 F 4
Uribe o **CO** 60-61 C 6
Uribe, La o **CO** 60-61 D 6
Uribia o **CO** 60-61 E 2
Uribicha o **BOL** 70-71 F 4
Uribici o **BR** 74-75 F 7
Urica o **YV** 60-61 J 3
Urich o **USA** (MO) 274-275 D 6
Urickij ☆ **KZ** 124-125 D 2
Urickoe o **RUS** 118-119 L 5
Urik ~ **RUS** 116-117 K 9
Uril ~ **RUS** 122-123 D 4
Uriman o **YV** 60-61 K 5
Urimará o **BR** 68-69 J 6
Urin o **PNG** 183 E 3
Urique, Río ~ **MEX** 50-51 F 4
Urjah, Kurun- o **RUS** 120-121 G 4
Urjum, ozero o **RUS** 124-125 L 1
Urjumkan ~ **RUS** 118-119 J 10
Urjumkanskij, hrebet ▲ **RUS** 118-119 J 10
Urjup ~ **RUS** 114-115 U 7
Urjupino o **RUS** 118-119 J 9
Urjupinsk o **RUS** 102-103 N 2
Urka ~ **RUS** 118-119 L 9
Urkan ~ **RUS** 118-119 N 9
Urkan ~ **RUS** 118-119 O 8
Urla ☆ **TR** 128-129 B 3
Urla-Burtja ~ **RUS** 96-97 K 8
Urluk o **RUS** 116-117 N 10
Urmatau hrebet ▲ **RUS** 96-97 K 7
Urmetan o **TJ** 136-137 L 5
Urmi ~ **RUS** 122-123 E 3
Urna ~ **RUS** 114-115 M 5
Urnes o **N** 86-87 C 6
Urnes, Stavkirke ··· **N** 86-87 C 6
Uročišče "Kontugaj" • **RUS** 96-97 K 8
Uroh ~ **RI** 164-165 F 5
Uromi o **WAN** 204-205 G 5
Uroševac o• **YU** 100-101 H 3
Urov ~ **RUS** 118-119 J 10
Urquhart Lake o **CDN** 20-21 Z 2
'Urr, al- o **Y** 132-133 C 6
Urre Lauquén, Laguna o **RA** 78-79 G 5
Ursano o **RI** 166-167 E 3
Ursine o **USA** (NV) 248-249 K 2
Ursulo Galván o **MEX** 52-53 K 2
Urt o **MAU** 148-149 E 6
Urtaovul o **UZ** 136-137 L 4
Urṭayyān o **KSA** 130-131 G 3
Uru ~ **ZRE** 210-211 L 4
Uru, Rio ~ **BR** 68-69 F 3
Uru, Rio ~ **BR** 72-73 F 3
Uruachic o **MEX** 50-51 E 4
Uruaçu o **BR** 72-73 F 3
Uruanã o **BR** 72-73 F 3
Uruapan del Progreso o• **MEX** 52-53 C 2
Uruara, Rio ~ **BR** 68-69 B 3
Uruaru, Cachoeira ~ **BR** 68-69 C 3
Urubamba o **PE** 64-65 F 8
Urubamba, Río ~ **PE** 64-65 F 8
Urubaxi, Rio ~ **BR** 66-67 E 3
Urubu, Cachoeira do ~ **BR** 72-73 F 2
Urubu, Ilha ⌒ **BR** 66-67 J 4
Urubu Grande, Rio ~ **BR** 68-69 D 7
Uruburetama o **BR** 68-69 J 3
Urucará o **BR** 66-67 J 4
Uruçu, Cachoeira do ~ **BR** 66-67 F 2
Urucu, Rio ~ **BR** 66-67 H 6
Urucu, Rio ~ **BR** 66-67 E 5
Uruçuca o **BR** 72-73 L 3
Uruçuí o **BR** 68-69 F 5
Uruçui, Serra do ▲ **BR** 68-69 F 6
Urucuia o **BR** 72-73 H 4
Urucuia, Rio ~ **BR** 72-73 H 4
Uruçui Preto, Rio ~ **BR** 68-69 F 6
Uruçui Prêto, Rio ~ **BR** 68-69 F 5
Uruçui Vermelho, Rio ~ **BR** 68-69 F 6
Urucum, Monte do ▲ **BR** 70-71 J 6
Urucuri, Ilha ⌒ **BR** 62-63 H 6
Urucuriana, Igarapé ~ **BR** 62-63 G 5
Uruena, Río ~ **RA** 76-77 E 4
Uru-Eu-Wau-Wau, Área Indígena X **BR** 70-71 F 2
Uruguai, Rio ~ **BR** 74-75 D 6
Uruguaiana o **BR** 76-77 J 5
Uruguay ■ **ROU** 78-79 L 2
Uruguay, Río ~ **RA** 78-79 K 2
Uruguinha o **BR** 62-63 J 5
Uruk = Erech .:.• **IRQ** 128-129 L 7
Uruljunguj ~ **RUS** 118-119 H 10
Uruma o **RI** 166-167 H 4
Uruma (Omba) ~ **RI** 166-167 H 4
Urumaco o **YV** 60-61 F 2
Urum aṣ-Ṣuġrā o **SYR** 128-129 G 4
Ürümqi ☆ **VRC** 146-147 H 4
Urungwe Safari Area ⊥ **ZW** 218-219 E 3
Urup ~ **RUS** 126-127 D 5
Urup, ostrov ⌒ **RUS** 122-123 O 6
Urup, proliv ≈ 122-123 O 5
Urupá, Rio ~ **BR** 70-71 F 2
Urupadi, Rio ~ **BR** 66-67 J 4
Urupês o **BR** 72-73 F 6
Urupuca, Rio ~ **BR** 72-73 J 5
'Urūq al-Awārik ∸ **KSA** 132-133 E 4
'Urūq ar-Rumaila ∸ **KSA** 132-133 E 3
'Urūq Ḥibāka ∸ **KSA** 132-133 F 3
'Urūq Subai' ∸ **KSA** 130-131 H 6
Ürür gol ~ **MAU** 148-149 E 2
Uruša o **RUS** (AMR) 118-119 L 8
Uruša ~ **RUS** 118-119 L 9
Urus-Martan o **RUS** 126-127 F 6
Urussu o **RUS** 96-97 H 6
Urusta, Moj- o **RUS** 120-121 N 3
Urutaí, Ilha ⌒ **BR** 62-63 J 6
Uru Uru, Lago o **BOL** 70-71 D 6
Uruwira o **EAT** 214-215 F 4
Urville, Île d' ⌒ **ARK** 16 G 31
Urville, Mer d' ≈ 16 G 15
Uryū-gawa ~ **J** 152-153 K 2
Urziceni o **RO** 102-103 E 5
Uržum ☆ **RUS** 96-97 G 5
Us ~ **RUS** 116-117 F 9
Usa o **J** 152-153 D 8
Usa ~ **RUS** 88-89 Y 4
Usa ~ **RUS** 108-109 J 8
Usa ~ **RUS** 114-115 U 7
Usa, Bol'šaja ~ **RUS** 108-109 L 8
Ušačy o **BY** 94-95 L 4
Usagara o **EAT** 212-213 D 5
'Usaila o **KSA** 130-131 J 5
'Ušaira o **KSA** 130-131 J 5
Uşak ☆ **TR** 128-129 C 3
Usakos o **NAM** 216-217 C 11
Ušakova, ostrov ⌒ **RUS** 84-85 q 2
Ušakovskoe o **RUS** 112-113 V 1
Usalgin ~ **RUS** 122-123 G 2
Usalin o **RI** 166-167 B 7
Usambara Mountains ▲ **EAT** 212-213 G 6
Ūšaral o **KZ** 124-125 M 5
Usa River o **EAT** 212-213 F 5
Usauer o **RI** 166-167 H 2
Uš-Bel'dir o **RUS** 116-117 J 10
Usborne, Mount ▲ **GB** 78-79 L 6
Uscal o **UZ** 136-137 F 3
Ušće o **YU** 100-101 H 3
Usedom ⌒ **D** 92-93 M 1
Useless Loop o **AUS** 176-177 B 3
Usemuare o **RI** 166-167 H 3
U.S. Energy Research and Development Administration xx **USA** (WA) 244-245 F 4
Usengi o **EAK** 212-213 E 4
'Usfān o **KSA** 132-133 A 3
Ušh ~ **RUS** 120-121 R 5
Ushaa o **Z** 218-219 B 2
Ushagat Island ⌒ **USA** 22-23 U 3
Usherville o **CDN** (SAS) 232-233 Q 3
Ushibuka o **J** 152-153 D 8
Ushuaia ☆ **RA** 80 F 7
Usilampatti o **IND** 140-141 G 6
Usim o **RI** 166-167 G 2
Usina Apiacás o **BR** 70-71 J 2
Usina São Francisco o **BR** 66-67 H 5
Usine o **RN** 198-199 C 3
Usino o **PNG** 183 C 3
Usinsk ☆ **RUS** 88-89 Y 4
Ušišir, ostrova ⌒ **RUS** 122-123 P 5
Usk o **CDN** (BC) 228-229 F 2
Usk o **USA** (WA) 244-245 H 2
Uškanij krjaž ▲ **RUS** 112-113 U 4
Uški, zaliv ≈ 120-121 M 4
Us-Kjuël' o **RUS** 118-119 P 4
Üsküdar o **TR** 128-129 C 2
Usmat o **UZ** 136-137 K 5
Ūsmat ☆ **UZ** 136-137 K 5
U.S. Navy's Strategic Radio and Communications Base • **AUS** 172-173 B 6
Usoke o **EAT** 212-213 D 6
Usol'e-Sibirskoe o **RUS** 116-117 L 9
Usolka ~ **RUS** 116-117 G 7
Usol'e ☆ **RUS** 114-115 D 5
Usol'ye Sibirskoye = Usol'e-Sibirskoe o **RUS** 116-117 L 9
Uson o **RP** 160-161 E 6
Uspallata o **RA** 78-79 E 2
Uspallata, Sierra de ▲ **RA** 78-79 E 2
Uspanapa, Río ~ **MEX** 52-53 G 3
Uspero o **MEX** 52-53 C 2
Usquil o **PE** 64-65 C 5
Ussel o **F** 90-91 J 9
Ussuri ~ **RUS** 122-123 E 5
Ussurijsk o **RUS** 122-123 E 7
Ussurka, Bol'šaja ~ **RUS** 122-123 F 6
Usta o **USA** (SD) 260-261 D 1
Usta Muhammad o **PK** 138-139 B 5
Ustamurot o **UZ** 136-137 J 3
Ust'-Barguzin o **RUS** 116-117 O 9
Ust'-Belaja o **RUS** 112-113 R 4
Ust'-Bel'skie gory ▲ **RUS** 112-113 R 4
Ust'-Bol'šereck ☆ **RUS** 122-123 R 2
Ust'-Cil'ma o **RUS** 88-89 W 4
Ust-Džeguta o **RUS** 126-127 D 5
Ust'-Džilinda o **RUS** 118-119 E 9
Ust'e o **RUS** 94-95 Q 2
Ust'e o **RUS** 116-117 G 7
Ust'-Èlegest o **RUS** 116-117 G 10
Ust'-Hajrjuzovo o **RUS** 120-121 R 5
Ust'-Hakčan o **RUS** 120-121 M 2
Ustica, Ísola di ⌒ **I** 100-101 D 5
Ust'-Ilga o **RUS** 116-117 M 8
Ust'-Ilimsk ☆ **RUS** 116-117 L 7
Ust'Ilimsk = Ust'-Ilimsk ☆ **RUS** 116-117 L 7
Ústí nad Labem o **CZ** 92-93 N 3
Ustinov = Iževsk ☆ **RUS** 96-97 H 5
Üstirt Šakyraj ▲ **KZ** 126-127 M 4
Ust'-Išim o **RUS** 114-115 L 6
Ust'-Jansk o **RUS** 110-111 V 4
Ustjurt, plato ▲ **UZ** 126-127 L 6
Ustjurtdagi Komsomol'sk o **UZ** 136-137 F 2
Ustjužina o **RUS** 94-95 P 2
Ustka o• **PL** 92-93 O 1
Ust'-Kada o **RUS** 116-117 K 8
Ust'-Kalmanka o **RUS** 124-125 N 2
Ust'-Kamčatsk ☆ **RUS** 120-121 U 5
Ust'-Kamenogorsk = Öskemen o **KZ** 124-125 N 4
Ust'-Kan o **RUS** (KRN) 116-117 F 7
Ust'-Kan o **RUS** (ROS) 124-125 O 3
Ust'-Kara o **RUS** 108-109 L 7
Ust'-Karenga o **RUS** 118-119 H 8
Ust'-Karsk o **RUS** 118-119 J 9
Ust'-Koksa o **RUS** 124-125 O 3
Ust'-Kujga o **RUS** 110-111 U 4
Ust'-Kulom o **RUS** 96-97 H 3
Ust'-Kut ☆ **RUS** 116-117 M 7
Ust'-Labinsk o **RUS** 102-103 L 5
Ust'-Lenskij zapovednik (učastok Del'tevyj) ⊥ **RUS** 110-111 P 3
Ust'-Lenskij zapovednik (učastok Sokol) ⊥ **RUS** 110-111 Q 3
Ust'-Luga o **RUS** 94-95 L 2
Ust'-Lyža o **RUS** 88-89 Y 4
Ust'-Maja o• **RUS** 120-121 F 3
Ust'-Mil' o **RUS** 120-121 E 4
Ust'-Nem o **RUS** 96-97 J 3
Ust'-Nera ☆• **RUS** 110-111 Y 7
Ust'-Njukža o **RUS** 118-119 K 7
Üštöbe o **KZ** 124-125 L 6
Ust'-Olenëk o **RUS** 110-111 M 3
Ust'-Omčug ☆ **RUS** 120-121 N 3
Ust'-Ordynsk Buryat Autonomous District = Ust'-Ordynskij Bur ▫ **RUS** 116-117 L 9
Ust'-Ordynskij ☆ **RUS** 116-117 M 9
Ust'-Pinega o **RUS** 88-89 Q 4
Ust'-Pit o **RUS** 116-117 E 6
Ust'-Reka o **RUS** 88-89 O 6
Ustrzyki Dolne o• **PL** 92-93 R 4
Ust'-Sobolevka o **RUS** 122-123 H 5
Ust'-Srednekan o **RUS** 120-121 P 2
Ust'-Tym o **RUS** 114-115 Q 5
Ust'-Uda ☆ **RUS** 116-117 L 8
Ustui Pass ▲ **PK** 138-139 C 2
Ust'-Ulagan ☆ **RUS** 124-125 Q 3
Ust'-Umal'ta o **RUS** 122-123 E 3
Ust'-Vaen'ga o **RUS** 88-89 R 5
Ust'-Vaga o **RUS** 88-89 R 5
Ust'-Voja o **RUS** (KOM) 88-89 Y 4
Ust'-Voja o **RUS** (KOM) 114-115 D 2
Ust'-Vyjskaja o **RUS** 88-89 T 5
Ust'-Vym' o **RUS** 88-89 V 5

406 Ul — Ust'-Vym'

Ventas con Peña Aguilera, Las o E 98-99 E 5
Ventersburg o ZA 220-221 H 4
Ventersdorp o ZA 220-221 H 3
Venterstad o ZA 220-221 G 5
Ventisquero, Cerro ▲ RA 78-79 D 6
Ventosa, La o MEX 52-53 G 3
Ventoux, Mont ▲ F 90-91 K 9
Ventspils ☆•• LV 94-95 G 3
Ventuari, Río ~ YV 60-61 H 5
Ventura o• USA (CA) 248-249 E 5
Venujeuo o RUS 108-109 O 6
Venus o USA (FL) 286-287 H 4
Venus o USA (NE) 262-263 H 2
Venustiano Carranza o MEX 52-53 H 3
Venustiano Carranza, Presa o MEX 50-51 J 4
Venustiono Carranza o MEX 52-53 C 2
Veppur o IND 140-141 H 5
Ver, Horej- o RUS 88-89 Y 3
Vera o BR 70-71 K 3
Vera o CDN (SAS) 232-233 J 3
Vera o RA 76-77 G 5
Vera o USA (TX) 264-265 E 5
Vera, Bahía ≈ 80 H 2
Vera, Cape ▲ CDN 24-25 b 2
Vera, Laguna o PY 76-77 J 4
Veracruz o MEX 50-51 B 1
Veracruz o• MEX 52-53 F 2
Veracruz ▫ MEX 52-53 E 1
Verada da Redenção ~ BR 68-69 G 7
Verada do Buriti ~ BR 68-69 G 7
Verada Tábua ou Rio Salitre ~ BR 68-69 H 7
Verado de Côcos ~ BR 72-73 H 2
Veranópolis o BR 74-75 E 7
Verao = Île Moso ⌒ VAN 184 II b 3
Verāval o IND 138-139 C 9
Verbano = Lago Maggiore o I 100-101 B 2
Verbena o USA (AL) 284-285 D 4
Verbljud, gora ▲ RUS 108-109 f 3
Verbrande Berg • NAM 216-217 C 10
Verchères o CDN (QUE) 238-239 M 3
Verchivceve o UA 102-103 J 3
Verchnie Jamki o RUS 112-113 L 2
Verchnjadzvimsk ☆ BY 94-95 K 4
Verchn'odniprovs'k o UA 102-103 J 3
Verdalsøra o N 86-87 E 5
Verde, Arroyo ~ RA 78-79 G 6
Verde, Bahía ≈ 78-79 H 5
Verde, Cay ⌒ BS 54-55 H 3
Verde, Laguna o RA 78-79 E 7
Verde, Península ⌣ RA 78-79 H 5
Verde, Punta ▲ EC 64-65 C 1
Verde, Río ~ BR 70-71 K 3
Verde, Río ~ BR 72-73 G 4
Verde, Río ~ BR 72-73 D 6
Verde, Río ~ BR 72-73 E 5
Verde, Río ~ MEX 50-51 K 7
Verde, Río ~ MEX 52-53 F 3
Verde, Río ~ MEX 52-53 C 1
Verde, Río ~ PY 70-71 J 6
Verde, Río ~ PY 76-77 H 2
Verde Grande, Río ~ BR 72-73 J 3
Verde Hot Springs o USA (AZ) 256-257 D 4
Verde Island ⌒ RP 160-161 D 6
Verde Island Passage ≈ 160-161 D 6
Verde River ~ USA 256-257 D 4
Verdigre o USA (NE) 262-263 H 2
Verdigris Lake o CDN (ALB) 232-233 F 6
Verdigris River ~ USA 262-263 L 7
Verdigris River ~ USA 264-265 J 2
Verdinho, Rio ~ BR 72-73 E 4
Verdon ~ F 90-91 L 10
Verdon-sur-Mer, le o F 90-91 G 9
Verdun o• F 90-91 K 7
Verdun o ROU 78-79 M 2
Verdun, Pampa ⊥ RA 80 E 3
Vereda Pimenteira ~ BR 68-69 G 6
Vereeniging o ZA 220-221 H 3
Veregin o CDN (SAS) 232-233 Q 4
Verena o ZA 220-221 J 2
Vereščagino o RUS (KRN) 114-115 T 2
Vereščagino ☆ RUS (PRM) 96-97 J 4
Verestovo, ozero o RUS 94-95 P 3
Vergara o ROU 74-75 D 9
Vergareña, La o YV 60-61 K 4
Vergas o USA (MN) 270-271 C 4
Vergel, El o MEX 50-51 F 4
Vergeleë o ZA 220-221 G 2
Vergement o AUS 178-179 G 2
Vergennes o USA (VT) 278-279 H 4
Vergi o EST 94-95 K 2
Vergne, La o USA (TN) 276-277 J 4
Verhalen o USA (TX) 266-267 D 2
Verhnee Ondomozero o RUS 88-89 P 3
Verhneimbatsk o RUS 114-115 U 3
Verhnejarkeevo ☆ RUS 96-97 J 6
Verhnekamskaja vozvyšennost' ▲ RUS 96-97 H 4
Verhnekarahbahskij kanal < AZ 128-129 M 2
Verhnekarelina o RUS 116-117 N 7
Verhnekolymskoe, nagor'e ▲ RUS 120-121 M 2
Verhnespasskoe o RUS 96-97 D 4
Verhne tazovskaja vozvyšennost' ▲ RUS 114-115 Q 3
Verhnetazovskij, zapovednik ⊥ RUS 114-115 R 3
Verhnetulomskij o RUS 88-89 L 2
Verhnetulomskoe Vodohranilišče < RUS 88-89 L 2
Verhneural'sk ☆ RUS 96-97 L 7
Verhneural'skoe vodohranilišče < RUS 96-97 L 7
Verhnevažskaja vozvyšennost' ▲ RUS 94-95 R 1
Verhneviljujsk ☆ RUS 118-119 K 4
Verhnevym'skaja grada ▲ RUS 88-89 V 4
Verhnezejsk o RUS 118-119 O 8
Verhnezejskaja ravnina ⌣ RUS 118-119 N 8
Verhnie Kigi ☆ RUS 96-97 L 6
Verhnie Tatyšly ☆ RUS 96-97 J 5
Verhnie Usugli ☆ RUS 118-119 G 9
Verhnij Balygyčan o RUS 112-113 H 5
Verhnij Baskunčak o RUS 96-97 E 9
Verhnij Enisej ~ RUS 116-117 F 10
Verhnij Kužebar o RUS 116-117 F 9
Verhnij Mefgin ~ RUS 122-123 D 3
Verhnij Paren' o RUS 112-113 M 5
Verhnij Suzun ~ RUS 124-125 N 2
Verhnij Toguzak ~ RUS 124-125 B 2
Verhnij Turukan ~ RUS 116-117 L 3
Verhnij Ufalej o RUS 96-97 M 5
Verhnij Uslon ☆ RUS 96-97 F 6
Verhnjaja Agapa ~ RUS 108-109 W 6
Verhnjaja Amga o RUS 118-119 N 6
Verhnjaja Angara ~ RUS 118-119 E 7
Verhnjaja Baiha ~ RUS 114-115 S 2
Verhnjaja Čunku ~ RUS 116-117 J 4
Verhnjaja Kočoma ~ RUS 116-117 N 5
Verhnjaja Kuènga o RUS 118-119 H 9
Verhnjaja Larba ~ RUS 118-119 L 8
Verhnjaja Mokla ~ RUS 118-119 J 8
Verhnjaja Pyšma ☆ RUS 96-97 M 5
Verhnjaja Salda ☆ RUS 96-97 M 4
Verhnjaja Sarčiha ~ RUS 114-115 U 3
Verhnjaja Tajmyra ~ RUS 108-109 c 4
Verhnjaja Tomba ~ RUS 116-117 N 2
Verhnjaja Viljujka ~ RUS 116-117 M 2
Verhnjaja Zolotica o RUS 88-89 Q 4
Verhojansk o RUS 110-111 T 6
Verhojanskij hrebet ▲ RUS 110-111 Q 5
Verhotupova, ostrov ⌒ RUS 120-121 V 4
Verhotur'e ☆ RUS 96-97 M 4
Véria o• GR 100-101 J 4
Verín o E 98-99 D 4
Verkhoyanskiy Khrebet = Verhojanskij hrebet ▲ RUS 110-111 Q 5
Verkola o RUS 88-89 S 5
Verkykerskop o ZA 220-221 J 3
Verlegenhuken ▲ N 84-85 K 2
Vermasse o RI 166-167 D 6
Vermelha, Serra ▲ BR 68-69 F 6
Vermelha, Serra ▲ BR 72-73 E 7
Vermelho, Rio ~ BR 68-69 C 5
Vermelho, Rio ~ BR 68-69 E 6
Vermelho, Rio ~ BR 68-69 J 7
Vermelho, Rio ~ BR 68-69 D 5
Vermelho, Rio ~ BR 72-73 E 3
Vermilion o CDN (ALB) 232-233 H 2
Vermilion o USA (OH) 280-281 D 2
Vermilion, Lake o USA (IL) 274-275 L 4
Vermilion Bay ≈ 268-269 H 7
Vermilion Bay o CDN (ONT) 234-235 K 5
Vermilion Hills ▲ CDN 232-233 M 5
Vermilion Lake o CDN (ONT) 234-235 L 4
Vermilion Lake o USA (MN) 270-271 F 3
Vermilion River ~ CDN 232-233 G 2
Vermilion River ~ USA 268-269 H 7
Vermillion o USA (SD) 260-261 K 4
Vermillion River ~ CDN 238-239 C 2
Vermillion River ~ USA 260-261 J 3
Vermillion River ~ USA 274-275 J 3
Vermillion, Rivière ~ CDN 236-237 P 5
Vermont o USA (IL) 274-275 H 4
Vermont ▫ USA 278-279 J 5
Vernal o USA (UT) 254-255 F 3
Vernalis o USA (CA) 248-249 C 2
Verner o CDN (ONT) 238-239 E 2
Verneuil-sur-Avre o F 90-91 H 7
Verneuk Pan o ZA 220-221 E 4
Vernia, La o USA (TX) 266-267 J 4
Vernoe o RUS 122-123 C 3
Vernon o CDN (BC) 230-231 K 3
Vernon o F 90-91 H 7
Vernon o USA (AL) 284-285 B 3
Vernon o USA (AZ) 256-257 F 4
Vernon o USA (CT) 280-281 O 2
Vernon o USA (FL) 286-287 D 1
Vernon o USA (IN) 274-275 N 6
Vernon o USA (LA) 268-269 H 4
Vernon o USA (OH) 280-281 F 2
Vernon o USA (TX) 264-265 E 4
Vernon o USA (UT) 254-255 C 3
Vernon, Lake < USA (LA) 268-269 G 5
Vernon Bridge o CDN (PEI) 240-241 N 4
Vernon Center o USA (MN) 270-271 D 7
Vernon Creek ~ USA 274-275 N 5
Vernon Hill o USA (VA) 280-281 G 7
Vernonia o USA (OR) 244-245 B 5
Vernon Islands ⌒ AUS 172-173 K 2
Vero Beach o USA (FL) 286-287 J 4
Verona o CDN (ONT) 238-239 J 4
Verona ☆•• I 100-101 C 2
Verona o USA (ND) 258-259 J 5
Verónica o RA 78-79 L 3
Veron Range ▲ PNG 183 G 3
Verret, Lake o USA (LA) 268-269 J 7
Versailles ☆••• F 90-91 J 7
Versailles o USA (IN) 274-275 N 5
Versailles o USA (KY) 276-277 L 2
Versailles o USA (MO) 274-275 F 6
Versailles o USA (OH) 280-281 B 3
Versalles o CO 60-61 C 5
Veršina-Tuojdah, gora ▲ RUS 110-111 W 7
Veršino-Darasunskij o RUS 118-119 G 9
Veršiny, Čelno- ☆ RUS 96-97 G 6
Versteende Woud • NAM 216-217 C 10
Vert, Cap ▲ SN 202-203 B 2
Verte, Rivière ~ CDN 240-241 G 3
Vertentes o BR 68-69 L 5
Vertientes o C 54-55 F 4
Vertijievka o UA 102-103 G 2
Vert Island ⌒ CDN (ONT) 234-235 P 6
Vértiz o RA 78-79 H 3
Verulam o ZA 220-221 K 4
Verviers o B 92-93 H 3
Verwoert Tunnels II ZA 218-219 E 6
Verwood o CDN (SAS) 232-233 N 6
Ves'egonsk o RUS 94-95 P 2
Vesele o UA 102-103 J 4
Veselovskoe o RUS 124-125 L 1
Veselovskoe vodohranilišče < RUS 102-103 M 4
Vesennij o RUS 112-113 N 3
Vešenskaja o RUS 102-103 M 3
Vesljana o RUS 88-89 V 5
Vesljana ~ RUS 88-89 V 5
Vesoul ☆ F 90-91 L 8
Vestaburg o USA (MI) 272-273 E 4
Vestbygd o N 86-87 C 7
Vesterålen ⌒ N 86-87 G 2
Vesterø Havn o DK 86-87 E 8
Vestfjorden ≈ 86-87 F 3
Vestfonna ⊂ N 84-85 L 3
Vestgrønland = Kitaa ▫ GRØ 26-27 b 5
Vestmannaeyjar ⌒ IS (RAN) 86-87 c 3
Vestmannaeyjar o IS (RAN) 86-87 c 3
Vestnik, buhta ≈ 122-123 R 3
Vestvågøy ⌒ N 86-87 F 2
Vesúvio ▲•• I 100-101 E 4
Veszprém o H 92-93 O 5
Veta, La o USA (CO) 254-255 K 6
Vetal o USA (SD) 260-261 E 3
Vetauua ⌒ FJI 184 III c 1
Veteran o CDN (ALB) 232-233 G 4
Vetlanda ☆• S 86-87 G 8
Vetluga o RUS (GOR) 96-97 D 5
Vetluga ~ RUS 96-97 E 4
Vetlužskij o RUS 96-97 D 5
Vetovo o BG 102-103 E 6
Vetrenyj pojas, krjaž ▲ RUS 88-89 N 5
Vetrivier ~ ZA 220-221 H 4
Vetryna o BY 94-95 L 4
Vetvejskij hrebet ▲ RUS 120-121 V 3
Vevay o USA (IN) 274-275 N 6
Veveno, Khor ~ SUD 206-207 L 5
Vévi o GR 100-101 H 4
Veyo o USA (UT) 254-255 B 6
Vezdehodnaja ~ RUS 108-109 j 4
Vézelay o••• F 90-91 J 8
Vežen ▲ BG 102-103 D 6
Vézère ~ F 90-91 H 9
Vi o S 86-87 H 5
Viacha o BOL 70-71 C 5
Viahtu o RUS (SHL) 122-123 K 3
Viahtu ~ RUS 122-123 J 3
Viai Island ⌒ PNG 183 C 2
Vialadougou o CI 202-203 G 5
Viale o RA 76-77 H 6
Viamão o BR 74-75 E 8
Vian o USA (OK) 264-265 K 3
Viana o ANG 216-217 B 4
Viana o BR (ESP) 72-73 K 6
Viana o BR (MAR) 68-69 F 3
Viana o BR (P) 62-63 J 6
Viana do Castelo o• P 98-99 C 4
Viangchan ★ LAO 158-159 G 2
Viangphoukha o LAO 156-157 B 6
Vianópolis o BR 72-73 F 4
Viar, Río ~ E 98-99 E 6
Viaréggio o I 100-101 C 3
Via River ~ PNG 183 E 3
Vibank o CDN (SAS) 232-233 P 5
Viboras, La o MEX 50-51 H 4
Viboras o USA (TX) 266-267 J 7
Víboras, Las o RA 76-77 E 3
Viborg o DK 86-87 D 8
Vic o E 98-99 J 4
Vicebck o BY 94-95 M 4
Vic-en-Bigorre o F 90-91 H 10
Vicência o BR 68-69 L 5
Vicente Franco o BR 68-69 E 3
Vicente Guerrero o MEX 52-53 L 1
Vicente Guerrero o MEX (DGO) 50-51 H 6
Vicente Guerrero o MEX (TLA) 52-53 E 2
Vicente Noble o DOM 54-55 K 5
Vicenza ☆••• I 100-101 C 2
Viceroy o CDN (SAS) 232-233 N 6
Vicertópolis o BR 72-73 E 6
Vichada, Río ~ CO 60-61 G 5
Vichadero o ROU 76-77 K 6
Vichy o• F 90-91 J 8
Vichy o USA (MO) 274-275 G 6
Vici o USA (OK) 264-265 E 2
Vicksburg o USA (AZ) 256-257 B 5
Vicksburg o USA (MS) 268-269 K 4
Vicksburg National Military Park • USA (MS) 268-269 K 4
Viçosa o BR (ALA) 68-69 K 6
Viçosa o BR (MIN) 72-73 J 6
Victoire o CDN (SAS) 232-233 L 2
Victor o USA (CO) 254-255 K 5
Victor o USA (ID) 252-253 G 3
Victor o USA (MT) 250-251 E 5
Victor o USA (NY) 278-279 D 6
Victor o USA (SD) 260-261 K 1
Victor, Lac o CDN (QUE) 242-243 G 2
Victor, Mount ▲ AUS 180-181 E 2
Victor Harbor o AUS 180-181 E 3
Victoria ▫ AUS 180-181 G 4
Victoria o BOL 70-71 D 2
Victoria o CDN (NFL) 242-243 P 5
Victoria ☆• CDN (BC) 230-231 F 5
Victoria o CO 60-61 D 5
Victoria ☆•• HK 156-157 J 5
Victoria o M 100-101 E 6
Victoria o RA 78-79 J 2
Victoria o RCH 78-79 C 5
Victoria o SME 62-63 G 3
Victoria ★• SY 224 D 2
Victoria o USA (KS) 262-263 G 6
Victoria o USA (MS) 268-269 L 2
Victoria o USA (TX) 266-267 K 5
Victoria o USA (VA) 280-281 H 7
Victoria, Isla ⌒ RCH 80 C 2
Victoria, La o YV (APU) 60-61 F 4
Victoria, La o YV (ARA) 60-61 H 2
Victoria, Lake o AUS 180-181 F 3
Victoria, Lake o EAT 212-213 D 4
Victoria = Limbé o• CAM 204-205 H 6
Victoria, Monte ▲ RCH 80 E 6
Victoria, Mount ▲ MYA 142-143 H 5
Victoria, Mount ▲ PNG 183 D 5
Victoria, Sierra de la ▲ RA 76-77 K 3
Victoria and Albert Mountains ▲ CDN 26-27 L 4
Victoria Beach o CDN (MAN) 234-235 G 4
Victoria Beach o CDN (NS) 240-241 K 6
Victoria Bridge o CDN (NS) 240-241 P 5
Victoria de Durango = Durango ☆• MEX 50-51 G 5
Victoria Falls ~••• Z 218-219 C 3
Victoria Falls o ZW 218-219 C 3
Victoria Falls National Park ⊥• ZW 218-219 C 3
Victoria Fjord ≈ 26-27 a 2
Victoria Head ▲ CDN 26-27 N 4
Victoria Highway II AUS 172-173 J 3
Victoria Island ⌒ CDN 24-25 O 5
Victoria Island ⌒ CDN (ONT) 234-235 O 6
Victoria Lake o CDN (NFL) 242-243 L 4
Victoria Land ⊥ ARK 16 F 16
Victoria Nile ~ EAU 212-213 C 2
Victoria Peak ▲ BH 52-53 K 3
Victoria Peak ▲ CDN (BC) 230-231 C 3
Victoria Peak ▲ USA (TX) 266-267 C 2
Victoria River ~ AUS (NT) 172-173 K 3
Victoria River ~ AUS 172-173 J 3
Victoria River ~ CDN 242-243 M 4
Victoria River Downs o AUS 172-173 K 4
Victorias o RP 160-161 E 7
Victoria Strait ≈ 24-25 V 6
Victoria Vale o AUS 174-175 G 6
Victoriaville o CDN (QUE) 238-239 O 2
Victoria West o ZA 220-221 F 5
Victorica o RA 78-79 G 4
Victorino o C 54-55 G 4
Victor Rosales o MEX 50-51 H 6
Victorville o USA (CA) 248-249 G 5
Victory, Mount ▲ PNG 183 E 5
Vičuga ☆ RUS 94-95 R 3
Vicuña o RCH 76-77 B 6
Vicuña, Estancia o RCH 80 F 7
Vicuña Mackenna o RA 78-79 G 2
Vicus • PE 64-65 B 4
Vida o USA (MT) 250-251 O 4
Vida o USA (OR) 244-245 C 6
Vidal o PE 64-65 F 3
Vidal o USA (CA) 248-249 K 5
Vidalia o USA (GA) 284-285 H 4
Vidalia o USA (LA) 268-269 J 5
Vidamlja o BY 94-95 H 5
Vidapanakallu o IND 140-141 G 3
Vidaurri o USA (TX) 266-267 K 5
Videira o BR 74-75 E 6
Vidhareidhi = Viðareiði o FR 90-91 D 1
Vidim o RUS 116-117 L 7
Vidin o BG 102-103 C 6
Vidisha o IND 138-139 F 8
Vidor o USA (TX) 268-269 G 6
Vidora o CDN (SAS) 232-233 J 6
Vidzy o BY 94-95 K 4
Viedgesville o ZA 220-221 J 5
Viedma ☆ RA 78-79 H 6
Viedma, Lago o RA 80 D 4
Vieira Grande, Canal do ~ BR 62-63 J 6
Vieja, Punta la ▲ RCH 78-79 C 3
Vieja, Sierra ▲ USA 266-267 C 3
Viejitas, Caño las ~ CO 60-61 F 6
Viejo, El o NIC 52-53 L 5
Viejo, Mission o USA (CA) 248-249 G 6
Viejo, Río ~ RA 76-77 F 5
Vielha e Mijaran o E 98-99 H 3
Viella-Mitg Arán = Vielha e Mijaran o E 98-99 H 3
Vienna o USA (GA) 284-285 G 4
Vienna o USA (IL) 276-277 G 3
Vienna o USA (MD) 280-281 L 5
Vienna o USA (MO) 274-275 G 6
Vienna o USA (VA) 280-281 J 5
Vienna o USA (WV) 280-281 E 4
Vienna = Wien ★•• A 92-93 O 4
Vienne o F 90-91 K 9
Vienne ~ F 90-91 H 8
Vientiane = Viangchan ★ LAO 158-159 G 2
Viento, Cordillera del ▲ RA 78-79 D 4
Viento, Puerto del ▲ E 98-99 E 6
Vientos, Los o RCH 76-77 C 3
Vientos, Paso de los ≈ 54-55 H 5
Vieques, Isla de ⌒ USA (PR) 286-287 Q 2
Vieques Passage ≈ 286-287 Q 2
Vieremä o FIN 88-89 J 5
Vierwaldstätter See o CH 92-93 K 5
Vierzon o F 90-91 J 8
Viesca o MEX 50-51 H 5
Viesite o LV 94-95 J 3
Vieste o I 100-101 F 4
Vietas o S 86-87 J 3
Vietnam = Viet Nam ▪ VN 156-157 D 7
Việt Trì ☆ VN 156-157 D 6
Viêt Vinh ☆ VN 156-157 D 5
Vieux-Comptoir, Lac du o CDN 38-39 F 2
Vieux-Comptoir, Rivière du ~ CDN 38-39 E 2
Vieux Fort o WL 56 E 5
View o USA (TX) 264-265 E 6
Vieytes o RA 78-79 L 3
Vigan ☆ RP 160-161 D 4
Vigan, le o F 90-91 J 10
Vigia o BR 62-63 K 6
Vigía, El o YV 60-61 F 3
Vigia Chico o MEX 52-53 L 2
Vigía de Curvaradó o CO 60-61 C 4
Vigía del Fuerte o CO 60-61 C 4
Vigil o USA (CO) 254-255 L 6
Vigo o E 98-99 C 3
Vihanti o FIN 88-89 H 4
Vihāri o PK 138-139 D 4
Vihorevka o RUS 116-117 K 7
Vihren ▲ BG 102-103 C 7
Vihti o FIN 88-89 H 6
Viisanmäki o FIN 88-89 J 5
Viitasaari o FIN 88-89 H 5
Viitna o•• EST 94-95 K 2
Vijayadurg o IND 140-141 E 2
Vijayanagar o IND 138-139 D 8
Vijayāpati o IND 140-141 G 6
Vijayapura o IND 140-141 G 4
Vijayapuri o IND 140-141 H 2
Vijayawada o• IND 140-141 J 2
Vik ☆ IS 86-87 d 3
Vik o N 86-87 C 6
Vikajärvi o FIN 88-89 J 3
Vikārābād o IND 140-141 G 2
Vikeke o RI 166-167 D 6
Vikenara Point ▲ SOL 184 I d 3
Vikersund ☆ N 86-87 D 7
Viking o CDN (ALB) 232-233 G 2
Vikna ⌒ N 86-87 E 4
Viksøyri ☆ N 86-87 C 6
Viktoria = Labuan o MAL 160-161 A 10
Viktorija, ostrov ⌒ RUS 84-85 U 2
Vikulova, mys ▲ RUS 108-109 H 4
Vila Aurora o BR 68-69 E 3
Vila Bela da Santíssima Trindade o BR 70-71 H 4
Vila Coutinho o MOC 218-219 H 2
Vila de Ribeira Brava o CV 202-203 B 5
Vila de Sal-Rei o CV 202-203 C 5
Vila de Sena o MOC 218-219 H 3
Vila do Maio o CV 202-203 C 6
Vila dos Remédios o BR 68-69 L 1
Vila Flor o ANG 216-217 C 6
Vilafranca del Penedès o E 98-99 H 4
Vila Franca de Xira o P 98-99 C 5
Vilagarcía de Arousa o• E 98-99 C 3
Vila Gomes da Costa o MOC 220-221 L 2
Vilaine ~ F 90-91 G 8
Vila Ipixuna o BR 68-69 E 3
Vilakalaka o VAN 184 II a 2
Vila Martins o BR 66-67 C 6
Vila Meriti o BR 66-67 H 5
Vilanandro, Tanjona ▲ RM 222-223 D 6
Vila Nazaré o BR 66-67 E 4
Vilanculos o MOC 218-219 H 5
Viljāni o•• LV 94-95 K 3
Vila Nova o ANG 216-217 D 6
Vila Nova o BR (PAR) 74-75 D 5
Vila Nova o BR (RSU) 74-75 D 8
Vila Nova da Fronteira o MOC 218-219 H 3
Vila Nova de Foz Côa o P 98-99 D 4
Vila Nova do Seles o ANG 216-217 C 5
Vilanova i la Geltrú o E 98-99 H 4
Vila Nova Laranjeiras o BR 74-75 D 5
Vila Nova Sintra o CV 202-203 B 6
Vila Porto Franco o BR 66-67 H 6
Vila-real o E 98-99 G 5
Vila Real o P 98-99 D 4
Vila Real de Santo António o P 98-99 D 6
Vilar Formoso o P 98-99 D 4
Vila Rica o BR 68-69 C 6
Vilarinho do Monte o BR 62-63 H 6
Vila Sagrado Coração de Jesus o BR 66-67 H 5
Vila Tambaquí o BR 66-67 E 4
Vila Tepequem o BR 62-63 D 4
Vila Velha o BR (APA) 62-63 J 4
Vila Velha o BR (ESP) 72-73 K 6
Vila Velha de Ródão o P 98-99 D 5
Vilavila o PE 70-71 B 4
Vilca o PE 64-65 E 8
Vilcabamba o EC 64-65 C 4
Vilcabamba • PE 64-65 F 8
Vilcabamba, Cordillera ▲ PE 64-65 F 8
Vilcanota, Cordillera de ▲ PE 70-71 A 3
Vilcas Huaman o PE 64-65 F 8
Vilčeka, Zemlja ⌒ RUS 84-85 f 2
Vilches o E 98-99 F 5
Vilcún o RCH 78 79 C 5
Vilcún, Río ~ RCH 78-79 C 5
Vilejka ☆ BY 94-95 K 4
Vilelas o RA 76-77 F 4
Vilhelmina o• S 86-87 H 4
Vilhena o BR 70-71 G 3
Viliga ~ RUS 120-121 R 3
Viliginskij, mys ▲ RUS 120-121 R 3
Viljandi ☆•• EST 94-95 J 2
Viljoenskroon o ZA 220-221 H 3
Viljučinskaja buhta ≈ 120-121 S 7
Viljuj ~ RUS 116-117 M 3
Viljuj ~ RUS 118-119 G 4
Viljujčan ~ RUS 118-119 G 4
Viljujsk ☆• RUS 118-119 K 4
Viljujskoe vodohranilišče < RUS 118-119 E 4
Vil'kickogo, ostrov ⌒ RUS 108-109 Q 5
Vil'kickogo, proliv ≈ 108-109 d 3
Vilkija o LT 94-95 H 4
Vil'kitskogo, Proliv = Vil'kickogo, proliv ≈ 108-109 d 3
Villa Abecia o BOL 70-71 E 7
Villa Ahumada o MEX 50-51 F 2
Villa Alcaraz o RA 76-77 H 6
Villa Alemana o RCH 78-79 D 2
Villa Ana o RA 76-77 H 5
Villa Angela o RA 76-77 G 4
Villa Atuel o RA 78-79 F 3
Villa Azueta o MEX 52-53 G 2
Villaba o RP 160-161 F 7
Villa Berthet o RA 76-77 G 4
Villablino o E 98-99 D 3
Villa Brana o RA 76-77 F 4
Villa Bruzual o YV 60-61 G 3
Villacañas o E 98-99 F 5
Villa Cañas o RA 78-79 J 3
Villa Candelaria o RA 76-77 F 5
Villa Carlos Paz o RA 76-77 E 6
Villacarrillo o E 98-99 F 5
Villach o A 92-93 M 5
Villa Constitución o RA 78-79 J 2
Villa Corona o MEX 52-53 C 1
Villa Coronado o MEX 50-51 G 4
Villa de Cazones o MEX 52-53 F 1
Villa de Cos o MEX 50-51 H 6
Villa de Cura o YV 60-61 H 2
Villa de García o MEX 50-51 J 5
Villa de Leiva o•• CO 60-61 E 5
Villa del Rosario o RA 76-77 F 6
Villa del Rosario o YV 60-61 E 2
Villa de Orestes o MEX 50-51 G 4
Villa de Reyes o MEX 50-51 J 7
Villa de Sari o MEX 50-51 D 3
Villadiego o E 98-99 E 3
Villa Dolores o RA 76-77 E 6
Villa Figueroa o RA 76-77 F 4
Villa Flores o MEX 52-53 H 3
Villafranca del Bierzo o E 98-99 D 3
Village Cove o CDN (NFL) 242-243 O 3
Village Creek ~ USA 268-269 F 6
Villa General Belgrano o RA 76-77 E 6
Villa General Güemes o RA 76-77 H 3
Villa General Roca o RA 78-79 F 2
Villa General San Martín o RA 76-77 C 6
Village of Yesteryear • USA (MN) 270-271 E 7
Villa Gesell o RA 78-79 L 4
Villa Gobernador Gálvez o RA 78-79 J 2
Villagran o MEX 52-53 D 1
Villaguay o RA 76-77 H 6
Villaguay Grande, Arroyo ~ RA 76-77 H 6
Villahermosa o MEX 52-53 C 1
Villahermosa o MEX (CAM) 52-53 K 3
Villahermosa ☆• MEX (TAB) 52-53 H 3
Villa Hidalgo o MEX (DGO) 50-51 G 4
Villa Hidalgo o MEX (JAL) 50-51 H 7
Villa Hidalgo o MEX (SON) 50-51 E 2
Villa Huidobra o RA 78-79 G 3
Villa Insurgentes o MEX 50-51 D 5
Villa Joyosa o E 98-99 G 5
Villa Juárez o MEX 50-51 J 6
Villa Larca o RA 78-79 G 2
Villalba o E 98-99 D 3
Villalbín o PY 76-77 H 4
Villaldama o MEX 50-51 J 4
Villa Lola o YV 60-61 K 4
Villalonga o RA 78-79 H 5
Villalpando o E 98-99 E 4
Villa Mainero o MEX 50-51 K 5
Villa María o RA 78-79 H 2
Villa Martín o BOL 70-71 D 7
Villamartín o E 98-99 E 6
Villa Mascardi o RA 78-79 D 6
Villa Mazán o RA 76-77 D 5
Villa Media Agua o RA 76-77 C 6
Villa Mercedes o RA 76-77 E 4
Villa Mills o CR 52-53 C 7
Villamontes o BOL 76-77 F 1
Villanow o USA (GA) 284-285 E 2
Villanueva o CO 60-61 E 2
Villanueva o MEX 50-51 H 6
Villa Nueva o RA 78-79 E 2
Villanueva o USA (NM) 256-257 K 3
Villanueva de Córdoba o E 98-99 E 5
Villanueva de los Castillejos o E 98-99 D 6
Villanueva de los Infantes o E 98-99 F 5
Villanueva y Geltrú = Vilanova i la Geltrú o E 98-99 H 4
Villa Ocampo o MEX 50-51 G 4
Villa Ocampo o RA 76-77 H 5
Villa O'Higgins o RCH 80 D 4
Villa Ojo de Agua o RA 76-77 F 5
Villa Oliva o PY (CEN) 76-77 J 3
Villa Oliva o PY (NEE) 76-77 J 4
Villa Ortega o RCH 80 E 2
Villapinzon o CO 60-61 E 5
Villarcayo o E 98-99 F 3
Villard o RH 54-55 J 5
Villardecierros o E 98-99 D 4
Villa Reducción o RA 78-79 H 2
Villa Regina o RA 78-79 F 5
Villa Rica o USA (GA) 284-285 F 3
Villarpando o DOM 54-55 K 5
Villarreal de los Infantes = Vila-real o E 98-99 G 5
Villarrica ☆ PY 76 77 J 3
Villarrica o RCH 78-79 C 5
Villarrica, Lago o RCH 78-79 C 5
Villarrica, Parque Nacional ⊥ RCH 78-79 C 5
Villarrica, Volcán ▲ RCH 78-79 D 5
Villarrobledo o E 98-99 F 5
Villa Salvadorita o NIC 52-53 L 5
Villa San Martín o RA 76-77 E 5
Villa Santa Rita de Catuna o RA 76-77 D 6
Villasimius o I 100-101 B 5
Villa Talavera o BOL 70-71 E 6
Villa Toquepala o PE 70-71 B 5
Villatoya o E 98-99 G 5
Villa Tunari o BOL 70-71 E 5
Villa Unión o MEX 50-51 J 3
Villa Unión o MEX (DGO) 50-51 G 6
Villa Unión o MEX (SIN) 50-51 F 6
Villa Unión o RA 76-77 C 5
Villa Valeria o RA 78-79 G 3
Villa Vásquez o DOM 54-55 K 5
Villavicencio ☆ CO 60-61 E 5
Villaviciosa o• E 98-99 E 3
Villazon o RA 76-77 E 2
Villebon, Lac o CDN (QUE) 236-237 L 5
Ville de Lameque o CDN (NB) 240-241 L 3
Villefranche-de-Rouergue o F 90-91 J 9
Villefranche-sur-Saône o F 90-91 K 9
Villeguera, La o YV 60-61 H 4
Ville-Marie o CDN (QUE) 236-237 J 5
Villemontel o CDN (QUE) 236-237 K 4
Villena o E 98-99 G 5
Villeneuve o CDN (ALB) 232-233 E 2
Villeneuve-sur-Lot o F 90-91 H 9
Ville Platte o USA (LA) 268-269 H 6
Villeroy o CDN (QUE) 238-239 O 2
Villeurbanne o F 90-91 K 9
Villicún, Sierra de ▲ RA 76-77 C 6
Villiers o ZA 220-221 J 3
Villisca o USA (IA) 274-275 D 4
Vilnes o N 86-87 B 6
Vilnius ★••• LT 94-95 J 4
Vil'njans'k o UA 102-103 J 4
Vil'nohirs'k o UA 102-103 J 3
Vilonia o USA (AR) 276-277 C 5
Vils ~ D 92-93 L 4
Vil'šany o UA 102-103 J 2
Vilyuyskoye Vodokhranilishche = Viljujskoe vodohranilišče < RUS 118-119 E 4
Vimieiro o P 98-99 D 5
Vimioso o P 98-99 D 4
Vimmerby ☆• S 86-87 G 8
Vina ~ CAM 204-205 K 5
Vina o USA (AL) 284-285 B 2
Vina, Chute de la ~• CAM 204-205 K 5
Viña, La o RA (CAT) 76-77 E 5
Viña, La o RA (SAL) 76-77 E 3
Viña del Mar o RCH 78-79 D 2
Vinalhaven o USA (ME) 278-279 N 4
Vinalhaven Island ⌒ USA (ME) 278-279 N 4
Vinanivao o RM 222-223 G 5
Vinaròs o E 98-99 H 4
Vinători o RO 102-103 C 5
Vincelotte, Lac o CDN 36-37 N 7
Vincennes o USA (IN) 274-275 L 6
Vincennes Bay ≈ 16 G 11
Vincent o USA (AL) 284-285 D 3
Vincent o USA (TX) 264-265 C 6
Vinces o EC 64-65 C 2
Vinchina o RA 76-77 C 5
Vinchina, Río ~ RA 76-77 C 5
Vindelälven ~ S 86-87 J 4
Vindeln o S 86-87 J 4
Vindhya Range ▲ IND 138-139 E 8
Vinegar Hill ▲ USA (OR) 244-245 G 6
Vine Grove o USA (KY) 276-277 K 3
Vineland o USA (CO) 254-255 L 5
Vineland o USA (NJ) 280-281 L 4
Viner Nejstadt, ostrov ⌒ RUS 84-85 f 2
Vingåker ☆ S 86-87 G 7
Vingerklip • NAM 216-217 C 10
Vinh ☆ VN 156-157 D 7
Vinhais o P 98-99 D 4
Vinh Bac Bô = Tonkin, Gulf of ≈ 156-157 E 6
Vinh Cam Ranh ≈ 158-159 K 5
Vinh Cây Dư'ơng ≈ 158-159 H 5
Vinh Diên Châu ≈ 156-157 D 7
Vinhedo o BR 72-73 G 7
Vinh Hy o VN 158-159 K 5
Vinh Kim o VN 158-159 K 3
Vinh Lọc ☆ VN 156-157 D 6
Vinh Long o VN 158-159 H 5
Vinh Pham Thiêt ≈ 158-159 K 5
Vinh Yên ☆ VN 156-157 D 6
Vinita o USA (OK) 264-265 J 2
Vinju Mare o RO 102-103 C 5
Vinkovci o HR 100-101 G 2
Vinnica = Vinnycja ☆ UA 102-103 F 3
Vinnycja ☆ UA 102-103 F 3
Vinnytsya = Vinnycja ☆ UA 102-103 F 3
Vinson o USA (OK) 264-265 E 4
Vinson, Mount ▲ ARK 16 F 28
Vinstra ☆ N 86-87 D 6
Vinsulla o CDN (BC) 230-231 J 3
Vinter Øer ⌒ GRØ 26-27 W 6
Vinton o USA (IA) 274-275 F 2
Vinton o USA (LA) 268-269 G 6
Vinton o USA (OH) 280-281 D 5
Vinukonda o IND 140-141 H 2
Vinza o RCB 210-211 E 5
Vinzili o RUS 114-115 H 6
Viola o USA (IL) 274-275 H 3
Viola o USA (KS) 262-263 J 7
Viola o USA (WI) 274-275 H 1
Violaineville o G 210-211 C 3
Violeta, La o RA 78-79 J 2
Viools drif o ZA 220-221 C 4
Viphya Mountains ▲ MW 214-215 G 7
Vipos, Río ~ RA 76-77 E 4
Vir o TJ 136-137 M 6
Virac ☆ RP 160-161 F 6
Viração, Cachoeira da ~ BR 62-63 G 6
Virachey o K 158-159 J 4
Virac Point ▲ RP 160-161 F 6
Viradouro o BR 72 73 F 6
Vira-e-Volta, Cachoeira ~ BR 68-69 C 3
Viraganur o IND 140-141 H 5
Virago Sound ≈ 228-229 B 2
Virangām o IND 138-139 D 8
Viranşehir ☆ TR 128-129 H 4
Virapalle o IND 140-141 H 3
Virār o IND 138-139 D 10
Virarājendrapet o IND 140-141 F 4
Virāwah o PK 138-139 C 7
Virden o CDN (MAN) 234-235 C 5
Virden o USA (IL) 274-275 J 5
Virden o USA (NM) 256-257 G 6
Virei o ANG 216-217 B 7
Virgem da Lapa o BR 72-73 J 4
Virgen, La o NIC 52-53 B 6
Virgilina o USA (VA) 280-281 H 7
Virgin Gorda ⌒ GB 56 C 2
Virgin Gorda ⌒ GB 286-287 R 2
Virginia o AUS 180-181 E 3
Virginia o USA (IL) 274-275 H 5
Virginia o USA (MN) 270-271 F 3
Virginia ▫ USA 280-281 G 6
Virginia o ZA 220-221 H 4
Virginia Beach o USA (VA) 280-281 L 7
Virginia City o USA (MT) 250-251 H 6
Virginia City o USA (NV) 246-247 F 4
Virginia Dale o USA (CO) 254-255 K 3
Virginia Falls ~ CDN 30-31 F 5
Virginiatown o CDN (ONT) 236-237 J 4
Virgin Islands ⌒ (VI) 286-287 R 2
Virgin Islands (United Kingdom) ▫ GB 286-287 R 2
Virgin Islands (United States) ▫ USA 286-287 R 2
Virgin Islands National Park ⊥ USA (VI) 286-287 R 2
Virgin Mountains ▲ USA 248-249 K 3
Virgin Passage ≈ 56 C 2
Virgin Passage ≈ 286-287 Q 2
Virgin River ~ USA 248-249 K 3
Virgolândia o BR 72-73 J 5
Virihaure o S 86-87 H 3
Virojoki = Virolahti o FIN 88-89 J 6
Virolahti o FIN 88-89 J 6
Viroqua o USA (WI) 274-275 H 1
Virovitica o HR 100-101 F 2
Virrat o FIN 88-89 G 5
Virtsu o EST 94-95 H 2
Viru o PE 64-65 C 6
Virudó o CO 60-61 C 5
Virudunagar o IND 140-141 G 6
Virunga, Parc National des ⊥••• ZRE 212-213 B 4
Vis o HR 100-101 F 3
Vis ⌒ HR 100-101 F 3

408 Ventas con Peña Aguilera, Las — Vis

Vis ~ NAM 220-221 C 2
Visaginas ☆ LT 94-95 K 4
Visalia o USA (CA) 248-249 E 3
Visayan Sea ≈ 160-161 E 7
Visayas ⌒ RP 160-161 E 7
Visby ☆•• S 86-87 J 8
Viscount o CDN (SAS) 232-233 N 4
Viscount Melville Sound ≈ 24-25 P 3
Višegrad o• BIH 100-101 G 3
Višera ~ RUS 88-89 V 5
Viseu ☆• P 98-99 D 4
Vishakhapatnam o•• IND 142-143 C 7
Visicsa, Río ~ BOL 70-71 D 6
Visim ~ RUS 114-115 F 3
Visimskij zapovednik ⊥ RUS 96-97 L 5
Visita o BR 66-67 H 6
Visite, La o RH 54-55 J 5
Višneva o BY 94-95 K 4
Višnevka ☆ KZ 124-125 H 3
Visočica ▲ HR 100-101 E 2
Visoko o BIH 100-101 G 3
Visrivier o ZA (CAP) 220-221 G 5
Visrivier ~ ZA 220-221 E 5
Visrivierafgronde Park ⊥ NAM 220-221 D 3
Visriviercanyon •• NAM 220-221 C 3
Visrivier Canyon Park, Ai-Ais and ⊥ NAM 220-221 C 3
Vista o CDN (MAN) 234-235 C 4
Vista o USA (CA) 248-249 G 6
Vista Alegre o ANG 216-217 C 4
Vista Alegre o BR (AMA) 66-67 C 6
Vista Alegre o BR (AMA) 66-67 E 3
Vista River ~ CDN 24-25 c 4
Visuvisu Point ▲ SOL 184 I c 2
Visviri o RCH 70-71 C 5
Vit ~ BG 102-103 D 6
Vita o CDN (MAN) 234-235 G 5
Vita o IND 140-141 F 2
Vitberget ▲ S 86-87 L 3
Vitebsk = Vicebck o BY 94-95 M 4
Viterbo ☆• I 100-101 D 3
Vitgenštejna, mys ▲ RUS 112-113 R 6
Vithalapur o IND 138-139 D 8
Vi Thanh o VN 158-159 H 6
Vitiaz Strait ≈ 183 D 3
Vitigudino o E 98-99 D 4
Viti Levu ⌒ FJI 184 III a 2
Vitim o RUS 118-119 F 6
Vitim ~ RUS 118-119 F 6
Vitimkan ~ RUS 118-119 E 8
Vitimskij o RUS 118-119 F 6
Vitimskij zapovednik ⊥ RUS 118-119 H 7
Vitimskoe ploskogor'e ⩊ RUS 118-119 F 9
Vitimskoye Ploskogor'ye = Vitimskoe ploskogor'e ⩊ RUS 118-119 F 9
Vitiones, Lago de los o BOL 70-71 H 6
Vitolište o MK 100-101 H 4
Vitória o BR 70-77 K 5
Vitor o PE 70-71 B 5
Vitoria o BR 68-69 B 3
Vitória ☆ BR 72-73 K 6
Vitória da Conquista o BR 72-73 K 3
Vitória de Santo Antão o BR 68-69 L 6
Vitória do Mearim o BR 68-69 F 3
Vitoria-Gasteiz o• E 98-99 F 3
Vitória Seamount ⩊ 72-73 M 6
Vitorino o BR 74-75 D 6
Vitorino Freire o BR 68-69 F 4
Vitoša, Naroden Park ⊥ BG 102-103 C 6
Vitré o F 90-91 G 7
Vitry-le-François o F 90-91 K 7
Vitshumbi o• ZRE 212-213 B 4
Vitsyebsk = Vicebck o BY 94-95 M 4
Vittangi o S 86-87 K 3
Vittel o• F 90-91 K 7
Vittichi, Río ~ BOL 70-71 E 7
Vittória o I 100-101 E 6
Vittorio Véneto o I 100-101 D 1
Vityaz Depth ⩊ 122-123 O 6
Viuda, Isla La ⌒ PE 64-65 C 6
Viudas de Oriente o MEX 50-51 H 6
Vivario o F 98-99 M 3
Viveiro o E 98-99 D 3
Vivi ~ RUS 116-117 H 4
Vivi, ozero o RUS 116-117 G 2
Vivian o CDN (MAN) 234-235 G 5
Vivian o USA (LA) 268-269 G 4
Vivian o USA (SD) 260-261 F 3
Vivo o ZA 218-219 E 6
Vivonne Bay ≈ 180-181 D 4
Vivoratá, Arroyo ~ RA 78-79 L 4
Vivorillo, Cayos ⌒ HN 54-55 D 7
Viwa ⌒ FJI 184 III a 2
Vižas ~ RUS 88-89 S 3
Vizcachillas, Cerro ▲ BOL 76-77 D 2
Vizcaíno, Desierto de ⩊ MEX 50-51 C 4
Vizcaíno, Península de ⌣ MEX 50-51 B 4
Vizcaíno, Reserva de la Biósfera El ⊥••• MEX 50-51 B 4
Vize, ostrov ⌒ RUS 84-85 p 3
Vizeu o BR 68-69 E 2
Vizianagaram o IND 142-143 C 6
Vizien, Rivière ~ CDN 36-37 N 5
Vizille o F 90-91 K 9
Vizinga o RUS 96-97 G 3
Vizzini o I 100-101 E 6
Vjalozero o RUS 88-89 N 3
Vjartsilja o RUS 88-89 L 5
Vjatka ~ RUS 96-97 H 4
Vjatskie Poljany ☆ RUS 96-97 G 5
Vjazemskij o RUS 122-123 F 5
Vjaz'ma ☆ RUS 94-95 O 4
Vjazniki o RUS 94-95 S 3
Vjosës, Lumi i ~ AL 100-101 G 4
Vlaanderen ▭ B 92-93 H 3
Vladičin Han o YU 100-101 J 3
Vladikavkaz ☆ RUS 126-127 F 6
Vladimir ☆••• RUS 94-95 R 3
Vladimirovka o KZ 124-125 F 2
Vladimirovka o RUS 122-123 K 3
Vladimirovo o RUS 122-123 K 4
Vladivostok o RUS 122-123 D 7
Vlaşca, Drăgăneşti- o RO 102-103 D 5
Vlasenica o BIH 100-101 G 2
Vlas'evo o RUS 122-123 J 2
Vlasovo o RUS 110-111 U 4
V. Lelija ▲ BIH 100-101 G 3
Vlieland ⌒ NL 92-93 H 2
Vliets o USA (KS) 262-263 K 5
Vlissingen o NL 92-93 G 3
Vlkolínec o••• SK 92-93 P 4
Vlorë ☆•• AL 100-101 G 4
Vltava ~ CZ 92-93 N 4
Vnutrennjaja guba ≈ 120-121 T 3
Vobkent o UZ 136-137 J 4
Voč' ~ RUS 96-97 J 3
Voca o USA (TX) 266-267 H 2
Vodla ~ RUS 88-89 O 6
Vodlozero, ozero o RUS 88-89 O 5
Vodnyj o RUS 88-89 W 5
Vodopadnyj, mys ▲ RUS 120-121 U 3
Vogan o RT 202-203 L 6
Vogar o CDN (MAN) 234-235 E 4
Vogelkop = Doberai Peninsula ⌣ RI 166-167 F 2
Vogulka ~ RUS 114-115 G 3
Vogul'skij Kamen', gora ▲ RUS 114-115 E 4
Vogvazdino o RUS 88-89 V 5
Vohémar = Iharana o RM 222-223 G 4
Vohilava o RM (FNS) 222-223 F 8
Vohilava o RM (FNS) 222-223 E 8
Vohilengo o RM 222-223 F 6
Vohimena o RM (TMA) 222-223 F 6
Vohimena ▲ RM 222-223 E 10
Vohimena, Tanjona ▲ RM 222-223 D 10
Vohipeno o RM 222-223 E 9
Vohitra ~ RM 222-223 F 7
Vohitraivo o RM 222-223 F 6
Võhma o EST 94-95 H 2
Võhma o•• EST 94-95 J 2
Vohma o RUS 96-97 E 4
Voi o EAK (COA) 212-213 G 5
Voi ~ EAK 212-213 G 5
Voi o VN 156-157 E 7
Voinjama ☆ LB 202 203 F 5
Voiron o F 90-91 K 9
Voisey Bay ≈ 36-37 T 6
Voja, Ust'- o RUS (KOM) 88-89 Y 4
Voja, Ust'- o RUS (KOM) 114-115 D 2
Vojampolka o RUS 120-121 S 4
Vojampolka (Matëraja) ~ RUS 120-121 S 4
Vojampolka (Žilovaja) ~ RUS 120-121 S 4
Vojejkov šel'fovyj lednik ⌒ ARK 16 G 13
Vojkarsyn'inskij massiv ▲ RUS 114-115 F 2
Vojkar ~ RUS 114-115 G 2
Vojnica o RUS 88-89 L 4
Vojvareto, ozero o RUS 108-109 P 7
Vojvodina ⩊ YU 100-101 G 2
Vojvož o RUS 88-89 X 5
Vokeo Island ⌒ PNG 183 C 2
Vokre, Hosséré ▲ CAM 204-205 K 4
Vol' ~ RUS 88-89 W 5
Volborg o USA (MT) 250-251 O 6
Volcán o PA 52-53 C 7
Volcán o RA 76 77 E 2
Volcán, El o RCH 78-79 D 2
Volcán Barú, Parque Nacionale ⊥•• PA 52-53 C 7
Volcán de Colima, Parque Nacional ⊥ MEX 52-53 C 2
Volčanka ~ RUS 108-109 Z 6
Volcano o USA (HI) 288 K 5
Volcans, Parc National des ⊥ ZRE 212-213 B 4
Volčansk o RUS 114-115 F 5
Volcán Tupungato, Parque Provincial ⊥ RA 78-79 E 2
Volčiha ☆ RUS 124-125 M 3
Volda ☆ N 86-87 C 5
Vol'dino o RUS 88-89 X 5
Volens o USA (VA) 280-281 G 7
Volga ~ RUS 94-95 N 3
Volga ~ RUS 96-97 E 10
Volga-Baltic Waterway = Volgo-Baltijskij kanal < RUS 94-95 P 1
Volgo-Baltijskij kanal < RUS 94-95 P 1
Volgodonsk o RUS 102-103 N 4
Volgo-Donskoi kanal < RUS 102-103 N 3
Volgograd = Zarizyn ☆• RUS 96-97 D 9
Volgogradskoe vodohranilišče < RUS (SAR) 96-97 E 8
Volgogradskoe vodohranilišče < RUS (VLG) 96-97 D 9
Volgogradskoye Vodokhranilishche = Volgogradskoe vodohranili < RUS 96-97 D 9
Volhov o RUS (LEN) 94-95 N 2
Volhov ~ RUS 94-95 N 2
Volimes o GR 100-101 H 6
Volksrust o ZA 220-221 J 3
Volna, gora ▲ RUS 112-113 H 5
Volnovacha o UA 102-103 K 4
Voločanka o RUS 108-109 a 6
Voločys'k ☆ UA 102-103 E 3
Volodarsk o RUS 94-95 S 3
Volodarskij ☆ RUS 96-97 F 10
Volodarskoe ☆ KZ 124-125 F 2
Volodino o RUS 114-115 S 6
Volodymyr-Volyns'kyj o UA 102-103 D 2
Vologda ☆• RUS 94-95 Q 2
Volokolamsk o• RUS 94-95 O 3
Volokonovka o RUS 102-103 K 2
Volokovaja o RUS 88-89 U 3
Volokvynejtkon, gora ▲ RUS 112-113 R 5
Volop o ZA 220-221 F 4
Vólos o• GR 100-101 J 5
Volosovo ☆ RUS 94-95 L 2
Volot o RUS 94-95 M 3
Volquart Boon Kyst ⌣ GRØ 26-27 o 8
Voišepahk, gora ▲ RUS 88-89 M 2
Vol'sk ☆ RUS 96-97 E 7
Volstruisleegte o ZA 220-221 F 6
Volta ▭ GH 202-203 L 6
Volta ~ GH 202-203 L 7
Volta Blanche ~ BF 202-203 K 4
Voltaire, Cape ▲ AUS 172-173 G 3
Volta Lake < GH 202-203 K 5
Volta Noire ~ BF 202-203 J 5
Volta Redonda o BR 72-73 H 7
Volta Region ▭ GH 202-203 L 5
Volta Rouge ~ BF 202-203 K 4
Volterra o I 100-101 C 3
Volturino, Monte ▲ I 100-101 E 4
Volturno ~ I 100-101 E 4
Voltzberg ▲ SME 62-63 F 3
Volubilis ∴•• MA 188-189 J 3
Vólvi, Límni o GR 100-101 J 4
Volyns'ka vysočyna ▲ UA 102-103 D 2
Volyns'kyj, Novohrad- o UA 102-103 E 2
Volyns'kyj, Volodymyr- o UA 102-103 D 2
Volzhskiy = Volžskij o RUS 96-97 D 9
Volžsk o RUS 96-97 F 6
Volžskij o RUS 96-97 D 9
Volžsko-Kamskij zapovednik ⊥ RUS 96-97 F 6
Vom o WAN 204-205 H 4
Vonavona = Parara ⌒ SOL 184 I c 3
Vonda o CDN (SAS) 232-233 M 3
Vondanka o RUS 96-97 E 4
Vondrove o RM 222-223 D 8
Vondrozo o RM 222-223 E 9
Von Frank Mountain ▲ USA 20-21 N 5
Vónitsa o GR 100-101 H 5
Von Lindequist Gate o NAM 216-217 D 9
Von Ormy o USA (TX) 266-267 J 4
Vontimitta o IND 140-141 H 3
Voon, Tarso ▲ TCH 198-199 H 2
Voortrekker fort • ZA 220-221 K 2
Vopnafjarðargrunn ⩊ 86-87 g 1
Vopnafjörður ≈ 86-87 f 2
Vopnafjörður o IS 86-87 f 2
Voranava ☆ BY 94-95 J 4
Voranga ~ RUS 118-119 L 3
Vorarlberg ▭ A 92-93 K 5
Vordingborg o• DK 86-87 E 9
Vóreio Egéo ▭ GR 100-101 K 5
Vorenža o RUS 88-89 N 5
Vorgašor o RUS 108-109 K 8
Vóries Sporádes ⌣ GR 100-101 J 5
Vøringfossen •• N 86-87 C 6
Vöring Plateau ⩊ 6-7 K 2
Vor'ja ~ RUS 114-115 G 3
Vorkuta ☆ RUS (KOM) 108-109 K 8
Vorkuta ~ RUS 108-109 K 8
Vorma ~ N 86-87 E 6
Vormsi saar ⌒ EST 94-95 H 2
Vorob'evo o RUS 114-115 O 6
Vorogovka ~ RUS 116-117 E 5
Vorona ~ RUS 94-95 S 5
Vorona ~ RUS 102-103 N 2
Voroncovka o RUS 118-119 F 6
Voroncovo o RUS 108-109 U 6
Voronet o••• RO 102-103 D 4
Voronež o RUS 102-103 L 2
Voronež ~ RUS 94-95 Q 5
Voronezh = Voronež o RUS 102-103 L 2
Voronina, ostrov ⌒ RUS 108-109 I a 2
Voron'ja ~ RUS 88-89 N 2
Voronov, mys ▲ RUS 88 89 R 3
Vorošilovgrad = Luhans'k ☆ UA 102-103 L 3
Vorotan ~ AR 128-129 L 3
Vorotynec o RUS 96-97 D 5
Vorožba o UA 102-103 J 2
Vorskla ~ RUS 102-103 J 2
Vorsma o RUS 94-95 S 4
Vorstershoop o ZA 220-221 F 2
Võrtsjärv järv o EST 94-95 K 2
Võru ☆•• EST 94-95 K 3
Vosburg o ZA 220-221 F 5
Vose o TJ 136-137 L 6
Vosges ▲ F 90-91 L 8
Voskopojë o• AL 100-101 H 4
Voskresenovka o RUS 122-123 C 3
Voskresensk ☆• RUS 94-95 Q 4
Voskresenskoe o RUS 94-95 P 3
Voskresenskoe o RUS 94-95 S 3
Voskresenskogo, buhta ≈ 108-109 X 4
Voss o USA (TX) 266-267 H 2
Vossavangen o• N 86-87 C 6
Vostočnaja, kosa ⌒ RUS 108-109 R 5
Vostočnaja Handyga ~ RUS 120-121 G 2
Vostočnoe Munozero o RUS 88-89 N 3
Vostočno-Sahalinskie gory ▲ RUS 122-123 K 3
Vostočnyj, proliv ≈ 110-111 H 2
Vostočnyj o RUS (ČUK) 112-113 W 3
Vostočnyj o RUS (SHL) 122-123 K 4
Vostočnyj hrebet ▲ RUS 120-121 S 7
Vostočnyj Kamennyj, ostrov ⌒ RUS 108-109 U 4
Vostočnyj Sinij, hrebet ▲ RUS 122-123 E 7
Vostočnyj Tannu-Ola, hrebet ▲ RUS 116-117 F 10
Vostok o ARK 16 F 11
Vostok o RUS 122-123 F 5
Votaw o USA (TX) 268-269 F 6
Votkinsk ☆ RUS 96-97 J 5
Votkinskoe vodohranilišče < RUS 96-97 J 5
Votkinskoye Vodokhranilishche = Votkinskoe vodohranilišče < RUS 96-97 J 5
Vot Tande ⌒ VAN 184 II a 1
Votuporanga o BR 72-73 F 6
Vouga o ANG 216-217 D 6
Vouga, Rio ~ P 98-99 C 4
Vouka o RCB 210-211 D 5
Voullagméni o GR 100-101 J 6
Vouzela o P 98-99 C 4
Vovča ~ UA 102-103 K 4
Vovčans'k o UA 102-103 K 2
Vovodo ~ RCA 206-207 G 5
Voxna o S 86-87 G 6
Voyageurs National Park ⊥ USA (MN) 270-271 F 2
Vože, ozero o RUS 94-95 Q 1
Vožega o RUS 94-95 R 1
Vožgora o RUS 88-89 U 4
Voznesens'k o UA 102-103 G 4
Voznesenskoe o RUS 94-95 S 4
Vozroždenie o RUS 96-97 F 7
Vozroždenija, ostrov ⌒ UZ 136-137 F 2
Vozroždenija otasi ⌒ UZ 136-137 F 2
Vozvraščenija, gora ▲ RUS 122-123 K 4
Vraca o BG 102-103 C 6
Vrangelja, mys ▲ RUS 120-121 H 6
Vrangelja, ostrov ⌒ RUS 112-113 U 1
Vranica ▲ BIH 100-101 F 2
Vrāška čuka, Prohod ▲ BG 102-103 C 6
Vrbas ~ BIH 100-101 F 2
Vrede o ZA 220-221 J 3
Vredefort o ZA 220-221 H 3
Vredenburg o ZA 220-221 C 6
Vredendal o ZA 220-221 D 5
Vredeshoop o NAM 220-221 D 3
Vreed-en-Hoop o GUY 62-63 E 2
Vreede Stein o GUY 62-63 E 2
Vriddhāchalam o IND 140-141 H 5
Vrigstad o S 86-87 G 8
Vrisia o GR 100-101 L 5
Vroolijk, Pulau ⌒ RI 164-165 L 4
Vršac o• YU 100-101 H 2
Vryburg o ZA 220-221 G 3
Vryheid o ZA 220-221 K 3
Vsesvjats'kyj kostel • UA 102-103 C 3
Vsevidof, Mount ▲ USA 22-23 M 6
Vsevidof Island ⌒ USA 22-23 M 6
Vsevoložsk ☆ RUS 94-95 M 1
Vstrečnyj o RUS 112-113 N 3
Vtoroj Kuril'skij proliv ≈ 122-123 R 3
Vuadil' o UZ 136-137 M 4
Vube o ZRE 212-213 A 2
Vui-Uata Nova Itália, Área Indígena ⨯ BR 66-67 C 4
Vuka ~ HR 100-101 G 2
Vukovar o• HR 100-101 G 2
Vuktyl ☆ RUS 114-115 D 3
Vulavu o SOL 184 I d 3
Vulcan o CDN (ALB) 232-233 E 5
Vulcano, Ísola ⌒ I 100-101 E 5
Vulcan Shoal ⌒ AUS 172-173 G 2
Vulkannyj hrebet ▲ RUS 112-113 N 3
Vulsinio = Lago di Bolsena o I 100-101 C 3
Vúlture, Monte ▲ I 100-101 E 4
Vulture Mine o USA (AZ) 256-257 C 5
Vul'vyveem ~ RUS 112-113 T 3
Vumba Gardens • ZW 218-219 G 4
Vumba Mountains ▲ ZW 218-219 G 4
Vũng Hòn Khói ≈ 158-159 K 4
Vũng Tàu o• VN 158-159 J 5
Vunisea o FJI 184 III b 3
Vuokatti o FIN 88-89 K 4
Vuolijoki o FIN 88-89 J 4
Vuollerim o S 86-87 K 3
Vuolvojaure o S 86-87 J 3
Vuotso o FIN 88-89 J 2
Vuranggo o SOL 184 I c 2
Vurnary o RUS 96-97 E 6
Vuxikou o VRC 154-155 L 6
Vwaza Game Reserve ⊥ MW 214-215 G 6
Vya o USA (NV) 246-247 F 2
Vyaparla o IND 140-141 H 2
Vybor o RUS 94-95 L 3
Vyborg ☆• RUS 94-95 L 1
Vyčegda ~ RUS 88-89 W 6
Vydrino o RUS 116-117 M 10
Vydropužsk o RUS 94-95 O 3
Vyezžij Log o RUS 116-117 F 8
Vygoniči o RUS 94-95 O 5
Vygozero o RUS 88-89 N 5
Vyhanaščanskoe, vozero o BY 94-95 J 5
Vyhodnoj, mys ▲ RUS 108-109 G 5
Vyja ~ RUS 88-89 S 5
Vyksa ☆ RUS 94-95 S 4
Vylkove o UA 102-103 F 5
Vym' ~ RUS 88-89 V 5
Vyngajaha ~ RUS 114-115 O 2
Vyngapurovskij o RUS 114-115 O 3
Vyra o RUS 94-95 L 2
Vys', gora ▲ RUS 112-113 H 5
Vyšhorod o UA 102-103 G 2
Vyšnij Voloček ☆ RUS 94-95 O 3
Vysokae o BY 94-95 H 5
Vysokaja, gora ▲ RUS 122-123 N 6
Vysokaja Gora ☆ RUS 96-97 F 6
Vysokaja gora ▲ RUS 120-121 V 4
Vysokaja Parma vozvyšennost' ▲ RUS 114-115 E 4
Vysokij, mys ▲ RUS (KOR) 112-113 R 6
Vysokij, mys ▲ RUS (SAH) 110-111 a 2
Vysokogornyj o RUS 122-123 H 3
Vytegra ☆• RUS 88-89 O 6
Vyvenka o RUS (KOR) 120-121 V 3
Vyvenka ~ RUS 112-113 P 6
Vyvenka ~ RUS 120-121 V 3

W

Wa o CI 202-203 F 6
Wa ☆• GH 202-203 J 4
Waaheen, togga ~ SP 208-209 G 3
Waajid o SP 212-213 J 2
Waal ~ NL 92-93 H 3
Waangyi-Garawa Aboriginal Land ⨯ AUS 174-175 D 6
Waar, Pulau ⌒ RI 166-167 H 3
Waara o RI 164-165 H 6
Waarlangier, Tanjung ▲ RI 166-167 G 5
Waat o SUD 206-207 L 4
Wababimiga Lake o CDN (ONT) 236-237 B 2
Wabag ☆• PNG 183 B 3
Wabakimi Lake o CDN (ONT) 234-235 O 4
Wabakimi Provincial Park ⊥ CDN (ONT) 234-235 O 4
Wabamun o CDN (ALB) 232-233 D 2
Wabamun Lake o CDN (ALB) 232-233 D 2
Wabana o CDN (NFL) 242-243 Q 5
Wabasca River ~ CDN 32-33 N 3
Wabash o USA (IN) 274-275 N 4
Wabasha o USA (MN) 270-271 F 6
Wabash River ~ USA 274-275 L 5
Wabash River ~ USA 274-275 L 6
Wabash River ~ USA 274-275 L 4
Wabash River ~ USA 274-275 N 4
Wabassi River ~ CDN 234-235 R 3
Wabbaseka o USA (AR) 276-277 D 6
Wabbwood o CDN (ONT) 238-239 D 2
Wabē Shebelē Wenz ~ ETH 208-209 E 5
Wabigoon Lake o CDN (ONT) 234-235 L 5
Wabinosh Lake o CDN (ONT) 234-235 O 4
Wabo o PNG 183 C 4
Wabron o CDN (BC) 230-231 K 2
Wabuda o PNG 183 B 5
Wabuda Island ⌒ PNG 183 B 5
Wabuk Point ▲ CDN 34-35 O 3
Waburton Bay o CDN 30-31 N 4
Wabuska o USA (NV) 246-247 F 4
Waccamaw, Lake o USA (NC) 282-283 J 6
Waccasassa Bay ≈ 48-49 G 5
Waccasassa Bay ≈ 286-287 G 2
Waccassa River ~ USA 286-287 G 2
Wachapreague o USA (VA) 280-281 L 6
Wach'īlē o ETH 208-209 D 6
Waci o RI 164-165 L 3
Waco o CDN 38-39 M 3
Waco o USA (TN) 276-277 H 5
Waco o USA (TX) 266-267 K 2
Waco, Lake o USA (TX) 266-267 K 2
Waconda Lake o USA (KS) 262-263 H 5
Waconia o USA (MN) 270-271 E 6
Wacuach, Lac o CDN 36-37 Q 7
Wad o PK 134-135 M 5
Wada'ah o SUD 200-201 B 6
Wadalai o PNG 183 F 5
Wad al Haddad o SUD 200-201 F 6
Wadamago o SP 208-209 H 4
Wad an-Nail o SUD 200-201 G 6
Wadau o PNG 183 D 3
Wadayama o J 152-153 F 7
Wad Bandah o SUD 200-201 C 6
Wad Ban Naqa o SUD 200-201 F 4
Wadbilliga National Park ⊥ AUS 180-181 K 4
Waddān o• LAR 192-193 G 3
Waddān, Jabal ▲ LAR 192-193 G 3
Waddell Bay ≈ 36-37 Q 3
Waddeneilanden ⌒ NL 92-93 H 2
Waddenzee ≈ 92-93 H 2
Waddikee o AUS 180-181 D 2
Waddington, Mount ▲ CDN 230-231 D 2
Waddy Point ▲ AUS 178-179 M 3
Wade o USA (MS) 268-269 M 6
Wade Lake o CDN 36-37 R 7
Wadena o CDN (SAS) 232-233 P 4
Wadena o USA (MN) 270-271 C 4
Wadesboro o USA (NC) 282-283 G 6
Wadeye o AUS 172-173 J 3
Wad Hāmid o SUD 200-201 F 4
Wadham Islands ⌒ CDN (NFL) 242-243 P 3
Wad Hassib o SUD 206-207 H 3
Wadhope o CDN (MAN) 234-235 H 4
Wadi o IND 140-141 G 2
Wādī Ĝimal, Ĝazīrat ⌒ ET 194-195 G 5
Wādī Halfā o SUD 200-201 E 2
Wādī Seidna o SUD 200-201 F 5
Wadley o USA (AL) 284-285 E 3
Wadley o USA (GA) 284-285 H 4
Wad Madani ☆ SUD 200-201 F 5
Wad Nafarein o SUD 200-201 F 6
Wadomari o J 152-153 C 11
Wad Rāwah o SUD 200-201 F 5
Wadsworth o USA (NV) 246-247 F 4
Wadsworth o USA (TX) 266-267 M 5
Waeldem o USA (TX) 266-267 K 4
Waenhuiskrans o ZA 220-221 E 7
Waeplau o RI 166-167 D 3
Waeputih o RI 166-167 D 3
Waerana o RI 168 E 7
Wafangdian o VRC 150-151 C 8
Wafra, al- o KWT 130-131 K 3
Wagait Aboriginal Land ⨯ AUS 172-173 K 2
Wagan o PNG 183 D 4
Wagar, Buuraha ▲ SP 208-209 G 3
Waga River ~ PNG 183 B 4
Wagau o PNG 183 D 4
Wagdari o IND 140-141 G 2
Wagener o USA (SC) 284-285 J 3
Wageningen o SME 62-63 F 3
Wager, Isla ⌒ RCH 80 C 3
Wager Bay ≈ 30-31 Z 3
Wageseri o RI 166-167 K 2
Wagga Wagga o AUS 180-181 J 3
Waġh, al- o KSA 130-131 E 4
Waghai o IND 138-139 D 9
Waghete o RI 166-167 J 4
Waġīd, Ġabal al- ▲ KSA 132-133 D 4
Wagin o AUS 176-177 D 6
Waglisla o CDN (BC) 228-229 F 4
Wagner o BR 72-73 K 2
Wagner o USA (SD) 260-261 H 3
Wagny = Ouana ~ G 210-211 D 4
Wagoner o USA (OK) 264-265 J 3
Wagon Mound o USA (NM) 256-257 L 2
Wagontire o USA (OR) 244-245 F 7
Wagram o USA (NC) 282-283 H 6
Wagrowiec o• PL 92-93 O 2
Wagwalcook o CDN (NS) 240-241 P 4
Waha o RI 164-165 H 6
Waha o USA (ID) 250-251 C 5
Wahabu o GH 202-203 J 4
Wahai, Al o LAR 192-193 J 3
Wahai o RI 166-167 E 3
Wahala o RT 202-203 L 6
Wah Cantonment o PK 138-139 D 3
Wahi o PK 134-135 M 5
Wahiawa o USA (HI) 288 G 3
Wahlbergøya ⌒ N 84-85 L 3
Wahlebone Cape ▲ USA 22-23 N 6
Wahlenbergfjorden ≈ 84-85 L 3
Wahoo o USA (NE) 262-263 K 3
Wahpeton o USA (ND) 258-259 L 5
Wahrān ☆•• DZ 188-189 L 3
Wahroonga o AUS 176-177 C 2
Wai o IND 140-141 E 2
Waiakoa o USA (HI) 288 J 4
Waialua o USA (HI) 288 J 3
Waialua o USA (HI) 288 G 3
Waian o RC 156-157 L 5
Waianae o USA (HI) 288 G 3
Waiāpi, Área Indígena ⨯ BR 62-63 H 5
Waiau o NZ 182 D 5
Waibula o PNG 183 F 5
Waidhān o IND 142-143 C 3
Waidhofen an der Thaya o A 92-93 N 4
Waidu o WAL 202-203 E 5
Waigen Lakes o AUS 176-177 K 3
Waigeo, Pulau ⌒ RI 166-167 F 2
Waihau Bay o NZ 182 F 2
Waihi o NZ 182 E 2
Waiji, Pulau ⌒ RI 166-167 F 2
Waikabubak o• RI 168 D 7
Waikaia o NZ 182 B 6
Waikaremoana o NZ 182 F 3
Waikawa o NZ 182 B 7
Waikelo o RI 168 D 7
Waikerie o AUS 180-181 E 3
Waikii o USA (HI) 288 K 5
Waikiki Beach <• USA (HI) 288 H 3
Wailapa o VAN 184 II a 2
Wailea o USA (HI) 288 J 4
Wailebe o RI 166-167 B 6
Wailua o USA (HI) 288 F 2
Wailua Falls ~• USA 288 J 4
Wailuku o• USA (HI) 288 J 4
Waimanalo Beach o USA (HI) 288 H 3
Waimanguar o RI 168 D 7
Waimate o NZ 182 C 6
Waimea o USA (HI) 288 G 3
Waimea Canyon ⌣• USA 288 F 2
Waimenda o RI 164-165 F 5
Waimiri Atroari, Área Indígena ⨯ BR 62-63 D 6
Wainganga ~ IND 138-139 G 9
Waingapu o RI 168 E 7
Waini River ~ GUY 62-63 E 1
Wainwright o CDN (ALB) 232-233 H 3
Wainwright o USA 20-21 L 1
Waiouru o NZ 182 E 3
Waipa o RI 166-167 J 3
Waipah o USA (HI) 288 G 3
Waipara o NZ 182 D 5
Waipawa o NZ 182 F 3
Waipio o USA (HI) 288 K 4
Waipoua Kauri Forest ⊥• NZ 182 D 1
Waipukang o RI 166-167 B 6
Waipukurau o NZ 182 F 4
Wair o RI 166-167 G 4
Wa'ir, Wādī al ~ LAR 192-193 H 4
Waira o PNG 183 C 4
Wairaha ~ SOL 184 I e 3
Wairoa o NZ 182 F 3
Wairunu o RI 166-167 B 6
Waisa o PNG 183 C 4
Waitakaruru o NZ 182 E 2
Waitaki o NZ 182 C 6
Waitaki River ~ NZ 182 C 6
Waitangi o• NZ 182 E 1
Waitara o NZ 182 E 3
Waitati o NZ 182 C 6
Waito o USA (MI) 272-273 O 3
Waitomo Caves • NZ 182 E 3
Waitsburg o USA (WA) 244-245 G 4
Waitville o CDN (SAS) 232-233 N 3
Waiuku o NZ 182 E 2
Waiwa o PNG 183 E 5
Waiwai o GUY 62-63 E 5
Waiwerang o RI 166-167 B 6
Waje o WAN 204-205 G 4
Wajima o J 152-153 G 6
Wajir o EAK 212-213 H 3
Waka o ETH 208-209 C 5
Waka o RI 168 E 7
Waka o USA (TX) 264-265 D 2
Waka o ZRE (EQU) 210-211 H 3
Waka o ZRE (EQU) 210-211 H 4
Waka, Tanjung ▲ RI 166-167 D 3
Wakaf Tapai o MAL 162-163 E 2
Wakami Lake Provincial Park ⊥ CDN (ONT) 236-237 F 5
Wakamoek o RI 166-167 F 2
Wakarusa River ~ USA 262-263 L 6
Wakasa-wan ≈ 152-153 F 7
Wakasawan Quasi National Park ⊥ J 152-153 F 7
Wakatin o RI 166-167 D 3
Wakatipu, Lake o NZ 182 B 6
Wakaw o CDN (SAS) 232-233 N 3
Wakay o SME 62-63 F 3
Wakaya ⌒ FJI 184 III b 2
Wakayama ☆ J 152-153 F 7
Wakde, Pulau ⌒ RI 166-167 K 2
Wakeeny o USA (KS) 262-263 G 5
Wakefield o CDN (QUE) 238-239 K 3
Wakefield o NZ 182 D 4
Wakefield o USA (MI) 270-271 J 4
Wakefield o USA (NE) 262-263 K 2
Wakefield o USA (RI) 278-279 K 7
Wakefield o USA (VA) 280-281 K 7
Wakefield River ~ AUS 180-181 E 3
Wake Forest o USA (NC) 282-283 J 5
Wakeham, Rivière ~ CDN 36-37 N 4
Wakeman River ~ CDN 230-231 C 2
Wakingku o RI 164-165 H 6
Wakinosawa o J 152-153 J 4
Wakkanai o J 152-153 J 2
Wakkerstroom o ZA 220-221 K 3
Waklarok o USA 20-21 H 5
Wako o PNG 183 E 4
Wakomata Lake o CDN (ONT) 238-239 B 2
Wakonassin River ~ CDN 238-239 C 2
Wakonda o USA (SD) 260-261 J 3
Wakoo o AUS 180-181 H 3
Wakool River ~ AUS 180-181 G 3
Wakopa o CDN (MAN) 234 235 D 5
Wakulla Springs • USA (FL) 286-287 E 1
Wakunai o PNG 184 I b 1
Wakusimi River ~ CDN 236-237 F 4
Wakwayokwastic River ~ CDN 236-237 H 3
Wala ~ EAT 212-213 D 6
Walachia ⩊ RO 102-103 D 6
Wäläjäpet o IND 140-141 H 4
Walakpa o USA 20-21 M 1
Walambele o GH 202-203 K 4
Wálamo, El o MEX 50-51 F 6
Walanae ~ RI 164-165 G 6
Wal Athiang o SUD 206-207 J 5
Wałbrzych ☆• PL 92-93 O 3
Walbundrie o AUS 180-181 J 3
Walcha o AUS 178-179 L 6
Walckenaer, Teluk ≈ 166-167 K 3
Walcott o CDN (BC) 228-229 H 2
Walcott o USA (WY) 252-253 M 5
Walcott Inlet ≈ 172-173 G 4
Wałcz o• PL 92-93 O 2
Waldburg o AUS 176-177 D 2
Waldburg Range ▲ AUS 176-177 D 2
Waldeck o CDN (SAS) 232-233 L 5
Walden o CDN (ONT) 238-239 D 2
Walden o USA (CO) 254-255 J 3
Walden o USA (NY) 280-281 M 2
Waldenburg o USA (AR) 276-277 E 5
Walden Ridge ▲ USA 276-277 K 5
Waldersee o CDN (MAN) 234-235 D 4
Waldheim o CDN (SAS) 232-233 M 3
Waldo o USA (AR) 276-277 B 7
Waldo o USA (FL) 286-287 G 2
Waldo o USA (OH) 280-281 C 3
Waldorf o USA (MD) 280-281 K 5
Waldport o USA (OR) 244-245 A 6
Waldron o CDN (SAS) 232-233 Q 5
Waldron o USA (AR) 276-277 A 6
Walea, Selat ≈ 164-165 H 4
Waleabahi, Pulau ⌒ RI 164-165 H 4
Waleakodi, Pulau ⌒ RI 164-165 H 4
Waleri o RI 168 D 3
Wales ▭ GB 90-91 F 5
Wales o USA 20-21 F 4
Wales o USA (UT) 254-255 D 4
Wales Island ⌒ CDN 24-25 c 6
Wales Island ⌒ CDN (BC) 228-229 D 2
Walewale o GH 202-203 K 4
Walfe, Chute ~ ZRE 210-211 J 6
Walgett o AUS 178-179 K 6
Walgra o AUS 178-179 E 1
Walgreen Coast ⌣ ARK 16 F 26
Walgun o AUS 172-173 E 7
Walhalla o USA (MI) 272-273 C 4
Walhalla o USA (ND) 258-259 K 3
Walhalla o USA (SC) 284-285 G 2
Walhalla Historic Site ∴ USA (ND) 258-259 K 3
Walikale o ZRE 212-213 B 4
Walir, Pulau ⌒ RI 166-167 G 4
Walis Island ⌒ PNG 183 B 2
Walk = Valga ☆• EST 94-95 K 3
Walker o USA (IA) 274-275 G 2
Walker o USA (MI) 272-273 D 4
Walker o USA (MN) 270-271 D 3
Walker o USA (SD) 260-261 E 1
Walker, Mount ▲ CDN 24-25 Z 4
Walkerbaai ≈ 220-221 D 7
Walker Baldwin Range ▲ CDN 24-25 S 3
Walker Bay ≈ 24-25 N 5
Walker Bay = Walkerbaai ≈ 220 221 D 7
Walker Creek ~ AUS 176-177 M 2
Walker Lake o CDN (NWT) 30-31 Y 2
Walker Lake o USA (AK) 20-21 N 3
Walker Lake o USA (NV) 246-247 G 5
Walker Mountains ▲ ARK 16 F 26
Walker Pass ▲ USA (CA) 248-249 F 4
Walker River ~ AUS 174-175 C 3
Walker River ~ USA 246-247 F 5
Walker River Indian Reservation ⨯ USA (NV) 246-247 G 4
Walkerston o AUS 178-179 K 1
Walkerton o CDN (ONT) 238-239 D 4
Walkerton o USA (IN) 274-275 M 3
Walkerville o AUS 180-181 H 5
Walkerville o USA (MI) 272-273 C 4
Wall o USA (SD) 260-261 D 2
Wall o USA (TX) 266-267 G 2
Wall, Mount ▲ AUS 172-173 C 7
Wallabi Group ⌒ AUS 176-177 B 4
Wallace o CDN (NS) 240-241 M 5
Wallace o USA (ID) 250-251 D 4
Wallace o USA (NC) 282-283 K 6
Wallace o USA (NE) 262-263 E 4
Wallaceburg o CDN (ONT) 238-239 C 6
Wallace River o CDN 30-31 W 5
Wallachisch Meseritsch = Valašské Meziříčí o CZ 92-93 O 4
Wallal Downs o AUS 172-173 E 5
Wallambin, Lake o AUS 176-177 D 5
Wallam Creek ~ AUS 178-179 J 5
Wallareenya o AUS 172-173 D 6
Wallaroo o AUS 180-181 D 2
Walla Walla o USA (WA) 244-245 G 4
Wallekraal o ZA 220-221 C 5
Wallenpaupack, Lake o USA (PA) 280-281 L 2
Wallhallow o AUS 174-175 C 5
Wallingford o USA (VT) 278-279 J 5
Wallis o USA (TX) 266-267 L 4
Walliser Alpen ▲ CH 92-93 J 5
Wallis Lake o AUS 180-181 M 2
Wallkill River ~ USA 280-281 M 2
Walløe, Kap ▲ GRØ 28-29 T 6
Wallonie ▭ B 92-93 H 3
Wallowa o USA (OR) 244-245 H 5
Wallowa Mountains ▲ USA (OR) 244-245 H 5
Walls of China, The • AUS 180-181 G 2
Wallula o USA (WA) 244-245 G 4
Wallumbilla o AUS 178-179 K 4
Walmanpa-Warlpiri Aboriginal Land ⨯ AUS 172-173 K 5
Walnut o USA (CA) 248-249 B 2
Walnut o USA (IL) 274-275 J 3
Walnut o USA (MS) 268-269 M 2
Walnut Canyon National Monument ∴ USA (AZ) 256-257 D 3
Walnut Cove o USA (NC) 282-283 G 4
Walnut Creek o USA (AZ) 256-257 C 4

Vis — Walnut Creek 409

Wel Jara o EAK 212-213 H 4
Welk'ītē o ETH 208-209 C 4
Welkom o ZA 220-221 H 3
Well o USA (KY) 276-277 K 3
Welland o CDN (ONT) 238-239 F 6
Wella-Sofon-Gari o RN 204-205 E 1
Wellawaya o CL 140-141 J 7
Wellesley Basin ⊥ CDN 20-21 U 5
Wellesley Islands ⌒ AUS 174-175 E 5
Wellesley Lake ⊖ CDN 20-21 V 5
Welling o CDN (ALB) 232-233 F 6
Wellington o AUS 180-181 K 2
Wellington o CDN (NS) 240-241 M 6
Wellington o CDN (ONT) 238-239 H 5
Wellington ★ NZ 182 E 4
Wellington o USA (AL) 284-285 E 3
Wellington o USA (CO) 254-255 K 3
Wellington o USA (KS) 262-263 J 7
Wellington o USA (NV) 246-247 F 5
Wellington o USA (OH) 280-281 D 2
Wellington o USA (TX) 264-265 D 4
Wellington o USA (UT) 254-255 E 4
Wellington o ZA 220-221 D 6
Wellington, Isla ⌒ RCH 80 C 4
Wellington, Lake ⊖ AUS 180-181 J 5
Wellington Bay ≈ 24-25 S 6
Wellington Caves • AUS 180-181 K 2
Wellington Channel ≈ 24-25 Z 3
Wellington Range ▲ AUS 176-177 F 3
Wellman o USA (TX) 264-265 B 5
Wells o CDN (BC) 228-229 N 3
Wells o USA (MN) 270-271 E 7
Wells o USA (NV) 246-247 L 2
Wells o USA (TX) 268-269 F 5
Wells, Lake ⊖ AUS 176-177 G 3
Wellsford o NZ 182 E 2
Wells Gray Provincial Park ⊥ CDN (BC) 228-229 O 4
Wells Lake ⊖ CDN 34-35 F 2
Wellstead o AUS 176-177 E 7
Wellston o USA (MI) 272-273 D 3
Wellston o USA (OH) 280-281 D 4
Wellsville o USA (MO) 274-275 G 5
Wellsville o USA (NY) 278-279 D 6
Wellsville o USA (UT) 254-255 D 2
Wellwood o CDN (MAN) 234-235 D 4
Welmel Shet' ~ ETH 208-209 E 6
Wel Meret < EAK 212-213 H 2
Welo ◻ ETH 208-209 C 6
Wels o A 92-93 N 4
Welsford o CDN (NB) 240-241 J 5
Welsford, Cape ▲ CDN 36-37 G 2
Welsh o USA (LA) 268-269 H 6
Welshpool o CDN (NB) 240-241 J 6
Welshpool o• GB 90-91 F 5
Welton o USA (AZ) 256-257 B 6
Welutu o RI 166-167 F 5
Welwel o ETH 208-209 G 5
Welwyn o CDN (SAS) 232-233 R 5
Womo o ZRE 210-211 H 4
Wembere ~ EAT 212-213 E 6
Wembi o RI 166-167 L 3
Wembley o CDN 32-33 L 4
Wemindji o CDN 38-39 E 2
Wen o SUD 206-207 H 4
Wenago o ETH 208-209 D 5
Wenaha Tucannon Wilderness Area ⊥ USA (WA) 244-245 H 4
Wenasaga River ~ CDN 234-235 K 4
Wenatchee o USA (WA) 244-245 F 3
Wenatchee Mountains ▲ USA 244-245 E 3
Wenceslao Escalante o RA 78-79 H 2
Wenchang o VRC (HAI) 156-157 G 7
Wenchang o VRC (SIC) 154-155 E 6
Wenchi o GH 202-203 J 6
Wenchiki o GH 202-203 L 4
Wench'it Shet' ~ ETH 208-209 D 3
Wenchuan o VRC 154-155 C 6
Wendell o USA (ID) 252-253 D 4
Wenden o USA (AZ) 256-257 B 5
Wendeng o VRC 154-155 N 3
Wendesi o RI 166-167 H 3
Wendi o RI 164-165 J 4
Wendi o VRC 156-157 G 6
Wendo o ETH 208-209 D 5
Wendou-Borou o RG 202-203 D 4
Wendover o USA (UT) 254-255 A 3
Wendover Range xx USA (UT) 254-255 B 3
Wenebegon Lake ⊖ CDN (ONT) 236-237 E 5
Wenga o ZRE 210-211 G 3
Weng'an o VRC 156-157 E 3
Wenge o ZRE 210-211 K 3
Weni o NEP 144-145 D 6
Wenlock ∴ AUS 174-175 G 3
Wenlock River ~ AUS 174-175 F 3
Wenona o USA (IL) 274-275 J 3
Wenona o USA (MD) 280-281 L 5
Wenquan o VRC 144-145 H 4
Wenshan o VRC 156-157 D 5
Wen Shang o VRC 154-155 K 4
Wenshui o VRC (GZH) 156-157 E 2
Wenshui o VRC (SHA) 154-155 G 3
Wentworth o AUS 180-181 F 3
Wentworth o USA (SD) 260-261 K 3
Wentworth Centre o CDN (NS) 240-241 M 5
Wentworth Springs o USA (CA) 246-247 E 4
Wentzel Lake ⊖ CDN (ALB) 30-31 M 6
Wentzel Lake ⊖ CDN (NWT) 30-31 M 2
Wentzel River ~ CDN 30-31 M 6
Wentzville o USA (MO) 274-275 H 6
Wenxi o VRC 154-155 G 4
Wen Xian o VRC 154-155 D 5
Wenzhen o VRC 156-157 K 2
Wenzhou o VRC 156-157 M 2
Wenzhou Wan ≈ 156-157 M 3
Weohyakapka, Lake ⊖ USA (FL) 286-287 H 4
Weott o USA (CA) 246-247 B 3
Wepener o ZA 220-221 H 4
Werda o RB 220-221 F 2
Werdër o ETH 208-209 G 5
Were Ilu o ETH 208-209 D 3
Wernadinga o AUS 174-175 E 6
Werner Lake o CDN (ONT) 234-235 J 4
Werota o ETH 208-209 C 3
Wer Ping o SUD 206-207 J 4
Werra ~ D 92-93 L 3
Werribee o AUS 180-181 H 4
Werrikimbie National Park ⊥ AUS 178-179 M 6
Werris Creek o AUS 178-179 L 6
Wertach ~ D 92-93 L 4
Wesel o D 92-93 J 3
Weser ~ D 92-93 K 2
Weskan o USA (KS) 262-263 E 6
Weslaco o USA (TX) 266-267 J 7
Weslemkoon o CDN (ONT) 238-239 H 4
Weslemkoon Lake ⊖ CDN (ONT) 238-239 H 3
Wesley o USA (ME) 278-279 O 4
Wesleyville o CDN (NFL) 242-243 P 3
Wessel, Cape ▲ AUS 174-175 D 2
Wessel Islands ⌒ AUS 174-175 D 2
Wesselsbron o ZA 220-221 H 3
Wessington o USA (SD) 260-261 H 2
Wessington Springs o USA (SD) 260-261 H 2
Wesson o USA (MS) 268-269 K 5
West o USA (MS) 268-269 L 3
West o USA (TX) 266-267 K 2
West = Ouest ◻ CAM 204-205 J 6
West Amatuli Island ⌒ USA 22-23 V 3
West Arm o CDN (ONT) 238-239 E 2
West Baines River ~ AUS 172-173 J 4
Westbank o CDN (BC) 230-231 K 4
West Bay ≈ 286-287 D 1
West Bay o CDN (NS) 240-241 O 5
West Bay o CDN (ONT) 238-239 C 3
West Bay o• GB 54-55 E 5
West Bend o CDN (SAS) 232-233 P 4
West Bend o USA (IA) 274-275 D 2
West Bend o USA (WI) 274-275 K 1
West Bengal ◻ IND 142-143 E 4
West Berlin o CDN (NS) 240-241 L 6
West Bijou Creek ~ USA 254-255 L 4
West Blocton o USA (AL) 284-285 C 3
Westboro o USA (WI) 270-271 H 5
Westbourne o CDN (MAN) 234-235 E 4
West Branch o USA (IA) 274-275 G 3
West Branch o USA (MI) 272-273 E 3
Westbridge o CDN (BC) 230-231 L 4
West Brook ~ CDN 242-243 M 1
Westbrook o USA (ME) 278-279 L 5
Westbrook o USA (MN) 270-271 C 6
Westbrook o USA (TX) 264-265 C 6
West Burke o USA (VT) 278-279 K 4
Westbury o AUS 178-179 H 2
West Butte ▲ USA (MT) 250-251 H 3
Westby o USA (MT) 250-251 P 3
Westby o USA (WI) 270-271 H 7
West Caicos ⌒ GB 54-55 J 4
West Canada Creek ~ USA 278-279 G 5
West Cape Howe ▲ AUS 176-177 D 7
West-Cape Province ◻ ZA 220-221 D 6
West Channel ~ CDN 20-21 X 2
West Chester o USA (OH) 280-281 E 3
West Chichagof Yakobi Wilderness ⊥ • USA 32-33 B 3
Westcliffe o USA (CO) 254-255 K 5
West Coast National Park ⊥ ZA 220-221 D 6
West Columbia o USA (SC) 284-285 J 2
West Columbia o USA (TX) 268-269 E 7
West Cote Blanche Bay ≈ 268-269 J 7
West Covina o USA (CA) 248-249 G 5
West Des Moines o USA (IA) 274-275 E 3
West End o BS 54-55 F 1
West End o GB 54-55 F 5
Westerberg o ZA 220-221 F 4
Westerland o D 92-93 K 1
Westerly o USA (RI) 278-279 K 7
Western ◻ EAK 212-213 E 3
Western ◻ EAU 212-213 C 3
Western ◻ GH 202-203 J 6
Western o USA (NE) 262-263 J 4
Western ◻ Z 218-219 B 2
Western Australia ◻ AUS 172-173 F 5
Western Creek ~ AUS 178-179 L 4
Western Desert = as-Sahrā' al-Ġarbīya ∴ ET 194-195 B 4
Western Desert = Sahrā' al-Ġarbīya, as- ∴ ET 194-195 B 4
Western Entrance ≈ 184 I b 2
Western Ghāts ▲ IND 10-11 G 7
Western Head ▲ CDN (NS) 240-241 K 7
Western Island ⌒ PNG 183 C 2
Western Kentucky Parkway II USA (KY) 276-277 H 3
Western Plains Zoo • AUS 180-181 K 2
Westernport o USA (MD) 280-281 G 4
Western Region ◻ GH 202-203 J 6
Western River ~ CDN 30-31 Q 2
Western Sahara ◼ WSA 196-197 C 2
Western Samoa = Samoa-i-Sisifo ◼ WS 184 V a 1
Western Samoa = Samoa-i-Sisifo ⌒ WS (WEF) 184 V a 1
Western Sayan Mountains = Zapadnyj Sajan ▲ RUS 116-117 E 9
Western Tasmania National Parks ⊥ ••• AUS 180-181 H 7
Western Thebes ∴ •• ET 194-195 F 5
Western Waigeo Pulau Reserve ⊥ • RI 166-167 F 2
Westerschelde ≈ 92-93 G 3
Westerville o USA (NE) 262-263 G 3
Westerville o USA (OH) 280-281 D 3
Westerwald ▲ D 92-93 J 3
West Falkland ⌒ GB 78-79 L 6
Westfall o USA (OR) 244-245 H 7
West Fargo o USA (ND) 258-259 L 5
Westfield o CDN (NB) 240-241 J 5
Westfield o USA (MA) 278-279 J 6
Westfield o USA (ND) 258-259 G 5
Westfield o USA (NY) 278-279 B 6
West Fork ~ USA 250-251 N 3
West Fork ~ USA 274-275 G 5
West Fork Big Blue River ~ USA 262-263 H 4
West Fork Des Moines ~ USA 274-275 D 1
West Fork Grand River ~ USA 274-275 D 4
West Fork River ~ USA 280-281 F 4
West Fork Trinity ~ USA 264-265 F 5
West Frankfort o USA (IL) 276-277 G 3
West Frisian Islands = Waddeneilanden ∴ NL 92-93 H 2
Westgard Pass ▲ USA (CA) 248-249 F 2
Westgate o AUS 178-179 J 4
Westgate o CDN (MAN) 234-235 B 2
West Glacier o USA (MT) 250-251 F 3
West Gletscher ⊂ GRØ 26-27 I 8
West Group ⌒ AUS 176-177 F 6
West Hamlin o USA (WV) 280-281 D 5
West Haverstraw o USA (NY) 280-281 M 2
West Hawk Lake o CDN (MAN) 234-235 H 5
West Helena o USA (AR) 276-277 E 6
West Hobolochitto Creek ~ USA 268-269 L 6
Westhoff o USA (TX) 266-267 K 4
West Holothuria Reef ⌒ AUS 172-173 G 2
Westhope o USA (ND) 258-259 F 3
West Ice Shelf ⊂ ARK 16 G 9
West Island ⌒ AUS (NT) 174-175 D 4
West Island ⌒ AUS (WA) 176-177 F 7
West Jordan o USA (UT) 254-255 C 3
West Kettle River ~ CDN 230-231 K 4
West Lafayette o USA (IN) 274-275 M 4
Westlake o USA (LA) 268-269 G 6
Westland National Park ⊥ ••• NZ 182 C 5
West Levant o USA (ME) 278-279 N 4
West Liberty o USA (IA) 274-275 G 3
West Liberty o USA (KY) 276-277 M 3
West Liberty o USA (OH) 280-281 C 3
West Linn o USA (OR) 244-245 C 5
West Lorne o CDN (ONT) 238-239 D 6
West Lunga ~ Z 214-215 C 7
West Lunga National Park ⊥ Z 214-215 C 7
Westmar o AUS 178-179 K 4
Westmeath o CDN (QUE) 238-239 J 3
West Memphis o USA (AR) 276-277 E 5
Westminster o USA (CO) 254-255 K 4
Westminster o USA (MD) 280-281 K 4
Westminster o USA (SC) 284-285 G 2
Westminster o ZA 220-221 H 4
Westmond o USA (ID) 250-251 C 3
West Monroe o USA (LA) 268-269 H 4
Westmoreland o AUS 174-175 E 5
Westmoreland o USA (KS) 262-263 K 5
Westmoreland o USA (TN) 276-277 J 4
Westmorland o USA (CA) 248-249 J 6
Westmount o CDN (NS) 240-241 P 4
West Mount Barren ▲ AUS 176-177 E 7
West Nicholson o ZW 218-219 E 5
Weston o USA (FL) 286-287 J 5
Weston o USA (ID) 252-253 G 4
Weston o USA (OR) 244-245 G 5
Weston o USA (WV) 280-281 F 4
Weston o USA (WY) 252-253 N 2
Weston-Super-Mare o GB 90-91 F 6
West Ossipee o USA (NH) 278-279 K 5
West Palm Beach o•• USA (FL) 286-287 J 5
West Plains o USA (MO) 276-277 D 4
West Point ▲ AUS (SA) 180-181 C 3
West Point ▲ AUS (TAS) 180-181 H 6
West Point o CDN (PEI) 240-241 L 4
Westpoint o GB 78-79 K 6
West Point o USA (IA) 274-275 G 4
West Point o USA (MS) 268-269 M 3
West Point o USA (NE) 262-263 K 3
West Point o USA (NY) 280-281 N 2
West Point o USA (TX) 264-265 B 5
West Point o USA (VA) 280-281 K 6
West Point ▲ USA (AK) 20-21 S 4
West Point ▲ WAN 204-205 H 6
West Point Lake < USA (GA) 284-285 E 3
West Poplar o CDN (SAS) 232-233 M 6
Westport o CDN (NFL) 242-243 M 3
Westport o CDN (ONT) 238-239 J 4
Westport o NZ 182 C 4
Westport o USA (CA) 246-247 B 4
Westport o USA (OR) 244-245 B 4
Westport o USA (WA) 244-245 A 4
Westport = Cathair na Mart o• IRL 90-91 C 5
West Prairie River ~ CDN 32-33 M 4
Westpunt o NA 60-61 G 1
Westray ⌒ GB 90-91 F 2
Westree o CDN (ONT) 236-237 G 5
West Richland o USA (WA) 244-245 F 4
West River ~ CDN 24-25 H 6
West River ~ USA 278-279 J 5
West Road River ~ CDN 228-229 K 3
West Saint-Modeste o CDN (NFL) 242-243 M 1
West Salem o USA (IL) 274-275 K 6
West Salem o USA (OH) 280-281 D 3
West Siberian Plain = Zapadno-Sibirskaja ravnina ⌣ RUS 10-11 G 2
Westside o USA (MS) 268-269 J 5
West Springfield o USA (PA) 280-281 F 2
West Taghkanic o USA (NY) 278-279 H 6
West Thumb o USA (WY) 252-253 H 2
West Travaputs Plateau ▲ USA 254-255 E 4
West Union o USA (IA) 274-275 G 2
West Union o USA (IL) 274-275 L 5
West Union o USA (OH) 280-281 C 5
West Union o USA (WV) 280-281 F 4
West Unity o USA (OH) 280-281 B 2
West Valley City o USA (UT) 254-255 C 3
West Vancouver o CDN (BC) 230-231 F 4
Westview o CDN (BC) 230-231 E 4
Westville o USA (IL) 274-275 L 4
Westville o USA (IN) 274-275 M 3
Westville o USA (OK) 264-265 K 3
Westville • USA (GA) 284-285 F 4
West Virginia ◻ USA 280-281 F 4
West Warwick o USA (RI) 278-279 K 7
West Wendover o USA (NV) 246-247 L 3
Westwold o CDN (BC) 230-231 K 3
Westwood o AUS 178-179 L 2
Westwood o USA (CA) 246-247 E 3
West Wyalong o AUS 180-181 J 2
West Yellowstone o USA (MT) 250-251 H 7
West York Island ⌒ 160-161 A 7
Wetalltok Bay ≈ 36-37 K 5
Wetan, Pulau ⌒ RI 166-167 E 5
Wetar, Pulau ⌒ RI 166-167 D 5
Wetar, Selat ≈ 166-167 C 6
Wetaskiwin o CDN (ALB) 232-233 E 3
Wete o EAT 212-213 G 6
Wete o ZRE 210-211 K 6
Wetetnagami, Lac ⊖ CDN (QUE) 236-237 M 4
Wetetnagami, Rivière ~ CDN 236-237 M 4
Wetherell, Lake ⊖ AUS 180-181 G 2
Wetmore o USA (CO) 254-255 K 5
Wetmore o USA (MI) 270-271 M 4
Wet Mountains ▲ USA 254-255 K 6
Weto o WAN 204-205 G 5
Wetonka o USA (SD) 260-261 H 1
Wettlet o MYA 142-143 J 4
Wet Tropics of Queensland ⊥ ••• AUS 174-175 H 5
Wetumka o USA (OK) 264-265 H 3
Wetumpka o USA (AL) 284-285 D 4
Wetzlar o• D 92-93 K 3
Wevok o USA 20-21 G 2
Wewahitchka o USA (FL) 286-287 D 1
Wewak ☆ PNG 183 B 2
Wewela o USA (SD) 260-261 G 3
Wewoka o USA (OK) 264-265 H 3
Wexford = Loch Garman ☆ IRL 90-91 D 5
Weyburn o CDN (SAS) 232-233 P 6
Weyland, Point ▲ AUS 180-181 C 2
Weymontachie Indian Reservation X • CDN (QUE) 236-237 P 5
Weymouth o CDN (NS) 240-241 K 6
Weymouth o• GB 90-91 F 6
Weymouth, Cape ▲ AUS 174-175 G 3
Weymouth Bay ≈ 174-175 G 3
Weyto o ETH 208-209 C 6
Whakatane o NZ 182 F 2
Whalan o USA (MN) 270-271 G 7
Whalan Creek ~ AUS 178-179 K 5
Whaleback Mining Area, Mount • AUS 172-173 D 7
Whale Bay ≈ 32-33 C 3
Whale Bay ≈ 158-159 E 5
Whale Cay ⌒ BS 54-55 G 2
Whale Channel ≈ 228-229 E 3
Whale Cove o CDN 30-31 X 4
Whale Island ⌒ USA 22-23 U 4
Whale Point ▲ CDN 36-37 F 2
Whaletown o CDN (BC) 230-231 E 3
Whangamata o NZ 182 E 2
Whanganui National Park • NZ 182 E 3
Whangarei o NZ 182 E 1
Wharfe ~ GB 90-91 F 4
Wharton o USA (TX) 266-267 L 4
Wharton, Península ⌣ RCH 80 C 4
Wharton Lake ⊖ CDN 30-31 T 3
Whatshan Lake ⊖ CDN (BC) 230-231 L 3
Wheatland o CDN (MAN) 234-235 C 4
Wheatland o USA (CA) 246-247 D 4
Wheatland o USA (NM) 256-257 M 4
Wheatland o USA (WY) 252-253 O 4
Wheatland Reservoir No.2 < USA (WY) 252-253 N 5
Wheatley o CDN (ONT) 238-239 C 6
Wheaton o USA (IL) 274-275 K 3
Wheaton o USA (MN) 270-271 B 5
Wheeler o USA (TX) 264-265 D 3
Wheeler o USA (WI) 270-271 G 5
Wheeler Lake < USA (AL) 284-285 C 2
Wheeler National Wildlife Refuge ⊥ USA (AL) 284-285 D 2
Wheeler Peak ▲ USA (NM) 256-257 K 2
Wheeler Peak ▲ USA (NV) 246-247 L 5
Wheeler Ridge o USA 248-249 E 4
Wheeler River ~ CDN 34-35 D 2
Wheelers Point o USA (MN) 270-271 D 2
Wheeling o USA (IN) 274-275 M 4
Wheeling o USA (WV) 280-281 F 3
Wheelock o USA (TX) 266-267 L 3
Whela Creek ~ AUS 176-177 D 3
Whelan, Mount ▲ AUS 178-179 E 2
Whewell, Mount ▲ ARK 16 F 17
Whidbey Island ⌒ USA (WA) 244-245 C 2
Whidbey Isles ⌒ AUS 180-181 C 3
Whim Creek o AUS 172-173 C 6
Whirlwind Lake ⊖ CDN 30-31 P 5
Whiskey Gap o CDN (ALB) 232-233 E 6
Whiskey Jack Lake ⊖ CDN 30-31 T 6
Whiskeytown ⊥ USA (CA) 246-247 C 3
Whisky Chitto Creek ~ USA 268-269 G 6
Whispering Pines o USA (CA) 246-247 C 5
Whistler o CDN (BC) 230-231 G 3
Whitbourne o CDN (NFL) 242-243 P 5
Whitby o CDN (ONT) 238-239 G 5
Whitby o• GB 90-91 G 4
Whitchurch o GB 90-91 F 5
White o USA (GA) 284-285 F 2
White, Lake ⊖ AUS 172-173 J 6
White, Mount ▲ AUS 176-177 F 3
White Bay ≈ 242-243 M 2
White Bear o CDN (SAS) 232-233 K 5
White Bear Lake o USA (MN) 270-271 E 5
Whitebear Point ▲ CDN 24-25 U 6
White Bear River ~ CDN 242-243 L 4
White Bird o USA (ID) 250-251 C 6
White Bluff o USA (TN) 276-277 H 4
White Butte ▲ USA (ND) 258-259 D 5
White Cape Mount ▲ USA (ME) 278-279 M 3
White Castle o USA (LA) 268-269 J 6
White Cay ⌒ BS 54-55 H 2
White City o CDN (SAS) 232-233 O 5
White City o USA (KS) 262-263 K 6
Whiteclay o USA (NE) 262-263 D 2
Whiteclay Lake ⊖ CDN (ONT) 234-235 P 4
White Cliff ▲ BS 54-55 J 3
White Cliffs o AUS 178-179 G 6
White crowned pigeons • BS 54-55 G 2
White Deer o USA (TX) 264-265 C 3
Whitedog o CDN (ONT) 234-235 J 4
White Earth o USA (MN) 270-271 C 3
White Earth o USA (ND) 258-259 E 3
White Earth Indian Reservation X USA (MN) 270-271 C 3
Whiteface o USA (MN) 270-271 F 3
Whiteface o USA (TX) 264-265 B 5
Whitefish o CDN (ONT) 238-239 D 2
Whitefish o USA (MT) 250-251 E 3
Whitefish Bay ⊖ USA (MI) 270-271 O 4
Whitefish Falls o CDN (ONT) 238-239 D 2
Whitefish Lake ⊖ CDN 30-31 Q 4
Whitefish Lake ⊖ USA (AK) 20-21 L 6
Whitefish Lake ⊖ USA (MN) 270-271 D 4
Whitefish Lake Indian Reserve X CDN (QUE) 238-239 D 2
Whitefish Point o USA (MI) 270-271 O 4
Whitefish Point ▲ USA (MI) 270-271 O 4
Whitefish Range ▲ USA 250-251 E 3
Whitefish River ~ CDN 30-31 H 3
Whitefish River ~ USA 270-271 M 4
Whitefish River Indian Reservation X CDN (ONT) 238-239 D 2
Whiteflat o USA (TX) 264-265 D 4
White Fox o CDN (SAS) 232-233 O 2
White Goat Wilderness ⊥ CDN (ALB) 232-233 B 3
Whitegull, Lac ⊖ CDN 36-37 R 7
Whitehall o USA (AR) 276-277 E 6
White Hall o USA (IL) 274-275 H 5
Whitehall o USA (IN) 274-275 M 5
Whitehall o USA (MI) 272-273 C 4
Whitehall o USA (MT) 250-251 G 6
Whitehall o USA (NY) 278-279 H 5
Whitehall o USA (WI) 270-271 G 6
White Hall State Historic Site • USA (KY) 276-277 L 3
White Handkerchief, Cape ▲ CDN 36-37 S 5
Whitehaven o USA (MD) 280-281 L 5
White Haven o USA (PA) 280-281 L 2
Whitehead o CDN (NS) 240-241 O 5
White Hills ▲ USA 20-21 Q 2
Whitehills Lake ⊖ CDN 30-31 W 3
Whitehorse ☆ • CDN 20-21 X 6
Whitehorse o USA (SD) 260-261 F 1
White Horse Pass ▲ USA (NV) 246-247 L 3
Whitehouse o USA (TX) 264-265 J 6
White Island ⌒ CDN 36-37 G 2
White Island ▲ NZ 182 F 2
White Lady • NAM 216-217 C 10
White Lake ⊖ AUS 176-177 F 2
White Lake ⊖ CDN (ONT) 236-237 C 4
White Lake ⊖ CDN (ONT) 238-239 J 3
White Lake o USA (SD) 260-261 H 3
White Lake o USA (WI) 270-271 K 5
White Lake ⊖ USA (LA) 268-269 H 7
White Lakes o USA (NM) 256-257 K 3
Whitelaw o CDN 32-33 L 3
Whitelock Mountains ▲ USA 256-257 F 6
Whitely o USA (TX) 264-265 C 4
Whiteman Range ▲ PNG 183 E 3
Whitemark o AUS 180-181 K 6
White Mountain o USA 20-21 J 4
White Mountains ▲ USA 20-21 R 4
White Mountains ▲ USA 248-249 F 2
White Mountains ▲ USA 278-279 K 4
Whitemouth o CDN (MAN) 234-235 H 5
Whitemud River ~ CDN 32-33 L 3
White Nile = al-Bahr al-Abyad ~ SUD 200-201 F 5
White Nile = Bahr al-Jabal ~ SUD 206-207 K 4
White Oak Creek ~ USA 264-265 K 5
White Oak Lake < USA (AR) 276-277 B 7
White Oak Mountain ▲ USA 276-277 B 6
White Oaks o USA (NM) 256-257 K 5
White Otter Lake ⊖ CDN (ONT) 234-235 M 5
White Owl o USA (SD) 260-261 D 2
White Pass ▲ USA (WA) 244-245 D 4
White Pigeon o USA (MI) 272-273 D 6
White Pine o USA (MI) 270-271 J 4
White Pine o USA (TN) 282-283 D 4
White Plains o LB 202-203 E 6
White Plains o USA (NY) 280-281 N 3
White River o CDN (ONT) 236-237 C 4
White River ~ CDN 20-21 U 5
White River ~ CDN 230-231 O 3
White River ~ CDN 236-237 B 4
Whiteriver o USA (AZ) 256-257 F 5
White River o USA (SD) 260-261 F 3
White River o USA (SD) 260-261 G 3
White River ~ USA 244-245 D 3
White River ~ USA 246-247 K 5
White River ~ USA 254-255 G 3
White River ~ USA 256-257 E 5
White River ~ USA 264-265 C 5
White River ~ USA 272-273 C 4
White River ~ USA 274-275 M 4
White River ~ USA 274-275 N 4
White River ~ USA 274-275 L 6
White River ~ USA 274-275 M 5
White River ~ USA 276-277 D 5
White River ~ USA 278-279 J 5
White River Junction o USA (VT) 278-279 J 5
White River Lake < USA (TX) 264-265 C 5
White River National Wildlife Refuge ⊥ USA (AR) 276-277 D 6
White Rock o CDN (BC) 230-231 G 4
White Rock o USA (NM) 256-257 J 3
White Rock o USA (SD) 260-261 K 1
Whitesail Lake ⊖ CDN (BC) 228-229 G 3
White Salmon o USA (WA) 244-245 D 5
Whitesand River ~ CDN 232-233 Q 4
White Sands Missile Range xx USA (NM) 256-257 J 5
White Sands National Monument ∴ USA (NM) 256-257 J 6
White Sands Space Harbor xx USA (NM) 256-257 J 5
Whitesboro o USA (TX) 264-265 H 5
Whites Brook o CDN (NB) 240-241 H 3
Whitesburg o USA (GA) 284-285 F 3
Whitesburg o USA (KY) 276-277 M 3
Whites City o USA (NM) 256-257 L 6
White Sea = Beloe more ≈ 88-89 O 4
White Sea-Baltic Canal = Belomorsko-Baltijskij kanal < RUS 88-89 N 4
White Settlement o USA (TX) 264-265 G 6
Whiteshell Provincial Park ⊥ •• CDN (MAN) 234-235 H 4
Whiteside, Canal ≈ 80 E 6
White Signal o USA (NM) 256-257 G 6
White Springs o USA (FL) 286-287 G 1
White Spruce o CDN (SAS) 232-233 Q 4
Whitespruce Rapids ~ CDN 30-31 T 6
White Star o USA (MI) 272-273 E 4
Whitestone River ~ CDN 20-21 V 4
White Strait ≈ 36-37 O 3
White Sulphur Springs o USA (MT) 250-251 J 5
White Sulphur Springs o USA (WV) 280-281 F 6
White Swan o USA (WA) 244-245 E 4
Whiteswan Lake Provincial Park ⊖ CDN (BC) 230-231 O 3
Whitetail o USA (MT) 250-251 O 3
White Tank Mountains ▲ USA 256-257 C 5
White Umfolozi ~ ZA 220-221 K 4
Whiteville o USA (NC) 282-283 J 6
Whiteville o USA (TN) 276-277 F 5
White Volta ~ GH 202-203 K 5
Whitewater o CDN (MAN) 234-235 C 5
Whitewater o USA (CO) 254-255 G 5
Whitewater o USA (KS) 262-263 J 7
Whitewater o USA (MT) 250-251 M 3
Whitewater o USA (WI) 274-275 K 2
Whitewater Baldy ▲ USA (NM) 256-257 G 5
Whitewater Bay ≈ 286-287 H 6
Whitewater Creek ~ CDN 232-233 L 6
Whitewater Lake ⊖ CDN (ONT) 234-235 O 4
Whitewater River ~ USA 276-277 F 3
White Woman Creek ~ USA 262-263 E 6
Whitewood o AUS 178-179 G 1
Whitewood o CDN (SAS) 232-233 Q 5
Whitewood o USA (SD) 260-261 C 2
Whitewright o USA (TX) 264-265 H 5
Whitfield o AUS 180-181 J 4
Whitharral o USA (TX) 264-265 B 5
Whitianga o NZ 182 E 2
Whiting o USA (IN) 274-275 L 3
Whiting River ~ USA 32-33 D 2
Whitkow o CDN (SAS) 232-233 L 3
Whitla o CDN (ALB) 232-233 G 6
Whitlash o USA (MT) 250-251 H 3
Whitley City o USA (KY) 276-277 L 4
Whitman o USA (NE) 262-263 E 2
Whitmann Mission National Historic Site • USA (WA) 244-245 G 4
Whitmire o USA (SC) 284-285 J 2
Whitmore Mountains ▲ ARK 16 E 0
Whitney o CDN (ONT) 238-239 G 3
Whitney o USA (NE) 262-263 C 2
Whitney o USA (TX) 266-267 K 2
Whitney, Lake < USA (TX) 264-265 G 6
Whitney, Lake < USA (TX) 266-267 K 2
Whitney, Mount ▲ USA (CA) 248-249 F 3
Whitney Point o USA (NY) 278-279 F 6
Whitney Turn o JA 54-55 G 5
Whitsett o USA (TX) 266-267 J 5
Whitsunday Island ⌒ AUS 174-175 K 7
Whitsunday Island National Park ⊥ AUS 174-175 K 7
Whitsunday Passage ≈ 174-175 K 7
Whittemore o USA (MI) 272-273 F 3
Whittier o USA 20-21 Q 6
Whittle, Cap ▲ CDN (QUE) 242-243 H 2
Whittlesea o AUS 180-181 H 4
Whittlesea o ZA 220-221 H 6
Whitula Creek ~ AUS 178-179 G 3
Whitwell o USA (TN) 276-277 K 5
Whitworth o CDN (QUE) 240-241 F 3
Wholdaia Lake ⊖ CDN 30-31 R 5
Whonnock o CDN (BC) 230-231 G 4
Why o USA (AZ) 256-257 C 6
Whyalla o AUS 180-181 D 2
Whycocomagh o CDN (NS) 240-241 O 5
Whycocomagh Indian Reserve X • CDN (NS) 240-241 O 5
Whymper, Mount ▲ CDN (BC) 230-231 E 5
Wiang Chai o THA 142-143 L 6
Wiang Sa o THA 142-143 M 6
Wiang Sa o THA 158-159 E 6
Wiarton o CDN (ONT) 238-239 D 4
Wiawer o EAU 212-213 D 2
Wia-Wia, National Reservaat ⊥ SME 62-63 G 2
Wiawso o GH 202-203 J 6
Wibaux o USA (MT) 250-251 P 5
Wichaway Nunataks ▲ ARK 16 E 0
Wichita o USA (KS) 262-263 J 7
Wichita Falls o USA (TX) 264-265 F 5
Wichita Mountains ▲ USA 264-265 F 4
Wichita Mountains National Wildlife Refuge • USA (OK) 264-265 F 4
Wichita River ~ USA 264-265 F 5
Wichita River, North ~ USA 264-265 E 5
Wichita River, South ~ USA 264-265 E 5
Wick o GB 90-91 F 2
Wickenburg o• USA (AZ) 256-257 C 5
Wickepin o AUS 176-177 D 6
Wickersham Dome ▲ USA 20-21 Q 4
Wickes o USA (AR) 276-277 A 6
Wickett o USA (TX) 266-267 E 2
Wickham o AUS 172-173 C 6
Wickham, Cape ▲ AUS 180-181 G 5
Wickham River ~ AUS 172-173 K 4
Wickliffe o USA (KY) 276-277 F 4
Wicklow = Cill Mhantáin ☆ IRL 90-91 D 5
Wicklow Mountains ▲ IRL 90-91 D 5
Wide Bay ≈ 22-23 S 4
Wide Bay ≈ 183 G 3
Widen o USA (WV) 280-281 F 5
Widener o USA (AR) 276-277 E 5
Wide Opening ≈ 54-55 F 2
Wide Ruins o USA (AZ) 256-257 F 3
Widgeegoara Creek ~ AUS 178-179 J 5
Widgee Mountain ▲ AUS 178-179 M 4
Widi, Kepulauan ⌒ RI 164-165 L 4
Widjefjorden ≈ 84-85 J 3
Wi Do ⌒ ROK 150-151 F 10
Widyān, al- ∴ 130-131 G 1
Wielbark o PL 92-93 Q 2
Wieliczka o••• PL 92-93 Q 4
Wieluń o• PL 92-93 P 3
Wien ★•• A 92-93 O 4
Wiener Neustadt o A 92-93 O 5
Wieprz ~ PL 92-93 R 3
Wierden o NL 92-93 J 2
Wiesbaden ☆• D 92-93 K 3
Wieskirche •• D 92-93 L 5
Wiga Hill ▲ WAN 204-205 K 3
Wiggins o USA (CO) 254-255 L 3
Wiggins o USA (MS) 268-269 L 6
Wigh, Al o LAR 192-193 F 5
Wignes Lake ⊖ CDN 30-31 R 5
Wigwam River ~ CDN 230-231 P 4
Wigwascence Lake ⊖ CDN (ONT) 234-235 O 2
Wikieup o USA (AZ) 256-257 B 4
Wikki warm Spring ~ • WAN 204-205 J 4
Wik'ro o ETH 200-201 J 6
Wikwemikong o CDN (ONT) 238-239 D 3
Wikwemikong Indian Reserve X CDN (ONT) 238-239 D 3
Wilber o USA (NE) 262-263 K 4
Wilberforce o CDN (ONT) 238-239 G 3
Wilberforce, Cape ▲ AUS 174-175 D 2
Wilbert o CDN (SAS) 232-233 J 3
Wilbrunga Range ▲ AUS 172-173 J 6
Wilbur o USA (WA) 244-245 G 3
Wilburton o USA (OK) 264-265 J 4
Wilcannia o AUS 178-179 G 6
Wilcock, Península ⌣ RCH 80 C 5
Wilcox o CDN (SAS) 232-233 O 5
Wilcox o USA (NE) 262-263 G 4
Wildcat Hill ▲ CDN (SAS) 232-233 Q 2
Wildcat Hill Wilderness Area ⊥ CDN (SAS) 232-233 P 2
Wildcat Peak ▲ USA (NV) 246-247 J 4
Wildcat River ~ USA 274-275 M 4
Wild Cove o CDN (NFL) 242-243 M 3
Wild Cove Pond ⊖ CDN (NFL) 242-243 M 3
Wilder o USA (ID) 252-253 B 3
Wilderness Corner o USA (VA) 280-281 J 5
Wilderville o USA (OR) 244-245 B 8
Wildhay River ~ CDN 228-229 Q 3
Wild Horse o CDN (ALB) 232-233 H 6
Wild Horse o USA (CO) 254-255 N 5
Wild Horse o USA (NV) 246-247 K 2
Wildhorse Creek ~ USA 264-265 G 4
Wild Lake ⊖ USA 20-21 P 3
Wildman Lagoon o AUS 172-173 K 2
Wildorado o USA (TX) 264-265 B 3
Wild Rice River ~ USA 270-271 B 3
Wild Rogue Wilderness Area ⊥ USA (OR) 244-245 B 8
Wildrose Station o USA (CA) 248-249 G 3
Wildwood o CDN (ALB) 232-233 C 2
Wildwood o USA (FL) 286-287 G 3
Wildwood o USA (NJ) 280-281 M 5
Wilge ~ ZA 220-221 J 3
Wilgus o USA (OH) 280-281 D 5
Wilhelm, Mount ▲•• PNG 183 C 3
Wilhelmina Gebergte ▲ SME 62-63 F 4
Wilhelmøya ⌒ N 84-85 M 3
Wilhelm-Pieck-Stadt Guben = Guben o D 92-93 N 3
Wilhelmshaven o D 92-93 K 2
Wilhelmstal o NAM 216-217 D 10
Wilhoit o USA (AZ) 256-257 C 4
Wilkes o ARK 16 G 12
Wilkes-Barre o USA (PA) 280-281 L 2
Wilkes Fracture Zone ≃ 14-15 R 8
Wilkes Land ∴ ARK 16 F 12
Wilkes Rise ≃ 222-223 E 2
Wilkie o CDN (SAS) 232-233 K 3
Wilkinson Lakes ⊖ AUS 176-177 M 4
Wilkins Strait ≈ 24-25 P 1
Will, Mount ▲ CDN 32-33 F 3
Willacoochee o USA (GA) 284-285 G 5
Willamette River ~ USA 244-245 C 6
Willamette River ~ USA 244-245 B 7

Wel Jara — Willamette River 411

Willandra Creek ~ **AUS** 180-181 H 2
Willandra Lakes Region ⊥ ··· **AUS** 180-181 H 2
Willandra National Park ⊥ **AUS** 180-181 H 2
Willapa Bay ≈ 40-41 B 2
Willapa Bay ≈ 244-245 A 4
Willapa Hills ▲ **USA** 244-245 B 4
Willard o **USA** (MO) 276-277 B 3
Willard o **USA** (NM) 256-257 J 4
Willard o **USA** (OH) 280-281 D 2
Willare Bridge Roadhouse o **AUS** 172-173 F 4
Willcox o **USA** (AZ) 256-257 F 6
Willcox Playa ⊂⊃ **USA** (AZ) 256-257 F 6
Willem Pretorius Wildtuin ⊥ **ZA** 220-221 H 4
Willemstad ☆ **NA** 60-61 G 1
Willen o **CDN** (MAN) 234-235 B 4
Willenberg o **PL** 92-93 Q 2
Willeroo o **AUS** 172-173 K 3
Willet o **USA** (NY) 278-279 F 6
William, Mount ▲ **AUS** 180-181 G 4
William A. Switzer Provincial Park ⊥ **CDN** (ALB) 228-229 R 3
William "Bill" Dannelly Reservoir ⊂⊃ **USA** (AL) 284-285 C 4
Williambury o **AUS** 176-177 C 1
William Creek o **AUS** 178-179 D 5
Williamez Peninsula ⌣ **PNG** 183 F 3
William H. Harsha Lake < **USA** (OH) 280-281 B 4
William Lambert, Mount ▲ **AUS** 176-177 H 2
William Point ▲ **CDN** 30-31 P 6
William River ~ **CDN** 30-31 P 6
Williams o **AUS** 176-177 D 6
Williams o **USA** (AZ) 256-257 C 3
Williams o **USA** (CA) 246-247 C 4
Williams o **USA** (MN) 270-271 D 2
Williamsburg o **USA** (IA) 274-275 G 3
Williamsburg o· **USA** (VA) 280-281 K 6
Williams Island ⌒ **BS** 54-55 F 2
Williams Junction o **USA** (AR) 276-277 C 6
Williams Lake o **CDN** (BC) 228-229 M 4
Williamson o **USA** (WV) 280-281 D 6
Williams Peninsula ⌣ **CDN** 36-37 R 3
Williamsport o **CDN** (NFL) 242-243 M 2
Williamsport o **USA** (AK) 22-23 U 3
Williamsport o **USA** (MD) 280-281 J 4
Williamsport o **USA** (PA) 280-281 J 2
Williams River ~ **AUS** 174-175 F 7
Williamston o **USA** (MI) 272-273 E 5
Williamston o **USA** (NC) 282-283 K 5
William's Town o **BS** 54-55 H 3
Williamstown o **USA** (KY) 276-277 L 2
Williamstown o **USA** (MA) 278-279 H 6
Williamsville o **USA** (MO) 276-277 E 4
William Weatherford Monument · **USA** (AL) 284-285 C 5
Willibert, Mount ▲ **CDN** 32-33 E 3
Willimantic o **USA** (CT) 280-281 O 2
Willingdon o **CDN** (ALB) 232-233 F 2
Willis o **USA** (NE) 262-263 K 2
Willis Group ⌒ **AUS** 174-175 L 5
Williston o **USA** (FL) 286-287 G 2
Williston o **USA** (ND) 258-259 D 3
Williston o **USA** (SC) 284-285 J 3
Williston o **ZA** 220-221 E 5
Williston Lake ⊂⊃ **CDN** 32-33 J 4
Willits o **USA** (CA) 246-247 B 4
Willmar o **CDN** (SAS) 232-233 Q 6
Willmar o **USA** (MN) 270-271 C 5
Willmore Wilderness Provincial Park ⊥· **CDN** (ALB) 228-229 P 3
Willochra ∴ **AUS** 180-181 E 2
Willochra Creek ~ **AUS** 178-179 D 6
Willow o **USA** 20-21 Q 6
Willow o **USA** (OK) 264-265 E 3
Willowbrook o **CDN** (SAS) 232-233 Q 4
Willow Bunch o **CDN** (SAS) 232-233 N 6
Willow Bunch Lake ⊂⊃ **CDN** (SAS) 232-233 N 6
Willow City o **USA** (ND) 258-259 G 3
Willow Creek o **CDN** (SAS) 232-233 J 6
Willow Creek ~ **CDN** 232-233 E 5
Willow Creek o **USA** (CA) 246-247 B 3
Willow Creek o **USA** (OR) 244-245 H 6
Willow Creek ~ **USA** 244-245 F 5
Willow Creek ~ **USA** 250-251 H 3
Willow Creek Pass ▲ **USA** (CO) 254-255 J 3
Willowdale o **USA** (OR) 244-245 E 6
Willow Lake ⊂⊃ **CDN** 30-31 K 4
Willowlake River ~ **CDN** 30-31 H 4
Willowmore o **ZA** 220-221 F 6
Willow Point o **CDN** (BC) 230-231 M 4
Willowra o **AUS** 172-173 L 6
Willowra Aboriginal Land Trust X **AUS** 172-173 L 6
Willow Ranch o **USA** (CA) 246-247 E 2
Willow River ~ **CDN** 32-33 N 4
Willow River ~ **CDN** 228-229 M 3
Willow River o **USA** (MN) 270-271 F 4
Willows o **CDN** (SAS) 232-233 N 6
Willows o **USA** (CA) 246-247 C 4
Willow Springs o **USA** (MO) 276-277 D 4
Willowvale o **ZA** 220-221 J 6
Willow Valley o **USA** (IN) 274-275 M 6
Will Rogers Memorial · **USA** (OK) 264-265 J 2
Wills, Lake ⊂⊃ **AUS** 172-173 J 6
Willsboro o **USA** (NY) 278-279 H 4
Wills Creek ~ **AUS** 178-179 E 2
Wills Creek Lake ⊂⊃ **USA** (OH) 280-281 E 3
Wills Point o **USA** (TX) 264-265 J 6
Willwood o **USA** (WY) 252-253 K 2
Wilma o **USA** (FL) 286-287 E 1
Wilmer o **USA** (AL) 284-285 B 6
Wilmington o **AUS** 180-181 E 2
Wilmington o **USA** (DE) 280-281 L 4
Wilmington o **USA** (IL) 274-275 K 3
Wilmington o **USA** (OH) 280-281 C 4
Wilmington o **USA** (VT) 278-279 J 6
Wilmington o· **USA** (NC) 282-283 K 6
Wilmore o **USA** (KY) 276-277 L 3
Wilmot o **USA** (AR) 276-277 D 7
Wilmot o **USA** (OH) 280-281 E 3
Wilmot o **USA** (SD) 260-261 K 1
Wilpattu National Park ⊥ **CL** 140-141 H 6
Wilpena Creek ~ **AUS** 178-179 E 6
Wilpena Pound · **AUS** 178-179 E 6
Wilsall o **USA** (MT) 250-251 J 6
Wilshaw Ridge ≃ 224 B 7
Wilson ∴ **AUS** 178-179 E 6
Wilson o **CDN** (ALB) 232-233 F 6
Wilson o **USA** (AR) 276-277 E 5
Wilson o **USA** (NC) 282-283 K 5
Wilson o **USA** (OK) 264-265 G 4
Wilson o **USA** (TX) 264-265 C 5
Wilson, Monte ▲ **PE** 64-65 D 9
Wilson, Mount ▲ **CDN** 30-31 E 4
Wilson, Mount ▲ **USA** (OR) 244-245 D 5
Wilson Bay ≈ 30-31 X 4
Wilson Buff Old Telegraph Station · **AUS** 176-177 K 5
Wilson Creek o **USA** (WA) 244-245 F 3
Wilson Creek ~ **USA** 244-245 G 3
Wilson Island ⌒ **CDN** (ONT) 234-235 Q 6
Wilson Island ⌒ **IND** 140-141 L 3
Wilson Lake ⊂⊃ **USA** (KS) 262-263 H 6
Wilson Lake < **USA** (AL) 284-285 C 2
Wilson River ~ **AUS** 172-173 H 4
Wilson River ~ **AUS** 178-179 G 4
Wilson River ~ **CDN** 30-31 X 4
Wilson's Creek National Battlefield Park ∴· **USA** (MO) 276-277 B 3
Wilson's Mills o **CDN** (QUE) 238-239 O 2
Wilsons Promontory National Park ⊥ **AUS** 180-181 J 5
Wilsonville o **USA** (NE) 262-263 F 4
Wilton o **USA** (AR) 276-277 A 7
Wilton o **USA** (ME) 278-279 L 4
Wilton o **USA** (ND) 258-259 G 4
Wilton o **USA** (WI) 270-271 H 7
Wiltondale o **CDN** (NFL) 242-243 L 3
Wilton River ~ **AUS** 174-175 C 4
Wiluna o **AUS** 176-177 F 3
Wimbledon o **USA** (ND) 258-259 J 4
Wimborne o **CDN** (ALB) 232-233 E 4
Wimico, Lake ⊂⊃ **USA** (FL) 286-287 D 2
Wimmera ⌣ **AUS** 180-181 G 4
Wimmera River ~ **AUS** 180-181 F 4
Winamac o **USA** (IN) 274-275 M 3
Winam Bay ≈ 212-213 E 4
Winburg o **ZA** 220-221 H 4
Winchelsea o **AUS** 180-181 G 5
Winchester o **CDN** (ONT) 238-239 K 3
Winchester o· **GB** 90-91 G 6
Winchester o **USA** (ID) 250-251 C 5
Winchester o **USA** (IL) 274-275 H 5
Winchester o **USA** (IN) 274-275 O 4
Winchester o **USA** (KY) 276-277 L 2
Winchester o **USA** (OR) 244-245 B 7
Winchester o **USA** (TN) 276-277 J 5
Winchester o **USA** (VA) 280-281 H 4
Winchester o **USA** (WI) 270-271 J 4
Winchester o **USA** (WY) 252-253 K 3
Winchester Bay o **USA** (OR) 244-245 A 7
Windabout Lake ⊂⊃ **AUS** 178-179 D 6
Windamere, Lake < **AUS** 180-181 K 2
Windarra Mine, Mount · **AUS** 176-177 G 4
Windber o **USA** (PA) 280-281 H 3
Wind Cave National Park ⊥ **USA** (SD) 260-261 C 3
Winder o **USA** (GA) 284-285 G 3
Winderie o **AUS** 176-177 C 2
Windermere o **CDN** (BC) 230-231 O 3
Windermere Lake ⊂⊃ **CDN** (ONT) 236-237 E 5
Windham o **USA** 32-33 D 3
Windhoek ★· **NAM** 216-217 D 11
Windidda o **AUS** 176-177 G 3
Windigo Bay ⊂⊃ **CDN** (ONT) 234-235 P 4
Windigo Lake ⊂⊃ **CDN** 34-35 L 4
Windigo Lake ⊂⊃ **CDN** (ONT) 234-235 M 2
Windigo River ~ **CDN** 34-35 L 4
Windigo River ~ **CDN** 234-235 M 2
Winding Stair Mountain ▲ **USA** 264-265 J 4
Windjana Gorge National Park ⊥ **AUS** 172-173 G 4
Windom o **USA** (MN) 270-271 C 7
Windom Peak ▲ **USA** (CO) 254-255 H 6
Windorah o **AUS** 178-179 G 3
Window on China · **RC** 156-157 M 4
Wind River ~ **CDN** 20-21 X 4
Wind River o **USA** (WY) 252-253 K 4
Wind River ~ **USA** 252-253 J 3
Wind River Indian Reservation X **USA** (WY) 252-253 J 3
Wind River Peak ▲ **USA** (WY) 252-253 J 4
Wind River Range ▲ **USA** 252-253 J 3
Windsor o **AUS** 176-177 E 4
Windsor o **CDN** (NFL) 242-243 N 4
Windsor o **CDN** (NS) 240-241 L 6
Windsor o **CDN** (ONT) 238-239 C 6
Windsor o **CDN** (QUE) 238-239 N 3
Windsor o **GB** 90-91 G 6
Windsor o **USA** (CO) 254-255 L 3
Windsor o **USA** (IL) 274-275 K 5
Windsor o **USA** (MA) 278-279 H 6
Windsor o **USA** (MO) 274-275 E 6
Windsor o **USA** (NC) 282-283 L 4
Windsor o **USA** (NH) 278-279 J 5
Windsor o **USA** (SC) 284-285 J 3
Windsor Ruins · **USA** (MS) 268-269 J 5
Windsorton o **ZA** 220-221 G 4
Windsorton Road o **ZA** 220-221 G 4
Windthorst o **CDN** (SAS) 232-233 Q 4
Windthorst o **USA** (TX) 264-265 F 5
Windward Islands ⌒ 56 E 4
Windy Bay ⊂⊃ **CDN** 30-31 M 5
Windy Corner ▲ **AUS** 176-177 H 1
Windygate o **CDN** (MAN) 234-235 E 5
Windygates o **CDN** (MAN) 234-235 E 5
Windy Harbour o **AUS** 176-177 D 7
Windy Lake ⊂⊃ **CDN** 30-31 T 5
Windy River ~ **CDN** 30-31 T 5
Winefred River ~ **CDN** 32-33 P 3
Winejok o **SUD** 206-207 H 4
Winesap o **USA** (WA) 244-245 E 3
Winfield o **CDN** (ALB) 232-233 D 3
Winfield o **CDN** (BC) 230-231 K 4
Winfield o **USA** (AL) 284-285 C 3
Winfield o **USA** (IA) 274-275 G 3
Winfield o **USA** (KS) 262-263 K 7
Wing o **USA** (ND) 258-259 G 4
Wingard o **CDN** (SAS) 232-233 M 3
Wingate o **USA** (TX) 264-265 D 6
Wingate Mountains ▲ **AUS** 172-173 K 3
Winger o **USA** (MN) 270-271 C 3
Wingham o **AUS** 178-179 M 6
Wingham o **CDN** (ONT) 238-239 D 5
Wingham Island ⌒ **USA** 20-21 S 6
Wingon o **MYA** 142-143 J 4
Winifred o **USA** (MT) 250-251 K 4
Winifred, Lake ⊂⊃ **AUS** 172-173 F 7
Winiperu o **GUY** 62-63 E 2
Winisk o **CDN** 34-35 O 3
Winisk Lake ⊂⊃ **CDN** (ONT) 234-235 Q 2
Winisk River ~ **CDN** 34-35 O 3
Winisk River ~ **CDN** 234-235 P 2
Winisk River Provincial Park ⊥ **CDN** 34-35 N 4
Wink o **USA** (TX) 266-267 D 2
Winkelmann o **USA** (AZ) 256-257 E 5
Winkler o **CDN** (MAN) 234-235 F 5
Winlock o **USA** (WA) 244-245 C 4
Winneba o **GH** 202-203 K 7
Winnebago o **USA** (MN) 270-271 D 7
Winnebago o **USA** (NE) 262-263 K 2
Winnebago, Lake ⊂⊃ **USA** (WI) 270-271 K 6
Winnebago Indian Reservation X **USA** (NE) 262-263 K 2
Winnecke Creek ~ **AUS** 172-173 K 5
Winnemucca o **USA** (NV) 246-247 H 3
Winnemucca Lake ⊂⊃ **USA** (NV) 246-247 F 3
Winnepegosis o **CDN** (MAN) 234-235 D 3
Winner o **USA** (SD) 260-261 G 3
Winnett o **USA** (MT) 250-251 L 5
Winnfield o **USA** (LA) 268-269 H 5
Winnibigoshish Lake ⊂⊃ **USA** (MN) 270-271 D 3
Winnie o **USA** (TX) 268-269 F 7
Winning o **AUS** 172-173 B 7
Winnipeg ☆· **CDN** (MAN) 234-235 F 5
Winnipeg, Lake ⊂⊃ **CDN** (MAN) 234-235 G 4
Winnipeg Beach o **CDN** (MAN) 234-235 G 4
Winnipesaukee, Lake ⊂⊃ **USA** (NH) 278-279 K 5
Winnsboro o **USA** (LA) 268-269 J 4
Winnsboro o **USA** (SC) 284-285 J 2
Winnsboro o **USA** (TX) 264-265 J 6
Winona o **USA** (AZ) 256-257 D 3
Winona o **USA** (KS) 262-263 E 5
Winona o **USA** (MI) 270-271 K 4
Winona o **USA** (MN) 270-271 G 6
Winona o **USA** (MO) 276-277 D 3
Winona o **USA** (MS) 268-269 L 3
Winooski River ~ **USA** 278-279 J 4
Winschoten o **NL** 92-93 J 2
Winslow o **USA** (AR) 276-277 A 5
Winslow o **USA** (AZ) 256-257 E 3
Winsted o **USA** (CT) 280-281 N 2
Winston o **USA** (NM) 256-257 H 5
Winston o **USA** (OR) 244-245 B 7
Winston-Salem o **USA** (NC) 282-283 G 4
Winter o **CDN** (SAS) 232-233 J 3
Winterberg o **D** 92-93 K 3
Winterberge ▲ **ZA** 220-221 G 6
Winter Brook o **CDN** (NFL) 242-243 P 4
Winter Garden o **USA** (FL) 286-287 H 3
Winter Harbour ≈ 24-25 R 3
Winter Harbour o **CDN** (BC) 230-231 A 3
Winterhaven o **USA** (CA) 248-249 K 7
Winter Haven o **USA** (FL) 286-287 H 3
Wintering Lake ⊂⊃ **CDN** (ONT) 234-235 Q 5
Winter Island ⌒ **CDN** 24-25 e 7
Winter Lake ⊂⊃ **CDN** 30-31 N 3
Winterland o **CDN** (NFL) 242-243 N 5
Winter Park o **USA** (CO) 254-255 K 4
Winter Park o **USA** (FL) 286-287 H 3
Winterport o **USA** (ME) 278-279 N 4
Winters o **USA** (CA) 246-247 D 5
Winters o **USA** (TX) 266-267 H 2
Winterset o **USA** (IA) 274-275 D 3
Winter Springs o **USA** (FL) 286-287 H 3
Winterthur o **CH** 92-93 K 5
Winterton o **ZA** 220-221 J 4
Winterveld ⩦ **ZA** 220-221 F 5
Winterville o **USA** (NC) 282-283 K 5
Winterville State Historic Site · **USA** (MS) 268-269 J 3
Winthrop o **USA** (ME) 278-279 M 4
Winthrop o **USA** (MN) 270-271 D 6
Winthrop o **USA** (WA) 244-245 E 2
Winton o **AUS** 178-179 G 2
Winton o **NZ** 182 B 7
Winton o **USA** (MN) 270-271 G 3
Winton o **USA** (NC) 282-283 L 4
Wintua o **VAN** 184 II a 3
Winyah Bay ≈ 284-285 L 3
Winyaw o **MYA** 158-159 E 3
Wipim o **PNG** 183 B 5
Wiradesa o **RI** 168 C 3
Wirawila o **CL** 140-141 J 7
Wirliyajarrayi Aboriginal Land X **AUS** 172-173 L 6
Wirmaf o **RI** 166-167 F 4
Wirrabara o **AUS** 180-181 E 2
Wirrulla o **AUS** 180-181 C 2
Wiscasset o **USA** (ME) 278-279 M 4
Wisconsin ◘ **USA** 270-271 G 6
Wisconsin Dells o· **USA** (WI) 274-275 J 7
Wisconsin Rapids o **USA** (WI) 270-271 J 6
Wisconsin River ~ **USA** 270-271 J 5
Wisconsin River ~ **USA** 274-275 H 1
Wisdom o **USA** (MT) 250-251 F 6
Wisdom, Lake ⊂⊃ **PNG** 183 D 3
Wisemans Ferry o **AUS** 180-181 L 2
Wisemen o **USA** 20-21 P 3
Wise River o **USA** (MT) 250-251 F 6
Wiseton o **CDN** (SAS) 232-233 L 4
Wishart o **CDN** (SAS) 232-233 P 4
Wishaw o **GB** 90-91 F 4
Wishek o **USA** (ND) 258-259 H 5
Wisil o **SP** 208-209 J 6
Wisła o **PL** (BIE) 92-93 P 4
Wisła ~ **PL** 92-93 P 1
Wiślany, Zalew ≈ 92-93 P 1
Wisłoka ~ **PL** 92-93 Q 3
Wismar o· **D** 92-93 L 2
Wismar o **GUY** 62-63 E 2
Wisner o **USA** (LA) 268-269 J 5
Wisner o **USA** (NE) 262-263 K 3
Wistaria o **CDN** (BC) 228-229 H 3
Wister o **USA** (OK) 264-265 K 4
Wister Lake < **USA** (OK) 264-265 K 4
Witagron o **SME** 62-63 F 3
Witbank o **ZA** 220-221 J 2
Witbooisvlei o **NAM** 220-221 D 2
Witchecan Lake ⊂⊃ **CDN** (SAS) 232-233 L 2
Witchekan Lake Indian Reservation X **CDN** (SAS) 232-233 L 2
Witfonteinrand ▲ **ZA** 220-221 H 2
Withfish River ~ **CDN** 236-237 H 4
Withington, Mount ▲ **USA** (NM) 256-257 H 5
Withlacoochee River ~ **USA** 284-285 G 6
Witjira National Park ⊥ **AUS** 178-179 C 4
Wit Kei ~ **ZA** 220-221 H 5
Witkoppies ▲ **ZA** 220-221 J 3
Witkransnek ▲ **ZA** 220-221 G 5
Witless Bay o **CDN** (NFL) 242-243 Q 5
Witney o **GB** 90-91 G 6
Witputz o **NAM** 220-221 C 3
Witrivier o **ZA** 220-221 K 2
Witsand o **ZA** 220-221 E 7
Witt, De o **USA** (AR) 276-277 D 6
Witt, De o **USA** (IA) 274-275 H 3
Wittabrenna Creek ~ **AUS** 178-179 F 5
Witteberge ▲ **ZA** 220-221 H 4
Witteberge ▲ **ZA** 220-221 E 6
Witteberge ▲ **ZA** 220-221 F 6
Witteklip o **ZA** 220-221 G 6
Witten o **USA** (SD) 260-261 F 3
Wittenberg o **USA** (WI) 270-271 J 6
Wittenberge o **D** 92-93 L 2
Wittenoom o **AUS** 172-173 D 7
Wittenoom Gorge ⌣· **AUS** 172-173 D 7
Wittingen o **D** 92-93 L 2
Wittlich o **D** 92-93 J 4
Wittman o **USA** (AZ) 256-257 C 5
Witts Springs o **USA** (AR) 276-277 C 5
Wittstock o· **D** 92-93 M 2
Wittyah, Al o **LAR** 192-193 D 1
Witu o **EAK** 212-213 H 5
Witu o **PNG** 183 E 3
Witu Islands ⌒ **PNG** 183 E 3
Witvlei o **NAM** 216-217 E 11
Witwater o **NAM** 220-221 B 2
Witwater o **ZA** 220-221 D 5
Witwatersberge ▲ **NAM** 216-217 C 11
Witwatersrand ▲ **ZA** 220-221 H 2
Wivenhoe, Lake < **AUS** 178-179 M 4
Wizzard Breakers ⌒ **SY** 224 B 4
W.J. van Blommesteinmeer ⊂⊃ **SME** 62-63 G 3
Władysławowo o· **PL** 92-93 P 1
Wlingi o **RI** 168 E 4
Włocławek ☆· **PL** 92-93 P 2
Włodawa o **PL** 92-93 R 3
Włoszczowa o **PL** 92-93 P 3
Wobulenzi o **EAU** 212-213 D 3
Woburn o **CDN** (QUE) 240-241 E 5
Woden o **USA** (IA) 274-275 E 1
Woe o **GH** 202-203 L 7
Woëvre ⩦ **F** 90-91 K 7
Wofikehn o **LB** 202-203 G 7
Wogadjina Hill ▲ **AUS** 176-177 F 1
Woganakai o **PNG** 183 F 3
Wogerlin Hill ▲ **AUS** 176-177 D 6
Wohlthat Mountains = Wohlthatmassivet ▲ **ARK** 16 F 2
Woinui, Selat ≈ 166-167 H 2
Woitape o **PNG** 183 D 5
Wokam, Pulau ⌒ **RI** 166-167 H 4
Woko National Park ⊥ **AUS** 178-179 L 6
Wolbach o **USA** (NE) 262-263 H 3
Wolcott o **USA** (CO) 254-255 J 4
Wolcott o **USA** (NY) 278-279 E 5
Woleai Island ⌒ **FSM** 13 F 2
Woleu ~ **G** 210-211 C 3
Wolf o **USA** (OK) 264-265 E 4
Wolf, Isla ⌒ **EC** 64-65 B 9
Wolf, Volcán ▲ **EC** 64-65 B 9
Wolf Bay o **CDN** (QUE) 242-243 H 2
Wolf Creek ~ **AUS** 172-173 H 5
Wolf Creek o **USA** (MT) 250-251 G 5
Wolf Creek o **USA** (OR) 244-245 B 8
Wolf Creek o **USA** (TN) 282-283 E 5
Wolf Creek ~ **USA** 250-251 D 3
Wolf Creek ~ **USA** 264-265 D 2
Wolf Creek Meteorite Crater National Park ⊥ **AUS** 172-173 H 5
Wolf Creek Pass ▲ **USA** (CO) 254-255 J 6
Wolf Creek Reservoir ⊂⊃ **USA** (KS) 262-263 L 6
Wolfeboro o **USA** (NH) 278-279 K 5
Wolfe City o **USA** (TX) 264-265 H 5
Wolfe Island ⌒ **CDN** (ONT) 238-239 J 4
Wolfenbüttel o·· **D** 92-93 L 2
Wolfforth o **USA** (TX) 264-265 B 5
Wolf Hole o **USA** (AZ) 256-257 B 2
Wolf Lake ⊂⊃ **CDN** 20-21 Z 6
Wolf Lake o **USA** (IN) 274-275 N 3
Wolford o **USA** (ND) 258-259 H 3
Wolf Point o **USA** (MT) 250-251 O 3
Wolf Rapids ~ **CDN** 30-31 V 2
Wolf River ~ **CDN** 20-21 Y 6
Wolf River ~ **CDN** 232-233 B 2
Wolf River ~ **USA** 268-269 L 6
Wolf River ~ **USA** 270-271 J 5
Wolf River ~ **USA** 276-277 F 5
Wolf Rock, Pulau ⌒ **RI** 164-165 K 3
Wolfsburg o **D** 92-93 L 2
Wolfville o **CDN** (NS) 240-241 L 5
Wolgast o **D** 92-93 M 1
Wolgograd = Zarizyn ☆· **RUS** 96-97 D 9
Wolin ⌒ **PL** 92-93 N 2
Wolkefit Pass ▲ **ETH** 200-201 H 6
Wollaston, Islas ⌒ **RCH** 80 G 7
Wollaston Forland ⩦ **GRØ** 26-27 p 6
Wollaston Lake o **CDN** (SAS) 30-31 S 6
Wollaston Lake ⊂⊃ **CDN** (SAS) 34-35 E 2
Wollaston Peninsula ⌣ **CDN** 24-25 O 6
Wollemi National Park ⊥ **AUS** 180-181 L 2
Wollogorang o **AUS** 174-175 D 5
Wollomombi o **AUS** 178-179 M 6
Wollondilly River ~ **AUS** 180-181 L 3
Wollongong o **AUS** 180-181 L 3
Wolmaransstad o **ZA** 220-221 G 3
Wolo o· **RI** 166-167 K 3
Wologizi Range ⩦ **LB** 202-203 F 5
Wolong Daxiongmao Reserves ⊥ **VRC** 154-155 C 6
Wołów o **PL** 92-93 O 3
Wolowaru o **RI** 168 E 7
Wolseley o **CDN** (SAS) 232-233 P 5
Wolseley o **ZA** 220-221 D 6
Wolseley Bay o **CDN** (ONT) 238-239 E 2
Wolsey o **USA** (SD) 260-261 H 2
Wolstenholme, Cap ▲ **CDN** 36-37 L 3
Wolstenholme Fjord ≈ 26-27 Q 5
Wolstenholme Ø ⌒ **GRØ** 26-27 P 5
Wolsztyn o· **PL** 92-93 O 2
Wolverhampton o **GB** 90-91 F 5
Wolverine River ~ **CDN** 20-21 a 2
Wolverine River ~ **CDN** 30-31 V 6
Wolwefontein o **ZA** 220-221 G 6
Woman River o **CDN** (ONT) 236-237 F 5
Woman River ~ **CDN** 236-237 F 5
Wombil Downs o **AUS** 178-179 J 5
Wonderfontein o **ZA** 220-221 J 2
Wonder Gorge ⌣· **Z** 218-219 E 2
Wondinong o **AUS** 176-177 E 3
Wondiwoi, Pegunungan ▲ **RI** 166-167 H 3
Wonegizi Mountain ▲ **LB** 202-203 F 6
Wonenara o **PNG** 183 C 4
Wongalarroo Lake ⊂⊃ **AUS** 178-179 H 6
Wongan Hills o **AUS** 176-177 D 5
Wonganoo o **AUS** 176-177 F 3
Wonga Wongué o **G** 210-211 B 4
Wonga-Wongué, Parc National du ⊥ **G** 210-211 B 4
Wonga Wongué, Réserve de ⊥ **G** 210-211 B 4
Wongoondy Wheat Bin o **AUS** 176-177 C 4
Wŏnju o **ROK** 150-151 F 9
Wonnangatta River ~ **AUS** 180-181 J 4
Wono o **RI** 164-165 F 5
Wonogiri o **RI** 168 D 3
Wonoka o **AUS** 178-179 E 6
Wonosari o **RI** 168 D 3
Wonosobo o **RI** 168 C 3
Wonreli o **RI** 166-167 D 6
Wonsan o **KOR** 150-151 F 8
Wonthaggi o **AUS** 180-181 H 5
Wonyulgunna Hill ▲ **AUS** 176-177 E 2
Wood o **USA** (SD) 260-261 F 3
Wood, Isla ⌒ **RA** 78-79 H 5
Wood, Islas ⌒ **RCH** 80 F 7
Wood, Mount ▲ **USA** (MT) 250-251 K 6
Woodall Mountain ▲ **USA** (MS) 268-269 M 2
Woodanilling o **AUS** 176-177 D 6
Wood Bay ≈ 16 F 17
Wood Bay ≈ 24-25 G 6
Woodbine o **USA** (GA) 284-285 J 6
Woodbine o **USA** (IA) 274-275 C 3
Woodbridge o **AUS** 180-181 J 7
Woodbridge o· **GB** 90-91 H 5
Wood Buffalo National Park ⊥ ··· **CDN** 30-31 N 6
Wood Buffalo River ~ **CDN** 32-33 O 3
Woodburn o **AUS** 178-179 M 5
Woodburn o **USA** (IN) 274-275 O 3
Woodburn o **USA** (OR) 244-245 C 5
Woodburry o **USA** (GA) 284-285 F 4
Woodbury o **USA** (GA) 284-285 F 4
Woodbury o **USA** (TN) 276-277 J 5
Wood Creek ~ **CDN** 34-35 N 3
Woodenbong o **AUS** 178-179 M 5
Woodfjorden ≈ 84-85 H 3
Woodford o **AUS** 178-179 M 4
Woodfords o **USA** (CA) 246-247 F 5
Woodgate o **AUS** 178-179 M 3
Woodgreen o **AUS** 178-179 C 2
Wood Islands ⌒ **AUS** 172-173 G 4
Wood Islands o **CDN** (PEI) 240-241 N 5
Woodi Woodi Mining Centre · **AUS** 172-173 E 6
Woodlake o **USA** (CA) 248-249 E 3
Wood Lake o **USA** (NE) 262-263 F 2
Woodland o **USA** (CA) 246-247 D 5
Woodland o **USA** (ME) 278-279 O 3
Woodland o **USA** (TX) 264-265 J 5
Woodland o **USA** (WA) 244-245 C 5
Woodland Beach o **USA** (DE) 280-281 L 4
Woodland Caribou Provincial Park ⊥ **CDN** (ONT) 234-235 H 3
Woodland Park o **USA** (CO) 254-255 K 5
Woodlands o **AUS** 176-177 E 2
Woodlark Island = Murua Island ⌒ **PNG** 183 G 5
Woodlawn o **CDN** (ONT) 238-239 J 3
Woodleigh (Old Homestead) o **AUS** 176-177 C 3
Wood Mountain o **CDN** (SAS) 232-233 M 6
Wood Mountain ▲ **CDN** (SAS) 232-233 M 6
Woodnorth o **CDN** (MAN) 234-235 B 5
Woodridge o **CDN** (MAN) 234-235 G 5
Wood River ~ **CDN** 228-229 Q 4
Wood River ~ **CDN** 232-233 L 6
Wood River o **USA** (NE) 262-263 H 4
Wood River ~ **USA** 20-21 Q 4
Woodroffe, Mount ▲ **AUS** 176-177 L 3
Woodrow o **CDN** (SAS) 232-233 M 6
Woodrow o **USA** 20-21 Q 6
Woodruff o **USA** (SC) 284-285 H 2
Woodruff o **USA** (UT) 254-255 D 2
Woodruff o **USA** (WI) 270-271 J 5
Woodruff Lake ⊂⊃ **CDN** 30-31 R 5
Woods, Lake ⊂⊃ **AUS** 174-175 B 5
Woods, Lake of the ⊂⊃ **CDN** (ONT) 234-235 J 5
Woodsboro o **USA** (TX) 266-267 K 5
Woodsfield o **USA** (OH) 280-281 E 4
Woodside o **CDN** (MAN) 234-235 E 4
Woods Lake ⊂⊃ **CDN** 36-37 R 7
Woods Lake < **USA** (TN) 276-277 J 5
Woods Landing o **USA** (WY) 252-253 M 5
Woodson o **USA** (TX) 264-265 E 5
Woods Peak o **AUS** 174-175 H 5
Woodstock o **AUS** (QLD) 174-175 J 6
Woodstock o **AUS** (QLD) 178-179 F 2
Woodstock o **CDN** (NB) 240-241 H 4
Woodstock o **CDN** (ONT) 238-239 E 5
Woodstock o **USA** (AL) 284-285 C 3
Woodstock o **USA** (IL) 274-275 K 2
Woodstock o **USA** (NY) 278-279 G 6
Woodstock o **USA** (VA) 280-281 H 5
Woodstock o **USA** (VT) 278-279 J 5
Woodstock 23 Indian Reserve X· **CDN** (NB) 240-241 H 4
Woodstock Dam < **ZA** 220-221 J 4
Woodstown o **USA** (NJ) 280-281 L 4
Woodsville o **USA** (NH) 278-279 J 4
Woodville o **CDN** (ONT) 238-239 G 4
Woodville o **NZ** 182 E 4
Woodville o **USA** (AL) 284-285 D 2
Woodville o **USA** (FL) 286-287 E 1
Woodville o **USA** (MS) 268-269 J 5
Woodville o **USA** (OH) 280-281 C 2
Woodville o **USA** (TX) 268-269 F 6
Woodward o **USA** (IA) 274-275 E 3
Woodward o **USA** (OK) 264-265 E 2
Woodward o **USA** (SC) 284-285 J 2
Woodworth o **USA** (ND) 258-259 H 4
Woody Island ⌒ **USA** 22-23 U 4
Woody Island Coulee ~ **USA** 250-251 L 3
Woody Point o· **CDN** (NFL) 242-243 L 3
Woogi o **RI** 166-167 K 3
Wooi o **RI** 166-167 H 2
Woolfield o **AUS** 178-179 G 1
Woolgoolga o **AUS** 178-179 M 6
Wooli o **AUS** 178-179 M 5
Woollett, Lac ⊂⊃ **CDN** 38-39 H 3
Woolly Hollow State Park ⊥ **USA** (AR) 276-277 C 5
Woolner o **AUS** 172-173 K 2
Woolnorth Point ▲ **AUS** 180-181 H 6
Woolocutty o **AUS** 176-177 E 6
Woolyeenyer Hill ▲ **AUS** 176-177 F 6
Woomelang o **AUS** 180-181 G 3
Woomera o **AUS** 178-179 D 6
Woomerangee Hill ▲ **AUS** 176-177 B 3
Woomera Prohibited Area X **AUS** 178-179 B 6
Woonsocket o **USA** (RI) 278-279 K 7
Woonsocket o **USA** (SD) 260-261 H 2
Woorabinda o **AUS** 178-179 K 3
Wooramel River ~ **AUS** 176-177 C 2
Wooramel Roadhouse o **AUS** 176-177 C 2
Woorkabing Hill ▲ **AUS** 176-177 D 6
Woorndoo o **AUS** 180-181 G 4
Wooster o **USA** (OH) 280-281 E 3
Wopasali o **PNG** 183 C 4
Wopmay Lake ⊂⊃ **CDN** 30-31 L 3
Wopmay River ~ **CDN** 30-31 L 3
Woqooyi Galbeed ◘ **SP** 208-209 F 3
Woraksan National Park ⊥· **ROK** 150-151 G 9
Worcester ☆· **GB** 90-91 F 5
Worcester o **USA** (MA) 278-279 K 6
Worcester o **ZA** 220-221 D 6
Worcester Range ▲ **ARK** 16 F 17
Worden o **USA** (MT) 250-251 L 6
Worden o **USA** (OR) 244-245 D 8
Wordie Bay ≈ 28-29 D 2
Wordie Gletscher ⊂ **GRØ** 26-27 o 6
Wordsworth o **CDN** (SAS) 232-233 Q 6
Wori o **RI** 164-165 J 3
Worin o **PNG** 183 D 4
Workai, Pulau ⌒ **RI** 166-167 H 5
Work Channel ≈ 228-229 D 2
Workington o **GB** 90-91 F 4
Worland o **USA** (WY) 252-253 L 2
World's Largest Mineral Hot Springs · **USA** (WY) 252-253 K 3
Worms o· **D** 92-93 K 4
Wortham o **USA** (TX) 266-267 L 2
Worthington o **CDN** (ONT) 238-239 D 2
Worthington o **USA** (MN) 270-271 C 7
Worthington o **USA** (OH) 280-281 C 3
Worthville o **USA** (KY) 276-277 K 2
Wosi o **RI** 164-165 K 4
Wosimi o **RI** 166-167 H 3
Wosnesenski Island ⌒ **USA** 22-23 Q 5
Wostok o **CDN** (ALB) 232-233 F 2
Wosu o **RI** 164-165 G 5
Wotap, Pulau ⌒ **RI** 166-167 F 5
Wotu o **RI** 164-165 G 5
Woumbou o **CAM** 206-207 B 6
Wounded Knee o **USA** (SD) 260-261 D 3
Wounded Knee Battlefield · **USA** (SD) 260-261 D 3
Wour o **TCH** 198-199 G 2
Wouri ~ **CAM** 204-205 H 6
Wouri, Wādī ~ **TCH** 198-199 G 2
Wowoni, Pulau ⌒ **RI** 164-165 H 6
Woyamdero Plain ⩦ **EAK** 212-213 G 3
Wozhang Shan ▲ **VRC** 156-157 C 4
Wrangel Island = Vrangelja, ostrov ⌒ **RUS** 112-113 U 1
Wrangell o **USA** 32-33 D 3
Wrangell, Cape ▲ **USA** 22-23 C 6
Wrangell Island ⌒ **USA** 32-33 D 3
Wrangell Mountains ▲ **USA** 20-21 T 6
Wrangell-St. Elias N.P. & Preserve & Glacier Bay N.P. ⊥ ··· **USA** 20-21 T 6
Wray o **USA** (CO) 254-255 N 3
Wreck Cove o **CDN** (NS) 240-241 P 4
Wren o **USA** (OR) 244-245 B 6
Wrens o **USA** (GA) 284-285 H 3
Wrentham o **CDN** (ALB) 232-233 F 6
Wrexham o **GB** 90-91 F 5
Wriedijk o **SME** 62-63 G 3
Wright o **RP** 160-161 F 7
Wright o **USA** (KS) 262-263 G 7
Wright o **USA** (WY) 252-253 N 3
Wright Brothers National Memorial · **USA** (NC) 282-283 M 5
Wright City o **USA** (OK) 264-265 J 4
Wrightson, Mount ▲ **USA** (AZ) 256-257 E 7
Wrightsville o **USA** (AR) 276-277 C 6
Wrightsville o **USA** (GA) 284-285 H 4
Wrightsville Beach o **USA** (NC) 282-283 K 6
Wrightwood o **USA** (CA) 248-249 G 5
Wrigley o **CDN** 30-31 H 4
Wrigley Gulf ≈ 16 F 24
Writing Rock ∴ **USA** (ND) 258-259 D 3
Wrocław ☆·· **PL** 92-93 O 3
Wrotham Park o **AUS** 174-175 G 5
Wrottesley, Cape ▲ **CDN** 24-25 L 3
Wrottesley Inlet ≈ 24-25 Y 5
Wroxton o **CDN** (SAS) 232-233 R 4
Września o **PL** 92-93 O 2
Wschowa o· **PL** 92-93 O 3
Wu'an o **VRC** 154-155 J 3
Wuasa o **RI** 164-165 G 4
Wubin o **AUS** 176-177 D 5
Wubu o **VRC** 154-155 G 3
Wuchang o **VRC** (HEI) 150-151 F 5
Wuchang o **VRC** (HUB) 154-155 J 6
Wuchiu Yü ⌒ **RC** 156-157 L 4
Wuchuan o **VRC** (GDG) 156-157 G 6
Wuchuan o **VRC** (GZH) 156-157 E 2
Wuchuan o **VRC** (NMZ) 148-149 K 7
Wuda o **VRC** 154-155 E 2
Wudalianchi o **VRC** (HEI) 150-151 F 3
Wudalianchi · **VRC** (HEI) 150-151 F 3
Wudang Shan ▲ ··· **VRC** 154-155 G 5
Wudang Shan ⊥ **VRC** (HUB) 154-155 G 5
Wudangshan · **VRC** 154-155 G 5
Wudang Zhao · **VRC** 154-155 G 1
Wudaogou o **VRC** 150-151 F 2
Wuday'ah o **KSA** 132-133 E 5
Wudil o **WAN** 204-205 H 3
Wuding o **VRC** 156-157 C 4
Wuding He ~ **VRC** 154-155 F 2
Wudu o **VRC** 154-155 D 5
Wufeng o **VRC** 154-155 G 6
Wugang o **VRC** 156-157 G 3
Wugong o **VRC** 154-155 F 4
Wugong Ci · **VRC** 156-157 G 7
Wugong Shan ▲ **VRC** 156-157 J 3
Wuhai o **VRC** 154-155 E 2
Wuhan ☆· **VRC** 154-155 J 6
Wuhe o **VRC** 154-155 K 5
Wuhu o **VRC** 154-155 L 6
Wuhua o **VRC** 156-157 J 5
Wüjang o **VRC** 144-145 B 4
Wuji o **VRC** 154-155 J 2
Wu Jiang ~ **VRC** 156-157 F 2
Wukari o **WAN** 204-205 H 5
Wulai · **RC** 156-157 M 4
Wulff Land ⩦ **GRØ** 26-27 a 2
Wulgo o **WAN** 198-199 G 6
Wuli o **VRC** 144-145 J 3
Wulian o **VRC** 154-155 L 4
Wulian Feng ▲ **VRC** 156-157 C 3
Wuliaru, Pulau ⌒ **RI** 166-167 F 5
Wulichuan o **VRC** 154-155 G 5
Wulik River ~ **USA** 20-21 J 3
Wuling Shan ▲ **VRC** 156-157 F 3
Wulingshan Z.B. ⊥· **VRC** 154-155 K 1
Wulingyuan ··· **VRC** 156-157 G 2
Wulo Kode o **ETH** 208-209 C 5
Wulong o **VRC** 156-157 E 2
Wuluhan o **RI** 168 E 4
Wulur o **RI** 166-167 E 5
Wum o **CAM** 204-205 J 5
Wumeng Shan ▲ **VRC** 156-157 C 4
Wuming o **VRC** 156-157 F 5
Wunagak o **SUD** 206-207 L 4
Wundanyi o **EAK** 212-213 G 5
Wundowie o **AUS** 176-177 D 5
Wunen o **RI** 166-167 K 3
Wuning o **VRC** 156-157 J 2
Wunna ~ **IND** 138-139 G 9
Wunnummin Lake o **CDN** 34-35 M 4
Wunnummin Lake ⊂⊃ **CDN** (ONT) 234-235 O 2
Wun Rog o **SUD** 206-207 J 4
Wun Shwai o **SUD** 206-207 J 4
Wuntau o **SUD** 206-207 L 3
Wuntho o **MYA** 142-143 J 4
Wupatki National Monument ∴ **USA** (AZ) 256-257 D 3
Wuping o **VRC** 156-157 K 4
Wuppertal o **D** 92-93 J 3
Wuppertal o **ZA** 220-221 D 6
Wuqi o **VRC** 154-155 F 3
Wuqia o **VRC** 146-147 B 6
Wurarga o **AUS** 176-177 D 4
Wurno o **WAN** 198-199 B 6
Wurtele o **CDN** (ONT) 236-237 G 3

412 Willandra Creek — Wurtele

Wuruma Reservation < AUS 178-179 L 3
Würzburg ○ ·· D 92-93 K 4
Wuse ○ WAN 204-205 H 4
Wushan ○ VRC (ANH) 154-155 K 5
Wushan ○ VRC (GAN) 154-155 D 4
Wushan ○ VRC (SIC) 154-155 F 6
Wushao Ling ▲ VRC 154-155 C 3
Wusheng Guan ▲ VRC 154-155 J 6
Wushi ○ VRC (GDG) 156-157 F 6
Wushi ○ VRC (XUZ) 146-147 D 5
Wushishi ○ WAN 204-205 G 4
Wushizen ○ VRC 156-157 F 6
Wusuli Jiang ~ VRC 150-151 K 4
Wutai ○ VRC 154-155 H 2
Wutaishan ▲ VRC 154-155 H 2
Wutan ○ VRC 156-157 G 2
Wutongqiao ○ VRC 156-157 C 2
Wutung ○ PNG 183 A 2
Wuwei ○ VRC (ANH) 154-155 K 6
Wuwei ○ VRC (GAN) 154-155 C 3
Wuwu ○ PNG 183 D 4
Wuxi ○ VRC (JIA) 154-155 M 6
Wuxi ○ · VRC (SIC) 154-155 F 6
Wuxu ○ VRC 156-157 F 5
Wuxuan ○ VRC 156-157 F 5
Wuxue ○ VRC 156-157 J 2
Wuyang ○ VRC 154-155 H 5
Wuyi ○ VRC 156-157 C 3
Wuyiling ○ VRC 150-151 G 3
Wuyishan ○ VRC (FUJ) 156-157 L 3
Wuyi Shan ▲ VRC 156-157 K 3
Wuyishan · VRC (FUJ) 156-157 K 3
Wuyishan Z.B. ⊥ VRC 156-157 K 3
Wuyuan ○ VRC 148-149 J 7
Wuzhai ○ VRC 154-155 G 2
Wuzhi ○ VRC 154-155 H 4
Wuzhi Shan ▲ VRC 156-157 F 7
Wuzhi Shan ▲ VRC (HAI) 156-157 F 7
Wuzhong ○ VRC 154-155 E 2
Wuzhou ○ VRC 156-157 G 5
Wyaaba Creek ~ AUS 174-175 G 5
Wyabing ○ AUS 176-177 E 6
Wyaconda River ~ USA 274-275 G 4
Wyagamack, Lac ⊂ CDN (QUE) 240-241 C 3
Wyalkatchem ○ AUS 176-177 D 5
Wyalusing ○ USA (PA) 280-281 K 2
Wyandotte Caves ∴ · USA (IN) 274-275 M 6
Wyandra ○ AUS 178-179 H 4
Wyangala, Lake ⊂ AUS 180-181 K 2
Wyara, Lake ⊂ AUS 178-179 H 5
Wyarno ○ USA (WY) 252-253 M 2
Wycheproof ○ AUS 180-181 G 4
Wyemandoo Hill ▲ AUS 176-177 E 4
Wyena ○ AUS 178-179 J 1
Wyeville ○ USA (WI) 270-271 H 6
Wylie Scarp ⊥ AUS 176-177 G 6
Wyllie's Poort ○ ZA 218-219 E 6
Wyloo ○ AUS 172-173 C 7
Wymark ○ CDN (SAS) 232-233 L 5
Wymer ○ USA (WA) 244-245 E 4
Wymore ○ USA (NE) 262-263 K 4
Wynbring ○ AUS 176-177 M 5
Wyndham ○ AUS 172-173 J 3
Wyndmere ○ USA (ND) 258-259 K 5
Wynndel ○ CDN (BC) 230-231 N 4
Wynne ○ USA (AR) 276-277 E 5
Wynnewood ○ USA (OK) 264-265 G 4
Wynniatt Bay ≈ 24-25 Q 4
Wynot ○ USA (NE) 262-263 J 2
Wynyard ○ AUS 180-181 H 6
Wynyard ○ CDN (SAS) 232-233 O 4
Wyola ○ USA (MT) 250-251 M 6
Wyola Lake ⊂ AUS 176-177 L 4
Wyoming ○ CDN (ONT) 238-239 C 6
Wyoming ○ USA (IL) 274-275 J 3
Wyoming ○ USA (MI) 272-273 D 5
Wyoming ○ USA (MN) 270-271 E 5
Wyoming □ USA 252-253 J 4
Wyoming Peak ▲ USA (WY) 252-253 H 4
Wyoming Range ▲ USA 252-253 H 3
Wyperfeld National Park ⊥ AUS 180-181 F 3
Wyralinu Hill ▲ AUS 176-177 G 6
Wyseby ○ AUS 178-179 K 3
Wyszków ○ PL 92-93 Q 2
Wytheville ○ USA (VA) 280-281 E 7
Wyżyna Małopolska ⌣ PL 92-93 Q 3

X

Xaafuun = Dante ○ SP 208-209 K 3
Xaafuun, Raas ▲ SP 208-209 K 3
Xagquka ○ VRC 144-145 J 5
Xaidulla ○ VRC 138-139 F 1
Xainza ○ VRC 144-145 G 5
Xai-Xai ☆ MOC 220-221 L 2
Xakriabá, Área Indígena X BR 72-73 H 3
Xalin ○ SP 208-209 J 4
Xalpatláhuac ○ MEX 52-53 E 3
Xa Mát ○ VN 158-159 J 5
Xambioá ○ BR 68-69 D 5
Xambrê, Rio ~ BR 72-73 D 7
Xam Hua ○ LAO 156-157 D 6
Xamindele ○ ANG 216-217 B 3
Xá-Muteba ○ ANG 216-217 D 4
Xandel ○ ANG 216-217 D 4
Xangongo ○ ANG 216-217 C 8
Xánthi ○ GR 100-101 K 4
Xanthos ··· TR 128-129 C 4
Xanxerê ○ BR 74-75 D 6
Xapuri ○ BR 70-71 C 2
Xapuri, Rio ~ BR 70-71 C 2
Xarar ○ SP 208-209 J 6
Xarardheere ○ SP 208-209 H 6
Xarlag ○ VRC 154-155 F 2
Xar Obot ○ VRC 148-149 O 5
Xarrama, Rio ~ P 98-99 C 5
Xassengue ○ ANG 216-217 E 5
Xateturu, Cachoeira ~ BR 68-69 B 5
Xàtiva ○ E 98-99 G 5
Xau, Lake ○ RB 218-219 C 5
Xaudum ~ RB 216-217 F 9
Xavante ou Rio das Vertentes, Rio ~ BR 68-69 C 7
Xavantes, Represa de < BR 72-73 F 7
Xavantes, Serra dos ▲ BR 72-73 F 2
Xavantina ○ BR 72-73 D 6
Xavantinho, Rio ~ BR 68-69 C 7
Xayar ○ VRC 146-147 F 5
Xebert ○ VRC 150-151 D 5
Xêgar ○ VRC 144-145 F 6
Xeitongmoin ○ VRC 144-145 G 6
Xel-Há ∴ · MEX 52-53 L 1
Xenia ○ USA (IL) 274-275 K 6
Xenia ○ USA (OH) 280-281 C 4
Xerente, Área Indígena X BR 68-69 D 6
Xeriuni, Rio ~ BR 66-67 F 3
Xerokambos ○ GR 100-101 L 7
Xert ○ E 98-99 H 4
Xeruã, Rio ~ BR 66-67 C 6
Xiabande ○ VRC 150-151 E 5
Xiachuan Dao ⌒ VRC 156-157 H 6
Xiahe ○ VRC 154-155 C 4
Xiamen ○ · VRC 156-157 L 4
Xi'an ☆ ·· VRC 154-155 F 4
Xianfen ○ VRC 154-155 G 4
Xianfeng ○ VRC 156-157 F 2
Xiangcheng ○ VRC (HEN) 154-155 J 5
Xiangcheng ○ VRC (HEN) 154-155 H 5
Xiangcheng ○ VRC (SIC) 144-145 M 6
Xiangfan ○ VRC 154-155 H 5
Xianggang = Hong Kong □ HK 156-157 J 5
Xianghuang Qi ○ VRC 148-149 L 6
Xiang Jiang ~ VRC 156-157 H 3
Xiangkhoang ○ LAO 156-157 C 7
Xiangmihu · VRC 156-157 H 5
Xiang Ngeun ○ LAO 156-157 C 7
Xiangning ○ VRC 154-155 G 4
Xiangshan ○ VRC 156-157 M 2
Xiangsha Wan · VRC 154-155 F 1
Xiangshui ○ VRC 154-155 L 4
Xiangtan ○ VRC 156-157 H 3
Xiangtangshan Shiku · VRC 154-155 J 3
Xiangxiang ○ VRC 156-157 H 3
Xiangyin ○ VRC 156-157 H 2
Xiangyun ○ VRC 156-157 H 2
Xiangzhou ○ VRC 156-157 F 5
Xianju ○ VRC 156-157 M 2
Xianning ○ VRC 156-157 J 2
Xianshan Gang ≈ 156-157 M 2
Xiantao ○ VRC 154-155 H 6
Xianxia Ling ▲ VRC 156-157 L 2
Xianyang ○ VRC 154-155 F 4
Xianyou ○ VRC 156-157 L 4
Xiaochi ○ VRC 156-157 J 2
Xiaogan ○ VRC 154-155 H 6
Xiaohe ○ VRC 154-155 F 5
Xiaojiahe ○ VRC 150-151 J 4
Xiaojin ○ VRC 154-155 C 6
Xiaokouzi · VRC 154-155 D 2
Xiaomei Guan ▲ VRC 156-157 J 4
Xiaonanchuan ○ VRC 144-145 K 3
Xiaoniao Tiantang · VRC 156-157 H 5
Xiaoshan ○ VRC 154-155 M 6
Xiao Shan ▲ VRC 154-155 G 4
Xiaowutai Shan ▲ VRC 154-155 J 2
Xiao Xian ○ VRC 154-155 K 4
Xiapu ○ VRC 156-157 L 3
Xiasi ○ VRC 156-157 E 4
Xia Xian ○ VRC 154-155 G 4
Xiaxiyu ○ VRC 154-155 J 2
Xiayi ○ VRC 154-155 K 4
Xiazhai ○ VRC 156-157 D 4
Xiazhuang ○ VRC 154-155 J 5
Xiazi ○ VRC 156-157 E 3
Xichang ○ VRC (GXI) 156-157 F 6
Xichang ○ VRC (SIC) 156-157 C 3
Xichong ○ VRC 154-155 D 6
Xichou ○ VRC 156-157 D 5
Xichuan ○ VRC 154-155 G 5
Xicoténcatl ○ MEX 50-51 K 6
Xicotepec de Juárez ○ MEX 52-53 F 1
Xide ○ VRC 156-157 C 2
Xie, Rio ~ BR 66-67 D 2
Xiezhou Guandi Miao · VRC 154-155 G 4
Xifeng ○ VRC (GAN) 154-155 E 4
Xifeng ○ VRC (GZH) 156-157 E 3
Xigangzi ○ VRC 150-151 F 3
Xigazê ○ ·· VRC 144-145 G 6
Xihua ○ VRC 154-155 J 5
Xiis ○ SP 208-209 H 3
Xiji ○ VRC 154-155 D 4
Xi Jiang ~ VRC 156-157 G 5
Xijin SK ⊂ VRC 156-157 F 5
Xijir Ulan Hu ⊂ VRC 144-145 H 3
Xijishui ○ VRC 154-155 D 3
Xikou ○ VRC (JXI) 156-157 J 2
Xikou ○ VRC (ZHE) 156-157 M 2
Xilamuren Caoyuan · VRC 148-149 K 7
Xi Liao He ~ VRC 150-151 D 6
Xilin ○ VRC 156-157 D 4
Xilinhot ○ VRC 148-149 N 6
Xilinji = Mohe ○ VRC 150-151 D 1
Xilitla ○ MEX 50-51 K 7
Xime ○ GNB 202-203 C 4
Xin'anjiang Sk. ⊂ VRC 156-157 L 2
Xin Barag Youqi ○ VRC 148-149 N 3
Xin Barag Zuoqi ○ VRC 150-151 B 3
Xinbin ○ VRC 150-151 E 7
Xincai ○ VRC 154-155 J 5
Xinchang ○ VRC 156-157 M 2
Xincheng ○ VRC 154-155 J 2
Xinchuan Gang ≈ 154-155 M 5
Xindeng ○ VRC 156-157 L 2
Xindong ○ VRC 156-157 G 5
Xinduqiao ○ VRC 154-155 B 6
Xinfeng ○ VRC (GDG) 156-157 J 4
Xinfeng ○ VRC (JXI) 156-157 J 4
Xinfengjiang SK ⊂ VRC 156-157 J 5
Xingalool ○ SP 208-209 J 4
Xingan ○ VRC 156-157 J 3
Xing'an ○ VRC 156-157 G 4
Xingcheng ○ VRC 150-151 C 7
Xinge ○ ANG 216-217 E 4
Xingguo ○ VRC 156-157 J 3
Xinghua ○ VRC 154-155 L 5
Xingjiejie ○ VRC 156-157 E 5
Xingkai Hu ⊂ VRC 122-123 E 6
Xingkai Hu ⊂ VRC 150-151 J 5
Xinglong ○ VRC 154-155 K 1
Xinglong ○ VRC 156-157 G 7
Xinglong-Shan Z.B. ⊥ VRC 154-155 C 4
Xingning ○ VRC 156-157 J 4
Xingod ○ SP 208-209 J 5
Xingpan ○ VRC 156-157 F 6
Xingren ○ VRC 156-157 D 4
Xingrenbu ○ VRC 154-155 D 3
Xingshan ○ VRC 154-155 G 6
Xingtai ○ VRC 154-155 J 3
Xingtang ○ VRC 154-155 J 2
Xingu, Parque Indígena do X BR 68-69 B 7
Xingu, Rio ~ BR 68-69 B 5
Xingu, Rio ~ BR 72-73 D 2
Xinguara ○ BR 68-69 D 5
Xingwen ○ VRC 156-157 D 2
Xing Xian ○ VRC 154-155 G 2
Xingxingxia ○ VRC 146-147 M 5
Xingxiuhai · VRC 144-145 L 3
Xingyi ○ VRC 156-157 D 4
Xinhe ○ VRC 146-147 F 5
Xinhuang ○ VRC 156-157 F 3
Xining ☆ VRC 154-155 B 3
Xiniujiao ○ VRC 156-157 F 6
Xinji ○ VRC 154-155 J 3
Xinjie ○ VRC 156-157 D 5
Xinjin ○ VRC (LIA) 150-151 C 8
Xinjin ○ VRC (SIC) 154-155 C 6
Xinlong ○ VRC 154-155 B 6
Xinmin ○ VRC 150-151 D 7
Xinning ○ VRC 156-157 G 3
Xinping ○ VRC 156-157 B 5
Xinshao ○ VRC 156-157 G 3
Xintai ○ VRC 154-155 K 4
Xintian ○ VRC 156-157 H 4
Xinxiang ○ VRC 154-155 H 4
Xinxim, Rio ~ BR 68-69 B 6
Xinxing ○ VRC 156-157 H 5
Xinxing ○ VRC 156-157 F 7
Xinxu ○ VRC 156-157 E 5
Xinyang ○ VRC 154-155 J 5
Xinye ○ VRC 154-155 H 5
Xinyi ○ VRC (GDG) 156-157 G 5
Xinyi ○ VRC (JIA) 154-155 L 4
Xinying ○ VRC 156-157 F 7
Xinyu ○ VRC 156-157 J 3
Xinyuan ○ VRC 146-147 F 4
Xinzhao Shan ▲ VRC 154-155 E 2
Xinzhelin SK ⊂ VRC 156-157 J 2
Xinzheng ○ VRC 154-155 H 4
Xinzhou ○ VRC 154-155 H 2
Xinzuotang ○ VRC 156-157 J 5
Xionger Shan ▲ VRC 154-155 G 4
Xiongyuecheng ○ VRC 150-151 D 7
Xipamanu, Rio ~ BR 70-71 C 2
Xipaotai · VRC 150-151 D 7
Xipembe, Rio ~ MOC 218-219 G 5
Xiping ○ VRC (HEN) 154-155 G 5
Xiping ○ VRC (HEN) 154-155 H 5
Xique-Xique ○ BR 68-69 G 7
Xishan · VRC (HUB) 154-155 J 6
Xishan · VRC (YUN) 156-157 C 4
Xishaqundao = Paracel Islands ⌒ 158-159 L 2
Xishuangbanna ⊥ · VRC 142-143 L 4
Xishuangbanna Z.B. ⊥ · VRC 142-143 M 5
Xishui ○ VRC (GZH) 156-157 E 2
Xishui ○ VRC (HUB) 154-155 J 6
Xistral ▲ E 98-99 D 3
Xi Taijnar Hu ⊂ VRC 144-145 H 2
Xitole ○ GNB 202-203 C 4
Xituo ○ VRC 154-155 F 6
Xi Ujimqin Qi ○ VRC 148-149 N 5
Xiushan ○ VRC 156-157 L 2
Xiushan ○ VRC 156-157 F 2
Xiushui ○ VRC 156-157 J 2
Xiuwen ○ VRC 156-157 E 3
Xiuwu ○ VRC 154-155 H 4
Xiuyan ○ VRC 150-151 D 7
Xiuying ○ VRC 156-157 G 7
Xiwu ○ VRC 144-145 L 4
Xixabangma Feng ▲ VRC 144-145 E 6
Xixia ○ VRC 154-155 G 5
Xi Xian ○ VRC 154-155 G 3
Xixiang ○ VRC 154-155 E 5
Xixia Wangling · VRC 154-155 D 2
Xixón = Gijón ○ E 98-99 E 3
Xixona ○ E 98-99 G 5
Xiyang ○ VRC 154-155 H 3
Xlacah ∴ · MEX 52-53 K 1
Xochiapa ○ MEX 52-53 G 3
Xochicalco ∴ · MEX 52-53 E 2
Xochimilco ○ ·· MEX 52-53 E 2
Xochob ∴ · MEX 52-53 K 2
Xom Dôn ○ VN 158-159 H 2
Xom Thôn ○ VN 158-159 H 2
Xopoto, Rio ~ BR 72-73 J 6
X-Pichil ○ MEX 52-53 K 2
Xpujil ∴ · MEX 52-53 K 2
Xuan'en ○ VRC 154-155 F 6
Xuanhan ○ VRC 154-155 E 6
Xuanhua ○ VRC 154-155 J 1
Xuân Lộc ○ VN 158-159 J 5
Xuanwei ○ VRC 156-157 D 3
Xuanzhong Si · VRC 154-155 H 3
Xuanzhou ○ VRC 154-155 L 6
Xuchang ○ VRC 154-155 H 4
Xuddur ☆ SP 208-209 F 6
Xudun ○ SP 208-209 H 4
Xuebao Ding ▲ VRC 154-155 C 5
Xuefeng Shan ▲ VRC 156-157 G 3
Xueshan ▲ VRC 154-155 D 3
Xugana Lodge ○ RB 218-219 B 4
Xumishan Shiku · VRC 154-155 D 3
Xunantunich ∴ · BH 52-53 K 3
Xungru ○ VRC 144-145 E 6
Xun He ~ VRC 154-155 F 5
Xunhua ○ VRC 154-155 C 4
Xun Jiang ~ VRC 156-157 G 5
Xunke ○ VRC 150-151 G 3
Xunwu ○ VRC 156-157 J 4
Xun Xian ○ VRC 154-155 J 4
Xunyang ○ VRC 154-155 F 5
Xunyi ○ VRC 154-155 F 4
Xupu ○ VRC 156-157 G 3
Xuro Co ⊂ VRC 144-145 F 5
Xushui ○ VRC 154-155 J 2
Xuwan ○ VRC 154-155 J 6
Xuwen ○ VRC 156-157 G 6
Xuyi ○ VRC 154-155 L 5
Xuyong ○ VRC 156-157 D 2
Xuzhou ○ VRC 154-155 K 4

Y

Yaak ○ USA (MT) 250-251 D 3
Yaak River ~ USA 250-251 D 3
Yaamba ○ AUS 178-179 L 2
Ya'an ○ VRC 156-157 C 2
Yaaq Braaway ○ SP 212-213 J 3
Yaba-Hita-Hikosan Quasi National Park ⊥ J 152-153 D 8
Yabassi ○ CAM 204-205 H 6
Yabayo ○ CI 202-203 G 7
Yabe ○ J 152-153 D 8
Yabebyry ○ PY 76-77 J 4
Yabelo ○ ETH 208-209 D 6
Yabelo Wildlife Sanctuary ⊥ ETH 208-209 D 6
Yabia ○ ZRE 210-211 J 2
Yabiti ~ DY 202-203 L 4
Yabo ○ YV 60-61 K 3
Yabrin ○ KSA 130-131 L 6
Yabucoa ○ · USA (PR) 286-287 Q 2
Yabuli ○ VRC 150-151 G 5
Yabus ~ ETH 208-209 B 4
Yabuyanos ○ PE 64-65 F 2
Yacambú, Parque Nacional ⊥ YV 60-61 G 3
Yacata ⌒ FJI 184 III c 2
Yachats ○ USA (OR) 244-245 A 6
Yacheng ○ VRC 156-157 F 7
Yachting Region ·· 56 E 5
Yacimiento Río Turbio ○ RA 80 D 5
Yaciretá, Ilha ⌒ PY 76-77 J 4
Yacoraite, Río ~ RA 76-77 E 2
Yacuiba ○ BOL 76-77 F 1
Yacuma, Río ~ BOL 70-71 D 4
Yadat, Wādī ~ SUD 200-201 G 4
Yadé, Massif du ▲ RCA 206-207 B 5
Yadgir ○ IND 140-141 G 2
Yadibikro ○ CI 202-203 H 6
Yadiki ○ IND 140-141 G 3
Yadkin River ~ USA 282-283 G 5
Yadkin River ~ USA 282-283 G 4
Yadma ○ KSA 132-133 D 4
Yadong ○ VRC 144-145 G 7
Yadua ⌒ FJI 184 III b 2
Yaeng ○ THA 158-159 F 2
Yafase ○ RI 166-167 L 3
Yafo, Tel Aviv- ☆ IL 130-131 D 1
Yafran □ LAR 192-193 E 2
Yafran ☆ ·· LAR (Yaf) 192-193 E 1
Yagati ○ IND 140-141 G 4
Yaghan Basin ≃ 6-7 C 14
Yagishiri-tō ⌒ J 152-153 J 2
Yagoua ○ CAM 206-207 B 3
Yagradagzê Shan ▲ VRC 144-145 K 3
Yaguachi Nuevo ○ EC 64-65 C 3
Yaguajay ○ C 54-55 F 3
Yagual, El ○ YV 60-61 G 4
Yaguaraparo ○ YV 60-61 K 2
Yaguari, Arroyo ~ RA 76-77 H 5
Yaguarón, Río ~ ROU 74-75 D 9
Yaguas ○ EC 66-67 B 4
Yaguas, Río ~ PE 66-67 B 4
Yahekou ○ VRC 154-155 H 5
Yahk ○ CDN (BC) 230-231 N 4
Yahualica ○ MEX 50-51 H 7
Yahuma ○ ZRE 210-211 J 3
Yahyalı ☆ TR 128-129 F 3
Yaibrai ○ VRC 154-155 C 2
Yaita ○ J 152-153 H 6
Yajalón ○ MEX 52-53 H 3
Yajiang ○ VRC 154-155 B 6
Yaka ○ RCA 206-207 D 6
Yakabindie ○ AUS 176-177 F 3
Yakak, Cape ▲ USA 22-23 H 7
Yakamul ○ PNG 183 B 2
Yakana ○ ZRE 210-211 J 3
Yakassé-Attobrou ○ CI 202-203 J 6
Yakatograk ○ VRC 146-147 H 6
Yakavlang ○ AFG 134-135 M 1
Yakeshi ○ VRC 150-151 C 3
Yakfıkebir ☆ TR 128-129 H 2
Yakima ○ USA (WA) 244-245 E 4
Yakima Firing Center xx USA (WA) 244-245 E 4
Yakima Firing Range · USA 244-245 E 4
Yakima Indian Reservation X USA (WA) 244-245 D 4
Yakima River ~ USA 244-245 E 3
Yakmach ○ PK 134-135 K 4
Yako ○ BF 202-203 J 3
Yakobi Island ⌒ USA 32-33 B 2
Yakoma ○ ZRE 206-207 E 6
Yakoun River ~ CDN 228-229 B 3
Yaku ○ J 152-153 D 9
Yakumo ○ J 152-153 J 3
Yaku-shima ⌒ J 152-153 D 9
Yaku-shima National Park ⊥ ··· J 152-153 D 9
Yakutat ○ USA 20-21 V 7
Yakutat Bay ≈ 20-21 V 7
Yakutsk = Jakutsk ☆ ·· RUS 118-119 O 4
Yala ○ EAK (WE) 212-213 E 3
Yala ~ EAK 212-213 E 3
Yala ○ GH 202-203 K 4
Yala ○ THA 158-159 F 7
Yalaki ○ ZRE 210-211 J 3
Yalakom River ~ CDN 230-231 G 2
Yalape · PE 64-65 D 5
Yalardy ○ AUS 176-177 C 3
Yalata X AUS 176-177 L 5
Yalata Aboriginal Lands X AUS 176-177 L 5
Yalbalgo ○ AUS 176-177 C 2
Yalbyn ~ RUS 118-119 O 7
Yale ○ CDN (BC) 230-231 H 4
Yale ○ USA (MI) 272-273 G 4
Yale ○ USA (OK) 264-265 H 2
Yale ○ USA (WA) 244-245 C 4
Yaleko ○ ZRE 210-211 K 3
Yale Point ▲ USA (AZ) 256-257 F 2
Yalewa Kalou ⌒ FJI 184 III a 2
Yalgoo ○ AUS 176-177 D 4
Yalgorup National Park ⊥ AUS 176-177 C 6
Yali ~ BF 202-203 L 3
Yali ○ CO 60-61 D 4
Yali ○ NIC 52-53 L 5
Yaligimba ○ ZRE 210-211 J 2
Yalinga ○ RCA 206-207 F 5
Yallalong ○ AUS 176-177 C 3
Yalleroi ○ AUS 178-179 H 3
Yallingup Caves · AUS 176-177 C 6
Yallo ○ BF 202-203 J 3
Yalogo ○ BF 202-203 K 3
Yaloké ○ RCA 206-207 C 6
Yalong Jiang ~ VRC 156-157 B 2
Yalosemo ○ ZRE 210-211 J 3
Yaloogarrie Creek ~ AUS 172-173 K 6
Yaloupi ~ F 62-63 H 4
Yalova ☆ TR 128-129 C 2
Yaltubung ○ RI 166-167 E 5
Yalufi ○ ZRE 210-211 K 3
Yalu Jiang ~ VRC 150-151 E 7
Ya'lujiang Kou ≈ 150-151 E 8
Yālūr ○ AFG 136-137 M 6
Yamada ○ J 152-153 J 5
Yamagata ☆ · J 152-153 J 5
Yamaguchi ☆ J 152-153 D 7
Yamakawa ○ J 152-153 F 7
Yamal, Poluostrov = Jamal, poluostrov ⌣ RUS 108-109 N 7
Yamal Nenets Autonomous District=Jamalo-Neneckij avt. okrug □ RUS 108-109 N 7
Yamanashi ○ J 152-153 H 7
Yamarna X AUS 176-177 G 4
Yamarna Aboriginal Land X AUS 176-177 G 3
Yamasá ○ DOM 54-55 K 5
Yamasaki ○ J 152-153 F 7
Yamato Rise ≃ 152-153 F 5
Yamatosammyaku ▲ ARK 16 F 4
Yamatsuri ○ J 152-153 J 6
Yamba ○ AUS 178-179 M 5
Yamba ○ BF 202-203 L 3
Yambacoona ○ AUS 180-181 G 5
Yambah ○ AUS 178-179 B 2
Yambala ○ RCA 206-207 E 5
Yamba Lake ⊂ CDN 30-31 O 3
Yambala Koudouvélé ○ RCA 206-207 E 5
Yambata ○ ZRE 210-211 H 2
Yamba-Yamba ○ ZRE 210-211 L 6
Yambéring ○ RG 202-203 D 4
Yambi, Mesa de ⌣ CO 64-65 G 1
Yambio ○ SUD 206-207 J 6
Yambuya ○ ZRE 210-211 K 3
Yamdena, Pulau ⌒ RI 166-167 F 5
Yame ○ J 152-153 D 8
Yamethin ○ MYA 142-143 K 5
Yamin ○ IRQ 130-131 K 2
Yamin, Puncak ▲ RI 166-167 K 4
Yam Kinneret ⊂ IL 130-131 D 1
Yamma Yamma, Lake ⊂ AUS 178-179 F 4
Yamon ○ PE 64-65 C 5
Yamoussoukro ★ · CI 202-203 H 6
Yampa ○ USA (CO) 254-255 J 3
Yampa River ~ USA 254-255 G 3
Yampi Sound Mining Area · AUS 172-173 F 4
Yamsay Mountain ▲ USA (OR) 244-245 D 8
Yamtu, Tanjung ▲ RI 166-167 F 2
Yamuna ~ IND 142-143 B 3
Yamunanagar ○ IND 138-139 F 4
Yamur, Danau ○ RI 166-167 H 3
Yamzho Yumco ⊂ VRC 144-145 H 6
Yan ○ MAL 162-163 D 2
Yana ○ WAL 202-203 D 5
Yanaba Island ⌒ PNG 183 F 5
Yanac ○ AUS 180-181 F 4
Yanachaga-Chemillen, Parque Nacional ⊥ PE 64-65 E 7
Yanacu Grande, Río ~ PE 64-65 E 4
Yanadani ○ J 152-153 E 8
Yanagawa ○ J 152-153 D 8
Yanahuanca ○ PE 64-65 D 7
Yanai ○ J 152-153 E 8
Yanam ○ IND 140-141 K 2
Yan'an ○ VRC 154-155 F 3
Yanaoca ○ PE 70-71 B 4
Yanatili, Río ~ PE 64-65 F 8
Yanayacu ○ PE 64-65 E 4
Yanbu' al-Baḥr ○ KSA 130-131 F 5
Yanbu' an-Naḥl ○ KSA 130-131 F 5
Yancannia ○ AUS 178-179 G 6
Yancannia Creek ~ AUS 178-179 G 6
Yancannia Range ▲ AUS 178-179 G 6
Yancey ○ USA (TX) 266-267 H 4
Yanceyville ○ USA (NC) 282-283 H 4
Yanchang ○ VRC 154-155 G 3
Yancheng ○ VRC 154-155 M 5
Yanchep Beach ○ AUS 176-177 C 5
Yanchep National Park ⊥ AUS 176-177 C 5
Yanchi ○ VRC 154-155 E 3
Yanco Creek ~ AUS 180-181 H 3
Yanco Glen ○ AUS 178-179 F 6
Yanda Creek ~ AUS 178-179 H 6
Yandama Creek ~ AUS 178-179 F 5
Yandang Shan ▲ VRC 156-157 L 3
Yandangshan · VRC 156-157 M 2
Yandaxkak ○ VRC 146-147 J 6
Yandeearra ○ AUS 172-173 D 6
Yandeearra Aboriginal Land X AUS 172-173 D 6
Yandev ○ WAN 204-205 H 5
Yandina ○ SOL 184 I d 3
Yandon ○ MYA 158-159 C 2
Yandongi ○ ZRE 210-211 J 2
Yandun ○ VRC 146-147 M 4
Yanfeng ○ VRC 156-157 C 3
Yanfolia ○ RMM 202-203 F 4
Yang ○ THA 158-159 G 3
Yanga ○ CAM 210-211 E 2
Yanga ○ TCH 206-207 D 4
Yanga, Komin- ○ BF 202-203 L 4
Yangalia ○ RCA 206-207 E 5
Yangambi ○ ZRE 210-211 K 3
Yangara ~ TCH 198-199 J 2
Yangas ○ PE 64-65 D 7
Yangasso ○ RMM 202-203 H 3
Yangbajain ○ VRC (XIZ) 144-145 H 5
Yangbajain · VRC (XIZ) 144-145 H 5
Yangcheng ○ VRC 154-155 H 4
Yangchun ○ VRC 156-157 G 5
Yangcun ○ VRC 156-157 J 5
Yangdok ○ KOR 150-151 F 8
Yanggandu ○ RI 166-167 L 6
Yangjiang ○ VRC 156-157 G 6
Yanglin ○ VRC 156-157 C 4
Yangling ○ VRC 154-155 J 4
Yangmingshan National Park ⊥ · RC 156-157 M 4
Yangon ★ ·· MYA 158-159 D 2
Yangoru ○ PNG 183 B 2
Yangouali, Mare ⊂ DY 202-203 L 4
Yangpu Gang ≈ 156-157 F 7
Yangquan ○ VRC 154-155 H 3
Yangquangu ○ VRC 154-155 G 3
Yangqu Shan ▲ VRC 154-155 H 3
Yangshan ○ VRC 156-157 H 4
Yangshaocun Yizhi ∴ VRC 154-155 G 4
Yangshuo ○ · VRC 156-157 G 4
Yangtze = Chang Jiang ~ VRC 154-155 F 6
Yangxi ○ VRC 156-157 G 6
Yangxin ○ VRC 156-157 J 2
Yang-Yang ○ SN 202-203 C 2
Yangyuan ○ VRC 154-155 J 1
Yangzhou ○ · VRC 154-155 L 5
Yangzi'e Z.B. ⊥ VRC 154-155 L 6
Yanhe ○ VRC 156-157 F 2
Yanhu ○ VRC 144-145 D 4
Yanhuqu ○ VRC 144-145 D 4
Yanji ○ VRC 150-151 G 6
Yanjin ○ VRC 156-157 D 2
Yanjing ○ VRC 144-145 M 6
Yankari Game Reserve ⊥ WAN 204-205 J 4
Yankee ○ USA (NM) 256-257 L 2
Yankoman ○ GH 202-203 J 7
Yankton ○ USA (SD) 260-261 J 4
Yankton Indian Reservation X USA (SD) 260-261 H 3
Yanmen G ▲ VRC 154-155 H 2
Yannarie River ~ AUS 176-177 C 1
Yanomami, Parque Indígena X BR 60-61 K 6
Yanonge ○ ZRE 210-211 K 3
Yan Oya ~ CL 140-141 J 6
Yanqi ○ VRC 146-147 H 4
Yanqing ○ VRC 154-155 J 1
Yanqul ○ OM 132-133 K 2
Yanrey ○ AUS 172-173 B 7
Yanshan ○ VRC (HEB) 154-155 K 2
Yanshan ○ VRC (JXI) 156-157 K 2
Yanshan ○ VRC (YUN) 156-157 D 5
Yanshiping ○ VRC 144-145 J 4
Yanshou ○ VRC 150-151 G 5
Yansoribo ○ RI 166-167 G 2
Yantai ○ VRC 154-155 M 3
Yantaikekeulik ○ VRC 146-147 J 6
Yantara, Lake ⊂ AUS 178-179 G 5
Yanting ○ VRC 154-155 D 6
Yantis ○ USA (TX) 264-265 J 6
Yantou ○ VRC 156-157 M 2
Yantzaza ○ EC 64-65 C 3
Yanuca ⌒ FJI 184 III c 3
Yanwodao · VRC 150-151 J 4
Yanzikou ○ VRC 156-157 D 3
Yaodian ○ VRC (GAN) 154-155 E 4
Yaodian ○ VRC (SXI) 154-155 F 3
Yaolin D. · VRC 156-157 L 2
Yaoundé ★ · CAM 204-205 J 7
Yaowang Gang ≈ 154-155 M 5
Yaowang Hill · VRC 154-155 F 4
Yao Xian ○ VRC 154-155 F 4
Yapacana, Parque Nacional ⊥ YV 60-61 H 6
Yapacani, Río ~ BOL 70-71 E 5
Yapacaraí ○ PY 76-77 J 3
Yapen, Pulau ⌒ RI 166-167 J 2
Yapen, Selat ≈ 166-167 H 2
Yapero ○ RI 166-167 J 4
Yapeyú ○ · RA 76-77 J 5
Yappar River ~ AUS 174-175 F 6
Yappirala ○ IND 140-141 H 3
Yapul ○ IND 142-143 J 1
Yaputih ○ RI 166-167 E 3
Yaqaga ⌒ FJI 184 III b 2
Yaqeta ⌒ FJI 184 III a 2
Yaque del Norte, Río ~ DOM 54-55 K 5
Yaqui ○ MEX 50-51 D 4
Yaqui, Boca del ≈ 50-51 D 4
Yaqui, Río ~ MEX 50-51 E 3
Yar ≈ 166-167 K 5
Yar ○ RN 198-199 F 2
Yara ○ C 54-55 G 4
Yaraka ○ AUS 178-179 H 3
Yaraligöz Dağı ▲ TR 128-129 F 2
Yaras, Las ○ PE 70-71 B 5
Yarbo ○ CDN (SAS) 232-233 R 5
Yardarino Gas and Oil Field · AUS 176-177 C 4
Yarden, ha ~ IL 130-131 D 1
Yardımcı Burnu ▲ TR 128-129 D 4
Yaré Lao ○ SN 196-197 C 6
Yaren ★ NAU 13 H 3
Yargatti ○ IND 140-141 F 3
Yarí, Río ~ CO 64-65 F 2
Yarim ○ Y 132-133 D 6
Yaritagua ○ YV 60-61 G 2
Yarkant He ~ VRC 146-147 D 6
Yarkhun ~ PK 138-139 D 1
Yarle Lakes ⊂ AUS 176-177 L 5
Yarlung Zangbo Jiang ~ VRC 144-145 H 6
Yarmouth ○ CDN (NS) 240-241 J 7
Yarmouth ○ USA (ME) 278-279 L 5
Yarnell ○ USA (AZ) 256-257 C 4
Yaro Lund ○ PK 138-139 B 6
Yaroslavl' = Jaroslavl' ☆ ·· RUS 94-95 Q 3
Yarra ○ DY 204-205 E 3
Yarrabubba ○ AUS 176-177 E 3
Yarralin ○ AUS 172-173 K 4
Yarraloola ○ AUS 172-173 B 6
Yarram ○ AUS 180-181 J 5
Yarraman ○ AUS 178-179 L 4
Yarra Yarra Lakes ⊂ AUS 176-177 C 4
Yarrie ○ AUS 172-173 E 6
Yarronvale ○ AUS 178-179 H 4
Yarrowitch ○ AUS 178-179 L 6
Yarrowmere ○ AUS 178-179 H 1
Yarumal ○ CO 60-61 D 4
Yarvicoya, Cerro ▲ RCH 70-71 C 7
Yarysah ~ RUS 110-111 P 5
Yasa ○ ZRE 210-211 H 5
Yāsāt, al- ⌒ UAE 134-135 E 6
Yasawa ⌒ FJI 184 III a 2
Yasawa Group ⌒ FJI 184 III a 2
Yashi ○ WAN 198-199 C 6
Yashikera ○ WAN 204-205 E 4
Yasothon ○ THA 158-159 H 3
Yass ○ AUS 180-181 K 3
Yassıhöyük (Gordion) ∴ · TR 128-129 E 3
Yass River ~ AUS 180-181 K 3
Yāsūj ☆ · IR 134-135 D 3
Yasun Burnu ▲ TR 128-129 G 2
Yasuní, Parque Nacional ⊥ EC 64-65 D 2
Yasuni, Río ~ EC 64-65 D 2
Yata ○ BOL 70-71 D 3
Yata ~ RCA 206-207 F 4
Yata, Río ~ BOL 70-71 E 2
Yatağan ☆ TR 128-129 C 4
Yatako ○ BF 202-203 L 2
Yata-Ngaya, Réserve de faune de la ⊥ RCA 206-207 F 4
Yates ○ CDN (ALB) 232-233 B 2
Yates Center ○ USA (KS) 262-263 L 7
Yates River ~ CDN 30-31 L 6
Yatesville ○ USA (GA) 284-285 F 4
Yathkyed Lake ⊂ CDN 30-31 U 4
Yatolema ○ ZRE 210-211 K 3
Yatsushiro ○ J 152-153 D 8
Yatsushiro-kai ≈ 152-153 D 8
Yatsu-take ▲ J 152-153 H 7
Yatta ○ EAK 212-213 F 4
Yatta Gap ▲ EAK 212-213 G 5
Yatta Plateau ▲ EAK 212-213 G 5
Yatúa, Río ~ YV 66-67 D 2
Yauca ○ PE 64-65 E 9
Yauca, Río ~ PE 64-65 E 9
Yauco ○ USA (PR) 286-287 P 2
Yauhannah ○ USA (SC) 284-285 L 3
Yauli ○ PE 64-65 E 8
Yauri ○ PE 70-71 B 4
Yaurisque ○ PE 70-71 B 3
Yauyos ○ PE 64-65 E 8
Yāval ○ IND 138-139 E 9
Yavapai Indian Reservation · USA (AZ) 256-257 C 4
Yavari, Río ~ PE 66-67 B 5
Yavari Mirim, Río ~ PE 64-65 F 4
Yávaros ○ MEX 50-51 E 4
Yavatmāl ○ IND 138-139 G 9
Yavero ó Paucartambo, Río ~ PE 64-65 F 8
Yavineto, Río ~ PE 64-65 E 2
Yavita ○ YV 60-61 H 6
Yaviza ○ PA 52-53 F 7
Yavuzeli ☆ TR 128-129 G 4
Yawatahama ○ J 152-153 E 8
Yawatongguzlangar ○ VRC 144-145 D 2
Yawatoutou, Mont ▲ RT 202-203 L 6
Yawgu ○ GH 202-203 L 4
Yawimu ○ RI 166-167 K 5
Yawkey ○ USA (WV) 280-281 E 5
Yawngo ○ MYA 142-143 L 4
Yawri Bay ≈ 202-203 D 5
Yaxcaba ○ MEX 52-53 K 1
Yaxchilan · MEX 52-53 J 3
Yaxia ∴ · GCA 52-53 K 3
Yaxing ○ VRC 156-157 F 7
Yayama ○ ZRE 210-211 J 4
Yazd □ IR 134-135 E 3
Yazd ☆ · IR (YAZ) 134-135 F 3
Yazdān ○ IR 134-135 J 2
Yazdavān, Rūd-e ~ AFG 134-135 L 2
Yazlıca Dağı ▲ TR 128-129 K 4
Yazmān ○ PK 138-139 C 5
Yazoo City ○ USA (MS) 268-269 K 4
Yazoo National Wildlife Refuge ⊥ USA (MS) 268-269 K 3
Yazoo River ~ USA 268-269 K 3
Yby Yaú ○ PY 76-77 J 2
Ycliff ○ CDN (ONT) 234-235 M 4
Ydžidnjur, boloto ⊂ RUS 88-89 V 5
Ydžidparma vozvyšennost' ▲ RUS 114-115 E 3
Ydžyd-Patok ~ RUS 114-115 E 2
Ye ○ MYA 158-159 D 3
Yea ○ AUS 180-181 H 4
Yebawmi ○ MYA 142-143 J 3
Yebbi-Bou ○ TCH 198-199 J 2
Yebbi Souma ○ TCH 198-199 H 2
Yébenes, Los ○ E 98-99 F 5
Yébigué ~ TCH 198-199 H 2
Yebok ○ MYA 142-143 H 6
Yebya ○ MYA 142-143 J 5
Yecheng ○ VRC 146-147 C 7
Yecla ○ E 98-99 G 5
Yécora ○ MEX 50-51 E 3
Yedseram ~ WAN 198-199 G 6
Yedseram, River ~ WAN 204-205 K 3
Yeed ○ SP 208-209 F 6
Yeehaw Junction ○ USA (FL) 286-287 J 4
Yeelanna ○ AUS 180-181 C 3
Yeelirrie ○ AUS 176-177 F 3
Yegguebo ○ RN 198-199 F 3
Yegros ○ PY 76-77 J 4
Yegua Creek ~ USA 266-267 L 3
Yegua Creek, Middle ~ USA 266-267 K 3
Yeguada ○ PA 52-53 D 7
Yégué ○ RT 202-203 L 5
Yegyi ○ MYA 158-159 C 2
Yeha ○ ETH 200-201 J 5
Yei ○ SUD (SR) 206-207 K 6
Yei ~ SUD 206-207 K 6
Yeï Lulu, Col de ▲ RN 198-199 G 2

Wuruma Reservation — Yeï Lulu, Col de 413

Yeji ○ **GH** 202-203 K 5
Yeji ○ **VRC** 154-155 J 6
Yekaterinburg = Ekaterinburg ☆ **RUS** 96-97 M 5
Yekebaierqier ○ **VRC** 144-145 M 3
Yekepa ○ **LB** 202-203 F 6
Yekia ○ **TCH** 198-199 H 4
Yekokora ~ **ZRE** 210-211 H 3
Yelahanka ○ **IND** 140-141 G 4
Yelcho, Lago ⊖ **RCH** 78-79 C 7
Yelcho, Río ~ **RCH** 78-79 C 7
Yele ○ **WAL** 202-203 E 5
Yelets = Elec ○ **RUS** 94-95 Q 5
Yélimané ○ **RMM** 202-203 E 2
Yelkaturti ○ **IND** 138-139 G 10
Yell ⌒ **GB** 90-91 G 1
Yellabinna Regional Reserve ⊥ **AUS** 176-177 M 5
Yellāpur ○ **IND** 140-141 F 3
Yellow Creek ○ **CDN** (SAS) 232-233 N 3
Yellow Creek ○ **USA** (PA) 280-281 H 3
Yellow Creek ~ **USA** 274-275 E 5
Yellow Creek ~ **USA** 284-285 B 3
Yellowdine ○ **AUS** 176-177 E 5
Yellow Grass ○ **CDN** (SAS) 232-233 O 6
Yellowhead Highway II **CDN** (ALB) 228-229 R 3
Yellowhead Pass ▲ **CDN** (BC) 228-229 Q 4
Yellow Jacket Pass ▲ **USA** (CO) 254-255 H 3
Yellowknife ☆ • **CDN** 30-31 M 4
Yellowknife Bay ⊖ **CDN** 30-31 M 4
Yellowknife Highway II **CDN** 30-31 L 5
Yellowknife River ~ **CDN** 30-31 N 4
Yellow Mountain, The ▲ **AUS** 180-181 J 2
Yellow Pine ○ **USA** (ID) 252-253 C 2
Yellow River ~ **USA** 270-271 H 6
Yellow River ~ **USA** 284-285 D 5
Yellow River ~ **USA** 284-285 G 3
Yellow River ~ **USA** 286-287 C 1
Yellow River = Huang He ~ **VRC** 154-155 K 3
Yellow River Mission ○ **PNG** 183 A 2
Yellow Sea ≈ 150-151 D 10
Yellowstone Lake ⊖ **USA** (WY) 252-253 H 2
Yellowstone National Park ⊥ ··· **USA** (WY) 252-253 H 2
Yellowstone River ~ **USA** 250-251 P 4
Yellville ○ **USA** (AR) 276-277 C 4
Yelm ○ **USA** (WA) 244-245 C 4
Yelrandu ○ **IND** 142-143 B 7
Yelvertoft ○ **AUS** 174-175 E 7
Yelwa ○ **WAN** (PLA) 204-205 H 4
Yelwa ○ **WAN** (SOK) 204-205 F 3
Yema ○ **ZRE** 210-211 D 6
Yema Manshan ▲ **VRC** 146-147 N 6
Yemassee ○ **USA** (SC) 284-285 K 4
Yembo ○ **ETH** 208-209 C 4
Yemen = al-Yaman ■ **Y** 132-133 E 6
Yemnu ○ **PNG** 183 B 2
Yen ○ **CAM** 210-211 D 2
Yenagoa ○ **WAN** 204-205 G 6
Yenakiyeve = Jenakijeve ○ **UA** 102-103 L 3
Yenangyaung ○ **MYA** 142-143 J 5
Yên Bái ☆ **VN** 156-157 D 6
Yên Châu ○ **VN** 156-157 D 6
Yenda ○ **AUS** 180-181 J 3
Yendé Milimou ○ **RG** 202-203 F 5
Yendéré ○ **BF** 202-203 H 4
Yendi ○ **GH** 202-203 K 5
Yên Định ☆ **VN** 156-157 E 6
Yénéganou ○ **RCB** 210-211 D 5
Yenge ~ **ZRE** 210-211 H 4
Yengema ○ **WAL** 202-203 E 5
Yengil ○ **IND** 142-143 H 2
Yengisar ○ **VRC** 146-147 C 6
Yengo National Park ⊥ **AUS** 180-181 L 2
Yên Hung ○ **VN** 156-157 C 6
Yenice Irmağı ~ **TR** 128-129 E 2
Yenihisar ☆ **TR** 128-129 B 4
Yenişehir ☆ **TR** 128-129 C 2
Yenkis ○ **PNG** 183 B 3
Yên Ly ○ **VN** 156-157 D 7
Yéno ○ **G** 210-211 C 4
Yentna River ~ **USA** 20-21 P 5
Yeoford ○ **CDN** (ALB) 232-233 D 2
Yeola ○ **IND** 138-139 E 9
Yeo Lake ⊖ **AUS** 176-177 H 4
Yeoval ○ **AUS** 180-181 K 2
Yeovil ○ **GB** 90-91 F 6
Yeppoon ○ **AUS** 178-179 L 2
Yerba Buena ○ **PE** 70-71 B 5
Yercaud ○ **IND** 140-141 H 5
Yerevan = Erevan ★ **AR** 128-129 L 2
Yergara ○ **IND** 140-141 G 2
Yergeni = Ergeni ▲ **RUS** 96-97 D 9
Yeriho = Arīḥāl ☆ •• **AUT** 130-131 D 2
Yerington ○ • **USA** (NV) 246-247 F 5
Yerköy ○ **TR** 128-129 F 3
Yermala ○ **IND** 138-139 E 10
Yerupaja, Cerro ▲ **PE** 64-65 D 7
Yerushalayim = al-Quds ★ ··· **IL** 130-131 D 2
Yesan ○ **ROK** 150-151 F 9
Yesanpo • **VRC** 154-155 J 2
Yeshin ○ **MYA** 142-143 J 4
Yesildağ ○ **TR** 128-129 D 4
Yeşildağ ○ **TR** 128-129 D 4
Yeşilhisar ☆ **TR** 128-129 F 3
Yeşilırmak ~ **TR** 128-129 G 2
Yesilırmak ~ **TR** 128-129 G 2
Yeşilova ☆ **TR** 128-129 C 4
Yeso ○ **USA** (NM) 256-257 L 4
Yeso Arroyo ~ **USA** 256-257 L 4
Yesterday River ~ **CDN** 236-237 H 2
Yet ○ **ETH** 208-209 F 6
Yetman ○ **AUS** 178-179 L 5
Yetti ∸ **RIM** 196-197 G 2
Ye-u ○ **MYA** 142-143 J 4
Yeu, Île d' ⌒ **F** 90-91 F 8
Yevpatoriya = Jevpatorija ☆ • **UA** 102-103 H 5
Yewa, River ~ **WAN** 204-205 E 5
Yew Mountain ▲ **USA** 280-281 F 5
Ye Xian ○ **VRC** 154-155 H 5
Yeyik ○ **VRC** 144-145 D 2
Ygannja ~ **RUS** 110-111 W 4
Ygyatta ~ **RUS** 118-119 H 4
Yhú ○ **PY** 76-77 K 3
Yi'an ○ **VRC** 150-151 E 4
Yibin ○ **VRC** 156-157 D 2
Yichang ○ **VRC** 154-155 G 6
Yicheng ○ **VRC** (HUB) 154-155 H 6
Yicheng ○ **VRC** (SHA) 154-155 G 4
Yichuan ○ **VRC** (HEN) 154-155 H 4
Yichuan ○ **VRC** (SXI) 154-155 G 4
Yichun ○ **VRC** (HEI) 150-151 G 4
Yichun ○ **VRC** (JXI) 156-157 J 3
Yığılca ☆ **TR** 128-129 D 2
Yihuang ○ **VRC** 156-157 K 3
Yijun ○ **VRC** 154-155 F 4
Yilan ○ **VRC** 150-151 G 4
Yıldız Dağları ▲ **TR** 128-129 B 2
Yıldızeli ☆ **TR** 128-129 G 3
Yilehuli Shan ▲ **VRC** 150-151 D 2
Yiliang ○ **VRC** (YUN) 156-157 C 4
Yiliang ○ **VRC** (YUN) 156-157 D 3
Yilingyan • **VRC** 156-157 F 5
Yilong ○ **VRC** 154-155 E 6
Yilou ○ **BF** 202-203 K 3
Yima ○ **VRC** 154-155 G 4
Yimen ○ **VRC** 156-157 C 4
Yimni River ~ **PNG** 183 B 2
Yimuhe ○ **VRC** 150-151 C 1
Yinan ○ **VRC** 154-155 L 4
Yinchuan ☆ • **VRC** 154-155 E 2
Yindarlgooda, Lake ⊖ **AUS** 176-177 G 5
Yindi ○ **AUS** 176-177 G 5
Yingawunarri Aboriginal Land X **AUS** 172-173 K 4
Yingcheng ○ **VRC** 154-155 H 6
Yingde ○ **VRC** 156-157 H 4
Yinggehai ○ **VRC** 156-157 F 7
Ying He ~ **VRC** 154-155 J 5
Yingjing ○ **VRC** 156-157 C 2
Yingkou ○ **VRC** 150-151 D 7
Yingkou (Dashiqiao) ○ **VRC** 150-151 D 7
Yingshan ○ **VRC** (HUB) 154-155 H 6
Yingshan ○ **VRC** (SIC) 154-155 E 6
Yingshang ○ **VRC** 154-155 K 5
Yingtan ○ **VRC** 156-157 K 2
Yingui ○ **CAM** 204-205 J 6
Ying Xian ○ **VRC** 154-155 H 2
Yingxian Muta • **VRC** 154-155 H 2
Yining ○ **VRC** 146-147 E 4
Yinjiang ○ **VRC** 156-157 F 2
Yinnietharra ○ **AUS** 176-177 D 2
Yin Shan ▲ **VRC** 148-149 J 7
Yinxu ∴ • **VRC** 154-155 J 3
Yi'ong Co • **VRC** 144-145 K 5
Yi'ong Zangbo ~ **VRC** 144-145 K 5
Yipinglang ○ **VRC** 156-157 B 4
Yiqikai ○ **VRC** 144-145 M 3
Yirga Alem ○ **ETH** 208-209 D 5
Yirga Ch'efē ○ **ETH** 208-209 D 5
Yirol ○ **SUD** 206-207 K 5
Yirrkala X **AUS** 174-175 D 3
Yirshi ○ **VRC** 150-151 B 4
Yirūb = Ğarūb ○ **Y** 132-133 H 5
Yishan ○ **VRC** 156-157 F 4
Yishui ○ **VRC** 154-155 L 4
Yismala Giyorgis ○ **ETH** 208-209 C 3
Yitong ○ **VRC** 150-151 E 6
Yitulihe ○ **VRC** 150-151 C 2
Yity ○ **OM** 132-133 L 2
Yiwu ○ **VRC** (XUZ) 146-147 M 4
Yiwu ○ **VRC** (ZHE) 156-157 M 2
Yiwulüshan • **VRC** 150-151 C 7
Yi Xian ○ **VRC** (HEB) 154-155 J 2
Yi Xian ○ **VRC** (LIA) 150-151 C 7
Yixing ○ **VRC** 154-155 L 6
Yiyang ○ **VRC** (HUN) 156-157 H 2
Yiyang ○ **VRC** (JXI) 156-157 K 2
Yiyuan ○ **VRC** 154-155 L 3
Yizhang ○ **VRC** 156-157 H 4
Yizheng ○ **VRC** 154-155 L 5
Ylämaa ○ **FIN** 88-89 J 6
Ylikiiminki ○ **FIN** 88-89 J 4
Yli-Kitka ⊖ **FIN** 88-89 K 3
Ylitornio ○ **FIN** 88-89 G 3
Ylivieska ○ **FIN** 88-89 H 4
Yllymah ○ **RUS** 118-119 N 6
Ylöjärvi ○ **FIN** 88-89 G 6
Ymer Nunatakker ▲ **GRØ** 26-27 n 5
Ymer Ø ⌒ **GRØ** 26-27 n 7
Ymir ○ **CDN** (BC) 230-231 M 4
Ynahsyt ○ **RUS** 118-119 J 4
Yoa, Lac ○ **TCH** 198-199 K 3
Yoakum ○ **USA** (TX) 266-267 K 4
Yobe, Komadougou ~ 198-199 F 6
Yoboki ○ **DJI** 208-209 F 3
Yockanookany River ~ **USA** 268-269 L 4
Yoco ○ **YV** 60-61 K 2
Yocona River ~ **USA** 268-269 L 2
Yoder ○ **USA** (CO) 254-255 L 5
Yoder ○ **USA** (WY) 252-253 O 5
Yof ○ • **SN** 202-203 B 2
Yufur ○ **RI** 166-167 J 4
Yogan, Cerro ▲ **RCH** 80 F 7
Yogoum ○ **TCH** 198-199 J 4
Yog Point ▲ **RP** 160-161 F 5
Yogyakarta ☆ **RI** 168 D 3
Yohnnybli ○ **LB** 202-203 F 7
Yoho ○ **CDN** (BC) 230-231 N 2
Yoho National Park ⊥ ··· **CDN** (BC) 230-231 N 2
Yoichi ○ **J** 152-153 J 3
Yoiti-dake ▲ **J** 152-153 J 3
Yokadouma ○ **CAM** 210-211 E 2
Yokena ○ **USA** (MS) 268-269 K 4
Yokkaichi ○ **J** 152-153 G 7
Yoko ○ **CAM** 204-205 K 6
Yokoate-shima ⌒ **J** 152-153 C 10
Yokoboué ○ **CI** 202-203 H 7
Yokohama ○ **J** (AOM) 152-153 J 4
Yokohama ☆ • **J** (KAN) 152-153 H 7
Yokosuka ○ **J** 152-153 H 7
Yokote ○ **J** 152-153 J 5
Yola ○ **CAM** 206-207 B 6
Yola ☆ **WAN** 204-205 K 4
Yolla ○ **AUS** 180-181 H 6
Yolombo ○ **ZRE** 210-211 J 4
Yombi ○ **G** 210-211 C 4
Yomblon ○ **PE** 64-65 C 5
Yomou ○ **RG** 202-203 F 6
Yomuka ○ **RI** 166-167 K 5
Yonago ○ **J** 152-153 E 7
Yoneshiro-gawa ~ **J** 152-153 J 4
Yonezawa ○ **J** 152-153 J 6
Yong'an ○ **VRC** 156-157 K 4
Yongchang ○ **VRC** 154-155 B 2
Yongcheng ○ **VRC** 154-155 K 5
Yongchuan ○ **VRC** 156-157 D 2
Yongdeng ○ **VRC** 154-155 C 3
Yongding ○ **VRC** 156-157 K 4
Yŏngdŏk ○ **ROK** 150-151 G 9
Yongfeng ○ **VRC** 156-157 J 3
Yongfu ○ **VRC** 156-157 F 4
Yongjing ○ **VRC** 154-155 C 4
Yongji Qiao • **VRC** 156-157 F 4
Yŏngju ○ **ROK** 150-151 G 9
Yongkang ○ **VRC** 156-157 L 2
Yongle Gong • **VRC** 154-155 G 4
Yongle Qundao ⌒ **VRC** 158-159 L 2
Yongling ○ **VRC** 150-151 E 7
Yongning ○ **VRC** (GXI) 156-157 F 5
Yongning ○ **VRC** (NIN) 154-155 E 2
Yongofondo ○ **RCA** 206-207 F 6
Yong Peng ○ **MAL** 162-163 E 3
Yongping ○ **VRC** 154-155 F 3
Yongren ○ **VRC** 156-157 B 3
Yongsheng ○ **VRC** 142-143 M 2
Yongshun ○ **VRC** 156-157 F 2
Yongtai ○ **VRC** 156-157 L 4
Yongxin ○ **VRC** 156-157 J 3
Yongxing ○ **VRC** 156-157 H 3
Yongxiu ○ **VRC** 156-157 J 2
Yonibana ○ **WAL** 202-203 D 5
Yonkers ○ **USA** (NY) 280-281 N 3
Yonne ~ **F** 90-91 J 7
Yonoféré ○ **SN** 202-203 C 2
Yop, Pulau ⌒ **RI** 166-167 H 3
Yopal ○ **CO** 60-61 E 5
Yopales ○ **YV** 60-61 K 3
Yopei or Tamala Port ○ **GH** 202-203 K 5
Yopie ○ **LB** 202-203 F 6
Yopurga ○ **VRC** 146-147 C 6
Yorito ○ **HN** 52-53 L 4
York ○ **AUS** 176-177 D 5
York ○ **GB** 90-91 G 5
York ○ **USA** (AL) 284-285 B 4
York ○ **USA** (MT) 250-251 H 5
York ○ **USA** (ND) 258-259 H 3
York ○ **USA** (NE) 262-263 J 4
York ○ **USA** (PA) 280-281 K 4
York ○ **USA** (SC) 284-285 J 2
York ○ **WAL** 202-203 D 5
York, Cape ▲ **AUS** 174-175 G 2
York, Kap ▲ **GRØ** 26-27 R 6
Yorke Peninsula ◡ **AUS** 180-181 D 3
Yorketown ○ **AUS** 180-181 D 3
Yorkeys Knob ○ **AUS** 174-175 H 5
York Factory (abandoned) ○ **CDN** 34-35 K 2
York Haven ○ **USA** (PA) 280-281 K 3
Yorkrakine ○ **AUS** 176-177 D 5
York River ~ **CDN** 238-239 H 3
York River ~ **USA** 280-281 K 6
Yorkshire Dales National Park ⊥ **GB** 90-91 F 4
Yorkshire Downs ○ **AUS** 174-175 F 7
York Sound ≈ 172-173 G 3
Yorkton ○ **CDN** (SAS) 232-233 Q 4
Yorktown ○ **USA** (TX) 266-267 K 5
Yorktown ○ **USA** (VA) 280-281 K 6
Yorkville ○ **USA** (IL) 274-275 K 3
Yoro ☆ **HN** 52-53 L 4
Yoro, Montaña de ▲ **HN** 52-53 L 4
Yorobougoula ○ **RMM** 202-203 G 4
Yoron ○ **J** 152-153 C 11
Yoron-shima ⌒ **J** 152-153 C 11
Yorosso ○ **RMM** 202-203 H 3
Yorubaland, Plateau of ▲ **WAN** 204-205 E 4
Yosemite ○ **USA** (KY) 276-277 L 3
Yosemite National Park ⊥ ··· **USA** (CA) 248-249 E 2
Yosemite Village ○ **USA** (CA) 248-249 E 2
Yoseravi ○ **BOL** 70-71 F 6
Yoshii-gawa ~ **J** 152-153 F 7
Yoshino-gawa ~ **J** 152-153 F 7
Yos Sudarso, Teluk ≈ 166-167 L 3
Yŏsu ○ **ROK** 150-151 F 10
Yosua ○ **PNG** 183 B 3
Yotefa Nature Reserve ⊥ •• **RI** 166-167 L 3
Yōtei-san ▲ **J** 152-153 J 3
Youangarra ○ **AUS** 176-177 E 4
Yoube ○ **ETH** 208-209 G 5
Youbou ○ **CDN** (BC) 230-231 E 5
Youdunzi ○ **VRC** 146-147 K 6
Youghal = Eochaill ○ **IRL** 90-91 D 6
Youghiogheny River Lake ⊖ **USA** (PA) 280-281 G 4
Yougzhou ○ **VRC** 156-157 G 3
You Jiang ~ **VRC** 156-157 E 5
Youkounkoun ○ **RG** 202-203 D 3
Young ○ **AUS** 180-181 K 3
Young ○ **CDN** (SAS) 232-233 N 4
Young ○ **ROU** 78-79 L 2
Younghusband, Lake ⊖ **AUS** 178-179 D 6
Younghusband Peninsula ◡ **AUS** 180-181 E 4
Youngou ~ **RCA** 206-207 E 5
Youngs Cove ○ **CDN** (NB) 240-241 K 5
Youngstown ○ **CDN** (ALB) 232-233 G 4
Youngstown ○ **USA** (FL) 286-287 D 1
Youngstown ○ **USA** (NY) 278-279 B 5
Youngstown ○ **USA** (OH) 280-281 F 2
Young Sund ≈ 26-27 p 6
Yountville ○ **USA** (CA) 246-247 C 5
Youssef Ben Tachfine, Barrage < **MA** 188-189 G 6
Youssoufia ○ **MA** 188-189 G 4
Youvarou ○ **RMM** 202-203 H 2
You Xian ○ **VRC** 156-157 H 3
Youyang ○ **VRC** 156-157 F 2
Youyi Feng = Tavan Bogd ▲ **VRC** 146-147 H 1
Youyiguan ○ **VRC** 156-157 E 5
Yowa ~ **ZRE** 210-211 H 2
Yowah Creek ~ **AUS** 178-179 H 4
Yoya, Pampa de la ∸ **PE** 70-71 B 5
Yoyo National Park ⊥ **GH** 202-203 J 7
Yozgat ☆ **TR** 128-129 F 3
Ypsilanti ○ **USA** (MI) 272-273 F 5
Yreka ○ **USA** (CA) 246-247 C 2
Yrgyz ☆ **KZ** (AKT) 126-127 O 3
Yrgyz ~ **KZ** 126-127 O 3
Yr Wyddfa = Snowdon ▲ **GB** 90-91 E 5
Ysabel Channel ≈ 183 E 1
Ystad ○ • **S** 86-87 F 9
Ystannah-Hočo ○ **RUS** 110-111 N 3
Yštyk ○ **KS** 146-147 D 5
Ysyk-Köl, ozero ⊖ **KS** 146-147 C 4
Ytar, Sylgy- ○ **RUS** 112-113 H 3
Ytterhogdal ○ **S** 86-87 G 5
Yttygran, ostrov ⌒ **RUS** 112-113 Y 4
Ytyk-Kjuël' ☆ • **RUS** 120-121 E 2
Ytymdža ~ **RUS** 118-119 N 7
Yu, Pulau ⌒ **RI** 166-167 E 2
Yu'alliq, Ğabal ▲ **ET** 194-195 F 2
Yuanbao Shan ▲ **VRC** 156-157 F 4
Yuango ○ **VRC** 154-155 G 4
Yuanjiang ○ **VRC** (HUN) 156-157 H 2
Yuanjiang ○ **VRC** (YUN) 156-157 B 5
Yuan Jiang ~ **VRC** 156-157 G 2
Yuan Jiang ~ **VRC** 156-157 C 5
Yuanling ○ **VRC** 156-157 G 2
Yuanmou ○ **VRC** 156-157 B 4
Yuanping ○ **VRC** 154-155 H 2
Yuanshangdu Yizhi ∴ • **VRC** 148-149 N 6
Yuantan ○ **VRC** 154-155 K 6
Yuanyang ○ **VRC** 156-157 C 5
Yuat River ~ **PNG** 183 B 3
Yuba ○ **USA** (OK) 264-265 H 5
Yuba City ○ **USA** (CA) 246-247 D 4
Yuba Pass ▲ **USA** (CA) 246-247 E 4
Yūbari ○ **J** 152-153 J 3
Yūbari-gawa ~ **J** 152-153 K 3
Yūbari-santi ▲ **J** 152-153 K 3
Yuba River ~ **USA** 246-247 D 4
Yubdo ○ **ETH** 208-209 B 4
Yūbetsu ○ **J** 152-153 K 2
Yubetu-dake ▲ **J** 152-153 J 3
Yucaipa ○ **USA** (CA) 248-249 G 5
Yucatán ○ **MEX** 52-53 L 1
Yucatán □ **MEX** 52-53 K 1
Yucca ○ **USA** (AZ) 256-257 A 4
Yucca House National Monument • **USA** (CO) 254-255 G 6
Yucca Valley ○ **USA** (CA) 248-249 H 5
Yuci ○ **VRC** 154-155 H 3
Yucomo ○ **BOL** 70-71 D 4
Yudu ○ **VRC** 156-157 J 4
Yuechi ○ **VRC** 154-155 E 6
Yuelai ○ **VRC** 154-155 F 6
Yuelong ○ **VRC** 156-157 H 2
Yuelushan • **VRC** 156-157 H 2
Yuendumu X **AUS** 172-173 K 7
Yuendumu Aboriginal Land X **AUS** 172-173 K 7
Yuenkotang ○ **VRC** 144-145 C 4
Yueqing ○ **VRC** 156-157 M 2
Yuexi ○ **VRC** 154-155 K 6
Yueyang ○ **VRC** 156-157 H 2
Yueyaqan Mingshashan • **VRC** 146-147 M 5
Yufengshan • **VRC** 156-157 F 4
Yufle ○ **SP** 208-209 H 3
Yüglük Dağı ▲ **TR** 128-129 E 4
Yugorskiy Shar, Proliv = Jugorskij Šar, proliv ≈ 108-109 H 7
Yugoslavia = Jugoslavija ■ **YU** 100-101 G 3
Yuhe ○ **VRC** (SXI) 154-155 F 3
Yuhe ○ **VRC** (YUN) 156-157 D 3
Yuhua D. • **VRC** 156-157 K 3
Yuin ○ **AUS** 176-177 D 3
Yuinmery ○ **AUS** 176-177 E 4
Yu Jiang ~ **VRC** 156-157 F 5
Yuki ○ **ZRE** 210-211 G 5
Yuki River ~ **USA** 20-21 M 4
Yukon ○ **USA** (OK) 264-265 G 3
Yukon-Charley-Rivers National Preserve ⊥ **USA** 20-21 T 4
Yukon Delta ≈ 20-21 H 5
Yukon Delta National Wildlife Refuge ⊥ **USA** 20-21 H 5
Yukon Flats ⊥ **USA** 20-21 S 3
Yukon Plateau ▲ **CDN** 20-21 V 5
Yukon River ~ **USA** 20-21 P 4
Yukon Territory □ **CDN** 30-31 E 4
Yüksekova ☆ **TR** 128-129 L 4
Yukuhashi ○ **J** 152-153 D 8
Yulara ○ **AUS** 176-177 L 2
Yule, Mount ▲ **PNG** 183 D 5
Yuleba ○ **AUS** 178-179 K 4
Yulee ○ **USA** (FL) 286-287 H 1
Yule Island ⌒ **PNG** 183 D 5
Yule River ~ **AUS** 172-173 D 6
Yuli ○ **RC** 156-157 M 5
Yuli ○ **VRC** 146-147 H 5
Yuli ○ **WAN** 204-205 J 4
Yuli, River ~ **WAN** 204-205 J 4
Yulin ○ **VRC** (GXI) 156-157 G 5
Yulin ○ **VRC** (SHA) 154-155 F 2
Yulin Ku • **VRC** 146-147 M 5
Yulong Xue Shan ▲ **VRC** 142-143 M 2
Yulton, Lago ⊖ **RCH** 80 D 2
Yului ○ **PNG** 183 B 2
Yuma ○ **USA** (AZ) 256-257 A 6
Yuma ○ **USA** (CO) 254-255 N 3
Yuma Proving Ground xx **USA** (AZ) 256-257 A 5
Yumariba ○ **YV** 60-61 K 5
Yumbarra Conservation Park ⊥ **AUS** 176-177 M 5
Yumbe ○ **EAU** 212-213 C 2
Yumbel ○ **RCH** 78-79 C 4
Yumbi ○ **ZRE** (Ban) 210-211 F 4
Yumbi ○ **ZRE** (KIV) 210-211 L 4
Yumbo ○ **CO** 60-61 C 6
Yumen ○ **VRC** 146-147 N 6
Yumenguan ○ **VRC** (GAN) 146-147 L 5
Yumenguan • **VRC** (GAN) 146-147 L 5
Yumen Zhen ○ **VRC** 148-149 C 7
Yumin ○ **VRC** 146-147 F 2
Yumtang ○ **BHT** 142-143 F 2
Yuna ○ **AUS** 176-177 C 4
Yuna, Río ~ **DOM** 54-55 L 5
Yunak ☆ **TR** 128-129 D 3
Yunan ○ **VRC** 156-157 G 5
Yunaska Island ⌒ **USA** 22-23 L 6
Yuncheng ○ **VRC** (SHA) 154-155 G 4
Yuncheng ○ **VRC** (SHD) 154-155 J 4
Yundamindera ○ **AUS** 176-177 G 4
Yunfu ○ **VRC** 156-157 H 5
Yungang Shiku • **VRC** 154-155 H 1
Yungas ∸ **BOL** 70-71 D 5
Yungay ○ **PE** 64-65 D 6
Yungay ○ **RCH** 78-79 D 4
Yungui Gaoyuan ∸ **VRC** 156-157 C 4
Yunguyo ○ **PE** 70-71 C 5
Yungyang ○ **VRC** 154-155 H 5
Yunhe ○ **VRC** 156-157 L 2
Yunkai Dashan ▲ **VRC** 156-157 F 5
Yunkanjini Aboriginal Land X **AUS** 172-173 K 7
Yun Ling ▲ **VRC** 142-143 L 2
Yunlong ○ **VRC** 142-143 L 3
Yunmeng ○ **VRC** 154-155 H 6
Yunomae ○ **J** 152-153 D 8
Yuntaishan • **VRC** 154-155 L 4
Yunwu Shan ▲ **VRC** 156-157 G 5
Yunwu Shan ▲ **VRC** 148-149 N 7
Yun Xian ○ **VRC** (HUB) 154-155 G 5
Yun Xian ○ **VRC** (YUN) 142-143 M 3
Yunxiao ○ **VRC** 156-157 K 5
Yuping ○ **VRC** 156-157 F 3
Yupurari, Raudal ~ **CO** 66-67 B 2
Yuqian ○ **VRC** 154-155 L 6
Yuqing ○ **VRC** 156-157 E 3
Yuquanshan • **VRC** 154-155 G 6
Yura ○ **PE** 70-71 B 5
Yura, Río ~ **BOL** 70-71 E 7
Yura-gawa ~ **J** 152-153 F 7
Yurayaco ○ **CO** 64-65 D 1
Yuraygir National Park ⊥ **AUS** 178-179 M 5
Yurécuaro ○ **MEX** 52-53 C 1
Yurimaguas ○ **PE** 64-65 D 4
Yuriria ○ **MEX** 52-53 D 1
Yurua, Río ~ **PE** 64-65 F 6
Yuruan, Río ~ **YV** 62-63 D 2
Yurubí, Parque Nacional ⊥ **YV** 60-61 G 2
Yurungkax He ~ **VRC** 144-145 C 2
Yusala, Lago ⊖ **BOL** 70-71 D 4
Yuscarán ☆ **HN** 52-53 L 5
Yu Shan ▲ **RC** 156-157 M 5
Yushan ○ **VRC** 156-157 L 2
Yushan National Park ⊥ • **RC** 156-157 M 5
Yushe ○ **VRC** 154-155 H 3
Yushu ○ **VRC** (JIL) 150-151 F 5
Yushu ○ **VRC** (QIN) 144-145 L 4
Yūsuf, Bahr < **ET** 194-195 E 3
Yusufeli ☆ **TR** 128-129 J 2
Yusun Shoal ≃ 158-159 K 5
Yusupalik Tag ▲ **VRC** 146-147 J 6
Yutian ○ **VRC** 144-145 C 2
Yuto ○ **RA** 76-77 E 2
Yuwang ○ **VRC** 154-155 E 3
Yuxi ○ **VRC** 156-157 C 4
Yu Xian ○ **VRC** 154-155 H 2
Yuyao ○ **VRC** 154-155 M 6
Yuzawa ○ **J** 152-153 J 5
Yuzhno Sakhalinsk = Južno-Sahalinsk ☆ **RUS** 122-123 K 5
Yuzhnyy Ural = Južnyj Ural ▲ **RUS** 96-97 K 8
Yuzhou ○ **VRC** 154-155 H 4
Yvetot ○ **F** 90-91 H 7
Ywama ○ **MYA** 142-143 K 5
Ywathit ○ **MYA** 142-143 J 4
Ywathit ○ **MYA** 142-143 J 6
Ywathitke ○ **MYA** 142-143 H 5

Z

Za, Oued ~ **MA** 188-189 K 3
Zaachila ∴ • **MEX** 52-53 F 3
Zaalajskij hrebet ▲ **TJ** 136-137 M 5
Zaamar = Bat-Ölzijt ○ **MAU** 148-149 G 3
Zaamin ○ **UZ** 136-137 L 5
Zaanstad ○ **NL** 92-93 H 2
Zab, Monts du ▲ **DZ** 190-191 E 3
Zabadāni, az- ○ **SYR** 128-129 G 6
Žabaj ~ **KZ** 124-125 F 2
Zabajkal'sk ☆ **RUS** 118-119 H 11
Zabarğad, Ğazīrat ⌒ **ET** 194-195 H 6
Žabasak ○ **KZ** 126-127 O 2
Zabid ○ ··· **Y** 132-133 C 6
Zabid, Wādī ~ **Y** 132-133 C 6
Zābol □ **AFG** 134-135 M 2
Zābol ○ • **IR** 134-135 J 3
Zāboli ○ **IR** 134-135 J 5
Zabré ○ **BF** 202-203 K 4
Zaburun'e ○ **KZ** 96-97 G 10
Zaburunje cyganaky ≈ 96-97 G 10
Zabūt ○ **Y** 132-133 H 6
Žabysaj ~ **KZ** 126-127 O 3
Zabzugu ○ **GH** 202-203 L 5
Zacapa ☆ **GCA** 52-53 K 4
Zacapa ○ **HN** 52-53 K 4
Zacapu ○ **MEX** 52-53 D 2
Zacatal ○ **MEX** 52-53 J 2
Zacatecas □ **MEX** 50-51 H 6
Zacatecoluca ☆ **ES** 52-53 K 5
Zacatepec ○ **MEX** 52-53 E 2
Zacatlán ○ **MEX** 52-53 F 2
Zachariaes Bræ ⊂ **GRØ** 26-27 p 4
Zachary ○ **USA** (LA) 268-269 J 6
Zachidnyj Buh ~ **UA** 102-103 C 2
Zacoalco de Torres ○ **MEX** 52-53 C 1
Zacualpan ○ **MEX** 52-53 E 2
Zacualtipán ○ **MEX** 52-53 E 1
Zaculeu ∴ • **GCA** 52-53 J 4
Zad, Col du ▲ **MA** 188-189 J 4
Zadar ○ • **HR** 100-101 E 2
Zadetkale Kyun ⌒ **MYA** 158-159 E 5
Zadetkyi Kyun ⌒ **MYA** 158-159 E 6
Zadgaj ○ **MAU** 148-149 D 4
Zadié ~ **G** 210-211 D 3
Zadoi ○ **VRC** 144-145 K 4
Zadonsk ○ **RUS** 94-95 Q 5
Zadonsk, Severo- ○ **RUS** 94-95 Q 4
Zaër-Zaïa ∸ **MA** 188-189 H 4
Ẓafār ∴ • **Y** 132-133 D 6
Za'farāna ○ **ET** 194-195 F 3
Za'farāna, Ra's ▲ **ET** 194-195 F 3
Zafarqand ○ **IR** 134-135 E 2
Zafarwāl ○ **PK** 138-139 E 3
Zafra ○ •• **E** 98-99 D 5
Ẓafra, aẓ- ∸ **UAE** 132-133 J 2
Zagai Island ⌒ **AUS** 174-175 G 1
Żagań ○ • **PL** 92-93 N 3
Zagaoua ∸ **TCH** 198-199 K 5
Žagarė ○ •• **LT** 94-95 H 3
Zagastajn davaa ▲ **MAU** 148-149 C 3
Zagatala = Zaqatala ○ • **AZ** 128-129 M 2
Zāge ○ **IR** 134-135 C 2
Zaghouan ☆ **TN** 190-191 H 2
Zaghouan, Jebel ▲ **TN** 190-191 H 2
Zagné ○ • **CI** 202-203 G 6
Zagora ○ **MA** 188-189 J 5
Zagorsk = Sergiev Posad ☆ ··· **RUS** 94-95 Q 3
Zagorskij ○ **RUS** 122-123 K 5
Zagreb ★ • **HR** 100-101 E 2
Zagros Mountains = Zāgros, Kūhhā-ye ▲ **IR** 134-135 C 2
Zagustaj ○ **RUS** 118-119 E 10
Zaharenko ○ **RUS** 110-111 Y 7
Zaharodze ∸ **BY** 94-95 J 5
Zaharovka ○ **KZ** 124-125 G 4
Zaharovo ○ **RUS** 118-119 D 10
Zāhedān ○ **IR** (FAR) 134-135 E 4
Zāhedān ☆ **IR** (SIS) 134-135 J 4
Ẓāhira, aẓ- ∸ **OM** 132-133 K 4
Zahirābād ○ **IND** 140-141 G 2
Zahir Pir ○ **PK** 138-139 C 5
Zahl ○ **USA** (ND) 258-259 D 3
Zahla ☆ **RL** 128-129 F 6
Zahmet ○ **TM** 136-137 H 6
Ẓahrān, aẓ- ○ **KSA** 134-135 D 5
Ẓahrān al-Ğanūb ○ **KSA** 132-133 C 5
Zāḫū ☆ **IRQ** 128-129 K 4
Zaidiya, az- ○ **Y** 132-133 C 6
Zaidūn, Wādī z- ~ **ET** 194-195 F 5
Zaigraevo ○ **RUS** 116-117 O 10
Zaila ○ **ZRE** 214-215 C 5
Zainsk ☆ **RUS** 96-97 H 6
Zaïo ○ **MA** 188-189 K 3
Zaïre □ **ANG** 216-217 B 3
Zaïre ~ **ZRE** 210-211 E 6
Zaïre = Zaïre ■ **ZRE** 210-211 G 5
Zaječar ○ **YU** 100-101 J 3
Zajsan ○ **KZ** 124-125 O 5
Zajsan köli ⊖ **KZ** 124-125 N 4
Žajyndy ~ **KZ** 126-127 M 4
Zaka ○ **ZW** 218-219 F 5
Zakamensk ○ **RUS** 116-117 L 10
Zaki Biam ○ **WAN** 204-205 H 5
Zákinthos ○ **GR** 100-101 H 6
Zákinthos ⌒ **GR** 100-101 H 6
Zakobjakino ○ **RUS** 94-95 R 2
Zakopane ○ •• **PL** 92-93 P 4
Zakouma ○ **TCH** 206-207 D 3
Zakouma, Parc National de ⊥ **TCH** 206-207 D 3
Zakou Shankou ▲ **VRC** 144-145 M 2
Žaksy ☆ **KZ** 124-125 E 3
Žaksybaj ~ **KZ** 96-97 J 9
Žaksybaj, köli ⊖ **KZ** 124-125 C 3
Žaksybutaly, tau ▲ **KZ** 126-127 N 4
Žaksy-Kargaly ~ **KZ** 126-127 M 2
Žaksy-Kön ~ **KZ** 124-125 F 4
Žaksy-Kylyç kölder ⊖ **KZ** 126-127 P 4
Zala ○ **ANG** 216-217 C 3
Zala ○ **ETH** 208-209 C 5
Zalaa ○ **MAU** 148-149 D 5
Zalābiya ∴ • **SYR** 128-129 H 5
Zalaegerszeg ○ **H** 92-93 O 5
Zalaf, az ○ **SYR** 128-129 G 6
Zalamea de la Serena ○ • **E** 98-99 E 5
Zalanga ○ **WAN** 204-205 J 3
Zalari ☆ **RUS** 116-117 L 9
Zalău ☆ **RO** 102-103 C 4
Žalauly, köli ⊖ **KZ** 124-125 J 2
Žaldama ~ **KZ** 124-125 D 3
Zalegošč' ○ **RUS** 94-95 P 5
Zaleščyky ☆ **UA** 102-103 D 3
Zalesovo ○ **RUS** 124-125 O 1
Zalesskij, Pereslavl- ○ • **RUS** 94-95 Q 3
Ẓalim ○ **KSA** 130-131 H 6
Zalingei ○ **SUD** 198-199 L 6
Zaliouan ○ **CI** 202-203 G 6
Zaliv ○ **RUS** 116-117 F 7
Zalki ○ **IND** 140-141 F 2
Zallūm, az- ○ **KSA** 130-131 G 2
Ẓalmā', Ğabal aẓ- ▲ **KSA** 130-131 F 4
Zaltan ○ **LAR** 192-193 H 3
Zaltan, Bi'r ○ **LAR** 192-193 H 3
Žaltyr ○ **KZ** 124-125 F 3
Žaltyr, köl ⊖ **KZ** 96-97 G 10
Žaltyrköl ⊖ **KZ** 96-97 G 9
Zaluč'e ○ **RUS** 94-95 M 3
Zalut ○ **MYA** 158-159 E 4
Zal'vjanka ~ **BY** 94-95 J 5
Zama ○ **RN** 204-205 E 1
Zamak ○ **Y** 132-133 E 5
Zama Lake ⊖ **CDN** 30-31 K 6
Žamanajrykty, tau ▲ **KZ** 126-127 L 5
Žaman-Kön ~ **KZ** 124-125 F 4
Zamantı Irmağı ~ **TR** 128-129 F 4
Zamantı Irmağı ~ **TR** 128-129 G 3
Zamay ○ **CAM** 204-205 K 3
Žambaj aral ⌒ **KZ** 96-97 F 10
Zambales Mountains ▲ **RP** 160-161 D 5
Žambejiti ☆ **KZ** 96-97 H 8
Zambeze ~ **ANG** 214-215 B 6
Zambeze, Rio ~ **MOC** 218-219 H 3
Zambezi ○ **Z** (NTW) 218-219 B 1
Zambezi ~ **Z** 218-219 E 2
Zambézia □ **MOC** 218-219 H 3
Zambezi Deka ○ **ZW** 218-219 D 4
Zambezi Escarpment ∸ **ZW** 218-219 E 3
Zambezi National Park ⊥ **ZW** 218-219 C 3
Zambi, Rapids de ~ • **ZRE** 210-211 D 6
Zambia ■ **Z** 218-219 C 2
Zamboanga City ○ • **RP** 160-161 E 9
Zamboanga Peninsula ◡ **RP** 160-161 E 9
Zamboanguita ○ **RP** 160-161 E 8
Zambrano ○ **HN** 52-53 L 4
Zambrów ○ **PL** 92-93 R 2
Zambué ○ **MOC** 218-219 F 2
Žambyl ○ **KZ** (DZZ) 124-125 G 5
Žambyl ☆ **KZ** (DZA) 136-137 M 3
Zamfara ~ **WAN** 198-199 B 6
Zaminān ○ **IR** 134-135 K 5
Zamlat Amagraj ∸ **WSA** 196-197 C 2
Zamora ○ •• **E** 98-99 E 4
Zamora ☆ **EC** 64-65 C 4
Zamora ○ **MEX** 52-53 C 1
Zamora, Punta ▲ **PE** 64-65 C 6
Zamora, Río ~ **EC** 64-65 C 3
Zamość ☆ ··· **PL** 92-93 R 3
Zāmurān Pass ▲ **PK** 134-135 K 5
Zamuro, Punta ▲ **YV** 60-61 G 2
Zamuro, Sierra del ▲ **YV** 60-61 K 5
Zamyn-Uud = Borhojn Tal ○ **MAU** 148-149 K 6
Zamza ~ **RCA** 206-207 E 5
Zamzam, Wādī ~ **LAR** 192-193 F 2
Zan ○ **TCH** 206-207 D 3
Zanaaul ○ **KZ** 124-125 O 4
Žanadar'ja ~ **KZ** 136-137 H 3
Zanaga ○ **RCB** 210-211 D 5
Žaṇakala ☆ **KZ** 96-97 G 9
Žana Ķazan ○ **KZ** 96-97 F 9
Žaṇakorgan ☆ **KZ** 136-137 K 3
Žanaortalyk ○ **KZ** 124-125 J 5
Žanatas ○ **KZ** 136-137 L 3
Žaṇatas ○ **KZ** 136-137 L 3
Zanda ○ **VRC** 144-145 B 5
Zandamela ○ **MOC** 220-221 M 2
Zanderij ○ **SME** 62-63 G 3
Zandvoort ○ **NL** 92-93 H 2
Zane Hills ▲ **USA** 20-21 M 3
Zanelli, Cerro ▲ **RCH** 80 D 6
Zanesville ○ **USA** (OH) 280-281 D 4
Zanfla ○ **CI** 202-203 H 6
Zanğān □ **IR** 128-129 M 4
Zanğān ☆ • **IR** (ZAN) 128-129 N 4
Zangāreddigūdem ○ **IND** 142-143 B 7
Zangasso ○ **RMM** 202-203 H 3
Zangdo ○ **VRC** 144-145 F 5
Zanğğān Rūd ~ **IR** 128-129 N 4
Zangguy ○ **VRC** 144-145 B 2
Zangitas ○ **RA** 78-79 F 2
Zango ○ **WAN** 198-199 D 6
Zanna, Ğabal az- ○ **UAE** 134-135 E 6
Zanré ○ **BF** 202-203 K 3
Zanthus ○ **AUS** 176-177 G 5
Zantiebougou ○ **RMM** 202-203 G 4
Zanuľe ○ **RUS** 96-97 F 3
Zanvar Čāy ~ **IR** 128-129 L 3
Žanybek ☆ **KZ** 96-97 E 9
Zanzibar ☆ •• **EAT** 214-215 K 4
Zanzibar ○ **RB** 218-219 E 6
Zanzibar and Pemba □ **EAT** 214-215 K 3
Zanzibar Channel ≈ 214-215 K 3
Zanzibar Island ⌒ **EAT** 214-215 K 4
Zanzra ○ **CI** 202-203 G 6
Zaokskij ☆ **RUS** 94-95 P 4
Zaonežskij zaliv ⊖ **RUS** 88-89 N 5
Zao Quasi National Park ⊥ **J** 152-153 J 5
Zaoro-Songou ○ **RCA** 206-207 C 6
Zao-san ▲ **J** 152-153 J 5
Zaouatanlaz ○ **DZ** 190-191 G 8
Zaouia Sidi Moussa ○ **DZ** 190-191 F 6
Zaoyang ○ **VRC** 154-155 H 5
Zaozërnyj ☆ **RUS** 116-117 G 8
Zaozhuang ○ **VRC** 154-155 K 4
Zapadna Morava ~ **YU** 100-101 H 3
Zapadnoe ○ **KZ** 124-125 E 2
Zapadno-Karel'skaja vozvyšennost' ▲ **RUS** 88-89 L 5
Zapadno-Sahalinskie gory ▲ **RUS** 122-123 K 3
Zapadnye Saledy, hrebet ▲ **RUS** 114-115 E 2
Zapadnyj, mys ▲ **RUS** 112-113 U 1
Zapadnyj Kamennyj, ostrov ⌒ **RUS** 108-109 U 4
Zapadnyj Tannu-Ola, hrebet ▲ **RUS** 116-117 E 10
Zapai ○ **ZRE** 206-207 G 6
Zapala ○ **RA** 78-79 D 5
Zapaleri, Cerro ▲ **BOL** 76-77 D 2
Zapallar ○ **RCH** (COQ) 76-77 B 6
Zapallar ○ **RCH** (VAL) 78-79 D 2
Zapata ○ **USA** (TX) 266-267 J 7
Zapata, Península de ◡ •• **C** 54-55 E 3
Zapatosa, Ciénaga ⊖ **CO** 60-61 E 3
Zape ○ **MEX** 50-51 G 5
Zape, Río ~ **MEX** 50-51 G 4
Zapiga ○ **RCH** 70-71 C 6
Zapoľe ○ **RUS** 94-95 L 2
Zapoljarnyj ○ **RUS** 88-89 L 2
Zapopan ○ • **MEX** 52-53 C 1
Zaporizhzhya = Zaporižžja ☆ • **UA** 102-103 J 4
Zaporižžja ☆ • **UA** 102-103 J 4
Zaporože = Zaporižžja ☆ • **UA** 102-103 J 4
Zapotillo ○ **EC** 64-65 B 4
Zapotlanejo ○ **MEX** 52-53 C 1
Zapovednik Černye zemli ⊥ **RUS** 126-127 G 5
Zapovednik Kodrii ⊥ **MD** 102-103 F 4
Zapovednik Magadanskij ⊥ **RUS** 120-121 Q 4
Zapovednik ostrov Vrangelja ⊥ **RUS** 112-113 U 1
Zapovednyj ○ **RUS** 122-123 E 7
Zaqāziq, az- ☆ **ET** 194-195 E 2
Za Qu ~ **VRC** 144-145 K 4
Zar ○ **IR** 134-135 G 5

Zar o RIM 196-197 C 6
Zara ☆ TR 128-129 G 3
Zarabag o UZ 136-137 K 6
Zarafšon o UZ 136-137 J 4
Zarafšon ~ UZ 136-137 H 5
Zaragoza o• E 98-99 G 4
Zaragoza o MEX (CHA) 50-51 F 2
Zaragoza o MEX (CHA) 50-51 F 3
Zaragoza o MEX (COA) 50-51 J 3
Zaragoza o MEX (PUE) 52-53 F 2
Zaragoza o MEX (SLP) 50-51 J 6
Zarajsk ☆•• RUS 94-95 Q 4
Zarand o IR 134-135 G 3
Zarandului, Munții ▲ RO 102-103 C 4
Zaranğ ☆ AFG 134-135 J 3
Zaranou o• CI 202-203 J 6
Zarasai o•• LT 94-95 K 4
Zárate o RA 78-79 K 3
Zarautz o E 98-99 F 3
Zaraza o YV 60-61 J 3
Zarbulak o KZ 124-125 N 5
Zarcero o CR 52-53 B 6
Zard o PK 134-135 L 4
Zar Dašt, Rūdḫāne-ye ~ IR 134-135 G 4
Zarde, Kūh-e ▲ IR 134-135 D 2
Zareče o RUS 116-117 N 9
Zarembo Island ⌒ USA 32-33 D 3
Zare Šaran ☆ AFG 138-139 B 3
Žargalant o MAU 148-149 G 3
Žargalthaan o MAU 148-149 J 4
Zarghūn ▲ PK 134-135 M 3
Zarǧūnšahr o AFG 138-139 B 3
Zari o WAN 198-199 F 6
Zaria o• WAN 204-205 G 3
Zarične o UA 102-103 E 2
Zarinsk ☆ RUS 124-125 O 2
Zarizyn ☆• RUS 96-97 D 9
Zarja, poluostrov ⌣ RUS 108-109 Y 4
Zarja, proliv ≈ 110-111 V 2
Žarkamys o KZ 126-127 M 4
Žarly ~ RUS 96-97 L 8
Žarma o KZ 124-125 M 4
Zarmal o AFG 138-139 B 3
Zarqa ~ JOR 130-131 D 1
Zarqā o SUD 200-201 D 6
Zarqā', az ☆ JOR 130-131 E 1
Zarqā' Ḥadida o SUD 206-207 H 3
Zarqān o IR 134-135 E 4
Zarrin o IR 134-135 F 2
Zarrīnābād o IR 128-129 N 5
Zarrīnābād o IR 128-129 N 4
Zarrīne Rūd ~ IR 128-129 M 4
Zarrīnšahr o IR 134-135 D 2
Zaruma o EC 64-65 C 3
Zarumilla o PE 64-65 B 3
Zarza de Granadilla o E 98-99 D 4
Zarzaïtine o DZ 190-191 G 6
Zarzal o CO 60-61 C 5
Zarzis o TN 190-191 H 4
Zašeek o RUS 88-89 M 3
Zaskar ~ IND 138-139 F 3
Zaškiv ☆ UA 102-103 G 3
Zastron o ZA 220-221 H 5
Zasuľe o RUS 88-89 T 4
Žatec o CZ 92-93 M 3
Zatobol'sk ☆ KZ 124-125 C 2
Zatoka o UA 102-103 G 4
Zatoka Syvaš ≈ 102-103 H 4
Zaube o LV 94-95 J 3
Zaulič'e o BY 94-95 K 4
Zaunguzskie Karakumy ⊥ TM 136-137 E 4
Zaur, Ra's az- ▲ KSA 130-131 L 4
Zaur, Ra's az- ▲ KWT 130-131 L 3
Zauraľskoe plato ▲ RUS 124-125 B 2
Zavalla o USA (TX) 268-269 F 5
Zaväre o IR 134-135 E 2
Žavarthošuu o MAU 148-149 L 3
Zave o ZW 218-219 F 3
Zavety Il'iča o RUS 122-123 J 4
Zavhan o MAU 146-147 M 1
Zavhan gol ~ MAU 146-147 L 1
Zavhan gol ~ MAU 148-149 C 4
Zavhlant o MAU 148-149 I 4
Zavitaja ~ RUS 122-123 C 4
Zavitinsk o RUS 122-123 C 3
Zav'jalova, ostrov ⌒ RUS 120-121 O 4
Zavlaka o YU 100-101 G 2
Zavod, Gazimurskij ☆ RUS 118-119 J 10
Zavodoukovsk o RUS 114-115 J 6
Zavodskoj o RUS 126-127 F 6
Zavolže o RUS 94-95 S 3
Zavolžsk o RUS 94-95 S 3
Zawiga Katrina = Monastery of Saint Catherine ☆• ET 194-195 F 3
Zawilah o• LAR 192-193 F 4
Zāwiyat al Amwāt o ET 194-195 E 3
Zāwiyat al Izzīyāt o LAR 192-193 K 1
Zāwiyat al Mukhayla o LAR 192-193 K 1
Zayande Rūd ~ IR 134-135 E 2
Zayat o MYA 142-143 J 4
Zayatkì o MYA 142-143 K 6
Zayetkon o MYA 142-143 J 5
Zayü o VRC 144-145 L 6
Zayü Qu ~ IND 142-143 K 2
Zaza ~ C 54-55 F 3
Zaza ~ RUS 118-119 E 9
Zaza, Presa < C 54-55 F 4
Zazafotsy o RM 222-223 E 9
Zazamt, Wādī ~ LAR 192-193 F 2
Zaziatou o RN 204-205 E 2
Zažimčar ~ RUS 114-115 J 2
Zäzir, Oued ~ DZ 198-199 B 2
Zäzir, Oued ~ DZ 198-199 B 2
Zban o KZ 126-127 P 3
Zbayra, Oued ~ WSA 196-197 D 2
Zblewo o PL 92-93 P 2
Zbruč ~ UA 102-103 E 3
Ždanha o RUS 108-109 e 5
Ždanov = Maryupol' o UA 102-103 K 4
Ždanova ~ RUS 108-109 f 3
Ždanovka o RUS 96-97 E 8
Ždanovo o KZ 136-137 M 3
Ždanovsk = Bejlagan o AZ 128-129 M 3
Zdvinsk ☆ RUS 124-125 L 1
Zè o DY 204-205 E 5
Zealandia o CDN (SAS) 232-233 L 4
Zealand Station o CDN (NB) 240-241 J 4
Zēbāk o AFG 136-137 M 6
Zeballos o CDN (BC) 230-231 C 4
Zebediela o ZA 220-221 J 2
Zebulon o USA (NC) 282-283 J 5
Zednes ▲ RIM 196-197 E 3
Zeebrugge o B 92-93 G 3
Zeehan o AUS 180-181 H 6
Zeekoegat o ZA 220-221 J 2
Zeeland o USA (ND) 258-259 H 6
Zeerust o ZA 220-221 H 2
Zefat ☆ IL 130-131 D 1
Zefre o IR 134-135 E 2
Zegbeli o GH 202-203 L 5
Zegher, Hamādat ⊥ LAR 192-193 D 4
Zégoua o RMM 202-203 H 4
Zegrir, Oued ~ DZ 190-191 D 4
Zéguédéguin o BF 202-203 K 3
Zehner o CDN (SAS) 232-233 O 5
Zeidābād o IR 134-135 F 4
Zeil, Mount ▲ AUS 176-177 M 1
Zeitz o D 92-93 M 3
Zeja ☆ RUS (AMR) 118-119 N 9
Zeja ~ RUS 120-121 D 6
Zeja ~ RUS 122-123 B 3
Zejskij zapovednik ⊥ RUS 118-119 N 8
Zejsko-Bureinskaja ravnina ⌣ RUS 122-123 C 3
Zejskoe vodohranilišče ⊖ RUS 118-119 N 8
Žekog o VRC 154-155 B 4
Želanija, mys ▲ RUS 108-109 N 3
Želannoe o RUS 124-125 H 1
Zelenoborskij o RUS 88-89 M 3
Zelenodoľsk ☆ RUS 96-97 F 6
Zelenodoľs'k o UA 102-103 H 4
Zelenoe o KZ 96-97 G 9
Zelenogorsk o RUS 94-95 L 1
Zelenograd o RUS 94-95 P 4
Zelenogradsk ☆• RUS 94-95 G 4
Zelenokumsk o RUS 126-127 E 5
Zelenyj, ostrov ⌒ RUS 122-123 M 7
Zelenzukskaja o RUS 126-127 D 6
Železinka ☆ KZ 124-125 J 2
Železnodorožnyj o RUS (IRK) 116-117 L 7
Železnodorožnyj o RUS (RF) 94-95 G 4
Železnogorsk o RUS 94-95 O 5
Železnogorsk-Ilimskij ☆ RUS 116-117 M 7
Železnovodsk o RUS 126-127 E 5
Zeffana o DZ 190-191 E 4
Zelina o HR 100-101 F 2
Želkuar su kojmasy < KZ 124-125 B 2
Zell o USA (SD) 260-261 H 2
Žel'tau ▲ KZ 124-125 H 6
Želtau ▲ KZ 126-127 L 4
Želtèr (Tušig) o MAU 148-149 G 2
Želtye Vody = Žovti Vody o UA 102-103 H 3
Zelzate o B 92-93 G 3
Žemaičių Naumiestis o• LT 94-95 G 4
Zembin o BY 94-95 L 4
Zembra ⌒ TN 190-191 H 2
Zemio o• RCA 206-207 G 6
Zemite o LV 94-95 H 3
Zemlja Bunge, ostrov ⌒ RUS 110-111 X 2
Zemmora o DZ 190-191 C 3
Zemmour ⊥ WSA 196-197 D 2
Zémongo, Réserve de faune de ⊥ RCA 206-207 G 5
Zempoala ∴• MEX 52-53 F 2
Zendeğān o AFG 134-135 J 1
Zengcheng o VRC 156-157 H 5
Zengō ▲ H 92-93 P 5
Zenguele o ANG 216-217 C 3
Zenia o USA (CA) 246-247 B 3
Zenica o BIH 100-101 F 2
Zenkōji • J 152-153 H 6
Zenkovo o RUS 114-115 K 4
Žen̦terek o KZ 96-97 J 10
Zentsūji o J 152-153 E 7
Zenye o AFG 136-137 L 7
Zenza do Itombe o ANG 216-217 C 4
Žepče o BIH 100-101 G 2
Zephyr o USA (TX) 266-267 J 2
Zephyrhills o USA (FL) 286-287 G 3
Zepita o PE 70-71 C 5
Zepu o VRC 146-147 C 6
Zeralda o DZ 190-191 D 2
Zérauk o AFG 138-139 B 3
Zeravšan ~ UZ 136-137 H 5
Zeravšanskij hrebet ▲ UZ 136-137 K 5
Zerbst o D 92-93 M 3
Žerd' o RUS 88-89 S 4
Žerdevka o RUS 102-103 M 2
Zere, Gōd-e ⊖ AFG 134-135 J 4
Zerendi ☆ KZ 124-125 F 2
Zeribet el Oued o DZ 190-191 F 3
Zerkal'noe, ozero ⊖ RUS 124-125 M 2
Zerkel o USA (MN) 270-271 C 3
Zernograd o RUS 102-103 M 4
Zeroud, Oued ~ TN 190-191 G 3
Žešart o RUS 88-89 U 5
Žeskazgan ☆ KZ 124-125 E 5
Žeskazgan ☆ KZ 124-125 E 5
Zestafoni o GE 126-127 E 6
Zêtang o VRC 144-145 H 6
Žetikara o KZ 124-125 B 2
Žetikonyr kum ⊥ KZ 124-125 F 5
Zetimtov toglari ▲ UZ 136-137 J 3
Žetisaj ☆ KZ 136-137 L 4
Žetybaj o KZ 126-127 K 6
Žetykol', ozero ⊖ RUS 126-127 O 2
Žetysaj o KZ 136-137 L 4
Žezdi ☆ KZ 124-125 E 4
Žezdilı sukojmasy < KZ 124-125 E 5
Žezdy ~ KZ 124-125 E 5
Zêzere, Rio ~ P 98-99 D 5
Zezget, Gorges du • MA 188-189 K 3
Zgierz o PL 92-93 P 3
Zgorzelec o• PL 92-93 N 3
Zhabdün = Zhongba o VRC 144-145 E 6
Zhag'yab o VRC 144-145 L 5
Zhalantun o VRC 150-151 D 4
Zhalan Tun • VRC 150-151 D 3
Zhambyl = Žambyl ▲ KZ 136-137 M 3
Zhanang o VRC 144-145 H 6
Zhangbei o VRC 148-149 M 7
Zhangcun o VRC 154-155 J 5
Zhangguangcai Ling ▲ VRC 150-151 G 5
Zhanghe SK ⊖ VRC 154-155 G 6
Zhanghuang o VRC 156-157 F 6
Zhanghuang o VRC 156-157 F 5
Zhangjiachuan o VRC 154-155 E 4
Zhangjiagang o VRC 154-155 M 6
Zhangjiakou o VRC 154-155 J 1
Zhangping o VRC 156-157 K 4
Zhangpu o VRC 156-157 K 4
Zhangqiu o VRC 154-155 K 3
Zhangshu o VRC 156-157 J 2
Zhangwu o VRC 150-151 D 6
Zhangye o VRC 154-155 B 2
Zhangzhou o VRC 156-157 K 4
Zhanjiang o VRC 156-157 G 6
Zhaodong o VRC 150-151 E 4
Zhaojue o VRC 156-157 C 2
Zhao Ling ∴• VRC 154-155 F 4
Zhaoping o VRC 156-157 G 4
Zhaoqing o VRC 156-157 H 5
Zhaosu o VRC 146-147 E 4
Zhaotong o VRC 156-157 C 3
Zhao Xian o VRC 154-155 J 3
Zhaoyuan o VRC 150-151 E 5
Zhaozhou Qiao • VRC 154-155 J 3
Zha po Gang ≈ 156-157 G 6
Zhargun Khel o PK 138-139 C 3
Zhari Namco ⊖ VRC 144-145 E 5
Zharkent o KZ 124-125 M 6
Zhaxigang o VRC 144-145 B 4
Zhaxilhünbo Si • VRC 144-145 G 6
Zhecheng o VRC 154-155 J 4
Zheduo Shankou ▲ VRC 154-155 B 6
Zhehai o VRC 156-157 C 3
Zhejiang ◻ VRC 156-157 L 2
Zhejue o VRC 156-157 C 3
Zhelang o VRC 156-157 J 5
Zhen'an o VRC 154-155 F 5
Zhenba o VRC 154-155 E 5
Zhenbao Ding ▲ VRC 156-157 G 3
Zheng'an o VRC 156-157 E 2
Zhengfeng o VRC 156-157 D 4
Zhenghe o VRC 156-157 L 3
Zhengxiangbai Qi o VRC 148-149 M 6
Zhengxiong o VRC 156-157 D 3
Zhengyang o VRC 154-155 J 5
Zhengzhou ☆• VRC 154-155 H 4
Zhenhai o VRC 156-157 L 4
Zhenjiang o• VRC 154-155 L 5
Zhenkang o VRC 142-143 L 4
Zhenlai o VRC 150-151 D 5
Zhenping o VRC (HEN) 154-155 H 5
Zhenping o VRC (SXI) 154-155 F 6
Zhenyuan o VRC (GAN) 154-155 E 4
Zhenyuan o VRC (GZH) 156-157 F 3
Zhenyuan o VRC (YUN) 142-143 M 4
Zhexi SK ⊖ VRC 156-157 G 2
Zhezqazghan = Žeskazgan ☆ KZ 124-125 E 5
Zhicheng o VRC 154-155 G 6
Zhidan o VRC 154-155 F 3
Zhigon o VRC 144-145 D 5
Zhijiang o VRC 156-157 F 3
Zhijin o VRC 156-157 D 3
Zhijin D. • VRC 156-157 D 3
Zhimenda o VRC 144-145 L 4
Zhiqu = Tongtian He ~ VRC 144-145 K 3
Zhob o PK (BEL) 138-139 B 4
Zhob ~ PK 138-139 B 4
Zhoda o CDN (MAN) 234-235 G 5
Zhombe o ZW 218-219 E 4
Zhongba o VRC (GDG) 156-157 J 5
Zhongba o VRC (XIZ) 144-145 E 6
Zhongdian o VRC 142-143 L 2
Zhongjian Dao ⌒ VRC 158-159 L 3
Zhongjiang o VRC 154-155 D 6
Zhongning o VRC 154-155 D 3
Zhongshan o VRC (GDG) 156-157 H 5
Zhongshan o VRC (GXI) 156-157 G 4
Zhongwei o VRC 154-155 D 3
Zhong Xian o VRC 154-155 F 6
Zhongxiang o VRC 154-155 H 6
Zhongxin Gang ≈ 154-155 M 5
Zhongxingqiao o VRC 154-155 M 5
Zhorgbu o VRC 156-157 F 2
Zhoudang o VRC 154-155 J 6
Zhoukou o VRC 154-155 J 5
Zhoukoudian ∴••• VRC 154-155 J 2
Zhouning o VRC 156-157 L 3
Zhoushan o VRC 154-155 N 6
Zhoushan Dao ⌒ VRC 154-155 N 6
Zhoushan Qundao ⌒ VRC 154-155 M 6
Zhouzhi o VRC 154-155 F 4
Zhouzhi Z.B. ⊥• VRC 154-155 E 4
Zhowagoin o VRC 144-145 L 6
Zhuanghe o VRC 150-151 D 8
Zhucheng o VRC 154-155 L 4
Zhud o EC 64-65 C 3
Zhugqu o VRC 154-155 D 5
Zhuhai o VRC 156-157 H 5
Zhuji o VRC 156-157 M 2
Zhujiang Kou ≈ 156-157 H 5
Zhumadian o VRC 154-155 J 5
Zhuozhou o VRC 154-155 J 2
Zhuozi o VRC 154-155 H 1
Zhuozi Shan ▲ VRC 154-155 E 2
Zhushan o VRC 154-155 G 5
Zhuxi o VRC 154-155 F 5
Zhuzhou o VRC 156-157 H 3
Zhytomyr = Žitomyr o UA 102-103 F 2
Zia Indian Reservation ✗ USA (NM) 256-257 J 3
Ziama ▲ RG 202-203 F 5
Ziama Mansouria o DZ 190-191 E 2
Ziārat o PK 134-135 M 3
Žiar nad Hronom ☆ SK 92-93 P 4
Zia Town o LB 202-203 G 7
Ziba o EAT 212-213 D 6
Ziban ⊥ DZ 190-191 E 3
Zibār, Az- o IRQ 128-129 L 4
Zibo o VRC 154-155 L 3
Zichang o VRC 154-155 F 3
Zielona Góra ☆• PL 92-93 N 3
Zierikzee o NL 92-93 G 3
Ziftā o ET 194-195 E 2
Zigal'ga hrebet ▲ RUS 96-97 L 6
Žigalova ~ RUS 114-115 S 5
Žigalovo ☆ RUS 116-117 M 8
Žigansk o RUS 110-111 O 6
Žigerbent o TM 136-137 H 4
Zighan o LAR 192-193 K 5
Zighout Youcef o DZ 190-191 F 2
Zigon o MYA 142-143 J 4
Zigon o MYA 142-143 J 6
Zigong o VRC 156-157 D 2
Ziguéy o TCH 198-199 G 6
Zigui o VRC 154-155 G 6
Ziguinchor ☆ SN 202-203 B 3
Žigulëvskij zapovednik ⊥ RUS 96-97 F 7
Zihuatanejo o• MEX 52-53 D 3
Zijin o VRC 156-157 J 5
Zik'wala • ETH 208-209 D 4
Zilair ☆ RUS 96-97 K 7
Zilairskoe plato ▲ RUS 96-97 K 7
Zile ☆• TR 128-129 F 2
Zilfi, az- o KSA 130-131 J 4
Žilina o SK 92-93 P 4
Žilinda o RUS (SAH) 110-111 J 4
Žilinda ~ RUS 110-111 K 4
Zilkale o TR 128-129 J 2
Zillah o LAR 192-193 G 3
Zillah o USA (WA) 244-245 E 4
Zil'merdak hrebet ▲ RUS 96-97 K 7
Žiloj, ostrov ⌒ AZ 128-129 O 2
Zilupe o• LV 94-95 L 3
Zim o USA (MN) 270-271 F 3
Zima ☆ RUS (IRK) 116-117 L 9
Zima ~ RUS 116-117 K 9
Zimām, Wādī az ~ LAR 192-193 F 3
Zimapán o MEX 52-53 E 1
Zimatlán o MEX 52-53 F 3
Zimba o Z 218-219 D 3
Zimbabwe ■ ZW 218-219 D 4
Zimbabwe National Monument, Great ∴••• ZW 218-219 F 5
Zimnij o UA 102-103 K 3
Zimmerman o USA (MN) 270-271 E 5
Zimmi o WAL 202-203 E 6
Zimnicea o RO 102-103 D 6
Zimnij bereg ⌣ RUS 88-89 Q 4
Zimnij Bereg = Zimnij bereg ⌣ RUS 88-89 Q 4
Zimovniki o RUS 102-103 N 4
Zina o CAM 206-207 B 3
Zinacatepec o MEX 52-53 F 2
Zinapécuaro o MEX 52-53 D 2
Zinave, Parque Nacional de ⊥ MOC 218-219 G 5
Zinder ◻ RN 198-199 D 5
Zinder ☆• RN (ZIN) 198-199 D 6
Zinga Mulike o EAT 214-215 K 5
Zinğibār o Y 132-133 D 7
Ziniaré o BF 202-203 K 3
Zin'kiv o UA 102-103 J 2
Zinna o WAN 204-205 J 4
Zinzana o RMM 202-203 H 3
Zio ~ RT 202-203 L 6
Zion o USA (IL) 274-275 L 2
Zion National Park ⊥ USA (UT) 254-255 C 6
Zion Reservoir < USA (AZ) 256-257 F 4
Ziope o GH 202-203 L 6
Zipaquirá o CO 60-61 D 5
Zira ~ EAT 214-215 G 5
Ziraándaro o MEX 52-53 D 2
Ziracuaretiro o MEX 52-53 D 2
Zirapup o IND 138-139 F 7
Žirenkopa o KZ 126-127 L 2
Žirkovskij, Holm- o RUS 94-95 N 4
Žirnov o RUS 102-103 M 3
Žirnovsk o RUS 96-97 D 8
Ziro o IND 142-143 H 2
Žirokaja ~ RUS 112-113 J 5
Zitenga o BF 202-203 K 3
Žitomir = Žytomyr o UA 102-103 F 2
Zitong o VRC 154-155 D 6
Zitouna o DZ 190-191 F 2
Zittau o• D 92-93 N 3
Zitundo o MOC 220-221 L 3
Zitziana River ~ USA 20-21 P 4
Živinice o BIH 100-101 G 2
Ziway o ETH 208-209 D 5
Ziway Hāyk' ⊖ ETH 208-209 D 4
Ziwu L ▲ VRC 154-155 F 4
Zixi o VRC 156-157 K 3
Zixing o VRC 156-157 H 4
Ziyā Ābād o IR 128-129 N 4
Ziya He ~ VRC 154-155 K 2
Ziyang o VRC (SIC) 154-155 D 6
Ziyang o VRC (SXI) 154-155 F 5
Ziyuan o VRC 156-157 G 3
Ziz, Gorges du • MA 188-189 J 4
Ziz, Oued ~ MA 188-189 J 5
Zizah ☆• UZ 136-137 K 4
Zizhong o VRC 156-157 D 2
Zizhou o VRC 154-155 G 3
Zjudev, ostrov ⌒ RUS 126-127 G 5
Zlabings = Slavonice o CZ 92-93 N 4
Zlatica o BG 102-103 D 6
Zlatograd o BG 102-103 D 7
Zlatoust ☆ RUS 96-97 L 6
Zlatoustovsk o RUS 122-123 E 2
Zli o RIM 196-197 D 5
Zlín o CZ 92-93 O 4
Zlītan ◻ LAR 192-193 F 1
Zlītan ☆ LAR (Zli) 192-193 F 1
Žlobin o BY 94-95 M 5
Złoczew o PL 92-93 P 3
Złotów o• PL 92-93 O 2
Z'Malet el Emir o DZ 190-191 D 3
Zmeinogorsk o RUS 124-125 N 3
Zmertène, Oued ~ TN 190-191 G 4
Zmiev = Zmijiv o UA 102-103 K 3
Zmievka o RUS 94-95 P 5
Znaim = Znojmo o CZ 92-93 O 4
Znamenka o KZ 124-125 L 3
Znamenka o RUS 94-95 R 5
Znamenka o RUS (HKS) 116-117 E 8
Znamenka o RUS (SML) 94-95 O 4
Znamenskoe ☆ RUS 114-115 M 6
Znamjanka o UA 102-103 H 3
Žnin o• PL 92-93 O 2
Znisne = Žnin o• PL 92-93 O 2
Znojmo o CZ 92-93 O 4
Zoa o CAM 204-205 K 6
Zoar o ZA 220-221 E 6
Zoar Village State Memorial • USA (OH) 280-281 E 3
Zobia o ZRE 210-211 K 2
Zóbuè o MOC 218-219 H 2
Žodino = Žodzina o BY 94-95 L 4
Žodzina o BY 94-95 L 4
Zoébefang o CAM 210-211 C 2
Zoétélé o CAM 210-211 C 2
Zogang o VRC 144-145 L 6
Žogarg Tobyl sukojmasy < KZ 124-125 C 2
Zogbodomè o DY 204-205 E 5
Zogoré o BF 202-203 J 3
Zögstèj o MAU 148-149 F 4
Zohlaguna, Meseta de ▲ MEX 52-53 K 2
Žohova, ostrov ⌒ RUS 110-111 d 1
Zohre, Rūdḫāne-ye ~ IR 134-135 D 3
Zoigê o VRC 154-155 C 5
Zolfo Springs o USA (FL) 286-287 H 4
Zolotaja, Ust'- o RUS 116-117 F 9
Zolotaja Gora o RUS 118-119 N 8
Zolote o UA 102-103 L 3
Zolotica ~ RUS 88-89 Q 4
Zolotinka o RUS 118-119 M 7
Zolotoj hrebet ▲ RUS 112-113 U 4
Zolotonoša o UA 102-103 H 3
Zolotuha o RUS 96-97 E 10
Zomandao ~ RM 222-223 D 8
Zomba o• MW 218-219 H 2
Žomboj ☆ UZ 136-137 K 5
Zondor o UZ 136-137 J 5
Zongar Alatauy ▲ KZ 124-125 L 6
Zongga o VRC 144-145 E 6
Zongia o ZRE 210-211 K 2
Zongo o ZRE 206-207 D 6
Zonguldak ☆ TR 128-129 D 2
Zongwe o ZRE (SHA) 212-213 A 6
Zongwe o ZRE (SHA) 214-215 F 4
Zongyang o VRC 154-155 K 6
Žonkeldi o UZ 136-137 H 4
Zonkwa o WAN 204-205 H 4
Zonokoi o CI 202-203 J 6
Zonūz o IR 128-129 L 3
Zoo Baba o RN 198-199 F 3
Zöölön o MAU 148-149 D 2
Zoppo, Portella dello ▲ I 100-101 E 6
Zorgo o BF 202-203 K 3
Zorita o E 98-99 E 5
Zorkul', ozero ⊖ TJ 136-137 N 6
Zoro o WAN 204-205 J 3
Zoró, Área Indígena ✗ BR 70-71 G 2
Zorritos o PE 64-65 B 3
Zorzor o LB 202-203 F 6
Žosaly ☆ KZ 124-125 D 6
Zou ~ DY 202-203 L 6
Zouan-Hounien o CI 202-203 F 6
Zouar o• TCH 198-199 H 2
Zouarké • TCH 198-199 H 2
Zouérat o RIM 196-197 D 3
Zoūgh o RIM 196-197 G 6
Zouireg o DZ 190-191 E 4
Zoukoubouè o CI 202-203 G 6
Zoukouzou o RCA 206-207 E 5
Zoulabot o CAM 210-211 E 2
Zouloumo o RCA 206-207 E 6
Zoumri, Pic ▲ RN 198-199 F 2
Zouping o VRC 154-155 K 3
Zoupleu o CI 202-203 F 6
Zousfana, Oued ~ DZ 188-189 K 5
Zoushi o VRC 156-157 G 2
Zouzoudinga o RN 192-193 E 6
Žovti Vody o UA 102-103 H 3
Zrenjanin o• YU 100-101 H 2
Zū o AFG 136-137 M 6
Žuantöbe o KZ 124-125 F 6
Zuata o YV 60-61 J 3
Zuata, Río ~ YV 60-61 J 3
Zubair, Ǧabal ⌒ Y 132-133 C 6
Zubaybān o Y 132-133 D 6
Zubcov o RUS 94-95 O 3
Zubova Poljana o RUS 94-95 S 4
Zubovo o RUS 94-95 P 1
Zubrat Rašid o KSA 132-133 C 5
Zuca o MOC 220-221 L 2
Zudáñez, Río ~ BOL 70-71 E 6
Zuénoula ☆ CI 202-203 G 6
Zuera o E 98-99 G 4
Zuevka ☆ RUS 96-97 G 4
Zufār ⊥ Y 132-133 H 5
Zug ☆• CH 92-93 K 5
Zugdidi o GE 126-127 D 6
Zugspitze ▲•• D 92-93 L 5
Zugurma Game Reserve ⊥ WAN 204-205 F 4
Zuhra, az- o Y 132-133 C 6
Zuhūr, Wādī az- ~ OM 132-133 J 4
Žuja ~ RUS 118-119 H 6
Zújar, Río ~ E 98-99 E 5
Zujl o MAU 146-147 L 2
Zujl = Mönhbulag o MAU 148-149 F 4
Zukovka o RUS 94-95 N 5
Zula o ER 200-201 J 5
Zula Bahir Selat'ë ≈ 200-201 J 5
Zulia, El o CO 60-61 E 4
Zulia, Río ~ CO 60-61 E 3
Zuluma o Y 132-133 F 6
Žulumaj o RUS 116-117 K 9
Žuma ☆ UZ 136-137 K 5
Zumba o EC 64-65 C 4
Zumbagua o EC 64-65 C 2
Zumbo o MOC 218-219 F 2
Zumbro Falls o USA (MN) 270-271 F 6
Zumbrota o USA (MN) 270-271 F 6
Zumpango o MEX 52-53 E 2
Zumpango del Río o MEX 52-53 E 3
Zungeru o WAN 204-205 G 4
Zunhua o VRC 154-155 K 1
Zuni o USA (NM) 256-257 G 3
Zuni Indian Reservation ✗ USA (AZ) 256-257 F 4
Zuni Indian Reservation ✗ USA (NM) 256-257 G 3
Zun-Murèn ~ RUS 116-117 L 10
Zun-Torej, ozero ⊖ RUS 118-119 H 10
Zunyi o VRC 156-157 E 3
Zuo Jiang ~ VRC 156-157 E 5
Zuoquan o VRC 154-155 H 3
Zuoyun o VRC 154-155 H 1
Županova ~ RUS 120-121 S 7
Zuqur, az- ⌒ Y 132-133 C 6
Zur o MAU 116-117 G 11
Zurak o WAN 204-205 J 4
Žuravlëva, zaliv ≈ 108-109 Z 1
Žuravlëvo o RUS 114-115 S 7
Zuri, Río ~ BOL 70-71 D 5
Zürich ☆• CH 92-93 K 5
Zurich o USA (KS) 262-263 G 5
Zurich o USA (MT) 250-251 K 3
Zürichsee ⊖ CH 92-93 K 5
Zurmi o WAN 198-199 C 6
Zuru o WAN 204-205 F 3
Zuruahã, Área Indígena ✗ BR 66-67 D 6
Žūryn o KZ 126-127 M 3
Zuša ~ RUS 94-95 P 5
Zuta o USA (GA) 284-285 J 5
Zutiua, Rio ~ BR 68-69 E 4
Zutphen o• NL 92-93 J 2
Zuunbulag o MAU 148-149 M 4
Zuunharaa o MAU 148-149 H 3
Zuunmod ☆ MAU 148-149 H 4
Zuurberg National Park ⊥ ZA 220-221 G 6
Zuwa, River ~ WAN 204-205 K 3
Zuwārah ☆ LAR 192-193 E 1
Zuytdorp Cliffs ⊥ AUS 176-177 B 3
Zuytdorp National Park ⊥ AUS 176-177 B 3
Zvenigovo o RUS 96-97 F 5
Zvenyhorodka ☆ UA 102-103 G 3
Zveroboj, ostrov ⌒ RUS 108-109 V 4
Zvishavane o ZW 218-219 F 5
Zvolen o SK 92-93 P 4
Zvornik o• BIH 100-101 G 2
Zwartkop o ZA 220-221 E 5
Zwedru ☆ LB 202-203 F 6
Zwelitsha ☆ ZA 220-221 H 6
Zwettl o A 92-93 N 4
Zwickau o D 92-93 M 3
Zwingli o ZA 220-221 H 2
Zwoleń o PL 92-93 Q 3
Zwolle ☆• NL 92-93 J 2
Zwolle o USA (LA) 268-269 G 5
Zylan o KZ 126-127 O 4
Žylancykturme, üstirti ▲ KZ 124-125 D 3
Žylandytau ▲ KZ 126-127 P 2
Zymoetz River ~ CDN 228-229 F 2
Zypern ⌒ CY 128-129 E 5
Zyrjanka ☆• RUS (SAH) 110-111 c 7
Zyrjanka ~ RUS 110-111 b 7
Zyrjanovsk o KZ 124-125 O 4
Zyrjanskoe o RUS 114-115 T 6
Žytomyr o UA 102-103 F 2

Zar — Žytomyr 415

Contributors/Credits

MACMILLAN
A Simon & Schuster Macmillan Company
1633 Broadway, New York, NY 10019

Copyright © 1997 RV Reise- und
Verkehrsverlag Munich · Stuttgart,
Germany
Maps copyright © 1997 Geo Data,
Werder/H., Germany

First United States edition 1997

U.S. Edition
Publisher
  Nathalie Chapman

Editorial Director
  Geoff Golson

Cover Design
  Iris Jeromnimon

Library of Congress Cataloging-in-
Publication Data
Planet earth Macmillan world atlas.
    p.   cm.
  Includes index.
  ISBN 0-02-861266-3
  1. Atlases.   I. Macmillan Publishers.
G1021.P655 1997 ‹G&M›
912–DC20 96–33068 CIP MAPS

Cartography
Editors-in-Chief/Project Directors
  Dieter Meinhardt, Stuttgart
  Eberhard Schäfer, Stuttgart

Editor
  Christoph Lutze, Stuttgart

Editorial Staff
  Hannelore Anders, Werder/H.
  Marianne Bartsch, Leipzig
  Ralf van den Berg, Stuttgart
  Francesco Bover, Barcelona
  Markus Burkhardt, Leipzig
  Vaclav Cerny, Stuttgart
  Klaus Dorenburg, Leipzig
  Werner Drapak, Stuttgart
  Heinz Eckert, Leipzig
  Gisela Gaebler, Leipzig
  Karin Gehrmann, Werder/H.
  Kai Gründler, Leipzig
  Angela Jaehne, Werder/H.
  Eva-Maria Jahnke, Leipzig
  Erika Klimpel, Leipzig
  Karl-Heinz Klimpel, Leipzig
  Renate Krahl, Werder/H.
  Beate Laus, Stuttgart
  Uwe Lipfert, Leipzig
  Winfried Maigler, Stuttgart
  Frank Meitzen, Leipzig
  Heinz-Jürgen Newe, Stuttgart
  Hans-Jochen Poetzsch, Leipzig
  Folker Rhaesen, Leipzig
  Klaus Schaefer, Werder/H.
  Helmut Schaub, Stuttgart
  Irmgard Sigg, Stuttgart
  Rüdiger Werr, Stuttgart
  Gabriele Wiemann, Werder/H.
  Erwin Woska, Werder/H.

Cartography Relief Artists
  Kai Gründler, Leipzig
  Eberhard von Harsdorf, Siegsdorf
  Prof. Dr. Christian Herrmann, Karlsruhe
  Bruno Witzky, Stuttgart

Computer Cartographers
  Directors: Wolfgang Severin, Stuttgart
  Jörg Wagner, Stuttgart
  Andreas Westermann, Berlin

  Vitor Vicente Antunes, Berlin
  Antoinette Beckert, Berlin
  Kerstin Budig, Berlin
  Heike Czeglars, Stuttgart
  Joachim Drück, Stuttgart
  Friedrich Enßle, Berlin
  Joachim Eppler, Stuttgart
  Ramona Fabian, Leipzig
  Natascha Fischer, Stuttgart
  Gerhard Geller, Stuttgart
  Margot Graf, Leipzig
  Jana Grundke, Leipzig
  Beate Jankowski, Stuttgart
  Kristine Keppler, Stuttgart
  Gudrun Kolditz, Leipzig
  Doris Kordisch, Leipzig
  Ute Krasselt, Leipzig
  Hannelore Kühsel, Leipzig
  Hanno Lehning, Berlin
  Michael Menzel, Stuttgart
  Helga Mickel, Leipzig
  Karin Oelzner, Leipzig
  Ulrich Zeiler, Leipzig
  Kathrin Zimmer, Leipzig

Technology
  Director: Bernd Hlawatsch, Stuttgart

  Elke Bellstedt, Stuttgart
  Erika Rieger, Stuttgart
  Olaf Untermann, Stuttgart
  Walter Zimmermann, Stuttgart

Typesetting
  Directors: Gabriele Stuke, Stuttgart
  Jörg Wulfes, Stuttgart

  Frank Barchet, Stuttgart
  Thomas Ellinger, Stuttgart
  Karin Krüger, Leipzig
  Elfriede Salomo, Leipzig
  Hannelore Scherer, Leipzig
  Mario Spalj, Stuttgart
  Judith Winter, Tübingen

Final Checking
  Director: Hartmut Voit, Stuttgart

  Bernd Hilberer, Stuttgart

**Independent Contributors and
Consultants**
  Institut für Angewandte Geodäsie,
    Frankfurt/M.
  UNESCO, World Heritage Center, Paris,
    Vesna Vujicic
  Moscow Aerogeodetic Enterprise,
    Moscow,
    Dr. Alexander Borodko
  Academia Sinica, Nanking,
    Prof. Zhang Longsheng
    Mrs. Liu Xiaomei
  Kartografie Praha A.S., Prague,
    Jirí Kucera
  Cartographia Ltd, Sofia,
    Ivan Petrov
  Maplan Warszawa, Warsaw,
    H. Michal Siwicki
  Prof. Dr. Christian Herrmann, Karlsruhe
  Prof. Dr. Wilfried Fiedler, Munich
  Prof. Dr. Heinrich Lamping,
    Frankfurt/M.
  Kartographie Messer, Pfungstadt

  Internationales Landkartenhaus,
    Stuttgart
  Birgit Kapper-Wichtler, Buhlenberg
  Beate Siewert-Mayer, Tübingen
  Dr. Martin Coy, Tübingen
  Dr. Wolfgang Frank, Remshalden
  Martin Friedrich, Tübingen
  Henryk Gorski, Warsaw
  Jörg Haas, Rottenburg
  Ernst-Dieter Zeidler, Potsdam
  Peter Krause, Regensburg
  Studio für Landkartentechnik,
    Norderstedt
  Jochen Layer, Fellbach
  Angelika Palczynski, Heidelberg
  Susanne Priemer, Esslingen
  Maryland Cartographics, Columbia MD
  European Map Graphics,
    Finchampstead (Berkshire)
  GeoSystems, Lancaster PA
  Timothy J. Carter, Comfort TX

Text and Photo Division
Editor-in-Chief/Project Director
  Carlo Lauer, Prisma Verlag GmbH,
  Munich

Editor
  Armin Sinnwell, Prisma Verlag GmbH,
  Munich

Assistant Editor
  Raphaela Moczynski, Prisma Verlag
  GmbH, Munich

Photo Editor
  Sabine Geese, Prisma Verlag GmbH,
  Munich

Texts
  Dr. Ambros Brucker, Gräfelfing
  Dr. Christoph Schneider, Düsseldorf

Translation
  GAIA Text, Munich

Illustrations
Satellite Imagery
  GEOSPACE-Beckel Satellitenbilddaten,
  Bad Ischl, Salzburg
  © Satellite images:
    Geospace/Eurimage/Eosat
  © Original data: EOSAT 1994

Photographers
  Abbreviations: AKG – Archiv für Kunst
  und Geschichte; B&U – B&U International Picture Service; IFA – IFA-Bilder-
  team; TG – Transglobe Agency; TIB –
  The Image Bank; TSW – Tony Stone
  Worldwide

Photo credits
  I NASA; 1 (center left/cl) AKG; 1 (top to
  bottom) Hans Wolf/TIB, David W.
  Hamilton/TIB, Ben Simmons/TG, TIB,
  Albrecht G. Schaefer, Luis Castaneda/
  TIB), Rauh/PhotoPress, B&U, Magnus
  Reitz/TIB, Eric Meola/TIB; 17 (cl) AKG,
  17 (left column: top to bottom) Zefa,
  J. Gnass/Zefa, Norbert Rosing/Silvestris,
  Hansgeorg Arndt/Silvestris, W. Allgö-
  wer/TG, Norbert Rosing/Silvestris, TSW,
  Derek Trask/TG, 17 (right column: top
  to bottom) Scholz/Bavaria, Hunter/IFA,
  Kokta/IFA, Fuhrmann/PhotoPress, Do-
  novan Reese/TSW, Glen Allison/TSW,
  A. Schein/Zefa, John J. Wood/Photo-
  Press, Cosmo Condina/TSW, Chris
  Haigh/ TSW, Rob Boudreau/TSW; 57
  (cl) AKG, 57 (top to bottom) Koene/
  TG, Diaf/IFA, Michael Scott/TSW, Mar-
  tin Wendler/Silvestris, R. McLeod/TG,
  TIB, L. Veiga/TIB, Giuliano Colliva/TIB,

  A.N.T./Silvestris, R. McLeod/TG, A.N.T./
  Silvestris; 81 (cl) AKG, 81 (top to bottom) Damm/Zefa, Magnus Rietz/TIB,
  Jürgens Ost+Europa Photo, UPA/IFA,
  Jeff Hunter/TIB, Wolfgang Korall/Silve-
  stris, Konrad Wothe/Silvestris, Everts/
  IFA, A. Gallant/TIB, Backhaus/Zefa, Jür-
  gens Ost+ Europa Photo; 105 (cl) AKG,
  105 (left column: top to bottom) Jür-
  gens Ost+Europa Photo, Jürgens Ost+
  Europa Photo, Hubert Manfred/Bava-
  ria, Aberham/IFA, Ben Simmons/TG,
  Jürgens Ost+Europa Photo, A. Filatow/
  APN/Nowosti, Hubert Manfred/Bava-
  ria, Gerd Ludwig/Visum, 105 (center
  column: top to bottom) Jürgens Ost+
  Europa Photo, M. Theis/TG, Richard
  Elliott/TSW, Ben Edwards/TSW, Rolf
  Richardson/TG, Everts/IFA, David
  Sutherland/TSW, Hoa-Qui/Silvestris,
  Roland Birke/Agentur Hilleke, Alex Ste-
  wart/TIB, Andreas Gruschke/Agentur
  Hilleke, 105 (right column: top to bot-
  tom) B&U, Terry Madison/TIB, K. Strati-
  on/TG, Romilly Lockyer/TIB, IFA, Glen
  Hillson/TSW, Paul Chesley/TSW, Chris
  Haigh/TSW, Nigel Dickinson/ TSW,
  Bail/IFA, Paul Chesley/TSW; 169 (cl)
  Interfoto, 169 (top to bottom) Cle-
  mens Emmler, Gottschalk/IFA, Voll-
  mer/IFA, Albrecht G. Schaefer, Albrecht
  G. Schaefer, Siebig/IFA, P. Arnold/IFA,
  BCI/IFA; 185 (cl) AKG, 185 (left co-
  lumn: top to bottom) Kiepke/Photo-
  Press, Werner Gartung, Diaf/IFA, Erika
  Graddock/Silvestris, Hoa-Qui/Silvestris,
  Werner Gartung, Werner Gartung,
  Obremski/TIB, 185 (right column: top
  to bottom) Diaf/IFA, Aberham/IFA,
  Fiedler/ IFA, Sally Mayman/TSW, Her-
  bert Schaible/TIB, Nicholas Parfitt/TSW,
  Stefan Meyers/Silvestrsi, Chris Harvey/
  TSW, Aberham/IFA, Konrad Wothe/
  Silvestris, Hoa-Qui/Silvestris; 225 (cl)
  AKG, 225 (left column: top to bottom)
  M. Braunger/Agentur Hilleke, Wunsch/
  IFA, Hunter/IFA, Hans Schmied/Silve-
  stris, Georg French/Bavaria, Diaf/IFA,
  Glück/IFA, Hunter/IFA, Krämer/IFA, 225
  (center column: top to bottom) The Te-
  legraph/Bavaria, M. Braunger/Agentur
  Hilleke, Nowitz/IFA, Sunwind/Bavaria,
  Nägele/IFA, Krämer/IFA, Picture Fin-
  ders/Bavaria, Picture Finders/Bavaria,
  David Ball/Bavaria, Comnet/IFA, M.
  Braunger/Agentur Hilleke, 225 (right
  column: top to bottom) Osborne/IFA,
  PhotoPress, M. Braunger/Agentur
  Hilleke, Picture Finders/Bavaria, Helga
  Lade, Bavaria, BCI/IFA, M. Braunger/
  Agentur Hilleke, P. Graf/IFA, Oertel/IFA,
  FPG/Bavaria.

Production
Design, Layout
  Pro Design, Munich
  Typographischer Betrieb Walter Biering
  & Hans Numberger, Munich

Reproduction
  Worldscan, Munich

Repro Director
  Wolfgang Mudrak, Munich

Manufacture
  Bernhard Mörk, Stuttgart

General Manufacture
  Mohndruck
  Graphische Betriebe Gütersloh

Printed in Germany

10 9 8 7 6 5 4 3 2 1